Sunset

NATIONAL
GARDEN
BOOK

By the Editors of Sunset Books and Sunset Magazine

SUNSET BOOKS INC. • MENLO PARK, CALIFORNIA

Rugosa roses and catmint in a Pennsylvania garden

Sunset Books Inc.
President & Chief Executive Officer: Steve Seabolt
VP, Chief Financial Officer: James E. Mitchell
VP, Manufacturing Director: Lorinda Reichert
Director, Sales & Marketing: Richard A. Smeby
Editorial Director: Bob Doyle
Director of Finance: Lawrence J. Diamond
Production Director: Lory Day
Retail Sales Development Manager: Becky Ellis
Art Director: Vasken Guiragossian

Special acknowledgment and thanks
to Susan J. Maruyama

Staff for this book
Managing Editor: Suzanne Normand Eyre
Senior Editors: Susan Lang, John R. Dunmire, Philip Edinger,
    Joseph F. Williamson, Lance Walheim, Cynthia Overbeck Bix
Sunset Magazine Senior Editor, Gardening: Kathleen Norris Brenzel
Chief Copy Editor: Rebecca LaBrum
Assistant Copy Editor and Indexer: Carolyn McGovern
Assistant Editors: Jody Mitori, Tishana Peebles
Production Coordinator: Patricia S. Williams

Art Director: Alice Rogers
Computer Production: Elaine Holland, Phoebe Bixler, Joan Olson,
    Karen Teague
Botanical Illustrator: Mimi Osborne
Gardening Illustrators: Lois Lovejoy, Bill Oetinger
Map Design and Cartography: Reineck & Reineck, San Francisco
Photo Editor: Susan Friedman
Concept Design: Alex R. Arthur

Cover photograph: Cornus florida *'Rubra', Saxon Holt*
Title page photograph: Clematis on arbor, David McDonald
Endpapers photograph, hardcover edition: Broad beech fern,
    R. Todd Davis Photography

First printing March 1997

Printed in the United States.

Foreword

This book came about because gardeners across the United States and Canada—familiar with *Sunset's* popular *Western Garden Book*—asked for it time and again. Either they had moved east of the Continental Divide from places like Los Angeles or Denver, or they had gardening friends or relatives in Nantucket, New Orleans, or places in between. But whether these gardeners with ties to the West lived near a palm-fringed beach in Florida, in the suburbs of Chicago, on a ranch in Texas, or amid a forest of maples in Maine, they wanted information that addressed conditions specific to their regions. They wanted to understand the climates and soils in their own backyards. They wanted to know which plants would grow best for them and, at the same time, bring the most beauty to their gardens. Quite simply, they wanted eastern, midwestern, or southeastern versions of the book they fondly called the "Bible" of western gardening.

What sets this book apart from others is its system of climate zones, developed with help from university climatologists, the National Weather Service, and agricultural extension agents across North America. While other plant zoning schemes are based on winter minimums—a useful plant hardiness index—the *Sunset* system recognizes that other factors are just as important in determining how well a particular plant will grow in a given region. Summer highs, humidity, rainfall patterns, elevation, land formations, length of growing seasons, and proximity to oceans or other large bodies of water all play important roles.

The *Sunset* climate maps organize the United States and the southern part of Canada into 45 climate zones. For each entry in the A to Z Plant Encyclopedia, we note the zones where that plant grows best—so once you've found your zone on one of the 23 regional maps, you can easily learn whether the plants you want to grow will perform well for you.

The encyclopedia includes detailed information about more than 6,000 plants—some widely available and commonly grown, others harder to find but worth seeking out. But this book also contains much more. The Plant Selection Guide will help you choose the right plants for special situations—such as damp soil or deep shade—and for special purposes, such as providing winter interest or attracting birds and butterflies. The Practical Gardening Dictionary contains the latest advice on everything from watering and fertilizing plants to managing garden pests in environmentally friendly ways. And the Resource Directory lists, among other things, outstanding botanical gardens and mail-order suppliers of seeds and plants.

Like its predecessors, the *Sunset National Garden Book* recognizes gardening as an art, a science, and an adventure in communing with the natural world. We hope that it will guide you faithfully in your gardening efforts for years to come.

Kathleen N. Brenzel
Senior Editor, *Sunset Magazine*

CONTENTS

INTO THE GARDEN

A gallery of many kinds of gardens—gardens where family and friends gather, quiet solitary retreats, a repository for new and interesting plants, a place to express your style—an inspiration for your own garden.

THE 45 CLIMATE ZONES

Regional maps and descriptions of the gardening climate zones of the United States and Canada. Identifying your zone will make choosing plants from the next two chapters easier.

A GUIDE TO PLANT SELECTION

Twenty-eight plant lists, organized by theme and illustrated with hundreds of color photographs, to help you create special effects, tackle difficult landscaping situations, or lay out a basic garden framework.

A TO Z PLANT ENCYCLOPEDIA

PRACTICAL GARDENING DICTIONARY

RESOURCE DIRECTORY

INDEXES

INTO THE GARDEN
A Welcoming Spirit

Open the gate, step into the garden, and—magically—leave the rest of the world behind. It sounds too easy, but it really works, as generations of gardeners can attest. A garden is a place that has little to do with the hustle and bustle of day-to-day life. Enter, and you invite nature to reveal its power to soothe and inspire.

Gardens represent many things to many people. A garden can be a place where friends and family gather, or a quiet, solitary retreat. It can be a laboratory for experimentation or a place to express your personal style—formal or informal, traditional or cutting-edge contemporary.

Anyone, anywhere, can have a garden. It can be as small as a window box or as large as a country acre. It can thrive by the beach or in the desert, on the Eastern seaboard or the West Coast, on the prairies of the Midwest, on the Mississippi Delta, or high in the Rocky Mountains.

In the pages that follow, you'll see all kinds of gardens from all over North America. We hope you'll be inspired by the ways they express their creators' personalities and reflect the regions in which they grow.

High atop a New York City rooftop, a lush garden flourishes in containers (above). This collection includes such hardy plants as boxwood, weeping flowering cherry, purple salvia, and black-eyed Susan. On the facing page: Roses and clematis ramble over a gate in Vancouver, British Columbia, inviting visitors into the tranquil garden beyond.

GARDEN RETREATS

Leaving the Outside World Behind

A pleasant, well-planned garden has an almost magnetic appeal: who can resist a comfy chair under the trees, a sunny expanse of lawn, or a shaded table laid for a picnic by a brilliant flower bed?

Sometimes a garden makes you want to be alone—to savor a good book or just plain relax with nothing but bird song for company. Other times, you want to bring others along to share the flower color and fresh air. Perhaps you have conversation in mind, perhaps an alfresco meal. Whatever your pleasure, the garden is always there, waiting for you to step out and enjoy.

Relaxing in Style

A hammock between two trees meets almost everyone's notion of the easy life. It's all the more delightful in a lush woodland setting like this one.

Treetop Retreat

Overlooking the treetops, this woodland gazebo takes on the mood of the moment. On a misty Delaware morning, it's a sanctuary for welcoming the day with a quiet cup of tea; when sun warms the garden, it's a perfect place for a friendly get-together.

Poolside Pleasures

Like a tranquil stream in a woodland clearing, this shimmering, stone-edged pool and spa sit comfortably among the mixed plantings that surround them (below). They invite a quick dip or a long, relaxing soak.

Classical Charm

Reflecting the old-world charm of the Georgian-revival-style home it adorns (above), this Ohio garden calls to mind leisurely summer meals enjoyed beneath the fragrant wisteria vine. The Palladian-style "windows" are actually tall mirrors that add depth to the small, enclosed patio.

Summer Hideaway

The "roof" and "walls" of this whimsical child-size hideaway are really just a flowery tangle of 'Heavenly Blue' morning glories, climbing up and over a simple wooden frame. Looking out from the leafy enclosure, children and their grown-up guests can enjoy a vista of sunflowers, Gloriosa daisies, 'Gourmet Popcorn' white roses, and more.

A Quiet Corner

This well-placed chair invites the gardener to take a moment's rest and contemplate the morning's work. A lush cover of Japanese spurge provides a green and cooling carpet.

THE CREATIVE GARDEN
A Form of Expression

Some people paint, some cook, some play piano. But for many creative souls, gardening is the perfect mode of self-expression. The garden may express ideas about color or pattern, or be based on a favorite style. Always, the challenge is in choosing just the right plants to fulfill the theme and thrive in their setting and climate.

The gardens shown here reflect diverse approaches to style and mood. All of them, however, are delightful expressions of the visions and personalities of their creators.

Enchanted Garden

An exuberant jumble of pink, yellow, and purple—strawflower, toadflax, geranium, and more—adds to the Alice-in-Wonderland charm of this California artist's garden. The focal point is a handmade gateway. Plants on either side of the gate spill over brightly painted raised beds topped with blue tiles made by the artist. Design: Keeyla Meadows

Cottage Garden Fantasy

An unused shed in this Pennsylvania garden has been transformed into one gardener's vision of an old-fashioned cottage, complete with perennial border. Wooden latticework on the walls supports flourishing trumpet vines and clematis. Crowding all around in glorious profusion are traditional cottage garden flowers such as delphinium, nasturtium, and pansy.

Upon Reflection

Window on the world or mirror image? At first glance, it's hard to tell. The creator of this playful window-box setting has grouped an appealing mix of red zinnia, pink pelargonium, lamb's ears, and clematis beneath a wooden frame. (And yes— it's a mirror.)

Worth Repeating

Patterns are what the garden below is all about. In an original approach to planting an herb garden, the softly rounded forms of alternating gray- and green-leafed santolina create a pleasing checkerboard effect.

Set in Stone

Enigmatic faces lie partly concealed amid the subtle colors of 'Burgundy Lace' ajuga in this carefully laid-out pathway. The stepping-stones provide that touch of whimsy that's the hallmark of an imaginative gardener. Design: Marcia Donahue

Study in Perspective

Inspired by Japanese tradition, the garden at left brings together the strong forms of rock, the music of falling water, and the soothing greens and blues of evergreens. To create the illusion of a large-scale landscape, the deodar cedar and false cypress are kept small with skillful pruning that leaves them resembling full-grown trees. Design: Imazumi

Time Out

Nestled among a collection of herbs and backed by lush hydrangeas, this sundial is the focal point of its own little garden corner. Thyme creeps around its upper edge, while a scented geranium embraces the pedestal.

COLLECTORS' GARDENS
Showcasing Special Plants

One of the many small joys of gardening is growing special plants—old favorites you love, new varieties you've been meaning to try, or perhaps cuttings from the gardens of your friends. Many gardeners become specialists; they may delight in dahlias, for example, or make a science of collecting dwarf conifers or unusual succulents. For these aficionados, the garden is a kind of laboratory—a place for making fascinating discoveries as they nurture their most cherished plants.

Colorful Standout

Gorgeous, silken-flowered peonies are a joy to grow. Many, like this *Paeonia lactiflora*, bloom in dazzlingly brilliant colors.

Iris Walk

In this Texas garden, the Louisana iris is queen. These beauties thrive in water or in bogs. Here they edge a pond in a garden that's been transformed from an overgrown swamp into a showplace.

Bonsai Gallery

Displayed like the works of art they really are, bonsai plants form a living gallery in a Northwest garden. A quiet backdrop of Douglas firs, evergreen hedges, and weathered fences sets off the beautiful shapes and intricate patterns of Japanese maple, flowering crabapple, apple, and rhododendron.

Carpet of Gold

Amid the stately trees of this grand Delaware landscape, a sweep of golden daylilies follows the gentle slope down to water's edge. Massing so many plants of the same type and color makes a dramatic statement in any setting. Here, surrounded by shades of green, the patch of bright gold stands out in bold relief.

Hemerocallis
(Daylily)

Rose-lover's Dream

Roses are on many gardeners' lists of their particular favorites. Here, deep red and creamy beige climbing varieties billow above a bed of pastel delphiniums in an informal setting that is full of old-fashioned charm. A hidden wire lattice serves as a ladder for these vigorous climbers.

Viola Portrait

Annuals paint a cheerful portrait of summer in this Pennsylvania garden. Yellow, orange, violet, and white pansies (*Viola wittrockiana*) splash strokes of bright color across a canvas of green lawn running up to a shady pergola.

NATURE-LOVERS' GARDENS

A Link to the Natural World

When you're in the garden, the beauty of nature is immediate, not to be denied. Even the smallest patch of urban greenery and bloom somehow makes you feel in touch with the natural world. Many of today's gardens underscore this link by making themselves a part of their natural surroundings. In some gardens, this means incorporating touches of the surrounding landscape into the formal garden design. In others, it means totally blurring the lines, so that it's no longer clear where the garden ends and where the natural landscape begins.

Floral Boundaries

Many gardeners find charm in juxtaposing the wild and the tame. *Above:* A brilliant pink 'Early Dawn' rhododendron seems to have sprung up naturally at the boundary between the garden and the woods beyond. *Left:* A casual planting of purple coneflower invites butterflies to pause and sip. *Below:* Forming a colorful display against a dramatic Rocky Mountain backdrop, this border—a mixture of pansy, ox-eye daisy, dame's rocket, and *Campanula glomerata*—has the look of a Colorado meadow in bloom.

Natural Nook

Creeping and trailing plants in many shades of green peek from between the stones of a bench and sprout among the pavers in a secluded California hideaway. The garden takes on the look of a patch of ground left to nature's devices. Design: Roger Raiche

Seasonal Cycles

Part of the joy of a natural garden lies in watching the seasons transform the landscape. As the Japanese maples and other trees in this New York garden change color, autumn splendor lights the rocks and stepping-stones with brilliant reds and golds.

Canyon Outlook

Rimmed by rugged cliffs, a ranch garden in a remote New Mexico canyon is bordered by sunny spuria irises and tawny gaillardia. Blossoms grow thick around the traditional adobe *horno*, which the owners use for cooking. The rest of the garden is given over to the cultivation of exotic vegetables and herbs for use in restaurants of nearby Santa Fe.

Winter's Garden

Caught by an early Massachusetts snowstorm, a majestic apple tree, loaded with fruit, becomes a fairyland vision in red and white. Snowfalls reveal a garden's underlying structure, bringing out forms and lines that can give a familiar scene an entirely different appearance.

THE *45* CLIMATE ZONES *of the United States and Canada*

When an unfamiliar plant strikes your fancy, your first question is likely to be, "Can I grow it?" You may have no trouble learning its soil preference, its water needs, and whether it thrives in full sun or does better in a shadier spot—but this information accounts for only part of the answer. Influencing the entire can-I-grow-it issue is the matter of climate. Are your summers hot or mild, dry or humid? Is winter a time of snow and ice or one of coolness and rain—or does it feature shirtsleeves-and-golf weather? Do you experience the full range of four seasons, or is yours a two- or three-season region? You can modify soil, apply or withhold water, or create shade in an attempt to satisfy the needs of certain plants, but the weather—the year-round climate—is in true control of your garden. And if the climate isn't right, some plants may fail to prosper despite your best efforts.

It is easy to understand why gardens in balmy San Diego feature a different plant palette than those in snowy-winter cities like Buffalo or Montreal. Less easy to grasp, without considering climate, are the differences you encounter between plantings in, say, Seattle and Savannah, or in Santa Barbara and Miami. The first two cities have similar annual rainfall and winter lows—yet they are quite unlike in terms of summer heat. The second two are both virtually frostless, but they differ vastly in matters of humidity and precipitation.

With the 1954 publication of *Sunset's* first *Western Garden Book*, gardeners west of the Continental Divide had the chance to read plant descriptions keyed to a map that organized the West into a set of actual climate zones. Until that time, gardening references addressed plant adaptability only in terms of cold tolerance, following hardiness-zone maps created by the United States Department of Agriculture and the Arnold Arboretum based on winter low temperatures and annual first-frost dates. The statement "hardy through Zone 8," for instance, identified a plant that could withstand lows to 10°F/−12°C, but revealed nothing about its preference, if any, for the climate of the southeastern states over that of central California. To take another example, consider Washington's cool/damp Olympic Peninsula and California's hot/dry Central Valley. The system treated these regions alike, presenting gardeners in both areas with the same list of "hardy in Zone 9" (to 20°F/−7°C) plants. The *Western Garden Book* system, however, assigned these two regions to different zones, giving gardeners in each a far more accurate idea of which plants would and would not flourish for them.

In the *National Garden Book*, *Sunset* has taken another groundbreaking step, this time applying the results of climate research to those parts of the United States and Canada lying east of the Continental Divide. The result is 21 new climate zones—Zones 25–45, additions to the list of 24 zones already well established for the West.

WHAT MAKES CLIMATE?

Weather and climate are two different, although obviously related, occurrences.

Weather is a day-to-day happening, the conditions described in the daily reports we read in the newspaper or hear on the radio or TV. *Climate* refers to the prevailing weather conditions of a place, determined by averaging weather data over a period of years. Thus we say, "Monday's weather will be rainy," but "South Texas has a hot-summer climate."

To grasp the complexities (and, therefore, the importance) of climate, you need to know some weather basics and understand how weather patterns are influenced by topography.

Three factors have a general influence on climate:

Latitude. The farther north of the equator a place is, the colder its winters are likely to be, and the longer the wintry weather is likely to last.

Elevation. Temperatures in both summer and winter tend to decrease with elevation. Mountain locations are cooler in summer, colder in winter than adjacent lowlands.

Wind patterns. In the middle latitudes of the Northern Hemisphere, winds move in a general west-to-east direction. Various high-altitude air currents known as jet streams are important in weather creation; their speed and strength make them express conduits for air of all qualities—moist, dry, warm, cold. In their predictable latitudinal migration, they tend to dip farther south in winter and move more to the north in summer, following the movement of the sun. The so-called storm track follows the jet streams' path, accounting for rainy and dry seasons.

Several other, more localized factors modify the basic patterns:

Influence of the Pacific Ocean or the Gulf of Mexico. During much of spring, summer, and fall, winds passing across these bodies of water move air across the land masses adjoining them. From the Pacific, relatively cool, dry air travels eastward, its effects diminished or blocked by mountain ranges with a north-south alignment. From the Gulf, warm and moist air moves north and northeast, affecting land from the Midwest to the Atlantic seaboard. As you move farther northward, this Gulf air's influence is diminished, chiefly by distance—the reason why the western and northern Great Plains are dry.

Air carried from the Pacific affects continental weather in two important ways. A tropical storm track can move northeast across northern Mexico into the Southwest and Midwest. When it carries moisture, it brings rainfall to these areas; when it is dry, it arrives as dust bowl–style wind. Winter jet streams bring major moisture to the western United States and Canada.

Ocean currents. Warm currents flow through the Gulf of Mexico and, as the Gulf Stream, up the Atlantic coast. This warm water evaporates readily, resulting in humid air (air with a high water-vapor content) along the Gulf Coast and eastern seaboard. During summer, Gulf Stream waters affect the entire Atlantic seaboard; in winter, however, the stream leaves the coast at about Cape Hatteras, allowing the cold Labrador Current to reach that far south. The Southeast thus experiences relatively mild winters, while the Northeast (including its coastal regions) is cold.

Along the Pacific Coast, cold southward-moving ocean currents travel nearly to Mexico, where they are met by a warmer current moving north. Since cold water evaporates much less readily than warm water, air carried inland from the Pacific is relatively dry in summer.

Proximity to one or more of the Great Lakes. Like other large bodies of water, the Great Lakes tend to mitigate extremes in air temperature: they cool more slowly in fall and warm more slowly in spring than land masses do. Areas near the Great Lakes thus have milder winters and cooler summers than do points farther inland at similar latitudes. These bodies of water also produce heavier snowfall, predominantly on their southeastern shores and especially during the earlier part of winter. Buffalo and Cleveland are prime examples of "lake effect" snow recipients.

Location of mountain ranges. Mountains interfere with basic wind patterns and the movement of air masses. In some instances, they block progress; in others, they direct movement. They also tend to extract rain from moist air as it cools upon rising. A mountain range's height and alignment determine the extent of its influence; for more on this subject, see below.

WEATHER IN THE UNITED STATES AND CANADA

To understand the garden climates of the United States and Canada, it's crucial to understand two points. The first one is geographic: the great height and length of the mountain ranges in the West are critical in determining the movement of winds and air masses. The Rocky Mountains run from within Canada down to central Mexico; the Cascade–Sierra Nevada mountains extend from British Columbia well into southern California. In general, Pacific influence tends to remain west of the Cascade–Sierra Nevada axis,

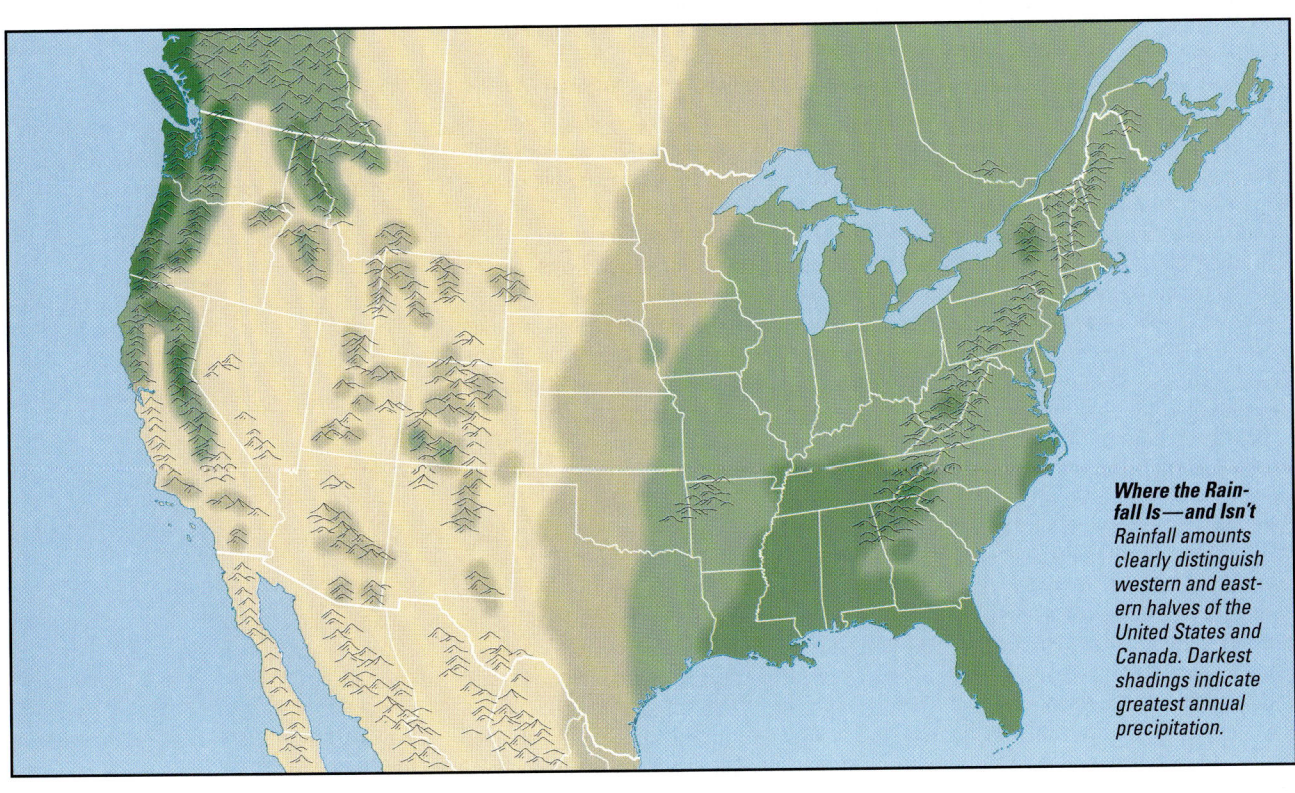

Where the Rainfall Is—and Isn't *Rainfall amounts clearly distinguish western and eastern halves of the United States and Canada. Darkest shadings indicate greatest annual precipitation.*

while Gulf and Atlantic influence stays east of the Rockies. The Appalachians and associated ranges, extending from Quebec in the north to a southern terminus in northern Georgia and Alabama, are old in comparison to western mountains and have been heavily weathered to much lower elevations. They have a far less significant influence on weather than the western mountains do.

The second point is climatological: air masses migrate according to predictable seasonal patterns. Our weather is dominated by semipermanent areas of high pressure that generally lie offshore. Air circulates around these highs in a clockwise direction, with air moving out from the center. In the Northern Hemisphere, the high-pressure areas lie far to the south in winter, near the Tropic of Cancer (latitude 23½° north). In summer, they move northward (to about 40° north) and lie off the Pacific and Atlantic coasts.

During summer, with high pressure offshore and low pressure over land, winds blow toward land. West of the Rockies, relatively cool, dry air comes inland. In the eastern United States and Canada, air circulation around the high-pressure area brings warm, moist air onshore, causing summer rainfall and typically warm, humid conditions. Periodically, colder air from the North Atlantic moves over land and encounters the warmer air, producing cooler temperatures and drizzle. When warm, moisture-laden air meets cooler air over the continent, the results can be dramatic. At best, the meeting produces spectacular thunderheads and rain; at its terrifying worst, it spawns tornadoes.

In winter, when the high-pressure masses again move south, the West Coast is open to storms coming in from the Pacific. West of the Cascade–Sierra Nevada ranges, this is the rainy season. In the eastern half of the continent, the south-lying high-pressure positions allow storms from the west (as well as cold arctic air) to dominate winter weather—with or without snow, depending on the air's moisture content.

Between the Rocky Mountains and the Cascade–Sierra Nevada chain lies the intermountain West, with its own particular climate: rain-shadow desert. In summer, the Rockies block moisture moving north from the Gulf of Mexico; in winter, eastward-moving Pacific storm systems drop much of their moisture on the western flanks of the Cascade-Sierra Nevada ranges, leaving little to fall in the intermountain lands to the east. The intermountain climate is thus dry and hot in summer, and likewise dry in

More than Cold and Wet

Fresh-water Lake Superior *(above)* and the not-always-peaceful Pacific Ocean *(below)* have something important in common: as large bodies of water they have large influences on weather.

winter—though some arctic air does influence the region then, bringing bone-chilling cold and some snow.

The preceding discussion highlights the summer-winter contrasts in North American weather patterns, since these differences underscore points critical to plant growth: amount and timing of rainfall; winter cold; presence or absence of summer humidity. But especially east of the Continental Divide, the quality and quirks of fall and spring transitional periods are also important. The give-and-take between cold arctic air masses and warm, moist air from the Gulf of Mexico is not an orderly minuet. With no interference from significant mountain ranges in this eastern half of the country, cold air can move south or southeastward with great suddenness. In fall, such a movement can bring a lethal freeze that puts an abrupt end to the summer growing season; in spring, it can stage an

equally devastating push that arrives well after plants have begun active growth—sometimes merely ruining the year's display, sometimes killing plants outright. This capricious tradeoff between cold and warm is an especially vexing feature in much of the mid-latitude Midwest, South, and East—and not only in spring and fall, but to some extent in winter as well. Another problem it brings to these regions is lack of a reliable snow cover, making winter protection necessary for possibly vulnerable shrubs and perennials.

THE 45 CLIMATE ZONES OF GARDENING

In the following 60 pages, the variety of United States and Canadian gardening is presented in 45 distinct climate zones. Zones 1–24 are the original, now well-established zones developed for western gardeners. Zones 25–45 cover the territory east of the Rockies, for the first time organizing this land mass into cohesive climatic regions as they relate to gardening.

Each description in the A to Z Plant Encyclopedia (beginning on page 161) states the zones in which that plant can be expected to thrive, given the garden culture it needs. Remember, too, that each garden has its own microclimates, areas in which exposure to sun, wind, and frost vary according to the terrain and the orientation of the house. Such microclimates may be critical to the survival of plants. For more, see "Frost and Freeze Protection" (page 564) and "Microclimate" (page 576).

In the climate zone descriptions that follow, each zone's growing season—the average number of days between the last frost in spring and the first frost in fall—is shown as a dark green band on a bar at the end of the zone description. The light green parts of the bands indicate shoulder seasons, when light frosts would not be likely to bother cool-season crops. Extra-mild zones have no shoulder season, since they rarely have killing frosts (28° F/−2°C or below).

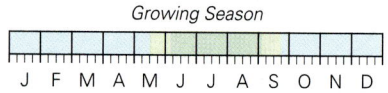

Growing Season

J F M A M J J A S O N D

Although growing season data offers a guide to the timing of some planting and choice of plants, it is just one piece of the climate puzzle. The expected growing season weather—hot, cool, wet, dry, windy—will affect plant success and your gardening practices.

Washington
Pages 22, 24

Montana
Pages 20, 22

Oregon
Pages 22, 27

Idaho
Page 22

Wyoming
Page 20

Northern
California
Page 28

California

Nevada
Page 20

Utah
Page 20

Colorado
Page 20

San
Francisco
Page 34

Central
California
Page 31

Los
Angeles
Page 38

California
Deserts
Page 44

Arizona
Page 46

New
Mexico
Page 48

San
Diego
Page 42

THE *24* CLIMATE ZONES *from the Western Prairie to the Pacific*

To find your garden's climate zone, start with this locator map and then turn to the page listed for your area. If you garden in a microclimate—a windy passage, thermal belt, cold pocket, hilltop, or canyon that's too small to register on the maps—adjust your climate zone accordingly.

At Home in Western Climates

Lack of summer rainfall and relatively low humidity favor plants from drier climates such as Bailey acacia *(Acacia baileyana)*, bearded irises like 'Beverly Sills', and orchid rockrose *(Cistus purpureus)*.

Though the western part of the continent embraces climates from alpine to desert, from dry prairie to seashore, the population is concentrated in those areas of the Far West and Southwest where winters are mild and summers are dry or only lightly visited by rain. Irrigation is a way of life for gardeners, and broad-leafed evergreen trees and shrubs dominate the landscape. Many gardens feature native plants—and plants from other dry-summer parts of the world—with water needs attuned to the western climate patterns.

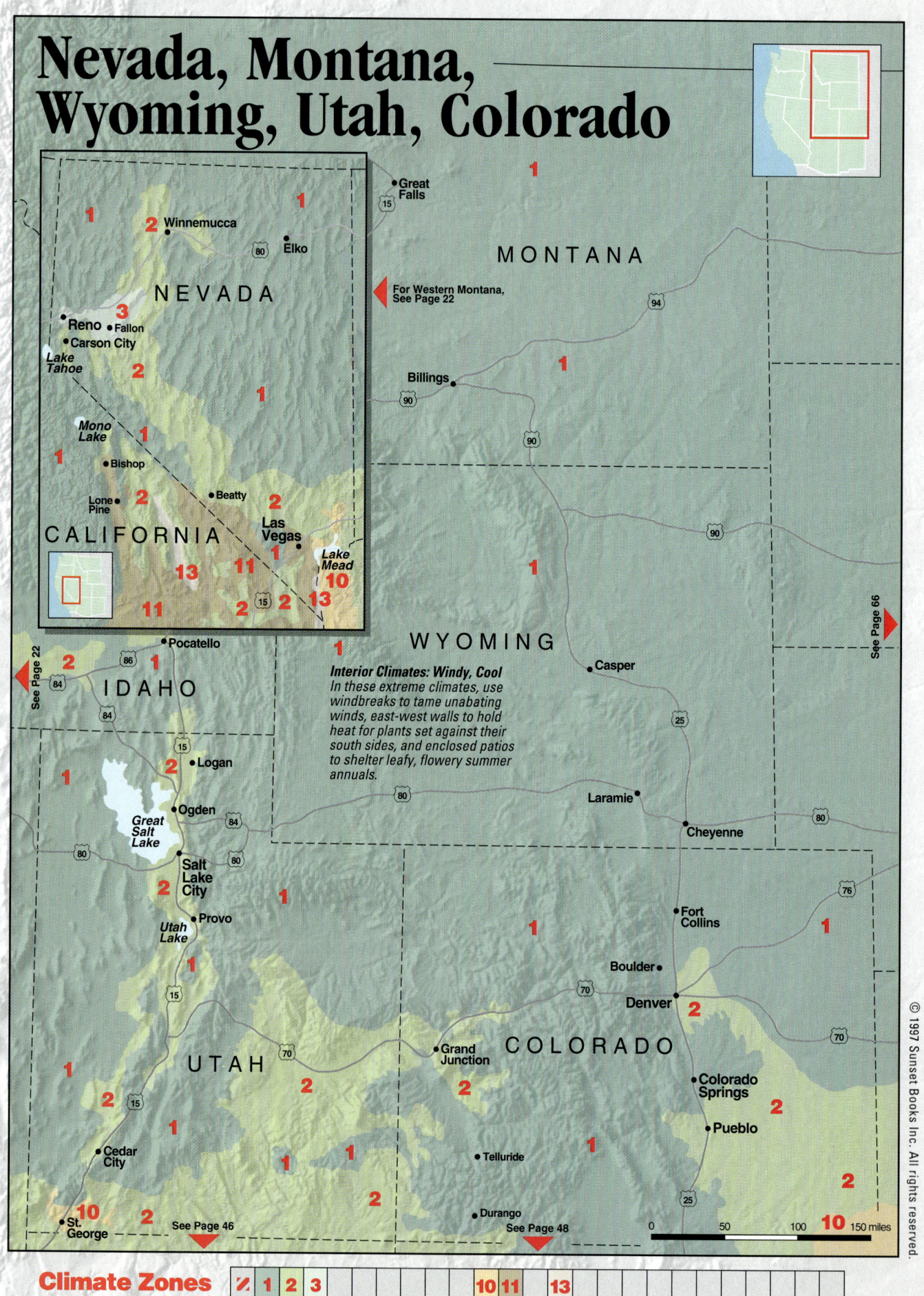

Nevada, Montana, Wyoming, Utah, Colorado

MONTANA

Great Falls

1

Winnemucca 2

Elko

NEVADA

1

For Western Montana, See Page 22

Billings

1

3

Reno Fallon

Carson City

Lake Tahoe

2

1

Mono Lake

1

Bishop

Lone Pine 2

Beatty

CALIFORNIA

2

Las Vegas 1

Lake Mead

13

11

10

11

2

13

WYOMING

1

Casper

Pocatello

2 1

IDAHO

Interior Climates: Windy, Cool
In these extreme climates, use windbreaks to tame unabating winds, east-west walls to hold heat for plants set against their south sides, and enclosed patios to shelter leafy, flowery summer annuals.

See Page 22

Logan 2

1

Ogden

Great Salt Lake

Laramie

Cheyenne

80

Salt Lake City

2

Provo

Utah Lake

1

Fort Collins

1

1

Boulder

Denver 2

1

UTAH

Grand Junction

2

2

COLORADO

Colorado Springs

2

Pueblo

1

1

Cedar City

1

Telluride

1

2

10

2

See Page 46

2

Durango

See Page 48

0   50   100   150 miles

10

St. George

20

Climate Zones 1 2 3 10 11 13

ZONE **1** Coldest Winters in the West

Zones 1, 2, and 3 are the snowy parts of the West—the regions where snow falls and stays on the ground (for a day, a week, or all winter) every year. Of the three snowy-winter climates, Zone 1 is by far the coldest.

The extreme winter cold of regions in Zone 1 can be caused by any or all of the three factors that create cold winters: latitude, influence of the continental air mass, and elevation (the higher you go, the colder it gets).

Growing Season

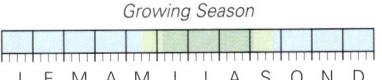

J F M A M J J A S O N D

In this zone, gardeners plant with a 75- to 150-day growing season in mind, though frosts can occur any night of the year. The zone's longer, more reliable growing seasons usually occur where large bodies of water, like Flathead Lake in Montana, moderate the winter cold.

Where Frost Is Never Far Away

Nestled in the Rocky Mountains, the town of Edwards, Colorado, has Zone 1 written all over it. High elevation, snow that's predictable, and a short growing season often combine to create a breathtaking background for a relatively small usable plant palette.

ZONE **2** Second-Coldest Western Climate

Here, as in Zone 1, snow is to be expected in winter. The chief difference between Zones 1 and 2 is that both record lows and average annual lows are lower in Zone 1 than in Zone 2. The difference is crucial: 'McIntosh' apples, for example, grow well in Zone 2, but not in Zone 1.

In Zone 2, windbreaks, trees planted for shelter, and heavy mulches can make it possible to grow plants that would otherwise perish from the effects of wind, cold, and winter sun. In addition, areas of Utah sheltered by the Wasatch Range and moderated by Great Salt Lake have milder winters than surrounding areas.

In the northerly latitudes and interior areas where the continental air mass rules supreme, determining which areas lie in Zone 2 and which lie in Zone 1 is mostly a matter of elevation. Notice that Zone 2 includes parts of the Snake River of Idaho, as well as the Grande Ronde and Burnt rivers of Oregon. It also extends along the Columbia and Spokane rivers in eastern Washington and to the lakes region of the Idaho panhandle. In Colorado, Zone 2 comprises the river valleys of the western portion of the state and the low-elevation plains in the southeast corner. Zone 2 covers about 20 counties of western Kansas. It also includes most of the high territory of New Mexico; only a small portion of the state lies in Zone 1. The Zone 2 areas in California and Arizona are at higher elevations, which are nevertheless not as cold as the higher

areas of Zone 1. During a 20-year period in Zone 2, annual low temperatures ranged from −3° to −34°F/−19° to −37°C.

Growing Season

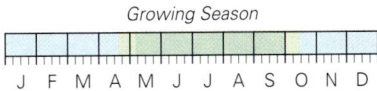

J F M A M J J A S O N D

High Interior Gardening

A meadow of thyme softens rock edges at Ohme Gardens in Wenatchee, Washington. As a ground cover, thyme is tough enough to take all the cold, ice, and snow that this part of Zone 2 can deliver and resilient enough to bounce back every spring.

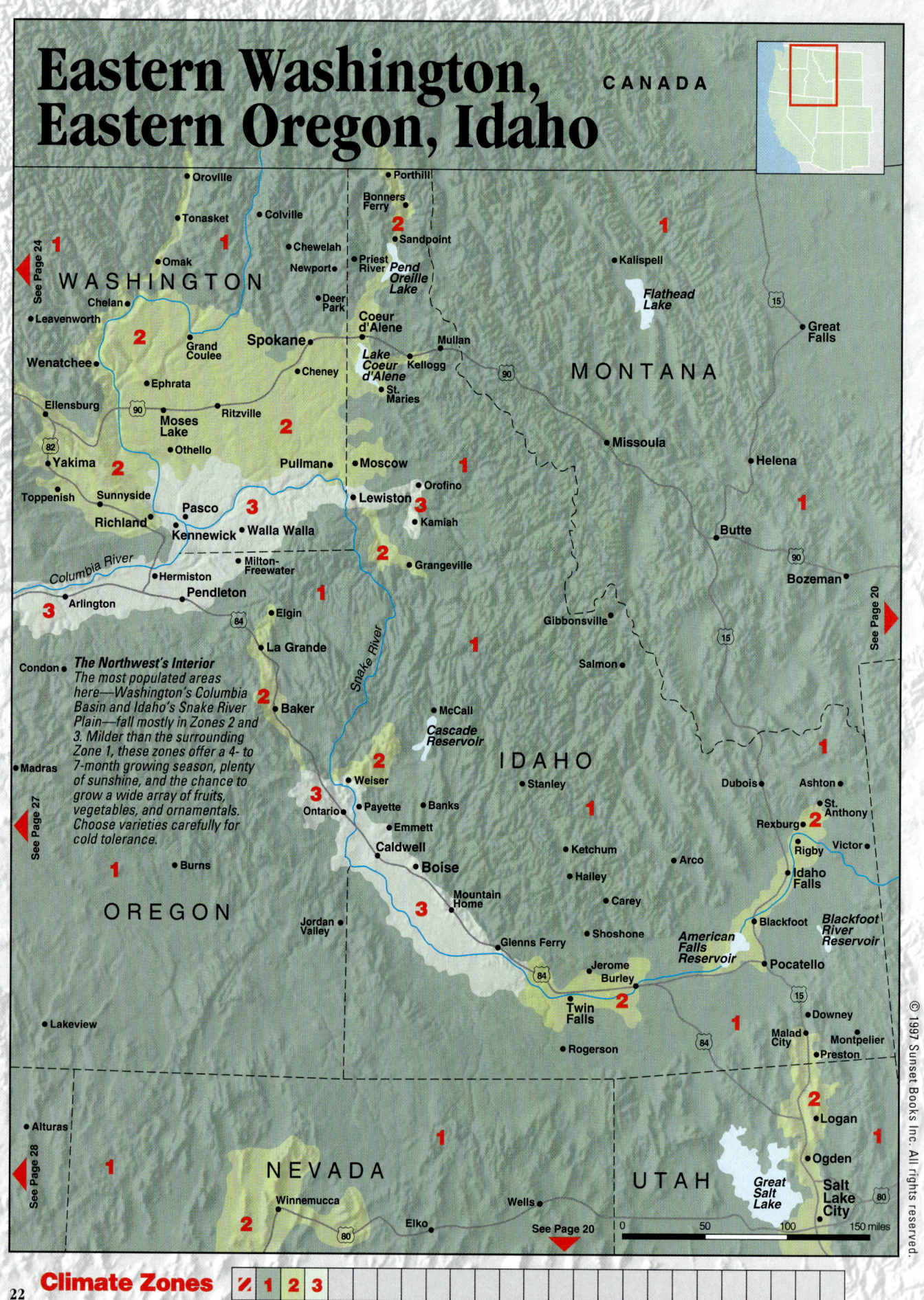

Eastern Washington, Eastern Oregon, Idaho

CANADA

WASHINGTON

Oroville
Tonasket
Colville
Chewelah
Omak
Newport
Chelan
Deer Park
Leavenworth
Wenatchee
Grand Coulee
Spokane
Ephrata
Cheney
Ellensburg
Moses Lake
Ritzville
Othello
Yakima
Pullman
Toppenish
Sunnyside
Pasco
Richland
Kennewick
Walla Walla
Columbia River
Hermiston
Milton-Freewater
Arlington
Pendleton
Elgin
La Grande

Porthill
Bonners Ferry
Sandpoint
Priest River
Pend Oreille Lake
Coeur d'Alene
Lake Coeur d'Alene
Mullan
Kellogg
St. Maries
Moscow
Lewiston
Orofino
Kamiah
Grangeville
Snake River

Kalispell
Flathead Lake
Great Falls

MONTANA

Missoula
Helena
Butte
Bozeman

The Northwest's Interior
The most populated areas here—Washington's Columbia Basin and Idaho's Snake River Plain—fall mostly in Zones 2 and 3. Milder than the surrounding Zone 1, these zones offer a 4- to 7-month growing season, plenty of sunshine, and the chance to grow a wide array of fruits, vegetables, and ornamentals. Choose varieties carefully for cold tolerance.

Condon
Madras
Baker
Weiser
Ontario
Payette
Banks
Emmett
Caldwell
Boise
Burns
Jordan Valley
Mountain Home
Glenns Ferry
Jerome
Burley
Twin Falls
Rogerson

OREGON

McCall
Cascade Reservoir
Stanley
Gibbonsville
Salmon

IDAHO

Ketchum
Hailey
Arco
Carey
Shoshone
American Falls Reservoir
Pocatello
Blackfoot
Blackfoot River Reservoir
Idaho Falls
Rigby
Victor
Rexburg
St. Anthony
Ashton
Dubois

Downey
Malad City
Montpelier
Preston
Logan
Ogden
Great Salt Lake
Salt Lake City

UTAH

Lakeview
Alturas
NEVADA
Winnemucca
Elko
Wells

See Page 24
See Page 27
See Page 28
See Page 20
See Page 20

0   50   100   150 miles

Climate Zones [hatch] 1 2 3

ZONE **3** Mildest of High-Elevation and Interior Climates

Cold Country's Banana Belt

Sheltered from Columbia Gorge winds by rows of poplars, commercial peach orchards *(above)* thrive in Zone 3, getting enough winter chill to set fruit and enough summer heat to ripen it. Columbine's exquisite flower *(below)* belies its toughness; some species are native to the intermountain West.

This is the mildest of the snowy-winter climates. East of the Cascades in the Northwest, the Zone 3 areas are the ones that are often called "banana belts." Of course, the only place you can grow the real, fruiting banana satisfactorily outdoors is in tropical climates such as Zone 25. But the comparatively mild winter temperatures of Zone 3 allow gardeners to grow such plants as common boxwood and winter jasmine.

The portion of Zone 3 from the Hood River to Lewiston is slightly lower in elevation than the surrounding Zone 2. The lower elevation, combined with the influence of Pacific air that spills over the Cascades and through the Columbia Gorge, moderates most winters. Much planting is based on winter lows of 10° to 15°F/−12° to −9°C. In an occasional winter, arctic air forces temperatures much lower. Such winters limit the selection of broad-leafed evergreens.

Absolute cold is not so much the enemy here as drying winds that dehydrate plants growing in frozen soil. Wind protection, mulching, shade, and careful late-autumn watering will help you grow many borderline evergreens.

In California, the Zone 3 areas often happen to be the lowest parts of the high mountains—where many cabin owners keep gardens. The zone also includes the Reno area of Nevada.

Over a 20-year period, minimum temperatures in Zone 3 ranged from 13° to −24°F/−11° to −31°C. While growing seasons can be shorter in Zone 3 than in Zone 2, winter minimum temperatures are always higher in Zone 3. In Walla Walla, Washington, the growing season lasts longer than in much of Zone 3—almost 220 days.

Growing Season

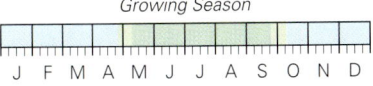

J F M A M J J A S O N D

Western Washington

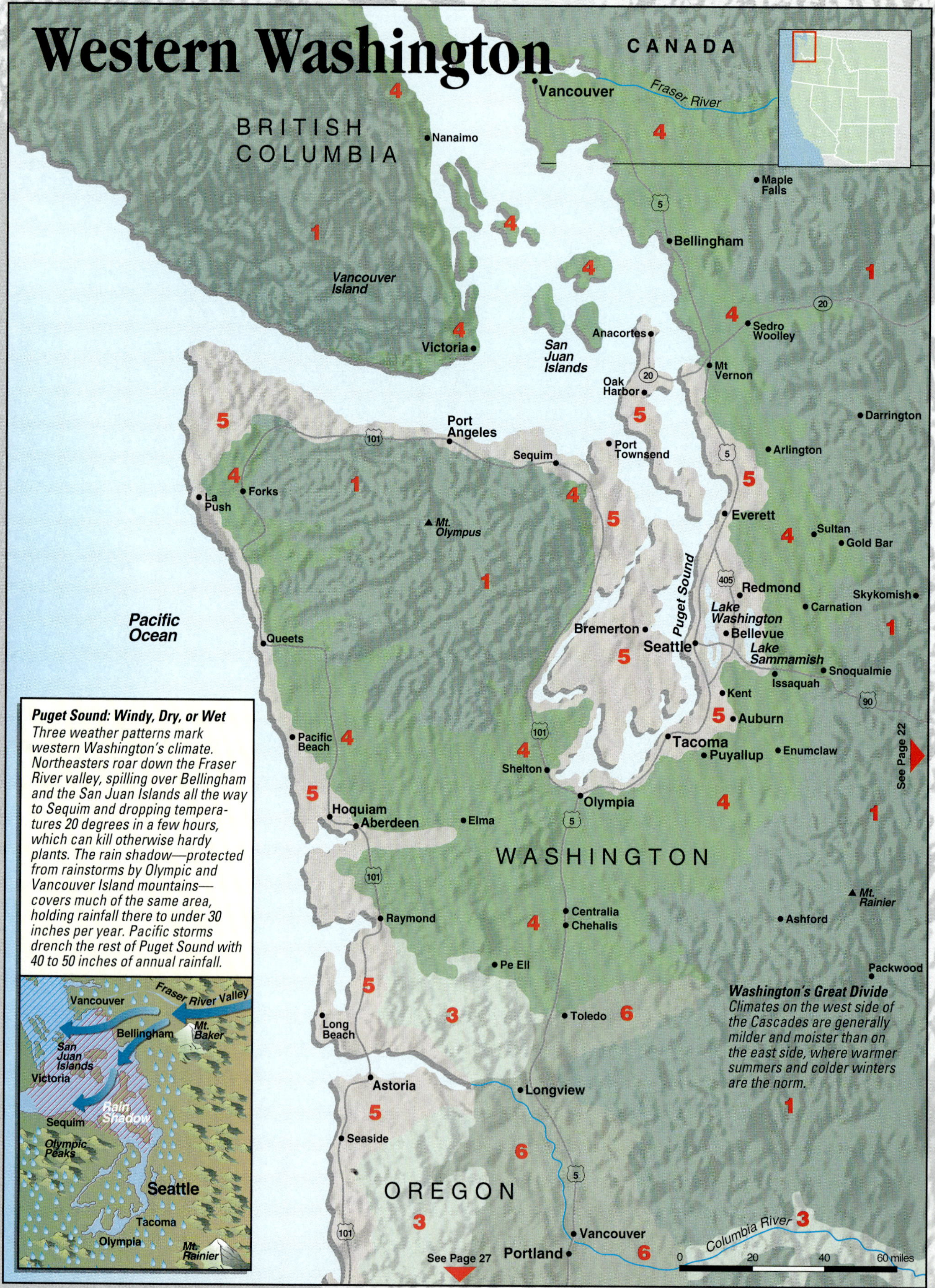

CANADA

BRITISH COLUMBIA

Fraser River

• Vancouver

• Nanaimo

Vancouver Island

• Maple Falls

US 5

• Bellingham

1

1

San Juan Islands

Anacortes

4

Victoria •

4

US 20

Oak Harbor

• Sedro Woolley

• Mt Vernon

US 20

• Darrington

5

Port Angeles

4

• La Push

• Forks

US 101

Sequim

• Port Townsend

5

• Arlington

5

5

• Everett

1

▲ Mt. Olympus

• Sultan
• Gold Bar

4

405

Pacific Ocean

• Queets

1

Puget Sound

Redmond

Lake Washington

• Skykomish

• Carnation

1

Bremerton •

Lake Sammamish

• Snoqualmie

Bellevue

Seattle

• Issaquah

5

90

• Kent

Puget Sound: Windy, Dry, or Wet

Three weather patterns mark western Washington's climate. Northeasters roar down the Fraser River valley, spilling over Bellingham and the San Juan Islands all the way to Sequim and dropping temperatures 20 degrees in a few hours, which can kill otherwise hardy plants. The rain shadow—protected from rainstorms by Olympic and Vancouver Island mountains— covers much of the same area, holding rainfall there to under 30 inches per year. Pacific storms drench the rest of Puget Sound with 40 to 50 inches of annual rainfall.

• Pacific Beach

4

• Shelton

101

5

Hoquiam
• Aberdeen

• Elma

Olympia

US 5

• Auburn

Tacoma
• Puyallup

• Enumclaw

4

1

WASHINGTON

▲ Mt. Rainier

• Centralia
• Chehalis

• Ashford

• Raymond

4

• Packwood

• Pe Ell

3

• Toledo

6

Long Beach

5

Washington's Great Divide
Climates on the west side of the Cascades are generally milder and moister than on the east side, where warmer summers and colder winters are the norm.

Fraser River Valley

Vancouver

• Longview

1

• Astoria

5

6

San Juan Islands

Bellingham

Mt. Baker

Victoria

Rain Shadow

Sequim

Olympic Peaks

Seattle

Tacoma

Olympia

Mt. Rainier

• Seaside

US 101

3

OREGON

See Page 27

Vancouver

3

US 5

Columbia River

3

6

Portland

0   20   40   60 miles

See Page 22

Climate Zones   1   3 4 5 6

ZONE 4   Cold-Winter Parts of Western Washington and British Columbia

One of the smallest climate zones in the West, Zone 4 is the region west of the Cascades whose climate gets considerable influence from the Pacific Ocean and Puget Sound—but also from the continental air mass, or higher elevation, or both. The zone touches salt water only in Skagit, San Juan, and Whatcom counties and British Columbia, so the influence of marine air is less powerful than in other western zones.

Zone 4 differs from neighboring Zone 5 in that it has extremely low winter temperatures more frequently, a shorter growing season, and, in most locations, considerably more rainfall. No western zone grows better perennials and bulbs; people who like to grow woodland plants and rock plants love Zone 4.

Zones 4 and 5 can be found in the same neighborhood, a fact that explains much of the familiar northwestern talk about warm or cold gardens. Over a 20-year period, average winter lows in Zone 4 ranged from 19°F/−7°C down to −7°F/−22°C.

Growing Season

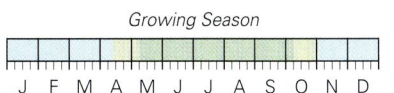

J F M A M J J A S O N D

Tulip Country

Washington's Skagit Valley has just the right soil and climate for growing commercial tulip crops, which wouldn't do as well in warmer climates. On the other hand, some of the more tender rhododendrons that Seattle grows would freeze here.

ZONE 5   Marine Influence Along the Northwest Coast and Puget Sound

Mild ocean air brings relatively warm winters to this area, which is on the same latitude as Duluth, Minnesota, and Bangor, Maine. The region is one of the world's great centers of rhododendron culture and rock gardens.

Over a 20-year period, minimum temperatures ranged from 28° to 1°F/−2° to −17°C. The occasional big freeze, with temperatures plummeting to near 0°F/−18°C, does considerable damage if it comes very early or very late, when plants are not conditioned for such cold. But these big freezes should not serve as the gauge of hardiness

Waterside Gardening

These astilbes and dogwoods thrive in a woodland garden near Lake Washington. The climate in Zone 5 is much like that of southern England, and the gardens here have benefited from England's long and successful search for more varied garden plants.

required for plants here; even normally tough native plants have been killed or injured by such freezes.

Many waterside areas show a very low heat accumulation in the summer. To grow heat-loving plants, pick out the hottest spots for them—a south wall or a west wall sheltered from cold winds will almost always supply such heat—and select peach and tomato varieties with low heat needs. The mildness in these areas favors flowering plants: It stretches out the bloom season of everything from fuchsias to calendulas.

The lowlands around Puget Sound and along the coast were once covered with forest, so native woodland plants like trillium, piggy-back plant, and a host of ferns thrive here, as do shade-tolerant trees like vine maples and dogwoods.

Growing Season

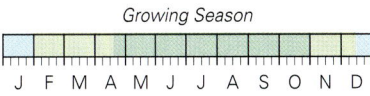

J F M A M J J A S O N D

ZONE 6 Willamette Valley

Warmer summers help distinguish the Willamette Valley climate from the climate of Zone 5. In the north, the Willamette can also have a much longer growing season: 279 days in Portland. The Coast Range tempers the coastal winds and somewhat reduces the rainfall, but the climate of the valley is still essentially maritime much of the year. This means that it gets much less winter cold and less summer heat than zones east of the Cascades.

This zone also stretches north along the Columbia River between Portland and Longview, then up the Cowlitz River a few miles.

Average lows are similar to those of Zone 5 — even slightly colder in some places — but summer highs average 5° to 9°F/−15° to −13°C warmer, warm enough to put sugar in the 'Elberta' peaches and to speed the growth of such evergreens as abelia and nandina. The long, mild growing season has made the Willamette Valley one

Growing Fields for Trees

The Portland area's long growing season, deep soil, and pronounced winter chill make it nearly perfect for growing nursery stock. These young shade trees in view of Mount Hood *(below)* will be dug and shipped to nurseries all over the United States.

Coated with Ice

Ice on plants, caused by ice storms blowing into Portland from cold eastern areas, is sublimely beautiful. But its weight can break tree branches and flatten meadow grasses against the ground, as shown here.

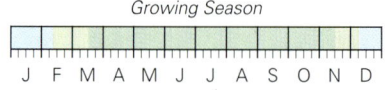

Growing Season

J F M A M J J A S O N D

of the West's best-known growing areas for berries, hazelnuts, and nursery stock. Many of the nation's fruit and shade trees, deciduous shrubs, and broad-leafed evergreens start life here.

Any mention of this zone must include roses and rhododendrons, both of which attain near-perfection here. Broad-leafed evergreens generally are at their best; choice azaleas and pieris join rhododendrons as the basic landscaping shrubs.

You'll encounter the zone's only anomaly east of Portland, where icy winter winds blow down out of the Columbia.

All in a Portland Dell

Rhododendrons are among the broad-leafed evergreens that mark Zone 6. They're shown off in Portland's Crystal Springs Rhododendron Garden *(above)*.

Western Oregon

See Page 24

Portland: Mild to Wild

In winter, when cold air builds east of the Cascades, winds can blast through Columbia Gorge at tree-ripping speed. They hit east Portland hard and usually curve south, sometimes icing up trees clear to Milwaukie. If you live in the Portland area east of Interstate 205, plant trees whose limbs bear up well in ice storms—for example, black walnut, ginkgo, linden, and sweet gum.

Vancouver
205
Columbia Gorge
Portland
Mt. Hood
Gresham
Mt. Scott
Milwaukie
Lake Oswego

WASHINGTON

Longview

Astoria

Seaside

Vancouver

Columbia River

Portland

Hood River

The Dalles

Garibaldi

Forest Grove

Milwaukie

Tillamook

Newburg

Mt. Hood

See Page 22

McMinnville

Willamette Valley Is Berry Country

The Willamette Valley is mild but sufficiently cool to make it one of the country's prime regions for growing boysenberries, blueberries, red raspberries, and such wine grapes as Chardonnay, Pinot Noir, and Riesling.

Lincoln City

Salem

Dallas

Newport

Albany

Corvallis

Waldport

Willamette River

Madras

OREGON

Florence

Redmond

Eugene

Springfield

Bend

Pacific Ocean

Reedsport

Drain

Cottage Grove

Oakridge

Coos Bay

Coquille

Roseburg

Bandon

Crater Lake

Port Orford

Rogue River

Upper Klamath Lake

Gold Beach

Grants Pass

Medford

Klamath Falls

Ashland

See Page 28

Brookings

CALIFORNIA

0   10   20   30 miles

Climate Zones

1   3   5 6 7   17

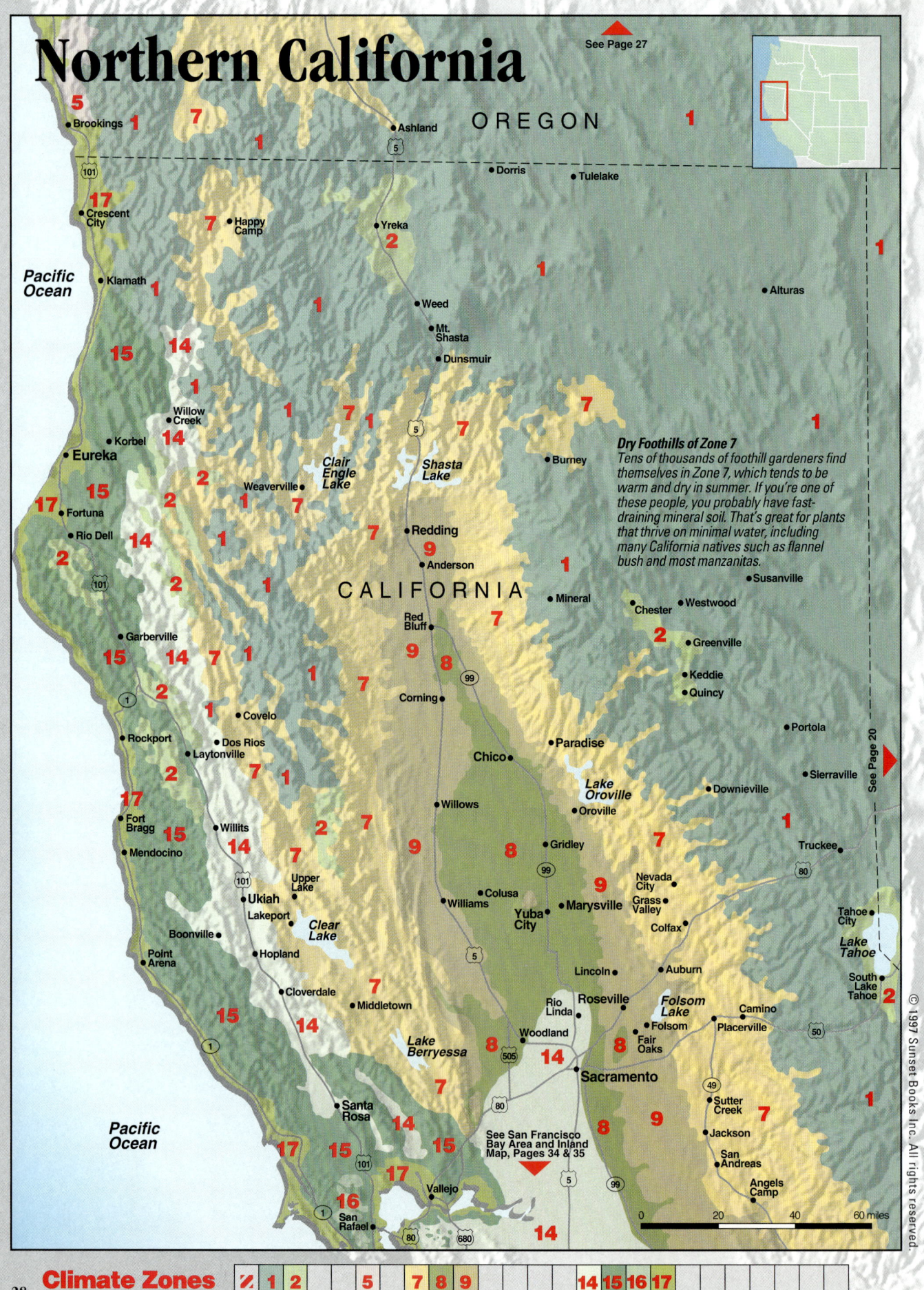

Northern California

See Page 27

OREGON

Pacific Ocean

CALIFORNIA

Pacific Ocean

Dry Foothills of Zone 7
Tens of thousands of foothill gardeners find themselves in Zone 7, which tends to be warm and dry in summer. If you're one of these people, you probably have fast-draining mineral soil. That's great for plants that thrive on minimal water, including many California natives such as flannel bush and most manzanitas.

See San Francisco Bay Area and Inland Map, Pages 34 & 35

See Page 20

Cities and towns labeled on the map: Brookings, Ashland, Crescent City, Dorris, Tulelake, Happy Camp, Yreka, Klamath, Weed, Alturas, Mt. Shasta, Dunsmuir, Willow Creek, Korbel, Eureka, Clair Engle Lake, Shasta Lake, Burney, Weaverville, Fortuna, Rio Dell, Redding, Anderson, Susanville, Chester, Westwood, Mineral, Garberville, Red Bluff, Greenville, Keddie, Quincy, Covelo, Corning, Rockport, Dos Rios, Laytonville, Chico, Paradise, Portola, Sierraville, Willows, Lake Oroville, Oroville, Gridley, Truckee, Fort Bragg, Willits, Mendocino, Nevada City, Grass Valley, Upper Lake, Ukiah, Colusa, Williams, Marysville, Colfax, Lakeport, Boonville, Clear Lake, Hopland, Yuba City, Tahoe City, Lake Tahoe, Point Arena, Cloverdale, Middletown, Lincoln, Auburn, South Lake Tahoe, Lake Berryessa, Woodland, Rio Linda, Roseville, Folsom Lake, Folsom, Camino, Placerville, Santa Rosa, Fair Oaks, Sacramento, Sutter Creek, Jackson, Vallejo, San Andreas, Angels Camp, San Rafael

Climate Zones

| 1 | 2 | 5 | 7 | 8 | 9 | 14 | 15 | 16 | 17 |

28

ZONE 7 California's Digger Pine Belt and Oregon's Rogue River Valley

At Home in the Foothills

Digger pines *(left)*, also called foothill or gray pines, mark much of Zone 7. Often you'll find them mixed with oaks, ponderosa pines, and even knobcone pines.

Zone 7 encompasses several thousand square miles in the regions west of the Sierra Nevada and Cascade ranges. Because of the influence of latitude, this climate is found at low elevations in a valley in Oregon (the Rogue Valley) but at middle elevations in California (the low mountains, most of which can be identified by native digger pines).

Hot summers and mild but pronounced winters give this area sharply defined seasons without severe winter cold or enervating humidity. The climate pleases plants that require a marked seasonal pattern to do well—peony, iris, lilac, and flowering cherry, for example. Deciduous fruit trees that require a marked seasonal pattern do well also; the region is noted for its pears, apples, peaches, and cherries.

Gardeners in a few spots around the San Francisco Bay will be surprised to find their gardens mapped in Zone 7, even though there isn't a digger pine to be seen. These are hilltop and ridge-top areas that are too high (and hence too cold in winter) to be included in milder Zones 15 and 16.

For such a big area, it is impossible to state exact low temperatures. But at weather-recording stations in Zone 7, the typical winter lows range from 23° to 9°F/ −5° to −13°C, and the record lows vary from 15° to −1°F/−9° to −18°C.

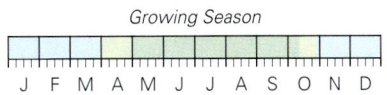
Growing Season
J F M A M J J A S O N D

Wild and Tamed Native Oaks

Valley oaks *(top)* dot grassy, rolling foothills in many parts of Zone 7. You can garden under native oaks if you limit your palette to plants that don't need summer water, such as airy grasses, sedges, and salvia *(above)*.

ZONE 8 Cold-Air Basins of California's Central Valley

Only a shade of difference exists between Zone 8 and Zone 9, but it's an important difference—crucial in some cases. Zone 9 is a thermal belt, meaning that cold air can flow from it to lower ground—and that lower ground is found here in Zone 8. Citrus furnish the most meaningful illustration. Lemons, oranges, and grapefruit, which flourish in Zone 9, cannot be grown commercially in Zone 8 because the winter nights are frequently cold enough to injure the fruit or the trees; the trees would need regular heating to deliver decent crops. The same winter cold can damage many garden plants.

Zone 8 differs from Zone 14, which it joins near the latitudes of north Sacramento and Modesto, in that Zone 14 occasionally gets some marine influence. Low temperatures in Zone 8 over a 20-year period ranged from 29° to 13°F/−2° to −11°C. Certain features that Zones 8 and 9 share are described under Zone 9.

Orchard Country

Cold air rolls off Zone 9 hillsides on winter nights and pools in the colder flatlands—Zone 8—below. Fruit trees that need chill, like these apple trees near Winters, grow best in the valleys.

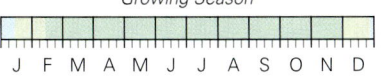
Growing Season
J F M A M J J A S O N D

ZONE 9 — Thermal Belts of California's Central Valley

As cited in the description of Zone 8, the biggest readily apparent difference between Zones 8 and 9 is that Zone 9, a thermal belt, is a safer climate for citrus than Zone 8, which is a cold-air basin. The same distinction, thermal belt versus cold-air basin, determines which species and varieties—hibiscus, melaleuca, pittosporum, and other plants—are recommended for Zone 9 but not for Zone 8.

Zones 8 and 9 have the following features in common: summer daytime temperatures are high, sunshine is almost constant during the growing season, and growing seasons are long. Deciduous fruits and vegetables of nearly every kind thrive in these long, hot summers; winter cold is just adequate to satisfy the dormancy requirements of the fruit trees. Fiercely cold, piercing north winds blow for several days at a time in winter, but they are more distressing to gardeners than to garden plants. You can minimize them with windbreaks.

Tule fogs (dense fogs that rise from the ground on cold, clear nights) appear and stay for hours or days during winter. The fogs usually hug the ground at night and rise to 800 to 1,000 feet by afternoon.

In the West, heat-loving plants such as oleander and crape myrtle perform at their peak in Zones 8 and 9 (and 14). Plants that like summer coolness and humidity demand some fussing; careful gardeners accommodate them by providing filtered shade from tall trees and plenty of moisture. In Zone 9, winter lows over a 20-year period ranged from 28° to 18°F/−2° to −8°C.

J F M A M J J A S O N D

For Zones 10 to 13—an area that includes the Southwest deserts, plus parts of Kansas, Oklahoma, and Texas—turn to pages 45–47.

True Heat-Lovers

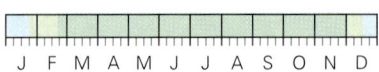

Oleanders thrive in the heat of Zones 8 and 9. But they don't do well where winter temperatures regularly plummet, preferring climates moderated by marine air.

The Tule Fog

Zone 9 hills rise into the clear air above the fog-shrouded flatlands of surrounding Zone 8. In winter, dense tule fogs can blanket both Zones 8 and 9 by afternoon, closing roads throughout the Central Valley. The picture above was taken near Bakersfield.

Central California

See Page 28

Mono Lake

14

See San Francisco Bay Area and Inland Map, Pages 34 & 35

580

Modesto

99

9

7

2

See Page 20

San Jose

280

15

15

7

Coyote

9

8

Mariposa

1

17

7

Felton

7

Morgan Hill

5

Merced

9

7

Santa Cruz

Gilroy

14

Watsonville

15

Los Banos

Chowchilla

Madera

9

7

Hollister

Dos Palos

Mendota

Herndon

Monterey Bay

16

14

7

Fresno

Sanger

Salinas

15

9

7

Monterey

16

15

9

8

Kingsburg

Soledad

15

99

Visalia

14

Hanford

1

Big Sur

7

King City

7

Tulare

7

Lindsay

San Ardo

Coalinga

8

Porterville

Bradley

9

Avenal

Central Valley—Apples with Oranges
Rich soils, a long and warm growing season, and a pronounced but mild winter make this a great food-growing region. From apples to oranges, nearly everything is possible.

16

Delano

9

See Page 44

17

San Simeon

Cambria

7

1

7

16

15

Atascadero

9

Wasco

Morro Bay

7

5

Bakersfield

1

San Luis Obispo

16

9

58

7

15

Pismo Beach

Taft

8

99

Tehachapi

Arroyo Grande

14

Nipomo

7

Maricopa

9

1

Pacific Ocean

17

3

3

11

15

Santa Maria

2

Lebec

16

1

18

15

Lompoc

14

2

3

5

Buellton

Santa Ynez

Solvang

16

23

18

Santa Barbara

20

Ojai

See Los Angeles and Inland Map, Pages 38 & 39

24

Carpinteria

21

Ventura

23

19

20

Oxnard

22

Malibu

Channel Islands

24

24

0   10   20   30 miles

Climate Zones 1 2 3 7 8 9 11 14 15 16 17 18 19 20 21 22 23 24

31

ZONE 14
Northern California's Inland Areas with Some Ocean Influence

Marine air moderates parts of Zone 14 that otherwise would be colder in winter and hotter in summer. The gap in Northern California's Coast Ranges created by San Francisco and San Pablo bays allows marine air to spill much farther inland than it can anywhere else. The same thing happens, but the penetration is not as deep, in the Salinas Valley. Zone 14 also includes the cold-winter valley floors, canyons, and land troughs in the Coast Ranges from Santa Barbara County to Mendocino County.

The milder-winter, marine-influenced areas in Zone 14 and the cold-winter inland valleys within Zone 14 differ in humidity. For example, lowland parts of Contra Costa County are more humid than Sacramento.

Fruits that need winter chilling do well here, as do shrubs needing summer heat (oleander, gardenia). Over a 20-year period, this area had lows ranging from 26° to 16°F/−3° to −9°C. Weather bureau records show all-time lows ranging from 20° to 11°F/−7° to −12°C.

Perfect for Vineyards

Vineyards blanket much of the land in Napa and Sonoma counties, producing hefty crops for wineries. The valley floors here are designated Zone 14.

Growing Season

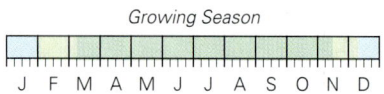

J F M A M J J A S O N D

ZONE 15
Chilly Winters Along the Coast Range

Zones 15 and 16 are areas of Central and Northern California that are influenced by marine air approximately 85 percent of the time and by inland air 15 percent of the time. Note that although Zone 16 is within the Northern California coastal climate area, its winters are milder because the areas in this zone are in thermal belts (explained on page 29). The cold-winter areas that make up Zone 15 lie in cold-air basins, on hilltops above the thermal belts, or far enough north that plant performance dictates a Zone 15 designation.

Many plants recommended for Zone 15 are not suggested for Zone 14 because they must have a moister atmosphere, cooler summers, milder winter weather, or all three conditions. But Zone 15 still receives enough winter chilling to favor some cold-winter specialties, such as herbaceous peonies.

Most of this zone gets a nagging afternoon wind in summer. Trees and dense shrubs planted on the windward side of a garden can disperse it, and a neighborhood full of trees can successfully keep it above the rooftops. Low temperatures over a 20-year period ranged from 28° to 21°F/−2° to −6°C, and record lows range from 26° to 16°F/−3° to −9°C.

Plenty of Moist Air, but Dry Air, Too

Zone 15 is moist enough for coast redwoods *(above left)* to thrive. Yet it's warm and dry enough to grow agave and cacti *(left)*. Both plantings were photographed at Sunset's Menlo Park headquarters; the redwoods, now towering more than 80 feet tall, were planted in 1952 from 7-gallon cans.

Growing Season

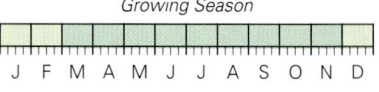

J F M A M J J A S O N D

ZONE 16 Central and Northern California Coast Thermal Belts

This benign climate exists in patches and strips along the Coast Ranges from western Santa Barbara County north to northern Marin County. It's one of Northern California's finest horticultural climates. It consists of thermal belts (slopes from which cold air drains) in the coastal climate area, which is dominated by ocean weather about 85 percent of the time and by inland weather about 15 percent.

Typical lows in Zone 16 over a 20-year period ranged from 32° to 19°F/0° to −7°C. The lowest recorded temperatures range from 25° to 18°F/−4° to −8°C. This zone gets more heat in summer than Zone 17, which is dominated by maritime air, and has warmer winters than Zone 15. That's a happy combination for gardening.

A summer afternoon wind is an integral part of this climate. Plant trees and shrubs on the windward side of your garden to help disperse it.

Growing Season

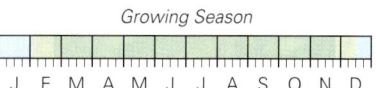

J F M A M J J A S O N D

Warm Slopes with a View

Parts of Zone 16, such as the Oakland-Berkeley hills *(left)*, practically never see a white frost. This zone gets more heat in summer than Zone 17 and has warmer winters than Zone 15—great for subtropicals like ginger lily *(below)*.

ZONE 17 Marine Effects in Northern California

The climate in this zone features cool, wet, almost frostless winters and cool summers with frequent fog or wind. The fog tends to come in high and fast, creating a cooling, humidifying blanket between the sun and the earth, reducing the intensity of the light and sunshine. Some heat-loving plants (citrus, hibiscus, gardenia) don't get enough heat to fruit or flower reliably.

In a 20-year period, the lowest winter temperatures in Zone 17 ranged from 36° to 23°F/2° to −5°C. The lowest temperatures on record range from 30° to 20°F/ −1° to −7°C. Of further interest in this heat-starved climate are the highs of summer, normally in the 60° to 75°F/16° to 24°C range. The average highest temperature of 12 weather stations in Zone 17 is only 97°F/36°C. In all the other Northern California climate zones, average highest temperatures on record are in the 104° to 116°F/40° to 47°C range.

Growing Season

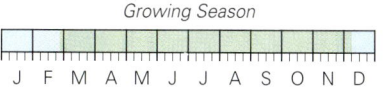

J F M A M J J A S O N D

Smell the Sea, See the Aloes

Zone 17's climate is dominated by the ocean about 98 percent of the time. You can see salt water from most areas in Zone 17, such as Pacific Grove, where mounding aloes and agaves with tall flower spikes bloom at the water's edge. This climate also favors fuchsias and commercially grown artichokes, Brussels sprouts, and Easter lilies.

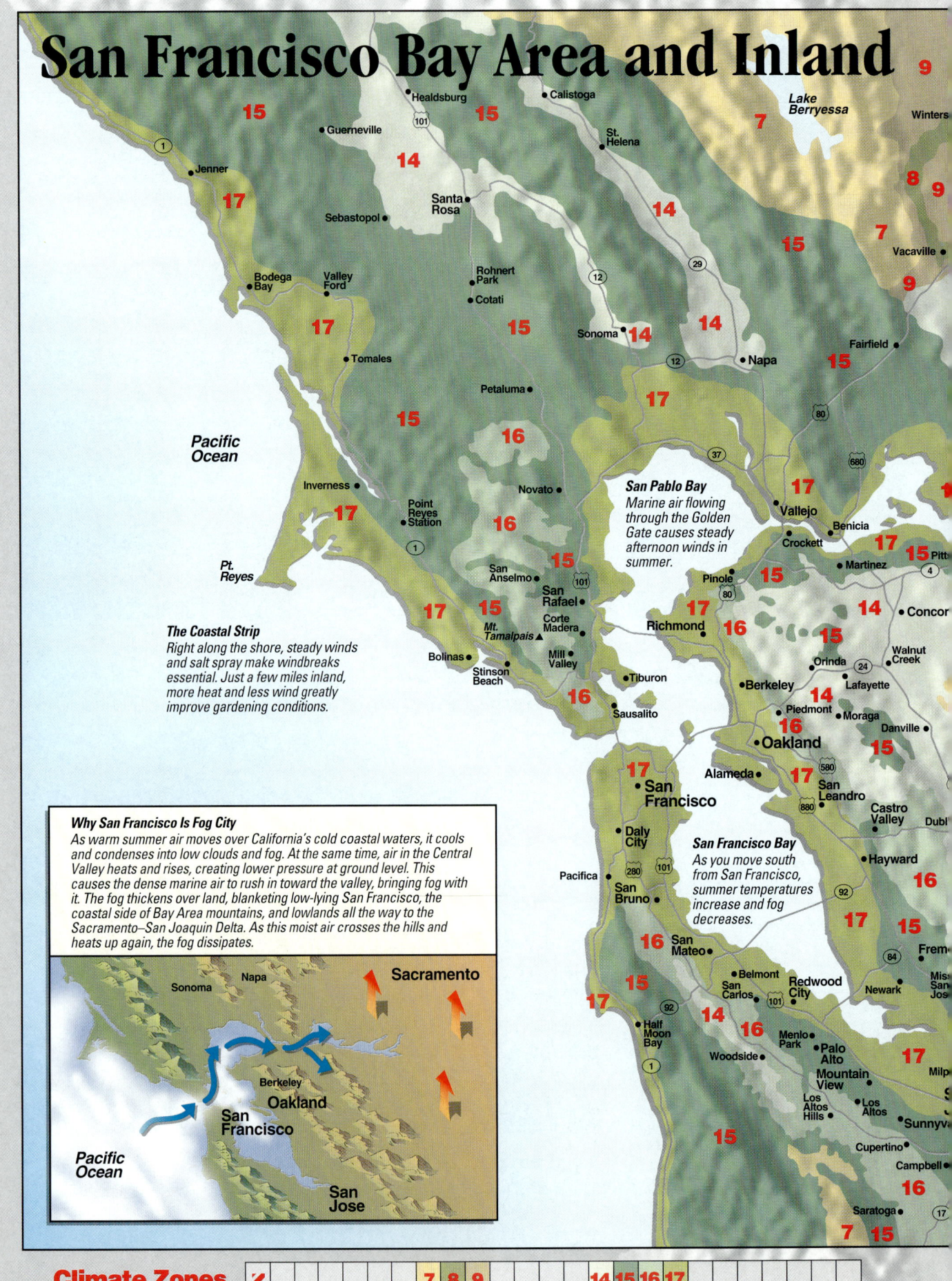

San Francisco Bay Area and Inland

Pacific Ocean

San Pablo Bay
Marine air flowing through the Golden Gate causes steady afternoon winds in summer.

The Coastal Strip
Right along the shore, steady winds and salt spray make windbreaks essential. Just a few miles inland, more heat and less wind greatly improve gardening conditions.

Why San Francisco Is Fog City
As warm summer air moves over California's cold coastal waters, it cools and condenses into low clouds and fog. At the same time, air in the Central Valley heats and rises, creating lower pressure at ground level. This causes the dense marine air to rush in toward the valley, bringing fog with it. The fog thickens over land, blanketing low-lying San Francisco, the coastal side of Bay Area mountains, and lowlands all the way to the Sacramento–San Joaquin Delta. As this moist air crosses the hills and heats up again, the fog dissipates.

San Francisco Bay
As you move south from San Francisco, summer temperatures increase and fog decreases.

Pacific Ocean

Sacramento
Sonoma
Napa
Berkeley
Oakland
San Francisco
San Jose

Map labels and climate zone numbers:

Healdsburg, Calistoga, Lake Berryessa, 9, Winters, 15, 15, Guerneville, 14, 7, St. Helena, Jenner, 17, Santa Rosa, 8, 9, Sebastopol, 14, 7, Vacaville, Bodega Bay, Valley Ford, Rohnert Park, Cotati, 15, 9, Tomales, 17, 15, Sonoma, 14, 14, Fairfield, 15, Napa, 15, Petaluma, 17, 16, Inverness, Novato, 80, 17, Point Reyes Station, 16, Vallejo, Benicia, Crockett, 17, 15, Pitts, Pt. Reyes, San Anselmo, 15, Pinole, 15, Martinez, 4, San Rafael, Corte Madera, 17, 16, 14, Concor, 17, 15, Bolinas, Mt. Tamalpais, Mill Valley, Richmond, 15, Walnut Creek, Stinson Beach, Tiburon, Orinda, Lafayette, 16, Sausalito, Berkeley, 14, Piedmont, Moraga, Danville, 16, Oakland, 15, 17, San Francisco, Alameda, 17, San Leandro, Castro Valley, Dubl, Daly City, 16, Hayward, Pacifica, San Bruno, 17, 15, 16, San Mateo, Belmont, San Carlos, Redwood City, Newark, Frem, 17, 14, 16, Menlo Park, Palo Alto, Milp, Half Moon Bay, Woodside, Mountain View, 17, Los Altos Hills, Los Altos, Sunnyva, 15, Cupertino, Campbell, 16, Saratoga, 7, 15

Climate Zones   7 8 9   14 15 16 17

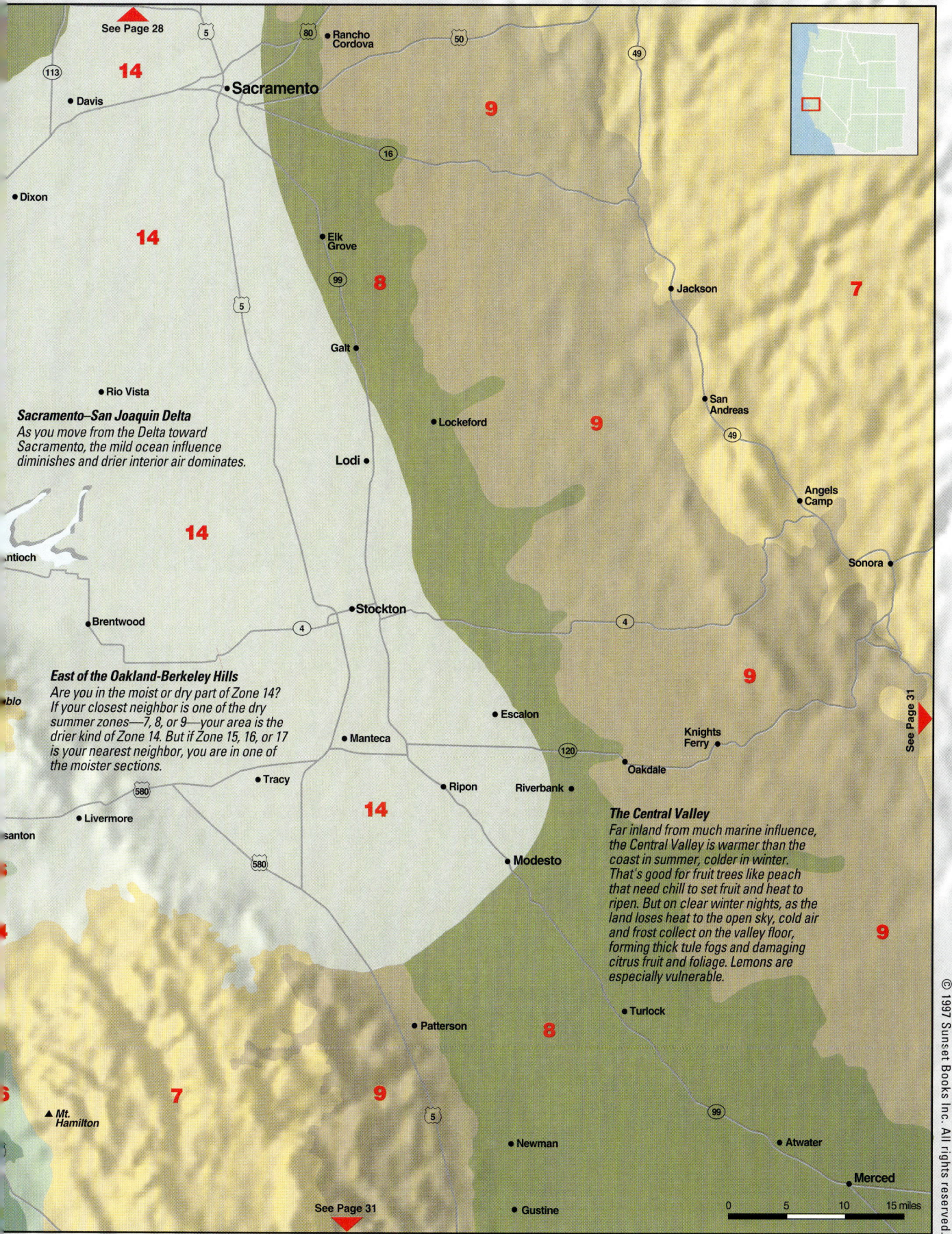

113

14

• Davis

• Dixon

5

80

• Rancho Cordova

50

Sacramento

49

9

16

• Elk Grove

99

8

• Jackson

7

• Galt

• Rio Vista

Sacramento–San Joaquin Delta
As you move from the Delta toward Sacramento, the mild ocean influence diminishes and drier interior air dominates.

• Lockeford

9

• San Andreas

49

• Angels Camp

5

• Lodi

ntioch

14

• Sonora

• Brentwood

4

Stockton

4

East of the Oakland-Berkeley Hills
Are you in the moist or dry part of Zone 14? If your closest neighbor is one of the dry summer zones—7, 8, or 9—your area is the drier kind of Zone 14. But if Zone 15, 16, or 17 is your nearest neighbor, you are in one of the moister sections.

9

ablo

• Escalon

• Manteca

Knights Ferry

See Page 31

120

• Oakdale

• Tracy

580

• Ripon

Riverbank

The Central Valley
Far inland from much marine influence, the Central Valley is warmer than the coast in summer, colder in winter. That's good for fruit trees like peach that need chill to set fruit and heat to ripen. But on clear winter nights, as the land loses heat to the open sky, cold air and frost collect on the valley floor, forming thick tule fogs and damaging citrus fruit and foliage. Lemons are especially vulnerable.

• Livermore

14

santon

580

• Modesto

9

6

7

▲ Mt. Hamilton

• Turlock

8

• Patterson

9

5

• Newman

99

• Atwater

Merced

See Page 31

• Gustine

0   5   10   15 miles

35

ZONE 18 Above and Below the Thermal Belts in Southern California's Interior Valleys

Zones 18 and 19 are classified as interior climates. This means that the major influence on climate is the continental air mass; the ocean determines the climate no more than 15 percent of the time.

Many of the valley floors of Zone 18 were once regions where apricot, peach, apple, and walnut orchards flourished, but the orchards have now given way to homes. Although the climate supplies enough winter chill for some plants that need it, it is not too cold for many of the hardier subtropicals like cymbidiums. It is too hot, too cold, and too dry for fuchsias but cold enough for tree peonies and many apple varieties, and mild enough for a number of avocado varieties. Zone 18 never supplied much commercial citrus (frosty nights called for too much heating), but home gardeners who can tolerate occasional minor fruit loss can grow citrus here.

Over a 20-year period, winter lows ranged from 28° to 10°F/−2° to −12°C. The all-time lows recorded in Zone 18 range from 22° to 7°F/−6° to −14°C.

Growing Season

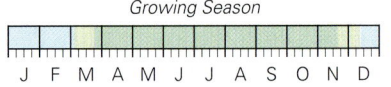

J F M A M J J A S O N D

Chilly Hilltops and Valleys

Zone 18 hilltops, like this one laced with houses, get more cold in winter and warmth in summer than the thermal belts (slopes and hillsides from which cold air drains) that make up Zone 19. Hilltops and cold-air basins get frost, thermal belts don't.

ZONE 19 Thermal Belts Around Southern California's Interior Valleys

Like that of Zone 18, the climate in this zone is little influenced by the ocean. Both zones, then, have a poor climate for such plants as fuchsias, rhododendrons, and tuberous begonias. Many sections of Zone 19 have always been prime citrus country—especially for those kinds that need extra summer heat in order to grow sweet fruit. Likewise, macadamia nuts and most avocados can be grown here.

The A to Z Plant Encyclopedia cites many ornamental plants for Zone 19 that are not

The Southland's Warm Slopes

Douglas iris, California poppies, and yellow meadowfoam splash the landscape with spring color at Rancho Santa Ana Botanic Garden in warm, dry Claremont, California. This garden also contains a wealth of evergreen natives, including ceanothus and manzanitas, that remain unscathed when winter temperatures drop into the 20s.

recommended for Zone 18, because of the milder winters in Zone 19. Plants that grow here, but not in Zone 18, include bougainvillea, several kinds of coral tree (*Erythrina*), livistona palms, Mexican blue and San Jose hesper palms (*Brahea armata, B. brandegeei*), giant Burmese honeysuckle, *Myoporum laetum*, several of the more tender pittosporums, and lady palm (*Rhapis excelsa*).

Winter lows over a 20-year period ranged from 27° to 22°F/−3° to −6°C, and the all-time lows measured at different weather stations range from 23° to 17°F/−5° to −8°C. Note that these are considerably higher than the temperatures in neighboring Zone 18.

Growing Season

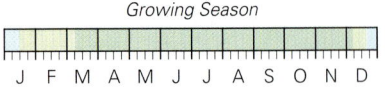

J F M A M J J A S O N D

ZONE 20   Cool Winters in Southern California's Sections of Occasional Ocean Influence

In Zones 20 and 21, the same relative pattern prevails as in Zones 18 and 19. The even-numbered zone is the climate made up of cold-air basins and hilltops, and the odd-numbered one comprises thermal belts. The difference is that Zones 20 and 21 get weather influenced by both maritime air and interior air. In these transitional areas, climate boundaries often move 20 miles in 24 hours with the movements of these air masses.

Because of the greater ocean influence, this climate supports a wide variety of plants. You can see the range of them at the Los Angeles State and County Arboretum in Arcadia. Winter lows over a 20-year period ranged from 28° to 23°F/−2° to −5°C. Record lows range from 21° to 14°F/−6° to −10°C.

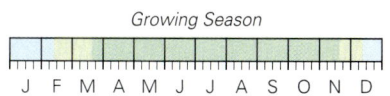

Growing Season

J F M A M J J A S O N D

Caution: Colliding Air Masses

In Zone 20 (but bordering Zone 21), the Los Angeles Arboretum is influenced by both marine and interior air. The result: everything from birches to palms grows here, as do relatively tender tropical trees like jacaranda, Moreton Bay fig, and tabebuia.

ZONE 21   Thermal Belts in Southern California's Sections of Occasional Ocean Influence

Where Oranges Meet Lilacs

Cold air drains from slopes above the Santa Clarita River near Moorpark, California, making them perfect for growing oranges *(left)*. Thermal belts such as these make it possible to grow plants in Zone 21 that would be too tender for Zone 20. Zone 21 is just cold enough for some lilacs. Varieties bred to grow and bloom with less winter chill than most lilacs require grow at Descanso Gardens in La Cañada–Flintridge *(below)*.

The combination of weather influences described for Zone 20 applies to Zone 21 as well. Your garden can be in ocean air or a high fog one day and in a mass of interior air (perhaps a drying Santa Ana wind from the desert) the next day.

Because temperatures never dip very far below 30°F/−1°C, this is fine citrus-growing country. At the same time, it's also the mildest zone that gets enough winter chilling for most forms of lilacs and certain other plants.

Over a 20-year period, winter lows at the weather-recording stations in Zone 21 ranged from 36° to 23°F/2°to−5°C. Record lows range from 27° to 17°F/−3° to −8°C.

Growing Season

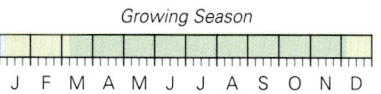

J F M A M J J A S O N D

Los Angeles and Inland

See Page 31

3

18

18

21

23

24

20 • Ojai

Santa
Barbara •

101

• Carpinteria

23

Saticoy •

Santa
Paula •

126

21

20

Fillmore •

21

18

19

Moorpark •

21

118

118 • Somis

Simi
Valley •

18

Thousan
Oaks •

23

• Ventura

24

101

Camarillo •

23

20

21

• Oxnard

1

22

23

*Pacific
Ocean*

Pacific Coast Highway

24

The Coast: Great for Fuchsias
*Coastal fogs and mild weather make
Zone 24 Southern California's best
fuchsia and tuberous begonia climate.
Scores of less well known plants from
Chile, New Zealand, the Canary Islands,
and the moister parts of South Africa do
well here for the same reason.*

Tracking the Santa Anas
*Every fall and winter, the Santa Ana wind revs up as the interior's cold,
heavy air flows downhill toward the Southern California coast. As this
air loses elevation, it compresses, heats up, dries out, and roars fero-
ciously through the passes behind Los Angeles and San Bernardino.
Cajon Pass and Soledad Canyon are two main routes, although the
wind is named for Santa Ana Canyon. When the Santa Ana wind hits
the Los Angeles basin, it's so hot and dry that it desiccates plants.
Sprinklers, windbreaks, and row covers help protect them. Santa Anas
usually play out near the coast, though sometimes they blow clear to
Santa Catalina Island. They reach as far north as Oxnard and as far
south as San Diego.*

Climate Zones

| 2 | 3 | | | | | | | | 11 | | | | | | 18 | 19 | 20 | 21 | 22 | 23 | 24 |

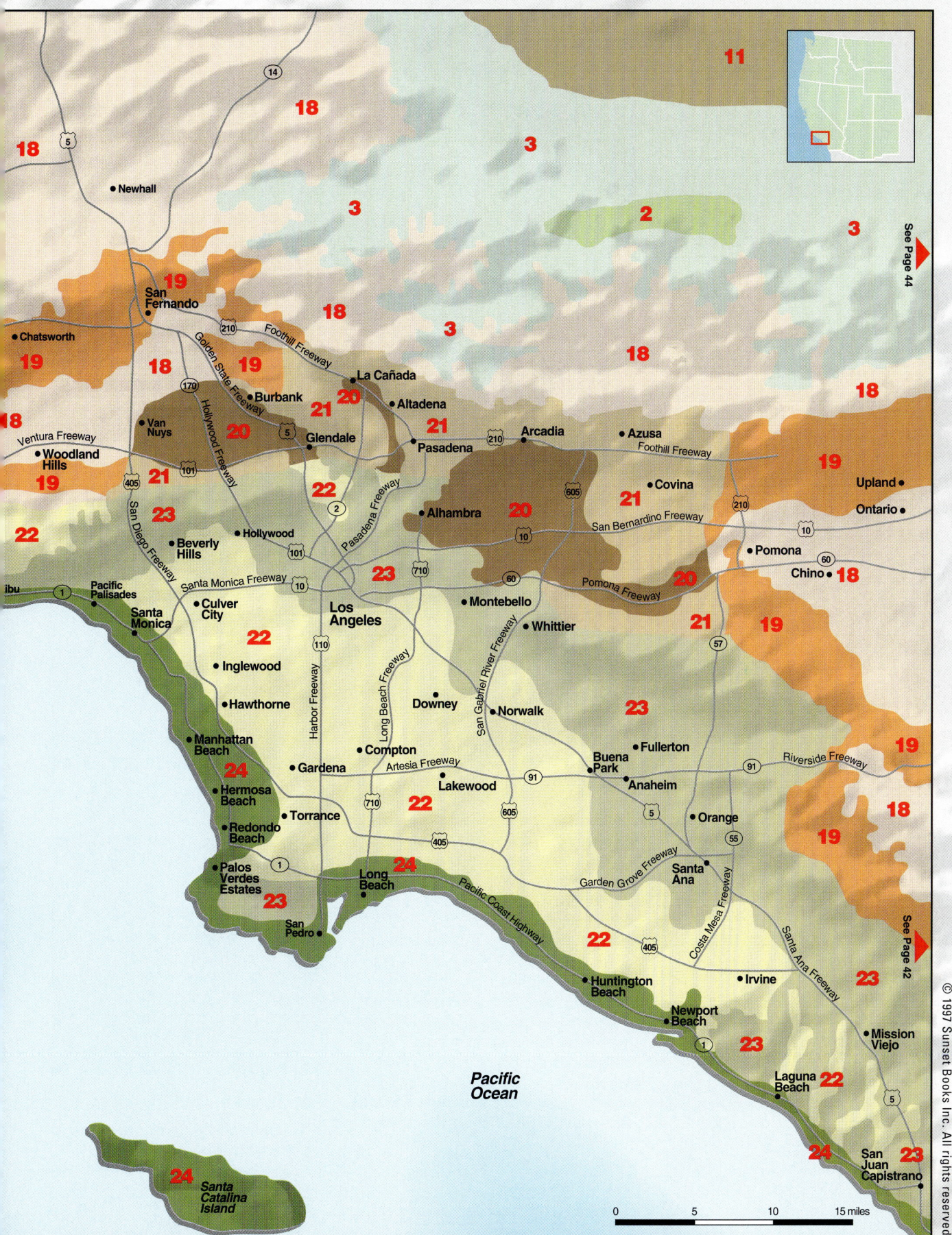

11

18

18

5

● Newhall

3

3

14

2

See Page 44

3

18

19
San
Fernando

● Chatsworth

18

210   Foothill Freeway

18

Golden State Freeway

19   19

La Cañada

18

19   18   170
Burbank   20   ● Altadena
21
Van Nuys   5   21
20   Glendale   610 Arcadia   ● Azusa
Hollywood Freeway   Pasadena   Foothill Freeway   18

● Woodland
Hills   19

101   ● Covina   19   Upland ●

22   21   22   605   21   210   Ontario ●

8

Ventura Freeway

San Diego Freeway   23   Hollywood   2   ● Alhambra   20   San Bernardino Freeway   ● Pomona   10
Beverly   10   60   Pomona Freeway   20   Chino ● 18
Hills   23   710   60   21

22

Santa Monica Freeway

Pacific
Palisades   ● Culver
City   Los
Angeles   ● Montebello   19
Santa
Monica   22   ● Whittier

Harbor Freeway   110   57

● Inglewood   23

● Hawthorne   Downey   ● Norwalk

San Gabriel River Freeway

● Manhattan   ● Gardena   Compton   Buena   ● Fullerton   19
Beach   24   Artesia Freeway   Park   ● Anaheim   91   Riverside Freeway   19
● Hermosa   Lakewood   91   ● Orange   18
Beach   710   22   605   825
● Redondo   405   ● Orange   55   19
Beach   1   Long   24   Garden Grove Freeway   Santa   18
Palos   Beach   Ana   ● Irvine
Verdes   Pacific Coast Highway   Costa Mesa Freeway   22
Estates   23   San   405   Santa Ana Freeway   23   See Page 42
Pedro   Huntington
Beach   Newport
Beach   23   ● Mission
Viejo

Pacific
Ocean   22   405   Laguna
Beach   22   5

24   23
San
Juan
Capistrano

24
Santa
Catalina
Island

0   5   10   15 miles

ZONE 22 — Cold-Winter Portions of Southern California's Coastal Climate

Areas falling in Zone 22 have a coastal climate (they are influenced by the ocean approximately 85 percent of the time). When temperatures drop in winter, these cold-air basins or hilltops above the air-drained slopes have lower winter temperatures than those in neighboring Zone 23.

Actually, the winters are so mild here that lows seldom fall below 28°F/−2°C. Annual winter lows recorded over 20 years ranged from 24° to 21°F/−4° to −6°C.

Gardeners who plant under overhangs or tree canopies can grow subtropical plants that would otherwise be burned by a rare frost. Such plants include bananas, tree ferns, and the like. The lack of a pronounced chilling period during the winter limits the use of such deciduous woody plants as flowering cherry and lilac. Many herbaceous perennials from colder regions fail here because the winters are too warm for them to go dormant.

Growing Season

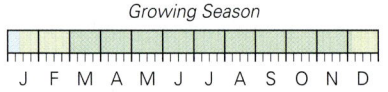

J F M A M J J A S O N D

Orange County's Coastal Canyons

Coastal canyons—narrow, steep-sided valleys that jut inland from the coast—are numerous in Orange County. The canyon floors, where cold air settles in winter, are in Zone 22, while the higher ground on either side falls into warmer Zone 23. Plants that thrive on the slopes can freeze in the canyon below.

ZONE 23 — Thermal Belts of Southern California's Coastal Climate

One of the most favored areas in North America for growing subtropical plants, Zone 23 has always been Southern California's best zone for avocados. Frosts don't amount to much here, because 85 percent of the time, Pacific Ocean weather dominates; interior air rules only 15 percent of the time. A notorious portion of this 15 percent consists of those days when hot, dry Santa Ana winds blow.

Zone 23 lacks either the summer heat or the winter cold necessary to grow pears, most apples, and most peaches. But it enjoys more heat than Zone 24. Gardenias and oleanders, for example, grow and flower more lustily here than in Zone 24.

Temperatures are mild here, but severe winters descend at times, resulting in a surprising spread of minimum temperatures. Over a 20-year period, lows ranged from 38° to 23°F/3° to −5°C. Record lows range from 28° to 23°F/−2° to −5°C.

Growing Season

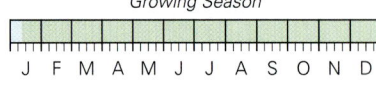

J F M A M J J A S O N D

The Avocado Belt

Delectable avocados *(above)* are a prime commercial crop in Zone 23, where the benign climate suits them perfectly. Cacti and fountain grass get plenty of sun in this garden in the Hollywood Hills *(far left)*, and more warmth than they would in Zone 24.

ZONE 24 Marine Influence Along the Southern California Coast

Stretched along Southern California's beaches, this climate zone is almost completely dominated by the ocean. Where the beach runs along high cliffs or palisades, Zone 24 extends only to that barrier. But where hills are low or nonexistent, it runs inland several miles.

This zone has a mild marine climate (milder than Northern California's maritime Zone 17), because south of Point Conception, the Pacific is comparatively warm. The winters are mild, the summers cool, and the air seldom really dry. On many days, the sun doesn't break through the high overcast until afternoon. Very tender plants like fuchsias find a good home here; they get along fine with only moderate summer heat. In this climate, gardens that include such plants as figs, rubber trees, and schefferas can become jungles.

Morning Coastal Fogs

In summer, high fog is one of Zone 24's regular features, rolling in off the ocean in the morning and burning off during the day *(below)***. It stretches the season for wildflowers, like these California poppies dotting a meadow at Santa Barbara Botanic Garden.**

Zone 24 is coldest at the mouths of canyons that channel cold air down from the mountains on clear winter nights. Several such canyons between Laguna Beach and San Clemente are visible on the map. Numerous smaller ones touch the coast between San Clemente and the Mexican border. Partly because of the unusually low temperatures created by this canyon action, the range of winter lows in Zone 24 is broader than you might think. In a 20-year period, lows ranged from 44° to 24°F/7° to −4°C. The all-time record lows range from 33° to 20°F/1° to −7°C. In other words, some weather stations in Zone 24 have never recorded a freezing temperature.

The all-time high temperatures here help define the total climate, but they aren't greatly significant in terms of plant growth. The average all-time high in Zone 24 is 105°F/41°C. Compare this with temperatures of Northern California's marine climate, Zone 17, which average 97°F/36°C, and Southern California's inland climates—Zone 22 at 111°F/44°C, Zone 20 at 114°F/46°C, and Zone 18 at 115°F/46°C.

Growing Season

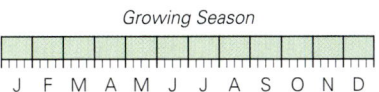

J F M A M J J A S O N D

Southern California Classic

At its best in frost-free Zone 24, bougainvillea can grow rampantly where conditions are good *(above)***. This one competes for light, heat, and space with an ornamental asparagus. Both can thrive here on rainfall alone.**

San Diego and Environs

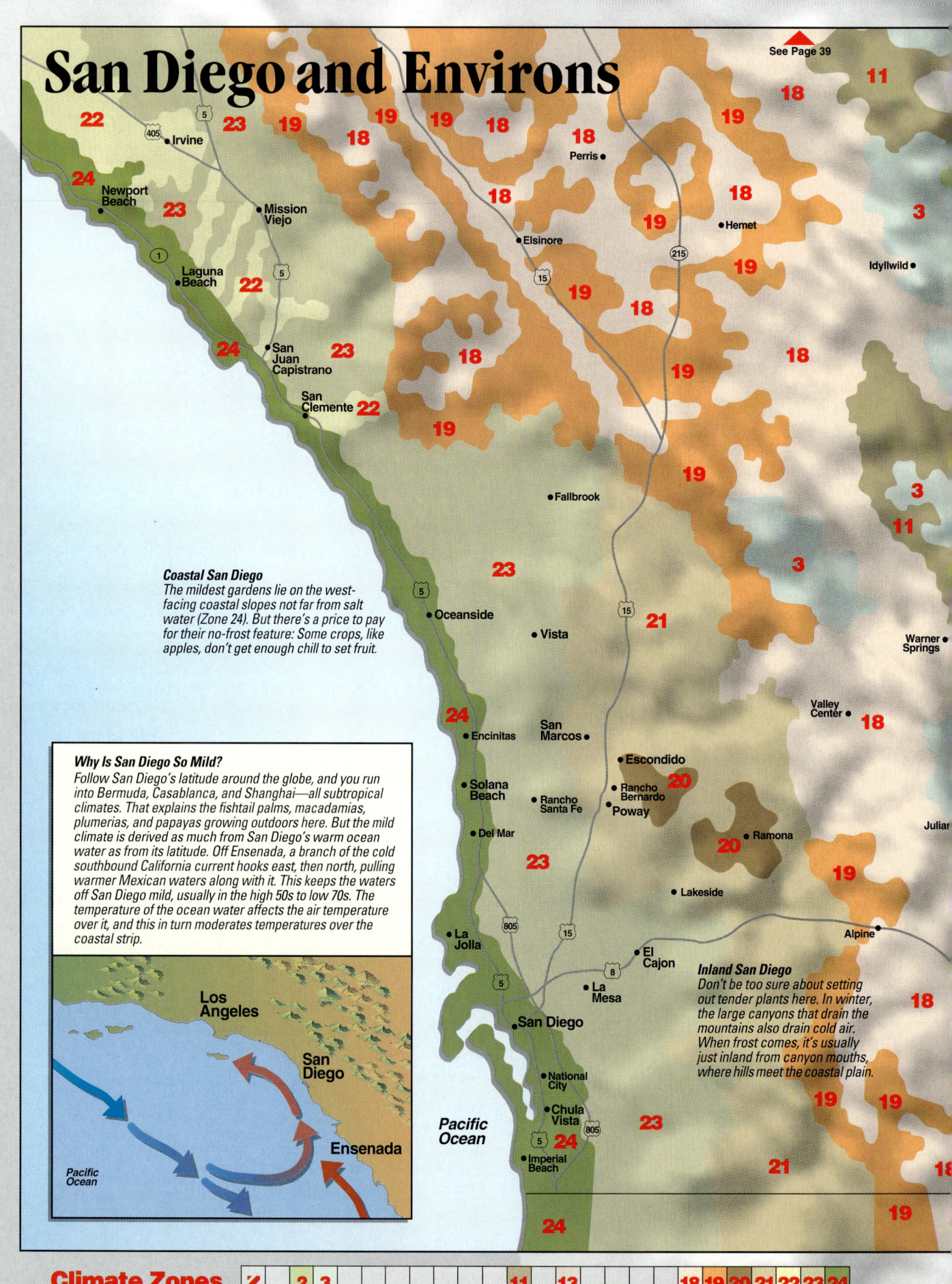

See Page 39

11
18
22   23   19   19   19   18   18   19
                                              Perris   18   3
24
Newport   18
Beach   23   Mission   Hemet
              Viejo   18   Idyllwild
                            Elsinore   19
                                                              19
Laguna
Beach   22   19   18
                                                              18
24   San
      Juan   23   18
      Capistrano   19
      San   18
      Clemente   22
                            19   3

                                                    19   3
                                                                  11
                                        Fallbrook

Coastal San Diego
The mildest gardens lie on the west-
facing coastal slopes not far from salt
water (Zone 24). But there's a price to pay
for their no-frost feature: Some crops, like
apples, don't get enough chill to set fruit.

                  23   3
            Oceanside   21   Warner
                        Vista   Springs

                                                    Valley
24   Center   18
Encinitas   San
              Marcos   Escondido
                                          20
Why Is San Diego So Mild?   Rancho
Follow San Diego's latitude around the globe, and you run   Solana   Bernardo
into Bermuda, Casablanca, and Shanghai—all subtropical   Beach   Rancho   Poway
climates. That explains the fishtail palms, macadamias,   Santa Fe
plumerias, and papayas growing outdoors here. But the mild   Del Mar   20   Ramona
climate is derived as much from San Diego's warm ocean
water as from its latitude. Off Ensenada, a branch of the cold   23
southbound California current hooks east, then north, pulling   Lakeside   19
warmer Mexican waters along with it. This keeps the waters
off San Diego mild, usually in the high 50s to low 70s. The   La
temperature of the ocean water affects the air temperature   Jolla   Alpine
over it, and this in turn moderates temperatures over the
coastal strip.   El
                                          Cajon   **Inland San Diego**
                                          La   Don't be too sure about setting
                                          Mesa   out tender plants here. In winter,
                                          San Diego   the large canyons that drain the
                                                    mountains also drain cold air.
                                                    When frost comes, it's usually
                                                    just inland from canyon mouths,
                                          National   where hills meet the coastal plain.   18
                                          City
Los   Chula
Angeles   Vista   19   19
              San
              Diego   **Pacific**   23
                      Ocean
              Ensenada   24   21   18
Pacific
Ocean   Imperial
                      Beach   19

                            24

Climate Zones   2   3   11   13   18 19 20 21 22 23 24

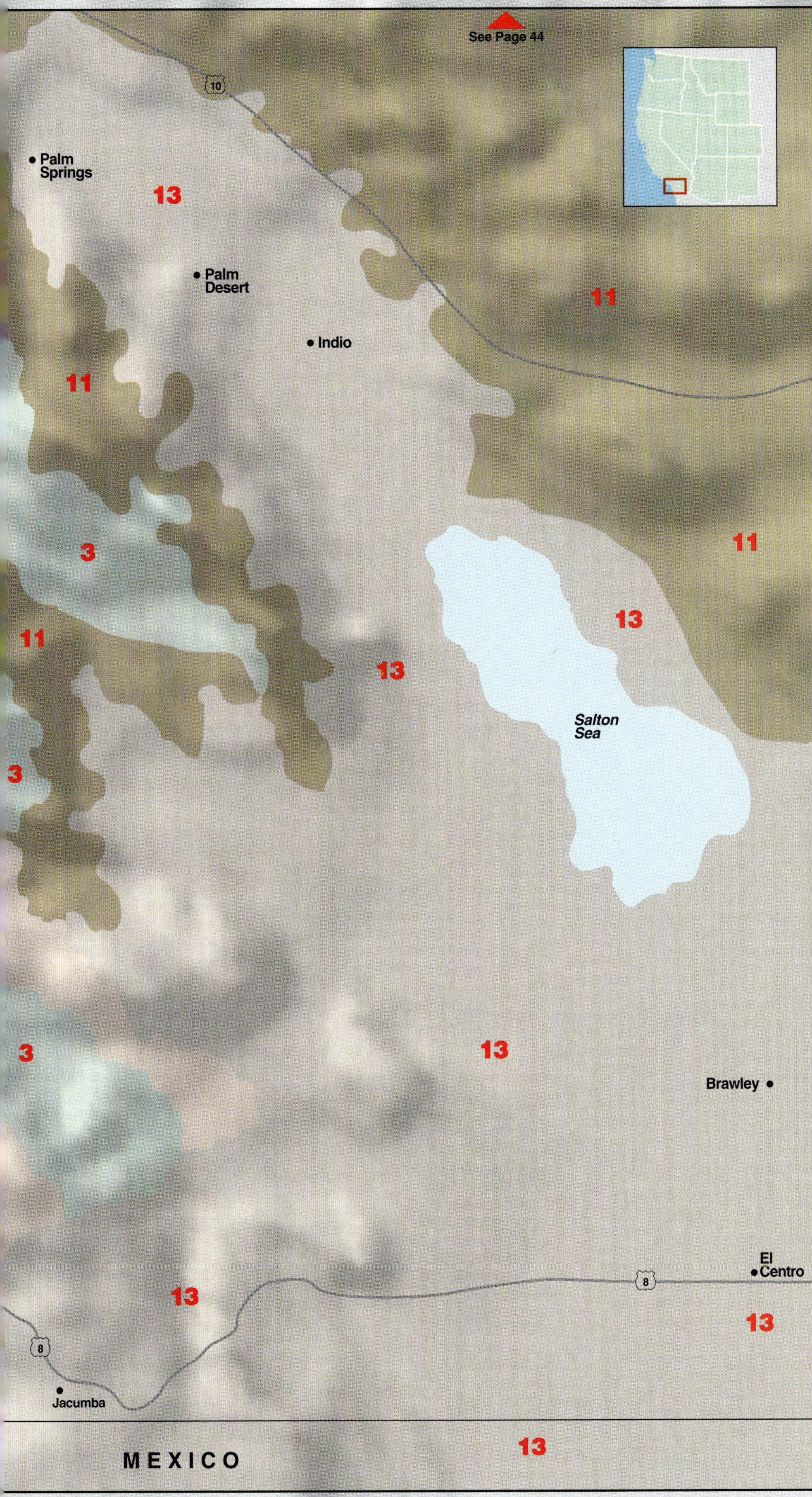

See Page 44

● Palm
Springs

13

● Palm
Desert

● Indio

11

11

11

3

11

3

13

13

11

13

*Salton
Sea*

3

13

Brawley ●

APPLE ALLEY BAKERY
JULIAN →
APPLE PIE

Coast to Desert

*Drive northeast from the San Diego area
and you'll pass through three very different
climates. Near the coast (Zone 24), such
tender plants as poinsettias, shown here
at Ecke Ranch in Encinitas, thrive outdoors.
In high-elevation Julian (Zone 3), apple
trees get enough winter chill to deliver
hefty crops. In Palm Desert (Zone 13), arid
conditions favor the growth of such tough,
unthirsty heat-lovers as gazania, spiky
ocotillo, and yellow-flowered brittlebush,
shown here at The Living Desert.*

El
● Centro

13

⑧

13

⑧

● Calexico

● Jacumba

13

MEXICO

13

0   5   10   15 miles

See Page 44 →

Southwest Deserts: Southern California

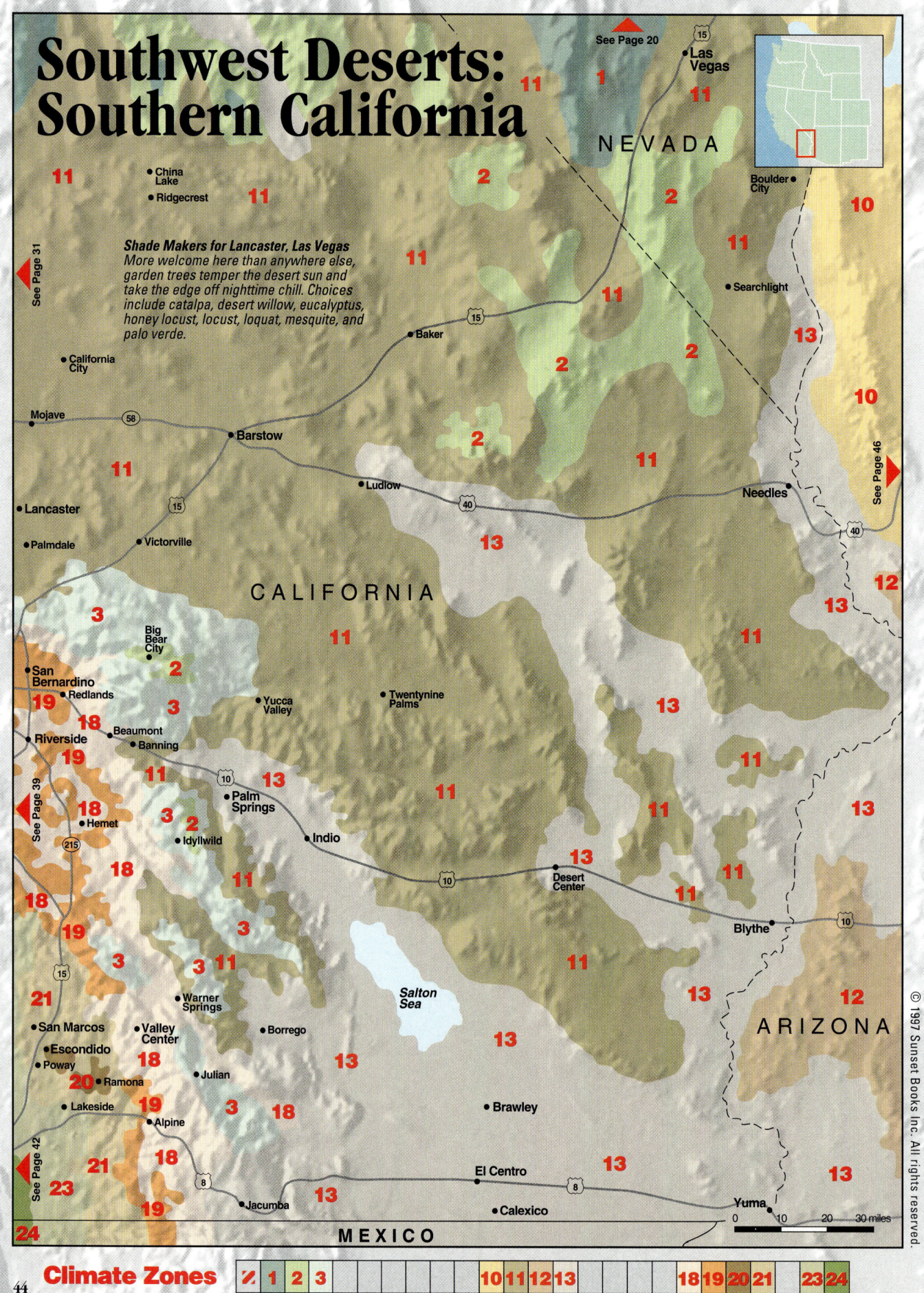

NEVADA

CALIFORNIA

ARIZONA

MEXICO

Shade Makers for Lancaster, Las Vegas
More welcome here than anywhere else, garden trees temper the desert sun and take the edge off nighttime chill. Choices include catalpa, desert willow, eucalyptus, honey locust, locust, loquat, mesquite, and palo verde.

See Page 20

See Page 31

See Page 46

See Page 39

See Page 42

China Lake
Ridgecrest
California City
Mojave
Barstow
Ludlow
Lancaster
Palmdale
Victorville
Big Bear City
San Bernardino
Redlands
Beaumont
Banning
Riverside
Hemet
Yucca Valley
Twentynine Palms
Palm Springs
Idyllwild
Indio
Desert Center
Warner Springs
San Marcos
Escondido
Poway
Ramona
Lakeside
Alpine
Julian
Valley Center
Borrego
Salton Sea
Brawley
El Centro
Calexico
Jacumba
Blythe
Needles
Searchlight
Boulder City
Las Vegas
Baker
Yuma

0   10   20   30 miles

Climate Zones   1 2 3   10 11 12 13   18 19 20 21   23 24

ZONE 10 — High Desert of Arizona, New Mexico, Kansas, Oklahoma, and Texas

Snowy Winters, Peppery Summers

Zone 10 gets enough winter chill to flock pampas grass *(far left)* and let you grow plants that need chilling—lilacs and deciduous fruits, for example. But it also gets plenty of summer heat for growing chilies, shown *(left)* drying on a pole in New Mexico.

This zone consists mostly of the 3,300- to 4,500-foot elevations in parts of Arizona, New Mexico, Kansas, Oklahoma, and Texas. It also includes parts of southern Utah and southern Nevada. It has a definite winter season; from 75 to more than 100 nights each year have temperatures below 32°F/0°C. In the representative towns of Albuquerque, Benson, and Douglas, average winter minimums range from 31° to 24°F/–1° to –4°C. Lows of 25° to 22°F/–4° to –6°C often come in April. The record low is –17°F/–8°C.

The cold winter season calls for spring planting and a spring-through-summer growing season. (In neighboring Zones 12 and 13, most planting is done in fall.) Distinguishing this climate from Zone 11 are more rain and less wind. Annual rainfall averages 12 inches, with half of that falling in July and August. In eastern Zone 10 (in the Pecos River drainage), the summer provides more precipitation than the winter.

Growing Season

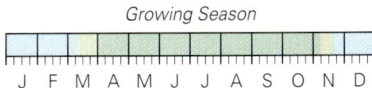

J F M A M J J A S O N D

ZONE 11 — Medium to High Desert of California and Southern Nevada

This zone shares some similarities with its extremely different neighbors—the cold-winter Zones 1, 2, and 3, and the subtropical low desert, Zone 13. Like Zones 1 to 3, Zone 11 has cold winters; like Zone 13, it has hot summers. Overall, it is characterized by wide swings in temperature. Hot summer days are followed by cool nights; freezing nights are often followed by daytime temperatures of 60°F/16°C. On average, there are 110 summer days above 90°F/32°C, with the highest temperatures recorded around 111° to 117°F/44° to 47°C. About 85 nights have temperatures below 32°F/0°C, with maximum lows from 11° to 0°F/–12° to –18°C.

If soil moisture is inadequate, the characteristic winds and bright sunlight may combine to dry out normally hardy evergreen plants, killing or badly injuring them.

Growing Season

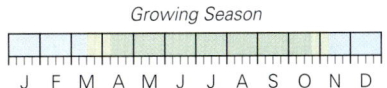

J F M A M J J A S O N D

Water Makes the Difference

Zone 11 is dry: oasis-like Las Vegas gardens *(above)* owe their existence to imported water. Yet wildflowers often make a dazzling show in Antelope Valley in spring *(left)*. Challenges for gardeners in Zone 11? Hot summer days, chilly nights, late spring frosts, and desert winds.

Southwest Deserts: Arizona

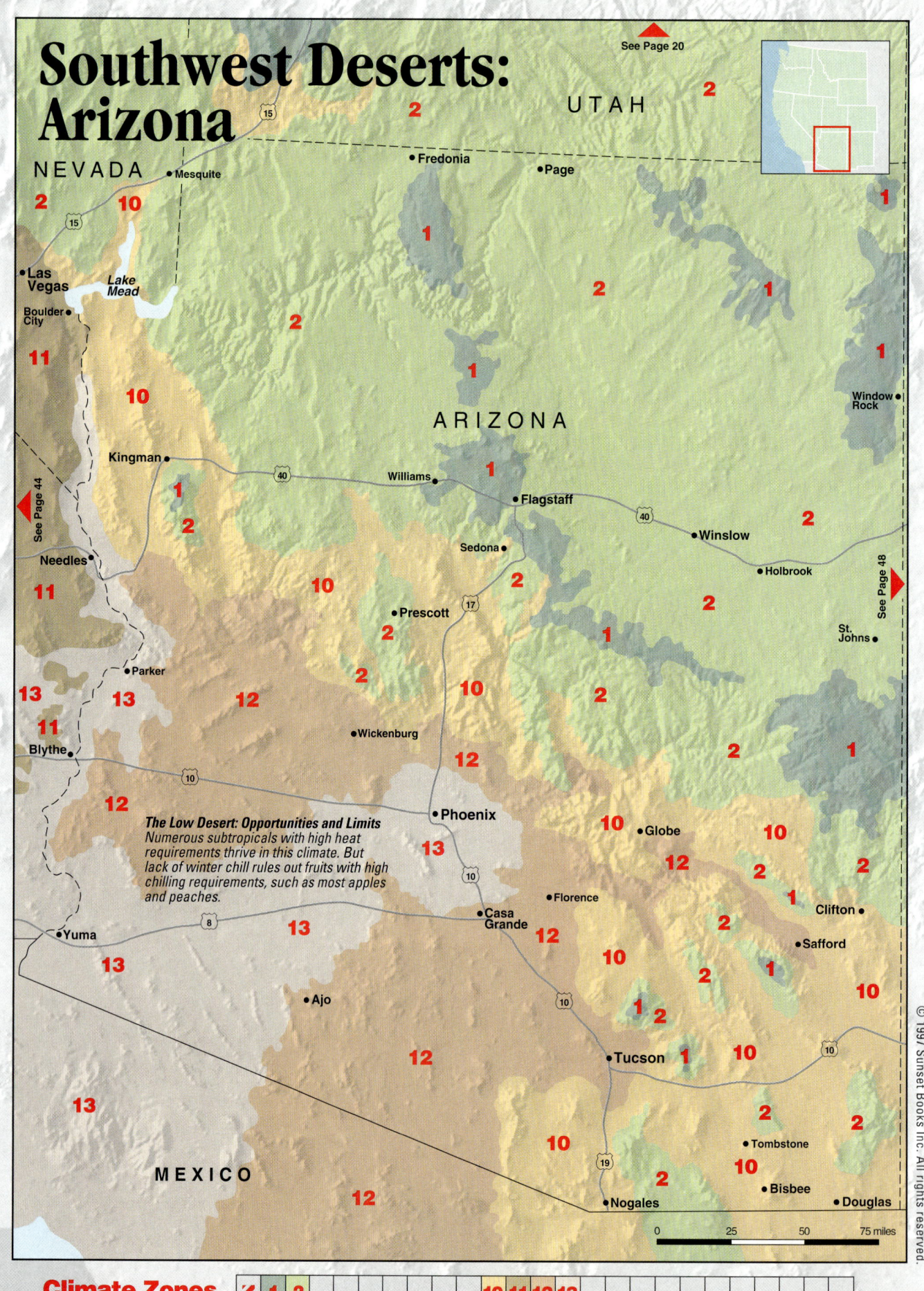

See Page 20

UTAH

NEVADA

ARIZONA

MEXICO

The Low Desert: Opportunities and Limits
Numerous subtropicals with high heat requirements thrive in this climate. But lack of winter chill rules out fruits with high chilling requirements, such as most apples and peaches.

Cities: Mesquite, Fredonia, Page, Las Vegas, Boulder City, Window Rock, Kingman, Williams, Flagstaff, Winslow, Sedona, Holbrook, Needles, Prescott, St. Johns, Parker, Wickenburg, Blythe, Phoenix, Globe, Yuma, Florence, Clifton, Casa Grande, Safford, Ajo, Tucson, Tombstone, Bisbee, Nogales, Douglas

See Page 44
See Page 48

0   25   50   75 miles

Climate Zones   1 2   10 11 12 13

ZONE 12 Arizona's Intermediate Desert

The crucial difference between Arizona's intermediate desert (Zone 12) and the low desert (Zone 13) is winter cold. But though the intermediate desert averages only 5 more freezing nights than the low desert (20 in Tucson compared with 15 in Phoenix and El Centro), it has harder frosts spread over a longer cold season. Seen another way, Zone 12 averages 8 months between freezes, 9 months between killing frosts (28°F/−2°C or lower). Zone 13, however, averages more than 11 months between killing frosts, when it gets them at all. Extreme lows of 6°F/−14°C have been recorded in Zone 12. The mean maximums in July and August are 5° to 6°F/3° to 4°C cooler than the highs of Zone 13.

Many subtropicals that do well in Zone 13 aren't reliably hardy here, but succeed with protection against the extreme winters.

Although winter temperatures are lower than in Zone 13, the total hours of cold are not enough to provide sufficient winter chilling for some deciduous fruits.

From March to May, strong winds (to 40 miles per hour) can damage young tender growth. Windbreaks help. Here, as in Zone 13 and the eastern parts of Zone 10, summer rains are to be expected and can be more dependable than winter rains. And as in Zone 13, the best season for cool-season crops (salad greens, root vegetables, cabbage family members) starts in September or October.

The Lush Arizona Desert

Saguaro, cholla, and organpipe cacti rise up out of a sea of yellow brittlebush flowers in southern Arizona's intermediate desert. Zone 12 supports a more lush, gardenlike flora than any other desert zone.

Growing Season

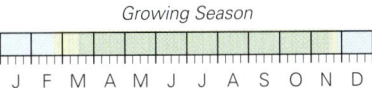

J F M A M J J A S O N D

ZONE 13 Low or Subtropical Desert Areas

Ranging from below sea level in the Imperial Valley and Death Valley to an elevation of 1,100 feet around Phoenix, Zone 13 is rightly classified as subtropical desert. Average summer maximum temperatures range from 106° to 108°F/41° to 42°C. Winters are short and mild. Frosts, anticipated from December 1 to February 15, are brief. Although the average minimum winter temperature is 37°F/3°C, with just 15 nights below freezing, lows of 19° to 13°F/−17° to −11°C have been recorded.

The gardening year begins in September and October for most vegetables and annuals, although crops like corn and melons are planted in late winter. Fall-planted crops grow slowly in winter, pick up speed in mid-February, and race through the increasing warmth of March and April. Spring winds and summer storms are a factor in gardening: the rains help with watering, and clouds shield plants from the sun.

Subtropicals in California

Winter lows and summer highs exclude some subtropicals from this zone, but ones like bauhinia *(above)*, date palms, and grapefruit thrive here. California fan palms and golden brittlebush bask in the sun in a canyon near Palm Springs *(left)*.

Growing Season*

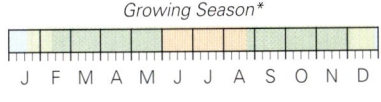

J F M A M J J A S O N D

*heat stops growth in summer

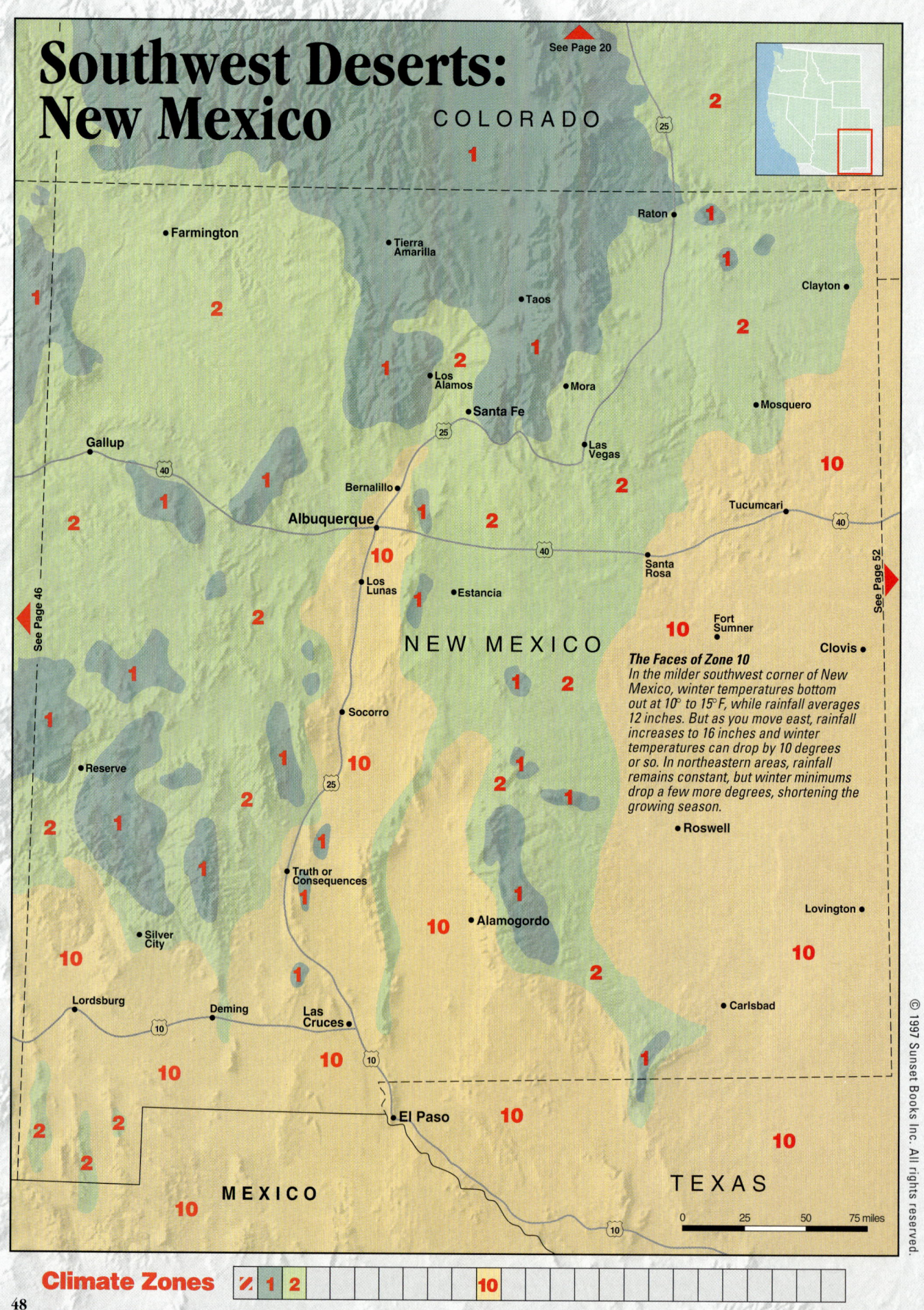

Southwest Deserts: New Mexico

See Page 20

COLORADO

The Faces of Zone 10
In the milder southwest corner of New Mexico, winter temperatures bottom out at 10° to 15° F, while rainfall averages 12 inches. But as you move east, rainfall increases to 16 inches and winter temperatures can drop by 10 degrees or so. In northeastern areas, rainfall remains constant, but winter minimums drop a few more degrees, shortening the growing season.

See Page 46

See Page 52

NEW MEXICO

TEXAS

MEXICO

0   25   50   75 miles

Climate Zones   1   2   10

The *21* Climate Zones *from the Midwest to the Atlantic*

To find your garden's climate zone, start with this locator map and then turn to the page listed for your area. If you garden in a microclimate—a windy passage, thermal belt, cold pocket, hilltop, or canyon that's too small to register on the maps—adjust your climate zone accordingly.

S ummer humidity, with rainfall distributed all through the grow- ing season: this is the climatic characteristic common through- out the eastern part of the United States and Canada. Gardens over the area reflect prevailing winter conditions. Where lows reach 0°F/–18°C or below, you'll find deciduous trees and shrubs plus cold-hardy perennials. As you travel toward the milder-winter parts of the Southeast, Gulf Coast, and Florida, you'll encounter more and more broad-leafed evergreens.

Attuned to Eastern Climates

Thriving in the eastern half of the continent are plants that demand good winter chill or moist humid summers. Among these are tulips *(Tulipa)*, native *Franklinia alatamaha*, and Oriental poppies *(Papaver orientale)*.

ZONE 25 South Florida and the Keys

Zone 25 boasts the mildest climate in the continental United States. In the mainland part of the region, winters are often frost-free, though temperatures do occasionally dip below freezing (lows range from 25° to 40°F/−4° to 4°C). The Florida Keys, at Zone 25's southern tip, are truly frost-free; in Key West, the lowest temperature on record is 41°F/5°C.

The warmth and high humidity here rule out certain slightly tender plants that grow well in other parts of the South and up the East Coast—camellias, for example.

Wherever you go in this part of Florida, you'll see tropical touches. Bananas and mangoes revel in the climate, too. And some plants thrive in Zone 25 that do not perform well (or even survive) in any other part of the country; among these are royal palm, coconut palm, royal poinciana, and large, thin-skinned West Indian avocados.

This zone gets plenty of rain, averaging 40 to 57 inches annually, although you will need to provide supplemental irrigation in the relatively low-rainfall months of December through March.

Soil is typically quite alkaline. Gardeners convert the native soil to a more friendly medium by excavating it and replacing it with trucked-in acid soil, or by mulching (with chipped prunings, melaleuca mulch, Florida peat), digging the mulch in, mulching some more, and so forth. It's an everlasting process, since the heat and moisture break mulches down quite rapidly.

Window on the Tropics

Beneath a cloudy South Florida sky, a variety of palms, tender trees, and shrubs line the water's edge. Warmth, ample rainfall, and humidity give these plants just the conditions they need to thrive.

Growing Season

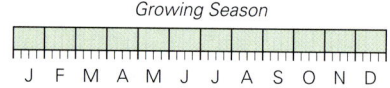

J F M A M J J A S O N D

ZONE 26 Central and Interior Florida

Gardeners in Zone 26 enjoy two horticultural worlds. They can grow many of the tropical trees and shrubs that thrive in neighboring Zone 25; they also succeed with many plants that flourish in the colder-winter climates to the north. Camellias thrive down through Tampa but begin to call it quits at Sarasota. Peaches are successful from Georgia south to Tampa. Pears, too, make it as far south as Tampa, but apples do well only as far as Ocala. Blackberries perform down to Fort Lauderdale, a few kinds of grapes to Miami.

Winter brings some frosts, but not many—typically about a dozen up in Daytona Beach, six in Orlando and Tampa, perhaps one in Fort Myers or West Palm Beach. Lows range from 15°F/−9°C at the north end of the zone to 27° to 30°F/−3° to −1°C at the south end. However, the region does experience the occasional arctic freeze: every few years, a mass of frigid air moves down the continent and spends 3 or 4 days over Florida. Such freezes are wicked indeed—but once the typical greenhouse-like weather returns, new plants will quickly grow in to replace any freeze victims.

Humidity is always high. Rainfall is heaviest in summer and early autumn, with annual averages varying from 46 inches in the north to 60 inches in the south.

Growing Season

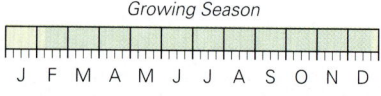

J F M A M J J A S O N D

Mild with a Bite

A horticultural odd couple? Maybe—but in central Florida, pines and palmettos grow side by side. Mild winters and year-round rainfall encourage tender perennials like black-eyed Susan vine (right), though periodic freezes exclude some of the truly tropical plants of Zone 25.

ZONE 27 The Lower Rio Grande Valley

Heaven for Heat-Lovers

Perfectly at home in warm Zone 27, heat-loving blanket flower makes a vivid sweep across an open field. Dead branch snags in trees along a watercourse testify to this region's seasonal and limited rainfall.

In this area of very humid summers and mild, usually frost-free winters, gardeners get two planting seasons each year: one in early fall for winter and spring flowers and vegetables, another in late February for summer crops. Tomatoes, peppers, and other vegetables considered summer crops elsewhere can be grown in either season. (To minimize whitefly damage to the winter tomato crop, however, delay planting until at least 2 weeks after the region's cotton growers have defoliated their crop.)

Texas commercial citrus is grown almost entirely in Zone 27—and home gardeners, too, can successfully raise sweet, juicy grapefruit and oranges. Home growers even have an advantage over commercial growers: the occasional severe freeze costs them only one or two trees, not an entire orchard.

For landscaping, gardeners can choose from a number of warm-climate plants, including split-leaf philodendron, *Ficus benjamina*, hibiscus, and *Tecomaria capensis* (Cape honeysuckle). Bougainvillea and oleander are popular, and there is growing interest in natives, especially palmettos.

Rain comes mostly in June, August, and September, typically totalling 23 to 26 inches per year. Winter lows are normally in the 30s and 40s, even slipping into the 20s at times. With daytime highs of at least 70°F/21°C (and often much hotter) ten months a year, the wind is a cooling friend—but plan your garden so that large, tough specimens can protect smaller, more delicate plants.

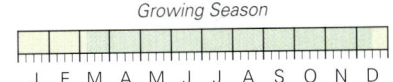

Growing Season

J F M A M J J A S O N D

ZONE 28 Northern Florida and the Gulf Coast

The Gulf of Mexico—North America's great humidity factory—is right at Zone 28's doorstep, so gardeners here must contend with rain, year-round humidity, and midyear high heat.

Annual rainfall is lowest at the Texas end of the zone, with a 30-inch average in Corpus Christi, and higher in the center and at the Florida end, with 64 inches in Mobile and 52 in Jacksonville. The Texas end does experience drought in some years, and gardeners there often wisely turn to native and other drought-resistant plants. In the zone's center and at its Florida end, however, drought is never a problem.

The high-rainfall part of Zone 28 is America's prime location for camellias and azaleas. Although this distinction might be shared with some zones on the West Coast, most of Zone 28 does seem to produce especially big, productive camellia and azalea plants—so big that they usually need

pruning to control size. Prune camellias right after bloom, azaleas by the Fourth of July. Zone 28 is also grand country for numerous subtropicals: palms, bananas, citrus, magnolia, jacaranda, bougainvillea, and many others.

You can grow roses here, but you may find coping with humidity-induced problems a full-time job. Due to diseases, weeds, and the long growing season (from 270 to 330 days), maintaining lawn grasses can be difficult as well. St. Augustine is the

easiest kind of grass to grow in the wetter sections, with Bermuda the top choice in the drier parts.

Winters are often entirely or nearly frost-free, but every 5 to 10 years, masses of arctic air (down to 20°F/−7°C or even lower) move down the continent and damage or kill many subtropicals in Zone 28.

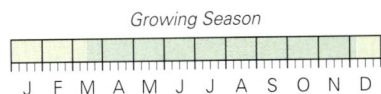

Growing Season

J F M A M J J A S O N D

A Natural Greenhouse

Beneath the spreading shelter of a southern live oak, Southern Indica Hybrid azaleas glow neon-bright. Though they do well in other climates, these plants perform at their peak in steamy Zone 28.

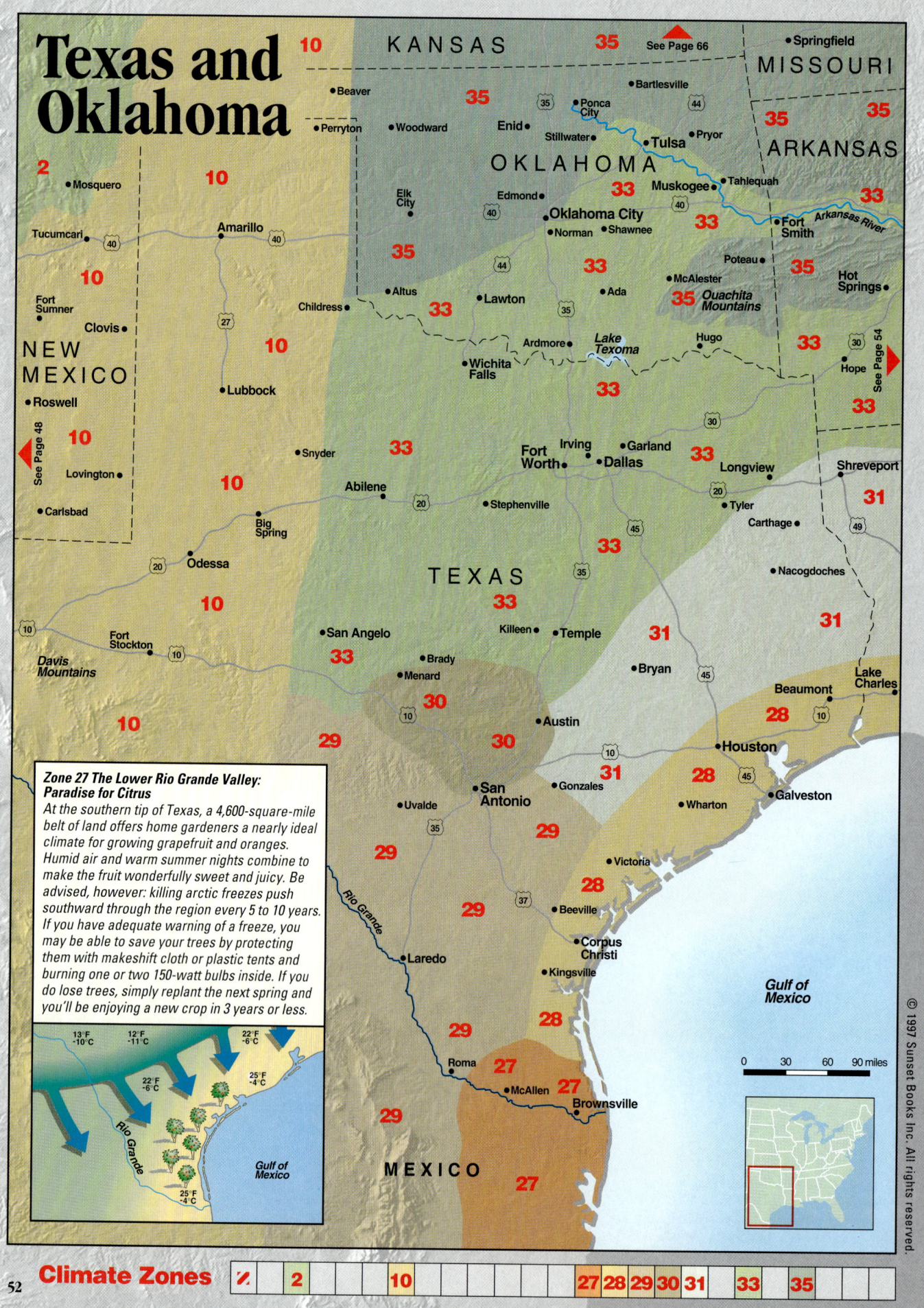

Texas and Oklahoma

10

KANSAS

35 See Page 66

•Springfield

MISSOURI

•Beaver

35

•Bartlesville

•Perryton

•Woodward

Enid

•Ponca City

•Pryor

•Tulsa

35

35

ARKANSAS

2

•Mosquero

OKLAHOMA

Stillwater

35

33 •Muskogee •Tahlequah

33

•Tucumcari

•Amarillo

Elk City

•Edmond

•Oklahoma City

33

•Fort Smith

Arkansas River

10

35

•Norman •Shawnee

33

Poteau•

35

•Hot Springs

•Fort Sumner

10

35

•Altus

33

•Lawton

•Ada

•McAlester

35 Ouachita Mountains

NEW MEXICO

•Clovis

•Childress

Ardmore

Lake Texoma

•Hugo

33

•Hope See Page 54

•Roswell

10

•Wichita Falls

33

33

•Lubbock

10

•Snyder

33

Fort Worth

•Irving •Garland

•Dallas

33

Longview•

•Shreveport

•Lovington

10

Abilene

•Stephenville

20

•Tyler

Carthage•

31

•Carlsbad

Big Spring

•Nacogdoches

•Odessa

10

TEXAS

33

31

Davis Mountains

Fort Stockton

•San Angelo

33

Killeen• •Temple

31

•Bryan

Lake Charles

•Beaumont

28

10

•Brady

•Menard

30

31

•Houston

28

•Galveston

10

•Austin

30

•Gonzales

29

•Wharton

28

See Page 48

See Page 54

Zone 27 The Lower Rio Grande Valley: Paradise for Citrus

At the southern tip of Texas, a 4,600-square-mile belt of land offers home gardeners a nearly ideal climate for growing grapefruit and oranges. Humid air and warm summer nights combine to make the fruit wonderfully sweet and juicy. Be advised, however: killing arctic freezes push southward through the region every 5 to 10 years. If you have adequate warning of a freeze, you may be able to save your trees by protecting them with makeshift cloth or plastic tents and burning one or two 150-watt bulbs inside. If you do lose trees, simply replant the next spring and you'll be enjoying a new crop in 3 years or less.

•Uvalde

San Antonio

29

31

28

•Victoria

29

37

•Beeville

28

Rio Grande

29

•Corpus Christi

•Kingsville

Gulf of Mexico

29

•Laredo

29

•Roma

27

•McAllen

27

•Brownsville

29

MEXICO

27

13°F -10°C 12°F -11°C 22°F -6°C

22°F -6°C 25°F -4°C

Rio Grande

25°F -4°C

Gulf of Mexico

0 30 60 90 miles

52   **Climate Zones**   **2**   **10**   **27 28 29 30 31**   **33**   **35**

ZONE 29 — Interior Plains of South Texas

Sometimes called the winter garden region of Texas, Zone 29 is especially hospitable to cool-season vegetable crops, such as spinach and the cole crops (cabbage, cauliflower, broccoli, and the like), and to cool-season flowers, primarily pansies and petunias.

All the hardier citrus are good performers here, especially satsuma mandarin and kumquat. In years when winters are particularly cold, however, citrus plants may

The Bridge to Western Deserts

Zone 29 is drier than the adjacent Gulf Coast—and the natural vegetation shows it. Here, small-leafed, drought-tolerant shrubs embrace a tough native yucca in its moment of glory.

need protection several times. Peaches can succeed in Zone 29 as well, but you'll need to choose varieties with a low chill requirement.

Bermuda and St. Augustine thrive as lawn grasses in years when rainfall is normal (20 to 25 inches annually). In times of drought, buffalo grass does well.

Winter lows normally range from 26° to 34°F/−3° to 1°C. In those infrequent years when freezing arctic air moves down through the central United States, temperatures have been known to drop as low as 6°F/−14°C.

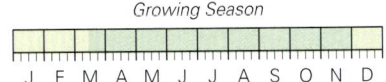
Growing Season

J F M A M J J A S O N D

ZONE 30 — The Hill Country of Central Texas

Garden Spot of Texas

The Texas Hill Country is wildflower heaven. Bluebonnet and fireweed *(above)* are two brilliant elements of the annual floral palette. A field carpeted with bluebonnets *(right)* captures the essence of the region's terrain and native flora.

Zone 30 owes its special gardening satisfactions to three physical factors. First, its elevation, ranging from 400 to 1,400 feet, is just high enough to give the winter a crisp tingle but not high enough to make snow an every-year event. Second, its distance from the Gulf of Mexico (150 to 280 miles) lets it enjoy some of the Gulf Coast's usually benign climate. Third, its location at about 30° north latitude puts it near enough to the equator for plenty of warmth, but not close enough to create a tropical climate.

The Hill Country's elevation makes it colder in winter and cooler in summer than the lower surrounding areas to the north, east, and south; the winter chill makes peaches, apples, wine grapes, wildflowers, and many garden perennials perform as they should. Although soils are generally

thin and alkaline, mild temperatures and adequate rainfall permit natural stands of live oak. The popular *Salvia greggii* is also native here.

Normal winter lows are around 20°F/−7°C. But in those rare years when a subzero air mass moves through, temperatures may drop as low as −2°F/−19°C, cold enough to kill tobira, photinia, Chinese tallow tree, and other shrubs and trees that thrive in Zone 30's ordinary winter temperatures.

The Hill Country gets plenty of rain during a normal year—about 35 inches, compared to 12 to 18 inches in the higher country to the west.

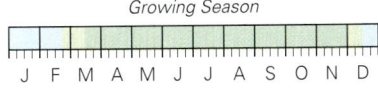
Growing Season

J F M A M J J A S O N D

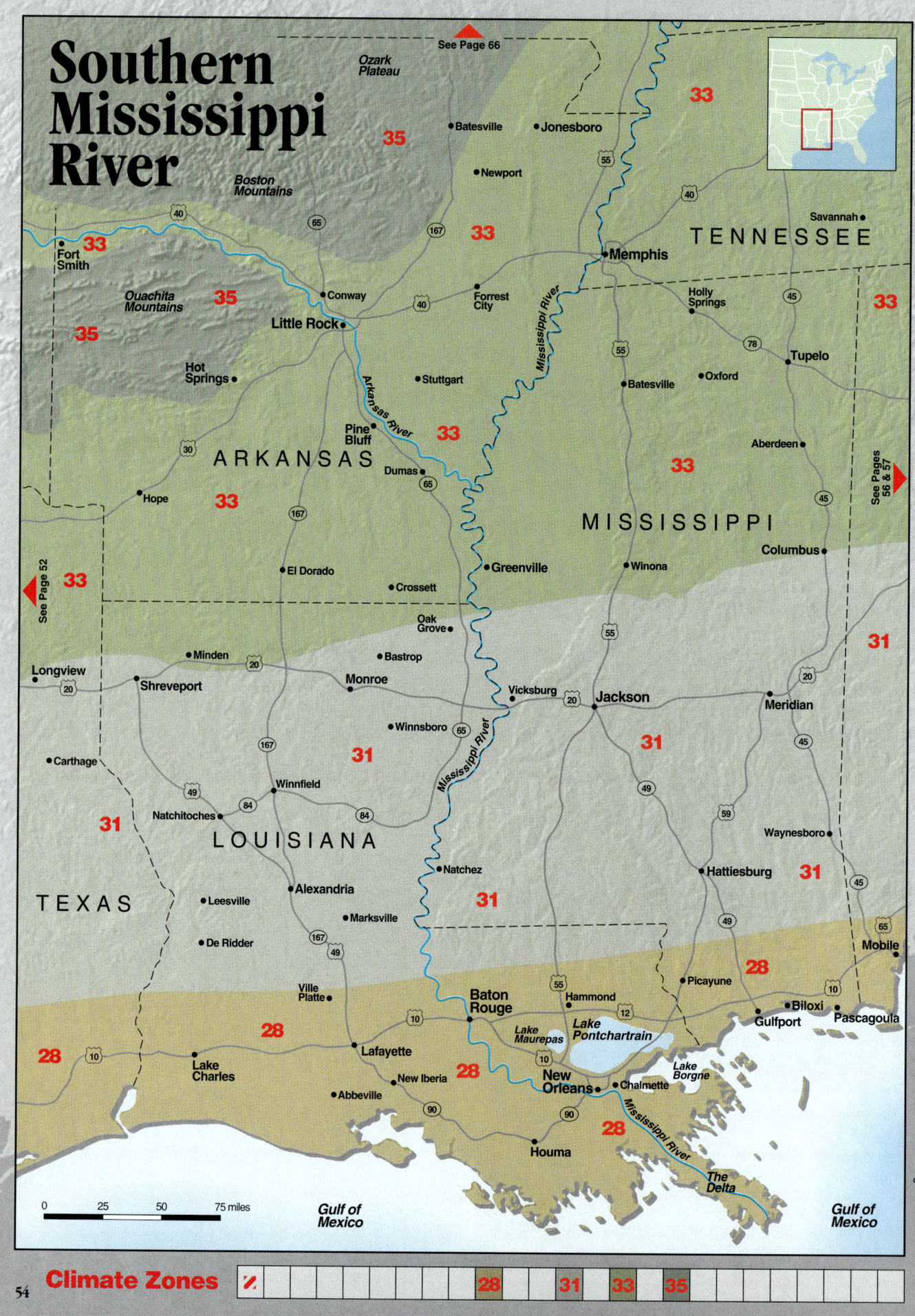

Southern Mississippi River

Ozark Plateau

35

Boston Mountains

See Page 66

33

Batesville • Jonesboro

• Newport

55

40

Savannah •

T E N N E S S E E

33

Fort Smith

Ouachita Mountains

35

35

40

65

167

33

Conway

40

Forrest City

Memphis

Holly Springs

45

78

33

Hot Springs •

Little Rock

55

Batesville •

Oxford •

Tupelo

Stuttgart •

A R K A N S A S

Pine Bluff

Arkansas River

33

Aberdeen •

See Pages 56 & 57

30

Dumas •

65

33

M I S S I S S I P P I

45

167

Hope •

33

Columbus •

See Page 52

33

El Dorado •

Crossett •

Greenville •

Winona •

31

Oak Grove •

55

Minden •

20

Bastrop •

Mississippi River

31

Longview •

20

Shreveport •

Monroe •

Vicksburg

20

Jackson •

Meridian •

Winnsboro •

65

31

45

167

• Carthage

59

49

Winnfield •

Waynesboro •

31

Natchitoches •

84

84

49

L O U I S I A N A

Hattiesburg •

31

Natchez •

31

T E X A S

Leesville •

Alexandria •

49

Marksville •

De Ridder •

167

49

Mobile •

Ville Platte •

55

Hammond

28

Picayune •

65

10

10

Baton Rouge

12

Biloxi •

28

Lafayette •

Lake Maurepas

Lake Pontchartrain

Gulfport •

Pascagoula •

Lake Charles

New Iberia •

28

New Orleans

Chalmette •

Lake Borgne

28

Abbeville •

90

Houma •

90

Mississippi River

28

The Delta

0   25   50   75 miles

Gulf of Mexico

Gulf of Mexico

54 **Climate Zones** | | | | | | **28** | | **31** | | **33** | | **35** | | | | | | |

ZONE 31   Interior Plains of Gulf Coast and Coastal Southeast States

Holding this large segment of the mild South together as a single climate zone are several critical meteorological measurements common to every part of the region. Throughout the zone, frost-free days number from 240 to 279. Typical last spring freezes come between February 27 and March 19; autumn's first freeze usually arrives between November 7 and December 3. During the hot, humid summers, average highs are all in the high 80s or low 90s; in winter, record lows (all resulting from south-moving arctic air) measure from 0° to 7°F/−18° to −14°C. Average annual rainfall measures 44 to 54 inches, and October is the least-rainy month.

Camellias and azaleas perform splendidly in Zone 31, as do various flowering dogwoods and magnolias—including the South's showy trademark tree, *Magnolia grandiflora*. Roses can grow well too, though they will require conscientious care. If you want to grow a palm tree, the least-risky choices are the hardiest ones:

Chamaerops humilis, the Mediterranean fan palm, or *Trachycarpus fortunei,* the windmill palm.

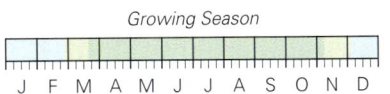

Growing Season

J F M A M J J A S O N D

Luxuriance from Heat and Moisture

In the lowland South, water is never far away: countless streams and rivers come together here as they flow to the ocean. The magnificent blossoms of southern magnolia *(above)* are this region's floral emblem.

ZONE 32   Interior Plains of Mid-Atlantic States; Chesapeake Bay, Southwestern Pennsylvania, Southern New Jersey

A Gardening Fusion of North and South

Zone 32's distinct seasons and reliable rainfall are ideal for the local deciduous shrubs and trees, among them the eastern redbuds and white dogwoods shown here. This part of Colonial America furnished many new plants to European gardens—and accepted countless Old World favorites in return.

For the most part, this region is a gardener's delight. It gets some snow, but usually not much; winter lows are typically in the 30s at the Georgia end of the zone, in the 20s north of Virginia. Thanks to the barrier of the Appalachians, arctic freezes rarely move through—but when they do, temperatures typically drop to 0° to 10°F/−18° to −12°C (record lows range from −9° to −17°F/−23° to −27°C). The growing season is long enough (180 to 240 days) and warm enough to offer grand gardening.

The northern cut-off line for Bermuda grass and traditional camellias runs through Zone 32. Both plants are popular in the zone's southern reaches, rare or entirely absent in Baltimore, Philadelphia, and Atlantic City. This is also the northernmost climate in which vegetables, flowers, and woody plants can be planted in fall as well as in spring.

Precipitation comes fairly evenly year-round; throughout the zone, the annual average is a consistent 40 to 50 inches.

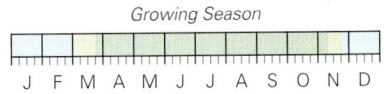

Growing Season

J F M A M J J A S O N D

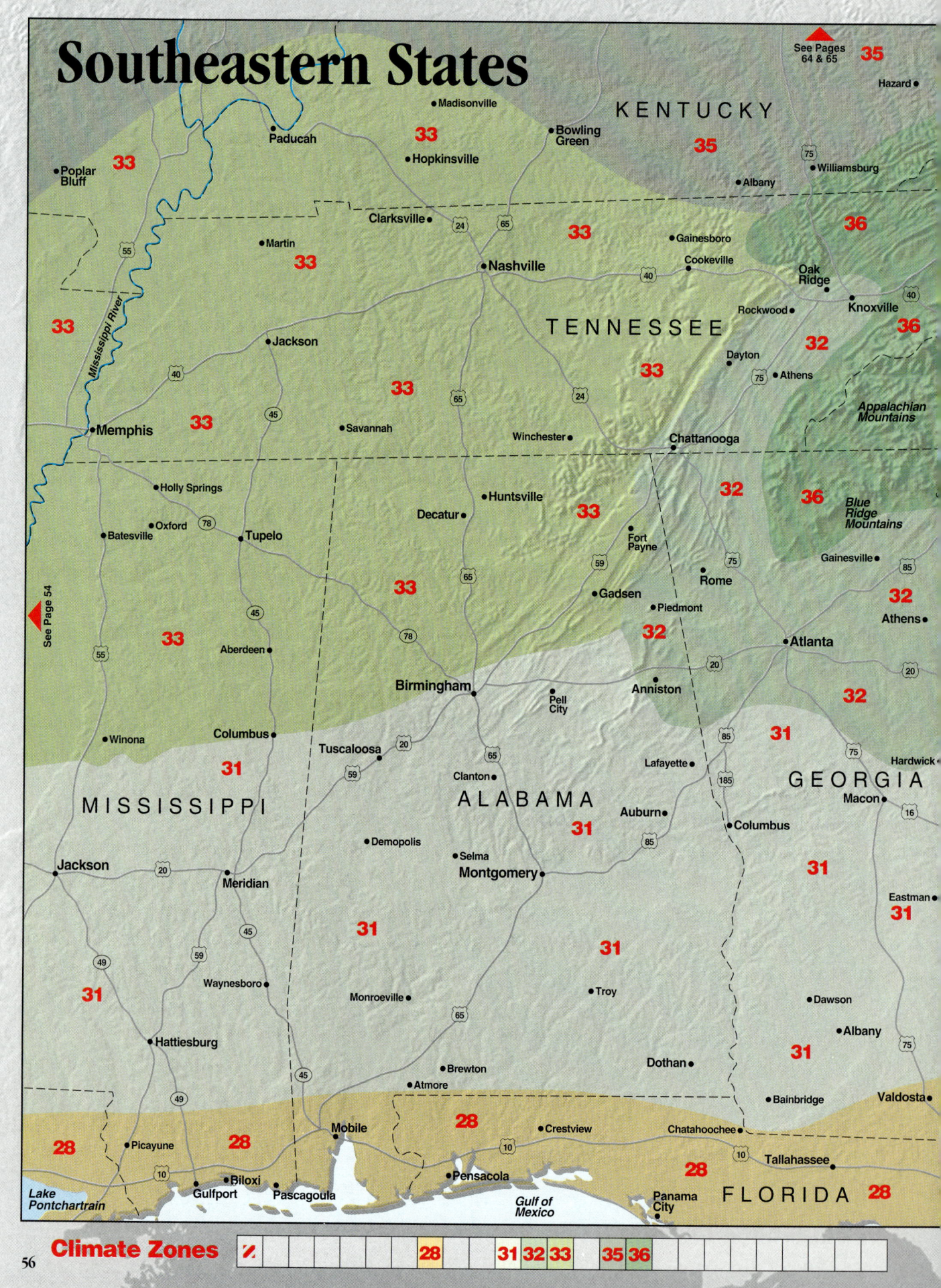

VIRGINIA

36

36 Appalachian Mountains

Blacksburg • • Roanoke

81

77

36

Marion • 81

Galax •

Johnson City •

181

77

36

Winston-Salem •

Greensboro •

Hickory •

40

Newton •

77

Asheville •

Charlotte •

Blue Ridge Mountains

26 85

Spartanburg •

Greenville •

385

Anderson •

26

Augusta •

Thomson •

Waynesboro •

31

31

Vidalia •

31

Douglas •

Waycross •

Okefenokee Swamp

Live Oak • Lake City •

301

32 29

See Page 71

32 95

Petersburg •

Hampton •

Portsmouth • Chesapeake •

Virginia Beach •

31

Emporia •

Franklin •

Elizabeth City •

Danville •

360

29

32

85

95

Durham •

40

32 Rocky Mount •

Raleigh •

Greenville •

31

NORTH CAROLINA

32

Goldsboro •

Kinston •

31

32

Fayetteville •

95

Jacksonville •

40

Morehead City •

31

Bennettsville •

Wilmington •

Camden •

95

20

Florence •

Columbia •

32

SOUTH CAROLINA

20

31

Barnwell •

26

Georgetown •

31

Moncks Corner •

28

Walterboro •

95

Charleston •

16

Hilton Head Island •

Savannah •

28

95

Jesup •

28

Brunswick •

28

Jacksonville •

See Pages 60 & 61

10

Atlantic Ocean

0   30   60   90 miles

57

ZONE 33 — North Texas and Southern Oklahoma to Northern Alabama and Central Tennessee

Gardeners and farmers in Zone 33, one of the four climate zones entirely contained between the arid West and the Appalachians, will always have to reckon with two prime forces: warm, moist air that moves northward from the Gulf of Mexico and extremely cold air that (in some winters) comes south from the arctic.

Winters here are not consistent in their degree of chill. Several years may go by with lows in the high teens to low 20s. Then comes a year when frigid air from the Far North sweeps through, dropping lows to somewhere between 0° to 15°F/−18° to −9°C. Cold fronts like these typically produce very rapid temperature shifts—from

From Plains to Mountains

Warm Gulf Coast air and arctic chill both help define the climate of Zone 33. Though there are no true mountains here, rugged terrain is common.

shirt-sleeve temperatures to near zero in just a few hours.

Gardeners take these big freezes in stride. Perhaps a new fig tree grows for four winters, untouched by freezes, bearing big crops each summer. Then comes an arctic blast that kills the whole thing to the ground. Alas, says the gardener; but the next year he or she may again plant a fig or something else that likes the local climate most of the time.

Rainfall, like winter chill, is inconsistent. In a normal year, annual averages range from 22 to 52 inches. In drought years, though, some parts of Zone 33 may record only half to two-thirds the normal rainfall.

Growing Season

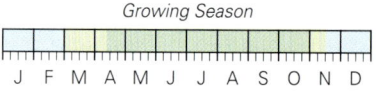

J F M A M J J A S O N D

ZONE 34 — Lowlands and Coast from Gettysburg to North of Boston

Zone 34 is the mildest region in the northeast corner of the United States. Winters here are so mild that some of the hardier camellias survive, along with many evergreen hollies, common boxwood, *Clerodendrum trichotomum,* and the hardier selections of *Magnolia grandiflora.*

This happy clime has predictable and temperate seasons, with generous precipitation year-round (30 to 50 inches annually). The weather here results from three major sources: first, cold air moving down from Canada in winter (though not as much as moves to some Great Lakes and midwestern areas); second, warm and moist air coming all the way up from the Gulf of Mexico; and third, some damp ocean air that occasionally moves inland from the North Atlantic.

In those winters when Zone 34 gets no freezing arctic air, winter minimums are in the low 20s; when arctic air moves in, lows range from −3° to −22°F/−19° to −30°C.

North of Philadelphia and Atlantic City, 12 National Oceanic and Atmospheric Administration stations typically record 100 or fewer days with freezing temperatures each year, and those 12 stations are all in Zone 34. La Guardia Airport records just 65 annual days of freezing temperatures; Central Park, 80; JFK Airport, 81; Mineola, NY, 85; Newark, NJ, 86; New Bedford, MA, 87; Jersey City, NJ, 89; Long Branch, NJ, 98; Boston, 98; Islip, NY, 98; Dobbs Ferry, NY, 99; and Bridgeport, CT, 100.

In elevation, most towns in this zone range from sea level to 600 feet—another factor resulting in milder winters here than in climates farther inland. New York, Newark, Boston, and Bridgeport lie essentially at sea level and get more marine air (bringing fog, mist, and moderate temperatures) than the zone's other cities do.

Growing Season

J F M A M J J A S O N D

North Atlantic Original

In contrast to the heavily populated areas around them, these Long Island pine barrens preserve a remnant of Zone 34's original coastal landscape.

ZONE **35** Ouachita Mountains, Northern Oklahoma, Southern Kansas to North-Central Kentucky and Southern Ohio

Throughout the central region of the United States and Canada, the climate in each area is determined by its latitude; by how much air from the Gulf of Mexico it gets midyear; and by how much arctic air it gets in winter. In Zone 35, these factors combine to produce a climate with hot, humid summers (with highs from 103° to 114°F/39° to 46°C) and winters with typical lows of 19° to 24°F/−7° to −4°C. When arctic air masses come through every few years, however, temperatures may drop as low as −20°F/−29°C.

Gardeners here enjoy success with a huge number of perennials; top-notch dependables include columbine, coreopsis, sunflower, hellebore, daylily, hosta, bee balm, peony, phlox, and Stokes' aster.

Many rhododendrons and azaleas do well in shady gardens, except in very windy areas and in those with alkaline soil. Roses do nicely, too; if adequately fertilized, they'll produce four or five flushes of bloom per year, though the fifth one is likely to be a bit weak.

Zone 35's normal annual rainfall is 36 to 42 inches. The growing season ranges from 150 to 240 days.

Growing Season

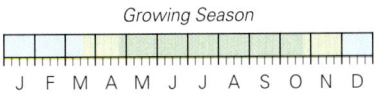

J F M A M J J A S O N D

Essential Midwest

Gardeners from coast to coast cherish heartland natives like these: purple coneflower, black-eyed Susan, and gayfeather *(above)*. Fertile farmland— and the occasional dramatic bluff, cliff, or rock formation—typify the region.

31
See Page 54
45
65
• Atmore 31
See Pages
56 & 57
28
Bainbridge 31

MISSISSIPPI
59

ALABAMA

See Page 54
49
• Picayune 28
Mobile •
28

• Crestview
10
Chattahoochee
10
• Tallahassee

10
• Biloxi
Gulfport
Pascagoula •
28
Pensacola •
Panama
City
28

28
LOUISIANA

Mississippi River

The
Delta

Gulf of
Mexico

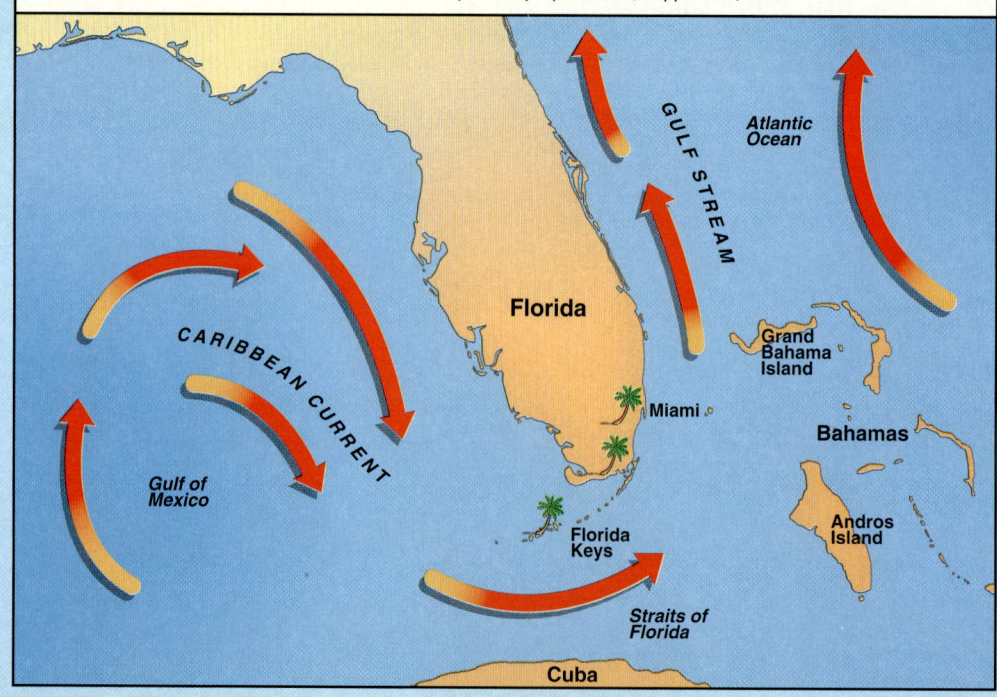

Southern Florida: America's Outdoor Greenhouse
The only spot in the continental U.S. that has never suffered a frost is the extreme southern tip of the Florida peninsula, along with the Florida Keys just off the coast. This exceptionally mild climate results largely from the area's latitude—its distance from the equator. Also keeping temperatures warm are the relatively warm waters in the Gulf of Mexico on the west and the warm Gulf Stream flowing in the Atlantic on the east. Many plants positively flourish in gardens here that do not really thrive outdoors anywhere else in the country (not even the mildest stretches of the southern California coast): coconut palm, royal poinciana, copper leaf, and others.

GULF STREAM

Atlantic
Ocean

CARIBBEAN CURRENT

Florida

Grand
Bahama
Island

Bahamas

Miami

Gulf of
Mexico

Andros
Island

Florida
Keys

Straits of
Florida

Cuba

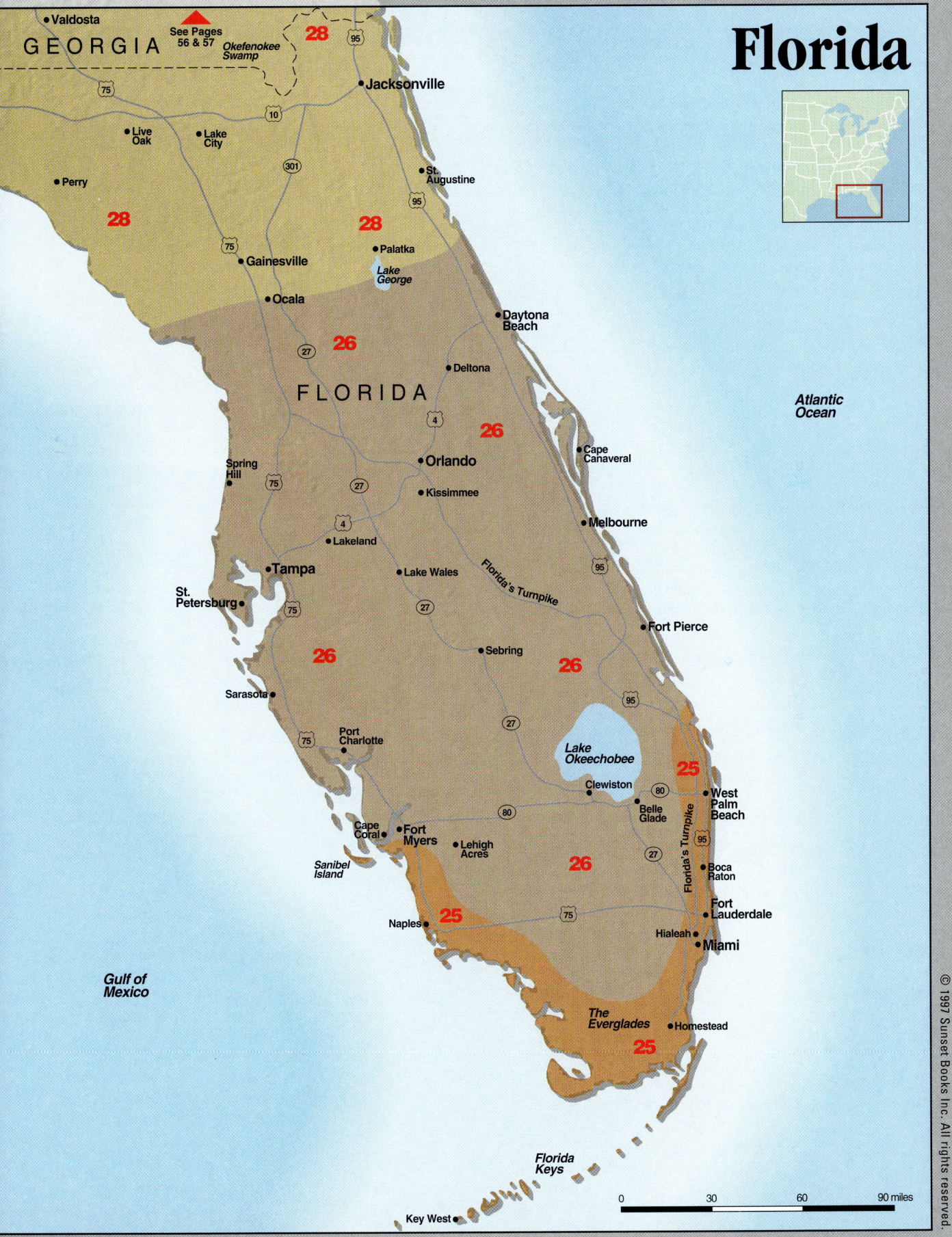

Florida

GEORGIA

Valdosta

See Pages 56 & 57

Okefenokee Swamp

28

28

75

Jacksonville

10

Live Oak

Lake City

St. Augustine

301

95

Perry

28

75

28

Palatka

Gainesville

Lake George

Ocala

Daytona Beach

27

26

FLORIDA

Deltona

4

26

Spring Hill

Orlando

Cape Canaveral

75

27

Kissimmee

4

Melbourne

Lakeland

Tampa

Lake Wales

95

St. Petersburg

Florida's Turnpike

75

27

Fort Pierce

26

Sebring

26

Sarasota

95

75

Port Charlotte

Lake Okeechobee

27

25

Clewiston

West Palm Beach

80

Cape Coral

Fort Myers

Lehigh Acres

80

Belle Glade

Florida's Turnpike

95

Boca Raton

Sanibel Island

26

27

Fort Lauderdale

75

Hialeah

Miami

Naples

25

The Everglades

Homestead

25

Gulf of Mexico

Atlantic Ocean

Florida Keys

0   30   60   90 miles

Key West

ZONE 36 Appalachian Mountains

In the eastern half of the United States, the Appalachian chain plays a part in determining the weather. When cold air masses move down through central North America, they don't always make it over or through the mountains—thus sparing the land on the lee (southeastern) side of the range some of the deep cold that settles to the west. When arctic air does make it up and over the Appalachians, it tends to warm up as it moves, so that winters on the mountains' southeast side are still milder than those to the west. Minimum temperatures range from 0° to −20°F/−18° to −29°C.

Within the Appalachians themselves, the higher elevation produces cooler summers and colder winters than in the surrounding regions. The area's biggest gardening challenge, though, lies in accommodating a weather pattern that crops up throughout winter and on into April: a few warm days will be followed by a freeze. Appalachian native plants can take this sort of inconsistency, and scores of handsome and enjoyable choices are sold by the region's native plant nurseries. Many of the hardier azaleas and rhododendrons also do well. The deciduous forests here are rich in species and luxuriant in growth, and an equally rich variety of shrubs and perennials flourishes beneath the trees.

The zone's second notable gardening problem, especially in the slightly lower elevations, is its sporadic rainfall, particularly between the end of the normally rainy spring and the beginning of winter. Again, native plants can help gardeners cope with this problem. Other solutions include double digging, incorporating ample organic matter in garden beds, mulching, and using drip and/or seepage irrigation.

The growing season varies from 120 to 160 days.

Highland Spring

Rising above the humid lowlands, the Appalachian and Blue Ridge Mountains offer both scenic grandeur and a climate perfectly suited to moisture-loving cool-climate plants such as spruces and Catawba rhododendrons.

Growing Season

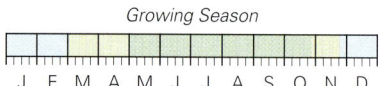

J F M A M J J A S O N D

ZONE 37 Hudson Valley and Appalachian Plateau

Covering parts of Pennsylvania, New York, and Connecticut, Zone 37 is too far inland to get much of the Atlantic's mild influence, but its elevation is low enough to let it largely escape the harshness of the neighboring mountains. Valleys in this zone are fine for gardening.

In the valleys, the last frosts of spring typically come in early or mid-May, while the first frosts of autumn arrive in early to mid-October. Over the region as a whole, the growing season varies from about 120 to 180 days.

Winters here are cold; low temperatures average in the high teens, though they may dip as low as −5° to −15°F/−20° to −26°C with the arrival of the occasional arctic air mass.

A wide range of trees, shrubs, vines, and perennials perform beautifully in Zone 37. Examples of sure-thing choices include this gardener's dozen: azalea, coreopsis, delphinium, flowering quince, hydrangea, lilac, mountain laurel, rhododendron, rudbeckia, Shasta daisy, spiraea, viburnum, and weigela.

Thanks to its location near a major metropolitan area, the Hudson Valley is increasingly popular among growers of quality produce for on-site sale to city buyers. Tomatoes can be planted in late April or early May and harvested from mid-July through August. Some discerning tomato fans claim that, variety for variety, tomatoes raised in the Hudson Valley clay-soil areas taste better than those grown anywhere else. Apples, the big commercial crop here, grow successfully in home gardens as well.

Civilized Countryside

Impressive, intimate, picturesque— all three words describe Zone 37's hills and valleys. Woodlands are everywhere, dotted with farmlands and blazing with warm color in autumn.

Growing Season

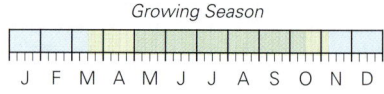

J F M A M J J A S O N D

ZONE 38 New England Interior and Lowland Maine

Gardeners here have only 4 or 5 months to work with: summers start quickly and end just as rapidly. Short though it is, the season offers some substantial horticultural pleasures. For one thing, growing cool-season lawn grass is supremely easy. When the locals say "just throw the seed on the ground and walk away," they're exaggerating only slightly. Another plus: regular rainfall often eliminates the need for irrigation, keeping moisture in the root zone throughout the growing season. (When rainfall is irregular, watering will be necessary in July and August.)

Zone 38 offers another advantage, too. Some of the native soils are just about perfect: slightly acidic and rich in organic matter. On the down side, the soil is incredibly rocky—and indeed, rock removal has always been part of New England gardening.

This area is world-famous for the autumn color of its deciduous trees, among them sugar maple, red maple, beeches, and oaks.

Picturesque, Rocky New England

New England has two faces. The rocky coastline tells a story of glaciation and erosion; interior valleys *(below)* offer fine farmland with even finer views.

Normal lows in Zone 38 range from −2°F/−19°C to perhaps 16° to 18°F/−9° to −8°C. Record lows (always due to arctic air) range from −19° to −30°F/−28° to −34°C. The cold means that most fruit trees become chancier as you move north within the zone. Apples make it all the way, but peaches and other stone fruits perform well only in the southern parts: either the trees themselves are not sufficiently cold-hardy, or the blossoms are killed by spring frosts in most years.

Hardier rhododendrons thrive here if carefully sited; exposure to the north keeps plants shaded in winter, avoiding freeze-and-thaw damage from southern sun. Provide protection from north winds.

Growing Season

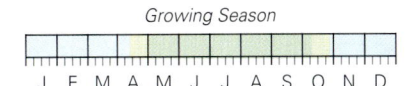

J F M A M J J A S O N D

Ohio River Valley

See Pages 68 & 69

Lake Michigan

MICHIGAN

96
41
Lansing

196

43

41
Rockford
41
94
39
South Haven
39
Kalamazoo
41
69

IOWA
Cedar Rapids
41
Clinton
90
39
Evanston
Chicago
94

380
Iowa City
Davenport
80
Aurora
55
Harvey
Joliet
80
Gary
Hammond
39
South Bend
80 90
Defiance

41
Kewanee
74
55
65
41
Plymouth
41

Galesburg
41
55
Logansport
Fort Wayne

Peoria
539

Bloomington
41
74
Lafayette
INDIANA
41
69
41

41
55
Quincy
41
Urbana Champaign
72
Crawfordsville
74
Tipton
Muncie
Greenville
70

See Page 66
Mississippi River
Jacksonville
72
Decatur
Springfield
ILLINOIS
57
35
Indianapolis
35

Bowling Green
35
Terre Haute
70
65
35
Cincinna

35
70
55
35
Effingham
70
35
Bloomington
65
74

Missouri River
St. Louis
Salem
64
64
35
Scottsburg
71
35

44
35
64
35
Jasper
64
Louisville
64
Lexing

55
Mississippi River
35
57
Carbondale
Marion
Anna
35
Evansville
Ohio River
Owensboro
65
Elizabethtown
35

MISSOURI
Cape Girardeau
24
33
Madisonville
KENTUCKY

35
Paducah
24
Bowling Green
33
35

Poplar Bluff
57
33
Hopkinsville
24
65

33
55
See Page 54
See Pages 56 & 57
Clarksville
Albany

Martin
33
TENNESSEE
33

Climate Zones 32 33 34 35 36 37 39 40 41 42 43

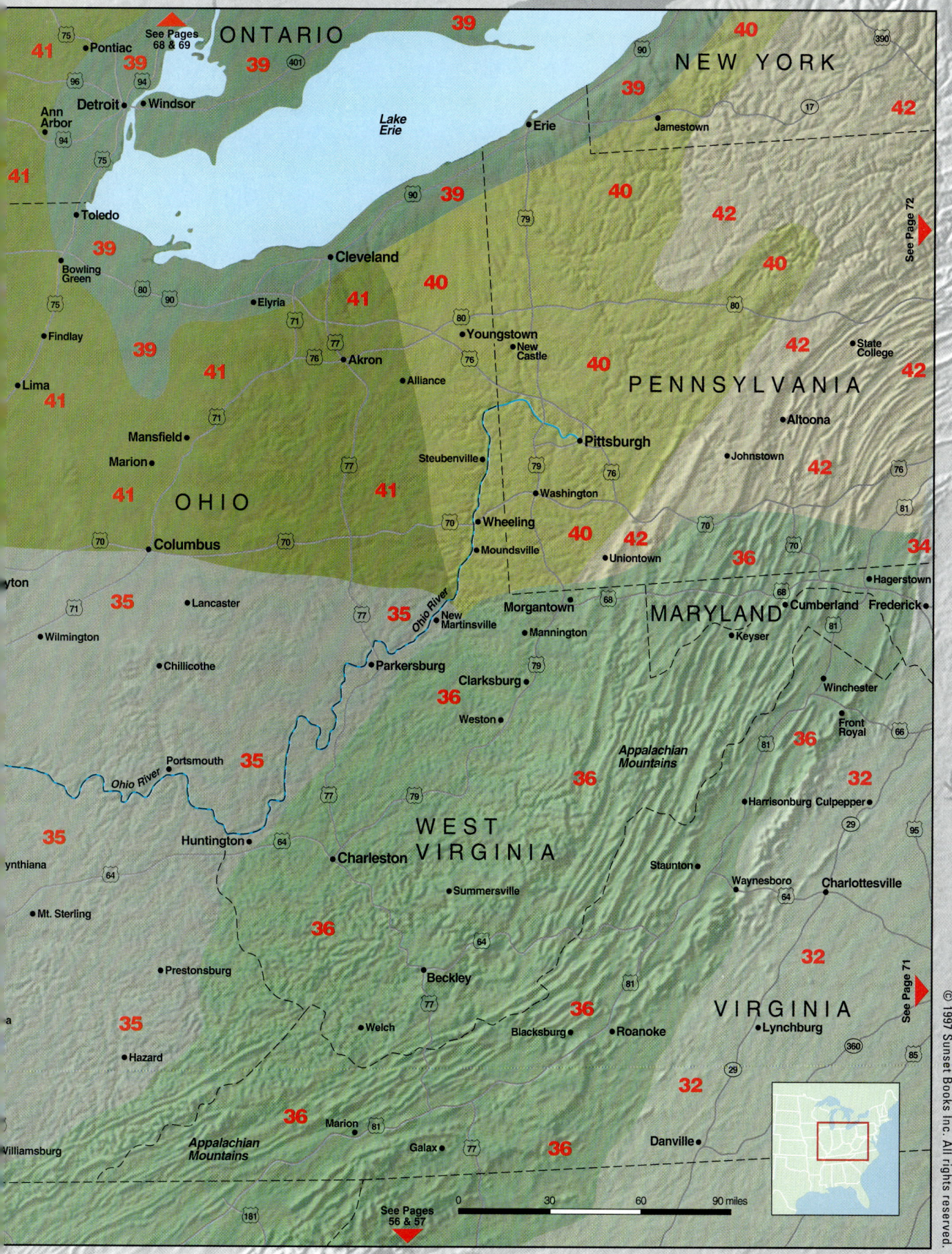

ONTARIO

NEW YORK

41 75 •Pontiac
See Pages
68 & 69
39 94
39 401

Ann
Arbor 96
Detroit •Windsor

41 75

•Toledo 94

•Bowling
Green 80 90

•Findlay 75

•Lima **41** **39**

Mansfield•

Marion•

41 **OHIO**

70 •Columbus

yton 71 **35**

•Wilmington

•Chillicothe

ynthiana 64

•Mt. Sterling

35

a

Williamsburg

Lake
Erie

39 •Erie

Jamestown•

90 •Cleveland

Elyria• 71

•Akron 76 77

Alliance•

Steubenville•

Wheeling

•Moundsville

New
Martinsville

•Mannington

•Parkersburg

Clarksburg•

Weston•

36

Portsmouth

Ohio River

Huntington•

•Charleston

Summersville•

36

•Prestonsburg

35

•Hazard

36

Appalachian
Mountains

Marion•

Galax•

See Pages
56 & 57

39

90 79

40 •Youngstown
New
Castle

76 **40**

•Pittsburgh

79

Washington•

40 **42** •Uniontown

68

Morgantown

79

36

36

Appalachian
Mountains

36

**WEST
VIRGINIA**

64

64 •Beckley

77

•Welch

Blacksburg•

81

36

77

40

40

PENNSYLVANIA

•State
College

•Altoona

•Johnstown

MARYLAND

•Keyser

81

Staunton•

VIRGINIA

36

Cumberland•

81

•Harrisonburg

32

29

Waynesboro•

64

•Roanoke

32

•Lynchburg

32

42

17

42

80

40

42

42

42

42

34

Hagerstown•

Frederick•

81

Winchester•

•Front
Royal 66

36

95

Culpepper•

29

Charlottesville•

360

85

32

Danville•

36

See Page 72

See Page 71

0   30   60   90 miles

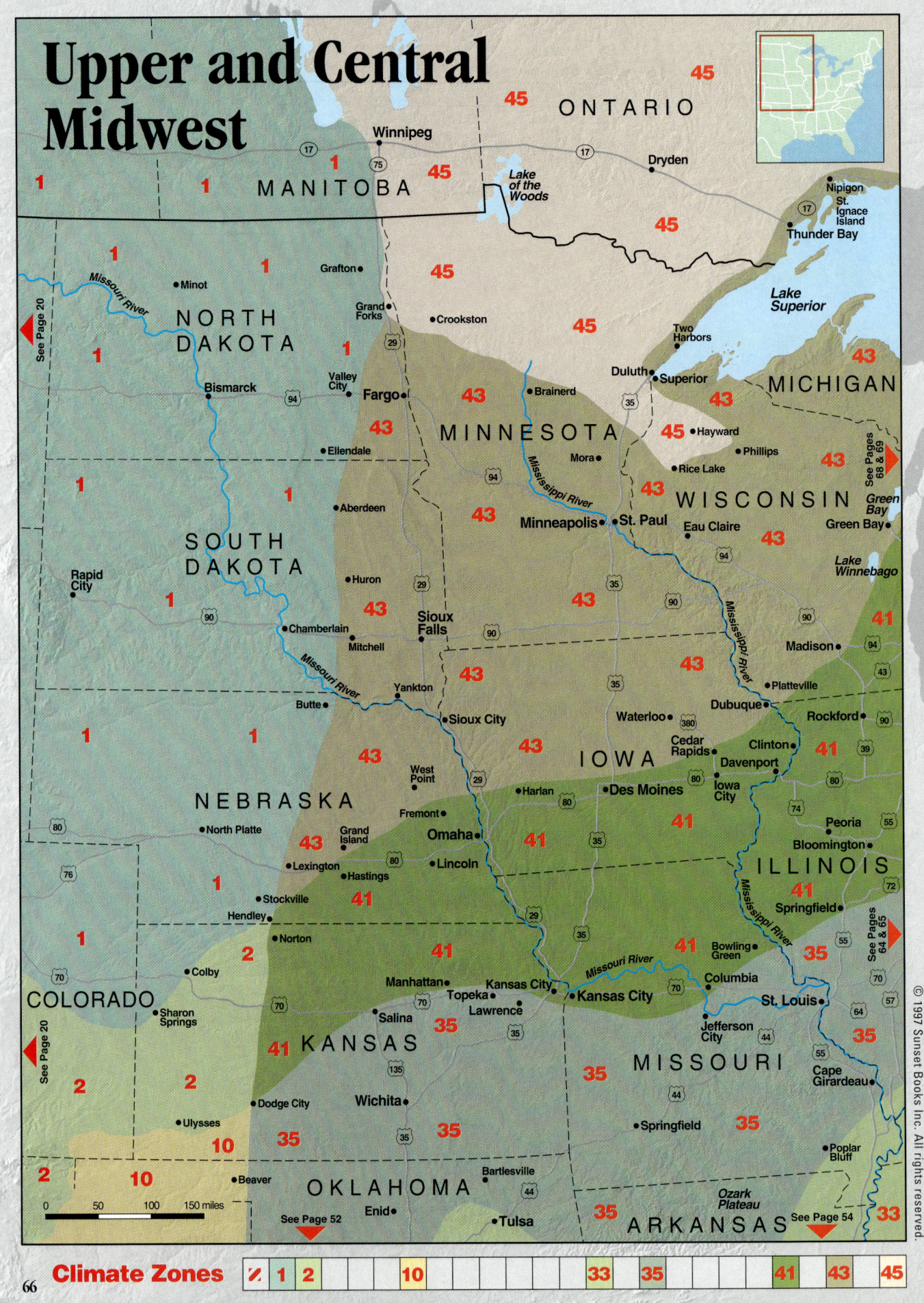

Upper and Central Midwest

ONTARIO

45   45

1   1   Winnipeg   1   45
MANITOBA

45   Dryden

Lake of the Woods

Nipigon
St. Ignace Island
Thunder Bay

45

1   1   Grafton   45

Minot

Grand Forks

Crookston

45   Lake Superior

NORTH DAKOTA

Two Harbors

Duluth   Superior   **MICHIGAN**   43

1   1   Valley City   1

Bismarck   Fargo

43   Brainerd

43

45   Hayward

See Pages 68 & 69

Ellendale

MINNESOTA

Mora

Rice Lake   Phillips

43

1   1   Aberdeen

43   43   **WISCONSIN**

Green Bay

SOUTH DAKOTA

Minneapolis   St. Paul   Eau Claire   43   Green Bay

Lake Winnebago

Huron

43   43   Madison   41

1   Chamberlain   Mitchell   Sioux Falls

43   Platteville

Butte   Yankton   43   43   Dubuque   Rockford

Waterloo

Sioux City   43   Cedar Rapids   Clinton   41

1   1   West Point   **IOWA**   Davenport

Harlan   Des Moines   Iowa City

43   Fremont   Peoria

NEBRASKA   Omaha   41   Bloomington

North Platte   Grand Island   Lincoln   41   **ILLINOIS**

43   Lexington   Hastings   41

1   Stockville   41   Springfield

Hendley

1   2   Norton   41   41   Bowling Green   35

Colby   Manhattan   Kansas City   Columbia

COLORADO   Sharon Springs   Topeka   Kansas City   St. Louis

2   2   Salina   Lawrence   Jefferson City   35

41   **KANSAS**   35   **MISSOURI**   Cape Girardeau

Dodge City   Wichita   35

2   Ulysses   Springfield   35

10   35   35   Poplar Bluff

2   10   Beaver   Bartlesville   Ozark Plateau   33

OKLAHOMA   Enid   35   **ARKANSAS**

Tulsa

See Page 20

See Page 52   See Page 54

0   50   100   150 miles

Missouri River   Mississippi River

66   **Climate Zones** | 1 | 2 | 10 | 33 | 35 | 41 | 43 | 45

ZONE **39** Shoreline Regions of the Great Lakes

From late spring through late fall and into the start of winter, the Great Lakes moderate the climate of some of the regions surrounding them—an effect felt more to the east and south of the lakes than to their north and west, since weather generally moves from west to east. Where this influence is strongest, a definably different garden climate exists, designated in this book as Zone 39.

Compared to the adjoining areas, Zone 39 has milder, later springs, and it is less likely to experience the late spring freezes that kill flower buds. It also has cooler summers and milder, longer autumns. The growing season varies from 180 to 210 days.

Year-round, gardens here—in Chicago, Detroit, Cleveland, and Buffalo, for example—experience an average of 21 fewer freezing days than do those located at the same latitude (41° to 42° north) but beyond the lakes' influence—such as in Sioux City, Madison, Lansing, Albany, and Worcester.

Winter lows range from 0° to 10°F/−18° to −12°C.

Inland Seashore

Where glaciers once held sway, the Great Lakes stretch for miles. And for miles around their shores, they help define the weather: Zone 39 enjoys milder winters and cooler summers than the regions farther inland.

Growing Season

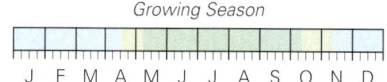

J F M A M J J A S O N D

ZONE **40** Inland Plains of Lake Erie and Lake Ontario

The second-mildest of the Great Lakes climates, Zone 40 covers parts of Ohio, Pennsylvania, New York, and Ontario. Typical winters see temperatures dropping to −10° to −20°F/−23° to −29°C; when arctic air moves in, lows may fall to −30°F/−34°C. The growing season begins in mid- to late May and ends in mid-September or soon thereafter.

Gardeners in Zone 40 can grow some fruits and berries: apples, pears, plums, blueberries, grapes. Nurseries sell about 60 kinds of ornamentals; those available in greatest variety are flowering crabapple, lilac, juniper, spiraea, maple, and viburnum.

Growing Season

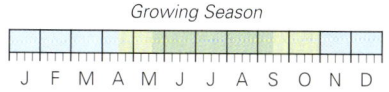

J F M A M J J A S O N D

Pastoral Sample

Water plants, grasses, and blooming wildflowers dot a marshy expanse in Erie National Wildlife Refuge. The glaciers that created this terrain of ponds and wetlands also left behind rich soils now used for cropland.

The Great Lakes

45   **45**   **43**   *Lake Superior*

MINNESOTA   • Two Harbors   **43**   • Houghton

45   **43**

Duluth • Superior

• Ashland   • Ironwood   **43**   • Marquette   Newberry

43   **45**   • Drummond   • Ishpeming

MICHIGAN   **43**   • Manistique

43   • Hayward   **45**   • Radisson   • Kingsford • Escanaba

• Mora   • Phillips   • Rhinelander

43   **43**

• New Richmond   **43**   • Merrill   **43**   Marinette

Minneapolis   • Holcombe   • Wausau   *Green Bay*   **41** • Sturgeon Bay Trav City

St. Paul   • Shawano   **43**

• Eau Claire   **43**   Green Bay

Mississippi River   • Marshfield

43   WISCONSIN   • Appleton   **41** • Manitowoc • Manistee **41**

Oshkosh *Lake Winnebago*   • Ludington

• La Crosse   Fond du Lac   • Sheboygan

43   **43**   *Lake Michigan*

• Reedsburg • Portage **43** • Beaver Dam

43   • Prairie du Chien   • Watertown   **41** Muskegon Gra Ra

IOWA   Madison   • Milwaukee   **41**

• Platteville   • Elkhorn **43** • Racine Holland

43   **41** Janesville **41**

• Dubuque   South Haven Kala

Mississippi River   • Rockford   **39** Th Ri

• Cedar Rapids • Clinton ILLINOIS   **39**

• Evanston • Chicago

41   **41**   Aurora   **39** South Bend

Davenport   **41** See Pages 64 & 65 • Harvey Gary • Hammond **41**

0 30 60 90 miles

See Page 66

See Pages 64 & 65

Climate Zones

| 39 | 40 | 41 | 42 | 43 | | 45 |

Is Chicago Really THE Windy City?

It's windy at times, yes. The Chicago area gets the continental wester-lies that blow across most of Illinois, as well as Lake Michigan's bit-ter cold winter winds and cooling summer breezes. But Chicago is not the windiest city in Illinois, nor even the windiest one on the Great Lakes: as many as half a dozen major lakefront cities get more and faster winds. Chicago's wind speeds average 10.3 miles per hour for the year (12 miles per hour in April, its windiest month). But in Mil-waukee, just 90 miles to the north, annual average wind speed is 11.6 miles per hour (13.1 miles per hour in the windiest month). Chicago does experience heavier snows than do cities farther from Lake Mich-igan. Cold winter winds pick up moisture as they move across the water—thus delivering more snow to Chicago than to communities farther inland.

ZONE 41

Southeast Nebraska and Northeast Kansas to Northern Illinois and Indiana, Southeast Wisconsin, Michigan, Northern Ohio

Here, as in Zone 33, the climate results from two primary forces: warm, moist air moving north from the Gulf of Mexico during spring, summer, and fall; and frigid arctic air descending from Canada in winter. A lesser (but still noteworthy) influence is the dry, usually warm air that sometimes moves in from the West or Southwest.

Average annual minimum temperatures range from 11° to 20°F/−12° to −7°C, with record lows from −26° to −37°F/−32° to −38°C. The growing season averages 120 to 180 days.

In parts of Illinois, Indiana, Michigan, Ohio, and Wisconsin, the Great Lakes do influence the weather (though their effect is not as strong here as it is in Zone 39). Areas of Zone 41 closer to the lakes have summers that are cooler, wetter, and later to arrive, while winters are somewhat milder and likewise later in arriving. Parts of Zone 41 west of the Mississippi have the hottest summers, while areas adjoining the Great Lakes have the fewest really hot days.

Zone 41 marks the northern boundary for many deciduous fruit trees (though not for apples and sour cherries), either because the trees are not hardy there or because springtime frosts kill the blossoms in most years.

Prairie Vignettes

Winter snow—a given in Zone 41—transforms spent rudbeckia blossoms into frosty candles *(above)*. As certain as the snow is the lush prairie spring *(below)*, with grasses and wildflowers springing from the deep, fertile midwestern soil.

Zone 41's temperature extremes vary from extremely cold to very hot (as high as 112°F/44°C)—conditions that rule out a number of popular permanent landscaping plants. Regional native plants, however, have the stamina and disposition to survive through every season. Handsome, durable natives of this area include, among many others, various kinds of columbine, gayfeather, and rudbeckia.

Originally much of this zone was tall-grass prairie, with a soil enriched by thousands of years of the slow decay of these grasses. Most of the area has been cleared for farming, and the preservation or restoration of prairie sites and a considerable interest in prairie gardens are quite recent. Soils, though fertile, often have a high lime content—ideal for lilacs and delphiniums, but difficult for rhododendrons and other acid-soil lovers. Grow the latter in raised beds heavily amended with peat moss or other organic matter. Protect these and other evergreens from freeze-and-thaw winters and harsh winds by mulching and using wind screens.

Growing Season

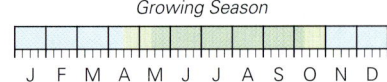

J F M A M J J A S O N D

Mid-Atlantic States

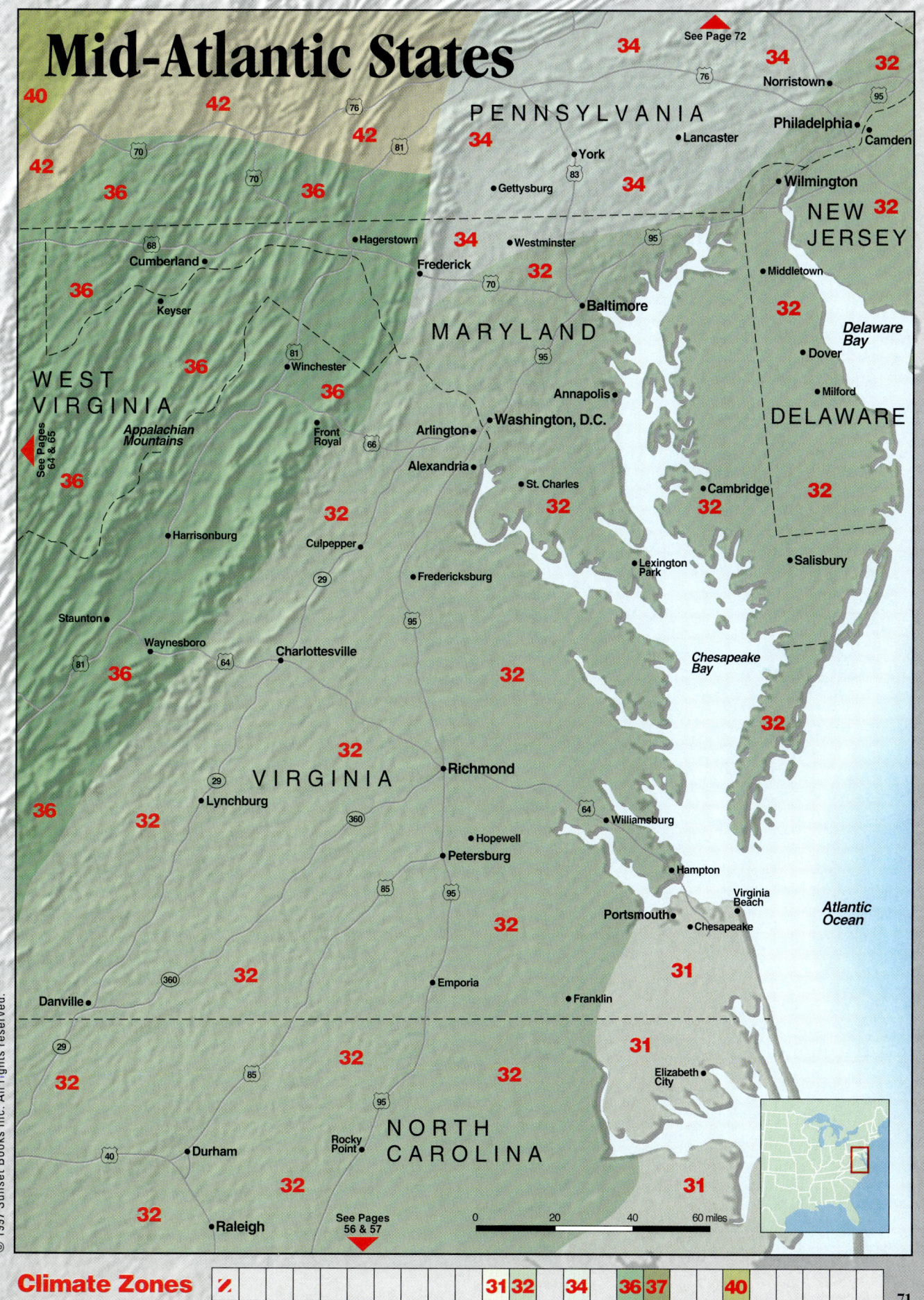

PENNSYLVANIA

NEW JERSEY

MARYLAND

DELAWARE

WEST VIRGINIA

Appalachian Mountains

VIRGINIA

NORTH CAROLINA

Delaware Bay

Chesapeake Bay

Atlantic Ocean

See Page 72

See Pages 64 & 65

See Pages 56 & 57

Cities and towns:
Norristown · Philadelphia · Camden · Lancaster · York · Gettysburg · Wilmington · Westminster · Hagerstown · Frederick · Middletown · Cumberland · Keyser · Baltimore · Dover · Milford · Annapolis · Washington, D.C. · Winchester · Arlington · Alexandria · Front Royal · St. Charles · Cambridge · Salisbury · Harrisonburg · Culpepper · Fredericksburg · Lexington Park · Staunton · Waynesboro · Charlottesville · Lynchburg · Richmond · Williamsburg · Hopewell · Petersburg · Hampton · Portsmouth · Virginia Beach · Chesapeake · Danville · Emporia · Franklin · Elizabeth City · Durham · Rocky Point · Raleigh

Route numbers: 76 · 70 · 81 · 68 · 95 · 83 · 29 · 66 · 64 · 360 · 85 · 40

Climate zone numbers shown: 40 · 42 · 34 · 32 · 36 · 31

Climate Zones 31 32 34 36 37 40

New York, Pennsylvania, New Jersey

45

QUEBEC

Ste.-Agathe-des-Monts **43**

45 15 Joliette **42** 40 30

Hull Laval Montreal **44**

Ottawa **43** Salaberry-de-Valleyfield St.-Jean-sur-Richelieu

43 **43** Cornwall 401 St.-Jean-sur-Richelieu 15 10

ONTARIO Massena *Lake Champlain*

42 Burlington 89

40 St. Lawrence **44**

Peterborough Kingston *Adirondack Mountains*

43 Belleville **39** 401 Watertown **38**

York Scarborough **39** **40** **44** 87

Toronto *Lake Ontario* Glens Falls

Kitchener Mississauga 81 Saratoga Springs

40 2 Hamilton *Oneida Lake* **42** Troy

Brantford St. Catharines QEW **39** Rochester Syracuse Utica Schenectady Albany

39 Niagara Falls 90 *Finger Lakes* **NEW YORK** 88 **37**

Buffalo Geneseo Ithaca Oneonta *Catskill Mountains* Hudson River

40 390 *Lake Erie* 42 *Finger Lakes* Kingston 87 **37**

Erie Jamestown 17 Corning Elmira Binghamton Poughkeepsie

39 17 17 81 84 Newburgh

40 79 **42** **42** Scranton *Pocono Mountains* 87 **34**

Youngstown Wilkes-Barre 380 80 *Long Island* 95

New Castle Williamsport 180 Stroudsburg 80 New York

40 **42** State College Hazleton **37** Paterson

Pittsburgh **PENNSYLVANIA** Altoona Bethlehem Newark See Pages 74 & 75

Steubenville 76 Johnstown *Appalachian Mountains* Allentown **34**

Washington 70 **42** **37** 78 9 Princeton

Wheeling **42** Lebanon Reading Trenton

Moundsville 76 81 Harrisburg 76 Pottstown **NEW JERSEY** *Atlantic Ocean*

40 83 **34** Norristown

36 Uniontown 79 70 York Lancaster Philadelphia Camden

36 Morgantown 68 Hagerstown Westminster 95 Wilmington **32**

WEST VIRGINIA Cumberland **36** **MARYLAND** Baltimore Middletown Vineland Atlantic City

Keyser 81 270 See Page 71 **32** **DELAWARE**

Winchester **32**

0 30 60 90 miles

Climate Zones

| | | | | | | 32 | 34 | 36 | 37 | 38 | 39 | 40 | | 42 | 43 | 44 | 45 |

See Pages 68 & 69

See Pages 64 & 65

See Page 76

ZONE **42** Mountains of Interior Pennsylvania and New York, St. Lawrence Valley

The United States part of Zone 42 is mountainous country, a continuation of the Appalachian range (Zone 36). Though lower in elevation than Zone 36, it is farther from the equator, so its minimum temperatures are lower. Winters are harsher and summers more humid than those in the surrounding areas. Still, numerous flowering native plants thrive to delight gardeners in this zone. You can grow excellent tomatoes here, too; plant them in late May for harvest in August and September. The growing season ranges from 90 to 120 days.

In Canada, much of the St. Lawrence Valley (as far north as 48° north latitude) experiences the general conditions just described, although the Canadian region of Zone 42 typically records lower temperatures than does the U.S. part. Over the zone as a whole, minimums range from −20° to −40°F/−29° to −40°C.

Rolling Hills, Fertile Farms

A field of wine grapes tumbles down a hillside above New York's Lake Cayuga. Sizable bodies of water like the Finger Lakes and St. Lawrence River create microclimates in the lands nearby.

Growing Season

J F M A M J J A S O N D

ZONE **43** Upper Mississippi Valley, Upper Michigan, Southern Ontario and Quebec

Here, as in Zones 41 and 33 to the south, gardening is influenced by two forces: warm, moist air moving north from the Gulf of Mexico in spring, summer, and fall (it reaches about as far as Minneapolis and St. Paul); and frigid arctic air coming south from Canada in winter.

Expected winter lows range from −20° to −30°F/−29° to −34°C, but in unusually cold years, temperatures may drop to −40°F/−40°C or lower. Given temperatures like these, the best shade trees for the region are its native maples, oaks, birches, and conifers, as well as some species from northern Europe and Asia. This far north, the one really dependable fruit tree is the

apple. Those that do best are early-ripening varieties on semidwarf rootstocks.

Tomatoes grown in this region are sweet and tasty. With the last frosts expected in late May, set out started plants in early June for harvest in late August and early September. The first frosts usually arrive in mid- to late September.

Roses bloom quite nicely during the summer. For many gardeners, the reward of warm-season blossoms is well worth the trouble of protecting the plants each autumn against winter's freezes. Or try Griffith Buck hybrids or other extra-hardy varieties.

Depending on the weather, lawns may well get through the summer without watering. An inch or more of rain each week will sustain the grass; less than that, and you'll need to water your lawn to keep it green.

Springtime, Short but Sweet

Native treasures like these trilliums are one lovely reward of a springtime stroll through northern woodlands *(above)*. Evergreen-fringed ponds *(below)* are a legacy of the glaciers which gave Minnesota its famous ten thousand (or more) lakes.

Growing Season

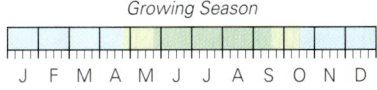

J F M A M J J A S O N D

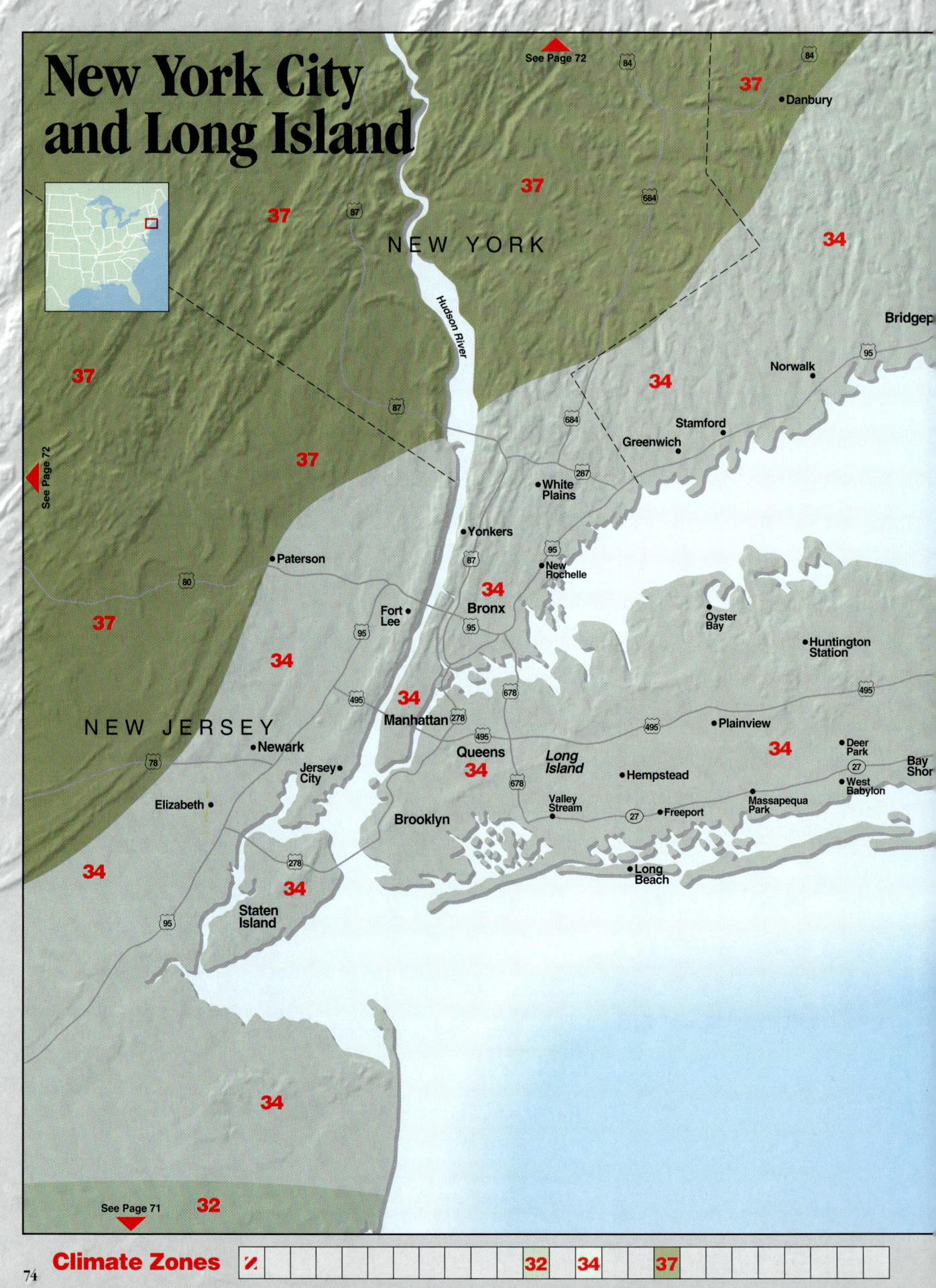

New York City and Long Island

See Page 72

37 Danbury

37

N E W Y O R K

37

34

Hudson River

Bridgep

37

Norwalk

34

Stamford

Greenwich

See Page 72

37

White
Plains

Yonkers

37

New
Rochelle

Paterson

34

Bronx

Oyster
Bay

Huntington
Station

Fort
Lee

34

34

Manhattan

37

34

Plainview

N E W   J E R S E Y

Queens

Long
Island

Deer
Park

34

Bay
Shor

Newark

34

Hempstead

West
Babylon

Jersey
City

Valley
Stream

Massapequa
Park

Elizabeth

Brooklyn

Freeport

34

Long
Beach

Staten
Island

34

34

See Page 71 **32**

Climate Zones   **32**   **34**   **37**

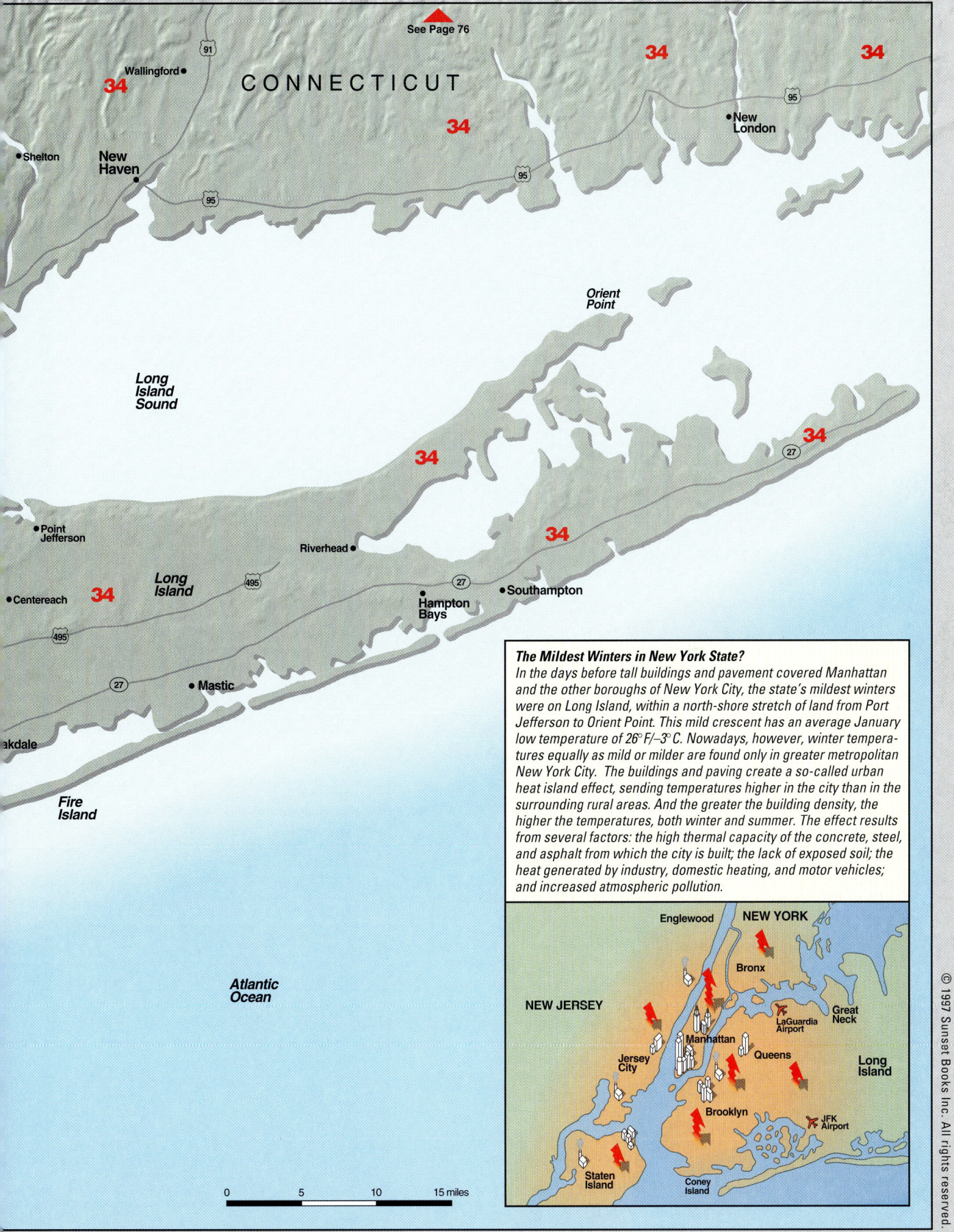

See Page 76

34

34

34

Wallingford •

34

C O N N E C T I C U T

34

• New
London

91

95

• Shelton

New
Haven

95

95

Orient
Point

95

Long
Island
Sound

34

27

34

• Point
Jefferson

Riverhead •

34

• Centereach

34

Long
Island

495

27

34

• Southampton

27

akdale

495

Hampton
Bays

27

• Mastic

Fire
Island

Atlantic
Ocean

The Mildest Winters in New York State?
In the days before tall buildings and pavement covered Manhattan and the other boroughs of New York City, the state's mildest winters were on Long Island, within a north-shore stretch of land from Port Jefferson to Orient Point. This mild crescent has an average January low temperature of 26° F/–3° C. Nowadays, however, winter temperatures equally as mild or milder are found only in greater metropolitan New York City. The buildings and paving create a so-called urban heat island effect, sending temperatures higher in the city than in the surrounding rural areas. And the greater the building density, the higher the temperatures, both winter and summer. The effect results from several factors: the high thermal capacity of the concrete, steel, and asphalt from which the city is built; the lack of exposed soil; the heat generated by industry, domestic heating, and motor vehicles; and increased atmospheric pollution.

Englewood   **NEW YORK**

Bronx

NEW JERSEY

Great
Neck

LaGuardia
Airport

Jersey
City

Manhattan

Queens

Long
Island

Brooklyn

JFK
Airport

Staten
Island

Coney
Island

0   5   10   15 miles

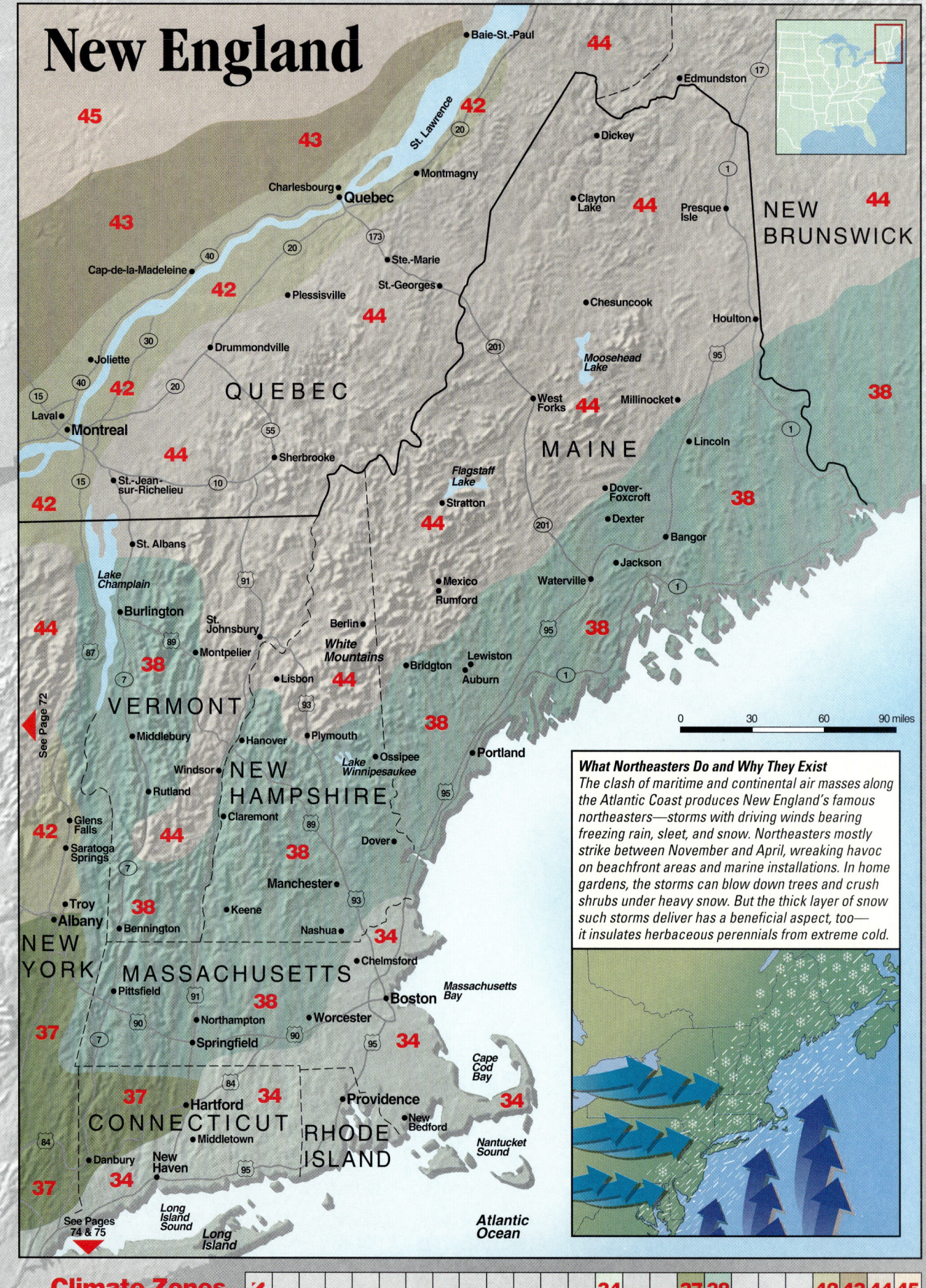

New England

Baie-St.-Paul
44
Edmundston
17
45
42
43
Dickey
St. Lawrence
20
Montmagny
Charlesbourg
Quebec
1
Clayton
Lake
44
Presque
Isle
NEW
BRUNSWICK
44
43
173
Ste.-Marie
St.-Georges
Cap-de-la-Madeleine
40
20
42
Plessisville
44
Chesuncook
Houlton
30
Drummondville
201
Moosehead
Lake
95
Joliette
40
42
20
QUEBEC
West
Forks
44
Millinocket
38
Laval
55
Montreal
MAINE
Lincoln
15
44
Sherbrooke
Flagstaff
Lake
Dover-
Foxcroft
38
St.-Jean-
sur-Richelieu
10
Stratton
44
Dexter
42
201
Bangor
St. Albans
Jackson
Lake
Champlain
91
Mexico
Rumford
Waterville
38
Burlington
St.
Johnsbury
Berlin
95
44
87
89
White
Mountains
38
Montpelier
Bridgton
Lewiston
7
Lisbon
44
Auburn
1
VERMONT
93
38
Middlebury
Hanover
Plymouth
Portland
Windsor
NEW
HAMPSHIRE
Lake
Winnipesaukee
Ossipee
125
Rutland
Claremont
Dover
42
Glens
Falls
44
89
Saratoga
Springs
7
38
Manchester
93
Troy
38
Keene
Albany
Bennington
Nashua
34
NEW
YORK
MASSACHUSETTS
Chelmsford
Massachusetts
Bay
Pittsfield
91
38
Boston
37
90
Northampton
Worcester
7
Springfield
90
95
34
Cape
Cod
Bay
84
37
34
Hartford
Providence
34
CONNECTICUT
Middletown
New
Bedford
RHODE
ISLAND
Nantucket
Sound
84
37
34
Danbury
New
Haven
95
Long
Island
Sound
Atlantic
Ocean
Long
Island

See Page 72

See Pages
74 & 75

What Northeasters Do and Why They Exist

The clash of maritime and continental air masses along the Atlantic Coast produces New England's famous northeasters—storms with driving winds bearing freezing rain, sleet, and snow. Northeasters mostly strike between November and April, wreaking havoc on beachfront areas and marine installations. In home gardens, the storms can blow down trees and crush shrubs under heavy snow. But the thick layer of snow such storms deliver has a beneficial aspect, too— it insulates herbaceous perennials from extreme cold.

0   30   60   90 miles

Climate Zones   34   37 38   42 43 44 45

ZONE **44** Mountains of New England and Southeastern Quebec

"Ski country" is what many people would call the southern half of Zone 44. Winters are very cold (with lows from −20° to −40°F/−29° to −40°C) and summers comparatively cool (highs from 60°F/16°C to 70°F/21°C or higher), thanks both to the region's northerly latitude and to its frequently high elevations. Mt. Washington (elevation 6,288 ft.), in the White Mountains, has been known to get freezing weather and snow during every month of the year.

But the region has its gardening life as well. If you want to grow a summer garden, wait until June 1 or the apparent last frost—and then plant immediately, since the year's first frost looms only about 3 months away (or even sooner, in the occasional extra-cold year). Get tomatoes and peppers into the ground as soon as possible, along with the hardier potatoes, broccoli, cauliflower, and cabbage.

Lawn grass grows well in May and June, then often slows a little in July. In August, cool, wet weather promotes fresh growth again.

Among roses, most popular hybrid teas, grandifloras, and floribundas are too tender to survive winters unless they are heavily protected. The most satisfactory roses for this climate are the hardiest species (such as *Rosa rugosa*) and cold-tolerant shrub roses developed in the Midwest and Canada.

Growing Season

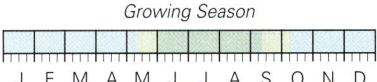

| J | F | M | A | M | J | J | A | S | O | N | D |

The Northeast's "Great Outdoors"

Firs, spruces, and tough deciduous trees like these snowy-trunked birches are quintessential elements of Zone 44's forests. A delight to hikers and wilderness buffs, the region poses a challenge to gardeners: its terrain is rocky, its soils shallow, and its growing season brief. Rugged *Rosa rugosa (left)* takes these conditions in stride.

ZONE 45   Northern Minnesota, Northwestern Wisconsin, Eastern Manitoba, Northern and Central Ontario and Quebec

No other garden climate in eastern North America matches Zone 45 for winter cold or briefness of the frost-free season. Temperatures often fall to $-30°$ to $-40°F/-34°$ to $-40°C$ (the lowest temperature ever reported in northern Minnesota is $-48°F/-44°C$). The soil freezes in early December—often to a depth of 5 to 6 feet—and thaws in mid-April.

The last spring frosts come in early or even mid-June, with the first frosts of fall arriving in early September. If you want to grow tomatoes, peppers, corn, and other frost-delicate crops, you'll need to choose short-season varieties.

Endless Panoramas

Gardening in Zone 45 requires careful planning—the choice of plants is limited and the growing season very short. Vast, open vistas are characteristic of this glacier-worn territory of large farms, widely spaced towns, and endless tracts of forest.

Among fruits and berries, good choices for Zone 45 are blueberries and native raspberries, cherries, and plums.

Gardeners in this region enjoy a number of dependable and beautiful flowering shrubs, including lilac, viburnum, and redtwig dogwood. Flowering trees are few, but two hawthorns, *Crataegus ambigua* and *C.* 'Toba', reliably show off their white flowers and red fruit. Spring-blooming bulbs perform beautifully; native wildflowers and rock garden plants are popular, too. The consistently low winter temperatures and a good snow cover aid in the survival of many perennials and low shrubs.

Broad-leafed evergreens are the major garden element lacking in this zone, but many conifers and berry-producing shrubs provide winter color. Recent work at the University of Minnesota has extended the cold tolerance of deciduous azaleas to $-40°F/-40°C$ in the Northern Lights Hybrids (such as 'Golden Lights,' 'Orchard Lights,' 'White Lights').

Growing Season

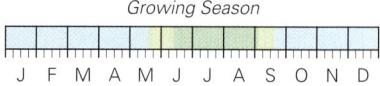

J F M A M J J A S O N D

A Guide to
PLANT SELECTION

The thousands of plants described in the A to Z Plant Encyclopedia (beginning on page 161) include an infinitely varied assortment of sizes, shapes, textures, and colors. The pleasure of choosing from this rich assortment is available to anyone with a sense of adventure and a bit of earth. But such abundance can sometimes lead to bewilderment. The lists of plants that follow, used with the plant encyclopedia, will help you to select the right plants, whether you are looking to achieve a special effect with flowers or foliage, tackling a difficult landscape situation, or starting out with the basics.

Perennials provide colorful display and flowers for cutting.

The symbols in the lists will help you choose plants most suitable for your garden. How much sun a plant needs for best performance is shown by one or more of three symbols:

☼ Grows best with unobstructed sunlight all day long or almost all day— you can overlook an hour or so of shade at the beginning or end of a summer day

◑ Needs partial shade—that is, shade for half the day or for at least 3 hours during the hottest part of the day

● Prefers little or no direct sunlight— for example, it does best on the north side of a house or beneath a broad, dense tree

A plant's approximate moisture needs are indicated by one or more of three symbols:

◌ Thrives with less than regular moisture—moderate amounts for some plants, little for those with greater drought tolerance

● Performs well with regular moisture—the soil doesn't become too wet or too dry

◕ Takes more than regular moisture— includes plants needing constantly moist soil, bog plants, and aquatic plants.

A plant's climate adaptability is shown after the ⚡. The numbers refer to the climate zones (see pages 16–78) where the plant will grow best. Other information, such as flower or leaf color, is explained in legends on the individual lists.

LANDSCAPE PLANTS
with Showy Flowers

Trees, shrubs, ground covers, and vines are the backbones of the garden, but that doesn't mean they only serve as a neutral backdrop to showy annuals and perennials. Many permanent landscape plants put on a striking show of blooms, which provide changing interest throughout the year. In this list, plants are arranged by the time of year in which they flower. Use it to plan your garden's permanent floral display according to season and flower color.

Aesculus carnea

Bauhinia

Chionanthus virginicus

Cornus florida 'Rubra'

Malus 'Liset'

SPRING
Trees

Aesculus
HORSECHESTNUT
NEEDS, ZONES VARY   **p. 169**

Bauhinia
BRAZILIAN BUTTERFLY TREE
☼ ◐ ◑ ⚡ ZONES VARY   **p. 204**

Catalpa
☼ ◐ ◑ ◑ ⚡ 3–24, 28–41   **p. 234**

Cercis
REDBUD
NEEDS, ZONES VARY   **p. 239**

Chionanthus virginicus
FRINGE TREE
☼ ◐ ◑ ⚡ MANY ZONES   **p. 245**

Cornus
DOGWOOD
☼ ◐ ◑ ⚡ ZONES VARY   **p. 262**

Crataegus
HAWTHORN
☼ ◑ ⚡ MANY ZONES   **p. 266**

Erythrina (some)
CORAL TREE
☼ ◐ ◑ ⚡ ZONES VARY   **p. 295**

Halesia
◐ ◑ ⚡ 2–9, 14–24, 31–41   **p. 326**

Laburnum
GOLDENCHAIN TREE
☼ ◐ ◑ ⚡ MANY ZONES   **p. 361**

Magnolia (most deciduous)
☼ ◐ ◑ ⚡ ZONES VARY   **p. 381**

Malus
CRABAPPLE
☼ ◐ ◑ ⚡ 1–21, 29–43   **p. 387**

Melaleuca (some)
☼ ◐ ◑ ⚡ ZONES VARY   **p. 393**

Prunus (flowering)
☼ ◐ ◑ ◑ ⚡ ZONES VARY   **p. 451**

Pyrus calleryana
☼ ◑ ⚡ MANY ZONES   **p. 459**

Tabebuia chrysotricha
GOLDEN TRUMPET TREE
☼ ◐ ◑ ⚡ 15, 16, 20–26   **p. 513**

SPRING
Shrubs

Abutilon (most)
FLOWERING MAPLE
☼ ◐ ◑ ◑ ⚡ 8, 9, 12–27   **p. 163**

Acacia (most)
☼ ◐ ◑ ⚡ ZONES VARY   **p. 163**

Alyogyne huegelii
BLUE HIBISCUS
☼ ◐ ◑ ⚡ 15–17, 20–27   **p. 176**

Berberis
BARBERRY
☼ ◐ ◑ ◑ ⚡ ZONES VARY   **p. 207**

Brunfelsia pauciflora
☼ ◐ ◑ ⚡ 12–17, 20–28   **p. 216**

Camellia (many)
◐ ◑ ◑ ⚡ MANY ZONES   **p. 224**

Chaenomeles
FLOWERING QUINCE
☼ ◐ ◑ ⚡ 2–21, 28–41   **p. 240**

Corylopsis
WINTER HAZEL
☼ ◐ ◑ ⚡ MANY ZONES   **p. 263**

For growing symbol explanations, please see page 79.

COLOR CODES: Each tint represents a range of colors, not a color match.

BLUE–PURPLE
WHITE–CREAM
PINK–RED
YELLOW–ORANGE

Laburnum

Prunus

Deutzia gracilis

Spring garden with white viburnum

Exochorda macrantha 'The Bride'

Kalmia latifolia

Mahonia aquifolium

Melaleuca nesophila

Daphne
NEEDS, ZONES VARY — p. 275

Deutzia (some)
☼ ◐ ● ⚡ MANY ZONES — p. 277

Erica (most)
HEATH
☼ ◐ ● ⚡ ZONES VARY — p. 291

Exochorda
PEARL BUSH
☼ ● ⚡ 2–9, 14–18, 31–41 — p. 302

Forsythia
☼ ● ● ⚡ MANY ZONES — p. 308

Jasminum (some)
JASMINE
☼ ◐ ● ⚡ ZONES VARY — p. 351

Kalmia latifolia
MOUNTAIN LAUREL
☼ ◐ ● ⚡ MANY ZONES — p. 358

Kolkwitzia amabilis
BEAUTY BUSH
☼ ● ● ⚡ MANY ZONES — p. 360

Leptospermum
TEA TREE
☼ ● ⚡ ZONES VARY — p. 366

Leucothoe
NEEDS, ZONES VARY — p. 368

Lonicera
HONEYSUCKLE
☼ ◐ ● ⚡ ZONES VARY — p. 376

Mahonia
NEEDS, ZONES VARY — p. 386

Melaleuca (some)
☼ ● ⚡ ZONES VARY — p. 393

Michelia figo
BANANA SHRUB
☼ ● ⚡ MANY ZONES — p. 396

Myrtus communis
MYRTLE
☼ ◐ ● ⚡ 8–24, 26–28 — p. 401

Philadelphus (some)
MOCK ORANGE
☼ ● ● ● ⚡ ZONES VARY — p. 427

Photinia
☼ ● ● ⚡ ZONES VARY — p. 430

Pieris
☼ ● ⚡ ZONES VARY — p. 432

Plumbago auriculata
CAPE PLUMBAGO
☼ ● ⚡ 8, 9, 12–28 — p. 441

Rhaphiolepis indica
INDIA HAWTHORN
☼ ◐ ● ● ⚡ MANY ZONES — p. 465

Rhododendron
AZALEA, RHODODENDRON
☼ ◐ ● ● ⚡ ZONES VARY — p. 465

Ribes (some)
CURRANT, GOOSEBERRY
☼ ◐ ● ⚡ ZONES VARY — p. 472

Rosa
ROSE
NEEDS, ZONES VARY — p. 473

Rosmarinus officinalis
ROSEMARY
☼ ● ⚡ 4–24, 26–32 — p. 480

Spiraea (some)
☼ ◐ ● ● ⚡ ZONES VARY — p. 502

Syringa
LILAC
☼ ◐ ● ⚡ ZONES VARY — p. 512

Tecoma stans
YELLOW BELLS
☼ ● ● ⚡ 10, 12, 13, 21–28 — p. 516

Viburnum (some)
NEEDS, ZONES VARY — p. 532

Weigela
☼ ◐ ● ⚡ MANY ZONES — p. 538

SPRING
Ground Covers, Vines

Allamanda cathartica
GOLDEN TRUMPET
☼ ● ⚡ 24–27 — p. 173

Bougainvillea
☼ ◐ ● ● ⚡ MANY ZONES — p. 212

Clematis (some)
☼ ● ⚡ ZONES VARY — p. 253

Clytostoma callistegioides
VIOLET TRUMPET VINE
☼ ◐ ● ● ⚡ 9, 12–28 — p. 256

Delosperma nubigenum
ICE PLANT
☼ ● ⚡ 2–24, 28–41 — p. 276

Distictis buccinatoria
BLOOD-RED TRUMPET VINE
☼ ◐ ● ● ⚡ 8, 9, 14–28 — p. 282

Drosanthemum
ICE PLANT
☼ ● ⚡ 14–27 — p. 284

Erigeron (some)
FLEABANE
☼ ◐ ● ⚡ ZONES VARY — p. 291

Rhododendron 'Bow Bells'

Rosa 'Belle Story'

Syringa

Tecoma stans

Clematis

Plant listings continue ▶

81

Lonicera japonica

Osteospermum fruticosum

Wisteria

Albizia julibrissin

Erythrina

Gelsemium sempervirens
CAROLINA JESSAMINE
☼ ◐ ● ◗ ✂ MANY ZONES   **p. 314**

Jasminum (some)
JASMINE
☼ ◐ ◗ ✂ ZONES VARY   **p. 351**

Lampranthus
ICE PLANT
☼ ◗ ✂ 14–26   **p. 363**

Lonicera (some)
HONEYSUCKLE
☼ ◐ ◗ ✂ ZONES VARY   **p. 376**

Macfadyena unguis-cati
CAT'S CLAW
☼ ◗ ✂ 8–29, 31   **p. 380**

Oenothera
EVENING PRIMROSE
NEEDS, ZONES VARY   **p. 407**

Osteospermum fruticosum
TRAILING AFRICAN DAISY
☼ ◗ ◗ ✂ ALL ZONES   **p. 411**

Potentilla (some)
CINQUEFOIL
☼ ◗ ◗ ✂ ZONES VARY   **p. 447**

Rosa
ROSE
NEEDS, ZONES VARY   **p. 473**

Solandra maxima
CUP-OF-GOLD VINE
☼ ◗ ✂ 17, 21–27   **p. 499**

Solanum jasminoides
POTATO VINE
☼ ◐ ◗ ◗ ✂ 8, 9, 12–27   **p. 499**

Vinca
PERIWINKLE
◐ ● ◗ ✂ ZONES VARY   **p. 534**

Wisteria
☼ ◗ ◗ ✂ ZONES VARY   **p. 538**

SUMMER
Trees

Albizia julibrissin
SILK TREE
☼ ◐ ◗ ◗ ✂ 4–23, 26–33   **p. 172**

Cassia leptophylla
GOLD MEDALLION TREE
☼ ◗ ◗ ✂ 21–25, 27   **p. 233**

Catalpa
☼ ◗ ◗ ◗ ✂ 3–24, 28–41   **p. 234**

Chilopsis linearis
DESERT WILLOW
☼ ◗ ✂ MANY ZONES   **p. 244**

Chionanthus retusus
CHINESE FRINGE TREE
☼ ◗ ◗ ✂ MANY ZONES   **p. 245**

Chitalpa tashkentensis
CHITALPA
☼ ◗ ✂ 3–24, 28–33   **p. 245**

Cordia sebestena
GEIGER TREE
☼ ◗ ✂ 24, 25, 27   **p. 260**

Cornus kousa
KOUSA DOGWOOD
☼ ◐ ◗ ✂ MANY ZONES   **p. 262**

Erythrina (some)
CORAL TREE
☼ ◗ ◗ ✂ ZONES VARY   **p. 295**

Jacaranda mimosifolia
JACARANDA
☼ ◗ ✂ 12, 13, 15–25, 27   **p. 351**

Lagerstroemia indica
CRAPE MYRTLE
☼ ◗ ✂ MANY ZONES   **p. 362**

Maackia
☼ ◗ ✂ ZONES VARY   **p. 380**

Magnolia grandiflora
SOUTHERN MAGNOLIA
☼ ◐ ◗ ✂ MANY ZONES   **p. 382**

Robinia ambigua 'Idahoensis'
IDAHO LOCUST
☼ ◗ ✂ 1–24, 29–45   **p. 472**

Sophora japonica
JAPANESE PAGODA TREE
☼ ◐ ◗ ✂ 2–24, 31–41   **p. 500**

Stewartia
☼ ◐ ◗ ✂ ZONES VARY   **p. 506**

Vitex agnus-castus
CHASTE TREE
☼ ◗ ✂ 4–33   **p. 535**

SUMMER
Shrubs

Abelia
☼ ◐ ◗ ✂ ZONES VARY   **p. 162**

Abutilon
FLOWERING MAPLE
☼ ◐ ◗ ◗ ✂ 8, 9, 12–27   **p. 163**

Alyogyne huegelii
BLUE HIBISCUS
☼ ◗ ◗ ✂ 15–17, 20–27   **p. 176**

Amorpha fruticosa
INDIGO BUSH
☼ ◗ ✂ 2, 3, 28–45   **p. 177**

Brunfelsia pauciflora
◗ ◗ ✂ 12–17, 20–28   **p. 216**

Buddleia davidii
BUTTERFLY BUSH
☼ ◐ ◗ ◗ ✂ MANY ZONES   **p. 217**

Chitalpa tashkentensis

Cordia sebestena

Magnolia grandiflora

Jacaranda mimosifolia

Buddleia davidii

For growing symbol explanations, please see page 79.

Caryopteris clandonensis

Erica cinerea

Hydrangea macrophylla

Hypericum 'Hidcote'

Jasminum nitidum

Caesalpinia
BIRD OF PARADISE
☼ ♦ ⚡ ZONES VARY   **p. 219**

Callistemon
BOTTLEBRUSH
☼ ♦ ♦ ⚡ 8, 9, 12–28   **p. 222**

Calluna vulgaris
SCOTCH HEATHER
☼ ♦ ⚡ MANY ZONES   **p. 222**

Caryopteris
BLUEBEARD
☼ ♦ ⚡ ZONES VARY   **p. 232**

Ceratostigma plumbaginoides
DWARF PLUMBAGO
☼ ◐ ♦⚡ MANY ZONES   **p. 239**

Clerodendrum
GLORYBOWER
◐ ♦ ⚡ ZONES VARY   **p. 255**

Clethra
◐ ♦♦♦⚡ ZONES VARY   **p. 256**

Daboecia
IRISH HEATH
☼ ♦ ♦ ⚡ ZONES VARY   **p. 274**

Deutzia (some)
☼ ◐ ♦ ⚡ MANY ZONES   **p. 277**

Erica (some)
HEATH
◐ ♦ ♦ ⚡ ZONES VARY   **p. 291**

Fuchsia
◐ ♦ ⚡ ZONES VARY   **p. 311**

Gardenia jasminoides
☼ ◐ ♦ ⚡ MANY ZONES   **p. 312**

Hibiscus
☼ ♦ ⚡ ZONES VARY   **p. 334**

Hydrangea
☼ ◐ ♦ ⚡ ZONES VARY   **p. 340**

Hypericum
ST. JOHNSWORT
☼ ◐ ♦♦ ⚡ ZONES VARY   **p. 341**

Jasminum (some)
JASMINE
☼ ◐ ♦ ⚡ ZONES VARY   **p. 351**

Justicia carnea
BRAZILIAN PLUME FLOWER
◐ ♦ ♦♦ ⚡ 8, 9, 13–27   **p. 358**

Lavandula
LAVENDER
☼ ♦ ⚡ ZONES VARY   **p. 365**

Lavatera
TREE MALLOW
☼ ♦ ⚡ ZONES VARY   **p. 366**

Leucophyllum
TEXAS RANGER
☼ ♦ ⚡ 7–24, 28–32, 35   **p. 367**

Melaleuca (some)
☼ ♦ ⚡ ZONES VARY   **p. 393**

Nerium oleander
OLEANDER
☼ ♦ ♦ ⚡ 18–31   **p. 405**

Philadelphus (some)
MOCK ORANGE
☼ ◐ ♦ ♦ ⚡ ZONES VARY   **p. 427**

Phlomis
JERUSALEM SAGE
NEEDS, ZONES VARY   **p. 428**

Potentilla
CINQUEFOIL
☼ ◐ ♦ ♦ ⚡ ZONES VARY   **p. 447**

Punica granatum
POMEGRANATE
☼ ♦ ♦ ⚡ 5–32   **p. 457**

Rosa (some)
ROSE
NEEDS, ZONES VARY   **p. 473**

Salvia (several)
SAGE
NEEDS, ZONES VARY   **p. 484**

Spiraea (some)
☼ ◐ ♦ ♦ ⚡ ZONES VARY   **p. 502**

Tecoma stans
YELLOW BELLS
☼ ♦ ♦ ⚡ 10, 12, 13, 21–28   **p. 516**

Tibouchina urvilleana
PRINCESS FLOWER
☼ ◐ ♦ ♦ ⚡ 16, 17, 21–27   **p. 520**

SUMMER
Ground Covers, Vines

Allamanda cathartica
GOLDEN TRUMPET
☼ ♦ ⚡ 24–27   **p. 173**

Antigonon leptopus
CORAL VINE
☼ ♦ ♦ ⚡ 12, 13, 18–30   **p. 181**

Bougainvillea
☼ ◐ ♦ ♦ ⚡ MANY ZONES   **p. 212**

Campsis
TRUMPET VINE
☼ ◐ ♦ ♦ ⚡ ZONES VARY   **p. 227**

Clematis (some)
☼ ◐ ♦ ⚡ ZONES VARY   **p. 253**

Delosperma cooperi
ICE PLANT
☼ ♦ ⚡ 3–24, 28–32   **p. 276**

Lavandula angustifolia

Philadelphus coronarius

Potentilla fruticosa

Allamanda

Lantana camara

Plant listings continue ▶

Mandevilla splendens 'Red Riding Hood'

Passiflora mollissima

Scaevola

Solanum jasminoides

Trachelospermum jasminoides

Distictis
TRUMPET VINE
☼ ◐ ● ⚡ ZONES VARY — p. 282

Jasminum (some)
JASMINE
☼ ◐ ● ⚡ ZONES VARY — p. 351

Lantana
☼ ● ⚡ 8–10, 12–30 — p. 363

Lonicera
HONEYSUCKLE
☼ ◐ ● ⚡ ZONES VARY — p. 376

Mandevilla
NEEDS, ZONES VARY — p. 391

Pandorea jasminoides
BOWER VINE
☼ ● ● ⚡ 16–27 — p. 414

Passiflora
PASSION VINE
☼ ● ● ⚡ ZONES VARY — p. 417

Petrea volubilis
QUEEN'S WREATH
☼ ◐ ● ⚡ 19–25 — p. 426

Plumbago auriculata
CAPE PLUMBAGO
☼ ● ⚡ 8, 9, 12–28 — p. 441

Podranea ricasoliana
PINK TRUMPET VINE
☼ ◐ ● ● ⚡ MANY ZONES — p. 443

Scaevola
☼ ● ● ⚡ 8, 9, 14–24 — p. 490

Solanum jasminoides
POTATO VINE
☼ ◐ ● ● ⚡ 8, 9, 12–27 — p. 499

Sollya heterophylla
AUSTRALIAN BLUEBELL CREEPER
☼ ◐ ● ⚡ 8, 9, 14–28 — p. 500

Trachelospermum jasminoides
STAR JASMINE
☼ ◐ ● ● ⚡ 8–32 — p. 523

Verbena
☼ ● ⚡ ZONES VARY — p. 531

FALL
Trees

Bauhinia blakeana
HONG KONG ORCHID TREE
☼ ● ● ⚡ MANY ZONES — p. 204

Chorisia
FLOSS SILK TREE
☼ ● ● ⚡ ZONES VARY — p. 246

Cochlospermum vitifolium
BUTTERCUP TREE
☼ ● ● ⚡ 25 — p. 257

Erythrina humeana
NATAL CORAL TREE
☼ ● ● ⚡ 12, 13, 20–27 — p. 295

Melaleuca (some)
☼ ● ⚡ ZONES VARY — p. 393

Prunus subhirtella 'Autumnalis'
☼ ● ● ⚡ MANY ZONES — p. 453

FALL
Shrubs

Abelia
☼ ◐ ● ⚡ ZONES VARY — p. 162

Alyogyne huegelii
BLUE HIBISCUS
☼ ● ● ⚡ 15–17, 20–27 — p. 176

Brugmansia
ANGEL'S TRUMPET
☼ ◐ ● ● ⚡ 16–27 — p. 216

Buddleia davidii
BUTTERFLY BUSH
☼ ◐ ● ● ⚡ MANY ZONES — p. 217

Caesalpinia
BIRD OF PARADISE
☼ ● ⚡ ZONES VARY — p. 219

Camellia sasanqua
◐ ● ● ⚡ MANY ZONES — p. 226

Cassia (some)
SENNA
☼ ◐ ● ⚡ ZONES VARY — p. 233

Cleyera japonica
◐ ● ⚡ MANY ZONES — p. 256

Erica (some)
☼ ◐ ● ⚡ ZONES VARY — p. 291

Fuchsia
◐ ● ⚡ ZONES VARY — p. 311

Hibiscus (some)
☼ ● ⚡ ZONES VARY — p. 334

Lavatera
TREE MALLOW
☼ ● ⚡ ZONES VARY — p. 366

Melaleuca (some)
☼ ● ⚡ ZONES VARY — p. 393

Nerium oleander
OLEANDER
☼ ● ● ⚡ 8–16, 18–31 — p. 405

Rosa (some)
ROSE
NEEDS, ZONES VARY — p. 473

Melaleuca nesophila

Brugmansia versicolor 'Charles Grimaldi'

Alyogyne huegelii

Fuchsia

*Lavatera
thuringiaca*

For growing symbol explanations, please see page 79.

Rosa 'Charmian'

Tibouchina urvilleana

Lonicera

Verbena

Bauhinia variegata 'Candida'

Salvia (some)
SAGE
NEEDS, ZONES VARY   **p. 484**

Tecoma stans
YELLOW BELLS
☼ ♦ ♦ ⚡ 10, 12, 13, 21–28   **p. 516**

Tibouchina urvilleana
PRINCESS FLOWER
☼ ☼ ♦ ⚡ 16, 17, 21–27   **p. 520**

FALL
Ground Covers, Vines

Antigonon leptopus
CORAL VINE
☼ ♦ ⚡ 12, 13, 18–30   **p. 181**

Clematis (some)
☼ ♦ ⚡ ZONES VARY   **p. 253**

Distictis buccinatoria
BLOOD-RED TRUMPET VINE
☼ ♦ ♦ ⚡ 8, 9, 14–28   **p. 282**

Lonicera (some)
HONEYSUCKLE
☼ ☼ ♦ ⚡ ZONES VARY   **p. 376**

Mandevilla (some)
☼ ☼ ♦ ⚡ ZONES VARY   **p. 391**

Plumbago auriculata
CAPE PLUMBAGO
☼ ♦ ⚡ 8, 9, 12–28   **p. 441**

Pyrostegia venusta
FLAME VINE
☼ ☼ ♦ ⚡ 13, 16, 21–27   **p. 459**

Verbena (some)
☼ ♦ ⚡ ZONES VARY   **p. 531**

WINTER
Trees

Acacia baileyana
BAILEY ACACIA
☼ ♦ ⚡ 7–9, 13–24, 26–28   **p. 163**

Bauhinia variegata
PURPLE ORCHID TREE
☼ ♦ ♦ ⚡ MANY ZONES   **p. 204**

Cochlospermum vitifolium
BUTTERCUP TREE
☼ ♦ ♦ ⚡ 25   **p. 257**

Erythrina (some)
CORAL TREE
☼ ♦ ♦ ⚡ ZONES VARY   **p. 295**

Michelia doltsopa
♦ ♦ ⚡ 14–28   **p. 396**

Prunus mume
JAPANESE FLOWERING PLUM
☼ ♦ ♦ ⚡ MANY ZONES   **p. 454**

WINTER
Shrubs

Camellia (many)
☼ ♦ ♦ ⚡ MANY ZONES   **p. 224**

Cassia (most)
SENNA
☼ ♦ ♦ ⚡ ZONES VARY   **p. 233**

Chaenomeles
FLOWERING QUINCE
☼ ♦ ♦ ⚡ 2–21, 28–41   **p. 240**

Chimonanthus praecox
WINTERSWEET
☼ ☼ ♦ ⚡ MANY ZONES   **p. 244**

Corylopsis
WINTER HAZEL
☼ ♦ ♦ ⚡ MANY ZONES   **p. 263**

Daphne (some)
NEEDS, ZONES VARY   **p. 275**

Erica (some)
HEATH
☼ ♦ ♦ ⚡ ZONES VARY   **p. 291**

Euphorbia pulcherrima
POINSETTIA
☼ ♦ ♦ ⚡ 13, 16–27   **p. 300**

Forsythia
☼ ♦ ♦ ⚡ MANY ZONES   **p. 308**

Hamamelis (most)
WITCH HAZEL
☼ ♦ ♦ ⚡ ZONES VARY   **p. 326**

Jasminum mesnyi
PRIMROSE JASMINE
☼ ☼ ♦ ⚡ 3–24, 26, 28–31   **p. 352**

Lonicera fragrantissima
WINTER HONEYSUCKLE
☼ ☼ ♦ ⚡ MANY ZONES   **p. 376**

Rhododendron (Azalea, some)
♦ ♦♦ ⚡ ZONES VARY   **p. 465**

Viburnum (some)
NEEDS, ZONES VARY   **p. 532**

WINTER
Ground Covers, Vines

Gelsemium sempervirens
CAROLINA JESSAMINE
☼ ☼ ♦♦ ⚡ MANY ZONES   **p. 314**

Jasminum (some)
JASMINE
☼ ☼ ♦ ⚡ ZONES VARY   **p. 351**

Pyrostegia venusta
FLAME VINE
☼ ☼ ♦ ⚡ 13, 16, 21–27   **p. 459**

Camellia

Chaenomeles

Daphne odora 'Marginata'

Forsythia

Viburnum tinus

ANNUALS
for Seasonal Color

Flowering annuals provide the quick, showy color that can bring almost instant drama to an otherwise quiet part of the garden. Available in every size and color imaginable, annuals make delightful fillers between shrubs, colorful companions to perennials, or stunning plantings just by themselves. Some plants on this list are biennials or perennials commonly grown as annuals. Cool-season annuals grow best in cool soils and mild temperatures—fall through spring in mild-winter climates. Warm-season annuals are planted after the last frost and generally grow best between late spring and fall.

Lathyrus odoratus

Antirrhinum majus

Calendula officinalis

Campanula medium

Chrysanthemum paludosum

COOL-SEASON ANNUALS

Antirrhinum majus
SNAPDRAGON
☼ ◐ ✹ ALL ZONES **p. 182**

Cabbage, kale, flowering
☼ ◐ ✹ ALL ZONES **p. 219**

Calendula officinalis
POT MARIGOLD
☼ ◐ ✹ ALL ZONES **p. 221**

Campanula medium
CANTERBURY BELL
☼ ◑ ◐ ✹ MANY ZONES **p. 228**

Centaurea cyanus
CORNFLOWER
☼ ◐ ✹ ALL ZONES **p. 237**

Chrysanthemum (several)
NEEDS, ZONES VARY **p. 246**

Clarkia amoena
GODETIA
☼ ◑ ◐ ✹ ALL ZONES **p. 253**

Consolida ambigua
LARKSPUR
☼ ◐ ✹ ALL ZONES **p. 259**

Cynoglossum amabile
CHINESE FORGET-ME-NOT
☼ ◐ ✹ ALL ZONES **p. 273**

Dianthus (some)
☼ ◑ ◐ ✹ 1–24, 30–45 **p. 278**

Dimorphotheca
AFRICAN DAISY
☼ ◐ ✹ ALL ZONES **p. 281**

Eschscholzia californica
CALIFORNIA POPPY
☼ ◐ ✹ ALL ZONES **p. 296**

Iberis umbellata
GLOBE CANDYTUFT
☼ ◐ ✹ ALL ZONES **p. 342**

Lathyrus odoratus
SWEET PEA
☼ ◐ ◐ ✹ ALL ZONES **p. 364**

Linaria maroccana
TOADFLAX
☼ ◑ ◐ ✹ ALL ZONES **p. 372**

Matthiola incana
STOCK
☼ ◑ ◐ ✹ ALL ZONES **p. 392**

Myosotis sylvatica
FORGET-ME-NOT
◑ ◐ ✹ 1–24, 32–45 **p. 401**

Nemesia strumosa
☼ ◐ ✹ 1–24, 28–45 **p. 404**

Papaver (some)
POPPY
☼ ◐ ◐ ✹ ZONES VARY **p. 415**

Primula (many)
PRIMROSE
☼ ◑◐ ◐ ◑◐ ✹ ZONES VARY **p. 448**

Schizanthus pinnatus
POOR MAN'S ORCHID
☼ ◐ ✹ MANY ZONES **p. 491**

Senecio hybridus
CINERARIA
◐ ◑ ◐ ✹ 16, 17, 22–24, 38 **p. 495**

Viola
PANSY, VIOLA
NEEDS, ZONES VARY **p. 534**

WARM-SEASON ANNUALS

Ageratum houstonianum
FLOSS FLOWER
☼ ◐ ◐ ✹ ALL ZONES **p. 170**

VERTICAL BAR: The band indicates blooming season in most zones.

	SPRING
	SUMMER
	FALL
	WINTER

Clarkia amoena

Eschscholzia californica

Nemesia strumosa

Papaver

For growing symbol explanations, please see page 79.

SPECIAL EFFECTS

Catharanthus roseus

Celosia

Helichrysum bracteatum

Heliotropium arborescens

Ipomoea

Lobelia erinus

Brachycome iberidifolia
SWAN RIVER DAISY
☼ ♦ ✓ ALL ZONES **p. 214**

Browallia speciosa
AMETHYST FLOWER
☼ ♦ ✓ ALL ZONES **p. 216**

Callistephus chinensis
CHINA ASTER
☼ ♦ ✓ ALL ZONES **p. 222**

Catharanthus roseus
MADAGASCAR PERIWINKLE
☼ ☼ ♦ ✓ ALL ZONES **p. 234**

Celosia
COCKSCOMB
☼ ♦ ✓ ALL ZONES **p. 237**

Cleome hasslerana
SPIDER FLOWER
☼ ♦ ✓ ALL ZONES **p. 255**

Convolvulus tricolor
DWARF MORNING GLORY
☼ ♦ ✓ ALL ZONES **p. 260**

Coreopsis tinctoria
CALLIOPSIS
☼ ♦ ✓ ALL ZONES **p. 261**

Cosmos
☼ ♦ ✓ ALL ZONES **p. 264**

Diascia barberae
TWINSPUR
☼ ☼ ♦ ♦ ✓ ALL ZONES **p. 279**

Eustoma grandiflorum
LISIANTHUS
☼ ☼ ♦ ✓ ALL ZONES **p. 301**

Gaillardia pulchella
BLANKET FLOWER
☼ ♦ ✓ ALL ZONES **p. 311**

Gomphrena
GLOBE AMARANTH
☼ ☼ ♦ ✓ ALL ZONES **p. 319**

Gypsophila elegans
☼ ♦ ✓ ALL ZONES **p. 325**

Helianthus annuus
COMMON SUNFLOWER
☼ ♦ ✓ ALL ZONES **p. 329**

Helichrysum bracteatum
STRAWFLOWER
☼ ♦ ✓ ALL ZONES **p. 329**

Heliotropium arborescens
COMMON HELIOTROPE
☼ ☼ ♦ ♦ ✓ ALL ZONES **p. 330**

Impatiens
BALSAM
NEEDS, ZONES VARY **p. 344**

Ipomoea
MORNING GLORY
☼ ♦ ♦ ✓ ZONES VARY **p. 346**

Lavatera trimestris
ANNUAL MALLOW
☼ ♦ ♦ ✓ ALL ZONES **p. 366**

Limonium (some)
SEA LAVENDER
☼ ♦ ✓ ZONES VARY **p. 371**

Lobelia erinus
☼ ☼ ♦ ♦ ✓ ALL ZONES **p. 375**

Lobularia maritima
SWEET ALYSSUM
☼ ☼ ♦ ✓ ALL ZONES **p. 376**

Mimulus hybridus
MONKEY FLOWER
☼ ♦ ♦ ✓ ALL ZONES **p. 396**

Nicotiana
☼ ♦ ✓ ALL ZONES **p. 406**

Petunia hybrida
PETUNIA
☼ ♦ ✓ ALL ZONES **p. 426**

Phlox drummondii
ANNUAL PHLOX
☼ ☼ ♦ ✓ ALL ZONES **p. 428**

Portulaca grandiflora
ROSE MOSS
☼ ☼ ♦ ♦ ✓ ALL ZONES **p. 446**

Salpiglossis sinuata
PAINTED TONGUE
☼ ♦ ✓ ALL ZONES **p. 484**

Salvia splendens
SCARLET SAGE
☼ ♦ ✓ ALL ZONES **p. 486**

Sanvitalia procumbens
CREEPING ZINNIA
☼ ♦ ♦ ✓ ALL ZONES **p. 488**

Scabiosa atropurpurea
PINCUSHION FLOWER
☼ ♦ ✓ ALL ZONES **p. 490**

Tagetes
MARIGOLD
☼ ♦ ✓ ZONES VARY **p. 513**

Thunbergia alata
BLACK-EYED SUSAN VINE
☼ ☼ ♦ ✓ ALL ZONES **p. 519**

Tithonia rotundifolia
MEXICAN SUNFLOWER
☼ ♦ ✓ ALL ZONES **p. 521**

Tropaeolum majus
GARDEN NASTURTIUM
☼ ☼ ♦ ✓ ALL ZONES **p. 525**

Verbena
☼ ♦ ✓ ZONES VARY **p. 531**

Zinnia
☼ ♦ ✓ ALL ZONES **p. 543**

Nicotiana

Petunia hybrida

Tagetes tenuifolia 'Lemon Gem'

Thunbergia alata

Verbena

Zinnia elegans

BULBS
and
Bulblike Plants

Some of a garden's showiest flowers appear from bulbs, corms, tubers, rhizomes, and tuberous roots (often lumped together as bulbs). These humble-looking structures store food, allowing the plants to survive underground until it's time to send out shoots and flowers. Bulbs thrive in many different environments. Daffodils and iris, for example, thrive equally well in both desert and mountain regions. Other bulbs have more specific growing needs. You can successfully grow many bulbs out of their range by planting them in containers and growing them indoors (amaryllis is a common example) or by providing a period of chilling in the refrigerator to simulate winter (in mild-winter climates crocus, hyacinths, and tulips should be chilled for 6 weeks).

Freesia

Anemone blanda

Cyclamen persicum

Hyacinthus orientalis

COLOR CODES: Each tint represents a range of colors, not a color match.

BLUE–PURPLE	
WHITE–CREAM	
PINK–RED	
YELLOW–ORANGE	

FALL PLANTED BULBS

Allium
ORNAMENTAL ALLIUM
☀ ☼ ♦ ⚡ ZONES VARY   **p. 173**

Amaryllis belladonna
NAKED LADY
☀ ♦ ⚡ 4–24, 28, 29   **p. 177**

Anemone
WINDFLOWER
NEEDS, ZONES VARY   **p. 179**

Arisaema
☀ ♦ ♦♦ ⚡ ZONES VARY   **p. 190**

Brodiaea
☀ ♦ ⚡ ZONES VARY   **p. 215**

Chionodoxa
GLORY-OF-THE-SNOW
☀ ♦ ⚡ 1–7, 14–20, 31–43   **p. 245**

Crocus
☀ ☼ ♦ ⚡ 1–24, 30–45   **p. 268**

Cyclamen (florists' types)
☀ ☼ ♦ ⚡ ZONES VARY   **p. 271**

Endymion
☀ ☼ ♦ ⚡ ZONES VARY   **p. 288**

Freesia
☀ ☼ ♦ ⚡ 8, 9, 12–24, 28   **p. 310**

Fritillaria
FRITILLARY
☀ ☼ ♦ ⚡ ZONES VARY   **p. 310**

Galanthus
SNOWDROP
☀ ☼ ♦ ⚡ MANY ZONES   **p. 312**

Hippeastrum
AMARYLLIS
☀ ☼ ♦ ⚡ 16, 17, 19, 21–28   **p. 336**

Hyacinthus orientalis
COMMON HYACINTH
☀ ☼ ♦ ⚡ ALL ZONES   **p. 339**

Hypoxis hirsuta
YELLOW STAR GRASS
☀ ☼ ♦ ♦ ⚡ 28–38   **p. 342**

Ipheion uniflorum
SPRING STAR FLOWER
☀ ☼ ♦ ⚡ 3–24, 27–34   **p. 346**

Iris
NEEDS, ZONES VARY   **p. 347**

Ixia
AFRICAN CORN LILY
☀ ♦ ⚡ 7–9, 12–24   **p. 350**

Leucojum
SNOWFLAKE
☀ ☼ ♦ ⚡ ZONES VARY   **p. 367**

Lilium
LILY
☼ ♦ ⚡ ALL ZONES   **p. 370**

Muscari
GRAPE HYACINTH
☀ ☼ ♦ ⚡ ZONES VARY   **p. 400**

Narcissus
DAFFODIL
☀ ☼ ♦ ⚡ ZONES VARY   **p. 402**

Oxalis (some)
NEEDS, ZONES VARY   **p. 412**

Paeonia (herbaceous)
PEONY
☀ ☼ ♦ ⚡ MANY ZONES   **p. 413**

Puschkinia scilloides
☀ ☼ ♦ ⚡ 1–11, 14, 29–43   **p. 458**

Iris

Narcissus

Lilium Asiatic hybrid

For growing symbol explanations, please see page 79.

Tulipa

Begonia

Dahlia

Gladiolus

Liatris

Ranunculus asiaticus
PERSIAN RANUNCULUS
☼ ● ✗ ALL ZONES — p. 462

Rhodohypoxis baurii
☼ ● ✗ 4–7, 14–24, 28–33 — p. 470

Scilla
SQUILL
☼ ◐ ● ✗ ZONES VARY — p. 492

Sparaxis tricolor
HARLEQUIN FLOWER
☼ ● ✗ 9, 12–24 — p. 501

Triteleia
☼ ● ✗ MANY ZONES — p. 525

Tritonia crocata
FLAME FREESIA
☼ ● ✗ MANY ZONES — p. 525

Tulipa
TULIP
☼ ● ✗ 1–24, 28–45 — p. 526

Watsonia pyramidata
☼ ● ✗ MANY ZONES — p. 537

Zantedeschia aethiopica
COMMON CALLA
☼ ● ● ✗ MANY ZONES — p. 542

WINTER-SPRING PLANTED BULBS

Begonia, tuberous
☼ ● ● ✗ 14–28 — p. 207

Caladium bicolor
FANCY-LEAFED CALADIUM
☼ ◐ ● ● ✗ 25–27 — p. 219

Canna
☼ ● ● ● ✗ 6–9, 12–31 — p. 227

Crocosmia
☼ ◐ ● ✗ 5–24, 28–39 — p. 268

Cyclamen (florists' types)
☼ ◐ ● ✗ ZONES VARY — p. 271

Dahlia
☼ ◐ ● ✗ ALL ZONES — p. 274

Gladiolus
☼ ● ✗ ZONES VARY — p. 317

Gloriosa rothschildiana
GLORY LILY
☼ ◐ ● ✗ 24–27 — p. 319

Hippeastrum
AMARYLLIS
☼ ◐ ● ✗ MANY ZONES — p. 336

Homeria collina
☼ ◐ ● ✗ 4–29 — p. 336

Hymenocallis
☼ ◐ ● ✗ 5, 6, 8, 9, 14–31 — p. 341

Liatris
GAYFEATHER
☼ ● ● ✗ MANY ZONES — p. 368

Lilium, Oriental hybrids
◐ ● ✗ ALL ZONES — p. 371

Polianthes tuberosa
TUBEROSE
☼ ◐ ● ✗ ALL ZONES — p. 443

Tigridia pavonia
MEXICAN SHELL FLOWER
☼ ◐ ● ✗ 4–31 — p. 520

Zantedeschia
CALLA
NEEDS, ZONES VARY — p. 541

Zephyranthes
ZEPHYR FLOWER
☼ ● ✗ ZONES VARY — p. 543

SUMMER PLANTED BULBS

Colchicum
MEADOW SAFFRON
☼ ● ✗ MANY ZONES — p. 258

Crocus (fall-flowering)
☼ ◐ ● ✗ 1–24, 30–45 — p. 268

Cyclamen (except florists' types)
☼ ◐ ● ✗ ZONES VARY — p. 271

Lycoris
SPIDER LILY
☼ ◐ ● ✗ ZONES VARY — p. 379

Sternbergia lutea
☼ ● ✗ MANY ZONES — p. 505

PLANT ANY TIME

Agapanthus
LILY-OF-THE-NILE
☼ ◐ ● ● ✗ ZONES VARY — p. 169

Clivia miniata
◐ ● ● ✗ 12–17, 19–27 — p. 256

Dietes
FORTNIGHT LILY
☼ ◐ ● ● ✗ 8, 9, 12–28 — p. 281

Hemerocallis
DAYLILY
☼ ◐ ● ✗ ALL ZONES — p. 331

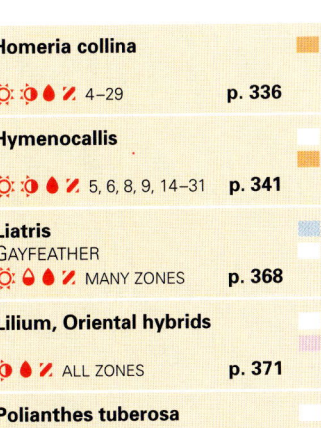
Colchicum

Crocus

Agapanthus 'Peter Pan'

Clivia miniata

Hemerocallis

AUTUMN FOLIAGE COLOR

Cercis canadensis 'Forest Pansy'

Cornus florida

Plants that change leaf color in fall do so in varying degrees, depending on the nature of the plant, the climate it grows in, and the exact weather each fall. Generally, the change is less pronounced in mild-winter areas than in cold-winter regions. The plants listed below display a notable autumn foliage change; many are worth planting for that reason alone. Leaf color can vary within a species, so it's best to shop for plants when they are changing color.

Acer saccharum (sugar maple) in autumn raiment

COLOR CODES: Each tint represents a range of colors, not a color match. ♣ indicates shrubs that can become small trees.

RED–PURPLE
YELLOW–ORANGE

Lagerstroemia indica

TREES

Acer (many)
MAPLE
☀ ◐ ♦ ♦ ✂ ZONES VARY   **p. 164**

Amelanchier
JUNEBERRY
☀ ◐ ♦ ♦ ✂ 1–6, 31–45   **p. 177**

Asimina triloba
PAWPAW
☀ ◐ ♦ ✂ MANY ZONES   **p. 194**

Betula
BIRCH
☀ ◐ ♦ ♦ ✂ ZONES VARY   **p. 208**

Carpinus
HORNBEAM
☀ ◐ ♦ ♦ ✂ ZONES VARY   **p. 231**

Carya ovata
SHAGBARK HICKORY
☀ ♦ ♦ ✂ 1–6, 28–44   **p. 232**

Catalpa
☀ ◐ ♦ ♦ ✂ 3–24, 28–41   **p. 234**

Celtis
HACKBERRY
☀ ◐ ♦ ♦ ✂ ZONES VARY   **p. 237**

Cercidiphyllum japonicum
KATSURA TREE
☀ ◐ ♦ ♦ ✂ MANY ZONES   **p. 239**

Cercis
REDBUD
NEEDS, ZONES VARY   **p. 239**

Chionanthus
FRINGE TREE
☀ ◐ ♦ ♦ ✂ ZONES VARY   **p. 244**

Cladrastis lutea
YELLOW WOOD
☀ ◐ ♦ ✂ 1–9, 14–16, 31–43   **p. 253**

Cornus (many)
DOGWOOD
☀ ◐ ♦ ✂ ZONES VARY   **p. 262**

Crataegus (some)
HAWTHORN
☀ ◐ ♦ ✂ MANY ZONES   **p. 266**

Fagus
BEECH
☀ ◐ ♦ ♦ ✂ ZONES VARY   **p. 302**

Franklinia alatamaha
☀ ◐ ♦ ✂ MANY ZONES   **p. 309**

Fraxinus (deciduous)
ASH
☀ ◐ ♦ ♦ ✂ ZONES VARY   **p. 309**

Ginkgo biloba
MAIDENHAIR TREE
☀ ◐ ♦ ✂ MANY ZONES   **p. 317**

Gleditsia triacanthos
HONEY LOCUST
☀ ♦ ♦ ✂ MANY ZONES   **p. 318**

Gymnocladus dioica
KENTUCKY COFFEE TREE
☀ ♦ ♦ ✂ MANY ZONES   **p. 325**

Halesia
◐ ♦ ✂ 2–9, 14–24, 31–41   **p. 326**

Koelreuteria bipinnata
CHINESE FLAME TREE
☀ ♦ ♦ ✂ 8–24, 26, 28–31   **p. 360**

Lagerstroemia indica
CRAPE MYRTLE
☀ ♦ ✂ MANY ZONES   **p. 362**

Larix
LARCH
☀ ♦ ✂ ZONES VARY   **p. 363**

Liquidambar
SWEET GUM
☀ ◐ ♦ ✂ ZONES VARY   **p. 373**

Larix decidua

Liquidambar styraciflua

Gleditsia triacanthos

Ginkgo biloba

Crataegus

For growing symbol explanations, please see page 79.

Liriodendron tulipifera
TULIP TREE
☼ ◑ ● ⚡ MANY ZONES   p. 373

Magnolia denudata
YULAN MAGNOLIA
☼ ◑ ● ⚡ MANY ZONES   p. 382

Malus 'Prairifire'
CRABAPPLE
☼ ● ● ⚡ 1–21, 29–43   p. 389

Metasequoia glyptostroboides
DAWN REDWOOD
☼ ● ⚡ 3–10, 14–24, 31–41 p. 395

Morus
MULBERRY
☼ ● ● ⚡ ZONES VARY   p. 399

Nyssa sylvatica
SOUR GUM
☼ ◑ ● ● ⚡ MANY ZONES   p. 407

Oxydendrum arboreum
SOURWOOD
☼ ● ⚡ MANY ZONES   p. 412

Persimmon

☼ ● ● ⚡ ZONES VARY   p. 425

Pistacia chinensis
CHINESE PISTACHE
☼ ● ⚡ MANY ZONES   p. 437

Populus (some)
POPLAR
☼ ● ⚡ ZONES VARY   p. 445

Prunus (deciduous)
☼ ● ● ⚡ ZONES VARY   p. 451

Pseudolarix kaempferi
GOLDEN LARCH
☼ ● ⚡ 2–7, 14–17, 32–41   p. 455

Ptelea trifoliata
WAFER ASH
☼ ◑ ● ● ⚡ MANY ZONES   p. 456

Pyrus (deciduous)
ORNAMENTAL PEAR
☼ ● ⚡ ZONES VARY   p. 459

Quercus (deciduous)
OAK
☼ ● ● ⚡ ZONES VARY   p. 459

Robinia
LOCUST
☼ ⚡ 1–24, 29–45   p. 472

Salix
WILLOW
☼ ● ⚡ ZONES VARY   p. 483

Sapium sebiferum
CHINESE TALLOW TREE
☼ ● ⚡ MANY ZONES   p. 488

Sassafras albidum
SASSAFRAS
☼ ● ⚡ 3–9, 14–17, 28–41   p. 489

Nyssa sylvatica

Persimmon

Pistacia chinensis

Populus tremuloides

Sorbus
MOUNTAIN ASH
☼ ◑ ● ● ⚡ ZONES VARY   p. 500

Styrax japonicus
JAPANESE SNOWBELL
☼ ◑ ● ⚡ MANY ZONES   p. 509

Taxodium
☼ ● ● ● ⚡ ZONES VARY   p. 515

Tilia
LINDEN
☼ ● ⚡ ZONES VARY   p. 520

Ulmus (most)
ELM
☼ ● ⚡ ZONES VARY   p. 528

Walnut
☼ ● ⚡ ZONES VARY   p. 536

Zelkova serrata
SAWLEAF ZELKOVA
☼ ● ● ⚡ MANY ZONES   p. 542

SHRUBS

Amelanchier
JUNEBERRY
☼ ◑ ● ● ⚡ 1–6, 31–45   p. 177 🌳

Aronia
CHOKEBERRY
☼ ◑ ● ● ⚡ ZONES VARY   p. 191

Berberis thunbergii
JAPANESE BARBERRY
☼ ◑ ● ● ⚡ 1–24, 28–41   p. 208

Blueberry
☼ ● ● ⚡ ZONES VARY   p. 211

Callicarpa
BEAUTYBERRY
☼ ● ● ⚡ MANY ZONES   p. 221

Calluna vulgaris
SCOTCH HEATHER
☼ ● ⚡ MANY ZONES   p. 222

Calycanthus
☼ ◑ ● ● ⚡ ZONES VARY   p. 223

Chaenomeles
FLOWERING QUINCE
☼ ● ● ⚡ 2–21, 28–41   p. 240

Chimonanthus praecox
WINTERSWEET
☼ ◑ ● ⚡ MANY ZONES   p. 244

Clethra alnifolia
SUMMERSWEET
◑ ● ● ⚡ 1–6, 31–43   p. 256

Cotinus coggygria
SMOKE TREE
☼ ● ⚡ 2–24, 29–41   p. 265 🌳

Pyrus calleryana

Quercus coccinea

Sorbus americanus

Berberis thunbergii 'Rose Glow'

Plant listings continue ▶

Euonymus alata

Hamamelis

Hydrangea quercifolia

Parrotia persica

Cotoneaster (most deciduous)
☼ ◐ ✿ ZONES VARY · · · · · · · · p. 265

Disanthus cercidifolius
☼ ◐ ◐ ✿ MANY ZONES · · · · p. 282

Enkianthus campanulatus
☼ ◐ ◐ ◐◐ ✿ MANY ZONES p. 288

Euonymus (several)
EUONYMUS
☼ ◐ ● ◐◐ ✿ ZONES VARY p. 298

Fothergilla
☼ ◐ ◐ ✿ MANY ZONES · · · · p. 308

Hamamelis
WITCH HAZEL
☼ ◐ ◐ ✿ ZONES VARY · · · · p. 326 ♣

Hydrangea quercifolia
OAKLEAF HYDRANGEA
☼ ◐ ◐ ✿ MANY ZONES · · · · p. 340

Ilex verticillata
WINTERBERRY
☼ ◐ ◐ ✿ 1–7, 31–43 · · · · · · p. 344

Itea virginica
VIRGINIA SWEETSPIRE
☼ ◐ ◐ ✿ MANY ZONES · · · · p. 350

Kerria japonica
☼ ◐ ● ◐ ✿ 2–21, 30–41 · · · p. 359

Lagerstroemia indica
CRAPE MYRTLE
☼ ◐ ◐ ✿ MANY ZONES · · · · p. 362

Leucothoe racemosa
SWEETBELLS
◐ ● ◐ ✿ 26, 28, 31–34 · · · p. 368

Lindera
SPICEBUSH
☼ ◐ ◐ ✿ ZONES VARY · · · · p. 372 ♣

Lonicera
HONEYSUCKLE
☼ ◐ ◐ ✿ ZONES VARY · · · · p. 376

Magnolia salicifolia
ANISE MAGNOLIA
☼ ◐ ◐ ✿ MANY ZONES · · · · p. 384

Nandina domestica
HEAVENLY BAMBOO
☼ ◐ ● ◐◐ ✿ 4–33 · · · · · · · · p. 402

Parrotia persica
PERSIAN PARROTIA
☼ ◐ ◐ ✿ MANY ZONES · · · · p. 416 ♣

Paxistema canbyi
☼ ◐ ◐ ✿ 1–10, 14–21, 32–43 p. 418

Philadelphus
MOCK ORANGE
☼ ◐ ◐ ◐ ✿ ZONES VARY · · · p. 427

Photinia villosa
☼ ◐ ● ◐ ✿ 1–6, 32–41 · · · · · p. 430 ♣

Prunus
☼ ◐ ◐ ◐ ✿ ZONES VARY · · · p. 451 ♣

Pseudocydonia sinensis
CHINESE QUINCE
☼ ◐ ✿ MANY ZONES · · · · · · p. 455 ♣

Punica granatum
POMEGRANATE
☼ ◐ ◐ ✿ 5–32 · · · · · · · · · · · p. 457 ♣

Rhododendron
AZALEA, DECIDUOUS
◐ ◐ ◐◐ ✿ MANY ZONES p. 465

Rhus
SUMAC
☼ ◐ ● ◐ ✿ ZONES VARY · · · p. 473 ♣

Rosa (some)
ROSE
NEEDS, ZONES VARY · · · · · · p. 473

Spiraea (many)
☼ ◐ ◐ ● ◐ ✿ ZONES VARY p. 502

Stephanandra incisa 'Crispa'
☼ ◐ ◐ ✿ 1–6, 32–43 · · · · · · p. 505

Stewartia
☼ ◐ ◐ ◐ ✿ ZONES VARY · · · p. 506 ♣

Syringa
LILAC
☼ ◐ ◐ ✿ ZONES VARY · · · · p. 512

Vaccinium
NEEDS, ZONES VARY · · · · · · p. 529

Viburnum (many)
NEEDS, ZONES VARY · · · · · · p. 532

Ziziphus jujuba
CHINESE JUJUBE
☼ ◐ ◐ ✿ 7–16, 18–24, 28–33 p. 544

VINES

Celastrus
BITTERSWEET
☼ ◐ ◐ ✿ ZONES VARY · · · · p. 236

Grape
☼ ◐ ◐ ✿ ZONES VARY · · · · p. 320

Parthenocissus
☼ ◐ ◐ ● ◐ ✿ ZONES VARY p. 416

Wisteria
☼ ◐ ◐ ◐ ✿ ZONES VARY · · · p. 538

Rhus typhina 'Laciniata'

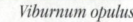

Stewartia

Viburnum opulus

Parthenocissus quinquefolia

Parthenocissus tricuspidata

For growing symbol explanations, please see page 79.

Acer davidii

TREES AND SHRUBS
for Winter Interest

E ven in the dead of winter, even in the coldest zones, you can have a lively landscape. With no flowers and foliage to steal the show, the beauties of stem, bark, and branch structure come to the fore. Locate these trees and shrubs strategically in your garden, and you'll create a landscape that transforms itself each winter into a striking display of color and sculptural beauty.

SPECIAL EFFECTS

Acer griseum

Platanus

Populus tremuloides

TREES

Acer davidii
DAVID'S MAPLE
☼ ◐ ♦ ♦ ⚡ MANY ZONES   p. 164

Acer griseum
PAPERBARK MAPLE
☼ ◐ ♦ ♦ ⚡ MANY ZONES   p. 164

Acer palmatum 'Sango Kaku'
CORAL BARK MAPLE
☼ ◐ ♦ ♦ ⚡ MANY ZONES   p. 165

Betula (most)
BIRCH
☼ ♦ ♦♦ ⚡ ZONES VARY   p. 208

Carya ovata
SHAGBARK HICKORY
☼ ♦♦ ⚡ 1–6, 28–44   p. 232

Lagerstroemia
CRAPE MYRTLE
☼ ♦ ⚡ ZONES VARY   p. 361

Pinus bungeana
LACEBARK PINE
☼ ♦♦ ⚡ 2–10, 14–21, 31–41   p. 434

Platanus
PLANE TREE, SYCAMORE
☼ ♦ ♦ ⚡ ZONES VARY   p. 438

Populus alba
WHITE POPLAR
☼ ♦ ⚡ 1–24, 30–45   p. 446

Populus tremuloides
QUAKING ASPEN
☼ ♦ ⚡ 1–7, 14–21, 32–45   p. 446

Prunus sargentii
SARGENT CHERRY
☼ ♦ ♦ ⚡ 2–7, 14–17, 32–41   p. 452

Prunus serrulata
JAPANESE FLOWERING CHERRY
☼ ♦ ♦♦ ⚡ 3–7, 14–20, 32–34   p. 452

Salix alba vitellina
WHITE WILLOW
☼ ♦♦ ⚡ 1–24, 30–45   p. 484

Salix matsudana tortuosa
HANKOW WILLOW
☼ ♦♦ ⚡ 3–24, 30–34, 39   p. 484

Stewartia
☼ ◐ ♦ ⚡ ZONES VARY   p. 506

Ulmus parviflora
CHINESE ELM
☼ ♦ ⚡ 3–24, 26–35, 37–39   p. 529

SHRUBS

Blueberry
☼ ♦♦ ⚡ ZONES VARY   p. 211

Cornus alba
TATARIAN DOGWOOD
☼ ◐ ♦ ⚡ 1–9, 14–24, 32–45   p. 262

Cornus sanguinea
BLOODTWIG DOGWOOD
☼ ◐ ♦ ⚡ 1–7, 31–45   p. 263

Cornus stolonifera
REDTWIG DOGWOOD
☼ ◐ ♦ ⚡ 1–9, 14–21, 31–45   p. 263

Corylus avellana 'Contorta'
HARRY LAUDER'S WALKING STICK
☼ ♦ ⚡ 2–9, 14–20, 32–41   p. 264

Cytisus
BROOM
☼ ♦ ⚡ ZONES VARY   p. 273

Euonymus alata
WINGED EUONYMUS
☼ ◐ ♦ ♦ ♦ ⚡ MANY ZONES   p. 298

Kerria japonica
☼ ◐ ♦ ♦ ⚡ 2–21, 30–41   p. 359

Leucothoe racemosa
SWEETBELLS
◐ ♦ ♦ ⚡ 26, 28, 31–34   p. 368

Syringa reticulata
JAPANESE TREE LILAC
☼ ◐ ♦ ♦ ⚡ 1–12, 14–16, 32–43   p. 512

Stewartia pseudocamellia

Ulmus parvifolia

Cornus stolonifera

Corylus avellana 'Contorta'

For growing symbol explanations, please see page 79.

COLORFUL FRUITS AND BERRIES

Viburnum plicatum tomentosum 'Mariesii'

The plants listed below offer a showy display of color in the form of fruit or berries that, depending on the plant, may be red, orange, yellow, purple, pink, blue, black, or white. Many produce this fruit in addition to striking flowers; in others, it comes as a surprise following an inconspicuous blossoming. Mountain ash, pyracantha, holly, and certain other plants produce fruits that especially appeals to birds. Trees like citrus and persimmon yield familiar edible crops.

Mandarin orange (citrus)

Crataegus

Malus 'Red Jade'

Persimmon

TREES

Amelanchier
JUNEBERRY
☼ ◑ ◐ ◐ ╱ 1–6, 31–45   **p. 177**

Citrus
☼ ◐ ╱ 8, 9, 12–27   **p. 250**

Coccoloba uvifera
SEA GRAPE
☼ ◐ ╱ 25–27   **p. 257**

Crataegus
HAWTHORN
☼ ◐ ╱ 2–12, 14–17, 28, 30–41   **p. 266**

Dipteronia sinensis
◑ ◐ ╱ MANY ZONES   **p. 282**

Eriobotrya japonica
LOQUAT
☼ ◐ ╱ 4–31   **p. 291**

Evodia daniellii
☼ ◐ ╱ 3–9, 14–24, 31–41   **p. 301**

Ilex (many)
HOLLY
☼ ◒ ◐ ╱ ZONES VARY   **p. 343**

Koelreuteria
☼ ◐ ◐ ╱ ZONES VARY   **p. 360**

Malus
CRABAPPLE
☼ ◐ ◐ ╱ 1–21, 29–43   **p. 387**

Persimmon
☼ ◐ ◐ ╱ ZONES VARY   **p. 425**

Sambucus
ELDERBERRY
☼ ◒ ◐ ╱ ZONES VARY   **p. 487**

Schinus terebinthifolius
BRAZILIAN PEPPER TREE
☼ ◐ ╱ 15–17, 19–27   **p. 491**

Sorbus
MOUNTAIN ASH
☼ ◑ ◐ ◐ ╱ ZONES VARY   **p. 500**

Syzygium paniculatum
BRUSH CHERRY
☼ ◐ ◐ ╱ 16, 17, 19–25   **p. 513**

SHRUBS

Actaea
BANEBERRY
◑ ◐ ◐ ╱ 1–5, 30–45   **p. 167**

Aronia
CHOKEBERRY
☼ ◒ ◐ ◐ ╱ ZONES VARY   **p. 191**

Berberis thunbergii
JAPANESE BARBERRY
☼ ◒ ◐ ◐ ╱ 1–24, 28–41   **p. 208**

Callicarpa bodinieri
BODINIER BEAUTYBERRY
☼ ◒ ◐ ◐ ╱ 3–9, 14–24, 29–41   **p. 221**

Carissa macrocarpa
NATAL PLUM
☼ ◒ ◐ ╱ 22–27   **p. 230**

Cestrum
◒ ◐ ╱ ZONES VARY   **p. 240**

Clerodendrum trichotomum 🌳
HARLEQUIN GLORYBOWER
◒ ◐ ╱ 7–9, 14–32   **p. 256**

Cornus kousa 🌳
KOUSA DOGWOOD
☼ ◒ ◐ ╱ MANY ZONES   **p. 262**

Cornus mas 🌳
CORNELIAN CHERRY
☼ ◒ ◐ ╱ 2–6, 32–41   **p. 262**

SYMBOL: 🌳 indicates shrubs that can become small trees.

Sorbus aucuparia

Aronia arbutifolia

Carissa macrocarpa

For growing symbol explanations, please see page 79.

Cotoneaster

Ilex verticillata

Mahonia lomariifolia

Nandina domestica

Pyracantha

Corylus
FILBERT, HAZELNUT
☼ ◑ ◆ ⚡ ZONES VARY   **p. 264**

Cotoneaster
☼ ◆ ⚡ ZONES VARY   **p. 265**

Duranta
SKY FLOWER
☼ ◆ ⚡ ZONES VARY   **p. 285**

Elaeagnus
☼ ◑ ◆ ◆ ⚡ ZONES VARY   **p. 287**

Euonymus (many)
EUONYMUS
NEEDS, ZONES VARY   **p. 298**

Hippophae rhamnoides
SEA BUCKTHORN
☼ ◆ ◆ ⚡ 1–5, 34, 37–45   **p. 336**

Ilex (many)
HOLLY
☼ ◑ ◆ ⚡ ZONES VARY   **p. 343**

Kolkwitzia amabilis
BEAUTY BUSH
☼ ◑ ◆ ⚡ 2–11, 14–20, 31–41   **p. 360**

Leycesteria formosa
HIMALAYAN HONEYSUCKLE
☼ ◑ ◆ ⚡ 4–6, 15–17, 31, 32   **p. 368**

Lindera
SPICEBUSH
☼ ◑ ◆ ⚡ ZONES VARY   **p. 372**

Lonicera (most shrubby types)
HONEYSUCKLE
☼ ◑ ◆ ⚡ ZONES VARY   **p. 376**

Lycium chinense
MATRIMONY VINE
☼ ◆ ◆ ⚡ 3–7, 31, 32, 34   **p. 379**

Mahonia
NEEDS, ZONES VARY   **p. 386**

Mitchella repens
◑ ● ◆◑ ⚡ 1–6, 28, 31–45   **p. 397**

Nandina domestica
HEAVENLY BAMBOO
☼ ◑ ◆ ◆ ⚡ 4–33   **p. 402**

Photinia serrulata
CHINESE PHOTINIA
☼ ◆ ◆ ⚡ 4–16, 18–22, 28–31   **p. 430**

Photinia villosa
☼ ◆ ◆ ⚡ 1–6, 32–41   **p. 430**

Punica granatum (some)
POMEGRANATE
☼ ◆ ◆ ⚡ 5–32   **p. 457**

Pyracantha
FIRETHORN
☼ ◆ ⚡ ZONES VARY   **p. 458**

Rhaphiolepis
☼ ◑ ◆ ◆ ⚡ MANY ZONES   **p. 464**

Rhus typhina
STAGHORN SUMAC
☼ ◆ ◆ ⚡ 1–10, 14–17, 31–45   **p. 472**

Ribes (some)
CURRANT, GOOSEBERRY
☼ ◑ ◆ ⚡ ZONES VARY   **p. 472**

Rosa (many, especially rugosas)
ROSE
NEEDS, ZONES VARY   **p. 473**

Sarcococca ruscifolia
SWEET BOX
◑ ● ◆ ◆ ⚡ 4–9, 14–24, 31   **p. 489**

Skimmia japonica
◑ ● ◆ ⚡ 4–9, 14–22, 31, 32   **p. 498**

Solanum pseudocapsicum
JERUSALEM CHERRY
☼ ◑ ◆ ◆ ⚡ 23–25, 27   **p. 499**

Symphoricarpos
SNOWBERRY
NEEDS, ZONES VARY   **p. 511**

Symplocos paniculata
SAPPHIREBERRY
☼ ◆ ⚡ 2–9, 14–17, 32–41   **p. 512**

Taxus
YEW
☼ ◑ ◆ ◆ ⚡ ZONES VARY   **p. 515**

Vaccinium
NEEDS, ZONES VARY   **p. 529**

Viburnum (many)
NEEDS, ZONES VARY   **p. 532**

PERENNIALS, VINES

Ampelopsis brevipedunculata
PORCELAIN BERRY
☼ ◑ ● ◆ ◆ ⚡ MANY ZONES   **p. 177**

Arum italicum
ITALIAN ARUM
◑ ● ◆ ⚡ 3–24, 28–34, 39   **p. 192**

Celastrus
BITTERSWEET
☼ ◆ ⚡ ZONES VARY   **p. 236**

Iris foetidissima
GLADWIN IRIS
☼ ◑ ◆ ● ⚡ 3–24, 32, 33   **p. 349**

Lonicera (some)
HONEYSUCKLE
☼ ◑ ◆ ⚡ ZONES VARY   **p. 376**

Ophiopogon jaburan
◑ ● ◆ ◆ ⚡ 5–9, 14–31   **p. 374**

Rosa rugosa

Skimmia japonica

Vaccinium (Blueberry)

Viburnum trilobum

Celastrus scandens

Plants with
COLORED FOLIAGE

Not all color comes from flowers or fruit. The plants listed below offer long-term garden accents in the form of colored leaves: gray or silver; bronze, red, or purple; yellow or gold; blue; and variegated. They can be used to enliven the basic green of other garden foliage, to form contrasting combinations with one another (such as gray and red), to complement flower colors in season, and to provide eye-catching focal points.

Achillea 'Moonshine'

Cerastium tomentosum

Artemisia 'Powis Castle'

Santolina chamaecyparissus

Teucrium fruticans

GRAY, SILVER
Trees

Acacia baileyana
BAILEY ACACIA
☼ ◑ ● 💧 ⚡ 7–9, 13–24, 26–28   **p. 163**

Elaeagnus angustifolia
RUSSIAN OLIVE
☼ ◑ ● 💧 💧 ⚡ MANY ZONES   **p. 287**

GRAY, SILVER
Shrubs

Artemisia

☼ ● 💧 ⚡ ZONES VARY   **p. 191**

Caryopteris clandonensis (several)
BLUE MIST
☼ ● 💧 ⚡ 3–7, 14–17, 29–41   **p. 232**

Elaeagnus 'Coral Silver'

☼ ◑ ● 💧 💧 ⚡ 2–24, 28–41   **p. 287**

Feijoa sellowiana
PINEAPPLE GUAVA
☼ ● 💧 ⚡ 7–9, 12–32   **p. 303**

Hippophae rhamnoides
SEA BUCKTHORN
☼ ● 💧 💧 ⚡ 1–5, 34, 37–45   **p. 336**

Juniperus (many)
JUNIPER
☼ ◑ ● 💧 💧 ⚡ ZONES VARY   **p. 353**

Salvia leucophylla
PURPLE SAGE
☼ ◌ ● ⚡ 8, 9, 14–17, 19–24   **p. 485**

Santolina chamaecyparissus
LAVENDER COTTON
☼ ● ● ⚡ MANY ZONES   **p. 488**

Teucrium fruticans
BUSH GERMANDER
☼ ● ⚡ 4–24   **p. 517**

GRAY, SILVER
Perennials

Achillea (many)
YARROW
☼ ● 💧 ⚡ 1–24, 26, 28–45   **p. 166**

Anaphalis
PEARLY EVERLASTING
☼ ◑ ● ● 💧 ⚡ ZONES VARY   **p. 178**

Antennaria
PUSSY TOES
☼ ● 💧 ⚡ MANY ZONES   **p. 181**

Centaurea

NEEDS, ZONES VARY   **p. 237**

Cerastium tomentosum
SNOW-IN-SUMMER
☼ ◑ ● 💧 ⚡ 1–24, 32–45   **p. 238**

Echeveria (many)

☼ ◑ ● ⚡ ZONES VARY   **p. 285**

Euryops

☼ ● ⚡ ZONES VARY   **p. 301**

Helichrysum petiolare
LICORICE PLANT
☼ ● 💧 ⚡ 16, 17, 22–24   **p. 330**

Lavandula (most)
LAVENDER
☼ ● ⚡ ZONES VARY   **p. 365**

Lychnis coronaria
CROWN-PINK
☼ ◑ ● ● 💧 ⚡ 3–9, 14–24, 30–34   **p. 379**

Origanum dictamnus
CRETE DITTANY
☼ ● ⚡ 8–24   **p. 410**

Panicum virgatum 'Heavy Metal'
SWITCH GRASS
☼ ◑ ● ● 💧 ⚡ MANY ZONES   **p. 414**

Centaurea cineraria

Echeveria

Helichrysum petiolare

Lychnis coronaria

For growing symbol explanations, please see page 79.

Perovskia
RUSSIAN SAGE
☼ ◐ ◖ ⚡ 3–24, 28–35, 37, 39 **p. 425**

Salvia chamaedryoides
☼ ◐ ◖ ⚡ 8, 9, 14–24, 27–31 **p. 485**

Salvia leucantha
MEXICAN BUSH SAGE
☼ ◐ ◖ ◗ ⚡ 10–24, 26–31 **p. 485**

Sempervivum
HOUSELEEK
☼ ◐ ◖ ◗ 2–24, 29–41 **p. 494**

Stachys byzantina
LAMB'S EARS
☼ ◐ ◖ ◗ ⚡ 1–24, 29–43 **p. 504**

Thymus (several)
THYME
☼ ◐ ◖ ◗ ⚡ ZONES VARY **p. 519**

Verbascum bombyciferum 'Arctic Summer'
☼ ◐ ◖ ⚡ 2–11, 14–24 **p. 531**

BRONZE, RED, PURPLE
Trees

Acer palmatum (some)
JAPANESE MAPLE
☼ ◐ ◖ ◗ ⚡ MANY ZONES **p. 165**

Acer platanoides (some)
NORWAY MAPLE
☼ ◐ ◖ ◗ ⚡ MANY ZONES **p. 165**

Cercis canadensis 'Forest Pansy'
EASTERN REDBUD
☼ ◐ ◖ ◗ ⚡ 2–20, 26, 28–41 **p. 239**

Cordyline australis 'Atropurpurea'
BRONZE DRACAENA
☼ ◐ ◖ ◗ 5, 8–11, 14–27 **p. 260**

Cotinus coggygria (some)
SMOKE TREE
☼ ◐ ◖ 2–24, 29–41 **p. 265**

Eriobotrya deflexa
BRONZE LOQUAT
☼ ◐ ◖ ◗ 8–28 **p. 291**

Fagus sylvatica (some)
EUROPEAN BEECH
☼ ◐ ◖ ◗ ⚡ 2–9, 14–24, 32–41 **p. 302**

Prunus blireiana
☼ ◐ ◖ ◗ 3–22, 32–34, 39 **p. 454**

Prunus cerasifera (some)
CHERRY PLUM
☼ ◐ ◖ ◗ MANY ZONES **p. 454**

BRONZE, RED, PURPLE
Shrubs

Berberis thunbergii (several)
JAPANESE BARBERRY
☼ ◐ ◖ ◗ ⚡ 1–24, 28–41 **p. 208**

Corylus avellana 'Fusco-rubra'
☼ ◐ ◖ ⚡ 2–9, 14–20, 32–41 **p. 264**

Sambucus nigra 'Purpurea'
BLACK ELDER
☼ ◐ ◖ ⚡ MANY ZONES **p. 487**

Spiraea bumalda (several)
☼ ◐ ◖ ◗ ⚡ MANY ZONES **p. 503**

BRONZE, RED, PURPLE
Perennials

Ajuga reptans (several)
CARPET BUGLE
☼ ◐ ◖ ⚡ 1–24, 26–45 **p. 171**

Astilbe 'Fanal'
☼ ◐ ◖ ◗ 1–7, 14–17, 32–45 **p. 196**

Caladium bicolor
FANCY-LEAFED CALADIUM
☼ ◐ ● ◖ ◗ ⚡ 25–27 **p. 219**

Canna (some)
☼ ◐ ◖◗ ⚡ 6–9, 12–32 **p. 227**

Euphorbia amygdaloides 'Purpurea'
☼ ◐ ◖ ◗ 3–24, 31–34 **p. 299**

Heuchera micrantha 'Palace Purple'
☼ ◐ ◖ ◗ ⚡ 2–11, 14–24, 31–43 **p. 334**

Pennisetum setaceum 'Rubrum'
☼ ◗ ⚡ MANY ZONES **p. 424**

Phormium tenax (several)
NEW ZEALAND FLAX
☼ ◐ ◖ ◗ ⚡ 14–28 **p. 430**

Sedum spathulifolium 'Purpureum'
☼ ◐ ◖ ⚡ 2–9, 14–24 **p. 494**

Sedum spurium (some)
☼ ◐ ◖ ⚡ 1–24, 29–43 **p. 494**

Sedum 'Vera Jameson'
☼ ◐ ◖◗ ⚡ 1–9, 14–24, 31–43 **p. 494**

YELLOW, GOLD
Trees

Acer shirasawanum 'Aureum'
GOLDEN FULLMOON MAPLE
☼ ◐ ◖ ◗ ⚡ MANY ZONES **p. 166**

Chamaecyparis lawsoniana (some)
PORT ORFORD CEDAR
☼ ◐ ◖ ◗ MANY ZONES **p. 241**

Gleditsia triacanthos 'Sunburst'
SUNBURST HONEY LOCUST
☼ ◐ ◖ ⚡ 1–16, 18–20, 32–43 **p. 318**

Cotinus coggygria

Berberis thunbergii 'Atropurpurea'

Ajuga reptans

Canna

Heuchera micrantha 'Palace Purple'

Acer platanoides

Salvia leucantha

Stachys byzantina

Acer palmatum 'Ever Red'

Cercis canadensis 'Forest Pansy'

Plant listings continue ▶

Chamaecyparis

Chrysanthemum parthenium 'Aureum'

Helichrysum petiolare 'Limelight'

Hosta

Taxus baccata 'Aurea'

Thuja plicata 'Aurea'
WESTERN RED CEDAR
☼ ◐ ♦ ♦ ☇ MANY ZONES   **p. 518**

YELLOW, GOLD
Shrubs, Perennials

Carex elata 'Bowles Golden'
☼ ◐ ♦ ☇ 1–9, 14–24, 28–45   **p. 230**

Chamaecyparis (some)
☼ ◐ ♦ ☇ ZONES VARY   **p. 241**

Chrysanthemum parthenium 'Aureum'
☼ ◐ ♦ ☇ 1–24, 28–45   **p. 248**

Helichrysum petiolare 'Limelight'
LICORICE PLANT
☼ ♦ ☇ 16, 17, 22–24   **p. 330**

Hosta (several)
PLANTAIN LILY
◐ ● ♦ ☇ MANY ZONES   **p. 337**

Juniperus (several)
JUNIPER
☼ ◐ ♦ ♦ ☇ ZONES VARY   **p. 353**

Ligustrum vicaryi
VICARY GOLDEN PRIVET
☼ ◐ ♦ ☇ 2–24, 32–41   **p. 370**

Milium effusum 'Aureum'
BOWLES' GOLDEN GRASS
◐ ● ♦♦ ☇ MANY ZONES   **p. 396**

Platycladus orientalis (several)
ORIENTAL ARBORVITAE
☼ ◐ ♦ ☇ 2–41   **p. 438**

Spiraea bumalda (several)
☼ ◐ ♦ ♦ ☇ MANY ZONES   **p. 503**

Taxus baccata (several)
ENGLISH YEW
☼ ◐ ♦ ♦ ☇ MANY ZONES   **p. 515**

Thuja occidentalis 'Rheingold'
AMERICAN ARBORVITAE
☼ ◐ ♦ ♦ ☇ MANY ZONES   **p. 518**

Viburnum opulus 'Aureum'
EUROPEAN CRANBERRY BUSH
☼ ◐ ♦ ☇ 1–9, 14–24, 29–43   **p. 533**

BLUE
Trees

Cedrus atlantica 'Glauca'
☼ ◐ ♦ ☇ 2–24, 31, 32, 34   **p. 236**

Chamaecyparis lawsoniana (some)
PORT ORFORD CEDAR
☼ ◐ ♦ ☇ MANY ZONES   **p. 241**

Cunninghamia lanceolata 'Glauca'
☼ ◐ ♦ ☇ 4–6, 14–21, 28, 31, 32   **p. 269**

Juniperus (some)
JUNIPER
☼ ◐ ♦ ♦ ☇ ZONES VARY   **p. 353**

Picea pungens (some)
COLORADO SPRUCE
☼ ◐ ♦ ♦ ☇ MANY ZONES   **p. 432**

BLUE
Shrubs, Perennials

Chamaecyparis lawsoniana (some)
PORT ORFORD CEDAR
☼ ◐ ♦ ☇ MANY ZONES   **p. 241**

Festuca ovina 'Glauca'
BLUE FESCUE
☼ ◐ ♦ ☇ 1–24, 29–45   **p. 304**

Hosta (several)
PLANTAIN LILY
◐ ● ♦ ☇ MANY ZONES   **p. 337**

Ilex meserveae
HOLLY
☼ ◐ ♦ ☇ MANY ZONES   **p. 343**

Ruta graveolens 'Jackman's Blue'
RUE
☼ ◐ ♦ ☇ 2–24, 30–41   **p. 482**

VARIEGATED
Trees

Acer negundo 'Variegatum'
VARIEGATED BOX ELDER
☼ ◐ ♦ ♦ ☇ MANY ZONES   **p. 165**

Acer palmatum 'Butterfly'
JAPANESE MAPLE
☼ ◐ ♦ ♦ ☇ MANY ZONES   **p. 165**

Cornus florida (several)
FLOWERING DOGWOOD
☼ ◐ ♦ ☇ MANY ZONES   **p. 262**

Fagus sylvatica 'Tricolor'
TRICOLOR BEECH
☼ ◐ ♦ ♦ ☇ MANY ZONES   **p. 303**

VARIEGATED
Shrubs

Aucuba japonica (several)
JAPANESE AUCUBA
◐ ● ♦ ☇ 4–24, 28–33   **p. 197**

Bougainvillea (some)
☼ ◐ ♦ ♦ ☇ MANY ZONES   **p. 212**

Cotoneaster horizontalis 'Variegatus'
☼ ◐ ♦ ☇ 2–11, 14–24, 31–41   **p. 265**

Daphne burkwoodii 'Carol Mackie'
☼ ◐ ♦ ♦ ☇ 2–6, 14–17, 31–41   **p. 275**

Daphne odora 'Marginata'
WINTER DAPHNE
◐ ♦ ☇ MANY ZONES   **p. 275**

Picea pungens

Ruta graveolens 'Jackman's Blue'

Cornus florida 'Welchii'

Daphne odora 'Marginata'

Bougainvillea 'Hawaii'

For growing symbol explanations, please see page 79.

Myrtus communis 'Variegata'

Pittosporum tobira 'Variegata'

Weigela florida 'Variegata'

Actinidia kolomikta

Elaeagnus pungens (some)
SILVERBERRY
☼ ◐ ● ◐ ✂ 4–24, 26–33   **p. 287**

Euonymus (some)
NEEDS, ZONES VARY   **p. 298**

Hydrangea macrophylla 'Tricolor'
GARDEN HYDRANGEA
☼ ◐ ● ✂ MANY ZONES   **p. 340**

Ilex (several)
HOLLY
☼ ◐ ● ✂ ZONES VARY   **p. 343**

Leucothoe fontanesiana 'Rainbow'
DROOPING LEUCOTHOE
◐ ● ● ✂ 4–7, 15–17, 32, 34   **p. 368**

Myrtus communis (several)
MYRTLE
☼ ● ✂ 8–24, 26–28   **p. 401**

Osmanthus heterophyllus 'Variegatus'
☼ ◐ ● ● ✂ MANY ZONES   **p. 411**

Pieris japonica 'Variegata'
LILY-OF-THE-VALLEY SHRUB
◐ ● ✂ 3–9, 14–17, 31–35, 37   **p. 432**

Pittosporum tobira (several)
TOBIRA
☼ ● ● ✂ 8–31   **p. 438**

Taxus baccata 'Stricta' (variegated form)
☼ ◐ ● ✂ 3–9, 14–24, 32, 33   **p. 515**

Viburnum tinus 'Variegatum'
☼ ◐ ● ✂ MANY ZONES   **p. 534**

Weigela florida 'Variegata'
☼ ◐ ● ● ✂ 1–11, 14–17, 32–41   **p. 538**

VARIEGATED
Vines, Ground Covers

Actinidia kolomikta
☼ ● ● ✂ 2–9, 15–17, 31–41   **p. 168**

Euonymus fortunei (some)
☼ ◐ ● ● ● ✂ 3–17, 28–41   **p. 298**

Hedera (some)
IVY
☼ ◐ ● ● ● ✂ ZONES VARY   **p. 328**

Lonicera japonica 'Aureo-reticulata'
GOLDNET HONEYSUCKLE
☼ ◐ ● ✂ 2–41   **p. 377**

Pachysandra terminalis 'Silver Edge'
◐ ● ● ✂ 3–10, 14–21, 32–41   **p. 412**

Vinca (some)
PERIWINKLE
◐ ● ● ✂ ZONES VARY   **p. 534**

VARIEGATED
Perennials, Annuals

Ajuga (several)
CARPET BUGLE
☼ ◐ ● ✂ 1–24, 26–45   **p. 171**

Cabbage, Kale, flowering
☼ ◐ ● ✂ ALL ZONES   **pp. 219, 358**

Caladium bicolor
FANCY-LEAFED CALADIUM
☼ ◐ ● ● ✂ 25–27   **p. 219**

Coleus hybridus
COLEUS
☼ ◐ ● ✂ ALL ZONES   **p. 258**

Helichrysum petiolare 'Variegatum'
LICORICE PLANT
☼ ● ✂ 16, 17, 22–24   **p. 330**

Hosta (many)
PLANTAIN LILY
◐ ● ● ✂ MANY ZONES   **p. 337**

Houttuynia cordata 'Variegata'
☼ ◐ ● ● ● ✂ MANY ZONES   **p. 338**

Impatiens, New Guinea hybrids
☼ ◐ ● ✂ ALL ZONES   **p. 344**

Iris 'Pallida Variegata'
NEEDS, ZONES VARY   **p. 348**

Lamium (several)
DEAD NETTLE
◐ ● ● ✂ 1–24, 32–43   **p. 363**

Liriope muscari (some)
LILY TURF
◐ ● ● ● ✂ 3–10, 14–33   **p. 374**

Miscanthus sinensis (several)
EULALIA GRASS
☼ ◐ ● ● ● ✂ 2–24, 29–41   **p. 397**

Phormium tenax (several)
NEW ZEALAND FLAX
☼ ◐ ● ● ✂ 14–28   **p. 430**

Physostegia virginiana 'Variegata'
FALSE DRAGONHEAD
☼ ◐ ● ✂ 1–24, 26–45   **p. 431**

Pulmonaria (several)
LUNGWORT
◐ ● ● ✂ 1–9, 14–17, 32–43   **p. 457**

Salvia officinalis 'Tricolor'
COMMON SAGE
☼ ● ✂ 2–24, 28–41   **p. 487**

Sedum sieboldii 'Variegatum'
◐ ● ✂ MANY ZONES   **p. 494**

Tulbaghia violacea (some)
SOCIETY GARLIC
☼ ● ✂ 13–24, 26–28   **p. 526**

Hedera helix 'Buttercup'

Caladium bicolor

Lamium

Pulmonaria

Tulbaghia violacea

Achillea

SHOWY PERENNIALS
for Beds and Borders

Year after year, these perennial garden mainstays provide spectacular flowers that inspire artists and photographers to attempt to capture their fleeting beauty. Perennials are distinguished from annuals and biennials by their longevity—they live for more than two years and usually bloom every year. Depending on the plant and the climate, they may be evergreen, or they may die to the ground every winter and regrow from the roots the next spring.

Perennial border

Alstroemeria

Armeria maritima

Aster novi-belgii

Aubrieta deltoidea

Acanthus mollis
BEAR'S BREECH
☼ ◐ ◐ ◐ ✄ MANY ZONES **p. 164**

Achillea
YARROW
☼ ◐ ✄ 1–24, 26, 28–45 **p. 166**

Aconitum
MONKSHOOD
☼ ◐ ◐ ✄ MANY ZONES **p. 167**

Adenophora
LADY BELLS
☼ ◐ ◐ ◐ ✄ MANY ZONES **p. 168**

Agapanthus
LILY-OF-THE-NILE
☼ ◐ ◐ ◐ ✄ ZONES VARY **p. 169**

Agastache
GIANT HYSSOP
☼ ◐ ◐ ◐ ✄ ZONES VARY **p. 170**

Alstroemeria
☼ ◐ ◐ ✄ MANY ZONES **p. 175**

Anaphalis
PEARLY EVERLASTING
◐ ◐ ◐ ◐ ✄ ZONES VARY **p. 178**

Anemone hybrida
JAPANESE ANEMONE
◐ ◐ ✄ 3–24, 30–39, 41 **p. 179**

Anthemis
☼ ◐ ◐ ◐ ✄ ZONES VARY **p. 181**

Aquilegia
COLUMBINE
☼ ◐ ◐ ✄ ZONES VARY **p. 186**

Arenaria montana
SANDWORT
☼ ◐ ◐ ✄ MANY ZONES **p. 190**

Armeria
THRIFT
☼ ◐ ◐ ✄ ZONES VARY **p. 191**

Aruncus
GOAT'S BEARD
☼ ◐ ◐ ◐ ✄ MANY ZONES **p. 193**

Asclepias tuberosa
BUTTERFLY WEED
☼ ◐ ◐ ◐ ✄ ALL ZONES **p. 194**

Aster
☼ ◐ ✄ ZONES VARY **p. 195**

Astilbe
FALSE SPIRAEA
☼ ◐ ◐ ✄ MANY ZONES **p. 196**

Aubrieta deltoidea
COMMON AUBRIETA
☼ ◐ ◐ ✄ MANY ZONES **p. 197**

Aurinia saxatilis
BASKET-OF-GOLD
☼ ◐ ◐ ✄ 1–24, 32–43 **p. 197**

Begonia, semperflorens
BEDDING BEGONIAS
◐ ◐ ◐ ✄ 14–28 **p. 206**

Campanula (some)
BELLFLOWER
☼ ◐ ◐ ◐ ✄ ZONES VARY **p. 227**

Cassia marilandica
WILD SENNA
☼ ◐ ◐ ◐ ✄ 1–10, 14, 28–43 **p. 233**

Catananche caerulea
CUPID'S DART
☼ ◐ ✄ ALL ZONES **p. 234**

Centaurea macrocephala
☼ ◐ ✄ 1–9, 14–24, 29–43 **p. 237**

Centranthus ruber
RED VALERIAN
☼ ◐ ◐ ◐ ✄ MANY ZONES **p. 238**

Cerastium tomentosum
SNOW-IN-SUMMER
☼ ◐ ◐ ✄ 1–24, 32–45 **p. 238**

COLOR CODES: Each tint represents a range of colors, not a color match.

BLUE-PURPLE
WHITE-CREAM
PINK-RED
YELLOW-ORANGE

Astilbe

Campanula persicifolia

Cerastium tomentosum

For growing symbol explanations, please see page 79.

Chelone glabra

☼ ◑ ◐ ◐◐ ⚡ MANY ZONES **p. 243**

Chrysanthemum

NEEDS, ZONES VARY **p. 246**

Chrysanthemum serotinum

☼ ◐ ⚡ 2–9, 14, 28–43 **p. 248**

Chrysopsis

☼ ◐ ◐ ⚡ MANY ZONES **p. 248**

Clematis recta

☼ ◐ ⚡ 1–6, 15–17, 31–45 **p. 254**

Convallaria majalis
LILY-OF-THE-VALLEY
◑ ◐ ⚡ 1–7, 14–20, 31–45 **p. 259**

Coreopsis

☼ ◐ ⚡ ZONES VARY **p. 260**

Cosmos atrosanguineus
CHOCOLATE COSMOS
☼ ◐ ⚡ 4–9, 14–24, 28–32 **p. 264**

Crambe cordifolia

☼ ◐ ⚡ MANY ZONES **p. 266**

Delphinium

☼ ◐ ⚡ ZONES VARY **p. 276**

Dianthus
PINK
☼ ◑ ◐ ⚡ 1–24, 30–45 **p. 278**

Dicentra
BLEEDING HEART
◑ ● ◐ ⚡ MANY ZONES **p. 279**

Dictamnus albus
GAS PLANT
☼ ◑ ◐ ⚡ 1–9, 31–45 **p. 280**

Digitalis
FOXGLOVE
◑ ◐ ⚡ ZONES VARY **p. 281**

Echinacea purpurea
PURPLE CONEFLOWER
☼ ◐ ⚡ 1–24, 26–45 **p. 286**

Echinops
GLOBE THISTLE
☼ ◐ ◐ ⚡ 1–24, 31–45 **p. 286**

Erigeron
FLEABANE
☼ ◑ ◐ ⚡ ZONES VARY **p. 291**

Erodium reichardii
CRANESBILL
☼ ◑ ◐ ⚡ MANY ZONES **p. 294**

Eryngium amethystinum
SEA HOLLY
☼ ◐ ⚡ 1–24, 26, 28–45 **p. 294**

Eupatorium

☼ ◑ ◐ ⚡ ZONES VARY **p. 299**

Euphorbia

NEEDS, ZONES VARY **p. 299**

Euryops pectinatus

☼ ◐ ⚡ 8, 9, 12–26 **p. 301**

Felicia amelloides
BLUE MARGUERITE
☼ ◐ ◐ ⚡ 8, 9, 13–24 **p. 304**

Filipendula

☼ ◑ ◐ ◐◐ ⚡ MANY ZONES **p. 307**

Gaillardia grandiflora
BLANKET FLOWER
☼ ◐ ⚡ ALL ZONES **p. 311**

Gaura lindheimeri
GAURA
☼ ◐ ◐ ⚡ 3–35, 37, 38, 39 **p. 313**

Gazania

☼ ◐ ◐ ⚡ 8–28 **p. 314**

Geranium
CRANESBILL
☼ ◐ ◐ ⚡ ZONES VARY **p. 315**

Gerbera jamesonii
TRANSVAAL DAISY
☼ ◑ ◐ ⚡ MANY ZONES **p. 316**

Geum

☼ ◑ ◐ ⚡ 1–24, 32–43 **p. 317**

Gypsophila

☼ ◐ ⚡ ZONES VARY **p. 325**

Helenium autumnale
COMMON SNEEZEWEED
☼ ◐ ⚡ ALL ZONES **p. 328**

Helianthemum nummularium
SUNROSE
☼ ◐ ⚡ 3–9, 14–24, 32, 34 **p. 329**

Helianthus
SUNFLOWER
☼ ◐ ⚡ ZONES VARY **p. 329**

Heliconia

◐ ◐◐ ⚡ 24, 25 **p. 330**

Heliopsis helianthoides
OX-EYE
☼ ◑ ◐ ◐ ⚡ MANY ZONES **p. 330**

Heliotropium arborescens
COMMON HELIOTROPE
☼ ◑ ◐ ⚡ ALL ZONES **p. 330**

Helleborus
HELLEBORE
◐ ◐ ◐ ◐◐ ⚡ ZONES VARY **p. 331**

Dicentra spectabilis 'Alba'

Erigeron karvinskianus

Eupatorium fistulosum 'Gateway'

Geranium

Helianthemum nummularium

Chrysanthemum maximum

Delphinium

Dianthus

Plant listings continue ▶

Penstemon gloxinioides 'Garnet'

Heliotropium arborescens 'Black Beauty'

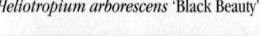

Hemerocallis

Lavandula

Hemerocallis
DAYLILY
☼ ◐ ◑ ✦ ALL ZONES · · · · · · · · · · p. 331

Heuchera
CORAL BELLS
☼ ◐ ◑ ✦ ZONES VARY · · · · · p. 333

Hibiscus moscheutos
ROSE-MALLOW
☼ ◑ ✦ 2–21, 26–41 · · · · · · · · p. 334

Hunnemannia fumariifolia
MEXICAN TULIP POPPY
☼ ◑ ✦ ALL ZONES · · · · · · · · · · p. 339

Iberis sempervirens
EVERGREEN CANDYTUFT
☼ ◑ ✦ 1–24, 31–45 · · · · · · · · p. 342

Inula
ELECAMPANE
☼ ◑ ◑ ◑ ✦ MANY ZONES · · · · p. 345

Iris
NEEDS, ZONES VARY · · · · · · · · p. 347

Kirengeshoma palmata
YELLOW WAX BELLS
◐ ◑ ✦ MANY ZONES · · · · · · · · p. 359

Knautia macedonica
☼ ◑ ✦ MANY ZONES · · · · · · · · p. 359

Kniphofia uvaria
RED-HOT POKER
☼ ◐ ◑ ◑ ✦ MANY ZONES · · · · p. 360

Lampranthus
ICE PLANT
☼ ◑ ✦ 14–26 · · · · · · · · · · · · · · p. 363

Lavandula
LAVENDER
☼ ◑ ✦ ZONES VARY · · · · · · · · p. 365

Liatris
GAYFEATHER
☼ ◑ ◑ ✦ MANY ZONES · · · · · · p. 368

Ligularia
◐ ◑ ◑ ✦ ZONES VARY · · · · · · · · p. 369

Limonium
SEA LAVENDER
☼ ◑ ✦ ZONES VARY · · · · · · · · p. 371

Linaria purpurea
TOADFLAX
☼ ◑ ✦ 2–24, 30–41 · · · · · · · · p. 372

Linum perenne
PERENNIAL BLUE FLAX
☼ ◑ ✦ 3–24, 32–34, 39 · · · · · p. 372

Lobelia cardinalis
CARDINAL FLOWER
☼ ◐ ◑ ◑ ✦ MANY ZONES · · · · p. 375

Lupinus
LUPINE
☼ ◑ ◑ ✦ ZONES VARY · · · · · · · p. 378

Lychnis chalcedonica
MALTESE CROSS
☼ ◐ ◑ ✦ MANY ZONES · · · · · · p. 378

Lysimachia clethroides
GOOSENECK LOOSESTRIFE
☼ ◐ ◑ ✦ MANY ZONES · · · · · · p. 379

Lythrum virgatum
PURPLE LOOSESTRIFE
☼ ◑ ✦ 1–9, 14–24, 29–43 · · · p. 380

Macleaya cordata
PLUME POPPY
☼ ◐ ◑ ◑ ✦ 1–24, 30–43 · · · · p. 381

Malva (most)
MALLOW
☼ ◐ ◑ ✦ ZONES VARY · · · · · · p. 391

Mirabilis jalapa
FOUR O'CLOCK
☼ ◐ ◑ ✦ ALL ZONES · · · · · · · · p. 397

Monarda
BEE BALM
☼ ◐ ◑ ◑ ✦ ZONES VARY · · · · p. 398

Nepeta
☼ ◐ ◑ ✦ 1–24, 32–43 · · · · · · p. 404

Nierembergia
CUP FLOWER
☼ ◑ ✦ ZONES VARY · · · · · · · · p. 406

Oenothera
EVENING PRIMROSE
NEEDS, ZONES VARY · · · · · · · · p. 407

Origanum
NEEDS, ZONES VARY · · · · · · · · p. 410

Osteospermum
AFRICAN DAISY
☼ ◑ ◑ ✦ ALL ZONES · · · · · · · · p. 411

Paeonia (herbaceous)
PEONY
☼ ◐ ◑ ✦ MANY ZONES · · · · · · p. 413

Papaver orientale
ORIENTAL POPPY
☼ ◐ ◑ ✦ MANY ZONES · · · · · · p. 415

Pelargonium
GERANIUM
☼ ◐ ◑ ◑ ✦ 8, 9, 12–24 · · · · · p. 423

Penstemon (many)
BEARD TONGUE
☼ ◐ ◑ ◑ ✦ ZONES VARY · · · · p. 424

Perovskia
RUSSIAN SAGE
☼ ◑ ✦ 3–24, 28–35, 37, 39 · · p. 425

Phlomis
JERUSALEM SAGE
NEEDS, ZONES VARY · · · · · · · · p. 428

Phlox
☼ ◐ ◑ ✦ ZONES VARY · · · · · · p. 428

Malva moschata

Nepeta

Oenothera berlandieri 'Woodside White'

Paeonia

Papaver orientale

For growing symbol explanations, please see page 79.

Physostegia virginiana

Platycodon grandiflorus

Primula

Prunella

Ratibida columnifera

Phygelius
CAPE FUCHSIA
☼ ◐ ● ⚡ 4–9, 14–32   **p. 430**

Physostegia virginiana
FALSE DRAGONHEAD
☼ ◐ ● ⚡ 1–24, 26–45   **p. 431**

Platycodon grandiflorus
BALLOON FLOWER
☼ ◐ ● ⚡ 1–24, 28–45   **p. 439**

Polemonium

◐ ● ● ⚡ MANY ZONES   **p. 443**

Potentilla
CINQUEFOIL
☼ ◐ ● ⚡ ZONES VARY   **p. 447**

Primula (many)
PRIMROSE
NEEDS, ZONES VARY   **p. 448**

Prunella
SELF-HEAL
☼ ◐ ● ⚡ 1–24, 29–43   **p. 450**

Pulmonaria
LUNGWORT
◐ ● ● ⚡ MANY ZONES   **p. 457**

Ratibida columnifera
MEXICAN HAT
☼ ● ⚡ 1–24, 26–43   **p. 463**

Romneya coulteri
MATILIJA POPPY
☼ ● ● ⚡ 4–12, 14–24   **p. 473**

Rudbeckia

☼ ◐ ● ● ⚡ ZONES VARY   **p. 481**

Salvia
SAGE
NEEDS, ZONES VARY   **p. 484**

Scabiosa
PINCUSHION FLOWER
☼ ● ● ⚡ ZONES VARY   **p. 490**

Scaevola

☼ ● ● ● ⚡ 8, 9, 14–24   **p. 490**

Sedum spectabile (varieties)

☼ ● ● ● ⚡ 1–24, 28–43   **p. 494**

Sedum telephium (varieties)

☼ ● ● ⚡ 1–24, 29–43   **p. 494**

Sidalcea
CHECKERBLOOM
☼ ● ⚡ 2–9, 14–24, 29–41   **p. 497**

Silene

NEEDS, ZONES VARY   **p. 497**

Sisyrinchium

☼ ◐ ● ● ⚡ ZONES VARY   **p. 498**

Solidago
GOLDENROD
☼ ◐ ● ⚡ ZONES VARY   **p. 499**

Solidaster luteus

☼ ◐ ● ⚡ MANY ZONES   **p. 499**

Stachys officinalis
BETONY
☼ ◐ ● ⚡ 1–24, 29–45   **p. 504**

Stokesia laevis
STOKES' ASTER
☼ ● ⚡ MANY ZONES   **p. 506**

Strelitzia reginae
BIRD OF PARADISE
☼ ◐ ● ⚡ 22–27   **p. 507**

Tagetes lemmonii

☼ ● ⚡ 8–10, 12–24, 27–29 **p. 514**

Teucrium chamaedrys
GERMANDER
☼ ● ⚡ 3–24, 28–34, 39   **p. 517**

Thalictrum
MEADOW RUE
◐ ● ⚡ ZONES VARY   **p. 517**

Thymus
THYME
☼ ◐ ● ⚡ ZONES VARY   **p. 519**

Trachelium caeruleum

☼ ◐ ● ⚡ 7–9, 14–28   **p. 523**

Tradescantia virginiana
SPIDERWORT
☼ ◐ ● ● ● ⚡ MANY ZONES **p. 524**

Trollius
GLOBEFLOWER
☼ ◐ ● ● ⚡ 1–6, 32–43   **p. 525**

Tulbaghia

☼ ● ⚡ 13–24, 26–28   **p. 526**

Verbascum
MULLEIN
☼ ● ⚡ ZONES VARY   **p. 531**

Verbena

☼ ● ⚡ ZONES VARY   **p. 531**

Veronica
SPEEDWELL
☼ ● ● ⚡ ZONES VARY   **p. 532**

Veronicastrum virginicum
CULVER'S ROOT
☼ ◐ ● ⚡ MANY ZONES   **p. 532**

Viola
VIOLA, PANSY
NEEDS, ZONES VARY   **p. 534**

Viola odorata
SWEET VIOLET
☼ ◐ ● ⚡ 1–24, 29–43   **p. 535**

Rudbeckia fulgida 'Goldsturm'

Sisyrinchium bellum

Solidago

Tagetes lemmonii

Thalictrum

Camellia reticulata 'Shot Silk'

Plants for
ESPALIERS

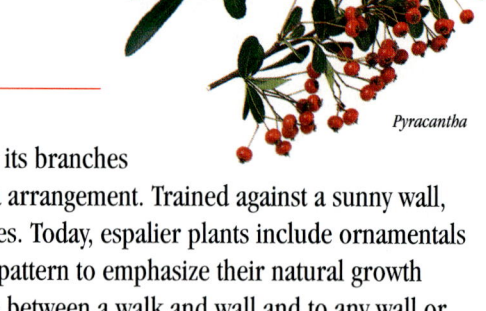

Pyracantha

The classic espalier is a fruit tree trained so that its branches grow in a flat plane, often in a rigid candelabra arrangement. Trained against a sunny wall, crops could be ripened early or in marginal climates. Today, espalier plants include ornamentals trained in a formal arrangement or in an irregular pattern to emphasize their natural growth habit. Espaliers are well-suited to the narrow space between a walk and wall and to any wall or fence where you want a tracery of branches, foliage, or flowers. The plants listed below are easy to espalier—strong enough to be self-supporting yet flexible enough to be guided.

Apple, 'McIntosh'

Cestrum

Orange (Citrus)

Fig, edible

Abutilon ❋
FLOWERING MAPLE
☼ 🌢 🌢 💧 ⚡ 8, 9, 12–27   **p. 163**

Apple ❋
☼ 🌢 ⚡ ZONES VARY   **p. 182** 🍎

Bauhinia galpinii ❋
RED BAUHINIA
☼ 🌢 🌢 ⚡ MANY ZONES   **p. 204**

Calliandra haematocephala ❋
PINK POWDER PUFF
☼ 🌢 🌢 ⚡ 22–27   **p. 221**

Callistemon citrinus ❋
LEMON BOTTLEBRUSH
☼ 🌢 🌢 ⚡ 8, 9, 12–28   **p. 222**

Camellia (some) ❋
🌢 🌢 🌢 ⚡ MANY ZONES   **p. 224**

Cestrum (some) ❋
🌢 🌢 ⚡ ZONES VARY   **p. 240** 🍎

Citrus ❋
☼ 🌢 ⚡ 8, 9, 12–27   **p. 250** 🍎

Cotoneaster ❋
☼ 🌢 ⚡ ZONES VARY   **p. 265** 🍎

Eriobotrya ❋
LOQUAT
☼ 🌢 🌢 ⚡ ZONES VARY   **p. 291** 🍎

Feijoa sellowiana ❋
PINEAPPLE GUAVA
☼ 🌢 ⚡ 7–9, 12–32   **p. 303** 🍎

Fig, edible ❋
☼ 🌢 ⚡ 4–9, 12–32   **p. 306** 🍎

Gardenia ❋
☼ 🌢 🌢 ⚡ ZONES VARY   **p. 312**

Hibiscus rosa-sinensis ❋
CHINESE HIBISCUS
☼ 🌢 ⚡ 9, 12, 13, 15, 16, 19–26   **p. 335**

Itea ilicifolia ❋
HOLLYLEAF SWEETSPIRE
☼ 🌢 🌢 ⚡ 4–24, 28, 31   **p. 350**

Magnolia grandiflora (smallest) ❋
SOUTHERN MAGNOLIA
☼ 🌢 🌢 ⚡ MANY ZONES   **p. 382**

Malus ❋
CRABAPPLE
☼ 🌢 🌢 ⚡ 1–21, 29–43   **p. 387** 🍎

Osmanthus fragrans ❋
SWEET OLIVE
☼ 🌢 🌢 🌢 ⚡ MANY ZONES   **p. 411**

Pear ❋
☼ 🌢 ⚡ ZONES VARY   **p. 421** 🍎

Persimmon ❋
🌢 🌢 🌢 ⚡ ZONES VARY   **p. 425** 🍎

Photinia fraseri ❋
REDTIP
☼ 🌢 🌢 ⚡ MANY ZONES   **p. 430**

Podocarpus (some) ❋
☼ 🌢 🌢 🌢 ⚡ ZONES VARY   **p. 442**

Pyracantha ❋
FIRETHORN
☼ 🌢 ⚡ ZONES VARY   **p. 458** 🍎

Pyrus kawakamii ❋
EVERGREEN PEAR
☼ 🌢 ⚡ 8, 9, 12–24   **p. 459**

Sarcococca ruscifolia
SWEET BOX
🌢 🌢 🌢 🌢 ⚡ 4–9, 14–24, 31   **p. 489**

Viburnum burkwoodii ❋
☼ 🌢 🌢 🌢 ⚡ MANY ZONES   **p. 533**

SYMBOLS: ❋ indicates plants that bear showy flowers; 🍎 indicates plants that bear showy fruit.

Magnolia grandiflora

Malus

Pear

For growing symbol explanations, please see page 79.

Citrus 'Bearss'

Chionanthus virginicus

Magnolia

Brugmansia versicolor 'Charles Grimaldi'

Clethra alnifolia

Corylopsis pauciflora

Gardenia jasminoides 'Radicans'

Daphne burkwoodii

Jasminum nitidum

FRAGRANT PLANTS

A garden's fragrance can be as memorable as its appearance; even years later, the scent of a particular blossom can evoke the memory of a past experience. Flower fragrance is usually most pronounced on warm and humid days and least noticeable when weather is dry and hot. Use fragrant plants where they're most likely to be noticed: in containers on a patio, or beneath a window so the pleasant aroma can drift into the house.

TREES

Chionanthus virginicus
FRINGE TREE
2–6, 15–17, 28–41 · **p. 245**

Citrus
8, 9, 12–27 · **p. 250**

Cladrastis lutea
YELLOW WOOD
1–9, 14–16, 31–43 · **p. 253**

Elaeagnus angustifolia
RUSSIAN OLIVE
MANY ZONES · **p. 287**

Laburnum watereri
GOLDENCHAIN TREE
MANY ZONES · **p. 361**

Magnolia (many)
ZONES VARY · **p. 381**

Malus (some)
CRABAPPLE
1–21, 29–43 · **p. 387**

Michelia doltsopa
14–28 · **p. 396**

Poncirus trifoliata
TRIFOLIATE ORANGE
8, 9, 12–27 · **p. 253**

Prunus (many deciduous)
ZONES VARY · **p. 451**

Robinia pseudoacacia
BLACK LOCUST
1–24, 29–45 · **p. 473**

Styrax obassia
FRAGRANT SNOWBELL
MANY ZONES · **p. 509**

SHRUBS

Bouvardia longiflora 'Albatross'
12, 13, 16, 17, 19–27 · **p. 213**

Brugmansia (several)
ANGEL'S TRUMPET
16–27 · **p. 216**

Buddleia
ZONES VARY · **p. 217**

Calycanthus floridus
CAROLINA ALLSPICE
MANY ZONES · **p. 223**

Carissa
22–27 · **p. 230**

Cestrum (some)
ZONES VARY · **p. 240**

Chimonanthus praecox
WINTERSWEET
4–9, 14–17, 28–34 · **p. 244**

Clerodendrum bungei
CASHMERE BOUQUET
5–9, 12–31 · **p. 255**

Clethra alnifolia
SUMMERSWEET
1–6, 31–43 · **p. 256**

Corylopsis
WINTER HAZEL
4–7, 15–17, 31–34 · **p. 263**

Cytisus
BROOM
ZONES VARY · **p. 273**

Daphne (many)
NEEDS, ZONES VARY · **p. 275**

Buddleia

Plant listings continue ▶

Jasminum polyanthum

Lavandula dentata

Lonicera japonica

Michelia figo

Philadelphus

Elaeagnus
☼ ◖ ● ♦ ✄ ZONES VARY — p. 287

Fothergilla
☼ ◖ ● ♦ ✄ 3–9, 14–17, 31–39 — p. 308

Gardenia
☼ ◖ ● ♦ ✄ ZONES VARY — p. 312

Hamamelis
WITCH HAZEL
☼ ◖ ● ♦ ✄ ZONES VARY — p. 326

Illicium
ANISE TREE
◖ ● ♦♦ ✄ 26, 28, 31, 32 — p. 344

Itea
SWEETSPIRE
☼ ◖ ● ♦ ✄ ZONES VARY — p. 350

Jasminum (some)
JASMINE
☼ ◖ ● ♦ ✄ ZONES VARY — p. 351

Lavandula (most)
LAVENDER
☼ ● ✄ ZONES VARY — p. 365

Lindera
SPICEBUSH
☼ ◖ ● ♦ ✄ ZONES VARY — p. 372

Lonicera
HONEYSUCKLE
☼ ◖ ● ♦ ✄ ZONES VARY — p. 376

Magnolia stellata
STAR MAGNOLIA
☼ ◖ ● ♦ ✄ 2–9, 14–24, 28–41 — p. 385

Michelia figo
BANANA SHRUB
◖ ● ✄ 9, 14–24, 26–29, 31, 32 — p. 396

Murraya paniculata
ORANGE JESSAMINE
☼ ◖ ● ✄ 21–27 — p. 399

Osmanthus (most)
☼ ◖ ● ♦ ✄ ZONES VARY — p. 410

Philadelphus (most)
MOCK ORANGE
☼ ◖ ● ♦ ✄ ZONES VARY — p. 427

Pittosporum tobira
TOBIRA
☼ ◖ ● ♦ ✄ 8–31 — p. 438

Plumeria
☼ ◖ ● ✄ ZONES VARY — p. 442

Rhaphiolepis 'Majestic Beauty'
☼ ◖ ● ♦ ✄ MANY ZONES — p. 465

Rhododendron alabamense
ALABAMA AZALEA
◖ ● ♦♦ ✄ 31–33 — p. 470

Rhododendron arborescens
SWEET AZALEA
◖ ● ♦♦ ✄ 32–41 — p. 470

Rhododendron 'Else Frye'
◖ ● ♦♦ ✄ MANY ZONES — p. 467

Rhododendron 'Fragrantissimum'
◖ ● ♦♦ ✄ MANY ZONES — p. 467

Rhododendron, Viscosum Hybrids
DECIDUOUS AZALEAS
◖ ● ♦♦ ✄ 3–7, 32–41 — p. 470

Ribes odoratum
☼ ◖ ● ✄ 1–10, 14–17, 33–45 — p. 472

Rosa (many)
ROSE
NEEDS, ZONES VARY — p. 473

Sarcococca
SWEET BOX
◖ ● ♦ ♦ ✄ ZONES VARY — p. 489

Skimmia japonica (esp. males)
◖ ● ♦ ✄ 4–9, 14–22, 31, 32 — p. 498

Syringa (many)
LILAC
☼ ◖ ● ✄ ZONES VARY — p. 512

Viburnum (several)
NEEDS, ZONES VARY — p. 532

VINES

Beaumontia grandiflora
EASTER LILY VINE
☼ ◖ ● ♦♦ ✄ MANY ZONES — p. 205

Clematis armandii
EVERGREEN CLEMATIS
☼ ◖ ● ✄ 4–9, 12–24, 28, 31, 32 — p. 254

Distictis laxiflora
VANILLA TRUMPET VINE
☼ ◖ ● ♦ ✄ 16, 22–27 — p. 282

Gelsemium sempervirens
CAROLINA JESSAMINE
☼ ◖ ● ♦ ✄ 8–24, 26, 28–33 — p. 314

Hoya carnosa
WAX FLOWER
◖ ● ♦ ✄ 15–25 — p. 339

Ipomoea alba
MOONFLOWER
☼ ◖ ● ♦ ✄ 15–17, 23–27 — p. 346

Jasminum (some)
JASMINE
☼ ◖ ● ♦ ✄ ZONES VARY — p. 351

Lonicera (some)
HONEYSUCKLE
☼ ◖ ● ♦ ✄ ZONES VARY — p. 376

Pittosporum tobira

Rosa 'Iceberg'

Passiflora alatocaerulea

Trachelospermum jasminoides

Cosmos atrosanguineus

For growing symbol explanations, please see page 79.

Crinum powellii 'Album'

Dianthus

Iris, tall bearded

Lilium 'Stargazer'

Mandevilla laxa
CHILEAN JASMINE
☼ ◐ ♦ ✂ MANY ZONES — **p. 391**

Passiflora alatocaerulea
PASSION VINE
☼ ♦ ♦ ✂ 5–9, 12–29 — **p. 417**

Stephanotis floribunda
MADAGASCAR JASMINE
◐ ♦ ✂ 23–25 — **p. 505**

Trachelospermum
STAR JASMINE
☼ ◐ ● ♦ ✂ ZONES VARY — **p. 523**

Wisteria

NEEDS, ZONES VARY — **p. 538**

PERENNIALS, ANNUALS, BULBS

Amaryllis belladonna
NAKED LADY
☼ ♦ ✂ 4–24, 28, 29 — **p. 177**

Centaurea moschata
SWEET SULTAN
☼ ♦ ✂ ALL ZONES — **p. 238**

Convallaria majalis
LILY-OF-THE-VALLEY
◐ ♦ ✂ 1–7, 14–20, 31–45 — **p. 259**

Cosmos atrosanguineus
CHOCOLATE COSMOS
☼ ♦ ✂ 4–9, 14–24, 28–32 — **p. 264**

Crinum

☼ ◐ ♦ ♦♦ ✂ 8, 9, 12–31, 33 — **p. 267**

Crocus chrysanthus

☼ ◐ ♦ ✂ 1–24, 30–45 — **p. 268**

Dianthus (some)
PINK
☼ ◐ ♦ ✂ 1–24, 30–45 — **p. 278**

Erysimum cheiri
ENGLISH WALLFLOWER
☼ ◐ ● ♦ ✂ MANY ZONES — **p. 294**

Freesia (some)

☼ ◐ ● ♦ ✂ 8, 9, 12–24, 28 — **p. 310**

Hedychium coronarium
WHITE GINGER LILY
☼ ◐ ●● ✂ 16, 17, 22–27 — **p. 328**

Heliotropium arborescens
COMMON HELIOTROPE
☼ ◐ ♦ ✂ ALL ZONES — **p. 330**

Hemerocallis lilio-asphodelus
LEMON DAYLILY
☼ ◐ ♦ ✂ 1–12, 14–24, 28–43 — **p. 332**

Hosta plantaginea
FRAGRANT PLANTAIN LILY
☼ ◐ ● ♦ ✂ MANY ZONES — **p. 337**

Hyacinthus
HYACINTH
☼ ◐ ♦ ✂ ALL ZONES — **p. 339**

Hymenocallis
☼ ◐ ♦ ✂ 5, 6, 8, 9, 14–31 — **p. 341**

Iberis amara
HYACINTH-FLOWERED CANDYTUFT
☼ ♦ ✂ ALL ZONES — **p. 342**

Ipomoea alba
MOONFLOWER
☼ ♦ ♦ ✂ 15–17, 23–27 — **p. 346**

Iris, bearded (many)
☼ ◐ ♦ ✂ 1–24, 30–45 — **p. 348**

Lathyrus odoratus
SWEET PEA
☼ ♦ ♦ ✂ ALL ZONES — **p. 364**

Lilium (many)
LILY
◐ ♦ ✂ ALL ZONES — **p. 370**

Matthiola
STOCK
☼ ◐ ♦ ✂ ALL ZONES — **p. 392**

Narcissus (many)
DAFFODIL
☼ ◐ ♦ ✂ ZONES VARY — **p. 402**

Nelumbo
LOTUS
☼ ◐ ♦ ✂ ALL ZONES — **p. 403**

Nicotiana
☼ ◐ ♦ ✂ ALL ZONES — **p. 406**

Paeonia (many)
PEONY
☼ ◐ ♦ ✂ ZONES VARY — **p. 413**

Phlox paniculata (esp. light colors)
SUMMER PHLOX
☼ ◐ ♦ ✂ 1–14, 18–21, 27–43 — **p. 429**

Polianthes tuberosa
TUBEROSE
☼ ◐ ♦ ✂ ALL ZONES — **p. 443**

Primula alpicola
MOONLIGHT PRIMROSE
☼ ◐ ● ♦ ✂ 3–6, 17, 34, 37 — **p. 449**

Primula vulgaris (some)
ENGLISH PRIMROSE
☼ ◐ ● ♦ ✂ MANY ZONES — **p. 450**

Reseda odorata
MIGNONETTE
☼ ◐ ♦ ✂ ALL ZONES — **p. 464**

Tropaeolum majus
GARDEN NASTURTIUM
☼ ◐ ♦ ✂ ALL ZONES — **p. 525**

Viola odorata
SWEET VIOLET
☼ ◐ ♦ ✂ 1–24, 29–43 — **p. 535**

Heliotropium arborescens

Nelumbo nucifera

Nicotiana

Phlox paniculata

Tropaeolum majus

Consolida ambigua

FLOWERS
for Cutting

A large bouquet of fresh flowers is a satisfying reward for your gardening efforts. Many kinds of flowers are good for cutting. The ones listed here will generally last a week in water. Annuals and biennials must be planted every year, although a few, such as larkspur and cosmos, may reseed themselves. Perennials and most bulbs provide flowers for cutting year after year. Peak flower season can come earlier or later than indicated, depending on climate and care.

Achillea and *Gaillardia*

Antirrhinum majus

Centaurea cyanus

Cosmos bipinnatus

ANNUALS, BIENNIALS

Antirrhinum majus
SNAPDRAGON
☼ ◕ ⚡ ALL ZONES **p. 182**

Calendula officinalis
POT MARIGOLD
☼ ◕ ⚡ ALL ZONES **p. 221**

Callistephus chinensis
CHINA ASTER
☼ ◕ ⚡ ALL ZONES **p. 222**

Centaurea cyanus
CORNFLOWER
☼ ◕ ⚡ ALL ZONES **p. 237**

Cleome hasslerana
SPIDER FLOWER
☼ ◕ ⚡ ALL ZONES **p. 255**

Consolida ambigua
LARKSPUR
☼ ◕ ⚡ ALL ZONES **p. 259**

Cosmos bipinnatus
☼ ◕ ⚡ ALL ZONES **p. 264**

Dianthus (some)
☼ ◑ ◕ ⚡ 1–24, 30–45 **p. 278**

Eustoma grandiflorum
LISIANTHUS
☼ ◑ ◕ ⚡ ALL ZONES **p. 301**

Gomphrena globosa
GLOBE AMARANTH
☼ ◑ ◕ ⚡ ALL ZONES **p. 319**

Gypsophila elegans
☼ ◕ ⚡ ALL ZONES **p. 325**

Helianthus annuus
COMMON SUNFLOWER
☼ ◕ ⚡ ALL ZONES **p. 329**

Helichrysum bracteatum
STRAWFLOWER
☼ ◕ ⚡ ALL ZONES **p. 329**

Helipterum roseum
PINK AND WHITE EVERLASTING
☼ ◕ ⚡ ALL ZONES **p. 331**

Lathyrus odoratus
SWEET PEA
☼ ◕ ⚡ ALL ZONES **p. 364**

Lavatera trimestris
ANNUAL MALLOW
☼ ◕ ◕ ⚡ ALL ZONES **p. 366**

Limonium sinuatum
☼ ◕ ⚡ ALL ZONES **p. 371**

Matthiola
STOCK
☼ ◑ ◕ ⚡ ALL ZONES **p. 392**

Nigella damascena
LOVE-IN-A-MIST
☼ ◑ ◕ ⚡ ALL ZONES **p. 406**

Phlox drummondii
ANNUAL PHLOX
☼ ◕ ⚡ ALL ZONES **p. 428**

Psylliostachys suworowii
☼ ◕ ⚡ ALL ZONES **p. 455**

Scabiosa (some)
PINCUSHION FLOWER
☼ ◕ ◕ ⚡ ZONES VARY **p. 490**

Tagetes (most)
MARIGOLD
☼ ◕ ⚡ ZONES VARY **p. 513**

Tithonia rotundifolia
MEXICAN SUNFLOWER
☼ ◕ ⚡ ALL ZONES **p. 521**

Zinnia
☼ ◕ ⚡ ALL ZONES **p. 543**

VERTICAL BAR: The green band indicates bloom time (most zones). An empty bar indicates the bloom time varies by variety.

SPRING	
SUMMER	
FALL	
WINTER	

Helianthus annuus

Lathyrus odoratus

Scabiosa atropurpurea

For growing symbol explanations, please see page 79.

Tagetes tenuifolia 'Lemon Gem'

Tithonia rotundifolia

Alstroemeria

Dahlia

Delphinium Magic Fountains strain

PERENNIALS, BULBS

Achillea filipendulina
FERNLEAF YARROW
☼ ◐ ☇ 1–24, 26, 28–45 **p. 166**

Alstroemeria
☼ ◔ ◐ ☇ MANY ZONES **p. 175**

Anemone coronaria
POPPY-FLOWERED ANEMONE
☼ ◔ ◐ ☇ 2–24, 30–41 **p. 179**

Anemone hybrida
JAPANESE ANEMONE
◔ ◐ ☇ 3–24, 30–39, 41 **p. 179**

Aster
☼ ◐ ☇ 1–24, 31–43 **p. 195**

Campanula (some)
BELLFLOWER
☼ ◔ ◐ ◐ ☇ MANY ZONES **p. 227**

Chrysanthemum (some)
NEEDS, ZONES VARY **p. 246**

Coreopsis (most)
☼ ◐ ☇ ZONES VARY **p. 260**

Dahlia
☼ ◔ ◐ ☇ ALL ZONES **p. 274**

Delphinium
☼ ◐ ☇ ZONES VARY **p. 276**

Dianthus (many)
☼ ◔ ◐ ☇ 1–24, 30–45 **p. 278**

Echinacea purpurea
PURPLE CONEFLOWER
☼ ◐ ☇ 1–24, 26–45 **p. 286**

Echinops
GLOBE THISTLE
☼ ◐ ◐ ☇ 1–24, 31–45 **p. 286**

Freesia
☼ ◔ ◐ ☇ 8, 9, 12–24, 28 **p. 310**

Gaillardia grandiflora
BLANKET FLOWER
☼ ◐ ☇ ALL ZONES **p. 311**

Gerbera jamesonii
TRANSVAAL DAISY
☼ ◔ ◐ ☇ MANY ZONES **p. 316**

Gladiolus
☼ ◐ ☇ ZONES VARY **p. 317**

Gypsophila paniculata
BABY'S BREATH
☼ ◐ ☇ MANY ZONES **p. 325**

Heliopsis helianthoides
OX-EYE
☼ ◔ ◐ ☇ MANY ZONES **p. 330**

Iris
NEEDS, ZONES VARY **p. 347**

Lavandula
LAVENDER
☼ ◐ ☇ ZONES VARY **p. 365**

Liatris
GAYFEATHER
☼ ◐ ◐ ☇ MANY ZONES **p. 368**

Lilium
LILY
◔ ◐ ☇ ALL ZONES **p. 370**

Limonium
SEA LAVENDER
☼ ◐ ☇ ZONES VARY **p. 371**

Narcissus
DAFFODIL
NEEDS, ZONES VARY **p. 402**

Phlox paniculata
SUMMER PHLOX
☼ ◐ ☇ MANY ZONES **p. 429**

Platycodon grandiflorus
BALLOON FLOWER
☼ ◔ ◐ ☇ 1–24, 26, 28–45 **p. 439**

Ranunculus asiaticus
PERSIAN RANUNCULUS
☼ ◐ ☇ ALL ZONES **p. 462**

Rudbeckia hirta
GLORIOSA DAISY
☼ ◔ ◐ ◐ ☇ 1–24, 26–43 **p. 481**

Scabiosa (some)
PINCUSHION FLOWER
☼ ◐ ◐ ☇ ZONES VARY **p. 490**

Solidago
GOLDENROD
☼ ◔ ◐ ☇ ZONES VARY **p. 499**

Stokesia laevis
STOKES' ASTER
☼ ◐ ☇ MANY ZONES **p. 506**

Thalictrum aquilegifolium
MEADOW RUE
◐ ◐ ☇ 2–10, 14–17, 31–41 **p. 517**

Tritonia
☼ ◐ ☇ MANY ZONES **p. 525**

Tulipa
TULIP
☼ ◐ ☇ 1–24, 28–45 **p. 526**

Veronica spicata
SPEEDWELL
☼ ◐ ☇ 1–9, 14–21, 31–43 **p. 532**

Zantedeschia
CALLA
NEEDS VARY, MANY ZONES **p. 541**

Gerbera jamesonii

Gladiolus

Liatris spicata

Platycodon grandiflorus

Echinacea purpurea

ORNAMENTAL GRASSES

Bamboo

Denizens of prairie, marsh, seashore, and forest, the ornamental grasses are enormously varied. In contrast to the familiar lawn grasses, these decorative cousins are not for mowing. Their beauty lies in their fountains and shaving-brushes of foliage, in their range of texture, color, and character. Many mount a significant floral display, producing reedlike stems with plumes or pendants of tiny floral structures. And some even offer colorful fall foliage.

Imperata cylindrica 'Rubra'

Calamagrostis acutifolia 'Stricta'

Festuca glauca

Helictotrichon sempervirens

Pennisetum orientale

Phalaris arundinacea 'Picta'

Stipa gigantea

Cortaderia selloana 'Pumila'

Arrhenatherum elatius bulbosum
BULBOUS OAT GRASS
2–7, 32, 34, 36–41 p. 191

Bamboo
ZONES VARY p. 199

Bouteloua gracilis
BLUE GRAMA GRASS
MANY ZONES p. 213

Briza maxima
RATTLESNAKE GRASS
ALL ZONES p. 215

Calamagrostis acutifolia 'Stricta'
FEATHER REED GRASS
2–24, 29–41 p. 220

Carex
SEDGE
1–9, 14–24, 28–45 p. 230

Chasmanthium latifolium
SEA OATS
1–24, 28–43 p. 242

Coix lacryma-jobi
JOB'S TEARS
12–24, 28–30 p. 258

Cortaderia selloana
PAMPAS GRASS
4–31, 33 p. 263

Cyperus
ZONES VARY p. 273

Deschampsia
HAIR GRASS
2–24, 28–41 p. 277

Festuca
FESCUE
1–24, 29–45 p. 304

Hakonechloa macra 'Aureola'
JAPANESE FOREST GRASS
2–9, 14–24, 31–41 p. 326

Helictotrichon sempervirens
BLUE OAT GRASS
2–24, 30–41 p. 330

Imperata cylindrica 'Rubra'
JAPANESE BLOOD GRASS
4–24, 26, 28, 31–33 p. 345

Juncus effusus
SOFT RUSH
1–24, 26–45 p. 353

Milium effusum 'Aureum'
BOWLES' GOLDEN GRASS
MANY ZONES p. 396

Miscanthus sinensis
EULALIA GRASS
2–24, 29–41 p. 397

Molinia caerulea
PURPLE MOOR GRASS
MANY ZONES p. 397

Muhlenbergia
ZONES VARY p. 399

Panicum virgatum
SWITCH GRASS
MANY ZONES p. 414

Pennisetum
FOUNTAIN GRASS
NEEDS, ZONES VARY p. 424

Phalaris arundinacea
RIBBON GRASS
MANY ZONES p. 427

Scirpus cernuus
FIBER OPTICS PLANT
7–28 p. 493

Setaria palmifolia
PALM GRASS
14–27 p. 496

Stipa
FEATHER GRASS
ZONES VARY p. 506

For growing symbol explanations, please see page 79.

Adiantum aleuticum

Asplenium scolopendrium

Athyrium nipponicum

Dennstaedtia punctilobula

FERNS
for Foliage Interest

Think of ferns, and you probably think of a lush and shady forest nook. What you may not imagine, though, is the stunning diversity that these typically shade-loving plants have to offer. In size, they range from forest-floor creepers to the majestic tree ferns that seem to belong to the age of dinosaurs. Their leaves (fronds) may look like a hand with outstretched fingers (palmate) or like feathers of a bird (pinnate); texture varies from silky-soft to thick and leathery. Most ferns have a filigree look, but some kinds have undivided fronds resembling green spearpoints.

Adiantum
MAIDENHAIR FERN
ZONES VARY — **p. 168**

Asplenium
ZONES VARY — **p. 195**

Athyrium
1–9, 14–24, 31–43 — **p. 197**

Cyathea cooperi
AUSTRALIAN TREE FERN
15–27 — **p. 271**

Cyrtomium falcatum
HOLLY FERN
5–9, 14–30 — **p. 273**

Davallia trichomanoides
SQUIRREL'S FOOT FERN
17, 23–27 — **p. 276**

Dennstaedtia punctilobula
HAY-SCENTED FERN
1–6, 31–45 — **p. 277**

Dicksonia
ZONES VARY — **p. 280**

Dryopteris
WOOD FERN
ZONES VARY — **p. 284**

Humata tyermannii
BEAR'S FOOT FERN
17, 23–27 — **p. 339**

Matteuccia struthiopteris
OSTRICH FERN
MANY ZONES — **p. 392**

Nephrolepis
SWORD FERN
ZONES VARY — **p. 404**

Onoclea sensibilis
SENSITIVE FERN
1–9, 14–24, 31–43 — **p. 409**

Osmunda
NEEDS, ZONES VARY — **p. 411**

Pellaea
CLIFF-BRAKE
ZONES VARY — **p. 423**

Platycerium
STAGHORN FERN
ZONES VARY — **p. 438**

Polypodium
ZONES VARY — **p. 444**

Polystichum
ZONES VARY — **p. 445**

Pteridium aquilinum
BRACKEN
1–10, 14–24, 28–43 — **p. 456**

Pteris
BRAKE
ZONES VARY — **p. 456**

Rumohra adiantiformis
LEATHERLEAF FERN
14–17, 19–27 — **p. 482**

Thelypteris
ZONES VARY — **p. 517**

Woodsia obtusa
1–6, 14–17, 31–43 — **p. 539**

Woodwardia
CHAIN FERN
ZONES VARY — **p. 539**

For growing symbol explanations, please see page 79.

Matteuccia struthiopteris

Nephrolepis cordifolia

Onoclea sensibilis

Osmunda cinnamomea

Dryopteris goldiana

PALMS

Whether they bring to mind a desert oasis or a tropical lagoon, there's no denying that palms are evocative. Their looks vary greatly: they may be single-trunked or clumping, fan- or feather-leafed, soft and graceful or stiff and architectural. In the milder zones where most palms thrive, use them to set a mood, create a contrast among other plants, or serve as stylish exclamation points in your landscape.

Rhapis excelsa

Neodypsis decaryi

Acoelorrhaphe wrightii
☼ ◖ ◗ ● ▨ 19–26   **p. 167**

Archontophoenix
☼ ◖ ◗ ● ◗ ▨ 21–25   **p. 189**

Brahea armata
MEXICAN BLUE PALM
☼ ◗ ▨ 10, 12–17, 19–24   **p. 214**

Brahea brandegeei
SAN JOSE HESPER PALM
☼ ◗ ▨ 19, 21–24   **p. 214**

Butia capitata
PINDO PALM
☼ ◗ ● ▨ 8, 9, 12–28   **p. 218**

Caryota
FISHTAIL PALM
☼ ◗ ● ▨ 23–25   **p. 232**

Chamaedorea
◖ ● ◗ ● ▨ 16, 17, 22–25, 26, 27 **p. 241**

Chamaerops humilis
MEDITERRANEAN FAN PALM
☼ ◖ ◗ ● ◗ ▨ 4–31   **p. 242**

Chrysalidocarpus lutescens
ARECA PALM
☼ ◗ ● ▨ 23–27   **p. 246**

Cocos nucifera
COCONUT PALM
☼ ◗ ● ▨ 25   **p. 257**

Howea
◖ ● ◗ ▨ 17, 21–25   **p. 338**

Jubaea chilensis
CHILEAN WINE PALM
☼ ◗ ● ▨ 12–24, 27–30   **p. 352**

Livistona
☼ ◗ ● ▨ 13–17, 19–27   **p. 375**

Neodypsis decaryi
TRIANGLE PALM
☼ ◖ ◗ ● ◗ ▨ 20–25   **p. 404**

Phoenix canariensis
CANARY ISLAND DATE PALM
☼ ◗ ● ▨ 9, 12–28   **p. 429**

Phoenix dactylifera
DATE PALM
☼ ◗ ● ▨ 9, 12–28   **p. 429**

Phoenix loureiri
☼ ◗ ● ▨ 9, 12–28   **p. 429**

Phoenix reclinata
SENEGAL DATE PALM
☼ ◗ ● ▨ 23–27   **p. 429**

Phoenix roebelenii
PYGMY DATE PALM
☼ ◗ ● ◗ ▨ 23–27   **p. 429**

Phoenix rupicola
CLIFF DATE PALM
☼ ◗ ● ▨ 17, 19–27   **p. 429**

Phoenix sylvestris
SILVER DATE PALM
☼ ◗ ● ▨ 14–17, 19–28   **p. 429**

Ptychosperma
◗ ● ▨ 23–25   **p. 456**

Rhapis
LADY PALM
☼ ◗ ● ◗ ▨ ZONES VARY   **p. 465**

Roystonea
ROYAL PALM
☼ ◗ ● ◖ ◗ ▨ 25   **p. 481**

Sabal
PALMETTO
☼ ◖ ◗ ● ▨ ZONES VARY   **p. 483**

Syagrus romanzoffianum
QUEEN PALM
☼ ◗ ● ▨ 12, 13, 15–17, 19–27   **p. 511**

Trachycarpus
PALMS
☼ ◖ ◗ ● ▨ ZONES VARY   **p. 523**

Washingtonia
☼ ◗ ● ◗ ▨ 8–30   **p. 537**

Brahea armata

Chamaerops humilis

Cocos nucifera

Phoenix canariensis

Sabal palmetto

Livistona chinensis

Washingtonia filifera

For growing symbol explanations, please see page 79.

Celastrus scandens and mockingbird

Plants that Attract
BIRDS

Watching birds enjoy your garden increases your enjoyment as well. Give feathered visitors a warm welcome by choosing plantings that provide favorite natural bird foods—seeds, berries, nectar. To keep the guests dropping in year-round, select your plants carefully, making sure the garden offers flowers, fruit, or seeds in every season.

FRUIT/SEED-EATING BIRDS
Ground Covers/Vines

Ampelopsis brevipedunculata
PORCELAIN BERRY
☼ ◐ ● ◑ ❀ 2–24, 28–41   **p. 177**

Celastrus scandens
AMERICAN BITTERSWEET
☼ ● ❀ 1–7, 10, 29–44   **p. 236**

Euonymus fortunei
☼ ◐ ● ◑ ❀ 3–17, 28–41   **p. 298**

Grape
☼ ● ❀ ZONES VARY   **p. 320**

Lonicera
HONEYSUCKLE
☼ ◐ ● ❀ ZONES VARY   **p. 376**

Parthenocissus
☼ ◐ ● ◑ ❀ ZONES VARY   **p. 416**

FRUIT/SEED-EATING BIRDS
Shrubs

Amelanchier
JUNEBERRY
☼ ◐ ● ◑ ❀ 1–6, 31–45   **p. 177**

Arctostaphylos uva-ursi
BEARBERRY
☼ ◐ ● ❀ MANY ZONES   **p. 189**

Aronia
CHOKEBERRY
☼ ◐ ● ◑ ❀ ZONES VARY   **p. 191**

Berberis
BARBERRY
☼ ◐ ● ◑ ❀ ZONES VARY   **p. 207**

Callicarpa
BEAUTYBERRY
☼ ◐ ● ◑ ❀ MANY ZONES   **p. 221**

Cornus
DOGWOOD
☼ ◐ ● ❀ ZONES VARY   **p. 262**

Cotoneaster
☼ ● ❀ ZONES VARY   **p. 265**

Elaeagnus
☼ ◐ ● ❀ ZONES VARY   **p. 287**

Euonymus
NEEDS, ZONES VARY   **p. 298**

Ilex
HOLLY
☼ ◐ ● ❀ ZONES VARY   **p. 343**

Leycesteria formosa
HIMALAYAN HONEYSUCKLE
☼ ◐ ● ❀ 4–6, 15–17, 31, 32   **p. 368**

Ligustrum
PRIVET
☼ ◐ ● ❀ ZONES VARY   **p. 369**

Lindera benzoin
SPICEBUSH
☼ ◐ ● ❀ 3–6, 31–41   **p. 372**

Lonicera
HONEYSUCKLE
☼ ◐ ● ❀ ZONES VARY   **p. 376**

Mahonia
NEEDS, ZONES VARY   **p. 386**

Malus sargentii
SARGENT CRABAPPLE
☼ ● ◑ ❀ 1–21, 29–43   **p. 390**

Myrica pensylvanica
BAYBERRY
☼ ● ◑ ❀ 3–7, 32–44   **p. 401**

Photinia
☼ ● ◑ ❀ ZONES VARY   **p. 430**

Prunus
☼ ● ◑ ❀ ZONES VARY   **p. 451**

Pyracantha
FIRETHORN
☼ ● ❀ ZONES VARY   **p. 458**

Ampelopsis brevipedunculata

Callicarpa dichotoma

Cornus stolonifera

Cotoneaster apiculatus

Ilex verticillata 'Afterglow'

Mahonia aquifolium

Myrica pensylvanica

Plant listings continue ▶

Pyracantha

Viburnum plicatum plicatum

Acer

Amelanchier canadensis

Juniperus communis

Rhamnus
☼ ◐ ◔ ⚡ ZONES VARY · p. 464

Ribes
☼ ◐ ◔ ⚡ ZONES VARY · p. 472

Rosa (some)
NEEDS, ZONES VARY · p. 473

Rosmarinus officinalis
ROSEMARY
☼ ◔ ⚡ 4–24, 26–32 · p. 480

Rubus
BRAMBLE
☼ ◐ ◔ ◔ ⚡ ZONES VARY · p. 481

Sambucus
ELDERBERRY
☼ ◐ ◔ ⚡ ZONES VARY · p. 487

Shepherdia
BUFFALOBERRY
☼ ◔ ◔ ⚡ 1–3, 7, 10, 33–45 · p. 496

Symphoricarpos
SNOWBERRY
NEEDS, ZONES VARY · p. 511

Vaccinium
NEEDS, ZONES VARY · p. 529

Viburnum
NEEDS, ZONES VARY · p. 532

FRUIT/SEED-EATING BIRDS
Trees

Abies
FIR
☼ ◐ ◔ ◔ ⚡ ZONES VARY · p. 162

Acer
MAPLE
☼ ◐ ◔ ◔ ⚡ ZONES VARY · p. 164

Alnus
ALDER
☼ ◐ ◔ ◔ ◐ ⚡ ZONES VARY · p. 174

Amelanchier
JUNEBERRY
☼ ◐ ◔ ◔ ⚡ 1–6, 31–45 · p. 177

Betula
BIRCH
☼ ◔ ◐ ◔ ⚡ ZONES VARY · p. 208

Carpinus
HORNBEAM
NEEDS, ZONES VARY · p. 231

Celtis
HACKBERRY
☼ ◐ ◔ ◔ ⚡ ZONES VARY · p. 237

Cornus
DOGWOOD
☼ ◐ ◔ ◔ ⚡ ZONES VARY · p. 262

Crataegus
HAWTHORN
☼ ◔ ◔ ⚡ MANY ZONES · p. 266

Elaeagnus angustifolia
RUSSIAN OLIVE
☼ ◐ ◔ ◔ ⚡ MANY ZONES · p. 287

Ilex
HOLLY
☼ ◔ ◔ ⚡ ZONES VARY · p. 343

Juniperus
JUNIPER
☼ ◐ ◔ ◔ ⚡ ZONES VARY · p. 353

Larix
LARCH
☼ ◔ ◔ ⚡ ZONES VARY · p. 363

Ligustrum lucidum
GLOSSY PRIVET
☼ ◐ ◔ ◔ ⚡ 5, 6, 8–31 · p. 369

Liquidambar styraciflua
AMERICAN SWEET GUM
☼ ◔ ◔ ⚡ 3–9, 14–37, 39 · p. 373

Magnolia
☼ ◐ ◔ ◔ ⚡ ZONES VARY · p. 381

Malus
CRABAPPLE
☼ ◐ ◔ ◔ ⚡ 1–21, 29–43 · p. 387

Morus
MULBERRY
☼ ◔ ◔ ⚡ ZONES VARY · p. 399

Myrica
WAX MYRTLE
☼ ◔ ◔ ◔ ◐ ⚡ ZONES VARY · p. 401

Picea
SPRUCE
☼ ◐ ◔ ◔ ⚡ ZONES VARY · p. 431

Pinus
PINE
☼ ◐ ◔ ◔ ⚡ ZONES VARY · p. 433

Prunus
☼ ◐ ◔ ◔ ⚡ ZONES VARY · p. 451

Quercus
OAK
☼ ◐ ◔ ◔ ⚡ ZONES VARY · p. 459

Sassafras albidum
SASSAFRAS
☼ ◔ ◔ ⚡ 3–9, 14–17, 28–41 · p. 489

Sorbus
MOUNTAIN ASH
☼ ◐ ◔ ◔ ⚡ ZONES VARY · p. 500

Thuja
ARBORVITAE
☼ ◐ ◔ ◔ ◔ ⚡ ZONES VARY · p. 518

Tsuga
HEMLOCK
☼ ◐ ◔ ◔ ◔ ⚡ ZONES VARY · p. 526

Crataegus

Malus 'Red Jewel'

Picea pungens

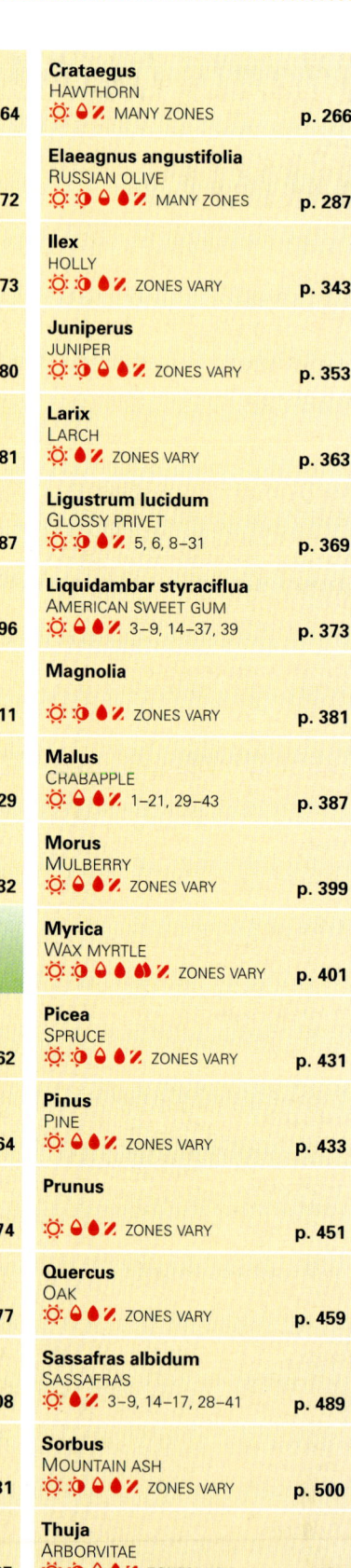

Quercus

Sorbus

For growing symbol explanations, please see page 79.

Cleome hasslerana

Iris

Kniphofia uvaria

Crocosmia crocosmiiflora

HUMMINGBIRDS
Annuals, Perennials, Bulbs

Alcea rosea — HOLLYHOCK — ALL ZONES — p. 172

Aloe — 8, 9, 12–27 — p. 174

Alstroemeria — MANY ZONES — p. 175

Antirrhinum majus — SNAPDRAGON — ALL ZONES — p. 182

Aquilegia — COLUMBINE — ZONES VARY — p. 186

Asclepias tuberosa — BUTTERFLY WEED — ALL ZONES — p. 194

Clarkia — ALL ZONES — p. 253

Cleome hasslerana — SPIDER FLOWER — ALL ZONES — p. 255

Crocosmia crocosmiiflora — MONTBRETIA — 5–24, 28–39 — p. 268

Delphinium — ZONES VARY — p. 276

Digitalis — FOXGLOVE — ZONES VARY — p. 281

Gladiolus — ZONES VARY — p. 317

Heuchera — CORAL BELLS — ZONES VARY — p. 333

Impatiens — BALSAM — NEEDS, ZONES VARY — p. 344

Ipomopsis aggregata — ZONES VARY — p. 346

Iris — NEEDS, ZONES VARY — p. 347

Kniphofia uvaria — RED-HOT POKER — MANY ZONES — p. 360

Lobelia cardinalis — CARDINAL FLOWER — MANY ZONES — p. 375

Lupinus — LUPINE — ZONES VARY — p. 378

Lychnis — ZONES VARY — p. 378

Monarda — BEE BALM — ZONES VARY — p. 398

Nicotiana — ALL ZONES — p. 406

Pelargonium — GERANIUM — 8, 9, 12–24 — p. 423

Penstemon (many) — BEARD TONGUE — ZONES VARY — p. 424

Phlox — ZONES VARY — p. 428

Phygelius capensis — CAPE FUCHSIA — 4–9, 14–31 — p. 430

Salvia (many) — SAGE — NEEDS, ZONES VARY — p. 484

Strelitzia reginae — BIRD OF PARADISE — 22–27 — p. 507

Tropaeolum majus — GARDEN NASTURTIUM — ALL ZONES — p. 525

Veronica — SPEEDWELL — NEEDS, ZONES VARY — p. 532

Zauschneria — CALIFORNIA FUCHSIA — 2–11, 14–24 — p. 542

Zinnia — ALL ZONES — p. 543

HUMMINGBIRDS
Ground Covers, Vines

Bean, scarlet runner — ALL ZONES — p. 205

Campsis — TRUMPET VINE — ZONES VARY — p. 227

Distictis buccinatoria — BLOOD-RED TRUMPET VINE — 8, 9, 14–28 — p. 282

Ipomoea quamoclit — CARDINAL CLIMBER — ALL ZONES — p. 346

Lupinus

Lychnis coronaria

Pelargonium

Penstemon gloxinioides

Salvia leucantha

Plant listings continue ▶

Campsis radicans

Zauschneria californica

Pyrostegia venusta

Strelitzia reginae

Lavandula

Lantana montevidensis

☀ ◐ ◑ ✂ 8–10, 12–30   **p. 363**

Lonicera
HONEYSUCKLE

☀ ◐ ◑ ✂ ZONES VARY   **p. 376**

Pyrostegia venusta
FLAME VINE

☀ ◐ ◑ ✂ 13, 16, 21–27   **p. 459**

Tecomaria capensis
CAPE HONEYSUCKLE

☀ ◐ ◑ ◑ ✂ 12, 13, 16, 18–28   **p. 516**

HUMMINGBIRDS
Shrubs

Abelia

☀ ◐ ◑ ✂ ZONES VARY   **p. 162**

Abutilon
FLOWERING MAPLE

☀ ◐ ◑ ◑ ✂ 8, 9, 12–27   **p. 163**

Acacia

☀ ◑ ✂ ZONES VARY   **p. 163**

Arctostaphylos uva-ursi
BEARBERRY

☀ ◐ ◑ ✂ MANY ZONES   **p. 189**

Bouvardia ternifolia

◐ ◑ ✂ 8–10, 12–28   **p. 213**

Buddleia

☀ ◐ ◑ ◑ ✂ ZONES VARY   **p. 217**

Caesalpinia

☀ ◑ ✂ ZONES VARY   **p. 219**

Calliandra

☀ ◑ ✂ ZONES VARY   **p. 221**

Callistemon citrinus
LEMON BOTTLEBRUSH

☀ ◑ ◑ ✂ 8, 9, 12–28   **p. 222**

Cestrum

◐ ◑ ✂ ZONES VARY   **p. 240**

Chaenomeles
FLOWERING QUINCE

☀ ◑ ✂ 2–21, 28–41   **p. 240**

Cotoneaster

☀ ◑ ✂ ZONES VARY   **p. 265**

Feijoa sellowiana
PINEAPPLE GUAVA

☀ ◑ ✂ 7–9, 12–31   **p. 303**

Fuchsia

◐ ◑ ✂ ZONES VARY   **p. 311**

Hibiscus

☀ ◑ ✂ ZONES VARY   **p. 334**

Kolkwitzia amabilis
BEAUTY BUSH

☀ ◐ ◑ ✂ 2–11, 14–20, 31–41   **p. 360**

Lavandula (many)
LAVENDER

☀ ◑ ✂ ZONES VARY   **p. 365**

Leucophyllum
TEXAS RANGER

☀ ◑ ✂ 7–24, 29–32   **p. 367**

Lonicera
HONEYSUCKLE

☀ ◐ ◑ ✂ ZONES VARY   **p. 376**

Ribes sanguineum
RED FLOWERING CURRANT

☀ ◐ ◑ ✂ 4–9, 14–24, 32, 34   **p. 472**

Rosmarinus officinalis
ROSEMARY

☀ ◑ ✂ 4–24, 26–32   **p. 480**

Sambucus
ELDERBERRY

☀ ◐ ◑ ✂ ZONES VARY   **p. 487**

Syringa
LILAC

☀ ◑ ✂ ZONES VARY   **p. 512**

Tecoma stans
YELLOW BELLS

☀ ◑ ✂ 10, 12, 13, 21–28   **p. 516**

Tecomaria capensis
CAPE HONEYSUCKLE

☀ ◐ ◑ ◑ ✂ 12, 13, 16, 18–28   **p. 516**

Weigela

☀ ◐ ◑ ✂ 1–11, 14–17, 32–41   **p. 538**

HUMMINGBIRDS
Trees

Aesculus
HORSECHESTNUT
NEEDS, ZONES VARY   **p. 169**

Albizia julibrissin
SILK TREE

☀ ◐ ◑ ✂ 4–23, 26–33   **p. 172**

Chilopsis linearis
DESERT WILLOW

☀ ◑ ✂ MANY ZONES   **p. 244**

Citrus

☀ ◑ ✂ 8, 9, 12–27   **p. 250**

Erythrina
CORAL TREE

☀ ◑ ◑ ✂ ZONES VARY   **p. 295**

Eucalyptus

☀ ◑ ◑ ✂ SEE CHART   **p. 296**

Lonicera

Tecomaria capensis

Weigela

Albizia julibrissin

Erythrina

For growing symbol explanations, please see page 79.

Asclepias tuberosa

Plants that Attract
BUTTERFLIES

Butterflies are always welcome garden visitors. Choose the right plants and you can encourage them to stay a while and return each year. Butterfly larvae (caterpillars) need food plants; adult butterflies need plants that offer nectar-bearing flowers. Sunny areas such as meadows that are sheltered from the wind and contain such amenities as leaf litter, rock crevices, brush piles, damp places, and even weeds are the most welcoming of gardens for butterflies. When you choose plants, keep in mind that not every plant will attract butterflies in every region. And never use pesticides, unless you can target the specific pest without harming the butterflies or their larvae.

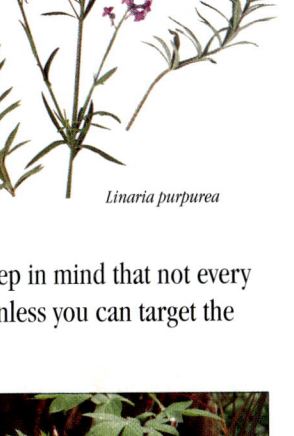
Linaria purpurea

Alcea rosea

Antirrhinum majus

Aster novi-belgii 'Carnival'

BUTTERFLY LARVAE
Annuals, Biennials, Perennials

Alcea rosea
HOLLYHOCK
☀ ◐ ✿ ALL ZONES — p. 172

Antirrhinum majus
SNAPDRAGON
☀ ◐ ✿ ALL ZONES — p. 182

Artichoke
☀ ◐ ✿ ZONES VARY — p. 192

Asclepias (esp. natives)
NEEDS VARY, ALL ZONES — p. 193

Aster
☀ ◐ ✿ 1–24, 31–43 — p. 195

Cleome hasslerana
SPIDER FLOWER
☀ ◐ ✿ ALL ZONES — p. 255

Dicentra
BLEEDING HEART
◑ ◐ ◐ ✿ 1–9, 14–24, 31–45 — p. 279

Digitalis purpurea
COMMON FOXGLOVE
◐ ◐ ✿ 2–24, 31–41 — p. 281

Eriogonum
WILD BUCKWHEAT
☀ ◐ ✿ 14–24 — p. 294

Foeniculum vulgare
COMMON FENNEL
☀ ◐ ✿ ZONES VARY — p. 307

Geum
☀ ◑ ◐ ✿ 1–24, 32–43 — p. 317

Helianthus
SUNFLOWER
☀ ◐ ✿ ZONES VARY — p. 329

Heliotropium arborescens
COMMON HELIOTROPE
☀ ◑ ◐ ✿ ALL ZONES — p. 330

Linaria purpurea
TOADFLAX
☀ ◑ ◐ ✿ 2–24, 30–41 — p. 372

Lupinus
LUPINE
☀ ◐ ◐ ✿ ZONES VARY — p. 378

Penstemon
BEARD TONGUE
☀ ◑ ◐ ◐ ✿ ZONES VARY — p. 424

Sidalcea
CHECKERBLOOM
☀ ◐ ✿ 2–9, 14–24, 29–41 — p. 497

Tropaeolum majus
GARDEN NASTURTIUM
☀ ◑ ◐ ✿ ALL ZONES — p. 525

Veronica
SPEEDWELL
NEEDS, ZONES VARY — p. 532

BUTTERFLY LARVAE
Ground Covers, Vines

Passiflora
PASSION VINE
☀ ◐ ◐ ✿ ZONES VARY — p. 417

Strawberry
☀ ◐◐ ✿ ALL ZONES — p. 507

Wisteria
☀ ◐ ◐ ◐ ✿ ZONES VARY — p. 538

Dicentra spectabilis

Helianthus

Passiflora alatocaerulea

Plant listings continue ▶

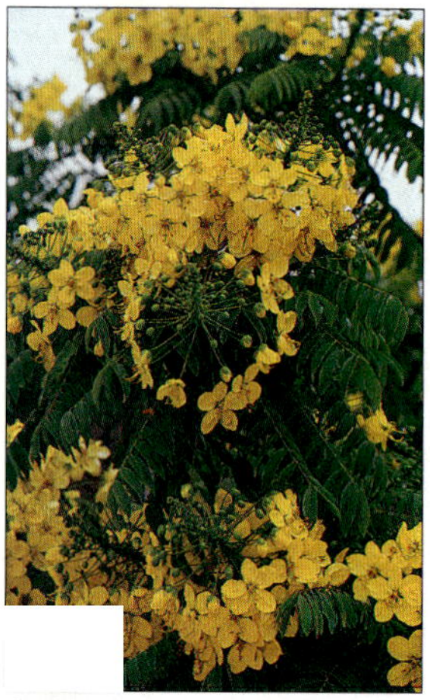

Cornus florida

BUTTERFLY LARVAE
Shrubs

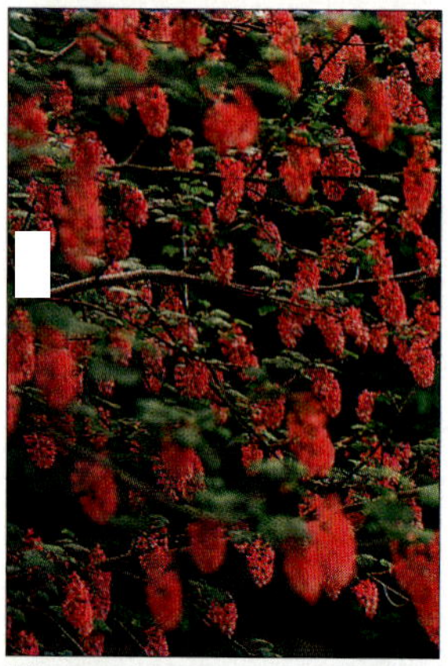

Cassia
SENNA
☼ ◐ ● ✎ ZONES VARY   **p. 233**

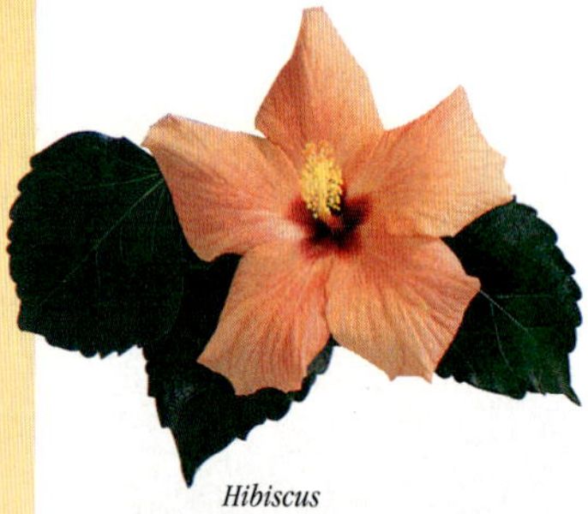

Ceanothus
☼ ◐ ● ✎ ZONES VARY   **p. 235**

Hibiscus
☼ ● ✎ ZONES VARY   **p. 334**

Lavatera
TREE MALLOW
☼ ◐ ● ✎ ZONES VARY   **p. 366**

Malva
MALLOW
☼ ◐ ● ✎ ZONES VARY   **p. 391**

Plumbago auriculata
CAPE PLUMBAGO
☼ ● ✎ 8, 9, 12–28   **p. 441**

Ribes
CURRANT, GOOSEBERRY
☼ ◐ ● ✎ ZONES VARY   **p. 472**

Rosa
ROSE
NEEDS, ZONES VARY   **p. 473**

Spiraea
☼ ◐ ● ● ✎ ZONES VARY   **p. 502**

Viburnum
NEEDS, ZONES VARY   **p. 532**

BUTTERFLY LARVAE
Trees

Aesculus
HORSECHESTNUT
NEEDS, ZONES VARY   **p. 169**

Betula
BIRCH
☼ ● ● ✎ ZONES VARY   **p. 208**

Celtis
HACKBERRY
☼ ◐ ● ✎ ZONES VARY   **p. 237**

Citrus
☼ ● ✎ 8, 9, 12–27   **p. 250**

Cornus
DOGWOOD
NEEDS, ZONES VARY   **p. 262**

Crataegus
HAWTHORN
☼ ● ✎ 2–12, 14–17, 28, 30–41   **p. 266**

Malus
CRABAPPLE
☼ ● ● ✎ 1–21, 29–43   **p. 387**

Pinus
PINE
☼ ● ● ✎ ZONES VARY   **p. 433**

Platanus
PLANE TREE, SYCAMORE
☼ ◐ ● ✎ ZONES VARY   **p. 438**

Populus
POPLAR
☼ ● ✎ ZONES VARY   **p. 445**

Prunus
☼ ● ● ✎ ZONES VARY   **p. 451**

Pseudotsuga menziesii
DOUGLAS FIR
☼ ◐ ● ● ✎ MANY ZONES   **p. 455**

Quercus
OAK
☼ ● ● ✎ ZONES VARY   **p. 459**

Salix
WILLOW
☼ ● ● ✎ ZONES VARY   **p. 483**

ADULT BUTTERFLIES
Annuals, Biennials, Perennials

Achillea
YARROW
☼ ● ✎ 1–24, 26, 28–45   **p. 166**

Agapanthus
LILY-OF-THE-NILE
☼ ◐ ● ● ✎ ZONES VARY   **p. 169**

Agastache
GIANT HYSSOP
☼ ◐ ● ● ✎ ZONES VARY   **p. 170**

Antirrhinum majus
SNAPDRAGON
☼ ● ✎ ALL ZONES   **p. 182**

Aquilegia
COLUMBINE
☼ ◐ ● ✎ ZONES VARY   **p. 186**

Armeria
THRIFT, SEA PINK
☼ ● ● ✎ ZONES VARY   **p. 191**

Asclepias tuberosa
BUTTERFLY WEED
☼ ● ✎ ALL ZONES   **p. 194**

Aster
☼ ● ✎ 1–24, 31–43   **p. 195**

Astilbe
FALSE SPIRAEA
☼ ◐ ● ✎ 1–7, 14–17, 32–45   **p. 196**

Borago officinalis
BORAGE
☼ ◐ ● ● ● ✎ ALL ZONES   **p. 212**

Bouvardia
NEEDS, ZONES VARY   **p. 213**

Cassia

Platanus

Pseudotsuga menziesii

Hibiscus

Ribes sanguineum

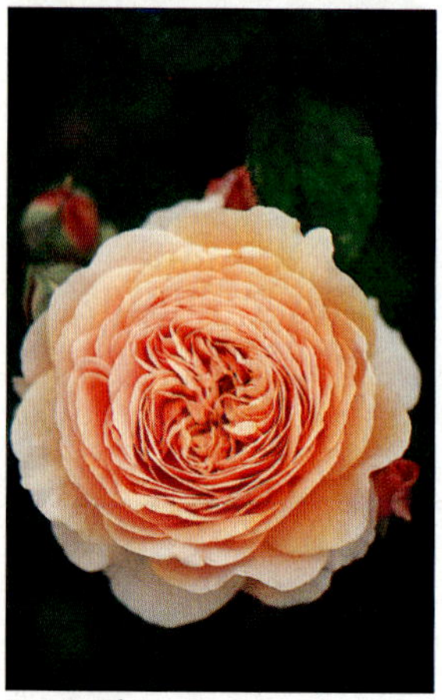

Quercus

Rosa 'Leander'

Achillea

For growing symbol explanations, please see page 79.

Armeria maritima

Centranthus ruber

Cosmos

Eryngium amethystinum

Catananche caerulea
CUPID'S DART
☼ ◑ ⚡ ALL ZONES   **p. 234**

Centranthus ruber
RED VALERIAN
☼ ◑ ◑ ⚡ 1–9, 12–24, 28–43   **p. 238**

Ceratostigma plumbaginoides
DWARF PLUMBAGO
☼ ◑ ◑ ⚡ 2–10, 14–24, 29–41   **p. 239**

Chelone
TURTLEHEAD
☼ ◑ ◑ ◑◑ ⚡ 3–9, 14–17, 28–43 **p. 243**

Chrysanthemum maximum
SHASTA DAISY
☼ ◑ ⚡ 1–24, 26, 28–43   **p. 247**

Coreopsis
☼ ◑ ⚡ ZONES VARY   **p. 260**

Cosmos
☼ ◑ ⚡ ZONES VARY   **p. 264**

Cynoglossum amabile
☼ ◑ ⚡ ALL ZONES   **p. 273**

Delphinium
☼ ◑ ⚡ ZONES VARY   **p. 276**

Dianthus
PINK
☼ ◑ ◑ ⚡ 1–24, 30–45   **p. 278**

Echinacea purpurea
PURPLE CONEFLOWER
☼ ◑ ⚡ 1–24, 26–45   **p. 286**

Echinops
GLOBE THISTLE
☼ ◑ ◑ ⚡ 1–24, 31–45   **p. 286**

Erigeron
FLEABANE
☼ ◑ ⚡ ZONES VARY   **p. 291**

Eryngium amethystinum
SEA HOLLY
☼ ◑ ⚡ 1–24, 26, 28–45   **p. 294**

Erysimum cheiri
ENGLISH WALLFLOWER
☼ ◑ ◑ ◑ ⚡ MANY ZONES   **p. 294**

Eupatorium
☼ ◑ ◑◑ ⚡ ZONES VARY   **p. 299**

Gaillardia grandiflora
BLANKET FLOWER
☼ ◑ ⚡ ALL ZONES   **p. 311**

Heliotropium arborescens
COMMON HELIOTROPE
☼ ◑ ◑ ⚡ ALL ZONES   **p. 330**

Hesperis matronalis
DAME'S ROCKET
☼ ◑ ◑ ⚡ ALL ZONES   **p. 333**

Iberis
CANDYTUFT
☼ ◑ ⚡ ZONES VARY   **p. 342**

Lathyrus odoratus
SWEET PEA
☼ ◑ ⚡ ALL ZONES   **p. 364**

Liatris
GAYFEATHER
☼ ◑ ◑ ⚡ 1–10, 14–24, 28–45   **p. 368**

Lobelia
☼ ◑ ◑ ◑◑ ⚡ ZONES VARY   **p. 375**

Lobularia maritima
SWEET ALYSSUM
☼ ◑ ◑ ⚡ ALL ZONES   **p. 376**

Monarda
BEE BALM
☼ ◑ ◑ ◑◑ ⚡ ZONES VARY   **p. 398**

Nepeta
☼ ◑ ◑ ⚡ 1–24, 30, 32–43   **p. 404**

Origanum vulgare
OREGANO
☼ ◑ ⚡ 1–24, 30–45   **p. 410**

Penstemon
BEARD TONGUE
☼ ◑ ◑ ◑ ⚡ ZONES VARY   **p. 424**

Pentas lanceolata
STAR CLUSTERS
☼ ◑ ⚡ ALL ZONES   **p. 424**

Phlox
☼ ◑ ◑ ⚡ ZONES VARY   **p. 428**

Primula vialii
☼ ◑ ◑ ◑◑ ⚡ MANY ZONES   **p. 450**

Prunella vulgaris
SELF-HEAL
☼ ◑ ◑ ⚡ 1–24, 29–43   **p. 450**

Ranunculus
NEEDS, ZONES VARY   **p. 462**

Rudbeckia hirta
GLORIOSA DAISY
☼ ◑ ◑ ◑ ⚡ 1–24, 26–43   **p. 481**

Salvia
SAGE
NEEDS, ZONES VARY   **p. 484**

Scabiosa
PINCUSHION FLOWER
☼ ◑ ◑ ⚡ ZONES VARY   **p. 490**

Sedum (tall)
STONECROP
NEEDS, ZONES VARY   **p. 493**

Solidago
GOLDENROD
☼ ◑ ◑ ⚡ ZONES VARY   **p. 499**

Erysimum cheiri

Lathyrus odoratus

Lobularia maritima

Rudbeckia hirta
'Marmalade'

Plant listings continue ▶

Salvia clevelandii

Abelia

Buddleia

Lantana

Mahonia aquifolium

Tagetes
MARIGOLD
☼ ◐ ♦ ⚡ ZONES VARY   **p. 513**

Tithonia rotundifolia
MEXICAN SUNFLOWER
☼ ♦ ⚡ ALL ZONES   **p. 521**

Verbena bonariensis
☼ ♦ ⚡ 8–24, 28–32   **p. 531**

Zauschneria
CALIFORNIA FUCHSIA
☼ ♦ ♦ ⚡ 2–11, 14–24   **p. 542**

ADULT BUTTERFLIES
Shrubs

Abelia
☼ ◐ ♦ ⚡ ZONES VARY   **p. 162**

Aralia spinosa
HERCULES' CLUB
☼ ◐ ♦ ♦ ⚡ 2–24, 28–41   **p. 188**

Buddleia
☼ ◐ ♦ ♦ ⚡ ZONES VARY   **p. 217**

Calluna vulgaris
SCOTCH HEATHER
☼ ♦ ⚡ 2–6, 15–17, 34, 36–41   **p. 222**

Caryopteris
BLUEBEARD
☼ ♦ ⚡ ZONES VARY   **p. 232**

Ceanothus
☼ ◐ ♦ ⚡ ZONES VARY   **p. 235**

Clethra alnifolia
SUMMERSWEET
◐ ♦ ♦ ♦ ⚡ 1–6, 31–43   **p. 256**

Eriogonum (some)
WILD BUCKWHEAT
☼ ♦ ⚡ 14–24   **p. 294**

Hebe
☼ ◐ ♦ ⚡ 14–24   **p. 327**

Hibiscus rosa-sinensis
CHINESE HIBISCUS
☼ ♦ ⚡ 9, 12, 13, 15, 16, 19–26   **p. 335**

Lantana
☼ ♦ ⚡ 8–10, 12–30   **p. 363**

Lavandula
LAVENDER
☼ ♦ ⚡ ZONES VARY   **p. 365**

Lonicera
HONEYSUCKLE
☼ ◐ ♦ ♦ ⚡ ZONES VARY   **p. 376**

Mahonia
NEEDS, ZONES VARY   **p. 386**

Philadelphus (single-flowered)
MOCK ORANGE
☼ ◐ ♦ ♦ ⚡ ZONES VARY   **p. 427**

Potentilla
CINQUEFOIL
☼ ◐ ♦ ⚡ ZONES VARY   **p. 447**

Rhododendron
◐ ♦ ♦♦ ⚡ ZONES VARY   **p. 465**

Rhus trilobata
SQUAWBUSH
☼ ♦ ♦ ⚡ 2, 3, 10, 31–41   **p. 471**

Ribes
CURRANT, GOOSEBERRY
☼ ◐ ♦ ⚡ ZONES VARY   **p. 472**

Rosmarinus officinalis
ROSEMARY
☼ ♦ ⚡ 4–24, 26–32   **p. 480**

Sambucus
ELDERBERRY
☼ ♦ ♦ ⚡ ZONES VARY   **p. 487**

Spiraea
☼ ◐ ♦ ♦ ⚡ ZONES VARY   **p. 502**

Syringa
LILAC
☼ ◐ ♦ ⚡ ZONES VARY   **p. 512**

Vaccinium
NEEDS, ZONES VARY   **p. 529**

Vitex agnus-castus
CHASTE TREE
☼ ♦ ⚡ 4–33   **p. 535**

ADULT BUTTERFLIES
Trees

Acer
MAPLE
☼ ◐ ♦ ♦ ⚡ ZONES VARY   **p. 164**

Aesculus
HORSECHESTNUT
NEEDS, ZONES VARY   **p. 169**

Albizia julibrissin
SILK TREE
☼ ◐ ♦ ♦ ⚡ 4–23, 26–33   **p. 172**

Apple
☼ ♦ ⚡ ZONES VARY   **p. 182**

Citrus
☼ ♦ ⚡ 8, 9, 12–27   **p. 250**

Salix
WILLOW
☼ ♦ ♦ ⚡ ZONES VARY   **p. 483**

Vitex
CHASTE TREE
☼ ♦ ⚡ ZONES VARY   **p. 535**

Philadelphus

Rhus trilobata

Spiraea bumalda

Aesculus carnea

For growing symbol explanations, please see page 79.

SPECIAL SITUATIONS

Plants that
RESIST DEER

Browsing deer are charming to watch, but they can do considerable damage to gardens. There are various ways you can attempt to discourage or repel deer, but the best tactic may be to grow plants that deer will find unpalatable. However, deer in different areas seem to have somewhat different tastes. To complicate the picture further, young plants may be eaten but older ones left alone; plants untouched in spring may be eaten in fall. As a final frustration, tastes change: what deer pass by one year they may find irresistible the next. Despite these variables, a number of plants can be considered "best bets" in deer country. These are listed below.

Albizia julibrissin

Acer palmatum 'Sango Kaku'

Ginkgo biloba

Melaleuca linariifolia

TREES

Abies
FIR
☼ ◑ ♦ ♦ ⟋ ZONES VARY   **p. 162**

Acer palmatum
JAPANESE MAPLE
☼ ◑ ♦ ♦ ⟋ MANY ZONES   **p. 165**

Albizia
NEEDS, ZONES VARY   **p. 172**

Cedrus
CEDAR
☼ ♦ ⟋ ZONES VARY   **p. 236**

Celtis
HACKBERRY
☼ ◑ ♦ ⟋ ZONES VARY   **p. 237**

Chamaecyparis
FALSE CYPRESS
☼ ◑ ♦ ⟋ ZONES VARY   **p. 241**

Crataegus
HAWTHORN
☼ ♦ ⟋ 2–12, 14–17, 28, 30–41   **p. 266**

Cupressus
CYPRESS
☼ ♦ ⟋ ZONES VARY   **p. 270**

Fig, edible
☼ ♦ ⟋ 4–9, 12–32   **p. 306**

Fraxinus
ASH
☼ ♦ ♦ ⟋ ZONES VARY   **p. 309**

Ginkgo biloba
MAIDENHAIR TREE
☼ ♦ ♦ ⟋ MANY ZONES   **p. 317**

Magnolia
☼ ◑ ♦ ⟋ ZONES VARY   **p. 381**

Melaleuca
☼ ♦ ⟋ ZONES VARY   **p. 393**

Olea europaea
OLIVE
☼ ♦ ⟋ 8, 9, 11–24   **p. 408**

Palms
NEEDS, ZONES VARY   **p. 413**

Picea
SPRUCE
☼ ◑ ♦ ♦ ⟋ ZONES VARY   **p. 431**

Pinus
PINE
☼ ♦ ♦ ⟋ ZONES VARY   **p. 433**

Podocarpus
☼ ◑ ♦ ♦ ⟋ ZONES VARY   **p. 442**

Pseudotsuga menziesii
DOUGLAS FIR
☼ ◑ ♦ ♦ ⟋ MANY ZONES   **p. 455**

Quercus
OAK
☼ ♦ ♦ ⟋ ZONES VARY   **p. 459**

Sequoia sempervirens
COAST REDWOOD
☼ ◑ ♦ ♦ ⟋ 4–9, 14–24, 32   **p. 495**

Tamarix
TAMARISK
☼ ♦ ⟋ ZONES VARY   **p. 514**

SHRUBS

Abelia grandiflora
GLOSSY ABELIA
☼ ◑ ♦ ♦ ⟋ 4–24, 28–35   **p. 162**

Aesculus californica
CALIFORNIA BUCKEYE
☼ ◑ ♦ ⟋ 4–10, 12, 14–24   **p. 169**

SYMBOLS: ⸙ indicates plants that are eaten in some areas; ✿ indicates plants whose flowers are sometimes eaten; ⊡ indicates plants that must be protected when young.

Browsing deer

Olea europaea

Picea

Plant listings continue ▶

Aesculus californica

Alyogyne huegelii

Anisodontea

Calluna vulgaris 'Spring Torch'

Lantana 'Radiation'

Alyogyne huegelii
BLUE HIBISCUS
☼ ● ● ◢ 15–17, 20–27   **p. 176**

Anisodontea
CAPE MALLOW
☼ ● ● ◢ 14–24, 28   **p. 180**

Bamboo
☼ ◐ ● ● ◢ ZONES VARY   **p. 199**

Berberis   ✎
BARBERRY
☼ ◐ ● ● ◢ ZONES VARY   **p. 207**

Buddleia
☼ ◐ ● ● ◢ ZONES VARY   **p. 217**

Buxus
BOXWOOD
☼ ● ● ● ◢ ZONES VARY   **p. 218**

Callistemon
BOTTLEBRUSH
☼ ● ● ◢ 8, 9, 12–28   **p. 222**

Calluna vulgaris
SCOTCH HEATHER
☼ ● ◢ 2–6, 15–17, 34, 36–41   **p. 222**

Cassia
SENNA
☼ ● ● ◢ ZONES VARY   **p. 233**

Chaenomeles
FLOWERING QUINCE
☼ ● ● ◢ 2–21, 28–41   **p. 240**

Cotoneaster   ✎
☼ ● ◢ ZONES VARY   **p. 265**

Daphne
NEEDS, ZONES VARY   **p. 275**

Elaeagnus
☼ ◐ ● ● ◢ ZONES VARY   **p. 287**

Erica
HEATH
☼ ◐ ● ◢ ZONES VARY   **p. 291**

Feijoa sellowiana
PINEAPPLE GUAVA
☼ ● ◢ 7–9, 12–31   **p. 303**

Gaultheria shallon
SALAL
☼ ● ◢ 3–7, 14–17, 21–24   **p. 313**

Grevillea
☼ ● ● ◢ ZONES VARY   **p. 324**

Hypericum
ST. JOHNSWORT
☼ ◐ ● ● ◢ ZONES VARY   **p. 341**

Ilex
HOLLY
☼ ◐ ● ◢ ZONES VARY   **p. 343**

Juniperus
JUNIPER
☼ ◐ ● ● ◢ ZONES VARY   **p. 353**

Kerria japonica
☼ ◐ ● ● ◢ 2–21, 30–41   **p. 359**

Lantana
☼ ● ◢ 8–10, 12–30   **p. 363**

Lavandula (some)   ✎
LAVENDER
☼ ● ◢ ZONES VARY   **p. 365**

Lavatera
TREE MALLOW
☼ ● ● ◢ ZONES VARY   **p. 366**

Leptospermum
TEA TREE
☼ ● ◢ ZONES VARY   **p. 366**

Mahonia   ✎
NEEDS, ZONES VARY   **p. 386**

Myrtus communis
MYRTLE
☼ ◐ ● ◢ 8–24, 26–28   **p. 401**

Nandina domestica   ✎
HEAVENLY BAMBOO
☼ ● ● ● ◢ 4–33   **p. 402**

Nerium oleander
OLEANDER
☼ ● ● ◢ 8–16, 18–31   **p. 405**

Plumbago auriculata
CAPE PLUMBAGO
☼ ● ◢ 8, 9, 12–28   **p. 441**

Potentilla   ✎
CINQUEFOIL
☼ ◐ ● ◢ ZONES VARY   **p. 447**

Pyracantha   ✎
FIRETHORN
☼ ● ◢ ZONES VARY   **p. 458**

Rhododendron (not azaleas)   ✎
☼ ● ● ◢ ZONES VARY   **p. 465**

Rhus
SUMAC
☼ ● ● ◢ ZONES VARY   **p. 471**

Ribes   ✎
CURRANT, GOOSEBERRY
☼ ◐ ● ◢ ZONES VARY   **p. 472**

Rosmarinus officinalis
ROSEMARY
☼ ● ◢ 4–24, 26–32   **p. 480**

Salvia   ✎
SAGE
NEEDS, ZONES VARY   **p. 484**

Sarcococca
SWEET BOX
☼ ● ● ● ◢ ZONES VARY   **p. 489**

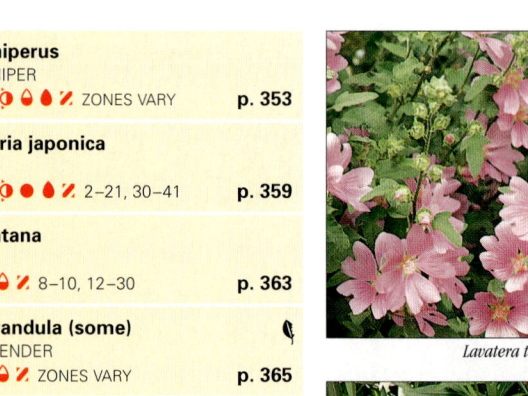
Lavatera thuringiaca

Nerium oleander

Rhododendron

Vaccinium ovatum

Ceratostigma plumbaginoides

For growing symbol explanations, please see page 79.

Gazania 'Burgundy'

Hedera

Sollya heterophylla

Acanthus mollis

Achillea millefolium hybrid

Syringa
LILAC
☀ ○ ◖ ◕ ◢ ZONES VARY **p. 512**

Teucrium
GERMANDER
☀ ◕ ◢ ZONES VARY **p. 516**

Vaccinium ovatum
EVERGREEN HUCKLEBERRY
☀ ◑ ● ◕ ◢ MANY ZONES **p. 529**

Viburnum
NEEDS, ZONES VARY **p. 532**

GROUND COVERS, VINES

Ajuga
CARPET BUGLE
☀ ◑ ◕ ◢ 1–24, 26–45 **p. 171**

Arctostaphylos uva-ursi
BEARBERRY
☀ ◑ ◕ ◢ MANY ZONES **p. 189**

Bougainvillea
☀ ◑ ◕ ◕ ◢ MANY ZONES **p. 212**

Ceratostigma plumbaginoides
DWARF PLUMBAGO
☀ ◑ ◕ ◢ 2–10, 14–24, 29–41 **p. 239**

Fragaria chiloensis
WILD STRAWBERRY
☀ ◕ ◢ 4–24 **p. 309**

Gazania
☀ ◕ ◕ ◢ 8–28 **p. 314**

Gelsemium sempervirens
CAROLINA JESSAMINE
☀ ◑ ◕ ◕ ◢ 8–24, 26, 28–33 **p. 314**

Hedera helix
ENGLISH IVY
☀ ◑ ◕ ◕ ◢ 3–34, 39 **p. 328**

Jasminum
JASMINE
☀ ◑ ◕ ◢ ZONES VARY **p. 351**

Lantana montevidensis
☀ ◕ ◢ 8–10, 12–30 **p. 363**

Pachysandra terminalis
JAPANESE SPURGE
☀ ● ◕ ◢ 1–10, 14–21, 31–43 **p. 412**

Solanum jasminoides
POTATO VINE
☀ ◑ ◕ ◕ ◢ 8, 9, 12–27 **p. 499**

Sollya heterophylla
AUSTRALIAN BLUEBELL CREEPER
☀ ◑ ◕ ◢ 8, 9, 14–28 **p. 500**

Tecomaria capensis
CAPE HONEYSUCKLE
☀ ◑ ◕ ◕ ◢ 12, 13, 16, 18–28 **p. 516**

Vinca
PERIWINKLE
☀ ● ◕ ◢ ZONES VARY **p. 534**

Wisteria
☀ ◕ ◕ ◢ ZONES VARY **p. 538**

PERENNIALS, BULBS

Acanthus mollis
BEAR'S BREECH
☀ ◑ ◕ ◕ ◢ 4–24, 28–32 **p. 164**

Achillea
YARROW
☀ ◕ ◢ 1–24, 26, 28–45 **p. 166**

Agave
NEEDS, ZONES VARY **p. 170**

Aloe
☀ ◑ ◕ ◕ ◢ 8, 9, 12–27 **p. 174**

Amaryllis belladonna
NAKED LADY
☀ ◕ ◢ 4–24, 28, 29 **p. 177**

Aquilegia
COLUMBINE
☀ ◑ ◕ ◢ ZONES VARY **p. 186**

Armeria
THRIFT
☀ ◕ ◕ ◢ ZONES VARY **p. 191**

Artemisia
☀ ◕ ◢ 1–24, 29–45 **p. 191**

Aster
☀ ◕ ◢ 1–24, 31–43 **p. 195**

Astilbe
FALSE SPIRAEA
☀ ◑ ◕ ◢ 1–7, 14–17, 32–45 **p. 196**

Begonia, tuberous
◑ ● ◕ ◢ 14–28 **p. 207**

Brachycome
SWAN RIVER DAISY
☀ ◕ ◢ ZONES VARY **p. 214**

Campanula poscharskyana
SERBIAN BELLFLOWER
☀ ◑ ◕ ◕ ◢ MANY ZONES **p. 229**

Carex
SEDGE
☀ ◑ ◕ ◕ ◢ 1–9, 14–24, 28–45 **p. 230**

Centaurea
NEEDS, ZONES VARY **p. 237**

Centranthus ruber
RED VALERIAN
☀ ◑ ◕ ◢ 1–9, 12–24, 28–43 **p. 238**

Aster frikartii

Astilbe arendsii hybrid

Brachycome

Aquilegia McKana hybrid

Campanula poscharskyana

Plant listings continue ▶

Carex

Erodium reichardii

Eschscholzia californica

Euphorbia martinii

Hemerocallis

Cerastium tomentosum
SNOW-IN-SUMMER
☼ ◐ ◗ ✎ 1–24, 32–45   p. 238

Chrysanthemum frutescens ❆
MARGUERITE
☼ ◗ ✎ 14–24, 26, 28   p. 246

Coreopsis
☼ ◗ ✎ ZONES VARY   p. 260

Crocosmia
☼ ◐ ◗ ✎ 5–24, 28–39   p. 268

Crocus
☼ ◐ ◗ ✎ 1–24, 30–45   p. 268

Cyclamen
☼ ◐ ◗ ✎ ZONES VARY   p. 271

Dahlia
☼ ◐ ◗ ✎ ALL ZONES   p. 274

Dicentra
BLEEDING HEART
☼ ● ◗ ✎ 1–9, 14–24, 31–45   p. 279

Dietes vegeta
☼ ◐ ◗ ◗ ✎ 8, 9, 12–28   p. 281

Digitalis
FOXGLOVE
◐ ◗ ✎ ZONES VARY   p. 281

Echinacea purpurea
PURPLE CONEFLOWER
☼ ◗ ✎ 1–24, 26–45   p. 286

Erigeron
FLEABANE
☼ ◐ ◗ ✎ ZONES VARY   p. 291

Erodium reichardii
CRANESBILL
☼ ◐ ◗ ✎ 7–9, 14–24, 31, 32   p. 294

Erysimum cheiri
ENGLISH WALLFLOWER
☼ ◐ ◗ ◗ ✎ MANY ZONES   p. 294

Eschscholzia californica
CALIFORNIA POPPY
☼ ◗ ◗ ✎ ALL ZONES   p. 296

Euphorbia
NEEDS, ZONES VARY   p. 299

Euryops
☼ ◗ ✎ ZONES VARY   p. 301

Felicia amelloides
BLUE MARGUERITE
☼ ◗ ✎ 8, 9, 13–24   p. 304

Ferns ✎
NEEDS, ZONES VARY   p. 304

Festuca ovina 'Glauca'
BLUE FESCUE
☼ ◐ ◗ ✎ 1–24, 29–45   p. 304

Freesia
☼ ◐ ◗ ✎ 8, 9, 12–24, 28   p. 310

Gaillardia grandiflora
BLANKET FLOWER
☼ ◗ ✎ ALL ZONES   p. 311

Geranium
CRANESBILL
☼ ◐ ◗ ✎ ZONES VARY   p. 315

Helichrysum
☼ ◗ ✎ ZONES VARY   p. 329

Helleborus
HELLEBORE
◐ ● ◗ ✎ ZONES VARY   p. 331

Hemerocallis
DAYLILY
☼ ◐ ◗ ✎ ALL ZONES   p. 331

Herbs (except basil)
NEEDS, ZONES VARY   p. 332

Iberis
CANDYTUFT
☼ ◗ ✎ ZONES VARY   p. 342

Iris
NEEDS, ZONES VARY   p. 347

Ixia
AFRICAN CORN LILY
☼ ◗ ✎ 7–9, 12–24   p. 350

Kniphofia uvaria ❦
RED-HOT POKER
☼ ◐ ◗ ◗ ✎ MANY ZONES   p. 360

Lamium maculatum
DEAD NETTLE
◐ ● ◗ ✎ 1–24, 32–43   p. 363

Limonium
SEA LAVENDER
☼ ◗ ✎ ZONES VARY   p. 371

Liriope and Ophiopogon
LILY TURF
◐ ● ◗ ◗ ✎ ZONES VARY   p. 373

Lithodora diffusa
☼ ◐ ◗ ✎ 5–7, 14–17, 32   p. 375

Lupinus
LUPINE
NEEDS, ZONES VARY   p. 378

Lychnis coronaria
CROWN-PINK
☼ ◐ ◗ ✎ 3–9, 14–24, 30–34   p. 379

Miscanthus sinensis
EULALIA GRASS
☼ ◐ ◗ ◗ ✎ 2–24, 29–41   p. 397

Kniphofia uvaria

Origanum laevigatum 'Hopley's'

Pennisetum setaceum

Penstemon gloxinioides

Phormium hybrid

For growing symbol explanations, please see page 79.

Romneya coulteri

Santolina chamaecyparissus

Stachys byzantina

Tagetes lemmonii

Monarda
BEE BALM
☼ ◐ ◔ ◔ ⚡ ZONES VARY   **p. 398**

Myosotis scorpioides
☼ ◔ ⚡ 1–24, 32–45   **p. 401**

Narcissus
DAFFODIL
☼ ◐ ◔ ⚡ ZONES VARY   **p. 402**

Nepeta
☼ ◐ ◔ ⚡ 1–24, 32–43   **p. 404**

Origanum
NEEDS, ZONES VARY   **p. 410**

Papaver orientale
ORIENTAL POPPY
☼ ◔ ◔ ⚡ 1–11, 14–21, 30–45   **p. 415**

Pennisetum setaceum
☼ ◑ ⚡ 8–24, 26–29   **p. 424**

Penstemon   🪶
BEARD TONGUE
☼ ◐ ◔ ◔ ⚡ ZONES VARY   **p. 424**

Phlomis fruticosa
☼ ◐ ◔ ⚡ 4–24, 31   **p. 428**

Phlox subulata
MOSS PINK
☼ ◐ ◔ ⚡ 1–17, 28–45   **p. 429**

Phormium
NEW ZEALAND FLAX
☼ ◐ ◔ ◔ ⚡ 14–28   **p. 430**

Romneya coulteri   🪶 🔲
MATILIJA POPPY
☼ ◔ ◔ ⚡ 4–12, 14–24   **p. 473**

Rudbeckia hirta
GLORIOSA DAISY
☼ ◔ ◔ ◔ ⚡ ZONES VARY   **p. 481**

Santolina
☼ ◔ ◔ ⚡ MANY ZONES   **p. 488**

Saxifraga
SAXIFRAGE
NEEDS, ZONES VARY   **p. 490**

Scabiosa (some)   🪶
PINCUSHION FLOWER
☼ ◔ ◔ ⚡ ZONES VARY   **p. 490**

Scilla
SQUILL
☼ ◐ ◔ ◔ ⚡ ZONES VARY   **p. 492**

Stachys byzantina
LAMB'S EARS
☼ ◐ ◔ ⚡ 1–24, 29–43   **p. 504**

Stipa
FEATHER GRASS
NEEDS, ZONES VARY   **p. 506**

Tagetes lemmonii   🔲
☼ ◔ ⚡ 8–10, 12–24, 27–29   **p. 514**

Thymus
THYME
☼ ◐ ◔ ⚡ ZONES VARY   **p. 519**

Tulbaghia violacea
SOCIETY GARLIC
☼ ◔ ⚡ 13–24, 26–28   **p. 526**

Verbena   🪶
☼ ◔ ⚡ ZONES VARY   **p. 531**

Veronica
SPEEDWELL
☼ ◔ ◔ ⚡ ZONES VARY   **p. 532**

Viola odorata
SWEET VIOLET
☼ ◔ ⚡ 1–24, 29–43   **p. 535**

Zantedeschia
CALLA
NEEDS VARY, MANY ZONES   **p. 541**

Zauschneria
CALIFORNIA FUCHSIA
☼ ◔ ◔ ⚡ 2–11, 14–24   **p. 542**

ANNUALS

Ageratum houstonianum
FLOSS FLOWER
☼ ◐ ◔ ◔ ⚡ ALL ZONES   **p. 170**

Campanula medium
CANTERBURY BELL
☼ ◐ ◔ ◔ ⚡ 1–9, 14–24, 31–45   **p. 228**

Catharanthus roseus
MADAGASCAR PERIWINKLE
☼ ◐ ◔ ⚡ ALL ZONES   **p. 234**

Clarkia amoena
GODETIA
☼ ◐ ◔ ◔ ⚡ ALL ZONES   **p. 253**

Impatiens   🪶
BALSAM
NEEDS, ZONES VARY   **p. 344**

Lupinus (some)
LUPINE
NEEDS, ZONES VARY   **p. 378**

Myosotis sylvatica
FORGET-ME-NOT
◐ ◔ ⚡ 1–24, 32–45   **p. 401**

Papaver rhoeas
SHIRLEY POPPY
☼ ◔ ◔ ◔ ⚡ ALL ZONES   **p. 415**

Scabiosa (some)
PINCUSHION FLOWER
☼ ◔ ◔ ⚡ ZONES VARY   **p. 490**

Senecio hybridus
CINERARIA
◐ ◔ ◔ ⚡ 16, 17, 22–24, 38   **p. 495**

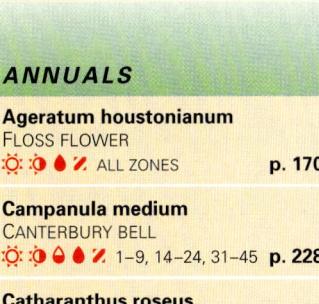

Clarkia amoena

Impatiens

Scabiosa

Thymus

Myosotis sylvatica

Franklinia alatamaha

Plants that TOLERATE SHADE

Shady spots, whether created by leafy trees, sun-blocking walls, or an overhead structure, are darker and cooler than sunny locations. Many plants that thrive in sunlight and warmth fail to prosper in the different environment that shade provides—either dwindling away or becoming leggy and sparse. In the lists below are trees, shrubs, ground covers, vines, perennials, bulbs, and annuals that prefer or accept some degree of shade.

Redwood bench in shade

SYMBOL: ✲ indicates plants that bear showy flowers.

TREES

Acer palmatum JAPANESE MAPLE		☼ ◐ 🌢 💧 Z MANY ZONES	**p. 165**
Cercidiphyllum japonicum KATSURA TREE		☼ ◐ 💧 Z MANY ZONES	**p. 239**
Cercis canadensis EASTERN REDBUD		☼ ◐ 💧 Z 2–20, 26, 28–41	**p. 239**
Davidia involucrata DOVE TREE	✲	☼ ◐ 💧 Z MANY ZONES	**p. 276**
Franklinia alatamaha	✲	☼ ◐ 💧 Z 2–6, 14–17, 31–35	**p. 309**
Halesia	✲	◐ 💧 Z 2–9, 14–24, 31–41	**p. 326**
Laurus nobilis SWEET BAY		☼ ◐ 🌢 Z 5–9, 12–24	**p. 365**
Palms (some)		NEEDS, ZONES VARY	**p. 413**
Podocarpus		☼ ◐ 🌢 💧 Z ZONES VARY	**p. 442**
Schefflera		☼ ◐ 💧 Z ZONES VARY	**p. 491**
Stewartia		☼ ◐ 💧 Z ZONES VARY	**p. 506**
Tree ferns		NEEDS, ZONES VARY	**p. 524**

SHRUBS

Abutilon FLOWERING MAPLE	✲	☼ ◐ 🌢 💧 Z 8, 9, 12–27	**p. 163**
Acanthopanax sieboldianus 'Variegatus'		☼ ◐ ● 🌢 💧 💧💧 Z MANY ZONES	**p. 163**
Actaea BANEBERRY		◐ ● 💧 Z 1–5, 30–45	**p. 167**
Aucuba japonica JAPANESE AUCUBA		◐ ● 🌢 Z 4–24, 28–33	**p. 197**
Brunfelsia pauciflora	✲	◐ 💧 Z 12–17, 20–28	**p. 216**
Buxus BOXWOOD		☼ ◐ ● 💧 Z ZONES VARY	**p. 218**
Camellia	✲	◐ 🌢 💧 Z MANY ZONES	**p. 224**
Clethra alnifolia SUMMERSWEET	✲	◐ 💧 💧💧 Z 1–6, 31–43	**p. 256**
Cleyera japonica	✲	◐ 💧 Z MANY ZONES	**p. 256**
Cordyline stricta	✲	◐ 💧 Z MANY ZONES	**p. 260**
Cycadaceae CYCADS		◐ 💧 Z ZONES VARY	**p. 271**
Daphne	✲	☼ ◐ 🌢 💧 Z ZONES VARY	**p. 275**

Laurus nobilis

Podocarpus henkelii

Abutilon

Brunfelsia pauciflora

Clethra alnifolia

Cycadaceae (*Cycas revoluta*)

For growing symbol explanations, please see page 79.

Fuchsia

Gardenia jasminoides

Hydrangea macrophylla

Pieris forrestii

Enkianthus campanulatus �
☼ ◑ ◐ 💧💧💧 ✂ MANY ZONES — **p. 288**

Euonymus fortunei
☼ ◑ ● ◐ 💧💧 ✂ 3–17, 28–41 — **p. 298**

Fatsia japonica
JAPANESE ARALIA
◑ ● ◐ ✂ 4–9, 13–31 — **p. 303**

Fothergilla ✳
☼ ◑ ● ◐ ✂ 3–9, 14–17, 31–39 — **p. 308**

Fuchsia ✳
◑ ● ◐ ✂ ZONES VARY — **p. 311**

Gardenia jasminoides ✳
☼ ◑ ● ◐ ✂ MANY ZONES — **p. 312**

Gaultheria ✳
◑ ● ◐ ✂ ZONES VARY — **p. 313**

Hamamelis ✳
WITCH HAZEL
☼ ◑ ● ◐ ✂ ZONES VARY — **p. 326**

Hydrangea ✳
☼ ◑ ● ◐ ✂ ZONES VARY — **p. 340**

Ilex ✳
HOLLY
☼ ◑ ● ◐ ✂ ZONES VARY — **p. 343**

Kalmia latifolia ✳
MOUNTAIN LAUREL
☼ ◑ ● ◐ ✂ MANY ZONES — **p. 358**

Leucothoe ✳
NEEDS, ZONES VARY — **p. 368**

Lindera ✳
SPICEBUSH
☼ ◑ ● ◐ ✂ ZONES VARY — **p. 372**

Loropetalum chinense ✳
☼ ◑ ● ◐ ✂ MANY ZONES — **p. 377**

Mahonia ✳
NEEDS, ZONES VARY — **p. 386**

Nandina domestica ✳
HEAVENLY BAMBOO
☼ ◑ ● ◐ ◐ ✂ 4–33 — **p. 402**

Osmanthus ✳
☼ ◑ ● ◐ ✂ ZONES VARY — **p. 410**

Philodendron selloum
◑ ● ◐ ◐ ✂ 25, 27 — **p. 428**

Pieris ✳
◑ ● ◐ ✂ ZONES VARY — **p. 432**

Pittosporum tobira ✳
TOBIRA
☼ ◑ ● ◐ ✂ 8–31 — **p. 438**

Rhapis
LADY PALM
◑ ● ◐ ✂ ZONES VARY — **p. 465**

Rhododendron ✳
AZALEA, RHODODENDRON
◑ ● ◐ ✂ ZONES VARY — **p. 465**

Ribes sanguineum
PINK WINTER CURRANT
☼ ◑ ● ◐ ✂ MANY ZONES — **p. 472**

Ruscus
BUTCHER'S BROOM
◑ ● ◐ ◐ ✂ 4–24, 28, 31, 32 — **p. 482**

Sarcococca
SWEET BOX
◑ ● ◐ ◐ ✂ ZONES VARY — **p. 489**

Skimmia japonica ✳
◑ ● ◐ ◐ ✂ 4–9, 14–22, 31, 32 — **p. 498**

Symphoricarpos (some) ✳
SNOWBERRY
NEEDS, ZONES VARY — **p. 511**

Taxus
YEW
☼ ◑ ● ◐ ◐ ✂ ZONES VARY — **p. 515**

Ternstroemia gymnanthera
◑ ● ◐ ◐ ✂ MANY ZONES — **p. 516**

Vaccinium ✳
NEEDS, ZONES VARY — **p. 529**

Viburnum (evergreen) ✳
NEEDS, ZONES VARY — **p. 532**

GROUND COVERS, VINES

Actinidia kolomikta
☼ ◑ ● ◐ ◐ ✂ 2–9, 15–17, 31–41 — **p. 168**

Aegopodium podagraria
BISHOP'S WEED
☼ ◑ ● ◐ ◐ ✂ MANY ZONES — **p. 169**

Akebia quinata
☼ ◑ ● ◐ ✂ 3–24, 29–41 — **p. 172**

Ampelopsis brevipedunculata
PORCELAIN BERRY
☼ ◑ ● ◐ ◐ ✂ 2–24, 28–41 — **p. 177**

Cissus
NEEDS, ZONES VARY — **p. 249**

Clematis (some) ✳
☼ ◑ ● ◐ ✂ ZONES VARY — **p. 253**

Pittosporum tobira 'Wheeler's Dwarf'

Skimmia japonica

Vaccinium ovatum

Aegopodium podagraria 'Variegata'

Plant listings continue ▶

Cornus canadensis

Parthenocissus tricuspidata

Alchemilla mollis

Astilbe

Aconitum

Cornus canadensis
BUNCHBERRY
1–7, 32–45   p. 262

Cymbalaria muralis
KENILWORTH IVY
MANY ZONES   p. 272

Euonymus fortunei
3–17, 28–41   p. 298

Fatshedera lizei
4–10, 12–32   p. 303

Fragaria chiloensis
WILD STRAWBERRY
4–24   p. 309

Glechoma hederacea
GROUND IVY
ALL ZONES   p. 318

Hedera
IVY
ZONES VARY   p. 328

Houttuynia cordata
MANY ZONES   p. 338

Lonicera (some)
HONEYSUCKLE
ZONES VARY   p. 376

Mitchella repens
PARTRIDGEBERRY
1–6, 28, 31–45   p. 397

Monstera deliciosa
SPLIT-LEAF PHILODENDRON
24–27   p. 398

Pachysandra terminalis
JAPANESE SPURGE
1–10, 14–21, 31–41   p. 412

Parthenocissus
ZONES VARY   p. 416

Rhoicissus capensis
EVERGREEN GRAPE
16, 17, 21–25   p. 471

Rubus pentalobus
4–6, 14–17, 31, 32   p. 481

Trachelospermum jasminoides
STAR JASMINE
ZONES VARY   p. 523

Vinca
PERIWINKLE
ZONES VARY   p. 534

PERENNIALS, BULBS, ANNUALS

Acanthus mollis
BEAR'S BREECH
4–24, 28–32   p. 164

Aconitum
MONKSHOOD
1–9, 14–21, 34–45   p. 167

Ajuga
CARPET BUGLE
1–24, 26–45   p. 171

Alchemilla
LADY'S-MANTLE
ZONES VARY   p. 172

Anemone
WINDFLOWER
NEEDS, ZONES VARY   p. 179

Aquilegia
COLUMBINE
ZONES VARY   p. 186

Arisaema
ZONES VARY   p. 190

Arum
ZONES VARY   p. 192

Aruncus
GOAT'S BEARD
1–9, 14–17, 31–43   p. 193

Asarum
WILD GINGER
ZONES VARY   p. 193

Aspidistra elatior
CAST-IRON PLANT
4–10, 12–31   p. 195

Astilbe
FALSE SPIRAEA
1–7, 14–17, 32–45   p. 196

Astrantia
MASTERWORT
3–9, 14–24, 31–41   p. 197

Begonia
14–28   p. 206

Bergenia
1–9, 12–24, 30–45   p. 208

Billbergia
12, 13, 16–27   p. 209

Bletilla striata
CHINESE GROUND ORCHID
4–9, 12–24, 26, 28–31   p. 210

Browallia
AMETHYST FLOWER
ALL ZONES   p. 216

Brunnera macrophylla
BRUNNERA
1–24, 31–45   p. 217

Caladium bicolor
FANCY-LEAFED CALADIUM
25–27   p. 219

Aruncus dioicus

Astrantia major 'Rubra'

Begonia foliosa 'Miniata'

Bergenia crassifolia

Brunnera macrophylla

For growing symbol explanations, please see page 79.

Campanula portenschlagiana

Clivia miniata

Corydalis cheilanthifolia

Dicentra spectabilis

Digitalis purpurea Foxy strain

Calceolaria herbeohybrida ❄
ALL ZONES **p. 220**

Campanula (some) ❄
BELLFLOWER
1–9, 14–24, 31–45 **p. 227**

Carex
SEDGE
1–9, 14–24, 28–45 **p. 230**

Cimicifuga ❄
1–7, 17, 32–45 **p. 249**

Clivia miniata ❄
KAFFIR LILY
12–17, 19–27 **p. 256**

Coleus hybridus ❄
COLEUS
ALL ZONES **p. 258**

Colocasia esculenta
ELEPHANT'S EAR
12, 16–28 **p. 258**

Convallaria majalis ❄
LILY-OF-THE-VALLEY
1–7, 14–20, 31–45 **p. 259**

Corydalis ❄
MANY ZONES **p. 263**

Crassula
8, 9, 12–28 **p. 266**

Cyclamen ❄
ZONES VARY **p. 271**

Cymbidium ❄
ALL ZONES **p. 272**

Dicentra (most) ❄
BLEEDING HEART
1–9, 14–24, 31–45 **p. 279**

Digitalis ❄
FOXGLOVE
ZONES VARY **p. 281**

Doronicum ❄
LEOPARD'S BANE
1–7, 14–17, 31–43 **p. 283**

Duchesnea indica ❄
INDIAN MOCK STRAWBERRY
1–24, 29–43 **p. 285**

Endymion ❄
ZONES VARY **p. 288**

Epimedium ❄
1–9, 14–17, 31–43 **p. 289**

Erythronium ❄
ZONES VARY **p. 295**

Ferns
NEEDS, ZONES VARY **p. 304**

Filipendula ❄
1–9, 14–17, 31–45 **p. 307**

Galax urceolata ❄
1–6, 31–43 **p. 312**

Galium odoratum ❄
SWEET WOODRUFF
1–6, 15–17, 31–43 **p. 312**

Gentiana ❄
GENTIAN
MANY ZONES **p. 315**

Geranium (some) ❄
CRANESBILL
ZONES VARY **p. 315**

Gillenia trifoliata ❄
4–6, 31–43 **p. 317**

Hakonechloa macra 'Aureola'
JAPANESE FOREST GRASS
2–9, 14–24, 31–41 **p. 326**

Heliconia ❄
24, 25 **p. 330**

Helleborus ❄
HELLEBORE
ZONES VARY **p. 331**

Hepatica ❄
LIVERLEAF
1–6, 28–45 **p. 332**

Heuchera ❄
CORAL BELLS
ZONES VARY **p. 333**

Heucherella tiarelloides ❄
1–9, 14–24, 31–45 **p. 334**

Hosta ❄
PLANTAIN LILY
MANY ZONES **p. 337**

Impatiens (most) ❄
NEEDS, ZONES VARY **p. 344**

Inula helenium ❄
ELECAMPANE
1–9, 14–24, 30–45 **p. 345**

Iris foetidissima ❄
GLADWIN IRIS
3–24, 32, 33 **p. 349**

Iris, crested ❄
17, 23, 24, 26–28 **p. 350**

Kirengeshoma palmata ❄
MANY ZONES **p. 359**

*Helleborus
orientalis*

Geranium 'Johnson's Blue'

Hakonechloa macra 'Aureola'

Heuchera 'Pewter Veil'

Hosta

Impatiens wallerana

Plant listings continue ▶

129

Lamium maculatum

Lilium Asiatic hybrid

Mertensia virginica

Polygonatum odoratum

Rehmannia elata

Senecio hybridus

Spigelia marilandica

Tradescantia

Trillium grandiflorum

Viola

Plant		Zones	Page
Lamium maculatum DEAD NETTLE	✳	1–24, 32–43	p. 363
Ligularia	✳	ZONES VARY	p. 369
Lilium LILY	✳	ALL ZONES	p. 370
Liriope LILY TURF	✳	ZONES VARY	p. 373
Lobelia (most)	✳	ZONES VARY	p. 375
Lysimachia	✳	ZONES VARY	p. 379
Meconopsis	✳	ZONES VARY	p. 393
Mertensia virginica VIRGINIA BLUEBELLS	✳	1–21, 31–45	p. 395
Milium effusum 'Aureum' BOWLES' GOLDEN GRASS		3–9, 14–17, 31–34, 39	p. 396
Mimulus hybridus MONKEY FLOWER	✳	ALL ZONES	p. 396
Myosotis FORGET-ME-NOT	✳	1–24, 32–43	p. 401
Nicotiana alata	✳	ALL ZONES	p. 406
Ophiopogon	✳	ZONES VARY	p. 373
Oxalis	✳	NEEDS, ZONES VARY	p. 412
Podophyllum		ZONES VARY	p. 443
Polemonium	✳	1–11, 14–17, 31–43	p. 443
Polygonatum SOLOMON'S SEAL	✳	1–7, 14–17, 28–43	p. 444
Primula PRIMROSE	✳	ZONES VARY	p. 448
Prunella SELF-HEAL	✳	1–24, 29–43	p. 450
Pulmonaria LUNGWORT	✳	1–9, 14–17, 32–43	p. 457
Rehmannia elata		7–10, 12–24, 31	p. 464
Rodgersia	✳	2–9, 14–17, 32–41	p. 473
Saxifraga SAXIFRAGE	✳	NEEDS, ZONES VARY	p. 490
Schizanthus pinnatus POOR MAN'S ORCHID	✳	MANY ZONES	p. 491
Senecio hybridus CINERARIA		16, 17, 22–24, 38	p. 495
Sisyrinchium	✳	ZONES VARY	p. 498
Smilacina racemosa FALSE SOLOMON'S SEAL		1–7, 14–17, 31–43	p. 498
Soleirolia soleirolii BABY'S TEARS		4–27	p. 499
Spigelia marilandica PINKROOT, INDIAN PINK	✳	4–6, 28–35	p. 502
Thalictrum MEADOW RUE		ZONES VARY	p. 517
Tiarella FOAMFLOWER		ZONES VARY	p. 519
Tolmiea menziesii PIGGY-BACK PLANT	✳	4–9, 14–17, 20–24	p. 521
Torenia fournieri WISHBONE FLOWER	✳	ALL ZONES	p. 522
Tradescantia		NEEDS, ZONES VARY	p. 523
Tricyrtis TOAD LILY	✳	ZONES VARY	p. 524
Trillium WAKE ROBIN	✳	1–6, 31–43	p. 524
Trollius GLOBEFLOWER	✳	1–6, 32–43	p. 525
Viola VIOLA, PANSY		NEEDS, ZONES VARY	p. 534

For growing symbol explanations, please see page 79.

Acer rubrum and birches

Betula populifolia

Magnolia virginiana

Nyssa sylvatica

Plants for
DAMP SOIL

S wamps, bogs, and marshes may be standard settings in gothic novels—but in your own backyard, they're distinctly lacking in romantic appeal. More often, they present problems that must be solved before you can plant or plan a garden. Fortunately, there are many attractive plants that will thrive in the oxygen-poor soils characteristic of these watery environs—as well as in damp ground alongside ponds and streams. Any of these "swamp creatures" may adapt to poorly drained soils, too, sparing you the trouble of extensively amending the soggier parts of your property.

TREES

Acer rubrum
SCARLET MAPLE
☼ ◑ ◊ ◊ ⚡ MANY ZONES — p. 165

Alnus
ALDER
☼ ◑ ● ◊ ◑ ⚡ ZONES VARY — p. 174

Betula
BIRCH
☼ ◑ ● ● ⚡ ZONES VARY — p. 208

Casuarina
BEEFWOOD
☼ ◑ ● ◑ ● ⚡ 8, 9, 12–26 — p. 234

Fraxinus latifolia
OREGON ASH
☼ ◑ ◊ ● ⚡ 4–24 — p. 309

Larix laricina
AMERICAN LARCH
☼ ◑ ⚡ 37–45 — p. 364

Liquidambar styraciflua
AMERICAN SWEET GUM
☼ ◑ ◊ ● ⚡ MANY ZONES — p. 373

Magnolia grandiflora
SOUTHERN MAGNOLIA
☼ ◑ ◑ ● ⚡ 4–12, 14–24, 26–32 — p. 382

Magnolia virginiana
SWEET BAY
☼ ◑ ◑ ● ⚡ MANY ZONES — p. 386

Melaleuca quinquenervia
CAJEPUT TREE
☼ ◑ ◊ ⚡ 9, 13, 15–17, 20–27 — p. 393

Nyssa sylvatica
SOUR GUM
☼ ◑ ◑ ◊ ◊ ⚡ MANY ZONES — p. 407

Pear
☼ ◑ ◊ ⚡ ZONES VARY — p. 421

Picea sitchensis
SITKA SPRUCE
☼ ◑ ◊ ◊ ⚡ 4–6, 14–17 — p. 432

Platanus
SYCAMORE
☼ ◑ ◊ ⚡ ZONES VARY — p. 438

Populus
POPLAR
☼ ◑ ⚡ ZONES VARY — p. 445

Quercus bicolor
SWAMP WHITE OAK
☼ ◑ ◊ ◊ ⚡ 1–3, 10, 32–43 — p. 460

Quercus nigra
WATER OAK
☼ ◑ ◑ ◑ ⚡ 26, 28–35 — p. 461

Salix
WILLOW
☼ ◑ ◑ ⚡ ZONES VARY — p. 483

Sambucus mexicana
BLUE ELDERBERRY
☼ ◑ ◑ ◊ ⚡ 1–10, 14–24 — p. 487

Sequoia sempervirens
COAST REDWOOD
☼ ◑ ◑ ◊ ⚡ 4–9, 14–24, 32 — p. 495

Taxodium
☼ ◑ ◊ ◑ ◑ ⚡ ZONES VARY — p. 515

Thuja occidentalis
AMERICAN ARBORVITAE
☼ ◑ ◑ ◊ ◑ ⚡ MANY ZONES — p. 518

SHRUBS

Aesculus parviflora
BOTTLEBRUSH BUCKEYE
☼ ◑ ◊ ⚡ 4–6, 31–41 — p. 169

Amelanchier
JUNEBERRY
☼ ◑ ◑ ◊ ◑ ⚡ 1–6, 31–45 — p. 177

Quercus bicolor

Taxodium

Aesculus parviflora

Plant listings continue ▶

Ilex verticillata

Itea

Leucothoe

Lindera

Aconitum

Andromeda polifolia
BOG ROSEMARY
☼ ◐ ◐ ▲ ✂ 1–5, 36–45   p. 178

Aronia arbutifolia
RED CHOKEBERRY
☼ ◐ ◐ ▲ ◐ ✂ 2–6, 31–41   p. 191

Calycanthus
☼ ◐ ● ▲ ✂ ZONES VARY   p. 223

Clethra alnifolia
SUMMERSWEET
◐ ▲ ◐ ✂ 1–6, 31–43   p. 256

Cornus stolonifera
REDTWIG DOGWOOD
☼ ◐ ▲ ✂ 1–9, 14–21, 31–45   p. 263

Gaultheria shallon
SALAL
◐ ▲ ✂ 3–7, 14–17, 21–24   p. 313

Hippophae rhamnoides
SEA BUCKTHORN
☼ ▲ ✂ 1–5, 34, 37–45   p. 336

Ilex verticillata
WINTERBERRY
☼ ◐ ▲ ✂ 1–7, 31–43   p. 344

Itea
SWEETSPIRE
☼ ◐ ▲ ✂ ZONES VARY   p. 350

Kalmia microphylla
WESTERN LAUREL
☼ ◐ ▲ ✂ 1–7, 16–17, 38–45   p. 359

Leucothoe
NEEDS, ZONES VARY   p. 368

Lindera
SPICEBUSH
☼ ◐ ▲ ✂ ZONES VARY   p. 372

Myrica gale
SWEET GALE
NEEDS, ZONES VARY   p. 401

Rhododendron vaseyi
PINKSHELL AZALEA
◐ ▲ ◐ ✂ 32–41   p. 470

Sabal minor
☼ ◐ ▲ ✂ 10, 12–17, 19–31   p. 483

Salix
WILLOW
☼ ◐ ✂ ZONES VARY   p. 483

Sambucus canadensis
AMERICAN ELDERBERRY
☼ ◐ ▲ ✂ MANY ZONES   p. 487

Thuja occidentalis
AMERICAN ARBORVITAE
☼ ◐ ▲ ◐ ✂ MANY ZONES   p. 518

Vaccinium
NEEDS, ZONES VARY   p. 529

Viburnum cassinoides
WITHE-ROD
☼ ◐ ▲ ✂ 1–10, 14–21, 31–43   p. 533

Zenobia pulverulenta
◐ ▲ ◐ ✂ 4–7, 14–17, 28–34   p. 543

PERENNIALS, BULBS

Aconitum
MONKSHOOD
☼ ◐ ▲ ✂ 1–9, 14–21, 34–45   p. 167

Actaea
BANEBERRY
◐ ● ▲ ✂ 1–5, 30–45   p. 167

Anaphalis
PEARLY EVERLASTING
☼ ● ▲ ◐ ✂ ZONES VARY   p. 178

Arisaema
◐ ● ▲ ◐ ✂ ZONES VARY   p. 190

Aruncus dioicus
GOAT'S BEARD
☼ ◐ ● ▲ ✂ 1–9, 14–17, 31–43   p. 193

Asclepias incarnata
SWAMP MILKWEED
☼ ▲ ✂ ALL ZONES   p. 193

Aster novae-angliae
NEW ENGLAND ASTER
☼ ▲ ✂ 1–24, 31–43   p. 196

Astilbe
FALSE SPIRAEA
☼ ◐ ▲ ✂ 1–7, 14–17, 32–45   p. 196

Athyrium otophorum
ENGLISH PAINTED FERN
◐ ● ▲ ◐ ✂ 1–9, 14–24, 31–43   p. 197

Caltha palustris
MARSH MARIGOLD
☼ ◐ ▲ ◐ ✂ 1–21, 31–45   p. 223

Carex
SEDGE
☼ ◐ ▲ ✂ 1–9, 14–24, 28–45   p. 230

Chelone glabra
☼ ◐ ▲ ◐ ✂ 3–9, 14–17, 28–43   p. 243

Chrysanthemum serotinum
☼ ▲ ✂ 2–9, 14, 28–43   p. 248

Cimicifuga racemosa
BLACK SNAKEROOT
☼ ◐ ● ▲ ✂ 1–7, 17, 32–45   p. 249

Cyperus
☼ ◐ ● ▲ ◐ ✂ ZONES VARY   p. 273

Equisetum hyemale
HORSETAIL
☼ ◐ ▲ ◐ ✂ ALL ZONES   p. 290

Aruncus dioicus

Astilbe

Carex

Cimicifuga racemosa

For growing symbol explanations, please see page 79.

Equisetum hyemale

Filipendula

Hibiscus moscheutos

Iris, Japanese

Eupatorium
☼ ◐ ◕ ◕ ╱ ZONES VARY   **p. 299**

Euphorbia palustris
☼ ◐ ◕ ◕ ◕ ╱ MANY ZONES   **p. 300**

Filipendula
☼ ◐ ◕ ◕ ◕ ╱ MANY ZONES   **p. 307**

Galium odoratum
SWEET WOODRUFF
◐ ● ◕ ◕ ╱ 1–6, 15–17, 31–43   **p. 312**

Geum rivale 'Lionel Cox'
WATER AVENS
☼ ◐ ◕ ◕ ╱ 1–24, 32–43   **p. 317**

Gunnera
◐ ◕ ◕ ╱ MANY ZONES   **p. 325**

Helianthus angustifolius
SWAMP SUNFLOWER
☼ ◕ ◕ ╱ 28–34   **p. 329**

Hibiscus moscheutos
ROSE-MALLOW
☼ ◕ ◕ ╱ 2–21, 26–41   **p. 334**

Houstonia caerulea
BLUETS
◐ ◕ ◕ ╱ 1–6, 31–43   **p. 338**

Inula helenium
ELECAMPANE
☼ ◕ ◕ ◕ ╱ 1–9, 14–24, 30–45   **p. 345**

Iris, Japanese
☼ ◐ ◕ ◕ ╱ 1–10, 14–24, 32–45   **p. 348**

Iris laevigata
☼ ◐ ◕ ◕ ╱ 1–10, 14–24, 32–45   **p. 349**

Iris, Louisiana
☼ ◐ ◕ ◕ ◕ ╱ 3–24, 26, 26–43   **p. 349**

Iris pseudacorus
YELLOW FLAG
☼ ◐ ◕ ◕ ◕ ╱ 1–24, 28–45   **p. 349**

Iris, Siberian
☼ ◐ ◕ ◕ ◕ ╱ MANY ZONES   **p. 349**

Iris versicolor
BLUE FLAG
☼ ◐ ◕ ◕ ╱ 1–9, 14–17, 28–45   **p. 350**

Iris virginica
SOUTHERN BLUE FLAG
☼ ◐ ◕ ◕ ╱ 3–9, 14–17, 28–43   **p. 350**

Juncus effusus
SOFT RUSH
☼ ◐ ◕ ◕ ╱ 1–24, 28–45   **p. 353**

Ligularia
◐ ● ◕ ◕ ╱ ZONES VARY   **p. 369**

Lobelia cardinalis
CARDINAL FLOWER
☼ ◐ ◕ ◕ ╱ MANY ZONES   **p. 375**

Lobelia syphilitica
☼ ◐ ◕ ◕ ╱ MANY ZONES   **p. 375**

Lysimachia
☼ ◐ ◕ ◕ ╱ ZONES VARY   **p. 379**

Mentha
MINT
☼ ◐ ◕ ╱ ZONES VARY   **p. 394**

Molinia caerulea
PURPLE MOOR GRASS
☼ ◐ ◕ ◕ ◕ ╱ MANY ZONES   **p. 397**

Monarda didyma
BEE BALM
☼ ◐ ◕ ◕ ◕ ╱ MANY ZONES   **p. 398**

Myosotis scorpioides
FORGET-ME-NOT
◐ ◕ ◕ ╱ 1–24, 32–45   **p. 401**

Petasites japonica
JAPANESE COLTSFOOT
☼ ◐ ● ◕ ◕ ◕ ╱ MANY ZONES   **p. 426**

Phyllostachys (most)
BAMBOO
☼ ◐ ◕ ◕ ◕ ╱ ZONES VARY   **p. 201**

Primula florindae
☼ ◐ ● ◕ ◕ ╱ 3–6, 17   **p. 449**

Primula japonica
☼ ◐ ● ◕ ◕ ╱ MANY ZONES   **p. 449**

Rodgersia
◐ ◕ ◕ ╱ 2–9, 14–17, 32–41   **p. 473**

Sanguinaria canadensis
BLOODROOT
◐ ● ◕ ◕ ◕ ╱ 1–6, 32–43   **p. 487**

Teucrium canadense
☼ ◐ ◕ ╱ 2–9, 14–17, 31–41   **p. 517**

Thelypteris palustris
MARSH FERN
◐ ● ◕ ◕ ◕ ╱ MANY ZONES   **p. 517**

Tradescantia virginiana
SPIDERWORT
☼ ◐ ● ◕ ◕ ◕ ╱ MANY ZONES   **p. 524**

Trollius
GLOBEFLOWER
☼ ◐ ◕ ◕ ◕ ╱ 1–6, 32–43   **p. 525**

Vernonia noveboracensis
IRONWEED
☼ ◐ ◕ ◕ ◕ ╱ MANY ZONES   **p. 531**

Zantedeschia aethiopica
COMMON CALLA
☼ ◐ ◕ ◕ ◕ ╱ MANY ZONES   **p. 542**

Ligularia

Lobelia cardinalis

Monarda didyma

Tradescantia virginiana

Trollius

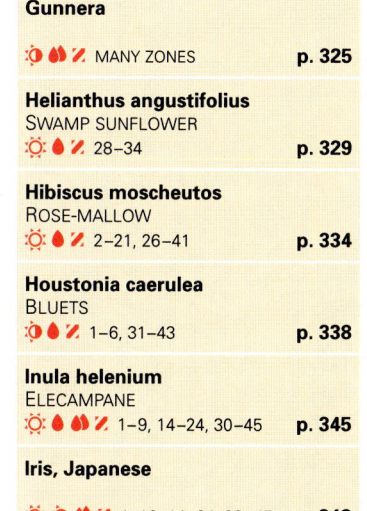

133

Plants for ARID GARDENS

Buddleia davidii

Lagerstroemia indica 'Rosea'

N ot all of the country receives rainfall that amounts to "regular watering." Scant rainfall totals, long dry seasons, or periodic drought years may leave gardeners slaves to watering or scrambling for supplies for garden use. Fortunately, many fine plants, once they are established in the garden, are naturally equipped to grow well with far less than regular water during the growing season. Here are some proven performers in all plant categories.

SYMBOLS: ✳ indicates plants that bear showy flowers; ♣ indicates shrubs that can become small trees.

Nerium oleander

Cedrus libani

TREES

Brachychiton ✳
☀ 🔴 ♦ ⚡ ZONES VARY — **p. 214**

Cassia leptophylla ✳
GOLD MEDALLION TREE
☀ 🔴 ♦ ⚡ 21–25, 27 — **p. 233**

Casuarina
BEEFWOOD
☀ 🔴 ♦ ⚡ 8, 9, 12–26 — **p. 234**

Cedrus
CEDAR
☀ 🔴 ♦ ⚡ ZONES VARY — **p. 236**

Celtis
HACKBERRY
☀ 🔴 ♦ ⚡ ZONES VARY — **p. 237**

Cercidium ✳
PALO VERDE
☀ 🔴 ♦ ⚡ 10–14, 18–20, 29 — **p. 239**

Chilopsis linearis ✳
DESERT WILLOW
☀ 🔴 ⚡ MANY ZONES — **p. 244**

Chitalpa tashkentensis ✳
CHITALPA
☀ 🔴 ⚡ 3–24, 28–33 — **p. 245**

Cupressus sempervirens
ITALIAN CYPRESS
☀ 🔴 ⚡ 4–24, 28–32 — **p. 270**

Elaeagnus angustifolia
RUSSIAN OLIVE
☀ 🔴 ♦ ⚡ MANY ZONES — **p. 287**

Fraxinus (most)
ASH
☀ 🔴 ♦ ⚡ ZONES VARY — **p. 309**

Gymnocladus dioica
KENTUCKY COFFEE TREE
☀ 🔴 ♦ ⚡ MANY ZONES — **p. 325**

Koelreuteria paniculata ✳
GOLDENRAIN TREE
☀ 🔴 ♦ ⚡ 2–21, 28–41 — **p. 360**

Lagerstroemia indica ✳
CRAPE MYRTLE
☀ 🔴 ♦ ⚡ MANY ZONES — **p. 362**

Laurus nobilis ✳
SWEET BAY
☀ 🔴 ♦ ⚡ 5–9, 12–24 — **p. 365**

Olea europaea ✳
OLIVE
☀ 🔴 ⚡ 8, 9, 11–24 — **p. 408**

Parkinsonia aculeata ✳
MEXICAN PALO VERDE
☀ 🔴 ♦ ⚡ 8–29 — **p. 415**

Pinus (many)
PINE
☀ 🔴 ♦ ⚡ ZONES VARY — **p. 433**

Pistacia chinensis
CHINESE PISTACHE
☀ 🔴 ♦ ⚡ 4–16, 18–23, 26, 28–33 — **p. 437**

Quercus (some)
OAK
☀ 🔴 ♦ ⚡ ZONES VARY — **p. 459**

Robinia ✳
LOCUST
☀ 🔴 ♦ ⚡ 1–24, 29–45 — **p. 472**

Sophora japonica ✳
JAPANESE PAGODA TREE
☀ 🔴 ♦ ⚡ 2–24, 31–41 — **p. 500**

Tilia tomentosa
SILVER LINDEN
☀ 🔴 ♦ ⚡ 2–21, 32–41 — **p. 520**

SHRUBS

Alyogyne huegelii
BLUE HIBISCUS
☀ 🔴 ♦ ⚡ 15–17, 20–27 — **p. 176**

Olea europaea

Parkinsonia aculeata

Koelreuteria paniculata

Sophora japonica

For growing symbol explanations, please see page 79.

SPECIAL SITUATIONS

Artemisia 'Powis Castle'

Callistemon citrinus

Cordia boissieri

Cytisus

Juniperus chinensis

Anisodontea
CAPE MALLOW
☼ ◐ ◐ ◢ 14–24, 28   **p. 180**

Arbutus unedo
STRAWBERRY TREE
☼ ◐ ◐ ◐ ◢ 4–24, 31, 32   **p. 188**

Artemisia

☼ ◐ ◢ 1–24, 29–45   **p. 191**

Buddleia davidii
BUTTERFLY BUSH
☼ ◐ ◐ ◐ ◢ MANY ZONES   **p. 217**

Calliandra tweedii

NEEDS, ZONES VARY   **p. 221**

Callistemon citrinus
LEMON BOTTLEBRUSH
☼ ◐ ◐ ◢ 8, 9, 12–28   **p. 222**

Caragana arborescens
SIBERIAN PEASHRUB
☼ ◐ ◢ 1–12, 35–45   **p. 230**

Caryopteris clandonensis
BLUE MIST
☼ ◐ ◢ 3–7, 14–17, 29–41   **p. 232**

Cassia (some)
SENNA
☼ ◐ ◐ ◢ ZONES VARY   **p. 233**

Cercis occidentalis
WESTERN REDBUD
☼ ◐ ◐ ◢ 2–24   **p. 239**

Chamaerops humilis
MEDITERRANEAN FAN PALM
☼ ◐ ◐ ◐ ◢ 4–31   **p. 242**

Cordia

☼ ◐ ◐ ◢ ZONES VARY   **p. 260**

Cotinus coggygria
SMOKE TREE
☼ ◐ ◢ 2–24, 29–41   **p. 265**

Cotoneaster

☼ ◐ ◢ ZONES VARY   **p. 265**

Cytisus
BROOM
☼ ◐ ◢ ZONES VARY   **p. 273**

Elaeagnus (some)

☼ ◐ ◐ ◐ ◐ ◢ ZONES VARY   **p. 287**

Euryops

☼ ◐ ◢ ZONES VARY   **p. 301**

Feijoa sellowiana
PINEAPPLE GUAVA
☼ ◐ ◢ 7–9, 12–32   **p. 303**

Genista
BROOM
☼ ◐ ◢ ZONES VARY   **p. 314**

Juniperus (some)
JUNIPER
☼ ◐ ◐ ◐ ◢ ZONES VARY   **p. 353**

Lantana

☼ ◐ ◢ 8–10, 12–30   **p. 363**

Lavandula
LAVENDER
☼ ◐ ◢ ZONES VARY   **p. 365**

Lavatera
TREE MALLOW
☼ ◐ ◐ ◢ ZONES VARY   **p. 366**

Leptospermum
TEA TREE
☼ ◐ ◢ ZONES VARY   **p. 366**

Leucophyllum
TEXAS RANGER
☼ ◐ ◢ 7–24, 28–32, 35   **p. 367**

Mahonia (most)

NEEDS, ZONES VARY   **p. 386**

Melaleuca (most)

☼ ◐ ◢ ZONES VARY   **p. 393**

Myrtus communis
MYRTLE
☼ ◐ ◐ ◢ 8–24, 26–28   **p. 401**

Nandina domestica
HEAVENLY BAMBOO
☼ ◐ ◐ ◐ ◐ ◢ 5–32   **p. 402**

Nerium oleander
OLEANDER
☼ ◐ ◐ ◢ 8–16, 18–31   **p. 405**

Phlomis
JERUSALEM SAGE
NEEDS, ZONES VARY   **p. 428**

Photinia serrulata
CHINESE PHOTINIA
☼ ◐ ◐ ◐ ◢ 4–16, 18–22, 28–31   **p. 430**

Pittosporum tobira
TOBIRA
☼ ◐ ◐ ◐ ◐ ◢ 8–31   **p. 438**

Plumbago auriculata
CAPE PLUMBAGO
☼ ◐ ◢ 8, 9, 12–28   **p. 441**

Portulacaria afra
ELEPHANT'S FOOD
☼ ◐ ◐ ● ◐ ◢ 8, 9, 12–27   **p. 446**

Punica granatum
POMEGRANATE
☼ ◐ ◐ ◐ ◢ 5–32   **p. 457**

Pyracantha
FIRETHORN
☼ ◐ ◐ ◢ ZONES VARY   **p. 458**

Rhamnus (most)

NEEDS, ZONES VARY   **p. 464**

Lavandula angustifolia 'Hidcote'

Lavatera assurgentiflora

Myrtus communis

Nandina domestica

Plumbago auriculata

Plant listings continue ▶

135

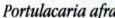

Portulacaria afra

Rosmarinus officinalis

Salvia leucantha

Tecoma stans

Bougainvillea

Rhus ☀
SUMAC
ZONES VARY · · · · · · **p. 471**

Rosa rugosa ☀
RAMANAS ROSE
· · · · 1–24, 32–45 **p. 480**

Rosmarinus officinalis ☀
ROSEMARY
· · · 4–24, 26–32 **p. 480**

Rubus ☀
BRAMBLE
ZONES VARY **p. 481**

Salvia (some) ☀
SAGE
NEEDS, ZONES VARY **p. 484**

Santolina chamaecyparissus ☀
LAVENDER COTTON
· · · MANY ZONES **p. 488**

Tecoma stans ☀
YELLOW BELLS ♣
· · · 10, 12, 13, 21–28 **p. 515**

Teucrium ☀
GERMANDER
· · ZONES VARY **p. 516**

Vitex agnus-castus ☀
CHASTE TREE ♣
· · 4–33 **p. 535**

GROUND COVERS, VINES

Antigonon leptopus ☀
QUEEN'S WREATH
· · · 12, 13, 18–30 **p. 181**

Arctostaphylos uva-ursi ☀
BEARBERRY
· · · MANY ZONES **p. 189**

Bougainvillea ☀
· · · · MANY ZONES **p. 212**

Calylophus hartwegii ☀
· · · MANY ZONES **p. 224**

Cerastium tomentosum ☀
SNOW-IN-SUMMER
· · · 1–24, 32–45 **p. 238**

Ceratostigma plumbaginoides ☀
DWARF PLUMBAGO
· · · · 2–10, 14–24, 29–41 **p. 239**

Delosperma ☀
ICE PLANT
· · ZONES VARY **p. 276**

Gazania ☀
· · · · 8–28 **p. 314**

Gelsemium sempervirens ☀
CAROLINA JESSAMINE
· · · · 8–24, 26–33 **p. 314**

Helianthemum nummularium ☀
SUNROSE
· · 3–9, 14–24, 32, 34 **p. 329**

Ipomoea acuminata ☀
BLUE DAWN FLOWER
· · · 8, 9, 12–28 **p. 346**

Lampranthus ☀
ICE PLANT
· · 14–26 **p. 363**

Lantana montevidensis ☀
· · 8–10, 12–30 **p. 363**

Macfadyena unguis-cati ☀
CAT'S CLAW
· · · · 8–29, 31 **p. 380**

Merremia tuberosa ☀
YELLOW MORNING GLORY
· · 24–27 **p. 395**

Phyla nodiflora ☀
LIPPIA
· · · 8–29 **p. 430**

Podranea ricasoliana ☀
PINK TRUMPET VINE
· · · · 9, 12, 13, 19–27 **p. 443**

Polygonum aubertii ☀
SILVER LACE VINE
· · 2–24, 31–41 **p. 444**

Rosa banksiae ☀
LADY BANKS' ROSE
· · · 4–33 **p. 479**

Rosmarinus officinalis (dwarf) ☀
ROSEMARY
· · 4–24, 26–32 **p. 480**

Verbena (most) ☀
· · ZONES VARY **p. 531**

Wisteria ☀
· · · ZONES VARY **p. 538**

PERENNIALS, BULBS, ANNUALS, ACCENTS

Achillea ☀
YARROW
· · 1–24, 26, 28–45 **p. 166**

Agapanthus ☀
LILY-OF-THE-NILE
· · · · ZONES VARY **p. 169**

Agave ☀
· · · · ZONES VARY **p. 170**

Aloe (most) ☀
· · · · · 8, 9, 12–27 **p. 174**

Amaryllis belladonna ☀
NAKED LADY
· · 4–24, 28, 29 **p. 177**

Gazania

Wisteria sinensis

Achillea taygetea

Coreopsis lanceolata

Euphorbia characias wulfenii

For growing symbol explanations, please see page 79.

Gaillardia

Geranium incanum

Kniphofia uvaria

Linum perenne lewisii

Oenothera berlandieri

Antennaria dioica ☀
PUSSY TOES
☀ 🔴 💧 MANY ZONES p. 181

Artemisia
☀ 🔴 💧 1–24, 29–45 p. 191

Baileya multiradiata ☀
DESERT MARIGOLD
☀ 🔴 💧 ALL ZONES p. 199

Baptisia
FALSE INDIGO
☀ 🔴 💧 1–24, 28–43 p. 203

Centranthus ruber ☀
RED VALERIAN
☀ 🌤 🔴 💧 1–9, 12–24, 28–43 p. 238

Coreopsis ☀
☀ 🔴 💧 ZONES VARY p. 260

Dietes ☀
FORTNIGHT LILY
☀ 🌤 🔴 💧 8, 9, 12–28 p. 281

Echeveria (most) ☀
☀ 🌤 💧 ZONES VARY p. 285

Euphorbia (most) ☀
NEEDS, ZONES VARY p. 299

Festuca ovina 'Glauca' ☀
BLUE FESCUE
☀ 🌤 🔴 💧 1–24, 29–45 p. 304

Gaillardia ☀
☀ 🔴 💧 ALL ZONES p. 311

Gaura lindheimeri ☀
GAURA
☀ 🔴 💧 3–35, 37, 38, 39 p. 313

Geranium incanum ☀
☀ 🌤 🔴 💧 14–24 p. 316

Hesperaloe parviflora ☀
☀ 🔴 💧 MANY ZONES p. 333

Iris, bearded ☀
☀ 🌤 💧 1–24, 30–45 p. 348

Kniphofia uvaria ☀
RED-HOT POKER
☀ 🌤 🔴 💧 MANY ZONES p. 360

Llatris ☀
GAYFEATHER
☀ 🔴 💧 1–10, 14–24, 28–45 p. 368

Limonium perezii ☀
☀ 🔴 💧 13, 15–17, 20–27 p. 371

Linum ☀
FLAX
☀ 🔴 💧 ZONES VARY p. 372

Melampodium leucanthum ☀
☀ 🔴 💧 MANY ZONES p. 393

Oenothera ☀
EVENING PRIMROSE
NEEDS, ZONES VARY p. 407

Pennisetum setaceum ☀
FOUNTAIN GRASS
☀ 🔴 💧 8–24, 26–29 p. 424

Penstemon (many) ☀
BEARD TONGUE
☀ 🌤 🔴 💧 ZONES VARY p. 424

Perovskia ☀
RUSSIAN SAGE
☀ 🔴 💧 3–24, 28–35, 37, 39 p. 425

Phormium ☀
NEW ZEALAND FLAX
☀ 🌤 🔴 💧 14–28 p. 430

Romneya coulteri ☀
MATILIJA POPPY
☀ 🔴 💧 4–12, 14–24 p. 473

Salvia (most) ☀
SAGE
NEEDS, ZONES VARY p. 484

Santolina ☀
☀ 🔴 💧 ZONES VARY p. 488

Sedum (many) ☀
STONECROP
NEEDS, ZONES VARY p. 493

Stachys byzantina ☀
LAMB'S EARS
☀ 🔴 💧 1–24, 29–43 p. 504

Stipa (some) ☀
NEEDS, ZONES VARY p. 506

Tagetes lemmonii ☀
MARIGOLD
☀ 🔴 💧 8–10, 12–24, 27–29 p. 514

Tithonia rotundifolia ☀
MEXICAN SUNFLOWER
☀ 🔴 💧 ALL ZONES p. 521

Verbascum ☀
MULLEIN
☀ 🔴 💧 ZONES VARY p. 531

Verbena (most) ☀
☀ 🔴 💧 ZONES VARY p. 531

Watsonia ☀
☀ 🔴 💧 ZONES VARY p. 537

Yucca (most) ☀
NEEDS, ZONES VARY p. 540

Zinnia grandiflora ☀
☀ 🔴 💧 ALL ZONES p. 543

Pennisetum setaceum

Perovskia 'Blue Spire'

Salvia coccinea

Watsonia

137

Plants for
WINDY AREAS

Calocedrus decurrens

Caragana arborescens

Strong winds can wreak havoc on plants. Wind causes water stress in plants by increasing transpiration and evaporation from leaves. A gale-force wind can defoliate or uproot plants, or snap off branches with such force that stems or trunks can split. Whether you live on the coast or inland, if wind is common in your area you'll want to choose plants that can take it. Listed below are plants tough enough to withstand strong winds, while still providing plenty of ornamental value in the garden. Some trees and large shrubs are tough enough to serve as windbreaks, allowing more delicate plants to thrive in their shelter.

Cupressocyparis leylandii

Elaeagnus angustifolia

Olea europaea

TREES

Acacia (some)
☀ ◐ ♦ ✂ ZONES VARY — **p. 163**

Acer campestre
HEDGE MAPLE
☀ ◐ ♦ ♦ ✂ 2–9, 14, 31–41 — **p. 164**

Acer platanoides
NORWAY MAPLE
☀ ◐ ♦ ♦ ✂ 1–9, 14–17, 30–43 — **p. 165**

Arbutus
NEEDS, ZONES VARY — **p. 188**

Broussonetia papyrifera
PAPER MULBERRY
☀ ♦ ♦ ✂ 3–24, 28–33 — **p. 216**

Calocedrus decurrens
INCENSE CEDAR
☀ ◐ ♦ ✂ MANY ZONES — **p. 223**

Caragana arborescens
SIBERIAN PEASHRUB
☀ ♦ ✂ 1–12, 35–45 — **p. 230**

Casuarina
BEEFWOOD
☀ ♦ ♦ ✂ 8, 9, 12–26 — **p. 234**

Celtis occidentalis
COMMON HACKBERRY
☀ ◐ ♦ ♦ ✂ 1–24, 30–45 — **p. 237**

Chamaecyparis lawsoniana
PORT ORFORD CEDAR
☀ ◐ ♦ ✂ MANY ZONES — **p. 241**

Chilopsis linearis
DESERT WILLOW
☀ ♦ ✂ 10–13, 18–21, 29, 30, 33 — **p. 244**

Cupressocyparis leylandii
☀ ♦ ♦ ✂ 3–24, 26, 28–34, 39 — **p. 270**

Cupressus
CYPRESS
☀ ♦ ✂ ZONES VARY — **p. 270**

Elaeagnus angustifolia
RUSSIAN OLIVE
☀ ◐ ♦ ♦ ✂ MANY ZONES — **p. 287**

Eucalyptus (most)
☀ ♦ ♦ ✂ SEE CHART — **p. 296**

Ficus rubiginosa
RUSTYLEAF FIG
☀ ♦ ✂ 18–27 — **p. 305**

Juniperus
JUNIPER
☀ ◐ ♦ ♦ ✂ ZONES VARY — **p. 353**

Lagunaria patersonii
PRIMROSE TREE
☀ ♦ ✂ 13, 15–26 — **p. 362**

Ligustrum lucidum
GLOSSY PRIVET
☀ ◐ ♦ ✂ 5, 6, 8–31 — **p. 369**

Maclura pomifera
OSAGE ORANGE
☀ ♦ ♦ ✂ 2, 3, 10–13, 29–41 — **p. 381**

Melaleuca
☀ ♦ ✂ ZONES VARY — **p. 393**

Olea europaea
OLIVE
☀ ♦ ✂ 8, 9, 11–24 — **p. 408**

Palms
NEEDS, ZONES VARY — **p. 413**

Parkinsonia aculeata
MEXICAN PALO VERDE
☀ ♦ ♦ ✂ 8–29 — **p. 415**

Picea abies
NORWAY SPRUCE
☀ ◐ ♦ ♦ ✂ MANY ZONES — **p. 432**

Melaleuca linariifolia

Picea abies

Pseudotsuga menziesii

For growing symbol explanations, please see page 79.

Buxus sempervirens 'Suffruticosa'

Chamaecyparis pisifera

Cotoneaster microphyllus

Juniperus chinensis

Callistemon

Pinus (many)
PINE
☼ ◐ ◖ ✂ ZONES VARY **p. 433**

Populus alba 'Pyramidalis'
BOLLEANA POPLAR
☼ ◖ ✂ 1–24, 30–45 **p. 446**

Populus fremontii
WESTERN COTTONWOOD
☼ ◖ ✂ 7–24 **p. 446**

Populus nigra 'Italica'
LOMBARDY POPLAR
☼ ◖ ✂ 1–24, 29–45 **p. 446**

Pseudotsuga menziesii
DOUGLAS FIR
☼ ◐ ◖ ◖ ✂ MANY ZONES **p. 455**

Quercus ilex
HOLLY OAK
☼ ◖ ◖ ✂ 4–24, 32 **p. 460**

Quercus phellos
WILLOW OAK
☼ ◖ ◖ ✂ MANY ZONES **p. 461**

Quercus virginiana
SOUTHERN LIVE OAK
☼ ◖ ◖ ✂ 4–31 **p. 461**

Roystonea
ROYAL PALM
☼ ◖ ◖ ✂ 25 **p. 481**

Sequoia sempervirens
COAST REDWOOD
☼ ◐ ◖ ✂ 4–9, 14–24, 32 **p. 495**

Thuja occidentalis
AMERICAN ARBORVITAE
☼ ◐ ◖ ◖ ✂ MANY ZONES **p. 518**

Thuja plicata
WESTERN RED CEDAR
☼ ◐ ◖ ◖ ✂ MANY ZONES **p. 518**

Ulmus pumila
SIBERIAN ELM
☼ ◖ ✂ 1–24, 26–45 **p. 529**

SHRUBS

Amelanchier alnifolia
SASKATOON
☼ ◐ ◖ ◖ ✂ 1–6, 31–45 **p. 177**

Artemisia
☼ ◖ ✂ 1–24, 29–45 **p. 191**

Berberis
BARBERRY
☼ ◐ ◖ ◖ ✂ ZONES VARY **p. 207**

Buxus
BOXWOOD
☼ ◐ ● ◖ ✂ ZONES VARY **p. 218**

Callistemon
BOTTLEBRUSH
☼ ◖ ◖ ✂ 8, 9, 12–28 **p. 222**

Carissa
☼ ◐ ◖ ✂ 22–27 **p. 230**

Chamaecyparis
FALSE CYPRESS
☼ ◐ ◖ ◖ ✂ ZONES VARY **p. 241**

Cotoneaster
☼ ◖ ✂ ZONES VARY **p. 265**

Elaeagnus
☼ ◐ ◖ ◖ ✂ ZONES VARY **p. 287**

Euonymus japonica
EVERGREEN EUONYMUS
☼ ◖ ◖ ✂ 4–20, 28–31 **p. 299**

Hippophae rhamnoides
SEA BUCKTHORN
☼ ◖ ◖ ✂ 1–5, 34, 37–45 **p. 336**

Juniperus
JUNIPER
☼ ◐ ◖ ◖ ✂ ZONES VARY **p. 353**

Laurus nobilis
SWEET BAY
☼ ◐ ◖ ✂ 5–9, 12–24 **p. 365**

Lavandula
LAVENDER
☼ ◐ ◖ ✂ ZONES VARY **p. 365**

Lavatera
TREE MALLOW
☼ ◖ ◖ ✂ ZONES VARY **p. 366**

Leptospermum
TEA TREE
☼ ◖ ✂ ZONES VARY **p. 366**

Leucophyllum
TEXAS RANGER
☼ ◖ ✂ 7–24, 28–32, 35 **p. 367**

Ligustrum japonicum 'Texanum'
☼ ◐ ◖ ✂ 4–31 **p. 369**

Lonicera tatarica
HONEYSUCKLE
☼ ◐ ◖ ✂ 1–9, 14–21, 32–43 **p. 377**

Myrica pensylvanica
BAYBERRY
☼ ◐ ◖ ✂ 3–7, 32–34 **p. 401**

Nandina domestica
HEAVENLY BAMBOO
☼ ◐ ● ◖ ◖ ✂ 5–33 **p. 402**

Nerium oleander
OLEANDER
☼ ◖ ◖ ✂ 8–16, 18–31 **p. 405**

Pittosporum tobira
TOBIRA
☼ ◐ ◖ ◖ ✂ 8–31 **p. 438**

Prunus (evergreen)
NEEDS, ZONES VARY **p. 451**

Lavatera thuringiaca 'Barnsley'

Leptospermum scoparium

Ligustrum japonicum 'Texanum'

Nandina domestica

Prunus lusitanica

Pittosporum tobira

Plant listings continue ▶

Bougainvillea

Viburnum dentatum

Delosperma cooperi

Lantana montevidensis

Carex elata 'Bowles Golden'

Chrysanthemum frutescens

Pyracantha
FIRETHORN
☼ ◐ ✂ ZONES VARY   **p. 458**

Rhamnus (some)
NEEDS, ZONES VARY   **p. 464**

Rhaphiolepis (most)
☼ ◐ ◐ ◐ ✂ MANY ZONES   **p. 464**

Rhus (some)
SUMAC
☼ ◐ ◐ ✂ ZONES VARY   **p. 471**

Rosmarinus officinalis
ROSEMARY
☼ ◐ ✂ 4–24, 26–32   **p. 480**

Viburnum cassinoides
WITHE-ROD
☼ ◐ ◐ ✂ 1–10, 14–21, 31–43   **p. 533**

Viburnum dentatum
ARROWWOOD VIBURNUM
☼ ◐ ◐ ✂ MANY ZONES   **p. 533**

GROUND COVERS, VINES

Arctostaphylos uva-ursi
BEARBERRY
☼ ◐ ◐ ✂ 1–9, 14–24, 34, 36–45   **p. 189**

Bougainvillea
☼ ◐ ◐ ◐ ✂ MANY ZONES   **p. 212**

Carpobrotus
ICE PLANT
☼ ◐ ✂ 12–27   **p. 231**

Delosperma
ICE PLANT
☼ ◐ ✂ ZONES VARY   **p. 276**

Drosanthemum
☼ ◐ ✂ 14–26   **p. 284**

Lampranthus
ICE PLANT
☼ ◐ ✂ 14–26   **p. 363**

Lantana
☼ ◐ ✂ 8–10, 12–30   **p. 363**

Tecomaria capensis
CAPE HONEYSUCKLE
☼ ◐ ◐ ✂ 12, 13, 16, 18–28   **p. 516**

PERENNIALS, ACCENT PLANTS

Agapanthus
LILY-OF-THE-NILE
☼ ◐ ◐ ◐ ✂ ZONES VARY   **p. 169**

Agave
☼ ◐ ◐ ✂ ZONES VARY   **p. 170**

Aloe
☼ ◐ ◐ ◐ ✂ 8, 9, 12–27   **p. 174**

Asparagus densiflorus 'Sprengeri'
SPRENGER ASPARAGUS
☼ ◐ ◐ ✂ 12–28   **p. 195**

Carex
SEDGE
☼ ◐ ◐ ◐ ✂ 1–9, 14–24, 28–45   **p. 230**

Cerastium tomentosum
SNOW-IN-SUMMER
☼ ◐ ✂ 1–24, 32–45   **p. 238**

Chrysanthemum frutescens
MARGUERITE
☼ ◐ ◐ ✂ 14–24, 26, 28   **p. 246**

Cortaderia selloana
PAMPAS GRASS
☼ ◐ ◐ ◐ ✂ 4–31, 33   **p. 263**

Euphorbia
NEEDS, ZONES VARY   **p. 299**

Euryops
☼ ◐ ✂ ZONES VARY   **p. 301**

Felicia amelloides
BLUE MARGUERITE
☼ ◐ ◐ ✂ 8, 9, 13–24   **p. 304**

Hemerocallis
DAYLILY
☼ ◐ ◐ ✂ ALL ZONES   **p. 331**

Kniphofia uvaria
RED-HOT POKER
☼ ◐ ◐ ◐ ✂ 3–9, 14–24, 28–34   **p. 360**

Limonium perezii
☼ ◐ ✂ 13, 15–17, 20–27   **p. 371**

Pelargonium
GERANIUM
☼ ◐ ◐ ◐ ✂ 8, 9, 12–24   **p. 423**

Phlomis
JERUSALEM SAGE
☼ ◐ ✂ ZONES VARY   **p. 428**

Phormium
NEW ZEALAND FLAX
☼ ◐ ◐ ✂ 14–28   **p. 430**

Salvia
SAGE
NEEDS, ZONES VARY   **p. 484**

Santolina
☼ ◐ ◐ ✂ MANY ZONES   **p. 488**

Yucca
NEEDS, ZONES VARY   **p. 540**

Zauschneria
CALIFORNIA FUCHSIA
☼ ◐ ◐ ✂ 2–11, 14–24   **p. 542**

Euphorbia seguierana niciciana

Euryops pectinatus 'Viridis'

Kniphofia uvaria

Phlomis russelliana

Agapanthus 'Peter Pan'

For growing symbol explanations, please see page 79.

Cornus stolonifera

Acer platanoides

Chamaecyparis pisifera

Coccoloba uvifera

Ilex opaca

Plants for
SEACOAST GARDENS

A walk on the beach is a pleasure in fine weather, but on less pleasant days, blustery, salt-laden winds can send you scurrying for shelter. Plants, unfortunately, have no escape: they have to tough it out. Even on the breeziest coastlines, though, some plants look fresh and healthy whatever the weather. A number of these sturdy choices are listed below.

TREES

Acer platanoides
NORWAY MAPLE
1–9, 14–17, 30–43   **p. 165**

Acer pseudoplatanus
SYCAMORE MAPLE
MANY ZONES   **p. 165**

Aesculus hippocastanum
COMMON HORSECHESTNUT
1–10, 12, 14–17, 32–43   **p. 169**

Casuarina
BEEFWOOD
8, 9, 12–26   **p. 234**

Chamaecyparis pisifera
SAWARA FALSE CYPRESS
MANY ZONES   **p. 241**

Coccoloba
SEA GRAPE
ZONES VARY   **p. 257**

Cocos nucifera
COCONUT PALM
25   **p. 257**

Cordia sebestena
GEIGER TREE
24, 25, 27   **p. 260**

Cordyline australis
5, 8–11, 14–27   **p. 260**

Crataegus crus-galli
COCKSPUR THORN
2–12, 14–17, 28, 30–41   **p. 267**

Cryptomeria japonica
4–9, 14–24, 32–34, 39   **p. 268**

Ilex opaca
AMERICAN HOLLY
MANY ZONES   **p. 344**

Melaleuca quinquenervia
CAJEPUT TREE
9, 13, 15–17, 20–27   **p. 393**

Olea europaea
OLIVE
8, 9, 11–24   **p. 408**

Picea sitchensis
SITKA SPRUCE
4–6, 14–17   **p. 432**

Pinus (many)
PINE
ZONES VARY   **p. 433**

Platycladus orientalis
ORIENTAL ARBORVITAE
2–41   **p. 438**

Quercus ilex
HOLLY OAK
4–24, 32   **p. 460**

Quercus virginiana
SOUTHERN LIVE OAK
4–31   **p. 461**

Sabal palmetto
CABBAGE PALM
12–17, 19–31   **p. 483**

Schinus terebinthifolius
BRAZILIAN PEPPER TREE
MANY ZONES   **p. 491**

Thuja occidentalis
AMERICAN ARBORVITAE
MANY ZONES   **p. 518**

Ulmus parvifolia
CHINESE ELM
3–24, 26–35, 37–39   **p. 529**

Ulmus pumila
SIBERIAN ELM
1–24, 26–45   **p. 529**

SHRUBS

Arctostaphylos uva-ursi
BEARBERRY
MANY ZONES   **p. 189**

Aronia arbutifolia
RED CHOKEBERRY
2–6, 31–41   **p. 191**

Cryptomeria japonica

Schinus terebinthifolius

Thuja occidentalis 'Woodwardii'

Plant listings continue ▶

Aucuba japonica

Buddleia alternifolia

Cornus stolonifera baileyi

Cotoneaster borizontalis

Elaeagnus pungens

Aucuba japonica
☼ ● ● ╱ 4–24, 28–33   **p. 197**

Baccharis halimifolia
SALT BUSH
☼ ● ╱ 26–41   **p. 198**

Berberis thunbergii
JAPANESE BARBERRY
☼ ● ● ● ╱ 1–24, 28–41   **p. 208**

Buddleia
☼ ● ● ● ╱ ZONES VARY   **p. 217**

Carissa macrocarpa
NATAL PLUM
☼ ● ╱ 22–27   **p. 230**

Chaenomeles
FLOWERING QUINCE
☼ ● ● ╱ 2–21, 28–41   **p. 240**

Clethra alnifolia
SUMMERSWEET
☼ ● ●● ╱ 1–6, 31–43   **p. 256**

Cornus stolonifera
REDTWIG DOGWOOD
☼ ● ● ╱ 1–9, 14–21, 31–45   **p. 263**

Cotoneaster
☼ ● ╱ ZONES VARY   **p. 265**

Cytisus
BROOM
☼ ● ╱ ZONES VARY   **p. 273**

Elaeagnus
☼ ● ● ● ╱ ZONES VARY   **p. 287**

Euonymus japonica
EVERGREEN EUONYMUS
☼ ● ● ● ╱ 4–20, 28–31   **p. 299**

Genista
BROOM
☼ ● ╱ ZONES VARY   **p. 314**

Hibiscus syriacus
ROSE OF SHARON
☼ ● ╱ 2–21, 26, 28–41   **p. 335**

Hippophae rhamnoides
SEA BUCKTHORN
☼ ● ● ╱ 1–5, 34, 37–45   **p. 336**

Ilex glabra
INKBERRY
☼ ● ● ● ╱ 3–24, 26, 28, 31–41   **p. 343**

Juniperus
JUNIPER
☼ ● ● ● ╱ ZONES VARY   **p. 353**

Lantana
☼ ● ╱ 8–10, 12–30   **p. 363**

Lavandula angustifolia
ENGLISH LAVENDER
☼ ● ╱ 4–24, 30, 32–34, 39   **p. 365**

Ligustrum amurense
AMUR PRIVET
☼ ● ● ╱ 1–24, 33–45   **p. 369**

Ligustrum ovalifolium
CALIFORNIA PRIVET
☼ ● ● ╱ 4–34, 39   **p. 370**

Lonicera nitida
BOX HONEYSUCKLE
☼ ● ● ╱ 4–9, 14–24, 28–32   **p. 377**

Lonicera pileata
PRIVET HONEYSUCKLE
☼ ● ● ╱ 3–9, 14–24, 31, 32   **p. 377**

Lycium chinense
MATRIMONY VINE
☼ ● ● ╱ 3–7, 31, 32, 34   **p. 379**

Melaleuca
☼ ● ╱ ZONES VARY   **p. 393**

Myrica pensylvanica
BAYBERRY
☼ ● ● ╱ 3–7, 32–44   **p. 401**

Myrtus communis
MYRTLE
☼ ● ● ● ╱ 8–24, 26–28   **p. 401**

Nerium oleander
OLEANDER
☼ ● ● ╱ 8–16, 18–31   **p. 405**

Pittosporum tobira
TOBIRA
☼ ● ● ● ╱ 8–31   **p. 438**

Rhamnus alaternus
ITALIAN BUCKTHORN
☼ ● ● ╱ 4–24, 31, 32   **p. 464**

Rhaphiolepis
☼ ● ● ● ╱ MANY ZONES   **p. 464**

Rhus
☼ ● ● ● ╱ ZONES VARY   **p. 471**

Rosa rugosa
RAMANAS ROSE
☼ ● ● ● ╱ 1–24, 32–45   **p. 480**

Rosmarinus officinalis
ROSEMARY
☼ ● ╱ 4–24, 26–32   **p. 480**

Shepherdia
BUFFALOBERRY
☼ ● ● ● ╱ 1–3, 7, 10, 33–45   **p. 496**

Spartium junceum
SPANISH BROOM
☼ ● ╱ 5–24   **p. 501**

Taxus cuspidata
JAPANESE YEW
☼ ● ● ● ╱ 2–6, 14–17, 32–41   **p. 515**

Viburnum cassinoides
WITHE-ROD
☼ ● ● ╱ 1–10, 14–21, 31–43   **p. 533**

Hibiscus syriacus

Juniperus chinensis

Nerium oleander

Rosa rugosa

Viburnum cassinoides

For growing symbol explanations, please see page 79.

Tecomaria capensis

Trachelospermum jasminoides

Artemisia 'Powis Castle'

Eryngium alpinum

Helianthemum nummularium

Viburnum dentatum
ARROWWOOD VIBURNUM
☼ ◐ ♦ ⚡ MANY ZONES   **p. 533**

Viburnum tinus
LAURUSTINUS
☼ ◐ ♦ ⚡ MANY ZONES   **p. 534**

VINES

Celastrus
BITTERSWEET
☼ ♦ ⚡ ZONES VARY   **p. 236**

Polygonum aubertii
SILVER LACE VINE
☼ ♦ ♦ ⚡ 2–24, 28–41   **p. 444**

Tecomaria capensis
CAPE HONEYSUCKLE
☼ ◐ ♦ ♦ ⚡ 12, 13, 16, 18–28   **p. 516**

Trachelospermum jasminoides
STAR JASMINE
☼ ◐ ♦ ● ⚡ 8–32   **p. 523**

Wisteria sinensis
CHINESE WISTERIA
☼ ◐ ♦ ♦ ⚡ MANY ZONES   **p. 539**

PERENNIALS, BULBS

Aloe arborescens
TREE ALOE
☼ ◐ ♦ ♦ ⚡ 8, 9, 12–27   **p. 174**

Armeria maritima
COMMON THRIFT
☼ ♦ ♦ ⚡ 1–9, 14–24, 33–43   **p. 191**

Artemisia (most)
☼ ♦ ⚡ 1–24, 29–45   **p. 191**

Asclepias tuberosa
BUTTERFLY WEED
☼ ♦ ⚡ ALL ZONES   **p. 194**

Aurinia saxatilis
BASKET-OF-GOLD
☼ ◐ ♦ ♦ ⚡ 1–24, 32–43   **p. 197**

Baptisia australis
BLUE FALSE INDIGO
☼ ♦ ⚡ 1–24, 28–43   **p. 203**

Cerastium tomentosum
SNOW-IN-SUMMER
☼ ◐ ♦ ⚡ 1–24, 32–45   **p. 238**

Chrysanthemum (most)
☼ ♦ ⚡ ZONES VARY   **p. 246**

Erigeron karvinskianus
SANTA BARBARA DAISY
☼ ◐ ♦ ♦ ⚡ 8, 9, 12–28   **p. 291**

Eryngium
SEA HOLLY
☼ ♦ ⚡ 1–24, 26, 28–45   **p. 294**

Euryops
☼ ♦ ⚡ ZONES VARY   **p. 301**

Felicia amelloides
BLUE MARGUERITE
☼ ♦ ♦ ⚡ 8, 9, 13–24   **p. 304**

Festuca ovina 'Glauca'
BLUE FESCUE
☼ ◐ ♦ ⚡ 1–24, 29–45   **p. 304**

Gypsophila
☼ ♦ ⚡ ZONES VARY   **p. 325**

Helianthemum nummularium
SUNROSE
☼ ♦ ⚡ 3–9, 14–24, 32, 34   **p. 329**

Hemerocallis
DAILY
☼ ◐ ♦ ⚡ ALL ZONES   **p. 331**

Heuchera sanguinea
CORAL BELLS
☼ ◐ ♦ ⚡ 1–11, 14–24, 31–45   **p. 334**

Hibiscus moscheutos
ROSE-MALLOW
☼ ♦ ⚡ 2–21, 26–41   **p. 334**

Hosta
PLANTAIN LILY
◐ ♦ ⚡ 1–10, 12–21, 28, 31–45   **p. 337**

Iberis sempervirens
EVERGREEN CANDYTUFT
☼ ♦ ⚡ 1–24, 31–45   **p. 342**

Kniphofia uvaria
RED-HOT POKER
☼ ◐ ♦ ♦ ⚡ 3–9, 14–24, 28–34   **p. 360**

Limonium
SEA LAVENDER
☼ ♦ ⚡ ZONES VARY   **p. 371**

Liriope and Ophiopogon
LILY TURF
◐ ♦ ♦ ♦ ⚡ ZONES VARY   **p. 373**

Lythrum virgatum
PURPLE LOOSESTRIFE
☼ ♦ ⚡ 1–9, 14–24, 29–43   **p. 380**

Pelargonium
GERANIUM
☼ ◐ ♦ ♦ ⚡ 8, 9, 12–24   **p. 423**

Phormium
NEW ZEALAND FLAX
☼ ◐ ♦ ♦ ⚡ 14–28   **p. 430**

Santolina
☼ ♦ ♦ ⚡ ZONES VARY   **p. 488**

Sedum
STONE CROP
NEEDS, ZONES VARY   **p. 493**

Stachys byzantina
LAMB'S EARS
☼ ◐ ♦ ♦ ⚡ 1–24, 29–43   **p. 504**

Hemerocallis

Hibiscus moscheutos

Lavandula angustifolia

Liriope

Santolina chamaecyparissus

Good Choices for ROCK GARDENS

Acer palmatum 'Dissectum'

Helianthemum nummularium

Small or tiny shrubs, miniature bulbous plants, annuals and perennials that form low tufts or creeping mats of foliage—these are the choices listed here. Classic European rock and alpine garden plants can be easily grown in the cool Pacific Northwest and some parts of the Northeast; but in climates made less favorable by heat, dryness, humidity, or cold call for a different assortment of plants. Read the climate zone adaptations carefully.

Picea glauca

Pinus mugo mugo

Pinus strobus 'Nana'

Berberis thunbergii 'Aurea'

TREES

Abies balsamea 'Nana'
DWARF BALSAM FIR
☼ ◑ ◌ ◌ ⚡ MANY ZONES   **p. 162**

Acer palmatum (dwarf)
JAPANESE MAPLE
☼ ◑ ◌ ◌ ⚡ MANY ZONES   **p. 165**

Betula pendula 'Trost's Dwarf'
☼ ◌ ◌◌ ⚡ 1–12, 14–24, 30–45   **p. 209**

Cedrus deodara (dwarf)
DEODAR CEDAR
☼ ◌ ⚡ 3–12, 14–24, 27–32   **p. 236**

Chamaecyparis obtusa (dwarf)
HINOKI FALSE CYPRESS
☼ ◑ ◌ ⚡ MANY ZONES   **p. 241**

Picea (many dwarf types)
SPRUCE
☼ ◑ ◌ ⚡ ZONES VARY   **p. 431**

Pinus densiflora
TANYOSHO PINE
☼ ◌ ◌ ⚡ 2–10, 14–17, 32–41   **p. 435**

Pinus mugo mugo
MUGHO PINE
☼ ◌ ◌ ⚡ 1–11, 14–24, 32–45   **p. 435**

Pinus strobus 'Nana'
DWARF WHITE PINE
☼ ◌ ◌ ⚡ 1–6, 32–41   **p. 436**

Pinus sylvestris (several)
DWARF SCOTCH PINE
☼ ◌ ◌ ⚡ MANY ZONES   **p. 437**

Thuja occidentalis (dwarf)
AMERICAN ARBORVITAE
☼ ◌ ◌ ◌ ⚡ MANY ZONES   **p. 518**

Tsuga canadensis (dwarf)
CANADA HEMLOCK
☼ ◌ ◌ ⚡ 3–7, 17, 32–43   **p. 526**

SHRUBS, SHRUBLETS

Andromeda polifolia 'Nana'
BOG ROSEMARY
☼ ◑ ◌ ⚡ 1–5, 36–45   **p. 178**

Berberis thunbergii (some)
JAPANESE BARBERRY
☼ ◑ ◌ ◌ ⚡ 1–24, 28–41   **p. 208**

Calluna vulgaris (dwarf)
SCOTCH HEATHER
☼ ◌ ⚡ 2–6, 15–17, 34, 36–41   **p. 222**

Cotoneaster (dwarf)
☼ ◑ ◌ ⚡ ZONES VARY   **p. 265**

Daboecia cantabrica
IRISH HEATH
☼ ◑ ◌ ◌ ⚡ MANY ZONES   **p. 274**

Erica (dwarf)
HEATH
☼ ◑ ◌ ◌ ⚡ ZONES VARY   **p. 291**

Gaultheria (most)
◑ ◌ ◌ ⚡ ZONES VARY   **p. 313**

Genista (several dwarf types)
DWARF BROOM
☼ ◌ ◌ ⚡ ZONES VARY   **p. 314**

Helianthemum nummularium
SUNROSE
☼ ◌ ◌ ⚡ 3–9, 14–24, 32, 34   **p. 329**

Hypericum coris
ST. JOHNSWORT
☼ ◑ ◌ ◌ ◌ ⚡ 4–24, 31, 32   **p. 341**

Ilex crenata (several dwarf types)
DWARF JAPANESE HOLLY
☼ ◑ ◌ ◌ ⚡ MANY ZONES   **p. 343**

Jasminum parkeri
DWARF JASMINE
☼ ◑ ◌ ◌ ⚡ 5–9, 12–24, 31   **p. 352**

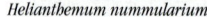

Calluna vulgaris

Cotoneaster

Erica cinerea

Teucrium chamaedrys

For growing symbol explanations, please see page 79.

Juniperus (many dwarf types)
JUNIPER
☼ ☼ ◐ ● ✂ ZONES VARY   **p. 353**

Pieris japonica (dwarf)
LILY-OF-THE-VALLEY SHRUB
☼ ● ✂ 3–9, 14–17, 31–35, 37   **p. 432**

Rhododendron
AZALEA, DWARF SATSUKI
☼ ● ◐ ✂ ZONES VARY   **p. 465**

**Rhododendron
(several dwarf types)**
☼ ● ◐ ✂ ZONES VARY   **p. 465**

Teucrium (low-growing)
GERMANDER
☼ ● ✂ ZONES VARY   **p. 516**

Vaccinium vitis-idaea minus
LINGONBERRY
☼ ● ● ✂ MANY ZONES   **p. 530**

PERENNIALS

Achillea (dwarf)
YARROW
☼ ● ✂ 1–24, 26, 28–45   **p. 166**

Aethionema
STONECRESS
☼ ● ✂ MANY ZONES   **p. 169**

Ajuga genevensis
CARPET BUGLE
☼ ◐ ● ✂ 1–24, 26–45   **p. 171**

Alchemilla alpina
LADY'S-MANTLE
☼ ◐ ● ✂ 1–6, 36–43   **p. 172**

Androsace
ROCK JASMINE
☼ ● ✂ 1–6, 14–17, 36–45   **p. 178**

Antennaria
☼ ● ● ✂ MANY ZONES   **p. 181**

Aquilegia (dwarf)
COLUMBINE
☼ ◐ ● ✂ ZONES VARY   **p. 186**

Arabis procurrens
☼ ● ✂ 1–10, 14–24, 31–45   **p. 187**

Arenaria
SANDWORT
☼ ◐ ● ✂ 1–9, 14–24, 32–45   **p. 190**

Armeria
THRIFT
☼ ● ● ✂ ZONES VARY   **p. 191**

Aster alpinus
☼ ● ✂ 1–4, 36–45   **p. 196**

Aubrieta deltoidea
COMMON AUBRIETA
☼ ● ● ✂ 1–9, 14–21, 36–43   **p. 197**

Aurinia saxatilis
BASKET-OF-GOLD
☼ ● ● ✂ 1–24, 32–43   **p. 197**

Calamintha nepetoides
CALAMINT
☼ ◐ ● ✂ 2–9, 14–24, 31–41   **p. 220**

Campanula (smallest)
BELLFLOWER
☼ ◐ ● ● ✂ 1–9, 14–24, 31–45   **p. 227**

Cerastium tomentosum
SNOW-IN-SUMMER
☼ ● ✂ 1–24, 32–45   **p. 238**

Delosperma
ICE PLANT
☼ ● ✂ ZONES VARY   **p. 276**

Dianthus (smallest)
PINK
☼ ◐ ● ✂ 1–24, 30–45   **p. 278**

Dodecatheon
SHOOTING STAR
NEEDS, ZONES VARY   **p. 282**

Draba
☼ ● ✂ 1–7, 32, 34, 36–43   **p. 283**

Dryas
☼ ● ✂ 1–6, 36–45   **p. 284**

Echeveria (many)
☼ ◐ ● ✂ ZONES VARY   **p. 285**

Erigeron (dwarf)
FLEABANE
☼ ◐ ● ✂ ZONES VARY   **p. 291**

Erinus alpinus
☼ ◐ ● ✂ MANY ZONES   **p. 291**

Eriogonum umbellatum
SULFUR FLOWER
☼ ● ✂ 1–24, 28–43   **p. 294**

Erodium reichardii
CRANESBILL
☼ ◐ ● ✂ 7–9, 14–24, 31, 32   **p. 294**

Euphorbia myrsinites
☼ ● ● ✂ 1–24, 31–43   **p. 300**

Gentiana
GENTIAN
☼ ◐ ● ✂ MANY ZONES   **p. 315**

Geranium (smallest)
CRANESBILL
☼ ◐ ● ✂ ZONES VARY   **p. 315**

Gypsophila (several dwarf types)
☼ ● ✂ ZONES VARY   **p. 325**

Hepatica
LIVERLEAF
◐ ● ● ✂ 1–6, 28–45   **p. 332**

Androsace sarmentosa

Antennaria neglecta

Armeria maritima

Campanula portenschlagiana

Dryas octopetala

Echeveria

Erigeron karvinskianus

Euphorbia myrsinites

Plant listings continue ▶

Saponaria ocymoides

Sempervivum arachnoideum

Crocus

Cyclamen coum

Muscari

Herniaria glabra
GREEN CARPET
☼ ◐ ● ♦ ⚡ ALL ZONES   **p. 333**

Heuchera
CORAL BELLS
☼ ◐ ♦ ⚡ ZONES VARY   **p. 333**

Iberis sempervirens
EVERGREEN CANDYTUFT
☼ ♦ ⚡ 1–24, 31–45   **p. 342**

Jasione laevis
SHEPHERD'S SCABIOUS
☼ ◐ ♦ ⚡ MANY ZONES   **p. 351**

Lewisia
☼ ◐ ♦ ⚡ 1–7, 14–17, 36–38   **p. 368**

Lithodora diffusa
☼ ◐ ♦ ⚡ 5–7, 14–17, 32   **p. 375**

Origanum (low-growing)
☼ ♦ ⚡ ZONES VARY   **p. 410**

Papaver alpinum
ALPINE POPPY
☼ ♦ ● ⚡ 3–9, 14–17, 32–41   **p. 415**

**Penstemon
(subshrubs or mat-forming)**
☼ ◐ ♦ ● ⚡ ZONES VARY   **p. 424**

Phlox (trailing or creeping)
☼ ◐ ● ♦ ⚡ ZONES VARY   **p. 428**

Polemonium reptans
◐ ● ♦ ⚡ 1–11, 14–17, 31–43   **p. 443**

Potentilla (some)
CINQUEFOIL
☼ ◐ ● ♦ ⚡ ZONES VARY   **p. 447**

Primula (most)
PRIMROSE
☼ ◐ ● ♦ ●♦ ⚡ ZONES VARY   **p. 448**

Pulsatilla vulgaris
PASQUE FLOWER
☼ ◐ ♦ ⚡ MANY ZONES   **p. 457**

Saponaria ocymoides
☼ ♦ ⚡ 1–11, 14–24, 33–45   **p. 489**

Saxifraga
SAXIFRAGE
NEEDS, ZONES VARY   **p. 490**

Sedum (many)
STONECROP
NEEDS, ZONES VARY   **p. 493**

Sempervivum
HOUSELEEK
☼ ♦ ● ⚡ 2–24, 29–41   **p. 494**

Silene acaulis
CUSHION PINK
☼ ◐ ♦ ⚡ MANY ZONES   **p. 497**

Thalictrum alpinum
MEADOW RUE
◐ ● ♦ ⚡ 2–10, 14–17, 32–41   **p. 517**

Thymus
THYME
☼ ◐ ♦ ⚡ ZONES VARY   **p. 519**

Veronica (mat-forming)
SPEEDWELL
NEEDS, ZONES VARY   **p. 532**

Woodsia obtusa
☼ ◐ ♦ ⚡ 1–6, 14–17, 31–43   **p. 539**

BULBS, BULBLIKE PLANTS

Allium (smallest)
ORNAMENTAL ALLIUM
☼ ◐ ♦ ⚡ ZONES VARY   **p. 173**

Chionodoxa
GLORY-OF-THE-SNOW
◐ ♦ ⚡ 1–7, 14–20, 31–43   **p. 245**

Crocus
☼ ◐ ♦ ⚡ 1–24, 30–45   **p. 268**

Cyclamen (except C. persicum)
☼ ◐ ♦ ⚡ ZONES VARY   **p. 271**

Freesia
☼ ◐ ♦ ⚡ 8, 9, 12–24, 28   **p. 310**

Galanthus
SNOWDROP
☼ ◐ ♦ ⚡ 1–9, 14–17, 31–45   **p. 312**

Iris (smallest)
NEEDS, ZONES VARY   **p. 347**

Muscari
GRAPE HYACINTH
☼ ◐ ♦ ⚡ ZONES VARY   **p. 400**

Narcissus (small)
DAFFODIL
☼ ◐ ♦ ⚡ ZONES VARY   **p. 402**

Rhodohypoxis baurii
☼ ♦ ⚡ 4–7, 14–24, 28–33   **p. 470**

Sternbergia lutea
☼ ♦ ⚡ MANY ZONES   **p. 505**

Tritonia
☼ ♦ ⚡ 9, 13–24, 26, 28, 29   **p. 525**

Tulipa (species only)
TULIP
☼ ♦ ⚡ ZONES VARY   **p. 526**

Zephyranthes
ZEPHYR FLOWER
☼ ♦ ⚡ ZONES VARY   **p. 543**

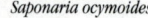

Geranium

Heuchera

Lewisia

Lithodora diffusa

Impatiens and *Lobelia*

Plants for
HANGING BASKETS
AND WINDOW BOXES

The charm of a garden in the air—whether it hangs suspended or perches at the edge of a window—derives from the choice of plants. You want a full (and probably colorful) display, with foliage that is lax enough to soften the edges of the container or even spill over it. Here's a selection of proven aerial artists, drawn from a variety of annuals, perennials, and woody plants.

Brachycome

Coleus hybridus

Convolvulus tricolor

Lobularia maritima

ANNUALS

Asarina antirrhinifolia
CLIMBING SNAPDRAGON
ALL ZONES — p. 193

Brachycome
SWAN RIVER DAISY
ZONES VARY — p. 214

Browallia
AMETHYST FLOWER
ALL ZONES — p. 216

Coleus hybridus
ALL ZONES — p. 258

Convolvulus tricolor
DWARF MORNING GLORY
ALL ZONES — p. 260

Evolvulus glomeratus
BLUE DAZE
24–27 — p. 302

Hypoestes phyllostachya
FRECKLE FACE
ALL ZONES — p. 342

Impatiens wallerana
BUSY LIZZIE
ALL ZONES — p. 344

Ipomoea tricolor
MORNING GLORY
ALL ZONES — p. 346

Lobelia erinus
ALL ZONES — p. 375

Lobularia maritima
SWEET ALYSSUM
ALL ZONES — p. 376

Mimulus hybridus
MONKEY FLOWER
ALL ZONES — p. 396

Nemesia strumosa
1–24, 28–45 — p. 404

Nemophila
1–24, 28–45 — p. 404

Petunia hybrida
GARDEN PETUNIA
ALL ZONES — p. 426

Phlox drummondii
ANNUAL PHLOX
ALL ZONES — p. 428

Portulaca grandiflora
ROSE MOSS
ALL ZONES — p. 446

Sanvitalia procumbens
CREEPING ZINNIA
ALL ZONES — p. 488

Schizanthus pinnatus
POOR MAN'S ORCHID
MANY ZONES — p. 491

Thunbergia alata
BLACK-EYED SUSAN VINE
23–27 — p. 519

Torenia fournieri
WISHBONE FLOWER
ALL ZONES — p. 522

Tropaeolum majus
GARDEN NASTURTIUM
ALL ZONES — p. 525

Verbena hybrida
GARDEN VERBENA
8–29 — p. 531

Viola
VIOLET
NEEDS, ZONES VARY — p. 534

Zinnia angustifolia
ALL ZONES — p. 543

Mimulus hybridus

Portulaca grandiflora

Tropaeolum majus

Plant listings continue ▶

Begonia, tuberous

Campanula isophylla

Epiphyllum

Helichrysum petiolare

Lamium maculatum 'Beacon Silver'

PERENNIALS, BULBS

Achimenes
ALL ZONES — p. 166

Asparagus densiflorus
12–28 — p. 194

Aurinia saxatilis
BASKET-OF-GOLD
1–24, 32–43 — p. 197

Begonia, semperflorens
14–28 — p. 206

Begonia, tuberous
14–28 — p. 207

Campanula isophylla
ITALIAN BELLFLOWER
MANY ZONES — p. 228

Campanula portenschlagiana
DALMATIAN BELLFLOWER
2–9, 14–24, 31–41 — p. 228

Campanula poscharskyana
SERBIAN BELLFLOWER
1–9, 14–24, 31–45 — p. 229

Ceropegia woodii
ROSARY VINE
21–27 — p. 240

Chlorophytum comosum
SPIDER PLANT
15–17, 19–27 — p. 245

Cymbalaria muralis
KENILWORTH IVY
MANY ZONES — p. 272

Epiphyllum
ORCHID CACTUS
8, 9, 14–28 — p. 289

Erigeron
FLEABANE
ZONES VARY — p. 291

Gazania
8–28 — p. 314

Glechoma hederacea
GROUND IVY
ALL ZONES — p. 318

Helichrysum petiolare
LICORICE PLANT
16, 17, 22–24 — p. 330

Iberis sempervirens
EVERGREEN CANDYTUFT
1–24, 31–45 — p. 342

Lamium maculatum
DEAD NETTLE
1–24, 32–43 — p. 363

Lotus berthelotii
PARROT'S BEAK
9, 15–24 — p. 377

Lysimachia nummularia
MONEYWORT
1–9, 14–24, 31–43 — p. 379

Nierembergia
CUP FLOWER
ZONES VARY — p. 406

Pelargonium peltatum
IVY GERANIUM
8, 9, 12–24 — p. 423

Primula (some)
PRIMROSE
ZONES VARY — p. 448

Saxifraga stolonifera
STRAWBERRY GERANIUM
4–9, 14–24, 29–32 — p. 490

Scaevola
8, 9, 14–24 — p. 490

Schlumbergera
16, 17, 21–27 — p. 492

Sedum morganianum
DONKEY TAIL
MANY ZONES — p. 494

Sedum sieboldii
4–9, 12, 14–24, 29–31 — p. 494

Senecio cineraria
DUSTY MILLER
4–24, 29–32 — p. 495

Senecio mikanioides
GERMAN IVY
14–24 — p. 495

Tradescantia albiflora
WANDERING JEW
12–28 — p. 523

Tradescantia fluminensis
WANDERING JEW
12–28 — p. 523

Vinca minor
DWARF PERIWINKLE
1–24, 28–43 — p. 534

SHRUBS, VINES

Abutilon megapotamicum
CHINESE LANTERN
8, 9, 12–27 — p. 163

Fuchsia hybrida
HYBRID FUCHSIA
15–17, 22–24 — p. 311

Hedera helix
ENGLISH IVY
3–34, 39 — p. 328

Nierembergia hippomanica

Pelargonium peltatum

Vinca minor

Abutilon megapotamicum

For growing symbol explanations, please see page 79.

GROUND COVERS
and Lawn Substitutes

Epimedium at base of tree

Lawn, the best-known ground cover, is unsurpassed as a surface to walk and play on. But where foot traffic is infrequent or undesirable, many other plants can offer much of a lawn's neatness and uniformity with considerably less maintenance. Ground covers run the gamut of foliage textures and colors, and many are noted for their colorful flowers. Some spread by underground runners or root as they grow. Others grow from clumps and must be planted close together to achieve the effect of a ground cover. Not all of them are low mats; some are knee-high or even taller. The taller ones function as barriers rather than as the green bridge a lawn provides.

Aegopodium podagraria 'Variegatum'

Alchemilla mollis

Antennaria dioica

Arctostaphylos uva-ursi

GROUND COVERS

Abelia grandiflora 'Prostrata' 🌿
4–24, 28–35 — p. 162

Achillea tomentosa 🌿
WOOLLY YARROW
1–24, 26, 28–45 — p. 166

Aegopodium podagraria 🌿
BISHOP'S WEED
MANY ZONES — p. 169

Ajuga reptans 🌿
CARPET BUGLE
1–24, 26–45 — p. 171

Akebia quinata ↻
FIVELEAF AKEBIA
3–24, 29–41 — p. 172

Alchemilla erythropoda 🌿
LADY'S-MANTLE
3–6, 36–40 — p. 172

Alchemilla glaucescens 🌿
LADY'S-MANTLE
3–6, 36–40 — p. 172

Anemone nemorosa 🌿
WOOD ANEMONE
1–9, 14–24, 30–43 — p. 179

Antennaria 🌿
PUSSY TOES
MANY ZONES — p. 181

Arabis 🌿
ROCKCRESS
1–10, 14–24, 31–45 — p. 187

Arctostaphylos uva-ursi 🌿
BEARBERRY
MANY ZONES — p. 189

Arenaria montana 🌿
SANDWORT
1–9, 14–24, 32–45 — p. 190

Armeria maritima 🌿
COMMON THRIFT
1–9, 14–24, 33–43 — p. 191

Aronia melanocarpa 🌿
BLACK CHOKEBERRY
1–6, 31–43 — p. 191

Artemisia (several) 🌿
1–24, 29–45 — p. 191

Aruncus aethusifolius 🌿
MANY ZONES — p. 193

Asarum 🌿
WILD GINGER
ZONES VARY — p. 193

Bamboo (some) 🌿
SEE CHART — p. 199

Bergenia 🌿
1–9, 12–24, 30–45 — p. 208

Bougainvillea ↻
MANY ZONES — p. 212

Calluna vulgaris (some) 🌿
SCOTCH HEATHER
2–6, 15–17, 34, 36–41 — p. 222

Camellia sasanqua (some) 🌿
MANY ZONES — p. 226

Campanula (some) 🌿
BELLFLOWER
1–9, 14–24, 31–45 — p. 227

Carex comans 🌿
NEW ZEALAND HAIR SEDGE
1–9, 14–24, 28–45 — p. 230

Carissa macrocarpa (some) 🌿
NATAL PLUM
22–27 — p. 230

SYMBOLS: The symbols indicate whether a plant is a shrub 🌿, perennial 🌿, or vine ↻.

Artemisia stellerana 'Silver Brocade'

Ajuga reptans

Asarum caudatum

Plant listings continue ▶

Bergenia

Carex comans

Cornus canadensis

Convallaria majalis

Corydalis lutea

Carpobrotus
ICE PLANT
☼ ◐ ♦ ∕ 12–27   **p. 231**

Cerastium tomentosum
SNOW-IN-SUMMER
☼ ◐ ♦ ∕ 1–24, 32–45   **p. 238**

Ceratostigma plumbaginoides
DWARF PLUMBAGO
☼ ◐ ♦ ∕ 2–10, 14–24, 29–41   **p. 239**

Chrysanthemum leucanthemum 'May Queen'
☼ ◐ ♦ ∕ 1–24, 28–43   **p. 246**

Chrysogonum virginianum
GOLDEN STAR
☼ ◐ ♦ ∕ 3–6, 28–32, 34–39   **p. 248**

Cissus (some)
NEEDS, ZONES VARY   **p. 249**

Conradina verticillata
CUMBERLAND ROSEMARY
☼ ◐ ♦ ∕ 4–9, 14–17, 31–33   **p. 259**

Convallaria majalis
LILY-OF-THE-NILE
◐ ♦ ∕ 1–7, 14–20, 31–45   **p. 259**

Cornus canadensis
BUNCHBERRY
◐ ♦ ♦ ∕ 1–7, 32–45   **p. 262**

Coronilla varia
CROWN VETCH
☼ ◐ ♦ ∕ 1–24, 28–45   **p. 263**

Corydalis
☼ ◐ ♦ ∕ MANY ZONES   **p. 263**

Cotoneaster (some)
☼ ◐ ♦ ∕ ZONES VARY   **p. 265**

Cymbalaria muralis
KENILWORTH IVY
☼ ◐ ♦ ♦ ∕ MANY ZONES   **p. 272**

Delosperma
ICE PLANT
☼ ◐ ♦ ∕ ZONES VARY   **p. 276**

Drosanthemum
☼ ◐ ♦ ∕ 14–27   **p. 284**

Dryas
☼ ◐ ♦ ∕ 1–6, 36–45   **p. 284**

Duchesnea indica
INDIAN MOCK STRAWBERRY
☼ ◐ ♦ ♦ ∕ 1–24, 29–43   **p. 285**

Epimedium
☼ ◐ ♦ ∕ 1–9, 14–17, 31–43   **p. 289**

Erica (some)
HEATH
☼ ◐ ♦ ∕ ZONES VARY   **p. 291**

Erigeron karvinskianus
SANTA BARBARA DAISY
☼ ◐ ♦ ∕ 8, 9, 12–28   **p. 291**

Erodium reichardii
CRANESBILL
☼ ◐ ♦ ∕ 7–9, 14–24, 31, 32   **p. 294**

Euonymus fortunei (varieties)
☼ ◐ ♦ ♦ ∕ 3–17, 28–41   **p. 298**

Euphorbia cyparissias
☼ ♦ ∕ 1–24, 28–43   **p. 300**

Festuca
FESCUE
☼ ♦ ∕ 1–24, 29–45   **p. 304**

Forsythia 'Arnold Dwarf', F. intermedia 'Goldtide'
☼ ♦ ♦ ∕ MANY ZONES   **p. 308**

Fragaria chiloensis
WILD STRAWBERRY
☼ ◐ ♦ ∕ 4–24   **p. 309**

Galax urceolata
◐ ● ♦ ∕ 1–6, 31–43   **p. 312**

Galium odoratum
SWEET WOODRUFF
☼ ◐ ♦ ∕ MANY ZONES   **p. 313**

Gardenia jasminoides 'Radicans'
☼ ◐ ♦ ∕ MANY ZONES   **p. 313**

Gaultheria (some)
◐ ♦ ∕ ZONES VARY   **p. 313**

Gazania
☼ ♦ ♦ ∕ 8–28   **p. 314**

Gelsemium sempervirens
CAROLINA JESSAMINE
☼ ◐ ● ♦ ♦ ∕ 8–24, 26–33   **p. 314**

Genista (some)
BROOM
☼ ♦ ∕ ZONES VARY   **p. 314**

Geranium
CRANESBILL
☼ ◐ ♦ ♦ ∕ ZONES VARY   **p. 315**

Glechoma hederacea
GROUND IVY
☼ ◐ ● ♦ ∕ ALL ZONES   **p. 318**

Gypsophila repens
☼ ♦ ∕ MANY ZONES   **p. 325**

Hedera
IVY
☼ ◐ ● ♦ ♦ ∕ ZONES VARY   **p. 328**

Helianthemum nummularium
SUNROSE
☼ ♦ ∕ 3–9, 14–24, 32, 34   **p. 329**

Epimedium

Euonymus fortunei

Festuca cinerea

Fragaria chiloensis

Galium odoratum

For growing symbol explanations, please see page 79.

Lonicera japonica

Helianthemum nummularium

Houttuynia cordata 'Variegata'

Lantana

Liriope spicata

Helleborus orientalis
LENTEN ROSE
MANY ZONES — p. 331

Hosta
PLANTAIN LILY
MANY ZONES — p. 337

Houttuynia cordata 'Variegata'
MANY ZONES — p. 338

Hypericum (low-growing)
ST. JOHNSWORT
ZONES VARY — p. 341

Iberis sempervirens
EVERGREEN CANDYTUFT
1–24, 31–45 — p. 342

Jasminum (some)
JASMINE
ZONES VARY — p. 351

Juniperus (low-growing)
JUNIPER
ZONES VARY — p. 353

Lamium maculatum (several)
DEAD NETTLE
1–24, 32–43 — p. 363

Lampranthus
ICE PLANT
14–26 — p. 363

Lantana (some)
8–10, 12–30 — p. 363

Leucothoe fontanesiana
DROOPING LEUCOTHOE
4–7, 15–17, 32–34 — p. 368

Liriope spicata
CREEPING LILY TURF
3–10, 14–34 — p. 374

Lonicera japonica
JAPANESE HONEYSUCKLE
2–41 — p. 377

Lotus berthelotii
PARROT'S BEAK
9, 15–24 — p. 377

Lysimachia
ZONES VARY — p. 379

Mahonia (some)
NEEDS, ZONES VARY — p. 386

Mazus reptans
MANY ZONES — p. 393

Mitchella repens
PARTRIDGEBERRY
1–6, 28, 31–45 — p. 397

Nandina domestica (some)
HEAVENLY BAMBOO
4–33 — p. 402

Nepeta faassenii
CATMINT
1–24, 30, 32–43 — p. 404

Nierembergia
CUP FLOWER
ZONES VARY — p. 406

Oenothera (many)
EVENING PRIMROSE
NEEDS, ZONES VARY — p. 407

Ophiopogon japonicus
MONDO GRASS
5–9, 14–32 — p. 375

Origanum (many)
NEEDS, ZONES VARY — p. 410

Oscularia
15–24 — p. 410

Osteospermum fruticosum
TRAILING AFRICAN DAISY
ALL ZONES — p. 411

Pachysandra terminalis
JAPANESE SPURGE
1–10, 14–21, 31–43 — p. 412

Parthenocissus quinquefolia
VIRGINIA CREEPER
1–24, 26–43 — p. 416

Passiflora
PASSION VINE
ZONES VARY — p. 417

Paxistima canbyi
1–10, 14–21, 32–43 — p. 418

Pelargonium peltatum
IVY GERANIUM
8, 9, 12–24 — p. 423

Penstemon (low-growing)
BEARD TONGUE
ZONES VARY — p. 424

Phlox (mat-forming)
ZONES VARY — p. 428

Polygonum (several)
KNOTWEED
NEEDS, ZONES VARY — p. 444

Potentilla (several)
CINQUEFOIL
ZONES VARY — p. 447

Pratia angulata
4–9, 14–24 — p. 448

Prunella
SELF-HEAL
1–24, 29–43 — p. 450

Pulmonaria (several)
LUNGWORT
1–9, 14–17, 32–43 — p. 457

Lysimachia nummularia

Nepeta faassenii

Ophiopogon japonicus

Oenothera berlandieri 'Siskiyou'

Phlox subulata

Plant listings continue ▶

Potentilla

Rosmarinus officinalis 'Prostratus'

Pratia angulata

Sarcococca hookerana humilis

Soleirolia soleirolii

Pyracantha (low-growing)
FIRETHORN
ZONES VARY **p. 458**

Ranunculus repens 'Pleniflorus'
CREEPING BUTTERCUP
MANY ZONES **p. 462**

Rhoicissus capensis
EVERGREEN GRAPE
16, 17, 21–25 **p. 471**

Rhus aromatica 'Gro-low'
1–3, 10, 31–43 **p. 471**

Rosa (some)
NEEDS, ZONES VARY **p. 473**

Rosmarinus officinalis (low)
ROSEMARY
4–24, 26–32 **p. 480**

Rubus pentalobus
4–6, 14–17, 31, 32 **p. 481**

Santolina
MANY ZONES **p. 488**

Saponaria ocymoides
1–11, 14–24, 33–45 **p. 489**

Sarcococca hookerana humilis
SWEET BOX
3–9, 14–24, 31, 32 **p. 489**

Saxifraga
SAXIFRAGE
NEEDS, ZONES VARY **p. 490**

Scaevola
8, 9, 14–24 **p. 490**

Sedum (many)
STONECROP
NEEDS, ZONES VARY **p. 493**

Senecio serpens
16, 17, 21–24 **p. 495**

Soleirolia soleirolii
BABY'S TEARS
4–27 **p. 499**

Sollya heterophylla
AUSTRALIAN BLUEBELL CREEPER
8, 9, 14–28 **p. 500**

Stachys byzantina
LAMB'S EARS
1–24, 29–43 **p. 504**

Stephanandra incisa 'Crispa'
1–6, 32–43 **p. 505**

Tanacetum densum amanii
3–24 **p. 514**

Taxus baccata 'Repandens'
SPREADING ENGLISH YEW
3–9, 14–24, 32–33 **p. 515**

Teucrium chamaedrys
GERMANDER
3–24, 28–34, 39 **p. 517**

Thymus
THYME
ZONES VARY **p. 519**

Tolmiea menziesii
PIGGY-BACK PLANT
MANY ZONES **p. 521**

Trachelospermum
STAR JASMINE
ZONES VARY **p. 523**

Vaccinium vitis-idaea
COWBERRY
MANY ZONES **p. 530**

Verbena
ZONES VARY **p. 531**

Veronica (several)
SPEEDWELL
NEEDS, ZONES VARY **p. 532**

Vinca
PERIWINKLE
ZONES VARY **p. 534**

Viola (several)
VIOLET
NEEDS, ZONES VARY **p. 534**

Waldsteinia fragarioides
BARREN STRAWBERRY
2–9, 14–17, 32–41 **p. 536**

WALK-ON LAWN SUBSTITUTES

Carex flacca
BLUE SEDGE
1–9, 14–24, 28–45 **p. 230**

Chamaemelum nobile
CHAMOMILE
1–24, 30–43 **p. 242**

Dichondra micrantha
8–10, 12–24, 28 **p. 279**

Hippocrepis comosa
(mat-forming)
8–26 **p. 336**

Phyla nodiflora
LIPPIA
8–29 **p. 430**

Sagina subulata
IRISH MOSS, SCOTCH MOSS
1–11, 14–24, 32–43 **p. 483**

Zoysia tenuifolia
KOREAN GRASS
7–10, 12–34 **p. 544**

Stachys byzantina

Teucrium chamaedrys

Thymus praecox arcticus

Vinca minor

Chamaemelum nobile

For growing symbol explanations, please see page 79.

Bougainvillea and nasturtium

VINES
and Vinelike Plants

Vines are some of the most tractable of plants. Unlike shrubs and trees, which have fairly rigid stems, the flexible stems of most vines can be guided to grow where you want them. You can train a vine to grow upward or outward (or both) on a flat, vertical surface; up and around a post or tree trunk; or up and over a pergola. Many will perform alternative duty as a ground cover.

Though vines are all tractable and long-limbed, they climb in different manners: some with tendrils, some by twining, some by clinging. Some have no means of attachment at all; they will climb only if you tie them to a support.

Lonicera sempervirens

Clytostoma callistegioides

Distictis buccinatoria

EVERGREEN

Plant	Common name	Showy	Zones	Page
Allamanda cathartica	GOLDEN TRUMPET	✲	24–27	p. 173
Beaumontia grandiflora	EASTER LILY VINE	✲	MANY ZONES	p. 205
Bignonia capreolata	CROSSVINE	✲	4–9, 14–24, 26–33	p. 209
Bougainvillea			MANY ZONES	p. 212
Cissus		✲	NEEDS, ZONES VARY	p. 249
Clematis armandii	EVERGREEN CLEMATIS	✲	4–9, 12–24, 28, 31, 32	p. 254
Clerodendrum thomsoniae	BLEEDING HEART GLORYBOWER	✲	22–28	p. 255
Clytostoma callistegioides	VIOLET TRUMPET VINE	✲	9, 12–28	p. 256
Distictis	TRUMPET VINE	✲	ZONES VARY	p. 282
Euonymus fortunei			3–17, 28–41	p. 298
Fatshedera lizei			4–10, 12–31	p. 303
Ficus pumila	CREEPING FIG	✲	8–28	p. 305
Gelsemium sempervirens	CAROLINA JESSAMINE		8–24, 26–33	p. 314
Hedera (many)	IVY	✲	ZONES VARY	p. 328
Jasminum (several)	JASMINE	✲	ZONES VARY	p. 351
Lonicera (several)	HONEYSUCKLE	✲	ZONES VARY	p. 376
Macfadyena unguis-cati	CAT'S CLAW	✲	8–29, 31	p. 380
Mandevilla 'Alice du Pont'			21–25	p. 391
Mandevilla splendens			21–25	p. 391
Pandorea		✲	16–27	p. 414
Passiflora	PASSION VINE	✲	ZONES VARY	p. 417
Petrea volubilis	QUEEN'S WREATH	✲	19–25	p. 426
Plumbago auriculata	CAPE PLUMBAGO	✲	8, 9, 12–28	p. 441
Podranea ricasoliana	PINK TRUMPET VINE	✲	9, 12, 13, 19–27	p. 443
Polygonum aubertii	SILVER LACE VINE	✲	2–24, 28–41	p. 444

SYMBOLS: ✲ indicates vines that bear showy flowers; ⟲ indicates perennial vines that are grown as annuals.

Lonicera heckrottii

Pandorea jasminoides

Passiflora caerulea

Plant listings continue ▸

Stephanotis floribunda

Thunbergia gregorii

Trachelospermum jasminoides

Akebia quinata

Parthenocissus tricuspidata

Wisteria floribunda

Ipomoea

Tropaeolum majus

Tropaeolum peregrinum

Pyrostegia venusta
FLAME VINE ☼
☀ ◐ ◉ ✂ 13, 16, 21–27　**p. 459**

Rhoicissus capensis
EVERGREEN GRAPE
☀ ◉ ✂ 16, 17, 21–25　**p. 471**

Senecio confusus
MEXICAN FLAME VINE ☼
☀ ◐ ◉ ✂ 13, 16–28　**p. 495**

Solandra maxima
CUP-OF-GOLD VINE ☼
☀ ◉ ✂ 17, 21–27　**p. 499**

Solanum jasminoides
POTATO VINE ☼
☀ ◐ ◉ ◉ ✂ 8, 9, 12–27　**p. 499**

Stephanotis floribunda
MADAGASCAR JASMINE ☼
◐ ◉ ✂ 23–25　**p. 505**

Tecomaria capensis
CAPE HONEYSUCKLE ☼
☀ ◐ ◉ ◉ ✂ 12, 13, 16, 18–28　**p. 516**

Thunbergia ☼
☀ ◐ ◉ ✂ ZONES VARY　**p. 519**

Trachelospermum
STAR JASMINE ☼
☀ ◐ ◉ ◉ ✂ ZONES VARY　**p. 523**

DECIDUOUS

Actinidia
KIWI
☀ ◐ ◉ ◉ ✂ ZONES VARY　**p. 167**

Akebia quinata
FIVELEAF AKEBIA ☼
☀ ◐ ◉ ◉ ✂ 3–24, 29–41　**p. 172**

Ampelopsis brevipedunculata
PORCELAIN BERRY
☀ ◐ ◉ ◉ ◉ ✂ 2–24, 28–41　**p. 177**

Antigonon leptopus
QUEEN'S WREATH ☼
☀ ◉ ◉ ✂ 12, 13, 18–30　**p. 181**

Aristolochia durior
DUTCHMAN'S PIPE ☼
☀ ◉ ◉ ◐ ◉ ✂ 1–24, 29–43　**p. 190**

Campsis
TRUMPET VINE ☼
☀ ◐ ◉ ◉ ◉ ✂ ZONES VARY　**p. 227**

Celastrus
BITTERSWEET
☀ ◉ ✂ ZONES VARY　**p. 236**

Clematis (most) ☼
☀ ◉ ✂ ZONES VARY　**p. 253**

Grape
☀ ◉ ✂ ZONES VARY　**p. 320**

Humulus lupulus
COMMON HOP ☼
☀ ◉ ✂ 1–24, 28–45　**p. 339**

Hydrangea anomala
CLIMBING HYDRANGEA ☼
☀ ◐ ◉ ✂ 2–21, 31–41　**p. 340**

Ipomoea
MORNING GLORY ☼
☀ ◉ ◉ ✂ ZONES VARY　**p. 346**

Lonicera (some)
HONEYSUCKLE ☼
☀ ◐ ◉ ✂ ZONES VARY　**p. 376**

Mandevilla laxa
CHILEAN JASMINE ☼
☀ ◐ ◉ ◉ ✂ MANY ZONES　**p. 391**

Parthenocissus
☀ ◐ ◉ ◉ ✂ ZONES VARY　**p. 416**

Passiflora (some)
PASSION VINE ☼
☀ ◉ ◉ ✂ ZONES VARY　**p. 417**

Rosa (climbers)
ROSE ☼
NEEDS, ZONES VARY　**p. 473**

Schizophragma hydrangeoides
JAPANESE HYDRANGEA VINE
☀ ◉ ◉ ✂ 4–9, 14–17, 31–34, 39　**p. 492**

Solanum wendlandii
COSTA RICAN NIGHTSHADE ☼
☀ ◐ ◉ ◉ ◉ ✂ 16, 21–25　**p. 499**

Wisteria ☼
☀ ◉ ◉ ✂ ZONES VARY　**p. 538**

ANNUALS

Asarina
CLIMBING SNAPDRAGON ☼
☀ ◐ ◉ ◉ ✂ ALL ZONES　**p. 193**

Bean, scarlet runner ☼
☀ ◉ ✂ ALL ZONES　**p. 205**

Cobaea scandens
CUP-AND-SAUCER VINE ☼
☀ ◉ ✂ ALL ZONES　**p. 257**

Dolichos lablab
HYACINTH BEAN ☼
☀ ◉ ✂ ALL ZONES　**p. 283**

Ipomoea (some)
MORNING GLORY ☼
☀ ◉ ◉ ✂ ZONES VARY　**p. 346**

Lathyrus odoratus
SWEET PEA ☼
☀ ◉ ✂ ALL ZONES　**p. 364**

Tropaeolum
NASTURTIUM ☼
NEEDS VARY, ALL ZONES　**p. 525**

For growing symbol explanations, please see page 79.

Clematis

Nandina domestica

Chaenomeles

Plants for
HEDGES AND SCREENS

Plants that maintain dense foliage from top to bottom are good candidates for providing a screen in your landscape. Some are knee-high shrublets, mainly useful for edging a walk or path; others are large shrubby trees that, grouped closely, can block an objectionable view or direct your attention to a focal point in the garden. Shearing can transform some of these plants into formal hedges.

SYMBOL: ♦♦♦ indicates plants that can be clipped into formal hedges.

Buxus

DECIDUOUS

Acanthopanax sieboldianus 'Variegatus'
☼ ◐ ● ♦ ♦ ♦ MANY ZONES **p. 163**

Acer campestre
HEDGE MAPLE
☼ ◐ ♦ ♦ 2–9, 14, 31–41 **p. 164**

Berberis thunbergii
JAPANESE BARBERRY
☼ ◐ ♦ ♦ ♦ 1–24, 28–41 **p. 208**

Caragana arborescens ♦♦♦
SIBERIAN PEASHRUB
☼ ♦ ♦ 1–12, 35–45 **p. 230**

Carpinus betulus ♦♦♦
EUROPEAN HORNBEAM
☼ ◐ ♦ ♦ 3–9, 14–17, 31–41 **p. 231**

Chaenomeles
FLOWERING QUINCE
☼ ♦ ♦ ♦ 2–21, 28–41 **p. 240**

Crataegus monogyna ♦♦♦
HAWTHORN
☼ ♦ ♦ 2–12, 14–17, 28, 30–41 **p. 267**

Elaeagnus angustifolia
RUSSIAN OLIVE
☼ ◐ ♦ ♦ ♦ MANY ZONES **p. 287**

Euonymus (some) ♦♦♦
NEEDS, ZONES VARY **p. 298**

Fagus sylvatica
EUROPEAN BEECH
☼ ◐ ♦ ♦ ♦ MANY ZONES **p. 302**

Hippophae rhamnoides
SEA BUCKTHORN
☼ ♦ ♦ ♦ 1–5, 34, 37–45 **p. 336**

Ligustrum (some) ♦♦♦
PRIVET
☼ ◐ ♦ ♦ ZONES VARY **p. 369**

Lonicera (shrubs)
HONEYSUCKLE
☼ ◐ ♦ ♦ ZONES VARY **p. 376**

Maclura pomifera
OSAGE ORANGE
☼ ♦ ♦ ♦ 2, 3, 10–13, 29–41 **p. 381**

Rhamnus frangula 'Columnaris' ♦♦♦
TALLHEDGE BUCKTHORN
☼ ◐ ♦ ♦ 1–7, 10, 11, 32–45 **p. 464**

Rosa (shrub)
ROSE
NEEDS, ZONES VARY **p. 473**

Salix purpurea 'Gracilis'
DWARF PURPLE OSIER
☼ ♦ ♦ ♦ 1–11, 34–43 **p. 484**

Viburnum opulus 'Nanum'
EUROPEAN CRANBERRY BUSH
☼ ◐ ♦ ♦ 1–9, 14–24, 29–43 **p. 533**

Weigela
☼ ◐ ♦ ♦ 1–11, 14–17, 32–41 **p. 538**

EVERGREEN

Abelia grandiflora
GLOSSY ABELIA
☼ ◐ ♦ ♦ 4–24, 28–35 **p. 162**

Bamboo (many)
☼ ◐ ♦ ♦ ♦ ZONES VARY **p. 199**

Berberis (some)
BARBERRY
☼ ◐ ♦ ♦ ♦ ZONES VARY **p. 207**

Buxus ♦♦♦
BOXWOOD
☼ ◐ ● ♦ ♦ ZONES VARY **p. 218**

Callistemon citrinus ♦♦♦
LEMON BOTTLEBRUSH
☼ ♦ ♦ ♦ 8, 9, 12–28 **p. 222**

Calocedrus decurrens
INCENSE CEDAR
☼ ◐ ♦ ♦ MANY ZONES **p. 223**

Carissa ♦♦♦
☼ ◐ ♦ ♦ 22–27 **p. 230**

Elaeagnus angustifolia

Rosa 'Showbiz'

Callistemon citrinus

Abelia grandiflora

Plant listings continue ▶

Elaeagnus pungens

Feijoa sellowiana

Hibiscus rosa-sinensis

Ilex

Leptospermum

Ligustrum japonicum

Myrtus communis

Chamaecyparis lawsoniana (several)
☼ ◐ ◑ ⚡ MANY ZONES **p. 241**

Citrus
☼ ◑ ⚡ 8, 9, 12–27 **p. 250**

Cotoneaster (some)
☼ ◑ ⚡ ZONES VARY **p. 265**

Cupressocyparis leylandii ♠♠♠
☼ ◐ ◑ ⚡ 3–24, 26, 28–34, 39 **p. 270**

Elaeagnus (some) ♠♠♠
☼ ◐ ◑ ◑ ⚡ ZONES VARY **p. 287**

Euonymus (most) ♠♠♠
NEEDS, ZONES VARY **p. 298**

Feijoa sellowiana
PINEAPPLE GUAVA
☼ ◑ ⚡ 7–9, 12–32 **p. 303**

Gardenia jasminoides
☼ ◐ ◑ ⚡ MANY ZONES **p. 312**

Hibiscus rosa-sinensis
CHINESE HIBISCUS
☼ ◑ ⚡ 9, 12, 13, 15, 16, 19–26 **p. 335**

Ilex ♠♠♠
HOLLY
☼ ◐ ◑ ⚡ ZONES VARY **p. 343**

Juniperus (shrub, columnar) ♠♠♠
JUNIPER
☼ ◐ ◑ ◑ ⚡ ZONES VARY **p. 353**

Laurus nobilis ♠♠♠
SWEET BAY
☼ ◐ ◑ ⚡ 5–9, 12–24 **p. 365**

Leptospermum (most) ♠♠♠
TEA TREE
☼ ◑ ⚡ ZONES VARY **p. 366**

Leucophyllum frutescens
TEXAS RANGER
☼ ◑ ⚡ 7–24, 28–32, 35 **p. 367**

Ligustrum (some) ♠♠♠
PRIVET
☼ ◑ ◑ ⚡ ZONES VARY **p. 369**

Mahonia (tall)
NEEDS, ZONES VARY **p. 386**

Murraya paniculata
ORANGE JESSAMINE
☼ ◐ ◑ ◑ ⚡ 21–27 **p. 399**

Myrtus communis ♠♠♠
TRUE MYRTLE
☼ ◐ ◑ ⚡ 8–24, 26–28 **p. 401**

Nandina domestica
HEAVENLY BAMBOO
☼ ◐ ◑ ◑ ◑ ⚡ 4–33 **p. 402**

Nerium oleander
OLEANDER
☼ ◑ ◑ ⚡ 8–16, 18–31 **p. 405**

Osmanthus (several)
☼ ◐ ◑ ◑ ⚡ ZONES VARY **p. 410**

Photinia
☼ ◐ ◑ ◑ ⚡ ZONES VARY **p. 430**

Pittosporum tobira ♠♠♠
TOBIRA
☼ ◐ ◑ ◑ ◑ ⚡ 8–31 **p. 438**

Podocarpus
☼ ◐ ◑ ◑ ⚡ ZONES VARY **p. 442**

Prunus (evergreen) ♠♠♠
☼ ◑ ◑ ⚡ ZONES VARY **p. 451**

Pyracantha
FIRETHORN
☼ ◐ ◑ ⚡ ZONES VARY **p. 458**

Rhamnus alaternus ♠♠♠
ITALIAN BUCKTHORN
☼ ◐ ◑ ◑ ⚡ 4–24, 31, 32 **p. 464**

Rhaphiolepis
☼ ◐ ◑ ◑ ⚡ MANY ZONES **p. 464**

Rosmarinus officinalis ♠♠♠
ROSEMARY
☼ ◑ ⚡ 4–24, 26–32 **p. 480**

Syzygium paniculatum ♠♠♠
BRUSH CHERRY
☼ ◐ ◑ ⚡ 16, 17, 19–25 **p. 513**

Taxus ♠♠♠
YEW
☼ ◐ ◑ ◑ ⚡ ZONES VARY **p. 515**

Tecoma stans
YELLOW BELLS
☼ ◑ ◑ ⚡ 10, 12, 13, 21–28 **p. 516**

Tecomaria capensis
CAPE HONEYSUCKLE
☼ ◐ ◑ ◑ ◑ ⚡ 12, 13, 16, 18–28 **p. 516**

Teucrium fruticans
BUSH GERMANDER
☼ ◑ ⚡ 4–24 **p. 517**

Thevetia
☼ ◑ ◑ ⚡ ZONES VARY **p. 518**

Thuja ♠♠♠
ARBORVITAE
☼ ◐ ◑ ◑ ◑ ⚡ ZONES VARY **p. 518**

Tsuga canadensis ♠♠♠
CANADA HEMLOCK
☼ ◐ ◑ ⚡ 3–7, 17, 32–43 **p. 526**

Viburnum (several)
NEEDS, ZONES VARY **p. 532**

Nerium oleander

Photinia fraseri

Tecomaria capensis

Tsuga canadensis

Viburnum tinus

For growing symbol explanations, please see page 79.

Woodland at Butchart Gardens

TREES

Acer davidii

The best trees are well suited to their sites. Patio trees are generally small, as trees go, and look good at close range. Many have showy flowers, fruit, or both; some have striking fall foliage or decorative bark. All are well-mannered: root systems are not likely to crack pavement; branches do not shed lots of leaves or drop messy fruit. All patio trees are fine candidates for garden planting, but the list of garden trees includes others of moderate size that fail to meet all the patio criteria. Some may shed leaves or fruit that would require frequent cleanup on a patio but pose no problem in a garden. Others may have roots that interfere with paving or other plantings.

Large landscape trees are generally too massive for small gardens but are worth planting on larger properties where their majesty can be appreciated.

Acer griseum

Bauhinia blakeana

PATIO TREES
Deciduous

Acer buergeranum
TRIDENT MAPLE
☼ ☼ ◐ ♦ ⚡ MANY ZONES   **p. 164**

Acer davidii
DAVID'S MAPLE
☼ ☼ ◐ ♦ ⚡ MANY ZONES   **p. 164**

Acer ginnala
AMUR MAPLE
☼ ☼ ◐ ♦ ⚡ MANY ZONES   **p. 164**

Acer griseum
PAPERBARK MAPLE
☼ ☼ ◐ ♦ ⚡ MANY ZONES   **p. 164**

Acer palmatum
JAPANESE MAPLE
☼ ☼ ◐ ♦ ⚡ MANY ZONES   **p. 165**

Acer pentaphyllum
☼ ☼ ◐ ♦ ⚡ MANY ZONES   **p. 165**

Acer truncatum
☼ ☼ ◐ ♦ ⚡ MANY ZONES   **p. 166**

Amelanchier
SERVICEBERRY
☼ ☼ ◐ ♦ ♦ ⚡ 1–6, 31–45   **p. 177**

Bauhinia blakeana
HONG KONG ORCHID TREE
☼ ◐ ♦ ⚡ 13, 19, 21, 23, 25–27   **p. 204**

Bauhinia forficata
BRAZILIAN BUTTERFLY TREE
☼ ☼ ◐ ♦ ♦ ⚡ 9, 12–23, 25–28   **p. 204**

Bauhinia variegata
PURPLE ORCHID TREE
☼ ◐ ♦ ⚡ 13, 18–23, 25–27   **p. 204**

Cercis
REDBUD
☼ ☼ ◐ ♦ ⚡ ZONES VARY   **p. 239**

Chilopsis linearis
DESERT WILLOW
☼ ◐ ♦ ⚡ 10–13, 18–21, 29, 30, 33   **p. 244**

Chionanthus
FRINGE TREE
☼ ◐ ♦ ⚡ ZONES VARY   **p. 244**

Chitalpa tashkentensis
CHITALPA
☼ ◐ ♦ ⚡ 3–24, 28–33   **p. 245**

Chorisia speciosa
☼ ◐ ♦ ⚡ 12–25, 26, 27   **p. 246**

Cladrastis lutea
YELLOW WOOD
☼ ◐ ♦ ⚡ 1–9, 14–16, 31–43   **p. 253**

Cornus florida
FLOWERING DOGWOOD
☼ ☼ ◐ ♦ ⚡ MANY ZONES   **p. 262**

Cornus kousa
KOUSA DOGWOOD
☼ ☼ ◐ ♦ ⚡ MANY ZONES   **p. 262**

Corylus (some)
FILBERT, HAZELNUT
☼ ☼ ◐ ♦ ⚡ ZONES VARY   **p. 264**

Cotinus coggygria
SMOKE TREE
☼ ◐ ♦ ⚡ 2–24, 29–41   **p. 265**

Crataegus
HAWTHORN
☼ ◐ ♦ ⚡ 2–12, 14–17, 28, 30–41   **p. 266**

Davidia involucrata
DOVE TREE
☼ ☼ ◐ ♦ ⚡ MANY ZONES   **p. 276**

Erythrina (most)
CORAL TREE
☼ ◐ ♦ ⚡ ZONES VARY   **p. 295**

Franklinia alatamaha
☼ ☼ ◐ ♦ ⚡ 3–6, 14–17, 31–35   **p. 309**

SYMBOL: 🌿 indicates plants whose roots may be invasive or break concrete.

Chilopsis linearis

Chionanthus retusus

Chitalpa tashkentensis

Plant listings continue ▶

Cotinus coggygria

Erythrina falcata

Lagerstroemia indica

Prunus

Laurus nobilis 'Saratoga'

Halesia carolina
SILVER BELL
☼ ◐ ♦ ✂ MANY ZONES   p. 326

Koelreuteria
☼ ♦ ♦ ✂ ZONES VARY   p. 360

Lagerstroemia indica hybrids
CRAPE MYRTLE
☼ ♦ ♦ ✂ MANY ZONES   p. 362

Magnolia (small)
☼ ◐ ♦ ✂ ZONES VARY   p. 381

Malus
CRABAPPLE
☼ ♦ ♦ ♦ ✂ 1–21, 29–43   p. 387

Oxydendrum arboreum
SOURWOOD
☼ ♦ ♦ ✂ MANY ZONES   p. 412

Parrotia persica
PERSIAN PARROTIA
☼ ♦ ♦ ✂ 3–6, 15–17, 31–41   p. 416

Prunus
FLOWERING CHERRY
☼ ♦ ♦ ✂ ZONES VARY   p. 451

Prunus cerasifera 'Purple Pony'
☼ ♦ ♦ ♦ ✂ MANY ZONES   p. 454

Prunus mume
JAPANESE FLOWERING PLUM
☼ ♦ ♦ ✂ 2–9, 12–22, 31–34, 39   p. 454

Pyrus salicifolia 'Pendula'
WEEPING WILLOW–LEAFED PEAR
☼ ♦ ✂ 2–9, 14–21, 32–41   p. 459

Sapium sebiferum
CHINESE TALLOW TREE
☼ ♦ ✂ MANY ZONES   p. 488

Stewartia (small)
☼ ◐ ♦ ✂ ZONES VARY   p. 506

Tabebuia
☼ ◐ ♦ ✂ 15, 16, 20–26   p. 513

PATIO TREES
Evergreen

Cassia leptophylla
GOLD MEDALLION TREE
☼ ♦ ♦ ✂ 21–25, 27   p. 233

Citrus
☼ ♦ ✂ 8, 9, 12–27   p. 250

Cordia boissieri
TEXAS OLIVE
☼ ♦ ♦ ✂ 8–28   p. 260

Eriobotrya deflexa
BRONZE LOQUAT
☼ ◐ ♦ ✂ 8–28   p. 291

Laurus nobilis 'Saratoga'
SWEET BAY
☼ ◐ ♦ ✂ 5–9, 12–24   p. 365

Leptospermum laevigatum
AUSTRALIAN TEA TREE
☼ ♦ ✂ 14–24   p. 366

Ligustrum lucidum
GLOSSY PRIVET
☼ ◐ ♦ ✂ 5, 6, 8–31   p. 369

Melaleuca quinquenervia
CAJEPUT TREE
☼ ♦ ✂ 9, 13, 15–17, 20–27   p. 393

Michelia doltsopa
◐ ♦ ✂ 14–28   p. 396

Nerium oleander
OLEANDER
☼ ♦ ♦ ✂ 8–16, 18–31   p. 405

Olea europaea (fruitless)
OLIVE
☼ ♦ ✂ 8, 9, 11–24   p. 408

Osmanthus fragrans
SWEET OLIVE
☼ ◐ ♦ ♦ ✂ MANY ZONES   p. 411

Palms (some)
NEEDS, ZONES VARY   p. 413

Photinia fraseri
REDTIP
☼ ♦ ♦ ✂ MANY ZONES   p. 430

Pittosporum tobira
TOBIRA
☼ ◐ ♦ ♦ ✂ 8–31   p. 438

Podocarpus gracilior
FERN PINE
☼ ◐ ♦ ♦ ✂ MANY ZONES   p. 442

Pyrus kawakamii
EVERGREEN PEAR
☼ ♦ ✂ 8, 9, 12–24   p. 459

Rhaphiolepis 'Majestic Beauty'
☼ ◐ ♦ ♦ ✂ MANY ZONES   p. 465

Rhus lancea
AFRICAN SUMAC
☼ ♦ ♦ ✂ 8, 9, 12–24, 29   p. 471

Schefflera actinophylla
QUEENSLAND UMBRELLA TREE
☼ ◐ ♦ ✂ 21–25, 27   p. 491

Schefflera pueckleri
☼ ◐ ♦ ✂ 19–25, 27   p. 491

Schinus terebinthifolius
BRAZILIAN PEPPER TREE
☼ ♦ ✂ 13, 14, 15–17, 19–27   p. 491

Thevetia thevetioides
GIANT THEVETIA
☼ ♦ ✂ MANY ZONES   p. 518

Sapium sebiferum

Cassia leptophylla

Nerium oleander

Thevetia thevetioides

Albizia julibrissin

For growing symbol explanations, please see page 79.

Brachychiton acerifolius

Laburnum

Magnolia soulangiana

Persimmon

SMALL TO MEDIUM GARDEN TREES
Deciduous

Albizia julibrissin
SILK TREE
☼ ◐ ♦ ⚡ 4–23, 26–33   **p. 172**

Betula ↻
BIRCH
☼ ♦ ♦♦ ⚡ ZONES VARY   **p. 208**

Brachychiton

☼ ♦ ♦ ⚡ ZONES VARY   **p. 214**

Carpinus
HORNBEAM
NEEDS, ZONES VARY   **p. 231**

Celtis
HACKBERRY
☼ ◐ ♦ ⚡ ZONES VARY   **p. 237**

Cercidiphyllum japonicum
KATSURA TREE
☼ ◐ ♦ ⚡ MANY ZONES   **p. 239**

Chilopsis linearis
DESERT WILLOW
☼ ♦ ⚡ MANY ZONES   **p. 244**

Fraxinus angustifolia 'Raywood'
RAYWOOD ASH
☼ ♦ ♦ ⚡ 3–9, 12–24, 29, 30   **p. 309**

Fraxinus holotricha

☼ ♦ ♦ ⚡ 4–24, 28–35, 37, 39   **p. 309**

Gleditsia triacanthos ↻
HONEY LOCUST
☼ ♦ ♦ ⚡ 1–16, 18–20, 32–43   **p. 318**

Laburnum
GOLDENCHAIN TREE
☼ ◐ ♦ ⚡ MANY ZONES   **p. 361**

Magnolia (many)

☼ ◐ ♦ ♦ ⚡ ZONES VARY   **p. 381**

Morus alba ↻
WHITE MULBERRY
☼ ♦ ♦ ⚡ 2–24, 26–41   **p. 399**

Nyssa sylvatica
SOUR GUM
☼ ◐ ♦ ♦ ⚡ MANY ZONES   **p. 407**

Parkinsonia aculeata
MEXICAN PALO VERDE
☼ ♦ ♦ ⚡ 8–29   **p. 415**

Persimmon

☼ ♦ ♦ ⚡ ZONES VARY   **p. 425**

Populus tremuloides ↻
QUAKING ASPEN
☼ ♦ ⚡ 1–7, 14–21, 32–45   **p. 446**

Prunus
FLOWERING PEACH
☼ ♦ ♦ ⚡ 2–24, 30–34, 39   **p. 451**

Punica granatum
POMEGRANATE
☼ ♦ ♦ ⚡ 5–32   **p. 457**

Pyrus calleryana
ORNAMENTAL PEAR
☼ ♦ ⚡ MANY ZONES   **p. 459**

Sophora japonica
JAPANESE PAGODA TREE
☼ ◐ ♦ ⚡ 2–24, 31–41   **p. 500**

Sorbus aucuparia
EUROPEAN MOUNTAIN ASH
☼ ◐ ♦ ♦ ⚡ MANY ZONES   **p. 500**

Stewartia pseudocamellia
☼ ◐ ♦ ⚡ MANY ZONES   **p. 506**

Styrax
☼ ◐ ♦ ⚡ ZONES VARY   **p. 509**

Tilia cordata
LITTLE-LEAF LINDEN
☼ ♦ ♦ ⚡ 1–17, 32–43   **p. 520**

Tilia euchlora
CRIMEAN LINDEN
☼ ♦ ♦ ⚡ 1–17, 32–43   **p. 520**

Tipuana tipu
TIPU TREE
☼ ♦ ⚡ MANY ZONES   **p. 521**

Vitex agnus-castus
CHASTE TREE
☼ ♦ ⚡ 4–33   **p. 535**

SMALL TO MEDIUM GARDEN TREES
Evergreen

Acacia baileyana
BAILEY ACACIA
☼ ♦ ⚡ 7–9, 13–24, 26–28   **p. 163**

Acacia smallii

☼ ♦ ⚡ 8, 9, 12–29   **p. 163**

Brugmansia
ANGEL'S TRUMPET
☼ ◐ ● ♦ ⚡ 16–27   **p. 216**

Callistemon citrinus
LEMON BOTTLEBRUSH
☼ ♦ ♦ ⚡ 8, 9, 12–28   **p. 222**

Callistemon viminalis
WEEPING BOTTLEBRUSH
☼ ♦ ♦ ⚡ 8, 9, 12–28   **p. 222**

Cornus capitata
EVERGREEN DOGWOOD
☼ ◐ ♦ ♦ ⚡ 8, 9, 14–20, 31   **p. 262**

Eriobotrya japonica
LOQUAT
☼ ◐ ♦ ♦ ⚡ 4–31   **p. 291**

Erythrina falcata

☼ ♦ ♦ ⚡ 19–25, 27   **p. 295**

Brugmansia

Populus tremuloides

Styrax japonicus

Tilia cordata

Callistemon citrinus

Plant listings continue ▶

159

Cornus capitata

Acer rubrum

Ginkgo biloba

Jacaranda mimosifolia

Ficus benjamina
WEEPING CHINESE BANYAN
13, 23–25, 27   **p. 305**

Ficus microcarpa
INDIAN LAUREL FIG
9, 13, 16–25, 27   **p. 305**

Ficus rubiginosa
RUSTYLEAF FIG
18–27   **p. 305**

Ilex (many)
HOLLY
ZONES VARY   **p. 343**

Lagunaria patersonii
PRIMROSE TREE
13, 15–26   **p. 362**

Magnolia (some)
ZONES VARY   **p. 381**

Melaleuca linariifolia
FLAXLEAF PAPERBARK
9, 13–24   **p. 393**

Prunus caroliniana
CAROLINA LAUREL CHERRY
7–24, 26–31, 32   **p. 451**

Sapindus drummondii
WESTERN SOAPBERRY
MANY ZONES   **p. 488**

LARGE LANDSCAPE TREES
Deciduous

Acer rubrum
SCARLET MAPLE
MANY ZONES   **p. 165**

Carya ovata
SHAGBARK HICKORY
1–6, 28–44   **p. 232**

Fagus sylvatica
EUROPEAN BEECH
MANY ZONES   **p. 302**

Ginkgo biloba
MAIDENHAIR TREE
MANY ZONES   **p. 317**

Gymnocladus dioica
KENTUCKY COFFEE TREE
MANY ZONES   **p. 325**

Jacaranda mimosifolia
JACARANDA
12, 13, 15–25, 27   **p. 351**

Liquidambar
SWEET GUM
ZONES VARY   **p. 373**

Liriodendron tulipifera
TULIP TREE
1–12, 14–23, 26, 28–41   **p. 373**

Pistacia chinensis
CHINESE PISTACHE
4–16, 18–23, 26, 28–33   **p. 437**

Platanus
SYCAMORE
ZONES VARY   **p. 438**

Quercus acutissima
SAWTOOTH OAK
2–7, 29–41   **p. 460**

Quercus (many)
OAK
ZONES VARY   **p. 459**

Robinia ambigua 'Idahoensis'
IDAHO LOCUST
1–24, 29–45   **p. 473**

Robinia pseudoacacia
BLACK LOCUST
1–24, 29–45   **p. 473**

Zelkova serrata
SAWLEAF ZELKOVA
3–21, 28–35, 37, 39   **p. 542**

LARGE LANDSCAPE TREES
Evergreen

Castanospermum australe
MORETON BAY CHESTNUT
18–22, 25–27   **p. 233**

Cedrus
CEDAR
ZONES VARY   **p. 236**

Cinnamomum camphora
CAMPHOR TREE
8, 9, 12–28   **p. 249**

Pinus nigra
AUSTRIAN BLACK PINE
MANY ZONES   **p. 436**

Pinus thunbergiana
JAPANESE BLACK PINE
MANY ZONES   **p. 437**

Pinus wallichiana
HIMALAYAN WHITE PINE
MANY ZONES   **p. 437**

Quercus ilex
HOLLY OAK
4–24, 32   **p. 460**

Quercus laurifolia
LAUREL OAK
25–33   **p. 461**

Quercus suber
CORK OAK
5–7, 8–16, 18–23   **p. 461**

Quercus virginiana
SOUTHERN LIVE OAK
4–31   **p. 461**

Sequoia sempervirens
COAST REDWOOD
4–9, 14–24, 32   **p. 495**

Tsuga canadensis
CANADA HEMLOCK
3–7, 17, 32–43   **p. 526**

Liquidambar

Robinia ambigua 'Idahoensis'

Cinnamomum camphora

Quercus suber

For growing symbol explanations, please see page 79.

The A to Z Plant
ENCYCLOPEDIA

Paeonia
Double Type

This encyclopedia describes a wide spectrum of plants—from majestic trees to small, gemlike perennials for rock gardens, from familiar summer annuals to such oddities as the succulent baseball plant. Many of the more than 6,000 plants included here are widely available; others are common in some regions, rare elsewhere.

Plants are listed alphabetically by scientific name (genus and species). Common fruits, vegetables, and berries are an exception; these are listed by common name (apple or pumpkin, for example). If you know only a common name, look that up—either in the plant encyclopedia or in the Index of Scientific and Common Names (pages 639–653)—to find a reference to the plant entry.

The scientific names we use are based on *Hortus Third* (New York: Macmillan, 1976) and the more recent *New Royal Horticultural Society Dictionary of Gardening* (London: Macmillan; New York: Stockton Press, 1992). Where the two authorities differ, we give both names with cross-references. We also have consulted local plant indexes. Although some scientific names may not be familiar to every reader, their use makes it easier for gardeners to speak a common language. (For help in understanding scientific names, see pages 632–633).

The sample entry below illustrates the format used throughout the encyclopedia. For the convenience of plant shoppers, former (and perhaps better-known) scientific names are shown in parentheses after the scientific name and are also cross-referenced. Next comes the plant's common name or names, followed by the family name in italics. The type of plant is described on the next line.

Climate adaptability is shown in the line that begins with ◢. The zone numbers refer to the climate zones (explained and mapped on pages 19–78) where the plant will grow. "Zones 14–24, 32–43,"

for example, gives the inclusive zones for which the plant is recommended. "All zones" means the plant will grow everywhere.

Recommended exposure is shown by one or more of the three symbols indicating how much sun a plant needs for best performance. ☼ means the plant grows best with unobstructed sunlight all day long or almost all day; you can overlook an hour or so of shade at the beginning or end of a summer day. ◐ means that the plant needs partial shade—shade for half the day or for at least 3 hours during the hottest part of the day. ● indicates that a plant prefers little or no direct sunlight—for example, it does best on the north side of a house or beneath a broad, dense-foliaged tree.

Approximate moisture needs, which can be supplied by irrigation or rainfall, are symbolized as follows. ◖ indicates the plant thrives with less than regular moisture—moderate amounts for some plants, little for those with greater drought tolerance. ◖ means the plant performs well with regular moisture: the soil shouldn't become too dry or too wet. ◖◖ means the plant takes more than regular moisture; this category includes plants requiring constantly moist soil (such as many ferns), bog plants (such as cardinal flower), and aquatic plants (such as pickerel weed). Many plants show a range; for example, ◖ ◖◖ means the plant can take regular moisture or wetter conditions.

If a plant or any of its parts is known to be poisonous, the toxicity is noted in the last line, next to the symbol ◖. Plants not marked with this symbol may have poisonous parts, but their toxicity is not well known.

The drawings that accompany the entries give a general idea of the appearance of one or more members of a genus. Not all members will necessarily look alike, so be sure to read the individual species descriptions.

Plant families are also included in the alphabetical listings. A family name may be omitted if only one member of the family is given in the plant encyclopedia; in these instances, the listed plant adequately illustrates family characteristics. When authorities differ on the correct names for certain plant families, we list both.

Throughout the encyclopedia are boxes offering advice on matters such as plant selection, planting and culture, and harvesting.

CONSOLIDA ambigua
(Delphinium ajacis)

LARKSPUR, ANNUAL DELPHINIUM

Ranunculaceae

ANNUAL

◢ ALL ZONES

☼ FULL SUN

◖ REGULAR WATER

◖ ALL PARTS, ESPECIALLY SEEDS, ARE POISONOUS IF INGESTED

Consolida ambigua

A

AARON'S BEARD. See HYPERICUM calycinum

ABELIA

Caprifoliaceae

EVERGREEN OR DECIDUOUS SHRUBS

ZONES VARY BY SPECIES

BEST IN SUN, TOLERATE SOME SHADE

REGULAR WATER

Graceful, arching branches densely clothed with oval, usually glossy leaves ½–1½ in. long; bronzy new growth. Tubular or bell-shaped flowers in clusters at ends of branches or among leaves. Though small, blossoms are plentiful

Abelia grandiflora

enough to be showy, mostly during summer and early fall. When blooms drop, they usually leave purplish or copper-colored sepals that provide color into the fall months. Leaves also may take on bronzy tints in fall.

To keep the shrub's graceful form, prune selectively; don't shear. The more stems you cut to the ground in winter or early spring, the more open and arching next year's growth will be.

Abelias are adaptable plants, useful in shrub borders, as space dividers and visual barriers, and near house walls; lower kinds are good bank or ground covers.

A. chinensis. Deciduous. Zones 4–24, 28–34. Grows to 4–5 ft. tall with fragrant, pink-tinted white flowers in summer and fall. Exceptionally attractive to butterflies.

A. grandiflora. GLOSSY ABELIA. Evergreen to semievergreen. Zones 4–24, 28–35. Hybrid of two species from China. Best known and most popular of the abelias. Grows to 8 ft. or taller; spreads to 5 ft. or wider. Flowers white or faintly tinged pink. Stems freeze at about 0°F/–18°C, but plant will usually recover to bloom the same year, making a graceful border plant 10–15 in. tall.

'Francis Mason' is a compact (3–4 ft. high and wide), densely branched variety, with pink flowers and yellow-variegated leaves. 'Golden Glow' is similar, but with entirely yellow foliage. 'Prostrata' is a low-growing (1½–2-ft.), smaller-leafed variety useful as ground cover, bank planting, low foreground shrub. 'Sherwoodii' grows 3–4 ft. tall, 5 ft. wide. Hybrid 'Edward Goucher' is less hardy (Zones 5–24, 28–32), lower growing (to 3–5 ft.), and lacier than its *A. grandiflora* parent, with small, orange-throated, lilac-pink flowers.

ABELMOSCHUS moschatus

SILK FLOWER

Malvaceae

ANNUAL

ALL ZONES

FULL SUN

REGULAR WATER

Bushy plant about 1½ ft. tall and wide, with deep green, deeply cut leaves. Five-petaled, 3–4½-in. flowers, cherry

Abelmoschus moschatus

red or pink with white centers, resemble tropical hibiscus. Likes good garden soil, heat, and a sunny location; blooms most profusely where summers are long and hot. Grow from seed sown outdoors as soon as ground is warm (or start indoors 6 to 8 weeks before transplanting outdoors). Flowering begins 100 days after sowing and continues to frost or cold weather. Can be grown as house plant in a 6-in. pot; set on a windowsill in bright light.

PRACTICAL GARDENING DICTIONARY
PLEASE SEE PAGES 545–616

ABIES

FIR

Pinaceae

EVERGREEN TREES

ZONES VARY BY SPECIES

FULL SUN OR LIGHT SHADE

REGULAR TO MODERATE WATER

Abies concolor

In nature, firs are tall, erect, symmetrical trees with uniformly spaced branch whorls. Though sometimes confused with spruces (*Picea*), they have softer needles that fall directly from the stems (spruces leave short pegs behind), and their large cones grow up rather than down. The cones shatter after ripening, leaving a spiky stalk. Most (but not all) native firs are high-mountain plants that grow best in or near their natural environments. Some species adapt well to warmer, drier conditions.

Christmas tree farms grow native firs for cutting, and nurseries in "fir country" grow a few species for the living Christmas tree trade. Licensed collectors in the Northwest dig picturesque, contorted firs at high elevations near the timberline and market them through nurseries as "alpine conifers." Use these in rock gardens; small specimens are good container or bonsai subjects. Birds are attracted by fir seeds.

A. balsamea. BALSAM FIR. Zones 3–7, 15–17, 36–38, 42–44. Native to northeastern U.S. Pyramidal tree to 50 ft.; dark green needles. Does not thrive in hot-summer climates, but where it is adapted, its legendary fragrance makes it a favorite for Christmas trees and wreaths. Dwarf variety 'Nana' is used as a rock garden or container plant.

A. concolor. WHITE FIR. Zones 1–9, 14–24, 34–37, 39, 41. Native to mountain regions of West and Southwest, but succeeds in the Northwest and humid-summer North and Northeast. Also does well in lower Midwest and in some lower-elevation areas of interior West. Grows 50–70 ft. tall in gardens. Bluish green, 1–2-in.-long needles; 'Candicans' is bluish white.

A. firma. JAPANESE FIR, MOMI FIR. Zones 4–6, 17, 32, 34. Native to Japan. Broadly pyramidal to 40–50 ft., with branches slightly above horizontal. Needles dark green above, lighter beneath. Can tolerate hot, moist climates.

A. fraseri. SOUTHERN BALSAM FIR, FRASER FIR, SOUTHERN FIR. Zones 36, 37. Native to higher, cooler elevations of the Appalachian Mountains. Attractive pyramidal tree resembling *A. balsamea* in both looks and fragrance. Widely grown as a Christmas tree where summers are not too hot.

A. homolepis. NIKKO FIR. Zones 32, 34, 36–38. Native to Japan. Broad, dense, rather formal fir to 80 ft. Needles are densely arranged, forward pointing. Adapted to warm, moist regions.

A. koreana. KOREAN FIR. Zones 3–9, 14–24, 32, 34, 39. Native to Korea. Slow-growing, compact, pyramidal tree seldom over 30 ft. Shiny, short green needles. Sets cones on young, small trees. 'Aurea', with gold-green foliage, is even smaller, slower growing.

A. lasiocarpa. ALPINE FIR, ROCKY MOUNTAIN FIR. Zones 1–9, 14–17. Native to high elevations in the western U.S. In the wild, if growing in good, moist soil, it is a narrow, steeple-shaped tree 60–90 ft. tall. In gardens, it loses its narrow shape and is typically much shorter. Needles are bluish green, 1–1½ in. long.

A. nordmanniana. NORDMANN FIR. Zones 3–11, 14–24, 32–37. Native to the Caucasus, Asia Minor, Greece. Vigorous, densely foliaged fir, 30–50 ft. tall and 20 ft. wide in cultivation. Dark green, shiny, ¾–1½-in.-long needles, with whitish bands beneath, densely cover branches. Adapts well to warm- and dry-summer western U.S. and humid mid-Atlantic and southeastern states, but does best with regular water. Will submit to long-term container growing.

A. pinsapo. SPANISH FIR. Zones 5–11, 14–24, 32, 33. Native to Spain. Thrives in warm, dry regions as well as cool, moist "fir country." Slow grower, reaching 50 ft. after many years. Thanks to its dense, symmetrical form, it's sometimes mistaken for a spruce. Stiff, deep green, ½–¾-in.-long needles are set uniformly around branches. 'Glauca' is blue gray.

A. procera (A. nobilis). NOBLE FIR. Zones 3–5, 15–17, 36, 37. Though this fir will grow satisfactorily—if slowly—in the Northeast, it performs best in its native Northwest range (Washington to northernmost California), where it is a narrow, graceful tree reaching well over 100 ft. in gardens. Blue-green, inch-long needles; short, stiff branches. Cones 6–10 in. long, 3 in. wide, with extended bracts.

ABUTILON

FLOWERING MAPLE, CHINESE BELLFLOWER, CHINESE LANTERN

Malvaceae

EVERGREEN VINE-SHRUBS

ZONES 8, 9, 12–27

PART SHADE IN HOT-SUMMER AREAS

REGULAR TO MODERATE WATER

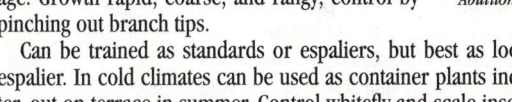

Abutilon hybridum

Mostly native to South America. Planted primarily for their flowers. Need good drainage. Growth rapid, coarse, and rangy; control by pinching out branch tips.

Can be trained as standards or espaliers, but best as loose, informal espalier. In cold climates can be used as container plants indoors in winter, out on terrace in summer. Control whitefly and scale insects with light oil spray.

A. hybridum. The best-known species. Upright, arching growth to 8–10 ft., with equal spread. Broad maplelike leaves. Drooping bell-like flowers in white, yellow, pink, and red. Main blooming season is spring, but white and yellow forms seem to bloom almost continuously.

A. megapotamicum. Vigorous growth to 10 ft. and as wide. Leaves are arrowlike, 1½–3 in. long. Flowers resembling red-and-yellow lanterns gaily decorate the long, rangy branches in spring and summer. This vine-shrub is more graceful in detail than in entirety but can be trained to an interesting pattern. Good hanging basket plant. 'Marianne' has superior form; 'Variegata' has leaves mottled with yellow; 'Victory' is compact and floriferous with small, deep yellow flowers.

A. pictum 'Thompsonii'. Similar to *A. hybridum* but foliage strikingly variegated with creamy yellow. Blooms almost continuously, bearing pale orange bells veined with red.

ABYSSINIAN BANANA. See ENSETE ventricosum

ABYSSINIAN SWORD LILY. See GLADIOLUS callianthus

ACACIA

Fabaceae (Leguminosae)

EVERGREEN OR DECIDUOUS SHRUBS OR TREES

ZONES VARY BY SPECIES

FULL SUN

MODERATE TO LITTLE WATER

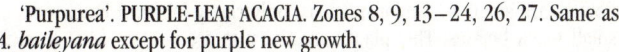

Acacia baileyana

Large group of shrubs or small trees native to tropics or warm regions of the world, notably Australia, Mexico, and the southwestern U.S. Many types are grown in California and the Southwest, and some have enjoyed use in the warmest southeastern climates. Acacias are relatively short lived (20–30 years on average), but all grow so rapidly that they reach good size in a few years. The various species produce yellow, cream, or white flowers; the blossoms of some are quite fragrant. All acacias are attractive to birds.

A. baileyana. BAILEY ACACIA (often called MIMOSA as cut flowers). Evergreen. Zones 7–9, 13–24, 26–28. Most widely planted acacia and among the hardiest to cold. Often grown as a multitrunked plant 20–30 ft. high. Feathery, finely cut, blue-gray leaves; thornless. Starts blooming when young, producing profuse, fragrant yellow flowers early in the year.

'Purpurea'. PURPLE-LEAF ACACIA. Zones 8, 9, 13–24, 26, 27. Same as *A. baileyana* except for purple new growth.

A. berlandieri. GUAJILLO. Deciduous. Zones 12, 13, 26–29. Southwestern native used as a shrub, hedge, or small tree. Thornless growth to about 15 ft. high. Fernlike foliage. Fragrant white flowers, rich in nectar, bloom winter to spring.

A. farnesiana. SWEET ACACIA. Deciduous. Zones 13–26. To 20 ft. high, with feathery foliage and thorny branches. Fragrant, deep yellow blossoms, borne nearly year-round, may freeze in a cold snap. Nurseries often sell the more cold-tolerant *A. smallii* under this name.

A. schaffneri. Deciduous. Zones 8, 9, 12–29. To about 18 ft., with curving branches like green tentacles and finely divided leaves hiding short thorns. Perfumed yellow balls in spring.

A. smallii (A. minuta). Deciduous. Zones 8, 9, 12–29. Finely divided foliage, thorny branches. Variable growth to 30–35 ft. high. Scented yellow puff balls produced in spring. Often sold as *A. farnesiana.*

ACALYPHA

Euphorbiaceae

EVERGREEN TROPICAL SHRUBS

ZONES 24, 25, 27; OR INDOORS

FULL SUN OR PARTIAL SHADE

REGULAR TO MODERATE WATER

Acalypha hispida

All three of the species described are tropical and quite tender; *A. wilkesiana* can be used as an annual. All need well-drained soil, bloom intermittently during warm months.

A. hispida. CHENILLE PLANT. Native to the East Indies. Grows outdoors only in the mildest frost-free climates; elsewhere, good in greenhouse or enclosed patio or, with heavy pruning, as house plant. Can grow to a bulky 10 ft. Heavy, rich green leaves to 8 in. wide. Flowers hang in 1½-ft.-long clusters resembling tassels of crimson chenille.

A. pendula. FIRETAIL. Resembles *A. hispida* in flower form but plant is much smaller; shorter tassels droop from trailing branches. Good in hanging basket.

A. wilkesiana (A. tricolor). COPPER LEAF. Native to South Pacific islands. Foliage more colorful than many flowers. Provides year-round interest in southern Florida, where it is an outdoor plant. Elsewhere, it is used as an annual, substituting for flowers from late summer to frost. Leaves to 8 in.; may be bronzy green mottled with shades of red and purple, red with crimson and bronze, or green edged with crimson and stippled with orange and red. In a warm, sheltered spot it can grow as a shrub to 6 ft. or more. Container plants need fast-draining potting mix, kept slightly dry through winter.

Acanthaceae. The acanthus family consists of herbs and shrubs, generally from warm or tropical areas. Many have showy flowers or foliage. Examples are bear's breech *(Acanthus)*, *Aphelandra*, and *Thunbergia*.

ACANTHOPANAX sieboldianus (Eleutherococcus sieboldianus)

Araliaceae

DECIDUOUS SHRUB

ZONES 2–10, 14–17, 28–41

SUN OR SHADE

MUCH OR LITTLE WATER

Acanthopanax sieboldianus

Grows 8–10 ft. tall and wide; erect, eventually arching stems have short thorns below each leaf. Leaves bright green, with five to seven leaflets 1–2½ inches long arranged like fingers on a hand. Clustered white

A

flowers are small and inconspicuous, only rarely followed by clusters of small black berries. This plant's great virtues are its somewhat tropical appearance and high tolerance for difficult conditions. It can thrive in bright sun or dense shade, with much or little water, in rich or poor soil. It is remarkably tolerant of urban air pollution. 'Variegatus', a showy 6–8-ft. plant with white-bordered leaflets, is grown more often than the species.

ACANTHUS mollis

BEAR'S BREECH

Acanthaceae

PERENNIAL

🌿 ZONES 4–24, 28–32

☼ ◑ FULL SUN OR PARTIAL SHADE

💧💧 REGULAR TO MODERATE WATER

Acanthus mollis

Native to southern Europe. Fast-growing, spreading plant with basal clusters of handsome, deeply lobed and cut, shining dark green leaves to 2 ft. long. Rigid 1½-ft. spikes of tubular whitish, lilac, or rose flowers with spiny green or purplish bracts top 2–3-ft. stems. Blooms late spring or early summer. Variety 'Oak Leaf' is very similar to species; 'Latifolius' has larger leaves, is hardier.

Cut back after flowering. To keep foliage through summer, cut off flower stalks and soak roots occasionally. Divide clumps between October and March. Plant where it can be confined; roots travel underground, making the plant difficult to eradicate. Effective with bamboo, large-leafed ferns.

ACCA sellowiana. See **FEIJOA sellowiana**

ACER

MAPLE

Aceraceae

DECIDUOUS OR EVERGREEN TREES OR SHRUBS

🌿 ZONES VARY BY SPECIES

☼ ◑ FULL SUN OR PARTIAL SHADE

💧💧 REGULAR TO MODERATE WATER

Acer palmatum

When you talk about maples, you're talking about many trees—large and midsize deciduous shade trees; smaller evergreen and deciduous trees; and dainty, picturesque shrubtrees. Maples of one type or another will grow over much of the country, the limiting factors being heat, dryness, and lack of winter cold. Southern California and low southwestern deserts are inhospitable to nearly all species, and only very tough or drought-tolerant types are worth trying in the lower Midwest. For a good fall leaf display, look for a maple that colors well in your area; visit local nurseries while the foliage is changing hue.

All maples prefer well-drained soil but must have moisture available in the root zone throughout their leafy period. Most have shallow, competitive roots, and the sizable ones cast dense shade; it's not easy to maintain a garden beneath them. They are subject to various problems, including anthracnose and verticillium wilt.

A. buergeranum. TRIDENT MAPLE. Deciduous tree. Zones 4–9, 14–17, 20, 21, 31–34. Native to China, Japan. Grows 20–25 ft. high. Roundish crown of 3-in.-wide, glossy, three-lobed leaves that are pale beneath. Fall color usually red, sometimes orange or yellow. Attractive flaking bark on older wood. Low, spreading growth; stake and prune to make it branch high. A decorative, useful patio tree and favorite bonsai subject.

A. campestre. HEDGE MAPLE. Deciduous tree. Zones 2–9, 14, 31–41. Native to Europe, western Asia. Slow growing to 70 ft., seldom over 30 ft. in cultivation. Usually rounded, dense habit. Leaves 2–4 in. wide, with three

to five lobes, dull green above; turn yellow in fall. 'Queen Elizabeth' has glossier foliage, more erect habit.

A. capillipes. Deciduous tree. Zones 3–9, 12, 14–24, 30–34, 39. Native to Japan. Moderate growth rate to 30 ft. Young branches red, turning brown with white stripes with age. Young leaves red; leafstalks and midribs red. Shallowly three-lobed leaves, 3–5 in. long; turn scarlet in fall. In warmer climates, does best in part shade.

A. cappadocicum. COLISEUM MAPLE. Deciduous tree. Zones 3–6, 31–34. Native to western Asia. Known here in its variety 'Rubrum', red coliseum maple. Grows to 35 ft.; forms compact, rounded crown. Leaves with five to seven lobes, 5½ in. wide. Bright red spring foliage turns rich dark green.

A. circinatum. VINE MAPLE. Deciduous shrub or small tree to about 25 ft. Zones 3–6, 14–17, 36, 37. In shaded West Coast forests, has a crooked, almost vinelike habit; in the open, becomes nearly symmetrical and upright, with one or several trunks. Leaves nearly circular, to 6 in. across, with 5–11 lobes; red tinted when new, light green as they mature, then orange, scarlet, or yellow in fall. Tiny reddish purple spring flowers are followed by red winged seeds. 'Monroe' has deeply cut foliage.

A. davidii. DAVID'S MAPLE. Deciduous tree. Zones 3–6, 15–17, 20, 21, 32–34. Native to central China. This 20–35-ft.-high maple is distinctive on several counts. Bark is shiny green striped with silvery white, particularly striking in winter. Leaves are glossy green, oval or lobed, 2–7 in. long, 1½–4 in. wide, deeply veined. New foliage bronze tinted; fall color of bright yellow, red orange, and purple. Clustered greenish yellow flowers showy in spring. Part shade in warmer areas.

Acer davidii

A. ginnala. AMUR MAPLE. Deciduous shrub or small tree. Zones 1–9, 14–16, 35–45. Native to Manchuria, north China, Japan. To 20 ft. high. Three-lobed, toothed leaves to 3 in. long, 2 in. wide. Striking red fall color. Clusters of small, fragrant yellowish flowers in early spring are followed by handsome bright red, winged seeds. Grown as staked, trained single-trunked tree or multiple-trunked tall shrub. 'Flame', 15–20 ft. tall, shows fiery red fall color. Tough trees, tolerating heat and cold.

A. griseum. PAPERBARK MAPLE. Deciduous tree. Zones 2–9, 14–21, 31–41. Native to China. Grows to 25 ft. or higher with narrow to rounded crown. In winter it makes a striking silhouette with bare branches angling out and up from main trunk, and cinnamon-colored bark peeling away in paper-thin sheets. Late to leaf out in spring; leaves are divided into three coarsely toothed leaflets 1½–2½ in. long, dark green above, silvery below. Inconspicuous red flowers in spring develop into showy winged seeds. Foliage turns brilliant red in fall unless caught by early frosts. Not drought tolerant.

A. japonicum. FULLMOON MAPLE. Deciduous shrub or small tree. Zones 3–6, 14–16, 31–35, 37, 39. Native to Japan. To 20–30 ft. Nearly round, 2–5-in.-long leaves cut into 7–11 lobes. Give regular moisture, part shade in warm regions. The following varieties are small, slow growing, and best placed as shrubs.

'Aconitifolium'. FERNLEAF FULLMOON MAPLE. Leaves are deeply cut, almost to leafstalk; each lobe is also cut and toothed. Fine fall color where adapted.

'Aureum'. GOLDEN FULLMOON MAPLE. See A. shirasawanum 'Aureum'

A. macrophyllum. BIGLEAF MAPLE. Deciduous tree. Zones 4–17. Native to stream banks, moist canyons, Alaska to California foothills. Broad-topped, dense shade tree 30–95 ft. tall—too big for small garden or street tree. Large (6–15-in.-wide) medium green leaves with three to five lobes; turn bright yellow to orange in fall. Small greenish yellow spring flowers are followed by tawny winged seeds hanging in long, chainlike clusters.

A. negundo. BOX ELDER. Deciduous tree. Zones 1–10, 12–24, 29–45. Native to most of U.S. Where you can grow other maples of your choice, do so. This is a weed tree of many faults—it seeds readily, hosts box elder bugs, suckers badly, and is subject to breakage. Fast growing to 60 ft., usually less. Leaves divided into three to five (or seven to nine) oval, 2–5-in.-long leaflets with toothed margins; yellow in fall.

'Flamingo'. Has white and pink leaf markings. Some shade in warm areas.

'Variegatum'. VARIEGATED BOX ELDER. Not as large or weedy as the species. Combination of green and creamy white leaves stands out in any situation. Large, pendent clusters of white fruit are spectacular.

A. nigrum. BLACK MAPLE. Zones 1–10, 14–20, 33, 35–45. Similar to sugar maple *(A. saccharum)*, but more resistant to heat and drought. Light green leaves turn yellow in fall. 'Greencolumn' can reach 65 ft. tall, 25 ft. wide.

A. palmatum. JAPANESE MAPLE. Deciduous shrub or tree. Zones 2–10, 12, 14–24, 31–41. Native to Japan and Korea. Slow growing to 20 ft.; normally many stemmed. Most airy and delicate of all maples. Leaves 2–4 in. long, deeply cut into five to nine toothed lobes. All-year interest: young spring growth is glowing red; summer's leaves are soft green; fall foliage is scarlet, orange, or yellow. Slender leafless branches in greens and reds provide winter interest. Japanese maples are inclined to grow in flat, horizontal planes, so pruning to accentuate this growth habit is easy. Plants fare best in filtered shade, though full sun can be satisfactory.

Grafted garden varieties are popular, but common seedlings have uncommon grace and usefulness: they are more rugged, faster growing, and more drought tolerant than named forms, and they stand more sun and wind. Grafted forms are usually smaller, more weeping and spreading in form, brighter in foliage color, and more finely cut in leaf. The following list includes the best known of the numerous varieties available.

'Atropurpureum'. RED JAPANESE MAPLE. Purplish or bronze to bronzy green leaves, brighter in sun. Color tends to fade in summer heat.

'Bloodgood'. Vigorous, upright growth to 15 ft. Deep red spring and summer foliage, scarlet in fall. Bark blackish red.

'Bonfire'. Orange-pink spring and fall foliage; twisted trunk, short branches, drooping branchlets.

'Burgundy Lace'. Leaves purplish, more deeply cut than those of 'Atropurpureum'; branchlets bright green.

'Butterfly'. Small (to 7-ft.) shrub with small bluish green leaves edged in white. Cut out growth that reverts to plain green. Needs some shade.

'Crimson Queen'. Small, shrubby, with finely cut reddish leaves that hold color all summer, turn scarlet before dropping off in fall.

'Dissectum' ('Dissectum Viridis'). LACELEAF JAPANESE MAPLE. Small shrub with drooping branches, green bark; pale green, finely divided leaves turn gold in autumn.

'Ever Red' ('Dissectum Atropurpureum'). Small mounding shrub with weeping branches. Finely divided, purple-tinged, lacy foliage turns crimson in fall.

'Filiferum Purpureum'. Mounding shrub to 10 ft. with threadlike leaf segments opening dark red and aging bronzy green.

'Garnet'. Similar to 'Crimson Queen' and 'Ever Red'; somewhat more vigorous grower.

'Ornatum' ('Dissectum Atropurpureum'). RED LACELEAF JAPANESE MAPLE. Like 'Dissectum' but with red leaves turning brighter red in autumn.

'Oshio Beni'. Like 'Atropurpureum' but more vigorous; has long, arching branches.

'Sango Kaku' ('Senkaki'). CORAL BARK MAPLE. Vigorous, upright, tree-like. Fall foliage yellow. Twigs, branches striking coral red in winter.

A. pentaphyllum. Deciduous tree. Zones 4–9, 14–17, 32. Rare plant to 20–30 ft., with leaves divided into five narrow, 3-in. leaflets spread like fingers on a hand. Medium green leaves turn pale orange to red in fall.

A. platanoides. NORWAY MAPLE. Deciduous tree. Zones 1–9, 14–17, 30–43. Native to Europe, western Asia. Broad-crowned, densely foliaged tree to 50–60 ft. Leaves five-lobed, 3–5 in. wide, deep green above, paler beneath; turn yellow in fall. Showy clusters of small, greenish yellow flowers in early spring. Very adaptable, tolerating many soil and environmental conditions. Once widely recommended, especially as street tree, but now strongly objected to because of voracious roots, self-sown seedlings, and aphid-caused honeydew drip and sooty mold. Here are some of the best horticultural varieties:

'Cavalier'. Compact, round headed, to 30 ft.

'Cleveland' and 'Cleveland II'. Shapely, compact, well-formed trees about 50 ft. tall.

'Columnare'. Slower growing and narrower in form than the species.

'Crimson King'. Holds purple foliage color until leaves drop. Slower growing, more compact than the species.

'Deborah'. Like 'Schwedler' but faster growing, straighter.

'Drummondii'. Leaves are edged with silvery white; unusual and striking. Some shade in warm areas.

'Faassen's Black'. Pyramidal in shape, with dark purple leaves.

'Globe'. Slow growing with dense, round crown; eventual height 20–25 ft.

'Green Lace'. Finely cut, dark green leaves; moderate growth rate to 40 ft.

'Jade Glen'. Vigorous, straight-growing form with bright yellow fall color.

'Parkway'. A broader tree than 'Columnare', with a dense canopy.

'Royal Red Leaf'. Another good red- or purple-leafed form.

'Schwedler' ('Schwedleri'). Purplish red leaves in spring turn to dark bronzy green, gold in autumn.

'Summershade'. Fast-growing, upright, heat-resistant selection.

A. pseudoplatanus. SYCAMORE MAPLE. Deciduous tree. Zones 2–9, 14–20, 31–41. Native to Europe, western Asia. Moderate growth to 40 ft. or more. Leaves 3–5 in. wide, five-lobed, thick, prominently veined, dark green above, pale below. No particular fall color. The variety 'Atropurpureum' ('Spaethii') has leaves that are rich purple underneath.

A. rubrum. RED MAPLE, SCARLET MAPLE, SWAMP MAPLE. Deciduous tree. Zones 1–9, 14–17, 26, 28, 31–44. Native to low, wet areas of eastern North America. Fairly fast growth to 60 ft. or more, 40 ft. or wider. Faster growing than Norway or sycamore maples. Red twigs, branchlets, and buds; quite showy flowers. Fruit dull red. Leaves 2–4 in. long, with three to five lobes, shiny green above, pale beneath; brilliant scarlet fall color in frosty areas. Often among the first trees to color up in fall. Very soil tolerant. Not at its best in urban pollution. Selected forms include the following:

'Armstrong' and 'Armstrong II'. Hybrids between red and silver maple. Tall, very narrow trees with often poor, orange to red fall color.

'Autumn Radiance'. Broad oval form, orange-red fall color.

'Bowhall'. Tall, narrow, cone shaped, with orange-red foliage color in fall.

Acer rubrum

'Columnare'. Tall, broadly columnar.

'Gerling'. Broadly pyramidal, to 35 ft. with 20-ft. spread.

'Karpick'. Narrow grower with red twigs, yellow to red fall color.

'Northwood'. Rounded form. Extremely cold hardy.

'October Glory'. Tall, round-headed tree; last to turn color in fall. Good color even in the South.

'Red Sunset'. Upright, vigorous branching pattern.

'Scarlet Sentinel'. Hybrid between red and silver maple. Columnar, fast-growing form.

'Schlesingeri'. Tall, broad, fast growing, with regular form; orange-red fall color.

'Shade King'. Very fast grower to 50 ft. Pale green foliage turns bright red in fall.

'Tilford'. Nearly globe-shaped crown if grown in the open; pyramidal when crowded.

'V. J. Drake'. Unusual fall color: leaf borders turn red and violet while center is still green. Leaves eventually turn completely red.

A. saccharinum. SILVER MAPLE. Deciduous tree. Zones 1–9, 12, 14–24, 26, 28–44. Native to eastern North America. Grows fast to 40–100 ft. with equal spread. Open form, with semipendulous branches; casts fairly open shade. Silvery gray bark peels in long strips on old trees. Leaves 3–6 in. wide, five lobed, light green above, silvery beneath. Autumn color is usually poor, pale yellow. Aggressive roots hard on sidewalks, sewers.

You pay a penalty for the advantage of fast growth: weak wood and narrow crotch angles make this tree break easily. Unusually susceptible to aphids and cottony scale. Many rate it among the least desirable of maples. Nevertheless, it is often planted for fast growth and graceful habit.

'Silver Queen'. More upright than the species, seedless. Bright gold fall color. ▶

'Wieri' ('Laciniatum'). WIER MAPLE, CUTLEAF SILVER MAPLE. Same as species but leaves are much more finely cut; provides open shade.

A. saccharum. SUGAR MAPLE. Deciduous tree. Zones 1–10, 14–20, 32–45. Native to eastern North America. The source of maple sugar in the Northeast, this tree is renowned for spectacular fall color in cold-winter climates. Moderate growth to 60 ft. and more, with stout branches and upright-oval to rounded canopy. Leaves 3–6 in. wide, with three to five lobes, green above, pale below. Brilliant autumn foliage ranges from yellow and orange to deep red and scarlet. Intolerant of road salt; also not suited to humid heat of the Deep South (though some selections succeed there). These are some of the most commonly available varieties.

'Arrowhead'. Erect pyramid with yellow to orange leaves in fall.

'Bonfire'. Tall, spreading tree with bright red fall foliage.

'Commemoration'. Heavy leaf texture; orange, yellow, and red fall color.

'Green Mountain'. Tolerant of heat and drought; autumn leaves are yellow to orange to reddish orange.

'Legacy'. Fast growing, drought resistant, and multihued in fall; the best variety for the South.

'Monumentale' ('Temple's Upright'). Narrow, erect form with yellow-orange fall leaves.

'Seneca Chief'. Narrow form, orange to yellow fall color.

A. shirasawanum 'Aureum'. GOLDEN FULLMOON MAPLE. Deciduous shrub or small tree. Zones 3–6, 14–16, 31–35, 37, 39. Leaves open pale gold in spring and remain a pale chartreuse yellow all summer. Some shade in warm areas.

A. tataricum. TATARIAN MAPLE. Deciduous shrub or small tree. Zones 1–6, 14–16, 34–43. Resembles *A. ginnala* in size and habit. Leaves toothed, lobed only on young plants, 2–3½ in. long. Winged seeds red in summer, showy; fall color yellow to reddish brown.

A. truncatum. Deciduous tree. Zones 1–9, 14–23, 32, 34–43. Native to China. Grows fairly rapidly to 25 ft. Like a small Norway maple with more deeply lobed leaves to 4 in. wide. Expanding leaves are purplish red, summer leaves green, autumn leaves dark purplish red. A good lawn or patio tree.

Aceraceae. The maple family consists of deciduous, rarely evergreen, trees and shrubs with paired opposite leaves and paired, winged seeds.

ACHILLEA

YARROW	
Asteraceae (Compositae)	
PERENNIALS	
🌿 ZONES 1–24, 26, 28–45	
☀ FULL SUN	
🌢 MODERATE WATER	

Achillea tomentosa

Yarrows are among the most carefree and generously blooming perennials for summer and early fall, several being equally useful in the garden and as cut flowers (taller kinds may be cut and dried for winter bouquets). Leaves are gray or green, bitter-aromatic, usually finely divided (some with toothed edges). Flower heads usually in flattish clusters. Drought tolerant once established. Cut back after bloom, dividing when clumps get crowded.

A. ageratifolia. GREEK YARROW. Native to Balkan region. Low mats of silvery leaves, toothed or nearly smooth edged. White flower clusters ½–1 in. across on stems 4–10 in. tall.

A. clavennae. SILVERY YARROW. Mats of silvery gray, silky leaves, lobed somewhat like chrysanthemum leaves. Loose, flat-topped clusters of ½–¾-in.-wide ivory white flower heads on 5–10-in.-high stems. Often sold as *A. argentea*.

A. filipendulina. FERNLEAF YARROW. Tall, erect plants 4–5 ft. high, with deep green, fernlike leaves. Bright yellow flower heads in large, flat-topped clusters. Dried or fresh, they are good for flower arrangements.

Several horticultural varieties are available. 'Gold Plate', a tall plant, has flower clusters up to 6 in. wide; 'Coronation Gold', to about 3 ft., also has large flower clusters. All types are less successful in Gulf Coast states than *A. millefolium*.

A. kellereri. Gray-green ferny leaves on a low (6-in.) plant. Clusters of flower heads look like tiny white daisies with yellow centers.

A. millefolium. COMMON YARROW, MILFOIL. This species may spread a bit or grow erect to 3 ft. Narrow, fernlike, green or gray-green leaves on 3-ft. stems. White flower clusters grow on long stems. 'Rosea' has rosy flower heads. One of the more successful garden varieties is 'Fire King', about 3 ft. tall with gray foliage and dark reddish flowers. 'Cerise Queen' has brighter red flowers. Hybrids, many of them named, have extended the color range. Summer Pastels and Debutante strains show white and cream to lighter shades of yellow and red; they can grow from seed. Galaxy exhibits deeper colors.

A LAWN-MEADOW DOTTED WITH WILDFLOWERS

That's the effect you get with common yarrow (*Achillea millefolium*) treated as a sometimes-mowed ground cover. Install in spring, like this: Prepare soil as for a new lawn. Use ½ lb. of seed per 1,000 sq. ft. Mix it with an equal amount of sand and broadcast the mix with a handheld spreader. Press seeds in with a lawn roller. Mow two to eight times a year (the less often you mow, the more flowers can form). Use a rotary mower at a 3–4-in. setting.

A. 'Moonshine'. Upright growth to 2 ft. Gray-green foliage and light yellow flowers. Like *A. taygetea* but flowers are deeper yellow.

A. ptarmica. Erect plant up to 2 ft. high. Narrow leaves with finely toothed edges. White flower heads in rather open, flattish clusters. 'The Pearl' has double flowers.

A. taygetea. Native to the eastern Mediterranean. Grows to 1½ ft. Gray-green, divided leaves 3–4 in. long. Dense clusters of bright yellow flower heads fade to primrose yellow—excellent contrast in color shades until it's time to shear off old stalks. Good cut flowers.

A. tomentosa. WOOLLY YARROW. Makes a flat, spreading mat of fernlike, deep green, hairy leaves. Golden flower heads in flat clusters top 6–10-in. stems in summer. 'Primrose Beauty' has pale yellow flowers; 'King George' has cream flowers. A good edging and a neat ground cover for small areas; used in rock gardens. Shear off dead flowers to leave attractive green mat.

ACHIMENES

Gesneriaceae	
TENDER PERENNIALS USUALLY GROWN IN POTS	
🌓 ● SHADE OUTDOORS; BRIGHT LIGHT INDOORS	
🌢 CAREFUL, FREQUENT WATER	

Achimenes

Native to tropical America. Related to African violet and gloxinia. Plants 1–2 ft. high, some trailing. Slender stems; roundish, crisp, bright to dark green, hairy leaves. Flaring tubular flowers, 1–3 in. across, in pink, blue, lavender, orchid, purple.

Sometimes grown in beds as ground cover in Zones 25 and 26, but more commonly used in containers—outdoors (protected from direct sun and wind) in window box, on porch or patio, under lath; or indoors (in bright light) in house or greenhouse. Plant rhizomes March–April, placing ½–1 in. deep in moist peat moss and sand. Keep in light shade at 60°F/16°C. When 3 in. high, set 6–12 plants in 6–7-in. fern pot or hanging basket, in potting mix of equal parts peat moss, perlite, leaf mold. In fall, dig rhizomes and let dry. Store in cool, dry place over winter; repot in spring.

ACIDANTHERA bicolor. See GLADIOLUS callianthus

ACOELORRHAPHE wrightii
(Paurotis wrightii)

Arecaceae (Palmae)

PALM

⬛ ZONES 19–26; OR INDOORS

☼ ◐ FULL SUN OR PARTIAL SHADE

🌢🌢 AMPLE WATER

Acoelorrhaphe wrightii

Native to the Florida Everglades, West Indies. Hardy to 20°F/–7°C. Handsome fan palm with several slender trunks topped by 2–3-ft.-wide leaves, green above, silvery below. Spines on leafstalks. Grows to 25 ft. tall in Florida, considerably less in dry-summer regions, where plant is somewhat difficult to establish. Tolerant of many soils. Can be grown as a house plant.

ACONITUM

ACONITE, MONKSHOOD

Ranunculaceae

PERENNIALS

⬛ ZONES 1–9, 14–21, 34–45

☼ ◐ FULL SUN OR PARTIAL SHADE

🌢 REGULAR WATER

⬥ ALL PARTS ARE POISONOUS IF INGESTED

Aconitum napellus

Leaves, usually lobed, in basal clusters. Flowers shaped like hoods or helmets, along tall, leafy spikes. Monkshood has a definite place in rich soil under trees, at the back of flower beds, or even at the edge of a bog garden. Substitute for delphinium in shade. Combines effectively with ferns, meadow rue, astilbe, and hosta.

Needs some winter chill. Hard to establish in warm, dry climates. Sow seeds in spring; or sow in late summer or early fall for bloom the next year. Moist, fertile soil for best growth and bloom. Divide in early spring or late fall, or leave undivided for years. Completely dormant in winter; mark site.

A. cammarum 'Bicolor'. Grows to 3 ft., with broad, branching spires of blue-and-white flowers in summer.

A. carmichaelii (A. fischeri). Native to central China. Densely leafy stems 2–4 ft. high. Leaves leathery, dark green, lobed and coarsely toothed. Blooms late summer into fall; deep purple-blue flowers form dense, branching clusters 4–8 in. long. 'Wilsonii' grows 6–8 ft. high, has more open flower clusters 10–18 in. long.

A. henryi (A. bicolor) 'Sparks'. Grows 4–5 ft. tall, with dark purple-blue flowers on a widely branching plant. Summer bloom.

A. napellus. GARDEN MONKSHOOD. Native to Europe. Upright leafy plants 2–5 ft. high. Leaves 2–5 in. wide, divided into narrow lobes. Flowers usually blue or violet, in spikelike clusters in late summer.

ACORUS gramineus

Araceae

PERENNIAL

⬛ ALL ZONES

☼ FULL SUN

🌢 MUCH WATER

Native to Japan, northern Asia. Related to callas, but fans of grasslike leaves more nearly resemble miniature tufts of iris. Flowers are inconspicuous. 'Ogon' has rich golden yellow leaves. 'Pusillus' is tiny, its

Acorus gramineus

green leaves seldom more than 1 in. long. It is used in planting miniature landscapes and dish gardens. 'Variegatus', with white-edged, ¼-in.-wide leaves to 1½ ft. long, can be planted in bog gardens or at pool edges. 'Variegatus' is also useful with collections of grasses, bamboos, or sword-leafed plants among gravel and boulders.

ACTAEA

BANEBERRY

Ranunculaceae

PERENNIALS

⬛ ZONES 1–5, 30–45

◐ ● PARTIAL OR FULL SHADE

🌢 REGULAR WATER

⬥ ALL PARTS ARE POISONOUS IF INGESTED

Actaea rubra

Woodland plants native to the U. S. and useful primarily for the wild or native plant garden, baneberries grow to 2½ ft. tall, with gracefully divided leaves somewhat like those of astilbe and clusters of small white blossoms in spring. Principal feature is the attractive (but poisonous) fruit that follows the flowers. Use as a background for smaller native plants. Give soil rich in humus.

A. alba (A. pachypoda). WHITE BANEBERRY, DOLL'S EYES. Showy ¼-in. berry is white with a dark spot at the end; berry stalks are swollen and red.

A. rubra. RED BANEBERRY. Similar to *A. alba*, but berries are somewhat larger, scarlet in color, and borne on slender stems.

ACTINIDIA

Actinidiaceae

DECIDUOUS VINES

⬛ ZONES VARY BY SPECIES

☼ ◐ FULL SUN OR PARTIAL SHADE

🌢🌢 REGULAR TO MODERATE WATER

Native to eastern Asia. Handsome foliage. Plant in rich soil. Supply sturdy supports for them

Actinidia deliciosa

to twine upon, such as a trellis, an arbor, or a patio overhead. You can also train them to cover walls and fences; guide and tie vines to the support as necessary. Thin occasionally to shape or to control pattern.

In winter, prune and shape plant for form and fruit production. Shape to one or two main trunks; cut out closely parallel or crossing branches. Fruit is borne on shoots from year-old or older wood; cut out shoots that have fruited for 3 years and shorten younger shoots, leaving from three to seven buds beyond previous summer's fruit. In summer, shorten overlong shoots and unwind shoots that twine around main branches.

A. arguta. HARDY KIWI. Zones 2–10, 12, 14–24, 28, 31–41. Much like *A. deliciosa* but with smaller leaves, flowers; fruit 1–1½ in. long, fuzzless (eat skin and all). Female varieties 'Ananasnaja' and 'Hood River' need male varieties for pollen. The rare variety 'Issai' is self-fertile. Fruiting is satisfactory even in mild winters.

A. deliciosa (A. chinensis). KIWI, CHINESE GOOSEBERRY VINE. Zones 4–9, 12, 14–24, 29–31. Twines and leans to 30 ft. if not curbed. Leaves 5–8 in. long, roundish, rich dark green above, velvety white below. New growth often has rich red fuzz. Flowers 1–1½ in. wide, opening creamy and fading to buff. Fruit egg size, roughly egg shaped, covered with brown fuzz. Green flesh edible and delicious, with hints of melon, strawberry, banana. Although single plants are ornamental, you need both a male and a female plant for fruit. The best female (fruiting) varieties are 'Chico' and 'Hayward' (similar, possibly identical varieties); 'Vincent' needs little winter chill and is a good variety for the mildest winter climates. 'Tomuri' is pollinator for 'Vincent'.

Harvest fruit in late October or November. Store at refrigerator temperature in plastic bags. Ripen fruit at room temperature as needed. ▶

A

A. kolomikta. Zones 2–9, 15–17, 31–41. Rapid growth to 15 ft. or more to produce a wondrous foliage mass made up of heart-shaped, 3–5-in.-long, variegated leaves. Male varieties are generally sold, since they are said to have better color than females. Some leaves are all white, some are green splashed with white, and others have rose, pink, or even red variegation. Color is best in cool spring weather. In warm regions, color is apparent only in light shade. Clusters of fragrant, small white flowers in early summer.

ADENIUM obesum

Apocynaceae

SHRUB, OFTEN GROWN AS HOUSE PLANT

⚡ ZONES 23–27; OR INDOORS

☼ FULL SUN

🌢 REGULAR WATER DURING GROWTH

☠ MILKY SAP IS POISONOUS IF INGESTED

Adenium obesum

Twisted branches grow from huge, fleshy, half-buried trunk or rootstock. Can reach 9 ft. tall outdoors. Leaves sparse; plant leafless for long periods. Clustered saucer-shaped blossoms are deep pink, 2 in. or more across. Cannot take frost or winter chill and cold soil. Relocate container plants to warm area when temperatures dip below 50°F/10°C. Needs heat, light, perfect drainage, regular water during growth, dryness during dormancy; in short, this is a plant for careful enthusiasts and collectors. In bloom, extremely showy; in eastern tropical Africa, where it is native, it is known as "desert rose" or "desert azalea."

ADENOPHORA

LADY BELLS

Campanulaceae (Lobeliaceae)

PERENNIALS

⚡ ZONES 1–10, 14–24, 30–43

☼◐ FULL SUN OR LIGHT SHADE

🌢🌢 REGULAR TO MODERATE WATER

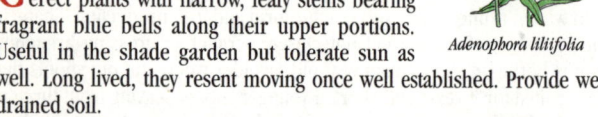
Adenophora liliifolia

Campanula relatives, mostly from the Far East; erect plants with narrow, leafy stems bearing fragrant blue bells along their upper portions. Useful in the shade garden but tolerate sun as well. Long lived, they resent moving once well established. Provide well-drained soil.

A. confusa. To 2½ ft., with deep blue flowers in mid- to late summer.

A. liliifolia. To 1½ ft., with pale blue (rarely white) flowers.

ADIANTUM

MAIDENHAIR FERN

Polypodiaceae

FERNS

⚡ ZONES VARY BY SPECIES

☼◐ PARTIAL OR FULL SHADE

🌢🌢 AMPLE WATER

Adiantum aleuticum

Most are native to tropics; some originate in North America. Stems thin, wiry, and dark; fronds finely cut; leaflets mostly fan shaped, bright green, thin textured. Plants need shade, steady moisture, and soil rich in organic matter. Leaves of even hardy varieties die back in hard frosts. Kinds listed as tender or indoor plants sometimes succeed in sheltered places in mild-winter areas.

A. aleuticum (A. pedatum aleuticum). FIVE-FINGER FERN, WESTERN MAIDENHAIR. Zones 1–9, 14–21, 36–40. Native to North America. Fronds fork to make a fingerlike pattern atop slender 1–2½-ft. stems. General effect airy and fresh; excellent in containers or shaded beds.

A. capillus-veneris. SOUTHERN MAIDENHAIR. Zones 5–9, 14–28, 31, 32, 34, 36, 37. Native to North America. To 1½ ft. tall, fronds twice divided but not forked.

A. hispidulum. ROSY MAIDENHAIR. Native to tropics of Asia, Africa. Indoor or greenhouse plant. To 1 ft. tall. Young fronds rosy brown, turning medium green, shaped somewhat like five-finger fern *(A. aleuticum)*.

A. jordanii. CALIFORNIA MAIDENHAIR. Zones 5–9, 14–24. Native to California, southern Oregon. Twice-divided fronds to 2 ft. tall.

A. peruvianum. SILVER DOLLAR MAIDENHAIR. Native to Peru. Indoor or greenhouse plant. To 1½ ft. or more in height. Segments of fronds quite large, to 2 in. wide.

A. raddianum (A. cuneatum, A. decorum). Native to Brazil. Tender fern for indoors or greenhouse. Fronds cut three or four times, 15–18 in. long. Many named varieties differing in texture and compactness. Grow in pots; move outdoors to a sheltered, shaded patio in summer. Varieties commonly sold are 'Fritz-Luthii', 'Gracillimum' (most finely cut), and 'Pacific Maid'.

A. tenerum. Native to New World tropics. Indoors or greenhouse. Long, broad fronds arch gracefully, are finely divided into many deeply cut segments ½–¾ in. wide. 'Wrightii' is similar or identical.

AECHMEA

Bromeliaceae

BROMELIADS

⚡ ZONES 22–27; OR INDOORS

◐ PARTIAL SHADE

🌢 UNIQUE WATER NEEDS AND MECHANICS

Aechmea fasciata

In frost-free areas, grow in pots, in hanging baskets, or in moss fastened in crotches of trees—always in shaded places with good air circulation. Can grow in ground, but be ready to bring indoors or cover during cold spells. Indoors or outdoors, soil should be fast draining but moisture retentive. Apply water regularly into cups within leaves. Put water on soil when it's really dry to the touch. Bromeliad specialists list dozens of species and varieties, and new hybrids appear frequently.

A. chantinii. Rosettes of leaves 1–3 ft. long, green to gray green banded with silver or darker green. Tall flower clusters have orange, pink, or red bracts; yellow-and-red flowers; white or blue fruit.

A. fasciata. Gray-green leaves crossbanded with silvery white. From the center grows a cluster of rosy pink flower bracts in which nestle pale blue flowers that change to deep rose. 'Silver King' has unusually silvery leaves; 'Marginata' has leaves edged with creamy white bands.

A. 'Foster's Favorite'. Hybrid with bright wine red, lacquered leaves about 1 ft. long. Drooping, spikelike flower clusters in coral red and blue. 'Royal Wine', another hybrid, forms an open rosette of somewhat leathery, glossy, light green leaves that are burgundy red beneath. Orange-and-blue flowers are borne in drooping clusters.

A. fulgens. Green leaves dusted with gray, 12–16 in. long, 2–3 in. wide. Flower cluster usually above the leaves; blossoms red, blue, and blue violet. *A. f. discolor* has brownish red or violet red leaves, usually faintly striped. Many hybrids.

A. pectinata. Stiff rosettes up to 3 ft.; leaves to 3 in. wide, strongly marked pink or red at bloom time. Flowers whitish and green.

A. weilbachii. Shiny leaves, green or suffused with red tones, in 2–3-ft.-wide rosettes. Dull red, 1½-ft. flower stalk has orange-red berries tipped with lilac.

FOR INFORMATION ON SELECTING PLANTS

PLEASE SEE PAGES 79–160

AEGOPODIUM podagraria

BISHOP'S WEED, GOUT WEED

Apiaceae (Umbelliferae)

DECIDUOUS PERENNIAL

☘ ZONES 1–9, 12, 14–24, 30–45

☀◐● SUN OR SHADE

◍ MODERATE WATER

Aegopodium podagraria
'Variegatum'

Very vigorous ground cover, especially in rich soil. Spreads by creeping underground rootstocks; best if contained behind underground barrier of wood, concrete, or heavy tar paper. Many light green, divided leaves make a low (to 6-in.), dense mass; leaflets are ½–3 in. long. To keep it low and even, mow it two or three times a year.

'Variegatum' is the most widely planted form. Leaflets are edged white, giving a luminous effect in shade. Pull plants that revert to solid green leaves. Can become invasive, but takes longer to do so than the species.

AESCULUS

HORSECHESTNUT, BUCKEYE

Hippocastanaceae

DECIDUOUS TREES OR LARGE SHRUBS

☘ ZONES VARY BY SPECIES

☀ FULL SUN

◍ REGULAR WATER, EXCEPT AS NOTED

◆ SEEDS OF ALL ARE SLIGHTLY TOXIC IF INGESTED

Aesculus carnea

Leaves are divided fanwise into large, toothed leaflets. Springtime flowers, in long, dense, showy clusters at the ends of branches, attract hummingbirds. Leathery fruit capsules enclose glossy seeds.

A. californica. CALIFORNIA BUCKEYE. Zones 4–10, 12, 14–24. Shrub or small tree, often multistemmed; 10–20 ft. or taller and wide spreading. Rich green leaves with five to seven 3–6-in.-long leaflets. Fragrant cream-colored flowers. Big, pear-shaped fruits split to reveal shiny brown seeds used in arrangements. Fully drought tolerant once established. In the wild, tree drops leaves by July, but if given water holds them until fall.

A. carnea. RED HORSECHESTNUT. Zones 1–10, 12, 14–17, 32–45. Hybrid between *A. hippocastanum* and *A. pavia*. To 40 ft. high and 30 ft. wide—smaller than *A. hippocastanum* and a better fit for small gardens. Round headed with large, dark green leaves, each divided into five leaflets; casts dense shade. Gets leaf scorch, defoliates in warm, humid regions. Bears hundreds of 8-in.-long plumes of soft pink to red flowers. 'Briotii' has rosy crimson flowers; 'O'Neill Red' has bright red blooms.

A. glabra. OHIO BUCKEYE. Zones 1–10, 12, 14–17, 32–43. To 40 ft., possibly taller, with dense, rounded form. Low branching, casts dense shade. Early to leaf out. Bright green expanding leaves mature to dark green, then turn yellow to orange in autumn. Flowers greenish yellow in 4–7-in. clusters. Prickly seed capsules enclose shiny brown buckeyes.

A. hippocastanum. COMMON HORSECHESTNUT. Native to Europe. Zones 1–10, 12, 14–17, 32–43. To 60 ft. high with a 40-ft. spread, this bulky, densely foliaged tree gives heavy shade. Leaves divided into five to seven toothed, 4–10-in.-long leaflets. Gets leaf scorch, defoliates in warm, humid regions. Spectacular flower show: ivory blooms with pink markings in 1-ft.-long plumes. Invasive roots can break up walks. 'Baumannii' has double flowers, sets no seeds.

A. parviflora. BOTTLEBRUSH BUCKEYE. Zones 4–6, 31–41. Native to southeastern U.S. Shrub to 12–15 ft. tall, spreading by suckers, with dark green leaves divided into five to seven 3–8-in.-long leaflets. Very showy white flower clusters (8–12 in. tall, 2–4 in. wide). Bright yellow fall foliage. Good choice for massing, shrub borders, or specimen planting.

A. pavia. RED BUCKEYE. Zones 3–9, 14–24, 30–34. Native to eastern U.S. Bulky shrub or tree to 12–20 ft., with irregular rounded crown. Nar-

row, erect 10-in. clusters of bright red or orange-red (rarely yellow) flowers. Best foliage for warm, humid climates.

AETHIONEMA

STONECRESS

Brassicaceae (Cruciferae)

PERENNIALS

☘ ZONES 1–9, 14–21, 32–45

☀ FULL SUN

◍ MODERATE TO LITTLE WATER

Aethionema warleyense

Native to Mediterranean region and Asia Minor. Choice shrublets, attractive in or out of bloom, best adapted to colder climates; a favorite among rock gardeners. Grow best in a light, porous soil with considerable lime. Bloom late spring to summer. Deadhead flowers.

A. schistosum. Erect, unbranched stems 5–10 in. high, densely clothed with narrow, slate blue, ½-in.-long leaves. Fragrant, rose-colored flowers; petals about ¼ in. long.

A. warleyense (A. 'Warley Rose'). Hybrid form; neat, compact plant to 8 in. high. Pink flowers in dense clusters. Widely used; only one planted to any extent in warmer climates.

AFRICAN BOXWOOD. See MYRSINE africana

AFRICAN CORN LILY. See IXIA

AFRICAN DAISY. See ARCTOTIS, DIMORPHOTHECA, OSTEOSPERMUM

AFRICAN IRIS. See DIETES

AFRICAN LINDEN. See SPARMANNIA africana

AFRICAN VIOLET. See SAINTPAULIA ionantha

AGAPANTHUS

LILY-OF-THE-NILE

Amaryllidaceae

PERENNIALS

☘ ZONES VARY BY SPECIES

☀◐ FULL SUN OR LIGHT SHADE

◍◍ REGULAR TO MODERATE WATER

Agapanthus orientalis

All form fountainlike clumps of strap-shaped leaves, from which rise bare stems ending in spherical clusters of funnel-shaped flowers in summer. Each bloom cluster resembles a burst of blue (sometimes white) fireworks.

Adaptable. Will bloom in full sun or light shade. Best in loamy soil but will grow in heavy soils. Thrive with regular water, but established plants in the ground year-round can grow and bloom without watering during prolonged dry periods. Divide infrequently; every 5 or 6 years is usually sufficient. In cold-winter areas, lift and store over winter and replant in spring. Superb container plants. Good near pools.

A. africanus. Evergreen. Zones 7–9, 12–31. Leaves shorter, narrower than those of *A. orientalis;* flower stalks shorter (to 1½ ft. tall) with blue flowers in fewer numbers (20–50 to a cluster). Often sold as *A. umbellatus.*

A. Headbourne Hybrids. Deciduous. Zones 3–9, 12–21, 28–31, warmer parts of 32. Flowers come in a range of blues and in white on 2–2½-ft.-tall stems above fairly narrow, rather upright foliage.

A. inapertus. Deciduous. Zones 3–9, 12–21, 28–31, warmer parts of 32. Deep blue blossoms in drooping clusters atop 4–5-ft. stems.

A. orientalis. Evergreen. Zones 7–9, 12–31. Most commonly planted. Broad, arching leaves in big clumps. Stems to 4–5 ft. tall bear up to 100 blue flowers. There are white ('Albus'), double ('Flore Pleno'), and giant blue varieties. Often sold as *A. africanus, A. umbellatus.*

A. 'Peter Pan'. Evergreen. Zones 7–9, 12–31. Outstanding dwarf. Foliage clumps 8–12 in. tall; profuse blue flowers top 1–1½-ft. stems.

A

AGASTACHE

GIANT HYSSOP

Lamiaceae (Labiatae)

PERENNIALS

⚡ ZONES VARY BY SPECIES

☼ ◐ FULL SUN OR PARTIAL SHADE

◗ ◖ REGULAR TO MODERATE WATER

Agastache foeniculum

Aromatic summer-blooming perennials somewhat resembling salvias, with whorls of purple, blue, or yellow flowers forming spikelike clusters. Provide well-drained soil.

A. barberi. Zones 8, 9, 14–24, 29, 30, warmer parts of 32. Woody-based perennial to 2 ft., with 2-in. leaves and reddish purple flowers on 6–12-in. spikes. 'Firebird' has coppery orange-red flowers, Purple-flowered 'Tutti-Frutti' is a good substitute for purple loosestrife *(Lythrum)*.

A. foeniculum. ANISE HYSSOP. Zones 2–24, 28–41. Erect, narrow clumping perennial to 5 ft., with anise- or licorice-scented foliage and dense clusters of lilac blue flowers on 4-in. spikes. Decorative and useful in perennial borders or herb gardens.

A. mexicana. Zones 14–24, 29. Grows to 2 ft., with 2½-in. toothed leaves and rose pink inch-long flowers on spikes to 1 ft. long. 'Champagne' has apricot flowers.

AGATHAEA coelestis. See FELICIA amelloides

Agavaceae. The agave family contains rosette-forming, sometimes treelike plants generally from dry regions. Flower clusters are spikes or spikelike; leaves often contain tough fibers.

AGAVE

Agavaceae

SUCCULENTS

⚡ ZONES VARY BY SPECIES

☼ ◐ FULL SUN OR PARTIAL SHADE

◗ MODERATE TO LITTLE WATER, EXCEPT AS NOTED

Agave attenuata

Succulents, mostly gigantic, with large clumps of fleshy, strap-shaped leaves. The flower clusters are big but not colorful. After flowering—which may not occur for years—the foliage clump dies, usually leaving behind suckers that make new plants. The plants shrivel from serious drought but plump up again when watered or rained on. In rainy climates, they must have good drainage.

A. americana. CENTURY PLANT. Zones 10, 12–30. Leaves to 6 ft. long, with hooked spines along the edges and a wicked spine at the tip; blue green in color. Be sure you really want one before planting it: the bulk and spines make it formidable to remove. After 10 years or more, the plant produces a branched, 15–40-ft. flower stalk bearing yellowish green flowers. There are several varieties with yellow- or white-striped leaves.

A. attenuata. Zones 20–27. Leaves 2½ ft. long, soft green or gray green, fleshy, somewhat translucent, without spines. Makes clumps to 5 ft. across; older plants develop a stout trunk to 5 ft. tall. Greenish yellow flowers dense on arching spikes to 12–14 ft. long. Will take poor soil but does best in rich soil with regular water. Protect from frost and hot sun. Statuesque container plant. Good near ocean or pool.

A. filifera. Zones 12–29. Rosettes less than 2 ft. wide; leaves are narrow, dark green, lined with white, and edged with long white threads.

A. parryi huachucensis. Zones 10, 12–30. Gray-green, 2–3-ft.-wide rosettes resemble giant artichokes. Tips of leaves fiercely spined. Makes offsets freely.

A. victoriae-reginae. Zones 10, 12, 13, 15–17, 21–30. Clumps only a foot or so across. The many dark green leaves are 6 in. long, 2 in. wide, stiff,

thick, with narrow white lines. Slow growing; will stand in pot or ground 20 years before flowering (greenish flowers on tall stalks), and then die.

AGERATUM, HARDY. See EUPATORIUM coelestinum

AGERATUM houstonianum

FLOSS FLOWER

Asteraceae (Compositae)

ANNUAL

⚡ ALL ZONES

☼ ◐ PARTIAL SHADE IN HOT CLIMATES

◗ REGULAR WATER

Ageratum houstonianum

Reliable favorite for summer and fall in borders and containers. Leaves roundish, usually heart shaped at the base, soft green, hairy. Tiny blue, white, or pink tassel-like flowers in dense clusters. A few tall types, such as 2½-ft. 'Blue Horizon', are sold but most varieties offered are low growers. Dwarf kinds (4–6 in. high) with blue flowers include 'Blue Blazer', 'Blue Danube' ('Blue Puffs'), 'Blue Surf', and 'Royal Delft'. Somewhat taller (9–12-in.) blues include 'Blue Mink' and 'North Sea'. Good varieties in other colors are 'Pink Powder-puffs' and white-blooming 'Summer Snow', both 9 in. high.

Best in rich, moist soil. Easy to transplant even when in bloom. Low growers make excellent edgings or pattern plantings with other similar-size annuals. Tall types provide good cut flowers.

AGLAONEMA

Araceae

PERENNIALS

⚡ ZONE 25, 27; OR INDOORS

☼ ◗ TOLERATE VERY LOW LIGHT

◖ AMPLE WATER

Aglaonema modestum

Tropical plants valued mostly for their ornamental foliage. Flowers resemble small, greenish white callas. Often used outdoors in containers or in north-side foundation plantings in mildest frost-free climates; elsewhere, they're house plants. Among the best plants for poorly lighted situations. In fact, few plants can get by on as little light as aglaonema; *A. modestum* is especially tolerant of low light.

Potted plants need a rich, porous potting mix; they thrive with lots of water but will get along with small amounts. Cut stems will grow for a long time in a glass of water. Exudation from leaf tips (especially those of *A. modestum*) spots wood finishes (as on tabletops).

A. commutatum. Grows to 2 ft. Deep green leaves to 6 in. long, 2 in. across, with pale green markings on veins. Flowers followed by inch-long clusters of yellow to red berries. *A. c. maculatum,* with many irregular, gray-green stripes on leaves, is the most common. 'Pseudobracteatum', 1–2 ft. tall, has white leafstalks and deep green leaves marked with pale green and creamy yellow. 'Treubii' has narrow leaves heavily marked with silvery gray.

A. costatum. Slow-growing, low plant with leaves to 8 in. long, 4 in. wide. Bright green spotted white and a broad white stripe along the midrib. 'Foxii' is similar or identical.

A. crispum (A. roebelenii). Robust plant with leathery leaves to 10 in. long, 5 in. wide, dark green with pale green markings. Sometimes sold as *A.* 'Pewter'.

A. modestum. CHINESE EVERGREEN. A serviceable, easily grown plant, in time forming substantial clumps with several stems 2–3 ft. high. Shiny dark green leaves to 1½ ft. long, 5 in. wide. Often sold as *A. simplex.*

A. 'Silver King' and **'Silver Queen'.** Both are heavy producers of narrow, dark green leaves strongly marked with silver. Both grow to 2 ft. 'Silver King' has larger leaves than 'Silver Queen'.

A

AGROPYRON

WHEATGRASS	
Poaceae (Gramineae)	
LAWN GRASSES	
✿ ZONES 1–3, 10, 41–45	
☼ FULL SUN	
⬤ MONTHLY SOAKINGS	

Agropyron smithii

Two kinds of wheatgrass, both basically pasture grasses, make reasonably attractive lawns in Rocky Mountains and on high plains. They can survive with 8–18 in. of rainfall per year, but when planted close and mowed at 2 in. they should be soaked to 18–20 in. every 30 days. Plant 2 lbs. per 1,000 sq. ft.

A. cristatum. CRESTED WHEATGRASS. Bunching grass rather than sod-forming grass. Fairway strain, used for low-maintenance, low-irrigation lawns, is shorter, denser, and finer than common kind.

A. smithii. WESTERN WHEATGRASS. Forms sod, but slowly. Tolerates great heat, cold, moderately alkaline soil.

AGROSTEMMA githago

CORN COCKLE	
Caryophyllaceae	
ANNUAL	
✿ ALL ZONES	
☼ FULL SUN	
⬤ REGULAR TO MODERATE WATER	
⬥ ALL PARTS ARE POISONOUS IF INGESTED	

Agrostemma githago

The species is an attractive weed of roadside and grain field. Variety 'Milas' is a superior plant with 3-in. flowers of deep purplish pink, lined and spotted with deep purple and centered with a white eye. Stems 6–12 in. long make it a good cut flower. Plants wispy but sturdy, 2–3 ft. tall. Sow seed in spring or early summer for summer and fall bloom in most climates; sow in fall for winter–spring bloom in warmest climates. Mass at rear of border, among shrubs, or in front of fence or hedge.

AGROSTIS

BENT, BENT GRASS	
Poaceae (Gramineae)	
LAWN GRASSES	
✿ ZONES 1–24, 34–45	
☼ FULL SUN	
⬤ AMPLE WATER	

Agrostis stolonifera

All except redtop make beautiful velvety lawns under proper conditions and with constant care. They need frequent close mowing, frequent feeding, occasional top-dressing, and much water. In hot weather they succumb to fungal diseases. Best putting greens are of bent grass.

A. gigantea. REDTOP. Coarser than other bents, not generally used in lawns. Has been used as quick-sprouting nurse grass in mixtures or for winter overseeding of Bermuda and other winter-dormant grasses.

A. stolonifera. CREEPING BENT. Premium lawn but requires the most care, including frequent mowing to ½ in. tall with special mower. Seed-grown strains include Emerald, Penncross, and Seaside. In some areas you can buy sprigs or sod of choice strains, Congressional, Old Orchard.

A. tenuis. COLONIAL BENT. More erect than *A. stolonifera;* somewhat easier to care for but still fussy. Astoria and Highland are best-known strains; latter is tougher, hardier, more disease resistant. Mow to ¾ in.

AILANTHUS altissima

TREE-OF-HEAVEN	
Simaroubaceae	
DECIDUOUS TREE	
✿ ZONES 2–24, 28–39	
☼ FULL SUN	
⬤⬤ REGULAR TO LITTLE WATER	

Ailanthus altissima

Native to China, but naturalized over much of the U.S. Fast growth to 50 ft. Leaves 1–3 ft. long are divided into 13–25 leaflets 3–5 in. long. Flowers on male trees are smelly. On female trees, the inconspicuous greenish flowers are usually followed by handsome clusters of red-brown, winged seedpods in late summer and fall; great for dried arrangements. Though often condemned as a weed tree because it suckers profusely and self-seeds, it must be praised for its ability to create beauty and shade under adverse conditions, including extreme air pollution and every type of difficult soil. It is the tree that survived against all odds in *A Tree Grows in Brooklyn.*

AIR PLANT. See KALANCHOE pinnata

Aizoaceae. This family of succulent plants includes all the ice plants and most of the so-called living stones.

AJUGA

CARPET BUGLE	
Lamiaceae (Labiatae)	
PERENNIALS	
✿ ZONES 1–24, 26–45	
☼ ◐ FULL SUN OR PARTIAL SHADE	
⬤ REGULAR WATER	

Ajuga reptans

One species is a rock garden plant; the others are ground covers. Of the latter, the highly variable *A. reptans* is better known and more useful, though it will escape into lawns unless contained. All bloom spring to early summer.

A. genevensis. Rock garden plant 5–14 in. high, does not spread by runners. Grayish, hairy stems and coarse-toothed leaves to 3 in. long. Flowers in blue spikes; rose and white forms are also sold.

A. pyramidalis. Erect plant 2–10 in. high; does not spread by runners. Stems, with long grayish hairs, have many roundish, 1½–4-in.-long leaves. Violet blue flowers are not obvious among the large leaves. 'Metallica Crispa' has reddish brown leaves with a metallic glint.

A. reptans. The popular ground cover ajuga. Spreads quickly by runners, making a mat of dark green leaves that grow 2–3 in. wide in full sun, 3–4 in. wide in part shade. Varieties with bronze- or metallic-tinted leaves keep color best in full sun. Flowers, usually blue, borne in 4–5-in.-high spikes. Plant in spring or early fall 6–12 in. apart. Mow or trim off old flower spikes. Subject to root-knot nematodes; also subject to rot and fungal diseases where drainage or air circulation is poor. Many varieties of this species are available, some sold under several names. The following are among the best choices.

'Alba'. Flowers are white.

'Purpurea'. Usually has somewhat larger leaves tinted bronze or purple. Often sold as 'Atropurpurea'.

'Rosea'. Pink flowers.

'Variegata'. Leaves edged and splotched with creamy yellow.

FOR INFORMATION ON YOUR CLIMATE ZONE
PLEASE SEE PAGES 16–78

A

AKEBIA quinata

FIVELEAF AKEBIA

Lardizabalaceae

DECIDUOUS VINE, EVERGREEN IN MILD WINTERS

☀ ZONES 3–24, 29–41

☀ ◑ ● SUN OR SHADE

💧 REGULAR WATER

Akebia quinata

Native to Japan, China, and Korea. Twines to 15–20 ft. Grows fast in mild regions, slower where winters are cold. Dainty leaves on 3–5-in. stalks, each divided into five deep green leaflets 2–3 in. long, notched at tips. Clusters of quaint dull purple flowers in spring are more a surprise than a show. The edible fruit, if produced, looks like a thick, 2½–4-in.-long, purplish sausage.

Give support for climbing; keep plant under control to prevent it from becoming rampant. Benefits from annual pruning. Recovers quickly when cut to the ground. For a tracery effect on post or column, prune out all but two or three basal stems.

A. trifoliata. THREELEAF AKEBIA. Like the above but with three instead of five leaflets per leaf.

ALASKA CEDAR. See CHAMAECYPARIS nootkatensis

ALBIZIA (Albizzia)

Fabaceae (Leguminosae)

DECIDUOUS TO SEMIEVERGREEN TREES

☀ ZONES VARY BY SPECIES

☀ ◑ FULL SUN OR PARTIAL SHADE

💧💧 WATER NEEDS VARY BY SPECIES

Albizia julibrissin

Twice-divided, finely textured foliage and powder-puff flowers that are attractive to birds.

A. distachya (A. lophantha). PLUME ALBIZIA. Semievergreen. Zones 15–17, 22–27. Native to Australia. Not as hardy as the better-known *A. julibrissin*. Often naturalizes in favorable climates. Needs no irrigation; will grow in pure sand at beach. Fast growing to 20 ft. Foliage is dark velvety green compared to the light yellowish green of *A. julibrissin*. The flowers in late spring are greenish yellow in fluffy, 2-in.-long spikes. Best as a temporary screen at beach while slower permanent planting develops.

A. julibrissin. SILK TREE. Deciduous. Zones 4–23, 26–33. Native to Asia from Iran to Japan. This is the "mimosa" of eastern U.S., though it's also grown in the West—it's one of the best sellers in inland valleys of Southern California. Rapid growth to 40 ft. with wider spread. Can be headed back to make a 10–20-ft. umbrella. Fluffy pink flowers like pincushions on ferny-leafed branches in summer. Light-sensitive leaves fold at night. 'Rosea' has richer pink flowers and is considered hardier. Silk tree does best with high summer heat. With regular water, it grows fast; on skimpy moisture, it usually survives but grows slowly, looks yellowish.

Unique flat-topped, spreading canopy makes it a good patio tree, despite fallen leaves, flowers, and pods. In many parts of the country, tree is short lived because of a wilt disease; check with a local nursery.

MAKE HOLLYHOCKS BLOOM TWICE

In July, after blooms fade, cut off flower stems just above the ground. Continue to feed and water the plants. Roots will push out another flush of growth, which will rebloom in September. This technique demands a lot from the plants, so feed two or three times during the regular growing season, and water as needed all along.

ALCEA rosea (Althaea rosea)

HOLLYHOCK

Malvaceae

BIENNIAL OR SHORT-LIVED PERENNIAL

☀ ALL ZONES

☀ FULL SUN

💧 REGULAR WATER

Alcea rosea

This old-fashioned favorite has its place against a fence or wall or at the back of a border. Old single varieties can reach 9 ft.; newer strains and selections are shorter. Big, rough, roundish heart-shaped leaves more or less lobed; single, semidouble, or double flowers 3–6 in. wide in white, pink, rose, red, purple, creamy yellow, apricot. Summer bloom. Destroy rust-infected leaves as soon as disease appears.

Chater's Double is a fine perennial strain; 6-ft. spires have 5–6-in. flowers. So-called annual strains (biennials treated as annuals) bloom first year from seed sown in early spring: Summer Carnival strain is 5–6 ft. tall with double 4-in. flowers; Majorette strain is 2½ ft. tall with 3–4-in. flowers; Pinafore strain (mixed colors) branches freely from base, has five to eight bloom stalks per plant. Sow seeds in ground in August or September for next season's bloom.

ALCHEMILLA

LADY'S-MANTLE

Rosaceae

PERENNIALS

☀ ZONES VARY BY SPECIES

☀ ◑ TOLERATE SUN IN COOL-SUMMER CLIMATES

💧 REGULAR WATER

Alchemilla mollis

Rounded pale green lobed leaves have a silvery look; after rain or overhead watering they hold beads of water on their surfaces. Summer flowers are yellowish green, in large branched clusters, individually inconspicuous but attractive as a mass. Useful for edgings in shady places, as ground cover and as soothing contrast to brightly colored flowers.

A. alpina. Zones 1–6, 36–43. Mat-forming plant creeping by runners, with flowering stems 6–8 in. tall. Leaves 2 in. wide, divided into five or seven leaflets.

A. erythropoda. Zones 3–6, 36–40. Resembles *A. glaucescens* but has more deeply lobed leaves and red-tinted flowering stems.

A. glaucescens (A. pubescens). Zones 3–6, 36–40. Dense grower. Flowering stems to 8 in. tall. Leaves nearly round; seven to nine lobes.

A. mollis. Zones 2–9, 14–24, 31–43. To 2 ft. or more, with equal spread, and nearly circular, scallop-edged leaves to 6 in. across.

ALDER. See ALNUS

ALDER BUCKTHORN. See RHAMNUS frangula

ALEURITES fordii

TUNG TREE, TUNG-OIL TREE

Euphorbiaceae

DECIDUOUS TREE

☀ ZONES 26–28

☀ FULL SUN

💧 REGULAR WATER

Aleurites fordii

Tree of rounded habit to 25 ft. or taller, with broadly oval, 5–10-in. leaves resembling those of catalpa. Clusters of 1-in. white flowers with pinkish or orange veins open as leaves expand. Following the blossoms are roundish, 2–3-.in.-wide fruits, valuable in producing the tung oil used in paints and varnishes. A handsome tree, but chiefly planted for its oil.

ALEXANDRA PALM. See ARCHONTOPHOENIX alexandrae

ALGERIAN IVY. See HEDERA canariensis

ALLAMANDA

Apocynaceae

EVERGREEN VINES OR SHRUBS

🌿 ZONES 24–27; OR ANNUAL OR GREENHOUSE PLANTS

☼ FULL SUN

💧 REGULAR WATER

◊ ALL PARTS ARE POISONOUS IF INGESTED

Allamanda cathartica

These handsome tropical plants tolerate very little frost and require considerable heat for proper growth; warm nights as well as warm days seem necessary. Both foliage and flowers are imposing. Year-round outdoor plants only in the mildest climates. Will succeed as annual vines anywhere with a long growing season; otherwise, greenhouse plants.

A. cathartica. ALLAMANDA, GOLDEN TRUMPET. Can grow to great heights as a vine, but often pinched back as a large free-standing shrub. Leaves are glossy, leathery, 4–6 in. long. Trumpet-shaped yellow flowers are 5 in. wide, 3 in. long. 'Hendersonii' has exceptionally attractive orange-yellow flowers.

A. schottii (A. neriifolia). BUSH ALLAMANDA. Shrubby, to 5 ft., with occasional climbing stems. Flowers 3 in. wide, tinted orange or reddish.

ALLIUM

ORNAMENTAL ALLIUM

Liliaceae

BULBS

🌿 ZONES VARY BY SPECIES; OR DIG AND STORE; OR GROW IN POTS

☼◑ FULL SUN OR PARTIAL SHADE

💧 REGULAR WATER DURING GROWTH AND BLOOM

Allium giganteum

About 500 species, all from the Northern Hemisphere. Relatives of the edible onion, peerless as cut flowers (fresh or dried) and useful in borders; smaller kinds are effective in rock gardens. Most ornamental alliums are hardy, sun loving, easy to grow; they thrive in deep, rich, sandy loam. Plant bulbs in fall. Lift and divide only after they become crowded. Alliums bear small flowers in compact or loose roundish clusters at ends of leafless stems 6 in.–5 ft. tall or more. Many are delightfully fragrant; those with onion odor must be bruised or cut to give it off. Various species provide flowers from late spring through summer, in white and shades of pink, rose, violet, red, blue, yellow. All alliums die to the ground after bloom, even in mild climates. In areas colder than stated hardiness, dig and store; or grow in pots and protect during winter.

A. aflatunense. Zones 1–24, 29–43. Round clusters of lilac flowers on stems 2½–5 ft. tall. Resembles *A. giganteum* but with smaller (2–3-in.) flower clusters; blooms in late spring.

A. atropurpureum. Zones 4–24, 28–34, 39. Stems to 2½ ft. tall carry 2-in. clusters of dark purple to nearly black flowers in late spring.

A. caeruleum (A. azureum). BLUE ALLIUM. Zones 1–24, 28–45. Cornflower blue flowers in dense, round clusters 2 in. across on 1-ft. stems. Late spring bloom.

A. carinatum pulchellum (A. pulchellum). Zones 3–24, 29–41. Tight clusters of reddish purple flowers on 2-ft. stems, late spring.

A. cepa. See Onion

A. christophii (A. albopilosum). STAR OF PERSIA. Zones 1–24, 29–43. Distinctive. Very large clusters (6–12 in. across) of lavender to deep lilac, starlike flowers with metallic sheen. Late spring bloom. Stems 12–15 in. tall. Leaves to 1½ ft. long, white and hairy beneath. Dried flower cluster looks like an elegant ornament.

A. giganteum. GIANT ALLIUM. Zones 3–24, 29–41. Spectacular ball-like clusters of bright lilac flowers on stems 5 ft. tall or more. Summer bloom. Leaves 1½ ft. long, 2 in. wide.

A. karataviense. TURKESTAN ALLIUM. Zones 1–24, 28–43. Large, dense, round flower clusters in midspring, varying in color from pinkish to beige to reddish lilac. Broad, flat, recurved leaves, 2–5 in. across.

A. moly. GOLDEN GARLIC. Zones 1–24, 28–43. Bright, shining, yellow flowers in open clusters on 9–18-in.-tall stems. Late spring bloom. Flat leaves 2 in. wide, almost as long as flower stems.

A. narcissiflorum. Zones 3–24, 29–41. Foot-tall stems with loose clusters of ½-in. bell-shaped, bright rose flowers, summer.

A. neapolitanum. Zones 4–24, 28–34, 39. Spreading clusters of large white flowers on 1-ft. stems bloom in midspring. Leaves 1 in. wide. Variety 'Grandiflorum' is larger, blooms earlier. A form of 'Grandiflorum' listed as 'Cowanii' is considered superior. Grown commercially as cut flowers.

A. ostrowskianum (A. oreophilum ostrowskianum). Zones 1–24, 28–43. Large, loose clusters of rose-colored flowers on 8–12-in. stems in late spring; two or three narrow, gray-green leaves. 'Zwanenburg' has deep carmine red flowers, 6-in. stems. Good for rock gardens, cutting.

A. porrum. See Leek

A. rosenbachianum. Zones 1–24, 29–43. Similar to *A. giganteum* but slightly smaller; blooms in late spring.

A. sativum. See Garlic

A. schoenoprasum. See Chives

A. scorodoprasum. See Garlic

A. sphaerocephalum. DRUMSTICKS, ROUND-HEADED GARLIC. Zones 1–24, 28–43. Tight, dense, spherical red-purple flower clusters on 2-ft. stems, early summer. Spreads freely.

A. tuberosum. CHINESE CHIVES, GARLIC CHIVES, ORIENTAL GARLIC. Zones 3–24, 28–41.

Allium tuberosum

Spreads by tuberous rootstocks and by seeds. Clumps of gray-green, flat leaves ¼ in. wide, 1 ft. long or less. Abundance of 1–1½-ft.-tall stalks bear clusters of white flowers in summer. Flowers have scent of violets, are excellent for fresh or dry arrangements. Leaves have mild garlic flavor, are useful in salads and cooked dishes. Grow like chives.

ALLOPLECTUS nummularia (Hypocyrta nummularia)

GOLDFISH PLANT

Gesneriaceae

INDOOR CONTAINER PLANT

◑ BRIGHT INDIRECT LIGHT

💧 FREQUENT WATER

Related to African violet, with similar cultural needs. Foot-long, arching branches closely set with shiny oval or roundish leaves to 2½ in. long.

Alloplectus nummularia

Flowers about 1 in. long, orange, puffy, and roundish, pinched at tip into pursed mouth like that of goldfish.

With ample warmth and humidity this plant will bloom year-round. Easy to root from tip cuttings; stems may root when in contact with damp soil mix. Because of arching, trailing growth, best in hanging pot.

ALLSPICE, CAROLINA. See CALYCANTHUS floridus

A

ALMOND

Rosaceae

DECIDUOUS TREES

⚘ BEST IN ZONES 8–10, 12–16, 19–21; LESS CERTAIN IN 29, 30, WESTERN PARTS OF 33, 35

☼ FULL SUN

💧 PERIODIC DEEP SOAKING

Almond

As a tree, almond is nearly as hardy as its close relative peach, but as a nut producer it is more exacting in climate adaptation. Performs best in regions with long, hot, dry summers; nuts will not develop properly in areas with cool summers or high humidity. Needs some winter chill but will suffer from late frosts, since it blooms earlier than peach. Most successful in the West, where commercial crop is grown. Possible, though less certain, in lower plains states and Texas; best bet here is a late bloomer such as 'Hall's Hardy' (developed in Kansas). Gardeners in these areas can graft peaches, nectarines, or plums onto almond branches and be assured of some crop even if almonds fail. In the West, gardeners can choose from many more varieties. Unless you select a self-fertile strain, you will need two varieties for pollination (they can be planted in the same hole if space is tight).

An almond tree grows to 20–30 ft. high, erect when young, spreading and dome shaped in age. Leaves are 3–5 in. long, pale green with gray tinge; flowers are palest pink or white. Fruit looks like a leathery, flattened, undersized green peach; in autumn, the hull splits to reveal the pit, which is the almond. To harvest, remove hulls, spread nuts in sun, and let dry for day or two. To test for dryness, shake nuts—kernels should rattle.

Adapts to all soils except heavy, slow-draining ones. Needs deep soil—at least 6 ft. Subject to attack by brown rot (causes fruit rot, twig dieback, cankers on trunk and branches) and mites (cause premature yellowing and falling of leaves). For ornamental relatives, see *Prunus*.

ALMOND, FLOWERING. See PRUNUS triloba

ALNUS

ALDER

Betulaceae

DECIDUOUS TREES

⚘ ZONES VARY BY SPECIES

☼ ◑ ● SUN OR SHADE

💧💧 AMPLE WATER

Alnus cordata

Moisture loving, thriving in moist or wet soils, even tolerating periodic flooding. Very fast growing. In all species, clusters of tassel-like, greenish yellow male flower catkins give interesting display before leaf-out. Female flowers develop into small woody cones that decorate bare branches in winter; these delight flower arrangers. Seeds attract birds.

A. cordata. ITALIAN ALDER. Zones 3–9, 14–24, 30–33. Native to Italy, Corsica. Young growth vertical; older trees to 40 ft., spreading to 25 ft. Heart-shaped, 4-in. leaves, glossy rich green above, paler beneath. Short deciduous period.

A. glutinosa. BLACK ALDER. Zones 1–10, 14–24, 30–43. Native to Europe, North Africa, Asia. Probably best as multistemmed tree. Grows to 70 ft. Roundish, 2–4-in., coarsely toothed leaves, dark lustrous green. Makes dense mass from ground up. Good for screen.

A. incana. WHITE ALDER, GRAY ALDER. Zones 1–6, 10, 36–45. Native to Europe and the Caucasus. Good tree for cold, wet sites. Forms a pyramid to 40–60 ft. high. Dull green leaves 2–4 in. long. Varieties are more often planted than the species; these include one with yellow leaves, one with a weeping habit, and many cut-leaf forms.

A. rhombifolia. WHITE ALDER. Zones 1–9, 14–21. Native to western U.S. Very fast growing to 50–90 ft. tall, 40 ft. wide. Branches spread out, then droop at tips. Coarsely toothed, 2½–4½-in. leaves are dark green above, paler green beneath. Very tolerant of heat and wind. Susceptible to tent caterpillars and borers in its native range.

ALOCASIA

ELEPHANT'S EAR

Araceae

PERENNIALS

⚘ ZONES 22–27; OR INDOORS

☼ FILTERED SUNLIGHT

💧 💧 AMPLE WATER

☣ PLANT JUICES ARE POISONOUS IF INGESTED

Alocasia macrorrhiza

Native to tropical Asia. Handsome, lush plants for tropical effects. Flowers like those of calla (*Zantedeschia*). Plant in wind-protected places or indoors. Provide ample organic matter in soil and light, frequent feedings. Tropical plant specialists sell many kinds with leaves in coppery and purplish tones, often with striking white veins.

A. amazonica. AFRICAN MASK. Leathery, deep bronzy green leaves to 16 in. long have wavy edges, heavy white main veins. This species is the one most commonly available as a house plant.

A. macrorrhiza. Evergreen at 29°F/–2°C; loses leaves at lower temperatures but comes back in spring if frosts not too severe. Large, arrow-shaped leaves to 2 ft. or longer, on stalks to 5 ft. tall, form a dome-shaped plant 4 ft. across. Tiny flowers on spike surrounded by greenish white bract. Flowers followed by reddish fruit, giving spike the look of corn on the cob.

A. odora. Similar to *A. macrorrhiza* but not quite as hardy. Flowers fragrant.

ALOE

Liliaceae

SUCCULENTS

⚘ ZONES 8, 9, 12–27

☼ ◑ LIGHT SHADE IN HOT-SUMMER AREAS

💧 💧 REGULAR TO LITTLE WATER

☣ LATEX BENEATH THE SKIN IS AN IRRITANT

Aloe arborescens

Aloes range from 6-in. miniatures to trees; all form clumps of fleshy, pointed leaves and bear branched or unbranched clusters of orange, yellow, cream, or red flowers. Most are South African. Showy, easy to grow in well-drained soil in reasonably frost-free areas. Need little water but can take more. Most kinds make outstanding container plants. Some species in bloom every month; biggest show midwinter through summer. Leaves may be green or gray green, often strikingly banded or streaked with contrasting colors. Where winters are too cool, grow in pots and shelter from frosts. Aloes listed here are only a few of the many kinds.

A. arborescens. TREE ALOE. Older clumps may reach 18 ft. Branching stems carry big clumps of gray-green, spiny-edged leaves. Flowers (early to midwinter) in long, spiky clusters, bright vermilion to clear yellow. Withstands salt spray. Tolerates shade. Foliage damaged at 29°F/–2°C, but plants have survived 17°F/–8°C.

A. barbadensis. See A. vera

A. saponaria. Short-stemmed, broad clumps. Broad, thick, 8-in.-long leaves with white spots. Clumps spread rapidly and may become bound together—dig up too-thick clumps and separate them. Branched flower stalk 1½–2½ ft. tall. Orange-red to shrimp pink flowers over long period.

Aloe saponaria

A. variegata. PARTRIDGE-BREAST ALOE, TIGER ALOE. Foot-high, triangular rosette of fleshy, triangular, dark green, 5-in.-long leaves strikingly banded and edged with white. Loose clusters of pink to dull red flowers intermittent all year.

A. vera (A. barbadensis). MEDICINAL ALOE, BARBADOS ALOE. Clustering rosettes of narrow, fleshy, stiffly upright leaves 1–2 ft. long. Yellow flowers in dense spike atop 3-ft. stalk, spring and summer. Favorite folk medicine plant used to treat burns, bites, inflammation, and a host of other ills. One of best for borderline areas.

ALONSOA

| MASK FLOWER |
| *Scrophulariaceae* |
| PERENNIALS USUALLY GROWN AS ANNUALS |
| ⚡ ALL ZONES |
| ☼ ◐ FULL SUN OR PARTIAL SHADE |
| 💧 REGULAR WATER |

Alonsoa warscewiczii

Barely hardy in the mildest climates (Zones 23–27), mask flowers are usually grown as summer bedding plants, as fillers in the perennial border, or as indoor or outdoor container plants. Sprawling or erect to 3 ft., freely branching, with wispy foliage and open clusters of oddly shaped, roundish flowers. All are fairly easy to grow from seed, blooming the first year if started early and continuing to frost or cold weather.

A. linearis. Flowers brick red.

A. meridionalis. Flowers are orange to dark red, somewhat less than 1 in. wide. Seed-grown Firestone Jewels strain has flowers ranging from white through yellow to salmon, pink, and red. 'Shell Pink' and 'Salmon' are offered as nursery plants.

A. warscewiczii. Flowers scarlet to peach with dark eye, to ½ in. across.

ALOYSIA triphylla (Lippia citriodora)

| LEMON VERBENA |
| *Verbenaceae* |
| DECIDUOUS OR PARTIALLY EVERGREEN HERB-SHRUB |
| ⚡ ZONES 9, 10, 12–31 |
| ☼ FULL SUN |
| 💧 REGULAR WATER |

Aloysia triphylla

May succeed in slightly colder climates if planted against warm wall. Legginess is the natural state of this plant; it's the herb that grew like a gangling shrub in grandmother's garden. Prized for its lemon-scented leaves. When you read of the scent of verbena in literature about the antebellum South, lemon verbena is the plant being described. Grows to 6 ft. or taller; narrow leaves to 3 in. long are arranged in whorls of three or four along branches. Bears open clusters of very small lilac or whitish flowers in summer. By pinchpruning you can shape it to give interesting tracery against wall. Or let it grow among lower plants to hide its legginess. Needs well-drained soil.

> **LEMON VERBENA LEAVES FOR FRAGRANCE AND FLAVOR**
>
> This plant is prized for its lemon-scented leaves, which scent the area around them in the garden. The long, shiny leaves add lemony flavor to teas and iced drinks. Dry the leaves for potpourri. When making apple jelly, try placing a big fresh leaf in the bottom of each glass or jar. For all these purposes, pick the fresh-looking leaves from near top of stem.

Well beyond its range, grow it as a house plant (pinch frequently) and let it spend warm months out-of-doors.

ALPINIA

| *Zingiberaceae* |
| PERENNIALS WITH RHIZOMES |
| ⚡ ZONES 14–29 |
| ◐ LIGHT SHADE |
| 💧 💧 AMPLE WATER |

Alpinia zerumbet

Evergreen in Zones 22–27. Roots hardy to about 15°F/−9°C. Tops die back in prolonged cool winter weather, but new shoots appear in spring. Need wind-free exposure, good soil. In order to bloom, alpinia must be established at least 2 years. Remove flowered canes yearly.

A. sanderae. VARIEGATED GINGER. To 3–4 ft. tall, with 8-in.-long leaves striped with white. Rarely blooms. A good container plant.

A. zerumbet (A. nutans, A. speciosa). SHELL GINGER, SHELL FLOWER. Native to tropical Asia and Polynesia. Grandest of gingers, best all-year appearance. To 8–9 ft. tall. Leaves shiny, 2 ft. long, 5 in. wide, with distinct parallel veins; grow on stems that are maroon at maturity. Waxy white or pinkish, shell-like, fragrant flowers marked red, purple, brown, in pendent clusters on arching stems in late summer. Most popular of the alpinias grown in Florida.

ALSOPHILA australis, A. cooperi. See CYATHEA cooperi

ALSTROEMERIA

| *Liliaceae* |
| PERENNIALS |
| ⚡ ZONES 5–9, 14–24, 26, 28, 31; WARMER PARTS OF 32, 34 |
| ◐ ☼ AFTERNOON SHADE IN HOT-SUMMER AREAS |
| 💧 REGULAR WATER |
| ◊ CAUSES DERMATITIS IN ALLERGIC PEOPLE |

Alstroemeria aurantiaca

Ligtu hybrids bloom on leafy stems 2–5 ft. tall, topped with broad, loose clusters of azalealike flowers in beautiful colors—orange, yellow, and shades of pink, rose, red, lilac, and creamy white to white; many are streaked and speckled with darker colors. Masses of color in borders from midspring to midsummer. Long-lasting cut flowers. Tops wither after bloom; flowerless shoots dry up even sooner.

Evergreen hybrids (Cordu, Meyer) have a long bloom season if spent flowering stems are pulled, not cut. Colors include white to pink, red, lilac, and purple, usually bicolored and spotted.

A Connecticut-bred group of hybrids called the Constitution Series has proved fairly hardy (with heavy mulching) along the Atlantic seaboard. Flowers are in the white to pink and purple color range, heavily marked with darker streaks.

A few nurseries offer 3–4-ft.-tall Peruvian lily (*A. aurea, A. aurantiaca*). 'Orange King' has orange-yellow, brown-spotted flowers; 'Lutea' has yellow flowers, 'Splendens' red. *A. psittacina (A. pulchella)* is 1–1½ ft. tall, more or less evergreen, with dark red flowers tipped green and spotted deep purple. It can be invasive.

All types grow best in cool, moist, deep, sandy to medium loam. Plant roots in fall; if you buy alstroemeria in a pot, you can plant outdoors any time in mild-winter climates. Set roots 6–8 in. deep, 1 ft. apart; handle brittle roots gently. Leave clumps undisturbed for many years because they reestablish slowly after transplanting. You can easily start alstroemerias by sowing seed where the plants are to grow or in individual pots for later transplanting. Sow in fall, winter, or earliest spring. All are hardy in cold-winter climates indicated if planted at proper depth and kept mulched in winter. Ligtu hybrids can be allowed to dry off after bloom. Evergreen kinds need moisture for continued bloom; cool summers also prolong bloom.

PICK ALSTROEMERIA FLOWERS IN A SPECIAL WAY

When you pick flowers of the evergreen kinds of alstroemeria, don't cut them. Instead, grasp each flower stem several inches above the soil and gently twist and pull upward to break the stem's base cleanly away from the rhizome. Cutting slows growth, but this technique encourages new bud growth and flower production.

ALTERNANTHERA ficoidea

Amaranthaceae

PERENNIAL TREATED AS ANNUAL

🌣 ALL ZONES

☼ FULL SUN

💧 REGULAR WATER

Alternanthera ficoidea
'Bettzickiana'

Colorful foliage somewhat resembles that of coleus. Plants grow 6–12 in. tall and should be planted 4–10 in. apart for colorful effect. Where winters are cold, plant only after soil warms up. Tolerates heat well. Keep low and compact by shearing. Grow from cuttings. Often sold as *A. bettzickiana*. 'Aurea Nana' is low grower with yellow-splotched foliage. 'Bettzickiana' has spoon-shaped leaves with red and yellow markings. 'Magnifica' is a red-bronze dwarf. 'Parrot Feather' and 'Versicolor' have broad green leaves with yellow markings and pink veins.

ALTHAEA rosca. See ALCEA rosea

ALUM ROOT. See HEUCHERA

ALYOGYNE huegelii
(Hibiscus huegelii)

BLUE HIBISCUS

Malvaceae

EVERGREEN SHRUB

🌣 ZONES 15–17, 20–27

☼ FULL SUN

💧💧 REGULAR TO LITTLE WATER

Alyogyne huegelii

Upright growth to 5–8 ft. Foliage deeply cut, dark green, rough textured. Flowers 4–5 in. across, lilac blue to deep purple, with glossy petals. Blooms off and on all year; individual flowers last 2 or 3 days. Hardy to about 23°F/−5°C. Pinch or prune as needed to keep it compact. Variable from seed. 'Santa Cruz' is good deep blue selection. 'Monterey Bay' is even bluer.

ALYSSUM

Brassicaceae (Cruciferae)

PERENNIALS

🌣 ZONES 1–24, 29–43

☼ FULL SUN OR JUST A LITTLE SHADE

💧 MODERATE WATER

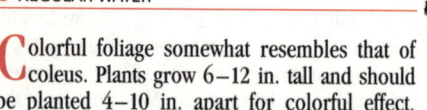
Alyssum montanum

Mostly native to Mediterranean region. Mounding plants or shrublets that brighten spring borders and rock gardens with their cheerful bloom. They thrive in poor, rocky, well-drained soil.

A. montanum. Stems to 8 in. high; leaves gray, hairy (denser on underside); flowers yellow, fragrant, in dense short clusters.

A. saxatile. See Aurinia saxatilis

A. wulfenianum. Prostrate and trailing, with fleshy, silvery leaves and sheets of pale yellow flowers.

ALYSSUM, SWEET. See LOBULARIA maritima

AMARACUS dictamnus. See ORIGANUM dictamnus

Amaranthaceae. The amaranth family largely consists of herbaceous plants, many of them weedy. Flowers are small and chaffy, often effective when massed.

AMARANTHUS

AMARANTH

Amaranthaceae

ANNUALS

🌣 ALL ZONES

☼ ☼ FULL SUN OR PARTIAL SHADE

💧 REGULAR WATER

Amaranthus caudatus

Coarse, sometimes weedy plants; a few ornamental kinds are grown for their brightly colored foliage or flowers. Sow seed in early summer—soil temperature must be above 70°F/21°C for germination.

Picked when young and tender, leaves and stems of many species (even some of the weedy ones) can be cooked like spinach, taking its place in hot weather. Some species have seeds that look like sesame seeds, have a high protein content, and can be used as grain.

A. caudatus. LOVE-LIES-BLEEDING, TASSEL FLOWER. Sturdy, branching plant 3–8 ft. high; leaves 2–10 in. long, ½–4 in. wide. Red flowers in drooping, tassel-like clusters. A curiosity rather than a pretty plant. One of the amaranths that produce grain.

A. hybridus erythrostachys. PRINCE'S FEATHER. To 5 ft. high with leaves 1–6 in. long, ½–3 in. wide, usually reddish. Flowers red or brownish red in many-branched clusters. Some strains grown as spinach substitute or for grain.

A. tricolor. JOSEPH'S COAT. Branching plant 1–4 ft. high. Leaves 2½–6 in. long, 2–4 in. wide, blotched in shades of red and green. Selections such as 'Early Splendor', 'Flaming Fountain', and 'Molten Fire' bear masses of yellow to scarlet foliage at tops of main stems and principal branches. Green-leafed strains used as spinach substitute under the name "tampala."

AMARCRINUM memoria-corsii
(A. 'Howardii')

Amaryllidaceae

BULB

🌣 ZONES 8, 9, 12–31; OR INDOORS

☼ ☼ FULL SUN OR PARTIAL SHADE

💧 REGULAR WATER

Amarcrinum memoria-corsii

Hybrid between belladonna lily (*Amaryllis belladonna*) and *Crinum moorei*. Flowering stems to 4 ft. carry very large clusters of soft pink, funnel-shaped, very fragrant, long-lasting flowers resembling belladonna lily. Late summer—early fall bloom. With year-round moisture, plant stays evergreen in mild climates. If no moisture is available, it simply endures until water comes, then starts growth and bloom. Can be grown as an indoor/outdoor plant or as a house plant. Scarce in nurseries; get offset bulbs from a friend.

Amaryllidaceae. The amaryllis family consists of herbaceous plants with strap-shaped leaves, bulbous or rhizomatous rootstocks, and clustered flowers (rarely a single flower) on top of a leafless stem.

AMARYLLIS belladonna (Brunsvigia rosea)

BELLADONNA LILY, NAKED LADY

Amaryllidaceae

BULB

✤ ZONES 4–24, 28, 29

☼ FULL SUN

◐ THRIVES ON WINTER RAINS

◆ BULBS ARE POISONOUS IF INGESTED

Amaryllis belladonna

Native to South Africa. Performs best in areas with warm, dry summers. Bold, straplike leaves in clumps 2–3 ft. across in fall and winter; foliage dies back during dormant period from late spring to early summer. In late summer, clusters of 4–12 trumpet-shaped, rosy pink, fragrant flowers bloom at tops of bare, reddish brown, 2–3-ft. stalks.

Grows in almost any soil as long as it is well drained. Gets all the moisture it needs from winter rains. Plant right after bloom period ends. In mild-winter areas, set tops of bulbs even with or slightly above ground level. In colder regions, choose a protected southern exposure and set bulbs slightly below ground level. Lift and divide clumps infrequently; may not bloom for several years if disturbed at wrong time. For plants with common name "amaryllis," see *Hippeastrum*.

A. hallii. See Lycoris squamigera

AMELANCHIER

JUNEBERRY, SHADBLOW, SERVICEBERRY

Rosaceae

DECIDUOUS SHRUBS OR SMALL TREES

✤ ZONES 1–6, 31–45

☼◐ FULL SUN OR PARTIAL SHADE

◐◑ REGULAR TO MODERATE WATER

Amelanchier laevis

Graceful, airy trees provide year-round interest. Drooping clusters of white or pinkish flowers in early spring, just before or during leaf-out, are showy, though short lived. These are followed in early summer by edible blueberry-flavored fruits excellent in pies—if you can get to them before the birds do. Purplish new spring foliage turns deep green in summer, then fiery in fall; drops to reveal attractive silhouette in winter.

Plant against dark background to show off form, flowers, fall color. Noninvasive roots and light shade make these good trees to garden under. Especially lovely in woodland gardens. All need a definite period of winter chill. Serviceberry is often pronounced "sarvisberry."

A. alnifolia. SASKATOON. Native to western Canada and mountainous parts of the western U.S. To 20 ft., spreading by rhizomes. 'Regent', 4–6 ft. tall, bears heavy crop of fruit in early summer. Red-and-yellow fall foliage.

A. canadensis. Narrowish, to 25 ft. tall, with short, erect flower clusters. Plants offered under this name may actually belong to other species.

A. grandiflora. APPLE SERVICEBERRY. Hybrid between *A. arborea* (similar to *A. canadensis* but larger) and *A. laevis*. Named selections—more than a dozen are available—may be sold under any of these species names. Most grow to 25 ft., with drooping clusters of white flowers opening from pinkish buds. 'Autumn Brilliance' has blue-green foliage that turns orange red in fall. 'Cole's Selection' and 'Princess Diana' are similar.

A. laevis. ALLEGHENY SERVICEBERRY. Native to eastern North America. Narrow shrub or small tree to 40 ft. with nodding or drooping, 4-in. white flower clusters. Leaves are bronzy purple when new, dark green in summer, yellow to red in autumn. Small black-purple fruit is very sweet.

AMERICAN SWEET GUM. See LIQUIDAMBAR styraciflua

AMETHYST FLOWER. See BROWALLIA

AMORPHA

Fabaceae (Leguminosae)

DECIDUOUS SHRUBS

✤ ZONES 2, 3, 28–45

☼ FULL SUN

◐ REGULAR TO MODERATE WATER

Amorpha fruticosa

Shrubs with leaves divided featherwise into many leaflets; 3–6-in.-long spikelike clusters of single-petaled flowers in early summer are blue or purple. In cold weather, plants may die back nearly to the ground; in warmer regions, they should be cut back severely to prevent lankiness. Tough and undemanding, withstanding heat and wind.

A. canescens. LEAD PLANT. Native to the high plains from Canada to Texas. About 3 ft. tall and wide, with silvery, downy foliage.

A. fruticosa. INDIGO BUSH, FALSE INDIGO. Native to eastern U.S. Lanky growth to 10–15 ft. tall, with light green foliage. Needs hard pruning in winter or early spring to maintain some degree of compactness.

AMPELOPSIS brevipedunculata

PORCELAIN BERRY

Vitaceae

DECIDUOUS VINE

✤ ZONES 2–24, 28–41

☼◐ SUN OR SHADE

◐◑ REGULAR TO MODERATE WATER

Ampelopsis brevipedunculata

Rampant climber with twining tendrils. To 20 ft. Large, handsome, three-lobed, 2½–5-in.-wide leaves are dark green. In warm climates, leaves turn red and partially drop in fall; more leaves come out, redden, and drop all winter. Many clusters of small grapelike berries turn from greenish ivory to brilliant metallic blue in late summer and fall. Needs strong support. Superb on concrete and rock walls or as shade plant on arbors. Invasive from seed; use with extreme caution near woods, natural areas. Attracts birds. Japanese beetles can be a problem. 'Elegans' has leaves variegated with white and pink. Smaller, less vigorous, and less hardy than the species, it is a splendid hanging basket plant.

Boston ivy and Virginia creeper, formerly included in genus *Ampelopsis*, are now placed under genus *Parthenocissus* because, unlike *Ampelopsis*, both have disks at ends of their tendrils.

AMSONIA

BLUE STAR FLOWER

Apocynaceae

PERENNIALS

✤ ZONES 3–24, 28–33

☼◐ FULL SUN OR LIGHT SHADE

◐ REGULAR TO MODERATE WATER

Amsonia tabernaemontana

Elegant milkweed relatives with narrow leaves and erect stems topped by clusters of small, star-shaped, pale blue flowers. Most bloom in late spring. All are tough plants that tolerate ordinary soil and occasional lapses in watering. Bright yellow fall foliage color is a bonus.

A. ciliata (A. hubrectii). To 2½–3 ft. tall, with crowded, needlelike (but soft), 2-in. leaves; has exceptional fall color.

A. illustris. Like *A. tabernaemontana* but has shiny, leathery leaves. ▶

A

A. tabernaemontana. To 2–2½ ft. tall, with narrow, willowlike foliage. 'Montana' is more compact and blooms earlier.

AMUR CHOKECHERRY. See PRUNUS maackii

Anacardiaceae. The cashew family includes evergreen or deciduous trees, shrubs, and vines with small, unshowy, but often profuse flowers. Foliage is attractive; fruits are sometimes showy or edible. Many have poisonous or irritating sap. Mango *(Mangifera)* and poison ivy *(Toxicodendron)* indicate the diversity of the family.

ANACYCLUS depressus (A. pyrethrum depressus)

MOUNT ATLAS DAISY
Asteraceae (Compositae)
PERENNIAL
◪ ZONES 3–24, 30–34, 39
☼ FULL SUN
◖ MODERATE TO LITTLE WATER

Anacyclus depressus

Slowly forms dense, spreading mat somewhat like *Chamaemelum.* Grayish leaves finely divided. Single daisylike flowers to 2 in. across, with yellow center disks and white ray-type petals (red on reverse side). Blooms in summer. Good in sunny, dry, hot rock gardens. May freeze in extremely severe winters or rot in cold, wet, heavy soil. Dislikes humidity.

ANAGALLIS

PIMPERNEL
Primulaceae
ANNUALS OR PERENNIALS
◪ ALL ZONES
☼ FULL SUN
◖ MUCH OR LITTLE WATER

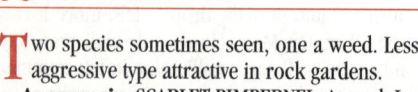
Anagallis monelli linifolia

Two species sometimes seen, one a weed. Less aggressive type attractive in rock gardens.
 A. arvensis. SCARLET PIMPERNEL. Annual. Low-growing weed with ¼-in. flowers of brick red. *A. a. caerulea* has deep blue, larger flowers.
 A. monelli. Perennial or biennial to 1½ ft., with ¾-in. flowers of bright blue. 'Pacific Blue' is a superior selection; 'Phillipsii' is compact, 1 ft. tall; *A. m. linifolia* has narrower leaves than the species.

ANAPHALIS

PEARLY EVERLASTING
Asteraceae (Compositae)
PERENNIALS
◪ ZONES VARY BY SPECIES
◐ ● PARTIAL OR FULL SHADE
◖ ◖ REGULAR TO MODERATE WATER

Anaphalis triplinervis

Furry gray foliage is the outstanding characteristic of the pearly everlastings. Most are mounding, heat-tolerant plants with erect, branching stems carrying attractively displayed (though not showy) clusters of papery daisies. These may be cut in summer for use in dried arrangements. Plants spread to form broad mats and are useful as foreground plants or in the rock garden. Since they withstand lower light than is typical for gray-leafed plants, they are ideal for semishady borders where other gray plants will fail. They are not fussy about soil, needing only reasonably good drainage.
 A. margaritacea. Zones 1–10, 14–17, 32–45. To 3 ft. high. Leaves, to 6 in. long, are green above, white and woolly beneath. Pearly white flowers

with yellow centers. *A. m. yedoensis (A. yedoensis, A. cinnamomea)* has smaller leaves than the species and brown-tinted flowers; it is less cold hardy (Zones 3–10, 14–17, 32–34, 39).
 A. triplinervis. Zones 2–10, 14–17, 32–41. Slightly shorter than *A. margaritacea,* with similar flowers and somewhat smaller, silvery leaves. 'Sulphur Light' has pale yellow blooms centered with deeper yellow.

ANCHUSA

Boraginaceae
ANNUALS, BIENNIALS, OR PERENNIALS
◪ ZONES VARY BY SPECIES
☼ FULL SUN
◖ ◖ REGULAR TO MODERATE WATER

Anchusa capensis

Related to forget-me-not *(Myosotis)* but larger and showier. Worth growing for vibrant blue color; rate high for purest blue among easier plants. Grow in well-drained soil. High humidity inhibits performance.
 A. azurea (A. italica). Perennial. Zones 1–24, 29–45. Coarse, open, spreading, 3–5 ft. tall. Leaves 6 in. or longer, covered with bristly hairs. Clusters of bright blue blossoms, ½–¾ in. across, bloom in summer and fall. Horticultural forms include 'Dropmore', gentian blue; 'Opal', sky blue; and 'Loddon Royalist' (a newer variety), rich blue. Not for small areas: once established, it is difficult to eradicate.
 A. capensis. CAPE FORGET-ME-NOT, SUMMER FORGET-ME-NOT. Biennial in Zones 7–24, 28; annual anywhere. Native to South Africa. To 1½ ft. high. Leaves narrow, to 5 in. long, ½ in. wide. Flowers bright blue, white throated, ¼ in. across, in clusters 2 in. long. Use for vivid clean blue in summer borders with marigolds, petunias.

ANDROMEDA polifolia

BOG ROSEMARY
Ericaceae
EVERGREEN SHRUB
◪ ZONES 1–5, 36–45
☼ ◐ FULL SUN OR LIGHT SHADE
◖ AMPLE WATER

Andromeda polifolia

Erect or spreading shrub, usually 4–6 in. tall, rarely to 1 ft. Narrow, leathery leaves are ½–2 in. long, dark green above, blue gray beneath. Flowers flask shaped, nodding, white to pink, up to eight in a cluster at top of stems. Plant requires strongly acid soil with ample moisture, sun (but with protection from hottest sun) or light shade. Connoisseur's plant for rock garden, pot culture, or streamside or bog garden. Varieties usually offered are 'Grandiflora', a dwarf form with blue-green leaves and large, creamy, pink-shaded flowers; and 'Nana', very compact and vigorous, with nearly round pink flowers.

ANDROSACE

ROCK JASMINE
Primulaceae
PERENNIALS
◪ ZONES 1–6, 14–17, 36–45
☼ FULL SUN
◖ MODERATE WATER

Androsace lanuginosa

Choice rock garden miniatures grown mostly by alpine plant specialists. Summer bloomers. All types require perfect drainage and are best adapted to gravelly banks in rock gardens. Protect from more aggressive rockery plants such as alyssum, rockcress, aubrieta. Rarely succeed in warm-winter areas.

A. lanuginosa. Trailing plant forms mats 3 ft. across. Silvery leaves to ¾ in. long, covered with silky white hairs. Pink flowers in dense clusters on 2-in. stems. *A. l. leichtlinii* has white flowers with crimson eye.

A. primuloides. Trailing; forms 4-in.-long runners. Leaves ½–2 in. long in rosettes covered with silvery hairs. Flowers pink, to ½ in. across, in clusters on 5-in. stems.

A. sarmentosa. Spreads by runners. Leaves to 1½ in. long, in rosettes, covered with silvery hairs when young. Flowers rose colored, ¼ in. across, in clusters on stems 5 in. tall. *A. s. chumbyi* forms dense clump, has woolly leaves.

ANEMONE

WINDFLOWER, ANEMONE
Ranunculaceae
PERENNIALS WITH TUBEROUS OR FIBROUS ROOTS
◢ ZONES VARY BY SPECIES
☼ ◐ ● EXPOSURE NEEDS VARY BY SPECIES
◆ REGULAR WATER
◊ ALL PARTS ARE POISONOUS IF INGESTED

Anemone blanda

A rich and varied group of plants ranging in size from alpine rock garden miniatures to tall Japanese anemones grown in borders; bloom extends from very early spring to fall, depending on species.

Of the species listed here, *A. blanda, A. coronaria,* and *A. fulgens* are grown from tubers; in general, tuberous types are short lived in warm regions, where they may best be treated as annuals. Plant them in a spot that gets some shade every day. Set out tubers October or November; in cold-winter areas, wait until spring to set out *A. coronaria* and *A. fulgens.* (Or, if planting in November, mulch with 6–8 in. of leaf mold or peat moss after first hard frost.) In warmer climates, some gardeners soak tubers of *A. coronaria* for a few hours before planting.

Plant tubers 1–2 in. deep, 8–12 in. apart, in rich, light, well-drained garden loam. Or start in flats of damp sand; set out in garden when leaves are a few inches tall. Keep soil moist. Protect from birds until leaves toughen. In high-rainfall areas, excess moisture induces rot.

A. blanda. Zones 2–9, 14–23, 30–41. Stems rise 2–8 in. from tuberous roots. Finely divided leaves covered with soft hairs. In spring, one sky blue flower, 1–1½ in. across, on each stem. Often confused with *A. apennina,* which has more pointed leaf segments. Grow with and among Japanese maples, azaleas, and other light shrubbery in partial shade. Associate with miniature daffodils, tulips, and scillas; or grow in pots. Selections with 2-in. flowers (in blue and other colors) on 10–12-in. plants include 'Blue Star', 'Pink Star', 'White Splendor', and purplish red 'Radar'.

A. canadensis. Zones 1–4, 32–45. Grows 1–2 ft. tall, with divided leaves and inch-wide white flowers springing in twos and threes from the upper leaf joints; summer bloom. Partial shade.

A. coronaria. POPPY-FLOWERED ANEMONE. Zones 2–24, 30–41. Tuberous rooted. Common large-flowered, showy anemone valued for cutting and for spectacular color in spring borders. Finely divided green leaves. Flowers red, blue, tones and mixtures of these colors, and white, 1½–2½ in. across, borne singly on 6–18-in. stems. Most popular strains are De Caen (with single flowers) and St. Brigid (with semidouble to double flowers). Full sun or partial shade.

A. fulgens. SCARLET WINDFLOWER. Zones 4–9, 14–24, 32–34. To 1 ft. high from tuberous roots. Leaves entirely or slightly divided. Flowers 2½ in. across, brilliant scarlet with black stamens, late spring or early summer. St. Bavo strain comes in unusual color range including pink and rusty coral. Partial shade.

Anemone coronaria

A. hybrida (A. japonica, A. hupehensis japonica). JAPANESE ANEMONE. Zones 3–24, 30–39, 41. A long-lived, fibrous-rooted perennial indispensable for fall color in partial shade. Graceful, branching stems

2–4 ft. high rise from clump of dark green, three- to five-lobed leaves covered with soft hairs. Flowers semidouble, in white, silvery pink, or rose. Many named varieties. Slow to establish but once started spreads readily if roots not disturbed. Mulch in fall where winters are extremely severe. Increase by divisions in fall or early spring or by root cuttings in spring. May need staking. Effective in clumps in front of tall shrubbery or under high-branching trees.

> ### WHICH SIDE OF AN ANEMONE TUBER IS UP?
> Locating the top side of an anemone tuber can be difficult because of its irregular shape. The important sign to look for is the depressed scar left by the base of last year's stem (sometimes you really have to search for it); plant the tuber with the scarred side up.

A. nemorosa. WOOD ANEMONE. Zones 1–9, 14–24, 30–43. To 1 ft., with creeping rhizomes, deeply cut leaves, and inch-wide white (rarely pinkish or blue) spring flowers held above the foliage. Spreads slowly to make an attractive woodland ground cover. Many named varieties exist; 'Allenii' has large blue flowers, and there are double forms. Partial to full shade.

A. pulsatilla. See Pulsatilla vulgaris.

A. quinquefolia. Zones 1–9, 14–17, 32–45. American native. Attractive woodland ground cover resembling *A. nemorosa,* with inch-wide white flowers in spring. *A. q. oregana* is similar, but blooms are sometimes blue or pink.

A. sylvestris. SNOWDROP ANEMONE. Zones 1–10, 14, 30–45. European native growing to 1½ ft. tall. White, fragrant, 1½–3-in. flowers appear in spring; attractive cottony seed heads follow. Partial to full shade.

A. vitifolia robustissima. Zones 3–7, 15–17, 30–39, 41. Vigorous plant to 6 ft. tall with single pink flowers in fall. Resembles *A. hybrida* on a larger scale. Partial shade. True name is probably *A. tomentosa.*

ANEMONELLA thalictroides

RUE ANEMONE
Ranunculaceae
PERENNIAL
◢ ZONES 4–8
◐ ● PARTIAL OR FULL SHADE
◆ REGULAR WATER

Anemonella thalictroides

D elicate woodland plant native to eastern North America. Grows to 9 in. high, with finely divided leaves resembling those of meadow rue *(Thalictrum).* Loose clusters of inch-wide white (usually) or pink flowers appear in early spring. Attractive for close-up viewing. The selection known as either 'Rosea Plena' or 'Schoaff's Double Pink' has long-lasting, fully double pink flowers like tiny roses.

ANETHUM graveolens

DILL
Apiaceae (Umbelliferae)
ANNUAL HERB
◢ ALL ZONES
☼ FULL SUN
◆ REGULAR WATER

Anethum graveolens

T o 3–4 ft. Soft, feathery leaves; umbrellalike, 6-in.-wide clusters of small yellow flowers. Seeds and leaves have pungent fragrance. Sow seed where plants are to be grown; for constant supply, sow several times during spring and summer. Thin seedlings to 1½ ft. apart. Sprouts and grows better in spring than summer.

A

An easy way to grow it in a casual garden is to let a few plants go to seed. Seedlings appear here and there at odd times and can be pulled and chopped as "dill weed." Use seeds in pickling and vinegar; use fresh or dried leaves with fish or lamb, in salads, stews, sauces.

ANGELICA archangelica

ANGELICA

Apiaceae (Umbelliferae)

BIENNIAL

🗡 ZONES 1–10, 14–24, 29–43

☼ PARTIAL SHADE

💧 REGULAR WATER

Angelica archangelica

To 6 ft. Tropical-looking plant with divided and toothed, yellow-green leaves 2–3 ft. long. Greenish white flowers in large umbrellalike clusters. Grow in moist, rich soil in partial shade. Cut flowers before buds open to prolong plant's life. Propagate from seed sown as soon as ripe in autumn.

> ## ANGELICA'S CULINARY USES
> Angelica leaves are good in salads; leafstalks can be cooked and eaten like celery. Both leafstalks and hollow flower stems can be candied and used to decorate pastries. The seeds are used commercially to flavor wines, vermouth, and liqueurs (Benedictine and Chartreuse).

ANGELONIA angustifolia

Scrophulariaceae

TENDER PERENNIAL OFTEN GROWN AS ANNUAL

🗡 ALL ZONES

☼☽ FULL SUN OR LIGHT SHADE

💧 REGULAR WATER

Angelonia angustifolia

Native to the American tropics. Perennial in Zones 25–27; elsewhere grown as an annual or a pot plant. Plants bushy, 1–1½ ft. tall, with narrow leaves and slender spikelike clusters of two-lipped blue, purple, or white flowers over a long period. Some say the foliage smells like apples. Cut back or divide plants if they become floppy. 'Alba' has white flowers, 'Blue Pacific' blue-and-white blossoms.

ANGEL'S HAIR. See ARTEMISIA schmidtiana

ANGEL'S TEARS. See NARCISSUS triandrus, SOLEIROLIA soleirolii

ANISE. See PIMPINELLA anisum

ANISE TREE. See ILLICIUM

ANISODONTEA

CAPE MALLOW

Malvaceae

EVERGREEN SHRUBS

🗡 ZONES 14–24, 28

☼ FULL SUN

💧💧 REGULAR TO LITTLE WATER

Anisodontea hypomandarum

These quick-growing South Africans are notable for producing vast quantities of flowers over a long period. Growth is rounded, rather open but freely branching, with small lobed leaves. Flowers are shaped like miniature individual hollyhock flowers and are borne throughout mild weather, year-round in mildest climates. Use in shrub perennial borders or in large containers.

A. capensis. Grows to 6 ft., with 1-in. lobed leaves and 1-in. flowers of purplish pink, with deeper veining and a dark basal spot. Probably identical to *A. hypomandarum*.

A. hypomandarum. To 6 ft. or more, with 1½-in. leaves and inch-wide pink flowers with dark veins and eyes. Flowering is continuous and profuse. Sometimes trained as single-trunk standards. 'Tara's Pink' has larger leaves and larger, lighter flowers.

A. scabrosa. To 6 ft., with aromatic leaves 2½–3 in. long and deep rosy purple flowers with darker eye spots.

Annonaceae. The annona family consists primarily of tropical trees and shrubs, many with edible fruit.

ANNONA cherimola

CHERIMOYA

Annonaceae

BRIEFLY DECIDUOUS SHRUB OR SMALL TREE

🗡 ZONES 21–25

☼ FULL SUN

💧 REGULAR WATER

Annona cherimola

Native to high elevations in tropics and consequently does not grow well in intense heat and high humidity. Hardy to about 25°F/–4°C. Grows fast first 3 to 4 years, then slows to make 15-ft. tree with 15–20-ft. spread. After tree has developed for 4 to 5 years, prune annually to produce bearing wood. Leaves dull green above, velvety-hairy beneath, 4–10 in. long; leaves drop in late spring. Thick, fleshy, 1-in., brownish or yellow, hairy flowers with a fruity fragrance begin opening about time of leaf drop and continue forming for 3 to 4 months. Pleasant near terrace.

To ensure fruit set, gather pollen on a brush and transfer it to the stigma of a freshly opened flower.

Large green fruits weigh ½–1½ lb. Skin of most varieties looks like short overlapping leaves; some show knobby warts. Pick when fruit turns yellowish green, then store in refrigerator until skin turns brownish green to brown. Skin is tender and thin. Handle fruit carefully. Creamy white flesh contains large black seeds. Flesh is almost custardlike; eat it with a spoon.

ANNUAL MALLOW. See LAVATERA trimestris

ANREDERA cordifolia
(Boussingaultia baselloides)

MADEIRA VINE

Basellaceae

PERENNIAL VINE

🗡 ZONES 12–28; OR DIG AND STORE IN ZONES 4–11, 29–33

☼ FULL SUN

💧 MODERATE WATER

Anredera cordifolia

Heart-shaped green leaves 1–3 in. long. Fragrant white flowers in foot-long spikes in late summer, fall. Climbs by twining; may reach 20 ft. in one season. Small tubers form where leaves join stems. Old-fashioned plant useful for summer screening of decks or other sitting areas. Can run rampant in mildest climates. In colder part of range, treat as you would dahlias: dig in fall and store tubers over winter.

ANTENNARIA

PUSSY TOES

Asteraceae (Compositae)

PERENNIALS

ZONES 1–3, 6, 7, 14–16, 36–45

FULL SUN

REGULAR TO LITTLE WATER

Antennaria dioica

Mat-forming plants with rosettes of woolly foliage and small furry puffs of flower heads. Tough and tolerant of heat and poor soil, they spread slowly but surely among rocks or along crevices in paving. Useful small-scale bulb cover or ground cover. Accept regular water if soil is well drained.

A. dioica. Inch-high gray mats produce pinkish white flower puffs. 'Rubra' has deep pink flowers.

A. neglecta. White flower puffs atop 3-in. stems.

ANTHEMIS

Asteraceae (Compositae)

PERENNIALS

ZONES VARY BY SPECIES

FULL SUN

REGULAR TO MODERATE WATER

Anthemis tinctoria

Aromatic foliage, especially when bruised. Leaves divided into many segments. Flowers daisylike or buttonlike. Some are weedy, but the following species are choice garden plants. All need good drainage.

A. carpatica (A. cretica carpatica). Zones 3–10, 14–24, 29–34. Green to gray-green mounds with 1½-in. white, yellow-centered daisies on 6-in. stems in spring and summer.

A. marschalliana (A. biebersteiniana). Zones 4–9, 14–24, 29–32. Rounded plant 1 ft. tall and as wide, with finely cut, fernlike, silvery leaves and 1-in. brilliant yellow, daisylike blooms in summer.

A. nobilis. See Chamaemelum nobile

A. punctata cupaniana. Zones 4–9, 14–24, 29–32. Foot-tall, spreading mounds of silvery foliage topped by a long show of white daisies.

A. tinctoria. GOLDEN MARGUERITE. Zones 1–11, 14–24, 30–45. Erect, shrubby. Grows to 2–3 ft. Angular stems. Light green, much-divided leaves. Golden yellow, daisylike flowers, to 2 in. across, bloom in summer and fall. Short lived; replant frequently. Grow from seed, stem cuttings, or divisions in fall or spring. Varieties include 'Beauty of Grallagh', golden orange flowers; 'E. C. Buxton', white with yellow centers; 'Kelwayi', golden yellow; 'Moonlight', soft, pale yellow.

ANTHRISCUS cerefolium

CHERVIL

Apiaceae (Umbelliferae)

ANNUAL HERB

ALL ZONES

PARTIAL SHADE

REGULAR WATER

Grows 1–2 ft. high. Finely cut, fernlike leaves resembling parsley; white flowers. Use like parsley, fresh or dried; flavor milder than parsley. Grow from seed in raised bed near kitchen door, in box near barbecue, or in vegetable garden. Quickly goes to seed in hot weather. Keep flower clusters cut to encourage vegetative growth.

Anthriscus cerefolium

ANTHURIUM

Araceae

PERENNIALS

ZONE 25; OR INDOORS

NO DIRECT SUN

AMPLE WATER; NEED HUMIDITY

Anthurium andraeanum

Native to tropical American rain forests. Exotic plants with handsome dark green leaves and lustrous flower bracts in vivid red, luscious pinks, or white. In southern Florida, they thrive outdoors in frost-free, shady spots, either in the ground or in pots. In all regions, they're no more difficult to grow as house plants than are some orchids.

The higher the humidity, the better. Anthurium leaves lose shiny texture and may die if humidity drops below 50 percent for more than a few days. Keep pots on trays of moist gravel, in bathroom, or under polyethylene cover. Sponge or spray leaves several times daily. For good bloom, plant by window with good light but no direct sun. Generally grow best at 80° to 90°F/27° to 32°C but will get along at normal house temperature. Growth stops below 65°F/18°C, is damaged below 50°F/10°C. Protect from drafts. Pot anthuriums in coarse, porous mix of leaf mold, sandy soil, and shredded osmunda. Give light feeding every 4 weeks.

A. andraeanum. Dark green, oblong leaves to 1 ft. long and 6 in. wide, heart shaped at base. Flower bracts spreading, heart shaped, to 6 in. long, surrounding yellow, callalike flower spike. Flower bracts, in shades of red, rose, pink, and white, shine as though lacquered. Bloom more or less continuously—plant may have from four to six flowers during the year. Flowers last 6 weeks on plant, 4 weeks after cut.

A. crystallinum. Leaves, up to 1½ ft. long, 1 ft. wide, are deep green with striking white veining. Flowers unexciting, with small, narrow, greenish bracts. Many similar anthuriums exist in florist trade; plants offered as *A. crystallinum* may be *A. clarinervium, A. magnificum,* or some other species.

A. scandens. Climbing or trailing plant to 2 ft., with 3-in.-long tapered oval leaves and small, fragrant greenish flowers, translucent lilac berries.

A. scherzeranum. Slow-growing, compact plant to 2 ft. Dark green leaves 8 in. long, 2 in. wide. Flower bracts broad, 3 in. long, deep red varying to rose, salmon, white. Yellow flower spikes spirally coiled. Easier to handle than *A. andraeanum* and often thrives under ordinary, good house plant conditions.

ANTIGONON leptopus

CORAL VINE, QUEEN'S WREATH, ROSA DE MONTANA

Polygonaceae

DECIDUOUS VINE

ZONES 12, 13, 18–30

FULL SUN

REGULAR TO LITTLE WATER

Antigonon leptopus

This native of Mexico revels in high summer heat, sun. Evergreen in warm-winter areas. Fast growing, climbing by tendrils to 40 ft. Foliage—dark green, 3–5-in.-long, heart-shaped or arrow-shaped leaves—is open and airy. Small rose pink flowers to 1½ in. long are carried in long, trailing sprays from midsummer to fall. In cold winters, leaves fall and most of top dies. Recovers quickly. Treat as perennial. Where winter temperatures drop below 25°F/–4°C, protect roots with mulch. There is a rare white variety 'Album', and a hot rose pink—nearly red—variety named 'Baja Red'; from seed the color of the latter is variable, but the best are as red as 'Barbara Karst' bougainvillea.

Widespread in Florida and parts of Central and Southeast Texas. Also a wonderful vine in the low deserts of California and Arizona, where it stays

A

green in summer heat if watered regularly. Give warmest spot in Southern California coastal gardens. Use the vine to shade patio or terrace, or let it drape its foliage and blossom sprays along eaves, fence, or garden wall.

ANTIRRHINUM majus

SNAPDRAGON

Scrophulariaceae

PERENNIAL USUALLY TREATED AS ANNUAL

🗡 ALL ZONES

☼ FULL SUN

💧 REGULAR WATER

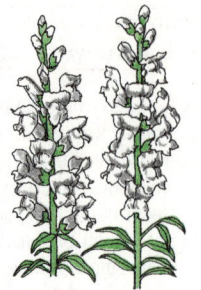
Antirrhinum majus

Among best flowers for sunny borders and cutting, reaching greatest perfection in spring and early summer. In regions with mild winters and hot summers, will bloom in winter and spring. Individual flower of basic snapdragon has five lobes, which are divided into unequal upper and lower "jaws"; slight pinch at sides of flower will make dragon open its jaws. Later developments include double flowers; the bell-shaped kind, with round, open flowers; and the azalea-shaped bloom, which is a double bellflower.

Snapping snapdragons in tall (2½–3-ft.) range include Pocket and Topper strains (single flowers) and Double Supreme strain. Intermediate (12–20 in.) are Cinderella, Coronette, Minaret, 'Princess White with Purple Eye', Sprite, and Tahiti. Dwarfs (6–8 in.) include Dwarf Bedding Floral Carpet, Kim, Kolibri, and Royal Carpet.

Bell-flowered strains include Bright Butterflies and Wedding Bells (both 2½ ft.); Little Darling and Liberty Bell (both 15 in.); and Pixie (6–8 in.). Azalea-flowered strains include Madame Butterfly (2½ ft.) and Sweetheart (1 ft.).

Sow seed in flats from late summer to early spring for later transplanting or buy started plants at nursery. Set out plants in early fall in mild-winter areas, spring in colder climates. If snapdragons set out in early fall reach bud stage before night temperatures drop below 50°F/10°C, they will start blooming in winter and continue until weather gets hot.

Valuable cut flowers. Tall and intermediate forms are splendid vertical accents in borders with delphinium, iris, daylily, peach-leafed bluebell (*Campanula persicifolia*), Oriental poppy. Dwarf kinds are effective as edgings and in rock gardens and raised beds, or pots.

FIVE WAYS TO AVOID SNAPDRAGON RUST

Snapdragons, like lawns, roses, and hollyhocks, can fall victim to rust (orange pustules on undersides of leaves). Here are five ways to avoid or minimize it: Start with rust-resistant varieties (even that's not foolproof). Keep plants well watered. Avoid overhead watering (or do it only in the morning or on sunny days). Feed regularly. If necessary, change planting locations from one year to the next.

APHELANDRA squarrosa

Acanthaceae

EVERGREEN SHRUB

🗡 ZONES 24, 25, 27; OR INDOORS

☼ ● PARTIAL OR FULL SHADE

💧 REGULAR WATER

Aphelandra squarrosa

Native to Mexico, South America. Popular for leaves and flowers. Large, 8–12-in.-long, dark green leaves strikingly veined with white. Green-tipped yellow flowers and waxy, golden yellow flower bracts make colorful upright spikes at tips of stems. 'Louisae' is best known, but newer varieties 'Apollo White' and 'Dania' are more compact and show more white venation. To make plant bushy, cut stems back to one or two pairs of leaves after flowering.

Grown as an accent with other tender shrubs in sheltered borders in warmest parts of Florida. Occasionally used outdoors in protected spots in Southern California gardens. If plant freezes, cut it to the ground; new shoots will appear when weather warms up. Indoors, provide morning (or filtered) sun and routine house plant care.

Apiaceae. This family, formerly known as Umbelliferae, comprises nearly 3,000 plants, most of them annuals and perennials. All have flowers in umbels—flat- or round-topped clusters whose individual flower stems all originate at a single point. Many are vegetables (carrot, parsnip, celery, fennel) or aromatic herbs (parsley, coriander, dill). Others are grown for ornament, such as wild buckwheat (*Eryngium*) and blue lace flower (*Trachymene*).

Apocynaceae. The dogbane family contains shrubs, trees, and vines with milky, often poisonous sap. Flowers are often showy and fragrant, as in *Plumeria* and oleander (*Nerium*).

Aponogetonaceae. Only the following genus is of importance in this small family of aquatic plants.

APONOGETON distachyus

CAPE PONDWEED, WATER HAWTHORN

Aponogetonaceae

AQUATIC PLANT

🗡 ALL ZONES

☼ ● FULL SUN OR PARTIAL SHADE

💧 LIVES IN WATER

Aponogeton distachyus

Native to South Africa. Suitable for small water gardens. Like miniature water lily, it produces floating leaves from submerged tuber. Leaves are long and narrow; ⅓-in.-long white, fragrant flowers stand above water in double-branched clusters. In hot-summer climates, blooms in cool weather and is dormant in hottest weather; where winters are cold, blooms in summer and is dormant in winter. Same culture as water lily (*Nymphaea*); will bloom in part shade.

APPLE

Rosaceae

DECIDUOUS FRUIT TREES

🗡 ZONES VARY BY VARIETY

☼ FULL SUN

💧 REGULAR WATER DURING FRUIT DEVELOPMENT

▶ SEE CHART

Apple

Most widely adapted deciduous fruit. Grows in home gardens and orchards from as far south as central Florida all the way north into Canada, and in every western climate. Fruit ripens from July to early November, depending on variety. Prime commercial growing areas include western New York, Shenandoah-Cumberland Valley, western Michigan, and valleys of Central Washington. To grow and fruit properly, most varieties require between 900 and 1,200 hours of 45°F/7°C or lower temperatures. In mild-winter regions, it's important to choose varieties with low winter chill requirement.

All apples except 'Golden Delicious' require cross-pollination for good fruit set. Certain varieties (triploids) do not produce fertile pollen and will

▶ page 185

APPLE

VARIETY	ZONES	RIPENING DATE	FRUIT	COMMENTS
'Anna'	7–24, 26–28, 30	Early. Sometimes a light second crop late in the season	Large, pale green blushed red. Crisp, sweet with some acid	Begins producing at a young age. Needs very little winter chill; useful in warmest winter areas. Good annual bearer. Use 'Dorsett Golden' as pollinator
'Braeburn'	1–9, 14–16, 34–43	Late	Medium size, orange red over yellow ground. Crisp, sweet-tart flavor. Stores well	Fruit drops in hot climates. Thin fruit to prevent bearing in alternate years. Very susceptible to mites
'Delicious' ('Red Delicious')	Sold wherever apples will grow. Best in 2, 3, 7	Midseason to late	Everybody recognizes pointed blossom end with five knobs. Color varies with strain and garden climate; best where days are sunny and warm, nights cool. Often older, striped kinds have better flavor than highly colored commercial strains	Many strains vary in depth and uniformity of coloring. 'Crimson Spur' is a popular home variety. All types susceptible to scab
'Dorsett Golden'	13, 17–24, 26–28, 30	Early	Medium to large, yellow or greenish yellow, sweet flavor. Good for eating fresh or cooking. Keeps a few weeks	Seedling of 'Golden Delicious' from Bermuda. Needs no winter chill. Good pollinator for 'Anna'
'Empire'	2, 3, 6, 7, 14–16, 34–43	Late midseason	Cross between 'McIntosh' and 'Delicious'. Small to medium, roundish, dark red. Flesh creamy white, juicy, crisp, mildly tart	Semispur growth habit. Good tree structure. Susceptible to spring frost damage
'Enterprise'	1–9, 14–16, 34–43	Late	Medium size, red blush, firm, sweet, good quality. Keeps well	Immune to scab but subject to preharvest fruit drop
'Fuji'	7–9, 14–16, 31–37, 39–42	Late	Medium to large, yellow-green ground with red stripes, firm, very sweet, excellent flavor. Stores exceptionally well	Tends to bear heavy crops in alternate years. Needs a long growing season (160 days) to ripen properly
'Gala'	4–9, 14–16, 30, 34–43	Early to midseason	Medium size, beautiful red-on-yellow color. Highly aromatic, firm, crisp, juicy, sweet, yellow flesh. Loses flavor in storage	Vigorous, heavy bearer with long, supple branches that break easily; provide support if necessary. Several color strains are available. Very susceptible to fireblight
'Ginger Gold'	2, 3, 6–16, 18, 30–43	Early midseason	Medium to large, yellow, firm, crisp, mild flavor. Resembles 'Golden Delicious'. Good keeper	One of the best early yellow apples. Ripens over 2–3-week period. Susceptible to mildew, especially in the South. Resistant to sunburn
'Golden Delicious' ('Yellow Delicious')	1–3, 7–11, 14–24, 34–43	Late midseason	Medium to large, clear yellow, though may develop skin russeting in some climates. Similar in shape to 'Delicious', with less prominent knobs. Highly aromatic, crisp. Excellent for eating fresh and cooking	Not related to 'Red Delicious'; different taste, habit. Long bloom season, heavy pollen production make it a good pollinator. Various strains available. Spurred types include 'Goldspur', 'Yelospur'
'Gold Rush'	3–16, 18, 19, 31–37, 39–42	Late	Medium size yellow, often with some russeting. Best after storage	Immune to scab; good resistance to powdery mildew; some resistance to fireblight
'Granny Smith'	4–11, 14–16, 32–35	Early midseason (late in cool-summer areas)	Large, bright to yellowish green, firm fleshed, tart. Good quality. Stores well, makes good pies, sauce	Australian favorite before it came to U.S. Chancy in cold areas because of late ripening
'Gravenstein'	Widely sold in 4–11, 14–24, 34–43, but best in 15–17	Early to midseason	Large, with brilliant red stripes over deep yellow ground. Crisp, aromatic, juicy. Excellent for eating; makes applesauce with character	Pollen-sterile, won't pollinate other varieties. Bears more heavily in alternate years. Susceptible to mildew in Zones 4–6. 'Red Gravenstein' is more highly colored

▶

A

APPLE

VARIETY	ZONES	RIPENING DATE	FRUIT	COMMENTS
'Honeycrisp'	1–16, 18, 19, 34–43	Midseason	Large, red (color not outstanding), firm, juicy. Remarkable crispness and sweetness after storage	Very cold hardy. Resistant to fireblight; somewhat resistant to scab
'Jonagold'	2–9, 14–16, 34–39, 41–43	Late midseason	Large, heavy red striping over yellow ground. Firm, mildly tart, juicy, fine flavor. A frequent taste-test favorite	Productive, medium-size tree. Heavy bearer. Pollen-sterile, won't pollinate other varieties. Not pollinated by 'Golden Delicious'. Best in cool climates
'Jonathan'	Sold everywhere, but best in 2, 3, 7, 34–43	Midseason	Small to medium, round-oblong. High-colored red. Juicy, moderately tart, crackling crisp, sprightly. All-purpose apple, good keeper	Subject to mildew. Somewhat resistant to scab. Popular in Midwest
'Liberty'	4–9, 14–16, 34–43	Late midseason	Medium size, heavy red blush. Crisp, fine sweet-tart flavor, dessert quality	Productive annual bearer. Can get mildew west of Cascades. Immune to scab; resists cedar-apple rust, fireblight. One of the best disease-resistant apples
'Lodi'	1–16, 18, 19, 34–43	Very early	Large, green to greenish yellow. Crisp, tart flesh good for pies, sauce	Vigorous tree, heavy bearer
'Macoun'	1–7, 34–39, 41–43	Late midseason	Medium size, red stripes on green ground. Sweet, crisp, juicy. Good dessert apple. A frequent taste-test winner	Large, upright tree fairly resistant to mildew. Thin for good fruit size. Drops badly when ripe. Grows best in cool regions. May bear more heavily in alternate years
'McIntosh'	2–6, 14–16, 34–39, 41–43	Midseason	Medium to large, bright red, nearly round. Snowy white, tender flesh. Excellent, tart flavor	Fine choice for cooler climates if given good care. Very susceptible to scab and preharvest drop. The selections 'Marshall' and 'Redmax' have high color
'Melrose'	1–7, 15, 16, 34–42	Late	Medium to large, roundish, red ground striped deeper red. Flesh white, mildly tart, aromatic	Cross between 'Jonathan' and 'Delicious'. Exceptional storage, good dessert apple. Somewhat mildew resistant. One of the best in Northwest. Ohio's official state apple
'Mutsu' ('Crispin')	4–9, 15, 16, 34–43	Late	Very large, greenish yellow to yellow blushed red. Flesh cream colored, very crisp, somewhat more tart than 'Golden Delicious'. Frequent taste-test winner. Excellent dessert and cooking apple with long storage life	Exceptionally large and vigorous tree. Pollen-sterile, won't pollinate other varieties
'Newtown Pippin' ('Yellow Newtown', 'Yellow Pippin')	1–11, 13–22, 32–36	Late	Large, green. Crisp and tart. Fair for eating, excellent for cooking	Large, vigorous tree. Excellent California central coast commercial variety. Often gets mildew in Zones 4–6
'Northern Spy' ('Red Spy')	1–3, 6, 7, 34, 37–43	Late	Large, red skinned. Tender, fine-grained flesh. Apple epicure's delight for sprightly flavor. Not attractive but excellent dessert, cooking apple. Keeps well	Slow to reach bearing age. 'Prairie Spy' is similar variety
'Paulared'	4–7, 34–43	Early	Large, red skinned, mild flavored. One of the best early apples	Good branch structure. Thrives in Northeast, Midwest, and Northwest (west of Cascades). Slightly resistant to scab
'Pristine'	3–16, 18, 19, 34–43	Early	Medium size, bright yellow skin, mildly tart white flesh. Good for eating, baking, sauce	Immune to scab; resistant to cedar-apple rust; somewhat resistant to powdery mildew, fireblight
'Redfree'	4–9, 14–17, 34–43	Early	Medium size, red skin, firm, crisp, good flavor	Heavy bearer. Immune to scab

APPLE

VARIETY	ZONES	RIPENING DATE	FRUIT	COMMENTS
'Rome Beauty' ('Red Rome')	3, 7, 10, 11, 34–43	Late	Large, round, smooth, red with greenish white flesh. Original 'Rome Beauty' supplanted by more uniformly red-skinned types like 'Red Rome'. Outstanding baking apple, only fair for eating fresh	Bears at an early age
'Spartan'	4–7, 15, 16, 34–43	Midseason	Medium size, dark red with purplish bloom. Crisp flesh. Good flavor similar to that of 'McIntosh'	Tree habit good; heavy bearing requires thinning the fruit
'Stayman' (often called **'Winesap'**)	1–7, 10, 11, 33–37, 39–41	Late	'Stayman' and 'Winesap' are actually two different apples. 'Stayman' (a 'Winesap' cross) is large, red with green and russet dots. 'Winesap' is smaller, all red. Both are fine grained, firm, juicy with lively flavor	Old-timers that still have their devotees
'Wealthy' ('Red Wealthy', **'Double Red Wealthy'**)	1–7, 34–43	Early midseason	Medium to large, rough, red. Flesh white with pink veining, firm, tart, juicy. Good cooking variety	Small, cold-hardy tree that tends to bear more heavily in alternate years. Not for hot climates
'Winter Banana'	4–9, 14–24, 34–43	Late midseason	Large, attractive, pale yellow blushed pink, waxy finish. Tender, aromatic	Accepts mild winters. Good pollinator for 'Delicious'. There is a 'Spur Winter Banana'

not fertilize either their own flowers or those of other apples. If you have a tree that is not bearing, graft a branch of another variety onto it or place fresh flower bouquets from another variety (in can of water) at base of tree. Don't use 'Gravenstein', 'Stayman,' or any other triploid (pollen-sterile) tree to pollinate an unfruitful tree.

An apple tree needs regular moisture while fruit is developing; you will have to make up for any lack of rainfall at this time with periodic deep soakings. The tree also needs full sun for best production, so don't crowd it into a partially shaded site. To have more than one variety in limited space, buy multiple-variety trees or dwarf trees.

Multiple-variety trees have three to five varieties grafted onto a single trunk and rootstock; they may be standard, dwarf, or semidwarf. You get not only a selection of varieties but also pollination, if needed.

In choosing varieties, remember that good apples are not necessarily red. Skin color is not an indicator of quality or taste. Make sure that eye appeal, slight taste preference, or name doesn't influence you to choose a difficult-to-grow variety. For example, if to your taste 'Golden Delicious' and 'Red Delicious' are nearly equal, consider differences in growing them. 'Golden Delicious' produces fruit without pollinator and comes into bearing earlier. It keeps well, while 'Red Delicious' becomes mealy if not stored at 35° to 40°F/2° to 4°C or lower. And it can be used for cooking, while 'Red Delicious' is principally an eating apple.

If you want nearly perfect fruit, the apple tree will need much care; however, as an ornamental tree it has more character, better form, and longer life than most deciduous fruit trees. It does best in deep, well-drained soil, but gets by in many imperfect situations.

The main insect pests are apple maggot, codling moth, and plum curculio, all of which infest the fruit. Codling moth is universal, while the other two pests are found mainly east of the Rockies. Traps may be enough to control these insects in a home garden. Diseases of apple are prevalent east of the Rockies—and good reason for gardeners there to plant resistant varieties (see chart). Apple scab causes hard, corky spots on fruit. Cedar-apple rust (spread from red cedars to apples) is responsible for orange spots on leaves and fruit, and subsequent defoliation and stunting of fruit. Powdery mildew causes twig dieback and russeting of fruit. Fungicidal sprays will help prevent all of these diseases. The bacterial disease fireblight produces blackening and dieback of growth. For timing of insect traps and fungicide sprays, consult your Cooperative Extension Office or a good local nursery.

Dwarf and spur apples. True dwarf apples (5–8 ft. in height and spread) are made by grafting standard apples on dwarfing rootstocks such as M9 and Bud 9. These trees take up little room and bear at a younger age than standard apples, but have shallow roots; they need the support of a post, fence, wall, or sturdy trellis to stand against wind and rain. They also need good soil and extra care in feeding and watering. Genetic dwarf apples are naturally small plants sometimes offered in the West.

Semidwarf trees are larger than true dwarfs but smaller than standard trees. They bear bigger crops than dwarfs and take up less space than standards. Many commercial orchards get high yields by using semidwarf trees and planting them close together. Semidwarf rootstocks reduce tree size by approximately the following factors: M26 and M7A are about half normal size; they may be espaliered or trellised if planted 12–16 ft. apart and allowed to grow 10–12 ft. tall. Trees on MM106 are approximately 65 percent of normal height; those on MM111 are 75 percent of normal height.

Rarely, growers offer trees dwarfed by double-working—grafting a piece of M9 trunk on vigorous rootstock, then grafting a bearing variety on this "interstock." The resulting dwarf is somewhat larger than a true dwarf tree and similar in size to a tree grown on an M26 rootstock.

Apples bear flowers and fruit on spurs—short branches that grow from 2-year or older wood. On spur-type apples, spurs form earlier (within 2 years after planting) and grow closer together on shorter branches, giving more apples per foot of branch. Spur apples are natural or genetic semidwarfs about two-thirds the size of normal apple trees when they are grafted on ordinary rootstocks. They can be further dwarfed by grafting onto dwarfing rootstocks; M7A and M26 give smallest trees, MM106 and MM111 somewhat larger ones.

Training and pruning apple trees. For most home use, plant dwarf or semidwarf trees for ease in maintenance and picking. Even commercial growers favor these smaller trees: closer spacing permits more trees to the acre and a heavier crop. Preferred style is pyramidal or modified leader, in which widely angled branches are encouraged to grow in spiral placement

A

around the trunk. Prune as little as possible during the first 5 or 6 years—just keep narrow-angled crotches from developing and don't let side branches outgrow the leader or secondary branches outgrow the primary branches.

Pruning of mature trees consists of removing weak, dead, or poorly placed branches and twigs, especially those growing toward the center of the tree (bearing is heaviest when some sun can reach the middle). Removing such growth will encourage development of strong new wood with new fruiting spurs (on apples, spurs are productive for about 3 years) and discourage mildew. If you have inherited an old tree, selective thinning of branches will accomplish the same goal.

Dwarf trees can be grown as espaliers tied to wood or wire frames, fences, or other supports. The technique requires manipulating the branches to the desired pattern and pruning out excess growth.

Recent arrivals are the colonnade apples. These develop a single spire-like trunk to 8 ft. tall, with fruiting spurs directly on the trunk or on very short branchlets. Total width does not exceed 2 ft. Five varieties are currently available: 'Emeraldspire', green-tinted yellow; 'Scarletspire', red and green; 'Crimsonspire', dark red; 'Ultraspire', red-blushed yellow green; and 'Maypole', a crabapple with deep pink blossoms and red fruit. Two varieties are needed for pollination. Easy to maintain, colonnade trees are attractive as accents or screen plants, or in containers.

For ornamental relatives, see *Malus.*

APRICOT

Rosaceae

DECIDUOUS FRUIT TREES

ZONES VARY BY TYPE; SEE BELOW

FULL SUN

PERIODIC DEEP SOAKINGS

Apricot

Though it's possible to grow one variety or another of standard market apricots in most of the West (Zones 3–24), best success and greatest choice of varieties come in Zones 8, 9, and 14. These areas are ideal for apricot growing—they have long, hot, dry summers, chilly winters with little risk of late frosts, and minimal chance of rain interfering with pollination. In other parts of the West, consult your Cooperative Extension Office or a local nursery for varieties adapted to your climate. Some varieties will need a pollinator.

Hardy varieties bred from Manchurian apricot (*Prunus armeniaca mandschirica*) succeed outside the normal range of apricots, though late frosts and high humidity can still make crops chancy. These hardy apricots—such as 'Chinese' ('Morton'), 'Giant Sureset', 'Goldcot', and 'Henderson'—are worth trying in Zone 2 and in adjacent areas of the plains states (Zones 35–41). Extra-hardy types—such as 'Manchu', 'Moongold', 'Sungold'—may succeed in Zone 43.

An apricot tree will grow to about 15 ft. high and wide. It is a good dual-purpose fruit and shade tree, easy to maintain; can also be trained as an espalier. The thin, roundish leaves to 3 in. long are reddish when new, maturing to bright green; the flowers are pink or white.

Apricot trees bear fruit on spurs that form on the previous year's growth and that remain fruitful for about 4 years. Some apricot varieties need a pollinator. Most varieties ripen their fruit from late spring into summer. To get a good crop of large apricots, do this: in midspring, thin excess fruit from branches, leaving 2–4 in. between individual fruits. Apricot trees need only moderate pruning: the goal is to conserve enough new growth (which will produce spurs) for a satisfactory quantity of fruit and to remove old, exhausted spurs.

Brown rot and bacterial canker are serious diseases affecting apricot. Your Cooperative Extension Office can give you a local timetable and directions for spraying trees (essential dates: during dormant season, before and after flowering, and at red-bud stage).

For ornamental relatives, see *Prunus.*

APRIUM and PLUOT

Rosaceae

DECIDUOUS FRUIT TREES

ZONES VARY BY TYPE; SEE BELOW

FULL SUN

PERIODIC DEEP SOAKINGS

'Flavor Delight' Aprium

These fruits are complex hybrids between apricot and plum; they combine characteristics of both fruits in varying degrees. Several are currently available, with more likely to appear in the future. Not yet widely tested, so zone listings are preliminary.

Aprium. Worth trying where standard market apricot varieties succeed (Zones 3–24). 'Flavor Delight' has sweet, bright yellow fruit similar to an apricot, but it's a little juicier and has a touch of plum flavor. Pollinate with any apricot or with 'Flavor Supreme' pluot. Late spring or early summer ripener. Tree similar to apricot tree; maintain as such.

Pluot. Zones 2, 3, 7–12, 14–23, 31, 32, 34, 36, 37, 39. Likely to succeed where 'Santa Rosa' plum does. Tree resembles plum tree and should be treated as such. Fruit is very sweet, closest in flavor to a plum. Mid- to late summer ripeners are 'Dapple Dandy', maroon-and-yellow mottled skin and creamy white flesh streaked with red; 'Flavor King', all-red fruit; and 'Flavor Queen', greenish yellow skin and golden flesh. 'Flavor Supreme', with green-and-maroon mottled skin and deep red flesh, ripens in late spring or early summer. 'Dapple Dandy' and 'Flavor Supreme' will pollinate any other pluot; or use a Japanese plum that blooms at the same time.

APTENIA cordifolia
(Mesembryanthemum cordifolium)

Aizoaceae

SHRUBBY PERENNIAL

ZONES 15–17, 21–27

LIGHT SHADE IN HOT CLIMATES

TAKES CONSIDERABLE DROUGHT

Aptenia cordifolia

Ice plant relative with trailing stems to 2 ft. long and profusion of inch-wide, heart-shaped or oval, bright green, fleshy leaves. Purplish red, inch-wide ice plant flowers in spring and summer. Though fleshy, looks less like ice plant than most. Use as trailer in rock garden, on slope or wall, or in hanging pot. Needs perfect drainage in hot, humid areas. 'Variegata' has white-bordered leaves. 'Red Apple', hybrid with *Platythyra haeckeliana,* has brighter red flowers, is good ground cover.

Aquifoliaceae. The holly family contains evergreen trees or shrubs with berrylike fruit. *Ilex* (holly) is the only important genus.

AQUILEGIA

COLUMBINE

Ranunculaceae

PERENNIALS

ZONES VARY BY SPECIES

FULL SUN OR FILTERED SHADE

REGULAR WATER

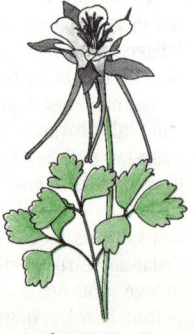

Columbines have a fairylike, woodland quality with their lacy foliage and beautifully posed flowers in exquisite pastels, deeper shades, and white. Erect, 2 in.–4 ft. high, depending on species

Aquilegia McKana Giant

or hybrid. Fresh green, blue-green, or gray-green divided leaves reminiscent of maidenhair fern. Slender, branching stems carry flowers to 3 in. across, erect or nodding, often with sepals and petals in contrasting colors; they usually have backward-projecting, nectar-bearing spurs. Some columbines have large flowers and very long spurs; these have an airier look than short-spurred and spurless kinds. Double-flowered types lack the delicacy of those with single blossoms, but they make a bolder color mass. Bloom season for columbines is spring, early summer.

Plants are not fussy about soil as long as it is well drained. On all columbines, cut back old stems for second crop of flowers. All kinds attract hummingbirds. Most columbines are not long-lived perennials; replace plants every 3 or 4 years. If you allow spent flowers to form seed capsules, you'll ensure a crop of volunteer seedlings. If you're growing hybrids, the seedlings won't necessarily duplicate the parent plants; seedlings from species (if grown isolated from other columbines) should closely resemble the originals. Leaf miners are a potential pest, especially on hybrids.

A. alpina. ALPINE COLUMBINE. Zones 1–9, 14–24, 32–45. Native to the Alps. Grows 1–2 ft. tall. Nodding, bright blue flowers to 2 in. across, with curved spurs to 1 in. long. Good rock garden plant. 'Hensol Harebell' is a cross between this species and *A. vulgaris;* flowers are deep blue on stems that may reach 3 ft. tall.

A. caerulea. ROCKY MOUNTAIN COLUMBINE. Zones 1–11, 14–24, 32–45. State flower of Colorado. Grows 1½–3 ft. high. Flowers upright, 2 in. or more across, blue and white. Spurs straight or spreading, to 2 in. long. This species is an important parent of many long-spurred hybrids.

A. canadensis. Zones 1–10, 14–24, 30–45. Native to much of eastern and central North America. Grows 1–2 ft. tall, occasionally taller. Red-and-yellow, 1½-in., nodding flowers have slightly curved, 1-in. spurs. Red color may wash out to pink in areas with warm nighttime temperatures. Less susceptible to leaf miners than most columbines. 'Corbett' (*A. c. flavescens*) has creamy yellow flowers.

A. chrysantha. GOLDEN COLUMBINE, GOLDEN-SPURRED COLUMBINE. Zones 1–11, 14–24, 32–45. Native to Arizona, New Mexico, and adjacent Mexico. One of showiest species. Large, many-branched plant to 3–4 ft. tall. Leaflets densely covered with soft hairs beneath. Upright, clear yellow, 1½–3 in. flowers, with slender, hooked spurs 2–2½ in. long. 'Silver Queen' has white flowers; double-flowered forms are white (sometimes pink-tinged) 'Alba Plena' and yellow 'Flore Pleno'.

A. flabellata. Zones 1–9, 14–24, 32–45. Native to Japan. Stocky, 9-in. plant with nodding lilac blue and creamy white flowers and hooked spurs to 1 in. long. Differs from most other columbines in having thicker, darker leaves with often overlapping segments. *A. f. pumila* is a very dwarf (4-in.) form. Good rock garden plants.

A. hinckleyana. HINCKLEY'S COLUMBINE. Zones 2–11, 14–24, 30, 33, 35, 41. Native to Big Bend country of Texas. To 1½–2 ft. high, with blue-gray foliage and long-spurred, chartreuse yellow flowers.

A. hybrids. Zones 2–10, 14–24, 32–43. Derived from several species. Preferred tall hybrid strains are graceful, long-spurred McKana Giants and double-flowering Spring Song (both to 3 ft.). Lower-growing strains include Biedermeier and Dragonfly (1 ft.); long-spurred Music (1½ ft.); and single to double, upward-facing Fairyland (15 in.). One of the most unusual hybrids is 2–2½-ft.-tall 'Nora Barlow', which has spurless, double, dahlialike flowers of reddish pink with a white margin.

A. longissima. Zones 1–11, 14–24, 30, 32–43. Native to southwest Texas and northern Mexico. Grows to 2½–3 ft. tall. Similar to *A. chrysantha*. Flowers numerous, erect, pale yellow, spurs very narrow, drooping, 4–6 in. long. 'Maxistar' is the variety most commonly offered.

A. saximontana. Zones 1–10, 14–24, 32–45. In effect, a miniature *A. caerulea*, 4–8 in. high.

A. vulgaris. EUROPEAN COLUMBINE. Zones 1–10, 14–24, 32–45. Naturalized in eastern U.S. Grows to 1–2½ ft. tall. Nodding, blue or violet flowers to 2 in. across; short, knobby spurs are about ¾ in. long. Many selections and hybrids, from single to fully double and either short spurred or spurless. Some nurseries offer a mix of flower forms in white and shades of pink, red, and violet.

ARABIS

ROCKCRESS

Brassicaceae (Cruciferae)

PERENNIALS

ZONES 1–10, 14–24, 31–45, EXCEPT AS NOTED

FULL SUN

MODERATE WATER

Arabis caucasica

Low-growing, spreading plants for edgings, rock gardens, ground covers, and pattern plantings. All kinds have attractive foliage and clusters of white, pink, or rose purple flowers that bloom in spring. Provide good drainage.

A. alpina. MOUNTAIN ROCKCRESS. Zones 1–7, 36–45. Low, tufted plant, rough-hairy, with leafy stems 4–10 in. high and basal leaves in clusters. White flowers in dense, short clusters. 'Rosea', 6 in. high, has pink flowers; 'Variegata' has variegated leaves. Plants sold as *A. alpina* are often really *A. caucasica*.

A. blepharophylla. CALIFORNIA ROCKCRESS, ROSE CRESS. Zones 5, 6, 15–17, 32, 34. Native to rocky hillsides and ridges along Northern California coast. Tufted plant 4–8 in. high. Basal leaves 1–2¾ in. long. Rose purple flowers, fragrant, ½–¾ in. wide, in short, dense clusters. Good in rock garden, containers.

A. caucasica (A. albida). WALL ROCKCRESS. Native Mediterranean region to Iran. Dependable old favorite. Forms mat of gray leaves to 6 in. high. White, ½-in. flowers almost cover plants in early spring. Excellent ground cover and base planting for spring-flowering bulbs such as daffodils and paper white narcissus. Start plants from cuttings or sow seeds in spring or fall. Provide some shade in hot climates. Short lived where winters are warm and summers humid.

'Variegata' has gray leaves with creamy white margins. 'Flore Plena' has double flowers; 'Rosabella' and 'Pink Charm' have pink blooms. Latter two are popular rock garden plants in cold climates.

A. ferdinandi-coburgii. Zones 3–10, 14–24, 31–43. Tight clumps to 4 in. Commonest form is 'Variegata', with leaves heavily edged and splashed with white.

A. procurrens. Creeping plant with 1–1¼-in. leaves and white flowers clustered on stems 4–12 in. tall.

A. sturii. Dense, fist-size cushions of small bright green leaves eventually grow into small mats. Clusters of white flowers on 2–3-in. stems. Some consider it among the finest rock garden plants.

***

Araceae. The arum family contains plants ranging from tuberous or rhizomatous perennials to shrubby or climbing tropical foliage plants. Leaves are often highly ornamental; while variable in shape, they tend to be arrow-like. Inconspicuous flowers cluster tightly on a club-shaped spadix within an often showy leaflike bract (spathe). Examples are *Anthurium,* calla *(Zantedeschia),* and *Philodendron.* Sap of many is highly irritating to mouth and throat.

ARACHNIODES simplicior

Dryopteridaceae

FERN

ZONES 4–24, 28–32

PARTIAL OR FULL SHADE

AMPLE WATER

Arachniodes simplicior
'Variegata'

Japanese fern sometimes known as holly fern. 'Variegata' is the variety usually grown. Grows 10–16 in. tall, with broadly triangular, once-divided fronds, deeply divided subdivisions. Base of each subdivision is yellow green, creating a strong two-tone effect. Winter-dormant in cold-winter regions, it remains green in milder climates.

ARALIA

Araliaceae

DECIDUOUS SHRUB-TREES OR PERENNIALS

⚡ ZONES 2–24, 28–41

☼ ◗ FULL SUN OR PARTIAL SHADE

🔴 ◖ REGULAR TO MODERATE WATER

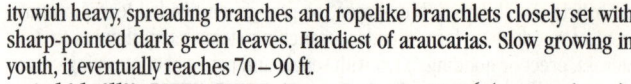

Aralia chinensis

Most are striking bold-leafed plants that may eventually grow to 25–30 ft. under ideal conditions. Often shrublike and multistemmed (because of suckering habit), especially in colder areas where they may grow to 10 ft. Branches are nearly vertical or slightly spreading, usually very spiny. Huge leaves, clustered at ends of branches and divided into many leaflets, have effective pattern value. White flowers, small but in such large, branched clusters that they are showy in midsummer, are followed by purplish berrylike fruit.

Grow in well-drained soil. Not good near swimming pools because of spines; even leafstalks are sometimes prickly. Protect plants from wind to avoid burning foliage.

A. chinensis. CHINESE ANGELICA. Only moderately spiny. Leaves 2–3 ft. long, divided into 2–6-in.-long toothed leaflets without stalks. Flower clusters grow 1–2 ft. wide.

A. elata. JAPANESE ANGELICA TREE. Native to northeast Asia. Similar to *A. chinensis* but leaflets are narrower, have fewer teeth. 'Variegata' has leaflets strikingly bordered with creamy white.

A. elegantissima. See Schefflera elegantissima

A. papyrifera. See Tetrapanax papyriferus

A. racemosa. SPIKENARD. Native to eastern U.S. Unlike the other species, a rhizomatous perennial to 6 ft., with long (2½-ft.) leaves divided into many coarse leaflets. Tiny white flowers are clustered into balls on branching stems. Tiny fruits are black or brown.

A. sieboldii. JAPANESE ARALIA. See Fatsia japonica

A. spinosa. HERCULES' CLUB, DEVIL'S WALKING STICK. Native to eastern U.S. Has a few usually unbranched spiny stems, each crowned by 2–6-ft. leaves. Tiny flowers form huge, branched clusters. Spreads by suckers. One of the most tropical-looking, genuinely hardy trees.

Araliaceae. The aralia family of herbaceous and woody plants is marked by leaves that are divided fanwise into leaflets or veined in pattern like the fingers of a hand. Individually tiny flowers are in round clusters or in large compound clusters. Examples are English ivy *(Hedera helix)*, Japanese aralia *(Fatsia japonica)*, and *Schefflera*.

ARAUCARIA

Araucariaceae

EVERGREEN TREES

⚡ ZONES VARY BY SPECIES

☼ FULL SUN

🔴 REGULAR WATER

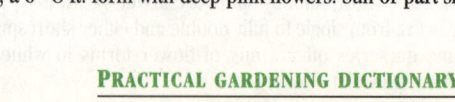

Araucaria araucana

These strange-looking conifers provide distinctive silhouette with their evenly spread tiers of stiff branches. Most have stiff, closely overlapping, dark to bright green leaves. All do well in a wide range of soils with adequate drainage.

These trees serve well as skyline trees, but they become so towering that they need the space they would have in a park. And they are not trees to sit under—with age they bear large, spiny, 10–15-lb. cones that fall with a crash. They thrive in containers for years.

A. araucana (A. imbricata). MONKEY PUZZLE TREE. Zones 4–9, 14–27; possible but unreliable in 28, 31, 32. Native to Chile. Arboreal odd-

ity with heavy, spreading branches and ropelike branchlets closely set with sharp-pointed dark green leaves. Hardiest of araucarias. Slow growing in youth, it eventually reaches 70–90 ft.

A. bidwillii. BUNYA-BUNYA. Zones 7–9, 12–25, 26 (protected sites), 27. Native to Australia. Moderate growth to 80 ft.; broadly rounded crown supplies dense shade. Two kinds of leaves: juvenile leaves are glossy, rather narrow, ¾–2 in. long, stiff, more or less spreading in two rows; mature leaves are oval, ½ in. long, rather woody, spirally arranged and overlapping along branches. Unusual house plant; very tough and tolerant of low light.

A. heterophylla (A. excelsa). NORFOLK ISLAND PINE. Zones 17, 21–25, 26 (protected sites), 27. Moderate growth rate to 100 ft., of pyramidal shape. Juvenile leaves rather narrow, ½ in. long, curved and with sharp points; mature leaves somewhat triangular and densely overlapping. Can be held in containers for many years—outdoors in mild climates, indoors anywhere.

Araucaria heterophylla

Araucariaceae. Coniferous trees with symmetrical branching habit and leaves that vary from needlelike to broad and leathery. *Araucaria* is the only representative in this book.

ARBORVITAE. See PLATYCLADUS orientalis, THUJA

ARBUTUS

Ericaceae

EVERGREEN TREES AND SHRUB-TREES

⚡ ZONES VARY BY SPECIES

☼ FULL SUN, EXCEPT AS NOTED

🔴 🔴 REGULAR TO LITTLE WATER

All types have ornamental bark, clusters of little urn-shaped flowers, decorative (and edible) fruit, and handsome foliage. Provide good drainage, especially if plant receives regular water.

A. 'Marina'. Zones 8, 9, 14–24. Hybrid of uncertain parentage. Tree to 40 ft., usually less. Resembles *A. unedo* but has larger leaves, rosy pink flowers in fall. Good garden substitute for *A. menziesii*.

Arbutus unedo

A. menziesii. MADRONE, MADRONA. Zones 3–7, 14–19. Suited only to its native habitat along Pacific Coast. Round-headed tree to 20–100 ft. tall. Most notable feature is smooth, reddish brown bark that peels in thin flakes. Leathery, 3–6-in.-long leaves are shiny dark green on top, dull gray green beneath. White to pinkish spring flowers. Red-and-orange berries ripen in autumn; they look like a small version of strawberry tree fruit.

A. unedo. STRAWBERRY TREE. Zones 4–24, 31, warmer parts of 32. Native to southern Europe, Ireland. Slow to moderate growth to 8–35 ft. tall and wide; tends to be a small shrub in Southeast, much larger in California. Trunk and branches have shreddy red-brown bark, become twisted and gnarled in age. Dark green, red-stemmed leaves 2–3 in. long. Clusters of flowers and fruit often appear simultaneously in fall and winter. Small, white or greenish white flowers; red-and-yellow, ¾-in. fruits resemble strawberries but are mealy and bland tasting. Varieties include 'Elfin King', a dwarf form (not over 5 ft. tall at 10 years old) that flowers and fruits nearly continuously; 'Compacta', seldom exceeding 10 ft.; and 'Oktoberfest', a 6–8-ft. form with deep pink flowers. Sun or part shade.

PRACTICAL GARDENING DICTIONARY

PLEASE SEE PAGES 545–616

ARCHONTOPHOENIX

Arecaceae (Palmae)

PALMS

⚡ ZONES 21–25; OR INDOORS

☼ ◐ FULL SUN OR PARTIAL SHADE

◐ ● REGULAR TO MODERATE WATER

Archontophoenix cunninghamiana

Called bangalow or piccabeen palms in Australia. They grow to 50 ft. or more, with 10–15-ft. spread. Handsome, stately, difficult to transplant when large. Where winds are strong, plant in lee of buildings to prevent damage. Young trees can't take frost; mature plants may stand 28°F/–2°C. They tolerate shade and can grow many years grouped under tall trees. Old leaves shed cleanly, leaving smooth green trunks. Feathery leaves on mature trees 8–10 ft. long, green above, gray green beneath. Good pot plant indoors or out.

A. alexandrae. ALEXANDRA PALM. Trunk enlarged toward base.

A. cunninghamiana (Seaforthia elegans). KING PALM. More common than *A. alexandrae.* Trunk not prominently enlarged at base. Clustered amethyst flowers are handsome. Highly recommended for nearly frost-free areas.

ARCTANTHEMUM. See CHRYSANTHEMUM arcticum

ARCTOSTAPHYLOS

MANZANITA

Ericaceae

EVERGREEN SHRUBS

⚡ ZONES VARY BY SPECIES

☼ ◐ FULL SUN OR LIGHT SHADE

● MODERATE WATER

Arctostaphylos uva-ursi

This enormous clan of evergreen shrubs is mostly native to the far West, especially California, where dozens of species and selections are grown as shrubs or ground covers. One species (the most widely grown), *A. uva-ursi,* is native to the northern regions of the world, extending south to the northern U.S. and down into California. All types have small white or pink urn-shaped flowers in late winter to early spring, followed by berrylike red or brown fruits. All require excellent drainage but can tolerate poor soil, preferring rocky or sandy, acid soils to heavy, rich ones.

A. columbiana. HAIRY MANZANITA. Zones 4–6, 15–17. Compact, low-growing shrub with reddish bark, 3-in.-long gray-green leaves, white flowers, and red-cheeked fruit. Form sold in Northwest is called 'Oregon Hybrid'.

A. densiflora. VINE HILL MANZANITA. Zones 7–9, 14–21. Generally low and spreading; outer branches root where they touch soil. Main stems slender and crooked. Reddish black, smooth bark. Small glossy green leaves; white or pink flowers. 'Howard McMinn' grows to 5–6 ft. tall, 7 ft. wide; 'Harmony' is similar but taller and broader. 'Sentinel' is upright to 6 ft. or taller, spreading to 8 ft.

A. 'Emerald Carpet'. Zones 6–9, 14–24. Dense, uniform carpet 9–14 in. tall, mounding slightly higher after many years. Tiny, oval bright green leaves. Small pink flowers not showy.

A. hookeri. MONTEREY MANZANITA. Zones 6–9, 14–24. Slowly forms a dense mound 1½–4 ft. high, spreading to 6 ft. or more. Small glossy green leaves, white to pinkish flowers, shiny bright red fruit, smooth red-brown bark. Good on hillsides. 'Monterey Carpet' is 1 ft. high, spreads by rooting branches to 12 ft. 'Wayside' grows 4 ft. tall, 8 ft. or wider.

A. manzanita. COMMON MANZANITA. Zones 4–9, 14–24. Grows 6–20 ft. high, spreads 4–10 ft. Picturesque crooked branching habit; purplish red bark. Small, broadly oval leaves. White to pink flowers in drooping clusters; fruit white, turning deep red. 'Dr. Hurd' is treelike form to

15 ft. tall and as wide or wider, with mahogany bark, large light green leaves, and white flowers.

A. uva-ursi. BEARBERRY, KINNIKINNICK. Zones 1–9, 14–24, 34, 36–45. Most widely adapted species. Good ground or bank cover at seashore, in mountains. Prostrate, spreading and rooting as it grows, eventually making broad mats a few inches deep. Small, glossy, leathery leaves are bright green, turning red or purplish in winter. White or pinkish flowers are followed by red or pink fruits. Slow to become established; mulch heavily between plants to keep down weeds until branches provide cover. Named, cutting-grown varieties provide uniform appearance in large plantings. These include:

'Alaska'. Flat grower with small, round dark green leaves.

'Massachusetts'. Small leafed, flat growing. Abundant pinkish white flowers, red fruit.

'Point Reyes'. Dark green leaves closely set along branches. Fairly tolerant of heat and drought.

'Radiant'. Leaves lighter green and more widely spaced than those of 'Point Reyes'. Heavy crop of large bright red fruit appears in fall, lasts into winter.

'Wood's Red'. Reliable producer of large bright red berries. Small dark green leaves turn reddish in cold weather.

ARCTOTIS

AFRICAN DAISY

Asteraceae (Compositae)

ANNUALS

⚡ ALL ZONES

☼ FULL SUN

● MODERATE WATER

Arctotis Hybrid

The term "African daisy" can refer to any of several plants; names and identities of the plants are often confused, even by seed companies and nurseries. *Arctotis* species have lobed leaves that are rough, hairy, or woolly; their flower heads usually have a contrasting ring of color around central eye. *Dimorphotheca* species (commonly used for mass flower color in winter) have smooth green foliage; their flowers are in the yellow-orange-salmon range or are white. Trailing ground cover African daisies and woody, shrubby white-and-blue African daisies are *Osteospermum.*

In cold-winter areas, the following annuals are planted in spring for summer bloom. In mild climates, they grow in winter and bloom from spring into early summer, with scattered bloom later. They do not withstand extreme heat and humidity.

A. hybrids. Most garden plants are hybrids 1–1½ ft. tall. Their 3-in. flowers come in white, pink, red, purplish, cream, yellow, and orange, usually with a dark ring around the nearly black eyespot. Will self-sow but tend to revert to orange. You can perpetuate colors you like by taking cuttings. Plants survive as perennials in mildest climates but bloom best in their first year.

A. stoechadifolia grandis. Bushy growth to 2 ft., with gray-green, slightly hairy leaves and 3-in. white daisies in which yellow ring surrounds deep blue central eye.

ARDISIA

MARLBERRY

Myrsinaceae

EVERGREEN SHRUBS OR SHRUBLETS

⚡ ZONES VARY BY SPECIES

☼ ● PARTIAL OR FULL SHADE

● REGULAR WATER

Ardisia japonica

Of the 150 species of evergreen shrubs in this genus, only the following two are commonly grown. Valued for foliage, beadlike fruits. ▶

A

A. crenata (A. crenulata, A. crispa). Zones 24–28; or indoors. In Florida, often grown in the ground on north side of buildings or in planters. Most familiar as 1½-ft. single-stemmed potted plant needing only routine house plant care. In large tub it can reach 4 ft. with nearly equal spread. In spring, spirelike clusters of tiny, ¼-in. white or pinkish flowers are carried above shiny, wavy-edged, 3-in.-long leaves. Flowers are followed in autumn by brilliant scarlet fruit that usually hangs on through winter.

A. japonica. Zones 5, 6, 15–17, 28–31. Low shrub that spreads as ground cover by rhizomes to produce succession of upright branches 6–18 in. high. Makes quality ground cover in shade. Leathery, bright green leaves, 4 in. long, are clustered at tips of branches. Forms with white or gold leaf variegation are sometimes sold. White, ¼-in. flowers, two to six in cluster, appear in fall, followed by small, round, bright red fruits that last into winter.

Arecaceae. It's difficult to generalize about any plant family as large and widespread as palms. Generally speaking, they have single, unbranched trunks of considerable height; some grow in clusters, though, and some are dwarf or stemless. The leaves are usually divided into many leaflets, either like ribs of a fan (fan palms) or like a feather, with many parallel leaflets growing outward from a long central stem (feather palms). But some palms have undivided leaves. This family was formerly called Palmae. See also Palms.

ARECA lutescens. See CHRYSALIDOCARPUS lutescens

ARECASTRUM romanzoffianum. See SYAGRUS romanzoffianum

ARENARIA

SANDWORT

Caryophyllaceae

PERENNIAL GROUND COVERS

✿ ZONES 1–9, 14–24, 32–45

☼ ◑ PARTIAL SHADE IN HOT CLIMATES

💧 REGULAR WATER

Arenaria montana

Low evergreen plants carpet ground with dense mats of mosslike foliage, have small white flowers in late spring and summer. They are often used as lawn substitutes, between stepping-stones, or for velvety green patches in rock gardens. Provide well-drained soil.

A. montana. Grows 2–4 in. high; weak stems up to 1 ft. long, usually covered with soft hairs. Leaves grayish, ½–¾ in. long. White flowers, 1 in. across, profuse in late spring or early summer. Good plant to let trail over sunny rock or tumble over low wall.

A. verna (A. v. caespitosa). See under Sagina subulata

ARGEMONE

PRICKLY POPPY

Papaveraceae

ANNUALS OR BIENNIALS

✿ ALL ZONES

☼ FULL SUN

💧 MODERATE TO LITTLE WATER

Argemone mexicana

Prickly-leafed and prickly-stemmed plants with large, showy poppy flowers. Native to desert or dry areas, Wyoming to Mexico and west to California. Grow easily from seed sown where plants are to bloom or from seed sown in pots; transplant gently. Need sun and good drainage. Bloom mostly in summer. To 3 ft.

A. intermedia. See A. polyanthemos

A. mexicana. Annual. Yellow to orange flowers.

A. platyceras. Annual. White flowers. Most common kind.

A. polyanthemos (A. intermedia). Annual or biennial. White flowers.

ARGYRANTHEMUM. See CHRYSANTHEMUM frutescens

ARISAEMA

Araceae

TUBEROUS-ROOTED PERENNIALS

✿ ZONES VARY BY SPECIES

☼ ● PARTIAL OR FULL SHADE

💧 💧 AMPLE WATER DURING ACTIVE GROWTH

Arisaema triphyllum

Eerie-looking woodland plants from the eastern U.S. and the Far East. All have leaves divided into segments and summer flowers somewhat resembling otherworldly callas, with a much-modified leaflike bract (spathe) surrounding a spike of minute flowers on a fleshy stalk (spadix). The native Jack-in-the-pulpit is a familiar example, but species from Asia attract connoisseurs of the odd. Fruits that follow the blossoms resemble small, bright red ears of corn. All die down in winter and tend to reappear late in spring. Use in the woodland garden or grow in pots for close-up viewing. All like rich soil, with abundant organic matter and plenty of water.

A. sikokianum. Zones 3–6, 31–41. Native to Japan. Grows to 20 in. Plant has two leaves, one with three leaflets, the other with five; leaflets grow 6 in. long, 4 in. wide. Flower stem, as tall (or nearly) as leafstalks, bears a 6-in. spathe—deep purple outside, yellowish within. Tip of spathe curves over a white spadix with a rounded, club-shaped tip.

A. speciosum. SHOWY COBRA LILY. Zones 4–6, 14–17, 31. Native to Himalayas, western China. Grows 2–3 ft., with a single 1½-ft. leaf bearing three leaflets with reddish edges. Leafstalk marbled dark purple. Spathe to 8 in., dark purple striped white. Whitish spadix terminates in a slender 2-ft. tail.

A. tortuosum. Zones 4–6, 14–17, 31, 32. Native to Himalayas, western China. Grows 3–4 ft. tall. Each leaf has 5–15 narrow leaflets. Green or purplish, 6-in. spathe is strongly curved downward at tip; green or purplish spadix thrusts out and upward in a strong curve.

A. triphyllum. JACK-IN-THE-PULPIT, INDIAN TURNIP. Zones 1–6, 26, 28, 31–43. Native to eastern North America. Each of the two 2-ft. leafstalks bears three 6-in. leaflets. Flowering stems, usually taller than leaves, carry a hooded spathe to 6 in., green or purple with white stripes (the pulpit), and a green or purple spadix (Jack). A common woodland plant. The name "Indian turnip" refers to the root. It contains calcium oxalate crystals that sting the tongue and throat, but is edible if thoroughly boiled.

ARISTOLOCHIA

Aristolochiaceae

DECIDUOUS OR EVERGREEN VINES

✿ ZONES VARY BY SPECIES

☼ ◑ ● EXPOSURE NEEDS VARY BY SPECIES

💧 💧 AMPLE WATER

Aristolochia elegans

Curiously shaped flowers in rather sober colors resemble curved pipes with flared bowls or birds with bent necks.

A. durior (A. macrophylla). DUTCHMAN'S PIPE. Deciduous. Zones 1–24, 29–43. Native to eastern U.S. Will cover 15 by 20 ft. in one season. Easily grown from seed. Kidney-shaped, 6–14-in.-long, deep green, glossy leaves are carried in shinglelike pattern to form dense cover on trellis. Blooms late spring to early summer. Flower is yellowish green, 3-in. curved tube that flares into three brownish purple lobes about 1 in. wide; flowers almost hidden by leaves. Thrives in full sun to heavy shade. Generous feeding and watering will speed growth. Cut back in winter if too heavy. Short lived in warm-winter areas. Will not stand strong winds.

A. elegans (A. littoralis). CALICO FLOWER. Evergreen. Zones 23–27; house or greenhouse plant elsewhere. Twines to 6 ft. or more. Wiry, slender stems; heart-shaped leaves 3 in. long. Whitish buds shaped like little pelicans open to 3-in.-wide, heart-shaped flowers of deep purple veined creamy white; summer bloom. Needs rich soil, partial shade.

Aristolochiaceae. This family includes *Aristolochia* and wild ginger (*Asarum*). All display odd-shaped flowers in low-key colors.

ARMERIA

THRIFT, SEA PINK

Plumbaginaceae

PERENNIALS

🌡 ZONES VARY BY SPECIES

☀ FULL SUN

💧💧 REGULAR TO LITTLE WATER

Armeria maritima

Narrow, stiff, evergreen leaves grow in compact tufts or basal rosettes; small white, pink, rose, or red flowers in dense globular heads. Main bloom period is spring to early summer, but removing faded flowers may prolong blooming into fall. Sturdy, dependable plants for edging walks or borders and for tidy mounds in rock gardens or raised beds. Attractive in containers. Need excellent drainage. Propagate by divisions or from seeds in spring or fall.

A. alliacea. Zones 3–9, 14–24, 32, 34–37. Leaf clumps 2–6 in. tall produce 8–16-in. flowering stalks with bright pink flowers. 'Leucantha' has white flowers.

A. arenaria (A. plantaginea). Zones 1–9, 14–24, 33–43. Leaves narrow, 2–6 in. long. Flowering stems 8–24 in. tall, with purplish pink or white blossoms.

A. girardii (A. juncea, A. setacea). Zones 6–9, 14–24, 32. Low, dense mounds of narrow, needlelike foliage produce lavender pink flowers.

A. juniperifolia (A. caespitosa). Zones 2–9, 14–24, 32, 34, 36–39. Stiff, needle-shaped leaves ½ in. long in low, extremely compact rosettes. Flowers rose pink or white on 2-in. stems. This little mountain native is very touchy about drainage; apply mulch of fine gravel around plants to prevent basal stem rot, especially in summer.

A. maritima (Statice armeria, Armeria vulgaris). COMMON THRIFT. Zones 1–9, 14–24, 33–43. Tufted mounds spreading to 1 ft. with 6-in.-long, stiff, grasslike leaves. Small white to rose pink flowers in tight clusters at top of 6–10-in. stalks. Blooms almost all year along Pacific Coast. 'Bloodstone' (rose red) and 'Cotton Tail' (white) are selections.

ARONIA

CHOKEBERRY

Rosaceae

DECIDUOUS SHRUBS

🌡 ZONES VARY BY SPECIES

☀ FULL SUN OR LIGHT SHADE

💧💧 MUCH OR LITTLE WATER

Aronia melanocarpa

Chokeberries, native to southern Canada and the eastern U.S., are tough, undemanding shrubs useful as fillers or background plantings. They tolerate a wide variety of soils and can thrive on much or little water. All tend to spread by suckering, but are somewhat leggy (good for planting beneath). Small white or pinkish flowers are followed by showy fruits that last well into winter. Fall foliage is brightly colored.

A. arbutifolia. RED CHOKEBERRY. Zones 2–6, 31–41. Clumping shrub to 6–8 ft., with many erect stems bearing shiny foliage that is rich

green above, paler beneath. Fruits are clustered, ¼ in. wide, brilliant red, long lasting. Fall foliage is also bright red; plants tend to color early. 'Brilliant' ('Brilliantissima') is a selected form with exceptionally fine fall color.

A. melanocarpa. BLACK CHOKEBERRY. Zones 1–6, 31–43. Lower growing than *A. arbutifolia*, to just 3–5 ft. tall, rarely taller. Purple-red fall color; shiny black ½-in. fruits.

ARRHENATHERUM elatius bulbosum 'Variegatum'

BULBOUS OAT GRASS

Poaceae (Gramineae)

PERENNIAL

🌡 ZONES 2–7, 32–34, 36–41

☀◐ FULL SUN OR PARTIAL SHADE

💧 REGULAR WATER

Arrhenatherum elatius bulbosum 'Variegatum'

With its narrow leaves boldly edged and striped in white, it is attractive in the perennial border or large rock garden and can brighten a dark place under trees or big shrubs. Makes a graceful foliage clump about 1 ft. high. Flowering stems in summer double the plant's height. Performs best in cool seasons and cool climates. If it flops over in heat, shear for fresh growth in fall. Clumps spread by rhizomes, which may periodically need curtailing. Divide and replant as needed.

ARTEMISIA

Asteraceae (Compositae)

PERENNIALS

🌡 ZONES 1–24, 29–45, EXCEPT AS NOTED

☀ FULL SUN

💧 MODERATE WATER

Artemisia abrotanum

Several species are valuable for interesting leaf patterns and silvery gray or white aromatic foliage. Most of those described here have woody stems; *A. dracunculus, A. frigida, A. lactiflora, A. ludoviciana albula,* and *A. stellerana* are herbaceous. Most kinds excellent for use in mixed border where white or silvery leaves soften harsh reds or oranges and blend beautifully with blues, lavenders, and pinks. Divide in spring and fall.

A. abrotanum. SOUTHERNWOOD, OLD MAN. Zones 3–24, 27–41. To 3–5 ft. Beautiful lemon-scented, green, feathery foliage; yellowish white flower heads. Use for pleasantly scented foliage in shrub border. Hang sprigs in closet to discourage moths. Burn a few leaves on stove to kill cooking odors.

A. absinthium. COMMON WORMWOOD. To 2–4 ft. Silvery gray, finely divided leaves with bitter taste, pungent odor. Tiny yellow flowers. Prune to get better-shaped plant. Divide every 3 years. Background shrub; good gray feature in flower border, particularly fine with delphiniums. 'Lambrook Silver' is a 1½-ft. form with especially finely cut, silver white leaves.

A. arborescens. Zones 7–9, 14–24, 29–31. To 3 ft. or a little more in height, 2 ft. wide, with silvery white, very finely cut foliage. Most attractive but more tender than other artemisias.

A. californica. CALIFORNIA SAGEBRUSH. Zones 3–24. Finely divided grayish white leaves on stems 1½–5 ft. tall. Loses leaves in extreme drought. 'Canyon Gray' and 'Montara' are superior selections.

A. caucasica. SILVER SPREADER. To 3–6 in. tall, spreading to 2 ft. in width. Silky, silvery green foliage; small yellow flowers. Bank or ground cover; plant 1–2 ft. apart. Needs good drainage. Takes extremes of heat and cold.

A. dracunculus. FRENCH TARRAGON, TRUE TARRAGON. Zones 3–24, 29–41. To 1–2 ft.; spreads slowly by creeping rhizomes. Shiny dark green,

A

narrow leaves are very aromatic. Flowers greenish white in branched clusters. Attractive container plant. Cut sprigs in June for seasoning vinegar. Use fresh or dried leaves to season salads, egg and cheese dishes, fish. Divide plant every 3 or 4 years to keep it vigorous. Propagate by divisions or by cuttings. Plants grown from seed are not true culinary tarragon.

A. frigida. FRINGED WORMWOOD. To 1–1½ ft. with white, finely cut leaves. Small yellow flowers. Young plants are compact; cut back when they become rangy.

A. lactiflora. WHITE MUGWORT. Tall, straight column to 4–5 ft. One of few artemisias with attractive flowers: creamy white in large, branched, 1½-ft. sprays in late summer. Leaves dark green with broad, tooth-edged lobes.

Artemisia dracunculus

A. ludoviciana albula (A. albula). SILVER KING ARTEMISIA. Bushy growth to 2–3½ ft., with slender, spreading branches and silvery white, 2-in. leaves. The lower leaves have three to five lobes; the upper ones are narrow and unlobed. Cut foliage useful in arrangements. 'Valerie Finnis' is a compact grower (to 2 ft. tall), with broader silvery leaves slightly lobed toward the tips.

A. pontica. ROMAN WORMWOOD. To 4 ft. Feathery, silver gray leaves. Heads of nodding, whitish yellow flowers in long, open, branched clusters. Leaves used in sachets.

A. 'Powis Castle'. Zones 4–24, 29–34. A hybrid, with *A. absinthium* as a probable parent. Silvery, lacy mound to 3 ft. tall, 6 ft. wide. Splendid background plant for bright flowers and tough enough to use as a bank or berm cover.

A. pycnocephala. SANDHILL SAGE. Zones 3–24. Native to beaches of Northern California. Rounded, somewhat spreading plant to 1–2 ft. tall; stems grow erect. Soft leaves—silvery white or gray, divided into narrow lobes—are crowded along branches. Very small yellow flowers. Becomes unkempt; replace every 2 years. 'David's Choice' is a compact plant to 1 ft. tall, 3 ft. wide.

A. schmidtiana. ANGEL'S HAIR. Forms dome, 2 ft. high and 1 ft. wide, of woolly, silvery white, finely cut leaves. Flowers insignificant. 'Silver Mound' is 1 ft. high.

A. stellerana. BEACH WORMWOOD, OLD WOMAN, DUSTY MILLER. Dense, silvery gray plant to 2½ ft. with 1–4-in. lobed leaves. Hardier than *Senecio cineraria* (another dusty miller), this artemisia is often used in its place in colder climates. Yellow flowers in spikelike clusters. 'Silver Brocade' is a superior, densely growing selection.

ARTICHOKE

Asteraceae (Compositae)

PERENNIAL VEGETABLE WITH LANDSCAPE VALUE

⚡ ZONES VARY; SEE BELOW

☀ FULL SUN

💧 REGULAR WATER TO PRODUCE CROP

Big ferny-looking plant with irregular, somewhat fountainlike form to 4 ft. high, 6–8 ft. wide. Leaves are silvery green. Big flower buds form at tops of stalks; they are the artichokes you cook and eat. If not cut, buds open into spectacular purple-blue, 6-in. thistlelike flowers that can be cut for arrangements (snip just before flowers are fully open).

Artichoke

Grown commercially in cool coastal California (Zone 17); produces fine, tender artichokes from September to May or all year. In Zones 8, 9, 14–16, 18–24, plant grows luxuriantly at least from spring through fall, and edible buds come as extra dividend in early summer only. In these areas, it is a dependable perennial crop grown from roots. Plant in winter or early spring, setting root shanks vertically with buds or shoots just

above soil line. Space 4–6 ft. apart. If grown only for ornamental value, can tolerate much drought. Cut off old stalks near ground level when leaves begin to yellow. Mulch in colder part of range.

Roots not routinely available beyond commercial growing areas. Crops have been raised from seed with some success in cool-summer, mild-winter areas of the Eastern Seaboard (Zones 34, 38). Start seed indoors 8 to 12 weeks before last frost; set outdoors when soil has warmed and frost danger is past. 'Green Globe' and 'Violetto' are ready to harvest the second summer after seeding; 'Imperial Star' produces first season, 90 to 100 days from transplant. Before first frost, cut stalks close to ground; protect with several inches of compost, manure, or straw. Replace plants every few years.

HOW TO EAT AN ARTICHOKE
To eat a whole artichoke, pull off each leaf, dip it in sauce or melted butter, and draw between your teeth to scrape off the tender base. Discard rest of leaf. When you reach the prickly center "choke," scoop it out and discard it. Cut the remaining "bottom" or "heart" into pieces to eat with a fork.

ARUGULA

ROCKET, ROQUETTE, RUGOLA

Brassicaceae (Cruciferae)

ANNUAL

⚡ ALL ZONES

☀ FULL SUN

💧 REGULAR WATER

Arugula

Leaves of this weedy plant supply 1–4-in.-long leaves, like small mustard leaves, that give a nutty zing to green salads. Pick small leaves; the bigger ones have sharp taste. Grows to 3 ft. high. Start from seed in winter or spring. Grows best in cool weather. Reseeds.

ARUM

Araceae

PERENNIALS WITH TUBEROUS ROOTS

⚡ ZONES VARY BY SPECIES

◑ ● PARTIAL OR FULL SHADE

💧 REGULAR WATER DURING ACTIVE GROWTH

🔥 SAP IS AN IRRITANT IF INGESTED

Arrow-shaped or heart-shaped leaves. Curious callalike blossoms on short stalks. Flower bract (spathe) half encloses thick, fleshy spike (spadix), which bears tiny flowers. Use in shady flower borders where hardy; *A. palaestinum* and *A. pictum* are sometimes used as indoor plants in colder climates.

Arum italicum

A. cornutum. See Sauromatum

A. italicum. ITALIAN ARUM. Zones 3–24, 28–34, 39. Arrow-shaped leaves, 8 in. long and wide, emerge in fall or early winter. Very short stem; white or greenish white (sometimes purple-spotted) flowers in spring and early summer. Spathe first stands erect, then folds over and conceals short yellow spadix. Dense clusters of bright red fruit follow. Lasting long after leaves have faded, these are the most conspicuous feature of the plant. They resemble small, bright red ears of shucked corn. In variety 'Pictum', leaves are veined with white.

A. palaestinum. BLACK CALLA. Zones 14–24. Leaves 6–8 in. long emerge in spring. The arrow-shaped spathe, about the same length, greenish outside, blackish purple inside, has a curved back that reveals the blackish purple spadix; spring and early summer. Potted plants bloom best when pot-bound.

A. pictum. Zones 7–9, 14–24, 28–31. Light green, heart-shaped, 10-in.-long leaves on 10-in. stalks appear in autumn, with or just after the flowers. Spathe is violet, green at base; spadix purplish black.

ARUNCUS

GOAT'S BEARD

Rosaceae

PERENNIALS

🌿 ZONES 1–9, 14–17, 31–43

☀️◑● CAN TAKE SUN IN COOL-SUMMER AREAS

💧 REGULAR WATER

Aruncus dioicus

Resemble *Astilbe*, with slowly spreading clumps of finely divided leaves topped in summer by plumy branched clusters of tiny white or creamy flowers. Good in perennial borders or at edge of woodland; especially handsome against a dark background. Require moist but not boggy soil.

A. aethusifolius. Deep green, finely divided leaves make foot-tall mounds. White flower plumes reach 16 in. Useful in rock garden, as edging or small-scale ground cover.

A. dioicus (A. sylvester). Grows to 6 ft., with a foam of white flowers in 20-in., much-branched clusters. 'Kneiffii' is half as tall, with more finely divided, almost ferny, leaves. 'Child of Two Worlds' ('Zweiweltenkind'), often sold as *A. chinensis,* grows to 5 ft.; branched flower clusters droop gracefully.

ARUNDINARIA. See BAMBOO

ARUNDO donax

GIANT REED

Poaceae (Gramineae)

PERENNIAL

🌿 ZONES 3–35, 39

☀️ FULL SUN

💧 AMPLE WATER

Arundo donax

One of largest grasses, planted for bold effects in garden fringe areas or by watersides. Also planted in hot-summer climates as quick windbreak or for erosion control. Often called a bamboo. Strong, somewhat woody stems, 6–20 ft. high. Leaves to 2 ft. long, flat, 3 in. wide. Flowers in rather narrow, erect clusters to 2 ft. high. 'Versicolor' ('Variegata'), less hardy than species (Zones 3–34), has leaves with white or yellowish stripes. Plants need rich soil. Protect roots with mulch in cold-winter areas. Cut out dead stems and thin occasionally to get look-through quality. Extremely invasive; plant only where you can control it. Can become a pest in irrigation ditches. Stems have some utility as plant stakes or, if woven together with wire, as fencing or shade canopy.

ASARINA

CLIMBING SNAPDRAGON, CHICKABIDDY

Scrophulariaceae

TENDER PERENNIALS OFTEN GROWN AS ANNUALS

🌿 ALL ZONES

☀️◑ CAN TAKE FULL SUN IN COOL-SUMMER AREAS

💧 REGULAR WATER

Asarina antirrhinifolia

Climbing, sprawling, or trailing tender plants with tubular flowers that flare at the mouth like snapdragons (a close relative). Perennials in Zones 17–27, but can be treated as annuals anywhere. Plants from early sowings will bloom in late spring and through the summer. Grow them on

a trellis or brushy twigs or in window boxes or hanging pots. They can also trail over a wall or serve as a small-scale ground cover.

A. antirrhinifolia. Flowers are lavender to purple, 1 in. long, with white throats marked yellow. A mixed-color seed strain offers red-and-yellow or blue-and-white flowers.

A. barclaiana. Vigorous grower to 8–10 ft., with white to pink or purple flowers. 'Angel's Trumpet' has 2-in. pink flowers.

A. scandens. Resembles *A. barclaiana,* with flowers that range from white to pink and dark blue.

ASARUM

WILD GINGER

Aristolochiaceae

PERENNIALS

🌿 ZONES VARY BY SPECIES

◑● PARTIAL OR FULL SHADE

💧💧 AMPLE WATER

Asarum caudatum

Roots and leaves of the wild gingers have a scent somewhat like that of ginger, but are not used as seasoning. Low, creeping plants with roundish or heart-shaped leaves, they make attractive woodland ground covers. Flowers are oddly shaped, with three spreading, leathery lobes that may be brownish, purplish, or greenish; hidden among the leaves, blossoms are curious rather than showy. Of the many species, only a few are available to gardeners. Asiatic species with fancily variegated leaves, now grown as connoisseur's plants in Japan, may eventually make their way here.

A. canadense. Zones 1–6, 31–45. Native to eastern North America. Deciduous, kidney-shaped, dark green leaves to 6 in. wide. Flowers are purplish brown. The hardiest species.

A. caudatum. Zones 4–6, 14–24, 31, 32. Native to the West Coast. Evergreen in warmer parts of range. Heart-shaped leaves 2–7 in. wide. Flowers reddish brown, the lobes elongated into tails. Where adapted, this is a valuable, quick-growing ground cover for shady places.

A. europaeum. Zones 2–6, 32–43. Native to Europe. Evergreen, shiny, kidney-shaped, dark green leaves 2–3 in. wide. Small brown flowers. Slow spreader.

A. shuttleworthii. Zones 4–6, 31–37, 39. Native to the Appalachians. Evergreen, 4-in. heart-shaped or roundish leaves usually variegated with silvery markings. Brown flowers with red spots. Slow growing. 'Callaway' spreads more quickly.

Asarum europaeum

Asclepiadaceae. Best-known family members are the milkweeds *(Asclepias),* but other garden plants also belong to this group, among them many succulents and some perennials and vines, including *Stephanotis.*

ASCLEPIAS

Asclepiadaceae

PERENNIALS

🌿 ALL ZONES

☀️ FULL SUN

💧💧💧 WATER NEEDS VARY BY SPECIES

⬥ ALL PARTS OF MANY SPECIES ARE POISONOUS IF INGESTED

Milkweeds are the best-known representatives of this group of plants. Just a few are cultivated in gardens; both of the following are native to the eastern U.S.

Asclepias tuberosa

A. incarnata. SWAMP MILKWEED. Grows 3–5 ft. tall, with narrow, long-pointed leaves and clustered pink flowers in joints of upper leaves. Needs plenty of moisture, even withstands wet soil. 'Ice Ballet', with white flowers, is a more compact 3½-ft. plant. ▶

A

A. tuberosa. BUTTERFLY WEED. Many stems to 3 ft. rise every year from perennial root. Broad clusters of bright orange flowers appear in midsummer, attracting swarms of butterflies. Prefers good drainage and moderate water. Flowers of Gay Butterflies strain are yellow to red. 'Hello Yellow' is a selected form with bright yellow flowers.

ASH. See FRAXINUS

ASH, MOUNTAIN. See SORBUS

ASIMINA triloba

PAWPAW

Annonaceae

DECIDUOUS TREE

ZONES 2–9, 14, 18–21, 28–41

FULL SUN, EXCEPT AS NOTED

REGULAR WATER

Asimina triloba

The pawpaw (sometimes known as Michigan banana) is the only hardy representative of a tropical family that has given us the cherimoya. It grows to 30 ft., generally broad and spreading when grown alone, but often narrow and erect in thickets that arise from suckering. In hot-summer climates, pawpaw suffers in full sun while very young and should have some shade in the first years. Leaves are oval, somewhat drooping, 4–10 in. long, medium green, turning bright yellow in fall. Foliage has an unpleasant odor when crushed. Flowers are large but not showy, purplish or brownish (sometimes green), with three prominent petals. Fruits are roughly oval, yellowish green turning brown, 3–5 in. long. The soft, custardlike flesh has a flavor somewhat like that of banana and a number of large brown seeds.

If possible, get grafted plants of named varieties such as 'Prolific' and 'Taylor'. Seedlings are highly variable.

ASPARAGUS, EDIBLE

Liliaceae

PERENNIAL VEGETABLE

ZONES 1–24, 29–45

FULL SUN

AMPLE WATER

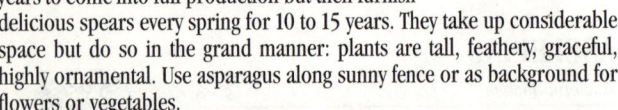
Edible Asparagus

One of most permanent and dependable of home garden vegetables. Plants take 2 to 3 years to come into full production but then furnish delicious spears every spring for 10 to 15 years. They take up considerable space but do so in the grand manner: plants are tall, feathery, graceful, highly ornamental. Use asparagus along sunny fence or as background for flowers or vegetables.

Seeds grow into strong young plants in one season (sow in spring), but roots are far more widely used. Set out seedlings or roots (not wilted, no smaller than an adult's hand) in fall or winter (mild climates), or in early spring (cold winters). Make trenches 1 ft. wide and 8–10 in. deep. Space trenches 4–6 ft. apart. Heap loose, manure-enriched soil at bottoms of trenches and soak. Space plants 1 ft. apart, setting them so that tops are 6–8 in. below top of trench. Spread roots out evenly. Cover with 2 in. of soil and water again.

As young plants grow, gradually fill in trench, taking care not to cover growing tips. Soak deeply whenever soil begins to dry out at root depth. Don't harvest any spears the first year; object at this time is to build big root mass. When plants turn brown in late fall or early winter, cut stems to ground. In cold-winter areas, permit dead stalks to stand until spring; they will help trap and hold snow, which will furnish protection to root crowns.

HOW TO BLANCH ASPARAGUS

Fresh white asparagus is a delicacy. It's not a special variety; blanching makes it white. In early spring before spears emerge, mound soil 8 in. high over a row of asparagus. When tips emerge from the top of the mounded soil, push a long-handled knife into the base of the mound to cut each spear well below the surface. Pull cut shoots out by the tips. Level mounds after the harvest season.

The following spring you can cut your first spears; cut only for 4 to 6 weeks or until appearance of thin spears indicates that roots are nearing exhaustion. Then permit plants to grow. Cultivate, feed, and irrigate heavily. The third year you should be able to cut spears for 8 to 10 weeks. Spears are ready to cut when they are 5–8 in. long. Thrust knife down at 45° angle to soil; flat cutting may injure adjacent developing spears. If asparagus beetles appear during cutting season, handpick them, knock them off the plant with water jets, or spray with rotenone or (carefully noting label precautions) malathion.

Asparagus seed and roots are sold as "traditional" ('Martha Washington' and others) and "all-male" ('Jersey Giant' and others). The latter kinds are bred to produce more and larger spears because they don't have to put energy into seed production. Such varieties still produce an occasional female plant.

ASPARAGUS, ORNAMENTAL

Liliaceae

PERENNIALS, SHRUBS, OR VINES

ZONES 12–28; OR INDOORS

FULL SUN OR PARTIAL SHADE

REGULAR WATER

Asparagus densiflorus
'Sprengeri'

There are about 150 kinds of asparagus besides the edible one—all members of the lily family. Best known of ornamental kinds is the fern asparagus (*A. setaceus*), which is not a true fern. Although valued mostly for handsome foliage of unusual textural quality, some of these species have small but fragrant flowers and colorful berries. Green foliage sprays are made up of what look like leaves. Needlelike or broader, these are actually short branches called cladodes. The true leaves are inconspicuous dry scales.

Most ornamental asparagus look greenest in partial shade but thrive in sun in cool-summer climates. Leaves turn yellow in dense shade. Plant in well-drained soil to which peat moss or ground bark has been added. Because of fleshy roots, plants can go for periods without water, but grow better when it comes regularly. Feed in spring with complete fertilizer. Trim out old shoots to make room for new growth. Will survive light frosts but may be killed to ground by severe cold. After frost, plants often come back from roots.

A. asparagoides. SMILAX ASPARAGUS. Much-branched vine with spineless stems to 20 ft. or more. Leaves to 1 in. long, sharp pointed, stiffish, glossy grass green. Small, fragrant white flowers in spring followed by blue berries. Birds feed on berries, drop seeds that sprout at random about the garden. (Plant also self-sows readily.) Roots are clusters of fleshy thongs and are nearly immortal, surviving long drought. Foliage sprays prized for table decoration. Becomes tangled mass unless trained. 'Myrtifolius', commonly called baby smilax, is a more graceful form with smaller leaves.

A. densiflorus. The species is less commonly grown than its forms. The following are the two most popular.

'Myers'. MYERS ASPARAGUS. Plants send up several to many stiffly upright stems to 2 ft. or more, densely clothed with needlelike deep green leaves. Plants have fluffy look. Good in containers. A little less hardy than Sprenger asparagus. Sometimes sold as *A. meyeri* or *A. myersii*.

'Sprengeri'. SPRENGER ASPARAGUS. Arching or drooping stems 3–6 ft. long. Shiny, bright green needlelike leaves, 1 in. long, in bundles. Bright red berries. Popular for hanging baskets or containers, indoors and out. Train on trellis; climbs by means of small hooked prickles. Used as billowy ground cover where temperatures stay above 24°F/–4°C. Takes full sun as well as partial shade; grows in ordinary or even poor soil. Will tolerate dryness of indoors but needs bright light. Sometimes sold as *A. sprengeri*. Form sold as 'Sprengeri Compacta' or *A. sarmentosus* 'Compacta' is denser with shorter stems.

A. meyeri, A. myersii. See *A. densiflorus* 'Myers'

A. officinalis. See Asparagus, Edible

A. plumosus. See *A. setaceus*

A. sarmentosus. See *A. densiflorus* 'Sprengeri'

A. setaceus (A. plumosus). FERN ASPARAGUS. Branching woody vine climbs by wiry, spiny stems to 10–20 ft. Tiny threadlike leaves form feathery dark green sprays that resemble true fern fronds. Tiny white flowers. Berries purple black. Dense, fine-textured foliage mass useful as screen against walls, fences. Florists use foliage as fillers in bouquets; holds up better than delicate ferns. Sometimes called emerald feather. Dwarf variety 'Nanus' is good in containers. 'Pyramidalis' has upswept, windblown look, is less vigorous than common fern asparagus.

A. sprengeri. See *A. densiflorus* 'Sprengeri'

ASPEN. See POPULUS

ASPEN DAISY. See ERIGERON speciosus macranthus

ASPERULA odorata. See GALIUM odoratum

ASPHODELINE lutea

YELLOW ASPHODEL, KING'S SPEAR

Liliaceae

PERENNIAL

☀️ ZONES 3–24, 29–33

☀️◐ FULL SUN OR PARTIAL SHADE

💧 REGULAR WATER

Asphodeline lutea

This rhizomatous rootstock forms a clump of dark green, grassy, 1-ft. leaves. The 3-ft. flower stalk is topped in spring by an 8-in. narrow cluster of yellow, fragrant flowers a little more than 1 in. across. These peer from a shag of buff or reddish brown bracts. Use it in perennial borders.

ASPIDISTRA elatior (A. lurida)

CAST-IRON PLANT

Liliaceae

PERENNIAL

☀️ ZONES 4–10, 12–31; OR INDOORS

☀️● TOLERATES VERY LOW LIGHT

💧 MODERATE WATER

Aspidistra elatior

Sturdy, long-lived evergreen foliage plant remarkable for its ability to thrive under conditions unacceptable to most kinds of plants. Leaf blades 1–2½ ft. long, 3–4 in. wide, tough, glossy dark green and arching, with distinct parallel veins; each blade is supported by a 6–8-in.-long grooved leafstalk. Inconspicuous brownish flowers bloom in spring close to ground. Although extremely tolerant, requiring minimal care, cast-iron plant grows best in porous soil enriched with organic matter and responds to feeding in spring and summer. Will grow in dark, shaded areas (under decks or stairs) anywhere, as well as in filtered sun—except in the desert, where it takes full shade only. A good

porch plant. Keep leaves dust free and glossy by hosing them off, or clean with a soft brush or cloth. Variegated form ('Variegata'), with leaves striped with white, loses its variegation if it is planted in soil that's too rich.

ASPIDIUM capense. See RUMOHRA adiantiformis

ASPLENIUM

Polypodiaceae

FERNS

☀️ ZONES VARY BY SPECIES

☀️● PARTIAL OR FULL SHADE

💧💧 AMPLE WATER

Asplenium bulbiferum

Widespread and variable group. These resemble each other only in botanical details and need for shade and liberal watering. Common name "spleenwort" refers to alleged medicinal value.

A. bulbiferum. MOTHER FERN. Zones 14 (protected), 15–17, 20–24; or house plant. From New Zealand. Graceful, very finely cut light green fronds to 4 ft. tall. Fronds produce plantlets that can be removed and planted. Hardy to 26°F/–3°C.

A. ebenoides (Asplenosorus ebenoides). SCOTT'S SPLEENWORT. Zones 1–6, 31–43. Hybrid between *A. platyneuron* and *A. rhizophyllum*. Small evergreen fern of variable appearance, with unevenly divided leaves.

A. nidus (A. nidus-avis). BIRD'S NEST FERN. Zone 25; or house plant. Native to Old World tropics. Tender fern with showy, apple green, undivided fronds to 4 ft. long, 8 in. wide, growing upright in cluster. Striking foliage plant. Grow potted plant indoors in winter, move to shady patio in summer.

Asplenium nidus

A. platyneuron. EBONY SPLEENWORT. Zones 1–6, 31–43. Native to eastern U.S. Evergreen, to 1½ ft. tall. Erect, once-divided dark green fronds have blackish brown midribs.

A. rhizophyllum (Camptosorus rhizophyllus). WALKING FERN. Zones 1–6, 31–43. Native to North America. An oddity with long, slender undivided fronds that taper to the tips; where they touch soil, tips take root and produce new plantlets. Needs some lime in the soil.

A. scolopendrium (Phyllitis scolopendrium). HART'S TONGUE FERN. Zones 2–6, 15–17, 31–41. Native to Europe (rare native in eastern U.S.). Strap-shaped leaves 9–18 in. long. Dwarf, crested, puckered, and forked varieties are collector's items. Needs humus; add limestone chips to acid soil. Good woodland plant, rhododendron and azalea companion; also fine pot plant.

A. trichomanes. MAIDENHAIR SPLEENWORT. Zones 1–6, 34–43. Native to much of the Northern Hemisphere. Delicate evergreen fern with narrow, bright green fronds 8–12 in. long. Leaflets are round or nearly so, only ½ in. long. Likes lime. Attractive in shady rock garden or on a wall where it can be seen close up.

ASTER

Asteraceae (Compositae)

PERENNIALS

☀️ ZONES 1–24, 31–43, EXCEPT AS NOTED

☀️ FULL SUN, EXCEPT AS NOTED

💧 REGULAR WATER

Aster frikartii

There are more than 600 species of true asters, ranging from alpine kinds forming compact mounds 6 in. high, to open-branching plants 6 ft. tall, to the odd tall climber. Flowers come in white or shades of blue, red, pink, lavender, or purple, mostly with yellow centers. Bloom is late summer to early fall, except as noted. Taller asters are invaluable for abundant color in large borders or among shrubs. Large sprays are effective in arrangements. Compact dwarf or cushion types make tidy edgings, mounds of color in rock gardens, good container plants.

Adapted to most soils. Most luxuriant in fertile soil. Few problems except for mildew on leaves in late fall. Strong-growing asters have invasive roots, need control. Divide clumps yearly in late fall or early spring. Replant vigorous young divisions from outside of clump; discard old center. Divide smaller, tufted, less vigorously growing kinds every 2 years.

A. alpinus. Zones 1–4, 36–45. Mounding plant 6–12 in. tall. Leaves ½–5 in. long, mostly in basal tuft. Several stems grow from basal clump, each carrying one violet blue flower 1½–2 in. across. Late spring to early summer bloom. Best in cold-winter areas. White and pink forms are uncommon.

A. amellus. ITALIAN ASTER. Sturdy, hairy plant to 2 ft. Branching stems with violet, yellow-centered flowers 2 in. across.

A. carolinianus. CLIMBING ASTER. Zones 26, 28–32. Unusual climber to 10–20 ft., with grayish green leaves and pink flowers aging to purplish blue. Fall bloom.

A. cordifolius. BLUE WOOD ASTER. Grows to 6 ft., with loose, branching clusters of inch-wide flower heads. 'Little Carlow' is lower growing (to 3½ ft). Sun or light shade.

A. divaricatus. WHITE WOOD ASTER. Broadly spreading plant with dark stems and a generous show of small flowers in pure white aging to pink. Thrives in shade.

A. ericoides. HEATH ASTER. To 3 ft., with narrow leaves and strong horizontal branching. Flower heads are small and profusely borne, in white, pink, or blue.

A. frikartii. One of the finest, most useful and widely adapted perennials. Hybrid between *A. amellus* and *A. thomsonii,* a hairy-leafed, lilac-flowered, 3-ft. species native to the Himalayas. Abundant clear lavender to violet blue single flowers are 2½ in. across. Open, spreading growth to 2 ft. high. Blooms early summer to fall—almost all year in mild-winter areas if dead flowers are removed regularly. May be short lived. 'Wonder of Stafa' and 'Mönch' are lavender blue favorites.

A. laevis. Zones 1–24, 31–45. To 3½ ft., with smooth, mildew-free foliage and clustered, 1-in. flower heads of deep purple blue.

A. lateriflorus. Zones 1–24, 31–45. Species grows to 4 ft.; garden selections are smaller, to 2½ ft. 'Horizontalis' is a twiggy, mounding plant with spreading branches bearing small pale blue flowers. Foliage turns purplish in fall, at height of flowering. 'Prince' is similar in form, with dark purple foliage and white flower heads centered in dark red.

A. novae-angliae. NEW ENGLAND ASTER. Stout-stemmed plant to 3–5 ft. with hairy leaves to 5 in. long. Flowers variable in color, pink to deep purple, 2 in. across. Good in wet areas. Reseeds

A. novi-belgii. NEW YORK ASTER. To 3 ft., similar to New England aster but with smooth leaves. Full clusters of bright blue-violet flowers.

Michaelmas daisy is the name applied to hybrids of *A. novae-angliae* and *A. novi-belgii.* They are tall (3–4 ft.), graceful, branching plants. Many horticultural varieties with flowers in white, pale to deep pink, rose, red, and many shades of blue, violet, and purple.

A. dumosus hybrids, sometimes known as Oregon-Pacific hybrids, are splendid garden plants developed by crossing some well-known Michaelmas daisies with a dwarf aster species native to the West. Dwarf, intermediate, and taller forms range in height from under 1 ft. to 2½ ft. Compact, floriferous, blooming late spring to fall. Many named varieties are available in white, blue, lavender, purple, rose, pink, cream.

A. pringlei. Eastern U.S. native known in cultivation through the variety 'Monte Cassino', a familiar florist's cut flower. Stems are long (sometimes to 5 ft.) and narrowish, freely set with very short branches bearing starry white, ¾-in. flower heads. Usually sold as *A. ericoides* 'Monte Cassino'.

A. tataricus. A giant (to 5–7 ft.) with 2-ft. leaves and sheaves of inch-wide blue flower heads in flat clusters in fall. Sun or shade.

A. yunnanensis 'Napsbury'. An improved garden variety of this Chinese species. Leaves dark green in basal tufts. Stems to 1½ ft., each bearing a single lavender blue, orange-centered flower. Blooms in late spring to early summer.

For the common annual or China aster, sold in six-packs at nurseries, see *Callistephus.*

Asteraceae. The sunflower or daisy family, one of the largest plant families, is characterized by flowers borne in tight clusters (heads). In the most familiar form, these heads contain two types of flowers—small, tightly clustered disk flowers in the center of the head, and larger, strap-shaped ray flowers around the edge. The sunflower *(Helianthus)* is a familiar example. The family was formerly called Compositae.

ASTILBE

FALSE SPIRAEA, MEADOW SWEET
Saxifragaceae
PERENNIALS
ZONES 1–7, 14–17, 32–45 (SEE BELOW)
FULL SUN OR PARTIAL SHADE
MOIST BUT NOT BOGGY SOIL

Astilbe arendsii

Valued for light, airy quality of plumelike flower clusters and attractive foliage, ability to provide color from late spring through summer. Leaves divided, with toothed or cut leaflets; leaves in some species simply lobed with cut margins. Small white, pink, or red flowers are carried in graceful, branching, feathery plumes held on slender, wiry stems ranging from 6 in. to 3 ft. or taller.

Astilbes are the mainstay of the shady perennial border, although in cool-summer climates they can withstand full sun if given plenty of moisture. Combine them with columbine, meadow rue, hosta, and bergenia in shady borders; with peonies, delphinium, and iris in sunnier situations. Effective at the edge of pools, along shady paths, and in containers. They require rich soil with ample humus. Cut off faded flowering stems and divide clumps every 4 to 5 years. Survival in coldest zones (1, 43, 45) depends on good snow cover.

A. arendsii. Most astilbes sold belong to this hybrid group or are sold as such. Most of the earliest blooming varieties belong to *A. japonica* and some of the later bloomers to *A. chinensis* or *A. thunbergii.* The plants differ chiefly in technical details. Here are some of the many varieties in use:

'Amethyst'. Late. Lavender, 3–4 ft.

'Bonn'. Early. Medium pink, 1½–2 ft.

'Bremen'. Midseason. Dark rose, 1½–2 ft.

'Bressingham Beauty'. Late midseason. Drooping pink clusters, 3 ft.

'Bridal Veil'. Midseason to late. Full white plumes, 3 ft.

'Deutschland'. Early. White, 1½ ft.

'Erica'. Midseason. Slender pink plumes, 2½–3 ft.

'Fanal'. Early. Blood red flowers, bronzy foliage, 1½–2½ ft.

'Hyacinth'. Midseason. Purplish pink, 2–3 ft.

'Koblenz'. Early to midseason. Bright red, 1½–2½ ft.

'Ostrich Plume' ('Straussenfeder'). Midseason to late. Drooping pink clusters, 3–3½ ft.

'Peach Blossom'. Midseason. Light salmon pink, 2 ft.

'Rheinland'. Early. Deep pink, 2–2½ ft.

'White Gloria'. Early to midseason. Creamy white, 2 ft.

A. chinensis. Resembles the *A. arendsii* hybrids, but generally blooms in late summer, grows taller, and tolerates dryness a little better. Varieties include:

A. c. davidii. Late, with dense, narrow pink plumes 3 ft. tall. Pink-flowered 'Finale' blooms latest, grows 18–20 in. tall.

A. c. taquetii 'Superba'. Bright pinkish purple flowers in spikelike clusters 4–5 ft. tall. 'Purple Candles' is deeper purple, slightly shorter.

A. simplicifolia. Grows to 16 in., with leaves merely cut or lobed instead of divided into leaflets. Known for its garden varieties. 'Sprite', the best known, is a low, compact plant with abundant pink, drooping, 1-ft. spires above bronze-tinted foliage; summer bloomer. 'Hennie Graefland' is similar, but grows a few inches taller and blooms somewhat earlier.

A. taquetii 'Superba'. See A. chinensis taquetii 'Superba'

ASTRANTIA

MASTERWORT

Apiaceae (Umbelliferae)

PERENNIALS

ZONES 3–9, 14–24, 31–41

FULL SUN OR PARTIAL SHADE

REGULAR WATER

Astrantia major

Flowers in dense, tight clusters surrounded by papery bracts resemble pincushions or, superficially, daisies. Flowers are attractive in arrangements and can be dried for winter use. Plants are useful in woodland gardens. Winter dormant even in mild climates.

A. carniolica. To 15–18 in. tall, with finely divided leaves. Bracts around flower heads shorter than in other species. 'Rubra' has dark red flowers with silvery accents.

A. major. Grows to 2–3 ft. tall, with inch-wide clusters of white and green or white and pink flowers.

A. maxima. Slightly larger than *A. major,* with pink flowers.

ATHYRIUM

Polypodiaceae

FERNS

ZONES 1–9, 14–24, 31–43

PARTIAL OR FULL SHADE, EXCEPT AS NOTED

AMPLE WATER

Athyrium filix-femina

Evergreen in mildest areas, these ferns turn brown after repeated frosts. Leave dead fronds on plant to provide mulch and to shelter emerging fronds in early spring, then cut back. Prefer rich, damp soil and shade. Propagate by dividing old clumps in early spring.

A. filix-femina. LADY FERN. Grows to 4 ft. or more. Rootstock rises up on older plants to make short trunk. Vertical effect; narrow at bottom, spreading at top. Thin fronds, finely divided. Vigorous; can be invasive. Tolerates full sun in constantly moist soil. Specialists stock many varieties with oddly cut and feathered fronds. In 'Frizelliae', divisions of fronds are reduced to balls; fronds look like strings of beads. 'Vernoniae Cristatum' has crested and feathered fronds.

A. nipponicum 'Pictum' (A. goeringianum 'Pictum'). JAPANESE PAINTED FERN. Fronds grow to 1½ ft. long, making a tight, slowly spreading clump. Leaflets are purplish at base, then lavender, then silvery greenish gray toward ends.

A. otophorum. ENGLISH PAINTED FERN. Actually a native of the Orient. It resembles Japanese painted fern, but its dark green fronds have a reddish or purple midrib.

A. pycnocarpon. GLADE FERN, SILVERY SPLEENWORT. Zones 1–6, 31–45. Attractive rosette-forming deciduous fern with once-divided fronds to 4 ft. long. New spring fronds are silvery light green; they turn darker in summer, then russet before dying back. Tolerates full sun in constantly moist soil.

AUBRIETA deltoidea

COMMON AUBRIETA

Brassicaceae (Cruciferae)

PERENNIAL

ZONES 1–9, 14–21, 36–43

FULL SUN OR LIGHT SHADE

REGULAR WATER

Aubrieta deltoidea

Native from eastern Mediterranean region to Iran. Low, spreading, mat-forming perennial; charming with other spring bloomers such as basket-of-gold, rockcress, perennial candytuft,

and moss pink. Ideal for chinks in dry stone walls or between patio flagstones. Grows 2–6 in. high, 1–1½ ft. across. Small gray-green leaves with a few teeth at top. Tiny rose to deep red, pale to deep lilac, or purple flowers. 'Novalis Blue' is a fine seed-grown variety.

Provide good drainage. Needs regular moisture before and during bloom; takes some drought later on. After bloom, shear off flowers before they set seed. Don't cut back more than half—always keep some foliage. After trimming, top-dress with mixture of gritty soil and bone meal. Sow seeds in late spring for blooms the following spring. Difficult to divide clumps; make cuttings in late summer. Short lived, especially in warm, humid regions.

AUCUBA japonica

JAPANESE AUCUBA

Cornaceae

EVERGREEN SHRUB

ZONES 4–24, 28–33

PERFORMS WELL IN DEEP SHADE

MODERATE WATER

Aucuba japonica

Native from Himalayas to Japan. Seedlings vary in leaf form and variegations; many varieties offered. Standard green-leafed aucuba grows at moderate rate to 6–10 ft. (sometimes 15 ft.) tall and almost as wide. Can be kept lower by pruning. Buxom shrub, densely clothed with polished, dark green, toothed leaves 3–8 in. long, 1½–3 in. wide.

Minute, dark maroon flowers in spring are followed by clusters of bright red, ¾-in. berries hidden in leaves in fall and winter. Both sexes must be planted to ensure fruit crop. Green-leafed 'Rozannie' is reportedly self-fertile.

Other green-leafed varieties include 'Longifolia' ('Salicifolia'), narrow willowlike leaves (female); 'Nana', dwarf to about 3 ft. (female); 'Serratifolia', long leaves, coarsely toothed edges (female).

Variegated varieties (usually slower growing) include 'Crotonifolia', leaves heavily splashed with white and gold (male); 'Fructu Albo', leaves variegated with white, berries pale pinkish buff (female); 'Picturata' ('Aureo-maculata'), leaves centered with golden yellow, edged with dark green dotted yellow (female); 'Sulphur', green leaves with broad yellow edge (female); 'Variegata', gold dust plant, best-known aucuba, dark green leaves spotted with yellow (male or female). 'Mr. Goldstrike' has heavier gold splashings.

Tolerant of wide range of soils. Requires shade from hot sun, accepts deep shade. Tolerates low light level under trees, competes successfully with tree roots. Gets mealybug and mites. Prune to control height or form by cutting back to a leaf joint (node).

All aucubas make choice tub plants for shady patio or in the house. Use variegated forms to light up dark corners. Associate with ferns, hydrangeas.

AURICULA. See PRIMULA auricula

AURINIA saxatilis (Alyssum saxatile)

BASKET-OF-GOLD

Brassicaceae (Cruciferae)

PERENNIAL

ZONES 1–24, 32–43

FULL SUN OR LIGHT SHADE

MODERATE WATER

Aurinia saxatilis

Stems 8–12 in. high; leaves gray, 2–5 in. long. Dense clusters of tiny golden yellow flowers in spring and early summer. Use as foreground plant in borders, in rock gardens, atop walls. Shear lightly (not more than half) right after bloom. Generally hardy but may be killed in extremely cold winters. Self-sows readily. Short lived in hot, humid areas. Varieties include 'Citrina' ('Lutea'), with pale yellow flowers; 'Compacta', dwarf, tight growing; 'Plena' ('Flore Pleno'), double flowered; 'Silver Queen', compact, with pale yellow flowers; 'Sunnyborder Apricot', with apricot-shaded flowers; 'Dudley Neville Variegated', with flower color similar to that of 'Sunnyborder Apricot' but leaves with whitish or creamy edges.

AUSTRALIAN BLUEBELL CREEPER. See SOLLYA heterophylla

AUSTRALIAN FLAME TREE. See BRACHYCHITON acerifolius

AUSTRALIAN TEA TREE. See LEPTOSPERMUM laevigatum

AUSTRALIAN TREE FERN. See CYATHEA cooperi

AUSTRALIAN WILLOW. See GEIJERA parviflora

AUSTRIAN BRIER. See ROSA foetida

AVOCADO

Lauraceae

EVERGREEN TREES

🌡 ZONES 9, 16–27, 28 (TEXAS)

☼ FULL SUN

🌢 LIGHT, FREQUENT WATERING

Avocado

Tropical fruit native to Mexico, Central and South America. Three races of avocado are grown, and numerous hybrids among them exist. The Mexican (hardiest, often surviving to 18°F/–8°C) and Guatemalan (hardy to 21° to 25°F/–6 to –4°C)) are grown in California in the zones indicated; the widely planted 'Fuerte' is a hybrid between the two. In Florida, the Mexican race is grown in colder parts of Central Florida, while Guatemalan and West Indian (most tropical, often perishing at temperatures below 25°F/–4°C) and their hybrids are cultivated southward. Mexican race seedlings are often grown in home gardens across South Texas.

Plants bloom in late winter and pollination is complex. Most varieties will produce some fruit if grown alone, but production is heavier when two or more varieties are planted. Fruit ripens from summer into winter, depending on variety. Guatemalan and West Indian fruits differ from Mexican in generally being larger with a lower oil content.

All avocado trees require good drainage; constantly wet soil encourages fatal root rot. Tree is shallow rooted; do not cultivate deeply. In the absence of rainfall, irrigate lightly and frequently enough to keep soil moist but not wet. A mulch is helpful; the tree's own fallen leaves can provide this. Scab disease can be a problem in Florida; choose resistant varieties.

When using avocado in the landscape, consider that most varieties will eventually grow quite large (to 40 ft.), produce dense shade, and shed leaves constantly throughout the year. Growth is rapid, but plants may be shaped by pinching terminal shoots. Avocado takes well to container culture, and varieties in marginal climates can be moved to protection during cold spells.

Principal California varieties include 'Mexicola' (hardiest); 'Bacon' (good home orchard variety); 'Fuerte' (the market favorite); 'Hass' (favorite in mild regions); and 'Wurtz' (dwarf tree for small garden or container).

Florida varieties include the hardy 'Brogdon', 'Gainesville', 'Mexicola', and 'Tonnage' (all moderately scab resistant); the somewhat less hardy 'Booth', 'Hall', 'Monroe' (all moderately scab resistant), and 'Choquette' (very scab resistant); and the least hardy 'Pollock', 'Ruehle', 'Simmonds', and 'Waldin' (all very scab resistant). Two hardy types setting good crops without cross-pollination are the commercial variety 'Lula' (susceptible to scab) and 'Taylor' (very scab resistant).

In Texas, 'Lula' is the commercial variety in the lower Rio Grande Valley. Most avocado trees in home gardens are varieties developed from Mexican race seedlings that survived cold winters. Check with a local nursery.

AZALEA. See RHODODENDRON

AZTEC LILY. See SPREKELIA formosissima

BABIANA

BABOON FLOWER

Iridaceae

CORMS

🌡 ZONES 4–24, 29–31, WARMER PARTS OF 32; OR DIG AND STORE

☼◐ FULL SUN OR VERY LIGHT SHADE

🌢 REGULAR WATER DURING GROWTH AND BLOOM

Babiana stricta

Native to South Africa. Spikes of freesialike flowers in blue, lavender, red, cream, and white in mid- to late spring. Leaves are strongly ribbed, usually hairy, in fans. Plant corms 4 in. deep, 3 in. apart, along border edge, paths, in rock gardens; also in deep pots. Regular water during growth, less after leaves turn yellow. In mild climates leave in ground several years. In coldest areas lift and store corms like gladiolus.

B. rubrocyanea. Spikes to 5–6 in. with six or seven flowers to a spike. Bottom half of each flower deep red, upper half royal blue.

B. stricta. Royal blue flowers on 1-ft. stems. Varieties in purple, lavender, white, and blue and white.

BABY BLUE EYES. See NEMOPHILA menziesii

BABY'S BREATH. See GYPSOPHILA paniculata

BABY SNAPDRAGON. See LINARIA maroccana

BABY'S TEARS. See SOLEIROLIA soleirolii

BACCHARIS

Asteraceae (Compositae)

EVERGREEN OR DECIDUOUS SHRUBS

🌡 ZONES VARY BY SPECIES

☼ FULL SUN

🌢🌢 WATER NEEDS VARY BY SPECIES

Baccharis halimifolia

Main value of these plants is toughness, ability to grow in difficult conditions. Withstand heat, wind, poor soil. Male and female flowers, borne on separate plants, are inconspicuous. Female plants produce cottony seed clusters that can make a mess when blown by wind. Grow male cultivars if available, or hoe out seedlings if they appear where you don't want them.

B. halimifolia. GROUNDSEL, SALT BUSH. Deciduous. Zones 26–41. Native from Massachusetts south to Florida and Texas. Grows 5–12 ft. tall and wide, with gray-green, coarsely toothed, 1–3-in. leaves. Tolerates saline soil in dunes, tidal flats, and ditches. Regular to moderate water.

B. pilularis. DWARF COYOTE BRUSH. Evergreen. Zones 5–11, 14–24. Native to central California coast. Dependable bank and ground cover for low-maintenance areas. Makes dense, rather billowy, bright green mat, 8–24 in. high and 6 ft. wide (or wider). Toothed, ½-in. leaves are closely set on branches. Moderate to little water. Male varieties include 'Twin Peaks', with small, dark green leaves, and 'Pigeon Point', which has larger, lighter green leaves and grows faster.

B

BACHELOR'S BUTTON. See CENTAUREA cyanus

BAILEYA multiradiata

DESERT MARIGOLD

Asteraceae (Compositae)

ANNUAL OR SHORT-LIVED PERENNIAL

⚡ ALL ZONES; BEST IN ARID REGIONS

☼ FULL SUN

💧 MODERATE WATER FOR BEST BLOOM

Baileya multiradiata

Western desert native displays inch-wide, bright yellow flower heads above gray foliage on 1–1½-ft. plants. Basic bloom period is spring through fall; year-round bloom is possible in mild-winter areas if plants receive periodic moisture. Self-sows.

BALD CYPRESS. See TAXODIUM distichum

BALLOON FLOWER. See PLATYCODON grandiflorus

BALLOTA pseudodictamnus

Lamiaceae (Labiatae)

SHRUBBY PERENNIAL

⚡ ZONES 8, 9, 14–24

☼ FULL SUN

💧 MODERATE TO LITTLE WATER

Ballota pseudodictamnus

Perennial of dense, rounded growth habit to 18–20 in., with opposite pairs of roundish, inch-wide, furry gray-green leaves. Whorls of small white flowers are less important than foliage and habit. Use in mixed perennial beds or bank plantings. Looks good with lavender, Jerusalem sage, and other Mediterranean perennials. Cut back hard in spring before new growth starts.

BALSAM. See IMPATIENS balsamina

Balsaminaceae. The touch-me-not family embraces herbaceous or shrubby plants with juicy stems, irregular flowers with spurs, and explosive seed capsules. *Impatiens* is the only important member.

BALSAM PEAR. See MOMORDICA charantia

BAMBOO

Poaceae (Gramineae)

GIANT GRASSES

⚡ SEE CHART FOR HARDINESS

☼ ◑ FULL SUN OR LIGHT SHADE

💧💧 REGULAR TO LITTLE WATER

▶ SEE CHART NEXT PAGE

Bambusa multiplex

Large, woody stems (culms) divided into sections (internodes) by obvious joints (nodes). Upper nodes produce buds that develop into branches; these, in larger bamboos, divide into secondary branches that bear leaves. Bamboos spread by underground stems (rhizomes) that, like the aboveground culms, are jointed and carry buds. Manner in which rhizomes grow explains difference between running and clump bamboos.

In running bamboos (*Arundinaria, Chimonobambusa, Indocalamus, Phyllostachys, Pleioblastus, Pseudosasa, Sasa, Sasaella, Semiarundinaria,* and *Shibataea*), underground stems grow rapidly to varying distances from parent plant before sending up new vertical shoots. These bamboos eventually form large patches or groves unless spread is curbed. They are generally fairly hardy plants from temperate regions in China and Japan, and they are tolerant of a wide variety of soils.

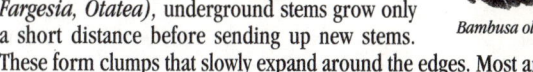

In clump bamboos (*Bambusa, Chusquea, Fargesia, Otatea*), underground stems grow only a short distance before sending up new stems.

Bambusa oldhamii

These form clumps that slowly expand around the edges. Most are tropical or subtropical.

See chart for hardiness. Figures indicate temperatures at which leaf damage occurs. Stems and rhizomes may be considerably hardier.

Plant container-grown bamboos at any time of year. Best time to propagate from existing clumps is just before growth begins in spring; divide hardy kinds in March or early April, tropical ones in May or early June. (Transplanting at other times is possible, but risk of losing divisions is high in summer heat or winter chill and wet soil.) Cut or saw out divisions with roots and at least three connected culms. If divisions are large, cut back tops to balance loss of roots and rhizomes. Foliage may wilt or wither, but culms will send out new leaves.

Rhizome cutting is another means of propagation. In clump bamboos, this cutting consists of the rooted base of a culm; in running bamboos, it is a foot-long length of rhizome with roots and buds. Plant in rich mix with ample organic material added.

Culms of all bamboos have already attained their maximum diameter when they poke through ground; in mature plants, they usually reach their maximum height within a month. Many do become increasingly leafy in subsequent years, but not taller. Plants are evergreen, but there is considerable dropping of older leaves; old plantings develop nearly weedproof mulch of dead leaves. Individual culms live for several years but eventually die and should be cut out.

Mature bamboos grow phenomenally fast during their brief growth period—culms of giant types may increase in length by several feet a day.

Phyllostachys aurea

Don't expect such quick growth the first year after transplanting, though. Giant timber bamboo, for example, needs 3 to 5 years to build up a rhizome system capable of supporting culms that grow several feet a day; growth during early years will be less impressive. To get fast growth and great size, water frequently and feed once a month with high-nitrogen or lawn fertilizer; to restrict size and spread, water and feed less. Once established, plants tolerate considerable drought, but rhizomes will not spread into dry soil (or into water). The accompanying chart lists two heights for each bamboo. "Controlled Height" means average height under dry conditions with little feeding, or with rhizome spread controlled by barriers. "Uncontrolled Height" refers to plants growing under best conditions without confinement.

Difficult to mass-produce and little known, most bamboos are hard to find in nurseries. Inquire about specialists in your area. The American Bamboo Society has chapters in various regions. Society members often propagate rare varieties for sales in connection with their meetings. Arboretum and botanical garden sales are another source. Plants may be offered under the principal name listed or under one of the synonyms. Plant names change so frequently that vendors cannot always keep up.

In the case of bamboo, disregard the rule of never buying root-bound plants: the more crowded the plant in the container, the faster its growth when planted. Both running and clump types grow well when roots are confined.

▶ page 203

BAMBOO

For explanation of height, see page 199; for Roman numerals I, II, III, and IV, see page 203. Hardiness is temperature at which leaf damage occurs.

B

NAME	ALSO SOLD AS	CONTROLLED (UNCONTROLLED) HEIGHT	GROWTH HABIT	STEM DIAMETER	HARDINESS	COMMENTS (GROWTH HABIT, CHARACTERISTICS, USES)
Arundinaria amabilis TONKIN CANE, TEASTICK BAMBOO		20–25 ft. (50 ft.)	Running	2½ in.	10°F/−12°C	III. Erect, thick-walled culms with small nodes. Beautiful, useful for wood
Bambusa beecheyana BEECHEY BAMBOO	*Sinocalamus beecheyanus*	12–20 ft. (20–40 ft.)	Clump	4–5 in.	15°F/−9°C	IV. Culms arch strongly for broad, graceful effect. Tropical looking. Scarce
B. multiplex	*B. glaucescens*	8–10 ft. (15–25 ft.)	Clump	1½ in.	15°F/−9°C	II. Branches from base to top. Dense growth. Hedges, screens. Less common than its varieties described below
B. m. 'Alphonse Karr' ALPHONSE KARR BAMBOO		8–10 ft. (15–35 ft.)	Clump	½–1 in.	15°F/−9°C	II. Similar to above, but culms are brilliantly striped green on yellow. New culms pinkish and green
B. m. 'Fernleaf' FERNLEAF BAMBOO	*B. nana, B. disticha*	6–10 ft. (10–20 ft.)	Clump	½ in.	15°F/−9°C	II. Closely spaced leaves, 10–20 to twig, give ferny look. Loses this look, grows coarser with rich soil, ample water
B. m. 'Golden Goddess' GOLDEN GODDESS BAMBOO		6–8 ft. (6–10 ft.)	Clump	½ in.	15°F/−9°C	II. Golden-stemmed variety with graceful, dense, arching growth. Good container or screen plant. Give tops room to spread
B. m. rivereorum CHINESE GODDESS BAMBOO		4–6 ft. (6–8 ft.)	Clump	¼ in.	15°F/−9°C	II. Solid culms arch gracefully. Tiny leaves in lacy, ferny sprays
B. m. 'Silverstripe'		20 ft. (40 ft.)	Clump	1½ in.	15°F/−9°C	II. Most vigorous of hedge bamboo varieties. Leaves have white stripes; occasional white stripes on culms
B. oldhamii OLDHAM BAMBOO, CLUMPING GIANT TIMBER BAMBOO	*Sinocalamus oldhamii*	15–25 ft. (20–55 ft.)	Clump	4 in.	15°F/−9°C	IV. Densely foliaged, erect clumps make it good plant for big, dense screens. Or use single plant for imposing vertical mass
B. textilis		15–20 ft. (20–40 ft.)	Clump	2 in.	13°F/−11°C	II or IV. Handsome, erect, reasonably hardy, rare. New culms blue green, sheaths green to orange
B. tuldoides PUNTING POLE BAMBOO		15–20 ft. (20–55 ft.)	Clump	2 in.	15°F/−9°C	IV. Prolific producer of slender, erect culms. Best as single plant
B. ventricosa BUDDHA'S BELLY BAMBOO		3–6 ft. (15–30 ft.)	Clump	2 in.	20°F/−7°C	II or IV. Stays small, produces swollen culms that give it its name only when confined in tubs or grown in poor, dryish soil. Otherwise a giant bamboo with straight culms
B. vulgaris vittata		15–25 ft. (50 ft.)	Clump	4 in.	30°F/−1°C	IV. Yellow culms have vertical green stripes. Used in well-lit interiors and mildest climates. Striking color. Rare
Chimonobambusa marmorea MARBLED BAMBOO (sometimes sold as "dwarf black bamboo")	*Arundinaria marmorea*	2–4 ft. (4–6 ft.)	Running	¼ in.	20°F/−7°C	III. New culm sheaths marbled cream and purplish. Older culms nearly black. Densely leafy; makes first-class hedge plant if roots are curbed

BAMBOO

For explanation of height, see page 199; for Roman numerals I, II, III, and IV, see page 203. Hardiness is temperature at which leaf damage occurs.

NAME	ALSO SOLD AS	CONTROLLED (UNCONTROLLED) HEIGHT	GROWTH HABIT	STEM DIAMETER	HARDINESS	COMMENTS (GROWTH HABIT, CHARACTERISTICS, USES)
C. quadrangularis SQUARE-STEM BAMBOO	*Bambusa quadrangularis*	10–15 ft. (20–30 ft.)	Running	1 in.	15°F/−9°C	III. Squarish culms have prominent joints, carry heavy whorls of branches. Valued for vertical effect
Chusquea coronalis		8–12 ft. (12–15 ft.)	Clump	¾ in.	28°F/−2°C	IV. Arching culms bear masses of tiny leaves on short whorled branches. Exceptionally attractive. Rare
Fargesia murielae	*Sinarundinaria murielae*	6–8 ft. (15 ft.)	Clump	¾ in.	−20°F/−29°C	II. One of two hardiest bamboos listed here. Light, airy, narrow clump, arching and drooping at top. Needs shade to look best. Rare
F. nitida FOUNTAIN BAMBOO	*Sinarundinaria nitida*	6–8 ft. (15–20 ft.)	Clump	¾ in.	0°F/−18°C	II. Light, airy, graceful, narrow clump, arching and drooping at top. Greenish purple culms mature to deep purplish black. Needs shade to look its best. Rare
Indocalamus tessellatus	*Arundinaria ragamowskii*	2–3 ft. (3–6 ft.)	Running	¼ in.	0°F/−18°C	Resembles *Sasa palmata*, but much lower growth, much longer leaves (2 ft.). Rapid spreader, best in shade. Rare
Otatea acuminata aztecorum MEXICAN WEEPING BAMBOO	*Yushania aztecorum, Arthrostylidium longifolium*	8–10 ft. (20 ft.)	Clump	1½ in.	15°F/−9°C	II. Extremely narrow leaves (6 in. by ⅛ in.) give lacy look. Foliage masses bend nearly to ground. Fairly drought resistant when established. Rare
Phyllostachys aurea GOLDEN BAMBOO		6–10 ft. (10–20 ft.)	Running	2 in.	0°F/−18°C	III. Erect, stiff culms, usually with crowded joints at base—good identifying mark. Dense foliage makes it good screen or hedge. Can take much drought but looks better with regular water. Good choice for growing in tubs
P. aureosulcata YELLOW GROOVE BAMBOO		12–15 ft. (15–25 ft.)	Running	1½ in.	−20°F/−29°C	III. Like more slender, more open golden bamboo. Young culms green with pronounced yellowish groove. One of two hardiest bamboos listed here
P. bambusoides GIANT TIMBER BAMBOO, JAPANESE TIMBER BAMBOO	*P. reticulata*	15–35 ft. (25–45 ft.)	Running	6 in.	0°F/−18°C	IV. Once commonest of large, hardy timber bamboos. Most perished during blooming period in 1960s–1970s. New plants from seed are available. Makes beautiful groves if lowest branches are trimmed off
P. b. 'Castillon'	*P. castillonis*	10–15 ft. (15–20 ft.)	Running	2 in.	0°F/−18°C	III. Yellow culms show green stripe above each branch cluster. Rare
P. heterocycla pubescens MOSO BAMBOO	*P. edulis*	20–40 ft. (40–60 ft.)	Running	8 in.	5°F/−15°C	IV. Largest of running timber bamboos. Gray-green, heavy culms; small, feathery leaves. Rare and hard to establish
P. meyeri		10–20 ft. (20–30 ft.)	Running	2 in.	−4°F/−20°C	III. Somewhat like *P. aurea* but lacks crowded basal joints. Hardy to cold
P. nigra BLACK BAMBOO		4–8 ft. (10–15 ft.)	Running	1½ in.	0°F/−18°C	III. New culms green, turning black in second year (rarely olive green dotted black). Best in afternoon shade where summers are hot
P. n. 'Henon'		50 ft. (54 ft.)	Running	3½ in.	0°F/−18°C	III. Much larger than black bamboo. Culms whitish green, not changing to black, rough to touch

B

BAMBOO

For explanation of height, see page 199; for Roman numerals I, II, III, and IV, see page 203. Hardiness is temperature at which leaf damage occurs.

NAME	ALSO SOLD AS	CONTROLLED (UNCONTROLLED) HEIGHT	GROWTH HABIT	STEM DIAMETER	HARDINESS	COMMENTS (GROWTH HABIT, CHARACTERISTICS, USES)
Pleioblastus argenteostriata		2–3 ft. (3–4 ft.)	Running	¼ in.	10°F/–12°C	I. Good light-colored ground cover for shade. Looks best cut back every year. White stripes on leaves
P. chino vaginata 'Variegata'		2–3 ft. (3–4 ft.)	Running	⅜ in.	10°F/–12°C	I. Graceful, densely foliaged. Slender leaves striped white
P. distichus DWARF FERNLEAF BAMBOO	*Sasa disticha*	1–2 ft. (2–3 ft.)	Running	⅛ in.	10°F/–12°C	I. Delicate in appearance. Tiny, two-ranked ferny leaves. Rampant; cut back to ground if rank or stemmy
P. pygmaea	*Sasa pygmaea*	½–1 ft. (1–1½ ft.)	Running	⅛ in.	0°F/–18°C	I. Aggressive spreader; good bank holder and erosion control. Can be mowed every few years to keep it from growing stemmy and unattractive
P. simonii SIMON BAMBOO, MEDAKE	*Arundinaria simonii*	10 ft. (20 ft.)	Running	1½ in.	0°F/–18°C	III. Vertical growth pattern, moderate spreader. Screens, hedges; garden stakes
P. s. variegatus		10 ft. (20 ft.)	Running	1½ in.	0°F/–18°C	III. Like *P. simonii* but some leaves have white striping
P. variegata DWARF WHITESTRIPE BAMBOO	*Sasa variegata, S. fortunei*	1–2 ft. (2–3 ft.)	Running	¼ in.	–10°F/–23°C	I. Fast spreader; curb rhizomes. Use in tubs or as deep ground cover
P. viridistriatus	*Arundinaria auricoma, A. viridistriatus*	1–2 ft. (2½ ft.)	Running	¼ in.	0°F/–18°C	I. Leaves 8 in. long, 1½ in. wide, strikingly variegated green and gold
Pseudosasa japonica ARROW BAMBOO	*Arundinaria japonica*	6–10 ft. (10–18 ft.)	Running	¾ in.	0°F/–18°C	III. Stiffly erect culms with one branch at each joint. Leaves large, with long, pointed tails. Rampant thick hedge in mild-winter climates; slow spreader where winters are cold, making dense, erect clumps
Sasa palmata PALMATE BAMBOO	Sometimes sold as *S. senanensis*	4–5 ft. (8–12 ft.)	Running	⅜ in.	0°F/–18°C	In class by itself. Grows bigger in moist or cool-summer areas than in very hot or dry areas. Broad, handsome leaves (to 15 in. long by 4 in. wide) spread fingerlike from stem and branch tips. Rampant spreader; curb it
S. veitchii		2–3 ft. (2–3 ft.)	Running	¼ in.	0°F/–18°C	I. Rampant spreader with large (7-in.-by-1-in.) dark green leaves that turn whitish buff all around the edges in autumn. Appropriate in Japanese gardens if curbed
Sasaella masamuneana		2–3 ft. (3–6 ft.)	Running	¼ in.	0°F/–18°C	I. Resembles *Sasa palmata,* but leaves are thickish, 6 in. long. Leaves of 'Albostriata' are boldly striped with creamy white
Semiarundinaria fastuosa NARIHIRA BAMBOO		8–10 ft. (12–25 ft.)	Running	1¼ in.	–4°F/–20°C	II or III. Rigidly upright growth. Slow spreader easily kept to a clump. Planted closely, makes tall, narrow, dense hedge or windbreak
Shibataea kumasaca		2–3 ft. (5–6 ft.)	Running	¼ in.	10°F/–12°C	III. Slow spreading, makes compact clumps of unbamboolike appearance. Leaves are short and broad (4 in. by 1 in.), distinctly stalked. Needs acid soil

Scale, mealybugs, and aphids are occasionally found on bamboo but seldom do any harm; if they excrete honeydew in bothersome amounts, spray with insecticidal soap or summer oil. To control mites, release predatory mites.

The chart classifies each bamboo by habit of growth, which, of course, determines its use in the garden. In Group I are the dwarf or low-growing ground cover types. These can be used for erosion control or, in small clumps (carefully confined in a long section of flue tile), in border or rock garden. Group II includes clump bamboos with fountainlike habit of growth. These have widest use in landscaping. They require no more space than the average strong-growing shrub.

Phyllostachys nigra

Clipped, they make hedges or screens that won't spread much into surrounding soil. When unclipped, they line up as informal screens or grow singly to show off their graceful form.

Bamboos in Group III are running bamboos of moderate size and more or less vertical growth. Use them as screens, hedges, or (if curbed) alone. Group IV includes the giant bamboos. Use running kinds for groves or for Oriental effects on a grand scale. Clumping kinds have a tropical look, especially if they are used with broad-leafed tropical plants. All may be thinned and clipped to show off culms. Thin clumps or groves by cutting out old or dead culms at the base.

Some of the smaller bamboos bloom on some of their stalks every year and continue to grow. Some bloom partially and at erratic intervals. Some have never been known to bloom. Others bloom heavily, set seed, and die. Giant timber bamboo (*Phyllostachys bambusoides*) and other species of *Phyllostachys* bloom at rare intervals of 30 to 60 years, produce flowers for a long period, and become enfeebled. They may recover very slowly or die. There is evidence that very heavy feeding and watering may speed their recovery.

> ### RUNNING BAMBOO CAN BE CONTAINED
> Make 2–3-ft.-deep barriers with strips of galvanized sheet metal, 30-mil plastic, or poured concrete; or plant in long flue tiles or bottomless oil drums. You can limit spread by periodically inserting a spade down to its full depth around the clump. New shoots break off easily; they do not resprout. Another way to limit spread of large running bamboos: Dig a foot-deep trench around plant and sever any rhizomes that grow into it; the trench will fill with a loose mulch of leaves. Sift through leaves with gloved hands to find roving rhizomes.

Bamboos are not recommended for year-round indoor culture, but container-grown plants can spend extended periods indoors in cool, bright rooms. You can revive plants by taking them outdoors, but it is important to avoid sudden changes in temperature and light.

There are several ways to eliminate unwanted bamboo. Digging it out with mattock and spade is the surest method, though sometimes difficult. Rhizomes are generally not deep, but they may be widespread. Remove them all or regrowth will occur. Starve out roots by cutting off all shoots before they exceed 2 ft. in height; repeat as needed—probably many times over the course of a year. Contact herbicide sprays that kill leaves have the same effect as removing culms. Full-strength glyphosate weed killer poured into freshly cut stumps is another good control.

BAMBURANTA. See CTENANTHE compressa

BAMBUSA. See BAMBOO

BANANA. See ENSETE, MUSA

BANANA PASSION VINE. See PASSIFLORA mollissima

BANANA SHRUB. See MICHELIA figo

BANEBERRY. See ACTAEA

BAPTISIA

FALSE INDIGO, WILD INDIGO

Fabaceae (Leguminosae)

PERENNIALS

🗡 ZONES 1–24, 28–43

☼ FULL SUN

🌢 MODERATE WATER

Native to eastern and midwestern U.S. The false indigos somewhat resemble lupines, but have deep taproots that enable them to survive difficult conditions. Long lived, they eventually become large clumps with many stems and bloom spikes.

Baptisia australis

They resent transplanting once established. Bluish green leaves are divided into three leaflets. Flower spikes to 1 ft. long top the plants in late spring or early summer. Flowers resemble small sweet peas and are followed by inflated seedpods; both flowers and pods are interesting in arrangements. Remove spent flowers to encourage repeat bloom.

B. alba. WHITE FALSE INDIGO. 3 ft. tall, with clusters of white flowers.

B. australis. BLUE FALSE INDIGO. Grows 3–6 ft. tall; flowers are indigo blue. 'Purple Smoke', a hybrid between this species and *B. alba*, grows 4½ ft. tall and has violet flowers with dark purple centers.

BARBERRY. See BERBERIS

BARLERIA

Acanthaceae

EVERGREEN SHRUBS

🗡 ZONES VARY BY SPECIES; OR INDOORS

☼◑ LIGHT SHADE IN HOTTEST AREAS

🌢 REGULAR WATER

Barleria obtusa

Outdoor plants in mild-winter regions; sometimes used as indoor/outdoor or house plants in colder regions. Grown for usually blue or purplish, tubular flowers produced in upper leaf joints. Plants have erect to spreading habit; pinch to keep compact or cut back hard after bloom to control size. Give rich, well-drained soil and plentiful, even moisture during active growth.

B. cristata. PHILIPPINE VIOLET. Zones 25, 26. To 4 ft. tall with leaves to 4 in. long. Dense spikes of 2-in. pale blue-violet (sometimes pink or white) flowers in summer. Tolerates shearing especially well and is often used for hedges.

B. obtusa. Zones 16–28. To 3 ft. tall with leaves to 3 in. long. Loose clusters of purplish blue, 1½-in. flowers in winter and spring.

BARREN STRAWBERRY. See WALDSTEINIA

BASEBALL PLANT. See EUPHORBIA obesa

BASIL. See OCIMUM

BASKET FLOWER. See CENTAUREA americana, HYMENOCALLIS narcissiflora

FOR INFORMATION ON SELECTING PLANTS

PLEASE SEE PAGES 79–160

BASKET-OF-GOLD. See AURINIA saxatilis

BASSWOOD. See TILIA americana

BAUHINIA

BRAZILIAN BUTTERFLY TREE

Fabaceae (Leguminosae)

EVERGREEN, SEMIEVERGREEN, OR DECIDUOUS TREES, SHRUBS

☑ ZONES VARY BY SPECIES

☼ B. FORFICATA TOLERATES JUST A LITTLE SHADE

◐◐ REGULAR TO MODERATE WATER

Bauhinia forficata

These flamboyant flowering plants have a very special place in Hawaii, central and southern Florida, and mild-winter areas of California and Arizona. Common to all garden bauhinias are twin "leaves," actually twin lobes. Not fussy about soil as long as it is reasonably well drained.

B. blakeana. HONG KONG ORCHID TREE. Partially deciduous for short period. Zones 13, 19, 21, 23, 25–27. Native to southern China. Umbrella-type growth habit, to 20 ft. high. Flowers are shaped like some orchids; colors range from cranberry maroon through purple and rose to orchid pink, often in same blossom. Flowers are much larger (5½–6 in. wide) than those of other bauhinias; they appear in late fall to spring. Gray-green leaves tend to drop off around bloom time, but the tree does not lose all of its foliage.

B. forficata. BRAZILIAN BUTTERFLY TREE. Evergreen to deciduous large shrub or tree. Zones 9, 12–23, 25–28. Native to Brazil. Probably hardiest bauhinia, though chancy in Zone 28. In spring and through summer, bears narrow-petaled, creamy white flowers to 3 in. wide. Deep green leaves, more pointed lobes than others. Grows to 20 ft., often with twisting, leaning trunk, picturesque angled branches. Short, sharp thorns at branch joints. Good canopy for patio. In intensely hot climates, give some afternoon shade; if unshaded, blooms tend to shrivel during day. Often sold as *B. corniculata* or *B. candicans.*

B. galpinii (B. punctata). RED BAUHINIA. Evergreen to semievergreen shrub. Zones 13, 15, 16, 18–23, 25–27. Native to South and tropical Africa. Brick red to orange flowers, as spectacular as those of bougainvillea, spring to fall. Sprawling, half-climbing, with 15-ft. spread. Best as espalier on warm wall. With hard pruning, can make splendid flowering bonsai for large pot or box.

B. purpurea. See B. variegata

B. variegata. PURPLE ORCHID TREE. Partially to wholly deciduous large shrub or tree. Zones 13, 18–23, 25–27. Native to India, China. Most frequently planted. Hardy to 22°F/–6°C. Spectacular street trees where spring is warm and stays warm. Wonderful show of light pink to orchid purple, broad-petaled, 2–3-in.-wide flowers, usually January to April. Light green, broad-lobed leaves generally drop in midwinter. Produces huge crop of messy-looking beans after blooming. Trim beans off if you wish—trimming brings new growth earlier. Inclined to grow as shrub with many stems. Staked and pruned, becomes attractive 20–35-ft. tree. 'Candida' is the same, but with white flowers. The species is commonly sold as *B. purpurea.*

BAY. See LAURUS, UMBELLULARIA californica

BAYBERRY. See MYRICA pensylvanica

BEACH WORMWOOD. See ARTEMISIA stellerana

BEAD PLANT. See NERTERA granadensis

FOR INFORMATION ON YOUR CLIMATE ZONE

PLEASE SEE PAGES 16–78

BEAN, BROAD

FAVA BEAN, HORSE BEAN

Fabaceae (Leguminosae)

ANNUAL

☑ ALL ZONES

☼ FULL SUN

◐ MODERATE WATER

◊ SOME PEOPLE HAVE SEVERE REACTIONS

Fava Bean

This bean (actually a giant vetch) was known in ancient and medieval times; it is a Mediterranean plant, while all other familiar beans are New World plants. Bushy growth to 2–4 ft. You can cook and eat immature pods like edible-pod peas; prepare immature and mature seeds in same way as green or dry limas.

Unlike true beans, this is a cool-season plant. In cold-winter areas, plant as early in spring as soil can be worked. In mild climates, plant in fall for late-winter or early-spring ripening. Matures in 120 to 150 days, depending on temperature. Space rows 1½–2½ ft. apart. Plant seeds 1 in. deep, 4–5 in. apart; thin to 8–10 in. apart. Watch for and control aphids.

Most people can safely eat fava beans, though a very few (principally of Mediterranean ancestry) have an enzyme deficiency that can cause severe reactions to the beans and even the pollen.

BEAN, DRY

Fabaceae (Leguminosae)

ANNUAL

☑ ALL ZONES

☼ FULL SUN

◐ REGULAR WATER AFTER SEEDLINGS EMERGE

Dry Bean

Same culture as bush form of snap bean. Let pods remain on bush until they turn dry or begin to shatter; thresh beans from pods, dry, store to soak and cook later. 'Pinto', 'Red Kidney', and 'White Marrowfat' belong to this group.

BEAN, GREEN. See BEAN, SNAP

BEAN, LIMA

Fabaceae (Leguminosae)

ANNUAL

☑ ALL ZONES

☼ FULL SUN

◐ REGULAR WATER AFTER SEEDLINGS EMERGE

Lima Bean

Like snap beans (which they resemble), limas come in either bush or vine (pole) form. They develop more slowly than string beans—bush types require 65 to 75 days from planting to harvest, pole kinds 78 to 95 days—and do not produce as reliably in extremely dry, hot weather. They must be shelled before cooking—a tedious chore but worth it if you like fresh limas.

Among bush types, 'Burpee's Improved Bush', 'Henderson Bush', and 'Fordhook 242' are outstanding; the last two are especially useful in hot-summer areas. 'Prizetaker' and 'King of the Garden' are fine, large-seeded climbing forms; 'Small White Lima', ('Sieva'), usually grown for drying, gives heavy yields of shelled beans. Grow like snap beans.

B

BEAN, SCARLET RUNNER

Fabaceae (Leguminosae)

PERENNIAL TWINING VINE GROWN AS ANNUAL

✿ ALL ZONES

☼ FULL SUN

💧 REGULAR WATER AFTER SEEDLINGS EMERGE

Scarlet Runner Bean

Showy and ornamental with bright scarlet flowers in slender clusters and with bright green leaves divided into three roundish, 3–5-in.-long leaflets. Use to cover fences, arbors, outbuildings; provides quick shade on porches. Pink- and white-flowered varieties exist.

Flowers are followed by flattened, very dark green pods that are edible and tasty when young but toughen as they reach full size. Beans from older pods can be shelled for cooking like green limas. Culture is same as for snap beans.

GROW A BEAN TEPEE

From July to September, children can play in the cool, shady confines of a bean tepee (it will be especially colorful if scarlet runner beans are used). Place a vertical 10-ft. center pole 1½ ft. deep in the soil. Pack it in well. Place bases of at least four 10-ft.-long bamboo poles (or other skinny wooden sticks) 4½ ft. out from base of center pole and tie their tops together 6–12 in. below top of center pole. In a circle just outside pole bases, plant the beans 1 in. deep and 1–3 in. apart. Train the vines up the outside of the tepee, keeping main stems out of its interior.

BEAN, SNAP

STRING BEAN, GREEN BEAN

Fabaceae (Leguminosae)

ANNUAL

✿ ALL ZONES

☼ FULL SUN

💧 REGULAR WATER AFTER SEEDLINGS EMERGE

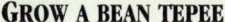
Snap Bean

Of all beans, the snap bean is the most widely planted and most useful for home gardens. Snap beans have tender, fleshy pods with little fiber; they may be green, yellow (wax beans), or purple. Purple kinds turn green in cooking. Plants grow as self-supporting bushes (bush beans) or as climbing vines (pole beans). Bush types bear earlier, but vines are more productive. Plants resemble scarlet runner bean, but white or purple flowers are not showy.

Plant seeds as soon as soil is warm, in full sun and good soil. The seeds must push heavy seed leaves through soil, so see that soil is reasonably loose and open. Plant seeds of bush types an inch deep and 1–3 in. apart in rows, with 2–3 ft. between rows. Pole beans can be managed in a number of ways: set three or four 8-ft. poles in the ground and tie together at top in wigwam fashion; or set single poles 3 or 4 ft. apart and sow six or eight beans around each, thinning to three or four strongest seedlings; or insert poles 1 or 2 ft. apart in rows and sow seeds as you would bush beans; or sow along sunny wall, fence, or trellis and train vines on web of light string supported by wire or heavy twine. Moisten ground thoroughly before planting; do not water again until seedlings have emerged.

Once growth starts, keep soil moist. In absence of rainfall, occasional deep soaking is preferable to frequent light sprinklings, which may encourage mildew. Feed after plants are in active growth and again when pods start to form. Pods are ready in 50 to 70 days, depending on variety. Pick every 5 to 7 days; if pods mature, plants will stop bearing. Mexican bean beetles are often a problem in the eastern U.S. A trap crop is an effec-

tive control: set out a few bean plants earlier than the bean crop you intend to harvest, wait until the trap beans are infested, and then dispose of them, pests and all. If the small, copper-colored beetles with 16 spots appear on your good crop, shake them loose onto a cloth, then discard it. Control aphids, cucumber beetles, and whiteflies as needed.

BEARBERRY. See ARCTOSTAPHYLOS uva-ursi

BEARD TONGUE. See PENSTEMON

BEAR'S BREECH. See ACANTHUS mollis

BEAR'S FOOT FERN. See HUMATA tyermannii

BEAUCARNEA recurvata

PONYTAIL, BOTTLE PALM

Agavaceae

SUCCULENT SHRUB OR TREE

✿ ZONES 13, 16–27; OR INDOORS

☼ FULL SUN

💧 MODERATE WATER

Beaucarnea recurvata

Base of trunk is greatly swollen. On young plants it resembles a big onion sitting on soil; on old trees in the ground, it can be a woody mass several feet across. Old plants can reach 15 ft. tall. Leaves cluster at ends of branches in dense tufts; arching and drooping, they measure 3 ft. or more in length, ¾ in. wide. Very old trees may produce large clusters of tiny, creamy white flowers.

Outdoors, give plants sun, well-drained soil, and infrequent deep watering during prolonged dry periods. They do exceptionally well as house plants if given good light and not overwatered. Mature plants have endured temperatures to 18°F/−8°C; young plants in containers freeze to death at a few degrees higher.

BEAUMONTIA grandiflora

HERALD'S TRUMPET, EASTER LILY VINE

Apocynaceae

EVERGREEN VINE

✿ ZONES 12, 13, 16, 17, 21–27

☼ ◐ FULL SUN OR LIGHT SHADE

💧💧 AMPLE WATER

Beaumontia grandiflora

Hardy to 28°F/−2°C. Rampant vine uses arching, semitwining branches to climb as much as 30 ft. and spread as wide. Large, dark green, 6–9-in., oval to roundish leaves, smooth and shiny above, slightly downy beneath, furnish lush tropical look. In spring and summer, bears trumpet-shaped, 5–8-in.-long, fragrant green-veined white flowers that look like Easter lilies. Needs deep, rich soil, ample water, and heavy feeding. Prune after flowering to keep it in scale, but preserve good proportion of 2- and 3-year-old wood; flowers are not borne on new growth. Frost-killed plants usually come back from the roots. Use as big espalier on warm, wind-sheltered wall, or train along eaves of house; sturdy supports are essential, since growth is so heavy. Good near swimming pools.

BEAUTYBERRY. See CALLICARPA

BEAUTY BUSH. See KOLKWITZIA amabilis

BEE BALM. See MONARDA

BEECH. See FAGUS

BEEFWOOD. See CASUARINA

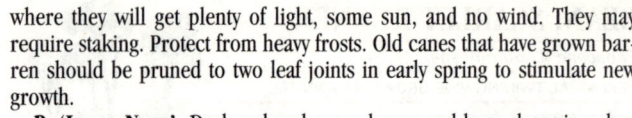

B

BEET

Chenopodiaceae

BIENNIAL GROWN AS ANNUAL

↗ ALL ZONES

☼ FULL SUN

🌢 REGULAR WATER

Raised for edible root and tender young leaves, beet grows best in relatively cool weather. In hot-summer climates, avoid extreme heat by sowing in early spring or late summer. In mild-winter regions, can be grown in fall and winter. Crop is

Beet

ready to harvest 45 to 65 days after seeding; sow at monthly intervals to have beets over a long season.

Grow in fertile, well-drained soil without lumps or rocks. Sow seed 1 in. apart and cover with ¼ in. of compost, sand, or vermiculite. Thin to 2 in. apart while plants are small—the thinnings (tops as well as roots) are edible. To keep roots tender, keep soil evenly moist. Begin harvesting when roots are 1 in. wide; complete harvesting before they exceed 3 in. (they will be woody if allowed to grow bigger). In cold climates, harvest all beets before hard frosts in fall.

Types with round, red roots include 'Detroit Dark Red' and 'Crosby's Egyptian' (old favorites) as well as many newer varieties. Novelties include 'Cylindra' and 'Forma Nova' (with long, cylindrical roots); there are also varieties with golden yellow or white roots.

BEGONIA

Begoniaceae

PERENNIALS

↗ ZONES 14–28, EXCEPT AS NOTED; OR OVERWINTER INDOORS OR TREAT AS ANNUALS

☼ ● BEST IN FILTERED SHADE

🌢 MOIST SOIL AND HUMID AIR

Perennials, sometimes shrubby, grown for textured, multicolored foliage, saucer-sized flowers, or lacy clusters of smaller flowers. Outdoors, most grow well in pots, in the ground, or in hanging baskets in filtered shade with rich, porous, fast-draining soil, consistent but light feeding, and

Tuberous Begonia

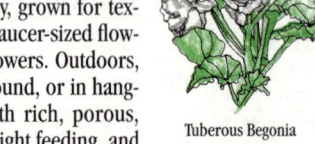

enough water to keep soil moist but not soggy. Most thrive as indoor plants, in greenhouse, or under lath. Some prefer terrarium conditions. Almost all require at least moderate humidity. (In hot dry-summer areas or indoors in winter, set pots in saucers filled with wet pebbles.)

Most can be propagated easily from leaf, stem, or rhizome cuttings. They also grow from dust-fine seed. Of the many hundreds of species and varieties, relatively few are sold widely.

Begonia enthusiasts group or classify the different kinds by growth habit, which coincidentally groups them by their care needs.

Hardy begonia. Unique among begonias is *B. grandis (B. evansiana, B. grandis evansiana)*. Suitable for Zones 3–33, it is the only begonia that is hardy outside the mildest parts of the U.S. Grows from a tuber; reaches 2–3 ft. tall, with branching red stems carrying large, smooth coppery green leaves with red undersides. Summer flowers are pink or white, borne in drooping clusters. Tops die down after frost; mulch to protect roots. Grow with ferns, hosta, bergenia, and similar shade plants.

Cane-type begonias. They get their name from their stems, which grow tall and woody and have prominent bamboolike joints. The group includes so-called angel-wing begonias. These erect plants have multiple stems, some reaching 5 ft. or more under the right conditions. Most bloom profusely with large clusters of white, pink, orange, or red flowers, early spring through autumn. Some are everblooming. When roots fill 4-in. pots, plants can be placed in larger containers or in the ground. Position plants

where they will get plenty of light, some sun, and no wind. They may require staking. Protect from heavy frosts. Old canes that have grown barren should be pruned to two leaf joints in early spring to stimulate new growth.

B. 'Irene Nuss'. Dark red-and-green leaves and huge drooping clusters of coral pink flowers.

Hiemalis begonias. Usually sold as Rieger begonias. Bushy, compact; profuse bloomers and outstanding outdoor or indoor plants. Flowers average about 2 in. across and appear over a long season that includes winter. On well-grown plants, green leaves and stems are all but invisible beneath a blanket of bloom. Give indoor plants plenty of light in winter. In summer, keep out of hot noonday sun. Water thoroughly when top inch of soil is dry. Don't sprinkle leaves. Plants may get rangy, an indication of approaching dormancy; if they do, cut stems to 4-in. stubs.

Multiflora begonias. Bushy, compact plants 1–1½ ft. tall. Abundant summer and fall blooms in carmine, scarlet, orange, yellow, apricot, salmon, pink. Includes Nonstop strain. All are essentially small-flowered, profuse-blooming tuberous begonias; for care, see Tuberous begonias.

Rex begonias. With their bold, multicolored leaves, these are probably the most striking of all foliage begonias. While many named varieties are grown by collectors, easier-to-find unnamed seedling plants are almost as decorative. The leaves grow from a rhizome; see Rhizomatous begonias for care. In addition, rex begonias should get high humidity (at least 50 percent) to do their best. In arid climates or indoors in winter, provide it by misting with a spray bottle, plac-

Rex Begonia

ing pots on wet pebbles in a tray, or keeping plants in greenhouse. When rhizome grows too far past edge of pot for your taste, either repot into slightly larger container or cut off rhizome end inside pot edge. Old rhizome will branch and grow new leaves. Make rhizome cuttings of the piece you remove and root in mixture of half peat moss, half perlite.

Rhizomatous begonias. Like rex begonias, these grow from a rhizome, a usually creeping stem-type structure at or near soil level. Although some have handsome flowers, they are grown primarily for foliage, which varies in color and texture among species and varieties. The group includes so-called star begonias, named for their leaf shape. Rhizomatous begonias perform well as house plants: give them bright light through a window and water only when the top inch or so of soil is dry. Plant them in wide, shallow pots. They flower from winter through summer, the season varying among specific plants. White to pink flowers appear in clusters on erect stems above the foliage. Rhizomes will grow over edge of pot, eventually forming a ball-shaped plant; if you wish, cut rhizomes back to pot. The old rhizome will branch and grow new leaves. Root the pieces of rhizome in mixture of half peat moss, half perlite.

B. masoniana. IRON CROSS BEGONIA. Large puckered leaves; known for chocolate brown pattern resembling Maltese cross on green background. Flowers insignificant.

Semperflorens begonias. Fibrous or bedding begonias. Dwarf (6–8-in.) and taller (10–12-in.) strains grown in garden beds or containers as if annuals, producing lots of small flowers spring through fall in a white-through-red range. Foliage can be green, red, bronze, or variegated. In mild climates, can overwinter, live for years. Thrives in full sun in coolest summer areas. Prefers broken shade elsewhere, but dark-foliaged kinds will take sun if well watered.

Shrublike begonias. This large class is marked by multiple stems that are soft and green rather than bamboolike as in the cane-type group. Grown for both foliage and flowers. Leaves are very interesting—some are heavily textured; others grow white or red "hairs"; still others develop a soft, feltlike coating. Most grow upright and bushy, but others are less erect and make suitable subjects for hanging baskets. Flowers in shades of pink, red, white, and peach can come any time, depending on species or variety. Care consists of repotting into larger container as the plant outgrows its pot. Some shrublike begonias can get very large—as tall as 8 ft. They require ample moisture—water when soil begins to dry on surface. Prune to shape; pinch tips to encourage branching.

B. 'Digswelliana'. Shrublike plant, 2–3 ft. high, with glossy leaves 2–4 in. long. Red flowers in clusters bloom almost continuously spring–fall.

B. foliosa. Inch-long leaves packed tightly on twiggy plant give fernlike look. Stems arch or droop to 3 ft. Flowers are small, white to red, everblooming in mild weather. 'Miniata' has rose pink to rose red flowers.

B. 'Richmondensis'. Exceeds 2 ft. tall, with arching stems carrying deep green, shiny, crisp leaves with red undersides. Vivid pink to crimson flowers develop from darker buds; nearly year-round bloom. Big and sturdy. Tolerant of sun and wind.

Trailing or climbing begonias. These have stems that trail or climb, depending on how you train them. They are suited to hanging basket culture or planting in the ground where well protected. Growing conditions similar to those for tuberous begonias, though trailing types are not lifted. Sporadic bloom during warm weather.

B. solananthera. Glossy light green leaves; fragrant white flowers with red centers.

Tuberous begonias. These magnificent large-flowered hybrids grow from tubers. Types range from plants with saucer-size blooms and a few upright stems to multistemmed hanging basket types covered with flowers. Except for some rare kinds, they are summer- and fall-blooming in almost any flower color except blue.

Grow tuberous begonias in filtered shade, such as under lath or in the open with eastern exposure. Not suited to areas of extreme heat and humidity. For best bloom in dry regions, mist with water several times a day. Watch for fuzzy white spots on leaves, which signal powdery mildew. In fall, when leaves begin to yellow and wilt, reduce watering. When stems have fallen off the plant on their own, lift tuber; shake off dirt; dry tuber in the sun for 3 days; and store in cool, dry place, such as a garden shed or garage, with its label until spring, when little pink buds will become visible. In April and May you can buy small seedling plants and plant them directly in pots.

Strains are sold as hanging or upright. The former bloom more profusely; the latter have larger flowers. Colors are white, red, pink, yellow, and peach; shapes are frilly (carnation), formal double (camellia), and tight-centered (rose). Some have petal edges in contrasting colors (picotee). Popular strains are Double Trumpet (improved rose form), Prima Donna (improved camellia), and Hanging Sensation.

HOW AND WHEN TO START BEGONIA TUBERS

In early February, place dormant tubers in shallow flats and cover ½–1 in. deep with coarse organic matter such as leaf mold. Water the flats regularly and keep them in broken shade (in mild climates) or under lights indoors (in cold-winter climates). As each plant reaches 3 in. high, repot into 8–10-in. pot with rich, humusy, fast-draining potting mix. Stake upright types. Water to keep potting mix moist but not soggy. Fertilize weekly with quarter-strength high-nitrogen fertilizer until mid-May; then switch to a bloom-producing fertilizer.

BELAMCANDA chinensis

BLACKBERRY LILY

Iridaceae

PERENNIAL WITH RHIZOME

☀ ZONES 1–24, 26, 28–43

☼ ◑ FULL SUN OR PARTIAL SHADE

🌢 REGULAR WATER

Belamcanda chinensis

Like its iris relatives, forms clumps of sword-shaped leaves in fanlike sheaves from slowly creeping rhizomes. In summer, zigzagging, 3–4-ft. stems carry sprays of 1½-in. yellowish orange flowers dotted with red. Each flower lasts only a day, but new blossoms keep opening for weeks. As blooms fade, rounded seed capsules develop; they split open to expose shiny black seeds resembling blackberries (hence the plant's common name). Cut seed-bearing stems for unique dried arrangements. Plant is effective in clumps in border. Plant rhizomes 1 in. deep in porous soil.

Blackberry lily was crossed with vesper iris (*Pardanthopsis dichotoma*, formerly *Iris dichotoma*) to create a group of hybrids, *Pardancanda norrisii*, sometimes called candy lily. This plant produces the same general effect as blackberry lily, but bears flowers in an expanded color range, including white, yellow, red, pink, and purple.

BELLADONNA LILY. See AMARYLLIS belladonna

BELLFLOWER. See CAMPANULA

BELLIS perennis

ENGLISH DAISY

Asteraceae (Compositae)

PERENNIAL OFTEN TREATED AS ANNUAL

☀ ZONES 1–24, 34–43

☼ ◑ LIGHT SHADE IN WARM AREAS

🌢🌢🌢 MODERATE TO LOTS OF WATER

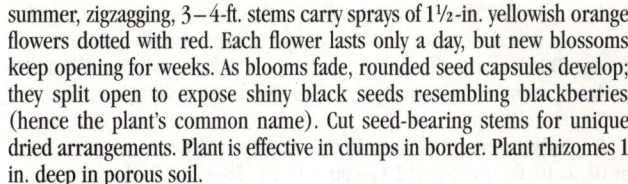

Bellis perennis

Native to Europe and Mediterranean region. The original English daisies are the kind you sometimes see growing in lawns. Plump, fully double ones sold in nurseries are horticultural varieties. Rosettes of dark green leaves 1–2 in. long. Pink, rose, red, or white double flowers on 3–6-in. stems, in spring and early summer. Edging or bedding plant; effective with bulbs.

BELLS-OF-IRELAND. See MOLUCCELLA laevis

BELLWORT. See UVULARIA

BELOPERONE. See JUSTICIA

BENT, BENT GRASS. See AGROSTIS

Berberidaceae. The barberry family contains both shrubs and herbaceous perennials. Barberry (*Berberis*) and heavenly bamboo (*Nandina*) are typical of the former; *Epimedium* of the latter.

BERBERIS

BARBERRY

Berberidaceae

EVERGREEN, SEMIEVERGREEN, DECIDUOUS SHRUBS

☀ ZONES VARY BY SPECIES

☼ ◑ FULL SUN OR LIGHT SHADE

🌢🌢 REGULAR TO MODERATE WATER

Berberis thunbergii

Ability of barberries, especially the deciduous species, to take punishment from climate and soil extremes makes them worth attention in all "hard" climates. They require no more than ordinary garden care. Vigorous growers can take a lot of cutting back for growth renewal; if plants are left to their own devices, some inner branches die and plants become ratty. The following species all bear yellow spring flowers and spiny branches typical of the genus. (Barberries with much-divided leaves are classified under *Mahonia* in this book.)

B. darwinii. DARWIN BARBERRY. Evergreen. Zones 5–9, 14–24, 31. Hardy to 10°F/−12°C. Showiest barberry. Fountainlike growth to 5–10 ft.

high and 4–7 ft. wide. Leaves small (1 in.), crisp, dark green, hollylike. Orange-yellow flowers are so thick along branches that it's difficult to see foliage. Berries dark blue and numerous—popular with birds. Wonderful as background for Oregon grape *(Mahonia aquifolium)*. Spreads by underground runners.

B. gladwynensis 'William Penn'. Evergreen; loses some of its leaves at 0° to 10°F/–18° to –12°C. Zones 1–24, 28–35, 39. Hardy to about –10°F/–23°C. Resembles *B. julianae* in general effect, but is faster growing, with denser growth to 4 ft. high and broader, glossier leaves. Good show of bright yellow flowers.

B. julianae. WINTERGREEN BARBERRY. Evergreen or semievergreen. Zones 4–24, 28–32. Hardy to 0°F/–18°C, but foliage damaged by winter cold. Dense, upright, to 6 ft., with slightly angled branches. Very leathery, spine-toothed, 3-in.-long, dark green leaves. Fruit bluish black. Reddish fall color. One of the thorniest—formidable as barrier hedge.

B. mentorensis. Evergreen; loses some or all leaves below about –5°F/–21°C. Zones 1–24, 28–41. Hardy to –20°F/–29°C. Hybrid with rather compact growth to 7 ft. and as wide. Leaves dark green, 1 in. long; beautiful red fall color in cold climates. Berries dull dark red. Easy to maintain as hedge at any height. Tolerates hot, dry weather.

B. thunbergii. JAPANESE BARBERRY. Deciduous. Zones 1–24, 28–41. Hardy to –20°F/–29°C. Graceful growth habit with slender, arching, spiny branches; if not sheared, usually reaches 4–6 ft. tall with equal spread. Dense foliage with roundish, ½–1½-in.-long leaves, deep green above, paler beneath, turning to yellow, orange, and red before they fall. Beadlike, bright red berries stud branches in fall and through winter. Hedge, barrier planting, or single shrub. Many attractive varieties include the following:

'Atropurpurea'. RED-LEAF JAPANESE BARBERRY. Plants sold as such vary in size and leaf color, from bronzy red to purplish red. Hold color all summer. Must have sun to develop color.

'Aurea'. Bright golden yellow foliage, best in full sun. Will tolerate light shade. Slow growing to 2½–3 ft.

'Cherry Bomb'. Resembles 'Crimson Pygmy', but taller (to 4 ft.), with large leaves and more open growth.

'Crimson Pygmy' ('Atropurpurea Nana'). Selected miniature form, generally less than 1½ ft. high and 2½ ft. wide as 10-year-old. Mature leaves bronzy blood red; new leaves bright red. Must have sun to develop color.

'Helmond Pillar'. Resembles 'Atropurpurea' but columnar in form; grows to 6 ft. tall, less than 1 ft. wide.

'Kobold'. Extra-dwarf bright green variety. Like 'Crimson Pygmy' in habit but fuller and rounder.

'Rose Glow'. New foliage marbled bronzy red and pinkish white, deepening to rose and bronze. Colors best in full sun or lightest shade.

'Sparkle'. To 5 ft. tall and 4–6 ft. wide, with rich green foliage that turns vivid yellow, orange, and red in fall.

BERCKMAN DWARF ARBORVITAE. See PLATYCLADUS orientalis

BERGENIA

Saxifragaceae

PERENNIALS

ZONES 1–9, 12–24, 30–45, EXCEPT AS NOTED

TOLERATE FULL SUN IN COOL-SUMMER AREAS

REGULAR WATER FOR BEST APPEARANCE

Bergenia crassifolia

Native to Himalayas and mountains of China. Thick rootstocks; large, ornamental, glossy green leaves, evergreen except in coldest areas. Thick leafless stalks, 1–1½ ft. high, bear graceful nodding clusters of small white, pink, or rose flowers. Strong, substantial textural quality in borders, under trees, as bold-patterned ground cover. Effective with ferns, hellebores, hostas, and as foreground planting for aucubas, rhododendrons, Japanese aralia.

Best performance in partial shade but will take full sun in cool-summer climates. *B. cordifolia* and *B. crassifolia* endure neglect, poor soil, cold, but respond to good soil, regular watering, feeding, grooming. Cut back yearly to prevent legginess. Divide crowded clumps and replant vigorous divisions.

B. ciliata (B. ligulata). Zones 4–9, 14–24, 29–34, 39. Choicest, most elegant. To 1 ft. Lustrous, light green leaves to 1 ft. across, smooth on edges but fringed with soft hairs; young leaves bronzy. White, rose, or purplish flowers bloom late spring, summer. Slightly tender; leaves burn in severe frost. Plants sold under this name may be garden hybrids.

B. cordifolia. HEARTLEAF BERGENIA. Leaves, to 1 ft. across, are glossy, roundish, heart shaped at base, with wavy, toothed edges. In spring, rose or lilac flowers in pendulous clusters partially hidden by leaves. Plant grows to 20 in. 'Morning Red' ('Morgenrote') has leaves with bronzy tones, dark red flowers.

B. crassifolia. WINTER-BLOOMING BERGENIA. Leaves dark green, 8 in. or more across, with wavy, sparsely toothed edges. Flowers rose, lilac, or purple in dense clusters on erect stems standing well above leaves. Plants 20 in. high. Blooms any time from midwinter to early spring, depending on climate.

B. hybrids. Many hybrids of English or German origin are available. Choices include 'Abendglut' ('Evening Glow'), with dark reddish leaves with crimped edges, dark red flowers; and 'Silberlicht' ('Silver Light'), with large, slightly toothed leaves and white flowers with pink tints.

BERMUDA, BERMUDA GRASS. See CYNODON dactylon

BETHLEHEM SAGE. See PULMONARIA saccharata

BETULA

BIRCH

Betulaceae

DECIDUOUS TREES

ZONES VARY BY SPECIES

FULL SUN

AMPLE WATER

Betula pendula

The white-barked European white birch—the tree that comes to mind when most people think of birches—has relatives that resemble it in graceful habit, thin bark that peels in layers, and small-scale, finely toothed leaves that turn from green to glowing yellow in fall. After leaf drop, the delicate limb structure, handsome bark, and small conelike fruit of birches provide a winter display.

All birches need ample moisture at all times. All are susceptible to aphids that drip honeydew; for that reason, these are not trees for a patio or to park a car under. Bronze birch borer is a pest mainly east of the Rockies, and birch leaf miner a problem in northern latitudes. These trees are generally too greedy for lawns.

B. albo-sinensis. Zones 3–11, 14–24, 31–34, 39. Native to western China. Tall tree (to 100 ft.) grown chiefly for beautiful pinkish brown to coppery bark covered with powdery gray bloom. Leaves 3 in. long. *B. a. septentrionalis* has flaking bark that is orange to orange brown.

B. jacquemontii (B. utilis jacquemontii). Zones 3–11, 14–17, 31–34, 39. Native to northern India. Tall, narrow tree with brilliant white bark. Grows about 2 ft. a year to 40 ft., then more slowly to an eventual 60 ft. Seedlings vary in bark color; buy grafted trees. Not thoroughly tested in the East, but promising.

B. lenta. SWEET BIRCH, BLACK BIRCH, CHERRY BIRCH. Zones 32, 34–40. Native to eastern U.S. Seldom sold. An attractive tree with shiny reddish to blackish brown bark; grows 40–50 ft. tall. Rich yellow fall foliage color. Most country children in the eastern states have tasted the bark, which has a sweet wintergreen flavor and was once used to make a soft drink known as birch beer.

B. maximowicziana. MONARCH BIRCH. Zones 3–9, 14–24, 31–34, 39. Native to Japan. Fast growing; open growth when young. Can reach 80–100 ft. Bark flaking, orange brown, eventually gray or white. Leaves up to 6 in. long. Plants sold under this name are not always the true species.

B. nigra. RIVER BIRCH, RED BIRCH. Zones 1–24, 26, 28–43. Native to eastern U.S. Very fast growth in first years; eventually reaches 50–90 ft. Trunk often forks near ground, but tree can be trained to single stem. Young bark is apricot to pinkish, very smooth, and shiny. On older trees bark flakes and curls in cinnamon brown to blackish sheets. Diamond-shaped leaves, 1–3 in. long, are bright glossy green above, silvery below. 'Heritage' has darker leaves and tan-and-apricot bark; keeps apricot color longer than the species. These are the best birches for hot, humid climates. Tolerate poor or slow drainage.

B. papyrifera. CANOE BIRCH, PAPER BIRCH. Zones 1–6, 37–45. Native to northern part of North America. Somewhat similar to *B. pendula* but taller (to 100 ft.), more open, less weeping, with a stouter trunk that is creamy white. Bark peels off in papery layers. Leaves are larger (to 4 in. long), more sparse. Excellent fall color. More resistant to bronze birch borer than *B. pendula.*

B. pendula. EUROPEAN WHITE BIRCH. Zones 1–12, 14–24, 30–45. Native from Europe to Asia Minor. Delicate and lacy. Upright branching with weeping side branches. Average mature tree 30–40 ft. high, spreading to half its height. Bark on twigs and young branches is golden brown. Bark on trunk and main limbs becomes white, marked with black clefts; oldest bark at base is blackish gray. Rich green, glossy leaves to 2½ in. long, diamond shaped, with slender tapered point. Often sold as weeping birch, although trees vary somewhat in habit and young trees show little inclination to weep. Very susceptible to bronze birch borer. The following are some of the varieties offered.

'Dalecarlica' ('Laciniata'). CUTLEAF WEEPING BIRCH. Leaves deeply cut. Branches strongly weeping; graceful open tree. Weeping forms are more affected by dry, hot weather than is the species. Foliage shows stress by late summer.

'Fastigiata' (*B. alba* 'Fastigiata'). PYRAMIDAL WHITE BIRCH. Branches upright; habit somewhat like Lombardy poplar. Excellent screening tree.

'Purpurea' (*B. alba* 'Purpurea'). PURPLE BIRCH. Twigs purple black. New foliage rich purple maroon, fading to purplish green in summer; striking effect against white bark. Best in cool to cold climates.

'Trost's Dwarf'. True dwarf (3 ft. tall and wide) for bonsai, container, rock garden. Needs excellent drainage.

'Youngii'. YOUNG'S WEEPING BIRCH. Slender branches hang straight down. Form like weeping mulberry's, but tree is more graceful. Decorative display tree. Trunk must be staked to desired height. Same climate limitations as that of 'Dalecarlica'.

B. platyphylla japonica. JAPANESE WHITE BIRCH. Zones 2–11, 14–24, 31–41. Native to Japan. Fast growth to 40–50 ft.; narrow, open habit. Leaves to 3 in. long, glossy green. Bark white. 'Whitespire' is a narrowly pyramidal, heat-tolerant selection resistant to bronze birch borer.

Betulaceae. The birch family includes deciduous trees and shrubs with inconspicuous flowers in tight clusters (catkins). Representatives are alder (*Alnus*), birch (*Betula*), filbert (*Corylus*), and hornbeam (*Carpinus*).

BIGNONIA capreolata

CROSSVINE

Bignoniaceae

EVERGREEN OR SEMIEVERGREEN VINE

🌿 ZONES 4–9, 14–24, 26–33

☀️◑ FULL SUN OR LIGHT SHADE

💧 REGULAR WATER

Bignonia capreolata

Native to the South and lower Midwest. Climbs rapidly to 30 ft. or more by tendrils and holdfast disks; useful for covering fences, poles, masonry walls, and outbuildings. Shiny dark green leaves consist of two

2–6-in. leaflets and a branching tendril; leaf cover is not dense. In winter, leaves turn purplish; they will fall off in severe weather. Clustered, 2-in., trumpet-shaped flowers, typically brownish red or brownish orange, appear in spring. 'Tangerine Beauty', with bright apricot orange flowers, is exceptionally bright colored and free blooming.

Bignoniaceae. The bignonia family includes vines (mostly), trees, shrubs, and (rarely) perennials or annuals—all with trumpet-shaped, often two-lipped flowers. The family gets its name from the genus *Bignonia*, which once included most of the trumpet vines; though most of these have been reclassified, they are often still sold as *Bignonia*. Listed below are the older names, followed by the new:

B. cherere. See Distictis buccinatoria
B. chinensis. See Campsis grandiflora
B. jasminoides. See Pandorea jasminoides
B. radicans. See Campsis radicans
B. speciosa. See Clytostoma callistegioides
B. tweediana. See Macfadyena unguis-cati
B. venusta. See Pyrostegia venusta
B. violacea. See Clytostoma callistegioides

BIG TREE. See SEQUOIADENDRON giganteum

BILLBERGIA

Bromeliaceae

EVERGREEN PERENNIALS

🌿 ZONES 12, 13, 16–27; OR INDOORS

◑ FILTERED SHADE

💧💧 AMPLE WATER DURING WARM WEATHER

Billbergia nutans

This pineapple relative is native to Brazil, where the plants grow as epiphytes on trees. Stiff, spiny-toothed leaves in basal clusters. Showy bracts and tubular flowers in drooping clusters. Usually grown in containers for display indoors or on patios. In mild climates, often grown under trees as an easy ground cover; in borders; or on limbs of trees or bark slabs, with roots wrapped in sphagnum moss and leaf mold. Excellent cut flowers.

Pot in light, porous mixture of sand, ground bark, or leaf mold. Need little water in winter, when growth is slow; large amounts during active growth in warm weather. Usually hold water in funnel-like center of leaf rosette, which acts as reservoir. When grown as house plants, give plenty of light and sun. Increase by cutting off suckers from base of plant. Specialists in bromeliads list dozens of varieties.

B. nutans. QUEEN'S TEARS. Deep green leaves to 1½ ft. long. Long spikes of rosy red bracts; drooping flowers with green petals edged deep blue. Vigorous. Makes offsets freely; easy to grow and propagate.

B. pyramidalis. Leaves to 3 ft. long, 2½ in. wide, with spiny-toothed margins. Flowers with red, violet-tipped petals and bright red bracts in dense spikes 4 in. long.

B. sanderana. Leaves leathery, to 1 ft. long, spiny toothed, dotted with white. Loose, nodding, 10-in.-long clusters of flowers with blue petals, yellowish green at the base; blue-tipped sepals, rose-colored bracts.

BIRCH. See BETULA

BIRCH BARK CHERRY. See PRUNUS serrula

BIRD OF PARADISE. See CAESALPINIA, STRELITZIA

BIRD OF PARADISE BUSH. See CAESALPINIA gilliesii

BIRD OF PARADISE, FALSE. See HELICONIA brasiliensis

BIRD'S FOOT TREFOIL. See LOTUS corniculatus

BIRD'S NEST FERN. See ASPLENIUM nidus

BISHOP'S HAT. See EPIMEDIUM grandiflorum

BISHOP'S WEED. See AEGOPODIUM podagraria

BITTER MELON. See MOMORDICA charantia

BITTERROOT. See LEWISIA rediviva

BITTERSWEET. See CELASTRUS

BLACK ALDER. See ILEX verticillata

BLACKBERRY

Rosaceae

DECIDUOUS SHRUBS OR VINES

🗲 ZONES 1 AND 2 IN WEST, 3–9, 14–41

☼ FULL SUN

🌢 REGULAR WATER

Blackberry

Blackberries grow in areas of North America where summers are not too hot and dry, and winters not too harsh. They thrive in cool, humid regions along the eastern and western coasts, as well as in the Great Lakes basin and in cool-night areas of moderate-elevation mountains. They are not adapted to the plains or high mountain states.

Varieties from the midwestern and eastern states tend to be hardy, upright, and stiff caned; they usually grow 4–6 ft. tall. Types in the West tend to be trailing; some of these are so distinctive that they have separate names (boysenberry, loganberry, marionberry, olallieberry). In the South, trailing kinds known as dewberries are often grown. Crosses between upright and trailing types are termed semierect.

All types bear fruit in summer. The fruit clusters of trailing varieties ripen earlier and are smaller and more open than those of erect or semierect types. For good crops, all blackberries need full sun; deep, well-drained soil; and regular water throughout the growing season. The fruit makes excellent pies, fine jams and jellies, tangy syrups, and even good wines.

Blackberries are subject to many pests and diseases, so start with healthy plants from a reputable supplier. Also look for resistant varieties. Because of their susceptibility to verticillium wilt, blackberries should not be planted where potatoes, tomatoes, eggplants, or peppers have grown in the last 2 years.

Blackberries are usually planted in spring. Set new bare-root plants an inch deeper than they grew at the nursery, their crowns covered with an inch of soil.

In general, erect and semierect types will grow throughout the West, except in desert regions, and in Zones 25–41 east of the Rockies. Trailing types are grown primarily in the West (Zones 4–9, 14–24); some types will succeed in Zones 28–32. When growing beyond certain hardiness, bury the first-year canes under a heavy mulch. In hard-winter areas, blackberries are best located on slight slopes with good air drainage. Northern exposures help keep plants dormant until spring freezes are past. Don't put plants where they will get standing water during the dormant season.

Though blackberry roots are perennial, the canes are biennial; they develop and grow one year, flower and fruit the second. Erect types can be tied to wire, though they don't need support. First-year canes can be headed back a little in midsummer to encourage side branches; the lateral branches can then be cut to 1 ft. long in early spring.

Trailing and semierect types are best grown on some kind of trellis. Train 1-year-old canes on the structure; after harvest, cut to the ground all canes that have fruited. The canes of the current season, those growing beneath the trellis, should now be trained onto it; thin to desired number of canes and prune to 6–8 ft., spreading them fanwise on trellis. Canes of semierect types often become more upright as plant matures.

The following includes some of the best blackberry varieties. (For ornamental relatives, see *Rubus.*)

'Arapaho'. Erect, thornless. Large, firm berries ripen at least 3 weeks before 'Navaho'. Disease resistant. Good variety for South.

'Black Satin'. Semierect, thornless, vigorous. Shiny black, very tart fruit. Good in Illinois, Ohio, Mid-Atlantic, Northeast.

'Boysen' and 'Thornless Boysen'. The western trailing type most commonly grown in other regions of the U.S. Large reddish berries with sweet-tart flavor, delightful aroma.

'Brazos'. Erect. Productive, disease resistant, with large, fairly firm, tart fruits. Well adapted to Texas, Gulf Coast states.

'Cascade'. Trailing. Classic wild blackberry flavor. For the West.

'Cherokee'. Erect, thorny. Firm berries with excellent flavor. Resists anthracnose. Good for South.

'Chester'. Semierect, thornless, heavy bearing, and resistant to cane blight. Very cold tolerant.

'Darrow'. Erect. A heavy bearer, with large fruit ripening over a long season. Reliable in Virginia, Northeast.

'Dirksen'. Semierect. Resistant to anthracnose, leaf spot, and mildew. Good variety for Illinois, Ohio, Mid-Atlantic.

'Illini Hardy'. Erect, very thorny. Cold-hardy variety introduced by University of Illinois. Good in Midwest, Northeast.

'Logan' and 'Thornless Logan'. Trailing. Light reddish berries tarter than 'Boysen'. For the West.

'Marion'. Trailing. Similar to 'Olallie' in berry size and quality. Good in coastal Northwest.

'Navaho'. Erect, thornless. Firm, sweet fruit ripening late. Disease resistant. Well suited to the South.

'Olallie'. Trailing. Big berries sweeter than 'Cascade' but with some wild blackberry sprightliness. Adapted from Oregon down the California coast; also good for the Gulf Coast.

'Smoothstem'. Semierect, thornless. Tart, large-seeded berries. Hardy from Maryland southward.

'Thornfree'. Semierect, thornless canes bearing large crop of tart berries. Productive in Oregon, and from Maryland south to North Carolina and west to Arkansas.

'Young' and 'Thornless Young'. Trailing. Sweeter than 'Boysen', though not as productive. Disease prone in South, less so in West.

BLACKBERRY LILY. See BELAMCANDA chinensis

BLACK CALLA. See ARUM palaestinum

BLACK-EYED SUSAN. See RUDBECKIA hirta

BLACK-EYED SUSAN VINE. See THUNBERGIA alata

BLACK LILY. See FRITILLARIA camschatcensis

BLACK SNAKEROOT. See CIMICIFUGA racemosa

BLADDERNUT. See STAPHYLEA

BLANKET FLOWER. See GAILLARDIA grandiflora

BLAZING STAR. See MENTZELIA

BLEEDING HEART. See DICENTRA

BLETILLA striata
(B. hyacinthina)

CHINESE GROUND ORCHID

Orchidaceae

TERRESTRIAL ORCHID

🗲 ZONES 4–9, 12–24, 26, 28–31, WARMER PARTS OF 32

☼ UNDER HIGH-BRANCHING TREES OR LATH

🌢 FREQUENT WATER DURING GROWTH

Bletilla striata

A terrestrial orchid native to China and Japan. Lavender, cattleya-like, 1–2-in. flowers, up to a dozen on 1½–2-ft. stem, produced for about 6 weeks beginning in May or June. Pale green leaves, three to six to a plant. 'Alba' is a white-flowered form.

Plant the tuberlike roots outdoors in early spring for spring and early summer bloom. Grow in pot or in ground under high-branching trees or under lath. Hardy to about 20°F/−7°C (to 0°F/−8°C if soil is well drained and plant is mulched). Dies back to ground each winter. In time will develop large clumps if grown in light shade and in a moist soil rich in humus. Can be divided in early spring before growth starts, but don't do it too often; blooms best when crowded.

BLOODLEAF. See IRESINE

BLOOD LILY. See HAEMANTHUS katherinae

BLOOD-RED TRUMPET VINE. See DISTICTIS buccinatoria

BLOODROOT. See SANGUINARIA canadensis

BLUEBEARD. See CARYOPTERIS

BLUEBELL. See ENDYMION, SCILLA

BLUEBERRY

Ericaceae

DECIDUOUS SHRUBS

ZONES VARY BY TYPE

FULL SUN

DON'T LET SOIL SURFACE DRY OUT

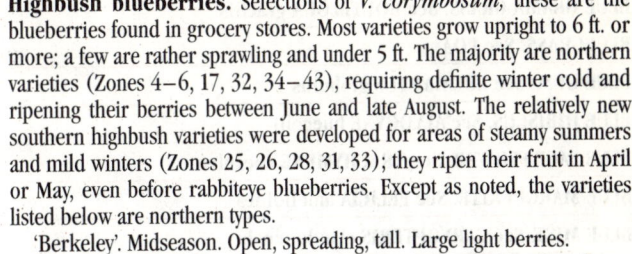

Blueberry

Native to eastern North America, blueberries thrive under conditions that suit rhododendrons and azaleas, to which they are related. Require sun and cool, moist, well-drained acid soil (pH 4.5–5.5). Outside their favored regions, either create proper soil conditions or grow plants in containers.

Most blueberries grown for fruit are also handsome plants suitable for hedges or shrub borders. Dark green or blue-green leaves change to red, orange, or yellow combinations in autumn. Spring flowers are tiny, white or pinkish, urn shaped. Summer fruit is very decorative.

Blueberries are available bare-root or in containers. Plant in early spring in cold regions, autumn in mild climates. Position crown so that it is no deeper than ½ in. below the ground. Grow at least two varieties for better pollination, resulting in larger berries and bigger yields per plant. Choose varieties that ripen at different times, for a long harvest season. Blueberries have fine roots near the soil surface; keep them moist but don't subject them to standing water. A 4–6-in.-thick mulch of sawdust, ground bark, or the like will protect roots and help conserve soil moisture. Don't cultivate around the plants.

Prune to prevent overbearing. Plants shape themselves but often produce so many fruit buds that berries are undersized and growth of plants slows down. Keep first-year plants from bearing by stripping off flowers. On older plants, cut back ends of twigs to point where fruit buds are widely spaced. Or simply remove some of oldest branches each year. Also get rid of all weak shoots. Plants don't usually have serious problems requiring regular controls in home gardens. Netting will keep birds from getting the berries before you do.

The following are the major types of blueberries grown. (For ornamental relatives, see *Vaccinium*.)

Lowbush blueberries. Zones 34, 37–45. Varieties of this ground cover species (*Vaccinium angustifolium*) exist, but seedlings or wild plants are most commonly cultivated. In Maine and Canada's Maritime provinces, fruit from wild plants is harvested in commercial quantities. Very sweet bluish black berries in summer. Plants grow from a few inches to 2 ft. tall; they spread by underground roots to cover large areas. They can thrive in poor, rocky, thin soil as long as it is acid and drains well. Rejuvenate plants by cutting all growth back to 1–2 in. every few years.

Lowbush has been hybridized with highbush varieties to produce very hardy types called half-high blueberries, growing to 2–4 ft. tall. The hybrids include 'North Country', 'Northblue', 'Northsky', and 'St. Cloud'.

Highbush blueberries. Selections of *V. corymbosum*, these are the blueberries found in grocery stores. Most varieties grow upright to 6 ft. or more; a few are rather sprawling and under 5 ft. The majority are northern varieties (Zones 4–6, 17, 32, 34–43), requiring definite winter cold and ripening their berries between June and late August. The relatively new southern highbush varieties were developed for areas of steamy summers and mild winters (Zones 25, 26, 28, 31, 33); they ripen their fruit in April or May, even before rabbiteye blueberries. Except as noted, the varieties listed below are northern types.

'Berkeley'. Midseason. Open, spreading, tall. Large light berries.

'Bluecrop'. Midseason. Erect, tall growth. Large berries. Excellent flavor. Attractive shrub.

'Blueray'. Midseason. Vigorous, tall. Large, highly flavored, crisp berries. Attractive shrub.

'Bluetta'. Early. More cold hardy than 'Earliblue', but fruit not as tasty.

'Collins'. Midseason. Erect, attractive bush. Small clusters of large, very tasty fruit.

'Concord'. Midseason. Upright to spreading growth. Attractive. Large berry, tart flavored until fully ripe.

'Coville'. Late. Tall, open, spreading. Unusually large leaves. Very attractive. Long clusters of very large light blue berries.

'Dixi'. Late. Not attractive plant—tall and open. Needs heavy pruning. Berries, among largest and tastiest, are medium blue, firm and sweet.

'Earliblue'. Early. Tall, erect. Large, heavy leaves. Large berries of excellent flavor.

'Elliott'. Late. Tall, upright. Medium to large berries of excellent flavor.

'Georgiagem'. Southern highbush. Very early. Moderately vigorous, upright. Medium-size, firm fruit of good flavor.

'Herbert'. Late. Vigorous, open, spreading. Among the biggest, best-flavored berries.

'Jersey'. Late. Tall, erect growing. Large light blue berries. Very bland.

'O'Neal'. Southern highbush. Very early. Large, flavorful berries.

'Patriot'. Midseason. Large, firm, tasty berries. Consistently high yields.

'Rancocas'. Midseason. Tall, erect, open, arching habit. Excellent shrub. Leaves smaller than most. Needs heavy pruning. Berries mild and sweet. Dependable old-timer.

'Sharpblue'. Southern highbush. Very early. Flavorful berries prone to bird damage. Attractive landscape plant.

'Weymouth'. Early. Ripens all berries quickly. Erect, medium height. Large dark blue berries of fair quality; lack aroma.

Rabbiteye blueberries. Zones 26 (upper portion), 28, 31, 33. Like southern highbush blueberries, these selections of the Southeast native *V. ashei* are adapted to hot, humid summers and mild winters. They are often taller than highbush plants, and they ripen their large light blue berries a little later—in May and June. Plant two or three varieties for good cross-pollination. Good fall color, even in warmest regions. The following list includes some of the most flavorful varieties.

'Brightwell'. Midseason. Hardy to frost. Firm berries.

'Climax'. Early. Upright, spreading. Good pollinator.

'Premier'. Early. Large, good-quality fruit.

'Tifblue'. Midseason to late. Vigorous, upright. Good commercial variety. Firm, excellent flavor. Tart until completely ripe.

'Woodward'. Early. Shorter, more spreading than other rabbiteyes. Rather soft berries, tart until fully ripe.

BLUE BLOSSOM. See CEANOTHUS thyrsiflorus

BLUE BUTTONS. See KNAUTIA arvensis

BLUE DAZE. See EVOLVULUS glomeratus

BLUE-EYED GRASS. See SISYRINCHIUM

BLUE-EYED MARY. See OMPHALODES verna

BLUE FESCUE. See FESTUCA ovina 'Glauca'

BLUE GINGER. See DICHORISANDRA thyrsiflora

B

BLUE GRAMA GRASS. See BOUTELOUA gracilis

BLUEGRASS. See POA

BLUE GUM. See EUCALYPTUS globulus

BLUE HIBISCUS. See ALYOGYNE huegelii

BLUE LACE FLOWER. See TRACHYMENE coerulea

BLUE MARGUERITE. See FELICIA amelloides

BLUE MIST. See CARYOPTERIS clandonensis

BLUE SPIRAEA. See CARYOPTERIS incana

BLUE STAR CREEPER. See LAURENTIA fluviatilis

BLUE STAR FLOWER. See AMSONIA

BLUETS. See HOUSTONIA caerulea

BLUEWEED. See ECHIUM vulgare

BOCCONIA cordata. See MACLEAYA cordata

BOG ROSEMARY. See ANDROMEDA polifolia

BOLTONIA asteroides

Asteraceae (Compositae)

PERENNIAL

⚡ ZONES 1–24, 28–45

☼ ◑ FULL SUN OR LIGHT SHADE

💧 REGULAR WATER

Boltonia asteroides

In late summer, tall stems bear broad, mounded clusters of small, yellow-centered white to blue flowers that much resemble Michaelmas daisies. Plants grow to 6 ft. or more; may be floppy with overhead watering. 'Snowbank' is more compact (to 5 ft. tall) and upright, with larger flowers of a clearer white. 'Pink Beauty' has lilac pink flowers. Plants survive in poor soil and with reduced water, but may bloom feebly on 2-ft. stems.

Bombacaceae. This tropical family of trees and shrubs includes two genera with very showy flowers: *Chorisia* and *Bombax*.

BOMBAX malabaricum

Bombacaceae

DECIDUOUS TREE

⚡ ZONES 24, 25

☼ FULL SUN

💧 REGULAR WATER

Bombax malabaricum

Native to Asian tropics. Unusual specimen tree to about 75 ft. tall. Distinguished by thick, buttressed trunk, prickly bark, and spectacular midwinter show of vivid red or orange, tulip-shaped flowers in clusters at branch ends. Tolerates various soils and light salt drift from the ocean.

BONESET. See EUPATORIUM perfoliatum

BONNET BELLFLOWER. See CODONOPSIS clematidea

Boraginaceae. The borage family consists of annuals and perennials (rarely shrubs or trees), most of which have small flowers in coiled clusters that straighten as bloom progresses. Forget-me-not (*Myosotis*) is a familiar example.

BORAGO officinalis

BORAGE

Boraginaceae

ANNUAL HERB

⚡ ALL ZONES

☼ ◑ ● SUN OR SHADE

💧💧 ● REGULAR TO MODERATE WATER

Grows 1–3 ft. high. Bristly, gray-green leaves up to 4–6 in. long are edible, with a cucumberlike flavor. Blue, saucer-shaped, nodding flowers in leafy clusters on branched stems.

Borago officinalis

Usually sown in spring after frost danger; best as a fall–spring crop in climates with mild winters and hot, humid summers. Tolerates poor soil. Seeds itself but doesn't transplant easily. Use small tender leaves in salads; you can also pickle them or cook them as greens. Cut flowers for arrangements or use as an attractive garnish. In dry climates, makes a good drought-tolerant ground cover and soil binder.

BOSTON FERN. See NEPHROLEPIS exaltata 'Bostoniensis'

BOSTON IVY. See PARTHENOCISSUS tricuspidata

BO-TREE. See FICUS religiosa

BOTTLEBRUSH. See CALLISTEMON, MELALEUCA

BOTTLE PALM. See BEAUCARNEA recurvata

BOTTLE TREE. See BRACHYCHITON populneus

BOUGAINVILLEA

Nyctaginaceae

EVERGREEN SHRUBBY VINES

⚡ ZONES 5, 6, 12, 13, 15–17, 19, 22–29

☼ ◑ LIGHT SHADE IN HOTTEST AREAS

💧💧 REGULAR TO MODERATE WATER

Reliably hardy in Zones 22–27, yet widely and satisfyingly grown in zones of minimum frost: 12, 13, 15–17, 19, 21, 28. Use has even extended into Zones 5, 6, and 29, thanks to low-growing shrubby types that can be purchased in full bloom

Bougainvillea 'San Diego Red'

in gallon cans and grown as container plants. They are used on terrace or patio as summer annuals and moved to a protected area over winter. Where frosts are routine, vines should be given protected warm wall or warmest spot in garden. If vines get by first winter or two, they will be big enough to take most winter damage and recover. In any case, flower production comes so quickly that replacement is not a real deterrent.

Bougainvillea's vibrant colors come not from its small inconspicuous flowers, but from the three large bracts that surround them. Vines make dense cover of medium-size, medium green leaves. Vigor and growth habit vary by species and variety. Plant in sun (in light shade in hottest areas) in early spring (after frosts), to give longest possible growing time before next frost.

Supply sturdy supports and keep shoots tied up so they won't whip in wind and strong gusts won't shred leaves against sharp thorns along stems.

Fertilize in spring and summer. In dry climates, water normally while plants are growing fast; then ease off temporarily in midsummer to promote better flowering. Don't be afraid to prune—to renew plant, shape, or direct growth. Prune heavily after bloom. On wall-grown plants, nip back long stems during growing season to produce more flowering wood. Shrubby kinds or heavily pruned plants make good self-supporting container shrubs for terrace or patio. Without support and with occasional corrective pruning, bougainvillea can make broad, sprawling shrub, bank and ground cover, or hanging basket plant.

PLANTING A BOUGAINVILLEA?

Watch those roots—they're fragile and do not knit easily. Here is how to keep the root ball intact during planting. Put the plant in an extra-wide planting hole, can and all. Insert blades of sharp, needle-nose shears into one of the drain holes and cut all the way around the can's bottom. Slide the detached bottom out from under the can. Then, make a cut down one side of can from the top to bottom. Make another cut on the opposite side. Fill in with soil around the root ball. Slide the two detached pieces up and out.

All of the following are tall-growing vines except those noted as shrubs. Double-flowering kinds can look messy because they hold faded flowers for a long time.

'Afterglow'. Yellow orange; heavy bloom. Open growth, sparse foliage.

'Barbara Karst'. Bright red in sun, bluish crimson in shade; blooms young and for long period. Vigorous growth. Fast comeback after frost.

'Betty Hendry' ('Indian Maid'). Basically red but with touches of yellow and purple. Blooms young and for a long period.

B. brasiliensis. See *B. spectabilis*

'Brilliant Variegated'. Spreading, mounding shrub. Leaves variegated with gray green and silver. Brick red bracts. Often used in hanging baskets, pots.

'California Gold' ('Sunset'). Deep golden yellow. Blooms young.

'Camarillo Festival'. Hot pink to gold blend.

'Cherry Blossom'. Double-flowered rose pink, with white to pale green centers.

'Crimson Jewel'. Vigorous shrubby, sprawling plant. Good in containers, as shrub, or as sunny bank cover. Lower growth, better color than 'Temple Fire'. Heavy bloom, long season.

'Crimson Lake'. See 'Mrs. Butt'

'Don Mario'. Large, vigorous vine with huge clusters of deep purple-red blooms.

'Hawaii'. ('Raspberry Ice'). Shrubby, mounding, spreading. Leaves have golden yellow margins. New leaves tinged red. Bracts red. Good hanging basket plant. Regardless of its tropical name, it's one of the hardiest.

'Isabel Greensmith'. Bracts variously described as orange, red orange, or red with yellow tinting.

'Jamaica White'. Bracts white, veined light green. Blooms young. Moderately vigorous.

'James Walker'. Big reddish purple bracts on big vine.

'La Jolla'. Bright red bracts, compact, shrubby habit. Good shrub, container plant.

'Lavender Queen'. An improved *B. spectabilis,* with bigger bracts, heavier bloom.

'Manila Red'. Many rows of magenta red bracts make heavy clusters of double-looking bloom.

'Mary Palmer's Enchantment'. Very vigorous, large-growing vine with pure white bracts.

'Mrs. Butt' ('Crimson Lake'). Old-fashioned variety with good crimson color. Needs lots of heat for bloom. Moderately vigorous.

'Orange King'. Bronzy orange. Open growth. Needs long summer, no frost.

'Pink Tiara'. Abundant pale pink to rose bracts over long season.

'Raspberry Ice'. See 'Hawaii'

'Rosea'. Large rose red bracts on large vine.

'Rosenka'. Can be held to shrub proportions if occasional wild shoot is pruned out. Gold bracts age pink.

'San Diego Red' ('San Diego', 'Scarlett O'Hara'). One of best on all counts: large, deep green leaves that hold well in cold winters; deep red bracts over long season; hardiness equal to old-fashioned purple kind. Vigorous, high climbing. Can be trained to tree form by staking and pruning.

'Southern Rose'. Lavender rose to pink.

B. spectabilis (B. brasiliensis). Hardy and vigorous. Blooms well in cool summers. Purple bracts.

'Tahitian Dawn'. Big vine with gold bracts aging to rosy purple.

'Tahitian Maid'. Extra rows of bracts give double effect to blush-pink clusters.

'Temple Fire'. Shrublike growth to 4 ft. high, 6 ft. wide. Partially deciduous. Bronze red.

'Texas Dawn'. Choice, vigorous plant. Purplish pink bracts in large sprays.

'Torch Glow'. An oddity: an erect, multistemmed plant to 6 ft. It needs no support. Reddish pink bracts close to stems are partially hidden by foliage.

'White Madonna'. Pure white bracts.

BOULDER RASPBERRY. See RUBUS deliciosus

BOUNCING BET. See SAPONARIA officinalis

BOUSSINGAULTIA. See ANREDERA cordifolia

BOUTELOUA gracilis

BLUE GRAMA GRASS, MOSQUITO GRASS

Poaceae (Gramineae)

BUNCHING GRASS

ZONES 1–3, 7–11, 14–24, 29, 30, 33, 35, 41, 43, 45

FULL SUN

MODERATE TO LITTLE WATER

Bouteloua gracilis

Ornamental perennial grass to 20 in. high, with very narrow, semievergreen leaves and 1½-in.-long, dark red to purple flower spikes. Spikes are held at right angle to slender stems and have the look of hovering mosquitoes. Also used as pasture grass. If mowed at 1½ in., makes a fair lawn requiring little maintenance or water; most useful in sunny, arid, alkaline-soil regions of Rocky Mountains and High Plains (Zones 1–3, 35, 41, 43, 45). Sow seed at 1 lb. per 1,000 sq. ft.

BOUVARDIA

Rubiaceae

EVERGREEN SHRUBS

ZONES VARY BY SPECIES

PARTIAL SHADE

WATER NEEDS VARY BY SPECIES

Bouvardia longiflora

Native to New Mexico, Arizona, Mexico, and Central America. Loose, often straggling growth habit. Showy clusters of tubular flowers. Sometimes grown in greenhouses in colder climates.

B. longiflora 'Albatross' (B. humboldtii 'Albatross'). Zones 12, 13, 16, 17, 19–27. Jasmine-scented, 3-in. snow-white blossoms on a weak-stemmed plant 2–3 ft. high. Flowers appear at almost any time; excellent in bouquets. Pinch out stem tips to make plant bushier. If soil is poor, grow in tubs or raised beds in rich, fast-draining soil mix. Regular water. 'Stephanie' is more compact and floriferous.

B. ternifolia (B. jacquinii). Zones 8–10, 12–28. To 6 ft. tall, with unscented, 1-in. red flowers. Though lacking the fragrance of *B. longiflora* 'Albatross', this species is hardier, easier to grow, and better looking after the flowers are gone. Drought tolerant. There are forms with pink, rose, or coral blossoms.

B

BOWER VINE. See PANDOREA jasminoides

BOWLES' GOLDEN GRASS. See MILIUM effusum 'Aureum'

BOWMAN'S ROOT. See GILLENIA trifoliata

BOX, BOXWOOD. See BUXUS

BOX ELDER. See ACER negundo

BOX HUCKLEBERRY. See GAYLUSSACIA brachycera

BOXTHORN. See LYCIUM chinense

BOYSENBERRY. See BLACKBERRY

BRACHYCHITON (Sterculia)

Sterculiaceae
EVERGREEN OR DECIDUOUS TREES
🗡 ZONES VARY BY SPECIES
☼ FULL SUN
◐ REGULAR TO LITTLE WATER

Brachychiton populneus

Native to Australia. All have woody, canoe-shaped fruits that delight flower arrangers but are merely litter to some gardeners. Grow in well-drained soil.

B. acerifolius (Sterculia acerifolia). FLAME TREE, AUSTRALIAN FLAME TREE. Deciduous for brief period. Zones 16–21, 23, 25–27. Hardy to 25°F/–4°C. When at its best, a most spectacular red-flowering tree reaching 60 ft. or more. Strong, heavy, smooth trunk, usually green. Leaves are handsome, glossy, bright green, 10-in.-wide fans, deeply lobed. Showiest flowering season usually late spring. Tree wholly or partially covered with great clusters of small, ¾-in., tubular, red or orange-red bells. Leaves drop before flowers appear in portion of tree that blooms.

B. populneus (Sterculia diversifolia). BOTTLE TREE. Evergreen. Zones 12–28. Moderate growth to 30–50 ft., 30-ft. spread. Common name from very heavy trunk, broad at base, tapering quickly. Leaves (2–3 in. long), a fresh green year-round, give general effect of poplar. They shimmer in breeze like aspens. Clusters of small, bell-shaped, white flowers in late spring noticeable close up. Appreciated in low and intermediate deserts, where it is frequently used as a shade tree and as a screen or windbreak. Susceptible to Texas root rot.

BRACHYCOME

SWAN RIVER DAISY
Asteraceae (Compositae)
ANNUALS AND PERENNIALS
🗡 ZONES VARY BY SPECIES
☼ FULL SUN
◐ REGULAR WATER

Brachycome iberidifolia

Neat, charming Australian daisies make mounds 1 ft. tall, 1½ ft. across, with finely divided leaves and a profusion of inch-wide flowers in spring and summer. Use in rock garden, at front of border, in containers or raised beds. Often spelled *Brachyscome*.

B. iberidifolia. Annual. All zones. Flowers are blue, white, or pink. Sow seed where plants are to grow. For best results in regions with mild winters and steamy summers, grow between fall and spring.

B. multifida. Perennial. Zones 14–24, 28. Very similar to *B. iberidifolia*. Blue flowers most common. Propagate by cuttings.

BRACKEN. See PTERIDIUM aquilinum

BRAHEA (Erythea)

Arecaceae (Palmae)
PALMS
🗡 ZONES VARY BY SPECIES
☼ FULL SUN
◐ VERY DROUGHT TOLERANT

Brahea armata

These fan palms from Mexico are somewhat like the more familiar washingtonias in appearance, but with important differences. All tolerate aridity.

B. armata. MEXICAN BLUE PALM. Zones 10, 12–17, 19–24. Hardy to 18°F/–8°C. Grows slowly to 40 ft. tall, with top spreading to 6–8 ft. Leaves silvery blue in color, almost white. Conspicuous creamy flowers. Takes heat and wind.

B. brandegeei. SAN JOSE HESPER PALM. Zones 19, 21–24. Hardy to 26°F/–3°C. Slow grower with slender, flexible trunk. Eventually tall; reaches 125 ft. in its native Baja California. Trunk sheds leaves when old. Leaves 3 ft. long, light gray green.

BRAKE. See PTERIS

BRAMBLE. See RUBUS

BRASSAIA actinophylla. See SCHEFFLERA actinophylla

Brassicaceae. The mustard, or cress, family contains many food plants and ornamentals as well as a number of weeds. The notable characteristic is a four-petaled flower resembling cross. Familiar members include all the cabbage group, radishes, turnips, stock *(Matthiola)*, and sweet alyssum *(Lobularia)*. This family was formerly called Cruciferae.

BRAZILIAN BUTTERFLY TREE. See BAUHINIA

BRAZILIAN FLAME BUSH. See CALLIANDRA tweedii

BRAZILIAN PLUME FLOWER. See JUSTICIA carnea

BRAZILIAN SKY FLOWER. See DURANTA stenostachya

BREYNIA disticha (B. nervosa)

SNOW BUSH
Euphorbiaceae
EVERGREEN SHRUB
🗡 ZONES 24–27; OR INDOORS
◐ PARTIAL SHADE
◐ REGULAR TO MODERATE WATER

Breynia disticha

Usually seen as a house plant or indoor/outdoor plant, except in the mildest frost-free climates. Open grower 3–4 ft. tall, with zigzag red branches set with ½–2-in. roundish leaves neatly arranged in two ranks. Leaves are liberally splashed with white; 'Roseo-Picta' has leaves splashed with white and pink. Likes humidity in the air and usually does poorly in hot, dry rooms.

FOR GROWING SYMBOL EXPLANATIONS PLEASE SEE PAGE 161

BRIMEURA amethystina
(Hyacinthus amethystinus)

Liliaceae

BULB

✿ ZONES 1–24, 29–43

☼ FULL SUN

● REGULAR WATER DURING GROWTH AND BLOOM

Brimeura amethystina

Bulbs, leaf rosettes exactly resemble small hyacinths. For rock gardens or naturalizing. Plants bloom in spring or early summer, bearing loose spikes of clear blue bells with paler blue streaks on 6–8-in.-tall stems. Plant in mid- to late autumn, 2 in. deep, 3 in. apart. Mulch in areas where winters are very cold.

BRIZA maxima

RATTLESNAKE GRASS, QUAKING GRASS

Poaceae (Gramineae)

ANNUAL

✿ ALL ZONES

☼ FULL SUN

●● MUCH TO LITTLE WATER

Briza maxima

Native to Mediterranean region. Ornamental grass of delicate, graceful form; used effectively in dry arrangements and bouquets. Grows 1–2 ft. high. Leaves are ¼ in. wide, to 6 in. long. Clusters of nodding, seed-bearing spikelets, ½ in. long (or longer), papery and straw colored when dry, dangle on threadlike stems. Spikelets resemble rattlesnake rattles. Scatter seed where plants are to grow; thin seedlings to 1 ft. apart. Often grows wild along roadsides, in fields. *B. media* is similar but perennial.

BROCCOLI

Brassicaceae (Cruciferae)

BIENNIAL GROWN AS ANNUAL

✿ ALL ZONES

☼ FULL SUN

● REGULAR WATER

Broccoli

Among cole crops (cabbage and its close relatives), broccoli is the best all-round choice for the home gardener; bears over long season, is not difficult to grow. Grows to 4 ft. and has branching habit. Central stalk bears cluster of green flower buds that may reach 6 in. in diameter. When central cluster is removed, side branches will lengthen and produce smaller clusters. Good varieties are 'Calabrese', 'Cleopatra', 'De Cicco', 'Green Goliath', 'Italian Green Sprouting'.

Broccoli is a cool-season plant that tends to bolt into flower when temperatures are high, so plant it to mature during cool weather. In mild climates plant in late summer, fall, or winter for winter or early spring crops. In cold-winter areas set out young plants about 2 weeks before last frost.

Young plants resist frost but not hard freezes. Good guide to planting time is appearance of young plants in nurseries. Young plants ready to be planted take 4 to 6 weeks to develop from seed. One pack of seed will produce far more plants than even the largest home garden can handle, so save surplus seed for later plantings. A dozen plants will supply a family of four.

Choose a sunny location; space plants 1½–2 ft. apart in rows and leave 3 ft. between rows. Keeps plants growing vigorously with regular deep irrigation during dry periods and one or two fertilizer applications before heads start to form. Harvest 50 to 100 days after setting out plants. Cut

heads before clustered buds begin to open, including 5–6 in. of edible stalk and leaves. Subject to same pests as cabbage.

BRODIAEA

Liliaceae

CORMS

✿ ZONES VARY BY SPECIES; OR GROW IN POTS

☼ FULL SUN

● REGULAR WATER DURING GROWTH AND BLOOM

Brodiaea elegans

Many are natives of the Pacific Coast, where they bloom in sunny fields and meadows in spring and early summer. Few grasslike leaves; a cluster of funnel-shaped or tubular, ½–2-in.-long flowers tops the stem during bloom. Good cut flowers. After bloom, plants die to the ground.

In nature they are often found in adobe soil, in areas where it rains heavily in winter and early spring and corms completely dry out in summer. They appreciate similar conditions in gardens; where you can't keep corms dry in summer, plant in sandy or gritty soil to lessen chance of rot. Plant corms 2–3 in. deep. In cold-winter areas grow in containers or mulch to protect from freezing and thawing.

Brodiaea includes many plants now listed under different names. Cross-references below will guide you to appropriate entries under *Triteleia*.

B. coronaria (B. grandiflora). HARVEST BRODIAEA. Zones 4–9, 14–24, 29, 30. Clusters of dark blue, inch-long flowers on 6–10-in. stems.

B. elegans. HARVEST BRODIAEA. Zones 1–9, 14–24, 29–43. Similar to B. *coronaria*, but taller (to 16 in.). Often seen as *B. grandiflora* or *B. coronaria*.

B. grandiflora. See B. coronaria. Another plant known by same name is *Triteleia grandiflora*.

B. laxa. See Triteleia laxa.

B. minor. Dark blue flowers on stems 3–4 in. long, rarely 1 ft. long.

B. 'Queen Fabiola'. See Triteleia 'Queen Fabiola'

B. tubergenii. See Triteleia tubergenii

BROMELIA balansae

HEART OF FLAME

Bromeliaceae

PERENNIAL

✿ ZONES 19–27

☼ FULL SUN

● REGULAR WATER

Bromelia balansae

Pineapple relative. Forms impressive cluster of 30–50 arching, saw-toothed leaves, glossy dark green above, whitish beneath. To 4 ft. tall, 4–6 ft. across. Center leaves turn bright scarlet in spring or early summer. From this center rises a stalk bearing a spike of rose-colored flowers margined with white. Needs warm nights to perform satisfactorily. Almost any soil if drainage is good. Feed lightly once or twice in summer.

FASTEN A BROMELIAD TO A TREE BRANCH

In mild-winter climates, bromeliad fanciers sometimes fasten these vibrant, junglelike plants to tree branches, packing sphagnum moss around the roots to hold moisture and encourage root growth. More often these plants are kept in pots of loose, fast-draining, highly organic growing mix. Feed lightly but infrequently and keep central cups filled with water.

B

Bromeliaceae. The bromelia, or pineapple, family; all its members are called bromeliads. Most bromeliads are stemless perennials with clustered leaves and showy flowers in unbranched or branched clusters. Leaves of many kinds are handsomely marked, and the flower clusters gain beauty from colorful bracts. Pineapple is the best-known example.

Bromeliads are considered choice house plants. Kinds most often grown indoors are, in their native homes, epiphytes: plants that perch on trees or rocks and gain their sustenance from rain and from whatever leaf mold gathers around their roots. These often have cupped leaf bases that hold water between rains. In mildest climates, many of these epiphytes grow well outdoors in sheltered places.

A few bromeliads (*Puya* and *Bromelia* are the best known) are terrestrial plants that resemble yuccas and thrive in the same conditions.

BRONZE DRACAENA. See CORDYLINE australis 'Atropurpurea'

BROOM. See CYTISUS, GENISTA, SPARTIUM junceum

BROUSSONETIA papyrifera

PAPER MULBERRY

Moraceae

DECIDUOUS TREE

☘ ZONES 3–24, 28–33

☼ FULL SUN

💧 💧 MUCH TO LITTLE WATER

Broussonetia papyrifera

Native to China and Japan. Common name comes from inner bark, used for making paper and Polynesian tapa cloth. Has been sold as *Morus papyrifera*. Valuable as shade tree where soil and climate limit choices. Tolerates heat, drought, strong winds, city pollution, and stony, sterile, or alkaline soils.

Moderate to fast growth to 50 ft., with dense, broad crown to 40 ft. across. Often considerably smaller and more shrublike in gardens. Suckering habit can be problem in rainy climates and highly cultivated gardens; very weedy in the South. Good in rough bank plantings. Smooth gray bark can become ridged and furrowed with age, as seen in handsome old specimens in Colonial Williamsburg. Heart-shaped, 4–8-in., rough leaves, gray and velvety beneath; edges toothed, often lobed when young. Flowers on male trees are catkins; on female trees, rounded flower heads are followed by red fruits if a male tree is growing nearby.

BROWALLIA

AMETHYST FLOWER

Solanaceae

ANNUALS, SOMETIMES LIVING OVER AS PERENNIALS

☘ ALL ZONES

☼ WARM SHADE OR FILTERED SUNLIGHT

💧 REGULAR WATER

Browallia speciosa

Choice plant for connoisseur of blue flowers. Bears one-sided clusters of lobelia-like blooms in brilliant blue, violet, or white; blue flowers are more striking because of contrasting white eye or throat. Blooms profusely in warm shade or filtered sunlight. Graceful in hanging basket or pots. Fine cut flower.

Sow seeds in early spring for summer bloom, in fall for winter color indoors or in greenhouses. Plants need warmth, regular moisture. You can lift vigorous plants in fall, cut back, and pot; new growth will produce flowers through winter in warm spot. Rarely sold as plants in nurseries; get seeds from specialists.

B. americana. Branching, 1–2 ft. high; roundish leaves. Violet or blue flowers ½ in. long, ½ in. across, borne among leaves. 'Sapphire', dwarf compact variety, dark blue with white eye, is very free blooming. This species and its variety are often listed in catalogs as *B. elata* or *B. e.* 'Sapphire'.

B. speciosa. Lives over as perennial in mild-winter climates. Sprawling, to 1–2 ft. high. Flowers dark purple above, pale lilac beneath, 1½–2 in. across. 'Blue Bells Improved', lavender blue, grows 10 in. tall, needs no pinching to make it branch. 'Marine Bells' has deep indigo flowers, 'Silver Bells' white flowers.

BRUGMANSIA (Datura)

ANGEL'S TRUMPET

Solanaceae

EVERGREEN TO SEMIEVERGREEN SHRUBS

☘ ZONES 16–27; OR GROW IN POTS

☼ ◑ ● SUN OR SHADE

💧 REGULAR WATER

◊ ALL PARTS ARE POISONOUS IF INGESTED

Brugmansia candida

Related to the annual or perennial jimsonweeds. All are large shrubs that can be trained as small trees. With their outsize leaves and big tubular flowers, they are dominating plants that will astonish your visitors. Main bloom period is summer and fall.

Provide sheltered position; wind tatters the foliage. Expect frost damage and unattractive winter appearance. Prune in early spring after last frost; cut back branchlets to one or two buds. Beyond hardiness range, grow in tubs and move to a frost-free site in cold weather. Tubbed plants can be wintered indoors with a little light and very little water.

B. arborea. Plants usually offered under this name are either *B. candida* or *B. suaveolens*. The true *B. arborea* has smaller flowers.

B. candida. Native to Peru. Fast and rank growing with soft, pulpy growth to 10–15 ft. (6 ft. or more in one season). Dull green, large leaves in the 8–12-in. range. Heavy, single or double white trumpets, to 8 in. long or more, are fragrant, especially at night. Shrub is showy in moonlight.

B. sanguinea. Native to Peru. Fast growing to 12–15 ft. Leaves bright green to 8 in. long. Trumpets, orange red with yellow veinings, about 10 in. long, hang straight down like bells from new growth. Rare.

B. suaveolens. Native to Brazil. Similar to *B. candida*, but leaves and flowers are somewhat larger and flowers less fragrant.

B. versicolor. To 15 ft. tall. Flowers white or peach colored. Named versions of uncertain origin include 'Charles Grimaldi' (pale orange yellow) and 'Frosty Pink' (cream deepening to pink).

BRUNFELSIA pauciflora (B. calycina)

Solanaceae

EVERGREEN SHRUBS

☘ ZONES 12–17, 20–28, EXCEPT AS NOTED

◑ PARTIAL SHADE

💧 REGULAR WATER

Brunfelsia pauciflora
'Floribunda'

Grown for showy clusters of white-throated, rich dark purple tubular flowers opening to a flat disk; spring and early summer bloom. In all but the warmest locations they lose most of their foliage for a short period. These handsome plants deserve extra attention—give them rich, well-drained soil, a constant supply of moisture, and regular feedings through the growing season. Prune in spring to remove scraggly growth and to shape. Use where you can admire the flower show. Good in containers; can also be grown in a greenhouse. The following are the forms available.

'Eximia' (*B. calycina eximia*). Somewhat dwarfed, compact version of 'Floribunda', a more widely planted variety. Flowers are a bit smaller but more generously produced.

'Floribunda'. YESTERDAY-TODAY-AND-TOMORROW. Common name comes from quick color change of blossoms: purple ("yesterday"), lavender ("today"), white ("tomorrow"). Flowers, several in a cluster and each flaring to 2 in. wide, profusely displayed all over plant. Oval leaves, 3–4 in. long, dark green above, pale green below. In partial shade plant will reach 10 ft. or more with several stems from base, but can be held to 3 ft. by pruning. Rather spreading habit.

'Macrantha' (*B. floribunda* 'Lindeniana', *B. grandiflora*). Zones 12, 13, 16, 17, 20–28. In addition to being less cold hardy, differs from the above in having fewer but larger flowers, 2–4 in. across. Also has a more slender habit and bigger leaves, to 8 in. long, 2½ in. wide.

Brunfelsia pauciflora 'Floribunda'

BRUNNERA macrophylla

	BRUNNERA
	Boraginaceae
	PERENNIAL
❁	ZONES 1–24, 31–45
☼ ◐	WILL TAKE FULL SUN IN COOL-SUMMER AREAS
♦	REGULAR WATER

Brunnera macrophylla

R eaches 1½ ft. tall; leaves heart shaped, dark green, 3–4 in. wide. Variegated forms also available. In spring, plants produce airy clusters of tiny clear blue forget-me-not flowers with yellow centers. Uses: informal ground cover under high-branching deciduous trees; among spring-flowering shrubs such as forsythia, deciduous magnolias; filler between newly planted evergreen shrubs. Freely self-sows once established. Planted seeds often difficult to germinate (try freezing them before sowing). Needs well-drained, moisture-retentive soil. Increase by dividing clumps in fall.

BRUNSVIGIA rosea. See AMARYLLIS belladonna

BRUSH CHERRY, AUSTRALIAN BRUSH CHERRY. See SYZYGIUM paniculatum

BRUSSELS SPROUTS

	Brassicaceae (Cruciferae)
	BIENNIAL GROWN AS ANNUAL
❁	ALL ZONES
☼	FULL SUN
♦	REGULAR WATER

A cabbage relative of unusual appearance. Mature plant has crown of fairly large leaves, and its tall stem is completely covered with tiny sprouts. Fairly easy to grow where summers are not too hot, long, or dry. 'Jade Cross Hybrid' is easiest to grow and most heat tolerant; 'Long Island Improved' ('Catskill') is standard market variety. You may have to grow your own from seed. Sow outdoors or in flats in April; transplant young plants in June or early July to sunny place. Sprouts are ready in fall. In mild climates plant in fall or winter for winter and spring use.

Brussels Sprouts

Treat the same as broccoli. When big leaves start to turn yellow, begin picking. Snap off little sprouts from bottom first—best when slightly smaller than golf ball. Leave little sprouts on upper stem to mature. After picking, remove only leaves below harvested sprouts. A single plant will yield from 50 to 100 sprouts. Subject to same pests as cabbage.

BUCHLOE dactyloides

	BUFFALO GRASS
	Poaceae (Gramineae)
	PERENNIAL GRASS
❁	ZONES 1–3, 10, 11; DRIER PARTS of 29, 30, 33, 35, 41, 43
☼	FULL SUN
♦	MODERATE TO LITTLE WATER

Buchloe dactyloides

M akes a low-maintenance, low-water-need lawn. Slow to sprout and fill in, it spreads rapidly by surface runners once established and makes matted, reasonably dense turf that takes hard wear and looks fairly good with very little irrigation during dry periods. Gray green from late spring to hard frost, straw colored through late fall and winter. Runners can invade surrounding garden beds. Given minimum water, it grows to 4 in. tall and requires little or no mowing. More water means higher growth, some mowing. Sow 2 lb. per 1,000 sq. ft. In absence of rain, soak occasionally to 1 ft. while grass is getting started. To start from sod, plant 4-in.-wide plugs 3–4 ft. apart in prepared soil in spring; cover should be complete in two seasons.

BUCKEYE. See AESCULUS

BUCKTHORN. See RHAMNUS

BUCKWHEAT. See ERIOGONUM

BUDDLEIA

	Loganiaceae
	EVERGREEN, SEMIEVERGREEN, OR DECIDUOUS SHRUBS
❁	ZONES VARY BY SPECIES
☼ ◐	FULL SUN OR LIGHT SHADE
♦♦	REGULAR TO MODERATE WATER

Buddleia davidii

O f the many species—all notable for flower color or fragrance, or both—these are the most commonly available. Grow in well-drained soil.

B. alternifolia. FOUNTAIN BUTTERFLY BUSH. Deciduous. Zones 2–24, 28–41. It can reach 12 ft. or more, with arching, willowlike branches rather thinly clothed with 1–4-in.-long leaves, dark dull green above, gray and hairy beneath. Blooms in spring from previous year's growth; profuse small clusters of mildly fragrant, lilac purple flowers make sweeping wands of color. Tolerates many soils; does very well in poor, dry gravels. Prune after bloom: remove some of oldest wood down to within few inches of ground. Or train up into small single- or multiple-trunked tree. So trained, it somewhat resembles a small weeping willow.

B. davidii. BUTTERFLY BUSH, SUMMER LILAC. Deciduous or semievergreen. Zones 3–24, 28–35, 37, 39. Fast, rank growth each spring and summer to 3, 4, or even 10 ft. Leaves tapering, 4–12 in. long, dark green above, white and felted beneath. In midsummer, branch ends adorned with small, fragrant flowers (lilac with orange eye) in dense, arching, spikelike, slender clusters 6–12 in. long or more. Needs good drainage and enough water to maintain growth but little else. Cut back plants heavily in late winter to early spring to promote strong new growth for good flowering. In cold climates, plants may freeze to the ground but will regrow each year from the roots. Many varieties are available with pink, lilac, blue, purple, or white flowers. Butterflies often visit flowers. ▸

C

B. globosa. ORANGE BUTTERFLY BUSH. Evergreen or semievergreen. Zones 4–24, 28–31. Grows 10–15 ft. tall. Fragrant orange-yellow flowers are tightly clustered in ¾-in. balls, which in turn are carried in narrow, spikelike 6–8-in. clusters. Blooms late spring or early summer. Flowers produced on previous year's wood, so prune as for *B. alternifolia.*

B. 'Lochinch'. Deciduous. Zones 3–24, 28–33. Hybrid between *B. davidii* and an Asian species. To 10–15 ft. tall. Displays woolly white new growth and branching foot-long clusters of intensely fragrant lilac blossoms with orange eyes. Produces summer flowers on current year's growth, so prune as for *B. davidii.*

B. pikei 'Hever' ('Hever Castle'). Deciduous. Zones 4–24, 28–31. Hybrid between *B. alternifolia* and a Himalayan species. Resembles a smaller *B. alternifolia,* with a profusion of fragrant, orange-centered lilac flowers in mid- to late spring. Leaves gray green. Prune as for *B. alternifolia.*

B. weyeriana 'Sungold'. Zones 3–24, 28–32. Hybrid between *B. davidii* and *B. globosa.* Resembles latter parent but deciduous and probably hardier, with somewhat less globular orange-yellow flower clusters. Blooms on old wood, so cut back after flowering as for *B. alternifolia.* (In coldest part of range, however, it freezes to the ground and so blooms on new wood.)

BUFFALOBERRY. See SHEPHERDIA

BUFFALO GRASS. See BUCHLOE dactyloides

BUGBANE. See CIMICIFUGA

BULL BAY. See MAGNOLIA grandiflora

BUNCHBERRY. See CORNUS canadensis

BUNNY EARS. See OPUNTIA microdasys

BUNYA-BUNYA. See ARAUCARIA bidwillii

BURRO TAIL. See SEDUM morganianum

BUTCHER'S BROOM. See RUSCUS aculeatus

BUTIA capitata

PINDO PALM

Arecaceae (Palmae)

PALM

⚡ ZONES 8, 9, 12–28

☼ ◑ FULL SUN OR LIGHT SHADE

💧 REGULAR WATER

Butia capitata

Native to Brazil, Uruguay, Argentina. Slow-growing, very hardy palm to 10–20 ft. Trunk heavy, patterned with stubs of old leaves; tree is more attractive if stubs are trimmed to the same length. Feathery, arching gray-green leaves. Long spikes of small flowers followed by showy clusters of yellow to red edible dates in summer.

BUTTERCUP TREE. See COCHLOSPERMUM vitifolium

BUTTERFLY BUSH. See BUDDLEIA

BUTTERFLY FLOWER. See SCHIZANTHUS pinnatus

BUTTERFLY WEED. See ASCLEPIAS tuberosa

BUTTERNUT. See WALNUT

BUTTONBUSH, BUTTON WILLOW. See CEPHALANTHUS occidentalis

BUTTONWOOD. See PLATANUS occidentalis

Buxaceae. The boxwood family comprises principally evergreen shrubs with inconspicuous flowers (fragrant in *Sarcococca*). Other members include boxwood *(Buxus)* and *Pachysandra.*

BUXUS

BOXWOOD, BOX

Buxaceae

EVERGREEN SHRUBS

⚡ ZONES VARY BY SPECIES

☼ ◑ ● SUN OR SHADE

💧 REGULAR WATER

Buxus microphylla japonica

Widely used for edging and hedging. When not clipped, most grow soft and billowing. All are easy to grow where adapted and therefore are often neglected. Often attacked by nematodes in Florida.

B. microphylla. This species is rarely planted. Its widely planted varieties include the following:

B. m. japonica. JAPANESE BOXWOOD. Zones 3–24, 26–34, 39. Hardy to −10°F/−23°C but poor winter appearance in cold areas. It takes dry heat and alkaline soil. Compact foliage (small, ⅓–1-in., round-tipped leaves) is lively bright green in summer, brown or bronze in winter in many areas. Grows slowly to 4–6 ft. if not pruned, making a pleasing informal green shrub. Most often clipped as low or medium hedge or shaped into globes, tiers, pyramids in containers. Can be held to 6-in. height as a hedge or border edging.

'Compacta'. Extra-dwarf plant with tiny leaves. Slow growing; good rock garden plant.

'Green Beauty'. Holds its deep green color in coldest weather and is considerably greener than *B. m. japonica* in summer heat.

'Kingsville Dwarf'. Exceptionally compact and low growing.

'Winter Gem'. Zones 3–24, 26–35, 37, 39. Hardiest of Japanese boxwoods.

B. m. koreana. KOREAN BOXWOOD. Zones 2–24, 26–41. Hardy to −20°F/−29°C. Slower and lower growing than Japanese boxwood. Leaves smaller (¼–½ in.). This species is noted for its hardiness and will live where others freeze.

'Tide Hill'. Hardy and maintains good green color—even in New England if sheltered from harsh winter wind. Slow grower to 3 ft. tall and twice as wide.

B. sempervirens. COMMON BOXWOOD. Zones 3–6, 15–17, 31–34, 39. Dies out in alkaline soils, arid hot-summer areas. Will grow to height of 15–20 ft. with equal spread. Dense foliage of medium-size, lustrous, dark green, oval leaves. Can be trained as a small tree. Plants labeled "American boxwood" will grow as described here.

'Suffruticosa'. This is the plant often referred to as "English boxwood." Slower growing than the species; to 4–5 ft. but generally clipped lower. Small leaves, dense form and texture. A variegated form with silver-edged foliage is available.

'Newport Blue'. Dense low grower with bluish green foliage.

'Vardar Valley'. Zones 3–6, 15–17, 31–35, 37, 39. Dark green foliage. Grows 2–3 ft. tall, nearly twice as wide. Considered hardiest common boxwood. Native to the Vardar Valley in Macedonia.

CABBAGE

Brassicaceae (Cruciferae)

BIENNIAL GROWN AS ANNUAL

⚡ ALL ZONES

☼ ◑ TOLERATE LIGHT SHADE IN HOT CLIMATES

💧 NEVER LET PLANTS WILT

Cabbage

Early varieties mature in 7 to 8 weeks from transplanting into garden; late varieties require 3 to 4 months. In addition to green cabbage you can get red and curly-leafed (Savoy) varieties. To avoid overproduction, set out a few plants every week or two or plant both early and late kinds. Time plantings so heads will form either before or after hot summer months. Sow seeds ½ in. deep about 6 weeks before planting-out time. Transplant to rich, moist soil, spacing plants 2–2½ ft. apart. Give frequent light applications of nitrogen fertilizer. Mulch helps keep soil moist and cool. Light frost doesn't hurt cabbage, but harvest and store before heavy freezes occur.

To avoid pest buildup, plant in different site each year. Row covers will protect plants from some pests such as cabbage loopers, imported cabbageworms, root maggots. Another way to prevent root maggots (a pest mainly in northern climates) is by ringing the base of the plant with a tar paper collar; the adult flies don't like to lay eggs on it. Collars also deter cutworms, which chew seedlings off at the base. *Bt* will control young larvae of loopers and cabbageworms if they get on the plants.

For ornamental relatives, see Cabbage, Flowering.

CABBAGE, FLOWERING

Brassicaceae (Cruciferae)

BIENNIAL GROWN AS ANNUAL

ALL ZONES

BEST IN FULL SUN, TOLERATE SOME SHADE

REGULAR WATER

Flowering cabbage and flowering kale are grown for their highly ornamental, highly colored leaf rosettes, which look like giant peonies in deep blue green, marbled and edged with white, cream, rose, or purple. Kale differs from cabbage in that its head is slightly looser and its leaf edges are more heavily fringed. Both are spectacular in the cool-season garden. They appreciate same soil, care, and timing as conventional cabbage. Plant 15–18 in. apart in open-ground beds, singly in 8-in. pots, or several in a large container. Colors are strongest after first frosts touch plants. Single rosette cut and placed on spike holder in bowl makes striking harvest arrangement. Foliage is edible raw or cooked and is highly decorative as a salad garnish.

Flowering Cabbage

CABBAGE PALM. See SABAL palmetto

Cactaceae. The cactus family contains a huge number of succulent plants (see also Succulents). Generally leafless, they have stems modified into cylinders, pads, or joints that store water in times of drought. Thick skin reduces evaporation, and most species have spines to protect plants against browsing animals. Flowers are usually large and brightly colored; fruit may also be colorful and is sometimes edible.

All (with one doubtful exception) are native to the Americas—from Canada to Argentina, from sea level into high mountains, in deserts or in dripping tropical rain forests. Many are native to drier parts of the West.

Cacti range in height from a few inches to 50 ft. Larger species are used to create desert landscapes. Smaller species are grown in pots or, if sufficiently hardy, in rock gardens. Many are easy-care, showy house or greenhouse plants. Large landscaping types require full sun, well-drained soil. Water newly planted cacti very little; roots are subject to rot before they begin active growth. In 4 to 6 weeks, when new roots are active, water thoroughly; then let soil dry before watering again. Reduce watering in fall to allow plants to go dormant. Feed monthly in spring, summer. For some larger kinds appropriate for garden use, see *Cephalocereus senilis, Cereus peruvianus, Echinocereus, Espostoa lanata, Opuntia.*

Smaller cacti for pot or rock garden culture usually have interesting forms and brightly colored flowers. Feed and water plants well during warm weather for good display; taper off on fertilizer to encourage winter dormancy. Use fast-draining soil mix. See *Chamaecereus sylvestri, Coryphantha vivipara, Echinopsis, Lobivia, Lobivopsis, Mammillaria.*

Showiest in flower are tropical cacti that grow as epiphytes on trees or rocks. These need rich soil with much humus, frequent feeding and watering, partial shade, and protection from frost. In all but the mildest cli-

mates, grow in lathhouse or greenhouse, or use as outdoor/indoor plants. See *Epiphyllum, Rhipsalidopsis, Schlumbergera.*

CAESALPINIA (Poinciana)

Fabaceae (Leguminosae)

EVERGREEN OR DECIDUOUS SHRUBS OR SMALL TREES

ZONES VARY BY SPECIES

FULL SUN

MODERATE TO LITTLE WATER

PODS AND SEEDS CAUSE SERIOUS ILLNESS

Caesalpinias grow quickly and easily in hot sun with light, well-drained soil and occasional, deep watering during periods of drought.

Caesalpinia gilliesii

C. gilliesii (Poinciana gilliesii). BIRD OF PARADISE BUSH. Evergreen shrub or small tree; drops leaves in cold winters. Zones 8–16, 18–28; occasionally seen in Zones 6, 7. Tough, interesting, fast growing to 10 ft., with finely cut, filmy foliage on rather open, angular branch structure. Blooms all summer; clusters of yellow flowers adorned with protruding, bright red, 4–5-in.-long stamens. Flowers attract hummingbirds.

C. mexicana. MEXICAN BIRD OF PARADISE. Evergreen shrub or small tree. Zones 12–16, 18–27. Moderately fast growth to 10–12 ft.; may be pruned to 6–8 ft. Foliage coarser than that of *C. pulcherrima.* Blooms year-round except in coldest months, bearing lemon yellow flower clusters 6 in. long, 4 in. thick.

C. pulcherrima (Poinciana pulcherrima). RED BIRD OF PARADISE, DWARF POINCIANA. Deciduous shrub; may be evergreen in mild winters. Zones 12–16, 18–27. Fast, dense growth to 10 ft. tall and as wide. Dark green leaves with many ¾-in.-long leaflets. Blooms throughout warm weather; flowers orange or red (rarely yellow), clustered, with long red stamens. Useful for quick screening. Acts as herbaceous perennial in colder part of range—freezes to ground but rebounds quickly in spring. Even if it doesn't freeze back, you can cut it back to ground in early spring to make more compact mound.

CAJEPUT TREE. See MELALEUCA quinquenervia

CALADIUM bicolor

FANCY-LEAFED CALADIUM

Araceae

TUBEROUS-ROOTED PERENNIAL

ZONES 25–27; OR DIG AND STORE OR GROW IN POTS

SOME VARIETIES ARE BRED FOR SUN

CAREFUL, FREQUENT WATERING

JUICES CAN CAUSE SWELLING IN MOUTH, THROAT

Caladium bicolor

Native to tropical America. Not grown for flowers. Entire show comes from large (to 1½-ft.-long), arrow-shaped, long-stalked, almost translucent leaves colored in bands and blotches of red, rose, pink, white, silver, bronze, and green. Most varieties sold in nurseries are derived from *C. bicolor*—usually 2 ft. tall, occasionally 4 ft. Most require shade. New sun-tolerant varieties include 'Red Flash', 'Fire Chief', 'Rose Bud', and 'White Queen'. Combine all types with ferns, coleus, alocasias, colocasias, and tuberous begonias.

Caladiums need rich soil, high humidity, heat (above 70°F/21°C during days and rarely below 60°F/16°C at night), and ample water. In warmest parts of Florida and Texas, tubers can remain in the ground all year. Elsewhere, dig and store after leaf dieback, or grow in pots and bring indoors during cold weather.

To grow in ground, plant tubers when days lengthen in spring; place tubers with knobby side up so tops are even with soil surface. Keep well watered and feed lightly throughout growing season. Foliage may be cut back in autumn. Where freezes are likely, dig tubers, remove most of soil, dry in semishade for 10 days, and store in dry peat moss or vermiculite at 50° to 60°F/10° to 16°C.

To grow in pots, start tubers indoors in March, outdoors in May. Pot in mix of equal parts coarse sand, leaf mold, and ground bark or peat moss. Use 5-in. pot for 2½-in. tuber, 7-in. pot for one or two large tubers. Fill pot halfway with mix; stir in heaping teaspoon of fish meal. Add 1 in. of mix, place tuber on top, cover with 2 in. of mix. Water thoroughly.

C. esculentum. See Colocasia esculenta

CALAMAGROSTIS acutifolia 'Stricta'

FEATHER REED GRASS

Poaceae (Gramineae)

PERENNIAL

🌿 ZONES 2–24, 29–41

☀️ FULL SUN

💧 REGULAR WATER

Calamagrostis acutifolia 'Stricta'

One of the most effective and handsome ornamental grasses. Erect, somewhat arching clumps of narrow, bright green leaves grow 1½–4 ft. in height. Evergreen in mild climates, partly so in colder areas. Upright flowering stems rise 3–4 ft. above foliage in late spring or early summer, remain upright until first snow. Green with purplish tones, they age to golden yellow, turn buff by winter.

CALAMINTHA

CALAMINT

Lamiaceae (Labiatae)

PERENNIALS

🌿 ZONES 2–9, 14–24, 31–41

☀️◐ FULL SUN OR LIGHT SHADE

💧 MODERATE WATER

Calamintha grandiflora

Perennials in the mint family with pleasant-scented foliage and pretty, tubular, two-lipped flowers borne in clusters. Herb fanciers brew tea from the leaves. Plants need well-drained soil.

C. grandiflora. Creeping rhizomes give rise to slender stems to 2 ft. tall. Summer flowers are pink, 1½ in. long. Better in partial shade than full sun. Forms with variegated leaves exist.

C. nepetoides. Bushy plant with many tough, slender, 1½-ft. stems that grow outward, then erect. The upper portion of the plant carries a profusion of ½-in. pale lilac to white flowers in late summer and fall.

CALAMONDIN. See CITRUS, Sour-Acid Mandarin

CALANDRINIA

Portulaceae

PERENNIALS USUALLY GROWN AS ANNUALS

🌿 ALL ZONES

☀️ FULL SUN

💧💧 REGULAR TO LITTLE WATER

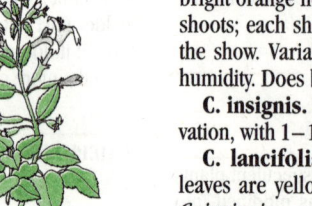

Calandrinia umbellata

Portulaca relatives with fleshy leaves and a profusion of brilliant, short-lived flowers that appear over a long period. Most are native to desert or semidesert areas of Chile and Peru, but one is native to southwestern U.S. Tolerate poor soils. Can take regular garden watering or extended periods of drought once established. Use as temporary fillers in rock gardens or flower borders, or as edgings in hot, dry areas. Easy from seed. Will survive winter in mildest climates.

C. ciliata menziesii. RED MAIDS. Native to California, Arizona. To 1 ft. or taller, with narrow, 2–4-in. leaves and ½-in. purplish red flowers in early spring. Common western wildflower seldom grown in gardens.

C. grandiflora. To 1–3 ft. tall, with leaves to 8 in. long. Stems tinged red. Bright magenta flowers, 1½ in. wide, in summer.

C. umbellata. To 6 in. high, with very narrow leaves less than ½ in. long. Bright magenta flowers, ¾ in. wide, in summer.

CALATHEA

Marantaceae

PERENNIALS

🌿 ZONE 25; OR INDOOR AND GREENHOUSE PLANTS

☀️● PARTIAL OR FULL SHADE

💧 REGULAR WATER

Calathea zebrina

Native to tropical America or Africa. Ornamental leaves, beautifully marked in various shades of green, white, and pink, arranged in basal tufts. Flowers of most are inconspicuous and of no consequence. Need high humidity and warm atmosphere (not under 55°F/13°C). Succeed outdoors in South Florida; elsewhere, they are greenhouse or indoor plants that can be brought outdoors in summer. Need porous soil, perfect drainage, frequent misting in dry atmosphere. Repot as often as necessary to avoid root-bound condition. Calatheas are often mistakenly called marantas.

C. crocata. ETERNAL FLAME. To 10 in. high. Leaves 6 in. long, 1–1½ in. wide, dark green above, purple beneath. Spikes 2 in. long, consisting of bright orange flower bracts that look like little torches. Clump has several shoots; each shoot dies after blooming, but new ones appear to keep up the show. Variable performance as house plant; subject to mites in low humidity. Does better in greenhouse.

C. insignis. Striking plant to 3–7 ft. in native rain forest, lower in cultivation, with 1–1½-ft.-long, yellow-green leaves striped olive green.

C. lancifolia. To 1½ ft. tall. Long (1–1½-ft.), narrow, wavy-edged leaves are yellow green banded with dark olive green. Usually sold as *C. insignis.*

C. louisae. To 3 ft. Foot-long dark green leaves heavily feathered with gray green along midrib.

C. makoyana. PEACOCK PLANT. Showy, 2–4 ft. high. Leaves have areas of olive green or cream above, pink blotches beneath. Silver featherings on rest of upper surface, corresponding cream-colored areas underneath.

C. ornata (C. majestica). Sturdy, 1½–3 ft. high. Leaves 2–3 ft. long, rich green above, purplish red beneath. Juvenile leaves usually pink striped between veins; intermediate foliage striped white. 'Roseo-lineata' has pink and white stripes at angle to midrib.

C. zebrina. ZEBRA PLANT. Compact plant to 1–3 ft. high. Elliptic leaves reach 1–2 ft. long, almost half as wide. Upper surfaces are velvety green with alternating bars of pale yellow green and olive green extending outward from midrib; undersides are purplish red.

CALCEOLARIA herbeohybrida

Scrophulariaceae

PERENNIAL GROWN AS ANNUAL

🌿 ALL ZONES

☀️● SHADE OUTDOORS; SUNNY SPOT INDOORS

💧 REGULAR WATER

Calceolaria herbeohybrida

This is florists' calceolaria, with masses of inch-long yellow to velvety red flowers, often spotted and marbled. Usually grown from seed sown in spring or summer in light, porous soil; plants ready for final potting or planting outdoors in a shady location in fall. If used as a house plant, needs a sunny spot. Can reach 2½ ft. tall, but the most popular strains are lower-growing Multiflora Nana and Multiflora, which grow 9–15 in. high. Plants are usually discarded after flowering but sometimes live over. Strain called Anytime tolerates high temperatures better than other strains do; start it indoors in late winter for summer bloom.

CALENDULAS IN COOKING

In times past, calendula leaves and flowers went into vegetable stews, and the vivid petals are still popular today for the tangy flavor they bring to salads, fish, and egg dishes. If cooked with rice, they give the grain a saffron color.

CALENDULA officinalis

CALENDULA, POT MARIGOLD

Asteraceae (Compositae)

ANNUAL

🌱 ALL ZONES

☀ FULL SUN

💧 MODERATE WATER

Calendula officinalis

Sure, easy color from late fall through spring in mild-winter areas; spring to midsummer in colder climates. Besides familiar daisylike, orange and bright yellow double blooms 2½–4½ in. across, calendulas come in more subtle shades of apricot, cream, and soft yellow. Plants somewhat branching, 1–2 ft. high. Leaves are long, narrow, round on ends, slightly sticky, and aromatic. Plants effective in masses of single colors in borders and parking strips, along drives, in containers. Long-lasting cut flowers.

Sow seed in place or in flats in late summer or early fall in mild-winter climates, spring elsewhere. Or buy seedlings at nurseries. Adapts to most soils if drainage is fast. Remove spent flowers to prolong bloom. Although it is an excellent pot plant, the common name is actually derived from the plant's earlier use as a "pot herb"—a vegetable to be used in the cooking pot.

Dwarf strains (12–15 in.) include Bon Bon (earliest), Dwarf Gem, and Fiesta (Fiesta Gitana). Taller (1½–2 ft.) are Kablouna (pompom centers with looser edges), Pacific Beauty, and Radio (quilled, "cactus" blooms).

CALIFORNIA BAY. See UMBELLULARIA californica

CALIFORNIA FAN PALM. See WASHINGTONIA filifera

CALIFORNIA FUCHSIA. See ZAUSCHNERIA

CALIFORNIA LAUREL. See UMBELLULARIA californica

CALIFORNIA POPPY. See ESCHSCHOLZIA californica

CALLA. See ZANTEDESCHIA

CALLIANDRA

Fabaceae (Leguminosae)

EVERGREEN SHRUBS

🌱 ZONES VARY BY SPECIES

☀ FULL SUN

💧 WATER NEEDS VARY BY SPECIES

Calliandra tweedii

Group of 250 or more species characterized by twice-divided, feathery foliage and very showy floral display of clustered stamens creating a powder puff effect. Grown as landscape plants in the warmest regions, in greenhouses in cold-winter climates.

C. haematocephala (C. inaequilatera). PINK POWDER PUFF, RED POWDER PUFF. Zones 22–27. Native to Bolivia. Grows fast to 10 ft. or more with equal spread. Among the most popular large flowering shrubs in Central Florida. Its beauty has carried it into areas harsher than those to which it is adapted; it will grow in Zones 13, 16–21, 28 if given special protection of overhang or warm, sunny wall. In form, it's a natural espalier. Foliage not as feathery as that of *C. tweedii;* leaflets longer, broader, and darker—glossy copper when new, turning to dark metallic green. Big puffs (2–3 in. across) of silky, watermelon pink stamens are produced in fall and winter. There is a rare white-flowered form. Needs light soil and regular water.

C. tweedii. TRINIDAD FLAME BUSH, BRAZILIAN FLAME BUSH. Best in Zones 22–27; satisfactory in Zones 15–21; freezes back but recovers in Zones 7–9, 12–14, 28. Graceful, picturesque structure to 6–8 ft. tall, 5–8 ft. wide. Lacy, fernlike leaves, divided into many tiny leaflets, scarcely hide branches. Flower clusters show as bright crimson pompoms at branch ends, midwinter to fall. Not fussy about soil. Takes regular to little water. Prune to thin and also to retain an interesting branch pattern. Often sold as *C. guildingii.*

CALLICARPA

BEAUTYBERRY

Verbenaceae

DECIDUOUS SHRUBS

🌱 ZONES 3–9, 14–24, 29–41, EXCEPT AS NOTED

☀ ◑ FULL SUN OR LIGHT SHADE

💧💧 REGULAR TO MODERATE WATER

Callicarpa bodinieri

These graceful shrubs with arching branches are cultivated for their pleasing fruit display. Small lilac flowers in summer are followed by tight clusters of small, round, lavender to violet purple fruits persisting into winter. Plants bloom and fruit on new wood, so prune in spring. In cold-winter areas, plants may freeze to the ground, but they come back from roots; in these regions, treat as herbaceous perennials and cut to the ground yearly. Beautyberry is effective in woodland gardens or massed in shrub borders.

C. americana. AMERICAN BEAUTYBERRY. Zones 4–9, 14–24, 26–32. To 6 ft. tall, with leaves to 6 in. long that turn purplish in fall. Fruits are purple. Biggest, coarsest foliage of the species listed here.

C. bodinieri. BODINIER BEAUTYBERRY. Grows to 6 ft. or more, with willowlike leaves to 5 in. long that turn pink or orange to purple in fall. Berries are violet. 'Profusion' is a heavy-fruiting variety.

C. dichotoma. PURPLE BEAUTYBERRY. To 3–4 ft. tall and slightly wider in sun (as tall as 8 ft. in shade), with slender branches sweeping the ground. Resembles a finer-textured *C. bodinieri.* Leaves to 3 in. long. 'Issai' is a select variety. *C. d. albifructus* is a white-fruited form.

C. japonica. JAPANESE BEAUTYBERRY. Upright, to 3–5 ft., with pink flowers, purple fruits. Leaves to 5 in. long; fall color varies from yellowish to deep reddish purple. 'Leucocarpa' has white fruits.

CALLIOPSIS. See COREOPSIS tinctoria

CALLIRHOE involucrata

POPPY MALLOW, WINE CUPS

Malvaceae

PERENNIAL

🌱 ZONES 1–3, 7–14, 29, 30, 32–35, 41, 43

☀ FULL SUN

💧💧 REGULAR TO LITTLE WATER

Callirhoe involucrata

Thick, fleshy root produces a spreading plant 6 in. tall by 2–3 ft. wide, with roundish, deeply cut leaves and quantities of 2-in. purplish red mallow flowers during hot weather. Needs superb drainage but survives in infertile soil and intense heat. Useful on hot slopes or areas that get little attention.

CALLISIA

Commelinaceae
PERENNIALS
⚘ ZONES 24–27; OR INDOORS
☼ ● PARTIAL OR FULL SHADE
💧 REGULAR WATER

Callisia elegans

They look like, and are related to, wandering Jew (*Tradescantia* and *Zebrina*). Can be grown outdoors in mildest-winter areas. Elsewhere, treat as house plants that can be brought outdoors in warm weather. For care, see *Tradescantia albiflora*.

C. elegans. Stems spread or reach upward instead of drooping, usually much less than maximum of 2 ft. Leaves thick, semisucculent, 3 in. long by 1 in. wide. Upper surfaces dark olive green with white pinstripes running lengthwise; undersides purple. Small flowers, not often seen.

C. fragrans. Leaves to 10 in. long make big rosettes that resemble loose-knit hen and chicks (*Echeveria*). Long runners produce miniatures of parent at tips. Makes massive hanging basket plant that is impressive rather than attractive. Branched clusters of fragrant flowers seldom produced. Offsets can be detached and set in shallow trays of water, the rosettes resting on pebbles or other support. They will root and grow for several months with no further attention, tolerating low light and humidity.

C. repens. This creeping, trailing plant is often sold as *Tradescantia* or as 'Little Jewel'. Closely spaced, thick, fleshy, shiny, bright green leaves an inch long or less make it attractive hanging pot plant. Small flowers bloom infrequently.

CALLISTEMON

BOTTLEBRUSH
Myrtaceae
EVERGREEN SHRUBS OR TREES
⚘ ZONES 8, 9, 12–28
☼ FULL SUN
💧💧 REGULAR TO MODERATE WATER

Callistemon citrinus

Fast-growing plants native to Australia. Colorful flowers, carried in dense spikes or round clusters, consist principally of long, bristlelike stamens—hence the common name "bottlebrush." Flowers followed by persistent woody capsules that sometimes look like bands of beads pressed into bark. Plants often severely damaged at 20°F /–7°C.

C. citrinus (C. lanceolatus). LEMON BOTTLEBRUSH. Most commonly grown bottlebrush; most tolerant of heat, cold, and adverse soils. Massive shrub to 10–15 ft., but with staking and pruning in youth easily trained into narrowish, round-headed, 20–25-ft. tree. Nurseries offer it as shrub, espalier, or tree. Narrow, 3-in.-long leaves coppery when new, vivid green at maturity. Bruised leaves smell lemony. Bright red, 6-in.-long brushes attract hummingbirds, appear in cycles throughout the year.

Variable plant when grown from seed. Cutting-grown selections with good flower size and color include 'Improved' and 'Splendens'. 'Compacta' makes a 4-ft. mound with smaller spikes. 'Violaceus' ('Jeffersii'), about 6 ft. tall and 4 ft. wide, has stiffer branching; narrower, shorter leaves; and reddish purple flowers fading to lavender. 'Mauve Mist' has the same flower color but grows taller, to 10 ft.

C. rigidus. STIFF BOTTLEBRUSH. Erect, sparse, rigid shrub or small tree to 20 ft. with 10-ft. spread. Leaves sharp pointed, gray green (sometimes purplish). Red flower brushes 2½–4½ in. long, spring and summer. Seed capsules prominent. Least graceful bottlebrush.

C. viminalis. WEEPING BOTTLEBRUSH. Shrub or small tree with pendulous branches. Fast growing to 20–30 ft. with 15-ft. spread. Leaves narrow, light green, 6 in. long. Bright red brushes late spring into summer, scattered bloom throughout year. As tree, needs staking, thinning of surplus branches to prevent tangled, top-heavy growth. Leaves tend to grow only at ends of long, hanging branches. 'Little John' is a superior dwarf form, 3 ft. tall and wide, with dense growth pattern and blood red flowers in fall, winter, and spring. 'Captain Cook' is a dense, rounded form to 6 ft. high, suitable for border, low hedge, or screen. 'McCaskillii' is denser in habit than others, more vigorous (to 20 ft. tall), and better in flower color and form.

Callistemon viminalis

CALLISTEPHUS chinensis

CHINA ASTER
Asteraceae (Compositae)
ANNUAL
⚘ ALL ZONES
☼ FULL SUN
💧 REGULAR WATER; AVOID OVERWATERING

Callistephus chinensis

Splendid cut flower and effective bedding plant when well grown and free of disease. Plants 1–3 ft. high. Some kinds are branching; others (developed mainly for florists) have strong stems and no side shoots. Leaves deeply toothed or lobed. Summer is bloom season. Many different flower forms: quilled, curled, incurved, ribbonlike, or interlaced rays; some have crested centers. Varieties classified as peony-flowered, pompom, anemone-flowered, ostrich feather. Colors range from white to pastel pink, rose pink, lavender, lavender blue, violet, purple, crimson, wine, and scarlet.

Plant in rich, loamy or sandy soil. After frosts, sow seed in place or set out plants started in flats. Keep growth steady; sudden checks in growth are harmful. Subject to aster yellows, a viral disease carried by leafhoppers. Discard infected plants. Spray or dust to control leafhoppers. All but wilt-resistant types are subject to aster wilt or stem rot, caused by parasitic fungus that lives in soil and is transmitted through roots into plants. Overwatering produces ideal condition for diseases, especially in heavy soil. Never plant in same location in successive years.

CALLUNA vulgaris

SCOTCH HEATHER
Ericaceae
EVERGREEN SHRUB
⚘ ZONES 2–6, 15–17, 34, 36–41
☼ FULL SUN
💧 REGULAR WATER

Calluna vulgaris

This, the true and only Scotch heather, has crowded, tiny, scalelike, dark green leaves and one-sided spikes of bell-shaped, rosy pink flowers. Garden varieties (far more common than wild kind) include dwarf ground cover and rock garden plants ranging from 2 in. to 3 ft. tall. Taller varieties make good backgrounds for lower kinds and are attractive cut flowers. Flower colors include white, pale to deep pink, lavender, and purple. Foliage—paler and deeper greens, yellow, chartreuse, gray, or russet—often changes color in winter. Most bloom in mid- to late summer; a few bloom into late fall. To prune, shear off faded flowers and branch tips immediately after bloom (with latest-flowering varieties, delay pruning until spring).

C

Heathers thrive in cool, moist climates—notably in the Pacific Northwest, on the Northern California coast, and in parts of New England—and also succeed in other areas that aren't too hot. They languish in heat, whether dry or extremely humid. Plants do best in sandy, peaty, fast-draining soil. Light feeding with acid plant food—once in late winter or early spring, a second time in late spring or early summer—will encourage good growth and bloom.

Here are a few of the scores of varieties obtainable from specialists. All begin blooming in summer, except as noted.

'Alba Jae'. Sprawler to 1½ ft., with bright green leaves, white flowers.

'Alba Plena'. Loose, medium green mound to 1 ft. Double white flowers. Fast growing.

'Aurea'. Spreading, twiggy, 8–12-in. plant with gold foliage turning russet in winter. Sparse purple bloom.

'Aureafolia'. Upright, to 1½–2 ft. Chartreuse foliage, tinged gold in summer. White flowers.

'Blazeaway'. Compact, 12–15 in., with pale foliage with apricot tints, emerging bronzy. Lavender flowers.

'Corbett Red'. Compact growth to 10 in. with dark green foliage. Violet red flowers.

'County Wicklow'. Mounding, 9–18 in., medium green. Pink double flowers from white buds.

'Dainty Bess'. Tiny gray leaves form mat 2–4 in. tall; shapes itself to rocks, crevices. Lavender flowers.

'Darkness'. Compact; to 1½ ft. Dark green foliage; dark purple flowers.

'David Eason'. Spreading mound, 1–1½ ft. Light green foliage; reddish purple flowers, October–November.

'Else Frye'. Erect plant to 2 ft. Medium green foliage; double white flowers.

'Foxii Nana'. Small mound to 6 in. Dark green foliage; purple flowers. A dwarf pincushion.

'Goldsworth Crimson'. Mounding, 1½–2 ft. Dark or smoky green foliage; crimson flowers, October–November.

'H. E. Beale'. Loose mound to 2 ft. Dark green foliage; soft pink double flowers. Long spikes are good for cutting.

'J. H. Hamilton'. Prostrate, bushy, to 9 in. Deep green foliage; profuse double pink bloom.

'Mair's Variety'. Erect, 2–3 ft. Medium green foliage; white flowers. Easy to grow, good background.

'Martha Herman'. Compact, to 4–9 in., with lime green leaves. White flowers.

'Minima Prostrata'. Nearly flat habit. Foliage dark green in summer, bronze in winter. Light rose purple flowers.

'Mrs. Pat'. Bushy, to 8 in. Light green foliage; pink new growth. Light purple flowers.

'Mrs. Ronald Gray'. Creeping mound, to 3 in. Dark green foliage; reddish purple flowers. Excellent ground cover.

'Mullion'. Tight mound to 9 in. Dark green foliage, rosy purple flowers. Fine ground cover.

'Nana'. Low, spreading, to 4 in. Dark green foliage; purple flowers. Often called carpet heather.

'Nana Compacta'. Tight mound to 4 in. Medium green. Purple flowers. Pincushion heather for rockery.

'Roma'. Compact, to 9 in. Dark green foliage; deep pink flowers.

'Searlei'. Bushy, 1–1½ ft. Yellow-green feathery foliage. White flowers.

'Silver King', 'Silver Knight', 'Silver Queen'. All grow 1–1½ ft. high, with light gray-green foliage and pink flowers.

'Tib'. Rounded, bushy, to 1–1½ ft. Medium green foliage; deepest rosy purple double flowers.

CALOCEDRUS decurrens (Libocedrus decurrens)

INCENSE CEDAR

Cupressaceae

EVERGREEN TREE

🌿 ZONES 3–12, 14–24, 32, 34, 36, 37

☼ ◐ FULL SUN OR LIGHT SHADE

💧 REGULAR WATER

Calocedrus decurrens

Unlike most of its native associates—white fir, Douglas fir, sugar pine—this Far West native adapts to many climates. Takes blazing summer heat, drought. Tolerates a variety of soils, but does best in deep, well-drained soil, especially if climate is humid. Symmetrical tree to 75–90 ft. with dense, narrow, pyramidal crown. Rich green foliage in flat sprays, reddish brown bark. Tree gives pungent fragrance to garden in warm weather. When open, the small, yellowish brown to reddish brown cones resemble ducks' bills. Good tree to make green wall, high screen, windbreak. May get a heart rot in some regions.

CALONYCTION aculeatum. See IPOMOEA alba

CALTHA palustris

MARSH MARIGOLD

Ranunculaceae

PERENNIAL

🌿 ZONES 1–21, 31–45

☼ ◐ ● SUN OR SHADE

💧 BOG OR MARSH PLANT IN NATURE

🔸 SAP IS AN IRRITANT

Caltha palustris

Native to eastern U.S., Europe, Asia. To 2 ft. tall, well adapted to edges of pools, ponds, streams, other moist situations. With sufficient water it can be grown in borders; good with bog irises, moisture-loving ferns. Green leaves 2–7 in. across, rounded with a heart-shaped base. Vivid yellow flowers are 2 in. across, in clusters. Lush, glossy foliage gives an almost tropical effect. Plant is vigorous; increase by divisions or sow seed in boggy soil. There is a double-flowered form.

Calycanthaceae. The calycanthus family contains shrubs with paired opposite leaves and flowers that somewhat resemble small water lilies—each bloom has an indefinite number of segments which are not easily defined as petals or sepals. *Calycanthus* and wintersweet (*Chimonanthus*) are typical.

CALYCANTHUS

Calycanthaceae

DECIDUOUS SHRUBS

🌿 ZONES VARY BY SPECIES

☼ ◐ ● SUN OR SHADE

💧 REGULAR WATER

🔸 SEEDS CAN PRODUCE CONVULSIONS

Calycanthus occidentalis

Deciduous shrubs, represented here by an eastern native and a western one. Both of these are bulky plants with lush foliage and flowers worthwhile for their fragrance and form.

C. floridus. CAROLINA ALLSPICE, STRAWBERRY SHRUB, SWEETSHRUB. Zones 3–9, 14–17, 28, 31–41. Native Virginia to Florida. Stiffly branched to 6–10 ft. tall and as wide or wider. Suckering, fast spreading.

C

Leaves oval to 5 in., glossy dark green above, grayish green beneath. Blooms at some time May–July, depending on climate and exposure. Flowers reddish brown, 2 in. wide, often with heady strawberry fragrance; carried at ends of leafy branchlets. Blooms followed by brownish, pear-shaped capsules, fragrant when crushed. Plant in shrub border or around outdoor living space where flower scent can be appreciated. Aroma varies, so buy when plants are in bloom. 'Michael Lindsay' is reliably fragrant. 'Athens' has yellow flowers.

C. occidentalis. SPICE BUSH. Zones 4–9, 14–22, 31, 32. Native along streams, moist slopes in California Coast Ranges and Sierra Nevada foothills. To 4–12 ft. high. Leaves 2–6 in. long, 1–2 in. wide, bright green, turning yellow in fall. Reddish brown flowers to 2 in. across, resembling small water lilies, appear April–August, depending on climate and exposure. Both flowers and bruised leaves have fragrance of old wine barrel. Can be trained into multistemmed small tree but is most useful as a background shrub or medium to tall screen. Easily grown from seed.

CALYLOPHUS hartwegii

Onagraceae

PERENNIAL

⚡ ZONES 2, 3, 10–13, WESTERN PARTS OF 33, 35, 41

☼ ◑ FULL SUN OR PARTIAL SHADE

💧 MODERATE WATER

Calylophus hartwegii

An evening primrose look-alike, this perennial grows 8 in. tall, 2 ft. across, and spreads by underground rhizomes. Yellow, 1-in. flowers appear over a long season, from spring well into fall. Plants are dormant in winter, when stems can be cut back.

CAMASSIA

CAMASS

Liliaceae

BULBS

⚡ ZONES 1–9, 14–17, 31, 32, 34, 39

☼ FULL SUN

💧💧 AMPLE WATER DURING GROWTH AND BLOOM

Camassia quamash

Most species native to moist meadows, marshes, fields in Northern California and Northwest. Starlike, slender-petaled blossoms are carried on spikes in late spring, early summer; grasslike basal leaves dry quickly after bloom. Plant in moist situation, fairly heavy soil, where bulbs can remain undisturbed for many years. Set bulbs 4 in. deep, 6 in. apart. To avoid premature sprouting, plant after weather cools in fall.

C. cusickii. Dense clusters of pale blue flowers on stems 2–3 ft. tall.

C. leichtlinii. Large, handsome clusters of creamy white flowers on stems 2–4 ft. tall. 'Alba' has whiter flowers than species, and 'Plena' has double greenish yellow blooms. *C. l. suksdorfii* is attractive blue form.

C. quamash (C. esculenta). Loose clusters of deep blue flowers on 1–2-ft. stems; flowers of 'Orion' are deeper blue, those of 'San Juan Form' deeper still.

CHOCOLATE CAMELLIA LEAVES

Camellia leaves make perfect "molds" for a pretty dessert garnish. Spread melted semisweet chocolate over undersides of washed, dried leaves; refrigerate or freeze until chocolate is hard, then carefully peel off leaves. Keep chocolate leaves chilled or frozen until you're ready to use them.

CAMELLIA

Theaceae

EVERGREEN SHRUBS OR SMALL TREES

⚡ ZONES 4–9, 12, 14–24, 26–31, AND WARMER PARTS OF 32 FOR MOST; HARDY TYPES THROUGHOUT 32

☼ BEST OUT OF STRONG SUN, EXCEPT AS NOTED

💧💧 REGULAR TO MODERATE WATER

Camellia hiemalis

Native to eastern and southern Asia. There are over 3,000 named kinds; range in color, size, and form is remarkable.

If you live in traditional camellia country, you are already aware of these splendid shrubs. If you are outside their generally recognized territory, take heart; bold gardeners are succeeding with camellias in such areas as the Delmarva Peninsula, the New Jersey shore, Long Island, coastal Connecticut, and Cape Cod. Although a few of the hardiest *C. japonica* varieties noted here are grown in these colder regions with careful attention to proper siting and winter protection, the newer hardy hybrids (see page 227) derived from *C. oleifera* (see page 226) represent a safer choice.

The following pages briefly discuss the cultural requirements of camellias and describe some of the lesser-known species as well as the widely distributed old favorites and new varieties. The plant descriptions include the unique cultural needs of species and varieties; general cultural requirements appear below.

Camellias need well-drained soil rich in organic material. Never plant camellias so trunk base is below soil line, and never permit soil to wash over and cover this base. Keep roots cool with 2-in.-thick mulch.

These make outstanding container plants—especially in wooden tubs and barrel halves. As a general rule, plant gallon-size camellias into 12–14-in.-wide tubs, 5-gallon ones into 16–18-in. tubs. Fill with a planting mix containing 50 percent or more organic material.

Camellias thrive and bloom best when sheltered from strong, hot sun and drying winds, though some species and varieties are more sun tolerant than others. Tall old plants in old gardens prove that camellias can thrive in full sun when they are mature enough to have roots shaded by heavy canopy of leaves. Young plants will grow better and bear more attractive flowers if grown under partial shade of tall trees, under lath cover, or on north side of a building. A few camellias need shade at any age.

Give regular to moderate water; in dry-summer climates, established plants (over 3 years old and vigorous) can survive on natural rainfall. Fertilize with a commercial acid plant food; read fertilizer label for complete instructions. Don't use more than called for. Better to cut amounts in half and feed twice as frequently. Don't feed sick plants. Poor drainage and excessive salts in water or soil are the main troublemakers. Best cure is to move plant into raised bed of pure ground bark or peat moss until it recovers.

Scorched or yellowed areas in center of leaves are usually due to sunburn. Burned leaf edges, excessive leaf drop, or corky spots usually indicate overfertilizing. Yellow leaves with green veins are signs of chlorosis; check drainage, leach, and treat with iron or iron chelates.

One disease may be serious: camellia petal blight. Flowers rapidly turn ugly brown. Browning at edges of petals (especially whites and pale pinks) may be caused by sun or wind, but if brown rapidly runs into center of flower, suspect petal blight. Sanitation is the best control. Pick up all fallen flowers and petals, pick off all infected flowers from plants, and dispose of in covered trash bin; encourage neighbors to do the same. Remove mulch (if you use one), haul it away, and replace with fresh one; a deep mulch (4–5 in.) helps keep spores of fungus from reaching the air.

Some flower bud dropping may be natural phenomenon; many camellias set more buds than they can open. Bud drop can be caused by overwatering, but more often by underwatering, especially during summer. It can also be caused by spells of very low humidity.

Some varieties bear too many flowers. To get nicest display from them, remove buds in midsummer like this: from branch-end clusters remove all but one or two round flower buds (leaf buds are slender); along stems, remove enough to leave single flower bud for each 2—4 in. of branch.

Prune after flowering. Remove dead or weak wood and thin when growth is so dense that flowers have no room to open properly. Prune at will to get form you want. Shorten lower branches to encourage upright growth. Cut back top growth to flatten lanky shrubs. Make cut just above scar that terminates previous year's growth (often a slightly thickened, somewhat rough area where bark texture and color change slightly). A cut just above this point will usually force three or four dormant buds into growth.

C. hiemalis. Includes number of varieties formerly listed as sasanquas but differing in their later and longer bloom and heavier-textured flowers. Four good examples:

'Chansonette'. Vigorous, spreading growth. Large, bright pink, formal double flowers with frilled petals.

'Shishi-Gashira'. One of the most useful and ornamental shrubs. Low growing with arching branches that in time pile up tier on tier to make compact, dark green, glossy-leafed plant. Leaves rather small for camellia, giving medium-fine foliage texture. Flowers rose red, semidouble to double, 2—2½ in. wide, heavily borne over long season—October—March in good year. Full sun or shade.

'Showa-No-Sakae'. Faster growing, more open than 'Shishi-Gashira'; willowy, arching branches. Semidouble to double flowers of soft pink, occasionally marked with white. Try this as espalier or in hanging basket.

'Showa Supreme'. Very similar to above but has somewhat larger flowers of peony form.

C. japonica. This is the plant most gardeners have in mind when they mention camellias. Naturally a large shrub or small tree, but variable in size, growth rate, and habit. Hundred-year-old plants may reach 20 ft. high and as wide, but most gardeners can consider camellias to be 6—12-ft. shrubs. Many are lower growing.

Following is a list of 17 varieties that are old standbys. Easily obtainable and handsome even in comparison with some of the newest introductions, they are plants for both beginners and advanced gardeners. The list specifies season of bloom as early, midseason, or late. The earliest types start blooming in November; the latest put on a show as late as May. Flower size is noted for each variety. Very large blossoms are over 5 in. across; large, 4—5 in.; medium large, 3½—4 in.; medium, 3—3½ in.; small, 2½—3 in.; and miniature, 2½ in. or less.

'Adolphe Audusson'. Midseason. Very large, dark red, semidouble flowers, heavily borne on a medium-size, symmetrical, vigorous shrub. Hardy. 'Adolphe Audusson Variegated' is identical but heavily marbled white on red.

'Alba Plena.' Early. Brought from China in 1792 and still a favorite large, white, formal double. Slow, bushy growth. Early bloom a disadvantage in cold or rainy areas. Protect flowers from rain and wind.

'Berenice Boddy'. Midseason. Medium semidouble, light pink with deeper shading. Vigorous upright growth. One of the most cold hardy.

'Covina'. Midseason—late. Medium, rose red, semidouble to rose-form flowers on a compact plant. Highly sun tolerant.

'Daikagura'. Early—late. Large, rose red, peony-type flowers on a dense, upright bush. Very long bloom season. 'Daikagura Variegated' is similar but has rose red flowers marbled with white.

'Debutante'. Early—midseason. Medium-large, peony-form flowers of light pink. Profuse bloom. Vigorous upright growth.

'Elegans' ('Chandler'). Also known as 'Chandleri Elegans'. Early—midseason. Very large anemone-form camellia with rose pink petals and smaller petals called petaloids, the latter often marked white. Slow growth

and spreading, arching branches make it a natural for espalier. Stake to provide height, and don't remove main shoot; it may be very slow to resume upward growth. A 100-year-old-plus variety that remains a favorite. Its offspring resemble it in every way except flower color: 'C. M. Wilson', pale pink; 'Shiro Chan', white, sometimes faintly marked with pink; and 'Elegans Variegated' (Chandler Variegated'), heavily marbled rose pink and white. A solid rose pink form is called 'Francine'. 'Elegans Champagne' has creamy-centered white flowers. 'Elegans Splendor' is blush pink edged white.

'Glen 40' ('Coquetti'). Midseason—late. Large formal double of deep red. One of best reds for corsages. Slow, compact, upright growth. Handsome even out of flower. Very good in containers.

'Herme' ('Jordan's Pride'). Midseason. Medium-large, semidouble flowers are pink, irregularly bordered white and streaked deep pink. Sometimes has all solid pink flowers on certain branches. Free blooming, dependable.

'Kramer's Supreme'. Midseason. Very large, deep, full peony-form flowers of deep, clear red. Some people can detect a faint fragrance. Unusually vigorous, compact, upright. Takes some sun.

'Kumasaka'. Midseason—late. Medium large, rose form to peony form, rose pink. Vigorous, compact, upright growth and remarkably heavy flower production make it choice landscape plant. Good cold hardiness. Takes morning sun.

'Magnoliaeflora'. Midseason. Medium semidouble flowers of pale pink. Many blossoms, good cut flower. Medium grower of compact yet spreading form. Hardy.

'Mathotiana'. Midseason—late. Very large, rose form to formal double, deep crimson, sometimes with purplish cast. Vigorous upright grower. Stands up well in hot-summer areas.

'Mrs. Charles Cobb'. Midseason—late. Large semidouble to peony-form flowers in deep red. Freely flowering. Compact plant with dense foliage. Best in warmer areas.

'Pope Pius IX' ('Prince Eugene Napoleon'). Midseason. A cherry red, medium-large formal double. Medium, compact, upright growth.

'Purity'. Late. White, medium, rose form to formal double, usually showing a few stamens. Vigorous upright plant. Late bloom often escapes rain damage.

'Wildfire'. Early—midseason. Medium, semidouble, orange-red flowers. Vigorous, upright plant.

The preceding 17 are the old classics in the camellia world. The following, all introduced since 1950, may supplant them in time:

'Carter's Sunburst'. Early—late. Large to very large pale pink flowers striped deeper pink. Semidouble to peony-form to formal double flowers on medium, compact plants.

'Drama Girl'. Midseason. Huge semidouble flowers of deep salmon rose pink. Vigorous, open, pendulous growth.

'Grand Slam'. Midseason. Large to very large flowers in glowing deep red. Semidouble to peony form. There is a form with variegated flowers.

'Guilio Nuccio'. Midseason. Coral rose, very large semidouble flowers with inner petals fluted in "rabbit-ear" effect. Unusual depth and substance. Vigorous upright growth. Many consider this variety to be the world's finest camellia. Variegated, fringed forms are available.

'Mrs. D. W. Davis'. Midseason. Spectacular, very large, somewhat cup-shaped flowers of palest blush pink open from egg-size buds. Vigorous, upright, compact plant with very handsome broad leaves. ▸

Flower Forms of *Camellia japonica*

Single   Semidouble   Formal Double   Peony Form   Anemone Form   Rose Form

C

'Nuccio's Gem'. Midseason. Medium-large, perfectly formed full formal double, white. Strong, full, upright grower.

'Nuccio's Jewel'. Midseason–late. Large, loose to full peony-form flowers are white with pink edging on petals.

'Nuccio's Pearl'. Midseason. Medium-size, full formal double flowers are white, with a rim of deep pink outer petals.

'Silver Waves'. Early–midseason. Large, semidouble white flowers have wavy-edged petals.

'Swan Lake'. Midseason–late. Very large, white, formal double to peony-form flower. Vigorous upright growth.

'Tiffany'. Midseason–late. Very large, warm pink flowers. Rose form to loose, irregular semidouble. Vigorous, upright shrub.

'Tom Knudsen'. Early–midseason. Medium to large dark red flowers with deeper red veining. Formal double to peony form to rose form.

C. oleifera. Large shrub or small tree to 20 ft. tall, with glossy, dark green leaves and fragrant, 2-in. white flowers in fall. Name means "oil bearing"; oil extracted from the large seeds has been used in China for cooking or as a hair conditioner. Possibly the hardiest of all camellias. A parent of hardy hybrids (see page 227).

C. reticulata. Some of the biggest and most spectacular camellia flowers occur in this species, and likely as not they appear on some of the lankiest and least graceful plants.

Camellia reticulata

Plants differ somewhat according to variety, but generally speaking they are rather gaunt and open shrubs that eventually become trees of considerable size—possibly 35–50 ft. tall. In gardens consider them 10-ft.-tall shrubs, 8 ft. wide. Leaves also variable but tend to be dull green, leathery, and strongly net-veined.

Culture is quite similar to that of other camellias, except that the plants seem intolerant of heavy pruning. This, in addition to their natural lankiness and size, makes them difficult to place in garden. They are at their best in light shade of old oaks, where they should stand alone with plenty of room to develop. They are good container subjects while young, but are not handsome out of bloom. They develop better form and heavier foliage in open ground. They are less hardy than *C. japonica* (not recommended for Zone 32). In marginal climates, grow them in containers so you can move them into winter protection, or plant beneath overhang or near wall.

Best-known varieties have very large, semidouble flowers with deeply fluted and curled inner petals. These inner petals give great depth to flower. All bloom late winter to early spring. The following varieties are the best choice for garden use:

'Buddha'. Rose pink flower of very large size; inner petals unusually erect and wavy. Gaunt, open; fast growth.

'Butterfly Wings'. Loose, semidouble flower of great size (reported up to 9 in. across), rose pink; petals broad and wavy. Growth open, rather narrow.

'Captain Rawes'. Reddish rose pink semidouble flowers of large size. Vigorous bushy plant with good foliage. Hardiest of reticulatas.

'Chang's Temple'. True variety is large, open-centered, deep rose flower, with center petals notched and fluted. 'Cornelian' is sometimes sold as 'Chang's Temple'.

'Cornelian'. Large, deep, irregular peony-form flowers with wavy petals, rosy pink to red, heavily variegated with white. Vigorous plant with big leaves; leaves are usually marked with white. This variety is often sold as 'Chang's Temple' or as 'Lion Head'. The true 'Lion Head' is not found in American gardens.

'Crimson Robe'. Very large, bright red, semidouble flowers. Petals firm textured and wavy. Vigorous plant of better appearance than most reticulatas.

'Purple Gown'. Large, purplish red, peony-form to formal double flowers. Compact plant with best growth habit and foliage in the group.

'Shot Silk'. Large, loose, semidouble flowers of brilliant pink with iridescent finish that sparkles in sunlight. Fast, rather open growth.

'Tali Queen'. Very large, deep reddish pink flowers of loose semidouble form with heavily crinkled petals. Plant form and foliage very good. This plant is often sold as 'Noble Pearl'; true 'Noble Pearl' is not available in the U.S.

C. sasanqua. Useful broad-leafed evergreens for espaliers, ground covers, informal hedges, screening, containers, and bonsai. Vary in form from upright and densely bushy to spreading and vinelike. Heights range from 1½ to 12 ft. tall. Leaves dark green, shiny, 1½–3½ in. long, a third as wide. Flowers heavily produced in autumn and early winter, short lived, rather flimsy, but so numerous that plants make a show for months. Some are lightly fragrant.

Most sasanquas tolerate much sun, and some thrive in full hot sun if soil is right and watering plentiful. They take drought very well. May be slightly less cold hardy than *C. japonica,* but garden conditions will determine survival. In camellia areas with much fall and winter rain and frost, such as the Pacific Northwest, sasanqua flowers are too often damaged to call the plants successful.

'Apple Blossom'. Single white flowers blushed with pink, from pink buds. Spreading plant.

'Cleopatra'. Rose pink semidouble flowers with narrow, curving petals. Growth is erect, fairly compact. Takes clipping well.

'Hana Jiman'. Large semidouble flowers white, edged pink. Fast, open growth; good espalier.

'Jean May'. Large double, shell pink. Compact, upright grower with exceptionally glossy foliage.

'Kanjiro'. Large semidouble flowers of rose pink shading to rose red at petal edges. Erect growth habit.

'Mine-No-Yuki' ('White Doves'). Large, white, peony-form double. Drops many buds. Spreading, willowy growth; effective espalier.

'Momozono-Nishiki'. Large semidouble flowers are rose, shaded white. Twisted petals.

'Narumigata'. Large, single, cupped flowers, white tinged pink.

'Setsugekka'. Large, white, semidouble flowers with fluted petals. Considerable substance to flowers; cut sprays hold well in water. Shrub's growth is upright and rather bushy.

'Tanya'. Deep rose pink single flowers. Tolerates much sun. Good ground cover.

'Yuletide'. Profusion of small, single, bright red flowers on dense, compact, upright plant.

C. sinensis (Thea sinensis). TEA. Dense, round shrub to 15 ft. with leathery, dull, dark green leaves to 5 in. long. A commercial crop in Asia, but grown ornamentally in the U.S. Fall flowers are white, small (1½ in. across), and fragrant. Takes well to pruning and can be trimmed as a hedge. Somewhat cold hardier than *C. japonica.*

C. vernalis. Certain camellias once classed as sasanquas have been placed here because they bloom later than sasanquas, are denser in growth and shinier in leaf, and have firmer-textured flowers. They are generally sold as sasanquas and are similar in cold hardiness. Best-known varieties, both to 9 ft. tall, are:

'Dawn'. Single to semidouble, small white flowers blushed pink. Dense, upright shrub of unusual hardiness.

'Hiryu'. Deep red, small, rose form. Dense, upright plant. 'Hiryu Nishiki' has white markings on flowers.

Higo camellias. These camellias, bred for 200 years in Japan but only now attracting attention in the United States, are probably varieties of *C. japonica* (and are equally cold hardy). They are generally compact plants with dense, heavy foliage and thick-petaled single flowers with broad, full brush of stamens in the center. In ideal Higo camellia, mass of stamens should be at least half the diameter of flower. Colors include white, pink, red; both solid and variegated. Many named varieties are already available in this country, and more are likely to appear.

Hybrid camellias. This term refers to camellias resulting from crosses between two or more species. Several categories of hybrids, described below, have been produced.

Medium-flowered hybrids. The first wave of hybridizing involved *C. japonica* and a floriferous small-flowered Chinese species. The resulting hybrids, most of them medium to large shrubs, are of generally good garden form, with foliage like that of *C. japonica* and abundant flowers. See *C. japonica* for explanations of bloom season and flower size terminology.

'Coral Delight'. Midseason. Coral pink semidouble flowers form garlands along the branches. Slow grower.

'Donation'. Midseason. Large semidouble flowers of orchid pink borne all along stems. Blooms young and heavily, on vigorous, upright, compact plant with slightly pendulous branches. Quite resistant to cold and sun. Appreciates a little shade in hot, dry areas. There is a variegated form.

'E. G. Waterhouse'. Midseason–late. Medium, full, formal double of excellent form. Light pink flowers heavily produced on vigorous, upright shrub.

'Fragrant Pink'. Midseason. Loose peony-form flowers on spreading bush. Flowers small, deep pink, very fragrant.

'Freedom Bell'. Midseason. Small to medium, semidouble, bell-shaped blooms of dark red open beneath branches.

'J. C. Williams'. Early–late. Medium-size single, cup-shaped pale pink flowers over very long season. Vigorous upright shrub with rather pendulous branches. This and the similar 'Mary Christian' and 'St. Ewe' have prospered in the Pacific Northwest and are worthy of trial elsewhere.

Large-flowered hybrids. The second wave of hybridizing, involving *C. reticulata*, produced plants that are more spectacular in blossom than the hybrids described above. See *C. japonica* for explanations of bloom season and flower size terminology.

'Flower Girl'. Early–midseason. Large to very large, semidouble to peony-form flowers of bright pink. Vigorous, upright growth. Profuse flowering and small leaves come from its sasanqua parent, big flowers from its Reticulata ancestor.

'Francie L.'. Midseason–late. Very large semidouble flowers with upright, wavy petals. Deep rose pink.

'Valentine Day'. Midseason–late. Large to very large, salmon pink, formal double flowers. Fast, upright grower.

'Valley Knudsen'. Midseason–late. Large to very large, deep orchid pink semidouble to loose peony form. Compact upright growth.

Hardy hybrids. Dr. William Ackerman, National Arboretum, Washington, D.C., and Dr. Clifford Parks, University of North Carolina, Chapel Hill, bred a number of species, especially the hardy *C. oleifera*, to produce hardy camellias. The hybrids withstand temperatures as low as −15°F/−26°C with little or no damage, provided they are given some shelter from winter sun and wind. Pink or white, 3½–4-in. flowers bloom October–November.

Varieties include 'Polar Ice', white, anemone form; 'Snow Flurry', white, anemone form; 'Winter's Charm', pink, peony form; 'Winter's Dream', pink, semidouble; 'Winter's Star', lavender pink, single; and 'Winter's Waterlily', white, formal double.

CAMPANULA

BELLFLOWER

Campanulaceae (Lobeliaceae)

MOSTLY PERENNIALS; SOME BIENNIALS OR ANNUALS

⚡ ZONES 1–9, 14–24, 31–45, EXCEPT AS NOTED

☼ ◑ TOLERATE FULL SUN IN COOLEST AREAS

💧 💧 REGULAR TO MODERATE WATER

▶ SEE CHART NEXT PAGE

Campanula isophylla

Vast and varied group (nearly 300 species) encompassing trailers, creeping or tufted miniatures, and erect kinds 1–6 ft. tall. Flowers generally bell shaped, but some star shaped, cup shaped, or round and flat. Usually blue, lavender, violet, purple, or white; some pink. Bloom period from spring to fall.

Uses are as varied as the plants. Gemlike miniatures deserve special settings—close-up situations in rock gardens, niches in dry walls, raised beds, containers. Trailing kinds are ideal for hanging pots or baskets, wall crevices; vigorous spreading growers serve well as ground covers. Upright growers are valuable in borders, for cutting, occasionally in containers.

In general, campanulas grow best in good, well-drained soil and cooler climates. Most species are fairly easy to grow from seed sown in flats in spring or early summer, transplanted to garden in fall for bloom the fol-

lowing year; also may be increased by cuttings or divisions. Divide clumps in fall every 3 to 4 years; some may need yearly division.

Campanulaceae. The campanula, or bellflower, family contains perennials or biennials, typically with bell-shaped or saucer-shaped flowers in shades of blue to purple, lilac, and white. This family includes plants formerly grouped under Lobeliaceae.

CAMPHOR TREE. See CINNAMOMUM camphora

CAMPSIS

TRUMPET CREEPER, TRUMPET VINE

Bignoniaceae

DECIDUOUS VINES

⚡ ZONES VARY BY SPECIES

☼ ◑ FULL SUN OR PARTIAL SHADE

💧 💧 REGULAR TO MODERATE WATER

Campsis radicans

Vigorous climbers that cling to wood, brick, and stucco surfaces with aerial rootlets. Unless thinned, old plants sometimes become top heavy and pull away from supporting surface. Will spread through garden and into neighbor's by suckering roots. If you try to dig up suckers, any remaining piece of root will grow another plant. Can be trained as big shrub or flowering hedge if branches are shortened after first year's growth. Use for large-scale effects, quick summer screen. All produce open, arching sprays of trumpet-shaped flowers in summer.

C. grandiflora (Bignonia chinensis). CHINESE TRUMPET CREEPER. Zones 4–12, 14–21, 28–32. Not as vigorous, large, or hardy as the American native *C. radicans*, but with slightly larger, more open scarlet flowers. Leaves divided into seven to nine leaflets, each 2½ in. long. 'Morning Calm' has peach-colored flowers.

C. radicans (Bignonia radicans). COMMON TRUMPET CREEPER. Zones 2–21, 26–41. Native to southeastern U.S. Most widely used in cold-winter areas. Hard freeze will kill to ground but new stems grow quickly. Leaves divided into 9–11 toothed leaflets, each 2½ in. long. Flowers, growing in clusters of 6–12, are 3-in.-long orange tubes with scarlet lobes that flare to 2 in. wide. Grows fast to 40 ft. or more, bursting with health and vigor. Blossoms of 'Flava' are yellow to pale orange.

C. tagliabuana. Zones 3–24, 26–34. Hybrid between the two above species. 'Mme. Galen', best-known variety, has attractive salmon red flowers. 'Crimson Trumpet' bears pure red blooms.

CANARY BIRD FLOWER. See TROPAEOLUM peregrinum

CANARY ISLAND BROOM. See GENISTA canariensis

CANDLE BUSH. See CASSIA alata

CANDOLLEA cuneiformis. See HIBBERTIA cuneiformis

CANDYTUFT. See IBERIS

CANNA

Cannaceae

TUBEROUS-ROOTED PERENNIALS

⚡ ZONES 6–9, 12–31, WARMER PARTS OF 32; OR DIG AND STORE

☼ FULL SUN

💧 💧 AMPLE WATER DURING GROWTH AND BLOOM

Canna

Native to tropics and subtropics. Best adapted to warm- to hot-summer climates; in areas where soil freezes deeply, lift and store roots over

▶ page 229

CAMPANULA

NAME, TYPE	GROWTH HABIT, SIZE	FOLIAGE	FLOWERS	USES, COMMENTS
Campanula alpestris (C. allionii) Perennial	Rosettes spring from creeping rhizomes. Stems 2–5 in. long	Leaves 2 in. long in rosettes	1¾ in. long, erect or horizontal, blue or white. Summer	Rock gardens, borders, edging
C. barbata Short-lived perennial or biennial	Clumps of erect stems, 4–18 in. high	Leaves mostly at base of stem, 2–5 in. long, narrow, hairy	Bell-shaped, lilac blue, bearded inside, 1 in. long, nodding. Few near top of each stem. Summer	Foreground in borders, rock gardens. Tap rooted; needs good drainage. White forms may appear from seed
C. carpatica (C. turbinata) TUSSOCK BELLFLOWER Perennial	Compact leafy tufts, stems branching and spreading. Usually about 8 in. tall, may reach 1–1½ ft.	Leaves smooth, bright green, wavy, toothed, 1–1½ in. long	Open bell- or cup-shaped, blue or white, 1–2 in. across, single and erect on stems above foliage. Late spring	Rock gardens, foreground in borders, edging. Variable in flower size and color. 'Blue Chips' and 'White Chips' good dwarf varieties. Easily grown from seed; sometimes sold as 'Blue Clips', 'White Clips'
C. elatines garganica (C. garganica) Perennial Zones 3–9, 14–24, 31–34, 39	Low (3–6 in. high), with outward spreading stems	Small, gray or green, sharply toothed, heart-shaped leaves	Flat, star-shaped, violet blue. One or a few at top of stem. Late spring to fall	Rock gardens. Usually sold as *C. garganica*. Somewhat like a miniature, prostrate *C. poscharskyana*
C. fragilis Perennial	Vinelike, trailing flower stems 12–16 in. long. Dies back to a tight basal rosette of leaves	Glossy oval leaves 1 in. across	Star-shaped, blue with white centers, 1½ in. across, in leaf joints at ends of branches. Late summer and fall	Choice spots in rock gardens or walls. Hanging containers. A plant for collectors, specialists
C. glomerata Perennial	Upright, with erect side branches to 1–2 ft.	Basal leaves broad, wavy-edged. Stem leaves broad, toothed. Both somewhat hairy	Narrow, bell-shaped, flaring at the mouth, 1 in. long, blue violet, tightly clustered at tops of stems. Summer	Shaded borders or large rock gardens. Plants have proportionately more foliage than flowers. Seed-grown strains Superba and Alba are deepest purple and white, respectively
C. isophylla ITALIAN BELLFLOWER, STAR OF BETHLEHEM Perennial Zones 4–9, 14–24, 31, 32	Trailing or hanging stems to 2 ft. long	Leaves heart-shaped, light green, toothed, 1–1½ in. long and wide	Pale blue, star-shaped, 1 in. wide, profuse in late summer and fall. Variety 'Alba' most popular, has white flowers, larger than the above. Variety 'Mayi' has gray, soft-hairy leaves, large lavender blue flowers	Hanging baskets, wall pots, tops of walls, rock gardens. Choice ground cover for small areas on slopes in mild-winter climates; indoor/outdoor plant in cold-winter areas. Grow from cuttings or from seed of Kristal strain, which blooms first year from winter sowing indoors
C. lactiflora Perennial Zones 3–9, 14–24, 31–34, 39	Erect, branching, leafy, 3½–5 ft. tall	Oblong, pointed, toothed leaves 2–3 in. long	Broadly bell-shaped to star-shaped, 1 in. long, white to pale blue in drooping clusters at ends of branches. Summer	Rear of borders in sun or partial shade. Endures even dry shade and is long lived. 'Loddon Anna' has pale pink flowers.
C. medium CANTERBURY BELL, CUP-AND-SAUCER Biennial or annual	Sturdy, hairy, leafy, with erect stems 2½–4 ft. tall	Lance-shaped basal leaves 6–10 in.; stem leaves 3–5 in., wavy-margined, lance-shaped	Bell-shaped or urn-shaped, 1–2 in. across, single or double, held upright in long, loose open clusters. Purple, violet, blue, lavender, pink, white. Late spring or early summer	Sow seed in May or June for bloom next year, or set out plants from nursery 15–18 in. apart. Good for cutting. 'Calycanthema', commonly called cup-and-saucer, is very popular. Annual variety with bell-shaped flowers (not cup-and-saucer) blooms in 6 months from seed
C. persicifolia PEACH-LEAFED BLUEBELL Perennial	Strong-growing, slender, erect stems 2–3 ft. tall. Plants leafy at base	Basal leaves smooth-edged, green, 4–8 in. long. Stem leaves 2–4 in. long, shaped like leaves of peach tree	Open, cup-shaped, about 1 in. across, held erect on short side shoots on sturdy stems. Blue, pink, or white. Summer	Choice plant for borders. Easy to grow from seed sown in late spring. 'Telham Beauty', old but still popular, has 3-in. blue flowers. 'Blue Gardenia' and 'White Pearl' have double flowers
C. portenschlagiana (C. muralis) DALMATIAN BELLFLOWER Perennial Zones 2–9, 14–24, 31–41	Low, leafy, mounding mats 4–7 in. high	Roundish, heart-shaped, deep green leaves with deeply toothed, slightly wavy edges	Flaring bell-shaped, violet blue flowers to 1 in. long; 2 or 3 on each semierect stem. Late spring into summer, sometimes blooming again in fall	Fine plant for edging or as small-scale ground cover. In warm regions best in partial shade. Spreads moderately fast; is sturdy, permanent, and not invasive. Easily increased by dividing. 'Resholt' has larger, darker flowers

CAMPANULA

NAME, TYPE	GROWTH HABIT, SIZE	FOLIAGE	FLOWERS	USES, COMMENTS
C. poscharskyana SERBIAN BELLFLOWER Perennial	Spreading, many branched, leafy, with semiupright flowering stems 1 ft. tall or taller	Long heart-shaped, irregularly toothed, slightly hairy leaves 1–3½ in. long, ¾–3 in. wide	Star-shaped, ½–1 in. across, blue-lilac or lavender. Spring to early summer. There also is a white-flowered form	Very vigorous. Shaded border near pools, shaded rock gardens, with fuchsias and begonias. Needs little water. Small area ground cover. Unlike other campanulas, thrives even in Zones 10–12
C. pyramidalis CHIMNEY BELLFLOWER Biennial or short-lived perennial Zones 4–9, 14–24, 31, 32	Sturdy upright stems, unbranched or branched at base, 4–6 ft. tall	Leaves nearly heart-shaped, about 2 in. long, with long stalks	Flat, saucer-shaped blue or white flowers, over 1 in. long, in dense spikes. Summer	Back of perennial borders, bays in big shrubbery borders, containers. Stake early to keep stems straight. In colder part of range, mulch around plants
C. raddeana Perennial Zones 2–9, 14–24, 31–41	Low growing, mat forming	Small, shiny, sharp-toothed, long-stemmed, dark green leaves	Bell-shaped, drooping, profuse on foot-tall stems; deep violet blue. Summer	Good in rock garden or foreground. Needs good drainage, some lime in acid soil
C. rapunculoides ROVER BELLFLOWER Perennial	Clumps of long-stemmed leaves send up 3-ft. spires of blue-purple bells	Leaves medium green, large, heart-shaped at base	Funnel-shaped flowers, 1 in. long. Sometimes pale blue or white. Summer	Tough, invasive plant, useful in difficult soils, climates. Don't locate near delicate plants
C. rotundifolia BLUEBELL OF SCOTLAND, HAREBELL Perennial	Upright or spreading, simple or with many branches, 6–20 in. tall	Leaves green or sometimes slightly grayish. Basal leaves roundish, long-stalked, 1 in. across. Stem leaves grasslike, 2–3 in. long. May dry up before blooming time	Broad, bell-shaped, bright blue, 1 in. across, one or a few nodding in open clusters. Summer	Flower color variable, sometimes in lavender, purple, or white shades. Rock gardens, borders, naturalized under deciduous trees. Self-sows in favorable situations
C. takesimana Perennial	Clumping, to 2 ft. high, spreading freely by underground runners	Large, roundish, toothed leaves	Large, drooping, bell-shaped, pale lilac with dark red spots inside. Early summer	Vigorous spreader. Useful in borders, but don't place near delicate plants

winter. An old favorite that can add a tropical touch in the right place. Large, rich green to bronzy red leaves resemble those of banana *(Musa)* or ti plant *(Cordyline terminalis)*. Spikes of large, showy, irregularly shaped flowers bloom on 3–6-ft. stalks in summer, fall. Many varieties in a wide range of sizes and shapes, in near-white, ivory, yellow, orange, pink, apricot, coral, salmon, and red. Bicolors include 'Cleopatra', with flowers strikingly streaked and spotted red on yellow. Low-growing strains are Grand Opera (26 in.), Pfitzer's Dwarf (2½–3 ft.), and Seven Dwarfs (1½ ft.); grow Seven Dwarfs strain from seed. There are forms with variegated leaves.

Most effective in groups of single colors against plain background. Grow in borders, near poolside, in large pots or tubs on terrace or patio. Leaves useful in arrangements; cut flowers do not keep well. Plant rootstocks in spring after frost danger is past, in rich, loose soil. Set 5 in. deep, 10 in. apart. Remove faded flowers after bloom. After all flower clusters have bloomed, cut stalk to ground.

CANTALOUPE. See MELON, MUSKMELON, CANTALOUPE

CANTERBURY BELL. See CAMPANULA medium

CAPE COWSLIP. See LACHENALIA

CAPE FORGET-ME-NOT. See ANCHUSA capensis

CAPE FUCHSIA. See PHYGELIUS

CAPE HONEYSUCKLE. See TECOMARIA capensis

CAPE MALLOW. See ANISODONTEA

CAPE MARIGOLD. See DIMORPHOTHECA, OSTEOSPERMUM

CAPE PONDWEED. See APONOGETON distachyus

CAPE PRIMROSE. See STREPTOCARPUS

Capparaceae. The caper family includes the caper plant *(Capparis spinosa)* as well as *Cleome basslerana*, commonly known as spider flower.

Caprifoliaceae. The honeysuckle family of shrubs and vines contains many ornamentals in addition to honeysuckle *(Lonicera);* among them are *Abelia, Viburnum,* and *Weigela.*

CARAGANA

PEASHRUB

Fabaceae (Leguminosae)

DECIDUOUS SHRUBS OR SMALL TREES

🔆 ZONES 1–12, 35–45

☼ FULL SUN

🔴 MODERATE TO LITTLE WATER

Caragana arborescens

Native to Russia, Manchuria, Siberia. Leaves divided into small leaflets. Spring flowers shaped like bright yellow sweet peas. Useful where choice is limited by cold, heat, wind, bright sun; nearly indestructible in desert, mountain, and prairie climates. Use as windbreak, clipped hedge, cover for wildlife.

C. arborescens. SIBERIAN PEASHRUB. Fast growing to 20 ft., with 15-ft. spread. Leaves to 3 in. long, each with four to six pairs of leaflets.

C. frutex. RUSSIAN PEASHRUB. To 10 ft.; leaves have one or two pairs of 1-in. leaflets.

CARAWAY. See CARUM carvi

CARDBOARD PALM. See ZAMIA furfuracea

CARDINAL CLIMBER. See IPOMOEA quamoclit

CARDINAL FLOWER. See LOBELIA cardinalis

CAREX

SEDGE	
Cyperaceae	
PERENNIALS	
✿ ZONES 1–9, 14–24, 28–45	
☼ ◐ MIDDAY SHADE IN HOT CLIMATES	
● CONSTANTLY MOIST SOIL	

Carex buchananii

Grasslike, clumping plants grown for foliage effect in borders, rock gardens, containers, water gardens. Long, narrow evergreen leaves are often striped or oddly colored. Specialists offer many varieties.

C. buchananii. LEATHER LEAF SEDGE. Curly-tipped, arching blades 2–3 ft. tall make clumps of striking reddish bronze. Use with gray foliage or with deep greens.

C. comans (C. albula). NEW ZEALAND HAIR SEDGE. Dense, finely textured clumps of narrow leaves are silvery green. Leaves, usually 1 ft. long, may reach 6 ft.; on slopes, they look like flowing water. Also sold as 'Frosty Curls'. 'Bronze' is similar but has coppery brown leaves.

C. conica 'Marginata'. A 6-in. dwarf sedge with white-margined leaves.

C. elata 'Bowles Golden'. Clumps up to 2 ft. have narrow leaves that emerge bright yellow in spring and hold some color until late summer. Needs much moisture; will grow in water.

C. flacca (C. glauca). BLUE SEDGE. Creeping perennial with blue-gray grasslike foliage 6–12 in. tall; evergreen only in mildest climates. Tolerant of many soils and irrigation schemes; best in moist soil. Not invasive but spreads slowly and can be clipped like a lawn. Endures light foot traffic, moderate shade, competition with tree roots.

C. morrowii expallida (C. m. 'Variegata'). VARIEGATED JAPANESE SEDGE. Drooping leaves striped with green and white make 1-ft. mound. Edging plant; single clumps attractive among rocks. 'Aurea-variegata' ('Goldband') has gold-striped leaves.

CARICA papaya

PAPAYA	
Caricaceae	
EVERGREEN TREE	
✿ ZONES 21, 23–27; OR IN GREENHOUSE	
☼ BENEFITS FROM REFLECTED HEAT IN WINTER	
● REGULAR WATER	

Carica papaya

Native to tropical America. Grows 20–25 ft. tall, with a straight trunk topped by crown of broad (to 2-ft.), fanlike, deeply lobed leaves on 2-ft.-long stems. Cream-colored flowers are inconspicuous; trees bear fruit when young. Self-fertile forms are sometimes available; otherwise, need both male and female trees to get fruit. To get most fruit, don't attempt to grow papaya as permanent tree. Keep a few plants coming along each year and destroy old ones.

Give plants regular supply of water and fertilizer in warm weather. Grow from seeds saved from fruit, or start with purchased plants.

CARISSA

Apocynaceae	
EVERGREEN SHRUBS	
✿ ZONES 22–27; SEE BELOW	
☼ ◐ TOLERATE SOME SHADE; FRUIT BEST IN SUN	
● REGULAR WATER	

Carissa macrocarpa

Their rightful climates are Zones 22–27, but so many gardeners find carissa appealing that these shrubs are grown in Zones 12, 13, 16–21, 28—far beyond safe limits. Excellent in ocean wind, salt spray. Easy to grow. Accept variety of soils. Prune to control erratic growth.

C. edulis. Native to Africa. Differs from widely grown *C. macrocarpa* in several ways. Shrubby or somewhat vinelike to 10 ft.; will grow to 30 ft. high and as wide. Glossy, bright green, red-tinged leaves to 2 in. long. Bears large clusters of pure white, fragrant flowers, opening from pink buds. Cherry-size fruit changes from green to red to purplish black as it ripens.

CARISSA'S TASTY FRUIT

Carissa macrocarpa, a plant of considerable beauty and function, also offers tasty and useful oval fruits. Pick them when they are 1–2 in. long and red. They're good eaten out of hand or in salads (skin and all). When people describe the taste, they most often use the word "cranberry." If you can pick enough at one time, you can make jelly, sauce, or pie from them. While picking, be wary of the plant's spines.

C. macrocarpa (C. grandiflora). NATAL PLUM. Native to South Africa. Fast-growing, strong, upright, rounded shrub of rather loose habit to 5–7 ft. (occasionally to 18 ft.). Lustrous, leathery, rich green, 3-in. oval leaves. Spines along branches and at end of each twig. White flowers, almost as fragrant as star jasmine and of same five-petaled star shape but larger (to 2 in. wide), appear throughout year, followed by fruit. Flowers, green fruit, and ripe fruit often appear together. Use as screen or hedge. Prune heavily for formal hedges, lightly for informal screen. Strong growth, spines discourage trespassers. Don't plant near walkways, where spines can be annoying to passersby. Widely used as an ocean-front plant in Florida. If you grow Natal plum outside Zones 22–27, give it same favorite spot you'd give bougainvillea—a warm wall facing south or west, preferably with overhang to keep off frost. It may also be grown as an indoor plant in good light. Many varieties are available.

'Boxwood Beauty'. Exceptionally compact growth to 2 ft. and as wide. Deep green leaves, like a large-leafed boxwood. Excellent for hedging and shaping. No thorns.

'Fancy'. Upright grower to 6 ft. Unusually large fruit, good show of flowers. Use as lightly pruned screen.

'Green Carpet'. Low growing to 1–1½ ft., spreading to 4 ft. or more. Smaller leaves than those of the species. Excellent ground cover.

'Horizontalis'. To 1½–2 ft., spreading, trailing. Dense foliage.

'Minima'. Slow growth to 1–1½ ft. tall, 2 ft. wide. Leaves and flowers both tiny.

'Prostrata'. Vigorous, to about 2 ft. and spreading. Good ground cover. Prune out growth that tends to grow upright. Can be trained as espalier.

'Ruby Point'. Upright grower to 6 ft. New leaves hold their red color through the growing season.

'Tomlinson'. Dwarf, compact growth to 2–2½ ft. high, 3 ft. wide. Shiny mahogany-tinted foliage, large flowers, wine-colored fruit. No thorns. Slow growing. Use as tub plant or for foundation plantings.

'Tuttle' ('Nana Compacta Tuttlei'). To 2–3 ft. high, 3–5 ft. wide. Compact, dense foliage. Heavy producer of flowers and fruit. Use as ground cover.

CARMEL CREEPER. See CEANOTHUS griseus horizontalis

CARNATION. See DIANTHUS caryophyllus

CAROB. See CERATONIA siliqua

CAROLINA ALLSPICE. See CALYCANTHUS floridus

CAROLINA JESSAMINE. See GELSEMIUM sempervirens

CAROLINA LAUREL CHERRY. See PRUNUS caroliniana

CARPENTERIA californica

BUSH ANEMONE

Philadelphiaceae (Saxifragaceae)

EVERGREEN SHRUB

ZONES 5–9, 14–24, 31

LIGHT SHADE

REGULAR TO LITTLE WATER

Carpenteria californica

Highly decorative California native accepts ordinary garden conditions, including regular moisture if soil is well drained. Slow growing to 3–6 ft., with many stems rising from base. Older bark is light colored and peeling; new shoots are purplish. Thick, narrow leaves are dark green above, whitish beneath, 2–4½ in. long. In late spring and summer, clusters of lightly scented, 1½–3-in., anemonelike white flowers with yellow centers appear at branch ends. Prune after flowering to shape or restrain growth. In marginal climates, grow against warm wall.

CARPET BUGLE. See AJUGA

CARPINUS

HORNBEAM

Betulaceae

DECIDUOUS TREES

ZONES VARY BY SPECIES

EXPOSURE NEEDS VARY BY SPECIES

REGULAR WATER

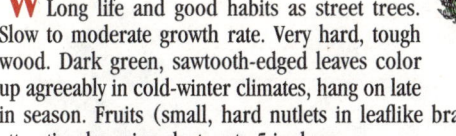

Carpinus betulus

Well-behaved, relatively small shade trees. Long life and good habits as street trees. Slow to moderate growth rate. Very hard, tough wood. Dark green, sawtooth-edged leaves color up agreeably in cold-winter climates, hang on late in season. Fruits (small, hard nutlets in leaflike bracts) are carried in attractive drooping clusters to 5 in. long.

C. betulus. EUROPEAN HORNBEAM. Zones 3–9, 14–17, 31–41. Excellent landscape tree to 40 ft. tall. Dense pyramidal form, eventually becoming broad with drooping outer branches. Handsome, furrowed gray bark somewhat similar to that of *C. caroliniana*. Very clean leaves, 2–5 in. long, turn yellow or dark red in autumn. Best in full sun, but tolerates light shade. 'Fastigiata' is the variety commonly sold; though name implies very upright growth, tree develops an oval-vase shape with age.

C. caroliniana. AMERICAN HORNBEAM. Zones 1–9, 14–17, 26, 28–43. Native from Nova Scotia to Minnesota, southward to Texas and Florida. Also known as blue beech and ironwood in its native range, where it is often found at forest edges or as understory plant along rivers and streams (in this location, it withstands periodic flooding). Those common names refer to the tree trunk, which is blue gray and smooth, with undulations that look like muscles flexing beneath the surface. To 25–30 ft. tall with round head; can be grown as single or multitrunked tree. Leaves, 1–3 in. long, turn mottled yellow and red in fall. Drops leaves before *C. betulus*. Does well in exposures from full sun to heavy shade. Best in natural gardens.

CARPOBROTUS

ICE PLANT

Aizoaceae

SUCCULENT PERENNIALS OR SUBSHRUBS

ZONES 12–27

FULL SUN

TAKE CONSIDERABLE DROUGHT

Carpobrotus chilensis

Trailing plants with coarse, fleshy leaves and summer blooms; useful for binding sand at the beach and for covering sunny banks (but not steep banks, since their weight when waterlogged could cause them to slide). Can rot in very wet conditions; can suffer dieback if severely stressed by lack of water or nitrogen during growth season. Scale insects can be a problem.

C. chilensis (Mesembryanthemum aequilaterale). Native along Pacific coast, Oregon to Baja California. The straight, three-sided leaves are 2 in. long; flowers lightly fragrant, rosy purple.

C. edulis (Mesembryanthemum edule). From South Africa. Leaves curved, 4–5 in. long. Flowers pale yellow to rose. Fruit edible but not particularly good.

CARRION FLOWER. See STAPELIA

CARROT

Apiaceae (Umbelliferae)

BIENNIAL GROWN AS ANNUAL

ALL ZONES

FULL SUN

MAINTAIN EVEN SOIL MOISTURE

Carrot

The variety to plant depends on the soil's condition: carrots reach smooth perfection only in good-textured soil free of stones and clods. Plant long market kinds only if you can give them a foot of this ideal, light soil. If you can provide only a few inches, plant half-long varieties such as 'Nantes' and 'Chantenay' or miniatures 'Amstel', 'Lady Finger', or 'Short 'n Sweet'.

Sow thickly in rows at least 1 ft. apart. Soil should be fine enough for root development and loose enough so crusting can't check sprouting of seeds. If crust should form, keep soil soft by sprinkling. Too much nitrogen or a lot of manure will make excessive top growth and cause forking of roots. Maintain even soil moisture; alternating dry and wet conditions cause split roots. To grow successive plantings, sow seed when previous planting is up and growing; in cold-winter climates, make last sowing 70 days before anticipated killing frost. When tops are 1–2 in. high, thin plants to 1½ in. apart; thin again if roots begin to crowd. After first thinning, apply narrow band of commercial fertilizer 2 in. out from the row. Begin harvest when carrots reach finger size, usually 30 to 40 days after sowing; most types reach maturity in 60 to 70 days. In mild-winter climates, carrots store well in the ground; dig as needed.

> ## CARROT THINNINGS TO EAT
> Carrot harvesting actually starts with thinning—the removal of excess seedlings when the tops are about 1–2 in. tall to make space for others to grow. Steam the tiny carrots in butter. Or chop the entire miniature plants, tops and all; add to tossed salads for a fresh surprise.

CARROT WOOD. See CUPANIOPSIS anacardioides

CARTHAMUS tinctorius

SAFFLOWER, FALSE SAFFRON

Asteraceae (Compositae)

ANNUAL

🗡 ALL ZONES

☼ FULL SUN

💧 MODERATE WATER

Carthamus tinctorius

This relative of the thistles is ornamental as well as useful. Erect, spiny-leafed stems, 1–3 ft. tall, bear orange-yellow flower heads above leafy bracts; inner bracts are spiny. Durable cut flower, fresh or dried. Grown commercially for oil extracted from the seeds. The dried flowers have been used for seasoning in place of true saffron, which they somewhat resemble in color and flavor. Sow seeds in place in spring after frosts. An ornamental spineless safflower is also available.

CARUM carvi

CARAWAY

Apiaceae (Umbelliferae)

BIENNIAL HERB

🗡 ALL ZONES

☼ FULL SUN

💧 REGULAR WATER

Carum carvi

Mound of carrotlike leaves, 1–2 ft. high, in first year. Umbrellalike clusters of white flowers rise above foliage in second year. Plant dies after seeds ripen in midsummer. Start from seed sown in place in fall or spring. Thrives in well-drained soil. Thin seedlings to 1½ ft. To harvest seed, pick dry heads and rub off seeds. Sift to remove chaff, dry thoroughly, and store in jars. Use dried seeds for flavoring pickles, vegetables, cookies, rye bread.

CARYA

PECAN, HICKORY

Juglandaceae

DECIDUOUS TREES

🗡 ZONES VARY BY SPECIES

☼ FULL SUN

💧💧 REGULAR TO MODERATE WATER

Carya illinoensis

Large trees with leaves divided featherwise into many leaflets, inconspicuous flowers, and nuts enclosed in husks that usually break away at maturity. Nuts of pecan and hickory are delicious, and the former is an important commercial crop. Trees are too large for smaller home plots, but are attractive where space is available. All develop deep taproots and should be planted while young and not moved later.

C. illinoensis. PECAN. Native to southern and central U.S. Grow for nut crop in Zones 8–10, 12–14, 18–20, 26–33, hardiest varieties in 35; may also be grown as an ornamental in Zones 4–7, 34, 36, 37, 39, 41. Graceful, shapely tree to 70 ft. tall and equally wide. Foliage like that of English walnut but prettier, with more (11–17) leaflets that are narrower and longer (4–7 in.); foliage pattern is finer textured, casts less shade. Trees need well-drained, deep soils (6–10 ft. deep); won't stand salinity. Prune to shape or remove dead wood.

Papershell pecans grow in hot climates; they need a 210-day growing season to ripen. 'Caddo', 'Elliot', 'Houma', 'Melrose', 'Stuart', and 'Sumner' are scab-resistant varieties suitable for the Southeast. Western papershells, recommended for drier regions from West Texas westward, include 'Western Schley' and 'Wichita'. Hardy northern varieties suitable for the Midwest

include the prevalent 'Major' as well as 'Fritz', 'Greenriver', and 'Peruque'. Most varieties need pollinators.

C. ovata. SHAGBARK HICKORY. Zones 1–6, 28–44. Grows to 60–100 ft. Most conspicuous feature is bark, which is gray and shaggy, with large plates curving out and away from the trunk. The hard-shelled nuts are sweet. Autumn foliage is an attractive yellow and brown. Wood is proverbially tough and hard. *C. laciniosa*, shellbark hickory, is a similar but smaller tree.

Caryophyllaceae. The pink family includes many garden annuals and perennials as well as a few weeds. Leaves are borne in opposite pairs at joints that are often swollen; leaves are often joined together at their bases. Pinks and carnations are typical representatives, along with snow-in-summer (*Cerastium*) and *Lychnis*.

CARYOPTERIS

BLUEBEARD

Verbenaceae

DECIDUOUS SHRUBS

🗡 ZONES VARY BY SPECIES

☼ FULL SUN

💧 MODERATE WATER

Caryopteris clandonensis

Valued for contribution of cool blue to flower borders from August to frost. Generally grown as shrubby perennials. If plant is not frozen back in winter, cut nearly to ground in spring. Cut back growth after each wave of bloom to encourage more flowers. Provide good drainage; can rot in wet soils.

C. clandonensis. BLUE MIST. Zones 3-7, 14–17, 29–41. Low-growing mound (to 2 ft. tall and wide) of narrow, 3-in.-long leaves. Clusters of small blue flowers top upper parts of stems. Selected forms 'Azure' and 'Heavenly Blue' have deep blue flowers. 'Dark Knight' and 'Longwood Blue' have deep blue flowers and silvery foliage. 'Worcester Gold' has yellow leaves, blue flowers.

C. incana (C. mastacanthus). COMMON BLUEBEARD, BLUE SPIRAEA. Zones 4–7, 14–17, 29–34. Taller than *C. clandonensis*, with looser, more open growth to 3–4 ft. Lavender blue flowers.

CARYOTA

FISHTAIL PALM

Arecaceae (Palmae)

PALMS

🗡 ZONES 23–25; OR INDOORS

☼◑ FULL SUN OR PARTIAL SHADE

💧 REGULAR WATER

Caryota ochlandra

Feather palms with finely divided leaves, the leaflets flattened and split at tips like fish tails. Tender. Native to Southeast Asia, where they grow in full sun. Indoors, need as much light as possible.

C. mitis. CLUSTERED FISHTAIL PALM. Slow grower to 20–25 ft. Basal offshoots eventually form clustered trunks. Foliage light green. Very tender; thrives only in ideal environment.

C. ochlandra. CANTON FISHTAIL PALM. Will probably reach 25 ft. Medium dark green leaves. Hardiest of the caryotas, it has survived to 26°F/–3°C.

C. urens. FISHTAIL WINE PALM. Single-stemmed palm to 100 ft. in Asia, to 15–20 ft. here with careful protection. If temperatures go below 32°F/0°C, it's certain to die. Dark green leaves. Avoid handling fruit with bare hands; invisible crystals can cause severe itching.

CASHMERE BOUQUET. See CLERODENDRUM bungei

CASSIA

SENNA

Fabaceae (Leguminosae)

EVERGREEN OR DECIDUOUS SHRUBS OR TREES AND
A PERENNIAL

⚘ ZONES VARY BY SPECIES

☼ FULL SUN

🌢🌢 REGULAR TO MODERATE WATER

Cassia splendida

The following tropical flowering shrubs and
trees from many lands provide numerous
landscaping choices for gardeners in southern-
most climates. *C. marilandica* is an exception: it's a perennial grown in
temperate regions. "Yellow" and "golden" are the words associated with
cassia. Blossoms may be yellow, bright yellow, egg-yolk yellow, deep yellow
gold. Flowering dates are approximate, since plants may bloom at any time
or scatter bloom over a long period. Many species have been reclassified
as *Senna*.

C. alata (Senna alata). CANDLE BUSH. Deciduous shrub. Zones 23,
25–27. Native to tropics. Grows 8–12 ft. tall and spreads wider. Golden
yellow flowers (1 in. wide) in big spikelike clusters, November–January.
Leaves divided into 12–28 leaflets 2½ in. long. Prune hard after bloom.

C. artemisioides (Senna artemisioides). FEATHERY CASSIA. Evergreen shrub. Zones 8, 9, 12–16, 18–23. Native to Australia. To 3–5 ft.;
attractive light, airy structure. Gray leaves divided into six to eight needlelike, 1-in.-long leaflets. Sulfur yellow, ¾-in. flowers, five to eight in a cluster, bloom January–April, often into summer. Prune lightly after flowering
to eliminate heavy setting of seed. More drought tolerant than other
species.

C. bicapsularis (Senna bicapsularis). Evergreen shrub. Zones 13,
22–27. Native to tropics. To 10 ft. Recovers after being killed to ground by
frost. Yellow, ½-in.-wide flowers in spikelike clusters, October–February,
if not cut short by frost. Leaflets roundish, rather thick, six to ten to a leaf.
Prune severely after flowering.

C. corymbosa (Senna corymbosa). FLOWERY SENNA. Evergreen
shrub. Zones 12, 13, 21–27. Native to Argentina. Naturalizes. To 10 ft. Yellow flowers in rounded clusters, spring to fall. Dark green leaves with six
narrow, oblong, 1–2-in. leaflets. Prune severely after flowering.

C. didymobotrya. Evergreen shrub. Zones 13, 22–27. Native to East
Africa. Naturalizes. Rangy grower to 10 ft. Leaflets 2 in. long, 8–16 pairs
per leaf. Yellow, 1½-in.-wide flowers in upright, dense clusters (to 1 ft.),
December–April. Thrives in heat. Foliage is smelly when cut or bruised,
but plant is nonetheless attractive in large wild gardens. Prune hard after
bloom. Also sold as *Senna didymobotrya* and *C. nairobensis*.

C. excelsa. CROWN OF GOLD TREE. Partially evergreen tree. Zones 12,
13, 19–27. Native to Argentina. Grows fast to 25–30 ft. Leaves divided into
10–20 pairs of 1-in.-long leaflets. Large bright yellow flowers in 12–16-in.-
long clusters, late summer, early fall. Prune hard after flowering.

C. fistula. SHOWER OF GOLD, GOLDEN SHOWER. Deciduous or partly
evergreen tree. Zones 25, 27. To 30–40 ft., with 2-ft. leaves divided into 3-
in. leaflets. Summer flowers are bright yellow, 2 in. wide, in drooping,
nearly 2-ft.-long clusters of 50 or more. Prune hard after bloom. Extremely
showy, but suitable only for warmest climates.

C. leptophylla. GOLD MEDALLION TREE. Nearly evergreen tree. Zones
21–25, 27. Native to Brazil. Most shapely and graceful of the cassias. Fast
growing to 20–25 ft.; open headed, low spreading, tending to weep. Shape
to single trunk or plant becomes very sprawling. Leaves with up to 12 pairs
of narrow leaflets. Deep yellow flowers to 3 in. wide, in 6–8-in. clusters in
July–August; scattered blooms later. Prune hard after flowering.

C. marilandica (Senna marilandica). WILD SENNA. Zones 1–10,
14, 28–43. Unlike most of its relatives, *C. marilandica* is a perennial,
dying back to the ground in winter. Grows 4–6 ft. tall. Feathery bright
green leaves; tall clusters of brownish yellow flowers at stalk ends in summer.

C. nairobensis. See C. didymobotrya

C. multijuga (Senna multijuga). Evergreen tree. Zones 22–25, 27.
Native to Brazil. Heavy-foliaged, much-branched tree to 15–20 ft. Some-
what brittle. Yellow, 2-in.-wide flowers in clusters in late summer and fall.
Leaves have 18–40 pairs of rather narrow leaflets that grow to ¾ in. long.
Prune hard after flowering.

C. splendida (Senna splendida). GOLDEN WONDER SENNA. Evergreen shrub. Zones 12, 13, 21–27. Native to Brazil. This name has been
applied to a number of cassias of varying growth habits. To 10–12 ft. high
and about as wide. Orange-yellow, 1½-in.-wide flowers in loose clusters at
branch ends, November–January. Other plantings of cassias with this
name, with bright yellow flowers, are strongly horizontal in branch pattern,
5–8 ft. high, spreading to 12 ft. wide. All must be severely pruned after
flowering.

C. surattensis (C. glauca or Senna surattensis). Evergreen shrub.
Zones 19–27. Grows fast to 6–8 ft. and spreads wider. Bright yellow flowers (¾ in. wide) in small clusters at branch ends, nearly all year.
Roundish, 1½-in.-long leaflets, 12–20 to each leaf. Does not need to be
pruned heavily. One of best for small gardens.

CASTANEA

CHESTNUT

Fagaceae

DECIDUOUS TREES

⚘ ZONES VARY BY SPECIES

☼ FULL SUN

🌢 REGULAR WATER

Castanea mollissima

The American chestnut (*C. dentata*) has
become nearly extinct as a result of chestnut blight, but other chestnuts
are available. They make wonderful, dense shade trees where there is
space to accommodate them and where their litter and rank-smelling
pollen won't be as noticeable— at large country places, for example. All
have handsome dark to bright green foliage. Small, creamy white flowers
in long (8–10-in.), slim catkins make quite a display in early summer.
The large edible nuts are enclosed in prickly burrs. Plant two or more
varieties to ensure cross-pollination and a substantial crop. Single trees
bear lightly or not at all. Somewhat drought tolerant.

C. mollissima. CHINESE CHESTNUT. Zones 2–9, 14–17, 28, 31–41.
Grows to 60 ft. with rounded crown that may spread to 40 ft. Leaves 3–7
in. long, with coarsely toothed edges. Most nursery trees are grown from
seed, not cuttings; hence, nuts are variable but generally of good quality.
Intolerant of alkaline soil.

C. sativa. SPANISH CHESTNUT. Zones 2–9, 14–17. Produces the nuts
sold commercially. Permitted only in the West, where chestnut blight is not
yet a problem. Larger, broader than *C. mollissima*; can reach 100 ft. high
with greater spread.

Dunstan hybrid chestnuts. Zones 2–9, 14–24, 28, 31–41. These
are offspring of American and Chinese chestnut parents, with characteristics intermediate between the two (the American chestnut is—or was—a
tall, broad timber tree with small but very sweet nuts). The hybrids seem
resistant to the blight and produce nuts equal to Spanish chestnuts in size
and sweeter in flavor.

CASTANOSPERMUM australe

MORETON BAY CHESTNUT

Fabaceae (Leguminosae)

EVERGREEN TREE

⚘ ZONES 18–22, 25–27

☼ FULL SUN

🌢 REGULAR WATER

Native to Australia. Beautiful in foliage; spectacular in flower. To 50–60 ft. tall, nearly as wide.
Large, shiny, dark green leaves are divided into
11–15 leaflets about 1½ by 5 in. Flowers bright red

Castanospermum australe

and yellow, in stiff spikes about 8 in. long. They grow from twigs, branches, and main trunk in summer. Seeds like chestnuts are occasionally roasted and eaten but don't taste very good.

CAST-IRON PLANT. See ASPIDISTRA elatior

CASTOR ARALIA. See KALOPANAX septemlobus

CASTOR BEAN. See RICINUS communis

CASUARINA

BEEFWOOD, SHE-OAK	
Casuarinaceae	
EVERGREEN TREES	
🌿 ZONES 8, 9, 12–26	
☀ FULL SUN	
🔴 REGULAR TO LITTLE WATER	

Casuarina equisetifolia

Native mostly to Australia. Long, thin, jointed, green branches look like long pine needles; true leaves are inconspicuous. Sturdy root system and ability, when damaged, to send up suckers from roots help these plants stabilize sandy soil near beaches, where tolerance of wind and salt makes them useful windbreaks as well. Also tolerate heat and wet or dry soils.

C. cunninghamiana. RIVER SHE-OAK. Tallest and largest. To 70 ft. Finest texture, with dark green branches.

C. equisetifolia. HORSETAIL TREE. Fast grower to 40–60 ft., 20 ft. wide. Has pendulous gray-green branches. This is the species widely used for ocean-front windbreaks, clipped hedges, and topiary in South Florida. Plants sold under this name may be *C. cunninghamiana* or hybrids between it and *C. glauca*.

CATALPA

Bignoniaceae	
DECIDUOUS TREES	
🌿 ZONES 3–24, 28–41	
☀◑ FULL SUN OR LIGHT SHADE	
🔴 REGULAR TO MODERATE WATER	

Catalpa speciosa

Catalpas are among the few truly deciduous trees that can compete in flower and leaf with subtropical species. Bloom in late spring and summer, bearing large, upright clusters of trumpet-shaped, 2-in.-wide flowers in pure white striped and marked with yellow and soft brown; flowers held above large, bold, heart-shaped leaves. Long, bean-shaped seed capsules, sometimes called Indian beans or Indian stogies, follow the blossoms.

Unusually well adapted to extremes of heat and cold, and to all soils. Where winds are strong, plant in lee of taller trees or buildings to protect leaves from damage. Some gardeners object to litter of fallen flowers in summer and seed capsules in autumn. Plants need shaping while young, seldom develop a well-established dominant shoot. Shorten side branches as tree grows. When branching begins at desired height, remove lower branches.

For the tree sometimes called desert catalpa, see *Chilopsis linearis*. Another tree sometimes mistakenly called catalpa is the very similar *Paulownia tomentosa*, or empress tree, with lavender flowers. *Paulownia* shows flower buds in winter; catalpa does not.

C. bignonioides. COMMON CATALPA, INDIAN BEAN. Native to southeastern U.S. Generally smaller than *C. speciosa*, 20–50 ft. according to climate or soil, with somewhat smaller spread. Leaves 5–8 in. long, often in whorls, give off odd odor when crushed. Chlorotic in alkaline soil. Yellow leaves of 'Aurea' are showier where summers are cool.

'Nana'. UMBRELLA CATALPA. A dense globe form usually grafted high on *C. bignonioides*. Almost always sold as *C. bungei*. It never blooms. Cut it back to keep it in scale.

C. erubescens 'Purpurea'. Selection of hybrid between *C. bignonioides* and a Chinese species. Tree resembles *C. bignonioides* parent. Young leaves and branchlets are deep blackish purple, turning purple-toned green in summer.

C. speciosa. WESTERN CATALPA. Native to central and southern Midwest. Round headed; 40–70 ft. tall. Leaves 6–12 in. long; no odor when crushed. Fewer flowers per cluster than for *C. bignonioides*. Early training and pruning will give tall trunk and umbrella-shaped crown.

Catalpa speciosa

CATANANCHE caerulea

CUPID'S DART	
Asteraceae (Compositae)	
PERENNIAL	
🌿 ALL ZONES	
☀ FULL SUN	
🔴 MODERATE WATER	

Catananche caerulea

Sturdy, free-flowering plant for summer borders and arrangements. Needs well-drained soil, not too much moisture; self-sows freely. Narrow gray-green leaves, 8–12 in. long, mostly at base of stem. Leafless, 2-ft. stems carry lavender blue, 2-in. flower heads reminiscent of cornflowers and surrounded by strawlike, shining bracts. Flowers dry well for everlasting bouquets. Remove faded flowers to prolong bloom. 'Alba' is white flowered.

> ### USEFUL IN MORE WAYS THAN ONE
>
> Madagascar periwinkle is a workhorse in the garden, bearing its colorful blooms over a long season and outlasting other summer annuals. It doesn't even need deadheading to keep the show going; the blossoms drop cleanly on their own. The plant's usefulness goes beyond the garden: in the 1950s, its alkaloids were discovered to be valuable in treating leukemia.

CATHARANTHUS roseus (Vinca rosea)

MADAGASCAR PERIWINKLE	
Apocynaceae	
PERENNIAL OFTEN GROWN AS ANNUAL	
🌿 ALL ZONES	
☀◑ FULL SUN OR PARTIAL SHADE	
🔴 MODERATE WATER	

Catharanthus roseus

Good for summer–fall color in hot climates. Thrives in dry or humid heat. Glossy leaves 1–3 in. long cover bushy plant 1–2 ft. high. Phlox-like flowers 1½ in. wide in pure white, white with rose or red eye, blush pink, clear cotton-candy pink, or bright rose. The Little series grows 8–10 in. high. Pacific and Cooler series are compact, 15-in. plants with large (2-in. or wider) flowers. The Tropicana series is early blooming (60 days from seed). Creeping strains, including the Carpet series, grow 4–8 in. tall, 1½ ft. wide. All types will bloom first season from seed sown early indoors, in greenhouse or cold frame. Nurseries sell plants in late spring.

Blooms all summer and keeps flowering after zinnias and marigolds have gone, until Thanksgiving if weather stays mild. Lives over in frost-free areas but may look ragged in winter. Self-sows readily. Provide good drainage and avoid overwatering.

CATMINT. See NEPETA faassenii

CATNIP. See NEPETA cataria

CAT'S CLAW. See MACFADYENA unguis-cati

CATTLEYA

Orchidaceae
EPIPHYTIC ORCHIDS
🗓 ZONES 25–27; OR GREENHOUSE OR INDOOR
  PLANTS
☀ LIGHT SHADE
💧 REGULAR WATER

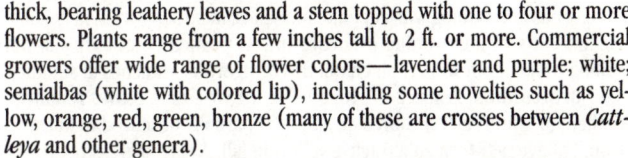
Cattleya

Native to tropical America. Most popular and best known of orchids. Showy flowers are used for corsages.

Species, varieties, and hybrids are too numerous to list here. All have pseudobulbs, 1–3 in. thick, bearing leathery leaves and a stem topped with one to four or more flowers. Plants range from a few inches tall to 2 ft. or more. Commercial growers offer wide range of flower colors—lavender and purple; white; semialbas (white with colored lip), including some novelties such as yellow, orange, red, green, bronze (many of these are crosses between *Cattleya* and other genera).

In mildest parts of Florida and Texas, potted plants are often left on terraces or under trees year-round; in Central Florida, they should be brought indoors during few cold nights. Indoors, all cattleyas grow best in greenhouse where temperature, humidity, and light can be readily controlled. However, they can be grown as house plants. Main requirements: (1) warm temperature (60°F/16°C at night, 70°F/21°C or higher during the day); (2) relatively high humidity (50–60 percent or more); (3) good light (20–40 percent of outside light with protection from hot midday sun). Color of orchid foliage should be light green, and leaves should be erect. When light intensity is too low, leaves turn dark green and new growth becomes soft. Also see Orchidaceae.

CAULIFLOWER

Brassicaceae (Cruciferae)
ANNUAL OR BIENNIAL GROWN AS ANNUAL
🗓 ALL ZONES
☀ FULL SUN
💧 REGULAR WATER

Cauliflower

Related to broccoli and cabbage; has similar cultural requirements but is more difficult to grow. Easiest in cool, humid regions. Where summers are hot, grow it to harvest well before or well after midsummer; also look for heat-tolerant varieties. Home gardeners usually plant one of the several 'Snowball' varieties or hybrids such as 'Early White Hybrid' and 'Snow Crown Hybrid'. An unusual variety is 'Purple Head', a large plant with a deep purple head that turns green in cooking. 'Romanesco' makes cone-shaped heads of light green flowerets that are less tightly packed than those of other cauliflowers. Considered to have a fine flavor.

Grow cauliflower like broccoli. Start with small plants; space them 1½–2 ft. apart in rows and leave 3 ft. between rows. Be sure to keep plants actively growing; any check during transplanting or later growth is likely to cause premature setting of undersized heads. When heads first appear, tie up the large leaves around them to keep them white. On self-blanching varieties, leaves curl over developing heads without assistance. Harvest heads as soon as they reach full size. Most varieties are ready in 50 to 100 days after transplanting; overwintering types may take 6 months. Cauliflower is subject to same pests as cabbage.

CEANOTHUS

Rhamnaceae
EVERGREEN OR DECIDUOUS SHRUBS
🗓 ZONES VARY BY SPECIES
☀ FULL SUN OR LIGHT SHADE
💧 LITTLE WATER, EXCEPT AS NOTED

Ceanothus americanus

Some 60 species and innumerable named varieties and hybrids exist, ranging in form from low-growing ground covers to tall shrubs. Most have clusters of showy blue flowers; a few bear white or pinkish blossoms. Bloom time is spring, except as noted. Foliage is typically evergreen. Most species thrive only where winters are not severe and where summers are not hot and humid, effectively limiting them to the West Coast. Two of the species described below are deciduous shrubs native to eastern and central North America.

C. americanus. NEW JERSEY TEA. Deciduous. Zones 2–6, 31–43. Probably the hardiest species. Dense, compact, rounded plant to 3 ft. tall, 5 ft. wide. Leaves are dark green, prominently veined. Tiny white flowers in 2-in. clusters at branch tips in summer. Attractive but not showy. Tough, tolerant plant for banks or wild areas. Regular to moderate water. Hybrids between this and tender blue *C. caeruleus* are occasionally tried. One, 'Gloire de Versailles', a tall deciduous shrub with light blue flowers, might survive in the zones noted above with special care.

C. 'Concha'. Evergreen. Zones 6–9, 14–24. Grows 6–7 ft. tall, to 8 ft. wide. Densely clad in dark green leaves. Dark blue flowers. One of best for gardens; tolerates summer water.

C. 'Dark Star'. Evergreen. Zones 4–9, 14–24. Grows 5–6 ft. tall, 8–10 ft. wide. Tiny dark green leaves; cobalt blue flowers. Similar to 'Julia Phelps'.

C. gloriosus. POINT REYES CEANOTHUS. Evergreen. Zones 4–6, 15–17. Grows 1–1½ ft. high, spreading 12–16 ft. Tough, spiny dark green leaves; light blue flowers. Does not do well in summer heat. 'Anchor Bay' is more densely leafed, spreads half the distance, and bears deeper blue blossoms. *C. g. exaltatus* 'Emily Brown' grows 2–3 ft. high and 8–12 ft. wide, has dark violet blue blooms.

C. griseus horizontalis. CARMEL CREEPER. Evergreen. Zones 4–9, 14–24. Handsome, glossy leafed; to 1½–2½ ft. high and 5–15 ft. wide. Light blue flowers. Sometimes suffers winter damage in colder part of range. 'Hurricane Point' grows 2–3 ft. high and spreads rapidly to 36 ft. wide. 'Yankee Point' is the same height but spreads only 8–10 ft.

C. 'Julia Phelps'. Evergreen. Zones 4–9, 14–24. Grows 4½–7 ft. tall, to 9 ft. wide. Tiny dark green leaves; indigo blue flowers. Similar to 'Dark Star'.

C. ovatus. Deciduous. Zones 2–6, 32–41. Grows 2–3 ft. tall, with shiny, dense foliage. White flowers in early summer are followed by bright red seed capsules. Regular to moderate water.

C. thyrsiflorus. BLUE BLOSSOM. Evergreen. Zones 3–9, 14–24. Among the hardiest of the evergreen species. Grows 6–21 ft. tall, 8–30 ft. wide. Glossy green leaves; spikelike clusters of light to dark blue blossoms. There are also varieties bearing white flowers. *C. t. repens* is a prostrate form.

CEDAR. See CEDRUS

CEDAR, EASTERN RED. See JUNIPERUS virginiana

CEDAR, INCENSE. See CALOCEDRUS decurrens

CEDAR, WESTERN RED. See THUJA plicata

CEDAR OF LEBANON. See CEDRUS libani

PRACTICAL GARDENING DICTIONARY
PLEASE SEE PAGES 545–616

CEDRUS

CEDAR

Pinaceae

EVERGREEN TREES

ZONES VARY BY SPECIES

FULL SUN

MODERATE WATER

Cedrus atlantica

These conifers, the true cedars, are stately specimen trees that look best when given plenty of room. Needles are borne in tufted clusters. Cone scales, like those of firs, fall from tree, leaving a spiky core behind. Male catkins produce prodigious amounts of pollen that may cover you with yellow dust on a windy day. Plant in deep, well-drained soil. All species are deep rooted and drought tolerant once established.

C. atlantica (C. libani atlantica). ATLAS CEDAR. Zones 2–24, 31, 32, 34. Native to North Africa. Slow to moderate growth to 60 ft. or more. Open, angular in youth. Branches usually get too long and heavy on young trees unless tips are pinched or cut back. In Zones 2–7, branches of any age tend to break in heavy snows. Growth naturally less open with age. Less spreading than other true cedars, but still needs 30-ft. circle.

Needles, less than 1 in. long, are bluish green. Varieties: 'Aurea', needles with yellowish tint; 'Glauca', silvery blue; 'Glauca Pendula', weeping form with blue needles; 'Pendula', vertically drooping branches. Untrained, spreading, informally branching plants are sold as "rustics." All types stand up well to hot, humid weather.

C. brevifolia. CYPRUS (or CYPRIAN) CEDAR. Zones 5–24, 32. Native to Cyprus. Resembles *C. libani* but is a smaller tree (to 50 ft.) with shorter needles (¼–½ in.) and smaller cones. Sometimes considered variety of *C. libani*. Very slow growing.

C. deodara. DEODAR CEDAR. Zones 3–12, 14–24, 27–32, favored sites of 33. (In Zones 32 and 33, best bet is an extra-hardy variety such as 'Shalimar'.) Native to the Himalayas. Fast growing to 80 ft., with 40-ft. spread at ground level. Lower branches sweep down to ground, then upward. Upper branches openly spaced, graceful. Nodding tip identifies it in skyline. Softer, lighter texture than other cedars. Planted in small lawn, it soon overpowers area. You can control spread of tree

Cedrus deodara

by cutting new growth of side branches halfway back in late spring. This pruning also makes tree more dense.

Although deodars sold by nurseries are very similar in form, many variations occur in a group of seedlings—from scarecrowlike forms to compact low shrubs. Needles, to 2 in. long, may be green or have blue, gray, or yellow cast. Following three variations are propagated by cuttings or grafting: 'Aurea', with yellow new foliage turning golden green in summer; 'Descanso Dwarf' ('Compacta'), a slow-growing form reaching 15 ft. in 20 years; and 'Pendula' ('Prostrata'), which grows flat on ground or will drape over rock or wall. Deodar cedar can be pruned to grow as spreading low or high shrub. Annual late-spring pruning will keep it in the shape you want. This is the best species for hot, humid climates.

C. libani. CEDAR OF LEBANON. Zones 3–24, 32, 34. Native to Asia Minor. To 80 ft., but slow—to 15 ft. in 15 years. Variable in habit. Usually a dense, narrow pyramid in youth. Spreads picturesquely as it matures to become majestic skyline tree with long horizontal arms and irregular crown. In young trees, needles, less than 1 in. long, are brightest green of the cedars; in old trees, they are dark gray green. Rather scarce and expensive because of time it requires to reach salable size. Routine garden care. No pruning needed. 'Sargentii' ('Pendula Sargentii') grows even more slowly, has a short trunk and crowded, pendulous branches; choice container or rock garden plant. 'Pendula' is a weeping form.

C. l. stenocoma. Zones 2–24, 32, 34, 35, 37. Hardiest of the cedars. More stiffly branched than species, with good green color.

Celastraceae. This family of evergreen or deciduous woody plants has undistinguished flowers, but fruit is often brightly colored. Bittersweet (*Celastrus*) and *Euonymus* are examples.

CELASTRUS

BITTERSWEET

Celastraceae

DECIDUOUS VINES

ZONES VARY BY SPECIES

FULL SUN

REGULAR WATER

Celastrus scandens

Grown principally for clusters of handsome summer fruit—yellow to orange capsules that split open to display brilliant red-coated seeds inside. Branches bearing fruit are much prized for indoor arrangements. Since birds seem uninterested in fruit, display extends into winter. To get fruit, you need a male plant near the female; self-fertile forms of *C. orbiculatus* are available.

Vigorous and twining with ropelike branches; need support. Will become tangled mass of intertwining branches unless pruned constantly. Cut out fruiting branches in winter; pinch out tips of vigorous branches in summer.

C. orbiculatus. Zones 2–7, 10, 29–41. To 30–40 ft. Leaves roundish, toothed, to 4 in. Fruit on short side shoots is partially obscured until leaves drop. Foliage may turn an attractive yellow in fall. A very aggressive grower that has escaped gardens and become a weed in the northeastern U.S.

C. rosthornianus (C. loeseneri). CHINESE BITTERSWEET. Zones 3–7, 10, 29–34. To 20 ft. Dark green, oval leaves to 5 in. long. Fruit heavily borne. Similar to *C. orbiculatus* but not as rampant.

C. scandens. AMERICAN BITTERSWEET. Zones 1–7, 10, 29–44. Native to eastern U.S. To 20 ft.; even higher if plant has something to grow on. If allowed to climb shrubs or small trees, it can kill them by girdling the stems. Leaves very light green, oval, toothed, to 4 in. Fruit in scattered dense clusters is held above leaves, looks showy before foliage falls.

CELERIAC

Apiaceae (Umbelliferae)

BIENNIAL GROWN AS ANNUAL

ALL ZONES

FULL SUN

KEEP SOIL EVENLY MOIST

Celeriac

A form of celery grown for its large, rounded, edible roots rather than for leafstalks; is usually displayed in markets as "celery root." Roots are peeled, then cooked or used raw in salads.

Growth requirements are same as for celery. Grow plants 6–8 in. apart in rows spaced 1½–2 ft. apart. Harvest when roots are 3 in. across or larger—in about 120 days. 'Giant Prague' and 'Alabaster' are recommended varieties.

CELERY

Apiaceae (Umbelliferae)

BIENNIAL GROWN AS ANNUAL

ALL ZONES

FULL SUN

KEEP SOIL EVENLY MOIST

Celery

Needs long period of warm but not high heat; not suited to hot, humid climates. Plant seeds in flats in early spring; where winters are mild, start in summer for winter crop. Seedlings are slow to reach planting size; to save time, purchase seedlings. Plant seedlings 6 in. apart in rows 2 ft.

apart. Enrich planting soil with fertilizer. Every 2 to 3 weeks apply liquid fertilizer with irrigation water. Work some soil up around plants as they grow to keep them upright. For whitened stalks, set bottomless milk carton, tar paper cylinder, or similar device over plants to exclude light from stalks (leaves must have sunlight). Or look for self-blanching varieties. Harvest 105 to 130 days after transplanting. Row covers will exclude many pests.

CELERY ROOT. See CELERIAC

CELOSIA

COCKSCOMB, CHINESE WOOLFLOWER

Amaranthaceae

ANNUALS

⚡ ALL ZONES

☀ FULL SUN

💧 MODERATE WATER

Celosia 'Cristata'

Richly colored tropical plants, some with flower clusters in bizarre shapes. Although attractive in cut arrangements with other flowers, in gardens celosias are most effective by themselves. Cut blooms can be dried for winter bouquets. Sow seed in place in late spring or early summer, or set out started plants.

There are two kinds of cockscombs, both derived from *C. argentea*, a species with silvery white flowers and narrow leaves to 2 in. or longer. One group, the plume cockscombs (often sold as *C.* 'Plumosa'), has plumy flower clusters. Some of these, like Chinese woolflower (sometimes sold as *C.* 'Childsii'), have flower clusters that look like tangled masses of yarn. Flowers come in brilliant shades of pink, orange red, gold, crimson. You can get 2½–3-ft.-high forms or dwarf, more compact varieties. The latter grow about 1 ft. high and bear heavily branched plumes.

The other group is the crested cockscombs (often sold as *C.* 'Cristata'). These have velvety, fan-shaped flower clusters, often much contorted and fluted. Flowers are yellow, orange, crimson, purple, and red. Tall kinds grow to 3 ft., dwarf varieties to 10 in. high.

CELTIS

HACKBERRY

Ulmaceae

DECIDUOUS TREES

⚡ ZONES VARY BY SPECIES

☀💧 FULL SUN OR PARTIAL SHADE

💧 MODERATE WATER

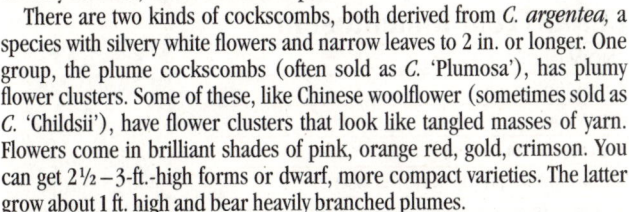

Celtis occidentalis

Related to elms and similar to them in most details, but smaller. All have virtue of deep rooting; old trees in narrow planting strips expand in trunk diameter and nearly fill strips without surface roots or any sign of heaving the sidewalk or curb. Good choice for street or lawn tree, even near buildings or paving. Canopy casts moderate shade in spring and summer; leaves turn yellow in fall. Mature trees have picturesque bark with corky warts and ridges. Small berrylike fruit attracts birds.

Hackberry is exceptionally tough, taking strong winds (stake young trees until well established), desert heat, and dry, alkaline soils. Bare-root plants, especially in larger sizes, sometimes fail to leaf out. Buy in containers or try for small bare-root trees with big root systems.

C. australis. EUROPEAN HACKBERRY. Zones 8–16, 18–20, 29–33. Moderate grower to 40 ft. in 14 to 15 years. In youth, branches are more upright than those of other hackberries. Never as wide spreading as *C. occidentalis;* dark green leaves, 2–5 in. long, more coarsely toothed and more sharply pointed. Has shorter deciduous period than *C. occidentalis.*

C. laevigata. SUGARBERRY, SUGAR HACKBERRY. Zones 7–14, 18–20, 28–35. Native to southern Midwest and South. Grows to 60 ft. or more with rounded crown. Similar to *C. occidentalis,* but resistant to witches'-broom (ugly clusters of dwarfed twigs). A desirable street or park tree.

C. occidentalis. COMMON HACKBERRY. Zones 1–24, 30–45. Native from Rocky Mountains to the Atlantic, north to Quebec and south to Alabama. Grows to form rounded crown 50 ft. high or more and nearly as wide. Branches are spreading and sometimes pendulous. Leaves oval, light green, 2–5 in. long, finely toothed on edges. Tree leafs out fairly late. Withstands urban pollution. Widely used in plains and prairie states, since it endures adverse conditions, including extreme cold, winds, soggy soil. Often disfigured by witches'-broom in the East and Midwest.

C. reticulata (C. douglasii). WESTERN HACKBERRY. Zones 1–24,; best in 1–3, 7–13, 18–21. Grows 25–30 ft. tall with similar spread. Has somewhat pendulous branches. Oval, tooth-edged leaves to 2½ in. long, pale beneath, strongly veined.

C. sinensis. CHINESE HACKBERRY, YUNNAN HACKBERRY. Zones 8–16, 18–20, 29–33. Similar in growth habit to *C. occidentalis,* but smaller. Leaves to 4 in. long, smoother and glossier than those of other hackberries, with scallop-toothed edges.

CENTAUREA

Asteraceae (Compositae)

PERENNIALS AND ANNUALS

⚡ ZONES VARY BY SPECIES

☀ FULL SUN

💧 MODERATE WATER, EXCEPT AS NOTED

Centaurea cineraria

Out of some 500 species, only dozen or so are widely cultivated. Of these, annuals are grown mainly for cut flowers; perennial kinds are used principally for soft, silvery foliage. All are relatively easy to grow. For best performance, add lime to acid soils. Sow seeds of annuals or set out plants of perennial kinds in spring (or in fall, in mild-winter climates).

C. americana. BASKET FLOWER. Annual. All zones. Native to central and southwestern U.S. To 5–6 ft. high, with rather rough, oval leaves to 4 in. long. Flower heads to 4 in. wide are rose pink, paler toward center. Good in arrangements, fresh or dried.

C. cineraria (C. candidissima). DUSTY MILLER. Perennial in Zones 8–30; annual anywhere. (This common name applies to many plants with whitish foliage; see Dusty Miller, page 285.) Compact plant to 1 ft. or more. Velvety white leaves, mostly in basal clump, are strap shaped, with broad, roundish lobes. Solitary 1-in. flower heads (purple, occasionally yellow) in summer. Trim back after flowering. Attracts bees.

C. cyanus. CORNFLOWER, BACHELOR'S BUTTON. Annual. All zones. To 1–2½ ft., branching if given sufficient space. Narrow gray-green leaves, 2–3 in. long. Flower heads 1–1½ in. across, blue, pink, rose, wine red, and white. Blue varieties are traditional favorites for boutonnieres. 'Jubilee Gem' is bushy, compact, 1 ft. tall, with deep blue flowers; Polka Dot strain has all cornflower colors on 16-in. plants. Sow seed in early spring in cold-winter areas, late summer or fall where winters are mild.

C. gymnocarpa. DUSTY MILLER. Perennial. Zones 8–30. Now considered a form of *C. cineraria. To* 1–3-ft.; white, feltlike leaves, somewhat resembling those of *C. cineraria* but more finely divided. Usually two or three purple flower heads at ends of leafy branches. Trim plants after bloom. Very drought tolerant.

C. hypoleuca 'John Coutts'. Zones 1–9, 14–24, 29–43. Resembles *C. montana* but has deeply lobed leaves and deep rose flower heads. Sometimes offered as a variety of *C. dealbata.*

C. macrocephala. Perennial. Zones 1–9, 14–24, 29–43. Coarse-foliaged, leafy plant 3–4 ft. tall, with 2-in. clusters of yellow flowers tightly enclosed at the base by papery, overlapping, shiny brown bracts. Flower heads resemble thistles. Use in fresh or dried arrangements.

C. montana. Perennial. Zones 1–9, 14–24, 29–43. Clumps 1½–2 ft. tall and as wide, with grayish green leaves to 7 in. long. Flowers resembling ragged 3-in. blue cornflowers top the stems. Divide every other year. Cool-season plant that is very weedy in North, less vigorous in warmer climates. Regular water.

C. moschata. SWEET SULTAN. Annual. All zones. Erect, branching at base, to 2 ft.; Imperialis strain to 3 ft. Green, deeply toothed leaves; thistle-like, 2-in. flower heads mostly in shades of lilac through rose, sometimes white or yellow. Musklike fragrance. Splendid cut flower. Sow seed directly on soil in spring or set out as transplants. Needs lots of heat.

CENTRANTHUS ruber (Valeriana rubra)

RED VALERIAN, JUPITER'S BEARD	
Valerianaceae	
PERENNIAL	
✿ ZONES 1–9, 12–24, 28–43	
☼ ◑ FULL SUN OR PARTIAL SHADE	
◈ MODERATE TO LITTLE WATER	

Centranthus ruber

Trouble-free plant; a weed in far western states. Self-sows prolifically because of small dandelionlike parachutes on seeds. Forms a bushy clump with upright stems to 3 ft. high bearing 4-in.-long bluish green leaves. Small, dusty crimson or rose pink flowers about ½ in. long in dense terminal clusters in late spring, early summer. 'Albus' is white. Plants give long, showy bloom in difficult situations. Will grow in poor, dry soils; accept almost any condition except damp shade. Cut off old flowering stems to shape plants, prolong bloom, and prevent seeding.

CENTURY PLANT. See AGAVE americana

CEPHALANTHUS occidentalis

BUTTONBUSH, BUTTON WILLOW	
Rubiaceae	
DECIDUOUS SHRUB OR SMALL TREE	
✿ ZONES 2–10, 14–21, 25–41	
☼ ◑ FULL SUN OR LIGHT SHADE	
◈◈ MOIST TO WET SOIL	

Cephalanthus occidentalis

Commonly called buttonbush in the East, button willow in the West. Remarkable for wide distribution—eastern Canada to Florida, Minnesota south through Oklahoma and west to California, with outposts in Cuba, Mexico, and Asia. Grows 3–15 ft. or taller, with rounded, rather open habit and bright green paired or whorled leaves 2–6 in. long. Leafs out late in spring. Creamy white, slender-tubed flowers crowded in rounded, 1–1½-in.-wide heads in late summer. Projecting stigmas produce a pincushion effect. Attracts butterflies. Useful for naturalizing in wet areas.

CEPHALOCEREUS senilis

OLD MAN CACTUS	
Cactaceae	
CACTUS	
✿ ZONES 21–24; OR INDOORS	
☼ FULL SUN	
◈ VERY LITTLE WATER	

Cephalocereus senilis

Native to central Mexico. Slender, columnar cactus growing slowly to 40 ft., usually much less. Covered with long, grayish white hairs. Yellow, 1½-in. spines. Old plants have 2-in.-long rose-colored flowers in April. Night blooming. Protect from hard frosts.

Good pot plant; older plants striking in cactus garden. Indoors, give it southern exposure.

CEPHALOTAXUS

PLUM YEW	
Cephalotaxaceae	
EVERGREEN SHRUBS OR TREES	
✿ ZONES 4–9, 14–17, 28, 31, 32	
☼ ◑ PARTIAL SHADE IN HOT-SUMMER AREAS	
◈ MODERATE WATER	

Cephalotaxus harringtonia

Slow-growing plants related to yews (*Taxus*); differ from yews in larger, brighter green needles and (on female plants only) larger fruit that resembles small green or brown plums. May not bear fruit in all areas. Very heat tolerant.

C. fortunei. CHINESE PLUM YEW. Big shrub or small tree to 10 ft. tall (rarely more), with soft, needlelike leaves up to 3½ in. long.

C. harringtonia. Spreading shrub or small tree to 10 ft. (possibly 20 ft.) tall, with needles 1–2½ in. long. Spreading ('Prostrata') and columnar ('Fastigiata') forms are sometimes seen. When young, the latter resembles Irish yew (*Taxus baccata* 'Fastigiata'). 'Korean Gold' has golden new foliage, columnar habit.

CERASTIUM tomentosum

SNOW-IN-SUMMER	
Caryophyllaceae	
PERENNIAL	
✿ ZONES 1–24, 32–45	
☼ ◑ PARTIAL SHADE IN HOT CLIMATES	
◈ REGULAR MOISTURE FOR FAST GROWTH	

Cerastium tomentosum

Low-growing plant that performs reliably everywhere except in hot, humid South. Spreading, dense, tufty mats of silvery gray, ¾-in.-long leaves. Masses of snow-white flowers, ½–¾ in. across, in early summer. Plant grows 6–8 in. high, spreads 2–3 ft. in a year. Use as ground cover on slopes or level ground, as bulb cover, in rock gardens, as edging for paths, between stepping-stones. Avoid extensive planting in prominent situations, since plant is not long lived.

In warmest areas, provide some shade. Takes any soil as long as drainage is good; standing water causes root rot. Set divisions or plants 1–1½ ft. apart, or sow seed. Feed two or three times a year to speed growth. Shear off faded flower clusters. May look a bit shabby in winter but revives rapidly in spring. Divide in fall or early spring.

CERATONIA siliqua

CAROB, ST. JOHN'S BREAD	
Fabaceae (Leguminosae)	
EVERGREEN SHRUB OR SMALL TREE	
✿ ZONES 9, 13–16, 18–24	
☼ FULL SUN	
◈ INFREQUENT, DEEP WATERING	

Ceratonia siliqua

Native to eastern Mediterranean region. Left to grow naturally, has bushy form with branches to ground; can be used as big hedge. Trained as tree, to 30–40 ft., with dense, round head. Dark green leaves divided into 4–10 round leaflets, each 2 in. long. Female trees produce (and drop) abundant 1-ft.-long, dark brown, leathery pods, which can be milled to a fine powder and used as a chocolate substitute. Roots break up sidewalks. Avoid overwatering, since plant is subject to root crown rot.

CERATOSTIGMA plumbaginoides

DWARF PLUMBAGO

Plumbaginaceae

PERENNIAL GROUND COVER

🌡 ZONES 2–10, 14–24, 29–41

☀️ ◑ FULL SUN OR PARTIAL SHADE

💧 MODERATE WATER

Ceratostigma plumbaginoides

Wiry-stemmed ground cover 6–12 in. high. In loose soil and where growing season is long, spreads rapidly by underground stems, eventually covering large areas. Bronzy green to dark green, 3-in.-long leaves turn reddish brown with frosts. Intense blue, ½-in. phloxlike flowers from July until first frosts. Most effective in early or midautumn, when blue flowers contrast with red autumn foliage. Blooms well only in areas with a long growing season. Semievergreen only in the mildest-winter areas; best to cut back after bloom. Dies back elsewhere; leafs out late in spring. In coldest climates, apply a winter mulch. When plants show signs of aging, remove old crowns and replace with rooted stems. Often sold as *Plumbago larpentae*.

For Cape plumbago, see *Plumbago auriculata*.

CERATOZAMIA mexicana

Zamiaceae

CYCAD

🌡 ZONES 21–27

◑ PARTIAL SHADE

💧 REGULAR WATER

Ceratozamia mexicana

Related to *Cycas revoluta* and similar in appearance. Trunk usually a foot high, 4–6 ft. in great age, a foot thick. Very slow growing. Leaves in whorl, 3–6 ft. long, divided featherwise into 15–20 pairs of foot-long, inch-wide leaflets. Striking in containers or protected place in open ground. Protect from frosts.

CERCIDIPHYLLUM japonicum

KATSURA TREE

Cercidiphyllaceae

DECIDUOUS TREE

🌡 ZONES 2–6, 14–16, 18–20, 32–41

☀️ ◑ FULL SUN OR LIGHT SHADE

💧 REGULAR WATER

Native to Japan. A specimen tree of many virtues if given regular moisture, especially during youth, and sheltered from intense sun and wind. Light, dainty branch and leaf pattern.

Cercidiphyllum japonicum

Foliage, always fresh looking, changes color during the growing season: new growth emerges reddish purple, becomes bluish green in summer, then turns yellow to apricot in autumn. To enhance fall color, water less frequently in late summer. Trees grown in acid soil will have the best color. Foliage of some katsura trees smells like burnt sugar on warm autumn days during leaf-fall.

Rather slow growing, eventually to 40 ft. or more. Pyramidal form when young; growth may remain upright or become more spreading with maturity. Some specimens have single trunk, but multiple trunks are more usual. Nearly round, 2–4-in. leaves neatly spaced in pairs along arching branches. Flowers inconspicuous. Brown bark somewhat shaggy on old trees. No serious pest or disease problems. There is a weeping form known as 'Pendulum' or 'Pendula'.

CERCIDIUM

PALO VERDE

Fabaceae (Leguminosae)

DECIDUOUS TREES

🌡 ZONES 10–14, 18–20, 29

☀️ FULL SUN

💧 MODERATE TO LITTLE WATER

Cercidium floridum

Tough, trouble-free trees native to deserts of California, Arizona. Valued for floral display, shade, colorful bark. Clusters of small flowers nearly hide the branches in spring. Lightly filtered shade is cast by intricate canopy of twigs rather than by tiny leaves, which are shed early. These trees attract birds.

C. floridum (C. torreyanum). BLUE PALO VERDE. In gardens, grows fast to 30 ft. tall and wide. Bright yellow flowers in 2–4½-in. clusters. Bluish green foliage; spiny bluish green branches.

C. microphyllum. LITTLELEAF PALO VERDE. Similar to *C. floridum*, but bark and leaves are yellowish green; flowers are paler yellow, in 1-in. clusters.

CERCIS

REDBUD

Fabaceae (Leguminosae)

DECIDUOUS SHRUBS OR TREES

🌡 ZONES VARY BY SPECIES

☀️ ◑ FULL SUN OR LIGHT SHADE

💧 REGULAR WATER, EXCEPT AS NOTED

Cercis canadensis

Valued for flowers, fruit, foliage. Clusters of small, sweet pea–shaped, rosy to purplish pink blossoms in early spring. Where plant is adapted, blooms are borne in great profusion on bare twigs, branches, sometimes even on main trunk. Flowers are followed by clusters of flat, beanlike pods that persist into winter. Attractive broad, rounded leaves are heart shaped at base. All provide fall color with first frosts. All are attractive in naturalized settings.

C. canadensis. EASTERN REDBUD. Zones 2–20, 26, 28–41. Native to eastern U.S. Largest (to 25–35 ft. tall) and fastest growing of the redbuds, and the most apt to take tree form. Round headed but with horizontally tiered branches in age. Rich green, 3–6-in.-long leaves have pointed tips. Small (½-in.-long), rosy pink flowers. Needs some winter chill to flower profusely. Valuable for filling the gap between the early-flowering fruit trees (flowering peach, flowering plum) and the crabapples and late-flowering cherries. Effective as specimen or understory tree. Varieties include 'Alba' (white flowers); 'Flame' (double pink flowers); 'Forest Pansy' (purple foliage, needs some shade in hot climates); 'Rubye Atkinson' (pure pink flowers); and 'Silver Cloud' (leaves marbled with white).

C. c. mexicana (C. mexicana). Zones 4–24, 26, 28–35. Includes plants from many sources in Mexico. Most widely distributed is a form with a single trunk to 15 ft., and leathery blue-green leaves and pinkish purple flowers.

C. chinensis. CHINESE REDBUD. Zones 4–20, 29–34. Native to China, Japan. Seen mostly as light, open shrub to 10–12 ft. Flower clusters (3–5 in. long) are deep rose, almost rosy purple. Leaves are sometimes glossier and brighter green than those of *C. canadensis*, with transparent line around the edge. 'Avondale' is a superior form with deep purple flowers. Full sun.

C. occidentalis. WESTERN REDBUD. Zones 2–24. Shrub or small tree 10–18 ft. tall and wide, usually multitrunked. All-year interest: magenta flowers in spring, handsome blue-green leaves and newly forming magenta seedpods in summer,

Cercis occidentalis

C

light yellow or red foliage in fall, and picturesque bare branches holding reddish brown seedpods in winter. Best floral display with some winter chill. Very drought tolerant; excellent for seldom-watered banks.

C. reniformis. Zones 3–9, 14–24, 29, 30, 33. Southwest native equivalent of eastern redbud. Leaves leathery, blue green, 2–3 in. wide, with rounded or notched tips. 'Alba' has white flowers. 'Oklahoma' has wine red flowers and thick, glossy, heat-resistant leaves.

C. siliquastrum. JUDAS TREE. Zones 3–19, 29–33. Native to Europe and western Asia. Performs best with some winter chill. Generally of shrubby habit to 25 ft., occasionally a taller, slender tree with single trunk. Purplish rose, ½-in.-long flowers; 3–5-in. leaves, deeply heart shaped at base, rounded or notched at tip. Fairly drought tolerant.

CEREUS peruvianus (C. uruguayanus)

Cactaceae

CACTUS

⚡ ZONES 16, 17, 21–28; OR INDOORS

☼ FULL SUN

💧 MODERATE TO LITTLE WATER

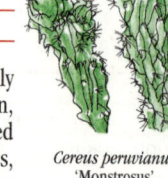

Cereus peruvianus 'Monstrosus'

Tall, branching, treelike cactus eventually reaching 30–50 ft. Striking bluish green, especially when young; ribbed with scattered spines. Flowers white, 6–7 in. long, 5 in. across, in June. Night blooming. Striking outline; effective in large containers. Protect from hard frosts. Variety 'Monstrosus' is smaller, slower growing than species, with ribs irregularly broken up into knobs and crests.

CEROPEGIA woodii

ROSARY VINE

Asclepiadaceae

SUCCULENT

⚡ ZONES 21–27; OR INDOORS

☼ PARTIAL SHADE

💧 REGULAR WATER

Ceropegia woodii

From South Africa. Little vine with hanging or trailing thin stems growing from tuberous base. Paired heart-shaped leaves—thick and succulent, ⅔ in. long, dark green marbled white. Little tubers that form on stems can be used to start new plants. Flowers small, dull pink or purplish, not showy but interesting in structure. Best in pots; stems may trail like a thin curtain or be trained on small trellis.

Other species are available from specialists: some are shrubby, some vining, and others stiffly succulent, but all of them have fascinating flower structure.

CESTRUM

Solanaceae

EVERGREEN SHRUBS

⚡ ZONES VARY BY SPECIES

☼ PARTIAL SHADE

💧 REGULAR WATER

☣ FRUIT AND SAP ARE POISONOUS IF INGESTED

All have showy, tubular flowers. Flowers and fruit attract birds. Fast growing, inclined to be rangy and top-heavy unless consistently pruned. Best in warm, sheltered spot. Feed generously. Add organic soil amendments before planting. Nip

Cestrum elegans

back consistently to maintain compact form; cut back severely after flowering or fruiting. In climates specified below, plants may freeze back in heavy frosts but will recover quickly.

C. aurantiacum. ORANGE CESTRUM. Zones 16, 17, 21–27. Native to Guatemala. Rare and handsome. To 8 ft. Brilliant show of clustered, 1-in.-long, orange flowers in late spring and summer, followed by white berries. Deep green, oval, 4-in. leaves.

C. elegans (C. purpureum). RED CESTRUM. Zones 13, 17, 19–27. Shrub or semiclimber to 10 ft. or higher, with arching branches, deep green 4-in. leaves. Masses of purplish red, 1-in.-long flowers in spring and summer, followed by red berries. Good espalier. 'Smithii' has pink flowers.

C. nocturnum. NIGHT JESSAMINE. Zones 13, 16–27. Native to West Indies. To 12 ft., with 4–8-in.-long leaves and clusters of creamy white flowers in summer; white berries. Powerfully fragrant at night—too powerful for some people.

C. parqui. WILLOW-LEAFED JESSAMINE. Zones 13–28. Native to Chile. To 6–10 ft. tall with many branches from base. Dense foliage of willowlike leaves, 3–6 in. long. Greenish yellow, 1-in.-long summer flowers in clusters. Berries dark violet brown. Not as attractive as other species in form, flowers, or fruit, but its perfume is potent. Leaves blacken in light frost. Best used where winter appearance is unimportant. In marginal climates, protect roots with mulch and treat as perennial.

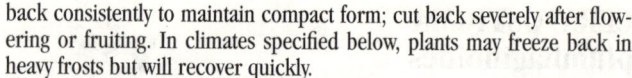

CESTRUMS FOR HUMMINGBIRDS

All cestrums come from the American tropics, and all have tubular flowers that attract the Americas' native nectar feeder, the hummingbird. Other birds enjoy these plants as well: warblers pierce the flowers to drink the nectar, and mockingbirds eat the berries.

CHAENOMELES

FLOWERING QUINCE

Rosaceae

DECIDUOUS SHRUBS

⚡ ZONES 2–21, 28–41

☼ FULL SUN

💧💧 REGULAR TO MODERATE WATER

Chaenomeles

Bloom time—as early as January where winters are mild—is the only time flowering quince calls attention to itself. The plant is bland-looking the rest of the year, though judicious pruning improves its looks. Blossoms are 1½–2½ in. across, single to semidouble or double, in colors ranging from soft to vibrant.

Practically indestructible shrubs with shiny green leaves (red tinged when young) and varying growth habit. Some grow to 10 ft. and spread wider; others are compact and low growing. Most are thorny, a few thornless. Some bear small quincelike fruit. All are useful as hedges and barriers. Easy to grow; tolerant of extremes in cold and heat, light to heavy soil. In humid regions, lower leaves may drop in summer. May bloom reluctantly in warm-winter areas. Prune any time to shape, limit growth, or gain special effects. Good time to prune is in bud and bloom season—use cut branches for indoor arrangements. New growth that follows will bear next year's flowers. Blossoms attract birds.

The following list of choice varieties notes both height and flower color. Tall types are 6 ft. and over; low are 2–3 ft. All are garden hybrids (some formerly called *Cydonia*); specialists can furnish even more varieties.

'Apple Blossom'. Tall. White and pink.

'Cameo'. Low, compact. Double, soft apricot pink.

'Contorta'. Low. White to pink; twisted branches. Good as bonsai.

'Corallina' ('Coral Glow'). Tall. Reddish orange.
'Coral Sea'. Tall. Large, coral pink.
'Enchantress'. Tall. Large, shell pink.
'Falconet Charlot'. Tall, thornless. Double, salmon pink.
'Hollandia'. Tall. Large red flowers; reblooms in fall.
'Jet Trail'. Low. Pure white.
'Low-n-White'. Low, spreading. White.
'Minerva'. Low, spreading. Cherry red.
'Nivalis'. Tall. Large, pure white.
'Orange Delight' ('Maulei'). Low, spreading. Orange to orange red.
'Pink Beauty'. Tall. Purplish pink.
'Pink Lady'. Low. Rose pink blooms from deeper-colored buds.
'Red Ruffles'. Tall, almost thornless. Large, ruffled, red.
'Rowallane'. Low. Darkest red.
'Snow'. Tall. Large, pure white.
'Stanford Red'. Low, almost thornless. Tomato red.
'Super Red'. Tall, upright. Large, bright red.
'Texas Scarlet'. Low. Tomato red.
'Toyo Nishiki'. Tall. Pink, white, pink and white, red all on same branch.

CHAIN FERN. See **WOODWARDIA fimbriata**

CHAMAECEREUS sylvestri (Echinopsis chamaecereus)

PEANUT CACTUS

Cactaceae

CACTUS

ZONES 8–10, 12–24; OR INDOORS

FULL SUN

REGULAR WATER DURING GROWTH AND BLOOM

Chamaecereus sylvestri

Native to Argentina. The cylindrical, ribbed, spiny, 2–3-in. joints of this dwarf cactus fall off easily and root just as easily. Profusely blooming in spring and early summer; even tiny rooted joints bloom. Flowers bright scarlet, almost 3 in. long. Great favorite with children.

CHAMAECYPARIS

FALSE CYPRESS

Cupressaceae

EVERGREEN SHRUBS OR TREES

ZONES VARY BY SPECIES

FULL SUN OR PARTIAL SHADE

REGULAR WATER

Chamaecyparis lawsoniana

False cypress is sometimes mistaken for arborvitae (*Thuja*), but leaf undersides of false cypress have white lines, while those of arborvitae are entirely green. Most false cypresses have two distinct types of leaves: juvenile and mature. Juvenile leaves (short, needlelike, soft but often prickly) appear on young plants and some new growth of larger trees. Mature foliage consists of tiny, scalelike, overlapping leaves. Cones are small and round.

All of the many varieties sold are forms of five species—one from the eastern U.S., two from the western U.S., and two from Japan. New varieties appear each year, while older ones lose market share. Many closely resemble each other and are often mislabeled. Many dwarf and variegated kinds are available, providing rich source of bonsai and rock garden material. All need good drainage and protection from wind.

C. lawsoniana. PORT ORFORD CEDAR, LAWSON CEDAR. Zones 4–6, 15–17, 32, 34, 39. The 60-ft. pyramidal western timber tree with lacy, drooping foliage is seldom seen in gardens. Blue-green forms include 'Allumii', slow growing to 30 ft.; 'Ellwoodii', dense, compact growth to 6–8 ft.; and 'Wisselii', to 15–18 ft., with twisted, irregular growth. Golden-leafed forms are 'Golden King', 'Lutea', and 'Stewartii', all conical to 30 ft. or more.

C. nootkatensis. NOOTKA CYPRESS, ALASKA CEDAR. Zones 4–6, 15–17, 36–40. Pyramidal tree to 80 ft., coarser than *C. lawsoniana*; stands poorer soil. 'Pendula', a weeping form, slowly grows to 10 ft., possibly to 30 ft.; it is the form most commonly sold in the eastern U.S.

C. obtusa. HINOKI FALSE CYPRESS. Zones 4–6, 15–17, 32–34, 36–41. There are dozens of golden, dwarf, and fern-leafed forms, but two varieties are the most important in landscaping. 'Gracilis', slender hinoki cypress, has slender, upright growth to 20 ft. with nodding branch tips; 'Nana Gracilis' is a miniature of the former to 4 ft. in height.

C. pisifera. SAWARA FALSE CYPRESS. Zones 4–6, 15–17, 32, 34, 39. Japanese tree to 20–30 ft., rarely seen except in its garden varieties. 'Cyano-Viridis' ('Boulevard') is a slow, dense bush to 6–8 ft., with silvery blue-green foliage. 'Filifera', to 8 ft., has drooping, threadlike branchlets; 'Filifera Aurea' has similar branchlets in yellow.

C. thyoides. WHITE CEDAR. Zones 4–6, 15–17, 28, 31, 32, 34, 36–42. Eastern U.S. timber tree, columnar to 75 ft. tall, found in wet sites in the wild. Garden forms include 'Andelyensis', dense, columnar, gray-green shrub to 10 ft., turning bronze in cold weather; and 'Heather Bun', broader than 'Andelyensis', turning intense plum purple in winter.

CHAMAEDOREA

Arecaceae (Palmae)

PALMS

ZONES 16, 17, 22–25, 26 (FOR SPECIES NOTED), 27; OR INDOORS

PARTIAL OR FULL SHADE

REGULAR WATER

Chamaedorea elegans

Generally slow-growing, small, feather-type palms. Some have single trunks, others clustered trunks. Leaves variable in shape. Good on shaded patio.

C. cataractarum. Single-stemmed palm growing slowly to 4–5 ft.; trunk speckled. Older plants take some frost.

C. costaricana. If well fed and liberally watered, develops fairly fast into bamboolike clumps of 8–10-ft. trunks. Good pot palm; will eventually need good-sized container. Lacy, feathery leaves 3–4 ft. long.

C. elegans. Often called parlor palm. The best indoor chamaedorea, tolerating crowded roots, poor light. Single stemmed; grows very slowly to eventual 3–4 ft. Occasionally douse tops of potted plants with water. Feed regularly. Groom by removing old leafstalks. Repot every 2 or 3 years, carefully washing off old soil and replacing with good potting mix. Plant three or more in container for effective display. Widely sold as *Neanthe bella*.

C. ernesti-augustii. Slow growing to 5 ft., with dark green leaves shaped like fish tails.

C. erumpens. Cluster-forming, bamboolike dwarf with drooping leaves. Slow grower to 4–5 ft.

C. geonomiformis. Fine palm for pots. Grows slowly to 4 ft. Broad oblong leaves are not feathery, but are deeply split at tips like fish tails.

C. glaucifolia. Slow growing to 8 ft. or more. Finely textured, feathery leaves, 4–6 ft. long, with bluish green tint on both sides (most marked on underside).

C. klotzschiana. Single-trunked palm, growing slowly to 4–5 ft. Handsome, dark green, feathery leaves. Hardy to 28°F/–2°C. Succeeds in Zone 26.

C. microspadix. Cluster palm with slender, ringed stems to 8 ft. Feathery leaves. One of hardier kinds; it takes very light frost.

C. radicalis. Slow-growing, single-stemmed plant to 4 ft. tall. Boldly patterned dark green leaves. Interesting, colorful seed formation. Will take temperatures down to 22° to 28°F/–6° to –2°C. Succeeds in Zone 26.

C. seifrizii. Cluster palm of dense, compact growth to 8–10 ft. Feathery leaves with narrow leaflets. Takes 28°F/–2°C.

C. tenella. Single trunk to 3–4 ft. Dark bluish green leaves are exceptionally strong, large, and broad; undivided but deeply cleft at ends.

C. tepejilote. Single trunk ringed with swollen joints like those of bamboo. Moderate growth to 10 ft.; leaves 4 ft. long, feathery.

CHAMAEMELUM nobile (Anthemis nobilis)

Chamaemelum nobile

CHAMOMILE

Asteraceae (Compositae)

EVERGREEN PERENNIAL

☀ ZONES 1–24, 30–43

☀◑ FULL SUN OR PARTIAL SHADE

◐ MODERATE WATER

Forms soft-textured, spreading, 3–12-in. mat of bright light green, finely cut, aromatic leaves. Most commonly grown form has small yellow buttons of summer-blooming flower heads; some forms have little daisylike flower heads. Makes lawn substitute if mowed or sheared occasionally. 'Treneague' is a nonflowering variety that needs no mowing. Also used between stepping-stones. Plant divisions 1 ft. apart.

Chamomile tea is made from dried flower heads, but sweeter, more flavorful tea comes from flowers of *Matricaria recutita (M. chamomilla)*.

CHAMAEROPS humilis

Chamaerops humilis

MEDITERRANEAN FAN PALM

Arecaceae (Palmae)

PALM

☀ ZONES 4–31

☀◑ FULL SUN OR PARTIAL SHADE

◐◐ REGULAR TO MODERATE WATER

Probably hardiest palm; has survived 6°F/–14°C. Clumps develop slowly from off-shoots, curving to height of 20 ft.; can also reach 20 ft. wide. Growth extremely slow in northern part of range. Leaves green to bluish green. Use in containers, mass under trees, grow as impenetrable hedge. Wind resistant.

CHAMOMILE. See CHAMAEMELUM nobile, MATRICARIA recutita

CHARD. See SWISS CHARD

CHASMANTHIUM latifolium (Uniola latifolia)

Chasmanthium latifolium

SEA OATS, BAMBOO GRASS

Poaceae (Gramineae)

PERENNIAL GRASS

☀ ZONES 1–24, 28–43

☀◑ PARTIAL SHADE IN HOT-SUMMER AREAS

◐ REGULAR WATER

Ornamental clump-forming grass. Broad, bamboolike leaves are topped by arching flowering stems, 2–5 ft. tall, carrying showers of silvery green flower spikelets that resemble flattened clusters of oats (or flattened armadillos). Flowering stems dry to an attractive greenish straw color and look good in dried arrangements. Clumps broaden slowly and are not aggressive like bamboo. Leaves turn brown in winter, when plants should be cut back almost to ground. Divide clumps when they become overgrown and flowering diminishes. Stake if flowering stems sprawl too far. Self-sows extensively and can become invasive.

CHASTE TREE. See VITEX

CHAYOTE

Chayote

Cucurbitaceae

ANNUAL OR PERENNIAL VINE

☀ ANNUAL IN ALL ZONES; PERENNIAL, 14–16, 19–28

☀ FULL SUN

◐ REGULAR WATER

Vine and leaves resemble those of squash, its relative. Grow this plant for its edible fruit; flowers are inconspicuous. Fruit is 3–8 in. long, green or yellow green, irregularly oval, grooved, with a large seed surrounded by solid meaty flesh. Large, fleshy tuberous roots are also edible. Chayote is also known as mirliton or christophine.

Needs rich soil. Climbs by tendrils; provide fence or trellis. In areas where fruit is sold in stores, buy in fall and allow to sprout in cupboard; then plant whole fruit edgewise, sprouted end at lowest point, narrow end exposed. If shoot is long, cut it back to 1–2 in. Plant two or more vines to ensure pollination. In mild climates, plant in February or March; in areas where roots may freeze, pot up in 5-gallon container and store until after frost. Plants can produce 20–30-ft. vine in first year, 40–50-ft. vine in second. Tops die down in frost. Bloom starts when day length shortens in fall; fruit is ready in a month. Well-grown plant can produce 200 or more fruits.

CHECKERBERRY. See GAULTHERIA procumbens

CHECKERED LILY. See FRITILLARIA meleagris

CHEIRANTHUS. See ERYSIMUM

CHELIDONIUM majus

Chelidonium majus

GREATER CELANDINE

Papaveraceae

PERENNIAL OR BIENNIAL

☀ ZONES 3–6, 31–41

☀◑ TOLERATES SUN IN COOL CLIMATES

◐ REGULAR WATER

Grows 2–3 ft. tall, with several erect stems rising from the rootstock. Leaves are attractively cut and lobed, smooth bright green. Profuse yellow to orange-yellow flowers to 1 in. wide; summer bloom. Orange sap is irritating to the skin. Self-sows freely and naturalizes (sometimes too well). Double-flowered 'Flore Pleno' also seeds itself freely. Both forms are best in wild gardens.

CHELONE

Chelone lyonii

TURTLEHEAD

Scrophulariaceae

PERENNIALS

☀ ZONES 3–9, 14–17, 28–43

☀◑ FULL SUN OR LIGHT SHADE

◐◐ AMPLE WATER

Leafy, clump-forming perennials related to penstemon. All are native to the eastern U.S. and grow in damp places in sun or light shade. Frequently used in bog gardens. All bloom in late summer and autumn. Common name comes from the oddly formed flowers—inch-long, puffy, and two lipped, with a fancied resemblance to a turtle's or snake's head. Useful for cut flowers, shade gardens, wild gardens.

C. glabra. Grows 2–3 ft. tall, occasionally much taller. Flowers are white or palest pink.

C. lyonii. Reaches 3 ft. tall. Rose pink flowers.

C. obliqua. To 2–2½ ft. tall, with deep pink flowers. The latest bloomer among these three species. 'Alba' is a compact, white-flowered variety.

CHENILLE PLANT. See ACALYPHA hispida

Chenopodiaceae. The goosefoot family contains many annuals and perennials (some of them weeds) and a few shrubs. Flowers are inconspicuous. Many will tolerate salty or alkaline soil, and some are useful food plants, notably beet and spinach.

CHERIMOYA. See ANNONA cherimola

CHERRY

Rosaceae

DECIDUOUS FRUIT TREES

⚡ ZONES VARY BY TYPE

☼ FULL SUN

🔴 REGULAR, DEEP WATERING

Both the sweet and sour cherries are useful and attractive trees in the home garden.

Fruiting Cherry

Sweet cherries. Most common market type. Main commercial growing areas are valleys of Oregon, Washington, and British Columbia in West, around the Great Lakes in East. High chilling requirement (need many hours below 45°F/7°C), thus not adapted to warm-winter regions. Can't take extreme summer heat or intense winter cold; freezes and heavy spring rains can damage crop. Trees 20–35 ft. tall, as broad in some varieties; at their best in deep, well-drained soil in Zones 2, 6, 7, 14, 15, 32, 34–37, 39.

Two trees are usually needed to produce fruit, and second tree must be chosen with care. No combination of these will produce fruit: 'Bing', 'Lambert', 'Royal Ann'. These varieties will pollinate any other cherry: 'Black Tartarian', 'Corum', 'Deacon', 'Hedelfingen', 'Republican', 'Sam', 'Stella', and 'Van'. However, because 'Lambert' blooms late, it is pollinated best by 'Republican'. 'Glacier', 'Lapins', 'Stella', and 'Sunburst' are self-fertile (a lone tree will bear).

Fruiting spurs are long lived, do not need to be renewed by pruning. Prune trees only to maintain good structure and shape. Fruit appears in late spring to early summer. Use netting to keep birds from eating the crop. For control of brown rot and blossom blight, apply a copper spray just as leaves fall in autumn, then a fungicide when first blooms appear and weekly during bloom. Resume fungicide program about 2 weeks before harvest. Dormant oil spray will control various pests, including scale insects and mites.

Varieties:

'Berryessa'. Fruit resembles 'Royal Ann' but is larger. Less likely to produce double fruit in hot weather. Early.

'Bing'. Top quality. Large, dark red, meaty fruit of fine flavor. Midseason.

'Black Tartarian'. Fruit smaller than 'Bing', purplish black, firm, sweet. Early.

'Chinook'. Fruit resembles 'Bing', ripens 4 to 10 days earlier.

'Corum'. Light-colored fruit with colorless juice, whitish flesh. Excellent flavor. Ripens 7 days before 'Royal Ann'.

'Deacon'. Large tree. Large to medium, firm, black fruit. Sweet, pleasant flavor. Ripens 7 days before 'Bing'.

'Glacier'. Large dark cherry; ripens 5 days ahead of 'Bing' and tastes better. Self-fertile.

'Hardy Giant'. Dark red fruit resembles 'Bing'. Late. Good pollinator, especially for 'Lambert'.

'Hedelfingen'. Medium-large black cherry. Ripens with 'Van', but fruit colors before maturity and needs early protection from birds. Early-bearing, productive tree. Not recommended for the West.

'Jubilee'. Resembles 'Bing', but fruit larger. Fewer double fruits. Early.

'Kansas Sweet' ('Hansen'). Large red cherry with semisweet flavor. Late.

'Lambert'. Very large, black fruit, very firm. Flavor more sprightly than 'Bing'. Late.

'Lapins'. Resembles 'Bing' but is self-fertile. Late.

'Mona'. Resembles 'Black Tartarian', but larger. Very early.

'Olympus'. Dark cherry, ripens after 'Bing'. Smaller fruit, larger crop. Pollinate with sour cherry 'Montmorency'.

'Rainier'. Has yellow skin with pink blush; ripens a few days before 'Bing'.

'Republican' ('Black Republican', 'Black Oregon'). Large, spreading tree. Small, round, purplish black fruit with dark juice, tender yet crisp texture. Good flavor. Late.

'Royal Ann' ('Napoleon'). Large, spreading tree, very productive. Light yellow fruit with pink blush; tender, crisp. Sprightly flavor. Midseason.

'Sam'. Vigorous tree. Large, firm, black fruit. Excellent flavor. Midseason.

'Stella'. Dark fruit like 'Lambert'; ripens a few days later. Self-fertile and good pollinator for other cherries.

'Sunburst'. Self-fertile cross between 'Stella' and 'Van'. Large black fruit, good tree structure. Early.

'Sunset'. Very late dark red cherry; late ripening lessens danger of cracking in late spring rains.

'Utah Giant'. Ripens with 'Bing' but is larger, sweeter; develops sweetness even before fully ripe. Holds color when processed. Pollinate with 'Van' or 'Stella'.

'Van'. Heavy-bearing tree. Shiny black fruit, firmer and slightly smaller than 'Bing'. Ripens slightly earlier than or at the same time as 'Bing'.

Sour cherries. Also known as pie cherries. More widely adapted than sweet cherries; succeed along the Atlantic Coast and farther north and south than sweet cherries do. Main commercial growing areas are in Michigan, New York, and Wisconsin. In home gardens and orchards, grow in Zones 1–9, 14–17, 33–43 in well-drained soil.

Sour cherry trees are smaller than sweet cherry trees—to about 20 ft. tall and spreading. They are self-fertile. There are far fewer types of sour cherries than sweet ones. 'Montmorency' and 'Early Richmond' are the preferred varieties, bearing small, bright red, soft, juicy, sweet-tart fruit. 'English Morello' is darker, with tarter fruit and red juice. 'Meteor' has fruit like 'Montmorency' but is a smaller tree. 'North Star', with red to dark red skin and yellow, sour flesh, is a small, very hardy tree.

CHERRY, FLOWERING. See PRUNUS

CHERRY PLUM. See PLUM and PRUNE, PRUNUS cerasifera

CHERVIL. See ANTHRISCUS cerefolium

CHESTNUT. See CASTANEA

CHICKABIDDY. See ASARINA

CHICORY

Asteraceae (Compositae)

PERENNIAL HERB

⚡ ALL ZONES, BUT DIFFICULT IN HOT-SUMMER AREAS

☼ FULL SUN

🔴 REGULAR TO MODERATE WATER

Chicory

Botanically known as *Cichorium intybus*. Dried ground roots can be roasted and used as substitute for coffee. Wild form grows as 3–6-ft. perennial roadside weed and is recognized by its pretty sky blue flowers that close by midday.

Grown for its leaves, it is known as chicory, endive, or curly endive; grown for its blanched sprouts, it's known as Belgian or French endive, endive hearts, or witloof ("white leaf"). For culture, see Endive.

Radicchio is the name given to a number of red-leafed chicories grown for salads. 'Rossa de Verona', or 'Rouge de Verone', is the best known. It forms lettucelike heads that color to a deep rosy red as weather grows cold in autumn or winter. Slight bitterness lessens as color deepens. Sow in early summer to mature in cold weather. Sow seeds of the similar 'Giulio' in spring to harvest in summer, 'Cesare' in midsummer for fall, winter harvest.

CHILEAN JASMINE. See MANDEVILLA laxa

CHILEAN WINE PALM. See JUBAEA chilensis

CHILOPSIS linearis

DESERT WILLOW, DESERT CATALPA
Bignoniaceae
DECIDUOUS SHRUB OR SMALL TREE
ZONES 10–13, 18–21, 29, 30, 33
FULL SUN
MODERATE TO LITTLE WATER

Native to desert washes and stream beds below 5,000 ft. Open and airy when trained as small tree. At first grows fast (to 3 ft. in a season), then slows down, leveling off at about 25 ft. With age it develops shaggy bark and twisting trunks. Drops leaves early, holds a heavy crop of catalpalike fruit through winter, and can look messy. But pruning can make it very handsome.

Chilopsis linearis

Narrow, 2–5-in.-long leaves. Trumpet-shaped flowers with crimped lobes look somewhat like those of catalpa. Flower color—pink, white, rose, or lavender, marked with purple—varies among seedlings; nurseries select most colorful. 'Burgundy' ('Burgundy Lace') has deep purplish red flowers. 'Cameo' is pure white with a yellow-striped throat. 'Pink Star' is light pink with some purple striping. All bloom in spring and often through fall. Attract birds.

CHIMONANTHUS praecox (C. fragrans, Meratia praecox)

WINTERSWEET
Calycanthaceae
DECIDUOUS SHRUB
ZONES 4–9, 14–17, 28–34
FULL SUN OR PARTIAL SHADE
MODERATE WATER

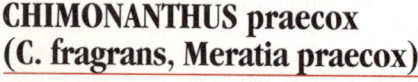

Native to China and Japan. Winter-blooming shrub with wonderfully spicy-scented blossoms. Needs some winter cold. Tall, open, slow growing to 10–15 ft. high and 6–8 ft. wide, with many basal stems. Flowers appear on leafless branches late winter to early spring, depending on climate; bloom lasts for many months if not frosted. Blossoms are 1 in. wide, with pale yellow outer sepals and smaller, chocolate-colored inner sepals. Tapered leaves are rough to the touch, medium green, 3–6 in. long and half that wide; turn yellow green in fall.

Chimonanthus praecox

In colder part of range, plant in sheltered site to prevent frost damage. In all areas, locate plant where its winter fragrance can be enjoyed. Some possible locations: near a much-used entrance or path, under a bedroom window. Keep plant lower by cutting back during bloom; shape as a small tree by removing excess basal stems; rejuvenate leggy plant by trimming to within a foot of the ground in late winter. Needs good drainage.

CHIMONOBAMBUSA. See BAMBOO

CHINA ASTER. See CALLISTEPHUS chinensis

CHINABERRY. See MELIA azedarach

CHINA FIR. See CUNNINGHAMIA lanceolata

CHINCHERINCHEE. See ORNITHOGALUM thyrsoides

CHINESE BELLFLOWER. See ABUTILON

CHINESE CABBAGE

Brassicaceae (Cruciferae)
BIENNIAL GROWN AS ANNUAL
ALL ZONES
TOLERATES LIGHT SHADE IN HOT CLIMATES
REGULAR WATER

Makes head somewhat looser than usual cabbage; sometimes called celery cabbage. Raw or cooked, it has more delicate flavor than cabbage. There are two kinds: pe-tsai, with tall, narrow heads; and wong bok, with short, broad heads. Favored pe-tsai variety is 'Michihli'; wong bok varieties include 'Springtime', 'Summertime', and 'Wintertime' (early to late maturing). Definitely cool-season crop; very prone to bolt to seed in hot weather or in long days of spring and early summer. In cold-winter regions, plant seeds directly in open ground in July; in August or September in milder climates. Sow seeds thinly in rows 2–2½ ft. apart and thin plants to 1½–2 ft. apart. Heads should be ready in 70 to 80 days. Subject to same pests as cabbage.

Chinese Cabbage

CHINESE CHIVES. See ALLIUM tuberosum

CHINESE ELM. See ULMUS parvifolia

CHINESE EVERGREEN. See AGLAONEMA modestum

CHINESE FLAME TREE. See KOELREUTERIA bipinnata

CHINESE FORGET-ME-NOT. See CYNOGLOSSUM amabile

CHINESE GROUND ORCHID. See BLETILLA striata

CHINESE LANTERN. See ABUTILON

CHINESE LANTERN PLANT. See PHYSALIS alkekengi

CHINESE PARASOL TREE. See FIRMIANA simplex

CHINESE PARSLEY. See CORIANDRUM sativum

CHINESE REDBUD. See CERCIS chinensis

CHINESE SCHOLAR TREE. See SOPHORA japonica

CHINESE SWEET GUM. See LIQUIDAMBAR formosana

CHINESE TALLOW TREE. See SAPIUM sebiferum

CHINESE WOOLFLOWER. See CELOSIA

CHIONANTHUS

FRINGE TREE
Oleaceae
DECIDUOUS SHRUBS OR SMALL TREES
ZONES VARY BY SPECIES
FULL SUN
REGULAR TO MODERATE WATER

Spectacular flowering plants requiring some winter chill. Earn common name from narrow, fringelike white petals on flowers that are borne in

Chionanthus retusus

impressive, ample, lacy clusters. There are male and female plants. Males have larger flowers. If both are present, female plants produce fruit like clusters of small dark olives, favored by birds. Broad leaves turn bright to deep yellow in fall. Both species tolerate city pollution.

C. retusus. CHINESE FRINGE TREE. Zones 3–9, 14–24, 28–34, 39. Grows to about 20 ft. tall; not quite as wide spreading as *C. virginicus*. Usually seen as a big multistemmed shrub, but can be grown as small tree. Produces pure white flower clusters to 4 in. long in late spring or early summer, 2 to 3 weeks before *C. virginicus*. Magnificent in bloom, something like a tremendous white lilac. Handsome gray-brown bark (sometimes golden on young stems) provides winter interest.

Chionanthus virginicus

C. virginicus. FRINGE TREE. Zones 2–6, 15–17, 28–41. Native Pennsylvania to Florida and Texas. Leaves and flower clusters often twice as big as those of *C. retusus,* and the blooms appear a little later. Slightly fragrant flowers are more greenish than white. Can reach 30 ft., but in cultivation usually 12–20 ft. high with equal spread. Variation in habit, from very shrubby and open to more treelike. In Zones 2–6, 38–41, where it grows very slowly (the most you can hope for is 12 ft. in 10 years), it is best used as an airy shrub; blooms profusely when just 2–3 ft. tall. One of the last deciduous plants to leaf out in spring. Susceptible to borers when growing in dry sites.

CHIONODOXA

GLORY-OF-THE-SNOW

Liliaceae

BULBS

✺ ZONES 1–7, 14–20, 31–43

☀ PARTIAL SHADE

🔴 REGULAR WATER DURING GROWTH AND BLOOM

Chionodoxa luciliae

Native to alpine meadows in Asia Minor. Charming small bulbous plants 4–6 in. high; among first to bloom in spring. Narrow basal leaves, two or three to each flower stalk. Blue or white, short, tubular, open flowers in loose spikes. Plant bulbs 3 in. deep in September or October in half shade; keep moist. Under favorable conditions, plants self-sow freely.

C. luciliae. Most generally available. Brilliant blue, white-centered, starlike flowers. 'Alba' offers larger white flowers; 'Gigantea' has larger leaves, larger flowers of violet blue with white throat.

C. sardensis. Deep, true gentian blue flowers with very small white eye.

CHITALPA tashkentensis

CHITALPA

Bignoniaceae

DECIDUOUS TREE

✺ ZONES 3–24, 28–33

☀ FULL SUN

🔴 MODERATE TO LITTLE WATER

Chitalpa tashkentensis

Fast growing to 20–30 ft. and as wide, this tree combines the larger flowers of its *Catalpa bignonioides* parent with the desert toughness and flower color of *Chilopsis linearis,* its other parent. Leaves are 4–5 in. long, an inch wide. Clusters of frilly trumpet-shaped flowers appear late spring to fall. 'Pink Dawn' has pink flowers, 'Morning Cloud' white ones. Culture same as for *Catalpa*.

FOR INFORMATION ON SELECTING PLANTS
PLEASE SEE PAGES 79–160

CHIVES

Liliaceae

PERENNIAL HERB

✺ ALL ZONES

☀ FULL SUN OR LIGHT SHADE

🔴 REGULAR WATER

Chives

Leaves are grasslike in general appearance but round and hollow in cross section. Clumps may reach 2 ft. in height but are usually shorter. Cloverlike, rose purple spring flowers are carried in clusters atop thin stems. Plant is pretty enough to use as edging in sunny or lightly shaded flower border or herb garden. Does best in moist, fairly rich soil. May be increased by divisions or grown from seed. Evergreen (or nearly so) in mild regions; goes dormant where winters are severe, but small divisions may be potted in rich soil and grown on kitchen windowsill. Chop or snip leaves; use as garnish or add to salads, cream cheese, cottage cheese, egg dishes, gravies, and soups for delicate onionlike flavor. For garlic chives (Chinese chives), see *Allium tuberosum*.

CHLOROPHYTUM

Liliaceae

PERENNIALS

✺ ZONES VARY BY SPECIES; OR INDOORS

☀ PARTIAL SHADE

🔴 REGULAR WATER

Chlorophytum comosum

Lily relatives with clumps of attractive evergreen foliage and small white or greenish flowers in long clusters.

C. bichetii. Indoor plant. Slow growing to an eventual 8–10 in. tall, 1½ ft. across. Leaves dark green with white stripes, shorter and relatively broader than those of *C. comosum,* gracefully recurved. Small white flowers on 8-in. stalks. Does not make runners. Bright indirect light. Water only when dry; feed occasionally to maintain good leaf color.

C. comosum. SPIDER PLANT. Indoor plant; ground cover in Zones 15–17, 19–27. Native to Africa. Forms 1–3-ft.-high clumps of soft, curving leaves like long, broad grass blades. 'Variegatum' and 'Vittatum', both striped white, are popular. Flowers white, ½ in. long, in loose, leafy-tipped spikes standing above foliage. Greatest attraction: miniature duplicates of mother plant, complete with root, at end of curved stems (as with strawberry plant offsets); these offsets can be cut off, potted individually. Excellent, easily grown house plant for fully lighted window, greenhouse. Ground cover or outdoor hanging basket plant in partial shade. As ground cover, set 2 ft. apart in diamond pattern. Plants will fill in area in same year. Often sold as *C. capense*.

CHOCOLATE LILY. See FRITILLARIA camschatcensis

CHOISYA ternata

MEXICAN ORANGE

Rutaceae

EVERGREEN SHRUB

✺ ZONES 7–9, 14–24, 26, 28, 31

☀ LIGHT SHADE IN HOT CLIMATES

🔴 MODERATE WATER

Choisya ternata

Fast growing to 6–8 ft. high and wide. Lustrous rich green leaves, held toward ends of branches, are divided into fans of three leaflets to 3 in. long. Clusters of fragrant white flowers, somewhat like small orange blossoms, open in very early spring and bloom continuously for a couple of months, then intermittently through summer. Sometimes called mock orange. Appealing to bees. Attractive informal hedge or screen. Needs fast drainage, neutral to acid soil. Hardy to about 10°F/−12°C. Subject to damage from sucking insects and mites. Foliage of 'Sundance' is yellow, gradually turning green.

CHOKEBERRY. See ARONIA

CHOKECHERRY. See PRUNUS virginiana

CHORISIA

FLOSS SILK TREE

Bombacaceae

EVERGREEN TO BRIEFLY DECIDUOUS TREES

🗡 ZONES VARY BY SPECIES

☀ FULL SUN

💧💧 REGULAR TO MODERATE WATER

Chorisia speciosa

Native to South America. Heavy trunks studded with thick, heavy spines. Young trunks are green, becoming gray with age. Leaves divided into leaflets like fingers of a hand; leaves fall during autumn flowering or whenever winter temperatures drop below 27°F/−3°C. Flowers large and showy, somewhat resembling narrow-petaled hibiscus blossoms. Provide fast drainage.

C. insignis. WHITE FLOSS SILK TREE. Zones 12, 13, 15–25, 26 (warm pockets), 27. To 50 ft. tall. Flowers white to pale yellow, 5–6 in. across.

C. speciosa. Zones 12–25, 26 (warm pockets), 27. Grows 3–5 ft. a year for the first few years, then slowly to 30–60 ft. tall. Flowers are pink, purplish rose, or burgundy. 'Los Angeles Beautiful', with wine red flowers, and 'Majestic Beauty', with rich pink flowers, are both grafted varieties.

CHRISTMAS BERRY. See HETEROMELES arbutifolia

CHRISTMAS CACTUS. See SCHLUMBERGERA bridgesii

CHRISTMAS FERN. See POLYSTICHUM acrostichoides

CHRISTMAS ROSE. See HELLEBORUS niger

CHRYSALIDOCARPUS
lutescens

ARECA PALM, CANE PALM, YELLOW PALM

Arecaceae (Palmae)

PALM

🗡 ZONES 23–27; OR INDOORS

☀◐● SUN OR SHADE

💧 REGULAR WATER

Chrysalidocarpus lutescens

Clumping feather palm of slow growth to 10–15 ft. or even taller. Graceful plant with smooth trunks and yellowish green leaves. Can take dense shade; intolerant of salt. Used in foundation plantings and as patio plant in warmest climates; house plant elsewhere. Tricky to maintain indoors, but a lovely palm. Prone to spider mites as a house plant. Often sold as *Areca lutescens*.

FOR INFORMATION ON YOUR CLIMATE ZONE
PLEASE SEE PAGES 16–78

CHRYSANTHEMUM

Asteraceae (Compositae)

PERENNIALS AND ANNUALS

🗡 ZONES VARY BY SPECIES

☀ BEST IN FULL SUN, EXCEPT AS NOTED

💧 REGULAR WATER, EXCEPT AS NOTED

Chrysanthemum frutescens

There are about 160 species of chrysanthemum, mostly native to China, Japan, and Europe. Included are some of most popular and useful of garden plants—top favorite being *C. morifolium*, whose modern descendants are known as florists' chrysanthemums. Botanists have split *Chrysanthemum* into many new genera. Growers may be slow to use new names, but some have begun to do so. The new names are listed immediately after the old.

C. arcticum (Arctanthemum arcticum). Perennial. Zones 1–24, 32–45. Very hardy autumn bloomer; forms clump with stems 6–12 in. high. Spoon-shaped leaves, usually three-lobed, 1–3 in. long, leathery in texture. White or pinkish flower heads 1–2 in. across. Developed from this species is a group of hybrids known as Northland daisies, with single flowers 3 in. across or more, in shades of pink, rose, rosy purple, and yellow. *C. arcticum* itself is primarily rock garden plant. Taller-growing varieties serve best in borders.

C. balsamita (Tanacetum balsamita). COSTMARY. Perennial. Zones 2–24, 28–41. Weedy plant with sweet-scented foliage that justifies its presence in herb garden (use leaves in salads and sachets). If leggy stems are cut back, gray-green basal leaves with tiny scalloped margins can make herb garden edging. Divide clumps and reset divisions in late summer or fall.

C. carinatum. SUMMER CHRYSANTHEMUM, TRICOLOR CHRYSANTHEMUM. Annual. All zones. Grows 1–3 ft. high, about 3 ft. wide. Summer and fall bloom; in mild-winter areas, can be planted for winter and spring bloom. Deeply cut foliage; showy, single, daisylike, 2-in.-wide flower heads in purple, orange, scarlet, salmon, rose, yellow, and white, with contrasting bands around dark center. Satisfactory, long-lasting cut flowers. Sow seeds in spring either in pots or in open ground. Where winters are mild, do sowing in fall. Court Jesters is an excellent strain.

C. coccineum (Pyrethrum roseum, Tanacetum coccineum). PYRETHRUM, PAINTED DAISY. Perennial. Zones 2–24, 33–41. Bushy plant to 2–3 ft., with very finely divided, bright green leaves and single, daisylike, long-stemmed flowers in pink, red, and white. Also available in double and anemone-flowered forms. Starts blooming in April in mild-winter climates, in May or June in colder areas; if cut back, blooms again in late summer. Excellent for cutting, borders. Needs summer heat to perform well (but does not take high humidity). Divide clumps or sow seeds in spring. Double forms may not come true from seed; they may revert to single flowers.

C. coronarium. CROWN DAISY. Annual. All zones. To 2½ ft., with light green, coarsely cut leaves and yellow daisies. A variety is the vegetable known as shungiku, chop-suey greens, or edible chrysanthemum; it can be cooked like spinach.

C. frutescens (Argyranthemum frutescens). MARGUERITE, PARIS DAISY. Short-lived shrubby perennial in Zones 14–24, 26, 28; grown as summer annual elsewhere. Bright green, coarsely divided leaves; abundant daisies 1½–2½ in. across in white, yellow, or pink. 'Snow White', double anemone type, has pure white flowers, more restrained growth habit; 'White Lady' and 'Pink Lady' produce buttonlike flower heads; 'Silver Leaf' has gray-green leaves and masses of very small white flowers. Also dwarf varieties. All types are splendid in containers and for quick effects in borders, mass displays in new gardens. For continued bloom, prune lightly at frequent intervals. In mild-winter areas, do not prune severely, since plants seldom produce new growth from hardened wood; replace every 2 to 3 years.

C. leucanthemum (Leucanthemum vulgare). OX-EYE DAISY, COMMON DAISY. Perennial. Zones 1–24, 28–43. European native naturalized in many places. To 2 ft., with bright green foliage, yellow-centered daisies from late spring through fall. 'May Queen' begins blooming in early spring.

C. maximum (C. superbum, Leucanthemum maximum, L. superbum). SHASTA DAISY. Perennial. Zones 1–24, 26 (northern portion), 28–43. Summer and fall bloomer. Original 2–4-ft.-tall Shasta daisy, with coarse, leathery leaves and gold-centered, white flower heads 2–4 in. across, has been largely superseded by varieties with larger, better-formed, longer-blooming flowers. They are available in single, double, quilled, and shaggy-flowered forms. All are white, but two show a touch of yellow. Some bloom May–October. Shasta daisies are splendid in borders and cut arrangements.

Following are some of the varieties available in nurseries:

'Esther Read', most popular double white, long bloom; 'Marconi', large frilly double; 'Aglaya', similar to 'Marconi', long blooming season; 'Alaska', big, old-fashioned single; 'Horace Read', 4-in.-wide, dahlialike flower; 'Majestic', large yellow-centered flower; 'Thomas Killin', 6-in.-wide (largest) yellow-centered flower.

'Cobham's Gold' has distinctive flowers in yellow-tinted, off-white shade. 'Canarybird', another yellow, is dwarf, with attractive dark green foliage.

Most popular varieties for cut flowers are 'Esther Read', 'Majestic', 'Aglaya', and 'Thomas Killin'.

Shasta daisies are easy to grow from seed. Catalogs offer many strains, including Roggli Super Giant (single) and Diener's Strain (double). 'Marconi' (double), also available in seed, nearly always blooms double. 'Silver Princess' (also called 'Little Princess' and 'Little Miss Muffet') is 12–15-in. dwarf single. 'Snow Lady' (single), an All-America winner, 10–12 in. tall, begins to bloom in 5 months from seed, then blooms nearly continuously.

Set out divisions of Shasta daisies in fall or early spring, container-grown plants any time. Thrive in fairly rich, moist, well-drained soil. Prefer sun, but do well in partial shade in hot-summer climates; double-flowered kinds hold up better in very light shade. In coldest regions, mulch around plants but do not smother foliage. Divide clumps every 2 to 3 years in early spring (or in fall in mild-winter areas). Shasta daisies are generally easy to grow but have a few problems. Disease called "gall" causes root crown to split into many weak, poorly rooted growing points that soon die. Dig out and dispose of affected plants; don't replant Shasta daisies in the same spot.

C. morifolium (Dendranthema grandiflorum). FLORISTS' CHRYSANTHEMUM. Perennial. Zones 2–24, 26 (northern portion), 28–41. The most useful of all autumn-blooming perennials for borders, containers, and cutting, and the most versatile and varied of all chrysanthemum species, available in many flower forms, colors, plant and flower sizes, and growth habits. Colors include white, yellow, red, pink, orange, bronze, purple, and lavender, as well as multicolors. Following are flower forms as designated by chrysanthemum hobbyists:

Chrysanthemum morifolium

Anemone. One or more rows of rays with large raised center disk or cushion. Center disk may be same color as rays or different. (Disbud to encourage very large flowers.)

Brush. Narrow, rolled rays give brush or soft cactus dahlia effect.

Decorative. Long, broad rays overlap in shingle effect to form broad, full flower.

Incurve. Big double flowers with broad rays curving upward and inward.

Irregular curve. Like above, but with looser, more softly curving rays.

Laciniated. Fully double, with rays fringed and cut at tips in carnation effect.

Pompom. Globular, neat, compact flowers with flat, fluted, or quilled rays. Usually small, they can reach 5 in. with disbudding.

Quill. Long, narrow rolled rays; like spider but less droopy.

Reflex. Big double flowers with rays that curl in, out, and sideways, creating shaggy effect.

Semidouble. Somewhat like single or daisy, but with two, three, or four rows of rays around a yellow center.

Single or daisy. Single row of rays around a yellow center. May be large or small, with broad or narrow rays.

Spider. Long, curling, tubular rays ending in fish-hook curved tips.

Spoon. Tubular rays flatten at tip to make little disks, sometimes in colors that contrast with body of flower.

Garden culture. It's easy to grow chrysanthemums, not so easy to grow prize-winning chrysanthemums. The latter need more water, feeding, pinching, pruning, grooming, and pest control than most perennials.

Plant in good, well-drained garden soil improved by organic matter and a complete fertilizer dug in 2 or 3 weeks before planting. In hot climates, provide shade from afternoon sun. Don't plant near large trees or hedges with invasive roots.

Set out young plants (rooted cuttings or vigorous, single-stem divisions) in early spring. When dividing clumps, take divisions from outside; discard woody centers. Water deeply at intervals determined by your soil structure—frequently in porous soils, less often in heavy soils. Too little water causes woody stems and loss of lower leaves; overwatering causes leaves to yellow, then blacken and drop. Aphids are the only notable pest in all areas. Feed plants in ground two or three times during the growing season; make last application with low-nitrogen fertilizer not less than 2 weeks before bloom.

Sturdy plants and big flowers are result of frequent pinching, which should begin at planting time with removal of new plant's tip. Lateral shoots will form; select one to four of these for continued growth. Continue pinching all summer, nipping top pair of leaves on every shoot that reaches 5 in. in length. On some early-blooming cushion varieties, or in coldest regions, pinching should be stopped earlier. Stake plants to keep them upright. To produce huge blooms, remove all flower buds except for one or two in each cluster—this is called disbudding.

Pot culture. Pot rooted cuttings February–April, using porous, fibrous, moisture-holding planting mix. Move plants to larger pots as growth requires—don't let them become root-bound. Pinch as directed above;

Flower Forms of *Chrysanthemum*

Anenome

Brush

Decorative

Incurve

Laciniated

Pompom

Reflex

Semidouble

Single

Spider

Spoon

C

stake as required. Plants need water daily in warm weather, every other day in cool conditions. Feed with liquid fertilizer every 7 to 10 days until buds show color.

Care after bloom. Cut back plants to within 8 in. of ground. Where soils are heavy and likely to remain wet in winter, dig clumps with soil intact and set on top of ground in inconspicuous place. Cover with sand or sawdust if you wish. Take cuttings from early to late spring (up until May for some varieties), or when shoots are 3–4 in. long. As new shoots develop, you can make additional cuttings of them. In cold-winter areas, store plants in cold frame or mulch them with a light, noncompacting material such as excelsior.

Off-season, potted chrysanthemums. Florists and stores sell potted chrysanthemums in bloom every day of the year, even though by nature a chrysanthemum blooms in late summer or fall. Growers force these plants to bloom out of season by subjecting them to artificial day lengths, using lights and dark cloths. You can plunge the potted flowering plants right into a garden bed or border for an immediate (but expensive) display, or you can enjoy them in the house while the flowers remain fresh and then plant them out. Either way, they will not bloom again at the same off-season time the next year. Instead, they will revert to their natural inclination and commence fall bloom once again.

Cut off flowers when they fade, leaving stems about 6–8 in. long. Remove soil clump from pot and break apart the several individual plants that were grown in the pot. Plant these individual plants. When new growth shows from the roots, cut off remainder of old flower stems.

C. multicaule (Coleostephus myconis). Annual. All zones. Broad-rayed, buttery yellow daisies 2½ in. across rise in spring above 6–8-in.-wide mats of bright green, fleshy foliage. Blooms best in cool weather; usually sold in fall, winter, early spring from six-packs or pots. Plants may live over a second year in cool-summer climates.

> ### BUTTER YELLOW DAISIES
> Where winters are mild, *Chrysanthemum multicaule* makes a great companion for bulbs in pots. Try it with Dutch iris—plant three bulbs in an 18-in. pot in October, and in the spaces between the bulbs plant three chrysanthemums from a six-pack. In March and April this pairing will give you a beautiful display of butter yellow and Wedgwood blue.

C. nipponicum (Nipponanthemum nipponicum). Perennial. Zones 2–24, 29–41. Resembles a large (up to 3-ft.), rounded, shrubby Shasta daisy with a dense mass of nearly succulent bright green leaves. White daisy flowers on long stems form in fall. In mild-winter regions, you may cut back after bloom. Where winters are cold, do not disturb plants until they put on strong new growth in spring; at that time, you may cut back partway to maintain compactness.

C. pacificum (Pyrethrum marginatum, Dendranthema pacificum). GOLD AND SILVER CHRYSANTHEMUM. Perennial. Zones 2–24, 28–41. Semitrailing and semishrubby, with stems to 2–3 ft. densely clad in lobed, dark green leaves apparently edged white (woolly white undersides show at edges). Broad clusters of yellow flowers appear in fall; lacking rays, they resemble clustered brass buttons. 'Pink Ice' is a pale pink–flowered variety with short petals. Use as bank or ground cover or at front of perennial border. In mild-winter regions, you may cut back after bloom. Where winters are cold, do not disturb plants until they put on strong new growth in spring; at that time, you may cut back partway to maintain compactness.

C. paludosum (Leucanthemum paludosum). Annual, sometimes living over for a second bloom season. All zones. In summer, bears white daisies 1–1½ in. wide on 8–10-in. stems above dark green, deeply toothed leaves. Look like miniature Shasta daisies.

C. parthenium (Tanacetum parthenium). FEVERFEW. Perennial. Zones 1–24, 28–45. Compact, leafy, aggressive; once favored in Victorian

gardens. Leaves have strong odor, offensive to some. Named varieties range from 1 to 3 ft. tall. 'Golden Ball' has bright yellow flower heads and no rays; 'Silver Ball' is completely double with only the white rays showing. In 'Aureum', commonly sold in flats as 'Golden Feather', chartreuse-colored foliage is principal attraction. Sow seeds in spring for bloom by midsummer, or plant from divisions in fall or spring. Can also grow from cuttings. Full sun or light shade.

C. ptarmiciflorum (Tanacetum ptarmiciflorum). DUSTY MILLER, SILVER LACE. Zones 16, 17, 19–24 as perennial; all zones as annual. To 6–10 in. tall, 8–10 in. wide. Very finely cut, silvery white leaves. Where hardy, produces white daisy flowers on 1½-ft. stems in summer. Somewhat drought tolerant.

C. rubellum (Dendranthema zawadskii). Perennial. Zones 1–24, 28–43. To 2 ft. tall, with finely cut leaves and pink flowers over a long blooming season beginning in late summer. 'Clara Curtis' is the best-known variety.

C. serotinum (C. uliginosum). Perennial. Zones 2–9, 14, 28–43. Grows 5–6 ft. tall, producing sheaves of 3-in., yellow-eyed white daisies in late summer. Useful for late flowers in back of perennial border. Can tolerate damp soil better than most daisies.

C. weyrichii (Dendranthema weyrichii). Perennial. Zones 2–6, 32, 34–41. Mat-forming; for rock garden. Leaves finely cut. Single daisies about 2 in. wide, with white to pink rays and yellow centers, appear just above foliage in autumn. 'Pink Bomb' has rosy pink rays, 'White Bomb' creamy white ones.

CHRYSOGONUM virginianum

GOLDEN STAR, GREEN AND GOLD

Asteraceae (Compositae)

PERENNIAL

✎ ZONES 3–6, 14–17, 28–32, 34–39

☼ ◗ PARTIAL SHADE IN WARMER AREAS

🔴 REGULAR WATER

Chrysogonum virginianum

Native to eastern U.S. Useful and attractive native plant for ground cover or foreground planting. Grows 8 in. tall and spreads freely. Bright green, toothed leaves, 1–3 in. long, make a good background for bright yellow flower heads. Blossoms have five rays, resemble stars more than daisies. Bloom is heavy in spring and fall, sporadic through summer months. Plant 1 ft. apart in rich soil high in organic matter for quick ground cover.

CHRYSOLARIX. See PSEUDOLARIX kaempferi

CHRYSOPSIS

GOLDEN ASTER

Asteraceae (Compositae)

PERENNIALS

✎ ZONES 1–14, 19–24, 28–43

☼ FULL SUN

🔴 🔴 REGULAR TO MODERATE WATER

Chrysopsis mariana

Perennials native to eastern and central U.S. Tough, somewhat coarse plants. Drought and heat tolerance makes them useful for poor, dry soils and hot situations, yet bright yellow daisylike flowers are showy enough for garden use. Late summer and fall bloom.

C. mariana. Grows to 2 ft. or possibly 3 ft. high, with large (9-in.) basal leaves, smaller stem leaves, tight clusters of 1½-in. flowers.

C. villosa. Taller than *C. mariana* (to 3–4 ft.), with smaller, somewhat more scattered flowers.

CHRYSOTHAMNUS nauseosus

RUBBER RABBITBRUSH, GRAY RABBITBRUSH

Asteraceae (Compositae)

DECIDUOUS SHRUB

ZONES 1–3, 7–16, 18–21

FULL SUN

VERY LITTLE WATER

Chrysothamnus nauseosus

Native to high desert and Rocky Mountain areas. Shrub to 6 ft., with narrow gray-green leaves that usually drop by flowering time in late summer, early autumn. Masses of golden yellow, fluffy flowers in broad, flat-topped clusters. Use in low-maintenance gardens, native plant gardens.

CICHORIUM intybus. See CHICORY

CIDER GUM. See EUCALYPTUS gunnii

CIGAR PLANT. See CUPHEA ignea

CILANTRO. See CORIANDRUM sativum

CIMICIFUGA

BUGBANE

Ranunculaceae

PERENNIALS

ZONES 1–7, 17, 32–45

PARTIAL SHADE IN WARMER AREAS

REGULAR WATER

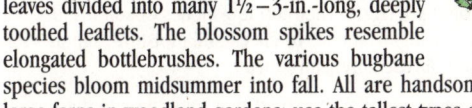

Cimicifuga racemosa

Stately, upright, slim spikes of small white flowers rise from clumps of shiny, dark green leaves divided into many 1½–3-in.-long, deeply toothed leaflets. The blossom spikes resemble elongated bottlebrushes. The various bugbane species bloom midsummer into fall. All are handsome planted among large ferns in woodland gardens; use the tallest types at the back of borders. Delicate, airy effect.

Best in rich, well-drained, moist soil. Will take considerable sun with plentiful water. Need some winter chill for best blooming. Clumps can remain undisturbed for many years. Divide in early spring before growth starts in cold-winter areas, in fall in milder climates. Dried seed clusters useful in flower arrangements.

C. japonica. Native to Japan. White flowers on purplish black, leafless stalks in autumn. About 3–4 ft. tall in bloom. 'Acerina' has white flowers opening from pink buds.

C. racemosa. BLACK SNAKEROOT. Native from Massachusetts south to Georgia and west to Missouri. Plant was once used medicinally by Native Americans. Flowering stems to 7 ft. tall. Starts blooming in midsummer in southern part of range, in late summer or early fall farther north.

C. ramosa. Fall bloomer with flowers on branched stems to 7 ft. tall. Narrow 1-ft. spires on each branch provide a long floral display. 'Atropurpurea' is lower growing (to 5 ft.), with dark reddish purple foliage.

C. simplex. KAMCHATKA BUGBANE. Native to Siberia and Japan. Fall bloomer, with plumes reaching 3–5 ft. high. 'White Pearl' has especially large flower spikes.

CINERARIA. See SENECIO hybridus

FOR GROWING SYMBOL EXPLANATIONS PLEASE SEE PAGE 161

CINNAMOMUM camphora

CAMPHOR TREE

Lauraceae

EVERGREEN TREE

ZONES 8, 9, 12–28

FULL SUN OR LIGHT SHADE

REGULAR WATER

Cinnamomum camphora

Native to China, Japan. Grows slowly to 50 ft. or more with wider spread. Aromatic foliage smells like camphor when crushed. Winter leaves are shiny yellow green. New foliage in early spring may be pink, red, or bronze, depending on tree. Usually strong structure, heavy trunk, and heavy, upright, spreading limbs. Beautiful in rain, when trunk looks black. Inconspicuous, fragrant yellow flowers in profusion in May, followed by small blackish fruits. Drops leaves quite heavily in March; flowers, fruits, and twigs drop later. Competitive roots make this tree a poor choice near garden beds. Most prone to a root rot (verticillium wilt) after wet winter or if planted in poorly drained soil.

CINNAMON FERN. See OSMUNDA cinnamomea

CINQUEFOIL. See POTENTILLA

CISSUS

Vitaceae

EVERGREEN VINES

ZONES VARY BY SPECIES

SUN OR SHADE

WATER NEEDS VARY BY SPECIES

Cissus antarctica

Related to Virginia creeper, Boston ivy, and grape, they are distinguished for their foliage. Flowers inconspicuous. Easy to grow. Useful near swimming pools. Take sun or shade outdoors, indirect light indoors.

C. antarctica. KANGAROO TREEBINE. Zones 16–25, 27. Native to Australia. A graceful vine, vigorous once established. To 10 ft. Medium green, shiny leaves, 2–3½ in. long and almost as wide, with toothed edges. When grown in the ground, it is very drought tolerant once established. Allow to climb or tumble down; for trellis, wall, or hillside. Good tub plant indoors or out.

C. capensis. See Rhoicissus capensis

C. rhombifolia. GRAPE IVY. Zones 13, 15, 16, 21–27 (needs all-year warmth). Native to South America. To 20 ft. Beautiful dark green foliage. Leaves divided into diamond-shaped leaflets 1–4 in. long, with sharp-toothed edges; show bronze overtones because of reddish hairs on veins beneath. Widely used indoors. Outdoors, it grows to good size and can be trained on trellis, pergola, or driftwood branches. Give regular water. 'Mandaiana' is more upright and compact than the species, with larger, more substantial leaflets. 'Ellen Danica' has leaflets shallowly lobed like an oak leaf; it grows more compactly than the species and has darker green, less lustrous leaves.

Cistaceae. Members of the rockrose family, grown primarily in the West, are evergreen shrubs with flowers that look something like single roses—small in sunrose (*Helianthemum*), large in rockrose (*Cistus*). Individual flowers are short lived, but plants bloom over a long season.

CISTUS

ROCKROSE

Cistaceae

EVERGREEN SHRUBS

ZONES 6–9, 14–24; EXPERIMENTAL IN 28–31

FULL SUN

MODERATE TO LITTLE WATER

Cistus purpureus

Native to Mediterranean region. In their favored dry-summer climate, these are care-free shrubs that perform beautifully with no fertilizer and little water. Bloom for a month or more in spring or early summer, producing a profusion of showy flowers. Tolerate seacoast conditions, desert heat, poor soil. Worth trying in the Southeast, but no guarantee of success there. If plants will be watered, provide excellent drainage. Periodically prune out a few old stems to keep plants neat; tip-pinch young plants to make them bushy.

C. hybridus (C. corbariensis). WHITE ROCKROSE. Grows 2–5 ft. high and almost as wide. Leaves to 2 in. long, gray green, crinkly; fragrant on warm days. Flowers 1½ in. across, white with yellow centers.

C. ladanifer (C. ladaniferus maculatus). CRIMSON-SPOT ROCK-ROSE. Compact, to 3–5 ft. high, with equal spread. Leaves to 4 in. long, dark green above, lighter beneath, fragrant. White, 3-in. flowers with dark crimson spot at base of each petal. 'Albiflorus' is an unspotted form. *C. l. latifolius* is 2 ft. high, with 3–4-in. pure white flowers. 'Blanche' (2 ft.) and 'Frank Birch' (6–8 ft.), both with very large (4-in.) pure white blossoms, are considered hybrids between *C. ladanifer* and *C. l. latifolius*.

C. laurifolius. Stiff, erect growth to 5 ft. Dark green, 3-in. leaves with pale undersides. Clusters of white, 2–2½-in.-wide flowers.

C. purpureus. ORCHID ROCKROSE. Compact grower to 4 ft. tall and wide. Leaves 1–2 in. long, dark green above, gray and hairy beneath. Reddish purple, 3-in. flowers with red spot at base of each petal.

C. salviifolius. SAGELEAF ROCKROSE. Wide-spreading shrub to 2 ft. high, 6 ft. across. Leaves light gray green, 1 in. long, crinkly, veined, crisp looking. Flowers 1½ in. wide, white with yellow spot at base of each petal; very profuse. Good bank or ground cover for rough situations. Usually sold as *C. villosus* 'Prostratus'.

CITRON. See CITRUS

CITRUS

Rutaceae

EVERGREEN TREES AND SHRUBS

ZONES 8, 9, 12–27 FOR MOST CITRUS; 7, 28–31 FOR HARDIEST TYPES; OR INDOORS

FULL SUN

DO NOT LET ROOT ZONE BECOME DRY OR SOGGY

Orange

As landscaping plants, they offer year-round attractive form and glossy deep green foliage; also bear fragrant flowers and decorative fruit in season. If you want quality fruit, your choice of varieties will depend on the total amount of heat available through the fruit-developing period (need varies according to type) and on the winter cold in your area.

Heat requirements. Generally, sweet-fruited varieties need moderate to high heat to form sugars, while sour-fruited types require less heat. Grapefruit demands the most heat; sweet oranges and mandarins need moderate heat; lemons will produce in mild-summer areas. Some citrus, such as satsuma mandarins, can't tolerate intense heat. Pigmented grapefruit and pummelos need heat to develop red color; without enough, the flesh looks white. Color in blood oranges isn't related to heat, but to chilly nights during ripening.

Hardiness. Citrus plants of one type or another are grown outdoors year-round in the southernmost parts of U.S. where summers are warm and winters mild. Lemons, limes, and citrons are most sensitive to freezes. Sweet oranges, grapefruit, and most mandarins and their hybrids are intermediate. Kumquats, satsuma mandarins, sour oranges, and calamondins are most cold resistant, withstanding temperatures in the high teens. Hardy citrus (see page 253) is available to gardeners just beyond the citrus belt.

Other factors affecting a tree's cold tolerance include preconditioning to cold (more endurance if exposed to cold slowly and if first freeze comes late), type of rootstock, location in garden. Prolonged exposure to freezing weather is more damaging than a brief plunge in temperature. All citrus fruit is damaged at several degrees below freezing, so choose early-ripening varieties in freeze-prone areas.

Anatomy. A citrus tree consists of two parts: scion (upper part of tree producing desirable fruit) and rootstock (lower few inches of trunk and the roots). These are joined at the bud union. Grafted trees begin bearing fruit in just a few years, contrasted with 10 to 15 years for seedling trees. Most varieties produce a single crop in fall or winter. Everbearing types (lemons, limes, calamondins) can produce throughout the year, though they fruit most heavily in spring. Plants don't go completely dormant, but their growth does slow in winter. Citrus fruit ripens only on the tree.

Tree size depends on category of citrus and sometimes on variety within category. Standard tree grows full size; dwarf is grafted onto rootstock that reduces size of tree but not of fruit. Dwarf trees are sold in California, Arizona, and through mail-order suppliers (these can't ship to commercial citrus-producing states). Standard trees are the norm in Florida, Texas, and along the Gulf Coast.

Drainage. Fast drainage is essential. In poorly drained soil, plant above soil level in raised beds or on soil mound. To improve drainage in average soil and water retention in sandy soil, dig in a 4–6-in. layer of organic matter (such as garden compost or aged sawdust) to depth of 1 ft.

Watering. Citrus trees need moist soil but never standing water. Though they require moisture all year, greatest demand is during active growth, usually from late winter or early spring through summer. Most critical when fruit is developing. Irrigate when top few inches of soil are dry but rest of root zone is still slightly moist. To check soil moisture, simply stick your finger in the soil; or use a moisture meter.

Fertilizing. Nitrogen is the main nutrient that must be supplied in all regions; if you garden in sandy soil, choose a complete fertilizer containing a full range of nutrients. Apply 2 oz. actual nitrogen the first year after newly planted tree puts on new growth; increase by 4 oz. each year for next few years; after fifth year, apply 1–1½ lb. yearly (use higher end of range for rainy-summer areas). To calculate pounds of actual nitrogen, multiply percentage of total nitrogen (as stated on fertilizer label) by weight of fertilizer.

Divide into several feedings throughout growing season (slow-release fertilizers, however, can be applied all at once). In freeze-prone areas, start feeding after last spring frost and stop in late summer.

Pests and diseases. Most problems are minor or can be solved by improving growing conditions. Unlike deciduous fruit trees such as apples or peaches, citrus trees do not need regular spraying. Some afflictions are more prevalent in certain regions: citrus leaf miner in Florida and Texas (apply horticultural oil spray); citrus thrips in Arizona (no control usually needed); greasy spot in hot, humid climates (use oil or copper fungicide spray). Check with Cooperative Extension Office, or local nurseries for problems you may encounter in your area.

Pruning. Commercial trees are allowed to carry branches right to ground. Production is heaviest on lower branches. Growers prune only to remove twiggy growth and weak branches or, in young plant, to nip back wild growth and balance plant. You can prune garden trees to shape as desired; espaliers of citrus are traditional. Lemons and sour oranges are often planted close and pruned as hedges. Many citrus plants are thorny, so wear gloves and long-sleeved shirt when picking fruit or pruning. In freeze-prone areas, don't prune in fall or winter.

Citrus in containers. Containers should have diameter of at least 1½ ft., though calamondin and 'Chinotto' sour orange can stay in 8–10-in. pots for years. Plant in light, well-drained soil mix. Daily watering may be necessary in hot weather. Use a slow-release fertilizer to keep nutrients from washing out with each watering.

Potted citrus can stay outdoors all year in mild-winter climates, but should be moved to protection if a freeze is predicted. In cold-winter regions, shelter plants in winter: a cool greenhouse is best, but a basement area or garage with good bright light is satisfactory.

Citrus as house plants. No guarantee of flowering or fruiting indoors (though plants are still appealing). 'Improved Meyer' and 'Ponderosa' lemons, 'Bearss' or 'Persian' lime, kumquats, calamondins, 'Rangpur' sour-acid mandarin most likely to produce good fruit. Locate no more than 6 ft. from sunny window, away from radiator or other heat source. Ideal humidity level is 50 percent. Increase air moisture by misting tree; also ring tree with pebble-filled trays of water. Water sparingly in winter.

SWEET ORANGE

Dense globes to about 25 ft. tall. Fruit usually stores on the tree for a few months.

'Washington'. Original navel variety from which the other navels developed. Seedless eating orange ripens early, fall into winter. In Texas and Florida, local selections sold simply as "navel" have better flavor.

'Cara Cara'. First rosy-fleshed navel, bearing at about same time as 'Washington'. Red in Florida, pink in warm areas of California. Other navel varieties include late bearers 'Lane Late' and 'Spring' (ripen 4 to 6 weeks after 'Washington'), available in California.

'Hamlin'. Early juice orange, nearly seedless, maturing fall into winter. Best in Arizona, South Texas, Florida.

'Jaffa' ('Shamouti'). Midseason (ripens winter into spring), nearly seedless eating orange from Israel. Grown in South Texas, Arizona, California.

'Marrs'. Low-acid, few seeds, ripening fall into winter. Arizona, South Texas.

'Parson Brown'. Early-ripening small juice orange, seedy, best in Florida.

'Pineapple'. Leading midseason orange in Florida; also grown in South Texas and Arizona. Fairly seedy but excellent for juicing. Tends to drop from tree after ripening.

'Trovita'. Midseason eating and juice orange. California, Arizona.

'Valencia.' This is the premier juice orange. Widely adapted, bearing nearly seedless fruit from midwinter in hottest areas to summer in coolest. 'Delta' and 'Midknight' are seedless selections ripening a little earlier. If grown in Florida, 'Rohde Red' has more highly colored flesh than the plain 'Valencia'.

Blood oranges. These are characterized by red pigmentation in flesh, juice, and (to a lesser degree) rind. Flavor has raspberry overtones. Need chilly nights during ripening; best in California inland valleys. Main varieties grown are 'Moro' (only one to color up near California coast), 'Sanguinelli', and 'Tarocco'.

SOUR ORANGE

Very ornamental trees with attractive leaves and big, perfumed, waxy white flowers. Clusters of deep red-orange, tart fruits ripen midfall to winter, hold for a year. For all citrus-growing regions.

'Bouquet de Fleurs' ('Bouquet'). Beautiful spreading tree 8–10 ft. high. Fragrant blooms used by French perfume makers. Nearly seedless fruit.

'Chinotto' (myrtle-leaf orange). Compact tree to 7 ft. or higher. Small, myrtlelike leaves and seedy fruit.

'Seville'. Thorny, upright to 20–30 ft. high. Seedy fruit makes superior marmalade.

MANDARIN

Small to medium-size trees (10–20 ft. tall) bearing juicy, loose-skinned, often flattened fruit; most produce in winter. Varieties with red-orange peel usually called tangerines. Many mandarins tend to bear heavily in alternate years.

'Clementine' (Algerian tangerine). Sweet, variably seedy flesh. Ripens early from fall into winter, holds well on tree. Light crop without a pollinator. California, Arizona, South Texas.

'Dancy'. Small, seedy fruit is traditional Christmas "tangerine." Needs high heat; best in Florida. Also grows in desert. Alternate bearer.

'Encore'. Very late, ripening spring into summer and holding on tree until fall. Sweet-tart, seedy fruit. Alternate bearer. California, Arizona, South Texas.

'Fremont.' Early variety with seedy, richly sweet fruit. Alternate bearer. California, Arizona, Upper Gulf Coast.

'Honey'. Midseason California variety with seedy, very sweet fruit. Different from 'Murcott' tangor, which is marketed as Honey tangerine. Alternate bearer. California, Arizona, South Texas, Upper Gulf Coast.

'Kara'. Springtime crop of sweet-tart fruit with varying seediness. Gets puffy soon after ripening. Alternate bearer. California.

'Kinnow'. Midseason variety with seedy fruit too sweet for some people. Holds fairly well on tree. Alternate bearer. California, Arizona.

'Mediterranean' ('Willow Leaf'). Midseason crop of sweet, aromatic, very juicy fruit gets puffy soon after ripening. Needs high heat. Alternate bearer. California, Arizona, South Texas, Upper Gulf Coast.

'Pixie'. Late variety with seedless, mild, sweet fruit. Alternate bearer. California, South Texas.

'Ponkan' (Chinese honey mandarin). Early crop of seedy, very sweet fruit. Alternate bearer. California, South Texas, Florida.

Satsuma. Very early mandarin with mild, sweet fruit that begins ripening in fall. Succeeds in areas too cold for most citrus. Ripe fruit deteriorates quickly on tree but keeps well in cool storage. Selections include 'Owari', 'Dobashi Beni', 'Okitsu Wase', and 'Kimbrough'. California, South Texas, Upper Gulf Coast, North Florida.

'Wilking'. Midseason variety with juicy, rich, distinctive flavor. Holds fairly well on tree. Alternate bearer. California, Arizona, South Texas.

MULTIPLE-VARIETY CITRUS PLANTS

The nursery offerings go by such names as cocktail citrus, salad citrus, and citrus medley. On these plants, which bear multiple kinds of fruit, several varieties (usually two or three) have been budded onto one stem. Such plants save space, but you must continually cut back the vigorous growers (limes, lemons, pummelos, grapefruit) so the weaker ones (oranges, mandarins) can survive.

MANDARIN HYBRIDS

These hybrids generally perform best in hot climates. Many were developed in Florida, where they produce outstanding crops.

Tangelo. Hybrid between mandarin and grapefruit. Best with a pollinator. Two main varieties. 'Minneola' bears winter crop of bright orange-red fruit (often with a noticeable "neck") with rich, tart flavor and some seeds. 'Orlando' produces mild, sweet, fairly seedy fruit about a month earlier than 'Minneola'.

Tangor. Hybrid between mandarin and sweet orange. Especially well adapted to sweet orange–growing areas of Florida. 'Murcott' is an alternate bearer with very sweet, seedy, yellowish orange fruit winter into spring; it's marketed under the name "Honey tangerine." 'Ortanique' has sweet, juicy, variably seedy fruit ripening spring to summer. 'Temple' bears winter to spring crop of sweet to tart, seedy fruit; needs high heat and is more cold sensitive than other tangors.

Other mandarin hybrids include the following:

'Ambersweet'. Result of crossing a hybrid of 'Clementine' mandarin and 'Orlando' tangelo with a midseason orange. Juicy fruit, borne fall to winter, is classified as an orange by fresh fruit marketers. Very seedy when grown near another variety.

'Fairchild'. Hybrid between 'Clementine' and 'Orlando'. Juicy, sweet fruit in winter. Best in desert. Bigger crop with a pollinator.

'Fallglo'. Somewhat cold sensitive, like its 'Temple' tangor parent. Juicy, tart, very seedy fruit ripening in fall. ▶

'Lee'. Hybrid between 'Clementine' and unknown pollen parent. Fairly seedy fruit matures fall to winter. Has best flavor if grown in Florida.

'Nova'. Cross between 'Clementine' and 'Orlando'. Juicy, richly sweet fruit fall to winter. Needs a pollinator.

'Page'. Parents are 'Clementine' and 'Minneola' tangelo. Many small, juicy, sweet fruits fall into winter. Few seeds, even with pollinator to improve fruit set.

'Robinson'. Hybrid between 'Clementine' and 'Orlando'. Very sweet fruit in fall. Quite seedy with a pollinator. Best flavor if grown in Florida.

'Sunburst'. Cross between 'Robinson' and 'Osceola' (an infrequently grown mandarin hybrid from Florida). Big, sweet, red-orange fruit in late fall. Nearly seedless without a pollinator. Best flavor in Florida.

'Wekiwa' (pink tangelo, 'Lavender Gem'). A cross between a tangelo and a grapefruit: looks like a small grapefruit but is eaten like a mandarin. Juicy, mild, sweet flesh is purplish rose in hot climates. Ripens late fall into winter.

SOUR-ACID MANDARIN

Both of these bear throughout the year in mild-winter climates; also fruit very well indoors.

Calamondin. A mandarin-kumquat hybrid with fruit like a very small orange but a sweet, edible rind. Juicy, tart flesh has some seeds. Variegated form is especially ornamental.

'Rangpur'. Often called Rangpur lime, though it's not a lime and doesn't taste like one. Fruit looks and peels like a mandarin. Less acid than lemon; flavor overtones make it a good base for punches and mixed drinks. 'Otaheite' (Tahiti orange) is an acidless form sold as a house plant.

PUMMELO

Forerunner of the grapefruit. Bears clusters of enormous round to pear-shaped fruit with thick rind and pith. Once peeled, fruit is just slightly bigger than a grapefruit. Different varieties have flavors from sweet to fairly acidic. Needs a little less heat than grapefruit. Ripens starting in winter in warmest areas.

'Chandler'. Pink-fleshed California variety.

'Hirado Buntan'. Pink-fleshed variety with sweetest flavor in Florida.

'Reinking'. White-fleshed California pummelo. It is not as sweet as 'Chandler'.

'Tahitian' ('Sarawak'). White fleshed; moderately acidic with lime undertone.

GRAPEFRUIT

Trees to about 30 ft. tall. Need heat for sweet-tart fruit. Good crops can be grown in the desert, but best in Florida, South Texas. Can ripen in as little as 6 months for fall and winter harvest, or take a year or longer in less heat.

'Duncan'. Oldest known grapefruit variety in Florida and the one from which all the others developed. Extremely seedy, white flesh with better flavor than modern seedless types. Good for juice.

'Flame'. Red flesh similar to that of 'Rio Red', slight rind blush, and few to no seeds. Now widely planted in Florida.

'Marsh' ('Marsh Seedless'). Main white-fleshed commercial variety. Seedless offspring of 'Duncan'. A pigmented form, 'Pink Marsh' ('Thompson'), doesn't hold its color well.

'Melogold'. Grapefruit-pummelo hybrid developed in California. Needs less heat than true grapefruit, but fruit doesn't hold as well on the tree. Seedless white flesh is sweeter than that of sister variety 'Oroblanco'; tree tolerates slightly more cold than 'Oroblanco'.

'Oroblanco'. Grapefruit-pummelo hybrid with same low-heat requirement as 'Melogold'. Fruit containing few to no seeds has a thicker rind and more sweet-tart flavor than 'Melogold'.

'Ray Ruby' and 'Henderson'. Almost identical seedless varieties have good rind blush and flesh pigmentation.

'Redblush' ('Ruby', 'Ruby Red'). Seedless with red-tinted flesh. Red internal color fades to pink, then buff by end of season.

'Rio Red'. Seedless variety with good rind blush and flesh nearly as red as that of 'Star Ruby'. More dependable fruit producer than 'Star Ruby'.

'Star Ruby'. Seedless variety with reddest color. Tree is prone to cold damage, erratic bearing, and other growing problems. Doesn't withstand desert heat.

LEMON

Low heat requirement. Bears fruit in cool-summer areas as well as in hot regions; will even produce indoors in northern climates.

'Bearss'. Selection of a Sicilian variety grown in Florida; no relation to 'Bearss' lime. Fruit similar to 'Eureka'. Some fruit all year, but main crop comes in fall and winter.

'Eureka'. Familiar lemon sold in grocery stores. Some fruit all year in mild climates. Big, vigorous, nearly thornless tree needs periodic pruning.

Lemon

'Improved Meyer'. Hybrid between lemon and sweet orange or mandarin. More cold tolerant than true lemon. Yellow-orange, juicy fruit with few seeds throughout year. Can grow 15 ft. tall, but usually considerably shorter. Not permitted in Arizona.

'Lisbon'. Fruit is similar to 'Eureka' (and is also sold in markets), but tree is bigger, thornier, and more cold tolerant. 'Lisbon Seedless' is the same without seeds. These are the best lemons for the desert. Some fruit all year in mild climates.

'Ponderosa' (American Wonder). Naturally dwarf, thorny lemon-citron hybrid. Seedy, thick-skinned, moderately juicy fruit weighing up to 2 lb. apiece. Some fruit all year. More susceptible to cold than true lemon. Thrives indoors.

'Variegated Pink' ('Pink Lemonade'). Sport of 'Eureka' with green-and-white leaves and green stripes on immature fruit. Light pink flesh doesn't need heat to develop color. Grows to about 8 ft. tall.

LIME

There's a lime for just about every area of the citrus belt warm enough for sweet oranges. Limes outperform lemons in Florida.

'Bearss' or 'Persian' ('Tahiti'). Big-fruited, seedless lime sold in grocery stores. Called 'Bearss' in West and 'Persian' or 'Tahiti' elsewhere. Some fruit all year. Needs less heat for fruiting and tolerates more cold than 'Mexican'. Plant grows 15–20 ft. tall.

'Kieffer'. Leaves are used in Thai and Cambodian cooking, as is bumpy, sour spring fruit. Available mainly in California.

'Mexican' ('Key', West Indian lime, bartender's lime). Very thorny plant to about 15 ft. high, bearing small, rounded, intensely flavored fruit all year. 'Mexican Thornless' is the same, minus the spines. Plants need high heat and are very cold sensitive.

'Palestine Sweet'. Shrubby plant with acidless fruit resembling that of 'Bearss' or 'Persian' and used in Middle Eastern, Indian, and Latin American cooking. Ripens fall or winter.

KUMQUAT

Shrubby plants 6–15 ft. or taller bear yellow to reddish orange fruits that look like tiny oranges. Eat whole and unpeeled—spongy rind is sweet, pulp is tangy. Best in areas with warm to hot summers and chilly nights during fall or winter ripening. Hardy to at least 18°F/–8°C.

'Marumi'. Slightly thorny plant with round fruit. Peel is sweeter than that of 'Nagami', but slightly seedy flesh is more acidic.

'Meiwa'. Round fruit is sweeter, juicier, and less seedy than that of other varieties. Performs better than other types in cool-summer areas. Considered the best kumquat for eating fresh. Nearly thornless.

'Nagami'. Main commercial variety. Oval-shaped, slightly seedy fruit is more abundant and sweeter in hot-summer climates. Thornless.

KUMQUAT HYBRIDS

Limequat. These 'Mexican' lime–kumquat hybrids are more cold tolerant and need less heat than lime parent. Good lime substitutes; edible rind like kumquat parent. Some fruit all year, but main crop comes from fall to spring. 'Eustis' fruit is shaped like big olive. 'Tavares' has elongated oval fruit and is a more compact, better-looking plant than 'Eustis'.

'Nippon' orangequat. Cold-tolerant cross between 'Meiwa' kumquat and satsuma mandarin with fairly low heat requirement. Small, round, deep orange fruit with sweet, spongy rind and slightly acidic flesh. Sweeter than kumquat when eaten whole. Ripens winter and spring, but holds on the tree for months.

CITRON

The first type of citrus to be cultivated. Small, thorny, irregular plants are grown for big, fragrant, unusual fruit; peel of fruit can be candied.

'Buddha's Hand'. Fruit is divided into "fingers" that contain all rind and no pulp. Some fruit all year. Tolerates no frost.

'Etrog'. More commonly planted citron. Tolerates no frost, though in South Texas often comes back after dying to the ground. Fruit resembles a big, warty-skinned lemon with dry pulp.

HARDY CITRUS

For areas beyond the citrus belt. Most are good choices for Zones 7, 28–31; some can be grown in even chillier regions. Hardiness figures apply to established plants conditioned to cold by the time freezes arrive.

Australian razzelquat. Shrubby plant with sweet-tart, rather dry fruit with lemon-lime flavor. Ripens in summer. Good for arid or humid climates to about 14°F/−10°C.

'Changsha' mandarin. Small tree with fruit similar to satsuma mandarin but not as tasty. Ripens from fall into winter. Sometimes grown in regions of Texas, Gulf Coast, and Southwest too cold for regular mandarin varieties. To about 5°F/−15°C.

Citrange. Hybrid between sweet orange and trifoliate orange. 'Morton' has fruit like slightly tart sweet orange. 'US-119' is newer and sweeter. Ripens late fall. Hardy to 5° to 10°F/−15° to −12°C.

Ichang papeda (Ichang lemon). Shrub or small tree bearing fruit like a lemon but with big seeds. Ripens early fall. Takes subzero temperatures (below 0°F/−18°C).

Khasi papeda. Small tree has fruit like a grapefruit but with a peppery tang. Ripens a few weeks after Ichang papeda. Hardiness listed at 15°F/−9°C, but reported to take considerably more cold.

Nansho daidai. Tough, thorny tree bearing big, orange-colored fruit with seedy, sour flesh eaten like a grapefruit or squeezed for juice. Ripens in fall. To at least 0°F/−18°C; withstands even lower temperatures with some protection.

'Thomasville' orangequat. Developed from a trifoliate orange, kumquat, and sweet orange. Small, nearly seedless fruit used as lime substitute if picked soon after ripening in fall. Left on tree, may become sweet enough to eat fresh. To about 0°F/−18°C.

Trifoliate orange. Extremely thorny deciduous shrub or small tree with fragrant flowers and inedible fruit makes an unusual specimen or barrier. To about −20°F/−29°C. 'Flying Dragon', a natural dwarf with curved thorns and twisted branches, survives to about −15°F/−26°C. Used as a dwarfing understock.

'Yuzu' ichandarin. Natural mandarin hybrid is a commercial variety in Japan. Shrubby plant has big-seeded yellow fruit with mildly sweet, lemony flavor ripening fall into winter. To about 0°F/−18°C.

CLADRASTIS lutea

YELLOW WOOD	
Fabaceae (Leguminosae)	
DECIDUOUS TREE	
🌿 ZONES 1–9, 14–16, 31–43	
☀ FULL SUN	
🔴 REGULAR WATER	

Native to Kentucky, Tennessee, and North Carolina. Slow growing to 30–50 ft. with broad, rounded head. Big leaves, 8–12 in. long, divided into many (usually 7–11) oval leaflets. Yellowish green new foliage turns to beautiful bright green in summer, then brilliant yellow in fall. Mature trees have handsome smooth gray bark; common name refers to color of freshly cut heartwood.

Cladrastis lutea

Tree may not flower until 10 years old and may skip bloom some years, but when floral display does come (possibly every 2 to 3 years), it's spectacular. In late spring to early summer, the tree produces big clusters (to 14 in. long) of fragrant white flowers that look like wisteria blossoms. ('Rosea' is pink flowered.) Blooms are followed by flat, 3–4-in.-long seedpods.

Even if it never blooms, yellow wood is useful and attractive as a terrace, patio, or lawn tree. It's deep rooted, so you can grow other plants beneath it. Tolerates alkaline soils. Established trees withstand some drought.

Prune when young to shorten side branches or to correct narrow, weak branch crotches, which are susceptible to breakage in ice storms. Usually low branching; you can remove lower branches entirely when tree reaches the height you want. Confine any pruning to summer, since cuts made in winter or spring bleed profusely.

CLARKIA (includes Godetia)

Onagraceae	
ANNUALS	
🌿 ALL ZONES	
☀◐ LIGHT SHADE IN HOTTEST CLIMATES	
🔴 KEEP SOIL MOIST FROM SEEDING TO FLOWERING	

Clarkia amoena

Native to western South and North America; especially numerous in California. They grow in the cool season, bloom in spring and early summer. Attractive in mixed borders or in mass displays, alone or with love-in-a-mist, cornflower, violas, sweet alyssum. Cut branches keep for several days; cut when top bud opens (others open successively).

Sow seed in place in fall (mild-winter areas) or spring. Seedlings are difficult to transplant, but volunteer seedlings grow very well. Best in well-drained soil without added fertilizer.

C. amoena (Godetia amoena, G. grandiflora). FAREWELL-TO-SPRING, GODETIA. Native California to British Columbia. Two wild forms: one coarse stemmed and sprawling, 4–5 in. high; the other slender stemmed, 1½–2½ ft. high. Tapered leaves are ½–2 in. long. On both forms, upright buds open into cup-shaped, slightly flaring, white, red, pink or lavender flowers, 2 in. across, usually blotched or penciled in crimson. Although seeds of named varieties are rarely sold in the U.S. (more available in England), strains of mixed colors are easy to find. Dwarf Gem grows 10 in. tall; Tall Upright reaches 2–3 ft.

C. unguiculata (C. elegans). CLARKIA, MOUNTAIN GARLAND. Erect, to 1–4 ft. Reddish stems, 1–1¾-in.-long leaves, 1-in.-wide flowers in rose, purple, white. Some varieties have double white, orange, salmon, crimson, purple, rose, pink, or creamy yellow flowers. Double-flowered kinds are ones usually sold in seed packets.

CLEMATIS

Ranunculaceae	
DECIDUOUS OR EVERGREEN VINES AND PERENNIALS	
🌿 ZONES VARY BY SPECIES	
☀ ROOTS NEED TO BE COOL; TOPS IN SUN	
🔴 REGULAR WATER	

Clematis armandii

Most of the 200-odd species are deciduous vines; the evergreen *C. armandii* and a few interesting freestanding or sprawling perennials and small shrubs are exceptions. All have attractive flowers, and most are spectacular. The flowers are followed by fluffy clusters of seeds with tails, often quite effective in flower arrangements. Leaves of vining kinds are dark green, usually divided into leaflets; leafstalks twist and curl to hold plant to its support.

Clematis are not demanding, but their few specific requirements should be met. Plant vining types next to a trellis, tree trunk, or open framework

C

to give stems support for twining. Provide rich, loose, fast-draining soil; add generous quantities of organic matter such as decomposed ground bark. Add lime only where soil tests indicate calcium deficiency.

To provide cool area for roots, add mulch, place large flat rock over soil, or plant shallow-rooted ground cover over the root area. Put in support when planting and tie up stems at once. Stems are easily broken, so protect them with wire netting if child or dog traffic is heavy. Clematis need constant moisture and nutrients to make their great rush of growth; apply a complete liquid fertilizer monthly during the growing season.

Pruning clematis sounds complicated, but it need not be; plants are forgiving and will quickly repair mistakes. Do remember that dormant wood can look dead, and take care not to make accidental cuts. Watch for healthy buds at leaf bases and preserve them. The basic objective is to get the greatest number of flowers on the shapeliest plant.

The type of pruning you do depends on when your plants flower. If you don't know what kind you have, watch them for a year to see when they bloom; then prune accordingly.

Spring-blooming clematis bloom only on the previous year's wood. Cut back a month after flowering to restrict sprawl, preserving main branches.

Summer- and fall-blooming clematis bloom on wood produced in the spring. In mild-winter climates, cut back in late fall after flowering or in early spring as buds swell; wait until spring in cold climates. For the first 2 to 3 years, cut to within 6–12 in. of the ground, or to two or three buds; cut to 2 ft. or less on older plants.

Clematis that bloom in spring and again in summer or fall bloom on old wood in spring, new wood later. Do only light, corrective pruning in fall or early spring; pinch or lightly shape portions that have bloomed to stimulate low branching and avoid a bare base.

Cut flowers are choice for indoors (float in bowl). Burn cut stems with match to make flowers last longer. Unless otherwise specified, flowers are 4–6 in. across.

C. alpina. Zones 1–6, 15–17, 31–43. To 8–12 ft., with dangling flowers borne singly on long stalks in spring. Flowers have four spreading, pointed, petal-like sepals and an inner cup of smaller modified stamens. Flowers may be blue, white, purple, pink, or red, depending on variety. 'Willy', pale pink, is best known. 'Helsingborg' is dark blue, 'Pamela Jackman' lavender blue.

C. armandii. EVERGREEN CLEMATIS. Zones 4–9, 12–24, 28, 31, warmer part of 32. Native to China. Fast growing to 20 ft. Leaves divided into three glossy dark green leaflets, 3–5 in. long; they droop downward to create strongly textured pattern. Glistening white, 2½-in.-wide, fragrant flowers in large, branched clusters in spring. 'Hendersoni Rubra' has light pink flowers.

Slow to start; races when established. Needs constant pruning after flowering to prevent tangling and buildup of dead thatch on inner parts of vine. Keep and tie up stems you want, and cut out all others. Frequent pinching will hold foliage to eye level. Train along fence tops or rails, roof gables. Allow to climb tall trees. Trained on substantial frame, makes privacy screen if not allowed to become bare at base.

C. chrysocoma. Zones 4–9, 14–24, 28, 31, 32. Native to western China. To 6–8 ft. or more in height; fairly open. Young branches, leaves, and flower stalks covered with yellow down. Flowers long stalked, white, shaded pink, 2 in. wide, in clusters from old wood in spring, with later flowers following from new wood. Will take considerable shade.

C. davidiana. See C. heracleifolia davidiana

C. dioscoreifolia (C. terniflora, C. paniculata, C. maximowicziana). SWEET AUTUMN CLEMATIS. Zones 3–9, 14–24, 26, 28–41. Native to Japan. Tall and vigorous (some would say rampant), forming billowy masses of 1-in.-wide, creamy white, fragrant flowers in late summer, fall. Attractive plumed seeds; self-sows freely. Dark green, glossy leaves divided into three to five oval leaflets, 1–2½ in. long. After bloom or in early spring, prune growth that has bloomed most recently to one or two buds. Good privacy screen, arbor cover.

C. durandii. Zones 2–9, 14–17, 31–41. Hybrid between *C. jackmanii* and *C. integrifolia*; a nonclimbing perennial. Scrambling rather than ascending, it should be tied to a support or permitted to ramble through a large shrub or sprawl in a large perennial border. Grows to 6 ft., with

4½–5-in. flowers in rich violet blue. Blooms over a long period in summer.

C. florida 'Sieboldii' (C. f. 'Bicolor'). Zones 3–9, 14–17, 31–39. Flowers 3–4 in. across, with a central puff of purple petal-like stamens, in summer. Vine is a somewhat delicate 8–12 ft. Not as rugged as other clematis, but bears striking flowers. 'Alba Plena' has double greenish white blooms.

C. heracleifolia davidiana (C. davidiana). Zones 1–9, 14–17, 31–43. Native to China. Woody-based perennial to 4 ft. high. Deep green leaves divided into three broad, oval, 3–6-in.-long leaflets. Dense clusters of 1-in.-long, tubular, medium to deep blue, fragrant flowers in summer. Use in perennial or shrub border.

C. integrifolia. Zones 1–9, 14–17, 29–43. Native to Europe and Asia. Woody-based perennial to 3 ft. with dark green, undivided, 2–4-in.-long leaves and nodding, urn-shaped, 1½-in.-long blue flowers in summer. 'Hendersonii' has larger flowers.

C. jackmanii. Zones 1–9, 14–17, 31–43. Series of hybrids between forms of *C. lanuginosa* and *C. viticella*. All are vigorous plants of rapid growth to 10 ft. or more in one season. The best known of the older large-flowered hybrids is known simply as *C. jackmanii*. It has a profusion of 4–5-in. rich purple flowers with four sepals. Blooms from early summer through fall, with heaviest bloom early in the season. Newer hybrids have larger flowers with more sepals, but none blooms as profusely. 'Comtesse de Bouchard' has silvery rose pink flowers; 'Mme. Edouard Andre' has purplish red blossoms. All flower on new wood; do best with severe pruning in early spring as buds begin to swell. Freeze to ground in cold-winter areas. (For more on large-flowered hybrid clematis, see discussion on page 255.)

C. lanuginosa. Zones 3–9, 14–17, 31–39. Native to China. A parent of many of the finest large-flowered hybrids. Grows only to about 6–9 ft. but produces magnificent display of large (6-in.) lilac to white flowers, May–July. Best known for its variety 'Candida', with 8-in. white flowers and light yellow stamens. Blooms on new and old wood. Prune only to remove dead or weak growth in early spring. Then, after first flush of flowers (March–April in favorable climates), cut back flowered portions promptly for another crop later in the summer.

C. macropetala. DOWNY CLEMATIS. Zones 1–9, 14–17, 31–43. Native to China, Siberia. Variable in size; may reach 6–10 ft. high. In early spring, produces 4-in. lavender to powder blue flowers that look double, resembling a dancer's tutu. Blooms are followed by showy bronzy pink, silvery-tailed seed clusters. 'Markham Pink' has lavender pink flowers. Prune lightly in late winter to remove weak shoots and limit vigorous growth to sound wood.

C. montana. ANEMONE CLEMATIS. Zones 3–9, 14–17, 31–39. Native to Himalayas, China.

Clematis montana

Vigorous to 20 ft. or more. Easy to grow. Massive early spring display of 2–2½-in. anemonelike flowers, opening white, turning pink. Flowers on old wood, so can be heavily thinned or pruned immediately after flowering to rejuvenate or reduce size.

'Tetrarose' has large rich mauve flowers. 'Elizabeth' has pale pink blooms with the fragrance of vanilla. 'Grandiflora', vigorous growth to 40 ft., bears abundant pure white blooms. *C. m. rubens*, to 15–25 ft., has crimson new leaves maturing to bronzy green; fragrant rose red to pink flowers are carried throughout vine. In *C. m. rubens* 'Odorata', the blossoms are vanilla scented.

C. paniculata. See C. dioscoreifolia

C. recta. Zones 1–6, 15–17, 31–45. Not a climber but a perennial to 4–5 ft., with a profusion of small (¾-in.), fragrant white flowers in summer. It resembles a mounding, sprawling version of *C. dioscoreifolia*. Profuse, attractive plumed seed heads follow the blossoms. 'Purpurea' has purple-tinted foliage.

C. tangutica. GOLDEN CLEMATIS. Zones 2–9, 14–17, 31–41. Native to Mongolia, northern China. To 10–15 ft., with gray-green, finely divided leaves. Bright yellow, 2–4-in., nodding, lantern-shaped flowers in great profusion from July to fall. They are followed by handsome, silvery-tailed seed clusters. Prune as for *C. dioscoreifolia*.

C. terniflora. See *C. dioscoreifolia*

C. texensis. SCARLET CLEMATIS. Zones 2–9, 14–17, 29–41. Native to Texas. Fast growing to 6–10 ft. Dense bluish green foliage. Bright scarlet, urn-shaped flowers to 1 in. long, early summer until frost. More tolerant of dry soils than most clematis. Hybrid 'Duchess of Albany' has flowers of bright pink shading to lilac at the edges.

C. viticella. Zones 2–9, 14–17, 31–41. Native to southern Europe, western Asia. To 12–15 ft. Purple or rose purple, 2-in. flowers in summer. Named varieties include 'Mme. Julia Correvon', rosy red, and 'Polish Spirit', deep purple blue with red center.

CLEMATIS IN HANGING BASKETS

Plant a bare-root clematis in a clay or wood hanging basket containing rich, loose, fast-draining soil mix (hold mix in pot with piece of window screen over drain hole). In mild-winter regions, plant in late winter; where winters are cold, wait until early spring. Keep in filtered shade or morning sun. Don't skimp on water or fertilizer. Spectacular, 4–5-in. flowers will spill over the basket's edge 5 months after planting. Provide frost protection in cold climates. Every year, shorten stems to 6–12 in. in late winter or early spring.

Large-flowered hybrid clematis. Best in Zones 2–9, 14–17, 31–41. Although well over a hundred varieties of large-flowered hybrid clematis are being grown today, your local nursery is not likely to offer more than a dozen of the old favorites. Mail-order catalogs remain the best source for collectors seeking the newest. Flowers on some of these may reach 10 in. wide. Most are summer bloomers.

Here are varieties to choose from—old favorites first, then newer offerings:

White. 'Henryi' and 'Candida' are standard. 'Marie Boisselot' or 'Mme. Le Coultre' (large, flat, round flowers) and 'Gillian Blades' (huge, star-shaped flowers) are newer.

Pink. 'Comtesse de Bouchaud', the standard pink, has these rivals: 'Charissima' (veined pink with deeper bars); 'Hagley Hybrid' ('Pink Chiffon'), shell pink with pointed sepals; and 'Lincoln Star' (pink with paler edges).

Red. Red clematis have deep purplish red flowers that are best displayed where the sun can shine through them, as on the top of a fence. 'Mme. Edouard Andre', 'Ernest Markham', and 'Red Cardinal' are standards. 'Ville de Lyon' has full, rounded, velvety flowers; 'Niobe' is the darkest red of all.

Blue violet. Mid-blue 'Ramona' is always popular. Other varieties are 'Edo Murasaki' (deep blue); 'General Sikorski' (huge, with faint red bar); 'Lady Betty Balfour' (dark blue); 'Mrs. Cholmondeley' (big, veined sky blue); 'Piccadilly' (purplish blue); 'Prince Philip' (huge purplish blue with ruffled edges); and 'Will Goodwin' (lavender to sky blue).

Purple. Classic *C. jackmanii* is the most popular. 'Purpureus Superba' ('Jackmanii Superba') is larger, somewhat redder. Others include 'Gypsy Queen' (deepest purple); 'Mrs. M. Thompson' (deep bluish purple with red bar); and 'Richard Pennell' (rosy purple).

Bicolor. 'Nelly Moser' (purplish pink with reddish center bar) is deservedly one of the most popular clematis. 'Carnaby' (white with red bar) and 'Dr. Ruppel' (pink with red bar) are newer and splashier.

Double. Fully double, roselike blooms in early summer on old wood are usually followed later by single or semidouble flowers on new wood. 'Belle of Woking' is silvery blue; 'Duchess of Edinburgh', white; 'Mrs. P. T. James', deep blue; 'Teshio', lavender; and 'Vyvyan Pennell', deep blue with lavender blue center.

CLEOME hasslerana (C. spinosa)

Cleome hasslerana

	SPIDER FLOWER
	Capparaceae
	ANNUAL
✎	ALL ZONES
☼	FULL SUN
💧	REGULAR WATER

Shrubby, branching plant topped in summer and fall with many open, fluffy clusters of pink or white flowers with extremely long, protruding stamens. Slender seed capsules follow blossoms. Short, strong spines on stems; lower leaves divided, upper ones undivided. Leaves and stems feel clammy to the touch, have a strong but not unpleasant smell. Reaches 4–6 ft. tall, 4–5 ft. wide. Thrives in heat, tolerates some drought. Grow in background, as summer hedge, against walls or fences, in large containers. Flowers and dry seed capsules are useful in arrangements.

Sow seeds in place in spring; they sprout rapidly in warm soil. A number of varieties can be grown from seed. In most cases color is indicated by variety name: 'Cherry Queen', 'Mauve Queen', 'Pink Queen', 'Purple Queen', 'Rose Queen', and 'Ruby Queen'. 'Helen Campbell' is snow-white. Plants self-sow to a fault.

CLERODENDRUM

Clerodendrum thomsoniae

	GLORYBOWER
	Verbenaceae
	EVERGREEN OR DECIDUOUS SHRUBS OR TREES
✎	ZONES VARY BY SPECIES
☽	PARTIAL SHADE
💧	REGULAR WATER

This relatively little known group of small trees, shrubs, and shrubby vines is cultivated for big clusters of showy, brightly colored flowers.

C. bungei (C. foetidum). CASHMERE BOUQUET. Evergreen shrub. Zones 5–9, 12–31. Native to China. Grows rapidly to 6 ft. tall; soft wooded. Prune severely in spring and pinch back through growing season to make 2–3-ft. compact shrub. Spreads by suckers, eventually forming thicket if not restrained. Big leaves (to 1 ft.), broadly oval with toothed edges, dark green above, with rusty fuzz beneath; ill smelling when crushed. Delightfully fragrant flowers in summer: ¾ in. wide, rosy red, in loose clusters to 8 in. across. Plant where it will be inconspicuous when out of bloom.

C. fragrans pleniflorum (C. philippinum pleniflorum). Evergreen to partly deciduous shrub. Zones 8, 9, 12–29. Coarse shrub spreading freely by root suckers unless confined. To 5–8 ft. (much less in containers), with 10-in. leaves like those of *C. bungei*. Flowers pale pink, double, in broad clusters that resemble florist's hydrangea; sweet, clean fragrance. Summer bloom.

C. paniculatum. PAGODA FLOWER. Evergreen shrub. Zones 25, 26. To 4 ft. or more, with roundish or oval leaves to 16 in. long and foot-long, branched, pyramidal clusters of small scarlet flowers.

C. speciosissimum. Evergreen shrub. Zones 22–28. Dense-growing and tall (to 12 ft.); can be kept to 4–5 ft. with pruning. Large, velvety leaves. Pyramidal, 1–1½-ft.-long clusters of small brilliant red flowers can appear at any time of year.

C. thomsoniae (C. balfouri). BLEEDING HEART GLORYBOWER. Evergreen vining shrub. In most protected spots of Zones 22–28; indoor/outdoor pot plant elsewhere. Native to West Africa. Leaves oval, 4–7 in. long, dark green, shiny, distinctly ribbed. Flowers are a study in color contrast—scarlet, 1-in. tubes surrounded by large (¾-in.-long) white calyxes, carried in flattish, 5-in.-wide clusters, late summer to fall. Will flower in 6-in. pot. Can grow to 6 ft. or more if left untrimmed. Give support for twining. Needs rich, loose soil mix, plenty of water with good drainage. Prune after flowering.

C. trichotomum. HARLEQUIN GLORYBOWER. Deciduous shrub-tree in Zones 7–9, 14–32; treat as herbaceous perennial in Zones 3–6, 33, 34. Native to Japan. Grows with many stems from base to 10–15 ft. or more; suckers freely. Leaves oval, to 5 in. long, dark green, soft, hairy. Fragrant clusters of white, tubular flowers almost twice as long as prominent, fleshy, ½-in.-long scarlet calyxes. Late-summer bloom. Calyxes hang on and contrast pleasingly with turquoise or blue-green, metallic-looking fruit. Give room to spread at top; plant under it to hide its legginess. *C. t. fargesii*, from China, is somewhat hardier and smaller; it has smooth leaves and green calyxes that later turn pink.

C. ugandense. Evergreen shrub. Zones 9, 14–29. To 10 ft. (usually much less), with glossy dark green, 4-in.-long leaves and 1-in.-long flowers with one violet blue petal and four pale blue ones. Pistil and stamens arch outward and upward. Summer bloom.

CLETHRA

Clethraceae

DECIDUOUS SHRUBS

⚘ ZONES VARY BY SPECIES

☼ PREFERS PARTIAL SHADE BUT ADAPTABLE

💧💧 AMPLE WATER

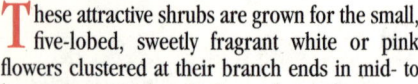
Clethra alnifolia

These attractive shrubs are grown for the small, five-lobed, sweetly fragrant white or pink flowers clustered at their branch ends in mid- to late summer. Fairly soil tolerant, but do best in moist, organic, slightly acid soil. Prefer partial shade but adapt well to less light as well as to full sun; need some shade where summers are very hot. No serious pest or disease problems. Routine pruning not required.

C. alnifolia. SUMMERSWEET, SWEET PEPPERBUSH. Zones 1–6, 31–43. Native to eastern U.S. As the common names imply, this shrub's outstanding feature is its display of flowers with a sweet, spicy scent. Summersweet grows 4–10 ft. tall (it's more apt to reach the upper end of the range in moist soil and in shade), with thin, strong branches forming a vertical pattern. The toothed, dark green, 2–4-in.-long leaves appear late in spring. In summer, each branch tip carries several 4–6-in.-long spires of tiny, gleaming white, perfumed blossoms. Fall foliage color ranges from golden yellow to brownish and can last for several weeks; old flower spikes hang on while the leaves are changing. Several varieties are commonly grown. 'Hummingbird' is a dense, compact plant; 'Paniculata' has clustered flower spires; 'Pink Spires' produces pale pink flowers from rose pink buds; 'Rosea' has pink buds opening pinkish white.

'Ruby Spice' has dark pink blooms. Tolerates seacoast conditions. Wonderful for borders, shade plantings. Prune in early spring, since flowers are produced on new growth. Spreads by suckers into a broad clump.

C. barbinervis. JAPANESE SWEET SHRUB. Zones 5–9, 14–24, 31–34, 39. Slow grower to 15–18 ft., with sharply toothed leaves that turn bright yellow in fall. Drooping, 4–6-in. clusters of fragrant white flowers. Attractive glossy gray to brown bark. Beautiful plant, but rarely grown in U.S.

CLEYERA japonica (Eurya ochnacea)

Theaceae

EVERGREEN SHRUB

⚘ ZONES 4–6, 8, 9, 14–24, 26, 28–31, WARMER PART OF 32

☼ PARTIAL SHADE

💧 REGULAR WATER

Cleyera japonica

Native to Japan and southeast Asia. Handsome foliage shrub related to camellia. Similar in

character to *Ternstroemia gymnanthera*, with which it is often confused in the nursery trade. Grows at moderate rate to 20 ft. tall, with graceful, spreading, arching branches. New leaves are beautiful deep brownish red. Mature leaves, 3–6 in. long, are glossy dark green with reddish midrib. Small clusters of fragrant, creamy white flowers in summer are followed by small, dark red, puffy berries that last through winter. Flowers and berries are attractive but not showy, don't form on young plants. 'Tricolor' (*C. fortunei*) has yellow-and-rose variegation on its foliage.

CLIFF-BRAKE. See PELLAEA

CLIMBING LILY. See GLORIOSA rothschildiana

CLIVIA miniata

Amaryllidaceae

TUBEROUS-ROOTED PERENNIAL

⚘ ZONES 12–17, 19–27; OR INDOORS

☼ ● PARTIAL OR FULL SHADE

💧 REGULAR WATER

Clivia miniata

Native to South Africa. Striking member of amaryllis family with brilliant clusters of orange, funnel-shaped flowers rising from dense clumps of dark green, strap-shaped, 1½-ft.-long evergreen leaves. Blooming period is December–April; most bloom March–April. Ornamental red berries follow flowers. French and Belgian hybrids have very wide, dark green leaves and yellow to deep red-orange blooms on thick, rigid stalks. 'Flame' is an exceptionally hot orange red. Solomone Hybrids have pale to deep yellow flowers.

In frostless areas or well-protected parts of garden, clivias are handsome in shaded borders with ferns, azaleas, other shade plants. Superb in containers; grow indoors in cold-winter climates. Plant with top of tuber just above soil line. Let clumps grow undisturbed for years. Container plants bloom best with regular fertilizing, crowded roots. Known as kaffir lily in some areas.

CLOVE PINK. See DIANTHUS caryophyllus

CLOVER. See TRIFOLIUM

CLYTOSTOMA callistegioides

VIOLET TRUMPET VINE

Bignoniaceae

EVERGREEN VINE

⚘ EVERGREEN IN ZONES 9, 12–28

☼ ◐ FULL SUN OR PARTIAL SHADE

💧💧 REGULAR TO MODERATE WATER

Clytostoma callistegioides

Formerly *Bignonia violacea, B. speciosa*. Strong-growing vine that will clamber over anything by tendrils; needs support on walls. Leaves divided into two glossy, dark green leaflets with wavy margins. Extended terminal shoots hang down in curtain effect. Trumpet-shaped flowers in violet, lavender, or pale purple, 3 in. long and nearly as wide at the top, in sprays at end of shoots, late spring to fall. Tops hardy to 20°F/–7°C, roots to 10°F/–12°C. Excellent vine for areas of Florida too cold for more tender bignonia relatives such as pandorea. Prune in late winter to discipline growth, prevent tangling. At other times of year, remove unwanted long runners and spent flower sprays.

COBAEA scandens

CUP-AND-SAUCER VINE

Polemoniaceae

TENDER PERENNIAL USUALLY GROWN AS ANNUAL

⚡ ALL ZONES

☼ FULL SUN

💧 REGULAR WATER

Cobaea scandens

Native to Mexico. Extremely vigorous growth to 25 ft. Bell-shaped flowers are first greenish, then violet or rose purple; there is also a white-flowered form. Called cup-and-saucer vine because 2-in.-long cup of petals sits in large, green, saucerlike calyx. Leaves divided into two or three pairs of oval, 4-in. leaflets. At ends of leaves are curling tendrils that enable vine to climb rough surfaces without support.

The hard-coated seeds may rot if sown outdoors in cool weather. Start indoors in 4-in. pots; notch seeds with a knife and press edgewise into moistened potting mix, barely covering seeds. Keep moist but not wet; transplant to warm, sunny location when weather warms up. Protect from wind. Blooms first year from seed. May not bloom until very late summer in coolest climates. In mild-winter areas (Zones 24–27), it lives from year to year, eventually reaching more than 40 ft. in length and blooming heavily spring–fall.

COBRA LILY, SHOWY. See ARISAEMA speciosum

COCCOLOBA

SEA GRAPE

Polygonaceae

EVERGREEN SHRUBS OR SMALL TREES

⚡ ZONES VARY BY SPECIES

☼ FULL SUN

💧 MODERATE WATER

Coccoloba uvifera

The quintessential seaside plants: tolerant of wind, sand, and salt, though tender to frost. Useful for windbreaks. Trunk and branches are thick and often picturesquely twisted. New leaves are reddish or coppery, mature leaves glossy green with reddish veins. Small, clustered white flowers are followed by drooping clusters of purple fruits that can be made into jelly. Control plant shape by pruning just before new growth emerges. Small plants in containers are sometimes used for bonsai.

C. diversifolia (C. laurifolia). PIGEON PLUM. Zones 25, 27. Can reach 40 ft. high. Similar to *C. uvifera*, but with shorter flower clusters, smaller fruits, and 2–4-in. oval leaves.

C. uvifera. Zones 25–27. Can grow to 30 ft. but is usually kept much lower. Nearly round leaves to 8 in. wide. Flowers in foot-long clusters; fruits ¾ in. wide.

COCHLOSPERMUM vitifolium

BUTTERCUP TREE

Cochlospermaceae (possibly Bixaceae)

DECIDUOUS TREE

⚡ ZONE 25

☼ FULL SUN

💧 REGULAR TO MODERATE WATER

Cochlospermum vitifolium

Slender, somewhat open and irregular tree native to Mexico and the American tropics. Starts blooming when young. Spring blossoms are very showy—bright yellow, 4 in. wide, carried in clusters on bare branches. Leaves that follow are broad, deeply lobed, to 1 ft. wide. Reaches

40 ft. but can be kept lower by hard pruning. Wood is soft and spongy. Easily propagated by cuttings; even good-size branches will root.

COCKSCOMB. See CELOSIA

COCKSPUR CORAL TREE. See ERYTHRINA crista-galli

COCKSPUR THORN. See CRATAEGUS crus-galli

COCONUT PALM. See COCOS nucifera

COCOS nucifera

COCONUT PALM

Arecaceae (Palmae)

PALM TREE

⚡ ZONE 25

☼ FULL SUN

💧 MODERATE WATER

Cocos nucifera

The coconut palm is both an economically valuable plant and a handsome ornamental, but it is hardy only in the warmest subtropical climates. Can reach 80 ft. but is usually much shorter, with a leaning or curving trunk and a crown of feathery, 20-ft. fronds. Flowers are not notable, but the fruit is the coconut of commerce. Sprouted coconuts are seen fairly often in large pots or tubs; such plants are attractive until they grow too large. Grows best near the shore, but does not absolutely require salt. Landscape use is limited by the risk that falling coconuts pose to passersby and by a potentially fatal plant disease, lethal yellows.

COCOS plumosa. See SYAGRUS romanzoffianum

CODIAEUM variegatum

CROTON

Euphorbiaceae

EVERGREEN SHRUB USUALLY GROWN AS HOUSE PLANT

⚡ ZONES 24–27; OR INDOORS

☼ ◐ 💧 SOME FORMS TAKE SUN, OTHERS SHADE

💧💧 AMPLE WATER

Codiaeum variegatum

Native to tropics. Can reach 6 ft. or more outdoors in frost-free climates; elsewhere, usually seen as single-stemmed house plant, 6–24 in. tall. Grown principally for coloring of large, leathery, glossy leaves, which may be green, yellow, red, purple, bronze, pink, or almost any combination of these colors. Leaves may be oval, lance shaped, or very narrow; straight edged or lobed. Dozens of named forms combine these differing features.

Outdoor exposure depends on the variety. Needs bright light, regular misting indoors; does well in a warm, humid greenhouse. Can be brought outdoors in warm season. Some people are sensitive to croton leaves.

CODONOPSIS clematidea

BONNET BELLFLOWER

Campanulaceae (Lobeliaceae)

PERENNIAL

⚡ ZONES 2–9, 14–17, 32–41

☼ ◐ TOLERATES SUN IN COOL-SUMMER CLIMATES

💧 MODERATE WATER

Codonopsis clematidea

Of the many attractive members of this group, *C. clematidea* is the only one generally grown in the U.S. It is a trailing or scrambling plant that will drape over a wall or hanging basket or, if supported by a shrub, twine to 2–2½-ft. Stems appear in spring from a tuberous root; they bear inch-long leaves and, at their tips, drooping, bell-shaped, inch-long light blue flowers with striking interior markings of orange and maroon. The plant has a slightly skunky odor when bruised. It prefers partial shade (though can take sun in cool climates) and soil with ample organic material. Don't neglect watering during protracted dry spells. Use in woodland garden or rock garden.

COFFEA arabica

COFFEE

Rubiaceae

EVERGREEN SHRUB

✂ ZONES 21–25, 27; OR INDOORS

◐ ● PARTIAL OR FULL SHADE

💧 REGULAR WATER

Coffea arabica

Native to East Africa. The coffee tree of commerce can be grown as a specimen or in shrub borders in mildest-winter regions; elsewhere, it's a handsome container plant for patios or large, well-lit rooms. Upright shrub to 15 ft., with evenly spaced tiers of branches clothed in shiny, dark green, oval leaves to 6 in. long. Small (¾-in.), fragrant white flowers are clustered near leaf bases. These are followed by ½-in. fruits—green when they first appear, then turning purple or red. Each fruit contains two seeds—coffee beans. Use same potting mix and care as for camellias. Protect from frosts.

COIX lacryma-jobi

JOB'S TEARS

Poaceae (Gramineae)

PERENNIAL GRASS

✂ ZONES 12–24, 28–30; ANNUAL IN COLDER CLIMATES

☼ ◐ FULL SUN OR PARTIAL SHADE

💧 REGULAR WATER

Coix lacryma-jobi

A curiosity grown for its ornamental "beads." Loose growing with smooth, prominently jointed stems to 6 ft. Sword-shaped leaves to 2 ft. long, 1½ in. wide. Outside covering of female flower hardens as seed ripens; becomes shiny, ¼–1½-in. bead in pearly white, gray, or violet. Beads can be strung into bracelets. Cut stems for winter arrangements before seeds dry and shatter.

COLCHICUM

MEADOW SAFFRON, AUTUMN CROCUS

Liliaceae

CORMS

✂ ZONES 1–9, 14–24, 29, 30, 33–43; OR INDOORS

☼ FULL SUN

💧 REGULAR WATER DURING GROWTH AND BLOOM

☢ ALL PARTS ARE HIGHLY POISONOUS IF INGESTED

Colchicum

Native to Mediterranean regions. Many species; sometimes called autumn crocus, but not true crocuses. Shining, brown-skinned, thick-scaled corms send up clusters of long-tubed, flaring, lavender pink, rose purple, or white flowers to 4 in. across in late summer, whether corms are sitting in dish on windowsill or planted in soil. When planted out, broad, 6–12-in.-long leaves show in spring, last for a few months, and then die

long before flower cluster rises from ground. Best planted where they need not be disturbed more often than every 3 years or so. Corms available during brief dormant period in July and August. The two best varieties are 'The Giant', single lavender, and 'Waterlily', double violet. Plant 3–4 in. deep. To plant in bowls, set upright on 1–2 in. of pebbles, or in special fiber sold for this purpose, and fill bowl with water to base of corms.

AUTUMN CROCUS IN A LAWN

Autumn crocus can add little clusters of lavender pink to a lawn in September. How to create such a picture: in midsummer, peel back small pieces of sod, plant corms in well-amended soil beneath, then lay sod back down and water well. For a more permanent splash of color every spring, plant purple Dutch crocus in fall.

COLEUS hybridus

COLEUS

Lamiaceae (Labiatae)

PERENNIAL TREATED AS ANNUAL OR INDOOR PLANT

✂ ALL ZONES

☼ ◐ MOST TAKE SHADE, SOME FULL SUN

💧 AMPLE WATER

Coleus hybridus

Native to tropics. Often sold as *C. blumei*. Grown for brilliantly colored leaves; blue flower spikes are attractive but spoil shape of plant and are best pinched out in bud. Leaves may be 3–6 in. long in large-leafed strains (1½–2 ft. tall), 1–1½ in. long in dwarf (1-ft.) strains. Colors include green, chartreuse, yellow, buff, salmon, orange, red, purple, brown, often with many colors on one leaf. The more red pigment in the leaves, the more sun tolerant the plant tends to be. 'Plum Parfait' and 'Burgundy Sun' are examples of varieties bred for full sun. Most coleus perform best in strong, indirect light or filtered shade.

Giant Exhibition and Oriental Splendor are large-leafed strains. Carefree is dwarf, self-branching, with deeply lobed and ruffled, 1–1½-in. leaves. Salicifolius has crowded, long, narrow leaves; plant resembles foot-high feather duster. Named cutting-grown varieties exist.

Useful for summer borders and as indoor/outdoor container and hanging basket plants. Plant in spring. Easy from seed sown indoors or, with protection, out-of-doors in warm weather. Easy from cuttings, which root in water as well as other media. Needs rich, loose, well-drained soil, warmth. Feed regularly with high-nitrogen fertilizer. Pinch stems often to encourage branching and compact habit; remove flower buds to ensure vigorous growth. To keep plants in sunny sites compact, shear by a third in midsummer. Recently renamed *Solenostemon scutellarioides*.

COLLARDS. See KALE

COLOCASIA esculenta (Caladium esculentum)

TARO, ELEPHANT'S EAR

Araceae

TUBEROUS-ROOTED PERENNIAL

✂ ZONES 12, 16–28; OR DIG AND STORE; OR GROW IN POTS

◐ BEST IN WARM, FILTERED SHADE

💧💧 AMPLE WATERING

☢ JUICES CAN CAUSE SWELLING IN MOUTH, THROAT

Colocasia esculenta

Native to tropical Asia and Polynesia. Fast growing to 6 ft. tall. Mammoth (to 2-ft.-long), heart-shaped, gray-green leaves add lush effect to any tropical planting within a single season. Flowers resemble giant callas but are seldom seen, except in southern Florida. The starchy roots are a staple food in Hawaii and the Pacific area in general; taro is occasionally grown for food production by Hawaiians and other Americans of Pacific Island descent.

In zones listed above, tubers can be left in ground; tops die down at 30°F/−1°C. Elsewhere, lift and store tubers or grow in containers; shelter over winter. Effective with tree ferns and other large-leafed tropical plants. Handsome in large tubs, raised beds, near swimming pools. Protect from wind, which tears leaves. Feed lightly once a month during growing season.

COLONIAL BENT. See AGROSTIS tenuis

COLUMBINE. See AQUILEGIA

COMFREY. See SYMPHYTUM officinale

COMMELINA

DAY FLOWER
Commelinaceae
TUBEROUS-ROOTED PERENNIALS

⚡ ZONES 7–9, 12–31; OR DIG AND STORE; OR INDOORS

☼ ◑ ● SUN OR SHADE

💧 AMPLE WATER

Commelina coelestis

Little-known tuberous-rooted perennials in the same family as the popular house plants known as wandering Jew. They are grown for their bright blue, three-petaled flowers; blossoms close in the afternoon, hence the common name day flower. Stems are fleshy and sheathed in stemless leaves; flower clusters, appearing over a long period in summer, emerge from a folded, leaflike bract (spathe). Roots are hardy in zones listed above, but should be lifted like dahlias where winters are colder. Plants may bloom the first year from seed. Day flower makes a satisfactory house or greenhouse plant.

C. coelestis. Clumps grow 1½−3 ft. tall, with 1-in. flowers.

C. dianthiflora. Resembles *C. coelestis,* but leaves are narrower, almost grassy-looking.

Commelinaceae. The spiderwort family is composed of herbaceous perennials, often fleshy, mostly tropical or subtropical. Wandering Jew (*Tradescantia albiflora* and *Zebrina*) and spiderwort (*Tradescantia virginiana*) are familiar examples. Flowers generally have three rounded petals.

Compositae. See Asteraceae

CONFEDERATE ROSE. See HIBISCUS mutabilis

CONRADINA verticillata

CUMBERLAND ROSEMARY
Lamiaceae (Labiatae)
SHRUBBY PERENNIAL

⚡ ZONES 4–9, 14–17, 31–33

☼ FULL SUN

💧 REGULAR WATER

Conradina verticillata

Native to sandy riverbanks of eastern Tennessee and Kentucky. Aromatic, freely branching plant that roots from trailing branches to make a small-scale ground cover. Dark green, narrow, needlelike leaves resemble those of rosemary (*Rosmarinus*) and have a minty scent. Lavender pink flowers top the 12−15-in. plant in spring or early summer.

CONSOLIDA ambigua (Delphinium ajacis)

LARKSPUR, ANNUAL DELPHINIUM
Ranunculaceae
ANNUAL

⚡ ALL ZONES

☼ FULL SUN

💧 REGULAR WATER

☠ ALL PARTS, ESPECIALLY SEEDS, ARE POISONOUS IF INGESTED

Consolida ambigua

Native to southern Europe. Upright, 1−5 ft. tall, with deeply cut leaves; blossom spikes densely set with 1−1½-in.-wide flowers (most are double) in white, blue-and-white, or shades of blue, lilac, pink, rose, salmon, carmine. Best bloom in cooler spring and early summer months. Giant Imperial strain has many 4−5-ft. vertical stalks compactly placed. Regal strain has 4−5-ft. base-branching stems, thick spikes of large flowers similar to perennial delphiniums. Super Imperial strain is base branching, has large flowers in 1½-ft. cone-shaped spikes. Steeplechase is base branching, has biggest double flowers on 4−5-ft. spikes, and is heat resistant. Sow seed where plants are to grow; fall planting is best except in heavy, slow-draining soils. Thin plants to avoid crowding, get biggest flowers.

CONVALLARIA majalis

LILY-OF-THE-VALLEY
Liliaceae
PERENNIAL GROWN FROM RHIZOME

⚡ ZONES 1–7, 14–20, 31–45; OR INDOORS

◑ PARTIAL SHADE

💧 REGULAR WATER

☠ ALL PARTS ARE POISONOUS IF INGESTED

Convallaria majalis

Graceful, creeping, 6−8-in.-high ground cover puts up one-sided, arching stems of small, nodding, delightfully sweet-scented, waxy white bells in spring. Pendent bells last only 2 to 3 weeks, but broad, bold, glossy green deciduous leaves are attractive throughout growing season. Bright red berries may appear in autumn; they, like the rest of the plant, are poisonous. Double- and pink-flowered forms are available, as is a variegated type with cream-striped foliage. All are charming in woodland gardens; use as carpet between camellias, rhododendrons, pieris, under deciduous trees or high-branching, not-too-dense evergreen trees. Where well adapted, lily-of-the-valley can become invasive—in fact, it has naturalized in many parts of the Northeast.

Plant clumps or single rhizomes (commonly called pips) in fall before the soil freezes. Give rich soil with ample humus. Set clumps 1−2 ft. apart, single pips 4−5 in. apart, 1½ in. deep. Cover yearly with leaf mold, peat moss, or ground bark. Large, prechilled pips for forcing available in December and January (even in mild-climate areas), can be potted for bloom indoors. After bloom, plunge pots in ground in cool, shaded area. When dormant, either remove plants from pots and plant in garden, or wash soil off pips and store in plastic bags in vegetable compartment of refrigerator until time to repot in December or January.

Convolvulaceae. The morning glory family contains climbing or trailing plants, usually with funnel-shaped flowers. Morning glories (*Convolvulus* and *Ipomoea*) are typical examples.

FOR INFORMATION ON SELECTING PLANTS

PLEASE SEE PAGES 79–160

CONVOLVULUS tricolor

DWARF MORNING GLORY
Convolvulaceae
ANNUAL
◢ ALL ZONES
☼ FULL SUN
◐ REGULAR WATER

Convolvulus tricolor

Native to southern Europe. Bushy, branching, and somewhat trailing, to 1 ft. high and 2 ft. wide. Leaves are small and narrow. In summer, plant is covered with 1½-in. funnel-shaped morning glory blossoms; usually blue with white-centered yellow throat, though color does vary. 'Blue Flash' and Rainbow Flash strain (mixed colors) are lower growing, reaching just 6 in. tall. All types are good as edging, against low trellis, or at top of wall. Nick tough seed coats with a knife and plant in place when soil has warmed up. In mild-winter climates, can be planted in fall for spring bloom.

COPPER LEAF. See ACALYPHA wilkesiana

CORAL BELLS. See HEUCHERA

CORALBERRY. See SYMPHORICARPOS orbiculatus

CORAL TREE. See ERYTHRINA

CORAL VINE. See ANTIGONON leptopus

CORDIA

Boraginaceae
EVERGREEN SHRUBS OR SMALL TREES
◢ ZONES VARY BY SPECIES
☼ FULL SUN
◐◑ WATER NEEDS VARY BY SPECIES

Cordia boissieri

These members of the forget-me-not family are trees or shrubs of tropical or subtropical origin with rough-surfaced, almost sandpapery leaves and showy flowers. Species grown in the U.S. include natives of the Southwest and tropical America.

C. boissieri. TEXAS OLIVE. Zones 8–28. Native to New Mexico, Texas, Mexico. Oval, grayish green, rough-surfaced leaves to 3 in. long. Clustered, 2½-in.-wide white flowers with yellow throats begin bloom in midspring and continue over a long season. May bloom again in autumn. Can be kept pruned low (3–5 ft.) or allowed to reach 8–10 ft. With training, can be made into a small tree. Regular to little water.

C. sebestena. GEIGER TREE. Zones 24, 25, 27. Native to the West Indies. Usually 10–15 ft. tall (possibly much taller), with dark green leaves 9–12 in. long and half as wide. Summer flowers are brilliant orange red, 2 in. wide, in large clusters at branch ends. Regular water.

CORDYLINE

Agavaceae
EVERGREEN PALMLIKE SHRUBS OR TREES
◢ ZONES VARY BY SPECIES
☼◑● EXPOSURE NEEDS VARY BY SPECIES
◐◑◭ WATER NEEDS VARY BY SPECIES

Cordyline australis

Woody plants with swordlike leaves, related to yuccas and agaves but usually ranked with palms in nurseries and in landscape. Good next to swimming pools. Often sold as *Dracaena;* for true *Dracaena,* see that entry.

C. australis (Dracaena australis). Zones 5, 8–11, 14–27. Hardiest of cordylines, to at least 15°F/–9°C. In youth, fountain of 3-ft.-long, narrow, swordlike leaves. Upper leaves are erect; lower leaves arch and droop. In maturity, 20–30-ft. tree, branching high on trunk, rather stiff-looking. Fragrant, ¼-in. flowers in long, branching clusters in late spring. For more graceful plant, cut back when young to force multiple trunks. Grows fastest in soil deep enough for big, carrotlike root. Full sun. Tolerates some drought. Used for tropical effects, with boulders and gravel for desert look, near seashore.

'Atropurpurea'. BRONZE DRACAENA. Like the above, but with bronzy red foliage. Slower growth. Combine with gray or warm yellowish green to bring out color.

C. stricta. Zones 13, 16, 17, 20–27; or indoors. Hardy to 26°F/–3°C. Slender, erect stems clustered at base or branching low. Swordlike, 2-ft.-long leaves are dark green with hint of purple. Lavender flowers in large, branched clusters, very decorative in spring. Will grow to 15 ft. but can be kept lower by cutting tall canes to ground; new canes replace them. Long cuttings stuck in ground root quickly. Needs some shade except in coolest-summer areas. Regular water. Fine container plant indoors or out; good for tropical-looking background in narrow areas, lanais, side gardens.

C. terminalis. TI PLANT. Zones 21–25, 27; or indoors. Many named forms with red, yellow, or variegated leaves. White, foot-long flower clusters. Plants are usually started from "logs"—sections of stem imported from Hawaii. Lay short lengths in mixture of peat moss and sand, covering about one-half their diameter. Keep moist. When shoots grow out and root, cut them off and plant them. Outdoors, ti plant reaches 6–8 ft. tall in frost-free locations where it receives ample water and soil stays warm; accepts considerable shade. Indoors, it takes ordinary house plant care; tolerates low light intensity.

GROOMING COREOPSIS

Early in the flowering season you can easily groom coreopsis by cutting off spent flowers with a pair of one-hand pruning shears. But by summer the dead flowers can outnumber the new until they're too much for one-hand shears. Cut back the waves of dead flowers with hedge shears. Such wholesale removals can bring on successive bloom.

COREOPSIS

Asteraceae (Compositae)
PERENNIALS AND ANNUALS
◢ ZONES VARY BY SPECIES
☼ FULL SUN
◐ MODERATE WATER, EXCEPT AS NOTED

Coreopsis tinctoria

Easily grown members of sunflower family yielding profusion of yellow, orange, maroon, or reddish flowers over long bloom season. Both annual and perennial kinds are easy to propagate—annuals from seed sown in place or in pots, perennials from seed or division of root crown. Tend to self-sow; seeds attract birds.

C. auriculata 'Nana'. Perennial. Zones 1–24, 26–45. Makes 5–6-in.-high mat of leaves 2–5 in. long. Under ideal conditions, it will spread by stolons to form a 2-ft.-wide clump in a year. Bright orange-yellow flower heads, 1–2½ in. wide, rise well above foliage. Long and profuse blooming season from spring to fall if you remove faded flowers. Best used in foreground of taller plants, in border, or as edging.

C. grandiflora. COREOPSIS. Perennial. Zones 1–24, 26, 28–43. Grows 1–2 ft. high, spreading to 3 ft.; leaves narrow, dark green, with three to five lobes. Bright yellow, 2½–3-in.-wide flowers bloom all summer, carried on long slender stems high above foliage. 'Sunburst' has large, semidouble flowers; it will bloom the first year from seed sown early in spring, then spread by self-sowing. 'Early Sunrise' is similar and even earlier to bloom. Both are tough enough for use in roadside beautification.

C. lanceolata. COREOPSIS. Perennial. Zones 1–24, 26, 28–45. Grows 1–2 ft. high. Leaves somewhat hairy, narrow, mostly in tuft near base. Flower heads 1½–2 in. across, yellow, on pale green stems, spring–summer. Some leaves on lower stem have a few lobes. When well established, will persist year after year. Excellent cut flower.

C. rosea. Perennial. Zones 2–24, 31–41. Finely textured plant 1½–2 ft. tall with pink, yellow-centered daisylike flowers from summer to fall. Unlike other species, prefers moist soil.

C. tinctoria. ANNUAL COREOPSIS, CALLIOPSIS. Annual. All zones. Slender, upright, 1½–3 ft. tall with wiry stems; much like cosmos in growth habit. Leaves and stems smooth. Flowers similar to perennial coreopsis, in yellow, orange, maroon, bronze, and reddish, banded with contrasting colors; purple-brown centers. Dwarf and double varieties. Flowers summer–fall, except where hot, humid weather shortens the show. Sow seed in place in full sun and dryish soil.

C. verticillata. Perennial. Zones 1–24, 26, 28–45. Plant is 2½–3 ft. tall, half as broad. Many erect or slightly leaning stems carry many whorls of finely divided, very narrow leaves. At top are 2-in. bright yellow daisies, freely borne over long summer and autumn season. One of the most tolerant of drought, neglect. 'Moonbeam', 1½–2 ft. tall, has pale yellow flowers; 'Zagreb', 1 ft. tall, has golden yellow flowers.

CORIANDRUM sativum

CORIANDER, CHINESE PARSLEY, CILANTRO

Apiaceae (Umbelliferae)

ANNUAL HERB

ALL ZONES

FULL SUN

REGULAR WATER

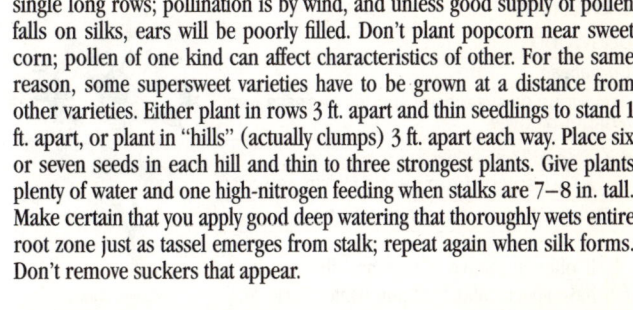
Coriandrum sativum

Grows 12–15 in. high. Delicate fernlike foliage; flat clusters of pinkish white flowers. Aromatic seeds crushed before use as seasoning for sausage, beans, stews, cookies, wines. Young leaves used in salads, soups, poultry recipes, and variety of Mexican and Chinese dishes. Grow in good, well-drained soil. Start from seed (including coriander seed sold in grocery stores); grows quickly, self-sows.

CORN

Poaceae (Gramineae)

ANNUAL

ALL ZONES

FULL SUN—ALWAYS

SPECIAL WATERING TIMES; SEE BELOW

Sweet Corn

Sweet corn is the one cereal crop that home gardeners are likely to grow; it requires considerable space but is still well worth growing. Once most sweet corn is picked, its sugar changes to starch very quickly; only by rushing ears from garden directly to boiling water can you capture full sweetness. Supersweet varieties of corn are actually sweeter than standard kinds and maintain their sweetness longer after harvest because of a gene that increases the quantity of sugar and slows its conversion to starch. A very few people find these varieties too sweet.

Corn needs heat, but suitable early hybrid varieties will grow even in cool-summer areas.

Adaptable, but grows best in deep, rich soils; good drainage is important. Give full sun. Sow seed 2 weeks after average date of last frost, and make three or four more plantings at 2-week intervals; or plant early, midseason, and late varieties. Plant corn in blocks of short rows rather than

single long rows; pollination is by wind, and unless good supply of pollen falls on silks, ears will be poorly filled. Don't plant popcorn near sweet corn; pollen of one kind can affect characteristics of other. For the same reason, some supersweet varieties have to be grown at a distance from other varieties. Either plant in rows 3 ft. apart and thin seedlings to stand 1 ft. apart, or plant in "hills" (actually clumps) 3 ft. apart each way. Place six or seven seeds in each hill and thin to three strongest plants. Give plants plenty of water and one high-nitrogen feeding when stalks are 7–8 in. tall. Make certain that you apply good deep watering that thoroughly wets entire root zone just as tassel emerges from stalk; repeat again when silk forms. Don't remove suckers that appear.

FOR THE TASTIEST EAR OF CORN

Check your crop when ears are plump and silks have withered; pull back husks and try popping a kernel with your thumb. Generally, corn is ready to eat 3 weeks after silks first appear. Kernels should squirt milky juice; watery juice means that corn is immature. Doughy consistency indicates overmaturity.

Corn earworm is a pest in all regions. Prevent by placing dropperful of mineral oil in tip of ear when silks have withered but before they turn brown. Or deter entry of worm by planting tight-husked varieties, or putting a clothes pin or rubber band on tip of husk. If damage occurs, just cut off damaged tips. European corn borer, a pest everywhere but Florida and the Far West, is most troublesome in the Midwest. Caterpillars tunnel into plant stalks and sometimes into ears. Place *Bt* or diazinon granules in leaf whorls on stalks.

Ornamental corn. Some kinds of corn are grown for the beauty of their shelled ears rather than for their eating qualities. Calico, Indian, Squaw, and rainbow corn are some names given to strains that have brightly colored kernels—red, brown, blue, gray, black, yellow, and many mixtures of these colors. Grow like sweet corn, but let ears ripen fully; silks will be withered, husks will turn straw color, and kernels will be firm. Cut ear from plant, including 1½ in. of stalk below ear; pull back husks (leave attached to ears) and dry thoroughly. Grow well away from late sweet corn; mix of pollen can affect its flavor.

Ornamental Corn

Zea mays japonica includes several kinds of corn grown for ornamental foliage; one occasionally sold is 'Gracilis', a dwarf corn with bright green leaves striped white.

Popcorn. Grow and harvest popcorn just like ornamental corn described above. When ears are thoroughly dry, rub kernels off cobs and store in dry place. White and yellow popcorn resemble other corn in appearance. Strawberry popcorn, *Popcorn* grown either for popping or for its ornamental value, has stubby, fat, strawberrylike ears packed with red kernels.

Cornaceae. The dogwood family consists of trees and shrubs with clustered inconspicuous flowers (sometimes surrounded by showy bracts) and berrylike fruit. *Aucuba* and dogwood (*Cornus*) are examples.

CORNELIAN CHERRY. See CORNUS mas

CORNFLOWER. See CENTAUREA cyanus

CORN PLANT. See DRACAENA fragrans

CORNUS

DOGWOOD

Cornaceae

DECIDUOUS OR EVERGREEN SHRUBS OR TREES AND
A GROUND COVER

ZONES VARY BY SPECIES

FULL SUN OR LIGHT SHADE, EXCEPT AS NOTED

REGULAR WATER, EXCEPT AS NOTED

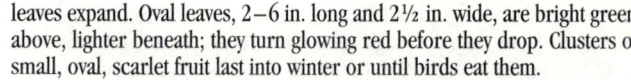

Cornus florida

All offer attractive foliage and flowers; some
have spectacular fruit and winter bark. Many
have bright fall foliage.

C. alba. TATARIAN DOGWOOD. Shrub. Zones 1–9,
14–24, 32–45. In
cold-winter areas its bare, blood red twigs are colorful against snow.
Upright to about 10 ft. high; wide spreading, eventually producing thicket
of many stems. Branches densely clothed with 2½–5-in.-long leaves to
2½ in. wide, deep rich green above, lighter beneath; red in fall. Small, fragrant, creamy white flowers in 1–2-in.-wide, flattish clusters in spring.
Bluish white to whitish small fruits.

Leaves of 'Gouchaultii' have yellow borders suffused with pink. 'Argen-
teomarginata' (*C.* 'Elegantissima') has showy green-and-white leaves on
red stems. 'Sibirica', Siberian dogwood, less rampant than species, grows to
about 7 ft. high with 5-ft. spread; has gleaming coral red branches in winter. In all types, new wood is brightest; cut back in spring to force new
growth.

C. alternifolia. PAGODA DOGWOOD. Shrub or small tree. Zones 1–6,
32–43. Multitrunked, to 20 ft. high. Strong horizontal branching pattern
makes attractive winter silhouette. Light green leaves turn red in fall. Small
clusters of creamy spring flowers are not showy. Blue-black fruit.

C. canadensis. BUNCHBERRY. Deciduous carpet plant. Zones 1–7,
32–45. Native to northern climates. It's difficult to believe this 6–9-in.-
high perennial is related to dogwoods when you see it under trees by lakes
and streams. Creeping rootstocks send up stems topped by whorls of oval
or roundish, 1–2-in.-long, deep green leaves that turn yellow in fall, die
down in winter. In late spring or early summer, plants bear small, compact
clusters of tiny flowers surrounded by (usually) four oval, ½–¾-in. pure
white bracts. Clusters of small, shiny red fruit appear in late summer.

For part or full shade in cool, moist climates, in acid soil with generous
amounts of humus or rotten wood. Considered hard to establish, but when
transplanted with piece of rotten log with bark attached, it establishes
readily. Excellent with rhododendrons, ferns, trilliums, lilies.

C. capitata. EVERGREEN DOGWOOD. Shrub or small tree. Zones 8, 9,
14–20, 31. Not reliably evergreen. To 20–30 ft. tall, with gray-green
leaves. Small flower clusters ringed by four to six yellowish bracts to 2 in.
long in late spring. Showy fall fruit is strawberrylike, crimson, 1-in. wide;
attracts birds.

C. controversa. GIANT DOGWOOD. Tree. Zones 3–9, 14, 18, 19,
31–34. From the Orient. Resembles big shrubby dogwoods in leaves,
flowers, and fruit but grows rapidly into magnificent 40–60-ft. tree with
picturesque horizontal branches. Luxuriant 3–6-in.-long oval leaves, 2–3
in. wide, are dark green above, silvery green beneath, glowing red in fall.
Creamy white spring flowers are not spectacular but so abundant they give
good show. They form in fluffy, flattish clusters 3–7 in. wide. Shiny, bluish
black, ½-in.-wide fruit, enjoyed by birds, ripens in late summer. Plant in
full sun for most flowers and best fall color.

C. florida. FLOWERING DOGWOOD, EASTERN DOGWOOD. Tree. Zones
2–9, 14–16, 26 (northern part), 28, 29, 31–41. Native to eastern U.S.,
from New England to central Florida. Has been called the most beautiful
native tree of North America. May reach 40 ft. high and wide, but 20–30 ft.
more common. Low-branching tree has fairly horizontal branch pattern
and upturned branch tips; makes beautiful winter silhouette. Old trees
broadly pyramidal but rather flat topped. Small springtime flower clusters
are surrounded by four roundish, 2–4-in.-wide bracts with notched tips.
White is the usual color in the wild, but named selections (see below)
come in pink shades to nearly red, in addition to white. Only white types
seem to succeed in Florida. Flowers almost cover trees in midspring before

leaves expand. Oval leaves, 2–6 in. long and 2½ in. wide, are bright green
above, lighter beneath; they turn glowing red before they drop. Clusters of
small, oval, scarlet fruit last into winter or until birds eat them.

Unfortunately, an anthracnose fungus has been infecting and destroying
these trees throughout their range. Dieback symptoms show up first in
lower branches and can spread to whole tree. Borers often attack trunks
and limbs of stressed trees. *C. florida* has been bred with *C. kousa* to produce more disease-resistant hybrids; see *C. rutgersensis*.

'Cherokee Chief'. Deep rosy red bracts, paler at base.

'Cherokee Princess'. Gives unusually heavy display of white blooms.

'Cloud Nine'. Blooms young and heavily. Produces better in cold climates than other varieties of *C. florida;* also tolerates heat and lack of winter chill better than other varieties.

'Pendula'. Drooping branches give it weeping look. White bracts.

'Pink Flame'. Leaves green and cream, deepening to dark green and
red. Bracts pink.

'Rainbow'. Leaves strongly marked bright yellow on green. Heavy
bloomer with large white bracts.

'Rubra'. Long-time favorite for its pink or rose bracts.

'Welchii'. TRICOLOR DOGWOOD. Best known for its variegated, 4-in.-
long leaves of creamy white, pink, deep rose, and green throughout spring
and summer; leaves turn deep rose to almost red in fall. Rather inconspicuous pinkish to white bracts are not profuse. Does best with some shade.

C. kousa. KOUSA DOGWOOD. Large shrub or small tree. Zones 3–9,
14, 15, 18, 19, 31–34. Native to Japan and Korea. Later blooming (late
spring or early summer) than other flowering
dogwoods. Can be big multistemmed shrub or
(with training) small tree to 20 ft. or higher. Delicate limb structure and spreading, dense horizontal growth habit. Lustrous, medium green leaves, 4
in. long, have rusty brown hairs at base of veins on
undersurface. Yellow or scarlet fall color.

Flowers along tops of branches show above
leaves. Creamy white, slender-pointed, 2–3-in.-
long, rather narrow bracts surround flower cluster,
turn pink along edges. In late summer–fall, red
fruit hangs below branches like big strawberries.
'Milky Way' is more floriferous and has pure white
bracts. 'Summer Stars' blooms later and is lavish
in bloom. 'Rosabella' has pink bracts. *C. k. chinensis,* native to China, has
larger leaves and larger bracts. This species is less susceptible to diseases
than *C. florida* and has been bred with the latter to produce resistant
hybrids; see *C. rutgersensis.*

Cornus kousa

C. mas. CORNELIAN CHERRY. Zones 2–6, 32–41. Pest-free dogwood
native to southern Europe and Asia. Usually an airy, twiggy shrub but can
be trained as a small tree, 15–20 ft. high. Provides a progression of color
throughout the year. One of earliest dogwoods to bloom, bearing clustered
masses of small, soft yellow blossoms on bare twigs in late winter or early
spring. Shiny green, 2–4-in.-long, oval leaves turn yellow in fall; some
forms turn red. Autumn color is enhanced by clusters of bright scarlet,
cherry-size fruits that hang on until birds get them. Fruits are edible and are
frequently used in making preserves. In winter, flaking bark mottled gray
and tan provides interest. 'Variegata' features leaves marbled creamy white.

C. nuttallii. PACIFIC DOGWOOD, WESTERN DOGWOOD. Tree. Zones
2–9, 14–20. Native to Pacific Coast. To 50 ft. tall, 20 ft. wide, with one
trunk or several. Gray branches in pleasing horizontal pattern. Blooms on
bare branches in spring, sometimes again on leafy ones in late summer;
flowers ringed by four to eight bracts, to 3 in. long, rounded or pointed,
white or tinged pink. Oval, 3–5-in. green leaves turn yellow, pink, and red
in autumn. Decorative red fruit in buttonlike clusters in fall. Dislikes routine garden watering, fertilizing, pruning; injury to tender bark provides
entrance for insects and diseases. Best in part shade.

C. rutgersensis. STELLAR DOGWOOD. Tree. Zones 3–9, 14, 15, 18, 19,
31–34. This hybrid between *C. florida* and *C. kousa* has greater disease
resistance than *C. florida.* Single-stemmed tree to about 20 ft. Bloom time
falls between the midspring bloom of *C. florida* and the late-spring or
early-summer bloom of *C. kousa;* flower bracts are produced with the

leaves. 'Stellar Pink' has pink bracts; 'Aurora', 'Galaxy', and 'Ruth Ellen' bear broad-bracted white flowers; 'Constellation' and 'Stardust' have narrower white bracts. 'Constellation' has the most upright growth habit; other varieties are more rounded. All have brilliant red fall leaves.

C. sanguinea. BLOODTWIG DOGWOOD. Shrub. Zones 1–7, 31–45. Big show comes in fall with dark blood red foliage and in winter with bare, purplish to dark red twigs and branches. Prune severely in spring to produce new branches and twigs for winter color. Grows as big multistemmed shrub to 12 ft. high, about 8 ft. wide. Dark green leaves 1½–3 in. long. Late-spring flowers are greenish white in 2-in.-wide clusters. Black fruit.

C. stolonifera (C. sericea). REDTWIG DOGWOOD, RED-OSIER DOG-WOOD. Shrub. Zones 1–9, 14–21, 31–45. Native to moist places, eastern North America and Northern California to Alaska. Another dogwood with brilliant show of red fall foliage and bright red winter twigs striking against a snowy backdrop. Grows rapidly as a big multistemmed shrub, 7–9 ft. high and wide spreading. Leaves oval, 1½–2½ in. long, fresh deep green. The plant blossoms throughout the summer months, bearing small, creamy white flowers in 2-in.-wide clusters among the leaves; blooms are followed by white or bluish fruits.

Use this adaptable native as a space filler on moist ground (good for holding banks) or plant it along property line as a screen. Spreads widely by creeping underground stems and rooting branches. To control spread, use a spade to cut off roots; also trim branches that touch ground. Shade tolerant.

C. s. baileya. 6–8 ft. tall; exceptionally bright red twigs in winter.

'Cardinal'. Cherry red stems; originated in Minnesota.

C. s. coloradensis. COLORADO REDTWIG. Native from Yukon to New Mexico and California; 5–6 ft. high. Brownish red stems. Its variety 'Cheyenne' is redder.

'Flaviramea'. YELLOWTWIG DOGWOOD. Yellow twigs and branches.

'Isanti'. A compact 5 ft. tall, with bright red stems.

'Kelseyi' ('Nana'). Seldom over 1½ ft. tall; not as red as the species.

'Silver and Gold'. Yellow stems; green leaves with creamy border.

CORONILLA varia

CROWN VETCH	
Fabaceae (Leguminosae)	
DECIDUOUS PERENNIAL GROUND COVER	
📏 ZONES 1–24, 28–45	
☼ FULL SUN	
💧 MODERATE WATER	

Coronilla varia

Related to peas, beans, and clovers. Creeping roots and rhizomes make it a tenacious ground cover. Straggling stems to 2 ft. high; leaves made up of 11–25 oval leaflets, ½–¾ in. long. Lavender pink flowers in 1-in. clusters soon become bundles of brown, slender, fingerlike seedpods. Dies back in winter, even in mild climates. For most attractive growth, mow early in spring. Too invasive and rank for flower beds. Use for covering erosion-prone banks and in fringes of garden. Once established, difficult to eliminate. 'Penngift' takes sun or shade.

CORTADERIA selloana

PAMPAS GRASS	
Poaceae (Gramineae)	
EVERGREEN GIANT ORNAMENTAL GRASS	
📏 ZONES 4–31, 33	
☼ FULL SUN	
💧💧💧 ANY AMOUNT OF MOISTURE	

Cortaderia selloana

Native to Argentina. Very fast growing in rich soil in mild climates; from gallon-can size to 8 ft. in one season. Established, may reach 20 ft. in height. Each plant is a fountain of saw-toothed, grassy leaves above which, in late summer, rise long stalks bearing 1–3-ft. white to chamois or pink flower plumes.

There is a chance that, under certain circumstances, this plant—like its truly worthless cousin *C. jubata*—may seed itself freely, releasing its seeds into the wind to germinate and grow wherever they land. The result is a multitude of unwanted seedlings that can crowd out more desirable plants. For this reason, nurseries in some areas no longer sell *Cortaderia* at all. Many horticulturists recommend against further landscaping with *C. selloana* and suggest removing it from gardens bordering wild lands, where it might threaten native plants. Grub out volunteer seedlings wherever they appear.

CORYDALIS

Fumariaceae	
PERENNIALS	
📏 ZONES 3–9, 14–24, 32–35, 37, 39–43	
☼ PARTIAL SHADE	
💧 MOIST, NOT SOGGY, SOIL	

Corydalis lutea

Handsome clumps of dainty, divided leaves much like those of bleeding heart (to which it is closely related) or maidenhair fern. Clusters of small, spurred flowers. Plant in rich, moist soil. Effective in rock crevices, in open woodland, near pool or streamside. Combine with ferns, columbine, bleeding heart, primrose. Divide clumps or sow seed in spring or fall. Plants self-sow in garden.

C. cheilanthifolia. Hardy Chinese native, 8–10 in. high, with fernlike green foliage. Clusters of yellow, ½-in.-long flowers in spring.

C. flexuosa. Recently introduced from western China. Forms 1-ft. mound of blue-green, fernlike foliage. Narrow, erect clusters of sky blue flowers borne in early spring and sporadically during the growing season. Selections include 'Blue Panda' and 'Pere David'.

C. lutea. Native to southern Europe. To 15 in. tall. Many-stemmed plant with masses of gray-green foliage. Golden yellow, ¾-in.-long, short-spurred flowers throughout summer.

C. solida. To 10 in. high, with erect clusters of up to 20 purplish red, 1-in.-long flowers in spring. Grows from tubers that are sometimes available from bulb catalogs.

CORYLOPSIS

WINTER HAZEL	
Hamamelidaceae	
DECIDUOUS SHRUBS	
📏 ZONES 4–7, 15–17, 31–34, EXCEPT AS NOTED	
☼ ◐ FULL SUN OR PARTIAL SHADE	
💧 REGULAR WATER	

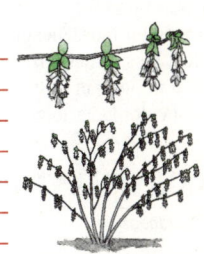

Corylopsis spicata

Valued for sweet-scented, bell-shaped, soft yellow flowers hanging in short, chainlike clusters on bare branches in spring. New foliage that follows is often tinged pink before turning bright green. Toothed, nearly round leaves somewhat resemble those of filbert (*Corylus*); fall color varies from none to poor to a good clear yellow. Rather open structure with attractive, delicate branching pattern. Give same soil conditions as for rhododendrons. Grow in wind-sheltered location in shrub border, at edge of woodland.

C. glabrescens. FRAGRANT WINTER HAZEL. Zones 4–7, 15–17, 31–35. Hardiest species. Grows 8–15 ft. high and wide. Can be trained as small tree. Flower clusters 1–1½ in. long.

C. pauciflora. BUTTERCUP WINTER HAZEL. Dainty plant to 4–6 ft. high, with spreading habit. Blossoms ¾ in. long, in clusters of two or three.

C. sinensis. To 15 ft. tall, with 3-in. flower clusters. 'Spring Purple' has purplish new growth that matures to green.

C. spicata. SPIKE WINTER HAZEL. New growth purple, turning bluish green. To 8 ft. high, spreading wider; 1–2-in.-long flower clusters, 6–12 blossoms per cluster.

CORYLUS

FILBERT, HAZELNUT

Betulaceae

DECIDUOUS SHRUBS OR TREES

ZONES VARY BY SPECIES

FULL SUN OR PARTIAL SHADE

REGULAR WATER, EXCEPT AS NOTED

Although filberts and hazelnuts are usually thought of as trees grown for their edible nuts (see Filbert, Hazelnut), the following types make pleasing ornamentals. The plants have separate female and male flowers: the female blossoms are inconspicuous, while the male ones, appearing in pendent catkins on bare branches in winter or early spring, are showy. Leaves are roundish to oval, with toothed margins.

Corylus avellana
'Fusco-rubra'

C. avellana. EUROPEAN FILBERT. Shrub. Zones 2–9, 14–20, 32–41. To 10–15 ft. high and wide. One of the species grown for nuts. Its ornamental varieties, including the following two, are more widely grown than the species.

'Contorta'. HARRY LAUDER'S WALKING STICK. Rounded to 8–10 ft. tall. Grown for fantastically gnarled and twisted branches and twigs, revealed after its 2–2½-in. leaves turn yellow and drop in autumn. Branches are used in flower arrangements. Plants are almost always grafted, so suckers arising from the base below the graft should be removed; they won't have contorted form.

'Fusco-rubra' ('Atropurpurea'). To 10–15 ft. high and wide, with 3–4-in. leaves in reddish purple.

C. colurna. TURKISH HAZEL. Tree. Zones 2–9, 14–20, 32, 34, 37, 39. Pyramidal in form; usually 40–50 ft. (possibly 75 ft.) tall and about half as wide, with leaves to 6 in. long. Can be grown as a single- or multitrunked tree. Flaking, mottled bark provides winter interest. Produces small, clustered nuts. Flourishes in areas with hot summers and cold winters. Attractive tree in its own right, and a parent (with *C. avellana*) of hybrids called trazels. Quite drought tolerant once established.

C. maxima. Shrub or tree. Zones 1–9, 14–17, 31, 32, 34, 36–41; also eastern parts of 33, 35. Native to southeastern Europe. One of the species grown for nuts. Suckering shrub to 12–15 ft. high; can be trained as small tree. Most widely grown ornamental form is 'Purpurea', which has leaves to 6 in. long in rich dark purple and heavily purple-tinted male catkins. Leaf color fades to green in hot climates.

CORYPHANTHA vivipara

Cactaceae

CACTUS

ZONES 1–24, 29, 30, 33, 35, 41, 43, 45; OR INDOORS

FULL SUN

REGULAR TO LITTLE WATER

Coryphantha vivipara

Native Alberta to north Texas. Has single or clustered globular, 2-in. bodies covered with little knobs bearing white spines. Showy purple flowers to 2 in. long. One of hardiest forms of cactus, taking temperatures far below 0°F/–18°C. Also thrives as a house plant. Usually sold as *Mammillaria vivipara*.

FOR INFORMATION ON YOUR CLIMATE ZONE
PLEASE SEE PAGES 16–78

COSMOS

Asteraceae (Compositae)

PERENNIALS AND ANNUALS

ALL ZONES, EXCEPT AS NOTED

FULL SUN

MODERATE WATER

Native to tropical America, mostly Mexico. Showy summer- and fall-blooming plants, open and branching in habit, with bright green divided leaves and daisylike flowers in many colors and forms (single, double, crested, and frilled). Heights vary from 2½ to 8 ft. Use for mass color in borders or background, or as filler among shrubs. Useful in arrangements if flowers are cut when freshly opened and placed immediately in deep cool water. Sow seed in open ground from spring to summer, or set out transplants from flats. Plant in not-too-rich soil. Plants self-sow freely, attract birds.

Cosmos bipinnatus

C. atrosanguineus. CHOCOLATE COSMOS. Tuberous-rooted perennial. Zones 4–9, 14–24, 28–32. Where winters are colder, dig and store as for dahlias. Grows to 2–2½ ft. tall, with coarsely cut foliage. Deep brownish red flowers, to nearly 2 in. wide, in late summer and fall, with a strong perfume of chocolate (or vanilla). Attractive with silvery-foliaged plants. Provide well-drained soil. Winter mulch is prudent in all but mildest regions.

C. bipinnatus. Annual flowers in white and shades of pink, rose, lavender, purple, or crimson, with tufted yellow centers. Heights to 8 ft. Modern improved cosmos include Sensation strain, 3–6 ft. tall, earlier blooming than old-fashioned tall kinds. Sensation varieties are 'Dazzler' (crimson) and 'Radiance' (rose with red center); white and pink are also available. 'Candystripe' has smaller (3-in.) white-and-rose flowers, blooms even earlier on smaller plants. Seashell strain has rolled, quilled ray florets like long, narrow cones.

C. sulphureus. YELLOW COSMOS. Annual. Grows to 7 ft., with yellow or golden yellow flowers with yellow centers. Tends to become weedy-looking at end of season. Klondike strain grows 3–4 ft. tall, with 2-in. semidouble flowers ranging from scarlet orange to yellow. Dwarf Klondike (Sunny) strain is 1½ ft. tall, with 1½-in. flowers.

COSTMARY. See CHRYSANTHEMUM balsamita

COSTUS

SPIRAL FLAG, GINGER LILY

Zingiberaceae

PERENNIALS

ZONES VARY BY SPECIES

LIGHT SHADE

AMPLE WATER DURING ACTIVE GROWTH

Related to true gingers (*Zingiber*) and other so-called gingers (*Alpinia, Hedychium*); like them, have fleshy rhizomes and stems bearing large leaves. In *Costus*, the leaves are spirally arranged around the stem. Flowers emerge from a tight, conelike cluster of colored bracts at stem ends in summer and fall.

Costus speciosus

Plants have sprawling, mounding habit. Native to tropical forest floor, they like light shade, but can stand full sun if roots are shaded. Use around foundation or near patio or pool; can be grown in large tubs. Plants are dormant in winter and need little water at that time. Provide a winter mulch.

C. speciosus. CREPE GINGER, MALAY GINGER. Zones 25–27. Clusters of stems grow to 6–8 ft. long, with 5–10-in. leaves. The flowering cone is 5 in. long, with green bracts tipped red. Crepelike white or pink flowers to 4 in. wide emerge from the cone two or three at a time.

C. spiralis. SPIRAL FLAG, SPIRAL GINGER. Zones 25, 27. Stems to 4–6 ft. long; 8-in. leaves. Orange flowering cone; pink to red, 1½-in. flowers.

COTINUS coggygria (Rhus cotinus)

SMOKE TREE

Anacardiaceae

DECIDUOUS SHRUB OR SMALL TREE

🗡 ZONES 2–24, 29–41

☼ FULL SUN

💧 MODERATE WATER

Cotinus coggygria

Unusual shrub-tree creating broad, urn-shaped mass usually as wide as high—typically 15 ft. tall, though it may eventually grow to 25 ft. Naturally multistemmed but can be trained to a single trunk. Common name derived from dramatic puffs of "smoke" from fading flowers: as the tiny, greenish blooms wither, they send out elongated stalks clothed in fuzzy lavender pink hairs. In the species, the roundish, 1½–3-in. leaves are bluish green in summer. Purple-leafed types are more commonly grown. Foliage of 'Purpureus' fades to green by midsummer; 'Royal Purple' (the variety with the deepest purple coloration) and 'Velvet Cloak' retain their purple leaves through summer. All types turn yellow or orange red in fall.

Plants are at their best under stress in poor or rocky soil. In cultivated gardens, provide fast drainage and avoid overly wet conditions.

A less widely grown American species is *C. obovatus,* American smoke tree. It is somewhat larger than C. *coggygria,* with bigger leaves; fall color is equally striking.

COTONEASTER

Rosaceae

EVERGREEN, SEMIEVERGREEN, DECIDUOUS SHRUBS

🗡 ZONES VARY BY SPECIES

☼ FULL SUN, EXCEPT AS NOTED

💧 MODERATE WATER

Cotoneaster apiculatus

Members of this genus range from low types used as ground covers to small, stiffly upright shrubs to tall-growing (18-ft.) shrubs of fountainlike form with graceful, arching branches. All grow vigorously and thrive with little or no maintenance, can tolerate poor soil and drought. White or pinkish springtime flowers resemble tiny single roses; though not showy, they are pretty because of their abundance. Usual color of fall and winter berries is red or orange red.

While some medium and tall growers can be sheared, they look best when allowed to maintain natural fountain shapes. Prune only to enhance graceful arch of branches. Keep medium growers looking young by pruning out portion of oldest wood each year. Prune ground covers to remove dead or awkward branches. Give flat growers room to spread. Don't plant near walk or drive where branch ends will need frequent cutting back.

Cotoneasters are useful if not striking shrubs, and can be attractive in the proper setting. Some are especially attractive in form and branching pattern *(C. congestus, C. horizontalis),* while others are notable for colorful, long-lasting fruit *(C. franchetii, C. microphyllus).* Trailing varieties make excellent ground cover plants.

C. acutifolius. PEKING COTONEASTER. Deciduous. Zones 1–3, 32–43. To 10 ft. tall and as wide, with glossy green foliage turning red in fall. Fruit is black. Useful as hedge or screen.

C. adpressus praecox. Deciduous. Zones 1–24, 29–43. To 1½ ft. tall, 6 ft. wide, with shiny leaves turning maroon red in fall. Profuse bright red, ½-in. fruit. Bank or ground cover. Tolerates some shade. *C. adpressus* is similar, somewhat smaller.

C. apiculatus. CRANBERRY COTONEASTER. Deciduous. Zones 1–24, 29–43. Best in cold-winter climates. Dense grower to 3 ft. tall, 6 ft. wide, with small round leaves turning deep red in autumn. Fruit is size of large cranberry, in clusters. Can take some shade. Use as bank cover, hedge, background planting.

C. congestus (C. microphyllus glacialis). PYRENEES COTONEASTER. Evergreen. Zones 3–24, 31–39. Slow grower to 3 ft., with dense, downward-curving branches, tiny dark green leaves, small, bright red fruit. Use in containers, rock gardens, above walls.

C. dammeri (C. humifusus). BEARBERRY COTONEASTER. Evergreen. Zones 2–24, 29–41. Fast, prostrate growth to 3–6 in. tall, 10 ft. wide. Branches root along ground. Leaves are bright, glossy green; fruit bright red. Many varieties differ somewhat in height, rate of growth. 'Coral Beauty' is 6 in. tall; 'Eichholz', 10–12 in. tall with a scattering of red-orange leaves in fall; 'Lowfast', 1 ft. tall; 'Skogsholmen', 1½ ft. tall. All are good ground covers in sun or partial shade and can drape over walls, cascade down slopes.

C. divaricatus. SPREADING COTONEASTER. Deciduous. Zones 2–24, 31–41. Stiff growth to 6 ft. tall and wide. Dark green leaves closely set on branches turn orange red in fall. Egg-shaped bright red fruits are ½ in. long. Informal hedge, screen, bank planting.

C. franchetii. Evergreen. Zones 3–24, 31–34, 39. Narrow habit to 10 ft. high with slender, erect stems arching outward toward the top. Foliage is gray green. Spring flowers are pinkish; orange-red fall fruits are long lasting.

C. horizontalis. ROCK COTONEASTER. Deciduous. Zones 2–11, 14–24, 31–41. Can be 2–3 ft. tall, 15 ft. wide, with stiff horizontal branches and many branchlets set in herringbone pattern. Leaves are small, round, bright green; turn orange and red before falling. Out of leaf very briefly. Showy red fruit. Effective when given enough room to spread; ugly when branches must be cut short to accommodate traffic. Fine bank cover or low traffic barrier. 'Variegatus' has leaves edged in white. *C. h. perpusillus* is smaller, more compact than species.

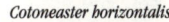
Cotoneaster horizontalis

C. lacteus (C. parneyi). Evergreen. Zones 4–24, 29–31. Graceful, arching habit to 8 ft. or more, with dark green leaves 2 in. long, clustered white flowers, and a heavy crop of long-lasting red fruit in 2–3-in. clusters. Best as informal hedge, screen, or espalier. Can be clipped as formal hedge, but form suffers.

C. microphyllus. ROCKSPRAY COTONEASTER. Evergreen. Zones 2–9, 14–24, 31–41. Its horizontal branches trail and root to 6 ft.; secondary branches grow erect to 2–3 ft. Leaves are very small (⅓ in.), dark green, gray beneath. Fruit is rosy red. *C. m. thymifolius,* a smaller plant, has even tinier leaves, with edges rolled under. Both are effective in rock gardens, on banks.

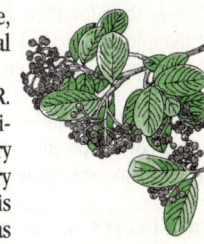
Cotoneaster lacteus

C. multiflorus. Deciduous. Zones 1–24, 31–43. Grows 6–10 ft. tall as spreading shrub or small tree with graceful arching and trailing branches. Dark green leaves are 2½ in. long. Clustered white flowers are showier than those of other cotoneasters. Pinkish red fruits follow.

C. salicifolius. WILLOWLEAF COTONEASTER. Evergreen or semievergreen. Zones 3–24, 31–34, 39. An erect, spreading shrub to 15–18 ft., with narrow, dark green, 1–3½-in.-long leaves and bright red fruits. Graceful screening or background plant but can self-sow and become invasive.

Better known are the trailing forms used as ground cover. 'Emerald Carpet' is 12–15 in. tall, to 8 ft. wide, with compact habit and small leaves. 'Autumn Fire' ('Herbstfeuer') grows to 2–3 ft. 'Repens' is similar in appearance; it is sometimes grafted to a tall stem of some other cotoneaster species and used as a weeping tree.

COTTONWOOD. See POPULUS

COTYLEDON

Crassulaceae

SUCCULENTS

☀ ZONES VARY BY SPECIES; OR INDOORS

☼ ☽ BEST IN LIGHT SHADE

💧 MODERATE TO LITTLE WATER

Cotyledon orbiculata

V arious sizes and appearances. Easily grown from cuttings and handsome in containers, raised beds, or open ground. In cold climates, can be grown in pots and protected in winter. House plants anywhere.

C. orbiculata. Zones 16, 17, 21–24. Shrubby, compact, to 3 ft. tall. Opposing pairs of fleshy leaves are 2–3 in. long, rounded, gray green to nearly white, narrowly edged red. Green-leafed forms are available. Flower stems rise above plant and carry clusters of orange, bell-shaped, drooping flowers in summer. Good landscaping shrub in mild climates and well-drained soils. Splendid container plant.

C. undulata. Zones 17, 23, 24. Striking 1½-ft. plant with broad, thick leaves thickly dusted with pure white powder. Leaf edges wavy. Flowers (spring and early summer) orange, drooping, clustered. Overhead watering washes off powder.

COWBERRY. See VACCINIUM vitis-idaea

COYOTE BRUSH, DWARF. See BACCHARIS pilularis

CRABAPPLE

Rosaceae

DECIDUOUS FRUIT TREES

☀ ZONES 1–21, 32–43

☼ FULL SUN

💧 REGULAR WATER DURING FRUIT DEVELOPMENT

C rabapple is a small, usually tart apple. Many kinds are valued more for their springtime flowers than for their fruit; these are flowering crabapples, described under *Malus*. One of the most popular crabapple varieties grown for fruit (used for jelly making and pickling) is 'Transcendent', with 2-in. red-cheeked yellow apples that ripen in summer. Red-fruited 'Maypole' is a newer colonnade apple variety. For information about colonnade types and general care, see Apple.

Crabapple

CRAB CACTUS. See SCHLUMBERGERA truncata

CRAMBE

Brassicaceae (Cruciferae)

PERENNIALS

☀ ZONES 3–9, 14–17, 31–35, 37, 39–41

☼ FULL SUN

💧 REGULAR WATER

T wo species of these big cabbagelike perennials are occasionally seen. Both have large, smooth leaves and much-branched clusters of small, honey-scented white flowers. They appreciate rich, well-drained garden soil and require considerable space.

Crambe cordifolia

C. cordifolia. Branching stems bearing dark green, 1-ft.-wide leaves on long stalks make 3-ft.-wide mounds. Flowering stem set with smaller leaves

can reach 8 ft. tall. Broad, branching flower cluster, up to 5 ft. wide, somewhat resembles a gargantuan baby's breath. Requires a big garden and leaves a big vacancy when summer flowering is finished; plug in annuals to fill the space. Use in big borders to astonish your friends.

C. maritima. SEA KALE. Branched, purplish stems carry blue-gray leaves up to 1 ft. wide. In early summer, sends up 1–2½-ft.-tall stem with flower clusters to 1½ ft. wide. Once widely used as a vegetable; blanch the leafstalks by placing large pots or boxes over the emerging plants.

CRANBERRY BUSH. See VIBURNUM trilobum

CRANESBILL. See ERODIUM reichardii, GERANIUM

CRAPE MYRTLE. See LAGERSTROEMIA

CRASSULA

Crassulaceae

SUCCULENTS

☀ ZONES 8, 9, 12–28; OR INDOORS

☼ ☽ 💧 PRODUCE FLOWERS IN SUN

💧 REGULAR WATER DURING ACTIVE GROWTH

Crassula ovata

M ostly from South Africa. Provide overhead protection in Zones 8, 9, 12–15, 18–21, 26, 28. All have succulent foliage; many have strange geometric forms. House plants anywhere.

C. arborescens. A shrubby, heavy-branched plant very like jade plant, but with gray-green, red-edged, red-dotted leaves. Summer flowers (usually seen only on old plants) are star shaped, white aging to pink. Good change of pace from jade plant; smaller and slower growing.

C. falcata. Grows to 4 ft. high. Fleshy, gray-green, sickle-shaped leaves are vertically arranged in two rows on stems. Dense clusters of scarlet flowers appear in late summer.

C. ovata (C. argentea). JADE PLANT. Top-notch house plant, large container plant, landscaping shrub in mildest climates. Sometimes sold as *C. portulacea*. Stout trunk, sturdy limbs even on small plants—and plant will stay small in small container. Can reach 9 ft. in time but is usu-

Crassula falcata

ally shorter. Leaves are thick, oblong, fleshy pads 1–2 in. long, glossy bright green, sometimes with red-tinged edges. 'Crosby's Dwarf' is a low, compact grower; variegated kinds are 'Sunset' (yellow tinged red) and 'Tricolor' (green, white, and pinkish). Clusters of pink, star-shaped flowers form in profusion, fall–spring. Good near swimming pools.

Crassulaceae. This large family of usually herbaceous (rarely shrubby) plants is familiar through sedums, sempervivums, and a host of other familiar succulents. Leaves are often in rosettes, as in the familiar hen and chicks (*Echeveria*).

CRATAEGUS

HAWTHORN

Rosaceae

DECIDUOUS TREES

☀ ZONES 2–12, 14–17, 28, 30–41, EXCEPT AS NOTED

☼ FULL SUN

💧 MODERATE WATER

T hese small trees, members of the rose family, are known for pretty flower clusters after leaf out in spring and for showy fruit resembling tiny apples in summer and fall, often into winter. Typically multitrunked, the

Crataegus laevigata

trees have thorny branches that need some pruning to thin out excess twiggy growth. Hawthorns attract bees and birds.

Will grow in any soil as long as it is well drained. Better grown under somewhat austere conditions, since good soil, regular water, and fertilizer all promote succulent new growth that is most susceptible to fireblight. The disease makes entire branches die back quickly; cut out blighted branches well below dead part. The rust stage of cedar-apple rust can be a problem wherever eastern red cedar (*Juniperus virginiana*) grows nearby. Aphids and scale are widespread potential pests.

C. ambigua. RUSSIAN HAWTHORN. Zones 1–10, 14, 32–45. Extremely cold hardy. Moderate growth to 15–25 ft. Vase form and twisting branches give attractive silhouette. Leaves to 2½ in. long, deeply cut. White flowers; profuse small red fruit.

C. 'Autumn Glory'. Hybrid origin. Vigorous growth to 25 ft. with 15-ft. spread. Twiggy, dense. Dark green leaves are similar to those of *C. laevigata* but more leathery. Clusters of single white flowers. Very large, glossy, bright red fruit, autumn into winter. Very susceptible to fireblight.

C. crus-galli. COCKSPUR THORN. Wide-spreading tree to 30 ft. Stiff thorns to 3 in. long. Smooth, glossy, toothed leaves are dark green, turning orange to red in fall. White flowers. Dull orange-red fruit. Most successful hawthorn for Oklahoma and adjacent Southwest. *C. c. inermis* is a thornless variety.

C. laevigata (C. oxyacantha). ENGLISH HAWTHORN. Native to Europe and North Africa. Moderate growth to 18–25 ft. high, 15–20 ft. wide. Best known through its varieties: 'Paul's Scarlet', clusters of double rose to red flowers; 'Double White'; 'Double Pink'. Double-flowered forms set little fruit. 'Crimson Cloud' ('Superba') has bright red single flowers with white centers, vivid red fruit. All have 2-in. toothed, lobed leaves lacking good fall color. Poorly adapted to hot, humid summers of southern states and much of Midwest; in these regions, trees are prone to leaf spot, which can defoliate them and shorten their life.

C. lavallei (C. carrierei). CARRIERE HAWTHORN. Zones 3–12, 14–21, 29–35, 37, 39. Hybrid origin. To 25 ft., with 15–20-ft. spread. Very handsome. More erect and open branching than other hawthorns, with less twiggy growth. Leaves dark green, leathery, 2–4 in. long, toothed; turn bronze red after first sharp frost and hang on well into winter. White flowers are followed by loose clusters of large orange to red fruit that lasts all winter. Fruit is messy on walks.

C. mollis. DOWNY HAWTHORN. Big, broad tree to 30 ft.; looks like mature apple tree. Leaves to 4 in. long, lobed, toothed, covered with down. Flowers white, 1 in. wide. Red fruit 1 in. across, also downy; fruit doesn't last on tree as long as that of other species, but has value in jelly making.

C. monogyna. Native to Europe, North Africa, and western Asia. Classic hawthorn of English countryside for hedges and boundary plantings. Little known in the U.S., except for upright variety 'Stricta', 30 ft. tall and 8 ft. wide. White flowers. Small red fruit in clusters, rather difficult to see. Very prone to fireblight, mites, and leaf diseases.

C. oxyacantha. See *C. laevigata*

C. phaenopyrum (C. cordata). WASHINGTON THORN. Native to southeastern U.S. Moderate growth to 25 ft. with 20-ft. spread. Graceful, open limb structure. Glossy leaves 2–3 in. long with three to five sharp-pointed lobes (like some maples); foliage turns beautiful orange, scarlet, or purplish in fall. Small white flowers in broad clusters. Shiny red fruit hangs on well into winter. Not successful in the hot-summer lower Midwest, but a choice hawthorn elsewhere. One of the least prone to fireblight.

C. pinnatifida. Native to northeastern Asia. To 20 ft. high, 10–12 ft. wide. Leaves lobed like those of *C. laevigata* but bigger and thicker; they turn red in fall. Tree has more open, upright habit than *C. laevigata*. Flowers white, ¾ in. wide, in 3-in. clusters. Fruit slightly smaller than that of *C. lavallei*.

C. punctata inermis. THORNLESS DOTTED HAWTHORN. Native to eastern and midwestern U.S. Essentially thornless, to 30 ft. high. Plentiful white flowers followed by large (¾-in.), long-lasting dark red fruits.

C. 'Toba'. Zones 1–10, 32–45. Canadian hybrid of great cold tolerance. To 20 ft. Leaves similar to those of *C. lavallei*. White flowers age to pink. Sets sparse large fruit.

C. viridis. GREEN HAWTHORN. Moderate growth to 25–30 ft., with broad, spreading crown. Clustered white flowers followed by red fruit.

'Winter King' is vase shaped, with silvery stems and larger fruit that lasts all winter; it's among the most attractive and trouble-free hawthorns.

CREEPING BENT. See AGROSTIS stolonifera

CREEPING BUTTERCUP. See RANUNCULUS repens 'Pleniflorus'

CREEPING JENNY. See LYSIMACHIA nummularia

CREEPING ZINNIA. See SANVITALIA procumbens

CRESS, GARDEN

Brassicaceae (Cruciferae)

ANNUAL

ALL ZONES

FULL SUN OR PARTIAL SHADE

AMPLE WATER

Garden Cress

It is sometimes called pepper grass and tastes like watercress. Easy to grow as long as weather is cool. Sow seed as early in spring as possible. Plant in rich, moist soil. Make rows 1 ft. apart; thin plants to 3 in. apart (eat thinnings). Cress matures fast; make successive sowings every 2 weeks up to middle of May. Where frosts are mild, sow through fall and winter. Try growing garden cress in shallow pots of soil or planting mix in sunny kitchen window. It sprouts in a few days, can be harvested (with scissors) in 2 to 3 weeks. Or grow it by sprinkling seeds on pads of wet cheesecloth; keep damp until harvest in 2 weeks.

CRETE DITTANY. See ORIGANUM dictamnus

CRINUM

Liliaceae

BULBS

ZONES 8, 9, 12–31, 33 (WARMER PARTS); OR GROW IN POTS

FULL SUN OR PARTIAL SHADE

AMPLE WATER DURING GROWTH AND BLOOM

ALL PARTS ARE POISONOUS IF INGESTED

Crinum powellii

Distinguished from their near relative amaryllis by long, slender flower tube that is longer than flower segments. Long-stalked cluster of lily-shaped, 4–6-in.-long, fragrant flowers rises in spring or summer from persistent clump of long, strap-shaped or sword-shaped leaves. Bulbs large, rather slender, tapering to stemlike neck; thick, fleshy roots. Bulbs generally available (from specialists) all year, but spring or fall planting is preferred.

Provide soil with plenty of humus. Set bulbs 6 in. under surface; give ample space to develop. Divide infrequently. In colder part of range, plant in sheltered, sunny sites and mulch heavily in winter. Move container-grown plants to frostproof location.

Excellent for tropical effect. Mail-order nurseries offer a wide selection. In the Deep South, a great many named varieties are obtainable.

C. bulbispermum (C. longifolium). Long, narrow, twisting gray-green leaves tend to lie on the ground. Flowers are deep pink.

C. 'Ellen Bosanquet'. Leaves are broad, bright green. Flowers are deep rose, nearly red.

C. moorei. Large bulbs with 6–8-in. diameter and stemlike neck 1 ft. long or more. Long, thin, wavy-edged, bright green leaves. Bell-shaped pinkish red flowers.

C. powellii. Resembles *C. moorei* (one of its parents) but has dark rose-colored flowers. 'Album' is a good pure white form, vigorous enough to serve as a tall ground cover in shade.

CROCOSMIA

Iridaceae

CORMS

🗡 ZONES 5–24, 28–39, EXCEPT AS NOTED; OR DIG AND STORE

☼ ◑ PART SHADE IN HOTTEST CLIMATES

💧 MODERATE TO LITTLE WATER

*Crocosmia
crocosmiiflora*

Native to tropical and southern Africa. Formerly called tritonia and related to freesia, ixia, sparaxis. Sword-shaped leaves in basal clumps. Small orange, red, yellow flowers bloom in summer on branched stems. Useful for splashes of garden color and for cutting. Where winter temperatures remain above 10°F/–12°C, needs no winter protection. Grow in sheltered location and provide winter mulch where temperatures dip to 0°F/–18°C. In colder areas, dig and store over winter.

C. crocosmiiflora (Tritonia crocosmiiflora). MONTBRETIA. A favorite for generations, montbretias can still be seen in older gardens where they have spread freely, as though native, producing orange-crimson flowers 1½–2 in. across on 3–4-ft. stems. Sword-shaped leaves to 3 ft., ½–1 in. wide. Many once-common named forms in yellow, orange, cream, and near scarlet are making a comeback. Good for naturalizing on slopes or in fringe areas.

C. hybrids. Zones 4–24, 26, 28–39. Sturdy plants with branching spikes of large flowers. Often called Masoniorum Hybrids. 'Lucifer' is 4 ft. tall, with bright red flowers. 'Solfatare', to 2 ft., has bronze-tinted foliage and pale orange-yellow flowers.

C. masoniorum. Leaves 2½ ft. long, 2 in. wide. Flowers flaming orange to scarlet, 1½ in. across, borne in dense, one-sided clusters on 2½–3-ft. stems that arch over at the top. Buds open slowly from base to tip of clusters, and old flowers drop cleanly from stems. Flowers last about 2 weeks when cut.

*Crocosmia
masoniorum*

CROCUS

Iridaceae

CORMS

🗡 ZONES 1–24, 30–45; BEST IN COLD CLIMATES

☼ ◑ FULL SUN OR PARTIAL SHADE

💧 REGULAR WATER DURING GROWTH AND BLOOM

Crocus vernus

Leaves are basal and grasslike—often with silvery midrib—and appear before, with, or after flowers, depending on species. Flowers with long stemlike tubes and flaring or cup-shaped petals are 1½–3 in. long; the short (true) stems are hidden underground.

Most crocus bloom in late winter or earliest spring, but some species bloom in fall, the flowers rising from bare earth weeks or days after planting. Mass them for best effect. Attractive in rock gardens, between stepping-stones, in containers. Set corms 2–3 in. deep in light, porous soil. Divide every 3 to 4 years. Won't naturalize where winters are warm.

C. ancyrensis. Flowers golden yellow, small, very early.

C. angustifolius. CLOTH OF GOLD CROCUS. Formerly *C. susianus*. Orange-gold, starlike flowers with dark brown center stripe. Starts blooming in January in warmest areas, in March in coldest climates.

C. chrysanthus. Orange yellow, sweet scented. Hybrids and selections of this plant range from white and cream through yellow and blue shades, often marked with deeper color. Usually even more freely flowering than *C. vernus,* but with smaller flowers. Spring bloom. Popular varieties are

'Blue Pearl', palest blue; 'Cream Beauty', pale yellow; 'E. P. Bowles', yellow with purple featherings; 'Ladykiller', outside purple edged white, inside white feathered purple; 'Princess Beatrix', blue with yellow center; and 'Snow Bunting', pure white.

C. imperati. Bright lilac inside, buff veined purple outside, saucer shaped. Early spring.

C. kotschyanus. Formerly *C. zonatus*. Pinkish lavender or lilac flowers in early fall.

C. sativus. SAFFRON CROCUS. Lilac. Orange-red stigma is true saffron of commerce. Interesting rather than showy. Autumn bloom. To harvest saffron, pluck the stigmas as soon as flowers open, dry them, and store them in glass or plastic vials. Stigmas from a dozen flowers will season a good-size paella or similar dish. To get continued good yield of saffron, divide corms as soon as leaves turn brown; replant in fresh or improved soil. Mark planting site with low-growing ground cover so you won't dig up dormant corms.

C. sieberi. Delicate lavender blue with golden throat. One of earliest.

C. speciosus. Showy blue-violet flowers in early fall. Lavender and mauve varieties available. Fast increase by seed and division. Showiest autumn-flowering crocus.

C. tomasinianus. Slender buds; star-shaped, silvery lavender-blue flowers, sometimes with dark blotch at tips of segments. Very early— January or February in milder climates.

C. vernus. DUTCH CROCUS. Familiar crocus in shades of white, yellow, lavender, and purple, often penciled and streaked. February–April (depending on climate). Most vigorous crocus, and only one widely sold in all areas.

CROSSVINE. See BIGNONIA capreolata

CROTON. See CODIAEUM variegatum

CROWN IMPERIAL. See FRITILLARIA imperialis

CROWN OF GOLD TREE. See CASSIA excelsa

CROWN OF THORNS. See EUPHORBIA milii

CROWN VETCH. See CORONILLA varia

Cruciferae. See Brassicaceae

CRYPTOMERIA japonica

JAPANESE CRYPTOMERIA

Taxodiaceae

EVERGREEN TREE

🗡 ZONES 4–9, 14–24, 32–34, 39

☼ FULL SUN

💧 REGULAR WATER

Cryptomeria japonica

Graceful conifer, fast growing (3–4 ft. a year) in youth. Eventually skyline tree with straight columnar trunk, thin red-brown bark peeling in strips. Foliage soft bright green to bluish green in growing season, brownish purple in cold weather. Branches, slightly pendulous, are clothed with ½–1-in.-long needlelike leaves. Roundish, red-brown cones ¾–1 in. wide. These trees are sometimes used in closely planted groves for a Japanese garden effect.

'Elegans'. PLUME CEDAR, PLUME CRYPTOMERIA. Quite unlike species. Feathery, grayish green, soft-textured foliage. Turns rich coppery red or purplish in winter. Grows slowly into broad-based, dense pyramid, 20–60 ft. high. Trunks on old trees may lean or curve. For Oriental effect, prune out some branches to give tiered look. For most effective display, give it space.

'Lobbii Nana' ('Lobbii'). Upright, dwarf, very slow to 4 ft. Foliage dark green.

'Pygmaea' ('Nana'). DWARF CRYPTOMERIA. Bushy dwarf 1½–2 ft. high, 2½ ft. wide. Dark green, needlelike leaves, twisted branches.

'Vilminiriana'. Slow-growing dwarf to 1–2 ft. Fluffy gray-green foliage turns bronze in late fall and winter. Rock garden or container plant.

CTENANTHE

Marantaceae

PERENNIALS

ZONES 23–25, 27; OR INDOORS

PARTIAL SHADE

AMPLE WATER

Ctenanthe compressa

Leaves are big feature; they may be short stalked, set along stem, or long stalked, rising from base only. Insignificant white flowers form under bracts in spikes at ends of branches. Use with other tropical foliage plants such as philodendron, alocasia, tree ferns. Plant in rich, moist soil; feed with liquid fertilizer.

C. 'Burle Marx'. Grows to 15 in. Leaves gray green above, feathered with dark green; maroon underneath. Leafstalks maroon. Tender; best grown as house plant, even in mildest climates.

C. compressa. BAMBURANTA. To 2–3 ft. high. Leathery leaves are oblong, lopsided, to about 15 in. long, waxy green on top, gray green beneath, held at angle on top of wiry stems. Often sold as *Bamburanta arnoldiana*.

C. lubbersiana (Maranta lubbersiana). To 2 ft. Yellow, 8-in. leaves with green markings.

C. oppenheimiana. GIANT BAMBURANTA. Compact, branching, 3–5 ft. high. Narrow, leathery leaves, dark green banded with silver above, purple beneath, set at angle on downy stalks. 'Tricolor' has showy cream patches along with the other colors.

CUCUMBER

Cucurbitaceae

ANNUAL VINE

ALL ZONES

FULL SUN

MAINTAIN EVEN SOIL MOISTURE

Cucumber

Each vine needs at least 25 sq. ft., but you can use a fence or trellis to conserve space. Both warm soil to sprout seeds and warmth for pollination are required.

There are long, smooth, green, slicing cucumbers; numerous small pickling cucumbers; and roundish, yellow, mild-flavored lemon cucumbers. Novelties include Oriental varieties (long, slim, very mild), Armenian cucumber (actually a long, curving, pale green, ribbed melon with cucumber look and mild cucumber flavor), and English greenhouse cucumber. This last type must be grown in greenhouse to avoid pollination by bees, with subsequent loss of form and flavor; when well grown it's the mildest of all cucumbers.

Bush cucumbers—varieties with compact vines—take up little garden space. Burpless varieties resemble hothouse cucumbers in shape and mild flavor but can be grown out-of-doors. Pickling cucumbers should be picked as soon as they have reached the proper size—tiny for sweet pickles (gherkins), larger for dills or pickle slices. They grow too large very quickly.

'Sweet Success' has quality of greenhouse cucumber but can be grown outdoors. Flowers are all female, but plants need no pollinator. Grow on trellis for long, straight cucumbers.

Plant seeds in sunny spot 1 or 2 weeks after average date of last frost. To grow cucumbers on trellis, plant seeds 1 in. deep and 1–3 ft. apart and permit main stem to reach top of support. Pick while young to ensure continued production.

Row covers will protect seedlings from various insect pests, including cucumber beetles and flea beetles; remove when flowering begins so that pollination can occur. Whiteflies are potential pest late in season; hose off plants regularly or hang yellow sticky traps. Misshapen fruit is usually due to uneven watering or poor pollination.

FRENCH CORNICHON PICKLES

For a gourmet pickle, buy seed of French cornichons from a specialty seed dealer. Plant when soil warms and all danger of frost is past; give full sun, fertile soil, consistent moisture. It's best to grow these little cucumbers on a trellis or in a 3-ft.-tall cage (two seedlings to a 14-in.-diameter cage). As plants mature, check daily for fruit. For pickling, take fruits at 1–2 in. long. Larger fruits, 2–2½ in., are best for eating fresh.

CUCUMBER TREE. See MAGNOLIA acuminata

Cucurbitaceae. The gourd family consists of vines with yellow or white flowers and large, fleshy, typically seedy fruits—chayote, cucumbers, gourds, melons, pumpkins, and squash.

CULVER'S ROOT. See VERONICASTRUM virginicum

CUNNINGHAMIA lanceolata

CHINA FIR

Taxodiaceae

EVERGREEN TREE

ZONES 4–6, 14–21, 28, 31, 32

FULL SUN

REGULAR WATER

Cunninghamia lanceolata

Native to China. Picturesque conifer with heavy trunk, stout, whorled branches, and drooping branchlets. Stiff, needlelike, sharp-pointed leaves are 1½–2½ in. long, green above, whitish beneath. Brown, 1–2-in. cones are interesting but not profuse. Grows at moderate rate to 30 ft. with 20-ft. spread. Becomes less attractive as it ages. Prune out dead branchlets. Among palest of needled evergreens in spring and summer; turns red bronze in cold winters. Protect from wind. 'Glauca', which has striking blue-gray foliage, is more widely grown and hardier than the species.

CUP-AND-SAUCER. See CAMPANULA medium

CUP-AND-SAUCER VINE. See COBAEA scandens

CUPANIOPSIS anacardioides

CARROT WOOD

Sapindaceae

EVERGREEN TREE

ZONES 16–26

FULL SUN

TOLERATES DRY OR DAMP CONDITIONS

Cupaniopsis anacardioides

Native to Australia. Slow to moderate growth to 40 ft.; glossy green leaves divided into six to ten leathery, 4-in.-long leaflets. Tolerates seacoast conditions, heat, drought, poor soil. As trees approach maturity, they may produce marble-size, leathery, yellow to orange fruit that splits but does not squash or stain. Some trees fruit heavily enough to be an annoyance, while others never fruit, for reasons not understood. Some feel that young trees selected for unusual vigor and broader-than-usual leaflets will produce less fruit than others; another theory is that trees under stress tend to develop more female flowers, hence more fruit. It is also believed that thinning out the tree every 2 years or so will result in production of young, nonfruiting wood. For several years, at least, an attractive, well-behaved tree. Consider underplanting with a ground cover deep enough to swallow the fruit drop. If you do so, be prepared to pull volunteer seedlings when they appear. Many landscape architects feel that the tree's virtues outweigh its faults.

CUP FLOWER. See NIEREMBERGIA

CUPHEA

Lythraceae

SHRUBBY PERENNIALS OR DWARF SHRUBS

✔ ZONES 16, 17, 21–29; ANNUALS IN COLDER AREAS

☼ ◑ POTTED PLANTS BEST IN LIGHT SHADE

🌢 REGULAR WATER

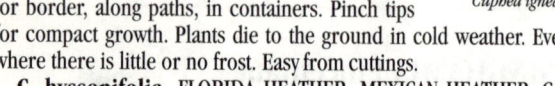
Cuphea ignea

Native to Mexico, Guatemala. Interesting for summer color in small beds, as formal edging for border, along paths, in containers. Pinch tips for compact growth. Plants die to the ground in cold weather. Evergreen where there is little or no frost. Easy from cuttings.

C. hyssopifolia. FLORIDA HEATHER, MEXICAN HEATHER. Compact shrublet 6 in.–2 ft. tall, with flexible, leafy branchlets. Leaves ½–¾ in. long, very narrow. Tiny summer flowers in pink, purple, or white are scarcely half as long as leaves.

C. ignea. CIGAR PLANT. Shrubby perennial. Leafy, compact, 1 ft. high and wide. Leaves narrow, dark green, 1–1½ in. long. Flowers tubular, ¾ in. long, bright red with white tip and dark ring at end (hence name "cigar plant"). Blooms summer and fall.

C. micropetala. Shrub or subshrub to 3 ft., with arching stems closely set with narrow, 5-in. leaves and topped by a slender, spikelike cluster of 1½-in. bright red flowers tipped in yellow. Blooms summer and fall.

CUPID'S DART. See CATANANCHE caerulea

CUP-OF-GOLD VINE. See SOLANDRA maxima

Cupressaceae. The cypress family differs from the pine and yew families in having leaves that are usually reduced to scales and cones with few scales. Cones may even be berrylike, as in junipers (*Juniperus*).

CUPRESSOCYPARIS leylandii

Cupressaceae

EVERGREEN TREE

✔ ZONES 3–24, 26, 28–34, 39

☼ FULL SUN

🌢 ◑ REGULAR TO MODERATE WATER

Cupressocyparis leylandii

Hybrid between *Chamaecyparis nootkatensis* and *Cupressus macrocarpa*. Grows very fast (from cuttings to 15–20 ft. in 5 years). Usually reaches 60–70 ft. in gardens. Most often planted as a quick screen. Long, slender, upright branches of flattened, gray-green foliage sprays give youthful tree narrow pyramidal form, though it can become open and floppy. Can be pruned into tall hedge, 10–15 ft. high, but will quickly get away from you without regular maintenance. Produces small cones composed of scales. Accepts wide variety of soil and climate conditions, strong wind. In warm-summer regions, loses stiff, upright habit and is subject to coryneum canker fungus.

Bagworms are a potential problem east of the Rockies. 'Naylor's Blue' has grayish blue foliage; 'Castlewellan' has golden new growth and narrow, erect habit; 'Emerald Isle' has bright green foliage on plant 20–25 ft. tall, 6–8 ft. wide.

CUPRESSUS

CYPRESS

Cupressaceae

EVERGREEN TREES

✔ ZONES VARY BY SPECIES

☼ FULL SUN

🌢 MODERATE WATER

Cupressus sempervirens

These conifers have tiny scalelike leaves, closely set on cordlike branches, and interesting globular, golf ball–size cones made up of shield-shaped scales.

C. arizonica. ARIZONA CYPRESS. Zones 5, 8–24, 26–31. To 40 ft., spreading to 20 ft. Seedlings variable, with foliage from green to blue gray or silvery. Rough, furrowed bark. *C. a. glabra* (often sold as *C. glabra*) is the same, but its bark is a smooth cherry red. Other forms include 'Blue Pyramid', a dense, blue-gray pyramid to 20–25 ft.; 'Gareei', with silvery blue-green foliage; and 'Pyramidalis', a compact, symmetrical grower. Mass trees for windbreak or screen.

C. sempervirens. ITALIAN CYPRESS. Zones 4–24, 28–32. Native to southern Europe, western Asia. Species has horizontal branches and dark green foliage, but variants are more often sold. 'Stricta' ('Fastigiata'), columnar Italian cypress, and 'Glauca', blue Italian cypress (really blue green in color), are classic Mediterranean landscape plants; both grow into dense, narrow trees to 60 ft. high. 'Swane's Golden', another columnar form, has golden yellow new growth.

CURRANT

Grossulariaceae (Saxifragaceae)

DECIDUOUS SHRUBS

✔ ZONES 1–6, 15–17, 34–43 FOR BEST FRUIT PRODUCTION

☼ ◑ 🌢 SOME SHADE IN HOT-SUMMER REGIONS

🌢 REGULAR WATER

Currant

Many-stemmed, thornless shrubs to 3–5 ft. high and equally wide, depending on vigor and variety. Attractive lobed, toothed leaves to 3 in. wide drop early in fall. Drooping clusters of yellowish flowers bloom in early spring, followed in summer by fruit used in jellies, jams, preserves.

Like other members of the *Ribes* tribe, currants may be hosts to white pine blister rust and are still banned in some areas where white pines grow; check with Cooperative Extension Office or a nursery for rules in your area. Black currants, derived from *R. nigrum* or *R. odoratum* (see descriptions under *Ribes*), are favored hosts. Rust-immune black currant hybrids are 'Consort', 'Coronet', and 'Crusader'; all have rich blackberry-like flavor and are good in jams and preserves. Red and white currants, derived from *R. sativum*, are less likely to be hosts; they are tart flavored and used mainly in jellies. Varieties include red-fruited 'Red Lake', 'Perfection', and 'Cherry' as well as 'White Imperial'.

Generally self-fertile. Do not grow where water or soil is high in sodium. Mulch well. Prune during dormant season. On red and white currants, cut to the ground stems older than 3 years; on black currants, remove stems older than 2 years. Older canes are often darker and peeling.

For ornamental relatives, see *Ribes*.

CUSHION PINK. See SILENE acaulis

CYATHEA cooperi

AUSTRALIAN TREE FERN

Cyatheaceae

TREE FERN

ZONES 15–27

PARTIAL SHADE IN HOT-SUMMER CLIMATES

REGULAR WATER

Cyathea cooperi

Fastest growing of the fairly hardy (to possibly 20°F/−7°C, but with damage to fronds) tree ferns. To an eventual 20 ft. tall, 12 ft. wide. At first, a low wide clump (can go from 1-ft. to 6-ft. spread in a year) before growing upward. Broad fronds are finely cut, bright green. Brownish hair on leafstalks and leaf undersurfaces can irritate skin; wear long sleeves, hat, neckcloth when grooming plants. Often sold as *Alsophila australis, A. cooperi,* or *Sphaeropteris cooperi.*

Cycadaceae. This is the best-known family in Cycadales, an order of slow-growing evergreen plants with large, firm, palmlike or fernlike leaves and conelike fruit. Most people think of them as a kind of palm.

Most are native to tropical regions. Some are subtropical, and among these, some are hardy enough to grow out-of-doors in mild-winter climates.

In addition to *Cycas circinalis* and *C. revoluta,* cycads include *Ceratozamia mexicana* and *Zamia pumila* (members of a related family, Zamiaceae).

CYCAS

Cycadaceae

CYCADS

ZONES VARY BY SPECIES

PARTIAL SHADE

REGULAR WATER

Cycas revoluta

These evergreen plants are neither ferns nor palms, but rather primitive, cone-bearing relatives of conifers. A rosette of dark green, featherlike leaves grows from a central point at the top of a single trunk (sometimes several trunks). Female plants bear conspicuous, red to orange, egg-shaped seeds. Use cycads for tropical effect.

C. circinalis. QUEEN SAGO. Zones 23–27. Native to Old World tropics. Beautiful specimen plant to 20 ft. tall. Graceful, drooping leaves to 8 ft. long atop unbranching trunk. Protect from frost.

C. revoluta. SAGO PALM. Zones 8–29; hardy to 15°F/−9°C. Native to Japan. In youth (2–3 ft. tall), has airy, lacy appearance of a fern; with age (grows very slowly to as high as 10 ft.), looks more like palm. Leaves are 2–3 ft. long (larger on very old plants), divided into many narrow, leathery segments. Tough, tolerant house or patio plant; also good subject for bonsai. Leaf spot disease is a problem in rainy climates.

CYCLAMEN

Primulaceae

TUBEROUS-ROOTED PERENNIALS

ZONES VARY BY SPECIES

FULL SUN OR PARTIAL SHADE

KEEP SOIL MOIST DURING GROWTH

Cyclamen persicum

Grown for pretty white, pink, rose, or red flowers carried atop attractive clump of basal leaves. Zones and uses for large-flowered florists' cyclamen (*C. persicum*) are given under that name. All other types are smaller flowered, hardier. They bloom as described in listings that follow; all lose their leaves during part of year.

Leaves may appear before or with flowers. Use the hardier types in rock gardens, in naturalized clumps under trees, or as carpets under camellias, rhododendrons, and large noninvasive ferns. Or grow them in pots out of direct sun.

All kinds of cyclamen grow best in fairly rich, porous soil with lots of humus. Plant tubers 6–10 in. apart; cover with ½ in. soil. (Florists' cyclamen is an exception to usual planting practice; upper half of tuber should protrude above soil level.) Best planting time is dormant period, June–August—except for florists' cyclamen, which is always sold as a potted plant rather than a tuber and is available in most seasons (although most are sold during the late fall–spring blooming period). Top-dress annually with light application of potting soil with complete fertilizer added, being careful not to cover top of tuber. Do not cultivate around roots.

Cyclamen grow readily from seed; small-flowered hardy species take several years to bloom. Older strains of florists' cyclamen needed 15 to 18 months from seed to bloom; newer strains can bloom in as little as 7 months. Grown out-of-doors in open ground, cyclamen often self-sows.

C. atkinsii. Zones 4–9, 14–24, 32. Crimson flowers on 4–6-in. stems, winter–early spring. Deep green, silver-mottled leaves. Also pink, white varieties.

C. cilicium. Zones 3–9, 14–24, 32–34. Pale pink, purple-blotched, fragrant flowers on 2–6-in. stems, fall–winter. Leaves are mottled. There is a white-flowered variety, 'Album'.

C. coum. Zones 3–9, 14–24, 32–34, 37. Deep crimson rose flowers on 4–6-in. stems in winter and early spring; round, deep green leaves. White, pink varieties.

C. europaeum. See C. purpurascens

C. hederifolium (C. neapolitanum). Zones 3–9, 14–24, 32–34, 37. Large light green leaves marbled silver and white. Rose pink flowers bloom on 3–4-in. stems, late summer–fall. There is a white variety. One of most vigorous and easiest to grow; very reliable in cold-winter climates. Set tubers a foot apart.

> ## AVOID WILD BULBS
>
> As a buyer of species cyclamen (any kind other than *C. persicum*), you should check to ascertain that the bulbs are commercially grown and not taken from the wild. Many bulb species are endangered and fast disappearing in their native habitats. Look for labels that mention "Holland" or "cultivated." In addition to cyclamen species, bulbs that have been dug in the wild for sale in the U.S. include *Eranthis, Galanthus, Leucojum,* and species *Narcissus.*

C. persicum. Wild ancestor of florists' cyclamen. Original species has deep to pale pink or white, 2-in. fragrant flowers on 6-in. stems. Selective breeding has resulted in large-flowered florists' cyclamen (the old favorites) and, more recently, smaller strains. Fragrance has disappeared, with rare exceptions.

Florists' cyclamen grows outdoors in Zones 16–24. Blooms late fall to spring; flowers crimson, red, salmon, purple, or white, on 6–8-in. stems. Kidney-shaped dark green leaves. Good choice for color in places occupied by tuberous begonias in summer. Must have shade in warm summer climates. Plants will lose leaves and go dormant in hot weather, but usually survive if drainage is good and soil not waterlogged.

Dwarf or miniature florists' cyclamens are popular; they are half or three-quarter-size replicas of standards. Careful gardeners can get these to bloom in 7 to 8 months from seed. Miniature strains (profuse show of 1½-in. flowers on 6–8-in. plants) include fragrant Dwarf Fragrance and Mirabelle strains.

C. purpurascens (C. europaeum). Zones 4–9, 14–24, 32. Distinctly fragrant crimson flowers on 5–6-in. stems, late summer–fall. Bright green leaves mottled silvery white; almost evergreen.

C. repandum. Zones 4–9, 14–24, 32. Bright crimson flowers with long, narrow petals on 5–6-in. stems in spring. Rich green, ivy-shaped leaves, marbled silver, toothed on edges.

C

CYDONIA. See CHAENOMELES

CYDONIA oblonga. See QUINCE, FRUITING

CYMBALARIA muralis (Linaria cymbalaria)

KENILWORTH IVY

Scrophulariaceae

PERENNIAL USUALLY GROWN AS ANNUAL

🌿 ZONES 3–24, 31, 32, 34, 36–39

◐ ● PARTIAL OR FULL SHADE

💧 REGULAR WATER

Cymbalaria muralis

Dainty creeper related to snapdragon. Leaves 1 in. wide or less, smooth, with three to seven toothlike lobes. Small lilac blue flowers carried singly on stalks a little longer than leaves. Trailing stems root at joints. Unshowy, but valuable as small-scale ground cover in cool, shady places or as decoration for terrarium or hanging basket. In ground, can be invasive, sometimes even sprouting in chinks of stone or brick wall.

CYMBIDIUM

Orchidaceae

TERRESTRIAL ORCHIDS

🌿 ALL ZONES—SUBJECT TO CONDITIONS BELOW

◐ BEST WITH HALF-SHADE

💧 KEEP SOIL MOIST DURING GROWTH

Miniature
Cymbidium

Native to high altitudes in southeast Asia, where rainfall is heavy and nights cool. Very popular because of their relatively easy culture. Except in frost-free areas, grow plants in containers in lathhouse, greenhouse, sunroom, or under overhang or high-branching tree. Excellent cut flower. Long, narrow, grasslike leaves form a sheath around short, stout, oval pseudobulbs. Long-lasting flowers grow on erect or arching spikes. Standard types usually bloom from February to early May. Bloom season for miniatures starts in September, is heaviest November–January.

For best bloom, give as much light as possible without burning foliage. Plants do well under shade cloth or lath. Let leaf color be your guide: plants with yellow-green leaves generally flower best; dark green foliage means too much shade. During flowering period, give plants shade to prolong bloom life, keep flowers from fading.

SOIL MIX FOR CYMBIDIUMS

If the store where you buy your cymbidiums doesn't offer a packaged cymbidium soil mix, here's a good one you can make: 2 parts composted bark, 2 parts peat moss, 1 part sand. Add a 4-in. pot of complete, dry fertilizer to each wheelbarrow of mix. Packaged or homemade, the medium should drain fast and still retain moisture.

Plants prefer 45° to 55°F/7° to 18°C night temperature, rising to as high as 80° to 90°F/27° to 32°C during day. They'll stand temperatures as low as 28°F/−2°C for short time only; therefore, where there's danger of harder frosts, protect plants with covering of polyethylene film. Flower spikes are more tender than other plant tissues.

Keep potting medium moist when new growth is developing and maturing—usually March–September. In winter, water just enough to keep bulbs from shriveling. On hot summer days, syringe foliage early in day.

Feed with complete liquid fertilizer high in nitrogen every 10 days to 2 weeks, January–July. Use low-nitrogen fertilizer August–December.

Transplant potted plants when bulbs fill pots. When dividing plants, keep minimum of three healthy bulbs (with foliage) in each division. Dust cuts with sulfur or charcoal to discourage rot.

Most cymbidium growers list only hybrids in their catalogs—large-flowered varieties with white, pink, yellow, green, or bronze blooms. Most have yellow throat, dark red markings on lip. Large-flowered forms produce dozen or more 4½–5-in. flowers per stem. Miniature varieties, about a quarter the size of large-flowered forms, are popular for their size, free-blooming qualities, flower color.

CYMBOPOGON citratus

LEMON GRASS

Poaceae (Gramineae)

PERENNIAL

🌿 ZONES 16, 17, 23–27; BRING INDOORS IN COLDER CLIMATES

☀ FULL SUN

💧 REGULAR WATER

Cymbopogon citratus

All plant parts are strongly lemon scented; widely used as an ingredient in Southeast Asian cooking. Very frost sensitive. Will usually live over in mild-winter zones listed above, but it is safer there and elsewhere to pot up a division and keep it indoors or in a greenhouse over winter. Clumps of inch-wide leaves grow 2–3 ft. tall. Sheathed leaf bases are nearly bulbous in appearance.

CYNODON dactylon

BERMUDA GRASS, BERMUDA

Poaceae (Gramineae)

LAWN GRASS

🌿 ZONES 8–10, 12–33, 35

☀ FULL SUN

◐ 💧 WATER LESS THAN MOST LAWN GRASSES

Cynodon dactylon

Subtropical fine-textured grass that spreads rapidly by surface and underground runners. Tolerates heat; looks good if well maintained. It turns brown in winter; some varieties stay green longer than others, and most stay green longer if well fed. Bermuda grass can be overseeded with cool-season grasses or dyed green for winter color. Needs sun and should be cut low; ½ to 1 in. is desirable. Needs thatching—removal of matted layer of old stems and stolons beneath the leaves—to look its best.

Common Bermuda is good minimum-maintenance lawn for large area. Needs feeding, careful and frequent mowing to remove seed spikes. Roots invade shrubbery and flower beds if not carefully confined. Can become extremely difficult to eradicate. Plant from hulled seed or sprigs.

Hybrid Bermudas are finer in texture and better in color than common kind. They crowd out common Bermuda in time but are harder to overseed with rye, bluegrass, or red fescue. Help them stay green in winter by feeding in September and October and by removing thatch. Useful in areas with short dormant season. Grow from sprigs (stolons), plugs, or sod.

'Tifdwarf'. Extremely low and dense; takes very close mowing. Slower to establish than others, but slower to spread where it's not wanted. Useful as small-scale ground cover on banks, among rocks.

'Tifgreen'. Fine textured, deep blue green, dense. Few seed spikes; sterile seeds. Takes close mowing; preferred for putting greens.

'Tifway'. Low growth, fine texture, stiff blades, dark green, dense, wear resistant. Slow to start. Sterile (no seeds).

'U-3'. More finely textured than common Bermuda but with obvious and unattractive seed spikes. Very tough. Grow from sprigs; not dependable from seed, tending to revert to mixture of many types. Not up to other hybrids in quality.

CYNOGLOSSUM amabile

CHINESE FORGET-ME-NOT

Boraginaceae

BIENNIAL GROWN AS ANNUAL

⚡ ALL ZONES; BEST IN COLDER CLIMATES

☼ FULL SUN

💧 REGULAR WATER

Cynoglossum amabile

Bedding, border, or wild garden plant, 1½–2 ft. high, with grayish green, soft, hairy, lance-shaped leaves. Loose sprays of blue, pink, or white flowers in spring, into summer where weather is cool. Not for hot, humid climates. Blossoms larger than those of forget-me-not (*Myosotis*), a relative. 'Firmament', most widely available, has rich blue flowers on compact, 1½-ft.-tall plant. Blooms first year from seed sown (preferably where plants are to grow) in spring. Hardy in mild-winter climates, where seeds can be sown in autumn.

Cyperaceae. Members of the sedge family superficially resemble grasses, but their stems are usually three-sided and their leaves are arranged in three ranks. They generally grow in wet places; *Carex* and *Cyperus* are examples.

CYPERUS

Cyperaceae

PERENNIALS

⚡ ZONES VARY BY SPECIES

☼ ◐ ● SUN OR SHADE

💧 BOG PLANTS IN NATURE

Cyperus papyrus

These are sedges—grasslike plants distinguished from true grasses by three-angled, solid stems and very different flowering parts. Valued for striking form, silhouette, shadow pattern.

Most kinds grow in rich, moist soil or with roots submerged in water, in sun or shade. Groom plants by removing dead or broken stems; divide and replant vigorous ones when clump becomes too large, saving smaller, outside divisions and discarding overgrown centers. In cold climates, pot up divisions and keep them over the winter as house plants.

C. alternifolius. UMBRELLA PLANT. Zones 8, 9, 12–31. Narrow, firm, spreading leaves arranged like ribs of umbrella at tops of 2–4-ft. stems. Flowers in dry, greenish brown clusters. Grows in or out of water. Effective near pools, in pots or planters, or in dry stream beds or small rock gardens. Self-sows. Can become weedy, take over a small pool. Dwarf form is 'Gracilis' ('Nanus').

C. papyrus. PAPYRUS. Zones 16, 17, 23–28. Tall, graceful, dark green stems 6–10 ft. high, topped with clusters of green threadlike parts to 1½ ft. long (longer than small leaves at base of cluster). Will grow quickly in 2 in. of water in shallow pool, or can be potted and placed on bricks or inverted pot in deeper water. Protect from strong wind. Also grows well in rich, moist soil out of water. Used by flower arrangers.

FOR GROWING SYMBOL EXPLANATIONS
PLEASE SEE PAGE 161

CYPHOMANDRA betacea (C. crassicaulis)

TREE TOMATO, TAMARILLO

Solanaceae

EVERGREEN OR SEMIEVERGREEN SHRUB

⚡ ZONES 14–27; OR INDOORS

☼ ◐ FULL SUN OR PARTIAL SHADE

💧 REGULAR WATER

Cyphomandra betacea

Fast growth to 10–12 ft. Treelike habit. Pointed oval leaves 4–10 in. long; small, pinkish summer and fall flowers. Winter fruit is red, 2–3 in. long, egg shaped, edible; has acid, slightly tomato-like flavor. If you find the fruit too tart, try stewing it with a little sugar, as the Australians do. Grow from seed like tomato. Shelter from frost; planting under eaves recommended in colder part of range. Control sucking insects.

CYPRESS. See *Cupressus.* True cypresses are all *Cupressus;* many plants erroneously called cypress are under *Chamaecyparis* and *Taxodium.*

CYPRESS, FALSE. See CHAMAECYPARIS

CYPRESS, SUMMER. See KOCHIA scoparia

CYPRESS VINE. See IPOMOEA quamoclit

Cypripedium. For tropical and subtropical orchids sold under this name, see *Paphiopedilum.* True cypripediums, the hardy lady's slipper orchids, are rare or endangered in the wild and extremely difficult to maintain in gardens. Most are collected from wild stands and seldom survive.

CYRTOMIUM falcatum

HOLLY FERN

Polypodiaceae

FERN

⚡ ZONES 5–9, 14–30; OR INDOORS

◐ ● PARTIAL OR FULL SHADE

💧 REGULAR WATER

Cyrtomium falcatum

Coarse-textured but handsome fern, 2–3 ft. tall, sometimes taller. Fonds large, dark green, glossy, leathery. Fully evergreen in mild climates. Takes indoor conditions well and thrives outside in milder areas; hardy to 14°F/−10°C. Provide good soil; take care not to plant too deeply. Protect from wind. 'Rochfordianum' has fringed leaflets.

CYTISUS

BROOM

Fabaceae (Leguminosae)

EVERGREEN, SEMIEVERGREEN, DECIDUOUS SHRUBS

⚡ ZONES VARY BY SPECIES

☼ FULL SUN

💧 MODERATE WATER

Cytisus battandieri

Most widely planted brooms belong here, but look for Spanish broom under *Spartium junceum,* other choice shrubs under *Genista.* Deciduous, semievergreen, or evergreen shrubs (many nearly leafless, but with green or gray-green stems). Sweet pea–shaped flowers, often fragrant. Plants tolerate wind, seashore conditions, and rocky, infertile soil. Prune after bloom to keep to reasonable size and form, lessen production of unsightly seedpods.

C. battandieri. ATLAS BROOM. Semievergreen or deciduous. Zones 4–6, 14–17, 31, 32. Fast growth to 12–15 ft. high and equally wide. Can be trained as small tree. Leaves divided into three roundish leaflets to 3½ in. long, 1½ in. wide, covered with silvery, silky hairs. Fragrant, clear yellow flowers in spikelike, 5-in. clusters bloom at the ends of branches during summer.

C. lydia. See Genista lydia

C. praecox. WARMINSTER BROOM. Zones 3–9, 12–22, 31–35, 37, 39. Deciduous. Compact growth to 3–5 ft. high and 4–6 ft. wide, with many slender stems. Plant resembles a mounding mass of pale yellow to creamy white flowers in spring. Small leaves drop early. Effective as informal screen or hedge, along drives, paths, garden steps. 'Allgold', slightly taller, has bright yellow flowers; 'Hollandia' has pink ones. 'Moonlight', formerly considered *C. praecox* variety, is now thought to be form of *C. scoparius.*

C. scoparius. SCOTCH BROOM. Evergreen. Zones 4–9, 14–22, 31–34. This species has given brooms a bad name in the West, where it escaped landscapes beginning in the early 20th century and spread into open land. Upright-growing mass of wandlike green stems (often leafless or nearly so) may reach 10 ft. Golden yellow, ¾-in. flowers bloom in spring and early summer.

Much less aggressive than the species are lower-growing, more colorful forms. Most of these grow 5–8 ft. tall: 'Burkwoodii', red blossoms touched with yellow; 'Carla', pink and crimson lined white; 'Dorothy Walpole', rose pink and crimson; 'Lena', lemon yellow and red; 'Lilac Time', lilac pink, compact plant; 'Lord Lambourne', scarlet and cream; 'Minstead', white flushed lilac and deep purple; 'Moonlight', pale yellow, compact plant; 'Pomona', orange and apricot; 'St. Mary's', white; 'San Francisco' and 'Stanford', red.

DABOECIA

IRISH HEATH
Ericaceae
EVERGREEN SHRUBS
⚡ ZONES VARY BY SPECIES
☼ ◐ TOLERATE FULL SUN IN COOL-SUMMER AREAS
💧 REGULAR WATER

Daboecia cantabrica

These members of the heath family bear ½-in.-long, egg-shaped flowers in spikelike clusters. They require fast-draining, acid soil and are most useful on hillsides and in rock gardens or natural landscapes.

D. azorica. Zones 8, 9, 14–24. Mounds to 6–10 in. tall. Closely set, bright green leaves ¼ in. long, broader than those of other heaths and heathers. Rosy red flowers bloom in spring or early summer, occasionally in fall.

D. cantabrica. Zones 3–9, 14–24, 32, 34, 39. Erect-stemmed, slightly spreading plant 1½–2 ft. tall, with larger leaves than those of *D. azorica.* Pinkish purple flowers in narrow, 3–5-in. clusters, late spring to early autumn; in warmer part of range, bloom begins earlier in spring. Cut back in fall to keep compact. Varieties include 'Alba', white; 'Praegerae', pure pink; 'Rosea', deep pink. 'William Buchanan' is a prostrate grower with reddish purple flowers; 'William Buchanan Gold' is similar but with some yellow variegation in the foliage.

DAFFODIL. See NARCISSUS

DAHLBERG DAISY. See DYSSODIA tenuiloba

DAHLIA

Asteraceae (Compositae)
TUBEROUS-ROOTED PERENNIALS
⚡ ALL ZONES; SEE BELOW
☼ ◐ LIGHT AFTERNOON SHADE IN HOTTEST AREAS
💧 REGULAR WATER

Dahlia Hybrid

Native to Mexico and Guatemala. Hardy to 20°F/−7°C; where winters are that mild, tubers can remain in the ground all year, though gardeners in all regions prefer to lift and store tubers. Through centuries of hybridizing and selection, dahlias have become tremendously diversified, available in numerous flower types and in all colors but true blue. Sketches illustrate types based on flower form as classified by American Dahlia Society.

Bush and bedding dahlias grow from 15 in. to over 6 ft. high. The tall bush forms are useful as summer hedges, screens, and fillers among shrubs; lower kinds give mass color in borders and containers. Modern dahlias, with their strong stems, long-lasting blooms that face outward or upward, and substantial, attractive foliage, are striking cut flowers. Leaves are generally divided into many large, deep green leaflets.

Planting. Most dahlias are started from tubers. Plant them after frost is past and soil is warm. Several weeks before planting, dig soil 1 ft. deep and work in organic matter such as ground bark or peat moss.

Dig holes 1 ft. deep and 3 ft. apart for most varieties; space largest kinds 4–5 ft. apart, smaller ones 1–2 ft. If you use fertilizer at planting time, thoroughly mix ¼ cup of complete fertilizer in bottom of hole, then add 4 in. of plain soil. For tall types, drive a 5-ft. stake into hole; place tuber horizontally, 2 in. from stake, with eye (growth bud) pointing toward it. Cover tuber with 3 in. of soil. Water thoroughly. As shoots grow, gradually fill hole with soil.

Dahlias also can be started from seed. For tall types, plant seeds early indoors; transplant seedlings into garden beds after frosts are over. For dwarf dahlias, sow seed in place after soil is warm, or buy and plant started seedlings from the nursery. Dwarf dahlias are best replaced each year, though they can be lifted and stored.

Thinning, pinching. On tall-growing types, thin to strongest shoot or two shoots (you can make cuttings of removed shoots). When remaining shoots have three sets of leaves, pinch off tips just above top set; two side shoots develop from each pair of leaves. For large flowers, remove all but terminal flower buds on side shoots. Smaller-flowered dahlias, such as pompoms, singles, and dwarfs, need only first pinching.

Plant care. Start watering regularly after shoots are aboveground, and continue throughout active growth. Dahlias planted in enriched soil don't need additional food. If soil lacks nutrients, side-dress plants with fertilizer high in phosphates and potash when first flower buds appear. Avoid high-nitrogen fertilizers: they result in soft growth, weak stems, tubers liable to rot in storage. Mulch to keep down weeds and to eliminate cultivating, which may injure feeder roots.

Cut flowers. Pick nearly mature flowers in early morning or evening. Immediately place cut stems in 2–3 in. of hot water; let stand in gradually cooling water for several hours or overnight.

Lifting, storing. After tops turn yellow or are frosted, cut stalks to 4 in. above ground. Dig around plant 1 ft. from center, carefully pry up clump with spading fork, shake off loose soil, and let clump dry in sun for several hours. From that point, follow either of two methods:

Method 1: divide clumps immediately. This saves storage space; freshly dug tubers are easy to cut, and eyes (growth buds) are easy to recognize at this time. To divide, cut the stalks with a sharp knife, leaving 1 in. of stalk attached to each tuber. Each tuber must have an eye in order to produce a new plant. Dust cut surfaces with sulfur to prevent rot; bury tubers in sand, sawdust, or vermiculite; and store through winter in cool (40° to 45°F/ 4° to 7°C), dry place.

Dahlia Flower Forms

Informal Decorative

Formal Decorative

Cactus

Semicactus

Collarette / Single

Ball

Anemone / Pompom

Method 2: leave clumps intact; cover them with dry sand, sawdust, peat moss, perlite, or vermiculite; store in cool, dry place. There is less danger of shrinkage with this storage method. About 2 to 4 weeks before planting in spring, separate tubers as described under method 1. Place tubers in moist sand to encourage development of sprouts.

In Zones 25 and 26, tubers tend to rot in long storage and should be replaced yearly.

DANDELION (Taraxacum officinale)

Cultivated Dandelion

Asteraceae (Compositae)

PERENNIAL

🗡 ZONES 1–24, 26–45

☀ FULL SUN

🌢 REGULAR WATER

A weed in lawns and flower beds, it can also be a cultivated edible-leaf crop. Seeds sold in packets. Cultivated forms have been selected for larger, thicker leaves than those of common weed form. Tie leaves together to blanch interiors; eat like endive. Add tender leaves to green salads; boil thick leaves like collards or other greens.

DAPHNE

Thymelaeaceae

EVERGREEN, SEMIEVERGREEN, DECIDUOUS SHRUBS

🗡 ZONES VARY BY SPECIES

☀◑ EXPOSURE NEEDS VARY BY SPECIES

🌢🌢 REGULAR TO MODERATE WATER, EXCEPT AS NOTED

◊ ALL PARTS, ESPECIALLY FRUITS, ARE POISONOUS IF INGESTED

Daphne odora 'Marginata'

Of the many kinds, three (*D. burkwoodii, D. cneorum, D. odora*) are the most widely grown; the others tend to be choice rock garden subjects with more limited distribution in the nursery trade. Although some daphnes are easier to grow than others, all require excellent drainage, cool soil (use a mulch or noncompetitive ground cover), careful watering during dry spells, and shelter from wind and extreme sun.

D. burkwoodii. Evergreen or semievergreen to deciduous. Zones 2–6, 14–17, 31–41. Hybrid with erect, compact growth to 3–4 ft. Densely set, narrow leaves; numerous small clusters of fragrant flowers (white aging to pink) around branch ends in late spring and again in late summer. 'Somerset' is 4–5 ft. tall, with pink flowers. 'Briggs Moonlight' has leaves of pale yellow with a narrow border of green. 'Carol Mackie' has gold-edged green leaves. Use in shrub borders, at woodland edge, as foundation planting. Full sun or light shade.

D. cneorum. GARLAND DAPHNE. Evergreen. Zones 2–9, 14–17, 31–41. Matting and spreading; less than 1 ft. high and 3 ft. wide. Good container plant. Trailing branches covered with narrow, 1-in.-long, dark green leaves. Clusters of fragrant rosy light pink flowers appear in spring. Choice

rock garden plant; give it light shade in warm areas, full sun in cool-summer areas. After bloom is through, top-dress with mix of peat moss and sand to keep roots cool and induce additional rooting of trailing stems.

Varieties include 'Eximia', lower growing than the species and with larger flowers; 'Pygmaea Alba', 3 in. tall, 1 ft. wide, with white flowers; 'Ruby Glow', with larger, more deeply colored flowers and with late-summer rebloom; and 'Variegata', with gold-edged leaves.

D. genkwa. LILAC DAPHNE. Deciduous. Zones 4–6, 16, 17, 31–34, 39. Erect, open growth to 3–4 ft. high and as wide. Before leaves expand, clusters of lilac blue, scentless flowers wreathe branches, making foot-long wands of blossoms. White fruit follows flowers. Leaves are oval, 2 in. long. Use in rock garden, shrub border. Full sun or light shade.

D. mantensiana. Evergreen. Zones 4–6, 15–17, 31–34, 39. Hybrid growing slowly to 1½ ft., spreading to 3 ft. Clusters of perfumed purple flowers at branch tips, late spring (and often through summer). Densely branched and well foliaged, it can be used in same way as low-growing azaleas. Leaves narrow, to 1¼ in. long. Full sun or light shade.

D. mezereum. FEBRUARY DAPHNE. Deciduous. Zones 2–7, 14–17, 31–41. Rather gawky, stiffly twigged, erect growth to 4 ft., with roundish, 2–3-in.-long, thin leaves. Plant in groups. Full sun or light shade. Fragrant reddish purple flowers in short stalkless clusters are carried along branches in mid- to late winter before leaf-out and continue into spring. 'Alba' is the same but is less rangy and has white flowers, yellow fruit.

D. odora. WINTER DAPHNE. Evergreen. Zones 4–10, 12, 14–24, 31; warmer parts of 32, 33. Prized for the pervasive fragrance of its flowers. Very neat, handsome plant usually to about 4 ft. high and spreading wider; has reached 8–10 ft. under ideal conditions. Rather narrow, 3-in.-long leaves are thick and glossy. Nosegay clusters of charming flowers—pink to deep red on outside, with creamy pink throats—appear at branch ends in winter.

Give this species good growing conditions, since it's the fussiest of the lot. Locate the plant where it will get midday shade. To avoid water mold root rot (the chief cause of failure), roots need well-aerated, neutral-pH soil. Dig planting hole twice as wide as root ball and one and a half times as deep; refill with mixture of 1 part soil, 1 part sand, and 2 parts ground bark. Top of root ball should remain higher than soil level. Feed right after bloom with complete fertilizer but not acid plant food. During dry periods, water just enough to keep plant from wilting.

'Alba'. Plain green leaves, white flowers. Terminal growth sometimes distorted by fasciation (cockscomb-like growths).

'Leucanthe'. Vigorous and relatively disease resistant, with dark green leaves and a profusion of pale pink flowers with white interiors.

'Marginata' ('Aureo-Marginata'). More widely grown than species. Leaves are edged with band of yellow.

DAPHNE PRUNING? IT'S SPECIAL

Correct the shape of a *D. odora* by cutting late-winter flower clusters to wear as corsages or for indoor display. Make cuts to outfacing buds to promote spreading, to infacing ones to promote upward growth. Cut stems of deciduous kinds for bouquets while they are in bud; put them in water indoors and buds will open.

DARMERA peltata
(Peltiphyllum peltatum)

UMBRELLA PLANT, INDIAN RHUBARB

Saxifragaceae

PERENNIAL

⚡ ZONES 3–7, 14–20, 32, 34, 36, 37; ALSO 1, 2 IN FAR WEST

☼ PARTIAL SHADE

💧 AMPLE WATER

Darmera peltata

Native to mountains of Northern California and southern Oregon. Large, round clusters of pink flowers on bare stalks to 6 ft. tall in spring. Shield-shaped leaves 1–2 ft. wide appear later on 2–6-ft. stalks. Stout rhizomes to 2 in. thick grow in damp ground or even into streams. A spectacular plant for pond, stream, or damp, cool woodland site.

DATE PALM. See PHOENIX

DATURA. See BRUGMANSIA

DAVALLIA trichomanoides

SQUIRREL'S FOOT FERN

Polypodiaceae

FERN

⚡ ZONES 17, 23–27; OR INDOORS

☼ PARTIAL SHADE

💧 REGULAR WATER

Very finely divided fronds to 1 ft. long, 6 in. wide, rise from light reddish brown, furry rhizomes (like squirrel's feet) that creep over soil surface. Hardy to 30°F/−1°C; can be used in mild-winter areas as small-scale ground cover in partly shaded areas. Best use in any climate is as hanging basket plant. Use light, fast-draining soil mix. Feed occasionally. For similar fern, see *Humata tyermannii*.

Davallia trichomanoides

DAVIDIA involucrata

DOVE TREE

Nyssaceae

DECIDUOUS TREE

⚡ ZONES 4–9, 14–21, 31, 32, 34

☼☼ PARTIAL SHADE IN HOT-SUMMER AREAS

💧 REGULAR WATER

Davidia involucrata

Native to China. In gardens, grows 20–40 ft. tall, with pyramidal to rounded crown and strong branching pattern. Has clean look in and out of leaf. Roundish to heart-shaped, 3–6-in.-long leaves are vivid green. Comes into bloom in spring; general effect is that of white doves resting among green leaves—or, as some say, like handkerchiefs drying on branches. Small, clustered, red-anthered flowers are carried between two large, unequal, white or creamy white bracts; one 6 in. long, other about 4 in. long. Because leaves are already present at bloom time, the large blossoms aren't as showy as smaller flowers of deciduous fruit trees. Trees often take 10 years to come into flower, and then may bloom more heavily in alternate years. Brown fruits about the size of golf balls hang on tree well into winter.

Plant this tree by itself; it should not compete with other flowering trees. Pleasing in front of dark conifers, where vivid green and white stand out.

DAWN REDWOOD. See METASEQUOIA glyptostroboides

DAY FLOWER. See COMMELINA

DAYLILY. See HEMEROCALLIS

DEAD NETTLE. See LAMIUM maculatum

DEERHORN CEDAR. See THUJOPSIS dolabrata

DELONIX regia

ROYAL POINCIANA, FLAMBOYANT

Fabaceae (Leguminosae)

PARTIALLY OR WHOLLY DECIDUOUS TREE

⚡ ZONE 25

☼ FULL SUN

💧 REGULAR WATER

Delonix regia

Flamboyant is a more apt common name than poinciana, which rightly belongs to another plant not described in this book. Wide-spreading, umbrella-shaped tree of rapid growth to 30 ft. and twice as wide. Fernlike leaves, finely cut into many tiny leaflets, give filtered shade. Large trusses of 4-in., orange to scarlet flowers with white markings put on a show in late spring or early summer. Blooms are followed by 2-ft. black seedpods, which hang on bare branches in winter. Easy to grow, but sensitive to cold.

DELOSPERMA

ICE PLANT

Aizoaceae

SUCCULENT PERENNIALS

⚡ ZONES VARY BY SPECIES

☼ FULL SUN

💧 TAKE CONSIDERABLE DROUGHT

Delosperma cooperi

This huge group of succulents includes two of the hardiest ice plants, described below. These and other types thrive in full sun with good drainage and just enough water to keep them looking bright and fresh.

D. cooperi. Zones 3–24, 28–31, warmer parts of 32. Grows 5 in. tall, 2 ft. wide. Brilliant, shining purple flowers all summer long. Tolerates 0°F/−18°C if protected by snow or mulch.

D. nubigenum. Zones 2–24, 28–41. Hardiest of all ice plants, it has withstood −25°F/−32°C. Barely 1 in. high, spreading to 3 ft. Fleshy, cylindrical, bright green leaves turn red in fall, then green up again in spring. Bright golden yellow flowers, 1–1½ in. wide, blanket plants in spring. Effective in rock gardens.

DELPHINIUM

Ranunculaceae

PERENNIALS, SOME TREATED AS ANNUALS

⚡ ZONES VARY BY SPECIES

☼ FULL SUN

💧 REGULAR WATER

Delphinium elatum

Most people associate delphiniums with blue flowers, but color range also includes white and shades of red, pink, lavender, purple, and yellow. Leaves are lobed or fanlike, variously cut and divided. Taller hybrids offer rich colors in elegant spirelike form. Blossoms of all types attract birds. All kinds are effective in borders and make good cut flowers; lower-growing kinds serve well as container plants. For annual delphiniums (larkspurs), see *Consolida ambigua*.

All kinds are easy to grow from seed. In mild-winter areas, sow fresh seed in flats or pots of light soil mix in July or August; set out transplants in October for bloom in late spring and early summer. (In mild-winter climates, most perennial forms are short lived, often treated as annuals. Definitely treat as fall-planted annuals in low desert and humid Deep South.) In cold climates, refrigerate summer-harvested seed in airtight containers until time to sow. Sow seed in March or April, set out transplants in June or July for first bloom by September (and more bloom the following summer).

Delphiniums need rich, porous soil and regular fertilizing. Improve poor or heavy soils by blending in soil conditioners. Add lime to strongly acid soils. Work small handful of superphosphate into bottom of hole before setting out plant. Be careful not to cover root crown.

HOW TO GROW CLOSE-TO-PERFECT DELPHINIUMS

When new shoots develop in spring, remove all but the two or three strongest and apply complete fertilizer alongside plants. Bait for slugs and snails. Stake flower stalks early. After bloom, cut back flower spikes, leaving foliage at the bottom; after new shoots are several inches high, cut old stalks to ground. Fertilize to encourage good second bloom in late summer, early fall.

D. ajacis. See Consolida ambigua

D. belladonna. Sturdy, bushy perennial. Zones 1–9, 14–24, 32, 34, 36–43. To 3–4 ft. Deeply cut leaves; short-stemmed, airy flower clusters. Varieties: 'Belladonna', light blue; 'Bellamosum', dark blue; 'Casa Blanca', white; 'Cliveden Beauty', deep turquoise blue. All have flowers 1½–2 in. across, are longer lived than tall hybrids listed under *D. elatum*.

D. cardinale. SCARLET LARKSPUR. Perennial. Zones 14–24. Native to California. Erect stems grow 3–6 ft. tall from deep, thick, woody roots. Leaves 3–9 in. wide, with deep, narrow lobes. Flowers 1 in. across, with scarlet calyx and spur and yellow, scarlet-tipped petals. Sow seed early for first-year bloom.

D. elatum. CANDLE DELPHINIUM, CANDLE LARKSPUR. Perennial. Zones 1–10, 14–24, 32, 34, 36–41. Along with *D. cheilanthum* and others, this 3–6-ft. Siberian species, with small dark or dull purple flowers, is parent of modern tall-growing delphinium strains such as spectacular Pacific strain.

Pacific strain delphinium hybrids (also called Giant Pacific, Pacific Hybrids, and Pacific Coast Hybrids) grow up to 8 ft. tall. They come in selected color series; members of these include 'Summer Skies', light blue; 'Blue Bird', medium blue; 'Blue Jay', medium to dark blue; 'Galahad', white with white center; 'Percival', white with black center. Other purple, lavender, pink named varieties also sold.

Like Pacific strain but shorter (2–2½ ft. tall) are the Blue Fountains, Blue Springs, and Magic Fountains strains. Even shorter is the Stand Up strain (15–20 in.). These shorter strains seldom require staking.

Other strains have flowers in shades of lilac pink to deep raspberry rose, clear lilac, lavender, royal purple, and darkest violet. Wrexham strain, tall growing with large spikes, was developed in England.

D. grandiflorum (D. chinense). CHINESE or BOUQUET DELPHINIUM. Short-lived perennial treated as biennial or annual. All zones. Bushy, branching, 1 ft. tall or less. Varieties include 'Dwarf Blue Mirror', 1 ft., upward-facing flowers of deep blue; and 'Tom Thumb', 8 in. tall, pure gentian blue flowers.

DENDRANTHEMA. See CHRYSANTHEMUM morifolium, C. rubellum, C. weyrichii

---

DENNSTAEDTIA punctilobula

HAY-SCENTED FERN

Dennstaedtiaceae

FERN

✂ ZONES 1–6, 31–45

◐ LIGHT SHADE

💧💧 REGULAR TO MODERATE WATER

Dennstaedtia punctilobula

Native from eastern Canada to the Gulf states. Deciduous fern with finely divided fronds to 2 ft. tall arising from creeping rhizomes. Spreads quickly to make an attractive ground cover. Crushed fronds smell like freshly cut hay. Tolerates full sun in cool-summer regions. If given adequate water, thrives even in poor, rocky soil. Can form mats that cover rocks. You may see it growing along the roadside or under rail fences in partly shaded areas.

DEODAR CEDAR. See CEDRUS deodara

DESCHAMPSIA

HAIR GRASS

Poaceae (Graminae)

PERENNIAL GRASSES

✂ ZONES 2–24, 28–41

☀◐ FULL SUN OR PARTIAL SHADE

💧💧 REGULAR TO MODERATE WATER

Deschampsia caespitosa vivipara

Ornamental clumping grasses with narrow, rough leaves obscured by clouds of yellowish flower panicles in late spring or early summer. Use in mass plantings. Best suited to cool-summer regions. Evergreen in warmer part of range, semievergreen in colder part.

D. caespitosa. TUFTED HAIR GRASS. Native to much of North America, but most garden varieties are imports from European nurseries. Dark green foliage. Purple-tinged greenish yellow panicles persist into winter. Fountainlike clumps typically 2–3 ft. high in bloom. Varieties with golden yellow flowers include 'Goldgehaenge', 'Goldschleier', 'Goldstaub'. 'Bronzeschleier' ('Bronzy Veil') has bronzy yellow blooms. *D. c. vivipara* has the darkest green foliage; instead of flowers, it produces plantlets that droop to the ground.

D. flexuosa. CRINKLED HAIR GRASS. Wiry, glossy green leaves in tight clumps 1–2 ft. high. Nodding, purple-tinged flowers mature to yellowish brown.

DESERT MARIGOLD. See BAILEYA multiradiata

DESERT WILLOW. See CHILOPSIS linearis

DEUTZIA

Saxifragaceae

DECIDUOUS SHRUBS

✂ ZONES 2–11, 14–17, 29–41

☀◐ FULL SUN OR LIGHT SHADE

💧 REGULAR WATER

They are best used among evergreens, where they can make a show when in bloom, then blend back in with other greenery during the rest of the year. Their mid- to late spring flowering coincides with that of tulips and Dutch iris.

Prune after flowering. With low- or medium-growing kinds, cut some of oldest stems to ground every other year. Prune

Deutzia rosea

tall-growing kinds severely by cutting back wood that has flowered. Cut to outward-facing side branches.

D. crenata. Native to Japan. Similar to *D. scabra,* but with white flowers.

D. elegantissima. Bears pink flowers on a 6-ft. shrub. 'Rosealind', 4–5 ft. tall and spreading, has deep rose flowers.

D. gracilis. SLENDER DEUTZIA. Native to Japan. To 6 ft. or less. Many slender stems arch gracefully, carry bright green, 2½-in., sharply toothed leaves and clusters of snowy white flowers. 'Nikko' (*D. g. nakaiana*) grows only 1–2 ft. tall by 5 ft. wide and has deep burgundy fall color; effective as ground cover, over walls, in rock gardens.

D. hybrida 'Pink-a-Boo'. Erect shrub to 6–8 ft. tall, 6 ft. wide, with large clusters of pink flowers.

D. rosea. Hybrid. Low growing (to 3–4 ft.), with finely toothed, 1–3-in. leaves. Flowers pinkish outside, white inside, in short clusters.

D. scabra. Native to Japan, China. This plant and its varieties are robust shrubs 7–10 ft. tall. Leaves oval, 3 in. long, dull green, roughish to touch, with scallop-toothed edges. Flowers are white or pinkish, in narrow, upright clusters. 'Pride of Rochester' has large clusters of small, frilled double flowers, rosy purple outside. 'Godsall' ('Godsall Pink') grows 4–6 ft. tall, bears pure pink double flowers.

DIANTHUS

PINK
Caryophyllaceae
PERENNIALS, BIENNIALS, AND ANNUALS
🌿 BEST IN ZONES 1–24, 30–45
☼ ◑ LIGHT AFTERNOON SHADE IN HOT AREAS
● REGULAR WATER

Over 300 species and extremely large number of hybrids, many with high garden value. Most kinds form attractive evergreen mats or tufts of grasslike green, gray-green, blue-green, or blue-gray leaves. Single, semidouble, or double

Dianthus caryophyllus

flowers in white and shades of pink, rose, red, yellow, and orange; many have rich, spicy fragrance. Main bloom period for most is spring into early summer; some rebloom later in season or keep going into fall if faded flowers are removed.

Among dianthus are appealing border favorites such as cottage pink and sweet William, highly prized cut flowers such as carnation (clove pink), and rock garden miniatures. Many excellent named varieties not mentioned here are available locally.

All kinds of dianthus thrive in light, fast-draining soil. Carnations, sweet William, and cottage pinks need fairly rich soil; rock garden or alpine types require gritty growing medium, with added lime if soil is acid. Avoid overwatering. Sow seed of annual or biennial dianthus in flats or directly in garden. Propagate perennial types by cuttings made from tips of growing shoots, by division or layering, or from seed. Perennials are often short lived, especially in humid Deep South, where they are often treated as annuals. Carnations and sweet William are subject to rust and fusarium wilt.

D. allwoodii. Group of modern pinks derived from *D. plumarius* and *D. caryophyllus*. Plants vary, but most have gray-green foliage and two blossoms on each stem; bloom over long period if deadheaded. Tend to be more compact and more vigorous than their *D. plumarius* parent. The many varieties include 'Aqua', which bears very fragrant, pure white double flowers on 10–12-in. stems. Plants sold as 'Allwoodii Alpinus' are the result of crossing *D. allwoodii* with dwarf species.

D. arenarius. Perennial. Tufted plant to 1½ ft. with narrow, grass green leaves and inch-wide fringed white flowers sometimes marked with green or purple. Highly fragrant; can tolerate some shade. 'Snow Flurries' has pure white flowers.

D. barbatus. SWEET WILLIAM. Vigorous biennial often grown as annual. Sturdy stems 10–20 in. high; leaves are flat, light to dark green,

1½–3 in. long. Dense clusters of white, pink, rose, red, purplish, or bicolored flowers, about ½ in. across, set among leafy bracts; not very fragrant. Sow seed in late spring for bloom following year. Double-flowered and dwarf strains are obtainable from seed. Indian Carpet strain is only 6 in. tall. Roundabout and Summer Beauty strains (1 ft.) bloom the first year from seed.

D. caryophyllus. CARNATION, CLOVE PINK. Perennial. There are two distinct categories of carnations: florists' and border types. Both have double flowers, bluish green leaves, and branching, leafy stems that often become woody at base.

Border carnations are bushier and more compact than florists' type, 12–14 in. high. Flowers 2–2½ in. wide, fragrant, borne in profusion. Effective as shrub border edgings, in mixed flower border, and in containers. Hybrid carnations grown from seed are usually treated as annuals, but often live over. 'Juliet' makes compact, foot-tall clumps with long production of 2½-in. scarlet flowers; 'Luminette', 2 ft. tall, is similar. Pixie Delight strain also is similar but includes full range of carnation colors. Knight series has strong stems, blooms in 5 months from seed; Bambino strain is a little slower to bloom. There is also a strain called simply Hanging Mixed, with pink- or red-flowered plants that sprawl or hang from pot or window box.

Florists' carnations are grown commercially in greenhouses, outdoors in gardens in mild-winter areas. Greenhouse-grown plants reach 4 ft., have fragrant, 3-in.-wide flowers in many colors—white, shades of pink and red, orange, purple, yellow; some are variegated. For large flowers, leave only terminal bloom on each stem, pinching out all other buds down to fifth joint, below which new flowering stems will develop. Stake to prevent sprawling. Start with strong cuttings taken from the most vigorous plants of selected named varieties. Sturdy plants conceal supports, look quite tidy.

D. chinensis. CHINESE PINK, RAINBOW PINK. Biennial or short-lived perennial; most varieties grown as annuals. Erect, 6–30 in. high; stems branch only at top. Stem leaves narrow, 1–3 in. long, ½ in. wide, hairy on margins. Basal leaves usually gone by flowering time. Flowers about 1 in. across, rose lilac with deeper colored eye; lack fragrance. Modern strains are compact (to 1 ft. tall or less) domes covered with bright flowers in white, pink, red, and all variations and combinations of those colors. 'Fire Carpet' is a brilliant solid red; 'Snowfire', white with a red eye. Telstar is an extra-dwarf (6–8-in.) strain. Petals are deeply fringed on some, smooth edged on others. Some flowers have intricately marked eyes. Sow directly in ground in spring, in full sun, for summer bloom. Pick off faded flowers with their bases to prolong bloom.

> ## THE STRONGLY FRAGRANT KINDS OF DIANTHUS
> In addition to cheerful colors and striking patterns, most dianthus offer a strong, spicy, clovelike scent. Among those especially known for fragrance are *D. arenarius,* border carnations, *D. gratianopolitanus,* and *D. plumarius.*

D. deltoides. MAIDEN PINK. Hardy perennial (even though it blooms in just a few weeks from seed) forming loose mats. Flowering stems 8–12 in. high, with short leaves. Flowers, about ¾ in. across, with sharp-toothed petals, are borne at end of forked stems. Colors include light or dark rose to purple, spotted with lighter colors; and white. Can tolerate a half day of shade. Blooms in summer, sometimes again in fall. Useful, showy ground or bank cover.

Varieties include 'Albus', pure white; 'Vampire', deep red; 'Zing', bright scarlet; 'Zing Rose', rose red. Microchip is a mixture including pinks, reds, and white, often with contrasting eyes.

D. gratianopolitanus (D. caesius). CHEDDAR PINK. Perennial. Neat, compact mound of blue-gray to green-gray foliage on weak, branching stems to 1 ft. long. Flowering stems erect, 9–12 in. high, bearing very fragrant, typically pink to rose single blooms with toothed petals. Bloom season lasts from spring to fall if flowers are deadheaded. Effective for ground cover, edging, rock gardens. Perform well in hot, humid South.

'Bath's Pink'. An old variety rediscovered and renamed. Blue-green mat about 4 in. high topped by 12–15-in. stems bearing fringed single blossoms of soft pink with a red eye. Blooms profusely in spring, sporadically through summer.

'Little Boy Blue'. To 1 ft. high, 2½ ft. wide, with intensely blue-gray leaves and single white flowers dotted pink.

'Little Joe'. Forms a clump of deep blue-gray foliage 4–6 in. high and about 6 in. across. Crimson single flowers. Especially effective with rock garden campanulas.

'Rose Bowl'. Very narrow leaves form a tight mat 2–3 in. high. Cerise rose flowers 1 in. across, carried on 6-in. stems.

'Spotty'. Resembles 'Rose Bowl', but the pink flowers are heavily spotted with white.

'Tiny Rubies'. Makes a low mat of gray-green foliage to 3 in. high, spreading to 4 in. Small, double, ruby red flowers on 4-in. stems.

D. plumarius. COTTAGE PINK. Perennial. Charming, almost legendary plant, cultivated for hundreds of years, used in developing many hybrids. Typically has loosely matted gray-green foliage. Flowering stems 10–18 in. tall; flowers spicily fragrant, single or double, with petals more or less fringed, in rose, pink, or white with dark centers. Highly prized are old laced pinks, with spicy-scented white flowers in which each petal is outlined in red or pink. Blooms summer–fall if deadheaded. Indispensable edging for borders or for peony or rose beds. Perfect in small arrangements and old-fashioned bouquets.

'Dad's Favorite'. Centuries-old variety with double flowers on 10-in. stems. Blooms are white with ruby red edge and maroon center.

'Essex Witch'. Semidouble rose pink flowers on 5-in. stems.

'Musgrave's White'. Classic variety two centuries old. Intensely fragrant single flowers, white with a pale green eye, on 1-ft. stems.

Diapensiaceae. The diapensia family contains a few perennials and tiny shrubs native to northern parts of the globe. Some, such as *Galax urceolata* and *Shortia,* are useful in shady gardens or rock gardens.

DIASCIA barberae

TWINSPUR

Scrophulariaceae

ANNUAL

ALL ZONES

PARTIAL SHADE IN HOT-SUMMER AREAS

REGULAR TO MODERATE WATER

Diascia barberae

Summer-blooming South African native related to snapdragon and foxglove. Rich salmon to coral pink flowers, ¾ in. across, each with two curving, hornlike spurs on back of lower petals. Blossoms borne in spikelike clusters at ends of slender, 6–12-in.-tall stems. Toothed leaves are small, shiny, dark green.

Sow seed directly in ground after last frost. Also easy to grow from cuttings. After first flush of flowers, cut stems back to foliage mound to encourage more blossoms. Good plant for rock gardens, borders, pots.

DICENTRA

BLEEDING HEART

Fumariaceae

PERENNIALS

ZONES 1–9, 14–24, 31–45

PARTIAL OR FULL SHADE, EXCEPT AS NOTED

REGULAR WATER

Dicentra spectabilis

Graceful, divided, fernlike foliage. Dainty flowers, usually heart shaped, in pink, rose, or white on leafless stems.

Combine handsomely with ferns, begonias, primroses, fuchsias, bergenias, hellebores. In general, bleeding heart needs rich, light, moist, porous soil. Never let water stand around roots. Foliage dies down even in mild-winter climates; mark clumps to avoid digging into roots in dormant season. Short lived in mild-winter areas.

D. eximia. FRINGED BLEEDING HEART. Native to northeastern U.S. Forms tidy, nonspreading clumps 1–1½ ft. high. Blue-gray, finely divided leaves at base of plant. Deep rose pink flowers with short, rounded spurs bloom midspring into summer. Cut back for second growth and occasional repeat bloom. 'Alba' has white flowers. 'Bacchanal' is nearly everblooming during the growing season, with deep red blossoms. Pink-flowered 'Bountiful' ('Zestful') is an everbloomer tolerating considerable sun. White-blossomed 'Langtrees' and deep pink 'Luxuriant' are long blooming; the latter can endure drier soil and stronger light than most. 'Snowdrift' is a long-blooming white.

D. formosa. WESTERN BLEEDING HEART. Native to moist woods along Pacific coast. Blue-green foliage. Leafless flower stalks 8–18 in. high, with clusters of pendulous pale or deep rose flowers on reddish stems, spring. 'Sweetheart' has light green leaves and beautiful white flowers spring–fall. 'Tuolumne Rose' has large blue-green leaves and tall clusters of large rose pink blooms. *D. f. oregana,* about 8 in. high, has translucent blue-green leaves, cream-colored flowers with rosy-tipped petals.

D. spectabilis. COMMON BLEEDING HEART. Native to Japan. Old garden favorite; showiest and largest-leafed of all bleeding hearts. Plants grow 2–3 ft. high; stems are set with soft green leaves. In late spring, rose pink, pendulous, heart-shaped flowers, 1 in. long or longer, with protruding white petals, are borne on one side of arching stems. 'Alba' ('Pantaloons') is a lovely pure white form. Both are beautiful with maidenhair ferns and in arrangements with tulips and lilacs. Plants generally die down and become dormant by midsummer; keep going longer in cool-summer climates if given adequate moisture. Plant summer-maturing perennials nearby to fill the gap. Best in partial shade.

DICHONDRA micrantha

Convolvulaceae

PERENNIAL GROUND COVER

ZONES 8–10, 12–24, 28

FULL SUN OR PARTIAL SHADE

REGULAR WATER

Dichondra micrantha

Ground-hugging plant that spreads by rooting surface runners. Small, round leaves look like miniature water lily pads. In shade and with regular moisture and nutrients, it can grow to 6 in. tall. Generally needs frequent mowing, but in sun and in areas subject to foot traffic—between stepping-stones, for example—stays low and seldom, if ever, needs mowing. Subject to flea beetle damage in many areas. Often sold as *D. carolinensis* or *D. repens.*

DICHORISANDRA thyrsiflora

BLUE GINGER

Commelinaceae

PERENNIAL

ZONES 25–27; OR INDOORS

PARTIAL OR FULL SHADE

AMPLE WATER

Dichorisandra thyrsiflora

Not a true ginger but rather a robust, upright-growing relative of wandering Jew (*Tradescantia, Zebrina*). Fleshy single or sparsely branched stems to 6–8 ft. arise from a fleshy rhizome. Long (6–12-in.), oval, deep green leaves are spirally arranged around the stem. Flowers are deep violet blue, in 6-in. spikes at tops of stems in late summer and fall. Tender except in nearly tropical climates, but grown as a house plant anywhere. Will bloom at 3 ft. tall in an 8-in. pot with bright indoor light. Easy to propagate by cuttings. Provide rich soil.

DICKSONIA

Dicksoniaceae

TREE FERNS

⚡ ZONES VARY BY SPECIES

☀ ◐ ● SOME SHADE IN HOTTEST CLIMATES

💧 REGULAR WATER

Dicksonia antarctica

Hardy, slow growing, from Southern Hemisphere. Easy to transplant and establish. See Ferns for culture.

D. antarctica. TASMANIAN TREE FERN. Zones 8, 9, 14–17, 19–26. Native to southeastern Australia, Tasmania. Hardiest of tree ferns; well-established plants tolerate 20°F/–7°C. Thick, red-brown, fuzzy trunk grows slowly to 15 ft. From top of trunk grow many arching, 3–6-ft. fronds; mature fronds are more finely cut than those of Australian tree fern (*Cyathea*).

D. squarrosa. Zones 17, 23–27. Native to New Zealand. Slender, dark trunk grows slowly to 20 ft. tall. Flat crown of 8-ft.-long, stiff, leathery fronds. Much less frequently grown than *D. antarctica*.

Dicksoniaceae. The dicksonia family of tree ferns differs from the other tree fern family, Cyatheaceae, only in technical details. One representative is *Dicksonia*.

DICTAMNUS albus

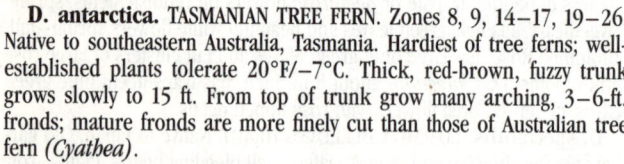

GAS PLANT, FRAXINELLA

Rutaceae

PERENNIAL

⚡ ZONES 1–9, 31–45

☀ ◐ FULL SUN OR PARTIAL SHADE

💧 REGULAR WATER

Dictamnus albus

Sturdy, long lived, extremely permanent in colder climates, needing little care once established. Forms clumps 2½–4 ft. high. In early summer, produces loose spires of blossoms at branch tips, each flower resembling a wild azalea with narrow petals and prominent, greenish stamens. Pink is the basic color, but nurseries offer lilac purple 'Purpureus' and white 'Albiflorus'. Seedpods that follow the blossoms can be left in place for fall interest. Attractive, glossy, olive green leaves with 9–11 leaflets, each 1–3 in. long, remain handsome throughout growing season. Plant emits strong lemony odor when rubbed or brushed against; however, the oils can cause allergic skin reactions in some people.

Effective in borders; combine with daylilies, Siberian iris, taller campanulas. Good cut flower. Divide infrequently; divisions are difficult to establish and often take 2 to 3 years before making a show. Propagate from seed (a slow process) sown in fall or spring, or from root cuttings in spring. Common name "gas plant" derives from this phenomenon: if a lighted match is held near flowers on warm, still evenings, volatile oil exuded from glands on that part of the plant will ignite and burn briefly.

DIDISCUS coeruleus. See TRACHYMENE coerulea

DIEFFENBACHIA

DUMB CANE

Araceae

PERENNIALS

⚡ ZONES 24–27; OR INDOORS

☀ ◐ ● SUN OR SHADE

💧 MODERATE WATER

⚠ SAP BURNS MOUTH, MAY PARALYZE VOCAL CORDS

Dieffenbachia amoena

Striking variegated evergreen foliage—colors varying from dark green to yellow green and chartreuse, with variegations in white or pale cream—is the main reason to grow dumb cane. In mildest-winter climates, plants will grow year-round outdoors, either in the ground as accents or in containers on the patio. Elsewhere, they're indoor foliage plants. Small plants generally have single stems, while older plants may develop multiple stems. Flowers resembling odd, narrow callas form on mature plants.

Outdoors, plants take sun or shade and moderate moisture. Indoors, provide ample northern light, water when soil surface feels dry, and turn pots occasionally. Give container plants well-drained potting soil, half-strength liquid fertilizer bimonthly in spring and summer. Underfed, underwatered plants show amazingly strong hold on life, recovering from severe wilting when better conditions come. Repotting is necessary when roots begin pushing plant up out of pot. Once repotted, plant usually sends out new basal shoots. Dumb cane will not withstand constant overwatering; sudden change from low to high light level will burn leaves. However, you can move plants into sheltered patio in summer. If plant gets leggy, air-layer it, or cut back and root the cuttings in water. If cut back to 6 in. above soil line, old, leggy plants will usually resprout with multiple stems.

D. amoena. To 6 ft. or more. Broad, dark green, 1½-ft.-long leaves with narrow, white, slanting stripes on either side of midrib.

D. bausei. To 3 ft. or more in height. Greenish yellow, 1-ft. leaves with deep green blotches and white flecks.

D. 'Exotica'. To 3–4 ft., with small leaves featuring dull green edges and much creamy white variegation. Midrib is creamy white.

D. maculata (D. picta). To 6 ft. or taller. Wide, oval green leaves, 10 in. or more in length, have greenish white dots and patches. 'Rudolph Roehrs' has leaves of pale chartreuse, blotched with ivory and edged with green. Foliage of 'Superba' is thicker and slightly more durable than that of species, with more creamy white dots and patches.

DIERAMA

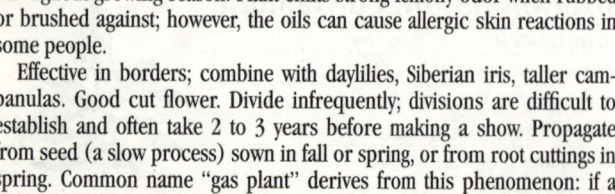

FAIRY WAND

Iridaceae

CORMS

⚡ ZONES 4–24

☀ FULL SUN

💧 REGULAR WATER

Dierama pulcherrimum

Native to South Africa. Evergreen; will die to the ground in extreme cold. Swordlike, 2-ft.-long leaves; slender, tough, arching stems 4–7 ft. tall, topped with pendulous flowers in purplish pink to pink and white. Blooms in spring in mildest climates, in summer in areas with colder winters. Effective against background of dark green shrubs or at end of pool where graceful form can be displayed. Divide only when necessary and include several corms in each division.

D. pendulum. Fits the general description above; has bell-shaped flowers.

D. pulcherrimum. As for *D. pendulum*, but flowers are more funnel shaped.

DIETES (Moraea)

FORTNIGHT LILY, AFRICAN IRIS

Iridaceae

PERENNIALS GROWING FROM RHIZOMES

🗡 ZONES 8, 9, 12–28

☼ ◑ FULL SUN OR PARTIAL SHADE

🌢🌢 BLOOM MORE FREELY WITH REGULAR WATER

Dietes vegeta

Fan-shaped clumps of narrow, stiff, irislike, evergreen leaves. Flowers like miniature Japanese iris appear on branched stalks throughout spring, summer, and fall, sometimes well into winter in mild areas. Each flower lasts only a day but is quickly replaced by another. Bloom bursts seem to come at 2-week intervals—hence the name "fortnight lily." Break off forming seedpods to increase flower production and prevent volunteer plants. Effective near swimming pools. Plant in any fairly good soil. Divide overgrown clumps in autumn or winter.

D. bicolor. To 2 ft. Flowers light yellow, about 2 in. wide, with maroon blotches. Cut flower stems to ground after all blossoms fade.

D. hybrids. 'Lemon Drops' and 'Orange Drops' are occasionally seen. These resemble *D. vegeta*, but flowers are creamy, with conspicuous yellow or orange blotches.

D. vegeta (*D. iridioides, Moraea iridioides*). To 4 ft., with 3-in.-wide, waxy white flowers with orange-and-brown blotch, purple stippling. 'Johnsonii' is robust variety with large leaves and flowers. Break off old blossoms individually to prevent self-sowing and prolong bloom, but don't cut off long, branching flower stems (these last from year to year). Instead, cut back to lower leaf joint near base of plant. Excellent in permanent landscape plantings with pebbles, rocks, substantial shrubs.

DIGITALIS

FOXGLOVE

Scrophulariaceae

PERENNIALS OR BIENNIALS

🗡 ZONES VARY BY SPECIES

◑ LIGHT SHADE

🌢 REGULAR WATER

🌢 ALL PARTS ARE POISONOUS IF INGESTED

Digitalis purpurea

Erect plants 2–8 ft. high, with basal rosette of hairy, gray-green leaves. Spires of tubular flowers shaped like fingers of glove in purple, yellow, white, pastels; bloom comes in spring and summer. After first flowering, cut main spike; side shoots will develop and bloom late in the season. In warmest climates, plants will usually die out in summer heat.

Provide rich soil. Sow seed in spring for bloom the following year. Set out plants in early spring in cold-winter areas, in fall in mild climates. Plants self-sow freely. Use for vertical display among shrubs or with ferns, taller campanulas, meadow rue. Hummingbirds like the flowers.

D. ferruginea. RUSTY FOXGLOVE. Biennial or perennial. Zones 1–24, 31–43. Very leafy stems to 6 ft. Leaves deeply veined. Flowers ¾–1¼ in. long, yellowish, netted with rusty red, in long, dense spikes.

D. grandiflora (*D. ambigua*). YELLOW FOXGLOVE. Biennial or perennial. Zones 1–24, 31–43. To 2–3 ft. high. Toothed leaves wrap around stem. Flowers are 2–3 in. long, yellowish marked with brown.

D. laevigata. Perennial. Zones 3–24, 31–34, 39. To 3 ft., with smooth, narrow dark green leaves and inch-long, creamy yellow flowers marked brownish purple.

D. lanata. GRECIAN FOXGLOVE. Perennial. Zones 2–24, 31–41. To 3 ft., with dark green leaves and narrow spikelike clusters of small flowers. Blossoms are cream colored, with purplish or brownish veining and a small near-white lip.

D. mertonensis. Perennial. Zones 1–24, 31–43. Spikes to 2–3 ft. high, bearing odd yet attractive coppery rose blooms. Though a hybrid between two species, it comes true from seed.

D. purpurea. COMMON FOXGLOVE. Biennial, sometimes perennial. Zones 2–24, 31–41. Naturalizes in shaded places. Variable, appears in many garden forms. Bold, erect, to 4 ft. high or more. Clumps of large, rough, woolly, light green leaves. Stem leaves have short stalks and become smaller toward top of plant; these leaves are source of digitalis, a valued but highly poisonous medicinal drug. Flowers 2–3 in. long, pendulous, purple, spotted on lower, paler side; borne in one-sided, 1–2-ft.-long spikes.

There are several garden strains. Excelsior, 5 ft., has fuller spikes than species, with flowers more horizontally held to show off interior spotting. Foxy, 3 ft., performs as an annual, blooming in 5 months from seed; Gloxiniiflora, 4 ft., has flowers that are individually larger and open wider than the species. Monstrosa, 3 ft., has an unusual trait: the topmost flower of each spike is open or bowl shaped and 3 in. wide. Shirley is a tall (6-ft.), robust strain in full range of colors. Volunteer foxglove seedlings are frequently white or light colors.

FOXGLOVES—SHOWY TOWERS

Flowers on spikes 3 ft. tall or more add charm and dimension to a garden. And foxgloves are perhaps the easiest of the towering flowering plants. An especially showy use for these plants is to fill a boxwood-edged flower bed with just one kind. Set the plants 1 ft. apart. Or mass them at the back of perennial borders.

DILL. See ANETHUM graveolens

DIMORPHOTHECA

AFRICAN DAISY, CAPE MARIGOLD

Asteraceae (Compositae)

ANNUALS

🗡 ALL ZONES; BETTER IN WARM-SUMMER CLIMATES

☼ FULL SUN

🌢 MODERATE WATER

Dimorphotheca sinuata

Gay, free-blooming plants with daisy flowers that close when shaded, during heavy overcast, and at night. Use in broad masses as ground cover, in borders and parking strips, along rural roadsides, as filler among low shrubs. Broadcast seed in early spring (late fall or early winter in mildest climates) where plants are to grow. Does best in light soil. For other plants known as African daisy, see *Arctotis* and *Osteospermum*.

D. aurantiaca. See D. sinuata

D. fruticosa. See Osteospermum fruticosum

D. pluvialis (*D. annua*). Branched stems to 16 in. high. Leaves to 3½ in. long, 1 in. wide, coarsely toothed. Flower heads 1–2 in. across; rays white above, violet or purple beneath; yellow center. 'Glistening White', dwarf form with flower heads 4 in. across, is especially desirable.

D. sinuata. Best known of annual African daisies; usually sold as *D. aurantiaca*. Plants 4–12 in. high. Leaves narrow, 2–3 in. long, with a few teeth or shallow indentations. Flower heads 1½ in. across, with orange-yellow rays, sometimes deep violet at base, and yellow center. Hybrids between this species and *D. pluvialis* come in white and shades of yellow, apricot, and salmon, often with contrasting dark centers.

PRACTICAL GARDENING DICTIONARY
PLEASE SEE PAGES 545–616

DIOON

Zamiaceae

CYCADS

ZONES VARY BY SPECIES

PARTIAL SHADE

REGULAR WATER

Dioon edule

Resemble *Cycas revoluta* and take same culture, but are less widely sold, more tender, and even slower growing. Male and female plants are separate.

D. edule. Zones 12, 13, 17, 19–27. Very slow. Eventually forms cylindrical trunk 6–10 in. wide, 3 ft. high. Leaves spreading, slightly arching, 3–5 ft. long, made of many leaflets toothed at tips or smooth edged. Leaves dusty blue green, soft, feathery on young plants; darker green, more rigid, hard, shiny on mature plants.

D. spinulosum. Zones 21–27. Slow growth to 12 ft. Leaves to 5 ft. long, with up to 100 narrow, spine-toothed, dark green, 6–8-in.-long leaflets. Protect from frosts.

DIOSPYROS. See PERSIMMON

DIPLADENIA amoena, D. splendens. See MANDEVILLA 'Alice du Pont'

DIPTERONIA sinensis

Aceraceae

DECIDUOUS SHRUB OR TREE

ZONES 4–6, 15–17, 20, 21, 31–34

PREFERS AFTERNOON SHADE

REGULAR WATER

Dipteronia sinensis

Unusual maple relative from central and western China; large shrub or tree to 30 ft. tall, 20 ft. wide. Leaves are in opposite pairs, as in maples, but are divided featherwise into 7–11 (rarely more) toothed, 3-in. leaflets. Leaves are coppery when they expand, maturing to bright green. Clusters of small greenish or whitish flowers are followed in autumn by large clusters of roundish winged fruits that turn from green to red.

DISANTHUS cercidifolius

Hamamelidaceae

DECIDUOUS SHRUB

ZONES 4–7, 14–17, 31–34

FULL SUN OR LIGHT SHADE

REGULAR WATER

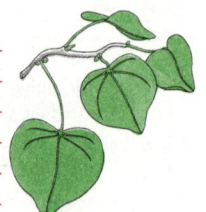

Disanthus cercidifolius

Native to Japan. This slender-branched shrub, to 10–12 ft. tall and broad spreading with age, is grown for its magnificent fall color. The nearly round, smooth, 2–4-in.-wide bluish green leaves turn shades of deep red and purple, often suffused with orange. Tiny, purplish fall flowers are mildly scented. Provide rich soil, light shade in hottest climates, and wind protection.

DISTICTIS

Bignoniaceae

EVERGREEN VINES

ZONES VARY BY SPECIES

FULL SUN OR PARTIAL SHADE

REGULAR WATER

Distictis buccinatoria

Spectacular vines for milder climates. Climb by tendrils and have trumpet-shaped flowers. To 20–30 ft. tall. Hardy to 24°F/−4°C.

D. buccinatoria (Bignonia cherere, Phaedranthus buccinatorius). BLOOD-RED TRUMPET VINE. Zones 8, 9, 14–28. Leaves have two oblong to oval leaflets 2–4 in. long. Clusters of 4-in.-long flowers stand out well from vine. Color is orange red fading to bluish red, with yellow throat. Flowers appear in bursts throughout year when weather warms. Effective on fence, high wall, arbor. Prune yearly to keep under control.

D. laxiflora (D. lactiflora, D. cinerea). VANILLA TRUMPET VINE. Zones 16, 22–27. Native to Mexico. More restrained than most trumpet vines and requires less pruning. Leaves, with two or three deep green, oblong, 2½-in.-long leaflets, make attractive pattern all year. The 3½-in., vanilla-scented trumpets, violet at first, fading to lavender and white, appear in generous clusters throughout warmer months, sometimes giving 8 months of bloom.

D. 'Rivers'. ROYAL TRUMPET VINE. Zones 16, 22–27. Plants sold under this name have larger leaves and flowers than other kinds and are much more vigorous. Substantial, glossy deep green leaves give them better winter appearance. Purple trumpets (to 5 in.) marked orange inside. Grows a little more slowly than *D. buccinatoria;* easier to keep neat. Sometimes labeled *D. riversii.*

Distictis 'Rivers'

DIZYGOTHECA elegantissima. See SCHEFFLERA elegantissima

DODECATHEON

SHOOTING STAR

Primulaceae

PERENNIALS

ZONES VARY BY SPECIES

EXPOSURE NEEDS VARY BY SPECIES

AMPLE WATER DURING GROWTH AND BLOOM

Dodecatheon bendersonii

Most of the shooting stars are native to the western U.S., but one grows successfully in the East. All are similar in form, with leaves forming a basal rosette and flowers carried in clusters on leafless stalks. Blossoms resemble small cyclamens, with swept-back petals and downward-thrusting stamens; color varies from white to pink, lavender, and magenta. All species die back completely at the onset of hot weather. All prefer rich, porous, well-drained soil.

D. hendersonii. Zones 3–11, 14–24, 32, 34. Typical western species has 6-in. leaves and white to magenta flowers on 1½-ft. stalks. Like other western species, seldom available at nurseries. Grow from seed from native plant specialists, or collect seed from wild plants native to your area. Give sun or partial shade.

D. meadia. Zones 1–6, 31–45. Native to the eastern U.S. Flower stalks to 1½ ft. bear many pink to white or purple flowers with prominent yellow stamens. Prefers part shade.

DODONAEA viscosa

HOP BUSH, HOPSEED BUSH

Sapindaceae

EVERGREEN SHRUB

ZONES 7–9, 12–27

FULL SUN OR LIGHT SHADE

REGULAR TO LITTLE WATER

Dodonaea viscosa

Tough shrub native to many mild-winter climates of the world. Tolerant of desert heat, ocean winds, poor soil. Rather billowy, to 15 ft. high and wide, with upright branching habit and narrow, willowlike, 4-in. leaves. With little water,

D

may remain under 10 ft.; with water and training, can be grown as small tree, though best used as informal hedge or accent group. Native Arizona green form is hardier and deeper rooted than purple-leaf forms. 'Purpurea', purple hop bush, has strongly bronze-tinted foliage that darkens in winter. 'Saratoga' has uniform rich purple leaves. Purple types need full sun to retain their color. Inconspicuous flowers followed in late summer by cream to pinkish winged seedpods.

DOGWOOD. See CORNUS

DOG-TOOTH VIOLET. See ERYTHRONIUM dens-canis

DOLICHOS lablab
(Lablab purpureus)

HYACINTH BEAN

Fabaceae (Leguminosae)

PERENNIAL VINE USUALLY GROWN AS ANNUAL

⚡ ALL ZONES

☼ FULL SUN

💧 REGULAR WATER

Dolichos lablab

T wining vine, with fast growth to 10 ft. Produces dense cover of purplish green leaves; each leaf divided fanwise into three broad, oval, 3–6-in.-long leaflets. Sweet pea–shaped purple or white flowers in loose, long-stemmed clusters stand out from foliage. Blossoms followed by showy edible pods in bright magenta purple; pods are velvety, beanlike, to 2½ in. long. Grow plants like string beans for quick screening. Needs good drainage.

DORONICUM

LEOPARD'S BANE

Asteraceae (Compositae)

PERENNIALS

⚡ ZONES 1–7, 14–17, 31–43

◑ PARTIAL SHADE

💧 REGULAR WATER

Doronicum cordatum

S ummer is the season for most yellow daisies, but this one bears its profusion of showy flowers in early to midspring. The 2–3-in. blooms on long, slender, branching stems rise from low, dense clumps of toothed, rounded to heart-shaped dark green leaves. Good cut flowers.

Most types die back by midsummer, so best used in a strictly spring-flowering scheme or where summer annuals can fill the gap. Combine with white, purple, or lavender tulips, blue violas or forget-me-nots; use in front of purple lilacs or with hellebores at edge of woodland or shade border. Mark location before plants die back; provide some moisture during dormancy. Divide clumps every 2 to 3 years; young plants bloom best. Tolerate full sun in cool-summer climates.

D. cordatum (D. caucasicum). Flower heads borne singly on 1–1½-ft. stems. 'Magnificum' and 'Finesse' a little taller, with bigger blossoms. Usually dies back in summer.

D. 'Mme Mason' ('Miss Mason'). Choice hybrid between *D. cordatum* and another species. Large, bright yellow daisies on 2½-ft. plant. Leaves are a little less toothed, flowers a little bigger than those of *D. cordatum;* plants also are less likely to die back in summer.

D. plantagineum. PLANTAIN LEOPARD'S BANE. Larger, coarser-leafed plant than the others, suitable for a wild garden. Each stout, 2½–3-ft.-tall

FOR INFORMATION ON SELECTING PLANTS
PLEASE SEE PAGES 79–160

---

stem bears a few 2–4-in.-wide flowers. 'Excelsum' ('Harpur Crewe') is taller than the species. Plants are dormant in summer.

DOROTHEANTHUS
bellidiformis

LIVINGSTONE DAISY

Aizoaceae

SUCCULENT ANNUAL

⚡ ALL ZONES

☼ FULL SUN

💧 TAKES CONSIDERABLE DROUGHT

Dorotheanthus bellidiformis

I ce plant, but unlike most others, an annual forming a pretty and useful temporary carpet. Trailing, a few inches high, with fleshy bright green leaves and daisylike, 2-in. flowers in white, pink, orange, red. Attracts bees. Sow seed in warm weather. Comes into bloom quickly. Tolerates poor, dry soil.

DOUGLAS FIR. See PSEUDOTSUGA menziesii

DOVE TREE. See DAVIDIA involucrata

DOXANTHA unguis-cati. See MACFADYENA unguis-cati

DRABA

Brassicaceae (Cruciferae)

PERENNIALS

⚡ ZONES 1–7, 32, 34, 36–43, EXCEPT AS NOTED

☼ FULL SUN

💧 REGULAR WATER

Draba aizoides

S ome 300 species native to mountainous or subarctic regions of the world. All are low, mat- or cushion-forming plants with tightly clustered, tiny leaves in rosettes and four-petaled yellow (rarely white) flowers in short, spikelike clusters. All require perfect drainage, dislike soggy soil. Can endure great cold. Use in rock gardens. These are just a few of the most commonly planted species:

D. aizoides. Native to mountains of southern Europe. Tufts of tiny rosettes make clumps 2–4 in. across. Flowering stems to 4 in. hold four to ten or more bright yellow flowers.

D. oligosperma. One of more than a dozen species native to the Rocky Mountain area. Makes silvery mats up to 1 ft. wide topped with yellow flowers.

D. sibirica (D. repens). Zones 1–7, 32, 34, 36–45. Native to Siberia, Greenland. Carpet-forming plant with trailing stems and a profusion of small yellow flowers in spring. Use in rock garden or between stepping-stones.

DRACAENA

Agavaceae

EVERGREEN, SMALL PALMLIKE TREES

⚡ ZONES VARY BY SPECIES; OR INDOORS

☼◑ FULL SUN OR PARTIAL SHADE

💧 MODERATE WATER

Dracaena draco

F oliage plants. Some show graceful fountain forms with broad, curved, ribbonlike leaves, occasionally striped with chartreuse or white. Some have very stiff, swordlike leaves. Outdoors, plant all but *D. draco* in a wind-protected site. Almost never flower as house plants. In containers, water only when top ½–1 in. of soil is dry. ▶

D

D. australis. See Cordyline australis

D. deremensis. Zones 24, 25, 27. Native to tropical Africa. Most commonly sold variety is 'Warneckii': erect, slow growing to an eventual 15 ft., with 2-ft.-long, 2-in.-wide leaves in rich green striped white and gray. 'Bausei' is green with white center stripe; 'Longii' has broader white center stripe; 'Janet Craig' has broad, dark green leaves. Compact versions of 'Janet Craig' and 'Warneckii' exist.

D. draco. DRAGON TREE. Zones 16, 17, 21–27. Native to Canary Islands. Stout trunk with upward-reaching or spreading branches topped by clusters of heavy, 2-ft.-long, sword-shaped leaves. Grows slowly to 20 ft. high and as wide. Makes odd but interesting silhouette. Clusters of greenish white flowers form at branch ends. After blossoms drop, stemmy clusters remain. Trim them off to keep plants neat.

D. fragrans. CORN PLANT. Zones 21, 23–25, 27. Native to West Africa. Upright, eventually to 20 ft. high, but slow growing. Heavy, ribbonlike, blue-green leaves to 3 ft. long, 4 in. wide. (Typical plant in 8-in. pot will bear leaves about 1½ ft. long.) 'Massangeana' has broad yellow stripe in center of each leaf. Other varieties with striped foliage are 'Lindenii' and 'Victoriae'.

D. marginata. Zones 21, 23–25, 27. Very easy to grow, very popular. Slender, erect, smooth gray stems to an eventual 12 ft. carry chevron markings where old leaves have fallen. Stems topped by crowns of narrow, leathery leaves to 2 ft. long, ½ in. wide. Leaves are deep glossy green with narrow margin of purplish red. If plant grows too tall, cut off crown and reroot it. New crowns will appear on old stem. 'Tricolor' ('Candy Cane') adds a narrow gold stripe to the green and red of the species.

Dracaena marginata

D. sanderana. Zones 21, 23–25, 27. Native to West Africa. Neat and upright, to a possible 6–10 ft., somewhat resembling young corn plant. Strap-shaped, 9-in.-long leaves striped with white.

DRAGON TREE. See DRACAENA draco

DROPWORT. See FILIPENDULA vulgaris

DROSANTHEMUM

Aizoaceae

SUCCULENT PERENNIALS

ZONES 14–27

FULL SUN

TAKE CONSIDERABLE DROUGHT

Drosanthemum floribundum

The two ice plants described here are often confused with each other, although they are quite different. In both, leaves are covered by glistening dots that look like tiny ice crystals. And both have typical ice plant flowers with many narrow petals, bloom in late spring and early summer, and endure poor soil.

D. floribundum. ROSEA ICE PLANT. Grows to 6 in. tall, but stems trail to considerable length or drape over rocks, walls. Best ice plant for reducing erosion on steep slopes. Pale pink, ¾-in. flowers make sheets of color; attract bees. Often sold as *D. hispidum*.

D. hispidum. To 2 ft. tall, 3 ft. wide, less inclined to stem-root than is *D. floribundum*. Showy, 1-in. purple flowers.

DRUMSTICKS. See ALLIUM sphaerocephalum

FOR INFORMATION ON YOUR CLIMATE ZONE
PLEASE SEE PAGES 16–78

DRYAS

Rosaceae

PERENNIALS

ZONES 1–6, 36–45

FULL SUN

MODERATE WATER

Dryas octopetala

Choice plants for rock gardens. Evergreen or partially so; somewhat shrubby at base, forming carpet of leafy creeping stems. Shiny white or yellow strawberrylike flowers, late spring–summer. Ornamental seed capsules with silvery white tails.

D. drummondii. To 4 in. high. Leaves oblong, 1½ in. long, white and woolly beneath. Flowers nodding, bright yellow, ¾ in. across.

D. octopetala. Mats to 2–3 ft. high. Leaves 1 in. long. Flowers white, 1½ in. across, erect.

D. suendermannii. Hybrid between the two species above. Leaves oblong, 1–1½ in. long, thick textured. Flowers yellowish in bud, white in full bloom, nodding.

DRYOPTERIS

WOOD FERN, SHIELD FERN, MALE FERN

Polypodiaceae

FERNS

ZONES VARY BY SPECIES

PARTIAL OR FULL SHADE

REGULAR WATER

Dryopteris dilatata

The wood or shield ferns number over 100 species and are found over most of the world, but only a few are generally offered by nurseries. Use them in shade or woodland gardens, where their fronds contrast with the coarser foliage of other perennials, especially such large-leafed plants as hosta and rodgersia. They prefer rich soil with adequate organic material and moisture.

D. affinis. SCALY MALE FERN. Semievergreen. Zones 4–9, 14–24, 31–34. Native to Europe and southwestern Asia. Grows to 5 ft. high. Finely cut fronds are chartreuse green with light brown scales when they unfold, dark green later.

D. carthusiana. (**D. spinulosa**). SPINULOSE WOOD FERN, TOOTHED WOOD FERN, SHIELD FERN. Evergreen, except in harsh winters. Zones 1–6, 34–43. Native to Europe, Asia, and North America. Coarsely cut yellowish green fronds grow 6–18 in. tall and have shaggy black scales on frond stem and lower part of midrib.

D. dilatata. BROAD BUCKLER FERN. Evergreen. Zones 1–6, 32, 34, 36–43. Native to many areas in Northern and Southern Hemispheres. Grows 1–2 ft. tall, possibly much more, with finely cut, widely spreading fronds.

D. erythrosora. AUTUMN FERN. Evergreen. Zones 4–9, 14–28, 31, 32. Native to China and Japan. Erect growth to 2 ft. One of the few ferns with seasonal color variation. Expanding fronds in spring are a blend of copper, pink, and yellow; they turn green in summer, then rusty brown in fall. Bright red spore cases, produced on leaf undersides in fall, are an attractive winter feature.

D. filix-mas. MALE FERN. Evergreen, sometimes becoming deciduous. Zones 1–9, 14–17, 31–45. Native to much of the Northern Hemisphere. Grows 2–5 ft. tall, with finely cut fronds to 1 ft. wide. 'Linearis Polydactyla' has narrow leaf divisions with spreading, fingerlike tips.

D. goldiana. GOLDIE'S WOOD FERN, GIANT WOOD FERN. Evergreen in milder climates, deciduous where winters are cold. Zones 2–6, 32–41. Robust grower to 4 ft., with arching fronds to 1½ ft. wide.

D. marginalis. MARGINAL SHIELD FERN, LEATHER WOOD FERN. Evergreen. Zones 2–6, 32–41. Grows 2–4 ft. tall. Finely cut, dark blue-green fronds.

D. wallichiana. WALLICH'S WOOD FERN. Evergreen. Zones 4–6, 15–17, 31–34. Native to India, China. Stately fern to 3 ft. (possibly 5 ft.) high. Finely cut fronds emerge bright golden green on scaly brown stems, later turn dark green.

DUCHESNEA indica

INDIAN MOCK STRAWBERRY
Rosaceae
PERENNIAL GROUND COVER
⚡ ZONES 1–24, 29–43
☼ ◑ ● SUN OR SHADE
◐ MODERATE WATER

Duchesnea indica

Grows like strawberry, with trailing stems that root firmly along ground. Bright green, long-stalked, evergreen to semievergreen leaves with three leaflets. Yellow, ½-in. flowers are followed by red, ½-in., insipid-tasting fruit that stands above foliage rather than under leaves as in true strawberry. Grows readily without much care. Best used as ground cover among open shrubs or small trees. Plant 1–1½ ft. apart. In well-watered garden, can become rampant invader. Attracts birds.

DUMB CANE. See DIEFFENBACHIA

DURANTA

Verbenaceae
EVERGREEN SHRUBS
⚡ ZONES VARY BY SPECIES
☼ FULL SUN
◐ REGULAR WATER
◐ BERRIES OF D. REPENS ARE POISONOUS IF INGESTED

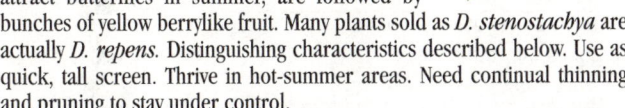

Duranta repens

Glossy green leaves arranged in pairs or whorls along stem. Attractive blue flowers in clusters attract butterflies in summer, are followed by bunches of yellow berrylike fruit. Many plants sold as *D. stenostachya* are actually *D. repens.* Distinguishing characteristics described below. Use as quick, tall screen. Thrive in hot-summer areas. Need continual thinning and pruning to stay under control.

D. repens (D. erecta, D. plumieri). SKY FLOWER, GOLDEN DEW-DROP, PIGEON BERRY. Zones 13, 16, 17, 21–27. Native to southern Florida, West Indies, Mexico to Brazil. Fast growing to 10–25 ft. Tends to form multistemmed clumps; branches often drooping and vinelike. Stems may or may not have sharp spines. Oval to roundish leaves are 1–2 in. long, rounded or pointed at tip. Tubular, violet blue flowers flare to less than ½ in. wide. Fruit clusters 1–6 in. long. 'Alba' has white flowers.

D. stenostachya. BRAZILIAN SKY FLOWER. Zones 13, 16, 21–23, 25, 27. Not as hardy as *D. repens;* seems to require more heat and is not at its best in coolest-summer areas. Makes neater, more compact shrub than *D. repens,* usually growing to about 4–6 ft. (under ideal conditions, 15 ft.). Stems are spineless. Leaves are larger (3–8 in. long) than those of *D. repens* and taper to long, slender point. Lavender blue flowers are also somewhat larger; fruit clusters grow to 1 ft. long.

DUSTY MILLER. This name is given to a number of plants with gray foliage. The dusty miller of one region may be unknown in another. Among the many dusty millers are *Artemisia stellerana, Centaurea cineraria, C. gymnocarpa, Chrysanthemum ptarmiciflorum, Lychnis coronaria, Senecio cineraria,* and *S. vira-vira.*

DUTCHMAN'S PIPE. See ARISTOLOCHIA durior

DYSSODIA tenuiloba (Thymophylla tenuiloba)

DAHLBERG DAISY, GOLDEN FLEECE
Asteraceae (Compositae)
ANNUAL; MAY LIVE OVER AS PERENNIAL
⚡ BEST IN ZONES 8–14, 18–20, 26, 30
☼ FULL SUN
◐ MODERATE WATER

Dyssodia tenuiloba

Southwest native. To 1 ft. high. Divided, threadlike leaves make dark green background for yellow flower heads, which look much like miniature golden marguerites. Use for massed display or pockets of color. Start in flats or plant in place, preferably in sandy soil. Blooms early summer to fall, to early winter in warm climates. In mildest regions, can be planted in fall for winter–spring bloom. Pull out plants that get ragged with age.

EASTER CACTUS. See RHIPSALIDOPSIS gaertneri

EASTER LILY CACTUS. See ECHINOPSIS

EASTER LILY VINE. See BEAUMONTIA grandiflora

ECHEVERIA

Crassulaceae
SUCCULENTS
⚡ ZONES VARY BY SPECIES
☼ ◑ FULL SUN OR PARTIAL SHADE
◐ MODERATE WATER, EXCEPT AS NOTED

Echeveria imbricata

All form rosettes of fleshy green or gray-green leaves, often marked or overlaid with deeper colors. Bell-shaped, nodding flowers, usually pink, red, or yellow, on long, slender, sometimes branched clusters. Good in rock gardens. Some make good house plants.

E. crenulata. Zones 17, 21–24; or house plant. Loose rosettes on short, thick stems. Pale green or white-powdered leaves to 1 ft. long and 6 in. wide, with wavy, crimped, purplish red edges. Flower clusters to 3 ft. high, with a few yellow-and-red flowers. Striking plant. Shelter from hottest sun; water frequently during warm weather.

E. elegans. HEN AND CHICKS. Zones 8, 9, 12–24. Tight, grayish white rosettes to 4 in. across, spreading freely by offsets. Flowers pink, lined yellow, in clusters to 8 in. long. Common, useful for pattern planting, edging, containers. Can burn in hot sun.

E. hybrids. Zones 8, 9, 12–24; or house plants. Generally have large, loose rosettes of big leaves on single or branched stems. Leaves are crimped, waved, wattled, or heavily shaded with red, bronze, or purple. All are splendid pot plants; they do well in open ground in mild-summer climates. Among them are 'Arlie Wright', with large, open rosettes of wavy-edged, pinkish leaves; 'Cameo', with large blue-gray leaves, each centered with a large raised lump of the same color; and 'Perle von Nürnberg', with pearly lavender blue foliage. Smaller, with short, close-set leaves, is 'Doris Taylor'; its leaves are densely covered with short hairs. Showy, nodding flowers are red and yellow.

E. imbricata. HEN AND CHICKS. Zones 8, 9, 12–24. Rosettes 4–6 in. across, saucer shaped, gray green. Loose clusters of small, bell-shaped, orange-red flowers. Makes offsets very freely.

E. secunda. HEN AND CHICKS. Zones 8, 9, 14–24. Gray- or blue-green rosettes, to 4 in. across. Makes offsets freely. *E. s. glauca (E. glauca),* its leaves faintly edged purple red, forms purplish blue-green rosettes.

E. setosa. Zones 17, 23, 24. Dense rosettes to 4 in. across are dark green, densely covered with white, stiff hairs. Flowers red, tipped with yellow. Good choice for rock gardens, shallow containers. Very tender.

E

ECHINACEA purpurea (Rudbeckia purpurea)

PURPLE CONEFLOWER

Asteraceae (Compositae)

PERENNIAL

ZONES 1−24, 26−45

FULL SUN

MODERATE WATER

Echinacea purpurea

Native to east-central U.S. Coarse, stiff plant, forming large clumps of erect stems 4−5 ft. tall. Bristly, oblong leaves are 3−8 in. long. Blooms over long period in mid- to late summer, bearing very showy flower heads with drooping, rosy purple rays and a beehivelike, orange-brown central cone. Flowering may continue sporadically until frost. If left in place, bristly seed heads hang on into winter; seeds are favored by finches.

'Bright Star' has 3−4-in. rosy pink rays. 'Magnus', 3 ft. tall, has horizontally spreading rays and a low, dark center cone; 'WFF Strain' is similar in appearance. 'White Swan' and 'White Lustre' have white rays around an orange-yellow cone.

Use on outskirts of garden or in wide borders with other robust perennials such as Shasta daisies, sunflowers, Michaelmas daisies. Generally does not need staking. Performs well in summer heat. Good cut flower. Deadheading prolongs bloom. Can self-sow. Divide crowded clumps (usually after about 4 years) in spring or fall.

ECHINOCEREUS

HEDGEHOG CACTUS

Cactaceae

CACTI

ZONES VARY BY SPECIES

FULL SUN

TAKE MUCH ARIDITY WHEN ESTABLISHED

Echinocereus engelmannii

Nearly 50 species of hedgehog cactus grow in the southwestern U.S. and northern Mexico, with some growing at fairly high elevations in Utah and Colorado, where they are subject to freezing temperatures. All have cylindrical, ribbed bodies in clumps; showy red, yellow, purple, or white flowers with many rows of petals; and fleshy fruit, edible in some species. Although hardy to cold in most zones, and often seen in collections, they are used in landscaping chiefly in desert or in Rocky Mountain or high plains gardens.

E. engelmannii. Zones 2, 3, 7, 10−24. Clumps grow to 3 ft. wide, 2 ft. tall. Flowers are 2−3 in. wide, lavender to deep purplish red. Inch-long red fruits are edible.

E. triglochidiatus. CLARET CUP. Zones 2, 3, 10, 11, 14, 18−23. Dense mounds, sometimes with hundreds of stems to 16 in. tall, each stem to 5 in. thick. Flowers are 3½ in. wide, orange to red; inch-long fruit pink to red.

ECHINOPS

GLOBE THISTLE

Asteraceae (Compositae)

PERENNIAL

ZONES 1−24, 31−45

FULL SUN

REGULAR TO MODERATE WATER

Echinops

Well-behaved, decorative thistles relatives for the perennial border. Rugged-looking, erect, rigidly branched plants 2−4 ft. tall with coarse, prickly, deeply cut gray-green leaves to 1 ft. long.

Distinctive flower heads are spherical, like golf ball−size pincushions stuck full of tubular metallic blue pins. Bloom midsummer to late fall.

Plants may be offered as *E. exaltatus, E. humilis, E. ritro,* or possibly *E. sphaerocephalus.* Whatever name you encounter, you're likely to get a plant closely resembling the general description above. 'Taplow Blue' is a select form 4 ft. tall. 'Veitch's Blue' has smaller, more numerous flower clusters on a somewhat shorter plant.

Grow from divisions in spring or fall, or sow seed in flats or open ground in spring. Combine with Michaelmas daisies, phlox, yellow and orange rudbeckias, sneezeweed. Given good, well-drained soil and plenty of moisture, plants may grow so vigorously that they need staking. Established plants tolerate dry periods. Flowers are excellent for dried arrangements, but they must be cut before they open, then dried upside down. Many types will rebloom if cut to the ground immediately after the flowers fade. Clumps can be left in place, undivided, for many years.

ECHINOPSIS

EASTER LILY CACTUS, SEA URCHIN CACTUS

Cactaceae

CACTI

ZONES 16, 17, 21−27; OR INDOORS

FULL SUN; INDOORS IN SUNNY WINDOW

REGULAR WATER SPRING THROUGH FALL

Echinopsis

Small (6−10-in.-high), cylindrical or globular cacti from South America, generally grown in pots. Big, long-tubed, many-petaled flowers in shades of white, yellow, pink, and red can reach 6−8 in. long. Free blooming in summer if given good light, frequent feeding, fast-draining soil. Many kinds, all showy and easy to grow. Give little or no water in winter.

E. chamaecereus. See Chamaecereus silvestri

E. eyriesii. Cylindrical plant 6−12 in. tall, with dark spines and large (8−10-in.-long, 2−4-in.-wide) white flowers. Eventually forms clumps.

E. hamatacantha. Spherical plant to 4 in. tall, with 3-in. red to yellow flowers.

ECHIUM

Boraginaceae

BIENNIAL OR SHRUBBY PERENNIAL

ZONES VARY BY SPECIES

FULL SUN

MODERATE TO LITTLE WATER

E. VULGARE IS POISONOUS IF INGESTED

Echium vulgare

Diverse plants with clusters of blue, purple, pink, or white clustered flowers. Do well in dry, poor soil but need good drainage. Where adapted, will self-sow freely. Good in seacoast gardens. Attract bees.

E. fastuosum (E. candicans). PRIDE OF MADEIRA. Shrubby perennial. Zones 14−24. Large, picturesque plant with many coarse, heavy branches 3−6 ft. high. Hairy, gray-green, narrow leaves form roundish, irregular mounds at stem ends. Blooms in spring, bearing little bluish purple flowers in large, spikelike, 1−2 -ft.-long clusters that stand out dramatically well above foliage. Developing spikes may be killed by late frosts.

E. vulgare. BLUEWEED, VIPER'S BUGLOSS. Biennial grown as an annual. All zones. Bushy plant to 1−3 ft. high. Lance-shaped dark green leaves are covered with stiff white bristles. Clusters of blue, white, or pink flowers in summer. Blooms first year from seed; sow in place in late winter or earliest spring (fall in mild climates). Can become a pest if seedlings are not removed; has naturalized in eastern North America.

EDELWEISS. See LEONTOPODIUM alpinum

EGGPLANT

Solanaceae

ANNUAL

ALL ZONES

FULL SUN

KEEP SOIL EVENLY MOIST

Eggplant 'Black Beauty'

F ew vegetable plants are handsomer than egg-plant. Bushes resemble little trees, 2–3 ft. high and equally wide. Big leaves (usually lobed) are purple tinged; drooping violet flowers are 1½ in. across. And, of course, big purple fruit is spectacular. Plants are effective in large containers or raised beds; a well-spaced row of them makes distinguished border between vegetable and flower garden. Most people plant large roundish or oval varieties such as 'Black Beauty', 'Burpee Hybrid', or 'Early Beauty'; the Japanese, who like their eggplant small and very tender, prefer long, slender variety usually sold as 'Japanese'. Specialists in imported vegetable seeds offer numerous colored varieties, including the full-size 'White Beauty' and a host of smaller varieties in a range of sizes (down to ½ in.) and colors, including white as well as yellow, red, green. Some of the smaller ones genuinely resemble eggs. All are edible as well as attractive.

Can be grown from seed (sow indoors 8 to 10 weeks before date of last expected frost), but starting from nursery-grown plants is much easier. Eggplant needs 2 to 3 months of warm days and nights (minimum night temperatures of 65°F/18°C) to produce a crop. Set plants out in sun in spring when frosts are over and soil is warm. Space 3 ft. apart in loose, fertile soil. Feed once every 6 weeks with commercial fertilizer. Keep weeds out. Prevent too much fruit setting by pinching out some terminal growth and some blossoms; three to six large fruits per plant will result. A second crop for late summer–fall harvest can be grown in southernmost climates.

If you enjoy tiny whole eggplants, allow plants to produce freely. Harvest fruits after they develop some color but never wait until they lose their glossy shine. Flea beetles are often a problem on young plants; grow under row covers until plants are big enough to tolerate leaf damage. Control aphids and whiteflies. For ornamental relatives, see *Solanum*.

EGLANTINE. See ROSA eglanteria

EICHHORNIA crassipes

WATER HYACINTH

Pontederiaceae

AQUATIC PLANT

ZONES 8, 9, 13–28; GROW AS ANNUAL IN COLDER CLIMATES

FULL SUN

LOCATE IN PONDS OR POOLS

Eichhornia crassipes

N ative to tropical America. Floating leaves and feathery roots. Leaves ½–5 in. wide, nearly circular in shape; leaf stems inflated. Showy flowers, carried many to a spike, are lilac blue, about 2 in. long; upper petals have a yellow spot in center. Needs warmth to flower profusely. Can become a pest where it is perennial; do not turn it loose in natural or large bodies of water. Prohibited in many mild-winter areas; check locally.

Elaeagnaceae. This family contains trees and shrubs with a coating of tiny silvery or brown scales on leaves (and sometimes on flowers) and with small, tart-tasting, single-seeded fruits. Flowers are not showy but can be fragrant. Most are tough plants from arid or semiarid climates.

ELAEAGNUS

Elaeagnaceae

DECIDUOUS, EVERGREEN SHRUBS OR SMALL TREES

ZONES VARY BY SPECIES

FULL SUN OR PARTIAL SHADE

REGULAR TO LITTLE WATER

Elaeagnus pungens

A ll are splendid screen plants. All grow fast when young, becoming dense, full, firm, and tough—and they do it with little upkeep. All tolerate seashore conditions, heat, and wind. Established plants will take considerable drought.

Foliage is distinguished in evergreen forms by silvery (sometimes brown) dots that cover leaves, reflecting sunlight to give plants a special sparkle. Deciduous kinds have silvery gray leaves. Small, insignificant, but usually fragrant flowers are followed by decorative fruit, typically red with silvery flecks. Evergreen kinds bloom in fall; in addition to their prime role as screen plants, they are useful as natural espaliers, clipped hedges, or high bank covers.

E. angustifolia. RUSSIAN OLIVE. Small deciduous tree. Zones 1–3, 7–14, 18, 19, 28, 30, 33, 35, 41, 43, 45. To 20 ft. high, but can be clipped as medium-height hedge. Angular trunk and branches (sometimes thorny) are covered by shredding dark brown bark that is picturesque in winter. Bark contrasts with narrow, willowlike, 2-in.-long silvery gray leaves. Very fragrant, small greenish yellow flowers in early summer are followed by berrylike fruit resembling miniature olives. Can take almost any kind of punishment, including hot summers, bitterly cold winters, drought, poor soil. Doesn't do as well in mild winters or either cool or very humid summers. Good background plant, barrier.

E. commutata. SILVERBERRY. Deciduous shrub. Zones 1–3, 35, 41, 43, 45. Native to Canada, northern plains, and Rocky Mountains. Upright to 12 ft., with open form and slender, spineless, red-brown branches that become coated with silvery scales. Oval leaves silvery gray on both surfaces. Tiny fragrant flowers in spring followed in early fall by dry, mealy, ⅓-in.-long oval fruits, also silver coated and a favorite of birds. Plant spreads by suckers to form colonies.

E. 'Coral Silver'. Zones 2–24, 28–41. Large shrub, evergreen in Zones 19–24, deciduous or partially deciduous elsewhere. Has unusually bright gray foliage, coral red berries in fall.

E. ebbingei (E. macrophylla 'Ebbingei'). Evergreen shrub. Zones 4–24, 26–33. Hybrid derived from *E. pungens*. More upright (to 10–12 ft.) than its parent, with thornless branches. Leaves 2–4 in. long, silvery on both sides when young, are later dark green above and silvery beneath. Tiny, fragrant, silvery flowers. Red fruit makes good jelly. 'Gilt Edge' has striking yellow margins on its leaves.

E. multiflora. Deciduous shrub. Zones 2–24, 28–41. To 6 ft.; leaves silvery green above, silvery and brown below. Small, fragrant spring flowers followed by attractive, ½-in.-long, bright orange-red berries on 1-in. stalks. Fruit is edible but tart, much loved by birds.

E. philippensis. LINGARO. Evergreen shrub or vine. Zones 25–27. Resembles *E. pungens*, but with longer arching branches 9–15 ft. long. Can be trained as a climber. Narrow, 2-in.-long leaves are silvery beneath. Exceptionally fragrant, ⅜-in. yellow flowers are followed by ¾-in. pink fruits that can be made into jelly.

E. pungens. SILVERBERRY. Large evergreen shrub. Zones 4–24, 26–33. Has rather rigid, sprawling, angular habit of growth to height of 6–15 ft.; can be kept lower and denser by pruning. Even tolerates shearing into hedge. Grayish green, 1–3-in.-long leaves have wavy edges and brown tinting from rusty dots. Branches are spiny, also covered with rusty dots. Overall color of shrub is olive drab. Oval fruit, ½ in. long, red with silver dust. Tough container plant in reflected heat, wind. Variegated forms listed below are more widespread than the species and have a brighter, lighter look in the landscape; they are less hardy than the species, however, and may suffer cold damage in Zone 32. Be sure to cut out growth that reverts to green. Effective barrier plantings: growth is dense and twiggy, and spininess is a help, yet plants are not aggressively spiny.

E

'Fruitlandii'. Leaves large, silvery.

'Maculata'. GOLDEN ELAEAGNUS. Leaves have gold blotch in center.

'Marginata'. SILVER-EDGE ELAEAGNUS. Silvery white leaf margins.

'Variegata'. YELLOW-EDGE ELAEAGNUS. Yellowish white leaf margins.

ELDERBERRY. See SAMBUCUS

ELECAMPANE. See INULA

ELEPHANT'S EAR. See ALOCASIA, COLOCASIA esculenta

ELEPHANT'S FOOD. See PORTULACARIA afra

ELM. See ULMUS

EMPRESS TREE. See PAULOWNIA tomentosa

ENDIVE

Asteraceae (Compositae)

BIENNIAL OR ANNUAL

⚡ ALL ZONES

☼ FULL SUN

💧 REGULAR WATER

Endive

Botanically known as *Cichorium endivia*. This species includes curly endive and broad-leaf endive (escarole). Forms rosette of leaves. Tolerates more heat than lettuce, grows faster in cold weather. Matures in 90 to 95 days. In cold-winter areas, sow seed June–August; in mild-winter climates, sow so that plants mature after summer heat. Space plants 10–12 in. apart in rows 15–18 in. apart. When plants have reached full size, pull outer leaves over center and tie them up; center leaves will blanch to yellow or white. 'Green Curled' is standard curly endive; 'Broad-leaved Batavian' is a good broad-leaf kind. Belgian or French endives are the blanched sprouts from roots of a kind of chicory. Roots are dug after a summer's growth, then stored in the dark to sprout. See Chicory.

ENDYMION
(Scilla, Hyacinthoides)

ENGLISH AND SPANISH BLUEBELLS, WOOD HYACINTH

Liliaceae

BULBS

⚡ ZONES VARY BY SPECIES

☼ ◑ FULL SUN OR PARTIAL SHADE

💧 REGULAR WATER DURING GROWTH AND BLOOM

Endymion non-scriptus

These spring bloomers are still popularly known as *Scilla* (and sold by most dealers as such), but the current botanical name is *Hyacinthoides*. They resemble hyacinths but are taller, with looser flower clusters and fewer, narrower leaves.

Climate may determine which of the following two species is better for you. Spanish bluebell is the better choice in warmer regions; the English species prefers definite winter cold and moderate to cool summers. When grown near each other, they often hybridize, producing intermediate forms. Plant in fall—3 in. deep in mild climates, to 6 in. deep where winters are severe. Propensity for reseeding makes these plants good choices for naturalizing. Plant informal drifts among tall shrubs, under deciduous trees, among low-growing perennials. Clumps can be divided in autumn. The plants also thrive in pots and are good for cutting.

E. hispanicus (Scilla campanulata, S. hispanica). SPANISH BLUE-BELL. Zones 1–11, 14–24, 28–43. Prolific, vigorous, with sturdy, 20-in. stems bearing 12 or more nodding bells about ¾ in. long. Blue is the most popular color, 'Excelsior' (deep blue) the most popular variety. There are also white, pink, and rose forms. The inch-wide, straplike leaves can look a little ratty before they die back.

E. non-scriptus (Scilla nonscripta). ENGLISH BLUEBELL, WOOD HYACINTH. Zones 3–6, 31–35, 37, 39–41. Fragrant flowers are narrower and smaller than those of Spanish bluebell, on 1-ft. stems that arch at the tip. Strap-shaped leaves are also narrower—only about ½ in. wide. 'Alba' is white flowered, 'Rosea' pink.

NATURALIZING A BLUEBELL PLANTING

Broadcast a handful of bulbs over an area and plant them where they fall. For a realistic effect, rearrange the bulbs before planting so they are closest together at one end of a group or toward the center—as though the colony originated at one spot and gradually increased outward. Mostly space bulbs about 6 in. apart.

ENGLISH DAISY. See BELLIS perennis

ENGLISH LAUREL. See PRUNUS laurocerasus

ENKIANTHUS campanulatus

REDVEIN ENKIANTHUS

Ericaceae

DECIDUOUS SHRUB

⚡ ZONES 2–9, 14–21, 31–41

☼ ◑ FULL SUN OR PARTIAL SHADE

💧 💧 AMPLE WATER

Enkianthus campanulatus

Native to Japan. Slow-growing, handsome shrub typically grows 6–8 ft. tall in cold-winter regions, but in milder climates, it may reach 20 ft. in 20 years. Stems are upright, with tiers of nearly horizontal branches; habit is narrow in youth, broad in age, but always attractive. Bluish green leaves, 1½–3 in. long and whorled or crowded at branch ends, turn brilliant yellow to orange and red in autumn. Since color varies, choose plants in fall during color change. Blooms in spring (at approximately the time leaves are developing), producing pendulous clusters of yellow-green, red-veined, ½-in.-long bell-shaped blossoms. *E. c. palibinii* has deep red blooms, 'Albiflorus' creamy white ones. Flowers of 'Red Bells' are rosier at the tips than those of the species.

Like rhododendrons, requires moist, well-drained, acid soil to which plenty of organic matter such as peat moss or ground bark has been added. Produces flowers on previous year's growth, so prune only to remove dead or broken branches. Plant in a location where silhouette and fall color can be enjoyed close-up.

ENSETE ventricosum
(Musa ensete)

ABYSSINIAN BANANA

Musaceae

LARGE, PALMLIKE PERENNIAL

⚡ ZONES 13, 15–27; OR INDOORS/OUTDOORS

☼ ◑ FULL SUN OR PARTIAL SHADE

💧 WATER FREQUENTLY TO SPEED GROWTH

Ensete ventricosum

Lush, tropical-looking, dark green leaves 10–20 ft. long, 2–4 ft. wide, with stout midribs, grow out in arching form from single vertical stem, 6–20 ft. high. Fast growing. Leaves easily shredded by winds, so plant in wind-sheltered place. Typically blooms 2 to 5 years after planting; inconspicuous flowers form within cylinder of bronze red bracts at end of stem. Plant dies to roots after flowering. Possible then to grow new plants from shoots at crown, but easier to discard, replace with new nursery

E

plants. 'Maurelii' has dark red leafstalks and leaves tinged with red on upper surface, especially along edges.

Plants die back in cold winters, regrow in spring. Attractive near swimming pools. Good container plants to grow outdoors in summer, indoors or in greenhouse over winter.

EPAULETTE TREE. See PTEROSTYRAX hispidus

EPIDENDRUM

Orchidaceae

EPIPHYTIC OR TERRESTRIAL ORCHIDS

🗡 ZONES 17, 21–27; OR INDOORS

☼ ◐ FULL SUN OR PARTIAL SHADE; SEE BELOW

🔴 REGULAR WATER, HIGH HUMIDITY

*Epidendrum
obrienianum*

All are easy to grow. Most species bear large clusters of blooms. On the whole they take same culture as cattleya. Those with hard, round pseudobulbs and thick, leathery leaves are tolerant of sun and aridity. Softer-textured (reed-stemmed) plants with thin, stemlike pseudobulbs do best with more shade and year-round moisture. Both types grow in ground bark or other orchid media.

Reed-stemmed types need abundance of sun to flower but also coolness and shade at roots. Mulch plants grown in the ground. If sun is too hot, foliage turns bright red and burns. Tip growth is damaged at 28°F/−2°C; plants are killed to ground at about 22°F/−6°C. In cold-winter areas, grow reed-stemmed plants in pots and move them indoors in winter.

Feed regularly with mild liquid fertilizer during growing season. Feed plants grown in pure ground bark at every other watering with high-nitrogen liquid fertilizer. Feed plants grown in other media monthly. When blooms fade, cut flower stem back to within one or two joints above soil.

E. cochleatum. Native to tropical America. Hardy to 25°F/−4°C. Pear-shaped pseudobulb 2–5 in. high, with one or more leaves as long as or longer than pseudobulb. Erect flower stem bears five to ten 2–3-in.-wide flowers. Narrow, twisted, yellow-green sepals and petals; purplish black lip (shaped like cockleshell) with lighter veins. Blooms at various times.

E. ibaguense (E. radicans). Native to Colombia. Erect, 2–4-ft., reed-like leafy stems. Dense, globular clusters of 1–1½-in. orange-yellow flowers with fringed lips are held at tips of slender stems well above foliage. Bloom season varies. Numerous hybrids in yellow, orange, pink, red, lavender, white; generally sold by color rather than by name.

E. obrienianum. Best known of reed-stemmed hybrids. Dense clusters of vivid red flowers, each the shape of miniature cattleya orchid, carried on slender stems 1–2 ft. above foliage.

EPILOBIUM. See ZAUSCHNERIA

EPIMEDIUM

Berberidaceae

PERENNIALS

🗡 ZONES 1–9, 14–17, 31–43

◐ PARTIAL SHADE

🔴 MODERATE WATER

*Epimedium
grandiflorum*

Low-growing plants with creeping underground stems and thin, wiry stems holding leathery leaves divided into heart-shaped leaflets to 3 in. long. Foliage is bronzy pink in spring, green in summer, bronzy in fall; whether it is evergreen, semievergreen, or deciduous depends on the species. Even in deciduous types, leaves last late into the year. In spring, plants produce loose spikes of small, waxy flowers like tiny columbines in pink, red, red orange, creamy yellow, or white. The flowers have four

petals, which may be spurred or hooded, and eight sepals—four inner ones resembling petals and four usually small, outer ones.

Use as ground cover under trees or among rhododendrons, azaleas, camellias; good in large rock gardens. Compete well with surface-rooted trees. Prefers partial shade, but tolerates heavy shade. Foliage, flowers long lasting in arrangements. Cut back foliage of semievergreen and deciduous types in late winter before bloom. Divide large clumps in spring or fall by severing tough roots with a sharp spade. Adaptable to containers.

E. alpinum. Evergreen. Rapidly spreading, 6–9 in. high, with small flowers. Like those of *E. rubrum*, the blossoms have red inner sepals and yellow petals.

E. cantabrigiense. Semievergreen hybrid. To 8–12 in. high, with olive-tinted foliage and small yellow-and-red flowers.

E. grandiflorum. BISHOP'S HAT, LONGSPUR EPIMEDIUM. Deciduous. About 1 ft. high. Flowers 1–2 in. across, shaped like bishop's hat; outer sepals red, inner sepals pale violet, petals white with long spurs. Varieties have white, pinkish, or violet flowers. 'Rose Queen', bearing crimson flowers with white-tipped spurs, is outstanding. 'White Queen', with silvery white blooms, is another good variety.

E. perralderianum. Evergreen. To 1 ft. tall and about 6 in. wide, with shiny leaves and bright yellow flowers. A hybrid of this species and *E. pinnatum colchicum* is *E. perralchicum* 'Frohnleiten', a 1½-ft. plant with large yellow flowers and leaves marked with brown in frosty weather.

E. pinnatum. Nearly evergreen. To 12–15 in. high. Flowers are ⅔ in. across, with bright yellow inner sepals and short red spurs. *E. p. colchicum* (often sold as *E. p. elegans*) is larger, with showier flowers.

E. rubrum. Semievergreen hybrid between *E. alpinum* and *E. grandiflorum*. To 1 ft. high. Flowers, borne in showy clusters, have bright crimson inner sepals, pale yellow or white slipperlike petals, upward-curving spurs. Rosy 'Pink Queen' and white 'Snow Queen' are desirable varieties offered by specialty nurseries.

E. versicolor. Semievergreen. Several hybrids of *E. grandiflorum* and *E. pinnatum* bear this name. Best-known selection is the vigorous 'Sulphureum', 12–20 in. high with clusters of light yellow flowers and leaves marked with brownish red.

E. warleyense. Evergreen hybrid. To 1 ft. high. Light green foliage; clusters of coppery orange-red flowers. Also known as 'Ellen Wilmott'.

E. youngianum 'Niveum'. Deciduous. Low-growing (6-12-in.) plant with pure white blossoms.

EPIPHYLLUM

ORCHID CACTUS

Cactaceae

CACTI

🗡 ZONES 8, 9, 14–28, WITH PROTECTION; OR INDOORS

◐ BEST UNDER LATH IN SUMMER OR UNDER TREES

🔴 REGULAR WATER IN SUMMER, LITTLE IN WINTER

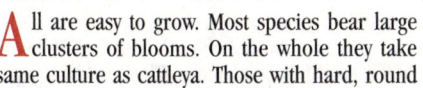

Epiphyllum Hybrid

Growers use *Epiphyllum* to cover a wide range of plants—epiphyllum itself and a number of crosses with related plants. All are tropical (not desert) cacti, and most grow on tree branches as epiphytes, like some orchids. Grow them in pots indoors; in lathhouse or shade outdoors in mild-winter climates. They need rich, quick-draining soil with plenty of sand and leaf mold, peat moss, or ground bark. Cuttings are easy to root in spring or summer. Permit the base of the cutting to dry for a day or two before potting it up. Overwatering and poor drainage cause bud drop.

In winter, epiphyllums need protection from frost. Most have arching (to 2 ft. high), trailing stems and look best in hanging pots, tubs, or baskets. Stems are long, flat, smooth, quite spineless, and usually notched along edges. Spring flowers range from medium size to very large (up to 10 in. across); color range includes white, cream, yellow, pink, rose, lavender, scarlet, and orange. Many varieties have blends of two or more colors. Feed with low-nitrogen fertilizer before and after bloom.

EPIPREMNUM aureum (Pothos aureus, Raphidophora aurea, Scindapsus aureus)

POTHOS

Araceae

EVERGREEN CLIMBING PERENNIAL

☀ ZONES 24, 25, 27; OR INDOORS

☀ ☀ ● SUN OR SHADE

● REGULAR WATER

Epipremnum aureum

Related to philodendron. Best known as a tough house plant with 2–4-in.-long, oval, leathery, dark green leaves splashed or marbled with yellow. Commonly used as an attractive trailer for pots, window boxes, larger terrariums; requires same care as vining philodendrons, but can take more sun and regular water. Outdoors and in greenhouses where it is given ample room, the plant becomes a big tropical vine with deeply cut leaves 2–2½ ft. long. Capable of climbing the tallest trees, the vine is sometimes used as a ground cover at the base of trees. Grows well in shade, but leaf color is better in full light.

EPISCIA

FLAME VIOLET

Gesneriaceae

PERENNIALS RELATED TO AFRICAN VIOLET

☀ ZONE 25; OR INDOORS

☀ ● FULL SHADE OUTDOORS; BRIGHT LIGHT INDOORS

● REGULAR WATER

Episcia cupreata

Low-growing tropical plants spread by strawberrylike runners with new plants at tips; provide an excellent display in hanging pots. Leaves 2–5 in. long, 1–3 in. wide; typically oval, velvety, beautifully colored. Flowers somewhat resembling African violets appear at scattered intervals through the year. Plants bloom well in high humidity of greenhouse, but will also grow as house plants if given bright light but no direct sun. In the warmest areas, potted plants can stay outdoors most of the year if given a shady, warm, wind-protected location.

E. cupreata. Red flowers. *E. c. viridifolia* has green leaves with creamy veins; 'Metallica', olive green leaves with pale stripes, red edges; 'Chocolate Soldier', chocolate brown, silver-veined leaves; and 'Silver Sheen', silver leaves with darker margins.

EQUISETUM hyemale

HORSETAIL

Equisetaceae

PERENNIAL

☀ ALL ZONES

☀ ☀ FULL SUN OR PARTIAL SHADE

● LOCATE IN MARSHY AREAS OR POOLS

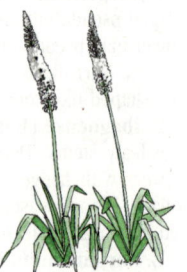
Equisetum hyemale

Rushlike survivor of Carboniferous Age. Slender, hollow, 4-ft. stems are bright green with black-and-ash-colored ring at each joint. Spores borne in conelike spikes at end of stem. Several species, but *E. hyemale* most common. Called horsetail because many of the species have bushy look from many whorls of slender, jointed green stems that radiate out from joints of main stem.

Although horsetail is effective in some garden situations, especially near water, use it with caution: it is extremely invasive and difficult to get rid of. Best confined to containers. In open ground, root-prune unwanted shoots rigorously and constantly.

Miniature *E. scirpoides* is similar, but only 6–8 in. tall.

ERANTHIS hyemalis

WINTER ACONITE

Ranunculaceae

TUBER

☀ ZONES 1–9, 14–17, 32–43

☀ PARTIAL SHADE

● REGULAR WATER DURING GROWTH AND BLOOM

Eranthis hyemalis

Charming buttercuplike plant 2–8 in. high, blooming in early spring, even before crocuses. Single yellow flowers to 1½ in. wide, with five to nine petal-like sepals; each bloom sits on a single, deeply lobed bright green leaf that looks like a ruff. Round basal leaves divided into narrow lobes appear immediately after flowers. All traces of the plant disappear by the time summer arrives. Ideal companion for other small bulbs or bulblike plants that bloom at the same time, such as snowdrop and Siberian squill.

Plant tubers in August or early September before they shrivel. If tubers are dry, plump them up in wet sand before planting. When dividing, separate into small clumps rather than single tubers. Plant tubers 3 in. deep, 4 in. apart, in moist, porous soil. Can reseed in shady, damp conditions.

DRAMATIC ACCENTS

Thanks to their impressive height, spikes of eremurus add a dramatic accent to sizable floral arrangements. Cut spikes when about a quarter of lower flowers are open; recut stems regularly to encourage upper buds to bloom. Spikes should last up to 10 days; remove wilted blossoms as new ones open.

EREMURUS

FOXTAIL LILY, DESERT CANDLE

Liliaceae

PERENNIALS

☀ ZONES 1–9, 14, 32–43

☀ FULL SUN

● MODERATE TO LITTLE WATER

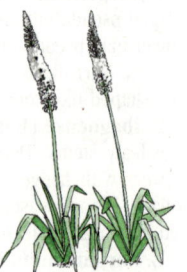
Eremurus himalaicus

Imposing lily relatives with spirelike flowering stems 3–9 ft. tall. Bell-shaped white, pink, or yellow flowers, ½–1 in. wide, massed closely in graceful, pointed spikes on upper third to half of stem. Plants bloom in late spring, early summer. Need winter cold to bloom well. Strap-shaped basal leaves in rosettes appear in early spring, fade away after bloom in summer. Magnificent in large borders against background of dark green foliage, wall, or solid fence. Dramatic in arrangements; cut when lowest flowers on spike open. Plant in rich, fast-draining soil; set crown just below surface in milder climates, 4–6 in. deep in colder ones. Handle thick, brittle roots carefully; they tend to rot when bruised or broken. When leaves die down, mark spot; don't disturb roots. Provide winter mulch in coldest areas.

E. himalaicus. To 3–8 ft. tall, with white flowers. Bright green leaves to 1½ ft. long.

E. robustus. To 6–9 ft. tall, with clear pink flowers lightly veined with brown. Dense basal rosettes of leaves to 2 ft. long.

E. Shelford hybrids. To 4–5 ft. tall; flowers in white and shades of buff, pink, yellow, and orange.

E. stenophyllus (E. bungei). To 3–5 ft. tall, with flowers in bright yellow aging to orange brown. Leaves to 1 ft. long.

FOR GROWING SYMBOL EXPLANATIONS
PLEASE SEE PAGE 161

ERICA

HEATH

Ericaceae

EVERGREEN SHRUBS

ZONES VARY BY SPECIES

FULL SUN EXCEPT IN HOTTEST CLIMATES

CONSISTENT, CAREFUL WATERING

SEE CHART NEXT PAGE

Erica carnea 'Springwood'

Evergreen shrubs with small, needlelike leaves and abundant, usually small flowers that may be bell shaped, urn shaped, or tubular. Native to many regions of the world; those from northern and western Europe are most widely used in American gardens. Various frost-tender species from South Africa are grown in mild-winter areas of California but are not suitable for the rest of the country. Intermediate in hardiness are heaths native to the Mediterranean and southern Europe; they are widely grown in the Northwest and Northern California.

The most common heaths—the hardy European species—tend to be fairly low growing. In suitable climates, fanciers sometimes plant the shortest types in masses for a Persian-carpet effect. If you select your heath and heather *(Calluna)* varieties carefully, you can have color all year.

All heaths need excellent drainage; most require acid soil (exceptions noted in chart). Sandy soil with organic matter such as peat moss and compost added is ideal; heavy clay is usually fatal. They are not heavy feeders; an annual sifting of compost may be enough. If plants lose color, give a light feeding of acid plant food in early spring. They will not tolerate standing water on roots or absolute dryness. Give light shade or afternoon shade in hot-summer climates. After flowers fade, shear or cut off spent flower spikes. Don't cut back into leafless wood, since new growth may not sprout. Heaths attract bees.

Ericaceae. The heath family contains shrubs and trees with rounded, bell-shaped, tubular, or irregular flowers, often showy, and fruits that are either capsules or berries. All share a preference, if not always a need, for acid soil with ample water and excellent aeration (a few plants from dry-summer climates are exceptions). Many are fine garden plants; azalea and rhododendron *(Rhododendron)*, blueberry, heath *(Erica)*, and heather *(Calluna)* are examples.

ERIGERON

FLEABANE

Asteraceae (Compositae)

PERENNIALS

ZONES VARY BY SPECIES

FULL SUN OR LIGHT SHADE

MODERATE WATER

Erigeron speciosus

Free-blooming plants with daisylike flowers; similar to closely related Michaelmas daisy, except that flower heads have threadlike rays in two or more rows rather than broader rays in a single row. White, pink, lavender, or violet flowers, usually with yellow centers, early summer into fall. Sandy soil. Cut back after flowering to prolong bloom.

E. karvinskianus. MEXICAN DAISY, SANTA BARBARA DAISY. Zones 8, 9, 12–28. Native to Mexico. Graceful, trailing plant 10–20 in. high. Leaves 1 in. long, often toothed at tips. Dainty flower heads ¾ in. across with numerous white or pinkish rays. Use as ground cover in garden beds or large containers, in rock gardens, in hanging baskets, on dry walls. Naturalizes easily; invasive unless controlled. 'Moerheimii' is somewhat more compact than species, with lavender-tinted flower heads.

E. speciosus. Zones 1–9, 14–24, 31–43. Native to Pacific Northwest coast. Erect, leafy stemmed, 2 ft. high. Flower heads 1–1½ in. across, with

dark violet or lavender rays. Hybrids are available; they have larger flower heads and come in white and pink as well as blue shades. Among these are azure blue 'Blue Beauty', violet blue 'Darkest of All', light violet 'Strahlenmeer', 'Pink Jewel' in various pink shades, carmine pink 'Förster's Liebling' (Förster's Darling), white 'Schneewittchen' ('Snow White').

ERINUS alpinus

Scrophulariaceae

PERENNIAL

ZONES 1–9, 14–17, 32, 34–43

FULL SUN OR PARTIAL SHADE

REGULAR WATER

Erinus alpinus

A short-lived perennial that reseeds itself freely, it can reach 1 ft. high, but usually grows in situations that restrict it to just 2–6 in. tall: in crevices in rock walls, in rock gardens, or between stepping-stones. Light green leaves are less than an inch long; narrow clusters of pink, purplish, or white flowers bloom in summer. Given the right conditions—cool, moist, not too sunny—it will reseed and form patches. It does not, however, become a pest. Especially attractive where flowers are at eye level, as on top of a wall or growing in chinks in the wall.

ERIOBOTRYA

LOQUAT

Rosaceae

EVERGREEN TREES OR LARGE SHRUBS

ZONES VARY BY SPECIES

FULL SUN OR PARTIAL SHADE

REGULAR WATER

Eriobotrya japonica

Both kinds have large, prominently veined, sharply toothed leaves. One bears edible fruit. Attractive to birds.

E. deflexa. BRONZE LOQUAT. Zones 8–28. Shrubby but easily trained into small tree form. New leaves have bright coppery color that they hold for a long time before turning green. Leaves aren't as leathery or as deeply veined as those of *E. japonica;* they are shinier and more pointed. Garlands of creamy white flowers attractive in spring. No edible fruit. Good for espaliers (not on hot wall), patio planting, containers. Fast growing.

E. japonica. LOQUAT. Zones 4–31. Tree is hardy to 20°F/–7°C; has survived 12°F/–11°C, but fruit often injured by low temperatures. Grows 15–30 ft. tall, equally broad in sun, slimmer in shade. Leathery, crisp leaves, stoutly veined and netted, 6–12 in. long, 2–4 in. wide. They are glossy deep green above and show rust-colored wool beneath. New branches woolly; small, dull white flowers, fragrant but not showy, in woolly 3–6-in. clusters in fall. Orange to yellow, 1–2-in.-long fruit ripens in winter or spring. Sweet, aromatic, acid flesh, with seeds (usually big) in center.

Plant in well-drained soil. In dry climates, it will thrive with no irrigation once established, but does better with regular moisture. Mulch over root zone. Prune to shape; if you like the fruit, thin branches somewhat to let light into tree's interior. If tree sets fruit heavily, remove some while it's small to increase size of remaining fruit and to prevent limb breakage. Fireblight is a danger; if leaves and stems blacken from top downward, prune back 1 ft. or more into healthy wood. Use as lawn tree; train as espalier on fence or trellis but not in reflected heat. Can be held in container for several years. Cut foliage is good for indoor decorating. Attracts bees.

Most trees sold are seedlings, good ornamental plants with unpredictable fruit quality; if you definitely want fruit, look for a grafted variety. Early-ripening 'Champagne', best in warm areas, has yellow-skinned, white-fleshed, juicy, tart fruit. Midseason 'Gold Nugget' has sweeter orange fruit. Early 'MacBeth' has exceptionally large fruit with yellow skin, cream flesh. 'Thales' is a late yellow-fleshed variety.

E

ERICA

NAME, ZONES, ORIGIN	GROWTH HABIT, SIZE	LEAVES	FLOWER COLOR, SEASON	COMMENTS
Erica arborea TREE HEATH Zones 15–17, 21–24 Southern Europe, North Africa	Dense shrub or tree to 10–20 ft., with one or many trunks, often with heavy burl at base	Bright green, ¼ in. long. New growth lighter	White, fragrant. Spring	Slow growing. Performs well enough in Zones 4–6 in years between big freezes. Burls are the "briar" used for making pipes
E. a. alpina	Dense, upright, fluffy-looking shrub to 6 ft.	As above	White. Spring	Slow to reach blooming age, but free blooming. Slightly hardier than above
E. australis SOUTHERN HEATH Zones 5–9, 14–24, 31, 32 Spain, Portugal	Upright, spired, 6–10 ft.	Dark green	Rosy or red. Clustered at ends of shoots. Spring	There is a white form, 'Mr. Robert'
E. canaliculata (usually sold as **E. melanthera** and often called Scotch heather) Zones 15–17, 20–24 South Africa	Bushy, spreading, but with general spired effect. To 6 ft.	Dark green above, white beneath	Pink to rosy purple. Fall, winter	Sometimes called Christmas heather because of winter bloom. Pink-flowered form is sold as 'Rosea', reddish purple form as 'Rubra'. Cut flowers last for weeks, whether stems are immersed in water or not
E. c. 'Boscaweniana' (sometimes sold as **E. melanthera 'Rosea'**)	Upright bush or small tree to 18 ft.	As above	Pale lilac pink to nearly white. Winter, spring	Like *E. canaliculata*, good source of cut flowers
E. carnea (**E. herbacea**) Zones 2–10, 14–24, 31, 32, 34, 36–39 European Alps	Dwarf, 6–16 in. Upright branchlets rise from prostrate main branches	Medium green	Rosy red. Winter, spring	Unsightly unless pruned every year. This and its varieties tolerate neutral or slightly alkaline soil
E. c. 'Ruby Glow'	To 8 in.	Dark green	Deep ruby red. Winter, spring	One of richest in color
E. c. 'Springwood' ('Springwood White')	Spreading, to 8 in. One of neatest heaths	Light green	White; creamy buds. Winter, early spring	Toughest, fastest-growing heath. More tolerant than others of hot, humid conditions
E. c. 'Springwood Pink'	Spreading mound, to 10 in.	Bright green	Pure pink. Winter, early spring	New growth pinkish rust. More tolerant than others of hot, humid conditions
E. c. 'Vivellii'	Spreading mound, to 1 ft.	Dark green; bronzy red in winter	Carmine red. Winter	Relatively tidy. Interesting for seasonal change in foliage color as well as for bloom
E. c. 'Winter Beauty' ('King George')	Bushy, spreading, compact, to 15 in.	Dark green	Deep, rich pink. Winter, early spring	Often in bloom at Christmas
E. ciliaris DORSET HEATH Zones 4–6, 15–17, 31, 32, 34, 39 England, Ireland	Trailing, 6–12 in.	Pale green	Rosy red. Summer	Good for massing
E. c. 'Mrs. C. H. Gill'	Spreading, to 1 ft.	Dark green	Deep red. Summer, early fall	Showy, bell-like flowers
E. c. 'Stoborough'	As above, but taller, to 1½ ft.	Medium green	White. Summer, early fall	Free blooming, showy
E. cinerea TWISTED HEATH Zones 4–6, 15–17, 31, 32, 34, 39 British Isles, northern Europe	Spreading mound, to 1 ft.	Dark green, dainty	Purple. Summer	Forms low mat; good ground cover
E. c. 'Atrosanguinea'	Low, spreading, bushy, to 9 in.	Dark green, dainty	Scarlet. Summer, early fall	Dwarf, slow growing

E

ERICA

NAME, ZONES, ORIGIN	GROWTH HABIT, SIZE	LEAVES	FLOWER COLOR, SEASON	COMMENTS
E. c. 'C. D. Eason'	Compact, to 10 in.	Dark green	Red. Late spring, summer	Outstanding; good summer flower display
E. c. 'P. S. Patrick'	Bushy, to 15 in.	Dark green	Purple. Summer	Long, sturdy spikes of large flowers
E. darleyensis 'Darley Dale' (E. mediterranea hybrida, E. purpurascens 'Darleyensis') Zones 2–10, 14–24, 31, 32, 34, 36–39	Bushy, to 1 ft.	Medium green	Light rosy purple. Fall to midspring	Tough, hardy plant that takes both heat and cold surprisingly well. Tolerates neutral soils. Hybrid between *E. carnea* and *E. mediterranea*
E. d. 'Furzey'	Bushy, 14–18 in.	Dark green	Deep rose pink. Winter, early spring	Spreading, vigorous plant
E. d. 'George Rendall'	Bushy, 1 ft.	Medium bluish green	Deeper purple than 'Darley Dale'. Fall to early spring	New growth gold tinted
E. d. 'Silberschmelze' ('Molten Silver', 'Alba', 'Mediterranea Hybrid White')	Vigorous, 1½–2 ft.	Medium green	White, fragrant. Winter, spring	Easy to maintain
E. 'Dawn' Zones 4–9, 14–24, 31, 32, 34, 39	Spreading mound, 1 ft.	Green; new growth golden	Deep pink. Summer, early fall	Excellent ground cover. Easy to grow. Hybrid between *E. ciliaris* and *E. tetralix*
E. mediterranea BISCAY HEATH Zones 4–9, 14–24, 31, 32 Ireland, France, Spain	Loose, upright, 4–7 ft.	Deep green	Lilac pink. Winter, early spring	Good background. Tolerates neutral soil. 'W. T. Rackliff' is pure white form with brown anthers
E. m. hybrida (see E. darleyensis 'Darley Dale')				
E. tetralix CROSS-LEAFED HEATH Zones 4–6, 15–17, 32, 34, 39 England, northern Europe	Upright, to 1 ft.	Dark green, silvery beneath	Rosy pink. Summer, early fall	Other heaths are more cold-tolerant. New growth yellow, orange, or red. Needs moister conditions than other heaths
E. t. 'Alba Mollis'	Upright, slightly spreading, to 1 ft.	Silvery gray	Clear white. Summer, early fall	Foliage sheen pronounced in spring, summer
E. t. 'Darleyensis'	Spreading, open growth, to 8 in.	Gray green	Salmon pink. Summer	Good color. Do not confuse with *E. darleyensis*, which blooms fall–midspring
E. vagans CORNISH HEATH Zones 3–6, 15–17, 20–24, 31, 32, 34, 39 Cornwall, Ireland	Bushy, open, to 2–3 ft.	Bright green	Purplish pink. Summer	Robust and hardy
E. v. 'Lyonesse'	Bushy, rounded, to 1½ ft.	Bright, glossy green	White. Summer, early fall	Best white Cornish heath
E. v. 'Mrs. D. F. Maxwell'	Bushy, rounded, to 1½ ft.	Dark green	Cherry pink or red. Summer, early fall	Outstanding for color and heavy bloom; widely grown
E. v. 'St. Keverne'	Bushy, rounded, to 1½ ft.	Light green	Rose pink. Summer, early fall	Heavy bloom. Compact if pruned annually

ERIOGONUM

WILD BUCKWHEAT

Polygonaceae

EVERGREEN SHRUBBY PERENNIALS

ZONES 14–24, EXCEPT AS NOTED

FULL SUN

MODERATE WATER

Eriogonum allenii

This large group has its greatest distribution in the West; only *E. allenii* and *E. umbellatum* are likely to be encountered in gardens in other regions. Individual blossoms are tiny but grow in broad-topped, often branched clusters, making domes of bloom above the rosettes of silvery-backed leaves. Bloom in spring and summer. Flowers age to an attractive tan or reddish brown and persist for a long time; good in dried arrangements. Wild buckwheats need excellent drainage and can endure poor, rocky soil and extreme heat and sun. They may self-sow. Difficult to transplant once established.

E. allenii. Zones 2–10, 14–17, 31–41. Native to rocky soils of Virginia and West Virginia. Grows 1½–2½ ft. tall, with bright yellow flowers.

E. arborescens. SANTA CRUZ ISLAND BUCKWHEAT. Native to California. Grows 3–4 ft. tall (sometimes to 8 ft.), spreading to 4–5 ft. or more. Shredding gray to reddish bark. Pale pink to rose blossoms.

E. giganteum. ST. CATHERINE'S LACE. California native. Like *E. arborescens* but with freer branching habit, whiter foliage, longer bloom.

E. grande rubescens (E. rubescens, E. latifolium rubescens). RED BUCKWHEAT. Native to California. Prostrate branches spread to 1–1½ ft., with upright tips to 1 ft. high. Rosy red blooms.

E. umbellatum. SULFUR FLOWER. Zones 1–24, 28–43. Native to the Rocky Mountains. Can occasionally reach 3 ft. tall and wide. Freely branching; in bloom, covered with a sheet of cream to yellow flowers. Dwarf forms make tight mats less than 1 ft. tall.

ERODIUM reichardii (E. chamaedryoides)

CRANESBILL

Geraniaceae

PERENNIAL

ZONES 7–9, 14–24, 31, 32

FULL SUN OR PARTIAL SHADE

REGULAR WATER

Erodium reichardii

Native to Balearic Islands and Corsica. Dainty-looking but tough plant, forming dense foliage tuft 3–6 in. high, 1 ft. across. Long-stalked, roundish, dark green leaves ⅓ in. long with scalloped edges. Profuse, cup-shaped, ½-in.-wide flowers with white or rose pink, rosy-veined petals notched at tips, spring–fall. Good small-scale ground cover, rock garden plant. A double-flowered pink and a single white form exist. Plant in porous soil. *E. chrysanthum* has silvery foliage and pale yellow flowers, and *E. petraeum crispum (E. foetidum)* has white flowers with lavender veins and a conspicuous purple spot on one petal.

ERYNGIUM

SEA HOLLY

Apiaceae (Umbelliferae)

PERENNIALS

ZONES 1–24, 29–43, EXCEPT AS NOTED

FULL SUN

MODERATE WATER

Eryngium amethystinum

Most are erect, stiff-branched, thistlelike plants with summer show of striking oval, steel blue or amethyst flower heads surrounded by spiny blue bracts. Upper leaves and stems are also sometimes blue. Make long-lasting cut flowers and dry well for winter arrangements. Leaves are sparse, dark green, deeply cut, spiny toothed. Plant in borders or in fringe areas in deep, well-drained soil. Taprooted plants are difficult to divide; propagate by root cuttings or sow seed in place, thinning seedlings to 1 ft. apart. Plants often self-sow.

Another group of sea hollies has long, narrow, spine-edged leaves that resemble those of yucca. One of these is native to the U.S.

E. alpinum. To 2 ft., with 2-in. flower heads and large, deeply cut blue bracts. 'Blue Star' is a choice variety.

E. amethystinum. Zones 1–24, 26, 28–45. To 2½ ft. tall, with 1-in. flower heads in rich blue above finely cut leaves.

E. planum. To 3 ft. high. Flowers heads small, freely borne, dark blue, with dark blue bracts.

E. variifolium. To 16 in., with small, rounded blue-gray flower heads and bluish white bracts. Thistlelike leaves are evergreen and heavily veined with white.

E. yuccifolium. RATTLESNAKE MASTER. Zones 1–24, 26, 29–43. Native to eastern and central U.S. Long (to 3-ft.), narrow, spiny-edged leaves in a basal rosette. Erect stems to 3–4 ft. branch toward top and carry small balls of white flowers without significant bracts.

> ## ERYNGIUM FLOWERS NEED LONGER STEMS
>
> Eryngium flowers have such dramatic form and unusual color, they call out to be used in arrangements. But their individual flower stems are too short (3–6 in.) to be seen in long-stemmed company. Cut florists' wire as needed, and fasten pieces to the stems with florists' tape. Eryngiums are everlastings; their stems don't need to be in water.

ERYSIMUM

WALLFLOWER

Brassicaceae (Cruciferae)

PERENNIALS AND BIENNIALS, SOME GROWN AS ANNUALS

ZONES VARY BY SPECIES

FULL SUN OR LIGHT SHADE

WATER NEEDS VARY BY SPECIES

Erysimum hieraciifolium

This genus swallowed up *Cheiranthus*, which included the old-fashioned, sweetly fragrant bedding wallflowers. All species have the typical clustered, four-petaled flowers that give the crucifers their name.

E. 'Bowles Mauve'. Perennial. Zones 4–6, 14–17, 22, 23, 30–32. Massed erect stems with narrow gray-green leaves form a plant to 3 ft. tall, 6 ft. wide; each stem is topped by 1½-ft.-long, narrow, spikelike clusters of mauve flowers. Best in areas with cool summers and mild winters, where bloom is practically continuous. Spring, summer bloom elsewhere. May be short lived. Moderate to little water. 'Wenlock Beauty' is smaller, with flowers varying from buff to purple in a single spike.

E. cheiri (Cheiranthus cheiri). ENGLISH WALLFLOWER. Perennial in Zones 4–6, 14–17, 22, 23, 32, 34, but usually grown as a biennial or an annual. Best suited to cool, moist regions, such as the coastal Northeast and the Pacific Northwest. Branching, woody-based plants 1–2½ ft. tall, with narrow bright green leaves and broad clusters of showy, delightfully sweet-scented flowers in spring. Blossoms are yellow, cream, orange, red, brown, or burgundy, sometimes shaded or veined with contrasting color. Sow seeds in spring for bloom the following year (some strains flower the first year if seeded early); or set out plants in fall or earliest spring. May self-sow. Regular water.

E. hieraciifolium (E. alpinum). SIBERIAN WALLFLOWER. Biennial or perennial (Zones 1–24, 32–43), frequently treated as an annual. This species (sometimes sold as *Cheiranthus allionii* or *E. asperum*) is more

E

widely grown in the eastern U.S. than is *E. cheiri*. Narrow-leafed, branching plants 1–1½ ft. tall, covered with fragrant, rich orange flowers in spring. Sow seeds or set out plants as for *E. cheiri*. Often self-sows. Regular water. 'Moonlight' has bright yellow flowers that open from red buds.

E. kotschyanum. Perennial (Zones 3–11, 14–21, 31–34), often treated as an annual in warm climates. Light green leaves form 6-in. mats from which rise scented, deep yellow flowers on 2-in. stems in spring. Moderate water. Use in rock garden or with other small perennials between paving stones. If plants hump up, cut out central portions, transplant them, and press original plants flat again. Divide clumps in fall.

ERYTHEA. See BRAHEA

ERYTHRINA

CORAL TREE

Fabaceae (Leguminosae)

DECIDUOUS OR NEARLY EVERGREEN TREES OR SHRUBS

⚡ ZONES VARY BY SPECIES

☼ FULL SUN

🌢🌢 REGULAR TO MODERATE WATER

◊ SEEDS ARE POISONOUS IF INGESTED

Erythrina caffra

Many species; known and used chiefly in normally frost-free areas of California, Arizona, and Florida. Only *E. crista-galli* and *E. herbacea* survive in colder regions. These trees are grown for their brilliant flowers, in colors ranging from greenish white through yellow, light orange, and light red to orange and red. The flat, beanlike pods that follow the flowers contain poisonous seeds. Leaves (divided into three leaflets) are usually shed in winter or spring. These are typically thorny plants with strong structural value, whether in or out of leaf.

E. acanthocarpa. TAMBOOKIE THORN. Deciduous shrub. Zones 19–25, 27. To 3 ft. tall (rarely 6 ft.). Bluish green leaflets to 1½ in. are as broad as long. Spring flower spikes are 7 in. long, 6 in. wide, with scarlet, yellow-tipped flowers. Thorny plant grows from large, thick tuberlike root.

E. americana. Deciduous tree (but may be evergreen in mildest areas). Zones 12, 13, 19–27. Native to Mexico; used as street tree in Mexico City. To 25 ft. tall. Resembles *E. coralloides* in habit and flowers.

E. bidwillii. Deciduous shrub. Zones 8, 9, 12–28. To 8 ft., sometimes treelike to 20 ft. or more, wide spreading. Hybrid origin. Spectacular display—2-ft.-long clusters of pure red flowers on long, willowy stalks from spring until winter; main show in summer. Cut back flowering wood when flowers are spent. Very thorny, so plant away from paths and prune with long-handled shears.

E. caffra (E. constantiana). KAFFIRBOOM CORAL TREE. Briefly deciduous tree. Zones 21–25, 27. Native to South Africa. Grows 25–40 ft. high, spreads to 40–60 ft. wide. Drops leaves in January; then angular bare branches produce big clusters of deep red-orange, tubular flowers that drip nectar. In March or earlier, flowers give way to fresh, light green foliage.

E. coralloides. NAKED CORAL TREE. Deciduous tree. Zones 12, 13, 19–27. Native to Mexico. To 30 ft. high and as wide or wider, but easily contained by pruning. Fiery red blossoms like fat candles or pine cones bloom at tips of naked, twisted, black-thorned branches in spring. At end of flowering season, 8–10-in. leaves develop, give shade in summer, turn yellow in late fall before dropping. Bizarre form of branch structure when tree is out of leaf is almost as valuable as spring flower display. Sometimes sold as *E. poianthes*.

E. crista-galli. COCKSPUR CORAL TREE. Zones 7–9, 12–17, 19–27, coastal areas of 28. Deciduous shrub or small tree 15–20 ft. high and wide in nearly frostless areas; perennial to 4 ft. in colder part of range. Native to eastern South

Erythrina crista-galli

America. First flowers form after leaves come in spring—at each branch tip is a big, loose, spikelike cluster of velvety, birdlike blossoms in warm pink to wine red (plants vary). Depending on environment there can be as many as three distinct flowering periods, spring through fall. Cut back old flower stems and dead branch ends after each wave of bloom.

E. falcata. Nearly evergreen tree. Zones 19–25, 27. Native to Brazil and Peru. Grows upright to 30–40 ft. high. Must be in ground several years before it flowers (may take 10 to 12 years). Rich deep red (occasionally orange-red), sickle-shaped flowers in hanging, spikelike clusters at branch ends in late winter, early spring. Some leaves fall at flowering time.

E. herbacea. CHEROKEE BEAN, CORAL BEAN. Zones 25–33. Native to southeastern states, Texas, northern Mexico. Perennial to 6 ft. tall in colder parts of range, deciduous shrub or small tree to 15 ft. tall in warmer zones. Bright red, 2-in. flowers in 8–12-in. spikes appear from spring to frost. Red seeds that follow are attractive and extremely poisonous.

E. humeana. NATAL CORAL TREE. Normally deciduous shrub or tree (sometimes almost evergreen). Zones 12, 13, 20–27. Native to South Africa. May grow to 30 ft. but begins to wear its bright orange-red flowers when only 3 ft. high. Blooms continuously from late summer to late fall, carrying flowers in long-stalked clusters at branch ends well above foliage (unlike many other types). Dark green leaves. 'Raja' is shrubbier and has leaflets with long, pointed "tails."

Erythrina humeana

E. lysistemon. Deciduous tree. Zones 13, 21–25, 27. Native to South Africa. Similar to *E. caffra* in size but slower growing. Light orange (sometimes shrimp-colored) flowers. Time of bloom varies greatly; may bloom intermittently from fall into spring, occasionally in summer. Many handsome black thorns. A magnificent tree of great landscape value. Very sensitive to wet soil. Sometimes erroneously sold as *E. princeps*.

E. sykesii. Deciduous tree. Zones 19–25, 27. Hybrid from Australia. Grows to 24–30 ft.; spreading habit. Showy red flowers in winter, before leaves. Unlike the other species, does not form pods.

E. variegata. Deciduous tree. Zones 25, 27. Native to Africa, Asia, Polynesia. Grows 20–30 ft. tall, with thick, prickly trunk and branches. Leaves have 3–8-in. leaflets. Profuse display of coral red flowers in late winter, early spring.

ERYTHRONIUM

Liliaceae

CORMS

⚡ ZONES VARY BY SPECIES

☼ ● PARTIAL OR FULL SHADE

🌢🌢 AMPLE WATER, EXCEPT AS NOTED

Erythronium tuolumnense

Spring-blooming, dainty, nodding, lily-shaped flowers 1–1½ in. across, on stems usually 1 ft. high or less. All have two (rarely three) broad, tongue-shaped, basal leaves, mottled in many species. All need some subfreezing temperatures. Plant in groups under trees, in rock gardens, beside pools or streams. Set out corms in fall, 2–3 in. deep, 4–5 in. apart, in rich, porous soil; plant corms as soon as you receive them, and don't let them dry out. No need to water the Western species during dormancy.

E. albidum. Zones 1–6, 32–43. Native from Minnesota to Ontario south to Texas. White flowers, flushed yellow at the base. Blooms later in spring than most of the other species. Leaves infrequently mottled silver green. Spreads slowly to form colonies.

E. americanum. Zones 1–7, 15–17, 28, 31–43. Native from Minnesota to Nova Scotia south to Florida. Shiny green leaves mottled brown and purple. Blooms in late spring at about the same time as *E. albidum*, bearing pale yellow blossoms sometimes flushed with purple. ▸

E. californicum. FAWN LILY. Zones 2–7, 14–17, 33–41. Native to Northern California and Oregon. Leaves mottled with brown. Flowers creamy white or yellow, with deeper yellow band at base.

E. dens-canis. DOG-TOOTH VIOLET. Zones 1–7, 15–17, 31–43. European species. Leaves mottled with reddish brown; purple or rose flowers on 6-in. stems. Specialists can supply named varieties with white, pink, rose, and violet blossoms. Needs more sun than others.

E. hendersonii. Zones 2–7, 14–17, 33–41. Native to Northern California and Oregon. Flowers, deeply curled back at tips, are light to deep lavender, deep maroon at base. Dark green leaves mottled with brown.

E. revolutum. Zones 2–7, 14–17, 33–41. Western native similar to *E. californicum*, with brown-and-white mottling on leaves. Large rose, pink, or lavender flowers are banded yellow at base. 'Rose Beauty' and 'White Beauty' are choice varieties.

E. tuolumnense. Zones 2–7, 14–17, 32 (colder parts), 33–41. Native to California. Solid green leaves. Flowers golden yellow, greenish yellow at base. Robust, with stems 12–15 in. tall. 'Kondo' and 'Pagoda' are extra-vigorous selections.

ESCHSCHOLZIA californica

CALIFORNIA POPPY

Papaveraceae

PERENNIAL OFTEN GROWN AS ANNUAL

⚡ ALL ZONES

☼ FULL SUN

◖◗ REGULAR TO LITTLE WATER

Eschscholzia californica

State flower of California, where it grows wild on hillsides and along roads. Free branching from base; stems 8–24 in. long. Finely divided, lacy blue-green leaves. In the wild, plants produce satiny-petaled, 2-in.-wide single flowers in colors ranging from pale yellow to deep orange. Garden forms available in yellow, pink, rose, flame orange, red, cream, and white. Sunset strain has single blooms, Mission Bells semidouble flowers, and Ballerina semidouble blooms with frilled and fluted petals. The Silk strain has bronze-tinted foliage and semidouble flowers in the full color range. Single-color varieties include 'Cherry Ripe', 'Milky White', and 'Purple-Violet'. Garden forms usually revert to the orange or yellow of wild plants when they reseed. Flowers of all types close at night and on overcast days.

In cold-winter areas, generally used as summer annual; pretty in cottage gardens, rock gardens. In mild climates, plants bloom from spring to summer and reseed freely; best suited for informal plantings and for naturalizing on hillsides, since foliage turns straw colored after bloom.

Does best in well-drained soil; in hot, humid regions, excellent drainage is essential. Sow seed where plants are to grow; brittle taproot makes it difficult to transplant successfully. Sow in early spring in cold-winter regions, in fall in milder climates. Birds are attracted to the seeds.

ESPOSTOA lanata

PERUVIAN OLD MAN CACTUS

Cactaceae

CACTUS

⚡ ZONES 12–24; OR INDOORS

☼ ◑ FULL SUN OR LIGHT AFTERNOON SHADE

◖ MODERATE TO LITTLE WATER

Espostoa lanata

Columnar cactus branching with age. Slow growing in pots, fairly fast to 8 ft. in open ground. Plant has light brown, bristly, ½–2-in.-long thorns, usually concealed in long, white hair that covers plant. Hair is especially long and dense near summit. Tubular, pink, 2-in.-long flowers in spring. Protect from hard frosts. Give bright light indoors.

EUCALYPTUS

Myrtaceae

EVERGREEN TREES OR SHRUBS

⚡ ZONES VARY; READ BELOW, AND SEE CHART

☼ FULL SUN

◖◗ REGULAR TO LITTLE WATER

▶ SEE CHART

Eucalyptus citriodora

Nearly all are native to Australia. Their drought tolerance makes them the most widely planted non-native trees in California and Arizona. They enjoy a limited but increasing success in the milder parts of the Pacific Northwest, where they may be cut down by hard freezes after several years of successful growth. In Florida, their success has been limited by the occasional sudden hard freeze, which kills eucalyptus along with orange trees and other subtropical plants. Lack of gradual hardening over a long, cool autumn makes the trees subject to fatal freezing at temperatures that would not materially harm the same trees in California. The Disney enterprises have grown lemon-scented gum trees *(E. citriodora)* to a height of 80 ft., only to lose them. One species, *E. torelliana*, is showing promise in South Florida. Another species, *E. cinerea*, is doing fairly well in South and Central Florida.

Outside of prime eucalyptus territory, you may wish to try your hand at growing the plants, if you enjoy experimenting. Plants are easily started from seed; most grow very rapidly, perhaps as much as 10–15 ft. in one year. Some are large trees with great skyline value; some are medium to large shrubs or multitrunked trees. Most bear small white or cream flowers that are conspicuous only in masses, while others have colorful, showy blooms. Some have leaves of unusual form, highly valued in floral arrangements. Nearly all have foliage that is aromatic when crushed. Most have two different kinds of leaves; those on young plants or young growth differ markedly from mature foliage.

In Victorian England, some species were grown as summer annuals for bedding out. In borderline climates, such bedded-out plants function today as perennials—tops are killed, but plants resprout vigorously the next year. Seed catalogs still offer seeds of many species for use as house plants—a concept amusing to Californians, who are accustomed to seeing many of the species tower over landscapes. Sow seeds in spring or summer, in flats or pots of prepared soil or planting mix. Keep flats shaded and water sparingly. As soon as seedlings are 2–3 in. tall, separate them carefully and transplant to pots or other containers. Spray lightly and frequently with dilute liquid fertilizer. Plant in open ground or large container when 6–12 in. tall; trees seldom thrive if roots have become pot-bound. Limbs subject to breakage on larger species, so choose planting site carefully.

The chart requires several cautionary notes. Size listed applies to plants growing in California, where only the most tender species are winter-killed; plants grown elsewhere are unlikely to reach such heights. Hardiness figures are not absolute. In addition to air temperature, you must take into account the plant's age (generally, the older the hardier); its condition; and the timing of the frost (24°F/–4°C following several light frosts is not as dangerous as the same low temperature following warm autumn and winter weather). Outside of California and Arizona, consider any eucalyptus a risk; occasional deep or prolonged freezes can kill even large trees. If you are committed to growing eucalyptus, don't hasten to remove apparently dead trees; although their appearance may be damaged, they could resprout from trunk or main branches.

EUCALYPTUS IN BOUQUETS

Though florists sell eucalyptus stems to include in arrangements, foliage you pick yourself is fresher and more fragrant. If you have an *E. cinerea*, clip the young foliage regularly for its gray-green, nearly round juvenile leaves. The silvery blue young foliage of *E. gunnii* is another attractive choice.

E

EUCALYPTUS

NAME	HARDINESS	FORM, SIZE	LEAVES, TRUNK	FLOWERS, FRUIT	COMMENTS
E. cinerea SILVER DOLLAR TREE	14° to 17°F/ −10° to −8°C	Small to medium tree growing 20–50 ft. high, nearly as wide. Irregular habit	Juvenile leaves gray green, roundish, 1–2 in. long, in pairs. Mature leaves long, narrow, green	Unimportant small white flowers. Grown for attractive juvenile foliage rather than blossoms	Cut back frequently for a supply of decorative foliage. Recovers from freezes if base of trunk is heavily mulched. Can be used as perennial in borderline climates
E. citriodora LEMON-SCENTED GUM	24° to 28°F/ −4° to −2°C	Tall, graceful tree to 60–80 ft. Lower half to two-thirds of tree is bare trunk	Leaves long (3–7 in.), golden green, lemon scented. Trunk white to pinkish	Small white flowers	Exceedingly attractive narrow tree; fast growing but tender
E. conferruminata (usually sold as **E. lehmannii**) BUSHY YATE	25° to 28°F/ −4° to −2°C	Small tree to 20–30 ft., flat topped, wide spreading	Light green, long oval, 2-in. leaves. Some turn red in fall	Apple green flowers in big (4-in.-wide) clusters open from horn-shaped buds	Fast-growing, dense tree for windbreak or seashore. Unpruned, branches touch ground
E. erythrocorys RED-CAP GUM	23° to 26°F/ −5° to −3°C	Small tree to 20–30 ft., usually with multiple trunks; or large bush	Thick, shiny, deep green, 4–7-in.-long, lance-shaped leaves	Bright red caps tilt up and fall off to reveal yellow flowers in clusters like shaving brushes	Can endure some drought or much water if drainage is good. Head back trunks to keep plant compact
E. ficifolia RED-FLOWERING GUM	25° to 30°F/ −4° to −1°C	Usually round-headed, single-trunked tree to 40 ft.; or a multi-stemmed big bush	Leaves 3–7 in. long, leathery, deep green; like rubber plant foliage	Spectacular 1-ft. clusters of red flowers (sometimes white, cream, pink, or orange). Heavy 1-in. seed capsules like dice cups	Prune seed capsules from young trees to avoid weighing down branches, spoiling form
E. globulus BLUE GUM	17° to 22°F/ −8° to −6°C	Tall tree to 150 ft., with heavy, straight trunk, big masses of foliage	Sickle-shaped, dark green leaves 7–10 in. long. Young leaves oval, silvery	Flowers white to yellowish. Warty seed capsules fall along with bark and leaves to make considerable litter	Good windbreak but greedy, messy, brittle. A smaller form, 'Compacta', grows to 30 ft.; it is densely branched, multitrunked
E. gunnii CIDER GUM	5° to 10°F/ −15° to −12°C	Medium to tall (40–70-ft.), dense, upright tree	Young foliage silvery blue green. Mature leaves 3–5 in. long, dark green	Small, creamy white flowers	One of the fastest growing and hardiest of eucalypts
E. macrocarpa	8° to 12°F/ −13° to −11°C	Erratic, sprawling shrub to 8–10 ft. Tries to be a vine, but stems are too stiff	Light gray-blue leaves 2–5 in. long sit close to stems in pairs	Golf ball–size buds open to fluffy pink, red, or white flowers that sit stalkless on branches; flowers round, flat topped, 4–7 in. wide. Followed by seed capsules 3 in. wide	Sprawling and awkward, but showy. For dry places. Can be espaliered on sunny fence or wall
E. pauciflora niphophila (**E. niphophila**) SNOW GUM	0° to 10°F/ −18° to −12°C	Small, wide-spreading, open tree to 20 ft. tall	Silvery blue, lance-shaped, 1½–4-in.-long leaves. Smooth white bark peels in patches. Red branches	Creamy white flowers followed by silvery seed capsules	Hardy, picturesque tree with attractive foliage and trunk
E. polyanthemos SILVER DOLLAR GUM	14° to 18°F/ −10° to −8°C	Slender, erect, fast-growing tree to 20–60 ft., with single or multiple trunks	Juvenile leaves gray green, nearly round, 2–3 in. wide. Mature leaves dark green, lance shaped	Small white flowers not noticeable. Grown for form and foliage, not flowers	Popular landscape and street tree in California. Can be used as perennial in borderline climates
E. torelliana CADAGA	Most likely 28° to 30°F/ −2° to −1°C	Straight-trunked tree 45–60 ft. tall, with rounded or spreading form	Leaves 3–6 in. long, dark green	Flowers white, profuse, showy	Fast-growing tree that flourishes in humid climates and likes water; is being grown in South Florida. Useful shelter belt tree
E. viminalis MANNA GUM	12° to 15°F/ −11° to −9°C	Tall, broad tree to 150 ft., with drooping, willowy branches	Light green, narrow, 4–6-in.-long leaves. Trunk whitish, with shedding bark	Small white flowers and seed capsules	Needs plenty of room; can create a significant silhouette

E

E

EUCOMIS

PINEAPPLE FLOWER

Liliaceae

BULBS

🌡 ZONES 4–29; OR DIG AND STORE; OR GROW IN POTS

☼ ◑ FULL SUN OR LIGHT SHADE

💧 REGULAR WATER DURING GROWTH AND BLOOM

Eucomis comosa

Unusual-looking plant: thick, 2–3-ft. spikes are closely set with ½-in.-long flowers and topped with clusters of leaflike bracts like a pineapple top. Bloom in summer, but persistent purplish seed capsules continue the show longer. Need rich soil with plenty of humus. Dormant in winter. Plant bulbs 5 in. deep; also fairly easy to grow from spring-sown seeds. Bulbs are hardy to about 5°F/–15°C; where winter temperatures are lower, dig and store bulbs or grow in pots and protect during cold weather. Divide clumps when they become crowded. Interesting potted plants for outdoor or indoor use. Good cut flower.

E. bicolor. To 2 ft.; flowers green, each petal edged with purple. Attractive leaves 1 ft. long, 3–4 in. wide, with wavy edges.

E. comosa (E. punctata). Thick spikes 2–3 ft. tall are set with greenish white flowers tinged pink or purple. Stems are spotted purple at the base. Leaves grow to 2 ft. long and are less wavy than those of *E. bicolor*.

EUCOMMIA ulmoides

HARDY RUBBER TREE

Eucommiaceae

DECIDUOUS TREE

🌡 ZONES 2–9, 14–41

☼ FULL SUN

💧 💧 REGULAR TO MODERATE WATER

Eucommia ulmoides

Though rubber can be made from the hardy rubber tree's sap, the process is not economically feasible. Instead, this tree is grown for its ornamental qualities. Attractive rounded habit; can reach 40–60 ft. in height, with nearly equal spread. Leaves resemble those of elm, but are glossier and more leathery. When a leaf is slowly torn in two, the sap from the veins congeals into threads of rubber, holding the two parts together. Summer foliage is attractive, fall color negligible. Flowers and fruit are not conspicuous. Requires good drainage but tolerates a wide variety of soils. Not troubled by pests.

EUGENIA

Myrtaceae

EVERGREEN SHRUBS OR TREES, MOSTLY TROPICAL

🌡 ZONES VARY BY SPECIES

☼ ◑ FULL SUN OR PARTIAL SHADE

💧 REGULAR WATER

Eugenia uniflora

Grown for attractive foliage, white flowers and edible "cherries." Grow in well-drained, rich soil. Best in moist atmosphere and sheltered spot. Some species have been reclassified; for *E. myrtifolia* and *E. paniculata*, see *Syzygium paniculatum*.

E. aggregata (Myrciaria edulis). CHERRY OF THE RIO GRANDE. Shrub or small tree. Zones 24–27. To 15 ft., with thick, smooth, dark green, 3-in. leaves. Fruit, to 1 in. long, ripens from orange red to deep purplish red. Good for pies.

E. braziliensis. GRUMICHAMA. Tree. Zones 25–27. Can reach 50 ft. (usually much less), with 5-in. leaves. Cherry-size fruit ages from dark red to black. Good for eating fresh or baking.

E. uniflora. SURINAM CHERRY, PITANGA. Shrub or small tree. Zones 21–27 (often killed to ground in Zone 26 but grows back). Very slow, open growth to 15–25 ft., usually to 6–8 ft. Leaves to 2 in. long, glossy coppery green deepening to purplish or red in cold weather. Fragrant flowers like little bottlebrushes. Fruit, size of small tomatoes, ripens from yellow to orange to deep red. Good for jams, jellies. Tolerates shearing into hedge, but at expense of fruit. Grafted varieties sometimes available.

EULALIA GRASS. See MISCANTHUS sinensis

EUONYMUS

Celastraceae

EVERGREEN, DECIDUOUS SHRUBS; EVERGREEN VINES

🌡 ZONES VARY BY SPECIES

☼ ◑ ● EXPOSURE NEEDS VARY BY SPECIES

💧 💧 REGULAR TO MODERATE WATER

Euonymus japonica

Deciduous and evergreen species are distinct; the characteristic squarish "hatbox" fruit provides the only hint that they're related. Deciduous types are valued for brilliant fall leaf color or prominent fruit; evergreen types, used mainly for landscape structure, include some of the most cold-tolerant broad-leafed evergreens. Most species tolerate a range of light conditions, from full sun to fairly deep shade; deciduous kinds with fall color give best display in sun. Scale can be a problem on any euonymus.

E. alata. WINGED EUONYMUS. Deciduous shrub. Zones 1–9, 14–16, 29–45. Though nursery tags may indicate a much smaller plant, the species can reach 15–20 ft. high and wide. Dense, twiggy, flat topped, with horizontal branching. Twigs have flat, corky wings that disappear on older growth. Though fruit is smaller and less profuse than that of *E. europaea*, fall color is impressive: the dark green leaves turn flaming red in autumn. (In shade, fall color is pink.) 'Compacta', a smaller plant (to 6–10 ft. high and a little narrower) with smaller corky wings, isn't quite as hardy. Use both species and variety as screen or alone, against dark evergreens for greatest color impact. 'Compacta' also makes a good unclipped hedge or foundation plant.

E. americana. STRAWBERRY BUSH. Deciduous shrub. Zones 4–6, 26, 28, 30–34, 39. Native to eastern and southern U.S. Many-stemmed, suckering shrub with green stems. To 6 ft. high. Leaves medium green, to 3 in. long, lacking the fall color of *E. alata*. Fruits are warty, bright red, up to ¾ in. in diameter. Tolerates much shade; use in native woodland plantings. Well-behaved plant.

E. europaea. SPINDLE TREE. Deciduous large shrub or small tree. Zones 1–9, 14–16, 31–45. Eventually reaches a possible 30 ft. tall; narrow when young, becoming rounded with age. Leaves are dark green; fall color varies from yellowish green to yellow to red. Fruits are the ornamental feature: a profusion of four-chambered, pink to red capsules open to reveal bright orange seeds. 'Aldenham' ('Aldenhamensis') produces profuse large pink capsules on long stems; 'Red Cascade' bears rosy red capsules. Full sun or partial shade. Scale is often a serious problem.

E. fortunei. Evergreen vine or shrub. Zones 3–17, 28–41. One of the best broad-leafed evergreens where temperatures drop below 0°F/–18°C. Trails or climbs by rootlets. If this plant is used as shrub, its branches will trail and sometimes root; if allowed to climb, it will be a spreading mass to 20 ft. or more. Prostrate forms can be used to control erosion. Leaves dark rich green, 1–2½ in. long, with scallop-toothed edges; flowers inconspicuous. Mature growth, like that of ivy, is shrubby and bears fruit; cuttings taken from this shrubby wood produce upright plants.

The varieties of *E. fortunei*, several of which are listed here, are better known than the species itself. Many nurseries still sell them as forms of *E. radicans*, which was once thought to be the species but is now considered to be another variety (see *E. f. radicans* below).

'Canadale Gold'. Compact shrub with light green, yellow-edged leaves.

'Colorata'. PURPLE-LEAF WINTER CREEPER. Same sprawling growth habit as *E. f. radicans,* though makes a more even ground cover. Leaves turn dark purple in fall and winter.

'Emerald Gaiety'. Small, dense-growing, erect shrub with deep green leaves edged with white.

'Emerald 'n Gold'. Similar to above, but with gold-edged leaves.

'Golden Prince'. New growth tipped gold. Older leaves turn green. Extremely hardy; good hedge plant.

'Greenlane'. Low, spreading shrub with erect branches, deep green foliage, orange fruit in fall.

'Ivory Jade'. Resembles 'Greenlane' but has creamy white leaf margins that show pink tints in cold weather.

E. f. radicans. COMMON WINTER CREEPER. Zones 4–9, 14–17, 28–34, 39. Tough, hardy, trailing or vining shrub with dark green, thick-textured, 1-in.-long leaves. Given no support, it sprawls; given masonry wall to cover, it does the job completely.

E. japonica. EVERGREEN EUONYMUS. Evergreen shrub. Zones 4–20, 28–31, warmer parts of 32. Upright, 8–10 ft. with 6-ft. spread, usually held lower by pruning or shearing. Flowers inconspicuous. Older shrubs attractive trained as trees, pruned and shaped to show their curving trunks and umbrella-shaped tops. Can be grouped as hedge or screen. Leaves very glossy, leathery, deep green, 1–2½ in. long, oval to roundish.

Though the species and its varieties are very tolerant of heat, unfavorable soil, and seacoast conditions, they're pest prone. Notorious for powdery mildew, except in Pacific Northwest; to lessen mildew risk, place in a full-sun location where air circulation is good. Plants are also very susceptible to scale insects, thrips, and spider mites.

Variegated forms are most popular; they are among the few shrubs that maintain variegations in full sun in hot-summer climates. There may be some confusion in plant labeling of variegated types.

'Aureo-variegata'. Leaves have brilliant yellow blotches, green edges.

'Grandifolia'. Plants sold under this name have shiny dark green leaves larger than those of the species. Compact, well branched, good for shearing as pyramids, globes.

'Microphylla' *(E. j. pulchella).* BOX-LEAF EUONYMUS. Compact, small leafed, 1–2 ft. tall and half as wide. Formal-looking; usually trimmed as low hedge.

'Microphylla Variegata'. Like 'Microphylla', but with leaves splashed white.

'Silver King'. Green leaves with silvery white edges.

'Silver Princess'. Like 'Microphylla Variegata', but 3 ft. tall, 2 ft. wide, with larger leaves.

'Silver Queen'. Green leaves with creamy white edges.

E. kiautschovica (E. patens). Semievergreen shrub. Zones 4–6, 30–35, 39. May retain leaves in warmest areas, drop them in coldest. About 8 ft. high and as wide or wider, with some low branches trailing on the ground and rooting. Relatively thin-textured, light green leaves and profusion of tiny, greenish cream flowers in late summer. Bloom followed by conspicuous pink to reddish fruits with red seeds. Two hybrids make good hedges: 'DuPont', a 4–6-ft.-high plant with large, dark green leaves; and 'Manhattan', an upright grower 6–8 ft. high with dark, glossy leaves.

EUPATORIUM

Asteraceae (Compositae)
PERENNIALS

⚡ ZONES VARY BY SPECIES
☀ ◐ LIGHT SHADE IN HOT-SUMMER AREAS
💧 AMPLE MOISTURE, EXCEPT AS NOTED

Eupatorium purpureum

Medium-size to towering perennials with large clusters of small flower heads at the tops of leafy stems. Except as noted, these species are native to the eastern and central U.S. and have become popular not only in wild gardens and restored meadows, but also in more ordered perennial borders. All are easy to grow. Remove faded flower heads to avoid seedlings. Divide clumps in spring or fall.

E. cannabinum. HEMP AGRIMONY. Zones 1–9, 14–17, 28–43. Native to Europe. Grows 5–6 ft. tall, with opposite pairs of deeply cut leaves and broad clusters of fluffy white, pink, or purple flower heads in summer. 'Album' bears white flowers, 'Plenum' pinkish purple blooms.

E. coelestinum. HARDY AGERATUM. Zones 1–9, 14–17, 25–43. Grows to 3 ft. tall, with freely branching stems set with pairs of 4-in. dark green, toothed leaves. Broad clusters of fluffy blue flowers exactly resemble those of the annual ageratum. Vigorous, freely spreading plant needs division every 3 years or so. Prefers ample moisture, but will not thrive in soggy soil in winter. Late to appear in spring; blooms from late summer until frost. The 1½–2-ft.-high 'Album' bears pure white flowers; 2-ft.-high 'Cori' has exceptionally clear blue blossoms and comes into bloom later than the species; 'Wayside Form' is more compact, growing to 15 in. high.

E. maculatum. JOE PYE WEED. Zones 1–9, 14–17, 28–43. Similar to *E. purpureum,* but smaller (to 6 ft. at most), with green stems speckled or blotched with purple. Flat-topped clusters of pink, purple, or white flowers bloom from midsummer to early fall.

E. perfoliatum. BONESET. Zones 1–9, 14–17, 28–45. Grows 3–5 ft. tall. The long (8-in.), narrow leaves are joined at their bases, so that the stem appears to grow through the leaves. Fluffy white flowers borne in flat-topped clusters. This plant is attractive in meadow restoration, but poisonous to cattle and thus considered a nuisance by ranchers. Likes moisture but tolerates considerable drought. In the past, this plant was thought to have medicinal value for people, helping to knit broken bones—hence the common name.

E. purpureum. JOE PYE WEED. Zones 1–9, 14–17, 28–45. Often sold as *E. fistulosum.* An imposing plant of damp meadows in the eastern U.S. Grows 3–9 ft. tall, with clumps of hollow stems and whorls of strongly toothed leaves to 1 ft. long. Leaves have a vanilla scent when bruised. Pale purple flowers, attractive to butterflies, appear in large, dome-shaped clusters in late summer or early fall. Variety commonly sold is 'Gateway', a sensible 5 ft. in height, with dusky purplish rose flowers at the top of purple stems.

EUPHORBIA

Euphorbiaceae
SHRUBS, PERENNIALS, ANNUALS, AND SUCCULENTS

⚡ ZONES VARY BY SPECIES
☀ ◐ ● EXPOSURE NEEDS VARY BY SPECIES
💧💧 REGULAR TO MODERATE WATER, EXCEPT AS NOTED
⚠ SAP IS POISONOUS IN SOME SPECIES

Euphorbia characias wulfenii

On euphorbia, what are called "flowers" are really groups of colored bracts. True flowers, centered in the bracts, are inconspicuous. Many euphorbias are succulents; these often mimic cacti in appearance and are as diverse as cacti in form and size. Only a couple of these are listed below, but specialists in cacti and succulents can supply scores of species and varieties. Plant euphorbias in well-drained soil. Give winter protection in cold climates.

E. amygdaloides. Perennial. Zones 3–24, 31–34. To nearly 3 ft., resembling a smaller *E. charasias* and also blooming late winter, early spring. 'Purpurea' has foliage heavily tinted purple, with bright green inflorescence. Best in sun, tolerates some shade. Dies back in winter.

E. biglandulosa. See E. rigida

E. characias. Evergreen perennial. Zones 4–24, 31, warmer parts of 32. Upright stems make dome-shaped bush 4 ft. tall. Narrow blue-green leaves crowded along stems. Clustered flowers make dense, round to cylindrical masses of chartreuse or lime green in late winter, early spring. Color holds with only slight fading until seeds ripen; then stalks yellow and should be cut out at base, since new shoots have already made growth for next year's flowers. *E. c. wulfenii (E. veneta),* the most common form, has broader clusters of yellower flowers. Both species and variety are fairly drought resistant and perform best in full sun.
▶

E

E. cotinifolia. CARIBBEAN COPPER PLANT. Evergreen shrub or tree. Zones 25, 27. Can become a small tree in frost-free areas, but is usually a multistemmed shrub. Long-stalked leaves to 4 in. long, 3 in. wide; 'Atropurpurea', the form commonly grown, has wine red leaves. Loose flower clusters have small white bracts; not showy. Likes sun, heat, good drainage; can't take frost. For a similar plant sometimes sold under this name, see *Synadenium grantii*.

E. cyparissias. Perennial. Zones 1–24, 28–43. Produces clumps of erect stems to 16 in. high (usually much less) from wide-roaming underground rhizomes. Narrow leaves to 1½ in. long are crowded on the stem to produce a feathery effect; stems somewhat resemble small pine trees. Clusters contain up to 18 greenish yellow or chartreuse yellow flowers, attractive over a long season in spring and summer. Covers ground rapidly and can become a pest among choice plants, but attractive along a road or at the edge of cultivated area. Can stand some shade but prefers sun. Needs little water once established. May become dormant in winter.

E. epithymoides (E. polychroma). Perennial. Zones 1–24, 26, 28–45. Neatly rounded hemisphere of deep green leaves symmetrically arranged on closely set stems. Each stem ends in a branching, rounded cluster of tiny flowers surrounded by bright yellow bracts. Effect is of a 1–1½-ft. gold mound suffused with green. Spring bloom. Displays good fall color (yellow to orange or red) before going dormant. Use in rock gardens, perennial borders. Needs some shade in hottest climates. Short lived, but reseeds.

E. fulgens. SCARLET PLUME. Evergreen shrub. Zones 24, 25, 27; or house or greenhouse plant. To 3–4 ft. tall, with drooping branches set with narrow, 2–4 in.-long leaves. Clusters of bright scarlet flowers line the branches in winter. Likes sun.

E. griffithii. Perennial. Zones 1–10, 14–24, 28–43. Erect stems to 3 ft., clad in narrow, medium green leaves and topped by clusters of brick red or orange bracts. Spreads by creeping roots but is not aggressive. Sun or light shade. Dies back in winter. 'Fireglow' is the variety commonly sold.

E. heterophylla. MEXICAN FIRE PLANT. Annual. All zones. To 3 ft. tall. Bright green leaves of varying shapes, larger ones resembling those of poinsettia; flowers unimportant. In summer, upper leaves are blotched bright red and white, giving appearance of second-rate poinsettia. Regular to little water. Useful in hot, dry, sunny borders in poor soil. Sow seed in place after frost danger is over.

E. lathyris. GOPHER PLANT, MOLE PLANT. Biennial. Zones 2–24, 28–41. Legend claims that it repels gophers and moles. Stems have poisonous, caustic milky juice; keep away from skin and especially eyes, since painful burns can result. Juice could conceivably bother a gopher or mole enough to make it beat a hasty retreat. Grows as tall single stem—to 5 ft. high by second summer, when it sets a cluster of unspectacular yellow flowers at the top. Flowers soon turn to seed, after which the plant dies. Long, narrow-pointed leaves grow at right angles to stem and to each other. Grow from seed. Give sun or shade, regular to little water.

E. marginata. SNOW-ON-THE-MOUNTAIN. Annual. All zones. To 2 ft. Leaves light green, oval; upper ones striped and margined white, uppermost sometimes all white. Flowers unimportant. Used for contrast with bright-colored bedding dahlias, scarlet sage, or zinnias, or with dark-colored plume celosia. Before using in cut arrangements, dip stems in boiling water or hold in flame for a few seconds. Sow seed in place in spring, in sun or partial shade. Thin to only a few inches apart, as plants are somewhat rangy.

E. martinii. Evergreen perennial. Zones 4–24, 31, 32. Hybrid between *E. amygdaloides* and *E. characias*. Resembles a compact *E. characias,* with dense clusters of chartreuse, brown-centered flowers in late winter, early spring. Has red stems in winter. Fairly drought resistant; takes full sun.

E. milii (E. splendens). CROWN OF THORNS. Woody perennial or subshrub; evergreen but sparsely leafed. Zones 21–27; or greenhouse, house, or summer pot plant. Shrubby, climbing stems to 3–4 ft., armed with long, sharp thorns. Leaves roundish, thin, light green, 1½–2 in. long, usually found only near branch ends. Clustered pairs of bright red bracts borne nearly all year. Many varieties and hybrids vary in form, size, and bract color (yellow, orange, pink). Train on small frame or trellis against

sheltered wall or in container. Grow in porous soil, in full sun or light shade. Salt tolerance makes it an ideal choice for oceanfront plantings.

E. myrsinites. Evergreen perennial. Zones 1–24, 31–43. Stems flop outward from central crown, then rise toward tip to 8–12 in. Leaves stiff, roundish, blue gray, closely set around stems. Flattish clusters of chartreuse to yellow flowers top stem ends in late winter, early spring. Cut out old stems as they turn yellow. Withstands cold and heat, but is short lived in warm-winter areas. Use in sunny rock gardens with succulents and gray-foliaged plants.

E. obesa. BASEBALL PLANT. Evergreen succulent. House plant or indoor/outdoor pot plant. Solid, fleshy, gray-green sphere (or short cylinder) to 8 in., with brownish stripes and brown dots that resemble stitching on a baseball. Flowers unimportant. Good drainage, bright light, warmth, no sudden temperature changes. Moderate to little water; keep dryish in winter.

E. palustris. Perennial. Zones 4–9, 14–17, 31–34. To 3 ft. (possibly 5 ft.) high, with many medium green, 2–3-in. leaves. Widely branching clusters of yellow flowers appear in spring, early summer. Will grow in sun or some shade, with regular to little water. Dies back in winter. Self-sows.

E. pulcherrima. POINSETTIA. Evergreen, semievergreen, or deciduous shrub. Zones 13, 16–27; or indoors. Native to Mexico. Leggy, to 10 ft. or taller. Coarse leaves grow on stiffly upright canes. Showy part of plant consists of petal-like bracts; true flowers in center are yellowish, inconspicuous. Red single form most familiar; less well known are red doubles and forms with white, yellowish, pink, or marbled bracts. Bracts of paler kinds often last until Easter. Poinsettia has typical milky euphorbia juice, but it is not poisonous; it is either completely harmless or at most mildly irritating to skin or stomach.

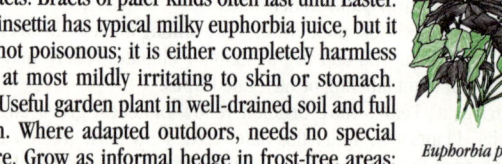

Euphorbia pulcherrima

Useful garden plant in well-drained soil and full sun. Where adapted outdoors, needs no special care. Grow as informal hedge in frost-free areas; where frosty (not severely cold), plant against sunny walls, in sheltered corners, under south-facing eaves. Thin branches in summer to produce larger bracts; prune them back at 2-month intervals for bushy growth (but often smaller bracts). To improve red color, feed every 2 weeks with high-nitrogen fertilizer, starting when color begins to show.

To care for holiday gift plants, keep them in a sunny window and avoid sudden temperature changes. Keep soil moist; don't let water stand in pot saucer. When leaves drop in late winter or early spring, cut stems back to two buds and reduce watering to a minimum. Store in a cool place until late spring. When frosts are past, set pots in sun outdoors. Plants will probably grow too tall for indoor use the next winter, but may survive winter if well sheltered. Start new plants by making late-summer cuttings of stems with four or five eyes (joints).

ENCOURAGING POTTED POINSETTIAS TO BLOOM

Plants bloom only when they experience long nights. Starting in October, move them into a closet each night for 14 hours (be sure they receive no light at all), then move them into light in the morning for a maximum of 10 hours. Continue this procedure for 10 weeks; you can have poinsettia blossoms by Christmas.

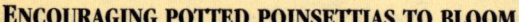

E. rigida (E. biglandulosa). Evergreen perennial or subshrub. Zones 4–24, 31. Stems angle outward, then rise up to 2 ft. Fleshy, gray-green leaves to 1½ in. long are narrow and pointed, their bases tightly set against stems. Broad, domed flower clusters in late winter or early spring are chartreuse yellow fading to pinkish. After seeds ripen, stems die back and should be removed; new stems take their place. Showy display plant in garden or container. Full sun.

E. robbiae (E. amygdaloides robbiae). MRS. ROBB'S BONNET. Evergreen perennial. Zones 4–24, 31, 32. Usually under 1 ft. high. The stems are closely set with leathery dark green leaves 1½–4 in. long, over 1 in. wide. Pale lime green flower clusters in late winter, early spring. Spreads slowly but surely from underground rhizomes. It can thrive in sun (but not the hottest sun) and in deep shade. Regular to little water.

E. seguierana niciciana. Evergreen perennial. Zones 4–24, 31–34. Resembles a delicate, fine-textured *E. characias*. To 1½ ft., with blue-gray, narrow, 1-in. leaves and chartreuse inflorescence in late winter, early spring. Full sun.

E. tirucalli. MILKBUSH, PENCILBUSH, PENCIL TREE. Zones 13, 23–25, 27; house plant or indoor/outdoor plant anywhere. Tree or large shrub to possible 30 ft. tall in open ground, usually much smaller. Single or multiple trunks support tangle of light green, pencil-thick, succulent branches with no sign of a leaf. Bleeds milky sap if cut. Flowers unimportant. Striking for pattern of silhouette or shadow. Very salt tolerant; often used as a hedge on ocean dunes in Florida. Just plant pieces of stem, water until established; requires no attention after that. As a house plant, thrives in driest atmosphere; needs all the light you can give it, routine soil, water, and feeding.

E. veneta, E. characias wulfenii. See E. characias

Euphorbiaceae. The euphorbia family contains annuals, perennials, shrubs, and an enormous number of succulents. Most have milky sap, and many have unshowy flowers made decorative by bracts or bractlike glands. Poinsettia *(Euphorbia pulcherrima)* is the best-known example.

EURYA

Theaceae
EVERGREEN SHRUBS

⚡ ZONES 4–6, 15–17, 21–24, 26, 28, 31, WARMER PARTS OF 32

☀️ LIGHT SHADE

💧💧 AMPLE WATER

Eurya emarginata

Native to Japan. Grown for refined foliage. Yellowish green flowers are insignificant and ill smelling but are present only on old plants. Slow growing to 6–8 ft. but easily kept to 3–4 ft. by pruning to side buds or branches. Give same conditions as azaleas.

E. emarginata. Branches rise at 45° angle from base of plant. Teardrop-shaped, dark green, leathery, ½-in.-long leaves are closely set on branches. *E. e. microphylla* has even tinier leaves—¼ in. long.

E. japonica. Leaves much larger (to 3 in. long) than those of *E. emarginata*. Cold weather gives them a purplish tint. 'Winter Wine' has more pronounced wine purple winter blush.

EURYOPS

Asteraceae (Compositae)
SHRUBBY EVERGREEN PERENNIALS

⚡ ZONES VARY BY SPECIES

☀️ FULL SUN

💧 MODERATE WATER

Euryops pectinatus

Native to South Africa. Leaves are finely divided; flower heads are daisylike. Long bloom season; keep old flowers picked off. Plants require excellent drainage. They thrive on buffeting ocean winds but are damaged by sharp frosts. Plants take well to container culture.

E. acraeus. Zones 8, 9, 12–24. Native to high South African mountains; hardier to frost than other species. Mounded growth to 2 ft. Leaves silvery gray, ¾ in. long. Inch-wide, bright yellow daisies cover plant in spring. Use in rock gardens.

E. pectinatus. Zones 8, 9, 12–26; can be grown as annual elsewhere. To 3–6 ft. high. Easy maintenance and extremely long flowering season

make it a good filler, background plant, or low screen. Leaves are gray green, deeply divided, 2 in. long. Bright yellow, 1½–2-in.-wide daisies on 6-in. stems bloom most of the year. Cut back in late spring or early summer to maintain compactness and limit size. Good pot plant. 'Viridis' is identical to the species but has deep green leaves. 'Munchkin' is a dwarf to 3 ft. tall, 4 ft. wide.

EUSTOMA grandiflorum (Lisianthus russellianus)

LISIANTHUS, TULIP GENTIAN, TEXAS BLUEBELL

Gentianaceae
BIENNIAL OR SHORT-LIVED PERENNIAL OFTEN GROWN AS ANNUAL

⚡ ALL ZONES

☀️◐ FULL SUN OR FILTERED LIGHT

💧 REGULAR WATER

Eustoma grandiflorum

Native to U.S. High Plains, but garden forms introduced from Japan. Plants grow better and have longer stems where nights are warm. Best cut flowers are produced in greenhouses.

In summer, clumps of gray-green foliage send up 1½-ft. stems topped by tulip-shaped, 2–3-in. flowers in purplish blue, pink, or white; plants bloom all summer if old blooms are cut off. Lion and Double Eagle strains have double flowers that look somewhat like roses. Heidi strain of F_1 hybrids are vigorous and long stemmed, and include yellow in addition to other flower colors. 'Red Glass' has rose red flowers. Picotee types are also available.

Buying started plants is easier, but lisianthus can be grown with much care from its dustlike seeds. Sprinkle seed on surface of potting soil; don't cover with soil. Soak well, then cover pot with glass or plastic until seeds germinate. At four-leaf stage (about 2 months), transplant three or four plants into each 6-in. pot. Needs good garden soil, good drainage, average fertilizer. Often grown as annual. Use in pots, border, cutting garden.

EVENING PRIMROSE. See OENOTHERA

EVERGREEN CANDYTUFT. See IBERIS sempervirens

EVERGREEN GRAPE. See RHOICISSUS capensis

EVERGREEN PEAR. See PYRUS kawakamii

EVERLASTING. See HELIPTERUM

EVODIA daniellii (Tetradium daniellii)

Rutaceae
DECIDUOUS TREE

⚡ ZONES 3–9, 14–24, 31–41

☀️ FULL SUN

💧 REGULAR WATER

Evodia daniellii

Native to northern China and Korea. Evodia is distantly related to citrus, but the leaves are more reminiscent of walnut. Grows to 30 ft. or taller and somewhat wider. The shiny dark green leaves are 1 ft. long or a little more, with five pairs of 2–5-in. leaflets plus a single leaflet at the end. Foliage is handsome throughout summer and early fall. No fall color; leaves drop while green. Blooms in early summer, bearing small white flowers in showy, 4–6-in., rather flat clusters; they are popular with bees. Fruits are small but attractive, aging from red to black. Although introduced nearly a century ago, the plant remains little known, despite its attractiveness, soil tolerance, and freedom from pests. ▶

E

F

A tree formerly known as *E. hupehensis* is now considered to be a somewhat less hardy form from southern China.

EVOLVULUS glomeratus

BLUE DAZE

Convolvulaceae

TENDER PERENNIAL OFTEN GROWN AS ANNUAL

🌡 ZONES 24–27; GROW AS ANNUAL IN COLDER CLIMATES

☀ ◐ FULL SUN OR LIGHT SHADE

💧 REGULAR WATER

Evolvulus glomeratus

Native to Brazil. Trailing stems to 20 in. are closely set with small gray-green leaves and spangled with blue morning glory flowers less than 1 in. wide. Flowers close in the evening and on darkly overcast days. Stems root where they touch the ground; cuttings root very easily in water or moist soil. Useful as a bedding plant, in summer borders, in hanging baskets. Often sold as *E. nuttallianus*.

EXACUM affine

GERMAN VIOLET, PERSIAN VIOLET

Gentianaceae

ANNUAL

🌡 ALL ZONES; OR INDOORS

◐ ● PARTIAL OR FULL SHADE

💧 💧 AMPLE WATER

Exacum affine

Small, rounded plant with egg-shaped, inch-long leaves and blue, sweet-scented, star-shaped flowers centered with tufts of bright yellow stamens. (A white variety is also available.) Sow seeds indoors in midwinter for summer bloom, in fall for spring bloom. Five plants in 5-in. pot make attractive showing. Needs rich soil. Good plant for house or cool greenhouse.

EXOCHORDA

PEARL BUSH

Rosaceae

DECIDUOUS SHRUBS

🌡 ZONES 2–9, 14–18, 31–41

☀ FULL SUN

💧 REGULAR WATER

Exochorda racemosa

Loose, spikelike clusters of 1½–2-in.-wide white flowers open from profusion of buds resembling pearls. Flowers bloom for a short time in spring, at about the same time the roundish, 1½–2-in.-long leaves expand. Foliage and arching growth suggest the related spiraea, but pearl bush's individual blossoms are considerably larger.

Showy during spring but undistinguished at other times of year, so choose your site accordingly. Prefers well-drained, acid soil; will take considerable neglect. Flowers are formed on previous year's growth, so prune after bloom to control size and form.

E. giraldii. Resembles the more widely grown *E. racemosa*, but with slightly smaller flowers and red tints in leaf veins and flower stalks.

E. macrantha. Hybrid between *E. racemosa* and another species. The only variety available, 'The Bride', is a compact shrub to about 4 ft. tall and as wide.

E. racemosa (E. grandiflora). COMMON PEARL BUSH. Native to China. Loose, open, slender; to 10–15 ft. tall and wide. In small gardens, remove lower branches to make upright, airy, multistemmed small tree.

Fabaceae. Previously called Leguminosae, the pea family is an enormous group containing annuals, perennials, shrubs, trees, and vines. Many are useful as food (beans, peas), while others furnish timber, medicines, pesticides, and a host of other products. Many are ornamental.

The best known kinds—sweet peas *(Lathyrus)*, for example—have flowers shaped like butterflies, with two winglike side petals, two partially united lower petals (called the keel), and one erect upper petal (the banner or standard). Others have a more regular flower shape *(Bauhinia, Cassia);* still others have tightly clustered flowers that appear to be puffs of stamens, as in acacia and silk tree *(Albizia)*. All bear seeds in pods (legumes). Many have on their roots colonies of bacteria that can extract nitrogen from the air and convert it into compounds useful as plant food; clovers *(Trifolium)* are a familiar example.

Fagaceae. The beech family contains evergreen or deciduous trees characterized by fruit that is either a nut enclosed in a cup, as in oak *(Quercus),* or a burr, as in beech *(Fagus)* and chestnut *(Castanea).*

FAGUS

BEECH

Fagaceae

DECIDUOUS TREES

🌡 ZONES VARY BY SPECIES

☀ ◐ FULL SUN OR LIGHT SHADE

💧 💧 REGULAR TO MODERATE WATER

Fagus sylvatica

Of the various beech types, those described here include a rarely seen Japanese species; a species native to the eastern U.S. that is widespread in nature but seldom planted in gardens; and the commonly planted European beech. Though all beeches are capable of growing to 90 ft. or more, they are usually considerably smaller. With the exception of selected horticultural varieties, they have a broad cone shape, with wide, sweeping lower branches that can reach the ground unless pruned off. Smooth gray bark contrasts well with glossy dark green foliage. Leaves color yellow to red brown in fall, then turn brown; many hang on the tree well into winter. Lacy branching pattern and pointed leaf buds provide an attractive winter silhouette. New foliage has a silky sheen. The nuts, enclosed in spiny husks, are edible but small; they will often fail to fill, especially on solitary trees.

All beeches cast heavy shade and have a dense network of fibrous roots near soil surface, inhibiting growth of lawn or other plants under the trees. Transplant from containers or, if moving an in-ground tree, dig with a substantial ball of earth. Give any good garden soil. Despite their size as trees, beeches can be closely planted and trimmed as dense, impassible hedges as low as 4 ft.

F. crenata. JAPANESE BEECH. Zones 2–6, 32–41. Leaves scallop edged, somewhat smaller than those of other beeches. Reddish brown fall color. Likes some shade in hot-summer areas, especially when young.

F. grandifolia. AMERICAN BEECH. Zones 1–6, 31–43. A stately tree and a principal component of the vast hardwood forests that once covered much of the eastern U.S. More tolerant of summer heat than the other two species described here and can be grown farther south. Leaves are toothed, 3–6 in. long; golden bronze fall color. Allow plenty of room for this tree.

F. sylvatica. EUROPEAN BEECH. Zones 2–9, 14–24, 32–41. Lustrous green leaves to 4 in. long, turning russet and bronzy in autumn. Many varieties, including the following:

'Asplenifolia'. FERNLEAF BEECH. Leaves narrow, deeply lobed or cut nearly to midrib. Delicate foliage on large, robust, spreading tree.

'Atropunicea'. COPPER BEECH, PURPLE BEECH. Leaves deep reddish or purple. Good in containers. Often sold as 'Riversii' or 'Purpurea'. Seedlings of copper beech are usually bronzy purple, turning bronzy green in summer.

'Fastigiata'. DAWYCK BEECH. Narrow, upright tree, like Lombardy poplar in form; 8 ft. wide when 35 ft. tall. Broader in great age, but still narrower than species.

'Laciniata'. CUTLEAF BEECH. Narrow green leaves, deeply cut.

'Pendula'. WEEPING BEECH. Irregular, spreading form. Long, weeping branches reach to ground, can root where they touch. Green leaves. Without staking to establish vertical trunk, it will grow wide rather than high.

'Purpurea Pendula'. WEEPING COPPER BEECH. Purple-leafed weeping form to 10 ft. tall. Splendid container plant.

'Tricolor'. TRICOLOR BEECH. Green leaves marked white and edged pink. Slow to 24–40 ft., usually much less. Foliage burns in hot sun or dry winds. Choice container plant.

'Zlatia'. GOLDEN BEECH. Young leaves yellow, aging to yellow green. Subject to sunburn. Good container plant.

FAIRY LILY. See ZEPHYRANTHES

FAIRY WAND. See DIERAMA

FALLUGIA paradoxa

APACHE PLUME

Rosaceae

PARTIALLY EVERGREEN SHRUB

ZONES 2–23

FULL SUN

MODERATE TO LITTLE WATER

Fallugia paradoxa

Native to western U.S., northern Mexico. Grows 3–8 ft. tall, with straw-colored branches and flaky bark. Small, clustered, lobed leaves are deep green on top, rusty beneath. White, 1½-in.-wide flowers like single roses in spring. Large clusters of feathery fruit follow the blooms; greenish at first, later tinged pink or reddish, they create a haze of soft, changing color through which you can see rigid branch pattern. Needs gritty, well-drained soil.

FALSE CYPRESS. See CHAMAECYPARIS

FALSE DRAGONHEAD. See PHYSOSTEGIA virginiana

FALSE INDIGO. See AMORPHA fruticosa, BAPTISIA

FALSE LUPINE. See THERMOPSIS

FALSE SOLOMON'S SEAL. See SMILACINA racemosa

FALSE SPIRAEA. See ASTILBE, SORBARIA

FAN PALM. See WASHINGTONIA

FAREWELL-TO-SPRING. See CLARKIA amoena

FARFUGIUM. See LIGULARIA tussilaginea

FATSHEDERA lizei

Araliaceae

EVERGREEN VINE, SHRUB, OR GROUND COVER

ZONES 4–10, 12–31, WARM PARTS OF 32

PARTIAL OR FULL SHADE

REGULAR WATER

Fatshedera lizei

Hybrid between Japanese aralia (*Fatsia japonica*) and English ivy (*Hedera helix*), with characteristics of both parents. Highly polished, 4–10-in.-wide leaves with three to five pointed lobes look like giant ivy leaves; plant also sends out long, trailing or climbing stems like ivy, though without aerial holdfasts. Fatshedera inherited shrubbiness from Japanese

aralia, though its habit is more irregular and sprawling than that of its parent. Several variegated forms exist.

Leaves are injured at 15°F/−9°C, tender new growth at 20° to 25°F/−7° to −4°C; seems to suffer more from late frosts than from winter cold. Give it protection from hot, drying winds. Good near swimming pools.

Fatshedera tends to grow in a straight line, but it can be shaped if you work at it. Pinch tip growth to force branching. About two or three times a year, guide and tie stems before they become brittle. If plant gets away from you, cut it back to ground; it will regrow quickly. If you use it as ground cover, cut back vertical growth every 2 to 3 weeks during growing season. Grown as vine or espalier, plants are heavy, so give them strong supports. Even a well-grown vine is leafless at base.

FATSIA japonica
(Aralia sieboldii, A. japonica)

JAPANESE ARALIA

Araliaceae

EVERGREEN SHRUB

ZONES 4–9, 13–31

PARTIAL OR FULL SHADE

REGULAR WATER

Fatsia japonica

Tropical appearance with big, glossy, dark green, deeply lobed, fanlike leaves to 16 in. wide on long stalks. Moderate growth to 5–8 ft. (rarely more); sparsely branched. Many roundish clusters of small whitish flowers in fall and winter, followed by clusters of small, shiny black fruit.

Grows in nearly all soils except soggy ones. Adapted to containers. During prolonged dry spells, wash occasionally with hose to clean leaves, lessen insect attack. Established plants sucker freely; keep suckers or remove them with spade. Rejuvenate spindly plants by cutting back hard in early spring. Plants that set fruit often self-sow.

A natural landscaping choice where bold pattern is wanted. Most effective when thinned to show some branch structure. Year-round good looks for shaded entryway or patio. Useful near swimming pools. 'Moseri' grows compact and low. 'Variegata' has leaves edged golden yellow to creamy white.

FAVA BEAN. See BEAN, BROAD

FAWN LILY. See ERYTHRONIUM californicum

FEATHERED HYACINTH. See MUSCARI comosum 'Monstrosum'

FEATHER GRASS. See STIPA

FEATHER REED GRASS. See CALAMAGROSTIS acutifolia 'Stricta'

FEIJOA sellowiana
(Acca sellowiana)

PINEAPPLE GUAVA

Myrtaceae

EVERGREEN SHRUB OR SMALL TREE

ZONES 7–9, 12–31, WARMER PARTS OF 32

FULL SUN

REGULAR WATER FOR BEST FRUITING

Feijoa sellowiana

From South America. Hardiest of so-called subtropical fruits. Normally a large multistemmed plant; if not pruned or killed back by frosts, reaches 18–25 ft., with equal spread. Can take almost any amount of pruning or training to shape as espalier, screen, hedge, or small tree. Oval leaves 2–3 in. long, glossy green above, silvery white beneath. Blooms in spring, bearing unusual inch-wide flowers with big tufts of red stamens and four fleshy white petals tinged purplish on inside. Petals are edible and can be added to fruit salads. Blossoms attract bees and birds.

Fruit ripens 4 to 5½ months after flowering in warmest regions, 5 to 7 months after bloom in cooler areas. Oval, grayish green, 1–4-in.-long fruit has soft, sweet to bland, somewhat pineapple-flavored pulp. Sometimes sold in markets under the name "feijoa" or "guava."

Improved varieties 'Beechwood', 'Coolidge', and 'Nazemetz' are self-fertile, although cross-pollination will produce a better crop. Single plants of seedlings or other named varieties may need cross-pollination.

FELICIA

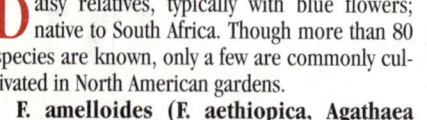

Asteraceae (Compositae)

SHRUBBY PERENNIALS AND ANNUALS

🌡 ZONES VARY BY SPECIES

☀ FULL SUN

🌢🌢 REGULAR TO MODERATE WATER

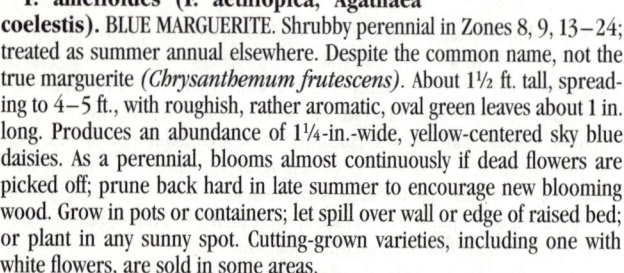

Daisy relatives, typically with blue flowers; native to South Africa. Though more than 80 species are known, only a few are commonly cultivated in North American gardens.

Felicia amelloides

F. amelloides (F. aethiopica, Agathaea coelestis). BLUE MARGUERITE. Shrubby perennial in Zones 8, 9, 13–24; treated as summer annual elsewhere. Despite the common name, not the true marguerite *(Chrysanthemum frutescens)*. About 1½ ft. tall, spreading to 4–5 ft., with roughish, rather aromatic, oval green leaves about 1 in. long. Produces an abundance of 1¼-in.-wide, yellow-centered sky blue daisies. As a perennial, blooms almost continuously if dead flowers are picked off; prune back hard in late summer to encourage new blooming wood. Grow in pots or containers; let spill over wall or edge of raised bed; or plant in any sunny spot. Cutting-grown varieties, including one with white flowers, are sold in some areas.

F. bergeriana. KINGFISHER DAISY. Annual. All zones. Forms a mat of somewhat hairy foliage to 6–10 in. high and about as wide. Blue daisies about 1 in. across bloom over a long period in summer and fall. Tolerates wind but not extreme heat. Sow seed in early spring (fall in warm-winter climates). Use in pots, window boxes, borders, as edging.

FELT PLANT. See KALANCHOE beharensis

FENNEL. See FOENICULUM vulgare

FERNLEAF YARROW. See ACHILLEA filipendulina

FERN PINE. See PODOCARPUS gracilior

FERNS. Large group of perennial plants grown for their lovely and interesting foliage. They vary in height from a few inches to 50 ft. or more, and are found in all parts of the world; most are forest plants, but some grow in deserts, in open fields, or near the timberline in high mountains. Most have finely cut leaves (fronds). They do not flower but reproduce by spores that form directly on the fronds.

Ferns are divided into several families, according to botanical differences. Such technical differences aside, these plants fall into several groups based on general appearance.

Most spectacular are tree ferns, which display their finely cut fronds atop a treelike stem. These need rich, well-drained soil, moisture, and shade (except in cool-summer regions, where they can take sun). Most tree ferns are rather tender to frost, and all suffer in hot, drying winds and in extremely low humidity. Frequent watering of tops, trunks, and root area will help pull them through unusually hot or windy weather. For several types of tree ferns, see *Cyathea cooperi, Dicksonia.*

Native ferns do not grow as tall as tree ferns, but their fronds are handsome and they can perform a number of landscape jobs. Naturalize them

in woodland or wild gardens; or use them to fill shady beds, as ground cover, as interplantings between shrubs, or along a shady house wall. Many of those native to eastern North America take extreme cold and are usually deciduous. For native ferns, see *Adiantum, Asplenium, Athyrium, Dennstaedtia punctilobula, Dryopteris, Onoclea sensibilis, Osmunda, Polystichum, Pteridium, Thelypteris, Woodsia, Woodwardia.*

Many ferns from other parts of the world grow well in the U.S.; although some are house, greenhouse, or (in mildest climates) lathhouse subjects, many are fairly hardy. Use them as you would native ferns, unless some peculiarity of habit makes it necessary to grow them in baskets or on slabs. Some exotic ferns will be found under *Adiantum, Arachniodes, Asplenium, Cyrtomium, Davallia, Humata, Nephrolepis, Pellaea, Platycerium, Polypodium, Polystichum, Pteris, Rumohra.*

All ferns look best if groomed. Cut off dead or injured fronds near ground or trunk—but don't cut back hardy outdoor ferns until new growth begins, since old fronds protect growing tips. Natives growing outdoors don't need it, but feed others frequently during growing season, preferably with light applications of organic-base fertilizer such as blood meal or fish emulsion. Mulch with peat moss occasionally, especially if shallow fibrous roots are exposed by rain or irrigation.

FESTUCA

FESCUE

Poaceae (Gramineae)

GRASSES

🌡 ZONES 1–24, 29–45

☀ FULL SUN, EXCEPT AS NOTED

🌢 REGULAR WATER; TOLERATE SOME ARIDITY

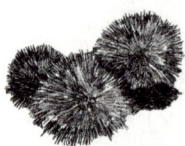

Festuca ovina 'Glauca'

Several of these clumping grasses are used for cool-season lawns, erosion control, or pasture; others have use as ornamental plants. Lawn fescues are classified as fine or coarse. All fescues need good drainage.

F. amethystina, F. cinerea, F. glauca. These grasses form tight clumps of narrow bluish or grayish leaves. All are similar to *F. ovina* 'Glauca' in appearance, culture, and uses; indeed, *F. o.* 'Glauca' may be the same plant as *F. amethystina* or *F. cinerea.* Named varieties abound; they vary in intensity of blue color and in height, ranging from 6–18 in. tall. 'Elijah Blue' is a popular powder blue variety.

F. elatior. TALL FESCUE. Coarse. Tall-growing (to 2½ ft.) pasture grass also used for erosion control when unmowed; or for moderately low-water-use lawns if planted close together and mowed to 2–3 in. high. Tough blades, tolerance of compacted soils make it good play or sports turf. Finer-textured strains are used as lawn grasses, either alone or mixed with bluegrass.

F. ovina. SHEEP FESCUE. Fine. Low-growing grass (to 1 ft.) with narrow, needle-fine, soft but tough leaves. *F. o. duriuscula*, hard fescue, is sometimes used as lawn grass. 'Glauca', blue fescue, forms blue-gray tufts 4–10 in. tall. Useful ground cover for sunny or partially shaded areas, on slopes or level ground. Cannot tolerate foot traffic. Clip back near to the ground after flowering or any time plants look shabby. Does not make solid cover and needs frequent weeding. Dig overgrown clumps, pull apart, and replant as small divisions. Set 6–15 in. apart, depending on desired effect.

F. rubra. RED FESCUE. Fine. Principal use is in blends with bluegrass or other lawn grasses. Also used to overseed Bermuda-grass lawns in winter. Blades narrow, dark green. Not fussy about soil; takes some shade. Used alone, tends to grow clumpy; mow to 1½–2½ in. high. The type most commonly sold is sometimes called creeping red fescue; it is one of most shade tolerant of good lawn grasses. Unmowed, all types of red fescue make attractive meadow on slopes too steep to mow.

FEVERFEW. See CHRYSANTHEMUM parthenium

FIBER OPTICS PLANT. See SCIRPUS cernuus

FICUS

Moraceae

EVERGREEN OR DECIDUOUS TREES, VINES, SHRUBS

ZONES VARY BY SPECIES

EXPOSURE NEEDS VARY BY SPECIES

REGULAR WATER

Ficus auriculata

The average gardener would never expect to find the commercial edible fig, small-leafed climbing fig, banyan tree, and potted rubber plant under one common heading—but they are classed together because they bear small or large figs (inedible in most species). Discussed below are ornamental plants; for edible figs, see Fig, edible.

F. auriculata (F. roxburghii). Briefly deciduous. Zones 20–25, 27. Native to India. Usually takes the form of large, spreading shrub or small tree to 25 ft. high and as wide. Leaves are unusually large—broadly oval to round, about 15 in. across. New growth is interesting mahogany red, turning to rich green. Leaves have sandpapery texture. Large figs are borne in clusters on trunk and framework branches. Can be shaped as small tree or espaliered. Beautiful in large container; good near swimming pools. Grow in wind-protected, sunny location.

F. benjamina. WEEPING CHINESE BANYAN. Evergreen tree. Zones 13, 23–25, 27; indoor plant anywhere. Native to India. To 30 ft. high and broadly spreading. Leathery, 5-in.-long leaves densely clothe drooping branches in shining green. Red figs. Grow in sun or shade in frost-free, wind-protected location. Often used as small tree

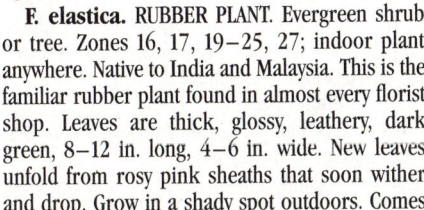

Ficus benjamina

in entryway or patio. Good as espalier or screen. In mildest climates, can be used as clipped hedge. Undoubtedly one of most popular house plants—thrives on rich, steadily moist (not wet) soil, frequent light feeding, and abundant light.

New plants are easy to start from semihardwood cuttings taken between May and July. 'Exotica' has wavy-edged leaves with long, twisted tips; it is often sold simply as *F. benjamina*.

F. carica. EDIBLE FIG. See Fig, Edible

F. deltoidea (F. diversifolia). MISTLETOE FIG. Evergreen shrub. Zones 19–25, 27; indoor plant anywhere. Native to Malaysia. Grows very slowly to 8–10 ft. high. Interesting open, twisted branch pattern. Thick, dark green, roundish, 2-in. leaves are sparsely stippled with tan specks on upper surface and a few black dots below. Attractive, small, greenish to yellow fruit borne continuously. Most often grown in containers as patio and house plant. Grow in part shade or strong diffused light.

F. elastica. RUBBER PLANT. Evergreen shrub or tree. Zones 16, 17, 19–25, 27; indoor plant anywhere. Native to India and Malaysia. This is the familiar rubber plant found in almost every florist shop. Leaves are thick, glossy, leathery, dark green, 8–12 in. long, 4–6 in. wide. New leaves unfold from rosy pink sheaths that soon wither and drop. Grow in a shady spot outdoors. Comes back quickly when cut to ground by frost. Can become a 40-ft. tree in mildest frost-free zones. One of most foolproof indoor pot subjects; takes less light than most big house plants.

If potted rubber plant becomes too tall and leggy, you can cut off top and select side branch to form a new main shoot or get a new plant by air layering top section. When roots form, cut branch section with attached roots and plant it in container.

'Decora' ('Belgica'). Considered superior to the species because of its broader, glossier leaves, bronzy when young.

Ficus deltoidea

Ficus elastica

'Rubra'. New leaves are reddish and retain red edge as rest of leaf turns green. Grown as shrub or small tree in Zones 22–25, 27.

'Variegata'. Leaves are long, narrow, variegated yellow and green. Variegation is interesting when viewed close up in container, but as an outdoor tree, plant has an unhealthy look.

F. lyrata (F. pandurata). FIDDLELEAF FIG. Evergreen shrub or tree. Zones 22–25, 27; indoor plant anywhere. Native to tropical Africa. Dramatic structural form with huge, glossy, dark green, fiddle-shaped leaves to 15 in. long and 10 in. wide, prominently veined. Highly effective as indoor pot plant. In protected outdoor position (sun or light shade), can grow to 20 ft., with trunks 6 in. thick. Good near swimming pools. To increase branching, pinch back when plant is young.

Ficus lyrata

F. macrophylla. MORETON BAY FIG. Huge evergreen tree. Zones 17, 19–27. Native to Australia. Grows to enormous dimensions. A tree in Santa Barbara, California, planted in 1877 is about 75 ft. tall and 150 ft. wide, with massive buttressed trunk and surface roots. Blunt, oval, leathery leaves, 10 in. long and 4 in. wide, glossy green above, brownish beneath. Rose-colored leaf sheaths appear like candles at branch ends. Inch-long figs are purple spotted with white. Full sun. Although tender when young, acquires hardiness with size. Shows damage at 24° to 26°F/−4° to −3°C. Plant only if you can give it plenty of room.

F. microcarpa (F. retusa). INDIAN LAUREL FIG. Evergreen tree. Zones 9, 13, 16–25, 27. Native to India, Malaysia. Grows at moderate rate to 25–30 ft. tall. Beautiful weeping form, with long, drooping branches thickly clothed with blunt-tipped, 2–4-in.-long leaves. Light rose to chartreuse new leaves, produced almost continuously, give tree a pleasing two-tone effect. Trim off lower trailing branches to reveal slim, light gray trunk supporting massive crown. Full sun.

F. m. nitida has dense foliage on upright-growing branches and is admirably suited to formal shearing. Leaves are clear lustrous green, similar in size to those of species. Prune at any time of year to the size or shape desired.

In some areas, both the species and variety are attacked by a thrips that curls new leaves, stippling them and causing them to fall. 'Green Gem' has thicker, darker green leaves and is apparently unaffected by the thrips.

F. pumila (F. repens). CREEPING FIG. Evergreen vine. Zones 8–28, protected parts of 29–32. Native to China, Japan, Australia. A most unfiglike habit; it is one of few plants that attaches itself securely to wood, masonry, or even metal in barnacle fashion. Because it is grown on walls, and thus protected, it is more often found in colder climates than any other evergreen fig. Grows in sun or shade; not for hot south or west wall.

Looks innocent enough in young stages, making a delicate tracery of tiny, heart-shaped leaves. Neat little juvenile foliage ultimately develops into large (2–4-in.-long), leathery leaves borne on stubby branches that bear large oblong fruit. In time, stems will envelop a three- or four-story building so completely that it becomes necessary to keep them trimmed away from windows. Safe to use this fig on houses if it is cut to the ground every few years; also control by removing fruiting stems from time to time as they form. Roots are invasive, probably more so than those of most other figs. 'Minima' has shorter, narrower leaves than species. Small, lobed leaves of 'Quercifolia' are like tiny oak leaves. 'Variegata' has standard-size leaves with creamy white markings.

F. religiosa. PEEPUL, BO-TREE. Briefly deciduous tree. Zones 13, 19, 21, 23–25, 27. Native to India. Large, upright; less spreading than *F. macrophylla*. Foliage is quite open and delicate, revealing structure of tree at all times. Bark is warm, rich brown. Roundish, pale green leaves are rather crisp and thin textured, 4–7 in. long with long tail-like point. They move easily even in slightest breeze, giving foliage a fluttering effect. Foliage drops completely in spring—a frightening experience for the gardener who has bought an "evergreen" fig. Full sun.

F. retusa. See F. microcarpa

F. roxburghii. See F. auriculata

F. rubiginosa. RUSTYLEAF FIG. Evergreen tree. Zones 18–27. Native to Australia. Grows to 20–50 ft., with broad crown, dense foliage, and single

F

or multiple trunks. Leaves about 5 in., deep green above, generally rust colored and woolly beneath. May develop hanging aerial roots that characterize many of the evergreen figs that grow in tropical environments. Full sun. A small-leafed form has been sold as *F. microphylla*.

F. r. australis varies from the species (if it varies at all) in having slightly less rusty leaves. 'El Toro' and 'Irvine' have exceptionally dark green leaves; 'Florida', widely distributed, has lighter green leaves. 'Variegata', with leaves mottled green and cream, is sometimes sold as a house plant.

> ### SUDDEN LEAF-SHEDDING ON A *FICUS BENJAMINA*?
> The problem is common and often results from the plant being moved to a new location. If the shedding problem begins shortly after a move, be patient; leaves usually grow back. If the leaves that fall are green, insufficient water is another possible cause; try to keep soil evenly moist. If the plant drops yellow leaves, overwatering may be to blame. Finally, if shedding is accompanied by a sweet smell and sticky leaves, look for scale insects and control them as needed.

FIG, EDIBLE

Moraceae

DECIDUOUS TREES

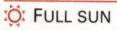 ZONES 4–9, 12–31, WARMER PARTS OF 32; OR IN POTS

☼ FULL SUN

🔴 REGULAR WATER

Edible Fig

For ornamental relatives, see *Ficus*. Grow fairly fast to 15–30 ft., generally low branched and spreading; where hard freezes are common, wood freezes back severely and plant behaves as a big shrub. Can be held to 10 ft. in big container, or trained as espalier along fence or wall.

Trunks heavy, smooth, gray barked, gnarled in really old trees, picturesque in silhouette. Leaves rough, bright green, with three to five lobes, 4–9 in. long and nearly as wide. Casts dense shade. Winter framework, tropical-looking foliage, strong trunk and branch pattern make fig a topnotch ornamental tree, especially near patio where it can be illuminated from beneath. Protect container plants in winter. Fruit drop is problem immediately above deck or paving.

Not particular about soil. In colder part of range, trees planted near south walls or trained against them benefit from reflected heat. Cut back tops hard at planting. As tree grows, prune lightly each winter, cutting out dead wood, crossing branches, and low-hanging branches that interfere with traffic. Pinch back runaway shoots any season. Avoid deep cultivation, which may damage surface roots; do not use high-nitrogen fertilizers, which stimulate growth at expense of fruit. If burrowing animals are a problem, plant trees in ample wire baskets.

Home garden figs do not need pollinating, and most varieties bear two crops a year. The first comes in June–July on last year's wood; the second and more important comes in September–October from current summer's wood. Ripe figs will detach easily when lifted and bent back toward the branch. Keep fruit picked as it ripens; protect from birds if you can. In late fall, pick off any remaining ripe figs and clean up fallen fruit.

Varieties differ in climate adaptability; most need prolonged high temperatures to bear good fruit, while some thrive in cooler conditions. The familiar dried 'Calimyrna' or imported Smyrna figs sold in markets require special pollinators (caprifigs) and special pollinating insect; not recommended for home gardens. Varieties with most tightly closed "eyes"— opening opposite stem end—resist invasion by dried fruit beetle, a pest in some areas. Such varieties are noted below.

'Alma'. Very sweet, medium-size fig with golden brown skin, amber-tan flesh. Closed eye.

'Brown Turkey' ('San Pedro', 'Black Spanish'). Adaptable to most fig climates; widely grown in Southeast. Good garden tree; small, cold hardy. Fruit has purplish brown skin, pinkish amber flesh; good for fresh eating. Closed eye.

'Celeste' ('Blue Celeste', 'Celestial'). The most widely grown fig variety in the Southeast; also grown in the West. Cold-hardy plant. Bronzy, violet-tinged skin, rosy amber flesh; good for fresh eating. Closed eye.

'Conadria'. Choice thin-skinned white figs blushed violet; white to red flesh, fine flavor. Best in hot areas; takes intense heat without splitting.

'Genoa' ('White Genoa'). Greenish yellow skin, strawberry to yellow flesh.

'Italian Everbearing'. Resembles 'Brown Turkey', but fruit is somewhat larger, with reddish brown skin. Good fresh or dried.

'Kadota' ('White Kadota'). Tough-skinned fruit has lemon yellow skin, light amber to yellow flesh. Commercial canning variety. Strong grower; needs little pruning. If pruned severely, will bear later, with fewer, larger fruits. Needs lots of heat.

'Magnolia' ('Brunswick'). Medium to large figs with reddish brown skin and amber to strawberry-colored flesh. A widely grown variety in the Southeast.

'Mission' ('Black Mission'). Large tree bearing purple-black figs with pink flesh; good fresh or dried. One of the most popular varieties in California; also grown in warm areas of Southeast. Closed eye.

'Osborn Prolific'. Medium to large fruit with purple-brown skin and white to amber, very sweet flesh. Good bearer in cool-summer areas.

'Texas Everbearing'. Medium to large figs with brownish yellow skin, strawberry-colored flesh. Closed eye.

'White Adriatic'. Medium to large, sweet white figs with yellowish green skin, strawberry pink flesh. Very drought tolerant.

FILBERT, HAZELNUT

Betulaceae

DECIDUOUS NUT TREES

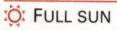 ZONES 2–7, 32, 34–43

☼ FULL SUN

🔴 REGULAR WATER

Filbert

For ornamental types, see *Corylus*. Those raised for nuts need winter chill for a good crop. Commercial orchards are in the Pacific Northwest, where named selections of European species (*C. avellana* and *C. maxima*) are grown. They produce the biggest, most flavorful nuts. The leading varieties include 'Barcelona', 'Butler', 'Du Chilly', 'Ennis', and 'Royal'. The growing range of European types is restricted, since their flower buds are damaged at 15°F/−9°C and they are susceptible to eastern filbert blight, a destructive and incurable bark disease.

Gardeners in the eastern U.S. can grow either the blight-resistant, hardier native hazelnuts (*C. americana* or *C. cornuta*) or European-American hybrids. The principal hybrids are 'Bixby', 'Buchanan', 'Potomac', and 'Reed'; these have inherited some of the blight resistance and cold hardiness of their American parents, but they bear typically smaller, somewhat less flavorful nuts than the European types. The nuts of American species are smaller and less flavorful still.

Most types grown for nuts are shrubby (10–18 ft. high) and will grow into thickets unless suckers are cleared out three or four times a year. For a boundary hedgerow, plant mixed varieties 4 ft. apart and permit suckers to grow. For best nut production, plant in deep, well-drained, fertile, slightly acid soil in a sunny spot (some afternoon shade is best in hottest climates). Since cross-pollination is necessary, plant at least two varieties (or two plants if growing a native). In the eastern U.S., don't plant a European variety if wild hazels are nearby; they carry the blight even though they themselves are unaffected. In the West, native hazels don't carry the disease. The blight is evident as rows of black dots on the trunk. As protection, spray copper and dormant oil together at bud break, usually late March, and again in mid-April and early May.

Nuts ripen by the end of August and drop in early fall. Harvest by picking them from the ground, then dry them in the sun for a few days. Squirrels are a nuisance, often picking the nuts before they ripen.

FILIPENDULA

Rosaceae

PERENNIALS

Zones 1–9, 14–17, 31–45, except as noted

Partial shade in warmer areas

Ample water

Filipendula rubra 'Venusta'

Like related *Astilbe,* have plumes of tiny flowers above coarsely divided leaves that look like fern fronds. Dormant in winter, even in mild-winter areas. Most species prefer moist to constantly damp soil. Use in borders, naturalistic landscapes, beside ponds. Plant in full sun in northern latitudes and where summers are cool; give partial shade where summers are warm to hot.

F. hexapetala. See *F. vulgaris*

F. purpurea. Zones 3–9, 14–17, 31–34, 39. Pink, 3–4-ft.-tall plumes rise above maplelike, 5–7-in. leaves. Varieties include 'Alba', with white plumes 2 ft. tall; 'Elegans', bearing 2-ft.-tall white flowers with red stamens; and 'Nana', with salmon pink plumes 12–15 in. tall.

F. rubra. QUEEN OF THE PRAIRIE. Given plenty of moisture and rich soil, can reach 8 ft. high in bloom; bears pink plumes. 'Venusta' has purplish pink flowers and is a little shorter, to 4–6 ft. high.

F. ulmaria. MEADOW SWEET, QUEEN OF THE MEADOW. To 6 ft. high, with 10-in. creamy white plumes. 'Flore Pleno', just 3 ft. tall, has dense plumes of double white flowers; 'Variegata' is similar, but with gold-speckled leaves. 'Aurea' is grown not for flowers but for bright golden leaves; protect from sun.

F. vulgaris (F. hexapetala). DROPWORT. White plumes on 3-ft. stems rise above 10-in., fernlike leaves with 1-in. leaflets. Double-flowered 'Flore Pleno' has heavier-looking plumes. Needs less water than the other species; also prefers full sun in all but the warmest regions.

FINOCCHIO. See **FOENICULUM vulgare azoricum**

FIR. See **ABIES**

FIRETAIL. See **ACALYPHA pendula**

FIRETHORN. See **PYRACANTHA**

FIRMIANA simplex (F. platanifolia)

CHINESE PARASOL TREE

Sterculiaceae

DECIDUOUS TREE

Zones 5, 6, 8, 9, 12–31, warmer parts of 32, 33

Full sun or morning sun

Regular water

Firmiana simplex

Native to China, Japan. Typically 30–45 ft. in gardens, usually slow growing, with unique light gray-green bark. Trunk often is unbranched for 4–5 ft. before dividing into three or more slender, upright, slightly spreading stems that carry lobed, tropical-looking, 1-ft. leaves. Each stem looks as if it could be cut off and carried away as a parasol. Large, loose, upright clusters of greenish white flowers appear at branch ends in early summer. Interesting fruit resembles two opened green pea pods with seeds

on margins. Goes leafless for long period in winter—an unusual trait for a tropical-looking tree.

Tolerates all soil types. Does well in patios and courtyards protected from wind. Useful near swimming pools.

FISHTAIL PALM. See **CARYOTA**
FIVE-FINGER FERN. See **ADIANTUM aleuticum**
FLAG. See **IRIS**
FLAMBOYANT. See **DELONIX regia**
FLAMEGOLD. See **KOELREUTERIA elegans**
FLAME OF THE WOODS. See **IXORA coccinea**
FLAME TREE. See **BRACHYCHITON acerifolius**
FLAME VINE. See **PYROSTEGIA venusta**
FLAME VIOLET. See **EPISCIA**
FLANNEL BUSH. See **FREMONTODENDRON**
FLAX. See **LINUM**
FLAX, NEW ZEALAND. See **PHORMIUM**
FLAXLEAF PAPERBARK. See **MELALEUCA linariifolia**
FLEABANE. See **ERIGERON**
FLORIDA HEATHER. See **CUPHEA hyssopifolia**
FLOSS FLOWER. See **AGERATUM houstonianum**
FLOSS SILK TREE. See **CHORISIA**
FLOWERING ALMOND, CHERRY. See **PRUNUS**
FLOWERING CRABAPPLE. See **MALUS**
FLOWERING MAPLE. See **ABUTILON**
FLOWERING NECTARINE, PEACH, PLUM. See **PRUNUS**
FLOWERING QUINCE. See **CHAENOMELES**
FLOWERY SENNA. See **CASSIA corymbosa**
FOAM FLOWER. See **TIARELLA**

IT FEEDS BENEFICIAL INSECTS

Common fennel is one of those prolific but valuable plants that provide pollen and nectar to beneficial insects when those insects aren't feeding on plant-damaging insects and mites. The good guys this plant sustains include hover flies, lacewings, ladybird beetles, paper wasps, and soldier bugs. It's also an important source of food for butterfly larvae.

FOENICULUM vulgare

COMMON FENNEL

Apiaceae (Umbelliferae)

PERENNIAL OR ANNUAL HERB

Zones vary by type

Full sun

Moderate water

Foeniculum vulgare

Two forms of fennel are commonly grown. One is a perennial, used for seasoning; the other is grown as an annual for its edible leaf bases.

The plain species is a perennial (Zones 3–24, 29–41), cultivated for licorice-flavored seeds and young leaves. Grows to 3–5 ft. tall. Similar to dill, but coarser. Yellow-green, finely cut leaves; flat clusters of yellow flowers. Bronze fennel ('Purpurascens', 'Smokey'), to 6 ft. tall, has bronzy purple foliage. Start from seed where plants are to be grown. Sow in light, well-drained soil; thin seedlings to 1 ft. apart. Use seeds to season breads; use leaves as garnish for salads, fish. Fennel often grows as a roadside or garden weed; it's attractive until tops turn brown, and even then birds like the seeds. New stems grow in spring from perennial root.

F. v. azoricum, called Florence fennel or finocchio, is grown as a summer annual in all zones. It is lower growing (to 2 ft. high) than the species, with larger, thicker leafstalk bases that are used as a cooked or raw vegetable.

FORGET-ME-NOT. See MYOSOTIS

FORSYTHIA

Oleaceae

DECIDUOUS SHRUBS

ZONES 2–16, 18, 19, 30–41; HARDIEST TYPES IN 1, 42, 43

FULL SUN

REGULAR TO MODERATE WATER

Forsythia intermedia

From late winter to early spring, these fountain-shaped shrubs' bare branches are covered with yellow flowers. During rest of growing season, medium green foliage blends well with other shrubs in background of border plantings. Leaves rounded, with pointed tips. Use as screen, espalier, or bank cover; or plant in shrub border. Branches can be forced for indoor bloom in winter.

Tolerate most soils; respond to fertilizer. Prune established plants after bloom: cut a third of branches that have bloomed down to ground; remove oldest branches, weak or dead wood. In coldest winter climates, the flower buds may be destroyed by temperatures of −15° to −20°F/−26° to −29°C. The most bud-hardy varieties are noted below.

F. 'Arnold Dwarf'. Grows 1½–3 ft. high, to 6 ft. wide. Flowers are sparse and not especially attractive, but plant is a useful, fast-growing ground cover in cold climates.

Hardy hybrids. The spate of cold-hardy introductions in recent years includes the following:

'Meadowlark'. Semiarching, to 6–9 ft. tall. Flower buds hardy to −35°F/−37°C. Bright yellow blooms. Grown commercially in the upper Midwest.

'New Hampshire Gold'. Mounding habit to 5 ft. high, with drooping golden yellow blossoms.

'Northern Sun'. Upright, to 8–10 ft. tall. Reliable bloomer in areas where winter temperatures often drop to −30°F/−34°C.

F. intermedia. The most widely grown forsythias belong to this hybrid group. Most grow 7–10 ft. tall and have arching branches; smaller selections are also included in the following list.

'Beatrix Farrand'. Upright to 10 ft. tall, 7 ft. wide. Branches thickly set with 2–2½-in.-wide flowers in deep yellow marked with orange.

'Fiesta'. Grows 3–4 ft. high. Deep yellow flowers followed by green-and-yellow variegated leaves that hold their color all summer long.

'Goldtide'. Compact growth to 20 in. tall by 4 ft. wide; profuse bright yellow flowers.

'Goldzauber' ('Gold Charm'). Erect to 6–8 ft. high, with large, deep yellow flowers.

'Karl Sax'. Resembles 'Beatrix Farrand' but is lower growing, neater, more graceful.

'Lynwood' ('Lynwood Gold'). Stiffly upright to 7 ft., with 4–6-ft. spread. Profuse tawny yellow blooms survive spring storms.

'Spectabilis'. Dense, upright, vigorous to 9 ft. Deep yellow flowers; buds are cold hardy.

'Spring Glory'. To about 6 ft. tall, with heavy crop of pale yellow flowers.

'Tetragold'. Grows 3–5 ft. high. Deep yellow blossoms.

F. mandschurica 'Vermont Sun'. Exceptionally bud hardy. Erect growing to 6–8 ft.; blooms earlier than other forsythias, bearing lemon yellow flowers. Not as showy as the forsythia hybrids.

F. ovata. KOREAN FORSYTHIA. Shrub to 4–6 ft., spreading wider. Early bloomer, with a profusion of bright yellow flowers about a week after *F. mandschurica* 'Vermont Sun'.

F. suspensa. WEEPING FORSYTHIA. Dense, upright growth habit 8–10 ft., with 6–8-ft. spread. Drooping, vinelike branches root where they touch damp soil. Golden yellow flowers. Useful large-scale bank cover. Can be trained as vine; if you support main branches, branchlets will cascade. 'Fortunei' is somewhat more upright, more available in nurseries.

F. viridissima. GREENSTEM FORSYTHIA. Stiff-looking shrub to 10 ft. with deep green foliage, olive green stems, greenish yellow flowers. 'Bronxensis' is slow-growing dwarf form to 16 in. tall, for smaller shrub borders or ground cover. *F. v. koreana (F. koreana)*, to 8 ft., has larger, brighter yellow flowers and attractive purplish autumn foliage.

FORTNIGHT LILY. See DIETES

FORTUNELLA margarita. See CITRUS, Kumquat

FOTHERGILLA

Hamamelidaceae

DECIDUOUS SHRUBS

ZONES 3–9, 14–17, 31–39

PARTIAL SHADE IN HOT-SUMMER AREAS

REGULAR WATER

Fothergilla major

Native to southeastern U.S. Grown principally for fall foliage color, but small, honey-scented white flowers in brushlike, 1–2-in. clusters on zigzagging stems are pretty in spring. Performs best in moist, well-drained, acid soil.

F. gardenii. DWARF FOTHERGILLA. Typically 2–3 ft. high (though it can grow considerably taller) and as wide or wider. Inch-long flower clusters appear before the 1–2½-in.-long leaves. Fall foliage intense yellow and orange red. 'Mt. Airy' is taller than the species, with larger flower clusters, deeper blue-green leaves, and better fall color. 'Blue Mist' also has bluish summer foliage.

F. major. Erect shrub to 9 ft. with roundish, 2–4-in.-long leaves turning yellow to orange to purplish red in autumn. Flowers appear with the leaves. Plant formerly known as *F. monticola* is now treated as this species.

FOUNTAIN GRASS. See PENNISETUM setaceum

FOUQUIERIA splendens

OCOTILLO

Fouquieriaceae

DECIDUOUS SHRUB

ZONES 10–13, 18–20

FULL SUN

VERY LITTLE WATER

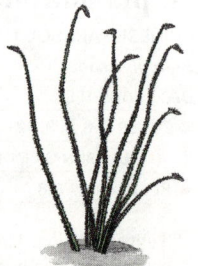

Fouquieria splendens

Native to Mojave and Colorado deserts east to Texas and south to Mexico. Many stiff, whip-like gray stems 8–25 ft. high, heavily furrowed and covered with stout thorns. Fleshy, roundish, ½–1-in.-long leaves appear after rains, soon drop. Tubular, ¾–1-in.-long red flowers in attractive foot-long clusters after spring or summer rains. Can be used as screening, impenetrable hedge, or for silhouette against bare walls. Needs excellent drainage. Cuttings stuck in ground will grow.

FOUR O'CLOCK. See MIRABILIS jalapa

FOXGLOVE. See DIGITALIS

FRAGARIA chiloensis

WILD STRAWBERRY, SAND STRAWBERRY

Rosaceae

EVERGREEN GROUND COVER

🗡 ZONES 4–24

☼ ◑ PARTIAL SHADE IN HOT-SUMMER AREAS

🌢 REGULAR WATER

Fragaria chiloensis

Native to Pacific beaches and bluffs, North and South America. One of the parents of commercial strawberries. Forms lush, compact mats 6–12 in. high. Dark green, glossy leaves have three tooth-edged leaflets. Leaves take on red tints in winter. Large (1-in.-wide) white flowers in spring, sometimes followed by bright red, ¾-in., seedy fruits in fall. Fruits are edible but not very tasty, although birds do find them appealing. For fruiting or garden strawberry, see Strawberry.

Plant rooted stolons in late spring or early summer. Nursery-grown plants can be planted any time. Set plants 1–1½ ft. apart. Mow or cut back annually in early spring to force fresh new growth and to prevent stem buildup.

FRANGIPANI. See PLUMERIA rubra

FRANKLINIA alatamaha (Gordonia alatamaha)

Theaceae

DECIDUOUS TREE

🗡 ZONES 3–6, 14–17, 31–35

☼ ◑ FULL SUN OR LIGHT SHADE

🌢 REGULAR WATER

Franklinia alatamaha

Unusual, very handsome tree once native to Georgia, but apparently extinct in the wilds before 1800. Open, airy form; may reach 30 ft., but more typically grows 10–20 ft. high. Tends to be fairly slender when grown with a single trunk, broad spreading with multiple trunks. Attractive dark gray bark has faint white vertical striping. Shiny dark green, spoon-shaped leaves, 4–6 in. long, turn orange and red in fall; they hang on for a long time before dropping. Fragrant, 3-in.-wide, five-petaled white flowers centered with clusters of yellow stamens open from round white buds in August–September, sometimes coinciding with fall foliage color. Blossoms resemble single camellias—not surprising, since franklinia and camellia belong to the same family. Flowers are followed by small, woody capsules split into ten segments, each containing five seeds.

Provide moist, rich, light, acid soil. Good drainage is critical. Grows well in light shade, but has best bloom and fall color in full sun. Easy to grow from seed, blooming in 6 to 7 years. Highly decorative lawn or patio tree. Use for contrast in azalea or rhododendron plantings. Performs better in northern part of range than in southern.

FRAXINELLA. See DICTAMNUS albus

PRACTICAL GARDENING DICTIONARY
PLEASE SEE PAGES 545–616

FRAXINUS

ASH

Oleaceae

DECIDUOUS TREES

🗡 ZONES VARY BY SPECIES

☼ FULL SUN

🌢 💧 REGULAR TO MODERATE WATER

Fraxinus ornus

Trees grow fairly fast, and most tolerate hot summers, cold winters, and various soils. In many areas, ashes are susceptible to a number of serious problems, including anthracnose and borers, so check before planting. They are chiefly used as street trees, shade trees, lawn trees, patio shelter trees.

In most cases, leaves are divided into leaflets. Male and female flowers (generally inconspicuous, in clusters) grow on separate trees in some species, on same tree in others. In latter case, flowers are often followed by clusters of single-seeded, winged fruit, often in such abundance that they can be a litter problem. When flowers are on separate trees, you'll get fruit on female tree only if it grows near male tree.

F. americana. WHITE ASH. Zones 1–11, 14–17, 28–43. Native to eastern U.S. Grows to 80 ft. or more, with straight trunk and oval-shaped crown. Leaves 8–15 in. long, with five to nine oval leaflets; dark green above, paler beneath. Foliage turns purplish in fall. Male and female flowers on separate trees, but plants sold are generally seedlings, so you don't know what you're getting. If you end up with both male and female trees, you will get a heavy crop of seed; both litter and seedlings can be problem.

Seedless selections include 'Autumn Applause' and 'Autumn Purple', both with exceptionally good, long-lasting purple fall color; 'Champaign County', a dense grower with no appreciable fall color; 'Greenspire', narrow upright habit, deep orange fall color; 'Rosehill', with bronzy red fall color; 'Royal Purple', upright, with purple autumn leaves; and 'Skyline', an upright oval with brown and purple fall color. *F. texensis*, a drought-tolerant and fairly pest-resistant tree growing 30–45 ft. high, is considered a variety of *F. americana*.

F. angustifolia (F. oxycarpa). Zones 3–9, 12–24, 29, 30. Fairly compact, small leafed, and fine textured, with delicate, lacy look. Apparently not grown in the U.S. except in its variety 'Raywood'—the Raywood or claret ash, a round-headed, compact, fast-growing tree to 25–35 ft. tall with purple-red fall color and no seeds.

F. excelsior. EUROPEAN ASH. Zones 1–11, 14–17, 30–43; best in colder part of range. Native to Europe, Asia Minor. Rounded-headed tree 60–80 ft. (possibly 140 ft.) tall. Black dormant buds. Leaves 10–12 in. long, divided into 7–11 oval, toothed leaflets, dark green above, paler beneath; do not change color but drop while green. 'Kimberley' is a seedless selection used as a shade tree. 'Pendula', weeping European ash, is a spreading, rather asymmetrical, umbrella-shaped tree with weeping branches that reach the ground.

F. holotricha. Zones 4–24, 28–35, 37, 39. Native to eastern Balkan Peninsula. Upright, rather narrow tree to 40 ft. Leaves have 9–13 dull green, 2–3-in.-long leaflets with toothed edges. Casts light filtered shade. Leaves turn yellow in fall, dry up, and sift down into lawn or ground cover, thus lessening litter. 'Moraine' is a neat, symmetrical tree with a rounded head and uniform bright yellow fall foliage; produces few seeds.

F. latifolia (F. oregona). OREGON ASH. Zones 4–24. Native to Sierra Nevada and along coast from Northern California to British Columbia. Grows 40–80 ft. tall. Light green leaves 6–12 in. long, divided into five to seven oblong to oval leaflets. Male and female flowers on separate trees.

F. ornus. FLOWERING ASH. Zones 3–9, 14–17, 28–34, 39; best in colder parts of range. Native to southern Europe and Asia Minor. Grows rapidly to 40–50 ft. with broad, rounded crown 20–30 ft. wide. Supplies luxuriant mass of foliage. Leaves 8–10 in. long, divided into 7–11 oval, medium green, 2-in.-long leaflets with toothed edges. Foliage turns to soft shades of lavender and yellow in fall. In spring, displays quantities of fluffy, branched, 3–5-in.-long clusters of fragrant white to greenish white

F

blossoms followed by unsightly seed clusters that hang on until late winter unless removed.

F. pennsylvanica (F. lanceolata). GREEN ASH, RED ASH. Zones 1–6, 26, 28–45. Native to eastern U.S. Typically 50–60 ft. tall, forming irregular oval crown. Gray-brown bark; dense, twiggy structure. Bright green leaves 10–12 in. long, divided into five to nine rather narrow, 4–6-in.-long leaflets. Inconsistent yellow fall color. Takes wet soil and severe cold, but foliage burns in hot, dry winds. Male and female flowers on separate trees.

Seedless varieties include 'Bergeson', fast growing, cold tolerant; 'Emerald', round headed, not as cold hardy as other selections; 'Marshall', fast growing, tapered crown, fewer insect problems than species; 'Patmore', tolerant of extreme cold; 'Summit', upright habit, good golden yellow fall color; and 'Urbanite', pyramidal shape and bronze fall color.

F. quadrangulata. BLUE ASH. Zones 2–6, 33, 35–41. Native to central U.S. Grows rapidly to 60–80 ft. or more. Branches distinctly square, usually with flanges along edges. Oval, dark green leaflets (7–11 per leaf), 2–5 in. long, with toothed edges. Foliage turns purplish in fall. Fruit may become litter problem if you have both female and male trees.

F. velutina. ARIZONA ASH. Zones 8–24, 28–30. Withstands hot, dry conditions and cold to about −10°F/−23°C. Grows about 30 ft. (possibly to 50 ft.) tall. Pyramidal when young; spreading, more open when mature. Leaves divided into three to five narrow to oval, 3-in.-long leaflets; turn bright yellow in fall. Male and female flowers on separate trees.

'Rio Grande' is the variety most commonly grown in Texas. Its leaflets are larger and darker green than those of the species; they resist wind. 'Modesto' (Zones 3–24) is the most popular ash in California. It is a vigorous form to about 50 ft. tall and 30 ft. wide, with glossier leaves than species.

Fraxinus velutina 'Modesto'

FRECKLE FACE. See HYPOESTES phyllostachya

FREESIA

Iridaceae

CORMS

ZONES 8, 9, 12–24, 28; OR INDOORS

FULL SUN OR PARTIAL SHADE

REGULAR WATER DURING GROWTH AND BLOOM

Freesia Hybrid

Native to South Africa. Prized for rich perfume of flowers; white and yellow types tend to be more fragrant than those with blooms in other colors. Slender, branched stems grow 1–1½ ft. tall, about same height as lowest leaves; stem leaves shorter. Flowers tubular, 2 in. long, in one-sided spikes. Older variety 'Alba' has fragrant white or creamy blooms; newer, larger-flowered varieties with 1–1½-ft. stems are Tecolote and Dutch hybrids with white, pink, red, lavender, purple, blue, yellow, and orange flowers, mixed or in varieties named for single colors. Freesias will self-sow if faded flowers are not removed; volunteers tend to revert to cream marked with purple and yellow.

Freesias are hardy to 20°F/−7°C. In mild climates, plant corms 2 in. deep (pointed end up) in fall in sunny, well-drained soil. Plants dry up after bloom, start growing again in fall; they increase rapidly. In cold climates, plant 2 in. deep, 2 in. apart in pots; grow indoors in sunny window. Keep room temperature as cool as possible at night. Freesias are easily grown from seed sown in July–August; often bloom following spring. Flowering potted freesias grown from chilled and stored corms are available throughout the year.

FREMONTODENDRON (Fremontia)

FLANNEL BUSH

Sterculiaceae

EVERGREEN SHRUBS OR SMALL TREES

ZONES 7–24

FULL SUN

WILL TOLERATE VERY LITTLE SUMMER WATER

Fremontodendron 'California Glory'

Native to California. Fast growing to 6–20 ft. tall, usually irregularly shaped. Leathery leaves are dark green above, grayish or whitish and feltlike beneath. Very showy, brilliant yellow, saucerlike blossoms in spring. Followed by persistent conical seed capsules covered with bristly, rust-colored hairs; these can irritate skin. Plants are completely drought tolerant when established; they will accept occasional water during their normally dry period in summer only if drainage is excellent. Roots are shallow, so stake plants while young. Locate in front of a sunny wall in marginal climates. Usually short lived.

F. 'California Glory'. Hybrid between *F. californicum* and *F. mexicanum*. Flowers to 3 in. across, rich yellow inside, tinged red outside. Prolific bloom over long period.

F. californicum. COMMON FLANNEL BUSH. Eye-catching show of lemon yellow, 1–1½-in. flowers; tend to bloom all at once. Roundish unlobed or three-lobed leaves, 1 in. long.

F. mexicanum. SOUTHERN FLANNEL BUSH. Brilliant display of orange-tinted blossoms to 2½ in. across. Blooms less profusely than *F. californicum*, but flowers appear over a longer period. Leaves, to 3 in. long, have three to five distinct lobes.

F. 'San Gabriel'. Resembles 'California Glory', but leaves are more deeply cut (maplelike).

FRINGE BELLS. See SHORTIA soldanelloides

FRINGECUPS. See TELLIMA grandiflora

FRINGED WORMWOOD. See ARTEMISIA frigida

FRINGE HYACINTH. See MUSCARI comosum

FRINGE TREE. See CHIONANTHUS

FRITILLARIA

FRITILLARY

Liliaceae

BULBS

ZONES VARY BY SPECIES

FULL SUN OR LIGHT SHADE, EXCEPT AS NOTED

REGULAR WATER DURING GROWTH AND BLOOM

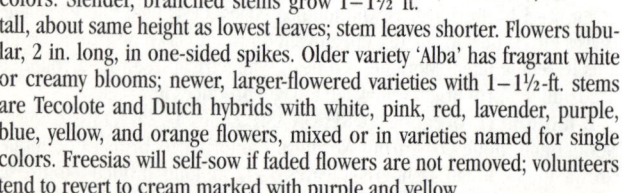

Fritillaria imperialis

In spring, unbranched stems, 6 in.–4 ft. high, are topped by bell-like, nodding flowers, often unusually colored and mottled. Use in woodland gardens, rock gardens, or borders. In fall, plant bulbs in porous soil with ample humus. Set smaller bulbs 3–4 in. deep; set largest (*F. imperialis*) 4–5 in. deep. Bulbs sometimes rest a year after planting or after blooming, so put in enough for a yearly display.

F. biflora. MISSION BELLS. Zones 3–7, 14–17. Native to California. Thrives in heavy clay soil. Grows 6–16 in. tall, with one to six brownish, 1½-in. flowers on each stem. 'Martha Roderick' has rusty orange flowers with a white center.

F. camschatcensis. BLACK LILY, CHOCOLATE LILY. Zones 1–7, 15–17, 38–43. Native to areas around northern Pacific Ocean, Japan to northwestern U.S. Grows 9–18 in. tall, with whorls of leaves around the stem; one to six dark purple to black bells per stem. Prefers part shade.

F. imperialis. CROWN IMPERIAL. Zones 1–7, 14–17, 32–43. Native to Europe. Stout stalk 3½–4 ft. tall, clothed with broad, glossy leaves and topped by circle of 2–3-in.-long bells in red, orange, or yellow; tuft of leaves above flowers. Bulb and plant have somewhat unpleasant odor.

F. meleagris. CHECKERED LILY, SNAKESHEAD. Zones 1–7, 15–17, 32–43. Native to damp meadows in Europe, Asia; tolerates occasional flooding. Showy 2-in. bells, checkered and veined with reddish brown and purple, atop 1–1½-ft. stems. Lance-shaped leaves are 3–6 in. long. There is a white-blossomed form.

F. michailovskyi. Zones 2–7, 14–17, 32 (colder parts), 33–41. Native to northeastern Turkey. Grows 6 in. tall; each stem bears one to five 1–1¼-in. bells that are purplish brown on the lower portion, bright yellow on the top half.

F. pallidiflora. Zones 1–7, 33–43. Native to Siberia, northern China. Slender stems 4–16 in. tall carry one to six (or more) pale yellow, green-tinted bells 1¼ in. long.

F. persica 'Adiyaman'. Zones 2–7, 14–17, 32 (colder parts), 33–41. Stems 2–3 ft. tall carry up to 30 deep plum purple, 1-in. flowers on upper half. Foliage is grayish. Plant is hardy and easy to grow—but in colder regions, emerging stems need protection from late frosts.

FUCHSIA

Onagraceae

EVERGREEN OR DECIDUOUS SHRUBS

ZONES VARY BY SPECIES

PARTIAL SHADE

REGULAR WATER

Fuchsia hybrida
Double Type

Popular, showy-flowered fuchsias are forms of *F. hybrida,* and are discussed under that heading. Other species are grown almost entirely by collectors, though the one described here, *F. magellanica,* is good for basic landscaping purposes. The following types bloom from early summer to first frost. Flowers are unscented, frequented by hummingbirds.

F. hybrida. HYBRID FUCHSIA. Here belong nearly all garden fuchsias. Zones 15–17, 22–24 have the best climates for growing fuchsias outdoors all year—cool summers with atmospheric moisture (such as morning fog) and virtually frostless winters. Zones 4–6, and coastal 38, have excellent growing-season climate, but plants will need garden protection or indoor shelter from winter cold. In Zones 7–9, 14, 20, 21, plants will need frequent summer misting or sprinkling to increase humidity and are likely to need frost protection in most winters. In other zones, fuchsias are either impossible due to summer heat and humidity or are grown (with some fussing) as summer annuals, in greenhouses, or as house plants.

Hundreds of varieties are available, with many color combinations. Sepals (top parts that flare back) are always white, red, or pink. Corolla (inside part of flower) may be almost any color possible within range of white, blue violet, purple, pink, red, and shades approaching orange. Flowers may be single- or double-petaled, varying in size from as small as a shelled peanut to as large as a child's fist. Plants vary from erect-growing shrubs 3–12 ft. high to trailing types grown in hanging containers.

Soil mix for containers or planting beds should be porous, water retentive, and rich in organic matter. In hot-summer climates, heavy mulching helps maintain soil moisture in beds. When foliage

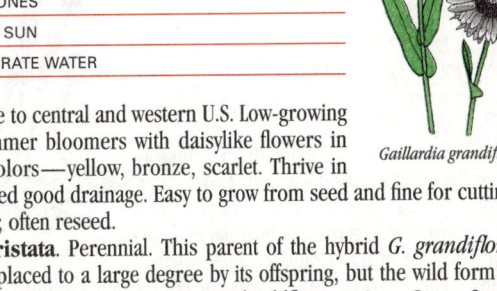
Fuchsia hybrida
Single Type

wilts in extreme heat, mist to cool it down. Apply light doses of complete fertilizer frequently. If plant becomes leggy, pinch branch tips to force side branching. Pick off old flowers as they start to fade.

Where frosts are light, fuchsias lose their leaves; sometimes tender growth is killed. Where freezes are hard, most plants die back to hard wood, sometimes to roots. A few varieties, including 'Royal Purple',

'Checkerboard', and 'Marinka', can stand outdoor exposures in winter in areas as cold as Zones 4–7. Protect outdoor fuchsias by mounding 5–6 in. of sawdust over roots. Store potted plants in greenhouse or cool basement; keep soil moist, but not soggy, all winter.

Fuchsias everywhere need some pruning in early spring. In frost-free areas, cut out approximately same volume of growth that formed the previous summer, leaving about two healthy leaf buds. In mild-frost regions, cut out all frost-damaged wood and enough additional wood to remove most of last summer's growth. In cold-winter regions, prune plants lightly before storing them; in early spring, cut back to live wood.

F. magellanica. Zones 3–9, 14–24, 31, 32. Many arching, 3-ft.-long stems loaded with drooping, 1½-in.-long, red-and-violet flowers. Leaves are oval, in groups of two or three, ½–1 in. long. Where winters are mild, can reach 20 ft. trained against wall. Treat as herbaceous perennial in cold-climate areas. Roots are hardy with mulching; tops will die back with the first hard frost.

Fumariaceae. This family consists of annuals and perennials, usually with irregularly shaped flowers. *Corydalis* and bleeding heart *(Dicentra)* are examples. This family is considered by many to be included in the poppy family (Papaveraceae).

FUNKIA. See HOSTA

GAILLARDIA

BLANKET FLOWER

Asteraceae (Compositae)

PERENNIALS AND ANNUALS

ALL ZONES

FULL SUN

MODERATE WATER

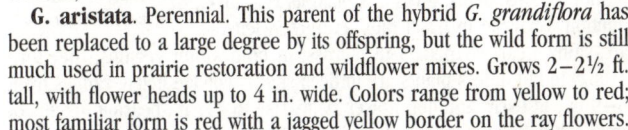
Gaillardia grandiflora

Native to central and western U.S. Low-growing summer bloomers with daisylike flowers in warm colors—yellow, bronze, scarlet. Thrive in heat, need good drainage. Easy to grow from seed and fine for cutting and borders; often reseed.

G. aristata. Perennial. This parent of the hybrid *G. grandiflora* has been replaced to a large degree by its offspring, but the wild form is still much used in prairie restoration and wildflower mixes. Grows 2–2½ ft. tall, with flower heads up to 4 in. wide. Colors range from yellow to red; most familiar form is red with a jagged yellow border on the ray flowers.

G. grandiflora. Perennial. Developed from native species *G. aristata* and *G. pulchella.* To 2–4 ft. high. Roughish gray-green foliage; flower heads 3–4 in. across, single or double petaled. Much variation in flower color: warm shades of red and yellow with orange or maroon bands. Exceptionally long bloom period for a perennial—from early summer until frost. Plants flower first year from seed. Can be short lived in hot, humid climates.

Many strains and varieties are available, including dwarf kinds and types with extra-large flowers. 'Goblin', 1 ft. tall, is an especially good compact variety with large, deep red flowers bordered in bright yellow. 'Goblin Yellow' is similar, but with yellow blooms. 'Baby Cole', another red-and-yellow type, grows 7–8 in. tall. The following varieties are all 2½ ft. tall: 'Burgundy', deep red; 'Tokajer', pure orange; 'Torchlight', yellow blooms bordered with red.

G. pulchella. Annual. To 1½–2 ft. high. Soft, hairy leaves. Bears 2-in.-wide flower heads in warm shades of red, yellow, gold; blossoms carried on long, whiplike stems. Easy to grow; sow seeds in warm soil after frost danger is past. 'Lorenziana' has no ray flowers (petals); instead, disc flowers are enlarged into little star-tipped bells, making blooms look like balls of bright fluff. Double Gaiety strain (1½ ft. tall) has flowers that range from near white to maroon; often bicolored. Lollipop strain is similar but only 10–12 in. tall.

GALANTHUS

SNOWDROP

Amaryllidaceae

BULBS

🌡 ZONES 1–9, 14–17, 31–45

☀☽ FULL SUN OR PARTIAL SHADE

💧 REGULAR WATER DURING GROWTH AND BLOOM

⚠ G. NIVALIS BULB IS POISONOUS IF INGESTED

Galanthus nivalis

Best adapted to cold climates. Closely related to *Leucojum* (snowflake) and often confused with it. White, nodding, bell-shaped blossoms are borne one per stalk. Inner flower segments have green tips; larger outer segments are pure white. Plants have two or three basal leaves. Use in rock gardens or under flowering shrubs; naturalize in woodland; or grow in pots. Plant in autumn, in moist soil with ample humus; set 3–4 in. deep, 2–3 in. apart. Do not divide often; when necessary, divide right after bloom.

G. elwesii. GIANT SNOWDROP. Globular bells to 2 in. long on 1-ft. stems; two or three strap-shaped, 1¼-in.-wide leaves, 4 in. long (elongating to as much as 1 ft. after bloom). March–April bloom in cold climates. In southern part of range (where better adapted than *G. nivalis*), blooms January–February.

G. nivalis. COMMON SNOWDROP. More delicate version of *G. elwesii*, blooming about a week earlier. Dainty, 1-in.-long bells on 6–9-in. stems; leaves very narrow.

GALAX urceolata (G. aphylla)

Diapensiaceae

PERENNIAL

🌡 ZONES 1–6, 31–43

◐ 💧 PARTIAL OR FULL SHADE

💧 REGULAR WATER

Galax urceolata

Native to mountain woodlands, Virginia to Georgia. Often used as ground cover, although it spreads slowly. Foliage, much used in indoor arrangements, gives this plant its real distinction. Growing in basal tufts, evergreen leaves are shiny, heart shaped, 5 in. across; in cold-winter regions, they turn bronzy in fall unless plants are in deep shade. Foliage height ranges from 6–9 in.; in early summer, flower stems rise to 2½ ft., bearing foxtails of small white flowers at their tips.

Grow in acid soil with much organic material—preferably mulch of leaf mold. Locate under plants that appreciate the same conditions: dogwood, rhododendron, azalea, pieris. Space 1 ft. apart.

GALEOBDOLON luteum. See LAMIUM galeobdolon

GALIUM odoratum (Asperula odorata)

SWEET WOODRUFF

Rubiaceae

PERENNIAL

🌡 ZONES 1–6, 15–17, 31–43

◐ 💧 PARTIAL OR FULL SHADE

💧 REGULAR WATER

Galium odoratum

Attractive, low-spreading perennial that brings to mind deep-shaded woods. Slender, square stems 6–12 in. high, encircled every inch or so by whorls of six to eight aromatic, bristle-tipped leaves. Clusters of tiny

white flowers show above foliage in late spring and summer. Leaves and stems give off fragrant, haylike odor when dried; used to make May wine.

In the shade garden, sweet woodruff is best used as ground cover or edging along path. Will spread rapidly in rich soil with abundant moisture—can become a pest if allowed to grow entirely unchecked. Self-sows freely. Can be increased by division in fall or spring.

GALTONIA candicans

SUMMER HYACINTH

Liliaceae

BULB

🌡 ZONES 4–32; OR DIG AND STORE

☽ PARTIAL SHADE

💧 REGULAR WATER DURING GROWTH AND BLOOM

Galtonia candicans

Native to South Africa. Straplike leaves, 2–3 ft. long; stout 2–4-ft. stems topped in summer with loose, spikelike clusters of fragrant white flowers—drooping, funnel-shaped, 1–1½ in. long, with three outer segments often tipped green. Plant behind low, bushy plants. Plant bulbs 6 in. deep in rich soil in fall; they will grow well for many years in mild-winter regions without lifting, dividing. In coldest zones, protect with a thick winter mulch; beyond hardiness range, dig and store.

GARDENIA

Rubiaceae

EVERGREEN SHRUBS

🌡 ZONES VARY BY SPECIES

☀☽ LIGHT SHADE IN HOT CLIMATES

💧 REGULAR WATER

Gardenia jasminoides

White, intensely fragrant flowers contrast sharply with shiny, leathery, dark green leaves. Double forms are classic corsage blooms. Gardenias do well in pots on patios or in greenhouses; don't make good house plants.

G. jasminoides (G. augusta). Zones 7–9, 12–16, 18–28, 31; with protection in 32, 33. Native to China. Glossy bright green leaves and usually double white flowers. Though hardy to 20°F/−7°C or even lower, plants fail to grow and bloom well without summer heat. In cool-summer areas, plant in full sun; take advantage of reflected heat from walls or pavement. In hot climates, give filtered shade or morning sun but light shade thereafter.

Soil should drain fast but retain water, too; condition it with plenty of organic matter such as peat moss or ground bark. Plant high (like azaleas and rhododendrons) and avoid crowding by other plants and competing roots. Mulch plants instead of cultivating. Feed every 3 to 4 weeks during growing season with acid plant food, fish emulsion, or blood meal. Prune to remove straggly branches, faded flowers. Control whiteflies, aphids, other sucking insects.

The many varieties are useful in containers or raised beds, as hedges, espaliers, low screens, or single plants.

'August Beauty'. Grows 4–6 ft. high and blooms heavily, midspring into fall. Large double flowers.

'Chuck Hayes'. Extra-hardy variety, possibly as cold tolerant as 'Klein's Hardy'. To 4 ft. high. Double flowers in summer, with heavy rebloom in autumn. Very heat tolerant.

'First Love' ('Aimee'). Somewhat larger shrub than 'August Beauty', with larger flowers. Spring bloom.

'Golden Magic'. Reaches 3 ft. tall, 2 ft. wide in 2 to 3 years, eventually larger. Extra-full flowers open white, gradually age to deep golden yellow. Spring through summer, peaking in midspring.

G

'Kimura Shikazaki' ('Four Seasons'). Compact plant 2–3 ft. tall. Flowers similar to those of 'Veitchii', but slightly less fragrant. Extremely long bloom season—spring to fall.

'Klein's Hardy'. Developed for cold-winter climates; hardy to 0°F/–18°C. To about 2–3 ft. high; tips are winter-killed. Single flowers in summer. Grow in a wind-protected site.

'Miami Supreme'. Grows to 6 ft. tall, with large double flowers (4–6 in. wide) in spring, periodic flowering through summer.

'Mystery'. Best-known variety; has 4–5-in., double white flowers, mid- to late spring or longer. Tends to be rangy and needs pruning to keep it neat. Can reach 6–8 ft.

'Radicans'. Grows 6–12 in. tall and spreads to 2–3 ft., with small dark green leaves and inch-wide double flowers in summer. Good small-scale ground cover, container plant. 'Radicans Variegata' has gray-green leaves with white markings.

'Veitchii'. Compact 3–4½-ft. plant with many 1–1½-in. fully double blooms midspring into fall, sometimes even during warm winter. Prolific bloom, reliable grower.

'White Gem'. At 1–2 ft. tall, useful for edgings, in containers, or in raised beds, where fragrance of single creamy white summer flowers can be appreciated.

G. thunbergia. Zones 16, 17, 21–27. Native to South Africa. Angular-branched shrub to 10 ft. tall, 20 ft. wide. Leaves to 6 in. long, dark green (nearly black). Single, long-tubed, 3–4 in. flowers in winter. Seems somewhat more tolerant of cool conditions and less-than-perfect soil than *G. jasminoides*, but tender to frost. With age, becomes more vigorous, flowers more profusely.

GARDENIA'S DEMANDS

Like a temperamental artist, the gardenia has its own set of rules. Fuss over them and the plants give beauty. Ignore them and they yellow and die. For thriving gardenias, provide warmth, regular water and feeding, and good soil drainage.

GARLAND FLOWER. See HEDYCHIUM coronarium

GARLIC

Liliaceae

BULB

⚡ ALL ZONES

☼ FULL SUN

💧 REGULAR WATER

For ornamental varieties, see *Allium*. Seed stores and some mail-order seed houses sell mother bulbs ("sets") for planting. In mild-winter areas, plant October–December for early summer harvest. Where winters are cold, plant early in spring. Break bulbs up into cloves and plant base downward, 1–2 in. deep, 2–3 in. apart, in rows 1 ft. apart. Harvest when leafy tops fall over; air-dry bulbs, remove tops and roots, and store in cool place. Giant or elephant garlic has unusually large (fist-size) bulbs and mild garlic flavor. Same culture as regular garlic.

Garlic

GARLIC CHIVES. See ALLIUM tuberosum

GAS PLANT. See DICTAMNUS albus

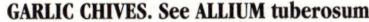

FOR INFORMATION ON SELECTING PLANTS
PLEASE SEE PAGES 79–160

GAULTHERIA

Ericaceae

EVERGREEN SHRUBS OR SHRUBLETS

⚡ ZONES VARY BY SPECIES

☼ PARTIAL SHADE

💧 REGULAR WATER

Gaultheria shallon

All have urn-shaped flowers and berrylike fruit. They need woodland soil. Smaller kinds are favored for rock gardens, woodland plantings. Larger types are good companions for other acid-soil shrubs such as rhododendrons and azaleas.

G. miqueliana. Zones 3–7, 14–17, 31–34. Native to Japan. Dense, twiggy shrub to 1 ft. tall, with leaves to 1½ in. long and half as wide. Tiny white flowers in summer are followed by white (sometimes faintly pink-tinted) berries a little less than ½ in. long.

G. ovatifolia. Zones 1–7, 14–17. Native to mountains in Northern California to British Columbia, east to northern Idaho. Spreading, trailing, with upright branches to about 8 in. high. Oval, leathery dark green leaves, ¾–1½ in. long, nearly as wide. Tiny white to pinkish flowers in summer. Bright red berries ¼ in. wide in fall and winter are edible, wintergreen flavored. Small-scale ground cover in woodland.

G. procumbens. WINTERGREEN, CHECKERBERRY, TEABERRY. Zones 1–7, 14–17, 32–45. Native Newfoundland to Manitoba, south to Georgia and Alabama. Creeping stems; upright branches to 6 in. tall, with 2-in., oval, glossy dark leaves clustered toward tips. Leaves turn reddish with winter cold. When bruised, foliage emits strong wintergreen odor. Small, pinkish white summer flowers followed by scarlet berries. Both fruit and foliage have flavor of wintergreen (or teaberry). Use as ground cover; plant 1 ft. apart. 'Macrocarpa' is a compact, profusely fruiting variety.

G. shallon. SALAL. Zones 3–7, 14–17, 21–24. Native from Central California coast to Alaska. Can reach 4–10 ft. tall in good growing conditions. Nearly round, glossy bright green leaves 1¾–4 in. long. Loose, 6-in.-long clusters of white or pinkish flowers on reddish stalks, spring. Edible black fruits resemble large huckleberries but are bland tasting; birds like them. Cut branches of this plant are sold by florists as "lemon leaves."

GAURA lindheimeri

GAURA

Onagraceae

PERENNIAL

⚡ ZONES 3–35, 37, 38 (coastal), 39

☼ FULL SUN

💧 REGULAR TO LITTLE WATER

Native to Texas and Louisiana. Airy plant growing 2¼–4 ft. high. Stalkless leaves, 1½–3½ in. long, grow directly on stems. Branching flower spikes bear many 1-in.-long white blossoms that open from pink buds closely set on stems. Long bloom period (often from late spring into fall), with only a few blossoms opening at a time. Blossoms age to rosy color, then drop off cleanly, but seed-bearing spikes should be cut to improve appearance, prevent overly enthusiastic self-sowing, and prolong bloom. 'Whirling Butterflies' is a bit shorter and more compact than the species, with larger flowers.

Gaura lindheimeri

Needs good drainage. Used widely in the South, since it takes heat and humidity very well, outlasting many other border plants. Legginess and sparse bloom may be a problem in that region. Blooms more profusely in the Southwest, where it is one of the few long-lived perennials. Taproot makes it very drought tolerant. Clumps never need dividing; for additional plants, let some volunteer seedlings grow.

GAYFEATHER. See LIATRIS

GAYLUSSACIA brachycera

BOX HUCKLEBERRY

Ericaceae

EVERGREEN SHRUB

🌿 ZONES 4–6, 32, 34, 36–39

◐ PARTIAL SHADE

🔴 REGULAR WATER

Gaylussacia brachycera

Native to mountains of Pennsylvania to Virginia, Kentucky, and Tennessee. Uncommon in cultivation, box huckleberry can make an attractive 6–18-in.-high ground cover in well-drained, acid soil with ample organic content. Leathery, glossy dark green leaves to 1 in. long show reddish tints in full sun, turn bronze or purple in winter. Tiny, urn-shaped white or pinkish flowers are followed by edible bluish black berries that ripen in mid- to late summer. Spreads by underground stems, eventually covering large areas. In nature, some single plants have spread to form patches blanketing several hundred acres; it has been estimated that such patches may have started their growth up to 10,000 years ago.

GAZANIA

Asteraceae (Compositae)

PERENNIALS; ANNUALS IN COLDER AREAS

🌿 ZONES 8–28

☀ FULL SUN

🔴🔴 REGULAR TO MODERATE WATER

Gazania 'Copper King'

Native to South Africa. Daisy flowers give dazzling color display during peak bloom in late spring, early summer. In mild areas, they continue to bloom intermittently throughout the year. Gazanias grow well in almost any soil. Feed once in spring with slow-acting fertilizer. Divide plants every 3 to 4 years. In cold areas, carry gazanias through winter by taking cuttings in fall as you would for pelargoniums.

There are basically two types: clumping and trailing. Clumping gazanias (complex hybrids between a number of species) form a mound of evergreen leaves—dark green above, gray and woolly beneath, often lobed. Flowers 3–4 in. wide, on 6–10-in.-long stems; they open on sunny days, close at night and in cloudy weather. You can buy clumping gazanias in single colors—yellow, orange, white, or rosy pink, with reddish purple petal undersides, often with dark blossom centers. Or you can get a mixture of hybrids (as plants or seeds) in different colors. Seed-grown kinds include Carnival (many colors, silver leaves); Chansonette (early blooming, compact; medium-size round flowers); Harlequin (many colors, eyed and banded); Mini-Star (compact, floriferous plants; named selections include 'Mini-Star Yellow', 'Mini-Star Tangerine'); Sundance (5-in. flowers, striped or banded); and Sunshine (big, multicolored flowers, gray foliage).

Named hybrids of special merit are 'Aztec Queen' (multicolored), 'Burgundy', 'Copper King', and 'Fiesta Red'; these are best used in small-scale plantings, although the last is sturdy enough for large expanses. 'Moonglow' is double-flowered bright yellow of unusual vigor; its blossoms, unlike most, stay open even on dull days.

Clumping gazanias serve as temporary fillers between young, growing shrubs and as a replaceable ground cover for relatively level areas not subject to severe erosion. Try in parking strips, as edgings along sunny paths, or in rock gardens.

Trailing gazanias (*G. rigens leucolaena*, formerly sold as *G. uniflora* or *G. leucolaena*) grow about as tall as clumping ones, but spread rapidly by long trailing stems. Foliage is clean silvery gray; flowers are yellow, white, orange, or bronze. New, larger-flowered hybrids are 'Sunburst' (orange, black eye) and 'Sunglow' (yellow). 'Sunrise Yellow' has large, black-eyed yellow flowers; leaves are green instead of gray. New hybrids are superior to older kinds in length of bloom, resistance to dieback. Trailing gazanias are useful on banks, level ground. Or grow them at top of wall and allow them to trail over. Attractive in hanging baskets.

GEIGER TREE. See CORDIA sebestena

GEIJERA parviflora

AUSTRALIAN WILLOW, WILGA

Rutaceae

EVERGREEN TREE

🌿 ZONES 8, 9, 12–24

☀ FULL SUN

🔴 MODERATE WATER

Geijera parviflora

Graceful, fine textured, to 30 ft. tall, 20 ft. wide. Main branches sweep up and out; little branches hang down. Distant citrus relative; called Australian willow because its 3–6-in.-long, narrow, drooping leaves give a weeping willow effect. Trouble-free patio, street, or grove tree. Noninvasive roots. Needs well-drained soil.

GELSEMIUM sempervirens

CAROLINA JESSAMINE

Loganiaceae

EVERGREEN VINE

🌿 ZONES 8–24, 26–33

☀ ◐ 🔴 BEST IN FULL SUN; TOLERATES SHADE

🔴 REGULAR WATER

☠ ALL PARTS ARE POISONOUS IF INGESTED

Gelsemium sempervirens

Native to southeastern U.S. Shrubby and twining vine; moderate growth rate to about 20 ft. Clean pairs of shiny, light green, 1–4-in.-long leaves on long, streamerlike branches. Semievergreen in colder part of range. Fragrant, tubular yellow flowers, 1–1½ in. long, in late winter, early spring. Sometimes flowers sporadically in fall. 'Pride of Augusta' ('Plena') is a double-flowered form.

On trellis, vine will cascade and swing in wind; when trained on house, makes delicate green curtain of branches. Often trained on fences and mailboxes. Can get top-heavy; in this case, cut back severely. Also used as ground cover, especially on banks; keep trimmed to 3 ft. high. For best bloom and densest growth, plant in full sun, though plant will tolerate shade.

GENISTA

BROOM

Fabaceae (Leguminosae)

DECIDUOUS OR EVERGREEN SHRUBS

🌿 ZONES VARY BY SPECIES

☀ FULL SUN

🔴 MODERATE TO LITTLE WATER

Genista lydia

Leaves often small and short lived. Green branches give deciduous or sparsely leafed plants an evergreen look. Flowers yellow, sweet pea shaped. Less aggressive than other brooms (*Cytisus, Spartium);* will not run wild. Smaller kinds attractive in rock gardens, bank plantings. Need good drainage; tolerate rocky or infertile soil.

G. aetnensis. MT. ETNA BROOM. Zones 8, 9, 14–24. Large shrub or small tree to 18 ft. or more, with graceful arching, weeping green branchlets, leafless or with very few tiny leaves during growing season. Branches are covered with blooms in summer. Doubtful if hardy much below 5°F/–15°C.

G. canariensis (Cytisus canariensis). CANARY ISLAND BROOM. Evergreen. Zones 8, 9, 14–24. Damaged at 15°F/–9°C but recovers quickly. Many-branched, upright shrub 6–8 ft. tall, 5–6 ft. wide. Bright green leaves divided into ½-in. leaflets. Fragrant flowers appear at ends of branches in spring and summer. The genista of florists.

G. fragrans. A white-flowered species not in the nursery trade. Plants sold under this name are *G. spachiana.*

G. lydia. Evergreen. Zones 4–6, 14–17, 32, 34. Nearly leafless shrublet, often sold erroneously as *Cytisus lydia.* Grows to 2 ft. high, with spreading habit. Makes a good ground cover. Profusion of flowers at ends of shoots in late spring. Sets little seed.

G. monosperma. BRIDAL VEIL BROOM. Zones 16, 17, 22–24. Upright growth to 20 ft. high, 10 ft. wide, with slender, graceful, gray-green, almost leafless branches. Fragrant white flowers in late winter, spring.

G. pilosa. Deciduous. Zones 3–22, 32, 34, 37. Fairly fast growing, ultimately reaching 1–1½ ft. tall with 7-ft. spread. Intricately branched, gray-green twigs. Roundish, ¼–½-in.-long leaves. Blooms in spring. 'Vancouver Gold' is best selection.

G. sagittalis. Zones 2–22, 32, 34, 37. Rather rapid grower to 1 ft. high, with wide spread. Leafless, upright, winged, bright green branchlets appear jointed. Makes sheet of golden flowers during bloom in late spring and early summer.

G. spachiana (G. racemosa). Evergreen. Zones 7–9, 14–24. Similar to *G. canariensis,* but with larger leaflets and longer, looser spikes of fragrant yellow flowers in late spring. Naturalizes where adapted. Often sold as *G. fragrans.*

G. tinctoria. DYER'S GREENWEED, WOADWAXEN. Deciduous. Zones 1–24, 32, 34, 37–43. Species grows to 6 ft., with undivided leaves to 2 in. long. 'Royal Gold', 2 ft. tall and as wide, is the only variety generally available; it bears yellow flowers on upright, 1–3-in.-long spikes in late spring or early summer. Cutting back after summer bloom will encourage some later flowering.

GENTIANA

GENTIAN

Gentianaceae

PERENNIALS

⚡ ZONES 1–6, 14–17, 34, 36–43, EXCEPT AS NOTED

☼ ◐ FULL SUN OR PARTIAL SHADE

🔴 REGULAR WATER

Gentiana acaulis

Low, spreading, or upright plants, generally with very blue tubular flowers. Though most are hard to grow, they are prized by rock garden enthusiasts. Need perfect drainage. Most require lime-free soil. If they thrive, they produce some of the richest blues in the garden.

G. acaulis. Leafy stems to 4 in. tall. Leaves 1 in. long. Rich blue flowers 2 in. long in summer. Grows well, but often fails to bloom.

G. andrewsii. CLOSED GENTIAN, BOTTLE GENTIAN. Zones 1–6, 14–17, 33–43. Native to eastern U.S. Fairly easy to grow in rich soil. Clump-forming plant to 2 ft. tall. Dark green leaves; dark blue flowers clustered at top of stem and in joints of upper leaves, in late summer or early fall. Flowers are usually fully closed, sometimes only partially closed.

G. asclepiadea. WILLOW GENTIAN. Native to Europe and western Asia. Similar to *G. andrewsii,* but the 1½-in. dark blue flowers open into stars. Flowers appear singly or in twos or threes in joints of upper leaves, in late summer or early fall. Appearance is that of arching, leafy spikes of blue flowers. Prefers partial shade. Not difficult. 'Alba' is a white form.

G. clusii (G. acaulis clusii). Similar to *G. acaulis,* but with larger flowers.

G. septemfida. Arching or sprawling stems 9–18 in. long. Oval leaves to 1½ in. long. Clusters of 2-in. dark blue flowers in late summer. Easy to grow. *G. s. lagodechiana* has sprawling stems that turn up at tips to display flowers at branch tips and among upper leaves.

G. sino-ornata. Trailing stems grow from 7-in. rosettes of bright green leaves; 2-in.-long flowers of brightest blue appear at stem ends in early fall. Fairly easy to grow in half shade.

G. verna. SPRING GENTIAN. Mat-forming plant 1½–4 in. tall. Dark blue, 1-in. flowers appear singly on short stems in spring. Difficult, fragile plant. Needs some lime.

Gentianaceae. The gentian family includes annuals and perennials from many parts of the world. Many have blue or purple flowers, including the gentians, Persian violet *(Exacum),* and *Eustoma.*

Geraniaceae. The cranesbill family of annuals and perennials (the latter sometimes shrubby) includes true geranium, *Erodium,* and *Pelargonium.*

GERANIUM

CRANESBILL

Geraniaceae

PERENNIALS

⚡ ZONES VARY BY SPECIES

☼ ◐ AFTERNON SHADE IN HOT-SUMMER AREAS

🔴 REGULAR WATER, EXCEPT AS NOTED

Geranium pratense

The common indoor/outdoor plant most people know as geranium is, botanically, *Pelargonium.* True geraniums, considered here, are hardy plants. Many types bloom over a long period, bearing flowers that are attractive though not as showy as those of pelargonium. Carried singly or in clusters of two or three, flowers have five overlapping petals that look alike. (Pelargonium blossoms also have five petals, but two point in one direction, the other three in the opposite direction.) Colors include rose, blue, and purple; a few are pure pink or white. Beaklike fruit that follows the flowers accounts for the common name "cranesbill." Leaves are roundish or kidney shaped, lobed or deeply cut; plants may be upright or trailing. Good in rock gardens, perennial borders; some are useful as small-scale ground covers.

The best climates for geraniums are cool- and mild-summer regions, where plants can grow in full sun or light shade. Give afternoon shade in hottest areas. All species appreciate moist, well-drained soil. Clumps of most types can be left in place for many years before they decline due to crowding; at that point, divide clumps in early spring. Increase plantings by transplanting rooted portions from a clump's edge.

G. argenteum. Zones 3–6, 32, 34, 39. To 3–5 in. high. Leaves basal, 1 in. across, with five to seven lobes; densely covered with silky, silvery hairs. Pink flowers with darker veins, 1½ in. across, with notched petals. Blooms late spring to early summer.

G. cantabrigiense. Zones 1–24, 31–43. Hybrid between *G. macrorrhizum* and *G. dalmaticum.* Similar to former, but with pink flowers. 'Biokovo' is white flowered. Blooms late spring to early summer.

G. cinereum. Zones 1–24, 31–43. To 6 in. tall, much wider, with deeply cut dark green leaves. Inch-wide pink flowers with darker veining appear late spring–summer. 'Ballerina' has lilac pink flowers with purple veining; blooms over a long summer season. 'Lawrence Flatman' has slightly larger flowers of a deeper color. *G. c. subcaulescens* has deep purplish red flowers with black centers.

G. clarkei 'Kashmir White'. Zones 3–9, 14–24, 31–39. Grows 2 ft. tall. Finely cut leaves; 1½-in. white flowers veined with pink. Blooms late spring to early summer.

G. dalmaticum. Zones 1–24, 31–43. Dwarf (6-in.) plant with glossy, 1½-in., finely cut leaves and bright pink, 1-in. flowers in spring. Useful in rock garden.

G. endressii. Zones 1–9, 14–24, 31–43. Bushy, 1–1½ ft. high. Leaves 2–3 in. across, deeply cut in five lobes. Flowers rose pink, about 1 in. across. Blooms late spring into fall in mild-summer areas; peters out in early summer in hot areas. 'Wargrave Pink' is a more compact form with salmon pink flowers. ▸

G

G. himalayense (G. grandiflorum). Zones 1–24, 31–43. Wiry, branching stems 1–2 ft. high. Leaves roundish, five lobed, long stalked, 1¾ in. across. Flowers in clusters, lilac with purple veins and red-purple eye, 1½–2 in. across. Blooms all summer. 'Birch Double' ('Plenum') has double flowers of somewhat lighter shade.

G. ibericum. Zones 1–9, 14–24, 31–37, 39–43. To 2 ft. tall, with 4-in., deeply cut leaves and 2-in. lavender blue flowers with purple veining. Late spring bloomer.

G. incanum. Zones 14–24. South African trailing ground cover plant 6–10 in. high. Spreads fast to make wide cushions of finely cut leaves; 1-in.-wide flowers of light magenta appear spring to fall. Least hardy of true geraniums. Cut back every 2 to 3 years to keep neat. Very drought tolerant.

G. 'Johnson's Blue'. Zones 3–9, 14–24, 30–39. Hybrid resembling *G. himalayense* parent, but leaves are more finely divided. Blue-violet, 2-in.-wide flowers appear spring to fall.

G. macrorrhizum. Zones 1–24, 30–43. To 8–10 in. high, spreading by underground roots. Inch-wide spring flowers are deep magenta; leaves with five to seven lobes are fragrant and have attractive autumn tints. Good ground cover for small areas, though it can overwhelm delicate smaller plants. 'Bevan's Variety' has deep reddish purple flowers, 'Cambridge' pure pink blooms. Other pinks include 'Ingwersen's Variety' and 'Marjorie's'. 'Spessart' ('Album') has white flowers with pink sepals and stamens.

G. maculatum. WILD CRANESBILL, SPOTTED CRANESBILL. Zones 1–24, 30–45. Native to eastern North America; the only commonly cultivated native cranesbill. To 2 ft. tall and somewhat narrower, with deeply lobed leaves and an abundance of lilac pink, 1–1½-in. flowers in spring to early summer. 'Album' has white blooms.

G. magnificum. Zones 3–9, 14–24, 30–39. Hybrid between *G. ibericum* and *G. platypetalum*. Dark violet blue summer flowers are similar to those of *G. platypetalum,* but larger. Grows to 2½ ft. high.

G. oxonianum. Zones 3–9, 14–17, 30–39. Hybrid between *G. endressii* and *G. sanguineum striatum*. 'Claridge Druce' is a vigorous spreader 2–3 ft. tall, 3 ft. wide, with finely cut grayish green leaves and large pink, dark-veined flowers blooming over a long period in summer.

G. phaeum. MOURNING WIDOW, BLACK WIDOW. Zones 2–9, 14–17, 32–41. Grows to 2 ft. high, with open clusters of dark purple (nearly black) flowers in late spring to early summer. Tolerates deep shade.

G. platypetalum. Zones 3–9, 14–24, 30–39. Grows 16 in. tall. Dark violet blue flowers to nearly 2 in. wide. Late spring bloomer.

G. pratense. Zones 1–7, 32–43. Common border perennial to 3 ft. Upright, branching stems; shiny green leaves, 3–6 in. across, deeply cut in seven lobes. Flowers about 1 in. wide, typically blue with reddish veins; often vary in color. Blooms late spring into summer. 'Mrs. Kendall Clark' has pale blue flowers with lighter veining.

G. psilostemon. Zones 2–9, 14–24, 30–41. Large (4-by-4-ft.) plant with big, deeply cut leaves and an early summer show of 1–1½-in. magenta flowers with darker centers. Leaves take on brilliant fall color.

G. renardii. Zones 2–9, 14–24, 30–41. Compact plant 1 ft. tall and as wide, with handsome gray-green, lobed leaves with deeply etched veins. Early summer flowers are white with faint purple veining; overall effect is pearly gray.

G. 'Russell Pritchard'. Zones 6–9, 14–24, 30, 31. Clumps under 1 ft. tall, with 2-in. light green leaves and deep purplish pink, ¾-in. flowers. Blooms over a long period, starting in late spring.

G. sanguineum. Zones 1–9, 14–24, 30–43. Grows 1½ ft. high; trailing stems spread to 2 ft. Leaves roundish, 1–2½ in. across, with five to seven lobes; turn blood red in fall. Deep purple to almost crimson flowers, 1½ in. wide, bloom from late spring well into summer. 'Album' is somewhat taller than species and has white flowers. *G. s. striatum* (*G. s.* 'Prostratum', *G. lancastriense*) is a dwarf form, lower and more compact, with light pink flowers heavily veined with red (its seedlings may vary somewhat); an excellent rock garden or foreground plant. Other 1–1½-ft. selections include 'John Elsley', pink with deeper pink veins; 'Max Frei', reddish purple; 'New Hampshire', deep purple; and 'Vision', reddish purple.

G. sylvaticum. Zones 2–9, 14–24, 31–41. Shade-loving plant to 3 ft. tall. Late spring to early summer flowers, 1 in. wide, range in color from bluish to reddish purple.

G. wallichianum. Zones 3–9, 14–24, 31–34, 39. Grows 1 ft. tall, 3 ft. wide. Lilac flowers with a white eye, throughout summer. 'Buxton's Variety' has pure blue flowers.

WHICH IS REALLY A GERANIUM?

Gardeners use the word "geranium" to speak of ivy geraniums, fancy-leafed geraniums, common geraniums, and scented geraniums, all of which botanically are species of *Pelargonium*. Botanists define *Geranium* by the fact that all have five identical-looking overlapping petals in their flowers. For the botanical definition of *Pelargonium,* see that entry.

GERBERA jamesonii

TRANSVAAL DAISY

Asteraceae (Compositae)

PERENNIAL

🌢 ZONES 8, 9, 12–24, 26–29; ANNUAL IN COLDER AREAS

☼ ◐ PARTIAL SHADE IN HOTTEST AREAS

🔴 REGULAR WATER

Gerbera jamesonii

Native to South Africa. Most elegant and sophisticated of daisies. Lobed leaves to 10 in. long spring from root crowns that spread slowly to form big clumps. Slender-rayed, 4-in. daisies (one to a stem) rise directly from crowns on 1½-ft., erect or slightly curving stems. Colors range from cream through yellow to coral, orange, flame, and red. Flowers are first rate for arrangements; cut them as soon as fully open and slit an inch at bottom of stem before placing in water. Blooms any time of year with peaks in early summer, late fall.

The wild Transvaal daisy was orange red. Plants sold as hybrids are merely seedlings or divisions in mixed colors. Specialists have bred duplex and double strains. Duplex flowers have two rows of rays and are often larger (to 5–6 in. across) on taller (2–2½-ft.) stems. In doubles, all flowers are rays and flowers vary widely in form—some flat, some deep, some swirled, some bicolored. Happipot strain has 4-in. flowers on 6-in. stems. Double Parade strain has double flowers on 7–10-in. stems. Blackheart and Ebony Eyes strains have dark-centered flowers.

All types need excellent drainage; if drainage is poor, grow plants in raised beds. Plant 2 ft. apart with crowns at least ½ in. above surface. Feed frequently. Keep old leaves picked off. Let plants remain until crowded; divide February–April, leaving two or three buds on each division. As house or greenhouse plant, grow in bright light with night temperature of 60°F/16°C.

Plant as seedlings from flats, as divisions or clumps, or from pots. To grow your own from seed, sow thinly in sandy, peaty soil at 70°F/21°C. Water carefully; allow 4 to 6 weeks to sprout. Takes 6 to 18 months to flower. Seed must be fresh to germinate well; seed specialists can supply fresh seed of single, double, or duplex strains. Doubles come about 60 percent true from seed.

GERMANDER. See TEUCRIUM

GERMAN IVY. See SENECIO mikanioides

GERMAN STATICE. See GONIOLIMON tataricum

GERMAN VIOLET. See EXACUM affine

Gesneriaceae. The gesneriads are perennials, usually tropical or subtropical, grown for attractive flowers or foliage. Although a few are rock garden perennials, most are grown as house plants. African violet (*Saintpaulia*) and gloxinia (*Sinningia*) are examples.

GEUM

Rosaceae

PERENNIALS

ZONES 1–24, 32–43

PARTIAL SHADE IN HOT AREAS

REGULAR WATER

Geum chiloense

Double, semidouble, or single flowers in bright orange, yellow, and red over long season (spring to late summer) if dead blooms are removed. Foliage handsome; leaves divided into many leaflets. Plants evergreen except in coldest winters. Good in borders and for cut flowers.

Ordinary garden soil; need good drainage. Grow from seed sown in early spring, or divide plants in autumn or early spring.

G. 'Borisii'. Plants sold under this name make 6-in.-high mounds of foliage and have foot-high leafy stems with bright orange-red flowers. Use in rock garden, front of border. True *G. borisii* has yellow flowers.

G. chiloense. Foliage mounds to 15 in. Leafy flowering stems reach about 2 ft.; flowers are about 1½ in. wide. Varieties include 'Dolly North', semidouble bright orange; 'Fire Opal', semidouble orange scarlet; 'Lady Stratheden', double yellow; 'Mrs. Bradshaw', double scarlet; 'Princess Juliana', double copper; and 'Red Wings', semidouble scarlet with exceptionally long spring to autumn bloom season. For the plant sold as 'Georgenberg', see *G. heldreichii*.

G. heldreichii (G. montanum heldreichii). Hybrid between *G. montanum* and another species. The 12–15-in.-high 'Georgenberg' has apricot-colored flowers.

G. montanum. Grows 4–8 in. tall, with one to three bright yellow, 1½-in.-wide flowers per stem. Useful in rock gardens.

G. reptans. Grows to 6 in. high and spreads by surface runners. Orange, 1½-in.-wide blossoms.

G. rivale. WATER AVENS. Lower growing than *G. chiloense* (to 1 ft. tall and as wide), with slightly nodding, ivory to pink flowers. 'Lionel Cox' has light yellow flowers.

G. triflorum. PRAIRIE SMOKE, OLD MAN'S WHISKERS. Native to North America. Stems to 20 in. tall bear clusters of nodding maroon flowers. Entire plant is often furry. Seeds have long, feathery gray "tails."

GIANT GARLIC. See GARLIC

GIANT REED. See ARUNDO donax

GIANT SEQUOIA. See SEQUOIADENDRON giganteum

GILLENIA trifoliata (Porteranthus trifoliatus)

BOWMAN'S ROOT

Rosaceae

PERENNIAL

ZONES 4–6, 31–43

PARTIAL SHADE

REGULAR WATER

Gillenia trifoliata

Woodland plant native from the north and northeastern U.S.; little seen but deserving of wider use. Forms clumps of stiffish, upright, somewhat branching stems set with nearly stalkless leaves divided into three narrow, tooth-edged leaflets. Grows to 3 ft. or a little taller. In early summer, bears starlike white or pink flowers with red sepals. Open branching at flowering time gives an airy effect despite the erect stems. Foliage turns bronze red in autumn. Likes rich soil with ample organic material.

GINGER. See ZINGIBER officinale

GINGER LILY. See COSTUS, HEDYCHIUM

GINKGO biloba

MAIDENHAIR TREE

Ginkgoaceae

DECIDUOUS TREE

ZONES 1–10, 12, 14–24, 28, 30–44

FULL SUN

REGULAR TO MODERATE WATER

Ginkgo biloba

Graceful tree, attractive in any season, especially in fall when leathery, light green leaves of spring and summer suddenly turn gold. Fall leaves linger (they practically glow when backlit by the sun), then drop quickly and cleanly to make golden carpet where they fall. Related to conifers but differs in having broad (1–4-in.-wide), fan-shaped leaves rather than needlelike foliage. In shape and veining, leaves resemble leaflets of maidenhair fern, hence tree's common name. Can grow to 70–80 ft., but most mature trees are 35–50 ft. May be gawky in youth, but becomes well proportioned with age—narrow to spreading or even umbrella shaped. Usually grows slowly, about 1 ft. a year, but under ideal conditions can grow up to 3 ft. a year.

Plant only male trees (grafted or grown from cuttings of male plants); female trees produce messy, fleshy, ill-smelling fruit in quantity. Named varieties listed below are male. Use as street tree, lawn tree. Plant in deep, loose, well-drained soil. Be sure plant is not root-bound in pot. Stake young tree to keep stem straight; young growth may be brittle, but wood becomes strong with age. In general, ginkgos are not bothered by insects or diseases, and they're very tolerant of air pollution, heat, and acid or alkaline conditions.

'Autumn Gold'. Upright, eventually rather broad and spreading.

'Fairmount'. Fast-growing, broadly pyramidal form. Straighter main stem than 'Autumn Gold', requires less staking.

'Princeton Sentry'. Fairly narrow, conical shape.

'Saratoga'. Erect, rounded, and somewhat smaller than other ginkgo varieties, with narrow leaves deeply split at the ends. Pendulous leaves give tree a graceful character.

GLADIOLUS

Iridaceae

CORMS

ZONES VARY BY TYPE; OR DIG AND STORE

FULL SUN

REGULAR WATER DURING GROWTH AND BLOOM

Gladiolus callianthus

All have sword-shaped leaves and tubular flowers, often flaring or ruffled, in simple or branching, usually one-sided spikes. Extremely wide color range. Bloom from spring to fall, depending on kind and time of planting. Superb cut flowers. Good in borders or beds behind mounding plants that cover lower parts of stems, or in large containers with low annuals at base. Thrips are a pest.

Plant in rich, sandy soil. Set corms about four times deeper than their height, somewhat more shallowly in heavy soils. Space big corms 6 in. apart, smaller ones 4 in. apart. Corms can be left in the ground from year to year in indicated zones; in colder areas, dig soon after first frost in autumn. Corms should be dried, then stored in single layer in flats or ventilated trays in a cool place (40° to 50°F/4° to 10°C).

Baby gladiolus. Zones 4–9, 12–24 for most; additionally, 2, 3, 33–41 for winter-hardy types. Hybrid race resulting from breeding red-flowered *G. colvillei* with other species. Flaring, 2½–3¼-in. flowers in short, loose spikes on 1½-ft. stems. Flowers white, pink, red, or lilac; solid or blotched

G

with contrasting color. When left in the ground, will form large clumps in border or among shrubs. Plant in fall or early spring for late spring bloom.

Butterfly gladiolus. See G. primulinus.

G. byzantinum (G. communis byzantinus). BYZANTINE GLADIO-LUS. Zones 4–9, 12–24, 29–31, warmer parts of 32. Mainly maroon, sometimes reddish or coppery, 1–3-in. flowers in groups of 6–12 on 2–3-ft. stems. Narrower leaves than garden gladiolus. Plant in early spring for summer bloom.

G. callianthus (Acidanthera bicolor). ABYSSINIAN SWORD LILY. Perennial in Zones 4–9, 12–24, 29–31, protected areas of 32, but flowering may be better if corms are dug and divided every year. Stems 2–3 ft. tall, bearing two to ten fragrant, creamy white flowers marked chocolate brown on lower segments. Each blossom 2–3 in. wide, 4–5 in. long. Excellent cut flowers. Plant in spring for bloom in late summer–fall. 'Murielae' is taller, with purple-crimson blotches.

G. primulinus (G. dalenii). Zones 4–9, 12–24, 29–31. The 3-ft.-tall African species with hooded, primrose yellow flowers is rarely grown, but the name has been applied to its hybrids with other gladiolus. Butterfly gladiolus strain also belongs here. Frilled, medium-size flowers have a satiny sheen, vivid markings in throat. Wiry, 2-ft. stems bear as many as 20 flowers; six to eight open at a time. Colors include bright and pastel shades and pure white. Plant in spring for summer bloom.

Summer-flowering grandiflora hybrids. GARDEN GLADIOLUS. Perennial in Zones 4–9, 12–24, 29–33, but usually lifted yearly even in those areas. Commonly grown garden gladiolus are a complex group of hybrids derived by variation and hybridization from several species. These are the best-known gladiolus, with widest color range—white, cream, buff, yellow, orange, apricot, salmon, red shades, rose, lavender, purple, smoky shades, even green shades. Individual blooms as large as 8 in. across. Stems are 4–5 ft. tall.

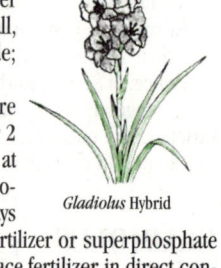

Newer varieties of garden gladiolus, to 5 ft. tall, have sturdier spikes bearing 12–14 open flowers at a time. They are better garden plants than older types and stand upright without staking. Another group, called miniature gladiolus, grows 3 ft. tall, with spikes of 15–20 flowers 2½–3 in. wide; useful in gardens and for cutting.

High-crowned corms, 1½–2 in. wide, are more productive than older, larger corms (over 2 in. wide). After soil has warmed in spring, plant at 1- to 2-week intervals for 4 to 6 weeks for progression of bloom. Corms bloom 65 to 100 days

Gladiolus Hybrid

after planting. If soil is poor, mix in complete fertilizer or superphosphate (4 lb. per 100 sq. ft.) before planting; do not place fertilizer in direct contact with corms. Treat with bulb dust (insecticide-fungicide) before planting. When plants have five leaves, apply complete fertilizer 6 in. from plants and water it in thoroughly. For cut flowers, cut spikes when lowest buds begin to open; keep at least four leaves on plants to build up corms.

GLECHOMA hederacea (Nepeta hederacea)

GROUND IVY	
Lamiaceae (Labiatae)	
PERENNIAL	
ALL ZONES	
☀ ◑ ● SUN OR SHADE	
● REGULAR WATER	

Glechoma hederacea

Trailing plant with neat pairs of round, scalloped, bright green or white-edged leaves 1½ in. across, spaced along stems. Small, trumpet-shaped blue flowers in spring and summer not especially showy. Sometimes planted as small-scale ground cover or used to trail from hanging basket. To 3 in. tall with stems trailing to 1½ ft., rooting at joints. Can become a pest in lawns.

GLEDITSIA triacanthos

HONEY LOCUST	
Fabaceae (Leguminosae)	
DECIDUOUS TREE	
ZONES 1–16, 18–20, 32–43	
☀ FULL SUN	
● REGULAR TO MODERATE WATER	

Gleditsia triacanthos

Native to eastern U.S. Fast growing, with upright trunk and spreading, arching branches. To 35–70 ft. tall. Bright green, fernlike leaves to 10 in. long are divided into many oval, ¾–1½-in.-long leaflets. Late to leaf out; leaves turn yellow and drop early in fall. Inconspicuous flowers followed by broad, 1–1½-ft.-long pods filled with sweetish pulp and hard, roundish seeds.

Foliage casts filtered shade, allowing growth of lawn or other plants beneath. Small leaflets dry up and filter into grass, decreasing raking chores. Not good in narrow area between curb and sidewalk, since roots of old plants will heave paving. Stake tree until good basic branch pattern is established. Tolerant of acid or alkaline conditions, salt, drought, cold, heat, wind. Does best in areas with sharply defined winters, hot summers. Combination of heat, humidity, and heavy soils in Southeast make most varieties poor performers in that region. Tree is susceptible to many pests, several of which are prevalent in humid-summer regions: mimosa webworm (chews leaves), pod gall midge (deforms foliage), honey locust borer (attacks limbs and trunks).

Trunks and branches of species are formidably thorny, and pods make a mess. Honey locusts for the garden are varieties of *G. t. inermis,* with no thorns and few or no pods. They include:

'Halka'. Fast growing, forms sturdy trunk early, has strong horizontal branching pattern. Can bear a heavy crop of seedpods.

'Imperial'. Spreading, symmetrical tree to about 35 ft. More densely foliaged than other forms; gives heavier shade.

'Moraine'. MORAINE LOCUST. Best known. Fast-growing, spreading tree with branches angled upward, then outward. Subject to wind breakage. Has greater resistance to webworms than do some of the newer selections.

'Rubylace'. Deep red new growth fading to bronzed green by midsummer, especially in warmest regions. Subject to wind breakage, webworm attack.

'Shademaster'. More upright and faster growing than 'Moraine'—to 24 ft. tall, 16 ft. wide in 6 years.

'Skyline'. Pyramidal and symmetrical.

'Sunburst'. Golden yellow new leaves; showy against deep green background. Summer color best in cooler climates. Defoliates early in response to temperature changes, drought. Prone to wind breakage. Very susceptible to foliage pests.

'Trueshade'. Rounded head of light green foliage.

GLOBE AMARANTH. See GOMPHRENA

GLOBEFLOWER. See TROLLIUS

GLOBE THISTLE. See ECHINOPS

GLOBULARIA

GLOBE DAISY	
Globulariaceae	
EVERGREEN PERENNIALS OR SHRUBS	
ZONES VARY BY SPECIES	
☀ FULL SUN	
● MODERATE WATER	

Globularia indubia

Globe daisies are mat-forming or mounding plants with leathery leaves and small blue flowers gathered into tight, round heads on stalks standing above the foliage. They are not true daisies, although the flower heads resemble rayless daisies or small powder puffs. Provide good drainage.

G. cordifolia. Woody-based perennial. Zones 3–9, 14–24, 32, 34, 35, 37, 39. To 5 in. tall and a foot wide, with dark green leaves on creeping, rooting stems. Blue flower heads in summer. Used in rock gardens.

G. indubia. Shrub. Zones 8, 9, 14–24. Hybrid. Forms a mound 1–2 ft. tall, 5 ft. wide, with lavender flower heads through summer and fall. Tough plant for hot, dry banks.

GLORIOSA DAISY. See RUDBECKIA hirta

GLORIOSA rothschildiana

GLORY LILY, CLIMBING LILY

Liliaceae

TUBEROUS-ROOTED PERENNIAL

🌿 ZONES 24–27; OR DIG AND STORE; OR GROW IN POTS OR GREENHOUSE

☀️ ◑ SUN OR FILTERED SHADE

💧 REGULAR WATER DURING GROWTH AND BLOOM

⬧ ALL PARTS ARE POISONOUS IF INGESTED

Gloriosa rothschildiana

Native to tropical Africa. Climbs to 6 ft. by tendrils on leaf tips. Lance-shaped leaves 5–7 in. long. Lilylike flowers 4 in. across with six wavy-edged, curved, brilliant red segments banded with yellow. Grow on terrace, patio; train on trellis or frame.

Set tubers horizontally about 4 in. deep in light, spongy soil. Start indoors or in greenhouse in February; set out after frosts. Feed with liquid fertilizer every 3 weeks. Tubers can remain in the ground in mildest-winter zones, though rotting is likely unless planting area is kept fairly dry. Where tubers cannot be protected and in colder regions, dig in autumn and store over winter. Potted tubers can be stored in pots of dry soil.

GLORYBOWER. See CLERODENDRUM

GLORY LILY. See GLORIOSA rothschildiana

GLORY-OF-THE-SNOW. See CHIONODOXA

GLOXINIA. See SINNINGIA speciosa

GLOXINIA, HARDY. See INCARVILLEA

GOAT'S BEARD. See ARUNCUS

GODETIA. See CLARKIA

GOLD DUST PLANT. See AUCUBA japonica 'Variegata'

GOLDEN ASTER. See CHRYSOPSIS

GOLDENCHAIN TREE. See LABURNUM

GOLDEN CUP. See HUNNEMANNIA fumariifolia

GOLDEN DEWDROP. See DURANTA repens

GOLDEN FLEECE. See DYSSODIA tenuiloba

GOLDEN GARLIC. See ALLIUM moly

GOLDEN GLOBES. See LYSIMACHIA procumbens

GOLDEN GLOW. See RUDBECKIA laciniata 'Hortensia'

GOLDEN LARCH. See PSEUDOLARIX kaempferi

GOLDEN MARGUERITE. See ANTHEMIS tinctoria

GOLDENRAIN TREE. See KOELREUTERIA paniculata

GOLDENROD. See SOLIDAGO

GOLDEN SEAL. See HYDRASTIS canadensis

GOLDEN SHOWER. See CASSIA fistula

GOLDEN STAR. See CHRYSOGONUM virginianum

GOLDEN TRUMPET. See ALLAMANDA cathartica

GOLDEN TRUMPET TREE. See TABEBUIA chrysotricha

GOLDEN WONDER SENNA. See CASSIA splendida

GOLDFISH PLANT. See ALLOPLECTUS nummularia

GOLD MEDALLION TREE. See CASSIA leptophylla

GOMPHRENA

GLOBE AMARANTH

Amaranthaceae

ANNUALS

🌿 ALL ZONES

☀️ ◑ FULL SUN OR PARTIAL SHADE

💧 MODERATE WATER

Gomphrena globosa

Stiffly branching plants 9 in.–2 ft. tall, covered in summer and fall with rounded, papery, cloverlike heads ¾–1 in. wide. These may be dried quickly and easily, retaining color and shape for winter arrangements. Narrow oval leaves are 2–4 in. long.

G. globosa. White, pink, red, lavender, or purple flower heads top 1-ft. stems. Dwarf varieties for use as edging or bedding plants are 9-in. 'Buddy' (purple) and 'Cissy' (white). 'Strawberry Fields' grows 2 ft. tall, has 1½-in. heads. Planted closely in large pots—six to a shallow 10-in. pot—makes a long-lasting living bouquet.

G. haageana. To 2 ft. tall, with heads of tightly clustered, bright orange bracts that resemble inch-wide pine cones. Tiny yellow flowers peep from the bracts. Sold as 'Haageana Aurea' or simply 'Orange'.

GONIOLIMON tataricum (Limonium tataricum)

GERMAN STATICE

Plumbaginaceae

PERENNIAL

🌿 ALL ZONES

☀️ FULL SUN

💧 MODERATE WATER

Goniolimon tataricum

Dense clumps of dark green, narrowly oval leaves arise from a woody rootstock. Leafless flower stalks rise to 1½ ft., forking repeatedly into a broad, domed cluster to 1½ ft. wide. Tiny flowers are light purplish to white. The entire inflorescence can be dried for winter flower arrangements. Plant is heat tolerant.

Goodeniaceae. Members of this small family of perennials and shrubs—principally from the Southern Hemisphere, notably Australia—have irregularly lipped flowers. *Scaevola* is the most widely grown example.

GOOSEBERRY

Grossulariaceae (Saxifragaceae)

DECIDUOUS SHRUBS

🌿 ZONES 1–6, 15–17, 34–43 FOR BEST FRUIT PRODUCTION

☀️ ◑ ● SOME SHADE IN HOT-SUMMER REGIONS

💧 REGULAR WATER

Gooseberry

For ornamental relatives, see *Ribes*. Same culture as currant; prune as for red and white currants. Like currant, prohibited in some areas

G

where white pines grow. Grown for pies, canning. Lobed, somewhat maple-like leaves. Fruit often striped longitudinally, decorative. 'Fredonia' is a fairly open plant producing large, dark red fruit. 'Oregon Champion', 3–5-ft. thorny bush with green fruit, bears heavily. 'Pixwell', extremely hardy and with few thorns, has pink fruit. 'Poorman' has red fruit sweet enough to eat off bush. 'Welcome' has medium large, dull red fruit with tart flavor; plants are productive, nearly spineless.

GOOSE PLUM. See PRUNUS americana

GOPHER PLANT. See EUPHORBIA lathyris

GORDONIA lasianthus

LOBLOLLY BAY

Theaceae

EVERGREEN TREE

⚡ ZONES 25–28, 31

☼ ◐ FULL SUN OR LIGHT SHADE

💧 AMPLE WATER

Gordonia lasianthus

Native to wet soils ("loblollies") of the coastal plain from Virginia to Louisiana. Narrow, erect, rather open-structured tree to 30–40 ft. tall, with shiny oval leaves 4–6 in. long. Attractive flowers up to 2½ in. wide bloom from midspring to midautumn; they look something like single white camellias and are enhanced by a big central brush of yellow stamens. Although wild trees grow in bogs, those in garden conditions seem to need perfect drainage as well as ample water. They are sometimes transplanted from the wild (with the owner's permission, of course), but are not considered easy to grow.

G. alatamaha. See Franklinia alatamaha

GOURD

Cucurbitaceae

ANNUAL VINES

⚡ ALL ZONES

☼ FULL SUN

💧 REGULAR DEEP WATERING

Gourd

Many plants produce gourds. One of most commonly planted is *Cucurbita pepo ovifera*, yellow-flowered gourd that produces great majority of small ornamental gourds in many shapes and sizes. May be all one color or striped. *Luffa aegyptiaca*, dish cloth gourd or vegetable sponge gourd, also has yellow flowers. Bears cylindrical gourds 1–2 ft. long, fibrous interior of which may be used in place of sponge or cloth for scrubbing and bathing. *Lagenaria siceraria (L. vulgaris)*, white-flowered gourd, bears gourds 3 in.–3 ft. long; these may be round, bottle shaped, dumbbell shaped, crooknecked, coiled, or spoon shaped.

All grow fast and will reach 10–15 ft. Sow seeds when ground is warm. Start indoors if growing season is short. Gourds need all the summer heat they can get to develop fruit by frost. If planting for ornamental gourd harvest, give vines wire or trellis support to hold ripening individual fruits off ground. Plant seedlings 2 ft. apart or thin seedlings to same spacing. You can harvest gourds when tendrils next to their stems are dead, but it's best to leave them on the vine as long as possible—until the gourds turn yellow or brown. They can even stay on the vine through frosts, but a heavy frost can discolor them. Cut some stem with each gourd so you can hang it up to dry slowly in a cool, airy spot. When thoroughly dry, preserve with coating of paste wax, lacquer, or shellac.

GOUT WEED. See AEGOPODIUM podagraria

GRAMA GRASS, BLUE. See BOUTELOUA gracilis

Gramineae. See Poaceae

GRAPE

Vitaceae

DECIDUOUS VINES

⚡ ZONES VARY BY VARIETY

☼ FULL SUN

💧 MODERATE WATER

▶ SEE CHART P. 322

Grape

For fruit, wine, shade, and fall color. A single grapevine can produce enough new growth every year to arch over a walk, roof an arbor, form a leafy wall, or provide an umbrella of shade over deck or terrace. Grape is one of the few ornamental vines with bold, textured foliage, colorful edible fruit, and dominant trunk and branch pattern for winter interest.

To get good-quality fruit, you must choose a variety that fits your climate, train it carefully, and prune it regularly.

There are several basic types of grapes. European grapes (*Vitis vinifera*) have tight skin, a generally high heat requirement, and cold tolerance to around 0°F/–18°C. These are the table grapes of the market, such as 'Thompson Seedless'. The classic wine grapes, such as 'Cabernet', 'Chardonnay', and 'Pinot Noir', are also European in origin. Although production of European wine grapes is increasing in the Northwest, Texas, tidewater Virginia, coastal Maryland, and eastern Long Island, these varieties are still grown primarily in California.

American grapes stem from *V. labrusca,* with some influence from other American native species and also often from *V. vinifera.* These are slipskin grapes of the 'Concord' type, which have a moderate summer heat requirement (as opposed to the European table grapes) and tolerate temperatures well below 0°F/–18°C. American grapes are used for jelly, in unfermented grape juice, and as flavoring for soft drinks; some wine, usually sweet, is also made from them. They grow throughout much of the U.S. but will not thrive in the Deep South; there, the grape of choice is the muscadine (*V. rotundifolia*), which bears large fruit in small clusters. Some muscadine varieties are self-fertile, while others require cross-pollination. (All other types of grapes are self-pollinating.)

Once established, grape vines grow rampantly. If all you want is a leafy cover for an arbor or patio, you need only train a strong vine up and over its support and thin out tangled growth each year. But most people plant grapes for fruit, even if they want shade as well. For good fruit production, you'll need to follow more careful pruning procedures.

Grapes are produced on stems that develop from 1-year-old wood—stems that formed the previous season. These stems have smooth bark; older stems have rough, shaggy bark. The purpose of pruning is to limit the amount of potential fruiting wood, ensuring that the plant doesn't produce too much fruit and that the fruit it does bear is of good quality.

There are several pruning methods for grapes. The two most widely used are spur pruning and cane pruning; see chart for recommended method for each variety. Either technique can be used for training grapes on arbors. Whichever method you choose, the initial steps—planting and creating a framework—are the same. (See illustrations on p. 321 for details.) Pruning should be done in the dormant season—winter or earliest spring, before the buds swell.

GRAPEFRUIT. See CITRUS

GRAPE HYACINTH. See MUSCARI

GRAPE IVY. See CISSUS rhombifolia

Grape Planting and Training

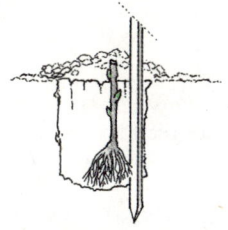

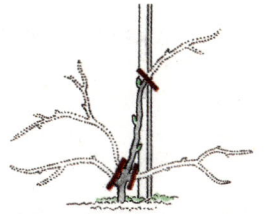

Planting: Plant bare-root grape deep in well-prepared soil, with only the top bud above soil level. Insert post or other support. Replace soil; cover exposed bud with lightweight mulch.

1st Summer: Let vine grow unchecked; don't try to train growth. The more leaves, the better the root development.

1st Winter: Select sturdiest shoot for trunk and remove all other shoots at their base. Shorten trunk to 3 or 4 lowest buds.

G

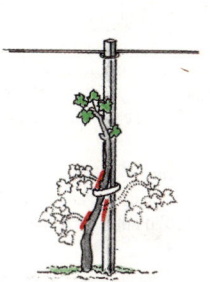

2nd Spring: Let buds grow into 6–8-in. shoots. Select a vigorous upright shoot to form the upper trunk, and tie loosely to post. Cut off all other shoots.

2nd Summer: When trunk reaches wire, cut its tip to force branching. Allow the 2 strongest developing shoots to grow, forming vine's arms; remove any others. Pinch any lateral shoots developing from arms to 10 inches long.

2nd Winter: Cut back all growth on trunk and arms; loosely tie arms to wire. Don't prune yet for fruit production; vines are too immature.

3rd Summer: Allow vine to grow. Remove any growth from trunk. Cane pruning and spur pruning differ from here on.

Cane Pruning from 3rd Winter: Cut back each arm to 12 buds; these will bear fruit the next summer. Select 2 strong lateral shoots near trunk and cut each to 2 buds; these are the renewal spurs. During next winter and every winter thereafter, remove fruiting canes at their base. Renewal spurs will have produced several new shoots from which new fruiting canes can be selected. Choose the 2 longest and strongest shoots and cut each to 12 buds; tie these shoots to wire. Select 2 next best shoots as renewal spurs and cut each to 2 buds.

Spur Pruning from 3rd Winter: Remove weak side shoots from arms. Leave strongest shoots (spurs) spaced 6–10 in. apart; cut each to 2 buds. Each spur will produce 2 fruit-bearing stems during next growing season. During next winter and every winter thereafter, remove upper stem on each spur and cut lower stem to 2 buds. Those buds will develop into stems that bear fruit the following summer.

Training on an Arbor

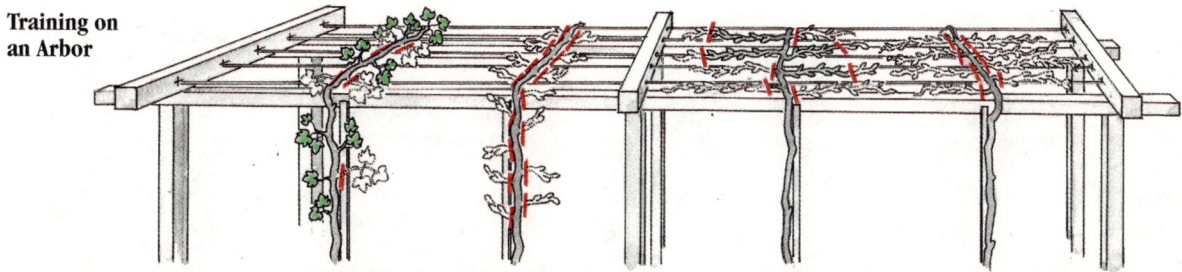

2nd Summer: When vine reaches top of arbor, bend it over and secure it as it grows across top. Remove side shoots to encourage tip to grow.

2nd Winter: Cut back main stem to point just beyond where you want the last set of branches. Cut off all side shoots. In spring, thin new shoots to 1 ft. apart.

3rd Winter, Cane Pruning: Cut back alternately to long canes (12 buds) and spurs (2 buds). Thereafter, follow cane pruning guidelines.

3rd Winter, Spur Pruning: Cut back each selected shoot (from previous summer's growth) to 2 buds. Thereafter, follow spur pruning guidelines.

GRAPE

G

VARIETY	ZONES	SEASON	PRUNING	COMMENTS
AMERICAN VARIETIES				
'Alden'	5–11, 13–22, 24, 34–40	Early midseason	Spur	Large, firm, seeded reddish blue grape with light muscat flavor. For fresh eating, wine. Very productive. Good fall leaf color. Protect below −15°F/−26°C
'America'	7–10, 14, 18–21, 23, 29–36	Midseason	Cane	Seeded black grape for fresh eating, wine, juice. May succeed in warmer parts of areas farther north, but often tends to be too acid
'Bluebell'	1–11, 14–22, 24, 34–43	Early	Cane	Seeded blue grape for fresh eating, juice, preserves. Good disease resistance. Hardy to at least −35°F/−37°C
'Buffalo'	1–11, 14–22, 24, 34–42	Early	Cane	Seeded blue table and juice grape with spicy flavor. Performs well after a late frost
'Campbell Early'	6–11, 13–22, 24, 32 (northern part), 34–42	Early midseason	Cane	Large seeded black grape of 'Concord' type for fresh eating, juice, wine. Colors before full sweetness develops; leave on vine a while. Tolerates heavy soil. In Zones 41 and 42, succeeds in areas with longest growing season
'Canadice'	1–11, 14–22, 24, 34–42	Early	Spur	Seedless red grape will ripen even in cool areas. Very heavy bearing. Cane pruning often recommended, but should be spur-pruned, possibly thinned, to prevent overcropping. Hardy to about −20°F/−29°C if not overcropped
'Champanel'	7 (warmer parts), 8–9, 14, 18–21, 23, 27, 29–31, 33, 35	Midseason	Cane	Seeded black juice grape colors before it is ripe; leave on vine to develop sweetness. Tolerates alkaline soil and Pierce's disease
'Concord'	6–11, 13–22, 24, 32 (northern part), 34–42	Midseason	Cane	Oldest cultivated American grape and the one most commonly used for juice, jelly. Seeded dark blue fruit. In Zones 41 and 42, succeeds in areas with longest growing seasons
'Diamond' ('Moore's Diamond', 'White Diamond')	6–11, 13–22, 24, 32 (northern part), 34–42	Early midseason	Cane or spur	Seeded white grape with sweet, refined flavor. For fresh eating, juice, wine. In Zones 41 and 42, succeeds areas with longest growing season
'Edelweiss'	1–11, 14–22, 24, 34–43	Early	Cane	Seeded white grape for fresh eating, juice. Pick as soon as ripe. Excellent disease resistance. Hardy to −30°F/−34°C
'Elvicand'	7 (warmer parts), 8–9, 14, 18–21, 23, 27, 28 (dryer parts), 29–35	Late midseason	Cane	Seeded red grape with spicy, peppery flavor. For fresh eating, juice, jelly. Good disease resistance. Tolerates alkaline soils
'Himrod'	1–11, 14–22, 24, 34–42	Very early	Cane	Firm, seedless white grape with spicy flavor. For fresh eating, raisins. Very vigorous, suited to arbors. Protect below −15°F/−26°C
'Interlaken'	1–11, 14–22, 24, 34–42	Very early	Cane or spur	Like 'Himrod', but sweeter and ripens a week earlier; vines are less vigorous but more productive. Protect below −15°F/−26°C
'Kay Gray'	1–11, 14–22, 24, 31–45	Early	Cane	Seeded white grape for table, juice, jelly. Hardy to −40°F/−40°C
'Lakemont'	5–11, 13–22, 24, 34–42	Early midseason	Cane or spur	Seedless white table grape with higher acid content than 'Himrod' or 'Interlaken'; keeps well in cold storage. Protect below −15°F/−26°C
'Manito'	6–11, 13–22, 24, 32 (northern part), 34–42	Early midseason	Cane	Seeded black table grape with fruity flavor. Widely adapted. In Zones 41 and 42, succeeds in areas with longest growing season
'New York Muscat'	1–11, 14–22, 24, 34–42	Early	Cane	Seeded blue-black grape with intense muscat flavor. For fresh eating, sweet wine. Moderately productive. Hardy to −20°F/−29°C
'Nitodal'	7–9, 14, 18–21, 23, 29–35	Midseason	Cane	Seeded reddish blue table grape. Good in limy soils, hot climates
'Price'	1–11, 14–22, 24, 34–42	Very early	Spur	Heavy crop of very sweet, seeded blue grapes with refined 'Concord' flavor. For fresh eating, fresh juice. Ripens even in coolest areas. Protect below −15°F/−26°C

GRAPE

VARIETY	ZONES	SEASON	PRUNING	COMMENTS
AMERICAN VARIETIES				
'Reliance'	5–11, 13–22, 24, 34–42	Early midseason	Cane or spur	Seedless red grape for fresh eating, fresh juice. May be ready to eat before it colors up. Reliable, heavy bearer. Hardy to about −25°F/−32°C
'Steuben'	6–11, 13–22, 24, 32 (northern part), 34–42	Midseason	Cane	Seeded blue grape with spicy flavor for fresh eating, juice. Very productive. Good disease resistance. In Zones 41 and 42, succeeds in areas with longest growing season
'Swenson Red'	1–11, 14–22, 24, 34–43	Early	Spur	Red or reddish blue grape with excellent strawberrylike flavor, small seeds. Clusters may have distinctive dumbbell shape; vines may take a few years to develop full vigor, yield. Hardy to −30°F/−34°C
'Valiant'	1–11, 14–22, 24, 31–45	Early	Cane or spur	Small seeded blue grape makes good cooked juice. Colors before full sweetness develops; leave on vine a while. Has survived −50°F/−46°C. Not very disease resistant. Cane-prune in coldest areas
'Vanessa'	5–11, 13–22, 24, 34–42	Early	Cane	Seedless red grape stands up to rain. Vines tend to have excess vigor
'Venus Seedless'	5–11, 13–22, 24, 34–41	Early	Cane	Large black grape, not always seedless. Flavor can be very good, aromatic, almost like muscat. For fresh eating, juice, jelly. Good fall leaf color
EUROPEAN VARIETIES				
'Centennial'	6–11, 14–22, 24	Late midseason	Cane	Big clusters of elongated, firm white grapes for fresh eating, raisins. Among the largest of the seedless grapes. May not be widely sold
'Dawn'	6–11, 14–22, 24	Early midseason	Cane	Very large, oval, seedless white table and raisin grape resists cracking and rain. May not be widely sold
'DOVine'	5–11, 14–22, 24	Very early	Cane	New seedless white grape developed for raisins; should also make a good, very sweet table grape. Name stands for "dried on vine"
'Early Muscat'	6–11, 14–22, 24	Early	Spur	Big clusters of oval, seeded yellow grapes with intense muscat flavor. For fresh eating, wine
'Flame'	5–11, 14–22, 24	Early	Cane or spur	Seedless red table and raisin grape resists cracking. Keep on dry side to reduce excess vigor
'Muscat Hamburg'	6–11, 14–22, 24	Midseason	Spur	Perhaps best of all muscat table grapes for intense, almost orangelike flavor. Also used for wine. Seeded blue-black fruit resists cracking
'Thompson Seedless'	7–11, 14–22, 24	Late midseason	Cane or spur	Big bunches of small, sweet, mild-flavored greenish amber grapes for fresh eating, raisins, wine. Best in hot-summer areas
MUSCADINE VARIETIES				
'Carlos'	7 (warmer parts), 8–9, 14, 18–21, 23, 26–33	Early to midseason	Spur	Seeded bronze grape with fine flavor. For juice, jelly, wine. Self-fertile
'Cowart'	7 (warmer parts), 8–9, 14, 18–21, 23, 26–33	Early to midseason	Spur	Large, seeded blue-black table and juice grape. Self-fertile
'Golden Isles'	7 (warmer parts), 8–9, 14, 18–21, 23, 26–33	Midseason	Spur	Seeded bronze grape for table, wine, juice. Self-fertile
'Jumbo'	7 (warmer parts), 8–9, 14, 18–21, 23, 26–33	Midseason to late	Spur	Huge black fruit. Needs pollinator
'Scuppernong'	7 (warmer parts), 8–9, 14, 18–21, 23, 26–33	Midseason	Spur	The original muscadine variety. Bronze, speckled grape with distinctive aroma and flavor. Needs pollinator
'Triumph'	7 (warmer parts), 8–9, 14, 18–21, 23, 26–33	Early midseason	Spur	Reliable, heavy crop of bronze to nearly yellow grapes with pineapple flavor. For juice, fresh eating, wine. Self-fertile

G

GRASSES. The grasses in this book are either lawn or ornamental plants—except for corn, the only cereal commonly grown in home gardens. They are described under entries headed by their botanical names; to find these, check lists below. (All bamboos, which are grasses, are charted under Bamboo.)

Lawn grasses are *Agropyron*, wheatgrass; *Agrostis*, bent grass, redtop; *Bouteloua*, blue grama grass; *Buchloe*, buffalo grass; *Cynodon*, Bermuda grass; *Festuca*, fescue; *Lolium*, ryegrass; *Paspalum*, bahia grass, seashore paspalum; *Poa*, bluegrass; *Stenotaphrum*, St. Augustine grass; *Zoysia*, zoysia.

Ornamental grasses are *Arrhenatherum*, bulbous oat grass; *Arundo*, giant reed; *Bouteloua*, blue grama grass; *Briza*, rattlesnake grass; *Calamagrostis*, feather reed grass; *Chasmanthium*, sea oats; *Coix*, Job's tears; *Cortaderia*, pampas grass; *Deschampsia*, hair grass; *Festuca*, fescue; *Hakonechloa*, Japanese forest grass; *Helictotrichon*, blue oat grass; *Imperata*, Japanese blood grass; *Milium effusum* 'Aureum', Bowles' golden grass; *Miscanthus*, eulalia grass, maiden grass, silver grass; *Molinia*, purple moor grass; *Muhlenbergia*, bamboo muhly, deer grass, muhly grass; *Panicum*, switch grass; *Pennisetum*, fountain grass; *Phalaris*, ribbon grass; *Setaria*, palm grass; and *Stipa*, feather grass, needle grass.

GRASS NUT. See TRITELEIA laxa

GRECIAN LAUREL. See LAURUS nobilis

GREEN AND GOLD. See CHRYSOGONUM virginianum

GREEN CARPET. See HERNIARIA glabra

GREVILLEA

Proteaceae

EVERGREEN SHRUBS OR TREES

⚡ ZONES VARY BY SPECIES

☼ FULL SUN

💧💧 WATER NEEDS VARY BY SPECIES

Native to Australia. Many species and hybrids. Plants vary in size and appearance, but generally have fine-textured foliage and long, slender, curved flowers, usually in dense clusters. Provide good drainage. Like other members of the protea family, sensitive to high levels of phosphorus in the soil. Fertilize lightly; avoid fertilizers with high phosphorus content. Intolerant of salt.

Grevillea robusta

G. banksii. Shrub or small tree. Zones 20–25, 27. Often sold as *G. banksii forsteri*. To 15–20 ft. Leaves 4–10 in. long, deeply cut into narrow lobes. Erect, 3–6-in.-long clusters of dark red flowers appear sporadically all year; bloom is heaviest in late spring. Showy used singly against high wall, near entryway, or grouped with other big shrubs. Freezes at 24°F/−4°C; takes wind. Much to little water.

G. 'Canberra'. Shrub. Zones 8, 9, 12–24. Open, graceful growth to 8 ft. tall, 12 ft. wide. Bright green, needlelike, 1-in. leaves. Clusters of red flowers in spring and intermittently at other times of year. Little water.

G. 'Constance'. Shrub. Zones 8, 9, 12–24. Orange-red bloomer similar to 'Canberra' but broader in growth. Little water.

G. lavandulacea. LAVENDER GREVILLEA. Shrub. Zones 15–24. Variable, but all forms are dense growers with ½-in. gray leaves. 'Billywing' grows 2½ ft. high, 6 ft. wide, with red-and-cream flowers in winter and spring. 'Penola' reaches 5 ft. high or taller, 8 ft. wide (wider if unpruned), with deep rose red flowers fall through spring. 'Tanunda' is 1½–3 ft. high, 3–6 ft. wide, with profuse coral pink flowers; main bloom winter, with occasional repeat bloom midsummer. Little water.

Grevillea 'Noellii'

G. 'Noellii'. Shrub. Zones 8, 9, 12–24. Probably a hybrid. To 4 ft. tall, 4–5 ft. wide. Densely clad with narrow, 1-in.-long, medium green glossy leaves. Clusters of pink-and-white flowers bloom in spring. Moderate water.

G. robusta. SILK OAK. Tree. Zones 8, 9, 12–27. Fast growing to 50–60 ft. (rarely 100 ft.). Symmetrical, pyramidal when young. Old trees broad topped, picturesque against skyline, usually with a few heavy, horizontal limbs. Fernlike leaves golden green to deep green above, silvery beneath. Heavy leaf fall in spring, sporadic leaf drop through rest of year. Large clusters of bright golden orange flowers in early spring. Wood is brittle, easily damaged in high wind. Young trees damaged at 24°F/−4°C; older ones hardy to 16°F/−9°C. Use for quick, tall screen; or clip as tall hedge. Much to little water. In cold climates, sometimes grown as pot plant or house plant and discarded when it gets too big.

GREWIA occidentalis

LAVENDER STARFLOWER

Tiliaceae

EVERGREEN SHRUB

⚡ ZONES 8, 9, 12–27

☼ FULL SUN

💧 REGULAR WATER

Grewia occidentalis

Usually sold as *G. caffra*. Native to South Africa. Fast-growing, sprawling habit. Tends to branch freely in flat pattern, making natural espalier if given some support. Becomes dense with pinching and pruning. Grows 6–10 ft. tall (sometimes higher), with equal spread if unstaked. Deep green leaves are 3 in. long. Flowers are 1 in. wide, starlike, lavender pink with yellow center. Main bloom comes in late spring, with scattered flowers into autumn.

GRISELINIA

Cornaceae

EVERGREEN SHRUBS

⚡ ZONES 9, 14–17, 20–24

☼ ☼ FULL SUN OR LIGHT SHADE

💧💧 REGULAR TO MODERATE WATER

Griselinia littoralis

Native to New Zealand. Upright form and thick, leathery, lustrous leaves. Flowers and fruit are insignificant. Always look well groomed. Good near swimming pools.

G. littoralis. A 50-ft. tree in New Zealand, but usually seen in U.S. as 10-ft. shrub of equal spread. Leaves roundish, 4 in. long. Dense, compact screen or windbreak. Fine beach plant, good espalier. 'Variegata' has leaves marked with cream.

G. lucida. Slower growing, smaller, more open and slender than *G. littoralis*, with larger (7-in.-long) leaves. Thrives in container. 'Variegata' has white markings on leaves.

GROUND CHERRY. See PHYSALIS peruviana

GROUND IVY. See GLECHOMA hederacea

GROUNDSEL. See BACCHARIS halimifolia

GRUMICHAMA. See EUGENIA braziliensis

GUAJILLO. See ACACIA berlandieri

GUAVA. See PSIDIUM

GUERNSEY LILY. See NERINE sarniensis

GUINEA GOLD VINE. See HIBBERTIA scandens

GUM. See EUCALYPTUS

G

GUNNERA

Gunneraceae

PERENNIALS

ZONES 4–6, 14–17, 20–24, 28, 31, 32

PARTIAL SHADE

CONTINUOUSLY MOIST SOIL

Gunnera tinctoria

Big, bold, awe-inspiring plant to 8 ft. high, with giant leaves (4–8 ft. across) on stiff-haired stalks 4–6 ft. long. Leaves are lobed, conspicuously veined; new sets grow every spring. In mild-winter areas, old leaves remain green for more than a year. In colder part of range, foliage dies back completely in winter; provide a thick winter mulch over crowns. Corncoblike, 1½-ft. flower clusters form close to roots. Tiny fruits are red.

Best suited to regions with relatively cool summers, not-too-cold winters. A challenge to grow in eastern U.S., but a conversation piece if it succeeds. Grow in rich, moist, organic soil; feed regularly. Use beside a pond, in a bog garden, or dominating a bed of low, fine-textured ground cover.

G. manicata. Leaves carried fairly horizontally. Spinelike hairs on leafstalks and ribs are red. Leaf lobes are flatter, lack frills of *G. tinctoria*.

G. tinctoria (G. chilensis). Lobed leaf margins are toothed and somewhat frilled. The leaves are held in a bowl-like way, half upright and flaring.

> ### DINOSAUR FOOD?
>
> Maybe not, but gunnera is such an exotic, jungly-looking plant that it's easy to imagine giant reptiles munching its huge leaves in a prehistoric forest. These statuesque plants are a good choice for anchors in mixed borders; they are striking at the edge of a pool, where their foliage will be mirrored in the water. Or try one in a large pot.

GYMNOCLADUS dioica

KENTUCKY COFFEE TREE

Fabaceae (Leguminosae)

DECIDUOUS TREE

ZONES 1–3, 7–10, 12–16, 18–21, 32–43

FULL SUN

REGULAR TO MODERATE WATER

Gymnocladus dioica

Native to eastern U.S. As a sapling, grows very fast, but slows down at 8–10 ft. Give it lots of space, since it ultimately reaches 60–100 ft. tall and 45–50 ft. wide. Unusual tree providing year-round interest.

Handsome bark is dark gray to deep brown with rough, scaly ridges. The relatively few heavy, contorted branches and stout twigs make bare tree picturesque in winter. Attractive 1½–3-ft.-long leaves, divided into many 1–3-in.-long leaflets, emerge late in spring, usually in May. They are pinkish when expanding, deep bluish green in summer. Fall color is usually not effective, though leaves sometimes turn an agreeable sunny yellow. In leaf, the tree casts light shade.

Male and female plants are separate. Narrow flower panicles at ends of branches in spring are up to 1 ft. long (and fragrant) on females, to 4 in. long on males. Blossoms on female trees are followed by flat, reddish brown, 6–10-in.-long pods containing hard black seeds. Pods persist through winter. Early settlers in Kentucky and Tennessee roasted the seeds to make a coffee substitute, giving the tree its common name.

Grows best in moist, rich, deep soil, but adapts to poor soil, drought, city conditions. Established tree can take much heat and cold. Prune in winter or early spring.

GYPSOPHILA

Caryophyllaceae

ANNUALS AND PERENNIALS

ZONES VARY BY SPECIES

FULL SUN

MODERATE WATER

Gypsophila repens

Much-branched slender-stemmed plants, upright or spreading, 6 in.–4 ft. tall, profusely covered in summer with small, single or double, white, pink, or rose flowers in clusters. Leaves blue green; few when plant is in bloom. Use for airy grace in borders, bouquets; fine contrast with large-flowered, coarse-textured plants. Dwarf kinds ideal in rock gardens, trailing from wall pocket or over top of dry rock walls.

Add lime to strongly acid soils. For repeat bloom on perennial species, cut back flowering stems before seed clusters form. Thick, deep roots of some perennial types difficult to transplant; do not disturb often.

G. cerastioides. Perennial. Zones 3–10, 14–21, 32, 34. Forms mat 3 in. tall, much broader, with gray leaves and clustered flowers varying from pink-veined white to pink. Use in rock garden, between paving stones.

G. elegans. Annual. All zones. Upright, 1–1½ ft. tall. Lance-shaped, rather fleshy leaves to 3 in. long. Profuse single white flowers ½ in. across or more. Pink and rose forms available. Plants live only 5 to 6 weeks; for continuous bloom, sow seed in open ground every 3 to 4 weeks from late spring into summer. Excellent cut flower.

G. paniculata. BABY'S BREATH. Perennial. Zones 1–10, 14–16, 18–21, 31–45. This is the classic filler in bouquets. Much branched to 3 ft. or more; leaves slender, sharp pointed, 2½–4 in. long. Single white flowers about $1/16$ in. across, hundreds in a spray. 'Bristol Fairy' is an improved form, more billowy, to 4 ft. high, covered with double blossoms ¼ in. wide. Florists' favorite variety is 'Perfecta', which bears larger flowers. 'Compacta Plena' is a double white dwarf 1½ ft. tall; other dwarfs are double pink 'Pink Star' (1½ ft. tall) and 'Viette's Dwarf' (12–15 in. high). Grow all types from root grafts or stem cuttings.

G. repens. Perennial. Zones 1–11, 14–16, 18–21, 31–43. Alpine native 6–9 in. high, with trailing stems 1½ ft. long. Leaves narrow, less than 1 in. long. Clusters of small white or pink flowers. Increase by cuttings in midsummer. Varieties include several 4-in.-high selections: white-flowered 'Alba' and pink-flowered 'Dubia' (with blooms borne on deep purplish stems) and 'Rosea'. Pink-blossomed 'Dorothy Teacher' is 2 in. high.

HABRANTHUS

Amaryllidaceae

BULBS

ZONES 8, 9, 14–28; OR GROW IN POTS

FULL SUN OR LIGHT SHADE

REGULAR WATER DURING GROWTH AND BLOOM

Habranthus robustus

Bulbous plants somewhat resembling miniature amaryllis *(Hippeastrum),* with narrow, grassy leaves and trumpet-shaped flowers. Native from Mexico to Argentina, but many are widely grown in Texas and naturalized there. Where soil freezes, grow in pots. Set with bulb tops at soil level. Plants can withstand some aridity. Use in rock gardens or naturalize.

H. andersonii (H. tubispathus). Flower stems reach 6 in., with inch-wide yellow flowers, coppery on the outside. 'Cupreus' is coppery orange. A bright yellow form with larger flowers is sold as *H. texanus*. Summer blooming.

H. robustus. Four-inch bright pink flowers are carried one or two to a stem. Bloom may occur any time from spring to fall.

HACKBERRY. See CELTIS

HAEMANTHUS katherinae
(Scadoxus multiflorus katherinae)

BLOOD LILY

Amaryllidaceae

BULB

☘ ZONES 21–27; OR INDOOR/OUTDOOR PLANT

☼ LIGHT SHADE

💧 REGULAR WATER DURING GROWTH AND BLOOM

Haemanthus katherinae

Tender South African plant closely related to amaryllis. Large (4-in.-diameter) white bulb stained red (hence common name). Broad, wavy-edged, bright green leaves, 12–15 in. long. Sturdy succulent stem 2 ft. tall, topped by large, round clusters of bright salmon blooms with protruding, showy red stamens; flower heads look like big pompoms.

Can grow in ground in frost-free regions, but even there it is usually grown in pots. In colder areas, grow in pots in greenhouse or sunny room, move to terrace or patio for bloom in late spring or early summer. Put one bulb in 10-in. pot in rich potting mix in winter or early spring. Set bulb with tip at soil surface; water sparingly; keep at 70°F/21°C. Can be moved outdoors to sheltered, lightly shaded spot when leaves appear (8 to 10 weeks). Water well; feed monthly with complete fertilizer. After bloom, gradually reduce watering; let plant dry out in cool, protected place. Do not repot next season. Simply add new potting mix on top of original soil; or tip out root ball, scrape off some soil, and replace with fresh mix.

HAKEA

Proteaceae

EVERGREEN SHRUBS OR TREES

☘ ZONES 9, 12–17, 19–24

☼ FULL SUN

💧 MODERATE TO LITTLE WATER

Hakea laurina

Native to Australia. Tough, attractive shrubs or small trees for difficult sites. Especially good for seacoast. Take poor soil.

H. laurina. SEA URCHIN, PINCUSHION TREE. Small, dense, rounded tree or large shrub to 30 ft. Narrow, gray-green, 6-in. leaves are often red margined. Showy flower clusters look like round crimson pincushions stuck with golden pins. Blooms winter, sometimes late fall.

H. suaveolens. SWEET HAKEA. Dense, broad, upright shrub to 10–20 ft. tall. Stiff, dark green, 4-in. leaves, branched into stiff, needlelike segments. Small, fragrant white flowers in dense, fluffy clusters, fall and winter. Can be pruned into tree form.

HAKONECHLOA macra
'Aureola'

JAPANESE FOREST GRASS

Poaceae (Gramineae)

PERENNIAL

☘ ZONES 2–9, 14–24, 31–41

☼ 💧 PARTIAL OR FULL SHADE

💧 REGULAR WATER

Hakonechloa macra 'Aureola'

Graceful, slender, leaning or arching stems to 1½ ft. carry long, slender leaves with gold stripes. (The basic species with all-green leaves is seldom grown.) Effect is that of a tiny bamboo. Spreads slowly by under-

ground runners. Needs good, well-drained soil. Choice plant for woodland garden or for close viewing in a container.

HALESIA

Styracaceae

DECIDUOUS TREES

☘ ZONES 2–9, 14–24, 31–41, EXCEPT AS NOTED

☼ PART SHADE

💧 REGULAR WATER

Elegant trees native to southeastern U.S. Give best flower display in areas with winter cold; grow best in cool, deep, humus-rich soil. Attractive in woodland gardens, with rhododendrons and azaleas planted beneath.

Halesia carolina

H. carolina (H. tetraptera). SNOWDROP TREE, SILVER BELL. Also grows in Zones 26, 28. Moderate growth to 30–40 ft., with 20–35-ft. spread. Lovely in mid-spring, when clusters of snow-white, ½-in., bell-shaped flowers hang along length of graceful branches just as leaves begin to appear. Oval, finely toothed, 2–5-in.-long leaves turn yellow in fall. Interesting four-winged brown fruits hang on almost all winter. Train plant to a single trunk when young or it will grow as a large shrub. Flowers show off to best advantage when you can look up into tree.

H. diptera. TWO-WINGED SILVER BELL. Small (to 20–30 ft. tall), rounded, usually multitrunked. Flowers resemble those of *H. carolina*, but are more deeply lobed and bloom a week or two later. Fruits resemble those of *H. carolina* but have two rather than four wings. *H. d. magniflora* is a more profuse bloomer.

H. monticola. MOUNTAIN SILVER BELL. Similar to *H. carolina* but larger, eventually to 60–80 ft. tall. Leaves are also bigger (3–6 in. long), but tree casts only moderate shade. Flowers, fruit are also somewhat larger. 'Rosea' has light pink flowers.

Hamamelidaceae. The witch hazel family contains deciduous (rarely evergreen) trees and shrubs. Some have showy flowers; these include *Fothergilla*, witch hazel (*Hamamelis*), *Loropetalum*. Many of the deciduous kinds have brilliant fall color; examples are sweet gum (*Liquidambar*), *Parrotia*.

HAMAMELIS

WITCH HAZEL

Hamamelidaceae

DECIDUOUS SHRUBS OR SMALL TREES

☘ ZONES VARY BY SPECIES

☼ ☼ FULL SUN OR PARTIAL SHADE

💧 MODERATE WATER

Hamamelis mollis

Medium-size to large shrubs, sometimes tree-like, usually with spreading habit and angular or zigzagging branches. Valued for bright fall foliage and interesting yellow to red blooms appearing in nodding clusters, usually in winter. Each flower consists of many narrow, crumpled petals; depending on whom you ask, blossoms resemble shredded coconut, mop heads, or spiders. Most types are fragrant and bloom over a long period. All appreciate rich, organic soil. Prune only to guide growth, remove poorly placed branches or suckers, or obtain flowering stems for winter bouquets.

H. intermedia. Zones 4–7, 15–17, 31–34, 39. Group of hybrids between *H. mollis* and *H. japonica*. Big shrubs (to 15 ft. high), blooming from late January in warmest part of range to mid-March in coldest areas. Often grafted; remove any growth originating from below graft. The following varieties are among the best:

'Allgold'. Upright shrub bearing deep yellow flowers, reddish at base; yellow fall foliage.

'Arnold Promise'. Late bloomer. Pure yellow, very fragrant flowers nearly conceal branches at peak of bloom. Exceptionally cold hardy.

'Carmine Red'. Spreading shrub with light red flowers; red-orange fall color. Vigorous.

'Diane'. Bright coppery red flowers with slight scent; fine ruddy gold fall color.

'Hiltingbury'. Spreading plant with pale copper blossoms; orange, red, and scarlet autumn leaves.

'Jelena' ('Copper Beauty', 'Orange Beauty'). Spreading plant with large leaves, large yellow flowers heavily suffused with red, and orange-red fall foliage.

'Magic Fire' ('Fire Charm', 'Feuerzauber'). Upright plant with fragrant blossoms of coppery orange blended with red.

'Moonlight'. Upright shrub with strongly perfumed blossoms of light sulfur yellow, red at base; yellow fall foliage.

'Primavera'. Late bloomer producing large quantities of sweet-scented, primrose yellow flowers. Vigorous.

'Ruby Glow'. Erect, with coppery red flowers and excellent rusty gold fall color.

'Sunburst'. Heavy crop of radiant yellow, unscented blooms.

H. japonica. JAPANESE WITCH HAZEL. Zones 4–7, 15–17, 31–34, 39. To 10–15 ft. tall, with loose, spreading habit. Fairly small, lightly scented yellow flowers, February–March. Chief distinction is brilliant fall foliage—shades of red, purple, and yellow. *H. j. flavopurpurascens* has yellow-orange flowers, purple at the base, and reddish yellow fall foliage. *H. j. arborea* is a larger form, to 20–25 ft. tall, with a profusion of yellow blossoms and yellow autumn leaves.

H. mollis. CHINESE WITCH HAZEL. Zones 2–7, 15–17, 31–34, 39. Moderately slow-growing shrub to 8–10 ft. or small tree that may eventually reach 30 ft. Roundish leaves, 3½–6 in. long, are dark green and rough above, gray and felted beneath; turn good clear yellow in fall. Sweetly fragrant, 1½-in.-wide, rich golden yellow flowers with red-brown sepals bloom on bare stems, February–March. Effective against red brick or gray stone. Flowering branches excellent for arrangements. 'Early Bright' is an early-blooming variety. 'Pallida' has pale yellow flowers; 'Coombe Wood' bears slightly larger, more highly scented blooms than the species.

H. vernalis. OZARK WITCH HAZEL. Zones 2–7, 15–17, 28, 31–41. Native to central and southern U.S. Slow-growing, rounded shrub to 10–15 ft., rarely taller. Leaves 2–5 in. long, medium to dark green, turning bright yellow in fall and holding for several weeks in favorable weather. Flowers are ½–¾ in. across, yellow (rarely orange or red), fragrant, and quite resistant to cold. Blooms January–March. 'Red Imp' has small red flowers.

H. virginiana. COMMON WITCH HAZEL. Zones 1–9, 14–16, 18–21, 31–43. Native to eastern North America. Sometimes to 25 ft. tall but usually 10–15 ft. high; open, spreading, rather straggling habit. Moderately slow growing. The bark is the source of the liniment witch hazel. Roundish leaves similar to those of *H. mollis* but not gray and felted beneath; turn yellow to orange in fall. Fragrant, ¾-in.-wide, golden yellow blooms appear October–November and tend to be lost in colored foliage.

HAMELIA patens

SCARLET BUSH

Rubiaceae

EVERGREEN SHRUB OR SMALL TREE

✿ ZONES 25–28

☀ SUN

💧 AMPLE WATER

Hamelia patens

Native from Southern Florida south to Central and South America. Gardenia and coffee relative growing to 9–10 ft. tall, possibly much taller, with whorls of oval, gray-green, 6-in. leaves. Leafstalks and flower stems are red. Clusters of ¾-in., tubular, orange to bright red flowers form at branch tips all summer long; thanks to shape and color of blossoms, plant

is also known as firecracker shrub. Flowers are followed by small dark red, purple, or black fruits much relished by birds. Likes lots of moisture but needs good drainage. Tolerant of salt.

HARDENBERGIA

Fabaceae (Leguminosae)

EVERGREEN SHRUBBY VINES

✿ ZONES VARY BY SPECIES

☀ ◗ PARTIAL SHADE IN HOT AREAS

💧 MODERATE WATER

Hardenbergia comptoniana

Native to Australia. Grow at moderate rate to 10 ft., climbing by twining stems. Attractive flowers shaped like pea blossoms, late winter to early spring. Need light, well-drained soil. Provide support for climbing and cut back after bloom to prevent tangling.

H. comptoniana. LILAC VINE. Zones 15–24. Light, delicate foliage pattern; leaves divided into three to five dark green, narrow, 2–3-in.-long leaflets. Long, narrow clusters of ½-in. violet blue blossoms. Where temperatures drop below 24°F/–4°C, plant under overhang.

H. violacea (H. monophylla). Zones 8–24. Vining or shrubby. Coarser texture than *H. comptoniana;* leaves usually undivided, 2–4 in. long. Flowers lilac or violet to rose or white. 'Happy Wanderer' is tough, vigorous selection with pinkish purple blooms. 'Rosea' has pink flowers.

HAREBELL. See CAMPANULA rotundifolia

HARE'S FOOT FERN. See POLYPODIUM aureum

HARRY LAUDER'S WALKING STICK. See CORYLUS avellana 'Contorta'

HART'S TONGUE FERN. See ASPLENIUM scolopendrium

HAWTHORN. See CRATAEGUS

HAY-SCENTED FERN. See DENNSTAEDTIA punctilobula

HAZELNUT. See CORYLUS, FILBERT

HEART OF FLAME. See BROMELIA balansae

HEATH. See DABOECIA, ERICA

HEATHER. See CALLUNA vulgaris

HEAVENLY BAMBOO. See NANDINA domestica

HEBE

Scrophulariaceae

EVERGREEN SHRUBS

✿ ZONES 14–24; 26 AS SHORT-LIVED PERENNIAL

☀ ◗ PARTIAL SHADE IN HOT AREAS

💧 REGULAR WATER

Hebe buxifolia

Closely related to *Veronica* and often sold under that name. Native to New Zealand. Generally fast growing. Most types are grown mainly for form and handsome foliage; those described here also give good summer flower display. Low hebes are useful for edgings or ground cover; taller ones make good shrubs. Good seacoast plants. Very susceptible to root rot; well-drained soil is essential. Shorten flowering stems considerably after bloom to keep plants compact.

H. buxifolia. BOXLEAF HEBE. Rounded, symmetrical, to an eventual 5 ft. high; easily shaped into 3-ft. hedge. Tiny deep green leaves densely cover branches. Clusters of small white flowers.

▶

H. elliptica (H. decussata). Much-branched shrub 5–6 ft. high. Medium green leaves 1½ in. long. Clusters of fragrant bluish flowers.

H. 'Patty's Purple'. To 3 ft. high. Stems wine red; tiny dark green leaves. Purple flowers on slender spikes. Resistant to root rot.

H. speciosa. SHOWY HEBE. Dense, broad, spreading habit; grows 2–5 ft. high. Stout stems bear dark green, glossy leaves, 2–4 in. long. Reddish purple flowers in 3–4-in. spikes. 'Imperialis' has reddish foliage, magenta flowers.

HEDERA

IVY

Araliaceae

EVERGREEN WOODY VINES

🌿 ZONES VARY BY SPECIES

☀️ ◑ ● SOME SHADE IN HOT AREAS

💧💧 REGULAR TO MODERATE WATER

Hedera helix

S preads horizontally over the ground; also climbs on walls, fences, trellises. Sometimes a single planting does both—wall ivy spreads to become surrounding ground cover or vice versa. Dependable, uniform, neat. Holds soil, discouraging erosion and slippage on slopes. Roots grow deep and fill soil densely. Branches root as they grow, further knitting soil.

Ivy climbs almost any vertical surface by aerial rootlets—a factor to consider in planting against walls that must be painted. Chain link fence planted with ivy soon becomes wall of foliage.

Ivy must have shade in hot climates. Its only real shortcoming is monotony. All year long you get nothing from it but green or green and white (except in the case of *H. helix* 'Baltica').

Thick, leathery leaves are usually lobed. Mature plants will eventually develop stiff branches toward top of vine that bear round clusters of small greenish flowers followed by black berries. These branches have unlobed leaves; cuttings from such branches will have same kind of leaves and will be shrubby, not vining. Such shrubs taken from variegated Algerian ivy are called "ghost ivy." The plain green *H. helix* 'Arborescens' is another variety of this shrubby type.

Most ivy ground covers need trimming around edges (use hedge shears or sharp spade) two or three times a year. Fence and wall plantings need shearing or trimming two or three times a year. When ground cover builds up higher than you want, mow it with rugged power rotary mower or cut it back with hedge shears. Do this in spring so ensuing growth will quickly cover bald look.

Many trees and shrubs can grow quite compatibly in ivy. But small, soft, or fragile plants will never exist for long with healthy ivy—it simply smothers them. Ivy can be a haven for slugs and snails; it also harbors rodents, especially when it is never cut back.

H. canariensis. ALGERIAN IVY. Zones 8, 9, 12–28. Shiny, rich green leaves 5–8 in. wide with three to five shallow lobes, more widely spaced along stems than on English ivy.

'Variegata'. VARIEGATED ALGERIAN IVY. Leaves edged with yellowish white; white edges are sometimes suffused with reddish purple in cold weather. Avoid extreme heat.

H. colchica. PERSIAN IVY. Zones 3–34. Oval to heart-shaped leaves, 3–7 in. wide, to 10 in. long (largest leaves of all ivies). Somewhat resembles Algerian ivy in large leaf size and glossiness, but is more cold-hardy. 'Dentata' is faintly toothed; 'Dentata Variegata' is marbled with deep green, gray green, and creamy white. 'Sulphur Heart' ('Paddy's Pride') has central gold variegation.

H. helix. ENGLISH IVY. Zones 3–34, 39; hardiest varieties in 35, 37, and warmer parts of 38 and 41. Dull dark green leaves with paler veins are 2–4 in. wide at base and as long, with three to five lobes. Not as vigorous as Algerian ivy, better for small spaces.

'Baltica', with whitish-veined leaves half as big as those of the species, is often considered hardiest variety of English ivy. Its leaves take on purplish

tone in winter. Other exceptionally hardy varieties are 'Bulgarica', 'Hebron', 'Rochester', 'Thorndale', and '238th Street'.

Many small- and miniature-leafed forms of English ivy are useful for small-area ground covers, hanging baskets, and training to form intricate patterns on walls and in pots. These varieties are also used to create topiary shapes—globes, baskets, animals—on wire frames. Some small-leafed forms are 'Hahn's Self Branching', light green leaves, dense branching, best in part shade; 'Conglomerata', a slow-growing dwarf; and 'Minima', leaves ½–1 in. across with three to five angular lobes. Other varieties include 'Buttercup', 'California', 'Fluffy Ruffles', 'Gold Dust', 'Gold Heart', 'Heart', 'Needlepoint', 'Ripple', 'Shamrock', and 'Star'; select for leaf color and shape. These are most often grown as house plants, but if planted in protected sites, most are hardy in Zones 3–34, 39.

HEDYCHIUM

GINGER LILY

Zingiberaceae

PERENNIALS

🌿 ZONES 16, 17, 22–27; OR INDOORS

☀️ ◑ FULL SUN OR LIGHT SHADE

💧 AMPLE WATER

*Hedychium
gardneranum*

F oliage is handsome under good growing conditions. Leaves are on two sides of stems but grow in a single plane. In late summer or early fall, richly fragrant flowers in dense spikes open from cone of overlapping green bracts at ends of stalks. Southern specialist growers offer dozens of species and selections in heights from 2 to 9 ft., in colors that range from white and cream through pink to red, and a host of yellows, oranges, and salmons.

Remove old stems after flowers fade to bring on fresh new growth. Useful in large containers, though potted specimens do not grow as tall as those in ground. Give soil high in organic matter. Frosts in mild-winter areas can kill plants to ground, but new stalks appear in early spring. Useful near swimming pools, with palms, ferns, other tropical-looking plants.

H. coronarium. WHITE GINGER LILY, GARLAND FLOWER. Native to India, Indonesia. Grows 3–6 ft. high. Leaves 8–24 in. long, 2–5 in. across. Wonderfully fragrant white flowers in 6–12-in.-long clusters; good cut flowers.

H. gardneranum. KAHILI GINGER. Native to India. Grows to 8 ft. high; 8–18-in.-long leaves 4–6 in. wide. Clear yellow flowers with red stamens, in 1½-ft.-long spikes.

H. greenei. Native to India. Grows to 5 ft., with orange-red flowers in 5-in. spikes.

HEDYOTIS caerulea. See HOUSTONIA caerulea

HELENIUM autumnale

COMMON SNEEZEWEED

Asteraceae (Compositae)

PERENNIAL

🌿 ALL ZONES

☀️ FULL SUN

💧 REGULAR WATER

Helenium autumnale

S pecies is rarely grown; plants sold as such are usually hybrids between *H. autumnale* and other species. Leaves 2–4 in. long, toothed. Numerous branching, leafy stems to 1–6 ft. high, depending on variety. Blooms over a long period from midsummer to early fall; flowers are daisylike, with rays in yellow, orange, red, or copper shades surrounding a pompomlike, typically brown center.

Blooms best in hot-summer areas. Trim off faded blossoms to encourage more flowers. Better looking with scant fertilizer. Taller varieties need staking and are best suited to back of borders. Divide all types every few years. Plants can take some neglect. Drought tolerant, but look better with regular moisture.

The following named varieties are sometimes offered. Tall types grow to 4–5 ft., compact ones to about 3 ft. high.

'Baudirektor Linne'. Tall. Velvety red petals and a brown center.
'Butterpat'. Tall. Light yellow blossoms with a deeper yellow center.
'Crimson Beauty'. Compact. Dusky deep red flowers.
'Cymbal Star' ('Zimbelstern'). Tall. Gold blooms touched with bronze.
'Dunkel Pracht'. Tall. Dark red blossoms with a brown center.
'Gold Kugel' ('Gold Ball'). Compact. Dark-centered yellow blossoms.
'Moerheim Beauty'. Compact. Coppery red petals around a brown center.
'September Gold'. Compact. Bright yellow blossoms.
'Sunball' ('Kugelsonne'). Tall. Lemon yellow rays, chartreuse centers.
'Waldtraut'. Tall. Copper-tinged rays surrounding a dark center.
'Wyndley'. Compact. Butter yellow petals around a lime yellow center.

HELIANTHEMUM nummularium

SUNROSE

Cistaceae

EVERGREEN SHRUBLETS

ZONES 3–9, 14–24, 32, 34

FULL SUN

MODERATE WATER

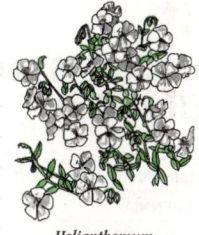
Helianthemum nummularium

Commonly sold under this name are a number of forms as well as hybrids between this species and others. They grow about 6–8 in. high and spread to 3 ft. Leaves ½–1 in. long; may be glossy green above and fuzzy gray beneath, or gray on both sides. Delightful late spring to early summer display of clustered, 1-in.-wide, single or double flowers in bright or pastel colors—flame red, apricot, orange, yellow, pink, rose, peach, salmon, or white. Each blossom lasts only a day, but new buds continue to open. Shear plants back after flowering to encourage repeat bloom.

Specialists offer many named varieties. Especially noteworthy is one sold as *H. apenninum* 'Roseum' or merely as 'Wisley Pink', with comparatively large, pure pink flowers that contrast nicely with the gray, furry foliage.

Let sunroses tumble over rocks, set in niche in dry rock wall, or grow in planters on sunny patio. Use them at seashore or in rock gardens; let them ramble over gentle slope. If used as ground cover, plant 2–3 ft. apart. In cold-winter areas, lightly cover plants with branches from evergreens in winter to keep foliage from dehydrating. Plants will be hardier if given soil that is not too rich (good drainage is essential, though) and kept on dry side; object is to encourage hard, nonsucculent growth.

HELIANTHUS

SUNFLOWER

Asteraceae (Compositae)

ANNUALS AND PERENNIALS

ZONES VARY BY SPECIES

FULL SUN

REGULAR WATER, EXCEPT AS NOTED

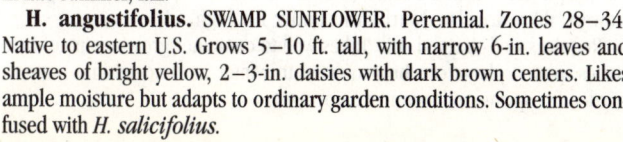
Helianthus annuus

Coarse, sturdy plants with bold flowers. Most are tough and widely adapted. Perennial kinds spread rapidly, may become invasive. Tall kinds not for tidy gardens, may need staking. All bloom in late summer, fall.

H. angustifolius. SWAMP SUNFLOWER. Perennial. Zones 28–34. Native to eastern U.S. Grows 5–10 ft. tall, with narrow 6-in. leaves and sheaves of bright yellow, 2–3-in. daisies with dark brown centers. Likes ample moisture but adapts to ordinary garden conditions. Sometimes confused with *H. salicifolius.*

H. annuus. COMMON SUNFLOWER. Annual. All zones. From this rough, hairy plant with 2–3-in.-wide flower heads have come many ornamental and useful garden varieties. Best-known form is coarse, towering (to 10 ft.) plant with small rays outside and cushiony center of disk flowers, 8–10 in. across. Usually sold as 'Mammoth Russian'. 'Sunspot' carries flowers of like size on 2-ft. plants. People eat the roasted seeds; birds like them raw and visit flower heads in fall and winter. For children, annual sunflowers are big and easy to grow and bring sense of great accomplishment. Sow seeds in spring where plants are to grow. Large-flowered kinds need rich soil.

H. atrorubens. DARK-EYED SUNFLOWER. Perennial. Zones 28–35, 37. Native to southeastern U.S. Grows 5–6 ft. tall, with coarse, bristly foliage and 2-in. yellow flower heads centered in dark purple. 'The Monarch' has semidouble flowers somewhat resembling the quilled flowers of a cactus-form dahlia.

H. maximilianii. Perennial. Zones 1–24, 27–43. Native to central and southwestern U.S. Clumps of 10-ft. stems clothed in narrow, 8–10-in. leaves and topped with narrow spires of 3-in. yellow flowers.

H. multiflorus (H. decapetalus). Perennial. Zones 1–24, 28–43. Hybrid between *H. annuus* and a perennial species. To 5 ft. high, with thin, toothed, 3–8-in.-long leaves and numerous 3-in.-wide flower heads with yellow centers. Excellent for cutting. 'Capenoch Star' has single lemon yellow flowers with a large central brown disk. 'Loddon Gold' ('Flore Pleno') is a double-flowered form with deeper yellow blooms.

H. salicifolius (H. orgyalis). Perennial. Zones 1–24, 28–43. Native to central U.S. Similar to *H. angustifolius*, but with narrower, more willowy, drooping leaves. The two species are sometimes confused in the nursery trade.

H. tuberosus. JERUSALEM ARTICHOKE. Perennial. Zones 2–24, 26–41. Also grown as a commercial crop; tubers are edible and sold in markets as sunchokes. Plants 6–10 ft. tall, with bright yellow flower heads. Oval leaves 8 in. long. Spreads readily and can become pest. Best to harvest tubers every year and save out two or three for replanting. If controlled, makes a good, quick temporary screen or hedge.

Helianthus tuberosus

SUNFLOWERS THAT MAKE THE CUT

For cut-flower bouquets, try these ten sunflower varieties, all excellent for arranging: 'Autumn Beauty', 'Big Smile', 'Color Fashion Mixed', 'Double Sun Gold', 'Inca Jewels', 'Italian White', 'Music Box', 'Sunrich Lemon', 'Sunrich Orange', and 'Valentine'.

HELICHRYSUM

Asteraceae (Compositae)

ANNUALS AND PERENNIALS

ZONES VARY BY SPECIES

FULL SUN

MODERATE WATER

Helichrysum bracteatum

Best known are the annual strawflowers used in both fresh and dried arrangements. Others, though little known, are choice plants for landscape use.

H. angustifolium. See *H. italicum*

H. bracteatum. STRAWFLOWER. Annual. All zones. Grows 2–3 ft. high with many flower heads; dwarf forms also available. Known as "everlasting" because pompomlike, 2½-in. summer flowers are papery and last indefinitely when dried. Also good in fresh arrangements. Flowers may be yellow, orange, red, pink, or white (seeds come in mixed colors). Strap-like leaves are medium green, 2–5 in. long. Plant seed in place in late spring or early summer (same time as zinnias). 'Dargan Hill Monarch' and 'Diamond Head' are shrubby perennial forms for mild-winter climates. Both have grayish green foliage and 3-in. golden yellow flower heads; the similar 'Cockatoo' has lemon yellow heads.

H. italicum (H. angustifolium). CURRY PLANT. Zones 13–24. Woody-based perennial. Spreading, branching to 2 ft. high, roughly as broad, with crowded, narrow, nearly white leaves to 1½ in. long. Leaves emit a strong fragrance of curry powder when bruised or pinched; though they are not used in curry, a few can add a pleasant aroma to a salad or meat dish. Bright yellow, ½-in. flower heads in clusters 2 in. across, midsummer to autumn.

H. petiolare. LICORICE PLANT. Perennial in Zones 16, 17, 22–24; can be grown as annual elsewhere. Woody-based plant with trailing stems to 4 ft. with white, woolly, inch-long leaves; insignificant flowers. Licorice aroma sometimes noticeable—in hot, still weather, for example, or when leaves are dry. 'Limelight' has luminous light chartreuse leaves; 'Variegatum' has foliage with white markings. All varieties are useful for their trailing branches, which will thread through mixed plantings or mix with other plants in large pots or hanging baskets.

H. subulifolium. Annual. All zones. Mound-shaped plant to 20 in. tall, with glossy green, 5-in. leaves and bright, shining, orange-yellow summer flowers 1½ in. wide. Excellent for fresh or dried cut flowers.

HELICONIA

Heliconiaceae
PERENNIALS
☀ ZONES 24, 25; OR IN GREENHOUSE
☼ LIGHT SHADE
♦ AMPLE WATER

Heliconia caribaea

Over 100 species of tropical American plants with growth habit resembling that of banana or canna. Evergreen leaves are large (sometimes very large) and plants form sizable clumps. Grown for big, showy, waxy flower clusters consisting of brightly colored bracts; small true flowers peep out from bracts. Clusters may be erect or drooping, from a few inches to several feet in length; used in spectacular tropical flower arrangements.

Need rich soil, heavy feeding, and ample water. Stems that have flowered should be cut away to make room for new growth. Beyond frost-free regions, grow plants in tubs and shelter them from winter cold. Potted plants can bloom any time; those in the ground flower in spring and summer.

H. brasiliensis (H. farinosa). FALSE BIRD OF PARADISE. Grows 3–5 ft. tall, with 2½-ft. leaves and erect clusters of red bracts enfolding white or red flowers.

H. caribaea. WILD PLANTAIN. Bananalike stems 6–15 ft. tall, with 5-ft. leaves and erect flower clusters to 1½ ft. Bracts are red or yellow, often marked with contrasting colors; flowers are white with green tips.

H. latispatha. Bananalike stem can reach 10 ft. high. Leaves to 5 ft. long; erect flower cluster up to 1½ ft. tall, with spiraling orange, red, or yellow bracts and green-tipped yellow flowers.

H. psittacorum. Highly variable species 4–8 ft. tall; leaves to 20 in. long. Bracts spread upward at 45° angle; red, sometimes shading to cream or orange, often multicolored. Flowers yellow, orange, or red, usually tipped dark green and white, in clusters to 7 in. long. Many named varieties are available.

H. schiedeana. Grows to a height of 6 ft., with leaves to 5 ft. long. Red or orange-red spiraling bracts enclose yellow-green flowers in a 1½-ft. flower cluster.

PRACTICAL GARDENING DICTIONARY
PLEASE SEE PAGES 545–616

HELICTOTRICHON sempervirens (Avena sempervirens)

BLUE OAT GRASS
Poaceae (Gramineae)
PERENNIAL
☀ ZONES 2–24, 30–41
☼ FULL SUN
♦ REGULAR WATER

Helictotrichon sempervirens

Evergreen, 2–3-ft. fountains of bright blue-gray, narrow leaves resemble giant clumps of blue fescue (*Festuca ovina* 'Glauca'), but are more graceful. Plants need full sun, good drainage. Combine with other grasses and broad-leafed plants, and with boulders in rock gardens. Pull out occasional withered leaves. Best appearance in cool end of range; becomes brown or gray in hot, humid summers.

HELIOPSIS helianthoides (H. scabra)

OX-EYE
Asteraceae (Compositae)
PERENNIAL
☀ ZONES 1–11, 14–24, 28–45
☼ FULL SUN OR LIGHT SHADE
♦ REGULAR TO MODERATE WATER

Heliopsis helianthoides

As species name implies, resembles true sunflower, *Helianthus*. Clump-forming perennial to 5 ft. tall and half as wide, with 6-in., rough-textured, medium green leaves. Bright orange-yellow flower heads are 3 in. wide or wider. Blooms from July until frost. Plants are usually offered as *H. scabra*, a subspecies of *H. helianthoides*. Some of the best varieties are: 'Ballerina', an early bloomer to 3 ft., with semidouble deep yellow flowers; 'Karat', to 3½ ft., with single bright yellow flowers; and 'Summer Sun', to 3 ft., with single blossoms in rich golden yellow. Divide clumps of all types every few years.

HELIOTROPE, GARDEN. See VALERIANA officinalis

HELIOTROPIUM arborescens (H. peruvianum)

COMMON HELIOTROPE
Boraginaceae
TENDER PERENNIAL, OFTEN TREATED AS ANNUAL
☀ ALL ZONES
☼ PARTIAL SHADE IN HOT-SUMMER CLIMATES
♦ REGULAR WATER
☠ ALL PARTS ARE POISONOUS IF INGESTED

Heliotropium arborescens

Old-fashioned plant grown for delicate, sweet fragrance of its flowers. In Zones 15–17, 23–26, shrubby perennial reaching 4 ft. tall; but in all regions, usually treated as summer bedding annual 1½–2 ft. high. Flowers are dark violet to white, arranged in tightly grouped, curved, one-sided spikes that form rounded, massive clusters. Veined leaves have darkish purple cast. 'Black Beauty' and 'Iowa' are varieties with deep purple flowers; there are also dwarf forms under 1 ft. high.

Requires well-drained soil. Takes well to container growing; in cold climates, potted plants can be protected in winter and moved into patio or garden for spring and summer enjoyment.

HELIPTERUM

EVERLASTING, SUNRAY

Asteraceae (Compositae)

ANNUALS AND PERENNIALS

🗲 ZONES VARY BY SPECIES

☼ ◑ EXPOSURE NEEDS VARY BY SPECIES

💧 REGULAR WATER

Helipterum roseum

A large Australian genus, mostly annual but with some perennials. All have daisylike flower heads with papery "petals" (ray florets) that retain their color and form when dried. Useful for winter arrangements and for garden color.

H. anthemoides. CHAMOMILE SUNRAY. Perennial. Zones 8, 9, 14–24. Forms a compact, gray-green mound 1 ft. tall, 2 ft. wide. Foliage has a chamomile scent when bruised. Blooms in late winter and early spring, with scattered bloom later; bright red buds open to white daisies ½–1 in. across. Takes full sun in mild climates; give some shade in hottest areas.

H. roseum (Acroclinium roseum). PINK AND WHITE EVERLASTING, PINK PAPER DAISY. Annual. All zones. Top-notch flower for cutting, drying. Grows 2 ft. tall, with scanty, narrow foliage and 1–2-in. pink or white daisies. Grow in full sun in warm soil, sowing seeds after frost where plants are to grow. Thin to 6–12 in. apart.

HELLEBORUS

HELLEBORE

Ranunculaceae

PERENNIALS

🗲 ZONES VARY BY SPECIES

☼ ● PARTIAL OR FULL SHADE

💧💧 REGULAR TO MODERATE WATER

⬧ ALL PARTS ARE POISONOUS IF INGESTED

Helleborus argutifolius

Distinctive, long-lived evergreen plants, blooming for several months in winter and spring. Basal clumps of substantial, long-stalked leaves, usually divided fanwise into leaflets. Flowers large, borne singly or in clusters, centered with many stamens. Good cut flowers; sear ends of stems or dip in boiling water, then place in deep, cold water.

Plant in good soil with lots of organic material added. Feed once or twice a year. Do not move often; plants reestablish slowly. Mass under high-branching trees on north or east side of walls, in beds bordered with ajuga, wild ginger, primroses, violets. Use in plantings with azaleas, fatsia, pieris, rhododendrons, skimmia, and ferns.

H. argutifolius (H. lividus corsicus, H. corsicus). CORSICAN HELLEBORE. Zones 4–24, 31, 32. Leafy stems to 3 ft. high. Pale blue-green leaves divided into three leaflets with sharply toothed edges. (Not to be confused with *H. lividus,* a rare plant with pale leaf veins and leaflets that have smooth edges or only a few fine teeth.) Clusters of large, firm-textured, light chartreuse flowers among upper leaves. In mild-winter areas, may flower late fall to late spring; in colder part of range, bloom holds off until early spring. After shedding stamens, flowers stay attractive until summer. Unlike other hellebores, this species can take some sun and is drought tolerant.

H. foetidus. Zones 3–9, 14–23, 30–34, 39. Grows to 1½ ft. high. Attractive leaves—leathery, dark green, divided into 7–11 leaflets. Blooms February–April; flowers 1 in. wide, light green with purplish margin, in large clusters at branch ends. Good with naturalized daffodils. Self-sows freely where adapted. As species name implies, plant parts emit a somewhat unpleasant odor when bruised.

H. niger. CHRISTMAS ROSE. Zones 1–7, 14–17, 32–45. Elegant plant to 1½ ft. tall, blooming at some time between December and early spring (timing depends on severity of winter). Though it's often planted in mild-winter climates, it seldom thrives there. Lustrous dark green leaves

divided into seven to nine leaflets with few, large teeth. White or greenish white, about 2-in.-wide flowers turn purplish with age. Named varieties are sometimes available. 'White Magic' has large white flowers that take on a hint of pink as they age.

H. orientalis. LENTEN ROSE. Zones 2–10, 14–24, 31–41. Much like *H. niger* in growth habit, but easier to transplant. Basal leaves with 5–11 sharply toothed leaflets. Blooming starts in late winter and continues into spring. Flowering stems branched, with leaflike bracts at branching points and beneath flowers. Blossoms are white, greenish, purplish, or rose, often spotted or splashed with deep purple. Lenten rose is often mistakenly sold under the name "Christmas rose," but it differs from true Christmas rose in flower color and in having many small teeth on leaflets. Self-sows freely.

HELXINE. See SOLEIROLIA

HEMEROCALLIS

DAYLILY

Liliaceae

PERENNIALS

🗲 ALL ZONES, EXCEPT AS NOTED

☼ ◑ FULL SUN OR LIGHT SHADE

💧 REGULAR WATER

Hemerocallis Hybrid

Tuberous, somewhat fleshy roots give rise to large clumps of arching, sword-shaped leaves—evergreen, semievergreen, or deciduous depending on type. Lilylike flowers in open or branched clusters at ends of generally leafless stems that stand well above foliage. Older yellow, orange, and rust red daylilies have mostly been replaced by newer kinds; both tall and dwarf varieties are available.

Although many species exist, only a few are offered by nurseries. Most of the daylilies available are hybrids; thanks to generations of crossing by scores of amateur and professional breeders, more than 20,000 named varieties have been registered by the American Hemerocallis Society, and hundreds more appear each year.

Use in borders with bearded iris, Michaelmas and Shasta daisies, red-hot poker, dusty miller, agapanthus. Mass on banks under high-branching, deciduous trees, along driveways and roadsides in country gardens. Group among evergreen shrubs, near pools, along streams. Plant dwarf daylilies in rock gardens, as edgings, low ground covers. Good cut flowers. Cut stems with well-developed buds; buds open on successive days, though each flower is slightly smaller than preceding one. Arrange individual blooms in low bowls. Snap off faded flowers daily.

Few plants are tougher or more trouble free than daylilies. They adapt to almost any kind of soil. Red-flowered daylilies need warmth to develop best color. Divide crowded plants in early spring or late fall.

H. altissima. Deciduous. Zones 3–10, 14–24, 26–34, 39. A lofty plant—leaves can grow to 5 ft. long, flower stems to 6 ft. high. Fragrant, 4-in. yellow flowers appear on branching stems in late summer and autumn. 'Statuesque' has 5-ft. stems, blooms in mid- to late summer.

H. fulva. TAWNY DAYLILY, COMMON ORANGE DAYLILY. Deciduous. To 6 ft. high, with leaves to 2 ft. long or longer; tawny orange-red, 3–5-in.-wide, unscented flowers in summer. Rarely sold, but commonly seen in old gardens and along roadsides; a tough, persistent plant suitable for holding banks. The double-flowered 'Kwanso' is sometimes seen. Both species and variety have been largely replaced by hybrids.

H. hybrids. Deciduous, evergreen, and semievergreen. Deciduous types go completely dormant in winter and are hardier than evergreen types; they are the plants of choice in cold-winter regions. Evergreen hybrids keep their leaves all year and are adapted to mild-winter regions. Semievergreen sorts may or may not retain leaves, depending on where they are grown.

▶

H

Modern hybrids grow 1–6 ft. tall and have flowers 3–8 in. across. Some have broad petals, others narrow, spidery ones; many have ruffled petal edges. Colors range far beyond the basic yellow, orange, and rusty red to pink, vermilion, buff, apricot, plum or lilac purple, creamy white, and near-white, often with contrasting eyes or midrib stripes that produce a bicolor effect. Many varieties are sprinkled with tiny iridescent dots known as diamond dust. Semidouble-flowered and double-flowered varieties exist.

To get what you want, buy plants in bloom (either in containers or in the field), or study specialists' catalogs, many of which have fine color photographs. To prolong the bloom season, look for reblooming (remontant) varieties; or select early, midseason, and late bloomers. Varieties listed as tetraploid (possessing twice the normal number of chromosomes) have flowers with unusually heavy-textured petals. Look for varieties that have received awards from the American Hemerocallis Society. The letters AM stand for Award of Merit, presented to ten varieties each year. HM means Honorable Mention, awarded to any plant receiving ten or more votes from the selection committee. SM stands for Stout Medal, the highest award a daylily can receive. SM winners include the long-blooming dwarf yellow 'Stella de Oro' and the free-blooming yellow tetraploid 'Mary Todd'. An old garden variety that retains its popularity amid the influx of new hybrid daylilies is 'Hyperion', a 4-ft.-tall plant with fragrant yellow flowers that bloom in midsummer.

H. lilio-asphodelus (H. flava). LEMON DAYLILY. Deciduous. Zones 1–12, 14–24, 28–43. To 3 ft. high, with 2-ft. leaves and fragrant, 4-in., pure yellow flowers in late May or June. Newer hybrids may be showier, but this species is still cherished for its delicious perfume and early blossom time.

HEMLOCK. See TSUGA

HEMP AGRIMONY. See EUPATORIUM cannabinum

HEN AND CHICKENS. See SEMPERVIVUM tectorum

HEN AND CHICKS. See ECHEVERIA

HEPATICA

LIVERLEAF

Ranunculaceae

PERENNIALS

ZONES 1–6, 28–45

PARTIAL OR FULL SHADE

REGULAR WATER

Hepatica americana

Low growers with leathery evergreen or semievergreen leaves and flowers consisting of petal-like sepals similar to those of some of the smaller anemones. (In fact, these plants were once classified as anemones.) Flowers appear early in spring, each rising on its own stalk above the clump of last year's leaves. A new crop of leaves follows bloom. Choice plants for woodland gardens or for the shaded rock garden. Little known in the U.S. except to wildflower fanciers, they are popular among plant collectors in Japan, where many varieties not yet grown here are cultivated.

H. acutiloba. Native to eastern U.S. Leathery 4-in. leaves divided into three sharp-pointed lobes. Flowers are lilac or white, ½–1 in. across, on stems 6–9 in. tall.

H. americana (H. triloba). Resembles the above, but leaves have rounded lobes and flowering stems are usually shorter, to 6 in. tall. Flowers typically light blue, but sometimes white or pink.

FOR INFORMATION ON SELECTING PLANTS

PLEASE SEE PAGES 79–160

HEPTACODIUM miconioides

SEVEN SONS FLOWER

Caprifoliaceae

DECIDUOUS SHRUB OR SMALL TREE

ZONES 3–6, 31–39, 41

FULL SUN OR LIGHT SHADE

REGULAR WATER

Heptacodium miconioides

This relative newcomer to the garden scene is a fountain-shaped shrub that eventually reaches 15–20 ft. tall, 8–10 ft. wide. It can be trained as a single- or multitrunked tree. Large, narrowly heart shaped leaves are shiny green, deeply veined. No appreciable fall color. Creamy white, fragrant flowers in large clusters at branch ends open over a long season in late summer or fall. Blooms are succeeded by even showier masses of small fruits with bright purplish red calyxes. Common name derives from number of individual flowers in each of the clusters forming part of the larger inflorescence. Even winter bark is picturesque: thin, pale tan strips peel away to reveal dark brown bark beneath.

Not fussy about soil and free of pests and diseases. A shrub of much promise; sometimes referred to as the crape myrtle of the North.

HERALD'S TRUMPET. See BEAUMONTIA grandiflora

HERB-OF-GRACE. See RUTA graveolens

HERBS. This category includes all plants that at some time in history have been considered valuable for seasoning, medicine, fragrance, or general household use. As you look through lists of plants, you can recognize certain herbs because they bear the species name *officinalis*—meaning sold in shops, edible, medicinal, recognized in the pharmacopoeia. Today's herb harvest is used almost entirely for seasoning foods.

Herbs are versatile. Some creep along the ground, making fragrant carpets. Others are shrublike. Many make attractive pot plants. However, quite a few do have a weedy look, especially next to regular ornamental plants. Many are hardy and adaptable. Although hot, dry, sunny conditions with poor but well-drained soil are usually considered best, some herbs thrive in shady, moist locations with light soil rich in humus.

Following are lists of herbs for specific landscape situations:

Kitchen garden. This can be a sunny raised bed near the kitchen door, planter box near the barbecue, or part of the vegetable garden. Plant basic cooking herbs: basil (*Ocimum basilicum*), chives, dill (*Anethum graveolens*), sweet marjoram (*Origanum majorana*), mint (*Mentha*), oregano (*Origanum vulgare*), parsley, rosemary (*Rosmarinus*), sage (*Salvia officinalis*), savory (*Satureja*), tarragon (*Artemisia dracunculus*), thyme (*Thymus*). The connoisseur may wish to plant angelica, anise (*Pimpinella anisum*), caraway (*Carum carvi*), chervil (*Anthriscus cerefolium*), coriander (*Coriandrum sativum*), common fennel (*Foeniculum vulgare*).

Ground cover for sun. Prostrate rosemary, mother-of-thyme (*Thymus praecox arcticus*), lemon thyme (*T. citriodorus*), or woolly thyme (*T. pseudolanuginosus*).

Ground cover for sun or partial shade. Chamomile (*Chamaemelum nobile*).

Ground cover for shade. Sweet woodruff (*Galium odoratum*).

Perennial or shrub border. Common wormwood (*Artemisia absinthium*), salad burnet (*Sanguisorba minor*), lavender (*Lavandula*), monarda, rosemary, scented geraniums (*Pelargonium*).

Hedges. Formal clipped hedge—santolina, germander (*Teucrium*). Informal hedge—lavender, winter savory (*Satureja montana*).

Herbs for moist areas. Angelica, mint, parsley, sweet woodruff.

Herbs for partial shade. Chervil, costmary (*Chrysanthemum balsamita*), lemon balm (*Melissa officinalis*), parsley, sweet woodruff.

Herbs for containers. Crete dittany (*Origanum dictamnus*), chives, costmary, lemon verbena (*Aloysia triphylla*), sage, pineapple sage (*Salvia elegans*), summer savory (*Satureja hortensis*), sweet marjoram, mint, small burnet.

Potpourris and sachets. Lavender, lemon balm, sweet woodruff, lemon verbena, monarda.

To dry leafy herbs for cooking, cut them early in day before sun gets too hot, but after dew has dried on foliage. (Oil content is highest then.) Leafy herbs are ready to cut from time flower buds begin to form until flowers are half open. (Exceptions: parsley can be cut any time; sage and tarragon may take on strong taste unless cut early in summer.) Don't cut perennial herbs back more than a third; annual herbs may be sheared back to about 4 in. from the ground. Generally you can cut two or three crops for drying during summer. Don't cut perennial herbs after September or new growth won't have chance to mature before cold weather.

Before drying, sort weeds and grass from herbs; remove dead or damaged leaves. Wash off loose dirt in cool water; shake or blot off excess moisture. Tie woody-stemmed herbs such as sweet marjoram or thyme in small bundles and hang upside down from line hung across room. Room should be dark (to preserve color), have good air circulation and warm temperature (about 70°F/21°C) for rapid drying to retain aromatic oils. If room is fairly bright, surround herb bundles with loose cylinders of paper.

For large-leafed herbs such as basil, or short tips that don't bundle easily, dry in tray with light wooden sides and window screen tacked to the bottom. On top of screen place double thickness of cheesecloth. Spread leaves out over surface. Stir leaves daily.

With good air circulation and low humidity, leafy herbs should be crumbly dry in a few days to a week. (If humidity is too high, try drying herbs in a paper bag in the refrigerator.) When herbs are dry, strip leaves from stems and store whole in airtight containers—glass is best—until ready to use. Label each container with name of herb and date dried. Check jars first few days after filling to make sure moisture has not formed inside. If it has, pour out contents and dry for a few more days.

To gather seeds, collect seed clusters such as dill, anise, fennel, caraway when they turn brown. Seeds should begin to fall out when clusters are gently tapped. Leave a little of stem attached when you cut each cluster. Collect in box. Flail seeds from clusters and spread them out in sun to dry for several days. Then separate chaff from seed and continue to dry in sun for another 1½–2 weeks. Store seed herbs same way as leafy ones.

HERCULES' CLUB. See ARALIA spinosa

HERNIARIA glabra

GREEN CARPET, RUPTURE WORT	
Caryophyllaceae	
PERENNIAL, SOMETIMES TREATED AS ANNUAL	
ALL ZONES	
SUN OR SHADE	
REGULAR WATER	

Herniaria glabra

Trailing plant under 2–3 in. tall with crowded, tiny, bright green leaves less than ¼ in. long. Bloom negligible. Where temperatures remain above −20°F/−29°C, grown as an evergreen perennial; foliage turns bronzy red in winter. In colder Zones 42–45, treated as an annual. Spreads well by rooting stems, but won't grow out of control. Use it between stepping-stones, on mounds, around rocks, or in parking strips. Endures occasional footsteps, but not constant traffic. Provide well-drained soil.

HESPERALOE parviflora

Agavaceae	
PERENNIAL	
ZONES 10–16, 18–21, 27–31, 33, 35	
FULL SUN	
MODERATE TO LITTLE WATER	

Hesperaloe parviflora

Native to Texas, northern Mexico. Makes dense, yuccalike clump of very narrow, swordlike, evergreen leaves 4 ft. long, about 1 in. wide. Pink to rose red, 1¼-in.-long, nodding flowers in slim, 3–4-ft.-high clusters bloom in early summer, with repeat bloom frequent in milder climates. On older plants, spikes can reach 8–9 ft. Good large container plant with loose, relaxed look. *H. p. engelmannii* is similar to species, but its 1-in.-long flowers are more bell shaped.

HESPERIS matronalis

DAME'S ROCKET	
Brassicaceae (Cruciferae)	
PERENNIAL OR BIENNIAL	
ALL ZONES	
FULL SUN OR LIGHT SHADE	
REGULAR WATER	

Hesperis matronalis

An old-fashioned, cottage-garden plant, freely branched, to 3 ft. tall and as broad, with 4-in., toothed leaves and rounded clusters of ½-in., four-petaled, lavender to purple flowers. Flowers resemble those of stock and are fragrant at night. Grows readily from seed and often self-sows. Old, woody plants should be replaced by young seedlings. White and double-flowered forms exist but are rare.

HETEROMELES arbutifolia (Photinia arbutifolia)

TOYON, CHRISTMAS BERRY, CALIFORNIA HOLLY	
Rosaceae	
EVERGREEN SHRUB OR SMALL TREE	
ZONES 5–24	
FULL SUN OR PARTIAL SHADE	
MODERATE WATER	

Heteromeles arbutifolia

Native to California. Dense shrub 6–10 ft. tall or multitrunked small tree 15–25 ft. tall; can be pruned to form small single-trunked tree. Thick, leathery, glossy dark green leaves 2–4 in. long, with bristly, pointed teeth. Small white flowers in flattish clusters, early summer. Bright red (rarely yellow) berries in clusters, fall into winter; birds relish them. Bees also attracted to plant. Though tolerates aridity, looks better with moderate water. *H. a. macrocarpa* has larger berries.

HEUCHERA

CORAL BELLS, ALUM ROOT	
Saxifragaceae	
PERENNIALS	
ZONES VARY BY SPECIES	
LIGHT SHADE IN HOTTEST AREAS	
REGULAR WATER	

Heuchera sanguinea

Compact, evergreen clumps of roundish leaves with scalloped edges. Slender, wiry stems 1–2½ ft. high bear open clusters of nodding, bell-shaped flowers ¼ in. or more across, in carmine, reddish pink, coral, crimson, red, rose, greenish, and white. Various types bloom between April and August. Flowers dainty, long lasting in cut arrangements, attractive to hummingbirds. Many recent introductions are grown more for leaf color than floral display.

Use in rock gardens or as ground cover; mass in borders or in front of shrubs; use as edging for beds of delphinium, iris, lilies, peonies, roses. Grow in well-drained, humus-rich soil. Divide clumps every 3 or 4 years in spring (division can be done in fall in mild-winter climates). Use young, vigorous, rooted divisions; discard older, woody rootstocks. Sow seed in spring.

H. americana. Zones 1–6, 15–17, 32–43. Foliage mound 1–2 ft. high. Leaves 1½–4½ in. wide, green mottled white. Flower stalks to 3 ft. high bear tiny greenish white blossoms. Varieties grown for handsome foliage include 'Garnet', deep red winter foliage, brighter red new foliage in spring; 'Lace Ruffles', ruffled and scalloped leaves mottled silvery white; 'Pewter Moon', purple leaves with strong central silvery zone; 'Pewter Veil', shining silvery leaves, small purple flowers; 'Ring of Fire', silvery, purple-veined leaves that develop a red rim in fall; 'Ruby Veil', 8-in. silvery leaves with veins that are red at leaf bases; and 'Velvet Night', deep bluish purple leaves.

H. brizoides. Zones 1–10, 14–24, 31–45. A group of hybrids between *H. sanguinea* and other species. As seed-grown plants, often called Bressingham Hybrids. Flowers come in white and shades of pink and red. 'June Bride' is a good white selection. 'Snowstorm' has deep reddish pink flowers above white-variegated leaves.

H. micrantha. Zones 2–11, 14–24, 31–43. Native to western U. S. Plant in protected spots in coldest part of range. Grows 1–2 ft. high. Long-stalked, roundish leaves are 1–3 in. long, hairy on both sides, toothed and lobed. Flowers are whitish or greenish, about ⅛ in. long, carried in loose clusters on leafy, 2–3-ft.-tall stems. Hybrid forms developed from *H. micrantha* are more widely adapted than the species itself. 'Palace Purple' has maplelike, rich brownish or purplish red leaves that retain their color all year; 'Ruffles' has leaves that are deeply lobed and ruffled around the edges.

H. sanguinea. CORAL BELLS. Zones 1–11, 14–24, 31–45. Native to Mexico and Arizona. Makes neat foliage tufts of round, 1–2-in. leaves with scalloped edges. Slender, wiry stems 1–2 ft. tall bear open clusters of nodding, bell-shaped bright red or coral pink flowers. Varieties with white, pink, or crimson flowers are available. 'Cherry Splash' and 'Frosty' display red flowers above variegated foliage.

HEUCHERELLA tiarelloides

Saxifragaceae

PERENNIAL

ZONES 1–9, 14–24, 31–45

LIGHT SHADE

REGULAR WATER

*Heucherella
tiarelloides
'Bridget Bloom'*

Hybrid between *Heuchera brizoides* and foam flower (*Tiarella cordifolia*). Combines the flowering habit of the *Heuchera* parent with the heart-shaped leaves of foam flower in a low, clumping, evergreen perennial. Foot-high stems bear narrow sprays of many tiny pinkish bells in late spring or early summer, with a possible second bloom in autumn. Good varieties include 'Bridget Bloom', which produces its shell pink flowers over a long period. 'Pink Frost', another long bloomer, has pink flowers and roundish, mottled gray-green leaves. All forms make a good ground cover for woodland or shaded rock garden. Provide humus-rich soil and good drainage.

FOR INFORMATION ON YOUR CLIMATE ZONE
PLEASE SEE PAGES 16–78

HIBBERTIA

Dilleniaceae

EVERGREEN SHRUBS AND VINES

ZONES VARY BY SPECIES

FULL SUN OR PARTIAL SHADE

REGULAR WATER

Hibbertia cuneiformis

Most are native to Australia, including these. All types have bright yellow flowers like wild roses. Low-growing species for rock garden are worth seeking, among them *H. vestita*, 6 in. high, 2–3 ft. wide, with tiny dark green leaves and comparatively large (1½-in.) blossoms. The following plants are more widely grown.

H. cuneiformis (Candollea cuneiformis). Shrub. Zones 13, 15–24. To 4 ft. tall and somewhat broader. Small polished green leaves are tapered at base and toothed at tip. Flowers carried all along new growth in spring. Prune after flowering to control outline. Requires exceptionally fast drainage. Tolerates wind.

H. scandens (H. volubilis). GUINEA GOLD VINE. Zones 16, 17, 21–24. Fast growing, shrubby, climbing by twining stems to 8–10 ft. In ideal climate, waxy dark green leaves are handsome all year. Flowers from spring into early fall. Can be grown as ground cover. Recovers quickly from light frosts.

HIBISCUS

Malvaceae

SHRUBS, PERENNIALS, AND ANNUALS

ZONES VARY BY SPECIES

FULL SUN

REGULAR WATER

Hibiscus rosa-sinensis

Seven species are commonly grown: one annual, one somewhat shrublike perennial, two deciduous shrubs, and three evergreen shrubs. Most of these are cultivated for big showy flowers, though one is raised for colorful foliage and another for food.

H. acetosella. RED-LEAF HIBISCUS. Sometimes grown from seed as an annual, but more often seen as a 5-ft.-tall evergreen shrubby perennial in Zones 25–27. The foliage, unlobed or lobed somewhat like a maple leaf, may be green or deep purplish red; only the red form is commonly grown, often as a coarse hedge. Cultivated for its foliage rather than the less conspicuous dark-centered red or yellow flowers. The plant may be better known as *H. eetveldeanus*.

H. eetveldeanus. See H. acetosella

H. huegelii. See Alyogyne huegelii

H. moscheutos. PERENNIAL HIBISCUS, ROSE-MALLOW. Perennial. Zones 2–21, 26–41. Largest flowers of all hibiscus, some reaching 1 ft. across, on a plant 6–8 ft. tall; bloom starts in late June and continues until frost. Oval, toothed leaves deep green above, whitish beneath. Plants die down in winter, even in mild climates. Feed at 6- to 8-week intervals during growing season. Protect from wind.

Seed-grown strains often flower the first year if sown indoors and planted out early. Southern Belle strain grows 4 ft. tall; Disco Belle, Frisbee, and Rio Carnival strains are 2–2½ ft. tall. Flowers, 8–12 in. wide, come in red, pink, rose, or white, often with a red eye. The many cutting-grown varieties include 'Blue River', 10-in. pure white flowers; and 'George Riegel', 10-in. ruffled pink blossoms with a red eye. Both of these varieties grow about 4 ft. high. Hybrid 'Lord Baltimore', to 6 ft. tall, produces 10-in. deep red flowers over an exceptionally long bloom period.

H. mutabilis. CONFEDERATE ROSE. Deciduous shrub. Zones 4–24, 26–31, warmer parts of 32. Shrubby or treelike in warmest climates, it behaves more like perennial in colder part of range, growing flowering branches from woody base or short trunk. Leaves broad, oval, with three to five lobes. Summer flowers 4–6 in. wide, opening white or pink and changing to deep red by evening. 'Rubrus' has red flowers. Double-flowered forms also exist. Whiteflies are a common pest.

H. rosa-sinensis. CHINESE HIBISCUS, TROPICAL HIBISCUS. Evergreen shrub. Zones 9, 12, 13, 15, 16, 19–26; provide overhead protection where winter lows frequently drop below 30°F/–1°C. Where temperatures go much lower, grow in containers and shelter indoors over winter; or grow as annuals, setting out fresh plants each spring. Also makes a good house plant that can be brought outdoors during the warm season.

One of showiest flowering shrubs. Reaches 30 ft. tall in tropics, but seldom over 15 ft. tall in the U.S., even in mildest climates. Glossy foliage varies somewhat in size and texture depending on variety. Growth habit may be dense and dwarfish or loose and open. Summer flowers single or double, 4–8 in. wide. Colors range from white through pink to red, from yellow and apricot to orange. Individual flowers last only a day, but the plant blooms continuously.

Requires excellent drainage; if necessary, improve soil or set plants in raised beds or containers. Fertilize monthly (potted plants twice monthly) April to early September, then let growth harden. To develop good branch structure, prune poorly shaped young plants when you set them out in spring. To keep a mature plant growing vigorously, prune out about a third of old wood in early spring. Pinching out tips of stems in spring and summer increases flower production. These are some of the many varieties available:

'Agnes Galt'. Big single pink flowers. Vigorous, hardy plant to 15 ft. Prune to prevent legginess.

'All Aglow'. Tall (10–15-ft.) plant has large single flowers with broad, gold-blotched orange petals, pink halo around a white throat.

'American Beauty'. Broad, deep rose flowers. Slow growth to 8 ft. tall. Irregular form.

'Bridal Veil'. Large pure white single flowers last 3 or 4 days. Plant 10–15 ft. tall.

'Bride'. Very large, palest blush to white flowers. Slow to moderate growth to open-branched 4 ft.

'Brilliant' ('San Diego Red'). Bright red single flowers in profusion. Tall, vigorous, compact, to 15 ft. Hardy.

'Butterfly'. Small, single bright yellow flowers. Slow, upright growth to 7 ft.

'California Gold'. Heavy yield of yellow, red-centered, single flowers. Slow or moderate growth to a compact 7 ft.

'Crown of Bohemia'. Double gold flowers; petals shade to carmine orange toward base. Moderate or fast growth to 5 ft. Bushy, upright. Hardy.

'Diamond Head'. Large double flowers in deepest red (nearly black red). Compact growth to 5 ft.

'Ecstasy'. Large (5–6-in.) single bright red flowers with striking white variegation. Upright growth to 4 ft.

'Fiesta'. Single bright orange flowers 6–7 in. wide; white eye zone at flower center edged red. Petal edges ruffled. Strong, erect growth to 6–7 ft.

'Fullmoon'. Double pure yellow flowers. Moderately vigorous growth to a compact 6 ft.

'Golden Dust'. Bright orange single flowers with yellow-orange centers. Compact, thick-foliaged plant 4 ft. tall.

'Hula Girl'. Large single canary yellow flowers have deep red eye. Compact growth to 6 ft. Flowers stay open several days.

'Itsy Bitsy Peach', 'Itsy Bitsy Pink', and 'Itsy Bitsy Red' are all tall (10–15-ft.) plants with small leaves and small (2–3-in.) single flowers.

'Jason Okumoto'. Semidouble scarlet-throated orange flowers surrounded by collar of large pink petals (blooms have a cup-and-saucer look). Grows 10–15 ft. tall.

'Kate Sessions'. Large red single flowers with broad petals; petal undersides tinged gold. Moderate growth to 10 ft. tall. Upright, open habit.

'Kona'. Ruffled double pink flowers. Vigorous, upright, bushy, to 15–20 ft. Prune regularly. 'Kona Improved' has fuller flowers of richer pink color.

'Kona Princess'. Small double pink flowers on a 6–7-ft. shrub.

'Morning Glory'. Single blush pink flowers changing to warmer pink with white petal tips. Grows 8–10 ft. tall.

'President'. Flowers single, 6–7 in. wide, intense red shading to deep pink in throat. Upright, compact, 6–7 ft. tall.

'Red Dragon' ('Celia'). Flowers small to medium, double, dark red. Upright, compact, 6–8 ft. tall.

'Ross Estey'. Flowers very large, single, with broad, overlapping petals of pink shading coral orange toward tips. Heavy-textured flowers last 2 or 3 days on bush. Vigorous grower to 8 ft. Leaves unusually large, ruffled, polished dark green.

'Vulcan'. Large single red flowers with yellow on back of petals open from yellow buds. Flowers often last more than a day. Compact grower, 4–6 ft. tall.

'White Wings'. Profuse, narrow-petaled, single white flowers with small red eye. Vigorous, open, upright to 20 ft.; prune to control legginess. A compact form with smaller flowers is available.

H. sabdariffa. ROSELLE, JAMAICA SORREL, JAMAICA FLOWER. Annual. All zones. Tall (4–5-ft.), narrowish plant. Leaves oval, with three to five lobes. Grown for fleshy red base of yellow flowers. These are used in making sauce, jelly, cool drinks, and teas; dried, they are known as Jamaica flowers. Flavor is reminiscent of cranberry or red currant. Plants need long, hot summer to ripen flowers. Bloom begins as days shorten; early frosts prevent harvests. Grow like tomatoes; space plants 1½–2 ft. apart in rows. Can be used as narrow temporary hedge.

H. schizopetalus. JAPANESE LANTERN HIBISCUS. Evergreen shrub. Zones 23–26. To 9 ft. tall, with drooping branches and 2½-in.-wide, deeply fringed, scarlet or pink flowers dangling from long stalks. Petals are strongly swept back and stamens are thrust out in shooting-star effect. Usually kept small and grown as a hanging basket plant. House or greenhouse subject in all but the mildest climates.

H. syriacus. ROSE OF SHARON, SHRUB ALTHAEA. Deciduous shrub. Zones 2–21, 26 (northern part), 28–41. To 10–12 ft. tall, upright and compact when young, spreading and open with age. Easily trained to single trunk with treelike top or as an espalier. Leaves medium size, often with three coarsely toothed lobes. Foliage emerges later in spring than does that of most other deciduous shrubs; drops in fall without coloring. Resembles a bush covered with hollyhock flowers from mid- or late summer until frost. Blossoms are single, semidouble, or double, 2½–3 in. across; some have a conspicuously contrasting red to purple throat. Single flowers are slightly more effective, opening somewhat wider, but tend to produce many unattractive capsule-type fruits—which tend to produce many unwanted seedlings.

Easy to grow. Prefers heat, tolerates some drought. Prune to shape; for bigger flowers, cut back previous season's growth in winter, cutting down to two buds. Where winter temperatures drop to –10°F/–23°C or lower, protect young plants with a winter mulch for first few years. The best varieties, some of them hard to find, include:

'Albus'. Single pure white 4-in. flowers.

'Anemoniflora' ('Paeoniflora'). Semidouble red blossoms with deeper crimson eye.

'Ardens'. Double purple flowers.

'Blue Bird'. Single blue blooms with deep red eye.

'Blushing Bride'. Double bright pink blossoms.

'Boule de Feu'. Double deep violet pink flowers.

'Coelestis'. Single violet blue flowers with reddish purple throat.

'Collie Mullens'. Double purplish lavender blossoms.

'Lucy'. Double deep rose flowers with red eye.

'Purpurea'. Semidouble purple blooms with red eye.

'Red Heart'. Single white blossoms with red eye.

'Woodbridge'. Single deep rose flowers with red eye.

Newer selections are sterile triploids, which have a long blooming season and set few or no seedpods. They include:

'Aphrodite'. Rose pink flowers with deep red eye.

'Diana'. Pure white blooms.

'Helene'. White flowers with deep red eye.

'Minerva'. Ruffled lavender pink blossoms with reddish purple eye.

HICKORY. See CARYA

HIMALAYAN HONEYSUCKLE, HIMALAYAN PHEASANTBERRY. See LEYCESTERIA formosa

HIMALAYAN POPPY. See MECONOPSIS betonicifolia

HINDU-ROPE PLANT. See HOYA carnosa

HIPPEASTRUM

AMARYLLIS

Amaryllidaceae

BULBS

✿ ZONES 16, 17, 19, 21–28; OR INDOORS

☀ ◑ LIGHT SHADE IN HOTTEST AREAS

💧 REGULAR WATER DURING GROWTH AND BLOOM

Hippeastrum Hybrid

Native to tropics and subtropics. Many species are useful in hybridizing, but only hybrids are generally available; these are usually sold as giant amaryllis or Royal Dutch amaryllis (though many are grown in South Africa or elsewhere). Named varieties or color selections in reds, pinks, white, salmon, near-orange, some variously marked and striped. Two to several flowers, often 8–9 in. across, form on stout, 2-ft. stems. Where plants are grown outdoors, flowers bloom in spring; indoors, they bloom just a few weeks after planting. Broad, strap-shaped leaves usually appear after bloom, grow through summer and disappear in fall if plants are dried off; otherwise, foliage is evergreen.

Newer forms include double-flowered varieties in white (some with red picotee edges), creamy yellow, or pink; miniatures, with 3–5-in. flowers topping 12–15-in. stems; and an unusual evergreen species, *H. papilio*, with 5-in. greenish white flowers heavily patterned with dark red.

All types are usually grown in pots. Plant November–February in rich, sandy mix with added bonemeal or superphosphate. Allow 2-in. space between bulb and edge of pot. Set upper half of bulb above soil surface. Firm soil and water it well; then keep barely moist until growth begins. Water regularly during growth and bloom. When flowers fade, cut off stem, keep up watering; feed to encourage leaf growth. When leaves yellow, withhold water, let plants dry out. Repot in late fall or early winter.

> ### ACHIEVE EARLY INDOOR BLOOM WITH AMARYLLIS
> A potted amaryllis bulb can be brought to bloom indoors in just a few weeks. Keep it in a warm, dark place until the roots have formed. Then move it to a warm, lightly shaded place where the air is not too dry. Increase watering as leaves form. Feed lightly every 2 weeks throughout the flowering period.

HIPPOCREPIS comosa

Fabaceae (Leguminosae)

PERENNIAL GROUND COVER

✿ ZONES 8–26

☀ FULL SUN

💧 REGULAR TO MODERATE WATER

Hippocrepis comosa

Forms evergreen mat 3 in. high; spreads to 3 ft. Leaves divided into 7–15 medium green, oval, ¼–½-in.-long leaflets. Flowers golden yellow, sweet pea shaped, ½ in. long, in loose clusters of 5–12. Blooms in spring; some repeat bloom in summer. Takes poor soils, but lusher looking with good soil. Roots bind soil on steep banks. Use for bank cover, in rock garden, as small-scale lawn substitute (mow once just after flowers fade). Set 1 ft. apart. Takes light foot traffic.

HIPPOPHAE rhamnoides

SEA BUCKTHORN

Elaeagnaceae

DECIDUOUS SHRUB OR SMALL TREE

✿ ZONES 1–5, 34, 37–45

☀ FULL SUN

💧 💧 REGULAR TO MODERATE WATER

Hippophae rhamnoides

Sea buckthorn is usually seen as an open, mounding shrub 8–10 ft. tall, although it can grow much taller. Spreads by suckering from roots. Branches are thorny. Leaves are narrow (¼ in. or less), to 3 in. long, silvery green to grayish green. Flowers are inconspicuous, but fruit on female plants is showy—bright orange, round or oval, to ⅓ in. long. Fruit lasts well through winter, apparently being too sour to appeal to birds. It can, however, be made into sauces or jam; it is high in vitamin C. To get fruit, you must have both male and female plants.

Sea buckthorn tolerates low temperatures, wind, poor soils (if they are reasonably well drained), and salt spray. A good screening plant for difficult situations.

HOGAN CEDAR. See THUJA plicata 'Fastigiata'

HOLLY. See ILEX

HOLLY FERN. See CYRTOMIUM falcatum

HOLLYHOCK. See ALCEA rosea

HOLLYHOCK, MINIATURE. See SIDALCEA

HOMERIA collina (H. breyniana)

Iridaceae

CORM

✿ ZONES 4–29; OR DIG AND STORE

☀ ◑ PARTIAL SHADE IN HOTTEST AREAS

💧 REGULAR WATER DURING GROWTH AND BLOOM

Homeria collina

Native to South Africa. First comes a single floppy, grasslike leaf. It is followed by 1½-ft., branching or unbranched stems bearing 2½–3-in.-wide flowers in golden yellow or muted orange. Plant becomes dormant after bloom. Needs good drainage, especially if corms will receive moisture during dormancy. In mild-winter regions, plant in winter for early spring bloom; in these climates, corms can stay in ground and be allowed to multiply freely. In colder climates, plant in spring for summer flowers; lift corms in late summer or early fall, store over winter. Can also be grown in pots.

HONEY LOCUST. See GLEDITSIA triacanthos

HONEYSUCKLE. See LONICERA

HONG KONG ORCHID TREE. See BAUHINIA blakeana

HOP. See HUMULUS

HOP BUSH, HOPSEED BUSH. See DODONAEA viscosa

HOP HORNBEAM. See OSTRYA

HOP TREE. See PTELEA trifoliata

HOREHOUND. See MARRUBIUM vulgare

HORNBEAM. See CARPINUS

HORSE BEAN. See BEAN, BROAD

HORSECHESTNUT. See AESCULUS

HORSERADISH

Brassicaceae (Cruciferae)

PERENNIAL

ZONES 2–24, 28–41

FULL SUN

REGULAR WATER

Horseradish

A large, coarse, weedy-looking plant grown for its large, white roots, which are peeled, grated, and mixed with vinegar or cream to make a condiment. Does best in rich, moist soils in cool regions. Grow it in some sunny out-of-the-way corner. Start with roots planted 1 ft. apart in late winter or early spring.

FRESH HORSERADISH

Through fall, winter, and spring, harvest pieces of horseradish roots from the outside of the root clump as you need them—that way you'll have your horseradish fresh and hot. Scrub and peel the roots, cutting away any dark parts; then grate them. Mix with vinegar, sweet cream, or sour cream—or simply sprinkle directly onto food.

HORSETAIL. See EQUISETUM hyemale

HORSETAIL TREE. See CASUARINA equisetifolia

HOSTA (Funkia)

PLANTAIN LILY

Liliaceae

PERENNIALS

ZONES 1–10, 12–21, 28, 31–45

PARTIAL OR FULL SHADE

REGULAR WATER

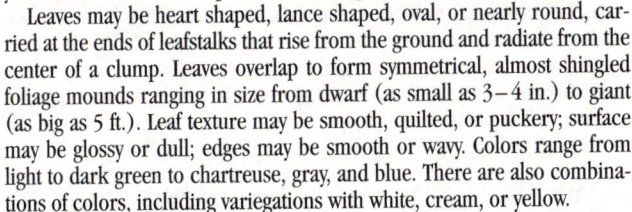

Hosta decorata

Their real glory is in their foliage. The thin spikes of blue or white, trumpet-shaped flowers that appear for several weeks in summer are a dividend. There is tremendous variety in leaf size, shape, and color among the available species and named varieties; to appreciate the selection fully, you'll need to consult a specialist's catalog or visit a well-stocked nursery.

Leaves may be heart shaped, lance shaped, oval, or nearly round, carried at the ends of leafstalks that rise from the ground and radiate from the center of a clump. Leaves overlap to form symmetrical, almost shingled foliage mounds ranging in size from dwarf (as small as 3–4 in.) to giant (as big as 5 ft.). Leaf texture may be smooth, quilted, or puckery; surface may be glossy or dull; edges may be smooth or wavy. Colors range from light to dark green to chartreuse, gray, and blue. There are also combinations of colors, including variegations with white, cream, or yellow.

New varieties enter the scene in ever-increasing numbers. In few plants have the species undergone so many name changes; to be sure you are getting the one you want, buy the plant in full leaf or deal with an expert. The plants listed below are just a few of the many possibilities.

Generally, hostas are shade lovers, though some will tolerate sun. Most will grow in considerable sun in cool-summer regions. All forms go dormant (collapse almost to nothing) in winter, even in mild climates. All are splendid companions for ferns and plants with fernlike foliage, such as bleeding heart. Good in containers. In ground, plants last for years; clumps expand in size and shade out weed growth. Feeding once a year will bring on extra leafy splendor. Blanket of peat moss around plants will prevent mud from splattering leaves. Where slugs or snails are a problem, provide protection or try reportedly resistant selections (those with heavily textured or waxy leaves are the best bets).

H. crispula. CURLED-LEAF HOSTA. Ovate, 7-in.-long, dark green leaves with wavy, uneven margins and drooping, curly leaf tips. Foliage mound to 1½ ft. high. Many lavender flowers early in the season. Plant is sometimes confused with *H. fortunei* 'Albo-marginata', which blooms later.

H. decorata (H. 'Thomas Hogg'). Foot-high mound of oval leaves, 6 in. long, bluntly pointed at tips, dull green with silvery white margins. Dark violet flowers early.

H. fortunei. May be an ancient hybrid affiliated with *H. sieboldiana*. Variable plant known mainly for its many selections offering a wide range of foliage color. Typically, plants are 1–1½ ft. high, with oval leaves to 1 ft. long and lilac flowers. Young leaves of 'Albo-picta' are yellow with uneven green border; the yellow fades by summer. Leaves of 'Albo-marginata' have an irregular yellow border that fades to white; late bloom. 'Hyacinthina' has large gray-green leaves edged with a fine white line.

H. hybrids. The following list includes some of the best, most widely grown hostas.

'Antioch'. Broad green leaves with wide, creamy white margins. Lavender flowers well above 1½-ft. foliage mound.

'August Moon'. Spade-shaped, lightly crinkled, bright chartreuse leaves in 1½-ft. mound. White flowers.

'Blue Angel'. Heavily veined blue-green leaves 16 in. long, nearly as wide, in an enormous 4-ft. mound. White flowers over long bloom period. Sun tolerant.

'Blue Wedgwood'. Slightly wavy-edged, strongly veined, heart-shaped leaves in 1½-ft. mound. Pale lavender flowers early.

'Chartreuse Wiggles'. Dwarf (6-in. high), with lance-shaped, wavy-edged, chartreuse-gold leaves. Lavender flowers late.

'Francee'. Broadly heart-shaped leaves to 6 in. long with striking white edges form a 1½–2-ft. mound. Lavender flowers late. Sun tolerant.

'Frances Williams' ('Gold Edge', 'Gold Circle'). Mound to 2½–3 ft. high, made up of round, puckered, blue-green leaves boldly and irregularly edged in yellow. Pale lavender flowers early.

'Ginko Craig'. Elongated, frosty green leaves with silver margins in a 1–1½-ft. mound. Abundant lavender flowers.

'Gold Edger'. Heart-shaped, 3-in., chartreuse-gold leaves. Foliage mound to 10 in. high. Masses of lavender flowers. Among the most sun tolerant; in fact, needs some sun for best color.

'Gold Standard'. Heart-shaped, bright golden leaves with a green margin form a 2-ft. mound. Pale lavender flowers. Sun tolerant.

'Hadspen Blue'. Low (1 ft.), with slightly wavy, broadly oval blue leaves. Slug-resistant foliage. Many lavender flowers.

'Halcyon'. Heart-shaped, heavy-textured, blue-gray leaves in a 1½-ft. mound. Short spikes of rich lilac blue flowers.

'Honeybells'. Wavy-edged, yellow-green leaves in 2–2½-ft. mound. Lightly scented, pale lilac flowers.

'Krossa Regal'. Big, leathery, frosty blue leaves arch upward and outward to make a 3-ft., vase-shaped plant. Slug-resistant foliage. Late bloom of lavender flower spikes can reach 5–6 ft.

'Piedmont Gold'. Broadly heart-shaped, heavily veined, slightly wavy-edged, 7-in. leaves of glowing chartreuse gold in a 2–2½-ft. mound. White flowers. Sun tolerant.

'Royal Standard'. Glossy light green leaves, elongated and undulated, in a 2-ft. mound. Fragrant white flowers. Sun tolerant.

'Shade Fanfare'. Leaves are pointed ovals to 7 in. long, green to gold with creamy white margin. Foliage mound to 1½ ft. high. Lavender flowers. Very sun tolerant.

'Sum and Substance'. Textured, shiny yellow leaves to 20 in. long form a mound to 3 ft. high, 5 ft. wide. Slug-resistant foliage. Lavender flowers. Very sun tolerant.

H. lancifolia (H. japonica). NARROW-LEAFED PLANTAIN LILY. Leaves glossy deep green, 6 in. long, and lance shaped, the bases tapering into the long stalks. Foot-high foliage mound. Pale lavender flowers late.

H. nakaiana 'Golden Tiara'. Foot-high mound of broadly heart-shaped leaves to 4 in. long, light green with gold edge. Purple flowers. Sun tolerant.

H. plantaginea (H. grandiflora, H. subcordata). FRAGRANT PLANTAIN LILY. Leaves glossy bright green, to 10 in. long, broadly oval with

H

parallel veins and quilted surface. Foliage mound 2 ft. high. Noticeably fragrant, large white flowers late. 'Aphrodite' is a double-flowered variety.

H. sieboldiana (H. glauca). Blue-green, broadly heart shaped leaves, 10–15 in. long, heavily veined and puckered. Many slender, pale lilac flower spikes nestle close to 2½-ft. foliage mound early in season. Foliage dies back early. 'Elegans' has the standard foliage, but leaves are covered in a blue-gray bloom; slug resistant.

H. sieboldii 'Kabitan'. Wavy, lance-shaped leaves to 5 in. long, chartreuse to yellow with thin green margins. White flowers rise above foot-high foliage mound.

H. tardiflora. Small plant (to 1 ft. high), with lance-shaped leaves to 6 in. long. Spikes of pale purple flowers, same height as foliage clump, come very late. More sun tolerant than most.

H. tokudama. Like *H. sieboldiana*, but smaller (to 1 ft.), with a more crepelike texture. Slug-resistant foliage. White flowers. 'Flavo-circinalis', with irregular yellow margins, is more sun tolerant than the species.

H. undulata (H. media picta, H. variegata). WAVY-LEAFED PLANTAIN LILY. Wavy-edged, narrowly oval leaves, 6–8-in. long, in a 1½-ft. mound. Typical leaf has a creamy white center stripe, the balance of the leaf being green. Foliage is used in arrangements. Pale lavender flowers. 'Albo-marginata' has creamy white margins on leaves. 'Erromena' is an all-green variety.

H. ventricosa (H. caerulea). BLUE PLANTAIN LILY. So named for violet blue blossoms, not for foliage color. Leaves are glossy deep green, broadly heart shaped, prominently veined, to 8 in. long, in a 2-ft. mound. Leaves of 'Aureo-maculata' are yellowish green with a green border. In 'Aureo-marginata' ('Variegata'), each leaf is green edged with creamy white; sun tolerant.

HOUSELEEK. See SEMPERVIVUM

HOUSTONIA caerulea (Hedyotis caerulea)

BLUETS, QUAKER LADIES

Rubiaceae

PERENNIAL

⚡ ZONES 1–6, 31–43

☼ LIGHT SHADE

🔴 REGULAR WATER

Houstonia caerulea

Creeping perennial making small (2–3-in.) mounds of tiny oval leaves. Flowers appear singly on 2–2½-in. stalks in late spring. The ½-in.-wide, four-lobed flowers are pale blue (sometimes white) with a yellow eye. Individually small, they are profuse enough to create a charming effect in a moist, lightly shaded garden. Use in rock gardens, around stepping-stones, or as carpet for large potted shrubs like camellia or aucuba. In the wild, thrives among mosses in light shade under tall oak trees. Will also grow in poor lawns. In cool-summer areas, tolerates considerable sun.

HOUTTUYNIA cordata

Saururaceae

PERENNIAL

⚡ ZONES 2–9, 14–24, 31–41

☼ ☽ 🔴 SUN OR SHADE

🔴🔴 AMPLE WATER

Houttuynia cordata

Underground rhizomes send up 2–3-in. leaves that look much like those of English ivy. When crushed, leaves give off a peculiar scent somewhat reminiscent of orange peel. Inconspicuous clusters of white-bracted flowers like tiny dogwood blossoms. Unusual ground cover that disappears completely in winter, even in mild climates. 'Variegata' ('Chameleon') has showy splashes of cream,

---

pink, yellow, and red on foliage. 'Plena' has more prominent flowers consisting of several rows of white bracts; leaves are plain green. Plants can spread aggressively in wet ground. Attractive in container or, if curbed, in shady garden. Can grow in standing water; good for pond sites.

HOVENIA dulcis

JAPANESE RAISIN TREE

Rhamnaceae

DECIDUOUS TREE

⚡ ZONES 4–9, 14–17, 31–35, 37

☼ FULL SUN

🔴 REGULAR WATER

Hovenia dulcis

Seldom-seen but attractive tree to 25–30 ft. high, probably taller with age. Branching is largely upright, resulting in a narrowish to rounded head. Broadly oval, shiny dark green leaves are 4–6 in. long, prominently marked by three veins running lengthwise. No real fall color. Clustered greenish white flowers are inconspicuous but fragrant. Blooms are followed in early autumn by small reddish fruits partially enclosed by their stalks; stalks swell into edible large, twisted, asymmetrical, fleshy red bodies with a sweet, faintly raisinlike flavor. Attractive lawn, garden, or small street tree. No serious pest or disease problems.

HOWEA

Arecaceae (Palmae)

PALMS

⚡ ZONES 17, 21–25

☼ PARTIAL SHADE

🔴 REGULAR WATER

Howea forsterana

Native to Lord Howe Island in the South Pacific. These feather palms are the kentia palms of florists, and are usually sold under the name "kentia." Slow growing, to eventual 35 ft. tall; with age, leaves drop to show clean, green trunk ringed with leaf scars. When using outdoors, plant under another tree. Give indirect light indoors.

Howeas are ideal pot plants—the classic parlor palms. Keep fronds clean and dust free to minimize spider mite problem.

H. belmoreana. SENTRY PALM. Less common than *H. forsterana*, smaller and more compact, with overarching leaves 6–7 ft. long. Withstands some watering neglect, drafts, dust.

H. forsterana. PARADISE PALM. Larger than *H. belmoreana*, with leaves to 9 ft. long and long, drooping leaflets.

HOYA

WAX FLOWER, WAX PLANT

Asclepiadaceae

EVERGREEN VINES

⚡ ONE SPECIES GROWS OUTDOORS, ZONES 15–25

☼ 🔴 PARTIAL OR FULL SHADE

🔴 REGULAR WATER, EXCEPT AS NOTED

Hoya carnosa

Thick, waxy, evergreen leaves and tight clusters of small waxy flowers. Grow in sunny window. Prefer rich, loose, well-drained soil. Bloom best when pot-bound; grown in pots even outdoors. Do not prune out flowering wood; new blossom clusters appear from stumps of old ones. Specialists list dozens of species and hybrids.

H. bella. House or greenhouse plant. Shrubby, small leafed, to 3 ft., with slender, upright branches that droop as they grow older. Tight clusters of purple-centered, white, ½-in. flowers in summer. Best in hanging basket.

H. carnosa. WAX FLOWER, WAX PLANT. Indoor plant or outdoors in Zones 15–25 with overhead protection—but even there it is quickly damaged by temperatures much below freezing. Vining to 10 ft. Leaves are oval, 2–4 in. long. Fragrant summer flowers in big, round, tight clusters; each ½-in.-wide blossom is creamy white, centered with five-pointed pink star. Red young leaves give extra color. In cool climates, let plant go dormant in winter, giving only enough water to keep it from shriveling. Outdoors, in mild climates, train on pillar or trellis in shade; indoors, train on wire in sunny window. 'Variegata' has leaves edged in white suffused with pink; it is not as vigorous or hardy as the green form. 'Exotica' shows yellow-and-pink variegation. 'Krinkle Kurl' has crinkly leaves closely spaced on short stems; it is often sold as 'Compacta' or as Hindu-rope plant.

HUCKLEBERRY. See VACCINIUM parvifolium

HUMATA tyermannii

BEAR'S FOOT FERN

Polypodiaceae

FERN

⚡ ZONES 17, 23–27; OR INDOORS

☼ PARTIAL SHADE

🌢 REGULAR WATER

Native to China. This small fern has furry, creeping rhizomes that look something like a bear's paws. Fronds 8–10 in. long, very finely cut, rising at intervals from the rhizome. Like *Davallia* in appearance and uses, but slower growing.

Humata tyermannii

HUMMINGBIRD FLOWER. See ZAUSCHNERIA

HUMULUS

HOP

Cannabaceae

PERENNIAL VINES

⚡ ZONES 1–24, 28–45

☼ FULL SUN

🌢 REGULAR WATER

Humulus lupulus

Extremely fast growth. Large, deeply lobed leaves attractive for summer screening on trellises or arbors. Plants sold in nurseries are typically female (sexes are separate); no pollinator required.

H. japonicus. JAPANESE HOP. To 20–30 ft. Flowers do not make true hops. 'Variegatus' has foliage marked with white. Flowers in greenish clusters like pine cones. Sow seeds in spring where plants are to grow. Roots are perennial; tops die back in fall.

H. lupulus. COMMON HOP. This plant produces the hops used to flavor beer. Grow from roots (not easy to find in nurseries) planted in rich soil in early spring. Place thick end up, just below soil surface. Furnish supports for vertical climbing. Shoots appear in midspring and grow quickly to 15–25 ft. by midsummer. Leaves with three to five lobes, toothed. Squarish, hairy stems twine vertically; to get horizontal growth, twine stem tips by hand. Light green hops (soft, flaky, 1–2-in. cones of bracts and flowers) form in late summer. They're attractive and have fresh, piny fragrance. Cut back stems to ground after frost turns them brown. Regrowth comes the following spring. Tender hop shoots can be cooked as a vegetable. 'Aureus' has attractive chartreuse leaves in spring; needs some shade in hot climates to prevent color from bleaching.

H. l. neomexicanus (H. americanus). Native to central and southern Rockies; scarcely differs from the cultivated hop noted above.

HUNNEMANNIA fumariifolia

MEXICAN TULIP POPPY, GOLDEN CUP

Papaveraceae

PERENNIAL, USUALLY TREATED AS ANNUAL

⚡ ALL ZONES

☼ FULL SUN

🌢 MODERATE TO LITTLE WATER

Related to California poppy (*Eschscholzia californica*). Bushy, open plant to 2–3 ft. high, with very finely divided blue-green leaves. Clear soft yellow, cup-shaped flowers with crinkled petals are about 3 in. across, bloom summer and early fall. Showy plant in masses. Blooms last for a week in water if cut in bud. Plant from nursery containers or sow seed in place in warm, sunny location; thin seedlings to 1 ft. apart. Reseeds. Needs excellent drainage.

Hunnemannia fumariifolia

HYACINTH BEAN. See DOLICHOS lablab

HYACINTHOIDES. See ENDYMION

HYACINTHUS

HYACINTH

Liliaceae

BULBS

⚡ ALL ZONES, BUT SEE BELOW

☼◑ FULL SUN OR HIGH SHADE

🌢 REGULAR WATER DURING GROWTH AND BLOOM

As garden plants, best adapted in cold-winter climates. Best used as annual plantings in warm-winter Southeast, Gulf Coast, low desert, and Southern California. Bell-shaped, fragrant flowers in loose or tight spikes rise from basal bundle of narrow bright green leaves. All are spring blooming. Where winters are cold, plant in September–October. In mild areas, plant October–December.

Hyacinthus orientalis

H. amethystinus. See Brimeura amethystina

H. azureus. See Muscari azureum

H. orientalis. COMMON HYACINTH. Grows to 1 ft., with fragrant, bell-shaped flowers in white, pale blue, or purple-blue. Two basic forms are the Dutch and the Roman or French Roman.

Dutch hyacinth, derived from *H. orientalis* by breeding and selection, has large, dense spikes of waxy, bell-like, fragrant flowers in white, cream, buff, and shades of blue, purple, pink, red, and salmon. The size of the flower spike is directly related to the size of the bulb. Biggest bulbs are desirable for exhibition plants or for potting; next largest size is most satisfactory for bedding outside. Small bulbs give smaller, looser clusters with more widely spaced flowers. These are sometimes called miniature hyacinths.

Set the larger bulbs 6 in. deep, smaller bulbs 4 in. Hyacinth bulbs have invisible barbs on their surfaces that can cause some people's skin to itch; after handling, wash hands before touching face or eyes. Hyacinths look best when massed or grouped; rows look stiff, formal. Mass bulbs of a single color beneath flowering tree or in border. Leave bulbs in ground after bloom, continue to feed. Flowers tend to be smaller in succeeding years, but maintain same color and fragrance.

Choice container plants. Pot in porous mix with tip of bulb near surface. After potting, cover containers with thick mulch of sawdust, wood shavings, or peat moss to keep bulbs cool, moist, shaded until roots well formed; remove mulch, place in full light when tops show. Also grow hyacinths in

H

water in special hyacinth glass, the bottom filled with pebbles and water. Keep in dark, cool place until rooted, give light when top growth appears; place in sunny window when leaves have turned uniformly green.

Roman or French Roman hyacinth *(H. o. albulus)* has white, pink, or light blue flowers loosely carried on slender stems; usually several stems to a bulb. Earlier bloom than Dutch hyacinths. These are well adapted to mild-winter areas, where they naturalize under favorable conditions. Where winters are cold (−10°F/−23°C or below), grow in pots for winter bloom.

HYDRANGEA

Hydrangeaceae (Saxifragaceae)

DECIDUOUS SHRUBS OR VINES

ZONES VARY BY SPECIES

SOME SHADE IN HOT-SUMMER CLIMATES

REGULAR WATER

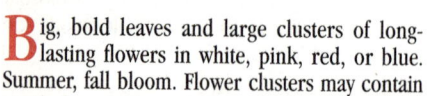

Hydrangea macrophylla

Big, bold leaves and large clusters of long-lasting flowers in white, pink, red, or blue. Summer, fall bloom. Flower clusters may contain sterile flowers (conspicuous, with large, petal-like sepals) or fertile flowers (small, starry petaled); or they may feature a cluster of small fertile flowers surrounded by ring of big sterile ones (these are called lace cap hydrangeas). Sterile flowers last long, often holding up for months, gradually changing in color. Effective as single plants, massed, or in tubs on paved terrace.

Easy to grow in rich, porous soil. Fast growing, so prune to control size and form. Most hydrangeas bloom on the previous year's wood and should be pruned after flowering. (No flowering will occur if flower buds are killed in cold winters.) *H. arborescens* blooms on new growth and should be pruned in the late dormant season. On all types, to get biggest flower clusters, reduce number of stems; for numerous medium-size clusters, keep more stems.

H. anomala. CLIMBING HYDRANGEA. Deciduous vine. Zones 2–21, 31–41. Climbs high by clinging aerial rootlets. Shrubby and sprawling without support. Roundish, 2–4-in.-long, green, heart-shaped leaves. Mature plants develop short, stiff, flowering branches with flat white flower clusters, 6–10 in. wide, in lace cap effect. Old plants have peeling, cinnamon-colored bark. *H. a. petiolaris (H. petiolaris)*, more common form in cultivation, differs hardly at all.

H. arborescens. SMOOTH HYDRANGEA. Deciduous shrub. Zones 1–21, 28–43. Upright, dense to 10 ft. Oval, grayish green, 4–8-in. leaves. In basic species, most flowers in a cluster are fertile; the few sterile ones are not plentiful enough for full lace cap effect. Much showier is 'Annabelle', which produces enormous (to 1-ft.) globular clusters of sterile white flowers on a plant about 4 ft. tall. 'Grandiflora' has 6-in. clusters on a similarly sized plant.

H. macrophylla (H. hortensia, H. opuloides, H. otaksa). BIGLEAF HYDRANGEA, GARDEN HYDRANGEA. Deciduous shrub. Zones 3–9, 14–24, 26, 28–33, 34 (warmer parts), 39. Symmetrical, rounded habit; grows to 4–8 ft. or even 12 ft. high. Thick, shining, coarsely toothed leaves to 8 in. long; white, pink, red, or blue flowers in big clusters. In many varieties, blue or pink is determined by soil pH—bluest color produced in acid soil, reddest in alkaline soil. Plants can be made (or kept) blue by applying aluminum sulfate to soil; plants can be kept red or made redder by liming the soil or applying superphosphate in quantity. Treatment must be started well ahead of bloom to be effective.

Great performer in areas where winters are fairly mild, but disappointing where plants freeze to ground every year (may never bloom under these conditions, since flower buds are produced on old wood). Protect in colder part of range by mounding soil or leaves over base of plants.

There are hundreds of named varieties, and plants may be sold under many names. Florists' plants are usually French hybrids, shorter (1–3 ft. tall) and larger flowered than old garden varieties. Among the hardier garden varieties are 'All Summer Beauty', 3–4 ft. tall, with flower heads

produced on current season's growth (unlike other bigleaf hydrangea varieties); 'Blue Wave', 6–7 ft. tall, with lace cap flowers; 'Domotoi', with double florets in large heads; 'Forever Pink', 3 ft. tall, with 4–5-in. flower heads; 'Goliath', with 15-in. flower heads; and 'Pia', a dwarf with tight clusters of heavy-textured small florets. Several lace cap varieties feature silver-variegated foliage: 'Silver Variegated Mariesii', 'Quadricolor', 'Tricolor', and 'Variegata'.

H. paniculata 'Grandiflora'. PEEGEE HYDRANGEA. Deciduous shrub. Zones 1–21, 31–43. Upright, of coarse texture. Can be trained as a 25-ft. tree, but best as a 10–15-ft. shrub. Leaves 5 in. long, turn bronzy in fall. Mainly fertile flowers in upright 10–15-in. clusters, white slowly fading to pinky bronze. 'Tardiva' blooms later, has more pyramidal clusters with a mix of sterile and fertile flowers.

H. quercifolia. OAKLEAF HYDRANGEA. Deciduous shrub. Zones 3–22, 26, 28, 31–41. Broad, rounded shrub to 6 ft., with handsome, deeply lobed, oaklike, 8-in.-long leaves that turn bronze or crimson in fall. Elongated clusters of fertile and sterile white flowers in late spring and early summer turn pinkish purple as they age. Improvements on the species are 'Snow Queen', with larger flower clusters, and 'Snowflake', with extra petals for double-flowered effect. Stems and flower buds may be damaged where temperatures go much below −10°F/−23°C; in these areas, plant is best grown for its handsome foliage. Makes an attractive container plant that can be protected in cold weather.

H. serrata. Deciduous shrub. Zones 3–9, 14–24, 28–34, 39. Similar to *H. macrophylla*, but generally a smaller plant with smaller leaves, smaller flowers, and more slender stems. The lace cap variety 'Blue Billow', 3 ft. tall, maintains blue color in most soils. 'Preziosa', to 4 ft., has round pink flower clusters that age to red.

Hydrangea quercifolia

Hydrangeaceae. The hydrangea family includes several woody-stemmed plants formerly listed under Saxifragaceae. *Hydrangea* and mock orange *(Philadelphus)* are examples.

HYDRASTIS canadensis

GOLDEN SEAL

Ranunculaceae

PERENNIAL

ZONES 3–6, 32–35, 37, 39

PARTIAL OR FULL SHADE

REGULAR WATER

Hydrastis canadensis

Native to eastern U. S. Roots are used in herbal remedies. Makes an unusual ground cover in woodland or shade gardens. Plant grows from a thick yellow rootstock, sending up two deeply lobed 8-in. leaves and a 1-ft. stalk topped by two smaller leaves and an inconspicuous whitish to yellowish green flower. The blossom is followed by a large, showy red berry that resembles an outsize raspberry, though it isn't edible. Plant will grow in ordinary good garden soil, but it prefers plenty of leaf mold or compost. A modestly attractive choice for native plant enthusiasts.

Hydrophyllaceae. The waterleaf family, largely but not entirely native to North America, includes annuals, perennials, and a few shrubs. Many have flowers in clusters shaped like a shepherd's crook. *Nemophila* is among the few kinds sometimes grown in gardens.

FOR GROWING SYMBOL EXPLANATIONS
PLEASE SEE PAGE 161

HYMENOCALLIS

Amaryllidaceae

BULBS

Hymenocallis narcissiflora

- ⚡ ZONES 5, 6, 8, 9, 14–31, EXCEPT AS NOTED; OR DIG AND STORE DECIDUOUS TYPES; OR GROW IN POTS
- ☼ ◐ FULL SUN OR PARTIAL SHADE
- ♦ REGULAR WATER DURING GROWTH AND BLOOM
- ◊ BULBS ARE POISONOUS IF INGESTED

Clumps of strap-shaped leaves like those of amaryllis. The 2-ft. stems bear several very fragrant flowers in summer; blooms resemble daffodils in having a center cup, but cup is surrounded by six slender, spidery segments. Deciduous species maintain foliage throughout summer if watered, then die back in fall. Unusual plants for borders or containers. Plant in rich, well-drained soil—in late fall or early winter in frostless areas, after frosts in colder climates. Set bulbs with tips 1 in. below surface. Deciduous sorts can be dug after foliage has yellowed (do not cut off fleshy roots), dried in an inverted position, and stored in open trays in a cool place.

H. festalis. Deciduous. Free flowering. Each stem bears four or more pure white flowers, the cup surrounded by very narrow curved segments. Leaves resemble those of *H. narcissiflora.*

H. latifolia (H. keyensis). SPIDER LILY. Evergreen. Zones 25–28. Native to Florida and the West Indies. Borne in clusters of 6–12, white flowers consist of 3-in. cup surrounded by 5-in.-long, spidery segments.

H. narcissiflora (Ismene calathina). BASKET FLOWER, PERUVIAN DAFFODIL. Deciduous. Leaves 1½–2 ft. long, 1–2 in. wide. White, green-striped flowers in clusters of two to five. Variety 'Advance' has pure white flowers, faintly lined with green in throat.

H. 'Sulfur Queen'. Deciduous. Primrose yellow flowers with light yellow, green-striped throat. Leaves like those of *H. narcissiflora.*

HYMENOSPORUM flavum

SWEETSHADE

Pittosporaceae

EVERGREEN SHRUB OR SMALL TREE

- ⚡ ZONES 8, 9, 14–24
- ☼ ◐ FULL SUN OR LIGHT SHADE
- ♦ INFREQUENT, DEEP WATERING

Hymenosporum flavum

Native to Australia. Slow to moderate growth to 20–40 ft., with 15–20-ft. spread. Graceful, upright, slender, open habit. In early summer, bears yellow flowers with pronounced fragrance of orange-blossom honey. Early training is necessary to correct two problems: first, branches spread out in almost equal threes, creating weak crotches that are likely to split; second, the glossy dark green, narrow leaves, 2–6 in. long, tend to cluster near ends of twigs and branches. Frequent pinching and shortening of growth in early years will result in stronger, denser plant. Best away from strong winds.

HYPERICUM

ST. JOHNSWORT

Hypericaceae

SHRUBS AND PERENNIALS, MOSTLY EVERGREEN

- ⚡ ZONES VARY BY SPECIES
- ☼ ◐ PARTIAL SHADE IN HOT AREAS
- ♦♦ REGULAR TO MODERATE WATER

Hypericum calycinum

Large group of shrubs and perennials bearing yellow flowers resembling single roses with prominent sunburst of stamens in center. Open, cup-shaped, five-petaled blooms range in color from creamy yellow to gold; flowers may be solitary or in clusters. Neat leaves vary in form and color. Plants are useful for summer flower color and fresh green foliage. Various kinds used for mass plantings, ground covers, informal hedges, borders. Perform especially well in mild, moist regions such as Pacific Northwest.

H. androsaemum. Semievergreen shrub. Zones 3–24, 31–34, 39. Shade-tolerant European native. To 3 ft. tall, with stems arching toward the top. Leaves to 4 in. long, 2 in. wide. Clusters of ¾-in., golden yellow flowers at tops of stems and at ends of side branches in summer. Blossoms are followed by berrylike fruits that turn from red to purple to black as they age. Useful as tall ground cover at edge of woods, on shaded slopes, in a wild garden.

H. beanii (H. patulum henryi). Evergreen shrub or perennial; more perennial-like in colder part of range. Zones 4–24, 31, 32. To 4 ft. tall, with light green, oblong leaves on graceful, willowy branches. Flowers brilliant golden yellow, 2 in. across, midsummer into fall. Good for low, untrimmed hedge, mass planting. Shabby winter appearance.

H. calycinum. AARON'S BEARD, CREEPING ST. JOHNSWORT. Evergreen to semievergreen shrublet; tops often killed in cold winters but come back in spring. Zones 3–24, 31–34. Grows to 1 ft. high and spreads by vigorous underground stems. Short-stalked leaves to 4 in. long are medium green in sun, yellow green in shade. Flowers bright yellow, 3 in. across throughout summer. A tough, dense ground cover that competes successfully with tree roots, takes poor soil. Fast growing; will control erosion on hillsides. May invade other plantings unless confined. Plant from flats or as rooted stems; set 1½ ft. apart. Clip or mow tops every 2 or 3 years during dormant season.

H. coris. Evergreen shrublet. Zones 4–24, 31, 32. Grows 6–12 in. or taller. Leaves narrow, ½–1 in. long, in whorls of four to six. Flowers yellow, ¾ in. across, in loose clusters, spring or early summer. Good ground cover or rock garden plant.

H. frondosum. Deciduous shrub; evergreen in mildest climates. Zones 3–24, 28–34, 39. Native to southeastern U.S. Grows 1–3 ft. tall, with mounding form. Blue-green leaves set off clusters of 1½-in. bright yellow flowers that bloom from midsummer to early autumn. 'Sunburst' forms a tight mound to 3 ft. tall and wide.

H. 'Hidcote' (H. patulum 'Hidcote'). Evergreen to semievergreen shrub; perennial that dies to the ground in coldest part of range. Zones 4–24, 31, 32. To 4 ft. tall in mildest climates; in cold areas, freezes keep height closer to 2 ft. Leaves 2–3 in. long. Yellow, 3-in.-wide flowers all summer. Very prone to root rot and wilt in warm, humid areas.

H. kouytchense. Semievergreen shrub. Zones 4–24, 31, 32. Twiggy, rounded growth 1½–2 ft. tall, 2–3 ft. wide. Pointed oval, 2-in. leaves; golden yellow, 2–3-in.-wide flowers, heavily produced in summer. Often sold as *H.* 'Sungold'.

H. moseranum. GOLD FLOWER. Evergreen shrub or perennial. Zones 3–24, 26, 28, 31, 32, 34. Hybrid plant. Where winters are mild, forms shrub to 3 ft. tall; in cold-winter areas, grows as hardy perennial that dies back each year. Moundlike habit with arching, reddish stems. Leaves 2 in. long, blue green beneath. Golden yellow flowers, 2½ in. across, are borne singly or in clusters of up to five. Blooms in summer, possibly into fall. Cut back in early spring. 'Tricolor' has gray-green leaves tinged with pink and edged in white.

H. patulum henryi. See H. beanii

H. reptans. Evergreen shrublet. Zones 3–6, 32, 34. Flat-growing plant that roots along ground. Leaves ¼–½ in. long, crowded along stems; flowers to 1¾ in. wide in summer. Rock garden plant. Protect from frosts in colder regions.

H. 'Rowallane'. Evergreen to semievergreen shrub; perennial that dies to the ground in coldest part of range. Zones 4–24, 31, 32. Upright and rather straggly growth to 3–6 ft. Flowers bright yellow, 2½–3 in. across, profuse in late summer and fall. Leaves 2½–3½ in. long. Remove older branches annually.

H. 'Sungold'. See H. kouytchense

HYPOCYRTA nummularia. See ALLOPLECTUS nummularia

HYPOESTES phyllostachya (H. sanguinolenta)

FRECKLE FACE, PINK POLKA-DOT PLANT

Acanthaceae

PERENNIAL TREATED AS ANNUAL OR HOUSE PLANT

✓ ALL ZONES AS ANNUAL

☼ ◐ FULL SUN OR LIGHT SHADE

💧 REGULAR WATER

Hypoestes phyllostachya

Though this tender plant is actually a perennial, it is almost always grown as bedding annual or house plant. Can reach 1–2 ft. tall. Slender stems bear oval, 2–3-in.-long leaves spotted irregularly with pink or white. A selected form known as 'Splash' has larger spots. Tiny, inconspicuous lavender flowers are not always produced. For indoor use, plant in loose, peaty mixture in pots or planters. Feed with liquid fertilizer. Pinch tips to make bushy.

Hypoxidaceae. The star grass family consists of a small number of perennial plants growing from corms or rhizomes. Flowers have six equal segments and resemble those of the lily and amaryllis families. Yellow star grass (*Hypoxis*) and *Rhodohypoxis* are the only two commonly seen.

HYPOXIS hirsuta

YELLOW STAR GRASS

Hypoxidaceae

PERENNIAL

✓ ZONES 28–38

☼ ◐ FULL SUN OR LIGHT SHADE

💧💧 REGULAR TO MODERATE WATER

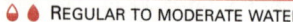

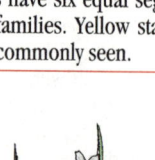

Hypoxis hirsuta

Native from Maine to Florida and west to Texas. Usually found in dryish woodlands, growing in sandy or stony soil in full sun or light shade. Grassy, somewhat hairy, 1-ft.-long leaves rise from a short, cormlike rhizome. In spring and early summer, a 1-ft.-tall stem carries from one to seven bright yellow, starlike, inch-wide flowers. A second bloom may follow later. Interesting primarily to native plant enthusiasts or rock gardeners.

HYSSOP, ANISE. See AGASTACHE foeniculum

HYSSOPUS officinalis

HYSSOP

Lamiaceae (Labiatae)

PERENNIAL HERB

✓ ZONES 1–24, 30–45

☼ ◐ FULL SUN OR LIGHT SHADE

💧💧 REGULAR TO MODERATE WATER

Hyssopus officinalis

Compact growth to 1½–2 ft. Narrow, glossy dark green, pungent-smelling leaves on woody-based stems. Profusion of dark blue flower spikes throughout summer and into autumn; not a dramatic show, but pleasant looking. Selections with white, pink, or lavender blooms are available, though they may be difficult to find.

Start from seed sown in early spring, or from stem cuttings in late spring or early summer. Once established, may self-sow. Tolerates some drought but will thrive with routine watering if drainage is good. Tolerates trimming as a low hedge or knot garden border. Peppery leaves sometimes used in cooking.

IBERIS

CANDYTUFT

Brassicaceae (Cruciferae)

PERENNIALS AND ANNUALS

✓ ZONES VARY BY SPECIES

☼ FULL SUN

💧 REGULAR WATER

Iberis sempervirens

Free-blooming plants with clusters of white, lavender, lilac, pink, rose, purple, carmine, or crimson flowers. Perennial candytufts bloom from early spring to summer; can be used as winter annuals in mildest climates. Annual species bloom in spring and summer; they are most floriferous where summer nights are cool. Use all types for borders, cutting; perennials for edging, rock gardens, small-scale ground covers, containers.

All types need well-drained soil. In early spring or (in mild climates) fall, sow seed of annuals in place or in flats; set transplants 6–9 in. apart. Plant perennials in spring or fall. After bloom, shear lightly to stimulate new growth.

I. amara. HYACINTH-FLOWERED CANDYTUFT, ROCKET CANDYTUFT. Annual. All zones. Fragrant white flowers in tight, round clusters that elongate into hyacinthlike spikes on 15-in. stems. Narrow, slightly fuzzy leaves.

I. gilbraltarica. Perennial. Zones 4–9, 13–24, 31, 32. Resembles *I. sempervirens* but is less hardy to cold and bears flatter clusters of light pinkish or purplish flowers, sometimes white near center.

I. sempervirens. EVERGREEN CANDYTUFT. Perennial. Zones 1–24, 31–45. Grows 8 in. to 1 ft. or even 1½ ft. high, spreading about as wide. Narrow, shiny dark green leaves are good looking all year. Pure white flower clusters carried on stems long enough to cut for bouquets. Lower, more compact varieties include 'Alexander's White', 6 in. tall, with fine-textured foliage; 'Kingwood Compact', also 6 in. high; 'Little Gem', 4–6 in. tall; and 'Purity', 6–12 in. tall, wide spreading. 'Snowflake', 4–12 in. tall and spreading to 1½–3 ft., has broader, more leathery leaves than the species; also has larger flowers in larger clusters on shorter stems. It is extremely showy in spring, with sporadic bloom through summer and fall. 'Snowmantle' is a similar vigorous variety. 'Autumn Snow' is a reliable spring and fall bloomer.

I. umbellata. GLOBE CANDYTUFT. Annual. All zones. Bushy plants 12–15 in. high. Lance-shaped leaves to 3½ in. long; flowers in pink, rose, carmine, crimson, salmon, lilac, and white. Dwarf strains Dwarf Fairy and Magic Carpet, available in the same colors, grow 6 in. tall.

ICE PLANT

Aizoaceae

SUCCULENT PERENNIALS, SUBSHRUBS, OR ANNUALS

✓ ZONES VARY; SEE INDIVIDUAL LISTINGS

☼ FULL SUN

💧 TAKE CONSIDERABLE DROUGHT

Delosperma cooperi

Once conveniently lumped together as *Mesembryanthemum*, but now classified under a number of separate names. Where hardy, they are among the most useful and colorful ground covers. In cold-winter climates, use them as house plants, in summer-flowering window boxes, or in hanging baskets. Feed lightly after bloom, again in autumn where winters are mild. All take most soils; won't take foot traffic.

Aptenia. Ground covers with small red flowers. Brightest green foliage in class.

Carpobrotus. Coarse, sturdy plants commonly used in California beach and highway plantings.

Delosperma. Good ground cover and bank cover. Two species (*D. cooperi* and *D. nubigenum*) are reliably hardy in cold-winter climates.

Dorotheanthus. Annuals for summer bloom.

Drosanthemum. Profuse pink or purple flowers, useful on steep banks.

Lampranthus. Large flowers; brilliantly colorful as ground cover, in rock gardens.

Mesembryanthemum. Annuals of little ornamental value are the only plants still classified under this name.

Oscularia. Dainty form, fragrance.

ILEX

HOLLY

Aquifoliaceae

EVERGREEN OR DECIDUOUS SHRUBS OR TREES

ZONES VARY BY SPECIES

FULL SUN OR PARTIAL SHADE

REGULAR WATER

Ilex aquifolium

Though English holly (*I. aquifolium*) is the most familiar in song and legend (and in Christmas wreaths), this species is entirely satisfactory only in the Pacific Northwest and in coastal northern California. In other areas, where temperatures cover a wider range, many other choices are better choices. These include evergreen species grown for their attractive foliage and fruit as well as deciduous types grown principally for showy autumn and winter berries. In size, hollies range from foot-high dwarfs to trees 40–50 ft. tall. More than 400 species and countless hybrids exist. Smaller hollies are attractive as foundation plantings or low hedges; larger evergreen kinds make attractive, impenetrable tall hedges or screens.

All holly plants are either male or female, and as a rule both sexes must be present for the female to set fruit. Varieties described below are female unless otherwise noted. A few are self-fertile; these are also noted.

Most hollies prefer rich, moist, slightly acid garden soil with good drainage. (A few exceptions are noted.) All appreciate a mulch to deter weeds and keep soil cool and moist. Though hollies will grow in sun or part shade, choose a sunny spot for best berry production and most compact growth. Principal pests are scale, bud moth, and leaf miner.

I. altaclarensis. Evergreen tree. Zones 3–24, 31–34. Hybrid between English holly and a species from the Canary Islands; resembles the former. 'Camelliafolia' has large, smooth-edged dark green leaves. 'J. C. Van Tol' bears regular crops of large dark red berries. 'Wilsonii' (also known as Wilson holly) can attain tree size, but is usually seen as a 6–8 ft. shrub; it has thick, leathery, rich green leaves up to 5 in. long.

I. aquifolium. ENGLISH HOLLY. Evergreen tree. Zones 4–9, 14–17, 32–34. The classic holly, but not the best choice for eastern or midwestern gardens. Dislikes poor drainage, low temperatures, cold drying winds, and high humidity coupled with high temperatures. Has succeeded in ideal locations, but chancy; *I.* 'Nellie R. Stevens' (see page 344) is a better choice for achieving similar effect. Among the hardiest English holly selections are 'Balkans', which is the most cold tolerant and has both male and female forms; 'Boulder Creek'; and 'Zero' ('Teufel's Weeping').

I. aquipernyi. Evergreen shrub or small tree. Zones 4–9, 14–24, 31–34. Hybrid between English holly and *I. pernyi*. May attain 20 ft. or more. The 2–4-in., spiny-edged leaves are closely set on branches. 'Aquipern' is a male selection; 'San Jose' and 'Brilliant' are female, with small red berries that set without pollination.

I. attenuata. Evergreen tree. Zones 4–6, 15–17, 26, 28–33. Hybrid between American holly (*I. opaca*) and a species native to the southeastern U.S. Dense, conical habit to 20–30 ft. tall; sparsely toothed foliage. 'East Palatka' and 'Foster's #2' (also known as Foster's holly) are widely planted female forms. 'Foster's #4' is a male plant. 'Nasa', a female holly, is known for its unusually narrow leaves.

I. cornuta. CHINESE HOLLY. Evergreen shrub or small tree. Zones 4–9, 14–24, 26–33, but needs long warm season to set fruit. Very tolerant of heat and drought. Dense or open growth to 10 ft. or taller. Leaves typically glossy, leathery, nearly rectangular, with spines at the four corners and at tip. Berries exceptionally large, bright red, long lasting. Selections rather than species usually grown; fruit set, leaf form, and spininess vary. In the following list, those setting fruit do so without pollination.

'Berries Jubilee'. Dome-shaped plant to 6–10 ft., with large leaves and heavy crop of large, bright red berries. Leaves larger, spinier than those of 'Burfordii', on smaller plant.

'Burfordii'. BURFORD HOLLY. To 15 ft. tall and wide. Leaves nearly spineless, cupped downward. Heavy fruit set. Useful as espalier.

'Carissa'. Dwarf to 3–4 ft. high and 4–6 ft. wide at maturity. Dense growth, small leaves. Use for low hedge. No berries. Has been known to revert to 'Rotunda', the form from which it was developed.

'Dazzler'. Compact, upright growth. Glossy leaves have a few stout spines along wavy margins. Loaded with berries.

'D'Or'. Resembles 'Burfordii' but has bright yellow berries.

'Dwarf Burford' ('Burfordii Nana'). Resembles 'Burfordii' but somewhat smaller, to about 8 ft. tall and wide. Densely covered with small (1½-in.), light green, nearly spineless leaves. Dark red berries.

'Rotunda'. DWARF CHINESE HOLLY. Compact grower to 3–4 ft. tall, 6–8 ft. wide at maturity. Usually does not produce berries. A few stout spines and rolled leaf margins between spines make the medium light green leaves nearly rectangular.

I. crenata. JAPANESE HOLLY. Evergreen shrub. Zones 2–9, 14–24, 28, 31–35, 37. Looks more like a boxwood than a holly. Dense, erect, usually 3–4 ft. high, sometimes to 20 ft. Narrow, fine-toothed leaves, ½–¾ in. long; berries are black. Extremely hardy and useful where winter cold limits choice of polished evergreens for hedges, edgings. Varieties include:

'Beehive'. Dense, compact mound with leaves ½ in. long, ¼ in. wide.

'Compacta'. Rounded shrub to 6 ft. tall. Dense habit, ¾-in. leaves. Many different plants sold under this name.

'Convexa'. Compact, rounded shrub to 4–6 ft. high, spreading wider. Leave are ½ in. long, roundish, cupped downward at the edges. Use clipped or unclipped. Many different plants sold under this name.

'Dwarf Pagoda'. Exceptionally slow growing and dense—to 1 ft. in 8 years. Leaves less than ½ in. long.

'Glory'. Male plant (no fruit). Dense, rounded growth. Extremely hardy.

'Green Island'. Open, spreading growth to 3 ft. tall and twice as wide.

'Helleri'. Dwarf variety to 1 ft. high, 2 ft. wide; larger after many years, to 4 ft. tall and 5 ft. wide.

'Jersey Pinnacle'. Compact, dense, erect. To eventual 8 ft. tall, 2 ft. wide.

'Mariesii'. Often labeled as dwarf less than 1 ft. high, but old plants often grow much taller. Usually grows only 8 in. in first 10 years; erect habit.

'Soft Touch'. Grows 2 ft. tall, 3 ft. wide. Unlike other varieties, has soft, flexible branches.

I. decidua. POSSUMHAW. Deciduous shrub. Zones 28–35, 37, 39. Native to southeastern U.S. To 6–10 ft.; possibly small tree to 20 ft. Pale gray stems; shiny dark green leaves to 3 in. long. Orange to red berries last into winter or spring. 'Warren's Red', eventually 15–20 ft. tall, bears a heavy crop of large red berries. 'Council Fire' is lower growing. For fruit production, need a male pollinator such as 'Red Escort' or any male variety of American holly, such as 'Jersey Knight'.

I. 'Ebony Magic'. Evergreen shrub. Zones 3–9, 12–24, 32, 34, 35, 37. Hybrid with pyramidal form. Grows 8–10 ft. tall, possibly to 20 ft. Blackish purple bark; shiny dark green, spiny-edged leaves. Large orange-red berries last through spring. 'Ebony Male' often used for pollination.

I. glabra. INKBERRY. Evergreen shrub. Zones 3–24, 26, 28, 31–41. Native to eastern North America. To 10 ft. tall, with thick, dark green (olive green in winter), spineless leaves and black berries. More widely available is the dwarf form 'Compacta'; it grows to 4 ft. but can be sheared to make a 2-ft. hedge. 'Densa', 'Nordic', and 'Shamrock' are other dwarf varieties.

I. latifolia. Evergreen tree. Zones 4–7, 15–17, 20–24, 26, 28, 31, warmer parts of 32. Native to China, Japan. Slow-growing, stout-branched plant to 50–60 ft. tall. Leaves are 6–8 in. long (largest of all hollies), dull dark green, leathery, fine toothed. Big clusters of large, dull red berries.

I. meserveae. Evergreen shrub. Zones 3–9, 14–17, 32, 34, 35, 37–39. Most plants in this category are hybrids between English holly and a cold-tolerant species from northern Japan. Apparently the hardiest of hollies that have true holly look. Dense, bushy plants 6–7 ft. tall, with purple stems and spiny, glossy blue-green leaves. Red-fruiting female varieties include 'Blue Angel', 'Blue Girl', and 'Blue Princess'; male pollinators include 'Blue Boy' and 'Blue Prince'. 'Golden Girl' has yellow berries.

I

Red-fruited 'China Boy' and 'China Girl', both to 10 ft. tall, are crosses between Chinese holly and the northern Japanese species. They are slightly hardier and tolerate more summer heat than the Blue series.

I. 'Nellie R. Stevens'. Evergreen shrub or small tree. Zones 4–9, 14–24, 28, 31, 32. Probably a hybrid between Chinese holly and English holly. Fast growing, densely conical to 15–25 ft. tall. Glossy, leathery, sparsely toothed leaves to 3 in. long. Sets fruit without a male holly, but forms a heavier crop if pollinated by male variety of Chinese holly.

I. opaca. AMERICAN HOLLY. Evergreen tree. Zones 3–9, 15, 16, 19–23, 26, 28, 31–35, 39. Native to eastern U.S. Slow growing to 50 ft. tall; pyramidal or round-headed form. Leaves 2–4 in. long, spiny margined, dull or glossy green. Red berries. Hundreds of named varieties exist. Among the best known are 'Dan Fenton', with large leaves glossier than those typical of the species; 'Jersey Delight' and 'Jersey Princess'; 'Jersey Knight', a male pollen source; 'Merry Christmas'; 'Stewart's Silver Crown', with leaves edged in cream and marbled with gray green; and 'Yellow Berry', with bright yellow berries.

Ilex opaca

I. pedunculosa. Evergreen shrub or small tree. Zones 3–9, 14–17, 32–35, 37, 39. Exceptionally hardy for a broad-leafed evergreen. Native to China, Japan. Grows to 15 ft. or taller; awkward shape when young. Narrow, smooth-edged leaves 1–3 in. long and half as wide. The ¼-in. bright red berries dangle on 1–1½-in.-long stalks in autumn.

I. pernyi. Evergreen tree. Zones 4–9, 14–24, 31, 32, 34. Native to China. Slow growth to 20–30 ft. Glossy, 1–2-in.-long leaves, square at base, one to three spines on each side; closely packed against branchlets. Red berries set tightly against stems.

I. verticillata. WINTERBERRY, BLACK ALDER, MICHIGAN HOLLY. Deciduous shrub. Zones 1–7, 31–43. Native to swamps of eastern North America. Unlike most hollies, thrives in boggy soils, but will succeed in any moist, acid, organic soil. To 6–10 ft. tall, rarely taller, eventually forming clumps by suckering. Leaves are oval, to 3 in. long and 1 in. wide. Female plants bear enormous crops of bright red berries that ripen in early fall and last all winter (or until they are eaten by birds). 'Afterglow' has orange to orange-red berries on a compact plant; 'Cacapon', 'Fairfax', and 'Winter Red' are standard-sized plants with dark red fruit; 'Red Sprite' is a large-berried dwarf selection. Pollinate with a male winterberry variety.

I. vomitoria. YAUPON. Evergreen shrub or small tree. Zones 3–9, 11–24, 26, 28, 31, 32, warmer parts of 33. Native to southeastern U.S. Tolerates extremely alkaline soils better than other hollies. To 15–20 ft. tall, with narrow, inch-long, shallowly toothed dark green leaves. Can be grown as standard or sheared into columnar form; good topiary plant. Tiny scarlet berries borne in profusion without pollinator. Varieties include:

'Nana'. DWARF YAUPON. Low shrub. Compact to 1½ ft. high and twice as wide. Refined, attractive. Formal when sheared.

'Pendula'. Weeping branches show to best effect when plant is trained as standard.

'Pride of Houston'. Large shrub or small tree, upright, freely branching. Use as screen or hedge.

'Stokes' ('Stokes Dwarf', 'Shillings'). Dark green, closely set leaves. Compact. Smaller growing than 'Nana'.

'Yawkey'. Yellow-berried form.

ILLICIUM

ANISE TREE

Illiciaceae

EVERGREEN SHRUBS OR SMALL TREES

✿ ZONES 26, 28, 31, 32

☾ ● PARTIAL OR FULL SHADE

💧 AMPLE WATER

Illicium floridanum

The anise trees are a little-used but attractive clan of shrubs or small trees noted for their anise-scented foliage and oddly shaped and col-ored flowers. Thick, leathery, glossy leaves; small flowers with many petal-like segments in early spring. Fruits that follow the blossoms are small, one-seeded pods arranged in a ring; the star anise of Chinese cookery is the fruit of *I. verum*, apparently not grown in the U. S. All like shade, ample moisture, and rich soil with abundant organic material. Big, bold foliage gives the impression of rhododendrons, so plants are useful for massing where rhododendrons will not thrive.

I. anisatum (I religiosum). ANISE SHRUB. Native to Japan. Grows 6–10 ft. (possibly 15 ft.) tall, with glossy 4-in. leaves and inch-wide creamy to yellowish green flowers.

I. floridanum. FLORIDA ANISE TREE. Native Florida to Louisiana. Reaches 6–10 ft. or more, with leaves to 6 in. long; inch-wide maroon flowers have a scent most people find unpleasant. 'Halley's Comet' has somewhat larger, redder flowers than species; 'Album' is white flowered.

I. parviflorum. SMALL ANISE TREE. Grows 8–15 ft. tall, with 4-in. olive green leaves and inconspicuous, ½-in. yellow-green flowers. Can form small colonies by suckering. More tolerant of sun and dry soil than other anise trees, but equally at home in damp shade.

IMMORTELLE. See XERANTHEMUM annuum

IMPATIENS

BALSAM, TOUCH-ME-NOT, SNAPWEED

Balsaminaceae

PERENNIALS AND ANNUALS

✿ ZONES VARY BY SPECIES

☀ ☽ ● EXPOSURE NEEDS VARY BY SPECIES

💧 REGULAR WATER

Impatiens wallerana

Of the hundreds of species, only the following are widely grown. Most of these are annuals or tender perennials treated as annuals; all are valuable for long summer bloom. Ripe seed capsules burst open when touched lightly and scatter seeds explosively.

I. balsamina. BALSAM. Summer annual. All zones. Erect, branching, 8–30 in. tall. Leaves 1½–6 in. long, sharply pointed, deeply toothed. Flowers large, spurred, borne among leaves along main stem and branches. Blossoms are solid colored or variegated, in shades of white, pink, rose, lilac, red. Compact, bushy, double camellia-flowered forms are most frequently used. Sow seeds in early spring; set out plants after frost in full sun (light shade in hot areas).

I. holstii. See I. wallerana

I. New Guinea hybrids. Perennials grown as summer annuals. All zones. A varied group of striking plants developed from number of species native to New Guinea, especially *I. hawkeri*. Plants can be upright or spreading; they usually have large leaves, often variegated with cream and red. Flowers are usually large (though not profuse); colors include lavender, purple, pink, red, orange. Many named kinds, ranging from spreading 8-in.-tall plants to erect 2-ft. types. 'Sweet Sue' and 'Tango', with bronzed foliage and bright orange, 2–3-in. flowers, can be grown from seed, as can Spectra hybrids. Grow in full sun or part shade. Good in pots, hanging baskets, borders.

I. oliveri (I. sodenii). POOR MAN'S RHODODENDRON. Perennial in Zones 15–17, 21–25, 27; greenhouse or indoor/outdoor container plant anywhere. Shrubby to 4–8 ft. tall, 10 ft. wide. Bears many slender-spurred lilac, pale lavender, or pinkish flowers 2¼ in. across. Glossy dark green leaves to 8 in. long in whorls along stems. Blooms in partial or deep shade; takes sun in cool-summer areas. Frosts kill it to ground, but it regrows in spring. Tolerates seacoast conditions.

I. sultanii. See I. wallerana

I. wallerana. BUSY LIZZIE. Perennial grown as summer annual. All zones. Includes plants formerly known as *I. holstii* and *I. sultanii*. Rapid, vigorous growth; tall varieties reach 2 ft. tall, dwarf kinds 4–12 in. high. Dark green, glossy, narrow, 1–3-in.-long leaves on juicy pale green stems. Flowers 1–2 in. wide, in all colors but yellow and true blue.

Strains exist in bewildering variety. Single-flowered kinds are best for massing or bedding; they nearly cover themselves with flowers. Doubles have attractive blooms like little rosebuds, but they don't match singles for mass show and are better grown in pots.

All types are useful for producing many months of bright color in partial or full shade. Grow from seed or cuttings; or buy plants in six-packs or pots. Space dwarf varieties 6 in. apart, big ones 1 ft. apart. If plants overgrow, cut them back as close as 6 in.—it's a tonic. New growth emerges in a few days; flowers cover it in 2 weeks. Plants often reseed in moist ground.

> ### AMERICA'S NUMBER-ONE BEDDING PLANT
> *Impatiens wallerana* does everything well and asks little. It's marvelously adaptable in shaded or semishaded landscapes; blooms prolifically from spring to late fall in beds, borders, pots, or hanging baskets.

IMPERATA cylindrica 'Rubra' ('Red Baron')

JAPANESE BLOOD GRASS

Poaceae (Gramineae)

PERENNIAL

🗂 ZONES 4–24, 26, 28, 31–33

☀️◐ FULL SUN OR PARTIAL SHADE

💧 REGULAR WATER

Imperata cylindrica 'Rubra'

Clumping grass with erect stems 1–2 ft. tall, the top half rich blood red. Striking in borders, especially where sun can shine through blades. Completely dormant in winter. Spreads slowly by underground runners. Rarely, if ever, flowers.

INCARVILLEA

HARDY GLOXINIA

Bignoniaceae

PERENNIALS

🗂 ZONES VARY BY SPECIES

☀️◐ LIGHT SHADE IN HOTTEST AREAS

💧 REGULAR WATER

Incarvillea delavayi

Not related to gloxinias but rather to the many trumpet vines (*Bignonia, Campsis,* and the like). These are showy perennials from high elevations in India, Tibet, and China. Only one species is commonly seen, but another merits use. All have showy trumpet-shaped flowers carried in long, spikelike clusters above leaves divided featherwise into many leaflets. Use in perennial borders or large rock gardens. Plants are deep rooted; they need reasonably deep soil and excellent drainage. In cold-winter regions, mulch plants after ground has frozen to prevent heaving.

I. arguta. Zones 4–6, 15–17, 31; can be treated as annual elsewhere. A species only recently available in this country. To 5 ft. tall, sometimes becoming shrubby at base. Stems may flop, but flower clusters rise above foliage. Leaves to 8 in. long. Blooms in summer, bearing clusters of up to 20 rose pink (rarely white), 1½-in. flowers. Plants will bloom first year from seed if started early.

I. delavayi. Zones 2–24, 31–41. Best known of the hardy gloxinias. Carrotlike roots are available from bulb growers in autumn; set them 8 in. deep in very well-drained soil. Leaves at base of plant are up to 1 ft. long. Bears 2½-in., yellow-throated, purplish pink flowers in early summer; blossoms are carried well above the foliage mass in an elongated spikelike cluster to 2 ft. tall. A white-flowered variety is available.

INCENSE CEDAR. See CALOCEDRUS decurrens

INDIA HAWTHORN. See RHAPHIOLEPIS indica

INDIAN MOCK STRAWBERRY. See DUCHESNEA indica

INDIAN PINK. See SPIGELIA marilandica

INDIAN RHUBARB. See DARMERA peltata

INDIAN TURNIP. See ARISAEMA triphyllum

INDIGO BUSH. See AMORPHA fruticosa, INDIGOFERA kirilowii

INDIGOFERA kirilowii

INDIGO BUSH

Fabaceae (Leguminosae)

SHRUBBY PERENNIAL

🗂 ZONES 2–9, 14–21, 31–41

☀️ FULL SUN

💧 REGULAR TO MODERATE WATER

Indigofera kirilowii

Native to northern China, Korea, Japan. To 3–4 ft. high, with somewhat fernlike, bright green foliage. Small sweet pea–shaped rosy pink flowers carried in erect 4–5-in. spikes over a long bloom period in summer. Not fussy about soil or water but requires reasonably good drainage. Where winters are cold, it is killed to the ground, but comes back to bloom the next summer. Even in mild-winter areas, plants are more compact and attractive when cut back hard in earliest spring. Similar species, *I. gerardiana* and *I. incarnata,* may occasionally be seen.

INKBERRY. See ILEX glabra

INSIDE-OUT FLOWER. See VANCOUVERIA planipetala

INTERRUPTED FERN. See OSMUNDA claytoniana

INULA

ELECAMPANE

Asteraceae (Compositae)

PERENNIALS

🗂 ZONES 1–9, 14–24, 30–45

☀️ FULL SUN

💧💧💧 WATER NEEDS VARY BY SPECIES

Inula ensifolia

The elecampanes are medium-size to large perennials with big, daisylike yellow flower heads characterized by many very narrow, sometimes drooping ray flowers around a central disk.

I. ensifolia. Grows to 2 ft. tall, making a dense, dark green clump of grassy leaves. Bright yellow daisies bloom at stem ends in late summer. 'Compacta' grows 8 in. high. Both species and variety need moderate water. Short lived in southern U.S.

I. helenium. Native to Europe and Asia; naturalized in North America. Can reach 9 ft.; leaves at base of plant may be 2½ ft. long, upper leaves smaller. Clusters of 1-in. flowers in summer. Roots were once employed medicinally. Takes moist or wet soil.

I. orientalis (I. glandulosa). Bushy growth to 1½–2 ft. tall. Orange-yellow, 3-in. flowers in summer. Regular water.

I. royleana. Exceptionally showy, with orange-yellow flowers to 5 in. across carried singly at tops of 2-ft. stems in late summer. Rays tend to droop. Regular water. Best where summer nights are cool.

IOCHROMA cyaneum

Solanaceae

EVERGREEN SHRUB

ZONES 16, 17, 19–24, 26

FULL SUN OR LIGHT SHADE

AMPLE WATER

To 8 ft. or more. Dull dark green, oval to lance-shaped leaves, 5–6 in. long. Clusters of purplish blue, tubular, drooping, 2-in.-long flowers in summer; flower color of seedlings may vary to purplish rose or pink. Buy plants in bloom to get color you want. Fast-growing, soft-wooded shrub that looks best espaliered or tied up against wall. Prune it hard after bloom; protect from hard frosts. Sometimes called *I. lanceolatum, I. purpureum, I. tubulosum.*

Iochroma cyaneum

IPHEION uniflorum (Brodiaea uniflora, Triteleia uniflora)

SPRING STAR FLOWER

Amaryllidaceae

BULB

ZONES 3–24, 27–34

FULL SUN OR PARTIAL SHADE

REGULAR WATER DURING GROWTH AND BLOOM

Native to Argentina. Flattish, bluish green leaves that smell like onions when bruised. Spring flowers 1½ in. across, broadly star shaped, pale to deep blue, on 6–8-in. stems. 'Wisley Blue' is a good bright blue selection. Edging, ground cover in semiwild areas, under trees, large shrubs.

Ipheion uniflorum

Plant 2 in. deep in any good soil in fall. Easy to grow; will persist and multiply for years. Prefers dry conditions during summer dormancy, but will accept water if drainage is good.

IPOMOEA

MORNING GLORY

Convolvulaceae

PERENNIAL OR ANNUAL VINES

ZONES VARY BY SPECIES

FULL SUN

REGULAR TO MODERATE WATER

This genus includes many ornamental vines and the sweet potato; it does not include the weedy plant known as wild morning glory or bindweed *(Convolvulus arvensis)*. The plants described here may self-sow, but they do not spread by nearly ineradicable underground runners as does wild morning glory.

Ipomoea tricolor

I. acuminata (I. leari). BLUE DAWN FLOWER. Perennial. Zones 8, 9, 12–28. Vigorous, rapid growth to 15–30 ft. Leaves dark green; flowers bright blue fading to pink, 3–5 in. across, clustered. Use to cover large banks, walls. Blooms in 1 year from seed; grows from cuttings, divisions, and layering of established plants.

I. alba (Calonyction aculeatum). MOONFLOWER. Perennial climber. Zones 15–17, 23–27; treated as summer annual in other zones. Fast growing (20–30 ft. in a season), providing quick summer shade for arbor, trellis, or fence. Luxuriant leaves 3–8 in. long, heart shaped, closely spaced on stems. Flowers fragrant, white (rarely lavender pink), often banded green, 6 in. across. Needs summer heat to bloom. Theoretically flowers open only after sundown, but they will stay open on dark, dull

days. Seeds are hard; abrade them or soak them for 1 or 2 days for faster sprouting.

I. batatas. See Sweet Potato

I. horsfalliae. Evergreen perennial. Zones 25–28. Dark green, deeply lobed, 1–5-in.-long leaves; 2-in. purple flowers in midwinter, with occasional repeat bloom in summer. More common form 'Briggsii' has deep purplish crimson flowers.

I. nil. MORNING GLORY. Summer annual. All zones. Includes rare large-flowered Imperial Japanese morning glories and a few varieties of common morning glory, including rosy red 'Scarlett O'Hara'. Early Call strain comes in a number of colors and is useful where summers are short. For culture, see *I. tricolor.*

I. pes-caprae. BEACH MORNING GLORY, RAILROAD VINE. Evergreen perennial. Zones 25, 26. Sprawling vine grows to great length, rooting at leaf joints as it runs. Leaves are fleshy, 1½–4 in. long, nearly round to kidney-shaped, notched at the tip. Summer flowers pink, 2 in. wide. Florida native useful as a ground cover on sandy salt-water beaches.

I. quamoclit (Quamoclit pennata). CYPRESS VINE, CARDINAL CLIMBER. Summer annual. All zones. Twines to 20 ft. Leaves 2½–4 in. long, finely divided into slender threads. Flowers are tubes 1½ in. long, flaring at mouth into five-pointed star; they are usually scarlet, rarely white.

I. tricolor. MORNING GLORY. Summer annual. All zones. Showy, single or double, funnel-shaped to bell-like flowers in solid colors of blue, lavender, pink, red, or white, usually with throats in contrasting colors; some bicolored or striped. Most types open only in morning, fade in afternoon. Bloom lasts until frost. Large, heart-shaped leaves.

Among most popular selections is 'Heavenly Blue', twining to 15 ft., with 4–5-in., pure sky blue flowers with yellow throat. Dwarf strain with white markings on leaves (known as Spice Islands or simply as Variegated) grows only 9 in. tall and spills to 1 ft. across; blooms in red, pink, blue, and bicolors.

Sow seed in place in full sun after frost. To speed sprouting, notch seed coat with knife or file (some growers sell scarified seed); or soak in warm water for 2 hours. For earlier start, start seed indoors, then set out plants 6–8 in. apart.

Use on fence or trellis or as ground cover. Or grow in containers; provide stakes or wire cylinder for support, or let plant cascade. For cut flowers, pick stems with buds in various stages of development, place in deep vase. Buds will open on consecutive days.

I. tuberosa. See Merremia tuberosa

IPOMOPSIS

Polemoniaceae

BIENNIALS OR SHORT-LIVED PERENNIALS

ZONES VARY BY SPECIES

FULL SUN

REGULAR TO MODERATE WATER

Erect single stems, finely divided leaves, and tubular red (or yellow-and-red) flowers. They are startling in appearance, best massed; individual plants are narrow. Sow seed in spring or early summer for bloom the following summer.

Ipomopsis aggregata

I. aggregata (Gilia aggregata). Biennial. Zones 1–24, 33–45. Native California to British Columbia, east to Rocky Mountains. To 2½ ft. tall. Flowers are red marked yellow (sometimes pure yellow), an inch or so long; borne in long, narrow clusters.

I. rubra (Gilia rubra). Biennial or perennial. Zones 7–9, 14–24, 26 (northern part), 28–31. Native to southern U.S. To 6 ft. tall. Flowers red outside, yellow marked with red inside.

FOR INFORMATION ON SELECTING PLANTS
PLEASE SEE PAGES 79–160

IRESINE

BLOODLEAF

Amaranthaceae

PERENNIALS

🌡 ZONES 22–25, WARMER PARTS OF 26, 27; OR INDOOR/OUTDOOR PLANTS

☀ FULL SUN

🔴 REGULAR WATER

Iresine herbstii

Tender, upright-growing plants to 2–3 ft. tall, grown for attractive leaf color; flowers are inconspicuous. Tolerate seacoast conditions. Good in containers. In areas beyond stated hardiness, plants must be wintered indoors or treated as annuals. Pinch tips for bushiness. Easy to propagate by stem cuttings in fall or spring.

I. herbstii. Oval to round leaves, 1–2 in. long, usually notched at tip. Leaves purplish red with lighter midrib and veins; or green or bronzy, with yellowish veins. Stems are always red.

I. lindenii. Densely foliaged plant with blood red, 2½-in.-long leaves, pointed instead of notched at tip.

Iridaceae. The large iris family includes many familiar (and unfamiliar) garden bulbs, corms, and fibrous-rooted perennials. Leaves are swordlike or grasslike, often in two opposing rows. Flowers may be simply arranged with six equal segments (as in *Crocus,* for example) or highly irregular in appearance (as in *Iris*).

IRIS

Iridaceae

BULBS AND RHIZOMES

🌡 ZONES VARY, ACCORDING TO SPECIES OR TYPE

☀ ◐ ● EXPOSURE NEEDS VARY BY SPECIES

🔴 🔴 🔴 WATER NEEDS VARY BY SPECIES

Tall Bearded Iris

A large and remarkably diverse group of from 200 to 300 species, varying in flower color and form, cultural needs, and blooming periods (although the majority flower in spring or early summer). Leaves swordlike or grasslike; flowers showy, complex in structure. The three inner segments (the standards) are petals; they are usually erect or arching but, in some kinds, may flare to horizontal. The three outer segments (the falls) are petal-like sepals; they are held at various angles from nearly horizontal to drooping.

Irises grow from bulbs or rhizomes. In floral detail, there are three categories: bearded (each fall bears a caterpillarlike adornment), beardless (each fall is smooth), and crested (each fall bears a comblike ridge instead of a full beard).

Tall bearded irises (and other bearded classes) are the most widely sold iris types; many new hybrids are cataloged every year. Specialty growers abound. A small number offer various beardless classes and some species. Retail nurseries carry bulbous irises for fall planting.

Iris borer is potentially serious pest. Found east of Rocky Mountains in Canada, south to Washington, D.C., west to Iowa, it is rare or absent where winter temperatures remain above 10°F/–12°C. This borer is the larval stage of a dull brown moth that appears in late summer and early fall. Eggs laid in fall in dry debris close to the soil hatch the following spring. Larvae feed on leaf margins as they work toward the rhizomes, which they consume, leaving hollow shells. Telltale signs of infestation in summer are small "sawdust" piles around plant base. Thorough cleanup of garden debris before winter is first step in control. In early spring when new iris leaves reach 6 in. high, spray plants and soil with dimethoate. Repeat weekly until 2 weeks after last bloom.

BULBOUS IRISES

Irises that grow from bulbs have beardless flowers. Bulbs become dormant in summer and can be lifted and stored until planting time in fall.

Dutch and Spanish irises. Zones 3–24, 30–34. The species that parented this group come from Spain, Portugal, Sicily, and northern Africa. (Dutch irises acquired their name because the hybrid group was developed by Dutch bulb growers.) Flowers come atop slender stems that rise up from rushlike foliage. Standards are narrow and upright; oval to circular falls project downward. Colors include white, mauve, blue, purple, brown, orange, yellow, and bicolor combinations—usually with a yellow blotch on falls. Dutch iris flowers reach 3–4 in. across, on stems 1½–2 ft. tall;

Dutch Iris

these are the irises sold by florists. Bloom period is March–April in warm climates, May–June in colder climates. Spanish irises are similar but have smaller flowers that bloom about 2 weeks after Dutch irises.

Plant bulbs 4 in. deep, 3–4 in. apart, in October–November; give full sun. Bulbs are hardy to about –10°F/–23°C, but in coldest adapted zones, apply a mulch in winter. Give regular water during growth. Bulbs can be left in the ground for several years where summers are dry; elsewhere, they should be lifted. After bloom, let foliage ripen before digging; store bulbs in cool, dry place for no more than 2 months before replanting. Dutch and Spanish irises are good in containers; plant five bulbs in a 5–6-in. pot.

The widely sold 'Wedgwood' is a Dutch hybrid hardy only in Zones 4–24, 30–32. Large flowers are lavender blue with yellow markings, blooming earlier than others (generally coinciding with 'King Alfred' daffodils). Bulbs are larger than those of average Dutch hybrid. Vigorous foliage is best masked by bushy annuals or perennials that will mature later in the season.

English irises. Zones 3–6, 15–17, 21–24, 32, 34, 39. The species (*I. latifolia*) from which named selections were made is native to the Pyrenees, where it grows in moist meadows. Early botanists first noticed the iris growing in southern England, where it had been taken by traders. Flowers are similar in structure to Dutch and Spanish irises, but falls are broader and decorated with a yellow hairline stripe. Colors include bluish purple, wine red, maroon, blue, mauve, white. Bloom time is early summer. Bulbs need cool, moist, acid soil; in fall, plant them 3–4 in. deep, 4 in. apart. Choose a partly shaded location in warm-summer areas, full sun where summers are cool. Because English irises don't need complete dryness after flowering, they can be left in the ground in suitable climates (bulbs are hardy to about –10°F/–23°C). Or they can be lifted and replanted.

Reticulata irises. Zones 3–24, 30–34; in pots in colder zones. Bulbs covered by a netted outer covering give the group its name. These are classic rock garden and container plants, the flowers (like small Dutch irises) appearing on 6–8-in. stems in March–April (late January–early February in mild areas). Thin, four-sided blue-green leaves appear after bloom. Available species include *I. reticulata*, with 2–3-in. violet-scented flowers (purple, in the usual forms), and bright yellow–flowered *I. danfordiae*. Pale blue–flowered *I. histrio* and large-flowered, blue-and-yellow *I. histrioides* may be carried by some specialists. Far more common are named hybrids such as 'Cantab' (pale blue with orange markings), 'Harmony' (sky blue marked yellow), 'J. S. Dijt' (reddish purple).

Bulbs are hardy to about –10°F/–23°C and need some subfreezing winter temperatures to thrive. Plant in autumn in well-drained soil in a sunny location; set bulbs 3–4 in. deep and as far apart. Bulbs need regular moisture from fall through spring. Soil should be kept dry during summer dormant period; in rainy climates, lift bulbs in summer or grow in pots so you can control moisture. Divide only when vigor, flower quality deteriorate. ▶

I

RHIZOMATOUS IRISES

Irises that grow from rhizomes (thickened, modified stems) may have bearded, beardless, or crested flowers; among this rhizomatous group are the most widely grown types. Leaves are swordlike, overlapping each other to form flat fans of foliage.

Bearded irises. Zones 1–24, 30–45. The most widely grown irises fall into the bearded group. Many species, varieties, and years of hybridizing have produced a vast array of beautiful hybrids. All have upright standards, flaring to pendent falls that have characteristic epaulettelike beards. Tall bearded irises are the most familiar of these, but they represent just one subdivision of the entire group.

Bearded irises need good drainage. They'll grow in soils from sandy to claylike, but in clay soils plant in raised beds or on ridges to assure drainage, avoid rhizome rot. Plant in full sun in cool climates; in hottest regions, they'll accept light shade during the afternoon. July–October is best planting period; plant during July–August in cold-winter zones, in September–October where summer temperatures are high. In regions with mild winters and cool to moderate summers, plant throughout this period. Space rhizomes 1–2 ft. apart; set with tops just beneath soil surface, spreading roots well. Growth proceeds from the leafy end of rhizome, so point that end in direction you want growth initially to occur. For quick show, plant three rhizomes 1 ft. apart. Water to settle soil, start growth. Thereafter, water judiciously until new growth shows plants have rooted; then water regularly until fall rains or frosts arrive. If weather turns hot, shade newly planted rhizomes to prevent sunscald, possible rot. Where winters are severe, mulch new plantings to prevent heaving from alternate freezing, thawing.

DIRECTING BEARDED IRIS

Rhizomes grow outward from the end with leaves; when planting, point that end in direction you want growth to take. For quick show, plant three rhizomes 1 ft. apart, two with growing ends pointed outward, the third aimed to grow into the space between them. On slopes, set rhizomes with growing end facing uphill.

From the time growth starts in late winter or early spring, water regularly until about 6 weeks after flowers fade; increases and buds for next year's flowers form during postbloom period. During summer, plants need less water: in warm climates, every other week is sufficient. For best performance, feed plants with moderate-nitrogen fertilizer as growth begins in spring, then again after bloom has finished. If spring weather is cool and moist, leaf spot may disfigure foliage; use appropriate fungicide at first sign of infection. Remove old and dry leaves in fall.

Clumps become overcrowded after 3 or 4 years; quantity and quality of bloom decrease. Lift and divide crowded clumps at best planting time for your area. Save large rhizomes with healthy leaves, discard old and leafless rhizomes from clump's center. Break rhizomes apart or use a sharp knife to separate. Trim leaves, roots to about 6 in., let cut ends heal for several hours to a day before replanting. If replanting in the same soil, amend it with plenty of organic matter.

Dwarf and median irises. These irises generally have flowers shaped like the familiar tall beardeds, but flower size, plant size, and stature are smaller. Median iris is a collective term for the categories standard dwarf, intermediate and border bearded, and miniature tall bearded.

Miniature dwarf bearded irises. Grow to 8 in. tall; flowers large for size of plant. Earliest to bloom of bearded irises (about 6 weeks before main show of tall beardeds). Hardy, need winter chill. Plants multiply quickly. Shallow root systems need regular moisture and periodic feeding.

Standard dwarf bearded irises. Grow 8–15 in. tall. Flowers and plants are larger than miniature dwarfs. Profuse bloom. Best with some winter chill.

Intermediate bearded irises. Grow 15–28 in., bear flowers 3–5 in. across. Flower later than dwarfs but 1 to 3 weeks before tall bearded irises. Most

are hybrids between standard dwarfs and tall bearded varieties, resemble larger standard dwarfs rather than border beardeds. Some give second bloom in fall.

Border bearded irises. Grow 15–28 in. tall—proportionately smaller versions of tall beardeds in the same great range of colors and patterns. Bloom period is same as for tall bearded.

Miniature tall bearded irises. Grow 15–28 in. high and flower with tall beardeds. But small flowers (2–3 in. wide), narrower foliage give them appearance of tall bearded irises reduced in every proportion. Good for cutting and arrangements—hence their original name, table irises.

Tall bearded irises. Among choicest perennials for borders, massing, cutting. Adapted in all climates, easy to grow. Flower in midspring, on branching stems 2½–4 ft. high. All colors but pure red and green; patterns of two colors or more, blends produce infinite variety. Countless named selections available. Modern hybrids often have elaborately ruffled, fringed flowers. Two variegated-foliage varieties are sold. Leaves of 'Palllida Variegata' (often cataloged as 'Zebra') are striped with cream; leaves of 'Argentea' have white stripes. Both bear smallish blue-lavender flowers on stems to 2 ft. high.

Remontant (or reblooming) tall bearded irises flower in mid- to late summer, fall, or winter, depending on variety and climate; in mild climates, some are nearly everblooming. Plants need fertilizer, regular moisture for best performance. Specialists' catalogs offer increasing numbers of remontant tall beardeds.

Aril and arilbred irises. The aril species and interspecies hybrids (characterized by an aril, or collar, on their seeds) offer strange and often remarkably beautiful flowers on unattractive plants. Exacting cultural requirements. Most species come from semidesert areas of the Near East and central Asia; plants need limy soil, perfect drainage, full sun, and no summer water (best suited to areas with scant or no summer rain). There are two main groups: *Oncocyclus* and *Regelias*. *Oncocyclus* include a number of species with huge, nearly globular flowers in lavender, gray, silver, maroon, and gold, often intricately veined and stippled with deeper hues. *Regelias* have smaller, narrower-petaled flowers, veined or unmarked. *Oncocyclus* are the most difficult to grow; somewhat easier are *Regelias* and hybrids between the two known as *Oncogelias*.

Arilbreds—hybrids between the arils and bearded irises—offer some of the arils' exotic beauty on plants nearly as easy to grow as tall beardeds, given well-drained, neutral to alkaline soil. Amount of aril ancestry can determine ease of culture: hybrids containing half aril ancestry or more usually are more demanding than those of one-quarter or three-eighths aril ancestry. Specialists' catalogs often state hybrid ancestries for this reason.

Beardless irises. Flowers in this group have smooth, "beardless" falls but otherwise differ considerably in appearance from one group or species to another. Rhizomes have fibrous roots (unlike fleshy roots of bearded types); most prefer or demand more moisture than bearded irises. Many can perform well from crowded clumps but will eventually need division. Timing varies; all should be dug and replanted quickly, keeping roots moist while plants are out of the ground.

The following five hybrid groups contain the most widely sold beardless irises. Also described are individual species (and their named selections) available from growers of specialty iris and perennials.

Japanese irises. Zones 1–10, 14–24, 32–45. Derived solely from *I. ensata* (formerly *I. kaempferi*), these irises feature sumptuous blossoms 4–12 in. across on slender stems to 4 ft. high. Flower shape is essentially flat. "Single" types have three broad falls and much-reduced standards, giving triangular flower outline; "double" blossoms have standards marked like the falls and about the same size and shape, resulting in circular flower outline. Colors are purple, violet, pink, rose, red, white—often veined or edged in contrasting shade. Plants have graceful, narrow, upright leaves with distinct raised midribs.

Iris ensata

Plants need much moisture during growing, flowering period. Acid to neutral soil and water are required. Plant rhizomes in fall or spring, 2 in. deep and 1½ ft. apart; or plant up to three per 12-in. container. Use in moist borders, at edge of pools or streams, or even in boxes or pots plunged halfway to rim in pond or pool during growing season.

Louisiana irises. Zones 3–24, 26–43. Approximately four species from the lower Mississippi River basin and Gulf Coast compose this group of so-called swamp irises. Graceful, flattish blossoms on stems 2–5 ft. tall, carried above and among leaves that are long, narrow, and unribbed. The range of flower colors and patterns is extensive—nearly the equal of tall beardeds.

Specialists offer a vast array of named hybrids; some may carry the basic species as well. *I. brevicaulis (I. foliosa)* has blue flowers with flaring segments carried on zigzag stems among the foliage. *I. fulva* has coppery to rusty red (rarely yellow) blossoms with narrow, drooping segments. *I. giganticaerulea* is indeed a "giant blue" (sometimes white) with upright standards and flaring falls; stems may reach 4 ft. or more, with foliage in proportion. *I. hexagona* also comes in blue shades with upright standards, flaring falls. *I. nelsonii,* a natural hybrid population derived from *I. fulva* and *I. giganticaerulea,* resembles the *I. fulva* parent in flower shape and color (but also including purple and brown tones) and approaches the *I. giganticaerulea* parent in size.

Plants thrive in well-watered, rich garden soil as well as at pond margins; soil and water should be neutral to acid. Locate in full sun where summers are cool to mild; choose light afternoon shade where summers are hot. Plant in late summer; set rhizomes 1 in. deep, 1½–2 ft. apart. Mulch for winter where ground freezes.

Pacific Coast irises. Best in Zones 4–24; grown with mixed success in 3, 32–34, 39, 41. Eleven species native to Pacific Coast states constitute a homogeneous group within the genus *Iris.* From several species, breeders have developed hybrids in a broad range of colors and patterns; flowers may be white, blue shades, pink, copper, brown, maroon, violet—many with elaborate veining or patterning. Foliage is narrow; clumps are like coarse grass. Slender flower stems grow 8 in.–2 ft., depending on variety.

Best conditions are sun to light shade, well-drained soil, moderate to scant water in summer. Intense heat coupled with water and poor drainage can be fatal; in clay soil, grow in raised beds in organically amended soil. Plant from containers any time, though spring, fall are best. Timing is critical in digging and replanting. Best moment is when new roots are starting to form (scrape away soil at plant base to check); this ranges from early fall in colder regions to midwinter in mild-winter areas.

Several species prominent in the ancestry of hybrids are sold by specialists. *I. douglasiana* is native to California coast from Santa Barbara north into Oregon. Evergreen leaves 1½–2 ft. long; stems 1–2 ft., sometimes branched, with flowers from purple through blue shades to white, cream. Tolerates less-than-perfect conditions. *I. innominata* comes from northwestern California and southwestern Oregon. Evergreen leaves; 8–12-in. stems bear flowers in yellow, orange, lavender, purple, blended brown, many attractively veined. Best in mild-summer regions, woodland or rock garden planting. *I. tenax* from Washington and Oregon makes grassy clumps of 1-ft. deciduous leaves. Flowers may be white, blue, purple, pink, cream, often veined in purple or brown. Best in regions with mild summers, some winter chill; the most promising species for gardens outside the Pacific Coast region.

Siberian irises. Zones 1–10, 14–23, 32–45. The most widely sold members of this group are named hybrids derived from *I. sibirica* and *I. sanguinea* (formerly *I. orientalis*). Clumps of narrow, almost grasslike leaves (deciduous in winter) produce slender stems up to 4 ft. (depending on variety), each bearing two to five blossoms with upright standards and flaring to drooping falls. Colors include white and shades of blue, lavender, purple, wine, pink, and light yellow.

Give plants full sun (partial or dappled shade where summer is hot), neutral to acid soil. Set rhizomes 1–2 in. deep, 1–2 ft. apart. In cold-winter regions, plant in early spring or late summer; in milder regions, plant in autumn. Water liberally from onset of growth until several weeks

after bloom. Divide infrequently—when clumps show hollow centers—at best planting time for your region.

Specialists may offer various Sino-Siberian species. Most feature drooping falls and erect to flaring standards. Predominantly yellow colors are found in *I. forrestii* and *I. wilsonii;* predominantly purple to violet flowers occur in *I. bulleyana, I. chrysographes, I. clarkei, I. delavayi,* and *I. dykesii.* These species and their hybrids perform best in Zones 4–6, 15–17, where climate is moist and relatively mild; some can be grown in cool-summer parts of Zones 36–41. Good, acid soil, regular moisture.

Spuria irises. Zones 2–24, 28–43. In flower form, the spurias resemble Dutch irises. Older members of this group had primarily yellow or white-and-yellow blossoms; *I. orientalis* (universally known as *I. ochroleuca*) has naturalized in many parts of the West and South, its 3–5-ft. stems bearing white flowers with yellow blotches on the falls. Dwarf *I. graminea* bears narrow-petaled, scented, blue-and-maroon blossoms on foot-high stems. Modern hybrids show a great color range: blue, lavender, gray, orchid, tan, bronze, brown, purple, earthy red, and near black—often with a prominent yellow spot on the falls. Flowers are held closely against 3–6-ft. stems, rising above handsome clumps of narrow, dark green leaves. Flowering starts during latter part of tall bearded bloom and continues for several weeks beyond.

Plant rhizomes in late summer or early fall in rich, neutral to slightly alkaline soil; choose a spot in full sun to partial light shade. Set rhizomes 1 in. deep, 1½–2 ft. apart. Plants need plenty of moisture from onset of growth through bloom period but little moisture during summer. Divide clumps infrequently (not an easy task); mulch clumps for winter where temperatures drop to −20°F/−29°C or lower.

I. foetidissima. GLADWIN IRIS. Zones 3–24, 32, 33. Native to Europe. Glossy evergreen leaves to 2 ft. make handsome foliage clumps. Stems 1½–2 ft. tall bear subtly attractive flowers in blue gray and dull tan; specialists may offer color variants in soft yellow and lavender blue, as well as a form with white-variegated leaves. Real attraction is large seed capsules that open in fall to show numerous round, orange-scarlet seeds; cut stems with seed capsules useful in arrangements. Grow in sun to shade in cool-summer regions, light or partial shade to full shade elsewhere. Extremely tolerant of aridity.

I. laevigata. Zones 1–10, 14–24, 32–45. Smooth, glossy leaves reach 1½–2½ ft. high, to 1 in. wide. Flower stems grow to about the same height, bearing violet blue blossoms with three upright standards and three drooping falls enlivened with yellow median stripes. Named color variants include white, magenta, and patterned purple-and-white. There also are varieties in which standards mimic falls in shape, pattern, and carriage, producing the effect of a double blossom. This is a true bog plant, growing best in constantly moist, acid soil—even in shallow water.

I. prismatica. Zones 3–6, 31–43. Foliage and flowers suggest a small Siberian iris. Typical form grows about 1 ft. high, bearing dainty purple-and-white blossoms on branching, sinuous stems. A pure white form also exists. *I. p. austrina,* from the southern Appalachians, is a bit taller and coarser, with lilac blue blossoms. Give plants full sun and moist (but not boggy), acid soil. Rhizomes spread widely, forming loose colonies rather than tight clumps.

I. pseudacorus. YELLOW FLAG. Zones 1–24, 28–45. Impressive foliage plant; under best conditions, upright leaves may reach 5 ft. tall. Flower stems grow 4–7 ft. (depending on culture), bear bright yellow flowers 3–4 in. across. Selected forms offer ivory and lighter yellow flowers, double flowers, variegated foliage, and plants with shorter and taller leaves. Plant in sun to light shade. Needs acid soil and more than average moisture; thrives in shallow water. Native to Europe but now found worldwide in temperate regions; seeds float, aiding plant's dispersal.

Several hybrids are excellent foliage plants with distinctive blossoms. All prefer ample water (but not pond conditions), sun to light shade. 'Holden Clough' perhaps has *I. foetidissima* as the other parent. Flowers, 3–4 in. across, are soft tan heavily netted with maroon veins; stems grow to 4 ft.; leaves reach 4–5 ft. but tips arch over. Two of its seedlings are similar but larger. 'Phil Edinger' grows to 4½ ft. with arching foliage; 4–5-in. flowers are brass colored, heavily veined in brown. 'Roy Davidson' is

I

similar, but flowers are dark yellow with fine brown veining and maroon thumbprint on falls.

I. unguicularis (I. stylosa). WINTER IRIS. Zones 4–9, 14–24, 31, warmer parts of 32. Native to Greece, the Near East, northern Africa. Dense clumps of narrow, dark green leaves. Depending on variety and mildness of winter, flowers appear from November to March. Typical form has lavender blue blossoms elevated on 6–9-in. tubes that serve as stems. Named selections vary in flower color (lighter and darker lavender, orchid pink, white) and in coarseness and length of foliage. Plants need neutral to acid soil, heat, and scant water during summer. In colder part of range, grow against sunny wall or house foundation to increase summer heat and lessen winter cold. Divide overcrowded clumps in early fall (mild-winter regions) or in late winter after flowering (colder regions). To reveal flowers (usually partly concealed by foliage), cut back tallest leaves in September. Slugs and snails are attracted to flowers.

I. versicolor. BLUE FLAG. Zones 1–9, 14–17, 28–45. Widely distributed North American species, found in bogs and swamps in the Great Lakes region, Ohio Valley, and the Northeast. Grows 1½–4 ft. tall; narrow leaves are thicker in the center but not ribbed. Shorter-growing forms have upright leaves, but foliage of taller types may recurve gracefully. The typical wild flowers are light violet blue, but lighter and darker forms exist; a wine red variant has been sold as 'Kermesina'. Selections include pink 'Rosea' and 'Vernal' and others with violet red flowers. Like *I. pseudacorus*, thrives in sun to light shade, in moist, acid soil or shallow water.

Specialty growers offer hybrids between *I. versicolor* and other species such as *I. ensata*, *I. laevigata*, and *I. virginica*. Violet-flowered 'Gerald Darby', a hybrid with *I. virginica*, has striking wine red stems.

I. virginica. SOUTHERN BLUE FLAG. Zones 3–9, 14–17, 28–43. In plant and flower, this species is similar to *I. versicolor*, but it has a more southerly distribution in the wild. Distinguishing floral feature is longer standards. Flower colors include light to dark blue, wine red, pink, lavender, and white. A plant sold as 'Giant Blue' is distinctly larger in all parts, approaching *I. pseudacorus* in size. Plant in moist, acid garden soil or grow in shallow water. In deep ponds, plant in large pots barely submerged beneath the surface.

Crested irises. Botanically placed with beardless irises, they represent a transition between beardless and bearded: each fall bears a narrow, comblike crest where a beard would be in bearded sorts. Slugs, snails are especially attracted to foliage, flowers. Several tender species and hybrids form bamboolike stems carrying foliage fans aloft; flower stems to 2 ft. are widely branched, bearing orchidlike sprays of fringed flowers in lavender to white with orange crests. These include *I. confusa*, *I. japonica*, *I. wattii*, and hybrids such as 'Nada' and 'Darjeeling'. Grow in sun where summer is cool, light shade elsewhere; plant in organically enriched soil. Regular water during growth. Reliable outdoors in Zones 17, 23, 24, 26–28; in other zones, grow in containers and move to shelter over winter.

I. cristata. Zones 3–6, 32–34, 39; hardy to –10°F/–23°C. Leaves 4–6 in. long, ½ in. wide. Slender, greenish rhizomes spread freely. Flowers white, lavender, or light blue with golden crests; specialty nurseries list named varieties. Give light shade, organically enriched soil, regular water. Divide just after bloom or in fall after leaves die down.

I. tectorum. ROOF IRIS. Zones 3–9, 14–24, 31–41. Foliage fans to 1 ft. tall look like those of bearded irises, but leaves are ribbed and glossy. Flowers suggest an informal bearded iris with fringed petals and crests in place of beards. Colors are violet blue with white crests, white with yellow crests; standards are upright at first, open out to horizontal as flower matures. Give plants organically enriched soil, light shade, regular water. Short lived in regions of hot, dry summers. Native to Japan, where it is planted on cottage roofs. Its hybrid with a bearded iris, 'Paltec', will grow with bearded irises. Height is about 1 ft., the lavender flowers suggesting a bearded iris with beards superimposed on crests.

IRISH MOSS. See SAGINA subulata

ISMENE calathina. See HYMENOCALLIS narcissiflora

ISOTOMA fluviatilis. See LAURENTIA fluviatilis

ITEA

SWEETSPIRE

Grossulariaceae (Saxifragaceae)

EVERGREEN OR DECIDUOUS SHRUBS

🗡 ZONES VARY BY SPECIES

☼ ◑ FULL SUN OR PART SHADE

💧 REGULAR WATER

Itea ilicifolia

Only a few of the ten or so species are cultivated in this country. Though they do not resemble one another in most details, they have in common small, scented flowers in elongated, narrow, tightly packed clusters.

I. ilicifolia. HOLLYLEAF SWEETSPIRE. Evergreen. Zones 4–24, 28, 31. Native to China. Graceful, open, arching shrub 6–10 ft. tall, occasionally much taller. Leaves are oval, glossy, 4 in. long, spiny toothed; bronze red when new, maturing to dark green. Small, lightly fragrant greenish white flowers are closely set in nodding or drooping clusters to 1 ft. long. Autumn bloom; flowering is sparse where winters are mild. Needs partial shade in hot-summer areas. Not striking, but a graceful plant of distinction. Attractive near water or espaliered along a fence or wall.

I. virginica. VIRGINIA SWEETSPIRE. Deciduous. Zones 3–6, 26, 28, 31–39. Native to eastern U.S. Erect shrub to 3–5 ft. tall or taller, spreading to form large patches where well adapted. Leaves are oval, dark green, to 4 in. long and 1½ in. wide. In fall, they turn purplish red or bright red; hang on the plant for a long time and may persist all winter in mild climates. Fragrant, ⅓–½-in., creamy white flowers are held in erect clusters; bloom in spring in the South, in summer farther north. 'Henry's Garnet' is a superior selection with 6-in. flower clusters and garnet red fall color. On 'Saturnalia', fall foliage is a mix of orange, purple, and wine red.

A variety known as 'Beppu' or 'Nana' may be in fact a form of *I. japonica*. It is lower growing (to 2½ ft.) than *I. virginica*, with somewhat smaller flowers. Spreads rapidly by suckers. Somewhat less hardy than *I. virginica*; may be injured at 0° to –10°F/–18° to –23°C.

ITHURIEL'S SPEAR. See TRITELEIA laxa

IVY. See HEDERA

IXIA

AFRICAN CORN LILY

Iridaceae

CORMS

🗡 ZONES 7–9, 12–24; OR DIG AND STORE; OR GROW IN POTS

☼ FULL SUN

💧 REGULAR WATER DURING GROWTH AND BLOOM

Ixia maculata

Garden kinds are hybrids of several South African species, notably *I. maculata*. Swordlike leaves. Wiry, 18–20-in. stems topped with spikelike clusters of 1–2-in. blooms in cream, yellow, red, orange, pink, all with dark centers.

Grows best in slightly alkaline soil; incorporate lime into acid soil before planting. Plant corms 2–3 in. deep. Where temperatures seldom fall below freezing, plant in fall for spring and summer bloom, or in spring for later summer bloom. In dry-summer areas, can be left undisturbed until planting becomes crowded or flowering declines. In areas of high rainfall or where corms are not hardy, treat as annual or dig and store until time to replant. Potted corms can be stored in pots of dry soil.

IXIOLIRION tataricum (I. montanum)

Amaryllidaceae

BULB

🌡 ZONES 3–11, 14–21, 29–33; OR DIG AND STORE; OR GROW IN POTS

☀ FULL SUN

💧 REGULAR WATER

Ixiolirion tataricum

Native to central Asia. Narrow, greenish gray leaves. Wiry, 12–16-in.-high stems bear loose clusters of violet blue, trumpet-shaped, 1½-in. flowers in spring. Set bulbs 3 in. deep. Plant in fall. In its coldest zones, needs a warm, sheltered site and mulch to protect leaves from spring frosts. In colder regions, plant in spring and treat as summer annual or dig after foliage dies back and store over winter. Where bulbs are left in ground, good drainage is essential to keep them from rotting over winter. Can also be grown in pots.

IXORA coccinea

IXORA, FLAME OF THE WOODS, JUNGLE FLAME

Rubiaceae

EVERGREEN SHRUB

🌡 ZONES 25–27; OR GREENHOUSE

☀ ◑ FULL SUN OR LIGHT SHADE

💧 REGULAR WATER

Ixora coccinea

The most commonly grown of this large and showy group of tropical shrubs. Long in cultivation, with many varieties featuring blossoms in shades of red, orange, pink, or yellow. Can reach 7–8 ft., but is usually kept to 4 ft. by occasional tip pinching or pruning. Whorled leaves are glossy and leathery. Flowers are 2 in. long and appear in large, dense clusters at branch tips throughout the warm months of the year. Prefers rich, somewhat acid soil well amended with organic material. Dies back after a freeze but recovers. Favorite decorative hedge or show plant in southern Florida; greenhouse plant in most of the country.

JACARANDA mimosifolia

JACARANDA

Bignoniaceae

DECIDUOUS OR SEMIEVERGREEN TREE

🌡 ZONES 12, 13, 15–25, 27

☀ FULL SUN

💧 MODERATE WATER

Jacaranda mimosifolia

Native to Brazil. Often sold as *J. acutifolia*. Grows 25–40 ft. high, 15–30 ft. wide. Open, irregular, oval headed; sometimes multitrunked or even shrubby. Finely cut, fernlike leaves, usually dropping in late winter. New leaves may grow quickly or branches may remain bare until tree comes into flower—usually in mid- to late spring, though blossoms may appear earlier or open at any time through the summer. Blossoms lavender blue, tubular, 2 in. long, in many 8-in.-long clusters. White-flowered 'Alba' is sometimes seen; it has lusher foliage, longer blooming period, and sparser flowers. All forms have roundish, flat seed capsules, quite decorative in arrangements.

Plant is fairly hardy after it attains some mature, hard wood; young plants are tender below 25°F/−4°C, but often come back from freeze to make multistemmed, shrubby plants. Takes wide variety of soils but does best in sandy soil. Often fails to flower in path of ocean winds or where heat is inadequate.

Stake to produce single, sturdy trunk. Prune to shape. Usually branches profusely at 6–10 ft.

JACK-IN-THE-PULPIT. See ARISAEMA triphyllum

JACOBEAN LILY. See SPREKELIA formosissima

JACOBINIA carnea. See JUSTICIA carnea

JACOB'S LADDER. See POLEMONIUM caeruleum

JADE PLANT. See CRASSULA argentea

JAMAICA FLOWER, JAMAICA SORREL. See HIBISCUS sabdariffa

JAPANESE ANGELICA TREE. See ARALIA elata

JAPANESE ARALIA. See FATSIA japonica

JAPANESE ASTER. See KALIMERIS pinnatifida

JAPANESE BLOOD GRASS. See IMPERATA cylindrica 'Rubra'

JAPANESE FLOWERING APRICOT, JAPANESE FLOWERING PLUM. See PRUNUS mume

JAPANESE LACE FERN. See POLYSTICHUM polyblepharum

JAPANESE PAGODA TREE. See SOPHORA japonica

JAPANESE RAISIN TREE. See HOVENIA dulcis

JAPANESE SILVER GRASS. See MISCANTHUS sinensis

JAPANESE SNOWBALL. See VIBURNUM plicatum plicatum

JAPANESE SNOWBELL, JAPANESE SNOWDROP TREE. See STYRAX japonicus

JAPANESE SWEET SHRUB. See CLETHRA barbinervis

JASIONE laevis (J. perennis)

SHEPHERD'S SCABIOUS

Campanulaceae (Lobeliaceae)

PERENNIAL

🌡 ZONES 3–9, 14–24, 31, 32, 34

☀ ◑ FULL SUN OR LIGHT SHADE

💧 REGULAR WATER

Jasione 'Blue Light'

Clump of deep green basal leaves produces 1½-ft.-tall, essentially bare stalks with a few smaller leaves along their lower part. Blooms from midsummer until frost, bearing clusters of small blue flowers that form a tight 2-in. ball at top of each stalk. Common name comes from flowers' resemblance to those of *Scabiosa*, the pincushion flower. Requires good drainage and non-acid soil. Use in rock garden or at front of perennial border. 'Blue Light' produces 1–2-ft. flowering stems, blooms over a slightly longer period than the species.

JASMINUM

JASMINE

Oleaceae

EVERGREEN, SEMIEVERGREEN, OR DECIDUOUS VINES OR SHRUBS

🌡 ZONES VARY BY SPECIES

☀ ◑ FULL SUN OR PARTIAL SHADE

💧 REGULAR WATER

Jasminum nitidum

When one thinks of fragrance, jasmine is one of the first plants that comes to mind. Yet not all jasmines are fragrant; and despite its common name, the intensely sweet-scented Confederate or star jasmine is not a true jasmine at all, but a member of the genus *Trachelospermum*. All jasmines thrive in regular garden soil and need frequent pinching and shaping to control growth. Low-growing, shrubby kinds make good hedges.

J. angulare. SOUTH AFRICAN JASMINE. Evergreen vine. Zones 16–24, 28. Leaves divided into three leaflets. Blooms in summer, bearing unscented white flowers in groups of three; flowers slightly more than 1 in. wide.

J. floridum. Evergreen or semievergreen, shrubby, sprawling, or half-climbing shrub. Zones 4–9, 12–24, 28, 31. To 3–4 ft. Leaves divided into three (rarely five) small leaflets, each ½–1½ in. long. Clusters of golden yellow, scentless, ½–¾-in. flowers over a long season in spring, summer, fall.

J. grandiflorum (J. officinale grandiflorum). SPANISH JASMINE. Semievergreen to deciduous vine. Zones 5–9, 12–24, 28, 29, 31. Rapid growth to 10–15 ft. Glossy green leaves with five to seven leaflets, each 2 in. long. Fragrant white flowers, 1½ in. across, in loose clusters. Blooms all summer. Spent flowers stay on plant. Gives open, airy effect along fence tops or rails.

J. humile. ITALIAN JASMINE. Evergreen shrub or vine. Zones 5–10, 12–24, 28–31. Erect, willowy shoots reach to 20 ft. and arch to make 10-ft. mound. Can be trained as shrub or, planted in a row, clipped as hedge. Light green leaves with three to seven leaflets, each 2 in. long. Clusters of fragrant, bright yellow, ½-in. flowers all summer. 'Revolutum' has larger, dull dark green leaves; flowers 1 in. across, up to 12 per cluster. Side clusters make even larger show.

J. magnificum. See J. nitidum

J. mesnyi (J. primulinum). PRIMROSE JASMINE. Evergreen shrub. Zones 3 (with shelter), 4–24, 26, 28–31. Long, arching branches 6–10 ft. long. Dark green leaves with three lance-shaped, 2–3-in. leaflets; square stems. Bright lemon yellow, unscented flowers to 2 in. across are semidouble or double, produced singly rather than in clusters. Main bloom in winter or spring; may flower sporadically at other times. Needs space. Best tied up at desired height and permitted to spill down in waterfall fashion. Use to cover pergola, banks, large walls. Can be clipped as 3-ft.-high hedge. In whatever form, plants may need occasional severe pruning to avoid brush pile look.

Jasminum mesnyi

J. multiflorum. DOWNY JASMINE. Evergreen vine often trained as shrub. Zones 21–24, 26, 28. Stems and leaves have a downy coating, producing an overall gray-green effect. Leaves up to 2 in. long. Clustered flowers are white; weakly scented. Often called star jasmine in Florida. Main bloom season comes in late winter or early spring.

J. multipartitum. AFRICAN JASMINE. Evergreen shrub. Zones 16–24. Sprawling growth to 2–3 ft. tall, 10 ft. wide. Pink buds at branch ends open into fragrant white summer flowers divided into 8–12 narrow segments.

J. nitidum. SHINING JASMINE, ANGELWING JASMINE. Evergreen to semievergreen vine. Zones 12, 16, 19–21, 26. Needs long, warm growing season to bloom satisfactorily. Not reliably hardy below 25°F/–4°C. Moderate growth to 10–20 ft. Leathery, uncut, glossy medium green leaves to 2 in. long. Very fragrant flowers shaped like 1-in. pinwheels open from purplish buds in late spring and summer. Flowers are white above, purplish beneath, borne in clusters of three. Responds well to drastic pruning. Good container plant. Can also be used as shrubby ground cover. Often sold as *J. magnificum*.

J. nudiflorum. WINTER JASMINE. Deciduous viny shrub. Zones 3–21, 30–34; best adapted in cold-winter climates. Unsupported, to 4 ft. high and 7 ft. wide; can grow to 15 ft. tall if trained on a trellis or wall. Slender, willowy green stems stand out in winter landscape. Unscented, bright yellow, 1-in.-wide flowers appear in winter or early spring before leaves unfold. Handsome glossy green leaves have three leaflets. Train like *J. mesnyi*. Good bank cover; spreads by rooting where stems touch soil. Attractive planted at top of retaining walls, with branches cascading over side. Cut back severely every few years to rejuvenate.

J. officinale. COMMON WHITE JASMINE, POET'S JASMINE. Semievergreen to deciduous twining vine. Zones 5–9, 12–24, 28, 29, 31. Resembles *J. grandiflorum* but covers more area (to 30 ft.) and is somewhat more tender. Very fragrant white flowers to 1 in. across; blooms all summer and into fall. Rich green leaves have five to nine leaflets, each up to 2½ in. long.

J. parkeri. DWARF JASMINE. Evergreen shrub. Zones 5–9, 12–24, 31. Dwarf, twiggy, tufted habit. To 1 ft. tall, 1½–2 ft. across. Leaves bright green, ½–1 in. long, made up of three to five tiny leaflets. Small, scentless yellow flowers borne profusely in spring. Good in rock gardens or pots.

J. polyanthum. Evergreen vine. Zones 5–9, 12–24, 28, 31. Fast-climbing, strong-growing vine to 20 ft. Finely divided leaflets. Dense clusters of highly fragrant flowers, white inside, rose colored outside. Blooms in late winter and spring; sporadic flowers rest of year. Prune annually to prevent tangling. Use as climber or ground cover; or grow in containers or hanging baskets.

J. sambac. ARABIAN JASMINE. Evergreen shrub. Zones 13, 21, 23–27. In Hawaii, it is also called pikake; it's a favorite flower for leis and is used in making perfume. In Asia, used in jasmine tea. To 5 ft. tall. Leaves undivided, glossy green, to 3 in. long. Blooms in summer, bearing clusters of powerfully fragrant, ¾–1-in. white flowers. Grow as small, compact shrub on trellis or in container. 'Grand Duke' has double flowers.

J. volubile. WAX JASMINE. Evergreen shrub or tall climber. Zones 22–25, 27. Glossy leaves. Fragrant white flowers throughout the year.

JERUSALEM ARTICHOKE. See HELIANTHUS tuberosus

JERUSALEM CHERRY. See SOLANUM pseudocapsicum

JERUSALEM SAGE. See PHLOMIS

JERUSALEM THORN. See PARKINSONIA aculeata

JEWEL MINT OF CORSICA. See MENTHA requienii

JOB'S TEARS. See COIX lacryma-jobi

JOE PYE WEED. See EUPATORIUM maculatum, E. purpureum

JOHNNY-JUMP-UP. See VIOLA tricolor

JONQUIL. See NARCISSUS jonquilla

JOSEPH'S COAT. See AMARANTHUS tricolor

JUBAEA chilensis (J. spectabilis)

Jubaea chilensis

CHILEAN WINE PALM

Arecaceae (Palmae)

PALM

🗡 ZONES 12–24, 27–30

☼ FULL SUN

🌢 MODERATE WATER

Slow grower to 50–60 ft. Feather-type leaves can reach 6–12 ft. long; flowers insignificant. Massive trunks are patterned with scars of leaf bases. Hardy for a palm (to 20°F/–7°C).

JUDAS TREE. See CERCIS siliquastrum

Juglandaceae. The walnut family consists of nut-bearing trees with leaves divided into many paired leaflets. Pecans and hickories (*Carya*), walnuts (*Juglans*), and wingnuts (*Pterocarya*) are examples.

JUGLANS. See WALNUT

JUJUBE. See ZIZIPHUS jujuba

JUNCUS effusus

SOFT RUSH

Juncaceae

PERENNIAL

🗇 ZONES 1–24, 26–45

☀ ◑ FULL SUN OR LIGHT SHADE

💧 AMPLE WATER

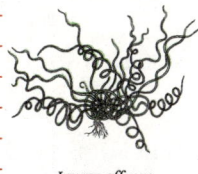

Juncus effusus
'Spiralis'

Somewhat resembles a grass. Round, leaflike stems are ⅛–¼ in. thick, to 2½ ft. tall, medium green turning brown with frost. Erect at first, they arch a little toward tips. Tiny, inconspicuous flowers are clustered at or near stem tips. 'Spiralis' has stems that coil in spirals. Use at edge of pond or stream, in the water, or among stones and pebbles.

JUNGLE FLAME. See IXORA coccinea

JUNIPERUS

JUNIPER

Cupressaceae

EVERGREEN SHRUBS AND TREES

🗇 ZONES VARY BY SPECIES

☀ ◑ SUN; MOST TOLERATE LIGHT SHADE

💧💧 REGULAR TO MODERATE WATER

▼ SEE CHART

Juniperus chinensis
'Kaizuka'

Large group of evergreen coniferous plants with fleshy, berrylike cones and foliage that is needlelike, scalelike, or both. Very widely used woody plants; there's a form for almost every landscape use. In the chart, junipers are grouped by common use and listed by botanical name; also noted are common names (if any) and any alternate names under which the plant may be sold at nurseries. If you can't locate a juniper in the first column, look for one of its alternate names in the next column to the right.

The ground cover group includes types ranging from a few inches to 2–3 ft. high. They are of two sorts: spreaders, which put down roots and spread out long, stiff branches; and creepers (mainly *J. horizontalis* varieties), which creep along the ground, rooting as they grow. If a spreader dies, the whole plant must be replaced;

Juniperus conferta

with a creeper, you may only lose the center. Low junipers are indispensable in rock gardens. As ground cover, space most varieties 5–6 ft. apart. In early years, mulch will help keep soil cool and weeds down.

Shrub types range from low to quite tall, from spreading to stiffly upright and columnar. You can find a juniper in almost any height, width, shape, or foliage color. Fewer tree types are grown; they are valued for picturesque habit. Many of the larger junipers serve well as screens or windbreaks in cold-winter areas.

Juniperus horizontalis

Junipers are subject to a number of pests and diseases. Among the most serious are bagworms (foliage is stripped from plant); blight (twig and branch dieback); twig borers (browning and dying branch tips); cedar-apple rust (disease alternating between junipers and apple trees causing twig dieback); juniper scale (no new growth, yellowed foliage); juniper webworm (webbing together and browning of foliage). To confirm a problem or decide on control measures, consult your Cooperative Extension Office or reputable local nursery.

JUPITER'S BEARD. See CENTRANTHUS ruber

JUSTICIA

Acanthaceae

SUBTROPICAL EVERGREEN SHRUBS

🗇 ZONES VARY BY SPECIES

☀ ◑ ● EXPOSURE NEEDS VARY BY SPECIES

💧 💧 WATER NEEDS VARY BY SPECIES

Justicia brandegeana

Includes plants formerly known as *Beloperone* and *Jacobinia*. Leaves are paired; flowers are tubular and tightly clustered.

J. brandegeana (Beloperone guttata). SHRIMP PLANT. Zones 12, 13, 15–17, 21–27, warmer parts of 28; anywhere as indoor/outdoor plant. Native to Mexico. Will form a 3- by 4-ft. mound but can be kept much lower. Egg-shaped, apple green leaves to 2½ in. long often drop in cold weather or if soil is too wet or dry. Moderate water. Tubular white flowers spotted with purple are enclosed in coppery bronze, overlapping bracts to form compact, drooping spikes 3 in. long, eventually lengthening to 6–7 in. Spikes somewhat resemble large shrimp; produced mainly spring to fall, sporadically rest of year. Flowers attract birds. Plants will take sun, but bracts and foliage fade there; maintain color better in partial shade. 'Chartreuse' has chartreuse yellow spikes that sunburn more easily than

▶ page 358

J (tab marker)

JUNIPER

NAME	ALSO SOLD AS	ZONES	SIZE, HABIT	CHARACTERISTICS
GROUND COVERS				
Juniperus chinensis 'Parsonii' PROSTRATA JUNIPER	*J. davurica* 'Parsonii' *J. prostrata* *J. squamata* 'Parsonii'	1–24, 26, 28–43	To 1½ ft. by 8 ft. or more. Spreading	Slow growing. Dense short twigs on flat, rather heavy branches
J. c. procumbens JAPANESE GARDEN JUNIPER	*J. procumbens*	1–24, 28–43	To 3 ft. by 12–20 ft. Spreading	Feathery yet substantial blue-green foliage on strong branches
J. c. p. 'Nana'	*J. compacta* 'Nana' *J. procumbens* 'Compacta Nana' *J. procumbens* 'Nana'	1–24, 28–43	To 1 ft. by 4–5 ft. Curved branches spreading in all directions	Shorter needles and slower growth than *J. c. procumbens*. Can be staked into upright, picturesque shrub
J. c. 'San Jose'	*J. c. procumbens* 'San Jose' *J. japonica* 'San Jose' *J. procumbens* 'San Jose'	1–24, 26, 28–43	To 2 ft. by 6 ft. or more. Prostrate, dense, spreading	Dark sage green with both needle and scale foliage. Heavy trunked, slow growing

JUNIPER

NAME	ALSO SOLD AS	ZONES	SIZE, HABIT	CHARACTERISTICS
GROUND COVERS				
J. c. sargentii SARGENT JUNIPER	*J. sargentii* *J. sargentii viridis*	1–24, 26, 28–43	To 3 ft. by 10 ft. Ground hugging, spreading	Gray-green or green foliage. Feathery. Classic bonsai plant. 'Glauca' has blue-green foliage; 'Viridis' has bright green foliage
J. c. 'Saybrook Gold'		1–24, 26, 28–43	2–3 ft. by 6 ft. Arching, spreading, with drooping tips	Rich yellow foliage
J. communis 'Effusa'		1–24, 31–45	To 1 ft. by 6 ft. Round, flat, spreading	Thin foliage shows off reddish brown stems
J. c. saxatilis	*J. c. montana* *J. c. sibirica*	1–24, 31–45	To 1 ft. by 6–8 ft. Prostrate, creeping	Variable gray, gray-green foliage. Upturned branchlets like tiny candles. Native alpine
J. c. 'Windsor Gem'		1–24, 31–45	To 8–10 in. by 6 ft., spreading	Similar to *J. c.* 'Effusa', but flatter, more open
J. conferta SHORE JUNIPER	*J. conferta littoralis.* Plants so named may be a grower's selected form	3–9, 14–24, 26–28, 31–34, 39	To 3 ft. by 6–8 ft. Prostrate, creeping	Bright green, soft needles. Excellent for seashore and will stand heat if given moist, well-drained soil. 'Blue Pacific' is denser, bluer, more heat tolerant. 'Emerald Sea' is bright green
J. davurica expansa 'Aureovariegata'	*J. chinensis* 'Alba'	1–24, 30–45	2–3 ft. by 4–5 ft. Mounding, spreading	Slow growing, with heavy, horizontal branches, patches of creamy yellow. Variegations can burn in hot sun
J. d. e. 'Parsonii'	*J. prostrata* *J. squamata* 'Parsonii'	1–24, 30–45	To 1½ ft. by 8 ft. or more, spreading	Dense, short twigs on heavy, horizontal branches
J. horizontalis 'Bar Harbor' BAR HARBOR JUNIPER	*J. h.* "Blue Rug"	1–24, 28, 31–45	To 1 ft. by 10 ft. Ground hugging, creeping	Fast growing. Feathery, blue-gray foliage turns plum color in winter. Foliage dies back in center to expose limbs as plant ages, especially in hot climates
J. h. 'Blue Chip'		1–24, 33–45	To 1 ft. by 8–10 ft., creeping	Silvery blue foliage
J. h. 'Blue Mat'		1–24, 31–45	9–12 in. by 6–7 ft., creeping	Dense mat of gray-green foliage
J. h. 'Douglasii' WAUKEGAN JUNIPER		1–24, 28, 31–45	To 1 ft. by 10 ft., creeping	Steel blue foliage turns purplish in fall. New growth rich green
J. h. 'Emerald Spreader'		1–24, 31–45	To 6 in. tall, creeping	Dense, feathery, bright green foliage
J. h. 'Glomerata'		1–24, 31–45	To 6 in. tall, creeping	Deep green turning plum color in winter. Scale foliage gives soft look
J. h. 'Hughes'		1–24, 31–45	To 6 in. tall, creeping	Showy silvery blue foliage
J. h. 'Huntington Blue'		1–24, 31–45	9–12 in. by 6–7 ft., creeping	Dense, bright blue-gray foliage
J. h. 'Marcellus'		1–24, 31–45	To 6 in. tall, creeping	Blue-gray, soft-textured foliage
J. h. 'Mother Lode'		1–24, 31–45	To 4 in. by 8–10 ft. Very flat juniper, creeping	Golden version of *J. h.* 'Wiltonii', the variety from which it was developed. Brilliant yellow foliage turns bronze yellow in winter
J. h. 'Plumosa' ANDORRA JUNIPER	*J. depressa plumosa*	1–24, 28, 31–45	To 1½ ft. by 10 ft., creeping	Gray green in summer, plum color in winter. Flat branches, upright branchlets. Plumy

J

JUNIPER

NAME	ALSO SOLD AS	ZONES	SIZE, HABIT	CHARACTERISTICS
GROUND COVERS				
J. h. 'Prince of Wales'		1–24, 28, 31–45	To 8 in. tall, creeping	Medium green foliage turns purplish in fall
J. h. 'Turquoise Spreader'		1–24, 28, 31–45	To 6 in. tall, creeping	Dense turquoise green foliage. Very flat
J. h. 'Wiltonii' **BLUE CARPET JUNIPER**	*J. h.* "Blue Rug"	1–24, 28, 31–45	To 4 in. by 8–10 ft. Very flat, creeping	Intense silver blue. Dense, short branchlets on long, trailing branches. Similar to *J. h.* 'Bar Harbor' but tighter; it rarely exposes limbs
J. h. 'Youngstown'		1–24, 31–45	To 1 ft. by 6 ft., creeping	Resembles *J. h.* 'Plumosa' but is flatter, more compact
J. h. 'Yukon Belle'		1–24, 31–45	To 6 in. tall, creeping	Silvery blue foliage. Extremely cold hardy
J. sabina 'Arcadia'		1–24, 31–45	To 1 ft. by 10 ft., spreading	Bright green, lacy foliage
J. s. 'Blue Danube'		1–24, 31–45	To 1½ ft. by 5 ft., spreading	Blue-green foliage
J. s. 'Broadmoor'		1–24, 31–45	To 14 in. by 10 ft. Dense, mounding, spreading	Soft, bright green foliage
J. s. 'Buffalo'		1–24, 31–45	8–12 in. by 8 ft. Lower than tamarix juniper. Very wide spreading	Soft, feathery, bright green foliage
J. s. 'Calgary Carpet'		1–24, 31–45	6–9 in. by 10 ft., spreading	Soft green foliage. Extremely cold hardy
J. s. 'Moor-Dense'		1–24, 31–45	To 1½ ft. by 8 ft., spreading	Resembles *J. s.* 'Broadmoor' but is denser. Has layered look
J. s. 'Scandia'		1–24, 31–45	To 1 ft. by 8 ft., spreading	Low, dense, bright green
J. s. 'Tamariscifolia' **TAMARIX JUNIPER, TAM**	*J. tamariscifolia*	1–24, 31–45	To 1½ ft. by 10–20 ft. Symmetrically spreading	Dense blue-green foliage. Widely used
J. scopulorum 'Blue Creeper'		1–24, 35, 41, 43	To 2 ft. by 6–8 ft., mounding, spreading	Bright blue-green color
J. virginiana 'Silver Spreader'	*J. v. prostrata*	1–24, 31–43	To 1½ ft. by 6–8 ft., spreading	Silvery green, feathery, fine textured. Older branches become dark green
SHRUBS				
J. chinensis 'Armstrongii' **ARMSTRONG JUNIPER**		1–24, 26, 28–43	To 4 ft. by 4 ft. Upright	Medium green. More compact than Pfitzer juniper
J. c. 'Blaauw' **BLAAUW'S JUNIPER, BLUE SHIMPAKU**		1–24, 26, 28–43	To 4 ft. by 3 ft. Vase shaped	Blue foliage. Dense. Compact
J. c. 'Corymbosa Variegata' **VARIEGATED HOLLYWOOD JUNIPER**	*J. c.* 'Torulosa Variegata' *J. c.* 'Kaizuka Variegata'	1–24, 26, 28–43	To 8–10 ft. Irregular cone	Creamy yellow variegation, can burn in hot sun. Growth more regular and slower than that of Hollywood juniper
J. c. 'Fruitland'		1–24, 26, 28–43	To 3 ft. by 6 ft. Compact, dense	Like Pfitzer juniper but more compact
J. c. 'Gold Coast'	*J.* 'Coasti Aurea'	1–24, 26, 28–43		Similar or identical to *J. c.* 'Golden Armstrong'

J

▶

JUNIPER

NAME	ALSO SOLD AS	ZONES	SIZE, HABIT	CHARACTERISTICS
SHRUBS				
J. c. 'Golden Armstrong'		1–24, 26, 28–43	To 4 ft. by 4 ft. Full, blocky	Between golden Pfitzer and Armstrong juniper in appearance
J. c. 'Hetzii' HETZ BLUE JUNIPER	*J. c. hetzi glauca* *J. glauca hetzi*	1–24, 26, 28–43	To 15 ft. Fountainlike	Blue-gray foliage. Branches spread outward and upward at 45° angle. Fast growing
J. c. 'Kaizuka' HOLLYWOOD JUNIPER	*J. c.* 'Torulosa'	1–24, 26, 28–43	To 15–30 ft. Irregular, upright	Rich green. Branches with irregular, twisted appearance. Give it plenty of room
J. c. 'Maney'		1–24, 26, 28–43	To 15 ft. Semierect, massive	Blue-gray foliage. Steeply inclined, spreading branches
J. c. 'Mint Julep'		1–24, 26, 28–43	4–6 ft. by 6 ft. Vase shaped	Mint green foliage, arching branches
J. c. 'Pfitzerana' PFITZER JUNIPER	*J. c.* 'Pfitzeriana'	1–24, 26, 28–43	5–6 ft. by 15–20 ft. Arching	Feathery, gray green. Sharp-needled foliage
J. c. 'Pfitzerana Aurea' GOLDEN PFITZER JUNIPER	*J. c.* 'Pfitzeriana Aurea'	1–24, 26, 28–43	3–4 ft. by 8–10 ft.	Blue-gray foliage with current season's growth golden yellow
J. c. 'Pfitzerana Compacta' NICK'S COMPACT PFITZER JUNIPER	*J. c.* 'Pfitzeriana Compacta'	1–24, 26, 28–43	To 2 ft. by 4–6 ft. Densely branched	Compact. Gray-green foliage
J. c. 'Pfitzerana Glauca'	*J. c.* 'Pfitzeriana Glauca'	1–24, 26, 28–43	5–6 ft. by 10–15 ft.	Silvery blue foliage. Arching branches
J. c. 'Sea Green'		1–24, 26, 28–43	4–5 ft. by 4–5 ft. Arching, fountainlike	Compact, dark green
J. sabina SAVIN JUNIPER		1–24, 31–45	Creeping or shrubby plant to 4–6 ft. by 5–10 ft.	Dark green foliage. Exceedingly tough plant
J. scopulorum 'Table Top Blue'		1–24, 35, 41, 43	To 6 ft. by 8 ft.	Gray. Massive. Flat-topped
J. squamata 'Blue Carpet'		2–24, 31–41	To 2 ft. by 4–6 ft.	Resembles *J. s.* 'Meyeri' in irregular branching habit, but is lower, more spreading and with bluer foliage
J. s. 'Blue Star'		2–24, 31–41	To 2 ft. by 5 ft. Moundlike	Regular branching. Silver blue foliage turns a little darker in winter
J. s. 'Holger'		2–24, 31–41	To 6 ft. by 6 ft.	Densely branched, broad, flat-topped. New growth yellow tipped
J. s. 'Meyeri' MEYER or FISHBACK JUNIPER		2–24, 31–41	6–8 ft. by 2–3 ft. Upright	Oddly angled stiff branches. Broad needles. Blend of green, gray, and reddish foliage. Retains old dead foliage
COLUMNAR TYPES				
J. chinensis 'Blue Point'		1–24, 26, 28–43	To 7–8 ft. Broadly columnar	Dense, blue-green scale and needle foliage
J. c. 'Blue Vase'		1–24, 26, 28–43	4–5 ft. by 3–4 ft.	Dense, blue-green scale foliage
J. c. 'Columnaris' CHINESE BLUE COLUMN JUNIPER SPINY GREEK JUNIPER	*J. c.* 'Columnaris Glauca' *J. excelsa* 'Stricta'	1–24, 26, 28–43	12–15 ft.	Blue-green, narrow pyramid. Prickly

J

JUNIPER

NAME	ALSO SOLD AS	ZONES	SIZE, HABIT	CHARACTERISTICS
COLUMNAR TYPES				
J. c. 'Hetz's Columnaris'		1–24, 26, 28–43	12–15 ft.	Rich green. Dense column. Scale foliage predominant, branchlets threadlike
J. c. 'Robusta Green'		1–24, 26, 28–43	To 20 ft.	Brilliant green, dense-tufted column
J. c. 'Spartan'	*J. c. densaerecta* 'Spartan'	1–24, 26, 28–43	To 20 ft.	Rich green, dense column
J. c. 'Wintergreen'		1–24, 26, 28–43	To 20 ft.	Deep green, dense-branching pyramid
J. communis 'Compressa'		1–24, 31–45	To 2 ft.	Dwarf, for rock gardens
J. c. 'Stricta' IRISH JUNIPER	*J. c. hibernica* *J. c. fastigiata*	1–24, 31–45	12–20 ft.	Dark green. Very narrow column with closely compact branch tips
J. scopulorum 'Cologreen'		1–24, 35, 41, 43	15–20 ft.	Narrow, bright green column
J. s. 'Gray Gleam'		1–24, 35, 41, 43	15–20 ft. in 30–40 years	Gray-blue, symmetrical column. Slow grower
J. s. 'Green Ice'		1–24, 35, 41, 43	To 15 ft. by 7–10 ft.	Dense branching, cold tolerance make it a good windbreak. Foliage is gray green; younger foliage paler
J. s. 'Medora'		1–24, 35, 41, 43	To 10 ft. by 2½ ft.	Slow growing, narrow, dense, bluish green
J. s. 'Pathfinder'		1–24, 35, 41, 43	To 25 ft.	Gray-blue, upright pyramid
J. s. 'Welchii'		1–24, 35, 41, 43	To 8 ft.	Silvery green. Very narrow spire
J. s. 'Wichita Blue'		1–24, 35, 41, 43	To 18 ft. or taller	Broad, silver blue pyramid
J. virginiana 'Cupressifolia' HILLSPIRE JUNIPER	*J. v.* 'Hillspire'	1–24, 28, 31–43	15–20 ft.	Dark green, compact pyramid
J. v. 'Idyllwild'		1–24, 28, 31–43	To 15 ft. by 7 ft.	Broad pyramid with dark green foliage. Use for screening
J. v. 'Manhattan Blue'	*J. scopulorum* 'Manhattan Blue'	1–24, 28, 31–43	10–15 ft.	Blue-green, compact pyramid
J. v. 'Skyrocket'	*J. scopulorum* 'Skyrocket'	1–24, 28, 31–43	10–15 ft.	Narrowest blue-gray spire
TREES				
J. recurva 'Coxii'		4–6, 15–17, 31–34	To 60 ft., usually much less	Erect with strongly weeping branches. Best in mild, moist climates
J. rigida 'Pendula' NEEDLE JUNIPER		3–9, 14–24, 31–34, 39	To 45 ft., usually much lower	Open growth, with drooping branchlets
J. scopulorum 'Tolleson's Blue Weeping'	*J. scopulorum* 'Repandens'	1–24, 35, 41, 43	To 20 ft. or more, 10 ft. wide	Blue-green, drooping branchlets make a graceful weeping tree. 'Tolleson's Green Weeping' is similar, but dark green. Plants are not well adapted to hot, humid climates
J. silicicola SOUTHERN RED CEDAR		25–31	To 25 ft.	Very similar to *J. virginiana*, though often more open and wide spreading. Grows in sand; frequently planted in rows and used as windbreak
J. virginiana EASTERN RED CEDAR		1–24, 26, 28, 31–43	40–50 ft. or more	Conical tree with dark green foliage that turns reddish in cold weather. Many varieties sold

J

357

do coppery bracts. To shape plant, pinch continuously in early growth until compact mound of foliage is obtained; then let bloom. To encourage bushiness, cut back stems when bracts turn black. Good for pot or tub, for close-up planting near terraces, patios, entryways.

J. carnea (Jacobinia carnea). BRAZILIAN PLUME FLOWER. Zones 8, 9, 13–27; anywhere as indoor/outdoor plant. Erect, soft-wooded plant with veined leaves to 10 in. long. Dense clusters of tubular pink to crimson flowers bloom on 4–5-ft. stems, midsummer to fall. Needs partial or full shade, rich soil, ample water. Cut back in early spring to encourage strong new growth. Tops freeze back at 29°F/–2°C.

KAFFIR LILY. See CLIVIA miniata, SCHIZOSTYLIS coccinea

KAHILI GINGER. See HEDYCHIUM gardneranum

KALANCHOE

Crassulaceae

SUCCULENTS

⚡ ZONES VARY BY SPECIES; OR INDOORS

☀️◐ FULL SUN OR PARTIAL SHADE

💧💧 REGULAR TO MODERATE WATER

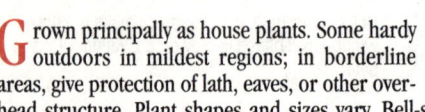
Kalanchoe blossfeldiana

Grown principally as house plants. Some hardy outdoors in mildest regions; in borderline areas, give protection of lath, eaves, or other overhead structure. Plant shapes and sizes vary. Bell-shaped flowers may be erect or drooping.

K. beharensis. FELT PLANT. Often sold as *Kitchingia mandrakensis.* Zones 21–25, 27. Stems usually unbranched, to 4–5 ft., possibly 10 ft. Thick, triangular to lance-shaped leaves—usually six to eight pairs of them—at stem tips. Each leaf 4–8 in. or more long and half as wide, covered with a dense, feltlike coating of white to brown hairs. Flowers not showy; foliage strikingly waved and crimped at edges. Hybrids between this and other species differ in leaf size, color, and degree of felting and scalloping. Striking in big rock garden, raised bed.

K. blossfeldiana. Some hybrids outdoors in Zones 17, 21–25, 27. Fleshy, shiny dark green leaves edged red; smooth edged or slightly lobed, 2½ in. long, 1–1½ in. wide. Small bright red flowers in big clusters held above leaves. Hybrids and named varieties come in dwarf (6-in.) and extra-sturdy (1½-ft.) sizes and in different flower colors, including yellow, orange, salmon. 'Pumila' and 'Tetra Vulcan' are choice dwarf seed-grown selections. Blooms winter, early spring. Popular house plant at Christmas.

K. daigremontiana. MATERNITY PLANT. Zones 23–25, 27. Upright, single-stemmed plant 1½–3 ft. tall. Leaves fleshy, 6–8 in. long, 1¼ in. wide or wider, gray green spotted red. Leaf edges are notched; young plants sprout in notches and may root on the plant. Clusters of small, grayish purple flowers.

K. manginii. Zones 23–25, 27. Hanging basket plant. Stems spreading or trailing, to 1 ft. long. Inch-long green leaves thick and fleshy. Drooping, inch-long flowers are bright red.

K. pinnata (Bryophyllum pinnatum). AIR PLANT. Zones 23–25, 27. Fleshy stems eventually 2–3 ft. tall. Leaves also fleshy. First leaves to form are undivided and scallop edged; later ones divided into three to five leaflets, these also scalloped. Produces many plantlets in notches of scallops. Leaves can be removed and pinned to curtain, where they will produce plantlets until they dry up. Flowers clustered, greenish white to reddish, to 3 in. long; not particularly attractive. Likes moisture.

K. tomentosa. Zones 23–25, 27. PANDA PLANT. Eventually 1½ ft. tall, branched. Leaves very fleshy, 2 in. long, densely coated with white, felty hairs. Leaf tips and shallow notches in leaves strongly marked dark brown.

K. uniflora. Zones 23–25, 27. Trailing plant, good in hanging baskets; inch-long, thick, fleshy leaves have a few scallops near rounded tips. Inch-long flowers are pinkish or purplish red.

KALE and COLLARDS

Brassicaceae (Cruciferae)

BIENNIAL GROWN AS ANNUAL

⚡ ALL ZONES

☀️◐ FULL SUN OR LIGHT SHADE

💧 REGULAR WATER

Kale

Vegetable crops that live 1 or 2 years. The type of kale known as collards is a large, smooth-leafed plant resembling a cabbage that does not form a head. Planted in early spring or late summer, collards will yield edible leaves in fall, winter, and spring. 'Georgia' and 'Vates' are typical varieties. Curly-leafed kales (such as 'Dwarf Blue Curled' and 'Dwarf Siberian') form compact clusters of tightly curled leaves; they make decorative garden or container plants and supply edible leaves as well. So-called flowering kale (similar to flowering cabbage) has brightly colored foliage, especially toward centers of rosettes; it is edible. For all types of kale and collards, harvest leaves for cooking by removing them from outside of clusters; or harvest entire plant. Far fewer pest and disease problems than most other cabbage-family crops.

KALIMERIS pinnatifida

JAPANESE ASTER

Asteraceae (Compositae)

PERENNIAL

⚡ ZONES 3–9, 14–24, 28–34, 39

☀️ FULL SUN

💧 REGULAR WATER

Kalimeris pinnatifida

Perennial similar to *Boltonia asteroides.* Grows to 5 ft. tall, with finely cut leaves 3½ in. long and half as wide. Daisylike long-stemmed, inch-wide flowers in open clusters bloom over a long period in summer. Blossoms are white, tinged pink or blue. 'Hortensis' is a pure white form with semidouble flowers on a 3-ft. plant.

KALMIA

Ericaceae

EVERGREEN SHRUBS

⚡ ZONES VARY BY SPECIES

☀️◐ FULL SUN OR PARTIAL SHADE

💧 REGULAR WATER

☣️ LEAVES AND FLOWER NECTAR ARE POISONOUS IF INGESTED

Kalmia latifolia

Elegant flowering shrubs related to rhododendron, with somewhat similar showy flower clusters. Notable difference is that each long flower stalk bears a small bud resembling a fluted turban; buds open to chalice-shaped blooms with five starlike points. Plants share rhododendron's need for moist atmosphere and well-drained acid soil rich in humus, but take more sun. They tolerate full shade but bloom better with some light.

K. latifolia. MOUNTAIN LAUREL, CALICO BUSH. Zones 3–7, 16, 17, 28 (northernmost Florida), 31–41. Native to eastern North America from Canada to Florida, west across the Appalachians into states drained by the Ohio–Mississippi river systems. Success diminishes the farther west you go into Zones 31, 33, 35, and 41, where summer heat, heavy soils do not suit it. Success also depends on plant source. Plants from southern forms grow better in warmer zones; those from northern seed sources grow better in cold-winter regions. Named selections are unlikely to perform well in all zones listed.

Slow growing to 6–8 ft. or taller, with equal spread. Glossy, leathery, oval leaves are 3–5 in. long, dark green on top, yellowish green beneath.

K

Blooms in late spring; typically bears 1-in.-wide light pink flowers opening from darker pink buds, but blossoms often have subtly different color in their throats and may have contrasting stamens. Flowers are carried in clusters to 5 in. across.

Many named varieties are available. 'Bay State' has coral flowers; 'Bullseye' bears dark purplish red blossoms with white centers; and 'Sarah' has pinkish red blooms opening from deep red buds. 'Olympic Fire' and 'Ostbo Red' have deep red buds opening to palest pink flowers. 'Pinwheel' produces flowers in a combination of deep red and white. Two dwarfs, both growing to 2–2½ ft. tall and 4–5 ft. wide, are 'Elf', with nearly white blossoms; and 'Tiddlywinks', with medium pink blossoms opening from deep pink buds.

K. microphylla (K. polifolia microphylla). WESTERN LAUREL, ALPINE LAUREL. Zones 1–7, 16–17, 38–45. Low plant has spreading branches with erect branchlets, small leaves (dark green above, whitish beneath), and rounded clusters of rose to purple, ½-in. flowers in summer.

Typical high-mountain form is 8–11 in. tall, with leaves up to ¾ in. long. A taller variety (to 2 ft. tall) with slightly larger leaves is *K. m. occidentalis;* it grows in coastal lowlands of California north to Alaska.

KALOPANAX septemlobus (K. pictus)

CASTOR ARALIA, TREE ARALIA

Araliaceae

DECIDUOUS TREE

ZONES 2–6, 32–41

FULL SUN

REGULAR WATER

Kalapanax septemlobus

Unusual in being the only hardy large tree in its family. Also notable for the tropical look conferred by big (7–10-in.) leaves with five to seven lobes. On young trees, leaves may exceed 1 ft. in width. Tree is 40–60 ft. tall, with a spiny trunk and relatively few coarse, spiny branches. Spines eventually disappear from trunk and larger branches. Open and gaunt in youth but eventually develops an attractive rounded habit. Tiny white flowers appear in large (1–2-ft.-wide), flattish clusters at branch ends. Tiny black fruits follow the blossoms; they are quickly consumed by birds.

KANGAROO TREEBINE. See CISSUS antarctica

KATSURA TREE. See CERCIDIPHYLLUM japonicum

KENILWORTH IVY. See CYMBALARIA muralis

KENTIA PALM. See HOWEA

KENTUCKY COFFEE TREE. See GYMNOCLADUS dioica

KENYA IVY. See SENECIO macroglossus

KERRIA japonica

Rosaceae

DECIDUOUS SHRUB

ZONES 2–21, 30–41

TAKES FULL SUN IN COOL-SUMMER AREAS

REGULAR WATER

Kerria japonica 'Pleniflora'

Native to China. Open, graceful, rounded shrub to 6 ft. tall. Slender stems are yellowish green to bright green in winter, providing welcome color in cold climates. Toothed, heavily veined, somewhat triangular, 2–4 in.-long, bright green leaves

unfold early in spring; turn yellow in fall. Flowers come in spring, sporadically into early summer; they look like small, single yellow roses. 'Pleniflora', more commonly planted than the species, has double golden, inch-wide blossoms and taller, suckering habit. 'Picta' has white-edged leaves, single yellow flowers. 'Kinkan' has yellow-striped stems, single yellow blooms.

Give kerria room to display its arching form. It blooms on previous year's wood. Prune heavily after flowering, cutting out branches that have bloomed, all dead or weak wood, and suckers. The green branches are a favorite subject in Japanese wintertime flower arrangements.

KINGFISHER DAISY. See FELICIA bergeriana

KING PALM. See ARCHONTOPHOENIX cunninghamiana

KING'S MANTLE. See THUNBERGIA erecta

KING'S SPEAR. See ASPHODELINE lutea

KINNIKINNICK. See ARCTOSTAPHYLOS uva-ursi

KIRENGESHOMA palmata

YELLOW WAX BELLS

Hydrangeaceae (Saxifragaceae)

PERENNIAL

ZONES 3–9, 14–24, 31–35, 37, 39

PARTIAL SHADE

REGULAR WATER

Kirengeshoma palmata

Attractive plant to 4–4½ ft. tall. Dark purplish or reddish stalks carry deeply lobed and toothed leaves to 8 in. across; flowers, in clusters of three, appear in joints of upper leaves and at top of stalks in late summer and early autumn. Blossoms drooping, narrowly bell shaped, 1½ in. long, pale yellow. A perennial of great elegance for partially shaded border or woodland garden.

KIWI, HARDY KIWI. See ACTINIDIA

KLEINIA. See SENECIO

KNAUTIA

Dipsacaceae

PERENNIALS

ZONES 3–10, 14–24, 31–35, 37, 39

FULL SUN

REGULAR WATER

Knautia macedonica

Related to pincushion flower (*Scabiosa*), with blossoms that are similar in structure—clustered in tight heads above ruffs of leafy bracts on bare stems. Leaves at base of plant are barely lobed, but upper leaves are deeply divided. The two species in cultivation are meadow plants that make few demands on the gardener; they are at home in cottage gardens, perennial borders, and meadow or roadside gardens. Flowers are good for cutting and can be dried for winter use.

K. arvensis. BLUE BUTTONS. Grows 1–4 ft. tall. Blue, 1½-in.-wide flower heads in summer.

K. macedonica. Grows 1½-2 ft. tall and as wide. Deep purplish red flower heads, early summer to fall.

FOR INFORMATION ON YOUR CLIMATE ZONE

PLEASE SEE PAGES 16–78

K

KNIPHOFIA uvaria (Tritoma uvaria)

RED-HOT POKER, TORCH-LILY, POKER PLANT

Liliaceae

PERENNIAL

ZONES 3–9, 14–24, 28–34

FULL SUN OR LIGHT SHADE

REGULAR TO MODERATE WATER

Kniphofia uvaria

Native to South Africa. Has been in cultivation long enough to give rise to garden varieties with some range in size, color. Typical plant is coarse, with large, rather dense clumps of long, grasslike leaves. Flower stalks (always taller than leaves) are about 2 ft. high in dwarf kinds, 3–6 ft. in larger kinds. The many drooping, orange-red or yellow, tubular flowers of the typical plant overlap, forming poker-like clusters 1 ft. long. Named varieties, in both dwarf and taller forms, come in soft or saffron yellow, creamy white, or coral. Flowers attract hummingbirds, are good in flower arrangements.

Plants require excellent drainage. Bloom spring and summer; exact flowering time depends on variety. Cut out flower spikes after bloom. Where winter temperatures drop to 0°F/–18°C or below, tie foliage over clump to protect growing points. In warmer areas, cut foliage to ground in autumn. Clumps will grow undisturbed for many years. To increase plantings, carefully dig and remove young plants from clump's edge. Useful in large borders with other robust perennials such as daylilies, globe thistle.

KNOTWEED. See POLYGONUM

KOCHIA scoparia

SUMMER CYPRESS

Chenopodiaceae

ANNUAL

ALL ZONES

FULL SUN

REGULAR WATER

Kochia scoparia

To 3 ft. high, with branches densely clothed with narrow, soft, light green leaves, making plant too dense to see through. Grow individually for its gently rounded form, or group plants for low, temporary hedge or edging. Can be sheared into any shape. Plant from seed. Tolerates high heat and will perform well in short-summer areas.

K. s. trichophylla. MEXICAN FIRE BUSH, BURNING BUSH. Same as above, but foliage turns red at first frost. Can reseed profusely enough to become pest; hoe out unwanted seedlings when small.

KOELREUTERIA

Sapindaceae

DECIDUOUS TREES

ZONES VARY BY SPECIES

FULL SUN

REGULAR TO MODERATE WATER

Koelreuteria paniculata

Small trees native to Asia. Noted for large, loose clusters of yellow flowers followed by fat, papery fruit capsules resembling little Japanese lanterns; capsules are used in arrangements. Good patio, lawn, or street trees. Very adaptable to different soils as long as soil is fairly well-drained. Control self-sown seedlings.

K. bipinnata (K. integrifoliola). CHINESE FLAME TREE. Zones 8–24, 26, 28–31; warmer parts of 32, 33. To 20–40 ft. or taller; spreading and eventually flat topped. Leaves 1–2 ft. long, divided into many oval leaflets; turn yellow for short time before dropping. Flower clusters in late summer are similar to those of *K. paniculata*, but 2-in. fruit capsules are more colorful: orange, red, or salmon, appearing soon after flowers and persisting into fall. Stake and prune tree to develop high branching. Roots deep, not invasive; good tree to plant under.

K. elegans (K. formosana, K. henryi). FLAMEGOLD. Zones 14–28. To 20–30 ft. tall, round headed. Similar to the other species, but not as cold hardy and less widely sold. Fall flowers are followed by pinkish capsules that hang on into December.

K. paniculata. GOLDENRAIN TREE. Zones 2–21, 28–41. To 20–35 ft., with 10–40-ft. spread. Open branching, giving slight shade. Leaves to 15 in. long with 7–15 oval, toothed or lobed leaflets, each 1–3 in. long. New leaves are purplish, turning bright green in summer; yellow to gold fall color unreliable. Very showy flower clusters, 8–14 in. long, in early to midsummer. Fruit capsules red when young, maturing to buff and brown shades; last well into autumn. Tree takes cold, heat, drought, wind. Prune to shape; can be gawky without pruning. Variety called 'Kew' or 'Fastigiata', to 25 ft. tall by 3 ft. wide, is occasionally offered.

KOHLRABI

Brassicaceae (Cruciferae)

BIENNIAL GROWN AS ANNUAL

ALL ZONES

FULL SUN

REGULAR WATER

Kohlrabi

Cool-season vegetable related to cabbage. Edible part is an enlarged, bulblike portion of the stem, formed just above soil surface. Standard varieties are 'Early White Vienna' and 'Early Purple Vienna'; these are similar in size and flavor, differing only in skin color. Other white varieties include disease-resistant 'Triumph' and early 'Grand Duke'. Plants are very fast growing, ready to harvest in 50 to 60 days from seed. Sow seed ½ in. deep in rich soil, about 2 weeks after average date of last frost. Follow first planting with successive sowings 2 weeks apart. In areas with warm winters, plant again in late fall and early winter. Space rows 1½ ft. apart; thin seedlings to 4 in. apart. Harvest when round portions are 2–3 in. wide; slice and eat raw, or cook like turnips. Not usually bothered by pests or diseases.

KOLKWITZIA amabilis

BEAUTY BUSH

Caprifoliaceae

DECIDUOUS SHRUB

ZONES 2–11, 14–20, 31–41

FULL SUN OR PARTIAL SHADE

REGULAR WATER

Kolkwitzia amabilis

Native to China. Graceful, upright growth to 10–12 ft.; arching form in partial shade, denser and shorter in full sun. Gray-green leaves to 3 in. long sometimes turn reddish in fall. Blooms heavily in mid- to late spring, bearing clusters of small, yellow-throated pink flowers. Blossoms are followed by conspicuous pinkish brown, bristly fruits that prolong color display. Brown, flaky bark gradually peels from stems during winter.

Adapts to many soils and climates. Flowers are borne on wood formed the previous year. Thin out oldest stems after blossoms have faded; or, to enjoy the fruit, prune lightly in early spring. Plant can be renewed by cutting to ground after bloom.

K

KOREAN FORSYTHIA. See FORSYTHIA ovata

KOREAN GRASS. See ZOYSIA tenuifolia

KUMQUAT. See CITRUS

Labiatae. See Lamiaceae

LABURNUM

GOLDENCHAIN TREE

Fabaceae (Leguminosae)

DECIDUOUS LARGE SHRUBS OR SMALL TREES

⚡ ZONES 3–9, 14–17, 34, 36–39

☼ ◗ AFTERNOON SHADE IN HOT AREAS

🔴 REGULAR WATER

🔻 SEEDPODS ARE POISONOUS IF INGESTED

Laburnum wateteri

Upright growth; usually pruned into single-stemmed tree, but can be shrubby if permitted to keep basal suckers and low branches. Green bark; bright green leaves divided into three leaflets (like clover). Handsome in bloom: in mid- to late spring, bears yellow, sweet pea–shaped flowers in hanging clusters like wisteria. Use as a single tree in lawn or border; group in front of neutral background; or space regularly in long border of perennials, rhododendrons, or lilacs.

Provide well-drained soil. Prune and trim regularly to keep tidy. If possible, remove seedpods; not only are they toxic, but a heavy crop drains the plant's strength. Trees perform best in northeastern U.S. and Pacific Coast states; they grow poorly or fail in lower Midwest and lower South.

L. alpinum. SCOTCH LABURNUM. To 30–35 ft. tall. Flower clusters 10–15 in. long. 'Pendulum' has weeping branches.

L. anagyroides. COMMON GOLDENCHAIN. To 20–30 ft. tall; often bushy and wide spreading. Flower clusters 6–10 in. long. Like *L. alpinum*, it has a weeping variety, 'Pendulum'.

L. watereri. Hybrid between the two preceding species. To about 25 ft. tall. Flower clusters 10–20 in. long. 'Vossii' is the most widely grown and most graceful variety; it can be espaliered.

LACHENALIA

CAPE COWSLIP

Liliaceae

BULBS

⚡ ZONES 16, 17, 23, 24; OR GROW IN POTS

☼ ◗ LIGHT SHADE IN HOT-SUMMER AREAS

🔴 REGULAR WATER DURING GROWTH AND BLOOM

Lachenalia bulbiferum

Native to South Africa. Strap-shaped, succulent leaves, often brown spotted. Tubular, pendulous flowers in spikes on thick, fleshy stems bloom in winter, early spring.

In the ground, best in mild-winter, dry-summer regions. In Zones 25–27, grow outdoors in containers (six in a 6-in. pot); protect from summer rain. Elsewhere, grow in pots in the house or greenhouse. Plant in late summer; set bulbs 1–1½ in. deep. Outdoors, water sparingly until growth starts, then give regular moisture until foliage yellows. Then gradually let plants dry out and keep as dry as possible until next fall. After planting for indoor bloom, water thoroughly and keep cool and dark until leaves appear; then bring into light, provide cool (50°F/10°C) night temperatures, and feed when flower spikes show. Store bulbs dry in pots over summer.

L. aloides (L. tricolor). Flowers yellow, inner segments tipped red, outer tipped green, on stems 1 ft. tall or less. Usually two leaves to a plant, 1 in. wide, as tall as flower stems or even taller. 'Aurea' has bright orange-yellow blooms; 'Nelsonii', bright yellow tinged green; 'Pearsonii', slightly taller, yellow orange with reddish orange buds and flower bases.

L. bulbiferum (L. pendula). Basal leaves to 2 in. wide. Flowers 1½ in. long, coral red and yellow, purple tipped, in spikes 12–15 in. tall. 'Superba', improved form, has orange-red flowers.

L. contaminata. Leaves bright green, to 9 in. long, nearly erect. Flower spikes to 8 in. long, narrow, packed with roundish, ½-in. flowers in white tinged red or brown.

LADY BELLS. See ADENOPHORA

LADY FERN. See ATHYRIUM filix-femina

LADY PALM. See RHAPIS

LADY'S-MANTLE. See ALCHEMILLA

LADY'S SLIPPER. See PAPHIOPEDILUM

LAELIA

Orchidaceae

EPIPHYTIC ORCHIDS

⚡ ZONES 16, 17, 21–27; OR GREENHOUSE OR HOUSE PLANTS

◗ FILTERED SHADE

🔴 REGULAR WATER

Laelia anceps

Resemble cattleyas in foliage and flowers. Most have blossoms in the white, pink, lavender, and purple range, though colors do include red, orange, and yellow. Grow on slab of tree bark or tree fern stem (hapuu), or in coarse bark or similar fast-draining material. Tack slabs on patio wall or hang from tree trunk; or grow in pots on patio. In zones listed, plants usually can be left outdoors in sheltered locations year-round; bring inside when frost is predicted. Indoor plants can be brought outdoors during warm season. During summer, feed several times with fish emulsion or fertilizer packaged especially for orchids. Let potting medium dry out between waterings.

L. albida. Fragrant blossoms carried two to eight per stem; flowers are transparent white, 2 in. wide, with yellow rib in throat and lavender flush in lip. Winter and early spring bloom. Oval, 1–2-in.-high pseudobulbs are topped by pair of narrow leaves to 9 in. long.

L. anceps. Flowers to 4 in. across, rose violet with yellow throat lined purple; carried two to six per stem. Fall and winter bloom. Four-sided pseudobulbs, 3–5 in. high, bear one or two 5–9-in.-long leaves. Repot as infrequently as possible.

L. autumnalis. Fragrant, 4-in., rose purple flowers with white at base of lip; borne three to nine on erect stem. Fall and winter bloom. Pseudobulbs are 2–4 in. high, bear two or three leathery, 4–8-in.-long leaves.

LAGENARIA. See GOURD

LAGERSTROEMIA

CRAPE MYRTLE

Lythraceae

DECIDUOUS SHRUBS OR TREES

⚡ ZONES VARY BY SPECIES

☼ FULL SUN

🔴 MODERATE WATER

Lagerstroemia indica

The crape myrtles are among the most satisfactory of plants for hot-summer regions: showy summer flowers, attractive bark, and (in many cases) brilliant fall color make them year-round garden performers. Long, cool autumns yield the

L

best leaf display; the first hard frost spoils the show. (In cool-summer regions, these plants flower less, and mildew is a more serious problem on susceptible varieties.)

Most crape myrtles seen in gardens are varieties of *L. indica* or hybrids of that species with *L. fauriei*. The latter species has recently attracted notice for its hardiness and exceptionally showy bark. Queen's crape myrtle, *L. speciosa*, grows only in the warmest gardens.

All crape myrtles bloom on new wood and should be pruned in winter or early spring to increase next summer's flowers. On small, shrubby forms, remove spent flower clusters and thin out small twiggy growth; to maintain compactness and eliminate leggy look, cut branches nearly to the ground in spring. On large shrubs and trees, shorten branches by 1–1½ ft. in spring if you need to limit their size. Heavy watering and any fertilizing in summer can significantly decrease hardiness in marginal climates.

L. fauriei. JAPANESE CRAPE MYRTLE. Zones 7–10, 12–14, 18–21, 25–31; warmer parts of 32, 33. Tree to 20–30 ft. with erect habit and outward-arching branches. Leaves light green, to 4 in. long and 2 in. wide, turning yellow in fall. Especially handsome bark: the smooth, gray outer bark flakes away to reveal glossy cinnamon brown bark beneath. Small white flowers are borne in 2–4-in.-long clusters; usually pauses after initial bloom, then flowers again in late summer. Resistant to mildew and best known as a parent of hardy, mildew-resistant hybrids with *L. indica*, though it is handsome in its own right. 'Fantasy', with even showier bark than the species, has a vase form—narrow below, spreading above. 'Kiowa' has outstanding cinnamon-colored bark that is uniform, not in patches.

L. indica. CRAPE MYRTLE. Zones 7–10, 12–14, 18–21, 25–31; warmer parts of 32. Shrub or tree where hardy, but capable of blooming from first-year regrowth if frozen to the ground. Behaves much like perennial in Zones 3–6, 33, 35. Variable in size (some forms are dwarf shrubs, others large shrubs or small trees) and habit (spreading to upright). Dark green leaves are 1–2½ in. long and somewhat narrower, usually tinted red on unfurling, often turning brilliant orange or red in fall. Crinkled, crepe-papery, 1–1½-in.-wide flowers in white or shades of pink, red, or purple are carried in dense clusters.

Trained as a tree, it develops an attractive trunk and branch pattern. Smooth gray or light brown bark peels off to reveal smooth, pinkish inner bark; winter trunk and branches seem polished.

The following list includes many of the best selections. Mildew can be a problem. Spray before plants bloom; or grow mildew-resistant hybrids of *L. indica* with *L. fauriei* (see list further down).

'Catawba'. Roundish, dense 6–10-ft. shrub (can be trained as a 15-ft. tree). Dark purple flowers. Orange-red fall color.

'Centennial'. Dwarf roundish shrub to 3 ft. high. Lavender flowers. Orange autumn foliage.

'Centennial Spirit'. Multistemmed large shrub or small tree to 20 ft. Dark red flowers. Orange-red fall color.

'Chica Pink' and 'Chica Red'. Compact, dense, 3–4 ft. tall and as wide. Bright pink or rosy red flowers. Yellow fall foliage.

'Glendora White'. Upright shrub to 9 ft. tall or, with training, a 25-ft. tree 20 ft. wide. White flowers. Red fall color.

'Peppermint Lace'. Somewhat erect shrub 6–7 ft. tall, or tree to 20 ft. high. Flowers are deep pink with a picotee edge of white. 'Prairie Lace' is similar in flower, but is a smaller (4–6-ft.) shrub. 'Queen's Lace', 12–14 ft. tall, is a hardier selection with similar flowers. All have red to red-orange fall foliage.

Petite series. These are semidwarf shrubs (5 ft. tall, 4 ft. wide) with names that describe their flower color: 'Petite Embers', 'Petite Orchid', 'Petite Pinkie', 'Petite Plum', 'Petite Red Imp', and 'Petite Snow'. Yellow fall foliage.

'Victor'. Compact shrub to 3 ft. tall. Dark red flowers. Red-tinged leaves turn reddish yellow in autumn.

The following are mildew-resistant hybrids between *L. indica* and *L. fauriei*. The products of a breeding program at the National Arboretum, they bear the names of Indian tribes.

'Acoma'. Spreading, arching shrub to 10 ft. tall and as wide. White flowers in 6–7 in. clusters. Reddish purple fall foliage.

'Comanche'. Large, spreading shrub to 12 ft. tall; can be trained as small tree. Bright red flowers. Reddish orange fall color.

'Hopi'. Shrubby plant 7 ft. tall, half again as wide. Pink flowers. Orange-red to dark red fall foliage.

'Muskogee'. Fast-growing large shrub or small tree to 20 ft. or more. Beige bark. Large clusters of lavender pink flowers. Red fall color.

'Natchez'. Fast-growing small tree to over 20 ft. tall and broad, with exceptionally handsome glossy brown bark. Large clusters of white flowers. Orange to red autumn foliage color.

'Seminole'. Shrub to 7–8 ft. tall and nearly as wide; can be trained into a 15–20 ft. tree. Large roundish clusters of pure medium pink flowers. Yellow fall color.

'Tonto'. Shrub to 8 ft. tall and 6 ft. wide, with beige bark. Bright magenta flowers.

'Tuskegee'. Small tree with multitrunked habit and horizontal branching; grows to 14 ft. high, 18 ft. wide. Deep pink to nearly red flowers. Orange-red fall foliage.

'Yuma'. Small multitrunked tree over 10 ft. tall and nearly as wide. Lavender flowers. Fall color yellowish to brownish red.

'Zuni'. Multistemmed shrub to 9 ft. tall and 8 ft. wide. Dark lavender (nearly purple) flowers. Orange-red to dark red fall foliage.

L. speciosa. QUEEN'S CRAPE MYRTLE. Zone 25. Large tree (to 80 ft. tall), with leaves 8–12 in. long, 4 in. wide. White to purple flowers are borne in clusters to 16 in. long. 'Majestic Orchid', a hybrid between this tree and *L. indica*, is as hardy as the latter. It grows 20 ft. tall and 15 ft. wide, with large clusters of deep orchid purple flowers and foliage that turns yellow in fall.

LAGUNARIA patersonii

PRIMROSE TREE, COW ITCH TREE

Malvaceae

EVERGREEN TREE

ZONES 13, 15–26

FULL SUN

MODERATE WATER

Lagunaria patersonii

Native to South Pacific and Australia. Rather fast growth to 20–40 ft. Young trees narrow and erect; old trees sometimes spreading, flat topped. Densely foliaged. Thick, oval, 2–4-in.-long leaves are olive green above, gray beneath. Blooms in summer, bearing hibiscuslike, 2-in.-wide, pink to rose flowers that fade to nearly white. 'Royal Purple' has purple blossoms. Brown seed capsules, popular with flower arrangers, hang on for a long time; they split into five sections, revealing bright brown seeds. Handle carefully; pods contain short, stiff fibers that can irritate skin.

Tolerates wide variety of soils and growing conditions. Resists ocean wind, salt spray; tolerates intense heat. Foliage is damaged at 25°F/−4°C but recovers quickly. Blooms best in coastal conditions. Plant individually as garden tree or in groups as showy windbreak or screen.

LAMB'S EARS. See STACHYS byzantina

Lamiaceae. Members of the mint family of herbaceous plants and shrubs are easily recognized by their square stems, leaves in opposite pairs, and whorled flowers in spikelike, sometimes branched, clusters. Many of the group are aromatic; the family contains most of the familiar kitchen herbs, including basil (*Ocimum*), mint (*Mentha*), oregano (*Origanum*), and sage (*Salvia*). Many have attractive foliage or flowers (*Coleus*, sage). This family was previously called Labiatae.

LAMIASTRUM galeobdolon. See LAMIUM galeobdolon

LAMIUM

DEAD NETTLE

Lamiaceae (Labiatae)

PERENNIALS

⚡ ZONES 1–24, 32–43

◐ ● PARTIAL OR FULL SHADE

🌢 REGULAR WATER

Lamium maculatum

Leaves in opposite pairs are heart shaped, toothed, marked with white. Clustered flowers are pink, white, or yellow. All are vigorous growers that thrive in shade. One species is used as a ground cover.

L. galeobdolon (Galeobdolon luteum, Lamiastrum galeobdolon). YELLOW ARCHANGEL. Upright to 2 ft., slowly spreading to form tight clumps. Yellow flowers are unimportant. Best-known selection is 'Herman's Pride', with leaves evenly streaked and spotted with white.

L. maculatum. DEAD NETTLE, SPOTTED NETTLE. Evergreen in mild climates but winter-deciduous elsewhere. Running or trailing perennial used as a ground cover or in hanging baskets. To 6 in. tall, spreading 2–3 ft. Grayish green leaves have silvery markings. Pink flowers bloom spring into summer. Species is vigorous, even weedy, and is planted less frequently than its choicer varieties. These include 'Beacon Silver', with pink flowers and green-edged, silvery gray leaves; 'White Nancy', a 'Beacon Silver' with white blooms; 'Chequers', with pink blossoms and green leaves with a white center stripe; and 'Pink Pewter', with abundant pink flowers above silvery leaves edged gray green. All varieties nicely light up shady areas of the garden. They need some periodic grooming to remove old, shabby growth.

LAMPRANTHUS

ICE PLANT

Aizoaceae

SUCCULENT SUBSHRUBS

⚡ ZONES 14–26

☼ FULL SUN

🌢 TAKE CONSIDERABLE DROUGHT

Lampranthus spectabilis

Most of the blindingly brilliant ice plants with large flowers belong to this genus. Plants erect or trailing, woody at base; fleshy leaves are cylindrical or three-sided. Select in bloom for the color you want. Cut back lightly after bloom to eliminate fruit capsules, encourage new leafy growth. Provide well-drained soil. Good at seashore. Attract bees.

L. aurantiacus. To 10–15 in. tall. Gray-green, inch-long, three-sided leaves. Flowers (midwinter into spring) 1½–2 in. across, bright orange. 'Glaucus' has bright yellow flowers; 'Sunman' has golden yellow flowers. Plant 15–18 in. apart for bedding, borders, low bank cover.

L. filicaulis. REDONDO CREEPER. Thin, creeping stems; finely textured foliage. Spreads slowly to form mats about 3 in. deep. Small pink flowers bloom in early spring. Use for small-scale ground cover, mound, or low bank cover.

L. productus. To 15 in. tall, spreading to 1½–2 ft. Gray-green, fleshy leaves tipped bronze. Purple, 1-in.-wide flowers. Blooms heavily early winter into spring; scattered bloom at other times. Plant 1–1½ ft. apart.

L. spectabilis. TRAILING ICE PLANT. Sprawling or trailing, to 1 ft. tall, 1½–2 ft. wide. Gray-green foliage. Makes carpets of gleaming color from late winter to spring. Flowers 2–2½ in. across, very heavily borne. Available in pink, rose pink, red, purple. Set plants 1–1½ ft. apart.

LANTANA

Verbenaceae

EVERGREEN SHRUBS

⚡ ZONES 8–10, 12–30; SEE BELOW

☼ FULL SUN

🌢 MODERATE WATER

☙ FRUITS ARE POISONOUS IF INGESTED

Lantana montevidensis

Fast growing, valued for profuse show of color over long season—every month of the year in frost-free areas. Light frosts merely keep plants in check. Heavier freezes—possible in Zones 8–10, 14, 29, 30—may seriously damage on kill plants in some (but not all) winters. In colder zones, grow lantana as a summer annual.

Prone to mildew in shade or during prolonged overcast weather. Prune hard in spring to remove dead wood and prevent woodiness. Feed lightly. Too much water and fertilizer cuts down on bloom. Shrubby kinds used as substitutes for annuals in beds or containers, as low hedges or foundation shrubs. Spreading kinds are excellent bank covers, will control erosion. Effective spilling from raised beds, planter boxes, or hanging baskets. Crushed foliage has a pungent odor that some people find objectionable.

L. camara. One of two species used in hybridizing. Coarse, upright to 6 ft. Rough dark green leaves. Yellow, orange, or red flowers in 1–2-in. clusters.

L. montevidensis (L. sellowiana). The other species used in breeding. This one is sold at nurseries. A little hardier than *L. camara*, it's a ground cover with branches trailing to 3 ft. or even 6 ft. Dark green, 1-in.-long leaves with coarsely toothed edges are sometimes tinged red or purplish, especially in cold weather. Rosy lilac flowers in 1–1½-in.-wide clusters. 'Lavender Swirl' is larger form that produces lavender, white, and mixed flower clusters. 'White Lightnin' is similar but has pure white flowers.

The following list gives some of the named kinds of lantana that are available. Some are merely forms of *L. camara*, or are hybrids between the forms. Others are hybrids between *L. camara* and *L. montevidensis*.

'Christine'. To 6 ft. tall, 5 ft. wide. Cerise pink. Can be trained into small patio tree.

'Confetti'. To 2–3 ft. by 6–8 ft. Blossoms mix yellow, pink, and purple.

'Cream Carpet'. To 2–3 ft. by 6–8 ft. Cream with bright yellow throat.

'Dwarf Pink'. To 2–4 ft. by 3–4 ft. Light pink. Rather tender.

'Dwarf White'. To 2–4 ft. by 3–4 ft.

'Dwarf Yellow'. To 2–4 ft. high and wide.

'Gold Rush'. To 1½–2 ft. by 4–6 ft. Rich golden yellow.

'Irene'. To 3 ft. by 4 ft. Compact. Magenta with lemon yellow.

'Lemon Swirl'. Slow growing to 2 ft. tall, 3 ft. wide. Yellow flowers, bright yellow band around each leaf.

'Radiation'. To 3–5 ft. high and wide. Rich orange red.

'Spreading Sunset'. To 2–3 ft. by 6–8 ft. Vivid orange red.

'Spreading Sunshine'. To 2–3 ft. by 6–8 ft. Bright yellow.

'Sunburst'. To 2–3 ft. by 6–8 ft. Bright golden yellow.

'Tangerine'. To 2–3 ft. by 6–8 ft. Burnt orange.

LARCH. See LARIX

LARIX

LARCH

Pinaceae

DECIDUOUS TREES

⚡ ZONES VARY BY SPECIES

☼ FULL SUN

🌢 REGULAR WATER

Larix decidua

Slender pyramids with horizontal branches and drooping branchlets. Needles (½–1½ in. long) soft to touch, in fluffy tufts. Woody, roundish cones, ½–1½ in. long, are scattered all along branchlets. Notable for color in spring and fall and for winter silhouette. In spring, new needle tufts are pale green and new cones bright purple red. In fall, needles turn brilliant yellow and orange before dropping. Winter interest is enhanced by many cones, which create a delightful polka-dot pattern against the sky. Best in regions with relatively cool summers and cool to cold winters. Not particular about soils. Plant with dark evergreen conifers as background or near water for reflection. Larches attract birds.

L. decidua (L. europaea). EUROPEAN LARCH. Zones 1–9, 14–17, 36–45. Moderate to fast growth to 30–60 ft. Summer foliage color is grass green. Branches of 'Pendula' arch out and down; branchlets hang nearly straight down.

L. kaempferi. JAPANESE LARCH. Zones 1–9, 14–19, 32, 34, 36–45. Fast growing to 60 ft. or more but can be dwarfed in containers. Summer foliage is a soft bluish green. 'Pendula' has long, weeping branches.

L. laricina. AMERICAN LARCH. Zones 37–45. Native to northern U.S. and much of Canada. Slow to medium growth to 40–80 ft. tall. Bright blue-green summer foliage. Grows well in moist to boggy soils.

LARKSPUR. See CONSOLIDA ambigua

LATHYRUS

SWEET PEA

Fabaceae (Leguminosae)

ANNUAL OR PERENNIAL VINES

⚡ ZONES VARY BY SPECIES

☼ FULL SUN

🌢◆ WATER NEEDS VARY BY SPECIES

Lathyrus odoratus

In this group is one of the best-known garden flowers—the delightfully fragrant and colorful sweet pea.

Throughout this book you will find flowers described as "sweet pea shaped." The flower of the sweet pea is typical of the many members of the pea family (Fabaceae). Each flower has one large, upright, roundish petal (banner or standard), two narrow side petals (wings), and two lower petals that are somewhat united, forming a boat-shaped structure (keel).

L. latifolius. PERENNIAL SWEET PEA. Zones 1–24, 29–45. Strong-growing vine up to 9 ft., with blue-green foliage. Flowers usually reddish purple, often white or pink. Single colors are sometimes sold. Blooms all summer if not allowed to go to seed. Plants grow with little care, tolerate aridity. May escape and become naturalized. Use as bank cover, trailing over rocks, on trellis or fence.

L. odoratus. SWEET PEA. Winter, spring, or summer annual. All zones, but performance is curtailed by heat. Bears many spikelike clusters of crisp-looking flowers with a clean, sweet fragrance, in single colors and mixtures. Color mixtures include deep rose, blue, purple, scarlet, white, cream, amethyst on white ground, salmon, salmon pink on cream. Sweet peas make magnificent cut flowers in quantity. Bush types offer cut flowers the same as vine types and require no training.

To hasten germination, soak seeds for a few hours before planting. Treat seeds with fungicide. Sow seeds 1 in. deep and 1–2 in. apart. When seedlings are 4–5 in. high, thin to at least 6 in. apart. Pinch out tops to encourage strong side branches. Where climate prevents early planting or soil is too wet to work, start three or four seeds in each 2¼–3-in. peat pot, indoors or in protected place, and set out when weather has settled. Plant peat pots 1 ft. apart, thinning each to one strong plant. This method is ideal for bush types. Never let vines lack for water; soak heavily. To prolong bloom, cut flowers at least every other day and remove all seedpods. Regular monthly feeding with commercial fertilizer will keep vines vigorous and productive.

For vining sweet peas, provide trellis, strings, or wire before planting. Seedlings need support as soon as tendrils form. Freestanding trellis run-

ning north and south is best. When planting against fence or wall, keep supports away from wall to give air circulation.

The following describes vine-type sweet peas (grouped by time of bloom) and bush types.

Early flowering. (Early Flowering Multiflora, Early Multiflora, formerly Early Spencers.) The name "Spencer" once described a type of frilled flower (with wavy petals) that is now characteristic of almost all varieties. "Multiflora" indicates that the plants carry more flowers per stem than the old Spencers did. The value of early-flowering varieties is that they will bloom in winter when days are short. (Spring- and summer-flowering types will not bloom until days have lengthened to 15 hours or more.) Where winter temperatures are mild, sow seeds in August or early September for late December or January bloom. Use these varieties for forcing in greenhouse. They are not heat resistant. Generally sold in mixed colors.

Spring flowering. (Spring-Flowering, Heat-Resistant Cuthbertson Type, Cuthbertson's Floribunda, Floribunda-Zvolanek strain.) Both mixtures and single-color named varieties are available in seed packets. Wide color range: pink, lavender, purple, white, cream, rose, salmon, cerise, carmine, red, blue. Royal or Royal Family is somewhat larger flowered and more heat resistant than the others. In mild-winter climates, plant between October and early January. Elsewhere, plant just as soon as soil can be worked.

Summer flowering. (Galaxy, Plenti-flora.) Available in named varieties and mixtures in wide color range. Heat resistant; bloom from early summer on. Large flowers are borne five to seven to each long stem. Heat resistance is not great enough for hottest summer areas.

Bush type. The so-called bush-type sweet peas are strong vines with predetermined growth, heights. Unlike vining types that reach 5 ft. and more, these stop their upward growth at 1–2½ ft. Suitable for all regions.

Bijou. To 1 ft. Full color range in mixtures and single varieties. Four or five flowers on 5–7-in. stems. Useful and spectacular in borders, beds, window boxes, containers. Not as heat resistant or as long stemmed as Knee-Hi; performs better in containers.

Cupid. Grows 4–6 in. tall, 1½ ft. wide. Trails on ground or hangs from container.

Jet Set. Bushy, self-supporting plants 2–3 ft. tall. All colors.

Knee-Hi. To 2½ ft. Large, long-stemmed flowers, five or six to the stem. Has all the virtues and color range of the spring-flowering types, on self-supporting, bush-type vines. Provides cutting-type flowers in mass display in beds and borders. Growth will exceed 2½ ft. where planting bed joins fence or wall. Keep in open area for uniform height. Follow same planting dates as for spring-flowering sweet peas.

Little Sweethearts. Rounded bushes, 8 in. tall, bloom over a long season. Full range of colors. Patio strain grows 9 in. tall. Snoopea (12–15 in.) and Supersnoop (2 ft.) need no support, come in full range of sweet pea colors.

GETTING SWEET PEAS OFF TO A FINE START

In less-than-perfect soil, prepare ground for sweet peas like this. Dig trench 1–1½ ft. deep. Mix 1 part peat moss or other soil conditioner to 2 parts soil. As you mix, add complete commercial fertilizer according to label directions. Backfill trench with mix; plant seeds in it.

Lauraceae. The laurel family contains evergreen and deciduous trees and shrubs with inconspicuous flowers and (usually) aromatic foliage. Fruits are fleshy, containing a single seed. Examples are avocado, camphor tree *(Cinnamomum),* and sweet bay *(Laurus).*

LAUREL. See LAURUS nobilis, PRUNUS

FOR INFORMATION ON SELECTING PLANTS
PLEASE SEE PAGES 79–160

LAURENTIA fluviatilis (Isotoma fluviatilis)

BLUE STAR CREEPER

Campanulaceae (Lobeliaceae)

PERENNIAL GROUND COVER

▨ ZONES 4–9, 14–24; GROW AS ANNUAL IN COLDER CLIMATES

☼ ◗ PARTIAL SHADE IN HOT AREAS

🌢 REGULAR WATER

Laurentia fluviatilis

C reeping, spreading plant that grows only 2–3 in. tall. Pointed, oval leaves ¼ in. long give plant look of baby's tears *(Soleirolia)*. Pale blue, starlike flowers, slightly broader than the leaves, spangle plantings in late spring and summer, with a scattering at other times. Can take light foot traffic. Plant pieces 6–12 in. apart for cover within a year. Feed lightly once a month, spring to fall. Recently renamed *Pratia pedunculata*.

LAURUS nobilis

SWEET BAY, GRECIAN LAUREL

Lauraceae

EVERGREEN SHRUB OR TREE

▨ ZONES 5–9, 12–24; OR GROW IN POTS

☼ ◗ FULL SUN OR PARTIAL SHADE

🌢 MODERATE WATER

Laurus nobilis

S low growth to 12–40 ft. Natural habit is compact, broad-based—often that of a multistemmed, gradually tapering cone. Leaves are leathery, aromatic, oval, 2–4 in. long, dark green; traditional bay leaf of cookery. Clusters of small yellow flowers are followed by ½–1-in.-long, black or dark purple berries. 'Saratoga' has broader leaves and a more treelike habit.

Not fussy about soil but needs good drainage. Tends to sucker heavily. Dense habit makes it a good large background shrub, screen, or small tree. Takes well to clipping into standards, hedges, or topiary shapes such as globes and cones. A classic formal container plant. In zones too cold for growing sweet bay in the ground, grow it in a container so it can be moved to the protection of a greenhouse or cool, well-lighted room when temperatures reach about 20°F/−7°C.

LAURUSTINUS. See VIBURNUM tinus

LAVANDIN. See LAVANDULA intermedia

LAVANDULA

LAVENDER

Lamiaceae (Labiatae)

EVERGREEN SHRUBS OR SUBSHRUBS

▨ ZONES VARY BY SPECIES

☼ FULL SUN

🌢 MODERATE WATER

Lavandula angustifolia

N ative to Mediterranean region. Prized for its fragrant lavender or purple flowers; those of some species are used for perfume, sachets. Aromatic grayish or gray-green foliage. Plant as hedge or edging, in herb gardens, or in borders with plants needing similar conditions—sunrose, nepeta, rosemary, santolina, verbena.

Lavenders require full sun, well-drained soil, little or no fertilizer. Their downfall is humidity accompanied by heat; they will succeed in cool coastal climates but not in steamy heat. Prune immediately after bloom to keep plants compact and neat. For sachets, cut flower clusters or strip flowers from stems just as color shows; dry in cool, shady place.

Since lavenders have been in cultivation for centuries and tend to interbreed, many varieties and hybrids have arisen, and names are difficult to sort out. Some of the names that follow may not agree with those you see on nursery labels.

L. angustifolia (L. officinalis, L. spica, L. vera). ENGLISH LAVENDER. Zones 4–24, 30, 32–34, 39. Hardiest species and the one most widely planted. The classic lavender used for perfume and sachets. To 3–4 ft. high and wide. Narrow, smooth-edged gray leaves to 2 in. long; lavender, ½-in.-long flowers in 1½–2-ft.-high spikes in late spring or summer. Many varieties exist, among them the following:

'Alba'. To 3 ft. high, with pure white flower spikes above gray-green foliage.

'Compacta' ('Compacta Nana', 'Dwarf Blue'). Dark blue flowers on an 8–12-in. plant.

'Grey Lady'. To 1½ ft. tall. Silvery gray foliage, lavender blue flowers.

'Hidcote'. To 15–20 in. tall. Deep purplish blue flowers, gray foliage.

'Irene Doyle'. To 1½ ft. high. Lavender blue flowers in summer; reblooms in early fall.

'Jean Davis'. Pale pink flowers above gray-green foliage on a 1½-ft. plant.

'Lavender Lady'. To 10 in. tall; gray foliage, lavender flowers. Fast grower, often blooming first year from seed.

'Mitcham's Gray'. Similar to 'Hidcote', but slightly taller and with lighter blue flowers.

'Munstead'. Compact plant to 1–1½ ft. Medium blue flowers. Long blooming; good for edging.

'Rosea'. Pink flowers on a 15-in. plant.

'Twickel Purple'. Dense, compact grower to 1½ ft. high, with heavy, thick spikes of light purple flowers.

L. dentata. FRENCH LAVENDER. Zones 8, 9, 12–24, 31. To 3 ft. tall. Narrow gray-green leaves, 1–1½ in. long, with square-toothed edges. Lavender purple flowers in short spikelike clusters, each topped with tuft of petal-like bracts. Long spring–summer flowering period; almost continuous bloom in mild-winter areas.

L. d. candicans, with somewhat larger leaves than the species, has dense grayish white down on young foliage.

L. intermedia. LAVANDIN. Zones 4–24, 30–34, 39. Group of hybrids between *L. angustifolia* and *L. latifolia*. All are vigorous, highly fragrant plants. About as hardy as English lavender parent, but more tolerant of warm, humid summers. Early to midsummer bloom. Includes 'Dutch', with 16-in. mounds of gray foliage and 3-ft. stems topped with dark purple flowers; 'Grappenhall', with dark violet spikes on 3½-ft. stems above 14-in. foliage mounds; 'Grosso', possibly the most fragrant of all, with compact, 8-in.-high mounds of silvery foliage and large, fat purple spikes on 2½-ft. stems; and 'Provence', a 2-ft. plant (to 3–4 ft. in bloom) with light purple flower spikes.

L. lanata. Zones 8, 9, 12–24, 31. Grows to 3 ft. tall. Woolly white stems and leaves. Leaves 2 in. long, ½ in. wide; flower spikes deep purple, 1–4 in. long. Bloom period same as for English lavender.

L. latifolia. SPIKE LAVENDER. Zones 4–24, 30, 32–34, 39. Much like English lavender in appearance, but with broader leaves and much-branched flower stalks. Bloom period same as for English lavender.

L. pinnata buchii, L. canariensis, L. multifida. Zones 16–24. Three very similar lavenders with deeply cut, almost fernlike leaves and tall flower stalks branching near the top, each branch carrying a short spike of deep purple flowers. They are nearly everblooming and are fine container subjects where frosts are too frequent or severe for year-round growing in the ground.

L. stoechas. SPANISH LAVENDER. Zones 4–24, 30, 31, warmer parts of 32. Stocky plant 1½–3 ft. tall, with narrow gray leaves ½–1 in. long. Flowers dark purple, about ⅛ in. long, in dense, short spikes, each topped with big tuft of purple, petal-like bracts. Blooms in late spring or early summer. *L. s. pedunculata* is the variety usually seen; it differs from the species in having flower stalks longer than the flower clusters themselves. 'Otto Quast', a long-stalked variety, has especially showy bracts.

L

LAVATERA

TREE MALLOW

Malvaceae

ANNUALS OR EVERGREEN SHRUBS

✂ ZONES VARY BY SPECIES

☼ FULL SUN

◐ ● REGULAR TO LITTLE WATER

Lavatera trimestris

Lavatera is named after the Lavater family of Zurich, but for many the word means "easy to grow." The flowers resemble single hollyhocks.

L. maritima (L. bicolor). Evergreen shrub. Zones 6–9, 14–24, 31. Quick, open growth to 6–8 ft., with gray-green, 2½-in. maplelike leaves and a summer-long show of light pink, 2–3-in. flowers with dark rose veining and a deep purple center. Cut back hard to keep it compact.

L. thuringiaca. Evergreen shrub. Zones 4–9, 14–24, 30–32. Resembles *L. maritima*, but growth is less open, leaves greener. Flowers are purplish pink, 3 in. across, nearly everblooming. The variety 'Barnsley' has lighter pink flowers paling to white centers. 'Rosea' has pink flowers.

L. trimestris. ANNUAL MALLOW. All zones; best in cool-summer regions. Reaches a height of 3–6 ft. from spring-sown seed. Satiny flowers to 4 in. across; named varieties in white, pink, rosy carmine. Bloom extends from midsummer to frost if spent flowers are removed to halt seed production. Colorful, fast-growing summer hedge or background planting. In mild-winter areas, can also be sown in fall for winter–spring bloom. 'Loveliness' grows 3–4 ft. high, bears deep rose blooms. More compact (2–3-ft.) varieties include 'Mont Rose', rose pink; 'Mont Blanc', white; and 'Silver Cup', bright pink.

LAVENDER. See LAVANDULA

LAVENDER COTTON. See SANTOLINA chamaecyparissus

LAVENDER MIST. See THALICTRUM rochebrunianum

LAVENDER STARFLOWER. See GREWIA occidentalis

LEAD PLANT. See AMORPHA canescens

LEADWORT. See PLUMBAGO auriculata

LEATHERLEAF FERN. See RUMOHRA adiantiformis

LEEK

Liliaceae

BIENNIAL GROWN AS ANNUAL

✂ ALL ZONES

☼ FULL SUN

● NEVER LET DRY OUT

Leek

An onion relative that doesn't form distinct bulb. Plants grow 2–3 ft. tall; their edible, mild-flavored bottoms resemble long, fat green onions. Leeks need very rich soil. Best in cool weather. Sow in early spring; in cold-winter areas, sow indoors and set out plants in June or July. When plants have considerable top growth, draw soil up around fat, round stems to make bottoms white and mild. Keep soil out of bases of leaves. Begin to harvest in late autumn. Where winters are cold, dig up plants with roots and plant them closely in boxes of soil in cool but frost-free location. Where winters are mild, dig as needed from late fall until spring. Any offsets may be detached and replanted. If leeks bloom, small bulbils may appear in flower clusters; plant these for later harvest. Not bothered by many pests and diseases that attack onions.

Leguminosae. See Fabaceae

LEMON. See CITRUS

LEMONADE BERRY. See RHUS integrifolia

LEMON BALM. See MELISSA officinalis

LEMON GRASS. See CYMBOPOGON citratus

LEMON-SCENTED GUM. See EUCALYPTUS citriodora

LEMON THYME. See THYMUS citriodorus

LEMON VERBENA. See ALOYSIA triphylla

LENTEN ROSE. See HELLEBORUS orientalis

LEONTOPODIUM alpinum

EDELWEISS

Asteraceae (Compositae)

PERENNIAL

✂ ZONES 1–9, 14–24, 36–43

☼ FULL SUN

● REGULAR WATER

Leontopodium alpinum

Short-lived rock garden plant 4–12 in. high, with woolly white foliage and small flower heads closely crowded on tips of stems; a collar of slender leaves radiates out from below each flower head like the arms of a starfish. The tiny bracts of flower heads, also white and woolly, are tipped with black. Blooms early summer. Needs excellent drainage, cool temperatures.

LEOPARD PLANT. See LIGULARIA tussilaginea 'Aureo-maculata'

LEOPARD'S BANE. See DORONICUM

LEPTOSPERMUM

TEA TREE

Myrtaceae

EVERGREEN SHRUBS OR SMALL TREES

✂ ZONES VARY BY SPECIES

☼ FULL SUN

● MODERATE WATER

Leptospermum scoparium
'Ruby Glow'

Native to New Zealand and Australia. In the U.S., commonly grown only in California. Both have small, somewhat prickly leaves and flowers like little roses distributed along the stems. Need good drainage and only moderate moisture. Heavy soil and excess moisture will cause root rot, and complete drying out will kill plants. Light shearing after bloom will keep plants shapely; regrowth is unlikely if you cut into bare wood.

L. laevigatum. AUSTRALIAN TEA TREE. Zones 14–24. To 30 ft. high and wide with a rounded but irregular shape, drooping branchlets, and shaggy-barked, multiple trunks. Gray-green to matte green, 1-in. leaves. Single white flowers in spring.

L. scoparium. NEW ZEALAND TEA TREE. Zones 14–24, 26; mixed success in Zone 28 (Florida and Georgia). Dense, erect, to 6–12 ft. high, with tiny needlelike green leaves. Profusion of white (rarely pink or red) flowers in spring or summer. True species is rarely seen, but varieties with single or double pink, red, or white blossoms are showy. Among most popular is 'Ruby Glow', upright to 6–8 ft., with dark foliage and double oxblood red flowers for overall red appearance. Good container plant.

FOR GROWING SYMBOL EXPLANATIONS

PLEASE SEE PAGE 161

LESPEDEZA thunbergii

SHRUB BUSH CLOVER

Fabaceae (Leguminosae)

DECIDUOUS PERENNIAL OR SHRUB

ZONES 3–9, 14–21, 30–34, 39

FULL SUN

MODERATE TO LITTLE WATER

Lespedeza thunbergii

Woody-based stems form a spreading, fountain-shaped plant 6 ft. tall and 10 ft. wide. Arching branches carry blue-green leaves with three 1½–2- in.-long leaflets. Blooms in late summer; drooping 6-in. clusters of rose pink, sweet pea–shaped flowers are carried in groups to form pendulous inflorescences 2–2½ ft. long. Cut plant to the ground in late fall or early spring; it will regrow rapidly and bear flowers on the new growth. Endures hot, dry sites and soil of low fertility. Needs good drainage. 'Gibraltar' is a more compact form (to 4½ ft.); 'Alba' has white flowers. Use among other shrubs or in large perennial borders.

LETTUCE

Asteraceae (Compositae)

ANNUAL

ALL ZONES

PARTIAL SHADE IN HOTTEST CLIMATES

REGULAR WATER

Lettuce

A short browse through a seed catalog, seed display rack, or selection of nursery seedlings will reveal enough variety to keep your salad bowl crisp and colorful throughout the growing season. There are four principle types of lettuce: crisphead, butterhead or Boston, loose-leaf, and romaine.

Widely sold in markets, crisphead is the most exasperating for home gardeners to produce. Heads form best when monthly average temperatures are around 55° to 60°F/13° to 16°C. In mild climates, this type of lettuce does well over a long season; in hot-summer areas, timing of planting is critical. Best varieties are various strains of 'Great Lakes', 'Imperial', and 'Iceberg'.

Butterhead or Boston types have loose heads with smooth green outer leaves and yellow inner leaves. Good varieties include 'Bibb' ('Limestone') and 'Buttercrunch'. 'Mignonette' ('Manoa') stands heat without bolting (going to seed).

Loose-leaf lettuce makes rosettes rather than heads. It withstands heat better than other types and is a summer mainstay in warm climates. Choice selections: 'Black-seeded Simpson', 'Oak Leaf', 'Slobolt', the red-tinged varieties 'Prizehead' and 'Ruby', and 'Salad Bowl', with deeply cut leaves.

Romaine lettuce has erect, cylindrical heads of smooth leaves, the outer ones green, the inner ones whitish. Tolerates heat moderately well. Try 'White Paris', 'Parris Island', 'Dark Green Cos', or 'Valmaine'.

Lettuces with bronzy to pinkish red leaves add color to a salad. 'Lollo Rosso', 'Red Sails', 'Red Oak Leaf', and 'Ruby' are loose-leaf varieties; 'Merveille des Quatre Saisons' and 'Perella Red' are butterheads; 'Rouge d'Hiver' is a romaine.

All types of lettuce need loose, well-drained soil. Sow in open ground at 10-day intervals for prolonged harvest. Barely cover seeds. Loose-leaf lettuce can be grown as close as 4 in. apart; thin all other types to 1 ft. apart. In cold-winter regions, begin sowing seed after frost, as soon as soil is workable; where summers are very short, sow indoors, then move seedlings outdoors after last frost. In mild-winter, cool-summer regions, sow in early spring for spring–summer harvest, then make further sowings in late summer or early fall for winter harvest. In mild-winter, hot-summer areas, grow only as a winter and early spring crop. Feed plants lightly and frequently.

LEUCANTHEMUM. See CHRYSANTHEMUM

LEUCOJUM

SNOWFLAKE

Amaryllidaceae

BULBS

ZONES VARY BY SPECIES

FULL SUN OR LIGHT SHADE

REGULAR WATER DURING GROWTH AND BLOOM

Leucojum aestivum

Strap-shaped leaves and nodding, bell-shaped, white flowers with segments tipped green. Easy to grow and permanent. Naturalize under deciduous trees, in shrub borders or orchards, or on cool slopes. Plant 4 in. deep in fall. Do not disturb until really crowded; then dig, divide, and replant after foliage dies down.

L. aestivum. SUMMER SNOWFLAKE. Zones 1–24, 29–43. Leaves 1–1½ ft. long. Stems 1½ ft. tall carry three to five 1-in. flowers. 'Gravetye Giant' is a bit taller and larger flowered than the species; it has as many as nine flowers per stem. In mild-winter areas, plants bloom November through winter; in colder regions, they bloom with daffodils.

L. vernum. SPRING SNOWFLAKE. Zones 1–6, 30–43. Flourishes in areas with definite winter cold; generally unsuccessful where temperatures remain above 20°F/–7°C. Leaves 9 in. long. In earliest spring, each foot-long stem bears a single large white flower (occasionally two per stem).

LEUCOPHYLLUM

TEXAS RANGER, SILVERLEAF

Scrophulariaceae

EVERGREEN SHRUBS

ZONES 7–24, 28–32; WARMER, DRIER PARTS OF 35

FULL SUN

MODERATE TO LITTLE WATER

Leucophyllum frutescens

Native to the Southwest and northern Mexico, these compact, slow-growing shrubs are highly useful and attractive in desert gardens. Most have silvery foliage and a good show of open bell-shaped flowers. They tolerate wind and heat, but often fail where humidity is high. Flowering may occur at varying times of year, often after summer showers. Use as clipped hedges, massed as tall ground cover, or in mixed dry-country gardens.

L. candidum. VIOLET SILVERLEAF. To 4–5 ft. tall, with small (½-in.) silvery leaves and deep purple flowers. 'Silver Cloud' blooms heavily. 'Thundercloud' is smaller (3–4 ft.) than the species.

L. frutescens. TEXAS RANGER, TEXAS SAGE, CENIZO. Grows to 6–8 ft., with silvery leaves and purple flowers. 'Compactum' is a dense grower to 3–4 ft. 'Green Cloud' has green leaves and deep violet flowers. 'White Cloud', with white flowers, has silvery foliage. 'Rain Cloud' is an erect grower.

L. laevigatum. CHIHUAHUAN SAGE. Grows 3–4 ft. tall and somewhat wider, with green leaves and blue-purple flowers.

L

LEUCOTHOE

Ericaceae

EVERGREEN OR DECIDUOUS SHRUBS

☒ ZONES VARY BY SPECIES

◐ ● PARTIAL OR FULL SHADE

◓ ◒ WATER NEEDS VARY BY SPECIES

◊ LEAVES AND NECTAR ARE POISONOUS IF INGESTED

Leucothoe fontanesiana

Related to *Pieris*. All have leathery leaves and clusters of urn-shaped white flowers. They need acid, woodsy, deep soil; do best in woodland gardens. Will tolerate full sun in cool climates if adequately watered. Best used in masses, since they are not especially attractive individually. Bronze-tinted winter foliage is a bonus.

L. axillaris. COAST LEUCOTHOE. Evergreen. Zones 3–7, 15–17, 26, 28–35, 37, 39. Native to southeastern U.S. Spreading, arching growth to 2–4 ft. tall, 3–6 ft. wide. Leathery leaves to 4 in. long are bronzy when new. Flower clusters 1–3 in. long droop along stems in spring. Takes regular water.

L. davisiae. SIERRA LAUREL. Evergreen. Zones 1–7, 15–17. Native to wet places in mountains of the Far West. Upright shrub to 3½ ft. high. Oblong or egg-shaped, glossy rich green leaves to 3 in. long. White flowers in erect 2–4-in. clusters in summer. Needs ample water.

L. fontanesiana (L. catesbaei). DROOPING LEUCOTHOE. Evergreen. Zones 4–7, 15–17, 32–34. Native to southeastern U.S. Slow grower to 2–6 ft. high; branches arch gracefully. Leaves are leathery, 3–6 in. long; they turn bronzy purple in fall (bronzy green in deep shade). Spreads from underground stems. Blooms in spring, bearing drooping clusters of slightly fragrant, creamy white flowers resembling lily-of-the-valley. 'Rainbow', 3–4 ft. high, has leaves marked yellow, green, and pink. 'Lovita' is smaller than the species (2 ft. tall, 4 ft. wide), with smaller, darker green leaves that turn mahogany red in winter. 'Scarletta' is similar in size to 'Lovita'; its leaves are brilliant red on expanding, deep green in summer, and deep red in late fall and winter.

The species and its varieties take regular water. Can be controlled in height to make 1½-ft. ground cover in shade; just cut older, taller stems to ground. Blooming branches make decorative cut flowers. Where summers are hot and humid, various leaf spot diseases can cause serious disfiguration or defoliation.

L. racemosa. SWEETBELLS. Deciduous. Zones 26 (upper half), 28, 31–34. Native to southeastern U.S. Grows 3–8 ft. tall, with 3-in. leaves that turn red before dropping from their red stems. White flowers in one-sided, 3-in. clusters form at ends of branches in late spring or early summer. A pink-flowering form is available. Endures dry shade.

LEVISTICUM officinale

LOVAGE

Apiaceae (Umbelliferae)

PERENNIAL HERB

☒ ZONES 4–9, 12–24, 29–33

☼ FULL SUN

◊ REGULAR WATER

Levisticum officinale

This herb is sometimes grown for the celery flavor of its seeds, leaves, and stems. Reaches 2–3 ft. tall, sometimes even 6 ft. high. Leaves are cut and divided, glossy deep green; small greenish yellow flowers are borne in flattish clusters. Grow from seeds or divisions.

PRACTICAL GARDENING DICTIONARY

PLEASE SEE PAGES 545–616

LEWISIA

Portulacaceae

PERENNIALS

☒ ZONES 1–7, 14–17, 36–38

☼ ◐ FULL SUN OR LIGHT SHADE

◊ LIGHT WATERING

Lewisia tweedyi

Beautiful, often difficult plants for rock gardens, collections of alpine plants. All need excellent drainage; plant with fine gravel around crowns to prevent rot. Of the many offered by specialists, these are outstanding:

L. cotyledon. Native to Northern California and southern Oregon. Rosettes of narrow, fleshy, evergreen leaves bear 10-in. stems topped by large, extremely showy clusters of 1-in. white or pink flowers striped with rose or red. Blooms spring to early summer. *L. c. howellii* is similar, but leaves are wavy edged and flowers somewhat larger. Can be grown in pots in fast-draining sterilized soil or growing mixes.

L. rediviva. BITTERROOT. Native to mountains of the West. State flower of Montana. Fleshy roots; short stems with short, succulent, strap-shaped leaves to 2 in. long that usually die back before flowers appear (seemingly from bare earth) in spring. Flowers, borne singly on short stems, look like 2-in.-wide rose or white water lilies. Not difficult if drainage is excellent.

L. tweedyi. Native to mountains, south-central Washington. Stunning big, satiny salmon pink flowers, one to three to a stem, bloom above fleshy, evergreen, 4-in. leaves. Prune out side growths to keep root crown open to air.

LEYCESTERIA formosa

HIMALAYAN HONEYSUCKLE, HIMALAYAN PHEASANTBERRY

Caprifoliaceae

DECIDUOUS SHRUB

☒ ZONES 4–6, 15–17, 31, WARMER PARTS OF 32

☼ ◐ FULL SUN OR LIGHT SHADE

◊ REGULAR WATER

Leycesteria formosa

Fast-growing shrub with stems that do not become woody until their second year. In most areas, freezes back and should be cut to ground in late winter or early spring. New growth rapidly reaches 6 ft. Stems are a handsome gray green turning bright green. Bright green leaves are paired, up to 6 in. long. Inflorescences are 4 in. long and form at branch tips and in upper leaf joints; the small purple or white flowers are less conspicuous than the deep purplish bracts that partially conceal them. Green berries that follow the blooms rapidly turn deep red, then purplish black; all three colors are present simultaneously. Birds are fond of the fruit. Do not allow plants to dry out.

LIATRIS

GAYFEATHER

Asteraceae (Compositae)

PERENNIALS

☒ ZONES 1–10, 14–24, 26, 28–45

☼ FULL SUN

◓ ◒ REGULAR TO MODERATE WATER

Liatris spicata

Showy plants native to eastern and central U.S. Basal tufts of narrow, grassy leaves grow from thick, often tuberous rootstocks. In summer or early fall, the tufts lengthen into tall stems densely set with slender leaves and topped by a narrow plume of small, fluffy purple (sometimes white) flower heads. Flowers of most species are unusual in opening from top of spike to bottom. Choice cut flowers.

These plants endure heat, cold, aridity, and poor soil. Fertilizing will give you larger flower spikes, but it also results in taller plants that need staking. Liatris is best used in mixed perennial borders, although the rosy purple color calls for careful placing to avoid color clashes.

L. callilepis. Plants grown and sold by Dutch bulb growers under this name are *L. spicata*.

L. ligulistylis. Grows 3–5 ft. tall, with reddish purple flowers that open from dark red buds.

L. microcephala. Only 12–14 in. tall, with grasslike leaves and rose purple flowers.

L. pycnostachya. KANSAS GAYFEATHER. To 4 ft. tall, with purple flowers. Likes moisture.

L. scariosa. To 2½ ft. high. The reddish purple flowers differ from those of most other gayfeathers in opening nearly all at once. Plant also prefers somewhat drier soil. 'September Glory' is taller, to 4–5 ft.; 'White Spire' is similar, but with white flowers.

L. spicata. Grows to 5 ft., with light purple flower heads tightly clustered in dense spikes. 'Alba' (3–4 ft.) is white flowered; 'Floristan White' (2–3 ft.) has a profusion of densely packed white blossom spikes good for cutting; 'Kobold' (2–2½ ft.) has deeper purple flowers and does not need staking; and 'Silvertips' (2½–3 ft.) has lavender flowers with a silvery finish.

LIBOCEDRUS. See CALOCEDRUS

LIGULARIA

Asteraceae (Compositae)

PERENNIALS

ZONES 3–9, 15–17, 32, 34, 36–43, EXCEPT AS NOTED

PARTIAL OR FULL SHADE

AMPLE WATER

Ligularia stenocephala 'The Rocket'

Stately perennials with big leaves (1 ft. wide or wider in most species) and daisy flowers in yellow to orange. All need rich soil, ample moisture, and some shade; they do not tolerate heat or low humidity. Good around pools, along stream beds, in bog gardens.

L. dentata. Zones 3–9, 15–17, 32, 34, 36–41. Grown primarily for attractive roundish leaves, heart shaped at base. Sends up 3–5-ft. stems topped by big, branching heads of orange daisies in mid- to late summer. 'Desdemona' and 'Othello' have deep purple leafstalks, veins, and leaf undersurfaces; upper surfaces of leaves are green.

L. hessei 'Gregynog Gold'. Clump of heart-shaped, toothed leaves gives rise to stems as tall as 6 ft., bearing conical spikes of yellow-orange flowers in mid- to late summer.

L. przewalskii. Similar to *L. stenocephala*, but leaves are deeply lobed and cut, flower stems are black, and bloom occurs a bit later.

L. stenocephala. Zones 3–9, 15–17, 32, 34, 36–41. Better known for flower spikes than foliage. Usually represented by variety 'The Rocket', with clumps of deeply cut leaves topped by tall (to 5-ft.), narrow spires of yellow daisies in early summer.

L. tussilaginea (L. kaempferi, Farfugium japonicum). Zones 4–10, 14–24, 32; house plant or indoor/outdoor in all zones. Choice foliage plant for shady bed or entryways. Good container plant. Top hardy to 20°F/–7°C; plant dies back to roots at 0°F/–18°C, puts on new growth again in spring. Leaves, typically 6–10 in. across, rise directly from rootstock on 1–2-ft. stems; flower stalks 1–2 ft. tall bear a few 1½–2-in.-wide flower heads with yellow rays. Speckled variety 'Aureo-maculata', leopard plant, has thick, rather leathery leaves blotched with cream or yellow; leaves are nearly kidney shaped, but with shallowly angled and toothed edges. 'Argentea' has deep green leaves irregularly mottled (particularly on edges) with gray green and ivory. 'Crispata' ('Cristata') has curled and crested leaf edges.

L. wilsoniana. GIANT GROUNDSEL. Zones 3–9, 15–17, 32, 34, 36–41. Clump of broadly triangular leaves is topped in mid- to late summer by 5–6-ft. stems carrying dense, columnar spikes of golden yellow flowers.

LIGUSTRUM

PRIVET

Oleaceae

DECIDUOUS OR EVERGREEN SHRUBS OR SMALL TREES

ZONES VARY BY SPECIES

FULL SUN OR PARTIAL SHADE

REGULAR WATER

LEAVES, FRUITS CAUSE GASTRIC DISTRESS IF INGESTED

Ligustrum lucidum

Most widely used as hedges, though one type is a street tree; can also be clipped into formal shapes and featured in tubs or large pots. All have abundant, showy clusters of white to creamy white flowers in late spring or early summer. Fragrance is described as pleasant to unpleasant (never wonderful or terrible). Flowers draw bees. Clipped hedges bear fewer flowers, since shearing removes most of the flower-bearing branches. Blossoms followed by small, berrylike blue-black fruits; birds eat them, thereby distributing seeds. Most privets are easily grown in any soil.

Nurseries sometimes misidentify certain privets. The plant sold as *L. japonicum* usually turns out to be the small tree *L. lucidum*. The true *L. japonicum* is available in two or more forms. The tall, shrubby kind is the true species; the lower-growing, more densely foliaged form is often sold as *L. texanum* and probably should be called *L. japonicum* 'Texanum'. The smaller-leafed hardy privets used for hedging are also often confused: *L. amurense*, *L. ovalifolium*, and *L. vulgare* look much alike, and any is likely to be sold as "common privet"—a name that belongs to *L. vulgare*.

L. amurense. AMUR PRIVET. Shrub. Zones 1–24, 33–45. Deciduous in coldest areas, where it is much used for hedge and screen planting. Partially evergreen in milder climates but seldom planted there. Much like *L. ovalifolium* in appearance, but foliage is less glossy.

L. ibolium 'Variegata'. Semievergreen to deciduous shrub. Zones 3–24, 31–41. Variegated form of a hybrid between *L. ovalifolium* and another Japanese privet. Resembles *L. ovalifolium* but has bright green leaves with creamy yellow edges.

L. japonicum. JAPANESE PRIVET, WAX-LEAF PRIVET. Evergreen shrub. Zones 4–31, warmer parts of 32. Dense, compact growth habit to 10–12 ft., but can be kept lower by trimming. Roundish oval leaves 2–4 in. long, dark to medium green and glossy above, distinctly paler to almost whitish beneath; have thick, slightly spongy feel. Excellent plant for hedges or screens, or for shaping into globes, pyramids, other shapes, or small standard trees. Sunburns in hot spells. In areas of caliche soil, or where Texas root rot prevails, grow it in containers. Often confused with its variety 'Texanum'.

'Howard' ('Howardii'). Two-toned shrub; leaves are yellow when new, aging to green. Both colors are usually present at once.

'Recurvifolium'. Leaves are somewhat smaller than in the species, wavy-edged, and twisted at the tip. Somewhat open grower.

'Rotundifolium' ('Coriaceum'). Grows 4–5 ft. high; has nearly round leaves to 2½ in. long. Partial shade in hot areas.

'Silver Star'. Grows 6–8 ft. high. Leaves are deep green, with gray-green mottling and startling creamy white edges. Provides a good contrast to deep green foliage.

'Texanum'. Very similar to the species but lower growing (to 6–9 ft.), with somewhat denser, lusher foliage. Useful as windbreak. Often sold as *L. texanum*.

'Variegatum'. Leaves have creamy white margins and blotches.

L. lucidum. GLOSSY PRIVET. Evergreen tree. Zones 5, 6, 8–31. Makes a round-headed tree that eventually reaches 35–40 ft. Can be kept lower as a big shrub or may form multitrunked tree. Glossy, 4–6-in.-long leaves are tapered and pointed, dark to medium green on both sides. They feel leathery but lack the slightly spongy feel of *L. japonicum*'s leaves. Flowers in especially large, feathery clusters followed by profusion of fruit. Fine lawn tree. Can grow in narrow areas; good street tree if not planted near pavement or where fruit will drop on cars (see disadvantages noted below). Performs well in large containers. Or plant 10 ft. apart for tall privacy screen. Useful as windbreak.

Before planting this tree, carefully weigh the advantages listed above against the disadvantages. Eventual fruit crop is immense; never plant where fruits will fall on cars, walks, or other paved areas (they stain). Fallen seeds (and those dropped by birds) profusely sprout in ground cover and will need pulling. Many people dislike the flowers' odor, and fruiting clusters are bare and unattractive after fruit drop.

L. ovalifolium. CALIFORNIA PRIVET. Semievergreen shrub. Zones 4–34, 39. Native to Japan. Grows rapidly to 15 ft. but can be kept sheared to any height. Dark green, oval, 2½-in.-long leaves. Set plants 9–12 in. apart for hedges. Clip early and frequently to encourage low, dense branching. Greedy roots. Well-fed, well-watered plants hold their leaves longest. Tolerates heat.

'Aureum'. GOLDEN PRIVET. Leaves have broad yellow edges. Sold as 'Variegatum'.

L. 'Suwannee River'. Evergreen shrub. Zones 4–31, warmer parts of 32. Reported to be hybrid between *L. japonicum* 'Rotundifolium' and *L. lucidum*. Slow growing to 1½ ft. tall in 3 years, eventually 3–4 ft.; compact habit. Leathery, dark green, somewhat twisted leaves; no fruit. Use as low hedge, foundation planting, in containers.

L. vicaryi. VICARY GOLDEN PRIVET. Deciduous shrub. Zones 2–24, 32–41. This one has yellow leaves; color is strongest on plants in full sun. To 4–6 ft. high, possibly to 12 ft. Best planted alone; color does not develop well under hedge shearing.

L. vulgare. COMMON PRIVET. Deciduous shrub. Zones 2–24, 30–41. To 15 ft., unsheared. Dark green leaves less glossy than those of *L. ovalifolium,* root system less greedy. Clusters of black fruit conspicuous on unpruned or lightly pruned plants. 'Lodense' ('Nanum') is a dense dwarf form that reaches only 4 ft. with equal spread.

LILAC. See SYRINGA

LILAC VINE. See HARDENBERGIA comptoniana

Liliaceae. The lily family contains hundreds of species of ornamental plants, as well as such vegetables as asparagus and the whole onion tribe. Most grow from bulbs, corms, or rhizomes. Flowers are often showy, usually with six equal-size segments.

LILIUM

LILY

Liliaceae

BULBS

⚡ ALL ZONES, EXCEPT AS NOTED, BUT MOST NEED WINTER CHILL FOR RECURRENCE

☼ ROOTS IN SHADE; TOPS IN SUN OR FILTERED SHADE

🌢 NEVER LET ROOT ZONE DRY OUT

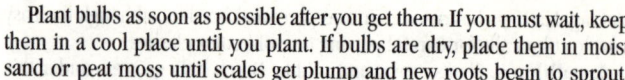

Lilium auratum

Most stately and varied of bulbous plants. For many years, only the species—the same plants growing wild in parts of Asia, Europe, and North America—were available, and many of these were difficult and unpredictable.

Around 1925, lily growers began a significant breeding program. They bred new hybrids from species with desirable qualities and also developed strains and varieties that were healthier, hardier, and easier to grow than the original species. They produced new forms and new colors; what is more important, they developed the methods for growing healthy lilies in large quantities. Today, the new forms and new colors are the best garden lilies, but it is still possible to get some desirable species.

Lilies have three basic cultural requirements: deep, loose, well-drained soil; ample moisture year-round (plants never completely stop growing); and coolness and shade at roots, with sun or filtered shade at tops where flowers form.

Plant bulbs as soon as possible after you get them. If you must wait, keep them in a cool place until you plant. If bulbs are dry, place them in moist sand or peat moss until scales get plump and new roots begin to sprout.

As noted above, lilies need deep, well-drained soil containing ample organic matter. If you want to plant in heavy clay or very sandy soil, add organic material such as peat moss, leaf mold, or composted ground bark. Spread a 3–4-in. layer of such material over the soil surface; broadcast complete fertilizer (follow directions for preplanting application) on top of it, then thoroughly blend both into the soil to a depth of at least 1 ft.

Before planting bulbs, remove any injured portions; then dust cuts with sulfur or an antifungal seed and bulb disinfectant. For each bulb, dig a generous planting hole (6–12 in. deeper than height of bulb). Place enough soil at bottom of hole to bring it up to proper level for bulb (see next paragraph). Set bulb with its roots spread; fill hole with soil, firming it around bulb to eliminate air pockets.

Planting depths vary according to size and rooting habit of bulb. General rule is to cover smaller bulbs with 2–3 in. of soil, medium bulbs with 3–4 in., and larger bulbs with 4–6 in. (but never cover Madonna lilies with more than 1 in. of soil). Planting depth can be quite flexible. It's better to err by planting shallowly than too deeply; lily bulbs have contractile roots that draw them down to proper depth. Ideal spacing for lily bulbs is 1 ft. apart, but you can plant as close as 6 in. for densely massed effect.

Lilies need constant moisture to about 6 in. deep. You can reduce watering somewhat after tops turn yellow in fall, but never allow roots to dry out completely. Flooding is preferable to overhead watering, which may help to spread disease spores. Pull weeds by hand if possible; hoeing may injure roots.

Viral or mosaic infection is a problem. No cure exists. To avoid it, buy healthy bulbs from reliable sources. Dig and destroy any lilies that show mottling in leaves or seriously stunted growth. Control aphids, which spread the infection. Control botrytis blight, a fungal disease, with appropriate fungicide. Gophers relish lily bulbs.

Wait until stems and leaves turn yellow before you cut plants back. If clumps become too crowded, dig up, divide, and transplant them in spring or fall. If you're careful, you can lift lily clumps at any time, even in bloom.

Lilies are fine container plants. Place one bulb in a deep 5–7-in. pot or five in a 14–16-in. pot. First, fill pot one-third full of potting mix. Then place bulb with roots spread and pointing downward; cover with about an inch of soil. Water thoroughly and place in deep cold frame or greenhouse that is heated (in colder climates) just enough to keep out frost. During root-forming period, keep soil moderately moist. When top growth appears, add more soil mixture and gradually fill pot as stems elongate. Leave 1-in. space between surface of soil and rim of pot for watering. Move pots onto partially shaded terrace or patio during blooming period. Later, if you wish to repot bulbs, do so in late fall or early spring.

Although the official classification of lilies lists eight divisions of hybrids and a ninth division of species, the following listings describe the lilies commonly available to gardeners. Advances in breeding are producing lilies with forms, colors, and parentage hitherto considered unlikely, if not impossible. Consult specialists' catalogs to learn about these new wonders, which are reaching the market faster than books can deal with them.

ASIATIC HYBRIDS

These are the easiest and most reliable for the average garden. Some have upward-facing flowers, while others have horizontally held or drooping flowers. Stems are strong, erect, and short (1½ ft.) to moderate (4½ ft.) in height. Colors range from white through yellow and orange to pink and red. Many have dark spots or contrasting "halos." They are the earliest to bloom (early summer). Examples are 'Enchantment', orange red spotted with black; 'Impala', bright yellow; 'Pink Floyd', creamy pink banded with rose pink; and 'Sancerre', pure white and unspotted.

AURELIAN HYBRIDS

Derived from Asiatic species, excluding *L. auratum* and *L. speciosum*. They have trumpet- or bowl-shaped flowers in midsummer. Flowers range from white and cream through yellow and pink, many with green, brown, or purple shading on their outer surfaces. Plants are 3–6 ft. tall, and each stem carries 12–20 flowers. Examples are 'Anaconda', coppery apricot; 'Black Dragon', white with maroon petal backs; 'Golden Splendour', yellow blooms from purple buds; and 'Thunderbolt', orange-apricot blossoms.

ORIENTAL HYBRIDS

The most exotic of the hybrids. Bloom midsummer–early fall, with big (to 9-in.) fragrant flowers of white or pink, often spotted with gold and shaded or banded with red. Most are tall, with nodding flowers, but a few are dwarf and have upward-facing blooms. Examples are 'Casablanca', pure white; 'Pink Ribbons', light rose banded and spotted with deep rose; and 'Stargazer', rose red with white margins.

SPECIES AND VARIANTS

L. amabile. To 3–4 ft. tall, with one to eight blooms per stem; flowers are fragrant, orange red, with dark purplish dots. Midsummer bloom.

L. auratum. GOLD-BAND LILY. Mid- to late summer bloom on 4–6-ft. plants. Flowers fragrant, waxy white spotted crimson, with golden band on each segment.

L. candidum. MADONNA LILY. Zones 4–9, 14–24, 30–33. Pure white, fragrant blooms on 3–4-ft. stems in late spring, early summer. Unlike most lilies, dies down soon after bloom, makes new growth in fall. Plant while dormant in August. Does not have stem roots; set top of bulb only 1–2 in. deep in sunny location. Bulb quickly makes foliage rosette that lives over winter, lengthens to blooming stem in spring. Subject to diseases that shorten its life. Cascade strain, grown from seed, is healthier than imported bulbs. The lily of medieval romance, a sentimental choice for many gardeners.

Lilium candidum

L. centifolium (L. leucanthemum centifolium). Grows 7–8 ft. high. Each stem bears 15–20 white flowers banded brownish purple on outside of petals. Late summer bloom.

L. cernuum. Only 12–20 in. tall, with lilac flowers often dotted dark purple. Midsummer bloom; perfectly hardy. Sun.

L. formosanum. Zones 14–28. Slender, 5-ft., purple-brown stems bear one to several fragrant, outward-facing, funnel-shaped blossoms in white flushed purple. Late summer bloom. Not as showy as modern hybrids, but one of the best for reliable recurrence in hot, humid regions.

L. henryi. Slender stems to 8–9 ft. topped by 10–20 bright orange flowers with sharply recurved segments. Midsummer bloom. Best in light shade.

L. lancifolium (L. tigrinum). TIGER LILY. To 4 ft. or taller with pendulous orange flowers spotted black. Late summer bloom. An old favorite; very easy to grow. Newer tiger lilies are available in white, cream, yellow, pink, and red, all with black spots.

L. lankongense. Zones 2–24, 28–41. Grows 4–6 ft. tall; stems bear up to 36 nodding, powerfully fragrant, pale to deep pink flowers with purple spots. Mid- to late summer bloom.

L. longiflorum. EASTER LILY. Zones 6–9, 14–24, 26–29; not for severe winter climates. Very fragrant, long, white, trumpet-shaped flowers on short stems. Usually purchased in bloom at Easter as forced plant. Set out in garden after flowers fade. Stems will ripen and die down. Plant may rebloom in fall; in 1 or 2 years, may flower in midsummer, its normal bloom season. Varieties include 'Ace', 1½ ft. tall; 'Tetraploid', 1–1½ ft. tall; 'Croft', 1 ft. tall; 'Estate', to 3 ft. tall. Recent hybridization has yielded pink, yellow, and red offspring. Don't plant forced lilies near other lilies; they may transmit a virus.

L. martagon. TURK'S CAP LILY. Purplish pink, recurved, pendent flowers in early summer on 3–5-ft. stems. This lily is slow to establish but is long lived and eventually forms big clumps. *L. m. album*, pure white, is one of the most appealing lilies. It is a parent of the Paisley hybrids, a group with flowers in yellow, orange, and mahogany shades, most with maroon spots.

L. pumilum. Each wiry, 1–1½-ft. stem carries 1–20 scented, coral red flowers. Blooms late spring–early summer. 'Yellow Bunting' is a brilliant yellow form.

L. regale. REGAL LILY. Superseded in quality by modern hybrid trumpet lilies but still popular and easy to grow. To 6 ft., with white, fragrant flowers in early to midsummer.

L. speciosum. Grows 2½–5 ft. tall. Large, wide, fragrant flowers with broad, deeply recurved segments, late summer; white, heavily suffused rose pink, sprinkled with raised crimson dots. 'Rubrum' is red, 'Album' pure white; there are also other named forms. Best in light shade (or at least afternoon shade); needs rich soil with plenty of leaf mold.

L. tigrinum. See L. lancifolium

LILY. See LILIUM

LILY-OF-THE-NILE. See AGAPANTHUS

LILY-OF-THE-VALLEY. See CONVALLARIA majalis

LILY-OF-THE-VALLEY SHRUB. See PIERIS japonica

LILY TURF. See LIRIOPE and OPHIOPOGON

LIME. See CITRUS

LIMEQUAT. See CITRUS, Kumquat Hybrids

LIMONIUM (Statice)

SEA LAVENDER

Plumbaginaceae

PERENNIALS, BIENNIALS, AND ANNUALS

⚡ ZONES VARY BY SPECIES

☼ FULL SUN

◔ MODERATE WATER

Limonium sinuatum

Large, leathery basal leaves contrast with airy clusters of small, delicate flowers on nearly leafless, many-branched stems. Tiny flowers consist of two parts: an outer, papery envelope (the calyx) and an inner part (the corolla) which often has a different color. For spring–summer bloom of annual kinds, sow indoors and move to garden when weather warms up. Or sow outdoors in early spring for later bloom. All tolerate heat and many soils but need good drainage. They often self-sow.

L. bonduellii. Annual or biennial. All zones. Grows 2 ft. tall, with 6-in. basal leaves lobed nearly to midrib. Flower stems are distinctly winged; calyx is yellow, tiny corolla deeper yellow.

L. gmelinii. Perennial. Zones 2–10, 14–24, 32–41. Basal rosette of spoon-shaped 5-in. leaves produces 2-ft., branching clusters of tiny blue flowers in mid- to late summer.

L. latifolium. Perennial. Zones 1–10, 14–24, 26, 28, 31–43. To 2½ ft. tall. Smooth-edged leaves to 10 in. long. Calyx is white and corolla bluish; pure white and pink kinds exist. Summer bloom. Vigorous plants may show a 3-ft.-wide haze of flowers.

L. perezii. Perennial. Zones 13, 15–17, 20–27. Rich green leaves up to 1 ft. long, including stalks. Calyx is rich purple, tiny corolla white. Flower clusters may be 3 ft. tall, nearly as wide. Long spring, summer bloom. First-rate beach plant.

L. sinuatum. Annual. All zones. Growth habit like *L. bonduellii*, with lobed leaves and winged stems, but calyx is blue, lavender, or rose and corolla is white. Widely grown as a fresh or dried cut flower.

L. suworowii. See Psylliostachys suworowii

L. tataricum. See Goniolimon tataricum

STATICE LASTS LONG FRESH OR DRIED

Cut for fresh bouquets after most flowers in each cluster have opened. For dried arrangements, cut after opening but before sun has faded them. With a rubber band, join several bunches together by stem bases; hang upside down in a dry spot out of bright sun until flowers dry.

Linaceae. The flax family of annuals, perennials, and shrubs displays cup- or disk-shaped flowers with four or five petals. Flowers are often showy. Individually short lived, they appear over a long season. Examples are flax (*Linum*) and yellow flax (*Reinwardtia*).

LINARIA

TOADFLAX

Scrophulariaceae

PERENNIALS AND ANNUALS

⚡ ZONES VARY BY SPECIES

☼ ◗ FULL SUN OR LIGHT SHADE

💧 MODERATE WATER

Linaria maroccana

Brightly colored flowers that resemble small, spurred snapdragons. Very narrow, medium green leaves. Easy to grow. Best in masses; individual plants are rather wispy.

L. cymbalaria. See Cymbalaria muralis

L. maroccana. BABY SNAPDRAGON, TOADFLAX. Annual. All zones. Grows to 1½–2 ft. high. Flowers in red-and-gold combination, rose, pink, mauve, chamois, blue, violet, or purple, blotched with different shade on the lip. Spur is longer than flower. Fairy Bouquet strain is only 9 in. tall and has larger flowers in pastel shades. Northern Lights strain blooms in reds, oranges, and yellows as well as bicolors. Seed in quantity for a show. Performs best during cool weather; sow in early spring after danger of frost is past (in fall in mild-winter climates), then again in late summer.

L. purpurea. Perennial. Zones 2–24, 30–41. Narrow, bushy, erect growth to 2½–3 ft. Blue-green foliage; violet blue flowers in summer. 'Canon Went' is a pink form. Short-lived in hot, humid regions, but volunteer seedlings ensure resupply.

LINDEN. See TILIA

LINDERA

SPICEBUSH

Lauraceae

DECIDUOUS SHRUBS OR SMALL TREES

⚡ ZONES VARY BY SPECIES

☼ ◗ FULL SUN OR PART SHADE

💧 REGULAR WATER

Lindera benzoin

Large deciduous shrubs grown principally for the beauty of their bright yellow fall foliage. Flowers are attractive but not showy: small, greenish yellow, clustered at the joints of leafless shoots in earliest spring. Female plants have attractive fruits, but these are seldom seen unless plants of both sexes are present. Common name refers to the foliage, which is strongly aromatic when bruised or crushed. Although too large for most gardens, spicebushes are effective at the edge of woodland or as space fillers. Need good drainage; tolerate some drought.

L. benzoin. SPICEBUSH. Zones 3–6, 31–41. Native to woodlands of eastern U.S. Grows 6–12 ft. tall and as wide. Light green leaves are 3–5 in. long, half as wide. Fall color and plant form are best in full sun; plants tolerate considerable shade but are loose and open if grown there. Fruit, noticeable after leaf fall, is bright red, ⅓–½ in. long. Species name describes the leaves' odor—a spicy scent reminiscent of benzoin, an aromatic gum once used in medicine and perfumery.

L. obtusiloba. JAPANESE SPICEBUSH. Zones 4–6, 31–34, 39. Native to Japan, Korea, and China. Larger than *L. benzoin* (10–20 ft. tall, somewhat narrower), with broader leaves (to 5 in. long, 4 in. wide). The shiny dark green leaves sometimes have a mitten shape, with one lobe or two as shallow divisions from the main leaf. Small (¼-in.) fruits turn from red to

black. Fall color is an exceptionally brilliant yellow that holds for 2 weeks or more and develops even in considerable shade.

LINGARO. See ELAEAGNUS philippensis

LINGONBERRY. See VACCINIUM vitis-idaea minus

LINNAEA borealis

TWINFLOWER

Caprifoliaceae

PERENNIAL

⚡ ZONES 1–7, 14–17, 36–45

◗ ● PARTIAL OR FULL SHADE

💧 REGULAR WATER

Linnaea borealis

Native to much of Northern Hemisphere. Delicate flat, glossy evergreen mats with 1-in.-long leaves. Spreads by runners. Paired flowers appear on 3–4-in. stems—pale pink, fragrant, trumpet shaped, ⅓ in. long. Collector's item or small-scale ground cover for woodland garden. Keep area around plants mulched with leaf mold to induce spreading. Tolerates sun in cool-summer climates.

LINUM

FLAX

Linaceae

PERENNIALS AND ANNUALS

⚡ ZONES VARY BY SPECIES

☼ FULL SUN

💧 MODERATE WATER

Linum perenne

These plants have erect, branching stems, narrow leaves, and abundant, shallow-cupped, five-petaled flowers that bloom from late spring into summer or fall. Each bloom lasts only a day, but others keep coming. The flax of commerce—*L. usitatissimum*—is grown for its fiber and seeds, which yield linseed oil.

Use in borders; some naturalize freely in uncultivated areas. Light, well-drained soil. Most perennial kinds live only 3 or 4 years and should be replaced regularly. Easy from seed; perennials also can be grown from cuttings. Difficult to divide.

L. flavum. GOLDEN FLAX. Perennial. Zones 3–24, 32–34, 39. Erect, compact, 12–15 in. tall, somewhat woody at base; grooved branches, green leaves. Flowers golden yellow, about 1 in. wide, in branched clusters. Often called yellow flax, a name correctly applied to closely related *Reinwardtia indica*. 'Compactum' is a smaller form.

L. grandiflorum 'Rubrum'. SCARLET FLAX. Annual. All zones. Bright scarlet flowers, 1–1½ in. wide, on slender, leafy, 1–1½ ft. stems. Narrow gray-green leaves. Also comes in a rose-colored form. Sow seed thickly in place in fall (in mild areas) or early spring. Quick color for borders or bulb cover. Good with gray foliage or white-flowered plants. Reseeds but doesn't become a pest. Often included in wildflower seed mixtures.

L. narbonense. Perennial. Zones 3–24, 32–34, 39. Wiry stems to 2 ft. high. Leaves blue green, narrow. Flowers large (1¾ in. across), azure blue with white eye, in open clusters. Best variety, 'Six Hills', has rich sky blue flowers.

L. perenne. PERENNIAL BLUE FLAX. Zones 3–24, 32–34, 39. Most vigorous blue-flowered flax. Stems to 2 ft., usually leafless below. Profuse bloomer, with branching clusters of light blue flowers that close in shade or late in the day. Self-sows freely.

LIPPIA citriodora. See ALOYSIA triphylla

LIPPIA repens. See PHYLA nodiflora

L

LIQUIDAMBAR

SWEET GUM

Hamamelidaceae

DECIDUOUS TREES

ZONES VARY BY SPECIES

FULL SUN

REGULAR TO MODERATE WATER

Liquidambar styraciflua

Valuable for form, foliage, fall color, and easy culture. Moderate growth rate; young and middle-aged trees generally upright, somewhat cone shaped, spreading in age. Lobed, maplelike leaves. Flowers inconspicuous; fruits are spiny balls that ornament trees in winter, need raking in spring.

Give neutral or slightly acid, improved garden soil; chlorosis in strongly alkaline soils is hard to correct (the reason why none of these trees is recommended for desert zones). Stake well. Prune only to shape. Trees branch from ground up and look most natural that way, but can be pruned high to expose a definite trunk.

Form surface roots that can be a nuisance in lawns or narrow parking strips. Good street trees in ample parking strip, however. Effective in tall screens or groves, planted 6–10 ft. apart. Brilliant fall foliage; fall color less effective in mildest climates or in mild, late autumns.

L. formosana. CHINESE SWEET GUM. Zones 4–9, 14–24, 26, 28–33. To 40–60 ft. tall, 25 ft. wide. Free-form outline; sometimes pyramidal, especially when young. Leaves with three to five lobes are 3–4½ in. across, violet red when expanding, then deep green. Yellow or red fall color.

L. orientalis. ORIENTAL SWEET GUM. Zones 5–9, 14–24, 26, 28, 31, 32. Native to Turkey. To 20–30 ft., spreading or round headed. Leaves 2–3 in. wide, deeply five lobed, lobes again lobed to produce a lacy effect. Leafs out early after short dormant period. Fall color varies from deep gold and bright red in colder regions to dull brown purple in warmer areas.

L. styraciflua. AMERICAN SWEET GUM. Zones 3–9, 14–37, 39. Native to eastern U.S. Grows to 60–75 ft. in gardens; much taller in the wild. Narrow and erect in youth, with lower limbs eventually spreading to 20–25 ft. Good all-year tree. Branching pattern, furrowed bark, corky wings on twigs, and hanging fruit provide winter interest. Leaves five to seven lobed, 3–7 in. wide; deep green in spring and summer, turning purple, yellow, or red in fall. Even seedling trees give good fall color, though color may vary somewhat from year to year. To get desired and uniform color, choose trees while they are in fall leaf or buy budded trees of a named variety, such as the following:

'Burgundy'. Leaves turn deep purple red, hang late into winter or even early spring if storms are not heavy.

'Festival'. Narrow, columnar. Light green foliage turns to yellow, peach, pink, orange, and red.

'Palo Alto'. Turns orange red to bright red in fall.

'Rotundiloba'. Lobes of leaves are rounded rather than sharp. Fall foliage is purple. Tree does not form fruit.

'Variegata'. Within a few weeks of unfurling, leaves develop streaks and blotches of yellow. They retain variegation throughout summer and early fall.

LIRIODENDRON tulipifera

TULIP TREE

Magnoliaceae

DECIDUOUS TREE

ZONES 1–12, 14–23, 26, 28–41

FULL SUN

REGULAR WATER

Native to eastern U.S. Fast growth to 60–90 ft., with eventual spread to 35–50 ft.; considerably larger in the wild. Straight, columnar trunk, with spreading, rising branches that form tall pyra-

Liriodendron tulipifera

midal crown. The 5–6 in. leaves are variously described as lyre shaped, saddle shaped, or truncated; they're like blunt-tipped maple leaves missing the end lobe. They turn from bright yellow green to bright yellow in fall.

Tulip-shaped flowers in late spring are 2 in. wide, greenish yellow, orange at base. Handsome at close range but not showy on the tree, since they are carried high up and well concealed by leaves. Trees don't usually bloom until they are 10 to 12 years old.

Nurseries may carry two slower-growing selections that are smaller than the species. 'Arnold' ('Fastigiata') has a rigidly columnar habit useful for narrow planting areas; it will bloom 2 to 3 years after planting. 'Majestic Beauty' has yellow-edged leaves.

Tulip trees thrive in deep, rich, well-drained neutral or slightly acid soil. Fairly weak wooded and subject to limb breakage from storms or ice; best used in wind-sheltered locations. Give them room; they make good large shade or lawn trees. Wide-spreading network of shallow, fleshy roots make them difficult to garden under. Control aphids as necessary.

LIRIOPE and OPHIOPOGON

LILY TURF

Liliaceae

EVERGREEN GRASSLIKE PERENNIALS

ZONES VARY BY SPECIES

SOME SHADE, EXCEPT AS NOTED

REGULAR TO MODERATE WATER

SEE CHART NEXT PAGE

Liriope muscari

These two plants are similar in appearance: both form clumps or tufts of grasslike leaves and bear white or lavender summer flowers in spikelike or branched clusters (quite showy in some kinds). Last well in flower arrangements. Use as casual ground cover in small areas. Also attractive as borders along paths, between flower bed and lawn, among rock groupings, or in rock gardens. Grow well along streams and around garden pools. They compete well with roots of other plants; try under bamboo or to cover bare soil at bases of trees or shrubs in ground or in large containers. None satisfactory as mowed lawn. Tolerate indoor conditions in pots or planter.

Provide filtered sun to full shade; take full sun in cool-summer regions. Plant in well-drained soil. Become ragged and brown with neglect; cut back shaggy old foliage before new leaves appear. Plants don't need heavy feeding. To increase, divide in early spring before new growth starts.

Plants look best from spring until cold weather of winter. Extended frosts may cause plants to turn yellow; they take quite a while to recover. Can show tip burn on leaves if soil contains excess salts or if plants are kept too wet where drainage is poor.

LISIANTHUS. See EUSTOMA

LITCHI chinensis

LITCHI, LITCHI NUT

Sapindaceae

EVERGREEN TREE

ZONES 21–25, 27

FULL SUN

REGULAR WATER

Litchi chinensis

Slow-growing, round-topped, spreading tree, 20–40 ft. tall. Leaves have three to nine leathery, 3–6-in.-long leaflets that are coppery red when young, dark green later. Inconspicuous flowers. When fruit is ripe, the brittle, warty rind surrounding it turns red. Fruit is sweet in flavor, juicy when fresh, raisinlike when dried.

Needs frost-free site, moist air, fertile acidic soil. Look for named varieties if you're interested in fruit production. 'Brewster', 'Groff', 'Kwai Mi', 'Mauritius', and 'Sweet Cliff' are grown.

L

LIRIOPE AND OPHIOPOGON

NAME	ZONES	GROWTH FORM	LEAVES	FLOWERS	COMMENTS
Liriope muscari BIG BLUE LILY TURF	3–10, 14–33	Forms large clumps but does not spread by underground stems. Rather loose growth habit, 1–1½ ft. high	Dark green. To 2 ft. long, ½ in. wide	Dark violet buds and flowers in rather dense, 6–8-in.-long spikelike clusters on 5–12-in.-long stems (resemble grape hyacinths). Followed by a few round, shiny black fruits	Profuse flowers held above leaves in young plants, partly hidden in older plants. 'Lilac Beauty' differs only in having paler violet flowers. Many other varieties
L. m. 'Border Gem'	3–10, 14–33	Dwarf clump to 8 in.	Leaves to 8 in. long	Lilac flowers	Use as edging. 'Little Beauty' is similar
L. m. 'Gold Banded'	3–10, 14–33	Large clump 1–1½ ft. high	Leaves broad, with narrow gold margins	Flowers as in *L. muscari*	Arching clumps
L. m. 'John Burch'	3–10, 14–33	Large clump 1–1½ ft. high	Leaves broad, chartreuse with wide green edging	Heavy flower spikes like cockscombs stand well above leaves	Performs best in full sun
L. m. 'Majestic'	3–10, 14–33	Resembles *L. muscari* but forms more open clumps and is somewhat taller growing	Similar to *L. muscari*	Dark violet flowers and buds in clusters that look somewhat like cockscombs, on 8–10-in.-long stems	Heavy flowering. Clusters show up well, held above leaves on young plants. 'Royal Purple' and 'Webster's Wideleaf' are similar
L. m. 'Monroe's White' ('Munroe's White')	3–10, 14–33	Large clump 1–1½ ft. high	Leaves broad, deep green	Flower spikes white, standing well above foliage	Prefers more shade than most. 'White on White' is similar, but with white leaf variegation
L. m. 'Samantha'	3–10, 14–33	Dwarf clump, to 10 in. high	Leaves dark green, narrow	Lavender pink flowers	Colors best in a warm spot
L. m. 'Silvery Sunproof'	3–10, 14–33	Open growth, strongly vertical, partly arching, 15–18 in. high	Foliage has gold stripes that turn white as leaves mature	Lilac flowers in spikelike clusters rising well above foliage	One of the best for open areas and for flowers. Leaves are whiter in sun; they become greener or yellower in part shade
L. m. 'Variegata' (may be sold as **Ophiopogon jaburan 'Variegata'**)	3–10, 14–33	Resembles *L. muscari*, but somewhat looser, softer	New leaves green, 1–1½ ft. long, edged with yellow; become dark green in second season	Violet buds and flowers in spikelike clusters well above foliage. Flower stalks 1 ft. high	Does best in partial shade. Sometimes sold as *L. exiliflora* 'Vittata'
L. spicata CREEPING LILY TURF	3–10, 14–34	Dense ground cover that spreads widely by underground stems. Grows 8–9 in. high	Narrow (¼-in.-wide), deep green, grasslike leaves, soft and not as upright as those of *L. muscari*. 'Silver Dragon' has white-striped leaves	Pale lilac to white flowers in spikelike clusters barely taller than leaves	To get best effect, mow every year in spring prior to new growth. Good ground cover for cold areas where *Ophiopogon japonicus* won't grow
L. s. 'Franklin Mint'	3–10, 14–34	Larger than species (12–15 in.)	Leaves broader than those of species	Flower spikes large, erect, pale lilac	Creeps like species, but has size and form of *L. muscari*
L. s. 'Silver Dragon'	3–10, 14–34	Similar in size to species	Leaves striped silvery white	Flowers pale purple on short spikes	Fine ground cover for shade, but slower growing and more sparse than species
Ophiopogon jaburan (often sold as **Liriope gigantea**)	5–9, 14–31	Eventually forms large clump growing from fibrous roots	Dark green, somewhat curved, firm leaves 1½–3 ft. long, about ½ in. wide	Small, chalk white flowers in nodding clusters, somewhat hidden by leaves. Metallic violet blue fruit	Fruit is very attractive feature; good for cutting. 'Vittatus' has leaves striped lengthwise with white, aging to plain green. Similar, perhaps identical, is *Liriope muscari* 'Variegata'

LIRIOPE AND OPHIOPOGON

NAME	ZONES	GROWTH FORM	LEAVES	FLOWERS	COMMENTS
O. japonicus MONDO GRASS	5–9, 14–31, warmer parts of 32	Forms dense clumps that spread by underground stems, many of which are tuberlike. Slow to establish as ground cover	Dark green leaves ⅛ in. wide, 8–12 in. long. 'Nana' and 'Kyoto Dwarf' have half-sized leaves in tight clumps. Slow, sure spreader	Flowers light lilac in short spikes usually hidden by the leaves. Blue fruit	Can be cut back. Easy to divide. Set divisions 6–8 in. apart. Roots will be killed at 10°F/−12°C. Looks best in partial shade
O. planiscapus 'Nigrescens' ('Nigricans', 'Arabicus', 'Ebony Knight')	5–9, 14–31, warmer parts of 32	Makes tuft 8 in. high and about 1 ft. wide	Leaves to 10 in. long. New leaves green but soon turn black	White (sometimes flushed pink) in loose spikelike clusters	Spreads slowly and does not make a solid cover. Interesting in containers. Valuable as novelty

LITHODORA diffusa

Boraginaceae

PERENNIAL

ZONES 5–7, 14–17, 32

WILL TAKE FULL SUN IN COOL-SUMMER AREAS

MODERATE WATER

Lithodora diffusa

Prostrate, somewhat shrubby, slightly mounded, broad mass 6–12 in. tall. Narrow evergreen leaves, ¾–1 in. long; both foliage and stems are hairy. In late spring (and often later), plant is sprinkled with tubular, brilliant blue flowers ½ in. long. Loose, well-drained, lime-free soil. Use in rock gardens, spilling over walls. Best suited to mild-summer climates. 'Heavenly Blue' and 'Grace Ward' are selected varieties. Formerly *Lithospermum diffusum* or *L. prostratum*.

LITHOSPERMUM. See LITHODORA

LIVERLEAF. See HEPATICA

LIVINGSTONE DAISY. See DOROTHEANTHUS bellidiformis

LIVISTONA

Arecaceae (Palmae)

PALMS

ZONES 13–17, 19–27

FULL SUN

REGULAR WATER

Livistona australis

Native from China to Australia. These fan palms somewhat resemble *Washingtonia* but generally have shorter, darker, shinier leaves. They are hardy to about 22°F/−6°C. All make good potted plants.

L. australis. AUSTRALIAN FAN PALM. In ground, grows slowly to 40–50 ft. Has clean, slender trunk with interesting-looking leaf scars. Dark green leaves 3–5 ft. wide.

L. chinensis. CHINESE FOUNTAIN PALM, CHINESE FAN PALM. Slow growing; 40-year-old plants are only 15 ft. tall. Self-cleaning (no pruning of old leaves needed) with leaf-scarred trunk. Roundish, bright green, 3–6-ft. leaves droop strongly at outer edges.

L. decipiens. To 30–40 ft. in 20 years. Stiff, open head of leaves green on top, bluish beneath, 2–5 ft. across; borne on long, spiny stems.

L. mariae. From hot, dry interior Australia. Grows slowly to 10–15 ft. tall. Leaves and leaf stems develop an attractive reddish tinge. Leaves 3–4 ft. wide.

LOBELIA

Campanulaceae (Lobeliaceae)

PERENNIALS OR ANNUALS

ZONES VARY BY SPECIES

PARTIAL SHADE IN HOTTEST CLIMATES

AMPLE WATER

MOST CONTAIN POISONOUS ALKALOIDS

Lobelia erinus

Distinct differences separate the annual lobelia from the most familiar perennial kinds; the former is blue and spreading, the others red or blue and upright. On all types, the tubular, lipped flowers resemble those of honeysuckle or salvia.

L. cardinalis. CARDINAL FLOWER. Perennial. Zones 1–7, 12–17, 26 (upper half), 28–45. Native to eastern U.S. and to a few sites in mountains of Southwest. Erect, single-stemmed, 2–4-ft.-high plant with saw-edged leaves set directly on the stems. Spikes of flame red, inch-long flowers in summer. A bog plant in nature, it needs rich soil and constant moisture through the growing season.

Crossbreeding between this species and *L. splendens* (*L. fulgens*), which is closely related, has resulted in a number of hybrids. 'Queen Victoria' and 'Royal Robe' have deep purple-red foliage and scarlet flowers; 'Heather Pink' has soft pink flowers.

L. erinus. Annual. All zones. Popular and dependable edging plant. Compact or trailing growth habit with leafy, branching stems. Flowers, ¾ in. across, are light blue to violet (sometimes pink, reddish purple, or white) with white or yellowish throats. Blooms from early summer to frost; lives over winter in mild areas. In mild-winter, hot-summer regions, grow it as a winter–spring annual. Takes about 2 months for seed sown in pots to grow to planting-out size. Moist, rich soil. Self-sows where adapted. Trailing kinds make a graceful ground cover in large planters or in smaller pots; the stems, loaded with flowers, spill over the edges.

'Cambridge Blue' has clear, soft blue flowers and light green leaves on compact 4–6-in. plant. 'Crystal Palace', also compact, has rich dark blue flowers, bronze green leaves. 'Rosamond' has carmine red flowers with white eyes. 'White Lady' is pure white. Three trailing varieties for hanging baskets or wall plantings are 'Hamburgia', 'Blue Cascade', and 'Sapphire'.

L. gerardii. Perennial. Zones 2–9, 14–17, 31–43. Hybrid between *L. cardinalis* and *L. syphilitica*; needs rich soil, constant moisture, part shade. 'Vedrariensis' grows to 4 ft., with coppery green foliage and bright royal purple flowers. 'Rosea', 2½ ft. high, has rose pink flowers. 'Ruby Slippers', 3 ft. tall, has dark red flowers.

L. syphilitica. Perennial. Zones 2–9, 14–17, 31–43. Native to eastern U.S. Leafy plants send up 3-ft. stalks set with blue flowers. Needs ample moisture, partial shade.

Lobeliaceae. See Campanulaceae

L

LOBIVIA

Cactaceae

CACTI

🌡 ZONES 16, 17, 21–27; OR INDOORS

☀◐ FULL SUN OR LIGHT SHADE

🌢 REGULAR WATER SPRING THROUGH FALL

Lobivia Hybrid

Small globular or cylindrical shapes with big, showy flowers in shades of red, yellow, pink, orange, purple, lilac. Flowers sometimes nearly as big as plants, like flowers of *Echinopsis* but shorter, broader. Many species offered. Usually grown in pots by collectors. Give porous soil, occasional feeding. Give little or no water in winter. Can grow indoors in bright light; bring outside in warm weather.

LOBIVOPSIS

Cactaceae

CACTI

🌡 ZONES 16, 17, 21–27; OR INDOORS

☀◐ BLOOM BEST IN FULL SUN

🌢 REGULAR WATER SPRING THROUGH FALL

Lobivopsis Hybrid

Hybrids between *Lobivia* and *Echinopsis*. Extremely free flowering with big, long-tubed flowers on small plants. Culture, hardiness same as for *Echinopsis*. Grow in fairly good-size pots (5-in. pot for a 3-in. plant); feed monthly in summer. Paramount Hybrids have blossoms in red, pink, orange, rose, and white. Some may show a dozen or more 6-in.-long flowers on a 3–4-in. plant. Keep cool and dry in winter.

LOBLOLLY BAY. See GORDONIA lasianthus

LOBULARIA maritima

SWEET ALYSSUM

Brassicaceae (Cruciferae)

ANNUAL

🌡 ALL ZONES

☀◐ BEST IN FULL SUN, TOLERATES LIGHT SHADE

🌢 REGULAR WATER

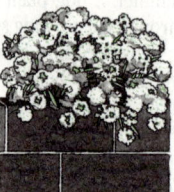

Lobularia maritima

Low, branching, trailing plant to 1 ft. tall, with narrow or lance-shaped leaves ½–2 in. long. Tiny, four-petaled white flowers crowded in clusters; honeylike fragrance. Blooms spring until frost in cold-winter regions; in mild climates blooms all year from self-sown seedlings. In hot, humid regions, may go dormant during hottest period but resume when weather cools. Seeds sometimes included in wildflower mixes or erosion-control mixes for bare or disturbed earth.

Easy, quick, dependable. Blooms from seed in 6 weeks; grows in almost any soil. Useful for carpeting, edging, bulb cover, temporary filler in rock garden or perennial border; between flagstones; in window boxes or containers. Attracts bees. If you shear plants halfway back 4 weeks after they come into bloom, new growth will make another crop of flowers, and plants won't become rangy.

Garden varieties better known than the species; these varieties self-sow too, but seedlings tend to revert to taller, looser growth, less intense color, and smaller flowers. 'Carpet of Snow' (2–4 in. tall), 'Little Gem' (4–6 in.), and 'Tiny Tim' (3 in.) are good compact whites. 'Tetra Snowdrift' (1 ft.) has long stems, large white flowers. 'Rosie O'Day' (2–4 in.) and 'Pink Heather' (6 in.) are lavender pinks. 'Oriental Night' (4 in.) and 'Violet Queen' (5 in.) are rich violet purples.

LOCUST. See ROBINIA

LOGANBERRY. See BLACKBERRY

LOLIUM

RYEGRASS

Poaceae (Gramineae)

ANNUAL OR PERENNIAL LAWN GRASSES

🌡 ZONES VARY BY SPECIES

☀ FULL SUN

🌢 REGULAR WATER

Lolium perenne

Not considered the choicest lawn grasses, but useful in special conditions and situations (lawns, pasture, soil reclamation). These are clumping, not running, grasses. To make tight turf, sow heavily. Ryegrass is often mixed with other lawn grass species for low-cost, large-area coverage in cool-summer climates. In Bermuda grass country, it is often sown in fall on reconditioned Bermuda lawns to give winter green.

L. multiflorum. ITALIAN RYEGRASS. All zones. Larger, coarser than perennial ryegrass. Basically an annual; some plants live for several seasons in mild climates. Fast growing, deep rooted. Hybrid between *L. multiflorum* and *L. perenne* is common or domestic ryegrass, often used as winter cover on soil or winter-dormant lawns.

L. perenne. PERENNIAL RYEGRASS. Zones 1–6, 15–17, 36, 38–45. Finer in texture than above, deep green with high gloss. Disadvantages are clumping tendency and tough flower and seed stems that lie down under mower blades. Advantages are fast sprouting and growth. Best in cool-summer climates. 'Manhattan' is finer, more uniform. Other varieties are 'Pennfine', 'Derby', 'Yorktown', 'Loretta'. Mow at 1½–2 in., higher in summer.

LONDON PRIDE. See SAXIFRAGA umbrosa

LONICERA

HONEYSUCKLE

Caprifoliaceae

EVERGREEN, SEMIEVERGREEN, OR DECIDUOUS SHRUBS OR VINES

🌡 ZONES VARY BY SPECIES

☀◐ FULL SUN OR LIGHT SHADE

🌢 MODERATE WATER

Lonicera periclymenum

These easy-to-grow plants exist in a great many species, most of them valued for tubular, often fragrant flowers. Vining kinds need support when they are starting out. When honeysuckles become overgrown, cut them to the ground; they regrow rapidly. Prune after flowering. Blossoms attract hummingbirds. Fruit provides food for many kinds of birds. Plants are generally not bothered by serious pests or diseases. Aphids are the chief problem, distorting buds and preventing flowering in parts of the Midwest and East.

L. brownii. Deciduous vine. Zones 1–7, 31–45. Hybrid between *L. sempervirens* and *L. hirsuta*, a little-grown vine from the northeastern U.S. 'Dropmore Scarlet', the only selection extensively grown, climbs to 9–10 ft. It has blue-green leaves, those on the upper stem joining at the base; clusters of tubular scarlet flowers appear from early summer to frost.

L. fragrantissima. WINTER HONEYSUCKLE. Deciduous shrub, semievergreen in mild-winter areas. Zones 2–9, 14–24, 31–41. Arching, rather stiff growth to 8 ft. Leaves oval, dull dark green above, blue green beneath, 1–3 in. long. Creamy white flowers, ½ in. long, in late winter and early spring. Flowers richly fragrant (like *Daphne odora*) but not showy.

L

Berrylike red fruit. Can be used as clipped hedge or background plant. Bring budded branches indoors for bloom.

L. heckrottii. GOLD FLAME HONEYSUCKLE, CORAL HONEYSUCKLE. Deciduous vine or small shrub, semievergreen in mild-winter climates. Zones 3–24, 30–35. Vigorous to 12–15 ft., with oval, 2-in., blue-green leaves. Free blooming from spring to frost. Clustered 1½-in.-long flowers, bright coral pink outside and rich yellow within, open from coral pink buds. Train as espalier or on wire along eaves.

L. hildebrandiana. GIANT BURMESE HONEYSUCKLE. Fast-growing evergreen vine. Zones 9, 14–17, 19–28. Big plant with 4–6-in., oval, glossy dark green leaves on supple, ropelike stems. Blooms in summer; tubular, fragrant flowers to 6–7 in. long open white, then turn yellow to dull orange. Blossoms are slow to drop. Plants occasionally have dark green, inch-wide, berrylike fruit. Thin out older stems occasionally and remove some of the growth that has bloomed. Striking along eaves, on arbor or wall.

L. japonica. JAPANESE HONEYSUCKLE. Evergreen, semievergreen, or deciduous vine, depending on climate. Zones 2–41. Rampant—even invasive in the Southeast. Deep green, oval leaves; purple-tinged white flowers with sweet fragrance, late spring into fall.

Several varieties are grown, all better known than the species itself. 'Aureo-reticulata', goldnet honeysuckle, has leaves veined yellow, especially in full sun. 'Halliana', Hall's honeysuckle, most vigorous and widely grown, climbs to 15 ft., covers 150 sq. ft.; flowers pure white changing to yellow, attractive to bees. 'Purpurea', probably same as *L. j. chinensis,* has leaves tinged purple underneath and purplish red flowers that are white inside.

Of the above, 'Halliana' is the most commonly used as bank and ground cover, for erosion control in large areas; as ground cover, set plants 2–3 ft. apart. Unless curbed, it can become a weed, smothering less vigorous plants, so prune severely (cut back almost to framework) once yearly to prevent undergrowth from building up. Can be trained as privacy or wind screen on chain link or wire fence. Tolerates drought and poor drainage.

L. maximowiczii sachalinensis. Deciduous shrub. Zones 2–9, 14–21, 32–41. These euphonious syllables denote an attractive dense, rounded shrub to 6–8 ft., with dark green leaves 1½–3 in. long and half as wide. The deep red, 1½-in.-long flowers are followed by red fruit. Fall color is bright yellow.

L. nitida. BOX HONEYSUCKLE. Evergreen shrub, deciduous in coldest part of range. Zones 4–9, 14–24, 28–32. To 4–6 ft. tall, with densely leafy branches. Tiny (½-in.), oval, shiny dark green leaves. Attractive bronze to plum-colored winter foliage. Late spring or early summer flowers are fragrant, creamy white, ½ in. long. Translucent blue-purple berries. Rapid growth, tending toward untidiness, but easily pruned as hedge or single plant. Takes salt spray. 'Baggesen's Gold' has golden foliage in sun.

L. periclymenum. WOODBINE. Evergreen vine in mild-winter areas, deciduous elsewhere. Zones 2–24, 30–41. Resembles *L. japonica* but is less rampant. Whorls of 2-in.-long, fragrant flowers in summer, fall. Blooms of 'Serotina' are purple outside, yellow inside. 'Berries Jubilee' has yellow flowers followed by profusion of red berries. 'Belgica' is less vining, more bushy than most, with abundant white flowers flushed purple, fading to yellow; flowers and red fruit come in large clusters. 'Graham Thomas' has white flowers that turn copper-tinted yellow.

L. pileata. PRIVET HONEYSUCKLE. Evergreen or semievergreen shrub. Zones 3–9, 14–24, 31, 32. Low, spreading plant to 3 ft. tall, with stiff horizontal branches. Dark green, 1½-in., privetlike leaves; small, fragrant white flowers in late spring; translucent violet purple berries. Good bank cover with low-growing euonymus or barberries. Does well at seashore. Give part or full shade in hot climates.

L. sempervirens. TRUMPET HONEYSUCKLE. Deciduous (retains some leaves during mild winters in warmer regions) twining vine, shrubby if not given support. Zones 2–41. From late spring into summer, bears showy, unscented, orange-yellow to scarlet flowers—trumpet shaped, 1½–2 in. long, carried in whorls at ends of branches. Scarlet fruit. Oval, 1½–3-in.-long leaves are bluish green beneath. 'Cedar Lane' (known by the name "coral honeysuckle" in Florida) is a vigorous selection with deep red

flowers. 'Sulphurea' has yellow flowers in late spring. For 'Dropmore Scarlet', see *L. brownii.*

L. tatarica. Deciduous shrub. Zones 1–9, 14–21, 32–43. Big, twiggy shrub to 10–12 ft. tall and wide, with bluish green foliage and white to pink flowers borne in pairs in late spring. Red berries follow. Most widely grown selection is 'Arnold Red', with dark red flowers. Too large for most gardens; use for shelter belt, screening, bird shelter.

L. xylosteum. Deciduous shrub. Zones 1–9, 14–21, 32–43. Mounding, arching growth to 10 ft. tall, 12 ft. wide. Grayish or bluish green leaves, white or pinkish flowers in late spring. Species is seldom seen. 'Claveyi' or 'Clavey's Dwarf' is most commonly grown; tends to stay 3–6 ft. tall, occasionally taller. Other dwarf selections are sometimes offered. All are useful for hedges or foundation plantings in harsh climates.

LOOSESTRIFE. See LYSIMACHIA punctata, LYTHRUM virgatum

LOQUAT. See ERIOBOTRYA

LOROPETALUM chinense

Hamamelidaceae

EVERGREEN SHRUB

✂ ZONES 6–9, 14–24, 26, 28, 31; BORDERLINE IN ZONES 4, 5, 32, 33

☀ ◑ FULL SUN OR PARTIAL SHADE

💧 REGULAR WATER

Loropetalum chinense

Generally 5–10 ft. tall. Neat, compact habit, with arching or drooping tiered branches. Leaves roundish, light green, soft, 1–2 in. long. Throughout the year, the occasional leaf turns yellow or red, providing a nice touch of color. White to greenish white flowers in clusters of four to eight at ends of branches. Each flower has four narrow, inch-long, twisted petals. Blooms most heavily in spring, but some bloom is likely at any time. 'Rubrum' ('Razzleberri') has purplish leaves and bright rosy pink flowers; 'Burgundy' is similar, if not identical.

Needs well-drained, nonalkaline soil. Subtly beautiful plant, good in foregrounds, raised beds, hanging baskets, woodland gardens, even maintained as a high ground cover.

LOTUS

Fabaceae (Leguminosae)

SHRUBBY PERENNIALS

✂ ZONES VARY BY SPECIES

☀ ◑ FULL SUN OR PARTIAL SHADE

💧 REGULAR WATER

Lotus berthelotii

Trailing stems, often completely prostrate. Leaves divided into leaflets. Flowers sweet pea shaped, in shades of red to yellow. (For plants with common name "lotus," see *Nelumbo.*)

L. berthelotii. PARROT'S BEAK. Zones 9, 15–24. Trailing perennial with stems 2–3 ft. long, thickly covered with silvery gray foliage and very narrow, 1-in.-long scarlet blossoms. Blooms in summer. Dies back in cold weather; suffers root rot in poor drainage. Space 2 ft. apart as ground cover; cut back occasionally to induce bushiness. Also very effective in hanging baskets, as cascade over wall or rocks.

L. corniculatus. BIRD'S FOOT TREFOIL. Zones 2–24, 28–41. Goes dormant where winters are cold. Use as ground cover or coarse lawn substitute. Makes mat of dark green, cloverlike leaves. Forms clusters of small yellow flowers in summer and fall. Seedpods at top of flower stems spread like bird's foot, hence common name. Sow seeds or set out plants. Should be mowed occasionally.

L. maculatus 'Gold Flash'. Zones 9, 15–24. Resembles *L. berthelotii* but has bright yellow flowers with striking orange-red markings. *L. mascaensis* is similar. Both require the same care and have the same uses as *L. berthelotii*.

LOVAGE. See LEVISTICUM officinale

LOVE-IN-A-MIST. See NIGELLA damascena

LOVE-LIES-BLEEDING. See AMARANTHUS caudatus

LUCKY NUT. See THEVETIA peruviana

LUFFA. See GOURD

LUMA apiculata

Myrtaceae

EVERGREEN SHRUB OR SMALL TREE

ZONES 14–24

FULL SUN

REGULAR TO LITTLE WATER

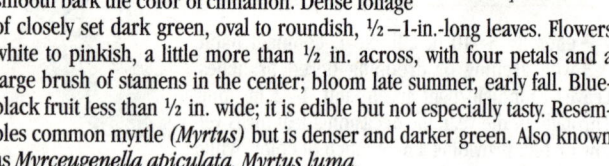
Luma apiculata

Fast growth to 6–8 ft. (possibly 20 ft.) tall, equally wide. Old plants develop beautiful, smooth bark the color of cinnamon. Dense foliage of closely set dark green, oval to roundish, ½–1-in.-long leaves. Flowers white to pinkish, a little more than ½ in. across, with four petals and a large brush of stamens in the center; bloom late summer, early fall. Blue-black fruit less than ½ in. wide; it is edible but not especially tasty. Resembles common myrtle (*Myrtus*) but is denser and darker green. Also known as *Myrceugenella apiculata, Myrtus luma*.

LUNARIA annua (L. biennis)

MONEY PLANT

Brassicaceae (Cruciferae)

BIENNIAL

ZONES 1–10, 14–24, 28–43

AFTERNOON SHADE IN HOT CLIMATES

REGULAR TO MODERATE WATER

Lunaria annua

Old-fashioned garden plant, grown for silvery, translucent circles (about 1¼ in. across) that stay on flower stalks and are all that remain of ripened seedpods after outer coverings drop with seeds. Plants are 1½–3 ft. high, with coarse, heart-shaped, toothed leaves. Spring flowers resemble wild mustard blooms but are purple or white, not yellow. There is a form with variegated leaves.

Plant in an out-of-the-way spot in poor soil or in a mixed flower bed where shining pods can be admired before they are picked for dry bouquets. Tough, persistent; can reseed and become weedy.

LUNGWORT. See PULMONARIA

HELP LUPINE SEEDS ALONG

Lupine seeds are hard coated and often slow to sprout. They will germinate faster if you soak them in hot water or scratch or nick the seed coats with a file before planting.

LUPINUS

LUPINE

Fabaceae (Leguminosae)

PERENNIALS, SHRUBS, AND ANNUALS

ZONES VARY BY SPECIES

FULL SUN

WATER NEEDS VARY BY SPECIES

Lupinus Russell Hybrid

Leaves are divided into many leaflets (like fingers of a hand). Flowers sweet pea shaped, in dense spikes at ends of stems. Hundreds of species, many of them native to western U.S.; occur in wide range of habitats, from beach sand to alpine rocks. The most commonly grown lupines are Russell Hybrids. Most lupines take poor conditions, but the hybrids prefer rich, slightly acidic, well-drained soil.

L. hartwegii. Annual. All zones. Native to Mexico. Grows 1½–3 ft. tall; comes in shades of blue, white, and pink. Easy to grow from seed sown in place in spring for summer bloom. Moderate water.

L. perennis. Perennial. Zones 1–6, 28–43. Native to eastern U. S. To 2 ft. high, with purple flowers in late spring or early summer. Regular water.

L. polyphyllus. Perennial. Zones 3–9, 14–21, 34, 37–39. Native to moist places along the West Coast. Grows 1½–4 ft. tall, with dense clusters of blue, purple, or reddish flowers in summer. One important ancestor of the Russell Hybrids. Ample water.

L. Russell Hybrids. RUSSELL LUPINES. Perennials. Zones 1–7, 14–17, 34, 36–45. Not suited to hot climates. Best in cool areas of the West Coast, Pacific Northwest, New England, northern tier of states and adjacent southern Canada, and higher elevations in mountains of the South. Large, spreading plants to 4–5 ft. tall, with long, dense spikes of flowers in late spring or early summer. Blooms in white, cream, yellow, pink, blue, red, orange, purple, and bicolors. Little Lulu and Minarette strains are smaller growing—to 1½ ft.

Grow from seed or buy started plants in flats or pots. Keep soil moist; give plants good air circulation to prevent mildew. Often short lived, even in mild climates. Self-sown seedlings won't resemble parents.

LYCHNIS

Caryophyllaceae

PERENNIALS AND ANNUALS

ZONES VARY BY SPECIES

FULL SUN OR LIGHT SHADE

WATER NEEDS VARY BY SPECIES

Lychnis coronaria

Hardy, old-fashioned garden flowers, all very tolerant of adverse soils. The different kinds vary in appearance but all offer eye-catching colors in summer. Plants are generally short lived and need to be replaced every few years.

L. arkwrightii. Perennial in Zones 2–9, 14–24, 31–41; sometimes grown as an annual. Complex hybrid involving several species. Remove faded flowers for repeat bloom. 'Dwarf Form' is a 10-in. plant with reddish green foliage and scarlet to orange-red flowers in few-flowered clusters. 'Vesuvius' is taller (to 2 ft.), with large orange-red flowers. Rich soil, regular water.

L. chalcedonica. MALTESE CROSS. Perennial. Zones 1–9, 11–24, 31–43. Loose, open, growing 2–3 ft. high, with hairy leaves and stems. Scarlet flowers in dense terminal clusters, the petals deeply cut. Plants effective in large borders with white flowers, gray foliage. There is a white variety, 'Alba'. Regular water.

L. coeli-rosa (Silene coeli-rosa, Agrostemma coeli-rosa, Viscaria coeli-rosa). Annual. All zones. Single, saucer-shaped, 1-in. flowers cover foot-tall plants over long summer bloom period. Blue and lavender are most common colors; white and pink are also available, most with contrasting lighter or darker eye spot. Leaves long, narrow, pointed. Good cut flowers. Sow seed in rich soil in early spring (in fall for winter and spring bloom in mild-winter climates). Regular water.

L. coronaria. CROWN-PINK, DUSTY MILLER, MULLEIN PINK, ROSE CAMPION. Perennial in Zones 3–9, 14–24, 30–34; treat as annual elsewhere. Grows 1½–2½ ft. tall, with attractive white, silky foliage and magenta to crimson flowers a little less than an inch across. Effective massed. 'Alba' has white flowers; 'Angel's Blush' bears white blossoms with a deep pink eye. All self-sow freely if fading flowers are not removed. Moderate water.

L. haageana. Perennial in Zones 2–9, 14–24, 31–41, but often treated as an annual. Red, orange, salmon, or white flowers carried in clusters of two or three blossoms throughout summer. Stems clothed in green leaves reach 1½ ft. high. Dies down shortly after bloom ceases. Mulch to protect against extreme heat or cold. Though a hybrid, it comes fairly true from seed. Regular water.

L. viscaria. Perennial. Zones 1–9, 11–24, 31–43. Compact, low, evergreen clumps of grasslike leaves to 5 in. long. Pinkish purple, ½-in. flowers on 1½–2-ft. stalks. 'Alba' has white blooms. Foot-high 'Splendens' has magenta blossoms; 'Splendens Flore Pleno' is similar but double flowered. Two deep red bloomers are 8-in. 'Atropurpurea' and 1½-ft. 'Zulu'. 'Alpina' is a 4-in. dwarf with rosy pink blooms. Regular to moderate water.

LYCIANTHES rantonnei (Solanum rantonnettii)

PARAGUAY NIGHTSHADE

Solanaceae

SEMIEVERGREEN SHRUB OR VINE

⚡ ZONES 12, 13, 15–27

☼ FULL SUN

💧 REGULAR TO MODERATE WATER

Lycianthes rantonnei

As freestanding plant makes 6–8-ft. shrub, but can be staked into tree form or, with support, grown as a vine to 12–15 ft. or more. Can also be allowed to sprawl as a ground cover. Bright green, oval leaves to 4 in. long; violet blue, yellow-centered, 1-in.-wide flowers throughout warm weather, often nearly throughout year. Wild species has flowers only half as large. 'Royal Robe' is more compact than the species, with a longer bloom season and darker purple flowers.

Informal, fast growing, not easy to use in tailored landscape. (If you use this plant there, prune it severely to keep neat.) In severe cold, leaf drop is heavy and branch tips may die back. In Zones 12, 13, place on protected patio.

LYCIUM chinense

MATRIMONY VINE, BOXTHORN

Solanaceae

DECIDUOUS SHRUB

⚡ ZONES 3–7, 31, 32, 34

☼ FULL SUN

💧💧 REGULAR TO MODERATE WATER

Lycium chinense

Arching, often vinelike shrub to 12 ft.; branches sprawl or creep unless supported. Stems are usually thornless. Diamond-shaped bright green leaves to 3 in. long; small purplish blue flowers followed by bright red to orange-red fruit that is eaten by birds. Not especially attractive, but useful for bank cover, where branches will take root. Can thrive in poor soil and in ocean wind. Can be invasive; do not locate near choice garden plants.

LYCORIS

SPIDER LILY

Amaryllidaceae

BULBS

⚡ ZONES VARY BY SPECIES

☼ ☽ FULL SUN OR LIGHT SHADE

💧 REGULAR WATER DURING GROWTH AND BLOOM

Lycoris radiata

Narrow, strap-shaped leaves appear in spring; in mild-winter climates, they sprout in autumn and live over to spring. Foliage ripens and dies down before bloom starts. Clusters of red, pink, or yellow flowers appear on bare stems to 2 ft. tall in late summer, fall. Flowers are spidery looking, with long stamens and narrow, wavy-edged segments curved backward.

Grow in garden beds (where bulbs will survive winter) or as pot plants. Some kinds are tender, some half hardy. Bulbs available July–August. Set 3–4 in. deep (note exception for *L. squamigera*) in good soil. Don't disturb plantings for several years. When potting, set with tops exposed. Don't use pots that are too large, since plants with crowded roots bloom best.

L. africana (L. aurea). GOLDEN SPIDER LILY. Zones 16, 17, 19–24, 26, 28; indoor/outdoor container plants. Bright yellow, 3-in. flowers.

L. radiata. Zones 4–9, 12–24, 27–33. Best known and easiest to grow. Coral red flowers with gold sheen; 1½-ft. stems. 'Alba' has white flowers. Will take light shade. Give protection in cold-winter climates.

L. sanguinea. Zones 4–24, 29–31. To 2 ft. tall, with 2–2½-in., bright red to orange-red flowers.

L. sprengeri. Zones 4–24, 29–33. Similar to *L. squamigera*, but with slightly smaller purplish pink flowers.

L. squamigera (Amaryllis hallii). Zones 3–24, 29–33. Clusters of fragrant, funnel-shaped, 3-in., pink or rosy lilac flowers on 2-ft. stems. Hardiest species; overwinters in colder regions if bulbs are planted 6 in. deep in protected location, as against a south wall.

LYSIMACHIA

Primulaceae

PERENNIALS

⚡ ZONES VARY BY SPECIES

☼ ☽ FULL SUN OR PARTIAL SHADE

💧 MODERATE WATER

Lysimachia nummularia

Most are vigorous perennials capable of spreading by underground roots beyond allotted limits, especially if water supply is plentiful; of those listed, only *L. ephemerum* is well behaved. See that the more aggressive types do not invade choicer plantings. They are useful for naturalizing in woodland edges or barely maintained areas. Except as noted, bloom is in summer.

L. barystachys. Zones 3–9, 14–21, 31–41. Grows to 2 ft. tall, with narrow leaves and spikes of white flowers that start out horizontal and gradually turn upright.

L. ciliata. Zones 1–9, 14–21, 28–43. Erect plant to 3 ft., with opposite or whorled oval, 5-in. leaves. Small, nodding yellow flowers appear in upper leaf joints. 'Atropurpurea' is similar, but with red leaves.

L. clethroides. GOOSENECK LOOSESTRIFE. Zones 1–9, 14–24, 32–45. Grows to 3 ft. high, with olive green foliage and gracefully curving spikes of white flowers.

L. ephemerum. Zones 3–10, 14–24, 32–41. Grows to 3 ft., making a neat clump of leathery gray-green foliage. Long, slender clusters of long-lasting white flowers. Not invasive.

L. nummularia. MONEYWORT, CREEPING JENNY. Zones 1–9, 14–24, 31–43. Evergreen creeping plant with long runners (to 2 ft.) that root at joints. Forms pretty light green mat of roundish leaves. Yellow flowers about 1 in. across form singly in leaf joints. Summer blooming. Best use is in corners where it need not be restrained. Will spill from wall, hanging basket. Good ground cover (plant 1–1½ ft. apart) near streams. 'Aurea' has yellow leaves, needs shade.

L. procumbens (L. congestiflora). GOLDEN GLOBES. Zones 8, 9, 14–24, 26. Trailing stems bend upward at tips. Leaves thick, to 2½ in. long. Branches end in clusters of bright yellow, inch-wide flowers that open from round buds. Blooms in spring, with some scattered bloom later. Use in hanging baskets or (with caution) as a ground cover.

L. punctata. LOOSESTRIFE. Zones 1–9, 14–24, 31–43. To 4 ft. tall. Erect stems have narrow leaves in whorls, with whorled yellow flowers on the top third.

Lythraceae. The loosestrife family is represented in this book by *Cuphea,* crape myrtle *(Lagerstroemia),* and purple loosestrife *(Lythrum). Lysimachia punctata,* whose common name is loosestrife, is in the primrose family.

LYTHRUM virgatum

PURPLE LOOSESTRIFE

Lythraceae

PERENNIAL

⚡ ZONES 1–9, 14–24, 29–43

☼ FULL SUN

💧 REGULAR WATER; TOO MUCH MOISTURE ENCOURAGES INVASIVENESS

Lythrum virgatum

Showy plant for pond margins or moist areas (but use with caution); also valued for cut flowers. The 2-ft.-wide clumps put up 2½–5 ft.-high stems. Narrow leaves clothe lower portion of stems; the upper 8–18 in. are densely set with ¾-in. magenta flowers in late summer and fall.

L. virgatum has a bad reputation with lovers of native plants, since seedlings spring up so freely that native vegetation is crowded out. Hybrids (often sold as varieties of *L. salicaria,* a similar plant), including 'Roseum Superbum', 'Morden's Pink', 'Morden's Gleam', 'Pink Spires', and 'Rosy Spires', are said to be sterile, but they may interbreed and become a nuisance. In some regions, it is illegal to plant purple loosestrife and its variants—and doing so is unwise, even if not outlawed, wherever plants have ample moisture throughout the year.

MAACKIA

Fabaceae (Leguminosae)

DECIDUOUS TREES

⚡ ZONES VARY BY SPECIES

☼ FULL SUN

💧 REGULAR WATER

Related to locust *(Robinia)* and yellow wood *(Cladrastis lutea),* maackias are medium-size trees with a slow to moderate growth rate. Leaves are divided featherwise into many leaflets. Small, sweet pea–shaped summer flowers are

Maackia amurensis

creamy or yellowish white, crowded into upright, spikelike clusters to 4–6 in. long. These are followed by flat, 2–3-in.-long seedpods. Plants are not fussy about soil and have no significant pest or disease problems.

M. amurensis. AMUR MAACKIA. Zones 1–10, 14–17, 32–43. Grows to a possible 60 ft., but may be only half that tall in gardens. Broad, rounded head; dark green foliage. Bark on trunk is an attractive bronze color, peels in curling flakes.

M. chinensis. CHINESE MAACKIA. Zones 2–10, 14–17, 32–41. Smaller (to 20–30 ft.) and shrubbier than *M. amurensis,* with leaves

divided into more and smaller leaflets. Foliage is silvery grayish green upon unfolding, then matures to dark green.

MACADAMIA

MACADAMIA NUT, QUEENSLAND NUT

Proteaceae

EVERGREEN TREES

⚡ ZONES 9, 16, 17, 19–25

☼ FULL SUN

💧 MODERATE WATER

Macadamia tetraphylla

Clean, handsome ornamental trees where frosts are light. Where best adapted (Zones 23–25), they produce clusters of hard-shelled, delicious nuts 3 to 5 years after planting. Most trees are sold under the name *M. ternifolia,* but they nearly always belong to one of the two species described below. 'Beaumont' ('Dr. Beaumont'), 'Cooper', and 'Vista' are hybrids between the two. Macadamia trees reach 25–30 ft. tall or taller, 15–20 ft. wide. Glossy, leathery leaves, 5–12 in. long, are good for fresh floral arrangements. Blooms in winter and spring, bearing small white to pink flowers carried in dense, 1-ft. clusters.

M. integrifolia. SMOOTH-SHELL MACADAMIA. Leaves are smooth edged. Nuts ripen late fall to May. Best near coast.

M. tetraphylla. ROUGH-SHELL MACADAMIA. Spiny leaves. More open tree than *M. integrifolia.* Nuts have thinner shells, appear fall through February. Best inland.

MACFADYENA unguis-cati

CAT'S CLAW, YELLOW TRUMPET VINE

Bignoniaceae

PARTLY DECIDUOUS VINE

⚡ ZONES 8–29, 31

☼◑ FULL SUN OR PARTIAL SHADE

💧 MODERATE TO LITTLE WATER

Macfadyena unguis-cati

Formerly known as *Doxantha unguis-cati* and *Bignonia tweediana.* Climbs high (to 25–40 ft.) and fast by hooked, clawlike, forked tendrils. Leaves divided into two oval, 2-in. glossy green leaflets. Blooms in early spring, bearing yellow trumpets to 2 in. long, 1¼ in. across. Vigorous; puts down roots where stems touch ground. Clings to any support—stone, wood, tree trunk. Suitable for covering chain link fence. Tends to produce leaves and flowers at stem ends; after bloom, prune hard to stimulate new growth lower down. Loses all leaves in cold winters.

MACLEAYA (Bocconia)

PLUME POPPY

Papaveraceae

PERENNIALS

⚡ ZONES VARY BY SPECIES

☼◑ SUN OR LIGHT SHADE

💧 REGULAR WATER

Macleaya cordata

These tall perennials are often still listed as *Bocconia,* a name properly belonging to their shrubby tropical relatives. The two species described below resemble each other. Both have creeping rhizomes; tall, erect stems; large, deeply lobed leaves like those of edible fig tree; and small flowers in large, branching clusters. These plants look tropical, and their value lies in size and struc-

M

ture rather than flower color. Can be invasive if not controlled; plant among shrubs rather than amid delicate perennials.

M. cordata. Zones 1–24, 30–43. To 7–8 ft. tall, with 3-ft.-wide clumps of grayish green, 10-in. leaves and clouds of tiny white to beige flowers. Considered somewhat less invasive than *M. microcarpa*.

M. microcarpa. Zones 2–24, 30–41. Similar to *M. cordata*, but with pinkish beige flowers. Flowers of 'Coral Plume' are more decidedly pink.

MACLURA pomifera

OSAGE ORANGE

Moraceae

DECIDUOUS TREE

◢ ZONES 2, 3, 10–13, 29–41

☼ FULL SUN

◗ REGULAR TO LITTLE WATER

Maclura pomifera

Native Arkansas to Oklahoma and Texas. Fast growth to 60 ft. tall (though often less), with spreading, open habit. Young branches are thornier than mature ones. Wood is orange in color and very hard. Medium green leaves to 5 in. long. If there's a male plant present, female plants may bear inedible, 4-in. fruits (so-called hedge-apples) that somewhat resemble bumpy, yellow-green oranges. Withstands heat, cold, wind, poor soil, moderate alkalinity, wet or dry conditions. Easily propagated by seed, stem cuttings, root cuttings; easily transplanted. Named varieties exist; 'Wichita' is nearly thornless. Useful as big, tough, rough-looking hedge or background. Prune to any size from 6 ft. up. Pruned high, becomes a shade tree.

MADAGASCAR JASMINE. See STEPHANOTIS floribunda

MADAGASCAR PALM. See PACHYPODIUM lamerei

MADAGASCAR PERIWINKLE. See CATHARANTHUS roseus

MADEIRA VINE. See ANREDERA cordifolia

MADRONE, MADRONA. See ARBUTUS menziesii

MAGNOLIA

Magnoliaceae

DECIDUOUS OR EVERGREEN TREES AND SHRUBS

◢ ZONES VARY BY SPECIES

☼◗ FULL SUN OR PARTIAL SHADE

◗ REGULAR WATER

▶ SEE CHART NEXT PAGE

Magnolia soulangiana

Magnificent flowering plants with remarkable variety in color, leaf shape, and plant form. Magnolias are discussed here by general appearance; the chart lists them alphabetically. New varieties and hybrids appear every year, but distribution is spotty in local nurseries. Mail-order specialists can supply many more kinds.

EVERGREEN MAGNOLIAS

To gardeners in mild-winter climates, the word "magnolia" usually means *M. grandiflora*, the classic southern magnolia with glossy leaves and huge, fragrant white flowers. Few trees can touch it for year-round beauty. And as cold-hardy selections have been developed in recent years, cultivation of this magnolia is spreading northward. Sweet bay *(M. virginiana)*, a hardier tree of smaller proportions, is nearly evergreen in the warmer parts of its range. The two species are parents of the evergreen hybrids

M. 'Freeman' and *M.* 'Maryland', which are similar to southern magnolia but slightly more cold tolerant.

DECIDUOUS MAGNOLIAS WITH SAUCER FLOWERS

This group includes the saucer magnolia *(M. soulangiana)* and its many varieties, often erroneously called tulip trees due to the shape and bright colors of their flowers. Also included here are the yulan magnolia *(M. denudata)* and lily magnolia *(M. liliiflora)*. All are hardy to cold, thriving in various climates—but all do poorly in hot, dry, windy areas, and early flowers of all forms are subject to frost damage. Related to these, but more tender to cold (and heat), are the big, spectacular Oriental magnolias from western China and the Himalayas—*M. campbellii*, *M. dawsoniana*, *M. sargentiana robusta*, *M. sprengeri* 'Diva'. Their early flowers are also subject to frost and storm damage.

DECIDUOUS MAGNOLIAS WITH STAR FLOWERS

This garden group includes *M. kobus*, *M. stellata* and its varieties (the star magnolias), and *M. salicifolia*. All are cold-hardy, slow-growing, early-blooming plants with wide climatic adaptability.

OTHER MAGNOLIAS

Less widely planted is a group of magnolias that bloom as leaves appear or after they unfurl; these are generally considered foliage plants or shade trees. Among them are *M. acuminata*, a big shade tree with inconspicuous flowers; *M. hypoleuca*, a big tree with large leaves and large but not noticeable flowers; and *M. fraseri* and *M. macrophylla*, medium-size trees with huge leaves and flowers.

MAGNOLIA CULTURE

Magnolia grandiflora

For any magnolia, pick planting site carefully. Virtually all magnolias are hard to move once established, and many grow quite large. The best soil for magnolias is fairly rich, well drained, and neutral to slightly acid; if necessary, add generous amounts of organic matter when planting. Although you can grow most magnolias in somewhat alkaline soil, the plants may develop chlorosis.

Magnolias never look their best when crowded, and they may be severely damaged by digging around their roots. Larger deciduous magnolias are at their best standing alone against a background that will display their flowers and, in winter, their strongly patterned, usually gray limbs and big, fuzzy flower buds. Small deciduous magnolias show up well in large flower or shrub borders and make choice ornaments in Oriental gardens. All magnolias are excellent lawn trees.

Balled-and-burlapped plants are available in late winter and early spring; container plants are sold any time. Do not set plants lower than their original soil level. Stake single-trunked or very heavy plants to prevent them from being rocked by wind, which will tear the thick, fleshy, sensitive roots. To avoid damaging the roots, set stakes in planting hole before placing tree. If you plant your magnolia in a lawn, try to provide a good-size area free of grass around the trunk. At least in the early years, keep a cooling mulch over the root area. Prevent soil compaction around root zone by keeping foot traffic to a minimum. Prune only when absolutely necessary; the best time is right after flowering, and the best technique is to remove the entire twig or limb right to the base. Magnolias seldom have serious pest or disease problems.

Magnoliaceae. The magnolia family contains evergreen and deciduous trees and shrubs with large, showy flowers, usually with a large number of petals, sepals, and stamens. Tulip tree *(Liriodendron tulipifera)*, *Michelia*, and magnolia are examples.

FOR INFORMATION ON SELECTING PLANTS
PLEASE SEE PAGES 79–160

M

MAGNOLIA

NAME	ZONES	TYPE	HEIGHT	SPREAD	AGE AT BLOOM	FLOWERS	USES, CHARACTERISTICS, COMMENTS
Magnolia acuminata CUCUMBER TREE	2–9, 14–21, 31–43	Decid-uous	60–80 ft.	25 ft.	12 yrs.	Small, greenish yellow, appear after leaves. Late spring, summer. Handsome reddish seed capsules, red seeds	Shade or lawn tree. Dense shade from glossy 5–9-in. leaves. Hardy to cold; dislikes hot, dry winds
M. a. cordata (M. cordata) YELLOW CUCUM-BER TREE, YEL-LOW MAGNOLIA	4–9, 14–21, 31–35, 37, 39	Decid-uous	To 35 ft.	To 35 ft.	12 yrs.	Larger (to 4 in.), chartreuse yellow outside, pure yellow within; appear as leaves start to expand. Mild lemon scent	Slow-growing lawn or border tree for large properties. Lower, shrubbier than *M. acuminata*. 'Miss Honeybee', with pale yellow flowers, is a good selection
M. campbellii	4–9, 14–21	Decid-uous	60–80 ft.	To 40 ft.	20 yrs. Grafts bloom young-er. Hybrid. 'Iolanthe' has 10-in. flowers, blooms at 2 ft. tall	Magnificent 6–10-in. bowls, deep rose outside, paler within. Central petals cupped over rose stamens. Very early flowering	Plant in lee of evergreens to protect flowers from strong winds. Make it focus of garden and give it room. 'Alba', 'Strybing White' are white forms; 'Hendricks Park', 'Late Pink' are good pinks; 'Charles Raffill' has very large, bright pink flowers, white inside
M. dawsoniana DAWSON MAGNOLIA	4–9, 14–21	Decid-uous	40–50 ft.	25–30 ft.	10 yrs. from grafts	Large (8–10 in.), white with rose shading. Narrow petals, slightly pendulous. Profuse bloom. Early flowering. Slight perfume	For big garden. Magnificent show; a little untidy close up. Very dark green leaves. Quite cold hardy when established; needs hardening off in fall. 'Chyverton' is selected salmon, fading pink
M. denudata (M. conspicua, M. heptapeta) YULAN MAGNOLIA	2–9, 14–24, 32–35, 37, 39	Decid-uous	To 35 ft.	To 30 ft.	6–7 yrs.	White, fragrant, sometimes tinged purple at base. Held erect; somewhat tulip shaped, 3–4 in. long, spreading to 6–7 in. Early; often a few in summer	Tends toward irregular form—no handi-cap in informal garden or at woodland edge. Place it where it can be shown off against dark background or sky. Leaves 4–7 in. long. Cut flowers striking in arrangements
M. 'Elizabeth'	3–9, 14–24, 31–35, 37, 39	Decid-uous	To 40 ft.	To 20 ft.	2–6 yrs. from grafts	Fragrant medium yellow flowers, 6–7 in. wide. Color is lighter in milder-winter regions	A hybrid between *M. acuminata cordata* and *M. denudata*. Grow as single-trunk specimen or multitrunk shrub-tree
M. fraseri (M. auriculata)	2–9, 14–21, 28, 31–35, 37, 39	Decid-uous	To 50 ft.	20–30 ft.	10–12 yrs.	Creamy to yellowish white, 8–10 in. wide. Bloom late spring, when leaves are full grown. Rose red, 5-in. seed capsules showy in summer	Single lawn tree or woodland tree. Leaves 16–18 in. long, parchmentlike, in whorls at ends of branches. Effect is that of parasols. Handsome dark brown fall color
M. 'Freeman' (and similar M. 'Maryland')	4–12, 14–24, 28–33	Ever-green	10–15 ft.	To 10 ft.	3–5 yrs. from grafts	White, 5 in. across, very fragrant. Summer	Narrow, dense, columnar evergreen tree. Hybrid between *M. virginiana* and *M. grandiflora*. Leaves like those of *M. grandiflora* but smaller. One very old tree has reached 50 ft. *M.* 'Maryland', another selection from the same cross, is more easily obtained
M. globosa	5–9, 14–21	Decid-uous	To 20 ft.	To 20 ft.	10 yrs.	White, fragrant, cupped or globe shaped, nodding or drooping. Late spring or early summer	Use as big shrub in lawn, at woodland edge, above a wall (so people can look up into flowers). Leaves 5–8 in. long, half as wide, rusty and furry beneath. Young trees prone to cold damage
M. grandiflora SOUTHERN MAGNOLIA, BULL BAY	4–12, 14–24, 26–33	Ever-green	To 80 ft.	To 40 ft.	15 yrs., some-times much less. 2–3 years from grafts or cuttings	Pure white, aging buff; large (8–10 in. across), powerfully fragrant. Carried throughout summer, fall	Street or lawn tree, big container plant, wall or espalier plant. Unpredictable in form and age of bloom. Grafted plants more predictable but need pruning to become single-trunked tree. Can grow as multitrunked tree. Glossy, leathery leaves, 4–8 in. long. Messy fruit

MAGNOLIA

NAME	ZONES	TYPE	HEIGHT	SPREAD	AGE AT BLOOM	FLOWERS	USES, CHARACTERISTICS, COMMENTS
M. g. 'Edith Bogue'	4–12, 14–24, 26–35, 37	Ever-green	To 35 ft.	To 20 ft.	2–3 yrs. from grafts	As in *M. grandiflora*. Young plants slower to come into heavy bloom than some other varieties	Shapely, vigorous tree, one of hardiest selections of *M. grandiflora*. Has withstood −24°F/−31°C. The one to try in coldest regions. Keep it out of strong winds
M. g. 'Little Gem'	7–12, 14–24, 26–33	Ever-green	Slow to 15–20 ft.	To 10 ft.	2 yrs. from grafts	Small (5–6 in. wide)	Good in containers, as espalier, in confined area. Half-size foliage, rusty beneath. Branches to ground
M. g. 'Majestic Beauty'	7–12, 14–24, 26–33	Ever-green	35–50 ft.	To 20 ft.	2 yrs. from grafts	Very large, to 1 ft. across, with 9 petals	Vigorous, dense-branching street or shade tree of broadly pyramidal form. Leaves exceptionally long, broad, and heavy. Most luxuriant of southern magnolias. 'Timeless Beauty' is more erect, denser
M. g. 'Russet'	4–12, 14–24, 26–32	Ever-green	Fast to 80 ft.	To 20 ft.	2 yrs. from grafts	Flattish, 10 in., last several days	Useful where fast-growing, narrow evergreen tree is needed. Densely foliaged. Narrow, glossy leaves with russet wool underneath
M. g. 'Samuel Sommer'	4–12, 14–24, 26–32	Ever-green	Fairly fast to 30–40 ft.	To 30 ft.	Same as *M. grandiflora*	Very large and full; to 10–14 in. across, with 12 petals	Leaves large, leathery and glossy, with heavy, rusty red felting on underside; very dark green above
M. g. 'San Marino'	4–12, 14–24, 26–32	Ever-green	Slow to 25 ft.	To 20 ft.	Same as *M. grandiflora*	Profuse show of 4-in. flowers	Grow as large shrub, small round-headed tree, espalier. Densely foliaged to ground unless shaped
M. g. 'St. Mary'	4–12, 14–24, 26–32	Ever-green	Usually 20 ft. Much larger in old age	To 20 ft.	Same as *M. grandiflora*	Heavy production of full-size flowers on small tree	Fine where standard-sized magnolia would grow too large too fast. Left alone, it will form a big, dense bush. Pruned and staked, it makes a small tree. Good for espalier and pots
M. g. 'Victoria'	4–12, 14–24, 26–32	Ever-green	To 20 ft.	To 15 ft.	2–3 yrs. from grafts	Same as *M. grandiflora*	Parent plant grew in Victoria, B.C. Withstands −10°F/−23°C with little damage, but plant out of wind. Foliage exceptionally broad, heavy, dark green. 'Pioneer' is as hardy
M. hypoleuca (M. obovata)	4–9, 14–21, 32–34	Decid-uous	To 50 ft.	To 25 ft.	15 yrs.	To 8 in. across, creamy, fragrant. Appear in summer after leaves expand	Only for big lawn or garden. Coarse texture
M. kobus KOBUS MAGNOLIA	2–9, 14–24, 32–41	Decid-uous	To 30 ft.	To 20 ft.	15 yrs.	White, to 4 in. across; early	Cold-hardy, sturdy tree for planting singly in lawn or in informal shrub and tree groupings. 'Wada's Memory'(*M. kewensis* 'Wada's Memory') blooms young, grows faster, has bigger flowers, coppery red new growth. *M. k. borealis* is much larger (to 75 ft.), with larger (6-in.) leaves
M. k. stellata (see M. stellata)							

MAGNOLIA

NAME	ZONES	TYPE	HEIGHT	SPREAD	AGE AT BLOOM	FLOWERS	USES, CHARACTERISTICS, COMMENTS
M. Kosar–De Vos Hybrids (the "Little Girl" series)	2–9, 14–24, 32–43	Decid-uous	To 12 ft.	To 15 ft.	4–5 yrs.	Flower color ranges from deep to pale purple (sometimes pink or white inside), depending on variety. Bloom in spring before leaf-out; sporadic rebloom in summer	Hybrids between *M. liliiflora* 'Nigra' and *M. stellata* 'Rosea'; bred to bloom later than *M. stellata* to avoid frost damage. Erect, shrubby growers bearing girls' names: 'Ann', 'Betty', 'Jane', 'Judy', 'Pinkie', 'Randy', 'Ricki', 'Susan'. Use in shrub border or singly in lawn
M. liliiflora (M. quinquepeta) LILY MAGNOLIA	2–9, 14–24, 28–41	Decid-uous	To 12 ft.	To 15 ft.	4–5 yrs.	White inside, purplish outside; about 4 in. across. Selections sold as 'Gracilis', 'Nigra', and 'O'Neill' are dark purple red outside, pink inside. Blooms over long spring, summer season	Good for shrub border; strong vertical effect in big flower border. Spreads slowly by suckering. Leaves 4–6 in. long. 'Royal Crown', hybrid with *M. veitchii*, has pink, candle-shaped buds that open to 10-in. flowers. Good cut flower if buds taken before fully open
M. loebneri	2–9, 14–24, 31–41	Decid-uous	Slow to 12–15 ft.; can reach 50 ft.	12–15 ft.	3 yrs.	Narrow, strap-shaped petals like those of *M. stellata*, but fewer, larger. Blossoms of some selections are fragrant. Early	Hybrids between *M. kobus* and *M. stellata*. 'Ballerina' is white with faint pink blush; 'Leonard Messel' has pink flowers, deeper in bud; 'Merrill' ('Dr. Merrill') is a free-flowering white, hardy in Zone 43. Taller 'Spring Snow' has pure white flowers. Use in lawn or shrub border, at woodland edge
M. macrophylla BIGLEAF MAGNOLIA	3–9, 14–21, 31–35, 37	Decid-uous	Slow to 50 ft.	To 30 ft.	12–15 yrs.	White, fragrant, to 1 ft. across, appearing in late spring and early summer, after leaves are out	Show-off tree with leaves 1–2½ ft. long, 9–12 in. wide. Needs to stand alone. Needs some shade in warm climates
M. salicifolia ANISE MAGNOLIA	2–9, 14–21, 32–41	Decid-uous	Slow to 18–30 ft.	To 12 ft.	2–10 yrs.	White, narrow petaled, to 4 in. across. Early	Usually upright with slender branches, graceful appearance. In front of trees, use as shrub border. Leaves (3–6 in. long) bronze red in fall. 'Kochanakee' and 'W. B. Clarke' are large flowered; bloom young and heavily. 'Miss Jack' has narrow, anise-scented leaves, blooms heavily
M. sargentiana robusta	5–9, 14–24	Decid-uous	To 35 ft.	To 35 ft.	10–12 yrs.; 8–10 yrs. from grafts	Huge (8–12-in.), mauve pink bowls that open erect, then nod. Fragrant. Early to mid-season	One of most spectacular of flowering plants. Leaves 6–8 in. long. Not for hot, dry areas. Must have ample room and protection from strong winds, which would tear early blooms. 'Caerhays Belle' and 'Marjory Gossler', hybrids of this and other large-flowered species, are vigorous trees with dinner plate–size pink flowers. Both are rare, choice
M. sieboldii (sometimes sold as **M. parviflora**) OYAMA MAGNOLIA	4–9, 14–24, 31–33	Decid-uous	6–15 ft.	6–15 ft.	5 yrs.	White, cup shaped, centered with crimson stamens; fragrant. Begin blooming in late spring, extend over long period	Good for small gardens. Buds like white Japanese lanterns. Nice planted upslope or at top of wall so people can look into flowers. Leaves 3–6 in. long. Best in partial shade
M. soulangiana SAUCER MAGNOLIA (often erroneously called TULIP TREE)	2–10, 12–24, 28–41	Decid-uous	To 25 ft.	To 25 ft. or more	3–5 yrs.	White to pink or purplish red, variable in size and form, blooming before leaves expand. Generally about 6 in. across. Late winter into spring	Lawn ornament, anchor plant in big corner plantings. Hybrid of *M. denudata* and *M. liliiflora*. Seedlings highly variable; shop for named varieties. Foliage good green, rather coarse; leaves 4–6 in. (or more) long

M

MAGNOLIA

NAME	ZONES	TYPE	HEIGHT	SPREAD	AGE AT BLOOM	FLOWERS	USES, CHARACTERISTICS, COMMENTS
M. s. 'Alba' ('Amabilis', 'Alba Superba')	2–10, 12–24, 28–41	Decid-uous	To 30 ft.	To 25 ft. or more	3–5 yrs.	Large, suffused purple, opening nearly pure white. Early	Same uses as for *M. soulangiana.* Rather more upright in growth than most
M. s. 'Alexandrina'	2–10, 12–24, 28–41	Decid-uous	To 25 ft.	To 25 ft. or more	3–5 yrs.	Large. Color highly variable, from almost pure white to dark purple. Midseason	Same uses as for *M. soulangiana.* Large, rather heavy foliage. Variable habit, flower color; choose trees in bloom to get color you want. Delayed
M. s. 'Brozzonii'	2–10, 12–24, 28–41	Decid-uous	To 25 ft.	To 25 ft. or more	3–5 yrs.	Large (to 8 in. across). White, very slightly flushed purplish rose at base. Early	One of handsomest whites. Large, vigorous plant
M. s. 'Burgundy'	2–10, 12–24, 28–41	Decid-uous	To 25 ft.	To 25 ft. or more	3–5 yrs.	Large, well rounded; deep purple halfway up to petal tips, then lightening to pink. Early	Earlier bloom than most makes it more susceptible to frost damage in cold areas
M. s. 'Coates'	2–10, 12–24, 28–41	Decid-uous	To 25 ft.	To 25 ft. or more	3–5 yrs.	Large, attractive; resemble those of *M. liliiflora* hybrid 'Royal Crown'. Midseason	Large, shrubby. Quick grower
M. s. 'Lennei' (M. lennei)	2–10, 12–24, 28–41	Decid-uous	To 25 ft.	To 25 ft. or more	3–5 yrs.	Very large, globe shaped, deep purple outside, white inside. Late	Spreading, vigorous plant with large leaves. Late bloom helps it escape frosts in cold areas
M. s. 'Lennei Alba' (M. lennei 'Alba')	2–10, 12–24, 28–41	Decid-uous	To 25 ft.	To 25 ft. or more	3–5 yrs.	Like those of *M. s.* 'Lennei', but white in color, slightly smaller, earlier (midseason)	Spreading, vigorous plant
M. s. 'Pink Superba'	2–10, 12–24, 28–41	Decid-uous	To 25 ft.	To 25 ft. or more	3–5 yrs.	Large, deep pink, white inside. Early	Best where late frosts are not a problem. Much like *M. s.* 'Alba' except for flower color
M. s. 'Rustica Rubra'	2–10, 12–24, 28–41	Decid-uous	To 25 ft.	To 25 ft. or more	3–5 yrs.	Large, cup shaped, deep reddish purple. Somewhat past midseason. Big (6-in.) seedpods of dark rose	Tall, vigorous grower for large areas. More treelike than many varieties.
M. s. 'San Jose'	2–10, 12–24, 28–41	Decid-uous	To 25 ft.	To 25 ft. or more	3–5 yrs.	Large, white flushed pink. Blooms Very early	Exceptionally early bloom puts it at risk for frost damage in cold areas
M. sprengeri 'Diva'	5–9, 14–24	Decid-uous	To 40 ft.	To 30 ft.	7 yrs. from grafts	To 8 in. wide, rose pink outside, white suffused pink with deeper lines inside. Scented. Early to midseason	One of brightest colors; erect, spectacular flowers. Buds more frost resistant than those of *M. sargentiana robusta.* Hybrids between this and *M. liliiflora* are 'Galaxy' (large purple flowers open late in spring) and 'Spectrum' (larger but fewer flowers). Both are small trees
M. stellata STAR MAGNOLIA	2–9, 14–24, 28–41	Decid-uous	To 10 ft.	To 20 ft.	3 yrs.	Very early, white, about 3 in. wide, with 19–21 narrow, strap-shaped petals. Profuse bloom in late winter, early spring. Some varieties are fragrant	Slow growing, shrubby; fine for borders, entryway gardens, edge of woods. Quite hardy, but flowers often nipped by frost in colder part of range. Fine texture in twig and leaf. Fair yellow-and-brown fall color
M. s. 'Centennial'	2–9, 14–24, 28–41	Decid-uous	To 10 ft.	To 20 ft.	3 yrs.	White, faintly marked pink, 5 in. across	Same uses as for *M. stellata.* Like an improved *M. s.* 'Waterlily'

M

▶

MAGNOLIA

NAME	ZONES	TYPE	HEIGHT	SPREAD	AGE AT BLOOM	FLOWERS	USES, CHARACTERISTICS, COMMENTS
M. s. 'Dawn'	2–9, 14–24, 28–41	Decid-uous	To 10 ft.	To 20 ft.	3 yrs.	To 40–50 pink petals	Same uses as for *M. stellata*
M. s. 'Rosea' PINK STAR MAGNOLIA	2–9, 14–24, 28–41	Decid-uous	To 10 ft.	To 20 ft.	3 yrs.	Pink buds; flowers flushed pink, fading to white. Very early	Same uses as for species. Various plants sold under this name. In cold regions, plant these early-flowering sorts in a northern exposure to delay bloom as long as possible, lessen frost damage
M. s. 'Royal Star'	2–9, 14–24, 28–41	Decid-uous	To 10 ft.	To 20 ft.	3 yrs.	White flowers with 25–30 petals. Fragrant. Blooms 2 weeks later than *M. stellata*	Same uses as for *M. stellata*. Faster growing
M. s. 'Rubra'	2–9, 14–24, 28–41	Decid-uous	To 10 ft.	To 20 ft.	3 yrs.	Rosy pink	More treelike in form than other *M. stellata* varieties
M. s. 'Waterlily'	2–9, 14–24, 28–41	Decid-uous	To 10 ft.	To 20 ft.	3 yrs.	White. Larger flowers than *M. stellata*; broader, more numerous petals. Fragrant	Faster growing than most star magnolias. Leaves modest in size (2–4 in. long); finer foliage texture than other magnolias
M. veitchii VEITCH MAGNOLIA	4–9, 14–24, 31, 32	Decid-uous	30–40 ft.	To 30 ft.	4–5 yrs.	Rose red at base, shading to white at tips, to 10 in. across. 'Rubra' has smaller, purple-red flowers. Early, before leaves emerge	Spectacular tree. Hybrid between *M. campbellii* and *M. denudata*. Fast growing and vigorous. Needs plenty of room and wind protection; branches are brittle. Blooms frequently frosted in Zones 31, 32
M. virginiana (M. glauca) SWEET BAY	4–9, 14–24, 26, 28–35, 37	Decid-uous to ever-green	10–20 ft. in north-ern part of range; to 60 ft. in south-ern part	To 20 ft.	8–10 yrs.	Nearly globular, 2–3 in. wide, creamy white, fragrant. June–Sept.	Prefers moist, acid soil. Grows in swamps in eastern U.S. Deciduous shrub in colder areas; big semiever-green to evergreen tree in colder climates. Leaves grayish green, nearly white beneath, 2–5 in. long
M. wilsonii WILSON MAGNOLIA	4–9, 14–24, 32–35, 37	Decid-uous	To 25 ft.	To 25 ft.	10 yrs.	White, with red stamens, pen-dulous, 3–4 in. across, fra-grant. Late spring	Blooms at 4 ft. and tends to remain shrubby. Plant high on bank where peo-ple can look up at flowers. Best in light shade. Rich purplish brown twigs; nar-row, tapered leaves, 3–6 in. long, with silvery undersides. Effect similar to that of *M. sieboldii*

MAHONIA

Berberidaceae

EVERGREEN SHRUBS

⚡ ZONES VARY BY SPECIES

☼ ◑ ● EXPOSURE NEEDS VARY BY SPECIES

◗ ◖ WATER NEEDS VARY BY SPECIES

Mahonia aquifolium

Related to *Berberis* and described under that name by some botanists. Easy to grow; good looking all year. Leaves divided into leaflets, usu-ally with spiny-toothed edges. Bright yellow flow-ers in dense, rounded to spikelike clusters, followed by blue-black (sometimes red), berry-like fruit. Generally disease resistant, though in some regions foliage may be disfigured by small looper caterpillars. All species attract birds.

M. aquifolium. OREGON GRAPE. Zones 2–12, 14–21, 31–41. Native British Columbia to Northern California. Erect growth to 6 ft. tall or taller; spreads by underground stems. Leaves 4–10 in. long, with five to nine very spiny-toothed, oval, 1–2½-in. leaflets that are glossy green in some forms, dull green in others. Young growth ruddy or bronzy; scattered mature red leaves. Purplish or bronzy leaves in winter, especially in cold-winter areas or where plants are grown in full sun. Spring flowers in 2–3-in. clusters along stems; edible blue-black fruit with gray bloom (makes good jelly).

'Compacta' averages about 2 ft. tall and spreads freely to make broad colonies. New leaves glossy, light to coppery green; mature leaves matte medium green. 'Orange Flame', 5 ft. tall, has bronzy orange new growth and glossy green mature leaves that turn wine red in winter.

M

Oregon grape can take any exposure, though it does best with some shade in hottest climates and wind protection in cold-winter areas. Plant in masses as foundation planting, in woodland, in tubs, as low screen or garden barrier. Control height and form by pruning; if any woody stems jut out too far, cut them down to ground (new growth fills in quickly). Needs little water.

M. bealei. LEATHERLEAF MAHONIA. Zones 3–12, 14–26, 28–34. To 10–12 ft., with strong pattern of vertical stems, horizontal foliage. Leaves are over 1 ft. long, divided into 7–15 broad, thick, leathery leaflets up to 5 in. long; leaflets grayish or bluish green above, olive green below, with spiny-toothed edges. Very fragrant flowers in erect, 3–6-in.-long, spikelike clusters at branch ends in earliest spring. Powdery blue berries. Truly distinguished plant against stone, brick, wood, glass. Takes sun in cool-summer areas; best in part shade elsewhere. Plant in rich soil with ample organic material. Regular water.

M. fortunei. Zones 7–9, 14–26, 28, 31. Native to China. Grows to 6 ft. Erect stems bear 10-in., dull matte green leaves with 7–13 spiny-toothed leaflets. Undersurface of leaves is yellowish green, with heavily netted veins. Flowers in short clusters; the purple-black berries seldom develop. Plant has an unusual stiff charm and is grown for form and foliage, not fruit. Sun to light shade. Moderate water.

M. lomariifolia. Zones 6–9, 14–26, 28, 31. Native to China. Showy plant with erect, little-branched stems to 6–10 ft. tall. Young plants often have a single, vertical unbranched stem; with age, plants produce more, almost vertical branches from near base. Clustered near ends of these branches are horizontally held leaves to 2 ft. long. In outline, leaves look like stiff, crinkly, barbed ferns; each has as many as 47 thick, spiny, glossy green leaflets arranged symmetrically along

Mahonia lomariifolia

both sides of central stem. Flowers in winter or earliest spring grow in foot-long, erect clusters at branch tips, just above uppermost cluster of leaves. Powdery blue berries. Prune stems at varying heights to induce branching. Needs shade at least in afternoon to keep deep green color. Regular water.

M. media. Zones 6–9, 14–24, 28, 31. Group of winter-blooming hybrids between *M. lomariifolia* and a Japanese species similar to *M. bealei*. Plants generally resemble *M. lomariifolia* and require the same conditions. Members of the group include 'Buckland', 'Charity', 'Faith', 'Hope', and 'Winter Sun'. 'Lionel Fortunescue' bears fragrant flowers in spikes to 16 in. long.

M. nervosa. LONGLEAF MAHONIA. Zones 2–9, 14–17, 32, 34. Native British Columbia to Northern California. Low shrub to 2 ft. tall (rarely to 6 ft. high). Spreads by underground stems to make good ground cover. Clustered at stem tips are 10–18-in.-long leaves with 7–21 glossy green, bristle-toothed, 1–3½-in.-long leaflets. Creates the impression of a stiff, leathery fern. Spring flowers in upright, 3–6-in.-long clusters. Blue berries. Best in shade; will take sun in cooler areas, becoming very compact. Use as woodland ground cover, facing for taller mahonias, low barrier planting. Moderate water.

M. repens. CREEPING MAHONIA. Zones 1–21, 32–34. Native British Columbia to Northern California, eastward to Rocky Mountains. Creeps by underground stems. To 3 ft. tall, with spreading habit. Dull bluish green leaves have three to seven spiny-toothed leaflets, turn bronzy in winter. Deep yellow spring flowers followed by blue berries in short clusters. Good ground cover in sun, partial shade. Needs little water.

MAIDEN GRASS. See MISCANTHUS sinensis 'Gracillimus'

MAIDENHAIR FERN. See ADIANTUM

MAIDENHAIR TREE. See GINKGO biloba

MAIDEN PINK. See DIANTHUS deltoides

MAJORANA hortensis. See ORIGANUM majorana

MALCOLMIA maritima

VIRGINIAN STOCK

Brassicaceae (Cruciferae)

ANNUAL

⬛ ALL ZONES

☼ FULL SUN

🔴 REGULAR WATER

Malcolmia maritima

Grows to 8–15 in., single stemmed or branching from base, covered with nearly scentless, four-petaled flowers from spring to fall. Colors include white, yellow, pinks, lilacs, and magenta. Leaves are oblong. Sow in place at any time except in hot or very cold weather. Like sweet alyssum (*Lobularia maritima*), this plant blooms only 6 weeks after seeds are sown. Give it moderately rich soil. Good bulb cover.

MALE FERN. See DRYOPTERIS

MALLOW. See MALVA

MALTESE CROSS. See LYCHNIS chalcedonica

MALUS

CRABAPPLE

Rosaceae

DECIDUOUS TREES, ONLY RARELY SHRUBS

⬛ ZONES 1–21, 29–43

☼ FULL SUN

🔴🔴 REGULAR TO MODERATE WATER

▶ SEE CHART NEXT PAGE

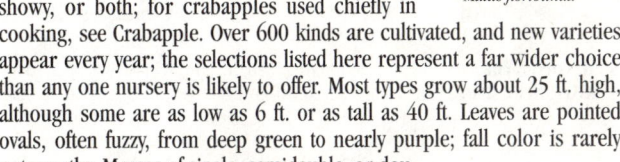

Malus floribunda

Valued for brief bloom of handsome white, pink, or red flowers and for fruit that is edible, showy, or both; for crabapples used chiefly in cooking, see Crabapple. Over 600 kinds are cultivated, and new varieties appear every year; the selections listed here represent a far wider choice than any one nursery is likely to offer. Most types grow about 25 ft. high, although some are as low as 6 ft. or as tall as 40 ft. Leaves are pointed ovals, often fuzzy, from deep green to nearly purple; fall color is rarely noteworthy. Masses of single, semidouble, or double flowers with a musky sweet scent appear in spring, usually before the foliage unfurls. Tiny red, orange, or yellow apples ripen from midsummer into autumn; in some varieties, the fruit hangs on until late in the season, after leaves drop. Blooming and bearing may occur more heavily in alternate years. Birds are fond of small-fruited types.

Malus sargentii

Plant bare-root trees in winter or early spring; set out container plants any time. Crabapples prefer good, well-drained, deep soil, but they will grow in rocky or gravelly soils and in conditions ranging from acid to slightly alkaline. More tolerant of wet soil than flowering cherries or other flowering stone fruits; also hardier and longer lived than flowering stone fruits. Adapt to a variety of climates, but not at their best in humid lower South or low desert. All need some winter chill.

Crabapples may be bothered by aphids, Japanese beetles, spider mites, or tent caterpillars, but these pests are minor compared with potential disease problems: fireblight, apple scab, cedar-apple rust, and powdery mildew. In most parts of their range, where humidity is high and persistent, disease resistance of crabapple varieties is of great importance if you wish to avoid spraying. Where long, dry summers are the rule, diseases are less of a problem. Disease resistance (or lack of it) is noted in the chart.

Crabapples are fine lawn trees. Planted near fences, they will heighten screening effect, provide blossoms and fruit, and still give planting room

▶ page 391

M

MALUS

NAME	SIZE, HABIT	FLOWERS	FRUIT	COMMENTS
'Adams'	Dense, round headed, to 20 ft.	Red buds open to single pink flowers	Red, over ½ in. wide, long lasting	Orange fall foliage. Good disease resistance
'Adirondack'	Columnar, to 10 ft. tall and 6 ft. wide	Red buds open to large waxy white flowers with red tinge	Red to orange red	Formal in appearance. High disease resistance
'Almey'	Upright, spreading, to 20 ft. (possibly taller)	Single scarlet flowers, white at base	Maroon, hangs on well	Purplish green foliage. Old-fashioned variety, very prone to disease except in areas of very low humidity. Newer, more resistant crabapples a better choice
'Ames White'	Dense, upright, to 20 ft.	Pink buds open to single white flowers	Yellow	High disease resistance
M. arnoldiana ARNOLD CRABAPPLE	Broad, to 20 ft. by 30 ft.	Red buds open to single pink flowers that fade to white; fragrant	Yellow and red	Susceptible to scab and fireblight
M. atrosanguinea CARMINE CRABAPPLE	Erect, dense, irregular, to 18 ft.	Single deep pink to red flowers; fragrant	Red turning brown; hangs on all winter	Summer foliage has purplish sheen. Moderate susceptibility to disease
'Brandywine'	Vigorous, shapely, to 15–20 ft. tall and wide	Double rose pink, fragrant	Yellowish green	Leaves have reddish cast. Moderate susceptibility to disease
'Callaway'	Attractive, round headed, to 25 ft.	Pink buds open to single white flowers	Deep red, large, long lasting	Low chilling requirement for bloom; good in southern gardens. High disease resistance
'Centurion'	Oval crowned, to 25 ft. tall and 15–20 ft. wide	Red buds open to single red flowers	Shiny deep red, long lasting	Blooms young. High disease resistance
'Coralburst'	Small, dense, to 8–15 ft.	Coral pink buds open to small double rose pink flowers	Reddish orange, small; scant crop	Sometimes grown as a shrub. Fair disease resistance
M. coronaria WILD SWEET CRABAPPLE	Short trunk; broad, round-headed crown. To 30 ft.	Pink buds open to single flowers in pure white or pink-tinged white; fragrant	Yellowish green, large	Late blooming. Susceptible to rust
M. c. 'Charlottae'	Resembles *M. coronaria*	Large double pale pink flowers	Fruit similar to that of *M. coronaria*	Orange-red fall color. Like *M. coronaria*, late blooming and susceptible to rust
'Dolgo'	Willowy, spreading, to 40 ft. tall and wide	Pink buds open to single white flowers	Purple red, large. Good flavor, can be used for jelly	Moderate disease resistance
'Donald Wyman'	Broad, to 20 ft. by 25 ft.	Pink to red buds open to single white flowers	Shiny bright red, small, long lasting	Lustrous foliage. Good disease resistance
'Dorothea'	Dense, round headed, to 25 ft. tall and wide	Red buds open to large semidouble pink flowers	Bright yellow, small	Susceptible to scab, fireblight
M. floribunda JAPANESE FLOWERING CRABAPPLE	Broad, dense, to 15–25 ft.	Deep pink buds open to single white flowers. Blooms fragrant, incredibly profuse	Yellow and red, small, do not last long	Moderate disease resistance
'Harvest Gold'	Vigorous, narrow, to 30 ft. tall and 15 ft. wide	Pink buds open to single white flowers. Late flowering	Yellow, showy, last until spring	High disease resistance
'Hopa'	Fast growth to 25 ft. by 20 ft.	Single rose red flowers; fragrant	Orange red, large, ripen and drop early. Good for jelly	Suckers freely. Old-fashioned variety, very prone to disease except in areas of very low humidity. Newer, more resistant crabapples a better choice

M

MALUS

NAME	SIZE, HABIT	FLOWERS	FRUIT	COMMENTS
M. hupehensis (M. theifera) TEA CRABAPPLE	Broad form; moderate growth to 15 ft. by 25 ft.	Single deep pink flowers fading to white; fragrant	Greenish yellow to red, small, not showy	Picturesque form and branching (branches are strongly angled from short trunk). Moderate disease resistance
'Indian Magic'	Round headed, to 15–20 ft. tall and wide	Red buds open to single deep pink flowers	Shiny red to orange, small, long lasting	Moderate susceptibility to disease
'Indian Summer'	Round headed, to 18 ft. tall and wide	Single rose red	Bright red, long lasting	Good orange-red fall foliage color. High disease resistance
M. ioensis PRAIRIE CRABAPPLE	Round headed, to 20–30 ft. tall and wide	Pink buds open to large single white flowers; fragrant	Dull yellow green, large	Susceptible to rust. Species rarely grown (see below)
M. i. 'Plena' BECHTEL CRABAPPLE	Round-headed, open, to 30 ft.	Double pink flowers; fragrant	Similar to species	Like species, highly susceptible to disease. *M. i.* 'Klehm's' is similar, but with higher disease resistance
'Jewelberry'	Dwarfish, dense, to 8 ft. by 12 ft.	Pink buds open to single white flowers	Shiny red, ½ in. wide, long lasting	Bears young. Moderate disease resistance
'Katherine'	Slow growing to 20 ft. tall and wide	Deep pink buds open to large double pink flowers that quickly fade to white	Yellow with red cheek, very small	Fair disease resistance
'Liset'	Roundish, dense, to 15–20 ft. tall and wide	Crimson buds open to single flowers of deep red to crimson	Dark red to maroon, persistent	Deep purplish green leaves. Fair disease resistance
'Madonna'	Narrow, erect, to 20 ft. by 10 ft.	Pink buds open to double white flowers. Long bloom season	Yellow with red cheek, small	Bronze new growth. Good disease resistance
M. micromalus (M. kaido) MIDGET CRABAPPLE	Slow growth to 20 ft. by 15 ft.	Red buds open to single pink flowers. Profuse bloomer	Red or greenish, not showy	Susceptible to disease
'Molten Lava'	Spreading, weeping, to 12 ft. tall and wide	Deep red buds open to single white flowers	Red orange, small, last well on tree	Attractive yellow winter bark. Good disease resistance
'Narragansett'	Broad, round headed, to 15 ft. tall and wide	Red buds open to single white flowers with faint touch of pink	Bright red, ½ in. wide, showy	High disease resistance
'Oekonomierat Echtermeyer' ('Pink Weeper') WEEPING CRABAPPLE	Moderate growth rate to 15 ft., with weeping branches	Red buds open to single purplish red flowers	Purplish to reddish to greenish brown	Purplish foliage becomes purplish green in summer. Any branches growing erect should be pruned out. Disease prone
'Pink Perfection'	Round headed, to 20 ft. tall and wide	Red buds open to large double pink flowers	Yellow, insignificant	Susceptible to scab
'Pink Princess'	Low, broad, to 15 ft. by 12 ft.	Single rose pink	Deep red, small, last well on tree	Reddish green foliage. Good disease resistance
'Pink Spires'	Narrowly upright to 25 ft.	Deep rose pink buds open to single rose pink flowers	Red purple, persistent	New foliage red, maturing to bronzy green. Moderate disease resistance
'Prairifire'	Round headed, to 20 ft. tall and wide	Red buds open to single deep pinkish red flowers	Small, dark red, persistent	Leaves emerge reddish maroon, turn dark green. High disease resistance
'Profusion'	Upright, spreading, to 20 ft. tall and wide	Deep red buds open to single, deep purplish pink flowers	Dark red, long lasting	Purple foliage matures to bronzy green. Moderate disease resistance

M

389

MALUS

NAME	SIZE, HABIT	FLOWERS	FRUIT	COMMENTS
'Purple Wave'	Broad, spreading, to 10–15 ft. tall and wide	Large single to semidouble rose red, fading to purplish pink	Dark purple red	Purplish foliage. Susceptible to scab, rust
M. purpurea 'Eleyi'	Irregular, open, to 20 ft. tall and wide	Single wine red flowers	Dark purple red. Profuse	Old-fashioned variety, very prone to disease except in areas of very low humidity. Newer, more resistant crabapples a better choice
'Radiant'	Broad, round headed, to 20 ft. tall and wide	Deep red buds open to single deep pink flowers	Bright red, colors early; long lasting	Young leaves reddish, turning to green. Susceptible to scab
'Red Baron'	Narrow (to 20 ft. by 12 ft.), broadening in age	Very deep red buds open to single reddish pink flowers	Shiny dark red	Susceptible to scab
'Red Jade'	Irregular, weeping form; to 15 ft. tall and wide	Small single white flowers	Bright red, heavy crop, holds well into fall	Moderate disease resistance
'Red Jewel'	Small, rounded, to 15 ft. by 12 ft.	Large single white flowers	Bright red, small, long lasting	Some disease resistance
'Red Silver'	Angular, irregular, to 30 ft. tall and wide	Single deep wine red flowers	Dark purplish red. Good for jelly	Reddish foliage silvered with silky hairs. Highly subject to scab in humid climates
'Robinson'	Dense, upright vase shape; to 25 ft.	Deep red buds open to single deep pink flowers	Dark red	Copper-tinged foliage. High disease resistance
'Royal Fountain'	Weeping, to 15 ft. tall and wide	Single rose red	Deep red	Purple leaves turn bronze in summer. Moderate disease resistance
'Royalty'	Upright, to 20 ft. tall	Single purplish crimson	Dark red	Foliage dark purple in spring, purplish green in summer, dark purple again in fall. Susceptible to scab, fireblight
M. sargentii SARGENT CRABAPPLE	Broad, dense, to 10 ft. by 20 ft.	Small single white flowers; fragrant. Profuse bloomer	Red, tiny, long lasting	Good disease resistance. 'Candymint' has pink flowers outlined in red. 'Rosea', a pink-flowered form, may be more disease prone than the species
'Snowdrift'	Rounded, dense, to 20–25 ft.	Red buds open to single white flowers. Long bloom season	Orange red, small, long lasting	Good disease resistance
'Strathmore'	Erect, narrow, to 20 ft. by 10 ft.	Single deep pink to reddish pink	Purplish red, small	Subject to scab in humid climates
'Strawberry Parfait'	Open, vase shaped, to 20 ft. by 25 ft.	Red buds open to single pink flowers edged in red; profuse bloomer	Yellow with red cheek	High disease resistance
'Sugar Tyme'	Upright, oval, to 18 ft. by 15 ft.	Light pink buds open to single white flowers; fragrant	Red, abundant, long lasting	High disease resistance
'Thunderchild'	Erect, oval, to 20 ft.	Single rose pink	Dark red	Purple foliage. Good disease resistance
'Weeping Candied Apple'	Weeping, to 10–15 ft.	Single red	Bright red, small, persist all winter	Good disease resistance
M. zumi calocarpa (**M. sieboldii zumi** **'Calocarpa'**)	Dense branching, rounded, to 25 ft. tall and wide	Single flowers open pale pink, fade to white; fragrant	Glossy bright red, small, last well on tree	Susceptible to fireblight

M

for primroses, spring bulbs, or shade-loving bedding plants. Prune only to build good framework, correct shape, or remove suckers. Crabapples can be trained as espaliers.

MALVA

MALLOW

Malvaceae

PERENNIALS OR BIENNIALS

✿ ZONES VARY BY SPECIES

☼ ◑ LIGHT SHADE IN HOTTEST AREAS

💧 REGULAR WATER

Malva alcea

Related to and somewhat resembling hollyhock (*Alcea*), but bushier, with smaller, roundish leaves. Easy to grow; need good drainage, average soil. Grow from seed; usually bloom first year. Use in perennial borders or for a quick tall edging. Plants not long lived.

M. alcea. Perennial. Zones 1–9, 14–24, 31–43. Grows to 4 ft. tall, 2 ft. wide. Saucer-shaped, 2-in.-wide pink flowers appear from late spring to fall. Common kind is 'Fastigiata', a narrower grower that looks much like a hollyhock.

M. moschata. MUSK MALLOW. Perennial. Zones 1–9, 14–24, 31–45. Erect, branching plant to 3 ft., with finely cut leaves and inch-wide (or somewhat larger) flowers, summer to fall. Entire plant emits a mild, musky fragrance if brushed or bruised. 'Rosea' has rose pink flowers; 2-ft.-tall 'Alba' is white flowered.

M. sylvestris. Perennial or biennial. Zones 1–9, 14–24, 31–45. Erect, bushy growth to 2–4 ft.; 2-in.-wide flowers appear all summer, often until frost. Common variety (often sold as *M. zebrina*) has pale lavender pink flowers with pronounced deep purple veining. 'Mauritiana' has deeper-colored flowers, often semidouble.

Malvaceae. The mallow family contains many hundreds of species of mainly herbaceous plants and some shrubs and trees, often with lobed leaves and showy flowers. Ornamental members include flowering maple (*Abutilon*), *Hibiscus*, hollyhock (*Alcea*), mallow (*Malva*), and checkerbloom (*Sidalcea*). Commercially, the family is important as the source of cotton.

MAMMILLARIA

Cactaceae

CACTI

✿ ZONES 8–24, 29, 30

☼ FULL SUN

💧 REGULAR WATER

Mammillaria

Specialists offer as many as a hundred species of these cacti. Plants are small (usually 2–6 in. high), cylindrical or globe shaped, either single stemmed or clustered; some elongate from spheres to cylinders as they age. Red, pink, or white flowers appear in a circle near top of plant. Most are grown by collectors as pot plants; their compact size makes them suitable for lath house or greenhouse, windowsill, tabletop display, or dish garden. Easy to grow in sun. Provide average or slightly sandy soil mixture. Give regular moisture during growing season; don't let go totally dry in winter.

For the plant sold as *M. vivipara*, see *Coryphantha vivipara*.

MANDARIN ORANGE. See CITRUS, Mandarin

FOR INFORMATION ON YOUR CLIMATE ZONE
PLEASE SEE PAGES 16–78

MANDEVILLA

Apocynaceae

EVERGREEN OR DECIDUOUS VINES

✿ ZONES VARY BY SPECIES

☼ ◑ PARTIAL SHADE IN HOTTEST AREAS

💧 REGULAR WATER

Mandevilla
'Alice du Pont'

Known for showy flowers, the genus *Mandevilla* includes plants that were formerly called *Dipladenia*. Flowers are saucer shaped, with tubular throats. Plants survive outdoors only in mildest regions; in colder climates, they are treated as annuals or grown indoors or in greenhouses.

M. 'Alice du Pont' (M. splendens, M. amabilis, Dipladenia splendens, D. amoena). Evergreen. Zones 21–25; may grow as root-hardy perennial in Zones 26, 27. To 20–30 ft., much less in pots or tubs (where it is usually grown). Twining stems; dark green, glossy, oval, 3–8-in.-long leaves. Clusters of pure pink, 2–4-in.-wide flowers appear among leaves, spring–fall. Even very small plant in 4-in. pot will bloom. Plant in rich soil and provide frame, trellis, or stake for support. Pinch young plant to induce bushiness.

M. boliviensis. Evergreen. Zones 24, 25. To 12 ft. as a vine; to 3 ft. tall, 5 ft. wide as a sprawling shrub. Glossy leaves. White flowers with yellow throats throughout the year.

M. laxa (M. suaveolens). CHILEAN JASMINE. Deciduous. Zones 4–9, 14–21, 28, 29, 31. Twines to 15 ft. or more. Leaves are long ovals, heart shaped at base, 2–6 in. long. Clustered summer flowers are white, 2 in. across, trumpet shaped, with powerful gardenialike fragrance. Provide rich soil. If plant becomes badly tangled, cut to ground in winter; it will bloom on new growth. Roots hardy to about 5°F/–15°C.

M. splendens (M. amabilis, M. 'Profusa', M. sanderi). Evergreen. Zones 21–25; may grow as root-hardy perennial in Zones 26, 27. Similar to 'Alice du Pont', with same bloom period. 'Red Riding Hood', with deep red flowers, and white-blossomed 'Summer Snow' are lower growing and shrubbier than the species. Superb in hanging baskets.

MANGIFERA indica

MANGO

Anacardiaceae

EVERGREEN TREE

✿ ZONES 23–25

☼ FULL SUN

💧 MAINTAIN STEADY SOIL MOISTURE

Mangifera indica

Large, attractive, fruit-bearing shade tree in South Florida. In mildest parts of Southern California, it often survives for years—but it may remain shrubby and is likely to fruit only in most favored, frost-free locations. Yellow to reddish flowers in long clusters at branch ends. Oval fruits to 6 in. long, green to reddish or yellowish, with large flat pit and peach-flavored flesh. Some say the flavor has varnish or turpentine overtones; this quality tends to be more prevalent in seedlings. Leaves are large (8–16 in. long) and handsome; often coppery red or purple when new, later turning dark green. Needs steady moisture but tolerates fairly poor, shallow soils. Fruit can cause a skin rash in some people.

MANGO. See MANGIFERA indica

MANZANITA. See ARCTOSTAPHYLOS

MAPLE. See ACER

MAPLE, FLOWERING. See ABUTILON

M

Marantaceae. The arrowroot family consists of tropical or subtropical herbaceous plants with fleshy rhizomes or tubers and highly irregular flowers. Most are grown for handsome foliage, a few for flowers. An example is *Calathea*.

MARGUERITE. See CHRYSANTHEMUM frutescens

MARIGOLD. See TAGETES

MARIGOLD, DESERT. See BAILEYA multiradiata

MARJORAM. See ORIGANUM

MARLBERRY. See ARDISIA

MARMALADE BUSH. See STREPTOSOLEN jamesonii

MARRUBIUM vulgare

HOREHOUND

Lamiaceae (Labiatae)

PERENNIAL HERB

⚡ ZONES 1–24, 26–45

☀ FULL SUN

💧💧 REGULAR TO LITTLE WATER

Marrubium vulgare

Grows 1–3 ft. high. Wrinkled, woolly, aromatic gray-green leaves; whorls of white flowers (similar to those of mint) on foot-long, branching stems. Needs little water but will take more if drainage is good; otherwise, not fussy about soil. Sow seeds in spring in flats; transplant seedlings to 1 ft. apart. As garden plant, invasive and rather weedy looking, but can serve as edging in gray garden. Used for medicinal purposes and in candy. Foliage lasts well in bouquets.

MARSH MARIGOLD. See CALTHA palustris

MASK FLOWER. See ALONSOA

MASTERWORT. See ASTRANTIA

MATILIJA POPPY. See ROMNEYA coulteri

MATRICARIA recutita (M. chamomilla)

CHAMOMILE

Asteraceae (Compositae)

ANNUAL

⚡ ALL ZONES

☀ FULL SUN

💧 MODERATE WATER

Matricaria recutita

This is the chamomile whose dried flowers yield a fragrant tea with overtones of pineapple. Plant grows 2–2½ ft. tall, with finely cut, almost fernlike foliage and daisylike white-and-yellow flower heads an inch wide or less. Summer bloom. Grows easily in full sun and ordinary soil from seed sown in late winter or spring. Becomes naturalized.

Plants or seeds sold as *Matricaria* 'White Stars', 'Golden Ball', and 'Snowball' are varieties of *Chrysanthemum parthenium*. Chamomile sold as walk-on ground cover is *Chamaemelum nobile (Anthemis nobilis)*. Its flowers yield medicinal-tasting, rather bitter tea.

MATRIMONY VINE. See LYCIUM chinense

MATTEUCCIA struthiopteris

OSTRICH FERN

Polypodiaceae

FERN

⚡ ZONES 1–10, 14–17, 32–45

☀ ◑ ● FULL SUN ONLY IN COOL, MOIST AREAS

💧 💧 AMPLE WATER

Matteuccia struthiopteris

Native to northern regions of North America. Hardy to extreme cold but an indifferent grower in mild-winter areas. Clumps are narrow at base, spread out at top like a shuttlecock. Unfolding young fronds (fiddleheads) are edible. Plant can reach 6 ft. in moist, moderate climates; grows only 1½–2 ft. tall in mountains where season is short, humidity low. Spreads by underground rhizomes. Dormant in winter. Attractive woodland or waterside plant. Needs rich soil.

MATTHIOLA

STOCK

Brassicaceae (Cruciferae)

BIENNIALS OR PERENNIALS GROWN AS ANNUALS

⚡ ALL ZONES

☀ ◑ FULL SUN OR LIGHT SHADE

💧 REGULAR WATER

Matthiola incana

Old-fashioned plants, especially well suited to the cottage garden. All have long, narrow gray-green leaves and luxuriant, scented flowers in erect, spikelike clusters. Best in cool weather.

M. incana. STOCK. Valued for fragrance, cut flowers. Oblong leaves to 4 in. long. Flowers single or double, 1 in. wide, with spicy-sweet scent. Colors include white, pink, red, purple, lavender, blue, yellow, cream. Blues and reds are purple toned; yellows tend toward cream.

Many strains available. Earliest bloomer is Trysomic Seven Weeks (blooms in 7 weeks), a branching plant to 12–15 in. tall. Ten Weeks, also branching, reaches 15–18 in. tall. Column stock and Double Giant Flowering are unbranched plants 2–3 ft. tall; they can be planted 6–8 in. apart in rows and are ideal for cutting. Giant Imperial strain is branched, 2–2½ ft. tall, comes in solid or mixed colors.

Stock needs light, fertile soil and good drainage. In cold-winter areas, plant in earliest spring to get flowers before hot weather; choose early bloomers. In mild-winter regions, plants set out in early fall will bloom in winter or early spring. Plants take moderate frost but will not set flower buds if nights are too chilly; late planting means bloom time will be delayed until spring. Where winter rainfall is heavy, plant in raised beds to ensure good drainage and prevent root rot.

M. longipetala bicornis. EVENING SCENTED STOCK. Foot-tall plant with lance-shaped leaves to 3½ in. long. Small purplish flowers are not showy, but emit a powerful fragrance at night. Winter annual in warmest regions.

MAY APPLE. See PODOPHYLLUM peltatum

MAYBUSH, MAYDAY TREE. See PRUNUS padus

MAYPOP. See PASSIFLORA incarnata

FOR GROWING SYMBOL EXPLANATIONS
PLEASE SEE PAGE 161

M

MAYTENUS boaria

MAYTEN TREE

Celastraceae

EVERGREEN TREE

ZONES 8, 9, 14–21, 25

FULL SUN

REGULAR TO MODERATE WATER

Maytenus boaria

Graceful, narrow-leafed tree with long, pendulous branchlets hanging down from branches; resembles a small-scale weeping willow. Slow to moderate growth to an eventual 30–50 ft. Provide good drainage; water deeply to keep tree from rooting near soil surface and invading planting beds. May partially defoliate after cold snaps or at bloom time in spring (flowers are inconspicuous), but recovers quickly. 'Green Showers' has weeping branchlets densely clad in deep green leaves that are a littler broader than those of most seedling trees.

MAZUS reptans

Scrophulariaceae

PERENNIAL

ZONES 3–9, 14–24, 28–34, 39

PARTIAL SHADE IN HOT CLIMATES

REGULAR WATER

Mazus reptans

Slender stems creep and root along ground, send up leafy branches 1–2 in. tall. Narrowish bright green leaves are 1 in. long, with a few teeth along edges. Spring and early summer flowers are purplish blue with white and yellow markings, ¾ in. across; they appear in clusters of two to five. In shape, flowers resemble those of *Mimulus*. Use in rock garden or as small-scale ground cover; needs rich soil. Takes heavy foot traffic between pavers. Evergreen in mild-winter climates; in colder areas, freezes to ground but usually recovers quickly in spring if protected over winter by snow cover or light mulch. Plant sold as *M. japonicus* 'Albiflora' is a white-flowering form of *M. reptans*.

MEADOW RUE. See THALICTRUM

MEADOW SAFFRON. See COLCHICUM

MEADOW SWEET. See ASTILBE, FILIPENDULA ulmaria

MECONOPSIS

Papaveraceae

PERENNIALS

ZONES VARY BY SPECIES

PARTIAL OR FULL SHADE

REGULAR WATER

Meconopsis betonicifolia

Ardent collectors and shade garden enthusiasts sometimes attempt the many species offered by specialist seed firms. Most are difficult, but the two listed here are not too hard to grow if given loose, acid soil and cool, humid, shady conditions. Best suited to Pacific Northwest; also do well on coast of Maine. Protect seaside plantings from wind. Plants self-sow without becoming invasive.

M. betonicifolia (M. baileyi). HIMALAYAN POPPY. Zones 4–6, 17, coastal 38. In the right climate, can reach 6 ft. tall, with abundant hairy leaves and silky, 3–4-in., sky blue poppies with yellow stamens; late spring or early summer bloom. In less favorable locales, it is a much squatter, shorter-lived plant with smaller flowers verging on mauve.

M. cambrica. WELSH POPPY. Zones 3–9, 14–17, 34, 38 (coastal area), 39. Easier to grow than above species. In summer, produces orange or yellow, 3-in. poppies on 1–2-ft. stems. Gray-green, divided leaves. Tolerates full sun, some drought.

MEDITERRANEAN FAN PALM. See CHAMAEROPS humilis

MELALEUCA

Myrtaceae

EVERGREEN SHRUBS OR TREES

ZONES VARY BY SPECIES

FULL SUN

MODERATE TO LITTLE WATER, EXCEPT AS NOTED

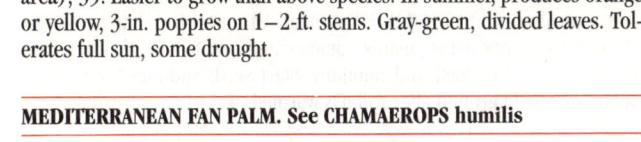

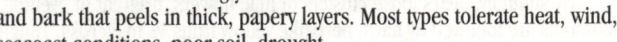

Melaleuca linariifolia

Native to Australia. Narrow, sometimes needle-like leaves and clustered flowers with prominent stamens. Since each cluster resembles a bottlebrush, some melaleucas are called bottlebrushes—though that name is more generally applied to *Callistemon*. Clusters of woody seed capsules are attached directly to branches. Many melaleucas have interestingly contorted branches and bark that peels in thick, papery layers. Most types tolerate heat, wind, seacoast conditions, poor soil, drought.

M. decussata. LILAC MELALEUCA. Large shrub or tree. Zones 9, 12–24. Grows 8–20 ft. tall, with equal spread. Brown, shredding bark. Tiny (½-in.-long) leaves closely set on arching, pendulous branches. Lilac to purple flowers in 1-in. spikes, late spring to summer.

M. linariifolia. FLAXLEAF PAPERBARK. Tree. Zones 9, 13–24. To 30 ft., with umbrellalike crown. White bark sheds in papery flakes. Slender branchlets. Stiff, needlelike leaves are bright green or bluish green, 1¼ in. long. Numerous fluffy spikes of small white flowers in summer.

M. nesophila. PINK MELALEUCA. Large shrub or tree. Zones 13, 16–24. Fast growth to 15–20 ft., possibly 30 ft. Grows naturally as small tree; if unpruned, produces gnarled, heavy branches that sprawl or ascend in picturesque patterns. Thick, spongy bark. Gray-green, roundish, 1-in. leaves. Small, roundish flowers produced at branch tips most of year; blossoms open mauve, then fade to white with yellow tips.

M. quinquenervia. CAJEPUT TREE. Tree. Zones 9, 13, 15–17, 20–27. Upright, open growth to 20–40 ft. Young branches pendulous. Trunk has thick, spongy, light brown to whitish bark that peels off in sheets (these sheets can be used to line wire hanging baskets). Leaves stiff, narrowly oval, 2–4 in. long, pale green; turn purplish with light frost. Young leaves have silky hairs. Yellowish white (sometimes pink or purple) flowers in 2–3-in. spikes, summer and fall. Can take much or little water. Has escaped from cultivation and become a pest in Florida, where it is commonly called punk tree. Usually sold as *M. leucadendra*.

MELAMPODIUM

Asteraceae (Compositae)

ANNUALS AND PERENNIALS

ZONES VARY BY SPECIES

FULL SUN

MODERATE WATER

Melampodium leucanthum

These tough, drought-tolerant plants produce masses of small daisies over a long period. Provide well-drained soil.

M. leucanthum. BLACKFOOT DAISY. Short-lived perennial. Zones 1–3, 10–13, 29, 30; western parts of 33, 35, 41, 43. To 1 ft. tall. Honey-scented white

M

daisies with yellow centers bloom in spring, summer, and (in mild climates) sporadically during winter.

M. paludosum. BUTTER DAISY. Annual. All zones. To 1½ ft. tall. Deep yellow daisies appear throughout summer and into fall; no deadheading required. Tolerates heat and humidity. Start seeds indoors for earliest bloom; or sow in ground after soil has warmed.

Melastomataceae. The melastoma family consists almost entirely of tropical shrubs and trees with strongly veined leaves and symmetrical flowers, such as princess flower (*Tibouchina*).

MELIA azedarach

CHINABERRY

Meliaceae

DECIDUOUS TREE

🗡 ZONES 6–31

☼ FULL SUN

🌢 MODERATE WATER

◈ FRUIT IS POISONOUS IF INGESTED

Melia azedarach
'Umbraculiformis'

To 30–50 ft. high, with spreading, irregular habit. Leaves 1–3 ft. long, cut into many toothed, narrow or oval leaflets 1–2 in. long. In spring or early summer, bears loose clusters of lilac flowers, fragrant in evening. Blossoms are followed by hard, berrylike yellow fruits ½ in. across. Tough tree that tolerates heat, wind, poor alkaline soil, drought; valuable where trees are hard to grow. Brittle wood makes it vulnerable to storm damage. In areas with year-round moisture, tends to self-sow and become a pest.

'Umbraculiformis', Texas umbrella tree, is less picturesque than the species. Grows to 30 ft., with dense, spreading, dome-shaped crown and drooping leaves.

MELIANTHUS major

HONEY BUSH

Melianthaceae

EVERGREEN SHRUB

🗡 ZONES 8, 9, 12–28

☼ ◑ PARTIAL SHADE IN HOTTEST CLIMATES

🌢🌢 REGULAR TO LITTLE WATER

Melianthus major

Soft-wooded plant of rapid growth to 12–14 ft., but easily kept much shorter. Irregular habit; stems semierect or sprawling and spreading. Boldly patterned foliage: grayish green, 1-ft.-long leaves divided into 9–11 strongly toothed leaflets. Foliage smells disagreeable when brushed or bruised. Foot-long spikes of reddish brown, 1-in. flowers in late winter, early spring. Use for tropical effect, sprawling over walls, as accent.

MELISSA officinalis

LEMON BALM, SWEET BALM

Lamiaceae (Labiatae)

PERENNIAL HERB

🗡 ZONES 1–24, 26–45

☼ ◑ SUN OR PARTIAL SHADE

🌢 REGULAR WATER

Melissa officinalis

Grows to 2 ft. Light green, heavily veined leaves with lemon scent. White flowers unimportant. Shear occasionally to keep compact. Likes rich soil. Very hardy; self-sows, spreads rapidly. Propagate from seed or root divisions. Leaves used in drinks, fruit cups, salads, fish dishes. Dried leaves help give lemon tang to sachets, potpourris.

MELON, MUSKMELON, CANTALOUPE

Cucurbitaceae

ANNUALS

🗡 ALL ZONES

☼ FULL SUN

🌢 WATER MOST WHEN PLANTS ARE YOUNG

Melon

The true cantaloupe, a hard-shelled melon, is rarely grown in the U.S. Principal types cultivated here are muskmelons ("cantaloupes") and late melons. (See Watermelon for information on that fruit.)

Muskmelons are ribbed, with netted skin and usually salmon-colored flesh; they are more widely adapted than late melons. Varieties include 'Hale's Best', 'Honey Rock', and the hybrids 'Ambrosia', 'Mainerock', 'Samson', and 'Saticoy'. Hybrids are superior to others in disease resistance and uniformity of size and quality. (Choosing varieties resistant to mildew and other diseases is particularly important in humid-summer regions.) Other muskmelons include small, highly perfumed types from the Mediterranean, such as white-fleshed 'Ha-Ogen' and orange-fleshed 'Chaca' and 'Charentais'.

Late melons are a varied group including honeydew, casaba, 'Crenshaw', 'Honey Ball', 'Golden Beauty', and 'Persian'. Because they need a longer growing season than muskmelons, they are less widely cultivated. They dislike high humidity and grow best in areas with hot, relatively dry summers.

To ripen to full sweetness, melons need steady heat for 2½–4 months. Sow seed 2 weeks after average date of last frost; don't rush the season, since melons are truly tropical plants and will perish in even light frost. In regions where summers are cool or relatively short, start plants indoors in peat pots a few weeks before last frost date, then plant outdoors in light, well-drained soil in warmest southern exposure. Row covers permit earlier planting outdoors. Black plastic mulch under melons warms soil, speeds harvest, helps keep melons from rotting.

You can grow melons on sun-bathed trellises, but heavy fruit must be supported in individual cloth slings. They are best grown in hills or mounded rows a few inches high at center; you will need to provide considerable space. Make hills about 3 ft. in diameter and space them 3–4 ft. apart; encircle each with a furrow for irrigation. Make rows 3 ft. wide and as long as desired, spacing them 3–4 ft. apart; make furrows for irrigation along either side. Plant seeds 1 in. deep—four or five seeds per hill, two or three seeds every 1 ft. in rows. When plants are well established, thin each hill to the best two plants; thin rows to one strong plant per foot. Fill furrows with water from time to time (furrows let you water plants without wetting foliage), but do not keep soil soaked. Feed (again in furrow) every 6 weeks.

To make melons taste sweeter, hold off watering a week or so before you expect to harvest the ripe fruit. To determine if a melon is ready for harvest, lift fruit and twist; it will slip off the stem if ripe. A pleasant, perfumy fragrance also indicates ripeness.

MENTHA

MINT

Lamiaceae (Labiatae)

PERENNIAL HERBS AND GROUND COVERS

🗡 ZONES VARY BY SPECIES

☼ ◑ SUN OR PARTIAL SHADE

🌢 REGULAR WATER

Mentha spicata

Spread rapidly by underground stems. Can be quite invasive. They grow almost anywhere but perform best in light, medium-rich, moist soil. Contain in pot or box to keep in bounds. Plants disappear in winter in colder part of range. Propagate from runners; replant every 3 years.

M. gentilis. GOLDEN APPLE MINT. Zones 3–24, 26–35, 37, 39. To 2 ft. Smooth, deep green leaves, variegated yellow. Flowers inconspicuous. Use in flavoring foods. Foliage excellent in mixed bouquets.

M. piperita. PEPPERMINT. Zones 1–24, 26–45. To 3 ft. Strongly scented, toothed, 3-in.-long leaves. Small purple flowers in 1–3-in. spikes. Leaves good for flavoring tea. *M. p. citrata*, called orange mint or bergamot mint, grows to 2 ft. and has broad, 2-in.-long leaves, small lavender flowers. It is used in potpourris or in flavoring foods. Crushed leaves have slight orange flavor.

M. pulegium. PENNYROYAL. Zones 4–24, 26–32. Creeping plant grows a few inches tall with nearly round 1-in. leaves. Small lavender flowers in tight, short whorls. Strong mint fragrance and flavor. Poisonous in large quantities but safe as a flavoring. Needs cool, moist site.

M. requienii. JEWEL MINT OF CORSICA. Zones 5–9, 12–24, 26–31. Creeping, mat forming, to only ½ in. high. Tiny, round bright green leaves give mossy effect. Tiny light purple flowers in summer. Delightful minty or sagelike fragrance when leaves are bruised or crushed underfoot.

M. spicata. SPEARMINT. Zones 1–24, 26–45. To 1½–2 ft. Dark green leaves, slightly smaller than those of peppermint; leafy spikes of purplish flowers. Use leaves fresh from garden or dried, for lamb, in cold drinks, as garnish, in apple jelly.

M. suaveolens. APPLE MINT. Zones 3–24, 26–35, 37, 39. Stiff stems grow 1½–2½ ft. tall. Rounded leaves are slightly hairy, gray green, 1–4 in. long. Purplish white flowers in 2–3-in. spikes. Leaves have apple-mint fragrance. 'Variegata', pineapple mint, has leaves with white markings, faint fragrance of pineapple. Species is usually sold as *M. rotundifolia*.

MENTZELIA

BLAZING STAR

Loasaceae

PERENNIALS, BIENNIALS, AND ANNUALS

ZONES 1–24, 29, 30; WESTERN PARTS OF 33, 35, 41, 43

FULL SUN

WATER NEEDS VARY BY SPECIES

Mentzelia lindleyi

Native to desert or semidesert areas of western U.S. Tolerate heat, wind, and poor soil, but require good drainage. Star-shaped yellow spring or early summer blossoms are large and showy.

M. laevicaulis. Biennial or short-lived perennial. Rough, ungainly plant to 3–3½ ft. tall, with narrow, 3–7-in.-long leaves. Spectacular pale yellow, 4-in. stars open in the evening; plant is often called evening star. Best used on bare banks. Little water.

M. lindleyi. Annual. To 1–4 ft. tall, usually narrow, sometimes spreading to 1½ ft. Light green, rough-textured leaves. Bright yellow flowers have orange or reddish center ring and big brush of yellow stamens. Sow seed in place in fall, winter, or earliest spring; give regular water until plants bloom, then reduce or stop watering. Use alone or in wildflower mixtures.

MERREMIA tuberosa (Ipomoea tuberosa)

YELLOW MORNING GLORY, WOOD ROSE

DECIDUOUS VINE

ZONES 24–27

FULL SUN

MODERATE WATER

Merremia tuberosa

Twines to 50–60 ft. unless cut down by frost. Leaves 6 in. long, divided into seven leaflets. Produces a fine warm-weather show of 2–4-in. golden yellow morning glories. These are followed by the wood roses used in dry arrangements: curious round, woody seed capsules surrounded by petal-like structures. *M. aurea* is similar, but it's smaller and has leaves divided into five leaflets.

MERRYBELLS. See UVULARIA

MERTENSIA virginica

VIRGINIA BLUEBELLS

Boraginaceae

PERENNIAL

ZONES 1–21, 31–45

PARTIAL OR FULL SHADE

REGULAR WATER

Mertensia virginica

A relative of forget-me-not *(Myosotis);* native to eastern U.S. Broadly oval, bluish green leaves form loose clumps that send up leafy, 1½–2-ft.-tall stems bearing loose clusters of nodding, 1-in. flowers. Buds are usually pink to lavender, but open to blue bells, sometimes with a pinkish cast. Appears and flowers early in spring; dies to ground soon after going to seed, usually by midsummer. Charming with naturalized daffodils or with ferns, trillium, bleeding heart in woodland garden.

Provide moist, rich soil. Use summer annuals to fill void after plants die back. Clumps can be left in place indefinitely; they will slowly spread. To get more plants, use volunteer seedlings or dig and divide clumps in early fall.

MESEMBRYANTHEMUM crystallinum

ICE PLANT

Aizoaceae

SUCCULENT ANNUAL

ALL ZONES

FULL SUN

TAKES CONSIDERABLE DROUGHT

Mesembryanthemum crystallinum

The least ornamental of many plants commonly called *Mesembryanthemum* or ice plant, this is now considered the only true *Mesembryanthemum*. Use in hanging baskets, window boxes. For other, showier kinds used as ground covers, see Ice Plant.

M. crystallinum is a sprawling plant a few inches tall and several feet wide. Oval, flat, stalked, fleshy leaves grow to 4 in. long, turn red when water stressed. Leaves are covered with tiny transparent blisters that glisten like flecks of ice. Foliage is edible and resembles New Zealand spinach in flavor. Inch-wide, white to pinkish flowers in summer. Easy to grow from seed. In warm, humid climates, provide well-drained soil.

METASEQUOIA glyptostroboides

DAWN REDWOOD

Taxodiaceae

DECIDUOUS CONIFER

ZONES 3–10, 14–24, 31–41

FULL SUN

BEST IN MOIST, NOT BOGGY SOIL

Metasequoia glyptostroboides

Thought to have been extinct for thousands of years, but found growing in a few isolated sites in China during the 1940s. Pyramidal tree bearing small cones. Soft, light green needles turn light bronze in autumn, then drop to reveal attractive winter silhouette. Branchlets tend to turn upward; bark is reddish in youth, becoming darker and fissured in age. Trees grow very fast in mild regions, moderately fast in cold-winter climates. They have reached about 90 ft., but they haven't been grown long enough in gardens to determine maximum height. Looks somewhat like bald cypress (*Taxodium distichum*), another deciduous conifer. While in leaf, also bears superficial resemblance to coast redwood (*Sequoia sempervirens*).

Grows best in good, organic, well-drained soil with regular water. Good lawn tree, though in time surface roots may interrupt smooth flow of turf. Not suited to arid regions or seacoast, since dry heat and salty ocean winds will burn foliage.

METROSIDEROS excelsus (M. tomentosus)

NEW ZEALAND CHRISTMAS TREE, POHUTUKAWA

Myrtaceae

EVERGREEN TREE OR LARGE SHRUB

ZONES 17, 23–25

FULL SUN

MODERATE TO LITTLE WATER

Metrosideros excelsus

Native to New Zealand. To 30 ft. or more; prune lower branches to get tree form. On young plants, leathery leaves are glossy green; on older ones, they are dark green above, white and woolly beneath. Big clusters of dark red flowers cover branch ends May–July (in December in New Zealand, hence the common name "Christmas tree"). Useful lawn tree or street tree (if given ample root space) in coastal gardens. 'Aurea' has yellow flowers.

MEXICAN BLUE PALM. See BRAHEA armata

MEXICAN DAISY. See ERIGERON karvinskianus

MEXICAN FAN PALM. See WASHINGTONIA robusta

MEXICAN FIRE BUSH. See KOCHIA scoparia trichophylla

MEXICAN FIRE PLANT. See EUPHORBIA heterophylla

MEXICAN FLAME VINE. See SENECIO confusus

MEXICAN HEATHER. See CUPHEA hyssopifolia

MEXICAN ORANGE. See CHOISYA ternata

MEXICAN PALO VERDE. See PARKINSONIA aculeata

MEXICAN SHELL FLOWER. See TIGRIDIA pavonia

MEXICAN SUNFLOWER. See TITHONIA rotundifolia

MEXICAN TULIP POPPY. See HUNNEMANNIA fumariifolia

MICHAELMAS DAISY. See ASTER novi-belgii

MICHELIA

Magnoliaceae

EVERGREEN SHRUBS OR TREES

ZONES VARY BY SPECIES

PARTIAL SHADE

REGULAR WATER

Michelia figo

Related to magnolias but bear numerous flowers among leaves rather than singly at branch ends. All need rich soil. Tolerate sun in cool-summer climates.

M. champaca. Tree. Zones 16–27. To 25–30 ft. tall, with large (to 10-in.-long) glossy leaves. Blooms off and on throughout the year, most heavily in winter and summer. Flowers many-petaled, pale orange, to 3 in. wide; national flower of Philippines. Rich, fruity fragrance is legendary.

M. doltsopa. Large shrub or tree. Zones 14–28. To about 40 ft. tall. May be bushy in form or narrow and upright; choose plant for desired

habit. Leaves thin, leathery, dark green, 3–8 in. long. Flowers open in winter from brown, furry buds that form in profusion among leaves near branch ends. Fragrant, 5–7-in.-wide, creamy or white blossoms with 12–16 petals; somewhat resemble flowers of saucer magnolia.

M. figo (M. fuscata). BANANA SHRUB. Zones 9, 14–24, 26–29, 31, warmer parts of 32. Slow, dense growth to 6–8 ft., possibly to 15 ft. Glossy, 3-in.-long, medium green leaves. Heaviest bloom in spring, but scattered flowers often appear throughout summer. Flowers 1–1½ in. wide, creamy yellow shaded brownish purple, resembling small magnolia blossoms. Powerful fruity fragrance like that of ripe bananas; scent is strongest in warm, wind-free spot. Choice plant for entryway or patio. 'Port Wine' has rose to maroon flowers.

MICROBIOTA decussata

SIBERIAN CARPET CYPRESS

Cupressaceae

EVERGREEN SHRUB

ZONES 1–10, 14–17, 32–45

PARTIAL SHADE IN HOTTEST AREAS

REGULAR WATER

Microbiota decussata

Native to Siberian mountains and hardy to any amount of cold. Neat, sprawling shrub that resembles a trailing arborvitae. Grows to 1½ ft. tall, 7–8 ft. wide, with many horizontal or trailing plumelike branches closely set with scalelike leaves. Foliage green in summer, turning purplish, reddish brown in winter. More shade tolerant than junipers. Needs excellent drainage. Use as a bank cover.

MIGNONETTE. See RESEDA odorata

MILFOIL. See ACHILLEA millefolium

MILIUM effusum 'Aureum'

BOWLES' GOLDEN GRASS

Poaceae (Gramineae)

PERENNIAL GRASS

ZONES 3–9, 14–17, 31–34, 39

LIGHT SHADE

AMPLE WATER

Milium effusum 'Aureum'

Attractive clumping grass to 2 ft. tall, usually less. Bright greenish gold leaves erect, then arching and weeping. Effective for spot of color in woodland garden, shaded rock garden.

MILKBUSH. See EUPHORBIA tirucalli

MIMOSA. See ACACIA baileyana, ALBIZIA julibrissin

MIMULUS hybridus

MONKEY FLOWER

Scrophulariaceae

SHORT-LIVED PERENNIAL GROWN AS ANNUAL

ALL ZONES

PARTIAL OR FULL SHADE

REGULAR WATER

Mimulus hybridus

Smooth, succulent, medium green leaves form a mound to 1–1½ ft. high. Showy, velvety flowers are thought to resemble a grinning monkey face; they are funnel shaped, 2–2½ in. long, with two "lips." Colors range from cream through rose, orange, yellow, scarlet, and brown, usually with heavy brownish maroon spotting or mottling. Best suited to cool, moist climates, where it tolerates full sun. Use in shady borders; or plant in hanging baskets or window boxes. Sow seed in spring for summer bloom, or set out plants for spring show.

MING ARALIA. See POLYSCIAS fruticosa

MINT. See MENTHA

MIRABILIS jalapa

FOUR O'CLOCK

Nyctaginaceae

TUBEROUS-ROOTED PERENNIAL

🌱 ALL ZONES; SEE BELOW

☼ FULL SUN

💧 MODERATE WATER

☠ ALL PLANT PARTS ARE POISONOUS

Mirabilis jalapa

Perennial in Zones 4–9, 12–32; frosts kill it to ground but roots survive. In colder climates, treat as summer annual; dig and store tuberous roots as you would dahlia roots. Strong, bushy habit gives this plant the substance and character of a shrub: erect, many-branched stems grow quickly to form a mounded clump 3–4 ft. high and wide. Deep green, oval, 2–6-in.-long leaves. Scented, trumpet-shaped flowers in red, yellow, or white, with variations of shades between. Blossoms open in midafternoon; bloom season runs midsummer through fall. Jingles strain is lower growing than old-fashioned kinds, has elaborately splashed and stained flowers in two or three colors. Four o'clock reseeds readily and has naturalized in many parts of the South.

MISCANTHUS

EULALIA GRASS, SILVER GRASS, MAIDEN GRASS

Poaceae (Gramineae)

PERENNIAL GRASSES

🌱 ZONES VARY BY SPECIES

☼☼ SUN OR LIGHT SHADE

💧💧 MUCH TO MODERATE WATER

Miscanthus sinensis

These are among the most popular ornamental grasses. All are large to very large clump-forming grasses; attractive flower clusters open as tassels and gradually expand into large plumes atop tall stalks in late summer or fall. Plumes are silvery to pinkish or bronze and last well into winter. Foliage is always graceful; may be broad or narrow, solid colored, striped lengthwise, or banded. In fall and winter, foliage clumps turn to shades of yellow, orange, or reddish brown, especially showy against snow or an evergreen background. Need little care. Cut back old foliage to the ground before new foliage sprouts in spring; divide clumps when vigor declines.

M. giganteus (M. floridulus). GIANT CHINESE SILVER GRASS. Zones 3–24, 29–34. Can reach 10–14 ft., with leaves to 2½ ft. long, 1½ in. wide. Silvery flower plumes rise another 1–2 ft. above foliage. Leaves turn purplish green in fall, then drop off, leaving tall bare stalks over winter.

M. sinensis. EULALIA GRASS, JAPANESE SILVER GRASS. Zones 2–24, 29–41. Variable in size and foliage. Flowers are held well above foliage clumps and may be cut for fresh or dry arrangements. All are attractive in borders or as focal points in a garden. Many varieties are obtainable; new ones come to market every year. Here are a few of the choicest:

'Adagio'. To 2–4 ft., with gray foliage and pink flowers aging white.

'Autumn Light'. To 5–6 ft. Late bloom; red autumn foliage.

'Cabaret'. Clumps reach 6 ft. Leaves are striped with white. Reddish plumes turn creamy with age.

M. s. condensatus 'Silver Arrow'. To 5–7 ft. White-striped leaves; silvery plumes.

'Cosmopolitan'. Narrow, erect, to 6 ft. or taller. Broad leaves have broad white stripes.

'Gracillimus'. MAIDEN GRASS. To 5–6 ft. Best-known variety. Reddish flowers borne late. Slender, weeping foliage with narrow white midrib turns orange or tan in the fall.

'Graziella'. To 5–6 ft., with narrow leaves and silvery plumes high above foliage. Orange fall color.

'Kirk Alexander'. Low growing (to 3 ft.); leaves horizontally banded with yellow. Tan flowers.

'Malepartus'. To 6–7 ft., with broad leaves that turn orange in fall. Rose pink plumes fade to silvery white.

'Morning Light'. To 4–5 ft. Leaves have white midrib and narrow stripes along leaf edges for overall silvery appearance. Reddish bronze flowers. One of the most elegant varieties.

'Purpurascens'. Foliage clumps 3–4 ft. tall turn reddish orange in fall. Silvery plumes.

'Strictus'. PORCUPINE GRASS. Narrow, erect, to 5–6 ft., with creamy stripes that run across leaves. Copper flowers. A little more cold hardy than the species.

'Yaku Jima'. Smaller grower (to 3–4 ft.). Slender green leaves; tan flowers.

'Zebrinus'. Broadly arching clumps to 5–6 ft.; leaves banded crosswise with yellowish white. Flowers are coppery pink, aging to white.

MISSION BELLS. See FRITILLARIA biflora

MITCHELLA repens

PARTRIDGEBERRY, TWINBERRY

Rubiaceae

EVERGREEN PERENNIAL

🌱 ZONES 1–6, 28, 31–45

☼● PARTIAL OR FULL SHADE

💧💧 AMPLE WATER

Mitchella repens

Attractive small, creeping evergreen plant native to much of eastern North America. Roundish leaves less than 1 in. long, borne in pairs along trailing, rooting, somewhat woody stems. Paired small white flowers appear in late spring or early summer; these are followed by bright red berries less than ¼ in. wide. Small-scale ground cover best seen near eye level—on a shady bank or above a wall. Provide steady moisture and soil with plenty of leaf mold or other organic matter.

MOCK ORANGE. See CHOISYA ternata, PHILADELPHUS

MOLE PLANT. See EUPHORBIA lathyris

MOLINIA caerulea

PURPLE MOOR GRASS

Poaceae (Gramineae)

PERENNIAL GRASS

🌱 ZONES 2–9, 14–17, 32–41

☼☼ FULL SUN OR LIGHT SHADE

💧💧 AMPLE WATER

Molinia caerulea
'Variegata'

Plant is long lived but slow growing, taking a few years to reach its full potential. Erect, narrow, light green leaves form a neat, dense clump 1–2 ft. tall and wide. In summer, yellowish to purplish flowers in narrow, spikelike clusters rise 1–2 ft. above clump; they turn to tan and last well into fall. Inflorescences are profuse, but have a narrow structure that gives clump a see-through quality; they make good cut flowers. In late fall, both leaves and flower clusters break off and blow away. 'Skyracer' has foliage clumps to 3 ft. tall; flowers bring it to 7–8 ft. 'Windspiel' is similar. Leaves of 'Variegata' are striped lengthwise with creamy white; foliage clump is 1–1½ ft. tall, with purple flowers adding 6–12 in.

MOLUCCELLA laevis

BELLS-OF-IRELAND, SHELL FLOWER
Lamiaceae (Labiatae)
ANNUAL
⚊ ALL ZONES
☼ FULL SUN
🌢 REGULAR WATER

Moluccella laevis

About 2 ft. high. Flowers are carried almost from base in whorls of six. Showy part of flower is large shell-like or bell-like, apple green calyx, very veiny and crisp textured; small white tube of united petals in center is inconspicuous. As cut flowers, spikes of little bells are attractive and long lasting, either fresh or dried; be sure to remove unattractive leaves.

Needs loose, well-drained soil. Doesn't perform well in hot, humid climates. Sow seed in ground in early spring for summer bloom; in mildest climates, can be sown in fall for winter bloom. If weather is warm, refrigerate seed for a week before planting. For long spikes, fertilize regularly.

MOMORDICA charantia

BALSAM PEAR, BITTER MELON
Cucurbitaceae
ANNUAL VINE
⚊ ALL ZONES
☼ FULL SUN
🌢 REGULAR WATER

Momordica charantia

Deeply lobed leaves; white, fringed flowers 1 in. across. Fruit to 8 in. long, cylindrical with tapered ends, ridged and warty, bright yellow when ripe, splitting to show scarlet seeds. Immature fruits cherished in Asian cooking despite bitter flavor. Showy ripe fruits are sometimes used in arrangements. Sprawls or climbs by tendrils. Sow seed when soil warms, feed generously, and provide a trellis or other support.

MONARDA

BEE BALM, OSWEGO TEA, HORSEMINT
Lamiaceae (Labiatae)
PERENNIALS
⚊ ZONES VARY BY SPECIES
☼ ◐ LIGHT AFTERNOON SHADE IN HOT AREAS
🌢🌢 AMPLE WATER

Monarda didyma

Bushy, leafy clumps spread rapidly at edges and can be invasive. Dark green leaves grow 4–6 in. long, have strong, pleasant odor like blend of mint and basil. In summer, upright square stems are topped by tight clusters of long-tubed flowers much visited by hummingbirds. Plant 10 in. apart. Divide every 3 or 4 years. Not long lived where winters are warm, summers long and hot. Prone to mildew and other leaf diseases in dry soils and in very humid regions.

M. didyma. Zones 2–11, 14–17, 30–41. Native to eastern U.S. Basic species has scarlet flowers surrounded by reddish bracts. Garden selections and hybrids include scarlet 'Adam', pink 'Croftway Pink' and 'Granite

Pink', 'Snow White', and dark red 'Mahogany'. A very old variety, 'Cambridge Scarlet', is still widely grown. Mildew-resistant varieties include 'Violet Queen' and pink 'Marshall's Delight'. If spent flowers are removed, all varieties bloom over long period of 2 months or more. Don't let soil dry out.

M. fistulosa. Zones 1–24, 28–45. Native from easternmost U.S. to Rocky Mountains. Lavender flowers to light pink encircled by whitish bracts are less showy than those of *M. didyma*. Best suited to wild garden.

MONDO GRASS. See OPHIOPOGON japonicus, under LIRIOPE and OPHIOPOGON

MONEY PLANT. See LUNARIA annua

MONEYWORT. See LYSIMACHIA nummularia

MONKEY FLOWER. See MIMULUS hybridus

MONKEY PUZZLE TREE. See ARAUCARIA araucana

MONKSHOOD. See ACONITUM

MONSTERA

Araceae
EVERGREEN VINES
⚊ ZONES 24–27; OR INDOORS
☼ FILTERED SHADE
🌢 REGULAR WATER

Monstera deliciosa

Related to philodendrons and resembling them in leaf gloss and texture. Most have cut and perforated foliage. Need rich soil. Outdoor growing restricted to warmest climates. For best results indoors, grow in container with good drainage, feed occasionally, and keep leaves clean. In poor light or low humidity, new leaves will be smaller. If tall plants get bare at base, replant in larger container and add younger, smaller plant to fill in; or cut plant back and let new shoots start.

M. deliciosa. SPLIT-LEAF PHILODENDRON. Eventually reaches great size if planted in open bed in greenhouse or outdoors. Should be given protection from frost, but recovers fairly quickly from frost damage. Long, cordlike roots that hang from stems root into soil, help support plant on trees or on moss logs. Leaves on youngest plants uncut; mature leaves heavy, leathery, dark green, deeply cut and perforated. Big plants may bear flowers something like callas, with a thick, 10-in. spike surrounded by a boatlike white bract. Often sold as *Philodendron pertusum*.

M. friedrichsthalii. SWISS CHEESE PLANT. Leaves smaller, thinner in texture than those of *M. deliciosa;* leaf edges are wavy, not deeply cut. Common name comes from series of oval holes on either side of leaf midrib.

HARVESTING MONSTERA FRUIT

If heat, light, and humidity are right, monstera flower spikes may ripen a year after bloom into edible fruits with a flavor reminiscent of banana, pineapple, and apple. The green, caplike rind knocks off easily when fruit is ripe, exposing the sticky fruit kernels; before that stage, the taste can be painfully caustic.

MONTBRETIA. See CROCOSMIA crocosmiiflora, TRITONIA

MOONFLOWER. See IPOMOEA alba

Moraceae. The mulberry family includes deciduous or evergreen trees, shrubs, and vines. Individual fruits are tiny and single-seeded but often aggregated into clusters. Fig *(Ficus)* and mulberry *(Morus)* are examples.

MORAEA IRIDIOIDES. See DIETES

MORAINE LOCUST. See GLEDITSIA triacanthos 'Moraine'

MORETON BAY CHESTNUT. See CASTANOSPERMUM australe

MORNING GLORY. See CONVOLVULUS tricolor, IPOMOEA, MERREMIA tuberosa

MORUS

MULBERRY

Moraceae

DECIDUOUS TREES

🗲 ZONES VARY BY SPECIES

☼ FULL SUN

💧 WATER NEEDS VARY BY SPECIES

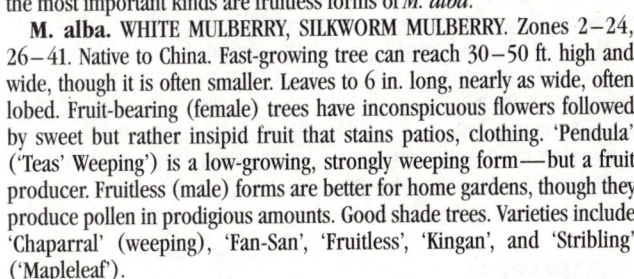

Morus alba

Leaves of variable form, size, and shape—often on same tree. Yellow fall color ranges from subdued to bright. Fruits look like miniature blackberries and are favored by birds. For creating shade in home gardens, the most important kinds are fruitless forms of *M. alba*.

M. alba. WHITE MULBERRY, SILKWORM MULBERRY. Zones 2–24, 26–41. Native to China. Fast-growing tree can reach 30–50 ft. high and wide, though it is often smaller. Leaves to 6 in. long, nearly as wide, often lobed. Fruit-bearing (female) trees have inconspicuous flowers followed by sweet but rather insipid fruit that stains patios, clothing. 'Pendula' ('Teas' Weeping') is a low-growing, strongly weeping form—but a fruit producer. Fruitless (male) forms are better for home gardens, though they produce pollen in prodigious amounts. Good shade trees. Varieties include 'Chaparral' (weeping), 'Fan-San', 'Fruitless', 'Kingan', and 'Stribling' ('Mapleleaf').

Plants tolerate heat, alkaline soil, seacoast conditions. They take some aridity, but grow faster with regular water. Difficult to garden under because of heavy surface roots.

M. australis 'Unryu' (M. bombycis 'Unryu'). CONTORTED MULBERRY. Zones 3–24, 29–34. Grows to 25 ft. tall, with twisted, contorted branches useful in dry floral arrangements or for winter silhouette. Fast growth means that branches may be cut freely with no harm to tree. Leaves to 6 in. long. Regular water.

M. nigra. BLACK MULBERRY, PERSIAN MULBERRY. Zones 4–24, 31–33. To 30 ft. tall, with short trunk and dense, spreading head. Heart-shaped leaves to 8 in. long. Large, juicy, dark red to black fruit. Takes some aridity. 'Black Beauty' is smaller, to 15 ft. tall. 'Illinois Everbearing' produces an early summer crop of fruit followed by a smaller autumn crop. 'Wellington' is a heavy-fruiting variety.

M. papyrifera. See Broussonetia papyrifera

M. rubra. RED MULBERRY. Zones 2–7, 26, 28–41. Native to eastern and central U.S. Well-behaved tree with upright, spreading habit. Somewhat resembles *M. alba*, but fruit is red in color, a bit larger, and better tasting. Best in rich, moist soil.

MOSES-IN-THE-BOAT, MOSES-IN-THE-CRADLE. See RHOEO spathacea

MOSS, IRISH and SCOTCH. See SAGINA

MOSS CAMPION. See SILENE acaulis, S. schafta

MOSS PINK. See PHLOX subulata

MOTHER FERN. See ASPLENIUM bulbiferum

MOTH ORCHID. See PHALAENOPSIS

MOUNTAIN ASH. See SORBUS

MOUNTAIN GARLAND. See CLARKIA unguiculata

MOUNTAIN LAUREL. See KALMIA latifolia

MOUNT ATLAS DAISY. See ANACYCLUS depressus

MOURNING BRIDE. See SCABIOSA atropurpurea

MOURNING WIDOW. See GERANIUM phaeum

MRS. ROBB'S BONNET. See EUPHORBIA robbiae

MUHLENBERGIA

Poaceae (Gramineae)

PERENNIAL GRASSES

🗲 ZONES VARY BY SPECIES

☼ ☀ FULL SUN OR LIGHT SHADE

💧 MODERATE TO LITTLE WATER

Muhlenbergia rigens

These slender-leafed, fall-flowering native grasses are showy enough to stand out in the garden. All require good drainage and resist heat and drought.

M. dumosa. BAMBOO MUHLY. Zones 8–24, 29. Native to Arizona, Mexico. To 3–6 ft. tall. Resembles bamboo, with narrow leaves and branching flower clusters on slender, woody stems. Flowers barely distinguishable from foliage.

M. filipes (M. capilaris). MUHLY GRASS. Zones 25–31. Native to coastal plains from North Carolina to Texas. Foliage clump to 2 ft. high. Reddish purple plumes increase height to 4–5 ft.

M. rigens. DEER GRASS. Zones 7–24. Native to California. Dense, tight clump to 3–4 ft. high. Slender yellow or purplish flower stalks are erect at first, then leaning; can reach 6 ft. tall.

MULBERRY. See MORUS

MULLEIN. See VERBASCUM

MULLEIN PINK. See LYCHNIS coronaria

MURRAYA paniculata (M. exotica)

ORANGE JESSAMINE

Rutaceae

EVERGREEN SHRUB

🗲 ZONES 21–27

☼ ☀ FULL SUN OR LIGHT SHADE

💧 REGULAR WATER

Murraya paniculata

Fast-growing plant to 6–15 ft. tall and wide. Good as hedge, filler, foundation plant. Sometimes grown as small single- or multitrunked tree. Open habit; graceful, pendulous branches with glossy dark green leaves divided into three to nine oval, 1–2-in. leaflets. Flowers are white, ¾-in. bells with jasmine fragrance. Blooms in late summer and fall, sometimes in spring. Mature plants have small red fruit. Needs rich soil, frequent feeding. Slowly recovers beauty after cold, wet winters. Attracts bees.

A dwarf variety is usually sold as *M. exotica*. It is slower growing, more upright and compact, reaching 6 ft. tall, 4 ft. wide. Leaves are lighter green, leaflets smaller and stiffer. Bloom is usually less profuse.

M

MUSA

BANANA

Musaceae

PERENNIALS, SOME TREELIKE IN SIZE

☀ ZONES VARY BY SPECIES; OR GREENHOUSE

☀◑ FULL SUN OR PARTIAL SHADE

🌢 AMPLE WATER

Musa paradisiaca seminifera

For most commonly grown bananas, see *Ensete*. Kinds described here include tall, medium, and dwarf plants, all fast growing. All have soft, thickish stems and spread by suckers or underground roots to form clumps. Spectacular long, broad leaves are easily tattered by strong winds, so plant in protected sites. Will usually regrow from roots if cut down by frost; in frost-prone areas, locate plants where their absence won't be conspicuous. Attractive near swimming pools. Can be grown in tubs and wintered indoors (cut tops off tall plants). Give rich soil; feed heavily.

M. acuminata 'Dwarf Cavendish' (M. cavendishii, M. nana). Zones 21–27. To 6–8 ft. tall, with leaves 5 ft. long, 2 ft. wide. Large, heavy flower clusters with reddish to dark purple bracts, yellow flowers. In warmest gardens, can bear sweet, edible 6-in. bananas. 'Enano Gigante' is similar, but its young leaves have red markings. Some authorities place these fruiting varieties under *M. paradisiaca*.

M. ensete. See Ensete ventricosum

M. maurelii. See Ensete ventricosum 'Maurelii'

M. paradisiaca (M. sapientum). Zones 16, 19–28. Many ornamental and edible forms. Most common type is often called *M. p. seminifera*. Large clump to 20 ft. tall, with leaves to 9 ft. Drooping flower stalk with powdery purple bracts; fruit (usually seedy and inedible) sometimes follows. Many varieties are available.

Musaceae. The banana family consists of giant herbaceous plants that resemble palm trees; the bases of the enormous leaves form a false trunk. *Ensete* and *Musa* are the only two members of the family.

MUSCARI

GRAPE HYACINTH

Liliaceae

BULBS

☀ ZONES VARY BY SPECIES

☀◑ FULL SUN OR LIGHT SHADE

🌢 REGULAR WATER DURING GROWTH AND BLOOM

Muscari armeniacum

Clumps of narrow, grassy, fleshy leaves appear in autumn and live through cold and snow. Small, urn-shaped, blue or white flowers in tight spikes appear in early spring. Plant 2 in. deep in fall, setting bulbs in masses or drifts under flowering fruit trees or shrubs, in edgings and rock gardens, or in containers. Very long lived. Lift and divide when bulbs become crowded. Plants self-sow under favorable conditions.

M. armeniacum. Zones 2–24, 29–43. Bright blue flowers on 4–8-in. stems above heavy cluster of floppy foliage. 'Cantab' is lower growing, has neater foliage, and produces clear light blue flowers later than species. 'Blue Spike' has double blue flowers in a tight cluster at top of spike.

M. azureum (Hyacinthella azurea, Hyacinthus azureus). Zones 2–24, 30–43. Between hyacinth and grape hyacinth in appearance. Stalks 4–8 in. high have tight clusters of fragrant, bell-shaped (not urn-shaped) sky blue flowers.

M. botryoides. Zones 1–24, 30–45. Most cold hardy of the commonly grown grape hyacinths. Medium blue flowers on 6–12-in. stems. 'Album' has white flowers.

M. comosum. FRINGE HYACINTH, TASSEL HYACINTH. Zones 2–24, 30–43. Unusual, rather loose clusters of shredded-looking flowers borne on 1–1½-ft. stems. In the species, blossoms are greenish brown on lower part of spike, bluish purple at top. 'Monstrosum' ('Plumosum'), feathered or plume hyacinth, bears violet blue to reddish purple flowers that look like shredded coconut.

M. latifolium. Zones 2–24, 32–43. Largest, possibly showiest of the grape hyacinths. Deep indigo blue flowers on 1-ft. stems. Plants have a single large leaf.

M. tubergenianum. Zones 1–24, 30–45. Stems to 8 in. tall. Flowers at top of spike are dark blue; those lower down are light blue.

MUSTARD

Brassicaceae (Cruciferae)

ANNUAL

☀ ALL ZONES

☀ FULL SUN

🌢 REGULAR WATER

Mustard

Curly-leaf mustard somewhat resembles curly-leaf kale in appearance. It is usually cooked like spinach or cabbage; young leaves are sometimes eaten raw in salads or used as garnishes. Mustard spinach (tendergreen mustard) has smooth dark green leaves. It ripens earlier than curly mustard and is more tolerant of hot dry weather. 'Red Giant' ('Chinese Red'), with large, crinkled leaves with strong red shadings, is handsome enough for a border. Use mustard spinach when young as a salad green; older leaves are useful as boiled greens.

Mustard is fast and easy to grow; it will be ready for the table 35 to 60 days after planting. Sow in early spring and make successive sowings when young plants are established. Thrives in cool weather but quickly goes to seed in summer heat. Sow in late summer for fall use. In mild-winter areas, plant again in fall and winter. Thin seedlings to stand 6 in. apart in rows. Harvest outer leaves as needed.

MYOPORUM

Myoporaceae

EVERGREEN GROUND COVERS, SHRUBS, SMALL TREES

☀ ZONES VARY BY SPECIES

☀ FULL SUN

🌢 MODERATE WATER

◊ FRUIT AND LEAVES CAN BE TOXIC

Myoporum laetum

Bell-shaped flowers attractive at close range but not showy; fruit small but colorful. Shiny dark green leaves with translucent dots. Tough and fast growing.

M. laetum. Shrub or small tree. Zones 8, 9, 14–17, 19–24. Temperatures below 24°F/–4°C can inflict severe damage. To 30 ft. tall, 20 ft. wide. Leaves to 4 in. long. If allowed to grow naturally, forms a billowing mass; if staked and pruned, makes attractive multitrunked tree. Can also make good ground cover if branches are pegged down so they'll root and spread. Clusters of small white summer flowers with purple markings are followed by small reddish purple fruit. Good seaside plant. 'Carsonii' is even faster growing than the species, with branches that are leafy all the way to base of plant; leaves are larger, broader, darker green.

M. parvifolium (M. p. 'Prostratum'). Ground cover. Zones 8, 9, 12–16, 18–24. To 3 in. high, 9 ft. wide, with a dense covering of small leaves. Tiny white summer flowers are followed by purple berries. Plant 6–8 ft. apart; plants will fill in within 6 months, rooting where the stems touch moist soil. Will not tolerate foot traffic. 'Burgundy Carpet' has red stems and purple new growth; 'Pink' is pink flowered; 'Putah Creek' grows 1 ft. high.

M

MYOSOTIS

FORGET-ME-NOT

Boraginaceae

PERENNIALS, BIENNIALS, AND ANNUALS

ZONES 1–24, 32–45

PARTIAL SHADE

REGULAR WATER

Myosotis sylvatica

Both forget-me-not species feature exquisite, typically blue springtime flowers, tiny but profuse. Grow easily and thickly as ground covers. They perform best in cool, moist growing conditions—in woodland gardens, around pond edges, and along stream banks, for example.

M. scorpioides. Perennial. Similar in most respects to *M. sylvatica*, but grows lower and blooms over an even longer season, and roots live over from year to year. Flowers, about ¼ in. wide, are blue with yellow centers, pink, or white. Bright green, shiny, oblong leaves. Plant spreads by creeping roots.

M. sylvatica. Annual or biennial. To 6–12 in. Soft, hairy leaves, ½–2 in. long, set closely along stem. Tiny, clear blue, white-eyed flowers to ⅓ in. wide loosely cover upper stems. Flowers and seeds profusely for a long season, beginning in late winter or early spring. With habit of reseeding, will persist in garden for years unless weeded out. Often sold as *M. alpestris*. Improved varieties are available, best of which are 'Blue Ball' and 'Royal Blue Improved'.

MYRICA

WAX MYRTLE, BAYBERRY

Myricaceae

EVERGREEN OR DECIDUOUS SHRUBS OR TREES

ZONES VARY BY SPECIES

FULL SUN OR PARTIAL SHADE

WATER NEEDS VARY BY SPECIES

Myrica pensylvanica

Several species are useful as screen plants, informal hedges, or roadside plantings. Foliage is pleasantly aromatic. Although none is showy in flower, female plants bear attractive (though not conspicuous) small fruits.

M. californica. PACIFIC WAX MYRTLE. Evergreen shrub or tree. Zones 4–6, 14–17, 20–24. Native to West Coast. At the beach, it's a low, flattened mass; out of wind, it's a big shrub or tree to 30 ft., usually with many upright trunks. Tolerates clipping into hedge. Branches are densely clad with tooth-edged, narrow, glossy leaves that are dark green above, paler beneath, to 4½ in. long. Birds enjoy the purplish, wax-coated nutlets. Moderate water.

M. cerifera. WAX MYRTLE. Evergreen shrub or tree. Zones 25, 26–28, 31, warmer parts of 32. Native to southeastern U.S. Grows to 15–20 ft., possibly taller. Leaves glossy dark green, to 3½ in. long. Grayish white fruits are heavily coated with a wax valued in candlemaking. Good specimen tree, hedge. Regular water.

M. gale. SWEET FERN, SWEET GALE. Deciduous shrub. Zones 1–5, 36–45. Native to much of the Northern Hemisphere. Dense, erect growth to as tall as 6 ft., more typically 2–4 ft. Grown for fragrant leaves, to 2½ in. long. Takes regular moisture or boggy conditions.

M. pensylvanica (M. caroliniensis). BAYBERRY. Deciduous to semievergreen shrub. Zones 3–7, 32–44. Native to eastern U.S. Dense, compact growth to 9 ft. Leaves to about 4 in. long, narrowish, glossy green, dotted with resin glands. Roundish fruit is covered with white wax—the bayberry wax used for candles. Tolerates seashore conditions—poor sandy or salty soil, wind. Fair tolerance for roadside salt. Regular water. *M. heterophylla* is similar to *M. pensylvanica*, but has somewhat larger leaves. Both species are semievergreen in the southern part of U.S., deciduous farther north.

MYROBALAN. See PRUNUS cerasifera

Myrsinaceae. This family consists of evergreen shrubs and trees with (usually) inconspicuous flowers, attractive foliage and habit, and sometimes showy fruits. Two representatives of the group are *Myrsine* and marlberry (*Ardisia*).

MYRSINE africana

AFRICAN BOXWOOD

Myrsinaceae

EVERGREEN SHRUB

ZONES 8, 9, 14–25

FULL SUN OR PARTIAL SHADE

MODERATE WATER

Myrsine africana

Grows 3–8 ft. high; slightly floppy when young, but stiffens into dense, rounded bush easily kept to a height of 3–4 ft. with pinching and clipping. Stems are vertical, dark red, closely set with very dark green, glossy, roundish, ½-in. leaves. Good for low hedges, topiary, foundation plantings, narrow garden beds, containers, cut foliage for arrangements.

Myrtaceae. The immense myrtle family of trees and shrubs is largely tropical and subtropical. Leaves are evergreen and often aromatic. Flowers are often showy, thanks to large tufts of stamens. Fruits may be fleshy (*Feijoa*) or dry and capsular (*Eucalyptus*). Other family members include myrtle (*Myrtus*), bottlebrush (*Callistemon*), and guava (*Psidium*).

MYRTLE. See MYRICA, MYRTUS, VINCA

MYRTUS communis

MYRTLE

Myrtaceae

EVERGREEN SHRUB

ZONES 8–24, 26–28

FULL SUN OR PARTIAL SHADE

MODERATE WATER

Myrtus communis

Rounded form to 5–6 ft. high, 4–5 ft. wide. Old plants can reach treelike proportions, to 15 ft. tall and 20 ft. across. Glossy bright green leaves are pointed, 2 in. long, pleasantly aromatic when brushed or bruised. White, sweet-scented, ¾-in. flowers with many stamens bloom in summer; these are followed by bluish black, ½-in. berries. Any soil, but good drainage is essential. Good formal or informal hedge or screen. Can also be trained to reveal attractive branches.

Named selections vary in foliage character and overall size. 'Variegata' fits basic description but has white-edged leaves. 'Boetica' is especially upright, with thick, twisted branches and larger, darker leaves. 'Buxifolia' has small leaves like a boxwood. Dwarf forms include 'Compacta', a small-leafed variety popular for edgings and low formal hedges; 'Compacta Variegata', similar but with white-margined foliage; and 'Microphylla', with tiny, closely set leaves.

NAKED LADY. See AMARYLLIS belladonna

PRACTICAL GARDENING DICTIONARY
PLEASE SEE PAGES 545–616

N

NANDINA domestica

HEAVENLY BAMBOO, SACRED BAMBOO

Berberidaceae

EVERGREEN OR SEMIDECIDUOUS SHRUB

☀ ZONES 4–33

☀ ◑ ● SUN OR SHADE; COLORS BETTER IN SUN

● ● REGULAR TO MODERATE WATER

Nandina domestica

Loses leaves at 10°F/−12°C; stems are damaged at 5°F/−15°C, but usually recovers fast. Belongs to the barberry family but is reminiscent of bamboo in its lightly branched, canelike stems and delicate, fine-textured foliage.

Slow to moderate growth to 6–8 ft. (you can keep plant to 3 ft. by pruning oldest canes to ground). Leaves intricately divided into many 1–2-in., pointed, oval leaflets, creating lacy pattern. Foliage expands pinkish and bronzy red, then turns to soft light green. Picks up purple and bronze tints in fall; often turns fiery crimson in winter, especially in sun and with some frost. Pinkish white or creamy white blossoms in loose, erect, 6–12-in. clusters at branch ends, late spring or early summer. If plants are grouped, shiny red berries follow the flowers; single plants seldom fruit heavily.

Needs afternoon shade in hottest climates. Best in rich soil with regular water, but its roots can even compete with tree roots in dry shade. Foliage may become chlorotic in alkaline soil. Most useful for light, airy vertical effects as well as for narrow, restricted areas. Good for hedge, screen, tub plant, bonsai. Dramatic with night lighting. Varieties include the following:

'Alba' (*N. d. leucocarpa*). Standard-size plant with creamy white berries and yellowish green foliage that turns yellow in fall. More subject to cold damage than the species.

'Compacta'. Lower growing than species (4–5 ft.), with narrower, more numerous leaflets; has very lacy look.

'Fire Power'. Compact plant to 2 ft. tall and wide. Red-tinged summer foliage turns bright red in winter.

'Harbour Dwarf'. Low growing (1½–2 ft.), freely spreading. Underground rhizomes send up stems several inches from parent plant. Orange-red to bronzy red winter color. Good ground cover.

'Moyers Red'. Standard-size plant with broad leaflets. Brilliant red winter color in regions getting frost.

'Nana' ('Nana Purpurea', 'Atropurpurea Nana'). To 1–2 ft. tall. Coarse-foliaged plant with somewhat cupped or crinkled leaflets. Purplish green in summer, purplish red in winter. A slow spreader best used as an individual plant in a container or against a background of rock or gravel to emphasize its domed habit.

'Woods Dwarf'. Rounded form to 3–4 ft. tall, densely foliaged, crimson orange to scarlet in winter.

NANKING CHERRY. See PRUNUS tomentosa

NARCISSUS

DAFFODIL

Amaryllidaceae

BULBS

☀ ZONES 1–24, 28–45, EXCEPT AS NOTED

☀ ◑ SUN; LATE KINDS LAST WELL IN LIGHT SHADE

● REGULAR WATER DURING GROWTH AND BLOOM

Narcissus—Daffodil

These spring-flowering bulbous plants are valuable in many ways. They are permanent, increasing from year to year; they stand up to cold and heat; they are useful in many garden situations; and they provide fascinating variety in flower form and color. Most offer early, midseason, and late varieties for extended bloom season, starting in winter in mildest climates. Most types are hardy to −30°F/−34°C (exceptions are noted). Finally, gophers and deer won't eat them—good news for gardeners in areas where those creatures are common.

Leaves are straight and flat (strap shaped) or narrow and rushlike. Flowers are composed of ring of segments (usually called petals) that are at right angles to the corona or crown (also called trumpet or cup, depending on its length) in center. Flowers may be single or clustered. Colors are basically yellow and white, but there are many variations—orange, red, apricot, pink, cream.

Flowers usually face sun; keep that in mind when selecting planting place. Use under trees and flowering shrubs, among ground cover plantings, near water, in rock gardens and patios, or in borders. Naturalize in sweeping drifts where space is available. Good in containers; fine cut flowers.

Plant bulbs as early in fall as you can get them. In warmest climates, however, wait until November so soil can cool. Look for solid, heavy bulbs. Number One double-nose bulbs are best; Number One round, single-nose bulbs are second choice. Plant with 5–6 in. of soil over tops of bulbs

Narcissus Divisions (Groups)

Trumpet

Large-cupped

Small-cupped

Double

Cyclamineus Hybrid

Tazetta

Poeticus Narcissus

Split Corona

Triandrus Hybrid

(4–5 in. for smaller bulbs). Set bulbs 8 in. apart and you won't have to divide for a number of years.

Let foliage mature and yellow naturally after bloom. Lift and divide clumps of daffodils when flowers get smaller and fewer in number; wait until foliage has died down. Don't forcibly break away any bulbs that are tightly joined to mother bulb; remove only those that come away easily. Replant at once, or store for only a short time—preferably not more than 3 weeks.

DAFFODILS IN CONTAINERS

For maximum show, set bulbs close together, the tips level with soil surface. Place pots in well-drained trench or cold frame and cover with 6–8 in. of moist peat moss, wood shavings, sawdust, or sand. Look for roots in 8 to 10 weeks (carefully tip soil mass from pot). Move pots with well-started bulbs to greenhouse, cool room, or sheltered garden spot to bloom. Keep well watered until foliage yellows; then plant in garden. You can sink pots or cans of bulbs in borders when flowers are almost ready to bloom, then lift containers when flowers fade.

Following are the 11 generally recognized divisions of daffodils and representative varieties in each division.

Trumpet daffodils. Trumpet is as long as or longer than surrounding flower segments. Yellows are the most popular; old variety 'King Alfred' best known, top seller, although newer 'Unsurpassable' and 'William the Silent' are superior. White varieties include 'Mount Hood', 'Cantatrice', 'Empress of Ireland'. Bicolors with white segments, yellow cup, include 'Spring Glory', 'Trousseau'. Reverse bicolors like 'Spellbinder' have white cup and yellow segments.

Large-cupped daffodils. Cups are more than one-third the length of flower segments, but not as long as segments. Varieties include 'Carlton' and 'Carbineer', yellow; 'Ice Follies', white; 'Binkie' and 'Mrs. R. O. Backhouse', bicolors.

Small-cupped daffodils. Cups less than one-third the length of segments. Less widely available; for specialists.

Double daffodils. 'Golden Ducat'; 'Mary Copeland', white and bright red; 'White Lion', creamy white and yellow; 'Texas', yellow and orange scarlet; 'Windblown', white and pale lemon.

Triandrus hybrids. Cups at least two-thirds the length of flower segments. Clusters of medium-size, slender-cupped, often nodding flowers. 'Thalia' is a favorite white with two or three beautifully proportioned flowers per stem. 'Silver Chimes' has six or more yellow-cupped white flowers per stem.

Cyclamineus hybrids. Early medium-size flowers with recurved segments. Gold, bright to creamy pale yellow, and white with yellow cup. Examples are 'February Gold', 'February Silver', 'Peeping Tom'.

Jonquilla hybrids. Clusters of two to four rather small, very fragrant flowers. Yellow (like 'Trevithian' and 'Suzy'), orange, ivory.

Tazetta and Tazetta hybrids. Hardy to about 10°F/–12°C. These are polyanthus or bunch-flowered daffodils with small-cupped white and yellow flowers in clusters. Good double varieties are 'Cheerfulness' (white) and 'Golden Cheerfulness'. Division also includes 'Geranium', paper white nar-

Narcissus tazetta 'Orientalis'

cissus, and *N. tazetta* 'Orientalis' (Chinese sacred lilies). These last three, along with 'Cragford' (white, scarlet cup) and 'Grand Soleil d'Or' (golden yellow), can be grown indoors in bowls of pebbles and water. Keep dark and cool until growth is well along, then slowly bring into light.

Poeticus narcissus. POET'S NARCISSUS. Late white flowers with shallow, broad yellow cups edged red. 'Actaea' is largest.

Species, varieties, and hybrids. Many species and their varieties and hybrids delight the collector. Most are small; some are true miniatures for rock gardens or very small containers.

N. asturiensis. Very early miniature trumpet flowers on 3-in. stems. Usually sold as *N.* 'Minimus'.

N. bulbocodium. HOOP PETTICOAT DAFFODIL. Hardy to –10°F/–23°C. To 6 in. tall, with little, upward-facing flowers that are mostly trumpet, with very narrow, pointed segments. Deep and pale yellow varieties.

N. cyclamineus. Hardy to –10°F/–23°C. Backward-curved lemon yellow segments and narrow, tubular golden cup; 6 in. high.

N. jonquilla. JONQUIL. Cylindrical, rushlike leaves. Clusters of early, very fragrant, golden yellow flowers with short cups.

N. triandrus. ANGEL'S TEARS. Clusters of small white or pale yellow flowers on stems to 10 in. Rushlike foliage.

Narcissus bulbocodium

Miscellaneous. This group serves as a catch-all for a variety of new flower forms. Typical are 'Baccarat', light yellow with deeper yellow corona cut into six equal lobes; and 'Cassata', white with ivory split corona, the segments of which lie flat along the petals.

NASTURTIUM. See TROPAEOLUM

NATAL IVY. See SENECIO macroglossus

NATAL PLUM. See CARISSA macrocarpa

NEANTHE bella. See CHAMAEDOREA elegans

NECTARINE. See PEACH and NECTARINE

NEEDLE GRASS. See STIPA

NELUMBO (Nelumbium)

LOTUS	
Nymphaeaceae	
AQUATIC PLANTS	
⚡ ALL ZONES	
☀️ ◐ FULL SUN OR PARTIAL SHADE	
🌢 LOCATE IN PONDS, WATER GARDENS	

These are water plants. If you acquire started plants in containers, put them in pond with 8–12 in. of water over soil surface. If you get roots, plant in spring, horizontally, 4 in. deep, in 1–1½-ft.-deep container of fairly rich soil. Place soil surface 8–12 in. under water. Huge round leaves attached at center to leafstalks grow above water level. Large fragrant flowers, growing above or below leaves, form in summer. Ornamental woody fruit, perforated with holes like a salt shaker, good for dried arrangements. Roots should not freeze; where freezing is possible, cover pond or fill it deeper with water.

Nelumbo nucifera

N. lutea (Nelumbium luteum). AMERICAN LOTUS. Similar to following but somewhat smaller in leaf and flower. Flowers are pale yellow.

N. nucifera (Nelumbium nelumbo). INDIAN or CHINESE LOTUS. Round leaves, 2 ft. or wider, carried 3–6 ft. above water surface. Pink, 4–10-in.-wide flowers carried singly on stems. Both tubers and seeds are esteemed in Chinese cookery, and the entire plant holds great religious significance for Buddhists. White, rose, and double varieties exist; dwarf forms suitable for pot culture are becoming available.

NEMESIA

Scrophulariaceae

ANNUALS

⬆ ZONES 1–24, 28–45; BEST IN COOL WEATHER

☼ FULL SUN

💧 REGULAR WATER

Nemesia strumosa

These South African natives are riotously colorful but somewhat touchy about weather—they don't like frost or heat. As summer annuals, they do best in cool-summer regions; succeed as winter–spring annuals in mild-winter climates. To enjoy a longer bloom season, remove fading flowers. Use as bedding plants, rock garden plants, in hanging baskets, as bulb covers.

N. strumosa. The wild species reaches 1½ ft. high, but plants sold under this name are usually more compact hybrids between *N. strumosa* and *N. versicolor*. Hybrids include all colors except green, as well as bicolors such as 'Mello Red and White' and blue-and-white 'KLM'. Several strains are available in mixed colors. All types bear small flowers in clusters up to 4 in. wide; blossoms are cup shaped, with an enlarged lower lip.

N. versicolor. Resembles *N. strumosa*, but color range contains more blue, yellow, and white. Flowers of 'Blue Gem' are a rich pure blue with a white center.

NEMOPHILA

Hydrophyllaceae

ANNUALS

⬆ ZONES 1–24, 28–45; BEST IN COOL WEATHER

☼◐ FULL SUN OR PARTIAL SHADE

💧 REGULAR WATER

Nemophila menziesii

Native to western U.S. Trailing plants 6–12 in. high, with bell-shaped flowers to 1 in. across. Pale green, hairy, fernlike foliage gives plants a delicate appearance. Often used as low cover for bulb beds. Broadcast seed as soon as ground is workable in spring; you can plant in fall in mild-winter regions. Quickly killed by heat and humidity. Will reseed in favorable conditions (cool, moist weather).

N. maculata. FIVE-SPOT NEMOPHILA. Flowers are white with fine purple lines; one large purple spot appears near tip of each of the five lobes.

N. menziesii (N. insignis). BABY BLUE EYES. Blooms as freely in gardens as in the wild, bearing sky blue blossoms with a whitish center. Two unusual color forms are 'Snow Storm' (*N. m. atomaria*), with white flowers liberally dotted with black spots; and 'Pennie Black' (*N. m. discoidalis*), with blackish purple flowers rimmed in white.

NEODYPSIS decaryi

TRIANGLE PALM

Arecaceae (Palmae)

PALM

⬆ ZONES 20–25

☼◐ FULL SUN OR PARTIAL SHADE

💧 REGULAR TO MODERATE WATER

Neodypsis decaryi

Native to arid parts of Madagascar, but can take regular moisture. Slow grower to 18–20 ft. Trunk is triangular in cross section because heavily keeled leaf bases grow in three ranks along the stem. Gray-green, featherlike fronds to 15 ft., strongly upright but arching at tips.

NEOREGELIA

Bromeliaceae

BROMELIADS

⬆ ZONES 21–27; OR INDOORS

◐● PARTIAL OR FULL SHADE

💧 KEEP WATER IN CUP AT BASE OF ROSETTE

Neoregelia carolinae

Bromeliads with rosettes of leathery leaves, often strikingly colored or marked; short spikes of usually inconspicuous flowers are buried in hearts of rosettes. Need light, open, fast-draining planting mix that holds moisture but does not exclude air. Feed lightly. Grow outdoors in sheltered, frost-free location; can be grown on tree branch with sphagnum moss around roots. Indoors, give strong indirect light.

N. carolinae. Many narrow, shiny leaves 1 ft. long, 1½ in. wide. Medium green leaves turn rich red at base as plant approaches bloom. 'Tricolor' has leaves striped lengthwise with white. Center turns bright red.

N. spectabilis. PAINTED FINGERNAIL PLANT. Leaves 1 ft. long, 2 in. wide are olive green with bright red tips. Plant takes on bronzy color in strong light.

NEPETA

Lamiaceae (Labiatae)

PERENNIALS

⬆ ZONES 1–24, 30, 32–43

☼◐ AFTERNOON SHADE IN HOT CLIMATES

💧 MODERATE WATER

Nepeta cataria

Vigorous, spreading, aromatic-leafed plants of the mint family. Sometimes used as a substitute for lavender in cold-winter climates. Will tolerate regular moisture if soil is well drained.

N. cataria. CATNIP. To 2–3 ft. high, with downy gray-green leaves and clustered lavender or white flowers at branch tips in late spring, early summer. Easy grower in light soil; reseeds readily. Attractive to cats; some fall into a rapturous frenzy, rolling wildly on the plants. Sprinkle dried leaves over cats' food or sew some into toy cloth mouse. Some people use catnip to flavor tea.

N. faassenii. CATMINT. Makes soft, gray-green, undulating mounds to 1½ ft. high in bloom. The small leaves (like those of catnip) are attractive to cats, who enjoy nibbling foliage and rolling in plantings. Loose spikes of lavender blue flowers in late spring, early summer. If dead spikes prove unsightly, shear them back; this may bring on another bloom cycle. Set 1–1½ ft. apart for ground cover. Often sold as *N. mussinii*. 'Dropmore Hybrid' is taller than the species (to 2 ft.); 'Six Hills Giant' is taller still (2–3 ft.).

N. hederacea. See Glechoma hederacea

N. sibirica. Dark green clump to 2–3 ft. high, topped by 10-in. spikes of bright blue flowers in early summer. 'Souvenir d'Andre Chaudron' ('Blue Beauty'), larger flowered than the species, is a compact grower to 1½ ft. high.

NEPHROLEPIS

SWORD FERN

Polypodiaceae

FERNS

⬆ ZONES VARY BY SPECIES; OR INDOORS

◐● PARTIAL OR FULL SHADE

💧 REGULAR WATER

Nephrolepis exaltata 'Bostoniensis'

Tough and easy to grow, these are the most widely used of all ferns. (For native western sword fern, see *Polystichum munitum*.) For house plants, provide well-drained fibrous soil, monthly applications of dilute liquid fertilizer, and strong indirect light.

N. cordifolia. SOUTHERN SWORD FERN. Zones 8, 9, 12–27. Will not take hard frosts. Bright green, narrow, upright fronds in tufts to 2–3 ft. tall. Fronds have closely spaced, finely toothed leaflets. Roots often have small roundish tubers. Plant spreads by thin, fuzzy runners and can be invasive if not watched. Tolerates poor soil and erratic watering. Good in narrow, shaded beds; can thrive in full sun with adequate water. Effective ground cover if adequately watered. Also used in pots and hanging baskets. Often sold as *N. exaltata*.

N. exaltata. SWORD FERN. Zones 23–25; or house plant. Taller than *N. cordifolia* (to 5 ft.), with broader fronds (to 6 in. wide). Most common are named selections grown as house plants. Best known is 'Bostoniensis', Boston fern; this is the classic parlor fern, with a spreading, arching habit and graceful, eventually drooping fronds broader than those of the species. Many more finely cut and feathery forms exist, including 'Fluffy Ruffles', 'Rooseveltii', and 'Whitmanii'.

N. obliterata. House plant. Native to northwestern Australia. A selection of this species called 'Kimberley Queen' has fronds to about 3 ft. in length. Plant habit is stiffer and more erect than that of *N. exaltata* 'Bostoniensis', and the plant is more tolerant of low humidity and both low and high light conditions.

NERINE

Amaryllidaceae

BULBS

🌿 ZONES 5, 8, 9, 13–28; OR INDOORS

☼ ◑ FULL SUN OR PARTIAL SHADE

🔴 REGULAR WATER DURING GROWTH AND BLOOM

Native to South Africa. Usually pot plants (good in cool greenhouses), but can grow outdoors all year round in mildest regions (hardy to at least 20°F/–7°C). Funnel-shaped flowers with six spreading segments bent back at tips, carried in rounded clusters. Bloom late summer or fall. Strap-shaped basal leaves (to 1 ft. long and 1 in. wide in the species described below) appear during or after bloom. Outdoors, plant bulbs 3 in. deep in well-drained soil and do not disturb or divide for several years.

Nerine curvifolia
'Fothergillii Major'

N. bowdenii. Flowers to 3 in., soft pink marked with deeper pink, in clusters of 8–12 on 2-ft. stems. Forms with taller stems and larger flower clusters come in deeper pink, crimson, and red. 'Crispa' is 1 ft. tall, has pale pink, wavy-edged segments; 'Pink Triumph' is a larger plant that blooms late.

N. curvifolia. Best-known representative of this species is variety 'Fothergillii Major', with clusters of 2-in. scarlet flowers overlaid with shimmering gold. Long stamens are topped by greenish yellow anthers. Bloom stalks reach 1½ ft. tall.

N. sarniensis. GUERNSEY LILY. Large clusters of iridescent crimson, 1½-in. flowers on 2-ft. stalks. Pink, orange, scarlet, and pure white varieties.

POTTED NERINE, BLOOMING IN AUTUMN

In late summer or early autumn, put one bulb in a 4-in. pot, or three in a 5–6-in. pot. Cover only the lower half of the bulb. Don't start watering until you see a flower stalk beginning to emerge. Water through winter and spring. In May, move pots outdoors to lightly shaded location. Withhold water from July until growth resumes. Do not repot until pots are quite crowded.

FOR INFORMATION ON SELECTING PLANTS
PLEASE SEE PAGES 79–160

NERIUM oleander

OLEANDER

Apocynaceae

EVERGREEN SHRUB

🌿 ZONES 8–16, 18–31

☼ BEST IN HEAT AND STRONG LIGHT

🔴🔴 REGULAR TO LITTLE WATER

🔶 ALL PARTS ARE POISONOUS IF INGESTED

Nerium oleander

Thrive where summers are warm and winters mild (plants are hardy to 15°F/–9°C). Moderate to fast growth; most varieties grow 8–12 ft. tall and wide. Ordinarily broad and bulky but easily trained into single- or multitrunked tree. Excellent screen, windbreak, border for road or driveway, tub plant. Narrow, 4–12-in.-long leaves are dark green, leathery, and glossy, attractive in all seasons; a form with golden variegation is sometimes available.

Flowers 2–3 in. across, clustered at twig or branch ends, from mid- to late spring continuing into autumn. Many varieties are fragrant. Forms with double and single flowers are sold; colors range from white to shades of yellow, pink, salmon, and red. 'Sister Agnes', single white, is most vigorous grower, often reaching 20 ft. tall; 'Mrs. Roeding', double salmon pink, grows only 6 ft. tall and has proportionally smaller, finer-textured foliage than big oleanders. Flowers of all double types hang on after bloom and turn brown. For the same luscious salmon pink as 'Mrs. Roeding' in blossoms that drop clean, try single-flowered 'Hawaii'.

'Petite Pink' and 'Petite Salmon' can easily be kept to 3–4 ft. with moderate pruning and make excellent informal flowering hedges, though they are not as cold hardy as regular oleanders. 'Little Red', bright red, is completely hardy—as are the following, intermediate in size between dwarfs and full-size plants: 'Algiers', deep red; 'Casablanca', white; 'Ruby Lace', bright red with 3-inch, wavy-edged individual flowers; and 'Tangier', soft pink. Even smaller (5–7 ft.) are red 'Marrakesh' and white 'Morocco'.

Oleanders need little water once established, but can take more. They are not at all particular about soil, even tolerating soil with relatively high salt content. In shade or ocean fog, however, they produce weak or leggy growth and few flowers.

Prune in early spring to control size and form. Cut out old wood that has flowered. Cut some branches nearly to ground. To restrict height, pinch remaining tips or prune them back lightly. To prevent bushiness at base, pull (don't cut) unwanted suckers. Oleander caterpillar sometimes defoliates plants in the Southeast.

Caution children against eating leaves or flowers; keep prunings, dead leaves away from hay or other animal feed; don't use wood for barbecue fires or skewers. Smoke from burning prunings can cause severe irritation.

For a plant called yellow oleander, see *Thevetia*.

NERTERA granadensis (N. depressa)

BEAD PLANT

Rubiaceae

PERENNIAL

🌿 ZONES 17, 22–24; OR INDOORS

◑ PARTIAL SHADE

🔴 KEEP SOIL MOIST, BUT NOT SOGGY

Nertera granadensis

Extremely tender, generally grown as house plant. Sometimes used as rock garden subject or small-scale ground cover. Prostrate habit. Tiny, smooth, rounded leaves make dense green mat an inch or so high; berry-like, ¼-in., bright orange fruit may last from midsummer into winter. Small green flowers are a lesser attraction. Plant in sandy loam with some leaf mold. Fine terrarium or dish garden plant.

NEW JERSEY TEA. See CEANOTHUS americanus

**NEW ZEALAND CHRISTMAS TREE.
See METROSIDEROS excelsus**

NEW ZEALAND FLAX. See PHORMIUM

NEW ZEALAND SPINACH. See SPINACH, New Zealand

NEW ZEALAND TEA TREE. See LEPTOSPERMUM scoparium

NICOTIANA

Solanaceae

TENDER PERENNIALS GROWN AS ANNUALS

ALL ZONES

FULL SUN OR PARTIAL SHADE

REGULAR WATER

ALL PARTS ARE POISONOUS IF INGESTED

Nicotiana alata

May live over in mild-winter areas. Upright-growing plants with slightly sticky leaves and stems. Usually grown for their fragrant flowers, which often open at night or on cloudy days; some kinds open during daytime. Flowers tubular, usually flaring at ends into five pointed lobes; grow near top of branched stems in summer. Large, soft, oval leaves. Some kinds reseed readily.

N. alata (N. affinis). Wild species is a 2–3-ft. plant with large, very fragrant white flowers that open toward evening. Seed is available. Selection and hybridization with other species have produced many garden strains that stay open day and night and come in colors ranging from white through pink to red (including lime green), but scent is not as strong as in the "unimproved" species.

Domino strain grows to 12–15 in. and has upward-facing flowers that can take heat and sun better than taller kinds. Nicki strain is taller (to 15–18 in.). The older Sensation strain is taller still (to 4 ft.) and looks more at home in informal mixed borders than as a bedding plant. Fragrance is erratic. If scent (especially during evening) is important, plant 'Grandiflora'.

N. langsdorffii. To 3–6 ft. tall. The branching stems are hung with drooping, inch-long, tubular light green flowers. No noticeable scent. Excellent for cutting.

N. sylvestris. To 5 ft. Intensely fragrant, long, tubular white flowers grow in tiers atop a statuesque plant. Striking in a night garden.

NIEREMBERGIA

CUP FLOWER

Solanaceae

PERENNIALS OR ANNUALS

ZONES VARY BY SPECIES

FULL SUN

REGULAR WATER

Nierembergia repens

Flowers are tubular but flare into saucerlike or bell-like cups. The first species listed here grows as a spreading mound; the other is a ground-covering mat. Both are covered with blooms during summer. Grow as perennials in mild-winter climate zones indicated below; grow as annuals in colder regions. Give light shade in hottest climates.

N. hippomanica violacea (N. h. caerulea). DWARF CUP FLOWER. Zones 8–31. Grows 6–12 in. high. Much-branched mounded plant, with very small, stiff leaves. Flowers are blue to violet. Trimming back plant after bloom to induce new growth seems to lengthen its life. Plants are shorter-lived in Gulf Coast gardens. 'Purple Robe' is common variety. 'Mont Blanc' bears white flowers.

N. repens (N. rivularis). WHITE CUP. Zones 5–9, 14–31. Prostrate 4–6-in. mat of bright green leaves. Blooms are white. For best performance, don't crowd it with more aggressive plants. Not as heat tolerant as dwarf cup flower.

NIGELLA damascena

LOVE-IN-A-MIST

Ranunculaceae

ANNUAL

ALL ZONES

FULL SUN OR PARTIAL SHADE

REGULAR WATER

Nigella damascena

Branching to 1–1½ ft. high. All leaves, even those that form under collar beneath each flower, are finely cut into threadlike divisions. Blue, white, or rose flowers, 1–1½ in. across, are borne singly at ends of branches in spring. Curious papery-textured, horned seed capsules lend airiness to bouquets or mixed borders, are very decorative in dried bouquets. 'Miss Jekyll', with semidouble cornflower blue blossoms, is an outstanding variety; 'Persian Jewels' is a superior strain in mixed colors.

Plants come into bloom quickly in spring and dry up in summer heat. Sow seed on open ground where plants are to grow; long taproot makes transplanting unsatisfactory. Seed as soon as ground is workable after last frost; can also be sown in fall in mild-winter climates. Self-sows freely.

NIGHT JESSAMINE. See CESTRUM nocturnum

NINEBARK. See PHYSOCARPUS

NORFOLK ISLAND PINE. See ARAUCARIA heterophylla

Nyctaginaceae. The four o'clock family includes annuals, perennials, shrubs, and vines with showy flowers or bracts. Examples are bougainvillea and four o'clock (*Mirabilis jalapa*).

NYMPHAEA

WATER LILY

Nymphaeaceae

AQUATIC PLANTS

ALL ZONES

PRODUCE FLOWERS IN SUN

LOCATE IN PONDS, WATER GARDENS

Nymphaea

Leaves float and are rounded, with deep notch at one side where leaf stalk is attached. Showy flowers either float on surface or stand above it on stiff stalks. Cultivated water lilies are largely hybrids that cannot be traced back to exact parentage. There are hardy and tropical types. Hardy kinds come in white, yellow, copper, pink, and red. Tropical types add blue and purple; recent introductions include an unusual greenish blue. Some tropicals in the white-pink-red color range are night bloomers; all others close at night. Many are fragrant.

When you buy water lilies, choose selections suitable for the depth of your pond; consult your supplier.

Hardy kinds are easiest for beginners. Plant them February–October in mild-winter areas, April–July where freezes prevail. Set 6-in.-long pieces of rhizome on soil at pool bottom or in boxes, placing rhizome in nearly horizontal position with bud end up. In either case, top of soil should be 8–12 in. below surface of water. Enrich soil with 1 lb. of complete dry fertilizer (3–5 percent nitrogen) for each lily. Groom plants by removing spent leaves and blooms. They usually bloom throughout warm weather and go dormant in fall, then reappear in spring. In very cold areas, protect by covering pond or filling it deeper with water.

Tropical kinds begin to grow and bloom later in summer but last longer, often up to first frost. Buy started tropical plants and set at same depth as hardy rhizomes. Tropical types go dormant but do not survive really low winter temperatures. Their best chance of long-term survival is in regions where orange trees grow. Where winters are colder, store dormant tubers in damp sand over winter or buy new plants each year.

Nymphaeaceae. The water lily family consists of aquatic plants, usually with floating leaves and flowers. Two examples are lotus (*Nelumbo*) and water lily (*Nymphaea*).

Nyssaceae. Deciduous trees from Asia and North America. Examples include sour gum (*Nyssa*) and dove tree (*Davidia*).

NYSSA sylvatica

SOUR GUM, BLACK GUM, TUPELO, PEPPERIDGE

Nyssaceae

DECIDUOUS TREE

🗡 ZONES 3–10, 14–21, 28, 31–41

☀ ◑ FULL SUN OR PARTIAL SHADE

💧 💧 REGULAR TO MODERATE WATER

Nyssa sylvatica

Native to eastern U.S. Slow to moderate growth to 30–50 ft. or more, spreading to 20–30 ft. Pyramidal when young; spreading, irregular, and rugged in age. Crooked branches and dark bark make dramatic picture against winter sky. Dark green, glossy, 2–5-in.-long leaves emerge rather late in spring. Plants have separate sexes. Both male and female trees bear inconspicuous flowers; females will bear fruit if a male is growing nearby (though males sometimes set some fruit as well). Fruits are bluish black, shaped like small olives; birds like them. In autumn, leaves turn yellow and orange, then bright red before dropping. This is among the best native trees for consistent, blazing fall color, even in mild-winter regions.

Prefers moist, deep, well-drained, acid soil, but tolerates poor drainage, some drought. Does not thrive in polluted air. Excellent specimen or shade tree; very attractive in naturalized landscapes. Select a permanent location, since this tree's taproot makes it difficult to move later on.

N. aquatica, water tupelo, is similar, but has larger leaves and fruits. It grows in areas subject to flooding.

OAK. See QUERCUS

OAT GRASS, BLUE. See HELICTOTRICHON sempervirens

OAT GRASS, BULBOUS. See ARRHENATHERUM elatius bulbosum 'Variegatum'

OCIMUM basilicum

SWEET BASIL

Lamiaceae (Labiatae)

ANNUAL HERB

🗡 ALL ZONES

☀ FULL SUN

💧 REGULAR WATER

Ocimum basilicum

Somewhat bushy plant to 2 ft. tall, with green, shiny, 1–2-in.-long leaves and spikes of white flowers. Forms with purple or variegated leaves have purple flowers. Most popular basil for cooking. Used fresh or dry, it gives a pleasant, sweet, mild flavor to tomatoes, cheese, eggs, seafood, salads. There is a small-leafed dwarf kind that thrives in containers.

'Dark Opal', with large, dark purple bronze leaves and small lavender pink flowers, is attractive enough for borders and mass plantings; especially pleasing with dusty millers or 'Carpet of Snow' sweet alyssum. It grows 1–1½ ft. high, about 1 ft. wide. Other good purple-leafed varieties include 'Red Rubin', uniform dark color; and 'Purple Ruffles', deeply fringed and ruffled leaf edges.

Sow seeds of any basil in early spring; make successive sowings 2 weeks apart to have replacements for the short-lived older plants. Or set transplants out after last frost. Space plants 10–12 in. apart. Fertilize once during growing season with complete fertilizer. Keeping flower spikes pinched out will prevent seeding and subsequent death of plant.

OCONEE BELLS. See SHORTIA galacifolia

O'CONNOR'S LEGUME. See TRIFOLIUM fragiferum

OCOTILLO. See FOUQUIERIA splendens

OCTOPUS TREE. See SCHEFFLERA actinophylla

OENOTHERA

EVENING PRIMROSE

Onagraceae

PERENNIALS

🗡 ZONES VARY BY SPECIES

☀ ◑ EXPOSURE NEEDS VARY BY SPECIES

💧 MODERATE WATER

Oenothera fruticosa

Valued for showy, four-petaled, silky flowers in bright yellow, pink, or white. Some types display their blossoms during the day, but others open in late afternoon and close the following morning. Carefree plants that grow in tough, rough places. Can withstand light shade.

O. fruticosa (O. tetragona). SUNDROPS. Zones 1–21, 30–45. Grows to 2 ft. high, spreading vigorously. Reddish stems and bright green foliage. Daytime display of 1½-in. bright yellow flowers all summer. Thrives in full sun or light shade. Leaves of 'Summer Solstice' turn purplish red in autumn. 'Fireworks', 1½ ft. high, has brownish-tinted leaves, red stems, and red flower buds.

O. macrocarpa (O. missouriensis). Zones 2–24, 30, 33–37, 39, 41. Prostrate, sprawling stems to 10 in. long. Soft, velvety, 5-in. leaves. Blooms in late spring and summer, bearing bright yellow, 3–5-in.-wide flowers that open in the afternoon. Large winged seedpods follow the flowers. Best in full sun. Showy plant for rock garden or front of border.

O. speciosa. MEXICAN EVENING PRIMROSE. Zones 3–24, 29, 30, 33. Often sold as *O. berlandieri* or *O. speciosa childsii*. Grows 10–12 in. high, with profuse showing of 1½-in. rose pink blooms in summer; flowers open in daytime, despite plant's common name. Stems die back after bloom. Spreads rapidly by underground stems and can invade other plantings. Full sun. 'Alba' is a white-flowered form; 'Woodside White' opens white but ages to pale pink; 'Siskiyou' is an especially vigorous, long-blooming variety with 2-in. light pink blossoms.

OKRA

Malvaceae

ANNUAL

🗡 ALL ZONES

☀ FULL SUN

💧 REGULAR WATER

Okra

Warm-season annual vegetable that grows well under same conditions as sweet corn. Plant when ground has warmed to 70°F/21°C. Soak seed 24 hours before planting to speed germination.

Fertilize at least once in spring. Allow 50 to 60 days from planting to harvest. Pods grow on large, erect, bushy plants with tropical-looking leaves. Harvest pods every 2 or 3 days. Best size is 1–3 in. long; overripe pods are tough, and they shorten plant's bearing life. In containers, variety 'Red River' has tropical look. In large tub in warm spot, a single plant can yield enough to make it worth growing.

OLD MAN CACTUS. See CEPHALOCEREUS senilis

Oleaceae. The olive family includes about 900 species of trees and shrubs with opposite leaves and flower parts usually in fours. Typical members include privet (*Ligustrum*), olive (*Olea*), and lilac (*Syringa*).

OLEA europaea

OLIVE

Oleaceae

EVERGREEN TREE

⚡ ZONES 8, 9, 11–24

☼ FULL SUN

💧 MODERATE WATER

Olea europaea

Hardy to 15°F/−9°C; best in areas with hot, dry summers. Slow growth to an eventual 25–30 ft. tall and wide. Can be trained to single or multiple trunks. Young trees put on height (if not substance) fairly fast. Smooth gray trunks and branches become gnarled and picturesque in maturity. Soft gray-green, willowlike foliage. Withstands heavy pruning. Yearly thinning shows off branch pattern; removing flowering-fruiting branches reduces or eliminates fruit crop, which is usually a nuisance. Growth is lushest in deep, rich soil, but tree tolerates poor soil.

The following varieties are most often used as landscape plants. 'Little Ollie' is a very dark green, dense shrub to 12 ft. high, excellent as hedge or screen; bears almost no fruit. 'Mission', hardier than others, is a commercial fruiting variety to 40 ft. tall. 'Swan Hill' grows to 30 ft. high; it has deep green leaves, little or no pollen, and no fruit.

OLEANDER. See NERIUM oleander

OLIVE. See OLEA europaea

OMPHALODES verna

BLUE-EYED MARY

Boraginaceae

PERENNIAL

⚡ ZONES 2–9, 14–21, 31–41

☼ LIGHT SHADE

💧 REGULAR WATER

Omphalodes verna

Attractive creeping perennial for shaded rock garden or woodland garden. Spreads slowly to become a small-scale ground cover. The 2-in. leaves are evergreen in milder parts of range. Spring flowers, ½ in. wide, are intense pure blue with a tiny white eye. Tolerates drought.

Onagraceae. Most members of the evening primrose family have flower parts in fours, but otherwise are diverse in appearance and structure. They include *Clarkia*, *Fuchsia*, *Gaura*, evening primrose (*Oenothera*), and California fuchsia (*Zauschneria*).

ONCIDIUM

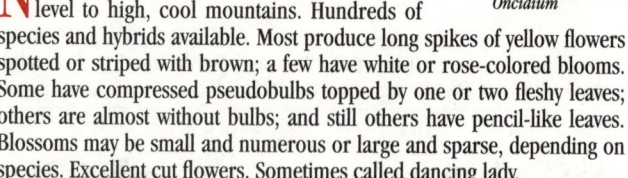

Orchidaceae

EPIPHYTIC ORCHIDS

⚡ ZONES 25–27; OR GREENHOUSE OR INDOOR PLANTS

☼ FILTERED SHADE

💧 REGULAR WATER

Oncidium

Native from Florida to Brazil, and from sea level to high, cool mountains. Hundreds of species and hybrids available. Most produce long spikes of yellow flowers spotted or striped with brown; a few have white or rose-colored blooms. Some have compressed pseudobulbs topped by one or two fleshy leaves; others are almost without bulbs; and still others have pencil-like leaves. Blossoms may be small and numerous or large and sparse, depending on species. Excellent cut flowers. Sometimes called dancing lady.

Outdoor plants in mildest climates: grow in pots or on slabs of bark attached to tree trunks, and bring indoors only when a freeze is imminent. Indoors, grow on a bright windowsill or in a greenhouse. Outside, treat as you would *Laelia*; indoors, treat like *Cattleya*. Also see Orchidaceae.

ONION

Amaryllidaceae

BIENNIAL GROWN AS ANNUAL

⚡ ALL ZONES

☼ FULL SUN

💧 REGULAR WATER

Onion

Grow onions from seed or sets (small bulbs). Sets are easiest for beginners, though seed gives larger crop for smaller investment and offers more choices in varieties. In mild climates, sets can be planted all winter long and through April; where winters are cold, planting can begin in early spring, as soon as soil is workable. Soil should be loose, rich, and well drained. Push sets just under soil surface so that point of bulb is visible; space a little wider than bulb size at maturity (closer if you want to harvest some as green onions). Sow seed ¼ in. deep, in rows 15–18 in. apart. In mild-winter regions, sow seed in fall and winter for winter–spring crop; in cold-winter areas, sow in early spring. When seedlings are pencil size, thin to same spacing as for sets, transplanting thinnings to extend planting. Trim back tops of transplants about halfway. In some areas, onion plants (field-grown, nearly pencil-size transplants or seedlings growing in pots) are available.

Onions are shallow rooted and need moisture fairly near the surface. Feed plants, especially early in season: the larger and stronger the plants grow, the larger the bulbs they form. Carefully eliminate weeds that compete for light, food, and water. When most of the tops have begun to yellow and fall over, dig bulbs and let them cure and dry on top of ground for several days. Then pull off tops, clean, and store in dark, cool, airy place.

Varieties differ in bulb size, shape, color, flavor, and storage life. Also keep in mind that onions form bulbs in response to day length. If you choose a type inappropriate for your area, it may make small premature bulbs or not bulb up at all. Long-day varieties need 14 to 16 hours of daylight and are grown in northern climates. They tend to be pungent and store well; examples are 'Early Yellow Globe', 'Ebenezer', 'Ruby', 'Southport White Globe', 'Sweet Spanish'. Short-day varieties require 10 to 12 hours of daylight and are grown in southernmost climes (Deep South, the Southwest, Southern California). They start making bulbs early in the year, tend to be sweet, and are poor keepers; examples are 'Bermuda', 'California Red', 'Granex', 'Super Sweet', 'Vidalia'. Intermediate-day types, requiring 12 to 14 hours of daylight, are suited to all growing areas; examples are 'Autumn Spice', 'Red Torpedo', 'Ringmaker'.

For ornamental relatives, see *Allium*.

O

ONOCLEA sensibilis

SENSITIVE FERN

Polypodiaceae

FERN

⚡ ZONES 1–9, 14–24, 31–43

☼ FULL SUN

🌢🌢 MOIST TO WET SOIL

Onoclea sensibilis

Native to eastern U.S. Coarse-textured fern with 2–4-ft. sterile fronds divided nearly to midrib; fertile fronds smaller, with clusters of almost beadlike leaflets. Fronds come from underground creeping rhizome that can be invasive. Dies to the ground in winter. Fronds seem coarse to many gardeners, but fern is useful for planting along streams and ponds. Takes regular moisture, but won't be as big as in wetter conditions. Called sensitive fern because it is among the first plants to show frost damage in fall.

OPHIOPOGON. See LIRIOPE and OPHIOPOGON

OPUNTIA

Cactaceae

CACTI

⚡ ZONES VARY BY SPECIES

☼ FULL SUN

🌢 MODERATE TO LITTLE WATER

Opuntia microdasys

Several species are native to the northern U.S. and Canada. Though perfectly hardy in the coldest winters, they need perfect drainage to survive winter freezes and thaws; best grown in raised beds. These species are not easy to identify because of frequent name changes by botanists. Among the hardiest are *O. compressa*, *O. fragilis*, and *O. polyacantha*, all small, clump-forming plants with showy bright yellow flowers. The more tender species described below include a widely grown landscape plant and a favorite house plant.

O. ficus-indica. Zones 8, 9, 12–29. Big shrubby or treelike cactus to 15 ft., with woody trunks and smooth, flat green joints. Few or no spines; has clusters of bristles. Bears 4-in.-wide yellow flowers in spring or early summer; the large red or yellow fruit that follows is sold in groceries in some areas. Within its range, a common hedge or screen plant.

O. microdasys. BUNNY EARS. Zones 12–24; or house plant. Fast growth to 2 ft. high, 4–5 ft. wide (much smaller in pots). Pads flat, thin, nearly round, to 6 in. across, velvety soft green with neatly spaced tufts of short golden bristles in polka-dot effect. 'Albispina' has white bristles. Small, round new pads atop larger old ones give plant silhouette of animal's head. A favorite with children.

ORANGE. See CITRUS

ORANGE CLOCK VINE. See THUNBERGIA gregorii

ORANGE JESSAMINE. See MURRAYA paniculata

ORANGEQUAT. See CITRUS, Kumquat Hybrids

Orchidaceae. The orchid family is probably the largest in the plant kingdom, with nearly 800 genera and over 17,000 species. Flowers have an unusual shape: one or more petals united to form a lip, and the stamens, style, and stigma united into a single organ, the column.

Best known are *Bletilla, Cattleya, Cymbidium, Epidendrum, Laelia, Oncidium, Paphiopedilum,* and *Phalaenopsis.*

Orchid growers' terms. Here are definitions of the orchid growers' terms you will encounter in this book.

Epiphytic. In nature epiphytic orchids cling to high branches of trees in tropical or subtropical jungles, deriving their nourishment from air, rain, and whatever decaying vegetable matter they can trap in their root systems.

Pseudobulb. Epiphytic orchids have thickened stems called pseudobulbs that store food and water and allow the plants to survive drought. These may be short and fat (like bulbs) or erect and slender. They vary from green to brown in color. Leaves may grow along pseudobulbs or from their tips.

Terrestrial. Some orchids (including most native orchids) are terrestrial and must grow in loose, moist soil rich in humus. They often occur in wooded areas but sometimes in open meadows as well. These orchids require constant moisture and food.

Sepals, petals, lip, and pouch. Segments of an orchid flower include three sepals and three petals; one of the petals, usually the lowest one, is called the lip. The lip is usually larger and more brightly colored than other segments. Sometimes it is fantastically shaped, with various appendages and markings. It may be folded into a slipperlike "pouch."

Rafts, bark. Nearly all orchids, terrestrial or epiphytic, are grown in pots. A few are grown on "rafts" (slabs of bark or wood), or in baskets of wood slats; a few natives are grown in open ground.

Potting and growing. Potting materials for cattleyas (the most commonly grown orchids) will work for most epiphytic orchids: osmunda fiber, hapuu (tree fern stem), or ground bark. Most popular now is bark, which is readily available, easy to handle, and fairly inexpensive. Use fine grade for pots 3 in. or smaller, medium grade for pots 4 in. or larger. It's sensible to use ready-made mixes sold by orchid growers; these are blended for proper texture and acidity.

Water plants about once a week—when mix dries out and becomes lightweight. Feed with a commercial water-soluble orchid fertilizer once every 2 weeks during growing season. To provide humidity for plants in house, fill a metal or plastic tray with gravel and add just enough water to reach almost to top of gravel. Stretch hardware cloth over tray, leaving an inch between gravel and wire for air circulation. Set pots on top. Maintain water level.

Temperature requirements. This list classifies orchids according to temperature requirements. Many cool-growing orchids are hardy enough to grow outdoors in mild-winter areas.

Temperate-climate orchids can be grown in pots on a window sill with other house plants, but will perform best if given additional humidity. An excellent method of supplying humidity is described in "Potting and growing," above. Most temperate-climate orchids can be moved outdoors in summer; place them in the shade of high-branching trees, on the patio, or in a lathhouse.

Warm-climate orchids need greenhouse conditions to provide the uniform warm temperatures and high humidity they require.

Cool-climate orchids: *Bletilla, Cymbidium, Epidendrum, Laelia, Paphiopedilum* (green-leafed forms). Some of these are hardy outdoors in mildest climates. Some are thoroughly hardy.

Temperate-climate orchids: *Cattleya, Epidendrum, Laelia, Oncidium, Paphiopedilum* (mottled-leafed forms).

Warm-climate orchid: *Phalaenopsis.*

ORCHID CACTUS. See EPIPHYLLUM

ORCHID TREE. See BAUHINIA

OREGANO. See ORIGANUM vulgare

OREGON GRAPE. See MAHONIA aquifolium

ORIENTAL ARBORVITAE. See PLATYCLADUS orientalis

O

ORIENTAL GARLIC. See ALLIUM tuberosum

ORIENTAL POPPY. See PAPAVER orientale

ORIGANUM

Lamiaceae (Labiatae)

PERENNIALS

☑ ZONES VARY BY SPECIES

☼ FULL SUN

◐ MODERATE TO LITTLE WATER, EXCEPT AS NOTED

Origanum majorana

Mint relatives with tight clusters of small flowers and foliage with a strong, pleasant scent. Bracts in flower clusters overlap, giving effect of small pinecones. Not fussy about soil type.

O. dictamnus (Amaracus dictamnus). CRETE DITTANY. Zones 8–24. Native to Mediterranean area. Aromatic herb with slender, arching stems to 1 ft. long. Thick, roundish, somewhat mottled, woolly white leaves to ¾ in. long. Flowers pink to purplish, ½ in. long; rose purple fruit in conelike heads. Blooms summer to fall. Shows up best when planted individually in rock garden, container, or hanging basket.

O. laevigatum. Zones 3–24, 32–34. Sprawling, arching plant, with stems rooting at joints; bears branching clusters of purple flowers. 'Herrenhausen' has lilac pink flowers and purplish leaves in cool weather; 'Hopley's' has large heads of deep purplish pink flowers. Useful in dry gardens as bank or ground cover.

O. majorana (Majorana hortensis). SWEET MARJORAM. Perennial in Zones 4–24, 29–31; treated as annual elsewhere. To 1–2 ft. Tiny, oval gray-green leaves; spikes of white flowers in loose clusters at top of plant. Grow in fairly moist soil. Keep blossoms cut off and plant trimmed to prevent woody growth. Propagate from seeds, cuttings, or root divisions. It's a favorite herb for seasoning meats, salads, vinegars. Use leaves fresh or dried. Often grown in container indoors on window sill in cold-winter areas.

O. onites. POT MARJORAM. Zones 8–24. To 2 ft. tall and as broad, with bright green aromatic leaves and flattish heads of tiny white or purplish flowers. Sometimes called Cretan oregano.

O. vulgare. OREGANO, WILD MARJORAM. Zones 1–24, 30–45. Upright growth to 2½ ft. Spreads by underground stems. Medium-size oval leaves; purplish pink blooms. Grow in medium rich soil; needs good drainage. Keep trimmed to prevent flowering. Replant every 3 years. Fresh or dried leaves are used in many dishes, especially Italian and Spanish ones. 'Compactum' is a few inches tall, spreads widely, and seldom flowers. It can be used as a ground cover.

ORNAMENTAL PEAR. See PYRUS

ORNITHOGALUM

Liliaceae

BULBS

☑ ZONES VARY BY SPECIES; OR DIG AND STORE; OR GROW IN POTS

☼ FULL SUN

◐ WATER NEEDS VARY BY SPECIES

✦ ALL PARTS, ESPECIALLY BULB, ARE POISONOUS IF INGESTED

Ornithogalum umbellatum

Leaves vary from narrow to broad and tend to be floppy. Flowers mostly star shaped, in tall or rounded clusters, appearing in late spring or early summer. Use in borders. In areas beyond their hardiness, bulbs can be lifted and stored during winter; or they can be grown in pots and protected.

O. arabicum. STAR OF BETHLEHEM. Zones 5–24. Handsome clusters of 2-in., white, waxy flowers with beady black pistils in centers. Stems 2 ft. tall. Floppy bluish green leaves to 2 ft. long, 1 in. wide. In cool-summer climates, bulbs may not bloom second year after planting because they lacked sufficient heat. In-ground planting best in dry-summer areas. Excellent cut flower. Moderate water.

O. thyrsoides. CHINCHERINCHEE. Zones 4–24. Tapering, compact clusters of white, 2-in. flowers with brownish green centers. Flower stems 2 ft. high. Leaves bright green, upright, to 1 ft. long, 2 in. wide. May survive colder winters if given sheltered southern or southwestern location and protected with mulch. Like *O. arabicum*, best in dry-summer areas. Long-lasting cut flower. Moderate water.

O. umbellatum. STAR OF BETHLEHEM. Zones 4–33. May naturalize once established and become a pest. Clusters of 1-in.-wide flowers, striped green on outside, atop 1-ft. stems. Grasslike leaves about as long as flower stems. Cut flowers last well but close at night. Regular water.

OSAGE ORANGE. See MACLURA pomifera

OSCULARIA

Aizoaceae

SUBSHRUBS

☑ ZONES 15–24

☼ FULL SUN

◐ MODERATE TO LITTLE WATER

Oscularia deltoides

Low plants with erect or trailing branches. To 1 ft. tall. Leaves very thick and fleshy, triangular, blue green with pink flesh. Fragrant flowers to ½ in. across in late spring, early summer. Best in pots, hanging baskets, rock gardens, borders. Can be used as small-scale ground cover. Sometimes grown as window box or pot plant in cold climates and protected during winter.

O. deltoides. Has purplish rose flowers.

O. pedunculata. Has paler, mauve pink flowers.

OSMANTHUS

Oleaceae

EVERGREEN SHRUBS

☑ ZONES VARY BY SPECIES

☼ ◐ FULL SUN OR PARTIAL SHADE

◐ REGULAR TO MODERATE WATER

Osmanthus fragrans

All have clean, leathery, attractive foliage and inconspicuous but fragrant flowers. Plants aren't particular about soil; once established, they are fairly drought tolerant.

O. delavayi (Siphonosmanthus delavayi). DELAVAY OSMANTHUS. Zones 4–9, 14–21, 26, 28, warmer parts of 31. Slow growing, graceful, to 4–6 ft., with arching branches spreading wider. Leaves dark green, oval, to 1 in. long, with toothed edges. Profuse clusters of four to eight white, fragrant flowers (largest of any osmanthus) in spring. Attractive all year. Easily controlled by pruning. Good choice for foundations, massing. Handsome on retaining wall where branches hang down. In hot-summer areas, give partial shade.

O. fortunei. Zones 5–10, 14–24, 28, 31, warmer parts of 32. Hybrid between *O. heterophyllus* and *O. fragrans*. Slow, dense growth to an eventual 20 ft. tall; often seen at height of about 6 ft. Leaves are oval, hollylike, up to 4 in. long. Small, fragrant white flowers bloom during fall. 'San Jose' is similar but has cream to orange flowers.

O. fragrans. SWEET OLIVE. Zones 8, 9, 12–24, 26 (northern part), 28–31. Moderate growth to 10 ft. and more with age. Broad, dense, compact. Can be pruned to upright growth where space is limited. Can be trained as small tree, hedge, screen, background, espalier, container plant. Pinch out growing tips of young plants to induce bushiness.

Leaves glossy, medium green, oval, to 4 in. long, toothed or smooth edged. Tiny white flowers have powerful sweet, apricotlike fragrance. Bloom is heaviest in spring and early summer, but plants flower sporadically throughout year in mild-winter areas. Give afternoon shade in hot-summer regions. *O. f. aurantiacus* has narrower, less glossy leaves than the species; its crop of wonderfully fragrant orange flowers is concentrated in early fall.

O. heterophyllus (O. aquifolium, O. ilicifolius). HOLLY-LEAF OSMANTHUS. Zones 3–10, 14–24, 28–33. Grows 8–10 ft. tall (possibly to 20 ft.), with 2½-in., spiny-edged leaves. Resembles English holly, but leaves appear opposite one another on stems. Fragrant white flowers in late fall and winter are followed by berrylike blue-black fruit in warmer regions.

'Goshiki'. Erect plant to 3½ ft. tall, 5 ft. wide. New leaves have pinkish orange markings that mature to yellow variegations on dark green. Flowers few to none.

'Gulftide'. Similar to 'Ilicifolius' but more compact.

'Ilicifolius'. Dense, symmetrical upright growth to 6–8 ft., eventually to 20 ft. Leaves dark green, strongly toothed, hollylike, to 2½ in. long. Fragrant white flowers in fall, winter, early spring. Good for screen, background.

'Purpureus' ('Purpurascens'). Same growth habit as species. Dark purple new growth, with purple tints through summer.

'Rotundifolius'. Slow growing to 5 ft. Roundish small leaves are lightly spined along edges.

'Variegatus'. Slow growing to 4–5 ft., with densely set leaves edged creamy white. Useful for lighting up shady areas. A bit less cold-tolerant than the species.

OSMUNDA

Osmundaceae

FERNS

⚡ ZONES VARY BY SPECIES

☼ ◐ ● EXPOSURE NEEDS VARY BY SPECIES

🌢🌢 DAMP TO WET SOIL

Osmunda regalis

Three species of large, coarse, imposing deciduous ferns useful in naturalistic plantings. All like plenty of moisture but can survive with less, responding with smaller, less vigorous growth. Rhizomes have heavy growth of matted brown roots—the source of the osmunda fiber used for potting orchids.

O. cinnamomea. CINNAMON FERN. Zones 1–6, 32–45. Fern with erect sterile fronds to as tall as 5 ft., arching outward toward the top. Spores are borne on a different sort of frond—narrow, erect, much shorter, turning cinnamon brown as spores ripen. Unfolding young fronds (fiddleheads) are harvested for food. Fronds turn showy yellow to orange in fall. Full or light shade.

O. claytoniana. INTERRUPTED FERN. Zones 1–6, 32–45. If given ample water, grows as tall as 5 ft., more typically to 3 ft. Shorter in dryish soils. Each frond is "interrupted" in the middle by several short brown spore-bearing segments. Full or light shade.

O. regalis. ROYAL FERN, FLOWERING FERN. Zones 1–9, 14–17, 26–45. Large fern (to 6 ft.) with twice-cut fronds, each leaflet quite large. Coarser in texture than most ferns. Tips of fronds have modified segments that somewhat resemble flower buds; these produce the spores. Leaves turn yellow to brown in fall. 'Cristata' has crested fronds; 'Purpurascens' has purplish red new growth and stems that remain purple throughout the season. Light shade, but will thrive in sun in wet soil, even in mud. Especially attractive beside streams or ponds.

OSTEOSPERMUM

AFRICAN DAISY

Asteraceae (Compositae)

SHRUBBY PERENNIALS OR ANNUALS

⚡ ALL ZONES

☼ FULL SUN

🌢🌢 REGULAR TO MODERATE WATER

Osteospermum fruticosum

South African plants closely related to *Dimorphotheca* and often sold as such. Perennials in Zones 8, 9, 12–26; elsewhere, treated as summer annuals. Profusion of daisylike flowers open only in sunlight. Medium green, narrowish oval leaves are smooth edged or with a few large teeth, 2–4 in. long. Plants look best with good garden soil and care, but will stand drought and neglect when established. Borders, mass plantings, slopes.

O. ecklonis (Dimorphotheca ecklonis). Grows 2–4 ft. tall, equally broad. Long stems bear 3-in. flower heads with white rays (tinged lavender blue on backs), dark blue center. Blooms early summer to frost.

O. fruticosum (Dimorphotheca fruticosa). TRAILING AFRICAN DAISY. Spreads rapidly by trailing, rooting branches. Will cover 2–4-ft. circle in a year; grows 6–12 in. high. Flowers to 2 in. wide, rays lilac above, fading nearly white by second day, deeper lilac beneath and in bud; dark purple center. As a perennial, blooms intermittently all year, most heavily in fall and winter. 'African Queen' and 'Burgundy' have purple blooms. 'Whirlygig' has unusual white-and-blue flower heads with spoon-shaped, white-tipped petals; each petal is pinched in middle to reveal blue underside.

OSTRICH FERN. See MATTEUCCIA struthiopteris

OSTRYA

HOP HORNBEAM

Betulaceae

DECIDUOUS TREES

⚡ ZONES VARY BY SPECIES

☼ ◐ FULL SUN OR LIGHT SHADE

🌢🌢 REGULAR TO MODERATE WATER

Ostrya virginiana

Hop hornbeams are so named because female flowers and fruit are enclosed in bractlike husks forming 1½–2½-in. clusters that resemble hops. Inch-long male catkins are attractive in winter. Trees are small to medium-size (seldom exceeding 40 ft.), slow growing. Foliage is dark green, turning yellow in fall. Attractive, but little used because of their slow growth—a fault to nurserymen, but a possible advantage to the gardener. Wood is hard, heavy, and dense.

O. carpinifolia. EUROPEAN HOP HORNBEAM. Zones 3–9, 14–17, 31–35, 37, 39. Scarcely differs from the more common American species, *O. virginiana.*

O. virginiana. AMERICAN HOP HORNBEAM, IRONWOOD. Zones 1–9, 14–17, 28, 31–43. Native to eastern North America, where it is an understory tree.

OSWEGO TEA. See MONARDA

OTATEA. See BAMBOO

FOR INFORMATION ON YOUR CLIMATE ZONE
PLEASE SEE PAGES 16–78

O

OXALIS

Oxalidaceae

PERENNIALS; SOME GROW FROM BULBS OR RHIZOMES

⚡ ZONES VARY BY SPECIES

☀ ◐ FULL SUN OR LIGHT SHADE, EXCEPT AS NOTED

💧 REGULAR WATER

Oxalis oregana

Leaves divided into leaflets; usually have three leaflets, like clover leaves. Flowers pink, white, rose, or yellow.

O. acetosella. WOOD SORREL, SHAMROCK. One of several plants known as shamrock. See Shamrocks.

O. adenophylla. Zones 4–9, 12–24, 30–32; container plant in colder-winter zones. Dense, low (4-in.-high), compact tuft of leaves, each leaf with 12–22 crinkly, gray-green leaflets. Flowers are 1 in. wide, on 4–6-in. stalks, bell shaped, lilac pink with deeper veins, in late spring. Plant roots in fall. Needs good drainage. Good rock garden plant or companion to bulbs such as species tulips or the smaller kinds of narcissus, in pots or in the ground.

O. oregana. REDWOOD SORREL, OREGON OXALIS. Zones 4–9, 14–24. Native to coastal forests from Washington to California. Creeping white roots send up velvety, medium green leaves 1½–4 in. wide on stems 2–10 in. high. Blooms in spring, sometimes again in fall; flowers to 1 in. across, pink or white veined with lavender. Interesting ground cover for partial shade to deep shade in mild-winter/cool-summer areas.

O. purpurea (O. variabilis). Zones 8, 9, 12–24, 29–31. Low growing (4–5 in. tall), with large leaves and rose red flowers an inch across. Spreads by bulbs and rhizomelike roots, but is not aggressive or weedy. Plant bulbs in early fall for late fall and winter bloom. Improved kinds sold under the name Grand Duchess; have larger flowers of rose pink, white, or lavender.

O. versicolor. Zones 6–9, 14–24; container plant in colder-winter zones. Bulbs give rise to erect or spreading stems up to 6 in. tall. Leaves bear three deeply notched leaflets less than ½ in. wide. Flowers are white, over 1 in. wide, with yellow throat and purplish margins. The variety commonly seen is 'Candy Cane', with white flowers striped red. Striped buds especially colorful. Plant in fall for spring bloom.

OX-EYE. See HELIOPSIS helianthoides

OXYDENDRUM arboreum

SOURWOOD, SORREL TREE

Ericaceae

DECIDUOUS TREE

⚡ ZONES 3–9, 14–17, 28, 31–35, 37, 39

☀ FULL SUN

💧 REGULAR WATER

Oxydendrum arboreum

Native from Pennsylvania and Ohio south to Florida, Mississippi, and Louisiana. Beautiful flowering tree with year-round interest. Slow growth to 15–25 ft., eventually to 50 ft. Pyramidal shape with slender trunk, rounded top, and slightly pendulous branches; handsome winter silhouette. Narrow, 5–8-in.-long leaves somewhat resemble peach leaves; they are bronze tinted in early spring, rich green in summer, orange and scarlet to blackish purple in autumn. Blooms in summer, with fragrant, bell-shaped, creamy white flowers in 10-in.-long, drooping clusters at branch tips. In autumn, when foliage is brilliantly colored, branching clusters of greenish seed capsules extend outward and downward like fingers; capsules turn light silver gray and hang on late into winter.

Grow in moist, acid, well-drained soil. Tolerates some drought, but not urban pollution. Will grow in partial shade, but best flowering and fall color in full sun. Among earliest and best trees for colorful autumn foliage in South. Not competitive; doesn't do well in lawns or under larger trees. Avoid underplanting with anything needing cultivation. Use as specimen in woodland garden, patio shade tree. Young plants make good container subjects.

OXYPETALUM caeruleum. See TWEEDIA caerulea

OYSTER PLANT. See RHOEO spathacea, SALSIFY

PACHISTIMA. See PAXISTIMA canbyi

PACHYPODIUM lamerei

MADAGASCAR PALM

Apocynaceae

SUCCULENT SHRUB

⚡ ZONE 25; OR INDOORS

☀ FULL SUN; BRIGHT LIGHT INDOORS

💧 WATER ONLY WHEN SOIL IS DRY

Pachypodium lamerei

Not a palm, though somewhat palmlike in appearance. Easy-to-grow plant with impressive silhouette: spiny, succulent, unbranched trunk 2–4 ft. high (as tall as 18 ft. under ideal conditions) is topped with a circle of strap-shaped leaves to 1 ft. long and 1–4 in. wide. Saucer-shaped white flowers to 4 in. wide are seldom seen; they usually appear only on large, old plants. Plant can be grown outdoors year round only in South Florida; elsewhere, it can be raised in a pot and summered outside or kept exclusively indoors as a house plant. Leaves usually drop in winter (specimens in South Florida and house plants may hold their foliage); plant needs no water until growth resumes.

PACHYSANDRA

SPURGE, PACHYSANDRA

Buxaceae

PERENNIAL GROUND COVERS

⚡ ZONES VARY BY SPECIES

☀ ● LIGHT TO HEAVY SHADE

💧 REGULAR WATER

Pachysandra terminalis

Two species of low-growing shrubby perennials used for ground cover in shady places. Slow but sure spreaders from underground runners, they are invaluable landscape plants. Hardy to cold; well able to compete with tree roots. Compact growth and clean, attractive foliage are their chief virtues. Flowers are not showy when viewed casually, but look attractive at close range. Provide moist, preferably somewhat acid soil, well amended with organic material. Too much sun causes yellowing foliage and poor growth.

P. procumbens. ALLEGHENY SPURGE, ALLEGHENY PACHYSANDRA. Zones 3–6, 15–17, 31–43. Deciduous in colder part of range, semievergreen to fully evergreen farther south. Not as widely available as the Japanese species below. Grows 6–12 in. high; grayish green leaves are 2–4 in. long and 2–3 in. wide, clustered near top of stem. Leaves often mottled with gray or brownish markings. Small white or pinkish flowers are fragrant. Spreads more slowly than *P. terminalis*.

P. terminalis. JAPANESE SPURGE, JAPANESE PACHYSANDRA. Evergreen. Zones 1–10, 14–21, 31–43. Grows 8–12 in. high. Shiny dark green leaves are 2–4 in. long and ½–1½ in. wide; upper half of leaf has shallowly toothed edges. Small white flowers are borne in 1–2-in. spikes. 'Green Carpet' is shorter and denser in growth than the species, with shinier, deeper green leaves. 'Green Sheen' has especially glossy leaves;

P

'Silver Edge' ('Variegata') has creamy-edged foliage; fast-spreading 'Cut Leaf' has deeply dissected leaves.

Japanese spurge can stand very heavy shade and is very widely used as a ground cover under trees. Plant 6 in. apart for reasonably quick cover; apply a mulch and keep moist until established. Performs better in northern part of range. Seldom bothered by pests, but a leaf blight can cause serious damage if it gets out of hand; control with fungicides and, if possible, by limiting overhead watering.

PAEONIA

PEONY

Paeoniaceae

PERENNIALS AND DECIDUOUS SHRUBS

ZONES VARY BY TYPE

AFTERNOON SHADE IN HOT CLIMATES

REGULAR WATER

Paeonia
Single Type

Although a few species may be found in specialists' lists or in seed exchanges, most garden peonies are hybrids. The two basic types are herbaceous and tree peonies. Herbaceous types die to the ground in late fall; they are mostly descendants of *P. lactiflora*. Tree (actually shrub) peonies flower from permanent woody branches; they are chiefly descendants of *P. suffruticosa*. All peonies are extremely long-lived plants of significant size, demanding more than ordinary care in site preparation. In return, they can provide outstanding garden beauty for as long as you live.

Herbaceous peonies are planted in fall (preferably) or earliest spring as bare-root plants: compact rhizomes with several "eyes" (growth buds) and thick, tuberous roots. Tree peonies, practically all of them grafted onto herbaceous peony roots, may be planted in the same way. Many growers now offer tree peonies as container plants from spring to fall (all year in mild-winter regions); they cost more than bare-root plants because of the time and labor involved in producing them.

Ideally, the planting site for peonies should be deeply dug several days before planting. Work in plenty of thoroughly decayed manure or compost and superphosphate; allow the soil to settle before planting. Set herbaceous peony roots with eyes 2 in. deep in cold climates, 1 in. deep in warmer regions; deeper planting will prevent flowering. Set tree peonies so that the graft line is 3–4 in. below the soil surface (the object is to get the shrubby top to root on its own). Mulch the first year after the ground has frozen. Plants are unlikely to bloom the first year, but should bloom every year after that if fertilized after the flowering period and again in fall (the American Peony Society recommends 8-8-8 and bonemeal).

During humid weather—particularly during cool, humid periods—the fungus disease botrytis is sometimes a problem: buds blacken and fail to develop, stems wilt and collapse. Prevent the problem by sanitation: in autumn, dispose of all leaves (also all stems on herbaceous peonies). As new growth emerges in spring, spray with copper fungicide.

WHY DIDN'T MY PEONY PUT ON A SHOW?

Poor flowering has many possible causes, including these: the plant is too young (wait a while); it was planted too deep or too shallow (lift during dormant season and replant at proper depth); flower buds were killed by a late freeze (wait until next year); extreme heat (plant early-flowering varieties); lack of nutrients (apply fertilizer); or the clump has been moved or divided too often (leave it alone).

Herbaceous peonies. Perennials. Zones 1–11, 14–16, 32–45. Bloom well only where they experience a period of pronounced winter chill. Grow to 3–4 ft. tall. Large blossoms borne in late spring or early summer are 4–6 in. (even up to 10 in.) across; many varieties have a refreshing old rose scent. Flowers fall into three basic categories: single or semidouble, with one or two rows of petals; Japanese, with a single row of petals and a large central mass of narrow petal-like segments called staminodes; and double, with full flowers composed of many petals. In hot-summer climates, singles and Japanese varieties tend to do better than full doubles. All profit from light afternoon shade where summers are very hot.

Provide support for the heavy flowers. All types are choice cut flowers; cut just as buds begin to open. Leave at least three leaves on every cut stem, and do not remove more than half the blooms from any clump. The object is to preserve leaf growth to nourish the plant for next year. Remove faded flowers from plants to prevent seed formation.

Varieties are too numerous to list. Three noteworthy doubles—all introduced more than a century ago and still popular—deserve mention because they are the ones most likely to be found in local garden centers and nurseries. These are 'Edulis Superba', bearing fragrant bright pink blooms with an outer ring of somewhat lighter petals; 'Felix Crousse', deep red; and 'Festiva Maxima', white with a few crimson flecks toward the center. These varieties have the added virtue of growing fairly well in the South. Enthusiasts can investigate dozens of others in catalogs.

There is no reason to divide a peony except to increase your stock. Dig in early fall, hose off soil, and divide into sections, making sure that each has at least three eyes; these appear at top of root cluster, at or near bases of past season's stems. Plant at once so that plants will get established before freezing weather.

P. tenuifolia 'Rubra Plena'. Perennial. Zones 1–11, 14–16, 32–43. DOUBLE FERN-LEAF PEONY. This herbaceous peony species plant has recently reentered the market. It grows only 1–1½ ft. tall, has exceedingly finely cut, fernlike foliage, and bears 3-in. double dark red flowers in early to midspring.

Tree peonies. Deciduous shrubs. Zones 2–12, 14–21, 31–43. Slow growth to an eventual 3–5 ft. tall, with handsome divided leaves and very large (to 10–12-in.) single to double flowers in early spring. They seldom reveal their true potential until they have spent several years in your garden, but the spectacular results are worth the wait. Relatively inexpensive imported small grafted plants are sometimes available, usually sold only

Paeonia
Double Type

by color (red, pink, white, yellow, purple); these are a good buy if you are very patient and can wait for them to attain good size. Catalogs offer named varieties of Japanese origin in white, pink, red, and purple. More recent and considerably more expensive (but worth it) are the yellow and orange hybrids resulting from crosses of *P. suffruticosa* with *P. delavayi* and *P. lutea*.

Tree peonies require less winter chill than herbaceous peonies. The flowers are fragile and should be sheltered from strong wind. Prune only to remove faded blooms and any dead wood. In coldest winter climates, shield from sun and wind with burlap curtain.

PAINTED DAISY. See CHRYSANTHEMUM coccineum

PAINTED FINGERNAIL PLANT. See NEOREGELIA spectabilis

PAINTED TONGUE. See SALPIGLOSSIS sinuata

Palmae. See Arecaceae

PALMETTO. See SABAL

PALMS. Most palms are tropical or subtropical; a few are surprisingly hardy (specimens are seen in Edinburgh, London, and southern Russia, as well as Portland and Seattle). Palms offer great opportunity for imaginative planting. In nature they grow not only in solid stands but also in company with other plants, notably broad-leafed evergreen trees and shrubs. They are effective near swimming pools.

Most young palms prefer shade, and all palms tolerate it; this fact makes them good house or patio plants when they are small. As they grow, they can be moved into sun or partial shade, depending on the species. Growth rates vary, but keeping plants in pots usually slows growth of faster-growing kinds. If temperatures are 60°F/16°C or higher, fertilize potted palms often; also wash them off frequently to provide some humidity and clean the foliage. Washing also dislodges insects, which (indoors, at any rate) are protected from their natural enemies and can increase at an unnatural rate.

To pot a palm, supply good potting soil, adequate drainage, and not too big a container. As with all potted plants, pot or repot a palm in a container just slightly larger than the one it's in.

Some shade-tolerant palms such as *Rhapis*, *Chamaedorea*, and *Howea* can spend decades in pots indoors. Others that later can reach great size —*Phoenix*, *Washingtonia*, *Chamaerops*—make charming temporary indoor plants but must eventually be moved.

Planting holes for palms should generally be the same depth as and 1–2 ft. wider than root ball. Amend the back fill with organic matter; water faithfully until established. From then on, palms need little maintenance; they thrive with reasonably fertile soil and adequate water. All tropical palms do their growing during warm times of year. Washing with a hose is beneficial, especially for palms exposed to dust and beyond reach of rain or dew; it helps keep down spider mites and sucking insects that find refuge in the long leaf stems.

Feather palms and many fan palms look neater when old leaves are removed after they have turned brown. Make neat cuts close to trunk, leaving leaf bases. Some palms shed old leaf bases on their own. Others, including *Syagrus* and *Chamaedorea*, may hold old bases. You can remove them by slicing them off at the very bottom of base (be careful not to cut into trunk).

Many palm admirers say that dead leaves of *Washingtonia* should remain on the tree, the thatch being part of the palm's character. If you also feel this way, you can cut lower fronds in a uniform way close to trunk, but leave leaf bases, which present a rather pleasant lattice surface.

Here are nine roles that the right kinds of palms can fill. Palms named in each listing are described under their own names elsewhere in this book.

Sturdy palms for park and avenue plantings and for vertical effects in large gardens: *Archontophoenix*, *Brahea*, *Cocos*, *Jubaea*, *Livistona*, *Phoenix canariensis*, *P. dactylifera*, *P. loureiri*, *P. rupicola*, *Ptychosperma elegans*, *Roystonea*, *Sabal* (tall species), *Syagrus*, *Washingtonia*.

Small to medium-size palms for sheltered areas in frost-free gardens: *Archontophoenix*, *Caryota*, *Chamaedorea*, *Chamaerops*, *Chrysalidocarpus*, *Howea*.

Small to medium-size palms for gardens in areas of occasional frosts: *Acoelorrhaphe*, *Brahea armata*, *Butia*, *Chamaedorea*, *Chamaerops*, *Livistona*, *Neodypsis*, *Phoenix roebelenii*, *Ptychosperma macarthuri*, *Trachycarpus*.

Hardiest palms, which will endure temperatures significantly below freezing: *Brahea armata*, *Chamaerops*, *Jubaea*, *Livistona*, *Phoenix canariensis*, *P. dactylifera*, *P. loureiri*, *Rhapis*, *Sabal mexicana*, *S. minor*, *S. palmetto*, *Trachycarpus*, *Washingtonia*.

Frost becomes more damaging to palms as it extends its stay and is repeated. Light frosts for half an hour may leave no damage, but the same frost during a period of 4 hours may damage some palms, kill others. Simplest damage is burned leaf edges, but frost may affect whole leaves, parts of trunks, or crown. Damage in crown is usually fatal (though some have recovered). Hardiness is also a matter of size; larger plants may pass through severe frosts unharmed while smaller ones perish.

PALMS AND POOLS: PERFECT PARTNERS

Palms are ideal for landscaping beside swimming pools because they do not drop leaves (though some drop fruit). Mature plants of *Phoenix reclinata* or *Chamaerops humilis*, with their curved trunks, create a tropical illusion. But whether palm trunks are curved or upright or topped with fan or feather leaves, they can create beautiful mirror effects in the water. Watch out for thorns on spiny types.

Salt-tolerant palms for seaside planting: *Butia*, *Chamaerops*, *Cocos nucifera*, *Phoenix canariensis*, *P. dactylifera*, *P. reclinata*, *Roystonea*, *Sabal blackburniana*, *S. palmetto*, *Washingtonia robusta*.

Palms for hot, dry climates: *Brahea armata*, *Butia*, *Chamaerops*, *Livistona chinensis*, *L. mariae*, *Phoenix canariensis*, *P. dactylifera*, *P. loureiri*, *P. sylvestris*, *Sabal mexicana*, *S. minor*, *Washingtonia*.

Palms to grow under lath or overhangs; or indoors: *Archontophoenix*, *Caryota mitis*, *C. ochlandra*, *C. urens*, *Chamaedorea*, *Howea*, young *Livistona*, *Phoenix reclinata* (when young), *P. roebelenii*, *Rhapis*, *Trachycarpus* (when young). Indoor palms should occasionally be brought outdoors into mild light.

Palms as underplantings: young palms, especially slow growers such as *Livistona chinensis* and *Chamaerops*, can be used effectively as plantings under tall trees. They'll stay low for 5 to 10 years. When they get too tall, move them to a location where you need height.

Palms for night lighting: thanks to their stateliness and spectacular leaves, all palms are good subjects for this. Backlight them, light them from below, or direct lights to silhouette them against light-colored wall.

PALO VERDE. See CERCIDIUM

PAMPAS GRASS. See CORTADERIA selloana

PANDA PLANT. See KALANCHOE tomentosa

PANDOREA

Bignoniaceae

EVERGREEN VINES

☘ ZONES 16–27

☼ ◐ PARTIAL SHADE IN HOT CLIMATES

💧 REGULAR TO MODERATE WATER

L eaves divided into glossy oval leaflets; clusters of trumpet-shaped flowers. Climb by twining. They are attractive even out of bloom.

Pandorea jasminoides

P. jasminoides (Bignonia jasminoides, Tecoma jasminoides). BOWER VINE. Fast to 20–30 ft. Slender stems, distinguished glossy medium to dark green foliage. Leaves have five to nine egg-shaped leaflets 1–2 in. long. Flowers white with pink throats, 1½–2 in. long, drop cleanly after June–October bloom. 'Alba' and the more vigorous 'Lady D.' have pure white flowers; 'Rosea' has pink flowers with rose pink throats. There is a form with variegated leaves. Plant in lee of prevailing wind. Prolonged freezes will kill it.

P. pandorana (Bignonia australis, Tecoma australis). WONGA-WONGA VINE. More vigorous than *P. jasminoides*; needs room to grow. Glossy foliage handsome in all seasons. Small (to ¾-in.-long) spring flowers are yellowish or pinkish white, usually with brownish purple spots in throat. Prune ends of branches heavily after bloom.

PANICUM virgatum

SWITCH GRASS

Poaceae (Gramineae)

PERENNIAL GRASS

☘ ZONES 1–11, 14–21, 28–43

☼ ◐ FULL SUN OR LIGHT SHADE

💧💧💧 MUCH TO LITTLE WATER

N ative to the tall grass prairie of the Midwest. Upright clump of narrow, deep green or gray-green leaves is topped by slender flower clusters; clump reaches 4–7 ft. high in bloom. Clusters open into loose, airy clouds of pinkish blossoms that fade to white, then brown. Foliage turns yellow in fall, gradually fades to beige. Both foliage and flowers persist all winter, providing interest in cold-weather gardens. 'Haense Herms' is grown for red fall foliage, 'Heavy Metal' for stiffly upright silvery blue leaves that turn bright yellow in autumn; both reach 4–5 ft. high.

Panicum virgatum

Plant tolerates many soils, moisture levels, and exposures, even salt winds. Attractive silhouette in winter. Use as accent in large informal flower border or as screening.

PANSY. See VIOLA

PAPAVER

POPPY

Papaveraceae

PERENNIALS AND ANNUALS

ZONES VARY BY SPECIES

FULL SUN

REGULAR TO MODERATE WATER

Papaver orientale

Poppies provide gay spring and summer color for borders and cutting. Give ordinary soil, good drainage; feed lightly until established. Perennials tend to be short lived. When using poppies as cut flowers, sear clipped stem ends in flame before placing in water.

P. alpinum (P. burseri). ALPINE POPPY. Perennial. Zones 3–9, 14–17, 32–41; best adapted to colder climates. Rock garden plant with basal foliage rosette and 5–8-in.-high flower stalk. Blue-green, nearly hairless, divided leaves. Spring flowers are 1–1½ in. across, come in white, orange, yellow, salmon. Blooms first year from seed sown in fall or early spring.

P. atlanticum. Perennial. Zones 3–9, 14–24, 32, 34, 37. To 1½ ft. high, with jagged-edged, softly hairy leaves to 6 in. long. Bright orange, 3-in. flowers in summer.

P. nudicaule. ICELAND POPPY. Short-lived perennial in Zones 1–6, 10, 32–45; grown as an annual in mild-winter Zones 7–9, 14–24, 26, (upper half), 28, 31. Divided leaves with coarse hairs. Slender, hairy stems 1–2 ft. high. Cup-shaped, slightly fragrant flowers to 3 in. across, in yellow, orange, salmon, rose, pink, cream, white. In cold-winter areas, sow seed in earliest spring for summer bloom; or set out summer-sown plants in autumn for bloom the following year. In mild climates, set out plants in fall for winter and early spring bloom. To prolong bloom, pick flowers frequently. Champagne Bubbles is most widely grown strain. Low-growing Wonderland strain (to 10 in.) comes in mixed or single colors. Oregon Rainbows has larger flowers than the species, in a wider color range that includes bicolors and picotees; outside of Northwest, produces many buds that fail to open. Misato Carnival strain has 6-in. flowers on 2–3-ft. stems.

P. orientale. ORIENTAL POPPY. Perennial. Zones 1–11, 14–21, 30–45. Needs winter chill for best performance. Height variable; some types are 16 in. tall, others reach 4 ft. Hairy, coarsely cut leaves. Single or double flowers are large to very large (to 11 in. across in some varieties); colors include white, pink, orange yellow, orange, scarlet, and dark red, usually with a dark blotch at base of each petal. A great many named varieties are sold; they bloom in late spring and early summer, then die back in midsummer. The sterile Minicap Hybrids from California were bred for greater heat tolerance and for profuse bloom over a longer period (2 to 4 months). In all types, new leafy growth appears in fall, lasts over winter, and develops rapidly in spring. Set sprawling plants such as baby's breath nearby to cover the bare areas after the poppies die down. Plant dormant roots in fall with tops 3 in. deep. Set container-grown plants flush with soil line. Provide good drainage and room for air circulation. Divide crowded clumps in August, after foliage has died down.

P. rhoeas. FLANDERS FIELD POPPY, SHIRLEY POPPY. Annual. All zones, but best where summers are cool. Slender, branching, hairy-stemmed plant 2–5 ft. high. Short, irregularly divided leaves; single or double flowers 2 in. or wider, in red, pink, white, orange, scarlet, salmon, bicolors. Selections bearing single scarlet flowers with a black base are sold as 'American Legion' or 'Flanders Field'. Angels' Choir strain offers double flowers in a wide range of colors on 2–2½-ft. stems. Broadcast seed mixed with fine sand. Sow successively for bloom from spring through summer. Take cut flowers when buds first show color. Remove seed capsules (old flower bases) weekly to prolong bloom season. Notorious self-sower.

P. somniferum. OPIUM POPPY. Annual. All zones. To 4 ft. tall, with virtually hairless gray-green leaves and usually double, sometimes single, 4–5-in. flowers in white or rosy shades (pink and red to purple). Late spring bloom. Large, decorative seed capsules. Opium is derived from the sap of the green seed capsules; ripe ones yield large quantities of the poppy seed used in baking. Because of its narcotic properties, this species is not as widely offered as many other types.

Papaveraceae. The poppy family of annuals, perennials, and shrubs displays showy flowers usually borne singly. In addition to *Papaver*, members include California poppy (*Eschscholzia*) and Matilija poppy (*Romneya*).

PAPAYA. See CARICA papaya

PAPER MULBERRY. See BROUSSONETIA papyrifera

PAPHIOPEDILUM

LADY'S SLIPPER

Orchidaceae

TERRESTRIAL ORCHIDS

INDOOR AND GREENHOUSE PLANTS, EXCEPT AS NOTED

INDIRECT LIGHT

KEEP SOIL MOIST AT ALL TIMES

Paphiopedilum insigne

Sometimes sold as *Cypripedium*, these terrestrial orchids are native to tropical regions of Asia. The group includes large-flowered hybrids grown commercially for cut flowers. Blooms are perky, usually one to a stem, occasionally two or more. Many of them shine as if lacquered. Flowers may be white, yellow, green with white stripes, pure green, or a combination of background colors and markings in tan, mahogany brown, maroon, green, and white.

Graceful, arching foliage (no pseudobulbs) is either plain green or mottled. Plain-leafed forms usually flower in winter, mottled-leafed forms in summer. Most plants obtained from orchid dealers are hybrids.

In general, mottled-leafed forms do best with temperatures of about 60° to 65°F/16° to 18°C at night, 70° to 85°F/21° to 29°C during the day. Plain-leafed forms require temperatures of 50° to 55°F/10° to 13°C at night, 65° to 75°F/18° to 24°C during the day. They have no rest period. Combine equal parts ground bark and sandy loam for a good potting medium. Don't plant in oversize pot; plants thrive when crowded. Hardiest kinds can be grown in pots indoors. Thrive in less light than most orchids require.

P. insigne. Can remain outdoors year-round only in Zone 25. Polished flowers on stiff, brown, hairy stems any time from October to March. Sepals and petals green and white, with brown spots and stripes; pouch reddish brown.

PAPYRUS. See CYPERUS papyrus

PARADISE PALM. See HOWEA forsterana

PARKINSONIA aculeata

JERUSALEM THORN, MEXICAN PALO VERDE

Fabaceae (Leguminosae)

DECIDUOUS TREE

ZONES 8–29

FULL SUN

REGULAR TO LITTLE WATER

Parkinsonia aculeata

Rapid growth at first, then slowing; eventually reaches 15–30 ft. high and wide. Yellow-

P

green bark, spiny twigs, picturesque form. Sparse foliage; leaves 6–9 in. long, with many tiny leaflets that quickly fall in drought or cold. Numerous yellow flowers in loose, 3–7-in.-long clusters. Long bloom season in spring; intermittent bloom throughout year.

Good tree for water-conserving gardens, since it grows in dry soil; also performs well in moist soil as long as it's well drained. Tolerates alkaline soil. Stake young trees and train for high or low branching. Requires minimal attention once established. As shade tree, it filters sun rather than blocking it. Litter drop is a problem on hard surfaces. Thorns and sparse foliage rule it out of tailored gardens. Flowering branches are attractive in arrangements.

PARROTIA persica

PERSIAN PARROTIA
Hamamelidaceae
DECIDUOUS SHRUB OR SMALL TREE
☘ ZONES 3–6, 15–17, 31–41
☼ FULL SUN
💧💧 REGULAR TO MODERATE WATER

Parrotia persica

Native to Iran. Slow growing to 30 ft. or more, but most often seen as a shrub or multi-trunked tree to 15 ft. Young trees are fairly upright; older ones are wide-spreading, rounded. Choice and colorful; attractive all year. Most dramatic display comes in autumn: leaves usually turn golden yellow, then orange or rosy pink, and finally scarlet. Attractive smooth, gray bark; in mature trees, it flakes off to reveal white, tan, and green patches beneath. Blooms in late winter or early spring before leaves open. Flowers have dense heads of red stamens surrounded by woolly brown bracts; blooming plants have an overall reddish haze. New foliage unfurls reddish purple, matures to lustrous dark green. Leaves are ¾ in. long, oval, shallowly toothed along upper half.

Prefers slightly acid soil but tolerates alkaline and chalky soils. Will also withstand light shade. Pest resistant.

PARROT'S BEAK. See LOTUS berthelotii

PARSLEY

Apiaceae (Umbelliferae)
BIENNIAL HERB TREATED AS ANNUAL
☘ ALL ZONES
☼◐ AFTERNOON SHADE IN HOT-SUMMER AREAS
💧 REGULAR WATER

Parsley

Attractive edging for herb, vegetable, or flower garden; also looks good in boxes or pots. Plants are 6–12 in. high, with tufted, finely cut, dark green leaves. Use leaves fresh or dried as seasoning, fresh as garnish. Most satisfactorily grown anew every year. Buy plants at nursery or sow seed in place (in spring in cold-winter climates; in fall or early spring where winter is mild; in early fall in low desert). Soak seed in warm water for 24 hours before planting. Even after soaking, it may not sprout for several weeks: according to an old story, parsley seeds must go to the devil and come back before sprouting. Thin seedlings to 6–8 in. apart.

THE SHOWY PARSLEY OR THE COOKING PARSLEY?

The Italian, flat-leafed parsley is the tastiest type for cooking. The curly varieties make the most attractive garnish and are appealing as a low border in a flower bed.

PARSNIP

Apiaceae (Umbelliferae)
BIENNIAL GROWN AS AN ANNUAL
☘ ALL ZONES
☼ FULL SUN
💧 MAINTAIN EVEN SOIL MOISTURE

Parsnip

Needs deep, well-prepared, loose soil for long roots; roots of some varieties are 15 in. long. In cold-winter areas, plant seeds in late spring and harvest in fall; leave surplus in ground to be dug as needed in winter. Cold makes the roots sweeter. In mild-climate areas, sow in fall and harvest in spring; in these areas, mature roots will continue to grow if they are left in ground, becoming tough and woody. Soak seeds in water 24 hours before planting to improve germination. Sow ½ in. deep in rows spaced 2 ft. apart; thin seedlings to 3 in. apart.

PARTHENOCISSUS (Ampelopsis)

Vitaceae
DECIDUOUS VINES
☘ ZONES VARY BY SPECIES
☼◐💧 SUN OR SHADE
💧 REGULAR WATER

Parthenocissus quinquefolia

Cling to walls by sucker discs at ends of tendrils. Superb and dependable orange to scarlet fall leaf color. Flowers are insignificant. Attractive to birds. Think twice before planting them against wood or shingle siding; they can creep under it, and their clinging tendrils are hard to remove at repainting time.

P. henryana. SILVERVEIN CREEPER. Zones 4–9, 14–17, 31, warmer parts of 32. Native to China. To 20 ft.; less aggressive growth than the other species. Leaves have five 1–2½-in.-long leaflets; they open purplish, then turn dark bronzy green with pronounced silver veining and purple undersides. Color is best in shade, fades to plain green in strong light. Leaves turn rich red in autumn. Clings to walls, but needs some support to get started. Also good spilling over walls or as a small-scale ground cover.

P. quinquefolia. VIRGINIA CREEPER. Zones 1–24, 26–43. Native to eastern U.S. Big, vigorous vine (to 30–50 ft. or more) that clings or runs over ground, fence, trellis, trees. Looser growth than *P. tricuspidata*; will drape its trailing branches over trellis, trees. Leaves divided into five separate 6-in. leaflets with saw-toothed edges; foliage turns bright to dull red in fall. Good ground cover on slopes; can control erosion. 'Engelmannii' has smaller leaves, denser growth.

P. tricuspidata. BOSTON IVY. Zones 2–24, 31–41. Native to China, Japan. Semievergreen in mild-winter areas. Even more vigorous than *P. quinquefolia*. Glossy leaves to 8 in. wide are variable in shape, usually three lobed or divided

Parthenocissus tricuspidata

into three leaflets; fall color varies from orange to burgundy. Clings tightly, grows fast to make dense, even wall cover. This is the ivy of the Ivy League; covers brick or stone in areas where English ivy freezes. In intensely hot regions, plant only on walls with northern or eastern exposure. Leaves of 'Beverly Brooks' and 'Green Showers' are larger than those of the species; leaves of 'Lowii' and 'Veitchii' are considerably smaller.

PARTRIDGEBERRY. See MITCHELLA repens

PASPALUM

Poaceae (Gramineae)

LAWN GRASSES

❖ ZONES VARY BY SPECIES

☼ FULL SUN

💧 REGULAR WATER

Paspalum vaginatum

Large genus comprising several species used for pasture or hay. Many (but not all) are native to coastal regions of the southeastern U.S. Many have been introduced from South America or Southeast Asia. Two are used as lawn grasses in warm regions.

P. notatum. BAHIA GRASS. Zones 25–32. Tough, rather coarse grass widely used for lawns in Florida. Needs little fertilizer and can endure periodic drought, but seedheads need frequent mowing to prevent unkempt look. Takes heavy foot traffic.

P. vaginatum. SEASHORE PASPALUM. Zones 17, 24–32. Native to sandy soils near the seashore from North Carolina to Texas. Finer textured than bahia grass and a deeper green; tolerates salty soil better than most grasses. Keep mowed close (to ¾ in.) with a reel mower. Seashore paspalum is usually sold as sod. Named varieties are available in some parts of the country.

PASQUE FLOWER. See PULSATILLA vulgaris

PASSIFLORA

PASSION VINE

Passifloraceae

EVERGREEN, SEMIEVERGREEN, OR DECIDUOUS VINES

❖ ZONES VARY BY SPECIES

☼ FULL SUN

💧💧 REGULAR TO MODERATE WATER

Passiflora alatocaerulea

Climb by tendrils to 20–30 ft.; bloom during warm weather. Flower parts can be seen to symbolize elements of the passion of Christ, hence plant's common name. The lacy crown represents a halo or crown of thorns; the five stamens, the five wounds; the ten petal-like parts, the ten faithful apostles.

Vigorous, likely to overgrow and tangle; to keep plant open and prevent buildup of dead inner tangle, prune annually after second year, cutting excess branches back to base or juncture with another branch. Tolerant of many soils. Favorite food of caterpillars of gulf fritillary butterfly.

Use vines on trellises or walls for their vigor and bright, showy flowers; or use as soil-holding bank cover. In cold-winter climates, use as greenhouse or house plants, training plants on a trellis or winding them on hoops of wire for wreath effect.

P. alatocaerulea (P. pfordtii). Evergreen or semievergreen. Zones 5–9, 12–29; dies to ground in colder part of range. Hybrid between *P. caerulea* and *P. alata*, a species not described here. Best known, most widely planted, probably least subject to damage from caterpillars. Three-lobed leaves 3 in. long. Fragrant, 3½–4-in. flowers, white shaded pink and lavender; deep blue or purple crown. Forms no fruit. In colder areas, give it a warm place out of wind, against wall or under overhang. Mulch roots in winter. Excellent windowsill bloomer.

P. caerulea. BLUE CROWN PASSION FLOWER. Evergreen or semievergreen. Zones 5–9, 12–29; dies to ground in colder part of range. Five-lobed leaves, smaller than those of *P. alatocaerulea.* Flowers also smaller, in greenish white with white-and-purple crown. Edible small, oval fruit with orange rind and red seeds.

P. edulis. PASSION FRUIT. Semievergreen. Zones 15–17, 21–25, 27. Leaves three lobed, deeply toothed, light yellow green. Flowers white with white-and-purple crown, 2 in. across. Fruit produced in spring and fall: deep purple, fragrant, 3 in. long, delicious used in beverages, fruit salads, sherbets. 'Nancy Garrison' is a hardier version. There is also a yellow-fruited variety.

P. incarnata. WILD PASSION VINE, MAYPOP. Deciduous. Zones 4–10, 12–33. Native to southeastern U.S. Hardiest of the passion flowers, surviving temperatures at least as low as –10°F/–23°C and possibly even lower. Dies to ground in colder part of range. Three-lobed leaves are 4–6 in. wide; freely produced flowers are 2–3 in. wide, white or pale lavender, with filaments banded in purple or pink. Yellow, 2-in. fruits are edible. Spreads vigorously from underground roots and can become an attractive pest. Although this plant is seldom sold in nurseries, it is easily grown from seed.

P. 'Incense'. Deciduous. Zones 5–31. Hardy to 0°F/–18°C; holds its leaves through short cold spells, dies to ground when weather turns colder. Hybrid between *P. incarnata* and an Argentinian species. Flowers are 5 in. wide, violet with lighter crown, with sweet pea–like fragrance. Egg-shaped, 2-in. fruit has fragrant, tasty pulp; when ripe, it turns from olive to yellow green, then drops.

P. jamesonii. Evergreen. Zones 14–28. Glossy, three-lobed leaves. Profusion of long-tubed (to 4-in.) salmon to coral flowers. Fast bank or fence cover. This and similar plants are sold as 'Coral Seas'.

P. 'Lavender Lady'. Evergreen. Zones 16–25, 27. Profuse show of 4-in. lavender purple flowers with deep violet crown.

P. mollissima. BANANA PASSION VINE. Evergreen. Zones 12–27. Soft green foliage; leaves three lobed, deeply toothed. Long-tubed pink to rose flowers 3 in. across. Yellow, 4–6-in.-long fruit. Rampant growth can be a plus or a minus: the plant's vigor makes it a good bank cover, but a problem if planted with trees or shrubs.

P. vitifolia. Evergreen. Zones 16, 17, 23–25. Grapelike, 6-in. deep green leaves set off bright red flowers 3½ in. long.

PASSION FRUIT. See PASSIFLORA edulis

PASSION VINE. See PASSIFLORA

PATRINIA

Valerianaceae

PERENNIALS

❖ ZONES 3–6, 15–17, 31–41

☼◐ EXPOSURE NEEDS VARY BY SPECIES

💧 REGULAR WATER

Patrinia triloba

Perennials with mounds of deeply cut or lobed leaves that produce stems bearing few or no leaves and flat-topped clusters of tiny yellow or white flowers. Summer bloom. They are useful for blending with other border perennials. Long-lasting cut flowers. All appreciate rich, well-drained soil.

P. scabiosifolia. Grows to 5–6 ft. and may require staking, but thinly foliaged flower stalks and open showers of yellow flower clusters give plant a see-through quality that makes it appropriate for either front or rear of border. Finely divided leaves to 6 in. 'Compact Selection' and 'Nagoya' grow only 1½–3 ft. tall. Cut flowers last several weeks and mix well with other kinds in arrangements. Full sun.

P. triloba. Grows 1 ft. tall and spreads slowly to make a small-scale ground cover. Glossy deep green, three- to five-lobed leaves are 2 in. long, finely divided. Yellow flowers. Grows best in light shade.

P. villosa. Leaves to 6 in. long, either divided or uncut. Sprawling flower stems to 1½ ft. hold showers of white blossoms. Full sun.

PRACTICAL GARDENING DICTIONARY
PLEASE SEE PAGES 545–616

PAULOWNIA tomentosa (P. imperialis)

EMPRESS TREE

Bignoniaceae

DECIDUOUS TREE

⚡ ZONES 3–9, 11–24, 31–35, 37, 39

☼ ◐ FULL SUN OR PARTIAL SHADE

💧 REGULAR WATER

Paulownia tomentosa

Native to China. Somewhat similar to catalpa in growth habit, leaves. Fast growth to 40–50 ft., with nearly equal spread. Heavy trunk and heavy, nearly horizontal branches. Foliage gives tropical effect: light green, heart-shaped leaves are 5–12 in. long, 4–7 in. wide. No significant fall color. Brown flower buds the size of small olives form in autumn and persist over winter; they open before the leaves in early spring, forming 6–12-in.-long, upright clusters of trumpet-shaped, 2-in.-long, fragrant flowers of lilac blue with darker spotting and yellow stripes on the inside. Flowers are followed by 1½–2-in. seed capsules shaped like tops; these remain on tree with flower buds. Does not bloom well where winters are very cold (buds freeze) or very mild (buds may drop off).

Performs best in deep, moist, well-drained soil, though it will grow in many soils. Tolerates air pollution. Protect from strong winds. Plant where falling flowers and leaves are not objectionable. Not a tree to garden under because of dense shade, surface roots. If tree is cut back annually or every other year, it will grow as billowy foliage mass with giant-size leaves up to 2 ft. long; however, such pruning will reduce or eliminate flower production.

PAUROTIS wrightii. See ACOELORRHAPHE wrightii

PAWPAW. See ASIMINA triloba

PAXISTIMA canbyi

Celastraceae

EVERGREEN SHRUB

⚡ ZONES 1–10, 14–21, 32–43

☼ ◐ PARTIAL SHADE IN HOT CLIMATES

💧 REGULAR WATER

Paxistima canbyi

Native to mountains of Virginia and West Virginia. Slowly forms a mat 9–12 in. high, 3–5 ft. wide. Leathery leaves, ¼–1 in. long and ¼ in. wide, are shiny dark green, turning bronzy in fall and winter. Insignificant flowers. Useful as low edging, ground cover. Best in well-drained soil.

PEA

Fabaceae (Leguminosae)

ANNUAL

⚡ ALL ZONES

☼ FULL SUN

💧 REGULAR WATER

Pea

Sometimes called garden or English pea to distinguish it from Southern pea (a category including black-eyed pea, cowpea, and crowder pea); for the latter, see Southern Pea.

Easy crop to grow when conditions are right, and delicious when freshly picked. Peas need coolness and humidity and must be planted at just the right time. If you have space and don't mind the bother, grow tall (vining) peas on trellises, strings, or screen; they reach 6 ft. or more and bear heavily. A good tall variety is 'Alderman'. Bush types are more commonly grown in home gardens; they require no support. Fine bush varieties are 'Green Arrow', 'Little Marvel', 'Morse's Progress No. 9', 'Freezonian', and 'Blue Bantam'. An unusually good vegetable (and one popular in Asian

cooking) is edible-pod snow or sugar pea; 'Mammoth Melting Sugar' is a tall vining variety, 'Dwarf Gray Sugar' a bushy one. 'Sugar Snap' is an edible-pod pea with full complement of full-size peas inside.

Peas need soil that is slightly acid to slightly alkaline, water retentive but fast draining. They are hardy and should be planted just as early in spring as ground can be worked. Where winters are mild and spring days quickly become too warm for peas, plant October–February, the later times applying where winters are coldest. Sow 2 in. deep in light soil, ½–1 in. deep in heavy soil or in winter. Moisten ground thoroughly before planting; do not supply supplemental irrigation until seedlings have broken through surface. Leave 2 ft. between rows and thin seedlings to stand 2 in. apart. Successive plantings several days apart will lengthen bearing season, but don't plant so late that summer heat will overtake ripening peas; most are ready to harvest in 60 to 70 days.

Plants need little fertilizer, but if soil is very light, give them one application of complete fertilizer. If weather turns warm and dry, supply water in furrows; overhead watering encourages mildew. Provide support for vining peas as soon as tendrils form. When peas begin to mature, pick all pods that are ready; if seeds ripen, plant will stop producing. Vines are brittle; steady them with one hand while picking with the other. Above all, shell and cook (or freeze) peas right after picking.

PEACH and NECTARINE

Rosaceae

DECIDUOUS FRUIT TREES

⚡ REGIONS VARY BY VARIETY

☼ FULL SUN

💧 REGULAR WATER

▶ SEE CHART

Peach

Trees of peach (*Prunus persica*) and nectarine (*P. p. nucipersica*) look alike and have the same cultural needs. Where fruit is concerned, nectarines differ from peaches in several respects: they have smooth skins; in some varieties, flavor is slightly different; and many are more susceptible to brown rot of stone fruit (see below for controls). Here we consider fruiting peaches and nectarines; for strictly flowering ones, see *Prunus*.

Peaches and nectarines of one variety or another can be grown in the Southeast, Mid-Atlantic, central and lower Midwest, temperate areas near the Great Lakes, California, and dry-summer areas of the Pacific Northwest and Intermountain West. Extra-hardy selections extend peach- and nectarine-growing into colder areas, such as the Northeast. Varieties tend to be regionally adapted; for the best choices for your area, see the chart and also consult local nurseries and your Cooperative Extension Office.

In most regions, crops ripen between June and September, depending on variety. For good harvests, trees need some winter chilling; most varieties require 600 to 900 hours of 45°F/7°C or lower temperatures during the dormant season. Only specially selected varieties with a low winter chill requirement do well in extremely mild-winter areas. Lack of winter chilling results in delayed leaf-out, a scanty crop, and eventual death of tree. In areas of late frosts, early-blooming varieties are risky. Plants also need clear, hot weather during the growing season; where spring is cool and rainy, they set few flowers, pollinate poorly, and get peach-leaf curl.

A standard-size fruiting peach or nectarine grows rapidly to 25 ft. high and wide; properly pruned trees are usually kept at a height of 10–12 ft. They start bearing large crops when 3 or 4 years old and reach peak production at 8 to 12 years. Natural or genetic dwarf trees, most of which grow 5–6 ft. tall and produce medium-size fruit, are useful in tubs and confined planting areas. With a few exceptions (see comments in chart), peaches and nectarines are self-fertile.

Peach and nectarine trees require good drainage, a regular fertilizing program, and heavier pruning than other fruit trees. When planting a bare-root tree that is an unbranched "whip," cut it back to 2–3½ ft. above ground (the thicker the trunk, the less severe the cutting back). New branches will form below cut. After first year's growth, select three well-

▶ page 421

P

PEACH and NECTARINE

VARIETY	ADAPTABILITY	FRUIT	COMMENTS
PEACHES			
'Babcock'	Coastal California	Small to medium. Freestone. Light pink skin blushed red, little fuzz. White flesh reddens near pit. Sweet flavor with some tang. Early	Old-timer. Low winter chill requirement. Thin heavily for good-size fruit
'Belle of Georgia'	Southeast, Mid-Atlantic, central and lower Midwest	Large. Freestone. Skin is creamy white blushed red; flesh is white. Fine flavor. Midseason	Vigorous tree; heavy bearer. Frost tolerant
'Biscoe'	Southeast, Mid-Atlantic, Northeast, lower Midwest	Medium to large. Freestone. Attractive red-and-yellow skin; deep yellow to orange flesh. Good flavor. Midseason	From North Carolina. Vigorous, productive
'Bonanza II'	Southeast, Mid-Atlantic, lower Midwest, Great Lakes, West	Large. Freestone. Skin orange flushed red; sweet yellow flesh. Midseason	Genetic dwarf 5–6 ft. high; showy flowers. Fruit is more flavorful than that of 'Bonanza', the original dwarf variety for home gardens
'Canadian Harmony'	Northeast, Great Lakes, central Midwest	Large. Freestone. Red-flushed yellow skin, little fuzz. Flesh yellow, slightly red at pit. Good flavor. Midseason	Large tree; extremely vigorous and productive
'Cresthaven'	Southeast, Mid-Atlantic, Great Lakes, central Midwest, West	Medium to large. Freestone. Golden yellow skin blushed red; yellow flesh. High-quality, firm fruit. Midseason to late	From Michigan. Blooms late. Fruit holds well on tree. Tasty fresh but also excellent for freezing, canning
'Dixiland'	Southeast	Large. Freestone. Yellow skin blushed red; little fuzz. Firm yellow flesh. Good quality. Late midseason	From Georgia. Vigorous, productive. Showy flowers
'Early Elberta' ('Improved Elberta', Gleason Elberta', 'Lemon Elberta')	Southeast, Mid-Atlantic, Great Lakes, central and lower Midwest, West	Better color and flavor than 'Elberta'; also ripens about 1 week earlier	Needs somewhat less heat and less winter chill than 'Elberta'; less subject to fruit drop. Thin heavily for good-size fruit
'Elberta'	Southeast, Mid-Atlantic, Great Lakes, central and lower Midwest, West	Medium to large. Freestone. Yellow skin blushed red; yellow flesh. Good quality. Midseason	From Georgia. Needs good amount of winter chill, high summer heat to ripen to full flavor
'Flordaking'	Southeast (warmer parts), Florida	Medium to large. Semicling. Firm yellow fruit. Early	Very vigorous. Good fruit if thinned well. Low winter chill requirement
'Garnet Beauty'	Southeast, Mid-Atlantic, Great Lakes, central Midwest	Medium to large. Semifreestone. Red-blushed yellow skin; yellow flesh streaked with red. Early	Earlier-ripening mutation of 'Redhaven' originating in Canada. Vigorous tree, heavy bearer
'Halberta' ('Hal-Berta Giant')	Central Midwest, West	Very large. Freestone. Very smooth yellow skin mottled and flushed red. Firm golden flesh. Ripens with 'Elberta' in midseason	From Illinois. Vigorous grower, but not very productive. Self-sterile; pollinate with another variety (but not 'J. H. Hale')
'Halehaven'	Southeast, Mid-Atlantic, Great Lakes, central Midwest, West	Medium to large. Freestone. Highly colored yellow fruit is firm, very sweet. Midseason	From Michigan. Flower and leaf buds are very winter hardy. Use fruit fresh or canned
'Harbrite'	Southeast (colder parts), Mid-Atlantic, Great Lakes	Medium to large. Freestone. Skin is yellow heavily flushed red; yellow flesh. Early	Heavy producer
'Harvester'	Southeast, Mid-Atlantic, lower Midwest	Medium-size. Freestone. Yellow fruit of excellent quality. Early	Has occasional low yields in some areas
'J. H. Hale'	Southeast, Mid-Atlantic, Northeast (warmer parts), Great Lakes, central Midwest	Very large. Freestone. Highly colored, fairly smooth-skinned yellow fruit of good quality. Fine keeper. Late midseason	Needs cross-pollination by another variety (but not 'Halberta')

P

▶

PEACH and NECTARINE

VARIETY	ADAPTABILITY	FRUIT	COMMENTS
PEACHES			
'LaFeliciana'	Southeast	Medium-size. Freestone. Yellow fruit of high quality. Early midseason	Originated in Louisiana
'Loring'	Southeast, Mid-Atlantic, Great Lakes, central and lower Midwest, West	Large. Freestone. Attractive yellow skin imbued with red, little fuzz. Moderately juicy yellow flesh. Good quality. Midseason	Vigorous. Showy flowers appear early; susceptible to frost
'Madison'	Southeast, Mid-Atlantic, Northeast, central Midwest, West	Medium-size. Freestone. Golden yellow skin blushed bright red. Firm golden flesh. Very good flavor. Midseason	Seedling of 'Redhaven' from Virginia. Good frost tolerance during bloom period. Heavy bearer
'Ouachita Gold'	Southeast, Mid-Atlantic, lower Midwest	Large. Freestone. Yellow fruit of good quality. Late	Heavy producer. Showy flowers
'Raritan Rose'	Southeast (colder parts), Mid-Atlantic, Northeast	Medium to large. Freestone. Red skin; somewhat soft white flesh streaked red. Midseason	From New Jersey. Vigorous, productive. Needs considerable winter chill
'Redglobe'	Southeast, Mid-Atlantic, lower Midwest, West	Medium to large. Freestone. Attractive red-flushed yellow skin, very fuzzy. Firm yellow flesh. Fair to good flavor. Midseason	Vigorous, productive. Flower buds tender to frost. Showy flowers. Fruit suitable for eating fresh, canning, or freezing
'Redhaven'	Southeast, Mid-Atlantic, Northeast, Great Lakes, central and lower Midwest, West	Medium-size. Freestone. Yellow skin blushed bright red. Firm yellow flesh. Good flavor. Early	Among best of all early peaches. Most important peach variety grown east of the Rockies. Very productive; needs thinning. Colors up early, so test for ripeness. Good fresh; freezes well
'Redskin'	Southeast, Mid-Atlantic, central and lower Midwest	Large. Freestone. Yellow skin with good red coloring; yellow flesh. High quality. Midseason	'Elberta' seedling from Maryland. Showy flowers. Fruit good for eating fresh, canning, or freezing
'Reliance'	Southeast (colder parts), Mid-Atlantic, Northeast, Great Lakes, central Midwest	Medium to large. Freestone. Yellow skin blushed dull medium red; yellow flesh can be fairly soft. Fair flavor. Midseason	Developed in New Hampshire. Very hardy; has produced crops after temperatures of −25°F/ −32°C. Showy flowers. Needs heavy thinning
'Rio Grande'	Southeast (warmer parts), California, Florida	Medium to large. Freestone. Red-blushed yellow skin. Firm yellow flesh. Mild flavor. Early	Low-chill variety from Florida. Productive tree with showy flowers. Fruit tends to vary in size and have an irregular surface
'Rio Oso Gem'	Southeast, Mid-Atlantic, central Midwest, West	Large. Freestone. Red-blushed yellow skin. Firm yellow flesh. Excellent flavor. Late midseason	Small tree is not vigorous. Large, showy flowers. Fruit freezes very well
'Wild Rose'	Southeast, Mid-Atlantic, Northeast, Great Lakes, central Midwest	Medium to large. Fairly smooth yellow-green skin mottled dull red. White flesh, red at stone. Good quality. Early midseason	Vigorous, moderately productive
NECTARINES			
'Fantasia'	Southeast, Mid-Atlantic, lower Midwest, West	Large. Freestone. Bright yellow-and-red skin. Firm yellow flesh. Midseason.	Vigorous. Showy flowers. Relatively low winter chill requirement
'Flavortop'	Southeast, Mid-Atlantic, lower Midwest, West	Large. Freestone. Skin is red with yellow undertone; flesh is yellow. Good flavor. Midseason	Vigorous, productive. Showy flowers
'Mericrest'	Northeast, Great Lakes, West	Medium-size. Freestone. Bright red skin; yellow flesh. Flavorful. Midseason	Winter-hardy variety from New Hampshire; may be as hardy as 'Reliance' peach. Good disease resistance
'Panamint'	Southeast (warmer parts), California	Medium to large. Freestone. Bright red skin; yellow flesh. Very good flavor. Midseason	Low chilling requirement
'Redgold'	Southeast, Mid-Atlantic, central Midwest, West	Large. Freestone. Deep red skin; golden yellow flesh. Good flavor. Midseason	Fair disease resistance

P

placed branches for scaffold limbs. Remove all other branches. On mature trees, in each dormant season, cut off two-thirds of previous year's growth by removing two of every three branches formed that year; or head back each branch to one-third its length; or head back some branches and cut out others. Trees can be trained as espaliers.

Peaches and nectarines tend to form too much fruit even with good pruning. When fruits are about 1 in. wide, remove (thin) some of the excess; remaining fruits should be 8–10 in. apart. If growth becomes weak and leaves yellowish, feed with nitrogen fertilizer.

Growing peaches and nectarines is not troublesome in areas with dry, hot summers and chilly winters. The trees require much more care in humid, mild-winter climates, where they are especially disease prone. Among the most serious ailments are peach leaf curl and brown rot of stone fruit. To control both diseases, practice sanitation (get rid of diseased plant parts) and give two dormant-season sprayings of fixed copper, Bordeaux mixture, or lime sulfur—the first after autumn leaf drop, the second in spring before buds swell. To control the diseases as well as scale insects, use sprays combining oil with either lime sulfur or fixed copper. Peach tree borer is the most serious insect pest; it tends to attack trees stressed by poor growing conditions or wounds, causing defoliation, branch dieback, and possibly death. Jellylike material exuding from base of tree is the first indication of the pest's presence. The insect holes will be evident at or just below ground level. Prevention through good growing conditions is the best control; if tree is attacked, consult local authorities for best treatment.

PEANUT

Peanut

Fabaceae (Leguminosae)

ANNUAL

☘ ZONES 2–42

☼ FULL SUN

🔴 REGULAR WATER

Best production where summers are long and warm. Tender to frost but worth growing even in cool regions. Plants resemble small sweet pea bushes 10–20 in. high. After bright yellow flowers fade, a so-called peg (shootlike structure) develops at each flower's base, grows down into soil, and develops peanuts underground. For best performance, give fertile, well-drained soil; sandy or other light-textured soil is ideal for penetration by pegs.

The four basic classes of peanuts are Virginia and Runner types, with two large seeds per pod; Spanish, with two or three small seeds per pod; and Valencia, with three to six small seeds per pod. Buy seeds (unroasted peanuts) from mail-order seed firms. Plant as soon as soil warms up, setting nuts 1½–2 in. deep. Sow seeds of Virginia and Runner peanuts 6–8 in. apart; sow Spanish and Valencia peanuts 4–6 in. apart. Fertilize at planting time. In 110 to 120 days after planting, foliage yellows and plants are ready to dig; loosen soil, then pull up plants. Cure peanuts on vines in warm, airy place out of sunlight for 2 to 3 weeks, then strip from plants.

PEANUT CACTUS. See CHAMAECEREUS sylvestri

PEAR (Pyrus communis)

Pear

Rosaceae

DECIDUOUS FRUIT TREES

☘ ZONES VARY BY VARIETY

☼ FULL SUN

🔴 REGULAR WATER

▶ SEE CHART NEXT PAGE

Most pears sold in markets and grown in gardens are varieties of this European species. Trees are long lived, pyramidal in form with strongly vertical branching; they grow 30–40 ft. tall, sometimes more. Pears on dwarfing understock make good small garden trees, excellent espaliers. Leaves of all types are leathery, glossy, bright green. Clustered white flowers are handsome in early spring. For ornamental relatives, see *Pyrus*.

To produce good crops, pears need at least 600 hours of winter chill (temperatures of 45°F/7°C or lower); most do better still with 900 hours. Their early bloom makes them prone to damage from spring frosts. In cold climates, trees are often planted in protected spots, such as on slopes.

Pears do best in well-drained loam, but they tolerate damp, heavy soil better than other fruit trees. They normally need cross-pollination for good fruit set; plant two or more varieties. Some types, notably 'Bartlett' and 'Comice', are self-fertile in many parts of California, but not usually self-fertile elsewhere. Train trees early to good framework of main branches; then prune lightly to keep good form, eliminate crowding branches. Harvest season is July to late October, depending on variety. Thinning the fruit is not usually necessary. Fruit should be picked when full size but unripe (green and firm), then put in a cool, dark place to ripen. If a pear is ready to harvest, the stem will snap free when you lift the fruit so that it is horizontal. If the stem stays intact, try again in a few days.

Most trouble-free pear growing occurs in warm, dry regions of California and Oregon, where commercial orchards are located. Since pears are highly subject to fireblight in warm, humid areas, it is more difficult to grow them for market in eastern fruit-growing regions. Home gardeners, however, have succeeded with pears east of the Rockies. In problem-prone areas, fireblight-resistant varieties offer the best chance of success. Fireblight can cause entire branches to die back quickly; as soon as you see blackened growth, cut it back to a growth bud or stem with green, healthy tissue, disinfecting pruning tools between cuts. To avoid heavy new growth, with resultant risk of fireblight, do not prune heavily in any one dormant season; also fertilize sparingly. Dormant oil sprays will control pear psylla and various other pests that may bother pear trees. Codling moth can ruin fruit; pheromone traps may be an effective control for one or two trees in a home garden.

PEAR, ASIAN or ORIENTAL

Asian Pear

Rosaceae

DECIDUOUS FRUIT TREES

☘ ZONES 3–12, 14–21, 32–41

☼ FULL SUN

🔴 REGULAR WATER

Descendants of two Asiatic species: *Pyrus pyrifolia* (*P. serotina*) and *P. ussuriensis*. Fruit differs from European pears in being generally round in shape, with flesh that is gritty, crisp, and firm to hard. Asian pears are often called apple pears because of their roundness and crispness, but they are not hybrids of those two fruits. All benefit from pollination by a second variety or by a European pear that flowers at the same time, such as 'Bartlett'. Unlike European varieties, they should be thinned to one pear per fruiting spur and should be picked ripe.

Because of their unpearlike texture and taste, fresh Asian pears should not be compared to European varieties, but they're valuable for mixing with other fruits and vegetables in salads. They require the same culture as European pears, but need fewer hours of winter chill (as few as 400) and are more resistant to fireblight. Varieties include 'Chojuro', 'Hosui', 'Ishiiwase', 'Kikusui', 'Niitaka', 'Nijisseki' ('Twentieth Century'), 'Okusan-kichi' ('Late Korean'), 'Shinko', 'Shinseiki' (self-fertile), 'Tsu Li', 'Ya Li', and 'Yakumo'.

PEARL BUSH. See EXOCHORDA

PEARLY EVERLASTING. See ANAPHALIS

PEASHRUB. See CARAGANA

PECAN. See CARYA

P

PEAR

NAME	ZONES	FRUIT	COMMENTS
'Anjou', 'd'Anjou' (**'Beurre d'Anjou'**)	2, 3, 6–9, 32–39	Medium to large, round or short necked, yellow to russeted yellow. Fine flavor. Late	Tree upright and vigorous. Tie down limbs for more consistent bearing. Moderately susceptible to fireblight. 'Red d'Anjou' is red-skinned selection
'Bartlett'	2–9, 14–18, 32–39	Medium to large, with short but definite neck. Thin skinned, yellow or slightly blushed, very sweet and tender. Midseason	Standard summer pear of fruit markets. Use any variety except 'Seckel' or 'Magness' to pollinate. Tree does not have the best form, is susceptible to fireblight. Nevertheless a good home variety
'Beirschmitt'	2–9, 14–18, 32–39	Seedling of 'Bartlett' and resembles that variety. Midseason	Moderately vigorous tree; a reliable producer. Susceptible to fireblight
'Bosc' (**'Beurre Bosc'**, **'Golden Russet'**)	2–9, 14–18, 32–39	Medium to large, quite long necked, interesting and attractive in form. Heavy russeting on green or yellow skin. Fine flavor. Though flesh is firm, fruit is juicy eaten fresh. Holds shape when cooked. Midseason	Large, upright, vigorous tree. Needs pruning in youth. Highly susceptible to fireblight
'Clapp Favorite'	2–9, 14–18, 32–39	Resembles 'Bartlett'. Soft, sweet. Early	Productive, shapely; good foliage. Highly susceptible to fireblight. 'Starkrimson' and 'Super Red Clapp' are related red-skinned varieties
'Colette'	2–9, 14–18, 32–39	Everblooming, bearing over a long season, from mid- or late September until frost. Firm; similar in size and shape to 'Bartlett'	Broad, short, shapely tree. Susceptible to fireblight
'Comice' (**'Doyenne du Comice'**, **'Royal Riviera'**)	3, 6, 7, 14–17, 32, 34, 36–39	Large to very large, roundish to pear shaped. Thick skinned, russeted greenish yellow, sometimes blushed. Superb flavor and texture. Late	Big, vigorous tree but slow to reach bearing age. Good crops when soil, climate, and exposure are right. Moderately susceptible to fireblight
'Duchess'	2–9, 14–18, 32–39	Large, with light yellow skin and juicy, spicy white flesh. Late	Self-fertile. Slow growing, but bears fruits when young. Susceptible to fireblight
'Fan Stil'	2–12, 14–21, 28–39	Medium-size, bell-shaped yellow fruit with slight red blush. Crisp, juicy; good fresh and cooked. Late	Asian pear hybrid. Vigorous, upright growth. Consistently large crops. Highly resistant to fireblight
'Kieffer'	2–12, 14–21, 28–39	Medium to large, oval; greenish yellow skin blushed dark red. Gritty in texture, fair in flavor. Late. Good for canning, baking	Asian pear hybrid. Quite resistant to fireblight. Most widely grown pear in the South
'Magness'	2–12, 14–21, 29–39	Large greenish, red-blushed, oval fruit with soft, sweet, juicy flesh. Late midseason	Highly resistant to fireblight. Does not form many flowers east of the Rockies. Will not pollinate other varieties
'Max-Red Bartlett'	2–9, 14–18, 32–39	Like 'Bartlett', but skin is bright red and flavor is somewhat sweeter	Red color extends to twigs and tints leaves. Susceptible to fireblight
'Moonglow'	2–9, 14–18, 29–39	Somewhat like 'Bartlett' in looks. Juicy, soft fruit of good flavor. Ripens 2 weeks before 'Bartlett'	Upright, vigorous, very heavy bearer. Highly resistant to fireblight
'Orient'	2–12, 14–21, 28–31, 32 (southern part), 33, 35	Large, bell-shaped fruit with russeted yellow skin. Firm, juicy, slightly sweet; good for canning, baking. Late	Asian pear hybrid. Heavy producer. Highly resistant to fireblight
'Seckel' ('Sugar')	2–9, 14–18, 32–39	Very small, very sweet, aromatic. Roundish to pear shaped; yellow-brown skin, granular flesh. Early midseason. A favorite for home gardens, preserving	Some resistance to fireblight. Any variety except 'Magness' and 'Bartlett' and its strains will do as a pollinator
'Sensation Red Bartlett'	2–9, 14–18, 32–39	Same as 'Bartlett', but with bright red skin over most of fruit. Midseason	Medium-size tree, less vigorous than 'Bartlett'. Susceptible to fireblight
'Winter Nelis'	2–7, 14–18, 32–39	Small to medium, roundish fruit with rough, dull green or yellowish skin. Very fine flavor. Late	Fruit not attractive, but a very fine keeper, fine for baking. Moderately susceptible to fireblight

P

PELARGONIUM

GERANIUM

Geraniaceae

SHRUBBY PERENNIALS

⚡ ZONES 8, 9, 12–24; OR GROW AS ANNUAL; OR INDOORS

☼ ◐ LIGHT SHADE IN HOT CLIMATES

💧 ● REGULAR TO MODERATE WATER

Pelargonium domesticum

Although "geranium" is used as a common name for *Pelargonium*, botanically speaking it's not really accurate. To the botanist, pelargoniums are perennials that endure light frosts but not hard freezes and have slightly asymmetrical flowers in clusters. Most come from South Africa. A true geranium, on the other hand, is one of many annual or perennial plants, most from the Northern Hemisphere, having symmetrical flowers borne singly or in clusters; some are weeds, some valued perennial border or rock garden plants.

To gardeners, the pelargonium is a Lady Washington (Martha Washington) pelargonium. A geranium is an ivy geranium, a common geranium, or a scented geranium, all of which are species or varieties of *Pelargonium*. Gardeners also use the word "geranium" for both true geraniums and true pelargoniums.

Pelargonium graveolens

Most garden geraniums can be divided among three species of *Pelargonium*: *P. domesticum*, Lady Washington pelargonium; *P. hortorum*, common geranium (this group also includes variegated forms usually referred to as fancy-leafed or color-leafed geraniums); and *P. peltatum*, ivy geranium. In addition, many other species have scented leaves.

These plants perform best in areas with warm, dry days and cool nights. Can be grown outdoors year-round in mildest California climates, where they bloom throughout warm weather. Elsewhere, they are popular annual bedding plants or house plants. In cold climates, move geraniums indoors before the first frost or take cuttings for next year.

All geraniums do well in pots. Common geraniums grow well in garden beds; Lady Washington pelargoniums are also planted in beds but tend to get rangy. Some varieties of Lady Washington are used in hanging baskets. Ivy geraniums are good in hanging containers, in raised beds, and as a bank or ground cover. Use scented geraniums in close-up situations—in pots or in ground (in mild areas). For good bloom on potted geranium indoors, place it in a sunny window or in the brightest light possible.

Pelargonium tomentosum

Plant in any good, fast-draining soil. Remove faded flowers regularly to encourage new bloom. Pinch growing tips while plants are small to force side branches. Geraniums in pots bloom best when somewhat pot bound. Aphids, whiteflies, and spider mites are common pests. Tobacco budworm may be a problem in some areas; suspect this pest if flowers are tattered or fail to open.

P. domesticum. LADY WASHINGTON PELARGONIUM, MARTHA WASHINGTON PELARGONIUM, REGAL GERANIUM. Erect or somewhat spreading, to 3 ft. More rangy than common geranium. Leaves heart shaped to kidney shaped, dark green, 2–4 in. wide, with crinkled margins, unequal sharp teeth. Large, showy flowers 2 in. or more across in loose, rounded clusters, in white and many shades of pink, red, lavender, purple, with brilliant blotches and markings of darker colors.

P. hortorum. COMMON GERANIUM, GARDEN GERANIUM. Most popular, widely grown. Shrubby, succulent stemmed, to 3 ft. or more; older plants grown in the open (in mild areas) become woody. Round or kidney-shaped leaves are velvety and hairy, soft to the touch, aromatic, with edges indistinctly lobed and scallop toothed; most varieties show zone of deeper color just inside leaf margin, though some are plain green. Fancy-leafed or

Pelargonium hortorum

color-leafed varieties have zones, borders, or splashes of brown, gold, red, white, or green in various combinations. Some also have highly attractive flowers. Single or double flowers are flatter and smaller than those of Lady Washington pelargonium, but clusters bear many more blossoms. Flowers are usually in solid colors. Many varieties in white and shades of pink, rose, red, orange, and violet.

There are also dwarf-growing, cactus-flowered, and other novelty kinds. Tough, attractive geraniums for outdoor bedding can be grown from seed, flowering the first summer. Widely available strains are Diamond and Elite (quick to reach bloom stage, compact, need no pinching); Orbit (distinct leaf zoning; broad, rounded flower clusters); and Sprinter (slow growing, very free flowering).

Pelargonium peltatum

P. peltatum. IVY GERANIUM. Trailing plants to 2–3 ft. or longer. Leaves rather succulent, glossy bright green, 2–3 in. across, ivylike, with pointed lobes. Inch-wide single or double flowers in rounded clusters of five to ten; colors include white, pink, rose, red, and lavender. Upper petals may be blotched or striped. Many named varieties. 'L'Elegante' has white-edged foliage; other varieties have white or yellow veins in leaves. Summer Showers strain can be grown from seed; it comes as a mixture of white, pink, red, lavender, and magenta.

Scented geraniums. Many aromatic species are available; all fall into the 1–3-ft.-high range and bear clusters of small blossoms in white or rosy colors (flowers are secondary to the foliage in appeal). The common name of each refers to the plant's fragrance. Types include apple (*P. odoratissimum*), lemon (*P. crispum*), lime (*P. nervosum*), peppermint (*P. tomentosum*), and rose (*P. capitatum, P. graveolens*). All such scented kinds are more tolerant of hot, humid summers than other types. Good for herb garden, edgings, front of borders, window boxes, hanging baskets. Peppermint geranium makes a good ground cover in frost-free gardens. Use fresh leaves of all types for flavoring jelly and iced drinks; use dried leaves in potpourri and sachets.

Pelargonium crispum

PELLAEA

CLIFF-BRAKE

Polypodiaceae

FERNS

⚡ ZONES VARY BY SPECIES; OR INDOORS

◐ FILTERED SHADE

● REGULAR WATER

Small plants; though not striking in appearance, they have charmingly detailed foliage. These two evergreen species are most commonly grown as house plants. Where hardy (both survive to 24°F/–4°C), they are sometimes rock garden plants.

Pellaea rotundifolia

P. rotundifolia. ROUNDLEAF FERN. Zones 14–17, 19–24. Small fern with spreading fronds to 1 ft. long. Nearly round leaflets, about ¾ in. across, are evenly spaced.

P. viridis (P. adiantoides). Zones 14–17, 19–25. Fronds to 2 ft. long; fresh green leaflets oval to lance shaped.

PELTIPHYLLUM peltatum. See DARMERA peltata

PENCILBUSH, PENCIL TREE. See EUPHORBIA tirucalli

FOR INFORMATION ON SELECTING PLANTS
PLEASE SEE PAGES 79–160

P

PENNISETUM

FOUNTAIN GRASS

Poaceae (Gramineae)

PERENNIAL GRASSES

⚡ ZONES VARY BY SPECIES

☀️ ☽ EXPOSURE NEEDS VARY BY SPECIES

💧 WATER NEEDS VARY BY SPECIES

Pennisetum setaceum

Fountain grasses are generally clump forming, with arching stems tipped with fat, furry flower plumes in summer. They are among the most graceful of ornamental grasses. Use them in containers, in perennial or shrub borders, as bank cover.

P. alopecuroides. Zones 3–24, 31–35, 37, 39. Bright green, 3–4-ft. foliage clumps are topped by pinkish plumes in early summer. Leaves turn yellow in fall, brown in winter. In 'Hameln', white plumes double the height of a 1–1½-ft. clump. In late summer, 'Moudry' has black plumes rising a foot or more above a 1½–2-ft. clump. 'Cassian' is a dwarf (2-ft.) selection with cream-colored flowers and yellow-tinted foliage that turns to orange and dark red in fall. Sun or light shade. Regular to moderate water. Can self-sow.

P. orientale. Zones 3–9, 14–24, 31–35, 37, 39. The 1–1½-ft. clumps of leaves are topped by pinkish plumes that stand a foot or more above the foliage. Plumes mature to light brown and foliage turns straw color in winter. Growing conditions are the same as for *P. alopecuroides.*

P. setaceum. Perennial in Zones 8–24, 26, 27, 28 (warmer parts), 29; treated as an annual elsewhere. Dense, rounded clump to 4 ft. high. Coppery pink or purplish flowers, borne on 3–4-ft. stems, are held within the foliage clump or just above it. Dies back in winter, even in mild climates. Full sun. Can take regular water, but is extremely drought tolerant when established. In arid climates, thrives in gravel beds and other dry sites. Seeds itself freely and threatens to crowd out native vegetation when planted near open country. To prevent seeding, cut plumes before seeds mature. 'Rubrum' ('Cupreum'), with reddish brown leaves and dark plumes, does not set seed.

PENNYROYAL. See MENTHA pulegium

PENSTEMON

BEARD TONGUE

Scrophulariaceae

PERENNIALS, EVERGREEN SHRUBS AND SHRUBLETS

⚡ ZONES VARY BY SPECIES

☀️ ☽ AFTERNOON SHADE IN HOT CLIMATES

💧 REGULAR TO MODERATE WATER

Penstemon gloxinioides

A few are widely grown; most are sold only by specialists. All have tubular flowers. Bright reds and blues are the most common colors, but there are penstemons in white and soft pinks through salmon and peach to deep rose, lilac, deep purple, and, rarely, yellow. Hummingbirds are attracted to the flowers. Of some 250 species, most are native to the western U.S. (of species described here, all but *P. digitalis* are western). Need fast drainage. Usually short lived (3 to 4 years). Hybrids and selections tend to be easier than wild species to grow alongside regular garden plants.

P. ambiguus. PRAIRIE PENSTEMON, SAND PENSTEMON. Shrubby perennial. Zones 2, 3, 7–15, 18–21, 30, 33, 35, 41. To 2 ft. high, with very narrow leaves and broad (rather than tall) clusters of white to pink flowers that resemble phlox. Early summer to early fall bloom.

P. barbatus. Perennial. Zones 1–24, 31–43. Needs some winter chill for best performance. Open, somewhat sprawling habit to 3 ft. high. Bright green, 2–6-in.-long leaves. Long, loose spikes of 1-in. red flowers in midsummer to early fall. Selections include 'Elfin Pink', bright pink flowers on 1-ft. spikes; 'Pink Beauty', pink flowers on 2–2½-ft. spikes; 'Prairie Dusk',

deep purple flowers on 2-ft. spikes; 'Prairie Fire', scarlet flowers on 2–2½-ft. spikes; 'Rose Elf', coral pink flowers on 2-ft. spikes, some rebloom; and 'Schooley's Yellow', lemon yellow flowers on 2-ft. spikes.

P. digitalis. Perennial. Zones 1–9, 14–24, 29–43. Native to much of the eastern and midwestern U.S. Perennial to 5 ft. tall. Leaves to 7 in. long; flowers to 1½ in. long in white or pink shades, often with faint purple lines. Spring to early summer bloom. 'Husker Red', 2½–3 ft. tall, has maroon leaves and pale pink flowers.

P. gloxinioides. BORDER PENSTEMON, GARDEN PENSTEMON. Perennial in mild West Coast gardens (Zones 7–9, 12–24); treated as an annual elsewhere. Specific name has no botanical standing, but is widely used to refer to a hybrid group . Compact, bushy, upright growth to 2–4 ft. Tubular summer flowers in loose spikes at stem ends, in almost all colors but blue and yellow. Varieties include lavender 'Alice Hindley' ('Lady Hindley'), pink-tipped white 'Apple Blossom', rose pink 'Evelyn', bright red 'Firebird', rosy red 'Garnet', white (sometimes pink-flushed) 'Holly White', white-throated 'Huntington Pink', dark purple 'Midnight', and pale-throated purple 'Sour Grapes'. Cut back for second bloom on side branches.

P. pinifolius. Shrublet. Zones 2–24. Spreading, 4–6 in. high (rarely to 2 ft.), with crowded needlelike leaves ¾ in. long. Coral to scarlet, 1½-in.-long flowers in summer. Rock garden, low border plant, small-scale ground cover. 'Mersea Yellow' has bright yellow flowers.

PENTAS lanceolata

STAR CLUSTERS

Rubiaceae

PERENNIAL USUALLY TREATED AS ANNUAL

⚡ ALL ZONES

☀️ ☽ FULL SUN OR PARTIAL SHADE

💧 REGULAR WATER

Pentas lanceolata

Grown as a perennial in Florida, where it is an easy source of nearly year-round color for semishady locations. Elsewhere, it is a summer annual. Spreading, multistemmed plant to 2–3 ft. tall. Leaves are long, somewhat hairy ovals; stems are topped by tight, 4-in.-wide clusters of small, star-shaped flowers in white, pink, lilac, or red. Remove dead flowers for a long bloom season. Feed monthly in summer. If growing as a house plant, give it as much sunlight as possible by setting in a bright west or south window.

PEONY. See PAEONIA

PEPINO. See SOLANUM muricatum

PEPPER

Solanaceae

PERENNIALS GROWN AS ANNUALS

⚡ ALL ZONES

☀️ FULL SUN

💧 REGULAR WATER

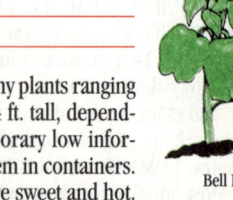

Bell Pepper

Peppers grow on attractive, bushy plants ranging from less than a foot high to 4 ft. tall, depending on variety. Use plants as temporary low informal hedge; or grow and display them in containers. The two basic kinds of peppers are sweet and hot.

Sweet peppers always remain mild, even when flesh ripens to red. This group includes big stuffing and salad peppers commonly known as bell peppers; best known of these are 'California Wonder' and 'Yolo Wonder'. Hybrid varieties have been bred for early bearing, high yield, or disease resistance. Big peppers are also available in bright yellow and purple (purple types turn green when cooked). Other sweet types are thick-walled, very sweet pimientos used in salads or for cooking or canning; sweet cherry peppers for pickling; and long, slender Italian frying peppers and Hungarian sweet yellow peppers, both used for cooking.

Hot peppers range from tiny (pea-size) types to narrow, 6–7-in.-long forms, but all are pungent, their flavor ranging from the mild heat of Italian peperoncini to the near-incandescence of 'Habañero'. 'Anaheim' is a mildly spicy pepper used for making canned green chiles. 'Long Red Cayenne' is used for drying; 'Hungarian Yellow Wax (Hot)', 'Jalapeño', and 'Fresno Chile Grande' are used for pickling. Mexican cooking utilizes an entire palette of peppers, among them 'Ancho', 'Mulato', and 'Pasilla'.

Peppers need a long, warm growing season, and in most areas must be set outdoors as seedlings if they are to produce fruit. Buy nursery plants, or sow seed indoors 8 to 10 weeks before average date of last frost. When weather warms up and night temperatures remain consistently above 55°F/13°C, set transplants outdoors, spacing them 1½–2 ft. apart. Fertilize once or twice after plants become established, before blossoms set. Sweet peppers are ready to pick when they have reached good size, but they keep their flavor until red-ripe. Pimientos should be picked only when red-ripe. Pick hot peppers when they are fully ripe. Possible pests include aphids, whiteflies, cutworms, pepper maggots, and Colorado potato beetles.

PEPPERMINT. See MENTHA piperita

PEPPER TREE. See SCHINUS

PEPPERWOOD. See UMBELLULARIA californica

PERICALLIS cruenta. See SENECIO hybridus

PERILLA frutescens

SHISO

Lamiaceae (Labiatae)

ANNUAL

☀ ALL ZONES

☀ ◑ FULL SUN OR LIGHT SHADE

🌢 REGULAR WATER

Perilla frutescens

Sturdy, leafy warm-weather plant to 2–3 ft. tall. Deeply toothed, egg-shaped leaves to 5 in. long. Kind most commonly seen has bronzy or purple leaves that look much like those of coleus. Leaves of Fancy Fringe strain are deeply cut and fringed, deep bronzy purple in color. Use leaves as vegetable or flavoring (they taste something like mint, something like cinnamon); fry long, thin clusters of flower buds as a vegetable in tempura batter. Extremely fast and easy to grow; self-sow freely. In Asia, seeds are pressed for edible oil.

PERIWINKLE. See CATHARANTHUS roseus, VINCA

PERNETTYA mucronata (Gaultheria mucronata)

Ericaceae

EVERGREEN SHRUB

☀ ZONES 4–7, 15–17, 32, 34

☀ ◑ PARTIAL SHADE IN HOT CLIMATES

🌢 REGULAR WATER

Pernettya mucronata

Compact growth to 2–3 ft., spreading by underground runners to form clumps. Small, glossy dark green leaves; some turn red or bronzy in winter. Tiny, bell-shaped white to pink flowers in late spring are followed by colorful, long-lasting berries in purple, white, red, rose, pink, or near black, all with a metallic sheen. You'll get more fruit if several plants are grown for cross-pollination. Grow in acid, peaty soil. Can be invasive; control by cutting roots with spade. Top often needs regular pruning to stay attractive. Use as informal low hedge or border, in tubs or window boxes.

PEROVSKIA

RUSSIAN SAGE

Lamiaceae (Labiatae)

SHRUBBY PERENNIAL

☀ ZONES 3–24, 28–35, 37, 39

☀ FULL SUN

🌢 MODERATE WATER

Perovskia 'Blue Spire'

Woody-based clump with many upright, gray-white stems clothed in gray-green foliage. Leaves are 2–3 in. long and deeply cut on lower part of stem, become smaller and merely toothed toward top of stem. Each stem is topped with a widely branched spray of small lavender blue flowers; when plants are in full bloom in late spring and summer, flowers form a haze above the foliage. To extend flowering period, trim off spent blossoms. Mature clumps may reach 3–4 ft. high, with equal spread.

Often sold as *P. atriplicifolia*, but plants in circulation are probably hybrids between that species and *P. abrotanoides*. Widely grown 'Blue Spire', with deep violet blue blooms, is sometimes sold as *P. atriplicifolia* 'Superba' or *P.* 'Longin'. 'Blue Mist' (earliest-flowering variety) and 'Blue Haze' bear lighter blue blossoms. 'Filagran' has silvery, very finely cut leaves. Mass plants or use them individually in borders. Plants take any soil, as long as it is well drained. Extremely resistant to heat and drought. Best in warm summers, even where weather is humid. Cut nearly to ground each spring before new growth starts.

PERSIAN VIOLET. See EXACUM affine

PERSIMMON (Diospyros)

Ebenaceae

DECIDUOUS FRUIT TREES

☀ ZONES VARY BY SPECIES

☀ FULL SUN

🌢🌢 REGULAR TO MODERATE WATER

Persimmon

Of the two types of persimmons grown, the native species is a bigger, more cold-tolerant tree than the Asian species; however, the Asian type bears larger fruit that is sold in markets. Neither species is fussy about soil.

American persimmon (*Diospyros virginiana*) is native from Connecticut to Kansas and southward to Texas and Florida. It grows best in Zones 3–9, 14–16, 18–23, 26 (northern part), 28–41. As a landscape tree, it is not as ornamental as the Asian species, and is probably best suited to wild gardens, where its tendency to form thickets from root suckers can be tolerated. Reaches 35–60 ft. tall, 20–35 ft. wide, with a broad, oval crown and attractive gray-brown bark fissured into a deep checkered pattern. Glossy, broad, oval leaves to 6 in. long turn yellow, pink, or reddish purple in fall. Fruit is round, yellow to orange (often blushed red), 1½–2 in. across; very astringent until soft-ripe, then very sweet. On wild species, fruit ripens in early fall after frost; some varieties do not require chill. Both male and female trees are usually needed to get fruit. 'Meader' is a self-fertile variety; its fruit is seedless if not pollinated.

> **TRY DRYING SOME PERSIMMONS**
>
> To dry persimmon fruit, pick it when hard-ripe with some stem remaining. Peel and hang by string in sun until it shrivels. Dried fruit has a flavor something like a date or very high quality prune.

Japanese or Oriental persimmon (*Diospyros kaki*) grows and fruits in Zones 6–9, 14–16, 18–23, 26 (northern part), 28–33. Reaches 30 ft. or more, with handsome, wide-spreading branch pattern. One of the best fruit trees for ornamental use; good small shade tree, espalier. Oval leaves,

6–7 in. long and 2–3½ in. wide, turn from glossy dark green to vivid yellow, orange, or red in autumn, even in mild climates. Brilliant orange, 3–4-in. fruits—the persimmons sold in markets—appear in fall and persist until winter unless harvested. This species sets fruit without pollination, though crops are often tastier and more abundant when pollinated. Varieties include:

'Chocolate'. Brown-flecked, very sweet flesh.

'Fuyu'. Nonastringent even when underripe; firm fleshed (like an apple), reddish yellow, about size of baseball but flattened like tomato. Similar but larger is 'Gosho', widely sold as 'Giant Fuyu'.

'Hachiya'. Shapeliest tree for ornamental use. This variety yields big (4-in.-long, 2½–3-in.-broad), slightly pointed persimmons. Pick before fully ripe to save crop from birds, but allow to become soft-ripe before eating; astringent unless mushy.

'Tamopan'. Very large, turban shaped, astringent until fully ripe.

PERUVIAN DAFFODIL. See HYMENOCALLIS narcissiflora

PERUVIAN LILY. See ALSTROEMERIA

PETASITES japonicus

JAPANESE COLTSFOOT, FUKI

Asteraceae (Compositae)

PERENNIAL

ZONES 3–9, 14–17, 31–41

☼ ◐ ● TAKES SUN IN COOL-SUMMER AREAS

🌢 AMPLE WATER

Petasites japonicus

Giant perennial for growing in perpetually-moist soil near the water. Creeping rhizomes give rise to huge (16-in.-wide), round leaves on long stalks; stalks are used as a vegetable (fuki) by the Japanese. Short spikes of fragrant white daisies appear in late winter before leaves emerge. Locate plant with care, since it is invasive and its thick rhizomes can be extremely difficult to eradicate. Varieties include 'Giganteus', with leaves up to 4 ft. wide on 5-ft. stalks, and 'Variegatus', with somewhat smaller leaves (to 2–3 ft.) boldly marked with creamy white.

PETREA volubilis

QUEEN'S WREATH

Verbenaceae

EVERGREEN VINE

ZONES 19–25

☼ ◐ FULL SUN OR LIGHT SHADE

🌢 REGULAR WATER

Petrea volubilis

Twines to 40 ft., but can be kept much smaller. Deep green leaves with sandpapery surface. Stunning display of purplish blue (occasionally white), star-shaped flowers in long, slender clusters, several times a year during warm weather. Although individually small, flowers are profusely borne. Sensitive to frost.

PETUNIA hybrida

PETUNIA

Solanaceae

TENDER PERENNIAL GROWN AS ANNUAL

ALL ZONES

☼ FULL SUN

🌢 REGULAR WATER

Petunia hybrida

Plants are low growing, bushy to spreading, with thick, broad leaves thaat are slightly sticky to the touch. Flower

form varies from single and funnel shaped to very double and heavily ruffled (like carnations); the many colors include cream, yellow, pure white, and the whole range from soft pink to deepest red, light blue to deepest purple. Bicolors and picotees are available, as are types with contrasting veins on the petals and those with fluted or fringed edges. In most zones, plants bloom throughout summer until frost. In Zones 12, 13, 25–27, they are done in by summer heat or humidity; in these areas, grow them for winter and spring color.

Plant in good garden soil. Single-flowered kinds tolerate alkalinity, will grow in poor soil if it's well drained. Plant 8–18 in. apart, depending on size of variety. After plants are established, pinch back halfway for compact growth. Feed monthly with complete fertilizer. Near end of summer (in all but Zones 12, 13, 25–27), cut back rangy plants by about half to force new growth. In humid weather, botrytis disease can damage blossoms and foliage of most petunias; Multifloras are somewhat resistant. Smog damage (spotting on seedling leaves), tobacco budworm (flowers look tattered or fail to open) may be problems in some areas.

Described below are the three classes of petunias (the long-standing Grandiflora and Multiflora classes and the new Milliflora) and the new ground cover variety. Petunias are generally labeled F_1 or F_2 hybrids. F_1 refers to first-generation hybrids, which are more vigorous and more uniform in color, height, and growth habit than their offspring, F_2 hybrids.

Hybrid Grandiflora. Of the three classes, these bear the largest flowers but bloom the least profusely. Sturdy plants to 15–27 in. high, 2–3 ft. wide. Flowers usually single, ruffled or fringed, to 4½ in. across, in pink, rose, salmon, red, scarlet, blue, white, pale yellow, or striped combinations. Fluffy Ruffles strain has the largest blossoms, to 6 in. across. Cascade, Countdown, and Supercascade series have a cascading growth habit that makes them good for hanging baskets. Magic and Supermagic strains give heavy bloom on compact plants, bearing large (4–5-in.-wide) single flowers in white, pink, red, blue. Double Hybrid Grandifloras with heavily ruffled flowers come in all petunia colors except yellow.

Hybrid Multiflora. Plants about same size as Grandifloras, but flowers are generally smooth edged and smaller (to 2 in. across), single or double. Neat, compact growth ideal for bedding, massed planting. Many named varieties in pink, rose, salmon, yellow, white, blue. Joy and Plum strains have single, satiny-textured flowers in white, cream, pink, coral, red, blue. 'Summer Sun' is a bright yellow petunia.

Hybrid Milliflora. Newest class of petunias, with smaller flowers and more dwarf habit than Multiflora. Fantasy strain makes neat, compact mound to 10 in. high, with plentiful 1–1½-in. blooms in pink, red, blue, ivory. Good for pots, hanging baskets, window boxes.

'Purple Wave'. The first-ever ground cover petunia, growing 4–6 in. high, with 4-ft. spread. Abundance of vivid purple, 2–3-in. blossoms. Good for banks, borders, containers, hanging baskets.

PHACELIA campanularia

CALIFORNIA DESERT BLUEBELLS

Hydrophyllaceae

ANNUAL

BEST IN ZONES 7–24; ALSO POSSIBLE IN 29, 30, WESTERN PARTS OF 33 AND 35

☼ FULL SUN

🌢🌢 REGULAR TO LITTLE WATER

Phacelia campanularia

Native to California deserts. Adaptable to most well-drained soils. Grows to 6–18 in. tall, with egg-shaped, coarsely toothed leaves and loose clusters of inch-long, bell-shaped, deep blue flowers. Blooms in spring. Sow directly in the ground in fall or earliest spring, or sow in pots and transplant while seedlings are very small.

PHAEDRANTHUS buccinatorius. See DISTICTIS buccinatoria

PHALAENOPSIS

MOTH ORCHID

Orchidaceae

EPIPHYTIC ORCHIDS

🌡 ZONE 25; OR INDOOR AND GREENHOUSE PLANTS

☼ FILTERED LIGHT

💧 KEEP SOIL MOIST AT ALL TIMES

Phalaenopsis

Epiphytic orchids with thick, broad, leathery leaves and no pseudobulbs. Long sprays of 3–6-in.-wide flowers in white, cream, pale yellow, or light lavender pink, spring–fall; some are spotted, barred, or have contrasting lip color. Leaves are rather flat, spreading to 1 ft. long. Flower sprays may be 3 ft. long. Cut faded sprays back to a node; secondary sprays may form.

Although very popular commercially, outside Zone 25 moth orchids are more for advanced amateurs than beginners. They require warmer growing conditions than most orchids (minimum of 60° to 70°F/16° to 21°C at night and 70° to 85°F/21° to 29°C during the day), fairly high humidity. Good location is near bathroom or kitchen window with light coming through a gauzelike curtain (foliage burns easily in direct sun). Give them same potting medium as for cattleyas (see Orchidaceae). When cutting flowers, leave part of main stem so another set of flowers can develop from dormant buds. Many lovely, large-flowered hybrids. Some smaller-flowered new hybrids give promise of being easier to grow, taking somewhat lower nighttime temperatures.

PHALARIS arundinacea

RIBBON GRASS, GARDENER'S GARTERS

Poaceae (Gramineae)

DECORATIVE PERENNIAL GRASS

🌡 ZONES 1–10, 14–24, 30–43

☼ ☼ FULL SUN OR PARTIAL SHADE

💧 💧 MUCH TO MODERATE WATER

Phalaris arundinacea

Tough, tenacious, bamboolike grass that spreads aggressively by underground runners to form spreading, 2–3-ft.-high clumps. Deep green leaves turn buff in fall. Airy flower clusters are white, aging to pale brown. 'Picta' has green leaves with longitudinal white stripes. The following selections are less invasive: 'Dwarf Garters', a slow spreader half as tall as the species; and 1½–2-ft.-high 'Mervyn Feesey' ('Feesey's Form'), with white variegation strongly blushed with pink.

PHASEOLUS coccineus. See BEAN, SCARLET RUNNER

PHILADELPHUS

MOCK ORANGE

Hydrangeaceae (Saxifragaceae)

DECIDUOUS SHRUBS, EXCEPT AS NOTED

🌡 ZONES VARY BY SPECIES

☼ ☼ PARTIAL SHADE IN HOTTEST AREAS

💧 💧 REGULAR TO MODERATE WATER

Philadelphus lemoinei

Grown for typically white, usually fragrant flowers that bloom in late spring or early summer. Four-petaled, 1–2-in. blossoms range from single through semidouble to double. Generally large, vigorous plants of fountainlike form with medium green foliage. Prune every year just after bloom, cutting out oldest wood and surplus shoots at base. To rejuvenate, cut to ground. Taller types are striking in lawns or as background and corner plantings; smaller kinds can be planted near foundations or used as low screens or informal hedges. Buy in bloom for best fragrance. Not fussy about soil, as long as drainage is good.

P. 'Buckley's Quill'. Zones 3–17, 30–34, 39. Dense, compact growth to 4–5 ft., with clusters of fragrant double flowers. Petals are narrow and pointed.

P. coronarius. SWEET MOCK ORANGE. Zones 2–17, 30–41. Old favorite. Strong growing, 10–12 ft. tall and wide. Oval, 1½–4-in.-long leaves. Clusters of very fragrant, 1½-in. flowers. 'Aureus' has bright golden leaves that turn yellow green in summer; it does not grow as tall as the species.

P. 'Galahad'. Zones 2–17, 30–41. Compact, rounded growth to 4–5 ft. tall. Large, fragrant single flowers.

P. gordonianus. See P. lewisii

P. lemoinei. Zones 3–17, 30–34, 39. This hybrid includes many garden varieties; most grow 5–6 ft. tall, and all have clusters of very fragrant flowers. Oval leaves to 2 in. long. Double-flowered 'Enchantment' is a well-known selection.

P. lewisii. WILD MOCK ORANGE. Zones 1–17, 30–43. Native to western North America. Erect, arching habit (tall race from west of the Cascades is often called *P. gordonianus*). Oval leaves 2–4 in. long. Large, satiny, fragrant single flowers. 'Goose Creek' is a double-flowered selection. Plants tolerate some aridity.

P. mexicanus. EVERGREEN MOCK ORANGE. Zones 8, 9, 14–24. Best used as vine or bank cover; long, supple stems with 3-in. evergreen leaves will reach 15–20 ft. if given support. Fragrant creamy flowers in small clusters.

P. purpureomaculatus. Zones 2–17, 30–41. Group of hybrids including moderate-size shrubs with flowers showing purple centers. 'Belle Etoile' grows upright to 5 ft. tall; fragrant, fringed, single flowers to 2½ in. Oval leaves to 2 in. long.

P. virginalis. Zones 2–17, 30–41. Another hybrid that has produced several garden varieties, usually with double flowers. Tall (6–8 ft.) varieties include 'Minnesota Snowflake' (reputedly hardy to −30°F/−34°C) and 'Virginal', both double, and 'Natchez', with 2-in. single flowers. Lower growing are double 'Glacier' (3–4 ft.) and 'Dwarf Minnesota Snowflake' (2–3 ft.).

PHILODENDRON

Araceae

EVERGREEN VINES AND SHRUBS

🌡 ZONES VARY BY TYPE; OR INDOORS

☼ ☼ ● EXPOSURE NEEDS VARY BY TYPE

💧 💧 MOIST, NOT SOGGY, SOIL

Philodendron domesticum

Philodendrons are tough, durable, fast-growing plants grown for their attractive, leathery, usually glossy leaves. They fall into two main classes; the list that follows indicates the class of each species and variety.

Arborescent and relatively hardy. These become big plants, reaching 6–8 ft. high (sometimes higher) and as wide, with large leaves and sturdy, self-supporting trunks. They will grow indoors but need much more space than most house plants. They grow outdoors in Zones 8, 9, 12–27, warmer parts of 28. As landscape plants, they do best in sun (some shade at midday where light is intense) but can survive considerable shade. Use them for tropical jungle effects or as massive silhouettes against walls or glass. Excellent in large containers, effective near swimming pools.

Vining or self-heading and tender. These forms can grow outdoors only in Zones 25 and 27, where they require partial or full shade. Elsewhere, they are house plants. Many kinds, with many different leaf shapes and sizes. Vining types do not really climb and must be tied to or leaned against a support until they eventually shape themselves to it. The support can be almost anything, but certain water-absorbent columns (sections of tree fern stems, wire and sphagnum "totem poles," slabs of bark) serve especially well, since they can be kept moist. Self-heading types form short, broad plants with sets of leaves radiating out from central point.

Whether in containers or open ground, a philodendron should grow in rich, loose, well-drained soil. House plant philodendrons grow best in good light (but not direct sun) coming through a window. Feed lightly and frequently for good growth and color. Dust leaves of indoor plants once a month.

It's the nature of most philodendrons—especially when grown in containers—to drop lower leaves, leaving bare stem. To fix a leggy philodendron, you can air-layer leafy top and, when it develops roots, sever it and replant it. Or cut plant back to short stub and let it start over again. Often the best answer is to throw out an overgrown, leggy plant and replace it with a new one. Aerial roots form on stems of some kinds; push them into soil or cut them off—it won't hurt plant.

Flowers may appear on old plants if heat, light, and humidity are high; they resemble callas, with a boat-shaped bract surrounding a club-shaped, spikelike structure. Bracts are usually greenish, white, or reddish.

Here are the kinds. Note that one great favorite—the so-called split-leaf philodendron—is not a philodendron at all, but a *Monstera*.

P. bipinnatifidum. Arborescent. Deeply cut 3-ft. leaves on upright trunks (leaning with age). Old plants may develop greenish cream inflorescences like giant (to 1-ft.-long) callas.

P. cordatum. See P. scandens oxycardium

P. domesticum. Vining. Usually sold as *P.* 'Hastatum'. Fairly fast, open growth. Leaves 1 ft. long, arrow shaped, deep green. Subject to leaf spot if kept too warm and moist. A number of selections and hybrids have become available; these are more resistant to leaf spot and tend to be more compact and upright. Some, possibly hybrids with *P. erubescens,* have much red in new foliage and in leafstalks. 'Emerald Queen' is a choice deep green, 'Royal Queen' a good deep red.

P. 'Lynette'. Self-heading. Makes tight cluster of foot-long, broadish, bright green leaves with strong patterning formed by deeply sunken veins. Good tabletop plant.

P. oxycardium. See P. scandens oxycardium

P. pertusum. See *Monstera deliciosa*. This is commonly sold as split-leaf philodendron.

P. scandens oxycardium. Vining. Most common philodendron, usually sold as *P. oxycardium* or *P. cordatum*. Heart-shaped, deep green leaves, usually 5 in. or less in length on juvenile plants, up to 1 ft. long on mature plants in greenhouses or outdoors. Easily grown (cut stems will live and grow for some time in vases of water). Thin stems will trail gracefully or climb fast and high. Train on strings or wires to frame a window or hang from a rafter, or grow on moisture-retentive columns.

P. selloum. Arborescent. Hardiest big-leafed philodendron used outdoors. Deeply cut leaves to 3 ft. long. 'Lundii' is more compact.

P. wendlandii. Self-heading. Compact clusters of 12 or more deep green, foot-long, broadly lance-shaped leaves on short, broad stalks. Useful where tough, compact foliage plant is needed for tabletop. *P.* 'Lynette' is similar.

Philodendron scandens oxycardium

PHLOMIS

JERUSALEM SAGE

Lamiaceae (Labiatae)

PERENNIALS OR SHRUBBY PERENNIALS

ZONES VARY BY SPECIES

FULL SUN, EXCEPT AS NOTED

MODERATE WATER

Mediterranean natives related to sage (*Salvia*). Erect stems are set with whorls of tubular flowers in yellow, purple, or lavender; late spring

Phlomis fruticosa

and early summer bloom. Tolerate poor soil as long as drainage is good. Withstand considerable drought, but do better with moderate water.

P. fruticosa. Zones 4–24, 31, warmer parts of 32. Shrubby growth to 4 ft. tall; woolly, gray-green, 6–8-in. leaves. Yellow, 1-in. flowers form ball-shaped whorls spaced along upper half of stems. Will produce several waves of bloom if cut back after each flowering. Evergreen in mild winters. Cut back by half in fall to keep plants compact. Tolerates light shade.

P. lanata. Zones 7–24. Dense, compact, shrubby plant to 2½ ft., with 1-in. woolly, wrinkled leaves and whorls of ½-in. yellow flowers. Nearly everblooming if old, faded stems are cut out.

P. russelliana. Zones 3–24, 30–34, 39. Spreads by runners, making clumps of large (to 8-in.), heart-shaped, furry leaves. Mats can be an effective weed-suppressing ground cover. Spikes with whorls of yellow flowers grow to 3 ft.

P. samia. Zones 3–24, 30–34, 39. Similar to *P. russelliana,* but with purplish pink flowers.

PHLOX

Polemoniaceae

PERENNIALS AND ANNUALS

ZONES VARY BY SPECIES

FULL SUN OR LIGHT SHADE, EXCEPT AS NOTED

REGULAR WATER, EXCEPT AS NOTED

Most are natives of North America. Except for *P. drummondii* (annual phlox), the species described here are perennial. The many types of phlox show wide variation in growth form, but all have showy flower clusters. Tall kinds are excellent border plants; dwarf forms are mainstays in the rock garden. Unless otherwise noted, plants perform well in average garden soil with regular moisture. Two major problems affect phlox: red spider mites (which attack almost all species) and powdery mildew (*P. paniculata* is especially susceptible to this).

Phlox paniculata

P. arendsii. Zones 1–17, 28–43. Hybrid between *P. divaricata* and *P. paniculata.* To 1½ ft. high, with 1-in.-wide blossoms in clusters to 6 in. across, early summer. Cut off faded flowers for later rebloom. 'Anja' has reddish purple blooms, 'Hilda' lavender ones, 'Suzanne' white blossoms with red eye.

P. bifida. SAND PHLOX. Zones 3–6, 31–34, 39. Clumps to 8–10 in. tall, with narrow light green leaves. Blooms spring–early summer, bearing profuse ½-in. lavender to white flowers with deeply notched petals. Likes full sun, excellent drainage. Drought tolerant.

P. carolina. See P. maculata

P. 'Chattahoochee'. See P. pilosa

P. divaricata. SWEET WILLIAM PHLOX. Zones 1–17, 28–43. To 1 ft. high, with slender, leafy stems and creeping underground shoots. Oval leaves 1–2 in. long. Blooms in spring, bearing open clusters of ¾–1½-in.-wide, somewhat fragrant blossoms in pale blue (sometimes with pinkish tones) varying to white. Use in rock gardens, as bulb cover. Give light shade and good, deep soil. Varieties include 'Arrowhead', with light lavender blue blossoms; 'Dirigo Ice', palest blue; 'Fuller's White'; *P. d. laphamii,* bright blue; and the compact 'London Grove', deep blue.

P. drummondii. ANNUAL PHLOX. All zones. Grows 6–18 in. tall, with erect, leafy stems more or less covered with rather sticky hairs. Flowers numerous, showy, in tight clusters at tops of stems. Bright and pastel colors (no blue or orange), some with contrasting eye. Tall strains in mixed colors include Finest and Fordhook Finest. Dwarf strains include Beauty and Globe, both with rounded flowers, and starry-petaled Petticoat and Twinkle. Bloom lasts from early summer until frost if faded flowers are removed. Plant in spring in cold regions, in fall in mild climates. Give full sun and light, rich loam.

P. glaberrima triflora. SMOOTH PHLOX. Zones 1–17, 28–43. To 1½–2 ft. tall, with smooth, narrow, 3-in.-long leaves. Lavender pink flowers in late spring. This species is mildew free.

P

P. maculata (P. carolina, P. suffruticosa). THICK-LEAF PHLOX. Zones 1–14, 18–21, 31–45. To 3–4 ft. tall. Early summer flowers about ¾ in. wide, in 15-in.-long clusters, in colors ranging from white with pale pink eye to magenta. Shiny, mildew-resistant foliage. Varieties include 'Alpha', rose pink; 'Delta', white with pink eye; 'Miss Lingard' (white; best-known variety); 'Omega', white with purplish pink eye; and 'Rosalinde', deep rose pink.

P. mesoleuca. CHIHUAHUAN PHLOX. Zones 4–24, 29, 30. To 6 in. high, 1½ ft. wide; growth tends to be straggly if plants are not tip pinched. Flower color varies from cream to yellow, orange, and red; late spring–summer bloom. Needs heat, good drainage, regular water during flowering season (best kept dry in winter). Plant is winter dormant even in warmest areas.

P. nivalis. TRAILING PHLOX. Zones 4–7, 31–34. Trailing plants form loose, 4–6-in.-high mats of narrow leaves. Pink or white, 1-in.-wide flowers in fairly large clusters, late spring–early summer. Excellent in rock gardens; needs good drainage. 'Camla' is a good salmon pink variety.

P. ovata. MOUNTAIN PHLOX. Zones 2–6, 31–41. To 15–20 in. tall, with smooth green, oval, mildew-free leaves to 6 in. long. Deep pink flowers in late spring.

P. paniculata. SUMMER PHLOX. Zones 1–14, 18–21, 27–43. To 3–5 ft. tall. Long, narrow, 2–5-in.-long leaves taper to a slender point. Fragrant, 1-in.-wide flowers in large, dome-shaped clusters throughout summer. Colors include white and shades of lavender, pink, rose, and red; blooms of some varieties have a contrasting eye. Plants do not come true from seed; most tend toward an uncertain purplish pink, though some are attractive. Thrives in full sun, but flower colors may bleach where conditions are intensely hot. Plants fare better in northern than southern climates. Mulch to keep roots cool. Divide plants every few years, replanting young shoots from outside of clump.

Very susceptible to mildew at end of bloom season. To minimize problem, provide good air circulation: don't crowd plants and keep only six to eight stems on a mature plant. Spray with fungicide if necessary. Mildew-resistant varieties include white-flowered 'David'; 'Eva Cullum', pink with red eye; and lilac pink 'Franz Schubert'.

P. pilosa. PRAIRIE PHLOX. Zones 1–17, 29–43. Forms a low (to 15-in.), mildew-free, semievergreen ground cover. Blue to pink or white blossoms in spring. 'Chattahoochee', now properly known as 'Moody Blue', has blue flowers with a red eye; 'Eco Happy Traveler' bears deep pink flowers; and 'Ozarkana' has light pink blooms with a white eye.

P. procumbens. Zones 1–17, 31–43. Hybrid between *P. stolonifera* and *P. subulata,* but less widely creeping than either. Forms a mound of semievergreen foliage 6–12 in. tall, with purplish pink flowers in spring. 'Millstream Hybrid' has lavender pink flowers; 'O.G.K.' has rose pink blooms; 'Variegata' has pink blossoms and leaves edged in creamy white.

P. stolonifera. CREEPING PHLOX. Zones 1–17, 31–45. Creeping, mounding plant to 6–8 in. high, with narrow evergreen leaves to 1½ in. long. Profusion of 1-in. lavender flowers in spring. Varieties include 'Blue Ridge', lavender blue; 'Bruce's White'; 'Sherwood Purple', deep lavender; and pink forms 'Home Fires', 'Melrose', and 'Pink Ridge'. Provide light shade.

P. subulata. MOSS PINK. Zones 1–17, 28–45. Stiffish, ½-in., needlelike, evergreen to semievergreen leaves on creeping stems; forms mat to 6 in. high. Blooms late spring or early summer, with ¾-in.-wide flowers that range in color from white through pink to rose and lavender blue. Makes sheets of brilliant color in rock gardens. Provide loose, not-too-rich soil, moderate water. Specialists offer two dozen or more varieties; many of these are actually selections of other low-growing species or hybrids between such species and *P. subulata*. One variety, 'Tamanonagalei' ('Candy Stripe'), has rose pink blossoms edged in white, good fall rebloom; it is more drought tolerant than the average moss pink.

P. suffruticosa. See P. maculata

FOR INFORMATION ON YOUR CLIMATE ZONE
PLEASE SEE PAGES 16–78

PHOENIX

DATE PALM

Arecaceae (Palmae)

PALMS

ZONES VARY BY SPECIES

FULL SUN, EXCEPT AS NOTED

REGULAR WATER

Phoenix canariensis

Mostly large feather palms, but one is a dwarf. Trunks patterned with bases of old leafstalks. Small yellowish flowers in large, hanging sprays. On female trees, blossoms are followed by clusters of dates—but only if the tree has been in the ground 3 to 6 years and if a male tree is nearby. Fruit does not always mature in Florida. Dates of two species are used commercially; those of other species don't have as much edible flesh. Date palms hybridize freely, so buy from a reliable nursery that knows seed or plant source.

P. canariensis. CANARY ISLAND DATE PALM. Zones 9, 12–28. Hardy to 20°F/–7°C; slow to develop new head of foliage after damage from hard frosts. Big, heavy-trunked plant to 60 ft. tall, with a great many gracefully arching fronds forming a crown to 50 ft. wide. Grows slowly until it forms trunk, then speeds up a little. Young plants do well in pots for many years, looking something like pineapples. Best planted on slopes, in parks and big spaces, along wide streets; not for small city lots. Takes seacoast conditions.

P. dactylifera. DATE PALM. Zones 9, 12–28. Leaves killed at 20°F/–7°C, but plants have survived 4° to 10°F/–16° to –12°C. Native to Middle East. Classic palm of movie desert oases. Very tall (to 80 ft.), with slender trunk and gray-green, waxy leaves; stiff, sharp-pointed leaflets. Suckers from base; natural habit is clump of several trunks. Bears dates of commerce; principal variety is 'Deglet Noor'. Too stiff and large for most home gardens. Does well at seaside, in desert.

Phoenix dactylifera

P. loureiri (P. humilis). Zones 9, 12–28. Hardy to 20°F/–7°C. Resembles smaller, more slender and refined *P. canariensis*. Slow grower to 10–18 ft. tall. Leaves dark green, flexible, to 10 ft. long. Does well in containers.

P. reclinata. SENEGAL DATE PALM. Zones 23–27. Expect trouble below 28°F/–2°C. Native to tropical Africa. Makes picturesque clumps from offshoots, with several curving trunks 20–30 ft. high. If you want a single-trunked tree, remove offshoots. Fertilize for fast growth. Good seaside palm.

P. roebelenii. PYGMY DATE PALM. Zones 23–27; or house plant. Native to Laos. Fine-leafed, small-scale, single-trunked palm; grows slowly to about 6 ft. Curved leaves form dense crown. Good pot plant. Does best in partial or full shade, but will not succeed in dark indoor corners.

Phoenix roebelenii

P. rupicola. CLIFF DATE PALM. Zones 17, 19–27. Hardy to 26°F/–3°C. From India. As stately as *P. canariensis*, but much smaller, reaching only 25 ft. tall. Slender trunk; lower leaves droop gracefully.

P. sylvestris. SILVER DATE PALM. Zones 14–17, 19–28. Hardy to 22°F/–6°C. Native to India. Beautiful palm with single trunk to 30 ft., tapering from wide base to narrow top. Thick, round crown of gray-green leaves. Fruit is used commercially for making date sugar.

PALMS FOR MANY USES

The various species of *Phoenix* can fill a number of roles. Some are good as stately sentinels along an avenue. Several are quite cold hardy, taking temperatures well below freezing. Some are salt-tolerant plants for seashore gardens; others flourish in hot, dry climates. For details, see Palms (pages 413–414).

PHORMIUM

NEW ZEALAND FLAX

Agavaceae

EVERGREEN PERENNIALS

⚡ ZONES 14–28, EXCEPT AS NOTED

☼ ◑ FULL SUN OR LIGHT SHADE

🌢🌢 MUCH OR LITTLE WATER

*Phormium tenax
'Variegatum'*

Big, dramatic plants composed of many sword-like, stiffly vertical leaves in fan pattern. Flower stems reach high above leaves, bearing clusters of 1–2-in. blossoms in dull red or yellow. Use as accent plants, near swimming pools. Sturdy, fast growing. Take poor drainage to a point; crown rot can be a problem in very poorly drained soil. Tolerate salt air and ocean spray, but not dune conditions. Good container plants. Increase by dividing large clumps.

P. colensoi (P. cookianum). Leaves 2½ in. wide, to 5 ft. long; less rigid than those of *P. tenax*. Flowers yellow or amber, on 7-ft. spikes. Useful for its moderate size. With *P. tenax,* a parent of numerous hybrids.

P. tenax. NEW ZEALAND FLAX. Large, bold plant tending to spread. Leaves to 9 ft. long, to 5 in. wide. Nursery plants in containers are deceptively small; allow enough room to accommodate mature plant. Reddish brown flower stalks bear many dark red to yellowish flowers. Variants in leaf color are available. Among these, 'Atropurpureum' is purple red; 'Bronze' is brownish red; 'Rubrum' has deepest coloring, dark purplish red; 'Variegatum' has green leaves striped with creamy white.

Numerous plants developed from *P. colensoi* and *P. tenax* are grown for their brightly colored foliage. They are smaller than *P. tenax* and thus better adapted to gardens of modest size. Less tolerant of cold and heat than either species: they are damaged by temperatures below 20°F/−7°C, and they need partial shade in intensely hot climates. Some are prevailingly yellow or apricot ('Apricot Queen', 'Golden Sword', 'Yellow Wave'), while others are dark purplish bronze ('Bronze Baby', 'Dark Delight'). Many are dazzling, with stripings and edgings of red, apricot, cream, green, or bronze ('Maori Chief', 'Maori Maiden', 'Maori Queen', 'Maori Sunrise', 'Sundowner'). A few are quite small ('Jack Spratt', 'Tom Thumb'). Some tend to revert to green or bronze; remove such growth at the base to preserve original color.

PHOTINIA

Rosaceae

EVERGREEN OR DECIDUOUS SHRUBS OR SMALL TREES

⚡ ZONES VARY BY SPECIES

☼ FULL SUN

🌢🌢 REGULAR TO MODERATE WATER

Photinia fraseri

Related to hawthorn, pyracantha. Densely foliaged plants, most with large, elliptical to oval leaves and bright-colored new growth. In early spring, all bear flattish clusters of small white flowers. Most types have red or black berries during fall and into winter. Evergreen species may suffer considerable damage if temperatures remain below 10°F/−12°C for prolonged periods. Good screens, background. Prune to shape; never allow new growth to get away and make long, bare switches. Attractive to birds. All are susceptible to fireblight; all but *P. fraseri* are subject to powdery mildew.

P. arbutifolia. See Heteromeles arbutifolia

P. fraseri. REDTIP. Evergreen shrub or small tree. Zones 4–24, 26 (northern part), 28, 30, 31, warmer parts of 32 and 33. Moderate to fast growth to 10–15 ft., spreading wider. Oval leaves to 5 in. long are bright, showy bronzy red when new, maturing to dark green. Flower clusters resemble those of *P. glabra* but are not followed by berries. Good espalier

or small single-stemmed tree. Cut branches excellent in arrangements. Resists mildew and heat. A fungus-induced leaf spot can be serious in the South, especially in humid weather; control with fungicide. Aphids may be a problem. Plant described here is properly known as 'Birmingham'; for many years, it was the only one sold, and the variety name was not attached. 'Indian Princess' (new growth is more orange than red) and 'Red Robin' are about half the size.

P. glabra. JAPANESE PHOTINIA. Evergreen shrub. Zones 4–24, 28–31, warmer parts of 32 and 33. Broad, dense growth to 6–10 ft. or more. Leaves oval, broadest toward tip, to 3 in. long. Coppery new growth; scattered leaves of bright red give touch of color through fall and winter. Summer pruning will restrict size of plant to neat 5 ft. and give continuing show of new foliage. Flowers with hawthorn fragrance in 4-in.-wide clusters. Berries red, turning black.

P. serrulata. CHINESE PHOTINIA. Evergreen shrub or small tree. Zones 4–16, 18–22, 28–31, warmer parts of 32 and 33. Broad, dense growth to 35 ft., but easily held to 10 ft. high and wide. Stiff, crisp, deep green leaves to 8 in. long, prickly along edges. Bright copper new growth; scattered crimson leaves in fall, winter. Flower clusters to 6 in. across. Bright red berries often last until winter. 'Aculeata' (often sold as 'Nova' or 'Nova Lineata') is more compact, has midrib and main leaf veins of ivory yellow.

P. villosa. Deciduous shrub or small tree. Zones 1–6, 32–41. Usually multistemmed, to 15 ft. tall and 10 ft. wide. The 1½–3-in.-long leaves are pale gold with rosy tints when expanding, dark green at maturity, bright red or yellow in fall. Flower clusters 1–2 in. across. Bright red fruit.

PHYGELIUS

CAPE FUCHSIA

Scrophulariaceae

PERENNIALS

⚡ ZONES 4–9, 14–31, WARMER PARTS OF 32

☼ ◑ FULL SUN OR LIGHT SHADE

🌢 REGULAR WATER

Phygelius capensis

Woody-based perennials that die to the ground in cold climates, remain shrubby in milder areas. Related to snapdragon and penstemon, but drooping flowers also suggest fuchsia. Plants grow 3–4 ft. tall and spread by underground stems or rooting prostrate branches. Tubular, curved flowers borne in loosely branched clusters at branch ends, summer–fall. Prune to keep plants neat; mulch roots in cold-winter regions. Species can be started from seed, but named varieties should be grown from cuttings or by layering branches.

P. aequalis. Flowers dusty rose, in pyramidal clusters. 'Yellow Trumpet' has showy pale yellow flowers.

P. capensis. More open and sprawling than *P. aequalis*, with open clusters of orange to red flowers.

P. rectus. Hybrid between the previous two species. 'African Queen' has deep salmon orange flowers; 'Moonraker' bears pale yellow blooms; 'Winchester Fanfare' has deep rose flowers with yellow throats.

PHYLA nodiflora (Lippia repens)

LIPPIA

Verbenaceae

PERENNIAL

⚡ ZONES 8–29

☼ FULL SUN

🌢🌢 REGULAR TO LITTLE WATER

Phyla nodiflora

Creeps and spreads to form flat, ground-hugging mat sturdy enough to serve as lawn. Gray-green leaves to ¾ in. long. Small lilac to rose

P

flowers in tight, round heads ½ in. across, spring–fall. Flowers attract bees; if you object to this, mow off tops. Dormant, unattractive in winter. Feed regularly, especially in early spring to bring it out of dormancy fast. Particularly useful in desert areas but subject to nematodes.

PHYLLITIS scolopendrium. See ASPLENIUM scolopendrium

PHYLLOSTACHYS. See BAMBOO

PHYSALIS

Solanaceae

PERENNIALS AND ANNUALS

⚡ ALL ZONES

☼ ◑ FULL SUN OR LIGHT SHADE

🔴 REGULAR WATER

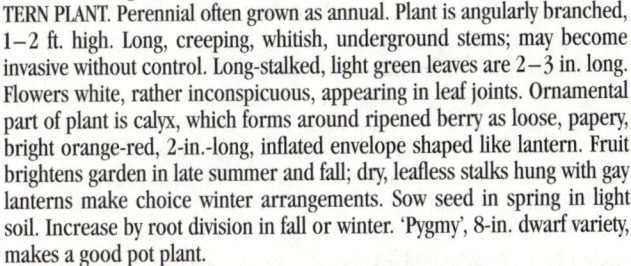
Physalis alkekengi

Fruit is surrounded by loose, papery husk (enlarged calyx of flower). First species below is ornamental; other two are edible.

P. alkekengi (P. franchetii). CHINESE LANTERN PLANT. Perennial often grown as annual. Plant is angularly branched, 1–2 ft. high. Long, creeping, whitish, underground stems; may become invasive without control. Long-stalked, light green leaves are 2–3 in. long. Flowers white, rather inconspicuous, appearing in leaf joints. Ornamental part of plant is calyx, which forms around ripened berry as loose, papery, bright orange-red, 2-in.-long, inflated envelope shaped like lantern. Fruit brightens garden in late summer and fall; dry, leafless stalks hung with gay lanterns make choice winter arrangements. Sow seed in spring in light soil. Increase by root division in fall or winter. 'Pygmy', 8-in. dwarf variety, makes a good pot plant.

P. ixocarpa. TOMATILLO. Annual of bushy, sprawling growth to 4 ft. Fruit about 2 in. wide, swelling to fill—or sometimes split—the baggy calyx. Fruit yellow to purple and very sweet when ripe, but usually picked green and tart and used (cooked) in Mexican cuisine.

P. peruviana. GROUND CHERRY, POHA. Tender perennial grown as annual. Bushy, 1½ ft. high. Leaves 2–4 in. long. Flowers bell shaped, ⅜ in. long, whitish yellow marked with five brown spots. Seedy yellow fruit is sweet, rather insipid; can be used for pies or preserves (remove papery husks before using in cooking). Grow in same way as tomatoes. Plants sprawl quite a bit and are slow to start bearing but are eventually productive where summers are long and warm. Several other species, including *P. pruinosa* and *P. pubescens,* are similar.

PHYSOCARPUS

NINEBARK

Rosaceae

DECIDUOUS SHRUBS

⚡ ZONES VARY BY SPECIES

☼ ◑ 🔴 SUN OR SHADE

🔴 🔴 REGULAR TO MODERATE WATER

Physocarpus capitatus

Ninebarks are so named because of their peeling bark, which strips off to reveal several layers. The plants resemble spiraeas and are closely related to them, bearing round clusters of tiny white or pinkish flowers in spring or early summer. All have lobed leaves. Of the species described below, only *P. monogynus* has good fall color. Prune plants as needed after bloom; rejuvenate by cutting old stems to the ground.

P. capitatus. Zones 1–3, 10. Native to mountains of western North America. To 8 ft. tall, with 2-in. leaves and dense clusters of white flowers.

P. monogynus. MOUNTAIN NINEBARK. Zones 1–3, 10, 33, 35, 41, 43. Rocky Mountain and High Plains native. To 3–4 ft. tall, with 1½-in. leaves

and few-flowered clusters of pinkish to white blossoms. Brilliant fall colors, typically orange and red.

P. opulifolius. COMMON NINEBARK, EASTERN NINEBARK. Zones 1–3, 10, 32–45. Native to eastern and central North America. Upright and spreading to 5–10 ft. tall and wide. Leaves to 3 in. Many white or pinkish flowers in each cluster. Varieties are more attractive than species. Leaves of 'Lutea' are yellow when plant is grown in sunlight, yellow green in shade; 'Dart's Gold' is similar but brighter. 'Nugget', a compact plant to 6 ft., has leaves that unfold golden yellow, gradually age to lime green, then turn gold again in fall. *P. o. intermedius* grows 4–5 ft. tall and has smaller, darker green leaves than species.

PHYSOSTEGIA virginiana

FALSE DRAGONHEAD, OBEDIENT PLANT

Lamiaceae (Labiatae)

PERENNIAL

⚡ ZONES 1–24, 26–45

☼ ◑ FULL SUN OR PARTIAL SHADE

🔴 REGULAR WATER

Physostegia virginiana

Slender, upright, leafy stems to 4 ft. Oblong leaves 3–5 in. long, with toothed edges and pointed tips. Funnel-shaped, 1-in.-long flowers in glistening white, rose pink, or lavender rose, carried in dense 10-in. spikes. Blooms from mid- to late summer into fall. Blossoms resemble snapdragons (hence the name "false dragonhead") and will remain in place if twisted or pushed out of position (hence the name "obedient plant"). The 3-ft. 'Bouquet Rose' has rose pink blossoms. The following varieties all grow 2 ft. high: rose pink 'Vivid'; white 'Summer Snow'; and 'Variegata', with bluish pink flowers and white-edged leaves.

Plant has a spiky form that makes it useful in borders, cut arrangements. Combine with taller fleabanes, pincushion flower, Michaelmas daisy. Stake taller stems to keep upright. Cut to ground after bloom. Vigorous and notoriously invasive; divide every 2 years to keep in bounds.

PICEA

SPRUCE

Pinaceae

EVERGREEN TREES OR SHRUBS

⚡ ZONES VARY BY SPECIES

☼ ◑ FULL SUN OR LIGHT SHADE

🔴 🔴 REGULAR TO MODERATE WATER

Picea pungens 'Glauca'

Like firs, spruces are pyramidal and stiff needled, with branches arranged in neat tiers. But unlike firs, they have pendent cones, and their needles are attached to branches by small pegs that remain after needles drop. Most spruces are tall timber trees that lose their lower branches fairly early in life as they head upward; their canopies thin out noticeably as they age. Many species have dwarf varieties useful as foundation plantings, for rock gardens, in containers. Spruces grow best in regions where summers are cool or mild, not hot and humid.

Check spruces for aphids in late winter; if the pests are present, take control measures promptly to avoid defoliation in spring. Other common pests of spruce are bagworms (in eastern and central U.S.), spruce budworm (in northern regions), pine needle scale, and spider mites.

Prune only to shape. If a branch grows too long, cut it back to a well-placed side branch. To slow growth and make it more dense, remove part of each year's growth to force side branches. When planting larger spruces, don't place them too close to buildings, fences, or walks; they need space. ▶

P

P. abies (P. excelsa). NORWAY SPRUCE. Zones 1–6, 14–17, 32–45. Native to northern Europe. Fast growth to 100–150 ft. Stiff, deep green, attractive pyramid in youth; ragged in age, as branchlets droop strongly and oldest branchlets (those nearest trunk) die back. Extremely hardy and wind resistant; valued for windbreaks in cold areas. Tolerates heat and humidity better than most spruces. 'Sherwoodii' is a rugged, picturesque shrub with compact but irregular growth habit; it was developed from a tree that at age 60 was only 5 ft. tall and 10 ft. across at base.

P. engelmannii. ENGELMANN SPRUCE. Zones 1–6, 10, 14–17. Native to western North America. Dense, slender pyramid, eventually exceeding 100 ft. tall and 30 ft. wide. Resembles blue-green forms of Colorado spruce, but has a narrower form and softer needles. Popular lawn tree in Rocky Mountain region.

P. glauca. WHITE SPRUCE. Zones 1–6, 14–17, 35–45. Native to Canada and northern U.S. Cone-shaped tree to 60–70 ft., dense when young, with pendulous twigs and silver-green foliage. Crushed needles have an unpleasant odor. Best where winters are very cold. The following two varieties are widely grown in gardens:

'Conica'. DWARF ALBERTA SPRUCE, DWARF WHITE SPRUCE. Also grows in Zones 32–34. Compact, pyramidal tree, slowly reaching 7 ft. in 35 years. Short, soft needles are bright grass green when new, gray green when mature. Needs shelter from drying winds (whether hot or cold) and from strong reflected sunlight. Popular container subject. Often sold as *P. albertiana*.

P. g. densata. BLACK HILLS SPRUCE. Zones 1–6, 35, 41, 43, 45. Slow-growing, dense pyramid; can reach 20 ft. in 35 years. 'Rainbow's End' is similar, but new growth is golden yellow.

P. omorika. SERBIAN SPRUCE. Zones 2–9, 14–17, 32, 34–41. Native to southeastern Europe. Narrow, conical, slow-growing tree to 50–60 ft. tall. Shiny dark green needles with silvery undersides. Retains branches to the ground for many years. Considered by some to be the most attractive spruce; one of the best for hot, humid climates. 'Nana' is a dwarf to 3–4 ft. tall (possibly to 10 ft. high), with short, closely packed needles.

P. orientalis. ORIENTAL SPRUCE. Zones 2–9, 14–17, 32–41. Native to Caucasus, Asia Minor. Dense, compact, cone-shaped tree with very short needles; grows slowly to 50–60 ft. high. Can tolerate poor soils if they are well drained, but may suffer leaf burn in very cold, dry winds. Highly rated by experts. 'Skylands', to 20 ft. tall, has yellow new growth in sun.

P. pungens. COLORADO SPRUCE. Zones 1–6, 10, 14–17, 32–45. The only spruce that will succeed in the Southwest and lower Midwest. Slow to moderate growth rate. In gardens, reaches 30–60 ft. tall, 10–20 ft. wide; in the wild, grows to a possible 100 ft. tall, 25–35 ft. across. Very stiff, regular, horizontal branches form a broad pyramid. Foliage of seedlings varies in color from dark green through all shades of blue green to steely blue. The following varieties have consistent color:

'Fat Albert'. Compact, erect, broad, formal-looking blue cone. Slow growth (to 10 ft. in 10 years) makes it a good living Christmas tree.

'Glauca'. COLORADO BLUE SPRUCE. Distinctive gray-blue color.

'Hoopsii'. Beautiful, striking silvery blue color. Fast growing; needs early training to encourage erect, cone-shaped habit.

'Koster'. KOSTER BLUE SPRUCE. Bluer than 'Glauca'; growth habit sometimes irregular.

'Moerheimii'. Same blue as 'Koster', but shape is more compact and symmetrical.

'Montgomery'. Broad cone growing slowly to 2 ft. high, with strikingly blue foliage.

'Pendula'. WEEPING BLUE SPRUCE. Gray blue, with weeping branchlets. Stake main trunk while plant is young.

'Thomsen'. Similar in color to 'Hoopsii'. Vigorous, symmetrical habit.

P. sitchensis. SITKA SPRUCE. Zones 4–6, 14–17. Native Alaska to California. Tall, pyramidal tree to 100–150 ft., with wide-spreading, horizontal branches. Short, prickly needles are bright green beneath, silvery white above. Very subject to Cooley spruce gall, a conelike growth on new shoots caused by adelgids, a type of aphid; treat as for scale.

PICKEREL WEED. See PONTEDERIA cordata

PIERIS

Ericaceae

EVERGREEN SHRUBS

ZONES VARY BY SPECIES

SOME SHADE, ESPECIALLY IN AFTERNOON

REGULAR WATER

LEAVES AND NECTAR ARE POISONOUS IF INGESTED

*Pieris
japonica*

Elegant in foliage and form all year, these plants make good companions for rhododendron and azalea, to which they are related. Whorls of leathery, narrowly oval leaves; clusters of small, typically white, urn-shaped flowers. Most plants form flower buds by autumn, so potential flower clusters are a subtle decorative feature over winter. Resembling strings of tiny greenish pink beads, the buds open late winter–midspring. New spring growth is often bright colored (pink to red or bronze), but matures to glossy dark green.

Same cultural needs as rhododendron and azalea. Need well-drained but moisture-retentive acid soil and summers that are cool to merely warm; do not thrive in hot, dry conditions. Choose a planting location sheltered from wind, where plants will get high shade or dappled sunlight at least during the warmest afternoon hours. Prune by removing spent flowers. Splendid in containers, in Oriental and woodland gardens, in entryways where year-round good looks are essential.

P. floribunda (Andromeda floribunda). MOUNTAIN PIERIS. Zones 3–9, 14–17, 32–37, 39. Compact, rounded shrub 3–6 ft. tall. Differs from the other species: new growth is pale green; mature leaves are dull dark green, 1½–3 in. long. Blossoms in upright clusters. Very hardy to cold. Tolerates sun, heat, and low humidity better than the others, but does not thrive in hot, humid regions.

P. 'Forest Flame' (P. 'Flame of the Forest'). Zones 3–9, 14–17, coolest parts of 32. Hybrid between *P. japonica* and a form of *P. forrestii*. Dense plant to 6–7 ft. high and ultimately as wide. Brilliant red new foliage fades to pink and cream, then matures to dark green. Blooms profusely, bearing broader, heavier flower clusters than those of *P. japonica*.

P. forrestii (P. formosa forrestii). CHINESE PIERIS. Zones 5–9, 14–17, coolest parts of 32. Dense, broad grower; reaches 10 ft. tall, with greater spread. Polished leaves to 6 in. long. New growth ranges from brilliant scarlet (in best forms) to pale salmon pink. Buy when plants are producing new growth to get good color; the best selections are sometimes offered as 'Bright Red'. Large, drooping flower clusters. Good espalier in shaded locations.

P. japonica (Andromeda japonica). LILY-OF-THE-VALLEY SHRUB. Zones 3–9, 14–17, 31–35, 37. Upright, dense, tiered growth to 9–10 ft. New growth is bronzy pink to red; mature leaves are glossy green, 3 in. long. Drooping clusters of white, pink, or nearly red flowers. Buds are often dark red. Many varieties, some rare. The following are grown for unusual habit or foliage:

'Bert Chandler'. New foliage turns from salmon pink through cream to white, then pale green.

'Compacta'. Grows to 6 ft. tall.

'Crispa'. Smaller than species (to 6–7 ft.), with handsome, wavy-edged leaves.

'Karenoma'. Compact growth to 3–6 ft., with upright flower clusters.

'Mountain Fire'. Fiery red new growth.

'Pygmaea'. Tiny dwarf less than 1 ft. tall, with very few flowers and narrow leaves to 1 in. long.

'Spring Snow'. Similar to 'Karenoma'.

'Variegata'. Slow grower with leaves marked with creamy white, tinged pink in spring. Prune out any green-leafed shoots.

The following varieties are grown principally for their flowers:

'Christmas Cheer'. Early-blooming bicolor with flowers in white and deep rose red; flower stalks are rose red.

'Coleman'. Pink flowers opening from red buds.

'Daisen'. Compact plant. Flowers are similar to those of 'Christmas Cheer', but leaves are broader.

P

'Dorothy Wyckoff'. Tall growing, with white flowers opening from deep red buds. Leaves turn purplish in winter.

'Pink'. Shell pink flowers fading to white.

'Purity'. To 3–4 ft. Late blooming; unusually large white flowers.

'Temple Bells'. Compact, tiered habit; a bit less cold tolerant than the species. Ivory flowers.

'Valley Rose'. Pink-and-white flowers; open habit.

'Valley Valentine'. Deep red buds and flowers.

'White Cascade'. Extremely heavy show of pure white blooms.

P. taiwanensis. Zones 5–7, 14–17. Similar to *P. japonica*, but flower clusters are somewhat larger and more erect. 'Snowdrift', a hybrid between this species and *P. japonica*, has unusually profuse pure white blooms.

PIGEON BERRY. See DURANTA repens

PIGEON PLUM. See COCCOLOBA diversifolia

PIGGY-BACK PLANT. See TOLMIEA menziesii

PIMPERNEL. See ANAGALLIS

PIMPINELLA anisum

ANISE

Apiaceae (Umbelliferae)

ANNUAL HERB

🌱 ALL ZONES

☀ FULL SUN

💧 REGULAR WATER

Pimpinella anisum

Forms a clump of bright green, toothed leaves. Flowering stems with narrow, feathery leaves elongate to 2 ft.; stems are topped by umbrellalike clusters of tiny white flowers. Use fresh leaves in salads; use seeds for flavoring cookies, cakes, breads, confections.

Grows quickly in warm weather, but needs about 4 months to grow and mature a seed crop. In coldest regions, sow seeds indoors, then set out young plants when frost danger is past. In mild-winter climates, sow directly in the ground in spring. (Where summers are very hot, sow in fall for spring harvest.) Plants are taprooted and do not transplant easily once they begin to put on size. Grow in light, well-drained soil.

Pinaceae. Members of the pine family are evergreen trees with narrow, usually needlelike leaves and seeds borne on the scales of woody cones. Pine *(Pinus)*, spruce *(Picea)*, true cedar *(Cedrus)*, larch *(Larix)*, Douglas fir *(Pseudotsuga menziesii)*, and hemlock *(Tsuga)* are examples.

PINCUSHION FLOWER. See SCABIOSA

PINCUSHION TREE. See HAKEA laurina

PINDO PALM. See BUTIA capitata

PINE. See PINUS

PINEAPPLE

Bromeliaceae

BROMELIAD; CAN BEAR FRUIT

🌱 ZONES 25–27; OR GREENHOUSE OR HOUSE PLANT

☀ ☀ FULL SUN FOR FRUIT

💧 REGULAR WATER

Plant is rosette of long, narrow leaves with saw-toothed edges. To grow it, cut leafy top from a market pineapple. Root base of top in water or fast-draining but moisture-retentive potting mix. When roots have formed, move pineapple to 7–8-in. pot of rich soil. Grow

Pineapple

outdoors only in warmest zones; elsewhere, grow in greenhouse or sunny room where temperature stays above 68°F/20°C. Water when soil is dry. Feed every 3 or 4 weeks with liquid fertilizer. Fruit forms (if you're lucky) in 2 years, on top of sturdy stalk in center of clump. Indoor-grown pineapple fruit is much smaller than commercial fruit. Sometimes available as a house plant is a variety with foliage variegated in pink, white, and olive green. Plants grown for foliage rather than fruit will take reduced light.

PINEAPPLE FLOWER. See EUCOMIS

PINEAPPLE GUAVA. See FEIJOA sellowiana

PINK. See DIANTHUS

PINK POLKA-DOT PLANT. See HYPOESTES phyllostachya

PINK POWDER PUFF. See CALLIANDRA haematocephala

PINKROOT. See SPIGELIA marilandica

PINK TRUMPET VINE. See PODRANEA ricasoliana

PINUS

PINE

Pinaceae

EVERGREEN TREES, RARELY SHRUBS

🌱 ZONES VARY BY SPECIES

☀ FULL SUN

💧💧 REGULAR TO LITTLE WATER

▶ SEE CHART NEXT PAGE

Pinus pinea

Pines are the great individualists of the garden, each species differing not only in its characteristics but also in way it responds to wind, heat, and other growing conditions. Cone size and shape are an identifying feature of pines; another is the number of long, slender needles in a bundle. Most species have needles in groups of two, three, or five. Those with two needles tend to be more tolerant of unfavorable soil and climate than three-needle species, and three-needle pines more so than five-needle ones. As a group, pines are more adaptable than spruces or firs.

Pines tend to be pyramidal in youth, becoming more open or round topped with age. They grow best in full sun and will thrive in most soils that are reasonably well drained. Too much water results in yellow needles (with the yellowing appearing first in the older needles) and a generally unhealthy appearance—and can even cause sudden death. Most pines are fairly drought tolerant; exceptions are typically among the five-needle species. Pines rarely need fertilizer, and trees that receive it generally produce undesirable, rank growth.

SPRING PRUNING TO SHAPE A PINE TREE

To fatten up a rangy pine or to keep a young one teddy-bear chubby, cut back the candles of new growth by half (or even more) when the new growth begins to emerge in spring. Leave a few clusters untrimmed if you want growth to continue along a branch.

A number of pests and diseases can afflict pines, but a healthy tree usually copes with such problems with little or no intervention. Trees most at risk are those weakened by drought or air pollution. Aphids, spider mites, scale, and bark beetles are possible wherever pines are grown. Most five-needle species are susceptible to white pine blister rust (a bark disease that can kill the tree), primarily in the Northeast and Northwest; currants and gooseberries are host plants to one part of the fungus's life cycle. In the Northwest, distorted or dead new shoots on two- and three-needle pines indicate an infestation of European pine shoot moth larvae. Aphids usually show their presence by sticky secretions, sooty mildew, and yellowing needles. Birds are attracted to seeds contained in pinecones.

▶ page 437

PINE

NAME, NATIVE HABITAT	ZONES	GROWTH RATE, SIZE	GROWTH HABIT	NEEDLES AND CONES	COMMENTS
P. aristata BRISTLECONE PINE High mountains of West; very local and widely scattered	1–11, 14–17, 36–43	Very slow to 20 ft., possibly as tall as 45 ft.	Dense, bushy, heavy trunked, with ground-sweeping branches. In youth, symmetrical, narrow crowned; has mature look even then	Needles: in 5s, 1–1½ in., dark green, whitish beneath flecked with white dots of resin. Cones: 3½ in., dark purplish brown	So slow growing it is good for years in containers, rock gardens. Good bonsai plant. Needles persist for many years, making crown extremely dense. Protect from winds in cold climates
P. banksiana JACK PINE From near the Arctic Circle southward to northern New York and Minnesota	1, 2, 34, 37–45. Extremely cold hardy	Slow to moderate growth to 30–50 ft., often less	Symmetrical in youth; later irregular, picturesque. Sometimes shrubby	Needles: in 2s, olive green, curved or twisted, to 2 in. Cones: 1–2 in., pointed, yellowish brown	Tolerates poor soil, even sand. Useful for windbreaks, soil conservation
P. brutia (P. halepensis brutia) CALABRIAN PINE Eastern Mediterranean, southern Russia, southern Italy	7–9, 11–24, 29, 30, 33. Cannot take temperatures much below 0°F/–18°C	Rapid, especially in youth, to 30–80 ft.	Denser, more erect than the related *P. halepensis*, closer to classic pine tree shape	Needles: in 2s, 5–6½ in., dark green. Cones: like those of *P. halepensis*, but not stalked or bent back	Faster growing and shapelier than *P. halepensis*, though form is less interesting in maturity. Thrives in heat, drought, wind, poor soils
P. bungeana LACEBARK PINE Northern and central China	2–10, 14–21, 31–41. Hardy to –20°F/–29°C	Slow to 75 ft.	Often multitrunked, spreading. Sometimes shrubby. Picturesque	Needles: in 3s, 3 in., bright green. Cones: 2–2½ in., yellowish brown	Smooth, dull gray bark flakes off like sycamore bark to show smooth, creamy white branches and trunk. Brittle limbs can break under heavy snow loads
P. canariensis CANARY ISLAND PINE Canary Islands	8, 9, 12–24. Has been severely damaged (even killed) at 10°F/–12°C; needles freeze at 20°F/–7°C	Fast to 60–80 ft., sometimes shorter	In youth a slender, graceful pyramid. Later a tiered structure; finally round headed	Needles: in 3s, 9–12 in., blue green in youth, dark green when older. Cones: 4–9 in., oval, glossy brown	Very young plants are gawky but soon outgrow their awkward phase. Drought tolerant
P. cembra SWISS STONE PINE Mountains of central Europe	1–7, 10, 32–45. Hardy to –35°F/–37°C	Extremely slow to 70 ft. or more	Spreading, short branches in narrow, dense pyramid; broad, open, and round topped in age	Needles: in 5s, 3–5 in., dark green. Cones: 3½ in., oval, light brown	Slow growth and dense, regular foliage make it a good plant for small gardens. Handsome in youth. Resistant to white pine blister rust
P. contorta BEACH PINE, SHORE PINE Pacific coastal area from Alaska to Northern California	4–9, 14–24. Hardy to 0°F/–18°C. Not at its best in hot, dry regions	Fairly fast to 20–35 ft.	Nursery trees compact, pyramidal, somewhat irregular. Trees grown along coast are dwarfed, contorted by winds	Needles: in 2s, 1¼–2 in., dark green, dense. Cones: 1–2 in., light yellow brown	Good looking in youth; densely foliaged, takes training well. One of the best pines for small gardens. Good in containers
P. c. latifolia (P. c. murrayana) LODGEPOLE PINE, TAMARACK Mountains of western United States	1–5, 15–17, 38–43. Hardy to –30°F/–34°C; not suited to arid regions or hot, humid areas	Rather slow to 80 ft., sometimes 150 ft	In gardens, rather irregular, open branched, attractive. Planted close together, trees are tall, slim trunked. Solitary trees in mountains are heavy trunked, narrow, dense	Needles: in 2s, 1½–3 in., yellow green. Cones: 1½ in., shiny brown, persist for many years	Mountain form of beach pine. Excellent in small garden, wild landscape, large rock garden
P. densiflora JAPANESE RED PINE Japan	2–10, 14–17, 32–41. Hardy to –20°F/–29°C	Rapid when young. May reach 100 ft., usually much less	Broad, irregular head. Often develops 2 or more trunks at ground level	Needles: in 2s, 2½–5 in., bright green or yellow green. Cones: 2 in., oval or oblong, tawny brown	Intolerant of hot, dry, or cold winds. 'Oculus-draconis', dragon eye pine, has 2 yellow bands on each needle; viewed endwise, branch has concentric green and yellow bands. 'Pendula' is dwarf, sprawling; good in rock gardens

P

PINE

NAME, NATIVE HABITAT	ZONES	GROWTH RATE, SIZE	GROWTH HABIT	NEEDLES AND CONES	COMMENTS
P. d. 'Umbraculifera' TANYOSHO PINE Japan	2–10, 14–17, 32–41. Hardy to −20°F/−29°C	Slow to moderate, 12–20 ft.	Broad, flat topped, with numerous trunks from base. Spread greater than height	Same as for *P. densiflora*	Good for containers, rock gardens, Oriental gardens. Showy, flaking red-orange bark on young branches
P. eldarica AFGHAN PINE Southwestern Asia	7–9, 11–24, 29, 30, 33. One of the best desert pines; also thrives near Pacific Coast	Same as for *P. brutia*	Same as for *P. brutia*	Same as for *P. brutia*	Something of a mystery pine; may be *P. brutia* from Afghanistan and Pakistan. Christmas Blue is a blue-green strain
P. elliottii SLASH PINE Coastal plains, South Carolina to Louisiana	25–29, 31	Fast, to possible 100 ft.	Dense, rounded crown	Needles: in 2s or 3s, to 1 ft., dark green, stiff. Cones: 3½–6 in., shiny brown	Not widely sold in nurseries; you are more likely to inherit one already growing on your property. Existing trees are worth keeping—they provide ideal open shade for azaleas, camellias. Adapted to acid-soil areas of East Texas. *P. e. densa* thrives in southern Florida
P. flexilis LIMBER PINE Mountains of northern Arizona, Utah, Nevada, southeastern California; eastern slope of Rockies, from Alberta to Texas. Grows at 5,000–11,000 ft.	1–11, 14–21, 32–43. Cold hardy. Good pine for the Midwest	Slow to moderate, to 20–30 ft. in gardens	Thick trunk, open round top, many limber branches that may droop at decided angle to trunk. Becomes dwarfed and more irregular at higher elevations	Needles: in 5s, to 3 in., slightly curved or twisted, dark green. Cones: to 5 in., oval or cone shaped, buff to buff-orange	Young plants rather straggly looking. Shapes well with shearing; can be used for bonsai. Good on rocky slopes. Tolerates wind, drought. 'Vanderwolf's Pyramid' has regular form, blue-green color
P. halepensis ALEPPO PINE Mediterranean region	8, 9, 11–24. Tender when young; older trees take temperatures near 0°F/–18°C	Moderate to rapid, to 30–60 ft.	Attractive as 2-year-old; rugged character at 5 years; in age, has open, irregular crown of many short, ascending branches	Needles: usually in 2s, 2½–4 in., light green. Cones: 3 in., oval to oblong, reddish to yellow brown	Can grow in poor soils under trying conditions: in desert heat, on seacoast, with little or no water. Better-looking trees can be found for less harsh climates
P. h. brutia (see **P. brutia**)					
P. heldreichii leucodermis (**P. leucodermis**) BOSNIAN PINE Balkans, Greece, Italy	2–11, 14–24, 34, 36–41. Very hardy to cold	Slow to 75 ft.	Erect, dense, oval to cone shaped	Needles: in 2s, short, stiff, dark green, persisting 5–6 years. Cones: 2–3 in., blue to bright brown, single or in clusters of 3	Pale gray bark. Slow growth, dense habit, and salt tolerance make it a good landscape tree, especially near ocean
P. koraiensis KOREAN PINE Korea and Japan	2–11, 14–21, 32 (cooler parts), 33–41. Very cold hardy	Slow growth to 30–50 ft., taller in old age	Loose cone shape, soft looking, branched to the ground	Needles: in 5s, 3–4½ in., bluish or grayish green. Cones: 3–6 in., cylindrical, bright brown	Attractive as single specimen or in groups. Very tolerant of soils and exposures. Relatively trouble free
P. mugo (**P. montana**) SWISS MOUNTAIN PINE Mountains of Spain, central Europe to Balkans	1–11, 14–24, 32–45	Slow to variable heights	Extremely variable. Prostrate shrub, low shrub, or pyramidal tree of moderate size	Needles: in 2s, 2 in., dark green, stout, crowded. Cones: 1–2 in., oval, tawny to dark brown	Generally a bushy, twisted, somewhat open pine. *P. m. pumilio* is an eastern European form, shrubby and varying from prostrate to 5–10 ft. high. Very susceptible to scale
P. m. mugo MUGHO PINE Eastern Alps and Balkan states	1–11, 14–24, 32–45	Slow to 4 ft.	From the start, a shrubby, symmetrical little pine. May spread in age	Needles: Same as for *P. mugo*, but darker green. Cones: Same as for *P. mugo*, but a little shorter	Widely used in rock gardens, containers. Pick plants with dense, pleasing form

P

PINE

NAME, NATIVE HABITAT	ZONES	GROWTH RATE, SIZE	GROWTH HABIT	NEEDLES AND CONES	COMMENTS
P. nigra (formerly **P. austriaca**) AUSTRIAN BLACK PINE Europe, western Asia	2–11, 14–21, 32 (cooler parts), 33–41. Hardy to −20°F/−29°C	Slow to moderate, usually not more than 40 ft. in gardens	Dense, stout pyramid with uniform crown. Branches in regular whorls. In age, broad and flat topped	Needles: in 2s, 3–6½ in., very dark green, stiff. Cones: 2–3½ in., oval, brown	Tree of strong character that will serve either as landscape decoration or as windbreak in cold regions. Tolerant of urban and seacoast conditions. Problem of dieback has been especially severe in Midwest
P. palustris LONGLEAF PINE Virginia to Florida and west to Mississippi, southeastern U.S. coast	25–28, 31. Can withstand 5°F/−15°C but is used to warmer winters	Slow for 5–10 years, then fast to 55–80 ft.	Gaunt, sparse branches ascend to form open, oblong head	Needles: in 3s, dark green; to 1½ ft. on young trees, to 9 in. on mature trees. Cones: 6–10 in., dull brown	Young plants look like fountains of grass. When taller, resemble green mops. Prefers deep soils (grows on sandy ridges in its native range). Timber tree in the South
P. parviflora JAPANESE WHITE PINE Japan and Taiwan	3–9, 14–24, 32–41. Will survive −20°F/−29°C	Slow to moderate, to 20–50 ft. or more	In open ground, a broad pyramid, nearly as wide as high	Needles: in 5s, 1½–2½ in., bluish to green. Cones: 2–3 in., reddish brown	Widely used as bonsai or container plant. There are blue-gray ('Glauca') and dwarf forms
P. pinea ITALIAN STONE PINE Southern Europe and Turkey	8, 9, 12–24, 29. Hardy to 10°F/−12°C	Moderate to 40–80 ft.	In youth, a stout, bushy globe; in middle life, has a thick trunk topped with umbrellalike crown of many branches. In age, broad and flat topped	Needles: in 2s, 5–8 in., bright green to gray green, stiff. Cones: 4–6 in., broadly oval, glossy chestnut brown	Excellent in beach gardens. Eventually too large for small gardens. Takes heat and drought when established. The pine of Renaissance paintings; also the source of pignolias (pine nuts)
P. ponderosa PONDEROSA PINE, WESTERN YELLOW PINE British Columbia to Mexico and east to Nebraska, Texas, northeast Oklahoma	1–10, 14–21, 35, 41, 43. Very hardy to cold	Moderate to rapid, to 50–60 ft. in 50 years, eventually to 150 ft. or more	In youth, straight trunked and well branched. Stately in age, with open branches in spirelike crown. Handsome plated bark	Needles: in 3s, 4–11 in., glossy yellow green to dark green, firm, in clusters at branch ends. Cones: 3–5 in., light brown to red brown, prickly	Important lumber tree. Bushy, attractive. Useful for groves, shelter belt; also good for bonsai or pots. Doesn't take desert heat and wind. *P. p. arizonica* has needles in 5s or 3s and 4s. *P. p. scopulorum*, from Rockies, has shorter needles, drooping branches
P. radiata MONTEREY PINE Central California coast	8, 9, 14–24. Not reliably hardy at temperatures below 15°F/−9°C. Best where summers are cool	Very fast to 80–100 ft. Puts on 6 ft. a year when young, reaches 50 ft. in 12 years	Shapely, broad cone in youth, then drops lower branches to develop rounded or flattish crown	Needles: in 3s or 2s, 3–7 in., bright green. Cones: 3–6 in., lopsided, light brown, clustered, persisting for many years	Often shallow rooted; can be blown down by strong winds. Prune to maintain denseness. Even in ideal climate, suffers from many pests, smog damage, water molds; lately a pitch canker has become a serious disease. Keep healthy with occasional deep watering, feeding
P. resinosa RED PINE Newfoundland to Manitoba, south to mountains of Pennsylvania, west to Michigan	1–3, 36–45. Withstands extremes of heat and cold, but best in colder climates	Moderate to 50–80 ft.	Short trunked, densely branched, eventually a dense oval	Needles: in 2s, 5–6 in., dark green. Cones: 3–6 in., light brown	Orange-red bark in youth, reddish brown plates in maturity. Attractive tree for difficult situations, poor soils. Use for windbreak, shelter belt, erosion control
P. strobus WHITE PINE, EASTERN WHITE PINE Newfoundland to Manitoba, south to Georgia, west to Illinois and Iowa	1–6, 32–41	Fast to 100 ft. or more	Symmetrical cone shape with horizontal branches in regular whorls. In age, broad, open, irregular. Fine textured, handsome	Needles: in 5s, 2–4 in., blue green, soft. Cones: 3–8 in., slender, often curved, light brown	Intolerant of strong winds, pollution, salts. Subject to white pine blister rust, white pine weevil (kills terminal shoots, causing tree to become bushy). Popular Christmas tree. Varieties include 'Fastigiata', among most beautiful of upright pines; 'Pendula', with weeping, trailing branches; 'Prostrata', a low, trailing form; 'Nana', suitable for pots, rock gardens for many years

P

PINE

NAME, NATIVE HABITAT	ZONES	GROWTH RATE, SIZE	GROWTH HABIT	NEEDLES AND CONES	COMMENTS
P. sylvestris SCOTCH PINE Northern Europe, western Asia, northeastern Siberia	1–9, 14–21, 32–45	Fast, then moderate to 70–100 ft.	In youth, a straight, well-branched pyramid. In age, irregular, open, and picturesque, with drooping branches	Needles: in 2s, 1½–3 in., blue green, stiff. Cones: 2 in., gray to reddish brown	Popular as Christmas tree and in landscaping. Showy red bark in maturity; sparse foliage. Pick young trees for good green winter color; some turn yellowish. Wind resistant. Garden forms include dwarfs 'Nana' and 'Watereri', weeping 'Pendula', columnar 'Fastigiata'
P. taeda LOBLOLLY PINE Southern New Jersey to Florida, East Texas and Oklahoma	26, 28–33	Fast to 50–90 ft.	Loose cone shape in youth; as it matures, loses lower branches to become a rather open-crowned tree	Needles: in 3s (rarely 2s), 6–10 in., dark yellowish green. Cones: 3–6 in., oval to narrowly conical, rust brown, in clusters of 2–5; scales are spine tipped	Tough tree, withstanding poor soils. Useful in Deep South for quick screening and shade. Adapted to acid-soil areas of East Texas. Widely planted for pulp, lumber
P. thunbergiana **(P. thunbergii)** JAPANESE BLACK PINE Japan	3–12, 14–21, 28–37, 39. Hardy to –20°F/–29°C	Fast in cool, moist climates; slow in arid regions. Height varies from 20 to 100 ft., depending on conditions	Spreading branches form broad, conical tree, irregular and spreading in age, often with leaning trunk	Needles: in 2s, 3–4½ in., bright green, stiff. Cones: 3 in., oval, brown	Handsome tree in youth. Takes well to pruning, even shearing. Excellent for bonsai or pots. Very salt tolerant. 'Majestic Beauty' stands up to smog. 'Thunderhead' is a dwarf (6 ft. at 10 years) with showy white winter buds and spring candles. Subject to nematodes
P. wallichiana **(P. griffithii,** **P. excelsa)** HIMALAYAN WHITE PINE Himalayas	4–6, 15–17, 32, 34, 37, 39. Needles turn brown at temperatures below –15°F/–26°C	Slow to moderate; reaches 40 ft. in gardens, 150 ft. in wild	Broad, conical, open. Often retains branches to the ground in age	Needles: in 5s, 6–8 in., blue green, drooping, soft. Cones: 6–10 in., light brown	Eventually large, but good form and color make it a good choice for featured pine in big lawn or garden. Resistant to white pine blister rust

All pines can be shaped, and usually improved, by pruning. The best time to prune is in spring, when needles start to emerge from the spires of new growth (the so-called candles). Cutting back partway into these candles will promote bushiness and allow some overall increase in tree size; cutting out candles entirely will limit size. Don't cut the tree's leading shoot unless you want to limit its height. Careful pruning will allow you to maintain pines as hedges or screens.

PISTACHE. See PISTACIA chinensis

PISTACIA chinensis

CHINESE PISTACHE

Anacardiaceae

DECIDUOUS TREE

ZONES 4–16, 18–23, 26, 28–33

FULL SUN

MODERATE WATER

Pistacia chinensis

Native to China. Slow to moderate growth to 30–60 ft. tall, with nearly equal spread. Young trees often gawky and lopsided, but older ones become dense and shapely if given reasonable care. Foot-long leaves consist of 10–16 paired dark green leaflets, each 2–4 in. long, ¾ in. wide. Good fall color even in mild climates: foliage turns luminous orange to red (sometimes shades of yellow). Only tree to color scarlet in the desert. Trees are either male or female; if the two sexes are grown near each other, the female will bear clusters of small red fruits that ripen to blue black.

Tolerant of a wide range of soils, including alkaline types. Where verticillium wilt is present, minimize risk by providing good drainage and by watering as little as possible during dry periods. Very drought tolerant. Stake young tree and prune for the first few years to develop a head high enough to walk under. Reliable tree for street, lawn, patio, or garden.

PITANGA. See EUGENIA uniflora

Pittosporaceae. The pittosporum family consists of evergreen shrubs, trees, and vines from Australia, New Zealand, and eastern Asia. Many have attractive flowers, foliage, or fruit. Sweetshade (*Hymenosporum*), *Pittosporum*, and Australian bluebell creeper (*Sollya*) are representatives.

PITTOSPORUM

Pittosporaceae

EVERGREEN SHRUBS AND TREES

ZONES VARY BY SPECIES

FULL SUN OR PARTIAL SHADE

REGULAR TO MODERATE WATER

Pittosporum tobira

Pittosporums are valued most for their foliage and form, though they also bear clusters of small, often sweetly fragrant flowers followed by fairly conspicuous fruits the size of large peas. All are basic, dependable shrubs or trees. Some make good clipped hedges; all have pleasing outlines when left unclipped. Excellent screens, windbreaks. Susceptible to aphids and scale insects; sooty black covering on leaves is a sure sign of infestation. Ripe fruits (usually orange) split open to reveal sticky seeds; fallen fruit can be a nuisance on lawns, paving.

P. crassifolium. Zones 9, 14–17, 19–24. Can attain 25 ft. in 8–10 years, but yearly pruning easily keeps it to 6–10 ft. tall and 6–8 ft. wide. Gray-green, 1–2-in.-long leaves with rounded ends are densely set on branches. Maroon flowers in late spring. Tolerates seaside conditions. 'Compactum' is a 3-ft. dwarf.

P. eugenioides. Zones 9, 14–17, 19–22. Often seen as high hedge or screen plant, but if left unpruned, it becomes a tree to 40 ft. tall and 20 ft. wide, with curving gray trunk. Wavy-edged, lance-shaped, 2–4-in. leaves; color may be yellowish or deep green. Fragrant yellow spring flowers. A form with leaves edged in creamy white is smaller, to just 10 ft.

P. phillyraeoides. WILLOW PITTOSPORUM. Zones 8, 9, 12–24. Slow growth to 20 ft. tall, 15 ft. wide. Weeping habit, with trailing branches and very narrow, 3-in.-long leaves. Small, fragrant, bell-shaped yellow flowers, late winter–early spring, followed by deep yellow fruit. Best as a specimen tree. More tolerant of heat, drought than other species.

P. tenuifolium (P. nigricans). Zones 9, 14–17, 19–24. Superficially similar to *P. eugenioides*, but with darker twigs and leafstalks; purple flowers; shorter, more oval, less wavy-edged, deeper green leaves; and greater tolerance for seacoast conditions. Selections available with dark purple or variegated leaves.

P. tobira. TOBIRA. Zones 8–31. Dense, rounded shrub, eventually reaching 10–15 ft. if not restricted by pruning. Lower limbs can be removed from older plants to make small trees. Whorls of leathery, narrowly elliptical, shiny dark green leaves to 5 in. long. Creamy white flowers, borne at branch tips in early spring, smell like orange blossoms. Very tolerant of seacoast conditions. 'Wheeler's Dwarf' grows to 2 ft. high; 'Variegata', to 5–10 ft., has gray-green leaves edged white. 'Turner's Dwarf' is a low plant with same foliage color as 'Variegata'.

P. undulatum. VICTORIAN BOX. Zones 16, 17, 21–26. Moderately fast to 15 ft., then slow to 30–40 ft. high and wide. Planted 5–8 ft. apart, can be kept to dense, 10–15-ft. screen by pruning (not shearing). Glossy green, lance-shaped, wavy-edged leaves to 6 in. long. Very fragrant creamy white flowers in early spring. Strong roots become invasive with age.

PLANE TREE. See PLATANUS

PLANTAIN LILY. See HOSTA

PLATANUS

PLANE TREE, SYCAMORE

Platanaceae

DECIDUOUS TREES

⚡ ZONES VARY BY SPECIES

☀ ◐ FULL SUN OR LIGHT SHADE

🔴 REGULAR WATER

Platanus acerifolia

All grow large, with heavy trunks and sculptural branch pattern. Older bark sheds in patches to reveal pale, smooth, new bark beneath. Big leaves (to 10 in. across) are rough surfaced and maplelike with three to five lobes; disappointing yellowish to brown autumn color. Ball-shaped brown seed clusters hang on threadlike stalks from bare branches through winter; these are prized for winter arrangements. Best in rich, deep, moist, well-drained soil. All are subject to anthracnose, which causes early leaf drop and twig dieback. Rake up and dispose of dead leaves, since fungus spores can overwinter on them.

P. acerifolia. LONDON PLANE TREE. Zones 2–24, 31–41. Hybrid between *P. occidentalis* and *P. orientalis,* and often sold under the latter name. Grows 30–40 ft. tall in 20 years; may reach an eventual 70–100 ft. tall, 65–80 ft. wide in gardens. Smooth, cream-colored upper trunk and limbs. Looks very handsome in winter. Tolerates many soils, stands up beautifully under city smog, soot, dust, reflected heat. Good avenue, street tree. Can fit smaller spaces when pollarded to create a low, dense canopy. 'Columbia' and 'Liberty' are resistant to both anthracnose and powdery mildew (can cause premature leaf drop). They are also somewhat resistant to cankerstain disease, which can kill branches or the entire tree. 'Bloodgood' resists anthracnose; 'Yarwood' is mildew resistant.

P. occidentalis. AMERICAN SYCAMORE, BUTTONWOOD. Zones 1–24, 26, 28, 31–43. Very hardy. Native to eastern U.S. Similar to *P. acerifolia;* but has whiter new bark and a longer leafless period. Irregular habit, contorted branches. Occasionally grows with multiple or leaning trunks. Old trees near streams sometimes reach huge size. Best in a large wild garden.

P. orientalis. See *P. acerifolia*

P. racemosa. CALIFORNIA SYCAMORE. Zones 4–24. Grows naturally along stream banks. Fast growth to 50–100 ft., often with multiple or leaning trunks. Bark flakes off in attractive patchwork of gray, white, green, and brown. Tolerates much heat, wind. For informal or wild garden.

PLATYCERIUM

STAGHORN FERN

Polypodiaceae

FERNS

⚡ ZONES VARY BY SPECIES

◐ PARTIAL SHADE

🔴🔴 REGULAR TO MODERATE WATER

Platycerium bifurcatum

Native to tropical regions, where they grow on trees; gardeners grow them on slabs of bark or tree fern stem, occasionally in hanging baskets or attached to trees. In the absence of rainfall, water only when slab or moss to which plant is attached is actually dry to the touch. Plant has two kinds of fronds. Sterile ones are flat, pale green, aging to tan and brown; they support plant and accumulate organic matter to help feed it. Fertile fronds are forked, resembling deer antlers.

P. bifurcatum. Zones 15–17, 19–27. From Australia and New Guinea. Surprisingly hardy; survives 20° to 22°F/−7° to −6°C with only lath structures for shelter. Fertile fronds clustered, gray green, to 3 ft. long. Makes numerous offsets that can be used in propagation. Often sold as *P. alcicorne*.

P. superbum. Zones 23–25. From Australia. Fertile and sterile fronds both forked, the former broad but divided somewhat like moose antlers. To 6 ft. long. Protect from frosts.

PLATYCLADUS orientalis (Thuja orientalis)

ORIENTAL ARBORVITAE

Cupressaceae

EVERGREEN SHRUB

⚡ ZONES 2–41

☀ ◐ FULL SUN OR LIGHT SHADE

🔴 REGULAR WATER

Platycladus orientalis

Foliage is carried in flattened sprays that are held vertically, forming a conical to pyramidal plant. Juvenile leaves are tiny and needlelike; mature leaves are minute, overlapping scales. Oval, ¾-in. cones are waxy blue green before ripening. Species (to 25 ft. high, 15 ft. wide) is rarely grown; nurseries offer more attractive, shrubbier selections 3–10 ft. high (see below). Widely used around foundations, by doorways or gates, in formal rows.

Less hardy to cold than American arborvitae *(Thuja occidentalis)*, but tolerates heat and low humidity better. Takes the place of American arborvitae in the South, lower Midwest, and Southwest. Tolerates many soils, but will not take boggy ones. Protect from strong winds. Bagworms (found in eastern U.S.) and red spider mites are potential pests. In Northwest, control blight of leaves and twigs by applying copper sprays in early fall and by destroying diseased growth.

'Aureus' ('Aureus Nana', 'Berckmanii'). DWARF GOLDEN ARBORVITAE, BERCKMAN DWARF ARBORVITAE. Dwarf, compact, golden, globe shaped, usually 3 ft. tall, 2 ft. wide. Can reach 5 ft.

'Bakeri'. Compact, cone shaped, with bright green foliage. Grows 5–8 ft. high in 10 years.

'Beverlyensis'. BEVERLY HILLS ARBORVITAE, GOLDEN PYRAMID ARBORVITAE. Upright, globe shaped to conical; somewhat open habit. Branchlet tips golden yellow. In time, can reach 10 ft. tall and wide. Give it room.

'Blue Cone'. Dense, upright, conical; good blue-green color. To 8 ft. tall, 4 ft. wide.

'Bonita' ('Bonita Upright', 'Bonita Erecta'). Rounded, full, dense cone to 3 ft. tall. Dark green with slight golden tinting at branch tips.

'Fruitlandii'. FRUITLAND ARBORVITAE. Compact, upright, cone shaped, with deep green foliage.

'Minima Glauca'. DWARF BLUE ARBORVITAE. Grows 3–4 ft. tall and as wide. Blue-green foliage.

'Raffles'. Resembles 'Aureus' but is smaller, denser in growth, brighter in color.

'Westmont'. To 3 ft. tall, 2 ft. wide. Green foliage has yellow tips through the growing season.

PLATYCODON grandiflorus

BALLOON FLOWER

Campanulaceae (Lobeliaceae)

PERENNIAL

ZONES 1–24, 26, 28–45

AFTERNOON SHADE IN HOT-SUMMER AREAS

REGULAR WATER

Platycodon grandiflorus

Inflated, balloonlike buds are carried on slender stalks at the ends of upright stems clad in broadly oval, 3-in. leaves. Buds open into 2-in., star-shaped blue-violet flowers with purple veins. Bloom begins in early summer and will continue for 2 months or more if spent blossoms (not entire stems) are removed. Double-flowered varieties are available, as are pink- and white-flowered types.

Plant is deep-rooted and takes 2 or 3 years to get well established. Dies back completely in fall, and new growth appears quite late in spring; mark position to avoid digging up fleshy roots. If you do unearth a root, replant it—or the pieces—right away.

PLECTRANTHUS

SWEDISH IVY

Lamiaceae (Labiatae)

PERENNIALS

ZONES 22–25; OR INDOORS

SHADE OUTDOORS; BRIGHT LIGHT INDOORS

REGULAR WATER

Plectranthus oertendahlii

Leaves somewhat thick, with scalloped edges and prominent veins. Small white or bluish flowers in spikes. In mildest climates, can be grown as ground cover or as trailing plants that drape over walls or planter edges. As greenhouse, lathhouse, or house plants, grow in hanging pot or wall container. Among eas-

iest plants to grow. Will root in water or soil. Many people remove flower buds before bloom to keep plants compact; others allow plants to bloom, then cut them back afterward. The following are the best known of many species and varieties:

BALLOON FLOWER IN BORDERS

With its decorative round buds, graceful star-shaped blossoms, and several-month-long bloom season, balloon flower is a nice choice for a summer border. Companion plants in shades of pink, deep to light blue, and white make for a lovely color combination; you might try astilbe, various kinds of bellflower *(Campanula)*, coral bells *(Heuchera)*, and mallow *(Malva)*. Lush foliage plants such as hosta are good partners, too.

P. australis. To 6 in. high; wide spreading. Shiny dark green leaves. Some forms have white-variegated foliage.

P. coleoides 'Marginatus'. To 2 ft. high; less trailing in habit than the others. Leaves green and gray green, edged in cream.

P. oertendahlii. To 6 in. high; wide spreading. Leaf veins are silvery above, purplish beneath. Leaf margins are purplish, scalloped.

PLEROMA. See TIBOUCHINA urvilleana

PLUM, FLOWERING. See PRUNUS

PLUM and PRUNE

Rosaceae

DECIDUOUS FRUIT TREES

ZONES VARY BY VARIETY

FULL SUN

PERIODIC DEEP SOAKINGS

SEE CHART NEXT PAGE

Plum

Like their cherry, peach, and apricot relatives, these are stone fruits belonging to the genus *Prunus;* for flowering plums, see pages 453–454. Three categories of edible plums and prunes are grown in the diverse climates of North America: European, Japanese, and hardy. They tolerate many soil types, but do best in fertile, well-drained soil. Plants bloom in late winter or early spring. Harvest season is from June into September, depending on variety.

The two most widely grown groups are European *(P. domestica)* and Japanese *(P. salicina)*. Damson plum *(P. insititia)* is often considered a type of European plum; it freely intercrosses with European plums. Prunes are European plum varieties with a high sugar content, a trait which allows them to be sun-dried without fermenting at the pit.

Compared to Japanese plums, European varieties as a group have a higher chill requirement, bloom later (and so are less subject to frost damage), ripen their fruit with less summer heat, and tend to be somewhat more cold hardy. European types are at their best in the Northeast and north-central states, but they also produce good crops in the West. Japanese plums are widely grown in the South and West. In the South, however, frost damage often results in inconsistent yields.

A third category dominates in regions with severe winters, especially the Dakotas, Minnesota, and the Canadian prairies. This is a complex group of hardy hybrids involving Japanese plum, several species of native American wild plums, and the native sand cherry *(P. besseyi)*. Varieties with fruit approaching the size and quality of Japanese plums are sometimes called Japanese-American

Plum

▶ page 441

PLUM and PRUNE

NAME, GROUP	ZONES	FRUIT	COMMENTS
EUROPEAN VARIETIES			
'Damson' ('Blue Damson', P. insititia)	2–23, 31–41	Small. Purple or blue-black skin, green flesh. Very tart flavor. Late	Makes fine jam and jelly. Strains of this variety are sold as 'French Damson', 'Shropshire'
'Earliblue'	2, 3, 32–41	Medium-size. Blue skin; tender green-yellow flesh. Early	Light to moderate producer. Slow to begin bearing
'Green Gage' (P. domestica italica)	2–12, 14–22, 31–41	Small to medium. Greenish yellow skin, amber flesh. Good flavor. Midseason	Very old variety; still a favorite for eating fresh, cooking, canning, or jam. Selected strain sold as 'Jefferson'
'Italian Prune' ('Fellenburg')	2–12, 14–18, 33–41	Medium-size. Sweet, purplish black. Late midseason	Excellent fresh and for canning; can be dried. 'Early Italian' ripens 2 weeks earlier
'Mount Royal'	34–44	Small to medium. Bluish black skin; meaty, tender, juicy, sweet yellow flesh. Midseason	Originated as a chance seedling discovered near Montreal, Canada. Vigorous, productive. Good-quality fruit for eating fresh, cooking
'President'	2–12, 14–20, 32–41	Large. Purplish blue skin, amber flesh. Attractive, but flavor not outstanding. Very late	Best for cooking, canning. Not for drying
'Stanley'	1–12, 14–22, 31–43	Large. Purplish black skin, yellow flesh. Sweet and juicy. Midseason	Good canning variety. Resembles larger 'Italian Prune'. Tends to overbear; best if fruit is thinned
'Sugar'	2–12, 14–22, 31–41	Medium to large. Dark blue. Very sweet, highly flavored. Early midseason	Good fresh, for home drying and canning. Tends to bear heavily in alternate years
JAPANESE VARIETIES			
'AU-Amber'	31–35	Medium-size. Red-purple skin, yellow flesh. Very sweet. Early	Developed at Auburn University, Alabama. Some tolerance of bacterial diseases. Early bloom often results in reduced yields
'AU-Producer'	31–35	Small to medium. Dark red skin, red flesh. Good quality. Midseason	Developed at Auburn University, Alabama. Some tolerance of bacterial diseases. Good yields
'Beauty'	2, 3, 6–10, 12, 14–20, 31–41	Medium-size. Bright red skin, amber flesh with scarlet streaks. Good flavor. Fruit softens quickly. Very early	Consistent heavy bearer
'Early Golden'	2, 3, 7–10, 32–41	Small to medium. Yellow fruit with good flavor. Early	Vigorous tree. Tends to bear heavily in alternate years. Fruit suitable for eating fresh, cooking
'Howard Miracle'	2, 3, 6–10, 14–20, 31–41	Medium-size. Yellow skin with red blush; yellow flesh with distinctive spicy, pineapplelike flavor. Midseason	Very vigorous. Fruit more acid than most Japanese plums, but truly distinctive in flavor
'Methley'	3–9, 14–24, 28–41	Medium-size. Reddish purple skin, dark red flesh. Sweet, mild flavor. Early	Bud-hardy, with early bloom. Good pollinator for other Japanese plum varieties
'Ozark Premier'	31–41	Very large. Red to purple skin, juicy yellow flesh. Very good flavor. Late midseason	Vigorous, productive. Fruit good for eating fresh, canning, cooking, jelly
'Santa Rosa'	2, 3, 7–12, 14–23, 28–41	Medium to large. Purplish red skin with heavy blue bloom, flesh yellow to dark red near skin. Rich, pleasing, tart flavor. Early	Important commercial variety for fresh eating. Good canned if skin is removed. Very prone to disease in Southeast; best in drier climates. 'Late Santa Rosa' follows by a month
'Satsuma'	2–12, 14–22, 31–41	Small to medium. Dull deep red skin; dark red, solid, meaty flesh. Mild, sweet flavor. Small pit. Early midseason	Preferred for jams and jellies. Sometimes called blood plum because of red juice. Tends to overbear, so thin fruit for best size
'Shiro'	2–12, 14–22, 32–41	Medium to large. Flavorful fruit with yellow skin and flesh. Early midseason	Heavy producer. Fruit good for eating fresh or cooking

P

PLUM and PRUNE

NAME, GROUP	ZONES	FRUIT	COMMENTS
HARDY HYBRIDS			
'Opata'	1–3, 35–45	Small. Purple skin, sweet green flesh. Late	Cherry-plum hybrid from South Dakota. Bush form. Upper branches often suffer winter injury in coldest areas, but lower branches usually fruit well. Fruit good fresh and for preserves
'Pipestone'	1–3, 35–43	Large. Tough red skin. Yellow flesh a little stringy but juicy and sweet. Midseason	Vigorous Japanese-American hybrid developed in Minnesota. Needs little heat to ripen. Very good for fresh eating and jam; good for jelly.
'Sapalta'	1–3, 35–45	Small. Red-purple skin, almost black flesh. Late	Cherry-plum hybrid developed in Canada. Bush form. Good for fresh eating, juice, canning, preserves
'Superior'	1–3, 35–43	Very large. Dark red, russeted skin. Firm yellow flesh, slightly tart near skin, dessert quality. Late midseason	Japanese-American hybrid developed in Minnesota. Tree comes into bearing early; prolific harvests. Good fresh and for jam, jelly
'Underwood'	1–3, 35–45	Medium to large. Dark red skin, amber flesh. Tender, juicy, sweet. Early	Vigorous Japanese-American hybrid developed in Minnesota. Good for fresh eating and jam, fair for jelly

hybrids; those with considerably smaller fruit that is closer in flavor to wild plums are often referred to as cherry-plum hybrids.

Most plum varieties are grafted onto another rootstock. Standard trees grow about 15 ft. high, dwarf trees about half that size. There is also an intermediate semidwarf category. Some of the hardy hybrids are trees; others have a bush form, to about 6 ft. high with spreading branches.

Plums come in many colors. The skin may be yellow, red, purple, green, blue, or almost black; the flesh may be yellow, red, or green. Japanese plums are the largest and juiciest of the lot, with a pleasant blend of acid and sugar; they are typically eaten fresh. European kinds are firmer fleshed and can be cooked or eaten fresh; prune varieties are used for drying or canning, but can also be eaten out of hand if you like the very sweet flavor. Many hardy plums are tasty fresh, while others are better cooked or made into preserves.

Train young trees to a vase shape. After selecting framework branches, cut back to lateral branches. If tree tends to grow upright, cut to outside branches; if it is spreading, cut to inside branches. Prune to avoid formation of V-shaped crotches. On types that produce excessive upright growth (mainly Japanese plums and Japanese-American hybrids), shorten shoots to outside branchlets. Mature European plum trees require limited pruning, mainly to thin out annual shoot growth. On bush-form hybrids, remove oldest shoots to the ground every few years.

SOME PLUMS NEED TO BE THINNED

Heavy bearing of Japanese varieties results in much small fruit and, possibly, damage to the tree. Thin fruit drastically as soon as it is big enough to be seen, spacing the plums 4–6 in. apart. Other plums do not require as much thinning as Japanese types do.

Most European plums don't require a pollinator, though they set fruit better when grown near other European varieties. Japanese plums generally produce better crops when cross-pollinated; plant two Japanese varieties. Cross-pollination of hardy plums is often difficult; ask local nurseries about effective and available pollinators for your area.

Plums are far easier to grow than peaches or apples, yet they are susceptible to some insect pests and diseases, especially east of the Rockies. Black knot (growths caused by a fungus) is a very common problem in the eastern U.S. Check with your Cooperative Extension Office for appropriate controls; the "knots" can also be removed to help reduce spread of disease. Peach tree borer may cause trouble. The more humid the climate, the more troublesome are plum curculio (which infests the fruit) and the diseases bacterial canker (which causes open wounds on trunk and branches) and brown rot of stone fruit. If you only have a few fruit trees, you may be able to control the curculio with traps. Dormant-season applications of sprays combining horticultural oil with lime sulfur or fixed copper will control brown rot and various insect pests such as scale; also prune trees to provide good air circulation. To reduce risk of bacterial canker, prevalent in the South, don't leave stubs when pruning and remove dead or broken branches right away.

Plumbaginaceae. The leadwort family consists of shrubs and perennials with clustered and funnel-shaped flowers: examples are thrift (*Armeria*) and two groups of plants commonly called plumbago (*Ceratostigma* and *Plumbago*).

PLUMBAGO auriculata (P. capensis)

CAPE PLUMBAGO, LEADWORT

Plumbaginaceae

EVERGREEN TO SEMIEVERGREEN SHRUB OR VINE

✔ ZONES 8, 9, 12–28

☀ FULL SUN

💧 MODERATE TO LITTLE WATER

Plumbago auriculata

If grown without a support, forms a sprawling, mounding bush to 6 ft. tall, 8–10 ft. wide; with support, can reach 12 ft. or more. Fresh-looking, light to medium green leaves, 1–2 in. long. Inch-wide flowers in phloxlike clusters, varying (in seedling plants) from white to clear light blue. Select plants in bloom to get color you want. Typically blooms spring–fall, but may flower throughout year in warm, frost-free areas. 'Alba' is white flowered; 'Royal Cape' has sky blue blooms.

Needs good drainage. Young growth blackens and leaves drop in heavy frosts, but recovery is good. Prune out damaged growth after frost danger is past. Slow to start, but tough. Good cover for bank, fence, hot wall; good

441

background and filler plant. Widely used as a hedge in central Florida. Withstands light salt drift from ocean. For other plants called plumbago, see *Ceratostigma.*

PLUMBAGO larpentae. See CERATOSTIGMA plumbaginoides

**PLUME CEDAR, PLUME CRYPTOMERIA.
See CRYPTOMERIA japonica 'Elegans'**

PLUME HYACINTH. See MUSCARI comosum 'Monstrosum'

PLUME POPPY. See MACLEAYA

PLUMERIA

Apocynaceae

DECIDUOUS SHRUBS OR SMALL TREES

🗡 ZONES VARY BY SPECIES

☀ ◗ FULL SUN OR HIGH SHADE

🌢 MODERATE WATER

Plumeria rubra

Handsome, useful plants with an open, gaunt character; they grow to 18 ft. tall, with leathery, pointed leaves clustered near the tips of thick branches. Bloom during warm weather, bearing clusters of large, showy, waxy, very fragrant flowers. All are easy to grow from cuttings. Tender to frost; won't take cold, wet soil. In frost-prone regions, grow in containers; when cold weather is expected, move to bright window for continued bloom or to a frost-free garage or shed. Feeding late in year will result in soft growth that will be nipped by lightest frosts.

P. alba. WHITE FRANGIPANI. Zones 24, 25. Narrow, lance-shaped, puckered leaves to 1 ft. long. Flowers 2½ in. wide, yellow with white center.

P. obtusa. SINGAPORE PLUMERIA. Zones 24, 25. Leaves dark green, 6 in. long, 2 in. wide, very glossy. White, 2-in. flowers.

P. rubra. PLUMERIA, FRANGIPANI. Zones 12, 13, 19, 21–25, 27. Thick leaves 8–16 in. long. Clusters of 2–2½-in.-wide red flowers. There are varieties with pink, yellow, or white blossoms.

PLUM YEW. See CEPHALOTAXUS

POA

BLUEGRASS

Poaceae (Gramineae)

PERENNIAL AND ANNUAL GRASSES

🗡 ZONES VARY BY SPECIES

☀ FULL SUN (EXCEPT FOR P. TRIVIALIS)

🌢 REGULAR WATER

Poa pratensis

One is the best-known cool-season lawn grass; the other two sometimes turn up in lawns, either intentionally or as an annual weed. Leaves of all have characteristic boat-prow tip.

P. annua. ANNUAL BLUEGRASS. All zones. Cool-season weed of lawns. Bright green, soft textured. Discourage it by maintaining thick turf of good grasses.

P. pratensis. KENTUCKY BLUEGRASS. Zones 1–11, 14–17, 32, 34–45. Rich blue-green perennial lawn grass. Many selections are available as seed or sod. Mow at 2 in. high in spring and fall, at 3 in. high in summer. Use alone or in mixture with other grasses.

P. trivialis. ROUGH-STALKED BLUEGRASS. Zones 1–11, 14–17, 32, 34–45. Fine-textured, bright green perennial meadow and pasture grass.

Occasionally used in shady lawn mixtures for its tolerance of shade and damp soil.

Poaceae. The grass family is undoubtedly the most important plant family in terms of usefulness to humans. All the world's important grain crops are grasses; the bamboos (giant grasses) are useful in building and crafts. Many grasses are used in lawns or as ornamental annual or perennial plants. Some botanists still use Gramineae as the family name for grasses.

PODOCARPUS

Podocarpaceae

EVERGREEN TREES OR SHRUBS

🗡 ZONES VARY BY SPECIES

☀ ◗ FULL SUN OR PARTIAL SHADE

🌢 🌢 REGULAR TO MODERATE WATER

Podocarpus gracilior

Versatile plants grown for good-looking foliage, interesting form; adaptable to many climates, many garden uses. Good screen or background plants. Foliage generally resembles that of yews (*Taxus*), to which these plants are related, but leaves of the better-known species are longer, broader, and lighter in color than those of yews. If a male plant is growing nearby, females bear fruit after many years, producing small fleshy fruits rather than cones. Grow well (if slowly) in most soils, though they may develop chlorosis where soil is alkaline or heavy and damp. Some botanists now divide these plants into three genera (*Afrocarpus, Nageia, Podocarpus*); in the following listings, new names are given in parentheses.

P. elongatus. See P. gracilior

P. gracilior (Afrocarpus gracilior). FERN PINE. Tree, often grown as espaliered vine or even as hanging basket plant. Zones 8, 9, 13–25, 26 (southern part), 27. To 20–60 ft. tall (70 ft. in its native East Africa). Among the cleanest, most pest-free trees for street, lawn, patio, garden; good hedge, big shrub, container plant.

Method of propagation determines growth habit. Plants grown from seed are upright when young, with 2–4-in.-long, ½-in.-wide, glossy dark green leaves somewhat sparsely set on branches. With age, they produce soft grayish to bluish green, 1–2-in.-long leaves that are more closely spaced on branches. Plants grown from cuttings or grafts of a mature tree retain the small, closely set leaves, but they have very limber branches and are often reluctant to produce strong vertical growth. These more willowy plants, suitable for espalier or growing as vines along fences, are often sold as *P. elongatus;* the larger-leafed, more upright kinds are sold as *P. gracilior.* The *P. elongatus* types eventually become upright trees, though their foliage mass persists in drooping for some time.

P. henkelii. LONG-LEAFED YELLOW-WOOD. Tree. Zones 8, 9, 14–25. Native to South Africa. Handsome, erect; grows slowly to 30–50 ft. Masses of drooping leaves 5–7 in. long, ⅓ in. wide.

P. macrophyllus. YEW PINE. Shrub or tree. Zones 4–9, 12–28, 31. Native to China, Japan. To 50 ft. tall, generally narrow and upright. Bright green leaves 4 in. long, ½ in. wide. Grow indoors or out, in tubs or open ground. Large shrub, screen, street or lawn tree (with staking and thinning). Limber enough to espalier. Easily pruned as clipped hedge, topiary. Very heat tolerant.

P. m. maki. SHRUBBY YEW PINE. Smaller, slower growing than species; reaches 6–8 ft. in 10 years. Dense, upright form. Leaves to 3 in. long, ¼ in. wide. One of the best container plants for outdoor or indoor use, and a choice shrub generally.

P. nagi (Nageia nagi). Tree. Zones 8, 9, 14–28. Slow growth to 15–20 ft. (80–90 ft. in its native Japan). Branchlets drooping, sometimes to a considerable length. Leaves 1–3 in. long, ½–1½ in. wide, leathery,

P

smooth, sharp pointed. More treelike in youth than other species. Makes decorative foliage pattern against natural wood or masonry. Plant in groves for slender sapling effect. Excellent container plant.

PODOPHYLLUM

Berberidaceae

PERENNIALS

ZONES VARY BY SPECIES

PARTIAL OR FULL SHADE

REGULAR WATER

RHIZOMES, LEAVES, STEMS, SEEDS POISONOUS IF INGESTED

Podophyllum peltatum

Odd herbaceous relatives of barberry, with thick, spreading underground rhizomes that send up stalks crowned with large, shield-shaped, deeply lobed leaves. Shoots with a single leaf are barren; those with two leaves bear a single 2-in.-wide flower (set between the leaves) followed by a juicy, 2-in.-long berry. Berries are edible but can have a powerful laxative effect. Attractive, slow-spreading deciduous ground cover plants for shady areas with rich, moist, woodsy soil.

P. hexandrum. Zones 3–6, 32–34, 37, 39. Native to Himalayas and China. Grows 1–1½ ft. high, with 10-in. umbrellalike leaves mottled brown. Leaves divided into three or five lobes, with each lobe further divided. White or pink flower; red berry.

P. peltatum. MAY APPLE, WILD MANDRAKE. Zones 1–6, 28–43. Native to eastern U.S. To 1½ ft. high. Leaves to 1 ft. across, divided into five to nine lobes. White flower; yellow berry. Leaves pushing up through the forest duff are one of the earliest signs of spring in eastern woodlands. Dies down completely in summer.

PODRANEA ricasoliana

PINK TRUMPET VINE

Bignoniaceae

EVERGREEN VINE

ZONES 9, 12, 13, 19–27

FULL SUN OR LIGHT SHADE

REGULAR TO MODERATE WATER

Podranea ricasoliana

Native to South Africa. Twining vine to 20 ft. Dark green leaves divided featherwise into three or four pairs of 2-in. leaflets. In spring or summer, loose clusters of flowers shaped like open trumpets appear at ends of new growth. Blooms are 2–3 in. wide, pink with red veins. Slow grower when young but speeds up as it matures. Likes heat, good drainage. Planting in sterilized, fertile soil is recommended in Florida, since plant is very subject to nematode damage there. May drop leaves in frost but can recover from roots even if top growth is frozen.

POHUTUKAWA. See METROSIDEROS excelsus

POINCIANA. See CAESALPINIA, DELONIX regia

POINSETTIA. See EUPHORBIA pulcherrima

POISON IVY, POISON OAK. See RHUS

POKER PLANT. See KNIPHOFIA uvaria

Polemoniaceae. The phlox family consists mostly of annuals and perennials, including many wildflowers; examples are *Ipomopsis* and *Phlox*. Cup-and-saucer vine *(Cobaea)* is another member.

FOR INFORMATION ON SELECTING PLANTS
PLEASE SEE PAGES 79–160

POLEMONIUM

Polemoniaceae

PERENNIALS

ZONES 1–11, 14–17, 31–43

PARTIAL OR FULL SHADE

REGULAR WATER

Polemonium caeruleum

Lush rosettes of finely divided fernlike foliage; clusters of bell-shaped flowers, spring–summer. Combine nicely with bleeding heart, bellflower, ferns, hellebore, hosta, and lilies. Need good drainage. Grow from seed or from divisions made after bloom or in spring. Listed below are the types most commonly available in nurseries. All are good under trees.

P. caeruleum. JACOB'S LADDER. Clusters of lavender blue, pendulous, 1-in.-long flowers on leafy, 1½–2-ft.-high stems.

P. 'Firmament'. Hybrid between *P. caeruleum* and *P. reptans*. To 20 in. high, with bright blue flowers.

P. foliosissimum. To 2½ ft. high, with leafy stems and lavender blue flowers enhanced by bright orange stamens. Native to western U.S.; short lived where summer heat is accompanied by high humidity.

P. reptans. Wildflower in eastern woodlands and midwestern plains. Best known though its variety 'Blue Pearl', a profusely blooming blue-flowered dwarf with spreading growth to 9 in. high, 1½ ft. wide. Good in shaded, dampish rock garden.

POLIANTHES tuberosa

TUBEROSE

Agavaceae

TUBEROUS-ROOTED PERENNIAL

ALL ZONES (SEE BELOW)

FULL SUN OR PARTIAL SHADE

REGULAR WATER DURING GROWTH AND BLOOM

Polianthes tuberosa

Native to Mexico. Noted for powerful, heady fragrance. Glistening white, tubular flowers are loosely arranged in spikelike clusters on stems to 3 ft. tall, late summer–fall. Long, narrow, grasslike basal leaves. Single forms are graceful, but double-flowered 'The Pearl' is most widely available; it's a good garden variety but not as long-lasting a cut flower as the single type.

To bloom year after year, tuberose needs a long (at least 4-month) warm season before flowering. Start indoors or plant outside after soil is warm. Set rhizomes 2 in. deep, 4–6 in. apart. If soil or water is alkaline, apply acid fertilizer when growth begins. Where winter temperatures remain above 20°F/–7°C, rhizomes may stay in ground all year, but many gardeners in these areas (and all those living in colder regions) dig rhizomes and store them over the winter. Dig plants in fall after leaves have yellowed; cut off dead foliage. Let rhizomes dry for 2 weeks, then store them in a cool (40° to 50°F/4° to 10°C), dry place. Tuberose can also be grown in pots and moved to a protected area during cold weather. Divide clumps every 4 years.

POLYANTHUS. See PRIMULA polyantha

Polygonaceae. The buckwheat family consists of annuals, perennials, shrubs, trees, and vines. Flowers lack petals, but sepals are often showy. Stems are jointed. Fruit is small, dry, single seeded. Representatives include wild buckwheat *(Eriogonum)*, rhubarb, knotweed *(Polygonum)*, and coral vine *(Antigonum)*. True buckwheat—the pancake flour kind—is *Fagopyrum*, a crop plant of no ornamental value.

POLYGONATUM

SOLOMON'S SEAL

Liliaceae

PERENNIALS

ZONES 1–7, 14–17, 28–43

WOODSY SHADE

REGULAR WATER

Polygonatum biflorum

Slowly spreading underground rhizomes send up stems that grow upright for a distance, then bend outward. On either side of the arching stems are broadly oval, bright green leaves arranged in nearly horizontal planes. Where leaves join stems, pairs or clusters of small, bell-shaped greenish white blossoms hang beneath the stems on threadlike stalks in spring. Small blue-black berries sometimes follow the flowers. Leaves and stems turn bright yellow in autumn before plant dies to the ground.

Attractive for form and flowers in woodland garden; good with astilbe, ferns, hellebore, hosta, wild ginger. Need loose, woodsy soil. Don't need dividing; to get more plants, remove rhizomes from a clump's edge in early spring. Attractive in containers. For false Solomon's seal, see *Smilacina*.

P. biflorum. Native to eastern North America. Bears 4-in. leaves on stems to 3 ft. tall. Flowers usually in pairs or threes.

P. commutatum. Carries 7-in. leaves on stems normally reaching 4–5 ft. high, possibly 7 ft. tall. Flowers in groups of two to ten. This species is considered to be a vigorous form of *P. biflorum*. It is sometimes sold as *P. canaliculatum*.

P. odoratum (P. japonicum). Native to Europe, Asia. To 3½ ft. tall, with 4–6-in. leaves. Scented flowers usually borne in pairs, sometimes singly. 'Variegatum' has white-edged leaves carried on stems that are dark red until fully grown.

POLYGONUM

KNOTWEED

Polygonaceae

EVERGREEN OR DECIDUOUS PERENNIALS AND VINES

ZONES VARY BY SPECIES

FULL SUN, EXCEPT AS NOTED

REGULAR WATER, EXCEPT AS NOTED

Polygonum cuspidatum compactum

Sturdy, sun-loving plants with jointed stems and small white or pink flowers in open sprays. Some kinds tend to get out of hand and need to be controlled.

P. affine. Evergreen perennial. Zones 4–9, 14–17, 31, 32. Tufted plant 1–1½ ft. tall. Leaves mostly basal, 2–4½ in. long, finely toothed, deep green turning to bronze in winter. Bright rose red flowers in dense, erect, 2–3-in. spikes, summer into fall. Informal border or ground cover. Tolerates some shade. 'Darjeeling Red' forms 3-in.-high mats with 10-in. spikes of flowers in deep pink aging to red; foliage turns red in fall. 'Dimity' has fatter, paler flower spikes. 'Superbum' is larger-leafed than the species, with somewhat taller spikes of pale pink flowers.

P. aubertii. SILVER LACE VINE. Evergreen in warmer part of range, deciduous in colder part. Zones 2–24, 28–41. Fast growing: can cover 100 sq. ft. in a season. Heart-shaped, glossy, wavy-edged leaves 1½–2½ in. long. Small, creamy white flowers appear in a frothy mass from late spring until fall. Use as quick screen on fences or arbors, on hillsides, at seashore. You can prune severely (to ground) each year; bloom will be delayed until well into summer. Drought tolerant.

P. baldschuanicum. BOKHARA FLEECEFLOWER. Deciduous vine. Zones 2–24, 31–41. Much like *P. aubertii* in appearance, growth, vigor, and uses. Fragrant pink flowers, borne in large, drooping clusters, are somewhat larger than those of *P. aubertii*.

P. bistorta 'Superbum'. Deciduous perennial. Zones 2–9, 14–17, 31–43. Forms a mound to 2½ ft. high, with leaves to 8 in. long. Flowers are pink aging to deep red, carried in dense, 4–6-in.-long, bottlebrushlike

spikes held well above the foliage. Blooms in early summer, with sporadic repeat bloom until frost. Leaves turn bright red in autumn.

P. capitatum. Evergreen perennial in Zones 8, 9, 12–24; summer annual elsewhere. Rugged, trailing ground cover to 8 in. high, spreading to 20 in. Leaves 1½ in. long; new leaves are dark green, old ones tinged pink. Foliage discolors and dies below 28°F/–2°C. Stems and small, round flower heads are pink. Blooms most of year in mild climates. Has invasive roots and also reseeds freely. Takes sun or shade. Drought tolerant.

P. cuspidatum (P. japonicum). JAPANESE KNOTWEED. Deciduous perennial. Zones 1–24, 31–43. Tough, vigorous plant forming large clumps of red-brown, wiry, 4–8-ft. stems. Leaves nearly heart shaped, to 5 in. long. Greenish white flowers in late summer and fall. Extremely invasive, so keep it away from choice plants. Useful in untamed parts of garden. Cut to ground in late fall or winter. Often called bamboo or Mexican bamboo because of jointed stalks.

P. c. compactum (P. reynoutria) is a lower, somewhat less rampant form, growing 10–24 in. high and spreading by creeping roots. In late summer, showy clusters of small, pale pink flowers open from red buds. Red-veined foliage turns red in fall before plant dies to the ground.

P. vacciniifolium. Evergreen perennial. Zones 4–7, 31, 32. Prostrate, with slender, leafy, branching red stems radiating 2–4 ft. Leaves ½ in. long, oval, turn red in fall. Rose pink late-summer flowers in dense, upright, 2–3-in. spikes on 6–9-in. stalks. Excellent bank cover or drapery for boulder in large rock garden.

P. virginianum (Tovara virginiana). Deciduous perennial. Zones 2–9, 14–17, 31–41. Native to eastern U.S. Rhizome produces upright, leafy stems to 2–3 ft. high; spreads aggressively. Late to leaf out in spring. Species is green-leafed; it is less often grown than forms with variegated foliage. 'Variegata' has green leaves marbled with creamy white. 'Painter's Palette' is similar, but with a V-shaped reddish mark in center of each leaf; new leaves are creamy white splashed with light green and pink. Give part shade; protect from wind.

Polypodiaceae. The polypody family contains the vast majority of ferns. They differ from other ferns only in technical details concerning spore-bearing bodies (sporangia).

POLYPODIUM

Polypodiaceae

FERNS

ZONES VARY BY SPECIES; OR INDOORS

PARTIAL OR FULL SHADE

AMPLE WATER

Polypodium aureum 'Mandaianum'

Widespread, variable group. Both types described here are tropical plants most commonly used in hanging baskets, often in the house or greenhouse. As with many ferns, reclassification has added new names, which are given below in parentheses.

P. aureum (Phlebodium aureum). HARE'S FOOT FERN. Zones 15–17, 19–27. Native to tropical America, including Florida. Heavy, brown, creeping rhizomes; coarse blue-green fronds 3–5 ft. long. Fronds drop if hit by frost, but plants recover fast. 'Mandaianum', sometimes called lettuce fern, has frilled and wavy frond edges. Both it and the species are showy.

P. subauriculatum 'Knightiae' (Goniophlebium subauriculatum 'Knightiae'). KNIGHT'S POLYPODY. Zones 24, 25. Native to tropical Asia. Gracefully drooping fronds to 3 ft. or longer, with fringed edges. Spectacular when well grown. Outdoor plants shed old fronds in spring, then quickly produce new ones.

FOR GROWING SYMBOL EXPLANATIONS

PLEASE SEE PAGE 161

POLYSCIAS

Araliaceae

EVERGREEN SHRUBS

ZONES 21–25; OR INDOORS

FULL SUN OR PARTIAL SHADE

REGULAR TO MODERATE WATER

Polyscias fruticosa
'Elegans'

Like many other aralia relatives, they are grown for their handsomely divided leaves; flowers are unimportant and seldom produced outside the tropics. Plants appreciate warmth and humidity. Outdoors, they need adequate water and protection from frost and mites. Often grown as hedges in South Florida. As house plants, they are considered fussy: they need fresh, fairly still air (they cannot tolerate drafts), good light but no direct sun, and enough water but not too much. Overwatering and mite damage are the two main causes of failure. Misting is useful, along with light feeding. If plants are doing well, don't move them. They will grow slowly, maintaining their shapeliness for years.

P. balfouriana (P. scutellaria 'Balfourii'). To 25 ft. tall. Species has green foliage. More commonly sold 'Marginata' bears white-edged leaflets. 'Pennockii' has white to pale green leaflets with irregular green spots.

P. fruticosa. MING ARALIA, PARSLEY PANAX. Grows 6–8 ft. tall. Leaves finely divided and redivided into multitude of narrow, toothed segments. 'Elegans' is a small, extremely dense-foliaged variety.

P. guilfoylei 'Victoriae'. To 15 ft. tall, with white-edged leaflets that are deeply slashed and cut.

POLYSTICHUM

Polypodiaceae

FERNS

ZONES VARY BY SPECIES

PARTIAL OR FULL SHADE

REGULAR WATER, EXCEPT AS NOTED

Polystichum munitum

Hardy symmetrical plants with medium-size, evergreen (except on *P. braunei*) fronds. Among most useful and widely planted ferns, they combine well with other plants and are easy to grow. Do best in rich, organic, well-drained soil. Use in shady beds, along house walls, in mixed woodland plantings.

P. acrostichoides. CHRISTMAS FERN. Zones 1–9, 14–24, 28–43. Native to eastern North America. Grows to 1–1½ ft., with dark green leaves that make a fine contrast to snow or to the brown of dead leaves at Christmas time. Stiff fronds remain upright until pushed over by heavy snow or hard frost. In coldest climates, plant appreciates a leaf mulch.

P. aculeatum. PRICKLY SHIELD FERN, HARD SHIELD FERN. Zones 3–9, 14–17, 31–35, 37, 39. Native to Europe. Grows 2–4 ft. tall. Glossy, firm, fairly upright, once- or twice-cut fronds; final segments are tipped by soft prickles. Pale young fronds make an attractive show against the dark green mature ones.

P. braunii. BRAUN'S HOLLY FERN. Zones 3–6, 32–41. Semievergreen to deciduous. Native to northern latitudes. Grows 1–3 ft. tall, with twice-divided fronds. Silvery green new growth.

P. munitum. SWORD FERN. Zones 2–9, 14–24, 36–38. Native to western North America. Leathery, shiny dark green fronds are 2–4 ft. long; erect, then spreading. Old plants may have 75–100 fronds. Established plants need little water.

P. polyblepharum. JAPANESE LACE FERN, TASSEL FERN. Zones 4–9, 14–24, 31–34, 39. Native to Asia. Handsome, dense, lacy. Resembles *P. setiferum* but is taller, darker green, and somewhat coarser; fronds are a little more upright (to 2 ft. high). Usually sold as *P. setosum*.

P. setiferum. SOFT SHIELD FERN. Zones 4–9, 14–24, 31–34, 39. Native to Europe. Finely cut fronds give effect of dark green lace, spread out in flattened vase shape. Many forms, 2–4½ ft. tall. 'Proliferum' makes

plantlets on midribs of older fronds; these can be used for propagation. Other fancy varieties are sometimes sold under the name "English fern."

P. setosum. See P. polyblepharum

POMEGRANATE. See PUNICA granatum

PONCIRUS trifoliata.
See Trifoliate Orange in Hardy Citrus under CITRUS

Pontederiaceae. The pickerel weed family contains aquatic or marsh plants with showy, usually blue flowers, among them pickerel weed (*Pontederia*) and water hyacinth (*Eichhornia*).

PONTEDERIA cordata

PICKEREL WEED

Pontederiaceae

AQUATIC PLANT

ALL ZONES

FULL SUN OR LIGHT SHADE

LOCATE IN PONDS, WATER GARDENS

Pontederia cordata

Grown as companion to water lilies; best planted in pots of rich soil placed in 1 ft. of water. Long-stalked leaves stand well above surface of water; these are heart shaped, to 10 in. long and 6 in. wide. Short spikes of bright blue flowers top 4-ft. (or shorter) stems. Gives wild-pond look to informal garden pool. Plant underwater at shorelines of natural ponds. Dormant in winter.

PONYTAIL. See BEAUCARNEA recurvata

POOR MAN'S ORCHID. See SCHIZANTHUS pinnatus

POOR MAN'S RHODODENDRON. See IMPATIENS oliveri

POPCORN. See CORN

POPLAR. See POPULUS

POPPY. See PAPAVER

POPPY, HIMALAYAN. See MECONOPSIS betonicifolia

POPPY MALLOW. See CALLIRHOE involucrata

POPULUS

POPLAR, COTTONWOOD, ASPEN

Salicaceae

DECIDUOUS TREES

ZONES VARY BY SPECIES

FULL SUN

REGULAR DEEP WATERING

Populus nigra 'Italica'

Fast-growing, tough trees, best suited to rural areas and fringes of large properties. They are almost signature trees in semiarid plains regions and westward into desert and intermountain territory. If they are planted in smaller gardens, their network of aggressive surface roots crowds out other plants, heaves pavement, and clogs sewer and drainage lines. Most poplars will sucker profusely if their roots are cut or disturbed. Plants are also subject to many pests and diseases. Nonetheless, some poplars are beautiful or distinctive enough to be widely sold despite their liabilities; many have good fall color.

P

Leaves of most poplars are roughly triangular, sometimes toothed or lobed. Pendulous catkins appear before spring leafout; those on male trees are denser textured. Female trees later bear masses of cottony seeds that blow about and become a nuisance; for that reason, male (seedless) varieties are offered in nurseries.

STAY OUT OF ROOT TROUBLE

Do not plant any kind of *Populus* near pavement, sewer lines, septic tanks, or their leach lines. Also keep them out of lawns and small gardens. Their roots are invasive, and they form suckers.

P. alba. WHITE POPLAR. Zones 1–24, 30–45. Native to Europe, Asia. Broad, wide-spreading tree to 40–60 ft. tall. Leaves are dark green above, white and woolly beneath, 2–5 in. long, usually with three to five lobes. A "lively" tree even in light breezes, with flickering white and green highlights. Poor fall color. Tolerates a wide range of soils. Suckers profusely. Seedless variety 'Pyramidalis', the Bolleana poplar (often sold as *P. bolleana*), forms a narrow column and has a birchlike white trunk.

P. balsamifera (P. candicans). BALM-OF-GILEAD. Zones 1–24, 30, 33, 35, 41–45. Native to northern climates. To 30–60 ft., broad topped. Leaves 4½–6 in. long. Two male selections are 'Idahoensis' ('Idaho Hybrid') and 'Mojave Hybrid'; both are large, fast-growing trees. The latter has nearly white bark.

P. canadensis. CAROLINA POPLAR. Zones 1–24, 30–43. Group of hybrids ranging in height from 40–150 ft. Toothed leaves to 4 in. long. Male varieties include fairly narrow 'Eugene' and disease-resistant 'Siouxland'.

P. fremontii. WESTERN COTTONWOOD, FREMONT COTTONWOOD. Zones 7–24. The cottonwood of desert waterholes and watercourses. To 40–60 ft. or taller, with 2–4-in.-wide, thick, coarsely toothed, glossy yellow-green leaves that turn bright lemon yellow in fall. 'Nevada' is a male variety.

P. nigra 'Italica'. LOMBARDY POPLAR. Zones 1–24, 29–45. Male selection of European native. Beautiful columnar tree to 40–100 ft., with upward-reaching branches. Bright green, 4-in. leaves turn beautiful golden yellow in fall. Few problems in cold-winter, dry climates. In other regions, however, tree is subject to a canker disease that will soon kill it; in these areas, it is best used as a quick, temporary screen. 'Afghanica'—also sold as 'Theves' and as *P. n. thevestina*—has white bark.

P. tremula. EUROPEAN ASPEN. Zones 1–3, 35–45. Similar to *P. tremuloides* but has somewhat darker bark and leaves that are more coarsely toothed. Seedless variety 'Erecta', sometimes called Swedish columnar aspen, is narrow like Lombardy poplar, but it has red fall color and is less prone to canker.

P. tremuloides. QUAKING ASPEN. Zones 1–7, 14–21, 32–45. Widely distributed in North America; native to northern latitudes and mountains. Tolerates poor soil; generally performs poorly or grows slowly at low elevations. To 40–50 ft. tall, 20–30 ft. wide; often grows with several trunks or in a clump. Smooth, pale gray-green to whitish bark. Dainty, round light green leaves flutter and quake with the slightest movement of air. Brilliant golden yellow fall foliage. Apt to suffer from sudden dieback or borers.

P. trichocarpa. BLACK COTTONWOOD. Zones 1–9, 14–24. Native along mountain streams and wet lowlands of coastal mountains of western North America. Tall, spreading tree, reaching 40 ft. in 15 years, 150–180 ft. in age. Heavy limbed, with dark gray, furrowed bark; wood very brittle. Leaves 3–5 in. across, deep green above and distinctly silver beneath; attractive when ruffled by breezes. Good golden yellow fall color.

PORCUPINE GRASS. See MISCANTHUS sinensis 'Strictus'

PORT ORFORD CEDAR. See CHAMAECYPARIS lawsoniana

PORTUGAL LAUREL. See PRUNUS lusitanica

PORTULACA

PORTULACA, ROSE MOSS
Portulacaceae
ANNUALS
✓ ALL ZONES
☀ ◐ FULL SUN OR VERY LIGHT SHADE
● REGULAR TO LITTLE WATER

Portulaca grandiflora

Low-growing plants with fleshy leaves and stems. Generally, the brilliant flowers open fully only in bright light and close by midafternoon in hot weather. Plants bloom from late spring until frost, though quality may decline in late summer. Thrive in high temperatures, intense sunlight. Drought tolerant; ideal for dry, sunbaked places. Not fussy about soil. Good for rock gardens, dry banks, edgings, hanging baskets. Plants don't require deadheading.

P. grandiflora. PORTULACA, ROSE MOSS. To 6 in. high, 1½ ft. across. Leaves cylindrical, pointed, 1 in. long. Trailing, branched reddish stems. Lustrous, roselike, 1-in.-wide flowers in red, cerise, rose pink, orange, yellow, white, pastel shades. Available as single colors or mixes, in either single-flowered or double strains. Prize Strain, Magic Carpet, Sunglo, Sunkiss are popular kinds. Afternoon Delight and Sundance strains stay open longer in the afternoon. Plants self-sow, though hybrid types don't come true from seed.

P. oleracea. PURSLANE. Unimproved form is a weed with tiny yellow flowers and edible stems and leaves. Warm weather and moisture encourage its growth. Control by hoeing or pulling before it goes to seed; don't let pulled plants lie about, since they can reroot or ripen seed.

A strain called Wildfire (sometimes offered as *P. oleracea* and sometimes as *P. grandiflora*, but actually a strain of *P. umbraticola*) is popular in the Deep South, Texas, and the Southwest. Plants have the broad, plump leaves of *P. oleracea*, but the 1–1½-in. single flowers come in white, bright shades of red, pink, magenta, lavender, yellow, orange, and peach, and bicolors. Each flower lasts only a day, but new flowers keep coming. Plants are a few inches tall and spread to 2 ft. Good temporary ground cover.

PURSLANE A WEED?

The French call it *pourpier*, the Mexicans call it *verdolaga*, and both cultures use it in cooking. You can use purslane in salad, soup, pork stew, tomato sauce, and scrambled eggs.

Portulacaceae. The portulaca family contains annuals, perennials, and a few shrubs, usually with succulent foliage and frequently with showy flowers. Examples are *Lewisia*, *Portulaca*, and elephant's food (*Portulacaria*).

PORTULACARIA afra

ELEPHANT'S FOOD
Portulacaceae
SUCCULENT
✓ ZONES 8, 9, 12–27
☀ ◐ ● SUN OR SHADE
● MODERATE TO LITTLE WATER

Native to South Africa. Can be grown outdoors but needs frost protection in Zones 8, 9, 12, 14, 15, 18–21, 26, 27. To 12 ft. tall and nearly as wide (usually much smaller in pots), with thick, juicy stems. Looks a bit like jade plant (*Crassula argentea*) and is some-

Portulacaria afra

P

times called miniature jade plant, but it's faster growing and more loosely branched, with more limber, tapering branches and smaller (½-in.-long) leaves. In South Africa, it bears clusters of tiny pink flowers; in the U.S., it seldom blooms.

Small specimens are good, easy pot plants. In frost-free or nearly frost-less areas, plant can be used as fast-growing informal screen or unclipped hedge, or cut back to make a high ground cover. Forms with variegated leaves ('Foliis Variegatis' and 'Variegata') are slower growing and smaller than the species. Another form has larger, inch-long leaves.

POSSUMHAW. See ILEX decidua

POTATO

Solanaceae

TUBEROUS-ROOTED PERENNIAL TREATED AS ANNUAL

⚡ ALL ZONES

☼ FULL SUN

🔴 EVENLY MOIST SOIL

⬢ GREEN SKIN AND RAW SHOOTS ARE TOXIC

Potato

For ornamental relatives, see *Solanum*. Though not the most widely grown home garden vegetables, potatoes can be very satisfying: 2 lb. of seed potatoes can yield 50 lb. of potatoes for eating. The many pests and diseases that beleaguer commercial growers are not likely to plague home gardeners. One of the most damaging insect pests is Colorado potato beetle, found mainly in the eastern U.S. To avoid disease problems, the best tactic is to start with certified disease-free starter potatoes or disease-resistant varieties.

Can be grown from minitubers (these are planted whole) or from seed potatoes that you cut into 1½-in.-sq. pieces, each with at least two eyes. Since minitubers are uncut, they are less likely to rot in the ground. Home gardeners have access to an increasing number of potato varieties, including types with red, yellow, or bluish purple skins, sorts with yellow flesh, and even all-blue kinds. Shapes vary from round to fingerlike. Some varieties mature faster than others, but most take about 3 months.

Potatoes need sandy, fast-draining, fertile soil; tubers become deformed in heavy, poorly drained soil. In cold-winter climates, plant as soon as soil is workable in spring. In mild-winter regions, plant in early spring for a summer crop, in late summer or early fall for a winter-into-spring crop. Potatoes can be planted in midwinter where frosts are not severe, as long as the soil isn't too wet from winter rains. Set minitubers or seed potato pieces 2 in. deep, 1–1½ ft. apart. Add loose soil as plant grows, taking care not to cover stems completely. The above-ground potato plant is sprawling and bushy, with much-divided dark green leaves somewhat like those of a tomato plant. Clustered inch-wide flowers are pale blue. Round yellow or greenish fruit is rarely seen.

Dig early potatoes (so-called new potatoes) when tops begin to flower; dig mature potatoes when tops die down. Dig carefully to avoid bruising or cutting tubers. Well-matured potatoes free of defects are the best keepers. Store in cool (40°F/4°C), dark place. Where ground doesn't freeze, late potatoes can remain in ground until needed. Dig before mild temperatures start them into growth again.

Another method of growing potatoes is to prepare soil so surface is loose, plant ½–2 in. deep, water well, and cover with a 1–1½-ft. layer of straw, hay, or dead leaves; surround with fence of chicken wire to keep loose material from blowing away. Potatoes will form on surface of soil or just beneath, requiring little digging. You can probe with your fingers and harvest potatoes as needed.

POTATO VINE. See SOLANUM jasminoides

POTENTILLA

CINQUEFOIL

Rosaceae

EVERGREEN PERENNIALS AND DECIDUOUS SHRUBS

⚡ ZONES VARY BY SPECIES

☼ ◑ SOME SHADE IN HOT CLIMATES

🔴 MODERATE WATER

Potentilla fruticosa

Hardy plants useful for ground covers and borders. Leaves are bright green or gray green, divided into small leaflets. Small, roselike, typically single flowers are cream to bright yellow; white; or pink to red. Cinquefoils generally are not at their best in hot, humid climates; they prefer cool nights and cool soils.

EVERGREEN PERENNIALS

These include creeping plants used as ground covers and sturdy clumping plants for use in rock gardens or perennial borders. Leaves are divided fanwise into leaflets and are reminiscent of strawberry foliage.

P. alba. Zones 1–9, 14–24, 32–43. To 4 in. high and spreading, with 2½-in. bright green leaves with five leaflets. White, 1-in.-wide flowers in early spring; occasionally reblooms.

P. atrosanguinea. Zones 1–9, 14–24, 31–43. Sprawling, mounding plant to 1½ ft. high, 2 ft. wide, with furry, three-leafleted leaves and 1-in. red blossoms in summer. A parent of several superior hybrids, including 1½-ft. 'Gibson's Scarlet'; 1-ft. 'Vulcan', with deep red flowers; and 15-in. 'William Rollisson', bearing semidouble bright orange blooms with a yellow center.

P. nepalensis. Zones 1–9, 14–24, 32–43. To 1–2 ft. high. Leaves divided into five roundish leaflets; branching clusters of 1-in. purplish red blossoms in summer. Varieties are superior to the species for borders, cut flowers. 'Willmottiae' ('Miss Willmott'), 10–12 in. high, has salmon pink flowers. 'Melton Fire', 12–15 in. high, bears bright red flowers with yellow blending to a deep red center.

P. recta 'Warrenii'. Zones 1–24, 21–43. To 15 in. tall, with leaves divided into five to seven leaflets. Profuse show of bright yellow, 1-in. flowers in late spring. Longer blooming and less weedy than the species. Tolerates a wide range of soils. Sometimes sold as *P. warrenii.* 'Macrantha' (which may be listed as *P. warrenii.* 'Macrantha') is the same or a very similar plant.

P. tonguei. Zones 2–24, 32–41. Hybrid between *P. nepalensis* and another species. Creeping plant with 1-ft.-long stems, leaves with three to five leaflets, and ½-in., red-centered apricot flowers.

P. tridentata 'Minima'. Zones 1–9, 14–17, 32–43. Creeping ground cover with shiny, 1-in. leaves divided into three leaflets. Foliage turns red in fall. Small white flowers in spring and summer resemble those of strawberry.

P. verna 'Nana'. Zones 1–24, 31–43. Botanists keep running with the name of this plant and nurserymen never catch up. It has been known as *P. crantzii* and *P. tabernaemontanii*. The first of these may be *P. villosa*; the second is now called *P. neumanniana*, which is probably the correct name for this dainty-looking yet tough and persistent creeper. Grows 2–6 in. high. Bright green leaves divided into five leaflets; butter yellow, ¼-in. flowers in spring and summer. Stands more water than most cinquefoils. May turn brown in cold winters. Fast-growing ground cover, bulb cover. Good lawn substitute for no-traffic areas. Subject to a disfiguring rust in some regions.

P. warrenii. See P. recta 'Warrenii'

DECIDUOUS SHRUBS

The shrubby potentillas, most often sold as named forms of *P. fruticosa*, are native to northern latitudes everywhere. They perform well in Zones 1–21, 32 (cooler parts), 34–45. All have leaves divided into three to seven leaflets; some are distinctly green on top, gray beneath, while others look more gray green all over. All bloom cheerfully from late spring to early fall.
▶

Fairly trouble-free. Best in well-drained soil with moderate water, but tolerate poor soils, drought, heat. Varieties with red or orange tinting should be lightly shaded, since they tend to fade quickly in hot sun. After the bloom period ends, cut out some of the oldest stems from time to time to make room for new growth. Here are some of the many varieties to be found in nurseries:

'Abbotswood'. To 3 ft., with dark blue-green leaves, 2-in. white flowers.

'Goldfinger'. Dense, dark green, to 3 ft. tall. Golden yellow, 1½-in. blooms.

'Goldstar'. Low mound to 2 ft., with 2-in. bright yellow flowers.

'Jackman's Variety'. To 4 ft. tall and somewhat wider, with 1½-in. bright yellow blossoms.

'Katherine Dykes'. Can reach 5 ft. but usually stays much lower; spreads at least as wide as high. Pale yellow, 1-in. flowers.

'Klondike'. Dense grower to 2 ft. high, with 1½–2-in. deep yellow flowers.

'Mount Everest'. Bushy, upright to 4½ ft.; 1½-in. pure white blossoms.

'Pixie Gold'. To 1–1½ ft. high, with ¾-in. yellow flowers.

'Primrose Beauty'. Silvery gray-green foliage on a 2–3-ft. plant. Pale yellow, 1½-in. flowers.

'Red Ace'. To 2 ft. high, 3–4 ft. wide. Flowers are 1½ in. wide, bright red with yellow center and yellow reverse. Flowers fade to yellow as they age (fading is very rapid in hot-summer climates or under poor growing conditions).

'Sunset'. To 2–2½ ft., with bright green foliage, 1½-in. yellow flowers shaded orange.

'Sutter's Gold'. To 1 ft. high, spreading to 3 ft. Clear yellow flowers about 1 in. across.

'Tangerine'. To 2½ ft. high, with 1½-in. bright yellow-orange blooms.

POTERIUM. See SANGUISORBA

POTHOS aureus. See EPIPREMNUM aureum

POT MARIGOLD. See CALENDULA officinalis

PRATIA

Campanulaceae (Lobeliaceae)

PERENNIALS

☀ ZONES 4–9, 14–24

☀ ◑ PART SHADE IN HOT CLIMATES

● REGULAR WATER

Small perennial plants with creeping, branching stems that root at the joints. All are useful low ground covers where soil is reasonably rich and well drained, but they require constant moisture. Small, closely set leaves and tolerance for an occasional footstep make them choice selections for use between stepping-stones. They resemble baby's tears *(Soleirolia)* in appearance, but have attractive flowers. Plants can be invasive where they are well adapted.

Pratia angulata

P. angulata. New Zealand native with tiny roundish leaves on short stems and white or bluish white, ¾-in. flowers on 2-in. stems. Flowers oddly shaped, with two-lobed upper lip, three-lobed lower lip. Summer bloom.

P. pedunculata. See Laurentia fluviatilis

PRICKLY PEAR. See OPUNTIA

PRICKLY POPPY. See ARGEMONE

PRIDE OF MADEIRA. See ECHIUM fastuosum

PRIMROSE. See PRIMULA

PRIMROSE TREE. See LAGUNARIA patersonii

PRIMULA

PRIMROSE

Primulaceae

PERENNIALS SOMETIMES TREATED AS ANNUALS

☀ ZONES VARY BY SPECIES OR TYPE

☀ ◑ ● TOLERATE FULL SUN IN COOL CLIMATES

● ◐ WATER NEEDS VARY BY TYPE

▶ SEE CHART

Primroses form a foliage rosette, above which rise circular, five-petaled flowers, each petal indented at the apex. Blossoms may be borne on individual stems, in clusters at stem ends, or in tiered, candelabralike clusters up the stem. Most are spring blooming, but some start flowering in mid- to late winter in mild climates, and a few bloom in early summer.

Primula malacoides

Specialists have organized the hundreds of species, selections, named hybrids, and hybrid strains into 34 sections, but primroses that are fairly easy to grow in home gardens are fewer in number. A combination of moist, rich soil and cool, humid air is ideal for primroses. Some types thrive with regular water, while others need damp or even boggy soil. Most require some winter chill (polyanthus hybrids are a notable exception).

Primula polyantha

Almost any primrose flourishes in the Pacific Northwest. The greater the summer heat, the more protection from direct sun primroses need. Filtered or dappled sunlight and high shade are preferred exposures. Where the climate is less than favorable, primroses are sometimes treated as annuals.

Specialty nurseries, mainly in the Northwest, offer seeds and plants of many kinds of primroses. Fanciers exchange seeds and plants through primrose societies.

Primulaceae. The primrose family of annuals and perennials has single or variously clustered flowers with five-lobed calyxes and corollas. Examples are rock jasmine *(Androsace)*, *Cyclamen*, and primrose *(Primula)*.

PRINCE'S FEATHER. See AMARANTHUS hybridus erythrostachys

PRINCESS FLOWER. See TIBOUCHINA

PRIVET. See LIGUSTRUM

PROSOPIS

MESQUITE

Fabaceae (Leguminosae)

EVERGREEN OR DECIDUOUS SHRUBS OR TREES

☀ ZONES 10–13, 27–30; ALSO WESTERN PART OF 33 AND 35

☀ FULL SUN

● ◐ REGULAR TO LITTLE WATER

Native to arid and semiarid areas of the U.S., Mexico, and South America. Much of their success is due to far-reaching roots that will travel great distances to tap into water. Established plants are highly drought tolerant, yet easily take regular lawn watering. In poor, rocky soil and without water, they will be shrubby. In deep soil where taproots can reach groundwater, they grow rapidly to about 30 ft. tall, with a picturesque, spreading canopy.

Prosopis glandulosa

▶ page 450

PRIMULA

NAME	ZONES	LEAVES	FLOWERS	COMMENTS
Primula acaulis (see **P. vulgaris**)				
P. alpicola MOONLIGHT PRIMROSE	3–6, 17, 34, 37	Long stalked, wrinkled, eventually forming wide clumps	Sulfur yellow (sometimes white or purple), spreading, bell shaped, in clusters on 20-in. stems. Powerfully fragrant. Summer	Somewhat tender in coldest areas. Regular water
P. auricula AURICULA	1–6, 17, 22–24, 32, 34, 36–40	Evergreen rosettes of broad, leathery, toothed or plain-edged, gray-green leaves, sometimes with mealy, powdery coating that spots and runs in rain	White, cream, yellow, orange, pink, rose, red, purple, blue, or brownish, with white or yellow eye; carried in clusters on 6–8-in. stems. Fragrant. Early spring	Usually grown in pots for display. Some choice named varieties have green or near-black flowers with rings of mealy powder or rims of contrasting color. Regular water
P. beesiana	2–6, 17, 34, 36–40	Long, tapering gradually into leafstalk; to 14 in. long (including stalk)	Somewhat variable, but usually reddish purple with yellow eye, in 5–7 dense whorls on 2-ft. stems. Mid- to late spring	Very deep rooted. Plentiful deep soakings
P. bulleyana	3–6, 15–17, 34, 37	Like those of *P. beesiana*, but with reddish midribs	Bright yellow, from orange buds. Whorls on 2-ft. stems open over long season, mid- to late spring	Plants disappear in late fall; mark the spot. Older plants can be divided after bloom or in fall. Showy at woodland edge. Regular water
P. denticulata	1–6, 34–43	About 6–12 in. long, only half grown at flowering time	Dense, ball-shaped clusters on foot-high, stout stems. Color ranges from blue violet to purple. Very early spring	Sometimes called drumstick primrose. Pinkish, lavender, and white varieties available. Not adapted to warm-winter areas. Regular water
P. florindae	3–6, 17	Broad, heart shaped, on long stems	Up to 60 yellow, bell-shaped, nodding flowers top 3-ft. stems in summer. Most fragrant and latest-blooming primrose	Will grow in a few inches of running water or in damp, low spot. Plants late to appear in spring. Hybrids have red, orange, or yellow flowers
P. japonica	2–6, 17, 32 (cooler parts), 34, 36–40	To 6–9 in. long, 3 in. wide	Stout stems to 2½ ft., each with up to 5 whorls of yellow-eyed purple flowers, late spring to early summer	'Miller's Crimson' is an excellent red variety. White and pink forms are also available. Needs lots of water; will grow at edge of pond, even in shallowest water
P. juliae hybrids (**Pruhonicensis hybrids**) JULIANA PRIMROSE	2–6, 14–17, 20–23, 32, 34–41	Bright green, in tuftlike rosettes	White, blue, yellow, orange-red, pink, or purple, borne singly or in clusters on 3–4-in. stems. Very early	Excellent for edging, woodland, rock garden. Regular water
P. malacoides FAIRY PRIMROSE, BABY PRIMROSE	8, 9, 12–24	Evergreen rosettes of soft, pale green, long-stalked leaves, 1½–3 in. long; oval with lobed and cut edges	White, pink, rose, red, lavender. Borne in loose, lacy whorls along numerous upright, 8–15-in. stems. Winter–spring	Grown as perennial in mild-winter areas of West. Treated as annual or pot plant elsewhere. Stands light frost. Regular water
P. obconica	4–9, 15–24	Evergreen, large, roundish, soft, hairy on long, hairy stems; hairs (except those of Freedom strain) may irritate skin	White, pink, salmon, lavender, reddish purple. 1½–2 in. wide, in large, broad clusters on stems to 1 ft. tall. Nearly everblooming in mild regions	Perennial, best treated as annual. Use for bedding where winters are mild, as house plant in cold regions. Regular water
P. polyantha POLYANTHUS PRIMROSES (often called English primroses; this is a group of hybrids)	2–10, 12–24, 32–41	Clumps of fresh green, tongue-shaped leaves to 8 in. long, resembling leaves of romaine lettuce	1–2 in. across, in large, full clusters on stems to 1 ft. high. Almost any color. Blooms from winter to early or midspring. Adaptable and brilliant. Miniature Polyanthus have smaller flowers on shorter stalks	Fine large-flowered strains include Clarke's, Concorde, Barnhaven, Pacific, Santa Barbara. Novelties include Gold Laced, with gold-edged mahogany petals. All excellent for massing, bulb companions, or containers. Treat as annuals in hot-summer areas. Regular water

P

PRIMULA

NAME	ZONES	LEAVES	FLOWERS	COMMENTS
P. pulverulenta	3–6, 17, 34, 37	A foot or more long, deep green, wrinkled	Red to red-purple, purple eyed, in whorls on 3-ft. stems thickly dusted with white meal. Late spring, summer	Bartley strain has flowers in pink and salmon range. A fine white with orange eye is available. Lots of water
P. sieboldii	2–6, 17, 34, 36–40	To 2–4 in. long, scalloped, toothed, on long, hairy stalks	Lilac with white eye, 1–1½-in. across, in clusters on 4–8-in. stems. Late spring	Hybrid strains available with white, pink, or purple flowers. All types usually go dormant after flowering, enabling them to endure hotter summers better than other sorts of primroses. This is an excellent variety for the Northeast. Regular water
P. sinensis CHINESE PRIMROSE	Greenhouse or indoor plant	Evergreen, on long stalks; roundish, lobed, toothed, soft, hairy, 2–4 in. long. Hairs may irritate skin	White, pink, lavender, reddish, and coral; about 1½ in. across, many clustered on 4–8-in.-tall stems. Stellatas have star-shaped flowers in whorls. Winter	Tender. Favorite European pot plant; imported seed available from specialists. Regular water
P. veris COWSLIP	2–6, 17, 32, 34–41	Similar to those of polyanthus primroses	Bright yellow, fragrant, ½–1 in. wide, in early spring. Stems 4–8 in. high	Naturalize in wild garden or rock garden. Charming but not as sturdy as polyanthus primroses. Regular water
P. vialii (**P. littoniana**)	2–6, 17, 34, 36–40	To 8 in. long, 1½–2½ in. wide, hairy, irregularly toothed; disappear in winter	Dense, narrow, 3–5-in.-long spikes of fragrant, ¼–½-in. wide flowers, violet blue opening from red buds. Stems erect, 1–2 ft. high. Late spring or early summer	Not long lived but quite easy from seed. Use in rock gardens. Rich, moist to damp soil
P. vulgaris (**P. acaulis**) PRIMROSE, ENGLISH PRIMROSE	2–6, 14–17, 21–24, 32–41	Tufted; much like those of polyanthus primroses	Flowers borne singly; vigorous garden strains often have 2 or 3 to a stalk. White, yellow, red, blue, and bronze, brown, and wine. Early spring	Double varieties available. Blues and reds especially desirable. Use in woodland or rock garden, as edging. Nosegay and Biedermeier strains are exceptionally heavy blooming. Regular water

Because plants hybridize freely, exact identification is sometimes difficult. All have dark bark and cast light, airy shade as sun filters through branches, spines, and tiny leaflets. Small spikes of tiny greenish yellow flowers appear in spring–summer; these are followed by 2–8-in., flat, beanlike pods.

P. alba. ARGENTINE MESQUITE. Nearly evergreen, shedding old leaves as new ones appear. Single-trunked tree with blue-green foliage and spines.

P. chilensis. CHILEAN MESQUITE. Two trees are sold under this name. The more common one is deciduous, with a dense canopy of deep green leaves. The true species is less dense, and it is deciduous only in areas with chilly winters.

P. glandulosa. TEXAS MESQUITE, HONEY MESQUITE. Deciduous. Tends to be multitrunked, with bright green leaves and drooping branchlets.

Proteaceae. The protea family of evergreen shrubs and trees is characterized by leathery leaves and irregular, somewhat tubular flowers in spikelike clusters or heads often surrounded by showy colored bracts. Many are attractive (*Grevillea*); one has edible nuts (*Macadamia*).

PRUNE. See PLUM and PRUNE

PRUNELLA

SELF-HEAL, HEAL-ALL
Lamiaceae (Labiatae)
PERENNIALS
ZONES 1–24, 29–43
FULL SUN OR LIGHT SHADE
REGULAR WATER

Prunella vulgaris

Creeping perennials that form low, dense mats of foliage from surface and underground runners. Tight spikes of gaping, two-lipped mint-type flowers appear in summer, rising above foliage on bare stems a few inches to 1 ft. tall. Names are much confused, but all these plants are tough, tolerant, and deep rooted. They are useful for small-scale ground cover and can endure the occasional footfall, but they are too invasive to risk planting near choice, delicate rock garden plants.

P. grandiflora. Largest species, with 4-in. leaves and purple flowers. Named varieties, sometimes sold as varieties of *P. webbiana*, include 'Pink Loveliness', 'Purple Loveliness' (lilac purple touched with white), and 'White Loveliness'.

P. vulgaris. Common species, with 2-in. leaves. Flowers are purple or pink. A form called *P. v. incisa* has deeply cut leaves.

P. webbiana. Similar to *P. grandiflora*, but with shorter leaves. There are purple and pink varieties.

PRUNUS

Rosaceae

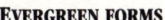

EVERGREEN OR DECIDUOUS SHRUBS OR TREES

ZONES VARY BY SPECIES

FULL SUN, EXCEPT AS NOTED

REGULAR TO MODERATE WATER

SEE CHARTS, PAGES 452–453, 454

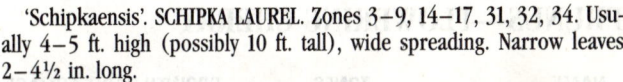

Fruit trees that belong to *Prunus,* the "stone fruits," are described under their common names. See Almond; Apricot; Aprium and Pluot; Cherry; Peach and Nectarine; Plum and Prune.

The ornamentals can be divided into two classes: evergreen and deciduous. Evergreens are

Prunus cerasifera

used chiefly as structure plants: hedges, screens, shade trees, street trees. Deciduous flowering trees and shrubs, closely related to the fruit trees mentioned above, are valued for their springtime display as well as for attractive shape and for form and texture of foliage. Many of these deciduous types offer a bonus of edible fruit.

EVERGREEN FORMS

The following useful and attractive evergreen species are all large shrubs or small trees.

P. caroliniana. CAROLINA LAUREL CHERRY. Zones 7–24, 26–31, warmer parts of 32. Native from North Carolina to Texas. As an upright shrub, it can be well branched from the base and useful as a clipped hedge or tall screen to 20 ft. high. Can be sheared into formal shapes. Trained as a tree, it is a broad-topped plant reaching 35–40 ft.; looks attractive with multiple trunks. Densely foliaged; leaves are glossy green, smooth edged, 2–4 in. long. Small, creamy white flowers in 1-in. spikes appear in late winter or spring, followed by black fruit to ½ in. wide. Flower and fruit litter can be a problem in paved areas. Very tolerant of heat, wind, drought. 'Bright 'n Tight' and 'Compacta' are denser than the species and reach only about 10 ft.

P. ilicifolia, P. lyonii. HOLLYLEAF CHERRY, CATALINA CHERRY. Zones 7–9, 12–24. Two similar plants that often hybridize when growing near each other. Hollyleaf cherry, *P. ilicifolia,* has glossy dark green, 2-in.-long, spiny-edged leaves similar to those of holly (though not as prickly). It is native to California's Coast Ranges. Catalina cherry, *P. lyonii,* native to California's Channel Islands, has smooth-edged or very faintly toothed leaves. Both bear narrow spikes of small white flowers, followed by dark red to black cherries with large pits and not much flesh. Catalina cherry has darker fruits and is the larger plant (to a possible 45 ft., compared to 30 ft. for hollyleaf cherry).

Both species can take extreme drought once established, but look best with occasional deep soakings. Need good drainage. Unusually high resistance to oak root fungus. Use as small trees, screen, or clipped hedge 3–10 ft. tall (set out plants 1½ ft. apart). Avoid planting near paved surfaces or parking areas, since fallen fruit causes stains.

P. laurocerasus. ENGLISH LAUREL. Zones 4–9, 14–24, 31, 32. Hardy to 5°F/–15°C; varieties listed below are hardier. Native from southeastern Europe to Iran. To 20 ft. tall, though generally seen as a lower clipped hedge. Leathery, glossy dark green leaves are 3–7 in. long, 1½–2 in. wide. Blooms in summer, bearing 3–5-in. spikes of creamy white flowers that are often hidden by leaves. Small black fruit appears in late summer and fall.

Where adapted, a fast-growing, greedy plant that's difficult to garden under or around. Regular water and nutrients will speed growth and keep top dense. Needs reasonably good drainage. Give partial shade in hot-summer areas. Tolerates salt spray. Stands heavy shearing but with considerable mutilation of leaves; best pruned by one cut at a time to remove overlong twigs just above a leaf. Best used as a tree or tall unclipped screen. The following are compact varieties:

'Otto Luyken'. Zones 4–9, 14–24, 31, 32. To 4 ft. tall, twice as broad. Leaves 2–4 in. long.

'Schipkaensis'. SCHIPKA LAUREL. Zones 3–9, 14–17, 31, 32, 34. Usually 4–5 ft. high (possibly 10 ft. tall), wide spreading. Narrow leaves 2–4½ in. long.

'Zabeliana'. ZABEL LAUREL. Zones 3–9, 14–21, 31, 32, 34. Narrow-leafed variety with branches angling upward and outward from base. Eventually reaches 6 ft., with equal or greater spread. More tolerant of full sun than species. Versatile plant; good for low screen, big foundation plant, bank cover (with branches pegged down), espalier.

Prunus laurocerasus 'Zabeliana'

P. lusitanica. PORTUGAL LAUREL. Zones 4–9, 14–24, 31, warmer parts of 32. Native to Spain, Portugal. Densely branched shrub 10–20 ft. high; or multitrunked spreading tree to 30 ft. or more. Trained to a single trunk, it is used as formal street tree. Glossy dark green leaves to 5 in. long, 2 in. wide. Small, creamy white flowers in 5–10-in. spikes in spring and early summer, followed by clusters of very small, bright red to dark purple fruit. Slower growing than *P. laurocerasus* and more tolerant of heat, sun, and wind. Very drought tolerant.

DECIDUOUS FLOWERING FRUIT TREES

Flowering cherry. Zones vary by type; see chart. Cultural needs of all are identical. They require full sun and fast-draining, well-aerated soil; if your soil is substandard, plant in raised beds. Prune only to remove awkward or crossing branches; pinch back the occasional overly ambitious shoot to force branching. You can cut during bloom time and use branches in arrangements. Early to midspring bloom, depending on variety.

All are good trees to garden under. Use them as their growth habit indicates: large, spreading kinds make good shade trees, while smaller ones are indispensable in Oriental gardens. Foliage may sustain damage from insect pests. Plants growing in heavy soil are sometimes subject to root rot (for which there is no cure); an afflicted tree will usually bloom, then send out new leaves that suddenly collapse.

Flowering nectarine. Zones 2–24, 30–34, 39. There is one important variety, 'Alma Stultz', a fast grower to 20 ft. high and wide. Blooms in early spring, covering itself with deliciously fragrant, 2–2½-in.-wide, waxy-petaled flowers in rosy white shaded pink, the color deepening with age. Flowers look something like azalea blossoms. Sparse crop of small, white-fleshed fruit is sometimes produced. Cultural needs and potential problems are the same as for peach.

Flowering peach. Identical to fruiting peach in size, growth habit, cultural needs, and potential problems, but more widely adapted. Flowering peach can be grown in Zones 2–24, 30–34, 39, though blossoms may be frost-damaged in cold climates and leaf-out may be delayed in warm-winter areas. Place trees where they will be striking when in bloom yet fairly unobtrusive out of bloom—behind evergreen shrubs, fence, or wall, for example. Heavy pruning is necessary for good show of flowers. Cut branches back to 6-in. stubs just after bloom or during bloom, using cut branches for arrangements. Multibranched new growth will be luxuriant by summer's end and will flower profusely the following spring. Bloom period is late winter–early spring.

The following varieties are strictly "flowering" in the sense that their blooms are showy and their fruit is either absent or worthless. In areas with late frosts, choose late bloomers; early bloomers are best in regions with hot, early springs.

'Early Double Pink'. Very early.

'Early Double Red'. Deep purplish red or rose red. Very early and brilliant, but color likely to clash with other pinks and reds.

'Early Double White'. Blooms with 'Early Double Pink'.

'Helen Borchers'. Semidouble clear pink, 2½-in.-wide flowers. Late.

'Icicle'. Double white flowers. Late.

'Late Double Red'. Later than 'Early Double Red' by 3 to 4 weeks.

'Peppermint Stick'. Double flowers striped red and white; may also bear all-white and all-red flowers on same branch. Midseason.

▶ page 453

P

PRUNUS—FLOWERING CHERRY

NAME	ZONES	GROWTH HABIT, FOLIAGE	HEIGHT, SPREAD	FLOWERS, SEASON, COMMENTS
Prunus 'Accolade'	2–9, 14–17	Small tree with spreading branches, twiggy growth pattern. Very vigorous	To 20 ft. or more, equally wide	Semidouble pink, in large drooping clusters. Early. Hybrid between *P. sargentii* and *P. subhirtella*
P. campanulata TAIWAN FLOWERING CHERRY	6–9, 14–23, 31, warmer parts of 32	Graceful, densely branched, bushy, upright, slender small tree	To 20–25 ft.; not as wide as high	Single, bell shaped, drooping, in clusters of 2–5. Striking color—electric rose, almost neon purple-pink. Blooms early, along with flowering peach. Good choice for warm-winter areas
P. 'Hally Jolivette'	3–7, 14–20, 31–34, 39	Dense, broad, shrubby	To 6–8 ft., eventually to 15 ft. Slow grower	Semidouble light pink. Early; relatively long bloom. Can be used in shrub borders. Hybrid between *P. subhirtella* and *P. yedoensis*
P. 'Okame'	4–9, 14–23, 31–33	Upright, oval, fast growing. Dark green, finely textured foliage. Yellow-orange to orange-red fall color	To 25 ft. tall, 20 ft. wide	Single pink. Very early. Hybrid between *P. campanulata* and another species
P. sargentii SARGENT CHERRY	2–7, 14–17, 32–41	Upright, spreading branches form rounded crown. Orange-red fall foliage	To 40–50 ft. or more; not as wide as high	Single blush pink, in clusters of 2–4. Midseason. 'Columnaris' is narrower and more erect than typical *P. sargentii*
P. serrula BIRCH BARK CHERRY	3–7, 14–16, 32 (cooler parts), 33, 34, 39	Round headed; narrow, willow-like leaves. Valued for its beautiful glossy mahogany red bark	To 30 ft. and as wide	Bark more important than small white flowers almost hidden by new leaves. Midseason. Not at its best in hot, humid areas
P. serrulata JAPANESE FLOWERING CHERRY	3–7, 14–20, 32–34	The species is known through its many cultivated varieties, some of which are listed below		
P. s. 'Amanogawa'	3–7, 14–20, 32–34	Columnar tree. Use as you would small Lombardy poplar	To 20–25 ft. tall, 8 ft. wide	Semidouble light pink, with deep pink margins. Early midseason
P. s. 'Beni Hoshi' ('Pink Star')	3–7, 14–20, 32–34	Fast grower with arching, spreading branches. Umbrella shaped in outline	To 20–25 ft. high and as wide	Single vivid pink; long, slightly twisted petals. Flowers hang below branches. Midseason
P. s. 'Kwanzan' ('Kanzan', 'Sekiyama')	3–7, 14–20, 32–34	Branches stiffly upright, forming inverted cone. Orange fall foliage	To 30 ft. high, 20 ft. wide	Large, double, deep rosy pink, in pendent clusters displayed before or with red young leaves. Midseason. Tolerates heat and humidity well
P. s. 'Royal Burgundy'	3–7, 14–20, 32–34	Habit similar to that of 'Kwanzan'. Reddish purple foliage	Same as 'Kwanzan'	Like those of 'Kwanzan', but deeper pink
P. s. 'Shirofugen'	3–7, 14–20, 32–34	Wide horizontal branching	To 25 ft. and as wide	Double, long stalked, pink, fading to white. Latest to bloom; flowers appear with coppery red new leaves
P. s. 'Shirotae' ('Mt. Fuji')	3–7, 14–20, 32–34	Strong horizontal branching	To 20 ft.; wider than high	Semidouble. Pink in bud; white when fully open, turning to purplish pink. Early
P. s. 'Shogetsu' ('Shimidsu Sakura')	3–7, 14–20, 32–34	Spreading growth, arching branches	To 15 ft.; wider than high	Semidouble and very double pale pink, often with white centers. Late
P. s. 'Snow Fountains' ('White Fountain')	3–7, 14–20, 32–34	Slightly curving trunk, branches weeping to ground. Yellow-and-orange fall foliage	To 6–12 ft. and as wide	Single white. Early
P. s. 'Snow Goose'	3–7, 14–20, 32–34	Erect, narrow at first, eventually becoming wider	To 20 ft. and as wide	Single white. Early. Reportedly disease resistant

P

PRUNUS—FLOWERING CHERRY

NAME	ZONES	GROWTH HABIT, FOLIAGE	HEIGHT, SPREAD	FLOWERS, SEASON, COMMENTS
P. s. 'Tai Haku'	3–7, 14–20, 32–34	Vigorous, with rounded crown. Good orange fall color	To 20–25 ft. and as wide	Largest blooms of any flowering cherry: single pure white, 2½ in. wide, appearing with bronzy new foliage. Late midseason
P. subhirtella 'Autumnalis'	2–7, 14–20, 32–41	Loose branching, bushy, with flattened crown, slender twigs	To 25–30 ft. and as wide	Double white or pinkish white. Often blooms during warm autumn or winter weather as well as in early spring
P. s. 'Pendula' SINGLE WEEPING CHERRY, WEEPING HIGAN CHERRY	2–7, 14–20, 32–41	Usually sold grafted at 5–6 ft. high on upright-growing under-stock. Graceful branches hang down, often to ground	To 15–25 ft. and as wide	Single small pale pink, in profusion. Early
P. s. 'Rosea'	2–7, 14–20, 32–41	Wide-spreading, horizontal branching	To 20–25 ft. high, spreading to 30 ft.	Single pink, opening from nearly red buds. Profuse, very early bloom
P. s. 'Whitcombii'	2–7, 14–20, 32–41	Same as *P.s.* 'Rosea'	To 30 ft. high, spreading to 35 ft.	Single pink fading to white. Early
P. s. 'Yae-shidare-higan' DOUBLE WEEPING CHERRY	2–7, 14–20, 32–41	Same as *P.s.* 'Pendula'	Same as *P.s.* 'Pendula'	Double rose pink. Midseason
P. yedoensis YOSHINO FLOWERING CHERRY	3–7, 14–20, 32–34, 39	Horizontal branches; graceful, open pattern	Fast to 40 ft., with 30-ft. spread	Single light pink to nearly white, fragrant. Early. Famous planting exists around the Tidal Basin in Washington, D.C.
P. y. 'Akebono' (sometimes called **'Daybreak'**)	3–7, 14–20, 32–34, 39	Same as *P. yedoensis*	To 25 ft. and as wide	Flowers pinker than those of *P. yedoensis*. Early

'Weeping Double Pink'. Smaller than other flowering peaches, with weeping branches. Requires careful staking and tying to develop main stem of suitable height. Midseason.

'Weeping Double Red'. Similar to above, but with deep rose red flowers. Midseason.

'Weeping Double White'. White version of weeping forms listed above.

Flowering plum. Zones vary by type; see chart. Flowers appear before leaves, from late winter to early spring. Less particular about soil than flowering cherries, nectarines, and peaches, but will fail if soil is water-logged for prolonged periods. If soil is boggy, plant in raised beds, 6–12 in. above grade. Little pruning is needed. Potential pests include aphids, borers, scale, tent caterpillars. Possible diseases include canker and leaf spots. The most ornamental flowering plums, including purple-foliaged varieties, are described in the chart; for additional flowering plums, see listings for *P. americana, P. cistena,* and *P. maritima.*

FLOWERING PLUM FOR INDOOR BLOOM

Branches of flowering plum (or flowering cherry, peach, or nectarine) are beautiful for indoor decoration. For the longest-lasting bloom, cut branches when buds first begin to show color or when they have just opened. Follow proper pruning procedures when you cut branches: prune to thin or shape (don't just hack indiscriminately); always cut back to a side branch; and never leave stubs. Place branches in a deep container of water, not in florist's foam; strip off any buds or flowers that will be below water level.

ADDITIONAL DECIDUOUS SPECIES

P. americana. WILD PLUM, GOOSE PLUM. Shrub or small tree. Zones 1–3, 10, 31–45. To 15–20 ft. high, forming thickets. Profusion of clustered white, 1-in. flowers appears before the dark green leaves emerge. Fruit yellow to red, to 1 in. wide, sour but good for jelly. Extremely tough and hardy.

P. besseyi. WESTERN SAND CHERRY. Shrub. Zones 1–3, 10, 30, 33, 35, 41, 43, 45. Native from Manitoba to Wyoming, south to Kansas and Colorado. To 3–6 ft. tall. Good show of white flowers in spring, followed by sweet black cherries used for pies, jams, jellies. Withstands heat, cold, wind, drought.

P. cistena. PURPLE-LEAF SAND CHERRY, DWARF RED-LEAF PLUM. Shrub. Zones 1–22, 32–45. Dainty, multibranched hybrid to 6–10 ft. high. Can be trained as single-stemmed tree; good for small patios. Bears white to light pink flowers as leaves emerge, then covers itself in red-purple foliage. May offer a summer crop of small blackish purple fruit. Pink-flowering 'Big Cis' forms a dense globe to 14 ft. high.

P. fruticosa. Like *P. besseyi,* but 2–3 ft. tall, with smaller red-purple fruit.

P. glandulosa. DWARF FLOWERING ALMOND. Shrub. Zones 2–10, 12, 14–19, 32–41. Native to China, Japan. In early spring, before leaves appear, the many slender stems are transformed into wands of blossoms. Typically sold are the double-flowered selections 'Alboplena' (white) and 'Sinensis' (pink), both with 1–1¼-in. blooms like fluffy pompom chrysanthemums. Plants grow 4–6 ft. high, with clumps of upright, spreading branches and light green, 4-in., willowlike leaves. Prune heavily during or after flowering to promote strong new growth for next year's bloom. Can be used as flowering hedge. Suckers freely. Fireblight can be a problem.

P. maackii. AMUR CHOKECHERRY. Tree. Zones 1–3, 10, 35–45. Native to Manchuria and Siberia; extremely hardy to cold and wind. To 25–30 ft.

P

PRUNUS—FLOWERING PLUM

NAME	ZONES	GROWTH HABIT	FOLIAGE, FLOWERS, FRUIT
P. blireiana (hybrid between **P. cerasifera 'Atropurpurea'** and **P. mume**)	3–22, 32–34, 39	Graceful, to 25 ft. high, 20 ft. wide. Long, slender branches	Leaves reddish purple, turning greenish bronze in summer. Flowers double, fragrant, pink to rose. Very little or no fruit
P. cerasifera CHERRY PLUM, MYROBALAN	3–22, 28, 31–34, 39	Used as rootstock for various stone fruits. Will grow to 30 ft. and as wide. The species is not widely grown; its purple- and red-leafed varieties are more popular	Leaves dark green. Flowers pure white. Small red plums, 1–1¼ in. across, are sweet but bland. Self-sows freely; some seedlings bear yellow fruit
P. c. 'Allred'	3–22, 28, 31–34, 39	Upright, slightly spreading, 20 ft. tall, 12–15 ft. wide	Red leaves, white flowers. Red, 1¼-in.-wide, tart fruit is good for preserves, jelly
P. c. 'Atropurpurea' (**P. 'Pissardii'**) PURPLE-LEAF PLUM	3–22, 28, 31–34, 39	Fast growing to 25–30 ft. high, rounded in form	New leaves copper red, deepening to dark purple, gradually becoming greenish bronze in late summer. White flowers. Sets heavy crop of small red plums
P. c. 'Hollywood' (hybrid between **P. c. 'Atropurpurea'** and Japanese plum **'Duarte'**)	3–22, 28, 31–34, 39	Upright grower to 30–40 ft., 25 ft. wide	Leaves dark green above, red beneath. Flowers light pink to white. Good-quality red plums 2–2½ in. wide
P. c. 'Krauter Vesuvius'	3–22, 28, 31–34, 39	To 18 ft. high, 12 ft. wide; upright, branching habit	Darkest foliage of all flowering plums. Light pink flowers, purple-black leaves. Little or no fruit
P. c. 'Mt. St. Helens'	3–22, 28, 31–34, 39	Upright, spreading, with rounded crown. Fast growth to 20 ft. high and wide	A sport of 'Newport', it grows faster and leafs out earlier; it has richer leaf color and holds it later in summer
P. c. 'Newport'	2–22, 28, 31–41	To 25 ft. high, 20 ft. wide	Purplish red leaves. Single pink flowers. Will bear a little fruit
P. c. 'Purple Pony'	3–22, 28, 31–34, 39	Genetic dwarf no taller than 10–12 ft. Available budded low or high	Deep purple foliage holds color throughout season. Single pale pink flowers. No fruit
P. c. 'Thundercloud'	3–22, 28, 31–34, 39	More rounded form than *P. c.* 'Atropurpurea'. To 20 ft. high and as wide	Dark coppery leaves. Flowers light pink to white. Sometimes sets good crop of red fruit

P

1–3, 10, 31–45. To 15–20 ft. high, forming thickets. Profusion of clustered white, 1-in. flowers appears before the dark green leaves emerge. Fruit yellow to red, to 1 in. wide, sour but good for jelly. Extremely tough and hardy.

P. besseyi. WESTERN SAND CHERRY. Shrub. Zones 1–3, 10, 30, 33, 35, 41, 43, 45. Native from Manitoba to Wyoming, south to Kansas and Colorado. To 3–6 ft. tall. Good show of white flowers in spring, followed by sweet black cherries used for pies, jams, jellies. Withstands heat, cold, wind, drought.

P. cistena. PURPLE-LEAF SAND CHERRY, DWARF RED-LEAF PLUM. Shrub. Zones 1–22, 32–45. Dainty, multibranched hybrid to 6–10 ft. high. Can be trained as single-stemmed tree; good for small patios. Bears white to light pink flowers as leaves emerge, then covers itself in red-purple foliage. May offer a summer crop of small blackish purple fruit. Pink-flowering 'Big Cis' forms a dense globe to 14 ft. high.

P. fruticosa. Like *P. besseyi*, but 2–3 ft. tall, with smaller red-purple fruit.

P. glandulosa. DWARF FLOWERING ALMOND. Shrub. Zones 2–10, 12, 14–19, 32–41. Native to China, Japan. In early spring, before leaves appear, the many slender stems are transformed into wands of blossoms. Typically sold are the double-flowered selections 'Alboplena' (white) and 'Sinensis' (pink), both with 1–1¼-in. blooms like fluffy pompom chrysanthemums. Plants grow 4–6 ft. high, with clumps of upright, spreading branches and light green, 4-in., willowlike leaves. Prune heavily during or after flowering to promote strong new growth for next year's bloom. Can

be used as flowering hedge. Suckers freely. Fireblight can be a problem.

P. maackii. AMUR CHOKECHERRY. Tree. Zones 1–3, 10, 35–45. Native to Manchuria and Siberia; extremely hardy to cold and wind. To 25–30 ft. tall. Main feature is handsome trunk bark, which is yellowish and peeling, like birch bark. Leaves strongly veined, rather narrow and pointed, to 4 in. long. Small white flowers in narrow clusters 2–3 in. long. Fruit is black, ¼ in. across.

P. maritima. BEACH PLUM. Zones 32, 34, 37–39. Native to Atlantic coast from Maine to Virginia. Suckering shrub to 6 ft. tall or taller, forming colonies. Dull green leaves are 1½–3 in. long, half as wide. White flowers are followed by ½–2-in., dark red to dark purple fruits that are cherished for preserves. Tolerates strong winds, salt spray.

P. mume. JAPANESE FLOWERING APRICOT, JAPANESE FLOWERING PLUM. Tree. Zones 2–9, 12–22, 31–34, 39. Blooms may be frosted in coldest areas. Neither true apricot nor true plum. Longer-lived, tougher, more trouble-free plant than other flowering fruit trees. Eventually develops into gnarled, picturesque 20-ft. tree. Leaves to 4½ in. long, broadly oval. Winter blossoms are small and profuse, with clean, spicy fragrance. Fruit is small, inedible. For profuse bloom on year-old wood, prune heavily; let tree grow for a year, then prune back all shoots to 6-in. stubs after bloom. The next year, cut back half the young growth to 6-in. stubs; cut back other half the next year. Continue this routine in succeeding years. Varieties include:

'Bonita'. Semidouble rose red.

'Dawn'. Large ruffled double pink.

'Peggy Clarke'. Double deep rose flowers with extremely long stamens

PSEUDOCYDONIA sinensis

CHINESE QUINCE

Rosaceae

DECIDUOUS SHRUB OR SMALL TREE

ZONES 3–10, 14–21, 30–34, 39

FULL SUN

REGULAR WATER

Pseudocydonia sinensis

Seldom seen, curious tree, usually 15–20 ft. high (rarely taller) and half as wide. Trunk is attractive, with bark that flakes off to reveal shades of brown, green, and gray. Trunks on old trees are often fluted. Roundish oval, dark green leaves to 4½ in. long turn yellow and red in fall. Spring bloom produces a scattering of flowers rather than a show—the pale pink, 1–1½-in. flowers are borne singly at ends of year-old twigs. Blossoms are followed by extraordinary fruits: fragrant yellow quinces to 7 in. long, weighing over a pound apiece. Fruits can be made into jam. Very susceptible to fireblight in warm, humid regions; control by pruning out damaged wood.

PSEUDOLARIX kaempferi (Chrysolarix kaempferi)

GOLDEN LARCH

Pinaceae

DECIDUOUS TREE

ZONES 2–7, 14–17, 32–41

FULL SUN

REGULAR WATER

Pseudolarix kaempferi

Slow growing to 40–70 ft. high, often nearly as broad at base. Wide-spreading branches, pendulous at tips, grow in whorls to form symmetrical, pyramidal tree. Foliage has a feathery look; 1½–2-in.-long, ⅛-in.-wide needles are clustered in tufts except near branch ends, where they are single. Needles are bluish green during growing season, then turn a magnificent golden yellow very briefly in autumn before dropping. Cones and bare branches make interesting winter patterns. Choose an open spot sheltered from winds. Best in deep, rich, well-drained, acid soil; performance is better in colder part of range. Fine for spacious lawns.

PSEUDOSASA. See BAMBOO

PSEUDOTSUGA menziesii (P. taxifolia)

DOUGLAS FIR

Pinaceae

EVERGREEN TREE

ZONES 2–7, 10, 14–17, 34–41

FULL SUN; TAKES PART SHADE IN YOUTH

REGULAR TO LITTLE WATER

Pseudotsuga menziesii

Of the five (possibly eight) species of *Pseudotsuga*, only this one grows over a wide territory and is much cultivated. Also a popular Christmas tree. Reaches 70–200 ft. tall in forests. Trees are cone shaped and foliaged to the ground when young, then lose lower limbs as they age. Soft, densely set, green or blue-green needles up to 1½ in. long radiate in all directions from the branches. Needles are sweetly fragrant when crushed. Ends of branches swing up. Pointed wine red buds form at branch tips in winter, open to apple green new growth in spring. Reddish brown, oval cones are about 3 in. long, have obvious three-pronged bracts. Unlike upright cones of true firs (*Abies*), these hang down.

Native range extends from Alaska through Northern California, eastward into the Rocky Mountains, and southward into northern Mexico. In coastal climates, tree is fast growing, feathery, dark green, with slightly drooping branchlets. Rocky Mountain form, *P. m. glauca*, is a blue-green tree that is slower growing, more cold tolerant, more compact, and stiffer than the species. This is the form that will succeed outside the Pacific Coast states. Compact, weeping, and other forms exist, but they are grown mostly in arboretums and botanical gardens. All tolerate wind and will grow in all soils except boggy ones.

PSIDIUM

GUAVA

Myrtaceae

EVERGREEN SHRUBS OR SMALL TREES

ZONES VARY BY SPECIES

FULL SUN OR HIGH SHADE

MODERATE WATER

Psidium cattleianum

White flowers (composed principally of brush of stamens). Berrylike fruit usually matures during warm months; it is good eaten fresh or used in jellies, purées, juice drinks. Does best in rich soil. Self-fertile, but may produce more fruit with a pollinator.

P. cattleianum (P. littorale). STRAWBERRY GUAVA. Zones 9 and 14 (in sheltered locations), 15–27. Moderate, open growth to 8–10 ft. as shrub; can be trained as multitrunked, 10–15-ft. tree. Especially beautiful bark and trunk—greenish gray to golden brown. Leaves glossy green, to 3 in. long; new growth bronze. Fruit is dark red (nearly black when fully ripe), 1½ in. wide, with white flesh and a sweet-tart, slightly resinous flavor. 'Lucidum', yellow strawberry guava or lemon guava, has yellow fruit, fairly dense growth.

P. guajava. GUAVA. Zones 23–25, 26 (warmer parts), 27. To 25 ft. tall, with strongly veined leaves to 6 in. long. May lose some of its leaves briefly in spring; new growth is an attractive salmon color. Fruit 1–3 in. across, with white, pink, or yellow flesh and a musky, mildly acid flavor. Most varieties of this species ripen in summer, but the old variety 'Redland' ripens in winter.

PSYLLIOSTACHYS suworowii (Limonium suworowii)

Plumbaginaceae

ANNUAL

ALL ZONES

FULL SUN

REGULAR WATER

Psylliostachys suworowii

Rosettes of narrow, 8-in.-long leaves produce 1½-ft.-tall spikes of tiny lavender pink flowers in summer. Spikes are very slender, single or branched, and cylindrical, reminiscent of furry rats' tails. They are excellent in flower arrangements, fresh or dry.

Sow seed indoors, or sow in ground when danger of frost is over; then transplant seedlings or thin them to 1 ft. apart. The plant may be offered as *Statice suworowii*.

FOR INFORMATION ON SELECTING PLANTS
PLEASE SEE PAGES 79–160

P

PTELEA trifoliata

WAFER ASH, HOP TREE

Rutaceae

DECIDUOUS SHRUB OR SMALL TREE

ZONES 1–6, 10, 28–43

SUN OR SHADE

REGULAR TO MODERATE WATER

Ptelea trifoliata

Dense, rounded shrub or small, low-branching tree to 10–20 ft. tall (usually less) and equally broad. Leaves are divided into three 2–5-in. leaflets, turn from dark green to yellow in fall. They contain oil glands and are pungently aromatic when bruised; most people find the odor pleasant. Late spring flowers are small, greenish white, inconspicuous but fragrant. Winged seeds are discs to 1 in. wide, surrounded by a thin, flat, nearly circular rim. They look like wafers and have been used as a substitute for hops (hence the two common names).

PTERIDIUM aquilinum

BRACKEN

Polypodiaceae

FERN

ZONES 1–10, 14–24, 26, 28–43

FULL SUN OR PARTIAL SHADE

ADAPTABLE

FRONDS ARE POISONOUS IF INGESTED

Pteridium aquilinum pubescens

A worldwide native, bracken is represented by various subspecies that differ in minor details. Coarse, much-divided fronds rise directly from deep, running rootstocks. Grows from 2 ft. high to as tall as 7 ft. under good conditions. Occurs naturally in many places and can be tolerated in untamed gardens, but beware of planting it: deep rootstocks can make it a tough, invasive weed. Do not gather fronds to cook as fiddleheads, since they contain a slow poison.

PTERIS

BRAKE

Polypodiaceae

FERNS

ZONES VARY BY SPECIES

PARTIAL OR FULL SHADE

MOIST, NOT SATURATED, SOIL

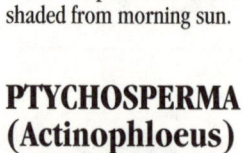
Pteris cretica

These are small evergreen ferns of subtropical or tropical origin, primarily used in dish gardens or in small pots; some are large enough for landscape use.

P. cretica. Zones 17, 23, 24, 25. To 1½ ft. tall, with comparatively few long, narrow leaflets. Numerous varieties exist: some have forked or crested fronds, while others are variegated. 'Wimsettii', a light green form with forked tips on mature plants, is so dense and frilly that it doesn't look like a fern.

P. 'Ouvrardii'. Zones 17, 22–25, 27. Dark green, 1–2½-ft.-tall fronds have extremely long, narrow, ribbonlike divisions.

P. quadriaurita 'Argyraea'. SILVER FERN. Zones 24, 25. From India. Fronds 2–4 ft. tall, rather coarsely divided, heavily marked white. Showy; unusual coloring for a fern. Protect from frost.

P. tremula. AUSTRALIAN BRAKE. Zones 16, 17, 22–25, 27. Extremely graceful, 2–4-ft. fronds on slender, upright stalks. Good landscape fern with excellent silhouette. Fast growing but tends to be short lived.

PTEROCARYA stenoptera

CHINESE WINGNUT

Juglandaceae

DECIDUOUS TREE

ZONES 4–24, 30–33

FULL SUN

REGULAR TO MODERATE WATER

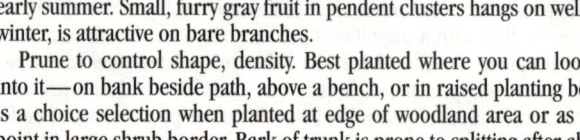
Pterocarya stenoptera

Fast to 40–90 ft., with heavy, wide-spreading limbs. Clearly shows its kinship to walnuts in its leaves: 8–16 in. long and divided into 11–23 finely toothed, oval leaflets. Foot-long clusters of small, single-seeded, winged nuts hang from branches. Good looking but has only one real virtue: it succeeds well in compacted, poorly aerated soil in play yards and other high-traffic areas. Aggressive roots make it unsuitable in garden or lawn. Volunteer seedlings can be a nuisance. *P. fraxinifolia*, Caucasian wingnut, is similar, with slightly larger leaflets, longer nut clusters.

PTEROSTYRAX hispidus

EPAULETTE TREE

Styracaceae

DECIDUOUS TREE

ZONES 3–10, 14–21, 31–41

PARTIAL SHADE IN HOT CLIMATES

REGULAR WATER

Pterostyrax hispidus

Native to Japan. Possibly reaches 40 ft., but more usually held to 15–20 ft. with 10-ft. spread. Trunk single or branched; branches open, spreading at top.

Light green leaves, gray green beneath, 3–8 in. long, rather coarse. Creamy white, fringed, lightly fragrant flowers in drooping clusters 4–9 in. long, 2–3 in. wide. Blooms in late spring or early summer. Small, furry gray fruit in pendent clusters hangs on well into winter, is attractive on bare branches.

Prune to control shape, density. Best planted where you can look up into it—on bank beside path, above a bench, or in raised planting bed. It is a choice selection when planted at edge of woodland area or as focal point in large shrub border. Bark of trunk is prone to splitting after abrupt winter temperature shifts. To minimize this tendency, plant where trunk is shaded from morning sun.

PTYCHOSPERMA (Actinophloeus)

Arecaceae (Palmae)

PALMS

ZONES 23–25

PARTIAL SHADE

REGULAR WATER

Ptychosperma macarthuri

Small-scale palms with slender, ringed trunks and feathery fronds toothed at apex. Often produce red fruits in warmest frost-free climates.

P. elegans. ALEXANDER PALM, SEAFORTHIA PALM, SOLITAIRE PALM. Native to Australia. Erect growth to 25 ft. tall, with a single trunk. Fronds to 8 ft. long.

P. macarthuri. MACARTHUR PALM. Native to New Guinea. Several clustered trunks to 10–15 ft. high. Fronds to 6½ ft. long. Often grown in containers.

PULMONARIA

LUNGWORT

Boraginaceae

PERENNIALS

ZONES 1–9, 14–17, 32–43

PARTIAL OR FULL SHADE

REGULAR WATER

Pulmonaria saccharata

Low-growing shade lovers with quiet charm. Many kinds have foliage attractively dappled with gray or silver. The long-stalked leaves are mostly in basal clumps, though there are a few on the flower stalks. Bear drooping clusters of funnel-shaped blue or purplish flowers in spring, just before leaves emerge or at the same time. After flowering finishes, more leaves emerge from the base. If you keep plants well watered, foliage will remain ornamental throughout the growing season.

All have creeping roots and can be used as small-scale ground covers in shaded areas. They associate well with ferns, azaleas, rhododendrons, blue scillas, pink tulips under spring-flowering trees. Divide every 4 or 5 years, either after flowering or in autumn.

P. angustifolia. COWSLIP LUNGWORT. Tufts of narrowish, unspotted, dark green leaves. Clustered pink buds open to dark blue flowers on 6–12-in. stems. 'Azurea' has sky blue flowers.

P. longifolia. Slender, silver-spotted deep green leaves to 20 in. long. Blooms a bit later than the other species. 'Bertram Anderson' has deep blue flowers; leaves remain attractive throughout season.

P. montana (P. rubra). Hairy, unspotted light green leaves to 20 in. long, 5 in. wide. Blooms very early in spring. Flowering stems can reach 16 in. Blossoms may be white, blue, or red, the last most commonly seen. Blooms of 1-ft. 'Redstart' are an odd shade between salmon and brick red.

P. 'Roy Davidson'. Hybrid between *P. saccharata* and *P. longifolia*. Resembles *P. l.* 'Bertram Anderson' but has slightly wider leaves and flowers that open pink and deepen to blue.

P. saccharata. BETHLEHEM SAGE. To 1½ ft. high and spreading to 2 ft. wide, with blue flowers and silvery-spotted leaves. Specialists usually offer named selections; the following are compact, foot-high plants. Flowers of 'Mrs. Moon' open pink and turn blue; 'Pierre's Pure Pink' has pink flowers; 'Sissinghurst White' has white blooms. 'Janet Fisk', another variety with blooms that turn from pink to blue, has leaves that are silvery almost all over.

PULSATILLA vulgaris (Anemone pulsatilla)

PASQUE FLOWER

Ranunculaceae

PERENNIAL

ZONES 1–6, 15–17, 36, 37, 39–45

FULL SUN OR LIGHT SHADE

REGULAR WATER

Pulsatilla vulgaris

Low-growing (8–12-in.-high) perennial from a woody rootstock. Basal leaves are 4–6 in. long and very finely cut, the segments covered with silky hairs. Each stem has several smaller, likewise silky leaves and is topped in spring by a cup-shaped, erect or nodding flower, 1½ to nearly 4 in. across, silky-hairy on the outer surfaces and centered with a yellow button of stamens. Flower color ranges from white through pink to bluish, purple, and red. Blooms are followed by fluffy seed clusters almost as showy as the flowers; each seed is topped by a long, twisting, feathery appendage. Plants need very well-drained soil. Best adapted to cool, moist climates.

PUMMELO. See CITRUS

PUMPKIN

Cucurbitaceae

ANNUAL VINE

ALL ZONES

FULL SUN

WATER AT FIRST SIGNS OF WILTING

Pumpkin

Related to gourds, melons, squash. Wide range of fruit size, depending on variety. One of the best for a jumbo-size Halloween pumpkin is 'Atlantic Giant'. 'Small Sugar' is a smaller pumpkin with finer-grained, sweeter flesh. 'Sweetie Pie' and 'Jack Be Little' are 3-in.-wide miniatures useful as decorations. 'Lumina' is a novelty white pumpkin with orange flesh; it weighs 10–12 lbs. Seeds of all kinds are edible, but the easiest to eat are those of hull-less varieties like 'Trick or Treat'.

Pumpkin vines need lots of room: a single vine can cover 500 sq. ft., and even bush types can spread over 20 sq. ft. Where the growing season is short, start plants indoors. In most areas, sow seeds outdoors in late spring after soil has warmed. For vining pumpkins, sow five or six seeds 1 in. deep in hills 6–8 ft. apart; thin seedlings to two per hill. For bush pumpkins, sow a cluster of three or four seeds 1 in. deep, 2 ft. apart, in rows spaced 3 ft. apart; thin seedlings to one or two plants per cluster. Water regularly during dry periods, but keep foliage dry to prevent leaf diseases. In late summer, slide wooden shingles or other protection under fruit to protect it from wet soil (this is not necessary if soil is sandy). Depending on variety, pumpkins are ready to harvest 90 to 120 days after sowing, when shell has hardened. They're usually picked after first frost kills the plant.

Pumpkins need rich soil, periodic fertilizer. They do not perform well in high heat and humidity. Subject to same pests and diseases as squash.

> ### GROW A GIANT PUMPKIN
> As plant grows, cut off all but two branches. When flowering begins, take off all but one flower on each branch (your aim: two branches with one pumpkin on each). Every 2 feet along each branch, put a 4-in. mound of soil over branch so roots can form there.

PUNICA granatum

POMEGRANATE

Punicaceae

DECIDUOUS SHRUB OR SMALL TREE

ZONES 5–31, WARMER PARTS OF 32

FULL SUN

REGULAR WATER FOR FRUIT PRODUCTION

Punica granatum

Bear showy summer flowers with ruffled petals surrounding central clump of stamens. Some varieties yield fruit in fall. Narrow leaves open bronzy, then turn glossy bright green to golden green; brilliant yellow fall color except in climates with very mild winters. All varieties tolerate great heat and a wide range of soils, including alkaline soil that would kill most plants. In coldest part of range, plant against south or west wall. Prune late in dormant season, since plant blooms on new wood. Nonfruiting varieties need little water once established.

'Chico'. DWARF CARNATION-FLOWERED POMEGRANATE. Compact bush can be kept to 1½ ft. tall if pruned occasionally. Double orange-red flowers over long season. No fruit. Excellent under lower windows, in containers, as edging.

'Legrellei' ('Madame Legrelle', 'California Sunset'). Dense 6–8-ft. shrub with double creamy flowers heavily striped coral red. No fruit.

'Nana'. DWARF POMEGRANATE. Dense shrub to 3 ft., nearly evergreen in mild winters. Blooms when a foot tall or less. Orange-red single flowers

P

followed by small, dry red fruit. Excellent garden or container plant; effective bonsai.

'Nochi Shibari'. To 8–10 ft. tall, with double dark red flowers.

'Tayosho'. To 8–10 ft. tall, with double light apricot flowers.

'Wonderful'. Best-known fruiting pomegranate. Grow as 10-ft. fountain-shaped shrub, tree, or espalier. Single orange-red flowers to 4 in. wide are followed by fruit with burnished red skin and red pulp. Will not fruit in cool-summer regions. Water deeply and regularly if fruit is important. Other fruiting varieties, only rarely seen, include yellow-blooming 'Sweet' and pink-blooming 'Fleshman', 'King', and 'Phil Arena's'; all have sweet pink pulp.

PURPLE CONEFLOWER. See ECHINACEA purpurea

PURPLE HEART. See SETCREASEA pallida 'Purple Heart'

PURPLE-LEAF PLUM. See PRUNUS cerasifera 'Atropurpurea'

PURPLE MOOR GRASS. See MOLINIA caerulea

PURPLE OSIER. See SALIX purpurea

PURSLANE. See PORTULACA oleracea

PUSCHKINIA scilloides

Liliaceae

BULB

✿ ZONES 1–11, 14, 29–43

☼ ☼ FULL SUN OR LIGHT SHADE

🌢 REGULAR WATER DURING GROWTH AND BLOOM

Puschkinia scilloides

Late winter or early spring bloomer closely related to squill (*Scilla*) and glory-of-the-snow (*Chionodoxa*). Performs best where ground freezes in winter. Bell-like flowers are pale blue or whitish with darker, greenish blue stripe on each segment, in spikelike clusters on 3–6-in. stems. Strap-shaped bright green leaves are broad, upright, a little shorter than flower stems. 'Alba' has white flowers. The most commonly sold variety is *P. s. libanotica*, a vigorous plant with pale blue, striped flowers like those of the species. Plant in autumn, placing 3–4 in. deep. Will grow for years without disturbance. Needs very little water during summer dormant period. Most effective in masses; good choice for naturalizing.

PUSSY TOES. See ANTENNARIA dioica

PYRACANTHA

FIRETHORN

Rosaceae

EVERGREEN SHRUBS

✿ ZONES VARY BY SPECIES

☼ FULL SUN

🌢 MODERATE WATER

Pyracantha coccinea

Grown for bright fruit, evergreen foliage (may be semievergreen in cold climates), variety of landscape uses, and ease of culture. All grow fast and vigorously, with habit from upright to sprawling; nearly all have needlelike thorns. All have glossy green leaves, generally oval or rounded at ends, ½–1 in. wide, 1–4 in. long. All bear flowers and fruit on spurs along wood of last year's growth. Spring flowers are small, fragrant, dull

creamy white, carried in flattish clusters; they're effective thanks to their profusion.

The real glory of firethorns is in the thick clusters of pea-size orange-red berries that light up the garden for months. Selections with red, orange, and yellow fruit are also available; if berry color is important, buy plants when in fruit. Depending on variety, berries color up from late summer to midautumn; some types hang on until late winter, when they're cleared out by birds, storms, or decay. Dislodge old withered or rotted berries with a water jet or an old broom.

As shrubs and ground covers, firethorns look better and fruit more heavily if allowed to follow their natural growth habit. Prune only occasionally to check wayward branches. Plants can be espaliered; they can also be sheared as hedges, though at the expense of much fruit. Tolerate most soils but should not be overwatered. Potential pests include aphids and scale insects. In humid regions, two serious problems are fireblight (which can kill the plant) and scab (which causes defoliation and turns fruit sooty); for best success, choose disease-resistant varieties.

P. coccinea. Zones 2–24, 26, 28–41. Very cold hardy. Rounded growth to 8–10 ft. high (20 ft. trained against wall). Red-orange fruit. Best known for its varieties, which include the following:

'Kasan'. Long-lasting orange-red berries. Spreading growth habit. Susceptible to scab.

'Lalandei' and 'Lalandei Monrovia'. Similar varieties with orange berries. Susceptible to scab.

'Wyattii'. Orange-red berries that color early. Very prone to fireblight and scab.

P. fortuneana (P. crenatoserrata, P. yunnanensis). Zones 4–24, 29–32. Vase-shaped plant to 15 ft. tall, 10 ft. wide. Limber branches make it a good choice for espalier. Orange to coral berries last through winter. 'Cherri Berri', to 10 ft. tall and 8 ft. wide, has deep red berries. 'Graberi', more upright than species, has huge clusters of dark red fruit.

P. hybrids. This category includes some of the most desirable firethorns. Plants vary in size, habit, and cold hardiness.

'Apache'. Zones 3–24, 29–33. To 5 ft. high and 6 ft. wide. Large bright red berries last well into winter. Resistant to fireblight and scab.

'Fiery Cascade'. Zones 3–24, 28–34, 39. To 8 ft. tall, 9 ft. wide; berries orange turning to red. Good disease resistance.

'Gnome'. Zones 2–24, 30–41. Very cold hardy. Densely branched, 6 ft. high, 8 ft. wide. Orange berries. Very susceptible to scab.

'Lowboy'. Zones 3–24, 29–33. Spreading plant to 2–3 ft. high. Orange fruit. Very prone to scab.

'Mohave'. Zones 3–24, 29–33. To 12 ft. tall and wide. Heavy producer of big orange-red fruit that colors in late summer and lasts well into winter. Resistant to fireblight and scab.

'Red Elf'. Zones 4–9, 12–24, 29–31. Densely branched, to 2 ft. high and wide, small enough for container culture. Long-lasting bright red fruit. Some disease resistance. Apparently the same as the plant sold as 'Leprechaun'.

'Ruby Mound'. Zones 4–9, 12–24, 29–31. Among the most graceful of ground cover firethorns. Long, arching, drooping branches make broad mounds 2½ ft. high, spreading to about 10 ft. Bright red fruit.

'Teton'. Zones 2–24, 29–41. Very cold hardy. Columnar growth to 12 ft. tall, 4 ft. wide. Golden yellow fruit. Resistant to fireblight and scab.

'Tiny Tim'. Zones 4–24, 29–31. Compact plant to 3 ft. high. Small leaves, few or no thorns. Red berries. Informal low hedge, barrier, tub plant.

'Watereri'. Zones 3–24, 29–33. To 8 ft. tall and wide. Very heavy producer of long-lasting bright red fruit.

'Yukon Belle'. Zones 3–24, 29–35, 37, 39. Cold-hardiest orange-fruited firethorn. Dense growth, to 6–10 ft. high and wide.

P. koidzumii. Unruly grower to 8–12 ft. tall and wide. Best known for its varieties, including these:

'Santa Cruz' ('Santa Cruz Prostrata'). Zones 4–24, 29–32. Low growing, branching from base, spreading. Easily kept below 3 ft. by pinching out the occasional upright branch. Red fruit. Plant 4–5 ft. apart for a ground cover or bank cover. Very resistant to scab.

'Victory'. Zones 4–24, 26, 28–32. Vigorous growth to 10 ft. tall, 8 ft. wide. Dark red berries color late in the year but hold on well. Resistant to scab.

'Walderi' ('Walderi Prostrata'). Zones 4–24, 29–31. Wide-spreading, low-growing ground cover (to 1½ ft. high, with a few upright shoots that should be cut out). Red berries. Plant 4–5 ft. apart for fast cover.

PYRETHRUM marginatum. See CHRYSANTHEMUM pacificum

PYRETHRUM roseum. See CHRYSANTHEMUM coccineum

PYROSTEGIA venusta
(P. ignea, Bignonia venusta)

FLAME VINE

Bignoniaceae

EVERGREEN VINE

 ZONES 13, 16, 21–27

☼ ◗ FULL SUN OR PARTIAL SHADE

◗ MODERATE WATER

Pyrostegia venusta

Native to South America. Fast growth to 20 ft. or more, climbing by tendrils; where well adapted, grows rampantly. Leaves consist of 2–3-in. oval leaflets. Impressive display of tubular, 3-in. orange flowers in clusters of 15–20 at branch ends; main bloom in winter. Plants growing in Florida sometimes form slender, 1-ft.-long fruit capsules. Tolerates many soils. In central Florida, most popular vine for covering fences and other structures. Prune right after bloom to restrain growth.

PYRUS

ORNAMENTAL PEAR

Rosaceae

EVERGREEN OR DECIDUOUS SHRUBS OR TREES

ZONES VARY BY SPECIES

☼ FULL SUN

◗ REGULAR WATER

Pyrus kawakamii

Fruiting pear is described under Pear. Following are ornamental species, grown for profuse flowers in late winter or early spring and for glossy, attractive leaves. Not fussy about soil, even growing well in heavy clay, but not at their best in shallow soil. Most are subject to fireblight (see Pear).

P. calleryana. Deciduous tree. Zones 2–9, 14–21, 28, 31–41. Needs some winter chill. To 25–50 ft. tall, with strong horizontal branching pattern; young growth is thorny. Broadly oval, scalloped, glossy dark green, leathery leaves to 1½–3 in. long; turn rich purplish red in fall. Clustered pure white flowers are ¾–1 in. wide. Very early bloom; late freezes may destroy flower crop. Fruit very small, round, inedible. Less susceptible to fireblight than most pears. Available varieties include:

'Aristocrat'. Pyramidal, with branches that curve upward (a more stable structure than that of 'Bradford'). Fall color ranges from yellow to red. Very subject to fireblight in the South.

'Bradford'. Original introduction. Strongly vertical limbs (with no central leader), the branching pattern spreading with age; mature trees have a tendency to split. Has reached 50 ft. high, 30 ft. wide.

'Capital'. Narrowly columnar. Coppery fall color.

'Chanticleer' ('Cleveland Select', 'Stone Hill'). Narrow but not columnar; about 40 ft. tall, 15 ft. wide. Fall color varies from orange to reddish purple. Resistant to fireblight.

'Redspire'. Forms a shorter, narrower pyramid than 'Aristocrat'. Has especially large blossom clusters and yellow to red fall color. Quite prone to fireblight.

'Trinity'. Round-headed form to 30 ft. tall. Orange-red fall color.

'Whitehouse'. Narrowly columnar. Red to reddish purple fall color. Often gets a disfiguring leaf spot.

P. communis. See Pear

P. kawakamii. EVERGREEN PEAR. Shrub or tree. Zones 8, 9, 12–24. Partially deciduous in coldest winters in coldest zones. Drooping branchlets; glossy, oval, pointed leaves. Clustered white flowers appear in masses in winter and early spring. Small, inedible fruit. Grows 12–30 ft. high. Without support, it is a broad, sprawling shrub or, in time, a multitrunked small tree. Easily espaliered. To train it as a tree, stake one or several branches and shorten side growth; keep staked until trunk is self-supporting. To build up framework limbs, shorten overlong, pendent branches to upward-facing growth buds or branchlets. Established, well-shaped plants need little pruning. Heavily pruned evergreen pears seldom flower. Tolerates many soils. Very subject to fireblight.

P. pyrifolia (P. serotina). SAND PEAR, JAPANESE SAND PEAR. Deciduous tree. Zones 2–9, 14–21, 32–41. To 40 ft. tall. Like the common fruiting pear in appearance, but leaves are glossier and more leathery. Fall color ranges from brilliant orange red to reddish purple. Small, woody, gritty fruit. Improved forms of this tree, *P. p. culta* and its varieties, are grown for fruit by the Japanese and are becoming popular in the U.S.

P. salicifolia 'Pendula'. WEEPING WILLOW-LEAFED PEAR. Deciduous tree. Zones 2–9, 14–21, 32–41. Elegant specimen plant to 15–25 ft. tall. Grown for silvery, willowlike foliage and beautiful weeping habit, showcased in winter when branches are bare. White flowers appear in early spring as silvery white new leaves emerge. Foliage slowly turns silvery green in summer. Fruit insignificant. Sometimes sold as 'Silver Frost'. Very susceptible to fireblight. Performance is better in cool climates.

QUAKER LADIES. See HOUSTONIA caerulea

QUAKING GRASS. See BRIZA maxima

QUAMOCLIT pennata. See IPOMOEA quamoclit

QUEEN OF THE MEADOW. See FILIPENDULA ulmaria

QUEEN OF THE PRAIRIE. See FILIPENDULA rubra

QUEEN PALM. See SYAGRUS romanzoffianum

QUEEN SAGO. See CYCAS circinalis

QUEEN'S TEARS. See BILLBERGIA nutans

QUEEN'S WREATH. See ANTIGONON leptopus, PETREA volubilis

Q

QUERCUS

OAK

Fagaceae

DECIDUOUS OR EVERGREEN TREES

ZONES VARY BY SPECIES

☼ FULL SUN

◗◗ SEE BELOW

Quercus coccinea

The oaks comprise 600 or so species of widely varying appearance and hardiness. Their common feature is the production of acorns—single nuts more or less enclosed in a cuplike organ made up of many closely set scales. Some oaks are widely planted over large parts of the country, while others have a limited range. Many wild-growing species may occur on rural or suburban properties but seldom, if ever, find their way into the nursery trade; these will not be discussed here.

Homeowners acquire oaks either by planting them or by inheriting trees that were present before the land was developed. Oaks that have been planted usually thrive without difficulty; inherited types probably require special attention. Protect trunks from earth-moving machinery with cribs of 2-by-4s or heavier timbers. Avoid piling excavated soil around trunks or above root systems (which extend somewhat beyond the branch spread); or provide drains for aeration and removal of excess water. Do not excavate or pave above the root zone without consulting a tree expert. Avoid compacting soil; when grading and other landscaping have been completed, be sure the tree has access to adequate water and air in the soil.

All oaks will take regular to moderate watering if they are planted out as young specimens. In summer-rainfall regions, mature trees will also take routine garden watering. In the West, native oaks have adapted their root systems to long, dry summers; heavy summer watering can cause serious root destruction. To safeguard such native trees, do not locate plantings too close to the trunk, and use only underplantings that require little or no summer water.

Caterpillars are the most serious potential pest of oaks. Gypsy moth caterpillars are most common in the East, oak moth larvae in the West. Heavy infestation can cause defoliation; serious attacks for 2 or more years in a row can weaken or even kill a tree. However, both these types of pests tend to be cyclical problems, striking perhaps every 7 to 10 years. If control becomes necessary, consult a professional arborist or tree service; oak trees are too large for the limited spray equipment available to the home gardener.

Oak wilt, a fungus disease, has killed millions of oaks east of the Rockies, especially in Texas and the Great Lakes states. It is spread by oak bark beetles and by contact between healthy and infected roots; starting from the treetop down, leaves wilt, turn dull, curl, dry, and drop. Avoid pruning in spring, when bark beetles are most active. Oak root fungus is a fatal disease of oaks in the West, also spread by contact with infected roots. In both regions, don't plant a new oak within the root zone of a tree that has died.

Q. acutissima. SAWTOOTH OAK. Deciduous. Zones 2–7, 29–41. Native to China, Korea, Japan. Moderate to fast growth to 35–45 ft. tall, usually with open, spreading habit. Deeply furrowed bark. Bristle-toothed, shiny dark green leaves are 3½–7½ in. long, a third as wide; they look like chestnut leaves. Foliage is yellowish on expanding, yellow to yellowish brown in fall; it may hang on late into winter. Fairly tolerant of various soils, though it prefers well-drained acid soil. Stands up well to heat and humidity. No serious problems. Good shade or lawn tree.

Q. agrifolia. COAST LIVE OAK. Evergreen. Zones 5, 7–24. Native to California's Coast Ranges. Round-headed, dense-foliaged tree to 20–70 ft. high, often with greater spread. Smooth dark gray bark; rounded, holly-like, 1–3-in. leaves. Attractive green all year unless leaves are devoured by oak moth larvae. Has greedy roots and drops almost all its old leaves in early spring. Despite its faults, a handsome and worthwhile shade or street tree. Can be sheared into a 10–12-ft. hedge.

Q. alba. WHITE OAK. Deciduous. Zones 1–6, 28, 31–43. Native from Maine to Florida, west to Minnesota and Texas. Slow to moderate to 50–80 ft., taller in the wild. Pyramidal when young; in maturity, a majestic round-headed tree, often broader than tall. Leaves are 4–8 in. long, dark green above, lighter beneath, with deep, rounded lobes. Folklore has it that when the emerging leaves are as big as a mouse's ear, it is time to plant corn. Fall color varies from brown to wine red. Best in rich, deep, moist, preferably acid soil. One of the handsomest oaks, useful for timber, flooring, and barrel-making, but not widely planted because of its ultimate size and slow growth. Where it occurs naturally, however, it is among the most cherished of trees; it is the oak associated with treaty signings and other historic events.

Q. bicolor. SWAMP WHITE OAK. Deciduous. Zones 1–3, 10, 32–43. Native Quebec to Georgia, west to Michigan and Arkansas. Slow to moderate growth to 50–60 ft., rarely taller, with equal or greater spread. Shallowly lobed or scalloped leaves are 3–7 in. long, a little more than half as wide, shiny dark green above, silvery white beneath. Fall color usually yellow, sometimes reddish purple. Bark of trunk and branches flakes off in scales. Tolerates wet soil; also thrives where soil is well drained. Drought resistant.

Q. coccinea. SCARLET OAK. Deciduous. Zones 2–24, 31–41. Native Maine to Florida, west to Minnesota and Missouri. Moderate to rapid growth in deep, rich soil. Can reach 60–80 ft. tall. High, light, open-branching habit. Bright green leaves are 3–6 in. long, a little more than half as wide,

with deeply cut, pointed lobes. Foliage turns scarlet where autumn nights are cold. Deep roots. Good street or lawn tree. Fine to garden under.

Q. douglasii. BLUE OAK. Deciduous. Zones 1–11, 14–24. Native to foothills around California's Central Valley. Low-branching, wide-spreading tree to 50 ft. high. Fine-textured light gray bark and shallowly lobed, oval, almost squarish leaves of a decided bluish green. Good in dry, hot situations. Attractive fall colors—pastel pink, orange, yellow.

Q. emoryi. EMORY OAK. Evergreen. Zones 10–13. Native to Arizona, New Mexico, Texas, northern Mexico. Handsome tree to 60 ft. (usually smaller in gardens). Leathery, oval, 2–3-in.-long leaves sometimes turn golden just before new growth starts in late spring. Grows well in low desert, tolerates a variety of soils. Needs periodic soaking in summer.

Q. falcata. SOUTHERN RED OAK, SPANISH OAK. Deciduous. Zones 28–35. Native from Virginia to Florida, westward to southern Illinois and Arkansas. Moderate growth to 70–80 ft., eventually with rounded crown. Leaves 5–9 in. long, sometimes longer, with sharp-pointed lobes varying in number from three to nine. Fall color not significant. Tolerates relatively poor and dry soils as well as occasionally flooded soils.

Q. frainetto. HUNGARIAN OAK, ITALIAN OAK. Deciduous. Zones 2–12, 14–21. Native to southern Europe. Erect, shapely tree to 100 ft. tall. Smooth dark gray bark. Glossy deep green leaves are large (to 8 in. long, 4 in. wide), with deeply cut lobes. Drought tolerant. Not for small properties.

Q. gambelii (Q. utahensis). ROCKY MOUNTAIN WHITE OAK. Deciduous. Zones 1–3, 10. Characteristic oak of Arizona's Oak Creek Canyon and Colorado foothills south of Denver. Grows slowly to 20–30 ft. (rarely to 50 ft.), often in colonies from underground creeping root system. Deeply fissured, dark gray to reddish brown bark. Dark green leaves, 3–7 in. long and half as wide, turn yellow, orange, or red in fall.

Q. garryana. OREGON WHITE OAK, GARRY OAK. Deciduous. Zones 4–6, 15–17. Native from British Columbia to Northern California. Slow to moderate growth to 40–90 ft., with wide, rounded canopy; branches are often twisted. Grayish, scaly, checked bark. Leathery, 3–6-in.-long leaves are dark glossy green above, rusty or downy beneath, broadly elliptical with rounded lobes. Deep, nonaggressive roots.

Q. hemisphaerica. See Q. laurifolia

Q. ilex. HOLLY OAK, HOLM OAK. Evergreen. Zones 4–24, warmer parts of 32. Native to Mediterranean region. Moderate growth to 40–70 ft. high, with equal spread. Though variable, leaves are generally 1½–3 in. long and a third as wide, either toothed or smooth edged, rich dark green above, yellowish or silvery beneath. Tolerates wind and salt air; will grow in areas with constant sea winds, but tends to be shrubby there. Good street or lawn tree. Can take clipping into formal shapes or hedges.

Q. imbricaria. SHINGLE OAK. Deciduous. Zones 3–6, 32–41. Native from Pennsylvania to Georgia, west to Nebraska and Arkansas. Slow growing and pyramidal in youth, eventually growing at a moderate rate into a rounded tree. Typical height is 50–60 ft., though tree sometimes reaches 100 ft. Shallowly ridged brown-gray bark. Oval, smooth-edged leaves are 2½–6 in. long, half as wide. Foliage is reddish on unfolding, dark glossy green in summer, yellowish brown to brownish red in autumn; often hangs on through winter. Thrives with pruning and can be trimmed into a hedge. Best in rich, deep, moist, well-drained soil; tolerates some drought.

The common name derives from one of the tree's uses: the wood was used for shingles. Sometimes called laurel oak because of its smooth, glossy leaves, but that name properly belongs to similar species *Q. hemisphaerica* and *Q. laurifolia*, less hardy evergreen or nearly evergreen oaks.

Q. kelloggii. CALIFORNIA BLACK OAK. Deciduous. Zones 5 (inland), 6, 7, 15, 16, 18–21. Native to mountains from southern Oregon to Southern California. Moderate growth to 30–80 ft., upright habit. Dark, furrowed, checked bark. Leaves 4–10 in. long, 2½–6 in. wide, with deep, bristle-pointed lobes. Leaves are soft pink or dusty rose when new, bright glossy green at maturity, yellow or yellow orange in fall. Good tree for spring and fall leaf color, attractive winter trunk and branch pattern.

Q. laurifolia. LAUREL OAK. Zones 25–33. Evergreen in southern part of range; loses leaves in winter in northern part. Native to coastal plain and piedmont from southern New Jersey to Florida, eastward to East Texas and southeast Arkansas. To 40 ft. or more in height, somewhat less in spread. Narrowly oval, smooth-edged, leathery leaves are shiny dark green, 1–4 in. long, ½–1¼ in. wide. *Q. hemisphaerica*, also called laurel oak, is similar. Both are useful street trees in the South, being smaller and less spreading than *Q. virginiana*.

Q. lobata. VALLEY OAK, CALIFORNIA WHITE OAK. Deciduous. Zones 1–9, 14–24. Native to interior valleys of California. Often reaches 70 ft. or taller, with equal or greater spread. Massive trunk and limbs with thick, ashy gray, distinctly checked bark. Limbs often picturesquely twisted; long, drooping outer branches sometimes sweep ground. Leaves deep green above, paler beneath, 3–4 in. long, nearly as wide, with deep, rounded lobes. Tolerates high heat, moderate alkalinity in its native range. Best in deep soils. Often seen with "oak balls"—big, corky spheres that result from insect activity but don't harm tree.

Q. macrocarpa. BUR OAK, MOSSY CUP OAK. Deciduous. Zones 1–11, 14–24, 29–45. Native from Nova Scotia to Pennsylvania, westward to Manitoba and Texas. Rugged-looking tree growing slowly to 60–80 ft. high and at least as wide. Deeply furrowed dark gray bark. Leaves are glossy green above, whitish beneath, 4–10 in. long and half as wide, broad at tip, tapered at base. Yellowish fall color. Large acorns form in mossy cups. Similar to *Q. bicolor* but faster growing, more tolerant of adverse conditions. Needs lots of room.

Quercus macrocarpa

Q. myrsinifolia. JAPANESE LIVE OAK. Evergreen. Zones 4–7, 14–24, 28–31, warmer parts of 32. Native to Japan, China. To 20–30 ft. tall and nearly as wide, usually round headed in age. Narrow, glossy dark green leaves 2½–4 in. long, toothed toward tip. Purplish new foliage. Unlike most oaks, it is graceful rather than sturdy; it's not easily recognized as an oak unless seen with its acorns. No serious problems.

Q. nigra. WATER OAK. Deciduous. Zones 26, 28–35. Native to lowland stream banks throughout southeastern U.S. Moderate to fast growth to 50–80 ft. tall, with conical or rounded canopy. Fairly narrow leaves, 1½–4 in. long, vary in shape from obovate to lobed; turn yellow to brown in fall, hang on late. Limbs subject to breakage by wind, snow, ice. Tolerates many soils, but not alkaline ones. Provide moist to wet conditions. Used as shade and street tree.

Q. palustris. PIN OAK. Deciduous. Zones 2–10, 14–24, 28–41. Native from Massachusetts to Delaware, westward to Wisconsin and Arkansas. Moderate to fairly rapid growth to 50–80 ft. Slender and pyramidal when young, open and round headed at maturity. Smooth brownish gray bark becomes shallowly ridged with age. Lower branches tend to droop almost to ground; if lowest whorl is cut away, branches above will adopt same habit. Only when fairly tall will it have good clearance beneath lowest branches. Glossy dark green leaves, 3–6 in. long and nearly as wide, are deeply cut into bristle-pointed lobes. In brisk fall weather, leaves turns yellow, red, and finally russet

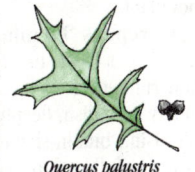

Quercus palustris

brown; may hang on in winter. Needs plenty of water; tolerates poorly drained soils. Widely used as lawn and street tree.

Q. phellos. WILLOW OAK. Deciduous. Zones 3, 4, 6–16, 18–21, 28–35. Native from New York to Florida, westward to Missouri and Texas. Fast to moderate growth to 50–90 ft. tall. Somewhat like *Q. palustris* in growth habit and spreading nature, this tree is grown and used in much the same way. Smooth gray bark becomes shallowly ridged in age. Leaves do not resemble those of other common oaks, but look more like willow leaves—2½–5 in. long, ⅓–1 in. wide, smooth edged. Foliage turns yellowish before falling; in warmer regions, dead leaves may hang on through winter. Most delicate foliage pattern of all oaks. Has no serious problems. Will tolerate poorly drained soils.

Quercus phellos

Q. prinus. CHESTNUT OAK, BASKET OAK. Deciduous. Zones 3–6, 31–41. Native from southern parts of Maine and Ontario southward to

South Carolina and Alabama. Moderate growth to an eventual dense, rounded 60–70 ft. Bark often quite dark, even nearly black, becoming deeply furrowed with age. Unlobed leaves with coarse, rounded teeth are 4–6 in. long, 1½–3½ in. wide; in fall, their deep yellowish green color changes to yellow or yellowish brown. This tree tolerates poor, dry, rocky soil but looks better and grows faster with adequate water, good soil. Does not tolerate wet soils.

Q. robur. ENGLISH OAK. Deciduous. Zones 2–12, 14–21, 32–41. Native to Europe, northern Africa, western Asia. Moderate growth to 40–60 ft. in gardens (to 90 ft. in wild), with rather short trunk and very wide, open head in maturity. Leaves 3–4½ in. long, half as wide, with three to seven pairs of rounded lobes. Leaves hold until late in fall and drop without much color change. 'Fastigiata', upright English oak, is narrow and upright (like Lombardy poplar) when young, branches out to broad, pyramidal shape when mature. Both this variety and the species are prone to mildew. Other varieties include 'Skymaster', a broad pyramid to 50 ft. tall and half as wide (narrower in youth); and 'Westminster Globe', a round-headed tree to 45 ft. tall and wide.

Q. rubra (*Q. r. maxima*, *Q. borealis*). RED OAK, NORTHERN RED OAK. Deciduous. Zones 1–12, 14–24, 31–45. Native from Nova Scotia to Pennsylvania, westward to Minnesota and Iowa. Fast growth to 60–75 ft. in gardens (over 100 ft. in wild). Broad, spreading branches and round-topped crown. With age, bark becomes quite dark and fissured. Leaves 5–8 in. long, 3–5 in. wide, with three to seven pairs of sharp-pointed lobes. New leaves and leafstalks are red in spring, turning dark red, ruddy brown, or orange in fall. Needs fertile soil and plenty of water. Stake young plants. High-branching habit and reasonably open shade make it a good tree for big lawns, parks, broad avenues. Deep roots make it good to garden under. Usually fairly trouble-free.

Q. shumardii. SHUMARD RED OAK. Deciduous. Zones 4–9, 12, 14–17, 26 (upper half), 28–35, 37, 39. Native from Kansas to southern Michigan, southward to North Carolina and Florida, westward to Texas. Similar to *Q. coccinea*, slightly less hardy. Yellow to red fall color. Tolerates drought, wide range of soils.

Q. suber. CORK OAK. Evergreen. Zones 5–7, 8–16, 18–23. Native to Mediterranean region. Moderate growth to 70–100 ft. high and as wide. Trunk and principal limbs covered with thick, corky bark (the cork of commerce). Toothed, 3-in. leaves are shiny dark green above, gray beneath. Good garden shade tree with interesting contrast between light-textured foliage and massive, fissured trunk. Needs good drainage. Fairly tolerant of various soils, but foliage is likely to turn yellow in alkaline soils. Established trees can take considerable drought. Value as street tree or park tree diminishes when children find out how easy it is to carve bark.

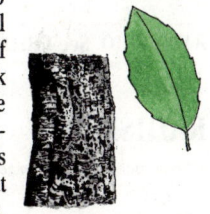

Quercus suber

Q. virginiana. SOUTHERN LIVE OAK. Evergreen; partly or wholly deciduous in cold-winter regions. Zones 4–31. Native from Virginia to Florida, westward to Texas. Signature tree of the South. Moderate growth to 40–80 ft. tall, with spreading, heavy-limbed crown up to twice as wide. Very long lived; with age, bark becomes very dark and checked. Smooth-edged, quite narrow leaves, 1½–5 in. long, shiny dark green above, whitish beneath. Old leaves are all shed in spring before new growth emerges. Tree is often draped with Spanish moss. Thrives on moisture and does best in deep, rich soil. Tolerates salt spray. Widely used as street tree in native range. Needs lots of space. A gall insect causes unsightly damage to leaves. Loss of trees to oak wilt has been severe, especially in Central Texas. Termites have killed many live oaks in New Orleans.

QUINCE, FLOWERING. See CHAENOMELES

QUINCE, FRUITING
(Cydonia oblonga)

Rosaceae

DECIDUOUS SHRUB OR SMALL TREE

🌿 ZONES 2–10, 14–24, 29–35, 37, 39

☼ FULL SUN

🔴 MODERATE WATER

Fruiting Quince

Slow to 10–25 ft. Unlike flowering quince (*Chaenomeles*), fruiting quince has thornless branches. Generally overlooked by planters of flowering fruit trees and home orchard trees, yet its virtues make common quince worth considering as an ornamental. Its winter form can be dramatic in pattern of gnarled and twisted branches. In spring, it bears white or pale pink, 2-in.-wide flowers at tips of leafed-out branches. Attractive, oval, 2–4-in. leaves, dark green above and whitish beneath; turn yellow in fall. Large, yellow, wonderfully fragrant fruit ripens in early fall.

Best in heavy, well-drained soil but tolerates wet soil. Avoid deep cultivation, which damages shallow roots and causes suckers. Prune only to form trunk and shape frame; thin out and cut back only enough to stimulate new growth. Do not use high-nitrogen fertilizer, as this results in succulent growth that is susceptible to fireblight. Remove suckers that sprout freely around the base of the tree; they rarely fruit and tend to weaken the tree.

Fruit is inedible when raw but useful in making jams and jellies. Fruit is also made into candy and blended with other fruits in pies. Some popular varieties are:

'Apple' ('Orange'). Old favorite. Round, golden-skinned fruit. Tender orange-yellow flesh.

'Cooke's Jumbo'. Large yellowish green fruit with white flesh. Can be nearly twice the size of other quinces.

'Pineapple'. Roundish, light golden fruit. Tender white flesh; pineapple-like flavor.

'Smyrna'. Round to oblong fruit with lemon yellow skin. Strong quince fragrance.

RADICCHIO. See CHICORY

RADISH

Brassicaceae (Cruciferae)

ANNUAL

🌿 ALL ZONES

☼ ☼ FULL SUN OR LIGHT SHADE

🔴 MAINTAIN EVEN SOIL MOISTURE

Radish

You can pull radishes for the table as early as 3 weeks after you sow the seed (the slowest kinds take 2 months). To grow well, they need moist soil and some added nutrients. Supply nutrients by blending rotted manure into soil before planting, or—about 10 days after planting—feed beside row as for carrots, or apply liquid fertilizer. Sow seeds as soon as ground can be worked in spring and at weekly intervals until warm weather approaches (heat causes plants to go to seed, with roots becoming bitter in the process). In mild areas, radishes make a fall and winter crop. Sow seeds ½ in. deep and thin to 1 in. apart when tops are up; space rows 1 ft. apart. Row covers will help protect against flea beetles, which attack foliage; will also deter root maggots by preventing adult flies from laying eggs.

Most familiar radishes are short, round, red or red-and-white types like 'Cherry Belle', 'Crimson Giant', and 'Scarlet White-tipped'. These should be used just as soon as they reach full size. Slightly slower to reach edible size are long white radishes, of which 'Icicle' is best known. Late radishes 'Long Black Spanish' and 'White Chinese' grow 6–10 in. long, can be stored in moist sand in a frost-free place for winter use. The last named,

along with 'Alpine Cross' and similar very large, mild radishes, are sold as daikon (pronounced "dye-con").

RANGPUR LIME. See CITRUS, Sour-Acid Mandarin

Ranunculaceae. The immense buttercup family numbers nearly 2,000 species, among them numerous ornamental annuals and perennials. Members include *Anemone*, columbine (*Aquilegia*), *Clematis*, *Delphinium*, hellebore (*Helleborus*), and *Ranunculus*. Many are poisonous if eaten.

RANUNCULUS

Ranunculaceae

PERENNIALS WITH TUBEROUS OR FIBROUS ROOTS

🌿 ZONES VARY BY SPECIES

☼ ☼ 🔴 EXPOSURE NEEDS VARY BY SPECIES

🔴 REGULAR WATER

Ranunculus asiaticus

A very large group (up to 250 species of widely different habit and appearance), but the two listed are the only ones grown to any extent.

R. asiaticus. PERSIAN RANUNCULUS, TURBAN RANUNCULUS. All zones (see below). Each large tuber produces many stalks to 1½ ft. or taller; in spring, each stalk bears one to four flowers, for a profuse show of blooms. Flowers are semidouble to fully double, 3–5 in. wide, in white and many shades of yellow, orange, red, pink, cream. Leaves are bright fresh green, almost fernlike. Popular strain is Tecolote Giants, available in single colors, mixed colors, and picotees. Bloomingdale is a dwarf (8–10-in.) strain.

Tubers are hardy to 10°F/–12°C; in Zones 4–9, 12–31, plant in fall for bloom in winter, early spring. Where winter temperatures fall below 10°F/–12°C, plant as soon as ground is workable in spring. Needs full sun, perfect drainage (if necessary, plant in raised beds). Set tubers with prongs down, 2 in. deep (½–1 in. deep in heavy soil), 6–8 in. apart. Tubers rot if overwatered before roots form; you can start them in flats of moist sand, then plant after sprouts appear. Cover young sprouts with netting to protect from birds. Where hardy, tubers can be left in ground, but they tend to rot if they get moisture during summer dormancy. Most gardeners in all regions lift tubers when foliage yellows, cut off tops, and store in cool, dry place. Nursery-grown seedlings are sold in some areas. Good pot plant.

R. repens 'Pleniflorus' (R. r. 'Flore Pleno'). CREEPING BUTTERCUP. Zones 1–11, 14–24, 28–43. Vigorous plant with thick, fibrous roots and runners growing several feet in a season, rooting at joints. Leaves glossy, roundish, deeply cut, toothed. Blooms in spring, bearing fully double, 1-in., button-shaped bright yellow flowers on 1–2-ft. stems. Ground cover in full sun to deep shade. Can be invasive. Basic species is single flowered and as aggressive as the variety (or more so).

RAPHIDOPHORA aurea. See EPIPREMNUM aureum

RAPHIOLEPIS. See RHAPHIOLEPIS

RASPBERRY

Rosaceae

DECIDUOUS SHRUBS WITH BIENNIAL STEMS

🌿 BEST IN ZONES 3–6, 15–17, 36–40, 42; ALSO COOLER PARTS OF 41 AND 43

☼ FULL SUN

🔴 REGULAR WATER

Raspberry

Most popular and heaviest bearing raspberries are red. There are two types: summer-bearing raspberries, which bear annually in summer on 2-year-old canes; and everbearing (also called fall-bearing) raspberries, which bear twice on each cane—in autumn of first year, then in summer of second year. In both types, fruit follows loose clusters of white flowers. For ornamental relatives, see *Rubus*.

Raspberries need winter chill or cold and a slowly warming, lingering springtime to reach perfection. In warmer zones outside of best raspberry climates, satisfactory production may come from plants grown in light shade. In Zone 28, 'Dorma Red' is the only good producer; in Florida Zones 25 and 26, the tropical mysore raspberry (*Rubus niveus*) bears black raspberry crops in winter and spring. Good drainage is essential; if your soil is heavy clay, consider planting in raised beds. Slightly acid soil (pH 6 to 6.5) is ideal. Water need is greatest during flowering and fruiting. Feed at bloom time.

Plants are erect; they can be grown as free-standing shrubs and staked, but they are most easily handled if tied to wires fastened between two stout posts. The lower wire should be at 2½ ft., the upper one at 4–5 ft. The best time to plant is late winter or early spring. Set plants an inch deeper than they grew originally; space them 2½–3 ft. apart, in rows 7–9 ft. apart. Cut back the cane that rises from the roots, leaving only enough (about 6 in.) to serve as a marker.

Summer-bearing varieties should produce three to five canes the first year; these will bear the next year and should be cut out at ground level after fruiting. Second-year canes will appear all around parent plant and even between hills and rows. Remove all except 5–12 closely spaced, vigorous canes that come up near the crown. Tie these to top wire. In spring, before growth begins, cut them back to 4½–5½ ft. Fruit-bearing laterals will appear from these canes.

Everbearing raspberries differ slightly in pruning needs; they fruit in their first autumn on top third of cane and in their second summer on lower two-thirds of cane. Cut off upper portion that has borne fruit and leave lower portion to bear next spring. Cut out cane after it has fruited along its whole length.

You can follow the example of growers who cut everbearing canes to the ground yearly in fall after fruiting is finished; wait until late winter in cold regions. You'll sacrifice one of the crops in return for easy maintenance and a prolonged crop in summer. Use a powerful rotary mower in a large berry patch.

To control anthracnose and other fungus diseases, spray with lime sulfur during the dormant season and again when bloom time begins; this will also help control many insect pests. Cane borer may attack canes; prune out and destroy any damaged canes below entry points (pinhead-size holes in canes at or near ground level).

The following varieties are summer bearing unless otherwise indicated:

'Bababerry'. Everbearing. Needs little winter chill, stands heat well.

'Boyne'. Very hardy variety bred in Manitoba. Early ripening. Subject to anthracnose.

'Canby'. Large, bright red berries. Thornless.

'Cuthbert'. Medium-size berries of good quality.

'Durham'. Everbearing. Medium-size, firm berries of good quality. Starts to ripen 2 weeks before 'Indian Summer'. Good in North.

'Fairview'. For coastal Northwest. Bears young and heavily. Early variety of good quality.

'Golden West'. Unlike the others, produces yellow berries. Excellent quality; tasty novelty.

'Heritage'. Everbearing. Small red berries are tasty, a bit dry.

'Indian Summer'. Everbearing. Small crops of large, tasty red berries. Fall crop often larger.

'Latham'. Older, very hardy variety for coldest regions. Mildews in humid-summer areas. Late ripening. Berries often crumbly.

'Meeker'. Large, firm bright red fruit on long, willowy branches.

'Newburgh'. Late-ripening variety. Large, light red berries. Takes heavy soil fairly well.

'New Washington'. Smallish fruit of high quality. Needs well-drained soil.

'Puyallup'. For west of the Cascades. Large, soft berries with very good flavor. Midseason.

'Ranere' ('St. Regis'). Everbearing. Small, bright red berries.

'September'. Everbearing. Medium to small berries of good flavor. Fall crop the heavier one.

'Summit'. Everbearing. Can bear the first year. Heavy producer.

'Sumner'. Early variety with some resistance to root rot in heavy soils. Fine fruit.

'Willamette'. Large, firm, dark red berries that hold color and shape well.

RASPBERRY, BLACK or BLACKCAP

Rosaceae

DECIDUOUS SHRUBS WITH BIENNIAL STEMS

ZONES 4–6, COOLER PARTS OF 32 AND 33, 34–43

FULL SUN OR LIGHT SHADE

REGULAR WATER

Black Raspberry

For ornamental relatives, see *Rubus*. Resemble regular red raspberry in many ways, but even less tolerant of mild climates. Blue-black fruit is firmer and seedier, with a more distinct flavor. Plants do not sucker from roots; new plants form when arching cane tips root in soil. No trellis needed. Head back new canes at 1½–2 ft. to force laterals. At end of growing season, cut out all weak canes and remove canes that fruited during current season. In late winter or early spring, cut back laterals to 10–15 in. on strong canes, 3–4 in. on weak ones. Fruit is produced on side shoots from these laterals. If you prefer trellising, head new canes at 2–3 ft. Subject to same pests and diseases as red raspberry.

Varieties usually sold are 'Cumberland', an old variety; 'Morrison', large berry on productive vine; and 'Munger', most popular commercial variety. 'Jewel', a recent introduction, is disease resistant and vigorous; tip-pinch at 5 ft. 'Sodus', purple raspberry, is a vigorous hybrid of red and black raspberry; head new canes at 2½–3 ft.

RATIBIDA

Asteraceae (Compositae)

PERENNIALS

ZONES 1–24, 26–43

FULL SUN

REGULAR WATER

Ratibida columnifera

Native to prairie and western states. Plants are stiffly erect, branched, roughly hairy, with deeply cut leaves. Flower heads resemble black-eyed Susan (*Rudbeckia*) but have fewer ray flowers and a round or cylindrical (rather than flat) central disc. Use in casual, natural-looking borders with grasses and other minimum-care perennials.

R. columnifera. MEXICAN HAT. To 2 ft. tall. Flowers have drooping ray flowers of yellow or brownish purple, and a tall, columnar brown disc. Effect is that of a sombrero with drooping brim.

R. pinnata. PRAIRIE or YELLOW CONEFLOWER. To 4 ft. tall, with yellow ray flowers and a nearly globular brown disc.

RATTAN PALM. See RHAPIS humilis

RATTLESNAKE GRASS. See BRIZA maxima

RATTLESNAKE MASTER. See ERYNGIUM yuccifolium

REDBUD. See CERCIS

RED-FLOWERING GUM. See EUCALYPTUS ficifolia

RED-HOT POKER. See KNIPHOFIA uvaria

RED MAIDS. See CALANDRINIA ciliata menziesii

REDONDO CREEPER. See LAMPRANTHUS filicaulis

REDTOP. See AGROSTIS gigantea

R

RED VALERIAN. See CENTRANTHUS ruber

REDWOOD, COAST REDWOOD. See SEQUOIA sempervirens

REDWOOD SORREL. See OXALIS oregana

REHMANNIA elata

Gesneriaceae

PERENNIAL

ZONES 7–10, 12–24, 31

SUN OR SHADE; BEST WITH SOME SHADE

REGULAR WATER

Rehmannia elata

Spreads by underground roots to form big clump of coarse, deeply toothed leaves. Stalks to 2–3 ft. tall are loosely set with 3-in.-long, tubular flowers that look something like big, gaping foxgloves. Common form is rose purple with yellow, red-dotted throat; there is a fine white-and-cream form that must be grown from cuttings or divisions. In mild-winter regions, it blooms from midspring well into fall and remains evergreen. In colder climates, bloom comes in summer. Long lasting as a cut flower. Provide rich soil.

REINWARDTIA indica (R. trigyna)

YELLOW FLAX

Linaceae

PERENNIAL

ZONES 8, 9, 12–28

FULL SUN OR PARTIAL SHADE

REGULAR TO MODERATE WATER

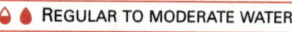

Reinwardtia indica

Shrublike form to 3–4 ft., with elliptical evergreen leaves 1–3 in. long. Brilliant yellow, 2-in., flaxlike flowers form in great profusion. Blooms do not last long, but for weeks new ones open daily. Blooms in late fall and early winter in mild-winter regions, in summer in colder part of range. Pinch to make more compact. Grow in fertile, well-drained soil. Spreads by underground roots. Increase by rooted stems; divide in spring.

RESEDA odorata

MIGNONETTE

Resedaceae

ANNUAL

ALL ZONES

PARTIAL SHADE IN HOT CLIMATES

REGULAR WATER

Reseda odorata

To 1½ ft. tall; rather sprawling habit. Light green leaves. Not particularly beautiful plant, but well worth growing because of remarkable spicy-sweet flower fragrance. Small greenish flowers tinged with copper or yellow, in dense spikes that become loose and open as blossoms mature. Sow seed in early spring—or late fall or winter in mildest climates. Successive sowings give long bloom period. Best in rich soil. Plant in masses to get full effect of fragrance, or spot a few in flower bed to provide fragrance to scentless plantings. Suitable for pots. Strains have longer flower spikes and brighter colors, but they are less fragrant.

FOR INFORMATION ON SELECTING PLANTS
PLEASE SEE PAGES 79–160

RETINISPORA pisifera. See CHAMAECYPARIS pisifera

Rhamnaceae. The buckthorn family of shrubs and trees has small, usually clustered flowers and fruits that are either drupes (single seeded, juicy) or capsules. Family members include *Ceanothus*, *Rhamnus*, and Chinese jujube (*Ziziphus*).

RHAMNUS

Rhamnaceae

EVERGREEN OR DECIDUOUS SHRUBS OR TREES

ZONES VARY BY SPECIES

FULL SUN OR PARTIAL SHADE, EXCEPT AS NOTED

MODERATE WATER

Rhamnus cathartica

Small, clustered flowers are rather inconspicuous; plants are grown for form and foliage. Used chiefly as background plantings, hedges. Berrylike, typically pea-size fruits attract birds; volunteer seedlings may be a nuisance.

R. alaternus. ITALIAN BUCKTHORN. Evergreen shrub. Zones 4–24, 31, 32. Fast, dense growth to 12–20 ft. or more, with equal spread. Oval, shiny bright green leaves to 2 in. long. Easily trained as single- or multitrunked small tree. Takes well to shearing, shaping. Black fruits. 'Variegata' ('Argenteo-variegata') grows 6–8 ft. tall, has creamy-edged foliage that looks striking against dark background (if branches with plain green leaves appear, cut them out or they'll quickly take over).

R. californica. COFFEEBERRY. Evergreen shrub. Zones 4–24. Basic species is a variably upright plant to 15 ft., with 3-in., glossy, oval leaves; it may be sold by specialists in western native plants, but two named selections are more often planted. 'Eve Case' is compact, rounded to 4–8 ft. high and wide; 'Seaview', to 6–8 ft. wide, can be kept to 1½ ft. high if upright growth is pinched out. Both have broadly oval leaves to 6 in. long and cherry-size fruits that turn from green to red to black.

R. cathartica. COMMON BUCKTHORN. Deciduous shrub or small tree. Zones 1–3, 32–45. To 15–25 ft. tall and wide. Glossy green, elliptical or oval leaves to 2½ in. long. Foliage drops late in season; fall color is poor. Short twigs often spine tipped. Black fruits. Tolerates drought, poor soil, wind. Useful hedge or small tree in coldest, driest regions. Full sun.

R. frangula. ALDER BUCKTHORN. Deciduous shrub or small tree. Zones 1–7, 10, 11, 32–45. To 10–12 ft. (possibly 18 ft.) tall and as wide. Oval or obovate leaves to 3 in. long, glossy dark green turning yellow in autumn. Fruits turn from greenish yellow to red orange, dark red, and then black. 'Columnaris', tallhedge buckthorn, grows 12–15 ft. tall, 4 ft. wide. Set 2½ ft. apart for a tight, narrow hedge that can be kept as low as 4 ft.

RHAPHIOLEPIS

Rosaceae

EVERGREEN SHRUBS

ZONES 8–10, 12–24, 26, 28–31; WORTH THE RISK IN ZONES 4–7, 32, 33

FULL SUN OR LIGHT SHADE

REGULAR TO MODERATE WATER

Rhaphiolepis indica

Where temperatures never (or very rarely) fall to 0°F/–18°C, these are among the most widely planted shrubs, and for good reason: their glossy, leathery leaves and compact growth habit make them attractive, dense background plants or informal hedges. They bloom profusely from late fall or midwinter to late spring, with flowers ranging in color from white to near red. Berrylike dark blue fruit (not especially showy) follows flowers. New leaves in tones of bronze and red often add more touches of color.

R

Most stay low. The taller kinds rarely reach more than 5–6 ft.; pruning can keep them at 3 ft. almost indefinitely. For bushy, compact plants, pinch back branch tips at least once yearly, after flowering. Plants in part shade are less compact and produce fewer flowers than those in full sun. Few pest problems, though aphids occasionally attack. Fireblight and a fungal leaf spot (in cool, wet weather) are possible disease problems. Good seacoast plants; tolerate salt drift.

R. delacouri. Pink-flowered hybrid of *R. indica* and *R. umbellata*. To 6 ft. tall. Small pink flowers in upright clusters. Leaves smaller than most.

R. indica. INDIA HAWTHORN. To 4–5 ft. high, with 1½–3-in.-long, pointed leaves and ½-in. white flowers tinged pink. Its varieties are widely grown and sold, although the species is not. Varieties differ mainly in color of bloom and in size and form of plant; there is variation even within a variety. Flower color is especially inconsistent. In warmer climates and exposures, blossoms are usually lighter; in general, bloom is paler in fall than spring. Varieties include the following:

'Ballerina'. Deep rosy pink flowers. Stays low (not much taller than 2 ft.) and compact (no wider than 4 ft.). Leaves take on reddish tinge in winter.

'Clara'. White flowers on compact plants 3–5 ft. high, about as wide. Red new growth.

'Dancer'. Clear pink flowers. Dense. To about 4 ft. tall.

'Enchantress'. Rose pink flowers. Grows 3 ft. tall, 5 ft. wide. A white form is called 'White Enchantress'.

'Indian Princess'. Light pink flowers. To 3 ft. high.

'Jack Evans'. Bright pink flowers. To about 4 ft. tall, with wider spread. Compact and spreading. Leaves sometimes have purplish tinge.

'Spring Rapture'. Compact 4-ft.-tall plant with rose red single flowers.

'Springtime'. Deep pink flowers. Vigorous, upright growth can reach 4–6 ft. high.

R. 'Majestic Beauty'. Fragrant light pink flowers in clusters to 10 in. wide. Leaves 4 in. long. Larger in every detail than others; can reach 15 ft. Thought by some to be hybrid between *Rhaphiolepis* and loquat (*Eriobotrya*). Use as background shrub or small tree with single or multiple trunk. Stake tree form carefully until it has formed a sturdy trunk. Thin branches to reduce wind resistance and minimize chances of plant blowing down.

R. umbellata (R. u. ovata, R. ovata). Easily distinguished from *R. indica* by its roundish, leathery, dark green leaves, 1–3 in. long. White flowers about ¾ in. wide. Vigorous plants 4–6 ft. tall, sometimes to 10 ft. Thick and bushy in full sun. This plant is sometimes called Yeddo hawthorn. 'Minor' is a dwarf, slow-growing form.

RHAPIS

LADY PALM

Arecaceae (Palmae)

PALMS

🌡 ZONES VARY BY SPECIES; OR INDOORS

◑ ● PARTIAL OR FULL SHADE

💧 REGULAR WATER

Rhapis excelsa

Fan palms that form bamboolike clumps with deep green foliage. Trunks covered with net of dark, fibrous leaf sheaths. Slow growing, choice, expensive. Several variegated forms exist, and fanciers are willing to pay very high prices for good examples. Good indoor plants; give indirect light.

R. excelsa. LADY PALM. Zones 12–17, 19–28. Hardy to 20°F/–7°C. Slow growing to 5–12 ft. tall, often much less. One of the finest container plants, it withstands poor light and neglect but responds quickly to better light and fertilizer.

R. humilis. RATTAN PALM, SLENDER LADY PALM. Zones 16, 17, 20–27. Hardy to 22°F/–6°C. Tall, bamboolike stems (to 18 ft.) give charming, graceful, tropical air. Larger, longer-leafed palm than *R. excelsa*.

RHIPSALIDOPSIS gaertneri (Schlumbergera gaertneri)

EASTER CACTUS

Cactaceae

CACTUS

🌡 ZONES 16, 17, 21–27; OR INDOORS

◑ PARTIAL SHADE

💧 REGULAR WATER

Rhipsalidopsis gaertneri

For culture and general description, see *Schlumbergera*. Much like *S. bridgesii*, but more upright or horizontal rather than completely drooping. Blooms in spring, often again in late summer or early fall. There are many varieties, with flowers in shades of pink and red. In marginal climates, protect under lathhouse or covered terrace. Good house plant; give bright light indoors and carry outdoors in warm season, if desired. Recently renamed *Hatiora gaertneri*, but not generally offered under that name.

RHODODENDRON (includes Azalea)

Ericaceae

EVERGREEN OR DECIDUOUS SHRUBS, RARELY TREES

🌡 SEE BELOW

◑ GENERALLY BEST IN FILTERED SHADE

💧💧 CONSTANTLY MOIST SOIL AND HUMID AIR

⬥ LEAVES ARE POISONOUS IF INGESTED

Rhododendron 'Trude Webster'

Approximately 800 species belong to this huge group. The International Register lists more than 10,000 named varieties, of which perhaps 2,000 varieties are currently available. Botanists have arranged species into series and subseries; one of these series includes plants called azaleas.

With careful selection, gardeners in all climates, even the coldest, hottest, and driest ones, can find ways to grow certain members of this genus (in containers or as house plants, if necessary). Rhododendrons generally do best in Zones 4–6, 15–17, 34, 37, and 39, though there are many exceptions. The climate adaptation of azaleas differs greatly from that of rhododendrons: for example, evergreen azaleas are grown extensively in the South and in Southern California, regions where rhododendrons require special attention. Overall, zones for azaleas vary widely, depending on the hybrid group or species; see the azalea listings (pages 468–470) for specifics.

Rhododendrons and azaleas have much the same basic soil and water requirements. They require acid soil. They need more air in the root zone than any other garden plants but, at the same time, they need a constant moisture supply. In other words, they need soil that is both fast draining and moisture retentive. Yellowing, wilting, and collapse of plants indicate root rot caused by poor drainage. Soils rich in organic matter have the desired qualities; improve your soil with liberal quantities of organic matter. Plant azaleas and rhododendrons with top of root ball slightly above soil level. Never allow soil to wash in and bury stems. Plants are surface rooters and benefit from a mulch such as pine needles, oak leaves, and wood by-products such as fir bark or chips. Never cultivate around these plants.

Sun tolerance of azaleas and rhododendrons differs by species and variety. Too much sun causes bleaching or burning in leaf centers, though most can take full sun in cool-summer areas. Ideal location is in filtered shade beneath tall trees; east and north sides of house or fence are next best. Too-dense shade results in lanky plants that bloom sparsely. Any fertilizing should be done immediately after bloom. ▶

R

Both rhododendrons and azaleas require special attention where soil and water are high in dissolved salts (as in the arid Southwest), or where soil is rich in lime (as in much of the Midwest). To avoid damage, plant in containers or raised beds and periodically leach the mix by heavy watering—enough to drain through mix two or three times. If leaves turn yellow while veins remain green, plants have iron deficiency called chlorosis; apply iron chelate to soil or spray with iron solution.

Though subject to many pests and diseases, plants are not usually beset by problems when well tended. Damage by root weevil adults, which notch leaves, is usually minor, but their larvae can girdle roots. Prevent new generations by controlling adults with contact insecticide. Lacebugs, which suck sap from leaf undersides, can be a severe problem in warm weather; spray with insecticidal soap or summer oil to control the wingless nymphs. Or use a systemic or contact insecticide to combat winged adults as well. Azalea petal blight fungus quickly ruins open blossoms of both azaleas and rhododendrons during warm, humid weather, turning the flowers brown and mushy. Because the spores form from resting bodies in petal debris from the previous year, thorough cleanup of infected blossoms will reduce infection both later in the season and in the following year. To control an infection, spray with a systemic insecticide; check with your Cooperative Extension Office for a specific recommendation.

Wind and soil salts burn leaf edges; windburn shows up most often on new foliage, salt burn on older leaves. Late frosts often cause deformed leaves. In extremely cold weather, sun and wind can severely damage plants; protect them by erecting a windbreak of burlap fastened to stakes. Protect roots against damage from alternate freezing and thawing by placing a mulch over the root system after the soil has frozen.

Prune evergreen azaleas by frequent pinching of tip growth from after flowering until July or August if you wish a compact plant with maximum flower production.

Prune large-flowered rhododendrons early in spring at bloom time if needed. Pruning in early spring will sacrifice some flower buds, but that is the best time for extensive pruning. Plant's energies will be diverted to dormant growth buds, which will then be ready to push out early in the growing season. Tip-pinch young plants to make them bushy; prune older, leggy plants to restore shape by cutting back to side branch, leaf whorl, or cluster of dormant buds. (Some varieties will not push new growth from dormant buds.) Clip or break off faded flower heads or spent clusters, taking care not to injure new buds and growth just beneath them.

KINDS OF RHODODENDRONS

Most people know rhododendrons as big, leathery-leafed shrubs with rounded clusters ("trusses") of stunning white, pink, red, or purple blossoms. But there are also dwarfs a few inches tall, giants that reach 40 or even 80 ft. in their native Southeast Asia, and a host of species and hybrids in every intermediate size, in a color range including scarlet, yellow, near-blue, and a constellation of blends of orange, apricot, and salmon.

The following sections list named varieties by categories, to give you some idea of their adaptability to different climates and garden roles. Many of them are described later. These are the generally available kinds, representing only a portion of the best rhododendrons grown throughout the country.

Ironclad hybrids for coldest winters. These can take temperatures to −25°F/−32°C: 'America', 'Boule de Neige', 'English Roseum', 'Ignatius Sargent', 'Nova Zembla', 'Parsons Gloriosum', 'PJM', 'President Lincoln', 'Roseum Elegans'.

Ironclad hybrids that tolerate hot summers. 'Anah Kruschke', 'Belle Heller', 'Cheer', 'Cynthia', 'English Roseum', 'Fastuosum Flore Pleno', 'Holden', 'Nova Zembla', 'PJM', 'Roseum Elegans', 'Scintillation'.

Vireyas for indoors and frost-free areas. The Vireya rhododendrons, from the tropics of Southeast Asia, manage nicely in frost-free and nearly frostless zones (17, 23–25, 27). They are also fine container plants (even indoors), so they can be grown in colder zones if brought inside for the winter. They need an especially fast-draining potting mix (many species are epiphytes in the wild); a combination of equal parts peat moss, coarse orchid bark, and perlite works well. Typically, plants flower on and off throughout the year rather than in one blooming season, bearing waxy-textured flowers in exciting shades of yellow, gold, orange, vermilion, salmon, and pink, plus cream, white, and bicolors. Species, named hybrids, and unnamed seedlings are offered by some specialty growers.

RHODODENDRON RATINGS AND HARDINESS

Each plant in the list that follows includes a two-number rating (3/3, for example) assigned by the American Rhododendron Society. Flower quality is shown first and shrub quality second; 5 is superior, 4 above average, 3 average, 2 below average, 1 poor.

The list also gives each plant a hardiness rating, which indicates minimum temperatures a mature plant can tolerate without serious injury. Heights given are for plants 10 years old; older plants may be taller, and crowded or heavily shaded plants may reach up faster.

The bloom time given is approximate and varies with weather and location. The bloom season starts as early as January (in mildest climates) and extends through August; most types are spring bloomers. In the list below, "very early" corresponds to winter; "early" to early spring; "midseason" to midspring; "late" to late spring; and "very late" to summer.

RHODODENDRONS IN CLAY OR ALKALINE SOIL?

They don't like it. Planting in raised beds that are 1–2 ft. above the original soil level is the simplest way to give these plants the conditions they need. Liberally mix organic material into top foot of native soil, then fill bed above it with a mixture that's 50 percent organic material, 30 percent soil, 20 percent sand. This mixture will hold air and moisture while allowing alkaline salts to leach through.

'A. Bedford'. 4/3. −5°F/−21°C. To 6 ft. Lavender blue with darker flare. Large trusses. Late midseason.

'America'. 3/3. −25°F/−32°C. To 5 ft. tall and wide. Dark red. Late.

'Anah Kruschke'. 2/3. −10°F/−23°C. To 5 ft. Lavender purple. Color not the best, but plant has good foliage, tolerates heat, is not fussy about soil. Midseason.

'Anna Rose Whitney'. 4/3. 5°F/−15°C. Compact grower to 5 ft., with excellent foliage. Big trusses in rich, deep pink. Midseason.

'Antoon Van Welie'. 3/3. −5°F/−21°C. To 6 ft. Carmine pink. Big trusses of 'Pink Pearl' type. Late midseason.

'Azurro'. 3/4. −15°F/−26°C. Compact plant to 4 ft. Rich purple with red blotch. Late.

'Belle Heller'. 4/3. −10°F/−23°C. To 5 ft. Pure white with gold blotch. Midseason. Sun and heat tolerant.

'Blue Diamond'. 5/4. 0°F/−18°C. Compact, erect growth to 3 ft. Small leaves. Lavender blue flowers cover plant early to midseason. Takes considerable sun in cool climates.

'Blue Ensign'. 4/3. −15°F/−26°C. Compact, well-branched, rounded plant to 4 ft. Leaves tend to spot. Lilac blue flowers have a striking dark spot in the upper petal. Midseason.

'Blue Peter'. 4/3. −10°F/−23°C. Broad, sprawling growth to 4 ft.; needs pruning. Large trusses of lavender blue flowers blotched with purple. Midseason.

'Boule de Neige'. 3/3. −25°F/−32°C. To 5 ft. Rounded plant with bright green leaves and snowball-like clusters of white flowers. Midseason.

'Bow Bells'. 3/4. 0°F/−18°C. Compact, rounded growth to 4 ft. Rounded leaves; bronzy new growth. Bright pink, bell-shaped flowers in loose clusters. Midseason.

R. carolinianum. 3/3. −25°F/−32°C. Native to mountains of the Carolinas and Tennessee. To 3–6 ft. tall and as broad or broader. Leaves turn purplish in cold winters. Tight clusters of pink flowers in midseason. 'Album' is similar but bears white flowers.

R. catawbiense. 3/3. −25°F/−32°C. Native to mountains from West Virginia to Alabama. To 5 ft., eventually much larger. Lavender purple

R

flowers in midseason. Ancestor of many heat-tolerant varieties. 'Album' has pink buds opening to white flowers with greenish yellow blotch.

'Cheer'. 3/3. −10°F/−23°C. Mound-shaped, glossy-leafed plant to 4 ft. Pink flowers. Early. Heat tolerant.

'Christmas Cheer'. 2/4. −5°F/−21°C. To 3 ft. Pink to white flowers in tight trusses. Very early bloom compensates for any lack in flower quality. Can take full sun.

R. chryseum. 2/2. −15°F/−26°C. Dwarf (1-ft.), densely branched plant with small leaves. Flowers are small, bright yellow bells, four or five to a cluster. Early midseason.

'Cilpinense'. 4/4. 5°F/−15°C. Low (to 2½-ft.) plant with spreading growth; small leaves. Funnel-shaped flowers of apple blossom pink fading white; loose clusters nearly cover plants early in season. Easy to grow. Effective massed. Protect blossoms from late frosts.

'Cinnamon Bear'. 5/5. −10°F/−23°C. Low, dense, to 4 ft. Rosy pink buds open to pink flowers. Midseason. Furry brown leaves an additional attraction.

'C.I.S.' 4/2. 10°F/−12°C. To 3 ft. Flowers are red in throat to cream yellow at edges, carried in large trusses. Midseason.

'Cotton Candy'. 4/4. 0°F/−18°C. To 6 ft. Large flowers in soft pink shades, carried in tall trusses. Midseason.

'Cunningham's White'. 2/3. −15°F/−26°C. An old-timer. To 4 ft. tall; white blooms with greenish yellow blotch. Late midseason.

'Cynthia'. 4/3. −15°F/−26°C. To 6 ft. Rosy crimson with blackish markings. Midseason. Old favorite for background. Heat tolerant.

'Dora Amateis'. 4/4. −15°F/−26°C. To 3 ft. tall. Compact, rather small-foliaged plant; spreading, good for foreground. Profuse bloomer with green-spotted white flowers. Early midseason.

'Elizabeth'. 4/4. 0°F/−18°C. Broad grower to 3 ft. tall, with medium-size leaves. Blooms very young. Bright red, waxy, trumpet-shaped flowers in clusters of three to six at branch ends and in upper leaf joints. Main show early; often reblooms in autumn. Very susceptible to fertilizer burn, salts in water. There is a red-leafed form.

'Else Frye'. 5/3. 15°F/−26°C. Long, limber growth makes this a natural for informal espalier. Considerable pinching needed for compact plant. Flowers are white with pink flush and gold throat. Early.

'English Roseum'. 3/4. −25°F/−32°C. Erect shrub to 6 ft. Lavender blooms with yellowish green petal blotches. Midseason. Hardy to both cold and heat.

'Fastuosum Flore Pleno'. 3/3. −10°F/−23°C. To 5 ft. Double mauve flowers in midseason. Dependable old-timer. Heat tolerant.

'Forsterianum'. 5/4. 20°F/−7°C. Open, rangy growth to 5 ft. Attractive glossy, red-brown, peeling bark and glossy leaves. Tubular, frilled, fragrant white flowers tinted pink. Very early; buds often damaged by frost in colder areas without overhead protection.

'Fragrantissimum'. 4/3. 20°F/−7°C. Large, powerfully fragrant, funnel-shaped white flowers touched with pink. Early midseason. Loose, open, rangy growth with bright green, bristly leaves. With hard pinching in youth, a 5-ft. shrub. Easily trained as espalier or vine, reaching 10 ft. or more. Can spill over wall. Grow as container plant in marginal climates; overwinter indoors in bright but cool room.

Rhododendron 'Fragrantissimum'

'Furnival's Daughter'. 5/4. −5°F/−21°C. To 5 ft. Bright pink flowers with deep red blotch. Midseason.

'Ginny Gee'. 5/5. −5°F/−21°C. Striking 2-ft. plant with small leaves, dense growth. Covered with small flowers in early midseason. Blooms range from pink to white, with striped and dappled patterns.

'Golfer'. 4/5. −15°F/−26°C. Low, broad, dense, to 1 ft., with silvery, furry coat on leaves. Bright pink. Midseason.

'Gomer Waterer'. 3/4. −15°F/−26°C. To 5 ft. White flushed lilac. Late midseason. Old-timer.

'Halfdan Lem'. 5/4. −5°F/−21°C. Well shaped, vigorous, to 5 ft. Luminous red trusses stand out against deep green foliage. Midseason.

'Hallelujah'. 5/5. −15°F/−26°C. To 4 ft. Rose red flowers in midseason stand above thick, beautiful forest green foliage. Takes full sun. Very strong grower. Fine-looking plant with or without flowers.

'Holden'. 3/3. −15°F/−26°C. Compact grower to 4 ft. Rose red flowers marked with deeper red. Midseason. Heat tolerant.

'Hong Kong'. 3/3. −20°F/−29°C. To 5 ft., with glossy green leaves and primrose yellow flowers. Probably the cold-hardiest true yellow. Midseason to late.

'Hotei'. 5/4. 5°F/−15°C. Compact, to 3 ft. Canary yellow flowers backed by a prominent calyx come only when plant is 6 to 8 years old. Closest of all varieties to a deep pure yellow. Midseason. Plant in well-drained soil only, since roots rot easily.

'Ice Cube'. 4/3. −20°F/−29°C. To 5 ft. Cone-shaped clusters of creamy white flowers with a small yellow flare. Midseason to late.

'Ignatius Sargent'. 2/2. −25°F/−32°C. To 5 ft., with open growth habit, large leaves. Deep rose pink flowers. Midseason to late.

'Janet Blair'. 4/3. −15°F/−26°C. Vigorous plant to 6 ft. tall and spreading. Large, ruffled pastel flowers blend pink, cream, white, and gold; rounded trusses. Midseason to late.

'Jean Marie de Montague'. 3/4. 0°F/−18°C. To 5 ft., with good foliage. Brightest scarlet red. Midseason.

'Johnny Bender'. 5/5. −5°F/−21°C. To 4 ft. Glossy dark green leaves set off blood red flowers. Midseason.

'Lem's Cameo'. 5/4. 5°F/−15°C. To 5 ft. Flowers in a blend of apricot, cream, and pink. Midseason.

'Lem's Monarch' ('Pink Walloper'). 5/5. 0°F/−18°C. Plant grows to 6 ft., takes on a treelike shape. Large, deep green leaves, darker at the edges, come in huge round trusses at midseason.

'Lem's Stormcloud'. 4/4. −15°F/−26°C. To 5 ft. Bright red flowers on large, erect trusses. Midseason.

'Leo'. 5/3. −5°F/−21°C. To 5 ft., well clothed in large dark green leaves. Rounded to dome-shaped trusses packed with rich cranberry red blooms. Midseason.

'Loder's White'. 5/5. 0°F/−18°C. Shapely growth to 5 ft. Big trusses of flowers are white tinged pink when they open, turn pure white as they mature. Midseason. Blooms freely even when young. Best white for most regions.

'Lodestar'. 4/4. −20°F/−29°C. To 5 ft. Large white or palest lilac flowers marked deep greenish yellow. Midseason to late.

'Lord Roberts'. 3/3. −10°F/−23°C. To 5 ft. Handsome dark green foliage and rounded trusses of black-spotted red flowers. Midseason to late. Plants grown in sun have more compact growth, bloom more profusely.

'Madame Mason' ('Madame Masson'). 3/3. −5°F/−21°C. To 5 ft. White with light yellow flare on upper petal. Late midseason. Needs pruning to keep it compact.

'Mars'. 4/3. −10°F/−23°C. To 4 ft. Dark red. Late midseason. Handsome form, foliage, flowers.

'Molly Ann'. 4/5. −10°F/−23°C. Compact grower to 2 ft. Rose-colored, upright trusses are set against round leaves. Midseason.

'Moonstone'. 4/4. −5°F/−21°C. Attractive, dense-growing dwarf to 2 ft. tall. Leaves neat, small, rounded. Flaring bells age from pale pink to creamy yellow. Early to midseason. Fine facing taller rhododendrons, as low foundation planting with 'Bow Bells'.

R. moupinense. 4/2. 0°F/−18°C. To 1½ ft., open, spreading. Small, oval leaves are deep red when new, then mature to green. White or pink flowers, spotted red. Very early.

'Mrs. Furnival'. 5/5. −10°F/−23°C. Compact growth to 4 ft. Tight, round trusses of clear pink flowers with light brown blotch in upper petals. Late midseason.

'Mrs. G. W. Leak' ('Cottage Gardens Pride'). 4/4. 5°F/−15°C. Strong growth to 5 ft. Deep pink with deep brown flare on upper petals. Midseason.

R. mucronulatum. 4/3. −25°F/−32°C. Deciduous azalealike rhododendron with open growth to 5 ft. Makes up for bare branches by very early bloom. Flowers are generally bright purple. There is a pink form, 'Cornell Pink'.

'Nova Zembla'. 3/3. −25°F/−32°C. To 5 ft. Profuse red flowers come late in the season. Hardy to both cold and heat.

'Paprika Spiced'. 4/3. 0°F/−18°C. To 3 ft. Flowers are a blend of yellow, pink, and orange, dotted with red. Midseason.

'Parsons Gloriosum'. 2/2. −25°F/−32°C. To 5 ft., upright but fairly compact. Pinkish lavender flowers. Midseason to late.

'Party Pink'. 4/4. −20°F/−29°C. To 5 ft., broad and spreading with broad leaves and large trusses of lavender pink flowers. Midseason to late.

'Patty Bee'. 5/5. −10°F/−23°C. Dense, moundlike growth to 1½ ft. Leaves are small, giving plant a finely textured look. Trumpet-shaped yellow flowers cover plant in midseason.

'Pink Pearl'. 3/3. −5°F/−21°C. To 6 ft. or more; open, rangy growth without pruning. Rose pink, tall trusses in midseason. Dependable grower and bloomer in all except coldest climates.

'PJM'. 4/4. −25°F/−32°C. To 4 ft. Lavender pink blooms come early. Foliage turns mahogany in winter. Takes heat as well as cold.

'President Lincoln'. 2/3. −25°F/−32°C. To 6 ft. Lilac-toned lavender pink with bronze blotch. Midseason to late.

'Purple Splendour'. 4/3. −10°F/−23°C. Informal growth to 4 ft. Ruffled, deep purple blooms blotched black purple. Midseason. Easy to grow.

R. racemosum. 3/3. −10°F/−23°C. Several forms include 6-in. dwarf, 2½-ft. compact upright shrub, and tall 7-footer. Small pink flowers in clusters of three to six all along stems. Early. Easy to grow; sun tolerant in cooler areas.

'Rainbow'. 4/3. 0°F/−18°C. Strong growth to 5 ft., with heavy foliage. Very showy flowers with light pink center and carmine petal edges. Early to midseason.

'Ramapo'. 3/4. −20°F/−29°C. Dense, spreading growth to 2 ft. in sun, taller in shade. New growth is dusty blue green. Violet blue flowers cover plant in midseason. Fine for rockeries.

'Rosamundi'. 2/3. −5°F/−21°C. Slow growing, compact, to 4 ft. high and wide. Ball-like trusses of pink flowers. Early.

'Roseum Elegans'. 2/3. −25°F/−32°C. Vigorous plant to 6 ft., with small trusses of pinkish lilac flowers. Midseason to late. Hardy to both cold and heat.

'Sapphire'. 4/4. 0°F/−18°C. Twiggy, rounded, dense shrublet to 1½ ft., with tiny gray-green leaves. Small, bright blue, azalealike flowers. Early.

'Sappho'. 3/2. −5°F/−21°C. To 6 ft. White with dark purple spot in throat. Midseason. Easy to grow; gangly without pruning. Use at back of border.

'Scarlet Wonder'. 5/5. −10°F/−23°C. Outstanding dwarf (to 2 ft. tall) of compact growth. Shiny, quilted foliage forms backdrop for many bright red blossoms. Midseason.

'Scintillation'. 4/5. −15°F/−26°C. Compact 5-ft. plant covered in lustrous, dark green leaves. Rounded trusses carry gold-throated pink flowers. Midseason. Heat tolerant.

'Sham's Candy'. 3/3. −20°F/−29°C. To 5 ft. with narrow deep green leaves. Cone-shaped trusses of deep pink flowers with yellow-green blotch. Midseason to late.

'Snow Lady'. 4/4. 0°F/−18°C. To 3 ft. Wide, flat, fragrant white flowers with black stamens. Early to midseason.

'Sumatra'. 4/4. −15°F/−26°C. Dwarf to 2 ft. tall. Deep pure red flowers. Midseason.

'Susan'. 3/4. −5°F/−21°C. To 4 ft., with handsome foliage. Silvery lavender flowers in large trusses. Midseason.

'Taurus'. 5/4. 0°F/−18°C. Vigorous, upright to 6 ft.; well covered with forest green leaves. Brilliant red flowers with black spotting on upper lobes come in large, round trusses. Midseason bloom comes only after plants reach 4 to 6 years old.

'Top Banana'. 4/4. 0°F/−18°C. Upright, vase-shaped plant to 4 ft. Clear, bright yellow. Midseason. Blooms at a young age (2 years).

'Trinidad'. 3/4. −20°F/−29°C. To 4 ft. Cream flowers edged in red. Midseason to late.

'Trude Webster'. 5/4. −10°F/−23°C. Strong 5-ft. plant, with large leaves. Huge trusses of clear pink flowers come in midseason. One of the best pinks.

'Unique'. 3/5. 5°F/−15°C. To 4 ft.; outstanding neat, rounded, compact habit. Apricot buds open to tight, rounded trusses in deep cream fading to light yellow. Early midseason.

'Unknown Warrior'. 3/2. 5°F/−15°C. To 4 ft. Light soft red, fading quickly when exposed to bright sun. Early to midseason. Easy to grow.

'Van Nes Sensation'. 3/4. 0°F/−18°C. To 5 ft. Pale lilac flowers in large trusses. Midseason. Strong grower.

'Vulcan'. 3/4. −5°F/−21°C. To 4 ft. Bright brick red flowers. Midseason to late. New leaves often grow past flower buds, partially hiding flowers.

R. yakushimanum. 4/4. −20°F/−29°C. Dense, spreading growth to 3 ft. Gray-felted new foliage; older leaves have heavy tan or white felt beneath. Clear pink bells changing to white. Late midseason. Selections range from 'Ken Janeck', a large (and large-leafed) form with very pink flowers, to 'Yaku Angel', with pink-tinged buds opening to pure white. There are also a number of hybrids that are as good in cold climates as they are in milder ones, among them 'Mardi Gras', 'Mist Maiden', 'Yaku Sunrise', and 'Yaku Princess' (this last selection is part of a good series of hybrids, all with monarchic names).

KINDS OF EVERGREEN AZALEAS

The evergreen azaleas fall into more than a dozen groups and species, though an increasing number of hybrids have such mixed parentage that they don't conveniently fit into any group. The following includes some of the most popular groups. Except as noted, bloom season is early (see "Rhododendron ratings and hardiness," page 466, for explanation of bloom season terms). In greenhouses, plants can be forced for winter bloom. Plant sizes vary within the groups.

Belgian Indica Hybrids. Zones 14–24. This is a group of hybrids originally developed for greenhouse forcing. Where lowest temperatures are 20° to 30°F/−7° to −1°C, many of them serve well as landscape plants. They have lush, full foliage and profuse large blossoms. Among the most widely sold are 'Albert and Elizabeth', white and pink; 'California Sunset', salmon pink with white border; 'Chimes', dark red; 'Mardi Gras', salmon with white border; 'Mission Bells', red semidouble; 'Mme. Alfred Sanders', cherry red; 'Orange Sanders', salmon orange; 'Orchidiflora', orchid pink; 'Paul Schame', salmon; and 'Red Poppy'. 'Violetta', deep purple, and 'William Van Orange', orange red, have pendent growth suitable for hanging baskets.

Beltsville Hybrids. Zones 4–9, 14–24, 31, 32, warmer parts of 33. Hardy to 0°F/−18°C. Similar to the Glenn Dale Hybrids. 'Casablanca Improved' is a large white single. 'Eureka' and 'Guy Yerkes' have pink flowers. 'Polar Bear' is an exceptionally hardy white.

Brooks Hybrids. Zones 8, 9, 14–24. Hardy to 20°F/−7°C. Bred in Modesto, California, for tolerance of hot, dry summers and for compactness and large flowers. Best known are 'Madonna', white; 'My Valentine', rose; 'Pinkie', pink; and 'Red Wing'.

Carla Hybrids. Zones 31, 32, warmer parts of 33. Hardy to 5° to 15°F/−15° to −9°C. Bred at North Carolina State University. Single to double flowers in pink, red, or white. Midseason bloom.

Gable Hybrids. Zones 4–9, 14–24, 31, 32, warmer parts of 33. Bred to produce azaleas of Kurume type that take 0°F/−18°C temperatures. In colder part of range, they may lose some leaves. Bloom heavily in midseason. Frequently sold are 'Caroline Gable', bright pink; 'Herbert', purple; 'Louise Gable', pink; 'Pioneer', pink; 'Purple Splendor'; 'Purple Splendor Compacta' (less rangy growth than 'Purple Splendor'); 'Rosebud', pink; and 'Rose Greeley', white.

Girard Hybrids. Zones 4–9, 14–24, 31–33. Hardy to −5°F/−21°C or somewhat colder. These originated from Gable crosses. Examples are 'Girard's Fuchsia', reddish purple; 'Girard's Hot Shot', orange red with orange-red fall and winter foliage; and 'Girard's Roberta', with 3-in. double pink flowers.

Glenn Dale Hybrids. Zones 4–9, 14–24, 31, 32, warmer parts of 33. Hardy to 0°F/−18°C. Developed primarily for hardiness, but they do drop some leaves in cold winters. Some are tall and rangy, others low and compact. Growth rate varies from slow to rapid. Some have small leaves like Kurume Hybrids; others have large leaves. Familiar varieties are 'Anchorite', orange; 'Aphrodite', pale pink; 'Buccaneer', orange red; 'Everest', white; 'Geisha', white with red stripes; 'Glacier', white; and 'Martha Hitchcock', white edged magenta.

Gold Cup Hybrids. Zones 14–24. Members of this group were originally called Mossholder-Bristow Hybrids. Plants combine large flowers of Belgian Indicas with vigor of Rutherfordiana Hybrids. Good landscape plants where temperatures don't go below 20°F/−7°C. Some popular varieties are 'Easter Parade', pink and white; 'Sun Valley', white; and 'White Orchid', white with red throat.

Greenwood Hybrids. Zones 4–7, 14–17, 32. Bred in Canby, Oregon, most of these are hardy and compact, with large double flowers. You can make them succeed in colder climates than they're bred for (to about 0°F/−18°C) by keeping them from drying out: it's desiccation, not freezing, that does them in. Some of the most popular varieties are 'Greenwood Orange'; 'Greenwood Rosebud', pink with a slight purple blush; 'Sherry', very deep red flowers and maroon winter foliage; 'Silver Streak', reddish purple flowers and white-edged leaves; and 'Sleigh Bells', single white flowers.

Kaempferi Hybrids. Zones 2–7, 31–34, 39. Based on *R. kaempferi*, the torch azalea, a cold-hardy plant with orange-red flowers. These are somewhat hardier than Kurume Hybrids, to −15°F/−26°C, taller and more open in growth, nearly leafless in coldest winters. Profuse bloom. Among those sold are 'Fedora', salmon rose; 'Holland', late, large red; 'John Cairns', orange red; and 'Palestrina', white.

Kurume Hybrids. Zones 5–9, 14–24, 28, 31. Hardy to 5° to 10°F/−15° to −12°C. Compact, twiggy plants, densely foliaged with small, glossy leaves. Small flowers are borne in incredible profusion. Plants mounded or tiered, handsome even out of bloom. Widely used as house plants. Grow well outdoors in half sun. Many varieties available; the most widespread are 'Coral Bells', pink; 'Hexe', crimson; 'Hino-crimson', bright red; 'Hinodegiri', cerise red; 'Sherwood Orchid', red violet; 'Sherwood Red', orange red; 'Snow'; and 'Ward's Ruby', dark red.

Kurume Evergreen Azalea

North Tisbury Hybrids. Zones 4–9, 14–24, 31–34. Hardy to about 0°F/−18°C. You can see a common, notable ancestry in most of these plants (*R. nakaharai*). Their low, spreading habit and very late bloom (into midsummer) make them naturals for hanging baskets and ground covers. Some of the best are 'Alexander', very hardy, with bronze fall foliage and red-orange flowers; 'Pink Cascade', pink; and 'Red Fountain', with dark red-orange blooms around the Fourth of July.

Robin Hill Hybrids. Zones 4–9, 14–24, 31, 32. Hardy to 5° to 10°F/−15° to −12°C. A large group that got its start more than 50 years ago. These medium-size plants bloom late; large flowers somewhat resemble those of Satsuki Hybrids. There are so many good ones—several with "Robin Hill" in their names—that it's hard to single out only a few. Try 'Betty Ann Voss', pink; 'Conversation Piece', pink with light center; 'Nancy of Robin Hill', pink with red blotch; 'Robin Hill Gillie', red orange; 'Hilda Niblett', light and deep pink and white.

Rutherfordiana Hybrids. Zones 15–24, 26 (northern part), 28. Greenhouse plants, good in garden where temperatures don't go below 20°F/−7°C and if given midday shade. Bushy 2–4-ft. plants with handsome foliage. Flowers intermediate between those of Kurumes and Belgian Indicas. Available varieties include 'Alaska', white; 'Constance', light orchid pink; 'Dorothy Gish', brick red; 'Firelight', rose red; 'L. J. Bobbink', orchid pink; 'Purity', white; 'Rose Queen', deep pink; and 'White Gish', pure white.

Satsuki Hybrids. Zones 4–9, 14–24, 28, 31, 32, warmer parts of 33. Includes azaleas referred to as Gumpo and Macrantha hybrids. Hardy to 5°F/−15°C. Plants low growing, some true dwarfs; many are pendent

enough for hanging baskets. Large flowers come late. Popular varieties: 'Bunkwa', blush pink; 'Flame Creeper', orange red; 'Gumpo', white; 'Gumpo Pink', rose pink; 'Hi Gasa', bright pink; 'Rosaeflora', rose pink; 'Shinnyo-No-Tsuki', violet red with white center.

Southern Indica Hybrids. Zones 8, 9, 14–24, 26, 28, 31. Varieties selected from Belgian Indica Hybrids for vigor and tolerance to sun. Most take temperatures of 10° to 20°F/−12° to −7°C, but some are damaged at even the upper end of that range. They generally grow faster, more vigorously, and taller than other kinds of evergreen azaleas. Many varieties are sold. Popular choices include 'Brilliant', carmine red; 'Duc de Rohan', salmon pink; 'Fielder's White'; 'Formosa' (also sold as 'Coccinea', 'Phoenicia', 'Vanessa'), brilliant rose purple; 'George Lindley Taber', light pink; 'Imperial Countess', deep salmon pink; 'Imperial Princess', rich pink; 'Imperial Queen', pink; 'Iveryana', white with orchid streaks; 'Little John',

'Fielder's White' Southern Indica Evergreen Azalea

a dense bush to 6 ft. (despite its name), with burgundy foliage and a few deep red flowers; 'Orange Pride', bright orange; 'Pride of Dorking', brilliant red; 'Southern Charm' (sometimes sold as 'Judge Solomon'), watermelon pink; and 'White April'.

R. mucronatum ('Indica Alba', 'Ledifolia Alba'). Zones 4–9, 14–24, 28, 31, 32. Spreading growth to 6 ft. (but usually 3 ft.); large, hairy leaves. White or greenish flowers 2½–3 in. across; early. 'Indica Rosea' ('Ledifolia Rosea') has white flowers flushed and blotched with rose; it blooms very early (about a month before the species). 'Sekidera' is white flushed reddish purple. 'Delaware Valley White' is slightly more cold tolerant.

KINDS OF DECIDUOUS AZALEAS

Very few deciduous shrubs can equal deciduous azaleas in show and range of color. Flowers of their evergreen relatives can't match these in the yellow, orange, and flame red range or in bicolor contrasts. Fall foliage is often brilliant orange red to maroon. Deciduous azaleas tend to be less particular about soil and watering than most evergreen types. Many deciduous species are native to the eastern and southern U.S., and one grows along the West Coast. Selections of these species and hybrids are increasingly popular. See "Rhododendron ratings and hardiness" (page 466) for bloom season terminology. In warm, humid regions, powdery mildew can be a serious problem for many Ghent, Knap Hill, and Mollis hybrids.

Ghent Hybrids. Zones 2–9, 14–17, 32–41. Many are hardy to −25°F/−32°C. Upright growth variable in height. Flowers generally smaller than those of Mollis Hybrids. Colors include shades of yellow, orange, umber, pink, and red. Midseason.

Knap Hill–Exbury Hybrids. Zones 2–9, 14–17, 32–41. Hardy to −25°F/−32°C. Plants vary from spreading to upright, from 4 to 6 ft. tall. Flowers are large (3–5 in. across), in clusters of 7–18, sometimes ruffled or fragrant, white through pink and yellow to orange and red, often with contrasting blotches.

Both Knap Hill and Exbury azaleas come from same original crosses; first crosses were made at Knap Hill (in England), and subsequent improvements were made at both Exbury (also in England) and Knap Hill. The "Rothschild" azaleas are Exbury plants. Ilam Hybrids are from same original stock, further improved in New Zealand.

Knap Hill–Exbury Deciduous Azalea

Midseason to late bloom. If you want to be sure of color and flower size, choose from named varieties. Some of the best are 'Cannon's Double', pink; 'Gibraltar', orange; 'Homebush', double deep pink; 'Klondyke', golden tangerine; and 'Oxydol', white with yellow markings. Don't automatically consider all seedlings inferior plants, however—but do select them in bloom. ▶

Mollis Hybrids. Zones 2–9, 14–17, 32–41. Hardy to −25°F/−32°C. Hybrids of *R. molle* and *R. japonicum*. Upright growth to 4–5 ft. high; 2½–4-in.-wide flowers are carried in clusters of 7–13. Blossom color ranges from chrome yellow through poppy red. New growth has a light skunky fragrance, but foliage turns a lovely yellow to orange in autumn. Very heavy bloom in midseason.

Northern Lights Hybrids. Zones 1–7, 34–45. Developed by the University of Minnesota; hardy to −40°F/−40°C. Grow 2–4 ft. tall, produce ball-shaped trusses of fragrant sterile flowers (they won't set seed) late in the season. Most widely available are 'Apricot Surprise', 'Orchid Lights', 'Rosy Lights', and 'White Lights'. Foliage can have the skunky odor of the group's Mollis ancestors.

Viscosum Hybrids. Zones 3–7, 32–41. Hardy to −15°F/−26°C. Hybrids between Mollis azaleas and *R. viscosum*. Deciduous shrubs with colors of Mollis but fragrance of *R. viscosum*. Late.

R. alabamense. ALABAMA AZALEA. Zones 31–33. Hardy to −5°F/−21°C. Native to Alabama, Georgia. Grows 5–6 ft. tall and spreads by suckering to form colonies. Highly fragrant white flowers usually blotched with yellow. Early.

R. arborescens. SWEET AZALEA. Zones 32–41. Hardy to −10°F/−23°C. Native to mountains from Pennsylvania to Alabama. Erect, open shrub to 8 ft. (possibly 20 ft.) tall. Fragrant white to pale pink flowers appear late, after leaves have expanded.

R. atlanticum. COAST AZALEA. Zones 4–6, 31–35, 37. Hardy to −15°F/−26°C. Native from Delaware to South Carolina. Suckering shrub to 3–6 ft. tall, with white to pink fragrant (and somewhat sticky) flowers early, before leaves expand (or as they expand).

R. austrinum. FLORIDA AZALEA. Zones 26 (northern part), 28, 31–33. Hardy to 5°F/−15°C. Native to northern and western Florida and southern parts of Georgia, Alabama, Mississippi. To 8–10 ft. tall, with fragrant flowers that may be pale yellow, cream, pink, orange, or red in color. Early.

R. bakeri. CUMBERLAND AZALEA. Zones 32–35, 37, 39. Hardy to −15°F/−26°C. Native to mountains of Kentucky, Virginia, Tennessee, Georgia, Alabama. Grows 3–8 ft. tall. Flowers range from yellow and orange to (usually) red. Late midseason. Does not tolerate heat.

R. calendulaceum. FLAME AZALEA. Zones 28, 31–41. Hardy to −25°F/−32°C. Native to mountain regions from southern Pennsylvania to Georgia. To 4–8 ft. or taller. Clusters of 2-in.-wide yellow, red, orange, or scarlet flowers. Late. A very important parent of many hybrid deciduous azalea races.

R. canadense. RHODORA. Zones 1–5, 33, 36–43. Hardy to −25°F/−32°C. Native from eastern Canada to Pennsylvania. Open, lanky shrub to 3–4 ft. Clusters of 1½-in. reddish purple flowers in early midseason as leaves expand. Needs cool climate.

R. canescens. PIEDMONT AZALEA. Zones 26 (northern part), 28, 31–33. Hardy to −5°F/−21°C. Native from North Carolina to Texas. Large (to 10-ft.), suckering shrub with fragrant white to pink or rose flowers. Early. Sun or shade.

R. flammeum. OCONEE AZALEA. Zones 31–34, 37. Hardy to −15°F/−26°C. Native to South Carolina, Georgia. Fairly compact shrub to 6 ft., with clusters of 1¾-in. flowers in midseason. Color is typically bright red but may vary to yellow or orange.

R. japonicum. JAPANESE AZALEA. Zones 3–7, 32–34, 39. Hardy to −10°F/−23°C. Upright, fast growth to 6 ft. tall. Salmon red flowers, 2–3 in. wide, are carried in clusters of 6–12. Midseason. *R. j. aureum* has rich yellow flowers.

R. luteum (R. flavum). PONTIC AZALEA. Zones 3–7, 14–17, 32–34, 39. Hardy to −15°F/−26°C. Native to Eastern Europe, Asia Minor. To 8 ft. Fragrant, single yellow flowers with darker blotch. Midseason.

R. oblongifolium. TEXAS AZALEA. Zones 28, 31–33. Hardy to −5°F/−21°C. Native to East Texas, Oklahoma, and Arkansas. To 6 ft. tall. Slightly fragrant white flowers to 1 in. long appear in midseason, after leaves emerge.

R. occidentale. WESTERN AZALEA. Zones 4–24. Hardy to −5°F/−21°C. Native to mountains and foothills of California and Oregon. Erect growth to 6–10 ft. high. Funnel-shaped flowers in clusters, midseason to late. Flower color varies from white to pinkish white with yellow blotch; in some kinds, blossoms are heavily marked with carmine rose. Fragrant. Superior cutting-grown plants with variety names are scarce but available and worth looking for. 'Centennial' ('Washington State Centennial') is especially noteworthy; orange and red buds open to large pale pink flowers with a large golden yellow flare.

R. periclymenoides (R. nudiflorum). PINXTERBLOOM AZALEA. Zones 31–35, 37, 39. Hardy to −15°F/−26°C. Native from Massachusetts to Ohio and North Carolina. Often called "honeysuckle" in its native range. Suckering shrub growing 2–3 ft. high (occasionally much taller). Pale pink (usually) to deep pink, fragrant, 1½-in. flowers appear in midseason, as leaves expand.

R. prinophyllum (P. roseum). ROSESHELL AZALEA. Zones 32–43. Hardy to −25°F/−32°C. Native from southern Quebec to Virginia, west to Missouri and Oklahoma. To 4–8 ft. tall, occasionally much taller; bright pink (sometimes white), 1½-in. flowers with strong clove fragrance. Blooms in midseason, before or with leaves. One of the parents of the extremely hardy Northern Lights Hybrids.

R. prunifolium. PLUMLEAF AZALEA. Zones 31–34, 37. Hardy to −15°F/−26°C. Native to Georgia and Alabama. To 10 ft., with orange-red to bright red flowers. This is the latest blooming of all azaleas.

R. schlippenbachii. ROYAL AZALEA. Zones 2–7, 14–17, 32–41. Hardy to −20°F/−29°C. Native to Korea. Densely branched shrub to 6–8 ft. Leaves in whorls of five at tips of branches. Large (2–4-in.), pure light pink, highly fragrant flowers in clusters of three to six. Early midseason. A white form is also available. Good fall color: yellow, orange, scarlet, crimson. Foliage resists mildew. Protect from full sun.

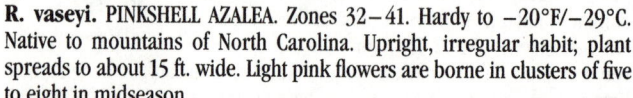

Rhododendron prunifolium

R. vaseyi. PINKSHELL AZALEA. Zones 32–41. Hardy to −20°F/−29°C. Native to mountains of North Carolina. Upright, irregular habit; plant spreads to about 15 ft. wide. Light pink flowers are borne in clusters of five to eight in midseason.

R. viscosum. SWAMP AZALEA. Zones 31–41. Hardy to −25°F/−32°C. Native to damp or wet ground, Maine to Alabama. To 5–8 ft. tall. Flowers are white (occasionally pink), 2 in. long, sticky on the outside, with a powerful clove scent. Very late.

RHODOHYPOXIS baurii

Hypoxidaceae

BULBLIKE TUBER

✎ ZONES 4–7, 14–24, 28–33; OR GROW IN POTS

☼ FULL SUN

♦ REGULAR WATER DURING GROWTH AND BLOOM

Rhodohypoxis baurii

Tufts of narrow, 2–3-in. leaves are nearly obscured by masses of 1-in. white, pink, or rose red flowers over a long spring–summer season. Dormant in winter. Tubers multiply quickly with good drainage, adequate water. In colder part of range, protect from winter rains or snow with pane of glass or shingle. If grown in pots, turn pots on side in winter or store over winter in cold frame. Excellent plant for rock garden, stone sink garden, or pots.

R

RHOEO spathacea (R. discolor)

MOSES-IN-THE-BOAT, OYSTER PLANT

Commelinaceae

PERENNIAL

ZONES 12–27; OR INDOORS

SUN OR SHADE

REGULAR WATER

Rhoeo spathacea

Stems to 8 in. high. Leaf tufts grow to 6–12 in. wide, with a dozen or so broad, sword-shaped, rather erect leaves that are dark green above and deep purple underneath. Flowers are interesting rather than beautiful; the small, white, three-petaled blooms are crowded into boat-shaped bracts borne down among leaves. 'Variegata' has leaves striped red and yellowish green.

Avoid overwatering; try to keep water out of leaf axils. Tough plant that takes high or low light intensity, casual watering, low humidity, heat. Most often used as a pot plant or in hanging baskets; grown as a ground cover and edging in Florida.

RHOICISSUS capensis (Cissus capensis)

EVERGREEN GRAPE

Vitaceae

TUBEROUS-ROOTED EVERGREEN VINE

ZONES 16, 17, 21–25; OR INDOORS

FULL SUN WITH SHADED ROOTS

REGULAR WATER

Rhoicissus capensis

Scallop-toothed leaves are roundish to kidney shaped, something like those of true grape in size and appearance. New stems and leaves are a rosy rust color, covered with red hairs. Upper surfaces of mature leaves are strong light green tinged with copper; undersides are rusty, hairy. Flowers insignificant. Slow-growing plant; makes a good overhead screen or ground cover in frost-free regions. Good house plant anywhere; tolerates low light indoors.

RHUBARB

Polygonaceae

PERENNIAL GROWN FROM RHIZOME

ZONES 1–11, 14–24, 26–45; BEST IN ZONES 1–11, 34–45

SOME SHADE IN HOTTEST CLIMATES

WATER FREELY DURING ACTIVE GROWTH

LEAVES ARE POISONOUS IF INGESTED; USE STEMS ONLY

Rhubarb

Big, elongated, heart-shaped, crinkled leaves and red-tinted leafstalks are showy enough to qualify for display spot in garden. Delicious leafstalks are used like fruit in sauces and pies. Flowers are insignificant, in spikelike clusters. Preferred varieties are 'Victoria', with greenish stalks; and 'Cherry' ('Crimson Cherry'), 'MacDonald', and 'Strawberry', all of which have red stalks.

Needs some winter chill for thick stems, good red color. Plant divisions (containing at least one bud) in late winter or early spring. Set tops of divisions at soil line; space 3–4 ft. apart. Permit plants to grow for two full seasons before harvesting. During next spring, you can pull off leafstalks for 4 or 5 weeks; older, huskier plants will take up to 8 weeks of pulling. Harvest leafstalks by grasping near base and pulling sideways and outward; do not cut with a knife, since cutting leaves a stub that will decay. Never remove all leaves from a single plant. Stop harvesting when slender leaf-

stalks appear. After harvest, feed and water freely; cut out any blossom stalks that appear. Plants won't die back completely in mildest winters.

In the Deep South and in the intermediate and low desert, treat as cool-season annual. In the Deep South, best started from seed and harvested twice: cut outer stalks in spring, remaining center stalks in fall. In desert, set out divisions in fall for winter–spring harvest (plants tend to rot in heat of late spring, summer).

RHUS

SUMAC

Anacardiaceae

EVERGREEN OR DECIDUOUS SHRUBS OR TREES

ZONES VARY BY SPECIES

FULL SUN

REGULAR TO LITTLE WATER

Rhus typhina

Of the ornamental sumacs, deciduous kinds are extremely hardy; they are noted for brilliant fall leaf color and, on female plants, showy clusters of (usually) red fruits. They tend to produce suckers, especially if their roots are disturbed by cultivation. Evergreen species are less hardy. All species of sumac thrive in almost any soil, as long as it is well drained; soggy soils can kill them.

R. aromatica. FRAGRANT SUMAC. Deciduous shrub. Zones 1–3, 10, 31–43. Native to eastern North America. Fast growing to 3–5 ft. tall, sprawling much wider. Leaves to 3 in. long, with three leaflets; fragrant when brushed against or crushed. Foliage turns red in fall. Tiny yellowish flowers in spring, small red fruit in late summer. Coarse bank cover, ground cover for poor or dry soils. Two available varieties are 'Gro-low' (to about 2 ft.) and 'Green Mound' (to 4 ft.).

R. cotinus. See Cotinus coggygria

R. glabra. SMOOTH SUMAC. Deciduous shrub or small tree. Zones 1–10, 14–17, 31–45. Native to much of North America. Upright to 10 ft., sometimes treelike to 20 ft. In the wild, spreads by underground roots to form large patches. Looks much like *R. typhina*, but usually grows lower and does not have velvety branches. Leaves divided into 11–23 rather narrow, 2–5 in.-long, toothed leaflets, deep green above and whitish beneath; turn scarlet in fall. Inconspicuous flowers are followed by showy, erect clusters of scarlet fruit that remain on bare branches from fall well into winter. Garden use same as for *R. typhina*. 'Laciniata' has deeply cut, slashed leaflets, giving it a fernlike appearance.

R. integrifolia. LEMONADE BERRY. Evergreen shrub. Zones 15–17, 20–24. Native to California. Generally 3–10 ft. high and as wide, rarely treelike to 30 ft. Dark green leaves are leathery, oval to nearly round, 1–2½ in. long. White or pinkish flowers in dense clusters, winter–spring. Small, flat, clustered fruit is reddish and gummy, with acid pulp that can be used to flavor drinks—hence the common name. Good plant for seacoast, espalier, clipped hedge, erosion control. Very susceptible to verticillium wilt.

R. lancea. AFRICAN SUMAC. Evergreen tree. Zones 8, 9, 12–24, 29. Hardy to 12°F/ –11°C. Slow growing to 25 ft. Open, spreading habit; graceful weeping outer branchlets. Train to single trunk or let grow as multi-trunked tree somewhat resembling olive. Dark green leaves are divided into three willowlike, 4–5-in.-long leaflets. Clusters of pea-size, berrylike, yellow or red fruit can be messy on pavement. Tolerates high heat. Can be clipped into hedge. Susceptible to Texas root rot.

R. ovata. SUGAR BUSH. Evergreen shrub. Zones 7–24. Native to dry slopes in California, Arizona. To 2½–10 ft. tall, upright or spreading. Glossy, leathery leaves, 1½–3 in. long, somewhat trough shaped and pointed at tips. Dense clusters of white or pinkish spring flowers are followed by small, reddish, hairy fruit coated with sugary secretion. Same landscape uses as *R. integrifolia*, but for inland areas rather than seacoast.

R. trilobata. SQUAWBUSH, SKUNKBUSH. Deciduous shrub. Zones 2, 3, 10, 31–41. Native from Illinois westward to Washington, California, Texas. Similar in most details to *R. aromatica*, but scent of bruised leaves is considered unpleasant by most people. Clumping habit makes it a natural low hedge. Brilliant yellow to red fall color.

R. typhina. STAGHORN SUMAC. Deciduous shrub or small tree. Zones 1–10, 14–17, 31–45. Upright to 15 ft. (sometimes 30 ft.) tall, spreading wider. Very similar to *R. glabra*, but branches are covered with short, velvety brown hairs and resemble a deer's antler "in velvet." Leaves divided into 11–31 toothed, 5-in.-long leaflets; foliage is deep green above, grayish beneath, turns rich red in fall. Tiny greenish blossoms in 4–8-in.-long clusters appear in early summer; these are followed by clusters of fuzzy crimson fruit that lasts all winter, gradually turning brown. 'Laciniata', with deeply cut leaflets, does not grow quite as large as the species and is said to have richer fall color.

Both *R. typhina* and *R. glabra* take extreme heat and cold. Big divided leaves give tropical effect; fall show is brilliant (for best effect, plant among evergreens). Bare branches make fine winter silhouette; fruit is decorative. Both species will grow in large containers. Their aggressive colonization by root suckers can be a problem, especially in small gardens.

ABOUT THE ITCHY RHUS RELATIVES

Poison ivy and poison oak were once members of *Rhus*, but they have now been reclassified as *Toxicodendron radicans* and *T. diversilobum*, respectively. Both can cause severe dermatitis on contact; even breathing smoke from burning plants can be harmful. If either plant is on your property (the three-leaflet leaves turn bright red in fall), destroy it with chemical brush killer.

RHYNCHOSPERMUM. See TRACHELOSPERMUM

RIBBON GRASS. See PHALARIS arundinacea

RIBES

CURRANT, GOOSEBERRY	
Grossulariaceae (Saxifragaceae)	
EVERGREEN OR DECIDUOUS SHRUBS	
ZONES VARY BY SPECIES	
FULL SUN OR PARTIAL SHADE	
MODERATE WATER	

Ribes odoratum

Those without spines are called currants; those with spines are known as gooseberries. The following species are grown ornamentally (though some bear edible fruit); see Currant and Gooseberry for strictly fruiting types. Members of this tribe are still banned in a few areas where white pines grow, because they are alternate hosts to white pine blister rust.

R. alpinum. ALPINE CURRANT. Deciduous. Zones 1–3, 10, 33–45. Native to Europe. Dense, twiggy growth to 4–5 ft. (rarely taller). Roundish, toothed, lobed, ½–1½-in.-wide leaves appear very early in spring. Flowers and fruit not showy. Good hedge. Dwarf forms are 'Green Mound' and yellow-leafed 'Aureum'.

R. aureum. GOLDEN CURRANT. Deciduous. Zones 1–11, 14–21, 33–45. Native to western U.S. Erect growth to 3–6 ft. tall. Light green, lobed, toothed leaves. Small, bright yellow spring flowers, usually with spicy fragrance, in 1–2½-in.-long clusters. Summer berries age from yellow to red to black.

R. nigrum. BLACK CURRANT. Deciduous. Zones 1–7, 34, 36, 38–43. To 6 ft. tall, with three-lobed, deep green, oddly scented leaves. Drooping clusters of whitish flowers turn to juicy, shiny black fruits with blackberry-currant (sweet-tart) flavor. Fruit used in jams, jellies, sauces. Rust-immune varieties include 'Consort', 'Coronet', and 'Crusader'.

R. odoratum. Deciduous. Zones 1–10, 14–17, 33–45. Similar to *R. aureum* but native to the Midwest and High Plains. Flowers have carnation fragrance. Old variety 'Crandall' has large, shiny black fruit with the rich, sweet-tart flavor of *R. nigrum*.

R. sanguineum. PINK WINTER CURRANT, RED FLOWERING CURRANT. Deciduous. Zones 4–9, 14–24, 32, 34. Native from British Columbia to Northern California. To 4–12 ft. tall, with 2½-in.-wide, maplelike leaves. Blooms in spring, producing small, deep pink to red flowers, 10–30 in each 2–4-in.-long, drooping cluster. Blue-black berries have a whitish bloom. Most commonly sold is *R. s. glutinosum* (more southerly in origin), with clusters of 15–40 flowers; pink, red, and white varieties are available. Needs excellent drainage where summers are warm and moist or humid.

R. speciosum. FUCHSIA-FLOWERING GOOSEBERRY. Nearly evergreen. Zones 8, 9, 14–24. Native to California. Erect grower to 3–6 ft. tall, with spiny, often bristly stems. Thick, maplelike, 1-in. leaves. Deep crimson to cherry red flowers, borne winter–spring, are drooping, fuchsialike, with long, protruding stamens. Gummy, bristly berries. Excellent barrier plant. Drought tolerant.

R. viburnifolium. CATALINA PERFUME, EVERGREEN CURRANT. Evergreen. Zones 8, 9, 14–24. Native to California. To 3 ft. tall, spreading to 12 ft. Wine red stems may root in moist soil. Roundish,

Ribes speciosum

1-in. dark green leaves are fragrant after rain or when crushed (some liken the scent to pine, others to apples). Light pink to purplish flowers, winter–spring. Red berries. Part shade in hot climates. Good on banks, under native oaks where watering is undesirable. Very drought tolerant.

RICE PAPER PLANT. See TETRAPANAX papyriferus

RICINUS communis

CASTOR BEAN	
Euphorbiaceae	
SHRUB USUALLY TREATED AS ANNUAL	
ALL ZONES	
FULL SUN	
REGULAR WATER	
SEEDS (OR BEANS) ARE HIGHLY POISONOUS	

Ricinus communis

Bold and striking plant. Can provide tall screen or leafy background in a hurry; grows to 6–15 ft. in a season. Where winters are mild, will live over and become quite woody and treelike. Should not be planted in areas where small children play—the poisonous seeds are attractive. Foliage or seeds occasionally cause severe contact allergies as well. To prevent seed formation, pinch off the burrlike seed capsules while they are small.

Large-lobed leaves are 1–3 ft. across on vigorous young plants, smaller on older plants. Unimpressive small, white flowers are borne in clusters on foot-high stalks in summer, followed by attractive prickly husks that contain seeds. Grown commercially for castor oil extracted from seeds. Many horticultural varieties: 'Zanzibarensis' has very large green leaves; 'Dwarf Red Spire' is lower-growing plant (to 6 ft.) with red leaves and seedpods.

ROBINIA

LOCUST	
Fabaceae (Leguminosae)	
DECIDUOUS SHRUBS OR TREES	
ZONES 1–24, 29–45	
FULL SUN	
MODERATE TO LITTLE WATER	
BARK, LEAVES, AND SEEDS ARE POISONOUS IF INGESTED	

Robinia pseudoacacia

Leaves divided like feathers into many roundish leaflets; clusters of sweet pea–shaped, white or pink flowers midspring to early summer.

Locusts are fairly fast growing and well adapted to dry, hot regions. Will take poor soil. Drawbacks: wood is brittle, roots aggressive, plants often spread by suckers.

R. ambigua. Name given to hybrids between *R. pseudoacacia* and *R. viscosa,* a seldom-grown pink-flowering locust. The following are best-known varieties:

'Decaisneana'. To 40–50 ft. tall, 20 ft. wide. Flowers like those of *R. pseudoacacia* but pale pink.

'Idahoensis'. IDAHO LOCUST. Tree of moderately fast growth to shapely 40 ft. Bright magenta rose flowers in 8-in. clusters; one of showiest of locusts in bloom.

'Purple Robe'. Resembles 'Idahoensis' but has darker, purple-pink flowers, reddish bronze new growth; blooms 2 weeks earlier and over a longer period.

R. pseudoacacia. BLACK LOCUST. Tree. Native to eastern and midwestern U.S. Fast growth to 75 ft., with rather open and sparse-branching habit. Deeply furrowed brown bark. Thorny branchlets. Leaves divided into 7–19 leaflets 1–2 in. long. Flowers white, fragrant, ½–¾ in. long, in dense, hanging clusters 4–8 in. long. Beanlike, 4-in.-long pods turn brown and hang on tree all winter.

Robinia pseudoacacia

Little valued in its native territory except as a source of honey and fence posts, it has been widely planted (and has subsequently escaped) in much of the western U.S. and in Europe. It manufactures its own fertilizer through nitrogen-fixing root nodule bacteria and can colonize the poorest soil. Given some pruning and training in its early years, it can be a truly handsome flowering tree, but locust borer limits its usefulness in many regions. Locust leaf miner is also a damaging pest in some areas.

Often used as street tree, but not good in narrow parking strips or under power lines. Wood is extremely hard; suckers are difficult to prune out where not wanted. Varieties include the following:

'Frisia'. New growth nearly orange; mature leaves yellow, turning greener in summer heat. Thorns and new wood are red.

'Pyramidalis' ('Fastigiata'). Very narrow, columnar tree.

'Tortuosa'. Slow growing, with twisted branches. Few flowers in blossom clusters.

'Umbraculifera'. Dense, round headed. Usually grafted 6–8 ft. high on another locust to create a living green lollipop. Very few flowers.

ROCKCRESS. See ARABIS

ROCKROSE. See CISTUS

RODGERSIA

Saxifragaceae

PERENNIALS

ZONES 2–9, 14–17, 32–41

PARTIAL SHADE

AMPLE WATER

Native to China, Japan. Large plants with imposing leaves and clustered tiny flowers in plumes somewhat like those of astilbe. Primary feature is handsome foliage, which often takes on

Rodgersia aesculifolia

bronze tones in late summer. Plants spread by thick rhizomes, need rich soil. Can tolerate full sun in cool-summer climates. The different species hybridize freely. Dormant in winter; provide winter mulch in cold climates. Showy in moist woodland or bog gardens.

R. aesculifolia. To 6 ft. Leaves are divided like fingers of hand into five to seven toothed, 10-in. leaflets; they resemble those of horsechestnut (*Aesculus*). Shaggy brown hairs on flower stalks, leaf stems, major leaf veins. White flowers.

R. henricii. Resembles *R. aesculifolia,* but leaves taper to a long point and flowers are purplish red.

R. pinnata. To 4 ft. Leaves have five to nine 8-in. leaflets. Red flowers.

R. podophylla. To 5 ft. Coppery green leaves divided into five 10-in. leaflets. Creamy flowers.

R. sambucifolia. To 3 ft. Leaves have up to 11 leaflets. Flat-topped flower clusters are white or pink.

R. tabularis (Astilboides tabularis). To 3 ft. Shield-shaped round leaves are 2 ft. wide. White flowers.

ROMNEYA coulteri

MATILIJA POPPY

Papaveraceae

PERENNIAL

ZONES 4–12, 14–24

FULL SUN

REGULAR TO LITTLE WATER

Romneya coulteri

Native to California. Large, shrublike plant sends up thick gray-green stems 6–8 ft. high, clothed in irregularly lobed leaves of the same color. Upper part of stems bear huge (to 9-in.) flowers often likened to giant-size fried eggs: the crepe-papery, slightly scented blossoms are white, centered with a cluster of golden stamens. Blooms late spring into summer, even into fall if given water. Takes regular garden irrigation (with good drainage), though established plants tolerate extreme drought. Will take any soil. Give plenty of room and do not locate near valued, more delicate plants, since rhizomes can be invasive. Cut nearly to ground in late fall.

ROSA

ROSE

Rosaceae

DECIDUOUS OR EVERGREEN SHRUBS

ALL ZONES, EXCEPT AS NOTED

FULL SUN OR LIGHT SHADE

REGULAR WATER, EXCEPT AS NOTED

The rose is undoubtedly the best-loved flower and most widely planted shrub in temperate parts of the world. Although mostly deciduous,

Hybrid Tea Rose 'Seashell'

can be evergreen in mild climates. Centuries of hybridizing have brought us the widest possible range of form and color. There are foot-high miniatures, tree-smothering climbers, flowers the size of a thumbnail or a salad plate, and all possible variations in between. Red, pink, and white are traditional rose colors, but you also find cream, yellow, orange, and blended and bicolor flowers, as well as magenta, purple, lavender, and even tan and brown.

Growing roses is not difficult, provided you choose types and varieties suited to your climate, buy healthy plants, locate and plant them properly, and attend to their basic needs—water, nutrients, any necessary pest and disease control, and pruning. Despite the delicate appearance of their blooms, roses are often quite resilient plants.

CLIMATE

Every year, the American Rose Society rates modern roses (and an increasing number of old roses) on a scale of 1 to 10. The higher the rating, based on a national average of scores, the better the rose. The highest rated roses are likely to perform well in most climates and so are good choices for novice growers. But a rating does not tell the entire story: a rose with a low rating may do especially well in certain regions but fail in others. The following general tips will help guide your selection.

In cool-summer areas, you should, if possible, avoid varieties having an unusually great number of petals. Many of these tend to "ball," opening poorly or not at all. Also, in the absence of heat, dark-colored flowers may appear "muddy" rather than clear and vibrant, while pastel colors are usually clear and attractive. The overcast and fog prevalent in many cool-summer areas also encourage foliar diseases—primarily mildew, rust, and black spot. Choose varieties noted for disease resistance; then be sure to plant them in open areas where air circulation is good.

In hot-summer areas, rose plants still grow vigorously, but flowers open rapidly. Varieties with few (under 30) petals may go from bud to flat-open blossom in several hours. Flowers with more petals take longer to open and stay attractive longer. Some colors fade readily, and dark reds may sunburn. Therefore, in hot-summer areas, roses are more satisfactory if they receive midday or afternoon shade. Avoid planting roses where they will receive reflected heat from light-colored walls or fences—especially in southern or western exposures. Best flowering is always in spring and fall (and in winter, in mildest zones); summer flower production may drop markedly as plants approach dormancy during intensely hot weather.

In cold-winter areas (Zones 1–3, 34–45), the widely marketed modern roses—hybrid teas, grandifloras, and floribundas—are not completely hardy; some form of winter protection is needed to guarantee their survival from year to year (see "Winter protection," page 476). Many of the old roses (usually those that flower in spring only) and a number of the species and their hybrids survive winters in the coldest zones with scant or no protection from the cold.

In any region, the best place to see roses suitable for your climate is a municipal or private rose garden. The varieties that are performing well are obviously good choices for your garden.

BUYING PLANTS

All roses are available as bare-root plants from late fall through early spring. In the warmer zones of the South and West, you may plant bare-root roses throughout winter. Where the soil freezes, either plant in fall before ground freezes (then protect plants over winter), or plant in early spring after soil has thawed.

The majority of modern roses sold are budded plants: growth eyes of the desired varieties are budded onto understock plants that furnish the root systems. The understocks are carefully selected to promote rapid top growth of the desired roses and make root systems capable of thriving in a wide range of soils and climates. However, many old roses, species and their hybrids, and virtually all miniatures are "own-root" plants raised from cuttings. Ultimately, it makes no difference whether the plant is budded or own-root: either can grow well and produce fine flowers. Budded plants do offer more uniform root quality than you find among own-root plants, and budded plants often are larger at time of purchase than are own-root ones. But both kinds will be equally husky within a year or two. Own-root roses have one advantage, however: if an own-root plant is killed to the ground by cold (or mowed down by accident), it will regrow from the roots as the rose you want, not as understock. Under similar conditions, regrowth from roots of the budded plant will be the understock rose rather than the desired variety.

Bare-root plants are the best buy, and they are graded 1, 1½, or 2 according to strict standards. Plants graded 1 and 1½ are the most satisfactory, number 1 being the best. Number 2 plants may take longer to develop into decent bushes than the huskier numbers 1 and 1½. Retail nurseries and mail-order suppliers of modern roses usually offer only number 1 plants, and they will often replace plants that fail to grow. Old roses, shrub roses, and species roses (most commonly available by mail order) may be offered as budded plants that conform to the numbered grading standards, but some growers offer own-root (not budded) plants that may or may not be up to number 1 size. Catalogs usually state what size plant to expect.

During bare-root planting time, retail nurseries also may offer a selection of "boxed" roses with root systems encased in cardboard cartons. Supermarkets, discount stores, and some retail nurseries sell dormant roses that have roots encased in moist material and enclosed in long, narrow bags. These packaged roses may be good value, but you should buy them as soon as they appear for sale. Those that are displayed indoors on store shelves may be dried out or encouraged into premature growth by the indoor heating. Be prepared, too, for a number of these bargain roses to be mislabeled.

If you wish to plant roses during their growing season, you can buy roses growing in containers. This way, you can see and evaluate unfamiliar varieties before purchase and quickly fill in gaps in your garden. But container roses are more expensive than bare-root plants. Best time to buy container-grown roses is in mid- to late spring—when plants are fairly well rooted in the containers and can be set out before stressful summer heat arrives. For standard bush and climbing roses, look for robust plants growing in large (preferably 5-gal.) containers; this guarantees that root systems will have received little or no pruning to fit the container. Also, try to buy only roses planted in containers toward the end of the most recent dormant season; they generally will be in better condition than plants that have been in containers for a year or more. Avoid plants showing considerable dead or twiggy growth. Miniature roses usually are sold in containers that range from 4-in. pots to 2-gal.

Grandiflora Rose 'Camelot'

cans. Healthy new growth and foliage are signs of a good miniature plant, regardless of container size.

The presence of a plant patent number on a variety's name tag is no assurance of quality. It simply means that for a variety's first 17 years in commerce, the patent holder receives a royalty on each plant sold. Many fine roses that bear no patent number on name tags once were patented but have been in commerce for longer than the 17-year patent lifespan.

LOCATION AND PLANTING

For best results, plant roses where they will receive full sun all day (exceptions noted under "Climate," page 473). Avoid planting where roots of trees or shrubs will steal water and nutrients intended for roses. To lessen any problem with foliar diseases, plant roses where air circulates freely (but not in path of regular, strong winds). Generous spacing between plants will also aid air circulation. How far apart to plant varies according to the growth habit of the roses and according to climate. The colder the winter and shorter the growing season, the smaller the bushes will be; where growing season is long and winters are mild, bushes can attain greater size. But some varieties are naturally small, others tall and massive—and those relative size differences will hold in any climate. In Zones 1–3, 34–45, you might plant most vigorous sorts 3 ft. apart, whereas the same roses could require 6-ft. spacing in milder zones.

Soil for roses should drain reasonably well; if it does not, the best alternative is to plant in raised beds. Dig soil deeply, incorporating organic matter such as ground bark, peat moss, or compost; this preparation will help aerate dense clay soils and will improve moisture retention of sandy soils. Add complete fertilizer to soil at the same time, and dig supplemental phosphorus and potash into planting holes; this gets nutrients down at the level where roots can use them.

Healthy, ready-to-plant bare-root roses should have plump, fresh-looking canes (branches) and roots. Plants that have dried out slightly in shipping or in nursery can be revived by burying them, tops and all, for a few days in moist soil, sand, or sawdust. Just before planting any bare-root rose, it is a good idea to immerse entire plant in water for several hours to be certain all canes and roots are plumped up. Plant according to directions for bare-root planting (see page 586), making sure that holes are large enough that you can spread out roots without bending or cutting them back. Just before planting, cut back broken canes and broken roots to below breaks. Set plant in hole so that bud union ("knob" from which canes grow) is just above soil level. Even growers in cold-winter climates find this successful, and plants produce more canes when planted this way, as long as plants are well protected during winter. After you have planted a rose and watered it well, mound soil, damp peat moss, or sawdust over bud union and around canes to conserve moisture. Gradually (and carefully) remove soil or other material when leaves begin to expand.

If you plan to plant new roses in ground where existing bushes have been growing for 5 or more years, dig generous (at least 1½-ft.-wide, 1½-ft.-deep) planting holes and replace old soil with fresh soil from another part of the garden. A condition known as "specific replant dis-

R

ease" inhibits growth of new roses planted directly in soil of established rose gardens.

ROUTINE CARE

All roses require water, nutrients, some pruning, and, at some point in their lifetimes, pest and disease control. (Exceptions are some antique and species roses that thrive on little water once established.)

Floribunda Rose 'Cathedral'

Water. For best performance, the most popular garden roses need watering at all times during the growing season. Inadequate water slows or halts growth and bloom. Water deeply so that entire root system is moistened. How often to water depends on soil type and weather. Big, well-established plants need more water than newly set plants, but you will need to water new plants more frequently to get them established.

Basin flooding is a simple way to water individual rose plants, and if you have a drip irrigation system, many plants can be watered this way at one time. In hot, dry regions, overhead sprinkling helps remove dust and freshen foliage, and provides partial control for aphids and spider mites; on the minus side, it washes off spray residues, may leave mineral deposits on foliage if water is hard, and in some areas may encourage foliar diseases by keeping foliage and atmosphere damp. If you sprinkle, do it early in the day to be sure foliage dries off by nightfall. Even if you irrigate in basins, give plants an occasional sprinkling to clean dust off foliage (if rain doesn't do it for you).

Mulch, spread 2–3 in. deep, will help save water, prevent soil surface from baking hard, keep soil cool in summer, deter weed growth, and contribute to healthy soil structure (well aerated, permeable by water and roots).

Nutrients. Regular applications of fertilizer will produce the most gratifying results. In mildest-winter climates (Zones 12–28), begin feeding established plants with complete commercial fertilizer in February. Elsewhere, give first feeding just as growth begins. Time fertilizer application in relation to bloom period. Ideal time to make subsequent feedings is when a blooming period has ended and new growth is just beginning for next cycle of bloom. Depending on expected arrival of freezing temperatures, stop feeding in late summer or fall, generally about 6 weeks before earliest normal hard frost. In mild-winter zones that experience little or no subfreezing temperatures, fertilizing may continue until mid-October for crop of late fall flowers.

Dry commercial fertilizer, applied to soil, is most frequently used. A variation on that type is slow-release fertilizer that provides nutrients over prolonged period; follow directions on package for amount and frequency of applications. Liquid fertilizers are useful in smaller gardens utilizing basin watering. Most liquid fertilizers can also be sprayed on rose leaves, which absorb some nutrients immediately.

Pest and disease control. Certain controls usually are needed during the growing season.

Principal rose pests are aphids, spider mites, and (in some areas) Japanese beetle, rose midge, and thrips. If you don't want to rely on natural predators, start controlling aphids when they first appear in spring and repeat as needed until they are gone or their numbers severely reduced. Spider mites are hot-weather pests capable of defoliating and weakening plants—especially those that are underwatered and weak. Best control for voracious Japanese beetle is at the grub stage. Likewise, rose midge larvae in the soil are the more vulnerable life-cycle stage, susceptible to applications of diazinon in granular or liquid drench form. Thrips do their damage inside flower buds, discoloring petals or disfiguring them so that buds may not open. Contact insecticide sprays can't reach most thrips hidden in petals; systemic insecticides are more successful.

Powdery mildew, rust, and black spot are the Big Three of foliar diseases. First line of defense for all three is thorough cleanup of all dead leaves and other debris during the dormant season; this is simplest right after you have pruned plants. Then, before new growth begins, spray plants and soil with dormant-season spray of horticultural oil or lime sulfur (calcium polysulfide). This will destroy many disease organisms (as well as insect eggs) that might live over winter to reinfect plants in spring. During the growing season, apply controls for diseases prevalent in your area. Preventive measures usually are recommended for disease control; unchecked infections can weaken plants, especially if defoliation occurs from rust or black spot.

Two other foliar diseases, anthracnose and downy mildew, can occur to a lesser extent on roses. Anthracnose is similar to black spot and responds to the same treatment. Downy mildew begins in the upper reaches of a plant after leaves have fully formed, appearing in moist weather when temperatures are below 80°F/27°C. Foliage of infected plants shows irregular, purplish blotches, then turns yellow (sometimes with patches of green remaining) and falls off. On stems, the fungus shows as purplish mottling; infected stems are likely to die by the end of the year without treatment. To combat downy mildew during the growing season, spray infected plants with a fungicide containing zinc and manganese. Where the disease has appeared, use a dormant spray containing zinc or copper after winter pruning and rose garden cleanup.

Chlorosis—evidenced by leaves turning light green to yellow while veins remain dark green—is not a disease but a symptom, usually of iron deficiency. Iron chelate corrects chlorosis most quickly; iron sulfate also is effective but slower to act.

Leaves that show irregular patterning in yellow or cream indicate that the plant is infected with a mosaic virus. Some plants show the virus consistently; others display symptoms just occasionally. Although plants may appear to grow with vigor, virus infection does impair overall strength and productivity—and it can make foliage unsightly. Fortunately, it is not transferable from plant to plant by insects or pruning; it is transmitted in propagation—from infected rootstock or budwood. Commercial rose producers now are diligently working to eliminate virused stock. If you have a virused plant that is growing poorly or is unattractive, remove it from the garden.

Pruning. Done properly each year, pruning will contribute to the health and longevity of your rose plants. Sensible pruning is based on several facts about the growth of roses. First, blooms are produced on new growth. Unless pruning promotes strong new growth, flowers will come on spindly outer twigs and be of poor quality. Second, the more healthy wood you retain, the bigger the plant will be; and the bigger the plant, the more flowers it can produce. Nutrients are stored in woody canes, so a larger plant is a stronger plant. Therefore, prune conservatively; never chop down a vigorous 6-ft. bush to 1½-ft. stubs unless you want only a few huge blooms for exhibition. (Exception: in Zones 1–3, 34–45, where plant may freeze back to its winter protection, you will remove dead wood in spring and may be left with equivalent of severely pruned plant.) Third, the best pruning time for most roses (certain climbers and shrub types excepted) is at the end of dormant season (January in mild climates to late February and early March in cold climates) when growth buds begin to swell. Exact time will vary according to locality.

General pruning guidelines. The following pruning practices apply to all roses except certain shrub and species roses. Special instructions for pruning those roses are included later in this section.

Use sharp pruning shears; make all cuts as shown in the Practical Gardening Dictionary under Pruning Cuts. Remove wood that is obviously dead and wood that has no healthy growth coming from it; branches that cross through the plant's center and any that rub against larger canes; branches that make bush appear lopsided; and any old and unproductive canes that strong new ones have replaced during past season. Cut back growth produced during previous year, making cuts above outward-facing buds (except for very spreading varieties: some cuts to inside buds will promote more height without producing many crossing branches). As a general rule, remove one-third to no more than one-half the length of previous season's growth (except in Zones 1–3, 34–45, as noted above). The ideal result is a V-shaped bush with relatively open center.

▶

R

If any suckers (growth produced from understock, not the rose variety growing on it) are present, completely remove them. Dig down to where suckers grow from understock and pull them off with downward motion; that removes basal growth buds that would have produced additional suckers in subsequent years. Let wound air-dry before you replace soil around it.

Be certain you are removing a sucker rather than a new cane growing from the bud union of the budded variety. Usually you can note a distinct difference in foliage size and shape, as well as in size of thorns, on sucker growth. If in doubt, let the presumed sucker grow until you can establish its difference from cane. A sucker's flowers will be different; a flowerless, climbing cane from a bush rose is almost certainly a sucker.

Consider cutting flowers as a form of pruning. Cut off enough stem to support flower in vase, but don't deprive plant of too much foliage. Leave on plant a stem with at least two sets of five-leaflet leaves. Prune to outward-growing bud or to five-leaflet leaf.

The most widely planted modern roses—hybrid teas and grandifloras—can be pruned successfully according to these guidelines. A few additional tips apply to other popular types:

Floribunda, polyantha, and many shrub roses are grown for quantities of flowers, so amount of bloom rather than quality of individual flower is the objective. Cut back previous season's growth only by one-fourth, and leave as many strong new canes and stems as plant produced. Most produce more canes per bush than do hybrid teas and grandifloras. If you have a hedge of one variety, cut back all plants to uniform height.

Climbing roses may be divided into two general types: those that bloom in spring only (including a large category known as natural climbers, discussed in "Climbing roses," page 477), and those that bloom off and on in other seasons as well as in spring (including the very popular climbing sports of hybrid tea roses). All climbers should be left unpruned for the first 2 or 3 years after planting; remove only dead, weak, and twiggy wood, allowing plants to get established and produce their long, flexible canes. Most bloom comes from lateral branches that grow from long canes, and most of those flowering branches develop when long canes are spread out horizontally (as along a fence). Types that bloom only in spring produce strong new growth after they flower, and that new growth bears flowers the following spring. Prune these climbers just after they bloom, removing oldest canes that show no signs of strong new growth. Repeat-flowering climbers (many are climbing sports of bush varieties) are pruned at the same time you'd prune bush roses in your locality. Remove oldest, unproductive canes and any weak, twiggy growth; cut back lateral branches on remaining canes to within two or three buds from canes.

Pillar roses are not quite bush or climber. They produce tall, somewhat flexible canes that bloom profusely without having to be trained horizontally. Prune pillar roses according to general guidelines for bush roses.

Tree roses, more properly called "standards," are an artificial creation: a bush rose budded onto a 2–3-ft.-high understock stem. Be sure to stake trunk securely to prevent its breaking from weight of bush it supports. A ½-in. metal pipe makes good permanent stake; use cross tie between stake and trunk to hold them secure. General pruning guidelines apply, with particular attention to maintaining symmetrical plant.

Miniature roses should be pruned back to at least half the height they attained during the previous year, removing all weak and twiggy stems. Some growers prune miniatures severely—back to the lowest outward-facing growth buds on the previous year's new stems.

Winter protection. Where winter low temperatures regularly reach 10°F/–12°C and lower, some winter protection is needed for nearly all modern roses. Low temperatures can kill exposed canes; repeated freezing and thawing will kill canes by rupturing cells; and winter winds can fatally desiccate exposed canes because plants are unable to replace moisture from frozen soil.

A healthy, well-ripened plant withstands harsh winters better than a weak and actively growing one. Prepare plants for winter by timing your last fertilizer application so that bushes will have ceased putting on new growth by expected date of first sharp frost. Leave the last crop of blooms

on plants to form hips (fruits), which will aid the ripening process by stopping growth. Keep plants well watered until soil freezes.

After a couple of hard freezes have occurred and night temperatures seem to remain consistently below freezing, mound soil over base of each bush to height of 1 ft. Get soil from another part of garden; do not scoop soil from around roses, exposing surface roots. Cut excessively long canes back to 2–4 ft. (the lower figure applies in the colder northern and midwestern regions); then, with soft twine, tie canes together to keep them from whipping around in wind. When mound has frozen, cover it with evergreen boughs, straw, or other fairly lightweight material that will act as insulation to keep mounds frozen. Your objective is to prevent alternate freezing and thawing of mound (and canes it covers), maintaining plant at constant temperature of 15° to 20°F/–9° to –7°C. A 3–4-ft.-high wire-mesh cylinder filled with noncompacting insulating material (such as straw, hay, oak leaves, or pine needles) may preserve much of the cane growth it encloses.

Polyantha Rose 'Margo Koster'

Remove protection in early spring when you are reasonably certain hard frosts will not recur. Gradually remove soil mounds as they thaw; do it carefully to avoid breaking new growth that may have begun sprouting under the soil. Use of manufactured styrofoam rose cones eliminates the labor of mounding and unmounding; just a bit of soil around the cone's base plus a rock or brick on top will hold it in place over the bush. Disadvantages are cost and limited availability of cones; the need to cut rose down to fit cone over it, perhaps requiring more severe pruning than is usually necessary; moisture condensation inside cone as days begin warming. To avoid condensation problem, get cones with removable tops that can be opened on warm late-winter days.

You should mound climbing roses in same manner, but in addition you need to protect all of their canes. Where winter lows range from –10° to 5°F/–23° to –15°C, wrap canes in burlap stuffed with straw or similar material for insulation. Where temperatures normally go below –10°F/ –23°C, remove canes from their support, gently bend them to ground, secure them in that position, and cover with soil. A wiser plan in such climates is to plant only climbers known to be successful in your area or reputed to be hardy in similar climates.

Standards (tree roses) may be insulated in the same manner as for climbers, but they still may not survive, since the head of the tree is the most exposed. Some rosarians wrap with straw and burlap, then construct a plywood box to cover the insulated plant. Others dig their standards each year and pack the roots loosely in soil or other medium in a cool garage, basement, or shed, then replant in spring. A simpler technique is to grow standards in large containers and move them in fall to cool shed or garage where temperatures won't drop below 10°F/–12°C.

TYPES OF ROSES

A renewed interest in old roses, continued developments of new hybrids, and breeding programs directed toward producing landscape shrubs have led to a greatly expanded offering of roses to the gardening public. For convenience, the following sections describe three broad categories: modern roses, old roses, and species and species hybrids.

Modern roses. Types described below constitute the majority of roses offered for sale and planted by hundreds of thousands each year. Those that have been All-America Rose Selections, recognized on the basis of their performance in nationwide test gardens, are indicated by "AARS"; those with an asterisk (*) before their names have been rated 8.0 or higher by the American Rose Society.

Hybrid teas. This, the most popular class of rose, outsells all other types combined. Flowers are large and shapely, generally produced one to a stem on plants that range from 2 ft. to 6 ft. or more, depending on the variety and climate. Many thousands of varieties have been produced since the first rose in the class, 'La France', appeared in 1867; hundreds are cataloged, and new ones appear each year. The most popular ones are listed in the following color groups:

Red: 'Chrysler Imperial' (AARS), *'Mr. Lincoln' (AARS), *'Olympiad' (AARS).

Pink: 'Bewitched' (AARS), 'Brigadoon' (AARS), *'Century Two', *'Color Magic' (AARS), *'Dainty Bess'(single), 'Duet' (AARS), *'First Prize' (AARS), *'Miss All-American Beauty' (AARS), 'Perfume Delight' (AARS), *'Royal Highness' (AARS), 'Secret' (AARS), 'Sheer Bliss' (AARS), *'Tiffany' (AARS), *'Touch of Class' (AARS).

Multicolors, blends: 'Broadway' (AARS), 'Chicago Peace', *'Double Delight' (AARS), *'Granada' (AARS), 'Just Joey', 'Medallion' (AARS), 'Rio Samba' (AARS), 'Seashell' (AARS), 'Voodoo' (AARS).

Orange, orange tones: 'Brandy' (AARS), *'Folklore', *'Fragrant Cloud', 'Tropicana' (AARS).

Yellow: *'Elina', 'Graceland', 'King's Ransom' (AARS), 'Oregold' (AARS), 'Midas Touch' (AARS), *'Peace' (AARS), 'Summer Sunshine', 'Sunbright'.

White: *'Garden Party' (AARS), 'Honor' (AARS), 'John F. Kennedy', *'Pascali' (AARS), *'Pristine'.

Lavender: 'Blue Girl', 'Blue Ribbon', 'Heirloom', *'Lady X', *'Paradise' (AARS).

Grandifloras. Vigorous plants, sometimes 8–10 ft. tall, with hybrid tea–type flowers borne singly or in long-stemmed clusters. Some are derived from crosses between hybrid teas and floribundas; others are just extra-vigorous, cluster-flowering segregates from ordinary hybrid tea ancestry. They're good for mass color effect, for number of cuttable flowers produced per plant, and as background or barrier plants.

Red: 'Love' (AARS), 'Olé'.

Pink, pink blends: *'Aquarius' (AARS), 'Camelot' (AARS), *'Earth Song', *'Pink Parfait' (AARS), *'Queen Elizabeth' (AARS), *'Sonia', *'Tournament of Roses' (AARS).

Orange, blends: 'Arizona' (AARS), 'Montezuma', 'Solitude' (AARS).

Yellow: *'Gold Medal'.

White: 'White Lightnin' (AARS).

Lavender: 'Lagerfeld'.

Floribundas. Originally developed from hybrid teas and polyanthas (see below), these are noted for producing quantities of flowers in clusters on vigorous and bushy plants. Plant and flower sizes are smaller than those of most hybrid teas. Some have flowers of elegant hybrid tea shape; others are more informal. These are plants for providing mass color. Use for informal hedges, low borders and barriers, as container plants.

Red: *'Europeana' (AARS), 'Impatient', *'Sarabande' (AARS), *'Showbiz' (AARS), *'Trumpeter'.

Pink: *'Betty Prior', *'Bridal Pink', 'Cherish' (AARS), 'Gene Boerner' (AARS), 'Pleasure' (AARS), *'Sexy Rexy', 'Sweet Inspiration' (AARS), *'Sweet Vivien'.

Orange, blends: *'Apricot Nectar' (AARS), 'Cathedral', *'First Edition' (AARS), 'Gingersnap', 'Marina', *'Orangeade', 'Redgold' (AARS), *'Summer Fashion'.

Yellow: *'Sun Flare' (AARS), *'Sunsprite'.

White: *'Evening Star', *'French Lace' (AARS), *'Iceberg', *'Ivory Fashion' (AARS).

Lavender: *'Angel Face' (AARS), 'Intrigue' (AARS).

Polyanthas. Original members of this class appeared in the late 19th century, the result of crosses with *R. multiflora.* Small flowers (under 2 in. across) come in large sprays; plants are vigorous and usually low growing, nearly everblooming, and quite disease resistant. 'Margo Koster' has coral orange, very double flowers that resemble ranunculus; it has sported to produce color variants in white, pink, orange scarlet, and red. 'The Fairy' produces huge clusters of small, light pink flowers on a plant that can reach 4 ft. high. 'China Doll' is a knee-high plant with larger, deeper pink flowers in smaller clusters. With light pruning two 19th-century classics make sizable bushes that resemble bushy Noisettes (see under "Old roses," page 478). 'Cécile Brunner' (often called the Sweetheart Rose)

has light pink flowers of perfect hybrid tea form; 'Perle d'Or' (sometimes called Yellow Cécile Brunner) is similar except for its apricot orange flower color.

Miniature roses. These are perfect replicas of modern hybrid teas and floribundas but plant size is reduced to 1–1½ ft. (grown in the ground) with flowers and foliage in proportion. Derived in part from *R. chinensis minima* (presumably through its forms 'Rouletii' and 'Pompon de Paris'), they come in all colors of modern hybrid teas. Plants are everblooming. Grow them outdoors in containers, window boxes, and rock gardens or as border and bedding plants. You can grow them indoors: pot in rich soil in 6-in. (or larger) containers, and locate in a cool, bright window. Miniatures are hardier than hybrid teas but still need winter protection in Zones 1–3, 34–45. Shallow roots demand regular water and fertilizer, mulch. Nearly all are own-root, cutting-grown plants.

Miniature Rose

Many new miniatures appear on the market each year. Among the best are these, all rated 8.5 or higher:

Red, orange: 'Orange Sunblaze', 'Peggy', 'Starina'.

Pink: 'Coral Sprite', 'Cupcake', 'Millie Walters', 'Pierrine', 'Pink Meillandina'.

Blends: 'Dreamglo', 'Earthquake', 'Jean Kenneally', 'Little Artist', 'Little Jackie', 'Loving Touch', 'Magic Carrousel', 'Minnie Pearl', 'Party Girl', 'Rainbow's End', 'Shortcake', 'Wow'.

Yellow: 'Morain', 'My Sunshine', 'Rise 'n' Shine'.

White: 'Pacesetter', 'Snowbride'.

Lavender, purple: 'Ruby Pendant', 'Winsome'.

Climbing roses. Modern climbing roses may be divided into two general categories: natural climbers (large flowered, except for miniatures) and climbing sports of bush roses (hybrid teas, grandifloras, floribundas, polyanthas, miniatures). Here are popular varieties of natural climbers:

Red: *'Altissimo' (single), 'Blaze', *'Don Juan', *'Dortmund', *'Dublin Bay', 'Solo', 'Tempo'.

Pink: 'Blossomtime', *'Clair Matin', *'Galway Bay', *'Hi Ho' (miniature), *'Jeanne Lajoie' (miniature), 'New Dawn', *'Pink Perpétué', *'Rhonda'.

Orange, blends: *'America' (AARS), *'Compassion', *'Handel', 'Joseph's Coat', *'Royal Sunset', 'Spectra'.

Yellow: 'Golden Showers' (AARS), 'Royal Gold'.

White: *'City of York', 'Lace Cascade', 'White Dawn'.

Here are popular varieties of climbing sports:

Red: 'Cl. Chrysler Imperial', 'Cl. Crimson Glory'.

Pink: 'Cl. Cécile Brunner' (polyantha), 'Cl. China Doll' (polyantha), 'Cl. Dainty Bess', 'Cl. First Prize', 'Cl. Queen Elizabeth'.

Orange, blends: 'Cl. Double Delight', 'Cl. Granada', 'Cl. Mrs. Sam McGredy', 'Cl. Peace'.

White: *'Cl. Iceberg'.

Climbing Rose 'Climbing Mrs. Sam McGredy'

Shrub roses. Significant breeding is under way to develop roses for general landscape use. These are collectively known as shrub roses. Emphasis is on plants that will provide attractive floral displays (even good-looking individual blossoms), disease-resistant foliage, and individuals that will survive cold winters with no special protection. Mail-order rose specialists lead the way in offering these plants, but retail nurseries are offering them more and more. Here is an overview of types available.

Hybrid musk roses. These were developed in the first three decades of the 20th century from the multiflora rambler 'Trier', which was distantly descended from the musk rose through the Noisettes. The hybrid musks are large (6–8-ft.) shrubs or small climbers that will perform well in dappled or partial shade as well as in sun. Most are nearly everblooming, with fragrant, clustered flowers in white, yellow, buff, pink shades, red. Popular varieties include 'Buff Beauty', buff apricot; 'Cornelia', coral; 'Felicia', pink;

'Kathleen', single pink, like apple blossoms; 'Penelope', salmon; 'Will Scarlet', red.

English roses. This is a rapidly expanding group of hybrids. England's David Austin has bred various old roses (albas, centifolias, gallicas) with modern roses in order to capture the forms and fragrances of old roses in repeat-flowering plants that offer the color range of modern hybrids. The group is extremely varied and includes low shrubs as well as plants that are determined to be climbers regardless of pruning. Many have Shakespearean or Chaucerian names; over 80 are in commerce. Popular varieties include 'Abraham Darby', pink-yellow-apricot blend, upright to climbing plant; 'Charles Austin', apricot, bushy plant; 'Fair Bianca', creamy white, spreading bush; 'Gertrude Jekyll', deep pink, tall and upright; 'Graham Thomas', rich yellow, tall plant; 'Mary Rose', rose pink, tall and upright; 'Othello', dusky dark red, tall bush or climber.

Ground cover roses. A number of European and American breeders are producing roses that spread their canes widely but build up to no more than 2 ft.—perfect for covering slopes, forming traffic-proof covers on level ground, or for container culture. Vigor, disease resistance, profusion of bloom are the hallmarks of these roses. Examples are 'Essex', 'Flower Carpet', 'Nozomi', 'Pink Bells', 'Rosy Carpet'.

Hardy roses. Two breeding programs have produced numerous varieties that will survive prairie and northern winters with virtually no special protection. Some of them resemble floribundas and grandifloras; ancestries include various hardy species plus modern hybrid teas and floribundas. Many of these feature country names: 'Country Dancer', 'Hawkeye Belle', 'Maytime', 'Prairie Princess'. Others are mostly larger shrubs to small climbers, derived in part from *R. rugosa;* most are cluster flowered, like large floribundas. Many are named for explorers: 'Alexander Mackenzie', 'Henry Kelsey', 'John Cabot', 'William Baffin'.

Patio roses. Larger than miniatures, smaller than floribundas, these plants (mostly of European origin) are bushy, profuse flowering, usually no more than 2 ft. tall. They're good providers of mass color as border and container plants. Examples are 'Amorette' and 'Hakuun', white; 'Minilights', soft yellow; 'Pink Pollyanna', pink; 'Yellow Jacket', yellow.

Other shrub roses. Many modern shrub roses of complex ancestry can't be pigeonholed into categories according to species affiliation or specific characteristic. The plants may be spreading or upright; they are usually 3 ft. or greater in height, and their flowers come in small to large clusters. These include such gems as 'Alchymist'; 'Ballerina' (classed as hybrid musk but more like a giant polyantha); 'Erfurt'; the various Meidiland roses ('Bonica', 'Pink Meidiland', 'Red Meidiland', 'White Meidiland'); 'Pearl Drift'; 'Sally Holmes'; and 'Sea Foam'. Check individual descriptions of catalog offerings to find appealing candidates that meet your specific landscape needs.

Old roses. Among rosarians, the dividing line between old and modern roses is 1867—the year that the first hybrid tea was introduced. Old roses are varieties that belong to the various rose classes that existed prior to 1867 (even though some varieties in these classes were introduced as late as the early 20th century). Old roses may be divided into two categories. The old European roses comprise the albas, centifolias, damasks, gallicas, and moss roses—the oldest hybrid groups derived from species native to Europe and western Asia. Most flower only in spring; many are hardy in the coldest climates with little or no winter protection. The second group contains classes derived entirely or in part from East Asian roses: Chinas, Bourbons, damask perpetuals, hybrid perpetuals, Noisettes, and teas. Original China and tea roses were brought to Europe from eastern Asia; 19th-century hybridizers greatly increased their numbers and also developed the other classes from crosses with European roses. Repeat flowering is a characteristic of these classes; hardiness varies, but nearly all need winter protection in coldest zones.

Alba roses. Developed from the *R. alba*, the White Rose of York, and associated with England's War of the Roses. Spring flowers range from single to very double, white to delicate pink. Upright plants are vigorous and long lived, with green wood and handsome, disease-resistant gray-green foliage.

Garden varieties include white 'Alba Semiplena' and these in shades of pink: 'Celestial', 'Great Maiden's Blush', 'Félicité Parmentier', and 'Königin von Dänemark'.

Centifolia roses. The roses often portrayed by Dutch painters; developed from *R. centifolia*, the cabbage rose. Plants are open growing with prickly stems; stems reach 6 ft. tall but arch with weight of blossoms. Intensely fragrant spring flowers typically are packed with petals, often with large outer petals that cradle a multitude of smaller petals within. Colors include white, pink shades. 'Rose des Peintres' is a typical rich pink cabbage rose; 'Paul Ricault' produces silken, deep pink flowers on an upright plant; 'Tour de Malakoff' is a tall, rangy plant with peonylike blossoms of pink fading to grayish mauve. Dwarf varieties (3 ft. or less) are 'Petite de Hollande', 'Pompon de Bourgogne', and 'Rose de Meaux'.

Damask roses. Originating with *R. damascena*. Plants reach 6 ft. or more, typically with long, arching, thorny canes and light or grayish green, downy leaves. The summer damasks flower only in spring; forms of these are cultivated to make attar of roses (used in the perfume industry). Available varieties include 'Celsiana', blush pink; 'Leda', white with crimson markings; 'Mme. Hardy', white; and 'Versicolor' ('York and Lancaster'), with petals that may be pink, white, or blend of pink and white. The autumn damask rose, *R. d.* 'Semperflorens' (*R. d. bifera*), flowers more than once in a year; slender buds open to loosely double, clear pink blossoms. This is the "Rose of Castile" of the Spanish missions.

Gallica roses. Cultivated forms of *R. gallica*, the French rose. Fragrant spring flowers run from pink through red to maroon and purple shades. Plants reach 3–4 ft. tall with upright to arching canes bearing prickles but few thorns and dark green, often rough-textured leaves. Grown on their own roots, these plants will spread into clumps from creeping rootstocks. Historic 'Officinalis', known as the Apothecary Rose, is presumed to be the "Red Rose of Lancaster" from the War of the Roses; flowers are semidouble, cherry red, on a dense, medium-height plant. Its sport, 'Versicolor'—generally known as 'Rosa Mundi'—has pink petals boldly striped and stippled red. Other gallicas include 'Belle de Crécy', pink aging to violet; 'Cardinal de Richelieu', slate purple; 'Charles de Mills', crimson to purple; and 'Tuscany', dark crimson with gold stamens.

Moss roses. Two old rose classes—centifolia and damask—include variant types that feature mosslike, balsam-scented glands that cover unopened buds, flower stems, and sometimes even leaflets. The moss of centifolias is soft to the touch; that of damask mosses is more stiff and prickly. Flowers are white, pink, red, often intensely fragrant. 'Communis' and 'Centifolia Muscosa' ('Muscosa') are typical pink centifolias with moss added; 'White Bath' is 'Centifolia Muscosa' done in white. Other available varieties are 'Comtesse de Murinais', pale pink to white; 'Gloire des Mousseux', deep pink; 'Mme. Louis Lévêque', salmon pink; 'Nuits de Young', dark red; 'William Lobb', dark red to purple. Repeat-flowering mosses include 'Alfred de Dalmas', creamy pink; 'Gabriel Noyelle', apricot; 'Henri Martin', red; and 'Salet', bright pink.

China roses. The first two China roses to reach Europe (around 1800) were really cultivated forms of *R. chinensis* that had been selected and maintained by Chinese horticulturists. Flowers were pink or red, under 3 in. across, in small clusters, on 2–4-ft.-high plants. 'Old Blush' ('Parson's Pink China'), one of the original two, is still sold; other available China roses include red 'Cramoisi Supérieur' ('Agrippina'), white 'Ducher', and crimson 'Louis Philippe'. China rose ancestry was the primary source of repeat-flowering habit in later 19th- and early 20th-century roses. Modern miniature roses owe their reduced stature to *R. chinensis minima*, presumably through its forms 'Rouletii' and 'Pompon de Paris'.

Bourbon roses. The original Bourbon rose was a hybrid between *R. chinensis* and the autumn damask (*R. damascena* 'Semperflorens'). Later developments were shrubs, semiclimbers, and climbers with flowers in white, pink shades, and red, mostly quite fragrant. Best known today are 'La Reine Victoria', 'Madame Ernst Calvat', 'Madame Pierre Oger', and 'Sou-

R

venir de la Malmaison' (all pink), and the supremely fragrant 'Madame Isaac Pereire' (magenta red). A famous Bourbon-China hybrid, 'Gloire des Rosomanes', gained widespread distribution as an understock (called "Ragged Robin") in commercial rose production. Occasionally it is offered as a hedge plant; growth is upright to fountainlike, with coarse foliage and semidouble, cherry red flowers throughout the growing season.

Damask perpetuals. This was the first distinct hybrid group to emerge, beginning around 1800, combining the China roses with old European rose types. Ancestries vary, but all appear to include China roses and the autumn damask (*R. damascena* 'Semperflorens'); generally they were known as Portland roses after the first representative, 'Duchess of Portland'. All are fairly short, bushy, repeat-flowering plants with centifolia- and gallica-like flowers. Among those sold are 'Comte de Chambord', cool pink; 'Duchess of Portland', crimson; 'Jacques Cartier', bright pink; and 'Rose du Roi', crimson purple.

Hybrid perpetuals. In the 19th and early 20th centuries, before hybrid teas dominated the catalogs, these were *the* garden roses. They are big, vigorous, and hardy to about −30°F/−34°C with minimal winter protection. Plants need more water and fertilizer than hybrid teas in order to produce repeated bursts of bloom. Prune high, thin out oldest canes, arch over remaining canes to encourage bloom in quantity. Watch for rust. Flowers often are large (to 6 or 7 in.), full, and strongly fragrant; buds usually are shorter, plumper than standard hybrid tea buds. Colors range from white through pink shades to red and maroon. Varieties still sold include 'Frau Karl Druschki', white; 'Général Jacqueminot', cherry red; 'Mrs. John Laing', rose pink; 'Paul Neyron', deep pink, peonylike flower; 'Ulrich Brünner Fils', carmine red.

Noisette roses. The union of a China rose (*R. chinensis*) and the musk rose (*R. moschata*) produced the first Noisette rose, 'Champneys' Pink Cluster', a repeat-flowering shrubby climber with small pink flowers in medium-size clusters. Crossed with itself and China roses, it led to a race of similar roses in white, pink shades, and red; crossed with tea roses, it yielded large-flowered, climbing tea-Noisettes. All are best in milder climates (Zones 6–9, 12–31). Small-flowered Noisettes include 'Aimée Vibert Scandens', white; 'Blush Noisette', light pink; and 'Fellenberg', cherry red. Larger-flowered tea-Noisettes are 'Alister Stella Gray', yellow; 'Crepuscule', orange; 'Lamarque', white; 'Madame Alfred Carrière', white; 'Maréchal Niel', yellow; and 'Rêve d'Or', buff apricot.

Tea roses. A race of elegant, virtually everblooming, relatively tender roses best in Zones 6–9, 12–31. Plants are long lived, building on old wood and disliking heavy pruning. Flowers are in pastel shades—white, soft cream, light yellow, apricot, buff, pink, and rosy red; flower character varies, but many resemble hybrid teas in flower quality. In crosses with hybrid perpetuals, tea roses were parents of the first hybrid teas. Available varieties include 'Duchesse de Brabant', warm pink, tuliplike; 'Lady Hillingdon', saffron; 'Maman Cochet', creamy rose pink; 'Marie van Houtte', soft yellow and pink; 'Mlle. Franziska Krüger', pink and cream to orange; 'Monsieur Tillier', dark pink and brick red; and 'White Maman Cochet', creamy white shaded pink. The cross of a tea and the tea ancestor *R. gigantea* produced 'Belle Portugaise' ('Belle of Portugal'), a rampant, spring-flowering climber bearing large pale pink blossoms.

Species and species hybrids. Among this diverse assemblage of wild species and their hybrids are excellent shrub and climbing roses, useful for mass floral effect and for attractiveness of plant and foliage.

R. banksiae. LADY BANKS' ROSE. Evergreen climber (deciduous in cold winters). Zones 4–33. Vigorous grower to 20 feet or more. Aphid resistant, almost immune to disease. Stems have almost no prickles; glossy and leathery leaves have three to five leaflets to 2½ in. long. Large clusters of small yellow or white flowers bloom in early to late spring, depending on zone. Good for covering banks, ground, fence, or arbor. The two forms sold are 'Lutea', with scentless, double yellow flowers; and *R. b. banksiae*

('Alba Plena' or 'White Banksia'), with violet-scented, double white flowers. The fragrant 'Fortuniana' (*R. fortuniana*) sometimes is sold as the double white banksia; it differs in having thorny canes, larger leaves, and larger flowers that come individually rather than in clusters.

R. bracteata. Evergreen climbing shrub with large, single creamy white blossoms. Zones 4–31, warmer parts of 32. Naturalized in southeastern U.S. Its celebrated offspring is 'Mermaid', an evergreen or semievergreen climber reliably hardy just in Zones 7–28. Vigorous (to 30 ft.), thorny, with glossy, leathery, dark green leaves and many single, creamy yellow, lightly fragrant flowers, 5 in. across, in spring, summer, fall, and intermittently through winter in mildest zones. Tough, disease resistant, thrives in sun or partial shade. Plant 8 ft. apart for quick ground cover; or use to climb wall (will need tying), run along fence, or climb tree.

R. eglanteria (R. rubiginosa). SWEET BRIAR, EGLANTINE. Deciduous shrub or climber. Zones 1–24, 30–45. Vigorous growth to 8–12 ft. Prickly stems. Dark green leaves have the fragrance of green apples, especially after rain. Flowers single, pink, 1½ in. across, appearing singly or in clusters in late spring. Red-orange fruit. Can be used as hedge, barrier, screen; plant 3–4 ft. apart and prune once a year in early spring. Can be held to 3–4 ft. Good hybrid forms are 'Lady Penzance', 'Lord Penzance'.

R. foetida (R. lutea). AUSTRIAN BRIER. Deciduous shrub. Zones 2–21, 32–41. Slender, prickly stems 5–10 ft. long, erect or arching. Leaves dark green, smooth or slightly hairy, especially susceptible to black spot; may drop early in fall. Flowers (mid- to late spring) are single, bright yellow, 2–3 in. across, with odd scent. This species and its well-known variety 'Bicolor', Austrian Copper rose, are the source of orange and yellow in modern roses. 'Bicolor' is a 4–5-ft.-tall shrub with brilliant coppery red flowers, their petals backed with yellow. Its form 'Persiana', Persian Yellow rose, has fully double, yellow blossoms.

All forms perform best in warm, fairly dry, well-drained soil and in full sun. Need reflected heat in cool-summer areas. Prune only to remove dead wood.

R. glauca (R. rubrifolia). Deciduous shrub. Zones 1–24, 30–45. Foliage, not flower, is the main feature of this species: the 6-ft. plant is covered in leaves that combine gray green and coppery purple. Small, single spring flowers are pink, forming small, oval hips that color red in fall.

R. harisonii. HARISON'S YELLOW ROSE. Deciduous shrub. Zones 1–24, 30–45. Thickets of thorny stems to 6–8 ft.; finely textured foliage; flowers (in late spring) profuse, semidouble, bright yellow, fragrant. Occasionally reblooms in fall in warmer climates. Showy fruit. Hybrid between *R. foetida* and *R. spinosissima*. Very old rose that was taken westward by pioneers from New York. Vigorous growing, disease free, hardy to cold, and (once established) resistant to aridity. Useful deciduous landscaping shrub.

R. hugonis. FATHER HUGO'S ROSE, GOLDEN ROSE OF CHINA. Deciduous shrub. Zones 2–24, 32–41. Dense growth to 8 ft. Stems arching or straight, with bristles near base. Handsome foliage; leaves deep green, 1–4 in. long, with 5–11 tiny leaflets. Blooms profusely in mid- to late spring. Branches become garlands of 2-in.-wide, bright yellow, faintly scented flowers. Useful in borders, for screen or barrier plantings, against fence, trained as fan on trellis. Will take high filtered afternoon shade. Prune out oldest wood to ground each year to shape plant, get maximum bloom.

R. laevigata. CHEROKEE ROSE. Evergreen climber. Zones 4–9, 12–31, warmer parts of 32. Native to Southeast Asia but widely naturalized in southern U.S., from which it gained its common name. Green stems with sharp, hooked thorns bear lacquered-looking, dark green leaves, each with three leaflets. Single white flowers to 3½ in. wide appear only in spring. Crossed with a tea rose, it produced 'Anemone', a mostly spring-flowering climber with soft, silvery pink, single flowers that resemble Japanese anemone blossoms. Its magenta pink sport is 'Ramona'.

R. moschata. MUSK ROSE. Deciduous shrub. Zones 4–32. Vigorous, arching plant is densely covered with matte-finish, mid-green foliage that turns butter yellow in late fall. Clustered, ivory white, single flowers appear in late spring, continue through summer; scent is delicious, somewhat like honey. *R. m. plena* has double blossoms, though their effect is lessened because inner petals wither before outer ones.

▸

R

R. moyesii. Deciduous shrub. Zones 3–10, 14–21, 32–34, 39. Large, loose shrub is best as background plant or featured shrub-tree specimen. Spring bloom is a glorious display of bright red single flowers to 2½ in. across, carried singly or in groups of two. A second display comes in fall, when the large, bottle-shaped hips ripen to brilliant scarlet. 'Geranium' is a selection with somewhat shorter, more compact growth and red flowers in clusters of up to five. The hybrid 'Sealing Wax' offers pink flowers, also on a smaller and more compact bush.

From a hybrid tea crossed with a form of *R. moyesii,* 'Nevada' makes a large, arching shrub with light green leaves and dark stems. In spring, stems are covered with 4-in., pink-tinted, single white flowers, with lesser displays following later in the year. 'Marguerite Hilling' is a pink sport.

R. multiflora. Deciduous shrub. Zones 1–24, 30–45. Arching growth on dense, vigorous plant 8–10 ft. tall and as wide. Susceptible to mildew, spider mites. Many clustered, small white flowers (like blackberry blossoms) in mid- to late spring; sweet fragrance akin to that of honeysuckle. Profusion of ¼-in. red fruit, much loved by birds, in fall. (Fruit display has a down side: profuse volunteer seedlings, which can put this rose in the "weed" category.) Promoted as hedge but truly useful for this purpose only on largest acreage—far too large and vigorous for most gardens. Spiny and smooth forms available; spiny form best for barrier hedge. Set plants 2 ft. apart for fast fill-in. Can help control erosion. One of the most widely used understocks in commerical rose production.

A number of distinctive climbing roses, known as multiflora ramblers, are hybrids of this species. Best known are several "blue ramblers": 'Bleu Magenta', crimson purple fading to gray violet; 'Rose-Marie Viaud', crimson purple to violet and lilac; 'Veilchenblau', maroon purple to gray lilac; and 'Violette', maroon purple to grayish plum.

R. roxburghii. CHESTNUT ROSE. Deciduous shrub. Zones 2–24, 26–41. Spreading plant with prickly stems 8–10 ft. long. Gray, peeling bark. Light green, very finely textured, ferny foliage; new growth bronze and gold tipped. Immune to mildew. Buds and fruit are spiny, like chestnut burrs. Flowers—generally double, soft rose pink, very fragrant—appear in mid- to late spring. Normally a big shrub for screen or border, but if stems are pegged down it makes good bank cover, useful in preventing erosion.

R. rugosa. RAMANAS ROSE, SEA TOMATO. Deciduous shrub. Zones 1–24, 32–45. Vigorous, very hardy shrub with prickly stems. To 3–8 ft. tall. Leaves bright glossy green, with distinctive heavy veining that gives them crinkled appearance. Flowers are 3–4 in. across and, in the many varieties, range from single to double and from pure white and creamy yellow through pink to deep purplish red, all wonderfully fragrant. Blooms spring, summer, early fall. Bright red, tomato-shaped fruit, an inch or more across, is seedy but edible and sometimes used in preserves.

All rugosas are extremely tough and hardy, withstanding hard freezes, wind, aridity, salt spray at ocean. They make fine hedges; plants grown on their own roots will make sizable colonies and help prevent erosion. Foliage remains quite free of diseases and insects, except possibly aphids. Among most widely sold rugosas and rugosa hybrids are 'Blanc Double de Coubert', double white; 'Frau Dagmar Hartopp', single pink; 'Hansa', double purplish red; 'Will Alderman', double pink. Two unusual rugosa hybrids are 'F. J. Grootendorst' and 'Grootendorst Supreme'; their double flowers with deeply fringed petals resemble carnations more than roses.

R. spinosissima (R. pimpinellifolia). SCOTCH ROSE, BURNET ROSE. Deciduous shrub. Zones 1–24, 32–45. Suckering, spreading shrub 3–4 ft. tall. Stems upright, spiny, bristly, closely set with small, ferny leaves. Handsome bank cover on good soil; helps prevent erosion. Spring flowers white to pink, 1½–2 in. across; fruit dark brown to blackish. Its form 'Altaica' can reach 6 ft. tall, with larger leaves and 3-in. white flowers garlanding branches. Several hybrids are noteworthy. 'Stanwell Perpetual' produces blush pink, double blossoms from spring to fall on a mounding, twiggy plant with small gray-green leaves. 'Frühlingsmorgen' is best known of several German hybrids; tall, arching bush bears large, single yellow flowers edged cherry pink and centered with maroon stamens. 'Golden Wings' makes a 6-ft. bush that flowers throughout the growing season; 4-in. blossoms are single, light yellow with red stamens.

R. wichuraiana. MEMORIAL ROSE. Vine. Deciduous in Zones 3–34, 39; evergreen or partially evergreen in Zones 4–32. Trailing stems grow 10–12 ft. long in one season, root in contact with moist soil. Leaves 2–4 in. long, with five to nine smooth, shiny, ¼–1-in. leaflets. Midsummer flowers are white, to 2 in. across, in clusters of six to ten. Good ground cover, even in relatively poor soil. Wichuraiana ramblers, produced in the first 20 years of this century, are group of hybrids between the species and various garden roses. Pink 'Dorothy Perkins' and red 'Excelsa' produce smothering spring displays of small, formless flowers that obscure the often-mildewed leaves. Larger, better-shaped flowers and glossy, healthier leaves are found in 'Albéric Barbier', creamy white; 'François Juranville', coral pink; 'Gardenia', light yellow; 'Paul Transon', coppery salmon; and 'Sander's White Rambler', white.

Rosaceae. The rose family contains an immense number of plants of horticultural importance. In addition to roses, family members include strawberry, bramble fruits (blackberry, raspberry), many flowering and fruiting trees (apple, crabapple, pear, plum), *Photinia,* firethorn *(Pyracantha),* and *Spiraea,* as well as other ornamental trees, shrubs, and perennials.

ROSA DE MONTANA. See ANTIGONON leptopus

ROSARY VINE. See CEROPEGIA woodii

ROSE. See ROSA

ROSE APPLE. See SYZYGIUM jambos

ROSELLE. See HIBISCUS sabdariffa

ROSE-MALLOW. See HIBISCUS moscheutos

ROSEMARY. See ROSMARINUS officinalis

ROSE MOSS. See PORTULACA

ROSE OF SHARON. See HIBISCUS syriacus

ROSMARINUS officinalis

ROSEMARY

Lamiaceae (Labiatae)

EVERGREEN SHRUB OR HERB

ZONES 4–24, 26–32, EXCEPT AS NOTED

FULL SUN

MODERATE TO LITTLE WATER

Rosmarinus officinalis

Basic species is 3–4 ft. high, rounded and a bit spreading, but generally with upward-sweeping branches. Narrow, almost needlelike, inch-long leaves usually glossy green above, grayish white beneath, aromatic when brushed or bruised. Bear small clusters of small, typically lavender blue flowers over long winter–spring bloom period. Plants must have well-drained soil in regions with summer rainfall and warm to hot temperatures. In western zones, they will accept regular watering (in well-drained soil) but will thrive with little or no supplemental water in all but the hottest-summer areas. Prune as needed, making all cuts to side branches or into leafy stems.

Selections include the following. Foliage of all types has culinary use.

'Alba'. Resembles basic species but bears white flowers.

'Arp'. The hardiest rosemary; takes temperatures to −10°F/−23°C. Found in Arp, Texas (Zone 33). Open grower to 4 ft. Bright blue flowers.

'Collingwood Ingram' *(R. ingramii)*. To 2–2½ ft. high, spreading to 4 ft. or more. Branches curve gracefully. Flowers in rich, bright shade of blue violet. Tallish bank or ground cover with high color value.

'Huntington Carpet' ('Huntington Blue'). To 1½ ft. high; spreads quickly yet maintains dense center. Pale blue flowers.

'Ken Taylor'. Resembles 'Collingwood Ingram' but is lower growing and has a greater tendency to trail.

'Lockwood de Forest' *(R. lockwoodii, R. forestii)*. Resembles 'Prostratus', but with lighter, brighter foliage and bluer flowers.

R

'Majorca Pink'. Erect shrub to 2–5 ft. Lavender pink flowers.

'Miss Jessup's Upright'. Very upright to 4 ft.; pale blue flowers. Suitable for formal herb gardens.

'Old Salem'. Dense, erect growth to 3 ft.; pale blue flowers. Fairly cold hardy under snow cover.

'Prostratus'. DWARF ROSEMARY. To 2 ft. high with 4–8-ft. spread. Will trail over wall or edge of raised bed to make curtain of bright to dark green. Pale lavender blue flowers. Slightly less cold hardy than most other types of rosemary.

'Tuscan Blue'. Rigid, upright branches to 6 ft. or taller grow directly from base of plant. Rich green leaves, blue-violet flowers. Makes an attractive tall, narrow screen.

ROWAN. See SORBUS aucuparia

ROYAL FERN. See OSMUNDA regalis

ROYAL POINCIANA. See DELONIX regia

ROYAL TRUMPET VINE. See DISTICTIS 'Rivers'

ROYSTONEA

ROYAL PALM

Arecaceae (Palmae)

PALM

ZONE 25

FULL SUN

AMPLE WATER

Roystonea regia

Native to the Caribbean region; widely planted in tropics around the world. Stately, symmetrical feather palms. Tall, smooth gray trunk is marked with rings and topped by a green crownshaft formed by the sheathing bases of the feathery fronds. Rapid growers; tolerate wind, even salt-laden ocean wind. Especially majestic planted in rows.

R. elata. FLORIDA ROYAL PALM. Native to southern Florida. Differs from *R. regia* in minor details. Considered by some to be a taller palm than *R. regia.*

R. regia. CUBAN ROYAL PALM. To 75 ft., with erect trunk swollen at base, tapering toward top, sometimes swollen toward middle. Arched, 9–20-ft.-long fronds with leaflets that stand out from the midrib at many angles.

RUBBER PLANT. See FICUS elastica

RUBBER TREE, HARDY. See EUCOMMIA ulmoides

Rubiaceae. The widespread and varied madder family contains herbs, shrubs, and trees with opposite or whorled leaves and (usually) clustered flowers. Among its members are *Bouvardia,* coffee *(Coffea), Gardenia,* and sweet woodruff *(Galium).*

RUBUS

BRAMBLE

Rosaceae

DECIDUOUS OR EVERGREEN SHRUBS OR GROUND COVERS

ZONES VARY BY SPECIES

FULL SUN OR LIGHT SHADE

REGULAR TO MODERATE WATER

Rubus deliciosus

Best known for edible members blackberry and raspberry (see separate entries), the brambles include many ornamental plants, most of them without prickles or thorns. Provide good drainage.

R. deliciosus. ROCKY MOUNTAIN THIMBLEBERRY, BOULDER RASPBERRY. Deciduous shrub. Zones 2–6, 10, 35–41. To 3–5 ft., with arching, thornless branches. Bright green, lobed leaves are nearly round. White spring flowers to 2–3 in. wide look like single roses. Fruit attracts birds. Hybrid between this species and *R. trilobus* is *R. tridel* 'Benenden', which grows 8–10 ft. tall.

R. pentalobus (R. calycinoides, R. fockeanus). Evergreen shrub, ground cover. Zones 4–6, 14–17, 31, 32. Creeping stems make a mat that spreads 1 ft. a year. Densely packed green leaves are ruffled, nearly round; look crinkled above, felty beneath. Some leaves turn red or bronze in winter or in full sun. Small white flowers like those of strawberry; edible salmon-colored berries. 'Emerald Carpet' is the selection most commonly seen.

RUDBECKIA

Asteraceae (Compositae)

PERENNIALS AND BIENNIALS

ZONES VARY BY SPECIES

FULL SUN OR LIGHT SHADE

REGULAR TO MODERATE WATER

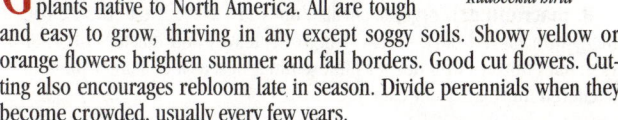

Rudbeckia hirta

Garden rudbeckias are descendants of wild plants native to North America. All are tough and easy to grow, thriving in any except soggy soils. Showy yellow or orange flowers brighten summer and fall borders. Good cut flowers. Cutting also encourages rebloom late in season. Divide perennials when they become crowded, usually every few years.

R. fulgida. Perennial. Zones 1–24, 28–43. To 3 ft. tall, with branching stems and 5-in.-long leaves. Yellow, 2–2½-in.-wide summer flowers with black to brown center. Spreads by rhizomes, forming large clumps. Varieties more often grown than species. Among most popular is *R. f. sullivantii* 'Goldsturm', bearing 3-in. black-eyed Susan flowers on 2–2½-ft. stems. Some nurseries offer the taller, more variable seed-grown Goldsturm strain.

R. hirta. GLORIOSA DAISY, BLACK-EYED SUSAN. Zones 1–24, 26–43. Biennial or short-lived perennial; often grown as annual because it blooms first summer from seed sown in early spring. To 3–4 ft. tall, with upright branching habit and rough, hairy stems and leaves. Daisylike single flowers 2–4 in. wide, with orange-yellow rays and purplish black center.

Gloriosa Daisy strain has 5–7-in.-wide single daisies in yellow, orange, russet, or mahogany, often zoned or banded. 'Irish Eyes' has golden yellow flowers with a light green center that turns brown as it ages. 'Pinwheel' has mahogany-and-gold flowers. 'Marmalade' (2 ft.) and 'Goldilocks' (8–10 in.) are lower growing, can be used at front of border or as ground cover. Gloriosa Double Daisy strain has somewhat smaller (to 4½-in.) double flower heads, nearly all in lighter yellow and orange shades.

R. laciniata. Perennial. Zones 1–24, 28–43. To 3 ft. tall, with deeply lobed, light green leaves. Blooms summer–fall, bearing 2–3½-in.-wide flowers with drooping yellow rays around a green central disc. Very heat tolerant. The following two varieties are more widely grown in gardens. 'Hortensia' ('Golden Glow'), to 6–7 ft. tall with double bright yellow flowers, makes a good summer screen or tall border plant. Aphids seem to like it. Does not seed, but spreads rapidly (sometimes aggressively) by underground stems and is easily divided. Less aggressive is 'Goldquelle', a 2½-ft.-tall plant with double yellow blooms.

R. maxima. Perennial. Zones 28–35, 37, 39. Large (to 5-in.) bluish gray leaves form a mound to 2–3 ft. tall and wide. In midsummer, 5–6-ft. stems bear flower heads with a 2-in. brown center cone and drooping yellow rays.

R. nitida. Perennial. Zones 3–9, 14–24, 28–35, 37, 39. Similar to *R. laciniata* but shorter. More widely grown than the species is 'Herbstsonne' ('Autumn Sun'), a 4–6-ft. plant bearing single yellow flower heads with a bright green central disc.

R. purpurea. See Echinacea purpurea

RUE. See RUTA graveolens

RUE ANENOME. See ANEMONELLA thalictroides

RUELLIA

Acanthaceae

EVERGREEN SHRUBS AND PERENNIALS

⚡ ZONES VARY BY SPECIES

☼ ◐ FULL SUN OR LIGHT SHADE

💧 REGULAR WATER

Ruellia brittoniana

Ruellias have opposite leaves and flaring bell-shaped flowers with five shallow lobes. They are grown outdoors in mild climates or cultivated in greenhouses.

R. 'Blue Shade'. Perennial. Zones 8, 9, 14–30. Low-growing plant (rarely more than 10 in. high) popular in Central Texas as a ground cover for light shade. Narrow, pointed-oval, olive green leaves; lavender blue flowers. Spreads fairly slowly.

R. brittoniana. Shrubby perennial. Zones 8, 9, 14–30. Mexican native naturalized in parts of the U.S. To 3 ft. high, with narrow leaves and 2-in. blue flowers. Should be contained (by an edging, for example), since it can be invasive. 'Katie' is a dwarf (10–12-in.) herbaceous variety.

R. macrantha. Evergreen shrub. Zones 21–27. Native to Brazil. To 3 ft. high, with paired dark green, 4-in., oval leaves and clusters of 3–4-in. rose pink flowers with deeper pink veining. Best as a container plant to be sheltered during frosty weather.

RUMOHRA adiantiformis

LEATHERLEAF FERN

Polypodiaceae

FERN

⚡ ZONES 14–17, 19–27

☼ ◐ FULL SUN OR PARTIAL SHADE

💧 REGULAR WATER

Rumohra adiantiformis

Fronds are deep glossy green, triangular, finely cut, to 3 ft. tall. They are firm in texture and last well in arrangements. Hardy to 24°F/–4°C. Usually sold as *Aspidium capense*.

RUPTURE WORT. See HERNIARIA glabra

RUSCUS

BUTCHER'S BROOM

Liliaceae

EVERGREEN SHRUBLETS

⚡ ZONES 4–24, 28, 31, 32

◐ ● BEST IN SHADE; TOLERATE SOME SUN

💧💧 REGULAR TO LITTLE WATER

Ruscus hypoglossum

Unusual leafless plants with some value as small-scale ground cover, curiosity, or source of dry arrangement material and Christmas greens. Not usually sold by nurseries, but rather passed around by gardeners. Flattened leaflike branches do work of leaves and bear tiny greenish white flowers in center of upper surfaces. If male and female plants are present, or if you have plant with male and female flowers, bright red (sometimes yellow), marble-size fruit follows the flowers. Plants spread by underground stems. Subject to chlorosis.

R. aculeatus. To 1–4 ft. tall, with branched stems. Spine-tipped "leaves" are 1–3 in. long, a third as wide, leathery, dull dark green. Fruit ½ in. across, red or yellow.

R. hypoglossum. To 1½ ft.; unbranched stems. "Leaves" to 4 in. long, 1½ in. wide, glossy green, not spine tipped. Fruit ¼–½ in. across. Spreads faster than *R. aculeatus*. A good small-scale ground cover.

RUSSELIA equisetiformis

CORAL FOUNTAIN

Scrophulariaceae

PERENNIAL

⚡ ZONES 19–27; OR INDOORS

☼ ◐ FULL SUN OR PARTIAL SHADE

💧 KEEP SOIL MOIST

Russelia equisetiformis

Hardy to about 32°F/0°C. Shrubby plant with trailing, bright green, practically leafless stems that look attractive spilling from a wall or hanging basket; stems can also be fastened to a trellis or wall. Many side branches bear a profusion of bright red, narrowly tubular flowers that look like little firecrackers; bloom lasts all spring and summer outdoors, goes on continuously in house or greenhouse. Give filtered light indoors. Needs regular fertilizing. Easy to propagate with pencil-size cuttings taken in spring.

RUSSIAN OLIVE. See ELAEAGNUS angustifolia

RUSSIAN SAGE. See PEROVSKIA

RUTABAGA. See TURNIP and RUTABAGA

Rutaceae. Besides rue *(Ruta)*, the rue family includes many perennials, shrubs, and trees, most important of which are the citrus clan. Most members have oil glands in leaves or other parts and are aromatic. Mexican orange *(Choisya)* and *Skimmia* are other notable members.

RUTA graveolens

RUE, HERB-OF-GRACE

Rutaceae

PERENNIAL HERB

⚡ ZONES 2–24, 30–41

☼ FULL SUN

💧💧 REGULAR TO MODERATE WATER

Ruta graveolens

To 2–3 ft., with aromatic, fernlike blue-green leaves. Small, greenish yellow flowers are followed by decorative brown seed capsules. Sow seeds in flats; transplant to 1 ft. apart. Needs good garden soil; add lime to strongly acid soil. Cut back in early spring to encourage bushiness. Seed clusters can be dried for use in wreaths or swags. 'Blue Beauty' and 'Jackman's Blue' are dense, compact varieties with fine blue-gray color. 'Blue Mound' and 'Curly Girl' are even more compact.

Rue owes its status as an herb to history and legend rather than to any medicinal or culinary use. It was once thought to ward off disease, guard against poisons, and aid eyesight. It was also used to make brushes for sprinkling holy water. Sap causes dermatitis in some people.

RYEGRASS. See LOLIUM

FOR INFORMATION ON YOUR CLIMATE ZONE

PLEASE SEE PAGES 16–78

R

SABAL

PALMETTO

Arecaceae (Palmae)

PALMS

⚡ ZONES VARY BY SPECIES

☀️ ◐ FULL SUN OR PARTIAL SHADE

🌢 MODERATE WATER

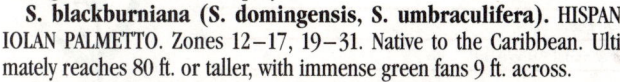

Sabal palmetto

Large, slow-growing, cold-hardy fan palms, some with trunks, some without. When plants are mature, large clusters of tiny flowers appear among leaves. Tolerate salt spray.

S. blackburniana (S. domingensis, S. umbraculifera). HISPAN-IOLAN PALMETTO. Zones 12–17, 19–31. Native to the Caribbean. Ultimately reaches 80 ft. or taller, with immense green fans 9 ft. across.

S. mexicana (S. texana). OAXACA PALMETTO. Zones 10, 12–17, 19–31. Native from Texas to Guatemala. Leaf stems hang on trunk in early life, then drop to show attractive, slender trunk. Grows 30–50 ft. high.

S. minor. Zones 10, 12–17, 19–31. Native to southeastern U.S. Leafy green palm; usually trunkless, but sometimes has trunk to 6 ft. tall. Old leaves fold at base, hang down like closed umbrellas.

S. palmetto. CABBAGE PALM. Zones 12–17, 19–31. Native from North Carolina to Florida. Grows slowly to an eventual 90 ft., with 5–8-ft. leaves that form a dense, globular head.

SAFFLOWER. See CARTHAMUS tinctorius

SAFFRON, MEADOW. See COLCHICUM

SAGE. See SALVIA

SAGE, RUSSIAN. See PEROVSKIA

SAGINA subulata

IRISH MOSS, SCOTCH MOSS

Caryophyllaceae

PERENNIAL

⚡ ZONES 1–11, 14–24, 32–43

☀️ ◐ FULL SUN OR PARTIAL SHADE

🌢 REGULAR WATER

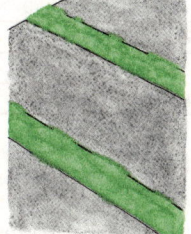

Sagina subulata

Of two different plants of similar appearance, *Sagina subulata* is the more common. The other is *Arenaria verna,* usually called *A. v. caespitosa.* Both make dense, compact, mosslike masses of slender leaves on slender stems. But *A. verna* has tiny white flowers in few-flowered clusters, while *S. subulata* bears flowers singly and differs in other technical details. In common usage, however, green forms of the two are called Irish moss, while golden green forms (*A. v.* 'Aurea' and *S. s.* 'Aurea') are called Scotch moss.

Both *Sagina* and *Arenaria* are grown primarily as ground covers for limited areas. They're useful for filling gaps between paving blocks. In cool-summer gardens, they can self-sow and become pests.

Although they look like moss, these plants won't grow well under conditions that suit true mosses. They need good soil, good drainage, and occasional feeding with slow-acting, nonburning fertilizer. They take some foot traffic and tend to hump up in time; control humping by occasionally cutting out narrow strips, then pressing or rolling lightly. Control slugs, snails, cutworms. Cut squares from flats and set 6 in. apart for fast cover. To avoid lumpiness, plant so that soil line of squares is at or slightly below the surface.

SAGO PALM. See CYCAS revoluta

ST. AUGUSTINE GRASS. See STENOTAPHRUM secundatum

ST. CATHERINE'S LACE. See ERIOGONUM giganteum

ST. JOHNSWORT. See HYPERICUM

SAINTPAULIA ionantha

AFRICAN VIOLET

Gesneriaceae

EVERGREEN PERENNIAL HOUSE PLANT

◐ ● FILTERED EARLY SUN, BRIGHT INDIRECT LIGHT

🌢 WATERING IS AN ART; SEE BELOW

Saintpaulia ionantha

Extremely popular house plant. Fuzzy, heart-shaped leaves with smooth edges grow in rosettes to 1 ft. wide. Pale lavender flowers grow in clusters of three or more. Hybrids and named varieties have leaves that are plain or scalloped, green or variegated; flowers are purple, violet, pink, white, or bicolored. Keep where temperatures average 60° to 70°F/16° to 21°C. Humidity should be high; if house air is quite dry, increase humidity around plants by setting each plant on a saucer filled with wet gravel.

African violets need a moisture-retentive yet fast-draining potting mix. You can buy packaged mixes composed specifically for African violets; if you prefer to concoct your own, use 3 parts peat moss to 1 part perlite and 1 part compost or sterilized loam. Don't use too large a pot; plants bloom best when roots are crowded.

Water plants from top or below, but avoid watering crown or leaves. Wick-irrigated pots work well. Use water at room temperature or slightly warmer, wet soil thoroughly, let potting mixture become dry to the touch before watering again. Don't let water stand in pot saucers for more than 2 hours after watering plants. If plant is well established, feed—only when soil is moist—with slightly acid fertilizer once every 2 to 4 weeks. Propagate from seeds, leaf cuttings, or divisions. Most common pests are aphids, cyclamen mites, thrips, and mealybugs. Keep spent leaves and flowers plucked off.

SALAL. See GAULTHERIA shallon

Salicaceae. The willow family consists of deciduous trees or shrubs with flowers in catkins and (generally) with silk-tufted seeds that blow about. Besides willow *(Salix),* examples are cottonwood and poplar *(Populus).*

SALIX

WILLOW

Salicaceae

DECIDUOUS SHRUBS OR TREES

⚡ ZONES VARY BY SPECIES

☀️ FULL SUN

🌢 LOTS OF WATER

Salix babylonica

Fast-growing, somewhat weak-wooded trees. Take any soil; most even tolerate poor drainage. All have shallow, invasive roots and are hard to garden under. Most are subject to borers, blights, cankers, and other problems. Weeping willows are best used as single trees near stream or lake, although they can, with training, become satisfactory shade trees for patio or terrace. They leaf out very early in spring and hold leaves late. Shrubby willows are grown mainly for catkins ("pussy willows") or colored twigs, as screen plants, or for erosion control on banks of streams and rivers. For this last purpose, types native to the region are best. The many willow species hybridize readily; as a result, names are much confused in the nursery trade. ▶

S

S. alba. WHITE WILLOW. Tree. Zones 1–24, 30–45. Upright growth to 75–100 ft. Yellowish brown bark. Narrow, 1½–4-in.-long leaves are bright green on top, silvery beneath; may turn golden yellow in fall. The following forms are valued for colorful twigs:

'Britzensis' ('Chermesina'). Young twigs turn radiant orange red in winter. For best display, cut back clump to about a foot high just before spring growth begins. Stems will grow as much as 8 ft. in a single season.

S. a. tristis (*S. babylonica aurea, S.* 'Niobe'). GOLDEN WEEPING WILLOW. Pendulous habit. To 80 ft. high; wider than tall. Young stems are bright yellow. Among the most attractive weeping willows.

S. a. vitellina. Brilliant yellow winter twigs. Cut back heavily, as for 'Britzensis'.

S. babylonica. WEEPING WILLOW. Tree. Zones 3–24, 26 (northern part), 28, 30–34, 39. To 30–50 ft., with equal or greater spread. Smaller than *S. alba tristis,* with longer (3–6-in.) leaves and even more pronounced weeping habit. Greenish or brown branchlets. 'Crispa' ('Annularis'), ringleaf or corkscrew willow, has leaves twisted and curled into rings or circles; it is a somewhat narrower tree than the species.

S. blanda. WISCONSIN WEEPING WILLOW. Tree. Zones 2–24, 30–41. To 40–50 ft. or more, spreading wider. Hybrid of *S. babylonica* but less strongly weeping, with broader leaves of a more bluish green color. 'Fan', fan giant blue weeping willow, is resistant to borers and blight.

S. caprea. FRENCH PUSSY WILLOW, PINK PUSSY WILLOW. Shrub or small tree. Zones 2–24, 30–41. To 25 ft. tall. Broad leaves 3–6 in. long, dark green above, gray and hairy beneath. Male plants produce fat, woolly pinkish gray catkins about 1 in. long in early spring before leaf-out. Can be kept to shrub size by cutting to ground every few years. 'Pendula', Kilmarnock willow, forms a trailing mound suitable for ground cover; it can also be grafted onto an upright trunk and used as a small weeping tree. 'Weeping Sally' is the female form.

S. discolor. PUSSY WILLOW. Shrub or small tree. Zones 1–24, 30–45. To 20 ft. tall. Slender stems are red brown; 2–4-in. leaves are bright green above, bluish beneath. Catkins of male plants (usually only kind sold) are the feature attraction—soft, silky, pearl gray, to 1½ in. long.

S. 'Flame'. Shrub or small tree. Zones 2–24, 30–41. Hybrid to 15–20 ft. high, with compact, dense habit. Branch tips curl upward and inward. Foliage turns a good golden yellow rather late in autumn. Spectacular orange-red bark in winter.

S. 'Golden Curls'. Shrub or small tree. Zones 3–24, 30–34, 39. Hybrid between *S. matsudana* 'Tortuosa' and *S. alba tristis.* To 30 ft. tall, with somewhat weeping and twisting branches, somewhat curled leaves, and bright yellow bark on new growth. After establishing a framework, cut back hard in winter to keep colorful new growth coming on.

S. gracilistyla. ROSE-GOLD PUSSY WILLOW. Upright, spreading shrub. Zones 3–24, 30–34, 39. To 6–10 ft. tall. Narrowly ovate, 2–4-in.-long leaves are gray green above, bluish green beneath. Male plants produce plump, 1½-in.-long, furry gray catkins with numerous stamens with rose-and-gold anthers. Cutting branches for arrangements will curb plant's size. Every 3 or 4 years, cut back whole plant to short stubs; you'll be rewarded by especially vigorous shoots with large catkins. *S. g. melanostachys* has black catkins with red anthers.

S. matsudana. HANKOW WILLOW. Tree. Zones 3–24, 30–34, 39. Upright, pyramidal growth to 40–50 ft. Narrow, bright green, 2–4-in.-long leaves. Can thrive on less water than most willows. 'Navajo', globe Navajo willow, is a large, spreading, round-topped tree to 70 ft. tall. 'Tortuosa', dragon-claw willow, grows 30 ft. tall and 20 ft. wide, has branches fantastically twisted into upright, spiraling patterns; it is valued for winter silhouette and for cut branches for arrangements. 'Umbraculifera', globe willow, reaches 35 ft. high and has an umbrella-shaped top with upright branches, drooping branchlets.

S. purpurea. PURPLE OSIER, ALASKA BLUE WILLOW. Shrub. Zones 1–11, 34–43. To 10–18 ft. high, with purple branches and narrow, 1–3-in. leaves that are dark green above, markedly bluish beneath. 'Gracilis' ('Nana'), dwarf purple osier, has slimmer branches and narrower leaves; it is usually grown as clipped hedge and kept 1–3 ft. high and wide.

S. 'Scarlet Curls'. Shrub or small tree. Zones 3–24, 30–34, 39. Resembles 'Golden Curls', but bark on new growth is red.

S. udensis 'Sekka' (*S. sachalinensis* 'Sekka'). JAPANESE FANTAIL WILLOW. Shrub or small tree. Zones 2–24, 30–41. Wide-spreading male plant to 10–15 ft. high. Narrow leaves are 2–4 in. long, green above, silvery beneath. Silvery catkins to 2 in. long. Main feature is the branch structure: branches are flattened, often 1–2 in. wide, twisted and curled, picturesque in arrangements.

SALPIGLOSSIS sinuata

Salpiglossis sinuata

PAINTED TONGUE
Solanaceae
ANNUAL
☀ ALL ZONES
☼ FULL SUN
🔴 REGULAR WATER

Upright, open habit, to 2–3 ft. tall. Sticky leaves and stems. Leaves to 4 in. long, narrowly oblong. Flowers much like petunias in shape and size (2–2½ in. wide), but more unusual in color—shades of mahogany red, reddish orange, yellow, purple and pink tones, marbled and penciled with contrasting color. Bolero (2 ft.), Friendship (15 in.), and Splash (2 ft.) are compact strains.

Provide rich, well-drained soil. Stake tall types. Pinch out tips of growing plants to induce branching. Best bloom in late spring and early summer, but regular deadheading will keep flowers coming until frost in cool-summer climates. Good background plant for border; handsome cut flower.

SALSIFY

Salsify

OYSTER PLANT
Asteraceae (Compositae)
BIENNIAL OFTEN GROWN AS AN ANNUAL
☀ ALL ZONES
☼ FULL SUN
🔴 REGULAR WATER

Grown for its edible root, which looks something like parsnip and has creamy white flesh that tastes a little like oysters. Plant grows to 4 ft. tall; leaves are narrow, grasslike. Plant in rich, deep, sandy soil, spaded deep. Culture is same as for parsnips. It takes 150 days to grow to maturity. Cooked, mashed salsify, mixed with butter and beaten egg, can be made into patties and sautéed until brown to make mock oysters. If plant is allowed to overwinter in mild climates, it will produce flower stalk topped by large head of lavender purple, dandelionlike flowers followed by white, cottony seeds.

SALT BUSH. See BACCHARIS halimifolia

SALVIA

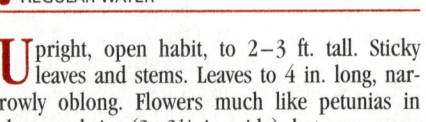
Salvia officinalis

SAGE
Lamiaceae (Labiatae)
ANNUALS, BIENNIALS, PERENNIALS, SHRUBS
☀ ZONES VARY BY SPECIES
☼ FULL SUN, EXCEPT AS NOTED
🔴 REGULAR WATER, EXCEPT AS NOTED
▶ SEE CHART

The sages, along with the ornamental grasses, became horticultural stars in the 1980s and 1990s. Botanical gardens and collectors have

▶ page 487

SALVIA

NAME, TYPE	ZONES	GROWTH HABIT	FLOWERS	COMMENTS
Salvia argentea SILVER SAGE Biennial	1–24, 26, 28–45	Flat 1-ft. rosette of white, furry, 6–8-in.-long leaves	Branched flowering stems to 4 ft.; white summer flowers, tinged pink or yellow	Use at front of border for striking foliage. Grow as an annual in colder climates
S. azurea grandiflora **(S. pitcheri)** Perennial	2–11, 14–24, 26 (northern part), 27–43	To 5 ft., with smooth or hairy, 2–4-in. leaves	Gentian blue, 1/2-in.-long blooms provide mass of color, summer–frost	Tolerant of heat, humidity. Not always permanent in wet winters
S. blepharophylla Shrubby perennial	14–24, 27–29	Mounding, spreading by underground stems, to 1 1/2 ft. tall	Brilliant red, nearly everblooming	Provides midheight mass of color over a long period
S. cacaliifolia Perennial	14–24, 27–29	Sprawling, to 3 ft. tall and much wider	Branching narrow clusters of pure blue, spring–fall	Appreciates some shade
S. chamaedryoides Perennial	8, 9, 14–24, 27–31	Low, mounding, spreading by underground runners	Silvery foliage a backdrop for bright blue summer flowers	Needs excellent drainage; endures some aridity
S. clevelandii Shrub	7–9, 14–24	Rounded shrub to 4 ft. Gray-green foliage has marvelous fragrance	Fragrant lavender blue flowers in tall, open spires, late spring, summer	Takes aridity. Look for choice compact named selections such as 'Allen Chickering' and 'Winifred Gillman'
S. coccinea Perennial, but usually a self-seeding annual	14–24, 26–30	Bushy, to 2–3 ft., with dark green furry leaves	Flowers red, in 4-in. spikes, spring–fall	'Brenthurst' is a pink form. 'Lady in Red' is a shorter selection good for foreground planting
S. elegans PINEAPPLE SAGE Perennial	8–24, 26–30	To 2–3 ft.; light green leaves have fruity scent and taste	Red flowers in short spikes, autumn	Use leaves in cool drinks, fruit salads
S. farinacea MEALY-CUP SAGE Perennial grown as annual	1–24, 26–45	Fast growth to 2–3 ft., grayish green leaves	Spikes of small blue flowers rise above foliage mound in summer	Plants are perennial where winter temperature remains above 10°F/–12°C. 'Mina' (1 ft.) and 'Victoria' (1 1/2 ft.) are dwarfs
S. greggii AUTUMN SAGE Shrub	8–24, 26–31	Erect, bushy, to 3–4 ft., with small medium green leaves	Forms with flowers in yellow, red shades, purple; spring–fall	Needs excellent drainage; drought tolerant. Light shade in hot climates
S. guaranitica Shrubby perennial	8, 9, 14–24, 26–31, warmer parts of 32	Bushy, spreading, to 5 ft., with dark green, 5-in. leaves	Dark blue, 2-in. flowers in 10-in. spikes, summer–fall	Lush plant likes some shade. 'Argentina Skies' has pale blue flowers. Grow as an annual in colder climates
S. involucrata Shrubby perennial	8–24, 27–30	Large plant (6 by 6 ft.), with dense foliage of velvety leaves	Foot-long clusters of rose pink flowers in late summer, fall	For large gardens. Light to dense shade. Annual in colder climates
S. leucantha MEXICAN BUSH SAGE Shrub	10–24, 26–31	To 3–4 ft., with graceful arching stems, grayish green foliage	Long velvety purple spikes set with small white flowers arch outward in summer, fall	Takes some aridity, sun or light shade. Cut old stems to the ground. All-purple and pink forms exist. Annual in colder climates
S. leucophylla PURPLE SAGE Shrub	8, 9, 14–17, 19–24	Erect or spreading shrub to 3–4 ft., much wider, with white, woolly leaves	Pink summer flowers in long, open clusters	Very drought tolerant. Use as bank cover. Selected forms are 'Point Sal' and 'Figueroa'
S. microphylla **(S. grahamii)** Shrub	8, 9, 14–24, 27–30	Somewhat open, rounded shrub to 3–5 ft.	Bright red flowers in 4–6-in. clusters, fall; bloom can be continuous in mild climates	Hybridizes freely with *S. greggii*
S. muelleri Shrub	8, 9, 14–24, 27–30	Resembles *S. greggii*, but lower, with narrow leaves	Short clusters of purple flowers spring–fall; almost everblooming in mild areas	Use in perennial borders
S. nemorosa Perennial	2–11, 14–24, 30–41	Narrow, erect plant to 3 ft., with narrow, 4-in., roughish leaves	Violet blue flowers in narrow spikes above foliage, summer–fall	Species rarely seen. 'East Friesland', 2 1/2 ft., is widely sold. Pink 'Rose Queen' is lower, not so vigorous. See also *S. superba*

SALVIA

NAME, TYPE	ZONES	GROWTH HABIT	FLOWERS	COMMENTS
S. officinalis COMMON SAGE Perennial	2–24, 26, 28–41	To 2½ ft., with aromatic, wrinkled gray-green leaves	Lavender blue flowers in short spikes above the foliage, summer	All varieties good for seasoning. 'Berggarten', nonflowering, has biggest leaves, is longest lived (but least pungent). Colored varieties are 'Icterina', yellow and green leaves; 'Purpurascens', purplish tints; and 'Tricolor', gray, white, and purplish pink. 'Nana' is a dwarf
S. patens GENTIAN SAGE Perennial	14–24, 27–29	To 2–3 ft., compact, with large, long-stalked leaves	Flowers 2 in. long, pure blue, in clusters to 16 in. long; summer, fall	Needs warm, well-drained site. Grow as an annual in colder climates. Fertilize for repeat bloom
S. pratensis MEADOW SAGE Perennial	2–11, 14–24, 30–41	To 3 ft., with large (6-in.), rough basal leaves	Spikes of lavender blue flowers on branching stems, spring	'Haematodes' is most commonly grown form. Makes a great show, but bloom period is short. Reseeds. Needs warm, well-drained site. Grow as an annual in colder climates
S. recognita Perennial	7–24, 29, 30	Gray-green leaves to 5 in. long; low foliage mass	Flowers pink, atop 2½–3-ft. stalks, spring	Showy plant for front of border
S. regla Shrub	14–24, 27–29	To 5 ft., possibly more, with bright green leaves	Flowers downy, 2 in. long, bright red or orange red, with persistent orange calyx, spring through fall	'Huntington' grows 4–5 ft. tall, 'Royal' 6–8 ft. tall
S. roemeriana Perennial	8–24, 27–30	Dense clump with soft, 1-in. leaves	Flowers scarlet, in loose clusters on branching 1-ft. stalks, spring–fall	Sun or part shade. Needs moderate water
S. sclarea CLARY Perennial or biennial	2–24, 27–41	Rough, gray-green, highly aromatic leaves to 8 in. long	Flowers white to lilac in big branching clusters to 3 ft., spring–summer	'Turkestanica' has pink flower stalks, white-and-pink flowers. Species and variety can be grown as annuals in all zones
S. sinaloensis Perennial	16, 17, 21–24, 27, 28	Low, spreading, 6–12 in. tall, with purplish tone	Flowers deep blue in short spikes, summer	Rock garden plant. Appreciates part shade
S. sonomensis Shrubby perennial	7, 14–24	Sprawling, mat-forming plant to 16 in. tall, much wider, with hairy leaves	Flowers lilac to blue in erect clusters, spring	Ground cover for hot, dry banks. Hard to maintain. 'Dara's Choice' is easier
S. splendens SCARLET SAGE Perennial usually grown as annual	All zones	Branched plant 1–3 ft. tall, depending on strain or variety, with bright green foliage	Flowers scarlet, in tall, dense clusters; also available in pink, purple, white, in tall or dwarf strains. Summer	Grow from seed or buy young plants from nurseries. Effective with gray-foliaged plants
S. superba Perennial	2–10, 14–24, 31–41	Erect, branched, 2–3-ft. plants with narrow leaves; narrow, erect flower spikes top each stalk	Flowers violet blue or purple, summer–fall	Closely related to *S. nemorosa*. Plants often sold under either name are 'Blue Hill', dark blue, tall, nearly everblooming; 'Lubeca', tall, early flowering, deep violet; 'May Night', low growing, with deep blue flowers; 'East Friesland' and 'Rose Queen' (see under *S. nemorosa*)
S. uliginosa Perennial	6–9, 14–24, 27–31, warmer parts of 32	Clumping plant with erect stems 6–7 ft. tall, with narrow, bright green, highly aromatic leaves	Flowers pale blue and white in erect, branched clusters to 5 in. long, summer–fall	Plant spreads by rhizomes to make big clumps. Divide from time to time. Much or little water. Provide winter protection
S. verticillata LILAC SAGE Perennial	2–11, 14–24, 30–41	Clumps 1½–2 ft. tall, composed of broad, hairy, heart-shaped leaves	Branched flower stalks to 2½ ft. carrying purple-blue flowers appear in summer (spring–fall in mild-winter areas)	Sun or light shade. 'Purple Rain' is a superior form with long, arching spikes of purple flowers
S. viridis (**S. horminum**) Annual	All zones	Single stemmed or branched plants to 1½ ft. tall	Flowers insignificant, but leaflike bracts in pink, white, or blue are showy in summer. Long-lasting cut flowers, fresh or dried	Claryssa is a superior selection

S

introduced scores of new species and selections from Mexico, South America, Eurasia, and Africa, along with superior forms of our native species. Some are annual bedding plants, others are border perennials, and still others serve as shrubs or ground covers. Where available as nursery plants, many of the tender perennials and shrubs are sometimes grown as annuals in cold-winter climates.

Flower colors range from white and yellow through pink to scarlet, and from pale lavender to true blue and dark purple. What they have in common is a floral arrangement in which whorls of two-lipped flowers are either distinctly spaced along the flower stalks or so tightly crowded they look like one dense spike. Inflorescences in some species are branched. Many salvias are aromatic, some strongly so; some are sweet scented, while others, such as common sage *(S. officinalis)*, have a more savory fragrance.

At least 60 species and an additional 40 to 50 selections are grown. The chart on pages 485–486 lists many of the best.

SAMBUCUS

ELDERBERRY

Caprifoliaceae

DECIDUOUS SHRUBS OR TREES

🌡 ZONES VARY BY SPECIES

☼ ◐ FULL SUN OR LIGHT SHADE

💧 REGULAR WATER, EXCEPT AS NOTED

⬥ UNCOOKED FRUITS OF RED-BERRIED SPECIES CAN CAUSE NAUSEA, VOMITING, DIARRHEA IF INGESTED

Sambucus canadensis

In their natural state, these are rampant, fast-growing, wild-looking plants—but they can be tamed to a degree. Use them as you would spiraea or other large deciduous shrubs. In large gardens, they can be effective as a screen or windbreak. To keep them dense and shrubby, prune hard: in late dormant season, cut back all previous year's growth to a few inches. New growth sprouts readily from stumps.

Elders are a confusing lot, and botanists in different regions tend to assign different names to the same plant. There are black-, blue-, and red-fruited elders; birds eat the fruit of all types, but the fruit of red-berried species can cause nausea in humans if consumed raw in large quantities.

S. canadensis. AMERICAN ELDERBERRY. Zones 1–7, 14–17, 26, 28, 31–45. Native to central and eastern North America. Spreading, suckering shrub to 6–8 ft. high. Foliage is almost tropical looking; each leaf has seven 2–6-in.-long leaflets. Flat, creamy white flower clusters to 10 in. wide in early summer, followed by tasty purple-black fruit. Fruit used for pies; both flowers and fruit used for wine. Strictly fruiting varieties include 'Adams', 'Johns', and many more; plant any two for pollination. Ornamental varieties include 'Aurea', with golden green foliage (golden in full sun) and red berries; and 'Laciniata', cutleaf or fernleaf elder, with finely cut foliage and dark berries.

S. mexicana (S. caerulea, S. glauca). BLUE ELDERBERRY. Zones 1–10, 14–24. Native to western U.S. Shrub 4–10 ft. high or spreading tree to 50 ft. tall. Leaves divided into toothed, 1–6-in. leaflets; five to nine leaflets per leaf. Small white or creamy white flowers in flat-topped, 2–8-in.-wide clusters in spring, summer. Clustered blue to nearly black berries, usually covered with whitish powder, follow the flowers. Fruit often used in jams, jellies, pies, wine. Tolerates drought.

S. nigra. BLACK ELDER, EUROPEAN ELDER. Zones 3–7, 14–17, 32–34, 39. Native to Europe, Africa, Asia. Resembles *S. canadensis* but grows larger (tree to 20–30 ft.) and bears less flavorful berries (which are usually mixed with other fruits in jellies). Species is rarely seen, but smaller-growing (6–8-ft.) ornamental forms are available. 'Alba Variegata' has white berries, leaves edged in creamy white. Types bearing the standard

FOR GROWING SYMBOL EXPLANATIONS

PLEASE SEE PAGE 161

purple-black berries include 'Aurea', with yellow new growth; 'Laciniata', with finely divided, fernlike leaves; and 'Purpurea' *(S. n. porphyrifolia)*, with deep purple leaves and pinkish flowers.

S. pubens. SCARLET ELDER. Zones 1–6, 34–43. Native to northern latitudes in North America. Shrubby plant, usually 2–4 ft. high, possibly reaching 15 ft. Leaves divided into five or seven 2–4-in.-long leaflets. Blooms in late spring, with tall (to 5-in.), loose flower clusters; inedible bright red fruit follows the flowers.

S. racemosa. RED ELDERBERRY, EUROPEAN RED ELDERBERRY. Zones 1–6, 34–43. Native to northern latitudes in North America, Europe, Asia. Bushy shrub 8–10 ft. tall. Leaves divided into five or seven smooth, sharply toothed leaflets. Small, creamy white flowers in dome-shaped clusters to 2½ in. wide, late spring into summer; inedible bright red berries. 'Plumosa Aurea' has finely divided golden leaves.

SAND CHERRY. See PLUM and PRUNE, PRUNUS

SANDHILL SAGE. See ARTEMISIA pycnocephala

SAND PEAR. See PYRUS pyrifolia

SAND STRAWBERRY. See FRAGARIA chiloensis

SANGUINARIA canadensis

BLOODROOT

Papaveraceae

PERENNIAL

🌡 ZONES 1–6, 32–43

◐ ☼ PARTIAL OR FULL SHADE

💧💧 AMPLE WATER

Sanguinaria canadensis

A North American native, this member of the poppy family gets its common name from the orange-red juice that seeps from cut roots and stems. Big, deeply lobed grayish leaves. Blooms in spring, bearing lovely (but ephemeral) white or pink-tinged, 1½-in. flowers carried singly on 8-in. stalks. Plant dies back in mid- to late summer. For damp, shaded rock or woodland garden where it can spread. 'Multiplex' has double flowers.

SANGUISORBA

BURNET

Rosaceae

PERENNIALS

🌡 ZONES VARY BY SPECIES

☼ ◐ LIGHT SHADE IN HOT CLIMATES

💧 REGULAR WATER

Sanguisorba canadensis

Perennials that grow from creeping rhizomes. Leaves are divided featherwise into toothed roundish or oval leaflets. Flowers are small, carried in dense, feathery spikes resembling small bottlebrushes. Often sold as *Poterium*.

S. canadensis. GREAT BURNET, CANADIAN BURNET. Zones 1–6, 15–17, 31–45. Bright green, 3–6-ft.-tall clumps put up 8-in. spikes of white flowers in late autumn. Dies to ground even in mild climates.

S. minor. GARDEN BURNET, SALAD BURNET. Zones 1–10, 14–21, 26 (northern part), 28, 30–43. Can grow to 1½ ft. tall, with roundish red flower heads 1 in. long, but is usually kept clipped to a few inches to maintain a supply of fresh new leaves for culinary use. Leaves have a light cucumberlike flavor and are used in salads, soups, cool drinks. Can be used as an edging for border planting or herb garden. Evergreen in all but the coldest-winter regions. ▶

S

S. obtusa. Zones 2–6, 15–17, 31–41. To 4 ft. tall, with grayish green leaves and 4-in. pink flower spikes in summer. Evergreen in all but the coldest winters.

SANSEVIERIA trifasciata

BOWSTRING HEMP, SNAKE PLANT, MOTHER-IN-LAW'S TONGUE

Agavaceae

EVERGREEN PERENNIAL

ZONES 13, 23–25; OR INDOORS

SHELTER FROM MIDDAY SUN

MODERATE WATER

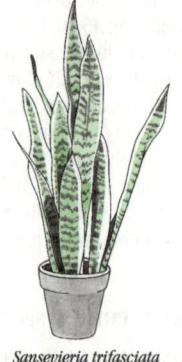

Sansevieria trifasciata 'Laurentii'

Grown outdoors all year in mildest-winter climates; indoor-outdoor or house plant anywhere. Often sold as *S. zeylandica*. Appreciated for thick, patterned leaves that grow in rosettes from thick rhizomes. Leaves to 4 ft. tall, 2 in. wide, rigidly upright or spreading slightly at top, dark green banded with gray green. 'Laurentii' is identical but has broad, creamy yellow stripes on leaf edges. Dwarf 'Hahnii' has rosettes of 6-in.-long, broad, triangular, dark green leaves with silvery banding; rosettes pile up to make a mass 1 ft. tall and wide. It's a good small potted plant or focus for dish garden.

First common name comes from use of tough leaf fibers as bowstrings; second comes from leaf banding or mottling, which resembles some snakeskins; third probably comes from toughness of leaves and plants' persistence under neglect. Erect, narrow clusters of greenish white, fragrant flowers seldom appear. Indoors, plants will grow in much or little light, seldom need repotting, and withstand considerable neglect—dry air, uneven temperatures, and light, capricious watering.

Other *Sansevieria* varieties and species are collectors' items; scores can be found in catalogs of succulent plant dealers.

SANTA BARBARA DAISY. See ERIGERON karvinskianus

SANTOLINA

Asteraceae (Compositae)

EVERGREEN SUBSHRUBS

ZONES 3–24, 27, 29, 30, 32–35, 39, EXCEPT AS NOTED

FULL SUN

REGULAR TO LITTLE WATER

Santolina chamaecyparissus

These have attractive foliage, a profusion of small, round, buttonlike flower heads in summer, and stout constitutions. Good as ground covers, bank covers, or low clipped hedges. Grow in any soil. All plants are aromatic if bruised and look best if kept low by pruning. Clip off spent flowers. Cut back to a few inches tall in early spring. May die to ground in coldest areas, but will come back from roots.

S. chamaecyparissus (C. incana). LAVENDER COTTON. Can reach 2 ft., but looks best clipped to 1 ft. or less. Brittle, woody stems are densely clothed with rough, finely divided, whitish gray leaves. Unclipped plants produce bright yellow flower heads. Set 3 ft. apart as ground cover, closer as edging for walks, borders, foreground plantings. Replace if woodiness takes over. 'Nana' is smaller than the species, to 1 ft. tall and 2–3 ft. wide. 'Lemon Queen', 2 ft. tall and wide, has lemon yellow flowers.

S. pinnata (S. ericoides). To 2–2½ ft. tall, with narrow, saw-edged dark green leaves and cream-colored flowers. *S. p. neapolitana*, 12–15 in. tall, has silvery foliage and bright yellow buttons.

S. rosmarinifolia (S. virens). Zones 4–24, 27, 29, 30, 32. To 2 ft., with narrow, green-and-silvery leaves like those of rosemary. Leaves may have tiny teeth or none at all. Bright yellow flowers.

SANVITALIA procumbens

CREEPING ZINNIA

Asteraceae (Compositae)

ANNUAL

ALL ZONES

FULL SUN

REGULAR TO MODERATE WATER

Sanvitalia procumbens

Not really a zinnia, but looks enough like one to fool most people. Grows only 4–6 in. high but spreads or trails to 1 ft. or more. Leaves are like miniature (to 2-in.-long) zinnia leaves. Flower heads nearly 1 in. wide, with dark purple-brown center and bright yellow or orange rays. Bloom lasts from midsummer until frost. Varieties are 'Mandarin Orange' and double-flowered 'Gold Braid'.

Needs good drainage. Resents transplanting, so sow seeds where plants will grow—as early as mid-March in mildest-winter climates, as late as May or even June where soil is slow to warm up. Heat resistant. Plant in hanging baskets or pots, or use as temporary filler in border, edging, or cover for slope or bank.

Sapindaceae. Members of the soapberry family are trees and shrubs with (usually) divided leaves, clustered small flowers (sometimes showy), and fruit that is berrylike, often showy. Some have edible fruit. Examples are carrotwood *(Cupaniopsis)*, hopbush *(Dodonaea)*, *Koelreuteria*, *Litchi*, and western soapberry *(Sapindus)*.

SAPINDUS drummondii

WESTERN SOAPBERRY

Sapindaceae

DECIDUOUS TREE

ZONES 7–10, 14, 18–21, 28–33, 35

FULL SUN

REGULAR TO MODERATE WATER

Sapindus drummondii

Native to south-central U.S. Attractive round-headed, spreading tree to 25–30 ft. tall, with 10–15-in. leaves divided into many 3-in. leaflets. Tiny yellowish white flowers in 8–10-in. clusters in early summer; these are followed by round, beadlike, ½-in. orange-yellow fruits that turn black in winter. Little grown in gardens, but useful for its tolerance of adverse conditions—poor, dry, stony soil, low-quality air, wind, occasional drought. Fruit drop and self-sown seedlings can be problems.

SAPIUM sebiferum

CHINESE TALLOW TREE

Euphorbiaceae

DECIDUOUS TREE

ZONES 8, 9, 12–16, 18–21, 26, 28–31

FULL SUN

REGULAR WATER

Sapium sebiferum

To 35 ft. tall and wide, with dense round or conical crown. Tends toward shrubbiness, multiple trunks, and suckering, but is easily trained to a single trunk. In colder areas, unripened branch tips freeze back each winter; new growth quickly covers damage, but may require thinning. Leafs out late in spring. Leaves are roundish, tapering to slender point, light green; fall color varies from yellow to brilliant red. Foliage is dense, but general effect is airy; leaves flutter in lightest breeze. Tiny yellowish flowers in spikes at branch tips develop into small, clustered, grayish white fruit with a waxy coating.

S

Grows in most soils but does somewhat better in mildly acid ones. In the southern U.S. coastal plain, conditions are so favorable that the tree is almost a weed. Prune only to correct shape. Stake young plants securely. Nice tree for lawn, street, patio, terrace; provides light to moderate shade. Good as a screen. Milky sap can be an irritant.

SHOP FOR SAPIUM FOR FLAMING COLORS

If a Chinese tallow tree grows in full sun and gets moderate autumn chill, its foliage can turn to brilliant, translucent neon red, plum purple, yellow-orange, or mixed colors. Select your tree while it is in fall color; some plants may show only an uninteresting purplish or yellow.

SAPONARIA

Caryophyllaceae

PERENNIALS

✿ ZONES VARY BY SPECIES

☼ FULL SUN

💧 REGULAR TO MODERATE WATER

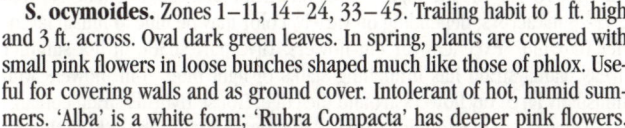

Saponaria ocymoides

Generally low growing; closely related to *Lychnis* and *Silene*. Easy to grow in well-drained soil. Useful as border or rock garden plants.

S. lembergii 'Max Frei'. Zones 3–6, 15–17, 32–34, 37. Hybrid between two Mediterranean species. Compact, trailing plant 6–15 in. tall, with blue-green foliage and a midsummer show of inch-wide, bright reddish pink flowers.

S. ocymoides. Zones 1–11, 14–24, 33–45. Trailing habit to 1 ft. high and 3 ft. across. Oval dark green leaves. In spring, plants are covered with small pink flowers in loose bunches shaped much like those of phlox. Useful for covering walls and as ground cover. Intolerant of hot, humid summers. 'Alba' is a white form; 'Rubra Compacta' has deeper pink flowers.

S. officinalis. SOAPWORT, BOUNCING BET. Zones 1–11, 14–24, 29–45. To 2 ft. tall, spreading by underground runners. Dark green leaves. Loose clusters of 1-in. red, pink, or white flowers in midsummer. If vigorously rubbed with water, plant produces suds. This is a tough plant; before the days of herbicides, it could be seen growing in the cinders along railroad rights-of-way. 'Rosea Plena', with double light pink flowers, is the common garden form. 'Rubra Plena' has crimson blooms that turn paler as they age.

S. pumilio (S. pumila). Zones 3–7, 14–17, 32–34, 37, 39. Forms a small, tight, bright green cushion to 1 ft. high, 2 ft. wide. Relatively large purplish pink flowers are borne singly on branch ends in spring, making a ring of blossoms around base of plant.

SAPPHIREBERRY. See SYMPLOCOS paniculata

SARCOCOCCA

SWEET BOX

Buxaceae

EVERGREEN SHRUBS

✿ ZONES VARY BY SPECIES

☼ ● PARTIAL OR FULL SHADE

💧 REGULAR TO MODERATE WATER

Sarcococca ruscifolia

Native to Himalayas, China. Grown for handsome, dark green, waxy foliage and for tiny, powerfully fragrant white flowers hidden in foliage in late winter or early spring. Small berrylike fruit. Useful in landscaping shaded areas—under overhangs, in entryways, beneath low-branching evergreen trees. They

---

maintain slow, orderly growth and polished appearance in deepest shade. Tolerate sun in cool-summer climates. Grow best in soil rich in organic matter; add peat moss, ground bark, or the like to planting bed. Scale insects are the only pests.

S. confusa. Zones 4–9, 14–24, 31. Similar to (and generally sold as) *S. ruscifolia*. However, latter has red fruit, while that of *S. confusa* is black.

S. hookerana humilis (S. humilis). Zones 3–9, 14–24, 31, 32. Low growing, seldom more than 1½ ft. high; spreads by underground runners to 8 ft. or more. Oval, pointed leaves (1–3 in. long, ½–¾ in. wide) are closely set on branches. Flowers are followed by glossy blue-black fruit. Good ground cover.

S. ruscifolia. Zones 4–9, 14–24, 31. Slow growth to 4–6 ft. high, 3–7 ft. wide. Will form natural espalier against wall, branches fanning out to create patterns. Leaves to 2 in. long, densely set on branches. Red fruit follows the flowers.

SARGENT CHERRY. See PRUNUS sargentii under PRUNUS, Flowering Cherry (chart)

SASA. See BAMBOO

SASSAFRAS albidum

SASSAFRAS

Lauraceae

DECIDUOUS TREE

✿ ZONES 3–9, 14–17, 28–41

☼ FULL SUN

💧 REGULAR WATER

Sassafras albidum

Native to eastern U.S. Grows rapidly to 20–25 ft. high, then more slowly to an eventual 50–60 ft. Often shrubby in youth; with age, becomes dense and pyramidal, with heavy trunk and rather short branches. Dark reddish brown, furrowed bark. Interesting winter silhouette. Leaves 3–7 in. long, 2–4 in. wide; they may be oval, mitten shaped, or lobed on both sides. Excellent fall color—shades of yellow, orange, scarlet, and purple. Yellow flowers aren't showy, but clusters outline the bare branches in early spring. Male and female flowers on separate trees; when the two sexes are grown near each other, the female tree bears dark blue, ½-in. berries on bright red stalks.

Pleasantly aromatic tree; bark of roots sometimes used for making tea, which has a flavor reminiscent of root beer. The tree's volatile oil, which contains safrole, is carcinogenic in animals; the bark is safrole-free.

Performs best in well-drained, nonalkaline soil; won't take prolonged drought. Hard to transplant. Tends to produce suckers, especially if roots are cut during cultivation. No serious pests or diseases.

SATUREJA

Lamiaceae (Labiatae)

ANNUALS AND PERENNIALS

✿ ZONES VARY BY SPECIES

☼ ◐ EXPOSURE NEEDS VARY BY SPECIES

💧 REGULAR TO MODERATE WATER

Satureja montana

Two of these aromatic plants serve many culinary purposes; the other has a long-standing reputation as a tonic.

S. douglasii (Micromeria chamissonis). YERBA BUENA. Perennial. Zones 4–9, 14–24. Native to the West Coast. To 6 in. high; slender stems root as they grow, spreading to 3 ft. Roundish, scallop-edged, 1-in.

S

leaves have strong minty scent; tea brewed from them was used as a tonic by early settlers. Small white or lavender-tinted flowers in spring, summer. Prefers part shade (tolerates full sun in cool climates). Use as a ground cover.

S. hortensis. SUMMER SAVORY. Annual. All zones. Upright to 1½ ft.; loose, open habit. Rather narrow, aromatic leaves to 1½ in. long; use fresh or dried as mild seasoning for meats, fish, eggs, soups, beans, vegetables. Whorls of tiny, delicate pinkish white to rose flowers appear in summer. Light, rich soil. Full sun. Good pot plant.

S. montana. WINTER SAVORY. Shrubby perennial. Zones 3–11, 14–24, 30–34, 39. Low, spreading, 6–15 in. high. Stiff, narrow to roundish leaves to 1 in. long; not as delicate in flavor as summer savory. Use leaves fresh or dried; clip at start of bloom season for drying. Profuse summer bloom; whorls of small white to lilac flowers, attractive to bees. Light, well-drained soil. Full sun. Use in rock garden, as dwarf clipped hedge in herb garden.

SAVORY. See SATUREJA

SAXIFRAGA

SAXIFRAGE

Saxifragaceae

PERENNIALS

⚡ ZONES VARY BY SPECIES

☼ ● EXPOSURE NEEDS VARY BY SPECIES

💧 REGULAR WATER

Saxifraga stolonifera

Some saxifrages are native to mountainous areas of North America; most are from Europe. They do best in rock gardens where summer heat and humidity are not intense. Require good drainage and light soil; rot easily in soggy soil. Most grow in full sun or light shade, but those listed here—all evergreen species—are shade plants.

S. rosacea (S. decipiens, S. sternbergii). Zones 3–7, 14–17, 32, 34. Cushion-forming, spreading plant—typical "mossy" type of saxifrage. Spreads fairly rapidly. Narrow, fleshy leaves are divided into three to five narrow lobes. In cold-winter climates, foliage turns crimson in late fall. In spring, flower stalks to 8–9 in. high display wide-open white flowers. Afternoon shade best in cool-summer areas; full shade essential where summers are hot. Many named varieties and hybrids exist, with flowers in pink, rose, and red. 'Carnival' has red flowers that fade to pink, then white.

S. stolonifera (S. sarmentosa). STRAWBERRY GERANIUM. Zones 4–9, 14–24, 29–32; house plant anywhere. Creeping plant that makes runners like strawberry. Nearly round, white-veined leaves to 4 in. across, pink underneath; blend well with pink azaleas. White flowers to 1 in. across, in loose, open clusters to 2 ft. tall, late summer–fall. Can be used as house plant in hanging baskets or pots; good ground cover where hard freezes are infrequent. Give bright indirect light indoors, partial or full shade outdoors.

S. umbrosa. Zones 3–7, 14–17, 32, 34. Rosettes of green, shiny, tongue-shaped leaves 1½ in. long. Blooms in spring, with open clusters of pink flowers on wine red stalks. Does best in full shade. Good ground cover for small areas; effective near rocks, stream beds. This species generally goes by the common name "London pride," but that name actually belongs to *S. urbium*, a hybrid between *S. umbrosa* and the similar *S. hirsuta*.

Saxifraga umbrosa

PRACTICAL GARDENING DICTIONARY

PLEASE SEE PAGES 545–616

Saxifragaceae. The saxifrage family once included a number of shrubs, but these now occupy their own families—Hydrangeaceae and Grossulariaceae (currants and gooseberries). Remaining in Saxifragaceae are a number of herbaceous plants, including *Astilbe, Bergenia,* coral bells *(Heuchera),* and of course saxifrage *(Saxifraga).*

SCABIOSA

PINCUSHION FLOWER

Dipsacaceae

ANNUALS AND PERENNIALS

⚡ ZONES VARY BY SPECIES

☼ FULL SUN

💧 REGULAR TO MODERATE WATER

Scabiosa caucasica

Stamens protrude beyond curved surface of flower head, giving illusion of pins stuck into a cushion. Bloom begins in midsummer, continues until frost if flowers are cut. Plants do not thrive in hot, humid climates, but they are easy to grow in cooler regions. Good in mixed or mass plantings. Excellent for arrangements.

S. anthemifolia. Perennial. Zones 15–24. Rounded, shrubby plants to 1½–2 ft. or more. Lavender blue or pink flowers, to 2 in. wide, stand well above the foliage clump.

S. atropurpurea. PINCUSHION FLOWER, MOURNING BRIDE. Annual in all zones; may persist as perennial where winters are mild. Usually sold as *S. grandiflora.* To 2½–3 ft. tall. Oblong, coarsely toothed leaves. Many long, wiry stems carry flowers to 2 in. wide or more, in colors ranging from blackish purple to salmon pink, rose, and white.

S. caucasica. PINCUSHION FLOWER. Perennial. Zones 1–10, 14–24, 32–43. To 1½–2½ ft. high. Leaves vary from finely cut to uncut. Flowers 2½–3 in. across; depending on variety, color may be blue to bluish lavender or white. Excellent for cut flowers. Give part shade in hot-summer areas. Fama strain has branching stalks of light blue, 3-in. flowers with unusually large ray flowers around the edge. House Hybrids strain contains a mixture of white and blue shades. 'Alba' is white flowered; 'Blue Perfection' bears lavender blue blooms with fringed petals.

S. columbaria. Perennial. Zones 4–24, 32–34. Better suited than *S. caucasica* to hot-summer, mild-winter areas of southwestern U.S. To 2 ft. tall. Finely cut gray-green leaves. Flowers to 3 in. across come in lavender blue, pink, or white, depending on the variety. 'Butterfly Blue' grows to 1 ft. high, bears 2-in. blooms. All types will bloom almost all year in the mildest-winter areas.

S. ochroleuca. Biennial or short-lived perennial. Zones 4–24, 32–34. To 2 ft. tall, with light yellow flowers to 2½ in. across.

S. stellata. Annual. All zones. To 1½ ft. tall. Many heads of pale blue, 1½-in. flowers; these quickly turn to papery bronze drumsticks, useful in dry arrangements.

SCADOXUS. See HAEMANTHUS katherinae

SCAEVOLA

Goodeniaceae

SHRUBBY PERENNIALS

⚡ ZONES 8, 9, 14–24; GROW AS ANNUALS IN COLDER CLIMATES

☼ FULL SUN

💧 REGULAR TO MODERATE WATER

Scaevola

Australian natives with fan-shaped flowers (all petals on one side) in blue shades. As evergreen perennials in mild climates, nearly everblooming. As annuals in colder regions, bloom late spring–frost. Good for hanging baskets, as ground covers, spilling over walls.

S. aemula. Fleshy-stemmed, sprawling plants used mainly in hanging baskets or to cascade over walls. Lavender blue, 1½-in. flowers produced along branches. Available mainly through varieties 'Blue Wonder' and 'Purple Fanfare' ('Diamond Head').

S. 'Mauve Clusters'. More wide spreading, smaller flowered than *S. aemula;* stems not as fleshy. Forms mats to 4–6 in. high, eventually 3–5 ft. across. Lilac mauve, ½-in.-wide flowers. Set plants 3 ft. apart for ground cover.

SCARLET BUSH. See HAMELIA patens

SCARLET LARKSPUR. See DELPHINIUM cardinale

SCARLET PLUME. See EUPHORBIA fulgens

SCHEFFLERA

Araliaceae

EVERGREEN SHRUBS OR SMALL TREES

⚡ ZONES VARY BY SPECIES; OR INDOORS

☼◑ LIGHT AFTERNOON SHADE IN HOT CLIMATES

🌢 REGULAR WATER

Schefflera actinophylla

Fast-growing, tropical-looking plants; long-stalked leaves divided into leaflets that spread like fingers of a hand. Summer bloom, showy in some species. All need rich, moisture-retentive, well-drained soil. Useful near swimming pools. Good container plants.

As house plants, give standard potting mix, occasional feeding, bright light but not direct sunlight. Let mix become dry between waterings. Wash leaves occasionally; mist plants to discourage mites. Unlikely to bloom indoors.

S. actinophylla (Brassaia actinophylla). QUEENSLAND UMBRELLA TREE, OCTOPUS TREE, SCHEFFLERA. Zones 21–25, 27; precariously hardy Zones 16–20, 26 with protection of overhang. As garden plant, grows fast to 20 ft. or more. "Umbrella" name comes from way giant leaves are held: horizontal tiers of long-stalked leaves are divided into 7–16 large (to 1-ft.-long) leaflets that radiate outward like ribs of umbrella. "Octopus" refers to showy arrangement of flowers in narrow, horizontally spreading clusters to 3 ft. long. Flowers age from greenish yellow to pink to dark red. Tiny dark purple fruit. Use for striking tropical effects, for silhouette, and for foliage contrast with ferns and other foliage plants. Cut out tips occasionally to keep plant from becoming leggy. Overgrown plant can be cut nearly to ground; it will branch and take better form.

S. arboricola (Heptapleurum arboricolum). HAWAIIAN ELF SCHEFFLERA. Zones 23–25. As outdoor plant can reach 20 ft. or more, with equal or greater spread, but easily pruned to smaller dimensions. Leaves dark green, much smaller than those of *S. actinophylla*, with 3-in. leaflets that broaden toward rounded tips. If stems are planted at angle, they continue to grow at that angle, which can give attractive multistemmed effects. Flowers yellowish aging to bronze, clustered in flattened spheres 1 ft. wide. Overall, gives a denser, darker, less treelike effect than *S. actinophylla*. Loves humidity.

Schefflera arboricola

S. elegantissima (Dizygotheca elegantissima). House plant in juvenile form, evergreen garden shrub as mature plant. Zones 16, 17, 22–25, 27. Leaves on juvenile plants are lacy looking, divided like fans into narrow (½-in.) leaflets with notched edges. Shiny dark green above, reddish beneath. As plants mature, leaflets grow to 1 ft. long, 3 in. wide.

S. pueckleri (Tupidanthus calyptratus). Zones 19–25, 27. To 20 ft., with single or multiple trunks. Leaves to 20 in. wide are divided fanwise into seven to nine glossy, bright green, stalked leaflets 7 in. long, 2½ in. wide. Resembles *S. actinophylla*, but branches from base and is denser in growth.

SCHINUS

PEPPER TREE

Anacardiaceae

EVERGREEN TREES

⚡ ZONES VARY BY SPECIES

☼ FULL SUN

🌢🌢 WATER NEEDS VARY BY SPECIES

◆ TOXICITIES ARE INVOLVED; SEE BELOW

Schinus terebinthifolius

Pepper trees are praised by some gardeners, heartily disliked by others. The two species discussed here are quite different from each other, though both are soil tolerant and leaves of both can cause dermatitis. Female trees bear fruit that attracts birds.

S. molle. CALIFORNIA PEPPER TREE. Zones 8, 9, 12–24, 28. Fast growth to 25–40 ft. tall and wide. Trunks of old trees are heavy and fantastically gnarled, with knots and burls that often sprout leaves or small branches. Heavy limbs; light, gracefully drooping branchlets. Bright green leaves divided into many narrow leaflets to 2 in. long. Drooping clusters of tiny yellowish white summer flowers are followed by rosy berries in fall, winter. Some gardeners object to messy litter, scale infestation, and greedy surface roots that make tree difficult to garden beneath. Handsome when used properly—planted away from paving, sewers, or drains and given room to spread. Can be killed by root rots, especially Texas root rot. Very drought tolerant.

S. terebinthifolius. BRAZILIAN PEPPER TREE, FLORIDA HOLLY. Zones 13, 14 (sheltered), 15–17, 19–27. Moderate growth to 30 ft. tall and wide; train to single or multiple trunks. Differs from *S. molle* in nonpendulous growth; in darker green, coarser, glossy leaves with 5–13 oval leaflets; and in very showy bright red berries around Christmas time. Much variation among trees. Select tree during fruiting season; look for the largest, showiest berries and best foliage. Dried berries are sold as pink peppercorns; eaten in quantity, they can cause gastric distress. Regular deep watering. Wood is subject to breakage, so shorten long, lanky limbs and thin canopy to let winds pass through. Prone to verticillium wilt. Self-sown seedlings are a problem in Florida. Attractive shade tree for patio or small garden.

SCHIZANTHUS pinnatus

POOR MAN'S ORCHID, BUTTERFLY FLOWER

Solanaceae

ANNUAL

⚡ BEST IN ZONES 1–6, 15–17, 21–24, 38, 39

☼ FILTERED SHADE

🌢 REGULAR WATER

Schizanthus pinnatus

Grows to 1½ ft. high. Great quantities of small orchidlike flowers, with varicolored markings on pink, rose, lilac, purple, or white background. Blossoms look quite showy against the plant's ferny foliage, make long-lasting cut flowers. Buy potted plants, or start seeds indoors about 4 weeks ahead of planting time (germination is slow). Sensitive to frost and heat. Plan for summer bloom where summer temperatures are moderate, for winter-spring bloom where summers are hot and winters normally frostless. Provide a wind-sheltered site. Good container plant. Often grown in greenhouses and conservatories.

S

SCHIZOPHRAGMA hydrangeoides

JAPANESE HYDRANGEA VINE

Hydrangeaceae

DECIDUOUS VINE

⚡ ZONES 4–9, 14–17, 31–34, 39

☼ PARTIAL SHADE

💧 REGULAR WATER

Schizophragma hydrangeoides

Resembles *Hydrangea anomala*, the climbing hydrangea. Climbs by holdfasts to 30 ft. Leaves are dark green, 3–5 in. long, oval, pointed, toothed. Broad clusters of flowers appear summer–fall; they resemble lace cap hydrangeas, but the showy white parts are the enlarged (to 1½-in.) sepals of the outermost flowers. In contrast to hydrangea, in which sterile flowers contain several showy sepals, sterile flowers of this plant have one sepal each. 'Moonlight' has blue-green foliage with a silvery cast. Use species or variety in shaded areas to climb masonry walls or trees.

SCHIZOSTYLIS coccinea

CRIMSON FLAG, KAFFIR LILY

Iridaceae

RHIZOMATOUS PERENNIAL

⚡ ZONES 5–9, 14–24, 26–29, 31; OR GROW IN POTS

☼ ◑ LIGHT SHADE IN HOT CLIMATES

💧💧 AMPLE WATER DURING ACTIVE GROWTH

Schizostylis coccinea

South African native hardy to 10°F/−12°C; in colder regions, grow in pots and protect in winter. Narrow, evergreen, 1½-ft.-long leaves resemble those of gladiolus. In autumn, slender 1½–2-ft. stems bear spikes of showy flowers—crimson, starlike, 2½ in. wide. Each blossom lasts 4 days, others follow; excellent cut flowers. Divide clumps when overgrown. Varieties include 'Alba', with white flowers; 'Mrs. Hegarty', pale pink; 'Oregon Sunset', watermelon red; 'Sunrise', bright pink; 'Viscountess Byng', soft pink. Water generously from spring through bloom; cut back on water at other times.

SCHLUMBERGERA

Cactaceae

CACTI

⚡ ZONES 16, 17, 21–27; OR INDOORS

☼ PARTIAL SHADE

💧 REGULAR WATER

Schlumbergera bridgesii

Schlumbergera truncata

In nature, these cacti live on trees like certain orchids. Plants are often confused in the nursery trade; many hybrids, selections differ principally in color. Remember, they come from the jungle—so give them rich, porous soil with plenty of leaf mold and sand. Feed frequently with liquid fertilizer, as often as every 7 to 10 days during growth and flowering. Give bright light indoors; if desired, set outdoors in partly shaded area in warm season.

S. bridgesii. CHRISTMAS CACTUS. Often sold as *Zygocactus truncatus* (which is actually an alternate name for *S. truncata*). Old favorite. Arching, drooping branches are made up of flattened, scallop-edged, smooth, bright green, spineless, 1½-in. joints. Grown right, plants may be 3 ft. across and may have hundreds of many-petaled, long-tubed, 3-in.-long, rosy purplish red flow-

ers at Christmas time. To ensure bud set for late December bloom, keep plant where it will receive cool night temperatures (50° to 55°F/10° to 13°C) and 12 to 14 hours of darkness per day during November.

S. gaertneri. See Rhipsalidopsis gaertneri

S. truncata (Zygocactus truncatus). CRAB CACTUS. Joints 1–2 in. long, sharply toothed, with two large teeth at end of last joint on each branch. Short-tubed scarlet flowers with spreading, pointed petals, fall and winter. Many varieties in white, pink, salmon, orange.

SCHOENOPLECTUS tabernaemontanus 'Zebrinus'

ZEBRA RUSH

Cyperaceae

GRASSLIKE PERENNIAL

⚡ ZONES 4–24, 28–32

☼ ◑ FULL SUN OR LIGHT SHADE

💧 AMPLE WATER

Schoenoplectus tabernaemontanus 'Zebrinus'

Zebra rush has simple, hollow, apparently leafless stems that are 2–4 ft. tall and banded horizontally with green and white. It will grow in several inches of water. Best used as a pool ornament. Stripes tend to fade late in season and in strong sun.

SCIADOPITYS verticillata

UMBRELLA PINE

Taxodiaceae

EVERGREEN TREE

⚡ ZONES 4–9, 14–24, 32–35, 37, 39

☼ ◑ AFTERNOON SHADE IN HOT CLIMATES

💧 REGULAR WATER

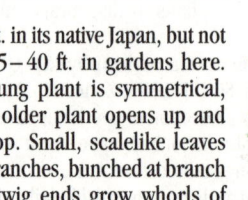

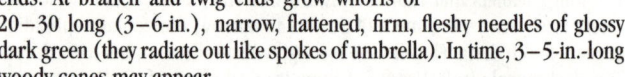

Sciadopitys verticillata

Grows to 100–120 ft. in its native Japan, but not likely to exceed 25–40 ft. in gardens here. Very slow grower. Young plant is symmetrical, dense, rather narrow; older plant opens up and branches tend to droop. Small, scalelike leaves grow scattered along branches, bunched at branch ends. At branch and twig ends grow whorls of 20–30 long (3–6-in.), narrow, flattened, firm, fleshy needles of glossy dark green (they radiate out like spokes of umbrella). In time, 3–5-in.-long woody cones may appear.

Choice decorative tree for open ground or container use. Plant in rich, well-drained, neutral or slightly acid soil. Leave unpruned, or thin to create Oriental effect. Good bonsai subject. Boughs are beautiful and long lasting in arrangements. These are trees for connoisseurs, scarce because of their extremely slow growth.

SCILLA

SQUILL, BLUEBELL

Liliaceae

BULBS

⚡ ZONES VARY BY SPECIES

☼ ◑ FULL SUN OR LIGHT SHADE

💧 REGULAR WATER DURING GROWTH AND BLOOM

⚠ ALL PARTS ARE POISONOUS IF INGESTED

Scilla siberica

All have basal, strap-shaped leaves and clusters of bell-shaped or starlike flowers in winter or spring. Best planted in informal drifts among shrubs, under deciduous trees, among low-growing spring perennials. Good in pots, for cutting. All but *S. peruviana* need some winter chill.

S

Plant cold-hardy species 2–3 in. deep, about 4 in. apart. All types are dormant in summer.

S. bifolia. Zones 2–11, 14–21, 30–41. First to bloom in early spring. Carries up to eight turquoise blue, inch-wide, starlike flowers on each 8-in. stem. There are white, pale purplish pink, and violet blue varieties. Each bulb produces only two leaves.

S. hispanica. See Endymion hispanicus

S. nonscripta. See Endymion non-scripta

S. peruviana. PERUVIAN SCILLA. Zones 14–17, 19–24, 26–29. Despite the name, a Mediterranean native. In late spring, clump of floppy leaves puts up foot-tall stems, each topped by a domed cluster of 50 or more purplish blue, starlike flowers. Bulbs go dormant only for a short time after leaves wither; replant then if necessary. Plant about 4 in. deep, 6 in. apart.

S. siberica. SIBERIAN SQUILL. Zones 1–7, 10, 33–45. Blooms very early, with loose spikes of intense blue flowers on 3–6-in. stems. 'Spring Beauty', with darker blue stripes, is choice. Also comes in white, purplish pink, and violet blue varieties.

S. tubergeniana (S. mischtschenkoana). Zones 1–11, 14–21, 29–43. Blooms in winter, at about same time as snowdrops and winter aconite. Flowers are pale blue with a darker blue stripe down center of each flower segment. Four or more flowers to each 4-in. stalk; three or more stalks to each bulb.

SCINDAPSUS pictus

Araceae

PERENNIAL VINE

INDOORS OR IN GREENHOUSE

☼ BRIGHT (BUT NOT STRONG) INDOOR LIGHT

🌢 REGULAR WATER; AVOID OVERWATERING

Scindapsus pictus

Resembles more familiar green-and-yellow pothos (*Epipremnum aureum*) in appearance, but the leaves are dark green mottled with gray green. Leaves are also thinner in texture and usually somewhat larger (to 6 in., compared with 2–4-in. leaves of pot-grown pothos). Flowers insignificant. 'Argyraeus' is most often grown; its markings are more prominent, larger, nearly silver, and leaves have a silky sheen. Fussier than pothos: needs perfect drainage, good atmospheric humidity, careful feeding, and light that is good but not too strong.

SCIRPUS cernuus (Isolepis gracilis)

FIBER OPTICS PLANT

Cyperaceae

GRASSLIKE PERENNIAL

✓ ZONES 7–28

☼ PARTIAL SHADE

🌢 AMPLE WATER

Scirpus cernuus

Grows to 6–10 in. high, usually less. Drooping, green, threadlike stems topped by small brown flower spikelets. Occasional division and resetting will keep it small. Ideal for edge of shallow pond; highly attractive for streamside effect in Japanese gardens. Good container plant.

SCOTCH BROOM. See CYTISUS scoparius

SCOTCH HEATHER. See CALLUNA vulgaris

SCOTCH MOSS. See SAGINA subulata

Scrophulariaceae. The figwort family consists principally of annuals and perennials. Most have irregular flowers, with four or five lobes often arranged as two lips. Some examples are snapdragon (*Antirrhinum*), *Calceolaria*, foxglove (*Digitalis*), *Nemesia*, beard tongue (*Penstemon*), and wishbone flower (*Torenia*).

SEA BUCKTHORN. See HIPPOPHAE rhamnoides

SEAFORTHIA elegans. See ARCHONTOPHOENIX cunninghamiana

SEA GRAPE. See COCCOLOBA

SEA HOLLY. See ERYNGIUM

SEA KALE. See CRAMBE maritima

SEA LAVENDER. See LIMONIUM

SEA PINK. See ARMERIA

SEASHORE PASPALUM. See PASPALUM vaginatum

SEA URCHIN. See HAKEA laurina

SEA URCHIN CACTUS. See ECHINOPSIS

SEDGE. See CAREX

SEDUM

STONECROP

Crassulaceae

SUCCULENT PERENNIALS

✓ ZONES VARY BY SPECIES

☼ ☼ FULL SUN OR LIGHT SHADE, EXCEPT AS NOTED

🌢 MODERATE TO LITTLE WATER, EXCEPT AS NOTED

Sedum rubrotinctum

They come from many parts of the world and vary in hardiness, cultural needs; some are among hardiest succulent plants. Some are tiny and trailing, others upright. Leaves fleshy, highly variable in size, shape, and color; evergreen unless otherwise noted. In cold climates, leaves of evergreen types may turn red. Flowers usually small, starlike, in fairly large clusters, sometimes brightly colored.

Smaller sedums are useful in rock gardens, as ground or bank cover, in small areas where unusual texture, color are needed. Some of the smaller types are prized by collectors of succulents, who grow them as potted or dish garden plants. Larger types good in borders or containers. Most propagate easily by stem cuttings—even detached leaves will root and form new plants. Soft and easily crushed, they will not take foot traffic; otherwise they are tough, low-maintenance plants. Set ground cover kinds 10–12 in. apart.

The botanically precise will note that several plants sold as *Sedum* have been reassigned to the genus *Hylotelephium*; changes are indicated below.

S. acre. GOLDMOSS SEDUM. Zones 1–24, 27–43. To 2–5 in. tall, with upright branchlets from trailing, rooting stems. Tiny light green leaves; clustered yellow flowers in spring. Extremely hardy but can get out of bounds, become a weed. Use as ground cover, between stepping-stones, or on dry walls.

S. album. Zones 1–24, 29–43. Often sold as *S. brevifolium*. Creeping plant 2–6 in. high. Leaves to ½ in. long, light to medium green, sometimes red tinted. White or pinkish summer flowers. Ground cover. Roots from smallest fragment, so beware of placing it near choice, delicate rock garden plants. 'Coral Carpet' has orange new growth, turns reddish bronze in winter.

S. anglicum. Zones 1–24, 29–43. Low, spreading plant 2–4 in. tall. Dark green leaves to ⅛ in. long. Pinkish white spring flowers. Ground cover.

S. brevifolium. Zones 8, 9, 14–24, 29. Tiny, slowly spreading plant to 2–3 in. high. Tiny (less than ⅛-in.), tightly packed leaves are gray white flushed with red. Pinkish or white summer flowers. Needs good drainage. Best in rock garden or with larger succulents in pots, containers, or miniature garden. Subject to sunburn in hot, dry places.

S. cauticolum (Hylotelephium cauticolum). Zones 1–11, 14–24, 29–43. Arching stems to 8 in. long are set with blue-gray, slightly toothed leaves. Clusters of small rose red flowers top stems in late summer or early fall. Dies to ground in winter.

S. dasyphyllum. Zones 2–24, 29–41. Low, spreading mat with tiny, closely packed gray-green leaves and small white flowers with pink streaks. 'Riffense' has especially plump, succulent, blue-gray leaves. Partial shade.

S. ellacombianum. Zones 1–11, 14–21, 29–45. Sometimes offered as a variety of *S. kamtschaticum*. Differs in being a shorter plant (to 6 in. high) with more compact growth, unbranched stems, and scalloped rather than toothed leaves.

S. guatemalense. See S. rubrotinctum

S. kamtschaticum. Zones 1–11, 14–21, 29–45. Trailing stems to 1 ft. long are set with thick, somewhat triangular, 1–1½-in., slightly toothed leaves. Summer flowers age from yellow to red. Useful in colder climates as small-scale ground cover, rock garden plant. 'Variegatum' has cream-edged leaves. *S. k. floriferum* is a more profuse bloomer than the species, with smaller, lighter yellow flowers. Its variety 'Weihenstephaner Gold' bears abundant bright yellow blossoms opening from red buds in late spring.

S. lineare. Zones 1–24, 29–43. Often sold as *S. sarmentosum*. Spreading, trailing, rooting stems to 1 ft. long, closely set with narrow light green leaves 1 in. long. Flowers yellow, star shaped, profuse in late spring, early summer. Ground cover. Vigorous spreader. 'Variegatum', with white-edged leaves, is a good container plant.

Sedum morganianum

S. morganianum. DONKEY TAIL, BURRO TAIL. Safely outdoors in Zones 17, 22–25; protect under lath or eaves in Zones 13–16, 18–21, 26, 27; house plant anywhere. Produces long, trailing stems that grow to 3–4 ft. in 6–8 years. Thick, light gray-green leaves overlap each other along stems to give braided or ropelike effect. Pink to deep red flowers (rarely seen) may appear from spring to summer. Because of long stems, most practical place to grow this plant is in hanging basket or wall pot; in mildest climates, try it at top of wall or in rock garden. Provide rich, fast-draining soil. Protect from wind and give half shade; water freely and feed two or three times during summer with liquid fertilizer.

S. rubrotinctum (S. guatemalense). PORK AND BEANS. Zones 8, 9, 12, 14–28. Sprawling, leaning stems 6–8 in. tall. Leaves like jelly beans, ¾ in. long, green with reddish brown tips, often entirely bronze red in sun. Reddish yellow spring flowers. Easily detached leaves root readily. Rock garden or potted plant, small-scale ground cover.

Sedum sieboldii

S. sarmentosum. See S. lineare

S. sieboldii (Hylotelephium sieboldii). Zones 4–9, 12, 14–24, 29–31, warmer parts of 32. Spreading, trailing, unbranched stems to 8–9 in. long. Leaves in threes, nearly round, stalkless, toothed in upper half, blue gray edged red. Plant turns coppery red in fall, dies to ground in winter. Each stem shows a broad, dense, flat cluster of dusty pink flowers in autumn. Beautiful rock garden or hanging basket plant. Light shade. 'Variegatum' has leaves marked yellowish white.

Sedum spathulifolium

S. spathulifolium. Zones 2–9, 14–24. Spoon-shaped blue-green leaves tinged reddish purple, packed into rosettes on short, trailing stems. Light yellow flowers, spring–summer. Ground cover, rock garden plant. Very drought tolerant. 'Cape Blanco' is a selected form with good leaf color. 'Purpureum' has deep purple leaves.

S. spectabile (Hylotelephium spectabile). Zones 1–24, 28–43. Upright or slightly spreading stems to 1½ ft. tall, well set with blue-green,

roundish, 3-in. leaves. Pink flowers in dense, 6-in.-wide, dome-shaped clusters atop stems in late summer, autumn. If stems are not cut after bloom, flower clusters mature into brownish maroon seed clusters atop bare stems. Dies to ground in winter. 'Brilliant' has deep rose red flowers, 'Carmen' is soft rose, 'Meteor' is carmine red, and 'Ruby Jewel' is deep maroon. Full sun. Regular to moderate water. Species resembles *S. telephium* in foliage and flowers, and in the developing seed heads that put on a long-lasting show.

S. spurium. Zones 1–24, 29–43. Low grower with trailing stems. Leaves thick, an inch or so long, nearly as wide, dark green or bronze tinted. Pink summer flowers in dense clusters at ends of 4–5-in. stems. For rock garden, pattern planting, ground cover. 'Coccineum', often known by the name "dragon's blood," has bronzy leaves, rosy red flowers.

S. telephium (Hylotelephium telephium). Zones 1–24, 29–43. To 2 ft. high. Resembles *S. spectabile*, but leaves are somewhat narrower. Like *S. spectabile*, it is showy over a long season, dies down in winter. 'Indian Chief' has deep pink flowers. Hybrid 'Autumn Joy' has blossoms of bright salmon pink turning to russet; hybrid 'Mohrchen' has rosy pink flowers and purple new growth. 'Atropurpureum' (often listed as a variety of *S. maximum*, a species no longer considered distinct from *S. telephium*) has burgundy leaves all season and dusty pink flowers. Full sun. Regular to moderate water.

S. 'Vera Jameson'. Zones 1–9, 14–24, 31–43. Hybrid with the habit and flowers of *S. sieboldii*, but with purple leaves.

SELF-HEAL. See PRUNELLA

SEMIARUNDINARIA. See BAMBOO

SEMPERVIVUM

HOUSELEEK

Crassulaceae

SUCCULENT PERENNIALS

🌡 ZONES 2–24, 29–41

☀ FULL SUN

💧💧 REGULAR TO LITTLE WATER

Sempervivum tectorum

Evergreen perennial plants with tightly packed rosettes of leaves. Little offsets cluster around parent rosette. Flowers star shaped, in tight or loose clusters, white, yellowish, pink, red, or greenish, pretty in detail but not showy. Summer bloom. Blooming rosettes die after setting seed, but easily planted offsets carry on. Many species, all good in rock gardens, containers, even in pockets on boulders or pieces of porous rock. Need good drainage.

S. arachnoideum. COBWEB HOUSELEEK. Tiny gray-green rosettes, ¾ in. across, of many leaves joined by fine hairs that give a cobweb-covered look to plant. Spreads slowly to make dense mats. Bright red flowers on 4-in. stems; seldom blooms.

S. tectorum. HEN AND CHICKENS. Rosettes gray green, 4–6 in. across, spreading quickly by offsets. Leaves tipped red brown, bristle pointed. Flowers red or reddish in clusters on stems to 2 ft. tall. Easy to grow in rock gardens, borders, pattern planting.

SENECIO

Asteraceae (Compositae)

PERENNIALS, SHRUBS, VINES

🌡 ZONES VARY BY SPECIES

☀◐● EXPOSURE NEEDS VARY BY SPECIES

💧💧💧 WATER NEEDS VARY BY SPECIES

Senecio cineraria

Daisy relatives that range from garden cineraria and dusty miller to vines, shrubs, perennials, succulents, even a few weeds. Succulents are often sold as *Kleinia*, an earlier name.

S. aureus. GOLDEN GROUNDSEL. Perennial. Zones 1–6, 29–43. Native to eastern North America. To 2 ft. high. Clump of bright green, toothed leaves is topped in spring by flat clusters of deep yellow, ½–1-in.-wide daisies. Full sun or part shade. Good bog garden plant.

S. cineraria. DUSTY MILLER. Shrubby perennial in Zones 4–24, 29–32; can be grown as annual in colder climates. To 2–2½ ft. tall and spreading. Woolly white leaves cut into many blunt-tipped lobes. Clustered heads of yellow or creamy yellow flowers at almost any season in mild-winter climates, during summer in colder regions. Gets leggy unless sheared occasionally. Full sun. Provide good drainage, moderate water. Striking in night garden.

WILL THE REAL DUSTY MILLER PLEASE STAND UP?

Many plants answer to the name; all have whitish, silvery, or grayish foliage, grow in full sun, and tolerate some drought. A number of plants are sold by this common name; the best known is *Centaurea cineraria*. Two are species of *Senecio*: *S. cineraria* and *S. vira-vira*. Others include *Artemisia stellerana* and *Lychnis coronaria*.

S. confusus. MEXICAN FLAME VINE. Zones 13, 16–28; dies to ground in mild frost but comes back fast from roots. Sometimes grown as summer annual in colder climates. Twines to 8–10 ft. Light green, rather fleshy leaves are 1–4 in. long, ½–1 in. wide, coarsely toothed. Large clusters of ¾–1-in., startling orange-red blooms with golden centers appear at branch ends; 'São Paulo' is deeper orange, almost brick red. Plants bloom all year where winters are mild. Provide light soil, regular water. Full sun or light shade. Use on trellis or column, let cascade over bank or wall, or plant in hanging basket.

S. greyi (Brachyglottis greyi). Evergreen shrub. Zones 5–9, 14–24. Spreading plant to 4–5 ft. high. Stiff, slightly curving stems bear leathery, 3½-in. leaves of gray green outlined in

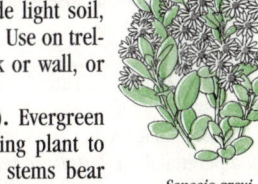

Senecio greyi

silvery white. Profuse summer bloom of 1-in. yellow daisies in flattish, 5-in. clusters; flowers contrast effectively with foliage. Full sun. Regular to moderate water. Prune out oldest growth yearly. Cut branches are long lasting in arrangements.

S. hybridus (S. cruentus, Pericallis cruenta). CINERARIA. Annual, best in Zones 16, 17, 22–24, 38; house plant or greenhouse plant anywhere. Valuable for bright colors in cool, shady places; not for hot climates. May persist or reseed where well adapted. Most common are large-flowered dwarf kinds usually sold as Multiflora Nana or Hybrida Grandiflora. These are compact, 12–15-in.-high plants with broad clusters of 3–5-in. daisies. Colors range from white through pink and purplish red to blue and purple, often with contrasting eyes or bands. Bloom late winter and early spring in mild-winter areas, spring and early summer elsewhere. Plants sold as *Cineraria stellata* are taller (2½–3 ft.), with looser clusters of smaller, star-like daisies. Give all types cool, moist (not soggy), loose, rich soil.

Senecio hybridus

S. leucostachys. See S. vira-vira.

S. macroglossus. KENYA IVY, NATAL IVY, WAX VINE. Evergreen vine in Zones 12, 13, 25; house plant anywhere. Twining or trailing vine to 6½ ft., with thin, succulent stems and thick, 2–3-in.-wide, waxy or rubbery leaves. Leaves are shaped like ivy leaves, with three, five, or seven shallow lobes. Tiny yellow daisies in summer. Leaves of 'Variegatum' are boldly splashed with creamy white. Outdoors, give part shade and moderate water. As house plant, grow in sunny window and water only when soil is dry.

S. mandraliscae (Kleinia mandraliscae). Succulent perennial. Zones 12, 13, 16, 17, 21–24; sometimes a pot plant in colder climates. Somewhat shrubby, with branches to 1–1½ ft. tall, spreading wider. Leaves

cylindrical, to 3½ in. long, slightly curved, strikingly blue gray. Use as ground cover where blue-gray effect is desired. Full sun. Moderate water.

S. mikanioides. GERMAN IVY. Vine. Zones 14–24; dies to ground in cold winters. House plant anywhere. Twines to 18–20 ft. outdoors. Ivy-like, roundish leaves with five to seven sharply pointed lobes, each ½–3 in. long. Winter flowers are small yellow daisies without rays. Good screen-

Senecio mandraliscae

ing vine or trailing plant for window boxes. Full sun or part shade. Moderate water. The plant is a weed in coastal California.

S. petasitis. VELVET GROUNDSEL, CALIFORNIA GERANIUM. Perennial. Zones 15–17, 21–24; greenhouse plant anywhere. Bulky plant to 6–8 ft. or taller, equally wide. Evergreen, tropical-looking leaves are large (to 8 in. across), lobed, fanlike, velvety to touch. Blooms in midwinter, bearing large clusters of small, daisylike, bright yellow flowers standing well above foliage mass. Full sun or light shade. Regular water. Prune hard after bloom to limit height and sprawl. Can be kept 2–4 ft. tall in tubs.

S. serpens (Kleinia repens). Succulent perennial. Zones 16, 17, 21–24. Like *S. mandraliscae*, but grows 1 ft. tall, with 1½-in.-long, light gray or bluish leaves. Full sun. Moderate water.

S. vira-vira (S. leucostachys, S. cineraria 'Candissimus'). DUSTY MILLER. Subshrub. Zones 4–24, 29–32. To 4 ft. tall, with broad, sprawling habit. Leaves like those of *S. cineraria* but more strikingly white and more finely cut into much narrower, pointed segments. Creamy white summer flowers are not showy. In full sun, it is brilliantly white and densely leafy; in part shade, it is looser and more sparsely foliaged, with larger,

Senecio serpens

greener leaves. Tip-pinch young plants to keep them compact. Moderate water.

SENSITIVE FERN. See ONOCLEA sensibilis

SENTRY PALM. See HOWEA belmoreana

SEQUOIA sempervirens

COAST REDWOOD

Taxodiaceae

EVERGREEN TREE

ZONES 4–9, 14–24, WARMER PARTS OF 32

FULL SUN OR LIGHT SHADE

REGULAR WATER

Sequoia sempervirens

Native to Coast Ranges, southern Oregon to Northern California. Tallest of the world's trees: some individuals in the wild are over 350 ft. tall. As landscape trees in their native range, redwoods grow rapidly but will reach only 70–90 ft. tall and 15–30 ft. wide in a gardener's lifetime. In less favorable areas, they grow more slowly and top out at perhaps 50 ft. Tree typically forms a symmetrical pyramid of soft-looking foliage. Flat, pointed, narrow leaves to 1 in. long, medium green on top, grayish beneath; leaves grow in one plane on both sides of stem, giving stem a featherlike look. Small brownish cones. Red-brown, fibrous-barked trunk goes straight up. A trunk with nearly parallel sides indicates a healthy tree; a struggling redwood develops a trunk with a noticeable taper. Somewhat variable habit, but most have branches that grow straight out from trunk and curve up at tips; from these main branches, branchlets droop slightly.

Becomes chlorotic in alkaline soil. However, it's normal for oldest leaves to turn from green to yellow to brown, then drop in late summer and early fall; short twigs also turn brown and drop. Where this tree is best adapted, it gets all the moisture it needs from fog drip.

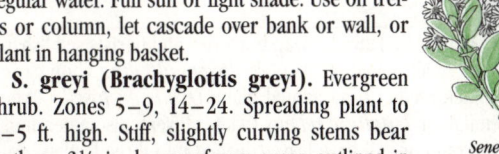

S

SEQUOIADENDRON giganteum (Sequoia gigantea)

BIG TREE, GIANT SEQUOIA

Taxodiaceae

EVERGREEN TREE

ZONES 1–23, 32, 34, 36–39

FULL SUN

MODERATE, DEEP WATERING

Sequoiadendron giganteum

Old specimens exceed 300 ft. tall and have the most massive trunk in the world (to 30 ft. in diameter), yet young trees ("young" in terms of a 3,000-year life span) are neat, handsome trees for larger gardens, reaching height of 60–100 ft. Foliage is gray green, each leaf a pointed scale overlapping the next like a prickly cypress. Dark reddish brown cones to 3½ in. long. Lower branches hang on for many years, forming a dense pyramid. Lowest branches sometimes root where they touch ground, forming secondary "trees" that blend into the original. Removing lower branches reveals a fissured, craggy trunk covered with dark red-brown bark. 'Pendulum' has drooping branches and must be staked to coax it into vertical habit.

Primary use is as featured tree in large lawn (roots may surface there) or other open space. Though native to semiarid mountains of central California, will tolerate the humid-summer region from southern New England through mid-Atlantic states. Succeeds better in eastern U.S. than *Sequoia sempervirens;* however, outside its natural habitat, it is subject to fungus diseases that can disfigure or kill it. Prefers deep soils. Requires excellent drainage in hot, humid regions.

SERVICEBERRY. See AMELANCHIER

SETARIA palmifolia

PALM GRASS

Poaceae (Gramineae)

PERENNIAL

ZONES 14–27

FULL SUN OR LIGHT SHADE

REGULAR WATER

Setaria palmifolia

This tropical-looking grass has long (1–3-ft.), wide (2–3-in.), pleated, deep green leaves in clumps 3–6 ft. tall. Evergreen in mild climates, but top freezes at 28°F/–2°C, resprouting if roots do not freeze. Use for tropical look along walks or in woodland plantings. Where adapted, it can seed itself and become a pest; remove flowers before seeds ripen.

SETCREASEA pallida 'Purple Heart' (Tradescantia pallida 'Purpurea')

PURPLE HEART, PURPLE QUEEN

Commelinaceae

PERENNIAL

ZONES 12–28; OR INDOORS

FULL SUN

MODERATE WATER

Setcreasea pallida 'Purple Heart'

Creeping plant related to wandering Jew. Stems a foot or more high, inclined to flop over. Leaves rather narrowly oval and pointed, strongly shaded with purple, particularly on undersides. Pale or deep purple flowers not showy. Use discretion in planting, since the vivid foliage can create a harsh effect. Pinch back after bloom. Generally

unattractive in winter. Frost may kill tops, but recovery is fast in warm weather. Outdoors, use as ground cover, bedding plant, or pot plant. Give house plants strong indirect light.

SEVEN SONS FLOWER. See HEPTACODIUM miconioides

SHADBLOW. See AMELANCHIER

SHALLOT

Liliaceae

SMALL ONIONLIKE BULB

ALL ZONES

FULL SUN

REGULAR WATER

Shallot

Prized in cooking for its distinctive flavor. Plant either sets (small dry bulbs) or nursery plants in fall in mild climates, early spring in cold-winter areas. Leaves 1–1½ ft. high develop from each bulb. Tiny lavender or white flowers sometimes appear. Ultimately two to eight bulbs will grow from each original bulb. At maturity (early summer if fall planted, late summer if spring planted), bulbs are formed and tops yellow and die. Harvest by pulling clumps and dividing bulbs. Let outer skin dry for about a month so that shallots can be stored for 4 to 6 months.

Some seed firms sell sets; nurseries with stocks of herbs may sell growing plants. If you use sets, plant so that tips are just covered. Golden brown skins of Dutch shallots enclose white cloves. Coppery skins of red shallots conceal purple cloves.

SHAMROCKS. Around St. Patrick's Day, nurseries and florists sell "shamrocks." These are small potted plants of *Medicago lupulina* (hop clover, yellow trefoil, black medick), an annual plant; *Oxalis acetosella* (wood sorrel), a perennial; or *Trifolium repens* (white clover), also a perennial. The last is most common. All have leaves divided into three leaflets, symbolic of the Trinity. They can be kept on a sunny windowsill or planted out, but they have little ornamental value and are likely to become weeds.

SHASTA DAISY. See CHRYSANTHEMUM maximum

SHELL FLOWER. See ALPINIA zerumbet, MOLUCCELLA laevis

SHELL GINGER. See ALPINIA zerumbet

SHE-OAK. See CASUARINA

SHEPHERDIA

Elaeagnaceae

DECIDUOUS SHRUBS

ZONES 1–3, 7, 10, 33–45

FULL SUN

REGULAR TO LITTLE WATER

Shepherdia argentea

Native to northern latitudes of North America. Tough plants for harsh growing conditions— withstand any amount of cold and wind, take most soils (including considerably alkaline ones), tolerate drought. Foliage grayish green during growing season; poor fall color. Flowers not showy. If both male and female plants are present, latter will bear small bright red or orange berries, sour but edible and used for jams and jellies. Birds like the fruit.

S. argentea. SILVER BUFFALOBERRY. Spreading, suckering plant grows 6–10 ft. (possibly 18 ft.) tall, with spine-tipped branchlets. Longish oval leaves to 1 in., silvery on both surfaces. Grayer appearance than *S. canadensis.*

S

S. canadensis. RUSSET BUFFALOBERRY. Rounded habit; grows 6–8 ft. tall. Leaves to 2 in. long, half as wide; they are green above and silvery with brown scales beneath, giving overall grayish green effect.

SHEPHERD'S SCABIOUS. See JASIONE laevis

SHIBATAEA. See BAMBOO

SHIELD FERN. See DRYOPTERIS, POLYSTICHUM

SHISO. See PERILLA frutescens

SHOOTING STAR. See DODECATHEON

SHORTIA

Diapensiaceae

PERENNIALS

Ⓩ ZONES 1–7, 31–39

☼ ● WOODSY SHADE

◖◗ AMPLE WATER

Shortia galacifolia

Beautiful, small spring-blooming evergreen plants that spread slowly by underground stems. *S. galacifolia* is native to the U.S.; the other two species are native to Japan. Intolerant of heat. Need acid, leafy, or peaty soil. Grow with azaleas or rhododendrons.

S. galacifolia. OCONEE BELLS. Native to mountains of North and South Carolina. Forms clump of glossy green, round or oval leaves 1–3 in. long, with scallop-toothed edges. Each of the many 4–6-in.-high stems is topped with a single, nodding, 1-in.-wide white bell with toothed edges.

S. soldanelloides. FRINGE BELLS. Round, coarsely toothed leaves form clumps similar to those of *S. galacifolia*, but flowers are pink to rose in color, with deeply fringed edges.

S. uniflora 'Grandiflora'. Like *S. galacifolia* but with indented and wavy-edged leaves and flowers that are large fringed bells of clear soft pink.

SHOWER OF GOLD. See CASSIA fistula

SHRIMP PLANT. See JUSTICIA brandegeana

SHRUB BUSH CLOVER. See LESPEDEZA thunbergii

SHUNGIKU. See CHRYSANTHEMUM coronarium

SIBERIAN CARPET CYPRESS. See MICROBIOTA decussata

SIBERIAN WALLFLOWER. See ERYSIMUM hieraciifolium

SIDALCEA

CHECKERBLOOM, MINIATURE HOLLYHOCK

Malvaceae

PERENNIAL

Ⓩ ZONES 2–9, 14–24, 29–41

☼ FULL SUN

◖ REGULAR WATER

Sidalcea malviflora

Most commonly grown forms are hybrids, typically 2–3 ft. high, with rounded, lobed leaves and silky-petaled 1–2-in. flowers like little hollyhocks. They include 'Brilliant', with carmine red flowers; 'Elsie Heugh', bright pink blossoms with fringed petals; and 'Loveliness', shell pink flowers. 'Party Girl', with deep pink blooms, is a little taller (to 3½ ft.). Plants bloom all summer if faded flowers are removed. These and other improved garden plants were developed mainly from *S. malviflora* (Zones 4–9, 14–24, 29–33), a species with bright pink or lavender pink flowers, and *S. candida*, a white-flowered native of the High Plains. Performance is best in cool, fairly dry climates. Provide good drainage. Divide clumps every few years.

SILENE

Caryophyllaceae

PERENNIALS

Ⓩ ZONES VARY BY SPECIES

☼ ● FULL SUN OR PARTIAL SHADE

◖ WATER NEEDS VARY BY SPECIES

Silene californica

Many species, some with erect growth habit, others cushionlike. Provide well-drained soil. For front of border, rock garden.

S. acaulis. CUSHION PINK, MOSS CAMPION. Zones 1–11, 14–16, 18–21, 32–45. Mosslike mat of small, narrow, bright green leaves. Reddish purple, ½-in. flowers, borne singly in spring. Regular water.

S. alpestris (S. quadrifolia). Zones 2–9, 14–24, 32–41. Low creeper to 8 in. high. Produces a fine show of small double white flowers in spring, with scattered bloom later. Moderate water.

S. californica. CALIFORNIA INDIAN PINK. Zones 7–11, 14–24. Loosely branching plant to 6–16 in. high. Somewhat sticky foliage. Flaming red, 1¼-in. flowers with cleft and fringed petals; spring bloom. In its native range, it is accustomed to going without water during summer.

S. coeli-rosa. See Lychnis coeli-rosa

S. schafta. MOSS CAMPION. Zones 2–9, 14–16, 18–21, 32–41. Forms tufts of upright, rather wiry stems to 6–12 in. high. Small, tongue-shaped leaves. Rose purple flowers, one or two to a stalk, late summer into fall. 'Splendens' is deep rose pink. Moderate water.

S. uniflora (S. vulgaris maritima). Zones 1–9, 14–24, 32–43. Forms a low cushion of gray-green foliage. Abundant white summer flowers; each flower is nearly enclosed by a balloonlike calyx. Moderate water.

S. virginica (Melandrium virginicum). FIRE PINK. Zones 1–9, 14–24, 32–43. Native to eastern and central U.S. Narrow, lance-shaped leaves in a clump to 2–3 ft. high. Clusters of crimson flowers with notched petals in late spring or early summer. Hybrid 'Longwood', with fringed, deep pink flowers, forms an evergreen mound to 8 in. high. Regular water.

SILK OAK. See GREVILLEA robusta

SILK TREE. See ALBIZIA julibrissin

SILVER BELL. See HALESIA carolina

SILVERBERRY. See ELAEAGNUS commutata, E. pungens

SILVER DOLLAR GUM. See EUCALYPTUS polyanthemos

SILVER FERN. See PTERIS quadriaurita 'Argyraea'

SILVER GRASS. See MISCANTHUS

SILVER LACE VINE. See POLYGONUM aubertii

SILVERLEAF. See LEUCOPHYLLUM

SILVER SAGE. See SALVIA argentea

SILVER SPREADER. See ARTEMISIA caucasica

SINARUNDINARIA. See BAMBOO, Fargesia

SINNINGIA speciosa (Gloxinia speciosa)

GLOXINIA

Gesneriaceae

TUBER

INDOOR/OUTDOOR OR HOUSE PLANT

● SHADE OUTDOORS; BRIGHT LIGHT INDOORS

◖ SEE INSTRUCTIONS BELOW

Sinningia speciosa

Leaves oblong, dark green, toothed, fuzzy, 6 in. or longer. Flowers are spectacular—large, velvety, bell shaped, ruffled on edges, in blue, purple, violet, pink, red, or white. Some flowers have dark dots or blotches, others contrasting bands at the flower rims. Leaves occasionally white veined. Tubers usually available December–March. Plant 1 in. deep in rich, loose mix. Water sparingly until first leaves appear; increase watering after roots form. Apply water around base of plant; don't water on top of leaves. When roots fill pot, shift to larger pot. Feed regularly during growth.

After bloom has finished, gradually dry off plants. Dig tubers and store in cool, dark place with just enough moisture to keep them from shriveling; or store tubers, soil and all, in pots until new growth starts. Repot in January–February.

SISYRINCHIUM

BLUE-EYED GRASS

Iridaceae

PERENNIALS

ZONES VARY BY SPECIES

FULL SUN OR LIGHT SHADE

REGULAR TO MODERATE WATER

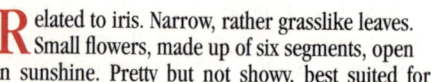

Sisyrinchium bellum

Related to iris. Narrow, rather grasslike leaves. Small flowers, made up of six segments, open in sunshine. Pretty but not showy, best suited for informal gardens or naturalizing.

S. angustifolium. Zones 1–6, 32–43. Native to eastern U.S. Grows 6–18 in. tall, with narrow dark green leaves and clusters of ½-in. blue flowers in summer.

S. bellum. Zones 4–11, 14–24. Native to coast of California. To 4–16 in. tall. Narrow green or bluish green leaves. Flowers purple to bluish purple, ½ in. across, early to midspring. Several named forms, many of them dwarf.

S. striatum. Zones 4–11, 14–24, 29–31. Larger than other species; attractive gray-green leaves 1 ft. long, to 1 in. wide. Useful for gray effect (old leaves age to black). Spikelike flower clusters to 2½ ft. tall, with many pale yellow, brown-streaked, ½-in. flowers in spring. Bloom will continue well into summer if old flower clusters are removed. If they are not removed, you may have hordes of unwanted plants the following year. 'Aunt May' ('Variegata') has cream-striped gray-green leaves.

SKIMMIA

Rutaceae

EVERGREEN SHRUBS

ZONES 4–9, 14–22, 31, 32

PARTIAL OR FULL SHADE

REGULAR WATER

Skimmia japonica

Slow growing and compact, with glossy, rich green leaves neatly arranged along the branches. In spring, tiny white flowers open from clusters of pinkish buds held well above foliage. Holly-like red fruit appears in fall and winter if pollination requirements are met. Individual plants are dense mounds; when massed, they form a solid foliage cover. Good under windows, beside shaded walks, flanking entryways, in containers. Blend well with all shade plants.

Prefer moist, highly organic, acid soils. Mites are the main pests; they give foliage a sunburned look. Thrips may also attack. Water mold is a problem in hot regions.

S. foremanii. Hybrid between *S. japonica* and *S. reevesiana*. Resembles *S. japonica* but is more compact, with broader, heavier, darker green leaves. Plants may be male, female, or self-fertile.

S. japonica. Variable in size. Slow growth to 2–5 ft. or taller, 3–6 ft. wide. Oval, blunt-ended leaves to 3–4 in. long and 1 in. wide, mostly clustered near twig ends. Flowers are borne in 2–3-in. clusters; they are larger

and more fragrant on male plants. If a male plant is present, female plants produce bright red berries—attractive enough to make planting both sexes worth the effort. A form with ivory white berries is available. Male variety 'Macrophylla' is a rounded, spreading shrub to 5–6 ft. tall, with large leaves and flowers.

S. reevesiana (S. fortunei). Dwarf, dense-growing shrub 2 ft. tall. Self-fertile, with dull crimson fruit. Fragrant flowers.

SKUNKBUSH. See RHUS trilobata

SKY FLOWER. See DURANTA repens, THUNBERGIA grandiflora

SMILACINA racemosa

FALSE SOLOMON'S SEAL, FALSE SPIKENARD

Liliaceae

PERENNIAL

ZONES 1–7, 14–17, 31–43

WOODSY SHADE

REGULAR WATER

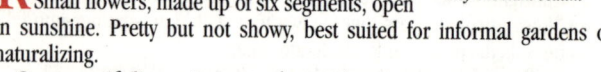

Smilacina racemosa

Commonly seen in shaded woods throughout much of North America. Grows 1–3 ft. tall; spreads by creeping rhizomes to form dense colonies. Each single, arching stalk has several 3–10-in.-long leaves with hairy undersides; foliage turns golden yellow in autumn. Stalks are topped by fluffy, conical clusters of small, fragrant, creamy white flowers in spring. Red autumn berries with purple spots follow the blooms; fruit is favored by wildlife. Good for naturalizing in wild garden. Needs rich, loose, moist, slightly acid soil. Resembles true solomon's seal (*Polygonatum*).

SMOKE TREE. See COTINUS coggygria

SNAKE PLANT. See SANSEVIERIA trifasciata

SNAKESHEAD. See FRITILLARIA meleagris

SNAPDRAGON. See ANTIRRHINUM majus

SNAPWEED. See IMPATIENS

SNEEZEWEED. See HELENIUM autumnale

SNOWBALL, FRAGRANT. See VIBURNUM carlcephalum

SNOWBELL. See STYRAX

SNOWBERRY. See SYMPHORICARPOS

SNOW BUSH. See BREYNIA disticha

SNOWDROP. See GALANTHUS

SNOWDROP TREE. See HALESIA carolina

SNOWFLAKE. See LEUCOJUM

SNOW GUM. See EUCALYPTUS pauciflora niphophila

SNOW-IN-SUMMER. See CERASTIUM tomentosum

SNOW-ON-THE-MOUNTAIN. See EUPHORBIA marginata

SOAPWORT. See SAPONARIA officinalis

SOCIETY GARLIC. See TULBAGHIA violacea

Solanaceae. Members of the potato family bear flowers that are nearly always star or saucer shaped and five petaled; fruits are berries or capsules. Plants are frequently rank smelling or even poisonous, but many are important food crops—eggplant, pepper, potato, tomato. Others are garden annuals, perennials, shrubs, or vines—amethyst flower (*Browallia*), *Cestrum*, *Nicotiana*, and *Petunia*, to name a few.

S

SOLANDRA maxima

CUP-OF-GOLD VINE

Solanaceae

EVERGREEN VINE

🌡 ZONES 17, 21–25, 26 (SOUTHERN PART), 27

☀ FULL SUN; SHADE ROOTS IN HOTTEST AREAS

💧 REGULAR, DEEP WATERING

Solandra maxima

Usually sold as *S. guttata*, a similar plant. Fast, sprawling, rampant vine to 40 ft.; fasten it to a support. Large, broad, glossy leaves 4–6 in. long. Blooms midwinter–early spring, intermittently at other times. Bowl-shaped flowers are 6–8 in. wide, golden yellow striped brownish purple.

Prune to induce branching and more flowers. Can be cut back to make rough hedge. Takes salt spray directly above tide line; stands wind, fog. Use on big walls and pergolas, along eaves, or as bank cover. For easy viewing inside the big flowers, encourage growth low on plant by tip-pinching. This vine is spectacular trained along swimming pool fence. Provide overhead protection in colder part of range.

SOLANUM

Solanaceae

EVERGREEN AND DECIDUOUS SHRUBS, VINES, PERENNIALS

🌡 ZONES VARY BY SPECIES

☀ ◑ FULL SUN OR PARTIAL SHADE

💧 ◑ REGULAR TO MODERATE WATER

☠ MANY SPECIES ARE POISONOUS IF INGESTED; MOST ARE SUSPECT

Solanum pseudocapsicum

In addition to eggplant and potato (described under those names), *Solanum* includes a number of ornamental plants, all with small, five-petaled, blue or white flowers; a few have decorative fruit.

S. crispum. Evergreen vine. Zones 8, 9, 12–27. Climbs to 12 ft. (sometimes remains shrubby), with leaves to 5 in. long, often wavy edged. In summer, bears 4-in. clusters of fragrant lilac blue flowers with yellow centers. Yellow fruit may be poisonous. May lose leaves in hard frost. 'Glasnevin' has deeper blue flowers in larger clusters.

S. jasminoides. POTATO VINE. Vine. Zones 8, 9, 12–27; evergreen in mild-winter areas. Twining habit; fast growth to 30 ft. Purplish-tinged leaves, 1½–3 in. long; 1-in.-wide flowers in pure white or in white tinged with blue, in clusters of 8–12. Nearly perpetual bloom, heaviest in spring. Grown for flowers or for light overhead shade. Cut back severely at any time to prevent tangling, promote vigorous new growth. Control rampant runners that grow along ground.

S. muricatum. PEPINO. Perennial. Zones 17, 24, 25, 27. Sprawling plant to 2 ft. high. Bright green, 3-in. leaves. Blue flowers followed in summer by football-shaped, greenish yellow fruit striped with purple. Fruit weighs ¼–1 lb., tastes like a cross between melon and cucumber. Grow like tomato.

S. pseudocapsicum. JERUSALEM CHERRY. Evergreen shrub. Zones 23–25, 27; annual or indoor/outdoor plant anywhere. To 3–4 ft. high (shorter if grown as an annual). Deep green, smooth, shiny leaves to 4 in. long. White flowers followed in autumn by fine show of scarlet (rarely yellow), ½-in. fruits that look like miniature tomatoes but are poisonous. In mildest-winter areas, the plant blooms, fruits, and seeds itself year-round. The many dwarf strains (to 1 ft. high) are more popular than taller kinds and bear larger fruit (to 1 in.).

S. rantonnetii. See Lycianthes rantonnei

S. seaforthianum. BRAZILIAN NIGHTSHADE. Vine; evergreen in mildest winter areas. Zones 16, 21–25. Leaves to 8 in. long, some undivided, others divided featherwise into leaflets. Clusters of violet blue, inchwide flowers in summer; small red fruits edible only to birds.

S. wendlandii. COSTA RICAN NIGHTSHADE. Deciduous vine. Zones 16, 21–25. Tall, twining vine with prickly stems. Leaves larger than those of other species (4–10 in. long), lower ones divided into leaflets. Loses leaves in low temperatures even without frost; slow to leaf out in spring. Big clusters of 2½-in., lilac blue flowers in summer. Use to clamber into tall trees, cover a pergola, decorate eaves of large house.

SOLEIROLIA soleirolii
(Helxine soleirolii)

BABY'S TEARS, ANGEL'S TEARS

Urticaceae

PERENNIAL

🌡 ZONES 4–27

☀ 💧 PARTIAL OR FULL SHADE

💧 REGULAR WATER

Soleirolia soleirolii

Creeping plant with tiny round leaves makes lush, 1–4-in.-high, medium green mats. Flowers inconspicuous. Tender, juicy leaves and stems are easily injured, but aggressive growth habit quickly repairs damage. Roots easily from pieces of stem and can become an invasive pest.

Freezes to black mush in hard frosts, but comes back. Cool-looking, neat cover for ferns or other shade-loving plants. Can be used to carpet terrariums or space under greenhouse benches. There is a golden green variety.

SOLENOSTEMON scutellarioides. See COLEUS hybridus

SOLIDAGO and SOLIDASTER

GOLDENROD

Asteraceae (Compositae)

PERENNIALS

🌡 ZONES 1–11, 14–21, 28–45, EXCEPT AS NOTED

☀ ◑ FULL SUN OR LIGHT SHADE

💧 MODERATE WATER

Solidago

Goldenrods are not as widely grown as they deserve, largely due to the mistaken belief that their pollen causes hay fever (in fact, other plants are responsible). Although a few of the hundred-plus species are weeds in many regions, many are choice garden plants. All have leafy stems rising from tough, woody, spreading rootstocks; all bear small yellow flowers in large, branching clusters from mid- or late summer into fall. All are tough plants that thrive in not-too-rich soil. Use in borders with black-eyed Susan or Michaelmas daisy, or naturalize in meadows. For a similar plant, try the goldenrod relative *Solidaster luteus*, also described below.

Solidago rugosa. Hairy-stemmed plant to 5 ft. tall, with flowers on widely branching, arching stems. 'Fireworks' makes a more compact, 4-ft. clump.

S. sphacelata 'Golden Fleece'. Zones 2–11, 14–21, 28–41. Stands just 1½–2 ft. high when in bloom. Low foliage mound makes it a good ground cover. Set 15 in. apart, plants will form a solid mat in a year.

S. virgaurea. To 3 ft. tall, with flower clusters in a tight spikelike inflorescence or a looser cluster with upright branches. Not as well known as its varieties or hybrids. 'Cloth of Gold', to 18–20 in. tall, has a long bloom season beginning in midsummer. 'Strahlenkrone' ('Crown of Rays') is a stiff, erect 2-footer with wide, flat, branched flower clusters. 'Goldenmosa', probably the best known, grows 2½–3 ft. tall, has very large flower clusters reminiscent of florists' mimosa.

Solidaster luteus. Hybrid of goldenrod and a perennial aster. To 2 ft. tall. Plant resembles goldenrod but has larger, softer yellow flowers like small asters. Unlike most goldenrods, needs staking to remain upright.

S

SOLLYA heterophylla (S. fusiformis)

AUSTRALIAN BLUEBELL CREEPER

Pittosporaceae

EVERGREEN SHRUB OR VINE

🌿 ZONES 8, 9, 14–28

☼ ◑ PARTIAL SHADE IN HOTTEST AREAS

💧 REGULAR WATER

Sollya heterophylla

Grows 2–3 ft. tall as a loose, spreading shrub; given support and training, climbs to 6–8 ft. Light, delicate foliage; narrow, glossy green, 1–2-in.-long leaves. Clusters of small, bell-shaped, brilliant blue flowers through most of summer. 'Alba' has white blooms. Use as ground or bank cover, in borders, over low walls, in containers. Prune frequently to encourage dense habit. Dies if drainage is poor.

SOLOMON'S SEAL. See POLYGONATUM

SOPHORA

Fabaceae (Leguminosae)

DECIDUOUS OR EVERGREEN TREES OR SHRUBS

🌿 ZONES VARY BY SPECIES

☼ ◑ FULL SUN OR PARTIAL SHADE

💧 MODERATE WATER

◈ SEEDS OF S. SECUNDIFLORA ARE POISONOUS IF INGESTED

Sophora japonica

Handsome flowering plants with showy, drooping clusters of sweet pea–shaped blossoms followed by seedpods. Leaves are divided into numerous leaflets.

S. japonica. JAPANESE PAGODA TREE, CHINESE SCHOLAR TREE. Deciduous tree. Zones 2–24, 31–41. To 50–75 ft. high and wide. Young wood smooth, dark gray green. Old branches and trunk gradually take on rugged look of oak. Dark green, 6–10-in. leaves are divided into 7–17 oval leaflets; no fall color. Small, yellowish white flowers are carried in branched, foot-long sprays at branch ends in summer. Pods are 2–3½ in. long, narrowed between big seeds for a bead necklace effect. Appreciates well-drained soil. Tolerates heat, drought, city conditions.

'Regent' is an exceptionally vigorous, uniform grower. Other varieties include 'Pendula', to 25 ft., with weeping branches; and 'Princeton Upright', similar to 'Regent' but more erect in habit. The spreading forms are good shade trees for lawn or patio, though stains from flowers and pods may be a problem on paved surfaces and parked cars.

S. secundiflora. MESCAL BEAN, TEXAS MOUNTAIN LAUREL. Evergreen shrub or tree. Zones 8–16, 18–24, 27–30. Naturally shrubby, but can be trained into 25-ft. tree with short, slender trunk or multiple trunks, narrow crown, upright branches. Very slow growth. Leaves 4–6 in. long, divided into seven to nine oval, glossy dark green leaflets. Sweet-scented violet blue flowers in drooping, 4–8-in. clusters reminiscent of wisteria; midwinter–early spring bloom. Silvery gray, woody, 1–8-in.-long seedpods open when ripe to show poisonous, bright red, ½-in. seeds. If possible, remove pods before they mature. Thrives in heat and alkaline soil, but needs good drainage. Choice small tree for street, lawn, patio. Untrained, it is a good large screen, bank cover, or espalier.

FOR INFORMATION ON SELECTING PLANTS
PLEASE SEE PAGES 79–160

SORBARIA

FALSE SPIRAEA

Rosaceae

DECIDUOUS SHRUBS

🌿 ZONES VARY BY SPECIES

☼ ◑ FULL SUN OR LIGHT SHADE

💧 REGULAR WATER

Sorbaria sorbifolia

These shrubs spread by suckering and will cover large areas if not curbed. Fernlike leaves are finely divided into many toothed leaflets; poor fall color. Foliage effect is lush, almost tropical, especially in rich, moist soil; in drier conditions, plant size is reduced. Stems are topped in summer by branching pyramidal clusters bearing clouds of tiny white blossoms that attract bees. These eventually fade to brown and are best cut off at that time. Thin clumps drastically or cut back almost to ground in early spring; blooms appear on new wood.

S. aitchisonii. Zones 3–10, 14–21, 32–34, 39. Larger overall than *S. sorbifolia*—grows 6–12 ft. tall, with leaves to 14 in. long and flower clusters to 1½ ft. long. Blooms mid- to late summer.

S. sorbifolia. Zones 1–10, 14–21, 32–45. Grows 3–8 ft. tall (possibly to 10 ft.), with foot-long leaves and foot-long flower clusters in early summer.

SORBUS

MOUNTAIN ASH

Rosaceae

DECIDUOUS TREES OR SHRUBS

🌿 ZONES VARY BY SPECIES

☼ ◑ FULL SUN OR LIGHT SHADE

💧💧 REGULAR TO MODERATE WATER

Sorbus aucuparia

Valued for showy flowers and showier fruit. Blossoms are grouped in broad, flat clusters scattered over foliage canopy in spring; they develop into hanging clusters of small, berrylike fruit that colors up in late summer or early fall. Fruit is typically red or orange red, but white, pink, and golden forms are occasionally available. Birds eat the fruit, but usually not until after leaves have fallen. Foliage is typically finely cut and somewhat fernlike, although some less widely planted species have undivided leaves. Some have good fall color; these are noted below.

Mountain ashes need some winter chill. Dislike of summer heat makes them poor candidates for planting in the lower Midwest, Southeast, Southwest, and much of California. Provide good, well-drained soil. Like many other members of the rose family, they are subject to fireblight. Borers and cankers are problems for trees under stress. Where adapted, they are good small garden or street trees, though fruit can be messy over paving.

S. alnifolia. KOREAN MOUNTAIN ASH. Tree. Zones 1–10, 14–17, 32–43. Broad, dense, to 40–50 ft. tall. The name *alnifolia* refers to the leaves, which are undivided (like those of alder); they are 2–4 in. long, toothed, dark green, turning yellow to orange in fall. Red-and-yellow fruit. Tolerates heat and humidity better than other mountain ashes.

S. americana. AMERICAN MOUNTAIN ASH. Tree, sometimes large shrub. Zones 1–6, 32–45. Native to mountains of eastern North America. To 30 ft. tall. Leaves to 10 in. long, divided into 11–17 leaflets; dark green above, paler beneath, turning yellow in fall. Orange-red fruit. Attractive in native range, but not considered a choice or long-lived tree elsewhere.

S. aria. WHITEBEAM. Tree. Zones 3–10, 14–17, 32–34, 39. To 30–45 ft. tall, with a dense crown of simple, undivided, 2–4-in.-long leaves—dark green above, whitish beneath. Variable fall color; best forms are yellow in autumn. Red or orange-red fruit.

S. aucuparia. EUROPEAN MOUNTAIN ASH, ROWAN. Tree. Zones 1–10, 14–17, 34–43. Naturalized in North America. To 20–40 ft. or taller. Sharply rising branches form a dense, oval to round crown. Leaves are 5–9 in. long, with 9–15 leaflets; they are dull green above, gray green below, turning tawny yellow to reddish in autumn. Orange-red fruit. 'Cardinal Royal' has especially large, bright red berries. 'Fastigiata' is a narrow, erect form; 'Blackhawk', another columnar form, is resistant to fireblight.

S. hupehensis. Tree. Zones 2–10, 14–17, 34–41. Eventually to a possible 50 ft. tall, usually much less. Leaves to 7 in. long, with 13–17 leaflets; turn orange red in fall. White fruit. The form in cultivation is fireblight-resistant 'Coral Cascade', with red fruit and red fall foliage.

S. hybrida. Tree. Zones 2–10, 14–17, 34–41. Hybrid of *S. aria* and *S. aucuparia*. Erect habit to 20–30 ft. Leaves are 2½–4 in. long; they have one or two pairs of leaflets at the base, but tips are merely lobed (like oak leaves). Red fruit.

S. reducta. Shrub. Zones 3–6, 14–17, 32–34, 39. To 2 ft. high, 3 ft. wide, spreading by underground runners. Leaves to 4 in. long, with 9–15 small leaflets; turn bronze red in autumn. Pink fruit. For rock garden or bonsai.

S. thuringiaca. Tree. Zones 3–6, 14–17, 34, 39. Hybrid between *S. aucuparia* and a species with undivided leaves. To 40 ft. tall, with leaves either deeply lobed and toothed or having one pair of leaflets beneath a large terminal leaflet. Bright red fruit.

S. tianshanica. TURKESTAN MOUNTAIN ASH. Shrub or small tree. Zones 3–10, 14–17, 34, 39. To 16 ft. tall. Leaves 5–6 in. long, with 9–15 leaflets. Bright red fruit. Neat form, slow growth; excellent plant for small garden. 'Red Cascade' is compact, oval crowned.

SORREL, WOOD or REDWOOD. See OXALIS

SOUR GUM. See NYSSA sylvatica

SOURWOOD. See OXYDENDRUM arboreum

SOUTHERN PEA

Fabaceae (Leguminosae)
ANNUAL
🗡 ALL ZONES (SEE BELOW)
☼ FULL SUN
🔴 REGULAR WATER

Southern Pea

The name "Southern pea" describes various hot-weather shelled beans, including black-eyed peas, cowpeas, crowder peas, and cream peas. A long-time staple of Southern cuisine, Southern peas grow somewhat like ordinary green peas ("garden" or "English" peas, to Southern gardeners), but their pods look more like lumpy string beans. They grow best in the long, sweltering summers of the Deep South, where they are ready for harvest about 65 days after sowing. In regions with cooler summers or a shorter growing season, best bets are early-bearing dwarf or bush varieties, although the yield may still be meager.

In ideal climate, wait until early summer nights are warm before sowing seeds; make successive sowings for a long harvest. Better to grow in poor soil than in rich, fertile soil. Sow 1 in. deep; plants will support each other if grown close together (2 in. apart, 3–4 ft. between rows). A space-saving trick is to intersperse peas with corn; the cornstalks provide a natural trellis for vining kinds of Southern peas to climb. Harvest for fresh peas when pods are plump, firm, and still green. Harvest for dry peas when pods turn yellow, tan, or purple; pods should rattle when shaken. Subject to attack by Mexican bean beetles; see Bean, Snap for control methods.

SOUTHERNWOOD. See ARTEMISIA abrotanum

SPANISH BAYONET. See YUCCA aloifolia

SPANISH BLUEBELL. See ENDYMION hispanicus

SPANISH BROOM. See SPARTIUM junceum

SPANISH DAGGER. See YUCCA gloriosa

SPARAXIS tricolor

HARLEQUIN FLOWER
Iridaceae
CORM
🗡 ZONES 9, 12–24; OR DIG AND STORE; OR GROW IN POTS
☼ FULL SUN
🔴 REGULAR WATER DURING GROWTH AND BLOOM

Native to South Africa. Makes a clump of sword-shaped leaves. Small, funnel-shaped flowers in spikelike clusters on 1-ft. stems over long period in late spring. Flowers come in yellow, pink, purple, red, and white, usually blotched and splashed with contrasting colors. Closely related to ixia and similar to it in uses and culture.

Sparaxis tricolor

SPARMANNIA africana

AFRICAN LINDEN
Tiliaceae
EVERGREEN SHRUB OR TREE
🗡 ZONES 15–27; OR INDOORS
☼ ◐ ● SUN OR SHADE
🔴 REGULAR WATER

Sparmannia africana

Fast to 10–20 ft.; usually grows as a thicket, multitrunked from base, especially if frosted back or pruned to control size. Slower, smaller in container or as house plant. Dense, coarse foliage: leaves are broad, angled, to 9 in. across, light green, heavily veined, velvety with coarse hairs. Clusters of white, 1–1½-in. flowers with brush of yellow stamens appear midwinter–early spring.

Feed regularly. Prune heavily every few years to give desired height and control legginess. Best used for furnishing bulk and mass near entryways, for screening, for combining with tropical foliage plants. Big leaves, easy cleanup make it a good choice near pools. Easily propagated by cuttings. Susceptible to spider mites. Indoors, takes ordinary house plant care and good light (but not direct sunlight).

SPARTIUM junceum

SPANISH BROOM
Fabaceae (Leguminosae)
NEARLY LEAFLESS SHRUB
🗡 ZONES 5–24
☼ FULL SUN
🔴 LITTLE WATER
◆ ALL PARTS ARE POISONOUS IF INGESTED

Many green, almost leafless stems form a gaunt, woody shrub to 6–10 ft. high; pruning fattens it up. Fragrant, 1-in., bright yellow flowers in clusters at branch ends over long bloom period—from early summer to frost in colder climates, from spring to late summer in warmer areas. Flowers followed by hairy seedpods. Good rough bank cover, but where best adapted is capable of crowding out other plants. In southernmost areas, caterpillars can be a serious pest, leaving plants without flowers or stems.

Spartium junceum

SPATHIPHYLLUM

Araceae

EVERGREEN PERENNIALS

ZONES 25, 27; 26 WITH FROST PROTECTION; OR INDOORS

PARTIAL OR FULL SHADE

REGULAR WATER

Spathiphyllum

Large, dark green leaves—carried erect on slender stalks that rise directly from soil— are oval or elliptical, narrowed to a point. Flowers resemble those of calla lily or anthurium, consisting of a central column of closely set tiny flowers surrounded by a leaflike white bract. Among the many varieties are 6-ft. 'St. Mary'; 1½-ft. 'Silver Streak', with matte green leaves with a silvery midrib and insignificant flowers; and 2-ft. 'Tasson', considered by some to be the surest bloomer.

Outdoors, use as pot plant or ground cover for shady areas. Among the few flowering plants that grow and bloom readily indoors. Place in good light but not a hot window. Provide loose, fibrous potting mix; feed weekly with dilute liquid fertilizer.

SPATHODEA campanulata

AFRICAN TULIP TREE

Bignoniaceae

EVERGREEN TREE

ZONES 21–25

FULL SUN

MODERATE WATER

Spathodea campanulata

Fast growing. Glossy leaves divided into four to eight pairs of leaflets. Branches end in clusters of spectacular tulip-shaped, 4-in., orange-scarlet flowers edged with yellow; typical bloom time is spring, but flowers may appear in any season. Plant grows rapidly and blooms young, but can be devastated by frosts. Give good drainage and a warm site. Can reach 50 ft., but such height likely only in truly frostless locations.

SPEARMINT. See MENTHA spicata

SPEEDWELL. See VERONICA

SPHAEROPTERIS cooperi. See CYATHEA cooperi

SPICE BUSH. See CALYCANTHUS

SPICEBUSH. See LINDERA

SPIDER FLOWER. See CLEOME hasslerana

SPIDER LILY. See LYCORIS

SPIDER PLANT. See CHLOROPHYTUM comosum

SPIDERWORT. See TRADESCANTIA virginiana

SPIGELIA marilandica

PINKROOT, INDIAN PINK

Loganiaceae

PERENNIAL

ZONES 4–6, 28–35

LIGHT SHADE

REGULAR WATER

ALL PARTS ARE POISONOUS IF INGESTED

Spigelia marilandica

Native to southeastern U.S. Woodland plant 1–2 ft. high, with stiff, erect stems set with pairs of glossy green, 4-in.

leaves. Clusters of 2-in., trumpet-shaped flowers; blossoms are red on the outside and yellow inside, facing upward to show a yellow five-pointed star at the mouth. Early summer bloom. Easy to grow if given light shade and moist, acid soil. With enough moisture, will tolerate full sun. Although once used medicinally, the plant is poisonous.

SPIKENARD. See ARALIA racemosa

SPINACH

Chenopodiaceae

ANNUAL

ALL ZONES

FULL SUN

KEEP SOIL EVENLY MOIST

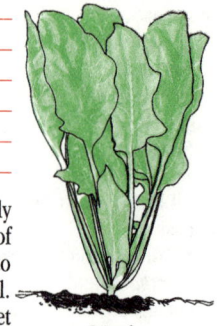

Spinach

Leafy cool-season vegetable. Matures slowly during fall, winter, and spring; long daylight of late spring and heat of summer make it go to seed quickly. Requires rich, fast-draining soil. Make small sowings at weekly intervals to get successive harvests. Space rows 1½ ft. apart. After seedlings start growing, thin plants to 6 in. apart. One feeding will encourage lush foliage. When plants have reached full size, harvest by cutting off entire clump at ground level. Leaf miner is often a pest.

SPINACH, NEW ZEALAND

Tetragoniaceae

PERENNIAL USUALLY GROWN AS ANNUAL

ALL ZONES

FULL SUN

REGULAR WATER

New Zealand Spinach

Warm-season vegetable used as substitute for true spinach, which needs cool weather to succeed. Harvest greens from plants by plucking off top 3 in. of tender stems and attached leaves. A month later, new shoots grow up for another harvest. Plant is spreading, 6–8 in. high. Evergreen perennial in mild-winter areas (most likely to live over in Zones 15–17, 21–24), but goes dormant in heavy frosts. Sow seed in early spring after frost danger is past. Feed once or twice yearly with complete fertilizer. Though heat and drought tolerant, also thrives in cool, damp conditions and even grows wild in some regions.

SPINDLE TREE. See EUONYMUS europaea

SPIRAEA

Rosaceae

DECIDUOUS SHRUBS

ZONES VARY BY SPECIES

FULL SUN OR LIGHT SHADE

REGULAR TO MODERATE WATER, EXCEPT AS NOTED

Spiraea bumalda 'Anthony Waterer'

Very widely planted shrubs varying in size, form, and flowering season. There are two distinct kinds of spiraeas: the bridal wreath type, with clusters of white flowers cascading down arched branches in spring or early summer; and the shrubby type, typically growing knee-high and bearing pink, red, or white flowers clustered at ends of upright branches in summer to fall.

Like other members of the rose family, these are subject to various pests and diseases, but tend not to be seriously bothered. Tough, easy to grow.

S

With few exceptions, not fussy about soil. Prune the mostly spring-blooming, bridal-wreath spiraeas after flowers have finished; cut to the ground wood that has bloomed. Prune the summer-blooming, shrubby spiraeas in winter or earliest spring; they generally need less severe pruning than bridal wreaths. If you remove spent flower clusters, plants will produce a second (but less lavish) bloom.

S. albiflora. See S. japonica 'Albiflora'

S. billardii. Zones 2–11, 14–21, 31–43. Hybrid between *S. douglasii* and a European species. Resembles *S. douglasii* in form, flowers, and requirement for acid soil and ample water. 'Triumphans' bears a profusion of purplish rose blossoms.

S. bumalda. Zones 1–11, 14–21, 31–43. Name given to a group of hybrids between varieties of *S. japonica*. All are low, shrubby spiraeas that bloom summer–fall. Selections include:

'Anthony Waterer'. Several forms; the best grows 3–4 ft. tall and slightly wider. All have flat-topped, carmine pink flower clusters and maroon-tinged foliage.

'Coccinea'. Like 'Anthony Waterer', but grows 2–3 ft. tall and bears brighter flowers.

'Dolchica'. To 1½–2½ ft. tall, with deeply cut leaves and bright pink flowers. Purplish new growth.

'Froebelii'. Resembles 'Anthony Waterer' but grows slightly taller.

'Goldflame'. Resembles 'Froebelii', but leaves are bronzy on unfolding, then yellow to chartreuse in summer and reddish orange before falling. Pink flowers. Prune out any green-leafed stems.

'Goldmound'. Compact 1–3-ft. shrub with yellow to chartreuse foliage, pink flowers. Sometimes considered a variety of *S. japonica*.

'Limemound'. Resembles 'Goldmound' but is somewhat hardier. Pink flowers; lime green foliage that turns orange red in fall.

S. cantoniensis (S. reevesiana). DOUBLE BRIDAL WREATH. Zones 4–11, 14–21, 26 (northern part), 28–33. Upright grower to 5–6 ft., with arching branches. White flowers wreathe leafy branches, late spring–early summer. In colder part of range, the small dark green leaves turn red in fall; in mild-winter areas, they remain on the plant without changing color. 'Lanceata' is the form commonly grown in southern climates.

S. douglasii. WESTERN SPIRAEA. Zones 1–9, 14–24. Native from West Coast to the Rockies. Suckering, clump-forming shrub 4–8 ft. tall. Leaves are dark green above, velvety white beneath. Pale to deep pink flowers form 8-in. clusters at branch ends in summer. Needs acid soil, ample water. Useful for wild plantings near streams.

S. japonica. Zones 2–9, 14–21, 32–41. Upright shrubby spiraea to 4–6 ft. tall, with flat clusters of pink flowers carried above sharply toothed, oval green leaves. Best known through its selections, which are typically lower than the species and bloom between summer and fall. These include:

'Albiflora' *(S. albiflora)*. Rounded, compact shrub 1–1½ ft. tall, with white flowers.

'Alpina'. DAPHNE SPIRAEA. Low (1-ft.) mound with pink flowers. Foliage turns red and orange in fall.

'Fortunei'. Unusually tall (to 5 ft.), with pink flowers.

'Little Princess'. Resembles 'Alpina' but is larger (to 2½ ft. tall).

'Magic Carpet'. To 1½–2 ft. tall. Reddish bronze new growth contrasts with chartreuse to yellow older foliage. Pink flowers.

'Neon Flash'. To 3–4 ft. tall, 4–5 ft. wide. Purplish-tinted foliage, bright rosy pink flowers.

'Norman'. To 1½–2 ft. tall, with deep pink flowers and dark purple autumn foliage.

'Shirobana' ('Shibori'). To 2–3 ft. tall, with flowers of white, light pink, and deep rose pink on the same plant.

S. nipponica tosaensis 'Snowmound'. Zones 1–11, 14–21, 32–43. Compact, spreading plant to 2–3 ft. tall. Profusion of white flowers in late spring or early summer. Narrow dark green leaves have little autumn color.

S. prunifolia 'Plena'. BRIDAL WREATH SPIRAEA, SHOE BUTTON SPIRAEA. Zones 2–11, 14–21, 31–41. Graceful, arching branches on a suckering, clump-forming plant to 6 ft. tall and wide. In early to midspring, bare branches are lined with small double white flowers resembling tiny roses. Small dark green leaves turn bright shades of red, orange, and yellow in autumn.

S. thunbergii. Zones 1–11, 14–21, 29–43. Showy, billowy, graceful shrub 3–5 ft. tall, with many slender, arching branches. Round clusters of small single white flowers appear all along bare branches in early spring. Blue-green, extremely narrow leaves turn soft reddish brown in fall.

S. tomentosa. HARDHACK, STEEPLEBUSH. Zones 1–3, 32–45. Native to eastern U.S. and northern Europe. Eastern equivalent of *S. douglasii*. Spreads by suckering to form thickets to 5 ft. tall. Rose pink flowers in 6-in. clusters, summer–fall. Best in acid soil with ample water. Useful in wild gardens.

S. trilobata 'Swan Lake'. Zones 1–11, 14–17, 32–43. Like a small version of *S. prunifolia* 'Plena'. To 3–4 ft. tall, with a massive show of tiny white flowers in mid- to late spring. Small leaves often have three lobes. 'Fairy Queen' is more compact, seldom exceeding 3 ft.

S. vanhouttei. Zones 1–11, 14–21, 29–43. Widely planted hybrid between *S. cantoniensis* and *S. trilobata*. The classic bridal wreath spiraea. Arching branches form a fountain to about 6 ft. high by 8 ft. or wider. Leafy branches are covered with circular, flattened clusters of single white blossoms in mid- to late spring, continuing into early summer in colder regions. Dark green foliage may turn purplish in fall.

SPIRAL FLAG. See COSTUS

SPLEENWORT. See ASPLENIUM

SPLIT-LEAF PHILODENDRON. See MONSTERA deliciosa

SPREKELIA formosissima

JACOBEAN LILY, ST. JAMES LILY, AZTEC LILY

Amaryllidaceae

BULB

⚡ ZONES 9, 12–24, 26–30; OR DIG AND STORE; OR GROW IN POTS

☀ FULL SUN

💧 REGULAR WATER DURING GROWTH AND BLOOM

Sprekelia formosissima

Often sold as *Amaryllis formosissima*. Native to Mexico. Foliage looks like that of daffodil. Stems 1 ft. tall, topped with dark crimson blooms resembling orchids: three erect upper segments and three lower ones rolled together into tube at base, then separating again into drooping segments. Plant in fall, setting bulbs 3–4 in. deep and 8 in. apart. Blooms 6 to 8 weeks after planting. Most effective in groups. In mild climates, may flower several times a year under conditions of alternating moisture and drying out. Where winters are cold, plant outdoors in spring; lift plants in fall when foliage yellows and store over winter (leave dry tops on). Or grow in pots like amaryllis (*Hippeastrum*); repot every 3 to 4 years.

SPRING STAR FLOWER. See IPHEION uniflorum

SPRUCE. See PICEA

SPURGE. See PACHYSANDRA

SQUASH

Cucurbitaceae

ANNUAL

⚡ ALL ZONES

☀ FULL SUN

💧 REGULAR WATER

Crookneck Squash

There are two forms of squash. Types planted for a warm-weather harvest and eaten in the immature state are called summer squash; this group includes scalloped white squash (pattypan squash), yellow crookneck and straightneck varieties, and cylindrical, green or gray zucchini or Italian squash. The other form is winter squash, grown for harvest in late summer or fall; it stores well and is used for baking and pies. Varieties come in many sizes, colors, and shapes (turban, acorn, and banana are a few); all have hard rinds and firm, close-grained, good-tasting flesh. In both forms of squash, blossoms and tiny, developing fruit at base of female flowers can be picked as delicacies.

Summer squash yields prodigious crops from just a few plants (within 50 to 65 days after sowing) and continues to bear for weeks. Vines are large (2½–4 ft. across at maturity) and need plenty of room; if space is limited, look for bush varieties. 'Early Summer Crookneck' and 'Early Prolific Straightneck' are good yellow summer squash. 'Early White Bush' (white) and 'Scallopini Hybrid' (green) are choice scalloped varieties. 'Ambassador Hybrid', 'Aristocrat Hybrid', and 'Burpee Hybrid' are productive zucchini varieties. Zucchini and scalloped squash also come in golden yellow variants. Novelties include 'Gourmet Globe', a round, striped zucchini, and 'Kuta', a whitish squash that can be eaten like summer squash at 6 in. or allowed to ripen into a 1-ft. winter squash.

Winter squash is planted and grown on vines like pumpkins, and typically needs more space than summer squash. Most are ready to harvest 60 to 110 days after sowing. Types for storing include the small 'Table Queen', 'Acorn', 'Butternut', and 'Buttercup', and the large 'Hubbard', 'Blue Hubbard', and 'Jumbo Pink Banana'. Spaghetti squash looks like any other winter squash, but when you open it after cooking, you find that the nutty-tasting flesh is made up of long, spaghetti-like strands. Winter squash doesn't grow well in high heat and humidity.

Bush varieties of summer squash can be planted 2 ft. apart in rows. If planted in circles (hills), they need more room; allow a 4-ft. diameter for each plant. Runner-type winter squash needs 5-ft. spacing in rows, 8-ft.-diameter hills. The few bush varieties of winter squash can be spaced as for bush varieties of summer squash. Provide rich soil, periodic fertilizer. Roots need regular moisture, but leaves and stems should be kept as dry as possible to prevent leaf diseases such as powdery mildew. Late squash should stay on vines until thoroughly hardened; harvest these with an inch of stem and store in cool place (about 55°F/13°C).

Pests include squash bug (set out boards or burlap as traps and destroy your catch each morning) and squash vine borer (plant early or late to avoid peak midsummer damage). Control cucumber beetles, which can spread incurable bacterial wilt disease as they chew holes in leaves and flowers.

SQUAWBUSH. See RHUS trilobata

SQUILL. See SCILLA

SQUIRREL'S FOOT FERN. See DAVALLIA trichomanoides

STACHYS

LAMB'S EARS, BETONY
Lamiaceae (Labiatae)
PERENNIALS
🌡 ZONES VARY BY SPECIES
☼ ◐ LIGHT SHADE IN HOT CLIMATES
🌢 MODERATE WATER

All have paired, typically rough or hairy leaves and spikelike clusters of small, usually two-lipped flowers. All are tough, tolerant plants. Of the 300-odd species, only a few are commonly grown. Provide well-drained soil. Plants often die out in center; divide and replant outer sections.

Stachys byzantina

S. byzantina (S. lanata, S. olympica). LAMB'S EARS. Zones 1–24, 29–43. Dense, ground-hugging rosettes of soft, thick, rather tongue-shaped, woolly white leaves to 4 in. long, 1 in. wide; clumps spread by surface runners. Some (not all) rosettes send up 1–1½-ft. flowering stems with small leaves and whorls of small purple flowers in late spring–early summer; these are attractive but become dowdy when they fade. Plant is

more useful for foliage effect, so many people cut off or simply pull out flowering stems. Continued rain can smash the plants down and make them mushy, and frost can damage leaves, but recovery is strong.

'Silver Carpet' does not produce flower spikes and is somewhat less vigorous than the species. 'Countess Helene von Stein', commonly called 'Big Ears' (the plant, not the countess), has longer, broader leaves than the species and produces fewer flowering stems. There are also harder-to-find lime green and variegated forms.

Use all forms for contrast with dark green foliage and with leaves of different shapes, such as those of strawberry or some sedums. Good edging plants for paths, flower beds; highly effective edgings for bearded iris. Excellent ground covers in high, open shade.

S. macrantha (S. grandiflora). BIG BETONY. Zones 1–24, 31–45. Dense, foot-high clump of long-stalked, heart-shaped, wrinkled, roughly hairy, scallop-edged green leaves to 3 in. across. Showy purplish pink flowers, carried two or three whorls to a spike, held 8 in. above leaves. Spreads rapidly in rich, moist soil. Most common form is 'Robusta', to 2 ft. high; its blossom spikes bear four or five whorls of flowers. 'Superba' has deep violet blossoms. 'Alba' is a white-flowered form.

S. officinalis. BETONY. Zones 1–24, 29–45. Similar to *S. macrantha*, but leaves are elongated (to 5 in. long) and may be hairy or nearly smooth. The purplish or dark red flowers are densely packed into short spikes atop leafy stems. Little grown except by herb fanciers, but white-blooming 'Grandiflora Alba' and pink-blooming 'Grandiflora Rosea' are attractive 2-ft. plants for perennial border or woodland edge.

STACHYURUS praecox

Stachyuraceae
DECIDUOUS SHRUB
🌡 ZONES 4–6, 14–17, 31–33
☼ ◐ FULL SUN OR LIGHT SHADE
🌢 REGULAR WATER

Stachyurus praecox

Slow to 10 ft., with spreading, slender, polished chestnut brown branches. Pendulous flower stalks 3–4 in. long, each with 12–20 unopened buds, hang from branches in fall–winter. In late winter, buds open into pale yellow or greenish yellow, bell-shaped flowers ⅓ in. wide. Greenish yellow, berrylike fruit in summer. Bright green, toothed leaves, 3–7 in. long, taper to sharp tip. Leaves often somewhat sparse. Fall color pleasant (but not bright) rosy red and yellowish. Grow under deciduous trees to shelter winter buds from heavy freezes.

STAGHORN FERN. See PLATYCERIUM

STAPELIA

STARFISH FLOWER, CARRION FLOWER
Asclepiadaceae
SUCCULENT PERENNIALS
🌡 ZONES 12, 13, 16–28; OR INDOORS
☼ FULL SUN
🌢 MODERATE WATER

Stapelia variegata

Plants resemble cacti, with clumps of four-sided, spineless stems. Summer flowers are large, fleshy, shaped like five-pointed stars; they usually have elaborate circular fleshy disc in center. Most smell like carrion, but odor is not usually pervasive enough to be offensive. They need cool, dry rest period in winter. Best managed in pots. Good desert succulent, tolerating extreme heat. Protect plants in areas where frosts can occur.

S. gigantea. Grow this plant as a remarkable novelty. Stems 9 in. tall. Brown-purple flowers marked in yellow are 10–16 in. wide, fringy edged.

S. variegata. Most common. Stems to 6 in. Flowers to 3 in. across, yellow heavily spotted and barred in dark purple brown. There are many hybrids and color variants. Flowers not strongly scented. Plant can take light frost.

STAPHYLEA

BLADDERNUT

Staphyleaceae

DECIDUOUS SHRUBS

☘ ZONES VARY BY SPECIES

☼ ◐ ● SUN OR SHADE

🔴 REGULAR WATER

Staphylea trifolia

Deciduous suckering shrubs with paired leaves divided into leaflets. Tightly clustered, greenish to yellowish white flowers bloom in spring or summer. Common name comes from the fruit, which is an inflated bladderlike capsule containing a few seeds; bladders are green, turning light brown. Plants tolerate a wide variety of soils. Most are too big for small gardens, but have their place at the woodland edge or in large shrub borders.

S. bumalda. JAPANESE BLADDERNUT. Zones 2–6, 31–41. To 4–6 ft. tall, with leaves divided into three 2½-in. leaflets. The off-white spring flowers, borne in 1–3-in. clusters, are followed by inch-long fruit.

S. colchica. COLCHIS BLADDERNUT. Zones 3–6, 31–35, 37, 39. To 12 ft. tall; leaves have three or five 3-in. leaflets. Yellowish white spring flowers in 2–4-in. clusters have a coconut fragrance. Fruit to 3 in. long.

S. pinnata. EUROPEAN BLADDERNUT. Zones 3–6, 31–35, 37, 39. To 10–15 ft. tall. Leaves have three to seven 4-in. leaflets. Drooping, 4–5-in. clusters of white flowers in early summer are followed by 1½-in. fruit.

S. trifolia. AMERICAN BLADDERNUT. Zones 1–6, 31–43. To 10–15 ft. tall, usually somewhat broader. Leaves have three 4-in. leaflets. Greenish white spring flowers in 1½–2-in. clusters, followed by 1–1½-in. fruit.

STAR CLUSTERS. See PENTAS lanceolata

STARFISH FLOWER. See STAPELIA

STAR JASMINE. See TRACHELOSPERMUM

STAR OF BETHLEHEM. See CAMPANULA isophylla, ORNITHOGALUM

STATICE. See LIMONIUM

STEEPLEBUSH. See SPIRAEA tomentosa

STENOLOBIUM stans. See TECOMA stans

STENOTAPHRUM secundatum

ST. AUGUSTINE GRASS

Poaceae (Gramineae)

PERENNIAL LAWN GRASS

☘ ZONES 12, 13, 18–31, WARMER PARTS OF 32

☼ ◐ FULL SUN; ENDURES SOME SHADE

🔴 REGULAR WATER

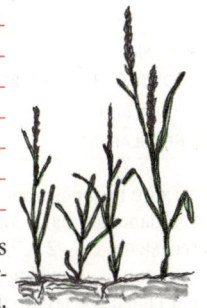

Stenotaphrum secundatum

Coarse-textured tropical or subtropical grass native to southeastern U.S. Spreads fast by surface runners that root at joints. Leaves dark green, to ³⁄₈ in. wide, on coarse, wiry, flattened stems. Turns brown during short winter dormancy, can creep into flower beds or other plantings, requires power mower to deal with heavy blades, produces thick thatch. On the plus side, it is easily removed from flower beds because of shallow roots, tolerates much wear, has few pests, and is fairly salt and shade tolerant. Plant from sod, plugs, or stolons. Mow to 3 in. high in summer, to 2 in. during cooler weather. A variegated form exists and is sometimes seen as a hanging basket plant.

STEPHANANDRA incisa

Rosaceae

DECIDUOUS SHRUB

☘ ZONES 1–6, 32–43

☼ ◐ FULL SUN OR LIGHT SHADE

🔴 REGULAR WATER

Stephanandra incisa

Mounding shrub 4–7 ft. tall, with arching branches that may root when they contact damp soil. Leaves are 1–2 in. long, deeply lobed, the lobes toothed; turn from bright green to dull reddish or purplish orange in autumn. Tiny white spring flowers, carried in loose, 1–2½-in. clusters, are not showy. Use for massing or informal hedge or screen, tall bank cover for weed and erosion control. More commonly used is 'Crispa', 2–3 ft. tall and 4–5 ft. wide, with good reddish purple fall color; useful bank or ground cover. Both species and variety dislike alkaline soil.

STEPHANOTIS floribunda

MADAGASCAR JASMINE

Asclepiadaceae

EVERGREEN VINE

☘ ZONES 23–25; OR INDOORS

◐ ROOTS IN SHADE, TOPS IN FILTERED SUN

🔴 REGULAR WATER

Stephanotis floribunda

Moderate growth to 10–15 ft. (taller if grown in open ground); can be kept small in pots. Needs warmth, support of frame or trellis. Waxy, glossy green leaves to 4 in. long. Funnel-shaped, waxy white flowers are very fragrant, 1–2 in. long, blooming in open clusters from June through the end of summer. A favorite flower for bridal bouquets.

As house plant, will bloom almost all year if given enough bright light but not direct sun; better suited to greenhouse. Allow indoor plants to rest by letting them dry out in winter; they will flower 6 weeks after resuming growth. Can be brought outdoors during warm season. Feed liberally; watch for scale, mealybugs.

STERCULIA. See BRACHYCHITON

Sterculiaceae. The sterculia family of shrubs and trees has flowers in which the calyx (the collective sepals), usually bowl shaped and five lobed, replaces the corolla (the collective petals) as the conspicuous element. Examples are *Brachychiton*, Chinese parasol tree (*Firmiana*), and flannel bush (*Fremontodendron*).

STERNBERGIA lutea

Amaryllidaceae

BULB

☘ ZONES 3, 7–10, 14–24, 26–33; OR GROW IN POTS

☼ FULL SUN

🔴 REGULAR WATER DURING GROWTH AND BLOOM

Narrow, 6–12-in. leaves appear in fall simultaneously with flowers and remain green for several months after blooms have gone. Golden yellow, 1½-in. flowers resemble large crocuses on 6–9-in. stems and provide a pleasant autumn surprise in borders or rock gardens, near pools. Good cut flowers. Dies to the ground in spring. Plant bulbs as soon as they become available (in

S

August or September). Set 4 in. deep, 6 in. apart. Clumps bloom well only after 2 or 3 years; wait at least 6 to 8 years before dividing.

In colder climates, grow in pots. Place four or five bulbs in a pot, setting them 2 in. deep. Don't be in a hurry to repot, since plants bloom better when pot-bound.

STEWARTIA

Theaceae	
DECIDUOUS SHRUBS OR TREES	
ZONES VARY BY SPECIES	
LIGHT SHADE IN HOT CLIMATES	
REGULAR WATER	

Stewartia koreana

These are all-season performers. They show off fresh green leaves in spring, white flowers like single camellias in summer, and colorful foliage in fall; winter reveals a distinctive pattern of bare branches and smooth bark that flakes off in varying degrees, depending on species. *S. koreana* and *S. pseudocamellia* have the showiest bark; it flakes off to show a patchwork of green, gray, brown, rust, terra-cotta, and cream.

Best in well-drained, acid soil with high content of organic matter. Good in woodland garden and as foreground specimens against backdrop of larger, darker-leafed trees. Success is limited to the Southeast, West Coast, and (with careful location) mid-Atlantic regions.

S. koreana. KOREAN STEWARTIA. Tree. Zones 4–6, 14–17, 20, 21, 32–34, 39. Pyramidal growth to 20–25 ft.; may eventually reach 50 ft. Leaves are 1–4 in. long, turn orange to red orange in fall. Flowers, carried on short stalks among leaves, reach 3 in. wide and have yellow-orange stamens. Probably a variety of *S. pseudocamellia.*

S. malacodendron. SILKY STEWARTIA. Shrub or small tree. Zones 4–6, 14–17, 20, 21, 31, 32. Native to southeastern U.S. (mainly to coastal plain). To 10–15 ft. tall and wide. Shoots and undersides of 2–4-in. leaves are downy. Blossoms are 3½ in. wide, have purple stamens with blue anthers. Bark not as effective as on other species.

S. monadelpha. TALL STEWARTIA. Tree. Zones 4–6, 14–17, 20, 21, 31–33. To 25 ft. tall, with slender, upward-angled branches. Leaves are 1½–3 in. long, turn brilliant red in fall. Flowers to 1½ in. wide. Older limbs and trunk have smooth, cinnamon brown bark.

S. ovata. MOUNTAIN STEWARTIA. Shrub or small tree. Zones 4–6, 14–17, 20, 21, 31–34, 39. Native to southeastern U.S. To 10–15 ft. tall and wide. Leaves grow 2–5 in. long, turn orange to scarlet in fall. Flowers, 3 in. wide, have frilled petals. Bark not as handsome as on other species. *S. o. grandiflora* has 4-in. flowers with lavender anthers; it will bloom even as a young plant.

S. pseudocamellia. JAPANESE STEWARTIA. Tree. Zones 4–6, 14–17, 20, 21, 32–34, 39. Forms a pyramid that may reach 30–40 ft. after many years. Leaves to 2½–3 in. long; fall color bronze to purple. Flowers are more cup shaped than those of *S. koreana;* they reach 2½ in. wide, have orange anthers.

STIGMAPHYLLON

ORCHID VINE	
Malpighiaceae	
EVERGREEN OR PARTIALLY DECIDUOUS VINES	
ZONES VARY BY SPECIES	
FULL SUN	
REGULAR WATER	

Stigmaphyllon ciliatum

Tall twiners of fairly fast growth to 20–30 ft. Leaves borne in pairs. Bright yellow, irregularly shaped flowers that somewhat resemble oncidium orchids arise in long-stalked clusters from upper portions of stems. Plants bloom most heavily in summer, but they may produce some flowers all year in mildest climates. Do best in rich soil. Provide support and prune out dead or straggling growth.

S. ciliatum. Zones 19–28; or house or greenhouse plant. Foliage open and delicate; plants easily kept small. Leaves heart shaped, 1–3 in. long, with a few long, bristly teeth on edges. Clusters of three to seven flowers 1½ in. across.

S. littorale. Zones 15–27. Larger, coarser vine than *S. ciliatum,* with larger (to 5-in.-long) oval leaves and larger clusters (10–20) of smaller flowers (1 in. across). Extremely vigorous; can climb to tops of tall trees.

STIPA

FEATHER GRASS, NEEDLE GRASS	
Poaceae (Gramineae)	
PERENNIAL GRASSES	
ZONES VARY BY SPECIES	
FULL SUN	
WATER NEEDS VARY BY SPECIES	

Stipa gigantea

Feather or needle grasses have large, open, airy inflorescences that can impart lightness and motion to the garden. Of the 150 or so species, a few have special merit.

S. gigantea. GIANT FEATHER GRASS. Zones 4–9, 14–24, 29–34. Clumps of narrow, arching leaves grow 2–3 ft. tall. Open, airy sheaves of yellowish flowers shimmer in a broad cloud reaching to 6 ft. in height and breadth. Regular water; established plants endure some drought.

S. pulchra. PURPLE NEEDLE GRASS. Zones 5, 7–9, 11, 14–24. One of the bunch grasses that once covered much of California's Central Valley and foothills—and pretty much restricted to wild gardens in its native range. Foliage reaches 1–1½ ft. high, flowering stems to 3 ft. Purplish flowers with long bristles mature, along with leaves, to golden yellow in summer. Plants then go dormant until winter rains arrive. No supplemental irrigation needed.

S. tenuissima. MEXICAN FEATHER GRASS, TEXAS NEEDLE GRASS. Zones 4–24, 29, 30, 33. Very thin bright green leaves form erect clumps that arch outward toward the top. Numerous thin flowering stems divide and redivide into almost hairlike fineness, green at first, then golden. Single or scattered clumps are effective among ground cover or boulders, on slopes. Larger plantings can create effective erosion control. Water regularly, but let soil dry out between irrigations. Can self-sow.

STOCK. See MATTHIOLA

STOKESIA laevis

STOKES' ASTER	
Asteraceae (Compositae)	
PERENNIAL	
ZONES 2–9, 12–24, 26, 28–43	
FULL SUN	
REGULAR WATER	

Stokesia laevis

Native to southeastern U.S. A rugged and most adaptable plant. Much branched, with stiff, erect stems 1½–2 ft. high. Smooth, firm-textured, medium green leaves, 2–8 in. long, sometimes toothed at base, evergreen (to semievergreen in cold climates). Leafy, curved, finely toothed bracts surround tight flower buds; in summer or early autumn, these open to 3–4 in.-wide, asterlike flower heads in blue, purplish blue, or white. Each blossom has a central button of small flowers surrounded by a ring of larger ones. Long-lasting cut flower. Grows best in well-drained soil. Provide winter cover of evergreen boughs or straw in coldest regions. Good in pots.

S

Choices include 10-in.-high 'Bluestone', medium blue; and the 1½-ft. tall varieties 'Blue Danube', with lavender blue blossoms and a long bloom season extending into winter in mildest climates; 'Klaus Jelitto', light blue; 'Silver Moon', white; and 'Wyoming', deep purple.

STONECRESS. See AETHIONEMA

STONECROP. See SEDUM

STRAWBERRY

Rosaceae

PERENNIALS

🌿 ALL ZONES

☀ FULL SUN

💧 REGULAR WATER

▸ SEE CHART NEXT PAGE

Strawberry

Plants have toothed, roundish, medium green leaves and white flowers. They grow 6–8 in. tall, spreading by long runners to about 1 ft. across.

June-bearing types produce one crop per year in late spring or early summer; generally, they are the highest-quality strawberries you can grow. Day-neutral or everbearing kinds flower and set fruit over a longer season. Their harvest tends to peak in early summer, then continue (often unevenly) through fall; the exact fruiting pattern depends on the variety. Everbearers put out fewer runners than June bearers.

Strawberries of one variety or another can be grown in every part of the U. S. and most of populous Canada, though success is difficult where soil and water salinity are very high. Varieties tend to be regionally adapted; check the accompanying chart for some of the best selections, and look for other good choices in local nurseries.

To bring in a big crop of berries, plant in rows—on flat ground if soil drains well, or on a raised mound (5–6 in. high) if soil is heavy or poorly drained. Set plants 14–18 in. apart in rows spaced 2–2½ ft. apart. For a small harvest, you can grow a dozen or so plants in a sunny patch in a flower or vegetable garden, or put them in boxes or tubs on the patio.

Planting season is usually determined by when local nurseries offer plants. In mild-winter areas, set out June bearers in late summer or fall for a crop the next spring; in colder climates, plant in early spring for harvest the following year. Set out everbearing plants in spring for summer–fall berries (in some areas, they may be available for fall planting); pinch off the earliest blossoms to increase plant vigor.

Plant carefully. The crown should be above soil level (a buried crown will rot); topmost roots should be ¼ in. beneath soil level (exposed roots will dry out). Mulch to deter weeds, conserve moisture, and keep berries clean.

Strawberry plants need about 1 in. of water per week throughout the growing season, even more moisture when bearing fruit. Drip irrigation is ideal to help reduce disease problems, but overhead irrigation is satisfactory. Feed June bearers twice a year—very lightly when growth begins and again, more heavily, after fruiting. Everbearing types prefer consistent light fertilization. Heavy feeding of either type in spring leads to excessive plant growth, soft fruit, and fruit rot.

Most varieties reproduce by runner plants; some make few or no offsets. Pinch off all runners to get large plants with smaller yields of big berries; let runner plants grow 7–10 in. apart for heavy yields of smaller berries. When your plants have made enough offsets, pinch off additional runners. Do not let the planting become too dense, since that leads to much lower yields, diseases, and poor-quality fruit.

Most perennially grown June bearers benefit greatly from renovation. After the harvest is over, cut off the foliage; you can use a lawn mower set high so it won't injure the crowns. If diseases were a problem, dispose of the leaves. Water and fertilize to encourage new growth. This is also a good time to reduce a dense planting by removing the old "mother" plants and leaving the younger, more productive "daughter" plants.

Some home gardeners are following the example of commercial growers who treat strawberries as annuals. Plants are installed in summer or early fall, usually with a plastic mulch; they are not allowed to make offsets. After harvest, the plants are removed and a new planting made. Benefits are healthier plants, fewer weeds, and bigger fruit. 'Chandler' is especially well adapted to this system, but almost any variety can be grown this way if planted at just the right time (you may have to experiment).

Strawberries need a winter mulch in cold climates. Cover the planting with a 4–6-in. layer of straw or other light, weed-free organic material. When temperatures warm in spring, rake the mulch between the plants.

Plants are subject to many diseases: fruit rots (botrytis, anthracnose, leather rot), leaf diseases (leaf spot, leaf scorch, leaf blight), crown diseases (anthracnose), root diseases (verticillium wilt, red stele, black root rot), and—especially in the Pacific Northwest—viruses. Root weevils, aphids, mites, and slugs and snails are among potential pests. To help reduce problems, install only certified disease-free plants; also remove diseased foliage and ripe or rotten fruit. Replace plants with new ones as they begin to decline, usually after 3 years.

See variety chart for choices in standard strawberries. Ornamental types suitable for full sun or light shade include varieties with white-and-green leaves grown mainly as ground covers, since they do not fruit well. 'Pink Panda', a hybrid between a strawberry and a potentilla, has typical strawberry foliage and an occasional tasty berry, but it is grown chiefly for the inch-wide pink flowers it bears from spring through fall.

STRAWBERRY BUSH. See EUONYMUS americana

STRAWBERRY GERANIUM. See SAXIFRAGA stolonifera

STRAWBERRY SHRUB. See CALYCANTHUS floridus

STRAWBERRY TREE. See ARBUTUS unedo

STRAWFLOWER. See HELICHRYSUM bracteatum

STRELITZIA

BIRD OF PARADISE

Strelitziaceae

EVERGREEN PERENNIALS

🌿 ZONES VARY BY SPECIES

☀◐ LIGHT SHADE IN HOTTEST AREAS

💧 REGULAR WATER

Strelitzia reginae

Tropical plants of extremely individual character. Both species are good to use by pools; they make no litter and seem to withstand some splashing. Endure temperatures to about 28°F/−2°C.

S. nicolai. GIANT BIRD OF PARADISE. Zones 22–25, 26 (southern part), 27; with protection, Zones 12, 13, northern part of 26. This one is grown for its dramatic display of leaves (similar to those of banana plants); flowers are incidental. Treelike and clumping, with many stalks to 30 ft. Gray-green, leathery, 5–10-ft. leaves are arranged fanwise on erect or curving trunks. Floral envelope is purplish gray, flower is white with dark blue tongue. Feed young plants frequently to push to full dramatic size, then give little or no feeding. Goal is to acquire and maintain size without lush growth and need for dividing. Keep dead leaves cut off and thin out surplus growth.

S. reginae. BIRD OF PARADISE. Zones 22–25, 26 (southern part), 27; under overhangs where heat can be trapped in Zones 9, 12–21, northern part of 26, and warmer parts of 28. Grown for its spectacular flowers, which bear a startling resemblance to tropical birds. Flowers combine orange, blue, and white, are borne on long, stiff stems; they appear intermittently throughout year, but flowering is best in cool season. Long lasting on plant and as cut flower. Trunkless plant grows 5 ft. high, with leathery, long-stalked, blue-green leaves to 1½ ft. long, 4–6 in. wide. Benefits

▸ page 509

STRAWBERRY

NAME	DESCRIPTION	ADAPTABILITY	RESISTANCE
JUNE-BEARING VARIETIES			
'Allstar'	Large, firm, light red fruit with good flavor. Consistent production	Widely adapted, but best in Mid-Atlantic, Northeast, eastern Canada, Great Lakes, Midwest	Resistant to red stele, verticillium wilt, leaf diseases
'Annapolis'	Early, consistent production of medium-large fruit	Mid-Atlantic, Northeast, eastern Canada, Great Lakes, Midwest	Resistant to red stele
'Apollo'	Good-size, firm, flavorful fruit. Fairly late	Southeast (also adapted to annual production there)	Tolerant of leaf diseases
'Atlas'	Firm berries with good aroma	Southeast	Tolerant of leaf scorch and leaf spot
'Benton'	Good crop of flavorful berries	Pacific Northwest	Virus tolerant, mildew resistant
'Camarosa'	Large, attractive, firm fruit over a long period	All regions in annual production	Susceptible to mites
'Cardinal'	Large, firm fruit with good flavor and color. Can be acidic	Southeast and lower Midwest	Susceptible to anthracnose
'Chandler'	Large juicy berries produced over long period. Very good flavor, good texture	California as perennial; all regions in annual production	Some resistance to leaf spot
'Delmarvel'	Early berry with excellent flavor. Moderate yields	Southeast, Mid-Atlantic	Some resistance to anthracnose. Resistant to red stele
'Earliglow'	Early crop of medium-size berries of excellent flavor and quality. Moderate yields	Widely adapted, but best in Southeast, Mid-Atlantic, Northeast, eastern Canada, Great Lakes, Midwest	Resistant to red stele. Tolerates fruit rot better than many other varieties
'Honeoye'	Large, firm fruit. Excellent, consistent production	Widely adapted, but best in Mid-Atlantic, Northeast, eastern Canada, Great Lakes, Midwest	Resistant to leaf diseases. Susceptible to red stele, verticillium wilt and, in the Pacific Northwest, viruses
'Hood'	Early, large, cone-shaped, bright red berries for fresh use, jam. Not the best variety for freezing	Pacific Northwest	Resists mildew. Susceptible to viruses
'Jewel'	Large, firm fruit with good flavor. Reliable producer	Widely adapted, but best in Mid-Atlantic, Northeast, eastern Canada, Great Lakes, Midwest	Resistant to leaf diseases. Reportedly tolerant of bacterial leaf spot. Susceptible to red stele
'Kent'	Large, firm, dark red fruit. Excellent production. Cold-hardy variety from Canada	Widely adapted, but best in Mid-Atlantic, Northeast, eastern Canada, Great Lakes, Midwest	Resistant to leaf diseases. Susceptible to red stele
'Northeaster'	Early crop of large berries with very good flavor	Northeast, eastern Canada, Great Lakes, Mid-Atlantic	Resistant to red stele
'Puget Reliance'	Large crop of big, tasty fruit; excellent flavor when processed. Vigorous plant	Pacific Northwest	Tolerant of viruses
'Rainier'	Berries of uniformly good size and excellent flavor. Good home garden variety	Pacific Northwest	Fair tolerance of root rot
'Redcrest'	Late crop of superior quality when processed for jam and jellies or frozen	Pacific Northwest	Susceptible to red stele and leaf diseases
'Sumas'	Early crop of large, attractive berries. Consistent producer	Pacific Northwest	Resists fruit rot
'Totem'	Juicy berries with excellent color and flavor. Outstanding for jam, jellies, and freezing. Productive. Late frosts can impair fruit set	Pacific Northwest	Resistant to red stele; tolerant of viruses. Holds berries off ground so fruit rot is less of a problem

S

STRAWBERRY

NAME	DESCRIPTION	ADAPTABILITY	RESISTANCE
JUNE-BEARING VARIETIES			
'Winona'	Reliable production of very good quality fruit in northern climates. Especially cold-hardy	Midwest	Resistant to red stele
DAY-NEUTRAL/ EVERBEARING VARIETIES			
'Quinalt'	Large, attractive fruit with very good flavor	Pacific Northwest	Resistant to viruses and red stele. Susceptible to botrytis
'Seascape'	Good production of large berries. Very good quality fresh; good quality for jam and freezing	Southeast, Pacific Northwest, California as perennial; annual production elsewhere	
'Selva'	Sweet fruit is large for everbearer	Southeast, Pacific Northwest, California as perennial; annual production elsewhere	Appears to have some resistance to red stele. Susceptible to spider mites, leaf spot in mild parts of Pacific Northwest
'Tribute'	Medium to large fruit with excellent flavor	All regions	Resistant to red stele and verticillium wilt. Susceptible to viruses in Pacific Northwest
'Tristar'	Medium-size berries with excellent flavor	All regions	Resistant to red stele and mildew. Moderately susceptible to viruses

greatly from frequent and heavy feedings. Divide infrequently, since large, crowded clumps bloom best. Good in containers. Recovers slowly from frost damage.

STREPTOCARPUS

CAPE PRIMROSE

Gesneriaceae

EVERGREEN PERENNIALS

🌿 ZONES 17, 22–24; OR HOUSE OR GREENHOUSE PLANTS

◐ ● PARTIAL OR FULL SHADE

💧 AMPLE WATER

Streptocarpus Hybrid

Related to gloxinias and African violets and look something like a cross between the two. Leaves are fleshy, sometimes velvety. Flowers are trumpet shaped, with long tube and spreading mouth. Long bloom season; some flower intermittently all year. Indoors, handle like African violets. Many species and hybrids of interest to fanciers; most widely available kinds are hybrids.

Large-flowered hybrids (Giant Hybrids). Clumps of long, narrow leaves and 1-ft.-high stems with long-tubed, 1½–2-in.-wide flowers in white, blue, pink, rose, red; often show contrasting blotches. Usually bloom after 1 year from seed. Wiesmoor hybrids are similar but grow taller (stems to 2 ft. high).

S. saxorum (Streptocarpella saxorum). Unlike other types; shrubby, much-branched perennial that makes a spreading mound of furry, gray-green, 1½-in.-long, fleshy leaves. Bloom comes in waves over much of year; the two-tone flowers are pale blue and white, 1½ in. wide, carried on 3–4-in. stems. Makes a splendid hanging container plant. Among hybrids developed from it, 'Concord Blue', with large flowers, blooms continuously.

STREPTOSOLEN jamesonii

MARMALADE BUSH

Solanaceae

EVERGREEN VINING SHRUB

🌿 ZONES 16, 17, 23–27

☀ ◐ FULL SUN OR PARTIAL SHADE

💧 REGULAR WATER

Streptosolen jamesonii

To 4–6 ft. tall and as wide; to 10–15 ft. trained against wall, bank, trellis. Ribbed, oval leaves to 1½ in. long. Large, loose clusters of 1-in.-wide, orange (sometimes yellow) flowers are carried at branch ends, spring–fall (even longer in frost-free areas). Grow in warm spot with fast drainage. Where frosts occur, protect plant; cut back dead wood after last frost. Effective spilling over a wall, lining garden stairs, in hanging basket.

Styracaceae. The storax family includes trees and shrubs with bell-shaped, usually white flowers. Members are *Halesia*, epaulette tree (*Pterostyrax*), and *Styrax*.

STYRAX

Styracaceae

DECIDUOUS TREES

🌿 ZONES VARY BY SPECIES

☀ ◐ FULL SUN OR PARTIAL SHADE

💧 REGULAR WATER

Styrax japonicus

Neat, well-behaved flowering trees of modest size for patios or lawns; make a nice contrast in front of larger, darker-leafed trees. Both the

S

species described below put on a spring show of white, bell-shaped flowers in hanging clusters. Easy to garden under, since roots are deep and nonaggressive. Provide good, well-drained, nonalkaline soil. Neither species will succeed in dry heat of the Southwest or lower Midwest.

S. japonicus. JAPANESE SNOWDROP TREE, JAPANESE SNOWBELL. Zones 3–10, 14–21, 32–34, 39. To 30 ft. tall, with slender, graceful trunk; branches often strongly horizontal, giving tree a broad, flat top. Oval, scallop-edged leaves to 3 in. long; turn from dark green to red or yellow in fall. Faintly fragrant, ¾-in. white flowers hang in small clusters on short side branches. Leaves angle upward from branches while flowers hang down, giving the effect of parallel green and white tiers. Prune to control shape; tends to be shrubby unless lower side branches are suppressed. Splendid tree to look up into; plant it in raised beds near outdoor entertaining areas, or on a high bank above a path. 'Pendula' ('Carillon') is a shrubby variety with weeping branches; 'Pink Chimes', also shrubby, is a more upright form with pink flowers.

S. obassia. FRAGRANT SNOWBELL. Zones 3–10, 14–21, 32–35, 37, 39. To 20–30 ft. tall, rather narrow. Oval to round, deep green, 3–8-in.-long leaves. Where frosts come very late, leaves may color yellow in autumn. Fragrant flowers to 1 in. long are carried in drooping, 6–8-in. clusters at branch ends and may be partly obscured by foliage. Blooms a little earlier than *S. japonicus*. Good against background of evergreens, or for height and contrast above border of rhododendrons and azaleas.

SUCCULENTS. Strictly speaking, a succulent is any plant that stores water in juicy leaves, stems, or roots to withstand periodic drought. Practically speaking, fanciers of succulents exclude such fleshy plants as epiphytic orchids and include in their collections many desert plants such as yuccas that are not fleshy. Although cacti are succulents, common consent sets them up as a separate category (see Cactaceae).

Most succulents come from desert or semidesert areas in warmer parts of the world. Mexico and South Africa are two very important sources. Some (notably sedums and sempervivums) come from colder climates, where they grow on sunny, rocky slopes and ledges.

Succulents are grown everywhere as house plants; in mildest-winter climates, many are useful and decorative as landscaping plants, either in open ground or in containers. When well grown and well groomed, they look good all year, in bloom or out. Although considered low-maintenance plants, they look shabby if neglected; they may live through extended drought but will drop leaves, shrivel, or lose color. Amount of irrigation needed depends on summer heat, humidity of atmosphere, rainfall level. Give plants just enough water to keep them healthy, plump of leaf, and attractive.

One light feeding at start of growing season should be enough for plants in open ground. Larger-growing and later-blooming kinds may require additional feeding.

Some succulents make good ground covers. Some are sturdy and quick growing enough for erosion control on large banks. Other smaller kinds are useful among stepping-stones or for creating patterns in small gardens. Most of these come easily from stem or leaf cuttings, and a stock can quickly be grown from a few plants. See *Echeveria*, ice plant, *Sedum*, *Senecio*.

Large-growing succulents have decorative value. See *Agave*, *Aloe*, *Cotyledon*, *Crassula*, *Echeveria*, *Kalanchoe*, *Portulacaria*, *Yucca*.

Many succulents have showy flowers. For some of the best, see *Aloe*, some species of *Crassula*, *Hoya*, ice plant, *Kalanchoe*.

Some smaller succulents are primarily collectors' items, grown for odd form or flowers. See smaller species of *Aloe*, *Ceropegia*, *Crassula*, *Echeveria*, *Euphorbia*, *Stapelia*.

A few words of caution to growers of succulents:

Variety of forms, colors, textures offers many possibilities for handsome combinations, but there's a fine line between successful grouping and jumbled medley. Beware of using too many kinds in one planting. Mass a few species instead of putting in one of each.

You can combine succulents with other types of plants, but plan combinations carefully. Not all plants look right with them. Consider also different cultural requirements.

SWEET POTATO

Convolvulaceae

PERENNIAL GROWN AS ANNUAL

ZONES 8–10, 12–14, 18–21, 26–33

BEST IN FULL SUN

REGULAR WATER

Sweet Potato

Not a potato, but the thickened root of a trailing tropical vine closely related to morning glory (*Ipomoea*). Bush and short vine varieties also available. Needs long, hot, frost-free growing season—easiest to grow in the South. Also requires well-drained soil (preferably sandy loam) and plenty of room. Start with certified disease-free slips (rooted cuttings) from a garden center or mail-order nursery. Look for resistant varieties. To avoid buildup of disease organisms in the soil, don't grow sweet potatoes in the same location 2 years in a row.

There are two classes of sweet potatoes. One has soft, sugary yellow-orange flesh (examples are 'Centennial', 'Gold Rush', 'Vineless Puerto Rico'); the other has firm, dry whitish flesh (members of this group include 'Yellow Jersey', 'Nemagold'). The sweet yellow-orange type is incorrectly labeled "yam" when sold in grocery stores. Most varieties are ready to harvest 110 to 120 days after planting.

Plant in late spring when soil temperature has warmed to 70°F/21°C. Work in a low-nitrogen fertilizer before planting; too much nitrogen produces leafy growth at the expense of roots. Set slips so that only stem tips

S

and leaves are exposed; space 1 ft. apart, in rows 3 ft. apart. To ensure good drainage, mark off rows and ditch between them to form planting ridges. Row covers provide added heat and keep out many pests. Harvest before first frost; if tops are killed by sudden frost, harvest immediately. Dig carefully to avoid cutting or bruising roots. Flavor improves in storage (starch is converted to sugar). Dry roots in sun, then cure by storing for 10 to 14 days in warm (about 85°F/29°C), humid place. Store in cooler environment (but not below 55°F/13°C) until ready to use.

Sweet potatoes are sometimes grown for decorative foliage—leaves are heart shaped in some varieties, cut or lobed in others. Ornamental variety 'Blackie' has deep purple leaves on purple stems; it is handsome in hanging baskets. 'Sulfur' is similar, but with bright yellow to chartreuse foliage.

SWEETSHADE. See HYMENOSPORUM flavum

SWEETSHRUB. See CALYCANTHUS floridus

SWEETSPIRE. See ITEA

SWEET SULTAN. See CENTAUREA moschata

SWEET WILLIAM. See DIANTHUS barbatus

SWEET WOODRUFF. See GALIUM odoratum

SWISS CHARD

Chenopodiaceae

BIENNIAL GROWN AS ANNUAL

🗡 ALL ZONES

☀ FULL SUN

🔴 REGULAR WATER

A form of beet grown for leaves and stalks instead of roots. One of the easiest and most practical of vegetables for home gardens. Sow big, crinkly, tan seeds ½–¾ in. deep in spaded soil, any time from early spring to early summer. Thin seedlings to 1 ft. apart. About 2 months after sowing (plants are generally 1–1½ ft. tall) you can begin to cut outside leaves from plants as needed for meals. New leaves grow up in center of plants. Yield all summer and seldom bolt to seed (if one does, pull it up and throw it away). In hotsummer, mild-winter areas, can be grown as fall–spring crop.

Regular green-and-white chard looks presentable in flower garden. 'Rhubarb' chard has red stems and reddish green leaves; it looks attractive in garden beds or containers. Its leaves are valuable in floral arrangements and tasty when cooked, too—sweeter and stronger flavored than green chard. Cook leaves and leafstalks separately, since stalks take longer.

Swiss Chard

SWISS CHEESE PLANT. See MONSTERA friedrichsthalii

SWITCH GRASS. See PANICUM virgatum

SWORD FERN. See NEPHROLEPIS, POLYSTICHUM munitum

SYAGRUS romanzoffianum (Arecastrum romanzoffianum)

QUEEN PALM

Arecaceae (Palmae)

PALM

🗡 ZONES 12, 13, 15–17, 19–27

☀ FULL SUN

🔴 REGULAR WATER

Syagrus romanzoffianum

South American palm with exceptionally straight trunk to 50 ft. Arching, bright glossy green leaves 10–15 ft. long; leaves break in high winds.

Grows quickly with fertilizer. May produce decorative orange dates. Subject to mites; wash young plants frequently. Damaged at 25°F/−4°C, but has recovered from 16°F/−9°C freeze. A good substitute for the more tender royal palm (*Roystonea*). Sometimes sold as *Cocos plumosa*.

SYCAMORE. See PLATANUS

SYMPHORICARPOS

SNOWBERRY, CORALBERRY

Caprifoliaceae

DECIDUOUS SHRUBS

🗡 ZONES VARY BY SPECIES

☀◐● EXPOSURE NEEDS VARY BY SPECIES

🔴 MODERATE WATER

Symphoricarpos albus

North American natives. Low growing, often spreading by root suckers. Small, pink-tinged or white flowers in clusters or spikes. Attractive round, berrylike fruit remains on stems after leaves drop in autumn; nice in winter arrangements, attracts birds. Use as informal hedge or to control erosion on slopes.

S. albus (S. racemosus). COMMON SNOWBERRY. Zones 1–11, 14–21, 32–45. Upright or spreading shrub 2–6 ft. tall. Leaves roundish, dull green, ¾–2 in. long (to 4 in. and often lobed on sucker shoots). Pink flowers in spring, followed by white fruit from late summer to winter. Best fruit production in sun. Not a first-rate shrub, but useful in its tolerance of poor soil, urban air, and shade. Withstands neglect.

S. chenaultii. Zones 1–11, 14–21, 32–43. Hybrid. Resembles parent *S. orbiculatus*, but red fruit is lightly spotted white and leaves are larger. 'Hancock' is 1-ft. dwarf valued as woodland ground or bank cover. High shade.

S. mollis. CREEPING SNOWBERRY, SPREADING SNOWBERRY. Zones 2–10, 14–24. Like *S. albus*, but usually less than 1½ ft. high, with earlier and sparser bloom, smaller fruit. Spreads like ground cover. Best in partial shade.

S. orbiculatus (S. vulgaris). CORALBERRY, INDIAN CURRANT. Zones 1–11, 14–21, 32–45. Resembles *S. albus*, but bears a profusion of small purplish red fruit in clusters. These are bright enough and plentiful enough to provide a good fall–winter show. Full sun.

SYMPHYTUM officinale

COMFREY

Boraginaceae

PERENNIAL HERB

🗡 ZONES 1–24, 26–43

☀◐ PARTIAL SHADE IN HOT-SUMMER AREAS

🔴 REGULAR WATER

☠ LEAVES ARE POISONOUS IF INGESTED

Symphytum officinale

Deep-rooted, clumping plant to 3 ft. high. Furry leaves with stiff hairs; basal leaves to 8 in. long or more, upper leaves smaller. Flowers not showy, ½ in. long, usually dull rose in color but sometimes white, cream, or purple. Leaves can be dried and brewed to make a medicinal tea, but this use is no longer recommended. In virtually frost-free climates, comfrey remains leafy through winter; elsewhere, it dies to the ground in fall. To keep leaf production high, cut out flowering stalks and mulch each spring with compost. Grow from root cuttings.

Although comfrey has a long history as a folk remedy, think hard before establishing it in your garden. Plant spreads freely from roots and is difficult to eradicate. Herb enthusiasts claim that comfrey accumulates minerals, enriches compost.

FOR INFORMATION ON YOUR CLIMATE ZONE
PLEASE SEE PAGES 16–78

S

SYMPLOCOS paniculata

SAPPHIREBERRY, SWEETLEAF

Symplocaceae

DECIDUOUS SHRUB

🗡 ZONES 2–9, 14–17, 32–41

☼ FULL SUN

🔴 REGULAR WATER

Symplocos paniculata

To 10–20 ft. tall; wider than tall in maturity. Can be trained as a low-branching or multitrunked small tree. Dark green leaves to 3½ in. long and half as wide. In late spring or early summer, 2–3-in. clusters of small, fragrant white flowers bloom on previous year's wood. Main draw is the autumn show of sapphire blue, ⅓-in. fruits that garland the branches. Berries are much appreciated by birds. Single plants set little or no fruit, so it's best to plant groups of seedlings; cutting-grown plants from a single parent are not self-fertile. Some growers sell groups of three seedlings as a single plant to ensure fruiting. Use for screening or as a feature in a large shrub border.

SYNADENIUM grantii

Euphorbiaceae

EVERGREEN SHRUB

🗡 ZONES 21–25; OR INDOORS

☼◐ FULL SUN OR LIGHT SHADE

🔴 MODERATE WATER

🔻 STEMS CONTAIN MILKY, POISONOUS SAP

Synadenium grantii

Can reach 8–12 ft. in warm, frost-free location, but usually grows much lower. Thick stems are clothed with dark green leaves to 4–7 in. long and half as wide. Form usually grown is 'Rubra', with deep purplish red leaves and clusters of red flowers at branch ends. Resembles *Euphorbia cotinifolia*, but easily distinguished from it by stalkless leaves that taper toward the main stems; leaves of *E. cotinifolia* have long stalks. Showy container plant.

SYRINGA

LILAC

Oleaceae

DECIDUOUS SHRUBS, RARELY SMALL TREES

🗡 ZONES VARY BY SPECIES

☼◐ LIGHT SHADE IN HOTTEST AREAS

🔴 REGULAR WATER

Syringa vulgaris

A garden staple in cold-winter regions, cherished for big, flamboyant, usually fragrant flower clusters at branch tips. Best known are common lilac (*S. vulgaris*) and its many varieties, but there are other species of great usefulness. All are medium-size to large shrubs with no special appeal when out of bloom. Individual flowers are tubular, flaring into four petal-like lobes (in single types) or into a clutch of "petals" (in double kinds). Floral show comes from number of small flowers packed into dense pyramidal to conical clusters. Depending on climate, bloom occurs from early spring (in the earliest kinds) to early summer, always after leaves have formed. Some forms bloom well with only light winter chill.

Provide well-drained, neutral to slightly alkaline soil; if soil is strongly acid, dig lime into it before planting. Most lilacs bloom on wood formed the previous year, so prune just after flowering ends. Remove spent flower clusters, cutting back to a pair of leaves; growth buds at that point will make flowering stems for next year. Renovate old, overgrown plants by cutting a few of oldest stems to the ground each year. For the few types that bloom on new growth, prune in late dormant season. Stem borer, scale, and leaf miner are the major pests; powdery mildew, leaf spot, and bacterial blight may be problems.

S. chinensis (S. rothomagensis). CHINESE LILAC. Zones 1–11, 14–16, 18–21, 32–43. Hybrid between common lilac and *S. persica*. To 15 ft. high, usually much less. More graceful than common lilac, with finer-textured foliage and twigs. Profusion of airy, open clusters of fragrant rose purple flowers. Does well in mild-winter, hot-summer climates. 'Alba' has white flowers.

S. hyacinthiflora. Zones 1–12, 14–16, 18–22, 32–43. Group of fragrant hybrids between common lilac and *S. oblata*, a Chinese species. Resemble common lilac, but generally bloom 7 to 10 days earlier. 'Assessippi' (single lavender), 'Excel' (single lilac blue), 'Grace McKenzie' (single lilac blue), and 'Mt. Baker' (single white) are very early blooming. Other varieties include 'Alice Eastwood' (double magenta), 'Blue Hyacinth' (single lavender), 'Clarke's Giant' (single lavender, larger flowers), 'Esther Staley' (single magenta), 'Gertrude Leslie' (double white), 'Pocahontas' (single purple), 'Purple Heart' (single purple), and 'White Hyacinth' (single white).

S. josikaea. HUNGARIAN LILAC. Zones 1–11, 14–16, 18–21, 32–43. Dense, upright growth to 12 ft. Dark green foliage. Lilac purple, slightly fragrant flowers in narrow clusters 4–7 in. long.

S. laciniata (S. persica laciniata). Zones 3–12, 14–16, 18–22, 31–35, 37, 39. To 8 ft. tall, with open habit and good rich green foliage color. Leaves to 2½ in. long, divided nearly to midrib into three to nine segments. Many small clusters of fragrant lilac-colored blooms.

S. meyeri 'Paliban'. Zones 1–9, 14–16, 32–43. Dense, neat habit to 4–5 ft. high, somewhat wider. Fine-textured, mildew-resistant foliage. Starts flowering when only a foot high. Profusion of reddish purple buds open to softly fragrant light pink flowers. Sometimes sold as *S. palibiniana* or *S. velutina*.

S. microphylla 'Superba'. Zones 2–11, 14–16, 18–21, 32–41. Compact grower to 7 ft. tall. Mildew-resistant leaves. Deep red buds open to fragrant, single bright pink flowers. Sometimes reblooms in September.

S. patula 'Miss Kim'. Zones 1–9, 14–16, 32–43. Dense, twiggy, rounded habit to eventual 8–9 ft., but stays at 3 ft. for many years. Sometimes grafted high to make standard tree. Purple buds open to very fragrant icy blue flowers. Leaves may turn burgundy in fall.

S. persica. PERSIAN LILAC. Zones 2–12, 14–16, 18–22, 31–41. Graceful, loose form to 6 ft. high, with arching branches and 2½-in.-long leaves. Many clusters of fragrant pale violet flowers appear all along branches.

S. prestoniae. Zones 1–11, 14–16, 33–45. Group of extra-hardy hybrids developed in Canada. Flowers come on new growth at the end of the lilac season, after common lilac has bloomed. Bulky, dense plants resemble common lilac, but they are shorter (to 6–10 ft.) and individual flowers are smaller and not particularly fragrant. Good selections include 'Donald Wyman' (dark rosy purple), 'Isabella' (lilac), 'Jessica' (violet), 'Minuet' (pale lilac), 'Miss Canada' (true bright pink), 'Nocturne' (bluish lilac), and 'Royalty' (purple to violet). For 'James MacFarlane' (sometimes sold as a member of this group), see *S. swegiflexa*.

S. reticulata (S. japonica, S. amurensis japonica). JAPANESE TREE LILAC. Zones 1–12, 14–16, 32–43. Can be grown as large shrub to 30 ft. tall, or easily trained as single-trunked tree. Smooth bark, something like cherry bark in glossiness. Leaves to 5 in. long. White flower clusters, to 1 ft. long, produced on new growth late in lilac season. Flowers showy, but scent is like that of privet flowers.

S. swegiflexa. Zones 3–9, 14–16, 32–34. Hybrid between two Chinese species, *S. reflexa* and *S. sweginzowii*; sometimes known by the name "pink pearl lilac." To 12 ft. tall. Deep reddish buds open to fragrant single pink flowers in clusters to 8 in. long. Blooms on new growth, 3 weeks after common lilac. 'James MacFarlane' is best-known variety.

S. vulgaris. COMMON LILAC. Zones 1–11, 14, 32–45. Can eventually reach 20 ft. tall, with nearly equal spread. Suckers strongly. Prune out suckers on grafted plants (no need to do so on own-root plants). Leaves roundish oval, pointed, dark green, to 5 in. long. Blooms in midspring, bearing pinkish or bluish lavender flowers in clusters to 10 in. long or more ('Alba' has pure white flowers). Fragrance is legendary; lilac fanciers

S

swear that the species and its older varieties are more fragrant than newer types. Excellent cut flowers.

Varieties, often called French hybrids, number in the hundreds. They generally flower a little later than the species and have larger clusters of single or double flowers in a wide range of colors. Singles are often as showy as doubles, sometimes more so. All lilacs require 2 to 5 years to settle down and produce flowers of full size and true color. Here are just a few of the many choice varieties:

'Charles Joly' (double dark purplish red), 'Miss Ellen Willmott' (double pure white), 'Ludwig Spaeth' (single reddish purple to dark purple), 'President Lincoln' (single Wedgwood blue), 'President Poincaré' (double two-tone purple), 'Sensation' (single wine red with white picotee edge), 'William Robinson' (double pink).

Newer hybrids include 'Krasavitsa Moskvy' ('Beauty of Moscow'), with large clusters of pink buds opening into double white flowers; 'Nadezhda' ('Hope'), with deep purple buds opening into lilac blue double flowers; and 'Primrose', with pale yellow blooms (paler in warm climates).

The Descanso Hybrids, developed to accept mild winters, perform exceptionally well in Zones 18–22; they are worthy of trial in the southeastern U.S. Best known is 'Lavender Lady'; other varieties include 'Blue Skies', 'Blue Boy', 'Chiffon' (lavender), 'Forrest K. Smith' (light lavender), 'Sylvan Beauty' (rose lavender), and 'White Angel' ('Angel White').

SYZYGIUM

Myrtaceae

EVERGREEN SHRUBS OR TREES

ZONES VARY BY SPECIES

BEST IN FULL SUN, TOLERATE SHADE

REGULAR WATER

Syzygium paniculatum

Closely related to *Eugenia* and usually sold as such in nurseries. Foliage rich green, often tinted coppery; new foliage brightly tinted. Flowers conspicuous for tufts of stamens that look like little brushes. Fruit is soft, edible, handsomely colored.

S. jambos (Eugenia jambos). ROSE APPLE. Zones 18–25, 27. Slow growth to 25–30 ft., usually much smaller and shrubby. Leaves 5–8 in. long, narrow, thick, shiny, coppery green; new growth pinkish. Greenish white flower brushes 2–3 in. across, carried in clusters at branch ends in spring. Sweetish, mild-flavored fruit is greenish or yellow (sometimes blushed pink), 1–2 in. wide, has fragrance of rose water. Slow growth means little or no pruning.

S. paniculatum (Eugenia myrtifolia, E. paniculata). BRUSH CHERRY, AUSTRALIAN BRUSH CHERRY. Zones 16, 17, 19–25. If left unclipped, makes a narrowish, single- or multitrunked tree to 30–60 ft. tall, with a dense foliage crown. Often clipped into formal shapes and hedges; also used as background or screening plant. Oblong, 1½–3-in.-long leaves in rich glossy green, often bronze tinged; reddish bronze new growth. Small, creamy white summer flowers are followed by showy, ¾-in. rose purple fruit, insipid if eaten raw but good in jellies. Several named varieties selected for good leaf color or dwarf form. Eugenia psyllid can cause defoliation; control is a predatory wasp.

TABEBUIA

Bignoniaceae

BRIEFLY DECIDUOUS, SOMETIMES EVERGREEN TREES

ZONES 15, 16, 20–26

FULL SUN OR LIGHT SHADE

REGULAR WATER

Tabebuia chrysotricha

Fast growth to 25–30 ft.; tend to have a gangly or irregular habit, especially in youth. Showy, trumpet-shaped flowers grow in rounded clusters

that become larger (up to 23 flowers) and more profuse as trees mature. Leaves dark olive green, usually divided into three to seven leaflets arranged like fingers of hand.

Useful as patio trees or as stand-alone flowering trees for display. Tolerate many soils and degrees of maintenance, but respond well to feeding. Good drainage essential. Stake while young and keep plants to single leading shoot until 6–8 ft. tall, then allow to develop freely. Hardy to about 24°F/–4°C.

T. chrysotricha. GOLDEN TRUMPET TREE. Sometimes sold as *T. pulcherrima*. Young twigs, undersides of leaves covered with tawny fuzz. Flowers are 3–4 in. long, golden yellow, often with maroon stripes in throat. Bloom heaviest in spring, when tree loses leaves for brief period. Sometimes blooms lightly at other times with leaves present.

T. heterophylla. PINK TRUMPET TREE. Sometimes grown as a large shrub. Summer blossoms are 2–3 in. long; color ranges from white to mauve, but dark pink is typical.

T. impetiginosa (T. ipe). PINK TRUMPET TREE. Lavender pink, 2–3-in.-long flowers have white throats banded with yellow. Blooms late winter, sometimes again late summer to fall. Does not bloom as a young tree.

TABERNAEMONTANA
divaricata (T. coronaria)

CRAPE JASMINE

Apocynaceae

EVERGREEN SHRUB

ZONES 25, 26

FULL SUN OR LIGHT SHADE

REGULAR TO MODERATE WATER

Tabernaemontana divaricata

Freely branching shrub with opposite pairs of glossy dark green leaves to 6 in. long. Branches form in pairs. Where branches fork, clusters of waxy white single flowers appear in summer; blossoms are 1½ in. wide, strongly fragrant at night. Double-flowered forms are available. More tender to frost than gardenia. Sometimes sold under its earlier name, *Ervatamia coronaria*.

TAGETES

MARIGOLD

Asteraceae (Compositae)

ANNUALS AND PERENNIALS

ZONES VARY BY SPECIES

FULL SUN

REGULAR WATER, EXCEPT AS NOTED

Tagetes erecta

Robust, free-branching, nearly trouble-free plants ranging from 6 in. to 4 ft. tall, with flowers from pale yellow through gold to orange and brown maroon. Leaves finely divided, ferny, usually strongly scented. Annuals will bloom early summer to frost if old flowers are picked off. Handsome, long-lasting cut flowers; strong aroma from leaves, stems, and flowers permeates a room, but some odorless varieties are available. Easy to grow from seed, which sprouts in a few days in warm soil; to get earlier bloom, start seeds in flats or buy flat-grown plants.

T. erecta. AFRICAN MARIGOLD, TALL MARIGOLD. Annual. All zones. Original strains were 3–4-ft.-tall plants with single flowers. Modern strains more varied; most have fully double flowers. They range from dwarf Guys and Dolls and Inca series (12–14 in.) through Galore, Lady, and Perfection (16–20 in.) to Climax (2½–3 ft.). Novelty tall strains are Odorless and First Whites (28–30 in.). 'Snowbird' (1½ ft.) is a white marigold with uniform habit and color. Triploid hybrids, crosses between African and French marigolds, have exceptional vigor, bear profusion of 2-in. flowers over a long bloom season. Generally shorter than other *T. erecta* strains, they range from 10-in. Nugget to 12–14-in. Fireworks, H-G, Solar, and Sundance.

T. filifolia. IRISH LACE. Annual. All zones. Mounds of bright green, finely divided foliage, 6 in. tall and as wide, resemble unusually fluffy, round ferns. Used primarily as edging plant for foliage effect, but tiny white flowers are attractive.

MAKE A TALL MARIGOLD PLANT STAND STRAIGHT

To make tall marigold plants stand as firmly as possible (perhaps stoutly enough not to need staking), dig planting holes extra deep, strip any leaves off lower 1–3 in. of stem, and plant with stripped portion below soil line.

T. lemmonii. Shrubby perennial. Zones 8–10, 12–24, 27–29. Native from southeastern Arizona (where it can reach 3 ft.) to southern Mexico and Central America, where it is a shrub to 6 ft. or taller, spreading as wide as it's high. Finely divided 4-in. leaves are aromatic when brushed against or rubbed—a strongly fragrant blend of marigold, mint, and lemon. Golden orange flower heads are carried at branch ends; bloom is sporadic all year, heaviest winter–spring. Damaged by frost in open situations; cut back to remove damaged growth or to correct shape and limit size. Takes aridity.

T. lucida. MEXICAN TARRAGON. Perennial in Zones 8–10, 12–24, 26–29, but usually grown as an annual in all zones. Single, usually unbranched stems grow to 2–2½ ft. Narrow, uncut, smooth dark green leaves have strong scent and flavor of tarragon. Unimpressive yellow flowers are less than ½ in. wide.

T. patula. FRENCH MARIGOLD. Annual. All zones. Varieties from 6–18 in. tall, in flower colors from yellow to rich maroon brown; flowers may be fully double or single, and many are strongly bicolored. Best for edging are the dwarf, very double Janie (8-in.), Bonanza (10-in.), and Hero (10–12-in.) series in a range of colors from yellow through orange to red and brownish red. The Aurora and Sophia series have flowers that are larger (2½ in. wide) but not as double.

T. tenuifolia (T. signata). SIGNET MARIGOLD. Annual. All zones. Infrequently planted. Smaller flower heads than French marigold, but incredibly profuse in bloom. Finely cut foliage. Golden orange 'Golden Gem' ('Ursula') and bright yellow 'Lemon Gem' both form 8-in. mounds.

TALLHEDGE BUCKTHORN. See RHAMNUS frangula 'Columnaris'

TAM. See JUNIPERUS sabina 'Tamariscifolia'

TAMARACK. See PINUS contorta latifolia

TAMARILLO. See CYPHOMANDRA betacea

TAMARIX

TAMARISK

Tamaricaceae

DECIDUOUS SHRUBS OR TREES

⚡ ZONES VARY BY SPECIES

☼ FULL SUN

🌢 MODERATE TO VERY LITTLE WATER

Tamarix ramosissima

These large shrubs or small trees are useful in areas where wind, salt, and poor soil are challenges, as in seacoast gardens. Only demands are sun and good drainage. Tend to be invasive in mild-winter climates and in rich soil; better behaved in more northerly regions. Tiny, scalelike, light green or bluish foliage on airy, arching, reddish branches; in spring or summer, narrow plumes of small pink or rose blossoms appear at branch ends. Prune regularly to maintain graceful effect. Locate where plant won't be prominent while out of leaf. There is much confusion in labeling of tamarisks in nurseries and among botanists.

T. parviflora. Zones 2–24, 28–43. To 12–15 ft. tall, usually not as wide. Light pink blossoms in late spring. Blooms on old wood; prune right after bloom.

T. ramosissima (T. pentandra). Zones 1–24, 28–45. To 10–15 ft. tall, usually not as wide. Rosy pink flowers in spring or early summer. Blooms on new wood; prune during late dormant season. 'Cheyenne Red' has deeper pink blooms than the species; 'Summer Glow' has bright pink flowers and blue-tinged foliage; 'Rosea' bears rich pink flowers later in summer.

TAMPALA. See AMARANTHUS tricolor

TANACETUM

Asteraceae (Compositae)

PERENNIAL HERBS

⚡ ZONES VARY BY SPECIES

☼ FULL SUN

🌢 REGULAR TO MODERATE WATER

Tanacetum vulgare

Most kinds of *Tanacetum* have finely divided leaves (often highly aromatic) and clusters of daisylike flower heads. Some have gray to nearly white foliage.

T. balsamita. See Chrysanthemum balsamita

T. coccineum. See Chrysanthemum coccineum

T. densum amanii. Zones 3–24. Sometimes sold as *Chrysanthemum haradjanii.* Low-growing plant spreading slowly to make broad mats. Leaves are finely cut, silvery white, featherlike in appearance. Small yellow flower heads appear a few inches above the mat. Use in rock garden, as small-scale ground cover in bright, sunny area with good drainage. Can withstand some dry spells when established. One of the whitest plants.

T. parthenium. See Chrysanthemum parthenium

T. ptarmiciflorum. See Chrysanthemum ptarmiciflorum

T. vulgare. TANSY. Zones 1–24, 26 (northern part), 28–43. Coarse garden plant to 3 ft. with finely divided bright green aromatic (some say smelly) leaves, and small yellow button flowers. Thin clumps yearly to keep in bounds. No longer used medicinally, though still grown in herb gardens. *T. v. crispum,* fern-leaf tansy, to 2½ ft., has finely cut foliage, is more decorative than the species.

TANGELO, TANGERINE, TANGOR. See CITRUS, Mandarin Hybrids and Mandarin

TANSY. See TANACETUM vulgare

TARO. See COLOCASIA esculenta

TARRAGON, FRENCH. See ARTEMISIA dracunculus

TARRAGON, MEXICAN. See TAGETES lucida

TASMANIAN TREE FERN. See DICKSONIA antarctica

TASSEL FERN. See POLYSTICHUM polyblepharum

Taxaceae. The yew family contains needle-leafed evergreens with single-seeded fruit surrounded by a fleshy coat. Yew (*Taxus*) is the most notable example.

Taxodiaceae. The taxodium family includes evergreen (and some deciduous) coniferous trees, usually with small cones containing two to six seeds on each scale. Members include *Cryptomeria,* dawn redwood (*Metasequoia*), umbrella pine (*Sciadopitys*), redwood (*Sequoia*), giant sequoia (*Sequoiadendron*), and *Taxodium.*

FOR GROWING SYMBOL EXPLANATIONS PLEASE SEE PAGE 161

TAXODIUM

Taxodiaceae

DECIDUOUS OR EVERGREEN TREES

❚ ZONES VARY BY SPECIES

☼ FULL SUN

🌢🌢🌢 MUCH OR LITTLE WATER

Taxodium distichum

Conifers of great size with shaggy, cinnamon-colored bark and graceful sprays of short, narrow, flat, needlelike leaves. Female flowers produce round, fragrant, 1-in. cones. The first two of the following species are native to the southeastern U.S., the third to Mexico; the U.S. natives adapt widely to much colder and drier climates. All are very tough, tolerant trees.

T. ascendens. POND CYPRESS. Deciduous. Zones 4–9, 12–24, 26, 28–41. Resembles bald cypress (*T. distichum*) in most details and is believed by some experts to be a variety of that species. Somewhat narrower and more erect than bald cypress; trunk not as strongly buttressed. Leafs out late in spring. In the wild, found on higher ground around ponds; doesn't actually grow in the water, as bald cypress does. 'Nutans' is the main form grown. 'Prairie Sentinel' is very narrow.

T. distichum. BALD CYPRESS. Deciduous. Zones 2–10, 12–24, 26, 28–43. Can grow into 100-ft.-tall, broad-topped tree in the wild, but young and middle-aged garden trees are pyramidal to 50–70 ft. high. Foliage sprays delicate and feathery, with narrow, about ½-in.-long leaves of a pale, delicate, yellow-toned green. Foliage turns orange brown before dropping. Interesting winter silhouette.

Any soil except strongly alkaline. Takes extremely wet conditions (even grows in swamps), but also tolerates rather dry soil. Trunk is buttressed near base. Develops knobby growths called "knees" when growing in waterlogged soil. Bagworms may be troublesome in some years. Requires only corrective pruning, to remove dead wood and unwanted branches. Outstanding tree for stream bank or edge of lake or pond.

T. mucronatum. MONTEZUMA CYPRESS. Evergreen in mild climates; partially or wholly deciduous in cold regions. Zones 5–10, 12–24, 29. With ample water, quickly attains 40 ft. in 14 years, then grows at a more moderate rate to reach an eventual 75 ft. Growth is slow under dry conditions. Extremely graceful, with strongly weeping branches. Has finer-textured, lighter-colored foliage than above two species. In colder part of range, foliage turns dull gold before falling very late in the year.

TAXUS

YEW

Taxaceae

EVERGREEN SHRUBS OR TREES

❚ ZONES VARY BY SPECIES

☼ ☽ FULL SUN OR PARTIAL SHADE

🌢🌢 REGULAR TO MODERATE WATER

🌢 FRUIT (SEEDS) AND FOLIAGE ARE POISONOUS IF INGESTED

Taxus baccata 'Stricta'

Yews are conifers—but they do not bear cones. Instead, they produce fleshy, scarlet (rarely yellow), cup-shaped, single-seeded fruit. In general, yews are more formal, darker green, and more tolerant of shade and moisture than most cultivated conifers. Long lived; tolerant of much shearing and pruning, since they sprout from bare wood. Excellent for hedges, screens.

Easily moved even when large, but since plants grow at a slow to medium rate, big ones are luxury items. They take many soils, but do not thrive in strongly alkaline or strongly acid ones. Do not take extreme heat. Reflected heat from hot south or west wall will burn foliage. Even cold-hardy kinds show needle damage when exposed to dry winds, very low temperatures. Only female plants produce berries, but many do so without

male plants nearby; varieties described below are female, except as noted. Subject to vine weevils, mealybugs, scale insects, various fungus diseases. During prolonged hot, dry weather, hose off plants every 2 weeks.

T. baccata. ENGLISH YEW. Zones 3–9, 14–24, 32, 33, warmest parts of 34. To 25–40 ft., sometimes taller, with wide-spreading branches forming broad, low crown. Needles ½–1½ in. long, dark green and glossy above, pale beneath; spirally arranged. Garden varieties are far more common than the species. These include:

'Adpressa'. Usually sold as *T. brevifolia*, name correctly belonging to the native western yew. Wide-spreading, dense shrub to 4–5 ft. high.

'Aurea'. Broad pyramid to 25 ft. tall after many years. New foliage is golden yellow from spring to fall, then turns green.

'Repandens'. SPREADING ENGLISH YEW. Long, horizontal, spreading branches make 2–4-ft.-high ground cover, spreading to 8–10 ft. after many years. Useful low foundation plant. Will arch over wall.

'Stricta' ('Fastigiata'). IRISH YEW. Dark green column to 20 ft. or taller. Has larger needles and more crowded, upright branches than does English yew. Branches tend to spread near top, especially in snowy regions or where water is ample. Branches can be tied together with wire. Plants that outgrow their space can be reduced by heading back and thinning; old wood sprouts freely. There is a form with yellowish white variegation on leaves.

T. brevifolia. WESTERN YEW, OREGON YEW. Zones 1–7, 14-17. Most trees sold under this name are actually *T. cuspidata* 'Nana'. True western yew is a rare, 50–60-ft. tree of northwestern woodlands. It has achieved some fame as the source of a drug used in treatment of some cancers. Not a garden tree.

T. cuspidata. JAPANESE YEW. Zones 2–6, 14–17, 32–41. To 50 ft. in Japan; usually grown as compact, spreading shrub in U.S. Needles ½–1 in. long, dark green above, tinged yellowish beneath; usually arranged in two rows along twigs, making flat or V-shaped spray. The two commonly grown varieties are:

'Capitata'. Plants sold under this name are probably ordinary *T. cuspidata* in its upright, pyramidal form. Dense growth to 10–25 ft., possibly taller. Can be held lower by pinching new growth. Fruits heavily.

'Nana'. Often sold as *T. brevifolia*. Slow-growing male variety to 3 ft. tall, 6 ft. wide in 20 years, eventually to a possible 20 ft. tall. Makes a good low barrier or foundation plant for many years.

T. media. Zones 2–6, 14–17, 32–41. Group of hybrids between Japanese yew and English yew. Intermediate between the two in color and texture. Of dozens of selections, these are among the most widely offered:

'Brownii'. Compact, rounded plant to 4–8 ft. tall, possibly larger. Male variety. Good low, dense hedge.

'Hatfieldii'. Broad column or pyramid to 10 ft. or taller; good dark green color. Male variety.

'Hicksii'. Narrow, upright grower to 10–12 ft. or taller; slightly broader at center than at top or bottom, widening with age.

TEA. See CAMELLIA sinensis

TEABERRY. See GAULTHERIA procumbens

TEA TREE. See LEPTOSPERMUM

TECOMA

Bignoniaceae

EVERGREEN SHRUB OR SMALL TREE

❚ ZONES 10, 12, 13, 21–28

☼ FULL SUN

🌢🌢 REGULAR TO MODERATE WATER

Various trumpet vines once lumped together as *Tecoma* now have different names. What remains is a showy large shrub or small tree.

T. australis. See Pandorea pandorana

T. capensis. See Tecomaria capensis

T. jasminoides. See Pandorea jasminoides ▶

Tecoma stans

T. stans (Stenolobium stans). YELLOW BELLS, YELLOW TRUMPET FLOWER, YELLOW ELDER. In mildest-winter areas, can be trained as tree. Where frosts are common, it is usually a large shrub. Much of wood may die back in winter, but recovery is quick in warm weather: rapid, bushy growth to 20 ft. Leaves divided into 5–13 toothed, 1½–4-in.-long leaflets. Flowers bright yellow, bell shaped, 2 in. across, in large clusters, late spring–winter. Needs heat, deep soil, fairly heavy feeding. Cut faded flowers to prolong bloom; prune to remove dead and bushy growth. Showy mass in large garden. Boundary plantings, big shrub borders, screening.

T. s. angustata is a hardier form, better adapted to Texas and desert Southwest. Has narrow leaflets, late spring–fall flowers.

TECOMARIA capensis (Tecoma capensis)

CAPE HONEYSUCKLE

Bignoniaceae

EVERGREEN VINE OR SHRUB

⚡ ZONES 12, 13, 16, 18–28; PROTECTED IN 14, 15

☼ ◑ ● FULL SUN OR LIGHT SHADE

🌢🌢 REGULAR TO MODERATE WATER

Tecomaria capensis

Native to South Africa. Can scramble 15–25 ft. if tied to support. With hard pruning, an upright shrub to 6–8 ft. Leaves divided into many glistening dark green leaflets. Blooms fall–winter, bearing compact clusters of tubular, 2-in., brilliant orange-red blossoms. 'Aurea' bears yellow flowers; it has lighter green foliage than the species, is smaller growing and less showy, and requires more heat to perform well.

Both species and variety need good drainage. Take wind, light salt drift. Use as espalier, bank cover (especially good on hot, steep slopes), coarse barrier hedge.

TELLIMA grandiflora

FRINGE–CUPS

Saxifragaceae

PERENNIAL

⚡ ZONES 4–9, 14–17

☼ ◑ PARTIAL SHADE IN HOT AREAS

🌢 REGULAR WATER

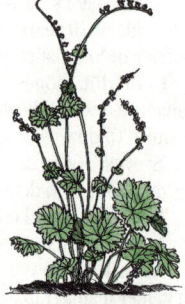
Tellima grandiflora

Pacific Coast native often confused with *Tiarella*. Creeping rootstocks send up roundish, lobed, light green, softly hairy leaves to 4 in. across on leafstalks to 8 in. long. Small, urn-shaped spring flowers with tiny fringed petals open green, age to deep red; though not showy, they are attractively arranged along tall (to 2½-ft.), slender stems. Provide rich, moist soil. Choice with ferns in woodland gardens.

TERNSTROEMIA gymnanthera (T. japonica)

Theaceae

EVERGREEN SHRUB

⚡ ZONES 4–9, 12–24, 26, 28, 29, 31, WARMER PARTS OF 32

☼ ◑ ● PARTIAL OR FULL SHADE

🌢🌢 AMPLE WATER

Ternstroemia gymnanthera

Takes a long time to reach 6–8 ft. and is usually seen as rounded plant 3–4 ft. tall and 4–6 ft. wide. Its appeal lies in its glossy, leathery foliage. Red-stalked, rounded oval to narrow oval leaves are 1½–3 in. long, bronzy red when new; when mature, they turn deep green to bronzy green to purplish red, depending on season, exposure, and plant itself. In deep shade, foliage tends to be dark green; with some sun, it may be bronzy green to nearly purple red. Red tints are deeper in cold weather.

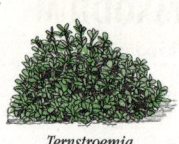
Ternstroemia gymnanthera

Summer flowers are ½ in. wide, creamy yellow, fragrant but not showy. Fruit (uncommon on small plants) resembles little yellow to red-orange holly berries or cherries, splits open to reveal shiny black seeds.

Grow in moist, well-drained acid soil. Tip-pinch to encourage compact growth. Use as basic landscaping shrub, informal hedge, tub plant, poolside plant. Good companion for camellias (to which it is related), azaleas, heavenly bamboo, pieris, ferns. Cut foliage keeps well.

In the Southeast, plants sold as *Cleyera japonica* usually are really *Ternstroemia gymnanthera*.

TETRADIUM daniellii. See EVODIA daniellii

TETRAPANAX papyriferus (Aralia papyrifera)

RICE PAPER PLANT

Araliaceae

EVERGREEN SHRUB

⚡ ZONES 15–28

☼ ◑ ● MIDDAY SHADE IN HOTTEST AREAS

🌢 REGULAR WATER

Tetrapanax papyriferus

Fast growing to 10–15 ft., often multitrunked. Big, bold, long-stalked leaves are 1–2 ft. wide, deeply lobed, gray green above, white-felted beneath, carried in clusters at ends of stems. Fuzz on new growth can irritate eyes and skin. Tan trunks often curve or lean. Big, branched clusters of creamy white flowers on furry tan stems show in winter.

Young plants sunburn easily, but older ones adapt. Plants seem to suffer only from high winds (which break or tatter leaves) and frost (foliage severely damaged at 22°F/–6°C, but recovers fast, often puts up suckers to form thickets). Digging around roots stimulates sucker formation; suckers may arise 20 ft. from parent plant. Use for silhouette against walls, on patios; combine with other sturdy, bold-leafed plants for tropical effect. Name comes from the thick pith of the stems, used to make Chinese rice paper.

TEUCRIUM

GERMANDER

Lamiaceae (Labiatae)

EVERGREEN SHRUBS OR PERENNIALS

⚡ ZONES VARY BY SPECIES

☼ FULL SUN

🌢 MODERATE WATER

Teucrium chamaedrys

Tough plants, enduring poor, rocky soils. They can't stand wet or poorly drained soils but will tolerate regular watering where drainage is good.

T. canadense. Perennial. Zones 2–9, 14–17, 31–41. Wild plant grows to 3 ft. tall, bearing white to rose flowers. The form offered in nurseries is a dwarf evergreen creeper to 8 in. high, with pale pink summer flowers.

T. chamaedrys. Shrubby perennial. Zones 3–24, 28–34, 39. To 1 ft. high, spreading to 2 ft.; many upright, woody-based stems densely set with toothed, ¾-in.-long, dark green leaves. Red-purple or white flowers in loose spikes (white-flowered form is looser). Use as edging, foreground, low clipped hedge, or small-scale ground cover. Shear back once or twice a year to force side branching. 'Prostratum' is 4–6 in. high, spreading to 3 ft. or more.

T. fruticans. BUSH GERMANDER. Shrub. Zones 4–24. Loose, silvery-stemmed plant to 4–8 ft. tall and as wide (or wider). Leaves 1¼ in. long, gray green above, silvery white beneath, giving overall silvery gray effect. Blooms almost year-round, bearing lavender blue flower spikes at branch ends. 'Azureum', to 3–4 ft. high and 6 ft. wide, has deeper blue flowers than the species. 'Compactum', to 3 ft. high, is relatively narrow and dense in habit, with deep blue blossoms. Thin and cut back in late winter, early spring.

T. gussonei (T. cossonii, T. majoricum). Shrubby perennial. Zones 8, 9, 14–24. Low mound to 3–8 in. tall, 1½–2 ft. across. Narrow gray leaves; dense heads of small, rosy purple flowers in a nearly unending show. Good rock garden plant.

T. marum. CAT THYME. Shrub. Zones 7–9, 14–24. To 1–1½ ft. tall. Densely clustered upright stems are closely set with tiny gray-green leaves. Blooms profusely in summer, when stems are covered with many deep pink or purplish flowers.

TEXAS MOUNTAIN LAUREL. See SOPHORA secundiflora

TEXAS OLIVE. See CORDIA boissieri

TEXAS RANGER, TEXAS SAGE. See LEUCOPHYLLUM frutescens

TEXAS UMBRELLA TREE. See MELIA azedarach 'Umbraculiformis'

THALICTRUM

MEADOW RUE	
Ranunculaceae	
PERENNIALS	
◢ ZONES VARY BY SPECIES	
☼ LIGHT SHADE	
◗ REGULAR WATER	

Thalictrum aquilegifolium

Foliage clumps, often blue green in color, resemble those of columbine. In late spring or summer, plants send up sparsely leafed stems topped by puffs of small flowers, each consisting of four sepals and a prominent cluster of stamens. Superb for airy effect; delicate tracery of leaves and flowers is particularly effective against dark green background. Pleasing contrast to sturdier perennials. Foliage good in flower arrangements.

Most meadow rues need some winter chill. All thrive in dappled sunlight at woodland edges and tolerate full sun in coolest regions. Grow in moist, humus-rich soil. Protect from wind. Divide clumps every 4 or 5 years.

T. alpinum. Zones 2–10, 14–17, 32–41. To 6–12 in. high, with green leaves, greenish purple sepals, yellow stamens. Good for rock garden.

T. aquilegifolium. Zones 2–10, 14–17, 32 (cooler parts), 33–41. To 2–3 ft. tall, with bluish green foliage. Earliest of the meadow rues to bloom. Clouds of fluffy stamens (the white or greenish sepals drop off) appear for a couple of weeks in mid- to late spring. Rosy lilac is the usual color; white and purple selections are available. If left in place, spent flowers are followed by attractive, long-lasting seed heads. Heat tolerant.

T. delavayi (T. dipterocarpum). CHINESE MEADOW RUE. Zones 2–10, 14–17, 31–41. To 3–4 ft. (even 6 ft.) tall, with thin, dark purple stems that need support. Green foliage. Lavender to violet sepals, yellow stamens. 'Hewitt's Double' has double lilac-colored flowers; bloom lasts 2 months or longer.

T. flavum glaucum (T. speciosissimum). Zones 2–10, 14–17, 31–41. To 3–5 ft. tall; stems need staking. Blue-green foliage; summer flowers similar to those of *T. aquilegifolium*, but color is lemon yellow. Heat tolerant.

T. minus. Zones 1–10, 14–17, 32–43. A somewhat variable species. The form most often sold reaches 3 ft. when in flower. Bluish green foliage; flowers consist of yellow stamens (greenish sepals drop off).

T. rochebrunianum. Zones 2–10, 14–17, 32–41. Forms green-foliaged clumps to 4–6 ft. tall, with sturdy stems that don't need staking. White or lavender sepals with pale yellow stamens. 'Lavender Mist', with violet sepals, is a superior selection.

Theaceae. The tea family consists of evergreen or deciduous trees and shrubs with leathery leaves and five-petaled flowers that have a large number of stamens. *Camellia, Franklinia,* and *Stewartia* are important representatives.

THEA sinensis. See CAMELLIA sinensis

THELYPTERIS

Thelypteridaceae (Polypodiaceae)	
FERNS	
◢ ZONES VARY BY SPECIES	
☼ ◗ PARTIAL OR FULL SHADE	
◗ ◗ AMPLE WATER	

Thelypteris palustris

The plants commonly sold under this name have undergone more name changes than is usual even for ferns. Botanically current names are noted in parentheses below; nurseries may not have caught up. Species grown in North America are deciduous and commonly thrive in shade, although some tolerate sun if moisture is plentiful. All have their place in fern collections or wild gardens.

T. hexagonoptera (Phegopteris hexagonoptera). BROAD BEECH FERN. Zones 1–6, 31–43. Medium green, triangular fronds to 1½–2 ft. long and wide. Fronds are once-divided, with each division deeply cut and toothed.

T. noveboracensis (Parathelypteris noveboracensis). NEW YORK FERN. Zones 1–6, 32–45. Pale green, 1–2-ft.-long fronds are once divided, with the segments deeply lobed. A vigorous colonizer, it can be used as a ground cover in shade—or even in full sun if kept moist.

T. palustris. MARSH FERN. Zones 1–6, 26, 28, 31–45. Spreads rapidly by rhizomes. Fronds occur singly or in tufts and are of two kinds: sterile and fertile. Sterile fronds are 6–24 in. long and half as wide, tapered at both ends, once-divided, with segments deeply lobed. Fertile fronds are 1–3 ft. long, sturdier and stiffer than the sterile ones.

T. phegopteris (Phegopteris connectilis). NARROW BEECH FERN. Zones 1–6, 32–43. Resembles *T. hexagonoptera*, but fronds are somewhat shorter and narrower.

THERMOPSIS

FALSE LUPINE, BUSH PEA	
Fabaceae (Leguminosae)	
PERENNIAL	
◢ ZONES VARY BY SPECIES	
☼ ◗ FULL SUN OR LIGHT SHADE	
◗ REGULAR WATER	

Thermopsis caroliniana

These easy-to-grow perennials resemble lupines. Silvery leaves are divided into leaflets that spread like fingers on a hand; erect, spikelike clusters of sweet pea–shaped yellow flowers appear in spring. Because of their tendency to spread by underground rhizomes, they are best in informal or wild gardens. Need little care. Somewhat drought resistant.

▶

T

T. caroliniana. Zones 1–9, 14–17, 28, 31–45. Native to the Carolinas and Georgia. To 3–4 ft. tall, with 10-in. flower clusters. More heat tolerant than the other species.

T. lupinoides. Zones 1–6, 34–45. Native to Eurasia, Alaska. To 2 ft. tall, with densely packed, 10-in. flower clusters.

T. montana. Zones 2–6, 33–41. Native to western North America. To 2–4 ft. tall, with 8-in. flower clusters.

THEVETIA

Apocynaceae

EVERGREEN SHRUBS OR SMALL TREES

ZONES VARY BY SPECIES

FULL SUN

REGULAR WATER

ALL PARTS ARE POISONOUS IF INGESTED

Thevetia peruviana

Fast-growing plants with narrow, glossy, deep green leaves and clusters of showy funnel-shaped flowers at branch ends. Thrive in heat; can take very little frost.

T. peruviana (T. neriifolia). YELLOW OLEANDER, LUCKY NUT. Zones 13, 21–27; with protection in 12, 14. Can be trained as 20-ft. tree or pruned into 6–8-ft. hedge, screen, or background planting. Leaves 3–6 in. long, with edges rolled under. Fragrant, 2–3-in., yellow to apricot flowers bloom almost any time (mostly summer–fall). Provide good drainage, wind protection. In colder part of range, mound dry sand 6–12 in. deep around base of stem; if top is then frozen, plant will recover quickly and new growth will bloom same year.

T. thevetioides. GIANT THEVETIA. Zones 22–25; with protection in 12, 13, 26. Open growth to 12 ft. tall and as wide. Leaves are darker green than those of *T. peruviana;* they resemble oleander leaves but are corrugated, heavily veined beneath. Large clusters of 4-in., brilliant yellow flowers bloom from summer to winter.

THRIFT. See ARMERIA

THUJA

ARBORVITAE

Cupressaceae

EVERGREEN SHRUBS OR TREES

ZONES VARY BY SPECIES

PARTIAL SHADE IN HOT-SUMMER AREAS

REGULAR TO MODERATE WATER

Thuja plicata

Neat, symmetrical, geometrical plants that run to globes, cones, cylinders. Juvenile foliage is feathery, with small, needlelike leaves; mature foliage is scalelike, carried in flat sprays. Foliage in better-known varieties is often yellow green or bright golden yellow. Urn-shaped cones with overlapping scales are ½ in. long, green turning brownish.

Although arborvitaes will take both damp and fairly dry soils, they grow best in well-drained soil. Need humidity and suffer in regions where summers are hot and dry. They are subject to some problems, including bagworms and heart rot. Generic name is sometimes spelled *Thuya.*

T. occidentalis. AMERICAN ARBORVITAE, EASTERN ARBORVITAE. Zones 1–9, 15–17, 21–24, 32–45. Native to eastern U.S. Upright, open growth to 40–60 ft., with branches that tend to turn up at ends. Leaf sprays bright green to yellowish green. Foliage turns bronze in severe cold.

PRACTICAL GARDENING DICTIONARY
PLEASE SEE PAGES 545–616

The species itself is seldom seen, but smaller garden varieties are common. Among these, the taller ones make good informal or clipped screens, while lower kinds are often used around foundations, along walks or walls, as hedges. Some good varieties are:

'Brandon'. Fast growth to 12–15 ft. tall, 3–4 ft. wide. Useful as screen.

'Douglasii Pyramidalis'. Vigorous-growing pyramid to 15 ft. or taller.

'Emerald' ('Emerald Green', 'Smaragd'). Neat, dense-growing, narrow cone to 10–15 ft. tall, 3–4 ft. wide. Holds its color throughout winter.

'Fastigiata' ('Pyramidalis', 'Columnaris'). Tall, narrow, dense, columnar plant to 25 ft. high, 5 ft. wide; can be kept lower by pruning. Good plant for tall hedges and screens (6 ft. or more), especially in cold regions and damp soils. Set 4 ft. apart for neat, low-maintenance screen.

'Globosa' ('Little Gem', 'Little Giant', and 'Nana' are similar varieties). GLOBE ARBORVITAE, TOM THUMB ARBORVITAE. Dense, rounded, with bright green foliage. Usually 2–3 ft. tall with equal spread; eventually larger.

'Nigra'. Tall, dense, dark green cone to 20–30 ft. tall, 4–5 ft. wide.

'Rheingold' ('Improved Ellwangeriana Aurea'). Cone-shaped, slow-growing, bright golden plant with a mixture of scalelike and needlelike leaves. Even very old plants seldom exceed 6 ft.

'Umbraculifera'. Globe shaped in youth, gradually becoming flat topped. At 10 years it should be 4 ft. tall and wide.

'Woodwardii'. Widely grown dense, globular shrub of rich green color. May attain considerable size with age, but it's a small plant over reasonably long period. If you can wait 72 years, it may be 8 ft. high by 18 ft. wide.

'Yellow Ribbon'. To 8–10 ft. tall, 2–3 ft. wide, with bright yellow foliage throughout the year.

T. orientalis. See Platycladus orientalis

T. plicata. WESTERN RED CEDAR. Zones 1–9, 14–24, 32–37, 39. Can reach over 200 ft. in coastal belt of Washington state; in gardens, typically grows to 50–70 ft. tall, 15–25 ft. wide. Slender, drooping branchlets, set closely with dark green leaf sprays. Unlike many forms of *T. occidentalis,* this species has foliage that does not discolor in cold weather. Single trees are magnificent in large lawns, but lower branches spread quite broadly and trees lose their characteristic beauty when these are cut off. An alternative to the more pest-ridden *Cupressocyparis leylandii.* A few varieties are:

'Aurea'. Younger branch tips golden green.

'Fastigiata'. HOGAN CEDAR. Very dense, narrow, erect; fine for tall screen.

'Hillieri'. Irregularly shaped dense, broad shrub with thick, short, heavy branches.

'Stoneham Gold'. Dense, slow-growing dwarf (6 ft. tall, 2 ft. wide) with orange new growth.

'Striblingii'. Dense, thick column 10–12 ft. tall, 2–3 ft. wide. For moderate-height screen planting or use as an upright sentinel.

'Virescens'. Narrow, fast growth.

'Watnong Green'. Fast growth; broad, conical form.

THUJOPSIS dolabrata

FALSE ARBORVITAE, DEERHORN CEDAR, HIBA CEDAR

Cupressaceae

EVERGREEN TREE

ZONES 3–7, 14–17, 32–37, 39

FULL SUN OR PARTIAL SHADE

REGULAR TO MODERATE WATER

Thujopsis dolabrata

Pyramidal, coniferous, often shrubby, of very slow growth to 30–50 ft. tall, 10–20 ft. wide. Foliage resembles that of *Thuja,* but twigs are coarser, glossy, branching in staghorn effect. Best where summers are cool, humid. Plant as single tree where foliage details can be appreciated. Slow growth makes it good container plant. 'Nana' is a dwarf variety to 3 ft. high; 'Variegata' has white branch tips.

THUNBERGIA

Acanthaceae

VINES OR SHRUBS

⚡ ZONES VARY BY SPECIES

☀ ◐ PARTIAL SHADE IN HOTTEST AREAS

🌢 REGULAR WATER

Thunbergia alata

Tropical plants noted for showy flowers. Some grow fast enough to bloom the first season and can thus be treated as annuals. Those grown as perennials are evergreen in mildest climates. Provide rich, well-drained soil. Good greenhouse plants.

T. alata. BLACK-EYED SUSAN VINE. Perennial vine grown as summer annual. May live over in Zones 23–27. Small, trailing or twining plant with triangular, 3-in. leaves. Flowers are flaring tubes to 1 in. wide in orange, yellow, or white, all with purple-black throat. Start seed indoors; set plants out in good soil in sunny spot as soon as weather warms. Use in hanging baskets or window boxes or as ground cover; or train on strings or low trellis.

T. erecta. KING'S MANTLE. Evergreen shrub. Zones 16, 21, 24–27. To 6 ft. tall, erect, sometimes twining, with dark green leaves. Velvety dark blue flowers with orange or cream throats (similar to gloxinia blossoms) appear in joints of upper leaves throughout summer and fall. *T. battiscombei* is similar, if not the same plant. 'Alba' is a white-flowering form.

T. grandiflora. SKY FLOWER. Perennial vine. Zones 16, 21–27. Vigorous twiner to 20 ft. or more, with 8-in., heart-shaped leaves. Slightly drooping clusters of tubular, flaring, 2½–3-in., delicate pure blue flowers. Blooms summer, fall. Takes a year to get started, then grows rapidly. Comes back to bloom in a year if frozen. Use to cover arbor, lathhouse, or fence; makes dense shade. There is a white variety. *T. laurifolia* is nearly identical to *T. grandiflora* in appearance and needs.

T. gregorii (T. gibsonii). ORANGE CLOCK VINE. Perennial in Zones 21–27; grow as summer annual elsewhere. Twines to 6 ft. tall or sprawls over ground to cover 6-ft. circle. Leaves 3 in. long, toothed. Flowers tubular, flaring, bright orange, borne singly on 4-in. stems. Blooms nearly all year in mildest areas, in summer where winters are cool. Plant 3–4 ft. apart to cover a wire fence, 6 ft. apart as a ground cover. Plant above a wall, over which vine will cascade, or grow in a hanging basket. Showy and easy to grow.

T. mysorensis. Perennial vine. Zones 16, 21–27. Tall climber with spectacular hanging clusters of gaping flowers that are red on the outside, yellow within; summer bloom. Clusters can reach several feet in length. Vine should be trained to overhead pergola or other support to permit flowers to hang unimpeded.

THYME. See THYMUS

THYMOPHYLLA tenuiloba. See DYSSODIA tenuiloba

THYMUS

THYME

Lamiaceae (Labiatae)

EVERGREEN SHRUBBY PERENNIALS

⚡ ZONES VARY BY SPECIES

☀ ◐ PARTIAL SHADE IN HOTTEST AREAS

🌢 MODERATE WATER

Thymus vulgaris

Members of the mint family with tiny, usually heavily scented leaves and masses of colorful little flowers in late spring or summer. Diminutive plants well suited to herb garden, rock garden; prostrate, mat-forming types make good ground covers for small spaces. Attractive to bees. Provide warm, light, well-drained soil; restrain plants as needed by clipping back growing tips.

T. citriodorus. LEMON THYME. Zones 1–24, 26, 28–43. Hybrid to 4–12 in. high; erect or spreading. Lemon-scented foliage; summer flowers of palest purple. Leaves of 'Argenteus' are splashed with silver, those of 'Aureus' with gold.

T. herba-barona. CARAWAY-SCENTED THYME. Zones 1–24, 30–43. Grows quickly to form a thick, flat mat of tiny dark green leaves with caraway fragrance. Clusters of rose pink flowers in midsummer.

T. lanuginosus. See T. pseudolanuginosus

T. praecox arcticus (T. serpyllum, T. drucei). MOTHER-OF-THYME, CREEPING THYME. Zones 1–24, 29–43. Main stems form a flat mat, with branches rising 2–6 in. high. Roundish dark green leaves; clusters of small, purplish white flowers in summer. Good for small areas or filler between stepping-stones where foot traffic is light. Soft and fragrant underfoot. Leaves can be used for seasoning and in potpourri. Among the many garden forms are the following:

'Album'. Pure white flowers.

'Coccineum'. Deep pink flowers.

'Linear Leaf Lilac'. Needlelike leaves, red stems, lilac flowers.

'Longwood'. Strong grower with furry gray leaves and 4-in. spikes of lilac flowers.

'Minus'. Tiny, dense, compact, slow-growing plant with pink flowers. 'Elfin' is even tinier.

'Pink Ripple'. Larger than the species. Lemon-scented foliage, salmon pink blooms.

'Reiter's'. Profuse rose red blooms.

T. pseudolanuginosus (T. lanuginosus). WOOLLY THYME. Zones 1–24, 30–43. Forms flat to undulating mat 2–3 in. high. Stems densely clothed with small, woolly gray leaves. Sparse, seldom-seen midsummer bloom of pinkish flowers in leaf joints. Becomes slightly rangy in winter. Use in rock crevices, between stepping-stones, to spill over bank or raised bed, to cover small patches of ground. 'Hall's Woolly' is not as furry but blooms more heavily.

T. vulgaris. COMMON THYME. Zones 1–24, 26, 28–43. To 6–12 in. high. Narrow to oval, gray-green leaves. Tiny lilac flowers in dense whorls in late spring or summer. Low edging for flower, vegetable, or herb garden. Good container plant. Use leaves fresh or dried for seasoning fish, shellfish, poultry stuffing, soups, vegetables. Many of the varieties, such as silver-variegated 'Argenteus', are not as hardy to cold as the species.

TI PLANT. See CORDYLINE terminalis

TIARELLA

FOAMFLOWER, SUGAR-SCOOP

Saxifragaceae

PERENNIALS

⚡ ZONES VARY BY SPECIES

◐ ● PARTIAL OR FULL SHADE

🌢 REGULAR WATER

Tiarella wherryi

Clump-forming perennials spread by rhizomes (and by stolons, in the case of *T. cordifolia*). Leaves arise directly from rhizomes; foliage is evergreen, though it may change color in autumn. Selections with year-round colorful foliage are becoming popular; look for new introductions in addition to ones described below. Narrow, erect flower stems carry many small white (sometimes pinkish) flowers. Useful in shady rock gardens; make pretty ground covers but will not bear foot traffic.

T. cordifolia. FOAMFLOWER. Zones 1–9, 14–24, 32–43. Rapid spreader. Forms foot-wide clumps of light green, lobed, 4-in. leaves that show red-and-yellow fall color. Flower stalks 1 ft. tall. Leaves of 'Dunvegan' are deeply cut and heavily veined with maroon; 'Slickrock' is a compact grower with 8-in. flower stalks.

T. trifoliata unifoliata (T. unifoliata). SUGAR-SCOOP, WESTERN FOAMFLOWER. Zones 1–7, 14–17. Dark green leaves are deeply cut and

T

toothed. Upright clusters of small white flowers on 16-in. stalks are followed by little fruits that look like sugar scoops.

T. wherryi (T. cordifolia collina). Zones 2–9, 14–24, 32–41. Resembles *T. cordifolia,* but has no stolons and spreads more slowly. Flower clusters are somewhat more slender; flowers are sometimes pink tinted. Leaves of 'Eco Red Heart' have dark red centers and veins. 'Oakleaf' has deeply lobed leaves, pink flowers.

TIBOUCHINA

PRINCESS FLOWER, GLORYBUSH, GLORY TREE

Melastomataceae

EVERGREEN SHRUBS OR TREES

✴ ZONES 25–27, EXCEPT AS NOTED

☼ ◑ PARTIAL SHADE IN HOT AREAS

● REGULAR WATER

Tibouchina urvilleana

Tropical trees and shrubs, most of Brazilian origin, with large, deeply veined, usually hairy leaves and big, showy, five-petaled purple flowers. Bloom is intermittent over a long period. Prefer rich, well-drained, slightly acid soil. The shrubs have a tendency to legginess and should be pruned lightly after every bloom cycle, somewhat more heavily in spring. They resprout quickly after heavy pruning. Pinch tips of young plants to encourage bushiness.

T. elegans. Shrub. To 6 ft. tall, with glossy green, 2-in. leaves and purple flowers 1½–2½ in. across.

T. grandifolia. Shrub. To 10 ft. tall, with 5–9-in.-long leaves and inch-wide violet flowers in 8–16-in.-long clusters.

T. granulosa. PURPLE GLORY TREE. To 40 ft., with broad, spreading habit. Leaves are 5–8 in. long. Purple, 2-in.-wide flowers come in clusters up to 1 ft. long. Has been attempted in mild-winter California gardens, where it has yet to prove itself; insufficient heat may be impediment.

T. urvilleana (T. semidecandra). PRINCESS FLOWER, PLEROMA. Shrub. Zones 16, 17, 21–27; with protection in Zones 14, 15. Open growth to 5–18 ft. high. Branch tips, buds, and new growth shaded with velvety hairs in orange and bronze red. Velvety, 3–6-in.-long leaves are often edged red; older leaves add spots of red, orange, or yellow, especially in winter. Clusters of brilliant royal purple, 3–5-in.-wide flowers. Protect from strong winds.

TIGER FLOWER. See TIGRIDIA pavonia

TIGRIDIA pavonia

TIGER FLOWER, MEXICAN SHELL FLOWER

Iridaceae

BULB

✴ ZONES 4–31; OR DIG AND STORE; OR GROW IN POTS

☼ ◑ PARTIAL SHADE IN HOTTEST AREAS

● REGULAR WATER DURING GROWTH AND BLOOM

Tigridia pavonia

Leaves narrow, ribbed, swordlike, 1–1½ ft. long; flower stalks (1½–2½ ft. tall) have shorter leaves. Showy, 3–6-in.-wide flowers have three large segments forming triangle, joined with three smaller segments to form center cup. Larger segments usually white or vivid solid color—orange, pink, red, yellow. Smaller segments usually spotted or blotched with darker colors. (Immaculata strain features solid colors, unspotted.) Plants bloom in summer; each flower lasts one day, but others follow for several weeks.

Plant in spring, after weather warms up. Plant in rich, porous soil, setting bulbs 2–4 in. deep, 4–8 in. apart. During active growth, feed every 2 weeks with mild solution of liquid fertilizer; or apply slow-release fertilizer

once, when bulbs break ground. Can be left in ground where hardy; divide every 3 or 4 years. In colder climates, dig and store bulbs after foliage turns yellow; break bulbs apart just before replanting in spring. Can also be grown in pots and protected in winter. Easily grown from seed and may bloom first year. Spider mites may require control; they cause yellowish or whitish streaks on foliage.

TILIA

LINDEN

Tiliaceae

DECIDUOUS TREES

✴ ZONES VARY BY SPECIES

☼ FULL SUN

● REGULAR WATER

Tilia cordata

Large, dense trees, usually taller than wide. All have irregularly heart-shaped leaves and small, fragrant, yellowish white flowers in drooping clusters, late spring–early summer. Flowers develop into nutlets, each with an attached papery bract. Stately good looks, moderate growth rate have made lindens favorite park and street trees in Europe.

Best growth in deep, rich, moist soil. In cold-winter areas, autumn color varies from negligible to good yellow. Young trees need staking and shaping; older trees require only corrective pruning. Aphids can cause disagreeable drip of honeydew and sooty mold.

T. americana. AMERICAN LINDEN, BASSWOOD. Zones 1–17, 31–45. Native to eastern and central North America. To 60–80 ft. tall, 30–50 ft. wide. Straight-trunked tree with a narrow crown. Dull dark green leaves to 4–6 in. long, nearly as wide. 'Redmond' is a pyramidal form with glossy foliage.

The southern native *T. heterophylla,* white basswood, was once considered a separate species but has now been merged with *T. americana.* It is less cold-hardy (Zones 3–17, 31–33) than the species and has silvery leaf undersides.

T. cordata. LITTLE-LEAF LINDEN. Zones 1–17, 32–43. The cold-hardiest linden. Native to Europe. Dense pyramid to 60–70 ft. or taller. Leaves 1½–3 in. long and as wide (or wider), dark green above, silvery beneath. Excellent medium-size lawn or street tree. Given space to develop its symmetrical crown, it can be a fine patio shade tree (but expect bees in flowering season). Can be sheared into hedges. Very tolerant of city conditions. Japanese beetle may be a problem in some regions. Selected forms include 'Chancellor', 'Glenleven', 'Greenspire', 'June Bride' (especially heavy bloomer), and 'Olympic'.

T. euchlora. CRIMEAN LINDEN. Zones 1–17, 32–43. Hybrid between *T. cordata* and another species. To 40–60 ft. tall, a little more than half as wide. Slightly pendulous branches. Leaves 2–4 in. long, rich glossy green above, paler beneath. Casts more open shade than *T. cordata.*

T. heterophylla. See T. americana

T. tomentosa. SILVER LINDEN. Zones 2–21, 32–41. Native to Europe, western Asia. To 50–70 ft. tall, a little more than half as wide. Leaves are 3–5 in. long, light green above, silvery beneath; they turn and ripple in the slightest breeze. More tolerant of heat and drought than other species. 'Sterling' has silvery young leaves and an especially handsome winter silhouette.

Tiliaceae. The linden family of trees and shrubs includes lavender starflower (*Grewia*) and African linden (*Sparmannia*), as well as linden trees (*Tilia*).

FOR INFORMATION ON SELECTING PLANTS

PLEASE SEE PAGES 79–160

TILLANDSIA

Bromeliaceae

PERENNIALS

⚡ ZONES 22–27; OR INDOORS

☼ ◑ EXPOSURE NEEDS VARY BY SPECIES

◐ ◕ WATER NEEDS VARY BY SPECIES

Tillandsia cyanea

These are bromeliads grown in pots of fast-draining, loose soil mix or as epiphytes on tree branches or slabs of bark. The best known is *T. usneoides*, the "Spanish moss" of southern U.S. Similar is Arizona native *T. recurvata*. In some, leaf rosettes are bright green; in others, they are gray and scaly or scurfy. Bright green ones need regular water and filtered light. Gray types need less water and are more sun tolerant. They are often mounted on plaques of wood or bark and used as wall ornaments indoors or outside (where hardy). Let potting mix dry out between waterings.

T. cyanea. Rosette of bright green, arching, 1-ft. leaves produces showy flower cluster: a flattened plume of deep pink or red bracts, from which violet blue flowers emerge one or two at a time for a long period.

T. ionantha. Miniature rosettes of 2-in.-long leaves covered with a silvery gray fuzz. Small, tubular flowers are violet; at bloom time, center of rosette turns red. Tough and undemanding plant.

T. lindenii (Vriesea lindenii). Like *T. cyanea,* but plume of bracts is green or green marked rose. As with other bromeliads, each rosette produces just one long-lasting inflorescence. Offsets replace original plant.

TIPUANA tipu

TIPU TREE

Fabaceae (Leguminosae)

SEMIEVERGREEN TREE

⚡ ZONES 12 (WARMEST AREAS), 13–16, 18–27

☼ FULL SUN

◐ REGULAR WATER

Tipuana tipu

Fast to 25 ft.; can eventually reach 35–50 ft. Hardy to 25°F/–4°C; well-ripened wood will take 18°F/–8°C with minor damage. Leaves divided into 11–21 oblong, 1½-in.-long, light green leaflets. Blooms late spring–early summer, bearing clusters of apricot to yellow, sweet pea–shaped flowers. Blooms followed by 2½-in. pods. Any soil except strongly alkaline. Flowers best in warm-summer areas out of immediate ocean influence. Good street tree or lawn tree. Useful shade canopy for patio or terrace, although flower litter can be a slight nuisance.

TITHONIA rotundifolia (T. speciosa)

MEXICAN SUNFLOWER

Asteraceae (Compositae)

PERENNIAL GROWN AS ANNUAL

⚡ ALL ZONES

☼ FULL SUN

◐ REGULAR WATER

Tithonia rotundifolia

Husky, gaudy, rather coarse plant with spectacular flowers, velvety green leaves. Grows rapidly to 6 ft. tall. Blooms from summer to frost, bearing 3–4-in.-wide flower heads with orange-scarlet rays and tufted yellow centers. Use as a temporary screen. 'Torch', to 4 ft., makes a bushy summer hedge. 'Goldfinger' and 'Sundance' are 3-footers for smaller gardens. All have inflated hollow stems; cut with care for bouquets to avoid bending stalks. Sow seed in place in spring, in well-drained, not-too-rich soil. Tolerant of drought, humidity, intense heat. Attractive to butterflies, hummingbirds.

TOADFLAX. See LINARIA

TOAD LILY. See TRICYRTIS

TOBIRA. See PITTOSPORUM tobira

TOLMIEA menziesii

PIGGY-BACK PLANT

Saxifragaceae

PERENNIAL

⚡ ZONES 4–9, 14–17, 20–24; OR INDOORS

◐ ● PARTIAL OR FULL SHADE

◐ ◕ TOLERATES WET SOIL

Tolmiea menziesii

Native to Coast Ranges from Northern California northward to Alaska. Chief asset is abundant production of attractive 5-in.-wide basal leaves—shallowly lobed and toothed, rather hairy. Leaves can produce new plantlets at junction of leaf stalk and blade. Tiny, rather inconspicuous reddish brown flowers top 1–2-ft.-high stems. Good ground cover for shade. As house plant, needs filtered light, cool temperatures, frequent watering. Mealybugs, spider mites are occasional pests. Makes handsome hanging basket plant. Start new plants any time of year: take leaf with plantlet and insert in moist potting mix so base of plantlet contacts soil.

TOMATILLO. See PHYSALIS ixocarpa

TOMATO

Solanaceae

PERENNIAL GROWN AS ANNUAL

⚡ ALL ZONES

☼ FULL SUN

◐ REGULAR WATER

Tomato

Easy to grow and prolific, tomatoes are just about the most widely grown of all garden plants, edible or otherwise. Amateur and commercial growers have varying ideas about how best to grow tomatoes; if your own particular scheme works, continue to follow it. But if you're a novice or you're dissatisfied with previous attempts, you may find the following useful.

First, choose varieties suited to your climate that will yield the kind of tomatoes you like on the kinds of plants that you can handle. Some varieties are determinate, others indeterminate. Determinate types are bushier and not as suitable for staking or trellising. Indeterminate ones are more vinelike, need more training, and generally have a longer bearing period. (Though the tomato plant is really a sprawling plant incapable of climbing, you'll often see it referred to as a "vine.") Plant a few each of early, midseason, and late varieties for production over a long period. Typically, six plants can supply a family of four with enough fruit to enjoy fresh and to use for processing.

Set out tomato plants in spring after frost danger is past and the soil has warmed. To grow your own plants from seed, sow seeds 5 to 7 weeks before you intend to set out plants. Sow in pots of light soil mix or in a ready-made seed starter (sold at garden supply stores). Cover seeds with ½ in. of fine soil. Firm soil over seeds. Keep soil surface damp. Place seed container in cold frame or sunny window—a temperature of 65° to 70°F/18° to 21°C is ideal, although a range of 50°F/10°C at night to 85°F/29°C in the day will give acceptable results. When seedlings are 2 in. tall, transplant them into 3- or 4-in. pots. Keep in sunny area until seedlings reach transplant size. When buying tomato plants, look for compact ones with sturdy stems; avoid plants that are tall for their pots or that already have flowers or fruit.

Plant in a sunny site in well-drained soil. Tomato plants prefer neutral to slightly acid soil; plan to add lime to very acid soil or sulfur to alkaline soil

T

the autumn before setting out plants. Space plants 1½–3 ft. apart (staked or trained) to 3–4 ft. apart (untrained). Make planting hole extra deep. Set seedlings in hole so lowest leaves are just above soil level. Additional roots will form on buried stem and provide a stronger root system.

Tomato management and harvest will be most satisfying if you train plants to keep them mostly off the ground (left alone, they will sprawl and some fruit will lie on soil, often causing rot, pest damage, and discoloration). Most common training method for indeterminate varieties is to drive a 6-ft.-long stake (at least 1 by 1 in.) into ground a foot from each plant. Use a soft tie to hold the plants to these stakes as they grow.

Slightly easier in the long run, but more work at planting time, is to grow each plant in wire cylinder made of concrete reinforcing screen (6-in. mesh). Screen is manufactured 7 ft. wide, which is just right for cylinder height; most indeterminate vines can grow to top of such a cylinder. Put stakes at opposite sides of cylinder and tie cylinder firmly to them. As vine grows, poke protruding branches back inside cylinder every week. Reach through screen to pick fruit.

Tomato plants need regular moisture at the root level. Since they are deep rooted, water heavily when you do water. If soil is fairly rich, you won't need to fertilize at all. But in ordinary soils, give light application of fertilizer every 2 weeks from the time first blossoms set until end of harvest; or give a single application of slow-release fertilizer.

Pests of tomato plants include Colorado potato beetles and whiteflies. If you see large green caterpillars with diagonal white stripes feeding upside down on leaf undersides, you have hornworms; handpick them or spray young caterpillars with *Bt*. Tomatoes are prone to a long list of diseases. Early blight (also called alternaria blight) shows up on leaves as dark spots with concentric rings inside, and on fruit as sunken lesions with same ring pattern. Sprays of liquid copper fungicide will control early blight and several other diseases; consult a local nursery or your Cooperative Extension Office for spray schedule. If plants are growing strongly, then suddenly wilt and die, the cause is probably verticillium wilt, fusarium wilt, or both. Pull and dispose of such plants. Diseases live over in soil, so plant in a different location every year and try varieties resistant to wilt or certain other diseases (see introduction to "Tomato varieties," below).

Some tomato problems—leaf roll, blossom-end rot, cracked fruit— are physiological; these can usually be corrected (or prevented) by maintaining uniform soil moisture. A mulch will help conserve moisture in very hot or dry climates.

If you have done everything right and your tomatoes have failed to set fruit in the spring, use hormone spray on blossoms. Tomatoes often fail to set fruit when night temperatures drop below 55°F/13°C. In chilly-night areas, select cold-tolerant varieties (especially small-fruited strains). Fruit-setting hormone often speeds up bearing in the earlier part of the season. Tomatoes can also fail to set fruit when temperatures rise above 100°F/38°C, but hormones are not effective under those conditions.

Harvest fruit when it is fully red and juicy; keep ripe fruit picked to extend season. When frost is predicted, harvest all fruit, both green and partly ripe. Store in a dry place out of direct sunlight at 60° to 70°F/16° to 21°C; check often for ripening.

TOMATO VARIETIES

Following are types of tomatoes you can buy as seeds or started plants. The number of varieties is enormous and increases every year. There are tomatoes for every taste and every region of the country. It's a good idea to consult a knowledgeable nursery, your Cooperative Extension Office, and other gardeners to find out which varieties will flourish in your local climate and soil.

If certain diseases or nematodes cause trouble locally, you may be able to grow varieties that resist one or more problems. Keys to resistance you may see on plant labels or in catalog descriptions include V (verticillium wilt), F (fusarium wilt), FF (Race 1 and Race 2 fusarium), T (tobacco mosaic virus), N (nematodes), A (alternaria leaf spot), and L (septoria leaf spot). For example, a variety labeled VFFNT resists verticillium wilt, two races of fusarium wilt, nematodes, and tobacco mosaic virus.

Main crop or standard tomatoes. 'Celebrity', 'Big Boy', and 'Better Boy' are widely grown. 'Heatwave' is popular in extremely hot climates. 'Ace'

and 'Pearson' are local favorites in California. Old varieties 'Marglobe' and 'Rutgers' are still popular in many regions.

Early tomatoes. These varieties set fruit at lower night temperatures than other tomatoes do. 'Early Girl', 'Burpee's Early Pick', 'Pilgrim', 'First Lady', and 'Dona' are representative. Such tomatoes are often successful in cool-summer climates.

Cool-summer tomatoes. These will ripen fruit where accumulated summer heat is too low for most tomatoes. 'Oregon Spring', 'Swift', 'Manitoba', and 'Stokesalaska' will grow in far northern and mountain areas. Nurseries in cool-summer areas may offer locally adapted varieties.

Hybrid tomatoes. Some suppliers tout certain tomatoes as hybrids. They are usually referring to first-generation offspring of controlled parent lines, sometimes indicated by F_1 after the name. These varieties are more predictable and uniform in growth and fruit quality. Some are giants like 'Beefmaster' and 'Big Beef', but hybrid paste tomatoes are also available.

Novelty tomatoes. Among these are yellow and orange varieties such as 'Orange Queen', 'Mountain Gold', 'Husky Gold', and 'Lemon Boy'. 'Caro Rich' is very high in vitamin A and beta carotene. Those who have a special taste for novelties can grow tomatoes with deep reddish brown flesh ('Black Prince'), white tomatoes ('New Snowball', 'White Beauty'), tomatoes with striped fruit ('Green Zebra', 'Tigerella'), and even one with fruit that is green when fully ripe ('Evergreen'). 'Long Keeper' will stay fresh in storage for 3 months, and 'Stuffer' and 'Yellow Stuffer' yield large, nearly hollow fruits that resemble bell peppers.

Large-fruited tomatoes. These grow to full size in areas where both days and nights are warm. Fruits can weigh a pound or even more. 'Beefsteak', 'Beefmaster', and 'Big Beef' are typical. 'Burpee's Supersteak Hybrid' can produce 2-lb. fruits, and 'Delicious' has produced a tomato weighing 7 lb. 12 oz.

Paste tomatoes. These bear prodigious quantities of small oval fruits with thick meat and small seed cavities. Sometimes called plum tomatoes, they are favorites for canning, sauces, and tomato paste. They are also good for drying. 'Roma', 'San Marzano', 'Viva Italia', and the yellow 'Italian Gold' are examples.

Small-fruited tomatoes. Fruits range in size from currants to large marbles. Shapes and colors are indicated by names: 'Red Cherry', 'Red Pear', 'Yellow Cherry', 'Yellow Pear'. Those with very small fruits include 'Sweet 100', 'Supersweet 100', 'Sweet Million', and 'Gardener's Delight'. Small-fruiting types that grow on small plants suitable for pots or hanging baskets include 'Tiny Tim', 'Small Fry', and 'Patio'.

Heirloom tomatoes. Varying in size, appearance, and plant habit, these represent old varieties that have been maintained by enthusiasts in different parts of the country. Most are grown for excellent flavor. 'Brandywine' is a currently popular heirloom variety.

TORCH-LILY. See KNIPHOFIA uvaria

TORENIA fournieri

WISHBONE FLOWER	
Scrophulariaceae	
ANNUAL	
✿ ALL ZONES	
◐ PARTIAL SHADE	
◆ REGULAR WATER	

Compact, bushy, to 1 ft. high. Blooms summer–fall; light blue flowers with deeper blue markings and bright yellow throats look like miniature gloxinias. Stamens arranged in wishbone shape. A white-flowered form is also avail-

Torenia fournieri

able. Sow seed in pots; transplant to garden after frosts. Prefers cool, moist soil and some shade (will tolerate full sun in coolest climates). Use in borders, pots, window boxes. In cold climates, plants in the ground can be lifted for winter bloom indoors in a sunroom.

TOUCH-ME-NOT. See IMPATIENS

TOVARA virginiana. See POLYGONUM virginianum

TOYON. See HETEROMELES arbutifolia

TRACHELIUM caeruleum

Campanulaceae (Lobeliaceae)

PERENNIAL

ZONES 7–9, 14–28; GROW AS ANNUAL IN COLDER CLIMATES

FULL SUN OR PARTIAL SHADE

REGULAR WATER

Trachelium caeruleum

Grows to 2½ ft. tall and wide. Clumps of stems are clothed with narrow, sharply toothed dark green leaves and topped by broad, dome-shaped clusters of tiny bluish violet flowers (good for cutting) over a long summer bloom season. If sown early, it will bloom first year (and so can be treated as an annual in colder climates). May self-sow in mild-winter climates. Tough, undemanding plant.

TRACHELOSPERMUM (Rhynchospermum)

STAR JASMINE

Apocynaceae

EVERGREEN VINES OR SPRAWLING SHRUBS

ZONES VARY BY SPECIES

SOME SHADE IN HOT AREAS

REGULAR WATER

Trachelospermum jasminoides

Ground covers, spillers, or climbers with delightfully fragrant, pinwheel-shaped blossoms in spring or early summer. They are among the most versatile and useful of shrubby plants. Cut stems exude a milky sap.

T. asiaticum. Zones 6–24, 26, 28–32. Twines to 15 ft. or sprawls on the ground with branchlets rising erect. Smaller, darker, duller green leaves than those of *T. jasminoides;* flowers also smaller, in creamy yellow or yellowish white.

T. jasminoides. STAR JASMINE, CONFEDERATE JASMINE. Zones 8–31, warmest parts of 32. Given support, a twining vine to 20 ft.; without support and with some tip-pinching, a spreading shrub or ground cover 1½–2 ft. tall, 4–5 ft. wide. New foliage is glossy light green; mature leaves are lustrous dark green, to 3 in. long. Profusion of 1-in. white flowers in small clusters on short side branches. Attractive to bees. 'Variegatum' has leaves bordered and blotched with white. As shrubby plant, use in raised beds or entry gardens, for edging along walks or drive, as extension of lawn, or as ground cover under trees and shrubs.

TRACHYCARPUS

Arecaceae (Palmae)

PALMS

ZONES VARY BY SPECIES; OR INDOORS

FULL SUN OR PART SHADE

REGULAR WATER

Trachycarpus fortunei

Fan-leafed palms of moderate size and great hardiness. Characteristic dense, hairy, black-

ish fiber grows on trunks; as trunks elongate, fiber falls off their lower portions. All can be grown as indoor potted palms.

T. fortunei. WINDMILL PALM. Zones 4–24, 26–31. Hardy to 10°F/–12°C or even lower temperatures. Native to China. Moderate to fast growth to 30 ft. in warm-winter areas; may eventually reach 60 ft. Trunk is dark, usually thicker at top than at bottom. Leaves 3 ft. across, carried on toothed, 1½-ft. stalks. May become untidy and ruffled in high winds. Sometimes sold as *Chamaerops excelsa.*

T. martianus. Zones 15–17, 19–27. Hardy to 22°F/–6°C. Native to Himalayas. Slower growing (to an eventual 45 ft. tall) and more slender than *T. fortunei.* Trunk is ringed with leaf scars.

T. takil. Zones 15–17, 19–27. Hardy to 20°F/–7°C. Native to western Himalayas. Very slow grower with heavy, inclined trunk. Can reach 20 ft., but is a dwarf (3–5 ft. tall) for many years.

TRACHYMENE coerulea (Didiscus coeruleus)

BLUE LACE FLOWER

Apiaceae (Umbelliferae)

ANNUAL

ALL ZONES

FULL SUN

REGULAR WATER

Trachymene coerulea

Upright stems to 2 ft. tall, clad with finely divided leaves. Numerous small, lavender blue flowers in 2–3-in.-wide, flat-topped clusters that are quite lacy in appearance. Good cut flower. Grow in light, rich, well-drained soil. Sow seeds in place (taproot makes transplanting difficult) in early spring for summer bloom. Does not perform well in heat. Where summers are hot and winters mild, sow in fall for winter–spring bloom.

TRADESCANTIA

Commelinaceae

PERENNIALS

ZONES VARY BY SPECIES; OR INDOORS

PARTIAL OR FULL SHADE, EXCEPT AS NOTED

WATER NEEDS VARY BY SPECIES

Tradescantia fluminensis

Most are long-trailing, indestructible plants, typically grown indoors in strong light (but not direct sun) or outdoors in shady sites. Usually seen in pots or hanging baskets, but can be used as ground covers—though the most vigorous, rambling types are likely to be invasive. Long-stemmed ramblers are often called inch plant or wandering Jew; the latter name is also applied to the related *Callisia* and (especially) *Zebrina.*

T. albiflora. WANDERING JEW, GIANT INCH PLANT. Zones 12–28; or house plant. Trailing, or sprawling and rooting at joints. Oblong, 2–3-in.-long leaves; small white flowers. 'Albovittata' has leaves finely and evenly streaked with white. 'Aurea' ('Gold Leaf') has chartreuse yellow foliage; 'Laekenensis' ('Rainbow') has bandings of white and pale lavender. Variegated forms are unstable and tend to revert to green, so keep solid green growth pinched out. Does best in well-drained soil with ample water. Trailing stems will live a long time in water, rooting quickly and easily. Renovate overgrown plants by cutting back severely or by starting new plants with fresh tip growth.

T. andersoniana. See T. virginiana

T. blossfeldiana. Zones 12–28; or house plant. Fleshy, furry stems spread and lean, but do not really hang. Leaves are shiny dark green above, furry and purple beneath, to 4 in. long. Flowers showier than those of most trailing or semitrailing tradescantias: clusters of furry purplish buds open into ½-in. pink flowers with white centers. Moderate water.

T

T. fluminensis. WANDERING JEW. Zones 12–28; or house plant. Rapid grower with prostrate or trailing habit. Succulent stems have swollen joints where 2½-in.-long, dark green, oval or oblong leaves are attached. Leaves of 'Variegata' are striped yellow or white. Tiny white flowers are not showy. Easy to grow; excellent for window boxes and dish gardens. Give ample water. A few stems placed in glass of water will live for a long time and will even grow.

T. navicularis. CHAIN PLANT. House plant. Compact, with short, barely trailing branches packed with fleshy, folded, brownish purple leaves. Miniature plants form along stems; detach for propagation. Tiny purple-red flowers. Treat as succulent: provide good drainage, avoid overwatering.

T. pallida 'Purpurea'. See Setcreasea pallida 'Purple Heart'

T. sillamontana. House plant. Short trailing or ascending branches with 2–2½-in. leaves densely coated with soft white fur. Tiny rose purple flowers. Moderate water.

T. virginiana. SPIDERWORT. Zones 1–24, 26, 28–43. Border perennial for sun or shade. Grows in 1½–3-ft.-tall clumps, with long, deep green, erect or arching grasslike foliage. Three-petaled flowers open for only a day, but buds come in large clusters and plants are seldom out of bloom during late spring, summer. Named garden varieties available in white, shades of blue, lavender, purple, gradations of pink from pale pink to near red. Ample water. May self-sow and become somewhat invasive in hot-summer climates. Divide clumps when crowded. Usually sold as *T. andersoniana.*

T. zebrina. See Zebrina pendula

TRAILING AFRICAN DAISY. See OSTEOSPERMUM fruticosum

TRANSVAAL DAISY. See GERBERA jamesonii

TREE ARALIA. See KALOPANAX septemlobus

TREE FERN. See CYATHEA cooperi, DICKSONIA

TREE MALLOW. See LAVATERA

TREE-OF-HEAVEN. See AILANTHUS altissima

TREE TOMATO. See CYPHOMANDRA betacea

TRICYRTIS

TOAD LILY
Liliaceae
PERENNIALS
⚡ ZONES VARY BY SPECIES
◐ PARTIAL SHADE
💧 AMPLE WATER

Tricyrtis hirta

Woodland plants that resemble false Solomon's seal (*Smilacina*) in foliage. Though not especially showy, the late summer–fall flowers are interesting—complex, heavily spotted, somewhat orchidlike. Each 1-in. flower has three petals and three sepals with a column of decorative stamens and styles rising from the center. Flowers appear at leaf bases and in terminal clusters. Need woodsy soil.

T. formosana. Zones 3–9, 14–17, 31–34, 39. May be the same as a species offered as *T. stolonifera.* To 2½ ft. tall; spreads by stoloniferous roots but is not invasive. Stems are more upright than those of *T. hirta*, and flowers are mostly in terminal clusters. Green leaves mottled with deeper green. Clusters of brown or maroon buds open to flowers in white to pale lilac densely specked with purple. Begins blooming a little earlier than *T. hirta.* Blossoms of 'Amethystina' are typically lavender blue spotted in dark red, with a white throat.

FOR INFORMATION ON YOUR CLIMATE ZONE
PLEASE SEE PAGES 16–78

T. hirta. Zones 2–9, 14–17, 32–41. To 3 ft. tall, with arching stems. Flowers, appearing in leaf joints all along the stems, are white to pale lilac, densely peppered with purple. 'Miyazaki' and 'Miyazaki Gold' are improved forms that bloom more profusely; the latter has yellow-edged leaves.

TRIFOLIUM

CLOVER
Fabaceae (Leguminosae)
PERENNIALS
⚡ ZONES VARY BY SPECIES
☀◐ FULL SUN OR PARTIAL SHADE
💧 REGULAR WATER

Trifolium repens

Scores of species, most of them field crops. All have ability to take nitrogen from air and put it into the soil through action of root bacteria. Two are perennials of garden importance as lawns or lawn substitutes. Leaves have three (rarely a lucky four) leaflets.

T. fragiferum. STRAWBERRY CLOVER. Zones 4–24. O'Connor's Legume, an Australian strain of this forage crop, is used as a ground or bank cover for its deep rooting (6–7 ft.) and tolerance of heat, aridity, and moderate salinity. Sow seed at 2–8 oz. per 1,000 sq. ft. Makes 6–7-in.-tall green mat.

T. repens. WHITE CLOVER, WHITE DUTCH CLOVER. All zones. Sometimes used to mix with lawn grass or dichondra seed. Can stain clothing of children who play on it; white flower heads attract bees. Prostrate stems root freely and send up lush cover of leaves with three ¾-in. leaflets. *T. r. minus* is one of the shamrocks.

TRILLIUM

WAKE ROBIN
Liliaceae
PERENNIALS
⚡ ZONES 1–6, 31–43
◐ PARTIAL OR FULL SHADE
💧 REGULAR WATER

Trillium grandiflorum

Bloom in early spring; need some winter chill. Each stem is topped with a whorl of three leaves; from center of these rises a single flower with three maroon or white petals. Plant the thick, deep-growing, fleshy rhizomes in shady, woodsy site. Left undisturbed, they will gradually increase. Plants die to the ground in mid- to late summer. In addition to species listed below, many others are offered by native plant specialists.

T. catesbaei (T. stylosum). Resembles *T. grandiflorum* but has pink flowers.

T. erectum. PURPLE TRILLIUM. To 2 ft. high, with 7-in. leaves and 2-in., erect, brownish purple flowers. Sometimes known by the name "stinking Benjamin" due to the odd odor of its flowers.

T. grandiflorum. Stout stems 8–18 in. high. Leaves 2½–6 in. long. Flowers are nodding, to 3 in. across, white aging to rose. 'Flore Pleno' has double flowers.

T. recurvatum. BLOODY BUTCHER. To 15 in. high. Leaves spotted in reddish purple; purple-brown flowers.

T. sessile. To 1 ft. high, with purple-spotted leaves and dark purplish red flowers. *T. s. luteum (T. luteum)* has yellow flowers with a faint lemon scent.

T. undulatum. PAINTED TRILLIUM. To 20 in. high, with upright or somewhat nodding, 1½-in. white flowers marked reddish purple within. Considered difficult; needs cool conditions, acid soil.

TRINIDAD FLAME BUSH. See CALLIANDRA tweedii

TRISTANIA

Myrtaceae

EVERGREEN TREES OR SHRUBS

☒ ZONES 15–17, 19–25

☼ FULL SUN

🌢 🌢 WATER NEEDS VARY BY SPECIES

Tristania conferta

Eucalyptus relatives with handsome foliage and brightly colored, shedding bark. Clusters of small flowers followed by woody capsules something like those of eucalyptus.

T. conferta (Lophostemon confertus). BRISBANE BOX. Tree. To 30–60 ft. tall. Rather upright when young, later becoming broad and rounded. Reddish brown bark peels to show lighter colored new bark beneath. Leathery, bright green, 4–6-in.-long leaves tend to cluster toward tips of branchlets. Creamy white summer flowers. Moderate to little water.

T. laurina (Tristaniopsis laurina). Shrub or tree. In 8 years, reaches 10 ft. tall, half as wide, with very dense, rounded crown. Can be kept shrubby by tip-pinching. Eventually much taller if trained as single-trunked tree. Mahogany-colored bark peels to show white new bark. Glossy green leaves to 4 in. long; clusters of small yellow flowers, late spring–early summer. Regular to little water.

TRITELEIA

Amaryllidaceae

CORMS

☒ ZONES 3–9, 14–24, 29, 30, 33

☼ SUN

🌢 REGULAR WATER DURING GROWTH AND BLOOM

Triteleia laxa

Plants under this name were formerly known as *Brodiaea*. General descriptions and culture are same as for *Brodiaea*, which differs only in technicalities. Spring–early summer bloom.

T. laxa (B. laxa). GRASS NUT, ITHURIEL'S SPEAR. Flower stalk to 2½ ft.; purple-blue, 1½-in. trumpets.

T. 'Queen Fabiola'. Flower stalk to 2½ ft. tall; deep violet flowers. Good cut flower.

T. tubergenii. Flower stalk to 2½ ft. tall; light blue flowers.

TRITOMA uvaria. See KNIPHOFIA uvaria

TRITONIA (Montbretia)

Iridaceae

CORMS

☒ ZONES 9, 13–24, 26, 28, 29; OR DIG AND STORE; OR GROW IN POTS

☼ FULL SUN

🌢 REGULAR WATER DURING GROWTH AND BLOOM

Tritonia crocata

Native to South Africa. Related to freesia, ixia, and sparaxis. Clumps of narrow, sword-shaped leaves give rise to branched stems carrying short, spikelike clusters of brilliant flowers in late spring. Long-lasting cut flowers.

Set corms 2–3 in. deep, 3 in. apart, in well-drained soil. Plant in fall where hardy, in early spring elsewhere. After bloom, foliage dies back. Corms can remain in the ground where hardy, but they are likely to rot unless planting area is kept fairly dry. Where corms cannot be protected and in colder regions, dig and store over winter or grow in pots. Good in rock gardens, borders.

T. crocata. Often called flame freesia. Stems to 1–1½ ft., bearing orange-red, funnel-shaped, 2-in. flowers. *T. c. miniata* has bright red blooms; 'Princess Beatrix' has deep orange flowers. Others come in white and shades of pink, salmon, yellow, and apricot.

T. hyalina. Bright orange flowers with narrower segments than those of *T. crocata*, with transparent area near base. A little smaller than *T. crocata*.

TROLLIUS

GLOBEFLOWER

Ranunculaceae

PERENNIALS

☒ ZONES 1–6, 32–43

☼ ☼ FULL SUN OR PARTIAL SHADE

🌢 🌢 AMPLE WATER

Trollius ledebouri

Clumps of finely cut, shiny dark green leaves put up 2–3-ft.-tall stems terminating in yellow to orange, roundly cupped to globe-shaped flowers. Some types begin blooming in spring, others in summer; remove faded flowers to prolong bloom. Excellent cut flowers.

Intolerant of drought, heat. Continually damp ground near a pond or stream is ideal planting site. If growing in regular garden bed, liberally amend soil with organic matter and keep well watered. Divide clumps when they thin out in the middle.

T. cultorum. Name given to a group of hybrids between T. *europaeus* and two Asiatic species. Grow 2–3 ft. tall and resemble T. *europaeus* in most details. Bloom comes at some time from spring into summer, depending on hybrid. Choices include 2-ft. 'Earliest of All', with pale orange-yellow blooms; 2-ft. 'Golden Queen', deep orange; and 2½-ft. 'Lemon Queen', soft yellow.

T. europaeus. To 1½–2 ft. tall. Globular, lemon yellow flowers, 1–2 in. across, in spring. Some varieties have orange blooms. Somewhat more tolerant of dry soil than other species.

T. ledebouri. Plant sold by nurseries under this name grows 3 ft. tall, bears 2-in., golden orange, cup-shaped flowers in summer. 'Golden Queen' reaches 4 ft., has 4-in. blossoms.

TROPAEOLUM

NASTURTIUM

Tropaeolaceae

ANNUALS

☒ ALL ZONES

☼ ☼ EXPOSURE NEEDS VARY BY SPECIES

🌢 REGULAR WATER

Tropaeolum majus

Distinctive appearance, rapid growth, and easy culture are three of nasturtiums' many strong points. Less conspicuous, but odd and pretty, is *T. peregrinum*, the canary bird flower.

T. majus. GARDEN NASTURTIUM. Two main kinds. Climbing types trail over the ground or climb to 6 ft. by coiling leaf stalks; dwarf kinds are compact, to 15 in. tall. Both have round, shield-shaped, bright green leaves on long stalks. Broad, long-spurred flowers, to 2½ in. across, have a refreshing fragrance, come in colors ranging through maroon, red brown, orange, yellow, and red to creamy white. Good cut flowers. Young leaves, flowers, and unripe seedpods have peppery flavor like watercress and may be used in salads.

Dwarf forms are most widely sold. You can get seeds of mixed colors in several strains, or a few separate colors, including cherry rose, mahogany, and gold. Both single- and double-flowered forms are available. All types are easy to grow in most well-drained soils; they do best in sandy soil. Sow in early spring; plants grow and bloom quickly, and will often reseed unless stopped by heat or humidity. In mild-winter, hot-summer areas, sow in fall

T

for winter–spring bloom. Full sun or light shade. Somewhat drought tolerant. Aphids can be a problem.

T. peregrinum. CANARY BIRD FLOWER. Climbs to 10–15 ft. Leaves are deeply five lobed. Flowers ¾–1 in. across, canary yellow, frilled and fringed, with green, curved spur. Sow in spring for bloom from summer until frost. Provide support, such as stakes or netting; or allow plant to climb into a shrub. Needs light shade. May live over in mild climates.

TRUMPET CREEPER, TRUMPET VINE. See CAMPSIS

TSUGA

HEMLOCK

Pinaceae

EVERGREEN TREES AND SHRUBS

⚡ ZONES VARY BY SPECIES

☼ ◐ FULL SUN OR PARTIAL SHADE

🔴 REGULAR WATER

Tsuga canadensis

These are mostly big trees with unusually graceful appearance. Branches horizontal to drooping. Needlelike leaves are banded with white beneath, flattened and narrowed at the base to form distinct, short stalks. Small, oval, medium brown cones hang down from branches. Bark is deeply furrowed, cinnamon colored to brown.

All hemlocks need some winter chill; all are shallow rooted. Best in acid soil and high summer humidity, with protection from hot sun and wind. Take well to heavy pruning; make excellent clipped hedges, screens. Easily damaged by salt and drought. Subject to various pests and diseases, but damage is not always serious if plants are well grown. Recently, a woolly adelgid (an aphid) has caused the decline and even death of many hemlocks.

T. canadensis. CANADA HEMLOCK. Zones 3–7, 17, 32–43. Native from Nova Scotia to Minnesota, southward along mountain ranges to Alabama and Georgia. Dense, pyramidal tree to 40–70 ft. or taller, half as wide. Tends to grow two or more trunks. Outer branchlets droop gracefully. Dark green needles, about ½ in. long, are mostly arranged in opposite rows on branchlets. Fine lawn tree or background planting; outstanding clipped hedge. 'Pendula', Sargent weeping hemlock, grows slowly to 10–20 ft. tall and twice as wide, with pendulous branches; with careful pruning, can easily be kept to handsome, 2–3-ft., cascading mound suitable for a large rock garden. Numerous other dwarf, weeping, and variegated selections are sold.

T. caroliniana. CAROLINA HEMLOCK. Zones 4–6, 32–41. Native to mountains in the southeast U.S. Resembles *T. canadensis* but is somewhat slower growing, a little stiffer in habit, and darker green in color. Longer needles are arranged all around the twigs instead of in opposite rows. More tolerant of polluted air and city conditions than *T. canadensis,* but not as well adapted to lowlands of eastern seaboard.

TUBEROSE. See POLIANTHES tuberosa

TULBAGHIA

Amaryllidaceae

PERENNIALS

⚡ ZONES 13–24, 26–28

☼ FULL SUN

🔴 REGULAR WATER

Tulbaghia violacea

Many narrow leaves grow from central point to make broad clumps, from which rise long stems bearing clusters of star-shaped flowers.

Evergreen in mild climates. Suffer frost damage at 20° to 25°F/–7° to –4°C, but recover quickly.

T. fragrans. Gray-green, 1-in.-wide leaves to 12–14 in. long or longer. Fragrant, lavender pink flowers, 20–30 on 1½–2-ft. stalk. Blooms midwinter–spring. Good cut flower.

T. violacea. SOCIETY GARLIC. Bluish green, narrow leaves to 1 ft. long. Rosy lavender flowers, 8–20 in cluster on 1–2-ft. stem. Some bloom most of year, with peak in spring and summer. Leaves, flower stems have onion or garlic odor if cut or crushed. Unsatisfactory cut flower for this reason (but can be used as seasoning). 'Variegata' has creamy stripe down the center of each leaf. 'Silver Lace' has white-margined leaves. 'Tricolor' is another variety with white-edged leaves; its foliage is suffused with pink in spring.

TULIPA

TULIP

Liliaceae

BULBS

⚡ ZONES 1–24, 28–45; BEST IN ZONES WITH DISTINCT WINTER CHILL

☼ FULL SUN

🔴 REGULAR WATER DURING GROWTH AND BLOOM

Darwin Hybrid Tulip

Tulips vary considerably in color, form, height, and general character. Some look stately and formal, others dainty and whimsical; a few are bizarre. Bloom comes at some time from March to May, depending on type.

Use larger tulips in colonies or masses with low, spring-blooming perennials such as aubrieta, basket-of-gold, candytuft, rockcress, or sweet William phlox, or with annuals such as forget-me-not, sweet alyssum, pansy, or viola. Plant smaller, lower-growing species in rock gardens, near paths, in raised beds, or in patio or terrace insets for close-up viewing. Tulips are superb container plants; the more unusual kinds, such as Double Early, Rembrandt, and Parrot strains, seem more appropriate for containers than for garden beds.

Nearly all hybrid tulips and most species (wild) tulips need an extended period of winter chill for best performance. But even in cold-winter regions, there's no guarantee of a good performance after the first year. Tulip bulbs form offsets that need several years to get to blooming size, but as the offsets mature, they draw energy from the mother bulb. The result is a decline in flowering. For this reason, most tulips are best treated as short-lived perennials. You can encourage repeat flowering by fertilizing with nitrogen before bloom and by allowing foliage to yellow and wither before removing it after bloom. In mild-winter areas, tulip bulbs should be prechilled in the refrigerator and the plants treated as annuals (in Zones 25–27, however, even prechilled bulbs usually fail to perform well). In areas with warm, wet summer soil, bulbs are prone to rot and shouldn't be expected to bloom for more than a year or two.

Bulbs can be planted under deciduous trees that leaf out after tulip flowers fade (good practice in hot-summer areas). Light shade helps prolong bloom of late-flowering kinds. Good light should come from overhead; otherwise, stems will lean toward light source. Rich, sandy soil is ideal, although tulips will grow in any good soil with fast drainage. They do not like soil where tulips were recently growing—choose an entirely different site, or put in fresh soil to the requisite planting depth. Set bulbs three times as deep as they are wide (a little shallower in heavy soils), from 4 to 8 in. apart depending on ultimate size of plant. Plant bulbs as early as mid-September in coldest areas, as late as December or January in warmer regions.

To protect tulips from burrowing animals, plant in baskets of ¼-in. wire mesh. Thwart ground squirrels and other animals that like to dig up bulbs by securing chicken wire over new plantings.

Tulips have been classified into many divisions; the most important of these are listed below, in approximate order of bloom.

T

Single Early tulips. Large single flowers of red, yellow, or white grow on 10–16-in. stems. Much used for growing or forcing indoors in pots. Also grown outdoors.

Double Early tulips. Double peonylike flowers to 4 in. across bloom on 6–12-in. stems. Same colors, same bloom season as Single Early tulips. In rainy areas, mulch around plants or surround with ground cover to keep mud from splashing short-stemmed flowers. Effective massed in borders for early bloom.

Darwin hybrids. Spectacular group bred from Darwin tulips and huge, brilliant species *T. fosterana*. Bloom before Darwins; have enormous, brightly colored flowers on 24–28-in. stems. Most are in scarlet-orange to red range; some have contrasting eyes or penciling; some measure 7 in. across. Pink, yellow, and white varieties exist.

Mendel tulips. Single flowers grow on stems to 20 in. tall. Bloom after Single Early and Double Early kinds, before Darwin tulips. Shades of white, rose, red, orange, yellow.

Triumph tulips. Single flowers on medium-tall (20-in.), sturdy stems. Bloom earlier than Darwin tulips and (like Mendel tulips) are valuable in providing continuity of bloom.

Darwin tulips. Most popular midseason tulips. Graceful, stately plants with large oval or egg-shaped flowers, square at base, usually with stems to 2½ ft. tall. Clear, beautiful colors of white, cream, yellow, pink, red, mauve, lilac, purple, maroon, and near black.

Breeder tulips. Large oval to globular flowers on stems to almost 3 ft. tall. Late blooming. Unusual colors include orange, bronze, purplish, mahogany—often overlaid with flush of contrasting shade. Called Breeders because Dutch growers once grew them primarily to breed the much-admired "broken" (variegated) tulips.

Lily-flowered tulips. Once included in Cottage division; now separate group. Flowers are long and narrow, with long, pointed segments. Graceful, slender stemmed, fine in garden (where they blend well with other flowers) or for cutting. Stems 20–26 in. tall. Late blooming. Full range of tulip colors.

Cottage tulips. Often called May-flowering tulips. About same size and height as Darwins. Flower form variable, long oval to egg shaped to vase shaped, often with pointed segments.

Double Late tulips (often called Peony-flowered). Large, heavy blooms like peonies. They range from 18 to 22 in. tall; flowers may be damaged by rain or wind in exposed locations.

The ten divisions above have recently been reclassified (and somewhat simplified), and you may now find tulips sold under the following names:

Single Early and Double Early. The earliest large tulips.

Triumph and Darwin hybrids. Midseason bloomers.

Single Late or May-flowering. Now includes Darwin and Cottage classes.

Double Late, Lily-flowered, and Novelty classes. These wind up the season. Novelty tulips (described below) include Rembrandt, Bizarre, Bybloems, and Parrot types.

Rembrandt tulips, Bizarre tulips, Bybloems (Bijbloemens). Because the streaks and variegations on these tulip flowers are caused by a transmittable virus, they can no longer be imported and should not be planted. Tulips now sold as Rembrandts are multicolor tulips of genetic, not viral, origin.

Parrot tulips. Late-flowering tulips with large, long, deeply fringed and ruffled blooms striped and feathered in various colors. Many have descriptive names, e.g. 'Blue Parrot', 'Red Parrot'. Good in containers, unusual cut flowers.

Three newer novelty groups are: Fringed tulips, variations from Single Early, Double Early, and Darwin tulips, finely fringed on edges of segments;

Viridiflora tulips, 10–20 in. tall, flowers edged or blended green with other colors—white, yellow, rose, red, or buff; and Multiflowered, three to six flowers on each 20–27-in. stem, flowers white, yellow, pink, and red.

In addition to divisions and groups described above, there are many classes covering species and species hybrids. Most important are:

Hybrids and varieties of *T. fosterana*, including huge, fiery red variety 'Red Emperor' ('Mme. Lefeber'), 16 in. tall.

Varieties and hybrids of *T. greigii* resemble those of *T. kaufmanniana*, with leaves usually heavily spotted and streaked with brown.

Varieties and hybrids of *T. kaufmanniana*, 5–10 in. tall, very early blooming, in white, pink, orange, and red, often with markings, some with leaves patterned brown.

Most species tulips—wild tulips—are low growing and early blooming with shorter, narrower leaves than garden hybrids, but there are exceptions. Generally best in rock gardens or wild gardens where plantings can remain undisturbed for many years.

Outstanding species are:

T. acuminata. Flowers have long, twisted, spidery segments of red and yellow on 1½-ft. stems. Late blooming.

T. batalinii. Single, soft yellow flowers on 6–10-in. stems. Very narrow leaves. Midseason.

T. clusiana. LADY or CANDY TULIP. Slender, medium-size flowers on 9-in. stems. Rosy red on outside, white inside. Grows well in mild-winter areas. Give sheltered position in colder areas. Midseason.

T. c. chrysantha (*T. stellata chrysantha*). To 6 in. tall. Outer segments rose carmine, shading to buff at base; inner segments are bright yellow. Midseason.

T. eichleri. Big scarlet flowers with black bases margined buff on 1-ft. stems. Early.

T. greigii. Scarlet flowers 6 in. across, on 10-in. stems. Foliage mottled or striped with brown. Early.

T. kaufmanniana. WATERLILY TULIP. Medium-large creamy yellow flowers marked red on outside and yellow at center. Stems 6 in. tall. Very early bloom. Permanent in gardens. Many choice named varieties.

Tulipa kaufmanniana

T. linifolia. Scarlet, black-based, yellow-centered flowers on 6-in. stems in midseason. Handsome with *T. batalinii*.

T. praestans. Cup-shaped, orange-scarlet flowers, two to four to 10–12-in. stem, in midseason. Variety 'Fusilier' is shorter, has four to six flowers to a stem.

T. saxatilis. Fragrant, yellow-based pale lilac flowers open nearly flat, one to three each 1-ft. stem. Early bloom. Good in warm-winter areas.

T. stellata chrysantha. See T. clusiana chrysantha

T. sylvestris. Yellow, 2-in. flowers, one or two on 1-ft. stem. Late. Good in warm-winter areas.

T. tarda (**T. dasystemon**). Each 3-in. stem has three to six upward-facing, star-shaped flowers with golden centers and white-tipped segments. Early.

T. turkestanica. Vigorous tulip with up to eight flowers on each slender, 1-ft. stem. Flowers slender in bud, star shaped when open, gray green on outside, off-white with yellow base inside. Very early bloom.

TULIPS IN MILD-WINTER REGIONS

Refrigerate bulbs in paper bags (away from ripening fruit) 6 weeks before planting. Plant between Christmas and mid-January. Mix low-nitrogen granular fertilizer into soil, then set bulbs 4–6 in. deep. Water sparingly until leaves emerge, then generously.

TULIP TREE. See LIRIODENDRON tulipifera, MAGNOLIA soulangiana

TUNG TREE, TUNG-OIL TREE. See ALEURITES fordii

TUPELO. See NYSSA sylvatica

TUPIDANTHUS calyptratus. See SCHEFFLERA pueckleri

TURNIP and RUTABAGA

Brassicaceae (Cruciferae)

BIENNIALS GROWN AS ANNUALS

ALL ZONES

FULL SUN

REGULAR WATER

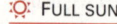

Turnip

Both are cool-season crops. Although turnips are best known for roots, foliage is also a useful green vegetable. Turnip roots come in various colors (white, white topped with purple, creamy yellow) and shapes (globe, flattened globe); some varieties are grown for leaves only. Rutabaga is a tasty turnip relative with large yellowish roots; its leaves are palatable only when very young, since they turn coarse as they mature. Turnip roots are quick growing and should be harvested and used as soon as big enough to eat; rutabaga is a late-maturing crop that stores well in the ground. Flavor of rutabaga improves with light frost.

Grow both in rich, loose, well-drained soil. In cold-winter areas, plant in early spring for early summer harvest, or in summer for fall harvest. In mild-winter areas, treat as fall–spring crops. Sow seeds ½ in. deep, 1 in. apart. Thin turnips to 2–6 in. apart for roots, 1–4 in. apart for greens. Thin rutabaga to 5–8 in. apart; it needs ample space for roots to reach full weight of 3–5 lb.

Roots of both turnip and rutabaga are milder flavored if soil is kept moist, become more pungent under drier conditions. Turnip roots are ready to harvest about 75 days after sowing, rutabaga in 90 to 120 days. Cabbage root maggot is a pest of turnip (it is less likely to infest rutabaga); see Cabbage for control.

TURTLEHEAD. See CHELONE

TWEEDIA caerulea (Oxypetalum caeruleum)

Asclepiadaceae

TWINING PERENNIAL

ZONES 14–27; OR GROW AS ANNUAL IN COLDER CLIMATES

FULL SUN

REGULAR WATER

Tweedia caerulea

Twining perennial to 3 ft. Can be grown as warm-season annual, blooming from late summer to fall from seed sown in early spring. Leaves are 4 in. long. Star-shaped, 1-in. flowers, pale blue aging to lilac, grow along the stems and at branch ends. Tip-pinch young plants to force branching. Good cut flower. Takes any well-drained soil.

TWINBERRY. See MITCHELLA repens

TWINFLOWER. See LINNAEA borealis

TWINSPUR. See DIASCIA barberae

FOR GROWING SYMBOL EXPLANATIONS
PLEASE SEE PAGE 161

UGNI molinae (Myrtus ugni)

CHILEAN GUAVA

Myrtaceae

EVERGREEN SHRUB

ZONES 14–24

PARTIAL SHADE IN HOT AREAS

REGULAR WATER

Ugni molinae

Slow to moderate growth to 3–6 ft. tall. Scraggly and open in youth, but matures into a compact, rounded plant. Small, oval, leathery leaves are dark green with bronze tints above, whitish beneath; leaf edges are slightly rolled under. Rose-tinted white flowers resembling little bottlebrushes appear in late spring, early summer. These are followed by purplish or reddish, ½-in., pleasant-tasting fruit that smells like apples and can be eaten fresh or used in jams and jellies. Tidy, restrained plant for patios, terraces, near walks and paths. Give neutral to acid soil.

Ulmaceae. The elm family contains trees and shrubs, usually deciduous, with inconspicuous flowers and fruit that may be nutlike, single-seeded and fleshy, or winged. Elm *(Ulmus)*, hackberry *(Celtis)*, and *Zelkova* are representative.

ULMUS

ELM

Ulmaceae

DECIDUOUS OR SEMIEVERGREEN TREES

ZONES VARY BY SPECIES

FULL SUN

REGULAR WATER

Ulmus americana

Once much-prized shade trees, elms have fallen on hard times. Dutch elm disease (spread by a bark beetle) has killed millions of American elms throughout North America and can attack most other elm species. Many of the larger elms are attractive fare for various beetles, leafhoppers, aphids, and scale, making them either time consuming to care for or messy (or both). Beyond their pest problems, elms have other drawbacks. Their root systems are aggressive and near the surface, making it difficult to grow any other plants beneath. Many types produce suckers. Branch crotches are often narrow, splitting easily in storms. Despite their flaws, elms are widely planted, valued for their fast growth, moderate shade, and environmental toughness. Researchers continue to devote much effort to finding disease-resistant varieties. All elms are fairly soil tolerant, and all have handsome oval leaves. Poor yellow fall color, except as noted.

U. alata. WINGED ELM. Deciduous. Zones 4–9, 14–17, 26, 28–33. Native to southeastern U.S. To 20–40 ft. tall, not quite as wide. Open, airy canopy. Leaves 1–2½ in. long, finely toothed, dark green turning pale yellow in fall. Common name derives from corky outgrowths ("wings") on twigs and young branches. Degree of winging varies among seedlings— the wings really stand out on some, while on others they're almost nonexistent. Your best bet is to get a cutting-grown tree from a parent with good bark characteristics. Clusters of small reddish seeds in spring. 'Lace Parasol' is a weeping form (to 8 ft. tall, 12 ft. wide after 45 years) now being introduced in the nursery trade.

U. americana. AMERICAN ELM. Deciduous. Zones 1–11, 14–21, 26, 28–45. Native to eastern North America. This majestic, arching tree once graced lawns and streets throughout its range, but it has been decimated by Dutch elm disease. Fast growth to 100 ft. or taller with nearly equal— sometimes greater—spread. Main branches upright, outer ones pendulous. Rough-surfaced, 3–6-in.-long, toothed dark green leaves; great variation in shade of yellow fall color. Leafs out very late where winters are mild. Papery, pale green seeds in spring are messy.

Long search for disease-resistant varieties with classic vase shape seems to have been fruitful. 'Valley Forge' and 'New Harmony' are currently being tested and should be made available to the public soon.

U. carpinifolia. SMOOTH-LEAFED ELM. Deciduous. Zones 2–11, 14–21, 31–41. Native to Europe. To 70–90 ft. tall, with upright branches, weeping branchlets. Shiny deep green leaves to 2–3½ in. long. Prone to many pests and diseases, though moderate in susceptibility to Dutch elm disease.

U. glabra. SCOTCH ELM. Deciduous. Zones 2–11, 14–21, 32–41. Native to Europe. Fairly upright habit to 70–100 ft. tall. Leaves 3–6 in. long, sharply toothed, rough surfaced, on very short stalks. Rarely planted today, but old trees are sometimes seen. 'Camperdownii', Camperdown elm, generally 10–20 ft. tall, has weeping branches that reach to ground and make a tent of shade. 'Pendula' is similar, but has a flatter top.

U. hollandica. DUTCH ELM. Deciduous. Zones 2–11, 14–21, 32–41. Group of hybrids between Scotch elm and smooth-leafed elm. Most grow to 100 ft. or taller and sucker freely. All are prone to Dutch elm disease.

U. parvifolia. CHINESE ELM, LACEBARK ELM. Semievergreen or deciduous, depending on winter temperatures and individual tree's heredity. Zones 3–24, 26–35, 37–39. Fast growth to 40–60 ft. tall. Extremely variable in form, but generally spreading, with long, arching, eventually weeping branchlets. On trunks of older trees, bark sheds in patches (somewhat as bark of sycamore does), creating beautiful mottling in many specimens. Leathery dark green leaves are ¾–2½ in. long, evenly toothed; mediocre display of yellow to reddish orange in fall. Good resistance to Dutch elm disease, elm leaf beetle, and Japanese beetle.

Reliably semievergreen to nearly evergreen varieties such as 'Brea', 'Drake', 'Sempervirens', and 'True Green' are widely sold in California and the Deep South. In colder regions, consult local authorities about hardy selections; some survive subzero temperatures. Two unusual dwarf varieties may interest bonsai specialists: 'Frosty', a shrub only 3 ft. high, has leaves edged with tiny white teeth; 'Hokkaido' is a very slow-growing miniature tree (to 1 ft. tall in 20 years) with tiny leaves.

A word of caution: A less desirable species, *U. pumila*, Siberian elm, is sometimes sold as Chinese elm.

U. procera. ENGLISH ELM. Deciduous. Zones 2–11, 14–21, 32–41. To 120 ft. tall. Tall trunk with wide-spreading or upright, dense crown of branches. Leaves 2–3½ in. long, sandpapery, medium green; hang on longer in autumn than those of American elm. Similar to American elm in susceptibility to Dutch elm disease. Suckers profusely.

U. pumila. SIBERIAN ELM. Deciduous. Zones 1–24, 26–45; used chiefly in Zones 1, 2, 10, 11, 43–45 where climate limits tree choices. To 50–70 ft. tall, not quite as wide. Leaves ¾–2 in. long, smooth, dark green. Endures cold, heat, aridity, and poor soil. Has brittle wood and weak crotches, and—though resistant to Dutch elm disease—is not a desirable tree. Possibly useful in holding soil against erosion; fast growth also makes it suitable for windbreak or shelterbelt. Papery, winged seeds disperse seedlings over wide area. Very susceptible to elm leaf beetles.

UMBELLULARIA californica

CALIFORNIA LAUREL, CALIFORNIA BAY, OREGON MYRTLE, PEPPERWOOD

Lauraceae

EVERGREEN TREE

☘ ZONES 4–10, 12–24

☼ ◐ ● SUN OR SHADE

◐ ● REGULAR TO LITTLE WATER

Umbellularia californica

Native to California, Oregon. In the wild, its form varies. On windy hillsides near coast, it is a huge, gumdrop-shaped shrub; in forests, it's a tall, free-ranging tree 75 ft. high, over 100 ft. wide. Dark green leaves to 5 in. long, 1 in. wide. Leaves

can be substituted for those of sweet bay (*Laurus nobilis*) in cooking, but they have a more pungent flavor. Clusters of tiny yellowish flowers give plant a yellowish cast in spring. Blossoms are followed by olivelike, purplish, inedible fruit. Because of litter, tree has limited use near paved areas. Tends to sucker and self-sow. Aggressive roots make it difficult to garden under. Often seen with sooty mold resulting from aphid or scale infestation. Nonetheless, it is useful for screen, background planting, tall hedges.

UMBRELLA PINE. See SCIADOPITYS verticillata

UMBRELLA PLANT. See CYPERUS alternifolius

UMBRELLA TREE, QUEENSLAND. See SCHEFFLERA actinophylla

UMBRELLA TREE, TEXAS. See MELIA azedarach 'Umbraculiformis'

Urticaceae. The nettle family, best known for stinging nettles (*Urtica*), also contains such ornamentals as baby's tears (*Soleirolia*).

UVULARIA

BELLWORT, MERRYBELLS

Liliaceae

PERENNIALS

☘ ZONES 1–7, 14–17, 32–43

☼ ● LIGHT OR DEEP SHADE

● REGULAR WATER

Uvularia grandiflora

Attractive woodland plants native to eastern and central North America. Underground rhizomes send up erect stems, nodding toward the tip. Leaves are smooth and bright green, held close to stems in two ranks. Drooping, bell-shaped, pale yellow flowers hang from joints of upper leaves in spring. Foliage remains attractive all summer, dies back in winter. For woodland or shaded rock garden with moist, acid soil. Doesn't make a bold show, but looks attractive close up.

U. grandiflora. To 2½ ft. tall, with gray-green foliage and 2-in. bells.

U. perfoliata. To 2 ft. tall, with blue-green leaves that seem to surround the stem. Bells are 1½ in. long.

VACCINIUM

Ericaceae

EVERGREEN OR DECIDUOUS SHRUBS

☘ ZONES VARY BY SPECIES

☼ ◐ ● EXPOSURE NEEDS VARY BY SPECIES

◐ ● ● WATER NEEDS VARY BY SPECIES

Vaccinium ovatum

Excellent ornamental shrubs with clusters of bell-shaped flowers and colorful, edible fruit that attracts birds. Species described here are evergreen shrubs; those described under Blueberry are deciduous. All require rich, organic, acid soil. Good for woodland gardens.

V. angustifolium. See Blueberry

V. ashei. See Blueberry

V. corymbosum. See Blueberry

V. macrocarpon. CRANBERRY. Zones 4–6, 32, 34, 36–45. Native from Newfoundland to Minnesota, south to North Carolina. Creeping plant 2–6 in. high, spreading and rooting from stems. Narrow, ¾-in.-long leaves are dark green in summer, turning coppery or purplish red in winter. Tiny pinkish spring flowers are followed by tart red fruits in autumn. Commercial producers grow cranberries in bogs—beds that can be flooded to control weeds and pests, provide winter protection, and make harvesting easier. Gardeners can use cranberry as an attractive small-scale ground cover in damp soil and full sun.

V. ovatum. EVERGREEN HUCKLEBERRY. Zones 4–7, 14–17. Native to Pacific Coast. Erect plant, growing 2–3 ft. tall in sun, 8–10 ft. high in shade. Young plants spreading, older ones taller than wide. Leathery, lustrous dark green leaves to 1¼ in. long; bronzy new growth. White or pinkish spring flowers are followed by black berries with whitish bloom, good in pies, jams, jellies, syrups. Can be trimmed into hedge or grown in pots. Cut branches are popular for arrangements. Accepts regular to moderate water, sun or shade.

V. vitis-idaea. COWBERRY, FOXBERRY. Zones 3–7, 14–17, 32, 34–41. Native to Europe. Slow growth to 1 ft. high, spreading to 3 ft. wide by underground stems. Glossy dark green leaves to 1 in. long; new growth often tinged bright red or orange. Clustered white or pinkish spring flowers followed by sour red berries something like tiny cranberries; these are valued for preserves, syrups. Handsome little plant for small-scale ground cover, informal edging around larger plantings. Needs moist or damp soil. Prefers part or full shade, but with ample water will take full sun in cool-summer areas. North American native *V. v. minus*, lingonberry, is hardier to cold, also growing in Zones 1, 2, 42–45. Has smaller leaves (to ½ in.), is attractive in pots.

Valerianaceae. The valerian family of perennial herbs (rarely shrubs), has clustered small flowers. In addition to *Valeriana*, members include red valerian (*Centranthus*) and *Patrinia*.

VALERIANA officinalis

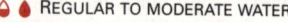

VALERIAN, GARDEN HELIOTROPE

Valerianaceae

PERENNIAL HERB

✿ ZONES 1–24, 26, 28–43

☼ ◑ FULL SUN OR PARTIAL SHADE

💧💧 REGULAR TO MODERATE WATER

Valeriana officinalis

Both true heliotrope (*Heliotropium*) and red valerian (*Centranthus ruber*) are more common than *Valeriana officinalis*. Tall, straight stems grow to about 4 ft. high; most leaves remain fairly close to ground. Leaves are light green, borne in pairs that are further divided into eight to ten pairs of narrow leaflets. Tiny, fragrant flowers are white, pink, red, or lavender blue, in rounded clusters at ends of stems. Plant spreads and can become invasive. Roots are strong smelling and are widely used in herbal preparations said to have sedative qualities. Start new plants from seeds or divisions. Grow in mixed herb or flower borders but don't allow it to crowd other plants. Use cut flowers in arrangements.

VALLOTA speciosa (Cyrtanthus purpureus, C. elatus)

SCARBOROUGH LILY

Amaryllidaceae

BULB

✿ ZONES 16, 17, 23–27; OR INDOORS

☼ BRIGHT INDIRECT LIGHT

💧 REGULAR WATER DURING ACTIVE GROWTH

Vallota speciosa

Native to South Africa. Strap-shaped evergreen leaves are 1–2 ft. long. Clusters of bright orange-vermilion, funnel-shaped, 2½–3-in.-wide flowers grow on 2-ft. stalks. Blooms summer and early fall. A white-flowered form is rarely available. Survives outdoors year-round where frosts are very light and infrequent, even succeeding in competition with tree roots. Excellent pot plant for patio or indoors. Plant June–July or just after flowering. Set bulbs with tips just below surface. Plant blooms best when roots are crowded. Fertilize monthly during active growth. Water regularly except during semidormant period in winter and spring, but never let plant dry out completely.

VANCOUVERIA

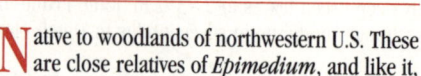

Berberidaceae

PERENNIALS

✿ ZONES VARY BY SPECIES

◑ PARTIAL SHADE

💧 REGULAR WATER

Vancouveria planipetala

Native to woodlands of northwestern U.S. These are close relatives of *Epimedium*, and like it, they are used as ground covers in shady spots. Bloom in late spring, early summer. Leaves are divided into numerous leaflets; cut foliage is attractive in bouquets. All species need cool, moist, acid conditions. Difficult to establish in hot-summer climates.

V. chrysantha. Evergreen. Zones 5, 6, 14–17. To 8–16 in. tall. Bronze-tinged gray-green leaves, 1½ in. long and wide. Small yellow flowers, 4–15 to the stalk, each flower ½ in. wide.

V. hexandra. Deciduous. Zones 4–7, 14–17, 19–24. To 4–16 in. tall. Leaflets are 1–2½ in. long, light green; fresh appearance all summer. Flower stalks usually topped with three drooping white flowers to ½ in. across, petals and sepals sharply bent backward.

V. planipetala (V. parviflora). INSIDE-OUT FLOWER. Evergreen; can be deciduous in colder part of range. Zones 4–7, 14–17. To 2 ft. tall. Light to medium green, 1½-in., shallowly lobed leaflets. White flowers are tiny—only about ⅛ in. wide—but are carried in large clusters (25–50 blossoms per cluster).

VANILLA TRUMPET VINE. See DISTICTIS laxiflora

VARIEGATED GINGER. See ALPINIA sanderae

VELTHEIMIA bracteata

Liliaceae

BULB

✿ ZONES 13, 16–25, 26 (WARMER PARTS), 27; OR INDOORS

◑ PARTIAL SHADE

💧 REGULAR WATER DURING GROWTH AND BLOOM

Veltheimia bracteata

Native to South Africa. There is some name confusion in the nursery trade; some plants sold as *V. capensis* or *V. viridifolia* are really *V. bracteata*. True *V. capensis* has pale pink flowers and bluish green leaves 1 ft. long, 1½ in. wide, whereas *V. bracteata* has pinkish purple flowers and shiny deep green, wavy-margined leaves about 1 ft. long and 3 in. wide. It is probable that all sold are *V. bracteata* or a variety of it.

Foliage makes this plant beautiful even when out of bloom. Blooms in late winter or early spring, when heavy clusters of green-tipped, tubular, drooping blooms resembling those of red-hot poker appear on stout, brown-mottled, 1-ft. stems.

Can go in the ground where temperatures remain above 25°F/−4°C, but usually grown in pots (either indoors or out). Plant in well-drained soil, setting bulbs with upper third above surface. Fertilize every 2 weeks throughout growing season. Provide wind protection; bring pots indoors when frost threatens. Allow plants to dry out during summer dormancy (in rainy-summer areas, this is easier to do when plants are in pots). Dig and divide only when growth becomes crowded.

VELVET GROUNDSEL. See SENECIO petasitis

PRACTICAL GARDENING DICTIONARY
PLEASE SEE PAGES 545–616

V

VERBASCUM

MULLEIN

Scrophulariaceae

BIENNIALS AND PERENNIALS

⚡ ZONES VARY BY SPECIES

☼ FULL SUN

🌢 MODERATE WATER

Verbascum bombyciferum
'Arctic Summer'

Large group of rosette-forming, summer-blooming plants that send up 1–6-ft. stems closely set with nearly flat, five-petaled, circular flowers about an inch across. Both foliage and stems are often covered in woolly hairs. Taller mulleins make striking vertical accents. Grow all in well-drained soil. Cut off spent flowers of perennial kinds to encourage a second round of blooming. Leave spikes of biennial species in place for reseeding. Mulleins self-sow freely—and some are downright weedy, such as the attractive roadside weed *V. thapsus*. Perennial species are short lived in hot, humid climates.

V. blattaria. MOTH MULLEIN. Zones 1–11, 14–24, 29–43. Biennial. Low clumps of smooth, dark green, cut or toothed leaves. Purple-centered, pale yellow or white flowers on stems 1½–2½ ft. high.

V. bombyciferum 'Arctic Summer'. Biennial. Zones 2–11, 14–24, 32–41. Foot-high rosettes of furry, gray-green, oval leaves. Powdery white stems to 6 ft. or more bear yellow flowers.

V. chaixii. Perennial. Zones 2–11, 14–24, 31–41. Leaves to 6 in. long, less conspicuously furry than those of *V. bombyciferum* 'Arctic Summer'. Red-eyed, pale yellow flowers in narrow, often branched spikes to 3 ft. high. 'Album' has white flowers with purple centers.

V. dumulosum. Perennial. Zones 7–9, 14–24. Dwarf to 1 ft. high, with velvety white leaves and short, branched spikes of purple-centered lemon yellow flowers. Hybrid 'Letitia' has a longer bloom season than the species.

V. hybrids. Perennials. Zones 3–10, 14–24, 32–34, 39. These include the Cotswold and Benary hybrids. Flower spikes in white, cream, and shades of pink or purple are carried on 3–4-ft. stems. Named selections in separate colors exist, such as the popular 'Pink Domino'.

V. olympicum. Perennial. Zones 3–10, 14–24, 32–34, 39. Large white leaves with soft, downy hairs form a rosette to 3 ft. across. Many stems to 5 ft. high carry bright yellow flower spikes.

V. phoeniceum. PURPLE MULLEIN. Perennial. Zones 1–10, 14–24, 32–43. Leaves are smooth on top, hairy underneath. Slender spikes of purple flowers on 2–4-ft. stems.

VERBENA

Verbenaceae

PERENNIALS, SOME GROWN AS ANNUALS

⚡ ZONES VARY BY SPECIES

☼ FULL SUN

🌢 MODERATE WATER

Verbena peruviana

Most produce their clusters of small, five-petaled, tubular blossoms in summer. Perennial species usually have purple flowers and are often treated as annuals. Low verbenas make good ground covers, hanging basket plants; taller sorts are good in borders. Most thrive in heat, tolerate drought. They dislike continually wet conditions, so provide good air circulation and well-drained soil. Most are susceptible to mildew and spider mites.

V. bipinnatifida. Perennial. Zones 1–24, 26 (northern part), 27–43. Native from Great Plains to Mexico. Grows 8–15 in. high, with finely divided leaves and blue flowers. Spreads by self-sowing in most climates.

V. bonariensis. Perennial in Zones 8–24, 28–31, warmer parts of 32; annual in colder climates. Native to South America, but naturalized in southeastern U.S. and California. Airy, branching stems to 3–6 ft. carry purple flowers. Leaves mostly in 1½-ft.-high basal clump. Plant's see-through quality makes it suited for foreground or back of border. Self-sows freely.

V. canadensis. Perennial in Zones 2–24, 28–41, but usually treated as annual in all zones. Native from Virginia to Florida west to Colorado and Mexico. To 1½ ft. high, with rosy purple flowers. There is a compact (6-in.-high) form suitable for rock gardens; white- and pink-flowering forms are also sold. 'Homestead Purple', to 6–10 in. high and spreading to 2 ft., has dark green leaves and deep purple flowers; it thrives in hot, humid climates. When growing the species or its varieties as perennials, provide good winter drainage; in colder part of range, cover with light winter mulch.

V. gooddingii. Short-lived perennial. Zones 7–24, 29, 30. Native to Southwest. To 1½ ft. high, spreading. Oval, deeply cut leaves. Heads of flowers, usually pinkish lavender, at ends of short spikes. Will bloom first summer from seed sown in spring. Can reseed where moisture is adequate. Tolerates desert heat.

V. hybrida (V. hortensis). GARDEN VERBENA. Short-lived perennial in Zones 8–29, but usually treated as annual in all zones. Many-branched plant 6–12 in. high, spreading to 1½–3 ft. Oblong, 2–4-in., bright green or gray-green leaves with toothed margins. Flowers in flat, compact clusters to 3 in. wide. Colors include white, pink, bright red, purple, blue, and combinations. Superior strains include Romance (6 in.) and Showtime (10 in.). Deep rose pink 'Showtime Trinidad' can withstand light frosts. If growing these plants as perennials, prune severely in winter or early spring.

V. peruviana (V. chamaedryfolia). Perennial in Zones 8–24, 29, 30, but usually treated as annual in all zones. Spreads rapidly, forming a very flat mat. Leaves are neat, small, closely set. Flat-topped clusters of scarlet-and-white flowers on slender stems cover foliage. Hybrids—with flowers in white, pinks, or reds—spread more slowly, have slightly larger leaves and stouter stems.

V. rigida (V. venosa). Perennial in Zones 3–24, 28–33; can be grown as annual. Native to South America, but naturalized in southeastern U.S. To 10–20 in. high, spreading. Rough, strongly toothed, dark green leaves to 2–4 in. long. Lilac to purple-blue flowers in cylindrical clusters on tall, stiff stems. Blooms in 4 months from seed. 'Flame', to 4 in. high, is a cutting-grown selection with bright scarlet flowers.

V. 'Sissinghurst'. Perennial. Zones 3–24, 29–33. Evergreen plant a few inches high and spreading to 4 ft. wide. Rose pink flowers.

V. 'Taylortown Red'. Perennial. Zones 3–24, 28–33. Evergreen spreader to 1 ft. tall, 6 ft. wide. Bright red flowers.

V. tenuisecta (V. erinoides). MOSS VERBENA. Perennial. Zones 7–9, 14–24, 28–31; annual in colder climates. Native to South America, but naturalized in Deep South. To 8–12 in. high, with finely cut leaves. Rose violet to pink flowers. 'Alba' is a white-flowered form. The species is sometimes offered as *V. pulchella gracilior*.

VERBENA, LEMON. See ALOYSIA triphylla

Verbenaceae. The immense verbena family contains annuals, perennials, shrubs, and a few trees and vines. Leaves are usually opposite or in whorls, flowers in spikes or spikelike clusters. Fruit may be berries or nutlets. Glorybower (*Clerodendrum*), *Lantana*, *Verbena*, and chaste tree (*Vitex*) are examples.

VERNONIA noveboracensis

IRONWEED

Asteraceae (Compositae)

PERENNIAL

⚡ ZONES 2–10, 14–17, 31–41

☼ ◐ FULL SUN OR LIGHT SHADE

🌢🌢🌢 MUCH TO LITTLE WATER

Vernonia noveboracensis

Seldom considered for gardens, this meadow plant is a handsome choice for the back of the border or for a contrasting color scheme with goldenrod and black-eyed Susan. Clumps of leafy stems to 6–8 ft. tall are topped in late summer by broad, flat clusters of fluffy, brilliant purple flower heads. These should be clipped off before they develop into the rust-colored seed clusters that give the plant its name (unless you want plant to naturalize from volunteer seedlings). Grows in wet or dry soils and needs no coddling.

VERONICA

SPEEDWELL

Scrophulariaceae

PERENNIALS

◢ ZONES VARY BY SPECIES

☼ FULL SUN, EXCEPT AS NOTED

♦♦ WATER NEEDS VARY BY SPECIES

Veronica prostrata

Handsome plants ranging from 4 in. to 2½ ft. in height. Small flowers (¼–½ in. across) in white, rose, pink, or pale to deep blue are massed for an effective color display. Use in sunny borders and rock gardens. Prostrate, mat-forming kinds are generally less tolerant of damp conditions than bushy kinds and should be watered less often. Named varieties are not easily assigned to a species; authorities differ. For shrubby plants sold as *Veronica*, see *Hebe*.

V. alpina. Zones 1–7, 14–17, 32–45. Creeping rootstock forms low rosette of foliage which sends up spikelike flower clusters in spring or early summer; in warmer part of range, often reblooms in fall. Varieties include 10-in. 'Alba', with white flowers; 10-in. 'Barcarolle', rose pink; and 1-ft. 'Corymbosa', deep blue. The hybrid 'Goodness Grows', 1–2 ft. tall, has an extra-long bloom period, producing violet blue blossoms from late spring to frost if old flowers are removed. Regular water.

V. gentianoides. GENTIAN SPEEDWELL. Zones 1–9, 14–21, 32–43. Creeping rootstock forms a dense mat of glossy dark green leaves, topped in spring by leafy stems carrying 10-in. spikes of ice blue flowers with darker veining. 'Variegata' has leaves marked with white. More tolerant of moist soils than other mat-forming species; do not let soil dry out.

V. grandis holophylla. Zones 1–7, 14–17, 32–43. Many stems to 2 ft. tall are densely clothed with waxy, glossy dark green leaves ending in spikelike clusters of blue flowers. These appear all summer if old clusters are deadheaded. 'Lavender Charm' ('Blue Charm') grows 1½–2 ft. tall. 'Icicle', to 1½ ft., has white flowers. Regular water.

V. incana. SILVER SPEEDWELL. Zones 1–7, 14–17, 32–43. Furry, silvery white, mat-forming foliage clumps. Deep blue flowers on 10-in. stems in summer. Varieties include 15-in. 'Minuet', with pink flowers; 10-in. 'Pavane', rose pink; 15-in. 'Red Fox', deep rose pink; 1½-ft. 'Saraband', deep blue; and green-leafed, 15-in. 'Romilley Purple', deep violet purple. Moderate to little water. Plants don't do well in very hot or rainy climates.

V. liwanensis. Zones 3–9, 14–24, 29, 30, 33. Evergreen creeping ground cover to 1 in. tall. In midspring, the tiny deep green leaves are concealed by a carpet of bright blue flowers. Use in rock garden, as bulb cover, between stepping-stones. Needs good drainage, only enough water to prevent wilting.

V. longifolia subsessilis (V. subsessilis). Zones 1–9, 14–21, 32–43. Clumps of upright stems to 2 ft. tall are topped in midsummer by spikes of deep blue flowers about ½ in. wide; deadhead to prolong bloom. Stems are leafy and rather closely set with narrow, pointed leaves. Regular water.

V. pectinata. Zones 1–9, 14–24, 33–43. Prostrate mat spreads by creeping stems that root at joints. Roundish, ½-in.-long leaves with scallop-toothed or deeply cut edges. Profuse spring or early summer bloom; flowers are deep blue with white centers, in 5–6-in. spikes among the leaves. 'Rosea' has rose pink flowers. Good in rock gardens or wall crevices. Full sun or part shade. Moderate to little water.

V. prostrata (V. rupestris). Zones 1–9, 14–24, 32–43. Small leaves to ¾ in. long. Tufted, hairy stems; some are prostrate and form mats of hairy foliage, while others grow upward to 8 in. tall and are topped by short clusters of pale blue flowers in late spring or early summer. 'Alba' bears white blooms, 'Mrs. Holt' pale pink ones. 'Trehane' has golden yellow leaves, bright blue flowers. Moderate to little water.

V. repens. Zones 3–9, 14–24, 29–34, 39. Shiny green, ½-in. leaves clothe prostrate stems, give mosslike effect. Clusters of tiny lavender to white flowers in spring. Good as a small-scale ground cover, filler between stepping-stones, or cover for small bulbs. Moderate to little water. Tolerates some shade.

V. saturejoides. Zones 1–9, 14–21, 32–43. Roundish, ½-in. leaves closely overlap on stems. Dark blue flowers in short, compact spikes appear in spring. Fine rock garden plant; stems spread by creeping roots. Moderate to little water.

V. spicata (V. austriaca, V. austriaca teucrium). Zones 1–9, 14–21, 28, 31–43. Rounded green clumps send up spikelike flower clusters to 2 ft. tall. Long summer bloom period if plants are deadheaded. 'Crater Lake', the old standby, grows to 15 in. tall, bears bright blue flowers. Other varieties include 'Blue Fox', to 20 in. high, and rosy pink 'Heidekind', to 10 in. high. All take regular water. Need good drainage, especially in the South.

V. 'Sunny Border Blue'. Zones 1–9, 14–21, 28, 31–43. Compact plant with crinkled foliage. Dark violet blue flowers in spires to 2 ft. tall over an exceptionally long bloom season, starting in late spring or early summer. Deadheading prolongs the show until frost. Regular water.

Veronica spicata

V. 'Waterperry' ('Waterperry Blue'). Zones 2–9, 14–21, 32–41. Low, trailing plant roots as it spreads. Leaves are roundish, bronze-tinted ovals ½ in. long. Round flowers in loose clusters are pale blue, veined deeper blue. Spring bloom is followed by sporadic flowering throughout summer and fall. Use for bulb cover, in rock garden, poolside. Mat-forming plant but prefers regular water.

VERONICASTRUM virginicum (Veronica virginica)

CULVER'S ROOT

Scrophulariaceae

PERENNIAL

◢ ZONES 1–9, 14–17, 32–43

☼ ◐ FULL SUN OR LIGHT SHADE

♦ REGULAR WATER

Veronicastrum virginicum

Native to eastern U.S. Resembles a very tall *Veronica*. Stems to 5–7 ft. high, clothed with whorls of toothed, 6-in., lance-shaped leaves. Stems branch in the upper portions and are topped by slender spikelike clusters (to 9 in. long) of tiny pale blue or white flowers. Pink varieties exist. Useful plant for background in large borders. Makes a striking pattern against dark background, such as tall hedge or woodland edge, but too much shade makes it floppy. Likes fertile, well-drained, slightly acid soil.

VIBURNUM

Caprifoliaceae

DECIDUOUS OR EVERGREEN SHRUBS, SMALL TREES

◢ ZONES VARY BY SPECIES

☼ ◐ FULL SUN OR PART SHADE, EXCEPT AS NOTED

♦ REGULAR WATER, EXCEPT AS NOTED

Viburnum opulus 'Roseum'

Large and diverse group of plants with clustered, sometimes fragrant flowers followed by single-seeded, often brilliantly colored fruit much appreciated by birds. In general, heaviest fruit set occurs when several different named varieties or seedlings that bloom at the same time are planted together. Some viburnums are valuable for winter flowers. Many deciduous kinds have poor or inconsistent fall color. Some evergreen types are used principally as foliage plants. A few species, as noted, can be grown as small trees.

Viburnums prefer slightly acid soil but are very tolerant, even accepting heavy soils. Many have a wide range of climate adaptability. Where summers are long and hot, most evergreen kinds look better with some sun protection. Prune to prevent legginess; some evergreen kinds can be sheared. Aphids, thrips, spider mites, scale, and root weevils are potential pests in many regions; nematodes are a problem in the South. However, plants are not usually seriously troubled. Keep any sulfur sprays off foliage.

V. bodnantense. Deciduous. Zones 4–9, 14–24, 31, 32. To 10 ft. or more. Oval leaves 1½–4 in. long are deeply veined, turn dark scarlet in fall. Loose clusters of very fragrant flowers, deep pink fading paler, bloom fall–spring. Red fruit is not showy. This plant is a hybrid; there are several varieties. Best known is 'Dawn' ('Pink Dawn'). Flower buds freeze in coldest winters.

V. burkwoodii. Deciduous in coldest areas, nearly evergreen elsewhere. Zones 2–12, 14–24, 31–41. Hybrid to 6–12 ft. tall, 4–8 ft. wide. Leaves to 3½ in. long, glossy dark green with white, hairy undersides; turn purplish red in cold weather. Very fragrant white flowers open in late winter or early spring from dense, 4-in. clusters of pink buds. Blue-black fruit is not showy. Early growth is straggly; mature plants are dense. Can be trained as espalier.

'Chenault' (*V. chenaultii*). Denser, more compact, slightly later blooming, more deciduous in mild climates than the species.

'Mohawk'. Zones 1–12, 14–24, 31–43. To 7 ft. tall. Red buds are showy long before they expand into white flowers. Bright orange-red fall color. Resistant to bacterial leaf spot.

V. carlcephalum. FRAGRANT SNOWBALL. Deciduous. Zones 3–11, 14–24, 31–34, 39. Hybrid plant to 6–10 ft. tall and wide. Leaves 2–3½ in. long, dull grayish green, downy beneath; turn reddish purple in autumn. Long-lasting, waxy white, perfumed flowers in showy, dense, 4–5-in. clusters in spring.

V. carlesii. KOREAN SPICE VIBURNUM. Deciduous. Zones 2–11, 14–24, 31–41. To 4–8 ft. tall and wide. Leaves are like those of *V. carlcephalum*; inconsistent reddish fall color. Sweetly fragrant, 2–3-in. clusters of white flowers open from pink buds in spring. Blue-black summer fruit is not showy. Best in part shade during summer, in sun during spring, winter. The hybrid 'Cayuga', hardy into Zones 1 and 43, grows 5 ft. tall and has white flowers opening from pink buds.

V. cassinoides. WITHE-ROD. Deciduous. Zones 1–10, 14–21, 31–43. Native to eastern and central North America. Attractive dense, rounded plant 5–6 ft. (possibly to 10 ft.) tall, with dull dark green leaves; red-orange to red-purple fall color. Flat clusters of white flowers bloom in late spring or early summer; these are followed by showy, mixed-color clusters of green, pink, red, and blue fruits that eventually turn black. Tolerates damp soil, wind, seacoast conditions.

V. davidii. Evergreen. Zones 4–9, 14–24; less satisfactory in 31, warmer parts of 32. Compact mound to 3–4 ft. high and wide. Handsome leaves are glossy dark green, deeply veined, to 6 in. long. Spring flowers in 3-in. clusters are white, opening from dull pinkish red buds. Blossoms are followed by very showy, metallic turquoise blue fruit. Use as foundation shrub or in foreground plantings.

V. dentatum. ARROWWOOD VIBURNUM. Deciduous. Zones 1–11, 14–21, 28, 31–45. Native from New Brunswick to Minnesota, south to Georgia. To 6–10 ft. tall (or taller) and as wide. Cream-colored flowers in late spring are followed by blue-black, ¼-in. fruit. Dark green, 4-in. leaves turn yellow, orange, or deep red in autumn. 'Morton' has deep burgundy fall color; 'Ralph Senior' and 'Synnestvedt' have red, yellow, and orange fall color. Plants tolerate heat, cold, and wet soil. Use as screen or tall hedge.

V. dilatatum. LINDEN VIBURNUM. Deciduous. Zones 3–9, 14–16, 32–34. To 8–10 ft. tall and not quite as wide. Nearly round, 2–5-in. gray-green leaves; inconsistent rusty red fall color. Tiny, creamy white, somewhat unpleasant-smelling flowers in 5-in. clusters, late spring or early summer. Showy bright red fruits are produced most heavily where summers are warm; they ripen in early fall, hang on into winter. Outstanding named varieties include the following:

'Catskill'. Compact growth to 5–8 ft. tall, 8–10 ft. wide, with smaller leaves than species. Dark red fruit. Fall color is a combination of yellow, orange, and red.

'Erie'. Rounded habit to 6 ft. tall, 10 ft. wide. Coral fruit. Leaves turn yellow, orange, and red in autumn. Highly disease resistant.

'Iroquois'. To 9 ft. tall, 12 ft. wide. Selected for heavy production of larger, darker red fruit. Orange-red to maroon fall foliage.

V. farreri (V. fragrans). Deciduous. Zones 3–9, 14–24, 31–35, 37, 39. Loose habit, to 8–12 ft. tall and as wide. Smooth green leaves are oval, heavily veined, 1½–3 in. long; turn soft russet red to reddish purple in fall. Fragrant white to pink flowers in 2-in. clusters appear before leaves open, in winter or early spring. Blossoms survive to 20° to 22°F/−7° to −6°C; they freeze in colder temperatures. Bright red fruit. Prune to prevent leggy growth. 'Album' has pure white flowers. Pink-flowered 'Nanum' is lower growing (to 2 ft.).

V. hybrids. This group includes plants of complex ancestry. The following, all spring bloomers, are widely offered:

'Chesapeake'. Semievergreen. Zones 3–12, 14–24, 31–34, 39. To 6 ft. tall, 10 ft. wide, with wavy-edged, glossy dark green leaves. Small, fragrant white flowers open from pink buds; dull red to black fruit follows.

'Conoy'. Evergreen. Zones 3–12, 14–24, 31–34, 39. Dense, rounded plant to 5 ft. tall, 8 ft. wide. Lustrous dark green leaves, whitish beneath; take on maroon tinge in winter in colder part of range. Creamy white, slightly fragrant flowers; long-lasting red berries. Tolerates shearing.

'Eskimo'. Semievergreen. Zones 3–12, 14–24, 31–35, 37, 39. Dense, compact habit to 5 ft. tall and wide. Shiny dark green foliage; unscented white flowers in 3–4-in., snowball-like clusters.

V. japonicum. Evergreen. Zones 5–10, 12, 14–24, 28–31. To 10–20 ft. tall; can be trained as small tree for background plantings. Leathery, glossy dark green leaves to 6 in. long. Sparse spring show of fragrant white flowers in 4-in. clusters. Red fruit is likewise sparse, but very attractive. Best with some shade in warmer areas. The hybrids 'Chippewa' and 'Huron' are hardier to cold (Zones 3–11, 14–21, 31–34, 39); both have semievergreen to deciduous, glossy green leaves that turn rich maroon and red in autumn.

V. juddii. Deciduous. Zones 2–9, 14–24, 31–41. Hybrid plant to 4–8 ft. tall. Bushier and more spreading than *V. carlesii* but similar to it in other respects, including fragrance.

V. lantana. WAYFARING TREE. Deciduous. Zones 2–9, 14–17, 33–41. Large (10–20-ft.), rounded, multistemmed shrub with 2–5-in. dark green leaves that turn an inconsistent purplish red in fall. Flat, 3–5-in. clusters of creamy flowers in midspring develop into yellow fruits that gradually age to red, then black; all colors are sometimes present at once. Berries of 'Mohican' hold their red color longest. This species tolerates drought and lime soils better than most other viburnums.

V. lentago. NANNYBERRY. Deciduous. Zones 1–9, 14–21, 32–45. Native to eastern and central North America. Will grow as single-trunked tree to 30 ft. tall or as massive shrub to lesser height. Creamy white flowers in flat, 4–6-in. clusters in spring. Edible fruit is red at first, turning to blue black. Glossy dark green, 2–4-in.-long leaves turn an inconsistent purplish red in fall. Good in dappled shade of taller trees, at woodland edge. Takes moist or dry soils.

V. macrocephalum macrocephalum (V. m. 'Sterile'). CHINESE SNOWBALL. Deciduous in coldest areas, nearly evergreen elsewhere. Zones 3–9, 14–24, 29–34, 39. To 12–20 ft. tall, with broad, rounded habit. Leaves oval to oblong, 2–4 in. long, dull green. Spectacular big, rounded, 6–8-in. flower clusters in spring (or anytime during warm weather) are composed of sterile blossoms that are lime green at first, changing to white. No fruit. Can be trained as espalier.

V. odoratissimum. SWEET VIBURNUM. Evergreen; briefly deciduous in colder part of range. Zones 15–24, 26–28; at some risk of frost damage in 8, 9, 14, 29. To 10–20 ft. tall; becomes treelike with age. Leaves bright green, 3–8 in. long, with glossy, varnished-looking surface. Conical, 3–6-in. clusters of white, lightly fragrant flowers in spring. Red fruit ripens to black. Good screen. 'Emerald Lustre' has larger leaves.

V. opulus. EUROPEAN CRANBERRY BUSH. Deciduous. Zones 1–9, 14–24, 29–43. To 8–15 ft. tall and wide, with arching branches. Lobed,

V

maplelike dark green leaves to 2–4 in. long and wider than long; fall color may be yellow, bright red, or reddish purple. Creamy white spring flowers consist of 2–4-in. clusters of small fertile blossoms ringed with larger sterile blossoms for a lace cap effect. Large, showy red fruit, fall–winter. Takes moist to boggy soils. Control aphids. Varieties include:

'Aureum'. To 10 ft. tall. Golden yellow foliage needs some shade to prevent sunburn.

'Compactum'. Same as *V. opulus* but smaller: 4–5 ft. high and wide.

'Nanum'. To 2 ft. tall, 2 ft. wide. Needs no trimming as low hedge. Cannot take poorly drained, wet soils. No flowers, fruit.

'Roseum' ('Sterile'). COMMON SNOWBALL. To 10–15 ft. Resembles *V. opulus,* but flower clusters are like snowballs: 2–2½ in. across, composed entirely of sterile flowers (so no fruit). Aphids are especially troublesome on this form.

V. plicatum plicatum (V. tomentosum 'Sterile'). JAPANESE SNOWBALL. Deciduous. Zones 3–9, 14–24, 31–35, 37, 39. To 8–15 ft. tall and wide. Oval, 3–6-in. long, strongly veined, dull dark green leaves turn purplish red in fall. Showy, 3-in. snowball-like clusters of white sterile flowers in midspring look like those of *V. opulus* 'Roseum', but this plant is less bothered by aphids. Horizontal branching pattern gives plant a tiered look, especially when in bloom: flower clusters are held above the branches, while leaves hang down. No fruit. Tolerates occasionally wet soils.

V. plicatum tomentosum. DOUBLEFILE VIBURNUM. Deciduous. Zones 3–9, 14–24, 31–35, 37, 39. A truly beautiful viburnum. Resembles Japanese snowball, but midspring flower display consists of clusters of small fertile flowers in flat, 2–4-in. clusters edged with 1–1½-in. sterile flowers in lace cap effect. Fruit is red aging to black, showy, not always profuse. Takes moist to wet soils. Selections include the following:

'Cascade'. To 10 ft. tall, with wide-spreading branches, large sterile flowers.

'Mariesii'. To 10 ft. tall, 12 ft. wide. Has larger flower clusters, larger sterile flowers than the species.

'Newport'. To 5–6 ft. tall and wide.

'Pink Beauty'. To 8–10 ft. tall, with light pink flowers that fade to white in warm temperatures.

'Shasta'. More horizontal habit than the species (to 10 ft. tall, 15 ft. wide), with large sterile flowers.

'Shoshoni'. To 5 ft. tall, 8 ft. wide.

'Summer Snowflake'. To 5–8 ft. tall. Blooms from spring to fall.

'Watanabe', 'Nana Semperflorens', and 'Fujisanensis' ('Mt. Fuji') are similar, if not identical, to 'Summer Snowflake'.

V. prunifolium. BLACK HAW. Deciduous. Zones 1–9, 14–21, 28–43. Native to eastern U.S. Upright to 15 ft. and spreading as wide. Can be trained as small tree. Common name comes from dark fruit and plant's resemblance to hawthorn (*Crataegus*). Oval, finely toothed leaves to 3 in. long turn purplish to reddish purple in autumn. Abundant clusters of creamy white flowers in spring are followed by edible blue-black fruit in fall, winter. Use as dense screen or barrier, attractive specimen shrub. Best in full sun. Tolerates drought.

V. rhytidophyllum. LEATHERLEAF VIBURNUM. Evergreen. Zones 3–9, 14–24, 32–35, 37, 39. Narrow, upright growth to 6–15 ft. tall. Leaves narrowish, to 4–10 in. long, deep green and wrinkled above, densely fuzzy underneath. Yellowish-white spring flowers in 4–8-in. clusters. Fruit is scarlet, aging to black. Tattered-looking plant where cold winds blow. Leaves droop in cold weather. Tolerates deep shade. Some find this plant striking; others consider it coarse. 'Alleghany' and 'Willowwood' are hybrids similar to the parent. Hybrid 'Pragense' has a finer texture than the parent.

Viburnum rhytidophyllum

V. rigidum. CANARY ISLAND VIBURNUM. Evergreen. Zones 15–24. Grows upright to 6–10 ft., with equal or greater spread. Resembles *V. tinus* but has larger flower clusters, larger leaves (to 6 in. long). Flowers bloom in late winter, early spring; these are followed by blue fruit that later turns black. Same uses as for *V. tinus.*

V. sargentii. Deciduous. Zones 1–9, 14–21, 33–43. Upright, rounded growth to 12–15 ft. tall and wide. Lobed, somewhat maplelike, 2–5-in.-long leaves. Foliage is bronze purple when new, dark green in summer; may turn yellow to red in autumn. White to cream blossoms in late spring; 2–4-in. clusters of small fertile flowers are edged with 1-in. sterile flowers in lace cap effect. Bright red fruit colors up in late summer and fall, hangs on into winter. 'Onondaga', to 6 ft. or taller, has foliage that emerges deep maroon and holds a maroon tinge when mature; its white lace cap flowers are tinged purple.

V. setigerum. TEA VIBURNUM. Deciduous. Zones 3–9, 14–21, 31–34, 39. To 8–12 ft. tall, rather erect, multistemmed, often bare at the base. (Plant lower shrubs around it for concealment.) Leaves, once used for making tea, are 3–6 in. long, dark green or blue green, turning purplish in fall. White spring flowers in 1–2-in. clusters are not striking, but heavy production of scarlet fruit makes this the showiest of fruiting viburnums.

V. suspensum. SANDANKWA VIBURNUM. Evergreen. Zones 12–24, 26, 28; risky in cold winters in Zones 8–10, 31. To 8–10 ft. tall and as broad. Leathery, oval, 2–4-in.-long leaves, glossy deep green above, paler beneath. White flowers in loose 2–4-in. clusters in early spring; some people find their fragrance objectionable. Red fruit ages to black; it is not long lasting. Moderate to little water. Serviceable screen or hedge. Watch for thrips, spider mites, aphids.

V. tinus. LAURUSTINUS. Evergreen. Zones 4–10, 12–23, 26, 28–31; 33 with some risk of frost damage. To 6–12 ft. tall, half as wide. Leathery, dark green, oval leaves to 2–3 in. long, with edges slightly rolled under. New stems wine red. Tight clusters of pink buds open to lightly fragrant white flowers, fall–spring. Bright metallic blue fruits last through summer. Dense foliage right to ground makes it good plant for screens, hedges, clipped topiary shapes. Susceptible to mildew, mites. Varieties include:

'Dwarf'. To 3–5 ft. tall, equally wide. Low screens, hedges, foundation plantings.

'Lucidum'. SHINING LAURUSTINUS. Zones 8, 9, 12–23, 26, 28, 29. Less cold hardy than species, with larger leaves. Mildew resistant.

'Robustum'. ROUNDLEAF LAURUSTINUS. Leaves coarser, rougher than those of species; flower buds less pink. Mildew resistant. Excellent small, narrow tree.

'Spring Bouquet' ('Compactum'). Upright to about 6 ft. tall; good for hedges. Leaves are slightly smaller, darker green than those of species.

'Variegatum'. Zones 4–9, 14–23, 26, 28–31. Leaves marbled with white and pale yellow.

V. trilobum. CRANBERRY BUSH. Deciduous. Zones 1–11, 14–20, 33–45. Native to Canada, northern U.S. To 10–15 ft. tall. Leaves look much like those of *V. opulus;* they emerge reddish tinged, mature to dark green, turn yellow to red purple in fall. White lace cap flowers appear in midspring, followed by fruit (edible in this species) similar to that of *V. opulus.* 'Compactum' grows 6 ft. tall; 'Wentworth' has berries larger than those of the species.

V. wrightii. Deciduous. Zones 3–9, 14–16, 32–34. Similar to *V. dilatatum* except for its larger leaves, which may turn a good red in fall. Useful tall hedge.

VICTORIAN BOX. See PITTOSPORUM undulatum

VINCA

PERIWINKLE, MYRTLE

Apocynaceae

PERENNIALS

ZONES VARY BY SPECIES

PARTIAL OR FULL SHADE

MODERATE WATER

Vinca minor

Trailing, arching stems that root where they touch the soil make these evergreen plants useful as ground and bank covers. Shiny dark green leaves are oval to oblong. Lavender blue, five-petaled, pinwheel-shaped flowers appear in leaf joints in spring. Tolerate sun if well watered.

V. major. Zones 5–24, 28–31, warmer parts of 32 and 33. The larger, more aggressive species. Leaves to 3 in. long, flowers to 2 in. across. Spreads rapidly; can be extremely invasive in areas that are sheltered and forested. Will mound up 1–2 ft. high. Shear close to ground occasionally to bring on new growth. A form with creamy leaf variegation exists.

V. minor. DWARF PERIWINKLE. Zones 1–24, 28–43. Miniature version of *V. major*, with smaller leaves and flowers and a height of just 6 in. More restrained, less likely to invade adjacent plantings. Among the many varieties are 'Alba', with white flowers; 'Atropurpurea', deep purple flowers and small leaves; 'Aureola', light blue flowers, yellow veins in leaf centers; 'Bowles' Variety', larger leaves, deeper blue flowers; 'Miss Jekyll', small grower with white flowers; 'Ralph Shugert', white-edged leaves, blue flowers, autumn rebloom. 'Sterling Silver' is a blue-flowered form with green leaves specked with pale green and edged in cream. 'La Grave' is similar to (if not the same plant as) 'Bowles' Variety'.

V. rosea. See Catharanthus roseus

VIOLA

VIOLA, VIOLET, PANSY
Violaceae
PERENNIALS, SOME TREATED AS ANNUALS
🌰 ZONES VARY BY SPECIES
☼ ◐ ● EXPOSURE NEEDS VARY BY SPECIES
💧 REGULAR WATER

Viola wittrockiana

Botanically speaking, violas, pansies, and violets are all perennials belonging to the genus *Viola*. However, pansies and violas are usually treated as annuals; they are invaluable for winter and spring color in mild-winter areas, for spring-through-summer color in colder climates. Pansies and violas provide mass color in borders and edgings, as ground covers for spring-flowering bulbs, and in containers. Violets are more often used as woodland or rock garden plants. Pansies and violas take sun or shade; except as noted, violets thrive in part or full shade.

V. blanda. SWEET WHITE VIOLET. Zones 1–10, 14–24, 29–43. Native to eastern North America. To 2–3 in. tall, spreading by runners. Fragrant early spring flowers are white veined purple, with sharply reflexed petals. Likes humus-rich soil.

V. cornuta. VIOLA, TUFTED PANSY. All zones as annuals; 2–10, 14–24, 29–43 for kinds grown as perennials. To 6–8 in. high, with smooth, wavy-toothed, somewhat oval leaves. Purple, pansylike flowers, about 1½ in. across, have slender spur. Modern strains and varieties have larger flowers with shorter spurs, in solid colors of purple, blue, yellow, apricot, ruby red, and white. Crystal strain has especially large flowers in clear colors. Set out nursery plants or sow seed as for pansy.

Some nurseries offer English violas—named varieties propagated by cuttings or division. These form clumps to 2 ft. wide and are reliably perennial. Varieties include 'Better Times', 2-in. yellow flowers; 'Columbine', creamy white flowers liberally splashed with purple; 'Etain', pale yellow flowers with purple borders; 'Mt. Spokane', white flowers with a shading of palest blue; and 'Whiskers', cream-colored flowers marked with thin purple lines.

V. cucullata (V. obliqua). MARSH BLUE VIOLET. Zones 1–9, 14–17, 32–43. Native to eastern and central North America. Leaves to 4 in. wide. Blue, ¾-in.-wide flowers in early spring. Good ground cover, but self-sows and can become a nuisance. 'Freckles' has white flowers liberally dotted with purple; comes true from seed.

V. hederacea. AUSTRALIAN VIOLET. Zones 7–9, 14–24, 29, 30. To 1–4 in. high; eventually covers several feet, spreading by runners at slow to moderate rate. Kidney-shaped leaves. Nearly spurless, ¼–¾-in. summer flowers come in white or in blue fading to white at petal tips. Plant goes dormant at about 30°F/–1°C. Use as ground cover in shade or in sun with abundant water.

V. labradorica. Zones 1–24, 29–45. Native to northeastern U.S., Canada, Greenland. Tiny violet 3 in. high or less, with roundish, 1-in. leaves tinged purple and tiny lavender blue flowers in spring. Spreads aggressively by runners and can invade choice small perennials; volunteer seedlings can earn it weed status. Useful small-scale ground cover in shade or filler between stepping-stones or paving blocks.

V. odorata. SWEET VIOLET. Zones 1–24, 29–43. The violet of song and story. Spreads by long runners at moderate rate. Dark green, heart-shaped leaves, toothed on margins. Fragrant, short-spurred flowers in deep violet, bluish rose, or white. Deep purple 'Royal Robe', a large plant with long stems (to 6 in.), is widely grown. 'Royal Elk' has single, fragrant, long-stemmed violet-colored flowers. 'Charm' grows in clumps, has small white flowers. 'Rosina' is pink flowered. Plant size varies from 2 in. for smallest varieties to 8–10 in. for largest.

Plants tolerate full sun in cool-summer areas. Remove runners and shear rank growth in late fall for better spring flower display. For heavy bloom, apply a complete fertilizer in very early spring, before flowering. In areas with mild winters and cool summers, these violets can become genuine pests if allowed to spread into other perennial plantings or lawns.

Parma violets are hybrids of imprecise ancestry but derived in part from *V. odorata*, which they resemble. Hardy to about 10°F/–12°C—possible outdoors in Zones 4–9, 14–24, 29–31. Flowers are very double and intensely fragrant. 'Duchesse de Parme' (lavender), 'Marie Louise' (deep violet), and 'Swanley White' represent the range of colors available. Plants prefer cool winters and mild summers. Beyond their hardiness range, grow these violets in containers and keep in a cool greenhouse (or cool indoor room) over winter.

V. palmata. EARLY BLUE VIOLET. Zones 1–7, 14–17, 32–43. Native to eastern U.S. Plants bear violet blue, white-centered violets on 8-in. stems in spring. Leaves are divided into several toothed lobes. Slow to spread.

V. pedata. BIRD'S-FOOT VIOLET. Zones 1–6, 31–43. Native to eastern North America. So named because its finely divided leaves resemble a bird's foot. Blooms early spring to early summer; inch-wide flowers on 4-in. stems are usually two-toned violet blue with darker veins. Forms clumps; does not spread by runners. Not as easy to grow as other violets; likes excellent drainage, filtered sun or high shade, acid conditions.

V. priceana. See V. sororia

V. sororia (V. priceana). CONFEDERATE VIOLET. Zones 1–11, 14–24, 29–43. Leaves are somewhat heart shaped, to 5 in. wide. Blooms spring–early summer; flowers are ½–¾ in. across, white, heavily veined with violet blue, flat-faced like pansies. No runners. Self-sows readily; best in woodland garden. Good ground cover among rhododendrons.

V. tricolor. JOHNNY-JUMP-UP. All zones as annual. To 6–12 in. tall, with oval, deeply lobed leaves. Purple-and-yellow spring flowers resemble miniature pansies. Flowers of 'Molly Sanderson' are so deep a purple that they appear black. Self-sows profusely. Like pansy, takes sun or shade.

V. t. hortensis. See V. wittrockiana

V. wittrockiana (V. tricolor hortensis). PANSY. All zones as annual. Many strains with flowers 2–4 in. across, in white, blue, mahogany red, rose, yellow, apricot, purple; also bicolors. Petals often striped or blotched; Crown and Crystal Bowl strains have unblotched flowers. Plants grow to about 8 in. high. F_1 and F_2 hybrids more free flowering, heat tolerant. To prolong bloom of pansies, pick flowers (with some foliage) regularly, remove faded blooms before they seed. In hot-summer areas, plants get ragged by midsummer and should be removed.

Set out nursery plants in spring for summer bloom in cold-winter climates; in fall for winter–spring (or longer) bloom in mild climates. Or start plants from seed. In cold climates, sow seed in mid- to late summer and overwinter seedlings in a cold frame until spring planting time; or sow seed indoors in January or February, plant out in spring. In mild-winter areas, sow in mid- to late summer, plant out in fall.

VIOLET. See VIOLA

VIOLET TRUMPET VINE. See CLYTOSTOMA callistegioides

VIPER'S BUGLOSS. See ECHIUM vulgare

V

VIRGINIA BLUEBELLS. See MERTENSIA virginica

VIRGINIA CREEPER. See PARTHENOCISSUS quinquefolia

VIRGINIAN STOCK. See MALCOLMIA maritima

VISCARIA coeli-rosa. See LYCHNIS coeli-rosa

Vitaceae. The grape family contains vines that climb by tendrils and produce berries. In addition to grape, best-known representatives are Boston ivy and Virginia creeper (both species of *Parthenocissus*).

VITEX

CHASTE TREE

Verbenaceae

DECIDUOUS OR EVERGREEN SHRUBS OR TREES

ZONES VARY BY SPECIES

FULL SUN

REGULAR WATER

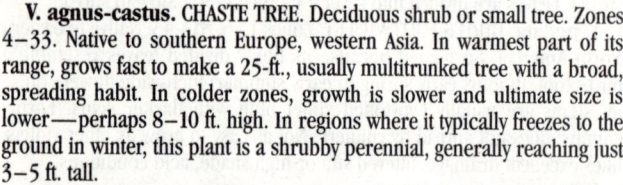

Vitex agnus-castus

Large group of mostly tropical and subtropical trees, only a few of which are grown in the U.S. They have handsome, divided leaves and clustered flowers. The deciduous species are root hardy and can be treated as perennials in colder parts of their range. All will tolerate seacoast conditions.

V. agnus-castus. CHASTE TREE. Deciduous shrub or small tree. Zones 4–33. Native to southern Europe, western Asia. In warmest part of its range, grows fast to make a 25-ft., usually multitrunked tree with a broad, spreading habit. In colder zones, growth is slower and ultimate size is lower—perhaps 8–10 ft. high. In regions where it typically freezes to the ground in winter, this plant is a shrubby perennial, generally reaching just 3–5 ft. tall.

Aromatic leaves are divided fanwise into five to seven narrow, 2–6-in.-long leaflets that are grayish green above, gray beneath. No real fall color. Small, fragrant, lavender blue flowers in 6–12-in. spikes at branch ends and in leaf joints, summer–fall. Varieties include 'Alba' and 'Silver Spire', with white flowers; 'Latifolia' (sometimes sold as *V. macrophylla*), a sturdy plant with large leaflets; and 'Rosea', with pinkish flowers.

Thrives in heat. Tolerant of various soils, but prefers well-drained soil. Good in shrub border. If trained high, makes a good small shade tree. Plants treated as perennials should be cut to within 1 ft. of ground in spring; they will bloom on new growth.

V. lucens. NEW ZEALAND CHASTE TREE. Evergreen tree. Zones 16, 17, 22–24. Slow to moderate growth to 40–60 ft. Divided leaves with three to five glossy, corrugated-looking, roundish, 5-in.-long leaflets. In winter, loose clusters of pink buds form in leaf joints; these open to lavender pink, 1-in. flowers during warm weather. Blossoms are followed by bright red fruits that resemble small cherries. Needs deep, rich soil and protection from frost while young.

V. negundo. Deciduous shrub or small tree. Zones 3–33. Native to southeast Africa, eastern Asia. Similar to *V. agnus-castus*, but a little larger and more cold hardy; 5–8-in. flower spikes aren't as showy. 'Heterophylla' has delicate-looking, finely lobed leaflets. In coldest areas, treat as perennial, as for *V. agnus-castus*.

VITIS. See GRAPE

FOR INFORMATION ON SELECTING PLANTS
PLEASE SEE PAGES 79–160

VRIESEA

Bromeliaceae

PERENNIALS

ZONES 22–25, 27; OR INDOORS

STRONG LIGHT BUT NOT DIRECT SUN

WATER LEAF BASES, DAMPEN MOSS

Vriesea hieroglyphica

Bromeliads with rosettes of long, leathery leaves and oddly shaped flower clusters. Grow as epiphytes in pockets of sphagnum moss on tree branches or in pots of loose, highly organic mix. Mist if grown in hot, dry rooms. Feed lightly and often.

V. hieroglyphica. Rosettes of 30–40 leaves, each 3 ft. long, 3 in. wide, dark green with pronounced cross-banding of blackish purple. Greenish flower spike with dull yellow flowers.

V. lindenii. See Tillandsia lindenii

V. splendens. FLAMING SWORD. Rosettes of up to 20 dark green, 1½-ft. leaves barred transversely with blackish purple. Flower stalk like a 1½–2-ft.-wide feather of bright red bracts from which small yellow flowers emerge. 'Chantrierei' is a brightly colored selection.

WAFER ASH. See PTELEA trifoliata

WAKE ROBIN. See TRILLIUM

WALDSTEINIA

BARREN STRAWBERRY

Rosaceae

PERENNIALS

ZONES 2–9, 14–17, 32–41

FULL SUN OR LIGHT SHADE

REGULAR WATER

Waldsteinia fragarioides

These creeping, strawberrylike, evergreen ground covers spread by runners to make 3–4-in.-high mats. Glossy bright green leaves are divided into three leaflets; in cold climates, they may take on bronze tones in winter. Yellow, ¾-in. flowers in spring and early summer are followed by tiny, inedible fruit. For fast cover, plant 1 ft. apart in well-drained soil. Do better in cool-summer areas than in regions where summers are hot and humid.

W. fragarioides. Native to eastern North America. Leaves larger than those of *W. ternata*, with leaflets to 3 in. long.

W. ternata. Native to Siberia, China, Japan. Similar to *W. fragarioides*, but has more compact growth and shorter leaflets (to 1½ in. long).

WALKING FERN. See ASPLENIUM rhizophyllum

WALLFLOWER. See ERYSIMUM

WALNUT (Juglans)

Juglandaceae

DECIDUOUS TREES

ZONES VARY BY SPECIES

FULL SUN

REGULAR WATER

Walnut

Large, spreading trees suitable for big properties. All produce oval or round, edible nuts in fleshy husks; those of native species have a wild flavor, those of English walnut are the ones sold commercially. Among the drawbacks of these trees are their large size; shallow, competitive roots

W

(roots of black walnut even inhibit growth of some other plants); and wind-borne pollen, which causes an allergic reaction in many people. Moreover, trees tend to be out of leaf for a long time—and they are often messy when in leaf (drip and sooty mildew from aphid exudations) and in fruit (husks from nuts can stain).

J. cinerea. BUTTERNUT. Zones 1–9, 14–17, 32–45. Native from New Brunswick to Georgia, west to Arkansas and North Dakota. To 50–60 ft. (possibly to 100 ft.) tall, with broad, spreading canopy. Resembles black walnut—but tree is smaller, leaves have fewer leaflets (11–19), and nuts are oval or elongated rather than round. Flavor is good, but shells are thick and hard to crack.

J. nigra. BLACK WALNUT. Zones 1–9, 14–21, 28–43. Native from Massachusetts to Florida, west to Texas and Minnesota. Can reach 150 ft. tall (though often attains only half that height in gardens), with high-branched, oval- to round-headed habit. Furrowed blackish brown bark. Leaves have 15–23 leaflets, each 2½–5 in. long. Richly flavored nuts, 1–1½ in. across, are thick shelled and very hard. Some varieties, however, are easier to crack. In hot, humid climates, a bacterial disease often causes tree to defoliate by late summer. Black walnut inhibits the growth of many other plants; consult your Cooperative Extension Office for a list of plants that will grow near it.

J. regia. ENGLISH WALNUT. Zones 4–9, 14–23, 29–33; some varieties in 1–3, 35–43. Native to southwest Asia, southeast Europe. To 60 ft. high, with equal spread. Fast growing, especially when young. Trunk and heavy, horizontal or upward-angled branches are covered with smooth gray bark. Leaves have five to seven (rarely more) 3–6-in.-long leaflets. This species bears the familiar walnuts sold commercially; most are produced in California, Oregon, and Washington.

Many varieties are available; choosing the right one is critical. In coldest part of range, choose a walnut described as Carpathian or Hardy Persian; most offered are seedlings, but grafted, named varieties exist. In areas with late frosts, get a variety that leafs out late and releases its pollen late, such as 'Hansen'. Other varieties will perform tolerably well in the hot, humid South, though they are subject to blights and rots; pecans are better suited to that climate. In mild-winter regions, grow a variety requiring little winter chill. Check with your Cooperative Extension Office or a local nursery for best choices in your area.

WANDERING JEW. See CALLISIA, TRADESCANTIA, ZEBRINA pendula

WARMINSTER BROOM. See CYTISUS praecox

WASHINGTONIA

Arecaceae (Palmae)

PALMS

ZONES 8, 9, 10 (WARMER PARTS), 11–30

FULL SUN

REGULAR TO LITTLE WATER

Washingtonia robusta

Native to California, Arizona, northern Mexico. These are fast-growing palms that quickly become too tall for most suburban gardens. They are best suited for planting on large properties, along avenues, or on parkways.

W. filifera. CALIFORNIA FAN PALM. To 60 ft., with thicker trunk than that of its Mexican cousin. Long-stalked, 3–6-ft. leaves stand well apart in open crown. As leaves mature, they bend down to form a petticoat of thatch. Hardy to 18°F/–8°C.

W. robusta. MEXICAN FAN PALM. Taller (to 100 ft.) than California fan palm, with slimmer, slightly curved or bent trunk. Head of foliage is more compact; leafstalks are shorter, with a red streak on the underside. Hardy to 20°F/–7°C. Good seacoast plant.

WASHINGTON THORN. See CRATAEGUS phaenopyrum

WATER AVENS. See GEUM rivale

WATERCRESS

Brassicaceae (Cruciferae)

PERENNIAL

ALL ZONES

FULL SUN OR PARTIAL SHADE

GROWS NATURALLY IN RUNNING STREAMS

Watercress

To 10–15 in. high. Small, roundish leaflets are edible, with a sharp, spicy flavor. Flowers are insignificant. Can be started from seed or cuttings. Plant seed in flats or pots; transplant seedlings to wet place in garden or to a wet stream bank, where they will grow rapidly. Or insert cuttings of watercress from the market into wet soil or near a stream; these root readily. (If you intend to plant watercress near a stream, make sure the water is free from pollution before you set out plants.) You can also grow watercress in pots of soil placed in a tub of water; change water at least weekly by running a hose slowly into tub. Plants are more cold hardy in water.

WATER HAWTHORN. See APONOGETON distachyus

WATER HYACINTH. See EICHHORNIA crassipes

WATER LILY. See NYMPHAEA

WATERMELON

Cucurbitaceae

ANNUAL

ALL ZONES

FULL SUN

WATER MOST HEAVILY WHEN PLANTS ARE YOUNG

Watermelon

Needs a long growing season, more heat than most other melons, and more space than other vine crops—about 8 ft. by 8 ft. for each hill (circle of seed). Other than that, culture is as described under Melon. Large varieties may need as many as 95 days of hot, sunny weather to mature. If your summers are short or cool, choose a smaller, earlier-ripening "icebox" variety that will produce in 70 to 75 days. Seed companies also offer yellow-fleshed kinds and seedless types. Unlike other melons, watermelon does not grow sweeter after harvest—it must be picked ripe. Three tests for ripeness: thumping the melon produces a "thunk"; underside of melon has turned from white to pale yellow; and tendril opposite stem has withered.

WATSONIA

Iridaceae

PERENNIALS

ZONES VARY BY SPECIES; OR DIG AND STORE DECIDUOUS TYPE

FULL SUN

REGULAR WATER

Native to South Africa. Somewhat similar to gladiolus, but flowers are smaller and more tubular, appearing on taller, branched stems. Narrow leaves to 2½ ft. long. Good cut flowers.

Watsonia pyramidata

Where hardy, leave undisturbed for many years, allowing large clumps to form. Divide only when quality declines.

W. beatricis. Evergreen. Zones 4–9, 12–24, 26, 28–31, warmer parts of 32. Bright apricot red, 3-in. flowers on somewhat branched, 3½-ft. stems in summer. Selected hybrids come in colors from peach to nearly scarlet.

W. pyramidata. Deciduous. Zones 4–9, 12–24, 26, 28, 29, 30. Rose pink to rose red, 2½-in. flowers in spikelike clusters on branched, 4–6-ft. stems, late spring–early summer. Many excellent large-flowered hybrids in pink, white, lavender, and red. Needs regular water during growth and bloom; can tolerate it during dormant season if soil is well drained. In cold climates, dig corms after foliage dies down; replant in early spring.

WAX FLOWER, WAX PLANT. See HOYA

WAX MYRTLE. See MYRICA

WAX VINE. See SENECIO macroglossus

WAYFARING TREE. See VIBURNUM lantana

WEDELIA trilobata

Asteraceae (Compositae)

PERENNIAL

✂ ZONES 12, 13, 21–27

☀ ◑ FULL SUN OR LIGHT SHADE

💧 REGULAR WATER

Wedelia trilobata

Trailing plant to 1½ ft. high that roots wherever stems touch damp earth. Fleshy evergreen leaves are dark glossy green, to 4 in. long and half as wide, with a few coarse teeth or shallow lobes toward tips. Inch-wide flower heads resemble tiny yellow zinnias or marigolds. Blooms almost year-round. Spreads fast; easily propagated by lifting rooted pieces or by placing tip cuttings in moist soil. Best in sandy, fast-draining soils but will take heavier soils if drainage is acceptable. If killed to ground by frost, it makes fast comeback. Tolerates high heat, seaside conditions. Plant 1½ ft. apart, feed lightly. Cut back hard if plantings mound up or become stemmy.

WEIGELA

Caprifoliaceae

DECIDUOUS SHRUBS

✂ ZONES 1–11, 14–17, 32–41

☀ ◑ FULL SUN OR LIGHT SHADE

💧 REGULAR WATER

Weigela florida

Valuable for lavish springtime display of funnel-shaped, 1-in.-long flowers. When weigelas finish blooming, their charm fades—they aren't attractive out of bloom. Most are rather stiff, coarse-leafed plants, becoming rangy unless pruned. No real fall color.

After flowering, cut back branches that have bloomed to unflowered side branches. Leave only one or two of these to each stem. Cut some of the oldest stems to ground. Thin new suckers to a few of the most vigorous. A simpler method you can employ every other year is to cut back entire plant about halfway just after blooms fade. Resulting dense new growth will provide plenty of flowers the next spring. Use as backgrounds for flower border, as summer screen, in mixed shrub border.

W. florida (W. rosea). Fast growth to 6–10 ft. tall, 9–12 ft. wide, with branches often arching to the ground. Leaves 2–4½ in. long, half as wide. Pink to rose red flowers are borne singly or in short clusters all along previous season's shoots. The many varieties and hybrids include:

'Bristol Ruby'. To 6–7 ft. tall and nearly as wide, with ruby red flowers. Some repeat bloom in midsummer and fall.

'Candida' ('Alba'). To 5 ft. tall, with white flowers tinged green.

'Java Red'. Compact growth to 2½–4 ft. Deep red flowers and red-tinted deep green foliage.

'Minuet'. Dwarf (to 2–3 ft. high), with purplish leaves and flowers that blend red, purple, and yellow.

'Newport Red' ('Vanicekii', 'Cardinal', 'Rhode Island Red'). To 6 ft. tall, with brilliant red flowers. Young stems are bright green in winter.

'Pink Delight'. Compact growth to 3–4 ft. tall. Deep pink flowers.

'Pink Princess'. Loose, open habit to 6 ft. tall. Lilac pink blossoms.

'Red Prince'. To 6 ft. tall, with nonfading red flowers; some rebloom in late summer.

'Variegata'. Compact growth to 4–6 ft. tall. Deep rosy red flowers; bright green leaves edged pale yellow to creamy white. Popular and showy.

W. middendorffiana. Dense, broad plant to 3–4 ft. tall. Dark green, wrinkled leaves 2–3 in. long, half as wide. Sulfur yellow flowers with orange markings are clustered at ends of branches. Best in cool, moist place; less rugged than other weigelas.

W. praecox. Similar to *W. florida*, but blooms several weeks earlier and grows to about 6 ft. tall. Pink to rose flowers with yellow throats.

WELSH POPPY. See MECONOPSIS cambrica

WESTERN RED CEDAR. See THUJA plicata

WESTERN SAND CHERRY. See PRUNUS besseyi

WESTERN SOAPBERRY. See SAPINDUS drummondii

WESTRINGIA fruticosa

Lamiaceae (Labiatae)

EVERGREEN SHRUB

✂ ZONES 8, 9, 14–24, 29

☀ FULL SUN

💧 MODERATE TO LITTLE WATER

Westringia fruticosa

Native to Australia. Spreading, rather loose growth to 3–6 ft. tall. Leaves medium green to gray green above, white beneath, slightly finer and filmier in texture than rosemary leaves. Small white flowers appear from midwinter through spring in colder areas, bloom throughout the year in milder climates. 'Wynyabbie Gem' produces light purplish flowers. Needs light, well-drained soil. Good near coast; wind tolerant.

WHEATGRASS. See AGROPYRON

WHITEBEAM. See SORBUS aria

WHITE CEDAR. See CHAMAECYPARIS thyoides

WHITE CLOVER, WHITE DUTCH CLOVER. See TRIFOLIUM repens

WHITE MUGWORT. See ARTEMISIA lactiflora

WILD GINGER. See ASARUM

WILD INDIGO. See BAPTISIA

WILD MANDRAKE. See PODOPHYLLUM peltatum

WILD MARJORAM. See ORIGANUM vulgare

WILD PLANTAIN. See HELICONIA caribaea

WILD PLUM. See PRUNUS americana

WILD STRAWBERRY. See FRAGARIA chiloensis

WILGA. See GEIJERA parviflora

WILLOW. See SALIX

WILLOW-LEAFED JESSAMINE. See CESTRUM parqui

WINDFLOWER. See ANEMONE

WINDMILL PALM. See TRACHYCARPUS fortunei

WINTER ACONITE. See ERANTHIS hyemalis

WINTERBERRY. See ILEX verticillata

WINTER CREEPER. See EUONYMUS fortunei

WINTERGREEN. See GAULTHERIA procumbens

WINTER HAZEL. See CORYLOPSIS

WINTERSWEET. See CHIMONANTHUS praecox

WISHBONE FLOWER. See TORENIA fournieri

WISTERIA

Fabaceae (Leguminosae)

DECIDUOUS VINES

⚡ ZONES VARY BY SPECIES

☼ FULL SUN, EXCEPT AS NOTED

💧💧 WATER YOUNG ONES WELL, OLDER ONES LESS

Wisteria sinensis

Twining, woody vines of great size, long life, and exceptional beauty in flower. So adaptable they can be grown as trees, shrubs, or vines. All have large bright green leaves divided into many leaflets, spectacular clusters of blue, white, or pinkish blossoms, and velvety, pealike pods to about 6 in. long. Fall color subdued, in yellow shades. Plants are not fussy about soil, but need good drainage; in alkaline soil, watch for chlorosis and treat with iron chelates or iron sulfate.

Often considered aggressive pests in the South, but such "nuisance" wisterias are usually untamed. In any region, pruning and training are important for control of size and shape and for bloom production. Let newly planted wisteria grow to establish framework you desire, either single-trunked or multitrunked. Remove stems that interfere with desired framework and pinch back side stems and long streamers. For single-trunked form, rub off buds that develop on trunk. For multiple trunks, select as many vigorous stems as you wish and let them develop; if plant has only one stem, pinch it back to encourage others to develop. Remember that main stem will become good-size trunk, and that weight of mature vine is considerable. Any support structure should be sturdy and durable; do not use a tree as a support.

Tree wisterias can be bought already trained; or you can train your own. Remove all but one main stem and stake this one securely. Tie stem to stake at frequent intervals, using plastic tape to prevent girdling. When plant has reached height at which you wish head to form, pinch or prune out tip to force branching. Shorten branches to beef them up. Pinch back long streamers and rub off all buds that form below head. Replace stakes and ties as needed. Wisterias can be trained as big shrubs or multistemmed, small, semiweeping trees; permit well-spaced branches to form the framework, shorten side branches, and nip long streamers. Unsupported plants make vigorous bank cover.

In general, wisterias do not need fertilizer. Prune blooming plants every winter: cut back or thin out side shoots from main or structural stems, and shorten back to two or three buds the flower-producing spurs that grow from these shoots. You'll have no trouble recognizing fat flower buds on these spurs.

In summer, cut back long streamers before they tangle up in main body of vine; save those you want to use to extend height or length of vine and tie them to support—eaves, wall, trellis, arbor. If old plants grow rampantly but fail to bloom, withhold all nitrogen fertilizers for an entire growing season (buds for the next season's bloom are started in early summer). If that fails to produce bloom the next year, you can try pruning roots in spring—after you're sure no flowers will be produced—by cutting vertically with spade into plant's root zone.

W. brachybotrys (W. venusta). SILKY WISTERIA. Zones 3–24, 32–35, 37, 39. Often sold as *W. b.* 'Alba'. Silky-haired leaves 8–14 in. long, divided into 9–13 leaflets. Flowers are white, very large, long-stalked, slightly fragrant, in short (4–6-in.) clusters that open all at once during leaf-out. 'Violacea' has purple-blue flowers. Older plants (especially in tree form) bloom remarkably profusely.

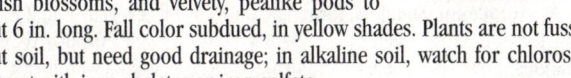

> ## WISTERIA SHOPPING TIP
> To get wisteria off to a good start, buy cutting-grown, budded, or grafted plants; seedlings may not bloom for years. With budded or grafted plants, watch for suckers during the first few years and remove them, or they may take over.

W. floribunda. JAPANESE WISTERIA. Zones 2–24, 26, 28–41. Often sold as *W. multijuga*. Leaves are 12–16 in. long, divided into 15–19 leaflets. Fragrant, 1½-ft. clusters of violet or violet blue flowers appear during leaf-out. Clusters open gradually, starting from the base; this prolongs bloom season but makes for a less spectacular burst of color than that provided by Chinese wisteria. Many varieties are sold in white, pink, and shades of blue, purple, and lavender, usually marked with yellow and white. 'Longissima' ('Macrobotrys') has long (1½–3-ft.) clusters of violet flowers. 'Longissima Alba' bears white flowers in 2-ft. clusters; 'Ivory Tower' is similar. 'Rosea' is a good lavender pink variety. 'Plena' has very full clusters of double flowers in deep blue violet. 'Texas Purple' blooms at an early age.

W. frutescens. AMERICAN WISTERIA. Zones 28–34. Native from Virginia to Florida and Texas. Leaves 7–12 in. long, divided into 9–15 leaflets. Less vigorous, thinner stems, later bloom, smaller pods than the other species. Fragrant, pale lilac flowers marked with yellow blotch appear in dense, 4–6-in.-long clusters in late spring–summer after leaf-out; blossoms are followed by 2–4-in. pods. White-flowered 'Nivea' blooms a little earlier than the species.

W. sinensis. CHINESE WISTERIA. Zones 3–24, 26, 28–35, 37, 39. Leaves are 10–12 in. long, divided into 7–13 leaflets. Plants bloom before leaves expand in spring. Clusters of violet blue, slightly fragrant flowers are shorter (to 1 ft.) than those of Japanese wisteria, but make quite a show by opening all at once nearly all along the cluster. 'Alba' is a white-flowered form. 'Caroline' and 'Cooke's Special' are grafted forms. Plants will bloom in sun or considerable shade.

WITCH HAZEL. See HAMAMELIS

WOADWAXEN. See GENISTA tinctoria

WONGA-WONGA VINE. See PANDOREA pandorana

WOODBINE. See LONICERA periclymenum

WOOD FERN. See DRYOPTERIS

WOOD HYACINTH. See ENDYMION non-scriptus

WOOD ROSE. See MERREMIA tuberosa

WOODRUFF, SWEET. See GALIUM odoratum

WOODSIA obtusa

BLUNT-LOBED WOODSIA, COMMON WOODSIA

Thelypteridaceae (Polypodiaceae)

FERN

⚡ ZONES 1–6, 14–17, 31–43

☼ ◐ FULL SUN OR LIGHT SHADE

💧 REGULAR WATER

Woodsia obtusa

Small deciduous fern. Fronds 12–15 in. long, 4 in. wide, bright green in shade, gray green in sun. May be once-cut (into deeply lobed segments)

or twice-cut. Fronds are produced throughout the growing season. Likes well-drained soil that is neutral or even slightly alkaline. Use in woodland or rock garden.

WOOD SORREL. See OXALIS acetosella

WOODWARDIA

CHAIN FERN

Blechnaceae (Polypodiaceae)

FERNS

ZONES VARY BY SPECIES

PART SHADE, EXCEPT AS NOTED

AMPLE WATER

Woodwardia fimbriata

Medium to large, usually coarse-textured ferns with rich green fronds. Name comes from chainlike pattern of spore cases beneath frond segments. Most like shade beneath canopy of tall trees, but some will withstand full sun if roots are kept wet.

W. areolata. Deciduous. Zone 28–41. Native to eastern and southeastern U.S. To 2½ ft. high, with deeply lobed fronds, the lobes finely toothed. Spore-bearing fronds are narrower. Can take considerable sun.

W. fimbriata. GIANT CHAIN FERN. Evergreen. Zones 4–9, 14–24. Native from British Columbia to Mexico. Can reach 9 ft. tall in moist forest sites; also seen in deserts where some shade and seepage exist. Usually 4–5 ft. tall in gardens. Fronds erect but spreading toward the top, twice cut but still somewhat coarse. Can take some sun in coolest areas.

W. virginica. Deciduous. Zones 26–41. Native to eastern and southern U.S. To 1–2 ft. tall, with twice-cut fronds that are bronzy green when they emerge. Likes wet soil and can even grow with roots submerged.

WORMWOOD. See ARTEMISIA

XANTHOCERAS sorbifolium

YELLOWHORN

Sapindaceae

DECIDUOUS SHRUB OR SMALL TREE

ZONES 1–3, 7–11, 14, 32–37, 40–43

FULL SUN

REGULAR WATER

Xanthoceras sorbifolium

Little-known plant worthy of greater garden use. Usually seen as a multistemmed shrub 8–10 ft. tall, but can attain stature of a small tree (20–25 ft.). Leaves are 1 ft. long, with many narrow, toothed dark green leaflets; they hang on late in fall. White, 1-in.-wide flowers appear in spring, clustered at branch ends or in joints of uppermost leaves; throat of each blossom has a yellow blotch that darkens to red. Flowers are followed by leathery, 2-in. pods filled with dark seeds; seeds are reminiscent of buckeyes. Tolerates wind, some drought. Needs summer heat for good growth and bloom. Propagate by seed or root cuttings.

XANTHORHIZA simplicissima

YELLOWROOT

Ranunculaceae

DECIDUOUS SHRUB

ZONES 1–6, 28, 31–43

SUN OR SHADE

AMPLE TO MODERATE WATER

Xanthorhiza simplicissima

Native to eastern U.S. Thicket-forming ground cover to 2–3 ft. high. Lacy, celerylike leaves usually divided into five toothed leaflets to

2½ in. long. Foliage is shiny bright green in summer, golden yellow and orange in autumn; drops fairly late. Roots and inner bark are yellow. Nodding clusters of tiny, star-shaped purplish flowers before spring leaf-out are attractive though not showy.

Extremely cold hardy. Prefers moist, well-drained, slightly acid soil, but tolerates heavy soils and dry sandy soils. Spreads fastest in damp, shady places; thrives along stream banks. Rejuvenate an overgrown planting by cutting it to the ground in spring. Plant root divisions in spring or fall. No serious pests or diseases.

XANTHOSOMA

Araceae

CORMLIKE TUBERS

ZONES 12, 13, 16, 17, 21–27; OR INDOORS

WARM FILTERED SHADE

AMPLE WATER

Xanthosoma violaceum

Tropical foliage plants related to *Alocasia*. All have big, arrow-shaped leaves on long stalks. Flowers clustered on spike surrounded by calla-like bract (spathe), usually greenish or yellowish and more curious than attractive. Use with ferns, begonias, schefflera. Grow in moist, rich, organic soil. Can also grow in standing water or submerged in pots. Protect from hard frosts.

X. sagittifolium. Trunklike stem to 3 ft. Dark green, 3-ft.-long leaves on 3-ft. stems. Spathes greenish white, 7–9 in. long.

X. violaceum. Stemless, forming clumps by offsets. Leaves to 2 ft. long, 1½ ft. wide, dark green above, lighter beneath, with purplish veins and margins, powdery appearance. Purple, 2½-ft. leafstalks with heavy, waxy, bluish or grayish cast. Large, yellowish white spathes.

XERANTHEMUM annuum

COMMON IMMORTELLE

Asteraceae (Compositae)

ANNUAL

ALL ZONES

FULL SUN

REGULAR WATER

Xeranthemum annuum

Grows to 2½ ft. tall. Everlasting flower; daisy-like heads of papery bracts to 1½ in. across in pink, lavender, white, shades of purple. Scant foliage is silvery green. Sow seed directly in the ground in spring for summer–fall bloom. Accepts almost any soil. Cut flowers can be dried for use in winter bouquets.

XYLOSMA congestum (X. senticosum)

Flacourtiaceae

EVERGREEN OR DECIDUOUS SHRUB OR TREE

ZONES 8–24, 26, 28, 31

FULL SUN OR PARTIAL SHADE

MODERATE WATER

Xylosma congestum

Basic landscape foliage plant, with loose, graceful, spreading habit to 8–10 ft. tall and as wide or wider. Can be trained as single or multitrunked small tree; often used as clipped or unclipped hedge. Leaves are shiny, yellowish green, long-pointed ovals, clean and attractive; new growth is bronzy. May

X

lose many (or all) leaves in hard frosts. Some plants are spiny. Flowers are insignificant and seldom seen. 'Compacta' grows slowly to half the size of species. Both species and variety tolerate heat, most soils.

YUCCA

Agavaceae

EVERGREEN PERENNIALS, SHRUBS, TREES

⚡ ZONES VARY BY SPECIES; OR INDOORS

☼ FULL SUN

◐◐◐ WATER NEEDS VARY BY SPECIES

Yucca whipplei

Yuccas grow over much of North America, and hardiness depends on species. All have tough, sword-shaped leaves and large clusters of white or whitish, rounded to bell-shaped flowers. Some are stemless, while others reach tree size. Best in well-drained soil.

Group with agaves, cacti, or succulents, or grow with various softer-leaved tropical foliage plants. Taller kinds make striking silhouettes, and even stemless species provide important vertical effects when in bloom. Some have stiff, sharp-pointed leaves; keep these away from walks, terraces, and other well-traveled areas. (Some people clip off the sharp tips with nail clippers.)

Young plants of some species can be used as indoor plants. They withstand dry indoor atmosphere and will grow well in hot, sunny windows. Buy gallon-can size or smaller; set out in garden ground when plants become too large for the house. Successful indoors are *Y. aloifolia* (but beware of sharp-pointed leaves), *Y. elephantipes, Y. filamentosa, Y. gloriosa, Y. recurvifolia.*

Y. aloifolia. SPANISH BAYONET. Zones 7–29, 31. Native to southern U.S. Slow growth to 10 ft. or more; trunk may be single or branched, sometimes sprawling in picturesque effect. Stems densely clothed in sharp-pointed leaves to 2½ ft. long and 2 in. wide (spiny leaf tips present a hazard if plant is near walkway). Leaves are dark green; in 'Variegata', they are marked with yellowish white. White flowers (sometimes tinged purple) to 4 in. across, carried in dense, erect clusters to 2 ft. tall in summer. Regular water.

Y. baccata. DACTIL YUCCA. Zones 1–24, 29, 30; western parts of 33, 35, 41, 43. Native to southwestern U.S. Foliage clump may have no stem or a short, prostrate one. Leaves to 2 ft. long, 2 in. wide, with fibers along the edges. Large, fleshy flowers in late spring are red brown outside, white inside, in dense, 2-ft.-long clusters. Fleshy fruit was eaten by Native Americans. Little water.

Y. elata. SOAPTREE YUCCA. Zones 7–24, 29, 30. Native to southwestern U.S., northern Mexico. Slow growth to 6–20 ft. tall, with single or branched trunk. Leaves to 4 ft. long, ½ in. wide. Tall spikes of white flowers in summer. Little water.

Y. elephantipes (Y. gigantea). GIANT YUCCA. Zones 12, 13 (protected from sun, hard frosts), 16, 17, 19–25. Native to Mexico. Fast growing (to 2 ft. per year), eventually 15–30 ft. tall, usually with several trunks. Leaves 4 ft. long, 3 in. wide, dark rich green. Striking silhouette alone or combined with other big-scale foliage plants; out of scale in smaller gardens. Large spikes of creamy white flowers in spring. Does best in good, well-drained soil with ample water.

Y. filamentosa. ADAM'S NEEDLE. Zones 1–24, 26–43. Native to southeastern U.S. Stemless. Stiff leaves grow to 2½ ft. long, 1 in. wide, with long, loose fibers at edges. Blooms late spring–summer; yellowish white, 2–3-in.-wide flowers, lightly fragrant in the evening, are carried in tall, narrow clusters to 4–7 ft. or taller. Similar in appearance to *Y. flaccida* and *Y. smalliana*. One of the hardiest, most widely planted yuccas in colder regions. Varieties include 'Concava Variegata', with cream-edged leaves tinted pink in cold weather; 'Ivory Tower', with outfacing rather than drooping flowers; 'Bright Edge', with leaves edged in yellow; and 'Garland Gold', with leaves having a broad gold center stripe. Regular water.

Y. flaccida. Zones 1–9, 14–24, 26–43. Native to southeastern U.S. Stemless. Differs from *Y. filamentosa* in having less rigid leaves, straight fibers on leaf edges, and somewhat shorter flower clusters. Regular water.

Y. glauca. SOAPWEED. Zones 1–24, 29, 30, 33, 35, 41, 43. Native to central and southwestern U.S. Stiff, narrow, 1–2½-ft.-long leaves form a clump 3–4 ft. wide. Stem is low or prostrate. Leaves are grayish green, edged with a hairline of white and a few thin threads. White summer flowers bloom on a spike 4–5 ft. tall. Regular water.

Y. gloriosa. SPANISH DAGGER, SOFT-TIP YUCCA. Zones 7–9, 12–32. Native to southeastern U.S. Much like *Y. aloifolia;* generally multitrunked to 10 ft. tall. In colder part of range, plant is usually stemless. Leaf points are soft and will not penetrate skin. Summer bloom. Good green color blends well with tropical-looking, lush plants. Needs regular water, but too much moisture may produce black areas on leaf margins.

Y. recurvifolia (Y. pendula). Zones 7–10, 12–24, 26–32. Native to southeastern U.S. Single, unbranched trunk to 6–10 ft. tall; may be lightly branched in age. Can be cut back to keep single trunked. Spreads by offsets to make large groups. Beautiful blue-gray-green leaves are 2–3 ft. long, 2 in. wide, sharply bent downward. Leaf tips are spined but bend to the touch; they are not dangerous. Less stiff and metallic looking than most yuccas. Large white flowers in late spring or early summer are borne in loose, open clusters 3–5 ft. tall. Easy to grow under all garden conditions.

Y. rostrata. Zones 7–24, 26, 27, 29, 30. Native to Mexico, extreme southwestern Texas. Notable feature is the trunk: 6–12 ft. tall, 5–8 in. thick, covered with soft gray fuzz (fibers remaining from old leaf bases). Needle-pointed leaves to 2 ft. long, ½ in. wide. Blooms in autumn, bearing 2-ft. clusters of white flowers on a 2-ft. stalk. Moderate to little water.

Y. smalliana. ADAM'S NEEDLE, BEAR'S GRASS. Zones 2–24, 26–43. Native to southeastern and south-central U.S. Similar to *Y. filamentosa,* but has narrower, thinner, flatter leaves and smaller individual flowers. Regular water.

Y. whipplei. OUR LORD'S CANDLE. Zones 2–24, 29. Native to California. Stemless, with dense cluster of rigid, 1–2-ft.-long gray-green leaves. Leaves are needle tipped, so don't locate the plant where people can walk into it. Flowering stems to 6–14 ft. long. Drooping, 1–2-in., creamy white blossoms in large, branched spikes 3–6 ft. long; summer bloom. Plants die after blooming and producing seed; new plants come from seeds or offsets. Little water.

Z

Zamiaceae. This family is closely related to the Cycadaceae, differing only in technical details; both families are generally considered to be cycads. *Ceratozamia, Dioon,* and *Zamia* are representatives.

ZAMIA

Zamiaceae (Cycadaceae)

CYCADS

ZONES 21–27; OR INDOORS

FILTERED SHADE

REGULAR WATER

Zamia furfuracea

Of 100 or so species, only the following two are often seen. They have short trunks usually marked with scars from old leaf bases; trunks may be completely or partially buried. Circular crowns of leaves resemble stiff fern fronds or small palm fronds. Grow in fast-draining soil amply enriched with organic material. Outdoor plants need filtered shade; house plants need strong interior light. Slow growing and costly, but will last many years with good care.

Z. furfuracea. CARDBOARD PALM. Native to Mexico. Short, sometimes subterranean trunk. Fronds up to 3 ft. long (usually much less) with as many as 12 pairs (usually fewer) of extremely stiff, leathery, dark green leaflets to 4½ in. long, 1½ in. wide. Leaflets may have a few teeth toward the tip.

Z. pumila (Z. floridana). COONTIE. Native to Florida, Cuba, West Indies. Short trunk is largely below soil level. Fronds to 3 ft. long, with as many as 30 pairs of dark green leaflets. Leaflets grow to 5 in long, are narrower than those of *Z. furfuracea.*

ZANTEDESCHIA

CALLA

Araceae

RHIZOMES

ZONES 5, 6, 8, 9, 12–29; OR DIG AND STORE; OR GROW IN POTS

PARTIAL SHADE IN HOT AREAS

WATER NEEDS VARY BY TYPE

Zantedeschia aethiopica

Native to South Africa. Basal clumps of long-stalked, shiny, rich green, arrow- or lance-shaped leaves, sometimes spotted white. Flower bract (spathe) surrounds central spike (spadix) that is tightly covered with tiny true flowers.

Common calla (*Z. aethiopica*) is basically evergreen, going only partly dormant even in colder parts of range. It is soil tolerant and will thrive in moist, even boggy, soil all year. It cannot withstand storage and so should be grown as a container plant where winter temperatures fall below 10°F/−12°C.

The other species described here die to the ground yearly. They need slightly acid soil and regular water during growth and bloom, followed by a resting period in which, ideally, water is withheld. In rainy climates, rhizomes will tolerate moisture if soil is well drained. Store potted rhizomes dry in their containers. Beyond their hardiness range, rhizomes of deciduous species can be dug and stored over winter, then replanted in spring.

Where callas are hardy, plant all types in fall, setting rhizomes of common calla 4–6 in. deep, those of other species 2 in. deep. Leave undisturbed until overcrowding causes a decline in vigor and bloom quality.

Z. aethiopica. COMMON CALLA. Forms large clump of unspotted deep green leaves 1½ ft. long, 10 in. wide. Pure white or creamy white, 8-in.-long spathes on 3-ft. stems appear mostly in spring and early summer. 'Green Goddess' is a robust variety with large spathes that are white at the base, green toward the tip. 'Hercules', larger than species, has big spathes that open flat, curve backward. 'Childsiana' is 1 ft. tall. 'Minor' grows 1½ ft. tall, with 4-in. spathes.

Z. albomaculata. SPOTTED CALLA. To 2 ft., with bright green, white-spotted leaves 1–1½ ft. long, 10 in. wide. Creamy yellow or white, 4–5-in.-long spathes have purplish crimson blotch at base. Spring–summer bloom.

Z. elliottiana. GOLDEN CALLA. To 1½–2 ft., with bright green, white-spotted leaves 10 in. long, 6 in. wide. Spathes 4–5 in. long, changing from greenish yellow to rich golden yellow, late spring or early summer. Tolerates full sun, even in hot-summer areas.

Z. pentlandii. Resembles *Z. albomaculata,* but leaves are unspotted and spathes (to 5 in. long) are deep golden yellow with a purple blotch at the base.

Z. rehmannii. RED or PINK CALLA. To 1–1½ ft., with narrow, lance-shaped, unspotted green leaves 1 ft. long. Pink or rosy pink spathes to 4 in. long in spring. 'Superba', a deeper pink, improved variety, is generally sold rather than species. Hybrids of this and other callas are available; flowers range through pinks and yellows to orange and buff tones, with some purplish and lavender tones on yellow grounds.

ZANTHOXYLUM piperitum

JAPAN PEPPER

Rutaceae

DECIDUOUS SHRUB OR SMALL TREE

ZONES 6–9, 14–17, 32–34, 39

FULL SUN

REGULAR WATER

Zanthoxylum piperitum

Native to China, Japan, Korea. Compact, dense growth to 8–20 ft. tall. Handsome dark green leaves 3–6 in. long, divided into 11–23 oval, 2-in.-long leaflets; may turn yellow in autumn. Flat, ½-in.-long spines grow in pairs along stems. Green flowers are inconspicuous. Small, aromatic red fruits have black seeds that are pulverized and used as a seasoning in Japan. Leaves have a peppery flavor, slightly numbing to the tongue; they too are used in Japanese cuisine, typically as a garnish floating on soups. Used this way, they are called sansho.

ZAUSCHNERIA (Epilobium)

CALIFORNIA FUCHSIA, HUMMINGBIRD FLOWER

Onagraceae

PERENNIALS OR SUBSHRUBS

ZONES 2–11, 14–24

FULL SUN

REGULAR TO LITTLE WATER

Zauschneria californica

Mainly California natives with profuse summer –fall bloom of trumpet-shaped, orange to scarlet flowers to 2 in. long; these attract hummingbirds. In most species, the narrow, gray to gray-green, ½–1½-in.-long leaves are evergreen in warmer part of range.

Nearly all spread by underground stems to make ever-larger colonies. Can be a nuisance in manicured gardens, but good for naturalistic plantings and hillsides. Plants can look ragged and ratty during winter; if cut to the ground, they resprout vigorously in spring.

Botanists have reclassified *Zauschneria* as *Epilobium,* reducing the number of species in the process. However, most nurseries sell the plants under the old name.

Z. californica (Epilobium canum canum). Stems upright or somewhat arching, 1–2 ft. tall, sometimes shrubby at the base. 'Alba' has white flowers; 'Solidarity Pink' bears soft pink blooms. 'Dublin' ('Glasnevin'), to 1 ft. tall, has scarlet blossoms; 'Etteri', to 6 in. high, has silvery leaves and scarlet flowers.

Z. cana (Epilobium canum canum). Differs from above species in its denser, more sprawling habit and in its more silvery leaf color.

Z. latifolia (Epilobium canum latifolium). Most widely grown form is 2-ft.-tall 'Arizonica', with broad, light green leaves and bright orange blossoms.

Z. septentrionalis (Epilobium septentrionale). Forms a mat of narrow, silvery gray-green leaves; bears orange-red flowers. Dies back yearly.

ZEBRA PLANT. See CALATHEA zebrina

ZEBRINA pendula (Tradescantia zebrina)

WANDERING JEW

Commelinaceae

PERENNIAL

ZONES 24–27; OR INDOORS

PARTIAL OR FULL SHADE

REGULAR WATER

Zebrina pendula

Has much the same growth habit and leaf shape as *Tradescantia fluminensis* but is not as hardy. Small clusters of flowers are purplish rose and white. Known mostly in its variegated forms. 'Quadricolor' has purplish green leaves with longitudinal bands of white, pink, and carmine red; 'Purpusii' has leaves of dark red or greenish red. Other varieties add white, pink, and cream to prevailing colors.

Use as ground cover in shady, frost-free sites. Good container plants for patio or house. When selecting a location indoors, remember that variegated plants need more light than all-green ones.

ZELKOVA serrata

SAWLEAF ZELKOVA

Ulmaceae

DECIDUOUS TREE

ZONES 3–21, 28–35, 37, 39

FULL SUN

REGULAR TO MODERATE WATER

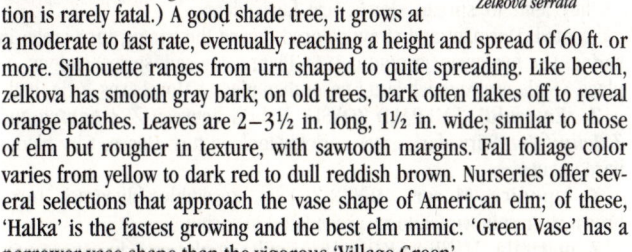
Zelkova serrata

Closely related to elms and sometimes used as a substitute for the ill-fated American elm, which has fallen victim to Dutch elm disease. (Zelkova, too, can get the disease, but the infection is rarely fatal.) A good shade tree, it grows at a moderate to fast rate, eventually reaching a height and spread of 60 ft. or more. Silhouette ranges from urn shaped to quite spreading. Like beech, zelkova has smooth gray bark; on old trees, bark often flakes off to reveal orange patches. Leaves are 2–3½ in. long, 1½ in. wide; similar to those of elm but rougher in texture, with sawtooth margins. Fall foliage color varies from yellow to dark red to dull reddish brown. Nurseries offer several selections that approach the vase shape of American elm; of these, 'Halka' is the fastest growing and the best elm mimic. 'Green Vase' has a narrower vase shape than the vigorous 'Village Green'.

Takes wide range of soils. Water deeply to encourage deep rooting; established trees are fairly tolerant of drought, wind. You will need to train and prune young trees to establish a good framework; thin out crowded ascending branches. Foliage may be visited by Japanese beetles and by elm leaf beetles if local elms have died.

FOR INFORMATION ON YOUR CLIMATE ZONE
PLEASE SEE PAGES 16–78

ZENOBIA pulverulenta (Andromeda speciosa)

Ericaceae

SEMIEVERGREEN TO DECIDUOUS SHRUB

ZONES 4–7, 14–17, 28–34

PARTIAL SHADE

AMPLE WATER

Zenobia pulverulenta

Native from North Carolina to Florida. Slow growth to 2–4 ft. or possibly 6 ft. tall, with open, loose, arching habit. Pale green leaves are 1–2 in. long, half as wide; new growth heavily dusted with bluish white powder for a pearly gray effect. Fall foliage is yellowish with a red tinge. White, bell-shaped, ½-in.-wide, anise-scented flowers bloom in loose clusters at ends of branches, late spring–early summer. Sometimes spreads by underground stems. Related to heaths and heathers; needs well-drained, acid soil.

ZEPHYRANTHES

ZEPHYR FLOWER, FAIRY LILY

Amaryllidaceae

BULBS

ZONES VARY BY SPECIES; OR GROW IN POTS

FULL SUN

REGULAR WATER DURING GROWTH AND BLOOM

Zephyranthes candida

Clumps of grassy leaves give rise to slender, hollow stems, each bearing a single funnel-shaped flower with six segments. Flowers of some kinds resemble lilies; those of other types look like crocuses. In the wild, flowers bloom after a rain (hence another common name, "rain lily"), and they may appear in the garden after a good soaking.

Need little care. Pretty in rock garden or foreground of border. Excellent pot plant for patio or greenhouse. Plant in late summer or early fall; set bulbs 1–2 in. deep. In borderline climates, mulch heavily over winter. Container plants bloom better when somewhat pot-bound.

Z. atamasco. Zones 4–9, 12–31, warmer parts of 32. Native to southeastern U.S. Semievergreen leaves to 1½ ft. long, ¼ in. wide. Pink-striped buds open to fragrant, crocuslike, pure white blossoms in midspring.

Z. candida. Zones 4–9, 12–32. Large clumps of glossy evergreen leaves to 1 ft. long. Glossy-textured, crocuslike flowers are 2 in. long, pure white outside, tinged rose inside, borne singly on stems as long as leaves. Blooms in late summer, early fall.

Z. citrina. Zones 7–9, 12–29. About the same size as *Z. candida* and blooms at the same time, but bears fragrant yellow flowers.

Z. grandiflora. Zones 7–9, 12–29. Rose pink, 4-in.-wide, lilylike flowers on 8-in. stems in summer. Blossoms are flat at midday, close in afternoon. Leaves to 1 ft. long.

Z. hybrids. Zones 6–9, 12–31. Most widely offered is *Z. ajax* (a cross between *Z. candida* and *Z. citrina*), a free-flowering plant with light yellow blossoms. Other hybrids available from mail-order specialists include 'Alamo', with deep rose pink flowers flushed yellow; 'Apricot Queen', yellow flowers stained pink; 'Prairie Sunset', large light yellow flowers suffused with pink; and 'Ruth Page', rich pink blooms.

Z. treatiae. Zones 12, 13, 25–29. Native to Florida. Pure white, crocuslike flowers open from red buds. Blooms 2 to 4 weeks before *Z. atamasco*. Gray-green leaves are extremely slender, reach 1 ft. long.

ZEPHYR FLOWER. See ZEPHYRANTHES

Z

Zingiberaceae. The ginger family contains tropical or subtropical perennials with fleshy rhizomes and canelike stems clothed with sheathing leaf stalks; usually bear large leaves. Flowers are irregular in form, in spikes or heads, often showy or with showy bracts. Many are aromatic or have fragrant flowers. Includes *Alpinia*, ginger lily *(Costus, Hedychium)*, and true ginger *(Zingiber)*.

ZINGIBER officinale

TRUE GINGER

Zingiberaceae

PERENNIAL WITH THICK RHIZOMES

🌿 ZONES 9, 14–28

🔅 PARTIAL SHADE

💧 WATER HEAVILY AFTER GROWTH STARTS

Zingiber officinale

Rhizomes are the source of ginger used in cooking. Stems 2–4 ft. tall. Narrow, glossy bright green leaves to 1 ft. long. Summer flowers (rarely seen) are yellowish green, with purple lip marked yellow; not especially showy. Ginger needs heat and humidity. Buy roots (fresh, not dried) at grocery store in early spring; cut into 1–2-in.-long sections with well-developed growth buds. Let cut ends dry, then plant just below surface of rich, moist soil; pot culture is common. Water cautiously until top and root growth are active. Feed once a month. Plants are dormant in winter; rhizomes may rot in cold, wet soil. Plant with tree ferns, camellias, fuchsias, begonias. Harvest roots at any time—but allow several months for them to reach some size.

ZINNIA

Asteraceae (Compositae)

ANNUALS AND A PERENNIAL

🌿 ALL ZONES

🔅 FULL SUN

💧 REGULAR WATER, EXCEPT AS NOTED

Zinnia elegans

Long-time garden favorites for colorful, round flower heads in summer and early fall. Hot-weather plants, they do not gain from being planted early, but merely stand still until weather warms up. Subject to mildew in foggy places, if leaves are habitually wet at night, and when autumn brings longer nights, more dew and shade. Sow seeds where plants are to grow (or set out nursery plants) May–July. Give good garden soil and feed generously. Most garden zinnias belong to *Z. elegans.*

Z. angustifolia. Annual. Compact plants to 16 in. tall. Leaves very narrow. Inch-wide flower heads are orange; each ray has a paler stripe. Blooms in 6 weeks from seed, continues late into fall. 'Classic' grows 8–12 in. tall, to 2 ft. wide. There are also white and yellow forms. Can be perennial in mild winters. Good in hanging baskets.

Z. elegans. Annual. Plant height ranges from 1–3 ft., leaves to 5 in.; flower head size from less than 1 in. to as much as 5–7 in. across. Forms include full doubles, cactus flowered (with quilled rays), and crested (cushion center surrounded by rows of broad rays); colors include white, pink, salmon, rose, red, yellow, orange, lavender, purple, and green.

Many strains are available, from dwarf plants with small flowers to 3-ft. sorts with large blooms. The Mini series and Thumbelina strain are extra-dwarf types (to 6 in. tall). Other small-flowered kinds on larger (1-ft.) but still compact plants are Cupid and Buttons; still taller (to 2 ft.) but small flowered are the Lilliputs. Dreamland and Peter Pan strains have 3-in. blooms on bushy dwarf plants to 1 ft.; Whirligig has large bicolored flowers on 1½-ft. plants. Large-flowered strains with 2–3-ft. plants include Border Beauty, Burpeeana California Giants, Dahlia-flowered, Giant Cac-

tus–flowered, Ruffles, State Fair, and Zenith. 'Rose Pinwheel', with single daisy-type rose pink flowers, is a 1½–2-ft.-tall hybrid between *Z. elegans* and *Z. angustifolia.*

Z. grandiflora. Perennial in Zones 14–24, 29; annual elsewhere. Native to high plains, the Southwest, Mexico. To 10 in. tall, spreading by seeds or runners. Leaves to 1 in. long, ⅛ in. wide. Flower heads are 1½ in. wide, bright yellow with orange eye. In its native range, it will bloom spring–fall if watered during dry season. Very drought tolerant once established.

Z. haageana. Annual. Plants compact, 1–1½ ft. tall; narrow, 3-in. leaves. Double strains Persian Carpet (1 ft. tall) and Old Mexico (16 in. tall) have flowers in mahogany red, yellow, and orange, usually mixed in the same flower head. Colorful, long blooming.

ZIZIPHUS jujuba

CHINESE JUJUBE

Rhamnaceae

DECIDUOUS SHRUB OR SMALL TREE

🌿 ZONES 7–16, 18–24, 28–33

🔅 FULL SUN

💧 MODERATE WATER

Ziziphus jujuba

Slow to moderate growth to eventual 20–30 ft. tall, with rounded habit. Usually grown as tree, but sometimes seen as large shrub. Spiny, gnarled, somewhat pendulous branches. Glossy bright green, 1–2-in.-long leaves with three prominent veins. Foliage may turn a good yellow in autumn. Clusters of small yellowish flowers bloom in late spring; these are followed in fall by shiny, reddish brown, ½–2-in.-long fruits with a sweet, applelike flavor. Candied and dried, fruits resemble dates. Two thornless, grafted varieties are 'Lang' (1½–2-in. fruits, bears young) and 'Li' (2-in. fruits).

Very decorative, but also tough—withstands drought, heat, saline and alkaline soils. Grows better in good garden soil. Thrives in lawns. Prune in winter to shape, encourage weeping habit, or reduce size.

ZOYSIA

Poaceae (Gramineae)

PERENNIAL GRASSES

🌿 ZONES 7–10, 12–34

🔅◐ THRIVE IN SUN, TOLERATE SOME SHADE

💧 REGULAR WATER

Zoysia tenuifolia

They tend to spread slowly, are fairly deep rooted. Dormant and straw colored during the winter; turn green in spring. Use for lawns, ground covers. Plant using sod, sprigs, stolons, or plugs. (Stolons give much faster cover than plugs.) Mow lawns ¾ in. high.

Z. 'Emerald'. EMERALD ZOYSIA. Hybrid between *Z. japonica* and *Z. tenuifolia.* Wiry, dark green, prickly-looking turf. Dense, wiry blades hard to cut.

Z. japonica 'Meyer'. MEYER ZOYSIA. Resembles bluegrass. Turns brown earliest in winter, turns green latest in spring.

Z. matrella. MANILA GRASS. Also similar to bluegrass in appearance. Holds color a little better than Meyer zoysia.

Z. tenuifolia. KOREAN GRASS. Creeping, fine textured, bumpy. Makes a beautiful grassy meadow or gives mossy Oriental effect in areas impossible to mow or water often.

ZUCCHINI. See SQUASH

ZYGOCACTUS. See SCHLUMBERGERA

Z

Practical Gardening
DICTIONARY

Gardening successfully requires a knowledge of techniques and materials, and an appreciation for the versatility of the plants that grow in your region. But it also demands a basic understanding of plant growth and its integral relationship to climate, soil, water, sunlight, nutrients, and the other organisms—both good and bad—that populate our gardens.

On the next 72 pages, you'll find definitions of common gardening terms; information on techniques, materials, tools, plant groups, and pests (animals, insects, diseases, and weeds); and all the helpful tips and illustrated step-by-step guidelines you'll need to garden successfully.

Acid Soil

An acid soil is one with a pH below 7. See Soil pH (p. 599).

Actual

In such phrases as "actual nitrogen," "actual" refers to the amount of the specified nutrient (by weight) contained in a fertilizer. For example, we sometimes recommend applying a cer-tain amount of actual nitrogen. To find out how to calculate "actual" nutrient contents from fertilizer labels, see the illustration below.

Aeration

Loosening or puncturing the soil by mechani-cal means to increase water penetration and air permeability is called aeration. Aerating can be as simple as cultivating around newly planted seedlings with a trowel or, in the case of lawns, can involve use of a gas-powered machine that removes small cores of soil from the turf. The response to aeration is generally improved plant growth.

Alkaline Soil

An alkaline soil is one with a pH above 7. See Soil pH (p. 599).

Annual

A plant that completes its life cycle in a year or less is called an annual. Seed germinates and the plant grows, blooms, sets seed, and dies—all in one growing season. Examples are most marigolds *(Tagetes)* and zinnias. The phrase "grow as an annual" or "treat as an annual" means to sow seed or set out plants in spring after the last frost, enjoy the plants from spring through fall, and pull them out or let the frosts kill them at the end of the year. Some plants that mild-winter (Zones 8–31) garden-ers treat as annuals are planted in fall, grow and bloom during winter and spring, and then are killed by summer heat.

Think of annuals as the real workhorses of the garden. Their lives are short, but that brief life-time is extremely productive. Annuals can bloom literally for months, from the moment the plants are mature enough to bear flowers until they are cut down by frost. In areas of no or mild frosts (Zones 8–31), certain annuals can brighten even a winter garden with blossoms. ▶

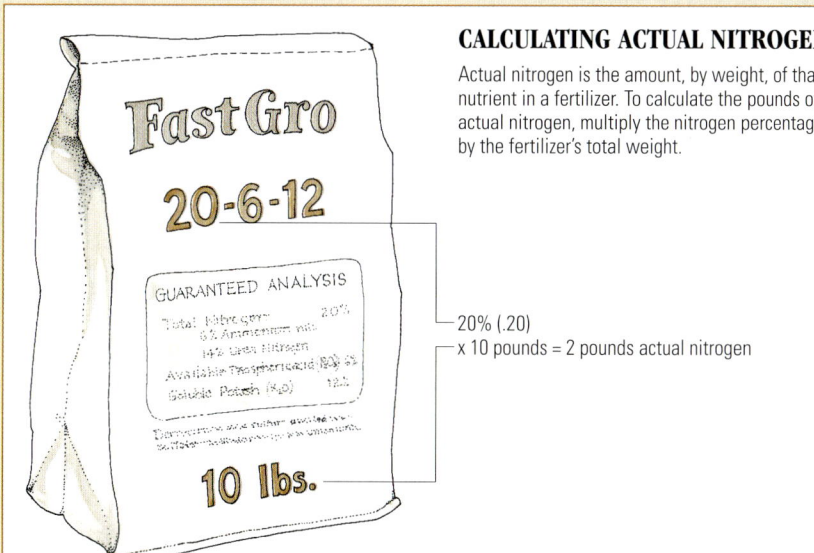

CALCULATING ACTUAL NITROGEN
Actual nitrogen is the amount, by weight, of that nutrient in a fertilizer. To calculate the pounds of actual nitrogen, multiply the nitrogen percentage by the fertilizer's total weight.

20% (.20)
x 10 pounds = 2 pounds actual nitrogen

B

Good soil, the foundation on which a successful annual planting is built, requires some advance preparation. Whether sowing seeds or setting out small plants, first refer to the soil preparation advice under Planting Techniques: Seeds (p. 584).

Planting and timing. Many gardeners prefer to sow their own annual seeds; you'll find guidelines for seed sowing under Planting Techniques: Seeds (p. 584). Or you can buy popular types and varieties already started at nurseries—sold in small individual containers, in packs of four or six, or in flats. The handling of these plants is discussed under Planting Techniques: Annuals and Perennials (p. 586).

In the mild-winter zones (8–31), there are two principal times of year for planting annuals: early spring, for those that bloom in late spring, summer, and fall (warm-season annuals); and late summer or fall, for the winter and early-spring bloomers (cool-season annuals). Both are periods of moderately cool temperatures preceding the sort of weather that favors development of annuals. Gardeners in cold-winter zones (1–7, 32–45) generally can plant only in spring to early summer.

The summer-flowering annuals need to establish roots before really warm days come along to hasten growth and bloom. Winter-blooming annuals should be set out while days are still warm enough for good plant growth but nights are lengthening. Winter annuals set out while days are longer than nights may perish or rush to maturity as stunted, poorly established plants. Favorite annuals are listed according to seasons of bloom in the charts beginning on page 86.

The secret to success with annual plantings is to keep the plants growing steadily. The keys to plant growth are watering, fertilizing, and grooming.

Watering. Sprinkling is an effective way to water annuals, although the spray of water may topple tall or weak-stemmed plants and promote certain diseases. A way to water annuals grown in rows or in block beds is to irrigate in furrows between the rows. However, furrow irrigation uses a lot of water and is not effective in very sandy soils. With a small bed of annuals, you may be able to hoe up a shallow dike around the bed and irrigate by flooding. Drip irrigation, using any of the various sorts of emitters available, offers a range of watering options. Mulching helps conserve water and reduce weeds. See Watering (p. 609) for detailed information on techniques.

Fertilizing. Mixing a complete fertilizer into the soil before planting annuals generally supplies enough nutrients to last at least half the growing season. In cold-winter zones (1–7, 32–45), an application of fertilizer after bloom is under way will carry annuals through their season. Where winters are warmer and the growing season for annuals is correspondingly

longer, give plants another fertilizer application in late summer.

If you didn't add fertilizer to your soil before planting annuals, give plants an application of a high-nitrogen complete fertilizer about 2 weeks after planting; then follow with a second application about 6 weeks after the first. In warmest zones, where growing seasons are longest, a third application may be in order 6 to 8 weeks after the second. For more about fertilizers, see Fertilizers (p. 561), and Nutrients, Basic (p. 577).

Grooming. To keep blooms coming all season long, you have to interrupt nature's seed-producing process by removing old blossoms before the plant can begin seed formation.

Anthracnose. See Leaf Spot   p. 575

Ants

By themselves, ants are not serious garden pests, although some types may damage young seedlings, and nests of others may disturb lawns and planting beds. However, they are closely associated with honeydew produced by sucking insect pests and are often the most visible clue that the pest is present. Ants can also interfere with the effectiveness of biological controls (p. 549). See Aphids for control measures.

Fire ants, common in mild-winter climates of the South and Southwest, do not directly damage plants but can be a serious nuisance because of their painful sting. Their raised mounds also disrupt lawns and planting beds. Various techniques have been used to make fire ants relocate their mounds, including drenching them with boiling or soapy water. Drenches containing pyrethrins or boric acid may also be effective. Some baits labeled for fire ants are effective, but they take time to work. The most effective control of fire ants is drenching or dusting the mound with an appropriately labeled pesticide, such as chlorpyrifos or diazinon. Repeat applications may be necessary.

Aphids

Aphids are soft, oval, pinhead- to match-head-size insects that cluster together on young shoots, buds, and leaves. They come in various colors—including green, pink, red, and black—with

and without wings (see photograph, p. 590).

Numerous creatures keep aphid populations in check; often the best tactic is to do nothing and watch natural controls go to work. Lacewings, ladybird beetles, syrphid flies, predatory midges, parasitic wasps, and even lizards and some small birds are among the many natural

aphid controls that may live in your garden. If you spray with a toxic insecticide, you risk killing the insect predators along with the problem.

Controls. Fortunately, you can get rid of most aphids with a blast of water from the hose. For greater effectiveness, wash them off with an insecticidal soap; the soap kills aphids but won't linger to harm other insects later.

The most troublesome aphids curl leaves around themselves or stay in protected places (inside a head of cabbage, for example). The best control for these aphids is anticipation: if you had them last year, expect them this year; hose or wash them off when the aphid colony is young and leaves are still open. You can also prevent aphids from reaching vegetables by planting under floating row covers (p. 596).

A dormant oil spray is effective in killing overwintering eggs of many species of aphids on trees and shrubs. On herbaceous plants, clean up old plant debris before growth starts in spring. If an aphid infestation is severe, spray with insecticidal soap, pyrethrum, rotenone, diazinon, malathion, or (on nonedible plants) acephate.

Ants often maintain aphid colonies, fighting off parasites and predators to feed on the sticky honeydew aphids produce. Getting rid of the ants often permits natural aphid controls to re-establish themselves. To keep ants out of plants, encircle trunks with bands of a sticky ant barrier, put out diazinon or chlorpyrifos granules, or use poisonous ant baits.

Backfill

Backfill soil is returned to a planting hole after a plant's roots have been positioned. Unless the native soil is heavy clay or very sandy, most plants will become established faster if backfill is simply the soil dug out to create the planting hole. In very sandy or heavy clay soils, mix the backfill with some organic soil amendments (p. 598) to improve its texture.

Bacterial Wilt

Bacterial wilt is a common disease of cucumbers, but it can also damage muskmelons, squash, and pumpkins. It is most troublesome east of the Rocky Mountains, particularly in the Midwest and Northeast. Bacterial wilt is prevalent during cool, moist weather and is usually spread by cucumber beetles feeding on plant foliage. Symptoms include rapid wilting and death of young seedlings. Older plants may wilt and die all at once, or they may go out stem by stem.

Check for presence of the disease by cutting a stem near the base. If thin strands of milky exudate form as you touch then slowly separate the ends of the stems, it's probably bacterial wilt.

Once a plant is infected with bacterial wilt, it will not recover. However, you can lessen the chance of infection by reducing the cucumber

B

beetle population (see p. 555) and by removing and destroying infected plants. There are also some vegetable varieties with varying degrees of resistance to bacterial wilt.

Bagworms

Bagworms, which are really moth larvae, or caterpillars, feed on the foliage of many trees and shrubs, usually starting from the top and working their way down, leaving devastation in their wake. Bagworms are most common east of the Rocky Mountains. See photograph, p. 590.

The individual caterpillars are not as noticeable as the dangling silken bags they create and drag along as they feed. During winter the bags are filled with up to 1,000 eggs. In spring the small brown caterpillars hatch and disperse to feed for a time, often blowing from tree to tree on thin threads. In summer each caterpillar tethers its bag to a twig and enters to pupate. In a few days the moths emerge. The wingless females remain in the bag, where they are joined by the black-winged males. After mating and laying eggs, the females die.

Spraying trees with *Bacillus thuringiensis (Bt)* is the preferred control for bagworms; however, it is effective only when the young caterpillars are feeding in spring. On smaller plants, you can hand-pick the bags in winter and burn them, but you have to be thorough to get adequate control. Malathion, diazinon, carbaryl, and acephate (on nonedibles) are also effective against bagworms.

Balled-and-Burlapped

Sometimes abbreviated B-and-B, balled-and-burlapped shrubs and trees are sold by some nurseries from late fall to early spring. The name comes from the large ball of soil around the roots, which is wrapped in burlap to hold it together. B-and-B plants usually cannot be offered bare-root. See Planting Techniques: Trees and Shrubs (p. 586) for planting instructions.

Bare-Root

In winter and early spring, nurseries offer many deciduous shrubs and trees, and some perennials, with all soil removed from their roots. For planting instructions, see Planting Techniques: Trees and Shrubs (p. 586) or Perennial (p. 579).

Bedding Plant

Plants (mainly annuals) suitable for massing in beds for their colorful flowers or foliage are called bedding plants.

Beneficial Insects. See Visual Guide to Identifying Biological Controls   p. 549

Bermuda Grass

A fine-textured and fast-growing perennial, Bermuda grass (see photograph, p. 614) is a well-established lawn grass and one of the most difficult garden weeds in low-elevation parts of California, Arizona, and New Mexico, and most of the Southeast as far north as Zones 35 and 36. Native to warm areas of the Old World, Bermuda grass spreads underground by rhizomes and aboveground by seeds and stolons. If not carefully confined, its rhizomes and stolons invade shrubbery and flower beds and can be difficult to eradicate once they are established.

Controls. If stray clumps do turn up in flower beds, pull or dig them up before they form sod. Be sure to remove all of the underground stem; otherwise, it can start new shoots. Or spray with fluazifop-butyl or sethoxydim, which can be applied over some ornamentals (check the label). Where patches are too big to be dug out of a lawn, apply glyphosate in summer or fall as Bermuda grass slows its growth (avoid desirable plants nearby). Repeat applications may be necessary.

Biennial

Plants called biennials complete their life cycle in 2 years. Two familiar biennials are foxglove *(Digitalis)* and Canterbury bells *(Campanula medium)*. Typically, you plant seeds in spring or set out seedling plants in summer or fall. The plants bloom the following spring, then set seed and die.

Bindweed

Also called wild morning glory, bindweed (see photograph, p. 615) grows in open, exposed areas—usually in loam to heavy clay—throughout the United States, but it is especially bothersome for gardeners in the Northwest, Northern California, the mountain states, and all but the Deep South of the eastern United States. Bindweed crawls over the ground and twines over and around other plants, com-

peting with them for nutrients and light. Its flowers appear in summer or early fall, before the plant goes dormant for winter.

When you pull bindweed, the stems break off, but frequently the deep roots and underground stems remain. The more you break it, the more it sprouts. If allowed to go to seed, bindweed becomes nearly impossible to control: its hard-coated seeds can sprout after lying dormant in the soil for years.

Controls. In midsummer, at the plant's peak growth but before it sets seed, spray isolated patches with glyphosate; repeat applications may be needed. If bindweed is intertwined with desirable plants, carefully paint its leaves with a herbicide.

Biological Pest Control. See Visual Guide to Identifying Biological Controls; and Pest Management   pp. 549, 580

Bird Protection

Most gardeners see birds as friends rather than enemies, but certain birds (crows in particular) at certain times can be nuisances: they eat newly planted seeds, tender seedlings, transplants, fruits, nuts, or berries.

Reflectors, fluttering objects, and scarecrows may reduce damage briefly, but birds soon become accustomed to them and resume their activities. The only surefire solution to bird depredation is to use screen or nylon or plastic netting material.

Broad-mesh netting (¾-inch) is popular for trees because it easily lets in air, water, and sunlight. It is commonly sold in most nurseries and garden centers. Enclose fruit trees with nets 2 or 3 weeks before fruit ripens; tie nets off where the lowest branches spring from the trunk. Remove netting to harvest.

For protecting sprouting seedlings and maturing vegetables, floating row covers (p. 596) are the easiest to use because they need no supports. Other options—which need to be supported with stakes and string, in tent fashion—are fine-mesh screen and nylon netting. If crows are the problem, chicken wire folded into a tent shape over the rows will provide protection.

Several species of sapsuckers, a type of woodpecker, often peck holes in the trunks of trees with sugary sap. They can create so many holes that the abundance of flowing sap and damaged bark weaken the tree, and it can die or be attacked by other pests.

The size of most trees makes it difficult to protect them from sapsuckers. If you can get up high enough, you can wrap the trunk with burlap or smear the sticky material used to trap ants around the holes.

In most areas it is illegal to shoot or poison nuisance birds. Check with your Cooperative Extension Office for alternative control measures for local bird species.

Blackberry

The blackberry can be a troublesome weed (but see p. 210 for garden varieties) almost anywhere in the United States but is particularly frustrating in mild-summer areas of the Pacific Northwest and the Northeast, and in the Southeast, turning up in flower beds, gravel paths, and lawns. See photograph, p. 615.

The roots are perennial, but the canes are biennial: they grow one year and flower and form fruit the next. Blackberry spreads rapidly by underground runners and seeds; birds eat the ripe, shiny berries in late summer and scatter the seeds willy-nilly across the landscape.

Controls. Pull out young plants in spring, before feeder roots develop. Cut back established plants during the summer growing season, when foliage is green (it's easier to dispose of fresh than dry). Wear heavy gloves; use a pick and shovel to dig up as many roots as possible.

Paint fresh shoots with glyphosate when 6 to 12 inches tall (spray only in isolated areas). Retreatment is usually necessary to control plants growing from dormant seeds, old and incompletely killed roots, and root crowns. Triclopyr can also be effective.

Black Spot. See Leaf Spot; and Visual Guide to Identifying Plant Problems   pp. 575, 590

Blanching

Tying outer leaves over the inner head or leaves of a plant to produce a lighter color or a milder flavor is termed blanching. It is most often done to keep heads of cauliflower white. See p. 194 for information on blanching asparagus.

Bolt

Annual flowers and vegetables that produce an elongated flower stalk are said to bolt. This happens most often when cool-season annuals and vegetables are set out too late in the year or when unseasonably hot weather rushes growth.

Bonsai

Bonsai (the word is Japanese) is one of the fine arts of gardening: growing carefully trained, dwarfed plants in containers selected to harmonize with the plants. The objective is to create in miniature scale a tree or landscape; often the dwarfed trees take on the appearance of very old, gnarled specimens. To get the desired effect, bonsai craftspeople meticulously wire and prune branches and trim roots.

Borers and Bark Beetles

In their larval stage, numerous types of beetles and some clearwing moths tunnel beneath or bore into the bark of many trees and shrubs. There they feed, girdling the trunk, cutting off the flow of water and nutrients, and weakening the plant structurally. The elm beetle also spreads Dutch elm disease (see p. 560).

Borers and bark beetles tend to attack trees stressed by drought, poor growing conditions, or wounds. The first signs of infestation are usually wilting, yellowing foliage on a single branch or limb. With borers you may also see small holes bordered by sawdust, excrement, or sap. The bark around the hole may feel spongy. Eventually the whole plant may die. Some species of borers and bark beetles attack below the soil line; then the evidence may be at the base of the plant. Many species are susceptible to borer attack. Ash, birch, lilac, dogwood, and fruits, nuts, and cane berries are particularly vulnerable.

Prevention is the best way to control borers and bark beetles. Keep plants healthy and growing vigorously. Avoid wounding tree trunks with weed-whips. Paint trunks of young trees white or use a commercial tree wrap to prevent sunburn (see Tree, p. 603). Prune in late fall or winter so wounds are healed by spring.

If borers or beetles are already present, prune out infested branches, making sure to cut well into healthy wood. You may be able to cut out individual borers with a knife, but you'll probably do more damage than good. Injecting parasitic nematodes into borer wounds may provide some control.

If timed properly to coincide with laying of eggs by adults, chemicals can help prevent infestations of bark beetles and borers. Chlorpyrifos, lindane (if available), and Thiodan are most commonly used.

Botanical Name

The Latin name of a plant is its botanical (scientific) name. Unlike common names, of which an individual plant may have many, a plant has only one correct botanical name, which it shares with no other. (The same common name—for example, dusty miller—may represent three or four different plants.) Asking for a plant by its botanical name (as listed in the Plant Encyclopedia) assures you of getting the plant you want. See also Plant Classification (p. 583). However, even botanical names can change with time.

Botrytis

Botrytis, also known as gray mold, is a fungus common in cool, moist weather. It usually starts out on plant debris and weakened or overcrowded plants and quickly spreads to other plants by splashing water or rain. Infections begin as small brown lesions that gradu-

ally grow larger, turning mushy and coating the plant with fuzzy gray mold. Fruit, foliage, stems, and flowers may be infected. Many plants are susceptible, especially strawberries, onions, tomatoes, camellias, tulips, lilies, and begonias.

To prevent botrytis, make sure plants have adequate room to grow and good air circulation. Rotate vegetable crops often. Water in the morning so plants dry quickly. Remove diseased plants or plant parts as soon as you see them. Keep the garden clean. Keep strawberries from touching the ground by planting through a plastic or thick organic mulch. Buy certified, disease-free onion sets. Chlorothalonil is an effective fungicide for plants listed on the label.

Bracts

Modified leaves called bracts may grow just below a flower or flower cluster. Bracts are usually green, but in some cases they are conspicuous and colorful, constituting what people regard as "flowers"; examples are bougainvillea, dogwood, and poinsettia.

Broadcast

To broadcast means to scatter seed or fertilizer over the soil surface. See Planting Techniques: Seeds (p. 584).

Broad-Leafed

The phrase "broad-leafed evergreen" refers to a plant that has green foliage all year but is not an evergreen conifer (such as a juniper) with needlelike or scalelike foliage. A broad-leafed weed is any weed that is not a grass.

Bud

The word "bud" has several definitions. A flower bud is one that develops into a blossom. A growth bud may be at the tip of a stem (terminal) or along the sides of a stem (lateral); these buds will produce new leafy growth (see Plant Anatomy and Growth, p. 583). To bud a plant is to propagate by a process similar to grafting.

Budding

Budding is a method of propagation in which a bud from one plant (the scion), is inserted into the bark of another related plant, usually a rootstock. This technique is commonly used to grow specific varieties of fruit trees and roses on desirable rootstocks.

Budding accomplishes the same result as grafting, but it is considerably easier to do and, for the novice, is more likely to be successful. In summer or early fall, when plants are actively growing, insert a growth bud from one plant under the bark of another plant of a related kind. If the plants are compatible and if you do

▶ page 550

Visual Guide to Identifying

BIOLOGICAL

CONTROLS

Using living organisms such as beneficial insects to destroy garden pests is called biological control. It is an effective way to reduce plant damage without using strong chemicals or sprays. Here are beneficial insects that are either common in gardens or can be released to reduce pest populations. Also described are other organisms that kill insect pests and a natural hormone product that hopelessly confuses them. For more information, see Pest Management (p. 580).

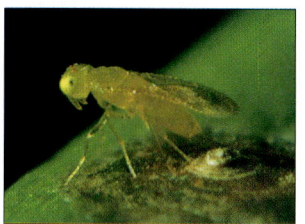

Scale Parasites
One tiny parasitic wasp *(Aphytis melinus)* attacks and kills red scale and other types of hard scale. *Metaphycus helvolus* attacks black scale and other hemispherical scales.

Cryptolaemus Beetle
The larvae and adults of the cryptolaemus beetle, a ladybird-beetle relative, feed on mealybugs.

Lacewings
Commonly found in gardens, both lacewing larvae and adults feed on a variety of insects and mites.

Predator Mites
Various species of mites feed on spider mites and sometimes thrips but do no damage to plants.

Fly Parasites
Tiny wasps (many species) that lay their eggs in the pupae of several types of flies, including houseflies, are very effective and most useful in controlling flies on ranches or farms.

Ladybird Beetle
The ladybird beetle (or ladybug, as most people know it) occurs naturally in gardens. Larvae *(left)* and adults feed on aphids, mealybugs, small worms, spider mites, and similar soft-bodied insects. Releasing ladybird beetles in your garden is often not effective because they fly away. They also migrate annually. If you do release them, do so in the evening because daylight encourages flight.

Whitefly Parasite
Several species of small wasps attack immature stages of whiteflies. Control of the greenhouse whitefly using *Encarsia formosa* requires average temperatures above 75°F/24°C. The wasps are most effective in greenhouses.

Trichogramma Wasps
Larvae of the tiny trichogramma wasp develop within the eggs of caterpillars and eat their way out, destroying the eggs. Adult wasps fly off to find new eggs to parasitize. Repeated releases are usually necessary to reduce a caterpillar infestation.

Semiochemicals
Insects use semiochemicals to communicate. Two general groups are commercially available: pheromones, which affect communications between insects, and kairomones, which affect feeding behavior. Both can be used to attract insects: sometimes to trap (possibly to monitor pest levels for precise timing of sprays) or confuse an insect pest; at other times, to lure beneficials into the garden. Semiochemicals are very target specific and are available for several common pests.

Parasitic Nematodes
Parasitic nematodes include several species of microscopic worms that seek out and eat their way into more than 250 soil-dwelling pests, such as grubs, weevils, sod webworms, and carpenter worms. Read directions carefully. Soil conditions and release techniques must be right for effectiveness.

Bacillus thuringiensis (Bt)
The bacterium *Bt* controls caterpillars (including wormlike budworms). After eating *Bt*-treated leaves, caterpillars die within 2 to 3 days. *Bt* can be used on all food crops up to harvest. Mixing it in alkaline water (pH 8 or higher) reduces its effectiveness. Apply it when caterpillars are small; reapply in 3 to 14 days. The strain for most caterpillars is *B. t. kurstaki*. Other available strains include *B. t. israeliensis* for mosquitoes and *B. t. tenebrionis* for Colorado potato beetle and elmleaf beetle. *Bt* is sold under several trade names.

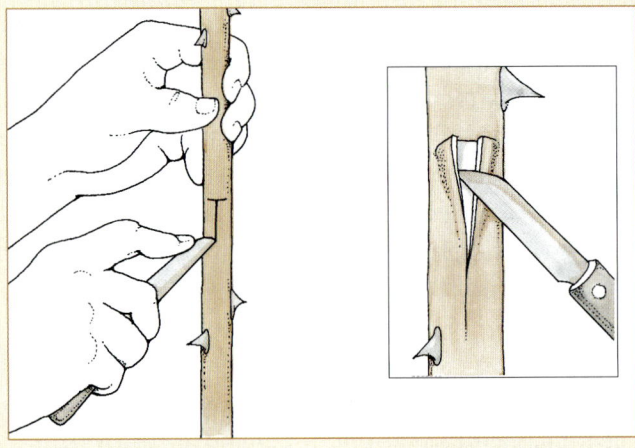

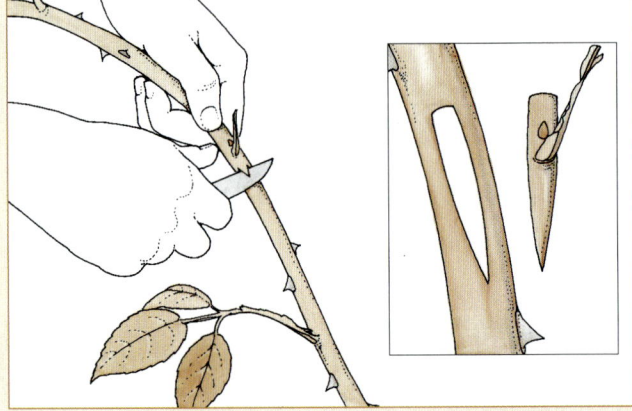

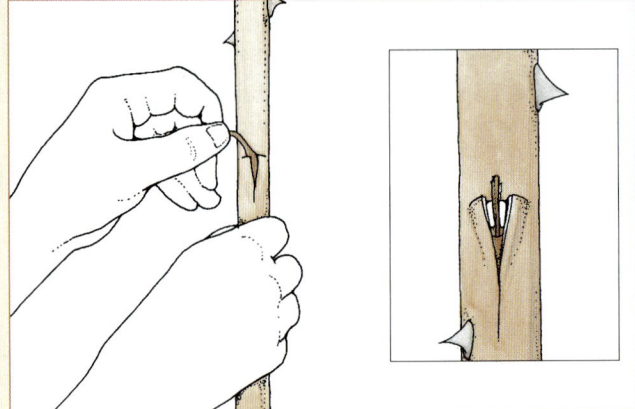

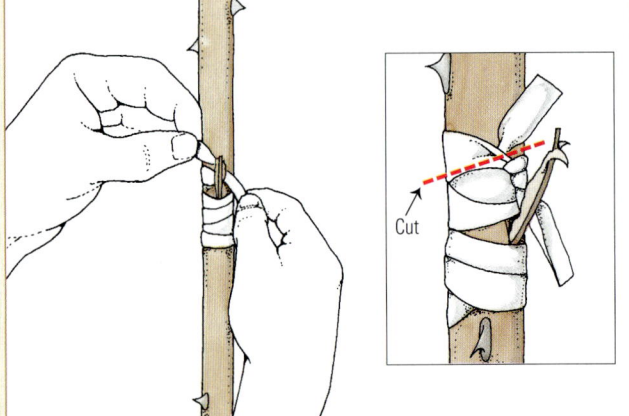

BUDDING

1 T-budding is fairly easy for the novice. Make T-shaped cut in branch ¼ to ½ inch in diameter; top of T should extend about one-third the distance around stem. Gently pry up corners where cuts meet.

2 Cut shield-shaped patch containing bud from selected bud-wood plant. Begin about ½ inch below bud and finish about 1 inch above it; leave a bit of wood attached to back of bud shield.

3 Push bud shield down between flaps of T-cut, being careful not to damage the bud. All of shield should fit beneath bark flaps.

4 Bind the operation snugly with plastic tape, starting beneath the bud and finishing above it so that tape overlaps in shingle fashion. Only bud itself should be exposed.

Cut above the inserted bud after the graft union has formed. This will force the bud to grow.

Cut

the budding carefully, the bud will unite with the stem into which it was inserted. Throughout fall and winter, the bud will remain plump but dormant; it will begin to grow in spring when all buds on the plant have a growth spurt. At that time, cut off the stem at a point just above the growing bud you inserted. See illustration.

Bud Union

The part of a plant where growth of the scion joins with the understock, generally 1 to 6 inches above the roots, is its bud union. It is an enlarged knob from which all major stems grow.

Bulbs

Bulbs are a very specialized group of perennial plants. Following popular usage, we call a number of plants bulbs that are not true bulbs—corms, rhizomes, tubers, and tuberous roots (see The Five Bulb Types illustration, p. 551). But whether true bulbs or bulblike plants, they all hold a reserve of nutrients in a thickened underground storage organ. This reserve almost guarantees that the bulb you purchase in summer or fall will bloom the following spring: all the nutrients the plant needs to complete its life cycle are in storage, waiting for the right combination of moisture and soil temperature to trigger the cycle's beginning phase.

Planting. Although the bulb you purchase from a nursery or commercial specialist is likely to be a sure first-season performer, performance in subsequent years will depend on the care you give it. As always, proper care begins with the soil. Most bulbs prefer soil that drains well yet retains a certain amount of water. See Soils (p. 600).

In planting true bulbs and most corms, the rule of thumb is to dig a hole about three times as deep as the bulb's greatest diameter. (To determine planting depths for the other "bulbs," see individual plant descriptions in the Plant Encyclopedia.) If you will be planting many bulbs in one bed, it may be easier to dig a trench or to excavate the bed to the desired planting depth than to dig individual holes.

Fertilizer. This is the time to add a complete fertilizer. Ones with controlled-release nitrogen are very effective. See Fertilizers (p. 561). If you plant bulbs in individual holes, dig up to a tablespoonful of fertilizer into the soil at the bottom of each hole, then cover with about 2 inches of soil and plant the bulb. Otherwise, dig fertilizer into the bottom of the trench or excavated bed.

Water. When all the bulbs are set in place and covered with soil, soak the area thoroughly. In some regions this initial watering, along with subsequent rain, will supply all the moisture bulbs will need until their leaves poke above the soil surface. But if you live in an arid climate or

THE FIVE BULB TYPES

True bulb and bulblet. A true bulb is a short underground stem (on solid basal plate) surrounded by modified fleshy leaves (scales) that protect and store food for use by the embryonic plant. Outer scales are dry and form papery covering (tunic).

The new bulb (often called an offset) is formed from a lateral bud on the basal plate; the old bulb may die or, like daffodils, keep coming back each year. Bulblets can be separated from the mother bulb and replanted to increase stock of the original plant. Bulbils are small bulbs that form in the axils of leaves, in flowers, or on stems of certain bulbous plants.

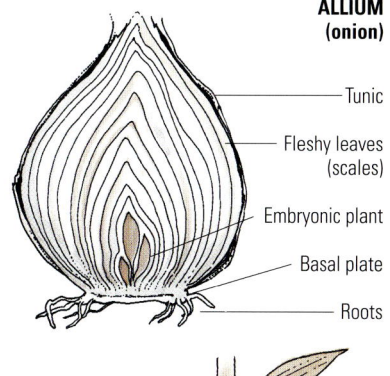

ALLIUM (onion)
- Tunic
- Fleshy leaves (scales)
- Embryonic plant
- Basal plate
- Roots

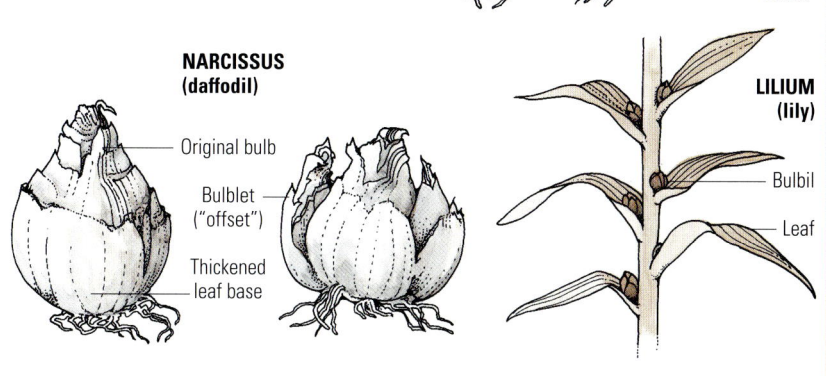

NARCISSUS (daffodil)
- Original bulb
- Bulblet ("offset")
- Thickened leaf base

LILIUM (lily)
- Bulbil
- Leaf

Corm and cormel. A corm is a swollen, underground stem base—solid tissue (in contrast to bulb scales) but with a basal plate from which roots grow. Growth point is on the corm's top; many corms have tunics that consist of dried bases of previous season's leaves. An individual corm lasts just one year. New corms form from axillary buds on the top of an old corm as it completes its growth cycle. Fingernail-size cormels will take 2 to 3 years to flower; larger corms should bloom the following year.

GLADIOLUS
- Dead leaf bases
- Basal plate
- Roots
- Cormels
- New corms
- Old corm
- Roots

Rhizome. A rhizome is a thickened stem that grows partially or entirely beneath the ground. Roots generally grow from the underside; the principal growing point is at the tip, although additional growing points will form along the rhizome's length. To divide, cut into sections that have visible growing points.

ZANTEDESCHIA (calla)
- Growth bud ("eye")

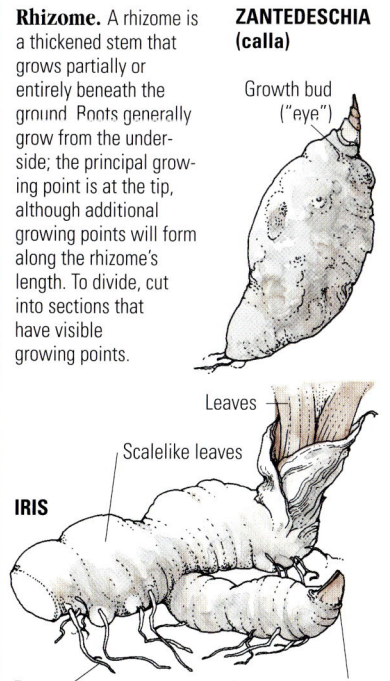

- Leaves
- Scalelike leaves
- **IRIS**
- Roots
- Growth bud ("eye")

Tuber. A tuber is a swollen, underground stem base, like a corm, but it lacks the corm's distinct organization. There is no basal plate, so roots can grow from all sides; multiple growth points are distributed over the upper surface—each is a scalelike leaf with a growth bud in its axil. An individual tuber can last for many years. Some (*Cyclamen,* for example) continually enlarge, but never produce offsets; others (such as *Caladium*) form protuberances that can be removed and planted separately. Divide tubers by cutting into sections that have growth buds.

BEGONIA (tuberous)
- Growth bud ("eye")

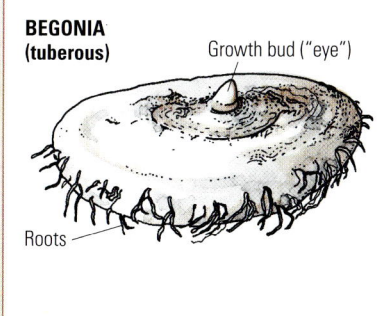

- Roots

Tuberous roots. Tuberous roots are actual roots (rather than stems) that are specialized to store nutrients. In a full-grown dahlia, daylily, or other tuberous-rooted plant, the roots grow in a cluster, with the swollen tuberous portions radiating out from a central point. Growth buds are at the bases of old stems rather than on the tuberous roots. To divide, cut apart so that each division contains both roots and part of the stem's base with one or more growth buds.

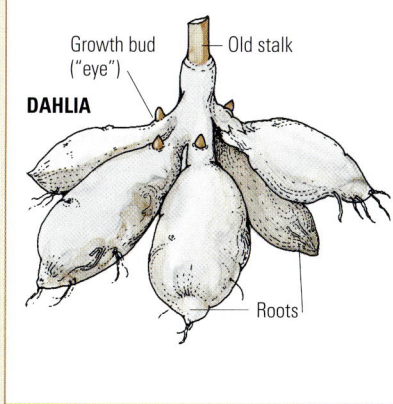

- Growth bud ("eye")
- Old stalk
- **DAHLIA**
- Roots

have an unusually dry winter, you will need to soak the bulbs periodically throughout the winter and into the blooming season. Summer-flowering bulbs need watering at least until they finish blooming.

The roots of bulbs grow below the depth at which you planted, so water, to do them any

good, must penetrate deep into the soil. (See Watering, p. 609, for specific advice on watering practices.) Mulching (p. 576) is also beneficial.

Care. Bulb plantings established for a year or more may benefit from application of a nitrogen fertilizer at the start of the growing season (as

recommended for perennials, p. 580). But the crucial moment for applying fertilizer comes after the blooms have faded.

When a bulb has finished flowering, much of its supply of stored nutrients is depleted. It must replenish those nutrients if it is to perform well the next year. For this reason, it is essential to

C

leave the foliage on the plant, even if it begins to look unsightly, until it has yellowed and can be pulled off easily. The leaves continue to manufacture food for the plant (see Plant Anatomy and Growth, p. 583). Cutting them off prematurely amounts to removing the next year's blossoms—or at least reducing their quantity and quality.

Furthermore, fertilizer application at this time helps bulbs form not only next year's flowers but also new bulbs that will increase the planting. Phosphorus and potassium—the nutrients emphasized in "bulb food"—are most useful now, although they must reach the root zone to be fully effective (see Nutrients, Basic, p. 577). In an established planting, you may be able only to scatter fertilizer over the soil surface, scratch it in, and hope that some phosphorus and potassium will reach the roots. Where bulbs are spaced far enough apart or in rows, you may be able to get fertilizer deep into the soil by digging narrow trenches or holes 8 inches deep, placing fertilizer at the bottom, and then filling with soil.

Caliche

A soil condition found in some areas of the arid Southwest, caliche is a deposit of calcium carbonate (lime) beneath the soil surface. For help in dealing with it, see Hardpan (p. 568).

Cambium. See Plant Anatomy and Growth p. 583

Caterpillars

Caterpillars are larvae of moths or butterflies. There are many types that feed on the foliage and fruit of a variety of plants. The most serious pests—including tomato hornworm (p. 522), bagworms (p. 547), oak worms (p. 460), borers (p. 548), tent caterpillar (p. 591), cabbage loopers (p. 219), and geranium budworms (p. 565)—are described in other parts of this book. As some of these names hint, not all caterpillars are hairy. Many are smooth skinned and more wormlike in appearance.

In general, the biological agent *Bacillus thuringiensis (Bt)* is the preferred control for most caterpillars. However, tall trees infested with caterpillars require high-pressure spray equipment for adequate coverage. This is true of the notorious gypsy moth, whose larvae (about 2 inches long, blackish with rows of blue and red spots, and tufts of fine hair on the sides) periodically defoliate a variety of trees and shrubs, particularly in the Northeast. Consult a local arborist or spray company for help.

Trichogramma wasps can also reduce caterpillar populations. Appropriately labeled chemical controls, such as carbaryl and acephate (on nonedibles) are also effective. You can often keep gypsy moth caterpillars out of trees by placing a band of burlap around the trunk. Leave the bottom of the burlap loosely attached so caterpillars can get underneath. During the day, they'll hide there where they can be easily collected. Keeping trees growing vigorously, with proper water and fertilizer, will help them recover from gypsy moth damage.

Catkin

A catkin is a slender, spikelike, and often drooping flower cluster.

Chelate

A chelate (pronounced key-late) is a complex organic substance that holds micronutrients (see Nutrients, Basic, p. 577), usually iron, in a form available for absorption by plants. Iron chelates, for example, are often used to cure chlorosis.

Chilling Requirement

Many deciduous shrubs and trees (fruit trees in particular), bulbs, and perennials need certain amounts of cold weather in winter to grow and bloom well the following year. Where winters are mild and these plants may get the necessary winter chill, their performance is often disappointing: plants leaf out late, fail to flower or fruit well, and often decline in health and vigor even to the point of dying. With some of these plants (apples and lilacs, for example), varieties have been developed that require less winter cold than is normal for the type. Gardeners in milder-winter areas should choose varieties with low chilling requirements. (Chilling requirement is measured in hours required at temperatures below 45°F/–7°C.)

Chlorosis

A systemic condition in which a plant's newer leaves turn yellow, chlorosis is usually caused by a deficiency of iron. (It occasionally results from lack of another mineral, such as zinc.) If the deficiency is mild, areas of yellow show up between the veins of the leaves, which remain a dark green (see photograph, p. 592). In severe or prolonged cases, the entire leaf turns yellow. Iron deficiency is only occasionally the result of a lack of iron in the soil; more frequently it is the result of some other substance (usually lime) making the iron unavailable to the plant.

To correct chlorosis, treat the soil with iron sulfate or with iron chelate (the latter has the important ability to hold iron in a form that is available to plants). Plants can also be treated with foliar sprays containing iron.

Cold Protection

At high elevations and in northern climates where soil freezes hard and temperatures drop below zero, tender plants will not thrive. But many gardeners do grow roses, and a few attempt broad-leafed evergreens: boxwood, *Euonymus,* holly, *Pieris,* and rhododendrons. All these plants need help to survive harsh winters.

With roses, which are basically deciduous, the aim is to keep roots and bud union alive and to preserve as many live canes as possible. For detailed instructions on winter protection for roses, see page 476.

Some broad-leafed evergreens will survive fairly low temperatures but succumb to windburn and sunburn when low temperatures, strong sun, and cold, drying winds combine forces. The greatest damage occurs when these plants transpire water from their leaves but can't replace the moisture because water in the soil is frozen.

Careful selection of garden location minimizes damage to tender broad-leafed evergreens. Locate these plants where bright sun—especially in early morning—will not strike frozen plants. To avoid rupturing plant tissues, thawing should be gradual. Above all, keep soil moist, and prevent alternate freezing and thawing with a thick mulch.

To protect an exposed evergreen (especially a newly planted one), shelter it with burlap, lath, plywood, Styrofoam, or cardboard secured on its windward side. A palisade of evergreen boughs stuck in the ground around the plant will offer further protection. See also Frost and Freeze Protection (p. 564).

COLD PROTECTION

Constructing a burlap screen on the windward side of recent plantings will buffer drying winds and reduce cold damage.

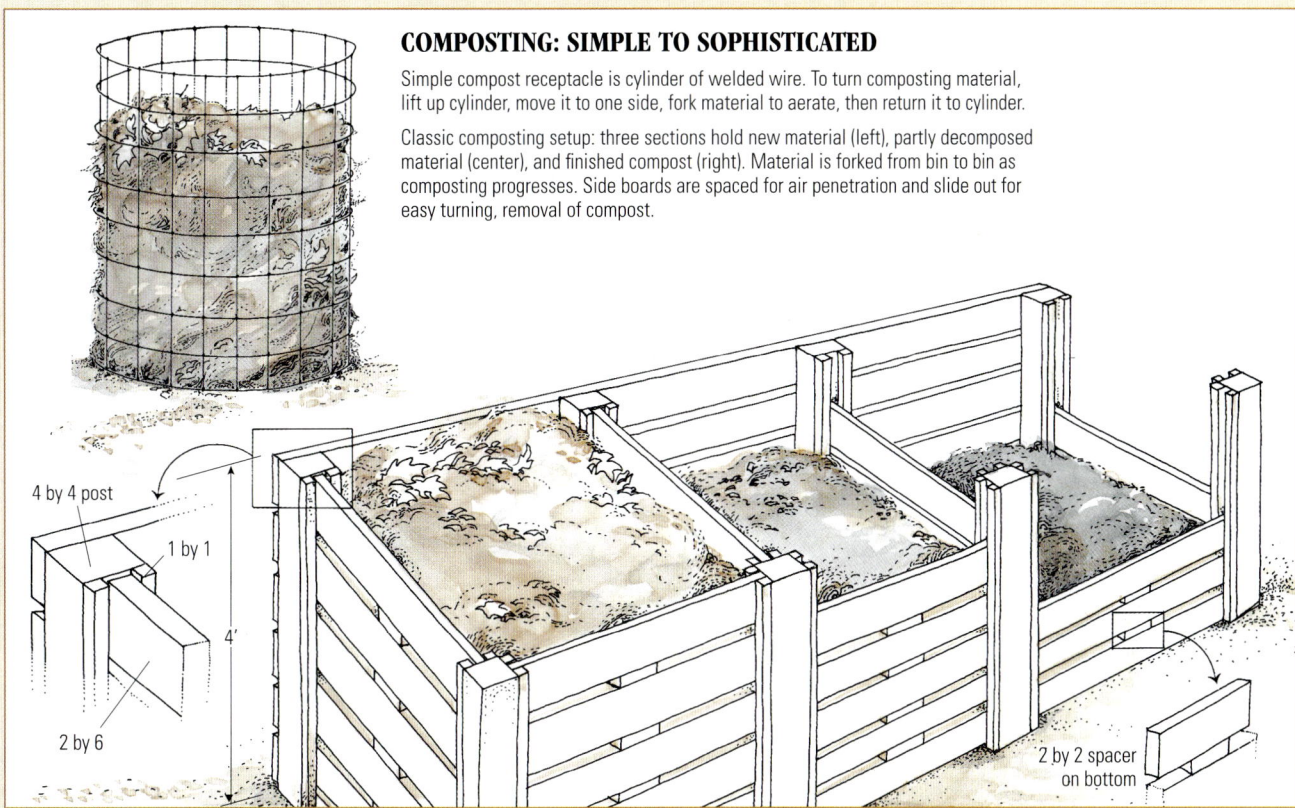

COMPOSTING: SIMPLE TO SOPHISTICATED

Simple compost receptacle is cylinder of welded wire. To turn composting material, lift up cylinder, move it to one side, fork material to aerate, then return it to cylinder.

Classic composting setup: three sections hold new material (left), partly decomposed material (center), and finished compost (right). Material is forked from bin to bin as composting progresses. Side boards are spaced for air penetration and slide out for easy turning, removal of compost.

4 by 4 post

1 by 1

4'

2 by 6

2 by 2 spacer on bottom

Cole Crops

A group of vegetables belonging to the cabbage family, cole crops include broccoli, Brussels sprouts, cabbage, kohlrabi, and cauliflower. They perform best in cool growing conditions and are planted in late summer or early spring.

Colorado Potato Beetles

Colorado potato beetles (see photograph, p. 591) occur almost everywhere in the United States, except for California and Nevada. Problems are most serious in the Midwest and along the East Coast. The ³⁄₈-inch adult beetle is easy to spot; the showy polka-dot vest and striped pants are a dead giveaway. The larvae are humped, yellow to orange red with a black head, and about ½ inch long. They hatch from clusters of bright yellow eggs laid on the undersides of leaves.

Both adult beetles and larvae feed voraciously on the leaves of vegetables and flowers. They prefer potato plants but will also eat peppers, tomatoes, eggplant, and nicotiana.

Sanitation will help keep Colorado potato beetles at bay. Discard plants after harvest and till the soil to expose overwintering adults. Hand-picking of adults, larvae, and egg clusters will also reduce pest numbers. Heavy mulching may keep overwintering adults from reaching plants in spring.

Bacillus thuringiensis tenebrionis is an effective biological control for Colorado potato

beetle larvae. Ladybird beetles, lacewings, spined soldier beetles, as well as many other beneficial insects, prey on the Colorado potato beetle. Rotenone, neem, and pyrethrum are botanical sprays to use against the adult insects. Several traditional chemicals are also labeled for control of the Colorado potato beetle, but the pest has become resistant to some. See Pest Management (p. 580).

Complete Fertilizer

Any plant food that contains all three of the primary nutrient elements—nitrogen, phosphorus, and potassium—is a complete fertilizer. See Fertilizers (p. 561).

Compost

Well-made compost is a soft, crumbly, brownish or blackish substance resulting from decomposition of organic material. It has limited value as a nutrient source but great value as an organic soil amendment (p. 598). Composting takes time, effort, and space. But if you have a ready supply of plant waste or a small garden that could be supplied by a continually maintained compost pile, the time and effort might be well spent. Remember, though, that a poorly maintained compost pile will be slow to yield its reward and may also breed flies and give off an obnoxious odor.

In its simplest and least efficient form, composting consists of piling up grass clippings, leaves, and other garden debris—plus vege-

table kitchen refuse—and permitting them to decompose. In 6 weeks to 6 months, depending on temperature, moisture, frequency of turning, and size of materials, the compost will have broken down sufficiently for use.

Composters. For the average garden, a better system is to stack the material for composting to a height of 4 to 6 feet inside an enclosure that has openings in its sides through which air can penetrate. A slatted bin or a wire-mesh cylinder (see illustration) will do the trick. Turn the piled-up material at least once a week to aerate the mass and to relocate pieces in various stages of decomposition. (Compost decomposes more rapidly in the heat and moisture of the pile's interior than on the outside.) Thoroughly moisten the pile as needed; it should be about as wet as a squeezed-out sponge. Adding a few handfuls of complete fertilizer with every sizable load of raw material hastens decomposition. Compost additives—or boosters, as they are sometimes called—have proven to be of little benefit.

A more sophisticated composting operation uses three receptacles, as shown in the illustration. Placing the receptacles side by side makes it simple to fork or shovel material from bin to bin. Prefabricated composters are also available for purchase.

Because large, coarse pieces decompose slowly, chop them up before adding them to the pile or omit altogether. A good mixture consists of green and dried materials in about equal proportions.

The serious composter might consider purchasing a compost grinder. Chopping up everything from leaves to thumb-thick branches into uniformly small fragments, these machines are a great aid to people who live beyond the service area of garbage collectors—particularly those who are prevented by ordinance from burning debris.

Conifer

Conifer is a more precise word for the plants that bear seeds in cones or modified conelike structures, such as cedars, cypresses, junipers, and pines. Leaves on most are narrow and needlelike or tiny and scalelike. Most but not all conifers are evergreen.

Container Gardening

Container plants generally require more attention than plants growing in the ground, but their potential advantages may make the extra care worthwhile. For the gardener with just a balcony or a paved patio, planting in containers is the only way to have a garden. And even those with garden space can use container plants to bring seasonal flowers onstage when colorful and remove them when past their prime. Other plants have such handsome foliage that they deserve to be grown in containers so they can be appreciated at close range throughout the year.

Container culture also lets you enjoy plants that aren't entirely suited to your garden conditions. You can grow acid-soil plants in regions where native soil is alkaline and plants that demand fast drainage even if your garden soil is clay. Plants too tender for your climate can be moved to shelter when cold weather comes, and plants sensitive to winter cold or summer heat may function well as container subjects indoors.

The routine extra attention container plants need falls into three categories: soil preparation, watering, and fertilizing. These plants also require periodic transplanting and replanting.

Soil mixes for containers. Container plants need soil that is porous and well drained but that retains moisture. The soil must allow roots to grow easily, and it must drain fast enough that roots don't suffocate in soggy soil. Yet the soil should retain enough moisture so that continuous watering isn't necessary.

Even the best garden soils fail to satisfy container soil requirements: in containers, garden soil inevitably forms a dense mass that roots can't penetrate easily, and it remains soggy for too long after watering. For these reasons, gardeners growing container plants turn to potting mixes.

Bagged soil mixes. You can purchase packaged potting mixes that are ready to use directly out of the bag. Formulations (listed on the bags) vary somewhat from brand to brand, but none contain actual soil. Look for a mix high in bark,

forest materials, or sphagnum peat plus vermiculite. A 2-cubic-foot bag of potting mix will fill a planter box 36 by 8 by 10 inches; it will also be enough to transplant 8 to 10 plants from 1-gallon nursery containers to separate 10- or 12-inch pots.

Homemade soil mixes. If you prefer to mix your own potting soil—or if you are planning a large-scale operation that would be too costly using packaged mixes—you can purchase the basic component materials and combine them yourself. There are countless possible formulations, but they all combine organic material (bark, peat moss, leaf mold, compost) and mineral matter (soil, sand, perlite, vermiculite) in proportions that produce the desired porosity, drainage, and moisture retention.

TRANSPLANTING CONTAINER-GROWN PLANTS

1 Tap pot gently against edge of workbench to free root ball. Pull apart coiled roots.

2 Set root ball into new pot partially filled with soil; top of root ball should be about an inch below pot's rim. Add soil around edges, firming lightly. Water thoroughly.

One time-honored basic container mixture consists of 1 part good garden soil (not clay), 1 part sand (river or builder's sand) or perlite, and 1 part peat moss or nitrogen-stabilized bark. For plants that prefer acid soil (such as rhododendrons, azaleas, and heather), alter the above mix to 2 parts peat moss or nitrogen-stabilized bark.

The use of soil-less mixes lessens the danger from soilborne diseases. But these mixes dry faster than those containing soil, and they will need more frequent fertilizer applications due to leaching from frequent watering. For a quantity of soil-less mix, combine ⅔ cubic yard of nitrogen-stabilized bark (or peat moss) and ⅓ cubic yard washed 20-grit sand; add to this 6 pounds of 0-10-10 dry fertilizer and 10 pounds dolomite or dolomitic limestone. For ways to increase the water retention of a potting soil, read about Soil Polymers (p. 600).

Watering. In hot, dry, windy weather you may need to water actively growing plants more than once a day; when the weather is cool, still, and overcast or if plants are semidormant, weekly (or even less frequent) watering may suffice. Test with your fingers: it's time to water if the soil is dry beneath the surface.

To water thoroughly, apply water over the entire soil surface until it flows out the pot's drainage holes. This guarantees moistening the entire soil mass and also prevents any potentially harmful salts from accumulating in the soil mix.

Note: If water comes out the drainage holes too fast, check to see if it is just running down the inside surface of the container and not through the soil. A root ball that has become too dry can shrink away from the sides of the container; when that happens, water will run around the root ball without penetrating it. To correct the problem, set the container in a tub of water and soak the plant until bubbles stop rising. If that method isn't practical, cork the container's drainage holes and then water the plant. Remove corks after the soil is soaked.

Fertilizing. Heavy and thorough watering leaches out plant nutrients from container soils, so regular fertilizer applications are required for best plant growth. Use either liquid or dry fertilizer according to label directions. The slow-release dry fertilizers, which release nutrients steadily over a period of time, don't need to be applied as often as other fertilizers. With other types, light and frequent applications give best results.

Transplanting. Shift a plant to a larger container when its root system fills the container in which it is growing; usually the first sign of this is roots protruding from drainage holes. Generally speaking, container plants should be shifted to a slightly larger container rather than to a much larger one, because you want to keep the soil mass fairly well filled with roots (unused soil in a container can stagnate and become a

C

haven for potentially harmful organisms). With fast-growing plants, it's safe to shift to a definitely larger container. And you can always put a number of small plants in a large container—their combined root systems will occupy the total soil mass.

When moving a plant to a larger container, select a new container that allows an inch or two of fresh soil on all sides of the root mass. If the plant's root ball appears compacted, cut it vertically with a sharp knife to encourage roots to move out into the new soil in the larger container. Make at least four equally spaced cuts about ¼ to 1 inch deep, depending on root ball size.

To keep an older plant in the same large container indefinitely, you can periodically root-prune the plant. During the plant's dormant period, gently turn it out of the container. Shave off an inch or two of the outer root mass on all sides and on the bottom with a sharp knife; then replant in the same container with fresh soil mix around and underneath the roots. See illustration.

Cool-Season Plants

Plants that thrive in cool weather are referred to as cool-season plants. They include some vegetables (cole crops, lettuce, spinach, peas), annual flowers (pansies, violas, calendula), and lawn grasses (bluegrass, tall fescue). See also Vegetable Gardening (p. 605), Annual (p. 545), and Lawns (p. 570).

Corm

Technically, a corm is a thickened underground stem capable of producing roots, leaves, and flowers during the growing season. See Bulbs (p. 550) and The Five Bulb Types illustration (p. 551).

Cover Crops

Sometimes referred to as "green manure," a cover crop is dug or tilled into the soil in early spring to return valuable organic matter and nitrogen to the soil. Legumes such as clover, cowpeas, and vetch are the most common cover crops.

Crabgrass

An infamous summer annual, crabgrass grows well in hot, damp areas. This shallow-rooted weed thrives in lawns and flower beds that receive frequent surface watering, in under-fed lawns, and in poorly drained fields. See photograph, p. 614.

Seeds germinate in early spring in southern climates, later in northern areas. As the plant grows, it branches out at the base; stems can root where they touch the soil. Seed heads form in mid- to late summer. As crabgrass declines in fall, it turns purplish, becoming especially noticeable in lawns.

In flower beds, pull crabgrass before it makes seeds. Keep lawns well fertilized and vigorous to provide tough competition for weeds; to dry out crabgrass roots, water lawns deeply but not frequently. In late winter or early spring, apply a granular pre-emergent herbicide—such as DCPA (Dacthal)—with a fertilizer spreader. Lawn care combination products include other effective controls. Use fluazifop-butyl or sethoxydim in ornamental plantings.

Crown

The crown of a tree is its entire branch structure, including foliage. In another usage, "crown" refers to the point at which a plant's roots and top structure join (usually at or near the soil line).

Cucumber Beetles

Two types of cucumber beetles are common garden pests over most of the United States. They are similar in appearance—about ¼ inch long and yellowish green—but one species has black spots on its shell, the other black stripes. They are appropriately named spotted and striped cucumber beetles.

Adult cucumber beetles feed on the foliage, flowers, fruit, and stems of a variety of plants, particularly members of the cucurbit family (Cucurbitaceae) of vegetables. Young seedlings are particularly vulnerable. Cucumber beetles also attack other vegetables and flowers like asters, dahlias, and roses. To make matters worse, they spread bacterial wilt to vine crops (see p. 546) as they feed. The small, ⅓-inch larvae feed on plant roots (especially corn roots) and stems.

Controlling cucumber beetles starts with good sanitation and prevention. Clean up and discard plant debris that might serve as over-wintering sites. Planting as early as possible in spring may help seedlings get established before the pest emerges. Some vegetable varieties are described as resistant to cucumber beetles. Use floating row covers to prevent adult beetles from reaching plants (see p. 596). They are most effective when supported by hoops. Make sure to remove the covers when plants are blooming so bees can reach the flowers for pollination.

Pyrethrum, rotenone, and sabadilla are useful botanical sprays for controlling cucumber beetles (see Pest Management, p. 580). Parasitic nematodes will reduce larvae populations. Carbaryl is one of several chemical controls labeled for cucumber beetles.

Cultivate

Cultivating is the process of breaking up the soil surface, often removing weeds in the process. It aerates the soil and improves plant growth. Increased aeration due to cultivation also allows the soil to warm earlier in spring and dry faster in wet weather.

Cuttings

Most gardeners who have propagated new plants have started cuttings from plant stems, roots, or leaves. Cuttings are of three types—softwood, semihardwood, and hardwood—depending on the maturity of the cutting material.

Softwood and semihardwood stem cuttings. Softwood stem cuttings, taken from spring until late summer, are the easiest and quickest-rooting stem cuttings. You take them during the active growing season from soft, succulent, flexible new growth. The steps are outlined in the illustration on the next page. You take semihardwood cuttings after the active growing season or after a growth flush, usually in summer or early fall. Growth is then firm enough that a sharply bent twig snaps (if it just bends, the stem is too mature for satisfactory rooting).

In addition to deciduous and evergreen shrubs and trees, many herbaceous or evergreen perennials may be propagated by softwood or semihardwood cuttings.

Choices of rooting medium are several, but all allow for easy water penetration and fast drainage. Pure sand (builder's sand or river sand) is the simplest medium but requires the most frequent watering. Better are half-and-half mixtures of sand and peat moss or of perlite and peat moss, or perlite or vermiculite alone.

Loss of water through the leaves that remain on the cuttings is the greatest threat to softwood and semihardwood cuttings. To minimize this water loss, provide a greenhouse atmosphere—high humidity—for the cuttings while they are striking roots. The easiest way is to place a plastic bag over the cuttings and container, then tie it around the container to confine humid air within the bag. Ventilate any of these improvised greenhouses for a few minutes every day or two.

When new growth forms on the cuttings, you can be fairly sure that they have rooted and can be transplanted.

Hardwood stem cuttings. Hardwood cuttings are best made during the fall-to-spring dormant season from wood of the previous season's growth. Many deciduous shrubs and trees can be increased from cuttings taken during the dormant season. See the illustration on the next page. ▸

C

SOFTWOOD STEM CUTTINGS

Take softwood and semihardwood stem cuttings during the growing season; cut below a leaf, remove lower leaves, dip cut in rooting hormone, then plant. Maintain high humidity around cutting (see text).

HARDWOOD STEM CUTTINGS

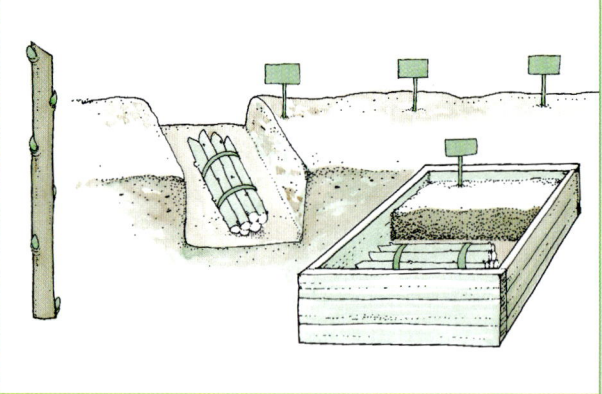

Take hardwood stem cuttings at onset of dormant season; make cut below a leaf bud, dip cut in rooting hormone. Refrigerate over winter in areas where the ground freezes; bury in a trench or soil-filled box outdoors in warmer climates.

LEAF CUTTINGS

Leaf cuttings will increase many succulents, African violets, *Sansevieria, Begonia,* and other plants. With some, cut veins and lay leaf flat on soil; others will grow from part of leaf inserted in soil.

ROOT CUTTINGS

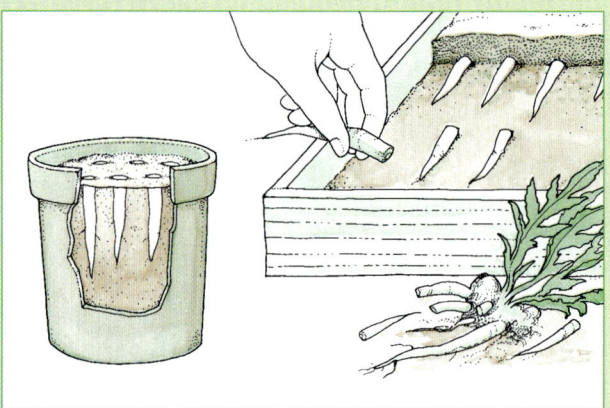

To make root cuttings, cut pencil- to finger-thick sections of roots; place them on their sides and cover with soil, or insert upright in soil with tops just at soil surface. Moisten, cover with plastic, and place in shade.

Hardwood cuttings may take longer to root and start growth than softwood cuttings, so you will want to put your hardwood cuttings where they can remain undisturbed.

During the winter the lower ends of the cuttings will begin to form calluses from which roots will grow. When weather starts to warm as spring approaches, dig out the cuttings and plant them in the open ground or in containers. Cuttings must be planted top side up; to be sure, make the top cut slanted, the bottom cut square.

Leaf cuttings. Some plants will root successfully from a leaf or portion of a leaf. See the illustration. New plants will sprout from the base of each leaf section or from the cut veins.

Root cuttings. Any plant that produces sprouts from its roots will grow from root cuttings. The technique is shown in the illustration. Check cuttings every week for moisture and for sprouts; remove the covering when growth shows.

Cutworms

A large variety of hairless larvae of night-flying moths make up the diverse group called cutworms. They feed at night and on overcast days, and most can cut off young plants at the ground—hence their name. In the daytime, they hide in the ground, curled up. Early in spring, the moths tend to lay eggs on garden weeds. The larvae begin feeding on the weeds, then move into garden plants when the weeds are destroyed.

Barriers. Susceptible seedlings should be protected from cutworms by putting a physical barrier around each seedling the day it sprouts or the day you plant it. One simple barrier is a cut-off milk carton sleeve: sink it 1 inch below soil level, allow 2 inches above, and provide at least an inch of space between the sleeve and the plant. As an extra precaution, put petroleum jelly or a sticky ant barrier on the upper edge.

Some cutworms crawl up into plants and eat buds, leaves, and fruit. One way to keep them out is to spread a sticky ant barrier around the base of each susceptible plant. If you have too many plants to easily employ barriers, try hand-picking cutworms at night. Or try trapping them by placing cardboard, plywood, wide boards, or heavy paper sacks in garden paths. During daylight, lift the traps and destroy the worms that have taken refuge beneath.

Cutworms in lawns. These are more difficult to eradicate. Your clue to infestation in grass or dichondra is small bare patches that grow rapidly in size day by day. If you're not sure the damage is from cutworms, drench a square yard with 1 tablespoon of dishwashing soap diluted in a gallon of water. That should bring the cutworms to the surface. Sometimes you can also see them with a flashlight at night.

Biological and chemical controls. Parasitic nematodes (p. 549) are the first line of defense against cutworms. *Bacillus thuringiensis* has limited effectiveness. To control seedling-eating cutworms, try dusting the ground where they feed with carbaryl or use carbaryl baits; for cutworms in lawns, apply diazinon, chlorpyrifos, or carbaryl.

Damping Off

In the most conspicuous type of damping off (a disease that can be caused by a number of different fungi), the stem of a seedling collapses at or near the soil surface, and the seedling topples. In some woody seedlings, infected plants may remain alive and standing for a while. Another type rots the seedling before it emerges from the soil or causes the seed to decay before sprouting.

Professional horticulturists practice careful sanitation, pasteurizing their soil mixes or using soil-less mixes. Home gardeners can take the following steps to reduce the occurrence of damping off:

- Buy seeds that have been treated with a fungicide, or dust them with one before planting.

- Provide good air circulation and ventilation (especially if growing seedlings indoors) to keep tops of seedlings dry and standing moisture to a minimum.

- Sow seeds or root cuttings in an inert (sterile) material rather than in garden soil: vermiculite, perlite, pumice, sand, sphagnum moss, and soil-less commercial mixes are all safe—at least the first time they are used.

You also can reduce problems by not planting too deeply or too close together and by avoiding overwatering.

A number of chemical fungicides help control damping off. Look for products that contain captan, or other properly labeled fungicides. But realize that one product may not be effective against all damping-off organisms. If one product doesn't work, switch to another.

Dandelion

Familiar as a lawn weed throughout the United States, dandelion is particularly troublesome in gardens in cold-winter climates. It grows from a deep, fleshy taproot that often breaks (and can regrow) when the weed is pulled out and spreads by dispersing windborne seeds and by sprouting root crowns (see photograph, p. 615). Flowering begins in spring and often continues until frost; in mild weather, seeds can germinate year-round.

Pull out young plants before the taproot has a chance to grow deep into the soil. On lawns, apply 2,4-D in spring and fall. Spray isolated plants with glyphosate or another properly registered herbicide.

Deciduous

Any plant that sheds all of its leaves at one time each year (usually in fall) is deciduous.

Deer Protection

With their soulful eyes and graceful gait, deer may be pleasant to watch, but they can make a garden ragged in no time by nipping off flower heads and nibbling tender leaves and new shoots. As wild plants dry out, deer spend more time looking for food in gardens on the fringes of suburbia. They develop browsing patterns, visiting tasty gardens regularly—most often in the evening. Fond of a wide array of flowering plants, especially roses, deer will eat foliage or fruit of nearly anything you grow for your table. For a list of plants deer usually ignore, see page 121.

Physical controls. Fencing is the most certain protection. On level ground, a 7-foot woven-wire fence will usually keep deer out, although some determined deer can jump even an 8-foot fence. A horizontal "outrigger" extension on a fence makes it harder for a deer to jump it. On a slope, you may need to erect a 10- to 11-foot fence to guard against deer jumping from higher ground. Because deer can jump high or jump wide—but not simultaneously—some gardeners have had success with a pair of parallel 5-foot fences, with a 5-foot-wide "no-deer's-land" between.

If you don't fancy a fortress garden, focus on individual plants (or areas). Put chicken-wire cages around young plants and cylinders of wire fencing around larger specimens. Cover raised beds with mesh, and use floating row covers (p. 596) on vegetables. It sometimes helps to keep a zealous (and vocal) watchdog in the yard, particularly during evening and nighttime hours.

Chemical controls. Commercial repellents can work if sprayed often enough to keep new growth covered and to replace what rain and watering wash away (though some repellents may make sticky, unsightly spots on flowers and foliage). Do not apply repellents to edible portions of plants unless approved by the label; some are not safe to eat. Some gardeners repel deer by hanging small cloth bags filled with blood meal among their plants; disadvantages are that blood meal attracts dogs and smells unpleasant, especially when wet.

Defoliation

The unnatural loss of a plant's leaves, usually to the detriment of the plant's health, is called defoliation. It may result from high winds that strip foliage away; intense heat (especially if accompanied by wind) that critically wilts leaves; drought; unusually early or late frosts that strike a plant still in active growth or just beginning growth; or severe damage by chemicals, insects, or diseases.

Dethatch

The process of removing dead stems (thatch) that build up beneath certain ground covers and lawn grasses is known as dethatching. It can be done by hand with a thatching rake or, in the case of lawns, with a gas-powered dethatcher, also called a vertical mower. It's usually performed in fall or early spring on cool-season lawns and in late spring for warm-season grasses. Followed up with fertilizer, the result is healthier, more vigorous growth.

Dieback

In dieback, a plant's stems die, beginning at the tips, for a part of their length. Causes are various: not enough water, nutrient deficiency, plant not adapted to climate in which it is growing, or severe insect, mite, or disease injury.

Diseases

Different kinds of organisms cause plant diseases. Most leaf, stem, and flower diseases result from bacteria, fungi, or viruses. The most prevalent soilborne diseases are caused by fungi.

Sometimes disease results from plants interacting with unfavorable environmental factors, such as air pollution, a deficiency or excess of nutrients or of sunlight, or the wrong climate (too hot, too cold, too dry, too wet). For information on symptoms and treatments of the most common nutrient deficiencies and excesses, see Chlorosis (p. 552) and Soil Salinity (p. 600), respectively. Exposure and climate preferences are spelled out for each plant listed in the Plant Encyclopedia. This discussion focuses on the various diseases that are caused by organisms.

Bacterial diseases. Bacteria are single-celled micro-organisms that are unable to manufacture their own food (as green plants do); those bacteria that cause plant diseases must obtain their nutrients from the host plants. ▶

D

Fungal diseases. Certain multicellular branching, threadlike organisms called fungi obtain their food parasitically from green plants, causing diseases in the process. Many fungi produce great numbers of tiny reproductive bodies called spores, which can be carried by wind or water from leaf to leaf and from plant to plant. Each spore, under the right conditions, will germinate and grow—producing new infections. Fungus diseases are among the most widespread of plant maladies, but many are controllable by good sanitation, planting resistant varieties, use of fungicides, and cultural practices.

Viral diseases. Ultramicroscopic viruses are capable of invading plant tissue and reproducing in it, usually at the expense of the host plant. Viruses may produce such symptoms as abnormalities in growth, color variegation of foliage, or "breaking" (color distortion) of blossoms.

In agriculture—especially among beans, citrus, sugar beets and cane, grapes, cucumbers, squash, potatoes, and tomatoes (to cite just a few)—virus-induced diseases are a serious threat because they affect vigor and productivity. In the home garden, a viral infection may or may not be detrimental. Undesirable viruses are those that cause an unattractive mottling on leaves or that stunt and yellow foliage; in some diseases, such as rose mosaic, the virus causes a striking foliage variegation but does not significantly reduce plant vigor. Some attractive plants—such as the various tulips that have bizarrely striped flowers and the variegated-leaf abutilon—owe their variegation to a virus.

There is no home cure at this time for a virus-infected plant, but you can reduce chances of a virus spreading to other plants in two ways. First, remove from your garden any plants that are severely stunted or mottled. Second, try to control the insects that carry viruses. Aphids are most efficient in spreading different kinds of viruses; leafhoppers and thrips can be vectors, too. And humans may spread viruses by vegetatively propagating virus-infected plants or by handling tobacco while working around plants (thereby spreading tobacco mosaic virus, which affects many plants in addition to tobacco).

DISEASE CONTROL

The first line of defense against plant diseases is prevention. Whenever possible, choose disease-resistant plants; make sure that planting locations and conditions don't encourage disease-producing organisms that are troublesome in your region.

Numerous packaged products are available for control of diseases. They can be categorized as preventatives (products that prevent diseases from occurring but are ineffective in controlling them once they are established), eradicants (materials that help control diseases—many simply protect new growth—once they are established), and systemics (materials that move inside the plant and act as preventatives, eradicants, or both). The controls described here are the ones most useful and commonly available. Several other products—generally less widely sold—are mentioned in the entries for the specific diseases they control.

The product descriptions that follow mention the common diseases each product controls, but these are usually just a few of the diseases listed on the product labels. (You may find a disease listed on a product label but not mentioned in these descriptions; that is because other products described for that disease usually are more effective.) You should also know that fungicide registrations change rapidly. Some products listed here may no longer be available or be labeled for the disease or plant mentioned. Check labels carefully.

Some products will control a disease on one plant but not on another; moreover, some products can do damage if applied to inappropriate plants. Read product labels carefully to be sure your plant is listed.

- **Captan:** Dust or wettable powder for prevention or eradication of damping off, leaf spots, and many other fungal diseases. Future registration limitations are possible.

- **Chlorothalonil (Daconil):** Multipurpose liquid fungicide for prevention of diseases on lawns, fruits, vegetables, and ornamentals.

- **Copper compounds:** A group of general-purpose fungicides and bactericides, most often used to prevent fireblight, peach leaf curl, and shot hole diseases.

- **Lime sulfur (calcium polysulfide):** Liquid preventative for various leaf spots, peach leaf curl, and powdery mildew. Often used as a dormant spray. Also controls some mites, scale insects, and thrips.

- **Sulfur:** Dust or wettable powder; one of the oldest fungicides. Used to prevent powdery mildew, scab, and rust.

- **Thiophanate-methyl:** Systemic, wettable powder effective against many plant diseases, including powdery mildew and black spot, of roses.

- **Triadimefon (Bayleton):** Wettable powder; systemic for prevention or eradication of powdery mildew, rust, and some lawn diseases; also effective against azalea petal blight.

- **Triforine (Funginex):** Liquid systemic for prevention and eradication of powdery mildew, rust, black spot, and a variety of other diseases. You must wear goggles and a face mask when using it.

Controls are listed alphabetically by generic name (name on the product label under "active ingredients") or common name; trade name (where different from generic name) appears in parentheses.

Divided Leaf

A leaf is said to be divided when it is separated into sections entirely or nearly to its stalk. In the first case, the sections are called leaflets; in the second, they are called lobes.

Dividing

The easiest way to propagate perennials, bulbs, and shrubs that form clumps of stems with rooted bases is by dividing. In fact, to keep these plants healthy and strong, it's necessary to divide them periodically. Each rooted segment or division is actually a plant in itself or is capable of becoming a new plant.

Division generally is done in autumn or early spring, when plants are dormant. In most climate zones, fall is the best time to divide perennials that bloom in spring or early summer, whereas early spring is better for those that blossom in late summer and autumn. But in the coldest zones, the spring-blooming perennials must be divided in early fall so that their roots will have a chance to grow before the coldest weather sets in.

To divide deciduous and semideciduous perennials, prune the foliage back to about 4 inches from the ground. With evergreen perennials, leave all young, healthy foliage, but remove all dead leaves. (See illustration, right.) Perennials that form a taproot and grow from a compact crown are best propagated by making stem cuttings (see Cuttings, p. 555) or by sowing seeds.

When decline in flower quantity and quality signals overcrowding of bulbs and bulblike plants (p. 550), let foliage ripen thoroughly before digging and separating the bulbs. Replant in well-prepared soil or store until the appropriate planting time.

Dormancy

The period when a plant's growth processes greatly slow down is called dormancy. It occurs in many plants with the coming of winter, as days grow shorter and temperatures drop. Dormancy can also occur during dry periods.

DIVIDING

Daylily

Shasta daisy

Iris

Dividing is an easy way to increase stock of many perennials and bulblike plants. Pull apart individual plants of clump-forming perennials (such as daylilies and Shasta daisies); break or cut apart separate plants of rhizomes (such as iris), some bulbs, and tuberous-rooted plants.

Dormant Spray

An insecticide or a fungicide applied to a plant during the season it is not putting on new growth is a dormant spray. Usually including, or composed only of, a dormant oil, a dormant spray is a very effective way to kill overwintering insects and disease organisms and reduce the necessity for multiple sprays during the growing season (see illustration at right).

Double Digging

A soil preparation approach, double digging helps to amend soil on the upper level and to break up soil on the lower level to allow roots to grow deeper. The classic procedure:

- Dig a trench one spade deep; set soil aside alongside trench.

- Dig down one spade's depth further in the same trench, mixing amendments with soil in lower level.

- Dig second trench by first; mix in amendments. Move amended soil to first trench.

- In second trench, dig one spade's depth more; mix in amendments.

- Continue to dig trenches in the same way.

Another, simpler method of double digging is shown in the illustration on page 560.

Double Flower

A double flower has a large number of petals that give the blossom an unusually full appearance. Many fruit trees with double flowers, including varieties of pomegranate, plum, and cherry, do not produce fruit and are commonly grown as ornamentals.

Drainage

Drainage refers to the movement of water through the soil in a plant's root area. When this happens quickly, the drainage is "good" or "fast," and the soil is "well drained"; when it happens slowly, the drainage is said to be "slow" or "bad," and the soil is "poorly drained." For plants to grow, water must pass through the soil. Plant roots need oxygen as well as water, and soil that remains saturated deprives roots of necessary oxygen. Fast drainage (water disappears from a planting hole in 10 minutes or less) is typical of sandy soils; slow drainage (water still remains in planting hole after several hours) is found in clay soils and where hardpan exists. Refer to Soils (p. 600) for more information on soil types and drainage.

Drip Line

The circle that could be drawn on the soil around a tree directly under the tips of its

SPRAYING DORMANT TREES

If diseases and insects have troubled your fruit or shade trees in the past, spray them while leafless (dormant). Use horticultural oil mixed with either lime sulfur or fixed copper. For complete coverage, spray branches (A), crotches (B), trunk (C), and ground within drip line (D).

D

outermost branches is called a drip line. Rainwater tends to drip from the tree at this point. The term is used in connection with feeding, watering, and grading around existing trees and shrubs.

Drought

Technically, a drought is a period of time during which a region gets less than what is considered normal precipitation. The word has been, and probably always will be, more appropriate in the East and Midwest than in the Far West.

In the Midwest and East, historically, every dry period has ended with the return of adequate rainfall. Such a period, with a beginning and an end, is a drought. But in the permanently arid West, the land is forever in a state of inadequate precipitation for local needs, so the midwestern and eastern sense of the word "drought"

E

SIMPLIFIED DOUBLE DIGGING

Remove spade's depth of soil; put it around sides. Spade soil amendments into next layer. Mix same kind of amendments into excavated soil as you replace it. Soil will be high at first.

as a temporary, abnormal condition is inappropriate in the West.

In heavily populated regions of the arid West, water is imported, usually over considerable distances, by pipelines and canals from reservoirs fed by rivers that are, themselves, fed by mountain streams. These populated areas depend on distant wintertime snowfall and rainfall for their supply of water. In years when precipitation is lower than normal and those reservoirs cannot provide adequate amounts of water, gardeners in irrigated arid areas must turn to a wide variety of water conservation approaches (p. 607). And as the West's population continues to grow, placing greater demands on limited water supplies, water conservation will become an everyday fact of life.

Drought Resistant, Drought Tolerant

Plants that can withstand long periods with little or no water, plants that have relatively low water requirements, or plants that are well adapted to the arid West are often described as drought resistant or drought tolerant. However, because water requirements vary greatly from plant to plant and from region to region (a plant that needs little water under cool coastal conditions may need a lot more in warmer inland areas), the phrases are often ambiguous and usually inappropriate. Soil conditions, exposure, degree of establishment, length of time without water, and other factors also affect a plant's water needs, its appearance, and its survival.

Dust

Dust defines a type of insecticide or fungicide—one so finely ground that it is dust—as well as its method of application. Applied in early morning when the air is still, the dust makes a large cloud, and the particles slowly settle as a thin, even coating over everything. The advantage of dusting over spraying is

convenience: no mixing, fast application, and easy cleanup. The disadvantage is that dust is difficult to apply to the undersides of the leaf surfaces.

Dutch Elm Disease

A devastating disease for decades confined to the East and Midwest, Dutch elm disease (abbreviated DED) spread slowly across the United States to reach the West in the early 1970s.

DED is spread primarily by the elm bark beetle, although it can also spread from infected trees to nearby healthy ones by natural root grafting. Normal transmission starts with beetle larvae that overwinter in dead and dying elm trees. When the young beetles emerge in spring, the sticky fungus spores adhere to their bodies; as the beetles migrate to healthy new elm growth to feed, they spread the fungus. The fungus spores begin to grow in feeding wounds, and the fungus moves through the water-conducting system of the tree. The first symptom of infection is usually wilted foliage (because water conductivity is interrupted); then leaves turn yellow and fall, and the tree dies.

DED is incurable at present, but sometimes its progress can be slowed. Removal of trees showing infection may help save other trees. (Do not save wood from infected trees.) If you have an elm you suspect has DED, call your county agricultural agent and report the symptoms. The agent should then advise you on the best course of action to take.

Earwigs

Gardeners in almost all areas may have occasional problems with earwigs. But chemical controls are necessary only in heavy infestations.

Earwigs will eat almost any soft materials. One common food is insects—such as aphids—which means that earwigs can be an important natural control of plant pests. Unfortunately, earwigs also feed on soft parts of plants, such as flower petals and corn silks. A large earwig population can significantly damage desirable plants.

Earwigs hide during the day but are active at night. When dawn comes, they scurry back into tight, cozy places. You can trap earwigs by providing the type of tight-fitting, moist shelter in which they like to spend the day. At night, put moistened rolled-up newspapers, rolls of corrugated cardboard, or short sections of garden hose on the ground; in the morning, dispose of the accumulated insects. You can also trap earwigs in a short cat food or tuna fish can filled with ½ inch of vegetable oil. Place several cans around the yard. Dispose of them as they fill.

Or you can buy earwig bait, which usually contains propoxur or carbaryl as the killing ingredient, and spread it around nonedible plants. If the lure in the bait is fish oil, however, it can also attract pets, which may be harmed by the active ingredient.

Epiphyte

Epiphytes grow on another plant for support but receive no nourishment from the host plant. Familiar examples of these plants are cattleya orchids and staghorn ferns. Epiphytes are often mistakenly called parasites; true parasites steal nourishment from the host.

Erosion Control

Many types of plants, certain landscape fabrics, and heavy mulches like straw can be used alone or in combination to prevent the erosion of soil by heavy rains or fast-moving water. When dealing with steep construction cuts or burned hillsides, it's best to get expert help. Your local Cooperative Extension Office or Natural Resource Conservation Service office can offer advice or recommend a soil engineer.

Espalier

A tree or shrub trained so that its branches grow in a flat pattern—against a wall or fence, on a trellis, along horizontal wires—an espalier may be formal and geometric or informal. The illustration below shows several espalier forms. For plants that espalier well, see page 104.

Established

A plant that is firmly rooted and producing a good growth of leaves is said to be established. Remember that an established plant needs time to re-establish itself after you transplant it.

Evapotranspiration

Abbreviated ET, evapotranspiration is the amount of water that transpires through a plant's leaves combined with the amount that evaporates from the soil in which the plant is growing. Measured in inches, ET can be used as a guideline for how much water a specific type of plant needs per day, per week, or per year. See its application for Lawns (p. 569).

Evergreen

An evergreen plant never loses all its leaves at one time. See also Broad-Leafed (p. 548) and Conifer (p. 554).

Eye

An undeveloped growth bud, an eye will ultimately produce a new plant or new growth. The eyes on a potato will, when planted, produce new potato plants. "Eye" is synonymous with one definition of Bud (p. 548).

Family. See Plant Classification   p. 583

Female Plant

A plant that produces fruit or seed but does not produce pollen is called a female plant.

Fertilize

In popular usage, fertilize has two definitions. To fertilize a flower is to apply pollen (the male element) to the flower's pistil (the female element) for the purpose of setting seed. (See Pollination, p. 589.) To fertilize a plant is to apply nutrients (plant food, usually referred to as fertilizer).

For fertilizer recommendations for specific plant types, see the appropriate entry in the Plant Encyclopedia.

Fertilizers

A visit to a nursery may reveal a bewildering selection of fertilizers for a variety of specified uses and with differing formulas. There are granular types packaged in cartons and sacks and liquid ones in bottles. An understanding of the basic fertilizer types will clear the confusion and help you select a product that meets your plants' needs.

The first distinction to draw is between dry and liquid forms. There are further differences between complete, simple, special-purpose, and organic fertilizers and between controlled-release, tablet, and combination products. The illustrations on pages 562 and 563 show several application methods.

Dry fertilizers. The majority of fertilizers sold are dry. You sprinkle or spread them onto a lawn; sprinkle them onto the soil around plants and scratch, rake, or dig them in; or apply them in subsurface strips. Dissolving when they contact water, the dry granules begin their fertilizing action quickly. But, depending on the fertilizer, they can last for several months.

Liquid fertilizers. Although the most widely sold fertilizers are the solid types, liquid fertilizers have certain attributes that recommend their use:

■ They are easy to use, especially on container plants.

■ There is little risk of burning a plant as long as you follow label directions for dilution.

■ The nutrients are available to the roots immediately.

Liquids are less practical than solids for large-scale use because they cost more and must be reapplied more often (their nutrients in solution leach through the root zone more rapidly).

Available in a variety of different formulations, liquid fertilizers include complete formulas and special types that offer just one or two of the major nutrients. All are made to be diluted with water: some are concentrated liquids; others are powder or pellets. Some liquid fertilizers are sold in ready-to-use, hose-end sprayers. Formulations for lawns may include herbicides for weed control.

Growers of container plants often use liquid fertilizers at half the strength and twice the frequency recommended so that plants receive a steadier supply of nutrients.

Foliar fertilizers. Some nutrients, particularly nitrogen in urea form and micronutrients (see Nutrients, Basic, p. 577), can be absorbed quickly through plant leaves. Many liquid or water-soluble fertilizers include rates for foliar feeding on their labels. In general, actively growing plants show the best response. But remember, foliar feeding is a quick fix and not a substitute for soil feeding. To avoid burning plant leaves, first make sure plants are well watered; don't apply foliar fertilizers if temperatures will rise above 85°F/29°C.

Complete fertilizers. Any fertilizer that contains all three of the primary nutrient elements—nitrogen (N), phosphorus (P), and potassium (K)—is called a complete fertilizer. Many fertilizer manufacturers put their product's N, P, and K percentages on the label, right under the product name, in big numbers—for example, 10-8-6. Without looking at the fine print under Guaranteed Analysis (always listed somewhere on a fertilizer label), you know that the fertilizer contains 10 percent total nitrogen, 8 percent phosphate (P_2O_5), and 6 percent potash (K_2O). See illustration on page 563.

F

POPULAR ESPALIER PATTERNS

Espalier training can take a number of different forms. Several common patterns are shown.

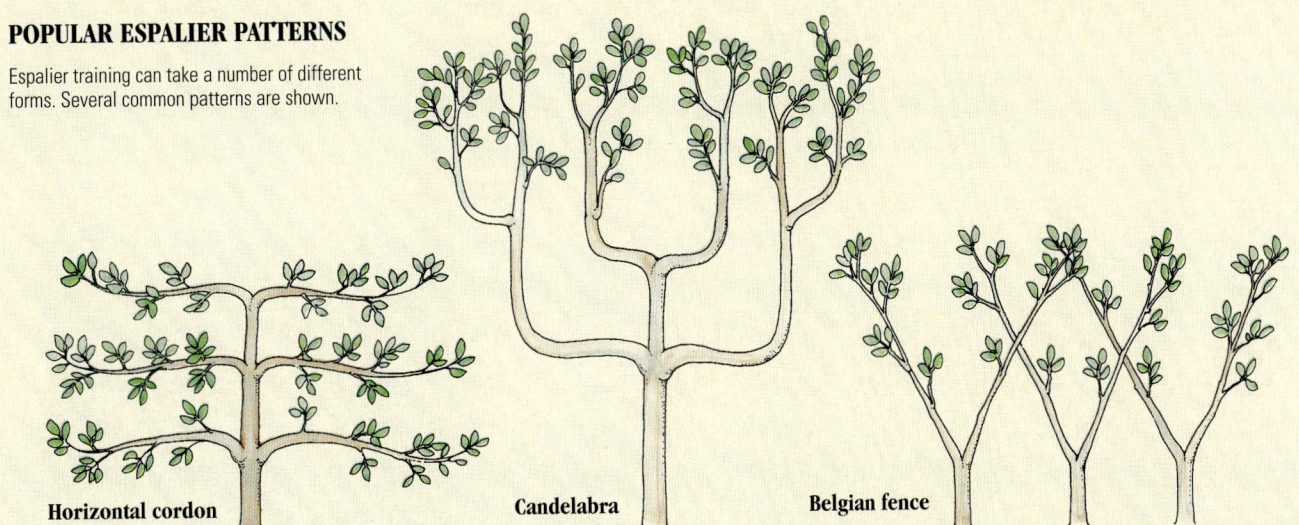

Horizontal cordon   Candelabra   Belgian fence

THREE WAYS TO FERTILIZE TREES

Surface feeding. In sandy soil or wet climates, broadcast granular fertilizer on the surface, by hand or using a spreader. Soak it in thoroughly with a sprinkler.

Root plug. With a soil-sampling tube or pipe, make 6- to 12-inch-deep holes 2 to 3 feet apart. Pour granular fertilizer into holes, fill with soil, and water well.

Root feeder. Insert a root feeder with a fertilizer tablet attached 6 to 12 inches deep every 4 to 6 feet; turn feeder on for about 5 minutes in each hole.

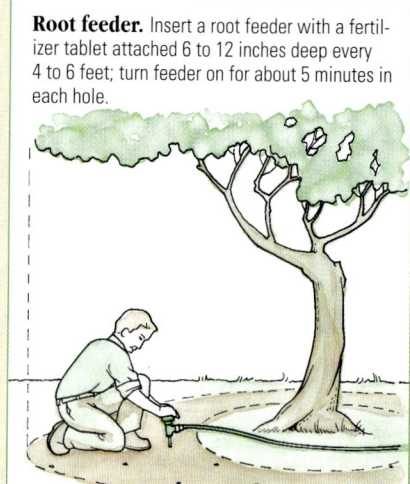

There are fertilizers with many different nutrient ratios on the market. Even when the percentages are the same on two different products, the formula by which one manufacturer arrives at its ratio can differ from others. (See Nutrients, Basic, p. 577.) The higher the numbers in the analysis, the stronger or more concentrated the fertilizer is (a 22-6-4 formula contains twice as much nitrogen as does an 11-6-4 fertilizer). And the higher the concentration (of N especially), the less you apply at one time.

Complete fertilizers are most useful when you work them into the soil where active roots can take up the phosphorus and potassium. If you want only the benefits of nitrogen, choose a nitrogen-only simple fertilizer.

Simple fertilizers. Simple fertilizers contain just one of the three major nutrients. Most familiar are the nitrogen-only types, such as ammonium sulfate (21-0-0), but you can find phosphorus-only and potassium-only fertilizers as well. Falling between the two extremes are "incomplete" types that contain two of the three major elements: N and P, N and K, or P and K.

Special-purpose fertilizers. Some packaged fertilizers are formulated for specific types of plants—"camellia food," "rhododendron and azalea food," and "rose food," for example. The camellia and rhododendron-azalea fertilizers belong to an old, established group, the acid fertilizers. Some fertilizers packaged for specific plants are done so for marketing purposes alone and are not necessarily based on the needs of that plant (compare, for example, the NPK ratios of three different brands of "tomato food").

All chemical fertilizers except calcium nitrate lower the pH of soil by producing acids as they decompose. Those that are especially acid producing are labeled "acid fertilizers" and are useful on acid-loving plants. They also are good for general-purpose fertilizing in alkaline-soil regions, to reduce alkalinity.

Organic fertilizers. The word "organic" simply means that the nutrients contained in the product are derived solely from the remains, part of the remains, or a by-product of a once-living organism. Cottonseed meal, blood meal, bonemeal, hoof-and-horn meal, and manures are examples of organic fertilizers. (Urea is a synthetic organic fertilizer—an organic-like substance manufactured from inorganic materials.) Most of these products packaged as fertilizers will have their NPK ratios stated on the package labels. Usually, an organic fertilizer is high in just one of the three major nutrients and low in the other two, although some are chemically fortified with the other nutrients. In general, the organics release their nutrients over a fairly long period. The potential drawback is that they may not release enough of their principal nutrient at a time to give the plant what it needs for best growth. Because they depend on soil organisms to release the nutrients, most organic fertilizers are effective only when the soil is moist and warm enough for the soil organisms to be active.

Although manure is a complete organic fertilizer, it is low in N, P, and K. Nutrient content

THREE WAYS TO FERTILIZE VEGETABLE TRANSPLANTS

Work dry fertilizer into soil with spading fork before planting.

Side-dress with narrow bands of dry fertilizer 5 to 6 inches from plants.

Liquid-feed in watering basins. (This is the most precise way to apply.)

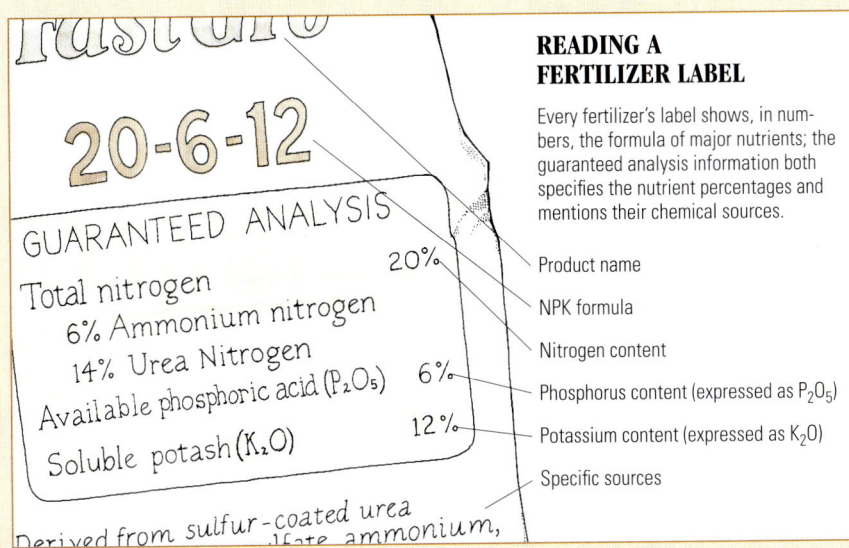

READING A FERTILIZER LABEL

Every fertilizer's label shows, in numbers, the formula of major nutrients; the guaranteed analysis information both specifies the nutrient percentages and mentions their chemical sources.

- Product name
- NPK formula
- Nitrogen content
- Phosphorus content (expressed as P_2O_5)
- Potassium content (expressed as K_2O)
- Specific sources

varies according to the animal species and its diet, but an NPK ratio of 1-1-1 is typical. Manures are best used as mulches or as soil conditioners, but only after they have been aged or composted. Some fresh manures have a high salt content, which will burn plants.

Controlled-release fertilizers. The beadlike granules of controlled-release fertilizers are balls of complete fertilizer coated with resin, sulfur, or another permeable substance. When the granules are moistened, as in normal watering, some of the fertilizer diffuses through its coating into the surrounding soil—a little bit with each watering—until the encapsulated fertilizer is used up. Some products are effective for 3 to 4 months; others, for 8 or more months. Scratch or dig the pellets into the soil so that they are covered. These are particularly useful for fertilizing container plants, which need frequent nutrient replenishment due to leaching from frequent watering.

Sticks, stakes, and tablets. Some fertilizers are compressed into hard cylinders or tablets; you push or hammer the sticks or stakes into the soil or drop the tablets into holes. Dissolving slowly in the presence of water, they yield nutrients gradually, sometimes for a year or more. These products are convenient (but expensive) for getting phosphorus and potassium to the regions of active root growth of established shrubs and trees.

Combination products. You can buy fertilizers combined with insecticides (chiefly for roses) or with weed killers, fungicides, or moss killers (all for lawns). These products are appropriate if you need the extra ingredient every time you fertilize; if not, it is more economical to buy it separately. Herbicides included in some combination products can damage plants whose roots are growing into areas where the product is applied. Read labels carefully.

Fire, Landscaping for

Wildfires are common in many parts of the United States, especially during periods of drought and in foothill and mountainous areas of the arid West. Unfortunately, many of these areas are heavily populated, and wildfires frequently result in loss of life and property. Although *everything* burns in a high-intensity fire, you can reduce the chances of fire destroying your home. Experts recommend the following steps:

- **Maintain a clear space around your home.** Ideally, the first 30 feet from your house should be clear of vegetation, but this is often not possible. If planted, it should be with plants that are not highly flammable (most are low-growing ground covers) and watered regularly to maintain a high moisture content. From 30 to 70 feet, plant low-fuel-

volume herbaceous perennials, such as gazania, poppy, and common yarrow. Keep watered and green all year, or let dry out and cut back. The next 30 feet should be free of highly combustible plants and kept pruned to reduce the buildup of dead wood.

- **Trim trees and shrubs near your house.** Trim tree limbs to 20 feet or more above the ground. Cut branches back to 15 to 20 feet from the house. Thin crowns of clustered trees, keeping trees 10 feet apart. Along the driveway, clear overhanging tree branches and prune bushy shrubs for fire-truck access.

- **Reduce fuel load.** Prune out all dead branches and remove dead plants. Cut grasses to about 4 inches after they turn brown. Cut back woody native chaparral yearly. Clear leaf litter from ground, rooftops, and gutters.

- **Select and position plants wisely.** Plants should be chosen not only for their low growth habit, low fuel volume, and high moisture content, but also for their aridity tolerance, deep-rooting habit, and compatibility with other plants in your garden and your native environment. Your local nursery staff or Cooperative Extension Office can help you select plants. Arrange plants in islands and avoid creating a fire ladder, where flames can easily jump from plant to plant to house.

- **Use fire-resistant building materials.** Check local codes for appropriate roofing materials. Consider using wood substitutes for fences and decks.

Fireblight

Troublesome in all parts of the United States, fireblight affects only the plants in the pome tribe of the rose family. When a flowering shoot of apple, cotoneaster, crabapple, hawthorn, pear, pyracantha, or quince dies suddenly and looks as though it has been scorched by fire (see photograph, p. 592), fireblight probably is the culprit.

The bacteria that cause fireblight survive in blighted twigs and cankers. In early spring—especially during moist weather, when temperatures are above 65°F/16°C—the bacteria are spread to open blossoms by rain and insects. Once in the blossoms, they are spread to other flowers by honeybees. Infection progresses from the blossoms down the shoots into the larger limbs, where dark, sunken cankers form. Bacteria also can enter a plant through any fresh wound in the foliage.

Controls. Wherever fireblight is a persistent problem, avoid growing susceptible plants, or plant resistant varieties (see Malus, p. 387; Pyrus, p. 459). If you grow susceptible plants,

BROADCASTING FERTILIZER BY HAND

Fill a bucket with the amount of granular fertilizer recommended on the package. Wearing gloves, distribute this in even bands as you walk slowly forward, using an underhand, sweeping toss; minimize overlap (too much fertilizer can burn).

take regular control measures. Commercial growers protect blossoms from infection by spraying at 4- or 5-day intervals during the flowering season with a fixed copper-based spray, but that is not practical for most gardeners.

Instead, control the bacteria once it has appeared by pruning out and burning the diseased twigs and branches as soon as you see them. Make cuts at least 10–12 inches below blighted tissue. Disinfect pruning shears between cuts with bleach or denatured alcohol. Avoid excess fertilizing with nitrogen.

Flat

A shallow box or tray used to start cuttings or seedlings is called a flat.

Flea Beetles

These tiny, oval jumping insects vary in color with the species, but most types are black, shiny bronze, or dark blue (see photograph, p. 591). Except for a species with a particular fondness for corn, all have an appetite for a broad range of edible plants, particularly seedlings. Dichondra lawns are also favorite feeding grounds.

Adult flea beetles riddle leaves with small holes, leaving the foliage dried and desiccated. Leaves often drop. Seedlings are most susceptible. The small white grubs feed on plant roots, leaving brown streaks in root crops such as potatoes.

Flea beetles are attracted to white; you can check for their presence by putting a white card or piece of paper among the plants or on the lawn. If they're there, they'll jump onto the white surface.

To control flea beetles, keep the garden clean and free of plant debris that might serve as overwintering sites. Till the soil in fall to expose grubs. Plant vigorous seedlings and cover vegetables with floating row covers to exclude adults. Parasitic nematodes are effective against grubs. Pyrethrum, rotenone, and sabadilla are useful botanical sprays. Diazinon and chlorpyrifos are useful chemical controls (see Pest Management, p. 580).

Foliar Fertilizer

A foliar fertilizer is one applied in liquid form to a plant's foliage in a fine spray. The nutrients it contains are absorbed through the plant's leaves. See Fertilizers (p. 561).

Forcing

Forcing is the process of hastening a plant along to maturity or a marketable state or of growing a plant to the flowering or fruiting stage out of its normal season. This is usually done by growing it in a greenhouse, where temperature, humidity, and light can be controlled.

Formal

The term "formal" means regular, rigid, and geometric. In gardening, it is variously applied to flowers form, methods of training, and styles of garden design. A formal double flower, as in some camellias, consists of layers of regularly overlapping petals. Examples of formal plant training are rigidly and geometrically structured espaliers (p. 561) and evenly clipped hedges. Formal gardens are those laid out in precise geometric patterns.

Frond

In the strictest sense, fronds are the foliage of ferns. Often, however, the word is also applied to the leaves of palms and is even used to designate any foliage that looks fernlike.

Frost

The most common type of frost occurs when low temperatures and humidity combined with clear, still nights cause surfaces (such as leaves or ground) to cool faster than the surrounding air, causing moisture to condense and freeze. Depending on the species of plant, the time of year, and the condition of the plant, a frost may or may not damage it. Because plants are actively growing in early fall and late spring, frosts at these times tend to be most damaging.

Frost and Freeze Protection

Virtually no place in the country is completely free from the threat of frost. From the dip below freezing that may hit San Diego or Miami once or twice in a decade to the occasional Big Freeze that sweeps down on the Deep South, these periodic deviations from the norm can wreak havoc on a landscape. Established plants that reach the limit of their cold tolerance in a particular zone's typical winter weather may suffer extensive damage—or they may die. Fortunately, there are ways to prepare for the occasional big chill and avert potential disaster in your garden. For information on protecting vegetables, see Extending Your Harvest, page 606.

Know your plants. Use trees, screen and hedge plants, and shrubs that are hardy enough for the extremes of your climate zone. Use the chancy or tender plants as fillers, as summertime display plants, in borders, or in areas of secondary interest. Locate these plants in sheltered sites, or grow them in containers and move them to sheltered sites when the weather turns cold.

Know your garden. Learn your garden's microclimates: discover which areas are warm and which are cool. Most dangerous for marginally hardy plants (and all tender vegetation) are stretches of open ground exposed to the air on all sides, particularly to the north. Hollows and low, enclosed areas that catch cold air as it sinks and hold it motionless also are poor choices. For iffy plants, the safest areas are under overhanging eaves (the best protection), lath structures, or branches of evergreen trees. Slopes from which cold air drains freely are safer than hollows and valley or canyon floors.

South-facing walls absorb heat during the day and radiate it at night, warming nearby plants. The warmest location of all is a south-facing wall with an overhang (see illustration). It gives maximum protection against frost, and in coolsummer/mild-winter climates, it supplies the warmth needed to stimulate buds, blossoms, and fruit of heat-loving plants such as bougainvillea, hibiscus, fig, and evergreen magnolia.

Condition plants and soil for frosts. Feed and water while plants are growing fastest, in late spring and early summer. To discourage production of new growth that would not have time to mature before cold weather hits, taper off nitrogen feeding in late summer. Actively growing plants are more susceptible to cold than are dormant or semidormant plants. Reducing water helps harden growth, but soil around plants should be moist at the onset of the frost season; moist soil holds and releases more heat than dry soil does.

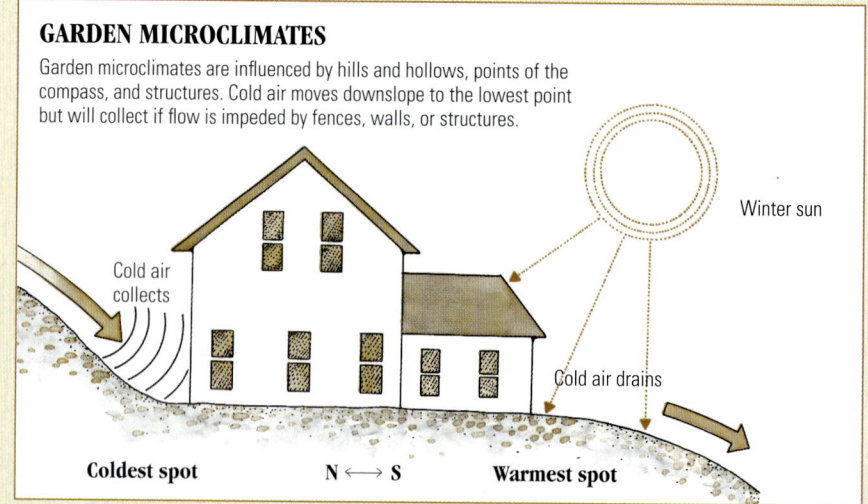

GARDEN MICROCLIMATES

Garden microclimates are influenced by hills and hollows, points of the compass, and structures. Cold air moves downslope to the lowest point but will collect if flow is impeded by fences, walls, or structures.

Winter sun

Cold air collects

Cold air drains

Coldest spot   N ⟷ S   Warmest spot

Some hardy plants have early blossoms that are damaged by spring frosts. Try to delay bloom of deciduous magnolias and some early rhododendrons beyond the time of heavy frosts by planting them with a north exposure or in the shade of high-branching deciduous trees.

Be especially watchful for frosts early in fall or in spring after growth is under way. These are much more damaging than frosts that occur while plants are semidormant or dormant. The warning signs are still air (tree branches motionless, smoke going straight up); absence of cloud cover (stars easily visible, very bright); low humidity (windshields and grass dry); and low temperature (45°F/7°C or less at 10 P.M.). If you notice these danger signs at bedtime, move any at-risk container plants under a porch roof or eaves or into a garage. Shelter any such plants that are in the ground: use burlap or plastic film—even evergreen boughs will help—secured over frames or stakes so that the covering material does not touch the plant. (Freezing is likely where the material touches foliage.) Remove coverings during the daytime.

After a frost. If plants have been damaged by frost, don't hurry to prune them. Premature trimming may stimulate new, tender growth that will be nipped by later frosts. And you may mistake still-alive growth for dead. Wait until new growth begins in spring; then remove only wood that is clearly dead.

Fungicide

Any material applied to plants to control fungus diseases is called a fungicide. See Diseases (p. 557).

Galls

Galls are growths on plant leaves and stems (see photograph, p. 590). Cause is usually abnormal cell growth stimulated by sucking insects like aphids or reactions to fungal, bacterial, or viral infections. Most leaf galls are harmless, although they may be unsightly. Galls on branches may be pruned off if they occur on smaller limbs. Large galls may be better left in place; pruning them out may harm the plant.

Genus. See Plant Classification   p. 583

Geranium (Tobacco) Budworm, Corn Earworm

The geranium budworm (properly, the tobacco budworm) is a first-rank garden pest in California and has appeared in damaging numbers in some mountain regions and mild-winter areas outside California. It is closely related to the corn earworm, which causes the brown mush atop ears of corn. Both are larvae of stout-bodied, dull-colored, night-flying moths.

GERMINATION OF A SEED

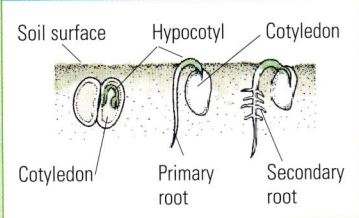

When conditions such as moisture, heat, and light are just right, the seed germinates.

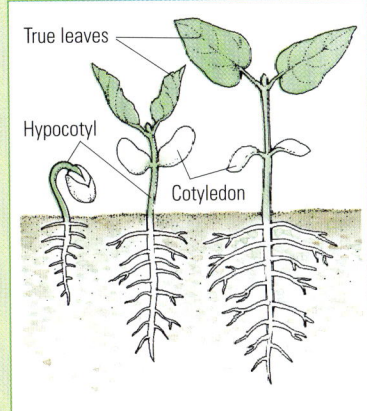

Some familiar plants—grasses, corn, orchids, lilies—have only one cotyledon and are called monocots. Plants with two cotyledons are called dicots.

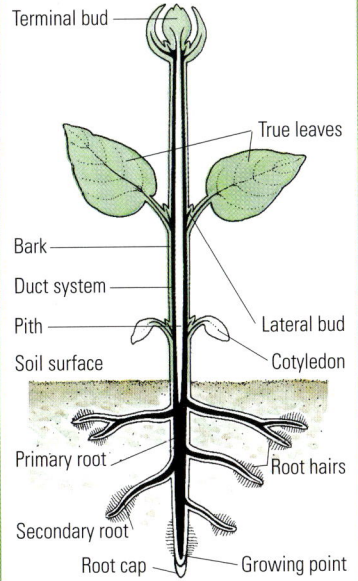

Germinating seed has primary root and cotyledons. Cotyledons sustain plant until true leaves and secondary roots appear.

The typical geranium budworm lives through the winter as a pupa in the soil. Then, in late April or May, a mature gray moth emerges and lays eggs on geranium (or rose or petunia) buds—one egg per bud. From the egg hatches a very small worm, which enters and feeds on the bud. As the worm grows, it consumes the bud and moves on to the rest of the plant, taking on the color of the plant tissue it eats. Once you see a hole in a bud, pick the bud, squash it, and discard it; this may destroy the young worm, which already will have damaged the potential blossom. For heavy infestations—where worms have outgrown the protective covering of flower buds—spray with *Bacillus thuringiensis,* pyrethrins, carbaryl, or acephate. Repeat weekly as needed. For ways to control corn earworm, see Corn (p. 261).

Germination

The sprouting of a seed is called germination. The process is explained in the illustration.

Girdling

The choking of a branch by a wire, rope, or other inflexible material, girdling occurs most often in woody plants that have been tightly tied to a stake or support. As the tied limb increases in girth, the tie fails to expand in diameter and cuts off supplies of nutrients and water to the part of the plant above the tie. If girdling goes unnoticed, the part of the plant above the constriction will die. The word "girdling" also applies to pest damage or to an encircling cut made through the bark of a trunk or branch to improve fruiting.

Gopher. See Pocket Gophers   p. 589

Grafting

Although many different grafting methods have been devised, all involve uniting a short length of stem—the scion—with a stock, which supplies the roots. The stock plant may be either a pencil-slim seedling to be grafted near ground level or an old fruit tree to be grafted at the top of its trunk or on its major limbs. Cleft grafting (see illustration, p. 566) is popular for converting old fruit and nut trees to new varieties. It is usually done to deciduous plants when they are dormant during winter.

With any grafting, it is crucial to align scion cambium with stock cambium. When that is done, the two cambiums will unite, the cuts will callus over, and the scion will be ready to grow. Use a very sharp knife to make all cuts; the cleaner the cuts, the better the chance for a successful union. When the operation is completed, cover the union with some sort of sealing agent to keep air from getting to the area.

G

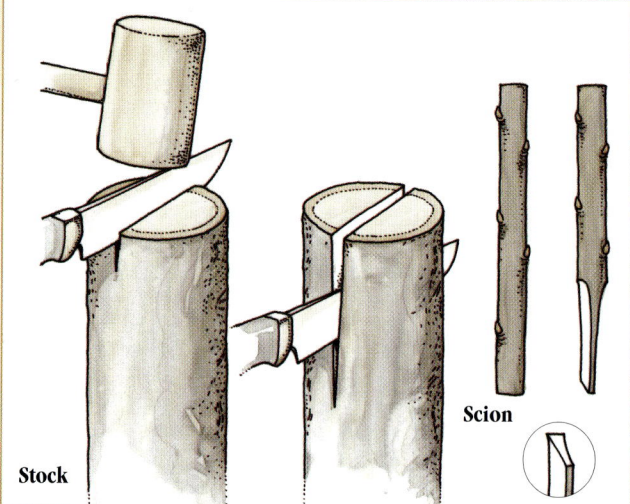

Stock

Scion

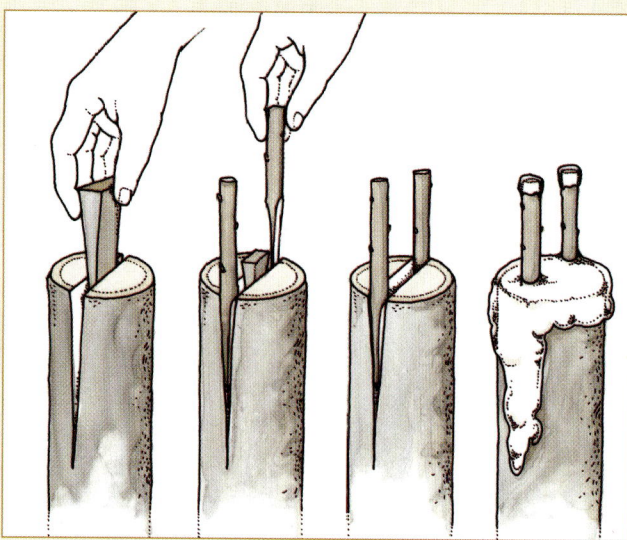

CLEFT GRAFTING

1 Prepare stock by splitting it several inches through a smooth, straight-grained section (so the split will be even). Shape one end of the scion into a long, gradually tapering wedge; outside edge of wedge should be slightly thicker than the inside (as shown in cross-section diagram).

2 Use a wedge to hold open the split in the stock while you work. Insert the scion (or two, as illustrated) into the stock, carefully placed so that cambium layers of stock and scions match. After the scions are properly placed, cover the entire union with grafting wax.

Grasshoppers

There are many different kinds, shapes, and sizes of grasshoppers. During their periodic outbreaks, grasshoppers can do devastating damage, especially in hot-summer areas. By preference, they lay their eggs in dry, undisturbed areas, such as in empty lots, but they also will lay eggs in gardens.

Eggs begin hatching from March to early June, depending on temperature and climate. Newly hatched nymphs resemble adults but are smaller and lack wings; these nymphs feed voraciously, sometimes stripping entire areas bare. When they mature and develop wings, they fly out and find new feeding areas.

Controls. When you are cultivating in fall, winter, and early spring, watch for and destroy egg clusters, which contain up to 75 cream or yellow rice-shaped eggs. In spring and early summer, while grasshoppers are still young and wingless, they are most vulnerable to chemicals and baits. Use malathion, diazinon, acephate, carbaryl, chlorpyrifos, or bran-and-carbaryl bait. Grasshoppers roost at night in hedges, tall weeds, and shrubs. Observe their evening behavior to locate roosting sites, then spray in these areas after dark.

Your best defense against large numbers of grasshoppers may be to protect desirable plants with floating row covers (p. 596) or netting.

In summer, when grasshoppers are mature and less vulnerable to chemicals, hand-pick them in early morning.

The disease-producing organism *Nosema locustae* causes grasshoppers to produce fewer eggs. Over large areas—on a ranch, for example—applying this commercially packaged material can help reduce grasshopper problems in later years.

Greenhouses

The ultimate in climate modification is a greenhouse. In such a structure, of glass or plastic, you can control temperature, humidity, and day length. Greenhouses are useful for:

- Wintering plants that are too tender for the normal outdoor winter low temperatures

- Starting seeds of annuals and vegetables early so that plants can be set out in the garden as soon as weather permits

- Starting cuttings and seeds that require the growth stimuli a greenhouse can provide

- Raising vegetables and flowers out of season (particularly when outside conditions are too cold), or maturing them earlier than would be normal if they were planted outdoors

- Growing specialty plants (orchids and tropical plants, for example) that cannot be grown outdoors because temperature or humidity or both are unfavorable

A greenhouse may be a simple lean-to constructed of plastic, a small bay window attachment on a house window, or a more elaborate separate structure with precise controls for regulation of heat, humidity, ventilation, and water.

Ground Bark

The bark of trees, ground up or shredded for use as a mulch, ground or path cover, or soil amendment, is known as ground bark. It may have other names in some areas.

Ground Covers

Gardeners select ground covers to blanket a prescribed area of soil and create a uniform appearance. The area may be just a 4- by 4-foot patch beneath a tree or it may run to an acre or more. The best-known ground cover is, of course, grass; you'll find information on choosing lawn grasses beginning on page 569. Other ground covers include perennials, shrubs, and vines—particular types that produce a relatively even surface (which may be as low as turf or as tall as 3 feet). Some matlike plants can be walked upon, although none will take the amount of foot traffic a lawn will tolerate.

Choosing a ground cover. Is the ground you want to cover level or sloping, sunny or shady, small or large in extent? Do you want a cover that will act as a barrier, or do you want to be able to walk across it? Will the ground cover have the space all to itself, or will it flow around shrubs, landscape boulders, or trees? And what about appearance: Do you prefer foliage only or green punctuated by colorful flowers or fruits? Answers to these questions will help you select the ground cover you need. Consider also the relationships that will exist between the ground cover and the adjacent landscape; take into account foliage textures and colors, as discussed in Selecting Shrubs (p. 597). Use the lists beginning on page 149 as a guide to more than 100 of the most popular ground covers.

General guidelines for planting and care of ground covers depend on whether the plants are perennials, shrubs, or vines. Each group has special requirements.

Planting and care of perennials. Many perennial ground covers root as they spread, in time forming dense, interlacing carpets; examples are *Vinca minor* and *Ajuga reptans.* Others spread much more slowly as they increase from clumps (*Liriope, Convallaria majalis*). Still another sort behaves more as a nonwoody shrub does, sending spreading branches out from the plant's base (*Nepeta faassenii, Iberis sempervirens*).

For all perennial ground covers, prepare the soil as recommended for sowing seeds (p. 584). Perennials that root as they spread may be sold in flats of rooted cuttings or in packs of small plants; those that spread from clumps generally appear in individual small pots or in 1-gallon containers. Spacing depends on the spread of the mature plant (see Plant Encyclopedia). Mulch plantings to conserve moisture, suppress weeds, and present a neat appearance while young plants develop. As plantings mature, some may need periodic shearing or light cutting back for neatness.

Planting and care of shrubs. Among the low-growing shrubs used for ground covers, you'll find three types: those that send out horizontal branches from a central point; those that begin at a central point but root from branches as they spread; and those—typified by *Hypericum calycinum*—that increase their territory by underground runners. Plants are sold in 1-gallon cans, small pots, or flats of rooted cuttings. Spacing depends on the ultimate spread of the plant (see Plant Encyclopedia). It typically ranges from 6 to 12 inches to more than 3 feet. If you plant rooted cuttings or plants from small pots, prepare the soil as directed for sowing seeds (p. 584); for 1-gallon container plants, follow the instructions for Plants in Containers (p. 587) under Planting Techniques: Trees and Shrubs. Apply mulch. As plantings mature, you may have to head back branches that grow above the desired foliage surface or that spread too far; you may also need to restrict the spread of those that increase by underground runners.

Planting and care of vines. Among vines used as ground covers are some that spread by rooting branches, such as ivy and euonymus, but most spread far and wide by extending their branches from a central point. Those vines that root as they spread may be sold in flats as rooted cuttings; most vines, however, are available in 1-gallon (or larger) containers. Planting and mulching directions are the same as for shrubs (above). As plants grow, you may need to do some untangling, thinning, or directing of growth to achieve even coverage. Mature plants may call for periodic heading back or shearing to maintain evenness and limit spread.

Growing Season

Specifically, the number of days between the average date of the last killing frost in spring and the average date of the first killing frost in fall is called the growing season. Used in general terms, the phrase also describes the period of time a plant is actively growing and not dormant.

Gummosis and Cankers

Gummosis (see photograph, p. 590) and canker are terms used to describe various bacterial or fungal diseases that usually cause oozing, sunken, woundlike lesions on the trunks or limbs of trees and shrubs, usually fruit trees. If the disease is serious enough, limbs above the lesions grow poorly, wilt, and may die.

Gummosis and cankers often start in wounds (including borer entry holes—see p. 548) or mechanical injuries (including pruning cuts) to the plant. In some cases, as with citrus, they can also be caused by overwatering, or by the tree trunk's being hit by sprinklers and kept overly wet. Using protective tree wraps or painting trunks of young trees white to prevent sunburn (see p. 604) will help prevent the diseases. So will good watering practices and keeping the plant as healthy as possible. Avoid wounding plants unnecessarily.

If healthy, many plants will naturally seal off cankers, preventing them from spreading. If the cankers occur in smaller limbs, prune out the limb well below the canker. Sterilize pruning shears with a 5 percent bleach solution between cuts. Larger cankers can often be cut out, but if they are too large, you may kill the plant by using this method. If you suspect that borers are present, take appropriate measures to control them (see page 548).

Consult your Cooperative Extension Office for specific chemical treatments to control cankers or gummosis.

Gypsum. See Soil Amendments, Inorganic p. 598

PLANTING AND CARE OF GROUND COVERS ON SLOPES

Sloping land frequently is prime territory for ground-cover planting: it is too steep to mow or to cultivate easily, and it is prone to erosion in the rainy season.

Planting technique. On a gentle slope, follow general Planting Techniques for the plant type, starting on page 584. On more steeply sloping land, however, the simplest method is to create a terrace for each plant, as shown in the illustration. These terraces create individual watering basins, but the high planting keeps the crowns of the plants from becoming saturated during waterings or buried if soil gradually washes downslope into the basin.

Care and training. Applying water is the most important aspect of care, at least when plants are young and becoming established. For sloping land, a drip irrigation setup (p. 610) provides the most thorough watering of each plant while minimizing or eliminating problems with water runoff or soil erosion that can result from watering with sprinklers.

After the ground cover is planted and watered in and a drip system is in place, mulch the entire area.

If you have planted vining plants to cover a bare slope, you may need to periodically untangle the growing stems and, more important at first, train some stems to grow upslope to achieve faster cover. To pin stems in place, use short lengths of wire bent into a U like a croquet wicket.

PLANTING ON A SLOPE

On a steep slope, set out plants on individual terraces with crowns high and watering basins behind the plants.

Harden Off

Hardening off is the process of adapting a plant that has been grown in a greenhouse, indoors, or under protective shelter to full outdoor exposure. Over a week or more, the plant is exposed to increasing intervals of time outdoors, so that when it is planted in the garden it can make the transition with a minimum of shock. "Hardened off" also refers to a plant's ability to withstand cold. See Frost and Freeze Protection (p. 564).

Hardpan

A tight, impervious layer of soil, hardpan can cause trouble if it lies at or near the surface. Such a layer can be a natural formation—in the Southwest, the most common natural hardpan layer is called caliche—or it can be created, such as when builders spread excavated subsoil over the surface and then drive heavy equipment over it. If the subsoil has a clay content and is damp while construction is going on, it can dry to a bricklike hardness. A thin layer of topsoil may conceal hardpan, but roots cannot penetrate the hard layer and water cannot drain through it. Planting holes may become water tanks: plants will fail to grow, be stunted, or die.

Planting in hardpan. If the hardpan layer is thin, you may be able to improve the soil by having it plowed to a depth of 12 inches or more. If plowing is impractical, you can drill through it with a soil auger when planting (see illustration). If the layer is too thick, a landscape architect can help you with a drainage system, which might involve sumps and drain tiles. To improve the soil over large planting areas, dig up the area to a depth of 18 inches or so with heavy equipment, then add organic matter and thoroughly mix it in. As a beneficial extra step, you can then grow a crop of some heavy-rooting grass, and after it grows, rototill it into the soil as additional organic material.

If drainage problems prove especially difficult or costly to surmount, consider installing raised beds for most of your garden plantings. Fill them with good, well-aerated soil, and make them deep enough to allow for root growth.

Hardy

A plant's hardiness is its resistance to, or tolerance of, frost or freezing temperatures (as in "hardy to −20°F/−29°C"). The word does not mean tough, pest resistant, or disease resistant. A half-hardy plant is hardy in a given situation in normal years but may freeze in coldest winters.

Heading Back

Cutting a 1-year-old shoot back to a bud or cutting an older branch or stem back to a stub or tiny twig is called heading back. See Pruning (p. 593).

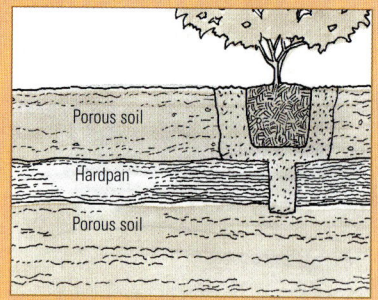

PLANTING OVER HARDPAN

For thin hardpan under shallow soil, dig down from planting hole to hardpan. Drill or chip to porous soil below. Backfill with porous soil.

Heavy Soil

A rather imprecise term, "heavy soil" refers to dense soil made up of extremely fine particles packed closely together. The term is used interchangeably with "clay" and "adobe." Such soils tend to be poorly aerated, slow to dry out, and overly wet. They often can be improved by adding organic matter. See Soils (p. 600).

Heeling In

Heeling in is a means of preventing roots of bare-root plants from drying out before you can set the plants out in the garden. The simplest approach is to dig a shallow trench in the shade, lay the plant on its side so that its roots are in the trench, and then cover the roots with soil, sawdust, or another material, moistened to keep the roots damp.

Henbit

Henbit, also known as dead nettle or bee nettle, is a weakly upright annual weed with lobed leaves and pink to purple flowers atop the stems in spring. It is a common weed in most of North America, particularly east of the Mississippi River. It can be especially troublesome in newly seeded lawns (see photograph, p. 614).

Seeds of henbit usually germinate in fall. Plants grow slowly over winter and become most obvious in spring. They are relatively easy to pull by hand, and numbers can be greatly reduced by late-winter or early-spring cultivation. Glyphosate is an effective herbicide for use outside lawn areas, where the weed can be treated alone. In lawns, keep the grass healthy and growing vigorously, or use an appropriately labeled weed-and-feed product.

Herb

The general term "herb" describes a variety of herbaceous plants valued for their flavor, fragrance, or medicinal purposes.

Herbaceous

Herbaceous, the opposite of woody, describes a plant with soft (nonwoody) tissues. In the strictest sense, it refers to plants that die to the ground each year and regrow stems the following growing season. In the broadest sense, it refers to any nonwoody plant—annual, perennial, or bulb.

Herbicide

A herbicide is a chemical used to destroy undesirable plants. See Weed Control (p. 613).

Honeydew

Aphids, scales, and whiteflies, as well as several other sucking insects, secrete a sticky substance called honeydew; certain ants (p. 546) and fungi (see Sooty Mold, p. 600) feed on honeydew, adding to the mess. Often honeydew from a tree will drip onto whatever is below: car, patio, or other plants. See entries for individual pests for control measures.

Horticultural Oil

A horticultural oil is a refined oil sprayed on plants to control insects. See Pest Management (p. 580).

House Plants

Plants that you keep indoors need careful attention to soil preparation, watering, and fertilizer application. The basics are outlined under Container Gardening (p. 554). Additional information appears below.

Soil. Container soil for house plants should be composed entirely of sterile materials—such as a prepared potting soil mix or a soil-less mix you make yourself. Potentially harmful organisms in garden soils pose a great threat to plant health when confined with roots in a limited soil mass and in the warmth and low light levels of a home.

Water. The best water for house plants is rainwater, but most people rely instead on water from the tap—which is usually satisfactory unless it contains quantities of harmful salts or is artificially softened with sodium. If you have a water softener, draw water for your house plants from an outside tap. If you must use softened water (or water that is high in alkaline salts), leach house plants completely about once a month. Thoroughly flush water through the soil several times, or set each plant in a sink or tub and let a trickle of water run through it for a while.

Light. Give house plants good light, but avoid the searing sun that comes through south and west windows. Unless you set plants back from such windows or moderate the sunlight with thin curtains, stick to a northern or eastern exposure. Plants grown for their flower display generally need more light than plants grown for foliage alone.

Humidity. Low humidity is the bane of most house plants, and low humidity goes hand in hand with heated rooms. Best places for plants are the cooler (but adequately lit) spots around the house; the higher humidity in bathrooms and kitchens favors growth. Avoid at all costs placing plants near hot-air registers.

Humus

The soft brown or black substance formed in the last stages of decomposition of animal or vegetable matter is called humus. Common usage, however, incorrectly applies the term to almost all organic materials that will eventually decompose into humus—sawdust, ground bark, leaf mold, and animal manures, for example.

Hybrid. See Plant Classification   p. 583

Insecticide

An insecticide is a material that kills or repels insects. See Pest Management (p. 580).

Iron Chelate. See Chelate   p. 552

Irrigation. See Watering   p. 609

Japanese Beetles

These coppery-colored beetles with metallic green heads attack a variety of plants, skeletonizing leaves and devouring flowers (see photograph, p. 591). Favorite foods include members of the rose family, zinnias, marigolds, and most vegetables. The small grayish white grubs feed on the roots of plants and are particularly troublesome in lawns (see p. 571). Japanese beetles are most common east of the Mississippi River but have also been found in Southern California.

Controlling Japanese beetles can take multiple approaches. Tilling the soil in fall will expose grubs to feeding birds. Floating row covers will exclude adults from vegetable plants. Floral-scented, sticky traps will attract Japanese beetles, but they can make matters worse by bringing in more pests than you had before. If you try these traps, keep them at least 100 feet away from plants to be protected.

Milky spore, a form of *Bacillus thuringiensis* is effective against grubs but tends not to reduce populations of adults, which will continue to move in from other areas. To reduce the number of adults, milky spore must be used over entire neighborhoods, not single gardens. Parasitic nematodes also kill grubs, but, as with milky spore, may not reduce numbers of adult beetles.

Insecticidal soaps, rotenone, and pyrethrum are effective against adult beetles. Traditional chemical controls include diazinon, chlorpyrifos, carbaryl, and acephate (on nonedibles).

Kikuyu Grass

A perennial grass, kikuyu can make a useful lawn in some coastal areas of the West but is a tough weed in others. Spreading rapidly by rhizomes and stolons, it eventually forms an impenetrable mat of wiry stems (see photograph, p. 614). Leaves are medium green and covered with fine hairs. To control kikuyu outside lawns, apply glyphosate.

Kudzu Vine

The woody kudzu vine spreads very rapidly, growing in some regions as much as 60 feet each year. This deep-rooted, perennial climbing vine can be found in the Southeast, where it was once welcomed for erosion control and as protein-rich animal fodder but has since become a weedy, aggressive, out-of-control nuisance.

Heavy, hairy, brown stems send the vine twining over shrubs and trees, which it can kill by shading them from needed sunlight. The woody stems carry large leaves with three leaflets, 3 to 6 inches long. Small red and purple flowers bloom in summer and produce long, hairy, flat pods containing seeds that are dispersed by birds (see photograph, p. 614).

Controlling kudzu vine is difficult; chemical control may be the best option. In late summer when the leaves are fully expanded, apply herbicide containing glyphosate or triclopyr. If the weed resprouts, repeat the treatment. Where kudzu vine has overrun shrubs and trees, cut off any runners and remove them before spraying. Or cut back climbing vines and paint undiluted glyphosate or triclopyr on freshly cut stumps.

Landscape Fabrics

Various fibrous or plastic materials called landscape fabrics can be rolled over the ground before planting to reduce weed growth and soil erosion. Use an old knife to make small X-shaped holes in the fabric for planting. Landscape fabrics are more attractive when covered with an organic mulch.

Lath

In gardening, lath designates any overhead plant-protecting structure (originally a roof of spaced laths) that reduces the amount of sunlight that reaches plants beneath or protects them from frost.

Lawn Problems. See Visual Guide to Identifying Lawn Problems   p. 571

Lawns

The well-manicured lawn is a time-honored tradition in most of America. Grass lawns, the ideal playing surface, add a sense of organization and unity to almost any landscape. But lawns are also high maintenance; to stay healthy, they need to be mowed, fertilized, and watered regularly. In the process, they use up valuable resources. Particularly in the arid West and Southwest, where water conservation is always a primary concern, gardeners are looking at grass lawns in a new light and finding ways to reduce their size, limit the amount of water they use, and even replacing them with plants that use less water.

In the East, Midwest, and South, most lawns are watered to supplement natural rainfall, but proper watering techniques are still important to keep the grass healthy, as well as to conserve water. Where lawns are prone to insects, weeds, and disease, there are also concerns about pollution of groundwater by nitrogen fertilizers and about the toxicity of excessive pesticide use.

All in all, it's difficult to deny the beauty and utility a lawn brings to a landscape, especially to a new home, which would otherwise be surrounded by bare soil while other landscape plants fill in. But keep in mind the time and resources a lawn requires and keep its size appropriate for the climate you live in and the ways the surface will be used.

Minimizing water use on lawns. Studies performed in the West revealed that as much as half of the water used by a typical single-family residence is applied outdoors—mostly to lawns—and that homeowners apply at least twice the water their lawns really need.

These startling facts have led many western communities to concentrate outdoor water conservation programs on providing more precise lawn-watering guidelines. Founded on evapotranspiration (ET)—a weather-based, localized measurement of how much water a plant uses and how much evaporates from the soil—these guidelines give you the average amount of water your lawn needs on a daily, weekly, or seasonal basis. If you live in an arid area, you can often obtain lawn-watering guidelines by contacting your local water department or Cooperative Extension Office.

Various alternatives to lawns are presented under Water Conservation (see p. 608, Evaluate Your Lawn). If, however, a lawn is a necessary component of your landscape (as a play surface, for example), you should consider these options: minimizing lawn size, choosing a grass adapted to your climate, installing a sprinkler system tailored to your lawn, and/or automating the watering with an electronic controller and moisture sensor (see Water Conservation, p. 608) so that the turf will receive no more than the minimum amount of water needed for good appearance.

Lawn care. Any good lawn—even if it is of drought-tolerant grasses—consumes much labor in preparation and subsequent care. You must prepare soil well, carefully sow seeds or plant live plants (sod, plugs, stolons), and then pamper the young lawn while it becomes established. Thereafter, routine maintenance involves mowing, watering, fertilizing, and controlling weeds and pests. On these pages we touch upon selecting grass type and installing the lawn; material on watering appears on pages 609–613. Further information on the various grasses appears in the Plant Encyclopedia: see the listing under Grasses, page 324, for the individual entries. For detailed information on lawn care—watering, mowing, fertilizing, weed and pest control—consult the Sunset book *Lawns*. For help in solving lawn problems, see Visual Guide to Identifying Lawn Problems, p. 571.

Lawn grasses. Climate should dictate your choice of a lawn grass in two ways. The first is water. If water supply is sufficient (especially in areas where summer rain is common), you can consider one of the high water consumers such as bluegrass, ryegrass, bent grass, or fine-textured fescue. Where water is scarce or supply is unpredictable, choose from among the drought-tolerant kinds.

The second climate factor to consider is temperature. Your summer heat and winter cold will direct you to either cool-season or subtropical grass types, as explained below.

Cool-season grasses. Cool-season grasses withstand winter cold, but most types languish in hot, dry summers. They are best adapted to the Northwest, Northeast, Midwest, and high-elevation areas where summer rains are common and high temperatures are not extreme.

These grasses are started from seeds sold either in blends of several different grasses or as individual types. Lawns of a single grass type will be the most uniform in appearance, most clearly expressing the characteristic you desire (fine texture or toughness, for example). The chief disadvantage of homogeneous lawns is that they may be wiped out by a pest infestation or disease to which they are susceptible or by extreme weather (drought or unusually high temperatures, for example). A blend of several kinds of grasses is safer. Those that survive to maturity will be the one, two, or three that do best given your soil conditions, climate, and maintenance practices.

When buying seed, consider both the kind of lawn you want and the cost to cover your area. Don't be fooled by the cost per pound. Choice, fine-leafed blends contain many more seeds per pound than do coarse, fast-growing blends; therefore, seeds of fine-textured grasses will cover a greater area per pound.

Subtropical grasses. Unlike the cool-season types, subtropical grasses grow vigorously during hot weather and go dormant in cool or cold winters. But even in their brown or straw-colored winter phase, they maintain a thick carpet that keeps mud from being tracked into the house. If you find their winter brownness offensive, they can be either dyed green or over-seeded with certain annual cool-season grasses that will stay green during mild winters.

The better subtropical grasses are grown from stolons, sprigs, plugs, or sod planted after the weather has warmed in mid- to late spring. Common Bermuda, hybrid Bermuda, and *Zoysia japonica* may be available in seed form, but seeding results are unsatisfactory and therefore the seeds are not widely offered. The hybrid Bermudas and St. Augustine grass cover quickly from runners; most zoysias are relatively slow. (Faster-growing zoysias are now becoming available as sod.) All can crowd out broad-leafed weeds. Hybrid Bermudas require frequent, close mowing and thatch removal.

"Water-conserving" grasses. Lawn grasses that thrive on less water than traditional Kentucky bluegrass can be broken up into three groups.

The first group is represented by the tall fescues, cool-season grasses that are grown from seed or sod planted in fall or early spring. Although slightly coarser in texture than bluegrass, turf-type tall fescues stay green year-round and are the turf of choice where a cool-season grass is desired. Newer dwarf tall fescue varieties have the added advantage of reducing mowing.

The second group of "water-conserving" grasses is made up of several specialties of the Rocky Mountains and high plains—wheatgrass *(Agropyron)*, blue grama grass *(Bouteloua)*, and buffalo grass *(Buchloe)*. Although widely used in the high-elevation West and the Great Plains, they are still being tested in many other areas. Each is described in the Plant Encyclopedia.

The third group consists of warm-season or subtropical grasses (see previous column), such as hybrid Bermuda. Thriving in hot summer weather, warm-season grasses can form an attractive turf on at least 20 percent less water than Kentucky bluegrass.

Instead of planting high-maintenance grasses, some gardeners approach the lawn as a natural meadow. This can be done by leaving native grasses like buffalo grass unmowed, or by planting a variety of low-growing plants (even wild-flowers) like silvery yarrow or creeping thyme.

▶ page 572

SECRETS OF A GREAT-LOOKING LAWN

Here are some tips for keeping a lawn healthy without wasting water.

- **Keep it small.** A small lawn means less work, and it takes less time and money to care for than a big one. It also demands less water. How much lawn do you really need? Studies show that for most activities, 600 square feet of lawn is plenty. Keep it a simple geometric shape so you can irrigate without overspray, and keep it fairly level to minimize runoff.

- **Choose the right grass.** Refer to the information on this page to select a lawn grass that is adapted to the climate you live in.

- **Water efficiently.** To encourage deep rooting and to conserve water, irrigate lawns as deeply and infrequently as possible. Where summer rainfall is plentiful, irrigate to supplement rainfall (most lawns need between 1 and 2 inches of water a week). In mild, dry-summer climates, twice-a-week watering should be adequate. In hotter climates, you may have to water more often. Check with local water agencies for ET guidelines on how much to apply. Apply less water during cooler months.

  Step on the grass. If the blades don't spring back from your footprint, it's time to water. You can also poke the soil with a screw-driver; if it doesn't penetrate easily, the lawn probably needs water (or the soil is compacted).

  Many sprinklers apply water faster than soil can absorb it. To prevent runoff, water in cycles. Let the sprinklers run until just before runoff or puddling occurs (often in 10 or 15 minutes); repeat the cycle in an hour. Also make sure your sprinklers are adjusted properly so they don't overshoot onto paving.

  To improve water penetration and reduce runoff, aerate and dethatch your lawn once a year.

- **Fertilize regularly.** Lawns are heavy feeders and require regular applications of high-nitrogen fertilizers. In acid soils, applying lime is also beneficial. Cool-season lawns should be fed throughout fall and spring. Feed warm-season lawns in the warm months of late spring and summer. If you cut back on watering because of drought, hold back on fertilizing, too.

- **Mow often.** To keep a lawn healthy, mow the grass when it's about a third taller than the recommended height. Grass is weakened if allowed to grow too long before mowing. Also, shorter clippings can be left on the lawn to decompose and add nitrogen to the soil. Set mowers to cut at these heights: hybrid Bermuda, ½ to 1 inch tall; bahia, tall fescue, and bluegrass, 2 to 3 inches; fine fescue, 1½ to 2½ inches; perennial rye, 1½ to 2 inches, St. Augustine, 2 to 3 inches.

Visual Guide to Identifying

LAWN PROBLEMS

The best advice for avoiding serious lawn problems is to keep your lawn healthy. Do this by following proper cultural techniques: watering, mowing, fertilizing, aerating, and dethatching on a regular basis. This page will help you correctly identify the more common lawn problems. For help identifying weeds in your lawn, see the Visual Guide to Identifying Weeds (pp. 614–615). For more information on lawn care, see page 570.

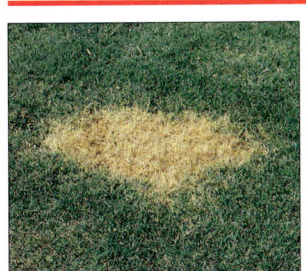

Problem: Small brown dead spots.

Cause, Solution: Dead spots circled by dark green grass may be caused by dog urine or gasoline spill from a mower. To prevent further damage, keep dogs off lawn and fuel mower on a paved surface. To repair damage, water area heavily to leach out salts or gasoline. Remove dead patch, along with 3 to 4 inches of soil beneath it. Fill hole with fresh soil; patch it with a fresh piece of sod, or reseed. Drought-stressed warm-season lawns may be infected with dollar spot. Improved cultural practices or appropriately labeled fungicide are control measures.

Problem: Small circular patches of dark green grass surrounding areas of dead or light-colored grass. Mushrooms may or may not be present.

Cause, Solution: Fairy ring, a fungus disease common in lawns growing in soil high in organic matter or including wood debris (boards or dead roots). To control, apply a nitrogen fertilizer and keep the lawn wet for 3 to 5 days. Aerate. There are no chemical controls.

Problem: Lawn has an uneven, washboard look with wavy ridges running in one direction.

Cause, Solution: Usually caused by running a power mower in the same direction every time you mow. Alternate mowing directions. It can also be caused by an unbalanced mower.

Problem: Bluegrass or ryegrass lawn has a yellowish to reddish brown color throughout. Small reddish pustules form in circular or elongated groups on older leaf blades and stems; blades eventually shrivel and die.

Cause, Solution: Rust. The best solution is to apply a high-nitrogen fertilizer, water, and mow more frequently. Several fungicides are labeled for control.

Problem: Yellow patches showing up in St. Augustine and zoysia grass lawns (also possible in bluegrass and creeping bent grass), especially in dry or drought-stressed locations. Patches eventually die.

Cause, Solution: Chinch bugs, small (¼-inch) gray-black insects that suck plant juices from grass blades, especially in hot weather. To confirm, push a bottomless can into the soil just where the grass is beginning to turn brown. Fill can with water. If lawn is infested, chinch bugs will float to the surface. Diazinon and chlorpyrifos are chemical controls.

Problem: Lawn looks striped or mottled yellow and dark green, often with brown dead streaks near edges.

Cause, Solution: Uneven fertilizer application: Parts of the lawn that received the right amount of fertilizer turn dark green, but portions that didn't, turn yellow. Areas that got too much burn and turn brown. To prevent streaking with a drop spreader, overlap wheel tracks so that no grass goes unfed. Burned areas along edges are usually caused by double dosing. To prevent, apply fertilizer around outside edges of lawn first, then go back and forth across middle. When you come to the edges, turn spreader off as you make the turn over part already fed.

Problem: Small dead patches in spring gradually enlarge as summer progresses. Whitish to buff-colored moths fly around lawn in a zigzag pattern at night.

Cause, Solution: Sod webworms. Larvae (gray caterpillars) feed on grass blades. To confirm, drench area of lawn with solution of 1 tablespoon dishwashing soap diluted in 1 gallon water. Larvae will come to surface. Treat if there are 15 or more webworms per square yard. Proper lawn care—watering, aeration, and dethatching—will reduce damage. Chlorpyrifos and diazinon are chemical controls.

Problem: Distinct, irregularly shaped brown patches. Symptoms most severe in late summer. Sections of dead turf can be pulled up like sod.

Cause, Solution: White grubs (beetle larvae) feeding on grass roots. Usually about 1 to 1½ inches long, the grubs curl into a C-shape when exposed. Parasitic nematodes are the biological control. Diazinon is an effective chemical control. Treat if there is more than one grub per square foot. Also see Japanese beetle, p. 569.

PLANTING A LAWN FROM SEED

1 Add to the seedbed organic soil amendments, commercial fertilizer, and any materials necessary to adjust soil's pH.

2 Thoroughly incorporate the amendments and fertilizers into the soil, using a rototiller (which is easier) or spading fork.

3 Remove all weeds and surface rocks with a rake or by hand; make sure seedbed is free of all such foreign matter.

4 Rake or drag the seedbed to establish a level, to smooth out soil, and to reveal any high or low spots that will need correcting.

The result is an open area that can be walked on but takes less maintenance and is less formal. Meadows combine particularly well with native plantings.

Lawns, Planting

A good lawn begins with a good environment for roots: the soil should be (1) of a texture easily permeable by water and roots to a depth of at least 8 to 12 inches, (2) well furnished with nutrients, and (3) neither highly acid nor overly alkaline.

If you're replacing an existing lawn, first make sure the old lawn, and any weeds it contains, are dead. The easiest way to do this is to get the old lawn growing vigorously (it may take several weeks of watering for a brown lawn), and spray it with a broad spectrum herbicide like glyphosate. digging dead sod into the soil makes for poor rooting, erratic water penetration, and irregular settling. It's better to rent a sod cutter and remove the old sod, or rent a power rake, tear up the old turf, and rake it up. If you remove the sod, you may have to add topsoil to raise the grade. Buy the best you can and blend it in with the existing soil to avoid an interface—a plane where two unlike soils meet (see Topsoil, p. 603).

Test soil. See Soil pH (p. 599) for information on how to determine your soil's acidity or alkalinity. If tests indicate a highly acid soil (pH below 6.0), add lime (calcium carbonate is best).

If the soil is highly alkaline (pH above 8.0), add iron sulfate or elemental sulfur. Iron sulfate is fast acting and will supply the iron that is lacking in alkaline soils.

Your Cooperative Extension Office or local nursery can recommend amounts and types of amendments that are best for adjusting soil pH in your area.

Add organic soil amendments. Nitrogen-stabilized soil amendments derived from sawdust and ground bark are available at most garden supply stores. Though more costly, these materials are easier to use than raw sawdust or bark products, which require additional nitrogen to hasten breakdown (see Soil Amendments, Organic, p. 598).

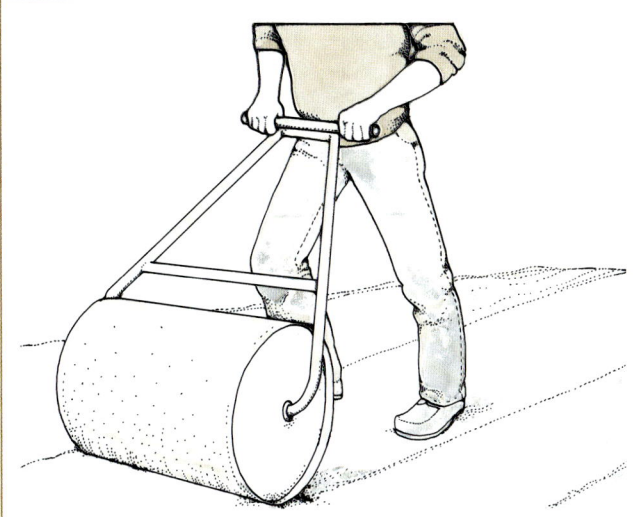

5 After raking and leveling, firm the seedbed with a full lawn roller; make passes in two directions.

6 Sow grass seed on a still, windless day; broadcast by hand or use mechanical seed sower. Then rake in seed lightly.

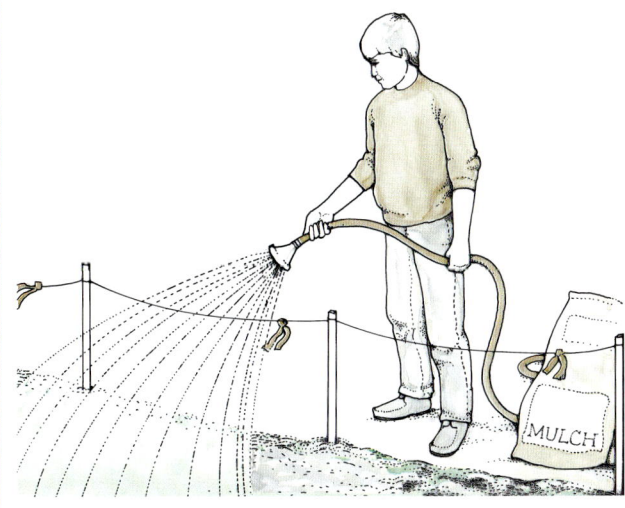

7 Apply mulch; keep seedbed moist until grass has germinated. Leave barrier around lawn until 8 weeks after first mowing.

8 A week after grass is up, begin pulling weeds (kneel on board to avoid denting lawn).

L

Blend in the amendment and nutrients thoroughly with a rototiller, making repeated passes until the mixture is completely uniform.

Mix nutrients into rooting area. Although you can't possibly add enough nitrogen to last the lifetime of your lawn, you should add enough to sustain the grass right after it sprouts. This can be added along with organic materials or spread on the finished seedbed. If your soil test or a local nurseryman indicates it's necessary, use a complete fertilizer, containing nitrogen, phosphorous, and potassium.

Smooth the seedbed. Steps are shown in the illustrations above. Usually you'll have to conform to surrounding paving, but if you have a choice, try to have a slight pitch away from the

house—a fall of 3 inches per 10 feet will provide good drainage. After raking and leveling, firm the seedbed with a full roller, making passes in two directions. Relevel if necessary.

Seed sowing. Although cool-season grasses may be sown in almost any month of the year in mild climates and from spring through fall in colder areas, fall and spring are usually best. Fall seeding reduces danger of heat injury. But to give grass a good start before heavy frosts come and soil turns cold, allow 6 weeks of 50° to 70°F/10° to 21°C temperatures. Fall seeding saves water, since fall and winter rains help germinate the seed and establish the roots. Spring seeding gives grass a long growing season in which to get established. On the other hand, late spring and summer heat calls for frequent hand watering during germination and careful irrigation and weeding later.

Pick a windless day for sowing, and sow seed as evenly as possible; a spreader or mechanical seeder will help. After sowing, rake in seed very lightly to ensure contact with seedbed. If you expect hot, dry weather or drying winds, put down a thin, moisture-holding mulch. Use 1/8 to 3/16 inch of peat moss; screened, aged sawdust; or use clean wheat straw and cover 50 percent of soil surfaces. To keep peat moss from blowing away (and to overcome its reluctance, when dry, to take up water), soak, knead, and pulverize it. After mulching, roll with an empty roller to press seed into contact with soil.

Water thoroughly, taking care not to wash out seed, and then keep seedbed dark with moisture until all the grass is sprouted. This may mean watering 5 to 10 minutes each day (sometimes two or three times a day, depending on the weather) for up to 3 weeks if your seed mixture contains slow-germinating kinds. Although a well-designed underground system may do the job without causing flooding or washouts, hand sprinkling is best.

Mow most grasses for the first time when blades are about a third higher than their recommended mowing height, or when they begin to take on a noticeable curvature. Be sure mower blades are sharp, and let sod dry out enough so that mower wheels will not skid or tear the turf.

Sod, sprigs, stolons, and plugs. Turf farms offer ready-made lawns in the form of sod. Compared with the cost of seeds, sod is expensive, but the saving in time and labor is considerable. Prepare a seedbed as for seeds, but make the surface about ¾ inch lower than the surrounding paving. Spread a layer of complete fertilizer (the amount the label suggests for new lawns), and then unroll sod on the prepared seedbed. Lay strips parallel, with strip ends pressed against each other, and with these seams staggered. Roll with a half-filled roller, and then water carefully until roots have penetrated deeply into the seedbed.

For sprigging—a method used to establish hybrid Bermudas and some bent grasses—prepare the seedbed as for seeds. To make the seedbed moist but of a good working consistency, presoak it. Make a series of parallel trenches 3 inches deep and 10 inches apart, take sprigs from plastic bags or tear from flats or sod, lay in trenches, and press soil back into trenches. Keep soil evenly moist until the sprigs root and begin to grow.

To plant stolons, broadcast them over the prepared seedbed at the rate of 3 to 5 bushels per 1,000 square feet. With a half-filled lawn roller, roll the broadcast stolons into the soil; then mulch with ½ inch of topsoil, peat moss, sawdust, or ground bark. Roll again, water thoroughly, and keep evenly moist until grass begins to grow.

To plant plugs of grass from flats, first cut the grass with a sharp knife into 2-inch squares. Then plant the plugs in prepared soil, spacing them evenly in all directions, about 12 to 15 inches apart.

Layering

In layering, a method of propagating plants, a branch is rooted while it is still attached to a plant. The two layering methods—ground layering and air layering—tend to be slow to produce results, but with some hard-to-root plants layering is more likely to be successful than is propagating from cuttings (p. 555). Because you don't remove the branch from the parent plant until it has formed roots, the original plant continues to keep the layer alive.

Ground layering. The technique for ground layering is shown in the illustration. Keep the soil around the layer moist, as you would for any cutting. When you are sure roots have formed (it may take more than a year; gently dig around the cut to check), cut the new plant free from the parent plant, dig it up, and move it to its intended location.

Air layering. The principle of air layering is the same as that of ground layering; the differ-

ence is that air layering is used for branches higher on a plant. It is especially useful with some large house plants. The technique is shown in the illustration.

If the rooting is successful, you'll see roots appearing in the sphagnum moss after several months. Then you can sever the newly rooted stem from the mother plant and pot it or plant it out on its own. At that time it is usually wise to halve the number of leaves—to prevent excessive loss of moisture through transpiration while the newly independent plant establishes itself. If no roots form, the branch will callus where it was cut, and new bark will eventually grow over the cut area.

Leaching

To understand leaching, think of brewing tea or coffee: when you pour hot water through tea leaves or ground coffee, you are leaching. You leach soil with water when you want to remove excess salts (see Soil Salinity, p. 600). In high-rainfall areas, rainwater leaches good nutrients as well as bad substances from the soil.

Leader

In a single-trunked shrub or tree, the leader is the central, upward-growing stem.

Leafburn

Leafburn occurs when there is damage to or destruction of a leaf's tissues from sunlight, chemicals (in the soil or on the leaves), strong wind, or lack of water. It usually starts as burnt-looking, dried-out tissue around the edges of the leaves. In bad cases, the whole leaf can dry out. Leafburn is very common among Japanese maples and azaleas.

Leaflet

Completely separated divisions of a leaf are called leaflets. They may be arranged like the fingers of a hand (palmate, fanwise) or like the divisions of a feather (pinnate, featherwise).

Leaf Miners

Leaf miner is a catchall term for certain moth, beetle, and fly larvae that tunnel within plant leaves, leaving twisting, tunnel-like trails on the surface (see photograph, p. 592). Adult leaf miners are rarely seen. Vegetables and some flowers and ornamentals can be infested. The damage is mostly cosmetic, although in some crops yields can be reduced. Some seedlings may die. In severe infestations, leaves may turn brown and drop.

The easiest way to protect vegetables is to plant them under floating row covers, thus preventing the adult insects from reaching the plants. Hand-picking infested leaves may help.

GROUND LAYERING

1 Select a low, flexible branch that can be bent into shallow hole. Cut halfway through it, put pebble in cut, and stake tip upright.

Pebble

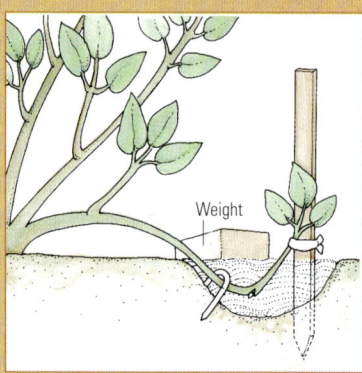

2 Secure prepared branch in shallow hole, using wire pin if needed. Brick or rock on soil also helps hold branch in place.

Weight

AIR LAYERING

Begin air layering below a node. Make a slanting cut (inserting matchstick to keep it open) or remove ring of bark. Dust cut with rooting hormone, encase in damp moss, and wrap with polyethylene to keep moss moist.

Node

L

Neem may prevent adults from laying eggs on the leaf surface. Chemical control is difficult once the insect is inside the leaf surface. Acephate, a systemic, may work on ornamentals.

In severe infestations, contact your local Cooperative Extension Office for specific identification of the pest and appropriate control measures.

Leaf Mold

Partially decomposed leaves—leaf mold— can be dug into the soil as an organic amendment. Oak leaf mold is the most familiar.

Leaf Rollers

The two most common leaf rollers—a group of larval garden pests—are the fruit-tree leaf roller and the oblique-banded leaf roller. Despite its name, the fruit-tree species feeds on oaks as well as fruit trees.

In spring, summer, or fall, adult moths lay egg clusters, which they cover with a waterproof cement. In some species, the eggs hatch early and overwinter in cracks in the bark of the host tree; other species don't hatch until spring. For the first few weeks after hatching, while the green larvae are about the size of long rice grains, they eat day and night. Then, when they are about half grown, they begin to hide during the daytime by folding leaves together (see photograph, p. 590); at night they crawl out and feed on the plant. When disturbed, they thrash about violently.

At maturity, the larvae pupate. From the pupa—a light brown or green segmented cylinder within the rolled-up leaf—emerges the adult moth. The oblique-banded leaf roller produces one or two generations a year; the fruit-tree leaf roller, just one.

Controls. A number of parasitic insects usually keep populations of leaf rollers low. Light infestations are easy to take care of physically: just pick off and destroy rolled leaves, or squash leaf rollers in place.

Use sprays only when leaf rollers threaten serious damage. The favored control is *Bacillus thuringiensis;* the surest chemical sprays are diazinon, carbaryl, and acephate.

Leaf Scar

Usually a rounded or crescent-shaped mark on a branch, a leaf scar indicates where a leafstalk was once attached.

Leaf Spot

Red, brown, yellow, or black spots on leaves and stems may be found on a number of different plants. On some *Prunus* plants, the spots drop out, leaving a "shot hole" appearance. Sometimes spots enlarge and coalesce, and then infected leaves drop; severe infections can defoliate some plants.

These symptoms represent several different diseases, including anthracnoses, black spot (familiar to rose growers), and scab, which affects some fruits. The fungus spores that cause these diseases are airborne or waterborne. Because the spores need free moisture to germinate, these diseases are far less serious in low-rainfall areas of the West than they are in areas with frequent summer rainfall or summer fog. Some types of leaf-spot fungi, activated by moisture during the winter rainy period, affect evergreen plants.

The source of these diseases is mainly live infected plants, although some disease-producing organisms can overwinter in plant refuse. Thorough garden cleanup each winter is important to lessen or eradicate infection. In addition, various fungicides may be labeled for use as sprays to control infections: chlorothalonil, captan, thiophanate-methyl, and triforine.

Three particular leaf-spot diseases are troublesome enough to warrant further explanation.

Anthracnose. Anthracnose fungi infect leaves and tender shoots as they emerge in spring; these fungi also infect older leaves, on which they produce large, irregular brown blotches and cause premature dropping of leaves (see photograph, p. 592). The fungi also cause twig dieback and canker on small branches; these blighted twigs and cankers will be a source of infection the following spring. Spores are spread by rain and by sprinkling; hence, the disease is most severe in wet springs and is checked by dry weather.

Your first attempt at control should be to eliminate sources of future infection: prune out all infected twigs and branches, if feasible. To prevent infection in spring, use chlorothalonil. Spray when leaves unfold, then two or three more times at 2-week intervals. Consult a commercial sprayer for help.

Some anthracnoses are very difficult to control, and sometimes it is necessary to live with them—especially if the disease affects a large tree. But the best approach is to grow plants that resist the disease. Among susceptible trees such as ash, Chinese elm, and sycamore, resistant cultivars are available.

Black spot. Black spot thrives where humidity runs high and summer rainfall is common. It is especially troublesome on roses in the Northwest and east of the Mississippi River. The fungus appears on leaves and stems as roughly circular spots of black with fringed edges, usually circled with yellow

(see photograph, p. 592). In severe cases, the plant will defoliate; unchecked infections, with repeated defoliation, can seriously weaken the host plant.

The black-spot fungus lives through winter in lesions on canes and on old leaves on the ground. In spring the fungus again becomes active and produces spores, which are then spread by splashing water to new leaves. Preventive control consists of planting resistant varieties and sanitation: clean up and destroy (burn or discard) old leaves in winter. Rose growers often have good luck controlling black spot with weekly applications of a baking soda–summer oil spray. To make the solution, mix 2 teaspoons baking soda and 2 teaspoons summer oil in a gallon of water. Otherwise, in spring, spray new foliage with triforine (the favorite of most rose growers), or chlorothalonil. Repeat sprayings will be needed as long as weather conditions favor the fungus's development.

Scab. Scab produces disfiguring lesions on apple and crabapple fruits and, when severe, can also cause defoliation. Another kind of scab occurs on loquats, pyracanthas, and toyons; still another infects willows. Scab is most prevalent in high-rainfall regions. The scab fungus (as well as the fungus that causes black spot on roses) differs from other leaf-infesting fungi in that the dark spots on leaves represent fungus growth on the foliage rather than dead tissue.

For control on deciduous trees, spray just before flower buds open with captan or thiophanate-methyl. Spray again when blossoms show color and again when three-quarters of the blossom petals have fallen. Whenever possible, try to avoid the problem by planting scab-resistant varieties of apple and crabapple. Scab on evergreen ornamentals is more difficult to control. Spray with appropriately labeled fungicide as needed; clean up all infected foliage debris.

Light Soil

The opposite of "heavy soil," the imprecise term "light soil" refers to soil composed of relatively large particles loosely packed together. The term is often synonymous with "sandy soil." See Soils (p. 600).

Loam

Gardeners call soil that is rich in organic material, does not compact easily, and drains well after watering loam. It is the ideal soil. See Soils (p. 600).

Macronutrients

Basic nutrients required by plants in relatively large amounts are called macronutrients. See Nutrients, Basic (p. 577).

Male Plant

A plant that produces pollen but does not produce fruit or seed is called a male plant. See Pollination (p. 589).

Manure

Manure is an organic material excreted by animals that is used as a fertilizer and an amendment to enrich the soil. See Soil Amendments, Organic (p. 598).

Mealybugs

Closely related to scale insects, mealybugs have an oval body with overlapping soft plates and a white, cottony covering (see photograph, p. 592). Unlike most scales, mealybugs can move around—at a very slow crawl. These pests suck plant juices, causing stunting or death. Often a black, sooty mold grows on the honeydew they excrete.

Mealybugs are prime house plant pests everywhere; outdoors they are particularly troublesome in areas with mild winters. For any infestation indoors or for a minor infestation outdoors, daub mealybugs with a cotton swab dipped in rubbing alcohol. Outdoors, hose plants with jets of water (or insecticidal soap) every 2 to 4 weeks to remove adult mealybugs, their eggs and young, and the black mold, which deters beneficial insects. Ants have the same symbiotic relationship to mealybugs as to aphids and scale insects; see Aphids (p. 546) for control.

Natural predators, such as ladybird beetles, can help control mealybugs—as can some commercially available predators such as cryptolaemus beetles and lacewings. Cryptolaemus beetle larvae are "sheep in wolves' clothing": they look like mealybugs but have chewing mouth parts and a ropey wax covering. See Visual Guide to Identifying Biological Controls (p. 549).

When mealybug infestations are heavy, spray with malathion, diazinon, acephate, or horticultural oil.

Microclimate

The climate of a small area or locality (such as a backyard or portion of it)—as opposed to that of a larger area, like a Sunset *National Garden Book* climate zone—is called a microclimate. The ability to recognize microclimates around your home—or if necessary, to create them—will influence which plants you choose and how well they grow in a particular area. Microclimates are influenced by hills and hollows, points of the compass, and structures. See also Frost and Freeze Protection (p. 564).

Micronutrients

Mineral elements required in small amounts for healthy plant growth are micronutrients. See Nutrients, Basic (p. 577).

Mites

To the naked eye, mites look like tiny specks of red, yellow, or green; in reality, they are tiny spider relatives (each has eight legs). Spider mites are especially troublesome in interior regions. The first (and sometimes only) sign of spider mite damage is yellow-stippled leaves (see photograph, p. 592). But there are many reasons for leaf yellowing. To confirm that mites are the problem, hold a piece of white paper beneath the stippled leaves and sharply rap the stem from which they are growing. If mites are present, the blow will knock some onto the paper—where they will look like moving specks. Some mites also make fine webbing across leaves (especially on the undersides) and around stems. Citrus bud mites distort lemon fruit and foliage in coastal areas of California. Control measures are rarely necessary.

Spider mite controls. If the plant is small, you might jet it thoroughly with water to wash off the mites; insecticidal soap added to a water spray will increase the spray's effectiveness. Dust that settles on leaves encourages mites, so continual hosing helps keep mite populations down. Increased humidity also helps. Drought-stressed plants are more prone to mites.

Many natural predators keep mites in check most of the time. Some of these predators—lacewing larvae and five different species of predatory mites—are bred and sold by biological control companies (see p. 549).

If you can't wash the plant or if washing is not effective, try spraying. Summer horticultural oils are especially effective because all stages of mites, including eggs, are killed. Sulfur can also be effective—but don't use in combination with oil sprays (it can be toxic to plants). If infestation is severe, outside California try dicofol (not registered in California).

Moles

Notorious pests in good soils throughout North America, moles have short forelegs pointing outward; large, flattened hands; and claws for digging tunnels.

Moles are primarily insectivorous, eating earthworms, bugs, and larvae (controlling Japanese beetle and other beetle grubs may reduce mole problems in lawns—see page 569), and only occasionally nibbling greens and roots. Irrigation and rain keep them near the soil surface, where they do the most damage as they tunnel: heaving plants from the ground, severing tender roots, and disfiguring lawns. A mole's main runways, which are used repeatedly, are usually from 6 to 10 inches underground and are frequently punctuated with volcano-shaped mounds of excavated soil. Shallower burrows, created while feeding, are used for short periods and then abandoned.

Controls. Trapping is the most efficient way to control moles. The spear- or harpoon-type trap is the easiest to set because you simply position the trap above the soil. A scissor-jaw trap must be carefully set into the main runway (probe with a sharp stick to find it); a wily mole will spring, heave out, or walk around a faultily set trap.

Due to their feeding habits, moles are very difficult to control with poison baits. And moles, like gophers, are difficult to control with toxic gas. To be successful with this method, place gas "mole bombs" directly in the main runways and block all holes. Be persistent with follow-up treatments.

You can dispatch a mole with a shovel blade, but you may wait a long time for a mole to appear. Your chances are best at dawn. If you see a mole scuttling along below ground (you'll notice the ground surface heaving), try the two-shovel method: block the runway in front of the mole with one shovel blade, and dig out the creature with the other.

Mulch

Any loose, usually organic material placed over the soil—such as ground bark, sawdust, straw, or leaves—is a mulch. The process of applying such materials is called mulching. A mulch can serve various functions. It may reduce evaporation of moisture from soil, reduce or prevent weed growth, insulate soil from extreme or rapid changes of temperature, prevent mud from splashing onto foliage and other surfaces, protect falling fruit from injury, or make a garden bed look tidy.

Naturalize

To plant out randomly, without a precise pattern, and leave in place to spread at will is called naturalizing (see illustration). Some plants have the capability to naturalize, meaning that they can spread or reseed themselves, growing as wildflowers do.

N

Nematodes

Nematodes are nonsegmented microscopic worms that live in the soil (see photograph, p. 592). Some types are beneficial (see p. 549), feeding on plant pests or aiding in nitrogen fixation (the process in which some plants, usually legumes, absorb nitrogen from the atmosphere and deposit it in the soil). Other nematodes are pests, feeding on plant roots and occasionally foliage.

Without a soil test, the presence of nematodes is hard to detect. And pest types are even harder to control. Infested plants (usually flowers and vegetables, but also woody plants) slowly deteriorate, grow poorly and become stunted, turn yellow, wilt, and often succumb. The symptoms are very similar to moisture stress. Roots will often have small bumps or nodules where the nematodes feed and inject toxins. But the nodules are not a sure sign of the presence of nematodes.

Nematodes are most common in sandy, moist soils in warm-summer climates, such as the Southeast. If you think they may be present, contact your local Cooperative Extension Office about testing procedures available in your area. Other than fumigating the soil, a difficult and dangerous procedure, there are few sure-fire control measures. Soil solarization may help. Rotating vegetable crops is also important. Some varieties of vegetables and flowers are described as being nematode resistant. Applying fast-acting nitrogen fertilizers to the soil may encourage beneficial organisms that feed on nematodes, reducing pest populations.

Nitrogen. See Nutrients, Basic   p. 577

Node

The joint in a stem where a leaf starts to grow is a node. The area of stem between joints is the internode.

Nutgrass, Yellow

An upright perennial weed that thrives in moist areas, yellow nutgrass can be identified by its bright green, 1/4-inch-wide leaves with a conspicuous midvein. Its flower head is golden brown (see photograph, p. 615). Small, roughly round tubers, or nutlets, may be found at the root tips. Nutgrass spreads by tubers or seed. Control can be difficult. Try glyphosate or another appropriately labeled herbicide.

Nutrient Deficiency

If soil drains well, has ample water, is neither too acid nor too alkaline, yet still fails to sustain plant growth well, it may be deficient in nutrients—most likely nitrogen.

Nutrients, Basic

In addition to light, air, water, and space for roots, growing plants need a supply of nutrients—elements necessary to carry out their life processes. Six nutrients, called macronutrients, are needed in relatively large amounts. The most commonly deficient macronutrient for all plants is nitrogen (chemical symbol N). Two others, phosphorus (P) and potassium (K), are often needed for annual plants, bulbs, and shallow-rooted perennials, including turf, but seldom needed for trees and deep-rooted shrubs and vines. These three nutrients are the basis for commercial fertilizers.

Micronutrients, so called because they are needed by plants only in very small quantities, are present in adequate amounts in most soils. Their availability to some plants may be inadequate, however, due to soil pH or another soil problem.   ▶

N

NATURALIZING BULBS

A number of bulbs, corms, and tubers can be planted in meadow, field, or light woodland situations where they will perform year after year as though they were wildflowers. By choosing bulbs that adapt to naturalizing and that thrive in your climate and location, you can enjoy an annual display with little more effort than it takes to plant them.

Selecting. Careful choice is the key to success with naturalizing. Read the description of each candidate in the Plant Encyclopedia to see if your choices will thrive under the conditions you can provide. Note especially the requirements for sun or shade. Also check moisture needs: Will the selected bulbs survive without supplemental water, or will you have to provide water during the dry months?

Planting. To achieve a naturalistic effect, plant bulbs in drifts, informal plant masses that appear to spread naturally from densely populated areas into more open areas. (See illustration.) If you plant spring-flowering bulbs in a grassy field or meadow you will mow, try to delay mowing the bulbs' area until bulb foliage has begun to yellow.

Flower size and quantity may decrease after bulbs have been in place for a number of years and become overcrowded. After flowering and foliage ripening, dig the bulbs, divide if needed, and replant when the time is right.

PLANTING BULBS IN DRIFTS

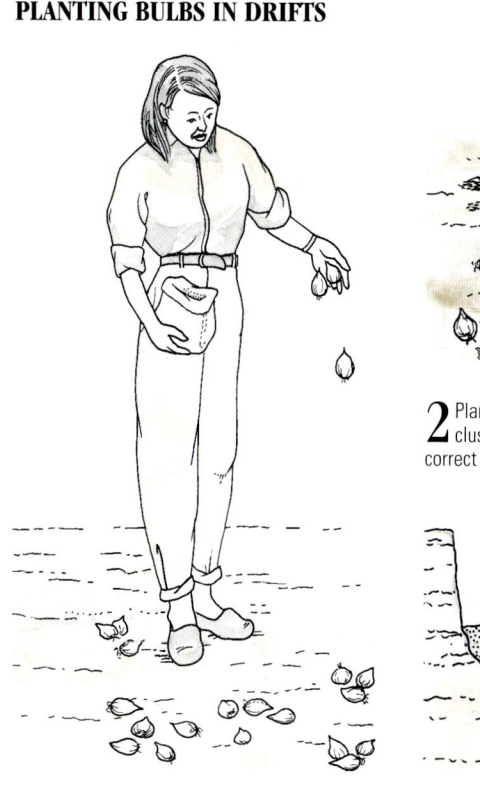

2 Plant each bulb where it falls—some in clusters, some farther apart. Bury each at correct depth for its species.

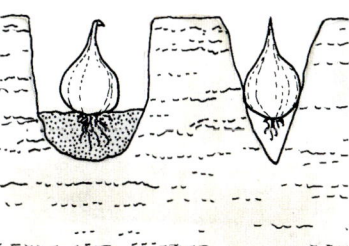

1 Toss handfuls of a single kind of bulb over the planting area, varying their density. Repeat with a second and third kind, if you like.

3 In hard ground, loosen the base of each hole so bulb rests on fine soil (left), not above an air pocket.

Nitrogen. The most commonly deficient nutrient, nitrogen, is not a mineral and hence is not present in the minute particles of soil from which plants derive their phosphorus, potassium, and other elements. All nitrogen must come from other sources: organic matter, air, water, or fertilizers. In nature, nitrogen comes primarily from decomposing organic material, which is generally in very short supply in some soils—especially in drier regions. Rainfall carries nitrogen from the atmosphere into the soil. Some groundwater may also contain nitrogen. In addition, specialized nitrogen-fixing bacteria that live on the roots of certain plants (legumes in particular) extract nitrogen from air between soil particles.

Plants use large quantities of nitrogen to form proteins, chlorophyll, and enzymes needed for plant cells to live and reproduce. When nitrogen is deficient, leaves yellow from their tips toward the stem, the plant yellows from the bottom upward, and growth is stunted (see photograph, p. 592).

Nitrogen can be absorbed by plant roots as nitrate, ammonium, or urea. Nitrate is soluble. Consequently, it can be easily lost by the leaching action of irrigation and rainfall. The ammonium ion, in contrast to nitrate, does not move through the soil with water. If applied to the soil surface, it must be converted to nitrate by soil organisms before it will move into the root zone. Urea is unique in that it moves with water, is converted to ammonium ion, and stays in the root zone until converted to nitrate. At that point it can be leached from the soil. Soil organisms also need nitrogen to thrive, and they, too, place demands on the available supply. For these reasons, many plants need supplemental nitrogen from time to time to grow as well as we expect them to.

Nitrogen fertilizers. The first of the three numbers shown on a fertilizer label indicates the percentage of nitrogen. In the natural course of events (with no supplemental fertilizer), nitrogen that comes into the soil as dead plant or animal material must undergo several chemical changes before it takes on the nitrate form plant roots can use. If a fertilizer's label says that all or most of the nitrogen contained is in either nitrate or nitric form, nitrogen will be released quickly and plants will be able to use it immediately. But if most of the nitrogen is in the ammonium form (ammonium sulfate, for example), nitrogen release will be slower—taking anywhere from 2 weeks to 3 months—but should be more sustained once it starts.

Ammonium nitrate consists of half ammonium nitrogen and half nitric nitrogen; it therefore yields some of its nitrogen quickly and some more slowly. Organic nitrogen—as in blood meal and IBDU (isobutylidene diurea)—first must go through a conversion to ammoniac nitrogen, which then is converted to nitrogen in the nitrate form. These are the slowest acting of the nitrogen sources. As a nitrogen source, organic matter is no more beneficial than inorganic sources because, ultimately, it is absorbed in the nitrate form. Organic fertilizers do, however, contribute organic matter to the soil, which can improve soil texture. See Soil Amendments, Organic (p. 598).

Note: If you add organic matter to your soil as a conditioner, the matter may be high in carbon compared with nitrogen. Soil organisms working to digest the high-carbon material may then compete with plants for the limited amounts of nitrogen available in the soil. For this reason, high-carbon (high-cellulose) soil conditioners—such as sawdust, wood shavings, ground bark, and straw—require special handling. One choice is to shop for and buy those materials in fortified form (with nitrogen already added to the material so that the organisms of decomposition will not take any nitrogen from the soil). If you get unfortified material, mix a nitrogen fertilizer with it.

Phosphorus. The second percentage of the three on a fertilizer label indicates the amount of phosphorus (expressed as phosphate, P_2O_5, and listed as available phosphoric acid) the product contains. Phosphorus availability is low in most soils; it does not move readily through the soil for roots to absorb. Soil particles that contain phosphorus ions release them "reluctantly" to the microscopic film of water (soil solution) surrounding them.

The phosphoric acid in a fertilizer ionizes in the soil to form phosphate compounds. Some of these compounds are useful to plants; others are so insoluble that plants cannot use them. When a phosphate fertilizer is simply spread on the soil and watered in, the phosphoric acid binds chemically to the mineral particles in only the top inch or two of soil. This means that surface applications of phosphorus fertilizers are largely ineffective, because they reach only surface roots.

For shallow-rooting annuals and perennials, including turfgrass and bulbs, many soils do not have sufficient amounts of phosphorus.

The most effective way to apply a fertilizer containing phosphorus is to concentrate it where roots can get at it. When you plant a lawn, annuals, or perennials (including bulbs), dig in superphosphate or a complete fertilizer that contains phosphorus as well as nitrogen and potash. Thoroughly mix the amount suggested in the label directions into what you estimate will be the root area for a few years to come. For seed planting, place the fertilizer beside the seed rows, a couple of inches to one side and a couple of inches below the seed level (following fertilizer label directions for amount per foot of row).

Potassium. The third percentage on a fertilizer label represents potassium (expressed as potash, K_2O). This element is described in various ways, such as "available or soluble potash" or "water-soluble potash." Plants remove from the soil more potassium than any other nutrient except nitrogen and calcium.

Potassium exists naturally in the soil in several forms, but plants can't use most of the natural soil potassium, even though it may be abundant. About 1 percent of the total soil potassium, called exchangeable potassium, acts as an important source for plants.

Potassium fertilization is often needed for annuals and perennials, but in most soils trees and shrubs seldom respond to its addition. Potassium deficiencies occur in soils that are acid, sandy, low in organic matter, and low in nutrient-holding capacity. If you suspect potassium deficiency on a woody plant, confirm it with your Cooperative Extension Agent or a knowledgeable nursery.

Like phosphorus, potassium is effective only if placed near roots, in their anticipated growth paths.

Calcium, magnesium, sulfur. Some fertilizers contain the important macronutrients calcium, magnesium, and sulfur; others do not. These elements are usually present in the soil in adequate supply, except that many soils of the high-rainfall areas of the Pacific Northwest and Southwest have a sulfur deficiency. There, sulfur can be readily leached away, just as nitrogen is. If you live in these areas, apply additional sulfur regularly to annual crops and lawns for optimum performance.

Calcium and sulfur often enter the soil in other kinds of garden products: lime (calcium), lime-sulfur fungicide and soil conditioner (calcium and sulfur), gypsum (calcium and sulfur), superphosphate (sulfur), and soil sulfur used for acidifying alkaline soils.

Calcium plays a fundamental part in cell manufacture and growth—most roots must have some calcium right at the growing tips. Magnesium forms the core of every chlorophyll molecule in the cells of green leaves. And sulfur acts with nitrogen in making new protoplasm for plant cells; it is just as essential as nitrogen, but its deficiency in the soil is not so widespread.

Iron, zinc, manganese. If soil is highly alkaline, as some soils in low-rainfall areas are, plants may not be able to absorb enough of these micronutrients. Gardeners can buy products to put on soil or spray on leaves to correct the deficiency. Some of these products are chelated—meaning that the iron, zinc, or manganese is in a form that can be used by the roots and is not susceptible to the fixing (a chemical binding process) that makes the native iron, zinc, or manganese unavailable.

Iron is essential to chlorophyll formation. Zinc and manganese seem to function as catalysts, or "triggers," in the utilization of other nutrients.

Oak Moth. See Plant Encyclopedia, *Quercus* p. 459

Oak Root Fungus

Oak root fungus *(Armillaria mellea)* can destroy a variety of woody garden plants, especially in the Southeast and low-elevation, nondesert regions of California. First symptoms may be dull or yellowed leaves and/or sparse foliage. Leaves may wilt and entire branches die; eventually, the affected plant succumbs.

To verify a problem as oak root fungus, check under the bark of the stem or trunk (or large roots) at or below ground level: between the bark and the hard wood, you'll find a mat of whitish fungus tissue. In late autumn or early winter, clumps of tan mushrooms may appear around infected plants (see photograph, p. 592). The fungus kills its host by gradually decaying the roots and moving into the main stem, where it girdles the plant; the aboveground part of the plant shows distress because its supply of water and nutrients is reduced and finally cut off.

Controls. Keep plants healthy—don't overwater those plants that are used to dry conditions, and don't underwater those that need moisture. You may be able to save lightly infected trees— or at least prolong their lives—by removing soil from their bases, exposing the juncture of roots and trunk or stems to the air, and cutting out all destroyed and infected tissue. More often, though, the disease runs its full course despite remedial action. The fungus lives for many years in the root systems of plants it has killed; roots of susceptible plants that contact infected roots will be invaded by the fungus. If you intend to replace a victim with a susceptible tree or shrub, thoroughly remove all infected roots from the soil. It's better to choose replacement plants such as the following: Japanese maple, ginkgo, jacaranda, *Mahonia aquifolium,* and nandina.

Offset

Some mature perennials may send out from their base a short stem, at the end of which a small new plant develops. The new plant is an offset. Some familiar examples are hen and chicks *(Echeveria),* hen and chickens *(Sempervivum),* and strawberry. See also Stolon (p. 601).

Organic Gardening

In simplest terms, organic gardening means using only materials derived from living things to grow plants. Such materials include organic fertilizers, soil amendments, and pest controls. The goals of organic gardening are to minimize impact on the environment, to reduce risks to people enjoying the garden, and to pro-

duce the healthiest food possible. However, the word "organic" is often considered a synonym for "safe," which is not always the case. Some organic pesticides, such as nicotine sulfate and rotenone, are toxic. Others, like pyrethrins, can cause allergic reactions in humans. Still others kill beneficial insects like bees as well as plant pests.

Organic Matter

Any material originating from a living organism—peat moss, ground bark, compost, or manure, for example—that can be dug into soil to improve its condition is referred to as organic matter. See Soil Amendments, Organic (p. 598).

Oxalis, Yellow (Yellow Wood Sorrel)

A very aggressive weed, yellow oxalis thrives throughout most of North America in sun or shade (see photograph, p. 614). It spreads quickly by seed. Seedlings start out from a single taproot, which soon develops into a shallow, spreading, knitted root system. Yellow flowers are followed by elongated seed capsules that open like popcorn as they dry, shooting seeds as far as 6 feet. In mowed lawns, clumps generally stay low and tight. In flower beds, they grow rangier and tangle up with desirable plants.

Control is difficult. Dig out small plants, or carefully spot-treat isolated plants with glyphosate. Once you have removed or killed plants, oryzalin is an effective pre-emergence control. Various herbicides included in lawn-care products also help control oxalis. Check labels carefully.

A vigorous, well-fertilized lawn provides tough competition for oxalis. Frequent surface watering encourages the shallow-rooted weed; water less frequently and more deeply.

Peach Leaf Curl

Named for its most widely grown host plant, the peach leaf curl fungus also infects nectarines. In early spring the emerging new leaves thicken and pucker along their midribs, producing the characteristic curling. The curled and distorted leaves may be tinged with red, pink, yellow, or white (see photograph, p. 590); later in the season, they may become covered with white spores that can be carried by the wind to other leaves or plants. Lodging in and on the buds of next year's growth, these spores become the source of next year's infection. By midsummer the curled leaves usually fall, and trees then produce new leaves. Successive years

of infection severely weaken a tree and decrease or eliminate fruit production.

The fungus overwinters on and in buds and on old, infected leaves, developing most rapidly during cool, moist winter or spring weather. Actual infection takes place when the bud scales (protective coverings on growth buds) first crack open—as early as December or as late as March, depending on the year, variety, and region. If buds swell early, they are susceptible to infection for several months, until active growth starts. Once leaf differentiation takes place, plants are resistant to infection.

Controls. For best control, protect buds with fungicide until they begin to swell. Spray with fixed copper (wettable powder) or lime sulfur at least once during the dormant season. Check with your local Cooperative Extension Office or local nursery for exact spray timing for your area. Normally, only one application is necessary around the first of the year. But repeat sprays may be necessary in some areas. Do not spray before the leaves drop or after buds have opened. You also can control infection by covering trees with plastic during rainy weather; this is easiest with genetic dwarf varieties. Picking off the whitish leaves on isolated plants may also stop the spread of peach leaf curl.

Peat Moss

A highly water-retentive, spongy organic soil amendment, peat moss is the partially decomposed remains of any of several mosses. It is somewhat acid in reaction, adding to soil acidity. Sphagnum peat moss is generally considered to be highest in quality. There is a sedge peat, not composed of mosses, which is not necessarily acid.

Perennial

A perennial is a nonwoody plant that lives for more than 2 years. The word is frequently used to refer to a plant whose top growth dies each winter and regrows the next spring, but some perennials keep their leaves all year.

Perennials are as diverse an assortment of plants as you'll find under one collective heading, yet all have two traits in common: (1) unlike shrubs, they are not woody; and (2) unlike annuals, they live from year to year. Typically, a perennial has one blooming season each year, from only a week to more than a month long. After blooming, the plant may put on new growth for the next year; it may die down and virtually disappear until the time is right, some months later, for growth to resume; or it may retain much the same appearance throughout the year.

Some perennials store reserve food for the next season in specialized underground tissues. These plants are discussed separately under Bulbs (p. 550).

Many of the popular perennials are grown for the beauty of their flowers, and any attractive

P

PLANTING A BARE-ROOT, MAIL-ORDERED PERENNIAL

1 Gingerly unwrap packaged plant, being careful not to damage roots. Look in packing material for a label and growing advice.

2 Gently pull moist packing material from roots, untangling them carefully. Many gardeners soak roots overnight in water.

3 Spread roots over cone of soil in the center of a generous planting hole. Refill hole, burying roots just to where new foliage emerges (crown).

foliage is merely a bonus. Conversely, a smaller group of perennials—artemisias, for example—are grown for their foliage alone, the flowers being inconsequential or even unattractive. Some perennials have evergreen foliage and are attractive throughout the year.

Garden uses. Like annuals, perennials provide color masses, but unlike annuals, they will bloom several years in a row without having to be dug up and replanted. Perennials are thus more permanent than annuals but less permanent than flowering shrubs. In fact, their semipermanence is a definite selling point. You can leave perennials in place for several years with little maintenance beyond annual cleanup, some fertilizing, and routine watering; but if you want to change the landscape, perennials are easy to dig up and replant—much more so than the average flowering shrub.

Planting. For instructions on planting most perennials, see Planting Techniques: Annuals and Perennials (p. 586). A number of popular perennials (irises, daylilies, peonies, Oriental poppies) and perennial fruits and vegetables (asparagus, rhubarb, and strawberries) are sold in nurseries or by mail as bare-root plants during their dormant periods. The roots of these bare-root perennials should be kept moist until planting. They also benefit from a several hours' soak in water before planting. For handling mail-order perennials, see illustration.

Before planting dormant, bare-root perennials, prepare the soil well, as recommended under Planting Techniques: Seeds (p. 584), and be sure to set out each plant at its proper depth; refer to individual entries in the Plant Encyclopedia for specific planting information. Be sure to spread roots out well in the soil, gently firm soil around them, and then water thoroughly to establish good contact between roots and soil. See illustration.

Care of established perennials. Feed perennials with a nitrogen fertilizer just prior to the normal growth cycle—in fall or late winter to early spring. Repeat after bloom.

With perennials that are periodically dug up, divided, and replanted, you can renew phosphorus and potassium when you prepare the soil for replanting. But even the "permanent" perennials, such as peonies, may appreciate replenishment of these nutrients from time to time. The best way to apply them is to use a complete fertilizer high in phosphorus and potassium: carefully dig it in, apply it in deep trenches, or use fertilizer stakes or tablets (see Fertilizers, p. 561).

Routine watering during the growth and bloom periods will satisfy most perennials. Exceptions are noted in the Plant Encyclopedia as preferring dry or unusually wet soil.

After a perennial has finished blooming, remove the old blossoms to prevent the plant's energy from going into seed production.

Later in the season (usually in fall), remove dead growth to minimize overwintering diseases and eliminate hiding and breeding places for insects, snails, and slugs.

Where the ground freezes in winter, many gardeners routinely mulch their perennials to protect them from alternate freezing and thawing. After the ground first freezes, apply a lightweight mulch that won't pack down into a sodden mass. Straw is one popular choice; evergreen boughs are good where available.

Digging, dividing, and replanting. Over time many perennials grow into such a thick clump that performance declines because the plants are crowded. When this happens, dig up the clump during its dormant period and divide it. See instructions under Dividing (p. 558).

Perlite

Perlite is a mineral expanded by heating to form very lightweight, porous white granules useful in container soil mixes to enhance moisture and air retention.

Pest Management

The notion of pest control—where control implies eradication—has been superseded by the concept of pest management. The management concept acknowledges that many perceived "problems" are natural components of gardens: the presence of pests doesn't necessarily spell trouble. In a diversified garden, most insect pests are kept in check by natural forces (such as predators and weather). If pests reach damaging levels, however, temporary intervention may be needed to restore a balance.

Because of this natural system of checks and balances in a garden, it makes sense to determine which form of intervention will return the situation to a normal balance with the least risk of destroying helpful (as well as harmless) organisms that maintain the equilibrium. Action choices range from doing nothing (giving nature a chance to correct the imbalance), or using restraints (washing plants, or repelling or physically destroying the damagers), to biological controls (improving the helpful side of nature's control system), and, as a last choice, chemical controls.

More and more gardeners are turning to physical restraints and biological controls (see Visual Guide to Identifying Biological Controls, p. 549) as a first line of defense against garden pests because they want natural gardens that are safer for children, pets, and wildlife. Yet almost all horticulturists acknowledge the need for at least occasional treatment with chemical controls. This approach—the preferred use of natural and mechanical controls, plus chemicals as a discretionary second choice—is called integrated pest management (IPM). Increasingly, IPM is being used in parks, city landscapes, and greenhouses.

The IPM approach. The following points explain how to implement IPM in your own garden.

- **Select well-adapted plants.** Choose plants that are adapted to your area and that are

INSECTICIDES

Insecticides carry one or more active ingredients in a liquid, powder, or granular form. Their availability is constantly shifting. New products continue to be developed and marketed. Existing products may be withdrawn from sale for home use if research reveals hazards to health or the environment.

On the label of each product is a list of plants and pests on which the control is registered for use. It is illegal to apply the control to a plant or pest not listed on the label.

- **Azadirachtin (neem).** A botanical insecticide from the African neem tree *(Azadirachta indica)*, this liquid spray is nontoxic to mammals; it stops feeding of many insects and prevents normal growth of immature insects. It has also shown to be effective against some fungal diseases, including black spot and powdery mildew. Neem has limited registration in some states.

- **Baygon (propoxur).** Common in earwig baits and wasp and hornet sprays, propoxur should not be used on edible crops.

- ***Bacillus thuringiensis (Bt).*** A biological control that paralyzes and destroys the stomach cells of the insects that consume it. Its various strains are toxic to caterpillars, mosquitoes, and some beetles. It works best on young larvae (see the Visual Guide to Identifying Biological controls, p. 549, for more information.).

- **Bendiocarb.** A dust, bendiocarb controls crawling pests (such as earwigs, pillbugs, and sowbugs) and some soil pests, including root weevils. It is not registered in all states.

- **Contact dusts.** Differing from insecticidal dusts, these powdered materials cling to, scratch, and destroy the waxy exterior of some pests. Diatomaceous earth, boric acid, and silica aerogels are among the most useful, but they can be hazardous to humans if inhaled.

  Use natural-grade, properly labeled diatomaceous earth to discourage ants, slugs, and snails. Boric acid, usually a dust or powder, is also available as a spray or paste and in baited traps. Silica aerogels dehydrate an insect's body, killing it. In the garden, apply as a dust for ants, fleas, and ticks.

- **Diazinon.** A broad-spectrum insecticide also widely used to control various lawn pests, diazinon is the only chemical control for soil pests in vegetable gardens. It is toxic to bees and birds.

- **Dursban (chlorpyrifos).** A control for certain borers in shade trees, lawn insects, and many other pests of ornamental plants, chlorpyrifos should not be used on vegetables.

- **Kelthane (dicofol).** Designed to control spider mites, dicofol may be found as one of the ingredients in multipurpose insecticides. It is not registered in California.

- **Malathion.** A broad-spectrum insecticide for use on both edible and ornamental crops, malathion is toxic to honeybees.

- **Mesurol (methiocarb).** An effective control for slugs and snails, methiocarb will also kill earthworms. It is not for use around edible crops.

- **Metaldehyde.** The most common slug and snail control, metaldehyde is usually the active ingredient in various baits and is also contained in some liquids. It may be used around vegetable and fruit crops, but it loses effectiveness in moist weather and after waterings. It can be toxic to pets.

- **Oil sprays.** Special, highly refined oils smother insects and their eggs. "Dormant oils" are used during winter or early spring for control of insects that overwinter on deciduous plants. "Summer oils" can be used after leaves have emerged and on woody evergreen plants such as citrus. Use in summer to control aphids, pear psylla, scale insects, mites, and eggs of some insects. Oils can burn sensitive leaves; test-spray on a small area of plant first.

- **Pyrethrum/pyrethrins.** Pyrethrum is a natural insecticide derived from *Pyrethrum* daisies. It is effective against many insects (especially quick knockdown of flying ones) but will break down within a few hours after exposure to sunlight. Pyrethrins are specific chemicals derived from the *Pyrethrum* daisy. Pyrethroids are synthetic versions, which are more toxic and last longer in the environment.

- **Rotenone.** A botanical insecticide derived from South American plants, rotenone dust is commonly used to control chewing insects on vegetables. It is fairly toxic to mammals and extremely toxic to fish.

- **Ryania.** A botanical insecticide derived from the powdered stem of a tropical shrub, ryania acts as a stomach poison, controlling codling moth, citrus thrips, corn earworm, and asparagus beetle. It is gentle on beneficials.

- **Sabadilla.** Made by grinding seeds of the sabadilla lily, this control acts as a stomach and contact poison against caterpillars, leafhoppers, and thrips. It has low toxicity to people but is highly toxic to birds. Sabadilla has limited registration in California.

- **Sevin (carbaryl).** This insecticide, commonly used in vegetable gardens, is effective against most chewing insects but generally not effective against sucking insects. It often increases problems with the latter pests by destroying their natural predators. Carbaryl is highly toxic to honeybees and earthworms.

- **Soaps.** These mixtures of special fatty acids are of low toxicity to humans but will control most small insects and mites. They are safe for use on edible plants and fast acting, but have no residual effectiveness. Soaps injure some plants. They are most effective in soft water. Once dry, soaps will not kill beneficials.

- **Sulfur.** Finely ground sulfur mixed with clay, talc, and gypsum is dusted over plants (or sometimes diluted with water and sprayed) to control mites, psyllids, and certain mildews. Never use when temperature will exceed 90°F/32°C.

- **Systemics.** These pesticides are absorbed by a plant's foliage or roots; insects that pierce the plant's external tissues and ingest the juices or chew the leaves are killed. Sprayed on the foliage, some systemics also kill insects on contact. Widely available are Cygon apply to leaves or soil; and Orthene (acephate)—apply only to leaves, since it is toxic to bees. None can be used on edible crops.

- **Thiodan (endosulfan).** This broad-spectrum insecticide is particularly effective against thrips, aphids, borers, fuchsia mites, and whiteflies. Its use is restricted in some areas.

Packaged pesticides are listed alphabetically by trade name or common name; the generic name, which you will find under "active ingredients" on the product label, appears in parentheses when it differs from the trade name.

P

ANATOMY OF A FLOWER

Among flowering plants, blossom form varies enormously. But this diversity obscures the fact that all flowers share a basic structural plan and that the structural elements always appear in the same order. The illustration shows a schematic flower and its parts, which are described below.

- **Receptacle** is the point where floral parts are attached to the tip of the specialized stem that bears the flower.

- **Sepals** make up the outer circle, or ring, of floral parts. Collectively, the sepals are known as the *calyx*.

- **Petals** form the next circle of flower parts, just inward from the sepals. In showy flowers, it is usually the petals that make the display. Petals may be separate, as in camellias and roses, or united into tubular, cupped, or bell-like shapes, as in rhododendrons and petunias. Collectively, the petals are called the *corolla* (and the calyx and corolla together are known as the *perianth*).

- **Stamens**, positioned inward from the petals, contain the male reproductive elements. Typically a stamen consists of a slender stalk (the filament) topped by an anther (most often a yellow color). The latter contains grains of pollen, which is the male element needed to fertilize the flower for it to produce seeds. See Pollination (p. 589).

- **Pistils**, found in the center of a flower, bear the female reproductive parts. Each pistil typically consists of an ovary at the base (in which seeds will form following pollination) and a stalklike tube called the style that rises from the ovary. The style is topped by a stigma, the part that receives the pollen.

A complete flower—a term that describes most of the flowers we grow—comprises all the parts described above. An incomplete flower lacks one or more of the floral parts, but those it does contain appear in the order listed. For more information on flowers and flower parts, see Single Flower (p. 598) and Double Flower (p. 559).

ANATOMY OF A COMPLETE FLOWER

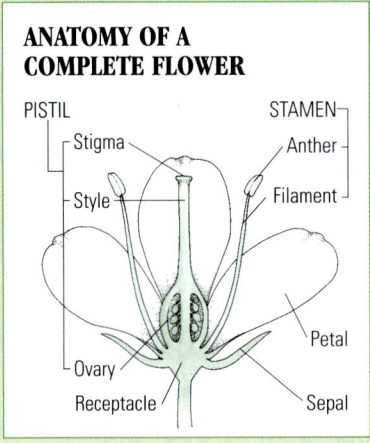

PISTIL — Stigma, Style, Ovary, Receptacle
STAMEN — Anther, Filament
Petal
Sepal

---

eases (p. 557). Before you purchase a chemical control and begin applying it, be sure you have correctly identified the problem. Only use a pesticide to solve a problem if both the pest and the plant it is preying on are listed on the pesticide's label. If you are at all uncertain, ask at a reputable local nursery or contact the nearest Cooperative Extension Office. Follow label directions exactly. For help identifying specific plant problems, see pages 590–592.

Biological controls. A number of living organisms can provide some measure of pest control. Many occur naturally in gardens (and may be eliminated by unwise pesticide use). For information on beneficial insects—insects that prey on garden insect pests—and other biological controls, see page 549.

Petals. See Plant Anatomy and Growth p. 583

Phosphorus. See Nutrients, Basic   p. 577

Pigweeds

The pigweeds are a family of summer weeds (*Amaranthus* species). Two of them, redroot pigweed, *A. retroflexus,* and prostrate pigweed, *A. blitoides,* are troublesome garden weeds throughout much of North America.

Redroot pigweed is an upright annual reaching 2 to 3 feet high, often with red striping on the stems, petioles, and roots. Green flower clusters with small hairy spines top the plant. Prostrate pigweed is a ground-hugging plant with many branched stems radiating from one taproot (see photograph, p. 615). Small leaves are medium green. Flowers are undistinguished.

The key to controlling pigweeds is to get them while they are small. Hoe or pull the young seedlings, which can come up any time there is sufficient moisture, as soon as you see them. The longer they stay in place, the harder they are to get out without breaking off the main stem, which will cause the plant to resprout. Traditional herbicides, including glyphosate, will also kill pigweeds.

---

resistant to your region's pest and disease problems. Plants stressed by inhospitable climate or from lack of water or nutrients are more vulnerable to damaging organisms than are their healthy, well-cared-for counterparts.

- **Adjust planting time.** If by planting early you can avoid a sure-thing pest, do so. Spider mites are most troublesome when the weather turns hot; plant beans early to avoid them. Keep records of planting dates and temperatures so you can make adjustments from season to season.

- **Try mechanical controls.** Hand-picking, traps, barriers, floating row covers, or a strong jet of water can reduce or thwart many pests, especially in the early stages of a potential problem. Cleanup of plant debris can remove the environment in which certain pests and diseases breed or overwinter.

- **Accept minor damage.** A totally pest-free garden is neither possible nor desirable. Allow natural control methods to play the major role in maintaining a healthy balance between pests and the beneficial (plus the harmless) insects and creatures that are normal garden components.

- **Solarize the soil.** Using the sun to heat the soil before planting is an effective way to reduce or eliminate soil-inhabiting pests. Just before the hottest time of the year (usually mid-July) and well before fall planting, till soil and remove weeds. Water soil, then lay 1½- to 2-mil clear plastic over it; anchor edges with soil. Leave in place for 4 to 6 weeks.

- **Use less toxic alternatives.** Release or encourage beneficial insects; use soaps, horticultural oils, botanical insecticides (such as natural pyrethrins), and one of several packaged forms of *Bacillus thuringiensis;* see the Visual Guide to Identifying Biological Controls (p. 549) for further explanation of these products. Realize that beneficial insects may take a while to reduce the pests they prey upon, and that you may have to use nonchemical controls at more frequent intervals than you would chemical controls. And although many natural insecticides have a relatively low impact on the environment, they can be harmful to humans if used carelessly. Follow label instructions exactly.

- **Use chemical preparations prudently.** Occasionally you will need to use a chemical control—especially for management of dis-

---

Pillbug, Sowbug

These two familiar creatures have sectioned shells and seven pairs of legs. Pillbugs roll up into black balls about the size of a large pea; sowbugs are gray and cannot roll up as  tightly. Their principal food is decaying vegetation, but they also will eat very young seedling plants and the skins of melons, cucumbers, squash, and berries—particularly if the fruits are overripe and have a break in the skin.

P

Mulching and composting encourage pill-bugs and sowbugs. If you sprout seeds near a compost pile or in heavily composted soil, you may get some pillbug and sowbug damage. You can apply carbaryl to the seedlings or to the ground where the pests are active. Or lift fruit off the ground on top of small saucers or boards, plastic mulch, or landscape fabric.

Pinching Back

Using thumb and forefinger to nip off the tips of branches is called pinching back. This basic pruning technique (p. 594) forces side growth, making the plant more compact and dense. It is especially useful with annuals, house plants, and shrubs.

Plant Anatomy and Growth

Knowledge about how plants grow is an important key to becoming a successful gardener. This background will make all aspects of plant culture more understandable. The box on the previous page explains the anatomy of a flower; the illustration below outlines the basics of plant growth.

Plant Classification

Botanists have classified the world's plants into an orderly, ranked system reflecting similarities among them. The plant kingdom is broken down into groups that are less and less inclusive: division, class, order, and then the groups defined on the next page, which are the ones of most significance to gardeners.

Family. Each plant belongs to a family, members of which share certain broad characteristics that are not always immediately evident. The rose family, for instance, includes such diverse plants as the rose, the apple tree, and the familiar perennial *Geum.* Most family names end in *-aceae* (Orchidaceae, Asteraceae, Liliaceae).

Genus. A plant family is divided into groups of more closely related plants; each group is called a genus (the plural is "genera"). Sometimes a family contains only one genus: for example, Ginkgoaceae contains only the genus *Ginkgo.* At the other extreme, the composite family (Asteraceae) contains around 950 genera. The first

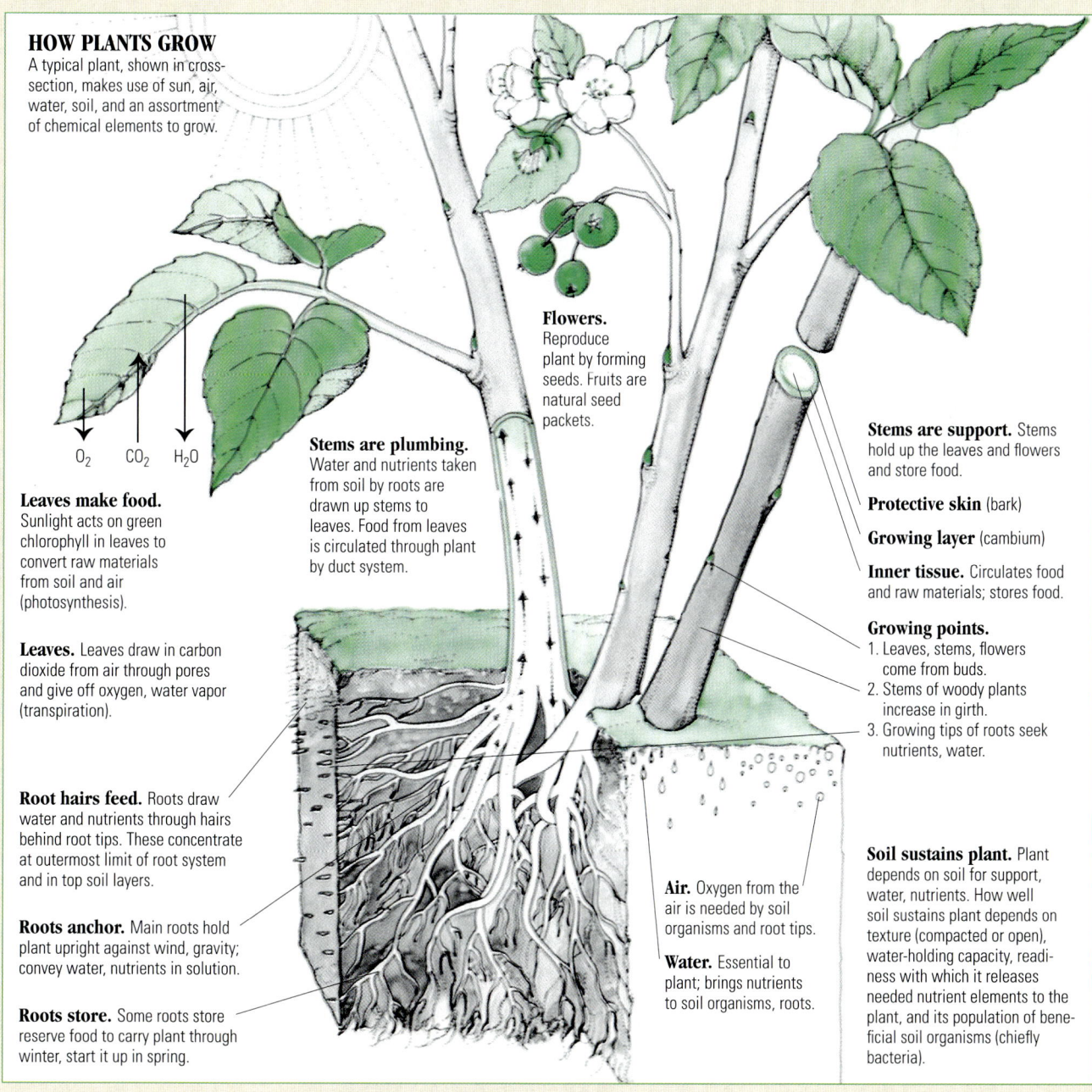

HOW PLANTS GROW
A typical plant, shown in cross-section, makes use of sun, air, water, soil, and an assortment of chemical elements to grow.

O_2 CO_2 H_2O

Leaves make food. Sunlight acts on green chlorophyll in leaves to convert raw materials from soil and air (photosynthesis).

Leaves. Leaves draw in carbon dioxide from air through pores and give off oxygen, water vapor (transpiration).

Root hairs feed. Roots draw water and nutrients through hairs behind root tips. These concentrate at outermost limit of root system and in top soil layers.

Roots anchor. Main roots hold plant upright against wind, gravity; convey water, nutrients in solution.

Roots store. Some roots store reserve food to carry plant through winter, start it up in spring.

Stems are plumbing. Water and nutrients taken from soil by roots are drawn up stems to leaves. Food from leaves is circulated through plant by duct system.

Flowers. Reproduce plant by forming seeds. Fruits are natural seed packets.

Air. Oxygen from the air is needed by soil organisms and root tips.

Water. Essential to plant; brings nutrients to soil organisms, roots.

Stems are support. Stems hold up the leaves and flowers and store food.

Protective skin (bark)

Growing layer (cambium)

Inner tissue. Circulates food and raw materials; stores food.

Growing points.
1. Leaves, stems, flowers come from buds.
2. Stems of woody plants increase in girth.
3. Growing tips of roots seek nutrients, water.

Soil sustains plant. Plant depends on soil for support, water, nutrients. How well soil sustains plant depends on texture (compacted or open), water-holding capacity, readiness with which it releases needed nutrient elements to the plant, and its population of beneficial soil organisms (chiefly bacteria).

P

word in a plant's botanical name is the name of the genus to which it belongs: for example, *Ginkgo, Liquidambar, Primula.*

Species. Each genus is subdivided into groups of individuals called species; the second word in a plant's botanical name designates the species. Each species is a generally distinct entity, reproducing from seed with only a small amount of variation. Species in a genus share many common features. When a third word occurs in a plant name, it indicates a variety, either botanical or horticultural. The botanical variety indicates a geographical or other variant of a given species that occurs in nature. This variety name is represented in italic *(Juniperus chinensis sargentii).* The botanical variety is sometimes called a subspecies. The horticultural variety is a plant of garden origin that has arisen by hybridization or selection. It is sometimes called a cultivar. It is represented in Roman type and is distinguished by being set off by single quotation marks or by the designation cv., thus: *Rosa* 'Chrysler Imperial' or *Rosa* cv. Chrysler Imperial. In common usage the term variety is used both for subspecies and cultivars.

Horticultural variety (clone or cultivar). This term is a name applied to a group of plants within a cultivated species that maintains its identity when propagated. Cultivars may be of different kinds. Those maintained by vegetative propagation (cuttings, grafting or budding, offsets, division, tissue culture are known as clones. Some cultivars are maintained by carefully selecting seed grown plants to assure uniformity. Many vegetable and flower varieties are of this kind *(Coreopsis grandiflora* 'Sunburst', eggplant 'Black Beauty'). Such seed-grown plants are known as open-pollinated varieties or cultivars.

Hybrid. A hybrid is plant resulting from a cross between two unlike plants, either within a species or between species, cultivars, subspecies, or (rarely) between different genera. An important class are the F_1 (first filial) hybrids, the first generation offspring of two carefully controlled parent lines. Notable for vigor and uniformity, they are extremely important in many vegetables and fruits. Seed saved from these hybrids will not come true in the next generation, but will produce a mixed lot of offspring. Hence new seed must be purchased and planted each year.

Strain. A strain is a variant of a cultivar that originates by mutation. It varies from its parent in some detail of color, size, or growth pattern. Many strains are especially desirable and acquire varietal (or cultivar) names of their own. 'Delicious' apple has yielded many such, including 'Crimson Spur Delicious' and 'Starkrimson Red Delicious'. When the term strain is used in this book for annuals, it describes a group of plants which are identical in growth habit, size, and general appearance but which differ only in color. The term series is, for

the purposes of this book, identical. Dazzler is a strain or series of Impatiens; plant and flower size are identical, but seeds are offered in 10 colors. In such a case, we use the term strain to describe Dazzler. Each individual color we consider a cultivar, hence Dazzler Impatiens, but Impatiens 'Dazzler Blush' or 'Dazzler Orange'.

Planting

Proper planting techniques depend on the type of plant—annual, perennial, shrub, tree, and so on—and how the plant is sold or propagated—as seed, bare-root, or in containers. Special techniques for various types of plants and planting approaches are explained in the entries that follow. To get plants off to a good start, you should also have an understanding of Soils (p. 600) and Soil Amendments (p. 598). Planting techniques for bulbs can be found under Bulbs (p. 550).

Planting Techniques: Seeds

In nature, seeds are scattered randomly from seed-bearing plants. And scattering, or broadcasting, seeds is a common method for planting seeds of lawn grasses and sometimes of wildflowers. To plant seeds of most garden plants, though, the gardener sows seeds more carefully in the open ground or in some sort of container.

You can buy seeds of most ornamental plants in three different forms. The traditional packaging is the seed packet, with a picture of the flower, fruit, or plant on the outside, the loose seeds within. You also can buy packets or packages of pelletized seeds: each seed is coated, like a small pill, to make handling and proper spacing easier. The third form is seed tapes—strips of biodegradable plastic in which seeds are embedded, properly spaced for growing to maturity. You just unroll the tape in a prepared furrow and cover it with soil. In all three cases, you will find planting instructions on the package.

In the open ground. One advantage of sowing seeds directly in the earth is that you usually avoid the need to transplant. The seeds germinate and grow into mature plants in one place. You may need to thin seedlings to prevent overcrowding, filling in a few sparse spots with thinned plants. But most of the seedling plants will need no handling once they break ground.

Gardeners commonly choose between two seed-sowing methods—broadcasting and row planting—depending on the results desired. Seeds planted in rows will probably need to be thinned later.

Broadcasting. Native wildflowers will make a reasonably good show if simply scattered—in time to catch fall rains—where they are to grow. But they will do even better if the ground is first cleared of weeds and grasses and pre-

TWO WAYS TO PLANT STRAIGHT

Lay a board on the soil surface; furrow or plant along its edge.

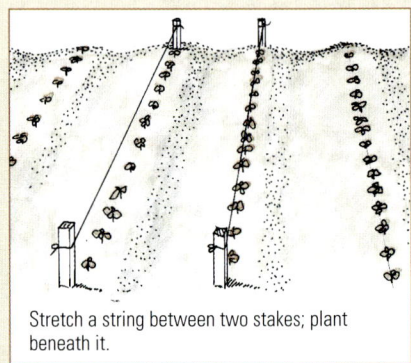

Stretch a string between two stakes; plant beneath it.

pared a bit by tilling and by adding organic amendments. If you plan to broadcast seeds in drifts or patterned plantings, or if you wish to sow a broad area with tough, easy-to-grow plants (such as sweet alyssum or California poppies), you can achieve a more even distribution by mixing the seed with several times its bulk of fine sand. After you have scattered the seeds—or seed-and-sand mixture—rake lightly, then carefully sprinkle the area with water. Cover the area with a very thin mulch (p. 576) to prevent the soil from crusting and to hide the seeds from predators. (Be prepared, though, for some loss to birds and, perhaps, to rodents.)

Most garden annuals and vegetables also can be sown in place, but they will benefit from a bit more attention than simple broadcasting calls for. With a fork, spade, or rototiller, prepare the seedbed, working in soil amendments (p. 598) and a complete fertilizer (read the label and apply the recommended amount). Smooth the prepared soil with a rake and moisten it well a few days before you intend to plant (if rains don't do the watering for you). Then follow the sowing and covering directions outlined for broadcasting.

Row planting. If you intend to grow vegetables or annuals in rows, prepare the soil as described previously. But you can omit the fertilizer and apply it, instead, at seeding time in furrows 1 inch deeper than the seeds and 2 inches on either side of the seed row (again, consult label recommendations for the proper amount of fertilizer per foot of row). Follow the seed packet instructions for optimum planting depth and

P

spacing of the rows, and lay them out in a north-south direction so that both sides will receive equal sunlight during the day. Use a hoe, rake, or stick to form the furrow; for perfectly straight rows, use a board or a taut string as a guideline. See illustration.

To sow seeds or seed pellets from packets, one of two methods will work best. Either tear off a small corner of the packet and tap the seeds out as you move the packet along the furrow or prepared seedbed; or pour a small quantity of seed into your palm, and then scatter pinches of seed as evenly as possible.

Thinning. When seedlings appear, thin excess plants (if necessary) so that those remaining are spaced as directed on the seed packet. Bare seeds scattered in furrows almost always come up too thickly; pelletized seeds are easier to sow at the proper spacing, and seed tapes do the spacing for you. Thin seedlings while they are still small. If you wait too long to thin them, plants will develop poorly, and it will be more difficult to remove one without disturbing those around it. Work quickly but gently, replanting the surplus seedlings elsewhere as you go.

In flats and containers. Many plants get off to a better start when they are sown in containers and later transplanted into place in the garden. Most nurseries stock seedling plants in flats or other containers, ready for you to plant. But you can start your own seedlings indoors or in a greenhouse—or in any location that is warmer than the out-of-doors and has adequate light. See illustration.

Choosing a container. Almost anything that will hold soil and has provision for drainage will do for a seed-starting container. Plastic or wooden nursery flats will accommodate the largest number of seeds; other choices are clay or plastic pots, peat pots, aluminum foil pans (the sort sold for kitchen use), Styrofoam or plastic cups, cut-down milk cartons, or shallow wooden boxes that you can make yourself.

Remember to punch holes for drainage in the bottom of any container that holds water; if you make your own wooden flats or boxes, leave about a ¼-inch space for drainage between the boards that form the container's bottom.

If you use containers that have held plants before, give them a thorough cleaning to avoid the possibility of infection by damping-off fungi, which destroy seedlings. A vigorous scrubbing followed by a few days of drying in the sun usually suffices.

Choosing a planting mix. Unless you plan a large-scale seed-planting operation, it's easiest to buy a prepared planting mixture for starting seeds. Nurseries carry a variety of such mediums—look for labels that say "potting soil." See Container Gardening (p. 554).

Sowing in a container. Gently firm the mixture into the container and level it off about ¾ to 1 inch from the top of the container. If the mix-

ture is powdery dry, water it thoroughly and wait a day or two to plant. Very fine seeds can be broadcast over the surface and covered with sand; larger seeds can either be planted in shallow furrows scratched into the surface or be poked in individually. Always remember that seeds should be planted no deeper than recommended on packet labels; a good general rule is to cover seeds to a depth equal to twice their diameter. Cover seeds with the proper amount of prepared mixture, press down gently but firmly, and then water. Direct watering of the soil surface can sometimes dislodge the seeds. Instead, place the container in a tub, sink, or bucket containing a few inches of water. The planting mix in the container will absorb enough water within a few hours. Thereafter, keep the seeding mixture moist but not soaking wet.

For slow-sprouting seeds or for plants whose seedlings develop slowly, you can sow seeds in a pot, and then tie a clear plastic bag around it. Place the pot where it receives good light but not direct sunlight. Air can get through the plastic, but water vapor cannot get out; seedlings will have enough moisture to complete germination without further watering. If you use this technique, be sure that your planting mixture is sterile and that the container has not been used for planting before.

Transplanting seedlings. When the new seedlings have developed their second set of true leaves, it's time to transplant or thin them. If you don't need many plants, you can thin them in place. Give them enough "elbowroom" (1½ to 2 inches between them) to grow larger before you plant them out in the garden. But if you want to save most of the plants that have germinated, you will need to transplant them to larger containers for growth to planting-out size. Preferably, transplant them into individual pots or cups; then when you plant out in the garden, they'll suffer a minimum of root disturbance.

First transplanting. Fill a new container with moist planting mix. Loosen the soil around the seedling plants (a kitchen fork or spoon is handy for this), and carefully lift out a seedling. Or lift a clump of seedlings and gently tease individual plants apart from the tangled mass of roots. Handle a seedling by its leaves to avoid bruising or crushing its tender stem. With a pencil, poke a hole in the new container's planting mix, place the seedling in the hole, and firm the soil around it. Water the transplant right away. Do this for each seedling plant until all are transplanted. Keep these plants out of direct sunlight for a few days, until they have adjusted.

Final transplanting. A few weeks to a month after the initial transplant, the seedlings should be ready to plant in the garden. During that month, you can help their development by watering once with a half-strength liquid fertilizer solution or by sprinkling lightly with a slow-acting fertilizer. ▸

For small seeds like lettuce, first mix ¼ package with 2 tablespoons sand. Scatter over moist potting mix in flat or aluminum pan with holes punched in bottom. Sprinkle with soil, firm, and water lightly. Set in protected area with bright light. Keep moist.

For large seeds like Swiss chard, sow in furrows made with a small stake. Sow according to label directions and water lightly. Set in protected area with bright light. Keep moist.

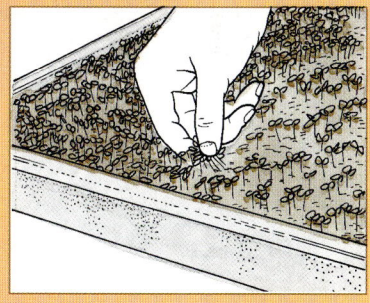

Thin seedlings of small, scatter-sown seeds (top drawing) to about 1 to 2 inches apart by snipping with scissors or pinching off with fingers.

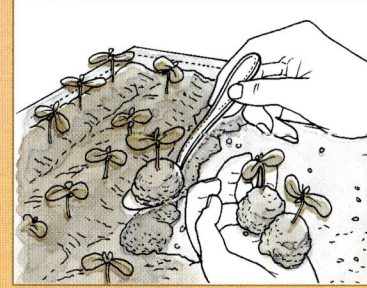

Transplant when seedlings have at least their second set of leaves. Scoop out with a kitchen spoon. Water regularly. If it's hot, shade plants.

P

THE PLANTING HOLE

All tree and shrub planting begins with digging a hole. Dig it so that sides taper outward into the soil and are roughened, not smoothly sculpted (use a spading fork to dig, or to roughen shovel-dug sides); this lets roots penetrate more easily into surrounding soil. To prevent or minimize settling of the plant after planting and watering, make the hole a bit shallower than the root ball or root system of the plant it will receive, then dig deeper around edges of the hole's bottom. This leaves a firm plateau of undug soil to support plant at proper depth.

Planting Techniques: Annuals and Perennials

B usy gardeners often forgo the pleasures of seed planting and buy seedlings of annuals, vegetables, and perennials at the nursery. Many of these plants—as well as some ground covers and hedge plants—are sold in plastic cell-packs, individual plastic pots, peat pots, and flats. Some perennials, perennial vegetables, and strawberries may also be sold bare-root during their dormant seasons; for planting instructions, see page 580.

You'll get the best results from small plants in pots and flats if you prepare the soil well, as you would for sowing seeds (see p. 584). Be sure not to let these plants dry out while they're waiting to be planted. For all small plants, plant so that the tops of their root balls are even with the soil surface.

From cell-packs. Plants in plastic cell-packs, with each plant in an individual cube of soil, are easy to remove. Push down with your thumb on the bottom of a soil cube, and remove the root ball with the other hand. See illustration, next page. If there is a mat of interwoven roots at the bottom of the root ball, tear it off—the plant will benefit from its removal. Otherwise, loosen the roots by pulling apart the bottom third of the root ball.

From pots. Plants in individual pots can be dislodged by placing one hand over the top of the container, with the plant stem between index and middle fingers, and then turning the container upside down. The plant and its root ball should slip out of the container into your hand.

From peat pots. If the plant is in a peat pot, plant it pot and all; the roots will grow through the pot. But make sure that the peat pot is moist before you plant it. A dry peat pot takes up moisture slowly from the soil, so roots may be slow in breaking through it. This can stunt the plant's growth or cause roots within the peat pot to dry out completely. Several minutes before transplanting, set the peat pot in a shallow container of water. Also be sure to cover the top of a peat pot with soil, because exposed peat acts as a wick to draw moisture out of the soil. If covering the peat would bury the plant too deeply, break off the top of the pot to slightly below the plant's soil level.

From flats. For plants in flats, a putty knife or spatula is a handy transplanting tool: separate the plants in the flat by cutting straight down around each one. Many gardeners prefer to separate individual plants out of flats gently with their fingers; they lose some soil this way, but keep more roots on the plant. If you work quickly, there will be little transplant shock.

Planting Techniques: Trees and Shrubs

A t all times of the year, you can purchase trees and shrubs for immediate planting: bare-root in the dormant season, balled-and-burlapped generally in the cooler months, and planted in containers the year around.

Bare-root plants. In winter and early spring, you can buy bare-root plants at many retail nurseries and receive them from mail-order nurseries. A great many of the deciduous plants are available bare-root: fruit and shade trees, deciduous flowering shrubs, roses, grapes, and cane fruits.

Why go out in the cold and wet of winter to buy and set out bare-root plants when you can wait until spring, summer, or fall and plant the same plants from containers? There are two valid reasons:

- You save money. Typically, a bare-root plant costs only 40 to 70 percent of the price of the same plant purchased in a container later in the year.

- The manner in which a bare-root tree or shrub is planted makes it establish itself faster and often better than it would if set out later from a container.

The advantage of bare-root planting is that, when you set out the plant, you can refill the planting hole with the backfill soil that you dug from the hole: the roots will grow in only one kind of soil. In contrast, when you plant from a container or balled-and-burlapped, you put two soils, usually with different textures, in contact with each other. The two different kinds of soil can make it difficult to get uniform water penetration into the rooting area.

PLANTING BARE-ROOT...

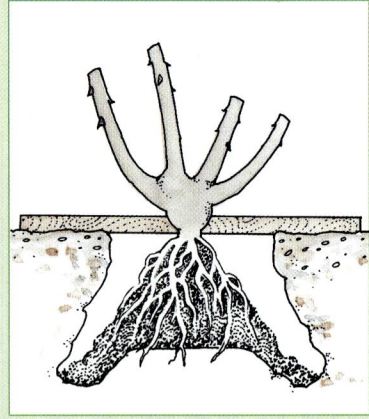

1 Make a firm cone of soil in hole. Spread roots over cone, positioning plant at same depth as (or slightly higher than) it was in growing field; use stick to check depth.

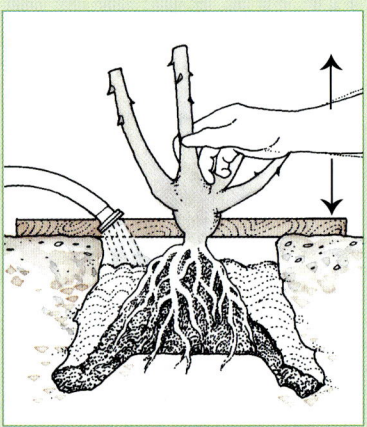

2 Fill in backfill soil nearly to top, firming it with your fingers as you fill. Then add water. If plant settles, pump it up and down, while soil is saturated, and raise it to proper level.

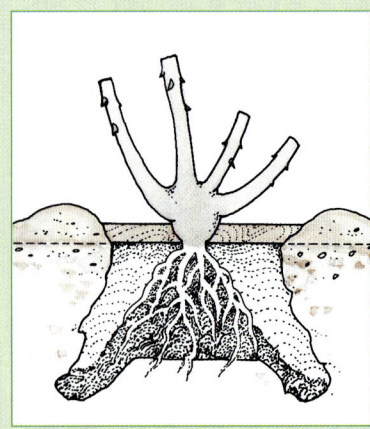

3 After plant is watered in and correct level has been established, fill in any remaining soil. When growing season begins, make ridge of soil around hole to form a watering basin.

P

…FROM A CONTAINER

1 Roots of container plants may have become coiled or matted. Spray soil off the outer few inches of root ball; then loosen and uncoil circling or twisted roots.

2 Spread roots out over firm plateau of soil, then add unamended backfill soil. Top of root ball should be about 2 inches above surrounding soil.

3 Make berm of soil to form watering moat. Irrigate gently—water should remain in moat rather than flood basin; objective is to keep trunk base dry.

…OR BALLED-AND-BURLAPPED

1 Set balled-and-burlapped plant into planting hole, placing root ball on firm plateau of undug soil; top of root ball then should be about 2 inches above surrounding soil.

2 Untie burlap and spread it out to uncover about half of root ball. Drive stake into soil alongside root ball before filling hole with backfill.

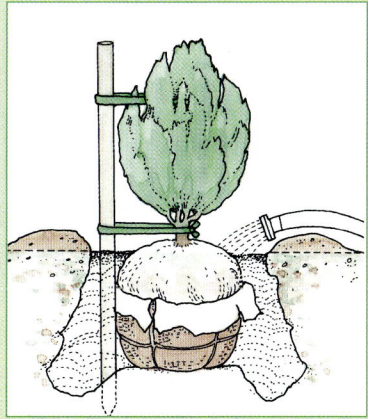

3 After firming in backfill soil, make berm of soil to form watering moat. Gently water in plant; then loosely tie plant to stake. Burlap will slowly decay.

Planting techniques. For successful bare-root planting, the roots should be fresh and plump, not dry or withered. Even if roots appear fresh and plump, it's a good idea to soak the root system overnight in a bucket of water before you plant.

Dig the planting hole broad and deep enough to accommodate roots easily without cramping, bending, or cutting them to fit. But cut back any broken roots to healthy tissue. In areas with shallow or problem soils, a wider hole will speed establishment. Follow the illustrations on page 586 to dig the planting hole and set out the bare-root plant.

After the initial watering, water bare-root plantings conservatively. Dormant plants need less water than actively growing ones, and if you keep the soil too wet, new feeder roots may not form. Check soil periodically for moisture (using a trowel, fingers, soil-sampling tube, or any pointed instrument) and water accordingly: if the root zone soil is damp, the plant doesn't need water.

When weather turns warm and growth becomes active, you will need to water more frequently. Do not overwater: check soil for moisture, as mentioned above, before watering. If hot, dry weather follows planting, shade the new plant at least until it begins to grow. And be patient—some bare-root plants are slow to leaf out. Many will not do so until a few warm days break their dormancy.

Plants in containers. Plants grown in containers are popular for many reasons. Most broad-leafed evergreen shrubs and trees are only offered growing in containers, and you can buy these plants in cans in all seasons. Available in a variety of sizes and prices, they are easy to transport and needn't be planted immediately. Furthermore, you can buy a container plant in bloom or fruit and see exactly what you are getting.

When shopping for container-grown plants, look for plants that have a generally healthy, vigorous appearance and good foliage. The root system should be unencumbered—that is, not badly tangled or constricted by the plant's own roots. Two signs of a seriously rootbound plant are roots protruding above the soil level and husky roots growing through the container's drainage holes. When selecting young trees, feel for circling roots around the trunk in the top two inches of soil. Additional indicators of crowded roots: plants that are large for the size of their containers, leggy plants, and dead twigs or branches. If you find any of these signs, look for another plant.

Removing plants from containers. Nurseries sell plants in a variety of containers—metal cans (1- and 5-gallon are standard sizes), plastic or fiber pots, clay pots, and wooden boxes for large specimen shrubs and trees. With straight-sided metal cans, have the cans slit down each side. The best time to cut cans is just

P

PLANTING FROM CELL-PACKS

1 Poke plants out of cell-pack by pushing on bottom of individual cell; let gravity help. If tight, run a knife between side of container and soil.

2 Lightly separate matted roots. If there's a pad of coiled-up white roots at the bottom, cut it off so roots will grow outward into soil.

3 Without squeezing roots, position plant in generous planting hole. Form a watering basin around each plant. Water each one separately, with a gentle flow that won't disturb soil or roots.

P

before you plant, but you may prefer to have the cans cut at the nursery before taking the plants home. Handle cut edges with care. If planting is delayed, keep the plants in a cool place (out of hot sun) and water often enough to keep roots moist (water gently so that you don't wash out soil). With tapered metal cans and plastic containers, you can easily knock the plants out of their containers; sharp taps on the bottom and sides will loosen the root ball so that the plant will slide out easily. With fiber pots, it's often easier to tear the pots away from the root ball.

Planting techniques. Follow the steps shown in the illustration on page 587 to set out plants from containers. After completing step 1, cut off any outside roots that seem to be permanently kinked. Set plant in hole, spread roots, and fill in around roots with unamended backfill, firming with your fingers until hole is about half full. Water thoroughly to eliminate air pockets. Finish filling the hole; then go to step 3. After plant-

ing, pump the plant up and down slightly to settle wet soil around the roots, and check to see that the top of the root ball remains about 2 inches above soil grade.

Balled-and-burlapped plants. Certain plants have roots that won't survive bare-root transplanting. Instead, they are dug with a ball of soil around their roots, the soil ball is wrapped in burlap (or another sturdy material), and the wrapping is tied with twine to keep the ball intact. These are called balled-and-burlapped (or B-and-B) plants. Available in this fashion are some deciduous shrubs and trees, such evergreen shrubs as rhododendrons and azaleas, and various conifers.

Treat B-and-B plants carefully: don't use the trunk as a handle; and don't drop them, because the root ball could shatter. Cradle the root ball well by supporting the bottom with one or both hands. If it is too heavy for one person to carry, get a friend to help you carry it in a sling of canvas or stout burlap.

Note: Many B-and-B plants are grown in clay or fairly heavy soil that will hold together well when the plants are dug up and burlapped. If your garden soil is medium to heavy in texture (heavier loam to clay), you can plant without amending the soil you return to the planting hole (called backfill soil). But when the B-and-B soil is more dense than the soil of your garden, there can be a problem in establishing the plant: its dense soil will not absorb water as quickly as the lighter garden soil around it. In such situations the soil ball around your B-and-B plant can become dry even when the garden soil is kept moist. To avoid this problem, amend the backfill as explained in the planting instructions that follow.

Planting techniques. Dig a hole twice as wide as the root ball and follow the instructions in the illustration on page 587. If the root ball is wrapped in burlap or another biodegradable fabric, you can leave it in place. But if a synthetic material encases the root ball, carefully remove it so that the roots can grow into the surrounding soil. Then fill the hole half full with backfill soil, firming it with your fingers or a stick.

If your soil is light to medium (and your B-and-B soil is heavier), mix one shovelful of organic amendment to each three shovelfuls of backfill soil. This will improve the water retention of the backfill soil, creating a transition zone between root ball and garden soil. Use peat moss, ground bark, nitrogen-fortified sawdust, or similar organic amendments—but not animal manures.

If you are setting out a B-and-B plant in a windy location, you should stake it. Drive the stake firmly into the soil beneath the planting hole on the side of the plant that faces the prevailing winds.

During the first couple of years after planting, pay close attention to watering—especially if the root-ball soil is heavier than your garden soil. Keep the surrounding garden soil moist (but never continuously soggy) so that the roots will grow out of the root ball into the surrounding soil as fast as possible.

Note: If a root ball becomes dry, it will shrink, harden, and fail to absorb water. Where there's a great difference between garden soil and root-ball soil, you can achieve better water penetration if you carefully punch holes in the root ball with a pointed instrument $\frac{1}{4}$ to $\frac{1}{2}$ inch wide. Or use a root irrigator (see Watering Devices, p. 610). After several years, when roots have grown out and become established in your garden soil, the difference between soil types won't matter.

Plant Problems. See Visual Guide to Identifying Plant Problems p. 590

Pleaching

I n pleaching, a method of training plant growth, branches are interwoven and plaited together to form a hedge or an arbor. Subsequent pruning merely maintains a neat, rather formal pattern. Trees that can be pleached include beech, apple, peach, and pear.

Pocket Gophers

Pocket gophers are serious garden pests in many parts of North America. Like little bulldozers, they dig out a network of tunnels—usually 6 to 18 inches below the surface—with strong, clawed forefeet. Tunnels near the surface are for gathering food; deeper ones are for sleeping, storing food, and raising young. Gophers eat roots, bulbs, and sometimes entire plants by pulling them down into their burrows. Well suited to burrow life, they have small eyes and ears that don't clog with dirt, and the flexibility needed to turn around in tight spaces.

The first sign of gopher trouble often is a fan-shaped mound of fresh, finely pulverized earth in a lawn or flower bed; this soil is a by-product of burrowing operations, brought to the surface through short side runs opening off the main burrow. A plug of earth is used to close the hole.

Controls. Trapping is the most efficient method of catching gophers. Avoid the temptation to place a single trap down a hole. Your chances of catching a gopher are much greater when you dig down to the main horizontal runway connecting with the surface hole and place two traps in the runway, one on either side of your excavation. Attach each trap to a stake on the surface with a chain or wire (this prevents a trapped gopher from dragging the trap farther into a burrow). The Macabee trap is the most effective. Box-type traps also work and are easier to set, but they require a larger hole to be dug for insertion.

When the traps are in place, plug the hole with a ball of carrot tops, fresh grass, or other tender greens; their scent attracts gophers. Next, place a board or soil over the greens and the hole to block all light. Check traps frequently, and clear tunnels if the gopher has pushed soil into the traps. Be persistent: a clever gopher may avoid your first traps.

Poison baits are very effective for the control of trapwise gophers. Probe for the deep burrows with a rod or sharp stick, insert bait, and close the hole. These baits are hazardous to other living things, so be sure not to spill any on the ground. And although poisoning of dogs and cats from eating poisoned gophers is rare, it can happen.

If your garden is subject to ongoing invasion by gophers from neighboring fields or orchards —or if all your trapping efforts fail—you can protect roots of young plants by lining the sides and bottom of planting holes with light-gauge chicken wire or hardware cloth.

Poison Oak, Poison Ivy

Poison oak *(Toxicodendron diversilobum)* is most common in California, western Oregon, and western Washington. In the open or in filtered sun, it grows as a dense, leafy shrub (see photograph, p. 615). Where shaded, as in coastal redwood country, it becomes a tall, climbing vine. Its leaves are divided into three leaflets, edges of which are scalloped, toothed, or lobed.

Very similar is poison ivy *(T. radicans),* which is very common east of the Rocky Mountains and also grows in eastern Oregon and eastern Washington. Poison ivy is commonly found in shady areas and along the edges of woodlands. It will grow as a sprawling plant until it finds something to climb on; then it becomes a clinging vine. Established plants bear clusters of pale green flowers in spring followed by small white berries.

The new growth of both poison oak and poison ivy is tinged red. Foliage turns bright orange to scarlet in fall—beautiful but to be avoided. It's hardest to identify the bare branches in winter and early spring; even brushing against these can cause the typical rash.

Poison oak and poison ivy are most effectively controlled with an appropriately labeled herbicide such as triclopyr or glyphosate.

Pollarding

In pollarding, a style of pruning, the main limbs of a young tree are drastically cut back to short lengths. Each dormant season following, the growth from these branch stubs is cut back to one or two buds. In time, branch ends become large and knobby. The result is a compact, leafy dome during the growing season and a somewhat grotesque branch structure during the dormant months. London plane tree *(Platanus acerifolia)* is most often subjected to this treatment.

Pollination

The transfer of pollen from stamens to pistil accomplishes pollination—which leads to seed formation and thus to a new generation of plants. Usually pollination happens by natural means—insects, birds, self-pollination, wind —although gardeners can transfer pollen from one flower to another to ensure fruit or to attempt a hybrid cross. An insect or animal that carries pollen from one part of a flower to another, or from one plant to another, is referred to as a pollinator.

Some plants produce separate male flowers (with stamens only) and female flowers (with pistils only). These may appear on the same plant (in pecans and walnuts, for example) or on separate plants (as in hollies). In the latter case, you need a male plant nearby to produce fruits on the female plant. To get a crop from some fruit and nut trees, you need to plant two varieties—either because a variety will not set fruit using its own pollen or because its own pollen will not be ripe when its pistils are receptive. A plant used to provide pollen for another plant is called a pollinator or pollenizer.

Potassium. See Nutrients, Basic	p. 577
Pot-Bound. See Root-Bound	p. 596

Potting Soil

A potting soil is a soil mix designed especially for plants growing in containers. See Container Gardening (p. 554).

Powdery and Downy Mildews

Powdery mildew and downy mildew are two diseases that are often confused. Powdery mildew first appears as small gray or white circular patches on plant tissue, spreading rapidly to form powdery areas of fungus filaments and spores (see photograph on p. 592). Powdery mildew can infect leaves, buds, flowers, and stems, depending on the exact kind of mildew and the host plant. It attacks young growth of some woody plants, such as roses and sycamores, and mature leaves of nonwoody plants such as dahlias, chrysanthemums, peas, beans, and squash. Infected leaves may become crumpled and distorted.

Powdery mildew spores are unique in that they can cause infection in the absence of moisture. Most powdery mildews (there are many kinds) thrive in humid air, but spores need dry leaves on which to become established. You're likely to find powdery mildew when days are warm and nights are cool; it also resurges when days shorten and cool, humid nights lengthen. No climate region escapes powdery mildew, but areas with summer rainfall generally have less mildew than dry-summer regions.

Some plants are notoriously mildew-prone *(Photinia glabra, Euonymus japonica,* and certain rose varieties, for example). Where powdery mildew is especially troublesome, it is best to exclude such plants from your garden or plant disease resistant varieties.

▶ page 593

P

Visual Guide to Identifying

PLANT PROBLEMS

Problems on plant leaves are often difficult to diagnose—there are so many possible causes, including insects, disease organisms, nutritional deficiencies, and cultural practices. Yet identifying the cause properly is the most important step in finding a solution. These pages will help you identify common maladies on plant leaves, so that you can refer to the entry for the pest to determine effective control measures. Also be sure to read Pest Management (p. 580).

DISTORTED LEAVES, STEMS, AND FRUIT

Peach Leaf Curl
Curled, distorted leaves   p. 579

Galls
Unusual growths   p. 565

Aphids
Wilted or malformed new leaves
          p. 546

Bagworm
Small, baglike nests, eaten foliage
          p. 547

Gummosis
Oozing liquid from branches, trunk   p. 567

Leaf Roller
Rolled or distorted leaves   p. 575

Thrips
Twisted, discolored, distorted leaves, flowers   p. 603

Tarnished Plant Bug
Blackened shoots, scarred fruit   p. 602

Flea Beetles
Small holes in leaves, foliage dried
p. 564

Gypsy Moth
Eaten leaves, plant defoliated
p. 552

Rose Chafer
Leaves chewed to lace, holes in flowers (roses and peonies are favorites); dead patches in lawn
p. 596

Tent Caterpillars
Eaten leaves, weblike nest
p. 602

Colorado Potato Beetle
Chewed leaves and flowers
p. 553

Slugs, Snails
Eaten leaves
p. 598

Japanese Beetle
Skeletonized leaves, eaten flowers
p. 569

Root Weevil
Notches in leaf edges
p. 596

Squash Bug
Eaten, wilted leaves
p. 601

WILTED AND DISCOLORED LEAVES

Bacterial Wilt
Wilted leaves, especially on cucumbers; prevalent in cold weather   p. 546

Mealybugs
White cottony masses
                                p. 576

Whiteflies
Whitish specks on leaf undersides
                                p. 613

Nitrogen Deficiency
Yellow leaves   p. 578

Spider Mites
Yellow stippling   p. 576

Leaf Miner
Tunnel-like trails in leaves   p. 574

Southern Blight
Wilted foliage, turns yellow, dies
                                p. 600

Nematodes
Wilted foliage, nodules on roots
                                p. 577

Iron Deficiency (Chlorosis)
Yellow leaves, green veins
p. 552

Oak Root Fungus
Dull yellow leaves, wilting, entire dead branches, possibly brown mushrooms at base in early winter   p. 579

Anthracnose
Irregular blotches of dead tissue, dropping leaves   p. 575

Scale
Bumps on stems, leaves   p. 597

Black Spot
Black spots with fringed edges   p. 575

Rust
Yellow-to-orange pustules on leaf undersides   p. 597

Sooty Mold
Black sticky mold that grows on leaves and twigs   p. 600

Fireblight
Dry, scorched leaves   p. 563

Verticillium Wilt
Leaf dieback   p. 606

Powdery Mildew
Small gray or white patches, distorted leaves coated with white powder   p. 589

FOUR WAYS TO PRUNE

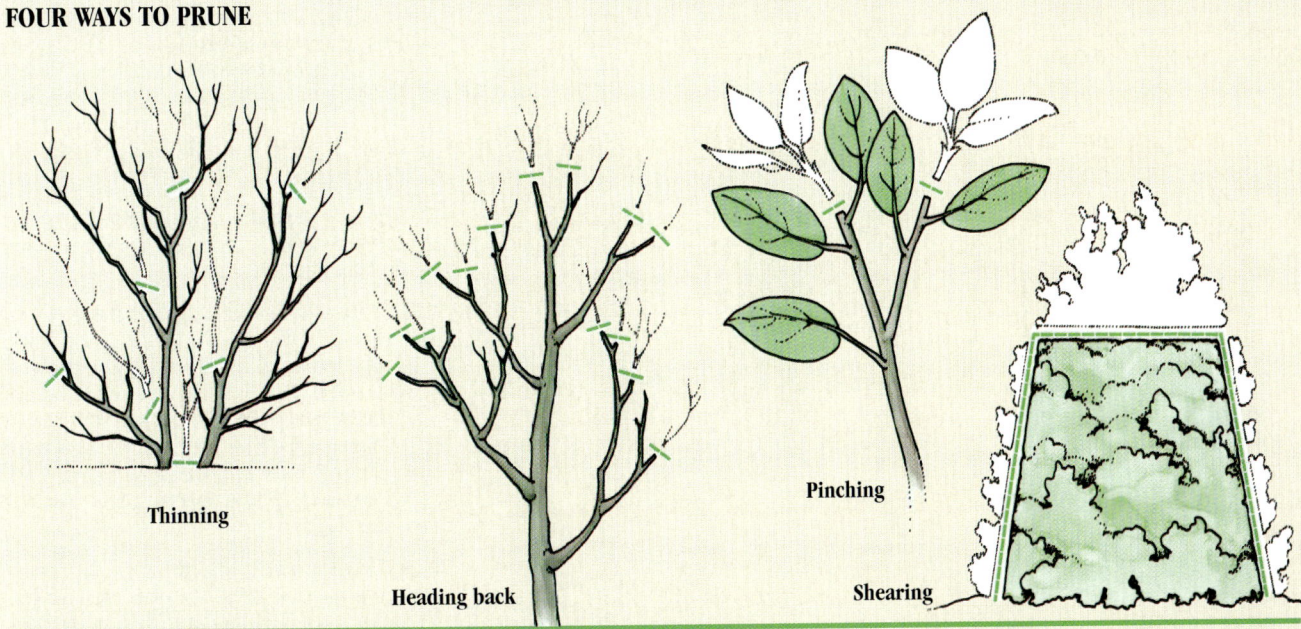

Thinning

Heading back

Pinching

Shearing

Downy mildew differs from powdery mildew in several ways. It is common in cool, moist conditions and spreads fastest on wet foliage. It can pop up almost anywhere in North America but becomes less serious where summers eventually warm up. It is particularly troublesome in cool-summer areas such as the Northeast and Northwest but, in general, is less common than powdery mildew. Downy mildew also differs from powdery mildew in that the white fuzzy fungus appears on the undersides of the leaves. The leaves develop yellow spots on top, then often dry, become brittle, and drop. Clusters of grapes (a common host) may also be infected and fail to ripen properly. Besides grapes, downy mildew also infects many vegetables, including peas and cucurbits, and flowers such as roses and pansies.

Controls. Several fungicides are effective at controlling powdery mildew. Triadimefon has been noted by rose growers as the most effective at both preventing and eradicating powdery mildew, although it has a tendency to shorten growth and can be difficult to find. Other helpful chemicals are triforine and thiophanate-methyl. Some rose growers have had good luck controlling powdery mildew by spraying plants with antitranspirant products or the baking soda/oil spray described for Black Spot, under Leaf Spot (p. 575). Overhead watering can also reduce problems with powdery mildew.

To control downy mildew, avoid overhead watering and irrigate early in the morning so foliage dries out quickly. Prune plants to keep them open for good air circulation. Clean up plant debris to prevent reinfection. Some plant species are available in varieties that resist downy mildew.

Controlling downy mildew with fungicides is difficult. Although several are labeled for control of downy mildew, not all are effective. Prevention through good cultural practices is the best method of control.

Propagation

In gardening usage, propagation refers to the many ways of starting new plants. These methods range from planting seeds to the more complicated arts of budding and grafting.

With the exception of seed sowing, all methods of starting new plants are known as vegetative propagation: the new plants that result will be identical to the parent plant. Vegetative propagation therefore maintains uniformity—ensuring, for example, that each plant of the rose 'Queen Elizabeth' is like every other.

Methods of propagating plants are described under their alphabetical listings: Budding (p. 548), Cuttings (p. 555), Dividing (p. 558), and Grafting (p. 565). Propagation by seed is described under Planting Techniques: Seeds (p. 584).

Pruning

Pruning is both a skill and an art. The skill is in making cuts that callus (form a thickened tissue that seals off wounds) properly and minimize the chance for decay. The art is in making cuts in the right places so that the plant takes on a handsome form and is prolific if grown for flowers or fruit.

No matter how much or how little pruning you do on an established plant, the objective is to modify the plant's growth. The modification can be done for any of the following reasons, singly or in combination:

- To maintain plant health by removing dead, diseased, or injured wood

- To control or direct growth

- To increase quality or yield of flowers or fruit

- To train young plants to position their main branches or to ensure strong structure

It shouldn't be necessary to cut back a plant continually to keep it in bounds. A plant that seems to require such treatment was the wrong choice for its garden location; the repeated cutting back only destroys the plant's natural beauty. Exceptions are pruning formal hedges, espaliering fruit trees, shaping topiary, and pollarding.

A word of caution: Pruning large trees over 10 to 15 feet high should be left to professional arborists or tree trimmers. They are properly trained and have the right equipment to do the job safely. To make sure you'll get the job done right, review pruning guidelines published by the International Society of Arboriculture. Your pruner should have a copy.

Pruning and growth. To understand how to approach the pruning of any plant, you need to know how growth occurs. Because all growth originates in buds, they are the first plant parts to consider.

The terminal growth bud develops at the end of a stem or branch. This bud causes the stem to grow in length.

Lateral buds grow along the sides of stems. These buds produce the sideways, or lateral, growth that makes a plant bushy.

Some plants may have latent buds—buds that lie dormant beneath the bark. Some of these buds may grow after pruning or injury removes the actively growing part of the stem.

Actively growing terminal buds produce hormones, called auxins, that stimulate their growth and, in many species, prevent lateral buds below them from growing during the current season. If the terminal bud is removed, either while the plant is growing or dormant, subsequent growth occurs from the uppermost lateral buds. These

P

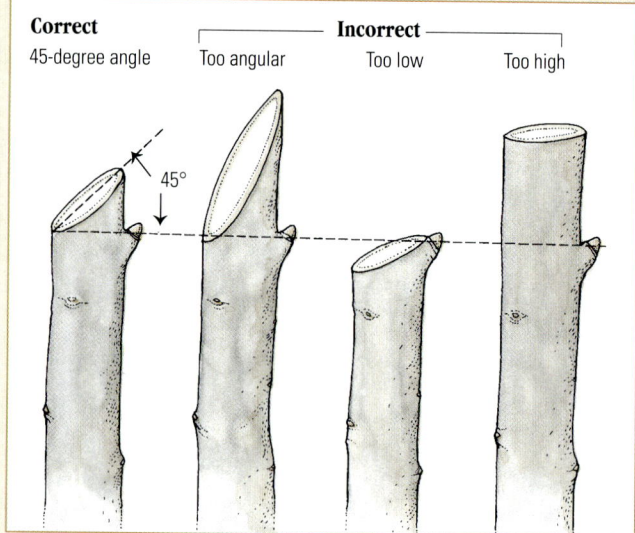

Correct
45-degree angle

— Incorrect —
Too angular   Too low   Too high

45°

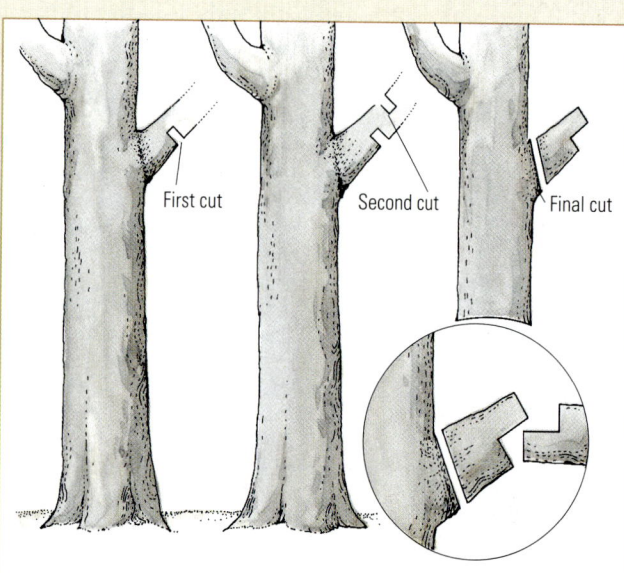

Correct

Blade

Cutting edge

Hook

Incorrect

Hook

Cutting edge

Blade

First cut

Second cut

Final cut

P

HOW TO MAKE A PRUNING CUT

A correct pruning cut has its lower point even with the top of a growth bud and slants upward at about a 45° angle.

HOW TO POSITION SHEARS

To make a proper close pruning cut, hold pruning shears with the blade closest to the growth that will remain on the plant. A stub results when you reverse the position and place the hook closest to the plant.

HOW TO REMOVE A LARGE LIMB

First, cut beneath branch, one-third to one-half through; then cut off limb beyond first cut. Finally, remove limb stub, cutting just outside bark ridges at limb's base as shown in circled inset illustration (or on a line bisecting top and bottom angles branch makes to trunk).

growth patterns and responses influence plant form and structural strength.

All pruning cuts, including pinching, should be made just above some growth—a growth bud, stem, or branch. For explanations of how to make proper cuts, see Pruning Cuts on the next page.

Types of pruning. All pruning methods have specific goals. Common approaches are explained in the illustration.

- **Thinning.** Thinning is the removal of a lateral branch at its point of origin or the shortening of a branch to a smaller lateral branch (at least 30 percent of the size of the branch being removed). Thinning serves to open a plant to sunlight—and reduce its size (if desired) while accentuating its natural form. In most cases thinning cuts are preferred over heading cuts.

- **Heading back.** This sort of pruning—also called cutting back—involves cutting a currently growing or 1-year-old shoot to a bud, or cutting an older branch back to a stub or a tiny twig. Pinching and shearing are forms of heading. With a few exceptions, including pruning fruit trees to establish main framework branches, shearing hedges to keep them compact, and pruning roses for flower production, heading is a less desirable type of pruning. The reason is simple: heading results in vigorous growth below the cut, usually from several to many buds, depending on the severity of the heading. While a plant that has been headed does become more compact, its natural shape is ruined and will be difficult to repair. In addition, new growth is often weakly attached and prone to breaking. Every year, scores of beautiful trees are ruined when they are headed back instead of thinned.

- **Pinching.** The first opportunity you have to control or direct plant growth is to remove—to pinch out—new growth before it elongates into stems. This is especially useful with young plants that you want to make bushier. For example, you can pinch all the terminal buds on every branch of a young fuchsia plant. This will force growth from buds that are at the leaf bases along the stems, creating perhaps two, three, or four new side branches instead of just one lengthening branch. When this happens, you get all-over growth. Conversely, if you want a plant to gain height, keep side growth pinched back so that the terminal bud on the main stem continues to elongate.

- **Shearing.** This is the only form of pruning that could be called indiscriminate. Ignoring all advice about cutting just above growing points, you instead clip the surface of densely foliaged plants. Shearing is the process that maintains the even surfaces of formal hedges and topiary work. Because the plants that normally are used for these purposes have buds and branches that are close together on their stems, every cut is close to a growing point.

Pruning cuts. After you understand how to approach a pruning job, you need to know how to make good pruning cuts. The first lesson: never leave a stub. Or to put it another way, always make a cut just above some sort of growth (a bud or a stem). To understand why this advice is given, think of a stem or branch as a conveying tube for water and plant nutrients. If you cut a branch some distance beyond its uppermost growing part, you leave nothing in the stub itself to maintain growth. The stub, no longer a part of the plant's active metabolism, withers and dies, although still attached to the plant. In time it will decay and drop off, leaving an open patch of dead tissue where it was attached. In contrast, when a cut is made just above a growing point, callus tissue begins to grow inward from the cut edges; in time, this tissue will cover the cut surface.

There is a right way to make pruning cuts—and there are several wrong ways, as the illustration on the previous page shows. You want to avoid leaving stubs, and you also want to avoid undercutting the bud or branch. The best cuts place the lowest part of the cut directly opposite and slightly above the upper side of the bud or branch to which you are cutting back.

Using pruning shears. When you cut with shears, be sure that the cuts are sharp: clean cuts callus over faster than cuts with ragged edges. Use shears that are strong enough for the job. If you can't get them to cut easily through a branch, the shears are too small, too dull, or both. Switch to a stronger pair of shears or use a pruning saw instead. With hook-and-blade pruning shears, remember to place the blade, not the hook, closer to the branch or stem that will remain on the plant. As illustrated on the next page, if the position of the shears is reversed, you will leave a small stub.

Using pruning saws. Pruning saws come in handy when you need to cut limbs that are too thick for shears or loppers, or when a plant's growth won't allow your hand and the shears to get into position to make a good cut.

Larger limbs—from wrist size upward—are heavy and need special care in removal. If you try to cut through one with a single cut, the branch is likely to fracture before you've finished the cut. The limb may fall, tearing wood and bark with it and leaving a large, ugly wound. To cut a larger limb safely, make it a three-step operation, as illustrated on the next page. The final cut should be made very carefully. For years, the recommended approach was to cut the branch flush to the trunk. That has changed slightly. To avoid decay, make the final cut slightly outside the branch bark ridge (the compressed bark in the branch crotch) and branch collar (the natural circles or ridges where the branch meets the trunk), as shown in the illustration on the next page. If no collar is visible, the angle of the cut should match the angle formed by the branch bark ridge and the axis of the trunk.

Pruning to shape. In shaping, your artistic side plays a role in determining what form a particular plant should take. Every plant has a natural shape; its growth tends to conform to a natural pattern, whether round, gumdrop-shaped, wide-spreading, vase-shaped, or arching. Observe what a plant's natural shape is, and then prune the plant in a manner that will allow the natural form to continue to develop. Remove any excess growth that obscures the basic pattern or any errant growth that departs from the natural form. Use thinning cuts.

When pruning to shape, make your cuts above a bud or side branch that points in the direction you'd like the new growth to take. If you have no preference, remember that generally it is better for a new branch to grow toward an open space than toward another branch. Also, it is generally better for growth to be directed toward the outside of the plant than toward its interior. Try to eliminate branches that cross and touch one another. Crossing branches may rub together, suffering injury, and are usually unattractive, especially in deciduous plants out of leaf.

Pruning for flower production. Flowering shrubs bloom either from new growth or from old wood, depending on the plant species. Before you prune, determine which sort of growth bears flowers. In this way, you can avoid inadvertently cutting out stems that would give you a flower display.

Most spring-flowering shrubs bloom from wood formed during the previous year. Wait until these plants have finished flowering before pruning them (or do some pruning by cutting flowers while they are in bud or bloom). Growth that the shrubs make after flowering will provide blooms for the next year.

Most summer-flowering shrubs bloom on growth from the spring of the same year. These are the shrubs you can prune during the winter dormant season without sacrificing the next crop of blooms.

A few shrubs bloom twice or throughout the growing season (many roses, for example). Spring flowers grow from old wood; later blooms come both from recent growth and from wood of previous years. During the dormant season, remove weak and unproductive stems and, if necessary, lightly head back remaining growth. During the growing season, prune as necessary to shape while you remove spent blossoms.

Pruning conifers. These evergreens fall into two broad classes: those with branches radiating out from the trunk in whorls and those that sprout branches in a random fashion. Spruce, fir, and most pines are examples of the whorl type; arborvitae, hemlock, juniper, and yew are examples of random-branching conifers. Pruning guidelines differ for the two groups.

On whorl-branching types, buds appear at the tips of new growth, along the lengthening new growth, and at the bases of new growth. You can cut back the new growth "candles" about halfway to induce more branching, or you can cut them out entirely to force branching from buds at their bases. The point to remember is that you must make cuts above potential growth buds or back to existing branches. Cutting back into an old stem—even one that still bears foliage—won't force branching unless you're cutting back to latent buds.

The random-branching conifers can be pruned selectively, headed back, even sheared; new growth will emerge from stems or branches below the cuts. But when you shorten a branch, don't cut into bare wood below green growth: most kinds (yew is an exception) won't develop new growth from bare wood.

Controlling height. Some conifers—chiefly the random-branching kinds, plus deodar cedar and hemlock—can be kept at a controlled size, either as dense specimens or as hedges. When growth reaches within a foot or so of the size you desire, cut back all but about 1 inch of the new growth. This will produce enough small side branchlets to make full, dense foliage. Once this bushy growth forms at the ends of the branches, you can hold the plant to a small size year after year by shortening new growth that develops and cutting out any wild shoots.

Repairing damaged trees. When a conifer has been damaged by cold or breakage, you may have to remove entire limbs. It's almost impossible to restore the natural shape, but you can often make the most of the situation by trimming or training the damaged plant into an unusual sculptural form. If the central leader has been damaged, you can stake one of the next lower branches vertically and train it as a new leader.

Pseudobulb

A thickened, aboveground modified stem is called a pseudobulb. Found in some orchids such as *Cymbidium*, it serves as a storage organ for nutrients.

Purslane

Purslane is a mat-forming annual weed. It thrives in damp or dry conditions and warm weather. Look for succulent, fleshy green-to-red stems and dark green leaves, often tinged with red; pale yellow flowers open on sunny mornings (see photograph, p. 614). Spreading by seeds and stem fragments that root in damp soil, this weed is easy to dig out. Chemical controls include glyphosate and appropriately labeled pre-emergence herbicides.

Ragweed

Ragweed, also called wild tansy or hogweed, is a particularly irritating weed because of the copious amounts of pollen it produces and the resulting hay fever it causes for millions of people in late summer and fall.

R

There are three troublesome species of ragweed: common ragweed, *Ambrosia artemisiifolia;* giant ragweed, *A. trifida;* and western ragweed, *A. psilostachya.* Common and western ragweed are similar-looking plants with ferny foliage on hairy stems, ranging from 1 to 6 feet high (western ragweed tends to be shorter and bushier). Greenish male flowers grow at the end of the stems, producing huge amounts of pollen. One important difference between the plants is that common ragweed is an annual and western ragweed is perennial, spreading by underground rhizomes.

Giant ragweed, an annual, grows taller—to 10 feet high—and has three-lobed leaves.

Ragweeds grow under a variety of conditions and are most prevalent in the central and eastern portions of the country, where summer rains are common. They are usually found growing on the edge of fields or vacant lots.

Young ragweed plants can easily be controlled by pulling, hoeing, or rototilling. Once the plants are older, they are harder to remove. Glyphosate is an effective herbicide for controlling ragweed.

Rhizome

A thickened modified stem, a rhizome grows horizontally along or under the soil surface (see illustration, p. 551). It may be long and slender, as in some lawn grasses, or thick and fleshy, as in many irises.

Rock Garden

Usually a constructed landscape, often on sloping ground, a rock garden contains natural-appearing rock outcrops and rocky soil surfaces. Plants commonly grown in rock gardens are listed on pages 144–146.

Root Ball

The network of roots and the soil clinging to them when a plant is lifted from the soil or removed from a container is called its root ball.

Root-Bound

When a plant grows for too long in its container, it generally becomes root-bound. With no room for additional growth, roots become tangled, matted, and grow in circles. Root-bound plants placed in the ground without having their roots untangled often fail to overcome their choked condition and don't grow well—or don't grow at all.

Rooting Hormone

A rooting hormone is a powder or liquid, containing growth hormones (auxins). It stimulates root formation on a cutting.

Root Rots, Water Molds

The diseases caused by the water-mold fungi are seldom mentioned as such. But they are indirectly referred to in directions that specify "infrequent but deep watering," "sharp drainage" or "well-drained soil," "good aeration," or "keeping a plant on the dry side." These phrases advise you how to avoid water molds.

Free water (excess water that fills the air spaces in the soil—see p. 609) can suffocate plant roots. But water can pass through the soil continuously without damaging roots if it carries air with it. The damage to roots from overwatering is, in almost all cases, not caused by water itself but by water-mold fungi that thrive when free water stands too long around roots —especially when soil is warm. Weakened or stressed plants are much more susceptible.

To offset problems caused by water-mold fungi, take steps to improve soil drainage (if necessary) for susceptible plants; see Soils (p. 600) for more information. And be sure not to overwater. The only symptom that almost always indicates a need for more water is wilting. Other signs—such as poor growth, dropping leaves, and yellowing—suggest other problems, including root rot. Planting in raised beds filled with soil-less potting mix that provides excellent drainage is also a good way to avoid root-rot problems.

Two chemicals, metalaxyl and fosetyl-al, have proven effective against water molds, but they are costly and often hard to find.

Roots. See Plant Anatomy and Growth p. 583

Rootstock

The rootstock is the part of a budded or grafted plant (see Budding, p. 548, and Grafting, p. 565) that furnishes the root system and sometimes part of the branch structure. "Understock" has the same meaning.

USING ROW COVERS

Row covers let you get the jump on the vegetable season or prolong it into fall. Cover traps heat, warming soil; light and water penetrate it, but insect pests and birds are excluded.

Root Weevils

Many species of root weevils are found throughout North America. From the moment they emerge in spring through fall, flightless gray or black adults eat notches from leaf edges of many plants—especially azaleas and rhododendrons, roses, and viburnums (see photograph, p. 591). In late summer, the weevils lay eggs on the soil or in folds of leaves. Eggs hatch into legless larvae with pinkish or whitish bodies and tan heads; these burrow into the soil and eat roots, particularly of strawberry plants. Controlling root weevils isn't easy. Floating row covers can exclude adults from vegetable plants. The botanical insecticide rotenone can also be effective against adults if sprayed at dusk. Use acephate to control adults (which feed only at night) on nonedible plants. Parasitic nematodes are effective for controlling larvae.

Rose Chafers

Rose chafers are slender, ½-inch-long beetles with long legs and light tan bodies (see photograph, p. 591). The adults feed in swarms, attacking flowering plants first (roses and peonies are favorites), then moving on to other plants. They eat holes in blossoms and chew leaves to lace. The slim, ¾-inch-long, white grubs attack lawns like other beetle grubs, but they prefer sandy soils. Dead patches of lawn are severed at the roots and easy to pull up.

Controlling rose chafers is similar to controlling Japanese beetles; however, milky spore is not effective against rose chafers. Row covers will protect flowers and vegetables. Rotenone, pyrethrum, and insecticidal soaps are less toxic pesticides for controlling adults. Regular tilling of the soil will expose grubs to birds. Parasitic nematodes also attack grubs.

Traditional chemicals include diazinon on lawns, carbaryl on vegetables, and acephate on ornamentals.

Rosette

Plants are said to grow in rosettes if their leaves are closely set around a crown or center—as in the case of hen and chicks (*Echeveria*) or hen and chickens (*Sempervivum*).

Row Covers

Several types of semitransparent materials, called row covers, are used to cover plants (see illustration). They trap heat, enhancing growth or providing frost protection, and exclude pests. See the box Extending the Season for Harvest (p. 606) under Vegetable Gardening.

R

SELECTING SHRUBS

In times past, homeowners sought out bulky shrubs for "foundation plantings," to provide transition from house to garden by hiding the unattractive house foundation. But with the disappearance of high foundations in many modern homes, shrubs have taken on new roles. Because they encompass such a diversity of sizes, shapes, and appearances, shrubs naturally can perform a great range of landscape functions well.

In choosing shrubs for your garden, don't be guided solely by flashy color or sentimental attachment. Keep in mind the following points:

■ **Adaptability.** No shrub will satisfy you unless it is suited to your climate, your soil, and your garden environment. Check specific descriptions in the Plant Encyclopedia.

■ **Plant size.** If you have a space for a 4-by-4-foot shrub but plant one that will reach 12 feet in all directions, you're bound to be unhappy in time. Remember that the most attractive shrubs (except those intended for sheared hedges) are those that are allowed to reach their natural size without severe restriction.

■ **Growth rate.** Hand in hand with knowledge of a plant's ultimate size should go the realization of how fast it will get there. Slow growth is the price you will have to pay for some of the most desirable shrubs, so place those plants where their slowness will not be detrimental to your plans.

■ **Texture.** The texture of individual leaves, as well as the texture of many leaves in mass, varies almost as much as do shrubs themselves. Shiny, dull, hairy or fuzzy, smooth, quilted—these qualities, combined with the size and shape of the leaf, give a plant its character. You can do much to highlight a shrub's inherent beauty if you consider how its foliage texture will complement that of neighboring plants and how it will relate to any nearby structure. If you capitalize on differences in texture—whether large leaves against small (or vice versa) or fine-textured against broad and stiff—the individual plants will have a chance to show off.

■ **Color.** Though many shrubs are planted for the floral display they will make, foliage colors are just as important in the landscape picture. See page 96 for lists of shrubs with leaves of different colors.

Much of the advice about plant texture also applies to choosing and combining foliage colors. Visualize the combinations and juxtapositions, remembering that too much of a good thing—color, in this case—produces not an artistic statement but a jumble.

Runner

A runner is a slender stem—sent out from the bases of certain perennials—at the end of which an offset develops. In common usage, however, the term "runner" has come to refer to either offsets or stolons.

Rust

One kind of rust is the notorious plague found on rose leaves; other kinds of rust colonize snapdragons, hollyhocks, and many other plants. Each type of rust is specific to a certain type of plant: rose rust will not infect hollyhocks, for example, and hollyhock rust will not infect roses. On roses, the fungus usually appears in late spring as yellow-to-orange pustules on undersides of older leaves. (Other rusts may be brownish or even purple.) As the infection progresses, leaf undersides become covered with powdery masses of spores (see photograph, p. 592), and upper surfaces display a yellow mottling. In advanced stages on some plants, entire leaves may turn yellow and drop.

Warm days, cool nights, and moisture (even heavy dew) encourage rust development; rain, sprinkling, and wind spread the fungus from plant to plant. Leaf surfaces must be wet for a minimum of 4 to 5 hours for spores to germinate and infect the plant. Prolonged hot, dry weather will usually halt rust development. The fungus can survive over winter on both live and dead leaves.

Controls. Rust prevention begins in winter. Thoroughly clean up fallen leaves and debris; remove any rust-infected leaves that remain on plants. During the rust season, choose from a number of fungicide sprays that kill the fungus. Triforine is favored by rose growers; triadimefon also is effective (although it has a tendency to shorten growth), as are chlorathalonil and wettable sulfur. If you water by overhead sprinkling, do it in early morning on sunny days so that leaves will dry quickly. For information on cedar-apple rust, see Apple, p. 185.

Salinity. See Soil Salinity	p. 600
Scab. See Leaf Spot	p. 575

Scale

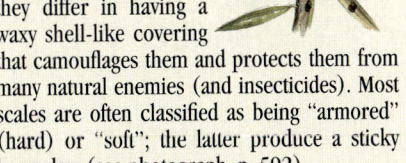

Scale insects can be a garden problem almost anywhere in North America. Closely related to mealybugs and aphids, they differ in having a waxy shell-like covering that camouflages them and protects them from many natural enemies (and insecticides). Most scales are often classified as being "armored" (hard) or "soft"; the latter produce a sticky honeydew (see photograph, p. 592).

An adult scale insect lives under its stationary waxy shell, which sticks to a plant. Running from the underside of the insect into the plant tissue is a tiny filamentous mouth part, through which the scale sucks plant juices. Scale eggs hatch beneath the stationary shell; then, sometime in spring or summer, the young crawl out from under the protective cover and seek their own feeding sites.

Controls. If scale infestation is light, you may control it by picking scales off the plant or scraping them off with a plastic scouring pad. On deciduous plants, you can kill some adult scales in winter with a dormant oil spray. Insecticides are effective against scales only during the juvenile "crawler" stage, before waxy shells develop. Effective at this time are summer oil spray, malathion, diazinon, acephate, and carbaryl. (To check for "crawlers," wrap sticky trap around infested branch and look for trapped crawlers.)

Many naturally occurring parasites and predators control or limit scale insect populations. Unless a valuable plant is in jeopardy from scale infestation, don't spray with an insecticide, because it can also kill the scale's natural enemies. *Aphytis* wasps, a parasite of some kinds of scale, are sometimes sold for release in the home garden. (See Visual Guide to Identifying Biological Controls, p. 549.) In dry regions, you can help scale-infested plants by hosing them off frequently: dust inhibits the various parasites and predators of scale insects.

Ants tend and protect scale insects as they do aphids. Refer to Aphids (p. 546) for ant control tips.

Scion

A scion is a bud or a short length of stem of one plant that is budded or grafted onto a rootstock of another. See Budding (p. 548) and Grafting (p. 565).

Seeds. See Germination; Plant Anatomy and Growth; and Planting Techniques: Seeds
pp. 565, 583, 584

S

Self-Branching

Certain annuals that produce numerous side growths and grow compactly without having to be pinched back are referred to as self-branching.

Sepals. See Plant Anatomy and Growth p. 583

Shot Hole. See Leaf Spot   p. 575

Shrub

A shrub is a woody plant that usually increases in size by growing new wood from older wood, as well as new stems from the plant's base. Unless specially trained, a shrub will have many stems that rise from ground level or close to it (in contrast to most trees, which grow a single trunk and branch higher up). Shrubs range from ankle-height dwarfs to multi-stemmed giants you can walk under; forms run from spreading to upright, from stiff to vinelike.

Whether a foot-high shrublet or a 15-foot shrub-tree, a shrub is planted to occupy a more or less permanent place in the garden. This permanence is perhaps a shrub's greatest virtue: after planting, you can expect years of enjoyment with little effort. For tips on selecting shrubs, see box on page 597.

Single Flower

The single flower type has the minimum number of petals for its kind, usually four, five, or six. (The basic number of petals for roses, for example, is five.)

Slugs, Snails

In many parts of the country, snails and slugs are the most troublesome garden pests. Similar creatures (a slug is simply a snail without a  shell), they feed on various plants by biting tissue with rasping mouths underneath their bodies (see photograph, p. 591). Both hide by day and feed at night, although they may be active during daytime hours on gray, damp days.

Nobody ever gets rid of slugs or snails for good. They always return—from neighbors' lots, on new plants, or even in new soil (often in container-grown plants) as eggs. The eggs look like clusters of 1/8-inch pearls; look for them under rocks, boards, and pots, and destroy those you find.

Chemical controls. The most popular controls are packaged baits containing metaldehyde or methiocarb in pellets, meal, or emulsion form. Metaldehyde is the most widely used, but its effectiveness is limited during periods of high humidity. Methiocarb, commonly used in slug bait, should not be used around fruits and vegetables. If you put out pellets, scatter them so there is space between them rather than making piles. And be careful using baits where dogs live or visit, because the bait can poison dogs, too. Never apply it when dogs are present: it may look as though you're putting out dry dog food.

Physical controls. Hand-picking is an easy way to control snails: you simply grab them by their shells and dispose of them however you wish. (Slugs are harder to pick up because they have no shell to grab. Some gardeners kill them with a 5 percent ammonia solution in a hand sprayer.) The best hunting time for slugs and snails is after 10 P.M.

You can also trap slugs and snails. One easy-to-set trap is a wide plank or piece of plywood elevated about an inch off the ground. Placed in an infested area, it offers a daytime hiding place—from which you can collect and dispatch the pests. Squash a slug or snail on the board's underside; this will attract other slugs and snails. Beer or a solution of sugar water and yeast appeals to slugs' fondness for fermented foods. Put the liquid in a saucer or other shallow container, and set it in the garden so the rim is even with the soil. Slugs will crawl into the dish and drown. Refill the container daily with fresh liquid.

You can prevent snails from damaging such plants as citrus by wrapping copper bands around the tree trunks. Snails and slugs will not cross this barrier.

Biological controls. Decollate snails feed on the brown garden snail, but, although they do not usually molest mature garden plants, they will feed on succulent leaves or berries near the ground, especially once the supply of brown garden snails has been depleted. Their sale is legal only in certain areas. Check with your Cooperative Extension Office before purchasing.

Soil Amendments, Inorganic

Various inorganic soil amendments may be useful in special situations. But because they provide no nourishment for micro-organisms in the soil, they are no substitute for organic amendments. Use inorganic materials only to supplement organic amendments when a specific need arises.

Physical amendments. This group of mineral amendments includes perlite, pumice, and vermiculite. These materials improve the texture of clay soils and increase the capacity of sandy soils to hold water and dissolved nutrients. But their relatively high cost limits use to small-scale projects: amending soil in containers or in small planting beds.

Perlite and pumice are hard, spongelike materials that are inert (as sand is), but their porosity makes them water absorbent. Soft-textured vermiculite (expanded mica) can absorb nutrients as well as water and will contribute some potassium and magnesium, which are essential to plant growth. Vermiculite breaks down after several years; perlite and pumice last considerably longer.

Chemical amendments. Included among the chemical amendments are lime and gypsum, both sold as fine powder or granules to be scattered over the soil surface and dug or tilled in. Although lime is the traditional remedy for raising the pH of overly acid soils, both lime and gypsum may improve some clay soils by causing the tiny clay particles to group together into larger units, or "crumbs." This produces larger spaces between particle aggregates, with a corresponding improvement in aeration and drainage.

Which material to use depends on the pH of your soil. Where soil is alkaline and high in sodium—the "black alkali" soils of the low-rainfall Southwest and West—gypsum (calcium sulfate) reacts with the sodium and clay particles to produce the larger soil crumbs. If your soil is acid—generally in regions of plentiful rainfall—lime is the material that might be useful. Lime adds calcium to soil; gypsum furnishes both calcium and sulfur. Either material may be used as a nutrient supplement in regions (such as parts of the Pacific Northwest and the Northeast) where these minerals sometimes are deficient.

Before using either lime or gypsum, check with your Cooperative Extension Office for advisability and guidelines.

Soil Amendments, Organic

Vital to the fertility of all soils—and particularly needed in sand and clay—is organic matter, the decaying remains of once-living plants and animals. Gardeners therefore incorporate organic soil amendments into their soil to improve or maintain the soil's texture and thereby encourage healthy root growth.

Advantages. Organic soil amendments immediately improve aeration and drainage of clay soils by acting as wedges between particles and particle aggregates. In a sandy soil, organic amendments help hold water and dissolved nutrients in the pore spaces, so the soil will stay moist and hold dissolved nutrients longer.

As organic matter decomposes, it releases nutrients, which add to soil fertility. But the nitrogen released by decaying organic matter isn't immediately available to plants. First it must be converted by soil micro-organisms (bacteria, fungi, molds) into ammonia, then into nitrites, and finally into nitrates, which can be absorbed by plant roots. See Nutrients, Basic (p. 577).

The micro-organisms that do this converting are living entities themselves and need a certain amount of warmth, air, water, and nitrogen to live and carry on their functions. Soil amendments, by improving aeration and water pene-

SOIL TEXTURE AND SOIL STRUCTURE

Clay particles are the smallest mineral component of a soil, sand particles are the largest, and silt represents the intermediate size. Clay and sand give their names to two soil types. A combination of the three particle sizes forms the basis for the soil called loam. See illustration.

Clay soils. Also called adobe, gumbo, or just "heavy" soils, clay soils are composed of microscopically small mineral particles. These tiny particles are flattened and fit closely together; pore spaces between particles (for air and water) also are small. But because small clay particles offer the greatest surface area per volume of all soil types, clay soils can contain the greatest volume of nutrients in soluble or exchangeable form (see Nutrients, Basic, p. 577). When clay soils get wet, drainage—the downward movement of water—is slow. This means that loss of soluble nutrients by leaching also is slow. And because of its high density, clay soil is the slowest to warm in spring.

Sandy soils. Sandy soils have comparatively large particles that are cube-shaped rather than flattened. The particle size and shape allow for much larger pore spaces between particles than clay soils have; consequently, sandy soils contain a lot of air, drain well, and warm quickly. In a given volume of sandy soil, the surface area of particles is less than that in the same volume of clay. The volume of soluble and exchangeable nutrients in sandy soil is therefore correspondingly less. And because sandy soil drains quickly, and hence leaches out nutrients faster than clay, plants in sand need watering and fertilizing more often than those in clay.

Loam. Loam is a gardener's term for soil intermediate between clay and sand. It contains a mixture of clay, silt, and sand particles, and in addition, is well supplied with organic matter. Thus loam—a compromise between the extremes of clay and sand—is the ideal gardening soil: draining well (but not drying too fast), leaching only moderately, and containing enough air for healthy root growth.

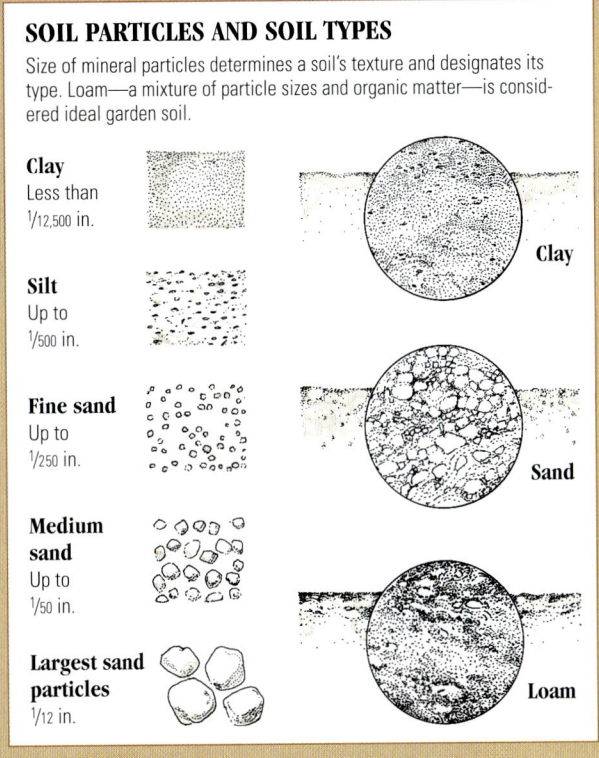

SOIL PARTICLES AND SOIL TYPES

Size of mineral particles determines a soil's texture and designates its type. Loam—a mixture of particle sizes and organic matter—is considered ideal garden soil.

Clay
Less than
1/12,500 in.

Silt
Up to
1/500 in.

Fine sand
Up to
1/250 in.

Medium sand
Up to
1/50 in.

Largest sand particles
1/12 in.

Clay

Sand

Loam

---

tration, also improve the efficiency of these organisms in making nitrogen available.

The final product of the action by soil bacteria and other organisms on organic materials is humus. By binding minute clay particles into larger crumbs, this soft, sticky material improves aeration and drainage. And in sandy soil, humus remains in pore spaces and helps hold water and nutrients.

Types of amendments. Because all organic materials are continuously being decomposed by soil organisms, even the best of soils will benefit from periodic applications of organic amendments. Included among organic soil amendments are ground bark, peat moss, leaf mold, sawdust and wood shavings, manure, compost (p. 553), and many other plant remains.

When you add organic amendments to your soil, be generous and mix them deeply and uniformly. For the most marked improvement, add a volume equal to 25 to 50 percent of the total soil volume in the cultivated area. Mix in thoroughly, either by spading and respading or by rototilling. The mixing will add air to the soil, and amendments will help keep it there.

Cautions. Organisms that break down organic materials need nitrogen to sustain their own lives. If they cannot get all the nitrogen they require from the organic material itself, they will draw upon any available nitrogen in the soil. This, in effect, "steals" the nitrogen that is vital to plants' roots; the result can be a temporary nitrogen depletion and reduced plant growth.

To raw wood shavings, ground bark, straw, or manure containing much litter (such as straw or sawdust), you will need to add nitrogen. After application, use 1 pound of ammonium sulfate for each 1-inch-deep layer of raw organic material spread over 100 square feet. A year later, apply half as much ammonium sulfate, and in the third and fourth years, use one-fourth as much.

Liberal and prolonged use of organic matter can significantly lower soil pH—that is, increase its acidity. Where soil already is neutral or acid, this can result, over a period of time, in an overly acid soil. A simple soil test (see entry on this page) will reveal your soil's pH.

Soil pH

Soil pH is a measurement of one aspect of the soil's chemical composition: the concentration of hydrogen ions (an ion is an electrically charged atom or molecule). The relative concentration of hydrogen ions is represented by the symbol pH followed by a number. A pH of 7 means that the soil is neutral, neither acid nor alkaline. A pH below 7 indicates acidity; one above 7 indicates alkalinity. The surest way to determine your soil's pH is to have the soil tested. See Soil Test (p. 600).

Acid soil. Most common in regions where rainfall is heavy, acid soil is often associated with sandy soils and soils high in organic matter. Most plants grow well in mildly acid soil, but highly acid soil is inhospitable.

East of the Mississippi River, most soils are on the acid side. In the West, overly acid soils are common in western Washington, in western Oregon, and along the north coast of California. Add lime to such soils only if a soil test indicates that it is needed and only in the quantity recommended by your Cooperative Extension Office. If you attempt to raise your soil's pH with lime, be sure that any fertilizers you use thereafter do not have an acid reaction.

Alkaline soil. Common in regions with light rainfall, alkaline soil is high in calcium carbonate (lime) or certain other minerals, such as sodium. Many plants grow well in moderately alkaline soil; others, notably camellias, rhododendrons, and azaleas, will not thrive there because the alkalinity reduces the availability of particular elements necessary for their growth.

Large-scale chemical treatment of highly alkaline soil is expensive and complex. A better

S

bet is to plant in raised beds or containers, using a good prepared soil mix.

Soils that are only slightly alkaline will support many garden plants. They can be made to grow acid-loving plants with liberal additions of peat moss, ground bark, or sawdust; fertilization with acid-type fertilizers; and periodic applications of chelates (see Chlorosis, p. 552).

Deep watering can help lessen alkalinity but is advisable only if the soil drains quickly.

Soil Polymers

Superabsorbent polymers are a recent development that can increase water retention of soils. Particularly useful in potting mixes, these gel-like polymers absorb hundreds of times their weight in water; in potting soil, the gel holds both water and dissolved nutrients for plant roots to use. Because the gel retains water that normally drains from the soil, plants still have a source of moisture when their potting soil becomes dry. This lets you stretch intervals between waterings. And plants grow better because the gel eliminates the wide fluctuations of moisture that can occur between waterings. Polyacrylamide gel is the longest-lasting kind. Mix the dry material with water to expand the particles; then add to potting mix in the proportion recommended by the manufacturer—usually about 1 pint gel to 6 pints potting mix.

Soils

An understanding of your soil is perhaps the most important aspect of gardening. It will guide you in watering and fertilizing your plants—in other words, in caring for them.

Soil is a mass of mineral particles mixed with air, water, and living and dead organic matter. The size (texture) and arrangement (structure) of the mineral particles greatly influence a soil's water- and nutrient-holding capacity, aeration, and ease of workability. The basic soil structure and texture—together with its pH and its content of organic matter, air, and nutrients—determine a soil's quality. For a discussion of soil texture and structure, see p. 599.

Soil Salinity

An excess of salts (salinity) in the soil is a widespread problem in coastal areas and arid parts of the West. These salts may be naturally present in the soil or they may come from water (especially softened water, which has a high sodium content), from fertilizers and chemical amendments, and from manures with high salt content. Where these salts are not leached through the soil by high rainfall or deep irrigation, they reach high concentrations in the root zone, inhibiting germination of seeds, stunting growth, and producing "salt burn"—scorched and yellowed leaves or browned and withered leaf margins.

Periodic, thorough leaching of the soil with water will lessen its salt content; but for effective leaching, drainage must be good.

Soil Test

A soil analysis will disclose your soil's pH (acidity or alkalinity) and also can reveal nutrient deficiencies. In some states, the Cooperative Extension Office can test your soil; if not, it should be able to direct you to commercial soil laboratories that can make such analyses. Many nurseries sell soil-test kits that can indicate definite problems.

Sooty Mold

A common black mold (see photograph, p. 592) that grows on leaves and twigs of trees and shrubs, sooty mold occurs when a fungus grows on honeydew secreted by sap-sucking insects such as aphids and scale. Wash or wipe the mold from leaves. Control the insects.

Southern Blight

A soilborne fungal disease that rots plant stems, southern blight thrives in the warm soils and wet weather of the Southeast (see photograph, p. 592). It is also known as southern wilt, sclerotium root rot, and mustard seed fungus; the last names refer to the organism's small yellow resting bodies.

Southern blight infects many flowers and vegetables, some shrubs, and occasionally lawns. White cottony growth appears on the plants' stems near the soil level and often spreads to the surrounding soil. The fungus gradually cuts off the flow of water through the stems. Plants rot at the base, wilt, turn yellow, and die.

Control is difficult. The fungus can survive in the soil for years without a host. Crop rotation and good sanitation are very important. Clean up all plant debris and discard infected plants, root ball and all. Avoid adding abundant organic matter to the soil, and till the soil in winter to bury overwintering resting bodies (sclerotium). Soil solarization may also help. PCNB (terriclor) is an affective fungicide for use on ornamental plants.

Sowbug. See Pillbug, Sowbug	p. 582
Species. See Plant Classification	p. 583

Specimen

As used by nursery staff, the term "specimen" refers to a tree or shrub large enough to make an immediate, significant contribution to a planting. "Specimen" may also refer to a single large plant in a conspicuous location.

Sphagnum

Various mosses native to bogs are called sphagnum. Much of the peat moss sold is composed partly or entirely of decomposed sphagnum. These mosses also are collected live and packaged in whole pieces, fresh or dried. They are used for lining hanging baskets and for air layering (p. 574).

Spike

A flowering stem with flowers directly attached (without any short flower stems) along its upper portion is a spike. The flowers open in sequence, typically beginning at the bottom of the spike. Familiar examples are *Gladiolus* and red-hot poker (*Kniphofia*). The term is often applied loosely to flower clusters that resemble spikes — especially to racemes, which differ in that each individual flower has its own short stem.

Spore

A spore is a simple type of reproductive cell capable of producing a new plant or fungus. Certain kinds of organisms (such as algae, fungi, mosses, and ferns) reproduce by spores.

Sport

A mutation—a spontaneous variation from the normal pattern—is called a sport. In horticulture, a sport is usually seen as a branch that differs noticeably from its parent plant. Examples include the spurred apple varieties that occur as limb sports on standard apple varieties and camellias propagated from branches that have shown changes in color or form of flowers.

Spotted Spurge

A demon in warm weather, the very aggressive summer annual spotted spurge grows from a shallow taproot in exposed areas such as sparse lawns, garden walks, and flower beds. It spreads fast; in as little as a month, each plant can produce several thousand seeds in clusters of tiny pinkish seed capsules. Oblong, ¼- to ⅜-inch leaves have reddish green undersides. Cut stems exude a milky juice. Plants turn red-orange and decline in fall (especially noticeable in lawns) as temperatures drop. Seeds germinate as early as January in warm-winter climates, and seedlings start active growth when temperatures climb in spring (see photograph, p. 614).

Control is difficult. Hoe out isolated plants early, before they produce seed, or spray them with glyphosate. On lawns (except dichondra), use a pre-emergence broad-leafed herbicide appropriately labeled to control spotted spurge. Watch for small plants in areas that have had problems in past years. A vigorous, well-fertilized lawn provides tough competition for spotted spurge. For cool-season lawn grasses, mowing the grass higher helps to discourage this weed.

Spur

Some fruit trees, particularly apples and cherries, bear their blossoms on a specialized short twig called a spur. Spurs are also short and saclike or long and tubular projections from a flower. The columbine *(Aquilegia)* is a familiar flower with pronounced spurs. Spurs can arise from either sepals or petals.

Squash Bugs

About ⅝ inch in length, squash bugs are a problem on many plants of the squash family. Damage is usually greatest on winter squash and pumpkin plants: the bugs can cause leaves to wilt completely and also will damage the fruit (see photograph, p. 591). Summer squash, melons, and cucumbers are seldom affected.

In spring, adult bugs lay their eggs on squash leaves. If you find a mass of hard brown eggs crowded together on a leaf underside, destroy them. Squash bugs spend nights under flat objects, so put out boards in the evening; in early morning, turn over the boards and kill the bugs (they can emit an unpleasant odor).

Carbaryl is an effective chemical control, but getting it applied to all the leaves is a problem—particularly on older plants with plenty of foliage. For best results, start control when plants are small or as soon as you see eggs. Sabadilla may also work.

Squirrels

Both ground and tree squirrels can be troublesome in gardens. Ground squirrels (see illustration) are capable of climbing trees, but they live in underground burrows where they store food, raise their young, and hide from predators. If a burrow is active, you'll see freshly excavated soil around the entrance (a hole about 4 inches wide). The animals wall themselves off when hibernating, but the plug isn't visible. Ground squirrels feed aboveground during the day, nibbling through tomato patches, digging up bulbs, gnawing roots and bark, and climbing trees after fruits and nuts.

Tree squirrels spend most of their life in trees; they build nests in branch crotches or take up residence in convenient holes in tree trunks. Active all year, these agile animals can easily jump a distance of 6 feet from limb to limb. They live largely on seeds, nuts, fruits, and bark; they also gnaw into buildings and invade attics.

Controls. Methods of controlling ground squirrels include using a baited (with a walnut, almond, or slice of orange tied to the trigger) box-type gopher trap placed outside the burrow. Anticoagulant types of poison bait are more effective with less effort. Baits should be placed in one or more bait stations near the squirrel burrows and must be available to the squirrel for at least a week to achieve maximum control. Before you try any of these approaches, check with your county agricultural agent or farm advisor: laws in some areas prohibit catching certain kinds of squirrels.

Metal guards around tree trunks can keep squirrels out of trees. Protect bulb beds with a cover of fine-mesh chicken wire.

Staking

Technically, staking is the practice of driving a stake or rod into the ground close to a plant to provide support for its stems. Whenever you stake a plant, make sure ties are loose enough so they don't restrict growth or girdle plant stems. See also Tree (p. 603).

Although often not done with a single stake, staking also refers to supporting tall flowers that may fall over without support (see illustration). For help in staking vegetables, see page 605.

Stamens. See Plant Anatomy and Growth
p. 583

Standard

A plant that does not naturally grow as a tree can be trained into a standard—a small treelike form with a single, upright trunk topped by a rounded crown of foliage. The "tree rose" is the most familiar example of a standard.

Stolon

A stolon is a stem that creeps along the surface of the ground, taking root at intervals and forming new plants where it roots—as opposed to offsets (p. 579), which may form at the ends of runners. Bermuda and St. Augustine grasses spread by stolons.

STAKING FLOWERS

Wire fencing cylinder
Good for bushy sprawlers

Bamboo stake and tie
Inexpensive and easy support for stems like those of delphinium

Metal hoop support
Widths range from 12 to 18 inches; plants grow through crossbars. Good for peonies

S

Stone Fruit

Fruits containing a single seed in the center—such as peaches, plums, and apricots—are stone fruits.

Strain. See Plant Classification   p. 583

Stress

Stress refers to a condition or conditions that endanger the health of a growing plant. Stress may stem from lack of water; too much heat, wind, or moisture; or low temperatures. What is stressful varies according to the particular plant and its needs. Stress shows up as wilting, loss or dulling of color in foliage, or browning of leaf edges. Causes of stress may not be immediately obvious; for instance, wilting may result not from lack of water but from destruction of roots caused by too much water—a common condition in house plants.

Subshrub

A subshrub is a type of plant, usually under 3 feet high and with more or less woody stems, that is sometimes grown and used as a shrub or perennial.

Sucker

In a grafted or budded plant, sucker growth originates from the rootstock rather than from the desired grafted or budded part of the plant. In trees, any strong vertical shoot growing from the main framework of trunk and branches is sometimes called a sucker, although the proper term is "watersprout."

Summer Oil

A summer oil is a highly refined horticultural oil (see Insecticides box, p. 581) that is sprayed on plants to control insect pests during the growing season.

Sunburn

Sunburn—damage to leaves, fruit, or bark from sunlight—may result from high temperatures, exposure of previously shaded bark to sun, or improper hardening off (p. 568) of transplants. Symptoms are most common on plant parts facing south, southwest, or west. They include cracked or split bark, wilting, bleached-out or yellowing foliage, and/or dead portions of leaves.

Protect newly set-out plants from strong sun and wind with temporary shelters. These can be as simple as a shingle lean-to on the sunny side of the plant or a small newspaper pup tent held down at the edges by a few handfuls of soil. Or they can be as elaborate as lath or burlap panels supported above the plants on low stakes.

Whichever type you choose, the object is to keep strong sun and wind from the young plants until the roots are able to do an efficient job of taking water from the soil to meet the plants' needs.

To protect newly planted trees, paint the exposed trunk with a white latex (water-based) paint or wrap it with a commercial tree wrap sold in nurseries. Tree branches and limbs newly exposed to sunlight following heavy pruning should also be painted with white latex paint.

Surface Roots, Feeder Roots

A plant's surface, or feeder, roots are the network of roots near the soil surface through which it absorbs most nutrients and water. Most are in the top 12 to 18 inches of the soil.

Systemic

A systemic is any chemical that is absorbed into a plant's system, either to kill organisms that feed on the plant or to kill the plant itself. There are systemic insecticides, fungicides, and weed killers.

Taproot

This main root grows straight down, like the root of a carrot or dandelion. In dry areas, some plants have very deep taproots to reach a deep water table.

Tarnished Plant Bugs

These fast-moving insects owe their name to their mottled brown coloring. A true bug, the tarnished plant bug has a shield-shaped body with a triangular arrangement of white spots on the thorax. The long-legged, ¼-inch-long adults have a black-tipped triangle at the end of each forewing; the nymphs are pale yellow (see photograph, p. 590). Both adults and nymphs suck sap from buds, fruit, and stems of most flowers, fruits, and vegetables, causing shoots to blacken and drop or become deformed. If feeding on fruit, the insects leave sunken, catfaced scars.

Prevent tarnished plant bugs by planting under floating row covers. Maintaining good sanitation and cleaning up plant debris will reduce the number of overwintering adults. If spined soldier beetles—beneficial insects that prey on the tarnished plant bug—are available, buy and release them. White sticky traps may also reduce pest numbers. Insecticidal soap, rotenone, and sabadilla are effective, as are carbaryl and malathion.

Tender

Tender is the opposite of hardy (p. 568). It denotes a low tolerance for freezing temperatures. Tender can also refer to seedlings that have not been properly hardened off to outdoor conditions (p. 568).

Tendrils

Twisting, threadlike projections, tendrils are found on some vines. They enable vines to cling to supports and climb.

Tent Caterpillars

Tent caterpillars form huge, weblike nests in many trees and shrubs (see photograph, p. 591). At night the caterpillars hide in the nest; during the day they venture out to feed on foliage, often defoliating entire plants. Other kinds of caterpillars are described on page 552.

The first thing to do to control tent caterpillars is to cut out the nest and destroy it. If that will seriously deform the plant, break up the nest with a stick and spray with an appropriately labeled insecticide. *Bacillus thuringiensis* is effective against young caterpillars. Several traditional insecticides are also effective against tent caterpillars. Hand-picking the white egg masses from branches and trunks in winter and early spring will help reduce pest numbers. A ring of sticky material around the trunk may also prevent caterpillars from crawling into the tree after overwintering in the soil. Releasing trichogramma wasps (see p. 549) may also reduce tent caterpillars.

Texas Root Rot

Texas root rot is a damaging and widespread disease in the semiarid and arid Southwest at elevations below 3,500 feet—from California's Imperial and Coachella valleys through Arizona and New Mexico and eastward into Texas. It is caused by a fungus *(Phymatotrichum omnivorum)* that destroys the outer portion of roots, thus cutting off the water supply to the upper parts of the plant.

The first symptom of the disease is a sudden wilting of leaves in summer, with the wilted leaves remaining attached to the plant. When this occurs, at least half the root system has already been damaged.

The fungus is favored by high temperatures and a highly alkaline soil low in organic matter. Fortunately, the fungus does not compete well with other soil-inhabiting organisms. Therefore, control measures focus on lessening alkalinity (by adding soil sulfur) and increasing the population of organisms that "crowd out" the fungus (by adding organic matter that decomposes rapidly). Contact your Cooperative Extension Office for specific recommendations.

Thatch

Thatch is a layer of dead stems that builds up beneath certain grasses and ground covers, reducing water and nutrient penetration. See Dethatch (p. 557).

S

Thinning Out

A pruning term, "thinning out" means to remove entire branches—large or small—back to the main trunk, a side branch, or the ground. The object is to give the plant a more open structure. See Pruning (p. 593).

When growing plants from seed, thinning out means removing excess seedlings so that those remaining are spaced far enough apart to develop well.

Thrips

Almost-microscopic pests (see photograph, p. 590), thrips feed by rasping soft flower and leaf tissue and then drinking the plant juices. In heavy infestations, both flowers and leaves fail to open normally, appearing twisted or stuck together and discolored. Look closely and you'll see stippled puckerings in flower or leaf tissue and the small black fecal pellets that thrips deposit while feeding. Leaves may take on a silvery or tan cast, distinguished from spider mite damage by the black, varnish-like fecal pellets on leaf undersides.

Thrips can be a problem starting in early to mid-spring, and they can breed rapidly, increasing in numbers as the season goes on. They are notoriously fond of white and light pink rose blossoms and of gladiolus leaves and flowers. Thrips also attack strawberries, onions, cabbage, and tomatoes.

The natural enemies of flower thrips are numerous, including ladybird beetles and larvae, green lacewing larvae, and predaceous thrips and mites. The Indian laurel fig variety 'Green Gem' is apparently resistant to Cuban laurel thrips, a common pest in the mild-winter West.

For serious thrips infestations on ornamental plants, try malathion, diazinon, chlorpyrifos, or acephate. On edible plants, use malathion or insecticidal soap.

Tools

A gardener needs good tools. The basics include a trowel, shovel, rake, hose, pruning shears, and probably a lawn mower. But there is much more to choose from, from the simple to the specialized. A trip to a well-stocked hardware or garden supply store will reveal a wealth of useful information and tools to make the hardest job easier. Select well-made tools that feel good in your hands. Maintain and store them properly, and they'll last for years.

Topdress

To topdress means to apply on the surface—usually referring to the spreading of an organic material, such as ground bark or manure, on the soil as a mulch. Sometimes it refers to application of manure on a lawn as a low-grade plant food.

Topiary

Topiary is the technique of pruning and training shrubs and trees into formalized shapes resembling such things as animals or geometrical figures.

Topsoil

Topsoil is the top layer of native soil, soil that is usually better for plant growth than what is beneath it. The term is often also used to describe good soil (see Soils, p. 600) sold at nurseries and garden supply stores.

Native topsoil can be nonexistent, only a few inches thick, or deeper. It is often removed to level ground during home construction or lost through erosion. See Erosion Control (p. 560).

If you must bring additional soil into the garden to fill in low spots or raise the level of your soil, don't add it as a single layer on top of existing soil. Instead, put down a portion of the new soil (up to half, depending on projected new depth) and mix it thoroughly with the existing soil by spading or rototilling. Then add the remaining new soil to bring the level up to the desired height and mix it thoroughly into the previously tilled soil. This extra work prevents formation of an interface—a barrier between the two dissimilar soils—that can slow or stop upward and downward movement of water.

If you purchase topsoil to add to your garden, try to find material that closely approximates your existing soil. Look for crumbly texture, and avoid very fine-textured clays and silts. Try to steer clear of saline soil (if it comes from good cropland, you can assume that salinity is no problem) and soil that contains seeds of noxious weeds or residue from herbicides.

Transpiration

The release of moisture (absorbed largely by plant roots) through the plant's leaves is transpiration. Temperature and humidity affect transpiration rate.

Transplanting

The process of digging up a plant and planting it in another location is transplanting. Transplanting is also sometimes used to describe planting from containers into garden soil or into larger pots.

Tree

No distinct line separates plants known as trees from those called shrubs. There are trees that reach 15 feet at maturity, but some shrubs reach up to 20 feet. Some of those shrubs will serve as small trees, particularly if the lower branches are removed.

Think of a tree as having a trunk topped by a foliage canopy. Some trees assume that aspect readily; others go through a prolonged, shrubby youth during which they maintain branches

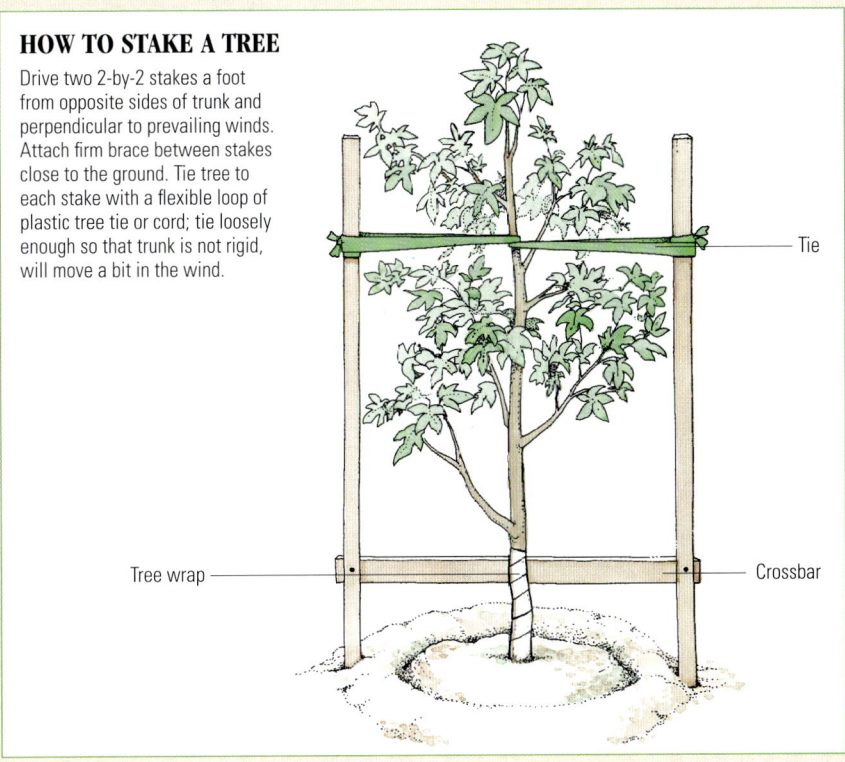

HOW TO STAKE A TREE

Drive two 2-by-2 stakes a foot from opposite sides of trunk and perpendicular to prevailing winds. Attach firm brace between stakes close to the ground. Tie tree to each stake with a flexible loop of plastic tree tie or cord; tie loosely enough so that trunk is not rigid, will move a bit in the wind.

Tie

Tree wrap

Crossbar

T

TIPS FOR SELECTING A TREE

Because trees are the largest plants in the landscape, it is no surprise that they require more years to reach mature height, or even to begin to fulfill your expectations, than other garden plants do. That fact underscores the importance of selecting just the right trees for your needs and desires. Consider these seven points:

- **Climate adaptability.** First be sure that any tree you consider is noted as being successful in your climate zone.

- **Garden adaptability.** If a tree will grow in your climate zone, read its cultural requirements and decide how well your garden can satisfy them.

- **Growth rate.** Different trees grow at different rates. Their speed—or lack of it—can be a crucial factor when you are choosing a tree to solve some garden problems. If, for example, you need a tree to screen hot sun from south-facing windows or to block an objectionable view, you may want one that will grow fast to do the job in a hurry. On the other hand, if you are choosing a tree only for the beauty of its flowers, you may be willing to wait a number of years before the plant assumes mature proportions.

- **Root system.** A tree with a network of greedy surface roots is a poor candidate for sharing a lawn or garden area; the tree will take most of the water and nutrients. But the same tree planted at the garden's edge or along a country drive may be an outstanding choice. Some trees grow surface roots that can lift and crack nearby pavement, a point to check out if you're choosing a tree for a patio, entryway, or parking strip.

- **Maintenance.** Notice words like "messy" or "litter" in a tree's description. Those words may refer to foliage, flower, or fruit drop; they may spell work if the litter gathers in a place that you want to keep neat, such as a lawn or a patio. But the same tree may pose no problem if grown toward the back of the garden or in a naturalistic setting so that litter can remain where it falls. In a region that receives regular high winds or consistent annual snowfall, avoid trees described as having weak or brittle wood or weak crotches. Such large, growing trees can be hazardous to people and property. And removing broken limbs can ruin the beauty of the tree as well as be costly.

- **Pest and disease problems.** Some trees may be plagued by particular insects or diseases in part of the region to which they are adapted. Often damage may be trivial. But if the action of a particular pest or disease will spoil your enjoyment of a tree (or compel you to wage eternal battle), you would be wise to plant a less troublesome one.

- **Longevity.** There are trees you can plant for your grandchildren to enjoy, and others that will grow quickly but slide into unattractive old age while the rest of your garden is still maturing. The short-lived trees are not necessarily less desirable, but they should be planted only where their removal won't be difficult or seriously compromise your overall garden design. Many attractive flowering trees will run their course in about 20 years but can be replaced by another of the same kind to fill the gap again within a few years. But if you want to screen out the neighboring high-rise for a long time, look for a tree that's likely to last as long as you will.

down to ground level. In time, though, most develop a canopy high enough to walk under.

Planting young trees. Some trees are sold with roots bare (no soil) during the dormant season, from late fall through early spring. Many of these trees, and others as well, are sold in containers or as balled-and-burlapped plants all year. Refer to Planting Techniques: Trees and Shrubs (p. 586) for planting instructions for all types.

Caring for young trees. Whether a tree flourishes or languishes can depend on the care you give it when it is young. Keep the following six guidelines in mind:

Water when young. For all trees, follow a regular watering schedule during the first several years. Even a drought-tolerant tree needs routine watering for the first year or two after planting so the roots can grow enough to carry the tree through dry periods. See Watering (p. 609) for advice on frequency, based upon your climate and soil type.

Wrap the trunk. A newly planted tree's trunk benefits from protection during at least the first year after planting. Drying winds; scorching sun; freezes; and physical damage by chewing dogs, scratching cats, gnawing wild animals (rabbits, deer, rodents), and careless lawn mowers can injure tender bark, resulting in anything from slowed growth to death. As a simple precaution, wrap the trunk with burlap (loosely tied) or a manufactured trunk wrapping. If animals are likely to be a problem, you can also encircle the

lower portion of the trunk with a cylinder of woven wire.

Stake only if necessary. If possible, it is better to leave a newly planted tree unstaked; the trunk will strengthen and thicken faster without additional support. But if a new tree is top-heavy enough to topple in a strong wind, stake it by the method shown in the illustration (proven best in university experiments). This technique strengthens the trunk by permitting some flexibility in the wind—but not so much that the tree will fall or tilt.

Whenever you encircle a trunk or limb with a nonexpandable tie (for staking or protection), be sure to check the tie several times each growing season. Before you might expect it, a tree can grow enough for the tie to constrict and damage the trunk. Remove the stakes as soon as possible. Don't leave them in place longer than a year.

Don't prune lower branches. Young trees increase in trunk girth faster if lower branches are allowed to remain on the trunk for several years. Cut back low branches only if they show signs of growing at the expense of higher branches that you intend for the tree's permanent framework. Then, in 3 to 5 years, remove the unwanted lower branches from the trunk.

Fertilize for the first few years. You may want to include young trees in a regular, annual fertilizer program for several years after you plant them. Ensuring a nitrogen supply (see p. 578) for the

springtime growth surge encourages young trees to establish themselves as quickly as possible.

After a tree has become established, it may grow satisfactorily with no further nutrient assistance. If it continues to put out healthy, vigorous new growth, fertilizer applications may be a waste of time, effort, and materials. (Exceptions are fruit and nut trees that are fertilized to ensure or enhance productivity; for specific guidelines, check your Cooperative Extension Office.) But if new growth appears weak, sparse, or unusually pale, or if the tree has much dieback (and you know that soil and watering practices are appropriate), supplemental nutrients may be in order. Other times of need are following periods of stress: a severe insect or disease attack (especially one that partially or entirely defoliates the tree) or tree damage that requires heavy pruning.

Most trees will continue to absorb nutrients and moisture after going dormant, so fall applications of nitrogen fertilizers can be effective, especially in cold-winter climates. However, if applied too early or to plants that are of borderline hardiness, fall fertilizer could promote cold-tender growth. In these cases, it's better to apply fertilizer about a month before the expected flush of late-winter or spring growth.

Watch for nitrogen deficiency. A tree that displays the poor growth symptoms mentioned above should benefit from the application of nitrogen (see p. 578 under Nutrients, Basic). One application may suffice, or you may need to extend treatment over several years; the tree's growth will be your guide. For a moderate application, measure the trunk diameter at 4 feet above ground, then multiply that number by 0.1; this gives you the pounds of actual nitrogen (see p. 545) to apply. For methods of applying fertilizer to trees, see the illustration Three Ways to Fertilize Trees (p. 562).

Truss

A cluster of flowers, usually rather compact, at the end of a stem, branch, or stalk is called a truss. The most familiar rhododendrons carry their flowers in trusses.

Tuber

A tuber is a fat underground stem from which a plant grows. It's similar to a rhizome (p. 596), but it is usually shorter and thicker and doesn't lengthen greatly as it grows. The world's most famous tuber is the potato.

Tuberous Root

A tuberous root—a thickened underground food storage structure—is an actual root (not a modified stem, as in the case of true tubers). Growth buds are in the old stems at the upper end of the root. The dahlia is a familiar example.

Underplanting

Planting one plant beneath another, such as a ground cover under a tree, is called underplanting.

Understock. See Rootstock   p. 596

Variegated

Leaves that are striped, edged, or otherwise marked with a color different from the primary color of the leaf are described as being variegated.

Variety. See Plant Classification   p. 583

Vegetable Gardening

Raising your own vegetables can be fun, fulfilling, and economical. But for the experience to be all three, you will need to invest some time in planning and, later, in maintenance.

Before you take a shovel to the soil, evaluate your needs. How many people do you hope to feed from your vegetable plot? It is all too easy to overplant and then work too hard to maintain a garden that produces a larger crop than you can use.

Make a list of vegetables you really like, and choose your plants from that list. Especially if your garden area is limited, raise only those plants that will give you a satisfactory return from the space they occupy. Melons, some squashes, and corn, for example, require large land areas relative to their edible yield. Beans, tomatoes, and zucchini, on the other hand, can overwhelm you with their bounty from a postage-stamp-size plot.

Location. Success with vegetables begins with choosing the right location for your garden. Vegetables need plenty of sunshine for steady growth, so be sure to plant them where they will receive at least 6 hours of sunlight each day. To avoid not only shade but also possible root competition, locate your vegetable patch at a distance from trees and large shrubs. If possible, choose a spot that is sheltered from regular high winds, which can dehydrate plants and therefore increase watering frequency. And avoid planting vegetables in low-lying areas that can become winter "frost pockets"—you want to aim for the longest possible growing season for the greatest productivity.

Level ground makes vegetable growing easier. You can run rows in north-south alignment so that plants receive an even amount of sunlight during the day. Level ground also gives you a choice among watering options—flooding, sprinkling, drip irrigation—with the least risk of runoff (see p. 610).

If you have to plant on sloping land, try to select a slope that faces south or southeast for maximum sunlight; plant the tallest vegetables on the north side of the plot to avoid shading shorter ones. Lay out rows along the slope's contours to minimize water runoff and erosion.

Planting. Most of the commonly grown vegetables are annual plants. Prepare your vegetable garden soil as described for seeds (p. 584).

In planting vegetables, you usually have two options: planting seeds or setting out young plants sold by a nursery. Seed planting is far more economical if you compute price per plant, but for a small garden, the purchase of young plants will not represent any great outlay. Realize that the earliest crops usually will come on plants set out as early as possible in the growing season (see Planting and Timing, p. 545, under Annual, and the Extending the Season for Harvest box, next page).

If you prefer to start from scratch, remember that seeds started indoors just before garden soil warms up enough to plant outdoors will be ready to set out at the very beginning of the growing season; see Planting Techniques: Seeds (p. 584) for seed-planting information. Nurseries and garden centers often have young plants available at the earliest moment it is advisable to plant outdoors.

Care. For the best possible crop, remember this one tip: keep plants growing. Be sure vegetable plants receive steady amounts of both

VEGETABLE SUPPORTS

To support cucumbers, squash, pole beans, and peas, drive in a row of metal fencing stakes 4 to 6 feet apart. Attach broad-mesh plastic netting to hooks in the fence posts.

To support a single tomato plant, tie plant to a wood stake—or surround it with a cylinder of welded wire fencing to minimize tying.

For a row of plants, use crossed pairs of bamboo poles tied together at the crosspole.

V

EXTENDING THE SEASON FOR HARVEST

Traditionally, gardeners wanting to extend nature's vegetable season have used glass or plastic covers to shelter young transplants from late frosts and, in the process, warm the soil. By planting earlier than their climate normally allowed, then protecting and warming the young plants, they brought vegetables to bearing size earlier.

Now gardeners can use row covers—made of polyethylene, polyester, or polypropylene—both to get a jump on the growing season and to extend it into the chill of autumn. Sold in rolls, these fabriclike covers are designed to be laid over vegetables at planting time (or over bearing plants toward the season's end), where they serve as miniature greenhouses—trapping heat, warming soil, and boosting growth. The various materials are extremely lightweight, transmit 80 to 95 percent of sunlight, and let both water and air pass through. Burying the cover's edges in soil or holding them securely against it also seals off plants from outside pests (although any insect pests already present on the plants will proliferate).

Laying row covers. To use row covers, just lay the material over rows of plants 1 to 3 feet wide, and secure the edges by burying them in the soil or holding them in place with 2-by-4s. Covers float on top of the plants without restricting or distorting growth.

Most gardeners who use row covers put them up for 4 to 6 weeks in early spring. As the weather turns warm, the covers come off: when the air temperature climbs to the 80°F/27°C, for example, it may be 110°F/43°C under the covers. But where frost can occur at any time during the growing season, gardeners cover plants on dangerous nights and days, and then remove covers on warm days. In cool-summer climates, they can use covers to mature warm-season vegetables that normally wouldn't receive enough heat to produce. And, at the end of a growing season, row covers can ripen the last crop of tomatoes, for example, that otherwise would remain green.

Watering covered crops. Because row covers are permeable to water, you can water covered plants by sprinkling—and rainfall gets through too. Young plants will be somewhat weighted down after a sprinkling but will pop back up once the material dries. The simplest system, however, is drip irrigation (p. 610).

water and nutrients; any check in growth detracts from productivity, quality, or both.

The basic advice for care after planting provided under Annual (p. 545) covers vegetables as well. The one difference is that, whereas you groom annuals to prolong flower production, you harvest vegetables to prolong crop production.

Part of the care for some vegetables is providing support for the vining or sprawling plants. Pole beans and peas, tomatoes, cucumbers, and melons, for example, benefit from support that raises them off the ground. Plants will produce larger crops, and the fruit won't rot due to contact with the soil. Four ideas for supporting vegetable plants are shown in the illustration (left). In regions with hot summers, avoid metal and wire constructions, because metal can heat up enough to burn plant parts that touch it.

Warm-season vs. cool-season vegetables. A distinct difference in the heat requirements for growth separates warm-season from cool-season vegetables and determines which of each are best adapted to your particular climate.

Warm-season vegetables, the summer crops, need warmth both to germinate and to form and ripen fruit. With nearly all of these vegetables, the fruit (rather than the leaves, roots, or stems) is the object of the harvest. The basic need of warm-weather vegetables is for enough growing heat—without significant cooling at night—both to keep plants growing steadily and to ripen the edible portions of the plants. Cool-season vegetables grow steadily at average temperatures 10° to 15° below those needed by warm-season crops. Many of them will endure some frost. But the most important difference is that you do not grow cool-season vegetables for their fruit or seeds: most of them are leaf or root crops. The exceptions are peas and broad beans (grown for edible seeds) and artichokes, broccoli, and cauliflower (grown for edible flowers).

Success with cool-season crops depends on bringing plants to maturity in the kind of weather that favors vegetative growth rather than flowering. In general, you plant in very early spring so that the crop will mature before summer heat settles in, or in late summer so that the crop matures during fall or even winter. In the warmer regions—Zones 12 to 31—many cool-season vegetables can be planted in fall to harvest either in winter or in early spring.

Vermiculite

The mineral mica is heated and puffed up to form vermiculite—lightweight, spongelike granules useful in conditioning container soils. Vermiculite granules hold both water and air.

Verticillium Wilt

Verticillium wilt is one of the most widespread and destructive plant diseases. The verticillium fungus invades and plugs the water-conducting tissues in the roots and stems of plants. A common symptom is wilting of one side of the plant. Leaves yellow, starting at their margins and progressing inward, and then turn brown and die. The dieback progresses upward or outward from the base of the plant or branch (see photograph, p. 592). Affected branches die. If you cut one of these branches, you may find that the sapwood (the outer layer of tissue just under the bark) is discolored—it frequently is streaked olive green, dark brown, or black. Development of the fungus is favored by cool, moist soil, but wilting of foliage may not show until days are sunny and warm and the plant is under water stress (the leaves transpire water faster than the diseased roots and stems can supply it).

The fungus can survive in the soil for years in the absence of susceptible plants. Even rotation (the growing of nonsusceptible plants in the infested soil) will not rid the soil of verticillium fungus. Highly susceptible crops—such as tomatoes, potatoes, cotton, strawberries, and various melons—frequently leave the soil infested.

Controls. Mildly affected plants may recover from an attack. You can aid recovery by deep but infrequent irrigation. If a plant has been neglected, apply fertilizer to stimulate new root growth. However, shrubs and trees showing lush growth should not be fertilized after the disease appears.

No measures will kill the fungus once it has invaded a plant. If you are planting shallow-rooted plants, you can control the fungus before you plant by having the soil fumigated. A commercial fumigation specialist will use chloropicrin (tear gas) or methyl bromide. But fumigation has not been successful with deep-rooted shrubs and trees.

The most certain solution to verticillium wilt is to grow wilt-resistant plants. Choices include cedar, cotoneaster, euonymus, holly, oleander, pyracantha, rhododendrons, and bulbs such as amaryllis, narcissus, and tulip. For additional advice on plants that resist verticillium wilt, contact your Cooperative Extension Office.

Vine

A vine is a more or less flexible shrub that doesn't stop growing in height or length (depending on whether you grow it vertically or horizontally). Most need some sort of support if they are to be anything more than a sprawling mass or a ground cover. But therein lies their usefulness: with their ability to wander and their willingness to be guided, they can find employment as decorative garden frosting; as emphasizers (or maskers) of architectural lines; or as sunscreens, windscreens, or view screens.

Choosing a vine. You've heard of "a clinging vine," but not all vines cling in the same manner—and some don't cling at all. Vines fall into

FOUR TYPES OF VINES

Vines climb by means of various natural devices. How a vine climbs will influence your choice of supports and training.

- **Twining vines.** New growth twists or spirals as it grows. It will twist around other growth, new or old, or around itself (and around nearby plants as well), requiring some thinning and guidance. Most twining vines have too small a turn circumference to encircle a large post; the best support is a cord or wire.

- **Vines with twining tendrils.** Specialized growths along the stems or at the ends of leaves reach out and wrap around whatever is handy—wire or rope, another stem of the vine, or another plant. Tendrils grow out straight until they make contact; then they contract into a spiral.

- **Clinging vines.** Special growths along the stems attach to a flat surface. Some clingers have tendrils with suction-cup discs at the ends; others have hooklike claws or tips on tendrils that hook into small irregularities or crevices of a flat surface. Still others possess small roots along the stems; these roots cling fast even to vertical surfaces.

- **Vines that require tying.** These vines have no means of attachment and must, therefore, be tied to a support. Some of these plants— climbing roses, for example—can anchor or stabilize themselves in adjacent shrubs or trees by means of their thorns. Others, such as *Fatshedera lizei*, are naturally sprawling and somewhat shrubby but will grow reasonably flat as long as you tie and train them.

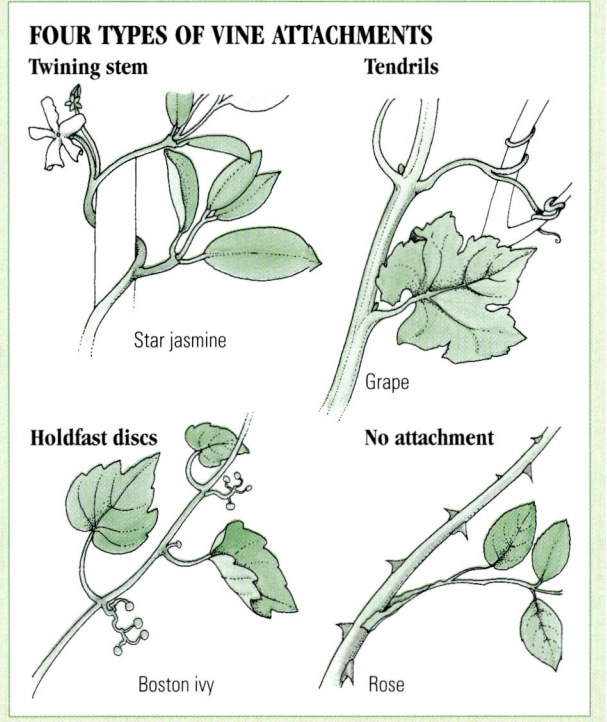

FOUR TYPES OF VINE ATTACHMENTS

Twining stem — Star jasmine

Tendrils — Grape

Holdfast discs — Boston ivy

No attachment — Rose

---

four general climbing types (see illustration). When you select a vine for a particular location or purpose, be sure to choose one whose mode of climbing suits the situation (see Vines and Vinelike Plants, p. 153).

Planting and care. Most vines are sold in containers (1 gallon or larger); a few are offered in small pots, and some deciduous kinds (roses and grapes, for example) are available bareroot. See Planting Techniques: Trees and Shrubs (p. 586) for container and bare-root planting guidelines.

Care after planting will depend on the particular vine you plant but almost certainly will involve some thinning, pruning, and training. Consult descriptions of individual vines in the Plant Encyclopedia for particulars of care.

Virus Diseases

Ultramicroscopic virus particles are capable of infecting plants and reproducing in them at the expense of the host. Insects and humans carry viruses from plant to plant.

Virus diseases are a serious threat to many agricultural crops, such as tomatoes, sugar beets, beans, citrus, and sugar cane. In the home garden, virus damage is seen in many forms. In some cases, such as in rose mosaic, the virus does not reduce the growth of the plant. The most common symptom is a mottled area on leaves or a stunting or general yellowing of the foliage. Viruses produce abnormalities in growth, variegation of foliage, or breaking (color distortion) of blossoms.

Although there is no cure at this time for a virus-infected plant, you can reduce the chance of a virus's entering a plant by controlling the insects that carry the virus. Aphids are most efficient in spreading different kinds of viruses; leafhoppers, thrips, and whitefly can be culprits too. Humans do a fair job of spreading these diseases by propagating infected plants from cuttings, budding or grafting, pruning or pinching diseased plants, and smoking or handling tobacco while working around plants (this can spread tobacco mosaic virus).

Warm-Season Plants

The term "warm-season plants" is used to describe plants that grow best in warm weather. These plants include summer vegetables, such as tomatoes, melons, and peppers; annual flowers like marigolds, petunias, and zinnias; and grass such as Bermuda grass. See also Vegetable Gardening (p. 605), Annual (p. 545), and Lawns (p. 569).

Watering Basin

A ridge of soil several inches high formed around a plant at its drip line is a watering basin. Water applied within the basin will thoroughly moisten the plant's root zone without runoff. Usually, you'll need to fill the basin more than once to ensure water penetrates deeply and wets the entire root zone. As plants get larger, basins need to be expanded to cover the larger

root area. If water accumulates in the basin, make a break in the edge to let the water drain.

Water Conservation

Most western gardeners work in a climate characterized by low rainfall, a long dry season, or both. Well over half the West's gardening population—excluding those living in California's north coast fog belt and in the area north of the Siskiyous and west of the Cascades—spend a good part of each year watering plants. And although the overall western water supply remains virtually fixed, more and more people are putting demands on that finite amount of water. Obviously, water management will be a continually increasing challenge. In eastern United States, periodic droughts and regional water shortages also can dictate water conservation. In fact, water is a limited resource everywhere and should be used wisely in the garden.

There are several ways to meet this challenge. Homeowners with established gardens can alter their watering practices—convert to drip irrigation systems, upgrade existing permanent systems with water-efficient sprinkler heads, refine watering schedules (perhaps aided by electronic controllers) to eliminate runoff and maximize penetration. Gardeners about to set out a new landscape—and those preparing to revamp an established one—can choose plants that, after they become established, don't need continual watering to survive the hot, dry months or periodic droughts. And any gardener can employ various water conservation measures.

W

Here are some tips to help you cut down on water consumption.

Know your plants. Most annual plants and perennials will need watering through the dry months. For best appearance, many lawns and other ground covers also will need regular watering. And the shallow-rooted garden favorites, such as azaleas, rhododendrons, and heathers, are likely to perish (or at least suffer) if their water supply is cut off. But numerous trees and shrubs—after they are established—can prosper on less-than-regular watering during the rainless months. See Plants for Arid Gardens (p. 134).

When water is scarce, think twice before you water any tree or shrub that has been in the ground for more than 2 years. Try extending the time between waterings for as long as the plants look presentable.

Learn to recognize drought stress. You can usually tell by a plant's leaves when it is becoming desperate for water. Most leaves will exhibit a dullness, loss of reflective quality, or curling edges just before they wilt. Wilted leaves, of course, are a certain tipoff. But a plant that has wilted is seriously dry, and you must supply water soon if the plant is to survive at all. In many cases, when an unwatered shrub or tree drops some of its leaves but doesn't wilt or even turn dull, it is simply employing natural mechanisms for surviving a drought. When regular water is supplied again, new leaves will grow.

Some plants, aside from those already mentioned, can't do without water during the dry season. Among these are lawn trees that have grown dependent on summer watering (particularly if their root systems extend only to the depth of the average lawn watering) and plants that are native to cool climates (Monterey pines and cypresses, for example) but are growing in hot inland gardens.

Evaluate your lawn. A lawn uses water at a rate disproportionate to the rest of your garden (see Lawns, p. 569). Re-evaluate your need for a lawn, or consider reducing its size. Alternatives to lawns are surfaces of gravel, brick, concrete, and wood decking. You can plant unthirsty ground covers, such as juniper, ivy, or *Baccharis*. If you must have a lawn, there are grasses that require less water than the more familiar types do (p. 570).

Locate plants wisely. Group plants with similar water needs so they can be irrigated together and so no plant will receive too much or too little water. This concept is called hydrozoning. You can cut water use if you use care in placing plants that need regular watering. Plant these "thirsty" plants where they will be shielded from drying summer winds, and restrict them to one part of the garden (perhaps close to the house, for easy maintenance and visual appeal). For most areas of your landscape, select water-conserving plants.

CONSERVING WATER ON A SLOPE

Individual basin
Make basin as wide as the root area. Build up on the low side to increase water-holding capacity.

Terracing
Headers help control runoff. Because surface reservoir is small, water must be applied slowly.

Conserve water on slopes. Plants on slopes can be a challenge to irrigate, since water can run downhill faster than it can seep into a plant's root zone. Make basins or terracing to channel water directly to plant roots (see illustration), preventing wasteful runoff.

Schedule your watering. If you water by sprinkling, wind and sun will cause water loss through evaporation even before the water reaches your plants. The best time for sprinkling is when it is windless and cool—during the night or earliest morning, when water pressure also is highest. An electronic controller (discussed later in this entry) will schedule such waterings without your having to alter your living schedule.

Mulch your plantings. A mulch placed over the ground occupied by a plant's roots will keep the soil beneath cool and moist longer than it would be if exposed to hot sun and drying wind. Mulched plants, then, are able to go longer between waterings than unmulched ones. Many materials have been tried and proven effective as mulches: compost, animal manures, ground bark, leaves, sawdust, straw, hoed or pulled weeds, and processing by-products (pomace, rice hulls, and cocoa hulls). Rocks and gravel also do the job. Black plastic sheeting, sold in rolls, conserves moisture and suppresses weeds. It is best for strawberries and other low-growing row crops. Lay strips of the plastic along both sides of a row of plants, or cut or punch holes in the plastic for each plant. Water penetrates this mulch only where there's a gap or cut in the plastic.

You can buy rolls of plastic materials (chiefly polypropylene fabric) that are permeable to water and air and have been specially manufactured for use as mulch. Ease of installation is their strong point: you just roll them out onto the soil. Some will last for 1 year, others are longer lived. But all are unattractive and should therefore be covered with a thin layer of organic mulch (which also forestalls degradation by sunlight).

Use electronic devices. The addition of an electronic controller, or timer, to your watering system assures you that the garden will be watered whether you're at home or away. But even more important, you can program watering schedules so that your plants receive no less and no more water than they need to thrive.

There are a variety of controllers available for home use, ranging from simple single-program, multiple-station versions to complex and versatile multiple-program, multiple-station sorts that can easily handle large areas containing plants with diverse water needs. Most are designed to operate on normal 110-volt household electrical current. For systems used in places where an electrical hookup would be difficult, there are battery-operated controllers.

Using an electronic controller, you can easily reduce runoff by setting cycles to run for a short period several times a day. With enough repetitions, water can penetrate to the desired depth.

Sensors. The flaw of electronic controllers is that they operate on a preset schedule regardless of weather: a controller could turn on the water during a rainstorm, or apply amounts of water appropriate for hot summer weather in cooler fall. Besides resetting a controller yourself, according to seasonal weather conditions, two electronic attachments can function as weather sensors to fine-tune the main control. A soil moisture sensor, linked to the controller, will trigger sprinkler operation only when the sensor indicates that soil moisture has dropped to the point where water is needed. And a rain shutoff device accumulates rainwater in a special collector pan, turning off the controller when the pan is filled to a prescribed depth, then triggering the controller to resume watering when the collected water has evaporated.

Watering

How often should I water? is perhaps the question most frequently asked by the novice gardener. No other question is quite so difficult to answer. "Give a plant as much water as it needs for healthy growth"—although accurate—is not really a helpful reply. The variable factors involved are many and complex: the needs of the particular plant, its age, the season, the weather (temperature, humidity, rainfall, and amount of wind), the nature of the soil, and the method of application. To ignore these factors and water by calendar or by clock may subject your garden to drought or drowning. But this much we can say: frequent light sprinkling and frequent heavy soaking alike are bad. Water thoroughly—and infrequently.

To understand this advice, it helps to know how water and soil interact, and what roots need for good health.

Watering depth and root growth. Roots develop and grow in the presence of water, air, and nutrients. Except for naturally shallow-rooted plants (rhododendrons and azaleas, for example), plants will root throughout the depth at which these essentials are found. If only the top foot of soil is kept well watered, roots develop primarily in the top foot. But under ideal conditions, roots of some plants can reach much deeper than that; see illustration. Even lawn grasses, frequently thought of as shallow rooted, can run roots from 10 to 24 inches deep. When shallow watering keeps a plant's roots near the surface, it can suffer severe damage if you go away for a long weekend and the weather turns hot, drying the top inches of soil. The plant will have no deep reserves of water to tap—and few roots with which to tap them, anyway.

Water penetration. A little water wets only a little soil, so you can't dampen soil to any depth by watering it lightly. Water moves down through the soil by progressively wetting soil particles. Once a particle has acquired its clinging film of water, every additional drop becomes "free" water—free to move and wet other particles. Although water moves primarily downward, it also moves laterally (to a much lesser extent), particularly in claylike soils. This lateral movement allows you to wet as much as a 12- to 18-inch diameter circle of soil (in heavier soils) with one drip emitter, or to water plants 6 to 9 inches on either side of a furrow or a soaker tube.

Because you should wet as much as possible of a plant's root zone when you water, it's important to understand water movement. You can see that in many soils a small watering basin around a shrub or tree is likely to encourage roots to remain within a small-diameter spread. You can also understand that an irrigation ditch 6 inches or more from a row of plants may not water the entire root area. And realizing that water moves primarily downward should affect the amount of water you give your plants: taking your soil type into account, apply enough for water to percolate down and penetrate the root zones. See illustration at the bottom of the next page.

Watering frequency. To maintain a healthy air-to-water ratio for plant roots, you shouldn't keep your soil constantly saturated. Water deeply but not too often (depending, of course, upon the various factors mentioned below that influence rate of soil drying). If damp soil remains low in oxygen for any length of time, both root development and nutrient absorption are reduced, slowing plant growth; at the same time, organisms harmful to the roots proliferate. Plants vary in their ability to tolerate such unfavorable conditions, but all plants (except water plants) need soil air.

If temperature, humidity, wind, and day length never varied, you could water your garden by the calendar. Weather conditions, however, will upset such a schedule at least part of the time. Under the influence of a hot, dry wind, plants use water so rapidly that shallow-rooted ones sometimes cannot absorb water from the soil fast enough to prevent wilting. In such weather, you need to water more frequently than a fixed schedule would call for. Conversely, when coolness or humidity prevails, you should water less frequently. The one watering rule that can be applied safely to all types of soils and climates is this: test the soil. If the top layer (3 to 4 inches) is dry—especially during the growing season—you probably need to water.

In winter, when the days are short and the sun is low on the horizon (diminishing light intensity and lowering plant water use), plants in leaf can exist for days or weeks on much less water than they demand in summer.

HOW DEEP DO ROOTS GROW?

Under ideal conditions, roots can reach the depths shown here. In most gardens, roots that reach two-thirds to three-quarters this depth are doing well. Most are concentrated in the upper third of this zone.

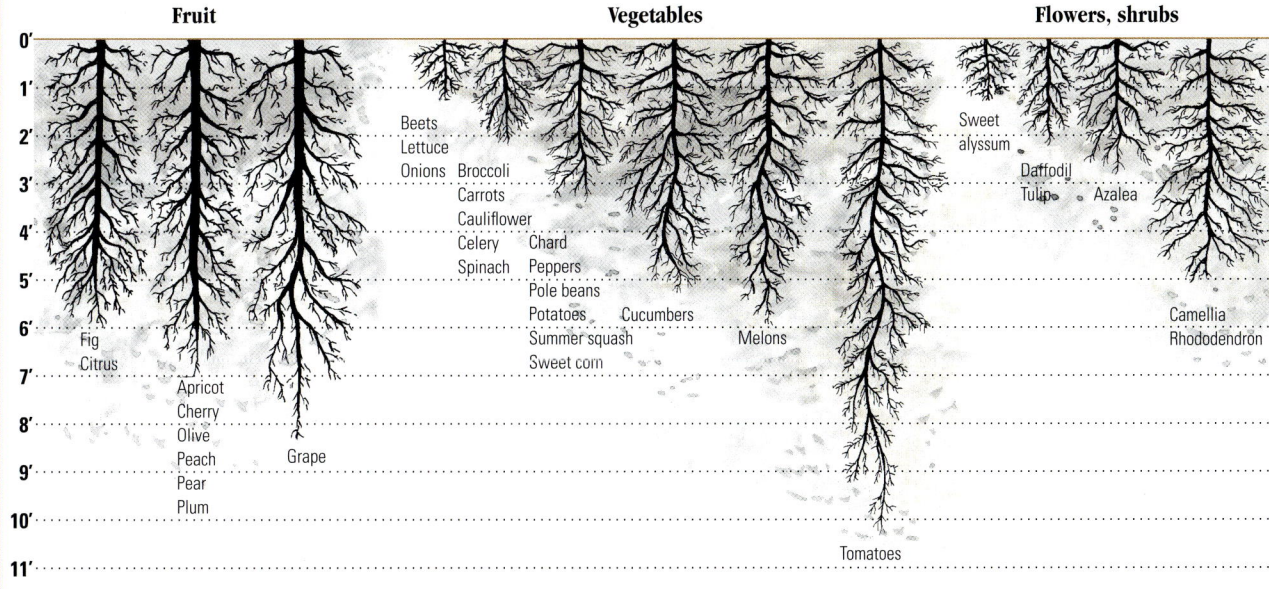

WATERING TO ENCOURAGE DEEP ROOTS

To wet a 4-by-5-foot flower bed to a depth of 2 feet*

Clay   Sprinkle for a total of 30 minutes. (If there is runoff, pause occasionally to let water soak in.)

Loam   Sprinkle bed evenly for 20 minutes.

Sand   Sprinkle for 10 minutes. Be sure to water the bed evenly from one side to the other.

*with hose delivering about 2 to 3 gpm (check your hose delivery with a watch and bucket of known volume)

To wet tree roots to a depth of 6 feet

Clay   Fill basin, let drain, repeat three more times.

Loam   Fill basin once, let drain completely, repeat.

Sand   Fill basin once. (If water soaks in so fast the basin won't fill, leave the hose on full—5 to 10 gpm—for 10 to 15 minutes for a 25-square-foot basin.)

4–6" deep

Watering Devices

A variety of sprinklers, soaker hoses, root irrigators, and drip irrigation systems can simplify watering.

Sprinklers. Nurseries, garden supply stores, and hardware stores sell a wide variety of sprinklers, both for attaching to the end of a garden hose and for incorporating into a permanent sprinkler system. Familiar types are the oscillating fan spray, the fountain of water (or fan of water in those manufactured to cover less than a full circle), the single- or multistream rotor sprinklers, and the "machine gun" impact types. Information about delivery rates, which can vary greatly, is available from the retailer or the manufacturer. Common to all sprinklers is an uneven distribution pattern, although the exact pattern varies from model to model.

Avoiding runoff. Runoff may occur when a sprinkler delivers water faster than some soils can absorb it. Inadequate water penetration results, even after extended watering. In a clay soil—especially on slopes—penetration can be so slow that more than 50 percent of the water is lost as runoff. In other words, you could easily sprinkle on 6 inches of water and have only 3 enter the soil.

The best way to avoid runoff is to alter your sprinkling procedure or change sprinkler heads—or possibly both. Slow the delivery rate so that the soil can absorb more of the water delivered to it. Or water at intervals, each time just to the runoff point, with a period between waterings so that the water will have a chance to soak in. Water as many times as necessary to get

the penetration you want. An electronic controller (p. 608) simplifies this operation.

You also can buy low-volume sprinkler heads that significantly cut the volume of water delivered; the decreased delivery rate more nearly matches the slower penetration rate of heavy soils. For the most even coverage, look for matched-precipitation sprinkler heads. These guarantee, for example, that a half-circle head will deliver just half as much water as a full-circle head, rather than deliver the same amount of water over a smaller area.

Another solution to the runoff problem—especially on steeply sloping ground—is to use a drip irrigation setup (discussed below). The low-volume delivery of various drip emitters and soaker tubing can eliminate runoff without sacrificing thorough penetration. If this approach is not practical, you can enhance water penetration for a particular plant by forming an irrigation basin around it.

Soil soaker hoses. Soaker hoses were the forerunners of drip irrigation—and still are quite useful for watering plants in rows. Attached to a hose nozzle, a long tube of canvas (or of perforated or porous plastic) seeps or sprinkles water along its entire length. You also can water trees and shrubs with a soaker by placing it in a circle around the plant, following the drip line. Simply position the soaker, attach the hose, and turn on the water for slow and steady water delivery. You will need to leave soakers on longer than you would a sprinkler.

Updated versions of soaker hoses are available for use with drip irrigation systems. They include several kinds of porous tubing: drip tubing with laser-drilled holes, double-walled

tubing, and soaker tubing that oozes water through its walls.

Root irrigators. Some special hose-end attachments can soak the soil beneath the surface. They are particularly useful for getting water deep into the soil on sloping land, where deep penetration without runoff can be a problem. They also can help trees root more deeply than they would with shallow watering. This may minimize pavement damage and uneven lawn surfaces caused by surface roots. In appearance and in effect, a root irrigator is like a giant hypodermic needle. You attach it to a hose, insert it into the root zone of a tree or shrub, and then turn on the valve: water flows through holes near the irrigator's tip, 12 to 18 inches below ground.

Drip irrigation. The term "drip irrigation" describes application of water not only by controlled-drip emitters but also by soaker tubing and miniature sprayers and sprinklers. What all these have in common is that they operate at low pressure and deliver a low volume of water compared with standard sprinklers. Because the water is applied slowly and near or on the ground, there should be no waste from runoff and little or no loss to evaporation. You place emitters so that water is delivered just where the plants need it, and you control penetration by varying the time the system runs or by varying the delivery capacity (in gallons per hour: gph) of the emitters you use. And you can regulate the volume of water to each plant by selecting the type and number of emitters you set for each one.

The chief advantage of drip irrigation systems is their flexibility. You can tailor them to water each plant with its own emitter(s), or you can distribute water over larger areas with microsprayers, minisprinklers, and porous tubing. A standard layout might include hookups to two or more valves, and could include many kinds of parts (see illustrations on the next page). Because lines are aboveground (they can be concealed by mulch) and are made of limber plastic, you can easily change line position and system layout, adding or subtracting emitters at will. About the only task drip irrigation isn't suited for is watering lawns.

You can set up a drip system to connect to a hose end; or you can make a permanent connection to your main water source, as you would for an underground, rigid-pipe setup. Such a permanent connection can be operated by an electronic controller (p. 608).

Emitters for drip systems. A number of different emitters are available—varying in shape, size, and internal mechanism—but all operate on the principle of dispensing water slowly to the soil. You can choose various flow rates, ranging from ½ to about 4 gph. Non-pressure-compensating emitters (the standard kind) work well on flat and relatively level ground,

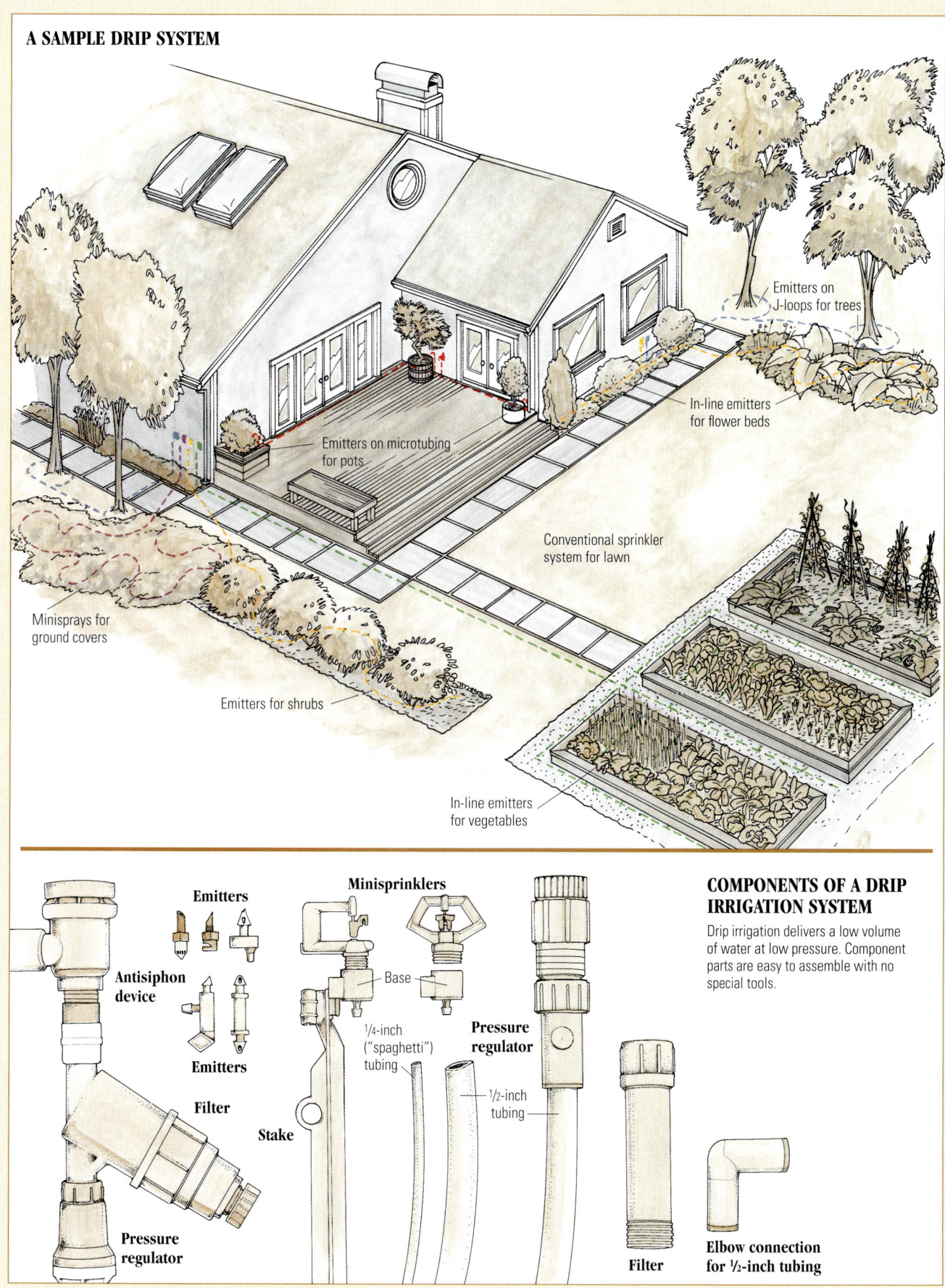

A SAMPLE DRIP SYSTEM

Emitters on J-loops for trees

In-line emitters for flower beds

Emitters on microtubing for pots

Conventional sprinkler system for lawn

Minisprays for ground covers

Emitters for shrubs

In-line emitters for vegetables

COMPONENTS OF A DRIP IRRIGATION SYSTEM

Drip irrigation delivers a low volume of water at low pressure. Component parts are easy to assemble with no special tools.

Emitters

Minisprinklers

Antisiphon device

Base

Emitters

¼-inch ("spaghetti") tubing

Pressure regulator

Filter

½-inch tubing

Stake

Pressure regulator

Filter

Elbow connection for ½-inch tubing

W

MEASURING SPRINKLER DELIVERY RATE AND DISPERSION

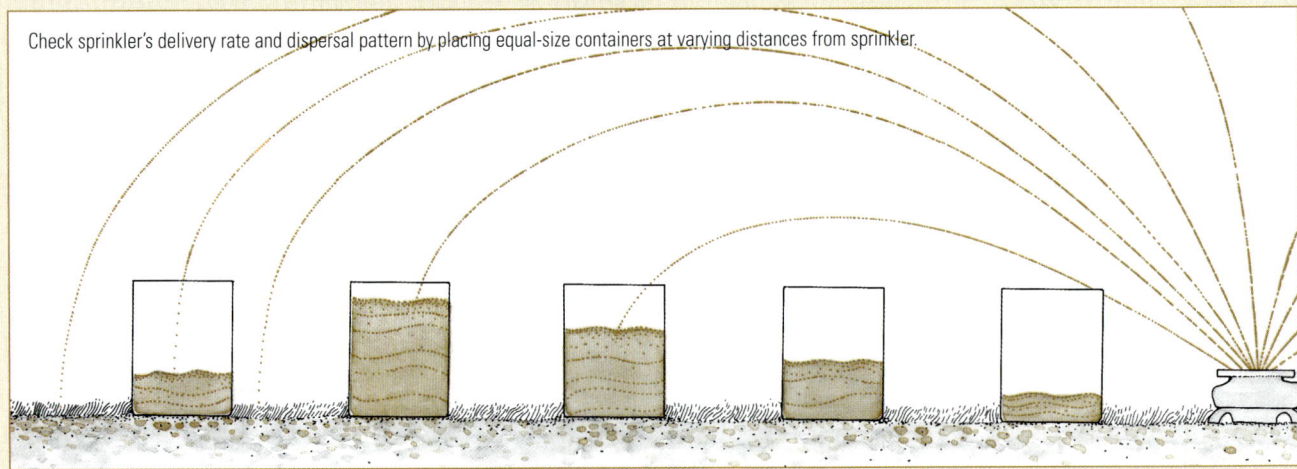

Check sprinkler's delivery rate and dispersal pattern by placing equal-size containers at varying distances from sprinkler.

and with lines not exceeding 200 feet in length. But when either gravity or friction (on hillsides or with long lines) will lower water pressure, choose pressure-compensating emitters. These will deliver the same amount of water throughout the system.

In addition to standard emitters that simply drip, you can buy a variety of other specialized emitters. Misters and foggers deliver a fine spray to increase humidity for plants like fuchsias and tuberous begonias. There are special setups for container plants. Microspray and minisprinkler heads offer low-volume equivalents of standard sprinkler-irrigation fixtures, delivering sprays of water over full- and partial-circle areas. These are useful for watering entire beds (where plants don't obstruct their flow and prevent even coverage). Just like regular sprinkler heads, however, they deliver water unevenly over the areas they cover. For even distribution, overlap their coverages by half. Flow rates are greater than those of drip emitters; you can find ones that deliver as little as 3 gph—and others that emit as much as 40 gph. Some operate at the water pressure used for drip emitters, but others require higher pressure. If you want to com-

bine these specialized emitters with standard drip emitters, be sure to check manufacturers' specifications for operating pressure.

Watering Techniques

Other than drip irrigation, there are really only two ways to apply water: by sprinkling or by flooding the ground. Many different sprinklers and soakers are available for use. Here are the basics of sprinkling and soaking.

Sprinkling. The simplest way to apply water evenly over a large surface is by sprinkling— essentially, producing artificial rainfall. Many plants, particularly those that like a cool, humid atmosphere, thrive with overhead sprinkling. Plants benefit from having dust rinsed off their leaves; sprinkling also discourages certain pests, especially spider mites.

But sprinkling has a negative side: it wastes water. Wind can carry off some water before it reaches the ground, and water sprinkled on, or running off onto, pavement is water lost. In areas where humidity is high, sprinkling encourages some foliage diseases (black spot and rust,

for example), although you can minimize the risk by sprinkling early in the morning so that leaves dry quickly as the day warms. Another potential drawback of sprinkling is that some plants with weak stems or heavy flowers bend and can break under a heavy load of water. For information on types of sprinklers, see page 610.

Application rates. To sprinkle effectively, you need to know the speed at which water penetrates in your soil and the water delivery rate of your sprinklers. Assume that 1 inch of rainfall (or sprinkling) will penetrate about 12 inches in sandy soil, 7 inches in loam, and 4 to 5 inches in clay. Therefore, if you want to water to a depth of 12 inches, you will need about an inch of sprinkling if your soil is sandy, or 2½ to 3 inches if your soil is clay.

To determine a sprinkler's delivery rate, place a number of same-size containers (such as coffee cans) at regular intervals outward from the sprinkler, and turn on the water. Note the length of time it takes to fill a container with an inch of water. In this process, you'll also learn the sprinkler's delivery pattern. That is, you'll notice that containers fill at an unequal rate. See illustration, above.

IRRIGATING VEGETABLES AND FLOWERS

Basins with sides 3 inches high hold water around large plants, such as tomatoes, peppers. On level ground, link basins to make watering easier.

Furrows 3 to 8 inches deep help irrigate straight rows. Bubbler on hose softens flow of water.

W

To achieve fairly even coverage, you'll have to overlap sprinkler coverage so that all areas watered receive approximately equal amounts.

Flooding. Flooding, or soaking, is an effective means of supplying sufficient water to the extensive and deep root systems of large shrubs and trees. Make a level basin for the plant by forming a ridge of soil several inches high around it at its drip line (p. 559). To water, simply fill the basin slowly. From the depth of water in a full basin, the length of time it takes to fill it, and knowledge of your soil type and absorption rate, you can calculate the time it will take to achieve the water penetration depth you desire.

If you grow vegetables or flowers in rows, you can build adjoining basins for large vegetables like squash or make furrows between rows (see illustration on previous page). Broad, shallow furrows are generally better than deep, narrow ones: there is less danger to roots in scooping out shallow furrows, and less likelihood that roots will be exposed by a strong flow of water. And a wide furrow will ensure soaking of a wide root area (remember that water in all except clay soils moves primarily downward). Do furrowing before root systems have developed and spread; if you wait, you may damage roots when you make even a shallow furrow.

From a water-conservation standpoint, furrow irrigation is much less efficient than drip irrigation. It also does not work well in sandy soils.

Watersprout. See Sucker   p. 602

Weed

Awild plant that grows out of place and competes with garden plants for water, nutrients, and space is a weed. See the Visual Guide to Identifying Weeds (pp. 614–615) for help in recognizing these problem plants.

Weed Control

Weed control is more than mere garden housekeeping. A weed-free garden is not only more attractive than a weed-filled one but also healthier. Weeds compete with garden plants for water, nutrients, light, and space. In some instances, they harbor insect and pathogen populations you'd rather live without.

You can control weeds several ways: physically (by pulling, hoeing, digging, mulching, or mowing) or chemically (with herbicides). The old slogan "Keep weeds from going to seed" goes far toward holding weed populations in check. In fact, preventing weeds from germinating in the first place by using mulches (p. 576), landscape fabrics (p. 569), or soil solarization (p. 582) is one of the best ways to control them.

Physical control. Pulling annual weeds by hand is sometimes necessary, especially when weeds grow among choice, shallow-rooted plants such as cyclamen, rhododendrons, and azaleas. Where damage to surface roots is not a risk, hoeing and cultivating furnish adequate weed control and, in roughing up the soil surface and breaking the crust, temporarily improve water penetration.

Many tools are available for weeding and cultivating. Common garden hoes and cultivating forks in a variety of sizes are useful for working among row crops, little garden plants, and shrubs. Scuffle hoes (flat-bladed, disk type, or U-shaped) are easier to use in close quarters or under spreading plants. As you push and pull them, they cut weeds without digging into roots of desirable plants.

For larger areas (orchards, roadsides, vacant lots), rototilling or disking will do the job, especially where there is no summer rain to germinate late weed crops. Either method will not only knock down weeds but also incorporate them into the soil, where they will decay to form humus. Weed-eaters knock down weed growth but leave severed tops on the ground; rotary mowers cut weeds and grind up the refuse in one operation. In many areas, weed control reduces the risk of fire (see Fire, Landscaping for, p. 563).

Chemical control. The herbicides, or chemical weed killers, were conceived as agricultural aids but years ago were welcomed into the home gardener's realm. These chemicals offer several approaches to weed control. Preplant herbicides are for use before you set out vegetables (if so labeled), bedding plants, or ornamentals. Pre-emergence herbicides applied to the soil will kill weed seeds as they germinate. Contact herbicides kill weeds onto which they are sprayed or sprinkled. Translocated herbicides contain an active ingredient that, when absorbed by a weed, moves to another part of the plant and interferes with its metabolism, causing the weed's death.

Chemical weed killers can, in certain situations, save the home gardener a great amount of time—especially if there is a severe weed problem to clear up or if the weeds are in difficult-to-work areas. Chemical controls are much more useful in established plantings (shrubs, ground covers, turf grasses) than among bedding plants. No herbicide should be used in a small vegetable garden after planting, although you can safely use a preplant herbicide to prepare the area for vegetables if it is labeled for that purpose.

Herbicide safety. You must use chemical herbicides with extreme care so that you run no risk of damaging other plants. Begin by identifying the weeds that are present. See the Visual Guide to Identifying Weeds (pp. 614–615) for help. (Check with a local nursery, farm advisor, or your Cooperative Extension Office for those you cannot identify.) Then choose the right product, labeled for your specific weed situation. Thoroughly read product labels for directions and cautions, and always follow directions to the let-ter. Some of these chemicals are so persistent that traces will remain in a sprayer even after rinsing. Play it safe: keep a separate sprayer just for applying weed killers. And always apply herbicides when there is no wind that could blow the spray onto ornamental or crop plants.

The herbicides listed on page 616 are the most widely available and useful in home gardens. Many other chemicals are most common in "weed and feed" fertilizer-herbicide combinations or in products for use on lawns. You will find these chemicals mentioned in the individual weed descriptions in this dictionary.

Weed Prevention

There are several effective ways to prevent weed seeds from germinating or weed plants from growing. You can plant annuals and vegetables close together so that their growth will shade out weeds. Ground-cover plantings—and ground-hugging plants beneath taller ones in a mixed planting—can blanket the soil so that even when weed seeds sprout, they'll have trouble getting the sunlight necessary to become established. Soil solarization (p. 582) is an effective method of weed control. And any sort of mulch (p. 576) materially cuts down on annual weed establishment; any weeds that do appear will be quite easy to remove. Landscape fabrics (p. 569) are designed to prevent weeds in ornamental plantings. Weeds can also be prevented with pre-emergence herbicides. See the box Weed Control with Herbicides (p. 616).

Wettable Powder

Afinely ground pesticide, wettable powder can be mixed in water and sprayed onto plants. Some kinds also can be dusted on, as described under Dust (p. 560).

Whiteflies

Aptly named, whiteflies are annoying winged insects (about 1/8 inch long) that fly up from a plant when you brush or touch it. Turn over an infested plant's leaf and you see winged adults, stationary pupae, and nymphs that suck plant juices and exude a sticky substance—and (with sharp eyes or a hand lens) tiny eggs and freshly hatched, mobile young (see photograph, p. 592).

Standard controls. Nature keeps whitefly populations in check most of the time: tiny wasp species (p. 549) are parasites of the nymphs and pupae, and some predatory creatures feed on them. When you spray with a chemical insecticide, you may also kill those parasites and predators—resulting in an increase of whiteflies. So
▶ page 616

W

Visual Guide to Identifying
WEODS

Uninvited and usually unattractive, weeds poke their scruffy leaves up into flower beds and lawns, ramble freely around the garden stealing moisture and nutrients from ornamental plants, and make a garden look unkempt. Some of them even jump fences to invade native plant habitats. Use this visual guide to help you identify common weeds. For controls, see the guidelines here, where provided, the individual weed entry, or Weed Control (p. 613).

Bermuda Grass
Warm-season grass that spreads by seed or underground runners   p. 547

Yellow Oxalis
Broad-leafed weed that thrives in sun or shade; deep taproot makes it hard to control   p. 579

Crabgrass
Well-known grassy weed common in lawns and flower beds; thrives in warm, wet soil   p. 555

Spotted Spurge
Low-growing, rapidly spreading broad-leafed weed that reproduces prolifically by seed   p. 600

Purslane *(Portulaca oleracea)*
Prostrate, broad-leafed weed with fleshy leaves and small yellow flowers   p. 595

Henbit
Annual weed particularly troublesome in eastern lawns   p. 568

Quack Grass
Aggressive perennial weed in gardens and lawns; herbicides are the most effective control

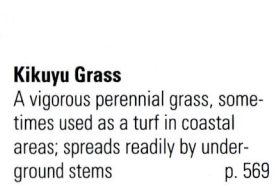

Kikuyu Grass
A vigorous perennial grass, sometimes used as a turf in coastal areas; spreads readily by underground stems   p. 569

Kudzu Vine
Aggressive, vining plant common in parts of the South   p. 569

Annual Bluegrass *(Poa annua)*
Common annual weed in lawns; easy to pull or hoe elsewhere   p. 442

Common Groundsel
Upright, broad-leafed perennial with small yellow flowers and puffball seed heads; hoe or pull young plants

Bindweed
Vining, broad-leafed weed with white flowers; tough to control because of its long-lived seeds and deep taproots
p. 547

Black Medic, Burclover
Two similar, low, spreading, broad-leafed weeds with small yellow flowers, usually annual, that are common in under-fertilized lawns and gardens; pull young weeds, increase nitrogen fertilizer in lawns

Poison Ivy
Sprawling, climbing plant most common in the East. Causes skin rash. Control with appropriate herbicide
p. 589

Ground Ivy
Aggressive, spreading perennial, often a weed in lawns. Hand-pulling and "Weed and Feed" products are best control
p. 318

Nutgrass (Nutsedge)
Grasslike perennial common to wet areas; yellow or purple flowering forms
p. 577

Dandelion
Edible, broad-leafed weed common to beds and lawns; hand-pull when young, or use appropriate herbicide
p. 557

Poison Oak
Vining, deciduous shrub that causes skin irritation; look for specifically labeled herbicides and note cautions
p. 589

Common Mallow
Deep-rooted, broad-leafed weed; mature plants hard to pull, so hoe or pull when young, or use appropriate herbicide

Blackberry
Difficult to kill, vigorously spreading perennial plant
p. 548

Pigweeds
Two species, upright and prostrate, of troublesome summer weeds
p. 582

Chickweed
Fast growing, prostrate, winter weed common in beds and lawns. Control similar to henbit

WEED CONTROL WITH HERBICIDES

Caution is the byword in using any chemical herbicide. Carefully read (and follow) label directions not only for application but also for the plants on which the product may be used (those not harmed by its proper application). The herbicide user can be held responsible for damage to neighboring properties resulting from uses not specified on the product label. If you have a particularly bad weed problem, consider contacting a commercial weed sprayer. They have a larger arsenal of sprays available.

Pre-emergence. Pre-emergence herbicides work by inhibiting growth of germinating weed seeds and very young seedlings. Apply them to weed-free soil; if weeds are already present, thoroughly remove the weeds or kill them with a translocated herbicide (see below). Common pre-emergents include:

- **DCPA (Dacthal).** Controls annual grasses and some broad-leafed weeds. Can be used on a wide variety of ornamental plantings, including turf.

- **EPTC (Eptam).** Controls a number of grasses and broad-leafed weeds among ornamental plants. Must be incorporated into soil immediately to reduce loss through vaporization.

- **Oryzalin (Surflan).** Controls annual grasses and many broad-leafed weeds (including spotted spurge and yellow oxalis) in some turf grasses and ornamental plantings.

- **Simazine.** Controls a wide variety of broad-leafed and grassy weeds among ornamentals and some crops. Effect is long lasting—could nearly fit into the total soil cleanup category. Not recommended for desert regions or sandy soils.

- **Trifluralin.** Controls many grasses and annual broad-leafed weeds in ornamental plantings.

Postemergence. Two types of weed killer act on growing weeds and other unwanted vegetation. The contact herbicides are effective when they touch the plant. Translocated herbicides must be absorbed by the plant, which they kill by interfering with plant metabolism; these are slower to show effectiveness than the contact kinds. Common postemergents include:

- **Fluazifop-butyl.** Translocated. Controls actively growing grassy weeds; best results when weeds are healthy and you add a surfactant (spreader-sticker) to the mixture. Can be sprayed over many ornamentals; see product label.

- **Glyphosate.** Translocated. Controls a great variety of actively growing vegetation: grasses, perennial weeds, woody plants (including poison oak); repeat application sometimes needed on perennial and woody plants. Effectiveness may be enhanced by addition of a surfactant (spreader-sticker).

- **Herbicidal soap (Superfast).** Contact. Made from selected fatty acids, like insecticidal soaps. Degrades quickly. Provides quick top-kill. Works best against annual weeds.

- **Sethoxydim (Poast).** Translocated. Controls annual grasses (but not annual bluegrass or hard fescue) in ornamental plantings. Should be applied at particular stage of weed growth; needs addition of an oil-based surfactant (spreader-sticker) to be effective.

- **Triclopyr (Brush-b-gon, Brush Killer).** Translocated. Used on hard-to-kill brush and weeds, such as blackberry and poison oak.

Total soil cleanup. Chemicals for total soil cleanup (prometon is the most common) have a broader-spectrum toxicity than the previous herbicides and/or a significant longevity in the soil. They are often misused. Follow the special application procedures outlined on the product label.

Packaged controls are listed alphabetically by generic name (the name you will find on the product label under "active ingredients") or common name; trade name (where different from generic name) appears in parentheses.

---

before you decide to use a chemical control, consider these options:

- Eliminate highly susceptible plants from your garden.

- Hose off infested plants, hitting both sides of all leaves to wash off adults and crawlers (newly hatched nymphs); repeat every few days. Insecticidal soap can be more effective than water, and it is less harmful than insecticides to natural enemies.

- Place yellow cards or stakes covered with sticky material among infested plants. The color attracts adult whiteflies; the sticky material captures and holds them.

- Buy and release in your garden a commercially reared natural parasite: *Encarsia formosa* wasps. They are parasites of the greenhouse whitefly (common species) and will kill them in a greenhouse or outdoors.

- On plants like squash, get rid of old, nonproductive yellow leaves in the center of the plant. These leaves carry many whitefly nymphs.

On edible plants, use pyrethrins or malathion. On nonedible plants, you can use systemics, neem, chlorpyrifos, or summer oils. Increase spray effectiveness by spraying at night, while whiteflies are resting.

Recent outbreaks of introduced species of whitefly, including the ash whitefly in California, are not effectively controlled with chemical sprays. Instead, massive releases of parasitic wasps by state agencies have been successful in bringing these annoying pests down to reasonable levels.

Cool-climate controls. In cold-winter climates whiteflies don't overwinter outdoors; all garden infestations originate from indoor plants or are imported as transplants. Inspect greenhouse and indoor plants and eliminate any whiteflies you find. When you buy new plants for your garden—particularly bedding plants, which may have started their lives in a greenhouse—carefully examine the undersides of leaves for the nymphs.

Wood Sorrel, Yellow. See Oxalis, Yellow
p. 579

Whorl

Whorls are composed of three or more leaves, branches, or flowers growing in a circle from a joint (node) on a stem or trunk.

Xeriscape

Derived from *xeros,* Greek for "dry," Xeriscape is a patented name that stands for water-conserving landscapes.

RESOURCE DIRECTORY

Gardeners in the United States and Canada can look to many sources for help and inspiration. Arboretums, fascinating plant collections, and great gardens throughout North America offer countless ideas for plant choices and garden design. Nurseries from Florida to Washington State provide a vast selection—everything from native grasses to roses, plumerias, and Christmas poinsettias—and catalogs make the list of possibilities even longer. And the variety is always expanding; annuals, perennials, and shrubs in new colors as well as new kinds of gourmet vegetables are introduced every year.

Botanical Gardens, Arboretums, and Estate Gardens

The many fine public gardens described on pages 618–625 range in size from a city block to hundreds of acres. Some were designed by outstanding landscape architects such as Frederick Law Olmstead, who helped plan the Arnold Arboretum by combining local native plants with the natural features of the site. Others were planted by visionaries like Cason Callaway, who was so inspired by a rare orange-red plumleaf azalea found in Pine Mountain, Georgia that he restored the area's rural landscape—and created Callaway Gardens.

Some public gardens mimic wild land, while others have a carefully tailored, formal design or present museum-style displays of labeled plants. If you're creating a new garden or adding to an existing one, a visit to a public garden can give you ideas to use at home: show-stopping flower combinations, innovative ways to plant vegetable beds, interesting container plantings. And of course, you can see which plants are best for your area and how they look when fully grown.

Mail-Order Catalogs

Nurseries and garden centers, too numerous to list in this resource directory, offer a wide variety of plants and seeds throughout the year. But sooner or later, adventurous gardeners may want to try growing novelties such as blue potatoes or chocolate-brown bell peppers. Many mail-order sources specialize in unusual or difficult-to-find varieties. The Native Seeds/SEARCH catalog, for instance, lists brown tepary beans (favored for vegetarian pâtés) and chiltepines (wild chilies best described as small round firecrackers). Some catalogs provide growing tips, recipes, or tidbits of gardening wisdom along with plant descriptions.

Catalogs can easily tantalize a reader into making unplanned purchases, but keep in mind that impulse buying is a surefire way to end up with a mishmash of a landscape. You'll get better results and better value for your dollar if you look before you leap. Before you buy, form a clear idea of your needs by assessing the space you want to fill, the amount of sun and shade it receives, and its soil conditions. Think about potential plant combinations; consider compatible bloom times and the plants' colors and heights as well as their water and fertilizer needs. And estimate how many plants you'll require.

Once you know your needs, read the catalog's plant descriptions carefully. These usually combine solid information with marketing tactics, so you can expect some jargon. Learning to decode a few typical words and phrases will help you shop more wisely.

"Start seeds indoors" describes seeds that require more care than usual. They may germinate slowly or need more warmth, or the seedlings may demand extra time or attention prior to being planted outdoors. Many perennials fall into this category. "Sow in place" usually means that the plant doesn't survive transplanting well; when you see this advice, it's wise to heed it.

When a vegetable is proclaimed "novel" or "unusual" or has "unique" color or shape, you know that flavor and texture are secondary. "Giant" is a clue that the vegetable so described may be better mounted above the fireplace than tossed into the cooking pan.

Watch out for anything "vigorous." This term sometimes implies that the vine, shrub, or vegetable in question is ready and able to outcompete most plants in its path. If space is limited, look instead for compact, bush, or dwarf varieties.

Plants that "self-sow readily" are usually annuals and biennials (but can be trees or shrubs) that you plant once, then have forever: a new crop of seeds germinates and grows each year with no help from you. Whether you wind up with a weed or a favorite companion depends, of course, on your liking for the plant—and on just how invasive it is.

Scientific Plant Names

In public gardens, nurseries, and catalogs, you'll most likely encounter Latin plant names. To learn what they mean and why they are important, see pages 632–633. How do you pronounce them? For guidelines, see pages 634–635.

BOTANICAL GARDENS
and Arboretums

Montreal Botanic Garden and Insectarium

Botanical gardens and arboretums display plants from around the world as well as local native species, often in landscape settings. Some have demonstration gardens filled with flowers, fruits, and vegetables; some include displays featuring irrigation devices, mulches, fencing, or paving. Many offer classes in gardening techniques, operate horticultural libraries, and sell hard-to-find plants. Some are living laboratories, overseeing the propagation and preservation of endangered plants. The botanical gardens and arboretums described below, listed alphabetically by region, are the major establishments (and a few less-well-known ones) that we have visited around the United States and Canada. Hours are subject to change.

CANADA

Montreal Botanical Garden and Insectarium
4101 Sherbrooke Street East
Montreal, Canada PQ H1X 2B2

(514) 872-1400

Open daily 9 to 6

Specialty: Chinese and Japanese gardens

The largest Chinese garden of its type outside of Asia is just one of the attractions at this 135-acre garden. Ten greenhouses display seasonal exhibitions as well as orchids and an impressive bonsai collection. The Leslie-Hancock Garden features rhododendrons and azaleas, in bloom from May to June.

Royal Botanical Gardens
RBG Center
680 Plains Road West
Burlington, Ontario L7T 4H4

(905) 527-1158

Open daily 9:30 to 6

Specialty: Lilacs, roses

The world's largest collection of lilacs, two acres of roses, 250,000 irises and 125,000 spring bulbs are part of this 2,700-acre garden. Tulips, annuals, and impatiens grow in the large rock garden. Other attractions include a medicinal garden, a scented garden, and a 40-acre arboretum.

University of British Columbia Botanical Garden
6804 S.W. Marine Drive
Vancouver, B.C., Canada V6T 1Z4

(604) 822-4208

Open mid-March to mid-October, daily 10 to 6

Specialty: Alpine plants, rhododendrons, and magnolias

Seventy acres of plants that thrive in Northwest gardens grow here. Giant Asian lilies are stunners in summer. The 1-acre Food Garden, a patchwork of raised beds, displays cool- and warm-season vegetables and espaliered fruit trees.

EASTERN STATES

Arnold Arboretum of Harvard University
125 Arborway
Jamaica Plain, MA 02130-3519

(617) 524-1718

Open daily from dawn to dusk

Specialty: Trees

The 265-acre Arnold Arboretum houses one of North America's finest collections of hardy trees, shrubs, and vines. Plants are grouped together by family in a natural landscape, Many special collections are here: among them is the Larz Anderson Bonsai Collection, including hinoki false cypresses which were imported from Japan in 1913 and have been in the United States longer than any other known bonsai. A popular mid-May attraction is the lilac collection, containing 250 kinds of lilacs.

Brooklyn Botanic Gardens
900 Washington Avenue
Brooklyn, NY 11225-1099

(718) 622-4433

Open April to September, Tuesday to Friday 8 to 6, weekends 10 to 6; October to March, Tuesday to Friday 8 to 4:30, weekends 10 to 4:30

Specialty: Gardens within one garden

Arnold Arboretum of Harvard University

This oasis allows viewers to escape from the middle of New York City into 52 acres of garden paradise. More than 12,000 kinds of plants are displayed. Highlights include a vast collection of Oriental flowering cherries, the Cranford Rose Garden, the Japanese Hill-and-Pond Garden, and a lily pool.

Cornell Plantations
One Plantations Road
Ithaca, NY 14850-2799

(607) 255-3020

Open daily from dawn to dusk
Specialty: Herbs and native plants
The botanical gardens, arboretum, and natural areas of Cornell University form Cornell Plantations, which totals more than 3,000 acres. The 50-acre botanical garden encompasses 14 separate gardens, including rhododendrons and azaleas, a garden tracing the evolution of vegetable gardening, and one of the country's top herb gardens. The 150-acre arboretum emphasizes native New York trees and shrubs and other cultivars hardy in central New York State.

New York Botanical Garden
Bronx, NY 10458-5126

(212) 220-8700

Open November to March, Tuesday to Sunday and Monday holidays 10 to 4; April to October, Tuesday to Sunday and Monday holidays 10 to 6

Founded in 1891, this 250-acre garden is one of the oldest and largest botanical gardens in the world. Visitors enjoy a river and waterfall, wetlands, a forest, and rock outcroppings. Among the 16 specialty gardens are the T. H. Everett Rock Garden, which displays thousands of mountain flowers, and the Peggy Rockefeller Rose Garden, which contains 2,700 rose bushes. Flowering trees and shrubs, including cherries and lilacs, are in bloom from April through June.

U. S. National Arboretum
3501 New York Avenue, NE
Washington, D. C. 20002

(202) 245-2726

Open daily 8 to 5; closed Christmas Day
Specialty: Bonsai and herb gardens
This national landmark contains 444 acres of fine collections, including the Gotelli Dwarf and Slow-Growing Conifer Collection, a 1,500-specimen gathering of firs, junipers, and pines. The National Herb Garden traces the history of herbs and explains their many uses. A Japanese garden, bonsai collection, and rose garden are other attractions.

GREAT LAKES

University of Minnesota Landscape Arboretum
3675 Arboretum Drive
Chanhassen, MN 55317

(612) 443-2460

Open daily 8 a.m. to dusk; closed major holidays. Extended hours seasonally
Specialty: Cold-hardy trees
This resource for cold-climate plants and trees encompasses 935 acres of rolling hills, native woods, restored prairie, and display gardens. Highlights are a Japanese wet garden composed of Minnesota-hardy plants, a hosta glade with more than 250 varieties, and a wildflower garden. The research at the arboretum has led to the development of fruit varieties that grow well in cold climates, among them apples, strawberries, and raspberries.

University of Wisconsin-Madison Arboretum
1207 Seminole Highway
Madison, WI 53711

(608) 263-7888

Open daily 7 a.m. to 10 p.m.

Specialty: Ecological restoration
This international authority on restoration comprises more than 1,200 acres of ecological communities devoted to returning plants to their natural environments. The main attractions include Curtis Prairie, the world's oldest restored prairie, and Greene Prairie. Also on display is the state's most extensive woody plant collection, including lilacs and flowering crabapples.

HAWAII

National Tropical Botanical Garden
Box 340
Lawai, HI 96765

(808) 332-7361

Call for opening times
Specialty: Tropical and native Hawaiian plants
The nation's only congressionally chartered tropical botanical garden. Located in a verdant valley near Poipu, the 186-acre garden contains the world's largest collection of native Hawaiian plants, many of them rare and endangered.

MIDWEST

Chicago Botanic Garden
1000 Lake Cook Road
Glencoe, IL 60022

(847) 835-5440

Open daily 8 a.m. to dusk;
closed Christmas Day

This garden encompasses 385 acres with 20 different garden areas. One of the highlights is a three-island garden composed of Midwestern natives displayed in Japanese style; each island symbolizes a different philosophy. Other areas of interest include native Illinois prairies, a rose garden, and a collection of aquatic plants.

Cleveland Botanical Garden
11030 East Boulevard
Cleveland, OH 44106

(216) 721-1600

Open daily from dawn to dusk
Specialty: Herb garden, native plants
Seven acres of landscaped grounds contain five different display gardens. The herb garden includes an English knot garden and more than 300 herb species; the rose garden features the best hybrids from northeast Ohio; the Japanese garden showcases

classic landscaping styles of Japan; the reading garden is filled with unusual plants; and the wildflower garden, threaded with walking trails, offers visitors a look at hundreds of native trees and flowers.

Hayes Regional Arboretum
801 Elks Road
Richmond, IN 47377

(765) 962-3745

Open Tuesday to Saturday 9 to 5, Sunday 1 to 5; closed Christmas Day and Easter Sunday

Specialty: Native trees

This 365-acre nature preserve contains 179 species of woody plants native to the region, along with 40 acres of Indiana's beech-maple forest. A nature center—housed in a converted dairy barn from 1833—displays exhibits. Visitors can also enjoy a bird sanctuary, hiking trails, and a 3-mile nature tour.

Missouri Botanical Gardens
4344 Shaw Boulevard
St. Louis, MO 63110

800-642-8842

Open Memorial Day to Labor Day daily 9 to 8, after Labor Day daily 9 to 5; closed Christmas Day

Specialty: Climatron greenhouse

The focal point of these gardens is the world-renowned Climatron, a geodesic-domed greenhouse, displays 24,000 square feet of tropical rain forest species, including cycads, palms, orchids, and ferns. The gar-

den is also home to a 14-acre Japanese strolling garden (the largest of its kind in the United States), an authentic Chinese garden, and 23 demonstration gardens.

Morton Arboretum
Route 53
Lisle, IL 60532

(630) 719-2400

Open daily 7 to 7 or dusk

Specialty: Northern Illinois–hardy trees

More than one million native and exotic trees, shrubs, vines, and woody plants are displayed on 1,700 acres. Some of the towering trees are older than the arboretum, which celebrates its 75th anniversary in 1997. Walking and driving trails wind through the grounds. Fall color is striking from September to November.

ROCKY MOUNTAIN STATES

Denver Botanic Garden
1005 York Street
Denver, CO 80206-3799

(303) 331-4000

Open Wednesday through Friday 9 to 5, Saturday through Tuesday 9 to 8; closed Christmas Day and New Year's Day

Specialty: Alpine rock garden plants

Set in the heart of the city with an exhilarating westward view of the Rocky Mountains, this 20-acre landscape is a year-round mecca for plant enthusiasts. In the tropical

Denver Botanic Garden

conservatory, brilliant bougainvilleas and orchids cure winter doldrums. Small theme gardens include a Japanese garden, a plains garden, and a formal herb garden. A 1-acre alpine rock garden, most colorful in May, features some 3,500 species of plants from the world's mountains.

Red Butte Garden and Arboretum/ State Arboretum of Utah
University of Utah
300 Wakara Way
Salt Lake City, UT 84133

(801) 581-5322; (801) 581-4747 (information hotline)

Open Tuesday through Sunday 10 a.m. to dusk, April through October; closed Mondays and Tuesdays, November through March

Wildflowers, flowering shrubs, and a large collection of dwarf conifers are among the displays located on 25 acres of developed gardens.

SOUTHERN STATES

Atlanta Botanic Gardens
1345 Piedmont Avenue
Atlanta, GA 30309

(404) 876-5859

Open April to October, Tuesday to Sunday 9 to 7; November to March, Tuesday to Sunday 9 to 6

Specialty: Tropical plants

This 30-acre garden includes 15 acres of outdoor landscaped gardens and 15 acres

Missouri Botanical Garden

Memphis Botanic Garden

of hardwood forest; displays include a rose garden, native plants, and carnivorous plants in a simulated bog. Visitors can also explore the Dorothy Chapman Fuqua Conservatory, which holds 7,000 tropical plants, including palms, cycads, ferns, epiphytes, and orchids.

Crosby Arboretum
1986 Ridge Road
Picayune, MS 39466
(601) 799-2311
Open Wednesday to Sunday 10 to 5; closed Thanksgiving Day, Christmas Day, and New Year's Day
Specialty: Native plants
The Native Plant Center is the focus of this 64-acre arboretum, which includes more than 300 species of indigenous trees and shrubs, as well as a collection of wildflowers and grasses found in south-central Mississippi and southeast Louisiana. Other features include pitcher plant bogs that contain numerous terrestrial orchids.

Memphis Botanic Gardens
750 Cherry Road
Memphis, TN 38117
(901) 685-1566
Open March to October, Monday to Saturday 9 to 6, Sunday 11 to 6; November to February, Monday to Saturday 9 to 4:30, Sunday 11 to 4:30
This garden holds more than 20 display gardens, including a Japanese Garden of Tranquillity and a sensory garden that focuses on the five senses—visitors can, for example, taste berries, listen to songbirds attracted to the garden, and see flowers grouped in warm and cool colors.

North Carolina Botanical Garden
University of North Carolina at Chapel Hill
CB 3375 Totten Center
Chapel Hill, NC 27599-3375
(919) 962-0522
Open mid-March to mid-November, weekdays 8 to 5, Saturday 9 to 6, and Sunday 10 to 6. Open mid-November to mid-March, weekdays 8 to 5
Specialty: Native plants
This center for research and conservation places special emphasis on plants native to the southeastern United States. The garden comprises almost 600 acres; standout features are the bogs, grasslands, and the Coker Arboretum (in the heart of the university campus), which contains about 580 species of trees and shrubs.

The State Botanical Garden of Georgia
2450 South Milledge Avenue
Athens, GA 30605
(706) 542-1244
Open daily 8 a.m. to dusk; closed major holidays
Specialty: Native and tropical plants
Under the direction of the University of Georgia, this garden covers more than 300 acres and includes 5 miles of nature trails, a three-story tropical conservatory, and a native flora garden. The international garden features an herb garden and a section on endangered plants of Georgia, complete with a bog garden.

SOUTHWEST

Dallas Arboretum and Botanical Garden
8617 Garland Road
Dallas, TX 75218
(214) 327-8263
Open March to October, daily 10 to 6, November to February, daily 10 to 5; closed major holidays
Specialty: Azaleas, perennials
This garden comprises 66 acres of landscaped grounds, including a 2-acre English-style ornamental perennial garden; shade-loving ferns in a misty dell; and a color garden with more than 15,000 chrysanthemums in the fall and more than 2,500 varieties of azaleas in the spring. There are also two historic mansions for visitors to explore.

The Desert Botanical Garden
1201 N. Galvin Parkway
Phoenix, AZ 85008
(602) 941-1225
Open 7 a.m. to 10 p.m. May to September, 8 to 8 October to April
Specialty: Plants of the Sonoran Desert
Displays on 145 acres of landscaped grounds focus mainly on plants and ecology of the Sonoran Desert. Trails snake among many kinds of cacti, including giant saguaros. Other displays feature desert natives of Mexico, Australia, and Africa. October through May is the best time to visit. Wildflowers add seasonal color.

Fort Worth Botanic Garden
3220 Botanic Garden Boulevard
Fort Worth, TX 76107
(817) 871-7686
(817) 871-7689 (recorded message)
Call for opening times
Specialty: A variety of gardens
Created in 1933 as a public relief project during the Depression, this 109-acre garden includes a Japanese garden, several rose gardens, a perennial garden, a fragrance garden and a cactus garden. A 10,000-square-foot conservatory displays tropical plants.

The Huntington Botanical Gardens

WEST COAST

Hoyt Arboretum
400 S.W. Fairview Boulevard
Portland, OR 97221

(503) 823-3655

Grounds open daily from dawn to dusk; visitor center open daily 9 to 3

Specialty: Conifers, shrubs

Trails crisscross this 175-acre site, leading through collections of trees from around the world and from the Pacific Northwest. Along the Redwood-Spruce Trail, Northwest natives such as Brewer's weeping spruce fill the air with woodsy fragrance. In spring, flowering cherries and magnolias are cloaked in bloom. Fall brings flaming glory to the arboretum's poplars, persimmons, and maples.

The Huntington Botanical Gardens
1151 Oxford Road
San Marino, CA 91108

(818) 405-2141

Open Tuesday through Friday noon to 4:30, Saturday and Sunday 10:30 to 4:30; closed major holidays

Specialty: Plants from around the world

More than 150 meticulously landscaped acres, showcasing one of the country's finest plant collections, surround the former mansion of the late railroad tycoon Henry E. Huntington. The plants—many of them rare—are displayed in separate gardens, including a jungle garden, palm garden, desert garden (a 12-acre spread featuring a large outdoor collection of cacti and succulents), camellia garden, rose garden, and Japanese garden. A Shakespeare garden features annuals and bulbs mentioned in the playwright's works.

Strybing Arboretum and Botanical Gardens
Golden Gate Park
Ninth Avenue and Lincoln Way
San Francisco, CA 94122

(415) 661-1316

Open weekdays 8:30 to 4:30, weekends and major holidays 10 to 5

Specialty: Plants from around the world, home demonstration gardens

In this 70-acre arboretum, plants are displayed in both residential settings and labeled collections. A 3-acre native plant section uses rocks, plant groupings, and low soil undulations to mimic creek beds and craggy terrain; in spring, it's carpeted with blooming poppies, Pacific Coast iris, and meadowfoam.

Washington Park Arboretum
2300 Arboretum Drive East
Seattle, WA 98112
Just off Lake Washington Boulevard East

(206) 543-8800

Open daily 7 a.m. to dusk

Specialty: Plants for western Washington

More than 200 acres of trees, shrubs, and bulbs. In January, wintersweet and witch hazel dot the landscape with color and spice the air with fragrance; midspring brings an explosion of bloom from flowering cherries, dogwoods, azaleas, and magnolias. In fall, Japanese maples and other deciduous trees in the Woodland Garden are ablaze with color.

Strybing Arboretum and Botanical Gardens

Butchart Gardens

ESTATE GARDENS
and Other Historic
Public Gardens

Left to posterity by pioneering gardeners and plant collectors, grand old estates and living museums throughout the United States and Canada celebrate flora and fauna of their own and other regions. A number of these public gardens (listed alphabetically by region) are described below. Visit them for gardening inspiration—and for the chance to view plants tested by time.

CANADA

Butchart Gardens
800 Benvenuto Avenue
Brentwood Bay, Victoria,
B.C., Canada V8M 1J8
(604) 652-4422
Call for opening times
Specialty: Flowering plants of all kinds
This 50-acre garden is one of the Pacific Northwest's top tourist destinations. It was begun in 1904 by Robert and Jenny Butchart in an old limestone quarry. Hundreds of bulbs bloom in midspring; in summer, hanging baskets overflow with flowers and garden beds blaze with color against a backdrop of flowering trees, shrubs, and a pond.

EASTERN STATES

Brookside Gardens
1500 Glenallan Avenue
Wheaton, MD 20902
(301) 949-8230
Open daily 9 to dusk; closed Christmas Day
This 50-acre public display garden features a variety of flowers that bloom throughout the seasons. The formal gardens are divided into three series: a perennial garden, a yew garden, and a round garden filled with plum trees and thousands of spring bulbs. At the fragrance garden, visitors can delight their senses by sniffing lavender, touching lamb's ears, and tasting mint. Other gardens include a rose garden, where the newest varieties grow, and tropical plant conservatories.

Longwood Gardens
Route 1, PO Box 501
Kennett Square, PA 19348
(610) 388-1000
Open daily 9 to 6
Eleven thousand different types of plants flourish throughout 1,050 acres of formal gardens, idea gardens, meadows, and woodlands. Some of the main attractions of the gardens are historic Peirce's Park, with trees planted by the Peirce family (the owners in around 1798); three fountains, with fountain shows during much of the year; and a 4-acre conservatory with 20 gardens under glass.

Wave Hill
675 W 252 Street
Bronx, NY 10471
(718) 549-3200
Open mid-May to mid-October, daily 9 to 5:30 (Wednesdays until dusk); mid-October to mid-May, daily 9 to 4:30
Originally built as a country home in 1843, Wave Hill is a 28-acre public garden in the Northwest Bronx that overlooks the Hudson River and the New Jersey Palisades. The flower garden, reminiscent of early 20th-century American gardens, exhibits perennials, annuals, bulbs, and vines; a wild garden is filled with plants from around the world; and the T.H. Everett Alpine House

Longwood Gardens

presents a collection of high-altitude and rock garden plants. Restored woodlands and meadow of native plants wrap around the estate's outer edge.

Winterthur Museum and Garden
Route 52
Winterthur, DE 19735
(800) 448-3883
Open Monday to Saturday 9 to 5:30, Sunday noon to 5:30; closed major holidays
Specialty: Rhododendrons and azaleas
Four generations of the duPont family have lived on this estate. Naturally landscaped meadows and woodlands surround the museum (the former manor house). Many Oriental woody species, especially rare rhododendrons and azaleas, help create spectacular displays. The pinetum includes crabapples, pines, tulip trees, and several rare species.

SOUTHERN STATES

Callaway Gardens
P.O. Box 2000
Pine Mountain, GA 31822
(800) CALLAWAY
Call for opening times
Specialty: Fruit and vegetable gardens
This 14,000-acre, year-round horticultural display garden grows hundreds of azaleas, hollies, rhododendrons, and wildflowers. Highlights include the Day Butterfly Center, filled with tropical plants and free-flying butterflies, and Mr. Cason's Vegetable Garden, one of the largest fruit and vegetable displays in the United States, with plants ranging from soybeans to fruit trees.

Cypress Gardens
2641 South Lake Summit Drive
Winter Haven, FL 33884
(941) 324-2111
Open daily 9:30 to 5:30; extended hours during special seasons
Specialty: Flower festivals
Considered Florida's first theme park, this entertainment center also includes lush botanical gardens. More than 8,000 varieties of plants and flowers from around the world grow on more than 200 acres. The park is particularly known for its four flower festivals: a spring festival of floral topiaries, a Victorian garden party with ivy topiaries, a chrysanthemum festival with more than 2½ million blooms, and a win-

ter festival featuring more than 40,000 poinsettias.

Fairchild Tropical Garden
10901 Old Cutler Road
Miami, FL 33156
(305) 667-1651
Open daily 9:30 to 4:30; closed Christmas Day
Specialty: Tropical plants
Nestled in Miami, this 83-acre tropical garden showcases exotic plants and trees, including a world-renowned collection of palms and cycads and many rare and endangered plants. The Moos Sunken Garden is a grotto with palms, ferns, orchids, and a waterfall. Plants from around the world are emphasized, including flowering trees, shrubs and vines, and bromeliads.

Magnolia Plantations and Gardens

Magnolia Plantations and Gardens
Rte. 4, Highway 61
Charleston, SC 29414
(803) 571-1266
Open daily 8 a.m. to dusk
Opened to the public in 1870, this garden on a former rice plantation is America's oldest man-made tourist attraction. A horticultural maze is modeled after those in 16th-century English gardens, but it uses camellias and holly instead of boxwood. Other features are a spring display of azaleas, a knot garden planted with herbs, a biblical garden, wetlands, and a wildlife refuge where all kinds of birds, animals, and reptiles live.

Marie Selby Botanical Gardens
811 S. Palm Avenue
Sarasota, FL 34236
(941) 366-5730
Open daily 10 to 5; closed Christmas Day
Specialty: Orchids
One of the world's largest collections of orchids, holding more than 6,000 living plants, can be found at this outdoor museum. Left to the community by Marie Selby, it is the only public garden in America that specializes in epiphytic plants. The estate's 11 acres display more than 20,000 plants, including cacti and succulents, palms, bromeliads, and bamboos.

Cypress Gardens

Massee Lane Gardens

Home of the American Camellia Society
One Massee Lane
Fort Valley, GA 31030

912-967-2358

Open April to November, Monday to Friday 9 to 4; December to March, Monday to Saturday 9 to 5, Sunday 1 to 5

Specialty: Camellias

The America Camellia Society's national headquarters is set on more that 9 acres planted with more than 1,000 camellia varieties and many rare species. Bloom time runs from November to March.

SOUTHWEST

National Wildflower Research Center

4801 La Crosse Avenue
Austin, TX 78739

(512) 292-4200

Open Tuesday to Sunday 9 to 5:30; closed major holidays

Specialty: Native plants

Founded by former First Lady Lady Bird Johnson, this 42-acre center in the Texas Hill Country is dedicated to preserving and re-establishing native wildflowers, grasses, vines, shrubs, and trees. Hike through a nature trail winding through a wildflower meadow and woodland; view garden flowers in a variety of landscape styles, from natural to formal. Other features include North America's largest rooftop rainwater collection system, a butterfly garden, and a children's garden.

WEST COAST

Bloedel Reserve

7571 N.E. Dolphin Drive
Bainbridge Island, WA 98110
45 minutes from downtown Seattle

(206) 842-7631

Open Wednesday through Sunday; closed major holidays. Reservations required

Specialty: Garden "rooms"

Gardens on 150 acres are crisscrossed by native woodland and dotted with meadows. The moss garden, reflection pool, bird marsh, English landscape, and Japanese garden offer glimpses of the styles that influence Northwest garden design.

Filoli

Canada Road
Woodside, CA 94062

(415) 364-2880

Open mid-February through first Saturday in November, Tuesday through Saturday plus second Sunday of each month; call for times and reservations

Specialty: Spring bulbs, roses, and rhododendrons

Magnificent formal gardens surround a stately, 36,000-square-foot Georgian manor house on a 654-acre estate about 25 miles south of San Francisco. Walls and hedges divide the 16-acre gardens into individual garden rooms, including a sunken garden with lily pond; a wild garden, where tall

Filoli

oaks shelter rhododendrons; and a rose garden planted with more than 500 bushes. The grounds are especially beautiful in midspring, when masses of tulips, spring annuals, flowering fruit trees, and a huge old wisteria burst into bloom.

The Living Desert

The Living Desert

47900 Portola Avenue
Palm Desert, CA 92260

(619) 346-5694

Open daily 9 to 5 (last admission 4:30); closed Christmas Day

Specialty: Plants and animals of the Southwest deserts

More than 1,200 acres include demonstration gardens, trails, a nursery, some 20 acres of developed gardens, live desert animals in realistic settings, and protected, preserved natural desert. Plants on display include tall California fan palms and groves of smoke trees.

Rhododendron Species Botanical Garden

2525 S. 336th Street
Federal Way, WA 98007

(206) 661-9377

Call for opening times

One of the most extensive collections of rhododendron species in North America, this garden covers some 24 acres and displays more than 400 species, many of them rare. Peak bloom is from late March to mid-May.

MAIL-ORDER SUPPLIERS

Antique roses

Tulips swirled with color like ribbon candy, watermelons splashed with yellow spots, red tomatoes with yellow stripes, red-brown cosmos that smell like chocolate: these are just a few of the plants that you may not find readily available in nurseries. But you can order them by mail. Among the hundreds of mail-order suppliers that have sizable catalogs, some old faithfuls continue to offer flowers and vegetables from A to Z. These top the list below. But an increasing number of suppliers are specialists—of roses, bulbs, fruits, native plants or grasses, ornamentals, seeds of gourmet herbs and vegetables, heirloom and open-pollinated (non-hybridized) seeds, or greenhouse plants.

Regardless of geographic location, these suppliers are prepared to ship far and wide. Many charge a modest price for their catalog—a small outlay considering the garden pleasure that can follow. Call or write to the companies for current catalog prices. Addresses and phone numbers are subject to change.

FLOWERS AND VEGETABLES FROM A TO Z

W. Atlee Burpee Company
300 Park Avenue
Warminster, PA 18974
(800) 888-1447
Seeds of flowers and vegetables; also lilies, fruit trees, and tools.

D.V. Burrell Seed Growers Co.
P.O. Box 150
Rocky Ford, CO 81067
(719) 254-3318
Good selection of vegetable seeds and annual flowers. Specialties are watermelon, cantaloupe, chilies, tomatoes, onions, corn, and popcorn.

Comstock, Ferre & Co.
P.O. Box 125
Wethersfield, CT 06109
(203) 529-3319
Older varieties of vegetables and disease-resistant newer varieties; seeds of annuals and perennials, and everlastings.

Ferry-Morse Seeds
Box 488
Fulton, KY 42041-0488
(800) 283-3400

Good selection of seeds, ranging from annuals to vegetables to herbs. Informative catalog with good plant descriptions.

Henry Field Seed & Nursery Co.
415 North Burnett
Shenandoah, IA 51602
(605) 665- 9391
A selection including a little of everything: vegetable and flower seeds, fruit and nut trees, shrubs, vines, and roses.

Gurney's Seed & Nursery
110 Capital Street
Yankton, SD 57079
(605) 665-1671

Sweet peas

A full range of plants and seeds, including vegetables and nuts, flowering trees, and shrubs.

Park Seed Co.
Cokesbury Road
Greenwood, SC 29647
(800) 845-3369; (803) 223-7333
Seeds, plants, bulbs; nearly 2,000 varieties of flowers and vegetables.

Spring Hill Nurseries Co.
6523 North Galena Road
Peoria, IL 61632
(309) 691-4616
Perennials, shrubs, roses, ground covers, summer-blooming bulbs, house plants, and preplanned garden schemes.

Stokes Seeds, Inc.
Box 548
Buffalo, NY 14240
(716) 695-6980
Annuals, herbs, perennials, and vegetables (including Chinese varieties).

Thompson & Morgan, Inc.
Box 1308
Jackson, NJ 08527-0308
(800) 274-7333
Rare and unusual varieties of annuals, bulbs, perennials, vegetables, and grasses.

Twilley Seed Co.
Box 65
Trevose, PA 19053
(800) 622-7333
Large selection of vegetables and flowers.

Vessey's Seeds, Ltd.
Box 9000, York
Charlottetown, PE, Canada C1A 8K6
(902) 386-7333
A variety of flowers and vegetables, with an emphasis on short-season varieties for Canada and New England.

Wayside Gardens
Hodges, SC 29695
(800) 845-1124
Unusual and hard-to-find perennials, bulbs (including tulips, daffodils, lilies), grasses, ornamental shrubs, trees, and vines. Varied collection of roses, including antique types and David Austin English roses.

White Flower Farm
Box 50
Litchfield, CT 06759-0050
(203) 496-9600
Begonias, dahlias, and lilies; also perennials, ornamental shrubs such as lilacs and roses, and some fruit trees.

ROSES

Antique Rose Emporium
Route 5, Box 143
Brenham, TX 77833
(409) 836-4293; (409) 836-9051
Old garden roses selected for fragrance and long bloom. Also have perennials.

Corn Hill Nursery
RR 5
Petitcodiac, NB, Canada E0A 2H0
(506) 756-3635
Own-root hardy old garden and modern shrub roses especially for northern climates; also a variety of trees and shrubs only for shipment within Canada.

Heirloom Old Garden Roses
24062 N.E. Riverside Drive
St. Paul, OR 97137
(503) 538-1576; fax (503) 538-5902
Catalog includes albas, Bourbons, damasks, hybrid musks, Noisettes; substantial collection of David Austin English roses.

Rosa 'Iceberg'

Heritage Rosarium
211 Haviland Mill Road
Brookville, MD 20833
(301) 774-2806
About 400 varieties of old garden, modern shrub, and species roses. Will root or bud your own roses and help with rose identification.

Hortico, Inc.
723 Robson Road
Watertown, ON, Canada L0R 2H1
(905) 689-6984
Over 700 varieties of modern, antique, and shrub roses.

Jackson & Perkins
Box 1028
Medford, OR 97501
(800) 292-4769; (503) 776-2000
Roses of every kind and color, plus perennials, garden accessories, and gifts.

Martin & Kraus
P.O. Box 12
Carlisle, ON, Canada L0R 1H0
(905) 689-2030
Winter-hardy roses, own-root and budded

Mendocino Heirloom Roses
Box 670
Mendocino, CA 95460
(707) 877-1888; (707) 937-0963
Eclectic list includes old garden and species roses on their own roots and a few newer roses, such as some from the 20s and 30s.

Nor'East Miniature Roses, Inc.
P.O. Box 307
Rowley, MA 01969
(800) 426-6485
Large selection of miniature roses and ministandards.

Pickering Nurseries, Inc.
670 Kingston Road
Pickering, ON, Canada L1V 1A6
(905) 839-2111
Catalog includes over 900 modern, old garden, and shrub roses.

Rosequus
40350 Wilderness Road
Branscomb, CA 95417
(707) 984-6959
Lists more than 200 old roses.

Roses of Yesterday and Today
802 Brown's Valley Road
Watsonville, CA 95076-0398
(408) 724-3537
Old and rare varieties of garden roses.

Sequoia Nursery
2519 East Noble Avenue
Visalia, CA 93292
(209) 732-0309
A selection of miniatures, old garden, shrub, and species roses.

Vintage Gardens
2833 Old Gravenstein Highway South
Sebastopol, CA 95472
(707) 829-2035
Old and extraordinary roses: hybrid perpetuals, Bourbons, Portlands, teas, Chinas, Noisettes, ramblers, climbers; also old hybrid teas, floribundas, miniatures.

BULBS, CORMS, AND TUBERS

Suppliers advise ordering bulbs as early as possible to obtain best selection.

A & D Peony and Perennial Nursery
6808 180th SE
Snohomish, WA 98290
(360) 668-9690
Daylilies, peonies, hostas, and perennials.

Jacques Amand Ltd., Bulb Specialists
Box 59001
Potomac, MD 20859
(301) 762-6601; (800) 452-5414
Spring- and summer-blooming allium, colchicum, crocus, tulips, and many others.

B & D Lilies
330 P Street
Port Townsend, WA 98368
(360) 385-1738; fax (360) 385-9996
Asiatic and Oriental hybrids, trumpets, and species lilies; also daylilies.

Lilium 'Casablanca'

Chuck Chapman Iris
11 Harts Lane
Guelph, ON, Canada N1L 1B1
An extensive list of many types of bearded irises.

Cooley's Gardens
Box 126–WG
Silverton, OR 97381
Offers 300 varieties of bearded irises.

The Daffodil Mart
Route 3, Box 794
Gloucester, VA 23061
(804) 693-3966
Enormous selection of bulbs, including novelty, miniature, and species daffodils.

Dutch Gardens
Box 200
Adelphia, NJ 07710
(908) 780-2713
Bulbs of all kinds for spring or summer bloom: anemones, crocus, iris, daffodils, dahlias, fritillarias, hyacinths, lilies, tulips.

Long's Gardens
P.O. Box 19
Boulder, CO 80306
(303) 442-2353
Comprehensive selection of tall and median bearded irises.

Louisiana Nursery
Rt. 7, Box 43
Opelousas, LA 70570
(318) 948-3696
Huge selection of daylilies and Louisiana and other irises. Different catalogs offer different plants, such as magnolias and other trees, shrubs, and vines.

McClure & Zimmerman
Box 368
Friesland, WI 53935
(414) 326-4220
Extensive list of bulbs, including many rare and hard-to-find varieties.

Grant E. Mitsch, Novelty Daffodils
Box 218
Hubbard, OR 97032
(503) 651-2742
Novelty daffodils; develops own hybrids.

Roris Gardens
8195 Bradshaw Road
Sacramento, CA 95829
(916) 689-7460
Irises of many kinds and colors.

John Scheepers, Inc.
Box 700
Bantam, CT 06750
(203) 567-0838
Spring- and summer-blooming bulbs of species narcissus, allium, amaryllis, hybrid lilies. Catalog has fine illustrations.

Schreiner's Gardens
3625 Quinaby Road
Salem, OR 97303
(503) 393-3232
Bearded irises, including tall, dwarf, median, and arilbreds.

Tulip and hyacinth bulbs
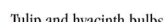

Swan Island Dahlias
Box 700
Canby, OR 97013
(503) 266-7711; fax (503) 266-8768
Dahlias of all kinds, colors, flower forms, and sizes.

Van Bourgondien Bros.
Box 1000
245 Farmingdale Road, Route 109
Babylon, NY 11702-0598
(800) 622-9997
Bulbs of many kinds, including amaryllis, daffodils, tuberous begonias, peonies, tulips, dahlias, Asiatic and Oriental hybrid lilies; also a large selection of perennials.

VanLierop Bulb Farm
13407 80th Street East
Puyallup, WA 98372-3608
(206) 848-7272
Many kinds of crocus, daffodils, hyacinths, tulips, and other bulbs. Selection includes Tazetta and poeticus daffodils, species tulips, and snowflakes (*Leucojum*).

FRUITS, NUTS, AND BERRIES

Chestnut Hill Nursery
Route 1, Box 341
Alachua, FL 32615
(904) 462-2820; (800) 669-2067
Specialty is blight-resistant chestnuts; also offers Oriental persimmons, hardy citrus, and figs.

Edible Landscaping
Box 77
Afton, VA 22920
(804) 361-9134
Fruit for Mid-Atlantic gardeners, from hardy kiwi to black currants and pawpaw. Catalog has good plant descriptions.

Northwoods Nursery
27635 S. Oglesby Road
Canby, OR 97013
(503) 266-5432; fax (503) 266-5431
Fruits of all kinds.

Raintree Nursery
391 Butts Road
Morton, WA 98356
(360) 496-6400
Hundreds of edible plants from all over the world, including fruits, nuts, and berries of all kinds. Specializes in disease-resistant varieties for home gardeners.

Lon J. Rombough
13113 Ehlen Road
Aurora, OR 97002-9745

(503) 678-1410

Lots of old and new varieties of wine and table grapes. Can't ship outside the United States, but will provide information on sources in other countries.

St. Lawrence Nurseries
Rd. 5, Box 324
Potsdam, NY 12676

(315) 365-6739

Informative catalog of organically grown, cold-hardy fruit and nut trees and other edible fruits, berries.

**Stark Brothers' Nurseries
& Orchards Co.**
Route 1, Box 272
Petersburgh, IL 62675

(314) 754-5511

Fruit trees of all kinds; specializes in 'Delicious' apples.

Imperata cylindrica 'Rubra'

NATIVES AND GRASSES

Appalachian Wildflower Nursery
Route 1, Box 275A
Reedsville, PA 17084

(717) 667-6998

Specializes in local native plants from known wild colonies.

Desert Moon Nursery
Box 600
Veguita, NM 87062

(505) 864-0614

Agaves, yuccas, other desert succulents, cacti; desert perennials such as blackfoot daisy and penstemon; wildflowers, shrubs, and trees.

Greenlee Nursery
301 E. Franklin Avenue
Pomona, CA 91766

(909) 629-9045

Large selection of ornamental and native grasses. Catalog includes tips on planting and care.

Niche Gardens
1111 Dawson Road
Chapel Hill, NC 27516

(919) 967-0078

Southeastern wildflowers and native plants; ornamental grasses and herbs.

Stock Seed Farms, Inc.
28008 Mill Road
Murdock, NE 68407-2350

(402) 867-3771; (800) 759-1520

A selection of seeds of prairie wildflowers and grasses native to the Midwest. Offers information on getting started.

Woodlanders, Inc.
1128 Colleton Avenue
Aiken, SC 29801

(803) 648-7522

Good selection of Southeastern native trees, vines, perennials, ferns, ground covers.

PERENNIALS, SHRUBS, AND TREES

Bluestone Perennials
7211 Middle Ridge Road
Madison, OH 44057

(216) 428-7535; (800) 852-5243

Perennials, grasses, ground covers. Small plants, good prices.

Brudy's Exotics
P.O. Box 820874
Houston, TX 77282-0874

(713) 963-0033; (800) 926-7333

Seeds for tropical trees, shrubs and fruits; plants of banana, bougainvillea, ginger, dwarf citrus, and others.

Busse Gardens
13579 10th Street N.W.
Cokato, MN 55321-9426

(612) 286-2654

Numerous hardy perennials, from astilbe and hosta to ferns and wildflowers.

Canyon Creek Nursery
3527 Dry Creek Road
Oroville, CA 95965

(916) 533-2166

Uncommon perennials; sizable salvia collection, hardy geraniums, euphorbias.

Carroll Gardens
Box 310
Westminster, MD 21158

(410) 848-5422; (800) 638-6334

Large selection of plants. Catalog provides good descriptions, information on plant culture.

Weigela florida 'Variegata'

Fairweather Gardens
Box 330
Greenwich, NJ 08323

(609) 451-6261

Ornamental trees and shrubs, viburnums, camellias, holly; very informative catalog.

ForestFarm
990 Tetherow Road
Williams, OR 97544

(503) 846-7269

Native plants, ferns, grasses, common and uncommon perennials, shrubs, and trees.

Gossler Farms Nursery
1200 Weaver Road
Springfield, OR 97478

(503) 746-3922

Strong witch hazel and magnolia collections; other unusual trees and shrubs.

Russell Graham, Purveyor of Plants
4030 Eagle Crest Road NW
Salem, OR 97304

(503) 362-1135

Small, family-run supplier of perennials such as alstroemeria, lilies, ferns, hardy cyclamen; also North American natives and companion plants.

Greer Gardens
1280 Goodpasture Island Road
Eugene, OR 97401
(503) 686-8266
Rhododendrons, maples, and rare stock.

Heronswood Nursery Ltd.
7530 288th Street NE
Kingston, WA 98346
(360) 297-4172
Unusual and hard-to-find trees, conifers, shrubs, perennials, vines, and grasses.

A High Country Garden
2902 Rufina Street
Santa Fe, NM 87505-2929
(800) 925-9387
Hardy and water-thrifty perennials for western gardens, including penstemon, prairie coneflower, *Zinnia grandiflora,* rock garden plants, native plants.

Klehm Nursery
4210 N. Duncan road
Champaign, IL 61821
(217) 359-2888; (800) 553-3715
Hostas, daylilies, irises, herbaceous and tree peonies, ferns, ornamental grasses.

Lamb Nurseries
Route 1, Box 460B
Long Beach, WA 98631
(360) 642-4856
Hardy perennials and rock garden plants; also kitchen herbs, species geraniums, hardy fuchsias, and more than 20 varieties of hardy violets.

Milaeger's Gardens
4838 Douglas Avenue
Racine, WI 53402-2498
(414) 639-2371
Large selection of perennials; also offers native plants. Catalog has good descriptions and illustrations.

Plants of the Southwest
Agua Fria, Route 6, Box 11A
Santa Fe, NM 87501
(505) 471-2212 (customer service);
(800) 788-7333 (mail order)
Grasses, perennials such as penstemon and ox-eye, shrubs, trees, and many kinds of wildflowers. Some Southwest and Rocky Mountain natives; also herbs and vegetables, including more than 30 varieties of chilies.

Shady Oaks Nursery
112 10th Avenue S.E.
Waseca, MN 56093
(507) 835-5033; (800) 504-8006
Shade plants of all kinds—ground covers, woodland plants, and especially hostas.

Siskiyou Rare Plant Nursery
2825 Cummings Road
Medford, OR 97501
(503) 772-6846
Alpine, rock garden, and woodland plants, including dwarf conifers and Japanese maples.

Surry Gardens
Box 145
Surry, ME 04864
(207) 667-4493
Perennials and rock garden plants; gentian, campanula, primula, thyme, veronica.

We-Du Nurseries
Route 5, Box 724
Marion, NC 28752
(704) 738-8300
Rock garden and woodland plants; offers Southern natives and unusual American, Japanese, Korean, and Chinese wildflowers.

Yucca Do Nursery
P.O. Box 450
Waller, TX 77484-0655
(409) 826-6363
Unusual trees, shrubs, and perennials; native plants.

SEEDS, GOURMET HERBS, AND VEGETABLES

The Cook's Garden
Box 535
Londonderry, VT 05148
(802) 824-3400; fax (802) 824-3027
Herb and vegetable seeds for the serious kitchen garden. Peppers, lettuces, and broccoli. Selections from France and Italy. Also seeds of flowers for cutting gardens.

DeGiorgi Seed Company
6011 N Street
Omaha, NE
68117-1634
(402) 731-3901
Herbs and vegetables; also annuals, perennials, wildflowers, grasses.

'Opal' basil

The Fragrant Path
Box 328
Ft. Calhoun, NE 68023
Wide selection of herbs and seeds of fragrant, rare, and old-fashioned plants.

Radishes, carrots

The Gourmet Gardener
8650 College Boulevard, Dept. 205SJ
Overland Park, KS 66210
(913) 345-0490
Herb, vegetable, and edible-flower seeds from around the world. Offerings include scented basils, radicchio varieties from Italy, Lebanese-type squash, and French heirloom tomatoes.

Johnny's Selected Seeds
310 Foss Hill Road
Albion, ME 04910
(207) 437-4301 (mail order)
Flowers and vegetables, including unusual corn, bean, and squash varieties and heirloom tomatoes.

Nichols Garden Nursery
1190 N. Pacific Highway
Albany, OR 97321-4598
(503) 928-9280
Herbs, Oriental greens, ornamental corn, hops, and much more.

Ronniger's Seed Potatoes
Star Route, Road 73
Moyie Springs, ID 83845
(208) 267-3265 (fax)
Large selection of seed potatoes, described by color, flavor, disease resistance, and

keeping qualities. Also offers Jerusalem artichokes, garlic, onions, shallots.

Sandy Mush Herb Nursery
Route 2, Surrett Coce Road
Leicester, NC 28748
(704) 683-2014
Wide selection of herb seeds and plants; also ornamental grasses and perennials.

Seeds West Garden Seeds, Inc.
Box 27057
Albuquerque, NM 87125-7057
(505) 242-7474
Untreated seeds of short-season, drought-tolerant vegetables, herbs, and flowers suitable for the arid West.

Shepherd's Garden Seeds
6116 Highway 9
Felton, CA 95018
(408) 335-6910
Vegetables, herbs such as scented basils, greens like arugula and French dandelion greens. Also flowers for fragrance, drying, or attracting beneficial insects; chilies; and sunflowers. Catalog includes recipes.

Story House Herb Farm
Route 7, Box 246
Murray, KY 42071
(502) 753-4158
Nearly 100 varieties of certified organic herbs for the kitchen garden.

Tomato Growers Supply Company
Box 2237
Fort Myers, FL 33902
(813) 768-1119
Tomato seeds for more than 250 varieties, from beefsteaks to cherry tomatoes.

Paste tomatoes

Totally Tomatoes
Box 1626
Augusta, GA 30903
(803) 663-0016
Tomatoes of all kinds and colors—orange, purple, yellow, yellow striped. Also some peppers.

Vermont Bean Seed Company
Garden Lane
Fair Haven, VT 05743-0250
(802) 273-3400

Numerous varieties of beans, cabbage, melons, corn, gourds, greens, and tomatoes, as well as other vegetables; also herbs and some flowers.

SEEDS—HEIRLOOM OR OPEN-POLLINATED (UNHYBRIDIZED)

Abundant Life Seed Foundation
Box 772
Port Townsend, WA 98368
(360) 385-5660
A nonprofit corporation that acquires, propagates, and preserves plants and seeds of native and naturalized flora of the Pacific Rim, with emphasis on species not commercially available. Offerings include grains and edible seeds, flowers, herbs, shrubs, trees, vegetables, and wildflowers.

Fox Hollow Herbs & Heirloom Seed Company
Box 148
McGrann, PA 16236
(412) 763-8247
Open-pollinated varieties of herbs and vegetables, garlic, shallots, Egyptian onion sets, and some old-fashioned garden flowers.

Garden City Seeds
1324 Red Crow Road
Victor, MT 59875-9713
(406) 961-4837
Heirloom and northern-acclimated vegetable seeds, asparagus roots, garlic, onion sets; also wildflowers, herbs, and cover crops.

High Altitude Gardens
Box 1048
Hailey, ID 83333
(208) 788-4363
All kinds of vegetables hardy enough for cold-climate gardens; offerings include tomatoes from Russia and Siberia and early peppers. Also wildflowers, native grasses, and herbs.

Lockhart Seeds, Inc.
3 N. Wilson Way
Stockton, CA 95205
(209) 466-4401
Vegetable seeds, including many open-pollinated varieties; everything from artichokes and asparagus to beans, carrots, onions, chilies, and tomatoes. Also herbs and Oriental vegetables. Minimum order of $10.

Native Seeds/SEARCH
2509 N. Campbell Avenue
Box 325
Tucson, AZ 85719
(602) 327-9123
A nonprofit seed conservation organization working to preserve the traditional crops of the Southwest and northern Mexico and their wild relatives. Catalog includes seeds of tepary beans, chilies, gourds, corn, herbs, unusual squashes, pumpkins with names like 'Hopi' and 'Acoma', tomatillos, and devil's claw for basketry.

'Bush Green' basil

Seeds Blüm
HC33 Idaho City Stage
Boise, ID 83706
(208) 342-0858 (for catalog price only);
fax (208) 338-5658
Nearly 1,000 open-pollinated vegetables, herbs, and flowers, including many unusual or heirloom varieties. Extensive listing of colored-flesh potatoes; more than 50 kinds of edible flowers.

Seeds of Change
Box 15700
Santa Fe, NM 87506-5700
(505) 438-8080 (mail order); fax (505) 438-7052
Many rare heirloom and traditional native vegetables, as well as a unique selection of flowers and medicinal and culinary herbs. Sizable collections of beans, corn, sunflowers, and tomatoes.

GREENHOUSE AND INDOOR PLANTS

Glasshouse Works
Box 97
Stewart, OH 45778-0097
(614) 662-2142
Enormous selection of exotic and tropical plants, including ferns, bromeliads, gingers, aroids, euphorbias. Specialty is variegated plants.

Logee's Greenhouses
141 North Street
Danielson, CT 06239
(203) 774-8038
Enormous collection of begonias and other kinds of greenhouse and exotic plants. Many can be grown outdoors in warmer climates.

DEMYSTIFYING
Scientific
Plant Names

Campsis radicans

S cientific plant names can be intimidating to gardeners. So why have they been used around the world for hundreds of years? Why do we use them in this book? And why do the plants sold at nurseries most often have scientific names printed somewhere on their labels? There's good reason: common names for plants are often confusing and misleading. A single common name can apply to different plants in different parts of the country or the world. It can be used for two or more plants that not only look different but vary tremendously in growth habit, needs, and bloom season.

Scientific Names Are Precise

Scientific names are more precise than common names. If you ask simply for "dusty miller," you may well get the response: "Which one?" All of the plants with that common name are perennials with silvery foliage, but they differ in other ways. Among the dusty millers, *Centaurea cineraria* has typically purple thistlelike flowers; *Senecio cineraria* has small yellow blooms; *Senecio vira-vira* bears white flowers; and *Lychnis coronaria* has magenta blossoms.

Other plants with the same common

Rudbeckia hirta

Thunbergia alata

name often are not at all similar. "Black-eyed Susan," for example, applies to a golden-flowered perennial (*Rudbeckia hirta*) and to a vine most often planted as a summer annual (*Thunbergia alata*). "Angel's tears" is a bulb grown for its clusters of white flowers (*Narcissus triandrus*) and is also a ground cover with inconspicuous flowers (*Soleirolia soleirolii*).

Multiple common names for a plant can also cause confusion. If you call a certain plant "sour gum," while another person knows it as "tupelo" and yet another says "pepperidge," you may not know you're all talking about the same tree—*Nyssa sylvatica.*

So the real reason for learning scientific names is a practical one: they provide the most accurate means we have for putting a verbal handle on a plant. You can't be sure what you are getting unless you order a plant by its scientific name.

Scientific Names Offer Clues

Scientific names, if you break them down, can tell you something about the plants. The first part of a scientific name is the genus name, which is usually a classical name. The second part is the species name, which is usually a descriptive word and often simple to decipher.

Descriptive words used again and again in species names are listed opposite. When you know the meanings of these words, many names become easy to understand and helpful in identifying plants. *Sollya heterophylla,* for example, combines *hetero* (heterogeneous or various) with *phylla* (leaves) to mean "various-size leaves." Some of the leaves are lanceolate and others oblong.

The common names that are direct translations are among the easiest to remember. Bigleaf hydrangea (*Hydrangea macrophylla*) does have large leaves. *Macro* means large, *phylla* means leaves.

Some of the scientific names are so much like English words that there is no question as to their meaning. *Prostratum, compacta, deliciosa, fragrans,* and *pendula* all say something immediately recognizable.

A GUIDE TO BOTANICAL NAMES

Color of Flowers or Foliage

albus—white
argenteus—silvery
aureus—golden
azureus—azure, sky blue
caeruleus—dark blue
caesius—blue-gray
candidus—pure white, shiny
canus—ashy gray, hoary
cereus—waxy
citrinus—yellow
coccineus—scarlet
concolor—one color
croceus—yellow
cruentus—bloody

Dodonaea viscosa 'Purpurea'

discolor—two colors, separate colors
glaucus—covered with gray bloom
incanus—gray, hoary
luteus—reddish yellow
pallidus—pale
purpureus—purple
rubens, ruber—red, ruddy
rufus—ruddy

Form of Leaf (*folius*—leaves or foliage)

acerifolius—maplelike
angustifolius—narrow
aquifolius—spiny
buxifolius—boxwood-like
ilicifolius—hollylike
laurifolius—laurel-like
parvifolius—small
populifolius—poplarlike
salicifolius—willowlike

Lavandula angustifolia 'Hidcote'

Shape of Plant

adpressus—pressing against, hugging
altus—tall
arboreus—treelike
capitatus—headlike
compactus—compact, dense
confertus—crowded, pressed together

contortus—twisted

decumbens—lying down

depressus—pressed down

elegans—elegant, slender, willowy

fastigiatus—branches erect and close together

humifusus—sprawling on the ground

humilis—low, small, humble

impressus—impressed upon

nanus—dwarf

procumbens—trailing

prostratus—prostrate

pumilus—dwarf, small

pusillus—puny, insignificant

repens—creeping

reptans—creeping

scandens—climbing

Where It Came From

A number of suffixes are added to place names to specify the habitat where the plant was discovered or the place where it is usually found.

africanus—of Africa

alpinus—of the Alps

australis—southern

borealis—northern

campestris—of the field or plains

canadensis—of Canada

canariensis—of the Canary Islands

capensis—of the Cape of Good Hope area

chilensis—of Chile

chinensis—of China

hispanicus—of Spain

hortensis—of gardens

indicus—of India

insularis—of the island

japonicus—of Japan

littoralis—of the seashore

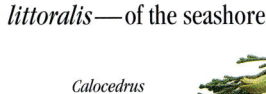

Calocedrus decurrens

montanus—of the mountains

riparius—of riverbanks

rivalis, rivularis—of brooks

saxatilis—inhabiting rocks

Plant Parts

dendron—tree

flora, florum, flori, florus—flowers

phyllus, phylla—leaf or leaves

Cestrum elegans

Zephyranthes grandiflora

Elaeagnus pungens

Ligustrum japonicum

Passiflora caerulea

Brachychiton acerifolius

Plant Peculiarities

armatus—armed

baccatus—berried, berrylike

barbatus—barbed or bearded

campanulatus—bell or cup shaped

ciliaris—fringed

cordatus—heart shaped

cornutus—horned

crassus—thick, fleshy

decurrens—running down the stem

densi—dense

diversi—varying

edulis—edible

floridus—free flowering

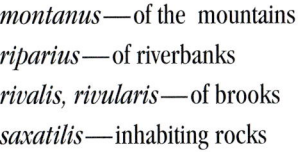

Hydrangea macrophylla

fruticosus—shrubby

fulgens—shiny

gracilis—slender, thin, small

grandi—large, showy

-ifer, -iferus—bearing or having; e.g., *stoloniferus,* having stolons

imperialis—showy

laciniatus—fringed or with torn edges

laevigatus—smooth

lobatus—lobed

longus—long

macro—large

maculatus—spotted

micro—small

mollis—soft, soft-haired

mucronatus—pointed

nutans—nodding, swaying

obtusus—blunt or flattened

officinalis—medicinal

-oides—like or resembling; e.g., *jasminoides,* like a jasmine

patens—open, spreading growth

pinnatus—constructed like a feather

platy—broad

plenus—double, full

plumosus—feathery

praecox—precocious

pungens—piercing

radicans—rooting, especially along the stem

Gardenia jasminoides

reticulatus—net-veined

retusus—notched at blunt apex

rugosus—wrinkled, rough

saccharatus—sweet, sugary

sagittalis—arrowlike

scabrus—rough feeling

scoparius—broomlike

OUR SPELLING	AS IN
a	hat, hand
ay	baby
ah	hall
ai	air
e	met, bed
ee	we
i	tin
ye	wine
o	hot
oe	romance
u	must, burr
oo	rumor
ew	human
uh	comma, consider, sinister, vapor, minus

PRONUNCIATION GUIDE

Scientific names are the universal language for plants, but they are pronounced differently in various parts of the world, even among English-speaking countries. Because these names come from Latin and Greek, there is no absolute, approved, obligatory pronunciation for them —we say them as we choose. What follows is a list of the most-often-used ways to say many scientific plant names.

Abutilon

A

Abelia—uh-BEE-lee-uh
Abutilon—uh-BEW-tuh-lon
    Acacia—uh-KAY-shuh
    Acer—AY-sir
    Achillea—ak-i-LEE-uh
    Achimenes—uh-KIM-muh-neez
    Aconitum—ak-oe-NYE-tuhm
    Actinidia—AK-ti-NID-ee-uh
    Adiantum—ad-ee-AN-tuhm
    Aesculus—ES-kew-luhs
    Agapanthus—ag-uh-PAN-thuhs
    Agave—uh-GAH-vay
    Ageratum—ah-JER-uh-tuhm
      (usually pronounced ad-juh-RAY-tuhm)
    Ailanthus—uh-LAN-thuhs
    Ajuga—uh-JEW-guh
    Alstroemeria—al-struh-MEE-ree-uh
    Amaryllis—am-uh-RIL-is
    Amelanchier—am-uh-LANG-kee-uhr
Anemone—uh-NEM-uh-nee
Anthurium—an-THU-ree-uhm
Aquilegia—ak-wuh-LEE-jee-uh
Arabis—AIR-uh-bis
Aralia—uh-RAY-lee-uh
Arctostaphylos—ahrk-toe-STAF-i-luhs
Arctotheca—ahrk-toe-THEE-kuh
Artemisia—ahr-tuh-MEE-zee-uh
Aspidistra—as-puh-DIS-truh
Astilbe—uh-STIL-bee

Aconitum

B

Babiana—bab-ee-AN-uh
Baccharis—BAK-uh-ris
Bauhinia—boe-HIN-ee-uh
Berberis—BUR-buh-ris
Bergenia—bur-GEN-ee-uh

Bougainvillea

Betula—BET-ew-luh
Bougainvillea—boo-guhn-VIL-ee-uh
Buddleia—BUD-lee-uh

C

Caladium—kuh-LAY-dee-uhm
Calceolaria—kal-see-oe-LAIR-ee-uh
Calendula—kuh-LEN-dew-luh
Callistemon—ka-li-STEE-muhn
Callistephus—ka-LIS-tuh-fuhs
Campanula—kam-PAN-ew-luh
Carpenteria—kahr-pen-TEER-ee-uh
Cattleya—KAT-lee-uh
Ceanothus—see-uh-NOE-thuhs
Celosia—see-LOE-shee-uh
Centaurea—sen-tah-REE-uh
Ceratonia—sair-uh-TOE-nee-uh
Ceratostigma—sair-ah-toe-STIG-muh
Cercidium—sir-SID-ee-uhm
Cercis—SIR-suhs
Chamaecyparis—kam-ee-SIP-uh-ris
Cheiranthus—kye-RAN-thuhs
Chelone—ke-LOE-nay
Chionanthus—kye-oe-NAN-thuhs
Chlorophytum—KLOER-oe-FYE-tuhm
Choisya—SHOY-zee-uh
Chrysogonum—kris-OG-uh-nuhm
Clematis—KLEM-uh-tis
Cleome—KLEE-oe-mee
Clivia—KLYE-vee-uh
Colchicum—KAHL-chi-kuhm
Convallaria—kon-vuh-LAIR-ee-uh
Convolvulus—kon-VOL-vew-luhs
Coreopsis—koer-ee-OP-suhs
Cotinus—koe-TYE-nuhs
Cotoneaster—kuh-toe-nee-AS-tuhr
Crataegus—kruh-TEE-guhs
Crocosmia—kroe-KOZ-mee-uh
Cuphea—KEW-fee-uh
Cymbidium—sim-BID-ee-uhm
Cynoglossum—sin-OE-GLOS-uhm

D

Daboecia—duh-BEE-shee-uh
Daphne—DAFF-nee
Deutzia—DOOT-zee-uh or DOYT-zee-uh
Dieffenbachia—deef-uhn-BAK-ee-uh
Dizygotheca—diz-uh-GOTH-ik-uh or diz-uh-goe-THEE-kah
Dracaena—druh-SEE-nuh
Dryopteris—drye-OP-ter-uhs
Duchesnea—dew-KEZ-nee-uh

E

Echeveria—ek-uh-VAIR-ee-uh
Echinacea—ek-uh-NAY-see-uh
Echinops—EK-uh-nops
Echium—EK-ee-uhm
Elaeagnus—el-ee-AG-nuhs
Epidendrum—ep-uh-DEN-druhm
Epiphyllum—ep-uh-FIL-uhm
Equisetum—ek-wuh-SEE-tuhm
Eremurus—air-uh-MEWR-uhs
Erica—ee-RYE-kuh (correct, but universally pronounced AIR-ik-uh)
Erigeron—ee-RIJ-uh-ron
Erythrina—air-i-THRYE-nuh
Eschscholzia—e-SHOELT-see-uh
Eucalyptus—ew-kuh-LIP-tuhs
Euonymus—ew-ON-uh-muhs
Exacum—EK-suh-kuhm
Exochorda—ek-so-KOER-duh

F

Fatshedera—fats-HED-uh-ruh
Feijoa—fuh-HOE-uh
Ficus—FYE-kuhs
Forsythia—for-SITH-ee-uh
Fragaria—fruh-GAIR-ee-uh
Fraxinus—FRAK-suh-nuhs
Fuchsia—FEW-shee-uh

G

Gaillardia—gay-LAHR-dee-uh
Gazania—guh-ZAY-nee-uh
Genista—je-NIS-tuh
Gentiana—jen-shee-AY-nuh
Gerbera—GUR-bur-uh
Geum—JEE-uhm
Gleditsia—gluh-DIT-see-uh
Gomphrena—gom-FREE-nuh
Grevillea—gruh-VIL-ee-uh
Gypsophila—jip-SOF-uh-luh

H

Halesia—HAYLZ-ee-uh
Hamamelis—ham-uh-MEE-luhs
Hebe—HEE-bee
Hedera—HED-uh-ruh
Helianthemum—hee-lee-AN-thuh-muhm
Helianthus—hee-lee-AN-thuhs
Heliopsis—hee-lee-OP-suhs
Heliotropium—hee-lee-oe-TROE-pee-uhm
Hemerocallis—hem-uh-roe-KAL-uhs
Heuchera—HEW-kuh-ruh
Hibiscus—hye-BIS-kuhs
Hippeastrum—hip-ee-AS-truhm
Hosta—HOS-tuh
Hydrangea—hye-DRAIN-jee-uh
Hymenocallis—hye-muh-noe-KAL-uhs
Hypericum—hye-PEER-i-kuhm

I

Iberis—eye-BEE-ruhs
Ilex—EYE-lex
Impatiens—im-PAY-shuhnz
Ipomoea—ip-oe-MEE-uh
Iresine—ir-uh-SYE-nee

Ilex

J

Jacaranda—jak-uh-RAN-duh
Jasminum—JAZ-muh-nuhm
Juniperus—joo-NIP-uh-ruhs

K

Kalanchoe—kal-an-KOE-ee
Kniphofia—nip-HOE-fee-uh
Kochia—KOE-kee-uh
Koelreuteria—ke-roo-TEE-ree-uh
Kolkwitzia—koel-KWIT-zee-uh

L

Lagerstroemia—lay-guhr-STREE-mee-uh
Lathyrus—LATH-uh-ruhs
Leptospermum—lep-toe-SPUR-muhm
Liatris—lye-AT-ruhs
Liriodendron—leer-ee-oe-DEN-druhn
Liriope—luh-RYE-oe-pee
Lobelia—loe-BEE-lee-uh
Lonicera—loe-NIS-uh-ruh

Lychnis—LIK-nis
Lysimachia—lye-suh-MAY-kee-uh

M

Macleaya—ma-KLAY-uh
Malus—MAY-lus
Mandevilla—man-duh-VIL-uh
Matthiola—ma-thee-OE-luh
Melaleuca—mel-uh-LOO-kuh
Metrosideros—MET-roe-SID-uh-ruhs
Mimulus—MIM-ew-luhs
Musa—MEW-zuh
Myosotis—mye-oh-SO-tuhs
Myrica—mi-RYE-kuh

N

Nandina—nan-DEE-nuh
Narcissus—nahr-SIS-uhs
Nerine—nuh-RYE-nee
Nerium—NEE-ree-uhm
Nicotiana—ni-koe-shee-AY-nuh
Nierembergia—nee-rem-BURG-ee-uh
Nyssa—NIS-uh

O

Olea—OE-lee-uh
Osmanthus—oz-MAN-thuhs
Osteospermum—os-tee-oe-SPUR-muhm
Oxalis—ok-SAL-is
Oxydendrum—OK-see-DEN-druhm

P

Pachysandra—pak-ee-SAN-druh
Papaver—puh-PAY-vuhr
Parthenocissus—PAHR-thuh-noe-SIS-uhs
Pelargonium—pel-ahr-GOE-nee-uhm
Pennisetum—pen-uh-SEE-tuhm
Penstemon—PEN-stuh-muhn
Philadelphus—fil-uh-DEL-fuhs
Photinia—foe-TIN-ee-uh
Phyla—FYE-luh
Phyllostachys—FIL-oe-STAK-ees
Physalis—FYE-suh-luhs
Picea—pye-SEE-uh
Pieris—pee-AIR-uhs
Pinus—PYE-nuhs
Pittosporum—pi-TOS-puh-ruhm,
  pi-tuh-SPOER-uhm
Platanus—PLAT-uh-nuhs
Platycladus—plat-i-KLAD-uhs
Podocarpus—poe-doe-KAR-puhs
Polianthes—pol-ee-AN-theez
Polygonatum—pol-ee-GON-uh-tuhm
Portulaca—por-tew-LAK-uh
Potentilla—poe-ten-TIL-uh
Primula—PRIM-ew-luh
Pseudotsuga—soo-doe-TSOO-guh
Pyrostegia—pye-roe-STEE-jee-uh
Pyrus—PYE-ruhs

Q

Quercus—KWER-kuhs

R

Ranunculus—ra-NUN-kew-luhs
Rhaphiolepis—raf-ee-OL-uh-puhs,
  raf-ee-oe-LEP-uhs
Rhoeo—REE-oe
Romneya—ROM-nee-uh
Rosmarinus—roez-muh-RYE-nuhs
Rudbeckia—rud-BEK-ee-uh

Rosmarinus

S

Salpiglossis—sal-pi-GLOS-uhs
Sanvitalia—san-vi-TAY-lee-uh
Scabiosa—skay-bee-OH-suh
Schefflera—SHEF-luh-ruh
Schizanthus—ski-ZAN-thuhs
Scilla—SIL-uh
Sempervivum—sem-per-VYE-vuhm
Senecio—suh-NEE-shee-oe
Sequoia—suh-KWOY-uh
Sinningia—si-NIN-jee-uh
Solandra—soe-LAN-druh
Soleirolia—soe-lee-uh-ROE-lee-uh
Spiraea—spye-REE-uh
Strelitzia—stre-LIT-see-uh
Symplocos—SIM-pluh-koes

T

Tagetes—tuh-JEE-teez
Taxodium—taks-OE-dee-uhm
Thuja—THOO-yuh
Thymus—TYE-muhs
Tibouchina—tib-oo-KYE-nuh
Tigridia—tye-GRID-ee-uh
Tolmiea—tol-MEE-uh
Trachelospermum—tra-kuh-loe-SPER-muhm
Tradescantia—trad-es-KAN-shee-uh
Tropaeolum—troe-PEE-uh-luhm
Tsuga—TSOO-guh

V

Vaccinium—vak-SIN-ee-uhm
Vancouveria—van-koo-VEE-ree-uh
Verbascum—vur-BAS-kuhm
Verbena—vur-BEE-nuh
Viburnum—vye-BUR-nuhm
Vinca—VING-kuh
Vitex—VEE-teks

Vinca minor

W–Z

Weigela—wye-JEE-luh
Xylosma—zye-LOZ-muh
Zantedeschia—zan-tuh-DES-kee-uh
Zephyranthes—zef-i-RAN-theez
Zizyphus—ZIZ-uh-fuhs
Zoysia—ZOY-see-uh

INDEX
Gardening Terms and Topics

INDEX
Scientific and Common Names

Italic page numbers refer to pages on which there are relevant photographs. The **boldface** page number after each scientific name refers to the plant's encyclopedia entry. The page number after a common name also refers to the encyclopedia entry; to find more page references to a common name, look under the scientific name in parentheses.

Acknowledgments

SPECIAL CONTRIBUTORS

Patricia P. Cobb
Department of Entomology
Alabama Cooperative Extension System
AUBURN UNIVERSITY
Auburn, AL

Steven M. Cohan
Executive Director
MEMPHIS BOTANIC GARDEN
Memphis, TN

Robert Crasweller
Tree Fruit Specialist
Department of Horticulture
PENNSYLVANIA STATE UNIVERSITY
University Park, PA

Miklos Faust
Plant Physiologist
UNITED STATES DEPARTMENT OF AGRICULTURE
Beltsville, MD

Chad Finn
Research Geneticist/Small Fruit Breeder
UNITED STATES DEPARTMENT OF AGRICULTURE
Corvallis, OR

Rick Foster
Department of Entomology
PURDUE UNIVERSITY
West Lafayette, IN

Duane Greene
Tree Fruit Specialist
Department of Plant and Soil Science
UNIVERSITY OF MASSACHUSETTS
Amherst, MA

Austin Hagen
Alabama Cooperative Extension System
AUBURN UNIVERSITY
Auburn, AL

Michael D. Henshaw
Alabama Cooperative Extension System
Double Springs, AL

David Himelrick
Specialist in Small Fruit Crops
Department of Horticulture
AUBURN UNIVERSITY
Auburn, AL

Jules Janick
Department of Horticulture
PURDUE UNIVERSITY
West Lafayette, IN

Jim McCausland
Garden Editor
SUNSET MAGAZINE

Thomas MacCubbin
Horticulturist
UNIVERSITY OF FLORIDA COOPERATIVE
   EXTENSION SERVICE
Orlando, FL

Craig Minor
Deciduous Tree Fruit Specialist
DAVE WILSON NURSERY
Hickman, CA

Phil Normandy
Plant Collections Manager
BROOKSIDE GARDENS
Kensington, MD

Marvin R. Pritts
Berries and Small Fruit Specialist
Department of Fruit and Vegetable Science
CORNELL UNIVERSITY
Ithaca, NY

Earl Puls, Jr.
Fruit Specialist
Department of Horticulture
LOUISIANA STATE UNIVERSITY
Baton Rouge, LA

Freddie Rasberry
Fruit and Nut Specialist
MISSISSIPPI STATE UNIVERSITY
Starkville, MS

Lon J. Rombough
Researcher and Consultant
Specialist in Grapes and Uncommon Fruits
Aurora, OR

George H. Taylor
Climatologist
OREGON STATE UNIVERSITY
Corvallis, OR

Roy L. Taylor
Executive Director
RANCHO SANTA ANA BOTANIC GARDEN
   (and former President of the Chicago
   Horticulture Society and Director of
   Chicago Botanic Garden)
Claremont, CA

William C. Welch
Extension Horticulture
TEXAS A&M UNIVERSITY
College Station, TX

CONSULTANTS

New England:

Nancy Adams
Dr. Lois Berg Stack
Thomas Buob
Thurston Handley
Donna Lamb
Sally Muspratt
Len Perry
David Seavey
Mandy Self
Roseann Sherry
Chris Strand
Richard Verville
Joann Wright

Mid-Atlantic States:

Susan Beebe
Robert Beyfuss
Dr. Toni Bilik
William Brown
Wayne Cahilly
Brian Caldwell
Joe Dektor
R. Edmonds
Brian Eshenauer
Tom Kirby
John Lankenau
Stephanie Mallozzi
Sue Mearing
Thomas Obourn
Dom Parise
Jeff Schulz
Steven VanderMark
Tom Whitlow
J. Craig Williams
Thomas Zundel

Southeast:

John K. Arbogas
Dr. David Bar-Zvi
David Barkely
Linda Blue
William Brown
Scott Byars
Scott Chadwell
Gerald Clingman
Paul Cooper
Terry Del Valle
Randall Drinkard
Frank Funderbunk
Robert Goerger
John Harris
Peter Heus
Randal Jackson
Bray McDonald
Wilma R. Penland
Ed Poenicke
Paul Thompson

Ann Upton
Jim Ward
Dr. Joe White
Dave Williams
Dee Wookey

Midwest:

Deborah Brown
Christy Bubolz
Gerald Draheim
John Fech
Steve Fouch
Barry Fugatt
Floyd Giles
Edward Hedborn
Greg Heilig
Jeff Iles
Ricky Kemery
Mark Kepler
Jack Kerrigan
Mohamad W. Khan
Dean Krauskopf
Karen Krueger
Ralph Kulm
Stephanie Larimer
Barbara Larson
Verna Litton
Chip Miller
Ann Munson
Don Neal
Krista Oakley
Sherry Rindels
David Robson
Dan Rogalla
Brenda Simons
Tom Tiddens
Celeste Vander Mey
Carl Wagner
Norman Warminski
Keith Zanziger

Rocky Mountain States:

Whitney Cranshaw
Ray Daugherty
Ginny McCamant
Kevin Mosley
Larry Sager
Lauren Springer

Southwest:

William Adams
Dr. Lynn Brandenberger
Mark Dimmitt
Valerie Edelbrook
Ron Gass
Steven George
Warren Jones
Michael W. Kilby
Darlene Locke
Terry Mikel

Charles Pingleton
Carol Shuler
Mark Terning
Larry Stein
Doug Welsh

Pacific Northwest:

Mark Albright
Arthur L. Antonelli
Wilbur Bluhm
Ron Brightman
Charles A. Brun
Chad Finn
Tonie Fitzgerald
Bill Hielscher
Donald G. Howse
Bill Janssen
Mareen Kruckeberg
Russell Link
Nicola Luttropp
Craig McConnell
Ray McNeilan
Dr. Pat Moore
Warren Manhart
Robert Norton
George Pinyuh
Melody Putnam
Diana Reeck
Robert L. Stebbins
Ted Van Veen

California and Nevada:

Maile Arnold
Dan Atkin
Michael Barclay
Tim Barnett
Mike Bodger
R. A. Brendler

Steve Brigham
Dorthy Bunch
William J. Carlos
Ann Chandler
Barrie Coate
Michelle Comeau
Richard Cowles
Dave Cudney
Dan Davids
Angela Dellavalle
Barbara Deutsch
Clyde Elmore
John and Cathy Etheridge
Susan Frommer
Rhonda Gildersleeve
Richard Harris
Eric A. Johnson
Elizabeth McClintock
Glenn McGourty
Rex Marsh
Jim Marshall
Luen Miller
Robert Morris
Kathy Musial
Eric Oglesby
Robert Raabe
Richard Schell
M. Nevin Smith
Ray Sodomka
John Steiner
Matthew Tekulsky
Paul Vossen
Judy Wigand
Christine Wotruba

Canada:

Andy Bootsma
Campbell G. Davidson
Bill Ingratta

We would like to thank the following people for their contributions to this book.

Cartographic production: Barton Wright. **Computer production:** Deborah Bates, Robert Kato, Bruce Mallon. **Design assistance:** Barbara Geisler, Elisa Tanaka, Debra Turner. **Technical support:** Phoebe Bixler. **Proofreaders:** Desne Border, Fran Haselsteiner, Stacey Lynn, David Sweet. **Miscellaneous illustrations:** Mary Davey Burkhardt, Ireta Cooper, Dennis Nolan.

If you would like to order additional copies of any of our books, call us at 1 (800) 643-8030 ext. 544 or check with your local bookstore.

Photography Credits

For pages with six or fewer photographs, each image has been identified by its position on the page: Left (L), center (C), or right (R); top (T), middle (M), or bottom (B). On other pages, such as those in "A Guide to Plant Selection" or the Dictionary Visual Guides, photographs are identified by their position in the grid (shown right). Photographs on the page edge are designated "tab"; those on the back cover, "back".

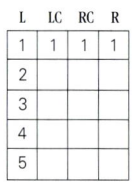

	L	LC	RC	R
1	1	1	1	1
2				
3				
4				
5				

Academy of Natural Sciences, Philadelphia/VIREO: 113 L1. **Ian Adams:** 50 BL; 51 BR; 62 T; 67 B, T; 73 BL. **L. Albee/Longwood Gardens:** 623 BL, BR. **Dariel Alexander:** 79. **George C. Anderson:** 9 TL. **Scott Atkinson:** 148 L1. **Val Atkinson:** 45 BR. **Tom Bean:** 78 B, T. **Steve Bentsen:** 51 T; 53 T. **Max Badgley:** 549 L1, L2, L3, LC2, R1, R2, RC1, RC2; 571 LC1, R3; 590 L3, LC2, RC1; 591 R2, R3; 592 L4, LC1, RC1, RC 5; 614 R1; 615 L3, R1, R2. **Bios (Klein-Hubert)/Peter Arnold, Inc.:** 90 R3. **Bios (W. Lapinski)/Peter Arnold, Inc.:** 95 R1. **T. Boyden:** 592 LC5. **Ron Boylan:** 614 R3. **Gary Braasch:** 26 T. **Marion Brenner:** 4 BR, RC; 33 TL, TR; 80 L2; 81 R5; 82 L4, R5; 83 L3, R5; 84 L2, L3, L4, R4; 85 R5; 86 L1, L2, L3, L5, R3, R4; 87 L3; 89 L1; 90 L1; 93 L3; 95 L3; 96 L3, R4; 97 L4; 98 L1, R1; 100 L3, R3; 101 R2; 102 R3; 103 R5; 104 L2, L3, R3; 105 L3; 108 L2; 115 R4; 116 R3; 118 R2; 119 L2, R1; 120 R1; 121 L2, L3, L4, R2, R3; 122 L1, L3, R1, R2, R4, R5; 123 L1, L2, L3, L5, R1, R2, R4, R5; 124 L1, L2, L3, L4 R1, R3, R4, R5; 125 L1, L2, L3, L4, R1, R2, R4, R5; 126, L4, R2; 127 L1, L4; 128 L3, L4, L5, R3, R4; 129 L1, L2, L5; 130 R1; 134 R2; 135 R3; 136 L2, R3; 137 R1; 138 R2, R4; 139 L2, R3, R6; 143 L3, R5; 145 L3, R4; 153 L3, L4; 154 L3, L5, R1, R2, R3; 156 R4; 157 L2, L3; 159 R3, R4, R5; 160 L1, R1, R5; 633 LC1, RC2; 634 L. **Kathy Brenzel:** 94 R4; 623 T. **Gerald Bricombe/The Image Bank:** 18 T. **Richard Brown:** 45 B. **Patricia J. Bruno/Positive Images:** 14 TL. **Karen Bussolini/Positive Images:** 9 BR. **Lisa Butler:** 21 T; 93 L4; 114 R3; 118 R4; 120 R2. **Scott Camazine:** 591 L1, L2, LC1. **James L. Castner:** 590 R2; 591 C2; 592 LC2; 614 RC3. **Peter Christiansen:** 617; 627 B. **Jack K. Clark/Comstock:** 592 R2, R5; 615 R4. **Jesse Clovis/WVU Biology Dept.:** 112 R3, R4. **Steve Cohan:** 37 B. **Comstock:** 590 RC2; 592 L2. **Ed Cooper:** 29 B; 32 T; 33 B; 47 T; 157 L1. **R. Cowles:** 571 R2; 591 C3; 592 L3, L5, R3; 614 L1, L3, RC2, R4. **Gary Cralle/The Image Bank:** 18 B. **Crandall & Crandall:** 571 LC2, RC2, RC3; 590 L1, LC1; 592 RC3, LC4; 614 RC1. **Whitney Cranshaw:** 615 RC3. **D. Cudney:** 615 L1, LC1, R3, RC1, RC2. **Claire Curran:** back LC; TR; 4 BL; 13 RT; 37 T; 40 BL; 43 T; 47 BL; 80 L3; 81 L4, R4; 82 L2, L5, R1, R4; 83 L5; 84 R2; 85 L1, L2, L5; 86 L4, R1; 87 L1, L2, L4, L5, L6, R2, R3, R4, R5; 88 R1; 89 L3, L4, L5, R5; 91 R4; 95 L4, L5; 96 R3; 99 L1, L2, R2; 101 L3; 102 L2, L3, L4; 104 R2; 105 L4, L5, R5; 106 L2, L3, L5, R1, R2, R3, R4; 107 L1, L2, L3, L4, R2, R3, R5; 108 L3, L4, R2; 109 L4, L5, R1, R2, R3, R4; 112 R5; 115 L1, L2; 117 R3; 118 L1, L4; 119 R3; 120 R4; 122 R3; 123 R3; 124 L5; 126 R4; 127 L2, R1; 128 L2; 129 R6; 130 R5; 134 R1, R4; 135 L1, L3, L5, R2; 136 L1, L5, R1; 139 L4; 142 R2; 143 R1, R3; 153 R2; 154 L1, L2; 155 L1, L4, L5, R2; 156 L2, L3, L4, L5, L6, R1, R2, R3, R5; 157 R3, R4; 158 L2, L3, R1, R2, R4, R5; 159 L1; 622 T; 627 T; 628; 632 BL, TL; 633 LC3, RC1, RC3. **Cypress Gardens:** 624 B. **R. Todd Davis Photography, Inc.:** 91 L1; 111 L1, L2, L4; 114 L4; 117 L2; 131 R1; 132 L2, R3; 141 L1; 142 L4; 148 L4; 150 L4. **Alan Detrick:** 132 R2. **William Dewey:** 30 T; 36 T; 37 ML; 40 T; 41 B, T; 115 L3; 116 L2, L4, L5, R4, R5; 120 L1, L4; 136 L4; 137 L3, R5; 140 L4; 153 L1. **Wally Eberhart/PHOTO/NATS:** 615 LC2. **Craig Engle:** 139 R2; 158 L4. **Fairchild Tropical Garden:** 50 T. **Derek Fell:** back TL; 9 TR; 10 L; 13 BR; 15 BL; 49 M; 82 R2; 83 L4, R2; 94 R3; 95 R5; 102 R1; 105 R1, R2; 110 L2; 112 L1, L2, L3, L4, R1; 116 L3, R2; 117 L1; 120 L2; 126 L1, R3; 127 R5; 131 L3, L4; 133 L1; 134 L2; 135 L2, L4; 141 L2, L4 L5, R2; 142 R1, R5; 144 R3; 148 L2; 590 L2, R1; 592 L1. **E. Ferguson:** 615 LC3. **Donna Ford-Werntz/WVU Herbarium:** 112 R2. **Galen D. Gates:** 59 B, T; 70 B, T. **Jeff Gnass:** 63 T. **Dan Guravich/ Researchers, Inc.:** 615 RC4. **Joe K. Hale:** 43 MR. **D. William Hamilton/ The Image Bank:** 16. **Harry Haralambou/Positive Images:** 10 B. **Jessie M.**

Harris: 83 R4; 120 R3; 130 R2; 132 L3; 133 L3; 142 L3, R4; 145 R2. **Hayes Arboretum:** 73 ML. **Margaret Hensel:** 15 BR. **Walter H. Hodge/Peter Arnold, Inc.:** 95 R4; 114 R4. **Saxon Holt:** 10 T, tab; 11 BL, TR, T, tab; 12 T; 14 BL; 19 L; 29 TR; 30 B; 80 L1, L4, L5, R4; 81 L1, L2, R3; 84 R3; 85 R1, R2, R3, R4; 90 L2, L4, R1, R2; 91 L2, L3, R2; 92 R3; 93 R4; 94 L2, L3, L4; 95 L1; 98 R3; 100 R1; 104 L1, L4; 107 R4; 110 L5, R4; 111 L3, L5, R1; 114 R1; 117 L3; 118 L3; 122 L2; 126 R1; 130 L3; 143 L1, L5; 144 L5; 145 L1; 146 R3, R5; 147 L2, L3, R2; 148 R2; 160 R4; 622 B; 625 R. **James Frederick Housel:** 12 BL. **Jerry Howard/ Positive Images:** 147 L1. **Jack Jennings/Missouri Botanical Garden:** 620 B. **Dr. Jerral Johnson:** 592 RC2. **Verna Johnston:** 29 TL. **B. Knoop:** 571 L1, RC1; 614, L2. **Stephen J. Krasemann/Peter Arnold, Inc.:** 114 L3. **Ray Krine/Grant Heilman Photo:** 591 R1. **M. Landis:** 90 L5; 92 R1. **Magnolia Plantations:** 624 T. **Charles Mann:** 12 M, tab; 13 tab; 14 tab; 15 T, tab; 19 R; 45 TL, TR; 47 BR; 80 R3; 82 L1; 83 L2, R1; 84 L5; 85 L3; 91 L4, R1; 92 R4; 94 R2; 95 R2; 96 R1, R5; 97 L1, L2, L3, R1; 98 L4; 99 L4; 101 L2; 102 R2, R4; 103 L1, L3, L5, R1, R4; 108 R4; 109 L2; 110 L4; 115 R5; 119 L1, L3, R2; 123 L4; 126 L2, L3; 128 R2; 129 R5; 130 R3; 132 L5; 133 R4; 134 R3; 135 R4; 136 R4; 137 L1, L4, L5, R4; 138 L1, L3; 140 L3; 143 L2; 144 L2, L3, R4; 148 R3; 151 R3, R5; 152 R1, R4; 155 L3; 157 L4, R2; 158 L1; 159 L2, L4, R2; 160 L3, L5, R3. **Jim McCausland:** 26 MR. **David McDonald:** 1; 21 B; 23 T; 25 B; 80 R1; 81 R1, R2; 82 L3; 86 R2; 88 L4, R3; 89 L2, R2, R4; 96 L2, L4; 97 R3, R4; 98 L2, L5, R4; 99 R1, R3, R4; 100 L2, L5; 101 R1, R4, R5; 103 R2; 104 R4; 109 L1; 113 L4, R3; 119 L4; 128 L1; 129 R2; 130 L2, L4, L5; 136 R5; 137 R2; 139 L1, L3, R1, R5; 140 L5, L6, R1, R2, R4; 144 R1, R5; 145 R3, R5; 146 L1, L2, L3, L4; 149 L3, L4, L5, R1, R3; 150 L1, L2, L3, L5, R1, R2, R3, R4, R5; 151 L2, L3, L4, R1, R2; 152 L1, L3, L4, L5, R2, R3; 153 R4; 154 R5; 155 R3; 156 L1; 159 L3; 615 L4; 620 T; 633 LC2. **Memphis Botanical Garden:** 621. **Montreal Botanical Garden:** 618 T. **Scott Millard:** 43 B. **Edward J. North:** 7; 11 BR. **Bart O'Brien:** 36 B. **Shep Ogden:** 630 T. **Jerry Pavia:** 90 L3; 92 L1, L4; 94 L1; 103 R3; 105 R4; 110 L3, R1; 113 R1; 114 R5; 116 R1; 133 L4; 142 L1; 149 L1; 151 L5; 629 L. **Joanne Pavia:** 146 R4. **Leonard G. Phillips:** 8 B; 13 T. **Norman A. Plate:** 40 BR; 77 L; 88 L5, R2; 89 R1; 625 B; 626 B, T; 631 B. **Rob Proctor:** 14 BR; 23 B. **Ed Reschke/ Peter Arnold, Inc.:** back RC; 95 R3; 138 R3. **Paul Resendez/Positive Images:** 131 L1. **James H. Robinson:** 591 L3. **Susan A. Roth:** back BR; 8 T; 49 L; 50 BR; 53 BL, BR; 58 B; 62 B; 77 R; 78 ML; 93 R1, R3; 95 L2; 96 R2; 97 R6; 100 R2; 114 L1; 115 R2; 127 R4; 132 R1, R4; 142 L2; 147 L5, R1; 148 R1. **Jim Schwabel/New England Stock:** 73 T. **Scotts Co.:** 571 L2, L3, R1. **Delilah Smittle/*Fine Gardening Magazine*:** 2. **Pam Spaulding/ Positive Images:** 131 R3; 132 L1. **Albert Squillace/Positive Images:** 111 R2, R3. **David M. Stone/ PHOTO/NATS:** 614 LC1. **Chris Strand/Arnold Arboretum:** 618 B. **Joseph G. Strauch, Jr.:** 14 TR; 84 L1; 90 R4; 91 R3; 92 L3; 93 L1, L2, R2; 101 R3; 105 L2; 110 R3; 113 L2, L3, R2, R4; 114 L5, R2; 128 R1, R5; 129 L3, L4, R3; 130 R4; 131 L2; 132 L4; 133 L2, R3; 134 L3, R5; 138 L2; 140 L2; 141 L3, R1, R3; 142 R3; 144 L4, R2; 145 L2; 146 R2; 147 L4; 148 L5, R4; 160 L2. **SuperStock, Inc.:** 110 L1. **K. Bryan Swezey:** 29 MR. **Michael S. Thompson:** 19 M; 49 R; 81 L3; 92 L2; 103 L2; 110 R2; 111 R4; 117 R2; 122 L4; 129 R3; 133 R5; 142 L5; 143 R2; 147 R3; 149 L2; 153 R1. **Larry Ulrich:** 55 B, TM; 58 T. **Michel Viard/Peter Arnold, Inc.:** 148 L3. **Paddy Wales:** back BL; 4 TL, TR; 6; 7 tab. **Keith Warren:** 26 B. **Darrow Watt:** 32 B, M; 88 L2; 108 L1; 549 LC1; 630 B; 631 T. **Marshall Webb/Shelburne Farms:** 63 B. **Stephen Whalen/Zephyr Pictures:** 43 ML. **Bob Wigand:** 8 tab; 9 BL, tab. **D. Wilder/Tom Stack & Assoc.:** 615 L2. **Doug Wilson:** 4 LC; 80 R2; 83 R3; 88 L3; 99 L3; 100 L4, R1; 102 R5; 115 R1; 117 L4; 118 R1; 120 L5; 127 R2; 140 R3; 146 R1; 629 R. **Tom Woodward:** 3; 5; 82 R3; 83 L1; 84 R1, R5; 85 L4; 87 R1, R6; 88 L1; 92 R5; 94 R1; 96 L1; 97 R2, R5; 98 L3, R2, R5; 99 R5; 102 L1; 103 L4; 104 L5, R1; 105 L1, R3; 106 L1, L4, R5; 107 R1; 108 R1, R3; 109 L3, R5; 114 L2; 115 L4, R3; 116 L1; 117 R1, R4; 118 L2, R3, R5; 119 R4; 120 L3; 121 L1; 122 L5; 124 R2; 125 R3; 127 L3, R3; 129 R1; 130 L1; 134 L1; 135 R1, R5; 136 L3; 137 L2, R3; 138 L4, R1; 139 L5, R4; 140 L1, R5; 144 L1; 145 R1; 149 R2; 151 L1, R4; 152 L2, R5; 153 L2, R3; 154 L4, R4; 155 L2; 157 R1; 158 L5, R3; 159 R1; 160 L4, R2; 592 R1, R4, RC4; 632 BR, TC, TR; 633 L1, R1, R2; 634 B, T; 635 B, M, T. **Cynthia Woodyard:** 13 BL; 92 R2; 100 L1; 133 R1, R3; 143 L4, R4; 155 R1. **Tom Wyatt:** 55 TR. **Linda Yonker:** 25 T. **Josephine Zeitlin:** 136 R2.